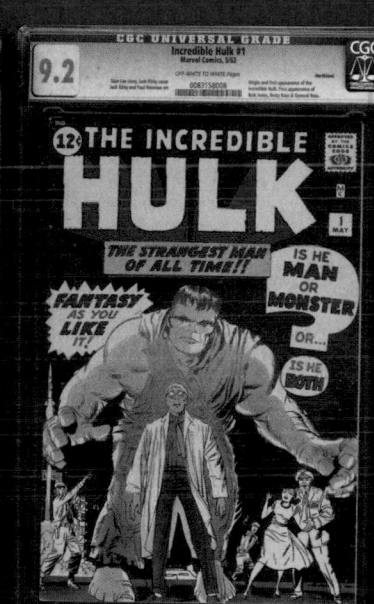

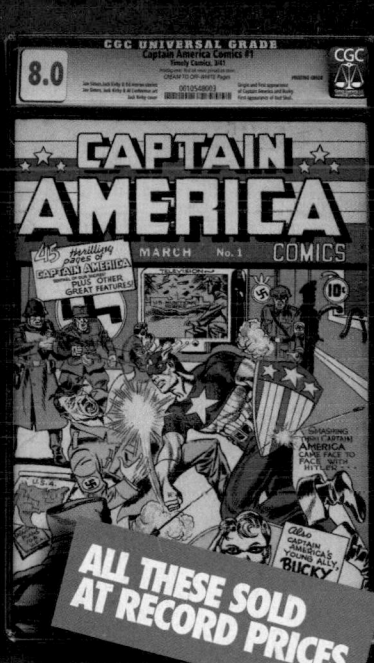

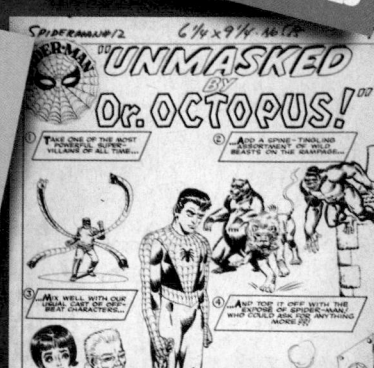

PEANUTS
$151,534
$41,264
$11,550
AMAZING! STARTLING!
SUPERMAN IS HERE!
A FLEISCHER STUDIOS CARTOON
TECHNICOLOR
AMERICANA & HAKE'S COLLECTIBLES
$19,898
7.5
Fantastic Four
THE GOERKE CO.
WELCOME
$10,350

Bill 'n' Anne Campbell
3501 Foxbriar Lane
Cibolo, TX 78108
Phone: (830)626-1077
e-mail: captainmarvel1940@satx.rr.com
THE FLASH
FASTEST MAN ALIVE
WONDER WOMAN
SENSATION COMICS
SUPERMEN OF AMERICA
ACTION COMICS
Radio and Box Top Premiums
(Rings, Badges, Decoders, Manuals)
Character Watches, Boxes, Inserts, Bands, Parts, Hands, Dials
Western Hero Items Including Cap Guns and Holsters
Comics, Big Little Books, Pop-Ups
Capt. Marvel, Capt. Midnight, Capt. Video, Buck Rogers, Tom Corbett Space Cadet, Doc Savage, Shadow, Tom Mix, Lone Ranger, Superman, Batman, Little Orphan Annie, Mickey Mouse, Donald Duck, Popeye, Howdy Doody, Hopalong Cassidy, Roy Rogers, G-Man, Gene Autry, Jack Armstrong, Davy Crockett, Paladin, Rin Tin Tin, Sgt. Preston, Zorro, Green Hornet, Sky King, Straight Arrow, Buster Brown, Flash Gordon
For personal collection: Capt. Marvel items wanted. Also especially need Whistle Bomb Ring, Big Bad Wolf and Donald Duck 1934 Wrist Watches with leather bands.
eBay Store: Bill and Anne's Wonderful Toys

STAR TREK II
THE WRATH OF KHAN
Admiral Kirk
Khan
Captain Terrell
SERIES 1
ACTION FIGURE ASST

ABOUT THE AUTHOR

Ted Hake is recognized as the founding father of America's collectibles industry. A collector from age seven beginning with coins and fossils, Hake's first presidential campaign item sales lists were issued from New York City while he was employed by General Electric at the 1964-65 New York World's Fair. In the Fall of 1965, he entered New York University's graduate film program and then in January, 1967 transferred to the Annenberg School for Communication at University of Pennsylvania, receiving his master's degree in 1968. While in Philadelphia, he founded Hake's Americana & Collectibles in 1967, the first auction house to specialize in 20th century American popular culture. His early initiatives in hundreds of collecting areas contributed significantly to establishing collectibles as a major pastime for millions of Americans. Over the years, Hake has shared his expertise by writing eighteen reference/price guides covering such subjects as presidential campaign artifacts, pinback buttons and vintage collectibles in the areas of advertising, comic characters, cowboy characters and television. His lifelong interest in Disneyana culminated in the publication of the *Official Price Guide to Disney Collectibles*, a comprehensive companion (10,000 color photos) to this book published 2007 in its second edition. He is a frequent guest on radio, was an appraiser on the first two seasons of the PBS series *The Antiques Roadshow* and is a featured expert on the History Channel's 2003 program History of Toys. In March, 2004, Hake sold his business which is now a division of Geppi's Entertainment Publications & Auctions and he continues as Chief Operating Officer. Hake's four annual catalogue and internet (www.hakes.com) auctions, homepage sales lists and books are produced at the company's home office in York, Pennsylvania.

OTHER BOOKS BY TED HAKE:

The Button Book
(out of print)

Buttons In Sets
With Marshall N. Levin

Collectible Pin-Back Buttons 1896-1986:
An Illustrated Price Guide
With Russ King

The Encyclopedia of Political Buttons 1896-1972
Political Buttons Book II 1920-1976
Political Buttons Book III 1789-1916

The Encyclopedia of Political Buttons: 2004 Revised Prices for Books I, II, III

Hake's Guide to Advertising Collectibles 100 Years of Advertising from 100 Famous Companies
(out of print)

Hake's Guide to Comic Character Collectibles An illustrated Price Guide to 100 Years of Comic Strip Characters
(out of print)

Hake's Guide to Cowboy Character Collectibles An Illustrated Price Guide Covering 50 Years of Movie & TV Cowboy Heroes

Hake's Guide to Presidential Campaign Collectibles
An Illustrated Price Guide to Artifacts from 1789-1988

Hake's Guide to TV Collectibles: An illustrated Price Guide
(out of print)

Official Hake's Price Guide to Character Toys,
Editions 1-6

Official Price Guide to Disney Collectibles
First Edition, 2005
Second Edition, 2007

Plate Collector's Handbook
with E. Ward Russell
(out of print)

Non-Paper Sports Collectibles: An Illustrated Price Guide
(with Roger Steckler)

Sixgun Heroes: A Price Guide to Movie Cowboy Collectibles
With Robert Cauler

A Treasury of Advertising Collectibles
(out of print)

For ordering information write the author at:
Hake's Americana & Collectibles
P.O. Box 12001 · York, PA 17402
Or visit: www.hakes.com
Or call: 866-404-9800 ext. 1635

THE OFFICIAL

Price Guide to POP CULTURE MEMORABILIA:

150 Years of Character Toys & Collectibles

First Edition

Ted Hake

FOR GEMSTONE PUBLISHING

J.C. Vaughn, Executive Editor & Associate Publisher
Brenda Busick, Creative Director • **Lindsay Dunn**, Editor
Tom Gordon III, Managing Editor • **Mark Huesman**, Production Coordinator
Diana Hundt, Advertising Assistant • **Courtney Jenkins**, Marketing Manager
Amanda Sheriff, Editorial Coordinator • **Heather Winter**, Office Manager

RANDOM HOUSE INFORMATION GROUP NEW YORK

HOUSE OF COLLECTIBLES

GEMSTONE PUBLISHING

GEMSTONE PUBLISHING, INC.

NOTICE: Values for items pictured in this book are based on author's experience, consultations with a network of advisors including collectors specializing in various categories, and actual prices realized for specific items sold through private sales and auctions, including the catalogues of Hake's Americana & Collectibles catalogue and internet bid auctions. The values offered in this book are approximations influenced by many factors including condition, rarity and demand, and they should serve as only guidelines, presenting an average range of what one might expect to pay for the items. In the marketplace, knowledge and opinions held by both sellers and buyers determine prices asked and prices paid. This is not a price list of items for sale or items wanted by the author or publisher. The author and the publisher shall not be held responsible for losses that may occur in the purchase, sale or other transaction of property because of information contained herein. Efforts have been made to present accurate information, but the possibility of error exists. Readers who believe they have discovered an error are invited to mail corrective information to the author, Ted Hake, at P.O. Box 12001, York, PA 17402. Verified corrections will be incorporated into future editions of this book.

COVER IMAGES

Front Cover: Charlie Brown ©2008 United Features Syndicate. Fred Flintstone ©2008 Hanna-Barbera. Woody Woodpecker ©2008 Universal Studios. Campbell's Kids © 2008 CSC Brands LP. Buck Rogers ©2008 Dille Family Trust. The Bionic Woman ©2008 Universal Studios. Mr. Peanut ©2008 Kraft Foods. SpongeBob SquarePants ©2008 Nickelodeon. The Beatles ©2008 Apple Corps, Ltd. Buddy Holly ©2008 Maria Elena Holly. All other characters ©2008 respective Copyright holders. All rights reserved.

THE OFFICIAL® PRICE GUIDE TO POP CULTURE MEMORABILIA: 150 YEARS OF CHARACTER TOYS AND COLLECTIBLES (1st Edition) is an original publication of Gemstone Publishing, Inc. and House of Collectibles. Distributed by The Random House Information Group, a division of Random House, Inc., New York and simultaneously in Canada by Random House of Canada Limited, Toronto. This edition has never before appeared in book form.

House of Collectibles
Random House Information Group
1745 Broadway
New York, New York 10019

www.houseofcollectibles.com

House of Collectibles is a registered trademark and the colophon is a trademark of Random House, Inc.

Published by arrangement with Gemstone Publishing.

ISBN: 978-0-375-72282-0

Printed in China.

10 9 8 7 6 5 4 3 2 1

HOUSE OF COLLECTIBLES

First Edition: October 2008

TOY CATEGORIES:

The following Disney categories were included in earlier editions of this work known as the *Official Hake's Price Guide to Character Toys*:

Bambi
Disney Characters Misc.
Disneyana Convention
Disneyland
Donald Duck
Dumbo
Mickey Mouse
Peter Pan
Pinocchio
Snow White & the Seven Dwarfs
Three Little Pigs
Toy Story
Uncle Scrooge
Winnie the Pooh
Zorro

These categories and over 100 additional Disney categories are part of the 10,000 items comprising the *Official Price Guide to Disney Collectibles* released in 2007 in its second edition.

ACKNOWLEDGEMENTS

Welcome to the first edition of *The Official Price Guide to Pop Culture Memorabilia: 150 Years of Character Toys & Collectibles*. Our guide has grown out of six editions, published since 1996, of *Hake's Price Guide to Character Toys*. Reasons for the title change are included in my introduction. What doesn't change are the ever expanding numbers of contributors, staff members and advertisers essential to presenting this body of information. We now have 16,000 collectible artifacts of our popular culture whose existance is documented in this book as to rarity and value by both experience and market results in a process I began four decades ago in 1967.

It's exciting to see this constantly growing number of contributors. We encourage new readers to report special items or suggest new categories for our next edition. For this edition, I'm pleased to acknowledge: Robert R. Barrett for his new fascinating information and review of the Tarzan section; Tom Gordon III for new sections on Masters of the Universe, Mego Superheroes and Transformers; Kathy Hammel and fellow researchers for new information on Howie Wing; Dan Morphy for updating his mechanical bank values; Jim Scancarelli for his unbroken string of additions to Amos 'n Andy and the Lone Ranger; Gene Seger for his comprehensive review and many contributions to the finest assemblage of Buck Rogers collectibles anywhere; John Snyder for embellishing many categories with new finds from his in-depth and superb character toy collection; Brent Taylor for sharing his results of concentrated study of the 1966 DC/Marvel "Superhero Club" numbered button series; and to Mike Wilbur, our specialist on the limited edition figure market.

Our original category histories, 305 of them in 1996, were researched and written by my late friend and noted pin-back button collector Marshall Levin. In our march to the present 461 categories, updates and new historical summaries have been researched by Dr. Arnold T. Blumberg, David Gerstein, Tom Gordon III, Charlie Roberts, J.C. Vaughn and myself.

Our six editions of *Hake's Price Guide to Character Toys* feature a

SPECIAL THANKS

Gary Alexander
Bob Allison
Ray Amati
Andy Anderson
Dave Anderson
Graeme Atkinson
Bob Baker
Charlie Balicki
Bob Barrett
Robert R. Barrett
Will Beierwaltes
Howard Bender
Arnold T. Blumberg
Steve Borock
Melissa Bowersox
Julian S. Bradfold II
Jaime Bramble
Robert Bruce
Scott Bruce
John Bruszewski
Terry Bruszewski
Patrick Buckley
Danton Burroughs
Jane Byrd
Joel S. Cadbury
Brian Callahan
Bill Campbell
Joe Caro
David Carr
Bob Cauler
Bob Cereghino
Ken Chapman
Mike Cherry
Tom Claggett
Russ Cochran
Bob Cook
Jerry Cook
Dan Coviello
Charles Crane
Lory Curtis
Joe Cywinski
Jimmy Dempsey
Jack Dixey
Ron Donnelly
Larry Doucet
Jerry Doxey
Mark Drennen
Bob Dziadosz
Ron Eccles
Tony Evangelista
Henry Ewald
Joe Fair
John Fawcett
Lee Felbinger
Ada L. Fitzsimmons
Don Flanagan
Matt Flynn
Keif Fromm
Bill Frost
Danny Fuchs
Everett Gamble
Josh Geppi
Steve Geppi
John Gilman
S. Harlan Glassman
Gordon Gold
Tony Goodstone
Tom Gordon III
Ralph Gould
Gary Greenberg
David Grisez
Rick Gronquist
Al Grossman
Bill Hagen
Robert Hall
Bruce Hamilton
Kathy Hammel
Jim Harmon
Phil Hecht
S. Leonard Hedeen
Joe Hehn
Robert Heide
Brian Heiler
Bob Hencey
Andy Hershberger
Bruce Hershenson
John Hintz
John Hone
David J. Howe
Bob Hritz
Mark Huesman
Bill Hughes
Bob Hummrich
Steve Ison
Jeanne Johnson
Jack Juka
Tom Kage
Doug Kaiser
Stephen A. Kallis, Jr.
Harvey Kamins
Bruce Kaufman
Fred L. King
Russ King
Pete Klaus
Walter Koenig
Al Konetzni
Bill Kozlowski
Rich Kozlowski
Dan Kubert
Ray La Briola
John C. La Monte
Hugh F. LaRue III
Bob Lesser
Richard Leibner
Andy Levison
Randy Lieberman
Don Lineberger
Carl Lobel
Larry Lowery
Howard Lowry
Leonard Maltin
Hy Mandelowitz
Don Maris
Barry Martin
Greg Mason

multitude of fascinating articles on specific characters and their creators. Value information in those editions is out of date, but the editions are available and the articles remain most informative. Our editorial content for this edition features an in-depth market report and article by John K. Snyder, Jr. and J.C. Vaughn, rarity and value charts by Tom Gordon III, Dick Tracy by Brandon DeStefano, Dogs & Cats (well-known ones, of course) by Lindsay Dunn and Courtney Jenkins, and information on Geppi's Entertainment Museum, where character collectibles are the star objects, by J.C. Vaughn.

Behind what's actually in this book are many people I'm also grateful to. For their care and support in this book process and always, special thanks to my wife Jonell and secretary Joan Carbaugh.

The initial source for so much of our information is Hake's Americana & Collectibles Auctions headed by General Manager Alex Winter. Most knowledgeable and so helpful to this book are Alex and his staff members: Mike Bollinger, Jack Dixey, Mark Herr, Terence Kean, Kelly McClain, Linda Snyder, Sarah Snyder, Deak Stagemyer and Sally Weaver.

Manipulating over 16,000 photos, 16,000 descriptions and 48,000 values, along with the editorial text into a coherent book is the responsibility of the Gemstone Publishing staff. My appreciation and amazement for how they do it goes particularly to Mark Huesman, Production Coordinator and Brenda

Syrocco-Style Superman Figure on Ashtray Base stands as one of the many rare iconic pieces of pop culture found in the pages of this book.

Bill Mastro
Harry Matetsky
Walter V. Matishak
Cory McClain
Jack Melcher
Richard Merkin
Paul Merolle
Peter Merolo
Rex Miller
Vall Miller
John Mlachnik
Pat Morgan
Dan Morphy
Peter Muldavin
Michael Naiman
DeWayne Nall
Gerald I. Nattboy
Curt Nelson
M. G. 'Bud' Norris
Anders Ogren
Richard Olson
Bob Overstreet
Ralph Perry
Don Phelps
Ralph Plumb
Ron Plotkin
Ed Pragler
Tony Raymond
Roger Reed
Harry Rinker
Charlie Roberts
Dave Robie
Robert Rogovin
Herb Rolfes
Scott Rona
Bruce Rosen
Barry Sadoff
Tommy Sage
Frank Salacuse
Michael Saler
Joe Sarno
Catherine Saunders-Watson
Jim Scancarelli
Jay Scarfone
Karl Schadow
Russ Sears
Gene Seger
Tony Seger
Gary Selmonsky
Brian Semling
Joe Semling
Maurice Sendak
Ken Sequin
Joel Siegel
Jim Silva
Joel Smilgis
Eugene M. Smith
David Smith
Herb Smith
John K. Snyder, Jr.
Deak Stagemyer
Joe Statkus
Larry Stidham
William Stillman
Dale Stratton
John Szuch
Brent Taylor
George Thomas
Harry Thomas
Charles Travis
Ernest Trova
Paul Troyer
Tom Tumbusch
Jim Ungerman
J.C. Vaughn
John Vavra
Jim Wagner
David Walsh
Jon R. Warren
Frank Weidner
Howard C. Weinberger
Jerry Weist
David Welch
Doug Wengel
Pat Wengel
Lizabeth West
Mike West
Mike Wilbur
Evelyn Wilson
Alex Winter
John Wise
Jim Wojtowicz
Henry Wroniarski
Joe Young
Debra Zakarin
Marc Zakarin
Larry Zdeb
Marco Zorrilla
Paul Zubritzky

Comment or suggestions for our next edition?

Contact:
Ted Hake
P.O. Box 12001
York, PA 17402

Busick, Creative Director. Thanks also to the entire Gemstone staff for their assistance in many ways: J.C. Vaughn, Executive Editor & Associate Publisher; Lindsay Dunn, Editor; Tom Gordon III, Managing Editor; Courtney Jenkins, Marketing Manager; Diana Hundt, Advertising Assistant; Amanda Sheriff, Editorial Coordinator and Heather Winter, Office Manager.

Another major thank you to Gemstone's iconic authority Bob Overstreet for sharing price information from *The Overstreet Comic Book Price Guide* on Big Little Books, Platinum Age comic books and promotional comic books. Each is a specialized section in Bob's definitive and comprehensive comic book reference now in its 38th edition. Additional contributions from John Clark, Joe McGuckin, Jeff Robison and Catherine Saunders-Watson are also appreciated. On our crew that spends a week just indexing this book, but not yet acknowledged, my sincere thanks to: Sally Campbell, Nancy Glatfelter, Mark Landis, Cory McClain and Sandy Robison.

Hake's Americana & Collectibles and Gemstone Publishing are both divisions of Geppi's Entertainment Publications & Auctions headed by John K. Snyder, Jr. John is a noted advocate for collecting in general and devoted collector of character collectibles in particular. His encouragement led to the first version of this book in 1996. For every edition since, he has made major contributions from his unique in-depth collection built with firm devotion to exemplary condition. John also closely monitors a multitude of popular culture collecting specialty areas and shares his overview by compiling our bi-annual Market Report.

All of our efforts to document popular culture collectibles in book form are realized by the commitment of Steve Geppi, President and CEO of Diamond Comic Distributors and Geppi's Entertainment Publications and Auctions. Steve's deep appreciation of the importance of popular culture is most apparent in the creation of Geppi's Entertainment Museum at Camden Yards in Baltimore. For highlights, read J.C. Vaughn's article on G.E.M. in this book.

The museum is first class in every way and a superb facility to showcase over two hundred years of popular culture artifacts that take the visitor from Benjamin Franklin's historic 1754 "Join, or Die" segmented snake newspaper cartoon to a movie poster from 2004 for Spongebob Squarepants. The museum is a marvelous visual presentation of important objects that informed and influenced the lives of our forefathers, ourselves and our children. If you enjoy this book, you must visit G.E.M. which takes the popular culture experience to the ultimate visual reality. My thanks to Steve and everyone who helped with this book. Our advertisers are also very important to continuing this process and we ask our readers to mention the Hake Guide when doing business with the outstanding firms supporting our efforts to document artifacts of American popular culture.

Ted Hake
March, 2008

Little Nemo Characters Bisque Figure Set

Two years ago, for the sixth time since 1996, I wrote an introduction to the *Official Hake's Price Guide to Character Toys*. That title grew out of *Hake's Price Guide To Character Toy Premiums*. Now, I'm pleased to introduce the first edition of the *Official Price Guide to Pop Culture Memorabilia: 150 Years of Character Toys & Collectibles*.

Why the change? To more accurately reflect the scope of our book as a compendium of artifacts embodying the American experience roughly since 1860. While we broadly define the word "toys," and retain it in our title, our book also covers celebrities, characters and events in addition to all our mediums of communication. The short list of communication mediums well represented by their artifacts among some 16,000 objects in 461 categories are: advertising, animation, children's literature, comic books, expositions, movies, music, newspapers, posters, pulps, radio, science fiction, television and, of course, toys, which broadly defined, are synonymous with many objects in the previously listed mediums.

The definition of "popular culture" in Webster's New Millennium Dictionary of English is: "contemporary lifestyle and items that are well known and generally accepted..." While certainly an accurate definition, it does little to communicate the multi-media depth and excitement of the American popular culture experience impacting the lives of successive generations and expanding worldwide. We believe the artifacts shown in our guide do precisely what the Webster's definition does not and thus our new title.

Over the three weeks I spent evaluating the artifacts from previous editions of this guide and pricing new additions in over one hundred categories added for this book, I had time to reflect on the days when I was the single source supplying collectors nationwide with 20th century pop culture collectibles. Long story short, the world of popular culture collecting essentially has gone from my auctions averaging a few hundred dollars each in 1967 to a collectibles industry exceeding the billion dollar mark. That's not just inflation; it's built on the interests, and in many cases passions, of millions of individual collectors. During my professional lifetime I've witnessed a collecting phenomenon begin, grow and just now start to mature as a market for the artifacts of our personal memories as well as artifacts of the cultural history that preceded us as individuals.

I see the 2006 opening of Geppi's Entertainment Museum at Camden Yards, Baltimore as a milestone in the appreciation of our popular culture heritage. G.E.M. showcases the importance and appeal of popular culture collectibles and clearly demonstrates how toys, in our early years, and later entertainments, in numerous forms, impact and influence our lives, just as they have the lives of our ancestors.

After being immersed in the collectibles business forty-two years and having expanded the collectibles in this guide from 5,000 to over 16,000, I am convinced the marketplace for popular culture collectibles is just emerging from its formative stage. The perspective of four decades has now clearly established the rarity of most objects and the appearance of these objects in the marketplace combined with their degree of appeal to collectors has determined the current values shown in this book. With help in a few special categories, the values are my considered opinion based on my historical view of an object's availability and popularity with collectors as well as thousands and thousands of actual sales.

It has fascinated me to see the exponential growth of interest in popular culture collectibles over the past four decades. First and foremost in growth, among the many collecting areas Hake's Americana & Collectibles Auctions serves, has been toys - a category we broadly define as entertainments and playthings in our auc-

1943 Batman Paper Mask.

tions, books and at Geppi Entertainment Museum. Numerous categories of toy collecting represented by only a handful of collectors when I began my auctions are now matured into nationwide clubs with their own reference books, conventions, publications and networks of specialized collectors and dealers. This infrastructure is the necessary bedrock of any sustainable broadly-collected specialty as it promotes vital communication among members, attracts enthusiastic new members and provides a stable marketplace. Toy collecting - be it mechanical banks, lunch boxes or wind-ups - has proven its appeal over many decades, among all age groups and flourished in a multitude of consumer society environments. As long as people appreciate objects with high levels of ingenuity, craftsmanship and emotional appeal, toys will be in the forefront of collecting. This fact will be recognized more and more in the future as today's mass media promotes the concepts of collecting to still large but increasingly segmented and targeted audiences.

Hobbies like collecting change our moods and routines. Time spent on a hobby is like exercise for the brain area called the *nucleus accumbens* which controls how we feel about life. Engaging in a hobby improves self-esteem, counters our tendency to feel defined by our job and benefits us both personally and professionally according to recent research. Two great attractions that make popular culture collecting an ideal hobby are the range of values from low to high and the fascinating options for specialization.

In the 1970s and 1980s, many people became popular culture collectors or dealers lured by what grandly may be called an asymmetry of knowledge. In other words, there was a relative absence of knowledge among the public that frequently resulted in a bargain for the buyer. This began to gradually change in the 1990s as publicity about pop culture collectible values, price guides and finally the internet proliferated. The original multi-link chain from the grass roots yard sale up to the most astute or high paying dealer and/or collector has now been condensed to typically just several links.

In fact, we are well past the days of greatest supply.There are less bargains and less new discoveries of vintage popular culture collectibles in the grass roots of America. However, emphatically, it is not true that there are less bargains overall. With the maturing of the marketplace comes the maturing of the original popular culture collectors of the late 1960s and 1970s. Today, much of the best material is coming out of collections formed then. The objects appear briefly on the auction block and most often immediately disappear into private collections where they may stay for the next forty to fifty years.The marketplace passes judgement on this parade, aided by books such as this, and sorts out the good, better and best.

Among pre-1960s pop culture collectibles, while there is limited demand for the most common objects in average condition that changes when an example in exceptional condition is offered and frequently yields a record price. Where rare objects are concerned, if condition isn't a detriment, record prices are commonplace. Yet these very record prices are most probably bargains in disguise. A casual look at the high ticket markets for fine art, antiques, coins and select merchanical banks will show that for their rarity and broadly recognized appeal, so many popular culture collectibles are indeed relatively under valued and hold great potential for appreciation.

As more collections are formed while at the same time the fresh supply of newly found artifacts decreases, the value of in-demand objects in the good, fine and near mint conditions we evaluate have risen substantially. Accordingly, the collector must decide for himself the balance between desirability, condition and price. If investment potential is part of the collecting rationale, then condition must be a prime consideration. As values of popular culture collectibles increase, the importance of accurate grading also increases. As a final word of advice to both sellers and buyers, quality (condition, demand and rarity) must justify the price applied to an object. In using this book, if an object is near mint "but" - it's not really near mint and that's not the guide price to focus on. That said, I urge readers to spend a few minutes on the following "Guide Values" section and our "Definitions: Good, Fine, Near Mint" as they apply to collectibles made of various materials.

All of us involved in producing this book hope you find it enjoyable and useful.

Ted Hake
March 2008

This guide is comprised of 461 categories in broad collecting specialties such as advertising characters, cereal companies, comic book, comic strip and cartoon characters, movies, music, pulps, sports, radio and television. The arrangement is alphabetical order by name of the character, company, person, product, program or publication. The most basic name form is used. This is particularly true for characters who often appear in multiple mediums with a variety of titles. For example, Radio Orphan Annie items are listed under the basic proper name Little Orphan Annie.

Each category is introduced with a history of the subject. The individual items are photo-illustrated and designated with a three letter abbreviation of the category name plus a sequential item number. These item numbers will change with each new edition of the guide to accommodate additions to each section while still maintaining chronological listings.

The photo caption code matches the code accompanying that item's description. Quotation marks in the item's title denote words actually appearing on the item. Where possible, the exact name used by the item's sponsor or maker is used in the title, although these words are not in quotations unless they actually appear on the item.

The rare 1940 Lone Ranger Prototype Secret Compartment Ring is just one of the many fascinating toy rings given away by companies to attract children to their products.

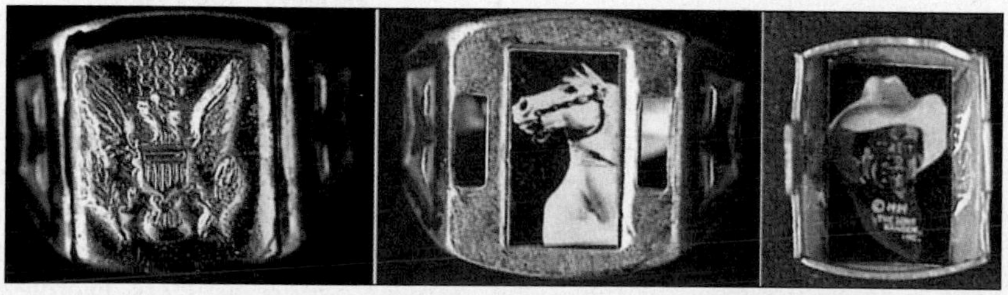

Date information is followed by the name of the sponsor issuer, if known, for the majority of the premium toys. However, this information is not listed for certain categories where it would merely be redundant. For example, Cracker Jack items are all issued by Cracker Jack and Ovaltine issued all Captain Midnight premiums between 1941-1989, with a few exceptions which are specified. In categories where sponsors are not noted, refer to the historical information introducing that category. Some items saw use both as store items and premiums. Where known, this type of information is included in the description.

Following the date and sponsor information, any descriptive text necessary to explain the item is included. The description ends with three values for the item in Good, Fine and Near Mint condition with a few exceptions where Near Mint examples do not exist. Also, items from the last two decades may have only a single value shown for Near Mint condition. It is most important to read the section defining these condition terms to properly understand and use the values specified for each item.

Buck Rogers Diecut Standup Store Display promoting both the character and also radio sponsor Popsicle from 1939.

TYPES OF ITEMS

Character toys are made from a diverse universe of materials and take an astonishing variety of forms from action figures to yo-yos (see types of items listing on pages 72-73).

Webster's New World Dictionary defines a toy as "any article to play with, especially playthings for children." Under this broad definition, we include both store-bought toys as well as those distributed as premiums by a sponsor. Premium toys may be included with product packaging or obtained by mail, sometimes requiring a small payment and/or proof of purchase of the sponsor's product.

The terms "character" and "comic" are also broadly defined. We include the vast range of entertainment-related subjects and personalities – both actual and created – that range from the Beatles to Superman.

The vast majority of catalogued items are of American origin. A few exceptions include *Doctor Who*,

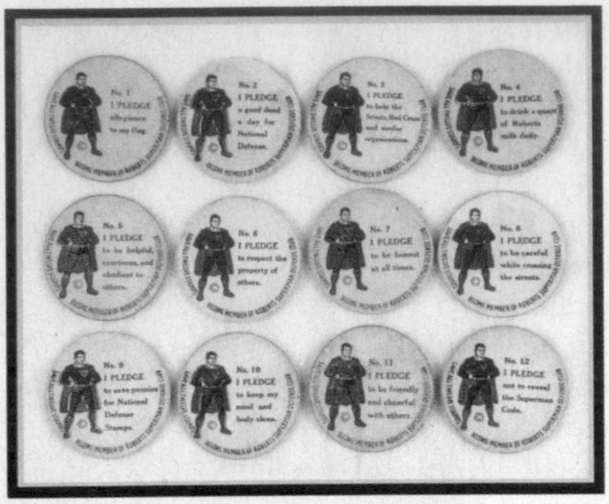

A complete set of Superman Defense Club Milk Bottle Lids from 1941. The twelve numbered lids each featured a "pledge" such as "I pledge not to reveal the Superman code."

with much merchandise originating in Great Britain, pinbacks from the 1960s and earlier produced in Australia, Canada and Great Britain for characters and programs originating in America, and foreign-produced items under authorized U.S. copyright such as 1930s character bisque figures made in Germany and Japan.

While *Guide* listings are comprehensive, they are selective and not all inclusive. Objects not included are not necessarily either common or rare.

DATING

Entries are dated as exactly as possible depending on available information and research. Most often the copyright date is used when this is obviously consistent with the date of issue. Other sources include toy catalogues, newspaper or comic book advertisements and other period sources. When objects are available over several years, the earliest known date is specified.

If an exact year is unknown, the item is dated to an approximate year or known exact decade. When a specific year or decade is open to question, the date is listed with the abbreviation c. for circa.

Within each category, the objects are listed chronologically by the earliest specific year, followed by the earliest approximated year, followed by those dated exactly or approximately to the earliest decade. The sequence repeats itself for each successive decade.

ABBREVIATIONS

Three abbreviations are used very frequently for recurring descriptive purposes:

c. = circa. An approximate date.

cello. = celluloid. Usually referring to a pinback button or other small collectible having a protective covering of this substance. The term and abbreviation are also used for convenience to indicate similar latter day substances, such as acetate or thin plastic, which gradually replaced the use of flammable celluloid coverings after World War II.

litho. = lithographed process. Usually referring to a pinback button or other small collectible with the design printed directly on metal, usually tin, rather than "cello" version wherein the design is printed on paper with a celluloid protective covering.

ADDITIONAL ABBREVIATIONS:

ABC = American Broadcasting Companies Inc.

BLB = Big Little Book series by Whitman Publishing Co.

BTLB = Better Little Book series by Whitman Publishing Co.

CBS = Columbia Broadcasting System, Inc.

KFS = King Features Syndicate

K.K. Publications = Kay Kamen Publications

MGM = Metro-Goldwyn-Mayer Studios, Inc.

NBC = National Broadcasting Company

NPP = National Periodical Publications, Inc.

RCA = Radio Corporation of America

WDE = Walt Disney Enterprises

WDP = Walt Disney Productions

SIZES

Many types of items come in standardized and typical sizes. Therefore, sizes are not specified for objects such as Big Little Books, comic books, folders, watches, etc. that match the expected dimensions. Sizes are only specified where it is deemed an important distinguishing factor for objects such as display signs, maps, posters, and standees, and when an item is known in more than one size. For pinback buttons and badges, sizes of two inches or more in diameter are always specified. Sizes are also included for selected pinbacks less than two inches in diameter.

GUIDE VALUES

Values in this guide are estimations of retail prices for each item in Good, Fine and Near Mint condition. The prices stated are based on the author's 42 years experience in auctioning and selling all types of popular culture artifacts. Factored in are results from other auctions, sales lists, show prices, transactions between individuals and advice from collectors and dealers with expertise in certain specialties.

Few vintage items are still truly Mint, so the highest grade listed for each item is Near Mint. However, there are those rare exceptions. Strictly Mint items with no traces of wear might command 25% or even more than the listed Near Mint value. Those items falling between the grades specified are termed Very Good or Very Fine. A reasonable approximation of value for these items would be the mid-point value between Good and Fine or Fine and Near Mint.

Original packaging, particularly if illustrated and appealing in design, is highly valued by many collectors. This applies usually to toys of a three-dimensional nature and includes mail order premiums. While premium mailer envelopes and boxes are not usually illustrated, the package often included an instruction sheet, order form or premium catalogue; collectors do consider these important. Thus, a wind-up toy illustrated original box or a "complete" premium package may add 50%-100% to the value of the basic toy. In many cases, the price guide evaluations take these options into account and specify separate values for toy and box or premiums complete as issued in mailer and Near Mint.

Jackie Robinson 1950 Metal Bust Bank was offered as a premium in Jackie Robinson comic books.

DEFINITIONS: GOOD, FINE, NEAR MINT

Value has three primary determining factors: rarity, demand and condition. Of these, condition is paramount. If a very rare, very desirable item has a significant condition problem, a large part of the potential buyer universe ceases to exist.

Accurately assessing an item's condition is a crucial step in using the Good, Fine and Near Mint prices specified in this guide. For any given item, from the years prior to collector issues intended to be preserved, the percentage of items still surviving in Near Mint condition is likely to be very small. This low supply coupled with collector demand for outstanding condition accounts for the disproportionately high values assigned to Near Mint examples versus those in Fine or Good. To correctly compare prices encountered in the marketplace with the values specified in this guide, the following condition definitions must be understood and applied. Condition issues vary according to an item's basic materials and those materials generally fall into the following four categories.

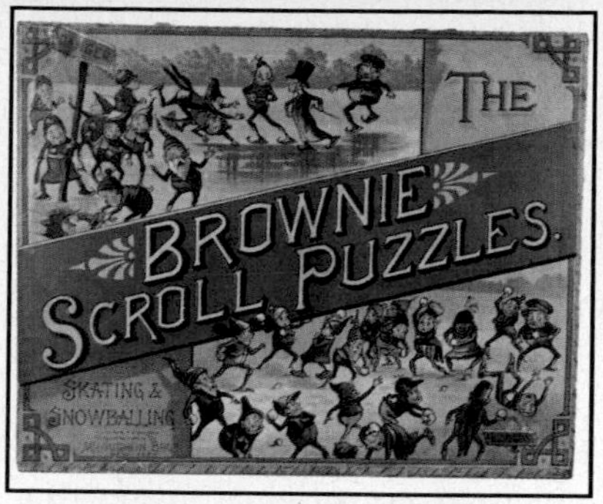

Brownie Scroll Puzzles Box from the 1890s. Pop culture collectibles will exhibit different forms of wear depending on the materials used in their construction.

PAPER/CARDBOARD

NEAR MINT: Fresh, bright original crisply-inked appearance with only the slightest perceptible evidence of wear, soil, fade or creases. The item should lay flat, corners must be close to perfectly square and any staples must be rust-free.

FINE: An above average example with attractive appearance but moderately noticeable aging or wear including: small creases and a few small edge tears; lightly worn corners; minimal browning, yellowing, dust or soiling; light staple rust but no stain on surrounding areas; no more than a few tiny paper flakes missing. Small tears repaired on blank reverse side are generally acceptable if the front image is not badly affected.

GOOD: A complete item with no more than a few small pieces missing. Although showing obvious aging, accumulated flaws such as creases, tears, dust and other soiling, repairs, insect damage, mildew, and brittleness must not combine to render the item unsound and too unattractive for display.

METAL

NEAR MINT: Item retains 90% or more of its original bright finish metallic luster as well as any accent coloring on the lettering or design.

Badges must have the original pin intact and rings must have near perfect circular bands. Any small areas missing original luster must be free of rust, corrosion, dark tarnish or any other defect that stands out enough to render the naked eye appearance of the piece less than almost perfect.

FINE: An average item with moderate wear to original luster but should retain at least 50%. There may be small, isolated areas with pinpoint corrosion spotting, tarnish or similar evidences of aging. Badges must have the original pin, although perhaps slightly bent, and rings must have bands with no worse than minor bends. Although general wear does show, the item retains an overall attractive appearance with noticeable luster.

GOOD: A well-used or aged item missing nearly all luster and color accents. Badges may have a replaced pin and ring bands may be distorted or obviously reshaped. There may be moderate but not totally defacing evidence of bends, dents, scratches, corrosion, etc. Aside from a replaced pin, completeness is still essential.

CELLULOID OR LITHOGRAPHED TIN PINBACK BUTTONS

NEAR MINT: Both celluloid and lithographed tin pinbacks retain the original, bright appearance without visual defects. For celluloid, this means the total absence of staining (known as foxing to button collectors). There can be no apparent surface scratches when the button is viewed directly; although when viewed at an angle in reflected light, there may be a few very shallow and small hairline marks on the celluloid surface. The celluloid covering must be totally intact with no splits, even on the reverse where the celluloid covering is folded under the collet. Lithographed tin buttons may have no more than two or three missing pinpoint-size dots of color and no visible scratches. Even in Near Mint condition, a button image noticeably off-center, as made, reduces desirability and therefore value to some price below Near Mint depending on the severity of the off-centering.

FINE: Both styles of buttons may have a few apparent scattered small scratches. Some minor flattening or a tiny dent noticeable to the touch, but not visually, is also acceptable. Celluloids may have a very minimal amount of age spotting or moisture stain, largely confined to the rim area, not distracting from the graphics and not dark in color. There may be a small celluloid split on the reverse by the collet, but the celluloid covering must still lay flat enough not to cause a noticeable bump on the side edge. Lithographed tin buttons may have only the slightest traces of paint roughness, or actual rust, visible on the front. A variation of the celluloid pinback is the celluloid covered pocket mirror which holds a glass mirror on the reverse rather than a fastener pin. Condition definitions for pocket mirrors match those for celluloid buttons except a fine condition item may have a clouded or smoked mirror and some streaks of missing silvering. A cracked mirror typically reduces desirability to the level of Good condition.

GOOD: Celluloid pinbacks may have moderately dark spotting or moisture stain not exceeding 25% of the surface area. There could be some slight evidence of color fade, a small nick on the front celluloid, or a small celluloid split by the reverse collet causing a small edge bump. Dark extensive stain, deep or numerous scratches and extensive crazing of the celluloid covering each render the button to a condition status of less than Good and essentially unsalable. Lithographed tin buttons must retain strong color and be at least 75% free of noticeable surface wear or they too fall into the likely unsalable range.

Large Celluloid Jointed Betty Boop Figure c. 1935. Celluloid items are difficult to locate in high-grade due to the fragile nature of the material.

OTHER MATERIALS

(Ceramic, Glass, Wood, Fabric, Composition, Rubber, Plastic, Vinyl, Etc.)

NEAR MINT: Regardless of the substance, the item retains its fresh, original appearance and condition without defect. Only the slightest traces of visually non-distracting wear are acceptable.

FINE: Each material has its inherent weakness in withstanding age, typical use or actual abuse.

Ceramic, porcelain, china, bisque

and other similar clay-based objects are susceptible to edge chips. These are acceptable if minimal. Glazed items very typically develop hairline crazing not considered a flaw unless hairlines have also darkened.

Glass is fragile and obviously susceptible to missing chips, flakes or hairline fractures but acceptable in modest quantity.

Wood items, as well as the faithful likeness composition wood, generally withstand aging and use well. Small stress fractures or a few small missing flakes are acceptable if the overall integrity of the item is not affected.

Fabric easily suffers from weave splits or snags plus stain spots are frequently indelible. Weaving breaks are generally acceptable in limited numbers but fabric holes are not. Stains may not exceed a small area and only a blush of color change.

Composition items, typically dolls or figurines, tend to acquire hairline cracks of the thin surface coating. This is commonly expected and normally acceptable to the point of obvious severity. Color loss should not exceed 20% and not involve critical facial details.

Rubber items, either of solid or hollow variety, tend to lose original pliability and evolve into a rigid hardness that frequently results in a warped or deformed appearance. Some degree of original flexibility is preferred or at least minimal distortion.

Plastic and vinyl items have a tendency to split at areas of high stress or frequent use. This is frequently expected and excused by collectors up to the point of distracting from overall appearance or function.

GOOD: Items of any material are expected to be complete and/or functional. Obvious wear is noticeable, but the item retains its structural soundness. Wear or damage must not exceed the lower limits of being reasonably attractive for display purposes.

COLLECTING MAKES SENSE

Much research and speculation on why people collect is in print. Here are a few thoughts on a related but different subject - why collecting in general and collecting toys and related pop culture objects in particular makes sense.

As we proceed through our lives, we all acquire a multitude of objects. Indeed, the acquisition of objects is one of the most basic human traits. Our cave men ancestors who put forth the effort to acquire that extra measure of food, fur, firewood, weapons and tools were the ones likely to survive the longest.

In today's society, most of us rather quickly and easily acquire the necessities for day-to-day living. Many of us have the time, energy, money and intellectual curiosity to acquire objects beyond the necessities. We are able to acquire objects that bring us a sense of satisfaction and enjoyment. Our lifetime accumulations make us all collectors in a general sense, but when we seek out, acquire and appreciate a particular type of object we have a focus, the hallmark of a true collector.

So why does collecting make sense? Many interests and pursuits share with collecting a wide range of psychological and emotional benefits. These may include simply providing a means of relaxation to offering opportunities for communication and interaction with people who share a common interest. The pursuits which bring these benefits often require financial expenditures. The bonus astute collectors realize is that rather than dissipating financial resources, they are actually increasing their wealth over time.

Since the mid-1960s, the buying and selling of new and old collectibles has grown to a multi-billion dollar industry. This is rather amazing considering that *Webster's New World Dictionary* defines "collectible" as: "any of a class of old things, but not antiques, that people collect as a hobby, specifically a thing of no great intrinsic value."

Collectors spending billions on

When it comes to collecting rare items, collectors sometimes need to have super strength and patience to locate key pieces. This 6' tall 1950 Superman Movie Standee would be a museum quality addition to any collection.

things "of no great intrinsic value" must have clear goals in mind and be rewarded with benefits or this economic activity would never have grown to its present level. If one's goals are solely financial, that person is more properly termed an investor rather than a collector. For collectors, financial benefits are often an important consideration and a positive bonus, but there are more important considerations.

Collectors feel passionate about the objects they seek and search for them with enthusiasm. The collector identifies with those objects emotionally. There is recognition intellectually of an item's historical importance or appreciation of its physical qualities. Sometimes, as with toy collecting, the emotional connection with objects is intensely personal.

Toys are most closely associated with childhood. Our memories of childhood, both the trials and triumphs, stay with us until our demise. Some say, in a negative way, that toy collectors are out to recapture their youth. The reality is that toy collectors never lost their youth. Toys are collected as a way to keep us in touch with our youth. Toy collections bring our past experiences to life in a physical form to be sensed visually and tactically and thus enhancing precious memories.

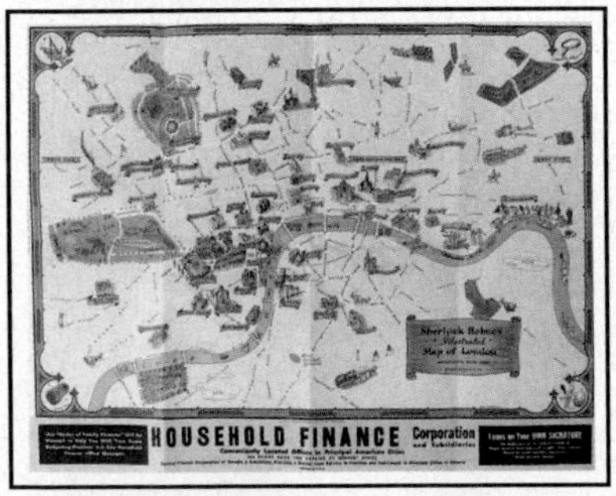

It is best to map out a strategy when deciding what to collect. This rare 1930s Sherlock Holmes map of London is highly desired by collectors.

Developing all the nuances of astute collecting and the evolution of a collector's focus takes time. The journey is rewarding in many ways. In contrast to our daily obligations and concerns, collecting is an adventure to be savored, a way to express and enjoy our passions. It makes sense.

FINDING IT

Even if a collector is precisely focused on what objects will be collected, he needs a framework of knowledge against which potential acquisitions may be evaluated. Honing these skills is an evolving process which should be an enjoyable journey of appreciation. The goal is to absorb the knowledge and develop the techniques that allow the collector to evaluate objects and recognize quality when it presents itself.

The resources to acquire this knowledge framework are both plentiful, and with the Internet, more accessible than ever. For toy collectors there are numerous museums, reference books such as this one covering a multitude of specialties to those on precisely defined subjects and clubs devoted to specific collectibles or favorite characters and personalities.

Many collector clubs publish member rosters and hold conventions. Find and meet collectors in the local area who share similar interests and travel to conventions, shows and in-person auctions. Observing and participating are the building blocks of an educated collector. An excellent source to learn about happenings in the world of vintage toys, along with new issues for collectors, is *Scoop!*, a free weekly e-newsletter sponsored by the publisher of this book, Gemstone Publishing (on the web at **http://scoop.diamondgalleries.com**).

When it comes to finding items, newer collectors who don't thoroughly know their items of interest are advised to know their dealer. Unlike Internet auction sites where both the authenticity and condition of items may be misrepresented, innocently or with malice, there are many nationally known sources for guaranteed authentic material such as Hake's Americana & Collectibles, Diamond International Galleries, Morphy Auctions and the dealers advertising in this guide.

As a collector's knowledge and confidence in his focus area grows, he may safely expand his searches for items with less concern about overpaying or purchasing reproductions. Although the odds of a significant find vary greatly, potential sources include garage sales, newspaper want ads, local auctions, single owner or multi-dealer retail stores, general or specialized show venues, Internet auction sites, and in person or catalogue/phone/Internet bidding specialized auctions with a field of nationwide or even worldwide bidders.

If the venue is an auction, some beforehand preparation is recommended. Is authenticity guaranteed or are items sold "buyer beware?" Know the terms of sale including bidding increments, applicable buyer's premium and returns policy. If at all possible, personally inspect items of interest. If that isn't possible, ask condition questions in advance or deal with auctioneers whose condition statements are known to be accurate and trustworthy. Decide in advance what each item of interest is worth to you. One approach is to pick an amount you would be happy to pay and a second amount as the maximum you are willing to pay. Remember to calculate and add in any buyer's premium the auction may require. Do not exceed your maximum without careful consideration. There are, however, those special items. Will the extra bid and money paid now to acquire a special piece have much future significance or will that be overshadowed by regret for a missed opportunity? The answer is part of the process of knowing ourselves and becoming astute collectors.

Tarzan Radio Club/Drink More Milk Brass Badge, 1936. It can be a jungle out there when trying to hunt down items. Collectors today have the advantage of being able to purchase items in person, at auctions, and online.

BUYING IT

When a purchase is made, the collector is putting his knowledge and instincts to the test. He is operating in a marketplace created by people with a shared interest in owning a particular object.

For vintage collectibles, as opposed to new creations designed for collector appeal, the rules of supply and demand are important, but actually secondary to the critical third factor of condition.

Supply, or rarity, is an assessment of availability. Vintage collectibles, for a variety of reasons, were produced in finite quantities and have various survival rates. Often, rarity is further increased as surviving examples enter collections to be held long-term. For example, many collections assembled in the 1960s and 1970s era of greater availability were brought to market in the 1990s and purchased by new owners who may hold them for a quarter century or longer.

Demand is an assessment of popular appeal. Levels of interest may vary over time and in some narrow specialties even be influenced by the actions of just a few individual collectors. The important issue for a person selecting a collecting focus is to find a subject with a demand level that results in a value structure comfortably in tune with available finances. Collecting goals must realistically match collecting resources. In establishing values, condition is the third and frequently most influential critical consideration. Rarity and demand being equal, an item with a significant condition problem results in the elimination of a large percentage of the potential buyers. An item in exceptionally choice Near Mint or Mint condition may add to the universe of potential buyers.

There are numerous additional factors that influence an item's perceived value. Among these are considerations of historical importance, provenance, physical size, aesthetic qualities and subject qualities that may attract interest from several distinct groups of collectors. On top of this, in auctions the unknown emotional motivations of competing bidders provide the wild card factor.

When the buying decision is imminent, reflect on whether the item conforms to your collecting focus. Does it grab your attention, pique your interest, spark your enthusiasm? Apply brutal, rigorous standards. You are taking one of many steps that together are going to play a big role in determining the future potential value of your collection. Try to buy the best example that fits your budget or that will likely ever present itself for purchase. Step up for important pieces. A few dollars "too much" now may quickly become irrelevant in terms of satisfaction and potential growth in value.

Restored items require the collector to balance many factors. How desirable do you find this item? Will an unrestored example likely be encountered soon? Is the restoration done professionally and not obvious? Is the piece sufficiently discounted in relation to an undamaged example? If the

Pinocchio Victor Record Button, 1940. When it comes to pop culture collectibles, there are items of every shape and size to fit any space or wallet.

answers fit your goals and standards, make the purchase.

Restoration takes many forms depending on the material substance of the object. From mending a box corner split, to filling in a rim flake, to the near total restoration of a lithographed tin image – nearly all things are possible for the professional restorer. The processes require skill, practice, and the correct materials. Many items are made worse, rather than better, by over-confident amateurs. Responsible sellers must volunteer the degree of restoration to potential buyers.

REPRODUCTIONS AND FANTASIES

Not all reproductions are created equally. Licensed or properly authorized reproductions, indelibly marked as such, allow people to own wonderful objects at reasonable prices. Unfortunately, other reproductions are created by people who deceive for profit. The collector's best defense is acquiring knowledge about a chosen specialty and patronizing dealers and auction houses who unconditionally guarantee their merchandise as authentic. Surprisingly, many big names in the auction world do not guarantee authenticity. Read the fine print prior to participating as a bidder.

Deceptive items may be broadly classified as fantasies or reproductions. In the mid-1970s, Hake's began using the term fantasy item to signify deceptive objects never licensed by the copyright owner, or an item that did not even exist during the time period that produced original and authorized collectibles. Fantasy collectibles are produced after the fact, typically when a person, character, movie, etc. becomes the subject of collector interest. The people making fantasy items intend them to appeal to, or intentionally defraud, collectors unaware of the item's unauthorized status and relative newness. Frequently such items bear illegitimate copyright notices and spurious dates. For most collecting specialties there are relatively few fantasy items and these can be identified easily. Fantasy items are most prevalent among Beatles collectibles, but there are Beatles specialty guides that warn collectors away from these deceptions.

Reproductions, undated and unmarked as such, will undoubtedly be encountered by active collectors. Unlike a fantasy item, the reproduction has its original, authentic counterpart. In some circumstances, a questionable item may be compared directly to a known original to determine any difference. Producing reproductions doesn't require ethics, but it does require some care and skill to produce a copy with most if not all of the distinguishing features of the original. Careful observation of originals, some appreciation of the materials and manufacturing techniques in use when the original was produced and a healthy degree of skepticism are potent weapons against reproductions. Copied items very seldom match all the characteristics of the original. If any doubts surface, postpone the purchase and get a second opinion, or at least obtain a written receipt with the seller's money-back guarantee of authenticity.

Here are a few basic warnings and tips to keep in mind regarding reproductions:

Tin Signs – Many authentic signs have been reproduced and many fantasy signs created. The reproductions are frequently executed

Four different fantasy buttons imply 1930s origin but none of these designs existed before the mid-1970s.

Star Wars Darth Vader Action Figure, 1978. For a collector, knowledge is power. Strengthen yourself with information and look out for the "Dark Side" which includes reproductions and fantasy items.

in a size different than the originals. Buyers need personal expertise or the guarantee of a reputable dealer knowledgeable in this area.

Framed Items - Covering an item with glass, or even shrink wrap, may hide a multitude of problems. A generous layer of grime or highly reflective glare may obscure the image enough to hide what proves to be a photocopy, color laser copy or printed reproduction.

Printed Items - Small single sheet paper items and cards are easy to reproduce. Color copies are particularly deceptive, but detectable on close inspection. Sometimes this technology is put to use to reproduce wrist or pocket watch dials as well as other deceptions. Both color and black/white reproductions of paper items sometimes reproduce small tears, creases or other flaws on the paper of the original item being copied. These defects may show on the copy while the paper used to produce the copy is actually not torn, not creased or otherwise flawed.

Pinback Buttons - Very few buttons were made in both celluloid and lithographed tin varieties. However, a small number of lithographed tin buttons have been reproduced as celluloids. Nearly all buttons described in this guide as lithographed tin (litho.) should be regarded with much suspicion if encountered as a celluloid version. Most button reproductions are celluloid copies made by photographing celluloid originals. This sometimes results in a slightly blurred appearance, sometimes the dot screen fills in on the reproduction and sometimes the covering of thin acetate is noticeably different than the celluloid of the 1950s and earlier. A shiny metal back does not prove much. The metal used now may quickly oxidize while the metal used in the 1960s and earlier may retain its shine. The presence or absence of a "union bug" does not determine authenticity.

To see many of the character buttons that have been reproduced, side by side with authentic examples, I recommend the website of collector Mark Lansdown (www.marklansdown.com/pinbacks). The site is devoted to vintage comic character buttons. In early 2006, Mark created a most helpful visual guide, which includes numerous fantasy buttons, so that collectors may easily see differences between authentic and copied buttons.

Metal Badges - These are more costly to copy than paper items or buttons but a limited number have been subject to reproduction. These are typically very exact copies of the front image. However, most originals had a soldered bar pin on the reverse while most reproductions feature a small oval metal plate joined to the badge with two small raised areas used to anchor the bottom bar of the pin to the oval plate. Nearly all badges with this style pin and plate are reproductions issued beginning around 1990.

Reproductions and fantasies are an annoying aspect of nearly all hobbies, but not cause for despair. In the normal course of enjoying and learning about a particular specialization, the ability to discern the small number of deceptive items is acquired almost automatically. Just proceed with a bit of caution at the outset and rely on fellow collectors

Obverses and reverses of the real and reproduction 1930s "Babe Ruth Boys Club" member badge from Esso gasoline. The original is on the left. On the right, note the oval back plate holding the pin on the reproduction. This oval plate style pin is a red flag to beware. Badges with this oval plate are almost certainly reproductions.

Genung's Store Advertising Button With Dick Tracy/Little Orphan Annie, 1930s. Classic multi-media pop culture characters never go out of fashion and stand the test of time.

for advice concerning reputable dealers.

TAKING CARE OF IT

When a collectible is acquired, the collector becomes its custodian, responsible for its well being. This is not much of a burden and in fact should be enjoyed, but there are some basic maintenance principles to apply.

First, remove any adhesive price tags as quickly as possible. The longer these are in place the more firmly they adhere. Also, an inked price may bleed through the tag and stain the item. In most cases, a few drops of adhesive solvent will do the item no harm. Let the solvent do its work for a few seconds and usually the tag will then easily lift off without taking along surface paper or paint.

If the seller marked the item with a price in pencil, it may be left alone or erased. Above all, don't

The Day The Earth Stood Still 5'Tall Movie Standee, 1951. Large oversized items are rare partly due to their size and the difficulty of proper storage. This is a factor not only in their survival rate, but also their value.

write the purchase price on the item. Record keeping should be done in a notebook or on the item's holder, not on the item itself.

Mylar bags are recommended for paper items with acidic paper such as comic books or pulp magazines. Pinbacks may go into glass covered "butterfly" mounts. However, these mounts in a stack create pressure and the glass may adhere to the paint on lithographed tin buttons. If this type of case is used, litho pinbacks should be stored separately in individual holders. Three dimensional objects are best stored on shelves in closed cases to protect them from accumulating dust and particularly tobacco smoke residue.

Collectibles in the home face their greatest threats when stored in attics and basements or any location that receives direct sunlight. Also dangerous to many printed items are fluorescent lights, which may fade colors very quickly. Any extreme - heat, light, moisture, smoke - presents dangers to be avoided. Glue, tape, pen and pencil should never be applied directly on the item. Do nothing to degrade it. Its future value depends in part on the custodial care it receives.

SELLING IT

Once acquired, some collectors abhor the thought of parting with a single object. The collection becomes a fortress with a one-way door. This approach is one extreme, but if it brings satisfaction, it's the correct approach for that collector.

Another approach is to test and fine-tune judgements by periodically entering the marketplace. This concept is particularly worthwhile

Supermen of Canada Felt Patch, 1940s. Although distributed by the thousands, remarkably many popular culture collectibles are today reduced to just several known examples.

for the more seasoned collector whose tastes and sense of appreciation has evolved over time. Being open to "trading up" and culling earlier mistakes will likely be a valuable learning experience and a financial benefit, at least in the long-term.

A collector may stay in touch with the retail marketplace without becoming a seller. This takes time and study, but is easily accomplished by attending shows or reviewing auction results. Entering the marketplace will likely provide different useful insights. Selling venues might include a hobby publication advertisement, taking a table at a show, consigning to an auction, listing items on public Internet auctions, and selling directly to a dealer or another collector.

The potential benefits of the selling experience may include: raising the collection's quality; establishing valuable relationships with dealers, auction houses and other collectors; receiving feedback on just how astute were the original purchases of the items now for sale; and a host of other insights to help continually refine collecting goals and skills.

MARKET REPORT

By John K. Snyder, Jr. & J.C. Vaughn

The market for vintage pop culture artifacts is strong.

Surrounded by the negative-minded economic prognosticators of the old media, that may seem like a bold statement, but the perceived turmoil of 2007 and early 2008 did nothing if not show us the strength we have in today's collectibles market.

While some speculated on dire circumstances in the general economy, the demand for high-end and rare vintage collectibles has seen record prices and increasing liquidity. Consider all the bad news we heard in this period: the subprime mortgage loan upheaval, the devaluation of the dollar, ups and downs in unemployment, the specter of inflation... The anxiety generated by this list and many other worries is utterly palpable to many people, but for all the supposed consensus of alleged experts, these events clearly did not impact our market in a meaningful way.

"Doin' The Howdy Doody With Bob Smith And Howdy Doody" Boxed Wind-Up by Unique Art, 1950s, 6.5" long by 5.5" tall tin litho with litho figures of Buffalo Bob 7" tall and Howdy Doody 8" tall.

In trying to understand why this market has performed so well, it is important to first clearly define what we mean by the term "Vintage Pop Culture Artifacts." A vintage pop culture artifact is an item, now characterized by excellence, maturity, enduring appeal, and scarcity, which was contemporary to and reflective of the lifestyle during the period in which it was produced. As a general rule, this area of study includes pieces that were not specifically created to be collectible but were instead intended to be used. While there are notable exceptions to this, this definition excludes what one might call mass-produced manufactured objects that attempt to meet an assumed demand among the collecting population.

Additionally, it is essential to recognize that a significant portion of the success experienced in this field is due to the fact that getting involved with vintage pop culture is an overwhelmingly positive pursuit. While there are incredible insights into history to be gleaned from the experience, it is first and foremost fun. Unlike bills or taxes, there are no penalties because the collector makes his own decisions. Collecting is a choice, and it is a choice that more and more people have made in recent years.

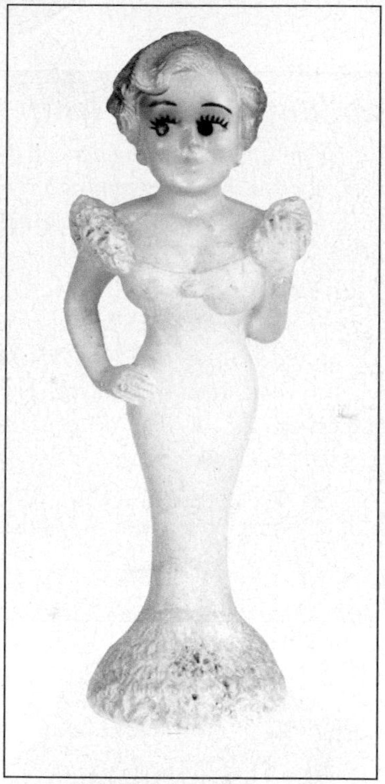

Mae West Painted Chalkware Figure, 14.5" tall, designed by Clarence DeWitt and made by William D. "Bill" Rainwater, 1936.

Market Awareness

There are three important factors that should be considered when evaluating the maturity of a

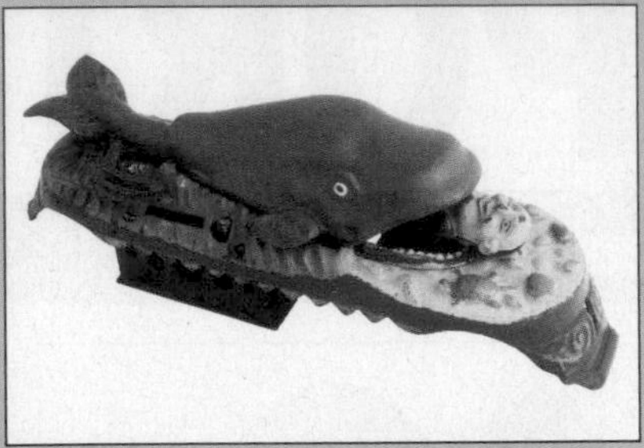

Banking on Cast Iron

The highly anticipated auction of the Steckbeck Mechanical Bank collection generated $7.7 million in a sale held Saturday, October 27, 2007 at Geppi's Entertainment Auctions' Morphy Auctions unit in Denver, Pennsylvania.

Expected to reach at least $5 million, the event's total made it the highest-grossing toy auction of all time. Fourteen banks sold for over $100,000 and the highest-selling bank, "Jonah and the Whale," brought in $414,000.

market: information, timing, and power.

Clearly, in an age when information is king, we have been given the keys to the kingdom. One can access the knowledge of a lifetime of historical study with a few clicks on the internet, and even the old media has taken an interest in what we do beyond the flash of headlines concerning record prices. Whether in print, on the radio or on television, information is readily available on just about every field of endeavor within the collecting community.

Timing, as they say, is everything. For the first time, vintage pop culture artifacts are postured as an alternative way to invest for those who were not previously collectors. While the steps to get to this point have been keenly noted over the years, it's truly staggering to realize how far the market has come in just the last decade or so. The increase in liquidity experienced is now widely accepted.

With the information at our disposal (and the timing, which we will assign to providence), the vintage pop culture market now has the power to communicate the many reasons the various niches and the field as a whole are so attractive.

Much of this has to do with the leadership in the business today. One does not have to ascribe altruistic motives to every single dealer, collector or historian to see that there are some excellent people at work, specialists who have labored long and hard to get the word out, set standards, and promote the hobby. Whether in the form of shows such as *Antiques Roadshow,* specialized internet sites like MegoMuseum.com, or price guides such as this one, there have been untold people working to document what went before so that collectors, dealers, and even simply interested observers can interact with confidence.

It has long been noted that the price of liberty is eternal vigilance, and it seems likely that this is a price we should all be willing to pay for a thriving market as well. We all owe it to ourselves to watch for negative behavior and its possible consequences for what we now enjoy. It seems that we must periodically address the absurd notion that once a generation for whom an item was made passes away, then that item will experience an irreversible decline in its desirability. A number of people, some of them quite sincere, have repeatedly advanced this notion, but their insistence can't make it true.

Setting aside for the moment obvious things like Impressionist paintings or Renaissance manu-

Our Gang Bisque Nodder Pair, circa 1930s, German, "Chubby Chaney" 3.5" tall and "Mary Ann Jackson" 3.25" tall.

Buck Rogers Canadian Club Member. Multi-Colored Button, 1937 (left), the rare Don Winslow Lt. Commander Badge (center), 1" tall, (while the Ensign rank badge is relatively common, this one is slightly larger and very rare), and the rarely seen Sgt. Preston of the Yukon Litho Button (right), c. 1949 by Green Duck, 1 3/8" litho, one of five known specimens.

scripts or cast iron mechanical banks, supply and demand will eventually dismiss this ill-conceived thought over the course of time. It is always wise, though, to challenge it whenever you see it arise. It has a very negative appeal, particularly in times filled with other uncertainties. We don't have to speculate on the motives of those who propagate this line of thinking. Instead, let's look at the basic evidence:

There is no one alive who was an adult in the main period of cast iron mechanical bank production. There are very few people alive who were even infants then either. Yet the demand has gone through the roof in the last decade. Why? Simply put, again, it's supply and demand. There are very few of these items available, regardless of condition. During the same period in which the supply has decreased, the general population has increased more than 300% in the United States alone. Add to that population an eager group of world wide collectors connected by telephone and the internet, and suddenly it's easy to understand why the potential pool of buyers is so much larger today than it ever was.

With today's seemingly insatiable hunger to connect with the past, vintage pop culture artifacts are more documented than ever before. The act of documenting them aids in the development of this awareness, and that awareness in turn can, and frequently does foster the demand.

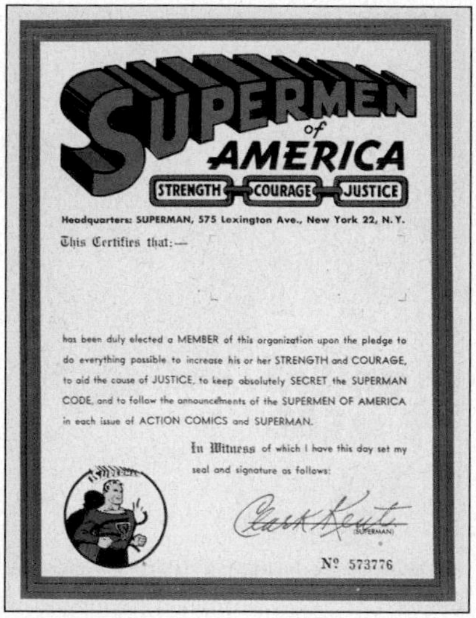

The last issued, 1965 version of the Supermen of America Club Kit Certificate, widely considered to be the smallest production run of the certificates in the series.

Character Time Pieces Keep Ticking

The market for character watches has been in a period of sustained growth for more than five years now, outdistancing fads and flashes-in-the-pan with steady interest and activity.

Key characters are always in demand as are rarely seen items like the Jay Ward Watch (with papers), which sold for $2,574.28 in 2007, but that wasn't anywhere near the top of the value chart.

"A top three list of character time pieces by value would be the 1936 Donald Duck Wristwatch ($12,000 in Near Mint), the 1934 Betty Boop Pocketwatch ($6,500), and the 1935 Popeye Pocketwatch ($6,500)," Toy Collector Magazine reported in late '07. "Rounding out a top ten list would be the 1934 Tom Mix Pocketwatch, the 1935 Tom Mix Wristwatch, the 1933 Mickey Mouse Clock Electric Version, the 1939 Donald Duck Pocketwatch with Mickey Decal, the 1939 Donald Duck Pocketwatch with Plain Metal Back, the 1935 Buck Rogers Pocketwatch, the 1930s Popeye Characters Alarm Clock, the 1949 Babe Ruth Wristwatch with Box, the 1933 Mickey Mouse Ingersoll Wristwatch, the 1940 Superman Wristwatch with Box, and the 1910 Happy Hooligan Painted Figural Clock."

Record-Breaking Mickey & Minnie Mouse

A pair of rare, giant display dolls of Walt Disney's Mickey Mouse and Minnie Mouse has shattered existing records by selling for $151,534.35 (including the buyer's premium) in the Hake's Americana & Collectibles auction that concluded Thursday, September 27, 2007. The 44" tall Mickey and 48" tall Minnie were promotional items for the highly acclaimed Charlotte Clark line of dolls from the early 1930s and were purchased by a private collector and longtime Hake's customer.

Following Mickey's successful introduction as a Clark doll in 1930, Minnie arrived in toy shops the following year. Together, the popular toys were produced in three sizes: 8.5", 13.5" and 18" – and only a significantly limited number of the largest ones were made for display purposes for prominent movie theaters, retail stores and the occasional photo shoot with Walt himself.

Made of stuffed velveteen, Clark's trademark material, Mickey is detailed with four 2" diameter natural pearl buttons, and Minnie wears a silk-like skirt with pantaloons that have lace accents. Each doll has a long, 32" tail.

[For more on the Disneyana market, pick up the current edition of Ted Hake's The Official Price Guide to Disney Collectibles, *Second Edition, now on sale.]*

The Results

Heritage Auction Galleries recorded an unparalleled year in 2007, ringing up nearly $600 million in auctions and sales in various fields. ComicLink broke $200,000 for a single comic book twice. The owners of Metropolis Collectibles believed sufficiently in the market to choose this period to launch ComicConnect, a new auction service. The prestigious antiquarian books house, Bloomsbury Auctions, based in London and Rome, opened their New York location with a series of successful events in rapid succession. Morphy Auctions netted $7.7 million in the sale of the Steckbeck Collection of Mechanical Banks.

Think about the different niches of collecting. How many can you think of that are not doing well?

Disneyana, the subject of our companion volume, *The Official Price Guide To Disney Collectibles* (Second Edition, now on sale) continues to perform spectacularly. Space adventure, particularly in the form of Buck Rogers, Flash Gordon, and the early science fiction television shows like *Space Patrol* and *Tom Corbett, Space Cadet* has attracted and sustained enthusiastic new attention. Classic, long-lived characters such as Popeye, Betty Boop, and superheroes like Batman, Superman and Spider-Man continue to thrive.

Presidential campaign artifact collecting is getting its usual quadrennial spike of new collectors and rare pinback buttons set records in nearly every auction.

Character watches, store displays, song sheets, club kits, statues, original comic book and comic strip art, dolls, rings, vinyl records, theatrical one-sheets, and many other specialties all attract broad interest. Coins and currency collectors set many new records. Aviation character collectibles have continued their revival of the past few years, with Jimmie Allen, Speed Gibson, Jack Armstrong, Hop Harrigan, and Captain Midnight items offering solid performance.

Five years ago in comic shops, one could find only Jeff Mariotte's *Desperadoes* periodically representing the Western genre. Today, though, we have the *Lone Ranger, Zorro, Bat Lash, Jonah Hex* and numerous other specials, one-shots, and mini-series. The enthusiasm for the new product has paralleled sustained interest in vintage pieces featuring other great twentieth century characters such as Hopalong Cassidy and Roy Rogers, and many of the collectors

This 17.5" x 21.5" framed store sign featuring "Hopalong Cassidy's Favorite Hot Cereal/Post's Wheat Meal," 1950s, is just one part of Hoppy's sustained resurgence.

doing the buying are far too young to have ever experienced them in their heyday.

Hoppy in particular should be singled out for comment due to the strength and longevity of his resurgence. Many different products endorsed by Bill Boyd's best known character have broken auction records while introducing new generations to his timeless brand of justice and morality. Certainly it's compelling to find a hero of yesteryear who wouldn't speak to a segregated audience, forcing a show promoter in Atlanta to allow equal access to a performance in a period when he could have just as easily bowed to the conventions of the day.

Older comic books (called the "Platinum Age" in the specialty market) are in a break-out period. *The Brownies* series, *Poor Li'l Mose*, *Yellow Kid*, *Foxy Grandpa*, *Buster Brown*, *Jeremiah Saddlebags*, *Obidiah Oldbuck* and *Bringing Up Father* have seen sometimes surprising growth.

Circa 1941-1943, this 42" long child's necktie has silk-screened "Captain Marvel" image and logo and represents a character who was actually more popular than Superman in that period.

Why We Do What We Do

There are two questions we all should ask ourselves. First, why are you collecting? Second, what legacy are you leaving?

As we've noted in other such market reports, the person who said that time is a constant probably didn't have email. When was the last time one of your friends lamented having too much time on his or her hands? With increasing frequency, we're seeing even our children's schedules regimented by school, organized functions, homework, and play dates. Add to that the chaos, confusion, distresses and demands of the adult world, and it's worse than an epidemic. It's a pandemic of tension, frustration and stress manifested in a struggle which results in the complete inability to make the activities of your life slow down.

Collecting offers us one means to not only slow things down for a moment or two, but to give us perspective on what's good for all of us. It may be one of those things that's so obvious that many of us missed it for years, but family members should be encouraged, whether in your own particular niche or another. Since we have recognized that vintage pop culture artifacts are a major key to understanding general history, shouldn't we take a generational approach to opening its mysteries (and its fun)? It's very easy to let the blind spirit of acquisition accidentally replace the fun-loving life-force that brought us into the

Peanuts Art Continues to Climb Charles Schulz's baseball-themed

Peanuts Art Continues to Climb

Charles Schulz's baseball-themed Peanuts *Sunday page, dated April 10, 1955, broke a record when it realized $113,525 in Heritage Auction Galleries' November 15-16, 2007 auction, continuing the trend of hefty prices for the late creator's originals.*

"Overall, this was a very strong auction for Schulz art, with a total of nine pieces - eight dailies and a Sunday - realizing a total of $279,630. Prices like these are a testament to the enduring popularity of this iconic artist, whose simple, heartfelt vision is still cherished by millions of people worldwide," said Ed Jaster, Vice-President of the Dallas-based firm. Heritage also brought in $77,000 with a selection of Peanuts *art in their August 2-4, 2007 auction.*

A 1954 daily strip in which Charlie Brown and Schroeder commemorate Beethoven's one-hundred-eighty-fourth birthday, sold for $27,738 at R&R Auctions in January 2008. Two months earlier, the August 16, 1966 daily featuring Snoopy as the World War One Flying Ace, realized $43,618

A Sunday page from August 1971 with a baseball theme was a hit at $67,800 at Philip Weiss Auctions, and a "Great Pumpkin" Sunday page from October 1962 brought $62,100 for the same auction house.

Big on Bats and Spiders

ComicLink has offered consistent reports of good times for Spider-Man and Batman. In their October 19, 2007 auction, the CGC-certified White Mountain pedigree copy of Amazing Fantasy #15, graded 9.4, sold for a record $227,000. The price was the highest price to date for which a comic book from the 1960s has ever sold in a public auction. The issue features the first appearance of Spider-Man. The CGC-certified White Mountain pedigree copy of the character's second appearance, Amazing Spider-Man #1, graded 9.6, sold on the site for $150,000, also a record price.

The company also reported the sale of a CGC-certified Batman #1, graded 9.0, for $280,000. The Batman #1 is the second highest price publicly paid for a comic book. Another CGC-certified copy of that issue, this one graded 8.0, sold on the site for $80,000.

game to start with, and a family's involvement is one check against that.

After all, we are at best custodians of these artifacts from another time. How we accept and handle the knowledge we gain and how we share our friendship will say more about us in the end than the quantity or monetary value of our acquisitions. How do we want to be remembered?

Steve Geppi, Ted Hake and the Gemstone Publishing and Hake's Americana & Collectibles staffs, and many other contributors have put a tremendous amount of work into this book, cataloging, describing, writing, editing, designing, proofing, and so on, because we love what we do. We hope you'll enjoy the results.

On the following pages you'll see a representative sampling of top sellers over the past two years in the character collectibles market.

John K. Snyder, Jr. is the President of Geppi's Entertainment Publications & Auctions. J.C. Vaughn is the Executive Editor & Associate Publisher of Gemstone Publishing.

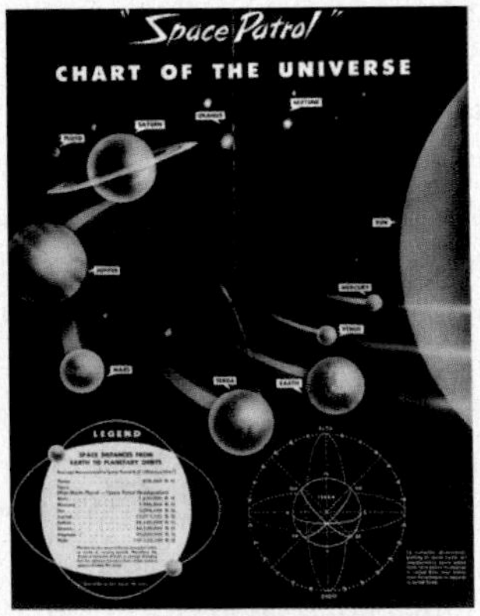

Space Patrol Club Chart of the Universe, 1952.

Information: MEGO-Style

Want to get beyond the record prices being paid today for MEGO action figures? It's easy enough to get caught up in the pursuit of the diminutive treasures, but if you're looking to feed your trivia hunger, then look no further than Benjamin Holcomb's MEGO 8" Super-Heroes: World's Greatest Toys!

The book is just plain awesome. The author spent four years researching and meticulously crafting a comprehensive guide to the figures, the play sets and the company that made them.

It is available through comic book retailers and at the TwoMorrows Publishing website, http://twomorrows.com.

A

Acrobat Cast Iron Bank in near mint condition $24,150
Action Comics #7 CGC certified 4.0......................$23,500
Alex Ross "Kingdom Come" Superman Painting 1996 in excellent condition......$10,120
Alex Schomburg Original Painted Cover Art to The Overstreet Comic Book Price Guide #10 ....$38,837.50
Alex Toth Black Canary Comic Book Page Original Art to Adventure Comics #418 1972 in Exc. $15,181.26
Alien Large Boxed Figure 1979 in excellent condition $650
American Cast Iron Bank in near mint condition $18,400
Astro Boy Sliding Tile Puzzle on Store Card in excellent condition $1106.88

B

Babe Ruth Club Button in near mint condition $200
Babe Ruth Esso Boys Club Badge in very fine condition $125
Babe Ruth Wristwatch in fine condition.......................$500
Batman 1943 March of Dimes - Infantile Paralysis Card in fine condition...............$2,187.30
Batman 1943 Paper Mask in very fine condition $1,800
Batman 1944 Color Transfers in fine condition $700
Batman 1944 Color Transfers in very good/fine condition..$460
Batman 1966 Painted Plaster Figural String Holder in excellent condition...........$2,277
Batman Creamy Peanut Butter Jar 1966 in excellent condition..$460
Batman Bond Bread Shelf Sign in very fine condition $1,016.40
Batman Bat-Phone by Marx in near mint condition with original box $1,254.29
Batman Bend-A-Bitty Bendee Toy On Card in very fine condition.........................$517.50
Batman and Joker Limited Edition 1989 Ken Melton Statues in mint condition $4,600
Batman 1966 Joker Eyes in very fine condition and on card $1,123.32
Batman Joker Bend-A-Bitty Bendee Toy On Card in very fine condition.........................$957.18
Batman Riddler Bend-A-Bitty Bendee Toy on Card in very fine condition $747.50
Batman Rocket Gun by Baravelli in very fine condition ..$1,707.75
Batman Robin Bend-A-Bitty Bendee Toy on Card in very fine condition $919.23
Batman Robin Boxed Hand Puppet in excellent condition..........................$2,760
Batman And Robin Boxed Banks in excellent condition $331.42
Batman 1966 Thermal Blanket in mint condition $757.68
Betty Boop and Her Pals Boxed Bisque Figures in near mint condition $1,075.25
Betty Boop Celluloid Nodder 1930s in fine condition.........................$517.50
Betty Boop c. 1930s Largest Size String Holder in excellent condition $1,927.27
Betty Boop c. 1930s Large Size String Holder in excellent condition..........................$910.80
Betty Boop c. 1930s Smallest Size String Holder in very fine condition $409.86
Big Little Mother Goose Book in very fine/near mint condition $948.75
Bismark Pig Cast Iron Bank in near mint+ condition ..$57,500
Bow-ery Mechanical Bank in near mint condition $86,250
Boy Robbing Birds Nest Bank with Box in near mint condition+ $51,750
Bonzo Bank Verse Variation Tin Bank c.1920s in near mint condition..........................$6,900
Bride of Frankenstein Aurora Model in near mint condition $345

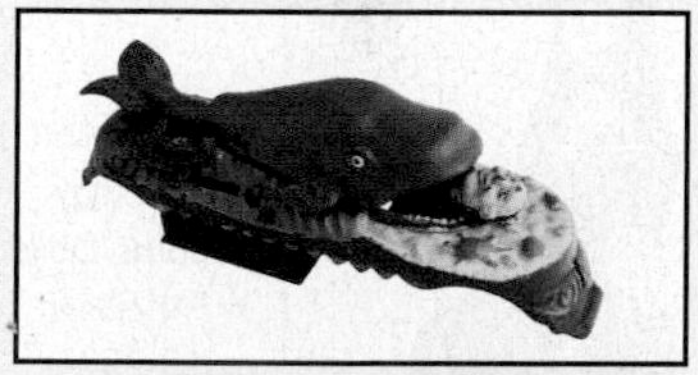

Jonah And The Whale Mechanical Bank in NM+ sells for a record $414,000

1914 Little Nemo Bisque Set in NM realizes $22,412

The Only Known Example of The Bride of Frankenstein D Style One Sheet Poster in FN+ on linen brought $334,600

Bride of Frankenstein 1938 Style D One Sheet in fine condition........................$334,600
Buck Rogers And Wilma 1933 Cocomalt Picture With Letter in fine condition $632.50
Buck Rogers Cocomalt Personalized Initial and Birthstone Premium Ring in excellent condition..........$361.66
Buck Rogers 25th Century Midget Caster Set in fine/ very fine condition $1,499.02
Buck Rogers Liquid Helium Water Pistol by Daisy in fine condition.........................$478.16
Buck Rogers 1935 Pocket Watch with Rare Box and Insert in very fine condition $5,014.24
Buck Rogers Ring of Saturn premium ring in fine condition $425
Buck Rogers 1939 Rocket Police Patrol Tin Wind-Up in very fine condition..........................$1,026
Buck Rogers 1935 School Bag in fine condition $1,802
Buck Rogers Strange World Adventures Club Serial Button near mint+ condition....$3,716.94
Buck Rogers Strange World Adventures Club Serial Button very fine+ condition $1,725
Buck Rogers Wilma Deering Pendant in very fine condition $1,094.23
Bugs Bunny Wristwatch with Box in very fine+ condition......$2,800
Bull and Bear Mechanical Bank in near mint condition $43,125
Bulletman Child's T-Shirt in fine+ condition $325
Buster Brown and Tige Original Art by R.F. Outcault in excellent condition $952
Buster Brown And Tige Painted Plaster String Holder in very fine condition $932.25
Butting Buffalo Mechanical Bank in near mint+ condition ..$37,375

C

Calamity Mechanical Bank with Box in near mint+ condition.........................$69,000
Captain Action Batman Accessory Set in fine condition $599.15
Captain America/Sentinels of Liberty Brass Badge in fine condition $600
Captain America Marx Scooter Friction Toy in Box in very fine+ condition..........................$2,530
Captain Battle Boy's Brigade Button in near mint condition $2,241.03
Captain Battle 1941 Comic Book Promotional Flier/Letter in excellent condition........$1,680
Captain Marvel Belt in very fine condition.......................$616
Captain Marvel Blue Felt Pennant in near mint condition..........$180
Captain Marvel E.Z. Code Finder in very fine condition $354.20
Captain Marvel Family Lead Figure Set c. 1954 by Timpo in excellent condition..........................$862.50
Captain Marvel Felt Club Patch in near mint condition..........$175
Captain Marvel Oil Painting by Artist Marc Swayze in near mint condition $3,516.70
Captain Marvel Rocket Raider Compass Ring Carded c.1946 in near mint condition on a fine condition card...................$2,213
Captain Marvel Rocket Raider Compass Ring in very fine+ $700
Captain Marvel Rocket Raider Compass Ring in very fine....$672
Captain Marvel Skull Cap in very fine condition $500
Captain Marvel Jr. Boxed Kerr Statue in fine condition ..$862.50
Captain Marvel Jr. 1946 Multi Products Figure in very fine condition...........................$1,800
Captain Marvel Jr. Felt Club Patch in very fine condition $225
Captain Midnight Mystic Sun God Ring with Story Folder in excellent condition $575
Captain Video Flying Saucer Ring Complete and Boxed in very fine condition $880.88

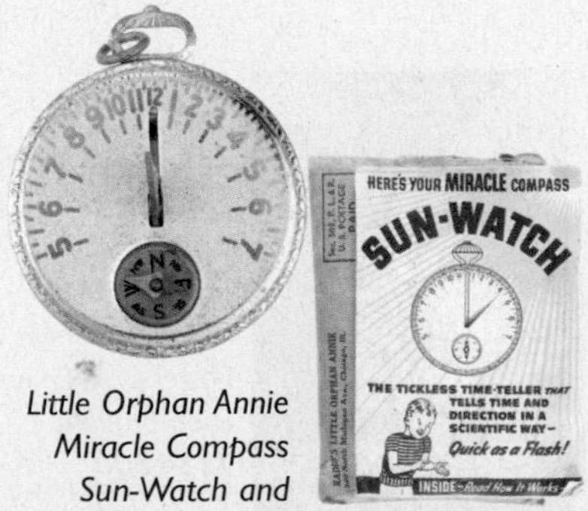

Little Orphan Annie Miracle Compass Sun-Watch and Mailer in NM+ Sold For $1,518

1920 Rare Tarzan Movie Serial Tinted Real Photo Button In Exc. Realized $3,686

Morticia And Wednesday Addams Dolls in FN closed at $3,232

Chandu Club Good Luck Ring c.1934 in NM+ Sold For $2,104.64
Charlie McCarthy Majestic Radio 1940 in very fine condition ..$677.60
Chimpanzee Cast Iron Bank in near mint+ condition ..$92,000
Chinaman In Boat Polychromed Lead Variant Bank c.1880s in near mint condition $103,500
Circus Cast Iron Bank in near mint+ condition $115,000
Clown, Harlequin, and Columbine Cast Iron Mechanical Bank c.1907 in near mint+ condition $103,500

D

Darky and Watermelon Cast Iron Mechanical Bank in near mint condition.......................$195,500
Darky Fisherman Lead Mechanical Bank in near mint condition $287,500
Davy Crockett Tool Kit 1954 in near mint condition..........$574
Davy Crockett Wristwatch by Bradley Time in Original Box in mint condition $1,490.72
DC Comics Promotional Glass in near mint condition..........$200
Devil Dogs Ring in very fine condition $120
Dick Tracy Animated Wristwatch with Rare New Haven Box in fine condition...............$1,092.50
Dick Tracy Aviation/Hostess Cap With Wing Badge Ad in excellent condition.........................$596.55
Dick Tracy Daily Strip Original Art by Chester Gould dated 11-20-1943 in very fine condition...........................$1,380
Dick Tracy Inspector General Badge in fine condition $700
Dick Tracy/Junior Button in near mint condition.............$450
Dick Tracy/Little Orphan Annie Genung's Store Advertising Button in very fine condition $1,150
Dick Tracy Tommy Gun Boxed in excellent condition ..$1,016.40
Dizzy Dean Premium Ring in near mint condition $300
Doc Savage Pulp Subscriber Portrait in fine condition ..$402.50
Don Winslow Squadron of Peace Ring in fine condition $650
Dudley Do-Right Metal Lunch Box With Thermos 1962 in very fine condition $1,574.28

E

Eagle 1941 Comic Club Button in near mint+ condition ..$632.50
E.C. Fan-Addict Club Kit 1954 Complete in excellent condition $1,128.38
Elvis Presley Handkerchief 1956 in very fine condition $300
Elvis Presley I.D. Bracelet in excellent condition $100
Elvis Presley Stitchless Wallet Display Sign in fine condition $846.03

F

Felix the Cat 1930s Scooter Wind-Up in fine condition $1,084.16
Felix Tin Wind-Up with Box c. 1920s in very good/fine condition.........................$929.78
Flash/Fastest Man Alive Button in very fine condition $1,848
Flash Gordon Clicker Tin Gun in very fine condition $550
Flash Gordon's Trip To Mars Linen-Mounted One-Sheet Poster 1938 Chapter 11 in excellent condition...........$4,025
Flash Gordon 1930s Sparkling Rocket Fightership Windup Boxed in excellent condition $2,713.43
Flip the Frog 1920s Mechanical Bank in NM+..................$57,500
Frank Buck 1932 Sterling Silver Movie Ring in near mint condition.........................$577.47
Frank Buck 1932 Silver Luster Movie Ring in near mint condition $325

Alex Schomburg Gouache on Board Painting Commissioned Cover For The Overstreet Comic Book Price Guide #10 in Exc. realized $38,837

War Of The Worlds Cast Metal Model From 1953 in Exc. sold for $9,382

The Shadow Radio Club Button From Kansas in NM brought $3,865

Frank Hawks/Melvin Purvis Secret Scarab Ring in near mint condition $862.50

Friends of the Phantom Shield Badge in very fine condition $225

Fu Manchu "The Shadow of Fu Manchu" Button in excellent condition $125

G

G-8 Battle Aces Pulp Premium Badge in very fine condition $862.50

Gene Autry Aluminum Friendship Ring in very fine condition $225

Gene Autry 1954 Lunchbox with Thermos and Rare Box in near mint/mint condition $1,808.95

Gene Autry Repeating Cap Pistol by Kenton in near mint condition with fine condition box $1,878.80

Gene Autry Six Shooter Wristwatch Boxed in excellent condition $948.64

Gene Autry Watch By Wilane Watch Company Boxed in excellent condition $885.50

Germania Exchange Cast Iron Mechanical Bank in near mint+ condition.......................$149,500

Gertie Animation Original Art by Winsor McCay 1914 in excellent condition...........$4,140

Ghost Rider Rare Premium Mask and Mailer 1953 in near mint condition $3,333.76

G.I. Joe Fire Fly Action Figure AFA 85 ....$2,100

G.I. Joe Snake Eyes Action Figure AFA 80 ....$1,725

G.I. Joe Storm Shadow Action Figure AFA 85 ....$2,247.22

Green Hornet Adventure Club Button in near mint condition $500

Green Hornet Loyalty Club Button in near mint condition $253

Green Hornet Large Oil Painting Set in near mint condition $1,725

Green Hornet Lenore Case Dairy Glass in near mint condition $596.29

Green Hornet Mike Oxford Dairy Glass in near mint condition $677.60

Green Hornet Secret Compartment Glow-In Dark Ring in fine condition.......................$400

Green Lama Club Kit Complete fine/very fine condition $1,120

H

Hal Foster Prince Valiant Original Sunday Page Panel dated 8-29-43 in excellent condition $2,710.40

Happy Hooligan Majolica Cookie Jar in excellent condition $712.10

Herman Munster Hand Puppet in fine/very fine condition $322.58

Hopalong Cassidy 1954 Metal Lunchbox with Thermos in excellent/near mint condition $1,382.94

Horrors of War Promotional Cards Lot of 10 with Over-Print Backs in very fine/excellent condition $2236.08

Horrors of War Yellow Wrapper in near mint condition..........$405

Howdy Doody Cookies Complete Premium Card Set in near mint/mint condition $560

Howdy Doody Flub-A-Dub Marionette in very fine/excellent condition.........................$360.52

Howdy Doody Jack-In-The Box Ring in near mint condition..........$500

Howdy Doody Tricycle Pull Toy in excellent condition......$508.60

Howdy Doody Wood Jointed Doll in fine+ condition $425

Howdy Doody Wrist Watch With Die-Cut Display 1954 in excellent condition $1,671.19

Howdy Doody 1954 Wristwatch by Ingraham with Rare Packaging and Box in near mint condition $1,626.99

Fantastic Four #1 CGC certified 7.5 with off-white to white pages sold for $19,898

1933 King Kong Grauman's Chinese Theatre Program in Exc. realized $4,144

Flip The Frog Bank in NM+ sold for $57,500

I

Incredible Hulk #1
CGC certified 6.5 ....$3,610

J

Jack Armstrong Adventures with The Dragon Talisman Complete Game in excellent condition $1,556.79

Jack Armstrong Secret Whistling Ring with Code Paper and Mailer in mint condition $1,120.53

Jay Ward 1969 Dudley Do-Right Snidely Whiplash Watch with 17 Jewels in mint condition..$695.75

Jiminy Cricket String Holder in excellent condition......$449.07

Joe Louis Portrait Ring in fine condition $650

Joe Louis Ring Promotional Sign in near mint condition $300

Jonah and The Whale Cast Iron Bank in near mint+ condition........................$414,000

Junior Justice Society of America Complete 1942 Club Kit in fine/very fine condition $1,644.50

Junior Justice Society of America 1942 Badge in fine condition $278.30

Junior Justice Society of America 1948 Badge in near mint condition..........................$985.60

Junior Justice Society of America 1945 Patch Variety in very fine condition..........................$573.90

K

Kellogg's Pep Cereal Box Featuring Superman/Pep Pins in fine condition $1,262.79

Kellogg's Pep Pin Comic Character Set in near mint condition $1,322.50

King Kong 1933 Grauman's Chinese Theatre Program $4,144.14

Krazy Kat Ignatz The Mouse Pull Toy in very fine condition $1,048.90

L

Little Lulu Painted Plaster Figural String Holder in excellent condition..........$569.25

Little Nemo Bisque Figurine Set 1914 in near mint condition $22,412.10

Little Nemo Cartoon Poster Winsor McCay Linen-Mounted 1911 in excellent condition $10,350

Little Sammy Sneeze 1905 Sunday Comics Reprint Book in fine condition $3,450

Lone Ranger Deputy Chief Badge in very fine condition $600

Lone Ranger 2004 Glow-In-The-Dark Secret Compartment Ring Lot in excellent condition $575

Lone Ranger Gum Inc. Premium Picture Set in very fine condition $1,530.81

Lone Ranger Merita Salesman's Club Pin 1938 in mint condition $632.50

Lone Ranger Miniature Sterling Silver Figure in excellent condition $575

Lone Ranger Glow-In-The-Dark Secret Compartment Ring Lot 2004 in excellent condition $575

Lone Ranger/Obey My Safety Rules Cardboard Sign in fine condition $580.03

Lone Ranger Punch-Out Book in excellent condition..........$632.50

Lone Ranger Signal Siren Flashlight Boxed with Store Display in excellent condition $1,118.04

M

Mad Magazine Type Character Pinback Button c.1896 Comfort Soap featuring an early version of an Alfred E. Neuman type character in fine condition $587.77

Mama Katzenjammer Cast Iron Bank c.1900s in near mint condition $74,750

Major Matt Mason standee 1967 excellent condition..$5,800

Mary Marvel Boxed Kerr Statue in near mint condition $1,150

Marvel Super-Heroes The Fantastic Four 1967 Jigsaw

1951 Space Patrol/Major Robertson/Ken Mayer Original Uniform from the Show in FN realized $16,675

Supermen of America Contest Prize Ring in FN sold for $6,325

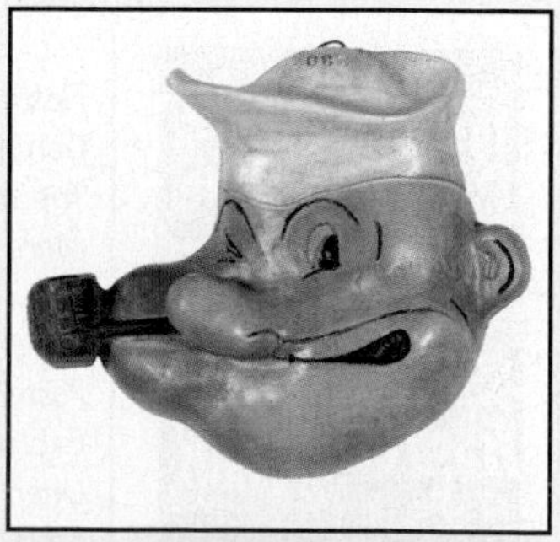

Popeye Figural String Holder in FN brought $4,048

Puzzle in near mint condition $1,265

Mego Aquaman Action Figure AFA 85 ....$1,100

Mego Green Arrow Boxed Action Figure in very fine condition..........................$287.50

Mego Robin Figure on Kresge Card in near mint condition $12,305.70

Mighty Thor Marx Friction Scooter Toy in excellent condition $2,530

Mikado Cast Iron Bank c. 1886 in NM+ $287,500

Morticia and Wednesday Addams Dolls from 1952 in fine condition $3,232.08

N

North Pole Cast Iron Bank c. 1910 in near mint+ condition $149,500

O

Operator #5 Premium Ring in very good condition $5,000

1938 Orphan Annie 1938 Miracle Compass Sun-Watch, Complete in near mint condition $1,320

Orphan Annie Secret Guard Magnifying Ring in near mint condition $2,012.50

Orphan Annie 1940s Wristwatch Boxed in very fine condition $490.82

P

Peanuts Daily Strip Art Dated 11-14-58 in excellent condition $13,751

Peanuts Daily Strip Art Dated 12-23-65 in fine condition..$21,275

Pez 1952 Advertising Sign in excellent condition $1,999.99

Pez Green Space Gun Dispenser in very fine condition $420.93

Pez Lion's Club Dispenser in excellent condition...........$2,972

Pez Make-A-Face Dispenser Complete and Loose in near mint condition..........................$1,800

Pez Vintage 1960s Candy Maker Molds in very fine condition......$560

Pez 1990s Psychedelic Hand Test Dispensers Lot of 7 in near mint condition........................$588.84

Pez Witch Regular Dispenser in excellent condition ..$2,054.72

Phantom's Club Member Club Button in near mint condition $230

Phantom Australian Rubber Ink Stamp Ring in near mint condition $644

Philadelphia Newspaper Comic Strip Promotional Booklet with Batman in excellent condition $10,950.02

Popeye Figural String Holder 1949 in fine condition $4,048

Popeye Bluto Figural String Holder in fine/very fine $1,782.50

Popeye Brutus 1930s Celluloid Figure in excellent condition $411.12

Popeye Express Tin Wind-Up Boxed in very fine condition $1,971.20

Popeye Knockout Bank in very fine condition $985.60

Popeye/Jeep 7" Tall Composition Figure in fine/very fine condition $609.84

Popeye/Jeep 13" Tall Composition Figure in fine/very fine condition $1,527.80

Popeye Olive Oyl Figural String Holder in very fine condition $2,087.25

Popeye/Olive Oyl Rare Pull Toy By Linemar in very fine condition $1,803.77

Popeye Nephew Poopeye Figural String Holder in very fine condition $1,683.72

Popeye Swee' Pea Figural String Holder in near mint condition ..$575

Popeye Swee' Pea Figural String Holder in fine condition ..$556.60

Popeye 1932 Tin Drummer by Chein in fine condition ..$1,584.05

Popeye Wimpy Figural String Holder in very fine condition $3,478.75

Pore Lil Mose Sunday Comics Reprint in good/very good

Flash Gordon's Trip To Mars One Sheet Poster in Exc. on Linen $4,025

Ingraham Howdy Doody Wristwatch in Exc. sold for $1,671

North Pole Bank in NM+ closed at $149,500

condition $862.50
Professor Pug Frogs Great Bicycle Feat Cast Iron Bank in near mint+ condition $103,500

Q

Quake Friendship Ring in near mint+ condition $550
Quake Volcano Whistle Ring in near mint condition $300
Quisp Figural Bank in excellent condition $625
Quisp Space Gun Ring in near mint condition $300

R

Rocket to the Moon Ring in very fine condition $200
Rocky and Bullwinkle Metal Lunchbox and Thermos in near mint condition $1,466.25
Roller Skating Cast Iron Bank in near mint condition $195,500
Roy Rogers 1950s Long Tom Rare Variation Cap Gun By Kilgore in very fine condition $1,008
Roy Rogers 1959-1960 Merchandise Catalogue in near mint condition $765.32
Roy Rogers Mineral City Demonstrator Boxed Display Playset in excellent condition $948.75

S

Sgt. Preston/Richard Simmons Full Size Hartland Figure in excellent condition $487.02
Sgt. Preston of The Yukon Litho. Button in near mint condition $1,985.08
Shadow Blue Coal Portrait Photo in very fine condition $350
Shadow Blue Coal Ring in near mint condition $400
Shadow High Quality Glazed Ceramic Figure in near mint condition..........................$727.38
Shadow Club Silvered Brass Lapel Stud in very fine+ condition $325
Shadow Glow-In-The-Dark Carey Salt Ring in mint condition $695.75
Shadow Hypno-Coin in excellent condition $560
Shadow Movie Club Button From Walter Gibson Estate in mint condition $5,834.08
Shadow Secret Society Glow-In-Dark Pinback Blue Variety in fine condition..........................$596.29
Shadow Radio Club Button from Kansas in near mint condition $3,361.55
Shirley Temple Plaster Carnival Statue in near mint condition $1,671.42
Shirley Temple String Holder in excellent condition......$367.25
Shock Gibson Volunteers Club Button in fine condition $300
Sky Birds Army Air Corps Ring in near mint condition..........$125
Sky King Aztec Emerald Calendar Ring in very good condition ..$400
Snookums Wind-Up Toy in very fine condition $322.58
Space Patrol Lunar Fleet Base Premium in excellent condition $2,300
Space Patrol Atomic Pistol/Flashlite Boxed in near mint+ condition $885.50
Space Patrol/Major Robertson/Ken Mayer Original Uniform from the television show 1951 in fine condition..........................$14,500
Space Patrol Magic Space Pictures Complete Set in excellent condition $1,043.62
Space Patrol Premium Trading Card Complete Set of 40 in excellent/near mint condition $4,437.62
Spider Pulp Ring in near mint condition $3,116.97
Spider Pulp Ring in fine condition............................$2,500
Spider Pulp Ring Box in very fine condition $500
Star Trek Astro-Helmet with Box in very fine condition $872.85
Star Trek Mission To Gamma VI

Winsor McCay Little Nemo Cartoon Poster in Exc. on Linen $10,350

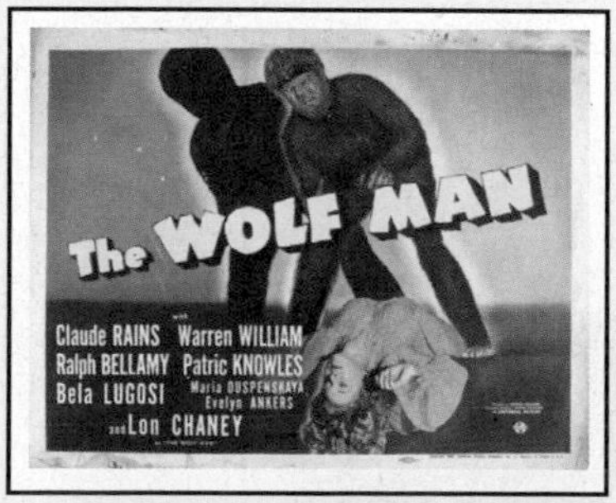

1941 The Wolf Man Title Lobby Card and Pair of Stills in VG/FN sold for $8,114

1942 Superman Fully-Painted Syroco-Style Promotional Figure in Exc. realized $6,325

Playset in fine condition $1,182.78

Star Trek Mugato Action Figure AFA 80 ....$1,426

Star Trek Romulan Action Figure AFA 60 ....$3,995

Star Trek Romulan Action Figure AFA70 ....$1,500

Star Trek Talos Action Figure AFA 85 ....$3,150.77

Star Wars Empire Strikes Back At-At AFA 75........................$1,508

Star Wars Darth Vader Limited Edition Bronze Statue by Bowen Designs #47/100 in excellent condition $6,501.29

Star Wars Darth Vader Action Figure AFA 90 on a 12 Back Card...................................$3,500

Star Wars Darth Vader Action Figure Loose AFA 90 with Telescoping Saber..........$2,999.99

Star Wars Early Bird Action Figure Set AFA 85....$3,150

Star Wars Droids Vlix Action Figure AFA 80..........$2,500

Star Wars Ben Kenobi Action Figure AFA 90 on a 23 Back Card $1,500

Star Wars Boba Fett Action Figure AFA 90 on a Return of The Jedi 45 Back Card $1,402.78

Star Wars Han Solo AFA 90 on a 12 Back Card $1,598.51

Star Wars Han Solo AFA 85 on a 12 Back Card $1,347.63

Star Wars Han Solo Laser Pistol AFA 90 ....$1,302

Star Wars Jawa Action Figure with Vinyl Cape in near mint condition $4,500

Star Wars Jawa Action Figure with Vinyl Cape AFA 80......$4,356

Star Wars Luke Sky Walker Double Telescoping Light Saber Action Figure AFA 85 ....$6,499.99

Star Wars Luke Sky Walker Action Figure AFA 90..........$2,500

Star Wars Empire Strikes Back Tie Bomber AFA 85 ....$2,150

Star Wars Power of The Force Yak Face Action Figure AFA 90 ....$2,299

Star Wars Power of The Force Anakin Skywalker Action Figure AFA 80 ....$5,500

Star Wars Power of The Force Anakin Skywalker Action Figure AFA 80 ....$3,100

Star Wars Power of The Force Anakin Skywalker Action Figure in excellent condition $2,225

Straight Arrow Nabisco Shredded Wheat Countertop Standee in excellent condition...........$1,008

Straight Arrow Prototype Pen Ring by Orin Armstrong in excellent condition $1,632.40

Strange Tales #117 Page 2 Original Art by Dick Ayres Featuring The Fantastic Four in excellent condition $862.50

Strange Tales #117 Page 6 Original Art by Dick Ayres Featuring The Fantastic Four in excellent condition..........$862.50

Superman #1 CGC certified 2.0 ....$20,000

Superman 1940s Bread Sign in excellent condition......$846.72

Superman Co-Creator/Artist Joe Shuster Original Art Action Comics #19 CoverRe-creation in near mint condition $15,180

Superman Die-Cut H-O Oats Advertising Sign in excellent condition $2,146.56

Superman 1949 Fo Lee Gum Badge in very good condition $2,651

Superman 1949 Fo Lee Gum Badge in fair condition $504

Superman 1940 Handkerchief in very fine condition $2,200

Superman 1940 Fleischer Cartoon Campaign Book in excellent condition..........................$3,186

Superman Milk Bottle Cardboard Disk Set of 12 in fine condition...............$3.262.44

Superman School Bag 1940s in fine condition $1,368.94

Superman Secret Chamber Ring With Superman Image on Top in excellent condition $4,312.50

Superman Silent Flame Lighter in fine condition $2,000

Superman Sunday Mail Comic

1962 Dudley Do-Right Metal Lunch Box With Thermos in VF brought $1,574

Mikado Cast Iron Bank in NM+ hits $287,500

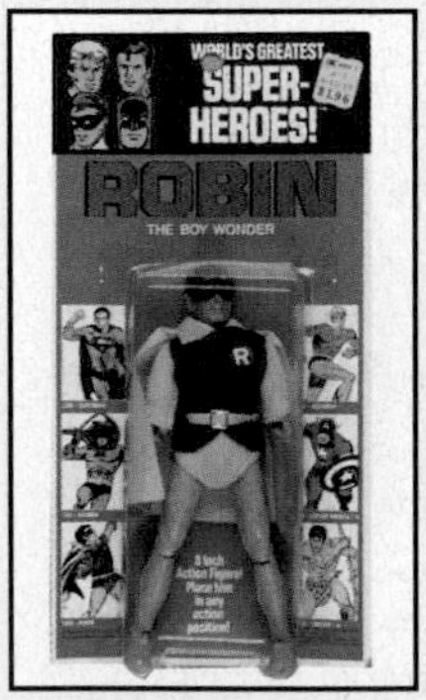

Mego Robin Figure on Kresge Card in NM sold for $2,831

Club Australian Button in fine+ condition $500
Superman Supertime Wristwatch 1950s Boxed in near mint condition............................$6,776
Superman Swan's Bread Certificate in very fine condition $1,000
Superman Syroco-Style Statue in fine condition $1,800
Superman Syroco-Style Fully-Painted Statue 1942 in excellent condition $6,325
Superman-Tim 1945 Franco Club Patch in near mint condition $840
Superman-Tim Pennant in near mint condition $517.50
Superman-Tim Premium Ring in fine condition $1,100
Superman-Tim Premium Ring in very good condition $824.33
Superman Turnover Tank Wind-Up Boxed by Marx in very fine condition.........................$765.33
Superman Wristwatch In Box in fine/very fine condition $2,465.13
Superman Wood And Composition Jointed Doll in fine condition $800
Supermen of America 1941 Club 7/8" Button in near mint condition $525
Supermen of America 1941 Club 7/8" Button in near mint condition.........................$402.50
Supermen of America 1940 Contest Prize Ring in fine condition $6,325

T

Tarzan 1920 Movie Serial Real Photo Button in near mint condition $3,206.50
Tarzan Radio Club Drink More Milk Premium Badge in fine condition $230
Tarzan Rescue Puzzle Game 1934 by Einson-Freeman in excellent condition........................$632.50
Tarzan The Tiger Universal's Gigantic Chapter Play Set Button in near mint condition $632.50
Tarzan Westworld Club Membership Card in very fine condition $588.33
Ted Williams Nabisco Cereal Premium Ring in very fine condition $309
Teenage Mutant Ninja Turtles #1 CGC certified 9.4..........$4,610.80
Tom Corbett Space Cadet Metal Lunchbox with Thermos in near mint condition $2,183.60
Tom Corbett Space Cadet Space Pistol Clicker Gun by Marx in very fine condition $1,080.78
Tom Corbett Space Cadet Wristwatch with Rocket Insert Box in near mint condition $1,010.23
Tom Mix Glow Belt Premium with Mailer and Instructions in fine condition $914.32
Tom Mix Ranch Boss Badge in fine+ condition $300
Toonerville Trolley 1922 Wind-Up in fine condition $626.18
Transformers Bumblebee AFA 85 ....$1,500
Transformers Hot Rod AFA 80 ....$2,025
Transformers Iron Hide AFA 90 ....$1,500
Transformers Megatron AFA 85 ....$3,950
Transformers Optimus Prime AFA 85 ....$3,500
Transformers Optimus Prime AFA 85 ....$2,499
Transformers Optimus Prime AFA 85 ....$1,775.01
Transformers Prowl AFA 85 ....$1,150
Transformers Soundwave AFA 80 ....$2,850

W

War of the Worlds Cast Metal Model from 1953 in excellent condition $8,159.92
Wizard of Oz 1915 Read the New Baum Book/The Scarecrow of Oz Button in very fine condition...........................$1,300
Wizard of Oz 1926 Club Member

Alex Toth Splash Page from Adventure Comics #418 in Exc. realized $15,181

1953 The Ghost Rider Rare Premium Mask and Mailer in NM brought $3,333

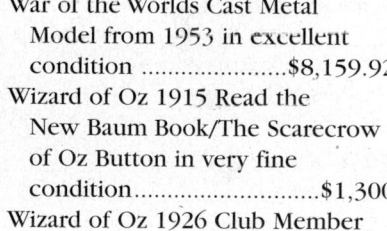

c. 1907 Clown, Harlequin, and Columbine Bank in NM+ sold for $103,500

Badge in good+ condition $450
Wizard of Oz Cowardly Lion String Holder in excellent condition $406
Wizard of Oz Jack Haley Movie Contest Button in very fine condition $800
Wizard of Oz Waddle Book 1934 Complete With Dust Jacket in Exc. $8,079.50
Wizard of Oz Wizard 1939 Promotional Glass in excellent condition $2,677.28
Wonder Woman Infantile Paralysis Card in excellent condition $1,757.55
Wonder Woman/Sensation Comics Button in very good condition..........................$406.06
Wonder Woman Super Queens Action Figure Boxed in near mint condition $4,871.26
Woody Woodpecker Wrist Watch in near mint condition $2,227.79

X

X-Men #1 CGC 5.0 ....$1,526.01

Y

Yellow Kid #2 CGC certified 3.0.......................$1,625
Yellow Kid #6 CGC certified 4.5.......................$2,979
Yellow Kid Child's Highchair in very fine condition $1,000
Yellow Kid High Admiral Button #137 Hawaii in fine condition $871.59
Yellow Kid Gum Card Set of 25 Cards in near mint condition $3,011.55
Yellow Kid For President McKinley Lapel Stud in near mint condition $1,800
Yellow Kid Soap Figure in very fine condition $400

1940s Superman School Bag in FN brought $1,573

Chinaman In Boat Polychromed Variant –Lead in NM sold for $103,500

1920s Bonzo Bank in NM sold for $6,900

Captain Marvel Rocket Raider Compass Ring First Seen Carded Example in NM on FN card brought $2,213

Wizard of Oz Waddle Book in Exc. realized $8,079

1934 Chandu Club Good Luck Premium Ring in NM+ closed at $2,104

Mama Katzenjammer Bank in NM+ brought $74,750

Alex Ross Kingdom Come Superman Painting in NM+ realized $10,120

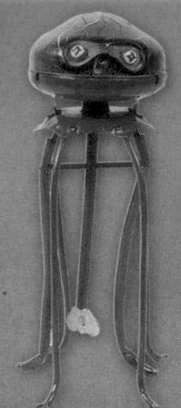

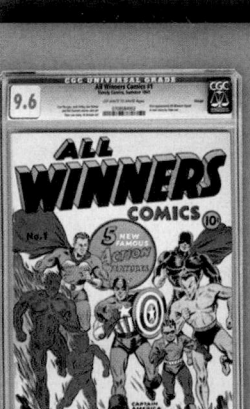

Through the Looking Glass: GEPPI'S ENTERTAINMENT MUSEUM

by J.C. Vaughn

Geppi's Entertainment Museum (GEM) is built around a walk-through timeline which takes visitors era by era through the history of popular culture in the United States, supporting and illustrating its viewpoints with thousands of rare and one-of-a-kind vintage pop culture artifacts ranging from dolls to cast iron mechanical banks, from movie posters and action figures to comic books and hundreds of other toys. Its walls are filled with a spectacular collection of original comic book and comic strip art, paintings and promotional pieces.

Covering each segment in its purview with a special room or exhibit, the museum details the momentous impact of comic characters on the children who connected with them. Chronicling the earliest comic characters through the highly recognized creations of recent years,

Mindy Geppi, Governor Robert Ehrlich, Steve Geppi, Dr. Arnold T. Blumberg, Wendy Kelman and John K. Snyder, Jr. at the grand opening of Geppi's Entertainment Museum.

the facility's different segments immerse partakers in its unique American experience.

In mid-2005, Steve Geppi, President and Chief Executive Officer of Diamond Comic Distributors, announced the formation of Geppi's Entertainment Museum, a 17,000 square foot facility at Camden Yards, which spotlights the role of entertainment and popular culture in the mainstream culture since the nation's founding.

A native of Baltimore's Little Italy section, Geppi started his first business, Geppi's Comic World, a retail outlet selling comic books, more than three decades ago. He then launched Diamond Comic Distributors, which is now the largest English-language distributor of comics in the world. He is the owner of *Baltimore* magazine, the nation's oldest city magazine, and is a minority owner of the Baltimore Orioles. In addition, he owns Geppi's Entertainment Publications & Auctions, which includes under its banner Diamond International Galleries, Hake's Americana & Collectibles, Morphy Auctions, and Gemstone Publishing. Geppi also owns Alliance Game Distributors and E. Gerber Products, which makes collector supplies. In late 2007, the NFL's Baltimore Ravens announced that the Club Level at M&T Bank Stadium was officially re-named The Geppi Entertainment Club Level, giving GEM even more visibility within the Camden Yards sports complex and the city.

"Over the years I have been fortunate enough to be in position to preserve, promote and present historical comic character collectibles in a variety of venues to the point at which this museum is the next logical step. Take a look around the museum and you'll see that the history of popular culture is so tightly woven into the social fabric of the United States of America that it parallels and reinforces mainstream history," Geppi said.

"From my earliest days in the comic book business – when I was a child, counting comics for a local store – I have always enjoyed sharing my excitement about the characters with other people. From my brother and the rest of my family, to my friends growing up in Baltimore's Little Italy, to the high profile acquaintances I have made in the business world, spreading the word has been a mission I've taken seriously," he said. "GEM is the next reasonable step in that mission. It is a showplace of ideas, a marketplace of thought and imagination."

Grand Opening – Part One

On Wednesday, September 6, 2006, Geppi's Entertainment Museum hosted a grand opening gala for the Baltimore and greater Maryland community including business, social and political leaders from around the region. Maryland's governor, Robert L. Ehrlich, State Superintendent of Schools Dr. Nancy Grasmick, and numerous other dignitaries represented the state.

Maryland Stadium

GEM Executive Vice President Melissa Geppi-Bowersox entertains guests at the grand opening gala.

Authority Chairman Bob McKinney served as master of ceremonies. He introduced the Governor, who talked about Steve Geppi's efforts to promote Baltimore and the state of Maryland through partnerships with the other tourist destinations and philanthropic efforts in the area. McKinney next introduced Geppi and his wife, Mindy, and lauded their civic accomplishments. Geppi explained that he planned to work together as a team with other museums and attractions to promote the city and state as tourist destinations.

"The connection between Steve's passion for this material and our ability to get the community at large interested in it just

Martin Luther King III was one of Steve Geppi's guests at the museum's opening.

GEM 4-1-1

Geppi's Entertainment Museum is now open to the public at 301 W. Camden Street, Baltimore, MD 21201, immediately next door to Oriole Park at Camden Yards, just across the street from the Baltimore Convention Center. GEM is situated on the second and third floors of Baltimore's historic Camden Station, right above another museum, Sports Legends at Camden Yards. Hours of operation are 10 AM to 5 PM daily (From October-March, the museum is closed on Mondays). GEM offers different membership levels for individuals, families, groups and corporations. Additional information is available by phone at (410)625-7060 or on GEM's website, http://www.geppismuseum.com

The Rooms

GEM's walk-through timeline is comprised of seven areas which are lined almost from floor to ceiling with vintage pop culture artifacts. An eighth room, "A Story in Four Colors," presents the museum's timeline concept in microcosm by showcasing comic books from the earliest American editions to the most recent.

THE ROOMS ARE AS FOLLOWS:
Pioneer Spirit [1776-1894]
Extra! Extra! [1895-1927]
When Heroes Unite [1928-1945]
America Tunes In [1946-1960]
Revolution [1961-1970]
Expanding Universe [1971-1990]
Going Global [1991-Present]

Governor Robert Ehrlich praises Steve and Mindy Geppi outside the historic Camden Station building before the official ribbon cutting ceremony.

became perceptibly more tangible," said GEM President John K. Snyder, Jr. as he surveyed reactions to the venue. "It will be great when even more people see the connections between popular culture and history."

Grand Opening – Part Two

Thursday, September 7, 2006, was the second of Geppi's Entertainment Museum's grand opening galas; this one focused on the collectibles industry.

Geppi himself served as master of ceremonies for the evening's events, and was joined on the podium by his wife, Mindy, DC Comics President and Publisher Paul Levitz, Dark Horse Comics President Mike Richardson, cartoonist Jerry Robinson, Brian Walker (representing his father, Mort Walker, who arrived later), fantasy artist Frank Frazetta, and activist Martin Luther King III.

Geppi thanked his staff for the incredible effort in developing and completing the museum, and lauded his entire family for their understanding and support during the process. He singled out daughter Melissa Geppi-Bowersox, who handled many of the arrangements for the two grand opening events. The Geppis were then joined by GEM President John K. Snyder, Jr., original museum Executive Director Wendy Kelman, and Curator Dr. Arnold T. Blumberg for the ceremonial ribbon cutting before the guests entered the museum.

The reactions came from many different perspectives, but most of them ended up in about the same place: "I have to come back and take more time here."

"I think [*Shi* creator and *Sgt. Rock* writer-artist] Billy Tucci really summed it up very well when he said Geppi's Entertainment Museum is going to make our industry look at its history in a whole new light," Snyder said.

Open to the Public

The following morning, Friday, September 8, 2006, the museum opened to the public, capping off a week of tremendous press coverage from print, radio, television and online outlets.

"The 17,000-square-foot space takes up the second and third floors of the former Camden train station here, whose main floor is home to the Sports Legends at Camden Yards museum. Geppi's Entertainment Museum celebrates the colorful characters and collectibles that have emerged from comic strips and comic books since the late 1800s. Its packed displays - of movie posters, animation cels, action figures, board games, advertisements and more - chronicle the evolution of these characters, often reflecting the periods of American history from which they emerged," *The New York Times* said.

"As you wander through the lobby wondering all along how much more impressive the rest of the exhibit could be, you receive your answer immediately on crossing the threshold into the museum's main hallway. The walls are easily 20 feet tall and are covered from top to bottom (well, about 3-4 feet from the floor) with posters, original artwork, cartoon cels, cereal boxes and virtually anything else you could imagine that has some sort of pop culture icon emblazoned on it. Far from being overwhelmingly busy, with seemingly disparate images that you might assume would be at odds with each other fighting for your attention instead coming together to form a tapestry telling the story of American culture," ComicBook Resources.com said.

"To tour the new Geppi's Entertainment Museum in Camden Station is to reunite with those legions of imaginary characters who have instructed generations of Americans from infancy to old age," said the *Baltimore Sun*.

Special Events

Whether one goes to see characters such as the Brownies, the Yellow Kid, Mickey Mouse, Superman, Hopalong Cassidy, or SpongeBob Squarepants, or the marketing incarnations of real life figures like Charles Lindbergh, Elvis Presley or Muhammad Ali, GEM delivers them not only in the form of its regular displays, but also in its changing exhibits.

An early example of these special events included "Finally in Full Color," a look at the changing role of African-American comic characters and creators in pop culture drawn from the collection of Professor William H. Foster III, a comic book historian and author of the book, *Looking for a Face Like Mine.*

Another was "The Force is With Us: 30 Years of Star Wars," which showcased collectibles from the entire Star Wars saga from the collection of Thomas G. Atkinson, Director of the Star Toys Museum.

"Scrooged!" celebrated the life and work of Scrooge McDuck creator Carl Barks (1901-2000) through a unique exhibition of original oil paintings, artwork and other memorabilia, including the complete original artwork for the comic story, "North of the Yukon."

Many additional events are planned throughout 2009 as well, and GEM staffers have even brought traveling exhibits to the Atlantique City antiques show in Atlantic City and to the New York Comic-Con, among other venues. As visitors to the museum discover, GEM's regular and changing exhibits are imbued with the same spirited, inventive and adventurous kind of learning that captures your mind as a child and stays with you through the rest of your life.

While the facility's staff is notably proud of their educational directives, the "fun" component of the museum isn't to be outdone either. GEM has also become a trendy location to host private occasions from weddings and Bar Mitzvahs to company parties and civic events. Groups numbering well into the hundreds have made it their home for an evening and come away, as one might expect, knowing they had a unique experience.

J.C. Vaughn is the Executive Editor and Associate Publisher of Gemstone Publishing.

The Staff

Coming from backgrounds which include education, publishing, pop culture auctions, travel and tourism, retailing, and many other specialties, the current GEM staff includes Stephen A. Geppi, CEO & Owner, John K. Snyder, Jr., President, Melissa Geppi-Bowersox, Executive Vice-President, Dr. Arnold T. Blumberg, Curator, Jeff Robison, Director of Administration, Andy Hershberger, Registrar, Julie Meddows, Associate Director of Sales & Marketing, Patricia Moore, Sales Associate, Ellen Caldwell, GEM Store Manager, Ben MacKrell, GEM Store Asst. Manager, Danielle Geppi-Patras, Facility Coordinator, and Laura Bevans, Office Manager.

(Top) Former Marvel Comics Editor-in-Chief Jim Shooter, DC Comics President and Publisher Paul Levitz, and Steve Geppi survey the crowd during the collectibles industry grand opening of GEM. (Above) Famed fantasy illustrator Frank Frazetta, Comics Buyer's Guide editor Maggie Thompson and writer-artist Billy Tucci

Calling

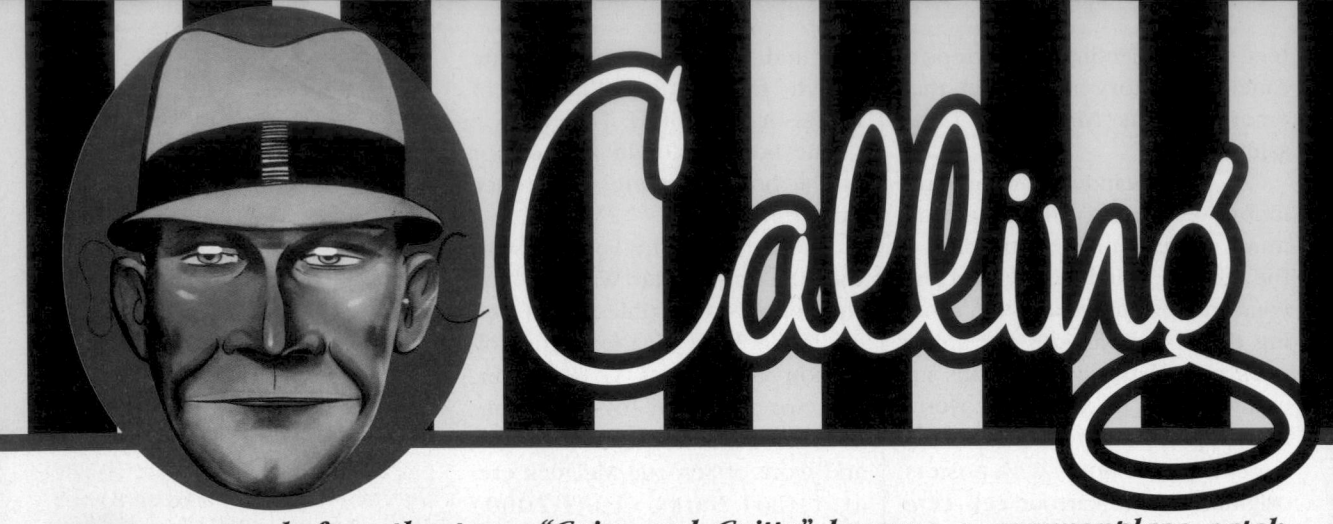

Long before the term "Grim and Gritty" became a commonplace catchphrase in comics, Chester Gould's* Dick Tracy *introduced America to one of the first streetwise crime fighters to appear in the Sunday funnies. A hard-nosed investigator, Tracy took the fight to the criminals with nothing more than his wits and his left hook, often going up against rogues that would give Batman a run for his money. Tackling controversial subjects, such as racketeering, extortion, rape and murder, Tracy fought against the culturally relevant crimes that were happening in the streets of major cities all over America.

An Overview

In the late-1920s and early-1930s, many Americans were facing some of the hardest times since those of the Great War (World War I). The stock market crash of 1929, which led the country into the economic downturn that would later be known as The Great Depression, had many seeking a way to escape the reality and drudgery of their daily lives. Some of this escapism came in the form of radio dramas, pulp novels and comic strips. The people were crying out, many unknowingly, for heroes to bring them salvation from the troubles and tribulations of their everyday lives. They would soon have a man-of-the-people hero to look up to.

In 1931, Chester Gould approached the *Chicago Tribune* with his idea for a crime-fighting character that mirrored the society that he was living in at the time. This hard-nosed crime-fighter, originally named Plainclothes Tracy, was Gould's answer to the violence and crime that surrounded him. Joseph Patterson, who was the head of the *Tribune* at the time, made the suggestion to Gould that he change the main character's name from Plainclothes to Dick, due to the fact that many referred to police detectives of the time as Dicks.

Above: Dick Tracy Paper Mask, 1933

Right: Dick Tracy First Chicago Tribune Promo, 1931. Can be seen at Geppi's Entertainment Museum

"I felt that it would either go to the top or fall on its face," said Gould in a 1980 interview with

Dick Tracy

By Brandon G. DeStefano

Max Allan Collins (reprinted in the first volume of *The Complete Chester Gould's Dick Tracy* from IDW Publishing). "I was afraid that Patterson might be offended by it because it was so rough, and say 'I don't like that,' and as it turned out, Patterson was wild about *Dick Tracy* from the beginning. That was the kind of stuff he wanted in his paper."

The first daily newspaper strip debuted on October 12, 1931 with a bang, literally, as Tess Trueheart, the love of Tracy's life, was kidnapped and her father was murdered by the gang of Big Boy Caprice. The violent nature of the crime, shown in graphic detail in the strip, prompted Dick Tracy to join the Plainclothesmen Squad and begin a lifelong job of fighting to uphold justice.

"[Selling papers] was the name of the game, and it still is today," said Gould of the violent nature of the strip.

Chester Gould: Creating Tracy

Tracy creator, Chester Gould, was born in Pawnee, Oklahoma in 1900 and first began to take interest in art at the behest of one of his high school teachers. After moving to Stillwater, Oklahoma in 1919, Gould began his higher education at Oklahoma A & M, which is now known as Oklahoma State University. Gould remained at A & M until 1921, when he transferred to Illinois' Northwestern University, graduating in 1923.

After college, Gould remained in the Chicago area and took courses in art, a subject that he never invested time in while at university. He quickly found work as a cartoonist, as he had been fascinated by comics from a very early age, and was hired by William Randolph Hearst's *Chicago Evening American*. While at the newspaper, he created the comic strips *Fillum Fables* and *The Radio Cats* in 1924. Later, he created a strip about the Windy City, appropriately titled, *Why It's a Windy City*. The strip was more of an editorial in comic strip form than an actual comic strip.

"I went to Mr. Curly [managing editor at the *American*] one day, and said that I'd got an idea for him, kind of Walter Winchell in cartoon, called *Why It's a Windy City*; I would interview big shots and businessmen," said Gould. "He said 'Sounds all right, give me a couple.' I had comments from all of the show [business] people that were in town; Eddie Cantor and Al Jolson, Ed Wynn, [and] a couple of the dramatic actors."

In 1931, Gould was hired away from the *Chicago Evening*

"Dick Tracy and The Wreath Kidnaping Case" Better Little Book, 1945.

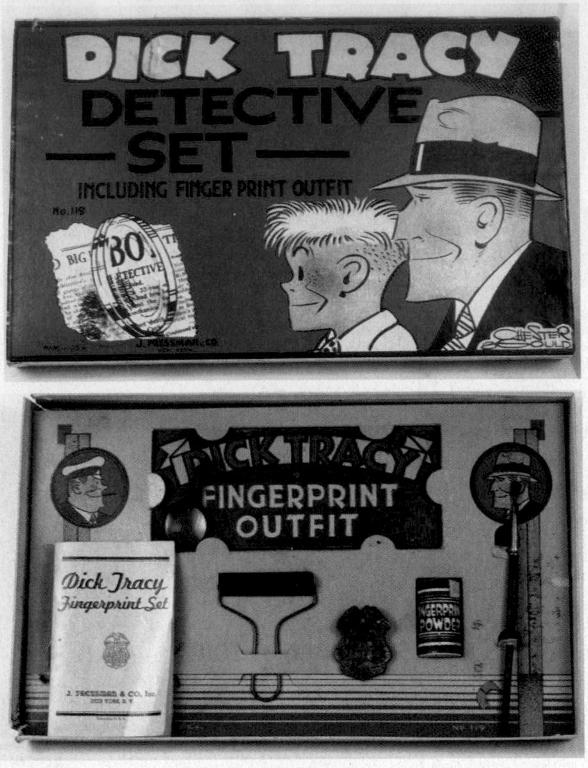

Dick Tracy Detective Set from 1930s.

American by the *Chicago Tribune* for his skills as a cartoonist. It was there that Gould introduced the world to *Dick Tracy*, a strip that he both wrote and drew, after being exposed to the unsavory headlines that topped the *Tribune* daily. Gould created the strip to heighten America's awareness of the growing problem of urban and organized crime, especially in major cities like New York, Chicago and Detroit. He spent endless hours creating a world for his character that mirrored the one in which he lived, creating a supporting cast of rogues, comrades, and even a love interest for Tracy, while bringing a reality to the stories that readers could identify with. In addition, Gould created a kid sidekick for Tracy, an adopted son named Junior, so that the image of a "good guy" would appeal to a larger audience (this was long before Jerry Robinson created Robin, the Boy-Wonder as Batman's ward).

Although Gould spent many hours creating characters for Tracy's world, he rarely spent much time in pre-planning the stories, preferring to create the adventures as he drew them. This approach allowed him to improvise and create plotlines on the fly to more accurately relate the stories to the real-world events happening across the country. It was the early 1930s, and crime was at an all-time high, with gangs from the North and South sides of Chicago making news on a daily basis. Dick Tracy answered the call of a real-life city begging for justice and peace from the daily dose of crime and violence.

The First Rogues Gallery

Dick Tracy was one of the first comic heroes to fight crime with no superpowers, yet had one of the most unique and bizarre rogues galleries in comics history. Tracy's rogues' gallery is as diverse as that of Batman and Spider-Man, but appeared in a time when most heroes were fighting nameless criminals or organizations.

Gould created a troupe of villains that ran amok in Tracy's Chicago. With such characters as The Blank, a gangster whose face was destroyed by a gunshot; The Claw, a violent criminal who made use of a hook that replaced one of his hands; Flattop, an assassin with a misshapen head; Haf-and-Haf, a criminal with half a scarred face (a precursor to Two-Face, maybe?); Little Face, a jewel thief with a tiny face and large head; Mumbles, a deadly killer who has nearly incoherent speech; and Pruneface, a Nazi agent and spy with a sun-damaged face; and of course the gang-leader, Big Boy Caprice, who appeared in the very first strip. Tracy's rogues could hold their own with just about any villains in comics today.

Built and modeled after real-life crime boss Al Capone, Big Boy Caprice was Gould's first villain to offer Tracy the means to join the fight against crime. Much to Gould's chagrin, Big Boy never generated as much attention as those who worked for him doing the dirty work. Though Big Boy was clearly the brains behind the organized crime operations that constantly kept Tracy on his toes, the head gangster rarely needed to sully his own hands, and without any facial deformities of his own to fall back on, unlike many of his henchmen, Caprice wasn't given nearly as much panel time as other

Dick Tracy strip villains.

Big Boy Caprice appeared in a few showdowns during the strip's forty-plus-year run, but never gained real popularity until Al Pacino's riveting silver screen portrayal of Big Boy Caprice in the 1990 Warren Beatty film, *Dick Tracy*, finally given his just due as a memorable Gould villain (although the social relevance of the character was long past).

One of the most popular of Big Boy's more colorful and bumbling henchmen was Pruneface. As one of the most deeply scarred, both physically and emotionally, Pruneface quickly emerges as one of the most memorable, thus warranting him a detailed back story. Although he didn't debut until 1942, which attested to his Nazi heritage and affiliation, he quickly rose to the top of Big Boy's organization and the attention of fans.

Dick Tracy One Sheet Movie Poster for "The Spider Strikes," 1937.

Despite his popularity and his quick rise to power within Big Boy's organization, Pruneface was killed in 1943, appearing to be frozen to death in a blizzard after being captured by Tracy. That same year, the nose-less Amazon wife of Pruneface (appropriately named Mrs. Pruneface) appeared in the strip and swore her revenge against Tracy for the loss of her "beloved" husband. Although she never succeeded in killing the detective, she quickly became a formidable opponent of Tracy's, at one point capturing him and driving a spike into his chest.

In the 1980s, writer Max Collins, who took over the strip after Gould retired, returned Pruneface to life and the forefront of Tracy's rogues' gallery. Pruneface still remains one of the most visually captivating characters in comics today.

Tracy's rogues' gallery began a phenomenon that continues to this day. Using eccentric characters with unique physical traits, Chester Gould was able to place his villains into the memories of his readers for the last 75 years.

Dick Tracy Police Station with Squad Car, 1952.

Tracy in the Media

Growing out of the daily and Sunday comic strips, *Dick Tracy* moved off the newsprint page and onto the silver screen appearing in many movie serials, television shows, cartoons and feature films. Beginning in 1937, the first of two 15-episode *Dick Tracy* movie serials debuted with a 20-minute episode shown at movie houses before the feature film.

Both *Dick Tracy* serials (from 1937) starred Ralph Byrd as the title character, Lee Van Atta as Junior and Kay Hughes as Gwen Andrews; but did not feature any of the rogues made famous by the *Tribune* strip. It wasn't until the 1945 film that any of the fan-favorite villains made their appearances.

The '45 short-film, *Dick Tracy, Detective*, starred Morgan Conway as Tracy, Anne Jeffreys as Tess Trueheart, Mickey Kuhn as Junior, Mike Mazurki as Splitface and Milton Parsons as Deathridge. The film opened on December 1, 1945 and continued to drive the popularity of the character in the newspaper strips.

Tracy next moved to the small screen in 1950 with a 30-minute

Dick Tracy Teaser Poster for Buena Vista Pictures, 1990.

television series that ran from '50 – '51. The series premiered on September 11, 1950 and starred 1937 serial star, Ralph Byrd, again as Dick Tracy, Angela Green as Tess Trueheart, Martin Dean as Junior, Lyle Talbot as The Brain (who replaced the less popular Big Boy Caprice), Alan Keys as Pruneface, John Cliff as Flattop and was narrated by William Woodson. The show built a loyal fan base due to the fact that many of the characters from the strip appeared regularly in the series.

Tracy would again appear on television a decade later in the form of the animated program, *The Dick Tracy Show*. Starring voice actors Everett Stone as Tracy, Benny Rubin as Flattop, Mel Blanc as Go-Go Gomez and a slew of other unaccredited talent for the remainder of the supporting character roles, the animated show was short-lived, only lasting one 11-epsiode season.

Tracy appeared in several other serials and series over the years, but arguably the most popular appearance of the character in a live-action feature was the 1990 Warren Beatty film. *Dick Tracy* exploded out of the box office bringing Tracy, Tess Trueheart and Big Boy Caprice to life in an all-new way. Featuring stunning performances by Beatty as Dick Tracy, Al Pacino as Big Boy, Glenne Headly as Tess Trueheart, Madonna as deadly-beautiful lounge singer, Breathless Mahoney, and Charlie Corsmo as The Kid (Junior), the film looked like a full-color moving comic strip. In addition to the main characters, Big Boy's gang was also brought to the screen in an amazing manner, showcasing Pruneface, Flattop, Shoulders, The Brow, Little Face, 88 Keys, Lips, Lefty Moriarty and many more.

Currently, the original Chester Gould strips are being reprinted in archive format by Max Collins and IDW Publishing in *The Complete Chester Gould's Dick Tracy*, and two volumes are now in print.

The Modern Impact of Dick Tracy

In January of 1946, the *Dick Tracy* comic strip changed the world forever with the introduction of a seemingly meaningless piece of cool gadgetry. Chester Gould introduced a seminal communications device for Tracy and members of the police force to stay in close contact with one another: the 2-way wrist radio.

This iconic piece of technology became one of the most recognizable items of the strip and is thought to be a precursor to the cellular phone technology (and ultimately push-to-talk technology as well) that we take for granted today. Gould again took this gadget to the next level in 1964 when Tracy's 2-way radio was upgraded to a 2-way wrist television, giving Tracy the ability to communicate

Right: Advertisement for Dick Tracy Aviation/Hostess Cap, 1939.
Below: Dick Tracy Aviation/Hostess Cap with Brass Badge, 1939.

visually with his fellow crime fighters.

Finally, in 1987, although Gould was no longer writing and drawing the strip, Tracy's communications device was upgraded again by Max Allan Collins to a wrist computer, similar to the PalmPilot and Portable Data Assistants (PDAs) used by millions of people today. Who would have imagined that 60 years later, a simple device, introduced to intrigue readers, would have had such an impact on the technology of today?

Chester Gould's street-wise detective was on a life-long mission to fight crime and bring justice to the streets of Chicago. Gould's creation inspired dozens of future crime-fighting characters, including Batman, James Bond, Adam Strange, the Rocketeer and many others, all of whom were just ordinary men using their brains, brawn and technology to make the world (or the galaxy, in Strange's case) a better place.

The Appeal of Dick Tracy

One of the most appealing aspects of *Dick Tracy* was its realistic, hard-hitting tone; its ability to bring reality into fiction. There was no fantasy involved in the early stories, because they were all related to what was actually going on in the world at the time. Gould saw no reason to add the fantastic to his stories because they were relevant to the time they were being published. Readers could relate to them because the battles that Tracy was fighting were going on right outside their very own windows and doors.

Dick Tracy is an American icon that has survived as a part of popular culture for more than 75 years. Few characters in American literature have as much bearing, appeal or relevance as that of the detective in the yellow fedora and overcoat.

Brandon DeStefano, a former Editor at Gemstone Publishing, is a freelance writer and editor for Empyre Studios.

A scarce 1938 "Inspector General" Brass Badge.

Dick Tracy Caramels Waxed Paper by Walter H. Johnson Co., Chicago, 1930s.

Dick Tracy/Junior Cello. Button, 1933.

One of the two "Blood Dailies" that helped popularize the toughness of Tracy's war on crime.

Pawing Through CATS & Add Character

The human-animal bond is a dynamic relationship that has existed for thousands of years. In fact, the human-canine bond is one of the oldest relationships in history, dating back 12,000 years. The transition of a dog from working companion to pet goes back to 600 to 1300 A.D and there is evidence of human-feline bonds that date back 9,500 years ago. Today, the majority of households in America own at least one pet. If one were to ask a dog owner about the health of their canine, most people would say that their dog's health and well-being is as important to them as their own. There's no question we humans love our pets, but what is it that bonds us to our animal friends?

Respected veterinarian, researcher and co-author of *Between Pets and People: The Importance of Animal Companionship*, Dr. Alan Beck wrote, "It is the loving devotion, the soft touch, the constant companionship, the attentive eye, and the uncritical ear of the pet," that is so attractive to many of us. Pets are not inclined to judge and are uncritically accepting, they give their love whole-heartedly, and are loyal even under the darkest of circumstances. The affection an animal provides is simple, unconditional and uncomplicated. Pets can be playmates and confidants for any age group, and can be life saving companions for those who are disabled. It is because of these qualities that humans and animals have happily co-existed for so many centuries.

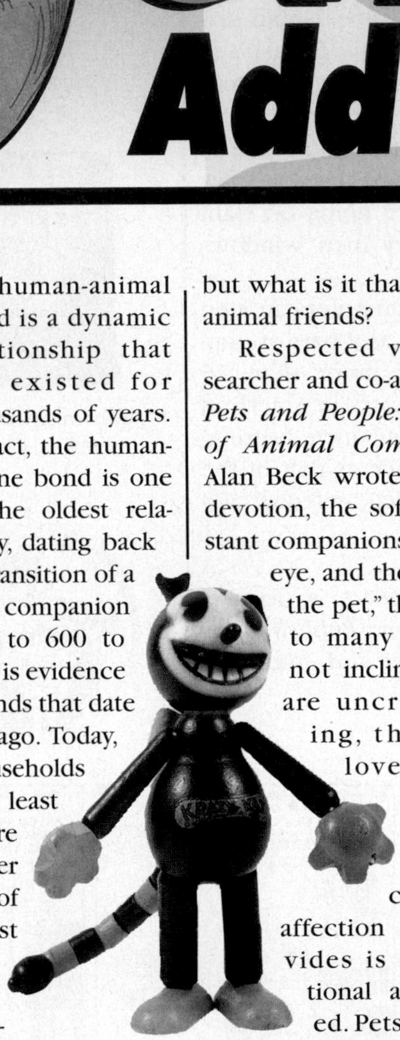

Krazy Kat Wood Jointed Doll from 1932.

Given the many reasons why animals have such appeal to humans, there's no wonder animals became an important part of pop culture identity. Comic character animals are amusing because creators of the entertainment world give these drawn and made-up animals humanistic personalities and characteristics. What makes animals who behave like humans so entertaining is that it is our furry friends reflecting our own strengths and weaknesses. Over the years, there have been a plethora of cats and dogs whose humorous antics have captured the hearts and imaginations of animal-lovers and entertainment buffs alike. One of the earliest pet cartoon characters was the beloved Krazy Kat, who was followed through history by favorites such as Lassie, Rin Tin Tin, and Garfield.

Pop Culture DOGS & Charm

By Lindsay Dunn & Courtney Jenkins

Krazy Kat

Created by the prolific humorist George Herriman more than 90 years ago, *Krazy Kat* has consistently topped polls and was even named the most important comic character by *The Comics Journal*. It all started in 1910, with Kokonino Kounty's Krazy Kat, Ignatz Mouse and Offissa Pupp starring in a series of tales that ran in the space beneath Herriman's daily strip *The Dingbat Family* (later called *The Family Upstairs*). By 1913, Herriman had dropped the Dingbats and expanded the *Krazy Kat* strip to a daily on its own, followed by a *Krazy Kat* Sunday page in 1916.

The strip's title character, Krazy Kat, a cat of indeterminate sex, was deeply smitten with Ignatz Mouse. Krazy's feelings, however, were not reciprocated, which set the stage for antics galore that usually resulted in Ignatz smacking Krazy's head with a brick. Krazy consistently took these gestures as signs of affection, which outraged Ignatz all the more and caused Offissa Pupp to keep a special eye on him for Krazy's sake. Only in Herriman's world would a mouse so blatantly and fearlessly assault a cat!

Often referred to as the most intellectual comic strip in history, Herriman's use of language is what gave the strip its tone. He took philosophical concepts and twisted them to fit into the world of his animal characters. Herriman's artwork was also very stylized and art-deco in appearance, adding to the general sophistication of the strip.

Comic art collectors the world over prize their *Krazy Kat* originals, which have been called visual poetry. e.e. cummings was one of many literary figures who wrote about Krazy, and a ballet based on the strip was created and staged in New York. It was Herriman's ingenious use of vocabulary that was primarily responsible for this, along with the huge irony that made every *Krazy* adventure wonderfully bizarre.

Another factor in Krazy's popularity was the characters' presence on the silver screen. While the screen versions carried none of the strip's wit or subtlety, their mere existence created a better public awareness of the characters. The cartoons first appeared in the late 1910s and had their heyday from 1929 until 1940.

Several manufacturers produced Krazy toys. The most successful was J. Chein. The company seemed to have a good relationship with the company responsible for the Krazy license, King Features, as they also had success with a line of

Above: Garfield "Attitude" Bobber Figure from 2003. Right: Krazy Kat Enameled Brass Pin Figural Pin from 1930s.

Popeye toys as well. Chein wasn't limited to just King Features characters, they made everything they could for children: pull toys, tin wind-up ducks, toy drums, globes and pails for the beach or mud pies.

Krazy toys were also manufactured by Knickerbocker, a company especially known for their dolls. They produced some of the most popular and highest quality dolls of their day. In addition to Krazy, they are also responsible for some of the best looking early Disney dolls in the collector's market.

The toy hobbyist knows that a good looking Krazy doll or toy is a real find. It isn't often that they come into the marketplace and when they do, they often reach top dollar. George Herriman's Krazy Kat is still krazy after all these years!

Lassie

An improbable superhero, Lassie, the brown and white collie with the communicative whimper and authoritative bark, showed fearless love and devotion to mankind, as well as to the animal kingdom. Through her exemplary heroism, courage and loyalty, Lassie became the one of the first ever animal rights advocates, elevating people's perceptions from dogs as mere pets to invaluable members of the family.

Lassie challenged the meaning of the term "man's best friend." As a tireless devotee to young male owners like Jeff and Timmy on the television series, Lassie was more accurately "child's best friend." The mid-20th century approach to educating children often included animals - plush, animated or live - and for nearly three decades, Lassie was a major proponent of that education.

Though many only associate the compassionate canine with television, Lassie first appeared in print as the protagonist in novelist Eric Knight's short story, *Lassie Come Home*. The 1938 story, which first appeared in *The Saturday Evening Post*, became a novel, which further explored the premise of a boy's devotion to his dog—and vice versa.

Following the success of the book, Hollywood took interest in the courageous collie and made *Lassie Come Home* a 1943 feature film, starring Roddy McDowell and Elizabeth Taylor.

Lassie became an icon after "her" (and we use quotes because television's Lassie was played by more than a half dozen dogs, and none were female) CBS debut on September 12, 1954. Her first family was the Millers: Jeff (played by Tommy Rettig), Ellen (Jan Clayton), and Grandpa (George Cleveland). Eventually, the Millers adopted an adorable boy named Timmy (Jon Provost).

As the series transitioned, the Millers sold their farm—with Timmy on it—to the Martins. Ruth (played both by Cloris Leachman and June Lockheart) and Paul (John Shepodd/Hugh Reilly) took Timmy and Lassie under their wings. Then, the Martins moved to Australia and left their dedicated "girl" with forest rangers Corey Stuart (Robert Bray), Scott Turner (Jed Allan) and Bob Erickson (Jack De Mave). The final season of the series found Lassie aimlessly roaming the world, seeking out friends in need of help and love.

At 17 seasons, Lassie was the longest running half-hour drama in television history. Though the last

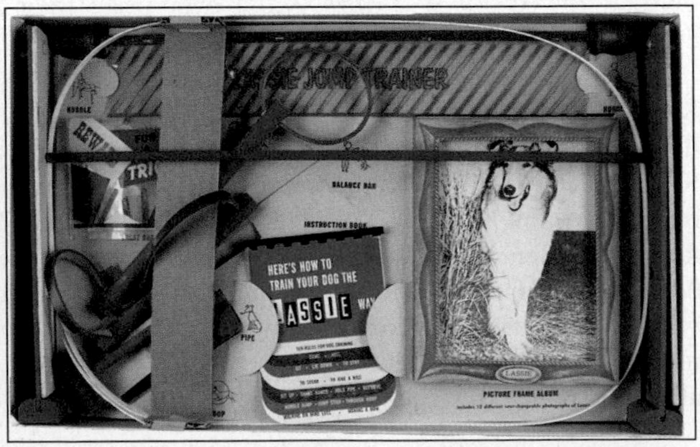

A 1950s "Lassie Trick Trainer" Dog Training Kit.

episode aired in 1971, Lassie's influence didn't end there. Throughout the years of her film and television career, she inspired thousands of Americans to purchase collies as pets. She also spawned a cartoon series, *Lassie's Rescue Rangers*, which ran from 1973-'75; three decades of comic books; Jeff's Collie Club; a forest ranger handbook and a host of buttons, badges and fan cards, all of which can be purchased and traded at auctions and collectibles shows today.

Rin Tin Tin

Credited as "the most recognized name in German Shepherd history," Rin Tin Tin became a film star in 1922, but the real-life, stranger-than-fiction story of Rinty dates back to 1918, when he was rescued from a bombed dog kennel in Lorraine, France during World War I.

On September 15, 1918, Corporal Lee Duncan found a litter of puppies in a newly bombed kennel, along with their mother, Betty. Duncan claimed two of the pups—a boy and a girl—and named them Rin Tin Tin and Nannette. The two pups the corporal claimed are the only two who survived. Then, during the process of transporting them back to his native Los Angeles, Nannette took ill and died.

Rin Tin Tin, however, proved to be tough and resilient. Three years later, Warner Brothers signed him for his first film, at Duncan's prompting. He was an immediate hit with fans who lauded his heroism and loyalty. His first endorsement was for Ken-L-Ration dog food and his picture graced millions of dog biscuit boxes.

As his career's height, Rin Tin Tin received nearly 10,000 fan letters a week! He died exactly one decade after his first film, having made 26 movies for Warner Brothers. Fortunately, Duncan bred Rin Tin Tin and several litters emerged from his line. One, named Junior, became his successor. Several dogs named Rin Tin Tin kept the lineage alive, constantly reinventing the character with shows like *The Adventures of Rin Tin Tin* (1954-1956) and *The New Adventures of Rin Tin Tin* in 1999.

Buttons, posters, stuffed animals and other memorabilia promoting the various television shows and films are now popular collectibles among Rin Tin Tin fans young and old.

Above: Rin Tin Tin "King of Canines" Button applying to his fame, rather than a movie title, 1930.
Below: Rin Tin Tin Toy Dog Premium plush and vinyl toy dog; Nabisco, 1954.

Above: Rin Tin Tin Magic Brass Ring, 1954.

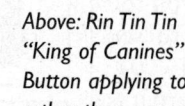

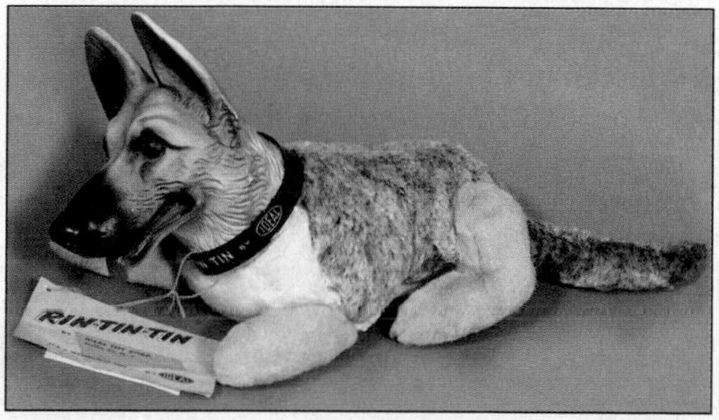

Top: Shredded Wheat Cereal 12 oz. Box Flat with Calvary Rifle Ballpoint Pen Offer, 1956.
Middle: Rin Tin Tin Insignia Patch, Nabisco peel-off stickers, 1958.
Bottom: Rin Tin Tin Color Litho. Button, sent to participants in Nabisco's 'Name The Puppy Contest.' 1956.

Garfield Die-Cut Display with Lapel Pins, 1978.

Garfield

Thank goodness for Garfield creator Jim Davis's short attention span. If he hadn't gotten bored with a little-known Garfield predecessor, Gnorm the Gnat, our favorite loafing, lasagna-lifting feline may never have come to be.

Limited Edition Garfield Figure with Watch, 1990s.

But in 1978, Davis did get around to trying out a non-insect comic strip star and the most famous cat ever to pounce on the funny pages was the remarkable result. What started out as a small-scale endeavor on Davis's part (he hoped for publication in 100 papers, 300 max.) has now become an incredible quarter-century empire. Today, Garfield appears in an astounding 2,750 papers. He also has a not-too-shabby merchandising line, worth the overweight cat's girth in billions.

Kittie Masters, a teacher in Indiana, who channeled her own personal long held interest in collecting into Garfield-themed classrooms, said it comes down to characteristics.

"He's honest. People don't like getting up in the morning. People don't like Mondays. People don't like diets. They do like to eat. I think he says a lot of things people are thinking, but he does it in a funny way," she said.

One might recall driving on the highway and looking over to see Garfield suction-cupped to the window of a passing car, but that is not all that's out there for Garfield fans. Collectors can pursue Pez dispensers, bobble heads, books, stuffed animals, figurines, watches, banks, playing cards, pins, animation cels and even globes!

Through their appreciation for the ephemera of these characters, collectors are passing the love of animals on to future generations, as well as a love of the cat and dog characters of the past. As long as the hobby of collecting continues, Krazy Kat, Lassie, Rin Tin Tin, and Garfield will remain pop culture icons for generations to come. The fact that these characters remain favorites among people of all ages emphasizes their collectible value, which in turn preserves the history of America's love affair with our pets and pop culture.

Stacia Brown and Jaime Bramble contributed to this article.

Above Right: Garfield Globe, 2001.
Right: Garfield "Smile" Bobber Figure from 2003.

PENELOPE PITSTOP
FRICTION CAR
THE ADDAMS FAMILY
CHARM & BUTTON
for CUFF LINKS-ORNAMENTS-LAPEL PINS and JACKET ZIPPERS
AMAZING MARVEL SUPER HEROES
5¢
Josie and the Pussycats
OFFICIAL MONKEES
5¢ each
8 DIFFERENT COMIC STRIPS & PUT-TO-GETHER ACTION FIGURES
AS SEEN ON T.V.
THE BEATLES IN THIS MACHINE
I SAW HER STANDING THERE
10¢
THE MIGHTY HERCULES
25¢
MAGIC RING
JUST LIKE THE MIGHTY HERCULES OWN RING
• GLOWS IN DARK
• SECRET COMPARTMENT
SAFE • HARMLESS
NO. 3109
SON OF GARLOO
PLAY BOTH ON LAND AND IN WATER
VOYAGE TO THE BOTTOM OF THE SEA
SUBMARINE SCOUT SET
AS SEEN ON T.V.
ROBIN
START A COLLECTION
SUCTION CUP BACK WILL STICK TO GLASS
PENGUIN
JOKER
10¢
A THINGMAKER ACCESSORY KIT FEATURING
The GREEN HORNET
THE GREEN HORNET STRIKES AGAIN! WILL HE LEAVE A CLUE?...IT'S UP TO YOU!
ACCESSORY PAK
PLASTIGOOP

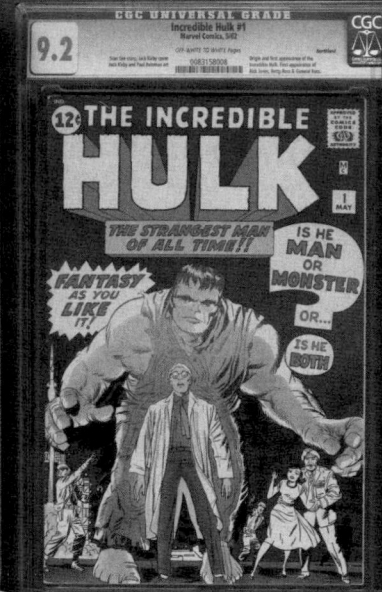

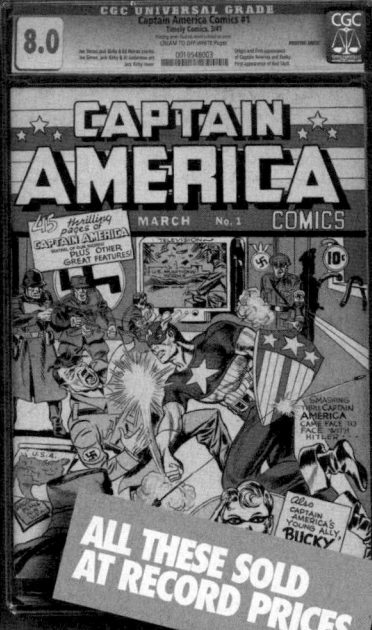

Batman and Wonder Woman Collectors

We buy pre 1975 Batman comics and memorabilia and Wonder Woman comics and memorabilia from all eras.

P.O. Box 604925
Flushing, NY 11360-4925
e-mail: batt90@aol.com
wwali@aol.com

© DC Comics 2001

Radio Spirits®

Let us take you back to the thrilling days of yesteryear with original radio broadcasts of

The Shadow	Superman
The Green Hornet	The Lone Ranger
Gunsmoke	Hopalong Cassidy
Sam Spade	Suspense
Inner Sanctum	Sherlock Holmes
Jack Benny	Jean Shepherd

Call 1-800-206-6454 for a **FREE** catalog, or Visit us today at www.RadioSpirits.com!

Walt Disney's ALICE in WONDERLAND

Always looking for items related to Walt Disney's Alice in Wonderland. Original art, books, paper items, movie memorabilia, toys, games, dolls, puzzles, watches, ceramics, novelties, advertising, you name it!

Especially looking for Evan K. Shaw teapots, Goebel, Zaccagnini, MCP, Weetman, Galigani, and other foreign figures.

Matt Crandall
P.O. Box 2998
Merrifield, VA 22116-2998
matt@alumni.caltech.edu

DIAMOND INTERNATIONAL GALLERIES

TWO GREAT RINGS!

$75.00 **The Spider Ring**

$75.00 **Operator 5 Ring**

Do you miss the action of the old pulps? Diamond International Galleries is pleased to offer you the chance to recapture that sense of adventure with a limited edition set of two of the more popular ring designs sought by today's collectors—The Spider Ring and the Operator 5 Ring! Both gold-toned, adjustable rings reproduce their classic designs in incredible exacting detail. Each is marked "repro" and numbered on the back. Both were originally limited to only 250 copies and now only a few sets remain!

You can get both rings for only $135 plus $4.50 shipping & handling.

Call Joe toll free now to order 888-355-9800 ext. 1626
(Or send check or money order to: Diamond International Galleries, 3679 Concord Rd., York, PA 17402.)

PRICING section

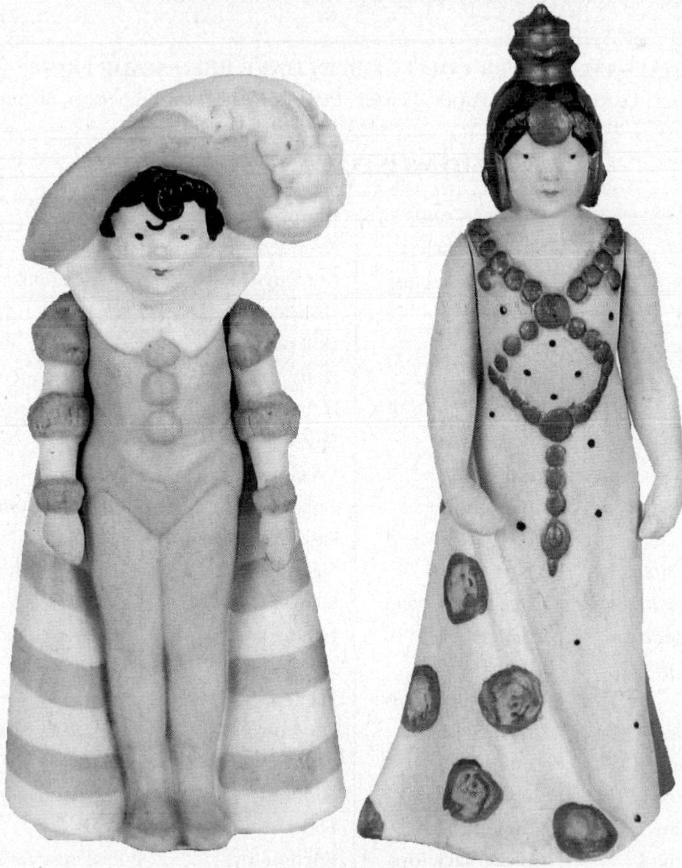

Little Nemo and the Princess Bisque Figures
LNE-14
(page 599)

The characters we love and collect have diverse origins, but there's a common thread that runs through the ones that become the most successful in the long run. It has almost nothing to do with artistic direction, the quality of the material, special effects or the rate of inflation. Instead it has to do with how well that character is marketed to the public.

A character may be introduced on a TV show, a cartoon, a newspaper comic strip, in a comic book, video game or feature film. From any one of these alone a fad, flash-in-the-pan, or short-lived hit may be created, but these things are rarely (if ever) sustained by only one medium.

Instead, it's most often the characters found in the greatest numbers of the categories listed on these two pages that will have the strongest connection in pop culture awareness. Each of those characters was the beneficiary of well-planned marketing and development programs which took them through just about every other available medium and type of product.

Using Superman as an example, *Action Comics* #1 (June 1938) launched Superman in comics. At its peak, its circulation was approximately 1.5 million copies per month. The daily newspaper strip (January 1939) first introduced the Man of Steel to adults, and in short order reached 20 million readers. The radio show (February 1940) had 22 million listeners three times a week. Clearly, while the comic book was the springboard, it wasn't the end game. Instead, it was merely a beginning. Through club kits, food products, trading cards, apparel, wind-up toys, action figures, watches, live events, posters, standees, radios, telephones and many other products, Superman transcended his relatively humble beginnings to become one of the most recognized characters in the world.

While there are varying levels of achievement for the huge number of characters created since Palmer Cox's success with the Brownies, it's difficult to think of any top characters that are not represented in a significant number of these categories.

TYPES OF MATERIALS CHARACTER COLLECTIBLES HAVE BEEN MADE FROM: Cardboard, Celluloid, Ceramic, Cloth, Glass, Leather, Metal, Paper, Plaster, Plastic, Resin, Rubber, Soap, String, Wood.

TYPES OF ITEMS INCLUDED IN THIS BOOK:

Action figures
Ads
Airplanes
Albums
Ash trays
Awards
Badges
Balloons
Balls
Bandannas
Banks
Battery toys
Bean bags
Beanie Babies
Beanies
Belts
Big Little Books
Billfolds
Binoculars
Blotters
Bobbing head dolls
Bookmarks
Books
Bottle caps
Bottles
Bowls
Boxes
Bracelets
Bubble bath soakies
Buses
Buttons
Calendars
Cameras
Candles
Candy
Candy containers
Candy machines
Car emblems
Cards
Cars
Casting sets
Catalogues
Cereal box premiums
Cereal boxes
Certificates
Chains
Charms
Christmas cards
Christmas lights
Circus premiums
Clickers
Clocks
Club kits
Coasters
Code books
Coins
Colorform sets
Coloring books
Coloring sets
Comic book stands
Comic books
Compasses
Concert programs
Cookie cutters
Cookie jars
Costumes
Coupons
Cracker Jack toys
Crayon sets
Cups
Cut-out books
Decals
Decoders
Detective kits
Dishes
Doll patterns
Dolls
Drawings
Envelopes
Eyeglasses
Fans
Fast food premiums
Figurines
Films
Fishing kits
Flashlights
Flickers
Flip books
Folders
Footwear
Forks
Friction toys
Games
Gasoline premiums
Glasses
Globes
Gloves
Golden books
Greeting cards
Gum cards
Gum wrappers
Gun holsters
Guns
Gyroscopes
Hair accessories
Handbags
Handbills
Handbooks
Handkerchiefs
Hats
Helmets
Ice cream lids
Ingots
Instructions
Jackets
Kaleidoscopes
Key chains
Kites
Knives
Labels
Lamps
Lariats
Leaflets
Letter openers
Letters
License plates
Lighters
Lithographs
Lobby cards
Locks
Lunch bottles
Lunch boxes
Magazines
Magic answer boxes
Magic sets
Magic slates
Magnets
Magnifiers
Mailers
Make-up kits
Manuals
Maps
Marbles

- Marionettes
- Masks
- Matches
- Mechanical toys
- Medals
- Membership cards
- Merchandise catalogs
- Microscopes
- Mirrors
- Mobiles
- Model kits
- Money clips
- Movie premiums
- Movie programs
- Movie viewers
- Mugs
- Musical instruments
- Napkins
- Necklaces
- Necktie slides
- Neckties
- Newsletters
- Newspaper premiums
- Newspapers
- Nightlights
- Noise makers
- Notepaper
- Original art
- Ornaments
- Package seeds
- Paddles
- Paint sets
- Paper money
- Paperbacks
- Paper dolls
- Paperweights
- Party supplies
- Patches
- Pedometers
- Pen holders
- Pencil boxes
- Pencil erasers
- Pencil holders
- Pencil sharpeners
- Pencils
- Pennants
- Pens
- Periscopes
- Pez
- Phonographs
- Photo frames
- Photos
- Pillows
- Pin Wheels
- Pinbacks
- Pinball Machines
- Pins
- Pitchers
- Placemats
- Planters
- Plaques
- Plates
- Playsets
- Pocket watches
- Pop-up books
- Post cards
- Posters
- Pottery
- Press books
- Printing sets
- Prints
- Product containers
- Projection equipment
- Prototypes
- Pull toys
- Pulps
- Punch-out sets
- Punching bags
- Puppets
- Puzzles
- Radio guides
- Radio premiums
- Radios
- Records
- Ribbons
- Rings
- Robots
- Rockets
- Rugs
- Rulers
- Salt & pepper shakers
- Sandbox toys
- Scales
- Scarves
- School bags
- Science kits
- Scissors
- Scrapbooks
- Scripts
- Sewing kits
- Sheet music
- Shirts
- Show tickets
- Signs
- Sirens
- Skates
- Sleds
- Snow domes
- Soap
- Song books
- Spaceships
- Sparklers
- Spinners
- Spoons
- Sporting goods
- Spurs
- Squeeze toys
- Stamps
- Standees
- Star finders
- Stickers
- Stools
- Straws
- Suspenders
- Sweaters
- Swords
- Tags
- Targets
- Tattoos
- Telephones
- Telescopes
- Thermometers
- Tie bars
- Tin containers
- Toothbrush holders
- Toothbrushes
- Tote bags
- Toy boats
- Toy chests
- Toy televisions
- Trains
- Transfers
- Trays
- Trucks
- TV guides
- TV premiums
- Umbrellas
- Valentines
- Videos
- Viewers
- Walkie talkies
- Wastebaskets
- Whistles
- Wind-up toys
- Wrappers
- Wrapping paper
- Wrist watches
- Writing paper
- Yearbooks
- Yo-yos

A SPECIAL NOTE ABOUT TOY-RELATED ARTWORK:

In most of the categories listed above, original artwork featuring comic characters was commissioned and used in packaging, displaying, and advertising the toys. These unique and often highly collectible pieces of art should be considered as very closely related to the products they were created to market. Among these types of art are advertising, animation (in numerous forms), comic book, comic strip, packaging, poster, and puzzle art. Examples of packaging art can range from book covers, such as the much sought after Big Little Book or Golden Book covers, to the actual package in which a toy is sold. Several types appear throughout the book.

Unless otherwise noted, prices listed for all items represent GOOD, FINE, and NEAR MINT conditions.

Ace Drummond

World War I air ace Eddie Rickenbacker created the story line for this aviation strip, with illustrations by Clayton Knight, for King Features in 1934. The strip was not a major success and was dropped in the late 1930s. A 13-episode adventure serial based on the strip was produced by Universal Pictures in 1936, with John King as Drummond and Noah Beery, Jr., as Jerry, his mechanic. Lon Chaney Jr. and Jean Rogers were also in the cast. The serial was released to TV in 1949.

ACE-1

ACE-2

❑ **ACE-1. Big Little Book #1177,**
1935. Store item by Whitman Publishing Company. - **$12 $36 $80**

❑ **ACE-2. "Ace Drummond" Cello. Button,**
1936. Universal Pictures. For 13-chapter movie serial "Ace Drummond" with added inscription "Capt. Eddie Rickenbacker's Junior Pilot's Club". - **$50 $175 $325**

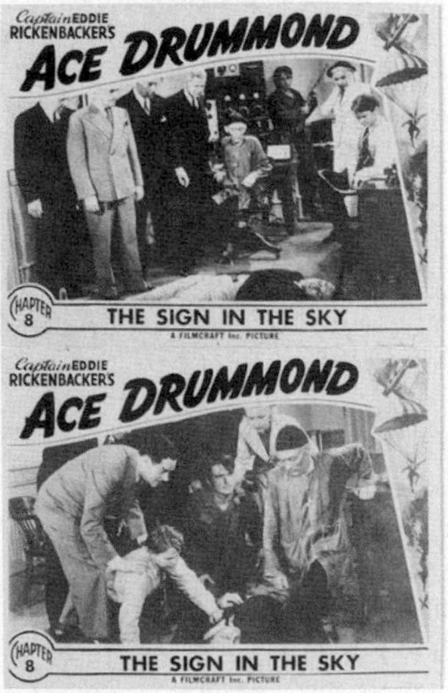

ACE-3

❑ **ACE-3. Lobby Cards,**
1936. Two 11x14" purpletone cards for original release of 13-chapter Universal serial. Both examples are for Chapter 8 "The Sign In The Sky." Each - **$20 $35 $70**

ACE-4

❑ **ACE-4. Movie Theater Giveaway Cards,**
1936. Universal Pictures. Ten shown from unnumbered set of 12. Each 2-3/8x3-1/4" browntone photo card. One depicts "Captain Eddie Rickenbacker" while others depict "Air Transport Progress." Examples seen have red ink stamp on reverse with theater name and starting date of serial. Each - **$8 $20 $35**

Addams Family

Cartoonist Charles Addams (1912-1988) was born in Westfield, New Jersey. Nicknamed "Chill" by his boyhood friends, the family's Victorian home resembled the Addams Family home of later fictional fame. Addams drew over 1,300 cartoons through his long career, highlighted by many appearances in *The New Yorker* magazine which published his first cartoon on February 6, 1932. He had a dark macabre sense of humor and was an excellent draftsman, which led to 15 reprint collections of his cartoons being published between 1942 and 1991. Interestingly, members of the Addams Family were only in 50 of his works.

ABC-TV aired *The Addams Family* between September 18, 1964 and September 2, 1966. The cast included: Carolyn Jones as Morticia, John Astin as Gomez, Jackie Coogan as Fester and Ted Cassidy playing a dual role as Lurch and Thing. Hanna-Barbera produced a Saturday morning cartoon series between September 8, 1973 and August 30, 1975 and a second series in 1992-1993. Orion Films released two live action films: *The Addams Family* in 1991 and *Addams Family Values* in 1993. Both features starred Anjelica Huston as Morticia, Raul Julia as Gomez and Christopher Lloyd as Uncle Fester. A new Broadway musical is planned for the 2009-2010 season. The dark humor of Charles Addams continues to bring laughter to millions worldwide.

ADF-1

❑ **ADF-1. Charles Addams Hardcovers With Dust Jackets Lot,**
1940s. Simon & Schuster. All are 8.25x11.5" with original dust jackets and feature Addams art. Numerous titles issued from 1940s through 1960s in numerous printings. For non-first edition with dust jacket typically - **$15 $35 $75**

ADF-2

❑ **ADF-2. "The Thing From The Addams Family" Boxed Battery Operated Bank,**
1964. Poynter Products Inc. 3.5x4.5x3.5" tall black hard plastic bank in box featuring illustrations of the Addams Family House. Copyright by Filmways TV Productions Inc. Bank is designed so that when a coin is placed in slot on top the bank rocks back and forth and a small green hand comes out and grabs the coin pulling it inside. Comes with 3x4" instruction sheet. Near Mint Boxed - **$225**
Loose - **$35 $65 $125**

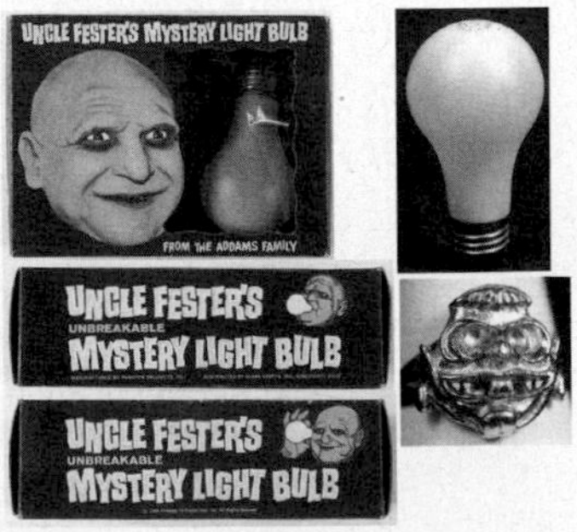

ADF-3

❑ ADF-3. "Addams Family Uncle Fester's Mystery Light Bulb" With Box,
1964. Poynter Productions Inc. 5.5x7.25x2.5" deep box has many illustrations of Fester with light bulb. Battery operated plastic light bulb is 4" tall with "UF" logo and Uncle Fester name. Bulb comes with "Mystery Ring" and "Foil Strips." Ring is adjustable goldtone metal depicting face of ghoulish character with jagged teeth. Strips are generic tin foil. Near Mint Boxed - **$500**
Bulb Only - **$25 $50 $100**
Ring Only - **$50 $100 $150**

ADF-4

ADF-5

❑ ADF-4. "The Addams Family/Morticia" Figure,
1964. Remco. 4.75" tall with molded plastic body, vinyl head with long rooted life-like hair. **$50 $100 $200**

❑ ADF-5. "The Addams Family/Lurch" Figure,
1964. Remco. 5.5" tall with molded plastic body and vinyl head. **$40 $75 $150**

ADF-6

❑ ADF-6. "The Addams Family" Puppet Set,
1964. Ideal. Puppets are 10.5" tall with silk-screened fabric bodies and vinyl heads. Each puppet has character name as well as body design. Morticia - **$35 $75 $150**
Gomez - **$35 $75 $150**
Uncle Fester - **$50 $100 $200**

ADF-7

❑ ADF-7. Addams Family Button Set,
1964. Filmways TV Productions. Each is 15/16" litho. Issued with various background colors as set of 12. Fester not shown.
Each - **$18 $30 $50**

ADF-8

❑ ADF-8. "Addams Family Haunted House" Aurora Model Kit,
1964. Near Mint Sealed - **$700**
Box Unsealed With Unused Parts - **$200 $400 $600**

ADF-9

❑ ADF-9. "The Addams Family View-Master" Set,
1965. - **$20 $40 $90**

ADF-10

❑ ADF-10. Addams Family Plastic Ring Figures,
1960s. Store item. Set of four, originally on card also holding attachment ring.
Each Ring With Base - **$3 $6 $10**

ADF-11

❑ ADF-11. "The Addams Family Uncle Fester" Boxed Figure,
1960s. Remco. 4.75x7.25x2.5" deep box holds 4.75" tall figure of hard plastic body with soft vinyl head depicting him holding a frog in one hand. Box interior is designed like a dungeon. Sticker on right corner of box reads "Stick To Dashboard." Near Mint Boxed - **$600**
Loose - **$100 $200 $300**

ADF-12

❑ ADF-12. "The Addams Family" Vending Machine Insert Paper,
1960s. 3x3-7/8" hexagonal-shaped glossy paper with images of the Addams Family house and portraits of its occupants. Reads "The Addams Family Twelve Different Buttons Collect! Trade! Save!" For series of 7/8" litho buttons featuring portraits of the characters.
$25 $50 $110

ADF-13

❑ **ADF-13. "The Addams Family" Lunch Box,**
1974. King-Seeley Thermos Co. 7x8.5x4" deep lunch box. Designed with images from the 1973 animated series by Hanna-Barbera. **$50 $125 $250**

ADF-14

ADF-15

❑ **ADF-14. Addams Family Cereal Box with "Cousin It" Flashlight Premium,**
1991. - **$6 $12 $35**

❑ **ADF-15. Addams Family Cereal Box with "Uncle Fester" Flashlight Premium,**
1991. - **$6 $12 $35**

ADF-16

ADF-17

❑ **ADF-16. Addams Family Cereal Box with "Lurch" Flashlight Premium,**
1991. - **$6 $12 $35**

❑ **ADF-17. Addams Family Cereal Box with "Thing" Flashlight Premium,**
1991. - **$6 $12 $35**

Admiral Byrd

Richard E. Byrd (1888-1957), American aviator and preeminent polar explorer, flew to the North Pole with Floyd Bennett back in 1926, made a spectacular transatlantic flight in 1927, and starting in 1928, led several important expeditions to Antarctica. The second such expedition featured weekly on-site short wave broadcasts--*The Adventures of Admiral Byrd*--over the CBS network from November 1933 to January 1935. The program was sponsored by Grape-Nuts Flakes.

ADM-1

❑ **ADM-1. Admiral Byrd Sheet Music & Booklet,**
1926. First is a 9.25x12" E.T. Paull color cover sheet music. "Top Of The World March." Eight pages. Second item is an 8.75x11.5", 36-page booklet titled "Highlights Of The Byrd/Antarctic Expedition." 1930 by the Tide Water Oil Co. Booklet consists of brown/white photos and text detailing Adm. Byrd's South Pole expedition. Cover artwork is blue/brown on tan.
Music - **$8 $15 $25**
Booklet - **$10 $20 $30**

ADM-2

ADM-3

❑ **ADM-2. "Conquerers Of The North Pole" Pamphlet,**
1927. Issued by John Wanamaker stores. Opens to 7-1/2x13-1/2". - **$15 $28 $50**

❑ **ADM-3. Commander Byrd Cello. Button,**
c. 1927. Identified "Commander Richard E. Byrd". - **$15 $35 $60**

ADM-4

❑ **ADM-4. Antarctic Expedition Medal,**
1928-1930. Features Admiral Byrd on front and an image of his plane with #NX4542 on wing. This was the plane that flew over the South Pole. - **$10 $20 $30**

ADM-5

ADM-6

❑ **ADM-5. Admiral Byrd Cello. Button,**
c. 1930. Profile picture inscribed "Rear Admiral Richard Evelyn Byrd, U.S.N." - **$20 $40 $75**

❑ **ADM-6. Admiral Byrd Historic Real Photo Button,**
c. 1930. Button is 1.25" and reads "First To Fly Over The South Pole Rear Admiral Richard E. Byrd, USN." - **$50 $150 $300**

ADM-7

❑ **ADM-7. "Commander Byrd's 'Floyd Bennett'" Cello. Buttons,**
1931. Bond Bread. 1-1/4" blue, black and white from set of six buttons picturing airplanes of famous aviators. One set has blank top rims while the second set has slogans promoting the virtues of bread. Second set is scarcer and images are the same as on the first set except button #4 pictures an autogiro.
Byrd Blank Rim - **$10 $23 $35**
Byrd Slogan Rim - **$15 $35 $55**

ADM-8

❑ **ADM-8. "Famous Flyers" Book with Dust Jacket,**
1931. Features Admiral Byrd on the cover and has a 46 page story of his life. - **$25 $55 $90**

ADM-9

❑ **ADM-9. "Little America Aviation & Exploration Club" Member's Card,**
1933. Sponsor unknown. Card is dated 1933-34 and has facsimile signature of "C. A. Abele Jr., President/With Byrd, At The South Pole." - **$23 $45 $80**

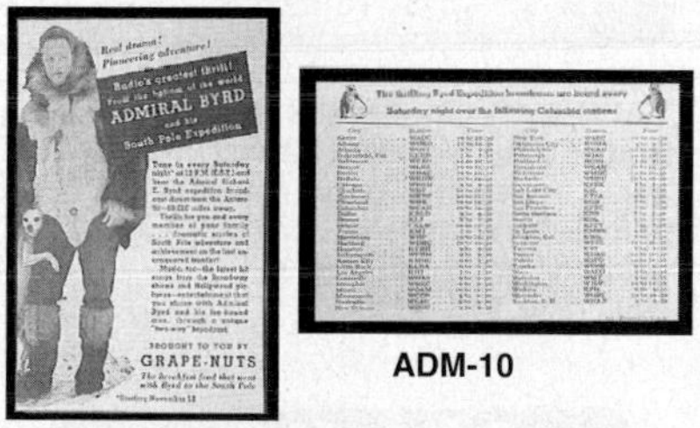

ADM-10

❑ **ADM-10. Radio Station Schedule Flyer,**
1933. Grape-Nuts. 3-1/2x5" with reverse listing of many cities, station call letters and times when the broadcasts were heard over Columbia stations. - **$10 $25 $55**

ADM-11

❑ **ADM-11. Admiral Byrd Radio Promo,**
1933. Scarce. Radio promo for gift map offered in exchange for 2 tops from Grape-Nuts packages. - **$22 $45 $85**

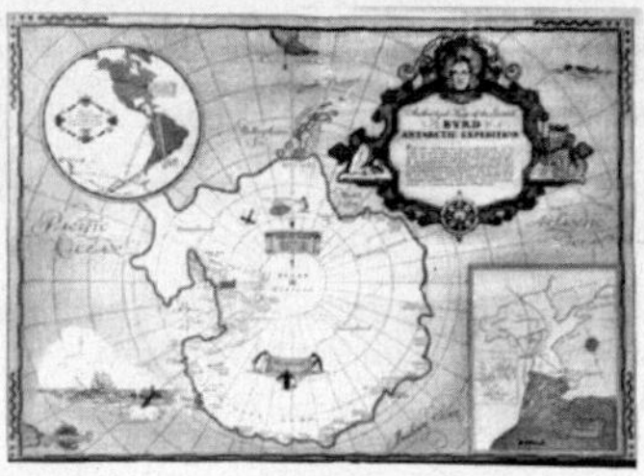

ADM-12

❑ **ADM-12. "Authorized Map Of The Second Byrd Antarctic Expedition",**
1933. General Foods. 18x24" opened. - **$40 $110 $160**

(FRONT ENLARGED)

ADM-13

(BACK)

❑ **ADM-13. Byrd Map Hard Cardboard Version,**
1933. Thick cardboard back with two hangers. - **$65 $145 $225**

ADM-14

❑ **ADM-14. "Trail Blazers" Watch,**
1933. - **$325 $650 $1100**

ADM-15

❑ **ADM-15. South Pole Radio News #2,**
1933. Grape Nuts Cereal premium. - **$22 $45 $80**

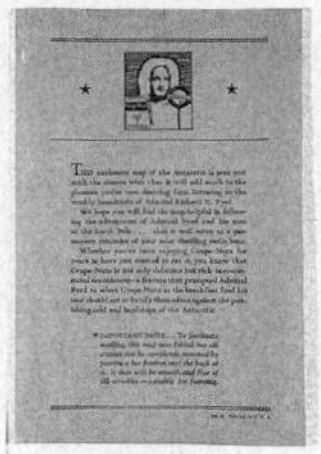

ADM-16 ADM-17

❑ **ADM-16. "South Pole Radio News" Photo Newspaper,**
1933. Grape-Nuts, "The Cereal Byrd Took To Little America". Issue #3 shown. At least three issues known.
Each - **$22 $45 $80**

❑ **ADM-17. Map Flyer,**
1933. Grape Nuts Cereal premium. Talks about receiving and using the map. - **$8 $18 $30**

ADM-18

❑ **ADM-18. "To The South Pole With Byrd" Booklet,**
1933. Ralston Purina Co. - **$15 $30 $45**

ADM-19

❑ **ADM-19. Byrd Expedition II Commemorative Cover,**
1933. 3.5x6.5" postal envelope commemorating "Landing, Bay Of Whales" and "Byrd Ice Party Ashore." - **$12 $22 $38**

ADM-20

❑ **ADM-20. "South Pole Picture Book,"**
1934. Softcover with 32 pages. Carries copyright of Capt. Ashley McKinley, third-in-command of the expedition. - **$12 $22 $40**

ADM-21

❑ **ADM-21. "The Romance Of Antarctic Adventure" Expedition Summary Book,**
1935. 48 pages. Includes numerous ads for food and household products. - **$15 $28 $45**

ADM-22

ADM-23

❑ **ADM-22. Byrd Expedition-Guernsey Club Award Medal,**
1935. 2-1/2" bronze with reverse text "For Distinguished Service To The Dairy Industry-In Commemoration By The American Guernsey Cattle Club May, 1935." Depicted cow was born December 19, 1933 during the second expedition, the farthest south recorded birth of any dairy animal. - **$30 $60 $125**

❑ **ADM-23. Magazine Cover Article,**
1936. May issue of "The Open Road For Boys" with article and photos from his 1929 expedition to Little America of South Pole. - **$15 $25 $45**

ADM-24

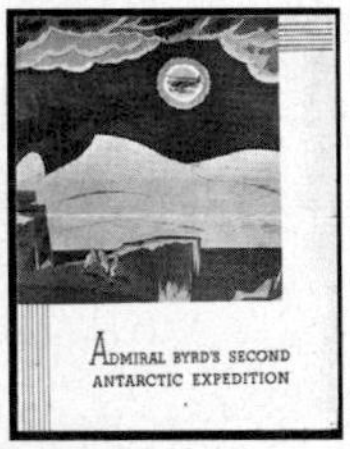

ADM-25

❑ **ADM-24. Blotter,**
1930s. Golden Guernsey Milk premium. - **$30 $50 $100**

❑ **ADM-25. Admiral Byrd Grape Nuts Booklet,**
1930s. - **$22 $45 $65**

ADM-26

❑ **ADM-26. "Byrd at the South Pole" Film,**
1930s. Movie Jecktor film #115 boxed. - **$20 $50 $100**

ADM-27

ADM-28

❑ **ADM-27. "Welcome Home" Cello. Button,**
1930s. Black and white 1-1/4". - **$20 $40 $70**

❑ **ADM-28. "Antarctica Service" Award Medal,**
1930s. Bar pin holds ribbon in shades of blue joined to 1-1/4" brass metal inscribed on reverse "Courage/Sacrifice/Devotion." - **$55 $110 $165**

Adventure Comics

Major Malcolm Wheeler-Nicholson got into the comic book publishing business in early 1935 with *New Fun.* Although sales weren't very good, he decided to try a second title. *New Comics* #1 appeared in late 1935 with paper covers and 80 pages of color and black and white stories and art. Siegel and Shuster began Federal Men in early 1936 and Sheldon Mayer and Walt Kelly also contributed. Starting with issue #12, the title became *New Adventure* and finally *Adventure Comics* with issue #32. Buttons and certificates were obtained by clipping a coupon from the comic and sending it with ten cents to Steve Carson at "J.F.M.C. Headquarters." Like *New Fun, Adventure Comics* was part of the foundation of DC Comics. DC cancelled the title in 1983.

ADC-1

ADC-2

❑ **ADC-1. "Special Operator" Cello. Button,**
c. 1937. New Adventure Comics magazine. - **$85 $160 $340**

❑ **ADC-2. Club Member Cello. Button,**
c. 1937. Inscribed "Special Operator/Junior Federal Men Club/New Adventure Comics Magazine." - **$45 $90 $200**

ADC-3

❑ **ADC-3. "Special Operator" Cello. Button,**
c. 1939. Adventure Comics magazine. - **$110 $275 $525**

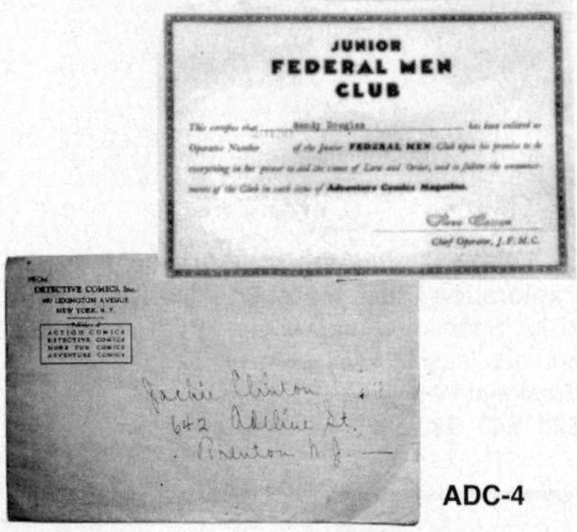

ADC-4

❑ **ADC-4. "Junior Federal Men Club" Member Certificate and Mailer,**
c. 1939. Adventure Comics magazine. Ink stamped Chief Operator's name "Steve Carson".
Certificate - **$135 $250 $435**
Mailer - **$30 $55 $110**

Advertising Misc.

Literally thousands of product makers in the past century have offered premiums in token or sporadic fashion. An absolute listing of all known advertising premiums would necessitate a massive set of volumes in book form while still leaving gaps of information lost in time. This section offers an overview of advertising premiums and similar items of established appeal to collectors. Represented are some of the most famous trademark characters of our popular culture. A more comprehensive listing is contained in *Hake's Guide To Advertising Collectibles/100 Years of Advertising From 100 Famous Companies* published in 1992.

ADV-1

ADV-2

❑ **ADV-1. J & P Coats Promo Calendar,**
1888. Thread ad shows dogs reading paper. Classic example of animals being used to promote products. - **$8 $15 $35**

❑ **ADV-2. Friends Oats Promo Booklet,**
1880s. Uses children to promote cereal products. - **$20 $40 $75**

ADV-3

ADV-4

❑ **ADV-3. J & P Coats Promo Card,**
1880s. Thread ad shows captured lion. Early use of animals, later used cartoon characters. - **$8 $15 $33**

❑ **ADV-4. J & P Coats Promo Card,**
1880s. Thread ad shows mice dressed up on front. Calendar on back. - **$8 $15 $33**

ADV-5

ADV-6

❑ **ADV-5. Quaker Oats Card,**
1890. - **$12 $22 $45**

❑ **ADV-6. Calendar Card,**
1891. Promotes Lucto Cereal on back of card. Sponsored by Reed & Carnrick. - **$10 $20 $40**

ADV-7

❑ **ADV-7. Hires Easel Card,**
1892. 5x6-1/2" diecut small counter sign with full color image. - **$60 $115 $200**

ADV-8

❑ **ADV-8. Roasted Oats Promo Card,**
1899. - **$12 $25 $50**

ADV-9

❑ **ADV-9. Friends Oats Promo Booklet,**
1890s. Front and back shown. - **$15 $30 $65**

(FRONT)

(BACK)

ADV-10

❑ **ADV-10. Frogs Thread J & P Coats Trade Card,**
1890s. - **$15 $30 $60**

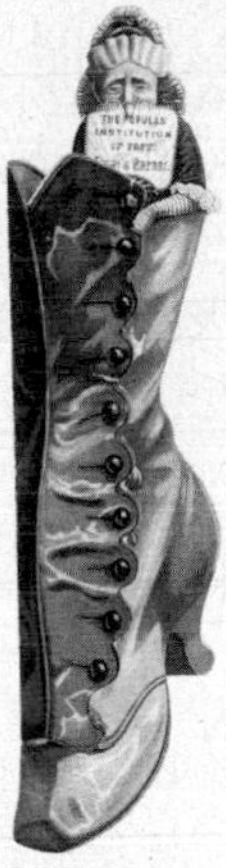

(CLOSED) ADV-11 (OPEN)

❑ **ADV-11. Mother Goose Series - Mother in Shoe Trade Card,**
1890s. Nestle's Chocolate. - **$33 $65 $125**

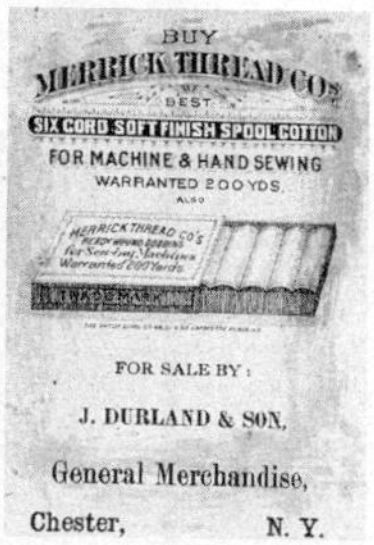

(FRONT) (BACK)

ADV-12

❑ **ADV-12. Spider's Spool Cotton Trade Card,**
1890s. - **$15 $30 $55**

ADV-13

ADV-14

❑ **ADV-13. Promo Card,**
1900. Domestic sewing machine ad card shows elves climbing trees. - **$10 $20 $45**

❑ **ADV-14. Wheatlet Cereal Standee,**
1900. Cereal and Flour Premium. 6" standee of girl in a long pink dress. - **$25 $50 $80**

ADV-15

ADV-16

❑ **ADV-15. Buffalo Bill Photo,**
c. 1900. Circus premium of famous star. - **$55 $120 $200**

❑ **ADV-16. Star Nursery Rhymes Book,**
1901. Star Soap premium. Twenty page book in color with beautiful art. - **$20 $40 $80**

ADV-17

❑ **ADV-17. Mapl-Flake Promo,**
1902. - **$10 $20 $40**

ADV-18

❑ **ADV-18. Mother Goose Series - Mother in Shoe Trade Card,**
1900s. Nestle's Food. - **$15 $30 $60**

ADV-19

❑ **ADV-19. Ceresota Mill Worker Cloth Doll,**
1912. 12" premium for Ceresota flour. - **$55 $90 $160**

(BOX FRONT)

(BOX BACK)

(SAMPLE CARDS)

ADV-20

❑ **ADV-20. "Going to Market" Playing Cards,**
1915. This card set was the first use of cards to promote multiple products. - **$80 $135 $260**

ADV-21

❑ **ADV-21. Circus Animals Booklet,**
1923. California Syrup premium. 16 pages. - **$35 $70 $140**

ADV-22

❑ **ADV-22. The Ad-ven-tur-ous Billy And Betty,**
1923. VanCamp Products. Fairy tales, 30 pages. Beautifully illustrated stories of Billy and Betty VanCamp. - **$20 $40 $80**

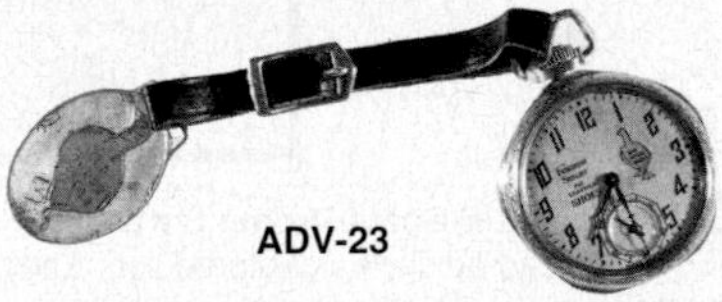

ADV-23

❑ **ADV-23. Red Goose Pocket Watch & Fob,**
1927. Watch - **$300 $600 $1150**
Fob - **$40 $75 $150**

ADV-24

❑ **ADV-24. Red Goose Alarm Clock,**
1920s. - **$300 $600 $1150**

ADV-25

❑ ADV-25. "Bing Bang Gun" Sign for July 4th,
1920s. 18" long sign with red lettering and red, yellow and black paper pop gun.
Sign - **$30 $60 $120**
Pop Gun - **$20 $40 $80**

ADV-26

❑ ADV-26. "Red Goose Shoes" Card Toy,
1920s. "Mov-I-Graff." 3-1/2x6-1/2" card featuring fine chain mounted on character face to form various facial images when card is jiggled or tapped. - **$12 $20 $35**

ADV-27

❑ ADV-27. Toy Army Tents,
1931. Colorful paper Army tents used with toy soldiers. Six different in box. Promotes different divisions of the Armed Services.
- **$85 $165 $400**

ADV-28

❑ ADV-28. Boy Scout Pocket Watch in Box,
1933. Has scout motto on hour and minute hands. Has scout badge as second hand and the words of the Scout Code of Honor around the dial. Scarce.
Watch - **$350 $750 $1250**
Box - **$250 $450 $650**
Complete - **$600 $1200 $1900**

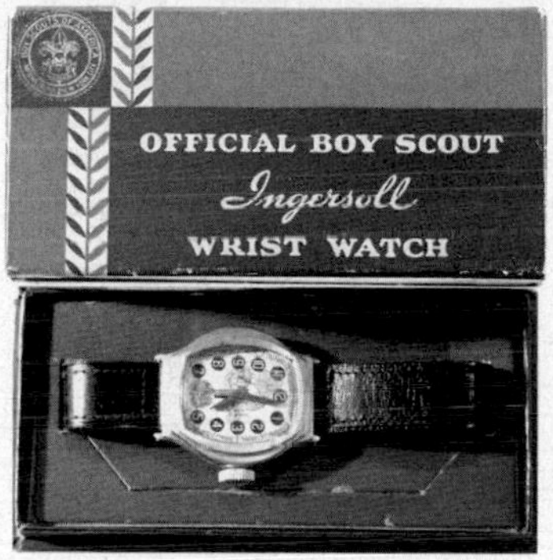

ADV-29

❑ ADV-29. Boy Scout Wrist Watch in Box,
1933. Has same make-up on dial as the pocket watch. Rare.
Watch - **$350 $750 $1250**
Box - **$300 $450 $650**
Complete - **$650 $1200 $1900**

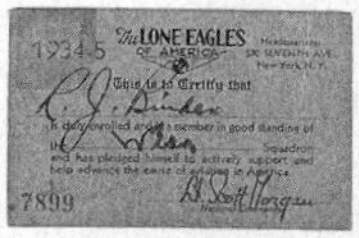

ADV-30

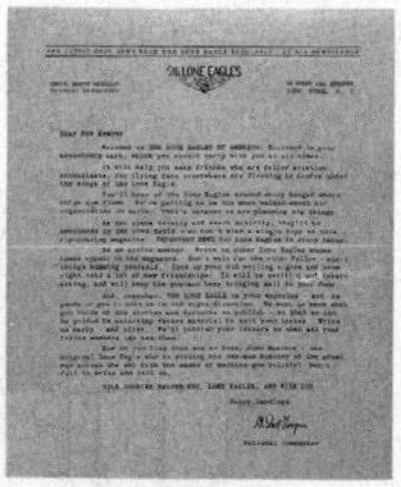

ADV-31

❑ ADV-30. Lone Eagles Club Card,
1934. Lone Eagles Magazine. -
$25 $65 $120

❑ ADV-31. Lone Eagles Of America Club Letter,
1934. National Lone Eagle Magazine. -
$18 $35 $65

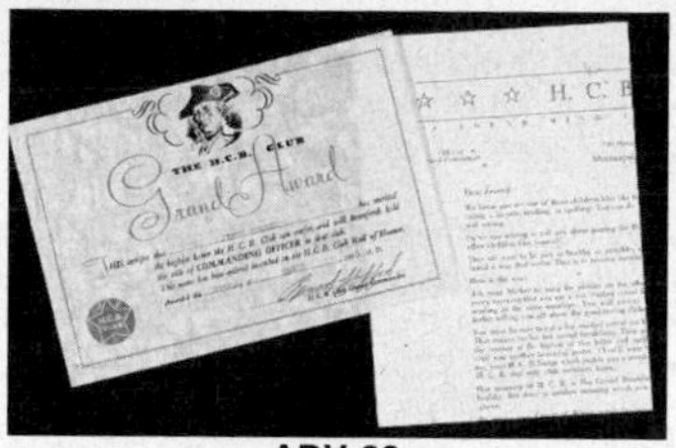

ADV-32

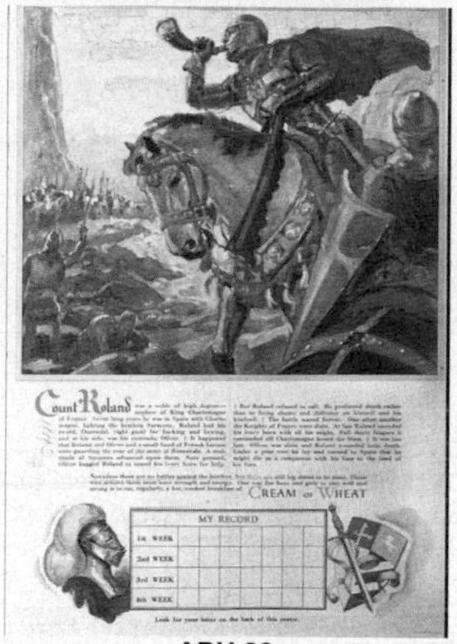

ADV-33

❑ ADV-32. H. C. B. (Hot Cereal Breakfast) Club Grand Award Certificate,
1935. Cream-of-Wheat premium. In addition to representing the club name, the H.C.B. initials had a secret meaning. Sworn to secrecy since 1934, our source decided in 2003 to reveal that H.C.B. also meant "Health Makes Colonels Brave." - **$22 $45 $65**

❑ ADV-33. H. C. B. (Hot Cereal Breakfast) Club Letter/Poster-on-Back,
1935. Cream-of-Wheat premium. -
$22 $45 $65

ADV-34

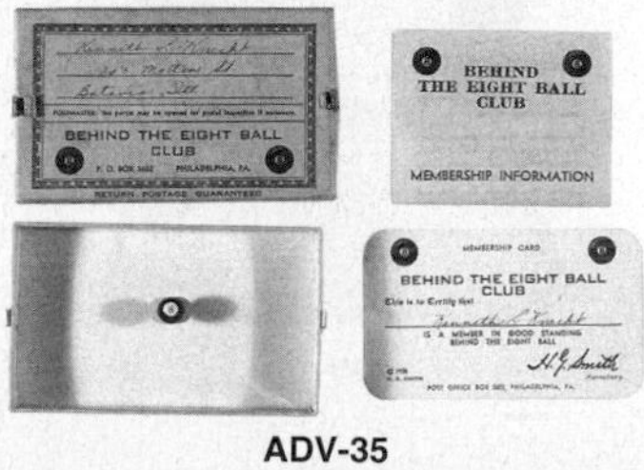

ADV-35

❑ **ADV-34. Kool-Aid Membership Card,**
1938. Kool-Aid Drink. Club card for Junior Aviation Corps. - **$15 $30 $50**

❑ **ADV-35. Behind The Eight Ball Club Kit,**
1938. National Salesman Club. Has rules, membership card, small plastic eight ball, and box. Complete - **$35 $75 $150**

ADV-36

❑ **ADV-36. Kraft 17" Standee,**
1938. Promotes Malted Milk and offers free 28" model of S.S. Normandie. From the Gordon Gold Archives. - **$135 $265 $500**

ADV-37

❑ **ADV-37. Earl Ortman's Model Planes Die Cut Standee,**
1938. Promotes Allsweet oleo and offers 4 different model planes. - **$225 $400 $750**

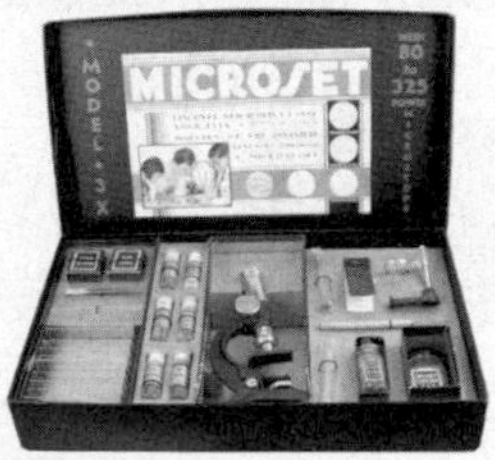

ADV-38

❑ **ADV-38. Microset Children's Microscope Set,**
1930s. Model 3X, distributed by Geo. Borgfeldt Corp. - same company that distributed early Disney toys. Also used as a prize.
- **$100 $200 $300**

ADV-39

ADV-40

❑ **ADV-39. Miller Wheat Flakes Cereal Sign 13x16 1/2"**
1930s. Wheat Flakes promotional for free punch-out rubberband gun. - **$65 $160 $250**

❑ **ADV-40. Butter-Nut Bread Aviator-Style Hat,**
1930s. Given away by bakeries. - **$22 $40 $65**

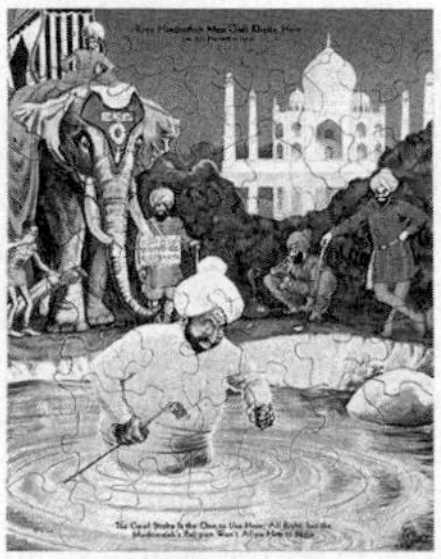

ADV-41

❑ **ADV-41. Richfield "Goofy Golf" Puzzle,**
1930s. Richfield Oil. Golf in India comical scene puzzle. - **$25 $50 $75**

ADV-42

❑ **ADV-42. Richfield "Goofy Golf" Puzzle,**
1930s. Richfield Oil. Golf in China comical scene puzzle with mailer. - **$30 $55 $85**

(COUPON)

(MEMBERSHIP CARD)

ADV-43

❑ **ADV-43. Airplane Model League Of America Coupon and Membership Card,**
1930s. American Boys Magazine.
Coupon for joining club. - **$6 $12 $22**
Club card. - **$18 $35 $55**

ADV-44

❑ **ADV-44. "Light Up A Kool" Willie Penguin Iron Cigarette Lighter,**
1930s. Cast metal. - **$115 $225 $360**

ADV-45

❑ **ADV-45. Rippled Wheat - Jack Dempsey 6" Standee,**
1930s. Die cut stiff cardboard counter sign. - **$75 $200 $400**

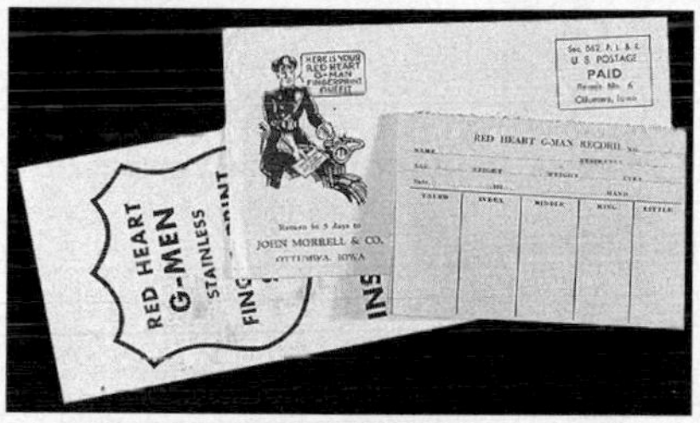

ADV-46

❑ **ADV-46. G-Men Fingerprint System (Red Heart),**
1930s. Instruction book. G-Man records and mailer. Gives children instructions on how to obtain fingerprints. Talks about capture of John Dillinger and gives advice from #1 G-Man J. Edgar Hoover. - **$65 $135 $250**

ADV-47

ADV-48

❑ **ADV-47. "Michelin" Plastic Ashtray,**
1930s. Likely produced into 1950s. - **$40 $75 $120**

❑ **ADV-48. Heinz Aristocrat Tomato Composition Figure,**
1930s. White base or black base. - **$70 $115 $175**

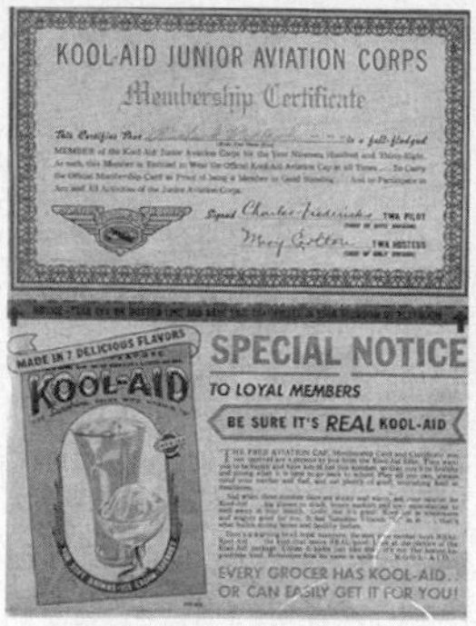

ADV-49

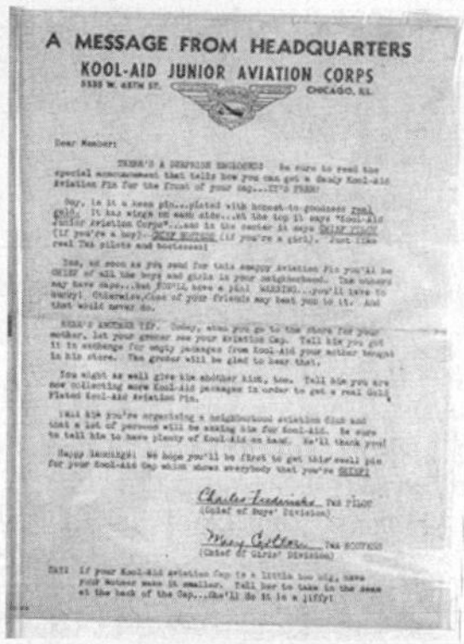

ADV-50

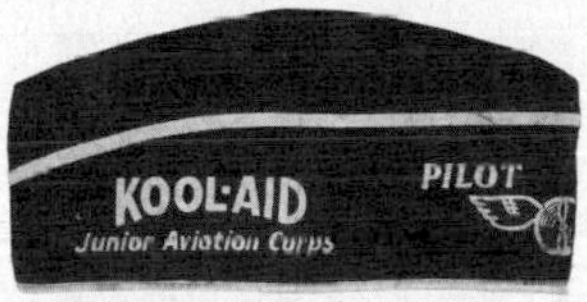

ADV-51

❑ **ADV-49. Kool-Aid 10x12" Promo,**
1930s. Has attached membership certificate for Junior Aviation Corps. - **$50 $100 $200**

❑ **ADV-50. T.W.A. Kool-Aid Club Instruction Form,**
1930s. - **$20 $40 $60**

❑ **ADV-51. Kool-Aid Aviation Club Cap,**
1930s. - **$35 $80 $120**

ADV-52

❑ **ADV-52. "Knot Hole League Of America" Patch and Card,**
1930s. Goudey Gum fabric patch plus member card for "Lou Gehrig" baseball club.
Patch - **$165 $265 $525**
Card - **$110 $185 $265**

ADV-53

ADV-54

❑ **ADV-53. Sunny Jim Cloth Doll,**
1930s. Force Cereal premium. - **$40 $70 $115**

❑ **ADV-54. Holsum Ranger Badge,**
1930s. Bread giveaway. - **$55 $110 $165**

ADV-55

❑ **ADV-55. Curtiss Candy Premium Puzzle,**
1930s. Puzzle titled "Singing in the Rain" shows kids eating Baby Ruth candy bars. With mailer. Complete - **$35 $85 $165**

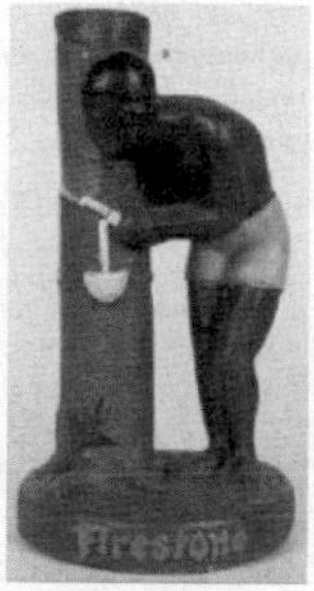

ADV-56

❑ **ADV-56. "Firestone" Plantation Worker Figurine,**
1930s. 5-3/4" tall painted hard rubber figurine on 3" diameter base. Issued to promote company's world-wide activities. - **$60 $135 $225**

ADV-57

❑ **ADV-57. "Butter-Nut Bread" Sign,**
1930s. 7x10" die-cut cardboard sign. - **$20 $40 $65**

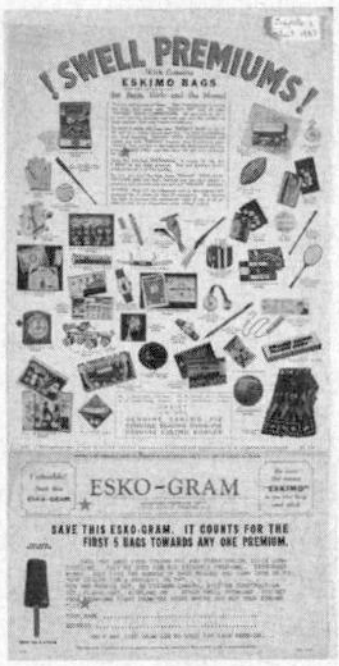

ADV-58

ADV-59

❑ **ADV-58. ESKO-GRAM Sign,**
1930s. With promo list that promotes premiums. - **$35 $85 $140**

❑ **ADV-59. Stamp Album For 48 Stamps,**
1940. Tydol Oil. - **$18 $35 $55**

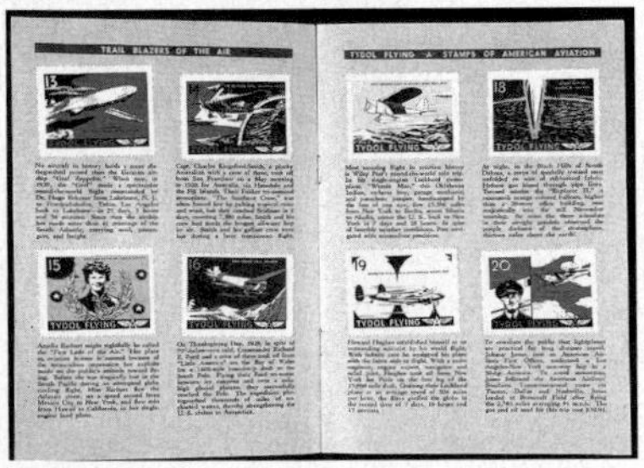

ADV-60

❑ **ADV-60. Stamps For Album,**
1940. Tydol Oil.
Each Loose or Mounted - **$1 $2 $4**

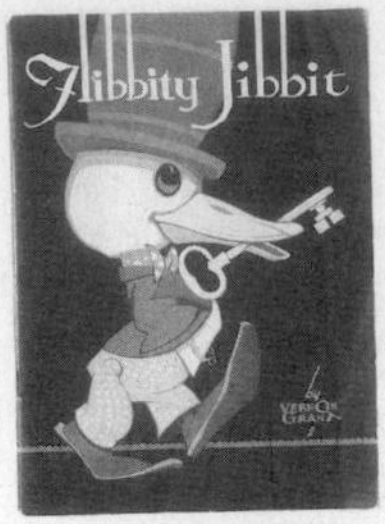

ADV-61

ADV-62

❑ **ADV-61. Flibbity Jibbit Book Premium,**
1943. Junkets Dessert premium. 32 pages. Vernon Grant art. - **$20 $40 $90**

❑ **ADV-62. Chiquita Banana Fabric Doll Pattern With Envelope,**
c. 1944. Kellogg's Corn Flakes. First version offered. Near Mint Packaged - **$165**
Loose Uncut - **$35 $55 $85**

ADV-63

❑ **ADV-63. Fearless Fosdick Matches,**
1949. Unused - **$10 $18 $33**

ADV-64

❑ **ADV-64. Dorothy Dix Food Advisor Booklet,**
1949. Sealtest. Four page radio premium. - **$15 $25 $40**

ADV-65

❑ **ADV-65. Macy's Red Star Club Badge,**
1940s. Scarce. - **$35 $65 $135**

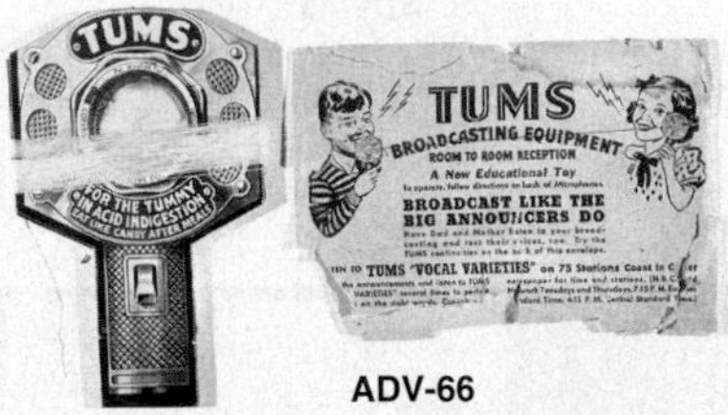

ADV-66

❑ **ADV-66. Tums Broadcasting Equipment,**
1940s. Radio premium with mailer. - **$30 $60 $90**

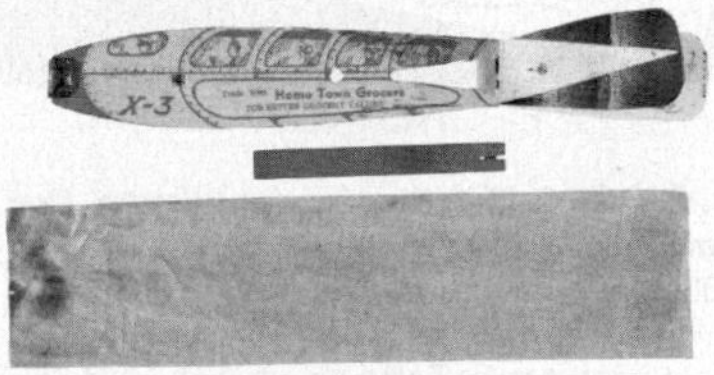

ADV-67

❑ **ADV-67. Rocket Gyro X-3 with Mailer,**
1940s. Sponsor Hometown Grocers. - **$35 $80 $135**

ADV-68

ADV-69

❑ **ADV-68. Red Goose Tin Whistle,**
1940s. Shoe premium. - **$10 $25 $40**

❑ **ADV-69. War Bond Matchbook Promo,**
1940s. Striking surface on Hitler's rear end. - **$30 $75 $150**

ADV-70 (DETAIL)

ADV-71

❑ **ADV-70. Pepsi-Cola Policemen Tin Sign,**
1940s. Lightly embossed litho. tin in red, white and blue, 3-1/2x21". - **$60 $135 $275**

❑ **ADV-71. "Pal" Cello. Button With Design By Al Konetzni, Prior To Career With Disney,**
1940s. 3" showing trademark man with lathered face. Design includes artist's "Alko" signature. - **$40 $80 $160**

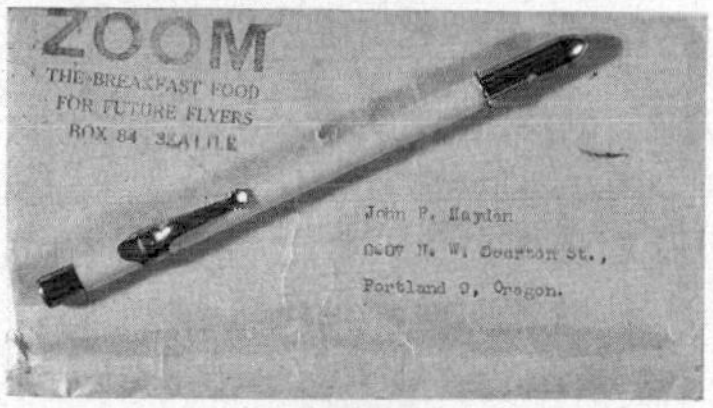

ADV-72

❑ **ADV-72. Zoom Bullet Pen And Mailer,**
1940s. Premium bullet yellow pen from Zoom Cereal for Future Flyers. - **$25 $50 $100**

ADV-73

❑ **ADV-73. Phillip Morris Counter Display,**
1940s. Four figure display with Johnny promoting candy and cigarettes. Rare.
- **$275 $550 $800**

ADV-74

ADV-75

❑ **ADV-74. Philip Morris 12" Tall Standee,**
1940s. 4" wide. Classic picture of Johnny , who always called out, "Call for Philip Morris." - **$115 $185 $300**

❑ **ADV-75. "Dr. Kool" Plaster Figure Paperweight,**
1940s. - **$55 $90 $160**

ADV-76

❑ **ADV-76. Life Magazine Scrap Book,**
1940s. Scarce. Sold for $1.00. - **$75 $150 $400**

ADV-77

❑ **ADV-77. RC Cola Sign,**
1940s. 13-1/4" x 10". Promotes Charm Beanies.
- **$55 $110 $165**

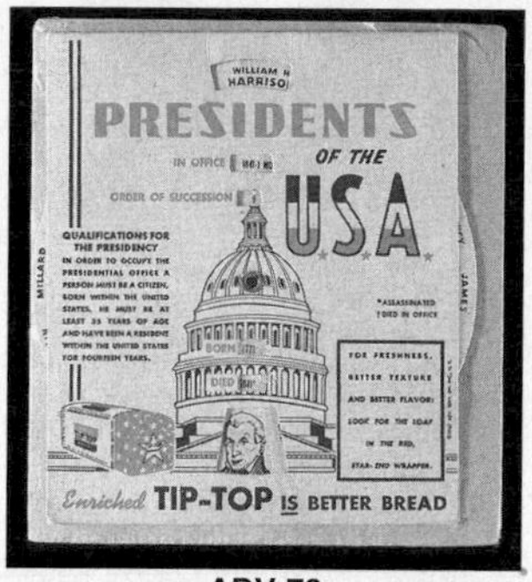

ADV-78

ADV-79

ADV-80

❑ **ADV-78. Tip-Top Bread Dial,**
1940s. Dial and window displays facts about Presidents of U.S. - **$12 $22 $38**

❑ **ADV-79. Good Humor "Captain" Safety Club button,**
1940s. Scarce - **$25 $50 $100**

❑ **ADV-80. "Junior Adventures" Club button,**
1940s. Premium from Marshall Field and Company. - **$15 $30 $75**

ADV-81

❑ **ADV-81. Wings Cigarettes Sign,**
1940s. Cardboard sign promotes 50 card premiums. - **$60 $125 $275**

ADV-82

❑ **ADV-82. Heinz Tomato Figure Likeness Salt & Pepper Set,**
c. 1940s. 4" tall ceramic figures obviously resembling Heinz tomato man although not credited. - **$60 $110 $185**

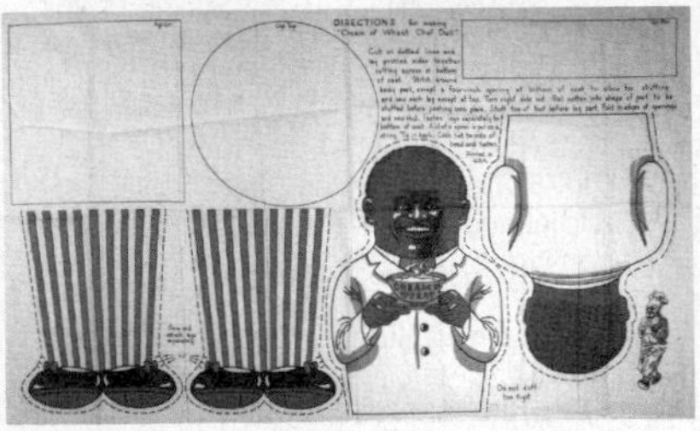

ADV-83

❑ **ADV-83. "Cream of Wheat Chef" Doll,**
1940s. Uncut cloth for stuffed doll. Large. -
$55 $110 $235

ADV-84

❑ **ADV-84. Fleer Gum Promo Booklet,**
1950. 12 pages with colorful pictures throughout. Front & back cover shown. - **$20 $45 $85**

ADV-85

❑ **ADV-85. Dubble Bubble Doodle Diary**
1950. Fleer. - **$18 $28 $55**

ADV-86

❑ **ADV-86. "Lennie Lennox" Figural Salt & Pepper Set,**
c. 1950. Each is 4-1/2" tall painted ceramic. Warren Products, Columbus, Ohio. -
$65 $125 $200

ADV-87

❑ **ADV-87. Kool Plastic Salt & Pepper Set,**
1951. Boxed - **$35 $65 $125**
Loose - **$18 $30 $40**

ADV-88

ADV-89

❑ **ADV-88. 7up "Fresh Up Freddie" Litho. Button,**
c. 1959. - **$12 $22 $50**

❑ **ADV-89. 7up "Fresh-Up Freddie" Soft Rubber Doll,**
c. 1959. - **$55 $110 $220**

ADV-90

❑ **ADV-90. Kool-Aid Soft Drink Stand,**
1950s. In colorful box with "How To..." booklet.
Boxed stand - **$110 $225 $350**
Booklet. - **$28 $55 $85**

ADV-91

❑ **ADV-91. Little Miss Sunbeam Standee,**
1950s. 40" x 27". - **$185 $375 $750**

ADV-92

❑ **ADV-92. Royal Crown Cola Postcard,**
1950s. Card offer for free carton of Royal Crown Cola. - **$10 $20 $30**

ADV-93

❑ **ADV-93. "Oscar Mayer" Plastic Weinermobile,**
1950s. "Little Oscar" figure rises and lowers. - **$75 $165 $285**

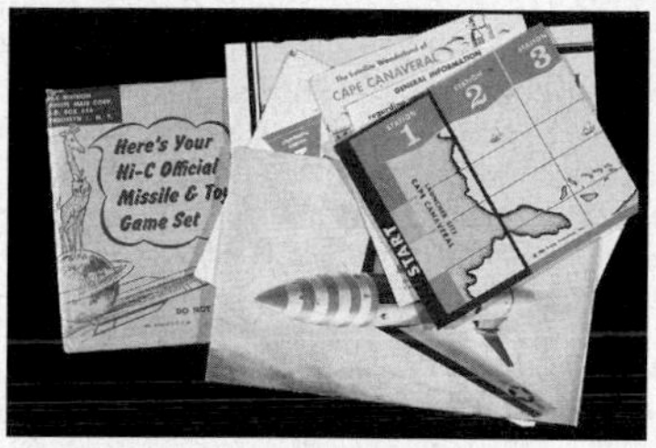

ADV-94

❑ **ADV-94. Missile Game Set,**
1950s. Consists of map, punch-outs, manual, instructions, game board, and mailer. Hi-C Minute Maid premium. - **$40 $80 $135**

ADV-95

❑ **ADV-95. Bardahl Detective Club 10x15" Sign,**
1950s. Rare. Shows all the villains. - **$50 $100 $250**

ADV-96

❑ **ADV-96. Bardahl Club Shield Litho. Tab,**
1950s. - **$15 $25 $40**

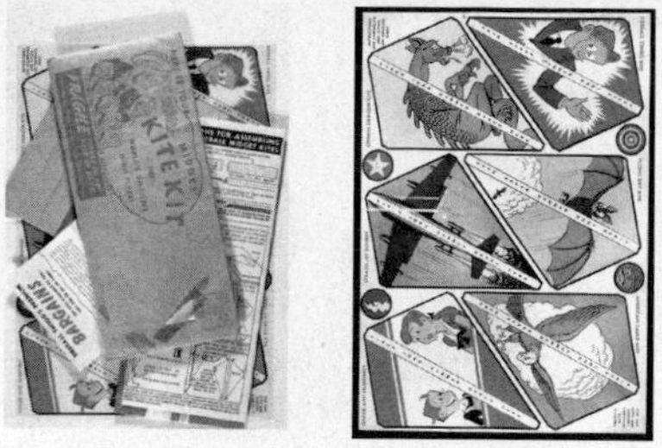

ADV-97

ADV-98

❑ **ADV-97. Fireball Twigg Midget Kite Kit with Mailer,**
1950s. 6 Kites. - **$45 $85 $185**

❑ **ADV-98. Grape-Nuts Flakes Fireball Twigg Kite Premium Sign,**
1950s. - **$40 $80 $165**

ADV-99

❑ **ADV-99. Register Dime Bank with Box,**
1950s. This was a very popular item used by children in the 1950s. Bankers used toys and TV characters to help entice children to save money, a habit they would take into adulthood.
Bank - **$18 $35 $60**
Box - **$30 $60 $125**

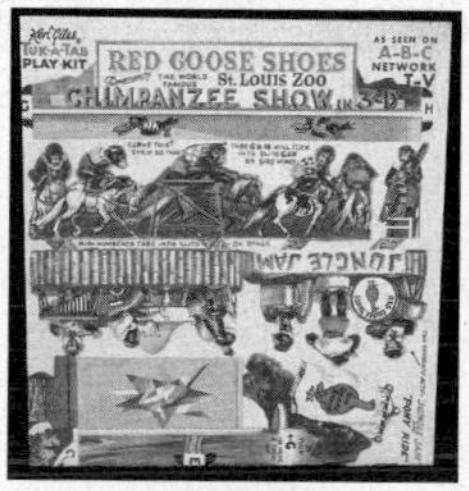

ADV-100

❑ **ADV-100. Red Goose Shoes,**
1950s. St. Louis Zoo punch-outs. - **$50 $100 $200**

ADV-101

❑ **ADV-101. Flap Happy Bird with Mailer,**
1950s. Post Toasties premium. - **$30 $65 $110**

ADV-102

ADV-103

ADV-104

ADV-105

ADV-106

❑ **ADV-102. Cheerio Yo-Yo Company Patch,**
1950s. Large Champion patch.
- **$50 $100 $170**

❑ **ADV-103. Cheerio Junior Instructor Patch,**
1950s. - **$15 $30 $65**

❑ **ADV-104. Cheerio Bronze Award Patch,**
1950s. - **$15 $30 $65**

❑ **ADV-105. 9 Trick Bronze Award Patch,**
1950s. - **$15 $30 $65**

❑ **ADV-106. 18 Trick Silver Award Patch,**
1950s. - **$20 $40 $90**

ADV-107

❑ **ADV-107. Esso Space Captain Sign (Silver Wings),**
1950s. Canada. - **$35 $65 $135**

ADV-108

❑ **ADV-108. Wild West Candy Box,**
1950s. Has Wild Bill Hickok card on back of box. - **$40 $110 $175**

ADV-109

❑ **ADV-109. Dubble Bubble Gum Premium Paddle Ball,**
1950s. By Fleer. - **$20 $40 $65**

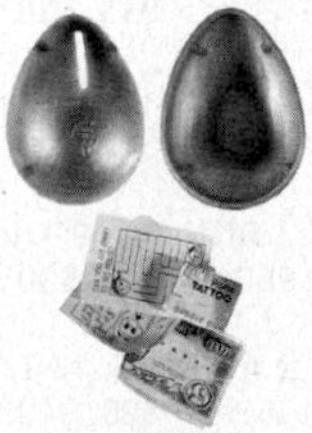

ADV-110 ADV-111

❑ **ADV-110. Red Goose Display Goose,**
1950s. Scarce. Goose lays plastic golden eggs. - **$450 $875 $1600**

❑ **ADV-111. Red Goose Gold Plastic Egg-Bank,**
1950s. Bank contained prize, connected to previous item. - **$12 $28 $45**

ADV-112

❑ **ADV-112. Bert And Harry Piel Ceramic Salt And Pepper Set,**
1950s. Piel's Beer. Bert is 3" tall salt, Harry is 4" tall pepper. - **$45 $85 $145**

ADV-113

❑ **ADV-113. "Toppie" Large Doll Premium,**
1950s. Top Value Stores. 11" tall by 14" long oilcloth. - **$50 $100 $185**

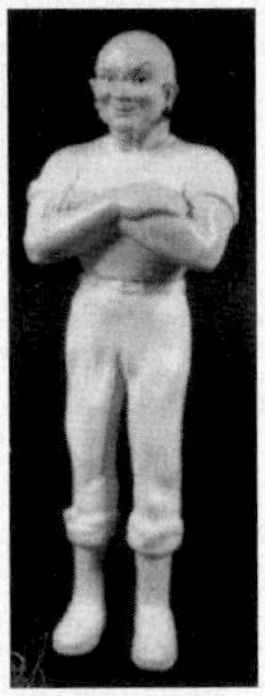

ADV-114 ADV-115

❑ **ADV-114. Marky Maypo Vinyl Figure,**
1961. Maypo Cereal. Came with unmarked 5" styrene bowl and 5" styrene spoon for $1 and box top. - **$40 $75 $150**

❑ **ADV-115. Mr. Clean Vinyl Doll,**
c. 1961. Procter & Gamble. - **$35 $75 $140**

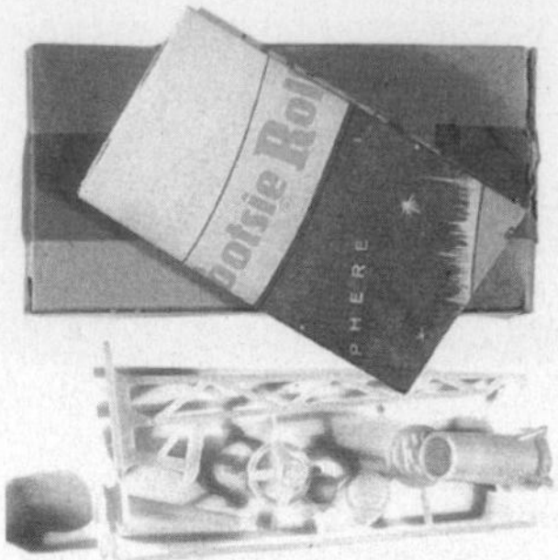
ADV-116

❑ **ADV-116. Astronaut -Orbit - Target Game,**
1962. Tootsie Roll premium. Plastic rocket with man and paper targets. Shows statistics of seven U.S. and Russian men who have been in space. Instruction and mailer enclosed.
Near Mint Boxed Unassembled - **$165**
Assembled With Target - **$30 $55 $85**

ADV-117

❑ **ADV-117. Esso "Happy Motoring" Coloring Book,**
1963. Esso/Humble Oil. 24 pages picturing national landmarks described by "Happy" Oil Drop character. - **$12 $22 $33**

ADV-118

❑ **ADV-118. Mr. Wiggle Vinyl Hand Puppet,**
1966. Premium from Jell-O, General Foods Corp. 3.5" bottom diameter by 6" tall hollow soft vinyl. - **$40 $70 $140**

ADV-119

❑ **ADV-119. "Naugahyde" Doll,**
1967. Issued by Uniroyal for naugahyde vinyl fabric. Many different color variations. -
$20 $35 $75

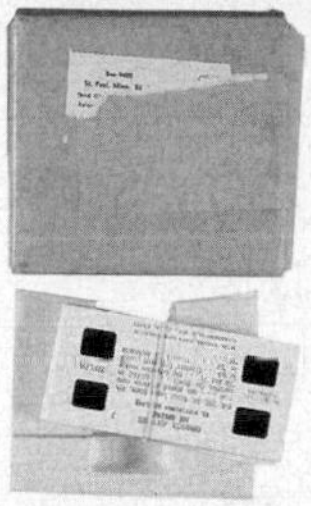

ADV-120

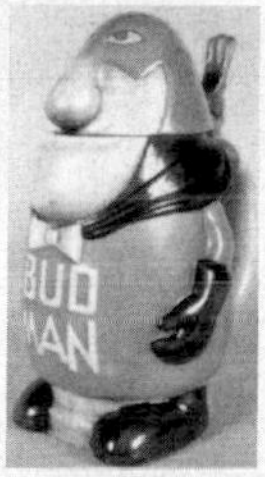

ADV-121

❑ **ADV-120. Football Movie Viewer And Slides,**
1969. Chiquita. 26 slides of photos of All Star football players like Bubba Smith, Mercury Morris, Joe Greene, Bob Lilly, and others. Also includes mailer and yellow plastic viewer. -
$85 $175 $300

❑ **ADV-121. "Bud Man" Ceramic Stein,**
c. 1969. Re-issued in 1990s. Original marked under base. Ceramarte made in Brazil. -
$80 $135 $225

ADV-122

❑ **ADV-122. Wheat Chex Magic Kit,**
1960s. 24 trick instruction book, includes items: 7 paper, 1 ring, 8 plastic, 3 wood, 3 metal. -
$35 $75 $135

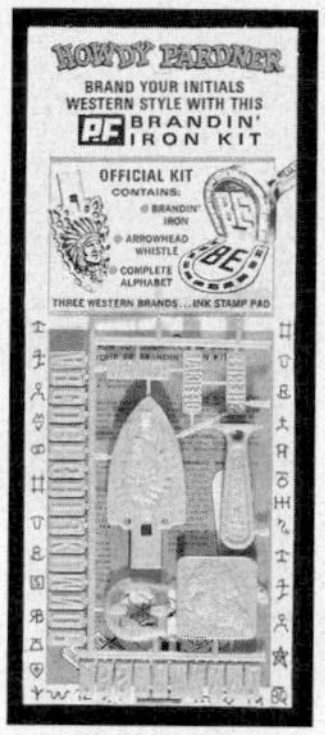

ADV-123

ADV-124

❑ **ADV-123. P.F. Branding Iron Kit With Whistle On Card,**
1960s. Scarce. B.F. Goodrich premium. Plastic kit with membership card on back. -
$40 $75 $135

❑ **ADV-124. SpaghettiOs Spoon Premium,**
1960s. - **$5 $12 $20**

ADV-125

❑ **ADV-125. Maypo Cello. Button,**
1960s. Classic cereal promotion with slogan, "I want my Maypo." Pinback shown from the promotion - **$15 $28 $55**

ADV-126

❑ **ADV-126. Esso "Happy" Oil Drop Punch Figure Card,**
c. 1960s. 5.25x8" rigid cardboard holding assembly cards for Esso symbolic figure. -
$20 $40 $75

ADV-127

ADV-128

❑ **ADV-127. Bud Man Foam Rubber Doll,**
c. 1970. - **$30 $60 $125**

❑ **ADV-128. "Chicken Hungry" Flexible Plastic Ring,**
1972. Red Barn System. - **$12 $22 $35**

ADV-129

ADV-130

❑ **ADV-129. Indian Sticker Badges,**
1972. Ovaltine premium. 6 different.
Each - **$6 $12 $20**

❑ **ADV-130. "Bazooka Joe" Cloth Doll,**
c. 1973. Bazooka Gum. 19" tall. - **$20 $40 $80**

ADV-131

❑ **ADV-131. "M&M's" Wall Clock,**
1979. Scarce. 15 1/2" tall. Wall clock has early version of the M&M boys. Premium offer.
With box - **$80 $160 $275**

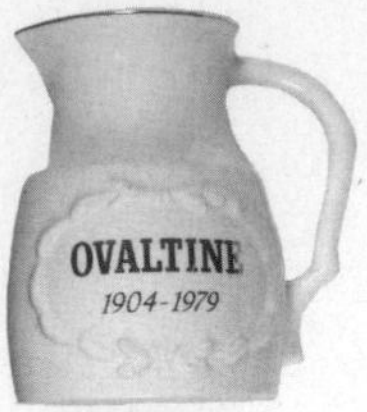

ADV-132

ADV-133

❑ **ADV-132. Ovaltine Premium Pitcher,**
1979. Celebrates 75 years (1904-1979) in business. - **$10 $25 $45**

❑ **ADV-133. Eskimo Pie Cloth Doll,**
1970s. 12" premium. - **$18 $35 $65**

ADV-134

ADV-135

ADV-136

❑ **ADV-134. Ben Franklin Stuffed Doll,**
1970s. Franklin Life Insurance Premium. - **$12 $28 $55**

❑ **ADV-135. "Burger Chef" Hand Puppet,**
1970s. Soft vinyl head with fabric chef hat and body. - **$22 $45 $80**

❑ **ADV-136. Tastykake Cloth Doll,**
1970s. Tastykake Bakery. - **$10 $25 $50**

ADV-137

❑ **ADV-137. "Where's the Beef?" Puzzle,**
1984. Wendy's Restaurants. 18"x 24" with box. 551 pieces. - **$10 $30 $60**

ADV-138

ADV-139

❑ **ADV-138. Raid Bug Plastic Wind-Up,**
1980s. - **$30 $60 $110**

❑ **ADV-139. Raid Battery Operated Plastic Robot With Remote Control,**
1980s. - **$110 $225 $335**

ADV-140

ADV-141

❑ **ADV-140. "Heinz" Talking Plastic Alarm Clock,**
1980s. Battery operated. - **$65 $155 $275**

❑ **ADV-141. Hershey "Messy Marvin Magic Decoder",**
1980s. Hershey's Chocolate Syrup. Mechanical cardboard with two diecut letter openings. - **$10 $18 $35**

ADV-142

❑ **ADV-142. Twinkie the Kid Anniversary Standee,**
1990. 4 ft. tall. - **$55 $110 $225**

ADV-143

❑ **ADV-143. "Oscar Mayer" Weinermobile,**
c. 1991. Re-issue without Little Oscar figure. - **$15 $28 $45**

ADV-144

❑ **ADV-144. A&W Root Beer Bean Bear Figures,**
1997. Orange shirt and hat. - **$22**
1998. Green shirt and hat. - **$18**

ADV-145

ADV-146

❑ **ADV-145. "Barnum Animals" Lion Bean Figure,**
1998. In box with tag. - **$16**

❑ **ADV-146. "Barnum Animals" Tiger Bean Figure,**
1998. In box with tag. - **$16**

ADV-147

ADV-148

❑ **ADV-147. Energizer Bunny Bean Bag,**
1998. - **$28**

❑ **ADV-148. "Hawaiian Punch" Doll,**
1998. With 2 tags. - **$32**

ADV-149

❑ **ADV-149. Pepsi Man Action Figure,**
1998. Japanese product has “Head Change” action. Sold in vending machines to promote the soft drink. - **$55**

ADV-150 ADV-151

❑ **ADV-150. Orioles Bear Beanie,**
1999. - **$12**

❑ **ADV-151. Taco Bell Bean Bag Dog,**
1999. With unbent tag - **$12**

ADV-152 ADV-153

❑ **ADV-152. FAO Schwarz Paddle Ball,**
1999. - **$22**

❑ **ADV-153. M&M's Sports Dispenser Figure,**
1999. Includes candy. - **$28**

ADV-154

❑ **ADV-154. Joe Camel Party Member Button,**
1990s. Very colorful 2 1/2" button shows probably the last cartoon-type character to ever promote cigarettes. - **$10 $18 $35**

ADV-155

❑ **ADV-155. Hot Wheels M&M's Racing Team Transporter,**
2001. In box. - **$22**

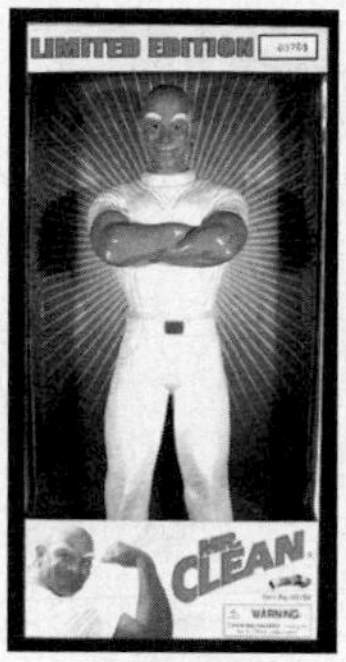

ADV-156

❑ **ADV-156. Mr. Clean Figure,**
2001. Limited edition in box. - **$30**

ADV-157

❑ **ADV-157. Bazooka Joe Wacky Wobbler Figure,**
2003. - **$18**

Air Juniors

One of the earliest radio clubs designed to encourage happy boys and girls to learn about flying airplanes and aspire to become pilots when they grew up, the *Air Juniors* club was formed in 1929. It was sponsored by the Commonwealth Edison Electric Shops. The project was promoted on the WENR Radio station broadcasting out of Chicago. The idea for the club piggy-backed on the popularity of Charles Lindbergh's flight from New York to Paris in May of 1927.

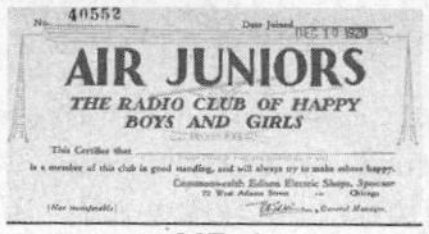

No. 40552 Date Joined DEC 10 1929

AIR JUNIORS

THE RADIO CLUB OF HAPPY BOYS AND GIRLS

This Certifies that

is a member of this club in good standing, and will always try to make others happy.

Commonwealth Edison Electric Shops, Sponsor

72 West Adams Street Chicago

(Not transferable) General Manager

AIR-1

AIR-2

❑ **AIR-1. Member's Card,**
1929. See AIR-3. - **$25 $65 $110**

❑ **AIR-2. Club Member Pin,**
1929. Scarce. - **$40 $100 $200**

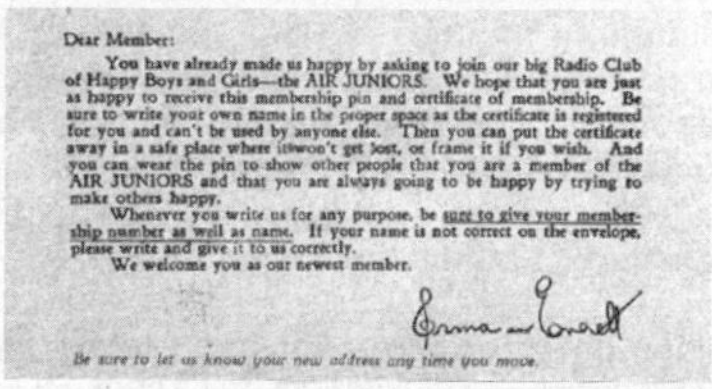

Dear Member:

You have already made us happy by asking to join our big Radio Club of Happy Boys and Girls—the AIR JUNIORS. We hope that you are just as happy to receive this membership pin and certificate of membership. Be sure to write your own name in the proper space as the certificate is registered for you and can't be used by anyone else. Then you can put the certificate away in a safe place where it won't get lost, or frame it if you wish. And you can wear the pin to show other people that you are a member of the AIR JUNIORS and that you are always going to be happy by trying to make others happy.

Whenever you write us for any purpose, be sure to give your membership number as well as name. If your name is not correct on the envelope, please write and give it to us correctly.

We welcome you as our newest member.

Be sure to let us know your new address any time you move.

AIR-3

❑ **AIR-3. Club Letter,**
1929. Membership card and letter came as a single piece for member to separate on perforated line. - **$20 $35 $65**

AIR-4

AIR-5

❑ **AIR-4. Mailer For Membership Card And Letter,**
1929. - **$15 $30 $50**

❑ **AIR-5. “Air Scouts” Member's Brass Pin,**
c. 1929. Same design as 1929 member's pin. Uncertain if title represents change in club's name or member's advancement to higher club rank. - **$55 $135 $240**

Al Jolson

Born Asa Yoelson, Al Jolson (1886-1950) and his family immigrated to America in 1894. Al began performing in vaudeville with his brother in 1901. To overcome his shyness, Jolson started working in blackface in 1904. He debuted on Broadway at the Winter Garden Theater in *La Belle Paree* in 1911, which made him a star.

Warner Brothers began casting the feature film *The Jazz Singer* in 1927. George Jessel was cast in the lead but wanted too much money and the part went to Jolson. He became the first star of "talking films," though he is virtually the only one who talks or sings in the movie. The success of *The Jazz Singer* led to international success for Jolson and also heralded the end of silent movies. Jolson's recording of *Sonny Boy* in the 1928 feature *The Singing Fool* became the world's first million selling record.

Jolson did a few more films and had moderate success on the radio in the 1930s and on Broadway in 1940, but entertaining the troops in WWII would lead to a last burst of fame for the charismatic performer. Columbia Pictures released *The Jolson Story* in 1946 and *Jolson Sings Again* in 1949. Larry Parks played the lead and lip-synched to recordings by Jolson himself. Al Jolson's current day fan base attests to his slogan "You Ain't Seen Nothin Yet."

ALJ-1

(AL JOLSON CLOSE-UP)

❑ **ALJ-1. Exhibit Postcard From 1929 Series "Star Pictures Stamp,"**
1929. 3.25x5.25" rare series. Stamp designs are in red and white borders with bluetone photos of various famous people. Reverse has denomination of 50 and coupon to clip off one corner. Pictured are Mix, Lindbergh, Ruth, Chaplin, Dempsey, Lloyd, Fairbanks and Jolson. **$100 $200 $300**

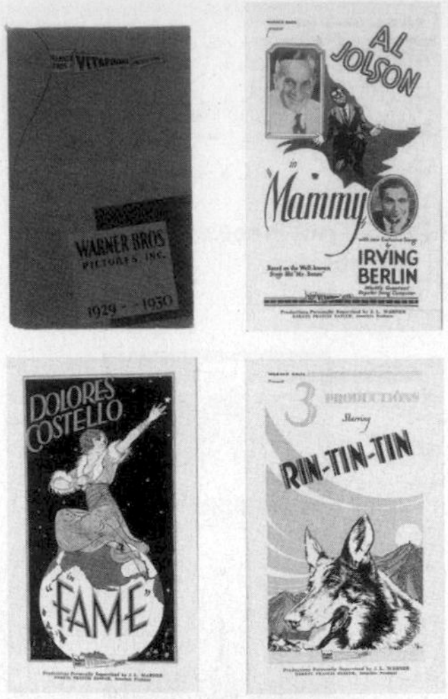

ALJ-2

ALJ-3

❑ **ALJ-2. Theater Preview Booklet,**
1929-30. Warner Bros. 4.25x7" with 122 pages. Has calendar pages on the left-hand side and studio/film information on the right-hand side. All films advertised are early sound films. Includes Jolson in "Mammy," John Barrymore, page on Rin-Tin-Tin Productions, etc. **$50 $100 $175**

❑ **ALJ-3. Child Star Of Al Jolson's "Sonny Boy" Movie Club Button,**
c. 1929. Philadelphia Badge. 1.25" color portrait on yellow background. Reads "Davey Lee Sonny Boy Club." - **$8 $15 $25**

ALJ-4

❑ **ALJ-4. "Al Jolson In Mammy" Rare Button,**
c. 1930. Philadelphia Badge. 7/8". **$50 $100 $225**

ALJ-5

❑ **ALJ-5. "Al Jolson In Hold On To Your Hats" Theater Program,**
1940s. 9x12", 16-page B&W stiff paper program. Contents include two-page biography of Jolson with photos, nice centerfold of pretty girls. **$8 $15 $30**

ALJ-6

❑ **ALJ-6. Milton Berle/Al Jolson Puppet Pair,**
1950s. National Mask And Puppet Co. Berle is 9.5" tall, Jolson is 9" tall in blackface to represent his 1927 role in famous first talking picture "The Jazz Singer." Cloth bodies, rubber heads, felt hands. Each - **$35 $75 $125**

ALJ-7

❑ **ALJ-7. "It's A Wonderful Life" Cast Signed First Day Cover,**
1977. 3.5x6.5" envelope postmarked October 6, 1977 from Hollywood, California for the "50th Anniversary of Talking Pictures 1927-1977." Envelope commemorates "The Jazz Singer," the first talking picture. Signed by director of 1946 holiday classic Frank Capra and stars James Stewart and Donna Reed. Near Mint
Autographed - **$400**
As Issued - **$5 $10 $20**

All In The Family

Produced by Norman Lear and based on the British TV show *Till Death Do Us Part,* CBS-TV aired *All In the Family* for nine seasons between January 12, 1971 and April 8, 1979. The show was re-titled *Archie Bunker's Place* in September 1979 and ran until 1983. The cast included Carroll O'Connor (1924-2001) as the bigoted racist Archie, Jean Stapleton as his frazzled "Dingbat" wife Edith, Sally Struthers as their daughter Gloria and Rob Reiner as liberal son-in-law (and Meathead!) Michael Stivic. The show was the first TV series taped before a live audience.

Set in Queens, New York, the program was number one in the Nielsens from 1971 to 1976 and won nine Emmy awards and four Golden Globes. Spin-off shows included "Maude" starring Bea Arthur which debuted September 12, 1972; "The Jeffersons" which debuted January 18, 1975 and ran 11 seasons; and a Hanna-Barbera cartoon series "Wait Till Your Father Gets Home" which ran for 49 episodes between 1972 and 1974.

The chairs used by Archie and Edith are in The Smithsonian Institute and the actual house shown in the opening of the show is located at 89-70 Cooper Ave. in the Glendale section of Queens. The show broke down many barriers, helping the country face prejudice on many levels. Like its theme song says – "Those Were The Days."

ALF-1

❑ **ALF-1. Archie Bunker Anti-Nixon Button,**
1971. 1.5" with slogan "Only Dingbats Support Phase II." Issued to protest Nixon's economic policies. - **$8 $15 $30**

ALF-2

ALF-3

❑ **ALF-2. "All In The Family" Product Sales Sheets,**
1972. Tandem Productions Inc. First is 8.5x11.75". Front photo shows display card and 7 different "Bunker For President" buttons in 2-1/8" and 3.5" size. Second is 8.5x11". Shows large store display containing assortment of buttons, bumper stickers, paste-ons and posters. Each - **$5 $10 $15**

❑ **ALF-3. Archie Bunker Campaign Buttons,**
1972. Tandem Productions Inc. Group of seven 7/8" litho vending machine buttons. Buttons are black with one accent color of either white, blue, yellow or green. Six feature photos and one is an illustration of Capitol building.
Each - **$2 $5 $10**

ALF-4

❑ **ALF-4. Archie Bunker For President Button Set,**
1972. Tandem Productions. Set of seven 1.5" diameter litho buttons in black and white on red, white and blue. Six have photos and one has illustration of Capitol building. Scarcer than 7/8" version. Each - **$3 $8 $15**

ALF-5

❑ **ALF-5. "Archie Bunker For President" Vending Machine Button Set With Insert Paper,**
1972. Creative House. Insert is 4.5" square glossy paper showing Archie and Edith. Advertises different vending machine items such as "Campaign Buttons, Mini-Stickers, Stamps, Signs." Set of 12 buttons, each 15/16" litho. Two include bluetone photos of Bunker and Edith and the rest feature campaign slogans. Insert - **$5 $12 $25**
Each Button - **$2 $5 $10**

ALF-6

ALF-7

❑ **ALF-6. "Archie Bunker For President" Beer Mugs,**
1972. T.P.I. First is 5" tall glazed ceramic showing Archie smoking cigar. Reverse slogan "Archie Bunker The Beer Party Candidate." Second is 5.5" tall glass showing Bunker. Reverse slogan "To The Rear March With Arch." Each - **$10 $20 $30**

❑ **ALF-7. Archie Bunker Campaign Button Pair,**
1972. Tandem Prod. Inc. 3.5". The one with the family reads "America's Foist Family," and the one with Edith reads "Behind Every Great Man There Is A Dingbat." Each - **$5 $10 $20**

ALF-8

❑ **ALF-8. Archie Bunker Campaign Button,**
1972. 3" litho reads "Archie Bunker Tells It Like It Was!" - **$5 $10 $20**

ALF-9

❑ **ALF-9. "Archie Bunker For President" Shield Pendant,**
1972. 2" tall flat brass with loop for chain. No maker or copyright. - **$20 $40 $80**

Alley Oop

V.T. Hamlin (1900-1993) began the daily comic strip on December 5, 1932 and followed with a Sunday page on September 9, 1934. Set in the prehistoric jungles of Moo, the cast includes Dinny the Dinosaur, King Guz and his advisor Grand Wizer, Foozy and Oop's girlfriend Ooola. The strip took a sudden turn on April 5, 1939 with the introduction of Dr. Wonmug and his time machine which brought Oop and Ooola to the 20th century and then sent them back in time for adventures with figures from history.

Dave Graue began assisting Hamlin with the art chores in 1950. Jack Bender and his wife Carole have been doing the strip since 2001.

A comic book fan award created by Ron Foss called "The Alleys" was given out between 1961 and 1969, and Oop was animated as a back-up feature on the 1971 "Archie" Saturday morning show.

The song *Alley Oop* by the Hollywood Argyles hit #1 on the 1960 pop music charts. It includes the lyric "He's The King Of The Jungle Jive" which rings true today.

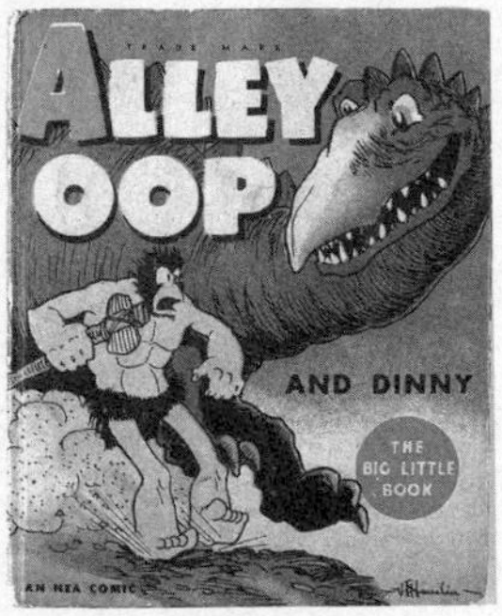

ALO-1

❑ **ALO-1. "Alley Oop And Dinny" Big Little Book,**
1935. Whitman. Book No. 763. - **$19 $57 $130**

ALO-2

❑ **ALO-2. "Alley Oop" Boxed Jungle Game,**
c. 1936. Whitman #2091. One of the first non-book Alley Oop items made. - **$225 $425 $875**

ALO-3

❑ **ALO-3. "The Game of Alley Oop",**
1937. - **$35 $65 $135**

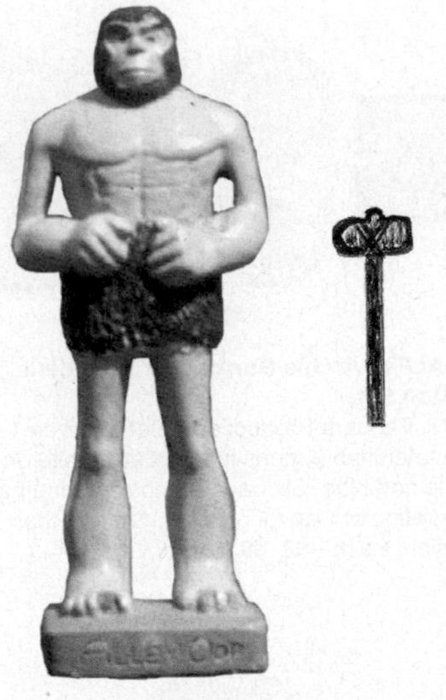

ALO-4

❑ **ALO-4. Alley Oop Product Statuette,**
1946. R.W. Kerr Co. 1.5x2x5.25" tall. Painted plaster figure made by company that made the famous Captain Marvel statuettes. Front base reads "Alley Oop" and back base has name of comic strip distribution syndicate. One of the rarest of the 1940s comic character figures. - **$1200 $2250 $3500**
With club/handle that fits inside arm - add **$250 $500 $1000**

ALO-5

❑ **ALO-5. "Alley Oop" 8-Pager,**
c. 1940s. 2.75x4" risque booklet with unauthorized "x-rated" comic story. - **$8 $15 $30**

ALO-6

❑ **ALO-6. "Alley Oop" Button,**
1973. Newspaper Enterprise Association. 3.5" portrait button with signature of artist printed over grass area at bottom and top rim reads "Alley Oop Series Number One." - **$10 $20 $40**

Alphonse and Gaston

"You first, my dear Gaston!" "After you, my dear Alphonse!" The Frederick Opper (1857-1937) pair of acutely polite Frenchmen and their friend Leon first appeared in the Hearst Syndicate Sunday pages in 1902. The strip was a hit with readers, but after 1904 the characters appeared only occasionally in Opper's other strips, particularly *Happy Hooligan* and *And Her Name Was Maud.* An early collection of color reprints was published by the *N.Y. American & Journal.* The American Mutoscope and Biography Company released comedy films in 1903.

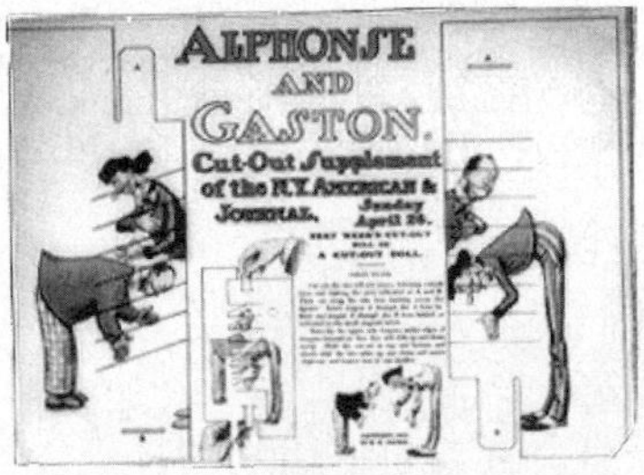

ALP-1

❑ **ALP-1. "Alphonse and Gaston" Cut-Out Supplement,**
1902. New York American & Journal newspaper. Uncut - **$45 $80 $140**

ALP-2

❑ **ALP-2. Alphonse And Gaston And Their Friend Leon Comic Strip Reprint Book,**
1903. The New York American And Journal. 10x15.25" with thin cardboard covers. Contains 40 sheets printed on one side, including black/white title page and 39 sheets in full color Sunday page reprints which comprise almost the entire year of 1903. Front cover specialty art by creator F. Opper. GD- **$500** FN - **$1800**

ALP-3

ALP-4

❑ **ALP-3. Cello. Button,**
1903. Advertises Omaha Grocers and Butchers picnic. - **$30 $55 $110**

❑ **ALP-4. Cello. Button,**
c. 1903. Advertises South Dakota State Fair. - **$20 $40 $85**

ALP-5

❑ **ALP-5. Early Handkerchief,**
c. 1903. - **$25 $45 $90**

ALP-6

❑ **ALP-6. Handkerchief,**
c. 1903. Probable store item. - **$25 $45 $90**

ALP-7

❑ **ALP-7. Cello. Button Without Imprint,**
c. 1903. - **$20 $40 $80**

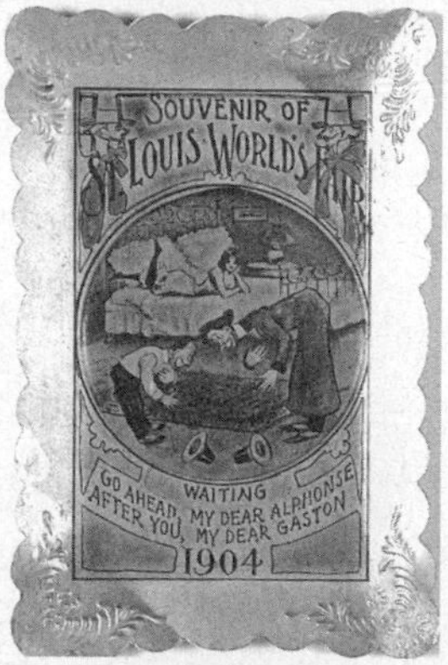

ALP-8

❑ **ALP-8. "St. Louis World's Fair" Naughty Souvenir Tray,**
1904. 3.25x4.75" aluminum with bw art and some brown accent color at top. - **$20 $40 $75**

ALP-9

❑ **ALP-9. Aluminum Cartoon Card,**
c. 1904. Store item set of 10 aluminum cards, only one featuring Alphonse & Gaston. Card pictures lady waiting at her bed as they deliberate who should go first. - **$35 $60 $115**

ALP-10

ALP-11

❑ **ALP-10. Gaston Tinted White Metal Charm,**
c. 1904. There is a matching Alphonse. Each - **$8 $15 $30**

❑ **ALP-11. Alphonse And Gaston Two-Sided Interchangable Picture Game,**
c. 1905. Green painted wood frame box is .5" deep by 5.5" square and holds 1.75" square wood blocks with paper illustrations of Alphonse, Gaston, Leon, Cop, Jockey, Uncle Sam. - **$100 $225 $450**

ALP-12

❑ **ALP-12. Postcard,**
1906. American Journal Newspapers. - **$10 $18 $30**

ALP-13

ALP-14

❑ **ALP-13. Alphonse Figural Ceramic Matchholder,**
c. 1910. 4.75" tall likeness figure depicted opening valise holder for matches. Unmarked, likely German. - **$60 $115 $200**

❑ **ALP-14. Alphonse & Gaston's Friend Leon Bisque Figure,**
c. 1910. Figure is 5.25" tall. Nice detail and paint on bisque. Yellow pants, bright green hat, polka dot shirt, striped pants. - **$50 $100 $175**

ALP-15

❑ **ALP-15. Gaston Cast Iron Nodder Toy,**
c. 1911. 6.25" tall replica of him in mule cart by Hubley Toys. - **$275 $550 $1600**

American Bandstand

It started in 1952 on WFIL, a Philadelphia ABC affiliate, and went on to become one of television's longest-running and most successful shows. Originally hosted by Bob Horn and titled "Bob Horn's Bandstand," the show got a new host on July 9, 1956. Dick Clark took the podium and brought *American Bandstand* to prime-time ABC on August 5, 1957 where it ran for 13 weeks from October through December. Since then, under various names and in different formats and time slots, Clark's program showcased thousands of contemporary bands, singers and dancers. He was inducted into the Rock and Roll Hall of Fame in 1993. Promotional items associated with the show typically carry an American Broadcasting Co. copyright.

AME-1

❑ **AME-1. Pre-Dick Clark "Bandstand Club Membership Card,"**
1955. Card is 2.25x4" for membership in "WFIL-TV Bandstand Club" and includes name of "Bob Horn" honorary president and the show's host. The show began as a local dance program in Philadelphia in 1952 moving to ABC in August, 1957 as a network program. - **$35 $50 $90**

AME-2

❑ **AME-2. Bandstand Yearbook,**
1955. WFIL-TV Philadelphia. Local program hosted by Bob Horn, pre-dating Dick Clark era. - **$35 $75 $125**

AME-3

❑ **AME-3. "Dick Clark Yearbook",**
1957. - **$15 $35 $70**
Mailer - **$6 $12 $25**

AME-4

❑ **AME-4. "Dick Clark American Bandstand" Metal Shield With Neck Chain,**
c. 1957. Brass luster depiction of dancing couple, musical instruments and musical notes. - **$30 $55 $110**

AME-5

AME-6

❑ **AME-5. "This Week Magazine" Cover Article,**
November 16, 1958. Sunday supplement magazine of various newspapers. - **$10 $15 $30**

❑ **AME-6. "Dick Clark Yearbook",**
c. 1959. - **$18 $35 $65**

AME-7

❑ **AME-7. "The Dick Clark Caravan Of Stars" Program,**
1959. Program is 9.5x12.5" with 24 pages.
- **$55 $110 $225**

AME-8

AME-9

❑ AME-8. "Dick Clark"/"IFIC" 3" Litho. Buttons,
1950s. Beech-Nut Gum, TV show sponsor. "Ific" is from slogan "Beech-Nut Gum Is Flavor-Ific."
Picture Version - **$18 $30 $45**
Initials Version - **$10 $15 $30**

❑ AME-9. Dick Clark Doll,
1950s. Store item by Juro. - **$160 $275 $435**

AME-10

❑ AME-10. Store Display With Jewelry,
1950s. Scarce. Displays 17 pieces including necklace, cuff links and tie clasps.
Complete - **$750 $1600 $2750**
Sign (without jewelry) - **$275 $650 $950**

AME-11

AME-12

❑ AME-11. "Platterpuss" Cat Cloth Doll With Tag,
1950s. Store item. 14" tall with tag inscription "Official Autograph Mascot/Dick Clark American Bandstand". - **$60 $115 $175**

❑ AME-12. "Secret Diary",
1950s. Store item. - **$25 $45 $90**

AME-13

AME-14

❑ AME-13. American Bandstand Patch of Dick Clark,
1950s. - **$5 $12 $25**

❑ AME-14. American Bandstand Ad Promo Display,
1950s. Promotes Vicks Cough Drops. - **$45 $80 $160**

AME-15

AME-16

❑ AME-15. Cello. Button,
1950s. WFIL-TV (Philadelphia). 1.25". - **$25 $50 $110**

❑ AME-16. Cardboard Record Case,
1950s. Store item. - **$30 $65 $135**

AME-17

❑ AME-17. "Dick Clark's Blinker Badge,"
1950s. Battery operated store item by Emenee musical toys. Near Mint Packaged - **$75**
Badge Only - **$15 $30 $50**

AME-18

AME-19

❑ AME-18. "American Bandstand" Dick Clark Autographed Card,
1950s. Color photo front with text on reverse, 2-1/4x3-1/2". - **$30 $60 $90**

❑ AME-19. "Because They're Young" Window Card,
1960. Columbia Pictures Corp. 14x22" card with images of Clark, Tuesday Weld and James Darren. - **$20 $40 $75**

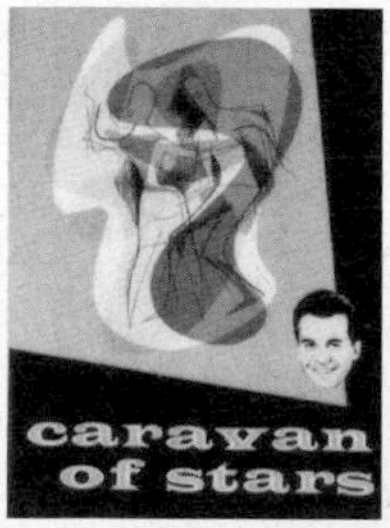

AME-20

AME-21

❑ AME-20. "Caravan Of Stars" Program,
c. 1964. - **$20 $35 $70**

❑ AME-21. "Where The Action Is" TV Show Program,
c. 1966. - **$15 $30 $55**

AME-22

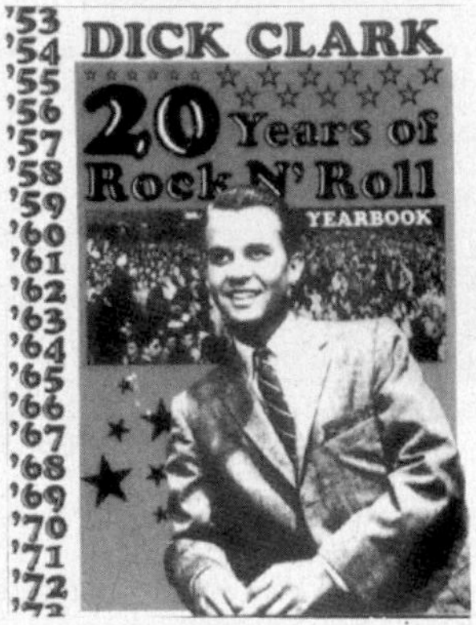

AME-23

❏ **AME-22. "Caravan Of Stars" Concert Program,**
1967. - **$18 $30 $65**

❏ **AME-23. "20 Years Of Rock And Roll Yearbook",**
1973. - **$15 $25 $45**

AME-24

❏ **AME-24. 20th Anniversary Dick Clark's American Bandstand Promotional Ashtray,**
1977. - **$10 $20 $35**

Amos 'n' Andy

Amos Jones and Andrew H. Brown, rustic blacks striving to succeed in the big city, were born in the imaginations of Freeman Gosden and Charles Correll, two white show business producers. Amos and Andy ran the Fresh Air Taxicab Co. and--together with George Stevens, the Kingfish of the Mystic Knights of the Sea Lodge--enchanted and entranced a huge radio audience in the 1930s. The program, probably the most successful radio series ever, was aired locally in Chicago beginning in March 1928 and went to the NBC network in August 1929. Sponsors included Pepsodent toothpaste until 1937, Campbell's soup until 1943, and Rinso soap, Rexall drugs and Chrysler automobiles. *The Amos and Andy Music Hall* ran on CBS radio from 1954 to 1960, and a prime-time television series with a black cast appeared on CBS from 1951 to 1953. Produced by Gosden and Correll and written by Joe Connelly and Bob Mosher, the black performers included Spencer Williams as Andrew H. Brown, Alvin Childress as Amos Jones, Johnny Lee as Algonquin J. Calhoun and Tim Moore as George (Kingfish) Stevens.

AMO-1

❏ **AMO-1. Correll & Gosden Photo Signed "Sam 'N' Henry" Pre-Amos 'N' Andy,**
c. 1926. 8x10" glossy black and white promo for WGN (Chicago) radio program featuring them as Sam and Henry characters to become later that year traditional Amos and Andy characters. Autograph to recipient was inked jointly by them. Same/Similar - **$165 $275 $575**

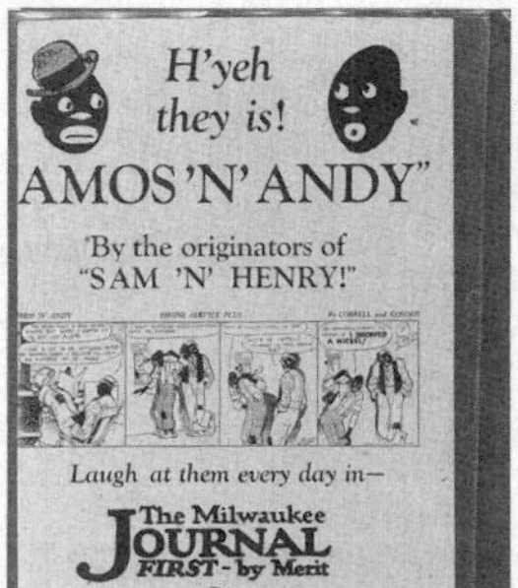

AMO-2

❏ **AMO-2. Newspaper Comic Strip Sign,**
1928. Imprinted for Milwaukee Journal. Black on orange insert sign for street newspaper vending box. - **$75 $150 $300**

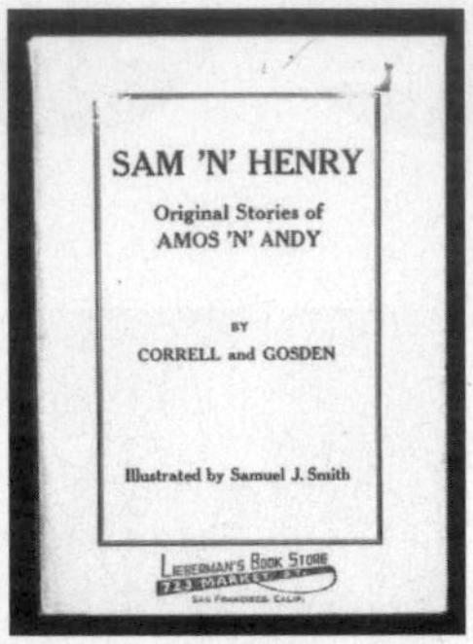

AMO-3

❏ **AMO-3. "Sam 'n' Henry Original Stories Of Amos 'n' Andy,"**
c. 1928. Softbound giveaway with 1926 Chicago Tribune copyright, published by Shrewsbury Publishing Co., Chicago. - **$30 $60 $110**

AMO-4

❏ **AMO-4. Fan Postcard,**
1929. Surebest Bread. Photo pictures actual portrayers of radio broadcast Amos and Andy. - **$22 $45 $85**

AMO-5

❏ **AMO-5. Amos 'N Andy Plaster Figures,**
1929. Matched pair, each having 3.5" diameter base and height of 7" to 7.5". Each is painted plaster done in caricature style. Back of each base has incised copyright reading "1929 By Frank Goodman." Underside of each has ink stamp reading "Midwest Novelty Company K.C. Mo." Each - **$110 $225 $325**

AMO-6 AMO-7

❑ AMO-6. "All About Amos 'n' Andy And Their Creators" Hardbound Book,
1929. Store item published by Rand McNally & Co. Striking black, white and orange dust jacket.
With Jacket **$60 $115 $240**
Without Jacket **$20 $35 $90**

❑ AMO-7. Cast Photo & Mailer,
1929. Pepsodent Co.
Photo Only - **$12 $25 $60**
With Mailer And Letter - **$45 $90 $160**

AMO-8 AMO-9

❑ AMO-8. Gosden & Correll Biography Folder,
1930. Accompanied Pepsodent cardboard standup figure set of two. - **$12 $22 $40**

❑ AMO-9. Pepsodent Cardboard Standup Figure Set,
1930. Each - **$30 $70 $135**

AMO-10

❑ AMO-10. "Amos 'N' Andy On The Screen" Movie Herald,
1930. R-K-O Radio Pictures. Double-fold leaflet, photos show front cover and both sides opened. - **$30 $50 $100**

AMO-11

❑ AMO-11. "Check and Double Check" Cardboard Standee,
1930. 9x9" die-cut in red, white and blue to promote their movie.. - **$100 $200 $400**

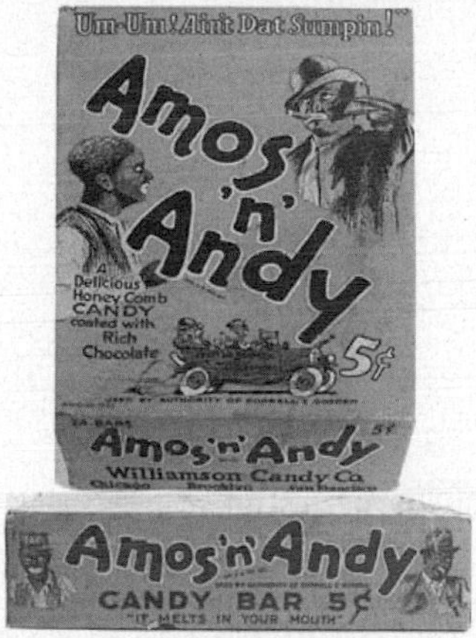

AMO-12

❑ AMO-12. Cardboard Candy Box,
1930. Williamson Candy Co. - **$115 $225 $450**

AMO-13

❑ AMO-13. Cardboard Countertop Standee,
1930. Williamson Candy Co. 5.5 x 11.25". - **$175 $400 $750**

AMO-14

❑ AMO-14. "Amos" and "Andy" Litho. Tin Wind-Up Toys,
1930. Store items by Marx. 11" tall. Made with either stationary or moving eyes.
Each - **$325 $750 $1550**

AMO-15

❑ AMO-15. "Amos 'n' Andy Card Party" Boxed Set,
1930. Store item by A. M. Davis Co.
Near Mint Complete Unused **$265**
Complete Used **$35 $60 $150**

(REGULAR VERSION)

AMO-16

(VARIANT)

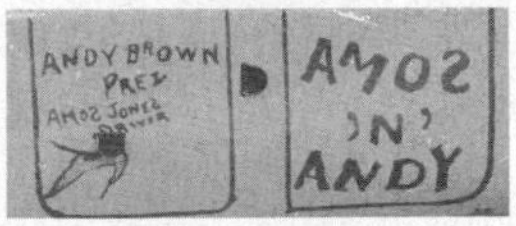

(DISTINGUISHING GRAPHICS ON LEFT SIDE OF VARIANT TAXI)

❑ **AMO-16. Amos 'n' Andy Fresh Air Taxi Tin Wind-Up,**
1930. Marx Toys. Sold boxed with 5x7-3/8" card of cut-out standup figures of Amos, Andy, dog and wastebasket. Rare variant exists with text reading "Andy Brown Prez Amos Jones Driver" on left hand side of car. Regular version has no text on that side.
Regular Version Taxi - **$325 $650 $1300**
Variant Version Taxi - **$450 $900 $1550**
Box - **$175 $350 $675**
Card - **$60 $115 $225**

AMO-17

❑ **AMO-17. "Amos 'n' Andy" Pencil Tablet,**
c. 1930. From series available through store. Each - **$30 $70 $135**

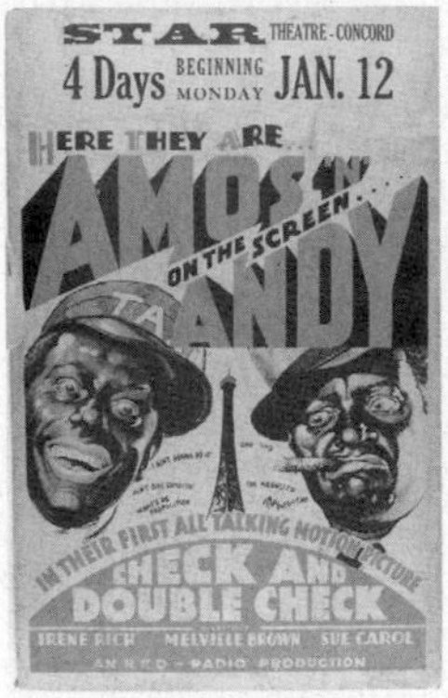

AMO-18

❑ **AMO-18. Amos 'N Andy Motion Picture Sign,**
1931. Sign is 14x22" stiff cardboard advertising Amos 'N Andy in their first motion picture "Check And Double Check." Sign features large dramatic images of both Amos and Andy and also the RKO radio tower. - **$325 $650 $1100**

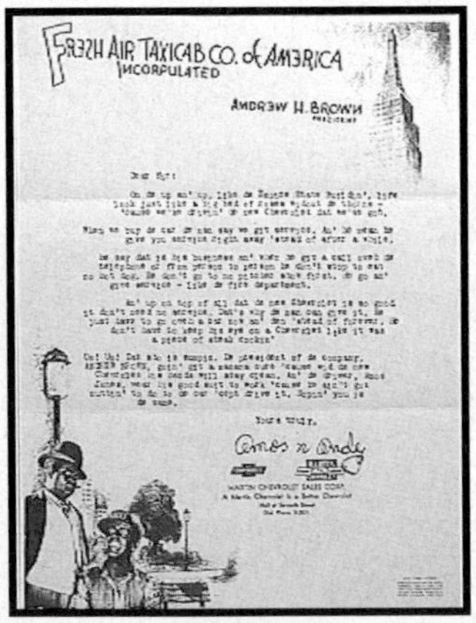

AMO-19

❑ **AMO-19. Chevrolet Car Dealer Promotion Letter,**
1931. Martin Chevrolet Sales Corp. Promotes products in dialect text on Fresh Air Taxicab Co. letterhead. - **$50 $95 $185**

AMO-20

❑ **AMO-20. Chevrolet Car Promotion Letter,**
1931. Martin Chevrolet Sales Corp. Similar to preceding item but different text and illustrations. - **$50 $95 $185**

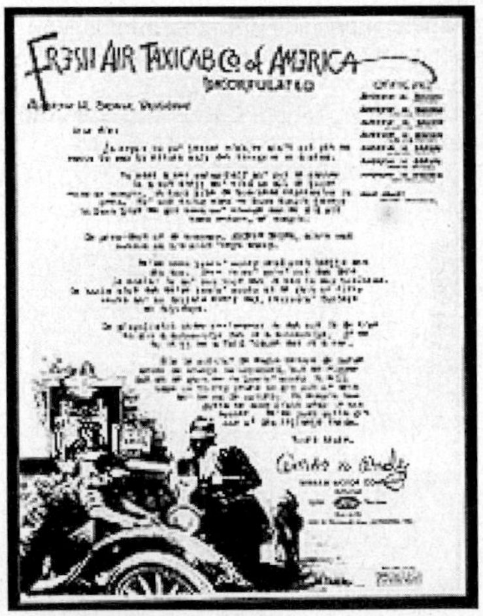

AMO-21

❑ **AMO-21. Ford Automobile Promotion Letter,**
1931. Ford Motor Co. local dealers. Promotion letter for Ford products in dialect text on Fresh Air Taxi Cab Co. letterhead. - **$50 $95 $185**

AMO-22

❑ **AMO-22. Sheet Music,**
1931. Check and Double Check movie theme. - **$20 $35 $75**

AMO-23

❑ **AMO-23. Christmas Card,**
1931. Hall Brothers. - **$25 $45 $95**

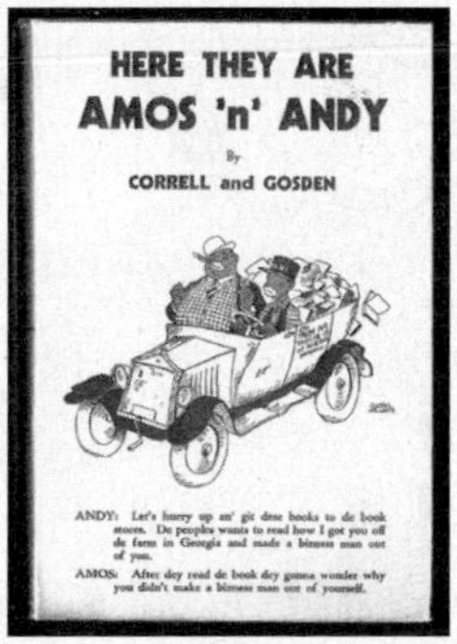

AMO-24

❑ **AMO-24. "Here They Are Amos 'n' Andy" Hardcover Book,**
1931. Store item published by Ray Long & Richard R. Smith, Inc., New York.
With Jacket - **$45 $85 $190**
Without Jacket - **$20 $35 $90**

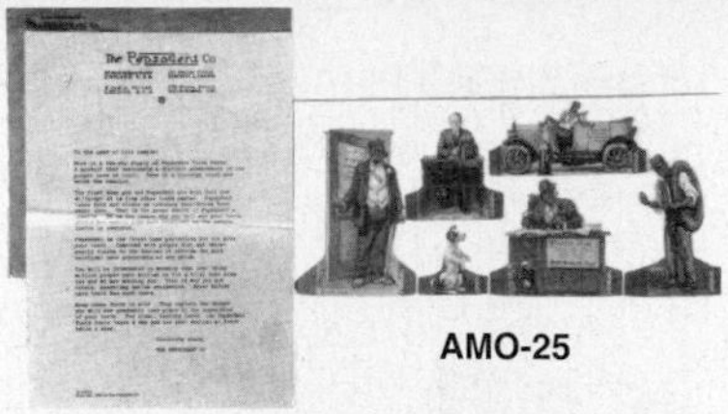

AMO-25

❑ **AMO-25. Cardboard Standup Figures With Letters And Envelope,**
1931. Set of six figures with two letters promoting Pepsodent toothpaste and urging dental visit. Near Mint In Envelope - **$475**
Each Standup - **$15 $30 $60**

AMO-26

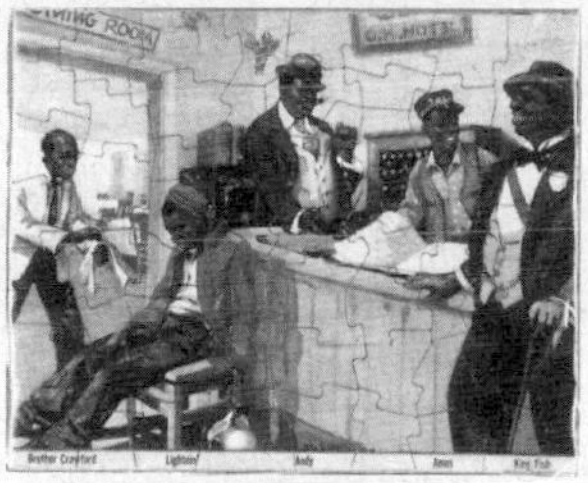

AMO-27

❑ **AMO-26. Candy Display Box,**
1931. Williamson Candy Company. Candy bars held in box on Amos' back. - **$165 $375 $700**

❑ **AMO-27. Puzzle,**
1932. Pepsodent Co. - **$35 $90 $150**

AMO-28

❑ **AMO-28. Radio Episode Script,**
December 25, 1935. Pepsodent. For episode "Amos' Wedding". - **$10 $25 $50**

AMO-29

❑ **AMO-29. Radio Theme Song Sheet Music,**
1935. Pepsodent Toothpaste, also store item.
Pepsodent Imprint - **$15 $30 $75**
Store Item - **$20 $35 $80**

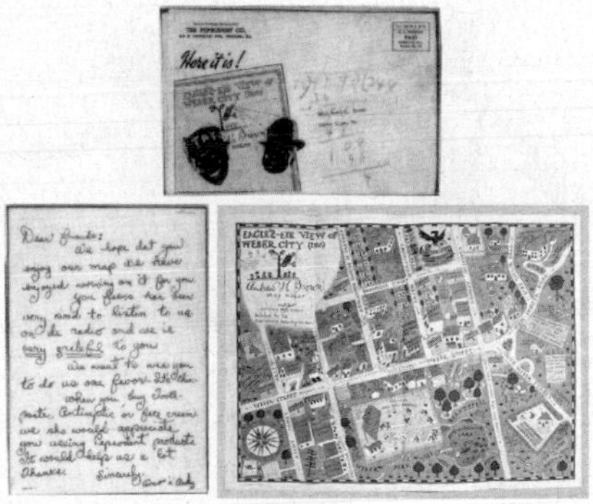

AMO-30

❑ **AMO-30. "Eagle's-Eye View Of Weber City (Inc.)" Map,**
1935. Pepsodent Co. Prize to each entrant of "Why I Like Pepsodent Toothpaste" contest.
Near Mint In Envelope - **$100**
Map Only - **$15 $30 $50**

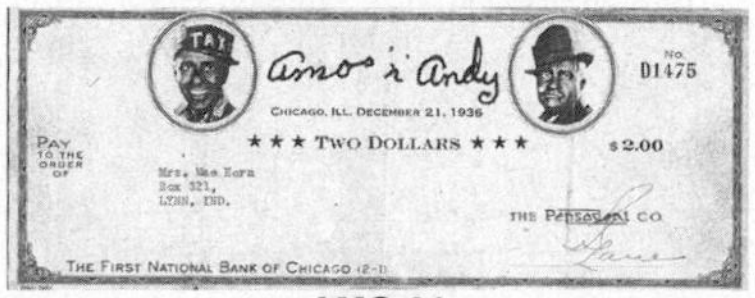

AMO-31

❑ **AMO-31. Pepsodent Contest Winner Check,**
1936. Rare. - **$315 $625 $1025**

AMO-32

❑ **AMO-32. "Campbell's Soup" 13x20" Paper Poster,**
c. 1938. - **$35 $70 $135**

AMO-33

AMO-34

❑ **AMO-33. "Amos" Wood Jointed Doll,**
1930s. Store item. - **$55 $135 $240**

❑ **AMO-34. "Andy" Wood Jointed Doll,**
1930s. Store item. - **$55 $135 $240**

AMO-35

❑ **AMO-35. Detroit Sunday Times Supplement Photo,**
1930s. - **$20 $35 $75**

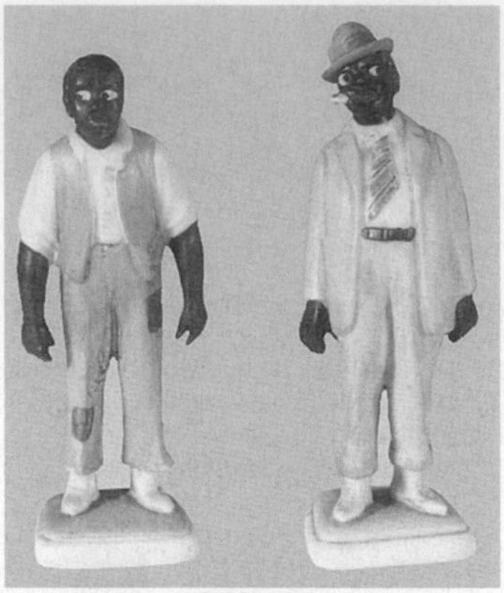
AMO-36

❑ **AMO-36. Bisque Figurines,**
1930s. Store item. Pair - **$160 $340 $550**

AMO-37

❑ **AMO-37. Wood Composition Figure Set,**
1930s. Probable store item. Beautifully colored 2x2x2-3/4" tall fully dimensional figures each with a 3/8" diameter cylindrical opening running vertically through the entire figure which may have held tube cigarette lighters. Only example we've seen so we are uncertain about the purpose of this opening which is only seen from the top or underneath views.
Value As Described Pair **$375 $750 $1300**

AMO-38

❑ **AMO-38. Portrait Button,**
1930s. Issuer unknown. 13/16" black and gray. Scarce. - **$55 $110 $220**

AMO-39

❑ **AMO-39. Promotional Sticker,**
1930s. "Shell 400, The 'Dry' Gas." 4-1/2" black and white including radio station call letters "KFRC." Diecut in shape of sponsor's logo. - **$25 $55 $110**

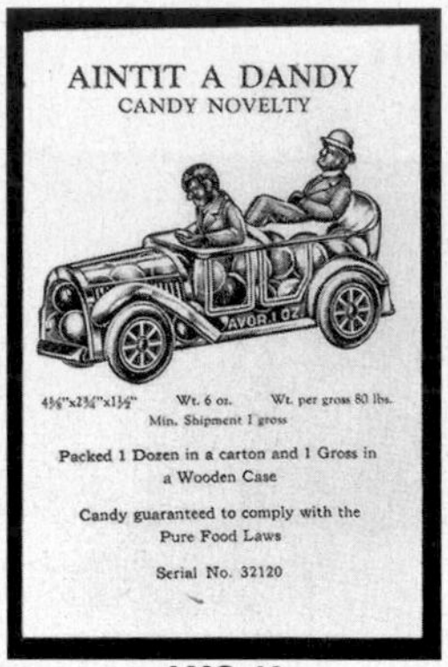

AMO-40

❑ **AMO-40. Glass Candy Container Advertising Postcard,**
1930s. Victory Glass Co. Pictures an unlicensed candy novelty called "Aintit A Dandy." Shown as next item. - **$20 $45 $85**

AMO-41

❑ **AMO-41. "Aintit A Dandy" Glass Candy Container,**
1930s. Victory Glass Co. Jeannette, PA. 1-1/2 x 4-5/8 x 2-3/4" tall. Amos in blue suit, Andy in red suit with brown derby, orange tires. Originally issued with metal base plate to hold candy in hollow taxi interior.
Container - **$125 $250 $400**
Base plate - **$25 $50 $100**

AMO-42

❑ **AMO-42. Photo Card,**
1930s. Exhibit card from numbered set of about 20. Each - **$10 $18 $30**

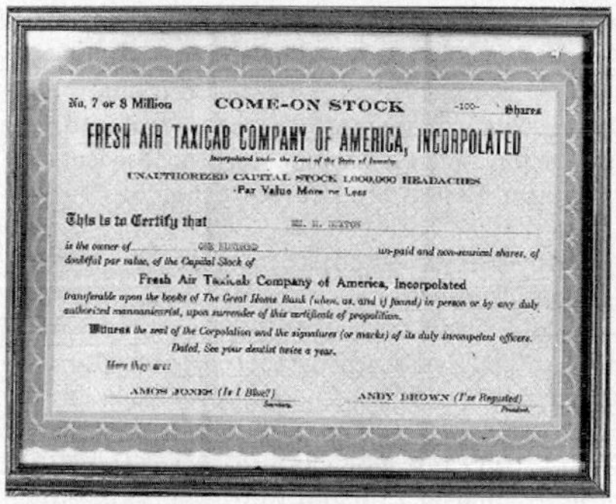

AMO-43

❑ **AMO-43. "Fresh Air Taxicab Company" Stock Certificate,**
1930s. Seen with advertising on bottom margin for "Ford Furniture Stores In Northwestern New Jersey." - **$75 $140 $275**

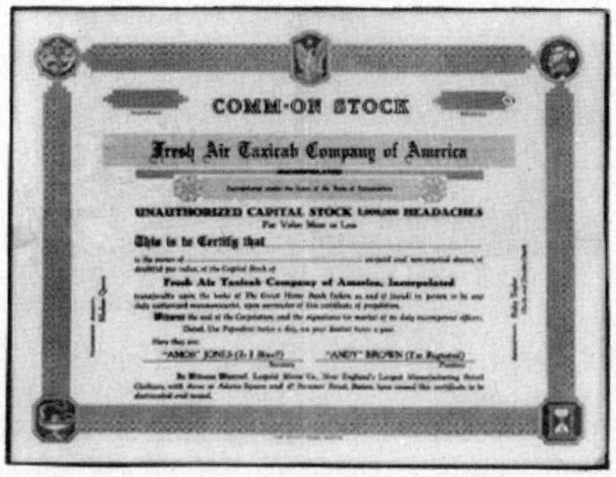

AMO-44

❑ **AMO-44. "Fresh Air Taxicab Company" Stock Certificate,**
1930s. - **$75 $140 $275**

AMO-45

❑ **AMO-45. "Fresh Air Taxicab Company" Stock Certificate,**
1930s. Cann Brothers & Kindig, Inc., Printers. - **$75 $140 $275**

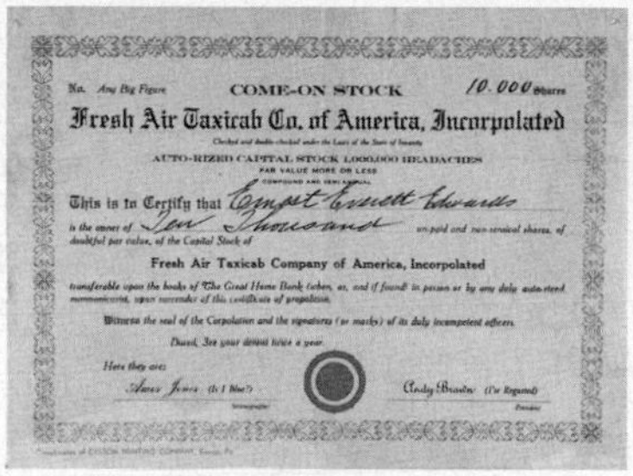

AMO-46

❑ **AMO-46. "Come-On" Stock Certificate,**
1930s. For the Fresh Air Taxicab Company. One of at least 4 varieties. - **$75 $140 $275**

AMO-47

❑ **AMO-47. Amos 'N' Andy 1¢ Candy Wrapper,**
1930s. Store item. Williamson Candy Co. "An Oh Henry Product." - **$50 $100 $200**

AMO-48

❑ **AMO-48. Amos 'N' Andy 5¢ Candy Wrapper,**
1930s. Williamson Candy Co. Orange and black with slogan "Um-Um! Aint Dat Sumpin." - **$50 $100 $200**

AMO-49

❑ **AMO-49. Candy Wrapper,**
1930s. Williamson Candy Co. 8x9" waxed paper titled in full "One Amos 'N' One Andy" for nickel candy product. - **$40 $85 $150**

AMO-50

❑ **AMO-50. Amos 'N' Andy 5¢ Candy Wrapper Redeemable For "Wise Crack Button",**
1930s. Williamson Candy Co. 6x8" wrapper in black, red and yellow. Bottom edge text reads, "Present 3 of these wrappers to the storekeeper from whom you purchased this bar and receive a WISE CRACK BUTTON. Enjoy Amos 'N Andy on your radio." See next item example button. - **$65 $125 $250**

AMO-51

❑ **AMO-51. "Free Ride In Fresh Air Taxi" Litho. Button,**
1930s. Amos 'N Andy Fresh Air Candy. From known series of 21 with a different slogan on each, including one example picturing the taxi. Each - **$18 $38 $70**

AMO-52

❑ **AMO-52. Lead Ashtray,**
1930s. Store item. - **$190 $350 $700**

AMO-53

❑ **AMO-53. Taxi And/Or Character Photos,**
1930s. Two 8x10" black and white glossies from series of at least six radio show promotional photos. Showing Taxi - **$20 $40 $80**
Taxi Not Shown - **$15 $30 $50**

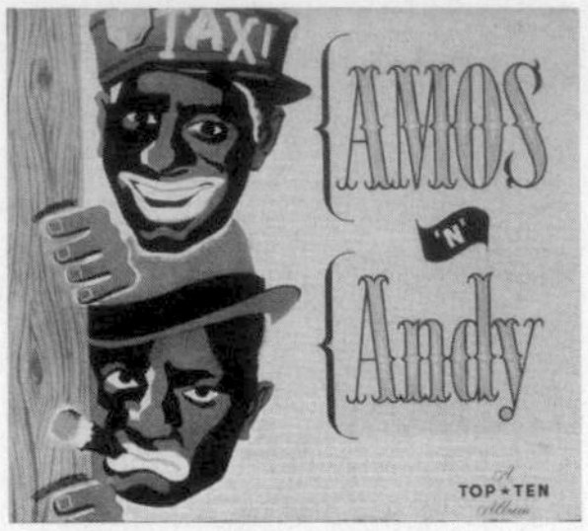

AMO-54

❑ **AMO-54. Amos and Andy Record Album,**
1947. Contains four 78 rpm records. Inside the front and back covers are write-ups of contents and a history of the radio show. Great picture of Amos and Andy on the inside front cover. Scarce. - **$65 $135 $225**

AMO-55

❑ **AMO-55. Paper Store Sign,**
1940s. Rexall drugstores. 11-1/2x36" in red, black and white. - **$55 $120 $190**

AMO-56

AMO-57

❑ **AMO-56. Amos and Andy Broadcast Sign,**
1940s. - **$115 $225 $500**

❑ **AMO-57. Amos and Andy Plenamins Promo Band,**
1940s. - **$30 $60 $90**

(Front) **AMO-58** (Back)

❑ **AMO-58. "The Best of Amos 'N' Andy" CD Box set,**
2001. Set is packaged in a box facsimile of an old style radio- **$18**

Andy Panda

The acquisition of "Su-Lin" the panda by the Brookfield Zoo in Chicago brought nationwide attention and gave animator Walter Lantz (1900-1994) the inspiration for a new cartoon character. *Life Begins For Andy Panda* was released September 9, 1939. He would appear in 29 cartoons between 1939 and 1949. Nominated for three Academy Awards, his voice was provided by Bernice Hansen 1939-1940, Sara Berner 1941-1944 and Walter Tetley until 1949. Andy's girlfriend Miranda Panda first appeared in 1941 in the comic book *Crackajack Funnies* #39 but she didn't appear on the big screen until the release of Andy's last cartoon *Scrappy Birthday* in 1949. Andy appeared in every issue of the *New Funnies* comic book series until 1962. A 1943 issue introduced his friend Charlie Chicken and their hometown of Lantzville.

Andy's career was upstaged a bit by the appearance of Woody Woodpecker in Andy's 1940 cartoon *Knock-Knock*, but Lantzville has proved to be an idyllic place for Andy's semi-retirement.

APD-1

❑ **APD-1. "Life Begins For Andy Panda" Storybook,**
1940. Universal Pictures Co. 5.5x6-5/8" hardcover contains 64 pages with text story on left pages and full page art on right pages. Rand McNally #316. Based on Walter Lantz Technicolor "Cartune." - **$20 $40 $75**

APD-2

❑ **APD-2. "New Funnies" Dell Gift Subscription Picture & Card With Envelope,**
1945. Dell Publishing Co. 8.5x10.5" envelope from "New Funnies" picturing Andy Panda , Raggedy Ann and Andy, Felix, Oswald and Eight Ball. Contents include 3.5x4.5" subscription notice. Card has Christmas art of Oswald, Andy Panda, Woody Woodpecker plus tiny Walter Lantz Productions copyright. Gift picture is 8x10.25" stiff paper image of Andy Panda and Homer Pigeon. Mailer - **$10 $20 $40**
Card - **$20 $40 $75**
Picture - **$25 $50 $100**

APD-3

APD-4

❑ **APD-3. "Andy Panda's Vacation All Pictures Comics" Better Little Book,**
1946. Whitman. Book No. 1485. Stories are comic book reprints. - **$12 $36 $78**

❑ **APD-4. "Andy Panda And The Mad Dog Mystery" Better Little Book,**
1947. Whitman. Book No. 1431. - **$11 $33 $72**

APD-5

❑ **APD-5. "New Funnies/Andy Panda" Cello. Button,**
1940s. New Funnies Comics. - **$40 $75 $125**

APD-6

❑ **APD-6. "Andy Panda Calliope" Tin Litho Flute,**
1940s. Kirchof, Newark, N.J. 7/8" diameter by 9-7/8" long with images of Andy, Oswald, Phooey Goose and Peterkin. Brown wood mouthpiece, red wood handle at base with wire rod to move to change pipe tones. One of his earliest items. - **$20 $40 $85**

APD-7

❑ **APD-7. Andy Panda "New Funnies" Walter Lantz Premium,**
1940s. 8x10" stiff paper picture. Comes with envelope featuring "New Funnies" characters Andy Panda, Raggedy Ann and Andy, Felix, Oswald Rabbit and Eight Ball.
Mailer - **$10 $20 $40**
Picture - **$25 $50 $100**

APD-8

❑ **APD-8. "The Oswald The Rabbit And Pepito Chickeeto Hop" & "Andy Panda Polka And Chilly Willy The Penguin" Records,**
1958. Cricket Records. Lot of two 7x7-1/8" color sleeves with 45-rpm records. Both records have text reading "A Woody Woodpecker Record" above song titles. Each - **$5 $10 $20**

APD-9

❑ **APD-9. Andy And Miranda Panda Glazed Ceramic Salt & Pepper Set,**
1958. Napco. Each is 4" tall with Napco black/gold foil stickers on underside. - **$25 $50 $85**

APD-10

❑ **APD-10. "Andy Panda" Wristwatch,**
1972. Walter Lantz. 1" diameter chrome case with attached dark blue vinyl band. Swiss made. - **$20 $40 $85**

Annie Oakley

Born in a log cabin in Ohio, Annie Oakley (1860-1926) was a skilled marksman even as a child. Nicknamed "Little Sure Shot," she joined the Buffalo Bill Wild West Show in 1885 and toured the world for 17 years. Her trick shooting was a consistent sensation and she continued setting and breaking records as late as 1920.

Hollywood began producing romanticized versions of the Annie Oakley legend as early as 1935. On the big screen she has been portrayed by--among others--Barbara Stanwyck, Betty Hutton, Gail Davis, and Geraldine Chaplin; on Broadway by Ethel Merman in *Annie Get Your Gun*; on television by Jamie Lee Curtis in a made-for-TV movie; and, memorably, by Gail Davis. Produced by Gene Autry Flying A Productions, the *Annie Oakley* television series with Davis (1925-1997) aired originally on ABC from January 1, 1954 to February 2, 1957, sponsored by Canada Dry, TV Time popcorn and Wonder bread. Cast members included Jimmy Hawkins as little brother Tagg, Brad Johnson as deputy sheriff Lofty Craig, Fess Parker as Tom Conrad and Shelley Fabares as Trudy. Annie's horse was Target. There was a brief revival in 1964-1965. *Annie Oakley* comic books appeared in the 1940s and 1950s. An annual Annie Oakley festival is staged in Greenville, Ohio.

ANN-1

❑ ANN-1. Movie Version "Annie Oakley" Dixie Ice Cream Picture,
1935. Pictures Barbara Stanwyck in title role from RKO Radio Pictures release. - **$15 $30 $65**

ANN-2

(ENLARGED VIEW)

❑ ANN-2. Movie "Annie Oakley" Lobby Hanger,
1935. RKO Radio Pictures. 17" tall diecut stiff paper string hanger assembled into rectangle bottom. Pictured is title star Barbara Stanwyck. - **$85 $165 $310**

ANN-3

❑ ANN-3. Canada Dry Ginger Ale "Free Carton" Coupon,
1954. Carton insert paper offering free carton for six bottle caps mailed to bottlers with offer expiring June 30. - **$12 $22 $35**

ANN-4

❑ ANN-4. "Annie Oakley And Tagg" Lunch Box And Bottle,
1955. Store item by Aladdin.
Box - **$85 $200 $425**
Bottle - **$30 $65 $115**

ANN-5 ANN-6

❑ ANN-5. "Annie Oakley And Tagg" Cello. Button,
c. 1955. Club issue by unknown sponsor. Also inscribed "Gail Davis/Member/Sharpshooter." - **$55 $90 $190**

❑ ANN-6. Annie Oakley Litho. Button,
c. 1955. - **$18 $28 $55**

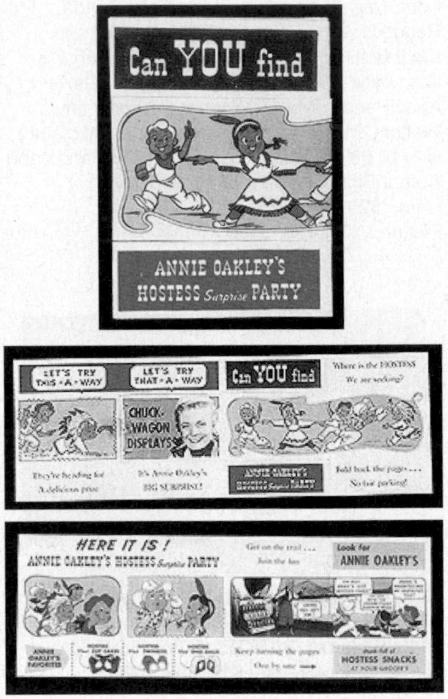

ANN-7

❑ ANN-7. "Hostess Surprise Party" Puzzle Folder,
c. 1955 Hostess Cupcakes. Leaflet with diecut strip panels to be arranged properly to reveal her as surprise hostess and her Hostess products. - **$18 $33 $65**

ANN-8

ANN-9

❑ ANN-8. Wonder Bread Flipper Badge,
c. 1955. Two-sided cardboard with pin fastener plus pull string for completion of front and back message "Annie Oakley Says Eat Wonder Bread." - **$15 $30 $65**

❑ ANN-9. Wonder Bread Coloring Contest Store Sign,
c. 1955. 6-1/2x12" cardboard placard for contest offering prize of tickets to live rodeo performance. - **$30 $60 $95**

ANN-10

❑ ANN-10. Wonder Bread Cardboard Badge,
c. 1955. 4" cardboard urging TV viewership. Back is blank with fastener pin at top margin, probable design for store clerk. - **$40 $75 $140**

ANN-11

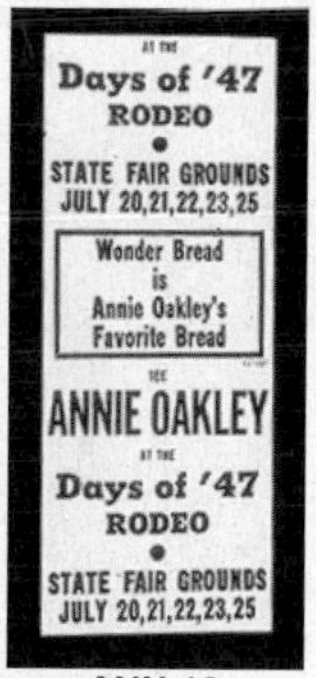

ANN-12

❑ ANN-11. Bread Loaf End Label,
c. 1955. Issued by Wonder Bread with b&w photo of Gail Davis as Annie Oakley.
Each - **$12 $22 $45**

❑ ANN-12. Wonder Bread Rodeo Announcement,
c. 1955. Waxed paper bread loaf insert strip for live performance in "Days Of '47 Rodeo" believed titled by commemorative nature year. - **$6 $12 $18**

ANN-13

ANN-14

❑ ANN-13. Annie Oakley Cello. Button,
c. 1955. Pictures Gail Davis. Australian issue. - **$32 $65 $120**

❑ ANN-14. Annie Oakley Cello. Button,
c. 1955. Pictures Gail Davis. - **$40 $70 $140**

ANN-15

ANN-16

❑ ANN-15. Annie Oakley Cello Button,
c. 1955. Pictures Gail Davis. - **$55 $120 $200**

❑ ANN-16. "Watch For Annie" Button,
c. 1955. 3" black, white and red target design with six simulated bullet holes. - **$18 $38 $80**

ANN-17

❑ ANN-17. Cowgirl Outfit,
c. 1955. Store item. Both vest and skirt have applied full color portrait patches.
Box (Not Shown) - **$35 $75 $150**
Playsuit - **$50 $100 $175**

ANN-18

ANN-19

❑ ANN-18. TV Show Promo Drinking Cup,
c. 1955. KTTV 11 Annie Oakley 7 P.M. Tues. co-sponsored by Laura Scutter Fine Foods. Thin paper cup is 3-1/4" tall. - **$8 $18 $35**

❑ ANN-19. Drawstring Lunch Box,
c. 1955. Issued by Aladdin. Vinyl over metal. Comes in blue or red background versions. - **$550 $1175 $1750**

ANN-20

❑ ANN-20. "Annie Oakley And Tagg" Ceramic Tile Paint Set Boxed,
c. 1955. Dexter-Wayne. Set of four picture tile plaques and color paint supplies. - **$30 $65 $135**

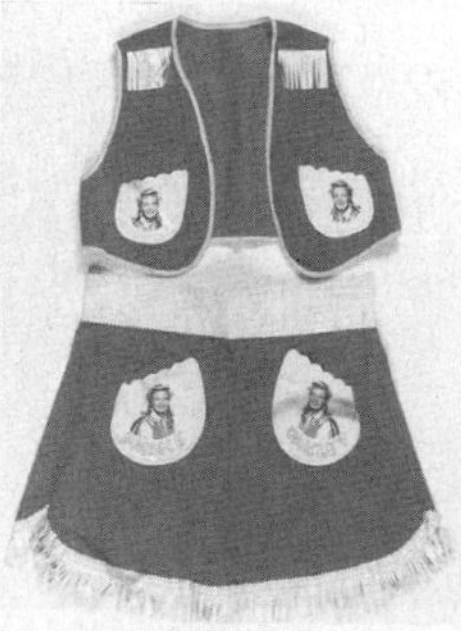

ANN-21

❑ ANN-21. "Annie Oakley" Cowgirl Playsuit,
c. 1955. 11x14" red corduroy vest with two 3x3" vinyl pockets showing Davis and 15x18" red corduroy skirt with vinyl waistband and fringe having two 4.5" pockets with color images of Davis and words "Annie Oakley."
Vest and Skirt - **$50 $100 $175**

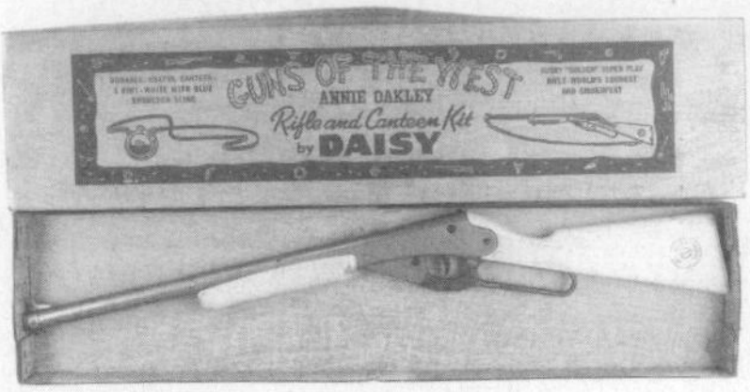

ANN-22

❑ **ANN-22. Annie Oakley Rifle Set,**
1956. Daisy. 32.5" long and 8" wide box holds Daisy Pop and Smoke Rifle with gold finish and gold Daisy logo on stock. Set also included blue sling and canteen. Box - **$75 $275 $350**
Rifle - **$75 $150 $300**

ANN-23

❑ **ANN-23. "Annie Oakley" Doll Book,**
1956. Photo cover cut-out doll book. - **$40 $75 $150**

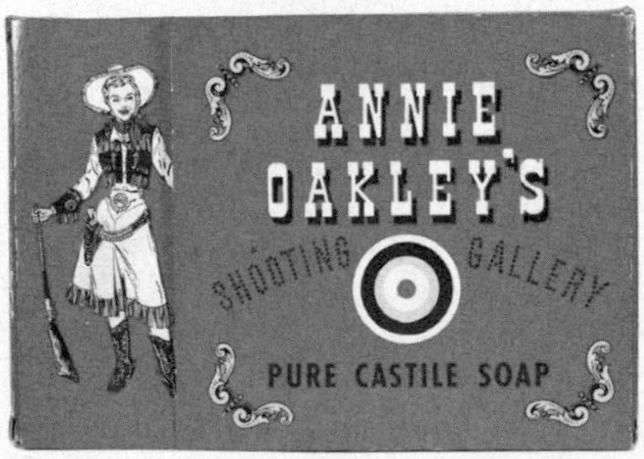

ANN-24

❑ **ANN-24. "Annie Oakley's Shooting Gallery Pure Castile Soap,"**
1950s. - **$75 $125 $175**

ANN-25

❑ **ANN-25. "Annie Oakley" Charm Bracelet,**
1950s. This bracelet is 7.75" long and has the following six charms-cowboy boot, stirrup, hat, rope, spur and one charm marked "Annie Oakley." - **$22 $45 $70**

ANN-26

❑ **ANN-26. Annie Oakley Hat,**
1950s. Store bought. Scarce. - **$35 $70 $175**

Archie

Archie Andrews, typical American teen, first appeared in December 1941 in *Pep Comics* and in more than 60 years has not yet aged a day. Inspired by the popularity of the "Andy Hardy" feature films, publisher John Goldwater and artist Bob Montana created Archie, his girlfriends Betty and Veronica, his pal Jughead, his rival Reggie, and dozens of other students at Riverdale High. They have appeared in comic books, a syndicated newspaper strip, paperback books, 15-and 30-minute radio shows (from 1943 to 1953 on the Mutual and NBC networks), and, starting in 1968, a continuing succession of TV cartoons on CBS or NBC. Archie became a merchandising success as well as a cartoon phenomenon: his bubble gum rock band even produced three hit songs.

The mid-1990s and early 21st century marked yet another upswing for the character and some of his more successful spin-offs. *Sabrina The Teenage Witch* debuted on ABC TV September 27, 1996, later moving to WB, and *Josie and the Pussycats* was released theatrically in 2001. Archie himself appears headed back to TV or the silver screen with both live action and animated projects in development. New music groups based on The Archies and Josie and the Pussycats are also being formed. 2007 marked the 65th anniversary of Archie's appearance in his own comic title.

ARC-1

❑ **ARC-1. Swift Co. Radio Program Letter,**
1947. 8.5x11" art and mimeographed text newsletter summarizing November 3 events on NBC radio program and urging listenership November 8 for solution of the events. Archie is pictured holding pack of sponsor's hotdogs. - **$45 $80 $145**

ARC-2

❑ **ARC-2. Final July Issue Of "Hi" Magazine Before Becoming Archie Magazine,**
1948. Diamond Sales Corporation. Clothing store promotion announcing forthcoming title change plus picturing cast members of radio show. Scarce. - **$60 $115 $225**

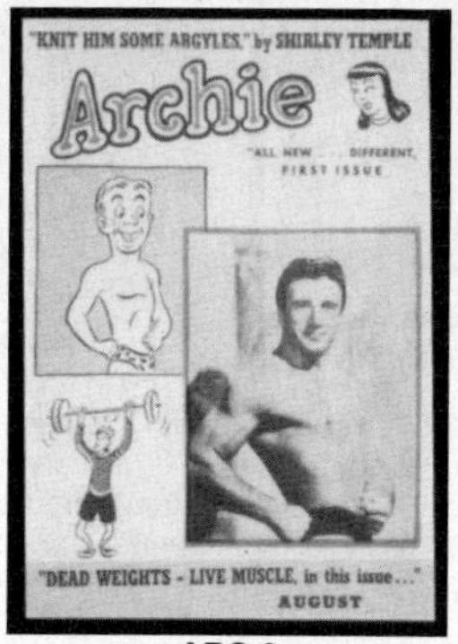

ARC-3

❑ **ARC-3. First Issue "Archie" Title Magazine,**
August 1948. Archie Comics Publications. Various store sponsor imprints on back. - **$50 $85 $190**

ARC-4

❑ **ARC-4. Magazines,**
1948. Archie Comics Publications Inc. Each - **$20 $30 $50**

ARC-5

❑ **ARC-5. "Archie Pin-Up Calendar,"**
1952. 6x9" calendar sheet obtained by mail coupon in back of Archie comic books. - **$18 $35 $80**

ARC-6

❑ **ARC-6. Bob Montana Personal Family Christmas Card,**
1956. Limited issue. - **$12 $25 $45**

ARC-7

❑ **ARC-7. "Archie Comics Blony Bubble Gum" Countertop Display Box,**
c. 1957. Topps Chewing Gum Inc. 8.25x8.25x3.25" deep box originally containing two hundred and forty pieces of bubble gum issued individually wrapped with Archie comic included with each piece. Box notes "Free Gift Inside." Lid features text only with "Archie Comics" name appearing only at top center of lid. Each side panel of box bottom has same design including portraits of Archie, Betty and Veronica. Text includes "Made Of Sugar 'N Spice 'N Everything Nice." - **$110 $225 $340**

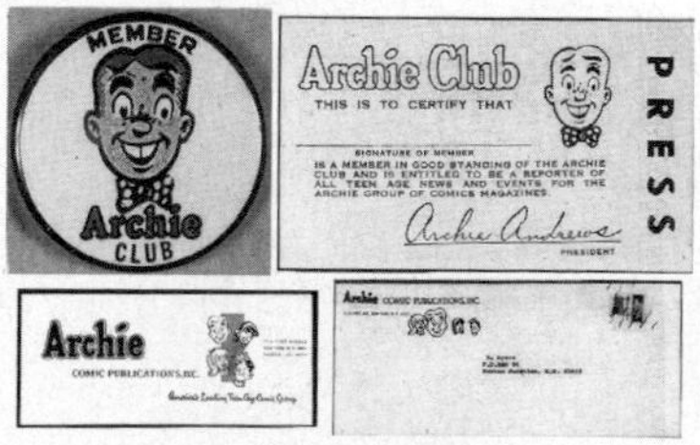

ARC-8

❑ **ARC-8. Comic Book Club Kit,**
1950s. Includes envelope, letter, card, cello. button. Set - **$35 $80 $135**

ARC-9

❑ **ARC-9. Promotional Match Pack,**
1950s. Promotes Archie magazines. - **$25 $50 $85**

ARC-10

❑ **ARC-10. "Archie's Girls Betty And Veronica Doll Book,"** 1964. Store item by Lowe Publishing Co. Unpunched - **$22 $45 $85**

ARC-11

❑ **ARC-11. Archies TV Show Record,**
1968. Came with colorful sleeve holder. Distributed by RCA Records. - **$30 $50 $90**

ARC-12

❑ **ARC-12. Archie's Car Model Kit in Box,**
1968. Aurora. Near Mint Boxed - **$185**
Built Unboxed - **$25 $50 $100**

ARC-13

❑ **ARC-13. Archie Spring-Loaded Plastic Head,**
1969. Post Cereals. - **$10 $20 $33**

ARC-14

❑ **ARC-14. "Post Super Sugar Crisp" Box With "The Archies Record",**
1969. Example from set of 4 boxes.
Each - **$30 $70 $125**

ARC-15

❑ **ARC-15. "Archie's Car" Premium Offer Cereal Box Flat,**
1969. Box held one of three Archie cars. Gordon Gold Archives. Near Mint Flat - **$400**
Used Complete - **$55 $165 $300**

ARC-16

❑ **ARC-16. Jughead's Hat Felt Beanie,**
1969. Post Raisin Bran and Toasties. -
$35 $70 $160

ARC-17

ARC-18

ARC-19

ARC-20

❑ **ARC-17. "Archie" Doll,**
c. 1969. Issuer unknown but possibly a Post Cereals premium. Stuffed cloth 19" tall. -
$25 $50 $100

❑ **ARC-18. Club Member Cello. Button,**
1960s. Version without accent border. -
$6 $12 $24

❑ **ARC-19. "Official Member Archie Club" Cello. Button,**
c. 1960s. For comic book club. - **$10 $20 $30**

❑ **ARC-20. Club Member Cello. Button,**
c. 1960s. One of at least two versions accented by rim color. - **$6 $12 $24**

ARC-21

❑ **ARC-21. Picture Or Slogan Litho. Buttons,**
1970. Store item vending machine set of 16.
Each Picture - **$3 $5 $12**
Each Slogan - **$2 $4 $6**

ARC-22

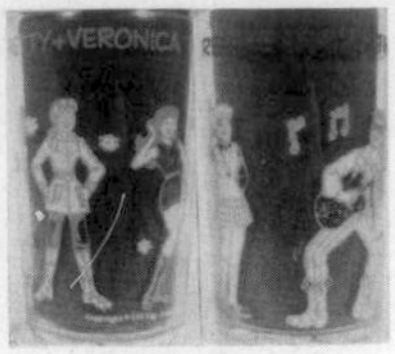

ARC-23

❑ **ARC-22. "Archies Gang!" Vending Machine Paper,**
1970. Archie Comic Publications Inc. Advertises vending items including 16 buttons and five booklets. - **$15 $28 $50**

❑ **ARC-23. Welch's Jelly Glasses,**
1971. Set of eight. Each - **$5 $10 $18**

ARC-24

ARC-25

❑ **ARC-24. Archie Doll with Original Tag,**
1987. - **$18 $45 $130**

❑ **ARC-25. Jughead Doll with Original Tag,**
1987. - **$15 $38 $115**

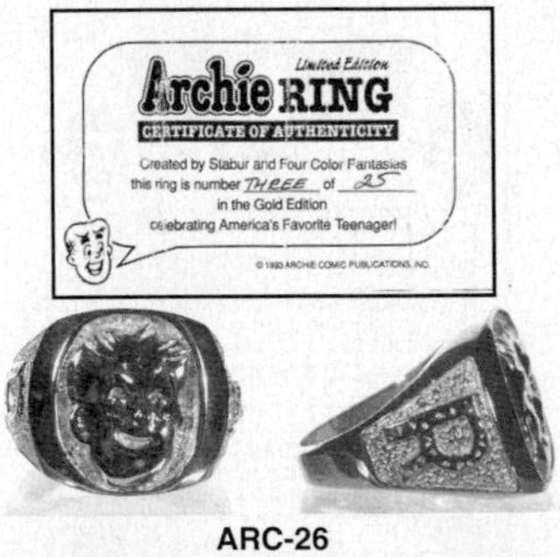

ARC-26

❑ **ARC-26. Archie Riverdale High Class Ring with Certificate,**
1993. Ring was offered on QVC in silver and 10K gold models. Edition of 50 silver rings sold out, but only 5 of the gold rings were made and sold from the planned edition of 25.
Silver Ring - **$150 $300 $650**
Gold Ring - **$800 $1100 $2200**

ARC-27

❑ **ARC-27. "Archie's Christmas Stocking" Toon Tumblers,**
2005. PopFun Merchandising. Four versions.
Clear glass tumbler with logos for Pepsi and the Mid-Ohio-Con. Edition of 450. - **$45**
Frosted glass tumbler with logos for Pepsi and the Mid-Ohio-Con. Edition of 175.- **$70**
Clear glass tumbler with logo for Mid-Ohio-Con. Edition of 200.- **$22**
Clear glass tumbler with no logos. Retail version. Edition of 200.- **$12**

Arthur Godfrey

Arthur Godfrey (1903-1983) served in the Navy as a radio operator from 1920 to 1924 and then with the Coast Guard from 1927 to 1930 including a brief stint on Baltimore radio billed as "Red Godfrey The Warbling Banjoist." He joined WFBR radio, then moved on to WRC in Washington, DC until 1934. He worked at CBS in New York and his moving live broadcast of President Roosevelt's funeral in 1945 led to the week-day morning *Arthur Godfrey Time* show and *Arthur Godfrey's Talent Scouts* which was simulcast on TV in 1948. *Arthur Godfrey And Friends* began in 1949. At the height of his fame in 1953, all three shows were on the air in the same week.

An accomplished pilot, Godfrey would fly his own plane from his Leesburg, Virginia home to New York City for broadcasts. His relaxed demeanor and ukulele playing, along with a folksy charm and a refusal to do commercials for products he didn't like, endeared him to his audience.

***Talent Scout* winners included the McGuire Sisters, The Chordettes, Julius LaRosa, Pat Boone and Patsy Cline. Sadly, Elvis Presley did not pass his April 1955 audition.**

Godfrey's theme song *Seems Like Old Times* is a good metaphor for the Arthur Godfrey era.

AGF-1

❑ **AGF-1. Arthur Godfrey Photo Ring,**
c. 1950. Convex clear plastic dome over black and white photo flanked by four-leaf clover and horseshoe designs on each side of adjustable band. Unknown sponsor. - **$85 $175 $300**

AGF-2

❑ **AGF-2. "Snow White And The Seven Dwarfs/Rinso" Store Sign,**
c. 1951. 17x22" stiff paper sign with portrait of Arthur Godfrey. Other characters shown are Snow White, Grumpy, Sleepy and Dopey. Also shows image of Rinso product and bottom margin reads "Get Entry Blanks Here." Godfrey's text reads "Play The Rinso Name Game/Just Identify These 4 Walt Disney Characters And Name The Rinso Bird." - **$50 $100 $150**

AGF-3

❑ **AGF-3. "TV Fan" First Issue,**
1953. 20th Century Books. 8.5x11" Vol. 1 #1 with 76 pages. Cover is in color and contents are black and white. Includes photos of stars and articles. Cover shows Lucille Ball and Arthur Godfrey. - **$15 $30 $60**

AGF-4

❑ **AGF-4. "Hartz" Sponsored Shows Store Signs,**
c. 1956. Hartz Mountain Products. Lot of three 1.25x6" thin plastic shelf signs for Winchell/Mahoney, Captain Kangaroo, Arthur Godfrey. Each features portrait illustrations and text for specific program. Each - **$5 $10 $15**

AGF-5

❑ **AGF-5. "Stork Club" Christmas Gift Box With Billingsley/Godfrey/ Downey Soap And More,**
1950s. 8.75x8.75x1.5" deep gold foil-covered box with lid reading "Merry Christmas." Inside lid reads "Stork Club Lipstick And Nail Enamel/ Nude Soap/Preferred By Sophisticated Stork Clubites/Presented To You By Sherman Billingsley/Arthur Godfrey/Morton Downey." Contents are three soap bars with raised portrait of each man and several other cosmetics. - **$20 $40 $100**

AGF-6

❑ **AGF-6. Arthur Godfrey TV Sponsor Endorsement Button,**
1950s. 1.25". Reads "I'm For Fiberglas." - **$10 $20 $40**

AGF-7

❑ **AGF-7. Arthur Godfrey Sponsor Ad Photo,**
1950s. Snow Crop Frozen Foods. Pictured are Godfrey and Teddy Snow Crop symbol character. - **$10 $18 $35**

AGF-8

❑ **AGF-8. Birthday Gift Cigarette Carton,**
1950s. Arthur Godfrey, Bing Crosby and Perry Como featured on empty gift box of Chesterfields. - **$30 $60 $115**

Atom Ant

Produced by Hanna-Barbera, Atom Ant was first seen on TV on September 12, 1965 on *The World Of Secret Squirrel And Atom Ant.* The cartoon show had character segments which included Morocco Mole, The Hillbilly Bears, Precious Pup and Squiddly Diddly.

The superhero ant, who flew and had super strength, was written by Michael Maltese, Tony Benedict and Warren Foster and animators included Irv Spence and Art Davis. His voice was provided by Howard Morris and Don Messick. His show ran a total of three seasons with 26 episodes. He appeared in a 1966 Gold Key comic and a 1990 video game. He may have been the inspiration for British punk rocker Stuart Goddard to adopt the stage name Adam Ant. "Up And At 'Em, Atom Ant!"

ATO-1

❑ ATO-1. "Secret Squirrel And Atom Ant" Three-Reel View-Master Pack With Story Booklet,
1966. 4.25x4-3/8" sleeve contains 3 reels plus story booklet with stories for Secret Squirrel, Atom Ant and Squiddly Diddly. Set B535. - **$8 $15 $35**

ATO-2

❑ ATO-2. "Hanna-Barbera's Atom Ant Play Fun" Activities Set,
1966. 8.75x12x1.5" deep box contains punch-out character pieces to assemble and play sheet along with crayons.
Near Mint Unused - **$75**
Used Complete - **$15 $30 $50**

ATO-3

❑ ATO-3. "Atom Ant" First Comic Book,
1966. Gold Key. First appearance of Atom Ant, Precious Pup and Hillbilly Bears in comic book form. - **$30 $90 $400**

ATO-4

ATO-5

❑ ATO-4. "Atom Ant Tricky Trapeze" Push Button Acrobat,
1960s. Kohner Brothers #4995. 5.25" tall. - **$10 $20 $40**

❑ ATO-5. "Punkin Puss" Figural Soap Container And Store Card,
1960s. Purex. 11.25" tall figure with name incised on base and paper band titled "Flintstones Fun Bath." Punkin Puss is not shown on band but Atom Ant leads the parade of characters. Bottle - **$10 $20 $30**
Band - **$5 $10 $20**

ATO-6

❑ ATO-6. Atom Ant Specialty Art,
1983. 9x12" sheet with 5.75x7.5" image and autograph area in black ink art. Signed at lower left "Best Wishes Don Arr Christensen." Executed in person at 1983 San Diego Convention. Near Mint Same Or Similar - **$75**

Aunt Jemima

Aunt Jemima Pancake Flour was formulated in 1889 in St. Joseph Missouri by newspaperman Chris L. Root, who based the product's name on a popular vaudeville song of the day "Aunt Jemima." Root sold out to Davis Milling Co. and it was the 1892 Columbian Exposition in Chicago that made Jemima a national figure. The R.T. Davis Mill & Manufacturing Co. hired Nancy Green, a black cook from Kentucky to stand outside its exposition booth and cook pancakes--more than a million, it is claimed--during the course of the fair. Ms. Green traveled the country making personal appearances as Aunt Jemima for the next 30 years until her death in 1923. Quaker Oats bought the product and name in 1924, and today there are over three dozen Aunt Jemima breakfast products. Various Aunt Jemima variety programs ran on CBS between 1929 and 1953 in either 5-minute or 15-minute versions. The trademark face has been re-drawn a number of times to cosmetically update the character's features.

AUN-1

❑ AUN-1. Cello. Button,
c. 1896. First issue is not inscribed "Pancake Flour."
Without Inscription - **$45 $115 $185**
With Inscription - **$32 $90 $135**

AUN-2

❑ AUN-2. "Aunt Jemima Pancake Flour" Paper Puzzle,
c. 1900. R. T. Davis Co. 3x4" diecut paper portrait card with string holding miniature paper pancake flour box. Reverse offers premium titled "Life History Of Aunt Jemima And A Set Of Her Pickaninny Dolls." - **$65 $135 $275**

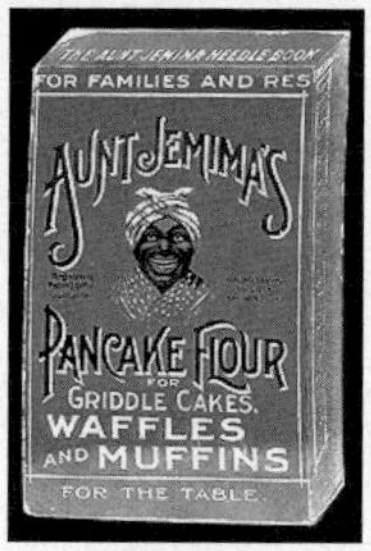

AUN-3

AUN-4

❑ **AUN-3. Needle Book With Doll Offer,**
c. 1910. Davis Milling Co. Diecut paper folder holding sewing needles and related plus panel ad for "Aunt Jemima Rag Doll Family." - **$55 $115 $200**

❑ **AUN-4. "Diana" Cloth Doll,**
c. 1910. Stuffed rag doll from family series inscribed near dress hem "A. J. Pancake Flour/Pickanniny Doll, Diana/Davis Milling Co., St. Joseph, Mo." - **$115 $225 $385**

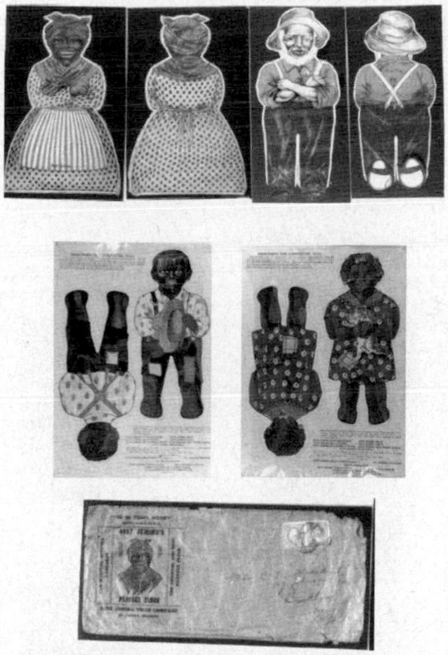

AUN-5

❑ **AUN-5. Aunt Jemima, Uncle Mose, Wade and Diana Doll Fabrics With Envelope,**
c. 1915. Scarce. Aunt Jemima Mills Co.
Near Mint Uncut In Mailer - **$2150**
Aunt Jemima Cut Or Assembled - **$165 $275 $700**
Others Cut Or Assembled - **$110 $215 $375**

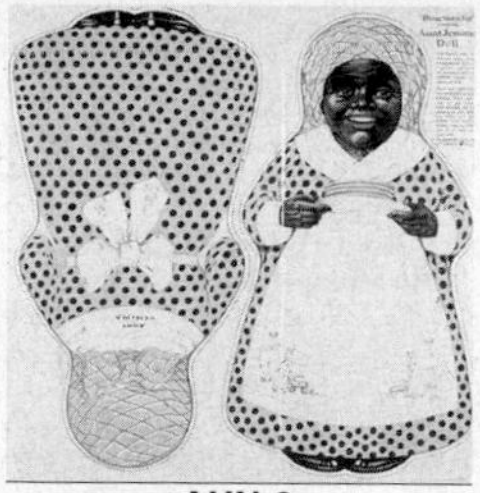

AUN-6

❑ **AUN-6. Cloth Doll,**
1929. Scarce. Near Mint Uncut - **$650**
Assembled - **$85 $190 $375**

AUN-7

❑ **AUN-7. "Ready-Mix For Pancakes" Store Display,**
c. 1940. 15x22" cardboard formed as oversized replica box of pancake mix with easel back. - **$115 $225 $350**

AUN-8

❑ **AUN-8. Premium Doll (unstuffed) and Instructions,**
1948. - **$65 $135 $225**

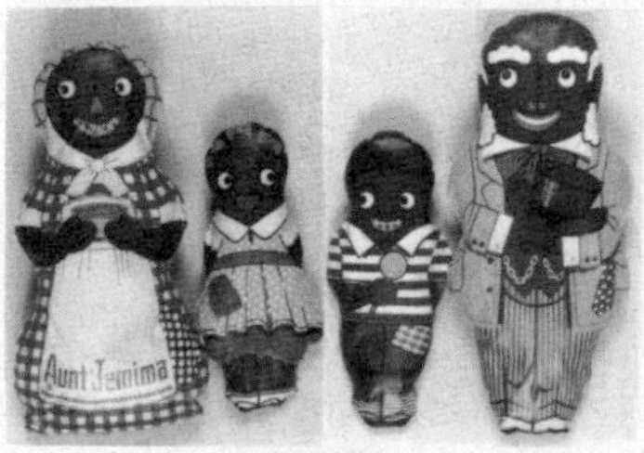

AUN-9

❑ **AUN-9. Vinyl Stuffed Doll Set,**
1948. Set of four - **$120 $240 $500**

AUN-10

❑ **AUN-10. Recipe Booklet Pair,**
1948-1949. Each 4x6" with 20 pages.
Each - **$10 $15 $30**

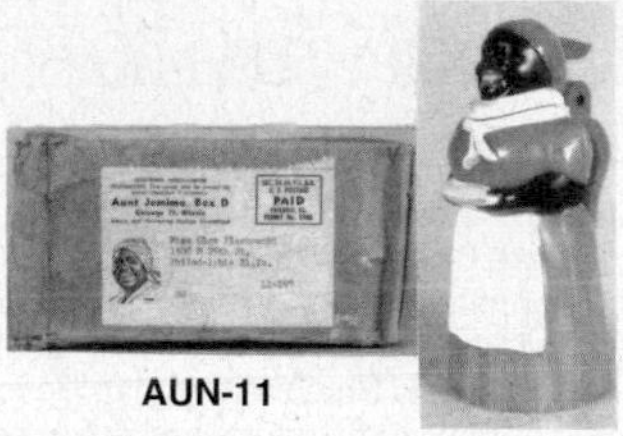

AUN-11

❑ **AUN-11. Plastic Syrup Pitcher With Box,**
c. 1949. Boxed - **$35 $80 $155**
Loose - **$20 $55 $95**

AUN-12

❑ **AUN-12. Hard Plastic Salt & Pepper Set,**
c. 1949. - **$18 $30 $65**

AUN-13

❑ **AUN-13. "Aunt Jemima Doll Family/Fun Book" Original Art Prototype Ad,**
1940s. 9-1/4x14-1/2" from the Gordon Gold Archives. Unique. - **$475**

AUN-14

❑ **AUN-14. "Pancake Days" Cardboard Pin-Back,**
c. 1952. Color portrait on rigid 4" cardboard. - **$20 $30 $75**

AUN-15

❑ **AUN-15. "Store Promotions Of The Quaker Oats Company" Fold-Out,**
1953. Color folder 7-1/2x11" opens to length of 34-1/2". Promotes "Circus Action Wild Animals" inserts with Muffets Shredded Wheat. Reverse promotes Aunt Jemima cream and sugar set. Gordon Gold Archives. - **$45 $85 $150**

AUN-16

❑ **AUN-16. "Aunt Jemima At Disneyland" Placemat,**
1955. Placemat is 9.5x14" textured paper from first year of Disneyland from the restaurant in Frontierland featuring both illustrations and photos of Aunt Jemima along with informative text. Title reads "A Story Of Aunt Jemima Yesterday, Today And Now/Aunt Jemima At Disneyland." - **$20 $40 $60**

AUN-17

❑ **AUN-17. Promotional Pinback,**
1950s. - **$10 $20 $32**

AUN-18

❑ **AUN-18. "Pastry Mix Set",**
1950s. Store item by Junior Chef. Complete - **$45 $80 $160**

AUN-19

❑ **AUN-19. Plastic Cookie Jar,**
1950s. - **$85 $300 $550**

AUN-20

❑ **AUN-20. Chrome Metal Cigarette Lighter,**
1960s. - **$30 $55 $110**

AUN-21

AUN-22

❑ **AUN-21. "Breakfast Club" 4" Litho Button,**
1960s. - **$18 $32 $55**

❑ **AUN-22. Litho. Tab With Color Portrait,**
1960s. - **$5 $10 $20**

Aunt Jenny

Known under a number of names--*Aunt Jenny, Aunt Jenny's Real Life Stories, Aunt Jenny's Thrilling Real Life Stories, Aunt Jenny's True-Life Stories*, and in Canada as *Aunt Lucy*--this 15-minute serial drama ran five times a week on CBS radio for almost 20 years, from 1937 to 1956. Jenny, played by Edith Spencer and Agnes Young, was assisted by her announcer Danny, played by Dan Seymour, in relating the troubles of her friends and neighbors, providing a golden thought of the day, and offering cooking tips, invariably involving Spry, her longtime sponsor.

AJR-1

❑ **AJR-1. Cast Member Photo With Mailer Envelope,**
c. 1937. Lever Brothers. Facsimile signature "Best Wishes/Dan Seymour-Sincerely Jennifer F. Wheeler (Aunt Jenny)". Mailer - **$6 $12 $20** Photo - **$12 $25 $45**

AJR-2

❑ **AJR-2. Fan Photo With Mailer,**
c. 1937. Lever Bros. 8x10" black and white with facsimile signature "Jennifer F. Wheeler (Aunt Jenny)". Mailer - **$6 $12 $20**
Photo - **$25 $45 $110**

AJR-3

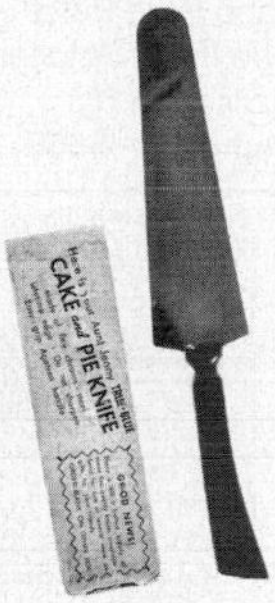

AJR-4

❑ **AJR-3. Cook Book,**
1942. Spry Cooking Oil. Fifty pages of recipes. - **$12 $25 $40**

❑ **AJR-4. Cake Knife With Advertising On Cardboard Cover,**
1940s. Scarce. - **$40 $110 $190**

AJR-5

AJR-6

❑ **AJR-5. Recipe,**
1940s. Spry Cooking Oil. Green premium cardboard disc - Coconut cake. - **$10 $20 $32**

❑ **AJR-6. "Complete Birthday Kit" With Mailer Box,**
1940s. Spry Cooking Oil. Contents include small candles, candleholders, cake frosting tints, cake recipe leaflet, birthday scroll piece for cake. - **$10 $15 $25**

AJR-7

AJR-8

❑ **AJR-7. "Old Home Recipes" Folder,**
1940s. Spry cooking oil. Unfolds to 3-1/2x13" sheet printed on both sides. - **$4 $8 $15**

❑ **AJR-8. "Favorite Recipes" Booklet,**
1940s. Spry cooking oil. 6x7" with 52 pages. - **$8 $15 $30**

AJR-9

❑ **AJR-9. "Aunt Jenny's Recipe Book-12 Pies Husbands Like Best",**
1952. Lever Brothers. - **$5 $12 $25**

AJR-10

❑ **AJR-10. Recipe,**
1950s. Spry Cooking Oil. Yellow premium cardboard disc - Cherry rolls. - **$10 $20 $30**

Babe Ruth

George Herman "Babe" Ruth (1895-1948), baseball legend and American national hero, began playing professionally in 1914 for the old Baltimore Orioles before being purchased by the Boston Red Sox. He was a formidable pitcher, but it was his bat that propelled him to greatness. He led the major leagues in home runs in 10 of the 12 years between 1919 and 1930, and in 1927 he hit a record 60. He played in the outfield for the New York Yankees from 1920 to 1935 and Yankee Stadium became known as "The House That Ruth Built." Movie appearances include: *Play Ball with Babe Ruth* (1920); *Heading Home* (1920); *Babe Comes Home* (1927); *Speedy* (1928); *Just Pals, Over the Fence, Perfect Control and Slide Babe, Slide* (all 1932); *Home Run on the Keys* (1936); *The Pride of the Yankees* (1942). The *Baby Ruth* candy bar, introduced in 1921 by the Curtiss Candy Company, owes much of its early success to the popularity of Ruth's name. He received no royalties. The Babe appeared on several network radio shows: *Play Ball* and *The Adventures of Babe Ruth* sponsored by Quaker cereals in 1934, the *Sinclair Babe Ruth Program* in 1937, *Here's Babe Ruth* in 1943 and *Baseball Quiz* in 1943 and 1944. Eleven issues of *Babe Ruth Sports Comics* were published by Harvey Publications from 1949 to 1951. Ruth was the subject of two feature films, *The Babe Ruth Story* (1948) and *The Babe* (1992). The Babe Ruth Birthplace & Official Orioles Museum in Baltimore, Maryland showcases his early years, playing career, and great moments in baseball history.

BAB-1

❑ **BAB-1. "Babe Ruth Song" Litho. Button,**
1928. Promotes sheet music for song following his 1927 record-breaking year of 60 home runs in season. - **$60 $125 $250**

BAB-2

❑ **BAB-2. "Smitty At The Ball Game" Strip Reprint Book Featuring Babe Ruth,**
1929. Cupples & Leon. 7x8.5" with 88 pages. Book features Babe Ruth as well as appearances by Grover Cleveland Alexander, Rogers Hornsby. GD - **$57** FN - **$229** VF - **$450**

BAB-3

❑ **BAB-3. "Babe's Musical Bat",**
c. 1930. German made store item. 4" long wood replica bat with insert harmonica reeds. -
$100 $190 $350

BAB-4

❑ **BAB-4. "Babe Ruth's Baseball Club" Display Sign,**
1934. Promotes Quaker Oaks ad campaign. Measures 20" x 29-1/2". - **$1100 $2200 $3850**

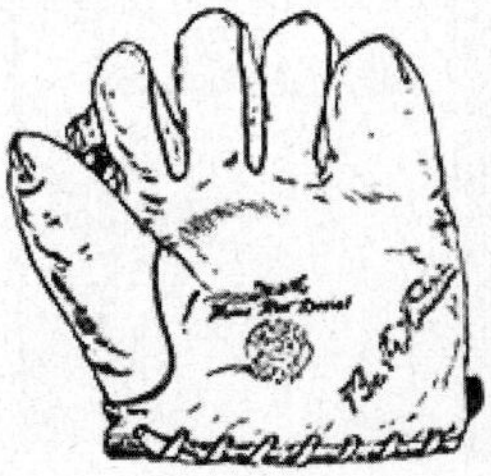

BAB-5

❑ **BAB-5. "Babe Ruth's Baseball Club" Contest Prize,**
1934. Quaker Puffed Wheat. Second prize in weekly contests of Babe Ruth model Spalding fielder glove with facsimile Ruth signature. -
$275 $500 $900

BAB-6

❑ **BAB-6. "Babe Ruth's Baseball Club" Contest Prize,**
1934. Quaker Puffed Wheat, also store item. Weekly contest third prize boxed Spalding "Babe Ruth Home Run Special" baseball.
Box - **$225 $500 $750**
Baseball - **$175 $450 $700**

BAB-7

BAB-8

❑ **BAB-7. Quaker Cereal "How To Throw Curves" Booklet,**
1934. - **$20 $45 $110**

❑ **BAB-8. Quaker Cereal "How To Knock Home Runs" Booklet,**
1934. Two additional "How To" booklets (not shown) are "Play The Infield" and "Play The Outfield". Each - **$20 $45 $110**

BAB-9

BAB-10

BAB-11

❑ **BAB-9. Cello. Baseball Scorer Fob,**
1934. Quaker Cereals. Pictures him in Yankee cap, back has scorer wheel. - **$85 $185 $475**

❑ **BAB-10. Cello. Baseball Scorer Fob,**
1934. Quaker Cereals. Pictures him in Boston Braves cap, back has scoring wheel. Made to replace version of him wearing Yankees cap shortly after the Yankees released him following the 1934 season. - **$75 $175 $450**

❑ **BAB-11. Quaker Cello. Club Button,**
1934. - **$35 $65 $110**

BAB-12

❑ **BAB-12. Quaker Oats Patches and Mailer,**
1934. The offer for the Babe Ruth patch included 2 other patches for your initials.
Babe Ruth Patch - **$330**
Two Initial Patches - **$220**
Mailer - **$110**
Complete - **$660**

BAB-13

BAB-14

❑ **BAB-13. Quaker Oats "Babe Ruth Hitting A Homer" Flip Booklet,**
1934. Pages flip for batting sequence. -
$135 $290 $500

❑ **BAB-14. "Ask Me" 3" Cello. Button,**
c. 1934. Store employee button promoting Quaker premium card game "Ask Me-The Game Of Baseball Facts". See BAB-16. -
$135 $290 $475

BAB-15

❑ **BAB-15. "Babe Ruth In The 'Home Run' A Miniature Movie" Flip-Book,**
c. 1934. Lion Brand, probable coffee product. 1-3/4x2-1/2" with black and white pages. -
$135 $290 $500

BAB-16

❑ **BAB-16. Ask Me Game,**
c. 1934. Rare. Quaker Cereals. Includes mailer, cards and instructions. See BAB-14.
Complete - **$425 $775 $1200**

BAB-17

❑ **BAB-17. Premium Photo,**
c. 1934. Quaker Oats. 8x10" black and white photo with facsimile inscription "To My Pal From 'Babe' Ruth." Bottom margin reads "Presented To Members Of Babe Ruth Baseball Club By The Quaker Oats Company, Makers Of Quaker Puffed Wheat And Puffed Rice." -
$65 $165 $325

BAB-18

❑ **BAB-18. Baseball Scorer,**
c. 1934. Quaker Cereals. Cardboard mechanical disk card. - **$45 $110 $200**

BAB-19

❑ **BAB-19. Babe Ruth Club Litho Button,**
c. 1934. Button is 7/8" with smiling photo, possibly issued by his Quaker Cereals club.
- $60 $125 $200

BAB-20

BAB-21

❑ **BAB-20. Quaker "Babe Ruth Champions" Brass Club Badge,**
1935. - **$25 $60 $100**

❑ **BAB-21. Quaker "Babe Ruth Champions" Cello. Club Button,**
1935. Pictures him in Boston cap. -
$60 $125 $200

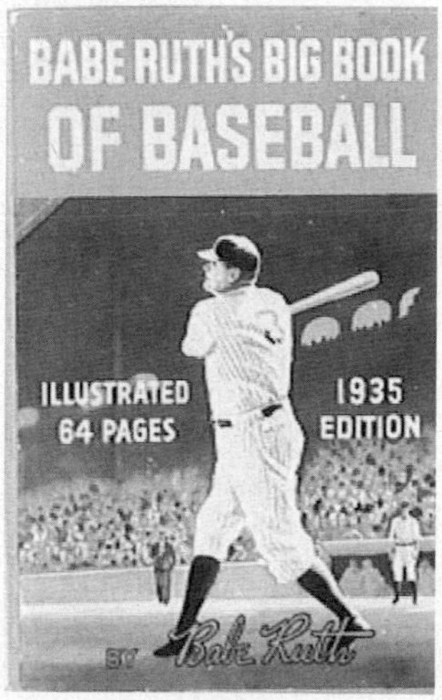

BAB-22

❑ **BAB-22. "Babe Ruth's Big Book Of Baseball",**
1935. Quaker Puffed Wheat And Puffed Rice, 5x7-1/2" with 64 pages of instructions on all facets of playing the game. - **$85 $190 $375**

BAB-23

BAB-23-Opposite side

❑ **BAB-23. Mail Order Premium Insert Sheet,**
1936. Quaker Cereals. 8x9" folded insert with one side showing six Babe Ruth premiums with expiration date of July 31, 1936. Opposite side offers "Photo-Statuettes Of Your Favorite Movie Stars." - **$45 $85 $165**

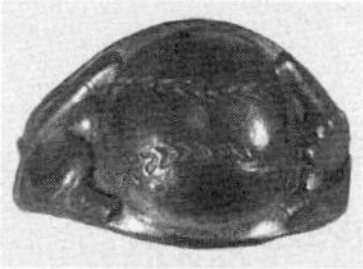

BAB-24

BAB-25

❑ **BAB-24. Babe Ruth Brass Ring,**
1935. Quaker Cereals. No inscriptions but Babe Ruth Club premium picturing baseball symbols. -
$65 $150 $265

❑ **BAB-25. Babe Ruth Brass Baseball Charms Bracelet,**
1935. Quaker Cereals. - **$80 $165 $300**

BAB-26

BAB-27

❑ BAB-26. "Babe Ruth" Cello./Steel Bat Replica Pocketknife,
1930s. Name inscribed on one side plus tiny baseball depiction. - **$65 $135 $325**

❑ BAB-27. "Babe Ruth" Brass Belt Buckle,
1930s. Store item by "Harris Belts" marked on reverse. - **$65 $150 $300**

BAB-28

❑ BAB-28. Club 3" Fabric Patch,
1930s. Possibly Quaker Cereals. -
$30 $55 $110

BAB-29

BAB-30

❑ BAB-29. "Esso Boys Club" Silvered Metal Badge,
1930s. Figural baseball accented in red/blue with inscription "Charter Member". -
$35 $75 $165

❑ BAB-30. "Play Ball With Babe Ruth" Cello. Button,
1930s. Universal Pictures. Promotion for "Christy Walsh All America Sports Reels" movie feature. - **$325 $775 $1850**

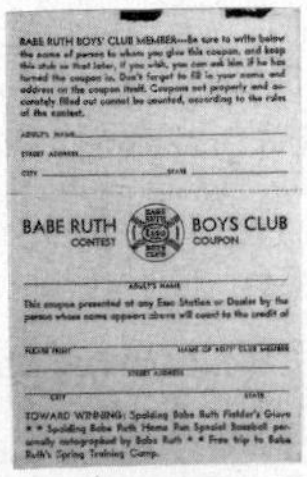
BABE RUTH CONTEST

BOYS CLUB COUPON

BAB-31

❑ BAB-31. Esso Gasoline "Babe Ruth Boys Club" Contest Coupon,
1930s. Offers premium for acquiring new members. See BAB-29. - **$15 $25 $50**

BAB-32

❑ BAB-32. "Bambino/The Real Ball Game" 4" Cello. Button,
1930s. For mechanical batting practice game based on Babe Ruth popular nickname by unidentified maker. - **$115 $275 $575**

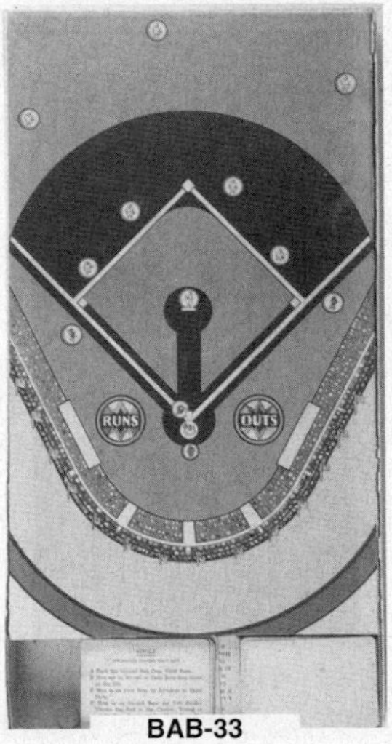

BAB-33

❑ BAB-33. "Babe Ruth's Baseball Game,"
1930s. Milton Bradley Co. 10.25x19x1.75" deep box comes with eighty-five 2.25x3.5" playing cards, 12 generic wood counter disks and instructions printed inside box lid.
- **$300 $600 $1200**

BAB-34

❑ BAB-34. "Babe Ruth As I Knew Him" Dell Magazine,
1948. Dedicatory issue of 50 pages including black and white career photos plus text by former teammate pitcher and life-time friend Waite Hoyt. - **$30 $55 $110**

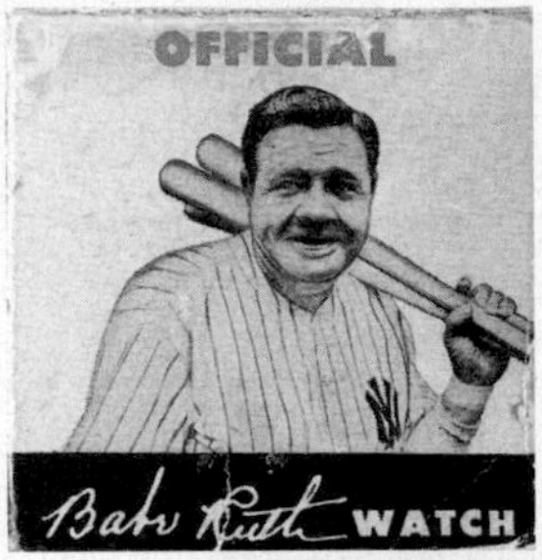

(BOX)

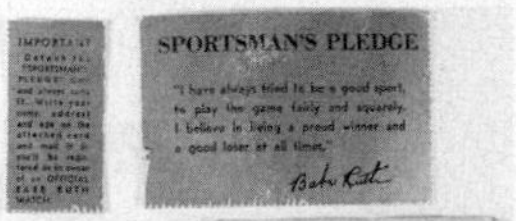

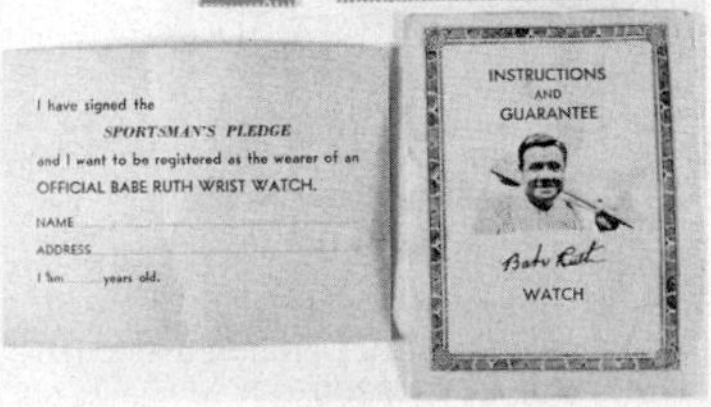

BAB-35

❑ BAB-35. "Official Babe Ruth Wrist Watch" With Display Case,
1949. Store item by Exacta Time. Plastic display case is replica baseball.
Near Mint In Case With Box, Coupons, Instructions, Pledge and Postcard - **$3500**
Watch Only - **$300 $675 $1300**

BAB-36

BAB-37

❑ BAB-36. Photo Charm,
1940s. 1" tall plastic looped frame inset by black and white photo. - **$12 $22 $45**

❑ BAB-37. "Babe Ruth" Plastic Ring,
1950. Inset picture of him swinging bat. From Kellogg's set of sixteen picturing sports and movie stars, airplanes and 19th century western personalities. - **$30 $60 $100**

BAB-38

❑ BAB-38. Look 'N See Gum Card,
1952. Issued by Topps. This is the stand-out card in the set and the only one to feature a sports figure. - **$35 $75 $165**

BAB-39

❑ BAB-39. "Hall Of Fame" Boxed Statuette,
1963. From series of 20 players.
Near Mint Boxed - **$150**
Loose - **$22 $45 $90**

BAB-40

❑ BAB-40. Hartland Figure,
1960s. 7.5" tall gesturing figure with removable bat by Hartland Plastics.
Complete With Bat - **$125 $175 $300**
Figure Without Bat - **$75 $125 $250**

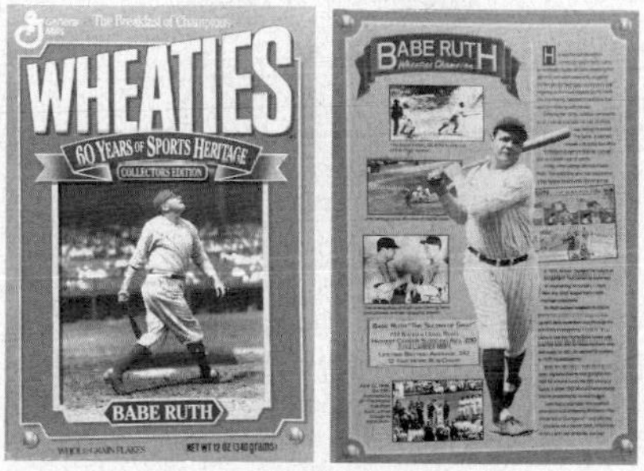

BAB-41

❑ BAB-41. Wheaties Cereal Box,
1992. From the set featuring "60 Years of Sports Heritage". Babe Ruth appears on front. Back has pictures and a write-up.- **$8 $12 $28**

BAB-42

❑ BAB-42. Commemorative Bank Car,
1995. 100th Anniversary product. Model car's window notes the Babe's 60 home runs hit in 1927. - **$55**

BAB-43

BAB-44

❑ BAB-43. Commemorative Baseball in Box,
1995. 100th Anniversary baseball. - **$33**

❑ BAB-44. Christmas Ornament with Tag,
1998. - **$18**

(THE BALL)

BAB-45

(3 VIEWS OF THE BOX)

❑ BAB-45. Babe Ruth Baseball in Box,
1999. Dark Horse Comics limited edition of 714. Signed by artist Monty Sheldon. - **$90**

BAB-46

BAB-47

❑ BAB-46. Figure on Card,
Late 1990s. Starting Lineup figure includes baseball card in package. - **$40**

❑ BAB-47. Raisin Bran Cereal Box
2001. Post Raisin Bran box features a "Babe Ruth Hall of Fame" card. - **$22**

Baby Snooks

Baby Snooks was a 7-year-old brat and America's radio listeners loved her. Born in the imagination of Ziegfeld Follies star Fanny Brice and written by Phillip Rapp and David Freeman, the irrepressible imp was introduced to the world on February 29, 1936, in *The Ziegfeld Follies of the Air,* a lavish 60-minute extravaganza on CBS. The program had a brief life but Baby Snooks was to appear continuously on one network program or another for the next 15 years including her own show *The Baby Snooks Show* in 1944. "Daddy" was played by actors including Frank Morgan, Alan Reed and Hanley Stafford. Child impersonator Lenore Ledoux was baby brother Robespierre. The series ended with Brice's untimely demise in 1951 at age 59. Sponsors included Maxwell House coffee, Post Toasties cereal, Sanka, Jell-O and Tums.

BSN-1

BSN-2

❑ **BSN-1. "Radio Guide" Magazine With Fannie Brice Cover,**
1938. - **$15 $25 $45**

❑ **BSN-2. "Fanny Brice's Baby Snooks Pops" Lollipop Pail,**
c. 1938. Store item by E. Rosen Co. 3" tall by 3-1/4" diameter litho. tin featuring three different images around perimeter. - **$65 $135 $250**

BSN-3

❑ **BSN-3. Composition/Wood/Wire "Flexy" Doll With Outfit And Tag,**
1939. Store item by Ideal Toy & Novelty Co. - **$115 $265 $500**

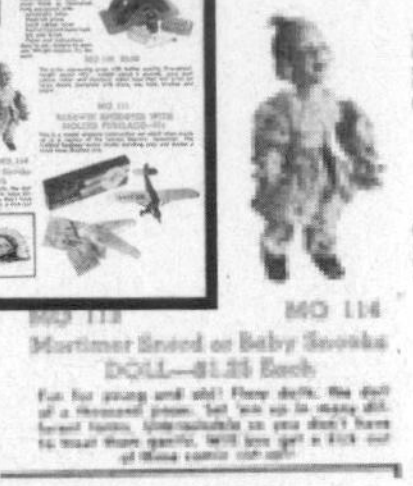

BSN-4

❑ **BSN-4. Ad for "Baby Snooks" Doll,**
1940. From the back cover of Blue Bolt #1 comic book. Was not offered after the first issue. - **$75 $100 $200**

BSN-5

❑ **BSN-5. Whitman Cut-Out Doll Book,**
1940. Store item. Designs by Queen Holden. - **$115 $225 $450**

BSN-6

BSN-7

❑ **BSN-6. "My Second Childhood" Cover Article,**
1944. May issue of "Tune In" national radio magazine including three-page article about "Baby Snooks" radio portrayal by Fannie Brice. - **$12 $18 $35**

❑ **BSN-7. Plastic Figure On Metal Bar Pin,**
c. 1940s. Figure finished in gold color. - **$25 $45 $85**

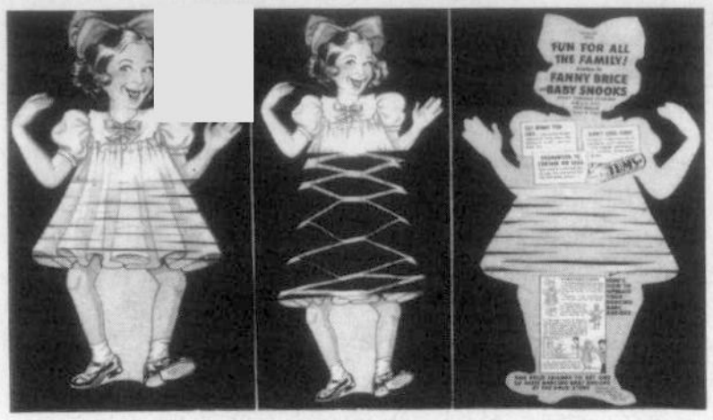

BSN-8

❑ **BSN-8. Cardboard Dancing Puppet,**
1950. Tums. Flexible diecut paper mid-section. - **$35 $80 $175**

BSN-9

❑ **BSN-9. Paper Store Sign With "Dancing Baby Snooks" Offer,**
1950. Tums. Full color 10x16". Gordon Gold archives. - **$60 $135 $250**

BSN-10

❑ **BSN-10. Cardboard Display Card With "Dancing Baby Snooks" Offer,**
1950. Tums. 3-1/2x6-1/2" with reverse instructions for inserting into display carton of product. Gordon Gold Archives. - **$35 $65 $110**

Bachelor's Children

Radio's beloved serial, *Bachelor's Children* tells the story of Dr. Bob Graham and the twin teenage girls he promised to raise. In true soap opera form, he eventually marries one of them. The popular series, which won awards for "realism," aired on CBS from 1936 to 1946, sponsored by Old Dutch cleanser, Wonder bread, and Colgate.

BCH-1

❑ **BCH-1. Story Synopsis Booklet With Station Listings,**
1937. Old Dutch Cleanser. 3-1/4x6-1/4" with 20 pages. - **$12 $25 $40**

BCH-2

❑ **BCH-2. "Bachelor's Children" Story Synopsis Book With Mailer,**
1939. Old Dutch Cleanser. 25-page hardcover including cast member photo plates.
Near Mint With Mailer - **$60**
No Mailer - **$8 $15 $30**

BCH-3

❑ **BCH-3. Wonder Bread Fan Newsletter,**
c. 1945. - **$12 $25 $50**

Bambi

See Ted Hake's *Official® Price Guide to Disney Collectibles*, Second Edition, formatted identically to this book but in full color evaluating over 9,000 Disney company and character collectibles from 1924 through 2006.

The Banana Splits

This imaginative live-action show consisted of four people wardrobed in outfits of Fleegle the dog, Bingo the gorilla, Drooper the lion and Snorky the baby elephant. The group was musically inclined in addition to adventuresome and appeared in 60-minute shows produced by Hanna-Barbera on NBC, sponsored by Kellogg's, from 1968 to 1970. The show's official title was a lengthy *Kellogg's of Battle Creek Presents The Banana Splits Adventure Hour*, though the title was shortened to *The Banana Splits & Friends Show* in syndication. Noted movie director Richard Donner got his start on the show. Characters were voiced by Paul Winchell (Fleegle), Daws Butler (Bingo), Allan Melvin (Drooper) and Don Messick (Snorky).

BSP-1

❑ **BSP-1. Thin Plastic Premium Hand Puppets,**
1968. Kellogg's Chocolate Flavored Kombos. Set consists of Fleegle, Bingo, Drooper and (not shown) Snorky. Each - **$12 $25 $50**

BSP-2

BSP-3

❑ **BSP-2. Record In Sleeve,**
1968. Kellogg's. Includes song "Doin' The Banana Split" and three others.
With Mailer - **$30 $60 $100**
No Mailer - **$15 $30 $60**

❑ **BSP-3. Record With Sleeve,**
1968. Kellogg's. Song "Tra-La-La Song" and three others.
With Mailer - **$30 $60 $100**
No Mailer - **$15 $30 $60**

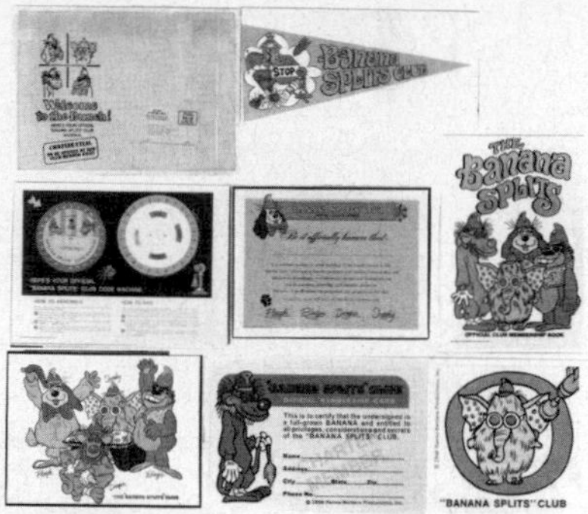

BSP-4

(enlarged coder)

❑ **BSP-4. Club Kit,**
1968. Mailing envelope plus pennant, membership book, code machine, certificate, group portrait, membership card, sticker.
Complete - **$100 $250 $400**
Code Card Only - **$30 $70 $135**

BSP-5

❑ **BSP-5. Banana Splits Character Stamp Pad Set,**
c. 1968. Kellogg's. Plastic case holding six character image ink stamp blocks plus instruction slip. - **$25 $60 $125**

BSP-6

❑ **BSP-6. Fleegle Plastic Mug,**
1969. Came with red plastic cereal bowl picturing the characters. Each - **$12 $25 $50**

BSP-7

❑ **BSP-7. Banana Buggy Aurora Model Kit,**
1969. Store item. Set consists of instructions, decal sheet, buggy, bench, figures of Fleegle, Bingo, Snorky, Drooper, along with eyeglasses and tails.
Near Mint Boxed Unassembled - **$400**
Built Model - **$55 $110 $165**
Box Only - **$35 $70 $115**

BSP-8

❑ **BSP-8. "Breakfast Set" Premium Offer Cereal Box,**
1969. Gordon Gold Archives.
Near Mint Flat - **$475**
Used Complete - **$110 $220 $350**

BSP-9

❑ **BSP-9. Cereal Box With "Banana Splits Pin-Up Posters" Offer,**
1969. This box held "Kellogg's Froot Loops" although offer was made on various Kellogg's product boxes. Gordon Gold archives.
Near Mint Flat - **$425**
Used Complete - **$80 $160 $290**

BSP-10

❑ **BSP-10. Fleer Gum "Tattoo" Vending Machine Card,**
1969.- **$12 $18 $35**

BSP-11

❑ **BSP-11. Frame Tray Puzzles Boxed Set,**
1969. Whitman. Four 8x10" puzzles. -
$40 $80 $175

BSP-12

❑ **BSP-12. Frame Tray Puzzle,**
1969. Whitman. 11.5x14.5" puzzle scene of them racing snowmobiles at North Pole. -
$12 $25 $50

BSP-13

❑ **BSP-13. NBC Promo Transparency,**
c. 1969. 4x5". - **$12 $18 $35**

BSP-14

❑ **BSP-14. The Banana Splits Tile Puzzle On Card,**
1960s. Card is 5x6" and holds 2.5x2.5x.25" thick black and white plastic puzzle by the Roalex Company. Carded - **$100 $200 $300**
Puzzle Only - **$30 $60 $115**

BSP-15

❑ **BSP-15. Banana Splits Plush Animal Pair,**
1970. Each is 7.25" tall depicting Drooper and Fleegle made by I.S. Sutton & Sons Inc. Each comes with felt hat and footwear. Drooper has vinyl glasses. 1x1.25" tags are secured to necks by strings. Each With Tags - **$70 $135 $240**

BSP-16

❑ **BSP-16. "Banana Splits Snorky" Large Stuffed Plush Doll,**
1970. Store item. 25" tall. - **$115 $225 $335**

BSP-17 BSP-18

❑ **BSP-17. Drooper Vinyl Figure,**
1971. Store item by Sutton.
Bagged - **$45 $65 $145**
Loose - **$25 $45 $90**

❑ **BSP-18. Fleegle Vinyl Figure,**
1971. Store item by Sutton.
Bagged - **$45 $65 $145**
Loose - **$25 $45 $90**

BSP-19

❑ **BSP-19. Button Set,**
1972. Hanna-Barbera copyright. Full color 1-1/4" buttons showing the group: Bingo, Drooper, Fleegle, and Snorky. Each - **$12 $22 $38**

BSP-20

❑ **BSP-20. 7-Eleven Plastic Cups,**
1976. Each - **$12 $22 $35**

Barbie

Until 1959, when Barbie first appeared, dolls were pretty much the same for hundreds of years. They were baby dolls to be mothered and nurtured by their youthful owners who would probably be mothers with their own real babies someday. Dolls came on the market with eyes that opened, movable arms and legs and finally dolls that wet and needed to be fed and changed–not too exciting. Barbie started a revolutionary trend; she wasn't a baby doll, but a young lady out in the world with fashionable clothes, cars, and boyfriends...and she had a bosom! Ruth Handler, Barbie's creator, has been quoted as saying "Barbie was originally created to project every little girl's dream of the future."

In the 1940s Ruth and Elliot Handler owned a company which made wood picture frames. Elliot began using the scraps to make doll furniture and in 1945 they joined with friend Harold Mattson to form Mattel: Matt for Mattson and El for Elliot. Barbie, named after the Handlers' daughter Barbara, was patented in 1958. Her clothes were designed by Charlotte Johnson and she was officially introduced at the New York Toy Show in 1959. Barbie's friend Ken, named after the Handlers' son Kenneth, came along in 1960. Her best friend Midge arrived in 1963. Little sister Skipper was introduced in 1964 as were her male friend Ricky and girlfriend Skooter. Barbie's first feature film "The Nutcracker" aired on CBS-TV Thanksgiving day 2001. On February 12, 2004 Barbie and Ken decided to spend some time apart after 43 years as a couple. Ruth Handler became president of Mattel in 1967 and passed away in April 2002. The Barbie product line by Mattel continues to rank among the most successful offerings of the toy industry.

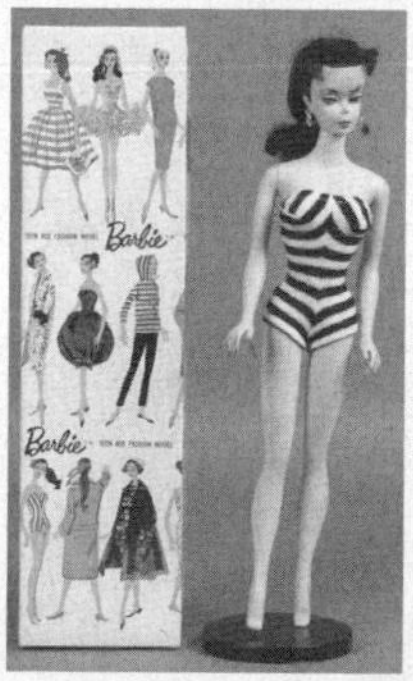

BAR-1

❑ **BAR-1. Barbie First Issue Boxed Doll,**
1959. 11-1/2" tall heavy vinyl solid body. White irises, pointed eyebrows. Soft ponytail in either blond or brunette. Black and white striped bathing suit. Has holes with metal cylinders in balls of feet to fit round-pronged stand. Gold hoop earrings.
Boxed Complete - **$2200 $4500 $7500**

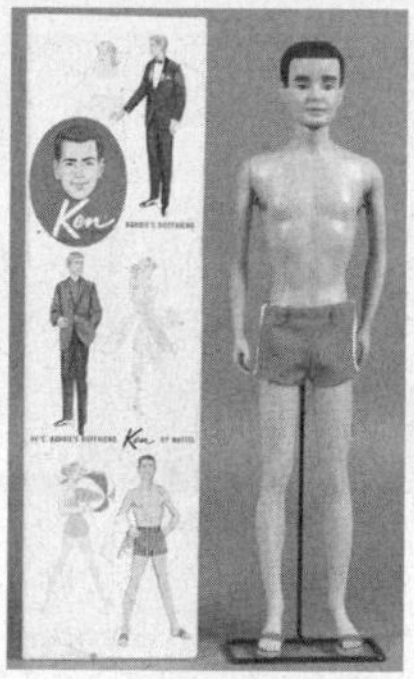

BAR-2

❑ **BAR-2. Ken First Issue Boxed Doll,**
1961. 12" tall. Straight legs, blue eyes, hard plastic hollow body, flocked hair. Red trunks and sandals. Wire display stand.
Boxed Complete - **$125 $250 $500**

BAR-3

❑ **BAR-3. "Barbie" Vinyl Lunch Box With Separate Thermos Compartment,**
1962. Lunch box is 8x8.75x3.5" vinyl made by Ponytail/Mattel. Lunch box has flap on side which reveals separate thermos compartment. Lunch box has vinyl carry straps, similar to that of a purse. - **$550 $1100 $1650**

BAR-4 BAR-5

❑ **BAR-4. "Barbie Play Ring" On Card,**
1962. Store item by Mattel. 4x6-1/2" card holds gold luster metal ring featuring Barbie profile surrounded by rhinestones.
Near Mint On Card - **$275**
Ring Only - **$40 $75 $150**

❑ **BAR-5. Metal Lunch Bottle,**
1962. Store item by King-Seeley. This bottle came with several different vinyl lunch boxes. - **$18 $35 $75**

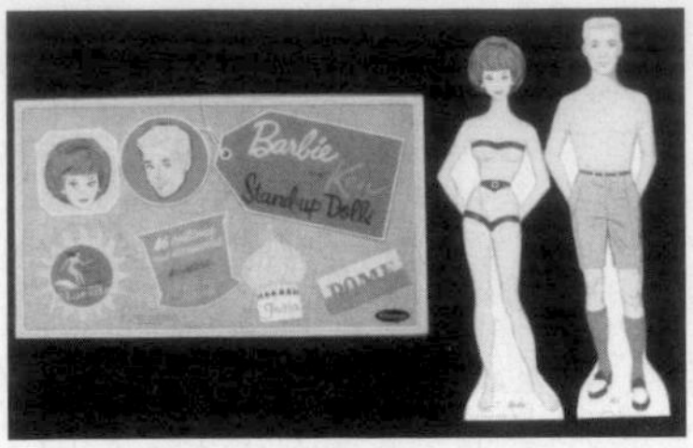

BAR-6

❑ **BAR-6. "Barbie & Ken Standup Dolls" Kit,**
1962. Store item by Whitman under Mattel copyright. Carrying case holds two diecut cardboard 9-1/2" tall figures. - **$40 $75 $135**

BAR-7

❑ **BAR-7. "Barbie's Keys To Fame" Game,**
1963. Store item by Mattel. - **$30 $55 $95**

BAR-8

❑ **BAR-8. Barbie And Ken Clothing Hanger Packs,**
c. 1963. Store item by Mattel. Barbie and Ken pack has red plastic hangers with 1963 copyright. Second pack has 1965 copyright with white plastic hangers for Barbie, Francie, Skipper and Scooter.
Each Sealed Pack - **$10 $20 $40**

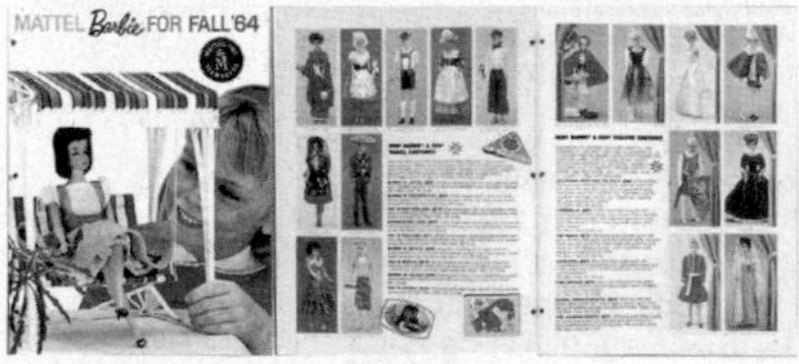

BAR-9

❑ **BAR-9. "Mattel Dolls For Fall '64" Retailer's Catalogue,**
1964. - **$45 $85 $145**

BAR-10

BAR-11

❑ **BAR-10. Fan Club Membership Card,**
1964.- **$12 $25 $50**

❑ **BAR-11. Wristwatch,**
1964. Store item. - **$50 $100 $200**

BAR-12

❑ **BAR-12. "Skipper" Vinyl Wallet,**
1964. Store item by Standard Plastics Products under license from Mattel. Comes with yellow or blue background. Each - **$20 $40 $75**

BAR-13

❑ **BAR-13. "Barbie" Magazine,**
March-April, 1965. One of a series by Mattel. Each - **$8 $15 $30**

BAR-14

❑ **BAR-14. Club Kit,**
1965. Mailing envelope holding cover letter, Barbie Magazine subscription coupon, club chapter application form, membership card, fabric peel-off sticker.
Near Mint Complete - **$185**

BAR-15

❑ **BAR-15. "World Of Fashion" Game,**
1967. Store item by Mattel - **$25 $40 $75**

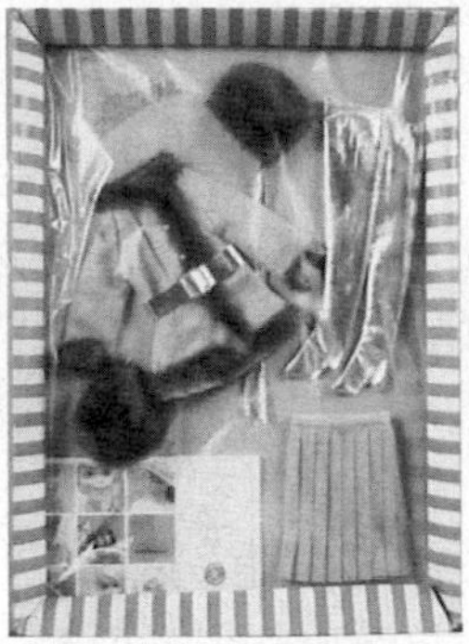

BAR-16

❑ **BAR-16. "Barbie & Stacey" Packaged Fashion Outfit,**
1967. Store item by Mattel. 9x11-1/2x1" deep package holds outfit for Barbie or "Barbie's British Friend." Sealed - **$40 $85 $150**

BAR-17

❑ **BAR-17. Barbie & Friends 6x10x30" Glass And Metal Mattel Electrical Display Sign,**
1960s. Florescent lighted. - **$150 $300 $500**

BAR-18

❑ **BAR-18. Special Edition of 1959 Barbie,**
1993. Boxed. - **$60**

BAR-19

❑ **BAR-19. Barbie and Ken Star Trek Gift Set,**
1996. Boxed. - **$85**

BAR-20

❑ **BAR-20. Space Camp Barbie in Box,**
1998. Boxed. - **$45**

BAR-21

❑ **BAR-21. "Barbie Loves Elvis" Gift Set,**
1999. - **$70**

BAR-22

❑ **BAR-22. "Barbie Loves Frankie Sinatra" Gift Set,**
1999. - **$50**

BAR-23

❑ **BAR-23. Becky Doll in Box,**
1999. Boxed. - **$35**

BAR-24

❑ **BAR-24. Barbie Ring and Earrings,**
1999. On card - **$12**

BAR-25

❑ **BAR-25. Becky Paralympic Champion Doll in Box,**
2000. Promotes races at Sydney 2000 Paralympic Games. - **$25**

BAR-26

❑ **BAR-26. President Barbie Doll in Box,**
2000. Toys 'R' Us Exclusive. Came in both a red box and a blue box. Each - **$35**

BAR-27

❑ **BAR-27. Barbie as Wonder Woman Collector Edition in Box,**
2000. DC Comics product. - **$85**

BAR-28

❑ **BAR-28. Barbie as Samantha from Bewitched - Collector Edition in Box,**
2001. From the 1960s TV show. - **$65**

BAR-29

❑ **BAR-29. Barbie as Wonder Woman Collector Edition in Box,**
2003. DC Comics product. - **$25**

Barney Google

"Barney Google, with his Goo-Goo-Googly Eyes," **the 1923 hit song by Billy Rose and Con Conrad, was about a feisty little sport in a top hat, the cartoon creation of Billy De Beck (1890-1942) that has been called one of the 10 greatest American comic strips of all time. The daily Barney strip first appeared in 1919 on the sports page of the Chicago Herald-Examiner, where he was soon joined by his pitiful racehorse Spark Plug. Readers loved them. Snuffy Smith, a mountain hillbilly, was introduced to the strip in 1934; his name was added to the title a few years later and by the mid-1940s he had taken full title. Fred Lasswell continued the strip after De Beck's death in 1942. Lasswell passed away in 2001 and the strip was taken over by Lasswell's long-time assistants John Rose and Mike Marland. A series of movie shorts was produced in the 1920s , Columbia produced four cartoons in 1935 and 1936, and a few animated TV cartoons were produced in the 1960s by Famous Studios.**

BNG-1

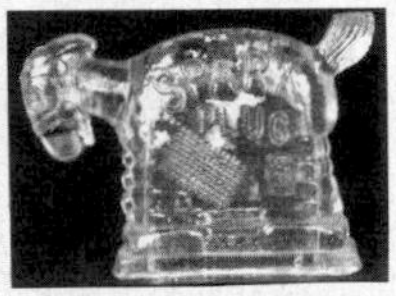

BNG-2

❑ **BNG-1. Fabric Doll,**
1922. Store item. - **$60 $165 $335**

❑ **BNG-2. "Spark Plug" Glass Candy Container,**
1923. Store item. Saddle blanket area originally had orange paint. - **$75 $150 $300**

BNG-3

❑ **BNG-3. Spark Plug Glass Figure,**
1923. Orange colored figure. Rare color variation. - **$125 $250 $500**

BNG-4

BNG-5

❑ **BNG-4. "Barney Google" Sheet Music,**
1923. Store item by Jerome Remick. - **$15 $30 $85**

❑ **BNG-5. "Barney Google And His Faithful Nag Spark Plug" Comic Strip Reprint Book,**
1923. First Barney Google title in Cupples & Leon series. GD - **$60** FN - **$240** VF - **$450**

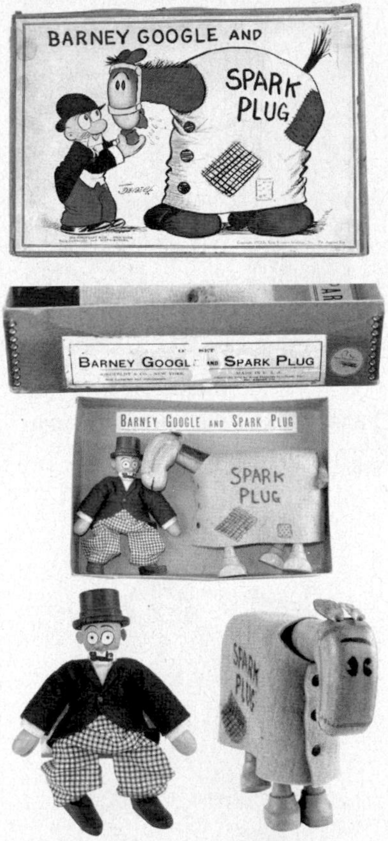

BNG-6

❑ **BNG-6. Boxed Set of Wooden Figures by Schoenhut,**
1923. Barney Google - **$225 $450 $900**
Spark Plug - **$225 $450 $900**
Box - **$300 $600 $1000**
Complete - **$750 $1500 $2800**

BNG-7

BNG-8

❑ **BNG-7. "Spark Plug" Wooden Pull Toy,**
1923. Store item. - **$75 $190 $325**

❑ **BNG-8. Google Character "Rudy" Wind-Up,**
1924. Nifty of Germany. 8.5" tall litho tin bird toy named along with creator's name DeBeck by decal on each side. When wound, neck and feet move while bottom of beak opens and closes. - **$325 $800 $1600**

BNG-9

❑ **BNG-9. Barney & Spark Plug Bisque,**
1924. Rare. Made in Germany. Some versions with paper label on bottom: "John Wanamaker, Philadelphia." Some versions include sponsor's name on base front. - **$110 $225 $450**

BNG-10

❑ **BNG-10. Barney Google On Spark Plug Wind-Up,**
1924. Nifty. 2.5x7x7" tall tin litho toy with built-in key. Toy travels forward, Barney rocks back and forth as Spark Plug moves his head and his tail wags. - **$650 $1300 $2250**

BNG-11

❑ **BNG-11. Barney Google And Spark Plug Scooter Race Pull Toy,**
1924. Nifty. 7.25x8x6" tall all tin litho. Barney is depicted atop a scooter while Sunshine rides Spark Plug. These two pieces have platform bases which are attached to the axles so that when toy is pulled along, they move as if racing one another. - **$1350 $2700 $4000**

BNG-12

❑ **BNG-12. Cello. Button,**
1924. The L.A. Examiner. 7/8" with color portrait. - **$35 $65 $135**

BNG-13

❑ **BNG-13. "Official Song Of The Secret And Mysterious Order Of Billygoats" Sheet Music,**
1928. - **$25 $45 $100**

BNG-14

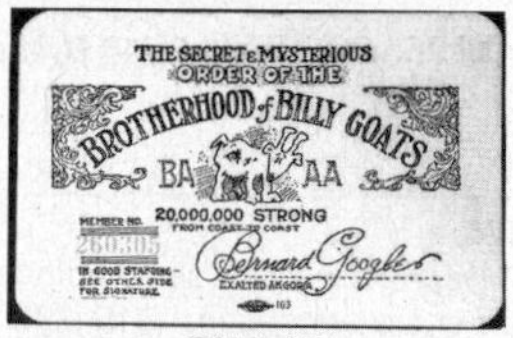

BNG-15

❑ **BNG-14. Brotherhood Of Bulls Membership Card,**
1920s. Scarce. Chicago Herald and Examiner. - **$35 $65 $135**

❑ **BNG-15. Brotherhood Of Billy Goats Membership Card,**
1920s. Scarce. Chicago Herald and Examiner. - **$35 $65 $135**

BNG-16

❑ **BNG-16. "16 Pages Of Fun/32 Comics In Colors" Promo Sign Featuring Barney And Spark Plug,**
1920s. 11x17" cardboard imprinted for Boston Sunday Advertiser. - **$125 $300 $600**

BNG-17

BNG-18

❑ **BNG-17. "The Atlanta Georgian's Silver Anniversary" Litho. Button,**
1937. Named newspaper. From set of various characters. - **$50 $115 $225**

❑ **BNG-18. "Sunday Herald And Examiner" Litho. Button,**
1930s. Chicago newspaper. From "30 Comics" set of various characters. - **$18 $35 $75**

BNG-19

BNG-20

❑ **BNG-19. Enamel On Silvered Brass Pin,**
c. 1930s.- **$ 55 $85 $175**

❑ **BNG-20. "Barney Google/Detroit Times" Cello. Button,**
1930s. Newspaper contest serial number issue from comic character series. - **$15 $30 $60**

BNG-21

❑ **BNG-21. Newspaper Contest Cello. Button,**
1930s. New York Sunday American. 1-1/4" in black, white and shades of red. - **$20 $35 $60**

BNG-22

❑ **BNG-22. "Barney Google/Snuffy Smith" Hand-Painted Plaster Salt & Pepper Set,**
c. 1943. Each is 2-3/4" tall. - **$20 $40 $75**

BNG-23

❑ **BNG-23. "Buy War Stamps" 14x18" Poster,**
c. 1944. U.S. Government. - **$60 $135 $225**

BNG-24

❑ **BNG-24. Snuffy Smith Hand Puppet,**
c. 1955. Store item by Gund. - **$20 $35 $75**

BNG-25

❑ **BNG-25. "Spark Plug" Marx Ramp Walker,**
1960s. Store item. 4" long plastic by Marx Toys. - **$45 $85 $145**

Bat Masterson

Born William Barclay Masterson, the real-life Bat Masterson (1853-1921) was a deputy with Wyatt Earp in Dodge City and also a sheriff, gambler, prize fight promoter and sports writer. Gene Barry, born as Eugene Klass in 1919, brought the character to life on NBC-TV in 108 episodes between October 8, 1958 and September 21, 1961.

Portrayed as a dapper dandy with his ever present cane and derby hat, Masterson used his cane (which concealed a sword) to defend the wrongly-accused while charming women along the way. Directors included Alan Crosland Jr. and Eddie Davis. Writers included Richard O'Connor and Don Brinkley. The popular theme song was written by Havens Wray and Bart Corwin. Reruns of the show are currently running on cable TV's *Encore Western* channel.

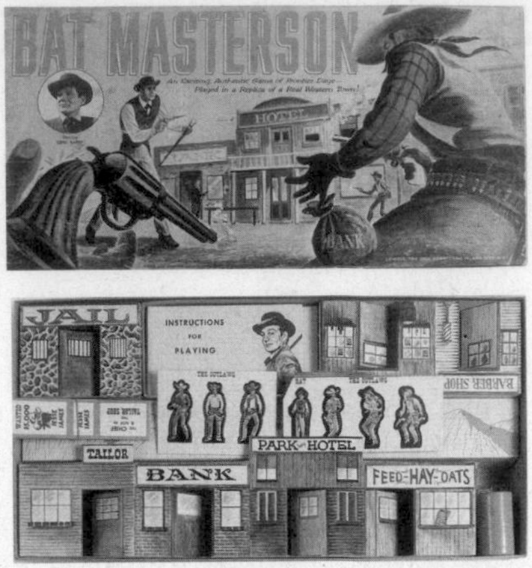

BTM-1

❑ **BTM-1. "Bat Masterson" Boxed Game,**
1958 Lowell Mfg. Corp. 10x19-7/8x2-1/8" deep box contains 19.25x19.5" gameboard, elaborate full color inserts designed like buildings on western street, punch-out figures of outlaws and Bat Masterson, instruction folder with Gene Barry art on front, cardboard tube, bag of playing pieces and six perforated cards. - **$25 $50 $100**

BTM-2

❑ **BTM-2. "Bat Masterson Holster Set With Cane And Vest",**
1958. Carnell Roundup. 13x18x2.75" deep die-cut display box for store display. Comes with 8" "Cowpoke Jr." gun by Lone Star. - **$150 $300 $600**

BTM-3

❑ **BTM-3. Bat Masterson Premium Cane With Leaflet And Mailer Tube,**
1959. Sealtest ice cream. 30" long black wood and silver plastic cane with mailer along with leaflet opening to 4-3/4x17" illustrated with instructions for cane twirling.
Tube - **$15 $30 $50**
Cane - **$30 $60 $125**
Leaflet - **$15 $30 $50**

BTM-4

❑ **BTM-4. Bat Masterson Cowboy Hat,**
1950s. Black with tag. - **$30 $60 $115**

BTM-5

❑ **BTM-5. "Bat Masterson" Vinyl Wallet In Box,**
1950s. Croyden. 3.25x4" wallet with image of Masterson and western scene. Clear plastic lid reads "Croyden Stitchless Wallet." Near Mint Boxed - **$125**
Wallet Only - **$20 $40 $65**

BTM-6

❑ **BTM-6. Bat Masterson/Sealtest Rare Sales Promo Gun,**
1950s. Marx. 3.5x5.5" card holds 3.75" metal cap gun with plastic grips. Card reads "Sure As Shootin' You Can Count On Sealtest For One Bang Up Profit Promotion After Another!"
Carded - **$50 $100 $165**

BTM-7

❑ **BTM-7. "Bat Masterson Jigsaw Puzzles,"**
1960. Colorforms. 13x17x1" deep box holds two puzzles. Text at bottom reads "Other Colorforms Bat Masterson Jigsaw Puzzles" available. - **$50 $100 $185**

BTM-8

❑ **BTM-8. "Pin-Up TV Heroes Pin-Up Badges" With Bat Masterson And Others,**
1960s. 5.25x8.25" card in plastic bag with header card reading "Fun-N-Play/John Henry Products 29 cents." Card holds four 2" tin embossed badges with 1.25" paper photos of Col. MacKenzie/MacKenzie's Raiders, Lt. Frank Ballinger/M Squad, Bat Masterson/Bat Masterson, Seth Adams/Wagon Train.
Near Mint Packaged - **$225**
Each Loose - **$10 $20 $40**

Batman

The legendary Batman--and the huge Bat-industry he was to spawn--was introduced in *Detective Comics* #27 of May 1939. Since then, the Caped Crusader and his sidekick, Robin the Boy Wonder, have battled crime and the forces of evil in comic strips, in live-action and animated cartoon TV series, on the radio, on prime-time network television, in comic books, 1940s movie serials, feature films and in the hearts of millions of fans, young and old. Artists Bob Kane and Jerry Robinson, and writer Bill Finger also produced an array of notable knaves, among them the Joker, Penguin, the Riddler and Catwoman. Notable Golden Age "ghost artists" included: Sheldon Moldoff, Jack Burnley, Fred Ray, Dick Sprang and Winslow Mortimer. Batman's two greatest successes were the 1966-1968 ABC television series with Adam West and Burt Ward as the Dynamic Duo and a string of famous actors as the various villains (which also spawned its own feature film--and the famous line "Some days you just can't get rid of a bomb."--starring the same regular cast of heroes and villains); and the 1989 blockbuster film starring Michael Keaton, Jack Nicholson, and Kim Basinger. This hit movie, directed by Tim Burton, was followed by three sequels: *Batman Returns* (1992), *Batman Forever* (1995), which handed the Bat-cowl from Keaton to Val Kilmer and featured Jim Carrey as the Riddler, and the lackluster *Batman and Robin* (1997), starring George Clooney as Batman, with Alicia Silverstone as Batgirl. These productions generated hundreds of toys, premiums, posters, games, models, dolls, etc. Holy Merchandise, Batman!

Batman presently stars in five monthly titles: *Batman*, *Detective Comics*, *Batman Confidential*, *Batman and the Outsiders*, and *All Star Batman and Robin, The Boy Wonder*. A fifth monthly title, *The Batman Strikes!*, was created as a stylistic companion to the character's animated adventures (see below).

Batman is currently featured with Superman in *Superman/Batman* and other Justice League characters in *Justice League of America*, and appears frequently in such related titles as *Birds of Prey*, *Catwoman*, *Nightwing*, and *Robin*, as well as in numerous specials and one-shots.

Debuting on Fox in 1992, *Batman–The Animated Series* featured a "Dark Deco" style and a superb voice cast including Kevin Conroy (Batman/Bruce Wayne), Mark Hamill (The Joker), and Efrem Zimbalist, Jr. (Alfred). The series ran for 85 episodes, the final season of which was under the title *The Adventures of Batman & Robin*. Three animated films, *Batman: Mask of the Phantasm* (theatrical release, 1993), *Batman: Sub-Zero* (direct-to-video release, 1998), and *Batman: Mystery of the Batwoman* (direct-to-video release, 2003) were also released. Episodes of a successor series, *The New Batman Adventures*, aired with re-broadcast episodes of the series as part of *The New Batman-Superman Adventures* on WB. Batman also appeared on the successful *Justice League Unlimited* animated series on Cartoon Network. Numerous lines of popular licensed toys have been produced in conjunction with this succession of animated incarnations.

A spin-off cartoon set in a darker future, *Batman Beyond*, debuted in 1999 and saw an elderly Bruce Wayne (again voiced by Kevin Conroy) guiding his young replacement,

Terry McGinnis (Will Friedle), against a variety of new and old villains. It ran 52 episodes over three seasons on WB and spawned one direct-to-video film, *Return of the Joker* (which featured the returning voice of Mark Hamill). The series also inspired a comic book limited series, an on-going monthly that ran 24 issues, and numerous toys.

Batman returned to animated adventures on the WB network with the Fall 2004 debut of *The Batman.* These new adventures take place during the early years of his crime-fighting career, showing his initial battles with his famous foes. The feature film *Batman Begins* starring Christian Bale, Katie Holmes and Michael Caine premiered in June 2005 with plenty of merchandising. Bale returned in the July 2008 sequel *The Dark Knight* to battle Heath Ledger's Joker.

BAT-1

❑ **BAT-1. Paper Mask,**
1943. Scarce. Philadelphia Record newspaper, probably others. Back announces new daily and Sunday comic strips. - **$450 $1600 $2400**

BAT-2

❑ **BAT-2. Paper Mask,**
1943. Same front and back design as BAT-1 except front has green type announcing start of movie serial at "State Theatre" and references feature movie "Deanna Durbin In 'Her's To Hold.'" - **$400 $1400 $2250**

BAT-3

❑ **BAT-3. Batplane Movie Promo,**
1943. Various sponsors. - **$950 $2000 $3500**

(1943 FRONT)

(1947 FRONT)

BAT-4

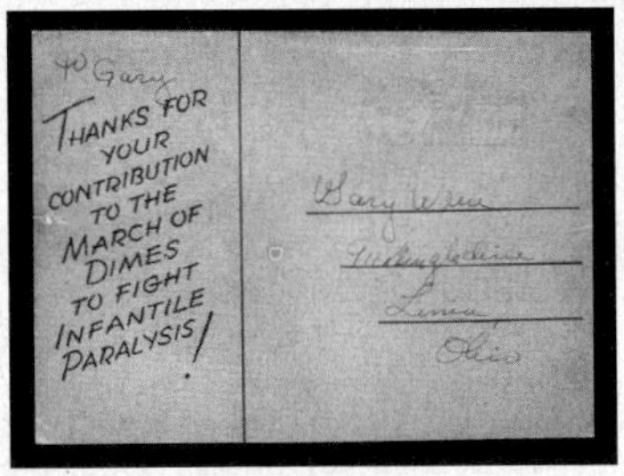

(BACK)

❑ **BAT-4. Batman Infantile Paralysis Card,**
1943. Scarce. March of Dimes premium. Small version offered in 1943, large version in 1947.
1943 version - **$1100 $2200 $3300**
1947 version - **$275 $550 $1100**

BAT-5

❑ **BAT-5. "Full Color Transfers",**
1944. Rare. Not a premium but earliest known merchandise (10 cents) item for Batman. Back of sheet has ad for Detective Comics. - **$350 $750 $1500**

BAT-6

❑ **BAT-6. "Batman's Last Chance" One-Sheet,**
1949. Columbia Pictures serial. - **$800 $1850 $2800**

BAT-7

❑ **BAT-7. "New Adventures of Batman & Robin Three-Sheet,**
1949. Columbia Pictures serial. - **$2500 $7000 $10,500**

BAT-8

❑ **BAT-8. Batman Sportsmanship Promo,**
1949. Scarce. National Comics Pub., Inc. - **$115 $225 $335**

BAT-9

❑ **BAT-9. Batman/Superman Christmas Card,**
1940s. Rare. - **$600 $1750 $2500**

BAT-10

❑ **BAT-10. DC Comics Fan Card,**
1960. - **$40 $85 $180**

BAT-11 BAT-12

❑ **BAT-11. "Crimefighter" 1-3/8" Litho. Button,**
1966.- **$8 $12 $20**

❑ **BAT-12. "Batman And Robin Deputy Crimefighter,**
1966. Cello. button 3-1/2", store item. - **$18 $32 $50**

BAT-13 BAT-14

❑ **BAT-13. Batman Beanie,**
1966. - **$15 $30 $60**

❑ **BAT-14. "Batman" Litho. Button,**
1966. From red, white and blue set of 14 in 7/8" size, also issued in similar set colored red, green, yellow, black.
Each - **$3 $8 $12**

BAT-16

❑ **BAT-16. Batmobile Model Kit in Box,**
1966. Aurora. With instructions.
Complete - **$500**

BAT-17

❑ **BAT-17. Batplane Model Kit in Box,**
1966. Aurora. With instructions.
Complete - **$225**

BAT-18

❑ **BAT-18. Batman Kellogg's OKs Cereal Box (Flat),**
1966. features Yogi Bear on front, Batman on back. Promotes Batman periscope premium. - **$450 $1050 $2000**

BAT-15

❑ **BAT-15. Batman Utility Belt,**
1966. Ideal Toy Corp. Belt includes Bat-Rocket Grenade, Bat-Storage Pouch, Bat-Rope, Bat-A-Rang, Dummy Transmitter, Bat-Cuffs, Bat-Gun Launcher, Batman Message Sender, and Bat-Signal Flash. Boxed Complete **- $5000 $10000 $20,000**

BAT-19

BAT-20

❑ BAT-19. Batman Periscope,
1966. Kellogg's OKs cereal premium. -
$40 $85 $135

❑ BAT-20. "Batman" Paperback Book,
1966. TV related. - **$10 $25 $40**

(FRONT) BAT-21 (BACK ENLARGED)

❑ BAT-21. Batman Kellogg's Frosted Flakes Box (Flat),
1966. promotes Batman printing set premium. -
$350 $950 $1450

BAT-22

❑ BAT-22. "Batman Golden Records" Boxed Set,
1966. N.P.P. Inc. Includes comic book, LP record, "Batman Official Member" gold and black litho. button, one of twelve different flicker rings and membership card with secret code.
Near Mint Boxed Set - **$275**
Comic - **$10 $30 $160**
Button - **$3 $8 $15**
Ring - **$10 $20 $50**
Card - **$10 $20 $50**

BAT-23

❑ BAT-23. "Batman Print Set,"
1966. Kellogg's Sugar Frosted Flakes. Plastic case holding six different plastic stamps and ink pad. Stamps picture Batman, Robin, Joker, Penguin, Riddler, Batmobile.
Near Mint Boxed - **$165**
Unboxed - **$20 $40 $70**

BAT-24

BAT-25

❑ BAT-24. "Batman And Robin Buttons" Vending Machine Display Paper,
1966. - **$12 $25 $40**

❑ BAT-25. "Batman" Lucky Charm Ad,
1966. Used in gumball display and machines.-
$18 $40 $60

BAT-26

❑ BAT-26. Batman 1" Size Litho. Button Set,
1966. Vending machines but scarcer than 7/8" size. 14 different.
Red/White/Blue Style Each - **$20 $35 $65**
Red/Green/Yellow Style Each - **$22 $38 $75**

BAT-27

❑ BAT-27. Contest Card With Three Picture Playing Pieces,
1966. Safeway Or Merit Gasoline. Shows both TV and comic book characters. -
$75 $150 $300

BAT-28

❑ BAT-28. "Batman Coins" On Card,
1966. Store item by Transogram.
Complete On Card - **$30 $60 $110**
Loose Coin - **$2 $3 $4**

BAT-29

BAT-30

❑ BAT-29. Fan Photo,
1966. Adam West and Burt Ward with facsimile signatures. - **$28 $45 $95**

❑ BAT-30. All Star Dairies 24x44" Cardboard Sign,
1966.- **$100 $200 $300**

BAT-31

❑ BAT-31. "Batman Ring Club" 4x5" Flicker Display Card,
1966. Showing both images. - **$45 $85 $150**

BAT-32

BAT-33

❑ BAT-32. Metal License Plate,
1966. Store item by Groff Signs. - **$15 $35 $65**

❑ BAT-33. Metal License Plate,
1966. Store item by Groff Signs. - **$15 $35 $65**

BAT-34

❑ BAT-34. Metal License Plate,
1966. Store item. - **$15 $35 $65**

BAT-35

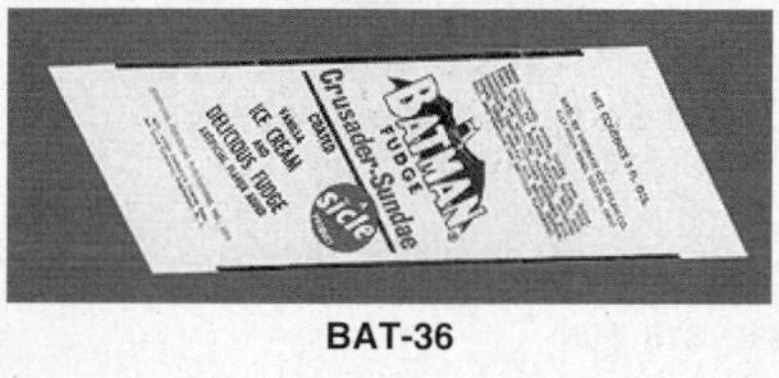

BAT-36

❑ BAT-35. Robin Flexible Rubber Ring,
1966. Vending machine issue. - **$15 $25 $45**

❑ BAT-36. "Batman Fudge Crusader-Sundae" Wrapper,
1966. Parallelogram waxed paper. -
$10 $18 $35

BAT-37

❑ BAT-37. "My Batman Collection" Metal Coin Set With Plastic Holders,
1966. Set of 20 coins.
Set In Holders - **$125 $225 $400**
Each Coin - **$3 $8 $15**

BAT-38 BAT-39

❑ BAT-38. Batman Poster 27x40",
1966. Toothpaste premium for TV show. -
$65 $150 $300

❑ BAT-39. Robin Poster 27x40",
1966. Toothpaste premium for TV show. -
$65 $150 $300

BAT-40

❑ BAT-40. Cardboard Mask,
1966. General Electric television. One mask on front, other on reverse. - **$8 $15 $30**

BAT-41

❑ BAT-41. "Batman & Robin Mask" Appliance Store Kit,
1966. Issued to promote General Electric television. Envelope originally held 50 thin cardboard flip masks printed on both sides plus pictured example 33x40" wall poster.
Envelope - **$8 $15 $30**
Poster - **$100 $250 $500**

BAT-42

❑ BAT-42. Batman/Magazine Promotion 3-1/2" Cello. Button,
1966. Authorized issue for Electronic Industries magazine. Probably a trade show item. -
$65 $185 $325

BAT-43

BAT-44

❑ BAT-43. Batman Mug,
1966. - **$10 $20 $35**

❑ BAT-44. Batman & Robin Glass Mug,
1966. Made in England. - **$30 $55 $85**

BAT-45

❑ **BAT-45. "All Star Ice Cream" Large Store Sign,**
1966. 24x44". - **$100 $200 $300**

BAT-46

❑ **BAT-46. "Corgi Batmobile" Complete Boxed First Issue,**
1966. Store item. Near Mint Boxed - **$725**
Car With Figures Only - **$90 $150 $275**

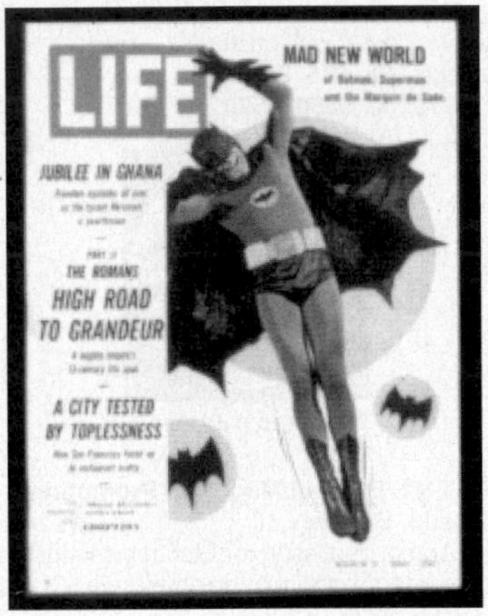

BAT-47

❑ **BAT-47. "Life" Magazine With Batman Cover Article,**
1966. March 11 issue. - **$10 $20 $40**

BAT-48

❑ **BAT-48. TV Guide With Batman Cover Article,**
1966. Has five-page article "Batty Over Batman?" - **$25 $40 $75**

BAT-49 BAT-50

❑ **BAT-49. Batman/Robin Clock Face Flicker Ring,**
1966. Vending machine issue. - **$30 $60 $100**

❑ **BAT-50. "Flicker Pictures" Vending Machine Display Paper,**
1966. - **$15 $35 $55**

BAT-51

❑ **BAT-51. Flicker Miniature Pictures,**
1966. Vending machine set of six.
Each- **$5 $12 $18**

BAT-52

❑ **BAT-52. Plastic Flicker Rings,**
1966. Set of 12 in either silver or blue base.
Silver Base Each - **$12 $25 $40**
Blue Base Each - **$5 $15 $25**

BAT-53

❑ **BAT-53. "Batman Candy & Toy" Boxes,**
1966. Store item by Phoenix Candy Co. Set of eight with front and back numbered pictures (1-16). Each Box - **$25 $55 $90**

BAT-54

❑ **BAT-54. Holloway Candies 17x22" Cardboard Store Sign,**
1966. Milk Duds, Black Cow, Slo-Poke candies. Offered three different coloring books with six-pack candy purchase. - **$150 $265 $385**

BAT-55 BAT-56

❑ **BAT-55. "Batman" English Cello. Button,**
1966. A&BC Chewing Gum Ltd. In addition to Robin (next item), the set includes an image of Batman flying through the air and one of Batman on a batwing design.
Each - **$20 $35 $75**

❑ **BAT-56. "Robin" English Cello. Button,**
1966. A&BC Chewing Gum Ltd. - **$20 $35 $75**

BAT-57 BAT-58

❑ **BAT-57. Batman Glass Tumbler,**
1966. - **$12 $18 $35**

❑ **BAT-58. Robin Glass Tumbler,**
1966. Same reverse side as Batman tumbler.- **$12 $18 $35**

(Front) BAT-59 (Back)

❑ **BAT-59. Coloring Book,**
1966. Holloway Candy. 4-1/4x4-3/4" 16 pages on newsprint. - **$10 $25 $75**

BAT-60

BAT-61

❑ **BAT-60. Pop Tarts Comic Booklet,**
1966. "The Mad Hatter's Hat Crimes" from set of six. - **$5 $15 $60**

❑ **BAT-61. Pop Tarts Comic Booklet,**
1966. "The Penguin's Fowl Play" from set of six. - **$5 $15 $60**

BAT-62

BAT-63

❑ **BAT-62. Pop Tarts Comic Booklet,**
1966. "The Catwoman's Catnapping Caper" from set of six. - **$5 $15 $60**

❑ **BAT-63. Pop Tarts Comic Booklet,**
1966. "The Man In The Iron Mask" from set of six. - **$5 $15 $60**

BAT-64 BAT-65

❑ **BAT-64. Batman Rubber Place Mat,**
1966. 18 3/4" wide and 13" tall. - **$30 $60 $100**

❑ **BAT-65. Robin Rubber Place Mat,**
1966. 18 3/4" wide and 13" tall. - **$30 $60 $100**

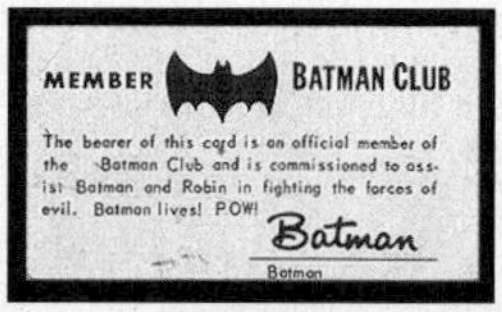

BAT-66

❑ **BAT-66. Club Card,**
1966. Membership card for TV show. - **$12 $25 $50**

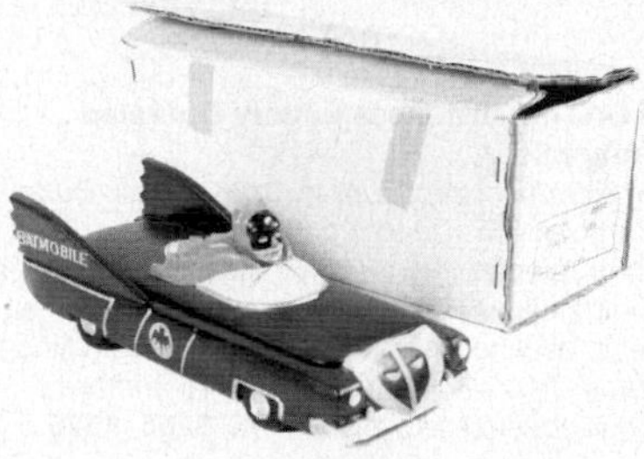

BAT-67

❑ **BAT-67. Batman In Batmobile Figural Ceramic Container Boxed,**
1966. National Periodical Publications Inc. 4x4x10" cardboard box contains 2-7/8x3x8.5" ceramic container made by Japanese company Lego. Container with lid is shaped like Batmobile from comic book "Batman" with him seated in cockpit. Tailfins have text "Batmobile" on each, bat symbol is on each door and bat battering ram is on hood.
Near Mint Boxed - **$750**
Car Only - **$200 $400 $600**

BAT-68

❑ **BAT-68. "Batman" Gum Card Countertop Display Box,**
1966. Topps Gum. 3.75x8x2" deep box originally contained 24 packs of cards for the first series. - **$165 $325 $550**

BAT-69

❑ **BAT-69. Batman 6 Ft. Standee,**
1966. Used to promote All Star Dairies. Art by Murphy Anderson. - **$125 $225 $400**

BAT-70

❑ **BAT-70. Batman Marionette,**
1966. 16" tall plastic and fabric figure with control unit by Hazelle Airplane Control Marionettes authorized by NPP copyright. - **$75 $150 $300**

BAT-71

❑ **BAT-71. "Batman Action Watch" Boxed,**
1966. Gilbert. 3x5x2" deep plastic case with insert holding bat-shaped watch with black/blue fabric band. Hands are designed as bat wings.
Box - **$50 $100 $200**
Contents - **$200 $400 $650**

BAT-72

❑ **BAT-72. Batman Portrait Wristwatch,**
1966. 1-1/8" metal case with dial face design including diecut circular paper with glossy varnish portrait plus glow hour numerals. Straps each feature a single bat symbol logo. Swiss made although no company or copyright indicated on the watch. Box marked ©NPP 1966 with guarantee card naming Luna Watch Service of New York. Box - **$750 $1500 $2500**
Watch - **$250 $500 $1000**

BAT-73

❑ **BAT-73. "Batman Dairy Chocolate" Paper Sign,**
1966. All Star Dairies. 14x21". -
$65 $125 $200

BAT-74

❑ **BAT-74. "Batman Peanut Butter" Jar,**
1966. Glass jar w/paper label color images of him and Robin. - **$35 $70 $110**

BAT-75

❑ **BAT-75. Japanese Friction Batmobile,**
c. 1966. Sanka, Japan. Car is 3.5x9x2-7/8" Tall. Tin litho version of the Batmobile done in red, white and blue. Features 3-D tin litho figure of Batman in cockpit plus image of Batman on hood of car, both wearing red/blue whereas his costume is gray/blue. Hood also features bat symbol with "Batman" in Japanese text. - **$140 $275 $550**

BAT-76

❑ **BAT-76. Japanese Battery Operated Batmobile,**
c. 1966. Alps, Japan. 4x11.5x2-7/8" tall. Bump-and-go action. Tin litho car has light-up red/green plastic panels with flashing lights and pinging sound. Features Batman and Robin sitting in dual cockpits with separate 3-D tin litho heads. Two silver bats adorn hood and area directly behind cockpits. - **$115 $265 $525**

BAT-77

❑ **BAT-77. Batman Pez Dispenser Box Display,**
c. 1966. Box is 5.5x7x4.25" deep with 10-3/8" insert for back. Held 24 Pez candy dispenser sets. Back insert features die-cut image of Batman's head and shoulders on a yellow to green background with Batman comic book title logo underneath the Pez logo. 1x2" bat symbol states "TV & Comic Strip Hero."
- **$1100 $1950 $3800**

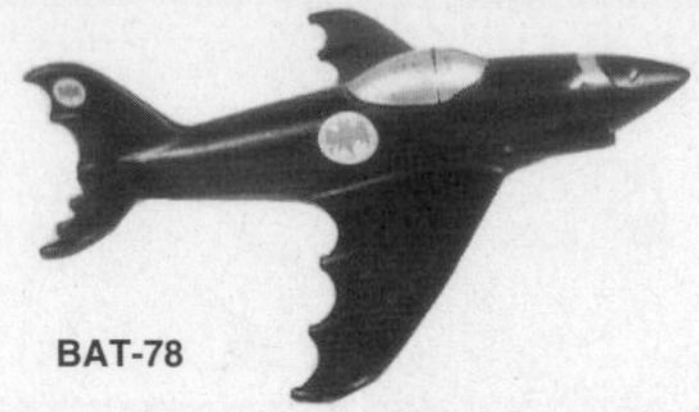

BAT-78

❑ **BAT-78. Large Plastic Free-Wheeling Airplane,**
c. 1966. Store item by Irwin. 19" long by 21" wide by 5" tall with name and image logo stickers. - **$115 $275 $525**

(STICKER, CARD, BUTTON SHOWN)
BAT-79

❑ **BAT-79. "Batman Club" Items,**
c. 1966. Ron Riley's Batman Club of WLS/WBKB-TV, Chicago. Includes 2" litho. button, 3-1/2" sticker plus card.
Button - **$5 $10 $15**
Sticker - **$10 $20 $40**
Card - **$15 $25 $50**

BAT-80

BAT-81

❑ **BAT-80. "Batman's Buddy" Cello. Button,**
c. 1966. Hy Vee grocery chain. - **$12 $22 $45**

❑ **BAT-81. "Curly Wurly/Blam" Litho. Button,**
c. 1966. English product. - **$15 $25 $50**

BAT-82

❑ **BAT-82. Newspaper Daily Strip Promo Sign,**
c. 1966. 10.5x13.75" cardboard announcing debut of comic strip in Los Angeles Herald Examiner. - **$135 $275 $475**

BAT-83

❑ **BAT-83. "Official Batman Fan Club" Australian Button,**
c. 1966. 1.25" red/white/blue on white for apparent sponsor "Heanor Derbys." - **$60 $110 $200**

BAT-84

❑ **BAT-84. "Batman & Robin" Australian Button,**
c. 1966. 1.5" cello black on cream design, possibly earlier than the TV craze era. - **$225 $450 $900**

BAT-85

BAT-86

❑ **BAT-85. Composition Bobbing Head Figure,**
c. 1966. Store item. - **$150 $400 $800**

❑ **BAT-86. "The Joker And His Pals Candy & Toy" Box,**
1967. Store item by Phoenix Candy Co. Eight different boxes in set.
Each Box - **$60 $125 $210**

BAT-87

❑ **BAT-87. Paper Mask/Menu,**
1968. 10x14" diecut folder with mask front opening to children's menu imprinted for local restaurant. - **$75 $150 $300**

BAT-88

❑ **BAT-88. High Relief Plastic 33x48" Store Display Sign,**
1969. Issued to promote Aurora Batmobile kit offered as premium by Burry's cookies. - **$375 $950 $1800**

BAT-89

❑ **BAT-89. "Batman And, Of Course, Robin" Movie Serial Re-Release 27x41 " Poster,**
1960s. Columbia Pictures. For reissue of original 1943 serial. - **$75 $150 $300**

BAT-90

❑ **BAT-90. Batmobile Tin Car with Box,**
1960s. Japan, battery operated. Complete - **$400**

BAT-91

❑ **BAT-91. "Ideal Official Batman & Justice League of America Play Set" Boxed,**
1960s. Ideal. Box is 15.5x27x7" deep and includes "Authentic Hand Painted Figures Of: Batman, Robin, Superman, Wonder Woman, Aqua Man, Flash, Joker, Sanctuary Mountain, Periscope, Weather Vane Key, Bat Car (Batmobile), Bat Plane and Launcher, Reflector Ray Weapon, Console, Robot, & Five Other Arch Enemies (The Key, Mouse Man, Kaltor, Brainstorm, Thunderbolt)." Boxed Complete - **$4500 $8500 $13,500**

BAT-92

❑ **BAT-92. Photo And Record,**
1960s. DC Comics. Photo reads "To All My Batman Fans-'Bats' Wishes Bob Kane." Record co-written by Kane titled "Have Faith In Me".
Pair - **$55 $95 $175**

BAT-93

❑ **BAT-93. "Send Batman To Viet-Nam" Button,**
c. 1970. 1-7/8" litho sold from series of about 16 different slogan buttons held in multi-compartment display box. - **$12 $25 $40**

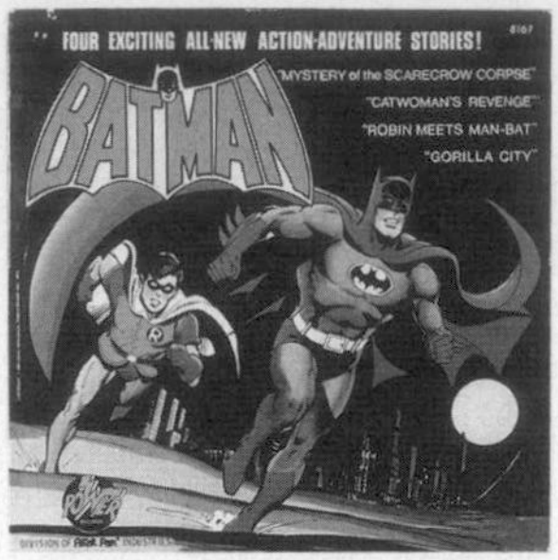

BAT-94

❑ **BAT-94. Batman Record,**
1975. Power Records, a division of Peter Pan Industries. Features "4 Exciting All-New Adventure Stories!" - **$8 $15 $30**

BAT-95

❑ **BAT-95. "Batman Mobile Bat Lab" Boxed Vehicle Set,**
1975. Store item by Mego. Large 8x14x7" tall hard plastic vehicle. Near Mint Boxed - **$800**
Used Complete - **$85 $150 $250**

BAT-96

❑ **BAT-96. Batman Diecut Enameled Brass Ring,**
1976. Store item made by Aviva. - **$5 $12 $20**

BAT-97 BAT-98

❑ **BAT-97. Batman Enameled Brass Ring,**
1976. Store item made by Aviva. - **$10 $18 $35**

❑ **BAT-98. Batman Enameled Brass Ring,**
1976. Store item made by Aviva. - **$5 $12 $20**

BAT-99

❑ **BAT-99. "Super Heroes Magnetic Dart Game",**
1977. Cheerios. - **$15 $30 $60**

BAT-100

❑ **BAT-100. Batman and Robin Yo-Yo,**
1978. Duncan. Sold in special container. - **$25 $40 $90**

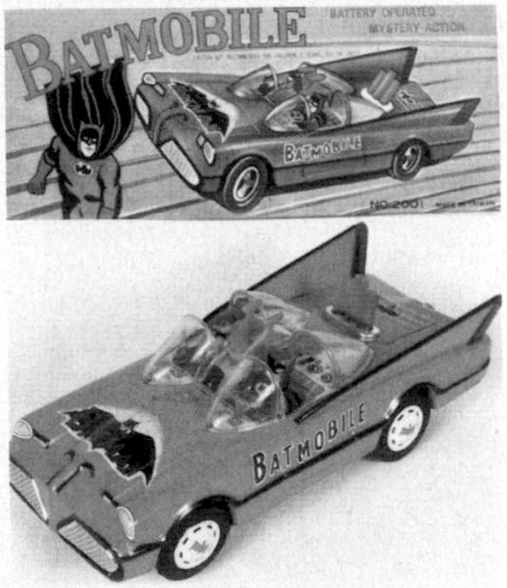

BAT-101

❑ **BAT-101. Batmobile Battery Operated Boxed Toy,**
1970s. 9.75" long mostly tin litho car in box with colorfully illustrated lid. Actions are bump-and-go plus blinking warning light and jet engine noise. Box - **$65 $125 $200**
Car - **$75 $140 $250**

BAT-102

❑ **BAT-102. "The Dark Knight" Plastic Display Sign With Press Release,**
1986. Promotes mini-series by Frank Miller.
Display - **$22 $40 $85**
Press Release - **$4 $8 $12**

BAT-103 BAT-104

❑ **BAT-103. Batman Button Collection,**
1989. Four on card. - **$40**

❑ **BAT-104. Large Button,**
1989. On card. - **$30**

BAT-105 BAT-106

❑ **BAT-105. Warner Brothers Limited Edition Batman Statue,**
1989. Offered only on the opening day of the Batman movie. Limited to 50, these were sculpted and hand-painted by Kent Melton. - **$800 $1800 $3200**

❑ **BAT-106. Warner Brothers Limited Edition Joker Statue,**
1989. Offered only on the opening day of the Batman movie. Limited to 50, these were sculpted and hand-painted by Kent Melton. - **$800 $1800 $3200**

BAT-107

❑ **BAT-107. Ralston Batman Cereal Box,**
1989. With plastic bank attached to box front. - **$15 $35 $55**

BAT-108

❑ **BAT-108. "Battery Operated Batman Motorcycle,"**
1980s. Tam Toys.
Near Mint Boxed **- $240**
Unboxed **- $40 $80 $145**

BAT-109

❑ **BAT-109. "Batman Returns" Promo Badge,**
1992. Each **- $3 $6 $15**

BAT-110

BAT-111

❑ **BAT-110. McDonald's Happy Meals 14x14" Plastic Translight Panel,**
1992. Depicts eight figures and vehicles. - **$30 $65 $120**

❑ **BAT-111. McDonald's Happy Meals 14x14" Plastic Translight Panel,**
1992. Depicts six cups. **- $20 $40 $60**

BAT-112

❑ **BAT-112. McDonald's Happy Meals 14x14" Plastic Translight Panel,**
1992. Depicts four vehicles. - **$20 $40 $60**

BAT-113

❑ **BAT-113. Batman Standee With Cups,**
1992. - **$125 $260 $425**

BAT-114

BAT-115

❑ **BAT-114. "Batman Returns" Cereal Box with Glow-In-The Dark Stickers Premium,**
1992. 4 differnet stickers.
Box - **$8 $15 $40**

❑ **BAT-115. "Batman Returns" Catch Game,**
1992. Back of box shown. - **$4 $8 $18**

(BOX FRONT)

(PUZZLE #1)

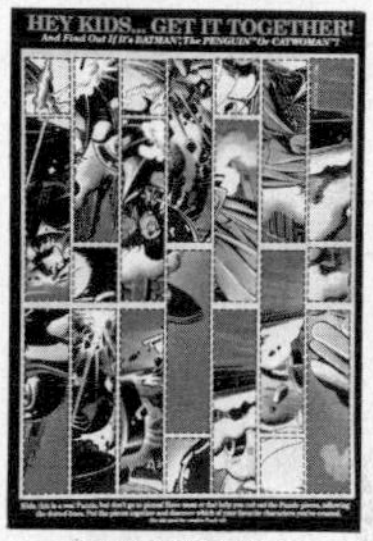

(PUZZLE #2)

(PUZZLE #3)

BAT-116

❑ **BAT-116. "Batman Returns" Cereal Box with Puzzle Box Back,**
1992. Three different puzzle backs.
Each - **$6 $12 $40**

BAT-117

BAT-118

❑ **BAT-117. "Batman Returns" Movie Cards,**
1992. Depicts 8 scenes. - **$30**

❑ **BAT-118. "Batman Returns" Print Portfolio,**
1992. Contains eight 11"x14" prints. - **$35**

BAT-119

BAT-120

❑ **BAT-119. "Robin" Resin Statue,**
1994. Limited to 3,900. Miniature version released in 1997. Boxed - **$350**

❑ **BAT-120. "The Joker" Resin Statue,**
1995. Limited to 4,650. Miniature version released in 1998. Boxed - **$320**

BAT-121

BAT-122

❑ **BAT-121. "Batman Forever" Promo Badge,**
1995. - **$3 $6 $12**

❑ **BAT-122. "Batman Forever" 3-D Viewer,**
1995. Has 21 3-D scenes from the movie on 3 discs. Projector is 7 1/2" tall. Stars of the movie are pictured on the back and sides of the box. - **$12 $30 $55**

BAT-123

BAT-124

❑ **BAT-123. "Batman Forever" Statue,**
1995. 14" tall with base. - **$150**

❑ **BAT-124. "Batman Forever" Robin Statue,**
1995. Warner Bros. Store exclusive. - **$115**

BAT-125

BAT-126

❑ **BAT-125. "Batman Forever" Riddler Statue,**
1995. - **$150**

❑ **BAT-126. "Batman Forever" Two Face Statue,**
1995. Warner Bros. Store exclusive by Kent Melton. - **$130**

BAT-127

BAT-128

❑ **BAT-127. Kellogg's Corn Pops Cereal Box,**
1995. 10.9 oz. box has offer for a "Batman Forever" baseball-style cap. - **$6 $12 $25**

❑ **BAT-128. "Batman Forever" Kellogg's Corn Pops 15 oz. Cereal Boxes,**
1995. 4 different boxes promote the movie. Each - **$8 $15 $35**

(Box front)

(Figures with reversed Bat logos)

(Corrected set)

BAT-129

❑ **BAT-129. "The History of Batman" Collection,**
1995. 3 figures in a display box. First set mistakenly reversed the colors of the yellow and black chest logos. Boxed- **$360**
Later corrected set boxed **- $150**

BAT-130

BAT-131

❑ **BAT-130. Batman "The Dark Knight Returns" Anniversary Resin Statue,**
1996. 10th Anniversary statue of Batman and Robin. Miniature version released in 1999. Limited to 5,500. - **$275**

❑ **BAT-131. "Poison Ivy" Ceramic Figure,**
1996. Warner Bros. catalog exclusive for promoting the next year's "Batman and Robin" movie. Limited edition of 1,250. - **$225**

BAT-132

❑ **BAT-132. Batman Cherryade Sugar Free Drink,**
1996. 3-1/4" tall. Brityic Soft Drinks Ltd., England. A Robin version also exists.
NM Full or Empty - **$25**

BAT-133

BAT-134

❑ **BAT-133. Batgirl Resin Statue,**
1997. Limited to 3,600. Miniature version released in 1999. Boxed - **$250**

❑ **BAT-134. Catwoman Resin Statue,**
1997. Limited to 3,700. Boxed- **$320**

BAT-135

❑ **BAT-135. Batman Movie Resin Statue,**
1997. From "Batman & Robin" movie. Cape is easily chipped. Figure is slightly off-balance because of the weight of the cape. 13 1/2" high counting the base. - **$190**

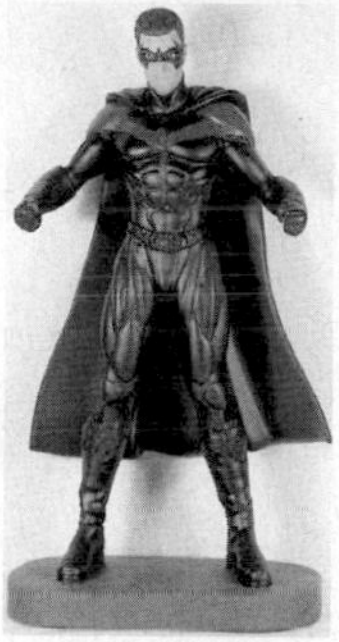

BAT-136

BAT-137

❑ **BAT-136. Robin Movie Resin Statue,**
1997. From "Batman & Robin" movie. Harder to find than the 1995 movie statue. - **$110**

❑ **BAT-137. Batgirl Movie Resin Statue,**
1997. From "Batman & Robin" movie. - **$160**

BAT-138

❑ **BAT-138. Mr. Freeze 13" Movie Resin Statue,**
1997. Has removable gun. This is tough to find, as many were broken in shipping from China. The base was not balanced correctly, causing the ankles to break. The gun handle also breaks easily. Warner Brothers stores did not reorder. Do not confuse with different Mr. Freeze made later. That statue is different in size and stance. - **$300**

BAT-139

❑ **BAT-139. Batman Movie Batarang Prop,**
1997. From "Batman & Robin" movie. Batarang is made of chrome plated spin cast metal. In display case of Mr. Freeze ice.
Limited edition of 500. - **$625**

BAT-140

❑ **BAT-140. "Batman & Robin" Movie Watches in Case,**
1997. Two watches feature photos of Batman and Mr. Freeze. Also includes limited metal cards of each character. Watches are in a silver metal presentation case with insert.
Limited edition of 500. - **$500**

BAT-141

BAT-142

❑ **BAT-141. Kellogg's Smacks Cereal Box,**
1997. Promotes "Batman & Robin" movie. Robin on front. - **$4 $8 $20**

❑ **BAT-142. Kellogg's Apple Jacks Cereal Box,**
1997. Promotes "Batman & Robin" movie. Mr. Freeze on front. - **$4 $8 $20**

BAT-143

❑ **BAT-143. Cocoa Krispies Cereal Box,**
1997. Promotes "Batman & Robin" movie. Herovision poster puzzle on back. - **$5 $10 $30**

BAT-144

❑ **BAT-144. Mr. Freeze Freezer Bars Box,**
1997. Promotes "Batman & Robin" movie. Limited edition box holds 24 bars. - **$8 $15 $35**

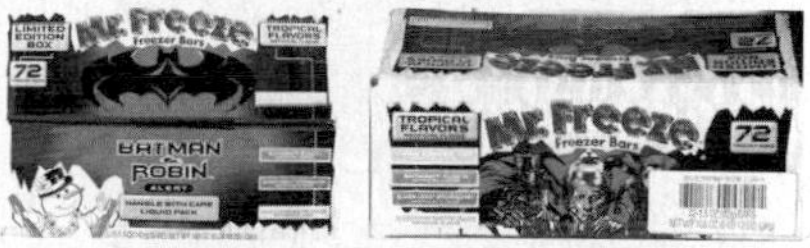

(TOP OF BOX) BAT-145 (FRONT OF BOX)

❑ **BAT-145. Mr. Freeze Freezer Bars Box,**
1997. Promotes "Batman & Robin" movie. Limited edition box holds 72 bars. - **$10 $25 $50**

BAT-146

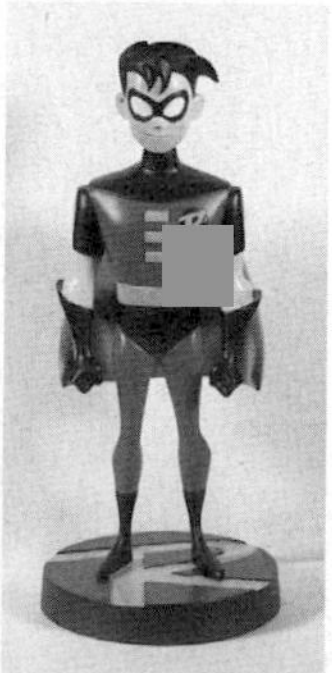

BAT-147

❑ **BAT-146. Batman Maquette,**
1998. From Superman/Batman Adventures animated series. Limited to 2,500. - **$340**

❑ **BAT-147. Robin Maquette,**
1998. Resin. From Superman/Batman Advs. animated series. Limited to 2,500. - **$250**

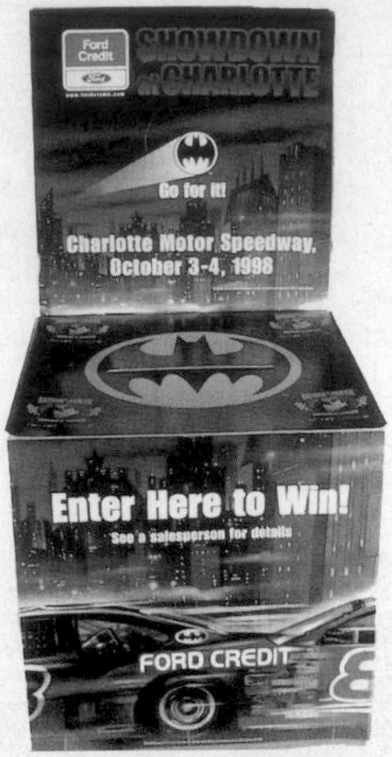

BAT-148

❑ **BAT-148. Promotional Display Box,** 1998. For the Charlotte Motor Speedway contest sponsored by Ford Credit. - **$25 $50 $115**

BAT-149

BAT-150

❑ **BAT-149. Classic Batman Figure with Card,** 1998. Has dark blue cape and card depicting cover of Batman #1. - **$30**

❑ **BAT-150. Classic Batman Figure with Card,** 1998. Has light blue cape and card depicting cover of Batman #4. - **$30**

BAT-151

BAT-152

❑ **BAT-151. Batman Bean Bag Figure,** 1998. Warner Bros. Store Exclusive. - **$18**

❑ **BAT-152. Robin Bean Bag Figure,** 1998. Warner Bros. Store Exclusive. - **$18**

BAT-153

BAT-154

❑ **BAT-153. Joker Bean Bag Figure,** 1998. Warner Bros. Store Exclusive. - **$12**

❑ **BAT-154. Penguin Bean Bag Figure,** 1998. Warner Bros. Store Exclusive. - **$12**

BAT-155

BAT-156

❑ **BAT-155. Catwoman Bean Bag Figure,** 1998. Warner Bros. Store Exclusive. - **$12**

❑ **BAT-156. Batman Resin Statue,** 1999. Warner Bros. Store Exclusive. - **$150**

BAT-157

BAT-158

BAT-159

❑ **BAT-157. Riddler Bean Bag Figure,** 1999. Warner Bros. Store Exclusive. - **$12**

❑ **BAT-158. Poison Ivy Bean Bag Figure,** 1999. Warner Bros. Store Exclusive. - **$12**

❑ **BAT-159. Harley Quinn Bean Bag Figure,** 1999. Warner Bros. Store Exclusive. - **$12**

BAT-160

BAT-161

❑ **BAT-160. Batgirl Bean Bag Figure,** 1999. Warner Bros. Store Exclusive. - **$12**

❑ **BAT-161. "Batman Beyond" Bean Bag Figure,** 1999. Warner Bros. Store Exclusive. - **$12**

BAT-162

BAT-163

BAT-164

❑ **BAT-162. Batman Miniature Figure,** 1999. In package. - **$33**

❑ **BAT-163. Robin Miniature Figure,** 1999. In package. - **$33**

❑ **BAT-164. Batgirl Miniature Figure,** 1999. In package. - **$33**

BAT-165 BAT-166 BAT-167

❑ **BAT-165. Joker Miniature Figure,**
1999. In package. - **$33**

❑ **BAT-166. Harley Quinn Miniature Figure,**
1999. In package. - **$33**

❑ **BAT-167. Penguin Miniature Figure,**
1999. In package. - **$33**

BAT-168 BAT-169 BAT-170

❑ **BAT-168. Riddler Miniature Figure,**
1999. In package. - **$33**

❑ **BAT-169. Mr. Freeze Miniature Figure,**
1999. In package. - **$33**

❑ **BAT-170. Poison Ivy Miniature Figure,**
1999. In package. - **$33**

BAT-171

BAT-172

❑ **BAT-171. Batman Walkie Talkies,**
2000. Warner Brothers Store exclusive. - **$65**

❑ **BAT-172. Batman 24" Statue on Base,**
2000. Warner Bros. Store Exclusive, sold only in New York City store which has since closed. Only a few were made. - **$85 $165 $350**

BAT-173

❑ **BAT-173. Batman Beyond Batmobile,**
2000. In box; from TV show. Fires 6 discs. - **$35**

BAT-174

BAT-175

❑ **BAT-174. Batgirl Resin Statue,**
2001. Styled from the animated series. Edition of 5,000. Boxed - **$150**

❑ **BAT-175. Batmite Resin Statue,**
2001. Edition of 1,400. Boxed - **$75**

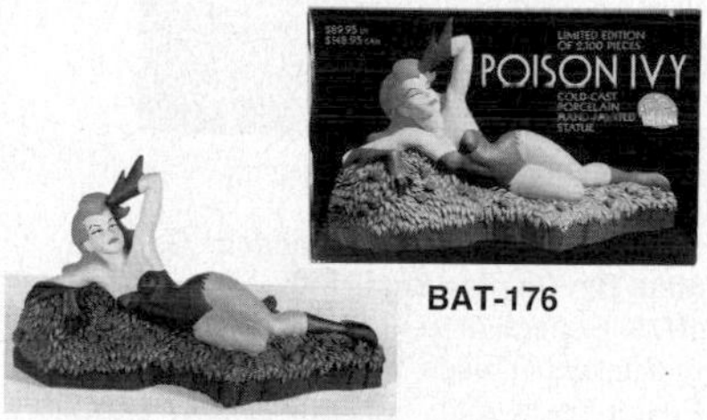

BAT-176

❑ **BAT-176. Poison Ivy Porcelain Statue,**
2001. Limited edition of 2100. Designed by Bruce Timm based on the animated series version. Boxed - **$125**

BAT-177

❑ **BAT-177. Batman Resin Statue,**
2001. Golden Age figure. Boxed - **$55**

Battlestar Galactica

Produced by Glen Larson, the two hour pilot for the TV show was released as a feature film in Canada and Europe in the summer of 1978. The ABC-TV series ran from September 17, 1978 through April 29, 1979. Each of the 21 episodes was budgeted at one million dollars, and top fantasy illustrator Frank Frazetta designed promotional posters. The cast included Lorne Greene as Commander Adama, Richard Hatch as Captain Apollo, Dirk Benedict as Lt. Starbuck. Daggit the robot dog provided comic relief. The basic plot had the last surviving warship Galactica trying to survive a threat by Cylon robots while searching for planet Earth. A follow-up series "Galactica 1980," aired briefly early in 1980 with Lorne Greene returning as the only original main cast member.

On December 8, 2003, the Sci-Fi Channel broadcast a two-part mini-series which led to a regular series of 52 episodes beginning January 14, 2005. The cast includes Edward James Olmos, Mary McDonnell and Katie Sackoff. The series has been one of the highest rated shows in *Sci-Fi Channel* history, and it won a 2006 Peabody Award.

BSG-1

❑ **BSG-1. Battlestar Galactica Rings,**
1978. Five rings each with clear acrylic over color photo with metal ring base. Bases vary in design. Ring bases for Commander Adama, Lt. Starbuck, Dagget have metal cut-out designs and adjustable brass luster bands. Imperious Leader is same design but silver luster. Cylon is brass luster and adjustable but without cutout designs. Each - **$5 $10 $20**

BSG-2

❑ **BSG-2. "Battlestar Galactica" Space Vehicles,**
1978. Larami Corp. One card is 6x9" with 3.75" long hard plastic "L.E.M. Lander" while the other two are 6x7" with 2.5" long die-cast metal and plastic "Galactic Cruiser" in two styles.
Each Carded - **$3 $6 $12**

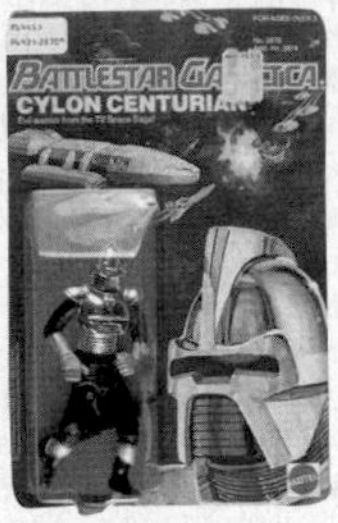

BSG-3

BSG-4

❑ **BSG-3. "Battlestar Galactica Cylon Centurion" Action Figure,**
1978. Mattel. Blister card contains 4.25" tall figure. Near Mint Carded - **$50**

❑ **BSG-4. "Battlestar Galactica Lucifer" Action Figure,**
1978. Mattel. Blister card contains 4.5" tall figure with translucent glitter head top. Second series. Near Mint Carded - **$85**

BSG-5

BSG-6

❑ **BSG-5. "Battlestar Galactica Boray" Action Figure,**
1978. Mattel. Blister card contains 4-1/8" tall figure with club. Second series. Near Mint Carded - **$95**

❑ **BSG-6. "Battlestar Galactica Baltar" Action Figure,**
1978. Mattel. Blister card contains 4" tall figure with blaster pistol. Second series. Near Mint Carded - **$85**

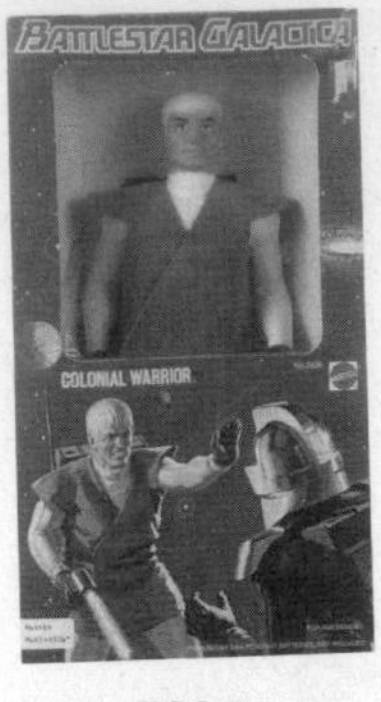

BSG-7

❑ **BSG-7. "Battlestar Galactica Colonial Warrior" Boxed Figure,**
1978. Mattel. 14" box holds 12.25" figure with fabric tunic and light-up ray gun powered by two "AA" batteries. Boxed - **$20 $40 $80**

BSG-8

❑ **BSG-8. "Battlestar Galactica" General Mills Bin Display Sign,**
1978. General Mills. Promotional sign for back of display bin reads "Free Battlestar Galactica Poster Yours With Two Purchases Of Any Of These Big G Cereals." - **$24 $50 $100**

BSG-9

❑ **BSG-9. Battlestar Galactica Button And Badge,**
c. 1978. Hewig & Marvic. 2.25" diameter litho button. Plastic badge is 1.25x3" with bar pin on back. Each - **$3 $6 $10**

BSG-10

❑ **BSG-10. "Battlestar Galactica Space Station Kit",**
1978. General Mills. Includes manual, punch-out control center, headset, activator card, patch, 11 mission cards, poster, four iron-on transfers.
Near Mint In Mailer - **$100**

BSG-11

❑ **BSG-11. "Battlestar Galactica" Lunch Box with Thermos,**
2001. - **$35**

Beany and Cecil

At the request of Charlotte Clark, an enterprising lady searching for a marketable product, the teenage artist Bob Clampett (1913-1984) designed the first Mickey Mouse doll in January, 1930.

Both Walt and Roy Disney were so pleased with the doll, they rented a house near the studio and set up Clark in the doll-making business. Clampett assisted for awhile, but really desired a studio job. Because there was no space for him at the tiny Hyperion studio, in 1931 Clampett left doll-making to work with Hugh Harman and Rudolf Ising as an animator on the Warner Brothers *Looney Tunes & Merrie Melodies* cartoon series. He helped develop Porky Pig with Friz Freleng in 1935 and became a director in 1937. He is also credited with the creation of Tweety Bird.

Always interested in puppetry, Clampett left Warner Bros. to create *Time For Beany* for TV station KTLA in Los Angeles. The show first aired on February 28, 1949 and ran 15 minutes a day, 5 days a week, until 1955.

The cast included Beany, Cecil The Seasick Serpent, Captain Horatio Huffenpuff, Dishonest John and the good ship Leakin' Lena. Stan Freberg voiced Cecil and Daws Butler, whose wife Myrtis designed Cecil, was the voice of Beany. The animated version, directed by Dick Kinney and former Disney Donald Duck director Jack Hannah first aired on network TV in January, 1962. Sponsored by the Mattel toy company, the show was titled *Matty's Funnies With Beany And Cecil.* The series moved from primetime to ABC-TV Saturday mornings on January 5, 1963 where it ran until 1967. A significant variety of licensed merchandise was produced, most items with copyrights of Mattel and Clampett. Current DVD sales prove it's still time for Beany.

B&C-1

❑ **B&C-4. "Beany And His Pals" Cast Photo,**
1949. Tea Time Candies. 8x10" glossy black and white. - **$25 $60 $135**

B&C-2

❑ **B&C-2. Early Beany & Cecil Hand Puppets,**
1949. Chemi-Plastic. Beany is 11" tall with fabric outfit, vinyl head, lifelike hair and felt beanie with plastic propeller. Cecil is 9.5" tall in vinyl with painted accents. Each - **$50 $150 $250**

B&C-3

❑ **B&C-3. Early Dishonest John And Captain Huffenpuff Hand Puppets,**
1949. Chemi-Plastics. Each puppet is about 9.5" tall with fabric bodies, felt hands and vinyl heads. Each - **$35 $100 $150**

B&C-4

❑ **B&C-4. Early Version Beany Hand Puppet,**
c. 1950. Sears store item. From era of KTLA-TV (Los Angeles) show "Time For Beany". - **$85 $225 $415**

B&C-5

❑ **B&C-5. "Beany" Boxed Hand Puppet,**
1952. Store item by Zany Toys.
Box - **$35 $60 $125**
Puppet - **$50 $90 $165**

B&C-6

❑ **B&C-6. Beany & Cecil Premium Card Set,**
1950s. H.P. Hood & Sons. Complete set of six 2.25x3-3/8" cards showing Beany, Cecil, Captain Huffenpuff, Dishonest John, Wong and Hunny Bear. Each - **$10 $20 $40**

B&C-7

❑ **B&C-7. Beany & Cecil Lamp With Shade,**
1950s. Alert Lamp Co. 10" tall figural lamp with solid painted plaster base. Back of base has incised Bob Clampett copyright. 7.5" tall stiff paper shade shows illustrations of Beany, Capt. Huffenpuff, Dishonest John, Wong and Hunny Bear. - **$250 $500 $1000**

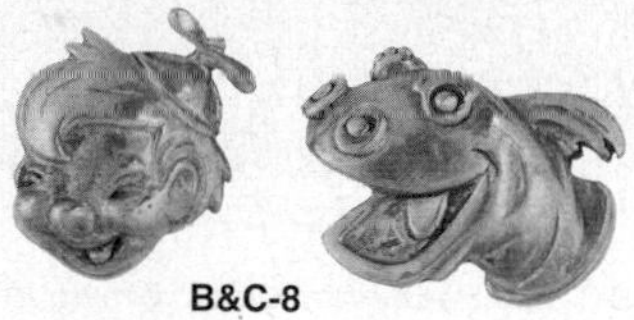

B&C-8

❑ **B&C-8. Beany & Cecil Cast Member Only Cufflinks,**
1950s. Set of cast metal cufflinks with relief design featuring heads of Beany & Cecil. Given to cast members who worked on the *Time For Beany* show. Rare. Pair - **$150 $300 $500**

B&C-9

B&C-10

❑ **B&C-9. "Beany And Cecil Ring Toss" Game,**
1961. Pressman Toy Corp. 14.5x19.5x2" deep box holds 13.5x13.5" tin litho base. Five wooden dowels have die-cut figures on top making them 7" tall. Also includes five 5" plastic rings and 4.5x7" instruction sheet. Boxed - **$40 $75 $125**

❑ **B&C-10. "Beany And Cecil Official Beany-Copter,"**
1961. Mattel Inc. 5.5" diameter by 4" tall beanie with two 5" propellers, winding mechanism and launch string. Label has image of Beany and Cecil along with Mattel logo. Complete unboxed - **$30 $60 $90**

B&C-11

❑ **B&C-11. "Cecil In The Music Box!",**
1961. Mattel. Box contains 5.5" tall music box with images of Beany & Cecil, Dishonest John, Captain Huffenpuff, Pop Gunn and Davey Crickett. When toy is wound a 4.5" tall cloth, spring-loaded figure of Cecil pops out.
Carton - **$20 $40 $75**
Music Box - **$30 $60 $100**

B&C-12

❑ **B&C-12. "Beany And Cecil" Brown Vinyl Variety Lunch Box,**
c. 1961. 3-7/8x9.25x7" tall brown vinyl lunch box. Right panel shows Dishonest John, left shows Captain Huffenpuff. - **$50 $125 $250**

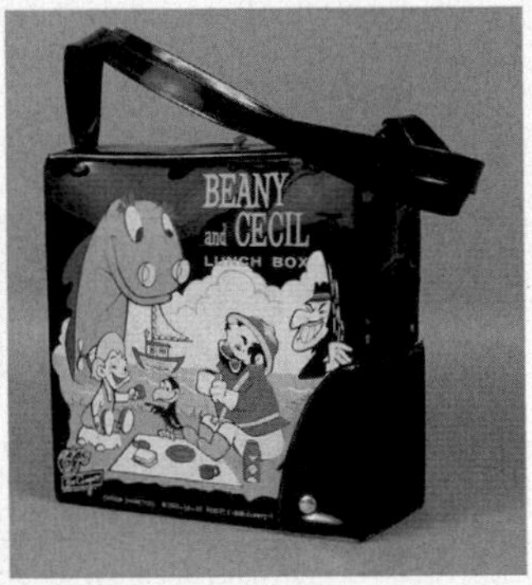

B&C-13

❑ **B&C-13. "Beany And Cecil Lunch Box" Large Size With Separate Thermos Compartment Black Variety,**
c. 1961. 10x10x3.5" deep lunch box with Clampett trademark logo shows characters from cartoon. Box - **$400 $800 $1500**
Bottle (Not Shown) - **$20 $40 $100**

B&C-14

B&C-15

❑ **B&C-14. "New! Beany & Cecil In '62!" Cello. Button,**
1962. Mattel Toys with Bob Clampett copyright. Probably from industry toy show. -
$50 $100 $200

❑ **B&C-15. Beany And Cecil Lunch Box,**
c. 1962. 3.5x8.5x8.75" vinyl over cardboard. "Bob Clampett" logo. - **$150 $300 $500**

B&C-16

❑ **B&C-16. "Beany & Cecil" Lunch Box And Thermos,**
1963. Vinyl lunch box is 6-7/8x9-1/8x4" deep. Left side shows Captain Huffenpuff, right side shows Dishonest John. 8" tall metal thermos shows 4 characters laughing.
Box - **$75 $150 $300**
Bottle - **$20 $40 $100**

B&C-17

❑ **B&C-17. "Seasons Greetings/The (Bob) Clampett Family" Personal Christmas Card,**
1960s. 4.5x5-7/8" card shows Bob Clampett and family along with character images including Beany & Cecil. - **$12 $25 $50**

The Beatles

The Beatles were Paul McCartney, John Lennon, George Harrison, and Ringo Starr (Richard Starkey), four lads from Liverpool, England, who became the dominant musical force of the turbulent 1960s and have remained cultural icons to this day. Considered "The Fifth Beatle," Pete Best was the Beatles drummer from late 1960 until August 15, 1963 when he was permanently replaced with Ringo. The Fab Four burst onto the American scene in an explosive live appearance on the Ed Sullivan Show on CBS-TV in February 1964, and though their last public concert was less than three years later, Beatles records and tapes still sell in the millions. Their movies--*A Hard Day's Night* (1964), *Help!* (1965) and the psychedelic animated feature *Yellow Submarine* (1968)--an animated Saturday morning series produced by King Features (1965-1969) and sponsored primarily by the A. C. Gilbert toy company, and comic books all added to the luster; but it was the brilliance and charm of the music that revolutionized rock and roll.

Half of the Fab Four have passed away; John Lennon on December 8, 1980 and George Harrison on November 29, 2001. In terms of lasting influence, The Beatles continue to sway not only music but pop culture in general. *A Hard Day's Night* is commonly considered to be one of the best rock and roll films ever made, while *Help!* is widely thought of as a precursor to the modern music video and a direct inspiration for the Monkees (see their category elsewhere in this book). With the release of *The Beatles Anthology I-III* (three 2-CD sets) and the companion video tape set, the surviving Beatles again set sales records around the world. These releases were accompanied by a large amount of Beatles merchandise, as well as the first new Beatles songs in years, mixing recently discovered Lennon vocals with new backing tracks by the surviving band members. Beatles memorabilia of all sorts, both original issues and later reproductions, are usually copyrighted NEMS Enterprises or SELTAEB.

BEA-1

❑ **BEA-1. Ashtray From "The Cavern" Early Beatles Venue,**
c. 1962-63. About 5-1/2" square by 5/8" deep glazed ceramic with 2-1/2x4" center scene inscribed "The 'Cavern'-Home Of The Mersey Sound." Group on stage resembles The Beatles and readable words on stage backdrop include "The Mersey Beet/ Rolling/The Fourmost/The Beatles." Marked on reverse "Prince William Warranted 22 Carat Gold/Made In England." - **$165 $375 $700**

BEA-2

❑ **BEA-2. Vinyl Doll Set,**
1964. Store item by Remco Plastics. Each has life-like hair.
Each - **$40 $75 $125**

BEA-3

❑ **BEA-3. "Beatle Dolls" 7x18" Paper Store Poster,**
1964. Remco Industries. - **$135 $275 $450**

BEA-4

❑ **BEA-4. "The Bobb'n Head Beatles" Boxed Set,**
1964. Store item. Composition figures by Car Mascots Inc.
Boxed Set - **$600 $1200 $2000**
Each Loose - **$125 $225 $350**

BEA-5

❑ **BEA-5. "The Beatles" Pillow,**
1964. 12x12x2-1/2" deep store item by Nordic House. One of three designs. Each - **$75 $140 $285**

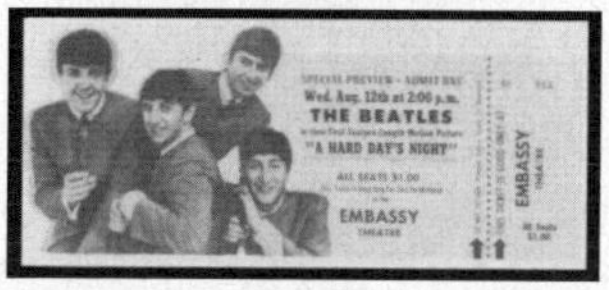

BEA-6

❑ **BEA-6. "The Beatles A Hard Day's Night" Movie Ticket,**
1964. Embassy Theater. - **$55 $110 $220**

BEA-7

❑ **BEA-7. Vinyl Overnight Case With Zippered Front And Handle,**
1964. Store item by Air Flite. Large item 12x13x5" deep.
Black Variety - **$200 $375 $725**
Red Variety - **$250 $525 $900**

BEA-8

BEA-9

BEA-10

BEA-11

BEA-12

❑ **BEA-8. First Series Gum Card Set,**
1964. Topps. Set of 60 numbered 1-60.
Set - **$50 $120 $300**

❑ **BEA-9. Second Series Gum Card Set,**
1964. Topps. Set of 55 numbered 61-115.
Set - **$50 $120 $300**

❑ **BEA-10. Third Series Gum Card Set,**
1964. Topps. Set of 50 numbered 116-165.
Set - **$50 $120 $300**

❑ **BEA-11. "Beatles Diary" Gum Card Set,**
1964. Topps. Set of 60. Set - **$60 $150 $360**

❑ **BEA-12. "Beatles Color Cards" Gum Card Set,**
1964. Topps. Set of 64. Set - **$50 $120 $300**

BEA-13

❑ **BEA-13. Calendar Cards,**
1964. Various advertisers.
Each - **$10 $15 $30**

BEA-14

❑ **BEA-14. Cincinnati Concert Program,**
1964. - **$30 $60 $120**

BEA-15

❑ **BEA-15. Topps Gum Wrapper,**
1964. - **$12 $25 $50**

BEA-16

❑ **BEA-16. "A Hard Day's Night" Movie Poster,**
1964. One sheet poster from the first Beatles film. Measures 41"x27". Produced by United Artists. - **$350 $675 $1100**

BEA-17

❑ **BEA-17. "Color Oil Portraits" Set Of 4,**
1964. Store item. Cut-out "Buddies Club" card on header.
Packaged With Uncut Card - **$75 $135 $210**

BEA-18

BEA-19

❑ **BEA-18. "Free/One Beatle Button" Ad Paper,**
1964. 5x7" glossy paper pennant printed on both sides including back offer for Beatles billfold. - **$85 $175 $335**

❑ **BEA-19. "I'm A Official Beatles Fan" Button,**
1964. Authorized issue in several variations all marked on rim curl "Copyright NEMS Ent. Ltd. 64" and Green Duck Co., Chicago-Made In U.S.A."
Litho. 4" Size - **$25 $55 $90**
Cello. 3-1/2" Size - **$18 $45 $75**
Litho. 1-3/8" Size - **$30 $85 $150**

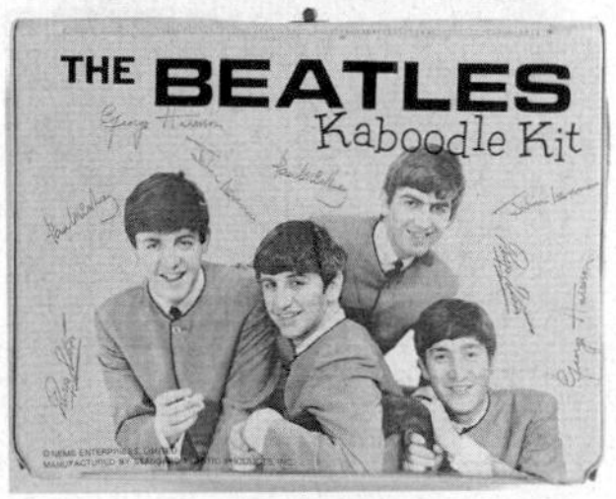

BEA-20

❑ **BEA-20. "The Beatles Kaboodle Kit,"**
1964. Vinyl lunch box is 7x9x4" deep by Standard Plastic Products Inc. Copyright NEMS Enterprises Ltd. Tan version - **$250 $500 $900**
Blue version - **$275 $600 $1000**

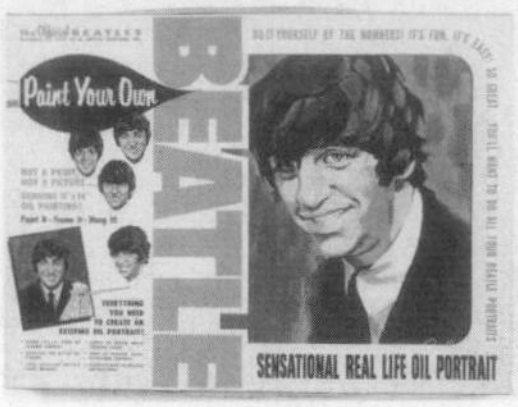

BEA-21

❑ **BEA-21. "Paint Your Own Beatle Ringo" Paint Set,**
1964. Artistic Creations Inc. 14x19" boxed set from a set of four, one for each "Beatle." This "Ringo" set includes 11x14" paint-by-number portrait board, 8 containers of oil paint and a 11x14" print of the finished portrait. Unused - **$275 $550 $825**

BEA-22

❑ **BEA-22. "The Beatles" Vinyl Carrying Case/Lunch Box,**
1964. Box is 7x9x4" deep by Air Flite. Copyright NEMS Enterprises Inc. - **$300 $700 $1200**

BEA-23

BEA-24

❑ **BEA-23. Vending Machine Litho. Button,**
1964. Set of nine (four pictures/five slogans) either in black/white/red, blue/orange, red/white/blue, or black/white/blue.
Pictures - **$3 $8 $15**
Slogans- **$3 $6 $10**

❑ **BEA-24. "Beatles Fan Club" Australian Button,**
c. 1964. 1.25" black/white/gray likely from the time of their 1964 Australian tour. - **$35 $70 $150**

BEA-25

❑ **BEA-25. "The Beatles" Charm Bracelet,**
c. 1964. Store item. - **$40 $75 $150**

BEA-26

❑ **BEA-26. "Beatles Sneakers By Wing Dings,"**
c. 1964. Near Mint Boxed - **$1000**
Box - **$100 $250 $400**
Sneakers - **$150 $300 $600**

BEA-27

❑ **BEA-27. "Official Fan Club News Bulletin",**
c. 1964. Includes six stapled photo pages. - **$30 $70 $135**

BEA-28

BEA-29

❑ **BEA-28. "Life Member" Fan Club Patch,**
c. 1964. - **$20 $50 $100**

❑ **BEA-29. "I Love" 3-1/2" Cello. Buttons,**
c. 1964. Each - **$12 $25 $55**

BEA-30

❑ **BEA-30. "The Beatles" Linen Wall Hanging,**
c. 1964. Store item marked "Pure Irish Linen/Alster." 20x31" with black and white portraits of them wearing dark burgundy suits against lavender background with white border. - **$75 $125 $250**

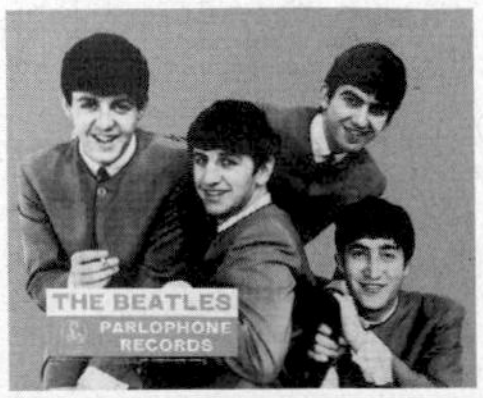

BEA-31

❑ **BEA-31. "Parlophone Records" Store Poster,**
c. 1964. E.M.I. Records Ltd., Great Britain. 12x15" stiff paper. - **$135 $250 $475**

BEA-32

❑ BEA-32. Cloth Handbag With Tag,
c. 1964. 10x10" bag issued in either vinyl or cloth with two-sided cardboard string tag attached to zipper pull.
Near Mint With Tag - **$900**
Bag Only - **$200 $400 $650**

BEA-33

❑ BEA-33. The Beatles Glasses Set,
c. 1964. Set of four 5.5" tall by 2.75" diameter glasses feature head and shoulder pictures of Beatles with names along sides. Around bottom are musical notes, records and guitar. Ringo glass is white, George is orange, Paul is yellow and John is white. Each - **$45 $85 $140**

BEA-34 BEA-35 BEA-36

❑ BEA-34. Flicker Ring Set,
c. 1964. Set of four.
Silver Base Each - **$12 $18 $35**
Blue Base Each - **$10 $15 $20**

❑ BEA-35. "Ringo Starr" Soaky Bottle,
1965. Colgate-Palmolive. Only Ringo and Paul were produced. - **$45 $85 $165**

❑ BEA-36. "Paul McCartney" Soaky,
1965. Colgate-Palmolive. Only Paul and Ringo were produced. - **$45 $85 $165**

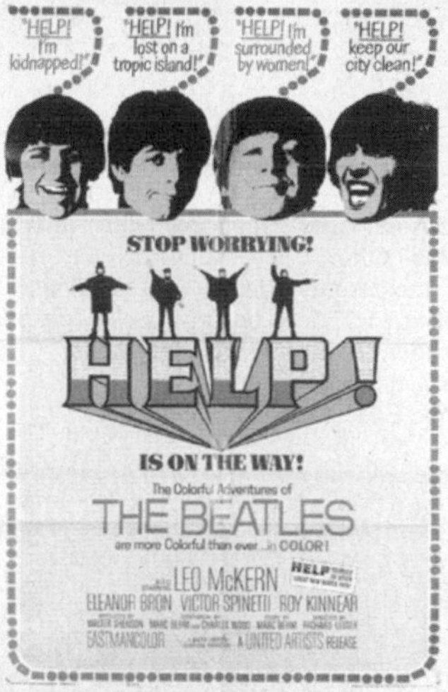

BEA-37

❑ BEA-37. "Help!" Movie Poster,
1965. One sheet poster from the Beatles' 2nd film. Measures 41"x27". - **$325 $650 $1050**

BEA-38

❑ BEA-38. Embossed Metal Lunch Box,
1965. Store item by Aladdin Industries Inc. - **$165 $375 $850**

BEA-39

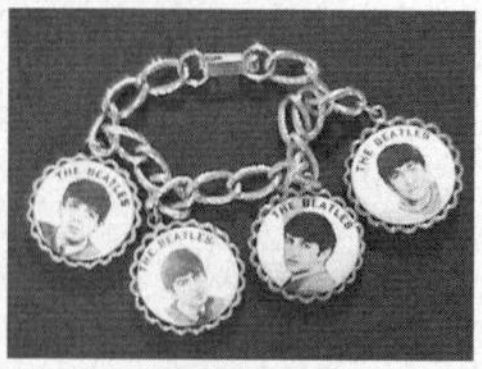

BEA-40

❑ BEA-39. Metal Lunch Box Bottle,
1965. Aladdin Industries Inc. Came with previous lunch box. - **$85 $225 $335**

❑ BEA-40. Bracelet With Celluloid Charms,
c. 1965. Store item. 6" long in brass luster with black and white celluloid portraits. - **$45 $90 $175**

BEA-41

❑ BEA-41. "The Beatles" Bracelet On Card,
c. 1965. Store item by Randall.
Near Mint Carded - **$200**
Bracelet Only - **$40 $75 $125**

BEA-42

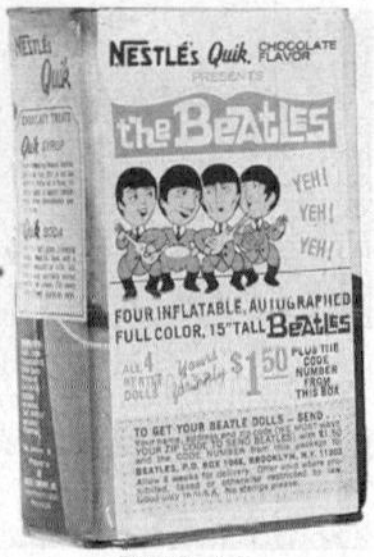

BEA-43

❑ BEA-42. "Help" Packaged Bandage,
c. 1965. Movie promotion on Curad bandage. - **$20 $35 $70**

❑ BEA-43. Nestle's Quik Container,
1966. Has offer for inflatable doll set. - **$225 $450 $800**

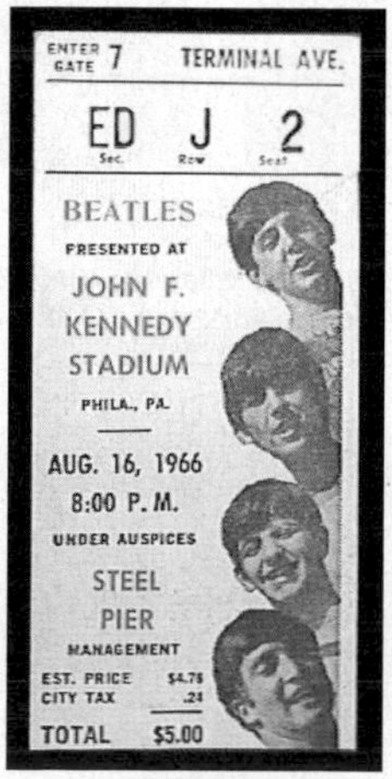

BEA-44

❑ BEA-44. Ticket Stub For JFK Stadium, Philadelphia,
1966. Black and white with red lettering. - **$80 $185 $350**

BEA-45

❑ BEA-45. "The Beatles Disk-Go-Case" Plastic 45 RPM Record Holder,
1966. Store item by Charter Industries. Issued in various colors. - **$50 $150 $300**

BEA-46

❑ BEA-46. Fan Club Christmas Record Postcard,
1966. The Beatles Bulletin/Official Publication Of The National Beatles Fan Club. 7x8-1/2" stiff cardboard with record on front inscribed "1966 Season's Greetings From The Beatles." - **$35 $70 $130**

BEA-47

❑ BEA-47. Beatles Inflatable Vinyl Dolls Set,
1966. Store item, also Nestle's Quik and Lux Soap. Each - **$25 $50 $100**

BEA-48

❑ BEA-48. "Go Go Beatles" Japanese Tote Bag,
c. 1966. Tag Only - **$20 $35 $85**
Bag Only - **$30 $60 $115**

BEA-49

❑ BEA-49. "Lux" Soap Box With "Inflatable Beatles" Offer,
1967. Lux Beauty Soap by Lever Brothers Co. 2-1/4x4x2-1/2" deep box has back panel offering set of four 15" tall inflatable vinyl dolls.
Near Mint Sealed - **$650**
Opened Box - **$125 $225 $400**

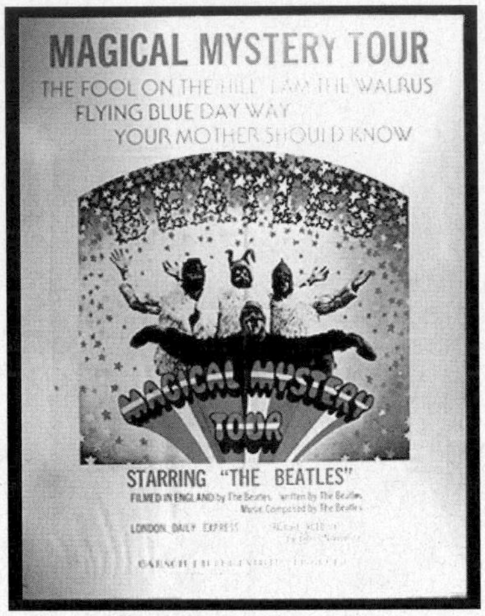

BEA-50

❑ BEA-50. "Magical Mystery Tour" Poster,
1967. 31" tall and 23" wide. Promotes the TV special filmed in England. - **$250 $500 $800**

BEA-51

❑ BEA-51. "Lucy In The Sky With Diamonds" Black Light Poster,
1967. Personality Posters. 22x30" paper vibrant design in day-glo red plus purple and orange image of Beatles in their Sgt. Pepper outfits plus Lucy of long flowing hair. Under black light only the letters "LSD" appear from title text. - **$55 $110 $225**

BEA-52

❑ BEA-52. "Sgt. Pepper's Lonely Hearts Club Band" 2-1/8" Litho. Button,
c. 1967. Great Britain issue for original record release although no copyright or company name. - **$20 $40 $75**

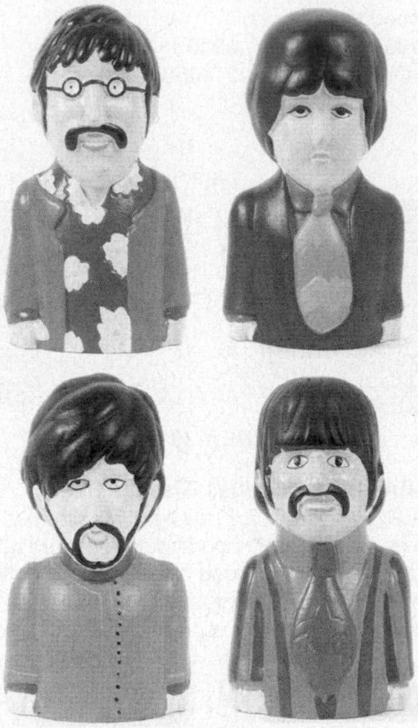

BEA-53

❑ BEA-53. Yellow Submarine Bank Set,
1968. Pride Creations Inc. 7.5" tall painted composition from set of four Beatle/Yellow Submarine role banks.
Lennon - **$150 $275 $500**
Other Three - **$100 $200 $400**

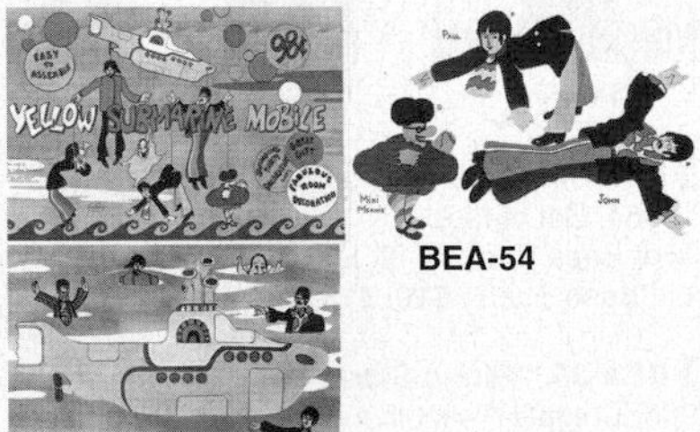

BEA-54

❑ BEA-54. Yellow Submarine Mobile,
1968. Stiff paper folder opening to 10x39" including picture of assembled model plus three panels of punch-out assembly pieces for Yellow Sub, all four Beatles, Boob and Mini Meanie. - **$85 $165 $325**

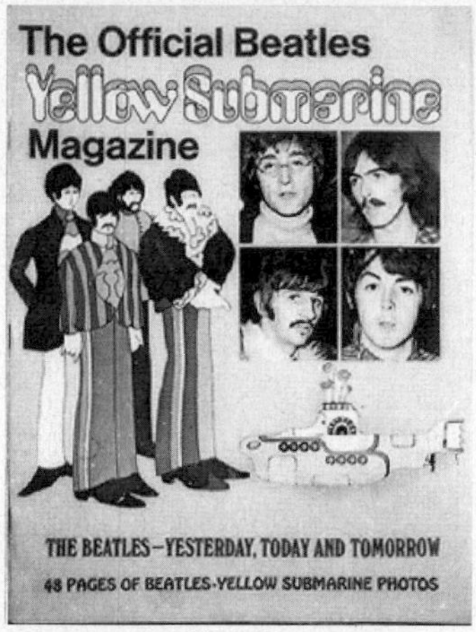

BEA-55

❑ **BEA-55. "Yellow Submarine Magazine",** 1968. Store item published jointly by Pyramid Publications and King Features. - **$30 $60 $120**

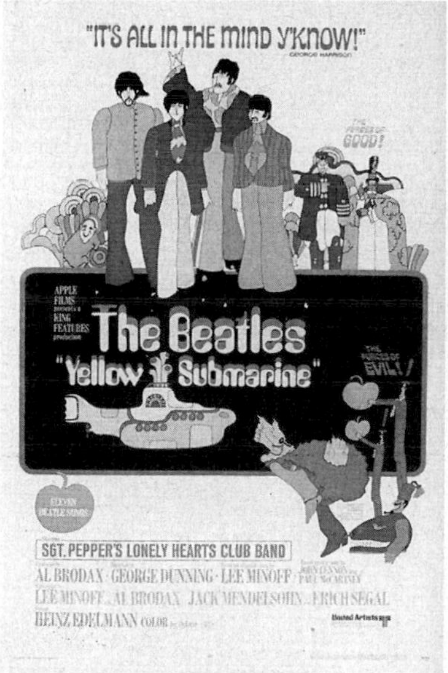

BEA-56

❑ **BEA-56. "Yellow Submarine" Movie Poster,**
1968. Earlier version of the one sheet poster. With its great graphics, it's one of the most sought after posters of the 60s. The apple at the left center mentions 11 Beatles songs.
United Artists. - **$350 $850 $1500**

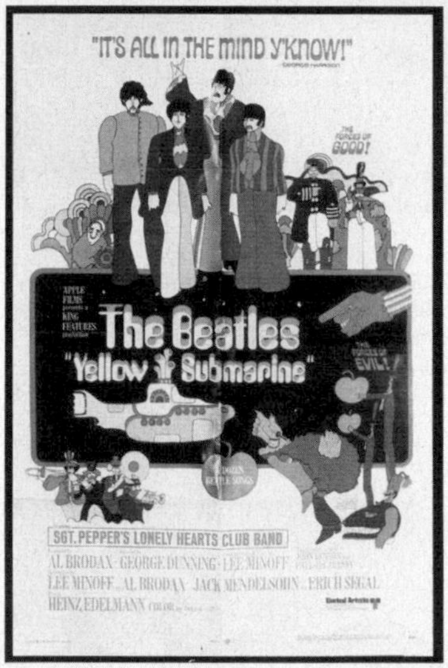

BEA-57

❑ **BEA-57. "Yellow Submarine" Movie Poster,**
1968. Later version of the one sheet poster has the apple moved to the center, now promoting a dozen Beatles songs. The pointing glove with a face was also added.
United Artists. - **$350 $850 $1500**

BEA-58

❑ **BEA-58. "Yellow Submarine" Lunch Box,** 1968. Store item by King-Seeley Thermos Co.
Box - **$150 $400 $800**
Thermos - **$100 $200 $400**

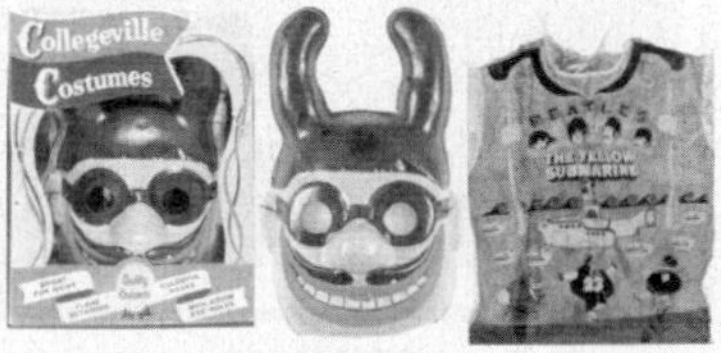

BEA-59

❑ **BEA-59. "Yellow Submarine" Blue Meanie Boxed Costume,**
1968. Store item by Collegeville Costumes.
Near Mint Boxed - **$700**
Costume and Mask Only - **$100 $200 $400**

BEA-60

❑ **BEA-60 "Yellow Submarine Inc." Straw,** 1968. No official copyright but art is 100% identical to that of the Beatles' Yellow Submarine. Issued by Sweetheart Straws.
Unopened - **$12 $25 $50**

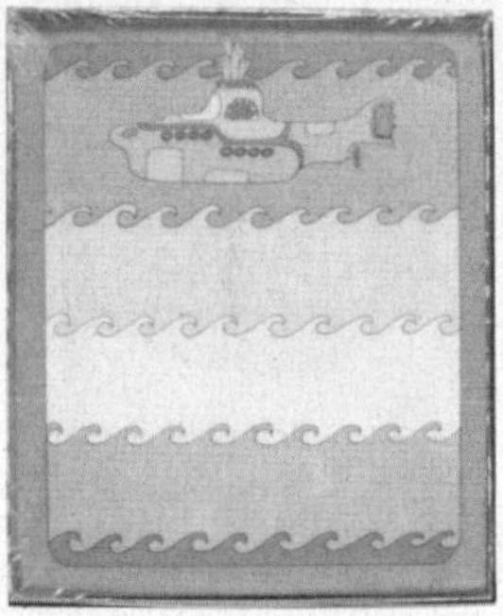

BEA-61

❑ **BEA-61. Yellow Submarine Stationery Set,** 1968. Store item by Unicorn Creations Inc. 18 different sets. Each Complete - **$40 $75 $115**

BEA-62

❑ **BEA-62. "The Beatles Yellow Submarine Bantam Pocket Picture Puzzle",** 1968. Store item by Jaymar. - **$45 $110 $225**

BEA-63

❑ **BEA-63. Yellow Submarine Pin Set,** 1968. Store item. Set - **$100 $200 $300**

BEA-64

❑ **BEA-64. Corgi "Yellow Submarine" Replica,**
1968. Near Mint Boxed - **$600**
Loose - **$100 $200 $300**

BEA-65

❑ **BEA-65. Yellow Submarine European Movie Theater Mobile,**
c. 1968. Two diecut thick cardboard pieces 17x25" and 6x10" for forming ceiling dangle mobile. Each piece is printed identically both sides with tiny inscriptions for French theater and possibly disco entertainment spot. - **$190 $400 $750**

BEA-66

❑ **BEA-66. Yellow Submarine Rub-Ons,**
1969. Nabisco Wheat (Or Rice) Honeys. Set of eight. Each - **$18 $28 $60**

BEA-67

❑ **BEA-67. John Lennon & Yoko "Give Peace A Chance" Button,**
1969. 3" cello color real photo without dot pattern of them holding placard "War Is Over!" Likely from July 1 recording of classic peace song. - **$150 $300 $600**

BEA-68

❑ **BEA-68. "The Swingers Music Set,"**
1960s. Unlicensed. Four figures, two standing microphones and drum set.
Boxed Complete - **$60 $115 $230**

BEA-69

BEA-70

❑ **BEA-69. Australian Fan Club Cello. Button,**
1960s. - **$35 $70 $125**

❑ **BEA-70. Rubber Figure Charms,**
1960s. Believed vending machine issue. Set of four, each 2-1/2" tall. Each - **$8 $12 $25**

BEA-71

❑ **BEA-71. "Let It Be" Poster,**
1970. Six sheet poster for the last of the Beatles' films. United Artists. - **$350 $675 $1050**

BEA-72

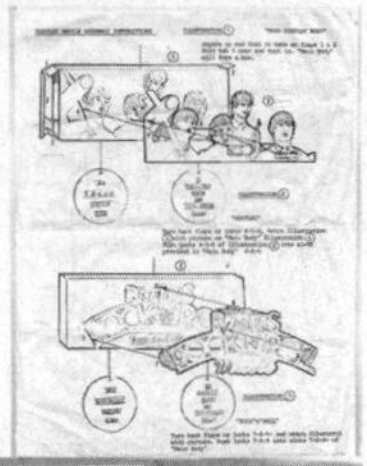

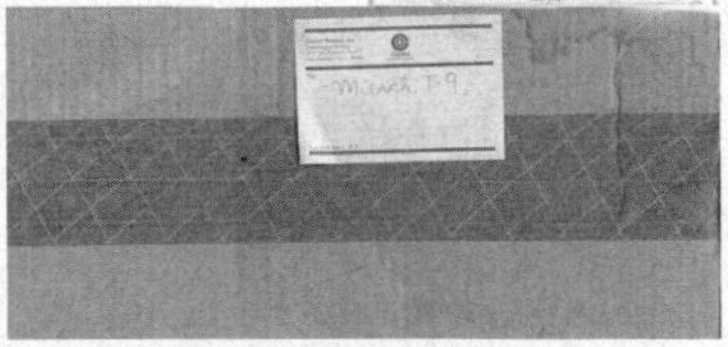

❑ **BEA-72. Promotional Mobile Set,**
1971. Capital Records promo. 5-piece mobile advertising a 2-record set. Comes with instructions and mailer.
5-Piece Mobile - **$100 $225 $450**
Instructions and Mailer - **$10 $25 $50**

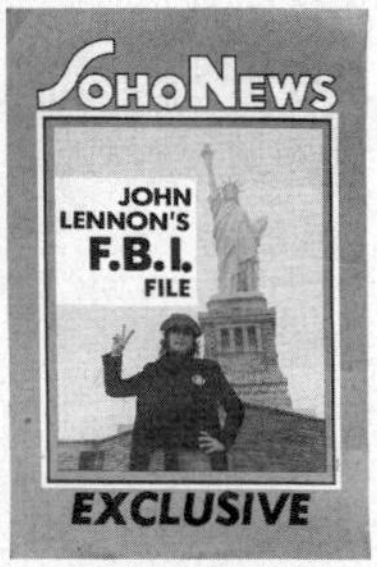

BEA-73

❑ **BEA-73. "Soho News" Sign With Lennon,**
c. 1975. 11x17" paper sign for New York newspaper announcing upcoming article of "Exclusive John Lennon's F.B.I. File." - **$40 $80 $160**

BEA-74

❑ **BEA-74. George Harrison Promotional Mobile,**
1976. Ganga Distributors. 8-sided ad piece promotes new album. Scarce - **$110 $225 $340**

BEA-75

❑ **BEA-75. "War Is Over" John & Yoko Gallery Poster,**
1970s. 20x30" paper inscribed in smaller text "If You Want It/Love And Peace From John & Yoko." Lower corner has certification seal for "Original Gallery Ad" 1970-1974. -
$135 $250 $450

BEA-76

❑ **BEA-76. "John Lennon" Figural Memorial Boxed Radio,**
c. 1980. Store item marked only "Made In Hong Kong." 8" vinyl figure in fabric outfit stands on 3-1/2x5x1-1/2" deep plastic base. He holds a silver microphone with white cord in one hand.
Near Mint Boxed - **$165**
Radio Only - **$35 $70 $115**

Beetle Bailey

Cartoonist Mort Walker, born in 1923, sold his first cartoon at age 11 and had 300 cartoons published by age 15. *Beetle Bailey* began as a daily comic strip on September 4, 1950 in 12 newspapers. Originally designed as a "slacker" college student, Beetle was recruited into the Army in 1951. Set in Camp Swampy, the cast includes: Killer The Ladies Man, Sgt. Snorkel and his dog Otto, Gen. Halftrack and his secretary Miss Buxley, Zero, Cookie The Cook and Lt. Sonny Fuzz. In 1970 Lt. Jack Flap became the first black character to integrate a modern white cast humor strip.

Walker won the National Cartoonists Society Reuben Award in 1953, and became president of the N.C.S. in 1970. A visit by Beetle to his sister in 1954 led to a popular new comic strip, *Hi And Lois* which was written by Walker and drawn by Dik Browne. The *Beetle Bailey* comic strip is in some 1,800 papers today, with Greg Walker assisting his father. Beetle has come a long way since he was known as "Spider" in college.

BBL-1 BBL-2

❑ **BBL-1. Beetle Bailey Bobbing Head Doll,**
1950s. - **$50 $100 $200**

❑ **BBL-2. Sgt. Snorkel Bobbing Head Doll,**
1950s. - **$50 $100 $200**

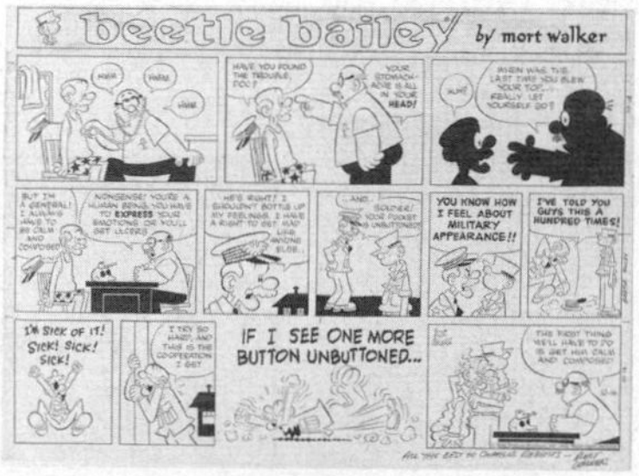

BBL-3

❑ **BBL-3. "Beetle Bailey" 1962 Sunday Page Original Art,**
1962. King Features Syndicate. 15.25x20-7/8" art board with 12.75x20.25" India ink image area with 12 panels. Art is signed in ink by artist-creator Mort Walker with additional ink inscription to the recipient. Same Or Similar -
$100 $200 $300

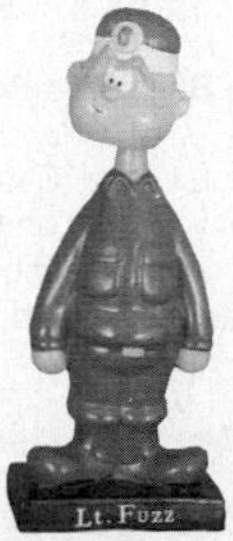

BBL-4

❑ **BBL-4. "Lt. Fuzz" Bobbing Head,**
1960s. 7.5" tall figure with name on base front. Bottom has KFS copyright. - **$45 $90 $165**

BBL-5

❑ **BBL-5. Beetle Baily Character Puppets,**
1960s. Gund Mfg. Co. Each puppet is about 10" tall with silk-screened fabric body and vinyl head. Puppets are Beetle Bailey, Sarge and Zero. Each - **$15 $30 $50**

BBL-6 BBL-7

❑ **BBL-6. Beetle Bailey 14" Doll,**
1984. King Features copyright.
With original tag - **$145**

❑ **BBL-7. Sgt. Snorkel Doll,**
1984. King Features copyright.
With original tag - **$145**

BBL-8

❑ **BBL-8. Beetle Bailey Limited Edition Ring,**
1993. KFS/The Hurst Corp. Sterling silver with raised Beetle Bailey portrait on top. Planned edition of 495 but only 20 numbered examples were produced. Mint As Issued - **$200**

BBL-9

❑ **BBL-9. Beetle Bailey PVC Set,**
2000. Copyright King Feature Syndicate. This seven figure set from Dark Horse features Beetle, Sarge, Otto, General Halftrack, Miss Buxley, Cookie and Lt. Flap. - **$50**

BBL-10

❑ **BBL-10. Beetle Bailey Resin Figure with Flag,**
2000. Limited Edition, 6 1/2" tall figure from Equity Marketing Inc. Boxed. - **$35**

Ben Casey

Airing on ABC-TV from October 2, 1961 until 1966, Vince Edwards (1928-1996) starred as the brooding neurosurgeon on the popular adult drama medical series. Co-stars included Sam Jaffe as Dr. Zorba, Bettye Ackerman as Dr. Maggie Graham, Jeanne Bates as Nurse Wills and John Zaremba as Dr. Harold Jensen. 153 episodes were televised, leading to two Emmy awards.

The series spawned a comic strip series by Neal Adams. The daily began November 26, 1962 and the Sunday page began September 20, 1964. Both ended July 31, 1966 but Neal Adams would go on to a highly successful career as a comic book artist. Vince Edwards also had a successful recording career, releasing six albums and a few singles on the Decca label.

The memorable opening of the show had Sam Jaffee saying "Man...Woman...Birth... Death...Infinity" as matching symbols appeared on a blackboard.

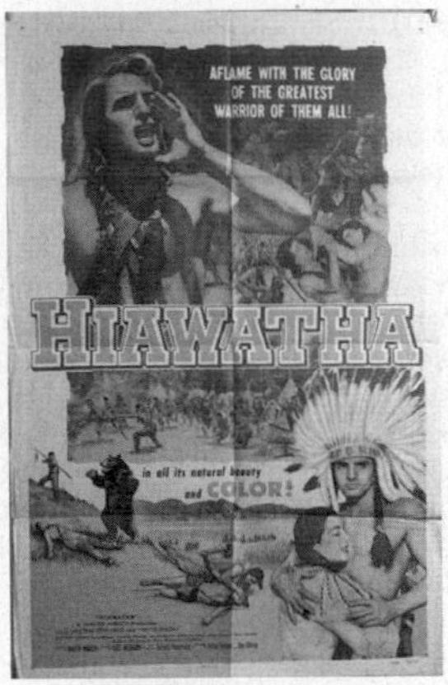

BEN-1

❑ **BEN-1. "Hiawatha Starring Vincent Edwards" Movie Poster,**
1953. Allied Artists. 27x41" with photos of Edwards as famous Indian. - **$10 $20 $40**

BEN-2

❑ **BEN-2. "Ben Casey Charm Bracelet",**
1962. Gerald Sears Co. 2.7x8.25" display card contains 6" long metal bracelet with gold luster. Bracelet has 5 figural symbol charms for male, female, life, death, infinity. Design reflects theme of the program's opening sequence.
Card - **$5 $10 $20**
Bracelet - **$10 $20 $30**

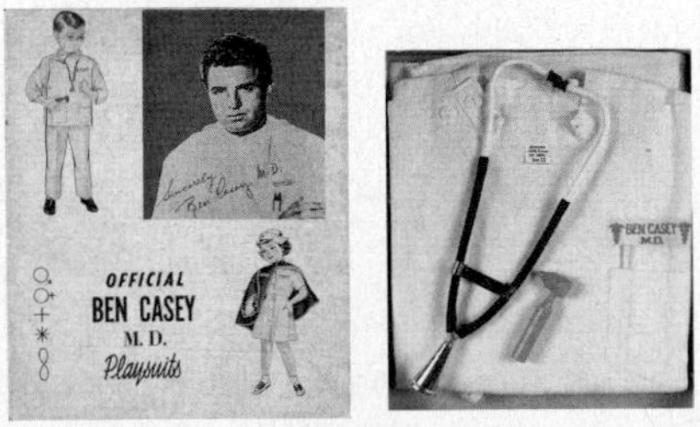

BEN-3

❑ **BEN-3. "Official Ben Casey M.D." Boxed Playsuit,**
1962. Pla-Master Play Suits. 10.5x12.5x1.5" deep box contains photo of Vince Edwards and illustration of boy and girl wearing doctor and nurse outfits. Outfit consists of white shirt with felt patch on chest reading "Ben Casey M.D." Accessories include wooden thermometer, plastic otoscope and plastic/rubber stethoscope. - **$20 $40 $75**

BEN-4

BEN-5

❑ **BEN-4. "Dr. Ben Casey M.D." Composition Bobbing Head,**
1960s. - **$45 $85 $165**

❑ **BEN-5. Vince Edwards As Ben Casey Button,**
1960s. 3.5" diameter button with portrait. - **$10 $20 $30**

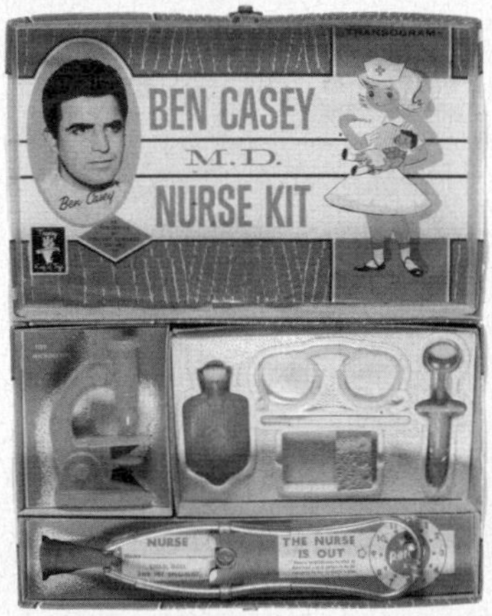

BEN-6

❑ **BEN-6. "Ben Casey M.D. Nurse Kit",**
1972. Transogram. 7.25x12x2.25" deep with brass handle and latch that holds toy microscope, hot water bottle, glasses, thermometer, syringe and stethoscope. - **$75 $150 $250**

Betty Boop

Max Fleischer created the Boop-Oop-a-Doop girl as an animated cartoon in the August 8, 1930 cartoon "Dizzy Dishes," the sixth installment of the "Talkartoon" series. Grim Natwick is most responsible for her design. The sexy little flirt, modeled on singer Helen Kane and actress Mae West, was an immediate success and became Paramount's leading cartoon feature. Along with her dog Bimbo and her pal Koko the clown, Betty vamped and sang her way through comedies and adventures throughout the 1930s. Production code censorship in 1934 forced Betty to wear a longer skirt with a less plunging neckline. Several actresses provided Betty's voice but Mae Questel is most closely identified with the character. King Features Syndicate ran a daily comic strip in 1934-1935, then released only Sunday comic strips until 1937, later published as an Avon paperback in 1975. A children's show, *Betty Boop Fables*, had a brief run on NBC radio in 1932-1933, and the cartoons were packaged for TV in 1956 and re-released in color in 1971. Many merchandised items appeared in the 1930s at the height of Betty's popularity. Her continuing appeal has produced an even wider range of licensed items from the 1980s to the present.

BTY-1

❏ **BTY-1. "Ko-Ko" The Clown Doll By Schoenhut,**
1920s. Doll is 11.5" tall with wood body and two-piece fabric outfit. Pinned to the outfit is 7/8" diameter button reading "Schoenhut All Wood Perfection Art Doll/Strong, Durable And Unbreakable/Made In U.S.A." but we are uncertain if doll was issued with button. Attached to front of outfit is fabric ribbon reading "Ko-Ko Out-Of-The-Inkwell Productions Fleischer Studios, N.Y. 1922-25." This is a later addition by a collector. - **$1100 $2200 $3300**

BTY-2

❏ **BTY-2. Movie Theater Premium Flip Movie Booklet,**
1932. Russell Theater Maysville, KY. 1-5/8x2-1/4" with 40 black and white pages. - **$65 $165 $300**

BTY-3

❏ **BTY-3. "Movie-Land Cut Ups" Boxed Puzzle Pair,**
1932. Store item by Wilder Co. 7.75x9" boxed set of two full color jigsaw puzzles also picturing Bimbo and Koko. - **$250 $575 $1000**

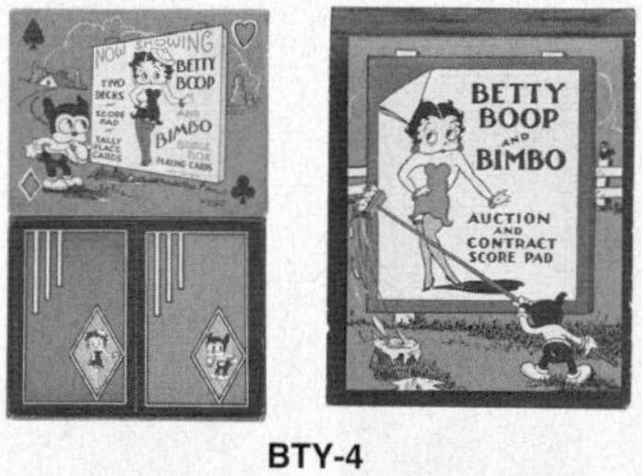

BTY-4

❏ **BTY-4. "Betty Boop And Bimbo Bridge Playing Cards,"**
c. 1932. Box measures 1x3.75x4.75" and holds 2-2/8x4.5" score pad and two 2.25x3.25" complete decks of cards. Shows Betty on billboard with Bimbo. Bottom of lid reads "Fleischer Studios." Score pad has illustration of Bimbo putting up billboard with Boop and reads "Betty Boop And Bimbo/Auction And Contract Score Pad." One deck has illustration of Betty in diamond -shape on green background, other is Bimbo on red background . - **$165 $325 $600**

BTY-5

❏ **BTY-5. "Betty Boop" Wood/Composition Doll By Cameo Doll Co.,**
c. 1932. Doll is 3.5x5.5x11.5" tall with wood body and arms, head and legs are painted composition. Doll wears fabric dress and underpants with flowers design. Attached to front is 1.5x1.75" fabric tag reading "Paramount Star Betty Boop." On chest is heart-shaped decal with "Betty Boop" name and copyright information. With Tag - **$550 $1100 $2200**
Without Tag - **$500 $1000 $2000**

BTY-6

BTY-7

❏ **BTY-6. Betty Boop/Gus Gorilla Fan Card,**
1933. Fleischer Studios. Autographed by Max Fleischer. Text refers to Paramount Pictures and NBC. Signed - **$40 $85 $200**
Unsigned - **$20 $50 $100**

❏ **BTY-7. Fleischer Studios Fan Card,**
c. 1933. Autographed by Max Fleischer. Text refers to Paramount, not NBC. - **$35 $80 $175**

BTY-8

❑ BTY-8. "Betty Boop" Rare Ingraham Pocket Watch,
1934. Metal case is 2" in diameter. Has incised design on back of case of Betty Boop with Bimbo and around them are a pair of stars and crescent moon. - **$2200 $4250 $7500**

BTY-9 BTY-10

❑ BTY-9. "Betty Boop in Snow White" Big Little Book #1119,
1934. Based on the Fleischer cartoon. Issued in softcover and hardcover format.
Softcover - **$50 $150 $350**
Hardcover - **$62 $186 $435**

❑ BTY-10. "Betty Boop in Miss Gulliver's Travels" Big Little Book #1158,
1935. Based on the Fleischer cartoon. -
$54 $162 $375

BTY11

❑ BTY-11. "Betty Boop's Movie Cartoon Lessons By Max Fleischer" Book,
c. 1935. Store item. Softcover 32-page illustrated guide "How To Make Movie Cartoons." -
$225 $450 $900

BTY-12

❑ BTY-12. "Betty Boop's Movie Theatre" Diecut Coloring Set Boxed,
c. 1935. 8.25" wide illustrated box lid has two diecut windows over crayons and larger diecut window opening around paper picture film that winds by wooden spools to show scenes from "Betty Boop's Circus." Paper filmstrip is designed for crayon coloring. -
$275 $550 $1000

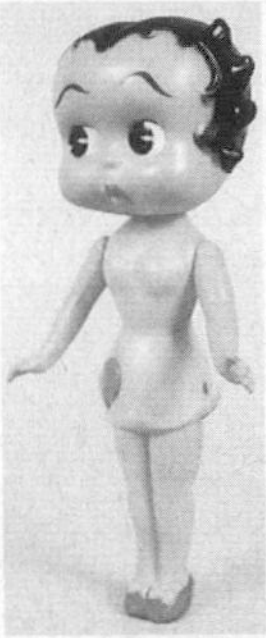

BTY-13 BTY-14

❑ BTY-13. Large Celluloid Jointed Figure,
c. 1935. Store item marked on reverse "Made In Japan." 7-3/4" tall with movable head and arms. -
$350 $700 $1300

❑ BTY-14. Enamel On Silver Luster Pin With Charm,
1939. Store item. 1-1/2" tall issued with the enamel on her dress in various single colors. Example shown has "New York World's Fair 1939" charm but also issued with other charms generally of a tourist destination nature.
With World's Fair Charm - **$50 $125 $250**
With Other Charm - **$35 $75 $175**
Version With Ankle-Length Dress and 1939 NYWF Charm - **$75 $175 $300**

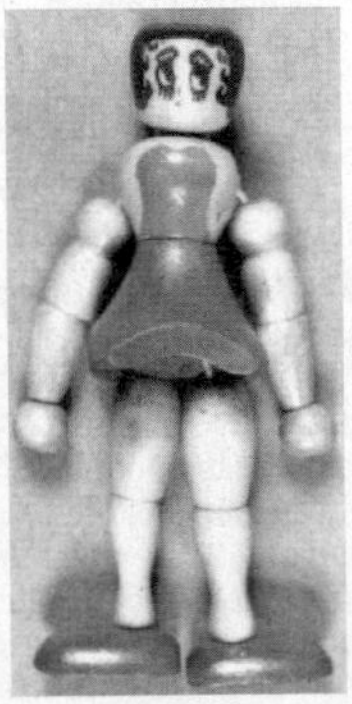

BTY-15 BTY-16

❑ BTY-15. Composition/Wood Jointed Doll,
1930s. Scarce in high grade. Store item by Cameo Products. 12-1/2" tall. -
$600 $1300 $2300

❑ BTY-16. Wood Jointed Doll,
1930s. Store item, 4-1/2" tall.- **$85 $165 $275**

BTY-17 BTY-18

❑ BTY-17 China Wall Pocket,
1930s. Store item. - **$80 $160 $275**

❑ BTY-18. Bisque Figure,
1930s. Store item. 3" size. - **$50 $100 $200**

BTY-19

❑ BTY-19. Betty Boop Bisque Figure With Movable Arms,
1930s. Bisque figure is 6" tall and marked "Copyright Betty Boop/Made In Japan."
- **$225 $450 $800**

BTY-20

❑ BTY-20. Betty Boop Boxed Figural Bisques,
1930s. Box is 1.5x3.5x5.5" with paper label holding four 3.25" tall figures of Betty each with different instrument. Includes horn, drum, accordian and violin. Name and copyright on back of each with "Made In Japan/Copyright Fleischer Studios" on bottom. Box - **$50 $100 $200**
Each Bisque - **$50 $100 $200**

BTY-21

❑ BTY-21. Betty Boop String Holder,
1930s. Painted plaster measuring 6x7x2.5" deep with recessed area in back to hold string. Hole at mouth, wire hanger at top reverse, as issued. Similar designs are known 6" tall and 10" tall. Small - **$100 $200 $400**
Medium - **$200 $400 $800**
Large - **$500 $1000 $1500**

BTY-22

❑ BTY-22. Mask,
1930s. "Bob-O-Link Shoes" ad on reverse. -
With ad - **$45 $75 $150**
Blank reverse - **$35 $65 $140**

BTY-23

❑ BTY-23. China Ashtray,
1930s. Store item. - **$85 $175 $265**

BTY-24

❑ BTY-24. Spanish Envelope,
1930s. Held transfer.
Envelope Only - **$12 $25 $45**
Complete - **$20 $35 $85**

BTY-25

❑ BTY-25. Betty Boop Postcard with Mickey Rooney,
1930s. - **$35 $80 $160**

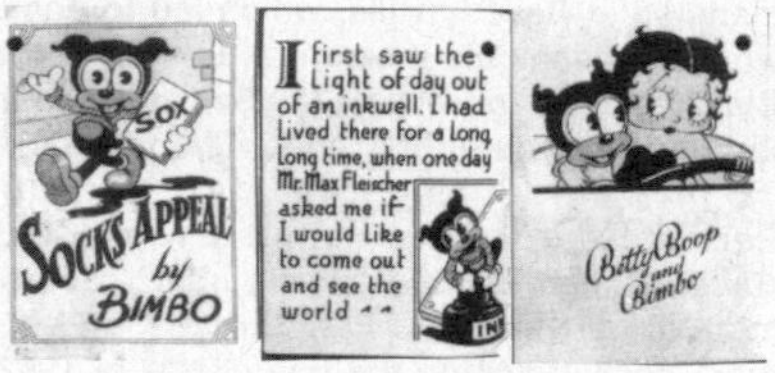

BTY-26

❑ BTY-26. "Socks Appeal By Bimbo" Booklet,
1930s. Given with pair of Bimbo socks. -
$65 $135 $225

BTY-27

BTY-28

BTY-29

❑ BTY-27. "Saturday Chicago American" Litho. Button,
1930s. From set of 10 various characters. -
$50 $100 $200

❑ BTY-28. "Ko-Ko/Max Fleischer's Talkatoons" Litho. Button #25,
1930s. Western Theater Premium Co. From numbered set of 50 either black, white, red or with additional yellow accent. - **$25 $50 $90**

❑ BTY-29. "Betty Boop" Cello. Button,
1930s. 1-1/4" in bright yellow, black and white with small copyright symbol "Fleischer Studios." Rare. - **$500 $1200 $3000**

BTY-30

BTY-31

❑ BTY-30. "Bimbo" Cello. Button,
1930s. Inscribed "A Paramount Star Created By Fleischer Studios". - **$40 $70 $150**

❑ BTY-31. Cello. Button,
1930s. Rim inscription "A Paramount Star Created By Fleischer Studios".- **$50 $100 $200**

BTY-32

❑ BTY-32. Rubber Eraser,
1930s. 2" wide printed top side in black on white rubber. Japan. - **$35 $75 $150**

BTY-33

❑ BTY-33. Betty & Koko Bisque Toothbrush Holder,
1930s. 5" tall painted figures in front of two slots for brushes. Curved base front is for toothpaste tube. Japan with Fleischer copyright. -
$325 $850 $1750

BTY-34

BTY-35

❑ **BTY-34. Carnival Doll,**
1930s. 14" tall painted chalkware on rounded base. - **$95 $200 $365**

❑ **BTY-35. Betty Boop Club Pinback,**
1980s. - **$15 $30 $60**

BTY-36

❑ **BTY-36. "Koko" Clown Figure,**
1990s. NM - **$80**

BTY-37

BTY-38

❑ **BTY-37. Ceramic Figure,**
2000. NM - **$40**

❑ **BTY-38. Wacky Wobbler Figure,**
2000. Black and white edition, limited to 3,000. NM - **$55**

The Beverly Hillbillies

Airing on CBS-TV, 274 episodes were shown between September 26, 1962 and May 23, 1971. The cast included the Clampett family, played by Buddy Ebsen as Jed, Irene Ryan as Granny, Donna Douglas as Elly May and Max Baer Jr. as Jethro. Created by Paul Henning who also wrote several episodes, directors included Richard Whorf and Robert Leeds.

The premise of the show had Jed Clampett discovering oil on the family's Ozark Mountain land and moving his family to a mansion in Beverly Hills, which led to some wonderful comedic moments. In reality, the Clampett mansion was at 750 Bel Air Road in Bel Air where outdoor scenes were filmed.

Series creator Paul Henning wrote *The Ballad Of Jed Clampett* theme song, recorded by Lester Flatt and Earl Scruggs, and the tune reached #44 on the pop charts in 1962. He also wrote the 1993 *Beverly Hillbillies* movie which starred Jim Varney, Cloris Leachman, Erika Eleniak and Lily Tomlin.

A DVD boxed set is due for release to which Jethro might exclaim "Wee Doggies!"

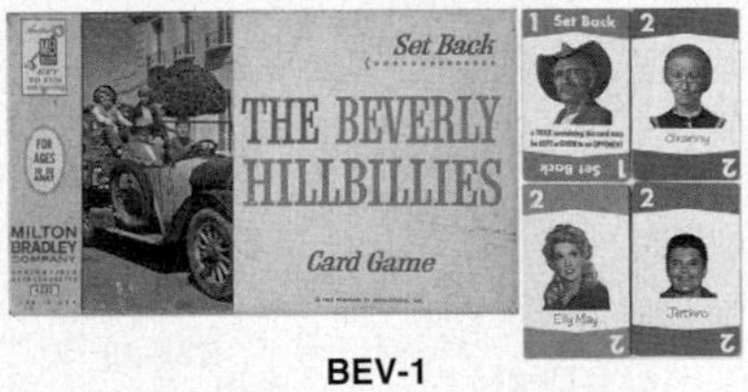

BEV-1

❑ **BEV-1. "The Beverly Hillbillies Card Game",**
1963. Milton Bradley. 6x10x1.5" deep box contains cast photo, deck of 42 cards, score pad, plastic storage tray with plastic chips. Cards feature Jed, Granny, Elly May and Jethro. - **$10 $20 $40**

BEV-2

❑ **BEV-2. "Elly May Of The Beverly Hillbillies Cut-Out Doll Book,"**
1963. Watkins Strathmore Co. 8.25x11" with 8 single-sided pages including two dolls and many outfits. Cover has doll image of Elly May. Back shows Beverly Hillbillies in their jalopy and Elly May doll in lingerie. Uncut - **$20 $40 $100**

BEV-3

❑ **BEV-3. "Kellogg's Corn Flakes" Cereal Box With Beverly Hillbillies Back,**
1963. 8.5x12.5x3" deep box with side panel offer for "Beverly Hillbillies Bubble Pipe" which could be obtained for 25-cents and one box top. Back panel has image of Beverly Hillbillies in their jalopy with information about differences in food production in 1947-1949 compared to 1963. Complete - **$50 $100 $200**

BEV-4

❑ **BEV-4. "The Beverly Hillbillies" Gum Card Set,**
1963. Topps. Set of 66, each 2.5x3.5". Fronts feature full color photos, backs have "Hillbillies Gags." Near Mint Set - **$400**
Each - **$1 $3 $6**

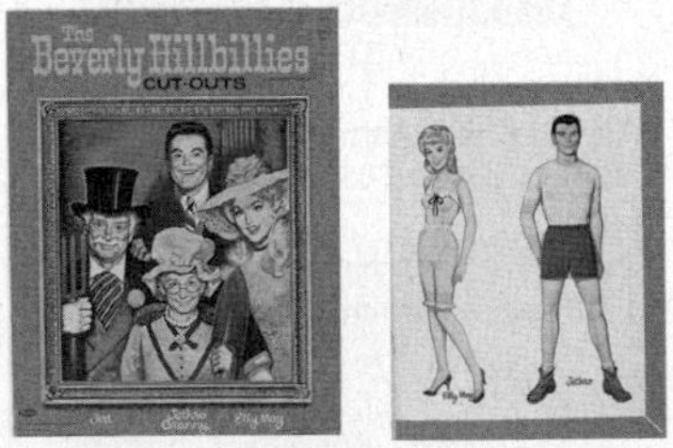

BEV-5

❑ **BEV-5. "The Beverly Hillbillies Cut-Outs" Paper Doll Book,**
1964. Whitman. 9.25x12" book with six single-sided pages and four punch-out dolls of Jed, Granny, Elly May and Jethro. Outfits include original hillbilly clothes and fine society clothes. Uncut - **$20 $40 $75**

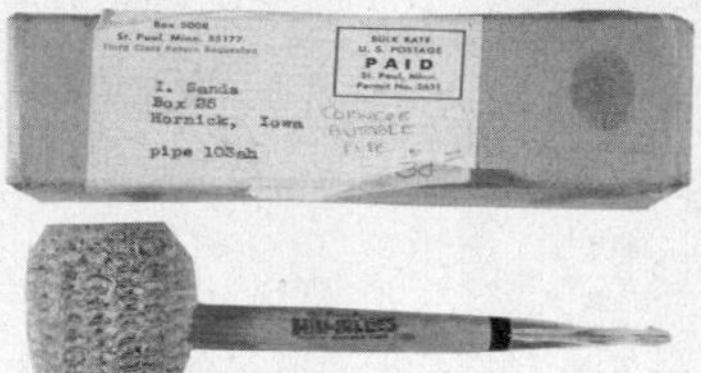

BEV-6

❑ **BEV-6. Beverly Hillbillies Pipe With Mailer,**
1965. TV premium. Corncob top pipe blows bubbles. - **$25 $50 $85**

BEV-7

❑ **BEV-7. "The Beverly Hillbillies" Sliding Tile Puzzle On Card,**
1960s. Roalex Company. 2.50x2.50x.25" thick plastic puzzle featuring Beverly Hillbillies characters. Puzzle is attached to 4.75x6" card that shows 5 images of puzzle in different positions.
Carded - **$100 $200 $300**
Puzzle Only - **$25 $50 $100**

BEV-8

❑ **BEV-8. "The Beverly Hillbillies" Cast-Signed Page,**
1960s. 10.25x13.5" magazine page showing Beverly Hillbillies in their jalopy signed in black felt tip pen by Donna Douglas, Buddy Ebsen, Max Baer and Irene Ryan who also added - "To Pat From Irene Ryan - Granny." Near Mint Same Or Similar - **$300**

Big Boy

In 1936 Bob Wian, running a little diner called Bob's Pantry in Glendale, California, added a double-decker cheeseburger to his menu. A few weeks later, according to legend, a chubby little neighborhood boy named Richard Woodruff walked in wearing oversized pants and suspenders. Wian was enchanted, dubbed him Big Boy, changed the name of the diner and began using an image of the boy as his advertising logo. Wian sold his first franchise to the Elias Brothers in Michigan in 1952, and other franchises quickly followed. The Elias Brothers of Warren, Michigan currently operates over 600 Big Boy restaurants in the US, Japan, Saudi Arabia, Thailand and Brazil. A giveaway comic book was started in 1956 and continued to 1996. Artists included Sheldon Moldoff, Manny Stallman and Sol Brodsky.

BIG-1

❑ **BIG-1. Big Boy Die-Cut Menu,**
1949. - **$22 $45 $90**

BIG-2

BIG-3

❑ **BIG-2. Big Boy Ad Card,**
1956. For Free comic. - **$15 $35 $85**

❑ **BIG-3. "Adventures Of The Big Boy" Comic Book #1,**
1956. Art by Bill Everett. - **$97 $291 $1400**

BIG-4

BIG-5

❑ **BIG-4. Ceramic Figural Ashtray,**
1950s. 3-3/4" diameter tray with 3" tall figure on rear edge. Marked only "Made In Japan." - **$80 $160 $265**

❑ **BIG-5. "Big Boy" Salt & Pepper Set,**
1950s. Pair of 4" tall ceramic figures. - **$75 $135 $235**

BIG-6

BIG-7

BIG-8

❑ **BIG-6. Early Litho. Button,**
1950s. Light green rim. - **$25 $45 $85**

❑ **BIG-7. "Nat'l Big Boy Club" Litho. Member Button,**
1960. - **$12 $25 $45**

❑ **BIG-8. Bobbing Head Figure,**
1960s. Painted composition figure with spring-mounted head. - **$200 $400 $750**

BIG-9

❑ **BIG-9. "Big Boy" Figural Bank,**
1960s. Hollow painted plaster with 3x4" oval base by 7.25" tall. Slot on back shoulders. - **$100 $200 $350**

BIG-10

❑ **BIG-10. Ceramic Salt & Pepper Set,**
1960s. - **$80 $160 $275**

BIG-11

❑ **BIG-11. Frame Tray Puzzle With Envelope,**
1960s. 6-1/4x9-1/4" with both sides in full color.
Near Mint With Envelope - **$100**
Puzzle Only - **$15 $30 $60**

BIG-12

❑ **BIG-12. "Manners Big Boy" Button,**
c. 1960s. 3.5" black/white cartoon art of him wearing "Manners" service cap. - **$20 $40 $75**

BIG-13

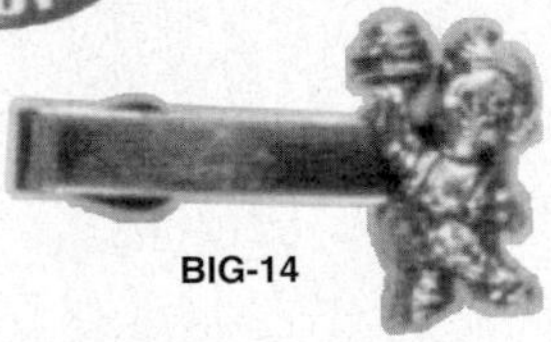

BIG-14

❑ **BIG-13. Club Member Litho. Button,**
c. 1960s. - **$10 $18 $30**

❑ **BIG-14. Silvered Metal Tie Bar,**
c. 1960s. "Big Boy" name on miniature figure. - **$12 $22 $45**

BIG-15

BIG-16

❑ **BIG-15. Vinyl Figure By Dakin,**
1970. - **$65 $135 $265**

❑ **BIG-16. "Adventures Of The Big Boy" Comic Book,**
1978. See The Overstreet Comic Book Price Guide for values of Issues #2 through #466.

BIG-17

❑ **BIG-17. Cloth Dolls,**
c. 1978. Dolls are Big Boy, Dolly and Nugget.
Each - **$10 $20 $40**

BIG-18

BIG-19

❑ **BIG-18. Vinyl Figure,**
1970s. - **$20 $35 $75**

❑ **BIG-19. Watch,**
1970s. - **$40 $80 $160**

BIG-20

BIG-21

❑ **BIG-20. Vinyl Figure Night Light,**
1970s. Electrical. - **$60 $115 $225**

❑ **BIG-21. Cloth Body Figure,**
1980. - **$15 $30 $50**

BIG-22

❑ **BIG-22. Limited Edition 50th Anniversary Watch in Box,**
1980. Produced by La Marque. Box snaps open and has "Big Boy" marked inside top. Big Boy name is on the dial. Boxed - **$375**

BIG-23

BIG-24

❑ **BIG-23. Limited Edition 5" Metal Figure,**
1980s. - **$22 $45 $95**

❑ **BIG-24. Big Boy Figure,**
1980s. - **$12 $25 $45**

BIG-25

BIG-26

❑ **BIG-25. Vinyl Figure,**
1980s. - **$12 $25 $45**

❑ **BIG-26. Commemorative Figure,**
1980s. - **$10 $20 $40**

BIG-27

BIG-28

❑ **BIG-27. Big Boy Figure,**
1990s. - **$10 $20 $45**

❑ **BIG-28. Bobbing Head Figure,**
1999. In box. NM - **$35**

Bill Barnes

Street & Smith began publication of its pulp "Bill Barnes, Air Adventurer" in February 1934. The title was changed to *Bill Barnes, Air Trails* in late 1935; then simply *Air Trails* from February 1937 to March 1939. He also appeared in the pulp *Doc Savage Magazine* in various 1939-1943 issues. Issues contained Bill Barnes air adventure stories, aviation news and features, and information on model planes. Barnes made his comic book debut in issue #1 of *Shadow Comics* in 1940 and had his own book from 1940 to 1943 under various titles: *Bill Barnes Comics*, *America's Air Ace Comics* and *Air Ace*.

BBR-1

BBR-2

❑ **BBR-1. "Bill Barnes Air Adventurer" Pulp Magazine,**
September 1935. Published by Street & Smith. - **$25 $45 $100**

❑ **BBR-2. "Bill Barnes/Air Adventurer" Gummed Paper Envelope Sticker,**
1930s. Street & Smith Co., publisher of Bill Barnes pulp magazine. - **$25 $40 $100**

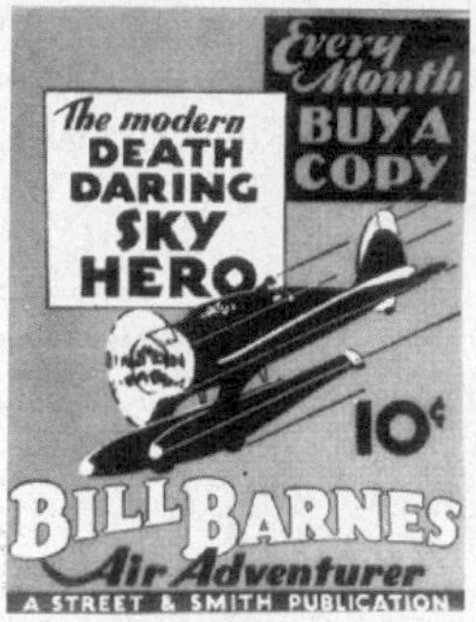

BBR-3

❑ **BBR-3. "Bill Barnes/Air Adventurer" 11x14" Window Card,**
1930s. Street & Smith Publications. Pictures example pulp magazine cover. - **$90 $185 $350**

BBR-4

❑ **BBR-4. "Bill Barnes Air Adventurer" Window Card,**
1930s. Street & Smith Publications. 10.5x13.5". - **$90 $185 $350**

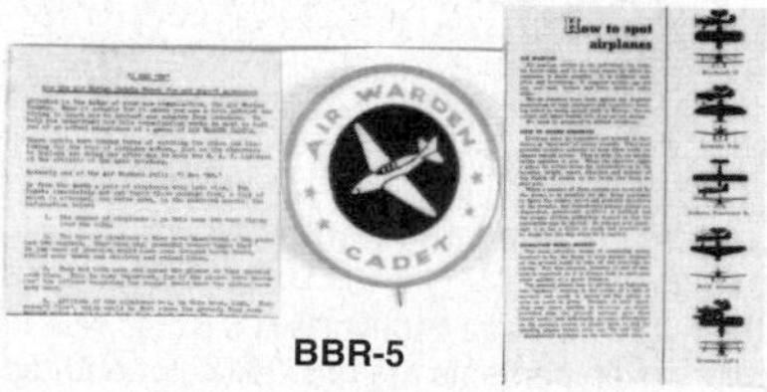

BBR-5

❑ **BBR-5. "Air Warden Cadets" Club Kit,**
c. 1943. Cello. Button - **$30 $60 $125**
Airplane Spotting Booklet - **$20 $40 $65**
Group Of Six Related Sheets - **$20 $40 $65**

Billy and Ruth

Billed as America's Famous Toy Children, Billy and Ruth and their dog Terry were the fictional stars of annual pre-Christmas toy catalogues published for the toy industry as early as 1936. Created by Philadelphia-based L.A. Hoeflich, the catalogues promoted the toys of different participating manufacturers. Retailers who subscribed to the service printed their own store information on the front cover and thus had a ready-made catalogue for their customers. In the late 1950s, as independent toy retailers went out of business, Billy and Ruth became casualties of the new marketplace.

BLR-1

❑ **BLR-1. Toy Catalogue,**
c. 1932. Various store imprints. 8-3/4x12" with 20 pages including Steelcraft, Lionel, Fisher-Price, Schoenhut, etc. - **$30 $60 $100**

BLR-2

❑ **BLR-2. "In Toy World With Billy And Ruth" Catalogue,**
1936. 32 pages of illustrated and priced period toys. - **$60 $110 $165**

BLR-3

BLR-4

BLR-5

❑ **BLR-3. Club Member's Cello. Button,**
c. 1936. Red on white 1-1/2". - **$18 $35 $70**

❑ **BLR-4. Promotional Cello. Button,**
c. 1936. - **$18 $35 $70**

❑ **BLR-5. Club Member Button,**
1940s. - **$25 $40 $60**

BLR-6

❑ **BLR-6. Christmas Toy Catalogue,**
1951. - **$20 $40 $80**

BLR-7

❑ **BLR-7. Christmas Toy Catalogue,**
1952. - **$20 $40 $80**

BLR-8

BLR-9

❑ **BLR-8. Christmas Toy Catalogue,**
1954. - **$20 $35 $70**

❑ **BLR-9. Christmas Toy Catalogue,**
1955. - **$20 $35 $70**

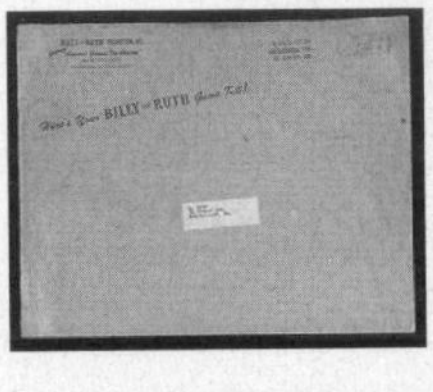

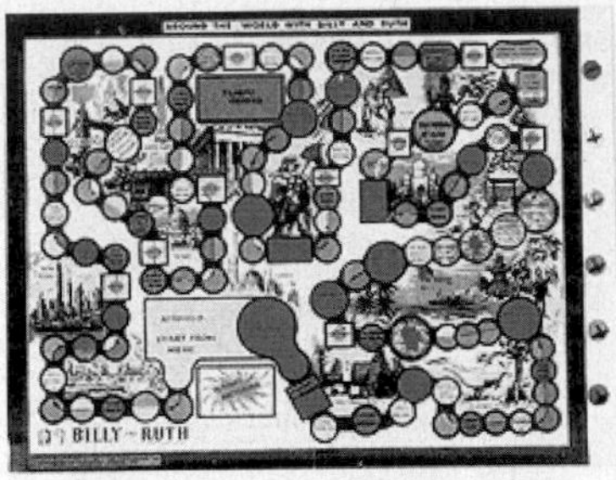

BLR-10

❑ **BLR-10. "Around The World With Billy And Ruth" Game Kit,**
1955. Billy And Ruth Promotion, Inc., Philadelphia. Mail envelope holding cover letter, instruction sheet, playing piece sheets to be scissored, paper playing board map opens to 13-1/2x17". Near Mint In Mailer - **$150**
Game - **$20 $35 $85**
Letter - **$8 $15 $35**

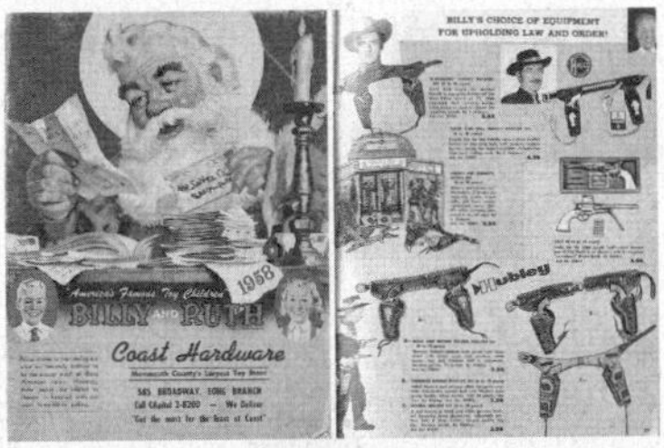

BLR-11

❑ **BLR-11. "Billy And Ruth 1958" Christmas Catalogue,**
1958. The 48-page catalogue is 8.5x11" with full color cover, contents are both full color and red, white and green. Pictured items include Disney TV pay phone, Popeye items of coloring set, target set and shooting game, Cheyenne game, Daisy guns and rifles, TV western gun and holster sets for Gunsmoke and Have Gun Will Travel, Gunsmoke MPC playset, vehicles, Lionel trains, etc. - **$20 $40 $80**

Billy Bounce

The weekly comic strip, drawn by noted *Wizard of Oz* illustrator W.W. Denslow began on November 11, 1901. Denslow drew the strip until August 1902 when C.W. Kahles took over. The strip continued until 1906. Apparently Billy Bounce earned some syndication beyond its home base of the *New York World*, as known premiums are mostly a few newspaper advertising pin-back buttons. A *Billy Bounce* hardcover book exists crediting W.W. Denslow, noted for his *Wizard of Oz* illustrations, as artist. Published in 1906 by M.A. Donohue and written by Dudley A. Bragdon, the book has 15 color plates.

BYB-1

BYB-2

❑ **BYB-1. "Compliments Of Billy Bounce" Cello. Button,**
1904. Pictured is W. W. Denslow character with copyright by T. C. McClure. - **$100 $250 $425**

❑ **BYB-2. "Philadelphia Press" Cello. Button,**
c. 1905. - **$90 $190 $350**

BYB-3

BYB-4

❑ **BYB-3. "Billy Bounce In The Sunday Sentinel" Cello. Button,**
c. 1905. Also comes with "Washington Times" imprint. - **$75 $175 $300**

❑ **BYB-4. "Billy Bounce" Hardcover Book,**
1906. Store item published by Donohue Co. Story by Denslow & Bragdon with pictures by Denslow (noted "Oz" artist). - **$100 $190 $350**

Black Flame of the Amazon

This radio adventure series was produced in California but apparently found air time only in the Midwest on the Mutual network. The syndicated program dramatized the adventures of explorer Harold Noice in the jungles of South America. Accompanied by his young friends Jim and Jean Brady, his aide Pedro, and the native guide Keyto, Noice did

battle with lawless types and dealt with wild animals and strange savage customs. Sponsors included Mayrose processed meats and Hi-Speed Gasoline. In Detroit the series aired on station WXYZ from February to May 1938, sponsored by Hi-Speed Gasoline.

BLF-1

❑ **BLF-1. Cardboard Ruler,**
1930s. Rare. Mayrose Meats. - **$60 $135 $240**

BLF-2

(ENLARGED VIEW)

❑ **BLF-2. Map 21 1/2 x 17",**
1930s. Rare. Radio show premium sponsored by Hi-Speed Gas. - **$220 $425 $650**

BLF-3

BLF-4

❑ **BLF-3. Stamp,**
1930s. Rare. Shows picture of Amazon warriors. One of 25 in set to place on map BLF-2. Each - **$5 $10 $20**

❑ **BLF-4. Paper Mask,**
1930s. Hi-Speed Gasoline. - **$30 $75 $150**

BLF-5

BLF-6

BLF-7

❑ **BLF-5. "Hi-Speed Explorer" Litho. Button,**
1930s. Hi-Speed gasoline. - **$10 $15 $30**

❑ **BLF-6. "Hi-Speed Explorer" Brass Compass Ring,**
1930s. - **$110 $250 $500**

❑ **BLF-7. "Paco Explorer" Litho. Club Button,**
1930s. - **$20 $45 $85**

Blondie

One of the world's most popular comic strips, Blondie was created by Chic Young (1901-1973) for King Features in 1930. This family comedy centers on the hectic misadventures of the Bumsteads--Blondie and Dagwood, their children Cookie and Alexander (originally Baby Dumpling), their dog Daisy and her pups, the neighbors Herb and Tootsie Woodley, Dagwood's boss Mr. Dithers and his wife Cora and the indestructible mailman Mr. Beasley. Notable ghost artists on the strip include: Alex Raymond, 1931-1933, who left to do *Flash Gordon* in 1934; Jim Raymond (Alex's brother) 1940's to 1970's; and Stan Drake 1980s. Dean Young, son of creator Chic Young, has been the writer for many years. Denis Lebrun is the current artist. The strip runs in 2300 newspapers worldwide. Hollywood turned out more than two dozen Blondie films with Penny Singleton and Arthur Lake in the lead roles and a half-hour radio program ran from 1939 to 1950, sponsored by Camel cigarettes, Super Suds and Colgate. Two TV series, in 1957 and again in 1968, failed to match the success of the strip or the movies. The term "Dagwood Sandwich" is so well known it became an entry in Webster's New World Dictionary.

BLD-1

❑ **BLD-1. "Baby Dumpling" Newspaper Button,**
1937. Litho for Blondie and Dagwood's offspring from series celebrating "Atlanta Georgian's Silver Anniversary." - **$50 $110 $225**

BLD-2

BLD-3

❑ **BLD-2. "Sunday Examiner" Newspaper Contest Litho. Button,**
1930s. Part of a set of various characters. - **$22 $45 $85**

❑ **BLD-3. "Blondie and Bouncing Baby Dumpling" Better Little Book #1476,**
1940. - **$10 $36 $78**

BLD-4

❑ **BLD-4. Esso Ad Folder,**
1940. - **$15 $30 $70**

BLD-5

❑ **BLD-5. Gasoline Promo Folder,**
1940. Esso Oil. Closed 5x7-1/2" sheet with full color cover and inner comic story that opens to final 10x15" with photo ad for lubrication services on reverse. - **$20 $40 $85**

BLD-6

❑ **BLD-6. "Blondie Goes To Leisureland" Paper Game,**
1940. Westinghouse Co. - **$25 $45 $100**

BLD-7

❑ **BLD-7. Daisy The Dog Stuffed Knickerbocker Doll With Original Tag,**
c. 1940. Store item. 8" tall with plastic strap collar. Text on tag refers to Columbia Pictures movie.
Doll - **$45 $125 $240**
Tag - **$15 $30 $60**

BLD-8 **BLD-9**

❑ **BLD-8. Blondie Playing Card Game,**
1941. King Features. Boxed. - **$25 $75 $150**

❑ **BLD-9. "Blondie, Cookie And Daisy's Pups" Better Little Book,**
1941. Whitman #1491. - **$10 $36 $78**

BLD-10 **BLD-11**

❑ **BLD-10. "Blondie Or Life Among The Bumsteads" Better Little Book,**
1944. Whitman #1466. - **$12 $36 $78**

❑ **BLD-11. "Blondie 100 Selected Top-Laughs" Book,**
1944. Store item published by David McKay Co. Reprint of 100 daily strips from late 1930s through early 1940s. - **$25 $45 $100**

BLD-12

❑ **BLD-12. Cut-Out Book,**
1944. Whitman. Paperdolls and clothing for Bumstead family members.
Uncut - **$55 $115 $250**

BLD-13 **BLD-14**

❑ **BLD-13. "Blondie - Papa Knows Best" Big Little Book #1490,**
1945. - **$11 $33 $72**

❑ **BLD-14. "Blondie and Dagwood in Hot Water" Big Little Book #1410,**
1946. - **$11 $33 $72**

BLD-15 **BLD-16**

❑ **BLD-15. "Comic Togs" Litho. Button,**
1947. From clothing maker series of various characters. - **$40 $75 $165**

❑ **BLD-16. "Blondie- Count Cookie in Too!" Big Little Book #1430,**
1947. - **$11 $33 $72**

BLD-17 **BLD-18**

❑ **BLD-17. "The Dagwood Sandwich" Boxed Tin Litho Kazoo,**
1947. Store item by Midwest Corp.
Box - **$60 $115 $220**
Toy Only - **$55 $110 $160**

❑ **BLD-18. "Blondie No Dull Moments" Better Little Book,**
1948. Whitman #1450. - **$11 $33 $72**

BLD-19 **BLD-20**

❑ **BLD-19. "Blondie and Dagwood- Everybody's Happy" Big Little Book #1438,**
1948. - **$11 $33 $72**

❑ **BLD-20. Dagwood Cello. Button,**
c. 1948. Philadelphia Inquirer newspaper. 1-1/4" dark red and cream from small set of comic character buttons issued to promote "Rotocomic" section. - **$50 $135 $250**

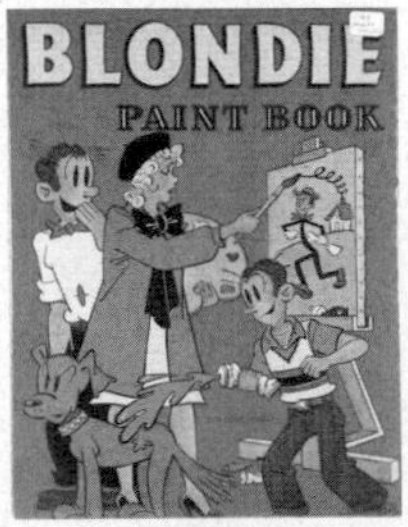

BLD-21 **BLD-22**

❑ **BLD-21. "Blondie- Fun For All" Big Little Book #1463,**
1949. - **$11 $33 $72**

❑ **BLD-22. "Blondie" Paint Book,**
1949. King Features copyright. - **$25 $65 $160**

BLD-23

❏ BLD-23. Blondie And Dagwood China Figures,
1940s. King Features Syndicate. 8" tall figures marked on base "Copyright KFS."
Each - **$55 $110 $160**

BLD-24

❏ BLD-24. "Dagwood the Driver" Tin Toy With Box,
1940s. Toy - **$250 $600 $1250**
Box - **$200 $300 $650**

BLD-25

BLD-26

❏ BLD-25. "Penny Singleton" Photo,
1940s. Radio and films Blondie portrayer. -
$12 $22 $45

❏ BLD-26. "Blondie" Coloring Book,
1950. King Features copyright. - **$25 $65 $160**

(Box)

(Blocks)

BLD-27

❏ BLD-27. "Blondie and Dagwood" Interchangable Blocks,
1951. With instructions in box. Family pictured on the front of the very colorful box. -
$75 $150 $250

BLD-28

BLD-29

❏ BLD-28. Refrigerators Advertising Cello. Button,
1960s. Westinghouse. 1-1/4" with Dagwood in red, white and blue patriotic outfit. -
$25 $55 $125

❏ BLD-29. Refrigerators Advertising Cello. Button,
1960s. Westinghouse. 1-1/4". Blondie wears red, white and blue patriotic outfit. -
$25 $55 $125

BLD-30

❏ BLD-30. Blondie and Dagwood Figures,
1983. 17" dolls have tags. Each - **$20 $45 $110**

BLD-31

❏ BLD-31. Daisy the Dog Plush Doll with Tag,
1985. - **$15 $35 $70**

Bob Hope

Born Leslie Townes Hope in Eltham, London on May 29, 1903, the family moved to Cleveland, Ohio in 1907 and Bob became a United States citizen. He boxed professionally under the name Packy West before going into vaudeville as a comedian in the early 1920s. Bob Hope went on to become one of the world's most beloved performers. His *Pepsodent Show*, which premiered on NBC in 1938, was one of radio's biggest hits for a dozen years. He made a series of successful "Road" movies with Bing Crosby and Dorothy Lamour from 1940 to 1962. He made countless TV appearances since 1950. He had also devoted much time and energy entertaining American troops all over the world. Hope was given a special Academy Award on five occasions, won the Kennedy Center Honors for Lifetime Achievement in the Arts (1985) and was accorded Honorary Knighthood (1998) by Queen Elizabeth II. He also sponsored the Bob Hope Desert Classic, an annual golf event for charity. At age 100, Hope passed away on July 27, 2003. Thanks for the memories, Bob.

BOB-1

BOB-2

❏ BOB-1. Post Card,
1930s. NBC Radio. - **$20 $40 $80**

❏ BOB-2. "They Got Me Covered" Book,
1941. Pepsodent toothpaste.
Book - **$12 $25 $50**
Mailer - **$10 $20 $30**

BOB-3

❑ **BOB-3. "Moonlight Becomes You" Song Sheet,**
1942. Featured in the movie hit "Road to Morocco" starring Bob Hope, Bing Crosby and Dorothy Lamour. - **$12 $20 $45**

BOB-4

❑ **BOB-4. "So This Is Peace" WWII Memoirs Book,**
1946. Simon and Schuster. Includes cartoon comparison of flying a P-38 plane to riding a bicycle pedaled by Superman. - **$12 $28 $55**

BOB-5

❑ **BOB-5. Bob Hope Figural Celebrity Mug,**
1940s. Figural painted and glazed ceramic mug is 5.5x4.5" tall. The handle to mug is that of a golf putter. From a celebrity series with bottom stamped "Hollywood Mugs-Barclay." Also has painted name of artist "Doya" on base.
- **$200 $400 $600**

BOB-6

BOB-7

❑ **BOB-6. Hair Pin Card,**
1940s. Store item. - **$12 $18 $40**

❑ **BOB-7. Framed Photo,**
1940s. From the war years. - **$20 $40 $70**

BOB-8

❑ **BOB-8. Hope-Lamour Birthday Card,**
1940s. Store item. - **$15 $30 $60**

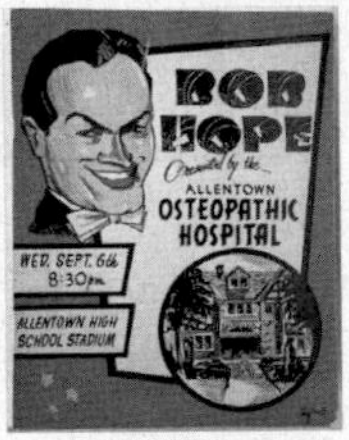

BOB-9

BOB-10

❑ **BOB-9. Hospital Visit Program,**
1950. Promotes a Bob Hope visit to a hospital. 78 pages containing several photos of Hope and a write-up. - **$10 $30 $65**

❑ **BOB-10. "Buttons and Bows" Song Sheet,**
1958. From the movie "Paleface" starring Bob Hope and Jane Russell. - **$12 $30 $65**

BOB-11

❑ **BOB-11. Bob Hope And Bing Crosby Figurines,**
c. 1950s. Each is 7-1/2" tall hollow ceramic figure standing on star-shaped base. Seen with underside of base either blank or ink stamped Wilfred Enterprises Holywood, Calif. Same company made Gene Autry item GAU-55.
Each - **$150 $300 $600**

BOB-12

BOB-13

❑ **BOB-12. Cigarette Lighter With 14K Gold Plate Finish,**
c. 1950s. Issuer unknown but made by "Florentine." - **$25 $40 $70**

❑ **BOB-13. Biography Booklet,**
c. 1960. NBC/Chrysler Corp. For Chrysler Theater series on NBC-TV. - **$12 $25 $40**

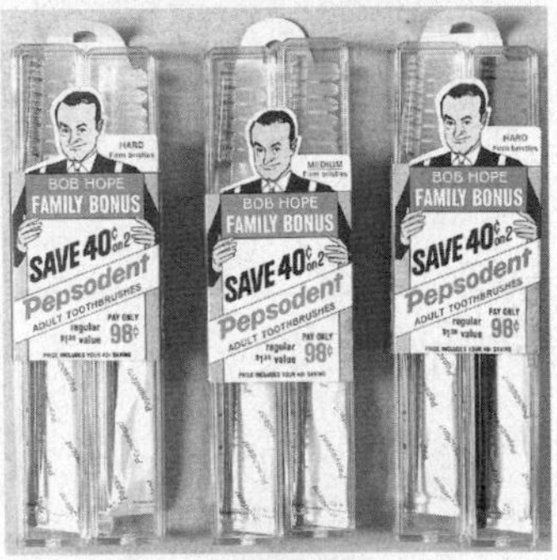

BOB-14

❑ **BOB-14. "Pepsodent" Toothbrush Containers With Hope Endorsement Sleeves,**
c. 1960. Three 2x6.5" plastic containers, each sleeved by Hope portrait and product endorsement by him. Each Double Pack With Slip Band Sleeve - **$12 $25 $40**

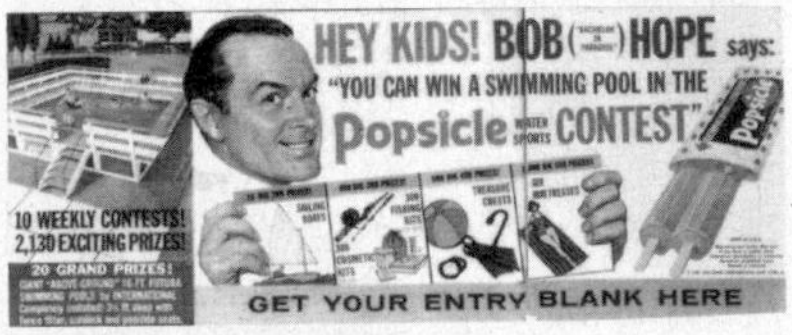

BOB-15

❑ **BOB-15. "Popsicle" 8x20" Contest Poster,**
1961. Joe Lowe Corp. Pictures water recreation prizes including grand prize of a swimming pool. - **$45 $85 $165**

BOB-16

❑ **BOB-16. "The World of Bob Hope" Premium Magazine,**
1969. NBC Television/Network/Texaco premium. 36 pages, mostly pictures. - **$10 $35 $80**

BOB-17

❑ **BOB-17. Health Care Promo Button,**
1960s. Black and white photo emphasizing "Health Care Is No Laughing Matter-August 17th." - **$12 $25 $45**

BOB-18

BOB-20

BOB-19

❑ **BOB-18. Bob Hope Veterans' Cause Photo,**
c. 1970. 3-1/2x3-1/2" card picturing him autographing veteran's leg cast with reverse inscription about craft kits given to hospitalized Vietnam veterans. - **$6 $12 $28**

❑ **BOB-19. "Vote Bob Hope" 3" Cello. Button,**
1976. NBC-TV. - **$15 $30 $55**

❑ **BOB-20. Plaster Statue,**
1979. Store item by Esco Products. 17" tall painted plaster from a series of personality statues. - **$30 $60 $115**

Bobby Benson

Bobby was the 12-year-old owner of a ranch in south Texas. With his cowgirl pal Polly and a cast of regulars, the *H-Bar-O Rangers* began on CBS October 17, 1932, created by Herbert Rice in Buffalo, New York. As long as the show was sponsored by H-O (Hecker's Oats) cereal, the ranch was called the H-Bar-O. When H-O dropped out as sponsor in 1936, the ranch became the B-Bar-B and the show continued until December, 1936. It was revived as *Bobby Benson and the B-Bar-B Riders* on the Mutual network from 1949 to 1955. Among the early cast members were Dead-End Kid Billy Halop as Bobby, Don Knotts and Al Hodge. A series of comic books was published by Magazine Enterprises from 1950 to 1953. Young artist Frank Frazetta did one of the covers.

BNS-1

BNS-2

❑ **BNS-1. Bobby Benson Star Badge,**
1932. 1st badge. Silver finish. Rare in any grade. - **$80 $160 $250**

❑ **BNS-2. Fan Club Photo,**
c. 1932. - **$20 $35 $60**

BNS-3

❑ **BNS-3. Display Sign,**
1933. Two sides. Promotes Bobby Benson premium money in Force cereal. Rare. 11" x 8-1/2". - **$250 $400 $535**

BNS-4

BNS-5

❑ **BNS-4. "H-Bar-O Transfer Book",**
1933. Paper cover holding strip of 12 sheets of transfer pictures to be cut apart and applied by water. - **$20 $65 $135**

❑ **BNS-5. H-Bar-O Ranger Belt,**
1933. H-O Cereals. Cowhide leather companion belt to BNS-8, unmarked and offered separately. - **$30 $60 $85**

BNS-6

❑ **BNS-6. H-Bar-O News,**
1933. Hecker H-O Co. 11x15" color print 16-page club newsletter edition including two center pages picturing 15 premiums. Pictured example is Vol. 1 #2. - **$20 $35 $75**

BNS-7

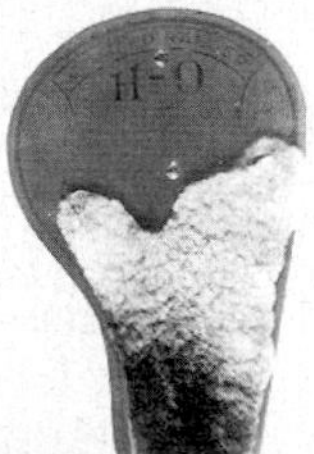

BNS-8

❑ **BNS-7. "H-Bar-O Ranger" Enameled Brass Star Badge,**
1933. Scarce. - **$85 $165 $265**

❑ **BNS-8. "H-Bar-O Ranger" Holster,**
1933. H-O Cereals. 7-1/2" long cowhide leather with wool cover panel, rear leather belt loop. See separately offered belt BNS-5. - **$45 $90 $175**

BNS-9

❑ BNS-9. "H-Bar-O Herald" Vol. 1 #1 Newspaper,
September 1933. Contents mention Benson radio broadcasts to begin September 18. - **$25 $40 $85**

BNS-10

❑ BNS-10. "H-Bar-O Rangers Club" Neckerchief,
1933. 20x32" issued by H-O Cereal. - **$20 $40 $80**

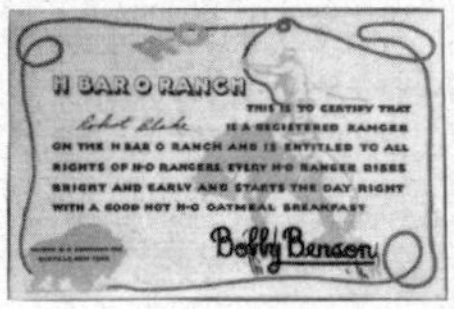

BNS-11

BNS-12

❑ BNS-11. Certificate,
1933. Hecker H-O Cereal. - **$15 $30 $70**

❑ BNS-12. Catalog,
1933. Hecker Oats Cereals. Six page color catalog. - **$35 $80 $135**

BNS-13

❑ BNS-13. "H-Bar-O Rangers Club" Cello. Button,
1933. - **$12 $20 $35**

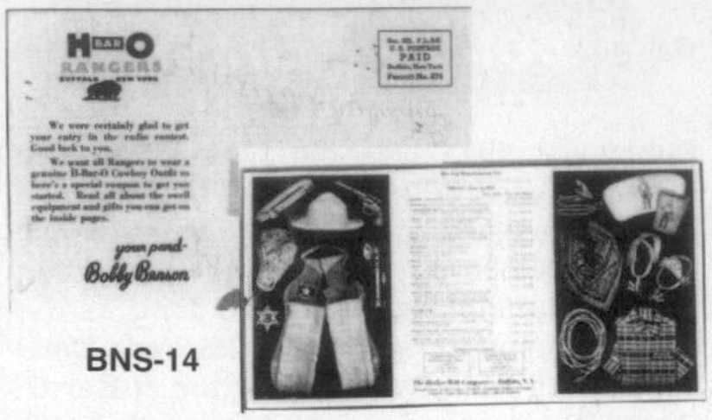

BNS-14

❑ BNS-14. "H-Bar-O Rangers/Bobby Benson" Premium Offer Folder,
1934. - **$30 $60 $110**

BNS-15

❑ BNS-15. H-Bar-O Newspaper Vol. 1 #3,
1934. Hecker Oats cereal. - **$20 $35 $75**

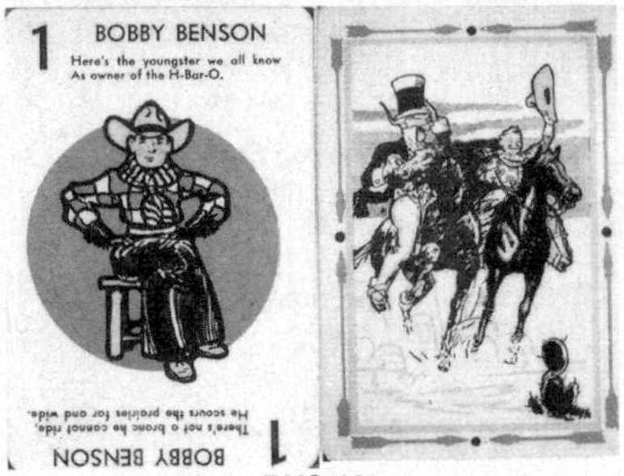

BNS-16

❑ BNS-16. "Bobby Benson's Game Circus,"
1934. Deck of 32 playing cards and instruction leaflet for 18 games.- **$30 $60 $100**

BNS-17

❑ BNS-17. "H-O" Cast Iron Cap Gun,
c. 1934. 7" long with cereal initials inscription on one side, offered in Bobby Benson premium folder of that year. - **$65 $150 $300**

BNS-18

❑ BNS-18. Code Rule,
1935. - **$30 $50 $100**

BNS-19

❑ BNS-19. Code Book,
1935. - **$18 $40 $80**

BNS-20

❑ BNS-20. Bobby Benson "B-Bar-B" Premium Humming Lariat,
c. 1935. Black and white with red accent color 2x4" with image of Bobby Benson on the front with lasso in hand. Back features cattle being lassoed and mentions B-Bar-B Riders.
- **$20 $35 $55**

BNS-21

BNS-22

❑ **BNS-21. "Bobby Benson In The Tunnel Of Gold" Booklet,**
1936. Hecker Cereals. - **$10 $30 $75**

❑ **BNS-22. "Bobby Benson And The Lost Herd" Book,**
1936. Hecker Cereals. - **$10 $30 $75**

BNS-23

❑ **BNS-23. Glass Bowl,**
1930s. Comes in green, yellow or red.
Each - **$12 $25 $40**

BNS-24

❑ **BNS-24. "Bobby Benson And The H-O Rangers In Africa" 19x25" Map,**
1930s. Map - **$125 $250 $400**
Envelope - **$30 $60 $120**

BNS-25

BNS-26

❑ **BNS-25. Star Junior Police Badge,**
1930s. Scarce. Gold badge with #808 which is number used on Bobby Benson premiums. - **$90 $170 $275**

❑ **BNS-26. "Special Captain" Cello. Club Rank Button,**
1930s. - **$25 $50 $90**

BNS-27

BNS-28

❑ **BNS-27. "Bobby Benson Ranger/H-Bar-O" Foil On Metal Badge,**
1930s. - **$30 $55 $110**

❑ **BNS-28. Fabric Scarf,**
1930s. Pictures and names the show's characters in white, dark brown and green on rose-colored background. - **$30 $75 $145**

BNS-29

❑ **BNS-29. Photos With Envelope,**
1930s. Ten different known. Photo not shown depicts Bart.
Envelope Or Each Photo - **$8 $15 $25**

BNS-30

❑ **BNS-30. Store Display Box With Glass Tumblers,**
1930s. Tumblers were obtained with two boxes of Force Toasted Wheat Flakes, six different characters.
Boxed Display - **$110 $275 $450**
Each - **$12 $20 $35**

BNS-31

BNS-32

❑ **BNS-31. "H-Bar-O Ranger" Enameled Brass Bracelet,**
1930s. - **$75 $125 $250**

❑ **BNS-32. "H-Bar-O Ranger/808" 2" Long Enamel Brass Tie Clip,**
1930s. Near Mint On Card With Mailer - **$325**
Tie Clip Only - **$45 $90 $145**

BNS-33

❑ **BNS-33. "20 Decals For You!" Mailing Folder,**
c. 1949. Folder text promotes program on Mutual Network. Folder holds four-panel strip of brilliant color decals. Complete - **$20 $50 $110**

BNS-34

❑ **BNS-34. B-Bar-B Riders Club Kit With Mailer Envelope,**
c. 1949. Contents of Bobby Benson humming lariat, photo, membership certificate.
Each Item - **$20 $50 $100**

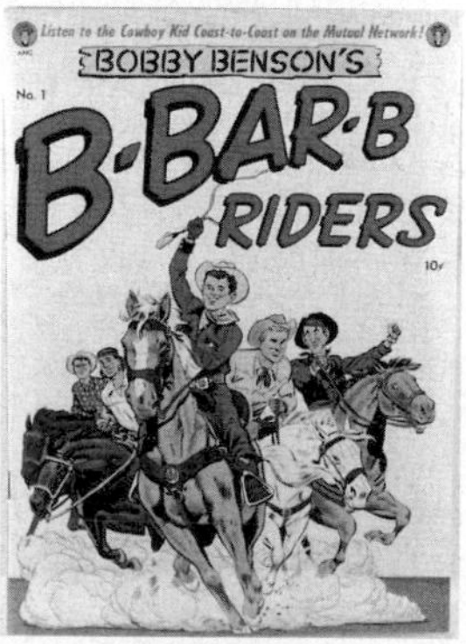

BNS-35

❑ **BNS-35. "Bobby Benson's B-Bar-B Riders #1" Comic Book,**
1950. Scarce. - **$41 $123 $575**

Bonanza

The story of the Cartwright family, set on their Ponderosa Ranch in Nevada in the 1860s, premiered on NBC in September 1959 and aired weekly until 1973--the second-longest Western series on television. One of the nation's most popular shows during most of the 1960s, it was also the first Western to be televised in color. The Ponderosa was a man's world, with Lorne Greene as the widowed father Ben and Pernell Roberts, Dan Blocker and Michael Landon as his sons Adam, Hoss and Little Joe. Roberts left the cast in 1965. Dan Blocker passed away suddenly in 1972 and the show ended early in 1973. The program often focused on the relationships between the characters rather than on typical Western violence. *Bonanza* is still being shown somewhere in the world every day. Special made-for-TV movie sequels including Michael Landon Jr. as a cast member are *Bonanza: The Return* (1993), *Bonanza: Under Attack* (1995) and *Bonanza: The Next Generation* (1998). The program's Nevada location north of Lake Tahoe, the Ponderosa Ranch, operated as an amusement park from 1968 until September 2004.

BON-1

BON-2

❑ **BON-1. "Bonanza Booster" 2-1/4" Cello. Button,**
c. 1960. - **$50 $100 $175**

❑ **BON-2. "TV Guide Cover Portrait",**
1961. Large high quality color matted photo from series sent to television stations. - **$30 $60 $145**

BON-3

❑ **BON-3. Arkansas Expo Sheet With "Bonanza" Stars,**
1962. 9x12" sheet printed on each side. - **$18 $30 $60**

BON-4

BON-5

❑ **BON-4. Fort Madison Iowa 2-1/4" Rodeo Button,**
1964. From series of event buttons beginning in 1957. - **$30 $60 $125**

❑ **BON-5. "Bonanza Days" 3" Cello. Button,**
1964. For celebration in site city of series, picturing all four original cast members. - **$35 $65 $135**

BON-6

❑ **BON-6. 33 RPM Record,**
1964. Chevrolet. - **$10 $18 $30**

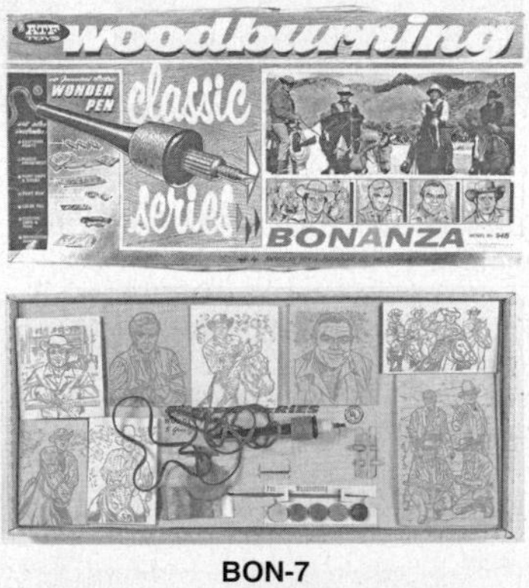

BON-7

❑ **BON-7. "Bonanza Woodburning" Set,**
1965. American Toy & Furniture Co. Inc. 12x25x1.75" deep box. Text includes "Classic Series/With Guaranteed Electric Wonder Pen/Set Also Includes/Additional Points. Plaque Assortment/Paint Chips & Brush/Paint Dish/Color Foil/Electric Cord & Plug/Instruction Manual." Set of eight plaques with red illustrations of all four Bonanza characters.
Near Mint Boxed - **$550**

BON-8

❑ **BON-8. "Ponderosa Ranch" Tin Cup,**
c. 1965. Visitors to tourist attraction Ponderosa Ranch purchased drinks in these. Pictures all four original stars. - **$8 $15 $30**

BON-9

BON-10

❑ **BON-9. "Bonanza" Enamel Diecut Brass Stickpin,**
c. 1965. European made, depicts Ben Cartwright on horseback. - **$15 $30 $50**

❑ **BON-10. "Adam" And "Joe" European Litho. 2-1/2" Stickpin Buttons,**
c. 1965. Each - **$18 $35 $75**

BON-11

❑ **BON-11. Real Photo European Stickpins Set,**
c. 1965. Four portrait pins featuring .75" brass luster frame around glossy photo without dot pattern. Likely Dutch with "Aster 32" on reverse.
Each - **$15 $30 $40**

BON-12

❑ **BON-12. "The Ponderosa Ranch Story" Booklet,**
1969. Ranch souvenir. - **$18 $28 $45**

BON-13

❑ **BON-13. "Ponderosa Ranch" Commemorative Beam Bottle,**
1969. 7" tall issued by James Beam Distilling Co. - **$20 $40 $80**

BON-14

BON-15

❑ **BON-14. Badge,**
1960s. Premium for TV series. Red stone in middle. - **$20 $40 $60**

❑ **BON-15. "Michael Landon/Little Joe" Fan Photo,**
1960s. - **$18 $30 $50**

BON-16

BON-17

❑ **BON-16. "Bonanza" Cello. Button,**
1960s. Australian issue picturing Lorne Greene. - **$40 $80 $135**

❑ **BON-17. Cast Members Premium Photo,**
1960s. Inscribed "Compliments Of Your Local Authorized Chevrolet Dealer." 8x10" glossy black and white. - **$10 $22 $40**

BON-18

❑ **BON-18. Bonanza Cast Restaurant Matches,**
1960s. Various franchises. Full color portrait of cast member on front with restaurant location on back.
Near Mint Unused Lorne Greene - **$22**
Near Mint Unused Michael Landon - **$33**
Near Mint Unused Dan Blocker - **$28**

BON-19

❑ **BON-19. Ben And Hoss Cartwright Sheriff Badges,**
1970s. Unmarked store item.
Each - **$25 $50 $85**

BON-20

BON-21

❑ **BON-20. Portrait Pins Made In Spain,**
1970s. Store items. 1" tall brass pin, each with mounted black and white glossy photo with color tinting on faces and outfits. Pictured are Lorne Greene, Michael Landon, Dan Blocker, Pernell Roberts. Each - **$12 $25 $40**

❑ **BON-21. "I Met Hoss Cartwright" Litho. Tin Tab,**
c. 1970s. Nickey Chevrolet, with backwards "K." - **$15 $30 $50**

Bonzo

English illustrator George Studdy (1878-1948) did art for various publications beginning in 1900, eventually turning to a more cartoonish style focusing on dogs. The *Studdy Dog* first appeared in *The Sketch* and on November 8, 1922 editor Bruce Ingram named him Bonzo. George Studdy's wonderful style and sense of humor made Bonzo immensely popular. He was featured in portfolios, books, figurines, games, puzzles, tableware, plush toys and literally hundreds of postcards. New Era Films produced 26 animated cartoons in 1924-1925 and Bonzo was one of the first neon signs put up in Piccadilly Circus in London in the 1920s.

The *American Weekly* newspaper supplement featured Bonzo on various full color covers from 1922 into the 1930s. The British published Dean Annuals featured him from 1935 into the late 1940s.

Today one can order hood ornaments, paperweights and trophies made from the original molds through the Lejeune Company.

BNZ-1

❑ **BNZ-41. "Bonzo" Glazed Cigarette Holder,**
1932. With "Studdy" - **$100 $200 $400**
Without "Studdy" - **$50 $100 $200**

BNZ-2

❑ **BNZ-2. Bonzo-like "I'm Salt/I'm Mustard/I'm Pepper" Glazed Ceramic Condiment Set,**
1930s. Unauthorized. Salt and pepper are each 3" tall with stoppers, mustard figure is 3.25" tall with removable head and ceramic spoon. - **$20 $40 $80**

BNZ-3

❑ **BNZ-3. Bonzo Vienna Bronze Style Tiny Metal Figure,**
1930s. 7/8" tall bronze figure of seated Bonzo. Example seen appears to read "Germany" under the base. - **$25 $50 $100**

BNZ-4

❑ **BNZ-4. Bonzo Brass Door Knocker,**
1930s. 1.5x5" back plate holds 1.5x3" unmarked, hinged Bonzo. - **$30 $60 $125**

BNZ-5

❑ **BNZ-5. Bonzo Bisque Figurine,**
1930s. 4" tall. Bottom reads "Made In Japan." - **$15 $25 $50**

BNZ-6

❑ **BNZ-6. "Bonzo's Annual" English Hardcover,**
1930s. Dean & Son Ltd. London. 8x10" with 124 pages. - **$35 $75 $175**

BNZ-7

❑ **BNZ-7. "Bonzo" Wood And Composition Doll,**
1930s. Doll is 3x3.5x7" tall. On chest is bone-shaped decal bearing his name, second decal appears on underside of one foot with his name and G.E. Studdy copyright.
- **$1000 $2000 $3000**

BNZ-8

❑ **BNZ-8. Mechanical "Bonzo Bank,"**
1930s. Bank is 2x3.5x7" tall tin litho marked "Bavaria" along with company logo that appears to be a double "S" in a circle. At bottom text reads "Press The Lever Lightly, Watch My Tongue Appear; Save A Penny Nightly, Make Your Fortune Here." - **$3000 $6000 $10,000**

Bozo the Clown

Bozo began his clowning around in 1946 on a kid's record album created by Alan Livingston, a former Capitol Records executive. Bozo's TV debut came in 1949 on Los Angeles television with Pinto Colvig, the voice on the records, playing the role. Colvig, who had actually been a circus clown, is also notable for being the voice of Goofy as well as Grumpy in Snow White for the Disney Studio. Numerous Capitol Record albums and Dell comic books built Bozo's reputation in the 1950s, and by the 1960s, syndicated television shows were hosted by nearly 200 Bozos in the U.S. and around the world including Willard Scott in Washington D.C.; now weatherman on *The Today Show.* Larry Harmon, an early Bozo, acquired the character rights in 1956 and licensed products since then carry his name. By the 1990s, Bozo shows were in steep decline. Chicago's station WGN, once home to the show with the most extensive production values, abandoned the successful weekday time slot in 1994 for Sunday morning at 7 A.M. and began mixing educational themes with pure clowning around. WGN taped the last Bozo show June 12, 2001.

BOZ-1

❑ **BOZ-1. "Bozo's Jungle Jingles" 78 RPM Record,**
1951. Capitol Records. Comes with colorful 4-page sleeve. - **$15 $30 $60**

BOZ-2

❑ **BOZ-2. "Bozo" The Clown Glazed Ceramic Figure,**
1950s. Figure has 3.75" diameter base and is 10.25" tall. Has name on sleeve. Holds dog under one arm. Opening at other hand, possibly produced as lamp, toothbrush holder or for holding simulated bunch of balloons. Copyright on back of base "C.R.I." (Capitol Records Inc.).
- **$20 $35 $70**

BOZ-3

❑ **BOZ-3. "I Am A Bozo Pal" Cello. Button,**
1950s. Serial number club button sponsored by WDSM-TV, Superior, Wisconsin. -
$15 $25 $40

BOZ-4

❑ **BOZ-4. "Bozo The Clown" Hassock,**
1950s. 10" tall store item by Knickerbocker. -
$30 $50 $90

BOZ-5

BOZ-6

❑ **BOZ-5. Bread Wrapper,**
c. 1950s. Colorful wrapper. - **$25 $50 $100**

❑ **BOZ-6. Soaky Toy,**
1965. - **$10 $25 $60**

BOZ-7

❑ **BOZ-7. Glass With Lid,**
1965. Held peanut butter. Set of five.
Each - **$10 $20 $33**
Lid - **$5 $10 $22**

BOZ-8

BOZ-9

❑ **BOZ-8. Mirror,**
1966. Promo for "Bozo Show." - **$10 $25 $50**

❑ **BOZ-9. "Bozo The Clown" Half Gallon Milk Carton,**
1968. London's Farm Dairy Inc. - **$12 $28 $55**

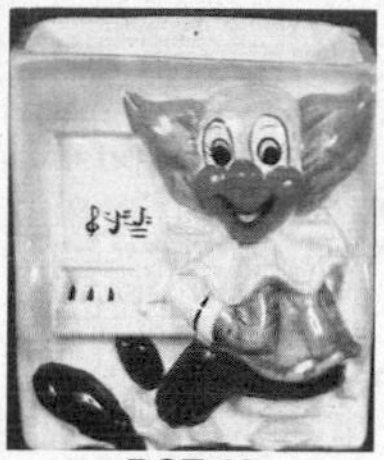
BOZ-10

BOZ-11

❑ **BOZ-10. Glazed Ceramic Planter,**
1960s. Store item. 5" tall depicting Bozo at piano. - **$25 $40 $80**

❑ **BOZ-11. "Bozo The Clown" Litho. Tin Button,**
1960s. Large, 3-1/2", colorful and scarce. -
$25 $50 $75

BOZ-12

❑ **BOZ-12. "Bozo The Clown Dancing Toy" Vinyl Wind-Up,**
1960s. Store item by Lakeside Toys. 5" tall in box with cellophane window.
Box - **$15 $25 $40**
Toy - **$20 $35 $50**

BOZ-13

BOZ-14

❑ **BOZ-13. Patch And Membership Card,**
1960s. TV promo for "Bozo Show." Store bought. - **$12 $25 $40**

❑ **BOZ-14. Plastic Push Puppet,**
1960s. Store item by Kohner. - **$15 $25 $50**

BOZ-15

BOZ-16

❑ **BOZ-15. Savings Club Of America Button,**
1960s. Capitol Records and Harmon copyrights. - **$22 $40 $70**

❑ **BOZ-16. Plaster Figure Bank,**
1960s. Large 18.5" tall painted figure with name on front base and reverse copyright by Capitol Records. - **$30 $60 $135**

BOZ-17

BOZ-18

❑ **BOZ-17. Plastic Portrait Ring,**
1960s. - **$20 $50 $90**

❑ **BOZ-18. "I Visited Bozo's Circus" Litho. Button,**
c. 1970s. WGN-TV (Chicago). - **$6 $12 $20**

BOZ-19

BOZ-20

❑ BOZ-19. Illuminated Plastic Snow Dome,
c. 1970s. Store item, battery operated. - **$45 $85 $165**

❑ BOZ-20. "Bozo Is Love" 3" Cello. Button,
c. 1970s. Various TV stations. Pictured example from Grand Rapids, Michigan. - **$5 $10 $20**

BOZ-21

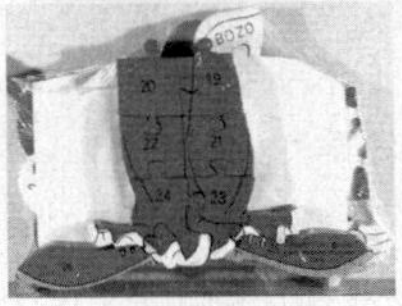

BOZ-22

❑ BOZ-21. Bozo Valentines in Box,
1996. 48 valentines with 3 cards on back of box. - **$20**

❑ BOZ-22. Bozo Block Puzzle,
1997. © Larry Harmon Pictues Corp. Figure is 11 1/2" tall when completed. - **$10 $20 $35**

BOZ-23

BOZ-24

❑ BOZ-23. Talking Bozo Bean Figure,
1999. 18" tall. Unstable printing on gloves. Ink rubs off easily. Ink rubs off nose too.
With tag and label - **$33**

❑ BOZ-24. Wacky Wobbler Figure,
2001. In box. - **$30**

BOZ-25

BOZ-26

❑ BOZ-25. Die-Cast Metal Car,
2000. Team Lightning. Carded - **$16**

❑ BOZ-26. Bozo Plush Doll,
2001. With tag. - **$28**

The Brady Bunch

Created and written by Sherwood Schwartz, the series ran on ABC-TV from September 26, 1969 through March 8, 1974 comprising five seasons and 117 episodes. The plot involved a widowed architect with three sons who marries a single mother with three daughters. The cast included Florence Henderson as Carol, Robert Reed (1932-1992) as Mike, Barry Williams as Greg, Christopher Knight as Peter, Mike Lookinland as Bobby, Maureen McCormick as Marcia, Eve Plumb as Jan, Susan Olsen as Cindy and Ann B. Davis as housekeeper Alice. The theme song was written by Sherwood Schwartz and Frank DeVol.

The series spawned a stage play, *The Real Live Brady Bunch* and Filmation produced an animated series between 1972 and 1974. NBC aired ten episodes of *The Brady Wives* which led to *The Brady Girls Get Married* two hour movie in 1981. CBS aired six episodes of *The Bradys* in 1990. Paramount released two feature films: *The Brady Bunch Movie* in 1995 and *A Very Brady Sequel* in 1996. The TV series still airs at least once a day somewhere in the world.

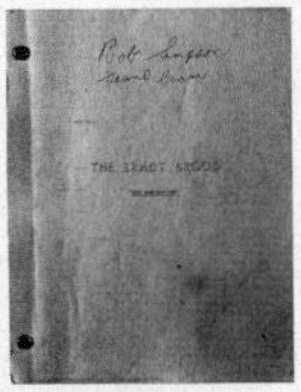

BRB-1

❑ BRB-1. Historic Brady Bunch Original TV Script For The First Episode Under Original Show Title "The Brady Brood,"
1968. 8.5x11". 43 pages on pink paper. Cover reads "The Brady Brood" followed by episode name "The Honeymoon." Title page reads "Last Final Revised Draft/First Episode October 2, 1968." - **$200 $500 $900**

BRB-2

❑ BRB-2. "TV Tab" With Brady Bunch Feature,
1970. 7.5x10.5" publication that was a supplement to western New York newspaper "Democrat and Chronicle" for week of November 15-21, 1970. Features one-page article on Ann B. Davis. - **$5 $10 $20**

BRB-3

❑ BRB-3. "The Brady Bunch" Lunch Box With Thermos,
1970. King-Seeley Thermos Co. 7x9x4" deep metal lunch box and 6.5" thermos with plastic cap. Shows classic images from the TV show.
Box - **$150 $300 $600**
Bottle - **$35 $75 $150**

BRB-4

❑ BRB-4. "The Brady Bunch Hex-A-Game,"
1973. Laramie Corp. 5x7.5" blister card with cast photo contains plastic hexagonal-shaped game pieces with stickers depicting different types of fruit. Carded - **$8 $15 $30**

BRB-5

❑ **BRB-5. "The Brady Bunch Magic Slate."**
1973. Whitman. 8.5x14" die-cut cardboard includes stylus. Has illustrations of the 8 family members and Alice. - **$20 $40 $65**

Breakfast Club

Don McNeill's *Breakfast Club*, a happy blend of Midwestern corn and audience participation, ruled morning radio for most of its 34 years on the air (1933 to 1968)--one of the longest-running network radio shows ever. The program, broadcast from Chicago, was essentially spontaneous and unrehearsed, combining contributions sent in by listeners, songs, prayers, marches around the breakfast table, poetry, anecdotes and occasional interviews with guest stars. There were many sponsors over the years. McNeill's familiar closing line-- "Be good to yourself"-- typified the warmth and charm of this popular and successful program. A TV simulcast in 1954 did not catch on. McNeill (1908-1996) jokingly ran for President in 1948.

BRK-1

❑ **BRK-1. Club Member Folder Kit,**
1944. Folder has contest and new member forms, comes with "Victory Garden" card.
Folder - **$20 $40 $70**
Card - **$8 $15 $30**

BRK-2

BRK-3

❑ **BRK-2. Don McNeill Club Book,**
1944. Says "Good Morning Breakfast Clubber & Good Morning to Ya" on cover. Contest rules & large photo of radio show cast & band. -
$15 $35 $70

❑ **BRK-3. "Don's Other Life..." Hardcover Book,**
1944. 7-7/8x9-1/4" with 64 pages credited as "By The First Lady Of The Breakfast Club Kay McNeill." - **$10 $25 $55**

BRK-4

BRK-5

❑ **BRK-4. Paper Sticker,**
1948. Full color 2x2-7/8" sticker gummed on reverse showing Woody Woodpecker carrying campaign sign. - **$5 $10 $15**

❑ **BRK-5. Don McNeill Featured In Radio Mirror Magazine,**
1948. July, 1948 issue features Don McNeill and family on cover with photos and major story about him on the inside. The Radio Mirror Magazine was to radio as TV Guide is to television. This issue is also important because it was one of the transition mags to also include television material. On the cover, note the small words after "Radio." Inside are the first photos of Buffalo Bob and Howdy Doody with a picture of the 1st 20-seat Peanut Gallery. The Howdy Doody marionette is the same as the one pictured on the pinback when Howdy was running for President and the Howdy photo is totally different than the one we are used to seeing. -
$30 $55 $85

BRK-6

BRK-7

❑ **BRK-6. "Don McNeill For President" Litho. Button,**
c. 1948. ABC Breakfast Clubs. - **$8 $12 $25**

❑ **BRK-7. "Don McNeill For President" Litho. Button,**
c. 1948. 2 1/2". Scarcer version. - **$15 $30 $60**

BRK-8

BRK-9

❑ **BRK-8. Club Charter Member Card,**
1940s.- **$10 $25 $50**

❑ **BRK-9. Fan Club Folder,**
1940s. - **$10 $25 $45**

BRK-10

❑ **BRK-10. Don McNeill's Breakfast Club Sign 12x36",**
1940s. Promotes radio show and victory bond drive in drug stores. - **$60 $135 $240**

BRK-11

BRK-12

❑ **BRK-11. Don McNeill Club Card,**
1940s. Postcard premium from the radio show. -
$15 $30 $50

❑ **BRK-12. "Don McNeill Sent Me" Litho. Button,**
c. 1950. Apparently to be worn to grocery or other retail store. - **$10 $18 $30**

BRK-13

BRK-14

❑ **BRK-13. Don McNeill's Breakfast Club Book,**
1953. Radio premium. "Twenty Years of Memory Time." - **$20 $45 $80**

❑ **BRK-14. "20 Years Of Corn" Booklet,**
c. 1953. - **$10 $20 $40**

BRK-15

BRK-16

❑ **BRK-15. "Kiddie Party Ideas" Booklet,**
1950s. Fritos. - **$30 $90 $160**

❑ **BRK-16. "Don McNeill/Himself Hide-Away" 2-1/4" Cello. Button,**
1950s. - **$12 $25 $50**

BRK-17

BRK-17. Various Yearbooks,
1940s-1950s. Issued annually.
❑ 1942 - **$10 $20 $60**
❑ 1947 - **$8 $15 $50**
❑ 1948 - **$8 $15 $50**
❑ 1950 - **$7 $15 $50**
❑ 1954 - **$7 $12 $45**

Breakfast in Hollywood

Radio veteran Tom Breneman was the host of *Breakfast at Sardi's* on the Blue network until he bought his own restaurant in 1943 and started broadcasting *Breakfast with Breneman.* The program, a variety show with audience participation, soon changed its name to *Breakfast in Hollywood* and aired on the ABC network with Breneman as host until his untimely death in 1948. Kellogg's cereals sponsored the show from 1945 to 1948. A United Artists film version was released in 1946 featuring Breneman, Bonita Granville, Beulah Bondi, Spike Jones, the King Cole Trio, and other Hollywood notables.

BHL-1

BHL-2

❑ **BHL-1. Tom Breneman's Book,**
1943.Fifty page premium for breakfast. Pictures Orson Welles, Jimmy Durante, Lum & Abner, Xavier Cugat and others. - **$20 $35 $50**

❑ **BHL-2. Premium Postcard,**
1943. Features Tom Breneman and Bob Hope.- **$10 $20 $30**

BHL-3

❑ **BHL-3. Tom Breneman's Booklet,**
1945. Ivory Flakes. Eight page premium features Hedda Hopper, Lum & Abner and others. Has "Breakfast in Hollywood" song on back. Has 25¢ cover. - **$15 $30 $60**

BHL-4

BHL-5

❑ **BHL-4. Tom Breneman's Ticket Postcard,**
1945.Premium ticket that can be used as postcard after attendance at show. - **$10 $20 $35**

❑ **BHL-5. "Tom Breneman's Magazine" First Issue,**
1948. Farrell Radio Magazine Inc. Volume 1 #1 from January with 128 pages. - **$12 $25 $50**

BHL-6

BHL-7

BHL-8

❑ **BHL-6. Tom Breneman's Peeks Book,**
1940s. Kellogg's Cereal. Photos of famous stars and a behind the scenes look at a movie breakfast in Hollywood - **$15 $35 $60**

❑ **BHL-7. Peeks Book Mailer,**
1940s. Kellogg's Cereal. - **$5 $10 $15**

❑ **BHL-8. Tom Breneman Standee,**
1940s. 10" tall. Promotes Pep cereal. Rare. - **$85 $175 $325**

Bringing Up Father

Cartoonist George McManus (1884-1954) drew *The Newlyweds* comic strip, also known as *Their Only Child/Snookums* between 1904 and 1916 but had a new idea. *Bringing Up Father* began as a daily strip on January 12, 1913 with a Sunday page following on April 14, 1918. The basic premise had Jiggs, Maggie and their lovely daughter Nora winning the Irish Sweepstakes. Jiggs went from being a laborer to wearing a tuxedo, playing cards and eating corned beef and cabbage with the boys at Dinty Moore's restaurant as Maggie and Nora constantly strive to bring him up to their perceived social standing.

Hearst's produced nine cartoons between 1916 and 1918 and also released two reel live action films 1920-1921. Gus Hill produced Broadway shows beginning in 1914 with various productions touring the country until 1928. MGM released a silent feature film in 1928 and Monogram released five feature films between 1946 and 1950.

Zeke Zekley was George McManus's assistant on the strip between 1935 and 1954, a period some consider the best with wonderful draftsmanship, art deco stylizations and great sight gags. After McManus passed away, numerous successors continued the strip including: Vernon Greene, Frank Fletcher, Hal Campagna and Frank Johnson. The strip ended on May 28, 2000 but is not forgotten by collectors.

BRF-1

❑ **BRF-1. "Bringing Up Father" Jiggs Cello Button,**
c. 1918. Issued with board game. 1/2".
- **$10 $20 $30**

BRF-2

❑ **BRF-2. George McManus Bringing Up Father Pre-1920 Daily Comic Strip Original Art,**
c. 1918. 7-3/8x19-1/8" thin art board has five 5.5x17.75" India ink panels. Signed in ink at bottom of last panel by creator "G. McManus." Same Or Similar - **$200 $400 $750**

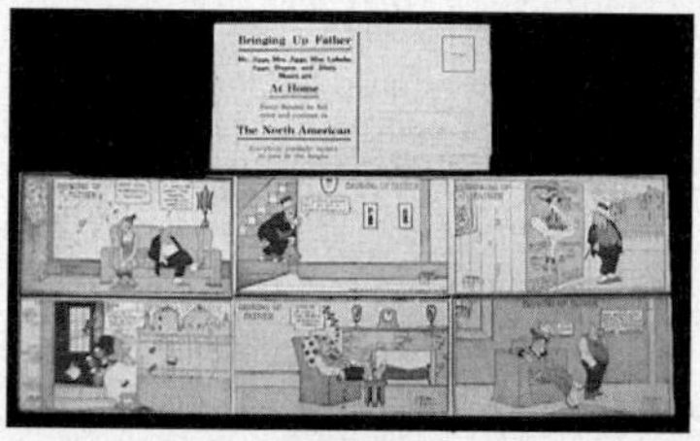

BRF-3

❑ **BRF-3. "Bringing Up Father At Home Every Sunday In The North American" Postcards,**
1919. The Star Co. promoting newspaper. Full color 3-5/8x6-5/8" with at least six known. Each - **$6 $18 $30**

BRF-4

BRF-5

❑ **BRF-4. Bringing Up Father Comic Strip Promo Diecut Jiggs Figure,**
c. 1920. 8-1/8" tall stiff paper with original pink string attached at die-cut hole on top of hat. Reverse text "Maggie And I Will Be With You In The Baltimore American Beginning October 7th." - **$15 $30 $60**

❑ **BRF-5. "Bringing Up Father Fifth Series" Comic Strip Reprint Book,**
1921. Cupples & Leon Co. 9-7/8x7-7/8" contains 48 pages of daily comic strip reprints. - **$25 $100 $250**

BRF-6

❑ **BRF-6. "Bringing Up Father 6th Series" Comic Strip Reprint Book,**
1922. Cupples & Leon Co. 9-7/8x9-7/8" contains 48 pages of comic strip reprints. - **$25 $100 $250**

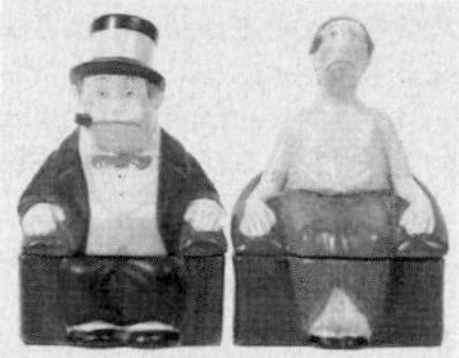

BRF-7

❑ **BRF-7. "Bringing Up Father" Ceramic Candy Dish Set,**
1923. Rare. 4" tall. Set - **$150 $300 $450**

BRF-8

❑ **BRF-8. "Bringing Up Father/Maggie/ Jiggs" Schoenhut Dolls In Original Box,**
1924. Distributed by George Borgfeldt & Co. 9x13x2.5" deep box with string attached to bottom to hold characters in place for display. Maggie figure is 9", Jiggs is 7" with painted composition heads, wooden bodies and fabric clothing. Both have jointed arms, legs and necks. Includes 3" wooden rolling pin and 2" wooden lunch bucket. Box - **$100 $200 $400**
Jiggs - **$125 $250 $500**
Maggie - **$125 $250 $500**

BRF-9

❑ **BRF-9. Bringing Up Father Maggie And Jiggs Boxed German Wind-Up Toy ,**
1924. Nifty. Box is 5.75x6.75x3" deep with illustrated paper label on the lid. Tin litho toy with built-in key is 2.5x7.25x5.25" tall. The outfits of both figures come in two totally different styles and on this one, Jiggs is depicted with striped pants and Maggie with polka dot skirt. On the other version, both are in a solid single color. Each 3.75" figure is attached to a wheeled platform and platforms are connected by a thin flat tin strip. Box - **$300 $600 $1200**
Toy Either Version - **$500 $1000 $1650**

BRF-10

BRF-11

❑ **BRF-10. "Bringing Up Father Series 9" Comic Strip Reprint Book,**
1925. Cupples & Leon Co. 9-7/8x9-7/8" contains 48 pages of daily comic strip reprints. - **$25 $100 $250**

❑ **BRF-11. "Bringing Up Father The Big Book" Hardcover,**
1926. Cupples & Leon. 10x10.25" with 142 pages featuring three regular issues of daily strips as single unit. Book - **$127 $508 $1000**
Dust Jacket - **$60 $225 $325**

BRF-12

❑ **BRF-12. Maggie/Jiggs/Daughter Large Painted Chalk Figures,**
c. 1920s. Ye Towne Gossip San Francisco, Calif. Figures are Maggie - 9.5" tall, Jiggs - 8.5" tall and Nora - 9" tall. Bottom of each is stamped "Copyrighted By Geo. McManus/Manufactured By Ye Towne Gossip San Francisco, Calif." Each - **$25 $50 $100**

BRF-13

❑ **BRF-13. Bringing Up Father Jiggs German Carnival Bumper Car Wind-Up,**
1920s. Tin litho toy is 3.5x4x5.25" with built-in key. Marked "Made In Germany."
- $1800 $3500 $6000

BRF-14

❑ **BRF-14. Sunday Comic Section 7x11" Cardboard Sign With Jiggs,**
1920s. Boston Sunday Advertiser. -
$50 $100 $200

BRF-15

❑ **BRF-15. "Bringing Up Father Series No. 18" Comic Strip Reprint Book,**
1930. Cupples & Leon Co. 9-7/8x9-7/8" with 48 pages of comic strip reprints. - **$40 $200 $375**

BRF-16

❑ **BRF-16. "Bringing Up Father In Gay New York" Song Folio With Crossword Puzzle,**
c. 1930. Harold Rossiter Music Co. 9.25x12.25" contains 16 pages of music for stage productions of various shows with copyright dates ranging from 1911 to 1930. - **$25 $50 $85**

BRF-17

❑ **BRF-17. "I Smoke Edgeworth Tobacco" Jiggs Figural Display,**
c. 1930. 10" tall painted plaster display. Front of base reads "Father." - **$150 $300 $600**

BRF-18

BRF-19

❑ **BRF-18. "Bringing Up Father" Reprint Book Rare High Number 20 In Series,**
1931. Cupples & Leon Co. 10x10" daily strip reprint book by McManus has 48 pages. - **$40 $200 $375**

❑ **BRF-19. "Bringing Up Father Series No. 22" Comic Strip Rare Reprint Book,**
1932. Cupples & Leon Co. 9-7/8x9-7/8" with 48 pages of comic strip reprints. - **$60 $300 $550**

BRF-20

❑ **BRF-20. "Bringing Up Father" Puzzle Box with 4 Puzzles,**
1932. Each Puzzle - **$10 $30 $45**
Box - **$30 $65 $110**

BRF-21

❑ **BRF-21. "Bringing Up Father" Reprint Book Rare High Number 23 In Series,**
1933. Cupples & Leon Co. 10x10" daily strip reprint book by McManus with 48 pages. - **$60 $300 $550**

BRF-22

❑ **BRF-22. Bringing Up Father Bisque Set,**
1934. King Features. Three 4" tall bisques with incised numbers for Jiggs (#266), Maggie (#268) and Nora (#267). Each - **$10 $20 $30**

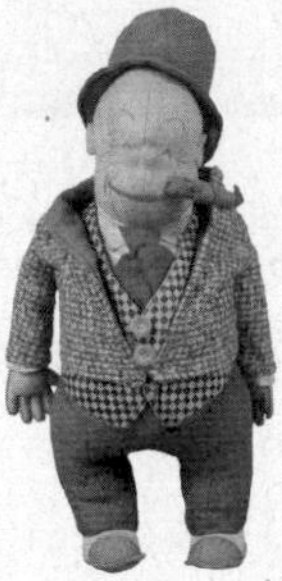

BRF-23

❑ **BRF-23. Jiggs Doll,**
1930s. 19.5" tall doll with felt body, hat, shoes, pants, hands, tie and cigar and oilcloth shirt and spats. - **$150 $300 $500**

BRF-24

❑ **BRF-24. "Bringing Up Father" Salt & Pepper Shakers,**
1930s. - **$75 $100 $200**

BRF-25

❑ **BRF-25. "Read America's Greatest Comics" Newsboy Apron With Jiggs,**
1930s. Philadelphia Sunday Ledger. 13-1/2x18" canvas fabric with neck strap and tie strings. -
$65 $165 $325

The Brownies

Palmer Cox (1840-1924) tried cartooning in San Francisco in the 1860s and early 1870s, then set up a studio in 1875 in New York City. He had some success being published in early *Life* humor magazines but his main claim to fame grew out of cartoons of Brownieland beginning in the *St. Nicholas* monthly children's magazine in February, 1883. Cox had been inspired by Scottish immigrant folk tales he heard as a boy in Granby, Canada. The frontispiece in the first book *The Brownies: Their Book* from 1887 reads: "Brownies, like fairies and goblins, are imaginary little sprites who are supposed to delight in harmless pranks and helpful deeds. They work and sport while weary households sleep and never allow themselves to be seen by mortal eyes." The Brownies world was a microcosm of society at its best and worst, all portrayed most skillfully through the mind and pen of Palmer Cox and his intricate work throughout the Victorian era and into the early 20th century. Two plays were produced in the 1890s and Palmer Cox built a 17-room home in Granby, Quebec in 1905 appropriately named Brownie Castle. He published 16 Brownie books in total. Brownieland complemented the times and most probably influenced the creation of *Little Nemo, Kewpies, Teenie-Weenies, Bucky Bug, Raggedy Ann* and other characters set in the world of fantasy. The Kodak Brownie camera, introduced in 1900 with a retail price of $1, gave the world an affordable way to document everyday life. Cox received no payment.

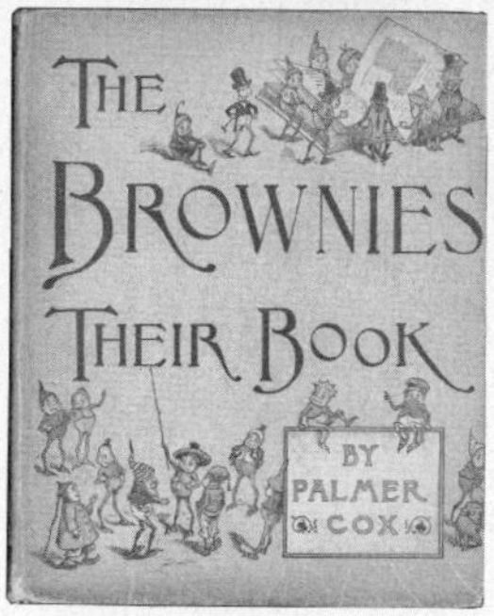

BRW-2

❑ **BRW-2. Hardcover Books,**
1887-1914. All came with dust jackets.
Book 1 - The Brownies: Their Book (1887) - **$200 $850 $1320**
Book 2 - Another Brownies Book (1890) - **$150 $635 $1000**
Book 3 - The Brownies at Home (1893) - **$125 $530 $825**
Book 4 - The Brownies Around the World (1894) - **$100 $425 $660**
Book 5 - The Brownies Through the Union (1895) - **$100 $425 $660**
Book 6 - The Brownies Abroad (1899) - **$100 $425 $660**
Book 7 - The Brownies in the Philippines (1904) - **$100 $425 $660**
Book 8 - The Brownies' Latest Adventures (1910) - **$100 $425 $660**
Book 9 - The Brownies Many More Nights (1914) - **$100 $425 $660**

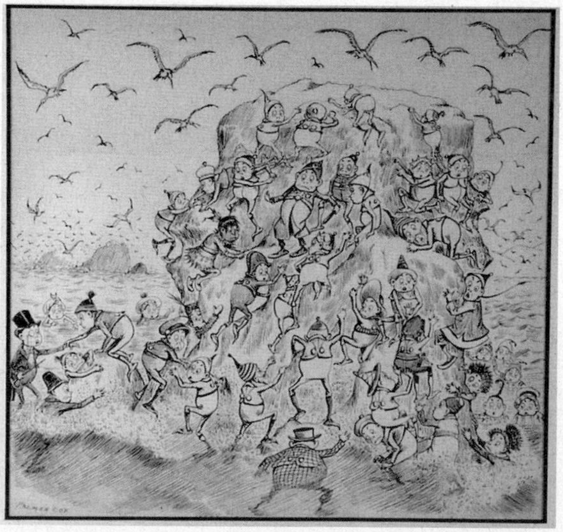

BRW-1

❑ **BRW-1. Original Pen and Ink Brownies Art by Palmer Cox,**
1880s. 46 characters shown, including Cox's favorite "The Dude" on the far left. Pen and ink originals are scarce; even rarer with his signature (found in the bottom left corner on this piece.) - **$3800**

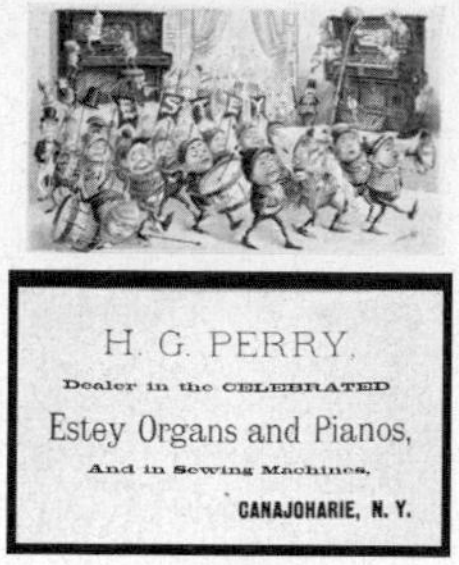

BRW-3

❑ **BRW-3. Estey Organs and Pianos Trade Card,**
1890. - **$15 $33 $65**

BRW-4

❑ **BRW-4. "Palmer Cox's Brownie Paper Dolls",**
1892. Brownies Chocolate Cream Drops.
Each - **$20 $45 $80**

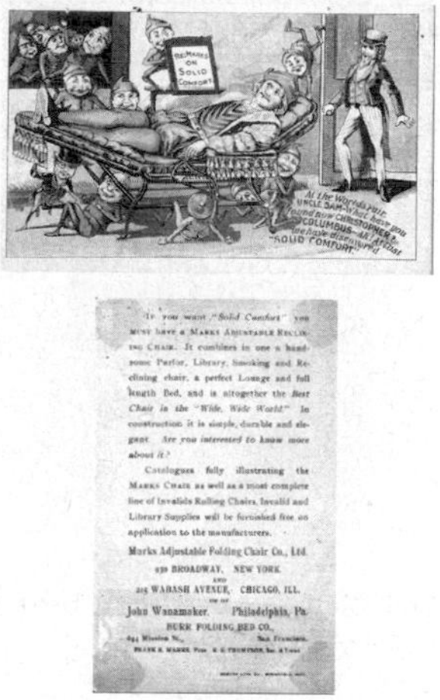

BRW-5

❑ **BRW-5. World's Fair Trade Card - Chairs,**
1892. - **$15 $35 $80**

BRW-6

❑ **BRW-6. World's Fair Pin, Needle & Thread Booklet,**
1892. - **$20 $40 $80**

BRW-7

❑ **BRW-7. Cloth Doll of "Highlander" Brownie,**
1892. Uncut - **$45 $90 $140**

BRW-8

❑ **BRW-8. Cloth Doll of "John Bull" England Brownie,**
1892. Uncut - **$45 $90 $140**

BRW-9

❑ **BRW-9. Cloth Doll of "Sailor" Brownie,**
1892. Uncut - **$45 $90 $140**

BRW-10

❑ **BRW-10. Cloth Doll of "Dude" Brownie,**
1892. Uncut - **$50 $100 $150**

BRW-11

❑ **BRW-11. Cloth Doll of "German" Brownie,**
1892. Uncut - **$45 $90 $140**

BRW-12

❑ **BRW-12. Cloth Doll of "Irishman" Brownie,**
1892. Uncut - **$45 $90 $140**

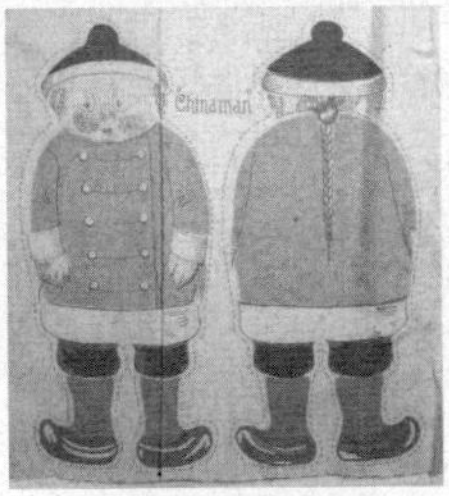

BRW-13

❑ **BRW-13. Cloth Doll of "Chinaman" Brownie,**
1892. Uncut - **$45 $90 $140**

BRW-14

❑ **BRW-14. Cloth Doll of "Canadian" Brownie,**
1892. Uncut - **$45 $90 $140**

BRW-15

❑ **BRW-15. Premium Booklet,**
1892. For Bee Soap. - **$80 $115 $175**

BRW-16

❑ **BRW-16. Metal Candy Tray,**
1893. Unusual image of Brownie with a gun as Policeman Brownie comes to the rescue.
- **$80 $160 $225**

BRW-17

❑ **BRW-17. World's Fair Trade Card - Stoves/Furnaces,**
1893. Scarce. - **$25 $60 $120**

BRW-18

❑ **BRW-18. Brownie Hinged Lid Metal Box,**
1893. Five Brownie figures on lid. Sold at World's Fair. - **$85 $170 $250**

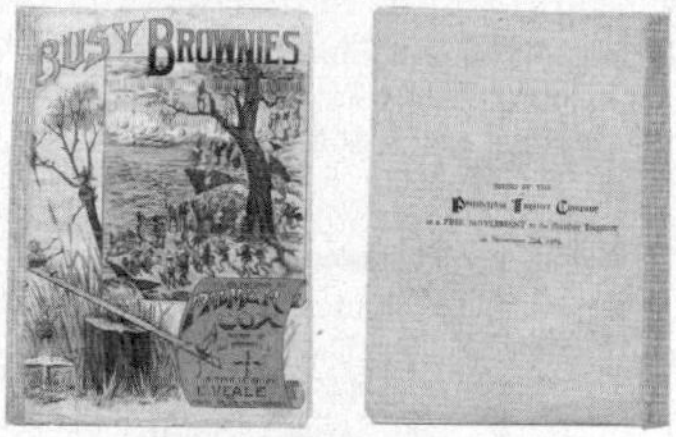

BRW-19

❑ **BRW-19. "Busy Brownies" Comic Giveaway,**
1896. Rare. 6 1/2 x 9". Various sponsors - this one sponsored by the **Philadelphia Inquirer** newspaper. - **$100 $250 $500**

BRW-20

❑ **BRW-20. Brownies "Snag Proof" Boot Advertising Calendar,**
1896. Calendar is 5.25x7". Calendar pad is complete from Oct. 1896 to Sept. 1897. Text includes "Snag-Proof Trademark/Lambertville Rubber Co./Lambertville, New Jersey/Jacob Trieschmann, Wellman, Ia., Sole Agent."
- **$60 $115 $175**

BRW-21

❑ **BRW-21. "Palmer Cox Primers" Booklets,**
1897. Jersey Coffee and others. Set of 12.
Each - **$25 $50 $85**
Brownie issue (smaller than BRW-19) - **$40 $75 $150**

BRW-22

❑ **BRW-22. "Brownie" Calendar Button,**
1897. - **$85 $175 $350**

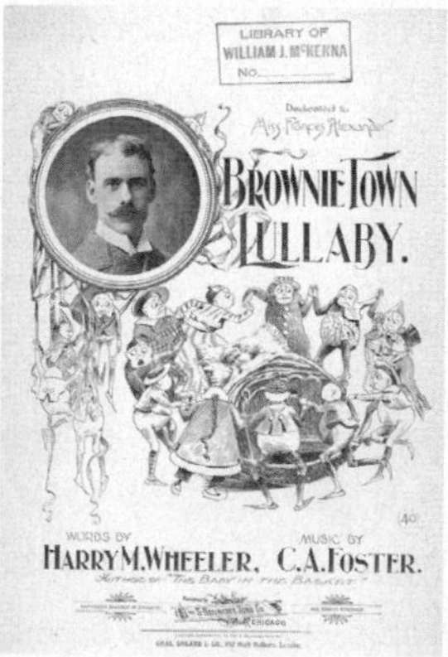

BRW-23

❑ **BRW-23. BrownieTown Lullaby Song Sheet,**
1898. - **$35 $85 $125**

BRW-24

❑ **BRW-24. "The Dude" 36" Figure,**
1899. Featured at the 1899 National Export Exposition in Philadelphia. Twelve different Brownies this size were made and two different (including this one) are known to have survived. These were made by the Schoenhut Company and were used to promote other contemporary Brownie products at the exposition.
Sold privately in 2006 for $9500.

BRW-25

❑ **BRW-25. Die-Cut Ad,**
1890s. Ad for free ring on back. - **$30 $55 $90**

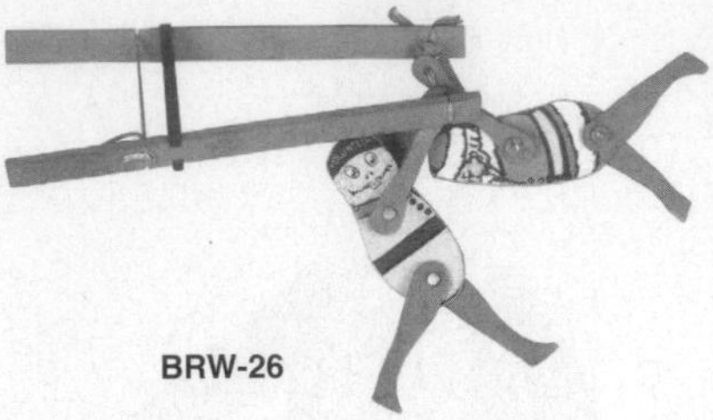

BRW-26

❑ BRW-26. Christmas Wood Toy,
1890s. Features Volunteer Brownie and Santa. - **$65 $135 $185**

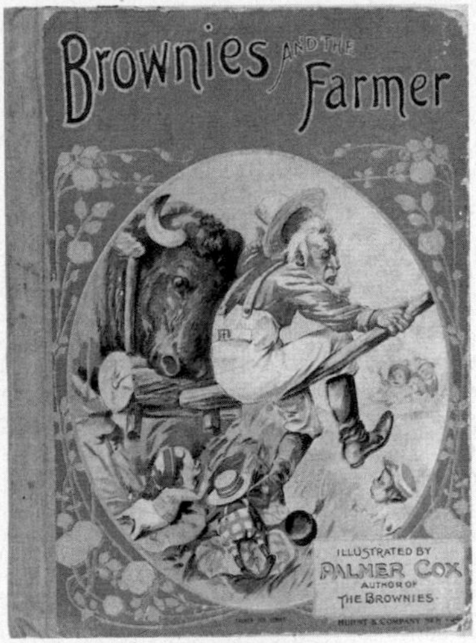

BRW-27

❑ BRW-27. "Brownies and the Farmer" Hardback Book by Palmer Cox,
1890s. Rare. The title was appropriate for the time as 85% of the U.S. population lived in rural areas. - **$125 $275 $500**

BRW-28

❑ BRW-28. Luden's Cough Drop 6x9" Sign,
1890s. Rare. Earliest known character die-cut sign ad. - **$350 $900 $1650**

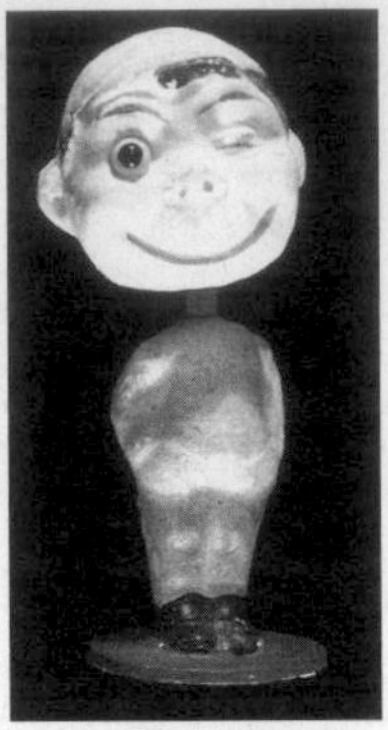

BRW-29

❑ BRW-29. Brownie Type Bobbing Head with Glass Eye,
1890s. Made in Germany. - **$125 $250 $450**

BRW-30 BRW-31

❑ BRW-30. The "Dude" Brownie Spoon,
1890s. Enameled figure on top. - **$30 $65 $110**

❑ BRW-31. Russian Brownie Spoon,
1890s. Enameled figure on top. - **$30 $65 $110**

BRW-32 BRW-33

❑ BRW-32. Scottish Brownie Spoon,
1890s. Enameled figure on top. - **$30 $65 $110**

❑ BRW-33. "Brownie" 'Sterling' Spoon,
1890s. Spoon is 3.5" long and marked "Sterling" on reverse. - **$30 $65 $110**

(CLOSE-UP)

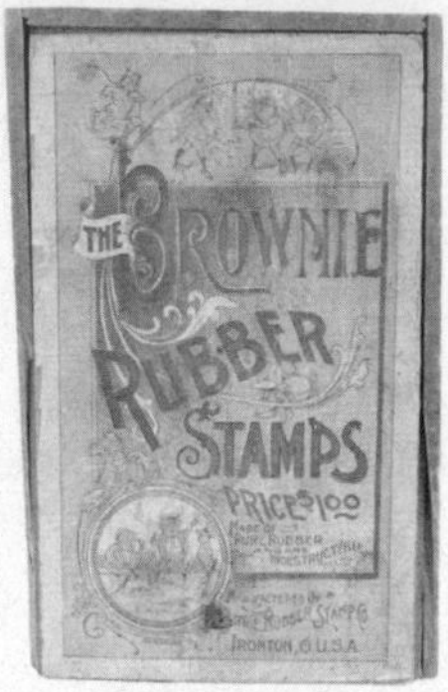

BRW-34

❑ BRW-34. Rubber Stamp Box Set,
1890s. Nineteen rubber on wood stamps with a pad of paper in box. - **$150 $250 $400**

BRW-35

❑ BRW-35. Hand-Painted Porcelain Lapel Stud,
1890s. Issuer unknown. 1-3/8" tall white porcelain with Brownie wearing a tam depicted in shades of brown. - **$35 $75 $150**

BRW-36

❑ BRW-36. Brass U.S. Brownie Charm,
1890s. "U.S." on belt buckle. - **$30 $60 $110**

BRW-37

❑ **BRW-37. Brownies "Smoker",**
1890s. For cheese. Shows many Brownies smoking pipes and other cigarettes. Rare. - **$265 $550 $1100**

BRW-38

❑ **BRW-38. Pitcher With Pewter Lid,**
1890s. - **$250 $500 $1000**

BRW-39

❑ **BRW-39. Candy Mold,**
1890s. - **$100 $200 $300**

BRW-40

❑ **BRW-40. Mandarin Figure,**
1890s. Candy container. - **$300 $475 $700**

BRW-41

❑ **BRW-41. "The Duke" Figure,**
1890s. Candy container. - **$300 $475 $700**

BRW-42

❑ **BRW-42. Pencil Holder,**
1890s. Children's school related pencil holder in shape of rolling pin. - **$75 $150 $225**

BRW-43

❑ **BRW-43. Bisque Figure,**
1890s. Features three Brownies riding a pig. Marvelous fine detail. Rare. - **$900 $1900 $3800**

BRW-44

❑ **BRW-44. "See-Saw" Dexterity Puzzle,**
1890s. Imprinted for Parkhurst-Duker Co. clothing, Quincy, Illinois . 1/2x1-1/2x3-1/2" cardboard frame holding glass over cardboard playing surface picturing three Brownies. Inner surface tilts adding to difficulty of placing three balls in holes. - **$65 $135 $265**

BRW-45 BRW-46

❑ **BRW-45. Brownies "Dutchman" Humidor,**
1890s. - **$215 $450 $775**

❑ **BRW-46. Brownies Floppy Cap Humidor,**
1890s. - **$215 $450 $775**

BRW-47 BRW-48

❑ **BRW-47. Brownies "German Cop" Humidor,**
1890s. - **$300 $600 $900**

❑ **BRW-48. Brownies "Prussian" Humidor,**
1890s. - **$300 $600 $900**

BRW-49

BRW-50

❑ BRW-49. Brownies "Turkish" Humidor,
1890s. - **$215 $450 $775**

❑ BRW-50. Brownies "Defender" Humidor,
1890s. - **$215 $450 $775**

BRW-51

❑ BRW-51. Brownies "Uncle Sam" Humidor,
1890s. - **$325 $650 $950**

BRW-52

BRW-53

❑ BRW-52. "Policeman" Candle Holder,
1890s. Figure is 7-1/2" tall. - **$150 $300 $600**

❑ BRW-53. "Policeman" Candle Holder,
1890s. Figure is 9" tall. - **$300 $600 $900**

BRW-54

❑ BRW-54. "Policeman" Candle Holder,
1890s. With openings for three candles.
- $400 $800 $1200

BRW-55

❑ BRW-55. "Villager" Candle Holder,
1890s. - **$100 $200 $400**

BRW-56

❑ BRW-56. "The Dude" Candle Holder,
1890s. With openings for three candles.
- $400 $800 $1200

BRW-57

BRW-58

BRW-59

❑ BRW-57. Brownie "White Apron" Candle Holder Figure,
1890s. - **$100 $200 $400**

❑ BRW-58. Brownie "Uncle Sam" Candle Holder Figure,
1890s. - **$150 $300 $600**

❑ BRW-59. Brownie "The Dude" Candle Holder Figure,
1890s. - **$125 $250 $500**

BRW-60

BRW-61

BRW-62

❑ BRW-60. Brownie "Defender" Candle Holder Figure,
1890s. - **$125 $250 $500**

❑ BRW-61. Brownie "Grey Hat" Candle Holder Figure,
1890s. - **$125 $250 $500**

❑ BRW-62. Brownie "Chinaman" Candle Holder Figure,
1890s. - **$150 $300 $600**

BRW-63

❑ **BRW-63. Brownie Ceramic German Mug With Metal Cap,**
1890s. Different characters around base. Has a thinner width of the two similar models. - **$125 $250 $500**

BRW-64

❑ **BRW-64. Brownie Ceramic German Mug With Metal Cap,**
1890s. Different arrangement of characters than preceeding mug. Thicker width of the two similar models. - **$125 $250 $500**

BRW-65

❑ **BRW-65. Brownie Stationery and Envelopes,**
1890s. One card and one envelope in each set. Set - **$10 $25 $50**

(BOX TOP)

(PROMO INSERT)

BRW-66

❑ **BRW-66. Boxed Block Set,**
1890s. With promo booklet insert.
- **$250 $450 $750**

BRW-67

❑ **BRW-67. Brownies Pins In Case,**
1890s. Stickpins in thermoplastic case designed to hold a photograph c. 1870s.
Pins each - **$18 $30 $55**
Case - **$40 $60 $90**

BRW-68

❑ **BRW-68. Candy Fig Box,**
1890s. - **$50 $150 $300**

BRW-69

❑ **BRW-69. "Brownie Member" Pinback,**
1890s. Rare. - **$35 $60 $115**

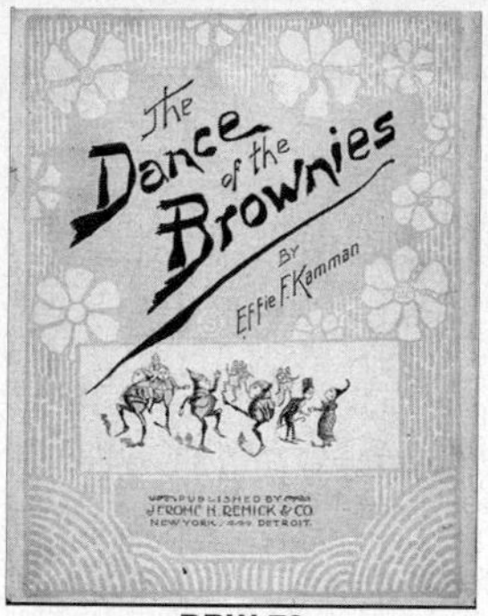

BRW-70

❑ **BRW-70. Brownies Song Book,**
1890s. - **$25 $60 $125**

BRW-71

❑ **BRW-71. Lion's Coffee Cut-Outs,**
1890s. Each - **$15 $30 $75**

BRW-72

❑ **BRW-72. Advertising Cards,**
1890s. Buttermilk Toilet Soap.
Each - **$15 $35 $75**

BRW-73

❑ **BRW-73. "Merry Christmas From The Brownies" Cardboard Box,**
1890s. Probably held candy or dates. -
$35 $65 $100

BRW-74

❑ **BRW-74. Brownie Soldier Bowl,**
1890s. Scene taken from "Toy Shop" story from 1887. - **$45 $90 $160**

BRW-75

❑ **BRW-75. Brownie Puzzles With Box,**
1890s. Two puzzles. Complete -
$225 $450 $900

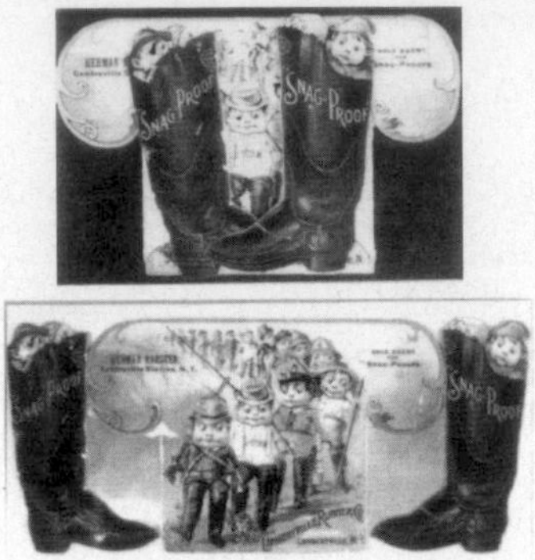

BRW-76

❑ **BRW-76. Advertising Trade Card,**
1890s. Snag-Proof Boots. Card opens to Brownies as sportsmen using boots. - **$25 $50 $100**

BRW-77

❑ **BRW-77. Brownie Stamps With Box,**
1890s. - **$75 $150 $300**

BRW-78

❑ **BRW-78. "Brownie" Picture Cards,**
1890s. Each. - **$15 $35 $65**

BRW-79

❑ **BRW-79. Christie's Biscuits Box Featuring The Brownies,**
1890s. Christie & Brown Company, Canada.
- **$250 $500 $750**

BRW-80 BRW-81

❑ **BRW-80. Metal Figure Stickpin,**
1890s. Tinted luster. - **$18 $30 $55**

❑ **BRW-81. Brownie Policeman Stickpin,**
c. 1900. 3/4" diecut brass figure accented in black and red on 2" brass stickpin. - **$18 $30 $55**

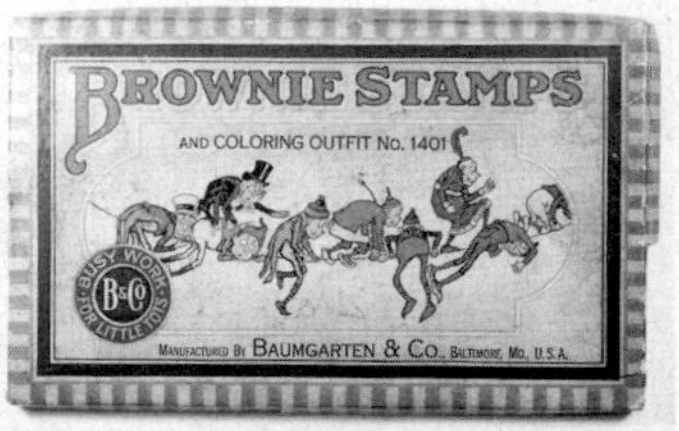

BRW-82

❑ **BRW-82. "Brownie Stamps And Coloring Outfit" Boxed,**
c. 1900. Baumgarten & Co., Baltimore. 6.5x10.5" boxed set of 12 different character ink stamps. - **$50 $100 $150**

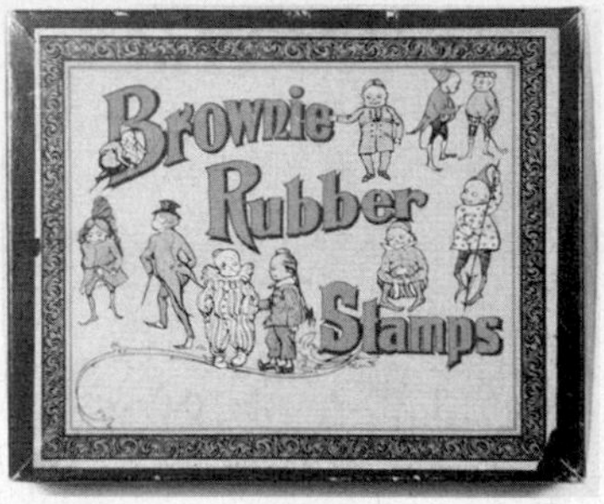

BRW-83

❑ **BRW-83. "Brownie Rubber Stamps" Boxed,**
c. 1900. No maker indicated. 5x6" boxed probable set of 10 different character ink stamps. - **$55 $110 $160**

(BOX)

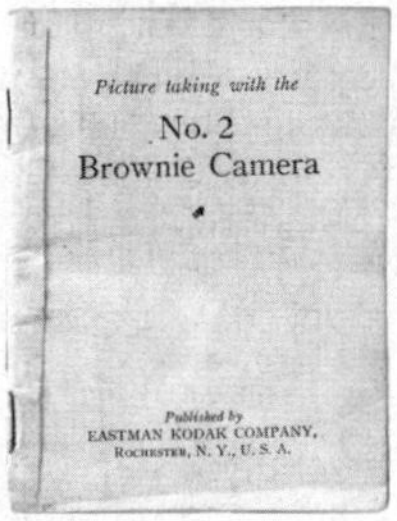

(INSTRUCTIONS)

(FRONT)

(BACK)

BRW-84

❑ **BRW-84. Early Brownie Camera in Box,**
c. 1901. With box and instructions.
- **$250 $400 $650**

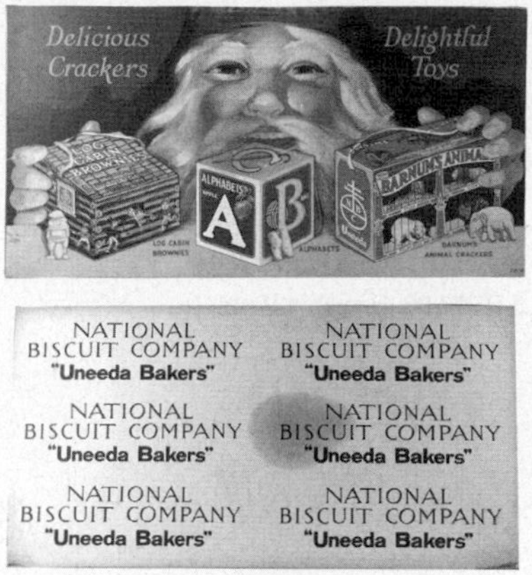

BRW-85

❑ **BRW-85. Brownies Sign,**
1902. 20-1/2 x 10-3/4" sign promoting National Biscuit Company products. - **$375 $750 $1500**

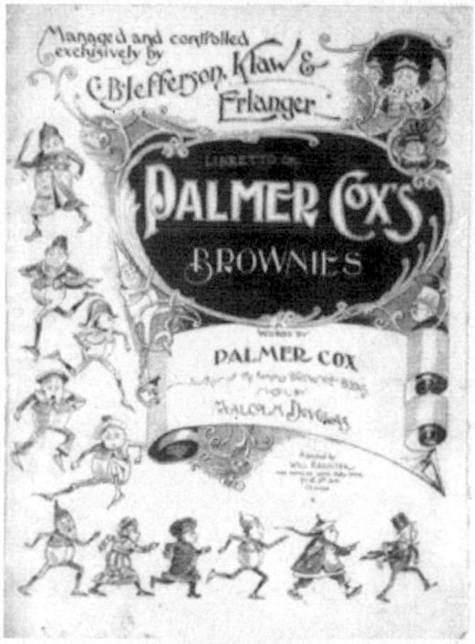

BRW-86

❑ **BRW-86. "Libretto Of Palmer Cox's Brownies" Booklet,**
c. 1904. 16-page song folio from stage production. - **$30 $65 $135**

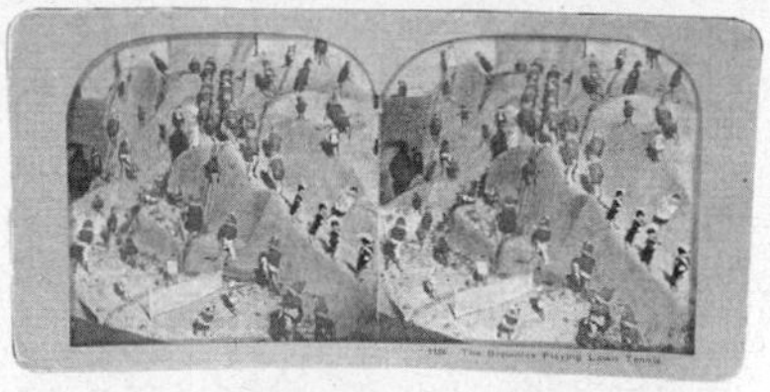

CLOSE-UP OF CARD

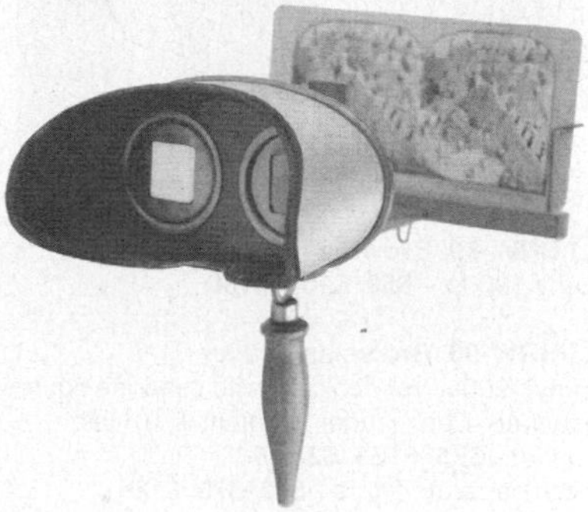

BRW-87

❑ **BRW-87. Stereoscopic Viewer and Card,**
c. 1910. Hand-held viewer with card #1186 depicting Brownies playing lawn tennis.
Viewer - **$30 $60 $120**
Card - **$35 $65 $130**

BRW-88

❑ **BRW-88. Brownie Stuffed Doll,**
Early 1900s. - **$75 $150 $225**

BRW-89

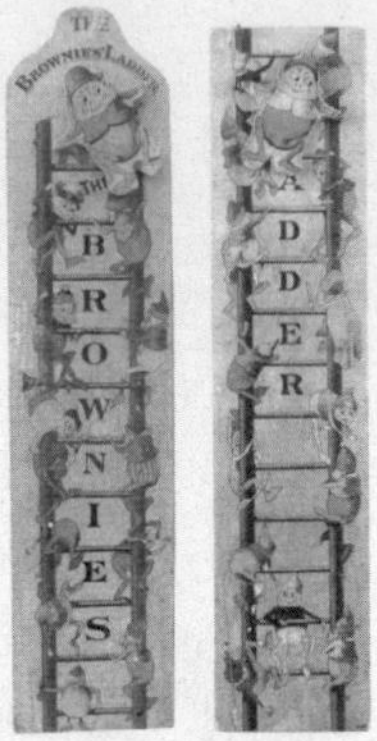

BRW-90

❑ **BRW-89. Brownie Hat,**
Early 1900s. - **$50 $100 $160**

❑ **BRW-90. Brownies Ladder,**
Early 1900s. Very colorful with separate figures attached. Each ladder segment is 16" tall.
Ladder - **$75 $135 $200**
Each separate figure - **$50 $75 $125**

BRW-91

❑ **BRW-91. Brownies China Plate,**
Early 1900s. - **$45 $90 $175**

BRW-92

❑ **BRW-92. Brownie Plate,**
Early 1900s. - **$75 $125 $200**

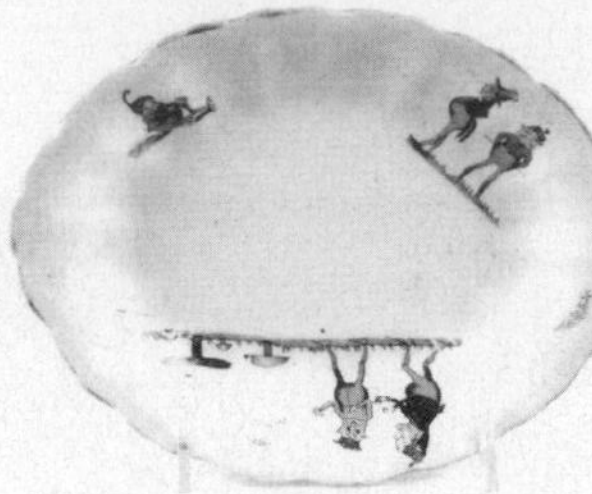

BRW-93

❑ **BRW-93. Brownie Plate,**
Early 1900s. - **$75 $125 $200**

BRW-94

❑ **BRW-94. Brownie Creamer,**
1900s. - **$50 $100 $200**

BRW-95

❑ **BRW-95. Brownie Creamer,**
1900s. - **$50 $100 $200**

BRW-96

❑ **BRW-96. Sports-Themed Cup and Saucer,**
Early 1900s. Cup and saucer feature images of fencing, boxing and baseball. - **$60 $120 $200**

BRW-97

❑ **BRW-97. Sports-Themed Bowl with Lid,**
Early 1900s. Features sporting images.
- **$100 $175 $300**

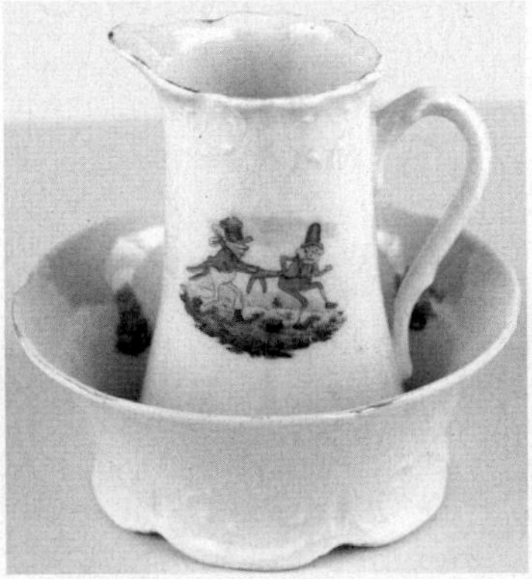

BRW-98

❑ **BRW-98. Brownie Creamer and Bowl,**
Early 1900s. - **$85 $140 $225**

BRW-99

❑ **BRW-99. Brownie Educational Toy,**
Early 1900s. Beautiful graphics include Brownie images emcompassing the frame and a Punch & Judy image. 8" x 9-1/2". - **$75 $150 $225**

BRW-100

❑ **BRW-100. Brownie Ruler,**
1900s. Mrs. Winslow Syrup premium. 8" long. - **$75 $125 $200**

BRW-101

BRW-102

❑ **BRW-101. Brownies China Plate,**
Early 1900s. Blue Edge. Scene taken from art in Brownie books. - **$35 $70 $140**

❑ **BRW-102. Brownies China Plate,**
Early 1900s. Gold Edge. Scene taken from art in Brownie books. - **$35 $70 $140**

BRW-103

❑ **BRW-103. Brownies Tin Button,**
1916. - **$50 $100 $200**

BRW-104

❑ **BRW-104. Log Cabin Brownies Box,**
1923. Rare. Ad for Chocolate Snaps on bottom of box. - **$125 $300 $500**

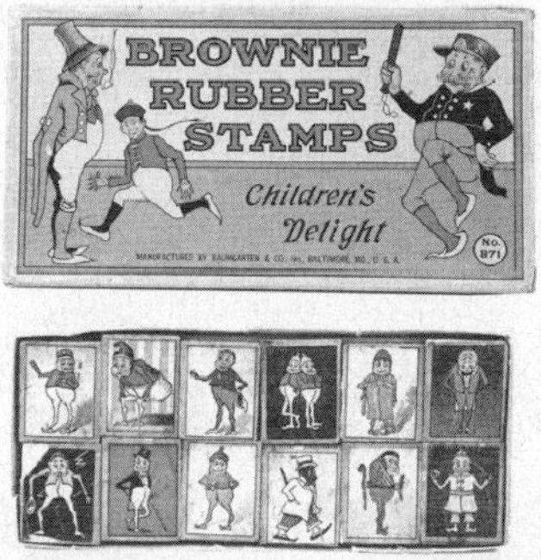

BRW-105

❑ **BRW-105. "Brownie Rubber Stamps" Box Set,**
1920s. Baumgarten & Co., Baltimore.
- **$100 $150 $225**

BRW-106

❑ **BRW-106. Brownies Ruler,**
1920s. - **$50 $100 $150**

BRW-107

❑ **BRW-107. Brownie Club Theater Pinback,**
c. 1920s. Not sure if related to Palmer Cox characters. - **$12 $25 $50**

BRW-108

❑ **BRW-108. Brownie Camera,**
1940s. In 1900, Kodak introduced the first boxed camera. In order to promote it to all age groups they called it the Brownie. Palmer Cox's Brownies were very popular at the time and the camera became an overnight success. The camera shown is a 1940s version.
Camera - **$30 $60 $100**
Box Showing Characters - **$75 $100 $200**

BRW-109

❑ **BRW-109. Brownie Indian Doll with Tag,**
1993. Made for the 100th Anniversary of the Brownies. - **$80**

Buck Jones

Movie serials, known then as chapter plays, blossomed in the 1930s, drawing countless thousands of youngsters to local movie palaces every Saturday to find out how their hero would save himself from the perilous predicament at the end of the previous episode. Buck Jones, with his horse known as Silver, was king of the Western serials. Charles Gebhart (1889-1942) was a cow-puncher, a mechanic, a soldier and a trick rider. Around 1917 he found work as a Hollywood stuntman. Three years later, as Buck Jones, he had his first starring role. In all, Buck Jones was to make more than 125 movies, but it was as the hero of six chapter

plays released between 1933 and 1941 that he was to find his greatest success. Kids everywhere waited breathlessly for the next Buck Jones serial. A radio series, *Hoofbeats*, sponsored by Grape-Nuts Flakes, ran for 39 episodes in 1937-1938. In the early 1940s Buck Jones starred with Tim McCoy and Raymond Hatton in Monogram Pictures' *Rough Riders* movies. On November 28, 1942 Jones was the guest of honor at a dinner at the Cocoanut Grove restaurant in Boston when a fire broke out. Nearly 500 people died and Buck Jones succumbed to his burns on November 30, 1942.

BKJ-1

❑ **BKJ-1. Club Booklet,**
1931. Columbia Pictures Corp. 4x6" black and white with 32 pages on bugle and harmonica playing along with information on club rank insignias and pledge text. - **$35 $65 $125**

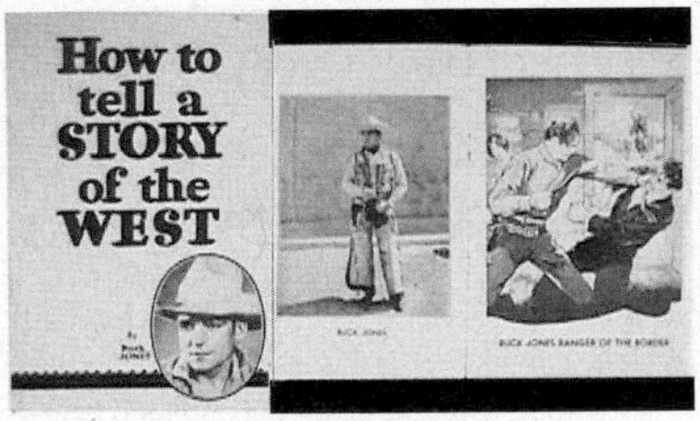

BKJ-2

❑ **BKJ-2. Club Booklet,**
1931. Columbia Pictures Corp. Similar to song booklet but devoted to storytelling techniques. - **$35 $65 $125**

BKJ-3

❑ **BKJ-3. "Rangers Club Of America" Cowboy Outfit,**
c. 1931. Hat - **$25 $50 $100**
Bandanna. - **$25 $50 $100**
Chaps, Includes Metal Rivet Accents And Club Logo - **$75 $150 $350**

BKJ-4

❑ **BKJ-4. Rangers' Club Newsletter,**
c. 1931. Columbia Pictures. - **$35 $75 $150**

Application for Membership
BUCK JONES' RANGER CLUB
I hereby apply for Membership and Agree to obey all Rules and Regulations.
Name.............................
Address.............................
Age............School............Grade............

BKJ-5

❑ **BKJ-5. Ranger's Club Member Application Card,**
c. 1931. - **$12 $20 $45**

BKJ-6

BKJ-7

❑ **BKJ-6. "Rangers' Club Of America" Cello. Button,**
c. 1931. Columbia Pictures. - **$20 $40 $80**

❑ **BKJ-7. "Buck Jones Rangers' Club Of America" Cello. Button,**
c. 1931. Version of blue photo with red rim. - **$35 $65 $110**

BKJ-8

❑ **BKJ-8. Ranger Club Card With Fabric Patch,**
c. 1931. Card - **$15 $30 $60**
Patch - **$20 $40 $80**

BKJ-9

❑ **BKJ-9. "Buck Jones' Ranger Club" Movie Cards,**
c. 1931. Columbia Pictures Corp. Black and white photo cards, each with club membership coupon on reverse.
Each - **$15 $30 $60**

BKJ-10

BKJ-11

❑ **BKJ-10. "Buck Jones Ranger" Enameled Brass Badge,**
c. 1931. Scarce. - **$100 $225 $425**

❑ **BKJ-11. "Buck Jones Rangers Club Of America" Leather Holster With Belt,**
c. 1931. Photo pictures embossed club symbol on holster cover panel. - **$80 $150 $300**

BKJ-12

BKJ-13

❑ **BKJ-12. Club Member's Large Brass Badge,**
c. 1931. Columbia Pictures. 1-1/2" with brass luster plus red and black enamel paint. - **$70 $150 $300**
Version with red trim - **$90 $185 $340**

❑ **BKJ-13. Club Member's Button,**
c. 1931. Columbia Pictures. - **$30 $60 $100**

BKJ-14

❑ **BKJ-14. Song Folio/Club Manual,**
1932. Published by Bibo-Lang. Copyright "Book No. 1" with club ranks, pledge, etc. -
$30 $70 $145

BKJ-15

BKJ-16

❑ **BKJ-15. Dixie Ice Cream Picture,**
1932. Movie scenes on reverse from "White Eagle." - **$20 $40 $80**

❑ **BKJ-16. "White Eagle" Movie Promo Card,**
1932. - **$25 $50 $90**

BKJ-17

❑ **BKJ-17. Big Thrill Gum Booklet,**
1934. Goudey Gum. Six in series.
Each - **$30 $65 $125**

BKJ-18

BKJ-19

❑ **BKJ-18. "The Red Rider" Cello. Button,**
1934. Universal Pictures. For 15-chapter movie serial "The Red Rider". - **$75 $150 $300**

❑ **BKJ-19. Dixie Ice Cream Picture,**
1935. - **$20 $40 $80**

BKJ-20

BKJ-21

❑ **BKJ-20. "Buck Jones In Ride 'Em Cowboy" Big Little Book,**
1935. Whitman Movie Edition #1116. -
$17 $51 $120

❑ **BKJ-21. "Buck Jones In The Fighting Rangers" Big Little Book,**
1936. Whitman #1188. - **$17 $51 $120**

BKJ-22

❑ **BKJ-22. "The Phantom Rider Of Hidden Valley" Sheet Music,**
1936. Sam Fox Publishing Co. Based on Universal film starring Buck Jones. -
$15 $30 $50

BKJ-23

❑ **BKJ-23. Photo-Statuette And Mailer Insert,**
1936. Quaker Cereals. 7x7-1/2" black and white stiff cardboard standup with fold-backs on lower corners. 20 stars were in the set and these are listed on the folder. Reverse of folder offers six Babe Ruth Premiums (see Babe Ruth section).
Buck Jones Statuette - **$15 $30 $60**
Insert - **$15 $30 $60**

BKJ-24

❑ **BKJ-24. "The Phantom Rider Club" Cello. Button,**
1936. Scarce. Universal Pictures. For 15-chapter movie serial "The Phantom Rider". -
$110 $265 $550

BKJ-25

BKJ-26

❑ **BKJ-25. Horseshoe Brass Badge,**
1937. Grape-Nuts Flakes. - **$15 $25 $50**

❑ **BKJ-26. "Buck Jones Club" Brass Ring,**
1937. Grape-Nuts Flakes. - **$65 $120 $235**

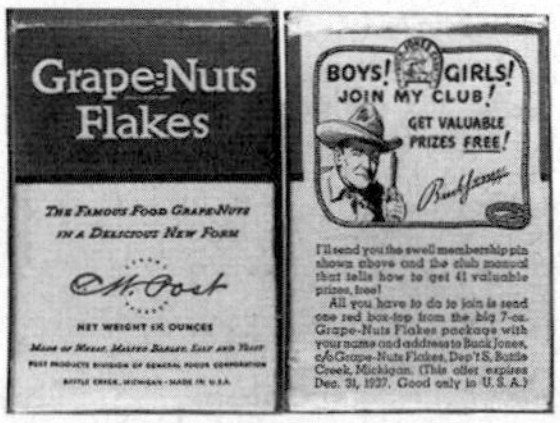

BKJ-27

❑ **BKJ-27. Club Membership Offer "Grape-Nuts Flakes" Sample Box,**
1937. 4" tall "New Package Adopted In 1936" with back panel ad expiring December 31, 1937. -
$100 $250 $475

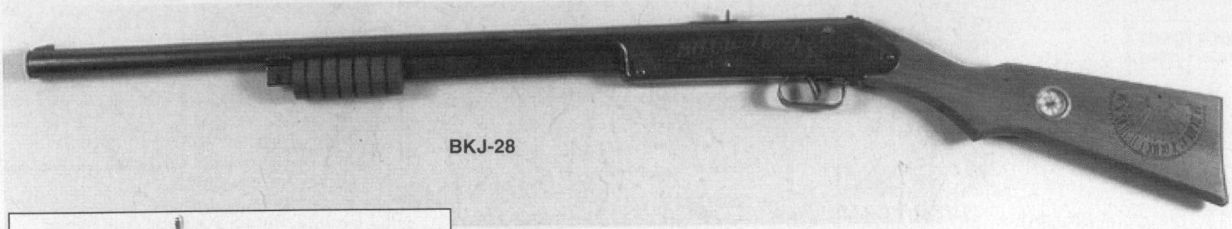

BKJ-28

❑ **BKJ-28. "No. 107 Daisy Buck Jones Special" Air Rifle,**
c. 1936. Store item by Daisy Mfg. Co., also used as premium. Compass and sundial on stock, sundial pointer often missing. - **$175 $325 $750**

BKJ-29

BKJ-30

❑ **BKJ-29. Grape-Nuts Flakes Premium Catalogue Folder Sheet,**
1937. Offers about 40 premiums with expiration date December 31. - **$15 $40 $85**

❑ **BKJ-30. Prize Folder,**
1937. Four page Grape-Nuts Flakes premium prize list - **$15 $40 $85**

BKJ-31

❑ **BKJ-31. Cello. Over Brass 3-1/4" Bullet Holder For Pencil,**
c. 1937. Grape-Nuts Flakes. Inscription "From Buck Jones To His Pal" followed by personalized name designated by orderer. -
$30 $60 $115

BKJ-32

❑ **BKJ-32. "Buck Jones Movie Book",**
1938. Daisy Mfg. Co. - **$30 $60 $125**

BKJ-33

BKJ-34

❑ **BKJ-33. "Buck Jones and the Killers of Crooked Butte" Better Little Book #1451,**
1938. - **$12 $36 $85**

❑ **BKJ-34. "Buck Jones and the Rock Creek Cattle Wars" Better Little Book #1461,**
1938. - **$12 $36 $85**

BKJ-35

BKJ-36

❑ **BKJ-35. "Buck Jones In The Cowboy Masquerade" Booklet,**
1938. Ice cream cone premium, Buddy Book #8. -
$39 $117 $275

❑ **BKJ-36. Buck Jones Framed Photo,**
1938. Columbia Pictures. From his movie "Stranger From Arizona" co-starring Dorothy Fay. - **$15 $25 $45**

BKJ-37

BKJ-38

❑ **BKJ-37. "Chicago Stadium Rodeo" Cello. Button,**
1930s. Single event issue. - **$50 $100 $200**

❑ **BKJ-38. Australian Issue Movie Cello. Button,**
1930s. Black and white real photo without dot pattern, 1". Two versions. Bottom rim reads "A Universal Star" or "The Red Rider."
Each - **$65 $150 $300**

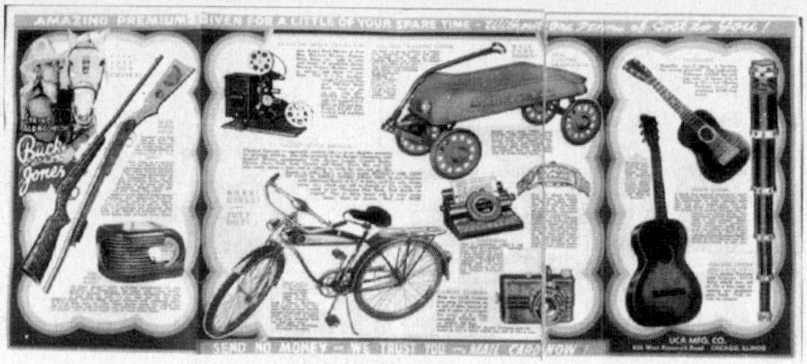

BKJ-39

❑ **BKJ-39. "UCA Salve" Premium Catalogue Folder Sheet,**
c. 1938. Has endorsement of Buck Jones and opens to 9x20" with air rifle only premium related to him. - **$35 $75 $140**

BKJ-40

BKJ-41

BKJ-42

❑ **BKJ-40. Photo,**
1930s. Sepia of him and horse Silver with facsimile autograph. - **$12 $25 $50**

❑ **BKJ-41. "For U.S. Marshal/Buck Jones" Cello. Button,**
1930s. - **$110 $225 $450**

❑ **BKJ-42. "Buck Jones Club" Cello. Button,**
1930s. Probably movie serial club. - **$60 $125 $225**

BKJ-43

BKJ-44

❑ **BKJ-43. Fan Photo,**
1930s. - **$12 $25 $50**

❑ **BKJ-44. Portrait Photo,**
1930s. Probably a premium. - **$12 $25 $50**

(CLOSE-UP)

BKJ-45

❑ **BKJ-45. "Buck Jones & Silver" Guitar,**
1930s. Guitar has 4x13x18" wood body and is 37" overall. Black and white image of Jones on horse with facsimile signature reading "Good Luck Buck Jones & Silver." Nicely made with mother-of-pearl inlay on frets.
- **$115 $225 $450**

(FRONT)

(BACK)

BKJ-46

❑ **BKJ-46. Photo Puzzle Card,**
1930s. Scarce. Movie premium. Very odd photo of Buck in deep thought, his cigarette smoke forming into the shape of his horse. Also note that his gun is pointed up towards him. Card is meant to be cut apart at lines on back and used as a puzzle. - **$35 $70 $130**

BKJ-47

❑ **BKJ-47. "Buck Jones Columbia Star" Figural Cast Metal Ashtray,**
1930s. Probable promotional item. 4-1/2" diameter by 6" tall. - **$260 $475 $875**

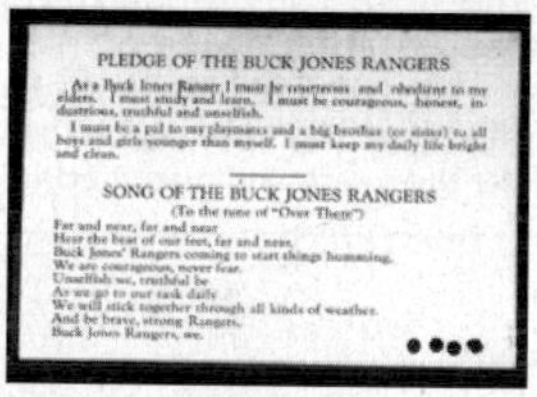

BKJ-48

❑ **BKJ-48. "Ranger's Club" Movie Serial Ticket,**
1930s. Front is designed for punching admittance to 15-chapter serial, back has Buck Jones Rangers Pledge and song lyrics. - **$35 $65 $110**

BKJ-49

BKJ-50

❑ **BKJ-49. Movie Serial Promotion Plaster Ashtray,**
1941. Universal. Issued for "Riders Of Death Valley", its stars listed on the 4x6" back panel from which an ashtray extends outward 3-1/2" at the bottom. - **$80 $160 $300**

❑ **BKJ-50. "Riders Of Death Valley Club" Cello. Button,**
1941. Universal Pictures. For 15-chapter movie serial "Riders Of Death Valley". - **$55 $100 $175**

Buck Rogers in the 25th Century

Buck Rogers was the first American comic strip to plunge into science fiction and it enjoyed great success after it was introduced in January 1929. The story was adapted by Phil Nowlan from his futuristic novel, illustrated by Dick Calkins and syndicated by the John F. Dille Co. Buck wakes after 500 years of suspended animation and, along with young Wilma Deering and the old scientist Dr. Huer, battles to save America and the earth from various enemies, in particular Killer Kane and Ardala Valmar, who want to conquer the world. The strip ran until 1967 (a companion Sunday strip appeared from 1930 to 1965) and both were revived in 1979 to 1983. A successful radio adaptation was broadcast from 1932 to 1947, sponsored first by Kellogg, then Cocomalt, Cream of Wheat, Popsicle and General Foods. A TV version had a brief run in 1950-1951 and a revised series, produced by Glen Larson and starring Gil Gerard and Erin Gray, debuted in 1979 and lasted two seasons. Movie adaptations appeared in 1939, with Buster Crabbe, and 1979 (released theatrically but also serving as the pilot for the Larson series). Crabbe had a memorable cameo in one episode of the '80s series. There have also been a variety of Big Little Books and comic books over the years and many reprints.

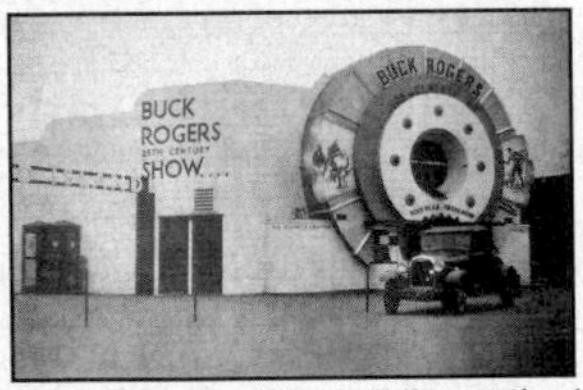

The Buck Rogers exhibit building at the 1934 Chicago World's Fair in the Enchanted Island area.

BRG-1

❑ BRG-1. "Amazing Stories" Pulp Magazine With First Buck Rogers Story ,
1928. Vol. 3 #5, August issue with story "Armageddon-2419 A.D." The cover illustration does not picture Buck Rogers, but a flying scientist from the magazine's lead story, "The Skylark of Space," by Edward Elmer Smith and Lee Hawkins Garby. (The Buck Rogers sequel "Airlords of Han" appeared here March, 1929. The cover of that issue does relate to the Buck Rogers story.) - **$600 $1250 $3500**

BRG-2

❑ BRG-2. "With My Very Best Regards" Fan Picture,
1929. Newspaper premium, black on green paper 6x9". Large 11-1/2x17-1/2" black on orange paper version appeared 1931.
Each - **$200 $500 $1000**

BRG-3

❑ BRG-3. Blotter In Full Color,
1930. Detroit Free Press. 3-3/8x8-3/8". - **$300 $600 $1200**

BRG-4

❑ BRG-4. "The Planet Venus" Coloring Sheet,
1931. Newspaper premium with art by Russell Keaton. Brown art on tan paper.
Uncolored - **$375 $700 $1400**
Colored - **$225 $450 $900**

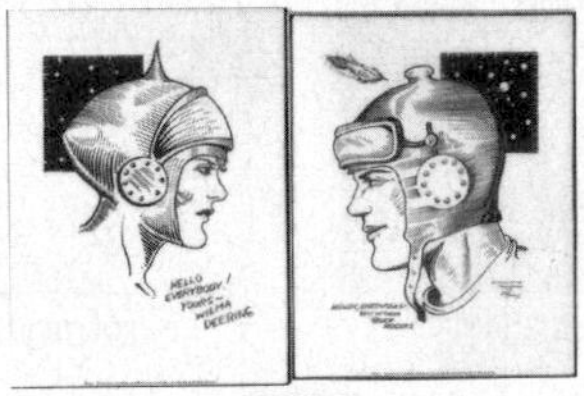

BRG-5

❑ BRG-5. Newspaper Comic Strip Portraits Premiums,
1932. Black and white, each about 8x10-1/2". Printed on buff paper. Both were reprinted in 1969 on white paper as part of promotion for book "*The Collected Works of Buck Rogers.*"
Each - **$200 $350 $700**

BRG-6

❑ BRG-6. "Pep" Leaflet With Radio Show Ad In Color,
1932. Kellogg's. - **$20 $40 $85**

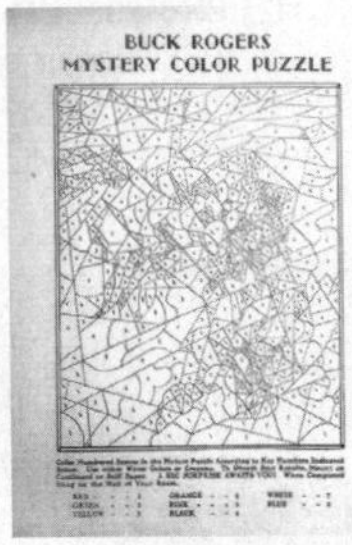

BRG-7

❑ BRG-7. "Mystery Color Puzzle" Paper Sheet,
1932. Newspaper offer in black and white 8-1/4x10-3/4". Reveals a giant bird. A 1931 puzzle is shown on page 27 in the book "The Aviation Art of Russell Keaton."
Uncolored - **$225 $475 $750**
Colored - **$150 $325 $625**

BRG-8

❑ BRG-8. "Bucktoy" Set Of Six Cut-Out Cards,
1932. Newspaper offer of set of six issued from 1932 to 1934. Stiff paper 2-3/8x5-5/8" in black and white (except Dr. Huer in green) to cut and color. Six others were used for Baltimore promotion, and of these, only 3 have been seen.
Each Uncut And Uncolored - **$125 $300 $600**
Each Uncut And Colored - **$95 $175 $300**
Each Cut And Colored - **$60 $85 $175**

BRG-9

❑ **BRG-9. Radio Broadcast Publicity Leaflet In Color,**
1932. Kellogg's Corn Flakes. Sponsorship indicated for Buck Rogers and Singing Lady programs. - **$35 $80 $150**

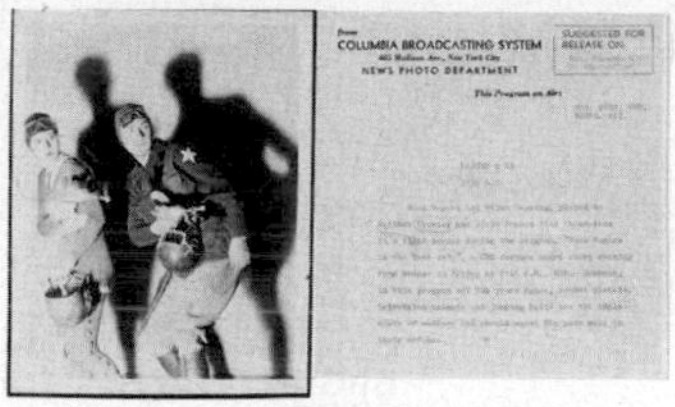

BRG-10

❑ **BRG-10. Buck & Wilma CBS Radio Publicity Photo,**
1932. 8x10" black and white glossy with reverse paper promo for program "Buck Rogers In The Year 2432" scheduled in early December just over a month from the program's debut November 7. - **$350 $700 $1100**

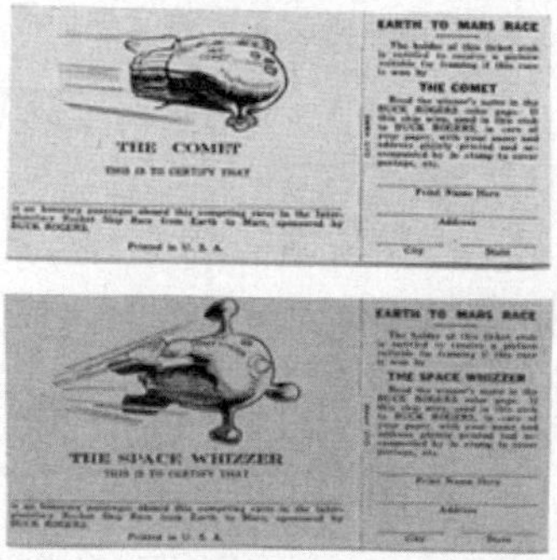

BRG-11

❑ **BRG-11. "Earth To Mars" Contest Tickets,**
1933. Various newspapers. 2-1/2x5-1/2" color tickets for competing rocketships named "The Comet" and "The Space Whizzer." Tickets also issued for third ship "The Rocket Flash" (the eventual winner). Those holding a ticket for winning ship signed and mailed the stub to receive "Picture Suitable For Framing" and winner's name would be printed in "The Buck Rogers Color Page." Each - **$150 $350 $600**

BRG-12

❑ **BRG-12. "The Rocket Flash" Contest Prize Picture,**
1933. Newspaper giveaway reading "Congratulations to YOU as one of the Buck Rogers fans who picked the winning ship in the race to Mars." 6x9" black and orange with art by Russell Keaton. Three different tickets, black on single card color stock, were issued; each pictures a different ship. Contest entrants selecting "The Rocket Flash" ship to win the Earth to Mars race received this picture. See previous item. - **$400 $900 $1750**

BRG-13

❑ **BRG-13. Origin Storybook,**
1933. Kellogg's. Reprinted in 1994 but no Kellogg's ad on back cover and printed in narrow format. Both are full color.
Near Mint With Envelope - **$625**
Loose - **$75 $150 $400**
White Paper Letter (2 Versions) Each - **$45 $90 $150**

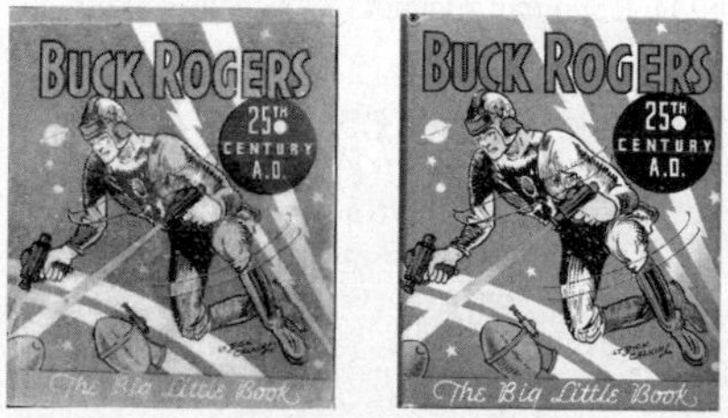

(Softcover) BRG-14 (Hardcover)

❑ **BRG-14. "Buck Rogers 25th Century A.D." BLB,**
1933. Softcover has Cocomalt ad on back cover. Sent boxed. The text for all BLBs were written by Dick Calkins and Rick Yager using scenes from the daily strip. See BRG-15.
Softcover (un-numbered) - **$27 $81 $190**
Hardcover Whitman #742 - **$43 $129 $300**

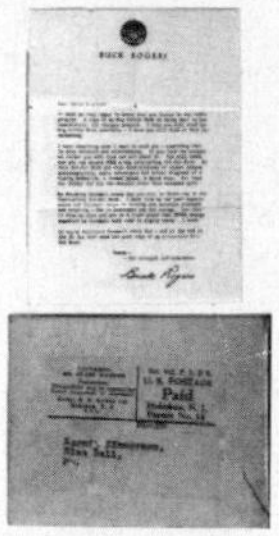

BRG-15

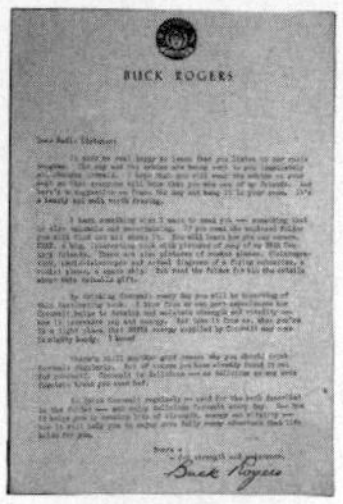

BRG-16

❑ **BRG-15. Mailer And Letter For Cocomalt BLB,**
1933. Accompanied softcover BRG-14.
Mailer - **$35 $75 $150**
Yellow Paper Letter - **$60 $140 $250**

❑ **BRG-16. "Solar System Map" Letter,**
1933. Cocomalt. Deep yellow paper. The text refers to fabric patch (see BRG-92) and map being sent separately and promotes the Cut-Out Adventure Book offer. - **$60 $140 $240**

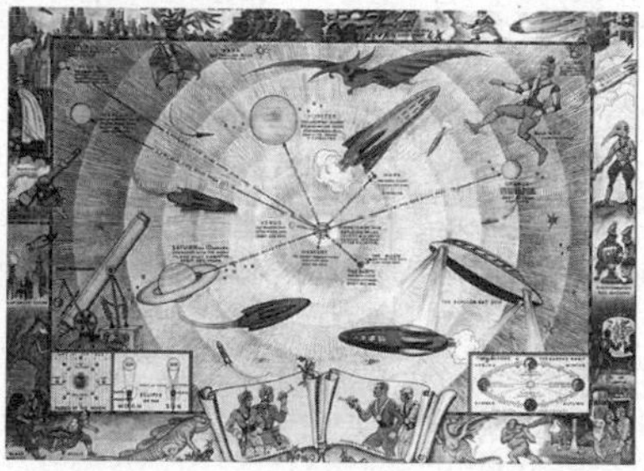
BRG-17

(ENLARGED VIEW)

❑ **BRG-17. Solar System Map 18x25",**
1933. Cocomalt. Sent rolled in a tube. Beware of 1970s color reproductions on glossy paper and color photo-copies. - **$325 $800 $1600**

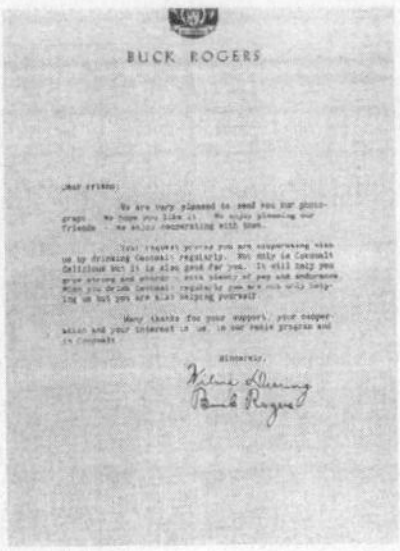

BRG-18

BRG-19

❑ **BRG-18. Buck And Wilma Cocomalt Browntone Picture,**
1933. Size 7-1/2" by 10". - **$75 $160 $300**
Blue Paper Letter - **$40 $80 $165**

❑ **BRG-19. Buck and Wilma Paper Masks,**
1933. Cocomalt. Made by Einson-Freeman. Note curly hair design on Wilma. An unlicensed store item marked "Made in Japan" without curly hair and on less slick paper was also issued. See BRG-145. Each - **$135 $250 $450**

BRG-21

❑ **BRG-21. Cocomalt "Buck Rogers Cut-Out Adventure Book" Order Folder,**
1933. Full color 9x13" Sent with BRG-14 and BRG-17. Also see BRG-20. - **$135 $275 $550**

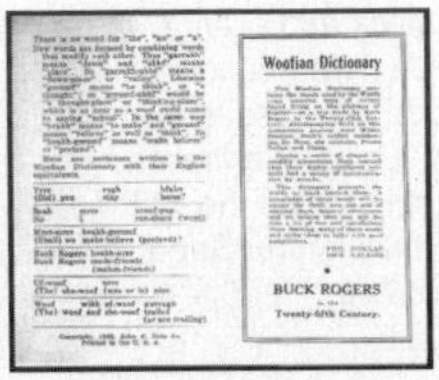

BRG-22

BRG-23

❑ **BRG-22. "Woofian Dictionary" Folder,**
1933. Newspaper offer containing words used by "Woofs," amazing animals living on the plateaus of Jupiter. Shown open. Beige paper. - **$150 $300 $600**

❑ **BRG-23. "Buck Rogers On The Air" Radio Station Listing Sheet,**
1934. Cocomalt. Three versions or more on blue or white paper, sizes vary.
Each - **$30 $65 $110**

BRG-24

❑ **BRG-24. "Buck Rogers" Cardboard Helmet,**
1934. Cocomalt. Helmet - **$135 $265 $500**

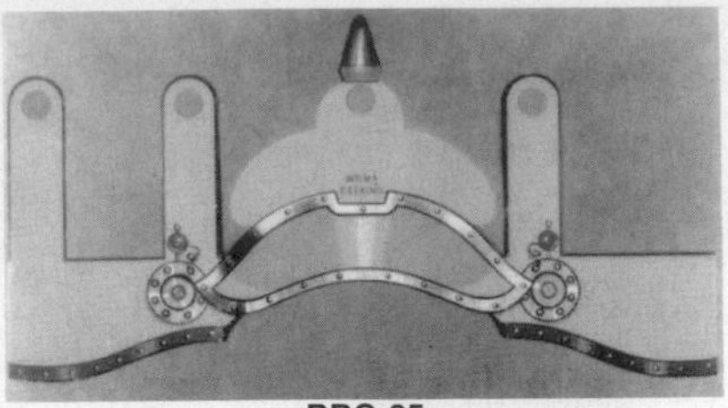

BRG-25

❑ **BRG-25. "Wilma Deering" Cardboard Helmet,**
1934. Cocomalt. Helmet - **$135 $265 $500**

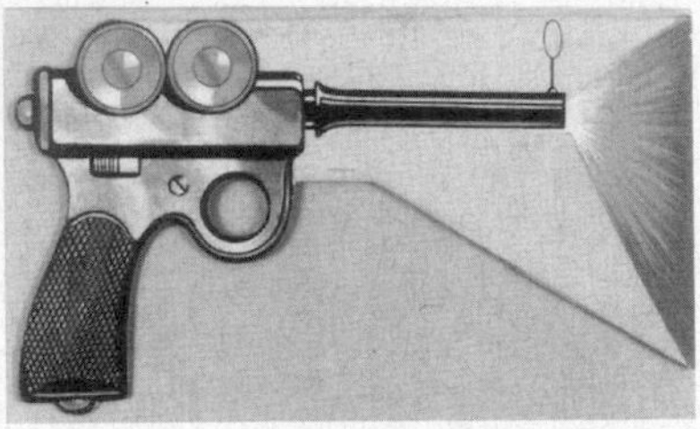

BRG-26

❑ **BRG-26. Cardboard Pop Gun,**
1934. Cocomalt. Came with Buck or Wilma paper helmet. See BRG-24-27.
Gun - **$90 $195 $385**

BRG-27

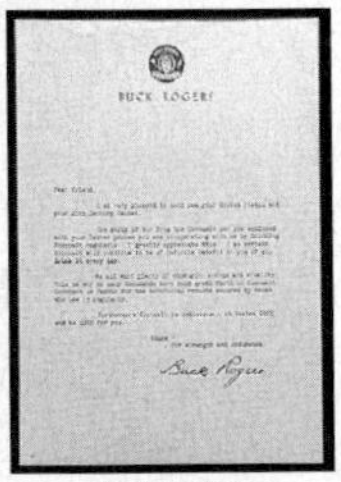

BRG-28

❑ **BRG-27. Large Mailer For Buck Or Wilma Helmet And Rocket Pistol,**
1934. Cocomalt. Both variations shown. See pistol BRG-26.
Black on tan mailer - **$65 $150 $300**
Full color mailer - **$125 $300 $600**

❑ **BRG-28. Letter Enclosed With Buck Or Wilma Helmet And Rocket Pistol,**
1934. Cocomalt. Blue paper letter. - **$60 $110 $185**

BRG-20

❑ **BRG-20. Cocomalt "Buck Rogers Cut-Out Adventure Book",**
1933. Rare. Came with letter and separate cardboard sheet for theater stage done in orange tones. Has 20 stand-ups. See order form BRG-21.
Complete Uncut - **$3000 $6000 $9000**
Complete, Figures Cut - **$700 $1400 $2400**

(2 VIEWS OF THE BOX)

BRG-29

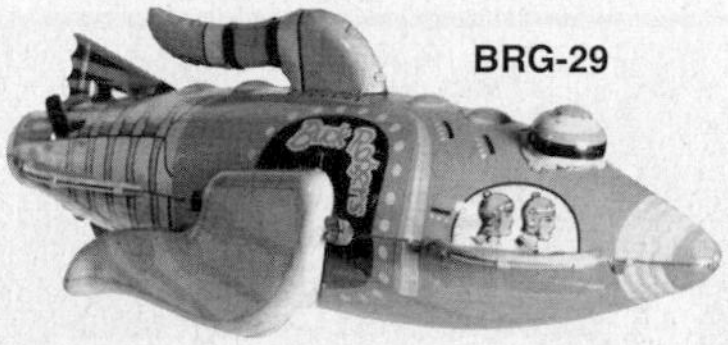

❏ BRG-29. "Buck Rogers" Tin Wind-Up Rocketship,
1934. Store item by Marx Toys. 12" long. Tail fin flint cover often missing or replaced. Toy came in colorful box. Toy Only - **$400 $800 $1600**
Box - **$425 $850 $1750**

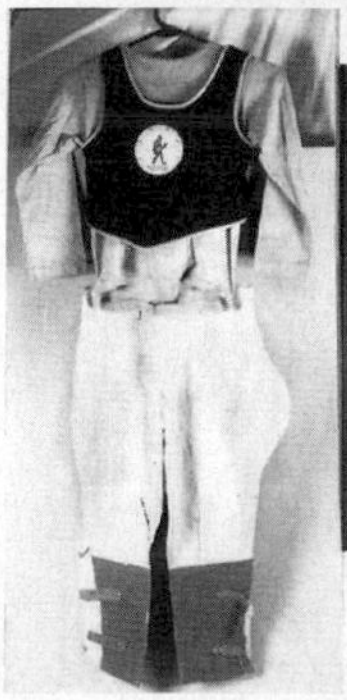

(PATCH ON VEST ENLARGED ABOVE)

BRG-30

❏ BRG-30. Child's Playsuit,
1934. Scarce. Store item and Cream of Wheat. Came with suede cloth helmet XZ-42. Jersey is orange. Sizes 4 to 14 made by Sackman Brothers. Playsuit also made for girls with khaki skirt.
Uniform, Complete Except Helmet - **$550 $1350 $2750**
Vest Only With Patch - **$225 $550 $1100**
Store Box Only - **$300 $675 $1200**

(KILLER KANE) (BUCK) (WILMA)

(ARDALA)

(LEAFLET)

BRG-31

❏ BRG-31. Killer Kane, Buck Rogers and Wilma Painted Lead Figures Set Plus Single Ardala,
1934. The set of three painted figures were given individually packaged in cellophane with a 5x5-5/8" sheet promoting the radio program. Recently discovered are two circa 1935 pedestaled metal figurines of Ardala and Buck Rogers (the latter we have not seen.) Ardala is 2.75" tall with copper colored finish over white metal, one hand on hip and one outstretched arm pointing downward. "J.F. Dille Co." is stamped into the base front and "Cocomalt" is stamped under the base. Ardala's design is a close match to cards 14 or 31 in the Buck Rogers card game. See BRG-98. Beware of recent alloy reproductions.
Near Mint Each Figure Sealed With Leaflet - **$300**
Each Loose Killer Kane, Buck Rogers or Wilma - **$50 $85 $150**
Each Leaflet - **$20 $40 $75**
Ardala - **$150 $300 $600**

(BOX FRONT)

(SIDE PANEL)

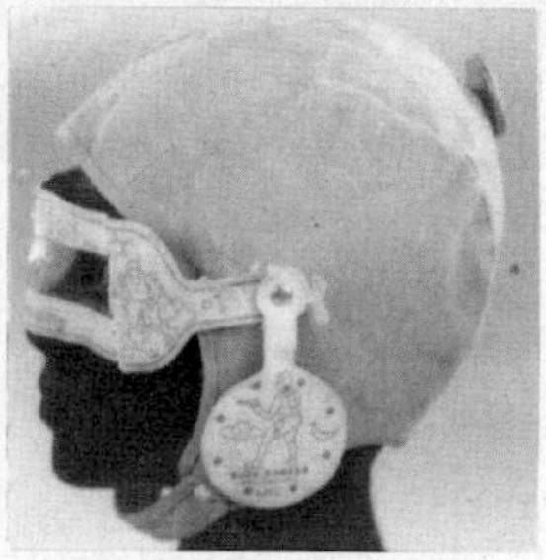

BRG-32

❏ BRG-32. "Buck Rogers 25th Century" Navigation Helmet by Daisy,
1934. Store item (brown suede cloth version) and Cream of Wheat (leather version). Suede version XZ-42 was included with previous item and came unboxed in three sizes. Leather version XZ-34 issued in 1935 came boxed in three sizes. Suede version has white or yellow cloth visor with cloth ear flaps. Leather version came with metal visor and metal flaps.
Each Helmet - **$300 $700 $1200**
XZ-34 Store Box - **$375 $725 $1400**

BRG-33

❏ BRG-33. Buck Rogers Gum Booklets,
1934. Big Thrill Chewing Gum. Six Buck Rogers titles from set of 24 booklets, with additional six each for Buck Jones, Dick Tracy and Tailspin Tommy. 2-3/8x3" with eight pages. Color covers with black and white scenes inside. Buck is shown on one corner of the Goudey Co. wrapper. Booklets are usually brittle from age.
Each Buck Rogers - **$24 $72 $170**

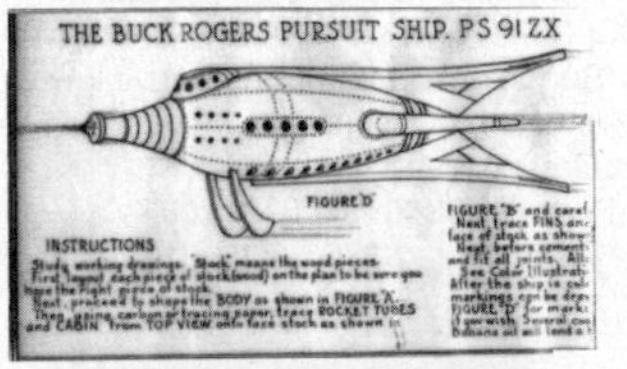

BRG-34

❑ BRG-34. Rocketship Balsa Wood Model,
1934. Six in set (#6 shown), each boxed ready-made or unfinished with color/bw instruction sheet. Sold in stores (Sears offered #1,3,and 4) or as newspaper premium. Only #4 "Super Dreadnought" was available (unfinished) as Cream of Wheat premium. The full set of models was completed by late 1935. Instruction sheets 11x17" were still available into the early 1940s. Boxes are 7-1/8" long. A 7th model ship was drawn but never released by Dille. All seven and others were seen at the 1934 Chicago World's Fair.
Each Boxed - **$325 $650 $1300**
Instruction Sheet - **$115 $265 $450**

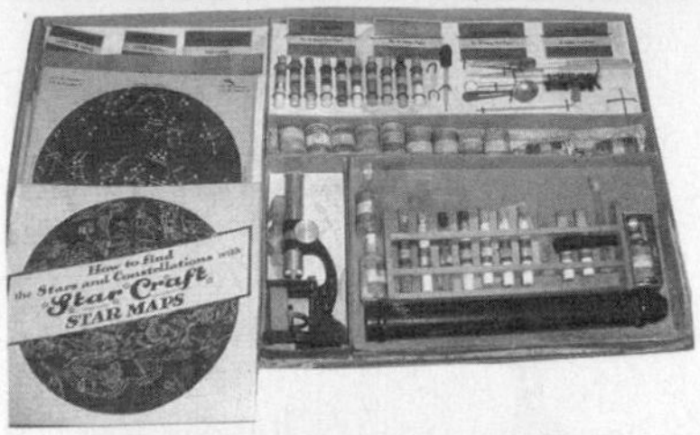

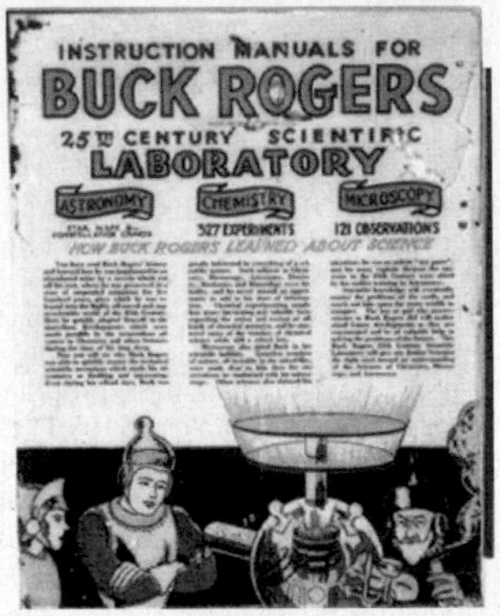

BRG-35

❑ BRG-35. Scientific Laboratory,
1934. Store item by Porter Chemical Co. Pictured are box, open box and envelope that held three instruction manuals. Many other items came in the large 17.5 x 31" x 3" deep set. Issue price of $15.00 limited sales, and few if any 100% complete sets are known. Set included generic microscope and Buck Rogers labeled telescope.
Empty Box - **$1000 $3000 $6500**
Complete (or nearly) - **$3000 $6000 $13,000**

(ENLARGED VIEW OF LABEL ABOVE)

BRG-36

❑ BRG-36. "Buck Rogers Telescope",
1934. Store item, part of Scientific Laboratory set. See BRG-35. Black covering, 14" long, not the later Cream of Wheat or Popsicle versions. - **$150 $500 $1000**

(COMBAT SET BOX)

(GUN BOX)

(HANDLE ENLARGED)

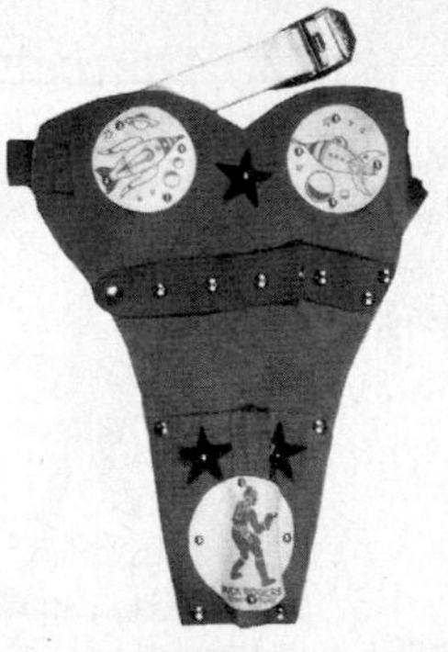

BRG-37

❑ BRG-37. Rocket Pistol XZ-31 and Holster XZ-33 by Daisy,
1934. Store item. Gun is 9.5" long with black finish and cocking handle. Box is red and black. The 9-3/4" three-color suede cloth holster and belt came unboxed or boxed with the gun, sold as XZ-32 "25th Century Combat Set." This box pictures Buck firing his pistol. A 25 x 38" dealer poster was also made.
Gun - **$125 $275 $550**
Holster - **$100 $200 $450**
Gun Box - **$350 $550 $825**
Combat Set XZ-32 Box - **$375 $600 $1150**

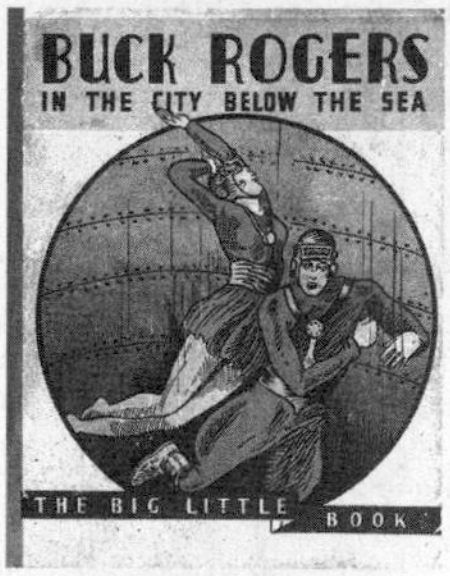

BRG-38

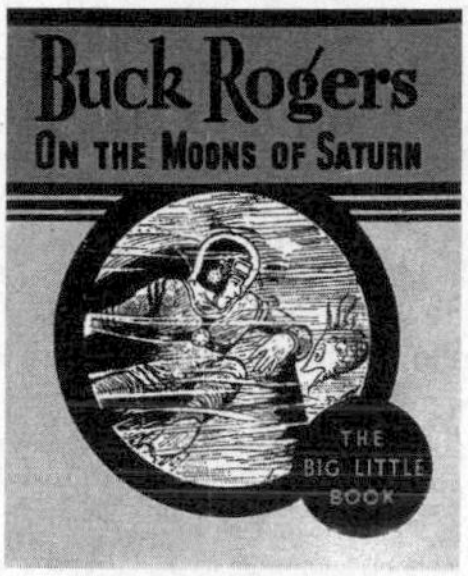

BRG-39

❑ **BRG-38. "Buck Rogers In The City Below The Sea" BLB #765,**
1934. Cocomalt. Whitman softcover premium version but has no Cocomalt advertising. Also issued as Whitman hardcover, both with same cover design. Softcover - **$58 $174 $410**
Hardcover - **$33 $99 $230**

❑ **BRG-39. "Buck Rogers On The Moons Of Saturn" BLB,**
1934. Cocomalt. No number Whitman softcover premium version but has no Cocomalt advertising. Also issued as Whitman #1143 hardcover, see next item. - **$58 $174 $410**

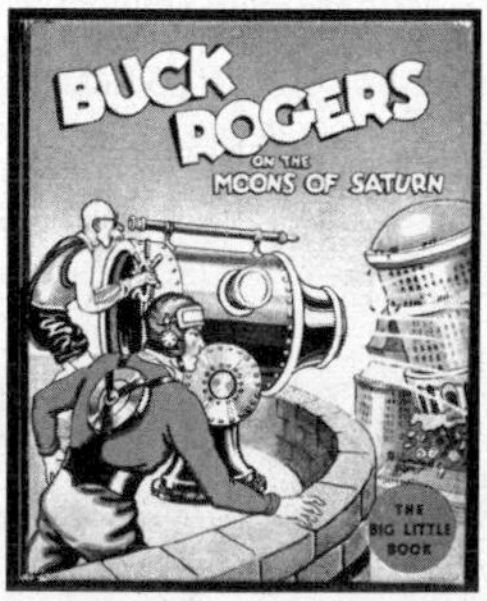

BRG-40

❑ **BRG-40. "Buck Rogers On The Moons Of Saturn" BLB #1143,**
1934. Whitman hardcover. - **$34 $102 $240**

BRG-41

BRG-42

❑ **BRG-41. Walgreen Drugstores World's Fair 2 For 1 Ticket,**
1934. For use at Chicago's "Island Midway" attractions including the "Buck Rogers Show." Upper portion of ticket stub with perforated coupons shown. - **$90 $200 $335**

❑ **BRG-42. "The Adventures Of Buck Rogers" Big Big Book,**
1934. Published by Whitman. #4057, 7x9-1/2" hardcover. Another edition with thinner paper exists, and because spine width was not changed, covers are less snug against the pages. - **$124 $372 $975**

BRG-43

❑ **BRG-43. "A Century Of Progress-I Was There" Brass Key Fob,**
1934. From Buck Rogers show at the fair during 1934 season. 1" holed as made. Giveaways included a pad and pencil set and a generic jigsaw puzzle. - **$200 $450 $750**

BRG-44

BRG-45

❑ **BRG-44. "A Century Of Progress" Chicago World's Fair Litho. Button,**
1934. Blue, orange and white 1-1/8" by Greenduck Co. - **$100 $300 $600**

❑ **BRG-45. Birthstone Initial Ring,**
1934. Cocomalt. Unmarked brass Buck Rogers tie-in issue and other non-Buck offers, top has personalized single initial designated by orderer. Also offered by Popsicle, 1939. - **$150 $325 $550**

(CASTER SET LID)

(CASTER SET OPEN)

(RAPAPORT CATALOG)

(RARE MOLD E-2507)

BRG-46

❑ **BRG-46. Electric Caster Set and Catalog,**
1934. Caster sets were store items by Rapaport Brothers. Sets were also made in 1935 for total of 3 different. Earliest box size is 7x18" then changed to 10x19". Pliers came with only one set and are scarce. There are only three catalog versions; one includes eight daily strips and photos of caster and mold sets. Caster sets were sold with one of eight molds. Two of the eight are rare. These are the Amphibian Squadron of Neptune (3 figures) and the recently discovered mold E-2507 Martian Stratosphere Patrol consisting of 3 extra-large figures depicting Martian Sky-Fighters, one with hand-held ray-gun, one advancing with disintegrator, and one riding a small rocket sled. Set shown lacks only four paint cans (red, yellow, blue, black.) Sets made were Electric, Midget and Caster Outfit. The eight molds make 22 figures.
Caster Set - **$575 $1400 $2500**
Catalog - **$110 $275 $450**
Typical Mold (Both Sides) - **$75 $125 $200**

HOW TO PLAY
BUCK ROGERS GAME

This game can be played by two, three, or four players. The object of this Buck Rogers game is to be first in reaching "Finis."

Each player spins the "Rocket Ship Direction Finder"—and then moves up the number of spaces indicated by the number on the card. If the player spins a 5, then he moves five spaces. If the player spins zero, then he loses his turn.

When a player lands on a space with special instructions, he must move according to those instructions.

If a player reaches a space already occupied then he must move back five spaces.

When you reach "Finis," yell "Buck Rogers," and win.

LUTZ & SHEINKMAN, INC., N. Y. C.

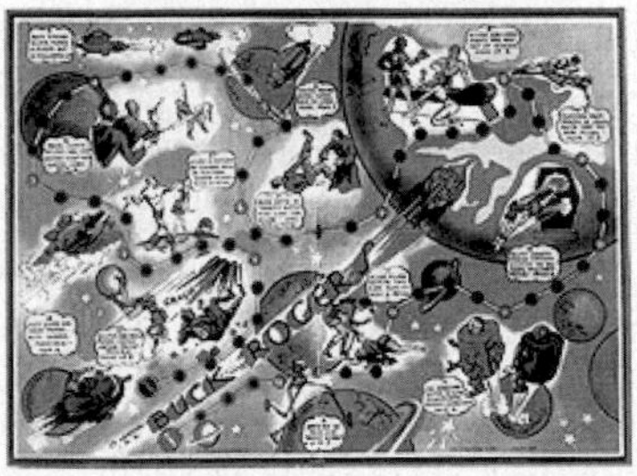

BRG-47

❑ BRG-47. "Buck Rogers Game Of The 25th Century A.D.",
1934. Colorful store item by Lutz and Sheinkman, Inc. with Stephen Slesinger copyright. Box holds 13x18" board with cardboard spinner, four cardboard markers in a punch-out frame, and instruction sheet.
Complete - **$300 $625 $1250**
Board Only - **$150 $300 $550**

BRG-48

❑ BRG-48. Rick Yager Personal Stationery,
1934. Scenes in blue. - **$60 $100 $200**

BRG-49

❑ BRG-49. Set of Three Colorful Board Games,
1934. Store item and Cream of Wheat premium. Came with 40 cards and 12 miniature bowling pin-shaped wood markers. Made by Lutz & Sheinkman. Instructions printed on game boards. Box size was 8-1/2"x17".
Complete Boxed Set - **$575 $1100 $1750**
Each Board - **$135 $300 $475**

BRG-50

❑ BRG-50. Macy's Train Ride Decal,
1934. New York department store. 2x4" red on blue. Rare. - **$125 $300 $600**

BRG-51

❑ BRG-51. Saturday Chicago American Litho. Button,
c. 1934. Multicolor on white 1" by Greenduck Co. - **$60 $140 $250**

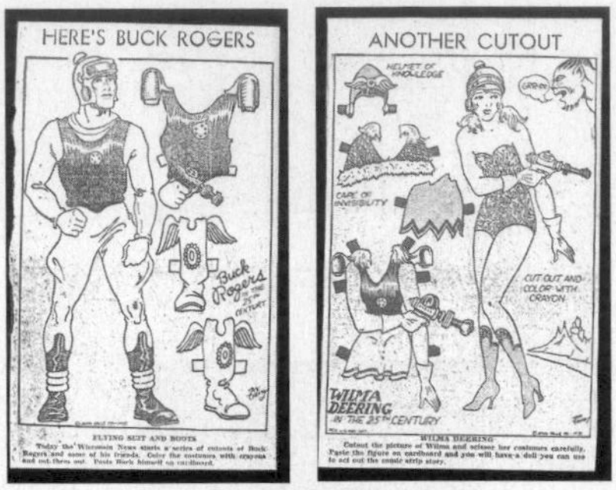

BRG-52

❑ BRG-52. Buck & Wilma Newspaper Cut-Outs,
1935. Wisconsin News. Two 4x7" black and white panels picturing them and their outfits to be scissored out and crayoned. Also printed in other papers during July, 1935.
Each Uncut - **$40 $85 $175**

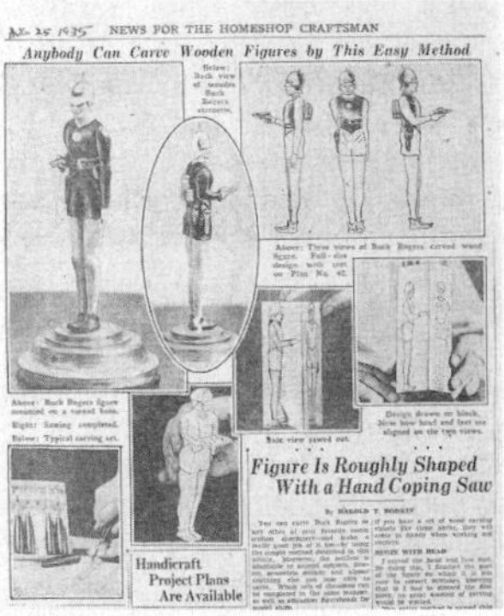
NEWS FOR THE HOMESHOP CRAFTSMAN
Anybody Can Carve Wooden Figures by This Easy Method
Figure Is Roughly Shaped With a Hand Coping Saw
Handicraft Project Plans Are Available

BRG-53

❑ BRG-53. Homeshop Craftsmen Model Figure Article,
1935. Detroit News. August 25 illustrated instruction article for carving wooden comic character figures using Buck Rogers as pictured example. Complete Article - **$30 $60 $100**

BRG-54

BRG-55

❑ **BRG-54. "Buck Rogers In The City Of Floating Globes" BLB,**
1935. Cocomalt premium by Whitman. Issued only as softcover with Cocomalt ad on back. An 8x10" color poster showing same cover scene was a Century of Progress giveaway sponsored by Amoco. - **$104 $312 $725**

❑ **BRG-55. "Tarzan Cups" Premium Booklet Featuring Buck Rogers,**
1935. Tarzan Ice Cream Cups or Lily Tulip brand. In the Big Little Book style, 1/2" thick, softcover only. From Whitman set of six different characters, each obtained for 12 cup lids. - **$150 $450 $1200**

BRG-56

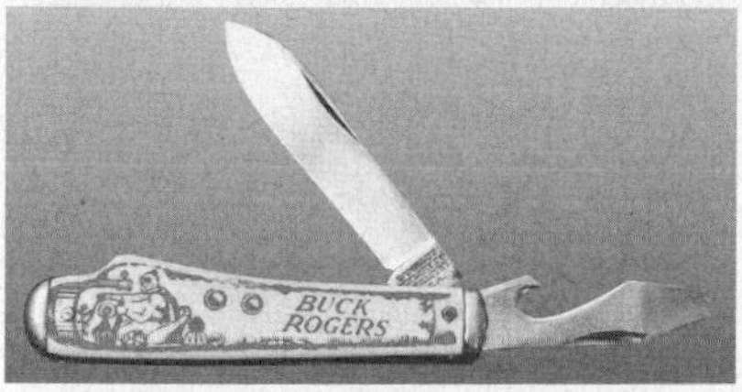

BRG-57

❑ **BRG-56. "Rocket Ship Knife" Box,**
1935. Scarce. Cream of Wheat and store item. Box Only - **$325 $650 $1300**

❑ **BRG-57. "Buck Rogers" Steel/Cello. Pocketknife,**
1935. Scarce. Store item produced by Adolph Kastor with manufacturer's name, Camillus Cutlery Co., on one of the two blades. Also a premium from Cream of Wheat. Same image on both grips in red, green or blue styles. Color easily worn off. - **$300 $600 $1200**

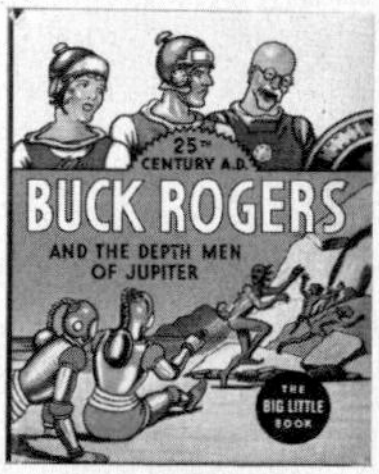

BRG-58

BRG-59

❑ **BRG-58. "Buck Rogers and the Depth Men Of Jupiter" BLB #1169,**
1935. Whitman hardcover. - **$33 $99 $230**

❑ **BRG-59. "Buck Rogers and the Doom Comet" BLB #1178,**
1935. Whitman hardcover. - **$31 $93 $220**

(COMBAT SET BOX)

(GUN BOX)

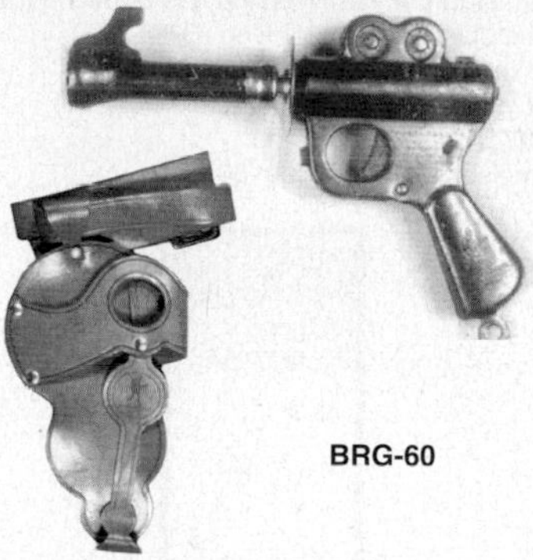
BRG-60

❑ **BRG-60. Rocket Pistol XZ-35 and Holster XZ-36 by Daisy,**
1935. Store item called "Wilma's Gun." Box is red and black. Gun is 7.5" long with black finish and cocking handle. Leather holster with round hole on holster front straps. Holster came with 30" leather belt. No box for holster alone, but gun, holster and belt were sold boxed as Combat Set XZ-37.
Gun - **$150 $300 $650**
Holster - **$75 $150 $300**
Gun Box - **$250 $450 $825**
Combat Set XZ-37 Box - **$375 $650 $1150**

BRG-61

❑ **BRG-61. Dille Syndicate Stationery,**
1935 and later. Buck Rogers scenes in black on red and rocket image in black and white. - **$65 $150 $265**

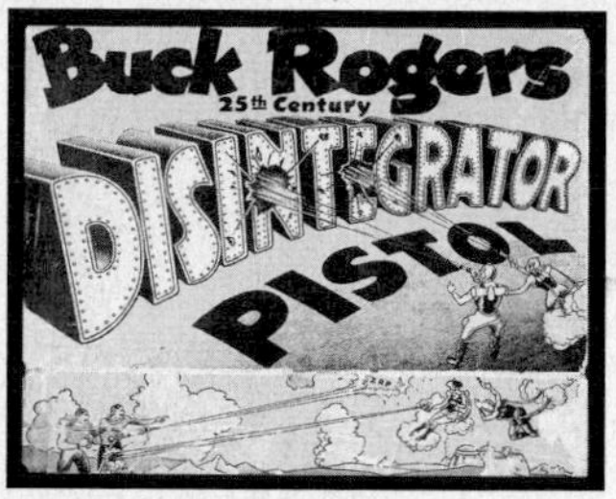

(GUN BOX)

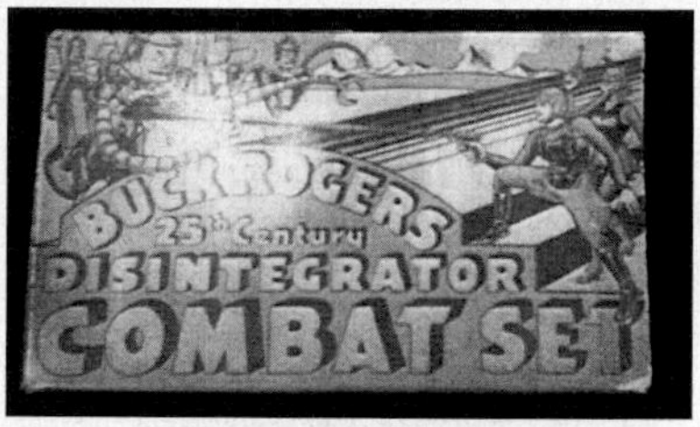

(COMBAT SET BOX)

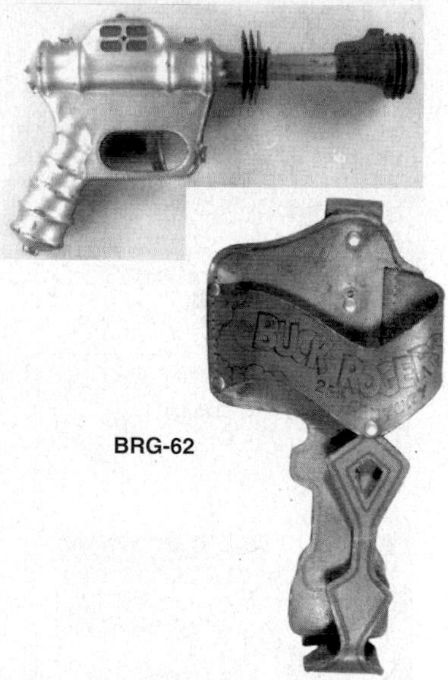

BRG-62

❑ **BRG-62. Disintegrator Pistol XZ-38 and Holster XZ-39 by Daisy,**
1935. Store item and Cream of Wheat. Used in 1939 as Popsicle premium. Copper finish, gun is 9.75" long. Flint produces spark. Leather holster with diamond-shaped hole on front strap. Holster came with 31" leather belt. No box for holster alone, but gun, holster and belt were sold boxed as Disintegrator Combat Set XZ-40. Gun box is yellow, Combat box is yellow and red, and is rare.
Gun - **$200 $400 $800**
Holster - **$150 $275 $500**
Gun Box - **$325 $600 $1050**
Combat Set XZ-40 Box - **$450 $825 $1350**

BRG-63

❑ **BRG-63. "Punch-O-Bag",**
1935. Morton's Salt premium by Lou Fox, Chicago. Came in 3"x5" envelope done in two design styles. Various colored balloons each showing a different character. Balloon typically missing or disintegrated. See BRG-190.
Envelope Only - **$35 $75 $135**

BRG-64

BRG-65

❑ **BRG-64. "Buck Rogers 25th Century Adventures" Printing Set,**
1935. Store item and Cream of Wheat. Set No. 4080 by StamperKraft Co. Includes 14 character stamps. - **$250 $600 $1200**

❑ **BRG-65. "Cosmic Conquests" Boxed Printing Set,**
1935. Store item by StamperKraft Co. Set #4090 with 22 character stamps. A set with 15 character stamps and alphabet was issued as #4090-S. See "Astral Heroes" set BRG-71.
Each Set - **$275 $675 $1300**

BRG-66

❑ **BRG-66. Pocketwatch,**
1935. Store item by Ingraham Co. Lightning bolt hands in copper color and case back pictures Comet Man. A 1971 version has brass hands and a blank case back. See (BRG-223).
Watch Only - **$300 $600 $1200**
Box With Golden Cardboard Insert - **$600 $1200 $2300**
Complete - **$900 $1800 $3500**

BRG-67

❑ **BRG-67. "Buck Rogers 25th Century Catalog,"**
1935. John Dille folder catalog of items available from company by mail order. Some items shown were also used as premiums. Black and white folder opens to 9x12". - **$115 $275 $550**

BRG-68

❑ **BRG-68. School Kit Bag,**
1935. Store item and Cream of Wheat premium. Three styles with frontal variations, made of suede cloth or leather. - **$600 $1350 $3250**

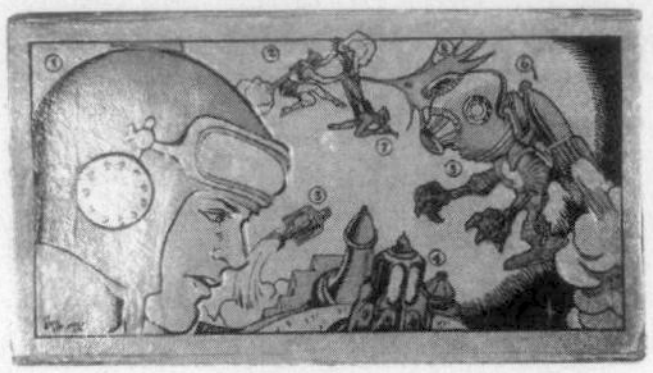

BRG-69

❑ **BRG-69. Pencil Box No. 35228,**
1935. Store item and Cream of Wheat premium. Red and blue, issued with contents. Between 1934 and 1938 at least 45 different boxes were made in various sizes and colors with 12 basic art scenes.
- **$75 $150 $300**

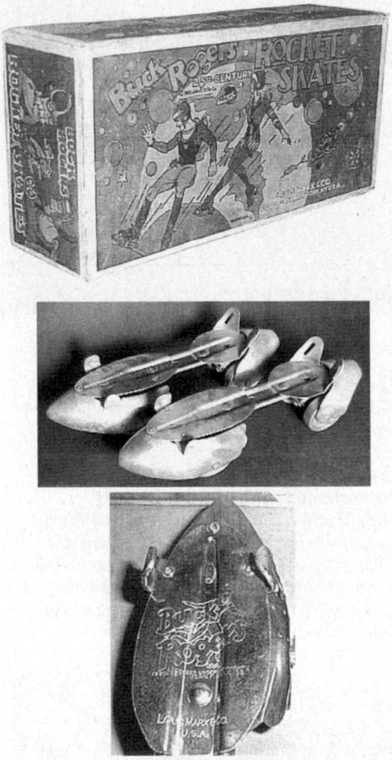

(ENLARGED VIEW OF FOOT PLATE)

BRG-70

❑ **BRG-70. Buck Rogers Rocket Skates,**
1935. Store item by Louis Marx. Pair of 11-1/2" long heavy steel roller skates with wheel coverings simulating a rocketship design. Shown in our photo without leather straps. Rear end of skates hold a 1" red jeweled reflector. Front of each foot plate has impressed image of Buck and his name "Buck Rogers" in large letters. Came with metal combination key and wrench to adjust clamps and tighten nuts. Rare.
Box - **$1100 $2250 $4500**
Skates - **$1200 $2500 $4000**

BRG-71

❑ **BRG-71. "Astral Heroes" Printing Set,**
1935. Store item by StamperKraft Co. Set number 4070 with seven character stamps.
See BRG-64 and BRG-65.
Complete Boxed - **$250 $650 $1250**

BRG-72

❑ **BRG-72. "Buck Rogers Paint Book",**
1935. Store item by Whitman Publishing Company. Whitman No. 679. Large 11-1/4x14" format. Has eight red and green pages with others in black and white. - **$175 $350 $850**

BRG-73

❑ **BRG-73. "Buck Rogers In The 25th Century" Cello. Button,**
c. 1935. Full color on dark blue 1" with Whitehead & Hoag Co. back paper. - **$40 $85 $150**

BRG-74

❑ **BRG-74. Dixie-Style Ice Cream Cup Lid,**
c. 1935. C.B.S. Radio. Red lettering on tan cardboard. Reads "Listen To Buck Rogers In The 25th Century On CBS!" - **$85 $165 $350**

BRG-75

❑ **BRG-75. "Ardala" Metal Alloy Figure By Britains,**
1936. Cream of Wheat. Full color paint. Each with moveable arm. Set (with name under base) of Buck, Wilma, Killer Kane, Ardala, Dr. Huer, Robot. Reproductions in metal made by DP Miniatures in 1989 do not have name under base.
Robot - **$400 $1000 $2000**
Others, Each - **$250 $500 $1000**

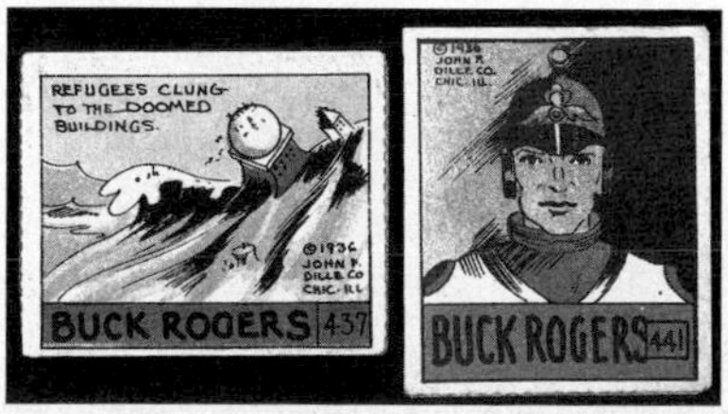

BRG-76

❑ **BRG-76. Cartoon Adventures Perforated Strip Cards,**
1936. Set of 24 (#425-448) from a larger set of 48 that includes 3 other newspaper comic characters. Cards are 2-1/4x2-3/4". Beware: card #442 has been reprinted.
Each In Buck Rogers Set - **$50 $100 $200**

BRG-77

❑ **BRG-77. Buck Rogers Standing On North America Picture,**
1936. Newspaper premium offered as "Dandy Picture Of Buck Rogers." Black and white 5-1/2x8-1/2" stiff paper. Example shown was later signed by the artist Dick Calkins. Scarce.
Unsigned - **$275 $600 $1000**

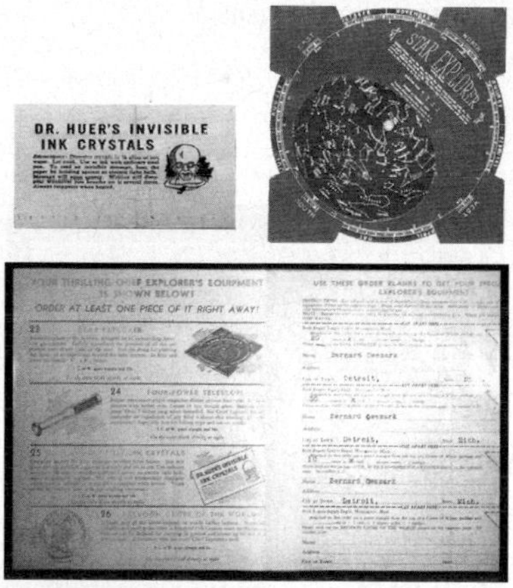

BRG-78

❑ **BRG-78. "Chief Explorer" Leaflet, "Star Explorer" Dial Device, and Dr. Huer's Ink Crystals**
1936. Cream of Wheat. Offers Chief Explorer badge (See BRG-95), Star Explorer (star finder device), Four-Power Telescope (smaller than one with Scientific Laboratory and not Popsicle version), Dr. Huer's Invisible Ink Crystals and Balloon Globe of the World. Also see BRG-194.
Leaflet - **$150 $300 $600**
Dial - **$125 $250 $400**
Crystals Envelope - **$100 $200 $300**

BRG-79

BRG-80

❑ BRG-79. Dixie Ice Cream Lid,
1936. Browntone photo. Inscribed for Cream of Wheat radio series. Lid also issued with Breyers Ice Cream imprint and others. A generic three-fold album with slots to hold the lids was available. Two color varieties.
Browntone - **$30 $65 $125**
Black and White - **$40 $80 $150**

❑ BRG-80. "Lite-Blaster" Flashlight,
1936. Cream of Wheat. Design in four colors. Rare. - **$800 $1600 $3500**

BRG-81

❑ BRG-81. Dixie Ice Cream Picture,
1936. Photo of Matthew Crowley, radio portrayer. Color, 8"x10", obtained by redeeming lids. - **$75 $165 $300**

BRG-82

❑ BRG-82. "Buck Rogers On The Air For Cream Of Wheat" Gummed Back Paper Sticker,
1936. Dark blue and yellow. 1-3/4x2-3/4". - **$65 $135 $275**

BRG-83

❑ BRG-83. "Irwin Projector" With Comic Character Films and Battery Operated Small Projector,
1936. Unmarked but offered as premium with six Buck Rogers film loops of 16mm black and white cartoon art (from group of 13 titles) in Cream of Wheat Buck Rogers Solar Scouts Club Manual. Films also issued on reels of four different lengths in 2-1/2" or 4" boxes.
Boxed Projector - **$60 $100 $175**
Each Boxed Film - **$8 $12 $20**

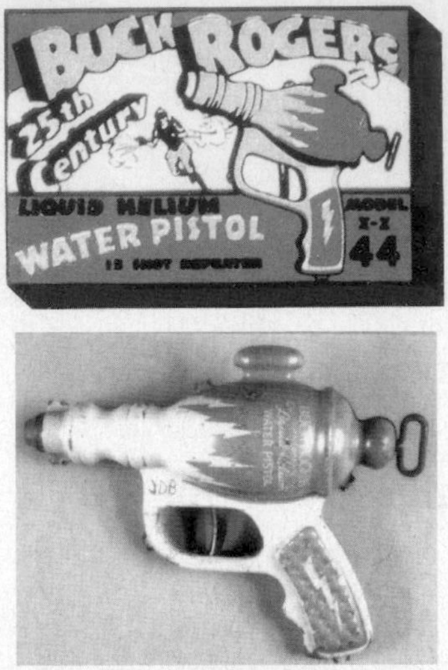

BRG-84

❑ BRG-84. Liquid Helium Water Pistol XZ-44 And Box By Daisy,
1936. Store item. Used in 1939 as Popsicle premium. No holster made. Gun examples are now non-functional due to aging of bladder. A red, yellow and black promotional flier was issued. Both boxes are in red and identical except box for copper gun says "New copper lacquer finish," or "Copper," stamped on box front. Gun is 7-1/4" long.
Red and Yellow Version - **$325 $850 $1850**
Copper Colored Version - **$375 $1000 $2100**
Box Only - **$400 $850 $1800**

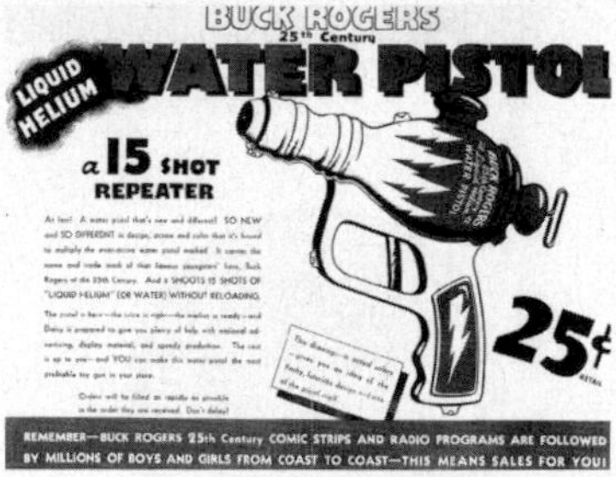

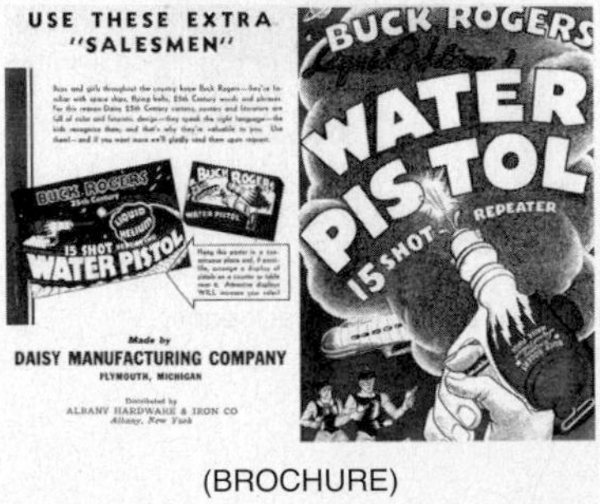

(BROCHURE)

(POSTER)

BRG-85

❑ **BRG-85. Water Pistol Promotional Flyer and Dealer Display Poster,**
1936. Daisy Mfg. Co. Brochure is full color 5-1/2x8-1/2" folder. Shown open, front and back. Poster size is unknown.
Brochure - **$150 $300 $600**
Poster - **$500 $1000 $2000**

BRG-86

BRG-87

❑ **BRG-86. "Buck Rogers and the Planetoid Plot" Big Little Book #1197,**
1936. Whitman hardcover. Also published in Portuguese as No. 12 in a set of generic titles. - **$31 $93 $220**

❑ **BRG-87. Decal Probably From Cream Of Wheat,**
1936. Black on gold, 1x1-1/4" with blue serial number on backing paper.
Unused - **$100 $200 $375**

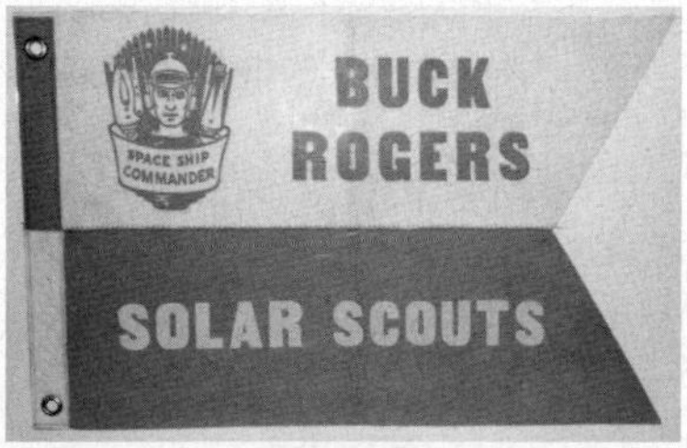

BRG-88

❑ **BRG-88. "Solar Scout" Premium Pennant,**
1936. Cream of Wheat. Rare. Ony 2 known. Has tag on back. 11x18" red and white cloth. - **$1200 $3400 $5000**

BRG-89

❑ **BRG-89. "Solar Scouts" Radio Club Manual,**
1936. Cream Of Wheat. Offers 18 premiums. Color cover with black and red illustrations. Centerfold held two orange pages with blank forms for new member recruitment. - **$100 $275 $600**

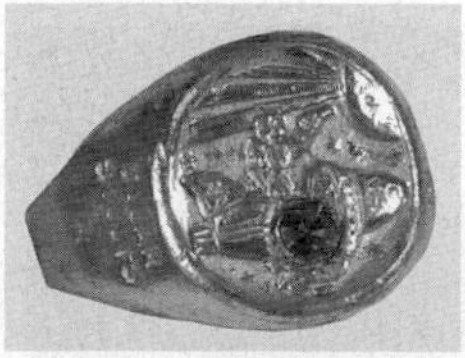

BRG-90

BRG-91

❑ **BRG-90. Repeller Ray Adjustable Brass Ring With Green Stone,**
1936. Scarce. Cream Of Wheat and newspaper premium offer. Original stone is faceted. Beware of replacements. Within Buck Rogers Solar Scouts club, also known as "Supreme Inner Circle" ring. Offered again from 1940 to 1942. - **$650 $2000 $4500**

❑ **BRG-91. Solar Scouts Member Brass Badge,**
1936. Cream of Wheat and newspaper premium offer. Facsimile Buck Rogers signature on reverse. Offered again from 1939 to 1942. At least three reverse varieties. Typical is "Made in U.S.A." Much scarcer is "Robbins Co. Attleboro Made in U.S.A." This version has a matte finish. Double guide value for this variety. Rarest is flat metal back without embossing and without any text. Triple guide value for this variety. - **$30 $60 $100**

BRG-92

❑ **BRG-92. "Solar Scouts" Sweater Emblem,**
1936. Cream of Wheat. Rare. Less than 10 known. Offered first with BRG-16. 3-1/2" red and blue on yellow felt. - **$1750 $5750 $8500**

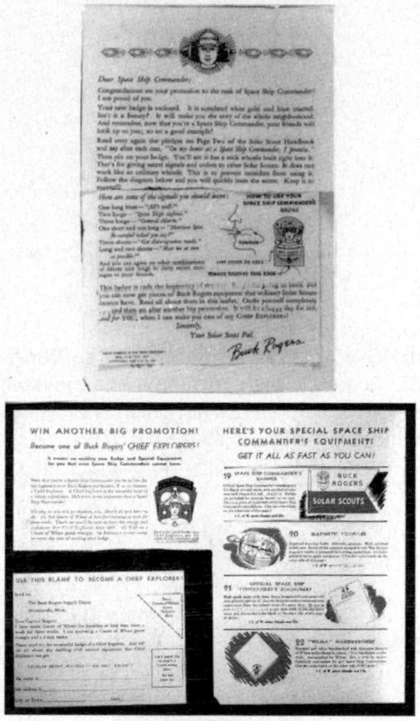

BRG-93

❑ **BRG-93. "Spaceship Commander" Leaflet,**
1936. Cream of Wheat. Offers badge, banner, magnetic compass, stationery, Wilma handkerchief. Leaflet - **$100 $200 $400**

BRG-94

BRG-95

❑ **BRG-94. "Spaceship Commander/Buck Rogers Solar Scouts" Silvered Brass Badge,**
1936. Cream of Wheat and newspaper premium offer. Metallic blue accent paint, holed at bottom to serve as whistle. Offered again from 1940 to 1942. - **$100 $250 $375**

❑ **BRG-95. "Chief Explorer/Buck Rogers Solar Scouts" Brass Badge,**
1936. Cream of Wheat and newspaper premium offer. Red enamel paint background. Badge inscribed on back "Awarded For Distinguished Achievement" with facsimile Buck Rogers signature. Offered again from 1940 to 1942. See BRG-78 and BRG-194. - **$125 $275 $425**

BRG-96

❑ **BRG-96. "Chief Explorer" Brass Badge,**
1936. Scarce. Cream of Wheat and newspaper premium offer. Variety with gold luster and no red enamel paint. - **$175 $375 $700**

BRG-97

❑ **BRG-97. Wilma Deering Brass Pendant With Chain,**
1936. Rare. Cream of Wheat and newspaper premium offer. Back inscription "To My Pal In The Solar Scouts". Offered again from 1940 to 1942; however, without her name on front and without her signature on reverse. - **$250 $600 $1200**

BRG-98

❑ **BRG-98. Boxed Card Game,**
1936. Store item by All-Fair. Box comes in two sizes, larger one shown. 35 full-color cards plus instruction card. Cards are in pairs except for Killer Kane. A few of these card poses are based on the Bucktoys. See BRG-8, and for Ardala only, see BRG-31. - **$200 $400 $800**

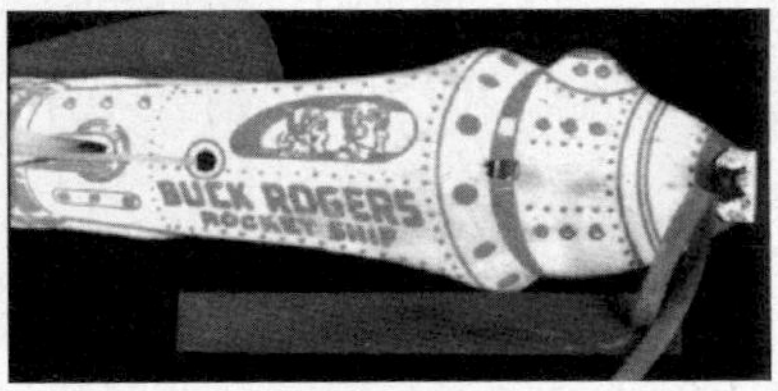

BRG-99

❑ **BRG-99. "Buck Rogers Rocketship" Balsa Flying Toy With Mailer Envelope,**
1936. Rare. Mrs. Karl's Bread by Spotswood Specialty Co., also Cream of Wheat premium. Envelope is plain, comes with wood stick and rubber band launcher. - **$185 $360 $750**

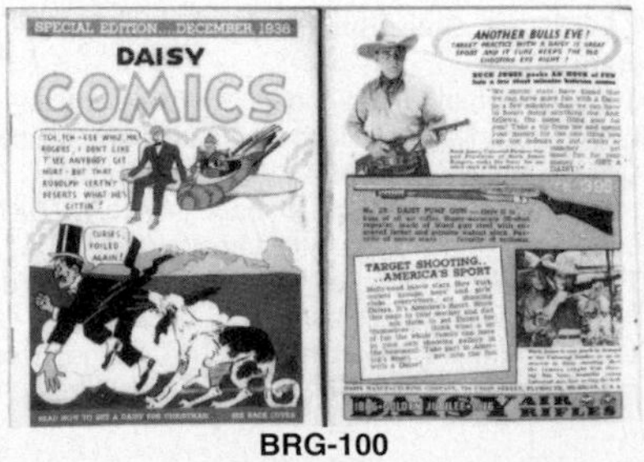

BRG-100

❑ **BRG-100. "Daisy Comics",**
1936. Daisy Mfg. Co. Contents include two-page Buck Rogers comic reprint and shows guns for him plus features on cowboys Buck Jones and Tim McCoy. Thinner and smaller format than a standard comic book. - **$34 $102 $425**

BRG-101

❑ **BRG-101. "25th Century Acousticon Jr." 2-1/4" Cello. Button,**
1936. Rare. Hearing aid device by Dictograph Products Co. Black, blue, red and fleshtone on white background. - **$600 $1800 $3750**

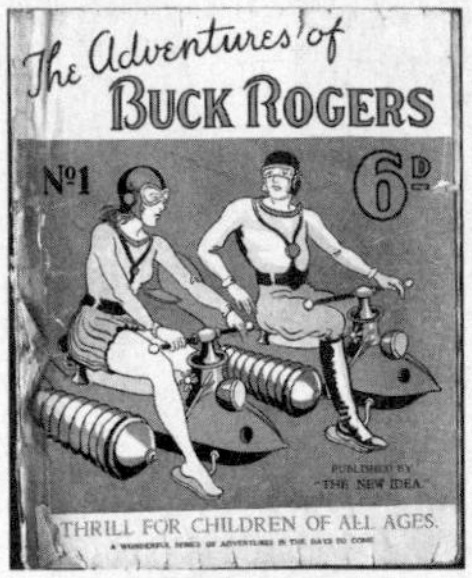

BRG-102

❑ **BRG-102. "The Adventures Of Buck Rogers" Australian Comic Book First Issue,**
1936. Fitchett Brothers. Large format 8.5x10.75" comic with 64 black and white pages featuring daily strip reprints by Dick Calkins. Strips are printed three per page with additional story text below each. 181 issues were published until 1953. All covers were in color with locally done original art. - **$125 $250 $500**

BRG-103

❑ **BRG-103. "Buck Rogers 25th. Century" Cello. Button,**
c. 1936. Issuer unknown. 1-1/2" black on blue picturing Buck with Dr. Huer peering over Buck's left shoulder. Only a couple examples known, both with staining. - **$350 $950 $2250**

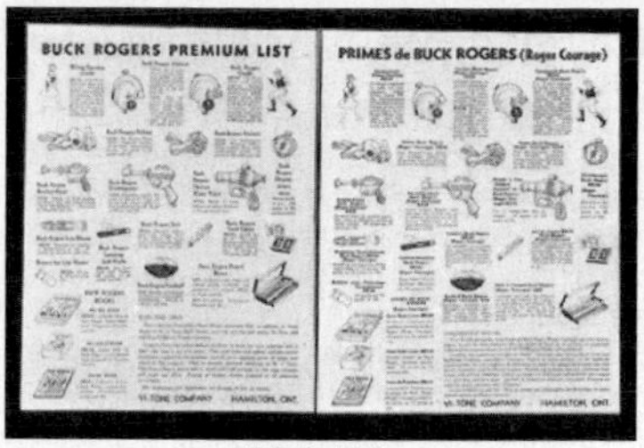

BRG-104

❑ BRG-104. Canadian "Buck Rogers Premium List,"
c. 1936. Vi-Tone Company Hamilton, Ont. 8-1/2x11" sheet in English on one side and French on the reverse side showing 19 premiums obtained by saving Vi-Tone and Egg-O Baking Powder coupons. Included are Buck and Wilma outfits, holsters, guns, Light Blaster, books, camping knife, Directoscope, card game, football game, pencil box. The French side has Buck Rogers name in English and identifies him as "Roger Courage." - **$125 $360 $725**

BRG-105

❑ BRG-105. Buck Rogers Fireworks Kit and Advertising Matchbook,
1937. National Fireworks. The company issued three large color folders which describe five sets of fireworks. The example kit shown here is titled "Battle of Mars."
Each Brochure (Not Shown) - **$200 $400 $800**
Each Boxed Kit - **$1500 $3000 $6000**
Matchbook Near Mint Complete - **$300**
Matchbook Empty Or Partial Contents - **$95 $175 $250**

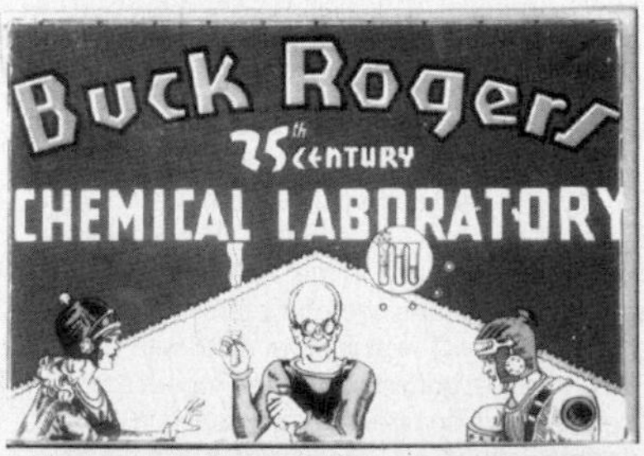

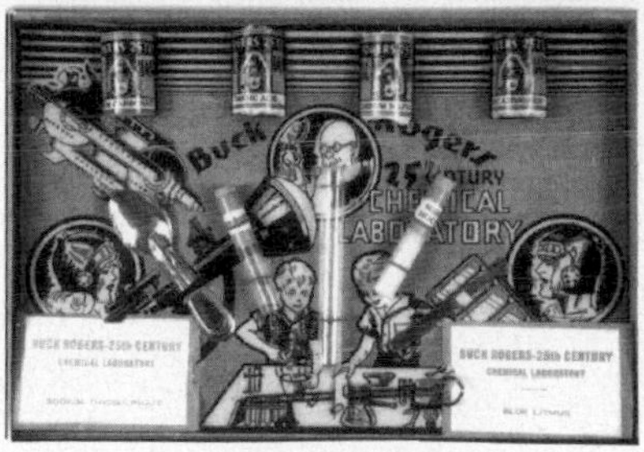

(SMALL SET)

(LARGE SET BOX LID)

BRG-106

❑ BRG-106. Chemical Laboratory Boxed Set,
1937. Store item in two sizes with four-section 6x16" instruction folder. By Gropper Mfg. Co. Small set is 8x12" and 1" deep. Large set size is uncertain. The large set features more detail on the box label.
Small Set - **$450 $850 $1700**
Large Set - **$625 $1300 $2250**
Instruction Booket - **$65 $125 $250**

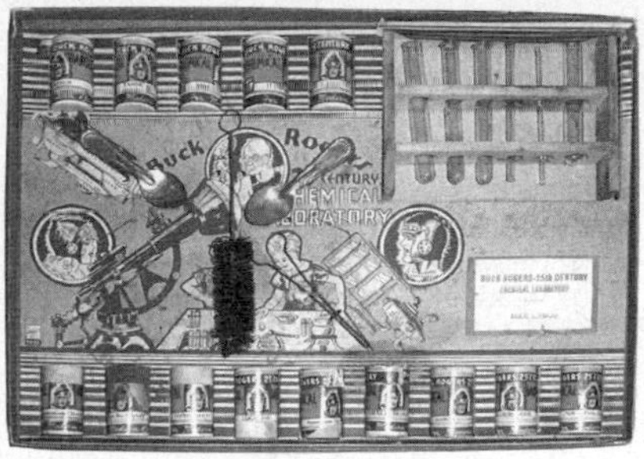

BRG-107

❑ BRG-107. "Outfit" Version "Chemical Laboratory,
1937. Gropper Mfg. Co. 12x16x1" deep. Titled differently and with different scene on label than previous two sets. - **$700 $1600 $2750**

BRG-108

❑ BRG-108. Secret Code Book,
1937. 3.5x5.5" spiral-bound pad with orange covers. Back cover has "Solar Scouts' Zodion Code" as used by them. - **$300 $600 $1200**

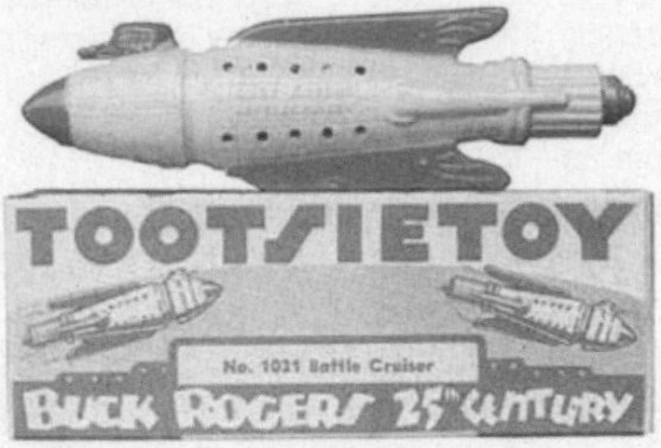

BRG-109

❑ BRG-109. Tootsietoy #1031 "Battle Cruiser",
1937. Metal "Buck Rogers Battle Cruiser TSDDM3030." Used as Popsicle premium in 1939. Earliest box shows three ships. Box shown in photo came into use in the 1940s. Ship had several color variations over the years. Reissued in early 1950s by Dowst in silver color with U.S. Air Force insignia but without Buck Rogers name. The reissue is scarce. Again reissued in 1960s, this time without Air Force insignia. Beware of removed 1950s decal. Slides on string.
Near Mint Boxed - **$600**
Loose - **$75 $175 $350**
1950s Reissue Loose - **$125 $200 $350**
1950s Reissue NM on Blister Card - **$400**
1960s Reissue NM on Blister Card - **$350**

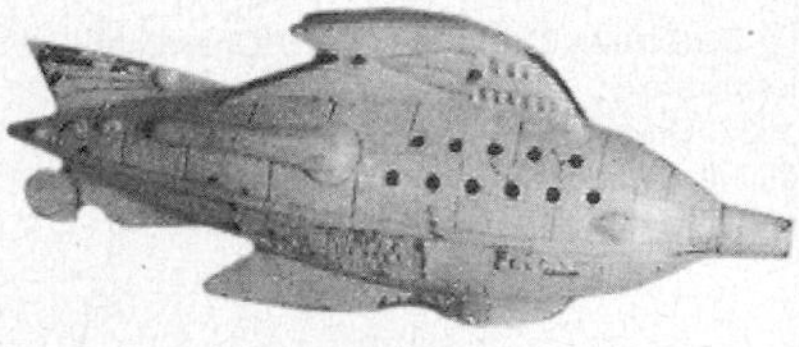

BRG-110

❑ BRG-110. "Earth Jupiter Transport NNS36" Metal Spaceship,
1937. Tootsietoy, perhaps intended as fourth rocketship in their series but may exist as prototype only. Slides on string. Seen in gray and sienna color. Design was used in 1942 daily strip art. - **$600 $1200 $1800**

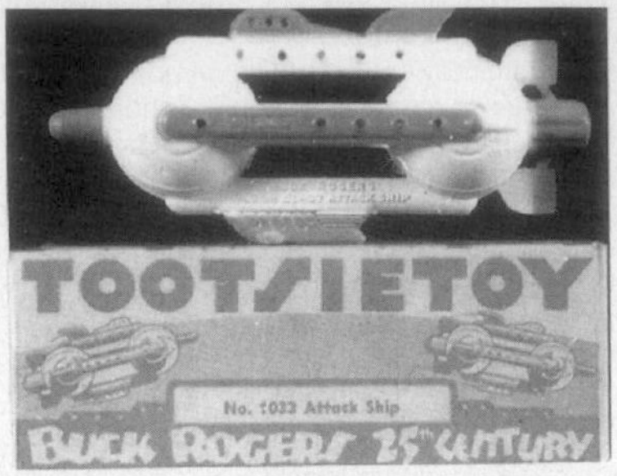

BRG-111

❑ BRG-111. Tootsietoy #1033 "Attack Ship",
1937. Metal "Buck Rogers Flash Blast Attack Ship TS 310 Z". Used as Popsicle premium in 1939. Earliest box shows three ships. Box shown in photo came into use in the 1940s. Ship had several color variations over the years. Reissued in early 1950s by Dowst in silver color with U.S. Air Force insignia but without Buck Rogers name. The reissue is scarce. Again reissued in 1960s, this time without Air Force insignia. Slides on string. Beware of removed 1950s decal.
Near Mint Boxed - **$600**
Loose - **$75 $175 $350**
1950s Reissue Loose - **$125 $200 $350**
1950s Reissue NM on Blister Card - **$400**
1960s Reissue NM on Blister Card - **$350**

(EXAMPLE OF EARLIEST BOX SHOWING THREE SHIPS)

BRG-112

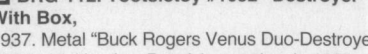

❑ BRG-112. Tootsietoy #1032 "Destroyer" With Box,
1937. Metal "Buck Rogers Venus Duo-Destroyer MK 24 L". Used as Popsicle premium in 1939. Earliest box shows three ships. Box shown in photo came into use in the 1940s. Ship had several color variations over the years. Reissued in early 1950s by Dowst in silver color with U.S. Air Force insignia but without Buck Rogers name. The reissue is scarce. Again reissued in 1960s, this time without Air Force insignia. Slides on string. Beware of removed 1950s decal.
See BRG-118. Single ship boxes are 4.75" long.
Near Mint Boxed - **$600**
Loose - **$75 $175 $350**
1950s Reissue Loose - **$125 $200 $350**
1950s Reissue NM on Blister Card - **$400**
1960s Reissue NM on Blister Card - **$350**

BRG-113

❑ BRG-113. "Buck Rogers" Silver Luster Belt Buckle,
1937. Store item by Reliable Belt Co. Came attached to brown leather belt, see next item.
Buckle Only - **$110 $225 $375**

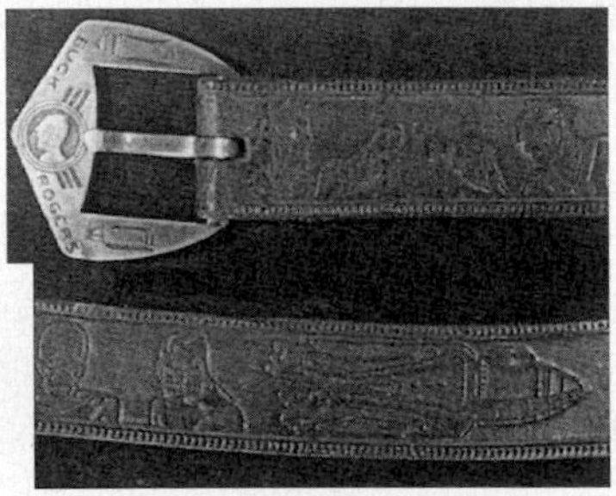

BRG-114

❑ BRG-114. "Buck Rogers" Buckle With Brown Leather Belt,
1937. Store item by Reliable Belt Co. Buckle is the same as preceding item but this example is attached to dark brown leather belt impressed with repeating images of Buck Rogers and other characters of the comic strip. 36" long. See box BRG-140. Buckle And Belt - **$225 $400 $700**

BRG-115

❑ **BRG-115. "Combat Game!",**
1937. Store item by Warren Paper Products Co. Set No. 110. Many full color pre-cut stiff thin cardboard pieces to form Rocket Ship Control Base with accessories of spaceships, guns and 11 standup characters. Total of 65 pieces plus instructions.
Boxed Complete - **$900 $2000 $3800**
Complete No Box - **$375 $800 $1750**

BRG-116

❑ **BRG-116. "Buck Rogers Rocket Rangers" Cello. Button,**
1937. Issuer unknown. 1-1/2" dark blue on white. Only a couple of examples known and the three examples we know about are all heavily stained. - **$425 $850 $1750**

BRG-117

❑ **BRG-117. Canadian Club Member Cello. Button,**
1937. Issuer unknown but 1" in blue/white/orange. Curl reads "Shaw Mfg. Toronto." - **$550 $1650 $3250**

BRG-118 (EXAMPLE OF 1937 BOX LID)

❑ **BRG-118. Buck Rogers Metal Figure 1-3/4" Tall,**
1937. Packaged with Tootsietoy rocketships. Sold only with both four ship boxed sets made in 1937 and 1940. Buck (Silver Color) Or Wilma (Gold Color) with respective name under base.
Each - **$135 $275 $550**

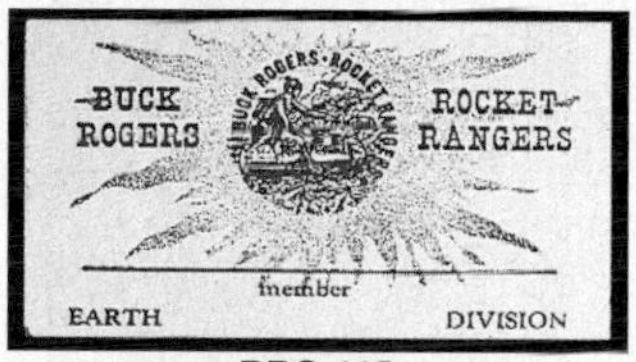

BRG-119

❑ **BRG-119. "Buck Rogers Rocket Rangers" Member Card,**
1937. Black and white card with yellow burst, same design as BRG-116. - **$55 $110 $225**

BRG-120

❑ **BRG-120. "Buck Rogers" Story Color Cover Pencil Tablet,**
1937. Store item. At least six in numbered series. Each has one different story chapter on cover and came in three different sizes.
Each - **$140 $325 $550**

BRG-121

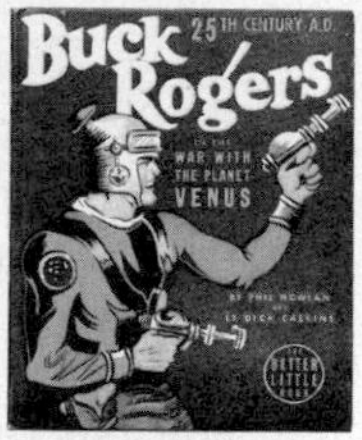

BRG-122

❑ **BRG-121. "Vicks Comics" Comic Book,**
1938. Vicks Chemical Co. published by Eastern Color Printing Co. 64 pages of stories printed earlier in Famous Funnies. Five pages relate to Buck Rogers, the others feature various characters. - **$58 $174 $840**

❑ **BRG-122. "Buck Rogers in the War with the Planet Venus" Better Little Book #1437,**
1938. Whitman, hardcover. - **$31 $93 $220**

BRG-123

❑ **BRG-123. Vicks And Other Premium Comic Books,**
c. 1938. Vicks Chemical Co. shown with their logo and same comic with local store imprint. These thin books reprinted stories from earlier Famous Funnies comic books. At least four additional similar thin versions were produced: one by Hecht, two by Pure Oil and one by Salerno. All were in color.
Each - **$21 $63 $260**

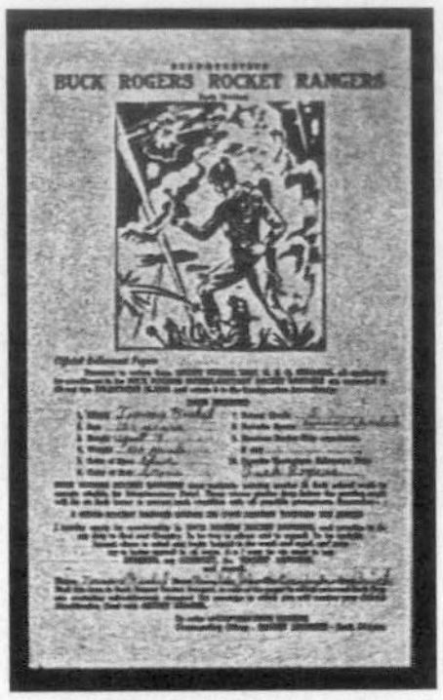

BRG-124

❑ **BRG-124. "Rocket Rangers" Enlistment Sheet,**
1939. Various newspapers. 7-1/4 x 10-1/2" black on yellow with text stating membership card will be sent upon receipt of this enlistment application. Also see BRG-126 and BRG-127. - **$100 $200 $400**

BRG-125

❑ **BRG-125. "Buck Rogers Rocket Police Patrol" Tin Wind-Up,**
1939. Store item by Marx Toys, 12" long. Tail fin flint cover often missing or replaced.
Toy Complete - **$450 $950 $2000**
Box (Text Only, No Art) - **$325 $700 $1200**

BRG-126

❑ **BRG-126. "Rocket Rangers" Club Member Card,**
1939. Pictures "Inter-Planetary Battle Cruiser" on yellow card. Each card acquired by sending offer coupon clipped from newspaper comic strip. Five later versions were on blue or white cards, the last issued in 1977. See cards for years 1944, 1946, 1952, 1958 and 1977. The 1939 card was used until 1942. All card sizes are 2-3/8" x 3-7/8".
This Version - **$90 $185 $375**

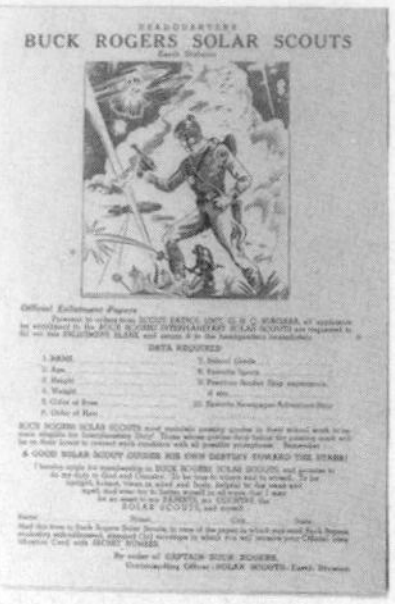

BRG-127

❑ **BRG-127. Solar Scouts Enlistment Form,**
1939. Newspaper issue. Art by Dick Calkins. Club was in name transition. Enlistment form uses "Solar Scouts" name but member's card uses "Rocket Rangers" name. 7-1/4x10-1/2". - **$90 $185 $360**

BRG-128

❑ **BRG-128. Movie Serial Press Book,**
1938-1939. Universal Studios. Eight pages printed in purple, green and white. Includes separate proof sheet with ads for all 12 chapters. Rare. - **$300 $600 $1100**

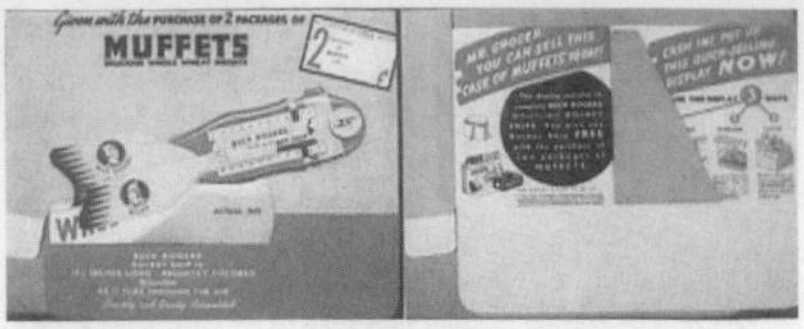

BRG-129

❑ **BRG-129. "Buck Rogers Whistling Rocketship" Premium Store Display,**
1939. Muffets cereal. Flattened size of 13-1/2x16-3/4" plus a 4" wide top panel missing from our illustrated example. This panel read "Free Buck Rogers Whistling Rocketship." Reverse shows how to assemble into three-dimensional form. See BRG-130. Gordon Gold Archives. - **$225 $450 $1000**

BRG-130

❑ **BRG-130. "Whistling Rocketship" Cardboard Punch-Out Assembly Kit In Color With Envelope,**
1939. Scarce. Muffets cereal. Example photo shows portrait details from tail fins. See BRG-129.
Unused With Envelope - **$300 $600 $1050**
Assembled - **$250 $500 $800**

BRG-131

❑ **BRG-131. "Buck Rogers Whistling Rocket Ship" Prototype Original Art,**
c. 1939. 16-1/4x21-1/2" in colored pencil. For a premium rocketship that was to be given away at movie theaters but was altered slightly and became the Muffets premium. Gordon Gold Archives. Unique. - **$2250**

BRG-132

❑ **BRG-132. "Buck Rogers/Muffets" Premium Rocketship Original Art Prototype Sign,**
c. 1939. Produced for 1939 Whistling Rocketship premium issued by Muffets Cereal. 15-3/4x20-1/2". Gordon Gold Archives. Unique. - **$1550**

BRG-133

❑ **BRG-133. Vintage Photostat Of Prototype Art,**
c. 1939. 5-1/2x8-1/2" pair of photostats mounted back to back picturing prototype artwork with reverse rocketship resembling the premium actually offered by Muffets. Gordon Gold Archives. Probably Unique. - **$350**

BRG-134

❑ **BRG-134. "Strange World Adventures Club" Serial Club Cello. Button,**
1939. Universal. Made by Philadelphia Badge Co. in blue and silver 1-1/4" design. Offered with a membership card by various theaters. One of the rarest and most desirable movie serial club buttons.
Button - **$1000 $2000 $4000**
Card - **$250 $500 $900**

BRG-135

❑ **BRG-135. "Gift List Radio News" Catalog,**
1939. Popsicle. Full color 7-1/2x10" with four pages. A different version was issued in 1940. Each - **$85 $175 $400**

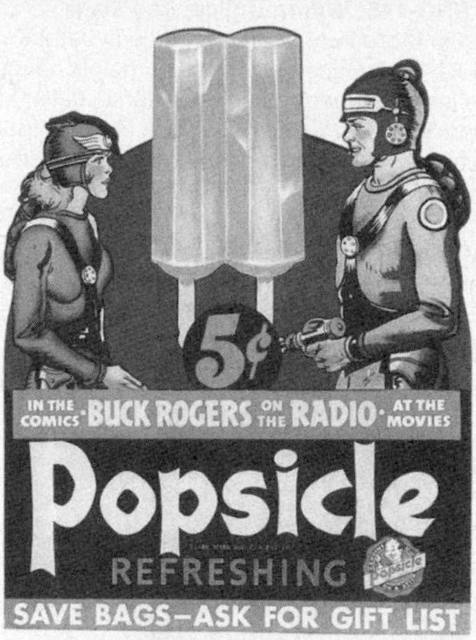

BRG-136

❑ **BRG-136. Diecut Standup Of Buck And Wilma,**
1939. Popsicle store display. 11x14" in superb color. - **$850 $1750 $4000**

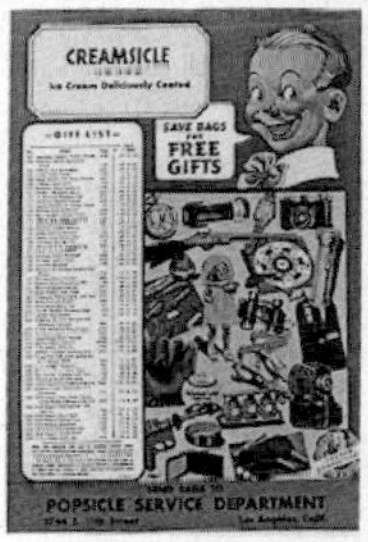

(CARD FRONT)

(CARD BACK)

(POSTER)

(DETAIL OF POSTER)

BRG-137

❑ **BRG-137. Creamsicle Gifts Dealer Instruction Card and Poster,**
1939. Card is 8-1/2x12" in color. Poster is 7-3/8x20" in color. See BRG-159. Detail of winged telescope shown. Card - **$200 $400 $800**
Poster - **$600 $1150 $2250**

BRG-138

❑ **BRG-138. Buck Rogers As Baseballer First Day Cover,**
1939. Mailing envelope commemorating centennial of organized baseball featuring cachet of Buck Rogers as a space batter. Cover has baseball commemorative stamp plus first day June 12 postmark from Cooperstown, New York, home of Baseball Hall of Fame. Cachet art is by Dick Calkins. - **$165 $325 $650**

BRG-139

❑ **BRG-139. "Buck Rogers" Comic Book First Issue,**
1939. Eastern Color Printing Co. #1 featuring Sunday strip reprints and cover art by Leonard Dworkins repeated front and back. Six issues published until 1943 - **$300 $900 $5000**

BRG-140

❑ **BRG-140. Red Belt Box,**
1930s. 7.75" long box only originally holding leather belt. All major panels have different Buck Rogers illustrations and one panel suggests box be retained and used for pencils and erasers at school. See belt BRG-114. Box Only - **$225 $450 $900**

BRG-141

❑ **BRG-141. Pop Gun With "Buck Rogers" Imprint,**
1930s. Waldman Bros. 6x8" colorful diecut cardboard pistol printed identically on both sides. Printed for comic strip readership in The Akron Times-Press (Ohio). Also issued was a revolver for the San Francisco Examiner. - **$95 $190 $375**

BRG-142

❑ BRG-142. "Eveready Book Of Radio Stars" With Buck Rogers,
1930s. National Carbon Co. 6x9" softcover with 48 pages. Contents include text for radio tubes plus majority is photos of radio personalities including page devoted to Buck Rogers with cast photo and text. A similar radio book was done by Libby in 1936. - **$60 $140 $250**

BRG-143

❑ BRG-143. School Map,
1930s. Rare. Probable Dixon Pencil Co. Yellow-tone, 8-1/2"x11" paper sheet came folded with Buck Rogers art in red border scenes on map of North America. (From 1936.)- **$300 $700 $1300**

BRG-144

❑ BRG-144. Newspaper Contest 1-1/4" Cello. Buttons,
1930s. "Buffalo Evening News" example pictures aviator character from early Buck Rogers daily newspaper strip. "Pittsburgh-Post Gazette" example pictures Buck Rogers. Both blue with flesh tone accent on white.
Buffalo - **$50 $100 $200**
Pittsburgh - **$115 $235 $400**

BRG-145

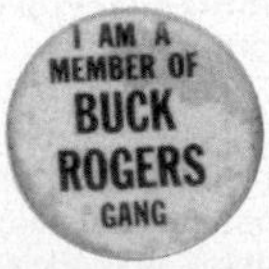

BRG-146

❑ BRG-145. Wilma Unlicensed Mask,
1930s. Store item, marked "Made In Japan". Unlike 1933 Cocomalt premium, hair is not curly and less slick paper stock resulted in duller color. See item BRG-19. A Buck Rogers "Made in Japan" matching version has not been seen. - **$75 $150 $350**

❑ BRG-146. "Buck Rogers Gang" Club Member Cello. Button,
1930s. Issuer unknown. 1-1/2" red on cream. - **$200 $400 $800**

BRG-147

❑ BRG-147. "Follow Buck Rogers" Cello. Button,
1930s. Washington Herald newspaper. Red type and blue image on white 1-1/4" from a set that includes other comic character strips appearing in the newspaper. - **$550 $1650 $3250**

BRG-148

❑ BRG-148. "The Hecht Co.'s Toy Land Funnies" Comic Book,
1930s. Hecht Department Store, Washington, D.C. 32 pages reprinting stories from earlier Famous Funnies comic books. Contains three Buck Rogers pages. Also published with other store logos. - (value will be based on future reported sales)

BRG-149

❑ BRG-149. "Lucky Coin",
1930s. Issuer unknown. 1-1/2" in the style of a "wooden nickel." - **$135 $275 $550**

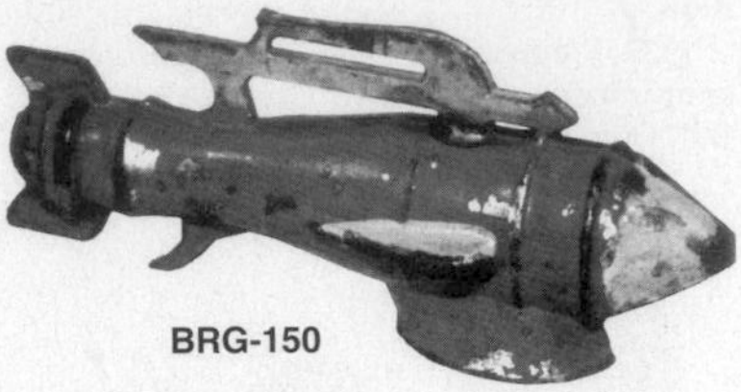

BRG-150

❑ BRG-150. Buck Rogers Style Rocketship,
1930s. Store item by Barclay in red, blue and yellow similar to Tootsietoy rockets. Other styles exist. - **$110 $225 $450**

BRG-151

BRG-152

❑ BRG-151. Matchbook,
1940. Popsicle/Creamsicle. "Starting May 4th" version for new radio sponsorship. Also issued with April 6th date for southern states. Blue background.
Empty or Incomplete - **$12 $25 $50**
Complete With All Matches - **$30 $60 $100**

❑ BRG-152. Matchbook,
1940. Popsicle. "Starting May 4th" version for new radio sponsorship. Also issued with April 6th date for southern states. Blue background.
Empty or Incomplete - **$12 $25 $50**
Complete With All Matches - **$30 $60 $100**

BRG-153

❑ BRG-153. "Onward School Supplies" 18x24" Colorful Paper Hanger Sign,
1940. Printed on both sides. A larger 18"x50" version came rolled on a wood dowel.
Small Version - **$200 $400 $800**
Large Version - **$450 $1100 $2250**

BRG-154

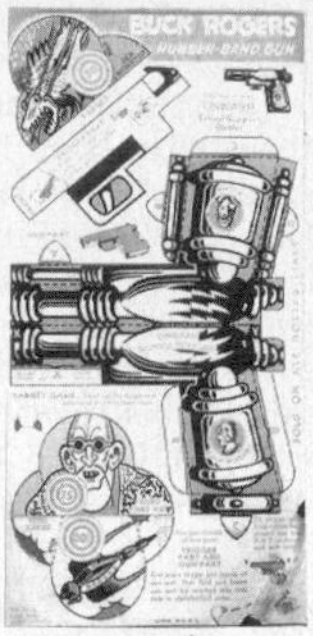

BRG-155

❏ BRG-154. School Supplies 11x16" Paper Store Poster,
1940. Onward School Supplies. Announces rubber band gun free with school supply purchase.- **$250 $500 $1000**

❏ BRG-155. Cardboard Punch-Out Rubber Band Gun,
1940. Onward School Supplies. Punch-out sheet includes standup targets of Sea Monster, Wing Bat Wu, Spaceship. 5x10" buff color thin cardboard with red and dark blue art.
Unpunched - **$90 $225 $350**

BRG-156

❏ BRG-156. "School Sale" Newspaper-Size Circular in Red and Blue,
1940. Photo examples show top half of front cover plus two illustration details. -
$50 $90 $150

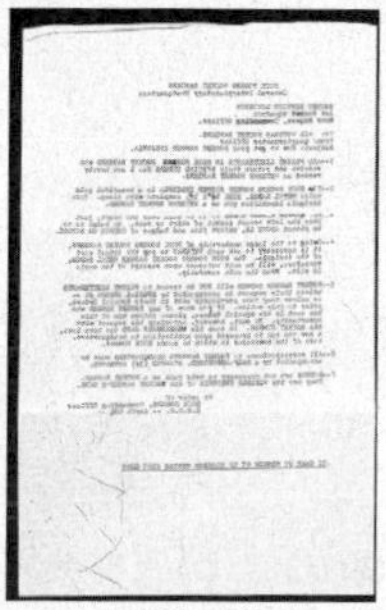

BRG-157

❏ BRG-157. Letter - How To Get Rocket Ranger Insignia,
c. 1940. Newspaper Premium. Have to hold up to mirror to read message. This letter, BRG-191 to BRG-194, and many others not shown, were offered in series by newspapers running the Buck Rogers daily strip and its associated club, the Rocket Rangers. All were sent folded. These letters were offered to young readers in 1939 through 1942, 1944, 1946, 1948 through 1950, 1952, and 1954. - **$45 $85 $125**

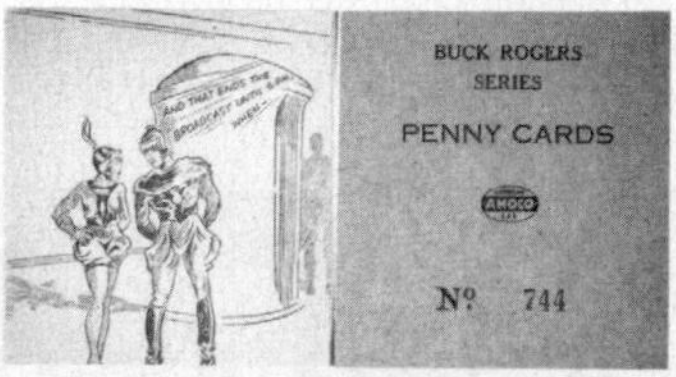

BRG-158

❏ BRG-158. Amoco Gasoline Penny Cards,
c. 1940. Black on cream thin cardboard 3x3". Many in series that include non-Buck Rogers characters. Images are pages out of Big Little Books. Display board was also available. Also issued by Sinclair and probably Texaco.
Each Buck Rogers - **$80 $135 $240**

BRG-159

❏ BRG-159. "Popsicle Pete's Free Gifts" Dealer Instruction Card,
1940. 8-1/2x12" in color. See BRG-137.
- **$200 $400 $800**

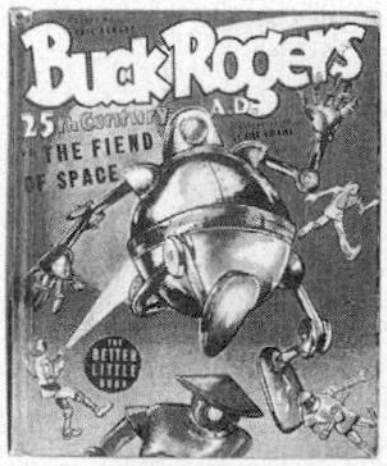

BRG-160

BRG-161

❏ BRG-160. "Buck Rogers Vs. The Fiend Of Space" BTLB,
1940. Whitman Better Little Book hardcover #1409. - **$31 $93 $220**

❏ BRG-161. "Buck Rogers and the Overturned World" Better Litttle Book #1474,
1941. Whitman, hardcover. - **$32 $96 $225**

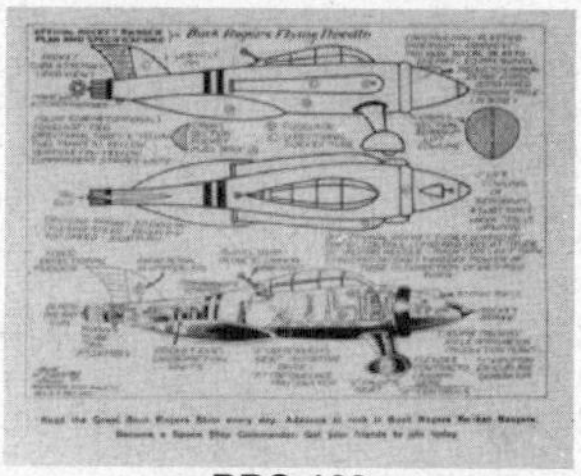

BRG-162

❏ BRG-162. "Flying Needle" Airship Diagram Sheet,
1941. Daily comic strip offer. For "Buck Rogers Rocket Rangers" club of aspiring "Spaceship Commander" readers. 8-1/2"x11", red on white, not a punch-out. - **$125 $275 $550**

BRG-163

❏ BRG-163. "Buck Rogers Ranger" Aluminum Dog Tag With Chain,
c. 1942. Rare. Item has 1935 copyright but probably issued a few years later. Black details wear off easily. - **$550 $1350 $2250**

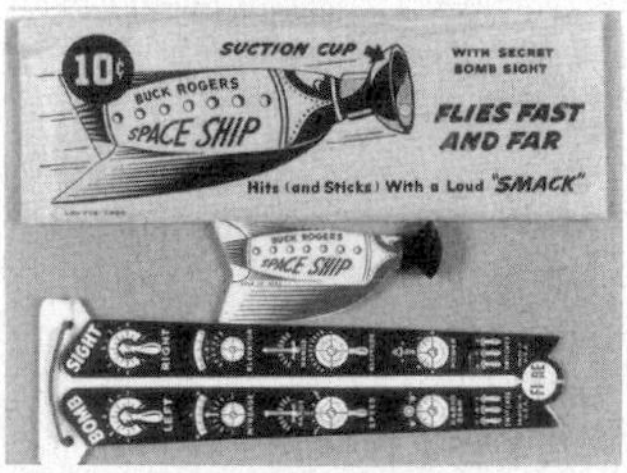

BRG-164

❏ BRG-164. Cardboard Spaceship With Envelope,
1942. Morton's Salt. Includes cardboard "Secret Bomb Sight". Suction cup nose stiffens with age. Bomb sight is dark blue with space ship red on white. Complete With Envelope - **$65 $150 $300**

BRG-165

BRG-166

❑ **BRG-165. "Buck Rogers and the Super-Dwarf of Space" Better Little Book #1490,**
1943. Whitman, hardcover. Has scenes only with no printed text. Buck Rogers 1943 comic book No. 6 had same story. - **$31 $93 $220**

❑ **BRG-166. "Rocket Rangers" Club Member Card,**
1944. Various newspapers. Same design as 1939 card but on blue card stock. - **$65 $125 $250**

BRG-167

❑ **BRG-167. Rocket Rangers Iron-On Transfers,**
1944. Newspaper premium. Set of three sent individually for Buck, Wilma and Rocketship. Photos show offer and two transfers. Transfers are red and blue on 3x6" tissue paper. Last photo is example of transfers with outlined image of Buck in green or blue, with or without orange details (4 versions), c. 1940 by Jitterprints.
Each Ranger Transfer - **$50 $100 $150**
Each Older Transfer - **$10 $25 $50**

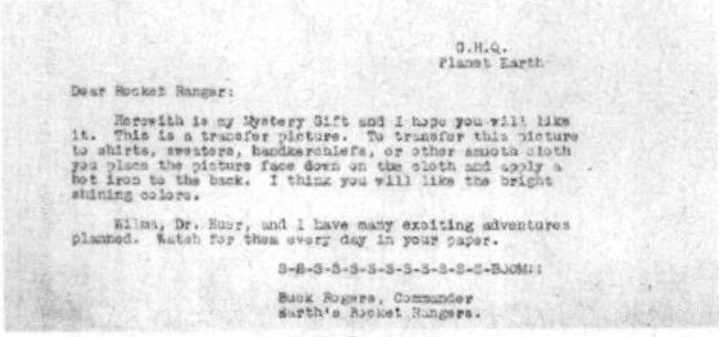

G.H.Q.
Planet Earth

Dear Rocket Ranger:

Herewith is my Mystery Gift and I hope you will like it. This is a transfer picture. To transfer this picture to shirts, sweaters, handkerchiefs, or other smooth cloth you place the picture face down on the cloth and apply a hot iron to the back. I think you will like the bright shining colors.

Wilma, Dr. Huer, and I have many exciting adventures planned. Watch for them every day in your paper.

S-S-S-S-S-S-S-S-S-S-S-S-BOOM!!

Buck Rogers, Commander
Earth's Rocket Rangers.

BRG-168

❑ **BRG-168. Transfer Picture Instruction Sheet,**
1944. Newspaper "Mystery Gift" addressed to "Dear Rocket Ranger." 4-1/4x8-1/2" white paper. - **$45 $85 $140**

BRG-169

❑ **BRG-169. Newspaper Strip Promotional Brochure,**
1944. John Dille Co. and National Newspaper Service. Text calls the strip "Public Fascinator No. 1-A" reverse lists ranks in the "Buck Rogers Rocket Rangers Club." Opens to 19x24". Various brochures on white or colored paper were issued throughout the run of the strip. - **$100 $220 $450**

BRG-170

❑ **BRG-170. "Atomic Bomber" Jigsaw Puzzle Boxed Set of Three,**
1945. Store item by Puzzle Craft Industries, Chicago. Each puzzle is 8-1/2x11" with art by Dick Calkins. Two versions of box lid. Exceptionally colorful. For color photo see the second edition of this book, page 711.
Each Puzzle Or Box - **$125 $250 $500**

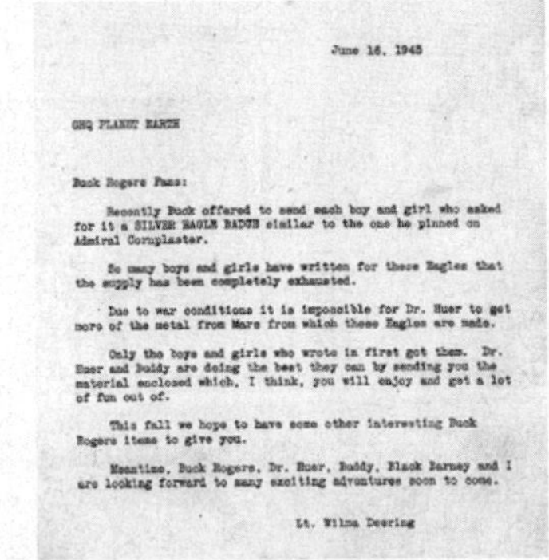

June 16, 1945

GHQ PLANET EARTH

Buck Rogers Fans:

Recently Buck offered to send each boy and girl who asked for it a SILVER EAGLE BADGE similar to the one he pinned on Admiral Cornplaster.

So many boys and girls have written for these Eagles that the supply has been completely exhausted.

Due to war conditions it is impossible for Dr. Huer to get more of the metal from Mars from which these Eagles are made.

Only the boys and girls who wrote in first got them. Dr. Huer and Buddy are doing the best they can by sending you the material enclosed which, I think, you will enjoy and get a lot of fun out of.

This fall we hope to have some other interesting Buck Rogers items to give you.

Meantime, Buck Rogers, Dr. Huer, Buddy, Black Barney and I are looking forward to many exciting adventures soon to come.

Lt. Wilma Deering

BRG-171

❑ **BRG-171. Silver Eagle Badge Letter,**
1945. Yellow paper letter 6-1/4x7" dated June 16, 1945. Text explains supply of badge is exhausted as "Due To War Conditions It Is Impossible For Dr. Huer To Get More Of The Metal From Mars From Which These Eagles Are Made." Letter says boys and girls will enjoy the Skyroads wings pin (see SRO-13) substituted item sent with this letter. Badge is extremely rare. No photo available.
Letter - **$110 $185 $375**
Badge - Undetermined

BRG-172

❑ **BRG-172. Atomic Pistol U-235 By Daisy,**
1945. Store item. Silver or black color finish. 9-3/4", came in yellow box. Flint produces spark. No holster made. A red, black and yellow promotional flyer was issued. See BRG-174 & 178.
Gun - **$135 $325 $600**
Box - **$165 $375 $700**
3-Page Story Folder - **$75 $135 $275**

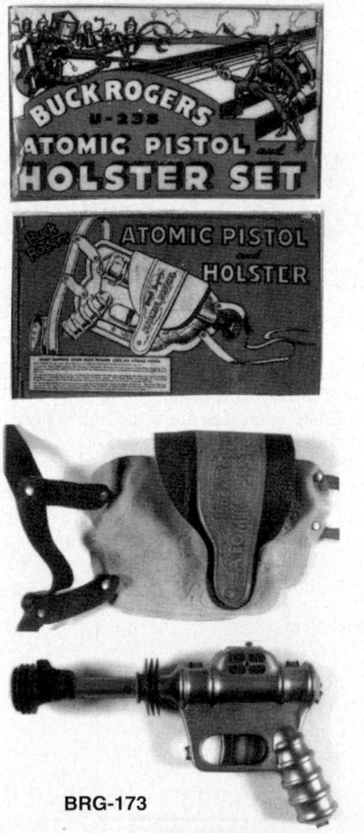

BRG-173

❑ **BRG-173. Atomic Pistol U-238 By Daisy,**
1946. Store item. Gold color finish. 9-3/4", came with holster in red and white box. Flint produces spark. Box style same as BRG-62 Combat Set box. Gun - **$165 $350 $625**
Leather Holster - **$150 $350 $675**
Box - **$175 $400 $725**
3-Page Story Folder **$75 $135 $275**

BRG-174

❑ **BRG-174. Atomic Pistol Promotional Flyer,**
1946. Daisy Mfg. Co. Three-fold full color 8-1/2x11" flyer. Both sides shown open. - **$125 $250 $500**

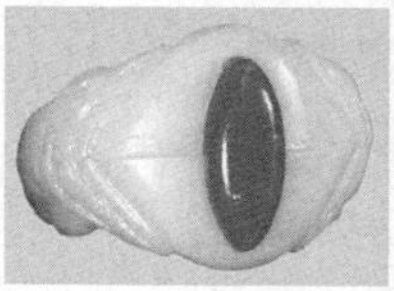
BRG-175

BRG-176

❑ **BRG-175. Glow-In-Dark Ring Of Saturn,**
1946. Post's Corn Toasties radio premium. White plastic topped by red plastic stone. - **$135 $250 $500**

❑ **BRG-176. "Ring Of Saturn" Instruction Folder,**
1946. Came with ring. Post's Corn Toasties radio premium. Red and black on white. Opens to 5-1/2"x9-1/4". - **$135 $250 $500**

BRG-177

❑ **BRG-177. "Rocket Rangers" Club Member Card,**
1946. Various newspapers. Shows flying ship on blue card stock. - **$75 $150 $265**

BRG-178

❑ **BRG-178. "Adventure Book,"**
1946. Daisy three-section folder issued with boxed guns Atomic Pistol U-235 and Atomic Pistol U-238. Folder in black and white reprints six daily newspaper comic strips. 3x15". - **$75 $135 $275**

BRG-179

❑ **BRG-179. Mailing Card For Conference With Dick Calkins Appearance,**
1946. 5x7" announcement mailer on green paper for October 22 appearance at a Toledo, Ohio high school to speak on "Five Centuries Ahead With Buck Rogers" and related topics. - **$45 $100 $175**

BRG-180

❑ **BRG-180. Post's Corn Toasties Cereal Box,**
1946. Rare. Post Cereal. Advertises radio program on The Mutual Network. Only two known.
Complete Box - **$650 $1300 $2650**
Back Panel Only - **$225 $350 $675**

BRG-181

❑ **BRG-181. Full Color Blotter,**
c. 1946. Chicago Herald-American. 3-5/8x8-1/2" newspaper promotional. - **$135 $260 $500**

BRG-182

BRG-183

❑ **BRG-182. "Daisy Handbook,"**
1946. Daisy Mfg. Co. The first of three booklets promoting Daisy products. Contents include 10 Buck Rogers daily newspaper strip reprints. 4-1/2"x5-1/4", 128 pages. - **$50 $135 $475**

❑ **BRG-183. John Larkin Fan Card,**
c. 1947. Issuer unknown. 3-1/2x5-1/2" black and white. Larkin portrayed Buck Rogers on radio 1946-1947. - **$35 $70 $115**

BRG-184

❑ BRG-184. Supersonic Two-Way Trans-ceiver,
1948. Store item made by Da-Myco. Box art by Rick Yager. Box 8x13-1/2". - **$225 $400 $800**

BRG-185

BRG-186

❑ BRG-185. Drawing Of Pluton,
1948. Newspaper premium with Rick Yager art in dark red on tan paper 8-1/2x11". Sent to readers who mailed in their own conception drawing.- **$165 $375 $750**

❑ BRG-186. Pittsburgh "Post-Gazette Sunday Funnies" Comic Book,
1949. Newspaper insert 16-page color comic including Buck Rogers and other characters. GD - **$400** FN - **$1200**

(1949)

(1950)

BRG-187

❑ BRG-187. Buck Rogers Five Trading Cards,
1949. Store item by Comic Stars, Inc. Full color 2-1/4x3-1/2" part of a set including other characters. Art by Murphy Anderson. In 1950, at least three more full color cards were done with Murphy Anderson art.
Each Buck - **$25 $45 $90**
Each Flame - **$20 $40 $80**

BRG-188

❑ BRG-188. Cardboard "Flying Saucer",
1949. Store item by unknown maker marked S. P. Co. Has metal rim and two convex surfaces, unlike a frisbee. Patent number on this item is incorrect. - **$65 $140 $260**

BRG-189

❑ BRG-189. Sonic Ray Gun Flier,
1949. Store item by Commonwealth Utilities Co. 8.5x11" full color sheet printed on both sides by illustrated announcement for toy gun retailed at $1.98. - **$35 $70 $135**

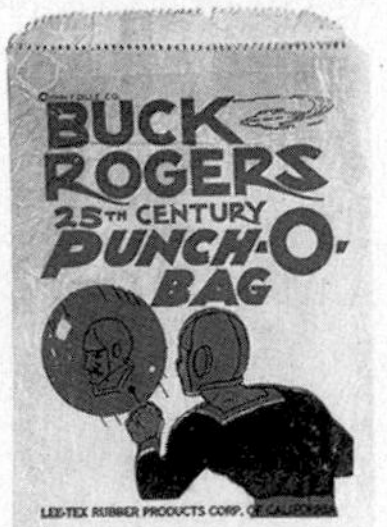

BRG-190

❑ BRG-190. "Punch-O-Bag,"
1940s. Store item from late 1940s by Lee-Tex Rubber Products Corp. Glassine bag 5x7" in red and blue held balloon usually missing or disintegrated. See BRG-63. - **$65 $150 $275**

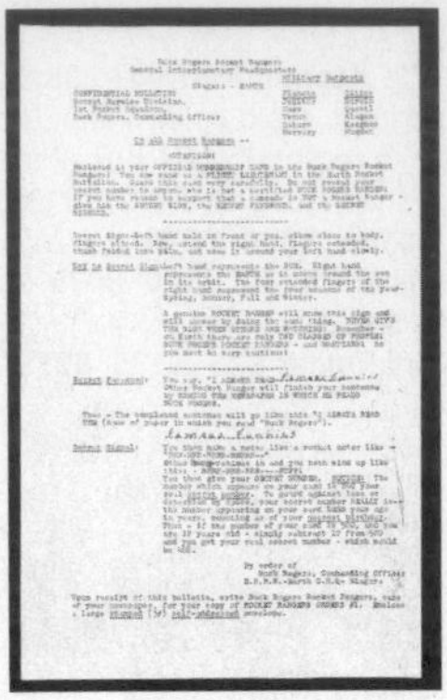

BRG-191

❑ BRG-191. Letter - How To Get Secret Signals,
1940s. Newspaper Premium. Came with membership card. - **$45 $85 $125**

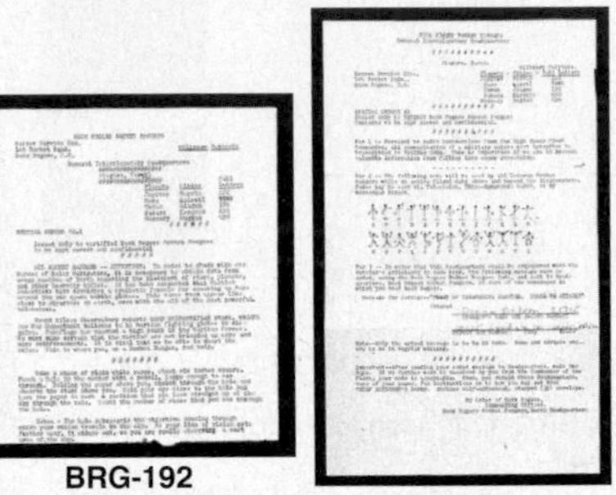

BRG-192

BRG-193

❑ BRG-192. Letter - Special Orders #1,
1940s. Newspaper Premium. Mars fighting globes described. - **$45 $85 $125**

❑ BRG-193. Letter - Special Orders #2,
1940s. Newspaper Premium. Shows secret code system. - **$50 $90 $135**

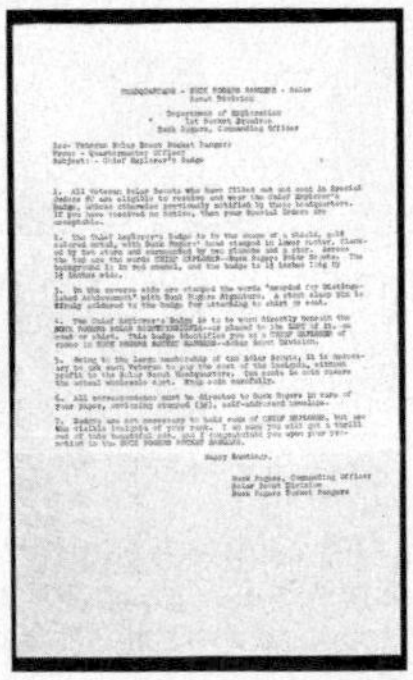

BRG-194

❑ BRG-194. Letter - Chief Explorer,
1940s. Newspaper premium. Talks about badge and Solar Scouts club information. See BRG-78 & BRG-95. - **$65 $135 $275**

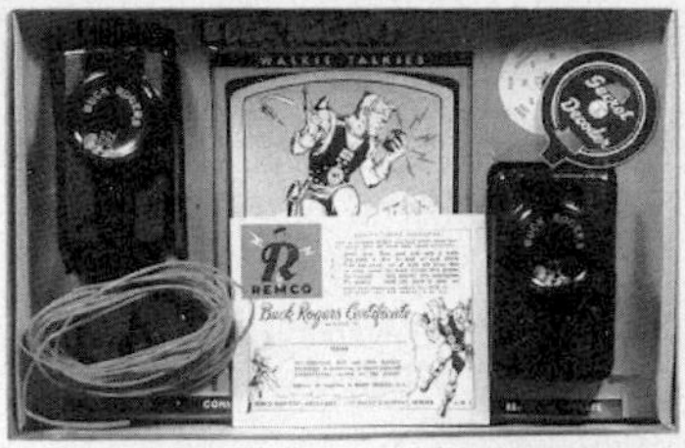

BRG-195

❑ **BRG-195. Electronic Walkie-Talkies,**
1952. Store item made by Remco. Box art by Murphy Anderson. 8-1/2x13x2" deep box holds "walkie talkie" units and box insert features cardboard secret decoder. - **$165 $375 $700**

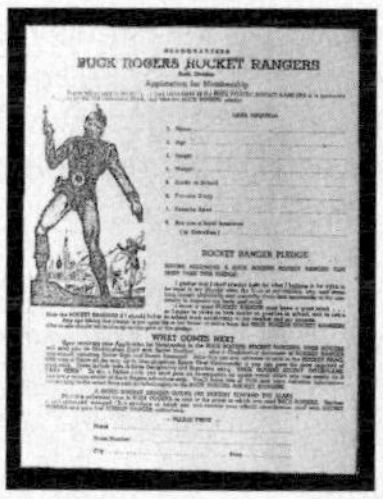

BRG-196

❑ **BRG-196. Rocket Rangers Application Form,**
1952. Newspaper issue. Art by Murphy Anderson. 8-1/2x11". - **$65 $150 $300**

BRG-197

❑ **BRG-197. "Rocket Rangers" Member Litho. Tin Tab,**
1952. Newspaper premium made by L.J. Imber, Chicago. 3/4x1-1/2" red, white and blue. - **$30 $90 $160**

BRG-198

❑ **BRG-198. "Rocket Rangers" Club Member Card,**
1952. Various newspapers. White card with red profile of Buck. Advertised in Famous Funnies comic books issues 211 to 217.- **$35 $75 $150**

BRG-199

❑ **BRG-199. Space Ranger Kit,**
1952. Sylvania Electric Products Inc. Six full color punch-out sheets, each 10-1/2x14-1/2". Kit includes string. One punch-out is a membership card. Unpunched In Envelope - **$100 $200 $400**

BRG-201

❑ **BRG-201. Sales Book for Space Ranger Kit,**
1952. Spiral binding, 10x14" with 36 black and white pages. Rare. From the Gordon Gold Archives. Near Mint - **$800**

BRG-200

❑ **BRG-200. Large Die-Cut Sign,**
1952. Promotes Sylvania and shows Space Ranger Kit pieces. From the Gordon Gold Archives. - **$1250 $2500 $4500**

BRG-202

❏ BRG-202. Space Ranger Kit Flyer,
1952. Sylvania TV. Red and black on 8x10-3/4" newsprint. - **$35 $65 $150**

BRG-203

❏ BRG-203. Ranger Kit Promo Photo,
1952. From the Gordon Gold Archives.
Near Mint - **$135**

BRG-204

❏ BRG-204. Sylvania TV Retailer's Sales Catalogue And Roster,
1952. 8-1/2x11" eight-page full color catalogue promotes use of the premium "Buck Rogers Space Ranger Kit." Roster is used to record names and addresses of children and parents visiting the store and given a kit. Gordon Gold Archives. Catalogue - **$135 $300 $500**
Roster - **$25 $50 $75**

BRG-205

❏ BRG-205. Large Display Poster,
1952. Promotes Space Ranger Kit premium from Sylvania. From the Gordon Gold Archives. - **$675 $1500 $3000**

BRG-206

❏ BRG-206. "Sylvania TV Buck Rogers Space Ranger Kit" Large Sales Promotion Four Page Folder,
1952. Issued by Sylvania Electric Products Inc. Black and white. Gordon Gold Archives.
- $65 $135 $250

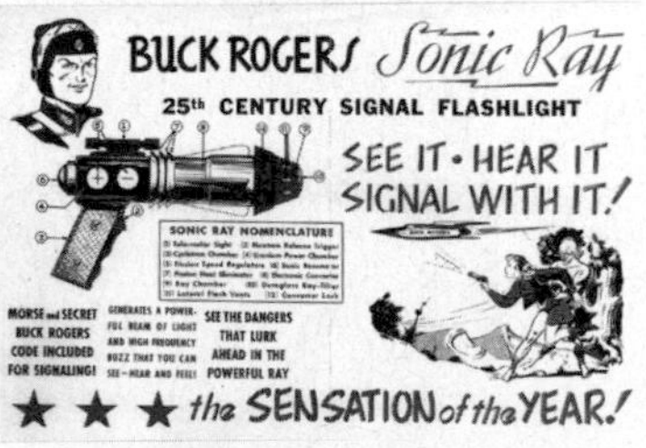

BRG-207

❏ BRG-207. Sonic Ray Signal Flashlight (Gun Style) Flyer,
1952. Store item by Norton-Honer Mfg. Co. 11x17" full color. Several other flyer styles exist. Gun made in various colors, each 7.25" long.
- $65 $135 $225

BRG-208

❏ BRG-208. Octopus Space Station Tray Puzzle,
1952. Store item by Milton Bradley. 10x14" originally sold with paper sleeve. Full color. Art by Rick Yager. A companion puzzle with art by Leonard Dworkins was never released.
Sleeve - **$35 $65 $100**
Puzzle - **$40 $75 $165**

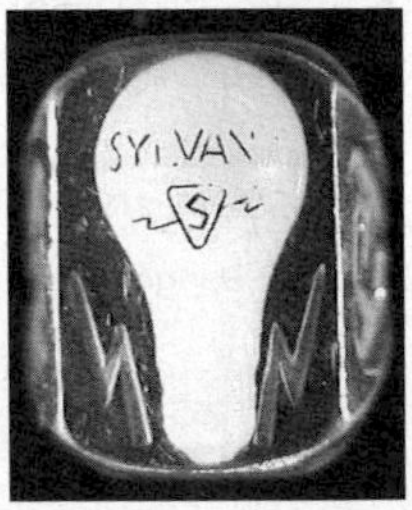

BRG-209

❏ BRG-209. Sylvania Glow-In-Dark Light Bulb Ring,
c. 1953. Sylvania was a Buck Rogers licensee around this time and used the character to promote their Halolight televisions. Although we've seen no paperwork linking this ring to Buck Rogers, the ring is accepted in the hobby as a Buck Rogers item. Bulb is white plastic mounted on brass base with adjustable bands. -
$265 $525 $1100

BRG-210

❑ BRG-210. Super Sonic Ray Gun Flyer,
1955. Store item by Norton-Honer Mfg. Co. 8-1/2x11" full color. Reverse shows three accessories. Items made in various colors.
Each **- $45 $90 $175**

BRG-211 BRG-212

❑ BRG-211. "Buck Rogers/Satellite Pioneers" Litho. Tin 2" Tab,
1957. Shown with stem unbent. Red and black on white made by Greenduck Co. This club lasted until 1967. **- $30 $60 $115**

❑ BRG-212. "Buck Rogers Satellite Pioneers" Member Card,
1958. Open from late 1957 through 1967. Various newspapers. White card with red scenes. 2-1/2x4-1/4". **- $35 $75 $150**

BRG-213

❑ BRG-213. "Satellite Pioneers Cadet Commission" Bulletin Folder,
1958. Various newspapers. Sent folded. 5-1/2x8-1/2". **- $40 $75 $140**

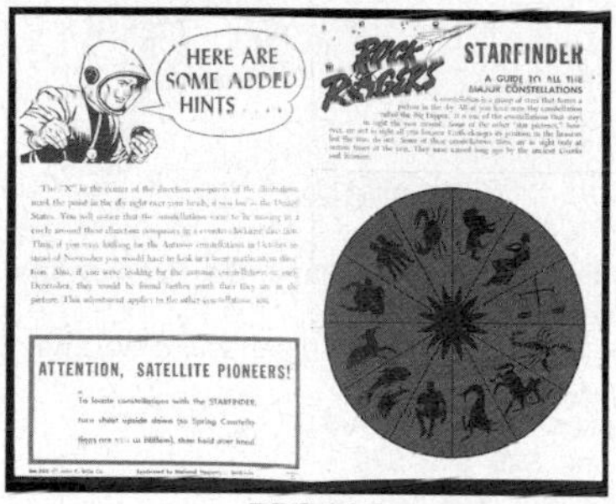

BRG-214

❑ BRG-214. Starfinder Folder,
1958. Newspaper premium. Satellite Pioneers Club. Guide to major constellations. 5-1/2x8-1/2". Sent folded. See BRG-216. **- $35 $70 $120**

BRG-215

❑ BRG-215. Satellite Pioneers Club Bulletin,
1958. Various newspapers. Cover portrait faces right. Includes blue "Map of the Solar System." 5-1/2x8-1/2". Sent folded. **- $35 $70 $120**

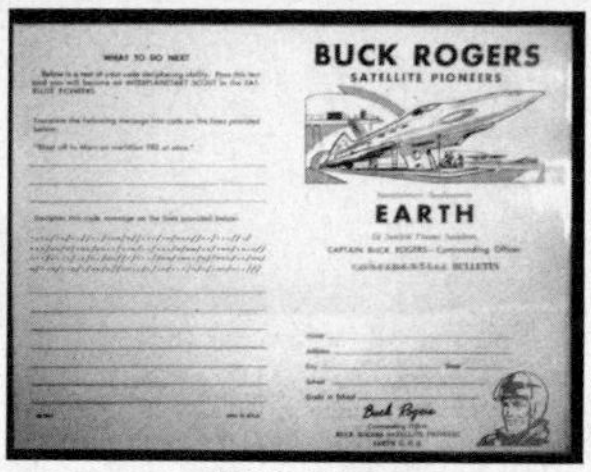

BRG-216

❑ BRG-216. "Satellite Pioneers" Bulletin,
1958. Newspaper premium. Secret Order No. 1 on pink paper mailed with Star Finder folder. 5-1/2x8-1/2". Sent folded. See BRG-214. -
$35 $70 $110

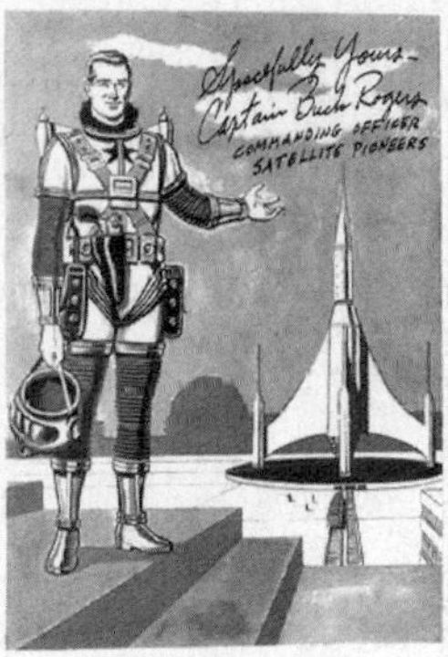

BRG-217

❑ BRG-217. "Satellite Pioneers" Picture Card,
1960. Offered by various newspapers. 3-1/2x5". Black and white. Art by Murphy Anderson.
- $45 $80 $160

BRG-218

❑ BRG-218. Captain Action & Action Boy Small Format Comic in Full Color,
1967. Ideal Toy & Novelty Co. Features Buck Rogers and other character accessory sets for use with Captain Action 12" figure. -
$12 $36 $215

BRG-219

❑ **BRG-219. Captain Action/Buck Rogers Full Color Plastic Flicker Ring,**
1967. Ideal Toys. Silver base marked "Hong Kong" came with boxed figure.
Silver "Hong Kong" Base - **$38 $50 $75**
Blue Base with "Disney" Name - **$12 $22 $45**
Silver "China" Modern Base - **$6 $12 $25**

BRG-220

❑ **BRG-220. Captain Action Card Game,**
1967. Kool-Pops/Kool-Aid. Buck Rogers and other characters on 36-card game. Full color cards came in separate mailing box.
Complete - **$35 $70 $100**

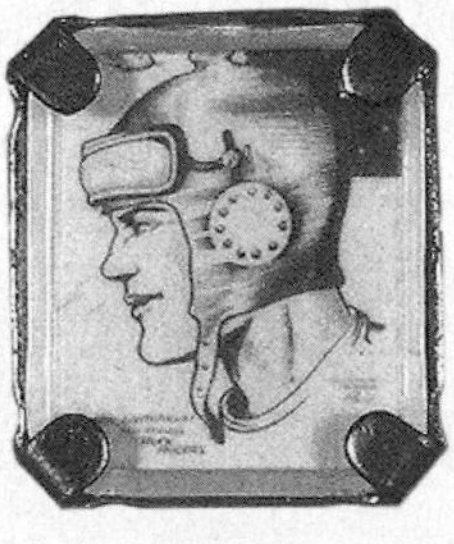

BRG-221

❑ **BRG-221. Buck Rogers Profile Ring,**
1960s. Issuer unknown. Brass base with black and white paper image under beveled edge plastic top. First example surfaced in late 1960s. No documentation known and possibly a fantasy creation but uncommon. - **$150 $350 $600**

BRG-222

❑ **BRG-222. Warren Paper Co. Promotional Items,**
1971. Color poster, stiff paper zap pistol and postcard. Poster 24x36".
Poster - **$25 $50 $100**
Pistol - **$20 $40 $90**
Postcard - **$10 $20 $40**

BRG-223

❑ **BRG-223. "Buck Rogers In The 25th Century" Revival Pocket Watch,**
1971. Box label marked Huckleberry Time Co. or Photorific Products, Inc. 2" diameter re-design of original 1935 pocket watch by Ingraham. Store item without Dille copyright. Boxed watches usually include a silver finish neck chain. This version was created by Robert Lesser. See BRG-66. Box - **$25 $50 $100**
Watch - **$125 $250 $500**

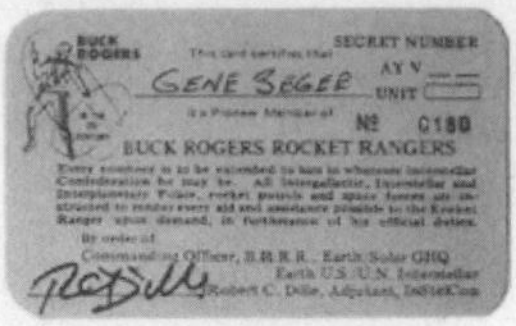

BRG-224

❑ **BRG-224. "Rocket Rangers" Club Member Card,**
1977. Red figure of Buck standing on blue card. Not offered through newspapers. -
$30 $70 $125

BRG-225

❑ **BRG-225. New York Times Special Features Sunday Strip Promotional Poster,**
1979. 16-1/2x21-1/2" full color on yellow background. Art by Gray Morrow. - **$35 $70 $120**

BRG-226

❑ **BRG-226. Television Series Promotional Poster,**
1979. Burger King. 17x22" color paper giveaway poster. - **$22 $40 $65**

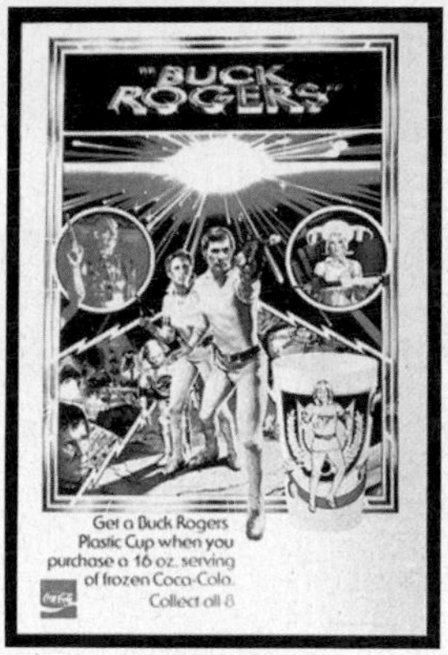

BRG-227

❑ **BRG-227. Television Series Plastic Cup Promotional Poster,**
1979. Burger King issue advertising Coca-Cola. 13x19" color paper poster advertising set of eight tumblers. - **$35 $60 $90**

BRG-228

❑ **BRG-228. "Buck Rogers Walking Twiki Robot,"**
1979. Store item by Mego. From set of seven different character figures.
Near Mint Boxed - **$60**
Loose - **$5 $10 $25**

BRG-229

❑ **BRG-229. "Buck Rogers Galactic Playset,"**
1979. Store item by HG Toys.
Near Mint Boxed - **$100**

BRG-230

❑ **BRG-230. "Buck Rogers" Cards/Sticker Set,**
1979. Issued by Topps. 88 cards and 22 stickers. Wrappers issued with three different left margin variations. Set was also offered in Australia by Scanlens. Included red announcement flyer. Near Mint Set - **$25**
Wrappers - **$1 $3 $6**

BRG-231

BRG-232

❑ **BRG-231. Coca-Cola Plastic Tumblers,**
1979. Distributed in theaters playing Buck Rogers movie. Eight different smaller size and five different larger size, each showing one character from the movie. Full color.
Small - **$5 $10 $15**
Large - **$15 $30 $50**

❑ **BRG-232. Coca-Cola Glass Tumblers,**
1979. Two sizes for four different characters. These may exist as test or prototypes only. Full color. Wilma glass has not been seen. The glasses seen are Buck Rogers, Twiki and Draco (with Martian Tigerman on one side.)
Near Mint Each - **$215**

BRG-233

BRG-234

❑ **BRG-233. "Adventures Of Big Boy" Comic Book,**
1979. Restaurant giveaway issue No. 270 with Buck Rogers movie skit. Various local restaurant logos used. - **$3 $9 $25**

❑ **BRG-234. "Star Of The '80s" 3" Metal Button,**
1979. Gottlieb pinball game advertising button, probably distributed at industry trade show. White and blue on black background. A 19x 28" color poster and an 11x17" die cut silvered folder were also made. - **$15 $30 $60**

BRG-235

❑ **BRG-235. Gottlieb Pinball Promo Poster,**
1979. 19" x 28". - **$15 $30 $50**

BRG-236

❑ **BRG-236. TV Board Game,**
1979. Milton Bradley. - **$30 $60 $120**

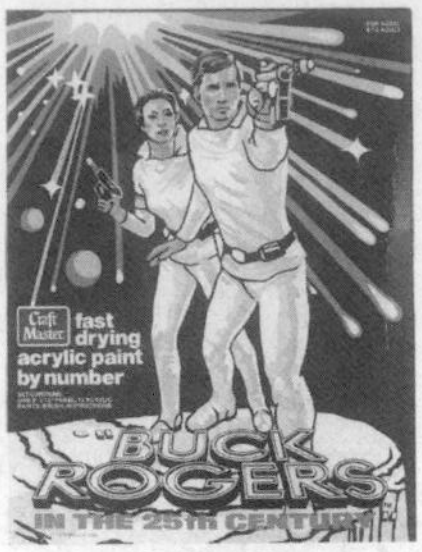

BRG-237

❑ BRG-237. Paint By Number Boxed Set,
1979. Craftmaster. Colorfully illustrated box containing 9x12" coloring panel, 12 paint tablets, brush. Near Mint - **$45**

BRG-238

❑ BRG-238. View-Master Reel Set,
1980. Three stereo view reels of color photos from TV show plus story booklet in 4.5" square envelope. Near Mint - **$28**

BRG-239

❑ BRG-239. Color Cards Set,
1980. Issued by Figurine Panini. Album and 240 smaller format cards. There is also a 1981 British offer that stipulated not for overseas distribution. Wrappers have 2 variations.
Near Mint Album - **$18**
Near Mint Card Set - **$22**

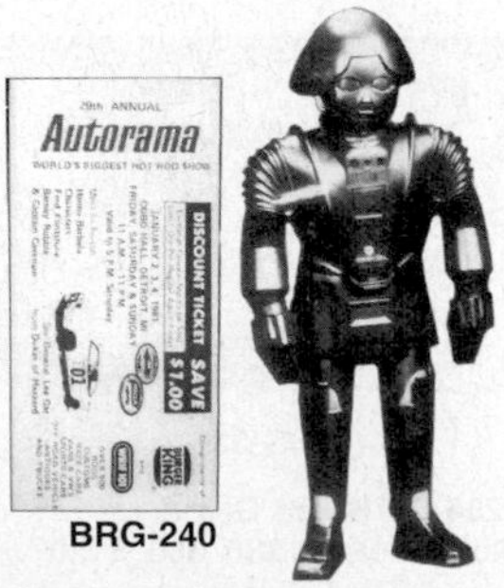

BRG-240

❑ BRG-240. Twiki Photo,
1981. Detroit 29th Annual Autorama show give-away 8x10" black and white photograph. Shown with admission discount ticket. - **$12 $25 $38**

BRG-241

BRG-242

❑ BRG-241. Color Postcard,
1981. Quick Fox 5x8" promo for Gray Morrow Buck Rogers book. - **$12 $25 $38**

❑ BRG-242. Buck Rogers Slurpee Video Game Plastic Tumbler,
1982. Southland Corporation. 1982 version has blue scene while 1983 version has red scene. From a set featuring various unrelated comic and game characters.
1982 Issue - **$10 $20 $30**
1983 Issue (Shown) - **$5 $10 $15**

BRG-243

❑ BRG-243. Cardboard Mobile,
1988. Issued by TSR. Full color packaged unassembled in 17x21" stiff envelope. - **$15 $30 $45**

BRG-244

❑ BRG-244. Movie/TV Show Armband Patch,
1980s. Issuer unknown. 4"x4" blue and black on white cloth. Band was worn on Buck and Wilma's right arm during 1979-81 TV series. - **$12 $20 $35**

BRG-245

BRG-246

❑ BRG-245. Bookmark,
1991. Issued by TSR. Full color 2-1/8x7-3/4". - **$5 $10 $18**

❑ BRG-246. Metal Badge and Cloth Insignia,
1994 (Badge, 1989). Both issued by TSR. Badge is 1-1/2" long in three colors; insignia is 1-3/4x3-3/8" silver and red on blue cloth.
Each - **$6 $12 $20**

BRG-247

❑ BRG-247. Cardboard Pog,
1995. Issued by Ektek Inc. 1-5/8" full color. Shows painting "War Against The Han" by Dennis Beauvais. - **$3 $4 $6**

BRG-248

❑ BRG-248. Wall Clock,
1990s. White plastic, 9.5" diameter, no brand name on clock. - **$30 $60 $125**

BRG-249

❑ BRG-249. Cloth Name Patch,
1990s. Issuer unknown. 2 x 4-1/4" orange/yellow stitched on black cloth. - **$6 $12 $20**

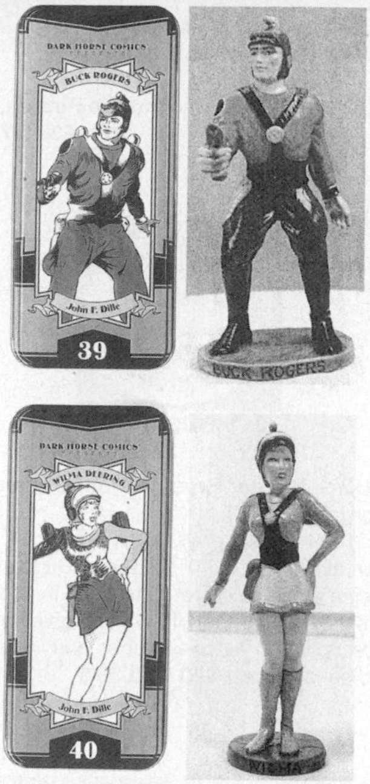

BRG-250

❑ **BRG-250. Buck & Wilma Figures From Limited Edition Series Of Comic Characters,**
2002. Dark Horse Comics store item. Each 5.25" molded figure is packaged in colorful lithographed tin box and limited to 600 each. Box lid interior holds folder and 1.25" cello portrait button. Buck Rogers #39 Mint Boxed - **$80**
Wilma Deering #40 Mint Boxed - **$70**

BRG-251 BRG-252

❑ **BRG-251. "Space Day 2003" Button,**
2003. 2-5/16" full color cello picturing actors Gil Girard and Erin Gray from 1979-1981 movie and TV series. Issued by New Mexico Museum of Space History, Alamogordo accompanied by 16x21" color poster. Button - **$10 $20 $35**
Poster - **$10 $20 $35**

❑ **BRG-252. "Wilma" From English Television Litho. Button Set,**
2004. Issuer unknown. Full color 1.25" with six different in set. A set of six magnets was also made. Each - **$2 $4 $8**

Meeting the Mongols

Sunken City of Atlantis, 1930

Martians Invade Jupiter, 1942

BRG-253

❑ **BRG-253. Buck Rogers "Floor Flyer" Space Ships,**
2005. Gearbox Toys. Set of three colorful metal and plastic space ships with wheels. Each on 5.25x7.5" blister card picturing the daily newspaper strip featuring that ship's appearance in the story. Each Near Mint Packaged - **$7**

Buffalo Bill Jr.

Gene Autry's *Flying A Productions* released 42 syndicated television episodes of the popular children's western series between March, 1955 and September, 1956. Set in 1890s Wileyville, Texas, the premise has orphan Buffalo Bill and his sister Calamity being adopted by Judge Wiley. Bill becomes marshal and promotes law and order, along with great stunt work and trick riding. The cast included Dick Jones as Bill, Nancy Gilbert as Calamity and Harry Cheshire as Judge Wiley. Dick Jones has a long Hollywood history, including the voice of *Pinocchio* in the 1940 animated feature and as co-star on the 1951-1953 *Range Rider* TV show playing Dick West.

Dell/Gold Key released 14 comic books between 1956 and 1965 with full color photo covers based on the *Buffalo Bill Jr.* series.

BUF-1

❑ **BUF-1. "Buffalo Bill Jr." Premium Transfer Set,**
1950s. Robin Hood Shoes. 5.5x7.5" envelope holds four transfer sheets in red/blue with black text to decorate a western shirt. Unused - **$8 $15 $30**

BUF-2

❑ **BUF-2. "View-Master Theatre" Diecut Display With Box,**
1950s. 14.25x18x.25" thick box contains 13.75x17" tall cardboard theater with screen area depicting Tarzan, Bugs Bunny, Woody Woodpecker, Rin Tin Tin, Buffalo Bill Jr., Dale Evans and others. - **$20 $40 $75**

BUF-3

BUF-4

❑ **BUF-3. "Buffalo Bill Jr. Weather Watch",**
1950s. Mars Candy. 1-5/8" thick aluminum disk designed as a watch. Cardboard litmus paper at center turns blue for fair weather or pink for rain. - **$15 $35 $65**

❑ **BUF-4. (Buffalo) Bill Jr. Brass Ring,**
1950s. Sides depict bucking horse and holster gun with buffalo on top. Probably from Mars Candy. - **$20 $35 $75**

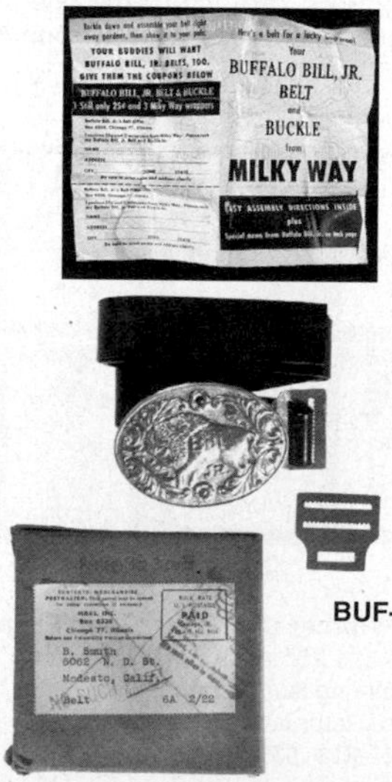

BUF-5

❑ **BUF-5. Buffalo Bill, Jr. Belt Buckle and Plastic Belt With Instructions,**
1950s. Milky Way. Near Mint Boxed - **$165**
Buckle Only - **$20 $30 $50**

Bugs Bunny

Probably the world's best-known rabbit, Bugs Bunny evolved into the brash character we know in the late 1930s in the Leon Schlesinger cartoon studios at Warner Brothers, dubbed "Termite Terrace" by its employees. The animation staff included Tex Avery, Friz Freleng, Chuck Jones, Bob Clampett and Virgil Ross. The unnamed rabbit first appeared in *Porky's Hare Hunt* released on April 30, 1938 and directed by Cal Dalton and Joseph Benson Hardaway. Ben Hardaway's nickname was Bugs and the rabbit already had his Bronx/Brooklyn accent. His maniacal laugh no doubt inspired Woody Woodpecker's laugh a few years later. He first uttered his memorable "Eh, what's up, Doc?" to Elmer Fudd in *The Wild Hare* in 1940, and the mischievous wabbit has been asking it ever since in the voice made famous by Mel Blanc. (Following Blanc's death, Jeff Bergman has occasionally voiced the wise-cwacking wabbit). Elmer was modeled after Arthur Bryan who did his voice.

Until 1969 the cartoons were released or produced by Warner Brothers. Bugs' first comic book appearance was in 1941 in the first issue of *Looney Tunes and Merrie Melodies* and a Sunday newspaper strip started in 1943. Many cartoons, comic books and animated TV specials in the years since have been accompanied by a seemingly endless parade of merchandise, usually copyrighted by Warner Brothers. In 1997 Bugs appeared on a U.S. postage stamp, and in 2002 Bugs ranked number one on *TV Guide's* list of the 50 greatest cartoon characters of all time

BUG-1

❑ **BUG-1. Warner Character Wood Plaques,**
1941. Six 4.5x5.25" laminated colorful wall plaques picturing Bugs Bunny, Daffy Duck, Elmer Fudd, Petunia Pig, Bookworm, Little Hoot. Each - **$18 $35 $70**

BUG-2

❑ **BUG-2. Animator Bob Clampett Personal Christmas Card,**
c. 1942. Inner design includes art of Clampett boiled in kettle stirred by Bugs. - **$70 $165 $265**

BUG-3

BUG-4

❑ **BUG-3. "Bugs Bunny All Picture Comics/Tall Comic Book,"**
1943. Whitman #530. 3-3/4x8-3/4" tall format with early comic book reprints. - **$28 $84 $195**

❑ **BUG-4. Bugs Bunny Paint Book,**
1944. Scarce in high grade and uncolored. - **$25 $65 $190**

BUG-5

BUG-6

❑ **BUG-5. Bugs Bunny All Pictures Comics,**
1944. Big Little Book #1435. - **$12 $36 $78**

❑ **BUG-6. "Bugs Bunny and His Pals" All Pictures Comics,**
1945. Big Little Book #1496. - **$12 $36 $82**

BUG-7

BUG-8

❑ **BUG-7. Figural Metal Bank,**
c. 1946. Store item. - **$65 $160 $250**

❑ **BUG-8. Bugs Bunny and the Pirate Loot,**
1947. Big Little Book #1403 - **$11 $33 $72**

BUG-9

❑ **BUG-9. Warner Bros. Cartoon Promotion Button,**
1947. 1-1/4" in red, gray, black and white. Shown along with 8x10" picture of Bugs as a magician pulling a carrot from a hat in Looney Tunes #74 (December, 1947) and given free for a subscription to "Looney Tunes and Merrie Melodies" comics. - **$20 $40 $75**

BUG-10

BUG-11

❑ **BUG-10. Bugs Bunny and Klondike Gold,**
1948. Big Little Book #1455 - **$11 $33 $72**

❑ **BUG-11. "Bugs Bunny in Risky Business" All Pictures Comics,**
1948. Big Little Book #1440. - **$11 $33 $72**

BUG-12

❑ **BUG-12. "Bugs Bunny And The Tortoise" Records Album,**
1948. Capitol Record Reader. Hardcover album of story and three 10" records keyed to the story. - **$12 $25 $50**

BUG-13

BUG-14

BUG-15

❑ BUG-13. "Bugs Bunny And The Giant Brothers" New Better Little Book,
1949. Whitman #706-10. - **$10 $30 $62**

❑ BUG-14. Bugs Bunny The Masked Marvel,
1949. Big Little Book #1465 - **$11 $33 $72**

❑ BUG-15. Color 8"x10" Picture,
1940s. Comic book premium from Dell. - **$30 $60 $100**

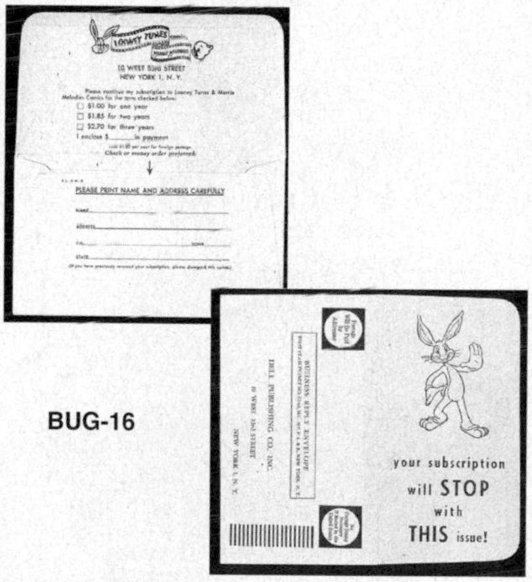

BUG-16

❑ BUG-16. Mailer,
1940s. Subscription mailer for Looney Tunes comic. - **$18 $33 $55**

BUG-17

❑ BUG-17. Bugs, Sniffles Cardboard Plaques,
1940s. Store items. Glows in the dark. Each - **$22 $40 $70**

BUG-18

BUG-19

❑ BUG-18. Rubber Squeaker Figure,
1940s. Store item by Oak Rubber Co. - **$30 $55 $120**

❑ BUG-19. Dell Comics Picture,
1940s. - **$20 $35 $70**

BUG-20

❑ BUG-20. Dell Comics Christmas Card,
1940s. - **$25 $55 $100**

BUG-21

❑ BUG-21. Bugs Bunny Animated Alarm Clock,
1940s. Metal case wind-up featuring dial face image of Bugs reclining with diecut arm holding carrot. This arm animates back and forth as if carrot is being eaten. - **$165 $300 $600**

BUG-22

❑ BUG-22. Dell Looney Tunes Comic Book Character Picture Strip,
1951. Dell Publishing Co. with Warner Bros. Cartoon Inc. copyright . Folder strip of five pictures, each about 6x8". - **$30 $55 $110**

BUG-23

❑ BUG-23. Original Comic Book Cover Art,
1951. 11 1/2"x16" Front and back cover art for Christmas Funnies #2. Early painted covers for Warner Bros. characters are rare. - **$3500**

BUG-24

BUG-25

❑ BUG-24. "What's Up Doc?" Litho. Button,
1959. Came on doll. - **$18 $30 $60**

❑ BUG-25. "Help Crippled Children" Litho. Tin Tab,
1950s. - **$3 $8 $12**

BUG-26

❑ BUG-26. Bugs Bunny Beanie,
1950s. - **$55 $125 $275**

BUG-27

BUG-28

❑ **BUG-27. "Bugs Bunny" Largest Version Stuffed Felt Doll,**
1950s. 19" tall toes to ears. - **$85 $165 $310**

❑ **BUG-28. Bugs Bunny Ceramic Planter,**
1950s. - **$20 $45 $70**

BUG-29

BUG-30

❑ **BUG-29. Bugs Bunny Painted Plaster Figural Bank,**
c. 1950s. Bank measures 4x4.5x14" tall. Bugs holds brightly colored carrot with paint accent on ears, eyebrows, cheeks, mouth and toes. Silver glitter added to ears and flower on top of head. - **$25 $45 $75**

❑ **BUG-30. "Magic Paint Book",**
1961. Post Sugar Coated Corn Flakes. Includes offer for Kool-Aid "Smiling Pitcher." - **$12 $25 $50**

BUG-31

❑ **BUG-31. "March Of Comics" #273,**
1965. Various sponsors. - **$5 $12 $22**

BUG-32

❑ **BUG-32. Figural Transistor Radio,**
1960s. Store item by Philgee International. Boxed 8.25" tall hard plastic figure radio.
Near Mint Boxed - **$70**
Radio Only - **$12 $25 $40**

BUG-33

BUG-34

❑ **BUG-33. Bugs Bunny "Happy Birthday Doc" Button,**
1960s. Button is 1.75". - **$12 $22 $45**

❑ **BUG-34. Talking Alarm Clock,**
1974. 17 1/2" tall. Says "Eh, Wake Up Doc." - **$18 $35 $85**

BUG-35

BUG-36

❑ **BUG-35. Club Member's Litho. Tin Button,**
1976. Has Warner Bros. copyright but no club sponsor indicated. Colorful 2-1/4". - **$15 $30 $55**

❑ **BUG-36. Mug and Premium Offer,**
1988. Mug comes with premium offer coupon for Bugs Bunny Vitamins.
Mug - **$6 $12 $33**
Paperwork - **$6**

BUG-37

❑ **BUG-37. Commemorative Figurine,**
1991. By Ron Lee. Bugs and Daffy shown in a scene from the cartoon "The Adventures of Robin Hood Bugs." Edition of 1250. - **$125**

(SERIES 1 BOX)

BUG-38

BUG-39

❑ **BUG-38. Comic Ball Cards Box,**
1990. Series 1 box with 34 packs of cards. Each silver-colored pack holds 12 cards. Each card has new artwork and stories from Chuck Jones.
Each pack - **$6**
Box - **$7 $15 $33**

❑ **BUG-39. Comic Ball Cards Box with Display,**
1990. Series 2 box with 34 packs of cards. Each silver-colored pack holds 12 cards.
Each pack - **$6**
Box - **$7 $15 $33**
Display - **$125**

BUG-40

❑ **BUG-40. "Space Jam" Cookie Jar,**
1996. With Bugs and Michael Jordan. - **$175**

(BOX)

(Two views of the action)

BUG-45

❑ **BUG-45. Large Electric Christmas Display,**
1997. Boxed. 2' 4" tall. Shows Bugs as Santa and the "Taz" as his reindeer. When working, characters spin in circle. - **$175**

BUG-41

BUG-42

❑ **BUG-41. "Space Jam" Figure with Tag,**
1996. Sold at theaters. - **$8 $18 $38**

❑ **BUG-42. U.S. Olympic 13" Resin Figure,**
1996. U.S. Olympic team special edition with official 4 1/2" x 3 1/2" Red, White and Blue tag. Made in China however! - **$12 $40 $60**

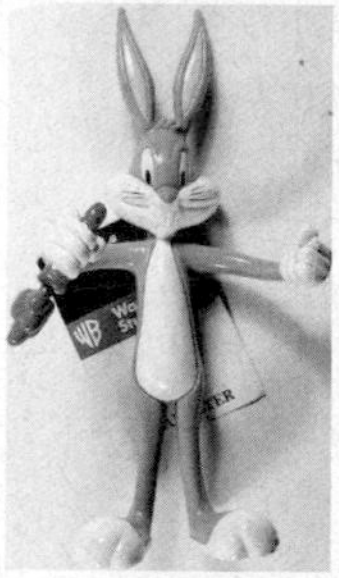

BUG-43

BUG-44

❑ **BUG-43. Bugs Flexible Figure with Tag,**
1997. 8" Warner store exclusive. Paint rubs off easily. - **$18**

❑ **BUG-44. Bugs Bunny Bobbing Head Figure,**
1997. Warner Brothers store. - **$10 $18 $45**

BUG-46

BUG-47

❑ **BUG-46. Bugs Bean Figure with 2 Tags,**
1997. - **$10**

❑ **BUG-47. Bugs Bunny Pencils on Card,**
1998. WIth free Bugs bookmark. - **$2 $3 $5**

BUG-48

BUG-49

❑ **BUG-48. Bugs Bunny Easter Bean Figure,**
1998. With tag. - **$20**

❑ **BUG-49. Bugs Bunny Stars and Stripes Bean Figure,**
1998. With tag. - **$20**

BUG-50

BUG-51

❑ **BUG-50. Snowman Bugs Bunny "Peace on Earth" Bean Figure,**
1998. With tag. - **$30**

❑ **BUG-51. Pencil Box,**
1999. - **$2 $4 $8**

Bullwinkle and Rocky

Rocky the flying squirrel and his pal Bullwinkle the moose were created by Jay Ward (1920-1989) and Alex Anderson in one of television's successful early animated cartoons. From 1959 to 1963 they battled the evil little Mr. Big and his cohorts Boris and Natasha in *Rocky and His Friends* on ABC, in *The Bullwinkle Show* from 1961 to 1964 on NBC and then back to ABC until 1973. Other regulars included Mr. Peabody the time-traveling beagle, his human friend Sherman, the inept Mountie Dudley Do-Right, his criminal foe Snidely Whiplash, and to a lesser degree, aliens Cloyd and Glidney. *Fractured Fairy-Tales*, offering skewed send-ups of classic folk and fairy-tales, was another regular feature of the show. Voice actors included: June Foray as Rocky, Natasha and Nell Fenwick; Bill Scott as Bullwinkle, Mr. Peabody and Dudley Do-Right; Hans Conried as Snidely Whiplash; Paul Frees as Boris and Captain Peachfuzz and Walter Tetley as Sherman. William Conrad was the main narrator and Edward Everett Horton narrated the Fractured Fairy Tales segments. Comic books started appearing in the early 1960s. A feature film starring Robert DeNiro (!) as Fearless Leader, Jason Alexander as Boris Badanov, and Rene Russo as Natasha had a disappointingly brief appearance in theatrical release in 2000 and has since made the leap to home video. Toys, games and other merchandise usually carry the copyright of P.A.T.-Ward Productions.

BUL-1

BUL-2

❑ **BUL-1. "P-F Flyers" Bullwinkle & Rocky 12x21" Cardboard Store Sign,**
c. 1959. B. F. Goodrich Co. Also promotes Rin-Tin-Tin, The Lone Ranger, Captain Gallant. -
$140 $275 $550

❑ **BUL-2. "Rocky and HIs Friends" Little Golden Book #408,**
1960. - **$12 $30 $80**

BUL-3

❑ **BUL-3. Original Cover Art for "Rocky and HIs Friends" Little Golden Book,**
1960. 12 1/2" x 10 1/2" painting. - **$3500**

BUL-4

BUL-5

BUL-6

❑ **BUL-4. Rocky The Flying Squirrel Glazed Ceramic Figure,**
1960. 4-3/4" tall store item. - **$45 $100 $200**

❑ **BUL-5. "Mr. Peabody" Glazed Ceramic Figural Bank,**
1960. Store item. 5-3/4" tall. - **$50 $110 $225**

❑ **BUL-6. "Mr. Sherman" Glazed Ceramic Figural Bank,**
1960. Store item. 5-7/8" tall. Japan. -
$50 $110 $225

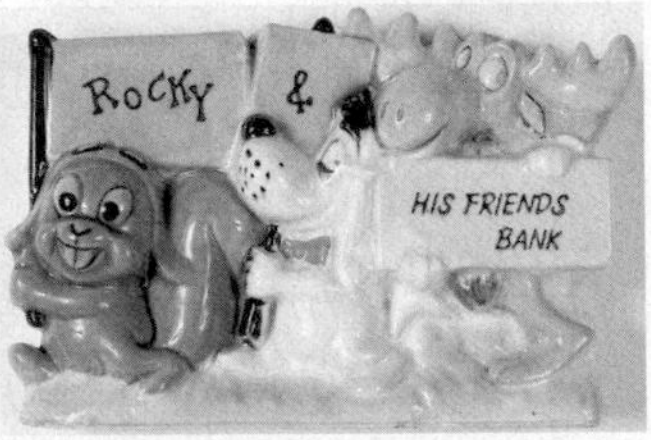

BUL-7

❑ **BUL-7. "Rocky & His Friends" Ceramic Figural Bank,**
1960. 6.25" wide front raised image of Rocky, Mr. Peabody and Bullwinkle. -
$75 $150 $300

BUL-8

BUL-9

❑ **BUL-8. Rocky Ceramic Figure Bank,**
1960. 5" tall with coin slot in top of tail. -
$55 $110 $225

❑ **BUL-9. "Bullwinkle Bank,"**
1960. Pat Ward. Glazed pottery bank measures 2.75x3.75x6" tall. Horizontal coin slot on shoulder. Photo example has souvenir sticker, not on most examples. - **$65 $125 $250**

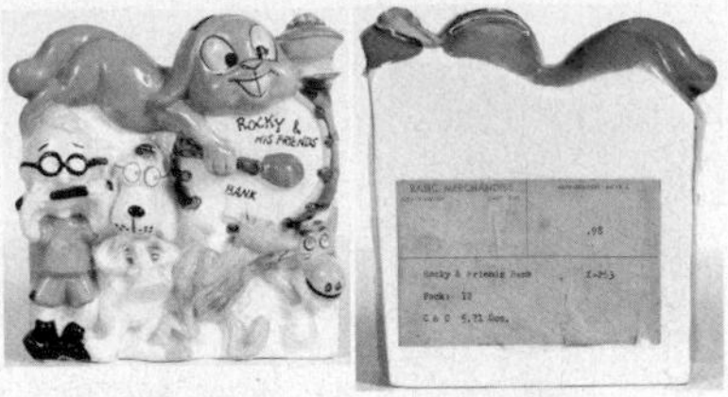

BUL-10

❑ **BUL-10. "Rocky And His Friends" Ceramic Bank,**
1960. 5.75" tall figural design of Rocky, Bullwinkle, Mr. Peabody, Sherman. -
$75 $150 $300

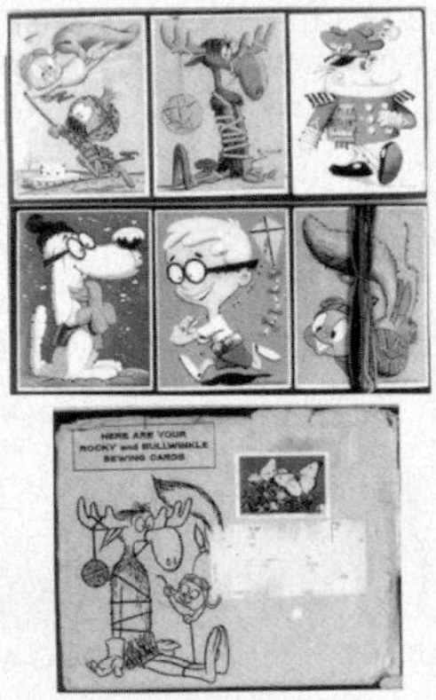
BUL-11

❑ **BUL-11. "Sewing Cards" Kit With Envelope,**
1961. Set of six cards for yarn threading.
Near Mint In Mailer - **$225**
Each Card- **$6 $12 $28**

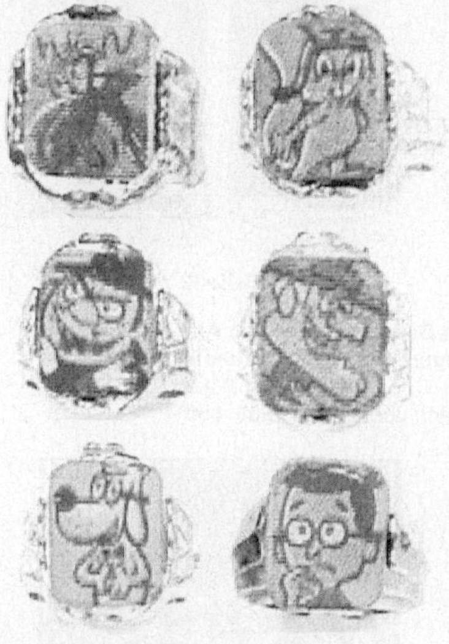

BUL-12

❑ **BUL-12. Jay Ward Character Flicker Rings Set,**
1961. Scarce rings distributed through vending machines. Each is on silvered plastic base although flickers have also been seen on modern bases marked "China." Two views of each character: Bullwinkle, Rocky, Boris, Dudley Do-Right, Sherman, Mr. Peabody.
Original Base Each - **$135 $265 $375**
Modern Base - **$80 $135 $220**

BUL-13

BUL-14

❑ **BUL-13. "March Of Comics" Booklet,**
1962. Child Life Shoes. Comic #233. -
$10 $30 $100

❑ **BUL-14. "Moosylvania" Litho. Tab And Decal,**
1962. Issuer unknown. 1-1/4" tall unfolded tab reads "The 52nd State" while 3-1/2" decal proclaims "Statehood." Each - **$6 $12 $18**

BUL-15

❑ **BUL-15. "Bullwinkle" Three Reel View-Master Pack With Story Booklet,**
1962. #B515. - **$12 $25 $50**

BUL-16

❑ **BUL-16. "Electric Quiz Fun Game",**
1962. General Mills. Battery operated. -
$30 $50 $100

BUL-17

❑ **BUL-17. "Bullwinkle Lunch Kit" Vinyl Lunch Box With Thermos,**
1963. Vinyl lunch box is 7x9x4" deep with 8" tall metal thermos with plastic cap. Manufactured by King-Seeley Thermos Company, P.A.T. Ward Productions. Box - **$200 $400 $800**
Thermos - **$100 $200 $300**

BUL-18

❑ **BUL-18. Bullwinkle's Safety Coloring Book,**
1963. General Mills. - **$12 $35 $70**

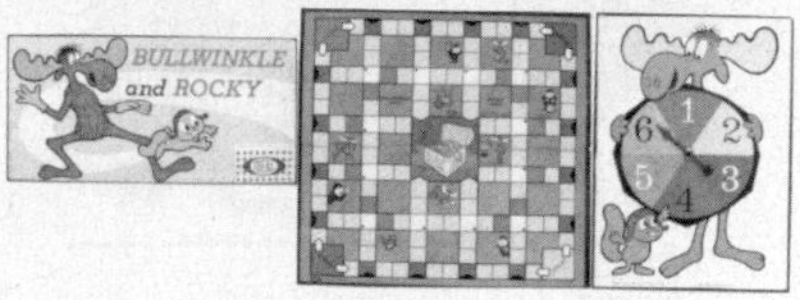

BUL-19

❑ **BUL-19. "Bullwinkle And Rocky" Boxed Game,**
1963. Ideal #2216-0-200. - **$35 $70 $135**

(CLOSE-UP)

BUL-20

❑ **BUL-20. Cheerios 21x28" Double-Sided Paper Sign,**
c. 1963. - **$50 $95 $185**

BUL-21

❑ **BUL-21. Bullwinkle's Mix 'N Match Game,**
1964. Cheerios. Set of six character cut-outs which comprised one of eight cut-out games on the back panels of the cereal boxes.
Each Box Used Complete - **$60 $125 $200**
Each Game Cut Complete - **$12 $25 $40**

BUL-22

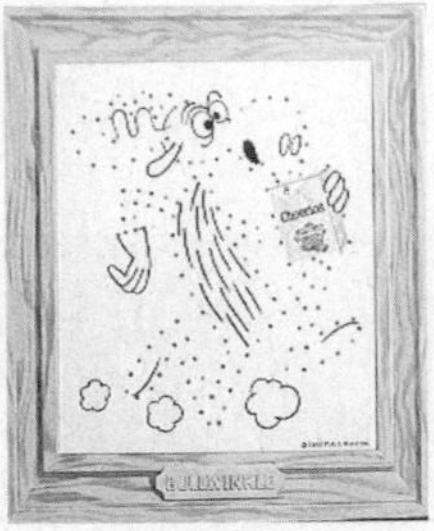
BUL-23

❑ **BUL-22. "Tattoo" Fleer Gum Wrapper,**
1965. Example from set with different tattoo images. - **$10 $18 $32**

❑ **BUL-23. "Bullwinkle" Follow The Colors Portrait,**
1966. Cheerios box back.
Used Complete Box - **$55 $110 $250**
Panel Only - **$10 $20 $40**

BUL-24

❑ **BUL-24. Bullwinkle With Cheerios Kid Drink Cup,**
1969. Cheerios premium made of Melmac. Other pieces in set believed to be plate and bowl. Each - **$10 $20 $40**

BUL-25

BUL-26

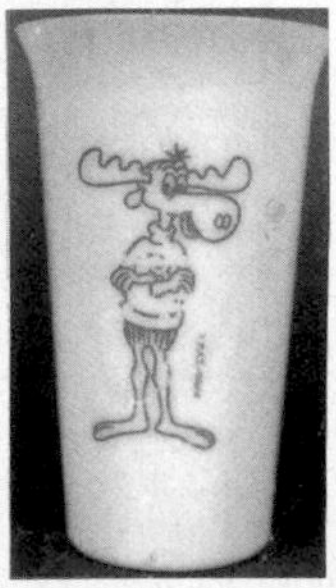
BUL-27

❑ **BUL-25. Bullwinkle And Cheerios Kid Store Clerk Cello. Button,**
1960s. 3" full color. - **$100 $200 $325**

❑ **BUL-26. Bullwinkle Trading Coin,**
1960s. Old London Dipsy Doodles and Corn Doodles. Numbered set of 60 plastic coins with paper inserts picturing Bullwinkle and other Jay Ward characters.
Each - **$3 $8 $15**

❑ **BUL-27. Plastic Tumbler,**
1960s. Issuer unknown. - **$15 $25 $50**

(BOTH PICTURED IN ADS)

BUL-28 BUL-29

❑ **BUL-28. T-Shirt,**
1970. Charlton Comics. - **$45 $100 $180**

❑ **BUL-29. Sweatshirt,**
1970. Charlton Comics. - **$65 $140 $225**

BUL-30

❑ **BUL-30. Fan Club Membership Card,**
1970. Charlton Comics. Part of fan club kit. - **$10 $15 $25**

BUL-31

❑ **BUL-31. "Bullwinkle Gum With Tattoos" Store Vending Machine,**
1973. 15.5" tall gum dispenser of clear glass on metal base centered on front by coin slot, turn handle, lift-up "Thank You" hinged dispenser lid. - **$165 $325 $550**

BUL-32

❑ **BUL-32. Bullwinkle And Rocky Dakin Figures In Cartoon Theater Boxes,**
1976. Each Near Mint Boxed - **$95**
Each Loose - **$18 $35 $50**

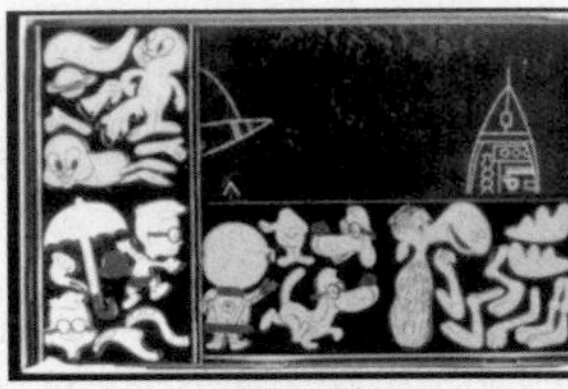
BUL-33

❑ **BUL-33. Colorforms Set ,**
1970s. Interior shown. - **$35 $65 $100**

BUL-34

BUL-35

❑ **BUL-34. Pepsi Collector Series Glasses,**
1970s. Each - **$10 $15 $20**

❑ **BUL-35. Bullwinkle Pez Dispenser,**
1970s. Issued with tan or yellow antlers and either brown or yellow body. - **$35 $125 $250**

BUL-36

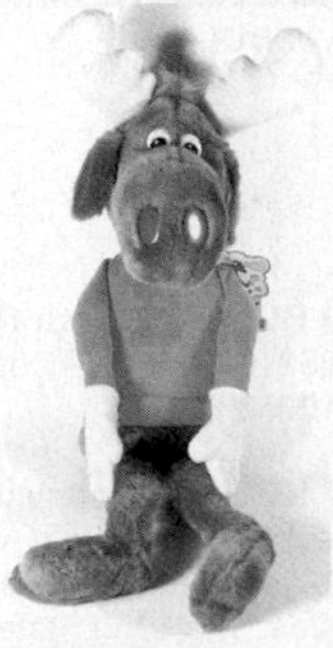
BUL-37

❑ **BUL-36. Rocky Plush Figure,**
1982. From Wallace Berrie & Company. With cloth hat and tag. - **$15 $40 $80**

❑ **BUL-37. Bullwinkle Plush Figure,**
1982. From Wallace Berrie & Company. 17" tall with tag. - **$15 $40 $80**

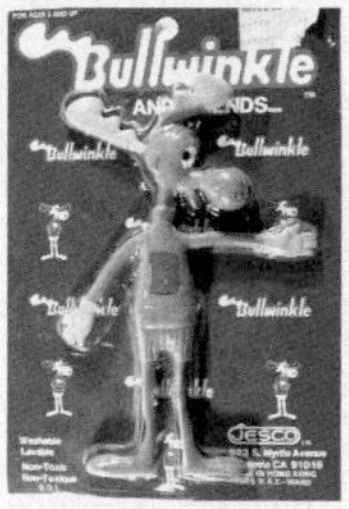

BUL-38

BUL-39

❑ **BUL-38. Bullwinkle Bendy on Card,**
1985. - **$8 $15 $40**

❑ **BUL-39. Rocky Ceramic Figure,**
1980s. 2 1/2" tall. - **$10 $22 $45**

BUL-40

❑ **BUL-40. Bullwinkle Bobbing Head Figure,**
1996. Ward Productions. - **$12 $35 $55**

BUL-41

❑ **BUL-41. Rocky & Bullwinkle Christmas Ornament,**
1996. Carlton Cards. - **$38**

BUL-42

❑ **BUL-42. Hot Wheels Car-Toon Friends Die-Cut Car Series,**
1998. Set includes Natasha's "Saltflat Racer," Rocky's "XT-3," Bullwinkle's "Double Vision," and Boris' "Lakester." On card. Each - **$9**

BUL-43

❑ **BUL-43. Mr. Peabody Plastic Figure,**
1999. Comes with tag. - **$12 $18 $40**

BUL-44

❑ **BUL-44. Mr. Peabody and Sherman Plush Dolls,**
1999. Large - **$30** each.
Small - **$15** each.

BUL-45

❑ **BUL-45. TV Ad 2-1/2" Cello. Button,**
c. 1990s. Channel 5, unidentified location. By Reno, Nevada maker without copyright. - **$10 $15 $25**

BUL-46

❑ **BUL-46. "The Adventures of Rocky and Bullwinkle" Flying Playset,**
2000. Promotes movie. Store bought. - **$28**

BUL-47

BUL-48

❑ **BUL-47. "The Adventures of Rocky and Bullwinkle" Plush Rocky Doll on Card,**
2000. Promotes movie. - **$28**

❑ **BUL-48. "The Adventures of Rocky and Bullwinkle" Talking Rocky Doll,**
2000. On card-type box. - **$28**

Burns and Allen

Longtime vaudeville stars, George Burns (1896-1996) and Gracie Allen (1906-1964), became a comedy team in 1922 and made a successful transition to radio in 1932 and broadcast continuously on CBS or NBC until Gracie decided to retire in 1958. George was the straight man, Gracie the scatterbrain and the show ranged from standup gags to situation comedy. The program also introduced Mel Blanc's Happy Postman character. Sponsors over the years included Robert Burns and White Owl cigars, Campbell's soup, Grape-Nuts Flakes, Chesterfield cigarettes, Hinds lotion, Hormel Packing Co., Swan soap, Maxwell House coffee and Block Drugs. They appeared in comedy shorts and feature films between 1929 and 1939 and a popular half-hour TV show aired from 1950 to 1958 on CBS. "Say goodnight, Gracie."

BUR-1

BUR-2

❑ **BUR-1. "Gracie Allen's Anniversary Gift To Guy Lombardo" Booklet,**
1933. General Cigar Co., maker of Robert Burns cigars. Humor dialogue between Gracie and George Burns on what to buy orchestra leader Lombardo for his fourth anniversary of radio broadcasts.- **$12 $25 $45**

❑ **BUR-2. Photo,**
1937. Philadelphia Record newspaper premium. - **$10 $25 $45**

BUR-3

BUR-4

❑ **BUR-3. Grape-Nuts 12x18" Sign,**
1930s. Scarce. Printed on both sides and with hanging cord. - **$325 $650 $1300**

❑ **BUR-4. Fan Photo,**
1930s. Campbell's Soups. - **$10 $25 $45**

BUR-5

BUR-6

❑ **BUR-5. Fan Photo,**
1930s. Columbia Broadcasting System. - **$10 $20 $40**

❑ **BUR-6. Radio Broadcast Listing Folder,**
1930s. Grape-Nuts. - **$18 $35 $60**

BUR-7

❑ **BUR-7. Radio Tubes Ad Folder With Punch-Out Figure,**
1930s. RCA Cunningham/Radiotrons. One panel of folder has cartoon punch-out figure of Burns and Allen with base for standing. Unpunched - **$20 $40 $60**

BUR-8

❑ **BUR-8. "Gracie Allen's Missing Brother" Boxed Jigsaw Puzzle,**
1930s. Store item by Commanday-Roth Co. Comes with leaflet describing the search for him in pictured crowd scene. Boxed - **$18 $35 $65**
Loose - **$10 $20 $40**

BUR-9

BUR-10

❑ **BUR-9. "How To Become President By Gracie Allen" Button,**
1940s. 1.25" bright red on white. - **$25 $45 $90**

❑ **BUR-10. "George Burns And Gracie Allen/Swan Soap" Display Sign,**
1940s. 11x14". - **$40 $70 $125**

BUR-11

❑ **BUR-11. "George Burns And Gracie Allen/Swan Soap" Display Sign,**
1940s. Cardboard sign is stiff 10x14" with bottom margin pair of folding tabs where sign fit between large cakes of Swan soap on a display. Text includes "Listen To George Burns & Gracie Allen Every Tues. Night." - **$40 $70 $125**

BUR-12

❑ **BUR-12. Paper-Mate Pen Standee,**
1953. The 32" x 30" standee promotes Paper-Mate Pens, a sponsor of Burns and Allen's CBS television show. - **$165 $375 $625**

BUR-13

❑ **BUR-13. "Motorola TV Coffee Servers" Boxed Set,**
1950s. Motorola, maker of TV sets. Offered at 99 cents per set, glass items by Pyrex. Boxed - **$30 $50 $90**

Buster Brown

Buster Brown was the creation of R. F. Outcault (1863-1925). The color strip first appeared in the Sunday New York Herald on May 4, 1902, a half-dozen years after Outcault's first great strip, *The Yellow Kid*, appeared in the New York World. Buster was a pint-size prankster, constantly bedeviling those around him, then resolving to behave better in the future. His ever-present companion was Tige, a Boston terrier with an evil toothy grin. The strip was a huge success and ran until 1920. A number of newspaper strip reprint books and advertising booklets featuring cartoon panels appeared in the early part of the century. Owning the rights and beginning in 1904 with the St. Louis World's Fair, Outcault sold merchandising rights to the Buster Brown character to more than 50 manufacturers of everything from bread to soap to harmonicas; today we can still buy Buster Brown shoes and children's clothes. Thomas Edison's film company produced a movie in 1904, and Universal issued a series of live-action shorts in the mid-1920s which co-starred Pete the Pit Bull as Tige. Complete with circle around his eye, Pete would go on to greater fame in the Our Gang shorts. A weekly drama based on the strip ran on CBS in 1929 and was revived as *Smilin' Ed McConnell's Buster Brown Gang* for NBC. It aired from 1943 to 1953, when it transferred to television, retaining Buster Brown Shoes as sponsor. On McConnell's death in 1954, Andy Devine took his place and the show was re-named *Andy's Gang*. The star of the show was Froggy the Gremlin. Jerry Maren, the Lollipop Kid in the *Wizard of Oz*, played Buster on TV and made personal appearances in costume. Buster Brown has been a rich source of toys, comic books and premiums for over a century and is still going strong. "Plunk your magic twanger, Froggy!"

BWN-1

❑ **BWN-1. "New York Herald/Young Folks" Cello. Button,**
c. 1902. Early newspaper issue. - **$100 $225 $450**

BWN-2

❑ **BWN-2. Newspaper Promo,**
1903. New York Herald promotion for its Sunday pages. Appeared in the March 27, 1903 Easter Edition. More information is on the back. - **$35 $65 $100**

BWN-3

❑ **BWN-3. "Buster Brown And His Bubble" Postcard,**
1903. From numbered set of 10. The Yellow Kid appears on cards 3, 6, 8, 9, and 10.
Buster Only Each - **$20 $35 $60**
With Yellow Kid - **$25 $45 $90**

BWN-4

❑ **BWN-4. Buster & Tige Figural Ceramic Touring Car,**
c. 1903. 5.5" long by 4.5" tall glazed likeness of them in touring car similar to common theme of Buster Brown postcards of the era. Probably German. - **$160 $325 $650**

BWN-5

❑ **BWN-5. "Brown's Blue Ribbon Book Of Jokes And Jingles",**
1904. Scarce. Brown Shoe Co. Considered the first comic book premium. This is the first of four books in a series titled *Jokes and Jingles*. This first book came in four versions. Earliest printings include Pore Li'l Mose, while later printings replace him with the Yellow Kid. See BWN-11 and BWN-25. - **$300 $1050 $1900**

BWN-6

❑ **BWN-6. Bloomingdale's Christmas Postcard,**
1904. One of the most sought-after of all Buster Brown cards. - **$65 $120 $210**

BWN-7

❑ **BWN-7. "Buster Brown's Experiences With Pond's Extract" Booklet,**
1904. - **$100 $250 $525**

BWN-8

BWN-9

❏ BWN-8. "Buster Brown Drawing Book,"
1904. Issued by Collins Bread. 3x4-7/8" with eight pages. - **$50 $150 $315**

❏ BWN-9. "Buster Brown Bread" Ad Cards,
1904. Back has imprint of baker in Lancaster, Pa. Each card is 3-1/2x5-3/8".
Each - **$20 $40 $80**

BWN-10

❏ BWN-10. "Buster Brown's Pranks" Comic Strip Reprint Book,
1905. Published by Frederick A. Stokes Co.
GD - **$400** FN - **$1450**

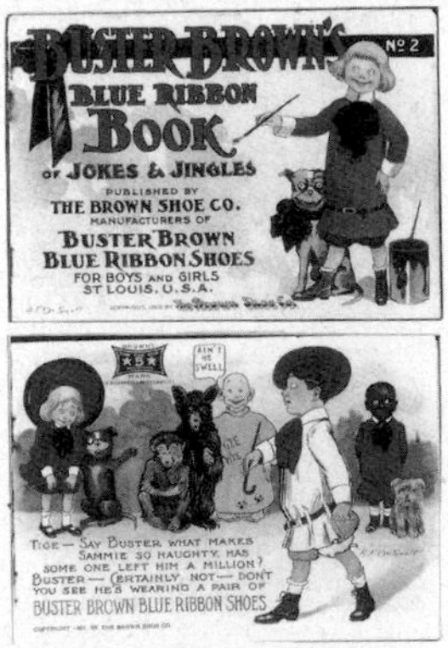

BWN-11

❏ BWN-11. "Buster Brown's Blue Ribbon Book Of Jokes & Jingles No. 2",
1905. One of earliest premium comic books. See BWN-5 and BWN-25. - **$200 $600 $1260**

BWN-12

BWN-13

❏ BWN-12. "Buster Brown Shoes" Cello. Pocket Mirror,
c. 1905. - **$110 $225 $380**

❏ BWN-13. Enamel And Brass Stickpin,
c. 1905. Initials on bottom edge stand for 'Buster Brown Blue Ribbon Shoes'. -
$65 $160 $275

BWN-14

❏ BWN-14. "Quick Meal Steel Ranges" Booklet,
c. 1905. - **$50 $150 $315**

BWN-15

❏ BWN-15. Original Watercolor of "Tige",
c. 1905. A small picture of Buster's sidekick Boston Terrier, signed by RF Outcault. - **$900**

BWN-16

❏ BWN-16. "Buster Brown Bread" Cello. Button,
c. 1905. Issued in both yellow and gray rim variations. - **$15 $30 $65**

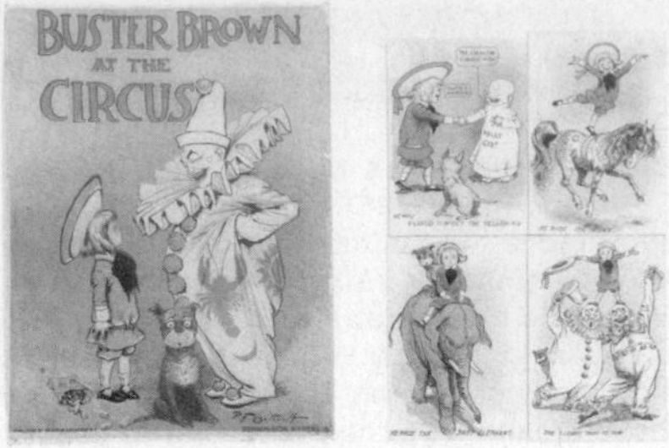

BWN-17

❏ BWN-17. "Buster Brown At The Circus" Card Game,
c. 1905. Artist-signed at lower right by creator R.F. Outcault. Text at bottom of art includes "Published By Selchow & Righter N.Y. Herald." Forty cards plus original instructions. Cards show Buster and Tige's visit to the circus with captions below. Yellow Kid, Tipsy, monkey and bear make appearances on individual cards. Boxed Complete - **$150 $300 $650**

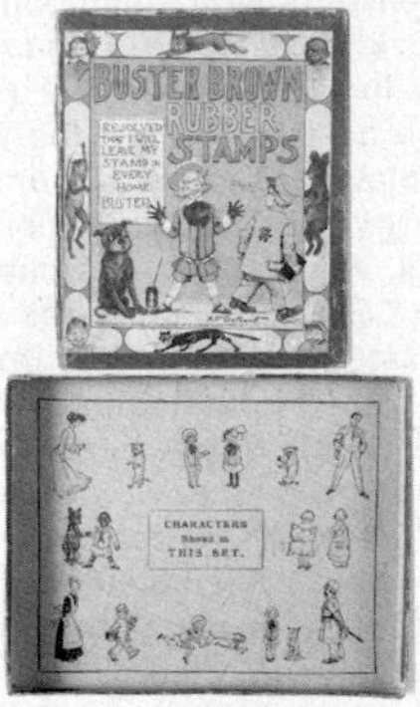

BWN-18

❏ BWN-18. "Buster Brown Rubber Stamps" And Others Boxed,
c. 1905. Graphic design labeled box containing 15 wood block stamps including character stamps for Outcault characters Yellow Kid and Poor Lil Mose. - **$135 $265 $475**

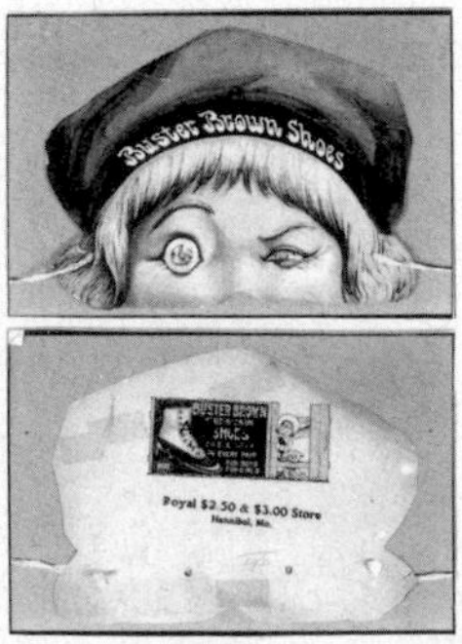

BWN-19

❏ BWN-19. Paper Mask,
c. 1905. - **$65 $150 $275**

BWN-20

❑ **BWN-20. "Buster Brown Stocking Magazine",**
1906. - **$40 $80 $140**

BWN-21

❑ **BWN-21. Drawing Book,**
1906. 3.5x4.75" booklet of inside pictures and tracing paper. - **$50 $150 $300**

BWN-22

❑ **BWN-22. "Buster Brown's Latest Frolics",**
1907. Comic strip reprint book published by Cupples & Leon Co. - **$163 $600 $1025**

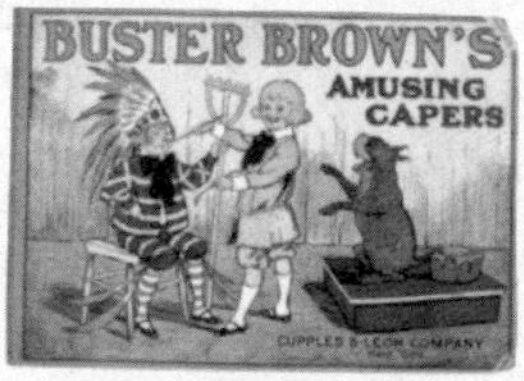

BWN-23

❑ **BWN-23. "Buster Brown's Amusing Capers" Comic Strip Reprint Book,**
1908. Cupples & Leon Co. - **$129 $475 $815**

BWN-24

❑ **BWN-24. Assortment of Postcards From Several Series,**
c. 1908. Buster Brown and his dog Tige.
Each - **$10 $20 $40**

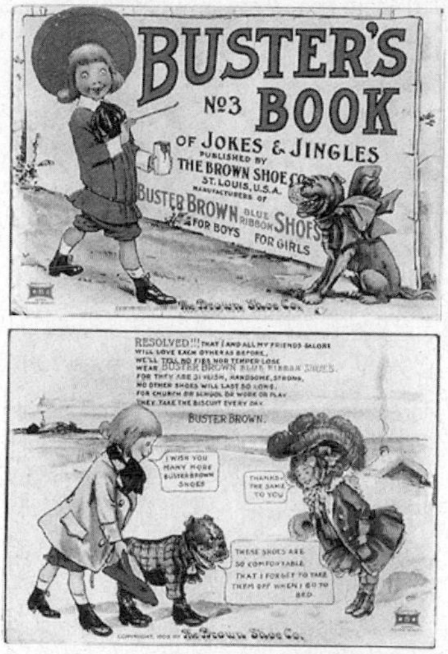

BWN-25

❑ **BWN-25. "Buster's Book Of Jokes And Jingles No. 3",**
1909. Third of four in series. See BWN-5 and BWN-11. - **$150 $400 $840**

BWN-26

BWN-27

❑ **BWN-26. "Buster Brown Shoes" Cello. Button,**
c. 1910. Red background. - **$70 $175 $300**

❑ **BWN-27. Black Background Version Cello. Button,**
c. 1910. - **$95 $225 $350**

BWN-28

❑ **BWN-28. "You Can't 'Buster Brown' Hose Supporter" Advertising Cello. Buttons,**
c. 1910. Buster Brown Hosiery. Examples also known with Buster hugging Tige and Buster falling down. Each - **$18 $30 $55**

BWN-29

❑ **BWN-29. "Buster Brown & Tige" Paperdoll With Envelope,**
c. 1910. Buster is 12" with 4 outfits and matching hats. 5" tige with dunce hat. 6.5x12" envelope. R.F. Outcault facsimile signature at bottom of envelope. Envelope - **$30 $65 $125**
Figures & Clothes - **$75 $135 $275**

BWN-30

❑ **BWN-30 "Buster Brown Cloth Party Game,"**
c. 1910. 7x9" envelope has illustration of Buster Brown and Tige with Outcault name below. Pin-the-tail-on-the-donkey type of game. Comes with 18x24" folded as issued oilcloth illustration with Outcault name at bottom, along with 12 bow ties as game pieces.
Envelope - **$35 $60 $125**
Fabric Uncut - **$80 $165 $275**
Fabric Cut Complete - **$55 $110 $175**

BWN-31

❑ **BWN-31. "Buster Brown's Hosiery" In Original Box With Labels,**
c. 1910. Box is 2x7.5x11.75" and holds six pair of socks. Each pair has its own sticker. Size 9.5.
Box - **$35 $65 $125**
Each Sock Pair with Labels - **$15 $30 $50**

BWN-32

❑ **BWN-32. Buster Brown Pencil Box With Colorful Three-Panel Cartoon Lid,**
c. 1910. Heavy black lacquered hinged box with lock measures 2.5x8.5x1" deep. Three color panel images. Bottom of box is marked "Germany." - **$60 $125 $200**

BWN-33

BWN-34

❑ **BWN-33. Buster Brown 4" Bisque Figure,**
c. 1910. With movable arms. - **$125 $350 $550**

❑ **BWN-34. Wood Whistle,**
c. 1910. Shoe Premium - **$25 $50 $110**

BWN-35

❑ **BWN-35. "Buster Brown Blue Ribbon Shoes" Watch Fob,**
c. 1910. Silvered white metal, 1-3/4" oval. - **$110 $220 $350**

BWN-36

BWN-37

❑ **BWN-36. "Buster Brown Shoes" Store Ad Fan,**
c. 1910. Diecut cardboard with wooden rod. Imprinted for various stores. - **$75 $150 $300**

❑ **BWN-37. Cigar Tin,**
c. 1910 Store item. Price includes lid. -
$450 $1100 $1800

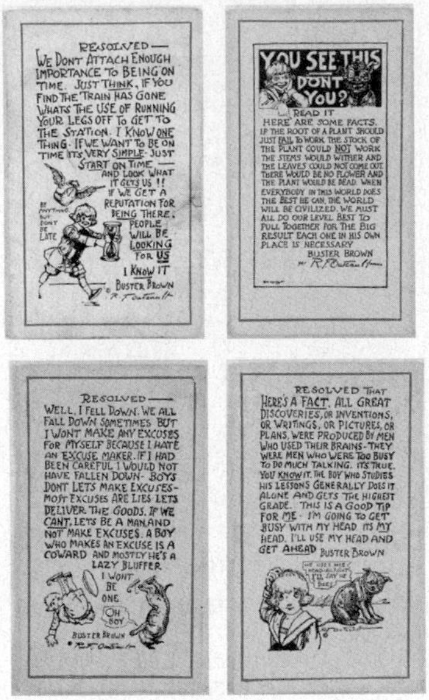

BWN-38

❑ **BWN-38. Bread Premium Cards,**
c. 1910. Scarce.
Each - **$15 $35 $65**

BWN-39

BWN-40

❑ **BWN-39. Entry Card For Pocketwatch Premium,**
c. 1912. - **$25 $45 $90**

❑ **BWN-40. Buster And Tige Pocketwatch,**
c. 1912. - **$300 $700 $1250**

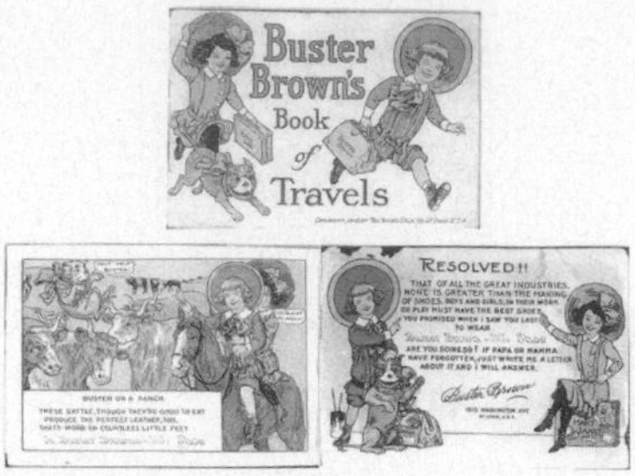

BWN-41

❑ **BWN-41. "Buster Brown's Book Of Travels",**
1912. Brown Shoe Co. 12 pages 3-1/2x5". - **$117 $408 $735**

BWN-42

❑ **BWN-42. "Buster Brown And His Chum Tige" Comic Strip Reprint Book,**
1915. Published by Frederick A. Stokes Co. - **$153 $535 $1000**

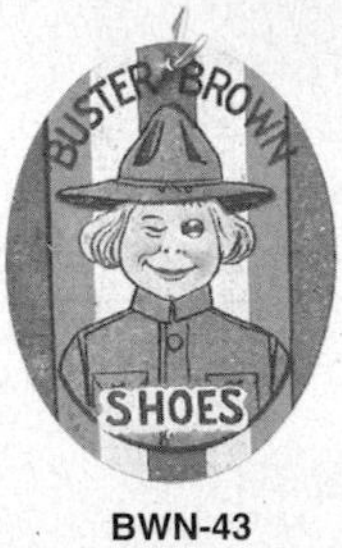

BWN-43

BWN-44

❑ **BWN-43. Celluloid Oval With Stickpin,**
c. 1917. Buster Brown Shoes. 1-3/8" tall with color portrait of Buster in Army uniform on red, white and blue background. - **$85 $165 $325**

❑ **BWN-44. Buster Brown Mirror,**
c. 1920. Shoe Premium. - **$45 $85 $170**

BWN-45

❑ **BWN-45. Buster Brown 2" Bisque Figure,**
1920s. Arms do not move. - **$55 $110 $160**

BWN-46

❑ **BWN-46. Happy Hooligan/Buster Brown-Like German Mechanical Toy,**
c. 1920. Spring-loaded tin mechanical toy is 1.75x4.5x6.75" tall with figure holding hammer to ring bell. This figure bears a resemblance to Happy Hooligan. When he is cocked and released, hammer hits anvil, yellow slide shoots up column to hit character at top who bears strong resemblance to Buster Brown. When character is hit, the ring in his hand flips to opposite side. - **$125 $250 $500**

BWN-47

❑ **BWN-47. "Buster Brown Walking Club" Oval Cello. Button,**
1920s. Includes "Tread Straight" trademark arrow symbol. - **$20 $50 $100**

BWN-48

❑ **BWN-48. "Health Shoes" Figural Pencil Case,**
1920s. 10.25" cardboard cylinder with wooden tip replica pencil. Cap removes for contents of traditional pencil, pen, ruler. - **$35 $70 $125**

BWN-49

❑ **BWN-49. "Shoe Game" Punch-Out With Sleeve,**
1920s. 7.25x7.5" paper instruction sleeve holding cardboard punch parts for ring toss game featuring Buster and Tige as rings target. - **$60 $135 $225**

BWN-50

❑ **BWN-50. Magic Kit,**
1934. Includes "Magic Ball, My Magic Ink, My Secret Ink, Trick Hospital Bandage".
In Mailer - **$20 $35 $80**

BWN-51

❑ **BWN-51. "Buster Brown" And Tige Figural String Holder,**
1938. 7x8x3" deep. Painted plaster. Rim of hat reads "1938 Buster Brown." Inside back area impressed letters read "Art W.I.E.H.L., 1938." Wire loop on back. - **$275 $550 $1100**

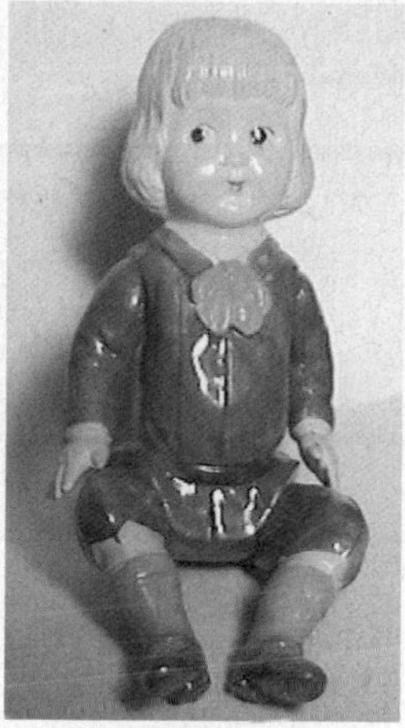

BWN-52

❑ **BWN-52. Jointed Celluloid Seated Figure,**
1930s. Issuer unknown. Beautifully colored figure with movable arms and legs but with legs molded in seated position. Comes in two sizes, either 3-1/4" tall or 5-1/4" tall as measured seated. Marked "Made In Japan" on reverse and may have Japan paper sticker under seat.
Each - **$75 $175 $350**

BWN-53

BWN-54

❑ **BWN-53. Cello. Fob,**
1930s. - **$60 $165 $325**

❑ **BWN-54. Litho. Tin Clicker,**
1930s. - **$18 $30 $60**

BWN-55

BWN-56

❑ **BWN-55. Felt Patch,**
1930s. - **$15 $30 $50**

❑ **BWN-56. Buster Brown Blotter,**
1930s. - **$20 $40 $65**

BWN-57

BWN-58

❑ **BWN-57. Tin Whistle,**
1930s. Shoe Premium - **$35 $75 $120**

❑ **BWN-58. Tin Whistle,**
1930s. - **$30 $60 $95**

BWN-59

❑ **BWN-59. Buster Brown Comics #1,**
1945. Scarce. Brown Shoe Co. No number and no date, covers refer to various shoe stores. - **$61 $183 $885**

BWN-60

BWN-61

❑ **BWN-60. Slide,**
1940s. Premium slide for neckerchief. - **$35 $70 $120**

❑ **BWN-61. Card,**
1940s. Buster Brown Shoes premium. When folded, eyes and mouth move when pulled. - **$22 $45 $65**

BWN-62

❑ **BWN-62. Toy Currency,**
c. 1940s. Various denominations collected for prizes. Each -**$6 $12 $18**

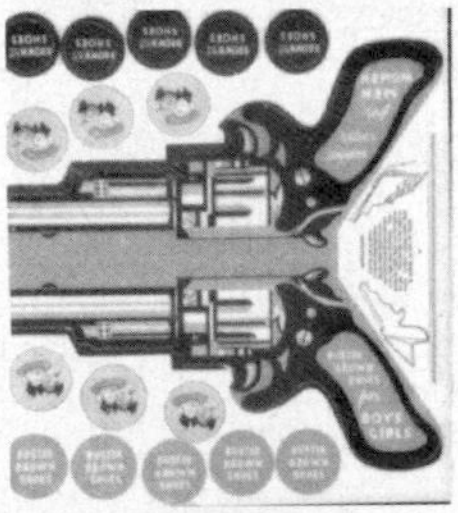

BWN-63

❑ **BWN-63. Punch-Out Gun Sheet,**
1940s. Unpunched - **$15 $30 $60**

BWN-64

❑ **BWN-64. Buster Brown Knife,**
1940s. Shoe premium, rare. - **$65 $140 $275**

BWN-65

❑ **BWN-65. 50th Anniversary Commemorative Coin,**
1954. Gold plastic medalet inscribed on both sides by text for 50 years of children's shoes. - **$5 $10 $15**

BWN-66

❑ **BWN-66. Buster Brown Beanie,**
1950s. - **$25 $45 $70**

BWN-67

❑ **BWN-67. Buster & Tige Figural Bank,**
1950s. 5" tall ceramic finished in glazed colors by unidentified maker. - **$110 $225 $360**

BWN-68

❑ **BWN-68. "Buster Brown Textiles Inc." Figural Cast Metal Award Bank,**
1964. 5" tall. - **$55 $110 $175**

BWN-69

❑ **BWN-69. Buster Brown Secret Agent Periscope,**
1960s. - **$25 $45 $90**

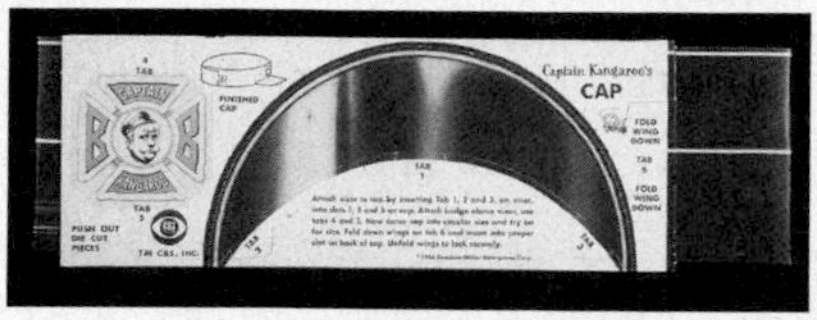

BWN-70

❑ **BWN-70. Buster Brown/Capt. Kangaroo Hat Punch-out,**
1960s. - **$20 $40 $75**

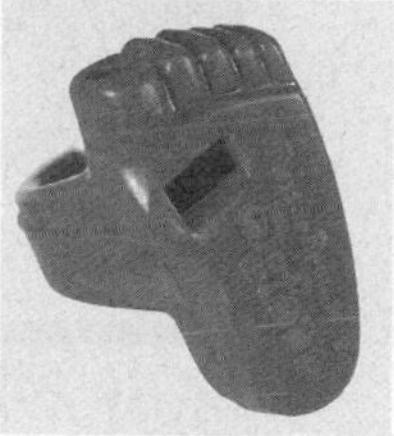

BWN-71 BWN-72

❑ **BWN-71. Plastic Flicker Ring,**
1960s. Image changes from Buster and Tige to "Stop" and "Go" signs. - **$15 $25 $40**

❑ **BWN-72. "Buster Brown Big Foot" Plastic Whistle Ring,**
1960s. Blowing into big toe creates whistling sound. - **$10 $15 $25**

BWN-73 BWN-74

❑ **BWN-73. Palm Puzzle,**
1960s. - **$8 $15 $30**

❑ **BWN-74. Child's Watch,**
1975. - **$25 $50 $100**

California Raisins

In the mid-1980s much of America was captivated by a bunch of cool raisins with an irresistible beat--the California Raisins had arrived. Created in clay by Will Vinton for the California Raisin Advisory Board (CALRAB) and animated for musical television commercials by the Claymation process, these diminutive sports were anything but dry. The commercials began in 1986, featuring the raisins' signature song *I Heard It Through The Grapevine.* The song was written by Norman Whitfield and Barrett Strong. Gladys Knight and the Pips originally recorded the song and Marvin Gaye had his first number one hit with it in 1968. Small vinyl figures of the raisins were widely promoted as premiums or giveaways by CALRAB. The group consists of: Ben Indasun, Tiny Goodbite, Justin X. Grape, Sugar E. Treat, Rye Stack and Delicious. Ray Charles and Michael Jackson starred as clay figures in a few commercials.

CAL-1

❑ **CAL-1. Musical Sandwich Toy,**
1987. Del Monte Fruit Snacks. Figural plastic with push button to play "Grapevine" song.
Boxed - **$18 $35 $75**
Unboxed - **$12 $25 $40**

CAL-2 CAL-3

❑ **CAL-2. Vinyl Bank,**
1987. - **$10 $20 $40**

❑ **CAL-3. Figure Keychain,**
1987. 3 1/4" tall. - **$3 $6 $15**

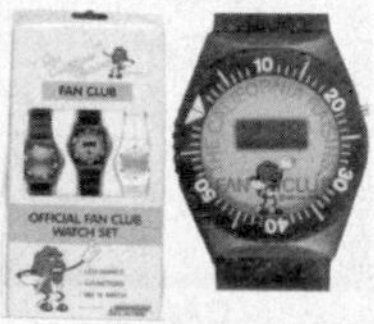

CAL-4 CAL-5

❑ **CAL-4. California Raisins "Duet" Music Toys On Card,**
1987. Store item by Imperial Toy Corp. - **$8 $15 $30**

❑ **CAL-5. "California Raisins Fan Club" Watch Set,**
1987. Nelsonic. Packaged - **$10 $20 $40**

CAL-6

❑ **CAL-6. Large Plaster Figure Bank,**
c. 1987. Unauthorized store or carnival item. 15" tall with 10" diameter. - **$25 $40 $95**

CAL-7

❑ **CAL-7. Store Display,**
1988. Hardee's Food Systems. Came with six vinyl figures. Complete - **$45 $80 $175**

CAL-8

❑ **CAL-8. "The California Raisins" Boxed Limited Edition Christmas Mug Set,**
1988. CALRAB. 3-3/8x5x15.5" tall colorful box has art of California Raisins ice skating and playing in snow. Has die-cut window with clear plastic revealing four cermaic mugs, each with different colorful scene of Raisins in Christmas and winter activities including one carrying gift, two pulling sled with Christmas tree, two building Raisin snowman, one sledding downhill. Each has designation "Limited Edition Christmas 1988." Near Mint Boxed - **$28**

CAL-9

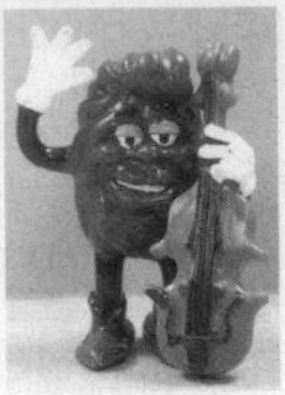

CAL-10

❑ **CAL-9. Girl Figure with Tambourine,**
1988. 2 3/4" tall. - **$4 $8 $20**

❑ **CAL-10. Figure with Bass Fiddle,**
1988. 2 3/4" tall. - **$4 $8 $20**

CAL-11

CAL-12

❑ **CAL-11. Valentine Boy Figure,**
1988. 2 3/4" tall. - **$4 $8 $20**

❑ **CAL-12. Valentine Girl Figure,**
1988. 2 3/4" tall. - **$4 $8 $20**

CAL-13

❑ **CAL-13. Figural Radio Boxed,**
1988. Colorfully illustrated box has diecut front window over 11" tall plastic radio likeness of one Raisin singer holding microphone in one hand. Figure has poseable arms and legs, radio is AM-FM. Near Mint Boxed - **$110**
Radio Only - **$18 $35 $70**

CAL-14

CAL-15

❑ **CAL-14. Vinyl Tote Bag,**
1988. - **$5 $10 $25**

❑ **CAL-15. Large Plush And Fabric Stuffed Doll,**
1980s. Store item with no apparent CALRAB licensing. Torso is about 8" diameter of maroon soft plush. - **$10 $20 $40**

Campbell Kids

Philadelphia artist Grace Wiederseim Drayton (1877-1936) created the Campbell Kids to promote the company's canned soup in 1904. She called them Roly-Polys, and after initial use in cards on Philadelphia streetcars the kids greeted the world at large in advertising in the *Ladies' Home Journal* in 1905. Since then the kids have had a long and distinguished promotional career in various forms, such as dolls, salt and pepper shakers, lunch boxes, etc., and in print advertising. In 1976 the kids were dressed in colonial costumes to mark the nation's bicentennial. Today's kids are a bit taller and thinner than the originals, but they're still easily recognized and still selling soup.

CAM-1

❑ **CAM-1. Early Postcards,**
1910. Jos. Campbell Co. Four numbered cards apparently published in a strip as small perforations mark the margins. Superb color art, probably by Grace Drayton but unsigned.
Each **- $15 $30 $65**

CAM-2

CAM-3

❑ **CAM-2. "Campbell's Menu Book,"**
1910. Softcover 48-page booklet of recipes for 30 days of the month based on 21 varieties of soups. Campbell Kids are pictured on cover and title page. - **$15 $30 $65**

❑ **CAM-3. Early Button By Campbell Kids Creator,**
c. 1911. Full color 7/8". Rim text reads "Member Kaptin Kiddo Klub" with tiny red text below image reading "Copyright The North American Company." This strip ran c. 1911-12 and was created by Grace Drayton. Has original backpaper reading "The Turr'ble Tales Of Kaptin Kiddo Appear Each Week In The Sunday North American." - **$10 $20 $30**

CAM-4

❑ **CAM-4. "The Optimist" Booklet,**
1932. Published monthly c. 1932-1940. Superb color cover. Each **- $12 $25 $45**

CAM-5

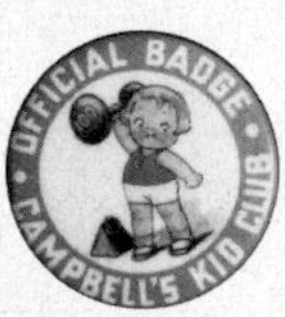

CAM-6

❑ **CAM-5. Place Cards With Envelope,**
c. 1930s. Set of three to be divided into six bridge tally place cards. Set **- $18 $30 $55**

❑ **CAM-6. "Campbell's Kid Club" Cello. Button,**
c. 1930s. 1-1/2" "Official Badge". -
$45 $120 $235

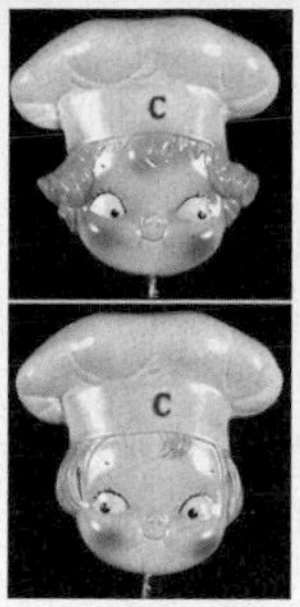

CAM-7

CAM-8

❑ CAM-7. Hot Pad Holders,
c. 1940s. Set of 5x5" painted plaster wall plaques with embedded wire hook hanger. Each - **$20 $40 $80**

❑ CAM-8. Campbell Kid Plaster Wall Plaque With Thermometer,
c. 1940s. - **$60 $100 $160**

CAM-9

CAM-10

❑ CAM-9. "I'm A Campbell Kid" Cello. Button,
c. 1950s. Variation of girl kid in western outfit. - **$15 $40 $80**

❑ CAM-10. "I'm A Campbell Kid" Cello. Button,
c. 1950s. Version of girl kid as milkmaid. - **$15 $40 $80**

CAM-11

CAM-12

❑ CAM-11. "I'm A Campbell Kid" Cello. Button,
c. 1950s. Version of boy kid as chef. - **$15 $40 $80**

❑ CAM-12. "I'm A Campbell Kid" Cello. Button,
c. 1950s. Version of boy kid as strongman. - **$15 $40 $80**

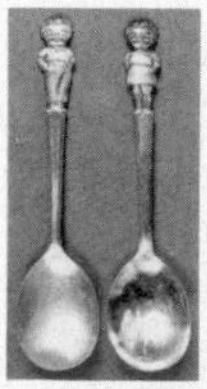

CAM-13

CAM-14

❑ CAM-13. Campbell Kids Silver Plate Spoons,
1950s. Each - **$8 $12 $15**

❑ CAM-14. Squeaker Doll,
1950s. 7" tall painted soft hollow rubber chef doll. - **$70 $135 $240**

CAM-15

❑ CAM-15. Tomato Soup And Fruit 17x22" Paper Store Sign,
ç. 1950s. Design includes chalkboard motif held by Campbell Kids. - **$25 $50 $100**

CAM-16

❑ CAM-16. "Toy Electric Mixer,"
1950s. Store item. Battery operated 5-1/2" tall tin toy. Boxed - **$25 $45 $85**

CAM-17

❑ CAM-17. "Campbell's Tomato Soup" Pillow With Mailer,
1960s. Made by U.S. Pillow Corp.
Near Mint Bagged - **$40**
Loose - **$6 $12 $25**

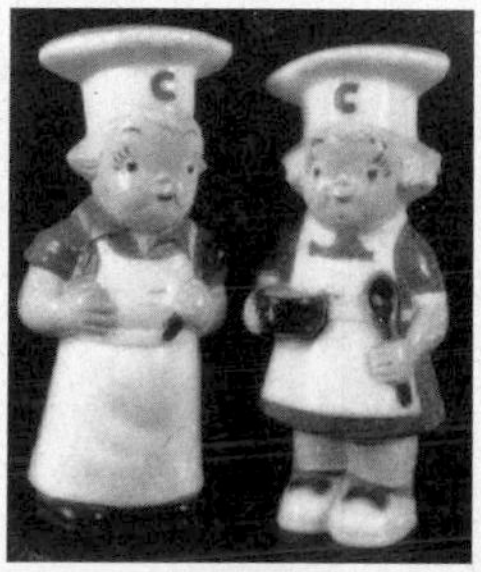

CAM-18

CAM-19

❑ CAM-18. Campbell Kid Plastic Salt & Pepper Set,
1960s. - **$18 $30 $60**

❑ CAM-19. "A Story Of Soup" Coloring Book,
1976. 11x14" official publication with 24 pages featuring Campbell Kids illustrating soup use from prehistoric times through present. - **$10 $20 $30**

CAM-20

❑ CAM-20. Bicentennial Doll Set,
1976. Pair of 10" vinyl dolls in fabric outfits offered as mail premium. Each - **$18 $35 $70**

CAM-21

❑ CAM-21. Boxed Dolls,
c. 1970s. Made by Product People. 7" tall painted soft vinyl boy and girl dolls in identical display carton.
Each Near Mint Boxed - **$100**
Each Loose - **$15 $30 $65**

CAM-22

❑ CAM-22. Cookie Jar,
1990s. - **$95**

Cap'n Crunch

Cap'n Crunch, a sweetened breakfast cereal that is supposed to stay crunchy down to the bottom of the bowl, was introduced in 1963 by Quaker Oats. In an unusual twist, the name of the cereal was also the name of the cartoon character created to promote it. The Cap'n was created in-house by Quaker and the TV ad campaign was designed by Jay Ward Productions, best known for Bullwinkle and Rocky animated cartoons. Other characters include Seadog, Jean LaFoote, Wilma the White Whale, Harry S. Hippo and Soggie. Other varieties of Crunch cereal include Crunchberries (1967); Peanut Butter Crunch (1969); Oops! All Berries (1997); and Oops! Choco Donuts (2002). There have been many premium offers and giveaways.

CRN-1

❑ CRN-1. "I'm Dreaming Of A Wide Isthmus" Comic Booklet,
1963. From set of three. Other titles are "Fountain of Youth" and "The Picture Pirates."
Each - **$5 $15 $75**

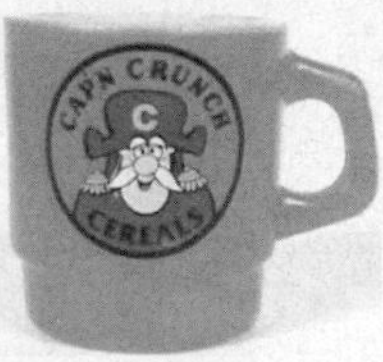

CRN-2

❑ CRN-2. Corporate Gift Mug,
1963. 3-1/2" tall red glass mug with color logo never available to the general public. -
$35 $60 $100

CRN-3

❑ CRN-3. Cereal Box Featuring Nine Rings Packaged One Per Box,
1964. Clockwise rings are titled: Compass Ring, Treasure Chest Ring, Pirate Gold Ring, Ship's Cannon Ring, Cutlass Ring, Pirate Puzzle Ring, Ship-In-Bottle Ring, Whistle Ring, Cap'n Crunch Statue Ring. Gordon Gold Archives.
Used Complete - **$225 $450 $775**

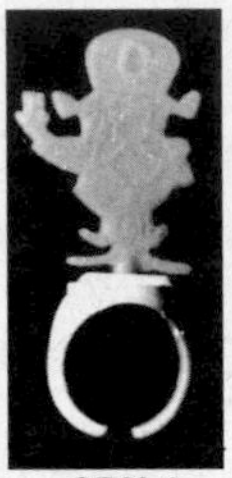

CRN-4

CRN-5

❑ CRN-4. Cap'n Crunch Statue Plastic Ring,
1964. - **$55 $110 $175**

❑ CRN-5. Ship's Cannon Plastic Ring,
1964. - **$35 $60 $100**

CRN-6

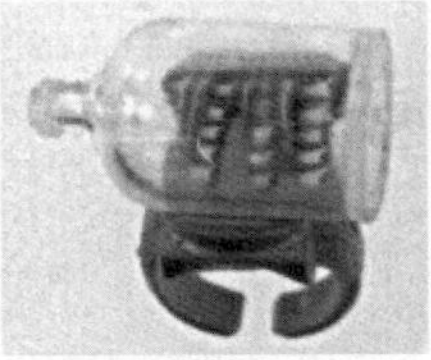

CRN-7

❑ CRN-6. Whistle Plastic Ring,
1964. - **$35 $55 $85**

❑ CRN-7. Ship-In-Bottle Plastic Ring,
1964. - **$35 $55 $85**

CRN-8

❑ CRN-8. Cereal Box With "Sea Battle Game" Back Panel,
c. 1964. Gordon Gold Archives.
Used Complete - **$125 $240 $450**

CRN-9

❑ CRN-9. Cereal Box With "Treasure Hunt Game" Back Panel,
c. 1964. Gordon Gold Archives.
Used Complete - **$135 $275 $475**

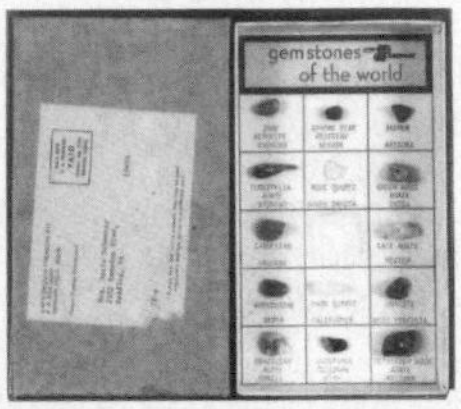

CRN-10

❑ CRN-10. "Treasure Kit",
c. 1965. Contains 14 "Gemstones Of The World." - **$15 $35 $70**

CRN-11

❑ CRN-11. Plastic Treasure Chest Bank,
1966. Came with padlock and key, 5 plastic pirate coins, insert tray useable as cereal bowl, pirate shovel (spoon), and treasure map.
Near Mint Complete - **$135**
As Bank, No Contents - **$12 $25 $50**

CRN-12

❑ CRN-12. Cereal Box With "Hat" Offer,
1968. Gordon Gold Archives.
Used Complete - **$175 $360 $600**

CRN-13

❑ **CRN-13. "Cap'n Crunch Coloring Book",**
1968. - **$10 $20 $45**

CRN-14

❑ **CRN-14. "Wiggle Figures" Offer Cereal Box,**
1969. Figures came one per box and offer pictures Cap'n Crunch and Seadog but additional figures were added to the series later. Gordon Gold Archives.
Box Used Complete - **$85 $165 $350**

CRN-15

❑ **CRN-15. "Wiggle Figure" Offer Cereal Box Flat,**
1969. Gordon Gold Archives.
Near Mint Flat - **$550**
Used Complete - **$85 $165 $350**

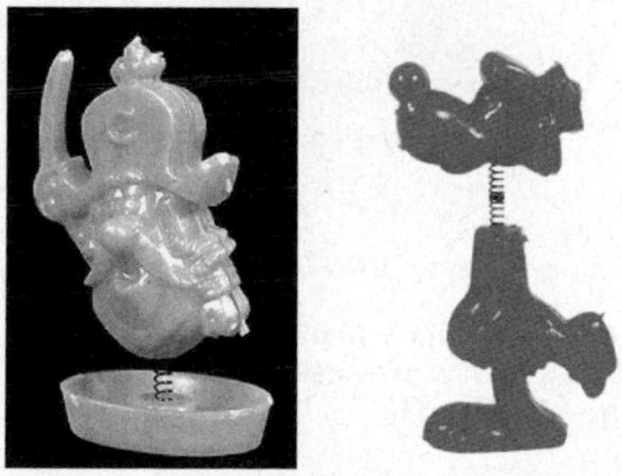
CRN-16

❑ **CRN-16. Cap'n Crunch Wiggle Figure,**
1969. Cap'n Crunch Berries. Six in set: Cap'n Crunch, Seadog, Jean LaFoote (pirate), Alfie (big boy with glasses), Little Boy (no glasses), Brunhilde (girl).
Cap'n Crunch, Seadog Near Mint Unassembled Each - **$70**
Others Near Mint Unassembled Each - **$50**
Cap'n Crunch, Seadog Assembled Each - **$18 $30 $50**
Others Assembled Each - **$12 $18 $35**

CRN-17

❑ **CRN-17. "Play Putty" Offer Cereal Box,**
1969. Silly Putty-like item was available free with three purchase seals.
Used Complete - **$70 $150 $235**

CRN-18

❑ **CRN-18. Cap'n Crunch Dally Log,**
1969. A combo desk calendar, engagement diary, and reference book. 120 pages. Quaker Oats gift to those who promoted cereal during 1968. - **$30 $80 $135**

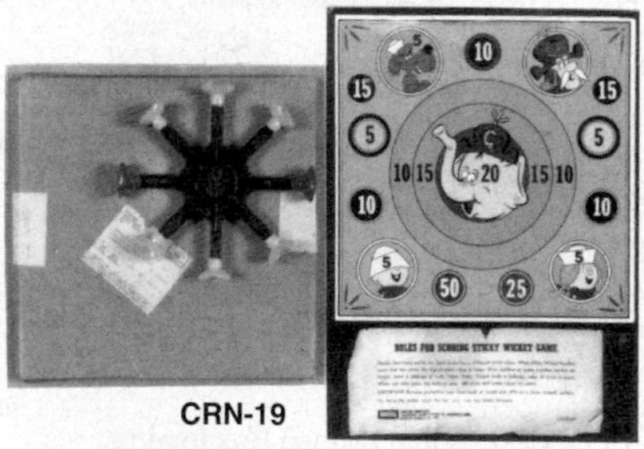
CRN-19

❑ **CRN-19. "Sticky Wicket" Target Game,**
1970. - **$12 $25 $50**

CRN-20

CRN-21

❑ **CRN-20. "Jean LaFoote" Vinyl Bank,**
1972. - **$35 $70 $140**

❑ **CRN-21. Vinyl Bank,**
1972. - **$30 $55 $100**

CRN-22

❑ **CRN-22. Seadog Spy Kit,**
1974. Kit - **$10 $20 $40**
Instructions - **$5 $10 $15**

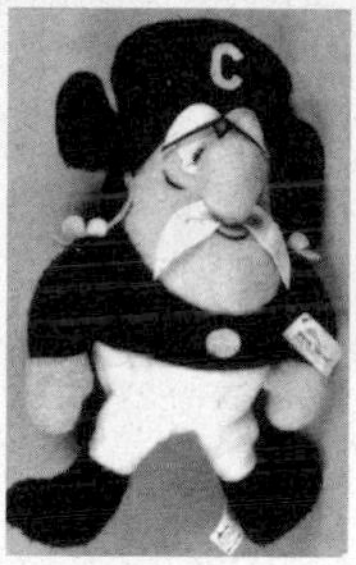
CRN-23

❑ **CRN-23. Fabric Doll,**
1976. - **$15 $30 $60**

CRN-24

❑ **CRN-24. Plastic Sea Cycle Model,**
1970s. Near Mint Boxed - **$45**
Assembled - **$12 $22 $35**

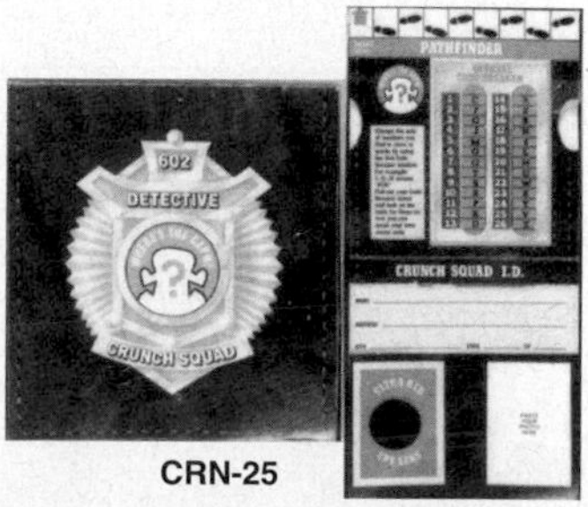

CRN-25

❑ **CRN-25. "Detective Crunch Squad" Paper Wallet,**
1970s. - **$10 $15 $30**

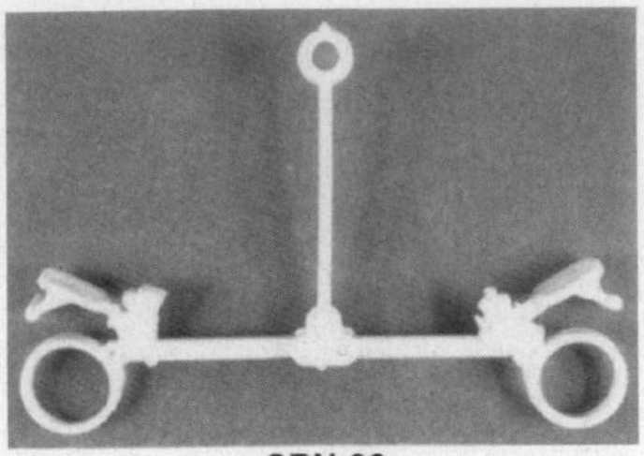

CRN-26

❑ **CRN-26. Finger Tennis Game,**
1970s. Plastic agility toy for two players. -
$6 $12 $20

CRN-27

❑ **CRN-27. "La Foote" Miniature Plastic Vehicles,**
1970s. Balloon operated for movement.
Each - **$6 $12 $20**

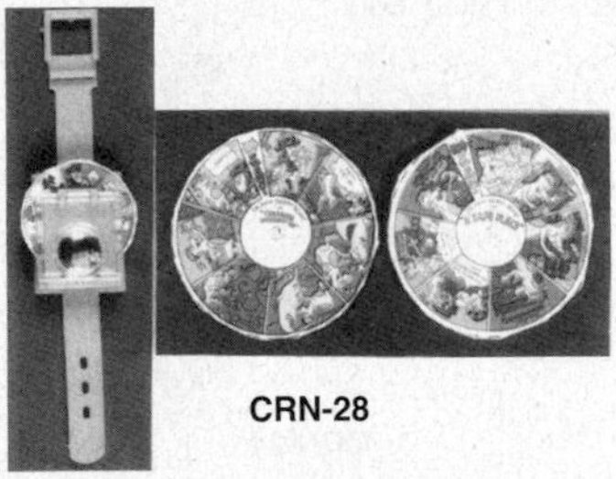

CRN-28

❑ **CRN-28. Story Scope With Disks,**
1970s. At least three disks cut from box backs.
Scope Unit - **$12 $25 $40**
Each Disk - **$3 $6 $12**

CRN-29

❑ **CRN-29. Cap'n Crunch Four Plastic Rings,**
1970s. Our photo shows illustration off cereal box back panel.
Guided Missile Ring - **$55 $110 $180**
I-Spy Glass Ring - **$50 $100 $155**
Brunhilde's Spin-It-Ring - **$70 $135 $200**
Carlyle's Rocket Ring (With Shooting Missile) - **$70 $135 $200**

CRN-30

❑ **CRN-30. "Smedley" Poster,**
1970s. 18.5x24" glossy paper featuring large image of Smedley within border picturing him and eight other characters including Cap'n Crunch, Seadog, LaFoote, Soggie. -
$15 $25 $50

CRN-31

❑ **CRN-31. Cap'n Crunch Box Inserts,**
c. 1981. Plastic mechanical toys of flying saucer and tennis game plus booklet "Crunch Berry Beast's Farm Animals Stamp Album."
Saucer Toy Near Mint Packaged - **$28**
Loose - **$6 $12 $20**
Tennis Game Toy Near Mint Packaged - **$28**
Loose - **$4 $10 $18**
Stamp Album - **$6 $12 $20**

CRN-32

❑ **CRN-32. "Surfer" Cereal Box With Premium,**
1983. Three different figures, each 1-1/2" tall with 3-1/2" long plastic foam "Surfboard" were packaged one per box.
Used Complete Box - **$40 $85 $150**
Premium Assembled Each - **$6 $12 $20**

CRN-33

❑ **CRN-33. "Cap'n Crunch" 15x17x21" Treasure Chest Toy Box,**
1987. Awarded as a contest prize. -
$35 $65 $130

CRN-34

❑ **CRN-34. Frame Tray Puzzle,**
1987. - **$3 $6 $12**

CRN-35

❑ **CRN-35. Crunch The Soggie Target Game,**
1987. Came with three balls covered with velcro strips. - **$6 $12 $18**

CRN-36

❑ **CRN-36. Flicker Button 2-1/4",**
1980s. - **$10 $18 $30**

CRN-37

❑ CRN-37. Cap'n Crunch Island Adventure Board Game,
1980s. Includes four 2" figures. - **$25 $50 $125**

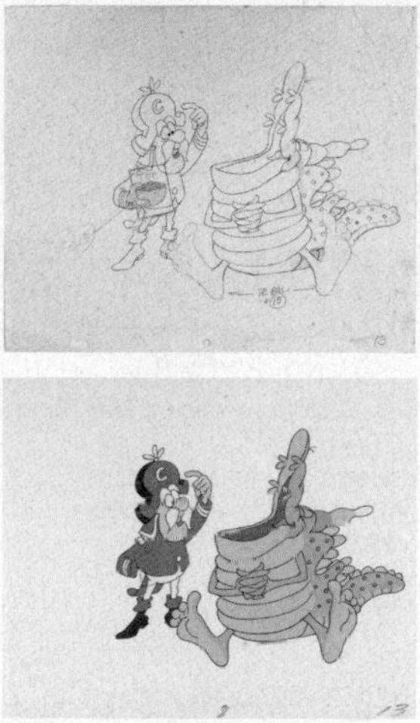

CRN-38

❑ CRN-38. Cap'n Crunch TV Commercial Animation Cel With Matching Pencil Drawing,
1980s. Acetate Sheet is 10.5x12.25" with well-centered 6x8.75" image of Cap'n Crunch looking puzzled as he observes a colorful green crocodile-like creature who has his head tilted back longing for some Cap'n Crunch cereal. Comes with same size white animation sheet with matching lead pencil drawing. Near Mint Similar - **$60**

CRN-39

❑ CRN-39. TV Commercial Animation Cel With Matching Pencil Drawing,
1980s. Similar Age And Quality Near Mint - **$85**

CRN-40

❑ CRN-40. "Crunch Island" Map,
1980s. 13x17" two-sided paper sheet printed one side in full color map tacked to wooden boards. Reverse is "Upper Crunch Island Coloring Map" to be crayoned. - **$10 $18 $30**

Captain Action

The Ideal Toy Company produced a series of jointed, posable dolls of Captain Action, his protégé Action Boy, and the villainous Dr. Evil in 1966-1968. The dolls were outfitted with costumes, boots, and assorted weaponry. Also offered were boxed character costumes and accessories, including flicker rings of Captain Action and his alter-ego superheroes Aquaman, Batman, Buck Rogers, Captain America, Flash Gordon, the Green Hornet, the Lone Ranger, the Phantom, Sgt. Fury, Spider-Man, Steve Canyon, Superman or Tonto. Kool-Pops offered a deck of Captain Action playing cards as a mail-order premium, and National Periodical published five Captain Action comic books in 1968-1969 with art by Wally Wood and Gil Kane. A new comic book from Moonstone debuted in Spring 2008.

In 1998, Playing Mantis restarted the Captain Action line. They produced the Captain Action and Dr. Evil dolls, along with costumes for Green Hornet, Kato, Flash Gordon and Ming. Later, they entered into an exclusive deal with Diamond Select Toys, and recently produced the Lone Ranger costume and the Kid Action doll. Soon to be released are costumes and accessories for Speed Racer, Racer X and Captain Terror. While they are similar to the old line, each is different with completely new packaging. In the future, all accessories will be marked so that they will be easy to distinguish from the 1960s originals. All of this activity can only help the market and create new interest in Captain Action products.

CAC-1

❑ CAC-1. "Captain Action" Store Sign,
1966. 12x19" glossy paper. -
$300 $650 $1750

CAC-2

❑ CAC-2. Catalogue Folder,
1966. Ideal Toy Corp. Opens to 9x12" picturing Captain Action nine different outfit sets. -
$30 $60 $115

CAC-3

❑ CAC-3. Captain Action Doll,
1966. Ideal Toys. Store bought.
Boxed With Accessories - **$1050**
Loose Figure - **$325**

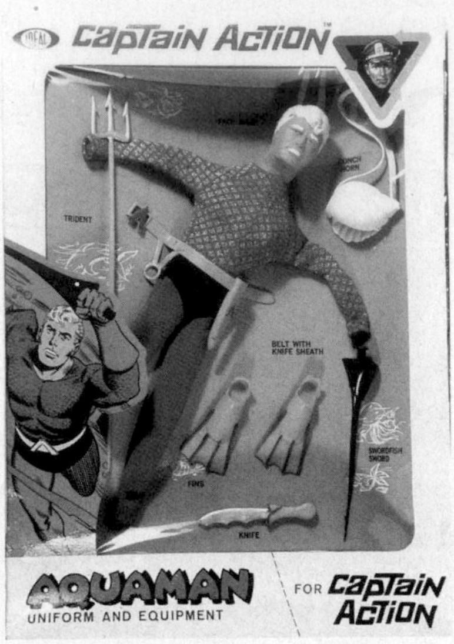

CAC-4

❑ **CAC-4. Captain Action "Aquaman" Set,**
1966. Uniform and equipment.
Boxed With Accessories - **$800**
Loose - **$225**

CAC-6

❑ **CAC-6. Captain Action "Captain America" Set,**
1966. Uniform and equipment.
Boxed With Accessories - **$1200**
Loose - **$325**

CAC-8

❑ **CAC-8. Captain Action "The Phantom" Set,**
1966. Uniform and equipment.
Boxed With Accessories - **$1000**
Loose - **$275**

CAC-5

❑ **CAC-5. Captain Action "Batman" Set,**
1966. Store item by Ideal.
Near Mint Boxed - **$1500**
Loose Complete - **$325**

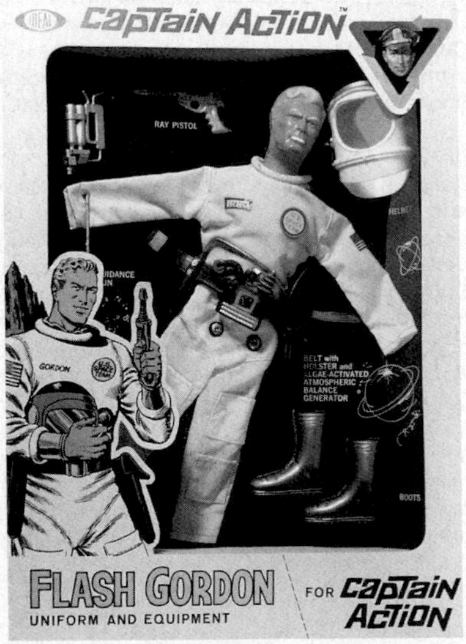

CAC-7

❑ **CAC-7. Captain Action "Flash Gordon" Set,**
1966. Uniform and equipment.
Boxed With Accessories - **$1100**
Loose - **$300**

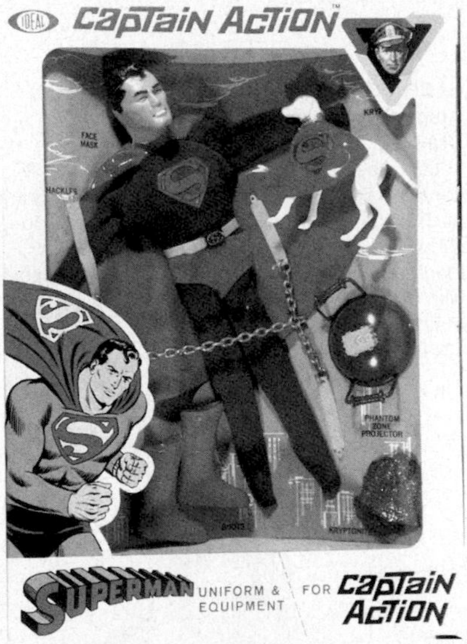

CAC-9

❑ **CAC-9. Captain Action "Superman" Set,**
1966. Uniform, equipment and caped Krypto the dog. The 1967 version came with a flasher ring as a bonus. Boxed With Accessories - **$1500**
Loose - **$350**

CAC-10

❑ CAC-10. Captain Action "Sgt. Fury" Set,
1966. Uniform and equipment.
Boxed With Accessories - **$900**
Loose - **$300**

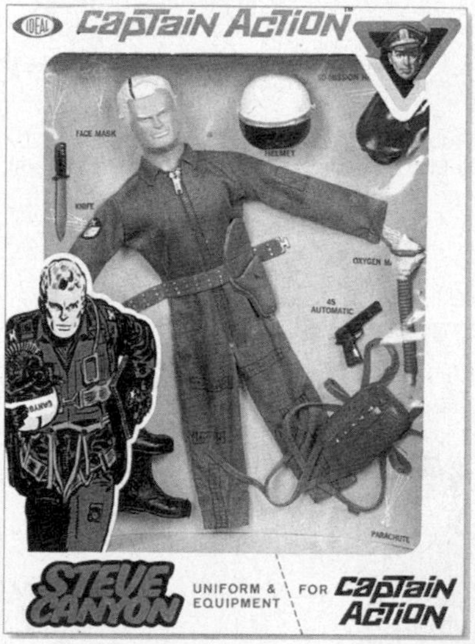

CAC-11

❑ CAC-11. Captain Action "Steve Canyon" Set,
1966. Uniform and equipment.
Boxed With Accessories - **$900**
Loose - **$275**

CAC-12

❑ CAC-12. Captain Action "Lone Ranger" Set,
1966. Store item by Ideal. Came with red shirt or blue shirt.
Set with red shirt - Near Mint Boxed - **$1400**
Loose Complete - **$400**
Set with blue shirt - Near Mint Boxed - **$2000**
Loose Complete - **$650**

CAC-13

❑ CAC-13. Captain Action "Lone Ranger" Set,
1967. Store item by Ideal with ring. Came with red shirt or blue shirt.
Set with red shirt - Near Mint Boxed - **$1500**
Loose Complete - **$500**
Set with blue shirt - Near Mint Boxed - **$2100**
Loose Complete - **$700**

CAC-14

❑ CAC-14. Captain Action "Sgt. Fury" Set,
1967. Uniform and equipment with ring.
Boxed With Accessories - **$950**
Loose - **$300**

CAC-15

❑ CAC-15. Captain Action "Tonto" Set,
1967. Store item by Ideal with ring.
Near Mint Boxed - **$1600**
Loose Complete - **$450**

CAC-16

❑ **CAC-16. Comic Book Style Catalogue,**
1967. Ideal Toy Corp. packaged with store bought items. 3-1/2x7", 32 pages in full color. - **$12 $36 $215**

CAC-18

❑ **CAC-18. Captain Action "Aqualad" Set,**
1967. Store item by Ideal. Near Mint Boxed - **$2300** Loose Complete - **$800**

CAC-17

❑ **CAC-17. Action Boy Boxed Figure,**
1967. Store item by Ideal.
Near Mint Boxed - **$1000**
Loose Complete - **$450**

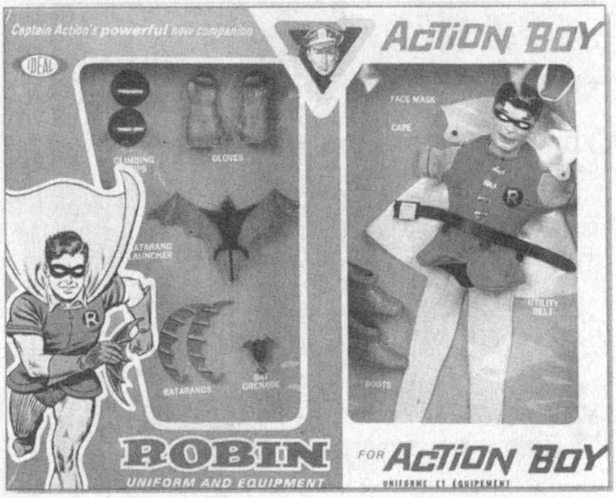

CAC-19

❑ **CAC-19. Captain Action "Robin" Set,**
1967. Store item by Ideal. Near Mint Boxed - **$2100** Loose Complete - **$800**

CAC-20

❑ **CAC-20. Superboy Accessory Set On Card,**
1967. Store item by Ideal. Near Mint Boxed - **$5000** Loose Complete - **$1200**

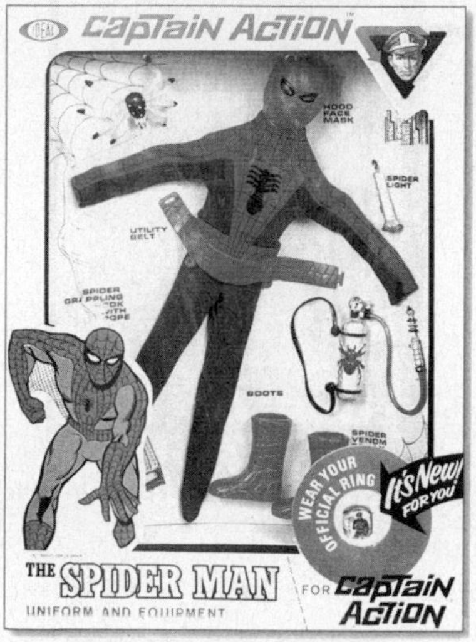

CAC-21

❑ **CAC-21. Captain Action "Spider-Man" Set,**
1967. Uniform and equipment with ring.
Boxed With Accessories - **$12,000**
Loose - **$400**

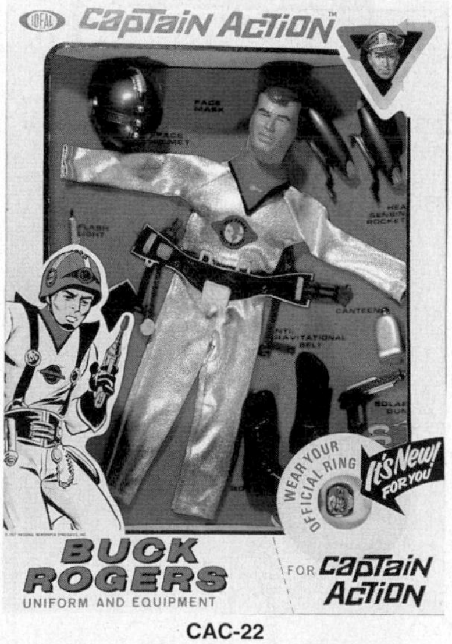

CAC-22

❑ **CAC-22. Captain Action "Buck Rogers" Set,**
1967. Uniform and equipment with ring.
Boxed With Accessories - **$2000**
Loose - **$450**

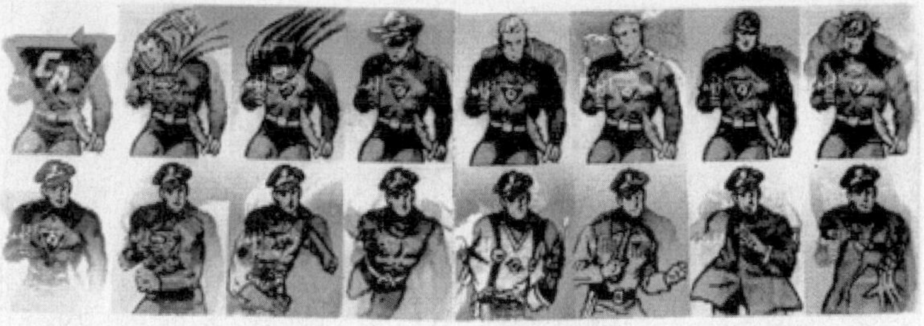

CAC-23

❑ **CAC-23. Uncut Flicker Ring Strip,**
1967. Vari-Vue Co. Strip of 16 flicker images alternating between Captain Action and other different action character outfits made for his use. - **$25 $40 $60**

CAC-24

❑ **CAC-24. Captain Action "Green Hornet" Set,**
1967. Uniform and equipment with ring.
Boxed With Accessories - **$6500**
Loose - **$1000**

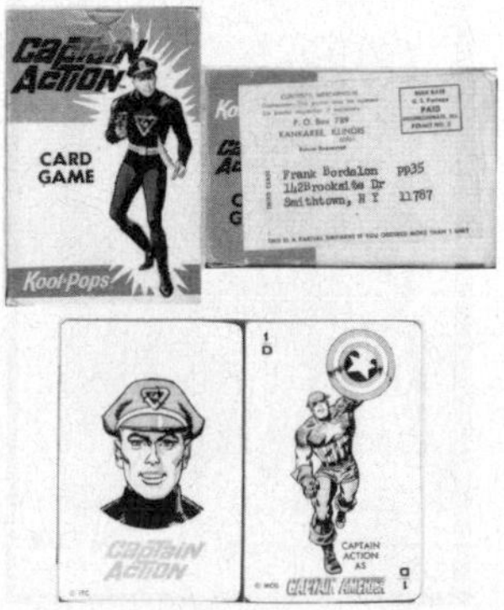

CAC-25

❑ **CAC-25. Kool-Pops "Captain Action" Card Game With Mailer Box,**
1967. - **$35 $70 $100**

CAC-26

CAC-27

CAC-28

CAC-29

❑ **CAC-26. Captain Action/The Lone Ranger Flicker Ring,**
1967. Ideal Toys. Silver base marked "Hong Kong" came with boxed figure. Silver "Hong Kong" Base - **$35 $60 $100**
Blue Base - **$10 $20 $35**
Silver "China" Modern Base - **$6 $12 $18**

❑ **CAC-27. Captain Action/Tonto Flicker Ring,**
1967. Ideal Toys. Silver base marked "Hong Kong" came with boxed figure. Silver "Hong Kong" Base - **$35 $60 $100**
Blue Base - **$10 $20 $35**
Silver "China" Modern Base - **$6 $12 $18**

❑ **CAC-28. Captain Action/The Phantom Flicker Ring,**
1967. Ideal Toys. Silver base marked "Hong Kong" came with boxed figure. Silver "Hong Kong" Base - **$35 $60 $100**
Blue Base - **$10 $20 $35**
Silver "China" Modern Base - **$6 $12 $18**

❑ **CAC-29. Captain Action/Batman Flicker Ring,**
1967. Ideal Toys. Silver base marked "Hong Kong" came with boxed figure. Silver "Hong Kong" Base - **$35 $60 $100**
Blue Base - **$10 $20 $35**
Silver "China" Modern Base - **$6 $12 $18**

CAC-30

❑ **CAC-30. Dr. Evil Doll,**
1967. Ideal Toys. Store bought. Arch-enemy of Capt. Action. Boxed With Accessories - **$1000**
Loose Figure - **$250**

CAC-31

❑ **CAC-31. Dr. Evil With His Disguises Set,**
1968. Rare 2nd issue. Commonly referred to as the "Lab Kit." Boxed With Accessories - **$4500**

CAC-32

❑ **CAC-32. "Captain Action" First Issue Comic Book,**
1968. Issue #1 for October-November by National Periodical Publications featuring his origin plus appearance by Superman. -
$7 $21 $110

CAC-33

❑ **CAC-33. Ming Costume for Dr. Evil Doll,**
1998. New series for return of Captain Action. Accessories in box. - **$50**

CAC-34

❑ **CAC-34. Lone Ranger Red Costume for Captain Action Doll,**
1998. Cover box has Carmine Infantino art. - **$40**

CAC-35

❑ **CAC-35. Kabai Singh Costume for Dr. Evil Doll,**
1999. Accessories in box. - **$40**

CAC-36

❑ **CAC-36. Kato Costume for Captain Action Doll,**
1999. - **$40**

CAC-37

❑ **CAC-37. Lone Ranger Blue Costume for Captain Action Doll,**
2000. Diamond Exclusive from Playing Mantis. - **$35**

CAC-38

❑ **CAC-38. Kid Action in Box,**
2000. Very low distribution. NM - **$35**

Captain America

World War II had begun but direct U.S. involvement was still nine months away when Captain America, created by Joe Simon and Jack Kirby, debuted in *Captain America Comics* #1 in March 1941. Steve Rogers, a 4-F desperate to serve his country volunteered to take the "Super Soldier Formula" which turned him into a one-man army. He battled the Nazi hordes (usually commanded by the nefarious Red Skull) and numerous other villains until January 1950, when his title was canceled. The comic was revived for a three-issue run in 1954, then went dormant until Marvel Comics' Stan Lee brought Cap into the modern era in *The Avengers* #4 (1964). A string of solo stories followed in *Tales of Suspense* #59, and the title was switched to *Captain America* with issue #100. That series ended with #454 and was followed immediately a number of other series leading to the current one, which began in 2005. In addition to being a member of The Avengers, Cap's partners have included James Buchanan "Bucky" Barnes (WWII era) and the Falcon ('70s & '80s), and other characters for shorter periods. The "Civil War" storyline that ran throughout Marvel titles in 2007 and events in his own series lead to the "Death of Captain America" in *Captain America* #25, which received major media attention. In *Captain America* #34, Steve Rogers was replaced by Bucky, long thought dead but most recently known as the Winter Soldier, as the new Captain America.

A 15-episode Republic Pictures serial starred Dick Purcell in 1944 (re-released in 1953). Two TV movies starred Reb Brown in 1979. A 13-episode cartoon series aired in 1966. Matt Salinger (son of author J.D. Salinger) went straight to home video in a 1989 film. A major release from Marvel Studios, originally slated for 2009, may be pushed back as a result of the 2007-2008 Writers Guild of America strike.

The Overstreet Comic Book Price Guide carries a list many of Captain America's other appearances, including *All-Select Comics*, *All-Winners Comics*, and *The Invaders*.

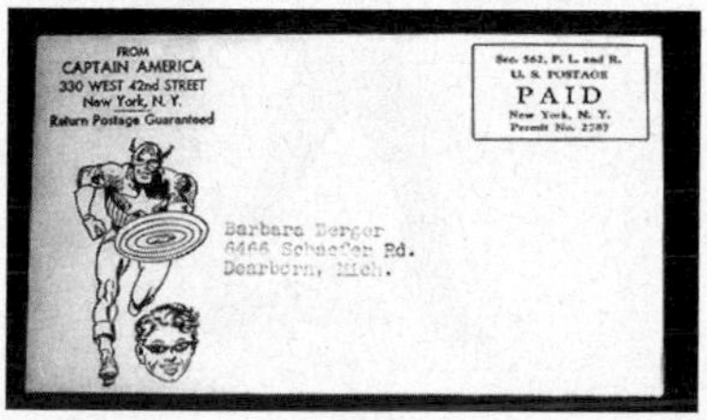

CAP-1

❑ **CAP-1. Mailing Envelope Version One,**
1941. "A" on helmet is below "G" of Guaranteed.-
$225 $450 $675

CAP-2

❑ **CAP-2. Membership Card Version One,**
1941. "A" on helmet is pointed. Blue color much lighter than version two, plus other differences in size and placement of type and words as well as amount of white shading on helmet. Design changed sometime between issuance of membership numbers 50,105 and 56,623. Art is by Joe Simon. - **$300 $750 $1400**

CAP-3

❑ **CAP-3. "Captain America/Sentinels of Liberty" Enameled Brass Badge (Version One),**
1941. - **$225 $575 $1200**

CAP-4

❑ **CAP-4. Membership Card Version Two,**
1941. "A" on helmet is squared off at the top. Blue color much darker than version one and other small differences. (See CAP-2). Art is by Al Avison. - **$300 $750 $1400**

CAP-5

❑ **CAP-5. Enameled Copper Member's Badge (Version Two),**
1941. Same size and inscription as CAP-3, but in copper rather than brass luster. -
$325 $675 $1350

CAP-6

❑ **CAP-6. Mailing Envelope Version Two,**
1941. "A" on helmet is below "g" of postage. -
$225 $450 $675

CAP-7

❑ **CAP-7. Mailing Envelope Version Three,**
1941. "A" on helmet is below the spacing between the words "Postage Guaranteed." Also, in the address the "W" of "west" is formed by two "V"s that overlap and form a tiny "V" at the center. At this time, it is not clear if this envelope was used with the Version One or the Version Two membership card and badge. -
$225 $450 $675

CAP-8

❑ **CAP-8. Three-Sheet Movie Poster,**
1944. Scarce. Republic Pictures serial. 41" by 81". - **$2200 $4500 $7250**

CAP-10

❑ **CAP-10. "Return Of Captain America" 27x41" Movie Poster,**
1953. Republic Pictures. Example is 1953 re-issue of 1944 serial. - **$200 $400 $750**

CAP-12

❑ **CAP-12. "Captain America" Movie Poster,**
1950s. 27x41" one-sheet for re-release of original 1944 Republic serial starring Dick Purcell in title role. - **$150 $225 $350**

CAP-13

❑ **CAP-13. "Captain America Game,"**
1966. Store item by Milton Bradley. - **$25 $45 $100**

CAP-9

❑ **CAP-9. "Captain America" Serial Poster,**
1944. Republic Studios. 27x41" one-sheet for Chapter 5 "Blade Of Wrath." - **$325 $650 $1200**

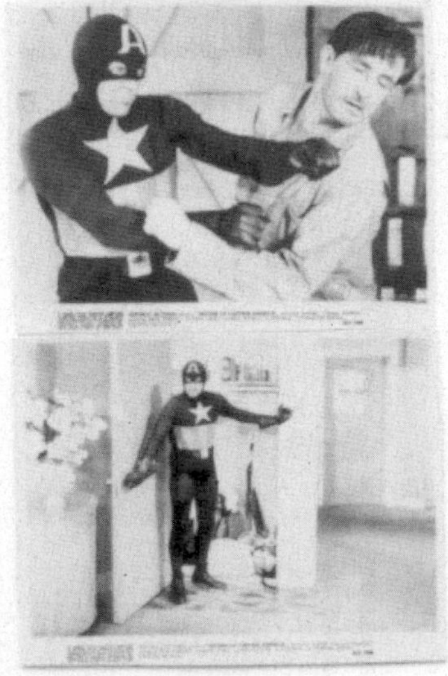

CAP-11

❑ **CAP-11. "Return Of Captain America" Movie Still Set,**
1953. Re-release of original 1944 serial with original title "Captain America."
Set - **$120 $200 $320**

CAP-14

❑ **CAP-14. Hand Puppet,**
1966. Ideal Toy Corp. 11" tall molded vinyl handcover puppet by Marvel Comics Group. - **$65 $135 $225**

CAP-15

❑ **CAP-15. Super-Flex Bendee Toy on Store Card,**
1966. Lakeside Toys. Copyright Marvel. 6 x 9" card contains a 6.25" tall figure made of pliable plastic with wire armature. - **$115 $225 $375**

CAP-17

CAP-16

❑ **CAP-16. "Captain America" 3-1/2" Cello. Button,**
1966. Store item. #3 from numbered series. See Marvel Comics section. Near Mint Bagged - **$75**
Loose - **$10 $20 $35**

❑ **CAP-17. Litho. Metal Bicycle Attachment Plate,**
1967. Store item by Marx Toys. - **$20 $40 $80**

CAP-18

CAP-19

❑ **CAP-18. Captain America Ring,**
1978. Store item by Marvel Comics Group. Part of a set marked with copyright symbol and "1978 MCG." Each - **$35 $70 $140**

❑ **CAP-19. "Keep Saving Energy" 2-1/2" Cello. Button,**
1980. Marvel Comics. - **$12 $25 $50**

CAP-20

❑ **CAP-20. "Captain America And The Campbell Kids" Comic Book,**
1980. Copyright by Marvel Comics and Campbell Soup Co. - **$2 $6 $12**

CAP-21

CAP-22

❑ **CAP-21. Pillow,**
1984. Captain America pictured on a large white pillow. Satin cloth. Very colorful. - **$15 $35 $80**

❑ **CAP-22. Watch on Card,**
1980s. - **$30 $50 $90**

CAP-23

❑ **CAP-23. Captain America Ring,**
1980s. Vitamins premium. - **$70 $145 $285**

CAP-24

❑ **CAP-24. Gum Ball Machine,**
1980s. Superior Toy Inc. Copyright Marvel. Plastic machine is 10" tall. Cap's upper body can be adjusted. - **$40 $65 $100**

CAP-25

CAP-26

❑ **CAP-25. 50th Anniversary Pin Set,**
1990. 1500 produced. Three in a holder.
Mint - **$100**

❑ **CAP-26. Limited Edition Of Badge In Holder,**
1990. Reverse inscribed "Captain America Is A Registered Trademark TM & ©1990 Marvel."
Mint - **$38**

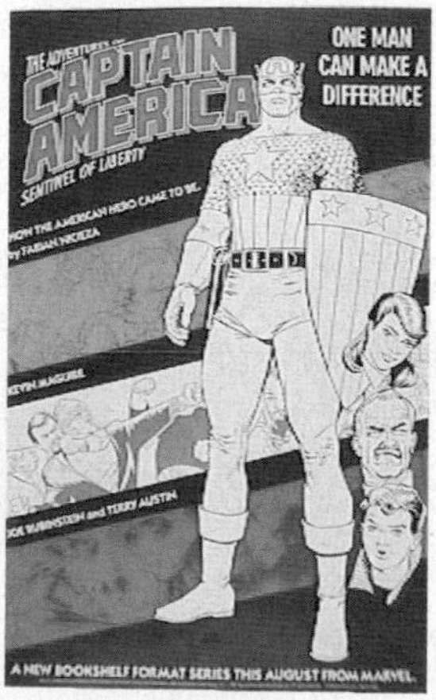

CAP-27

❑ **CAP-27. Store Poster,**
1991. Marvel Entertainment Group, Inc. 11x17" red, white and blue poster promoting "A New Bookshelf Format Series This August From Marvel." - **$10 $18 $35**

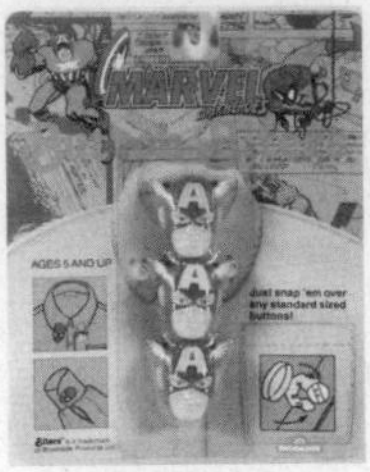

CAP-28

CAP-29

❑ **CAP-28. Button Biters,**
1990s. Produced by Brookside. - **$12**

❑ **CAP-29. Wastebasket,**
1999. - **$35**

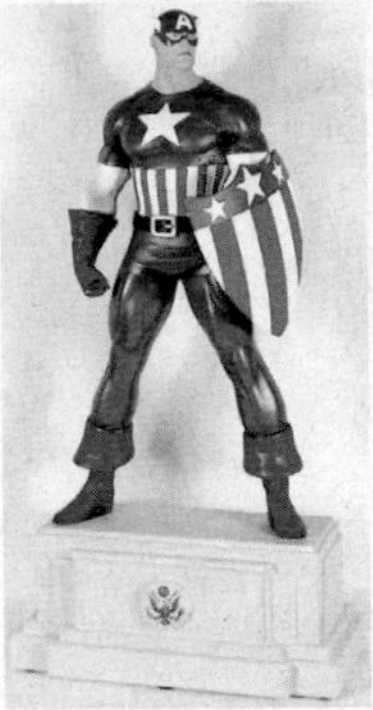

CAP-30 CAP-31

❑ **CAP-30. Golden Age Resin Statue,**
1999. Limited to 2,000. - **$275**

❑ **CAP-31. Modern Age Resin Statue,**
1999. Limited to 4,000. Miniature version released in 2001. - **$250**

CAP-32 CAP-33

❑ **CAP-32. "Red Skull" Mini-Bust,**
1999. Limited to 3,000. With clear base. - **$125**

❑ **CAP-33. "Bucky" Mini-Bust,**
2000. Bowen Designs. - **$40**

Captain Battle

Captain Battle had a brief run as a superpatriot comic book hero in the early 1940s. He made his first appearance in *Silver Streak Comics* #10 in May 1941, then in *Captain Battle Comics* from 1941 to 1943. Readers who promised to uphold the principles of Americanism and the Constitution could join the Captain Battle Boys' Brigade. Two issues of *Captain Battle Jr.* were published in 1943-1944. See related items in the Silver Streak section.

CBT-1

❑ **CBT-1. "Captain Battle Boys' Brigade" Cello. Button,**
1941. Scarce. Silver Streak Comics. -
$500 $1200 $2500

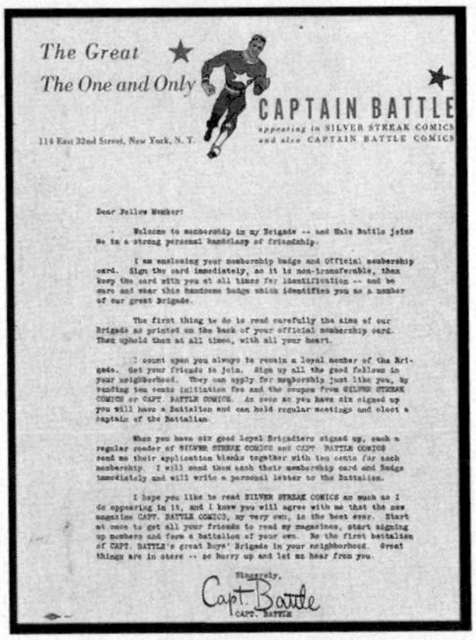

The Great
The One and Only
CAPTAIN BATTLE
appearing in SILVER STREAK COMICS
and also CAPTAIN BATTLE COMICS
114 East 32nd Street, New York, N. Y.

Dear Fellow Member!

Welcome to membership in my Brigade -- and Hale Battle joins me in a strong personal handclasp of friendship.

I am enclosing your membership badge and Official membership card. Sign the card immediately, as it is non-transferable, then keep the card with you at all times for identification -- and be sure and wear this handsome badge which identifies you as a member of our great Brigade.

The first thing to do is read carefully the aims of our Brigade as printed on the back of your official membership card. Then uphold them at all times, with all your heart.

I count upon you always to remain a loyal member of the Brigade. Get your friends to join. Sign up all the good fellows in your neighborhood. They can apply for membership just like you, by sending ten cents initiation fee and the coupon from SILVER STREAK COMICS or CAPT. BATTLE COMICS. As soon as you have six signed up you will have a Battalion and can hold regular meetings and elect a captain of the Battalion.

When you have six good loyal Brigadiers signed up, each a regular reader of SILVER STREAK COMICS and CAPT. BATTLE COMICS send me their application blanks together with ten cents for each membership. I will send them each their membership card and badge immediately and will write a personal letter to the Battalion.

I hope you like to read SILVER STREAK COMICS as much as I do appearing in it, and I know you will agree with me that the new magazine CAPT. BATTLE COMICS, my very own, is the best ever. Start at once to get all your friends to read my magazines, start signing up members and form a battalion of your own. Be the first battalion of CAPT. BATTLE's great Boys' Brigade in your neighborhood. Great things are in store -- so hurry up and let me hear from you.

Sincerely,
Capt. Battle
CAPT. BATTLE

CBT-2

❑ **CBT-2. Membership Kit Mailer, Letter and Card,**
1941. The 1-3/4" cello. club button came as part of this kit. The membership card has a list of 5 "Aims" printed on the reverse.
Mailer - **$50 $150 $350**
Letter - **$200 $350 $775**
Membership Card - **$200 $350 $775**

CBT-3

❑ **CBT-3. "Captain Battle Jr. #1" Comic Book,**
Fall 1943. Comic House Inc. First of two issues published for this title. Cover depicts Captain Battle Jr. fighting several Nazis in Berlin.
- $134 $402 $1950

Captain 11

Following the success of Captain Video and Space Patrol, the Rocket Ranger Club was formed in 1955. This club was designed to encourage children to watch Channel 11, KELO-TV in Sioux Falls, South Dakota. The show's long-time host was Dave Dedrick. Premiums issued for the club were only produced and distributed on a regional basis and are quite rare. The creed of the club focused on telling children to obey the laws and their parents at all times. The kit included a variety of decoders and planet credits, which enabled the young listeners to receive special messages and follow the exploits of the Rocket Ranger. The final show aired on December 28, 1996 and was repeated on January 1, 1997. After 41 years and 10 months it became the midwest's longest running children's program.

CVN-1

CVN-2

❑ **CVN-1. Membership Card,**
1955. - **$25 $50 $110**

❑ **CVN-2. Mailer,**
1955. - **$20 $35 $75**

CVN-3

❑ CVN-3. "Captain Eleven" Rare Club Button,
1955. Button is 7/8" with photo of show host. Button includes station call letters but printed as "KEL-O-LAND TV." - **$60 $125 $235**

CVN-4

❑ CVN-4. Membership Certificate And Creed,
1955. - **$35 $70 $140**

CVN-5

CVN-6

❑ CVN-5. Super Zoom Decoder,
1955. Rare. - **$90 $240 $450**

❑ CVN-6. Zoom Code Card,
1955. - **$50 $100 $200**

CVN-7

❑ CVN-7. Venus Credits Play Money,
1955. Six different. Each - **$8 $18 $35**

CVN-8

❑ CVN-8. Martian Credits Play Money,
1955. Seven different. Each - **$8 $18 $35**

Captain Ezra Diamond

Captain Diamond's Adventures aired on the NBC Blue radio network from 1932 to 1937, offering weekly tales of sea adventures as related by Captain Diamond in his lighthouse. Al Swenson played the Captain, and his young visitor each week was Tiny Ruffner. Diamond Salt was the sponsor.

CEZ-1

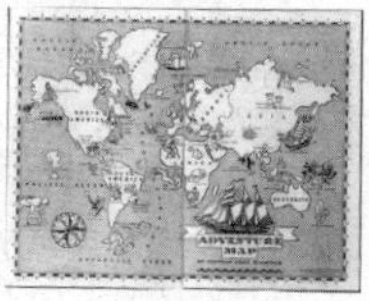

CEZ-2

❑ CEZ-1. "Adventure Map Of Captain Ezra Diamond" 17x22",
1932. - **$30 $60 $110**

❑ CEZ-2. "Adventure Map Of Captain Ezra Diamond" 16x22",
1933. - **$40 $80 $135**

CEZ-3

CEZ-4

CEZ-5

❑ CEZ-3. Cast Member Fan Photo,
c. 1933. White background version. - **$6 $12 $25**

❑ CEZ-4. Fan Photo Of Cast,
c. 1933. Black background version. - **$6 $12 $25**

❑ CEZ-5. Weather Forecast Card,
c. 1933. Lighthouse window area holds litmus paper. - **$22 $45 $65**

Captain Frank Hawks

Frank Hawks (1897-1938) was a skilled pilot and an air instructor for the army during World War I. Hawks gave future aviatrix Amelia Earhart her first plane ride on December 28, 1920. He set a number of speed records, including two in nonstop flights from Los Angeles to New York in 1929 and 1933. As a spokesman for Post cereals in the 1930s he made guest appearances on the radio and was always available to speak to the press. Boys and girls were urged to join Capt. Hawks' Sky Patrol to win free prizes. Ironically, Hawks was killed in an airplane crash.

CFH-1

❑ CFH-1. Sky Patrol Propeller Badge,
1935. Three ranks. Member - **$12 $18 $35**
Flight Lieutenant - **$18 $30 $65**
Flight Captain (scarce) - **$35 $70 $175**

CFH-2

CFH-3

❑ CFH-2. Club Manual,
1935. Post's 40% Bran Flakes. - **$22 $45 $100**

❑ CFH-3. Photo With Achievement Inscription,
c. 1935. Facsimile signature includes "Snapped Over The Andes At 19,000 Feet Altitude On May 4 1935". - **$30 $70 $145**

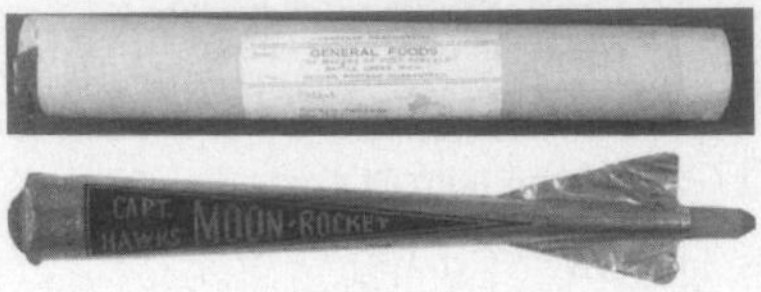

CFH-4

❑ **CFH-4. "Capt. Hawks Moon Rocket" Toy,**
c. 1936. Label on mailing tube reads "General Foods/The Makers Of Post Cereals." 10-3/4" long stiff cardboard tube with silver and blue paper covering, pair of aluminum tail fins and small wood plug inside tail end. Plug is removable and apparently blowing into the tube was meant to launch a red rubber ball from the front of the tube although the example we have seen was dried out. Front underside of tube has small wire loop for unknown purpose.
Mailer - **$25 $50 $100**
Rocket - **$80 $215 $325**

CFH-5

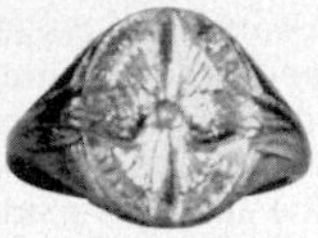

CFH-6

❑ **CFH-5. "Capt. Hawks Sky Patrol" Brass Ring,**
1936. Depicts portrait, cloud and propeller design. - **$65 $150 $350**

❑ **CFH-6. "Capt. Frank's Air Hawks" Brass Ring,**
1936. - **$50 $100 $300**

CFH-7

❑ **CFH-7. Air Hawks Wings Badge,**
1936. Three ranks.
Silver - "Member" - **$12 $18 $35**
Brass - "Squadron Leader" - **$18 $30 $70**
Bronze - "Flight Commander" - **$30 $70 $140**

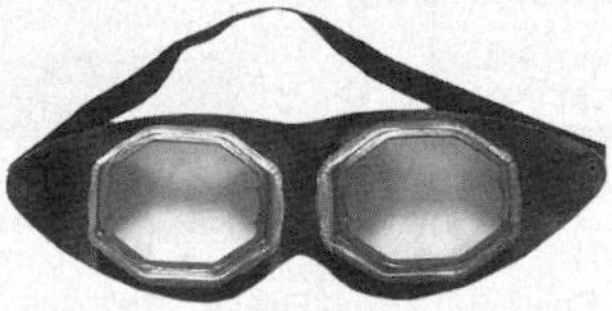

CFH-8

❑ **CFH-8. Goggles,**
1936. Rare. Premium obtained with 4 Post Bran Flakes box tops. - **$55 $90 $145**

CFH-9

CFH-10

❑ **CFH-9. "Air Hawks" Club Folder,**
1936. Post's 40% Bran Flakes. Eight pages of contents include illustrated premium offers, contest information on how to get 28 prizes. - **$22 $38 $65**

❑ **CFH-10. Fan Photo,**
c. 1936. - **$12 $28 $55**

CFH-11

❑ **CFH-11. One Sheet Poster,**
1937. For "The Mysterioius Pilot," Chapter 3 of the Columbia Pictures serial "Enemies of the Air" starring Frank Hawks. - **$125 $250 $500**

CFH-12

CFH-13

❑ **CFH-12. Sacred Scarab Ring,**
1937. Post's Bran Flakes. Scarab in green. Also issued for Melvin Purvis. - **$300 $650 $1200**

❑ **CFH-13. Sky Patrol Premium Booklet,**
1937. Post's 40% Bran Flakes. Offers eight premiums including club badge, manual, ring, ID bracelet. - **$25 $45 $90**

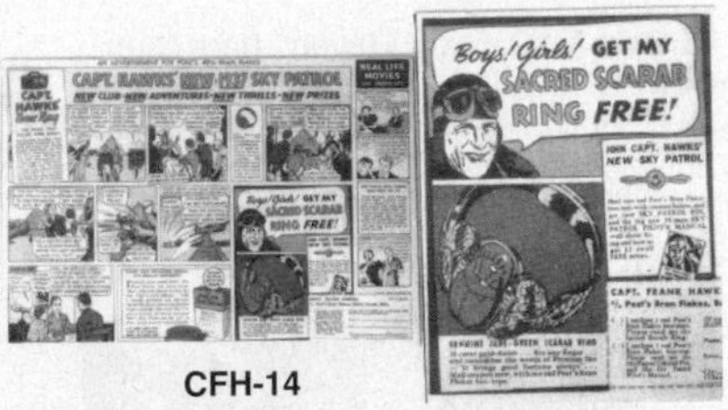

CFH-14

❑ **CFH-14. "Sacred Scarab Ring" Newspaper Ad,**
1937. Post's Bran Flakes. Ring offer expiration date December 31. Scarab in green, also issued for Melvin Purvis. Newspaper Ad. - **$12 $25 $40**

CFH-15

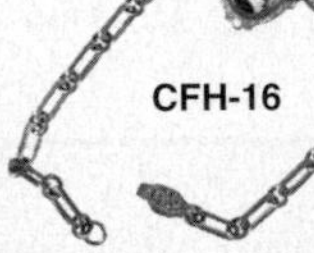

CFH-16

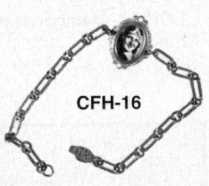

❑ **CFH-15. "Air Ace and the League of Twelve" BLB #1444,**
1938. - **$11 $33 $72**

❑ **CFH-16. Bracelet With Photo Picture,**
1930s. Rare. Assumed to be related to Capt. Hawks cereal campaign. - **$125 $250 $550**

CFH-17

❑ **CFH-17. Brass Paperweight and Perpetual Calendar,**
1940. - **$125 $250 $500**

Captain Gallant

Two-fisted Captain Gallant of the Foreign Legion, played by Olympic gold medalist and seasoned actor Buster Crabbe (1907-1983), premiered in a black-and-white series on NBC-TV in February 1955. Filmed originally in Morocco and later in Libya and Italy, the show was essentially a Western in Arab garb, with the Captain chasing camel thieves rather than cattle rustlers. Crabbe's son Cullen was featured as Cuffy Sanders, his ward. Fuzzy Knight played the bumbling sidekick. The show was sponsored by Heinz Foods until 1957, then by General Mills in repeats from 1960 to 1963. The following year the show was syndicated to local stations as *Foreign Legionnaire*. Items are usually copyrighted by Frantel Inc.

CGL-1

❑ **CGL-1. "Captain Gallant Hat" With Mailer,**
1955. H. J. Heinz Co. Fabric hat with cover letter, instructions and order coupon. Near Mint In Mailer - **$450**
Mailer Or Letter Only Each - **$25 $40 $75**
Hat Only - **$75 $150 $300**

CGL-2

❑ **CGL-2. Captain Gallant #1 Comic Book,**
1955. Heinz Foods. Membership certificate on back cover. Near Mint. - **$10**
See The Overstreet Comic Book Price Guide for values of other issues.

CGL-3

❑ **CGL-3. "Captain Gallant Of The Foreign Legion" Boxed Playset,**
1955. Store item by Marx. 14-3/4x23x3-1/4" deep box holds tin litho. building and wall sections with many hard plastic accessories including character figures of Captain Gallant and Cuffy. Complete - **$400 $800 $1650**

CGL-4

❑ **CGL-4. "Foreign Legionnaire" Button,**
1955. 1.25" cello rare version centered by blue-tone photo under dark blue text. -
$60 $140 $265

CGL-5 CGL-6

❑ **CGL-5. "Captain Gallant Holsum" Bread Button,**
1955. Shows Cuffy. 1.25". - **$50 $115 $200**

❑ **CGL-6. "Captain Gallant" Cuffy Cello. Button,**
1955. Holsum Bread. - **$60 $140 $265**

CGL-7

❑ **CGL-7. "Captain Gallant Desert Fort Game" Boxed,**
1956. Game consists of diecut cardboard pieces plus marbles. - **$65 $135 $250**

CGL-8

❑ **CGL-8. "Tim Magazine For Boys" Cover Article,**
June 1957. - **$18 $30 $50**

CGL-9

❑ **CGL-9. Captain Gallant And Cuffy Photos,**
1950s. Each - **$12 $28 $50**

CGL-10

❑ **CGL-10. "Junior Legionnaires" Club Card,**
1950s. - **$20 $50 $100**

CGL-11 CGL-12

❑ **CGL-11. "Junior Legionnaire" Litho. Tab,**
1950s. - **$15 $30 $65**

❑ **CGL-12. TV Sponsor Paper Store Pennant,**
1950s. P.F. footwear of B.F. Goodrich. - **$25 $60 $100**

CGL-13

❑ **CGL-13. "Captain Gallant Junior Legionnaire" Silvered Metal Badge,**
1950s. Cardboard insert photo. Probably came with store bought gun set and was sold off store display card or on individual card. - **$30 $60 $110**

CGL-14 CGL-15

❑ **CGL-14. Heinz Diecut Embossed Metal Member Badge,**
1950s. "57" numeral under flame image. For mounting on Heinz premium Legionnaire's hat. Scarce. - **$55 $110 $285**

❑ **CGL-15. "The Italy Star" Metal And Fabric Award Medal,**
1950s. Back has Captain Gallant logo and name. - **$25 $45 $100**

CGL-16 CGL-17

❑ **CGL-16. Foreign Legion Replica Award Medal,**
1950s. Fabric ribbon holding gold luster metal pendant with military motifs and "GRI" inscription. - **$25 $45 $100**

❑ **CGL-17. Foreign Legion Replica Award Medal,**
1950s. Fabric ribbon suspending silver luster metal pendant depicting cat-like animal killing dragon-like creature with commemorative date 1939-1945. - **$25 $45 $100**

CGL-18

❑ **CGL-18. "Captain Gallant" Holster,**
1950s. Came with belt in boxed set by Halco.
Boxed Complete - **$75 $150 $300**
Holster Only - **$30 $65 $125**

Captain Kangaroo

Bob Keeshan (1927-2004) had his first success on TV playing Clarabell on *The Howdy Doody Show* between 1947 and 1952. He would go on to greater success with *Captain Kangaroo* produced by Jack Miller, which first aired on CBS-TV on October 3, 1955. The simple premise had the gentle, grandfatherly Captain walking through the Treasure House. Puppeteer Cosmo Allegretti provided Bunny Rabbit, Mr. Moose and others and Hugh Brannum played the neighborly Mister Greenjeans. Another highlight of the show was the five minute *Tom Terrific* cartoons created by Gene Deitch at the Terrytoons studio. The cast featured Mighty Manfred the Wonder Dog and arch villain Crabby Appleton.

***Captain Kangaroo* was a weekday hour long show until 1981 when it became one half hour long. In 1982 it became a Saturday morning show. CBS cancelled the show in 1984 and it moved to PBS from 1985 until 1990. One of children television's most respected shows, the series was given six Emmy awards and three Peabody awards during its tenure.**

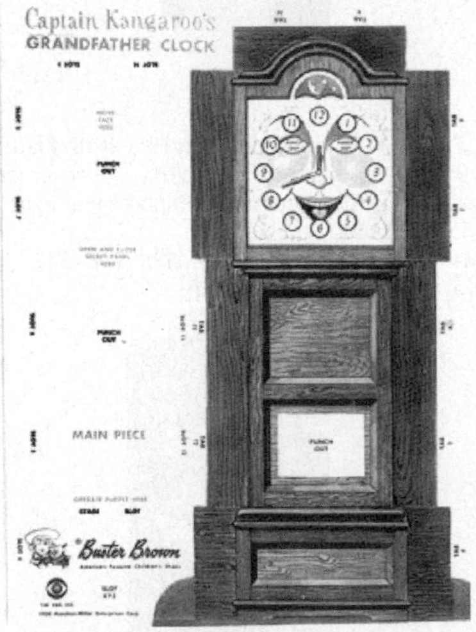

CPK-1

❑ **CPK-1. "Captain Kangaroo's Grandfather Clock" Punch-Out Sheet,**
1956. Buster Brown Shoes, copyright Keeshan-Miller Enterprises. Unpunched - **$20 $40 $75**

CPK-2

❑ CPK-2. "Captain Kangaroo" Large Boxed Doll,
1950s. Baby Barry Toy. 9x22x6" deep box holds 21" doll with molded vinyl head and hands, stuffed body, felt hat, jacket and pants plus cloth shirt with tie and vinyl collar. Jacket with brass buttons has small embossed tin shield badge with Captain Kangaroo's name and portrait. Feet are felt and vinyl covered and he wears vinyl suspenders. Box - **$25 $50 $100**
Doll - **$60 $110 $200**

CPK-3

❑ CPK-3. Captain Kangaroo Puzzle Postcard,
1950s. Kellogg's premium. 8 puzzle pieces. Prize for art drawing submitted to show. - **$30 $60 $110**

CPK-4

❑ CPK-4. "Captain Kangaroo" Cup,
1950s. Colgate toothpaste. Figural plastic with inset flicker eyes. - **$8 $15 $40**

CPK-5

❑ CPK-5. "Captain Kangaroo" Pull Toy With Wood Blocks,
1950s. Holgate Toys. 12x19x2.5" deep free-wheeling wood cart contains assortment of wood blocks in different shapes and colors. Has attached pull string with ball handle. - **$12 $25 $50**

CPK-6

❑ CPK-6. "Captain Kangaroo Puppet Theatre",
1950s. Rushton. 6x12.25x4" deep box with cellophane window contains three 5" puppets with cloth bodies and vinyl heads for Captain Kangaroo, Grandfather Clock and Mr. Greenjeans. Box - **$50 $100 $200**
Each Puppet - **$15 $30 $60**

CPK-7

❑ CPK-7. "Captain Kangaroo" Boxed Puppet,
1950s. Rushton. 10" tall puppet with vinyl head, fabric body, felt hands and bow tie in nicely illustrated box with cellophane window showing puppets, Mr. Greenjeans and Grandfather Clock. Box - **$20 $50 $125**
Puppet - **$15 $30 $60**

CPK-8

❑ CPK-8. "Captain Kangaroo" Hat,
c. 1960. 7" diameter by 3.5" deep. Likely a premium, issuer unknown. Stiff paper hat with adjustable band consisting of three pieces - body, brim and portrait badge with name and large initials "BB." - **$12 $25 $50**

CPK-9

❑ CPK-9. "Captain Kangaroo" Portrait Ring,
c. 1960. Aluminum ring with adjustable bands finished in bright gold luster with high relief portrait on top. - **$5 $15 $25**

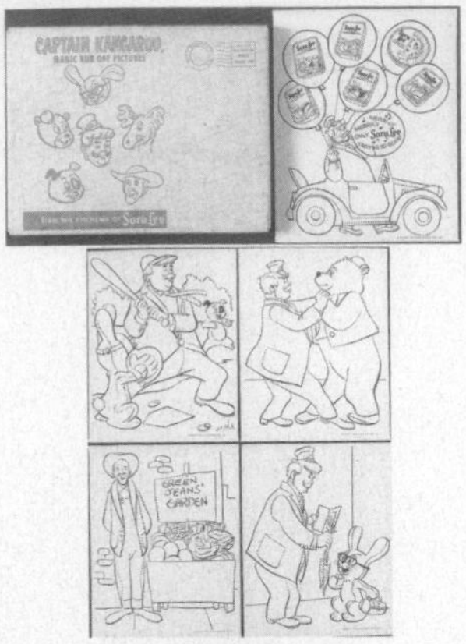

CPK-10

❑ **CPK-10. "Captain Kangaroo Magic Rub-Off Pictures",**
1960s. Sarah Lee. 7x8.5x1" deep box contains five 6.25x7.75" glossy cardboard pictures to be colored with crayon and then wiped off. Four photos of Captain Kangaroo and one of Mr. Greenjeans. Includes instruction sheet and generic crayons. Boxed Complete - **$15 $30 $60**

CPK-11

❑ **CPK-11. Captain Kangaroo Bob Keeshan Signed Card,**
1960s. 3x5" note card with blue felt tip pen signature "Bob Keeshan-Captain Kangaroo." Same Or Similar - **$50 $125 $250**

CPK-12

❑ **CPK-12. Captain Kangaroo Button,**
1990s. New York City TV station. 2.25" button reads "The Captain's Back On WCNY." - **$8 $15 $35**

Captain Marvel

Young Billy Batson, a homeless orphan, only had to utter the name of the wizard Shazam to be transformed into Captain Marvel, the World's Mightiest Mortal. Created by artist C. C. Beck and writer Bill Parker, Captain Marvel was introduced in *Whiz Comics* #2 in February 1940. It was a huge success, outselling all its competition and generating a Mary Marvel, Captain Marvel Jr., Uncle Marvel, several Lt. Marvels and Hoppy the Marvel Bunny. The Captain Marvel club was announced in *Whiz Comics* #23, on October 31, 1941.

The Captain subdued criminals and mad scientists for 13 years until a costly lawsuit for copyright infringement of the Superman character ended his run in 1954, but not before dozens of toys, novelties and premiums had been issued. Several comic book revivals and spinoffs have been published over the years. *The Adventures of Captain Marvel*, a 12-episode chapter play starring Tom Tyler as the Captain and Frank Coghlan Jr. as Billy was released by Republic Pictures in 1941. In 1974 a television series with Michael Gray as Billy was produced by Filmation Studios.

Ironically, Captain Marvel is now owned by DC Comics, publishers of *Superman*, and has enjoyed a recent resurgence. *The Power of Shazam!*, a 1994 hard cover graphic novel and 1995 monthly series of the same name, relaunched the character. He also appeared with the Justice Society in *JSA*. Mary Marvel has appeared as a pivotal figure in DC's weekly series *Countdown*. Captain Marvel, Jr. has appeared with various teams of young heroes in *Teen Titans* and *The Outsiders*.

The Marvel Family of characters continues to appear throughout the DC Universe, with Captain Marvel himself playing big roles in the mini-series *Kingdom Come* (1996) and *The Dark Knight Strikes Again* (2002). In 2007, Jeff Smith, the creator of the comic book *Bone*, revisited a very young Billy Batson's first adventure with the magic lightning with his high profile mini-series *Shazam!: The Monster Society of Evil*. At press time, a feature film is in pre-production.

CMR-1

❑ **CMR-1. Promotional Poster For Republic Pictures 12 Episode Captain Marvel Serial,**
1941. 27"x41". Advertised in press book. - **$1900 $3600 $6250**

CMR-2

❑ **CMR-2. Advs. of Captain Marvel Title & Scene Cards**
1941. Each chapter has 8 cards--one title card and seven scene cards (portraying action images from the film). The cards for Chapter 1 were in full color, while Chapters 2-12 were in duotone. Three of the seven scene cards for each chapter featured Captain Marvel and are considered more desirable. All 96 are rare.

❑ **Captain Marvel Title Card Chapter 1 - Color**
Scarce. Less than 10 known. - **$600 $1150 $1850**

❑ **Captain Marvel Title Cards Chapters 2-12 - Duotone**
Scarce. - **$110 $275 $500**

❑ **Captain Marvel Scene Card Chapter 1 - Color**
With Captain Marvel - **$165 $325 $525**
Without Captain Marvel - **$55 $110 $175**

❑ **Captain Marvel Scene Cards Chapters 2-12 - Duotone**
With Captain Marvel - **$115 $225 $310**
Without Captain Marvel - **$55 $85 $135**

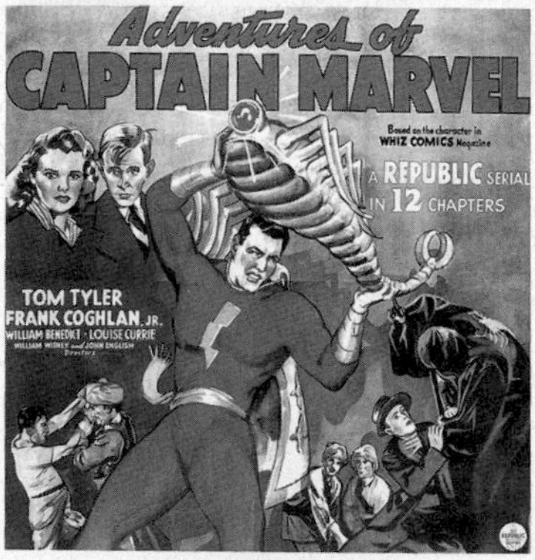

CMR-3

❑ **CMR-3. Adventures of Captain Marvel Six-Sheet Movie Poster,**
1941. Six-sheet and three-sheet posters were commonly created to span the entire run of a serial. Whereas a theater might have displayed a one-sheet for only the week that particular chapter was playing, the six-sheet would be displayed for the length of the serial. The Adventures of Captain Marvel Six-Sheet is rare, with less than 10 known. Full color. - **$3000 $7000 $11,000**

CMR-4

❑ CMR-4. Adventures of Captain Marvel One-Sheet Movie Posters
1941. Like most serials, the Captain Marvel one-sheets were created to promote the individual chapters of the serial.

❑ Chapter 1
Rare. Full color. Less than 10 known. Chapter 1 one-sheet does not have insert box as do Chapters 2-12; one, full poster image. -
$3250 $7500 $11,500

❑ Chapters 2-12
Scarce. Full color. One-sheets for Chapters 2-12 have insert boxes. Those with inserts featuring Captain Marvel are considered more desirable.With Capt. Marvel Insert -
$1100 $2250 $3500
Without Capt. Marvel Insert -
$550 $1100 $1750
Chapter 9 Showing Scorpion in Insert -
$1300 $2750 $4500

CMR-5

❑ CMR-5. Flyer for Spanish "Aventuras del Capitan Maravillas" Serial,
1941. Features the villain The Scorpion. -
$35 $65 $120

CMR-6

❑ CMR-6. Blotter 6",
1941. Rare. Promotes "The Adventures of Captain Marvel" 12 chapter serial. -
$250 $500 $950

CMR-7

❑ CMR-7. "Captain Marvel Club/Shazam" Club Litho. Button,
1941. - **$20 $40 $75**

(PUZZLE BOX)

(PUZZLE IMAGE)

CMR-8

❑ CMR-8. Boxed Picture Puzzle,
1941. Store item. 7-1/4x9-3/4x2" deep box contains puzzle that assembles to 13x17-1/2" titled "Captain Marvel Rides The Engine Of Doom" originally featured on the cover of Whiz #12
Box - **$55 $110 $165**
Puzzle - **$65 $140 $235**
Complete Box and Puzzle - **$120 $250 $400**

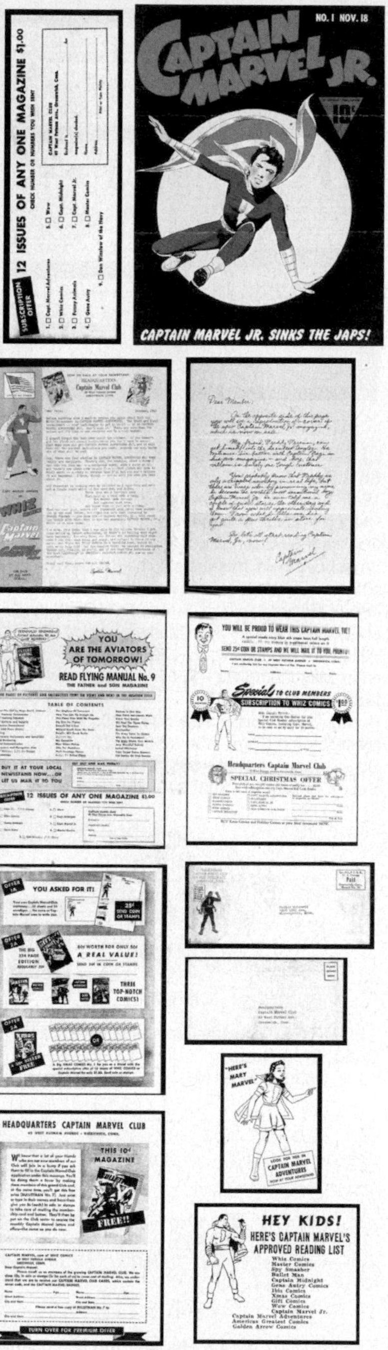

CMR-9

❑ CMR-9. Captain Marvel Jr. #1 Promotional Kit,
1942. Rare. Elaborate kit of 12 separate pieces plus mailing envelope. Includes full-color picture of front cover of Captain Marvel Jr. #1.
Complete - **$550 $1350 $1850**
Capt. Marvel Jr. Cover Promo Only -
$325 $650 $1150

CMR-10

❑ CMR-10. Membership Kit With Spy Smasher Tie-In,
1942. Kit includes envelope with "Remember Pearl Harbor" imprint, club member's cello. button, Whiz Comics subscription form, insert promoting Spy Smasher movie, membership card with secret code on reverse, insert with Captain Marvel's Secret Message which decodes as "Read all about Capt. Marvel Jr. in Master Comics. Gee Fellers it's great. On sale everywhere."
Near Mint Complete - **$565**
Button - **$20 $40 $75**
Subscription Form - **$20 $35 $60**
Membership Card - **$30 $60 $125**
Spy Smasher Insert - **$55 $110 $240**
Secret Message - **$20 $40 $65**

CMR-11

❑ CMR-11. "Captain Marvel Club/Shazam" Cello. Club Button,
1942. - **$30 $60 $100**

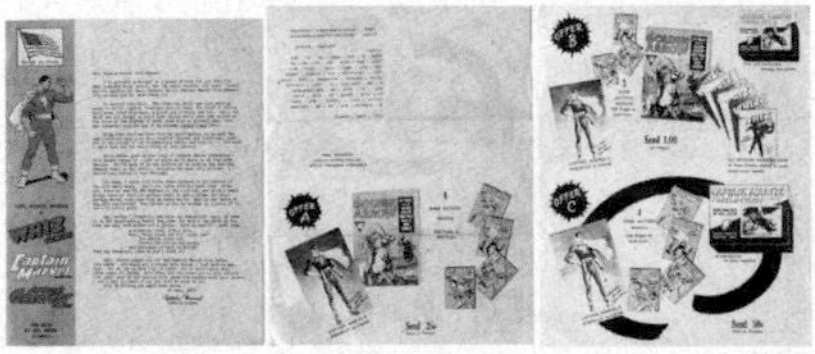

CMR-12

❑ CMR-12. Captain Marvel Club First Letter With Insert Sheet,
1942. Letter refers to story scheduled to appear in issue #13 of "Captain Marvel Adventures" and urges purchase for solution of the story. Slightly larger "Special Code Sheet" offers dime books, portrait picture, picture puzzle, Whiz Comics subscription by proper decoding.
Letter - **$50 $90 $175**
Offer Sheet - **$18 $30 $50**

CMR-13

❑ CMR-13.Club Letter With Inserts,
1942. November 1942 letter with order form for "E-Z Code Finder" and promo picture of Mary Marvel. Near Mint Complete **- $335**

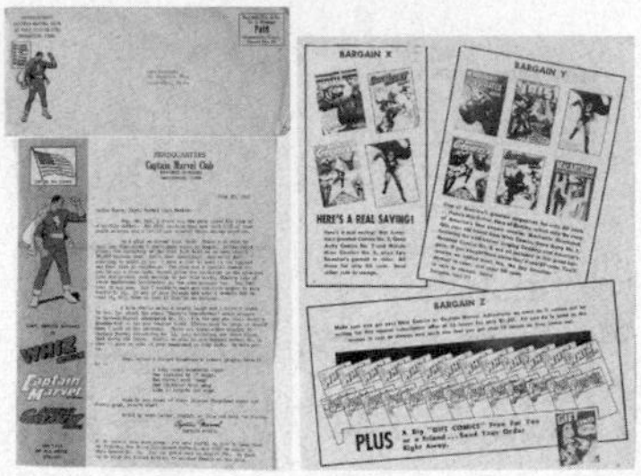

CMR-14

❑ CMR-14. Captain Marvel Club Second Letter With Insert Sheet,
1942. 8.5x10.75" letter dated July 20 announcing success of first letter from preceding June in addition to upcoming "Captain Marvel Adventures" issue #14. Second sheet is club application offering Golden Arrow comic, Spy Smasher portrait, other premiums by properly decoding. Letter - **$35 $80 $150**
Offer Sheet - **$12 $25 $35**

CMR-15

❑ CMR-15. Club Letters And "Secret Message" Sheets,
1942. Left envelope and letter is December, 1942 noting debut of Mary Marvel Comics and "Paste The Axis" contest. Right envelope and letter is undated. Mentions membership total of 200,000 and monthly letters but says "I Will Have To Stop This At Least Until The War Is Over." Also shown are two "Captain Marvel's Secret Message" sheets 2.75x4" and comic subscription offer 2.75x8.5".
Each Envelope And Letter - **$22 $40 $55**
Each Message Sheet - **$12 $18 $30**
Subscription Sheet - **$6 $12 $18**

CMR-16

CMR-17

❑ CMR-16. "Captain Marvel Comic Hero Punch-Outs Book",
1942. Store item by Samuel Lowe Co. - **$165 $325 $650**

❑ CMR-17. "Flying Captain Marvel" Punch-Out With Envelope,
c. 1942. Store item and club premium. Unused - **$20 $40 $75**

(FRONT) CMR-18 (BACK)

❑ CMR-18. Studio Prop Patch For Jacket,
c. 1942. RKO Studio Costume Dept. Reverse also reads "Max Berman & Sons Costume & Props." About 6" diameter. - **$275 $550 $900**

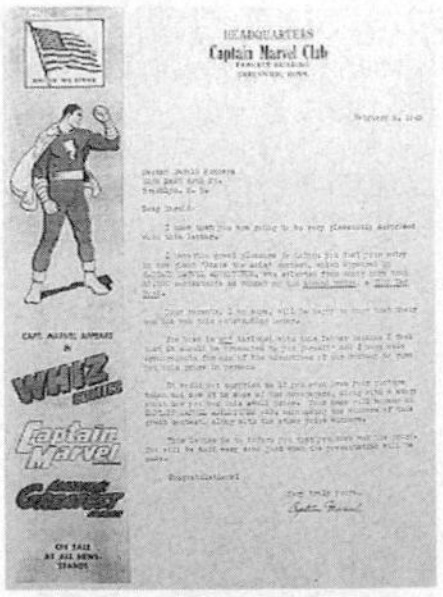

CMR-19

❑ CMR-19. "Paste The Axis" Letter To Second Prize Winner,
1943. Announces award of "$100 War Bond" and "Captain Marvel" states "I Have Made Arrangements For One Of The Executives Of Our Company To Give You This Prize In Person." - **$85 $165 $300**

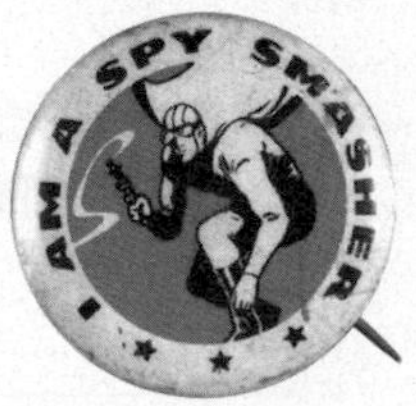

CMR-20

❑ CMR-20. Club Mailing February,
1943. Included Spy Smasher litho. button to make recipient an honorary member of Spy Smasher Victory Batallion, cover letter, sheet with new items including figure by Multi-Products, subscription offer coupon, Captain Marvel tie coupon, envelope.
Five Paper Items - **$120 $240 $360**
Spy Smasher Button **$20 $40 $65**

CMR-21

CMR-22

❑ CMR-21. "Secret Message Postcard",
1943. Scarce. - **$85 $200 $330**

❑ CMR-22. "E.-Z. Code Finder",
c. 1943. Scarce. - **$200 $375 $650**

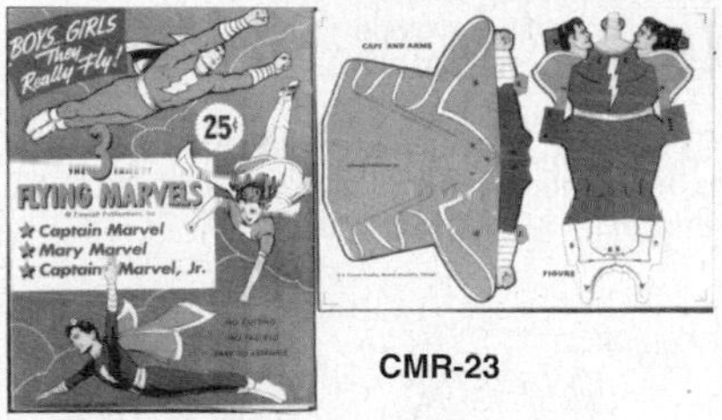

CMR-23

❑ CMR-23. "The Three Famous Flying Marvels" Punch-Outs,
1943. Store item and club premium.
Unused - **$25 $50 $80**

CMR-24

❑ CMR-24. World War II Navy Jacket Chest Patch,
1943. About 5-1/2" diameter featuring same design as cover of Captain Marvel #27. -
$325 $775 $1700

CMR-25

❑ CMR-25. "Captain Marvel Comic Story Paint Book",
c. 1943. Store item by Samuel Lowe Co. -
$75 $225 $1085

CMR-26

❑ CMR-26. "Magic Lightning Box" Punch-Out Paper Toy In Envelope,
c. 1943. Store item and club premium. Captain Marvel figure moves up and down inside box, scarcest item in punch-out series. -
$75 $150 $250

CMR-27 CMR-28

❑ CMR-27. Yellow Rectangular Patch,
c. 1943. Rare. Fawcett premium. -
$85 $225 $450

❑ CMR-28. Blue Rectangular Patch,
c. 1943. Fawcett premium. - **$50 $75 $140**

CMR-29

❑ CMR-29. "Captain Marvel's Fun Book",
1944. Store item and also available from Fawcett for 25¢. - **$36 $108 $450**

CMR-30

❑ **CMR-30. Christmas Letter To Members,**
1944. Cover letter plus sheet showing official items for 1945. Letter - **$30 $60 $100**
Premium Sheet - **$20 $40 $70**

CMR-31

❑ **CMR-31. Captain Marvel Military Felt Hat,**
1944. Rare. Less than five known. Captain Marvel on both sides of hat. - **$225 $450 $925**

CMR-32

CMR-33

CMR-34

❑ **CMR-32. "Captain Marvel Well Known Comics" Booklet,**
1944. Bestmaid give-away published by Samuel Lowe Co. - **$16 $48 $200**

❑ **CMR-33. "Captain Marvel Club/Shazam" Cello. Button,**
1944. Background around figure is blue rather than white as on 1942 version. - **$45 $90 $135**

❑ **CMR-34. Magic Picture,**
1944. Billy Batson's broadcast on front, says "Can you help Billy Batson". - **$80 $150 $250**

CMR-35

❑ **CMR-35. "Hoppy The Flying Marvel Bunny" Punch-Out Toy,**
c. 1944. Issued by Reed & Associates Inc.
Unpunched - **$30 $60 $100**

CMR-36

CMR-37

❑ **CMR-36. "Fawcett's Comic Stars",**
c. 1944. Store item with three metal stars depicting Captain Marvel, Hoppy The Marvel Bunny, Sherlock Monk.
Near Mint With Envelope - **$300**
Each Star - **$25 $50 $75**

❑ **CMR-37. "Captain Marvel Painting Book",**
c. 1944. Store item by L. Miller & Sons, London, England. - **$100 $150 $300**

CMR-38

CMR-39

❑ **CMR-38. "Captain Marvel's Rocket Raider" Paper Toy Kit,**
c. 1944. Store item and club premium.
Unused - **$20 $40 $75**

❑ **CMR-39. Punch-Out "Magic Eyes" Picture With Envelope,**
c. 1944. Store item and club premium.
Unused - **$20 $40 $75**

CMR-40

❑ **CMR-40 "One Against Many" Picture Puzzle,**
c. 1944. Store item and club premium. - **$25 $50 $85**

CMR-41

❑ **CMR-41. "Hoppy And Millie In Musical Evening" Cardboard Toy,**
c. 1944. Store item and club premium.
Unused - **$10 $25 $40**

CMR-42

❑ **CMR-42. "Buzz Bomb" Punch-Out Toy,**
c. 1944. Store item and club premium.
Unused - **$20 $40 $80**

CMR-43

❑ **CMR-43. "Shazam" Punch-Out Game With Envelope,**
c. 1944. Store item and club premium.
Unused - **$35 $70 $115**

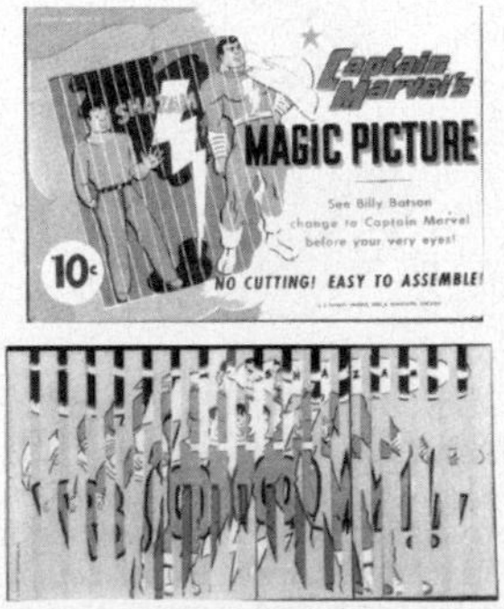

CMR-44

❑ **CMR-44. "Magic Picture" Cardboard Toy,**
c. 1944. Store item and club premium. Scarcer than others in series. Unused - **$45 $90 $180**

CMR-45

CMR-46

❑ CMR-45. "Captain Marvel, Jr. Ski Jump" Paper Assembly Toy In Envelope,
c. 1944. Store item and club premium. -
$20 $40 $60

❑ CMR-46. Toss Bag,
1945. Five varieties: Captain Marvel or Mary Marvel either flying or standing plus Hoppy.
Each - **$30 $65 $140**

CMR-47

❑ CMR-47."Captain Marvel Club" Christmas Letter With Order Form,
1945. Mentions first issue of "Marvel Family Comics." Offers 16 different premiums. -
$30 $55 $125

CMR-48

❑ CMR-48. "Flying Helicopter" Punch-Out Toy,
1945. Store item and probable premium by Reed & Associates.
Unpunched - **$90 $150 $300**

CMR-49

CMR-50

❑ CMR-49. Girl's Pink Felt Beanie,
1945. Rare. Marked Capt. Marvel with figure on front and back. Fawcett premium. -
$150 $300 $600

❑ CMR-50. Boy's Felt Beanie,
1945. Fawcett premium.
Black - **$150 $300 $600**
Blue - **$100 $200 $400**

CMR-51

CMR-52

❑ CMR-51. "Captain Marvel" Four Color Felt Patch,
1945. - **$85 $165 $330**

❑ CMR-52. "Mary Marvel" Four Color Felt Patch,
1945. - **$85 $165 $330**

CMR-53

❑ CMR-53. "Captain Marvel Jr." Four Color Felt Patch,
1945. 3.5x4" shield patch from series of four picturing Marvel family characters. -
$110 $225 $450

CMR-54

❑ CMR-54. Skull Cap,
1945. Scarce. Fawcett Premium. No brim. -
$125 $300 $650

CMR-55

❑ CMR-55. "Captain Marvel" Canadian Comic Book Glow-In-Dark Patch,
c. 1945. Anglo-American Publishing Co. Set of ten "Glo-Crests."
Captain Marvel - **$200 $450 $850**
Others: Commander Steel, Crusaders, Dr. Destiny, Freelance, Hurri-Kane, Kip Keene, Purple Rider, Red Rover, Terry Kane.
Each - **$40 $80 $165**

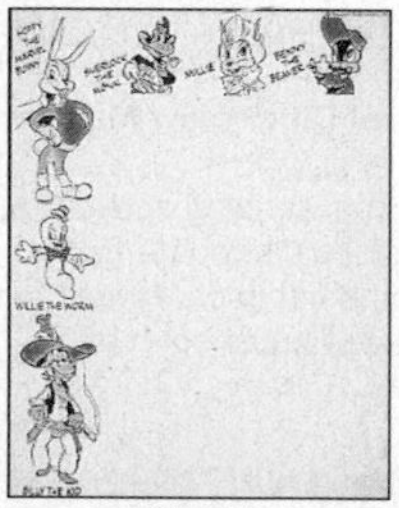
CMR-56

CMR-57

❑ CMR-56. Hoppy The Marvel Bunny Note Paper,
1946. Store item. From the same series as the Captain Marvel and Mary Marvel examples.
Scarce. Each Sheet - **$12 $25 $40**

❑ CMR-57. "Captain Marvel Club/Shazam" Litho. Button,
1946. Curl has text: "Copyright 1946 Fawcett Publications, Inc." - **$40 $75 $150**

CMR-58

❑ CMR-58. "Mary Marvel Notepaper" Boxed Set,
1946. Store item by Hobby Notes. Holds 18 sheets with envelopes.
Near Mint Boxed - **$850**
Each Sheet - **$12 $25 $40**

CMR-59

❑ CMR-59. "Mary Marvel Club" Member's Card,
1946. Card is captioned "Heroine Of Wow Comics." - **$135 $250 $500**

CMR-60

CMR-61

❑ **CMR-60. "Mary Marvel Club" New Member Letter,**
1946. Welcome letter acknowledging application receipt. Specifically mentions cardboard flip-style club badge and membership card was probably part of the package but is not mentioned. - **$75 $150 $275**

❑ **CMR-61. "Mary Marvel" Fabric Scarf,**
1946. Probable store item, maker unknown. - **$100 $200 $400**

CMR-62

❑ **CMR-62. "Mary Marvel Club Official Badge" Cardboard Flip-Pin,**
1946. 1-7/8" stiff cardboard with bar pin and string so piece can be flipped to show each side. A scarce badge for Mary's club members. - **$100 $200 $400**

CMR-63

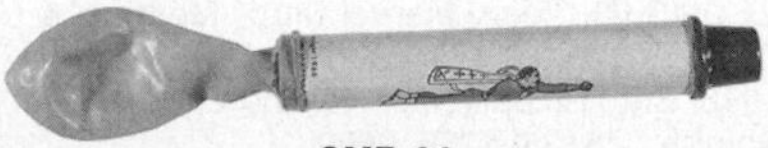

CMR-64

❑ **CMR-63. Whiz Wheaties Comic,**
1946. Thirty-two pages. Captain Marvel premium. Issued taped to Wheaties box.
GD - **$150** FN - **$600**
(not found above Fine condition)

❑ **CMR-64. Flute With Balloon,**
1946. - **$40 $80 $160**

CMR-65

❑ **CMR-65. "Shazam" Paper Pop-Up String Toy,**
1946. Fawcett Publications. - **$90 $165 $300**

CMR-66 CMR-67 CMR-68 CMR-69 CMR-70

❑ **CMR-66. Captain Marvel Syroco-Style 5" Figure,**
1945. Rare. Fawcett premium by Multi Products, Chicago. "Captain" spelled out on base. No box produced. 12 known. - **$2200 $4500 $7000**

❑ **CMR-67. Captain Marvel 5" Figure,**
1946. Rare. Fawcett premium by Kerr Co. of unknown blend of resin-like materials. "Capt." on base. No box produced. Less than 10 known. - **$2200 $4500 $7000**

❑ **CMR-68. Captain Marvel Jr. 5" Figure,**
1946. Fawcett premium by Kerr Co. of unknown blend of resin-like materials. No box produced. - **$400 $750 $1500**

❑ **CMR-69. Mary Marvel 5" Figure,**
1946. Fawcett premium by Kerr Co. of unknown blend of resin-like materials. Light color hair. No box produced. - **$400 $750 $1500**

❑ **CMR-70. Mary Marvel 5" Figure,**
1946. Rare. Similar to previous item. Hair may be light or dark. Wearing red dress with red belt and red lightning bolt. - **$1250 $2500 $3750**

CMR-71

CMR-72

❑ **CMR-71. Marvel Bunny 4 3/4" Figure,**
1946. Fawcett premium by Kerr Co. Rare. No box produced. - **$1500 $3500 $5250**

❑ **CMR-72. Marvel Bunny 6" Figure,**
1946. Fawcett premium by Kerr Co. of plastic. 20 known. Most examples have damaged or repaired ears. For C.C. Beck designed box in Near Mint, add $750. - **$500 $1500 $3000**

CMR-73 CMR-74 CMR-75

❑ **CMR-73. Captain Marvel 6-1/2" Figure,**
1946. Scarce. Fawcett premium by Kerr Co. of plastic. For C.C. Beck designed box in Near Mint add $750. - **$375 $875 $1500**

❑ **CMR-74. Captain Marvel Jr. 6-1/2" Figure,**
1946. Scarce. Fawcett premium by Kerr Co. of plastic. For C.C. Beck designed box in Near Mint add $750. - **$325 $600 $1150**

❑ **CMR-75. Mary Marvel 6-1/2" Figure,**
1946. Scarce. Fawcett premium by Kerr Co. of plastic. For C.C. Beck designed box in Near Mint add $750. - **$350 $650 $1300**

CMR-76

❑ **CMR-76. Statuettes Store Sign,**
1946. Rare. R. W. Kerr Co. Art by C. C. Beck. 6 known. - **$1350 $3300 $5500**

CMR-77

❑ **CMR-77. Magic Flute With Whistle on Card,**
1946. End piece in green or grey plastic.
Near Mint On Card - **$275**
Loose - **$35 $70 $140**

CMR-78

❑ **CMR-78. "Mary Marvel" Diecut Fiberboard Figure Badge,**
1946. Full color litho. paper front.
$75 $150 $300

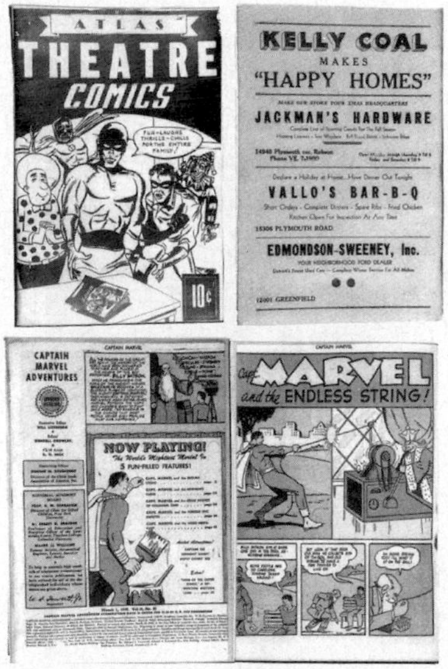

CMR-79

❑ **CMR-79. "Captain Marvel Adventures" Vol. 10 #55,**
1946. Scarce. Atlas Theater, Detroit. Theater replaced original cover of issue #55 with their own cover picturing generic heroes. -
$115 $325 $650

CMR-80

❑ **CMR-80. Tie-Clip,**
1946. On Card - **$40 $85 $155**
Clip Only - **$30 $60 $90**

CMR-81

CMR-82 **CMR-83**

❑ **CMR-81. Captain Marvel Glow-In-The-Dark Picture,**
1946. - **$75 $150 $340**

❑ **CMR-82. Captain Marvel Jr. Glow-In-The-Dark Picture,**
1946. - **$75 $150 $290**

❑ **CMR-83. Mary Marvel Glow-In-The-Dark Picture,**
1946.- **$75 $150 $290**

CMR-84 **CMR-85**

❑ **CMR-84. Hoppy Glow-In-The-Dark Picture,**
1946. Came unframed. - **$65 $100 $200**

❑ **CMR-85. "Captain Marvel Adventures" Wheaties Comic Book,**
1946. Copies were taped to box. Good - **$110**
Fine - **$450**

CMR-86

❑ **CMR-86. "Note Paper" Boxed Set,**
1946. Held 18 sheets and envelopes.
Near Mint Boxed - **$850**
Each Sheet - **$12 $25 $40**

CMR-87 **CMR-88**

❑ **CMR-87. "Captain Marvel" Litho. Button,**
1946. From set of 10 picturing Fawcett characters. - **$50 $125 $215**

❑ **CMR-88. "Mary Marvel" Litho. Button,**
1946. From set of 10 picturing Fawcett characters. - **$40 $110 $200**

CMR-89 **CMR-90**

❑ **CMR-89. "Captain Marvel Jr." Litho. Button,**
1946. From set of 10 picturing Fawcett characters. -**$50 $125 $215**

❑ **CMR-90. "Billy Batson" Litho. Button,**
1946. From set of 10 picturing Fawcett characters. - **$40 $110 $200**

CMR-91 **CMR-92**

❑ **CMR-91. "Hoppy The Marvel Bunny" Litho. Button,**
1946. From set of 10 picturing Fawcett characters. - **$30 $60 $110**

❑ **CMR-92. "Bulletman" Litho. Button,**
1946. From set of 10 picturing Fawcett characters. - **$20 $50 $100**

CMR-93

CMR-94

❑ **CMR-93. "Golden Arrow" Litho. Button,**
1946. From set of 10 picturing Fawcett characters. - **$20 $50 $90**

❑ **CMR-94. "Ibis" Litho. Button,**
1946. From set of 10 picturing Fawcett characters. - **$20 $50 $90**

CMR-95

CMR-96

❑ **CMR-95. "Nyoka" Litho. Button,**
1946. From set of 10 picturing Fawcett characters. - **$20 $50 $90**

❑ **CMR-96. "Radar" Litho. Button,**
1946. From set of 10 picturing Fawcett characters. - **$20 $50 $90**

CMR-97

❑ **CMR-97. "Mary Marvel" Felt Patch,**
1946. Scarce. Fawcett Publications. - **$85 $225 $425**

CMR-98

❑ **CMR-98. Captain Marvel Felt Club Patch,**
1946. - **$40 $80 $165**

CMR-99

❑ **CMR-99. Captain Marvel Jr. Felt Patch,**
1946. Blue - **$30 $60 $125**
Dark Green (Scarce) - **$60 $175 $350**

CMR-100

❑ **CMR-100. Felt Pennant,**
1946. Blue - **$50 $100 $175**
Yellow - **$75 $150 $275**
Green (With White Back) - **$100 $200 $385**

CMR-101

❑ **CMR-101. Plastic Keychain Fob,**
1946. Back inscription "This Certifies That The Holder Of This Key Ring Is A Bonafied Member Of The Captain Marvel Club". - **$30 $75 $160**

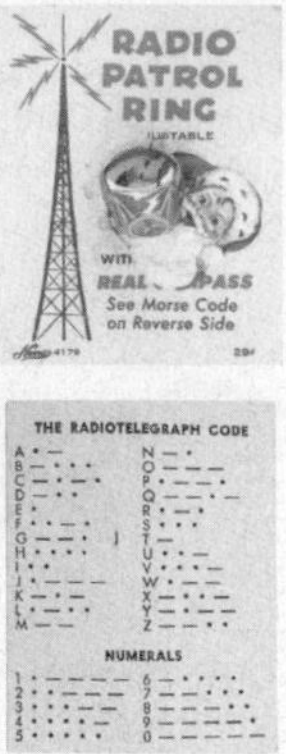

CMR-102

❑ **CMR-102. Rocket Raider Compass Ring,**
c. 1946. Red and black enamel paint on brass, unmarked but attributed to Captain Marvel. We suspect ring manufacturer (or Fawcett) sold surplus rings to another distributor and thus ring is known on a 2.75 x 3.5" card titled "Radio Patrol Ring" with "The Radiotelegraph Code" on the reverse. Only known example of card has a Santa Claus sticker added at center.
Ring - **$350 $700 $1600**
Card - **$150 $300 $600**

CMR-103

❑ **CMR-103. Captain Marvel Club Premiums Ad,**
1946. Fawcett Publications. Comic book page offering six premiums including set of 10 character litho. buttons picturing Marvels and other Fawcett adventure characters. - **$3 $6 $12**

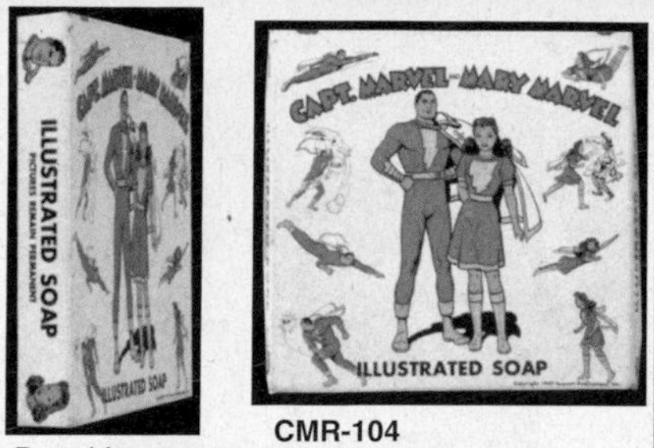

Box side

CMR-104

❑ **CMR-104. Capt. Marvel and Mary Marvel Illustrated Soap Box,**
1947. Illustrated Soap Co., Brooklyn, N.Y. Rare.
Box only - **$175 $350 $700**

CMR-105

❑ **CMR-105. Box Set of Race Cars,**
1947. Store item by Automatic Toy Co.
Numbered set of four.
Boxed With Keys - **$1400 $2750 $4500**
Each Car Loose, No Keys - **$135 $265 $575**

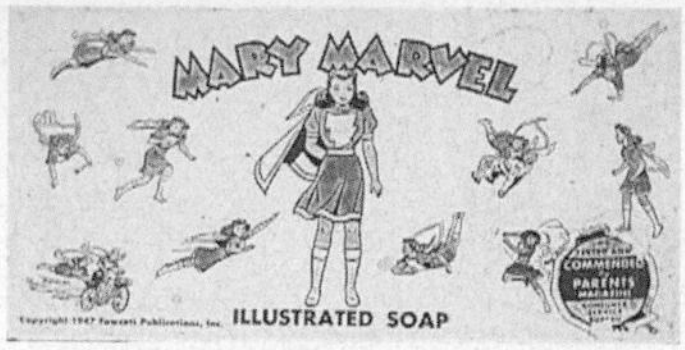

CMR-106

❑ **CMR-106. "Mary Marvel Illustrated Soap" Boxed,**
1947. Probable store item by Illustrated Soap Inc., Brooklyn, N.Y. This box holds three soap bars, each with different color decal. Also issued was three-bar set with Captain, Jr. and Mary.
Each Complete Box - **$200 $400 $750**

CMR-107

❑ **CMR-107. Sweater,**
1947. Store item by Somerset Knitting Mills, Philadelphia. - **$125 $250 $500**

(CLOSE-UP OF ART)

CMR-108

❑ **CMR-108. School Bag,**
1947. 11x13.5" canvas fabric with shoulder strap. A second version has a handle instead of a strap. Front pouch pocket has action art and his name. Either version - **$400 $800 $1600**

CMR-109

❑ **CMR-109. Hoppy And Captain Marvel Brunch Bags,**
1947-48. Store items. Captain Marvel has color image on red and is from 1947 while Hoppy has color image on dark green and is from 1948. Both are scarce.
Captain Marvel - **$325 $650 $1350**
Hoppy - **$550 $1100 $1650**

CMR-110

❑ **CMR-110. "Captain Marvel" Watch,**
1948. Store item and probable premium. Made in two sizes. Box - **$125 $250 $500**
Watch - **$100 $200 $400**

CMR-111

❑ **CMR-111. "Captain Marvel And Billy's Big Game" Comic Book,**
1948. Vital. 3.5x7" format 24-page full color comic from set of 18. Story is football theme involving Billy Batson as player on "Captain Marvel Club" squad. - **$85 $165 $375**

CMR-112

❑ **CMR-112. Marvel & Other Comic Books Store Sign,**
c. 1948. Miller's Kibbles/Miller's Dog Food. 8.5x17" paper ad for 18 different comics offered individually in bags of dog food. Six example comic covers are shown including one of Captain Marvel and another resembling Hoppy The Marvel Bunny although named "Super Rabbit." - **$125 $250 $500**

CMR-113

❑ **CMR-113. "Mary Marvel" Wristwatch,**
1948. Fawcett Publications copyright.
Box - **$150 $300 $600**
Watch - **$125 $250 $500**

CMR-114

CMR-115

CMR-116

❑ **CMR-114. "Capt. Marvel Jr." Wristwatch,**
1948. Scarce. Offered by the Fawcett Club and not known with a box. Luminous hands and blue, green, or red plastic strap.
- **$350 $700 $1350**

❑ **CMR-115. "Shazam-Captain Marvel Club" Litho. Button,**
1948. Fawcett Publications. - **$40 $85 $160**

❑ **CMR-116. Captain Marvel Braces" On Display Card,**
1948. Store item by Dunhill. Card includes punch-out "Official Badge" reading "Captain Marvel Shazam." Complete - **$200 $400 $800**

CMR-117

(CLOSE-UP OF THE CAPT. MARVEL CORNER IMAGE)

(A ?NECESSARY? WARNING IN THE FINE PRINT)

❑ **CMR-117. Captain Marvel Play Cape,**
1948. Only one known. This one shown is in Fine + condition. - **$650 $1300 $2750**

CMR-118

❑ **CMR-118. Captain Marvel & Others Blotter Pad,**
1948. Imprinted for J. T. Flagg Knitting Co. by publisher Brown & Bigelow Co. Cello. cover also pictures Red Ryder, Little Beaver, Gene Autry. - **$85 $165 $300**

CMR-119

❑ **CMR-119. "Hoppy The Marvel Bunny An Animated Novelty Book",**
c. 1948. Store item by John Martins House Inc., Kenosha, Wis. Spiral binding with four pop-ups. Rare. - **$115 $225 $450**

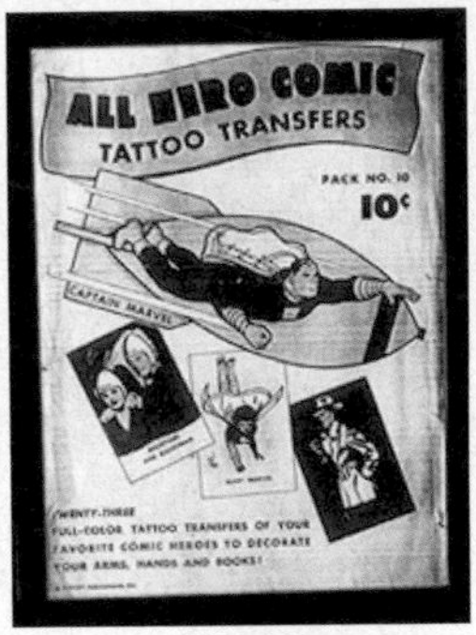

CMR-120

CMR-121

❑ **CMR-120. "All Hero Comic" Tattoo Transfers Pack,**
c. 1948. Fawcett Publications. Retail packet of 23 with envelope sample images of Captain Marvel, Bulletgirl and Bulletman, Mary Marvel, Radar. - **$85 $165 $300**

❑ **CMR-121. Captain Marvel Club Button,**
1949. English Club. 1 1/4" cello. button. - **$275 $550 $950**

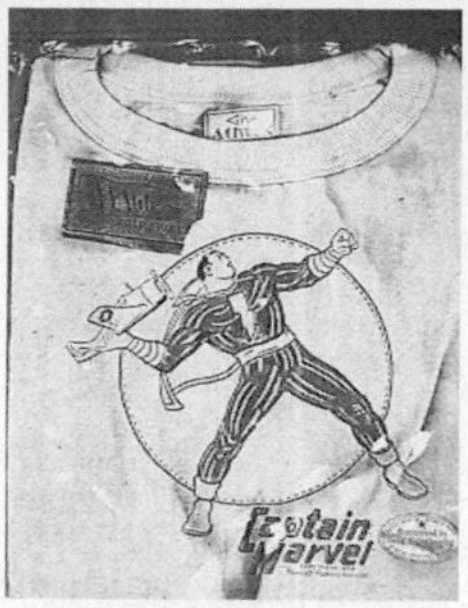

CMR-122

CMR-123

❑ **CMR-122. "Captain Marvel" Polo Shirt,**
1949. Store item by Flagg Polo Shirt. Rare, particularly near mint with company and Good Housekeeping labels. - **$165 $375 $875**

❑ **CMR-123. Portrait Picture,**
1940s. Comes with blank bottom margin or with "Capt. Marvel Appears Monthly In Whiz Comics." A third variety is known with text on reverse promoting movie serial.
Blank Margin - **$45 $85 $150**
Text Margin - **$60 $110 $190**
Text Reverse - **$85 $140 $230**

CMR-124

CMR-125

❑ **CMR-124. Merchandise Sheet,**
1940s. Regularly issued by Captain Marvel Club. - **$15 $30 $45**

❑ **CMR-125. Captain Marvel Club Membership Ad,**
1940s. Fawcett Publications. Comic book page ad offering Secret Code Finder, Magic Membership Card, Official Club Button. - **$10 $20 $30**

CMR-126

❑ **CMR-126. Captain Marvel Shirt,**
1940s. - **$325 $650 $1100**

CMR-127

CMR-128

❑ **CMR-127. "Mechanix Illustrated" Subscription Offer,**
1940s. Fawcett Publications. Comic book page ad utilizing Captain Marvel as promoter for sister publication by Fawcett. - **$10 $20 $30**

❑ **CMR-128. "Captain Marvel's Radar Racer" Punch-Out In Envelope,**
1940s. From series by Reed & Associates, copyright by Fawcett Publications. Assembly parts are for race car pictured on envelope.
Unpunched - **$75 $150 $300**

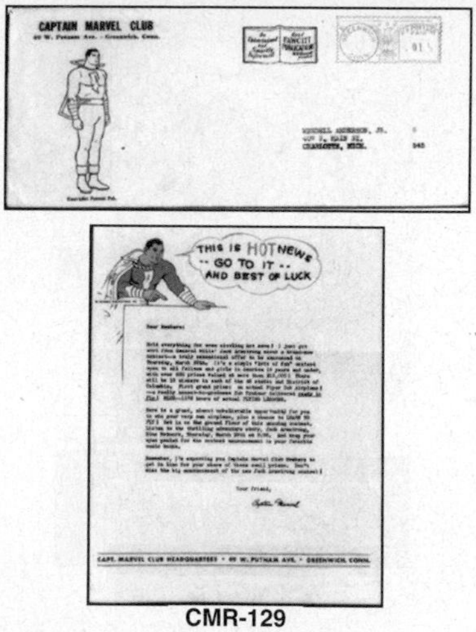

CMR-129

❑ **CMR-129. Club Letter With Envelope,**
1940s. Text for Jack Armstrong contest by Wheaties offering actual Piper Cub airplane as grand prize.
Envelope - **$25 $50 $75**
Letter - **$35 $70 $125**

CMR-130

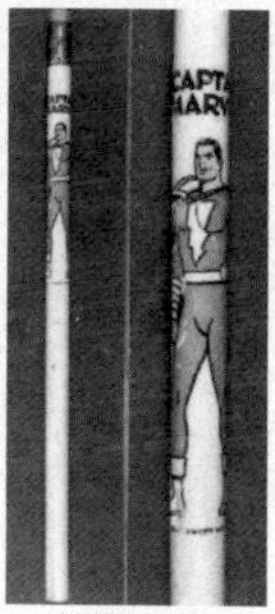

CMR-131

❑ **CMR-130. Club Letter,**
1940s. Example of many sent to club members. - **$15 $40 $80**

❑ **CMR-131. Pencil,**
1940s. Scarce. - **$50 $150 $300**

CMR-132

❑ **CMR-132. "Comic Heroes Iron-Ons" Packet,**
1940s. Envelope held 24 transfers.
Complete In Envelope - **$110 $165 $275**

CMR-133

❑ CMR-133. "War Stamps Savings Book" Envelope,
1940s. Held World War II savings stamp booklet. Included with mailings to club members. - **$125 $250 $400**

CMR-134

❑ CMR-134. "Jig-Saw" Puzzle #1,
1940s. Store item by L. Miller & Son Ltd., England. Boxed - **$45 $90 $200**

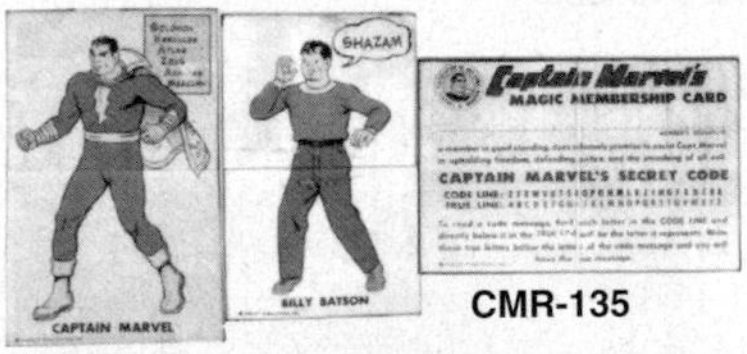

CMR-135

❑ CMR-135. "Magic Membership Card",
1940s. - **$45 $110 $185**

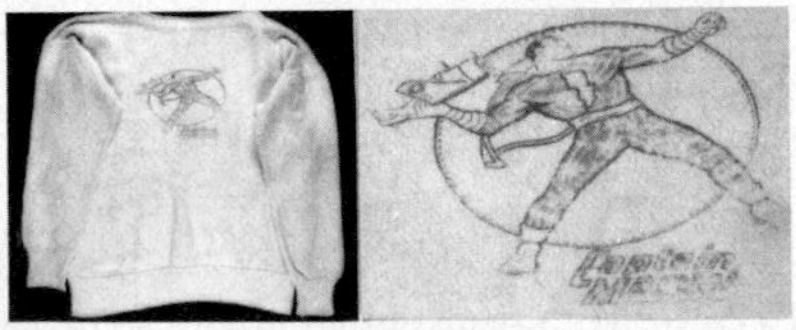

CMR-136

❑ CMR-136. Child's Sweatshirt,
1940s. Scarce. - **$125 $250 $500**

CMR-137

❑ CMR-137. "Mechanix Illustrated" Magazine Subscription Handbill,
1940s. Captain Marvel pictorial endorsement for magazine subscription. Included with mailings to club members. - **$20 $40 $80**

CMR-138

❑ CMR-138. "Magic Whistle" Diecut Cardboard,
1940s. American Seed Co., Lancaster, Pennsylvania. Working whistle that opens to show premiums earned by selling seed products. - **$35 $85 $165**

CMR-139

❑ CMR-139. "Magic Whistle" Envelope,
1940s. Reverse depicts generic premiums. Envelope Only - **$65 $125 $225**

CMR-140

❑ CMR-140. "Mary Marvel" Mailing Envelope,
1940s. Envelope is 4x9.5" and features Mary Marvel portrait and Fawcett copyright and text "Special Message For You From Mary Marvel." - **$150 $300 $450**

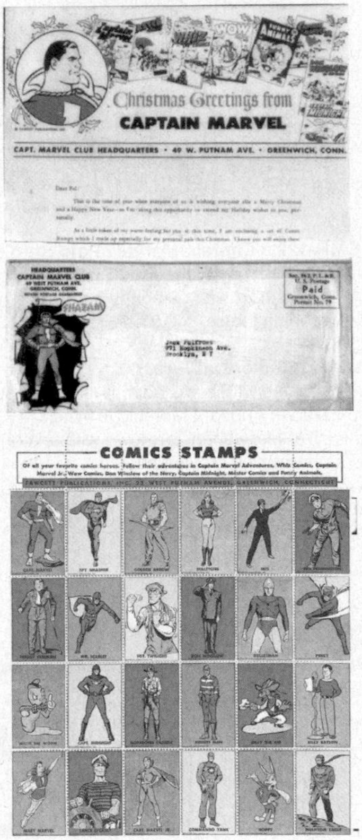

CMR-141

❑ CMR-141. Club Christmas Kit In Mailer Envelope,
1940s. Came with cover letter and sheet of 24 Fawcett character gummed stamps.
Near Mint In Mailer - **$425**
Letter - **$30 $60 $100**
Stamp Sheet - **$85 $165 $300**

CMR-142

❏ **CMR-142. Australian "Captain Marvel Coloring Book,"**
1940s. Book is 7.75x8.5" published by Larry Cleland Pty. Ltd., Melbourne, Fawcett Publications Inc. Has 24 pages.
- $60 $125 $250

CMR-143

❏ **CMR-143. Captain Marvel Carnival Statue,**
1940s. 15.25" tall painted hollow plaster figure including lightning bolt emblem on chest rather than Superman emblem as same mold was used for both characters. Figure otherwise is finished in red outfit with blue cape. -
$125 $275 $500

CMR-144

CMR-145

❏ **CMR-144. "Captain Marvel/Shazam" Cello. On Silvered Brass Pencil Clip ,**
1940s. - **$25 $50 $100**

❏ **CMR-145. "Captain Marvel" Power Siren,**
1940s. Store item. Red plastic siren whistle with metal loop ring. - **$50 $100 $150**

CMR-146

❏ **CMR-146. Captain Marvel Picture,**
1940s. 8x10" glossy black and white with facsimile signature by him but no publication markings. - **$70 $145 $200**

CMR-147

CMR-148

❏ **CMR-147. "Captain Marvel And The Good Humor Man" Movie Comic,**
1950. Jack Carson on cover. - **$48 $144 $625**

❏ **CMR-148. "Captain Marvel And The Lieutenants Of Safety" Comic Book #1 ,**
1950. Rare. Fawcett Publications/Ebasco Services. - **$200 $600 $1600**

CMR-149

❏ **CMR-149. "The Boy Who Never Heard Of Captain Marvel" Comic Booklet,**
1950. Bond Bread. Pocket size comic with 24 pages. Two other titles in series are "Captain Marvel And The Stolen City" and "Captain Marvel Meets The Weatherman."
Each - **$23 $69 $290**

CMR-150

CMR-151

❏ **CMR-150. "Captain Marvel And The Lieutenants Of Safety" Comic Book #2 ,**
1950. Rare. Fawcett Publications/Ebasco Services. - **$86 $258 $1250**

❏ **CMR-151. "Captain Marvel And The Lieutenants Of Safety" Comic Book #3 ,**
1951. Rare. Fawcett Publications/Ebasco Services. - **$86 $258 $1250**

CMR-152

❏ **CMR-152. Captain Marvel And Mary Marvel Lead Figures,**
1954. Store item by Timpo. Captain Marvel Jr. was also issued. Originals by this English firm have hollow bodies but reproductions are known with solid bodies. Each - **$75 $200 $350**

CMR-153

❏ **CMR-153. Tattoo Transfers,**
1955. Pack Number 2 shown. - **$35 $70 $150**

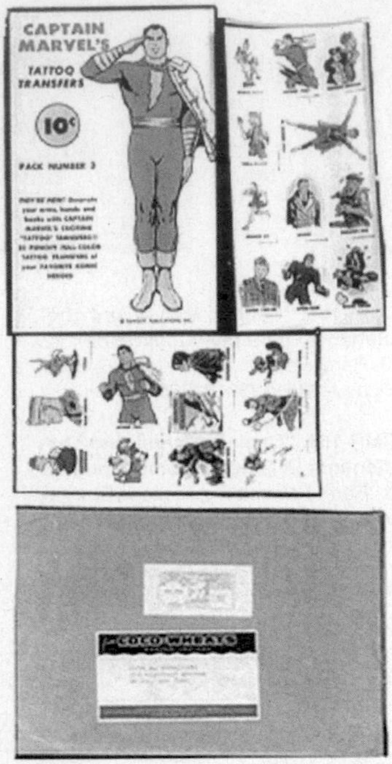

CMR-154

❑ CMR-154. Coco-Wheats "Tattoo Transfers" Kit With Mailer Envelope,
1956. Mailer - **$10 $20 $30**
Illustrated Inner Envelope With Two Sheets - **$35 $70 $150**

CMR-155

CMR-156

❑ CMR-155. "Captain Marvel Club" Cello. Button,
c. 1968. Mostly red, yellow and black 1-3/4". Button first appeared in the late 1960s and carries no sponsor or maker information. Several years later, Captain Marvel resurfaced in 1973 in DC Comics' *Shazam* #1. - **$10 $25 $50**

❑ CMR-156. "Shazam Is Coming" 4" Cello. Button,
1972. N.P.P. Inc. - **$15 $40 $80**

CMR-157

❑ CMR-157. Shazam Plate,
1973. Very limited. - **$25 $50 $100**

CMR-158

❑ CMR-158. Unauthorized Reproduction "Captain Marvel Club" Button,
c. 1975. 1" diameter. In 2007, an eBay seller wrote that he produced 1000 of these buttons "more than 30 years ago." We include for informational purposes because the button is undated and deceptive. In our opinion, value is nil.

CMR-159

❑ CMR-159. "Shazam!" Card Game,
1977. On display card. - **$10 $20 $40**

CMR-160

❑ CMR-160. "Shazam!" Puzzle,
1978. - **$10 $20 $60**

CMR-161

CMR-162

❑ CMR-161. "Power of Shazam" Sign,
1994. 19x35" sign promoting the return of Captain Marvel to comics. - **$25 $40 $80**

❑ CMR-162. Bean Bag Figure,
1999. Warner Bros. Store Exclusive. - **$25**

CMR-163

CMR-164

❑ CMR-163. Action Figure,
1999. DC Super-Heroes Collection. Display stand is included. - **$28**

❑ CMR-164. "Kingdom Come" Resin Statue,
1999. Sculpted by Alex Ross, based on his rendition of Capt. Marvel in the comic mini-series. Statue is copper-colored. Boxed - **$260**

CMR-165

❑ **CMR-165. Billy Batson/Captain Marvel Action Figures,**
2000. With sound chip in box. - **$60**

CMR-166

❑ **CMR-166. Full Color Resin Statue,**
2001. 9 1/2" tall. Full color hand painted statue from the Kingdom Come comic series. Designed and sculpted by Alex Ross. - **$200**

Captain Midnight

A shadowy plane and a mysterious pilot...diving furiously from the night sky...Captain Midnight and his Secret Squadron battled the sinister forces of evil on radio during most of the 1940s. Created by writers Robert Burtt and Wilfred Moore, the program originated as a syndicated show in 1938 over WGN in Chicago, sponsored by the Skelly Oil Co. and broadcast in the Midwest. The following year it went national on the Mutual network sponsored by Ovaltine, which had just dropped Little Orphan Annie. Captain Midnight's Secret Squadron was one of radio's major producers of premiums. For an Ovaltine seal and a dime kids became Secret Squadron members. Decoder badges, pins, patches, mugs, maps, booklets, wings and rings followed in great profusion until the show closed in 1949.

The Captain made his first comic book appearance in *The Funnies* #57 in July 1941, moved to *Popular Comics* a year later and had his own book from September 1942 to September 1948. A 15-episode serial starring David O'Brien was released by Columbia Pictures in 1942. The *Captain Midnight* TV series premiered in 1953, starring Richard Webb as the American superhero and aired for four years on ABC and CBS, still sponsored by Ovaltine, still offering Secret Squadron mugs and decoder badges. The Secret Squadron logo, SS, was changed to SQ.

In the late 1950s, after Ovaltine declined to give up the copyrighted Captain Midnight name, the show was syndicated in reruns as *Jet Jackson, Flying Commando.* In 1988 Ovaltine offered a Captain Midnight SQ Secret Squadron watch in exchange for a proof-of-purchase seal.

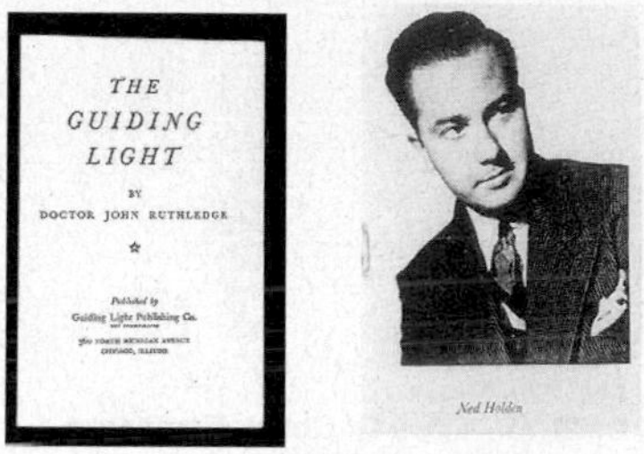

CMD-1

❑ **CMD-1. Radio Portrayer Photo In "The Guiding Light" Booklet,**
1938. Guiding Light Publishing Co./Ovaltine. Radio program synopsis booklet picturing Ed Prentiss, the radio voice of Captain Midnight on Mutual Network although identified by "Ned Holden" name of Guiding Light character. - **$45 $90 $220**

CMD-2

❑ **CMD-2. Skelly Large 36x84" Cardboard Display Sign,**
1939. Rare. Has three brass grommet holes to aid in displaying. - **$1200 $2500 $4500**

Captain Midnight's
FLIGHT PATROL REPORTER
BOYS! GIRLS! FOLLOW CAPTAIN MIDNIGHT ALL SUMMER IN FLIGHT PATROL NEWSPAPER!
CHUCK AND PATSY SEND FLIGHT PATROL MEMBERS GREETINGS
CALL AT YOUR SKELLY SERVICE STATION FOR NEXT ISSUE, OUT SOON

CMD-3

Captain Midnight's
FLIGHT PATROL REPORTER
SPARTAN BOMBER FOR FLIGHT PATROL MEMBERS
CHUCK AND PARTY MAKE SWIFT TOUR OF MEXICO CITY
HOW TO GET YOUR SPARTAN BOMBER
Amazingly Modern Plane with 32-inch Wingspan and Exploding Bombs Now Ready for Distribution
HERE'S YOUR BIG, SPEEDY SPARTAN BOMBER

CMD-4

❑ **CMD-3. Skelly Oil "Flight Patrol Reporter" Vol. 1 #1 Newspaper,**
Spring 1939. Six issues between Spring 1939 and March 1940. First Issue - **$35 $100 $200**
Other 5 Issues - **$30 $90 $165**

❑ **CMD-4. Skelly Oil "Flight Patrol Reporter" Vol. 1 #2 Newspaper,**
June 15, 1939. - **$30 $90 $165**

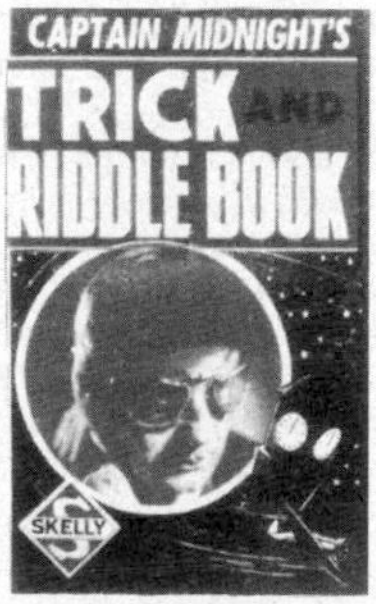

CMD-5

❑ **CMD-5. "Trick And Riddle Book",**
1939. Skelly Oil Co. - **$25 $60 $135**

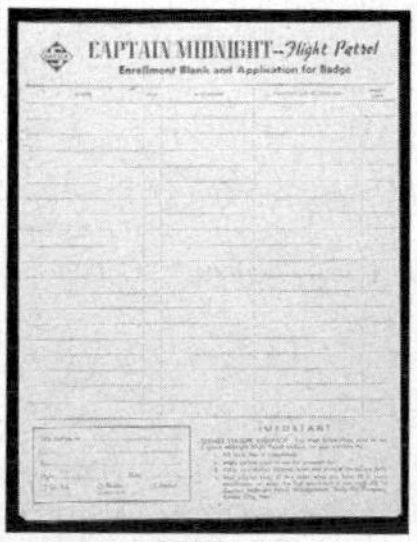

CAPTAIN MIDNIGHT—Flight Patrol
Enrollment Blank and Application for Badge

CMD-6

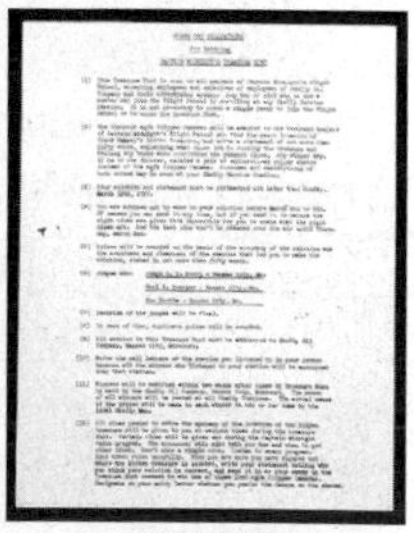

CMD-7

❑ **CMD-6. Flight Patrol Badge Application,**
1939. Skelly Oil Co. - **$45 $95 $200**

❑ **CMD-7. Treasure Hunt Rules,**
1939. Skelly Oil Co. - **$55 $110 $225**

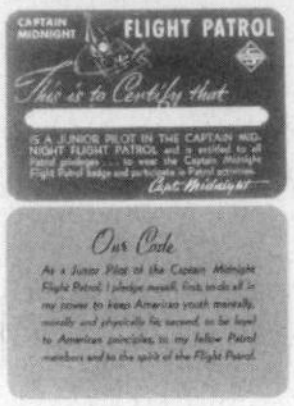

CMD-8

CMD-9

❑ **CMD-8. Membership Card,**
1939. Skelly Oil Co. - **$30 $80 $160**

❑ **CMD-9. "Air Heroes" Stamp Album,**
1939. Skelly Oil. Holds 16 stamps.
Empty - **$15 $30 $60**
Complete - **$30 $75 $150**

CMD-10

CMD-11

❑ **CMD-10. Portrait Photo,**
1939. Skelly Oil Co. - **$25 $75 $150**

❑ **CMD-11. "Happy Landings" Photo,**
1939. Skelly Oil Co. Captain Midnight with Patsy and Chuck. Bottom left margin says "Compliments of Skelly Oil Co." A reproduction exists. On the reproduction, both letter "i"s in "Compliments" and "Oil" are missing the dot. Also, the tonal contrast of the photo is much lighter than the original. - **$25 $65 $120**

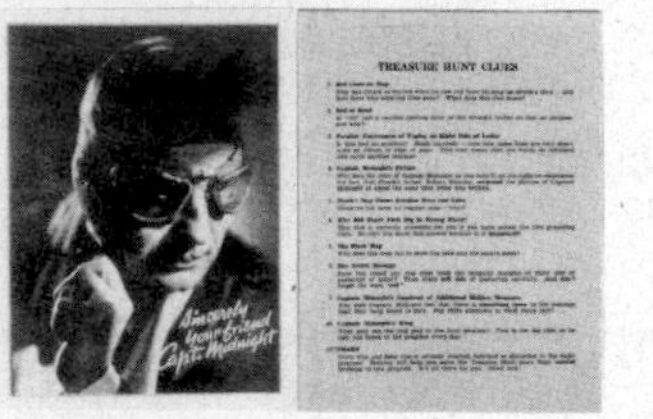

CMD-12

❑ **CMD-12. Portrait Photo With Treasure Hunt Back,**
1939. Skelly Oil Co. - **$75 $150 $275**

CMD-13

CMD-14

❑ **CMD-13. "Chuck Ramsey" Portrait Photo,**
1939. Skelly Oil Co. - **$30 $75 $140**

❑ **CMD-14. Unmarked Known As 'Chuck's Treasure Map' 9x11".**
1939. Skelly Oil Co. - **$90 $200 $400**

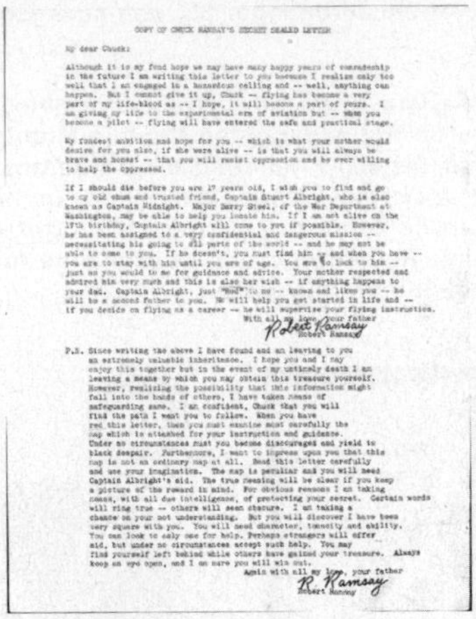

COPY OF CHUCK RAMSAY'S SECRET SEALED LETTER

My dear Chuck:

Although it is my fond hope we may have many happy years of comradeship in the future I am writing this letter to you because I realize only too well that I am engaged in a hazardous calling and -- well, anything can happen. But I cannot give it up, Chuck -- flying has become a very part of my life-blood as -- I hope, it will become a part of yours. I am giving my life to the experimental era of aviation but -- when you become a pilot -- flying will have entered the safe and practical stage.

My fondest ambition and hope for you -- which is what your mother would desire for you also, if she were alive -- is that you will always be brave and honest -- that you will resist oppression and be ever willing to help the oppressed.

If I should die before you are 17 years old, I wish you to find and go to my old chum and trusted friend, Captain Stuart Albright, who is also known as Captain Midnight. Major Barry Steel, of the War Department at Washington, may be able to help you locate him. If I am not alive on the 17th birthday, Captain Albright will come to you if possible. However, he has been assigned to a very confidential and dangerous mission -- necessitating his going to all parts of the world -- and he may not be able to come to you. If he doesn't, you must find him -- and when you have -- you are to stay with him until you are of age. You are to look to him -- just as you would to me for guidance and advice. Your mother respected and admired him very much and this is also her wish -- if anything happens to your dad. Captain Albright, just "Red" to me -- knows and likes you -- he will be a second father to you. He will help you get started in life and -- if you decide on flying as a career -- he will supervise your flying instruction.

With all my love, your father
Robert Ramsay
Robert Ramsay

P.S. Since writing the above I have found and am leaving to you an extremely valuable inheritance. I hope you and I may enjoy this together but in the event of my untimely death I am leaving a means by which you may obtain this treasure yourself. However, realizing the possibility that this information might fall into the hands of others, I have taken means of safeguarding same. I am confident, Chuck that you will find the path I want you to follow. When you have red this letter, then you must examine most carefully the map which is attached for your instruction and guidance. Under no circumstances must you become discouraged and yield to black despair. Furthermore, I want to impress upon you that this map is not an ordinary map at all. Read this letter carefully and use your imagination. The map is peculiar and you will need Captain Albright's aid. The true meaning will be clear if you keep a picture of the reward in mind. For obvious reasons I am taking means, with all due intelligence, of protecting your secret. Certain words will ring true -- others will seem obscure. I am taking a chance on your not understanding. But you will discover I have been very square with you. You will need character, tenacity and ability. You can look to only one for help. Perhaps strangers will offer aid, but under no circumstances accept such help. You may find yourself left behind while others have gained your treasure. Always keep an eye open, and I am sure you will win out.

Again with all my love, your father
R. Ramsay
Robert Ramsay

CMD-15

❑ **CMD-15. "Copy Of Chuck Ramsay's Secret Sealed Letter" From His Dad,**
1939. Skelly Oil. 8.5x11" facsimile typed letter from Robert Ramsay to son Chuck. From first year of premiums including references to aviation life and "Captain Stewart Albright," also known as Captain Midnight. - **$135 $240 $475**

CMD-16

CMD-17

❑ **CMD-16. Mysto-Magic Weather Forecasting Flight Wings Badge,**
1939. Skelly Oil Co.
With litmus paper - **$20 $45 $80**
Without litmus paper - **$15 $35 $50**

❑ **CMD-17. "Flight Patrol Commander" Brass Badge,**
1939. Rare. Skelly Oil Co. One of the rarest Captain Midnight badges. - **$600 $1400 $2500**

CMD-18

CMD-19

❑ **CMD-18. Skelly Oil "Fly With Captain Midnight" Radio Sponsorship Announcement Brochure,**
1940. Pictures Captain Midnight, Chuck, Patsy, Steve, Ivan Shark. Skelly president announces show with list of midwest stations. -
$125 $325 $600

❑ **CMD-19. Skelly Flight Patrol Member Card,**
1940. - **$60 $110 $225**

CMD-20

❑ **CMD-20. Membership Card,**
1940. Skelly Oil Co. - **$30 $80 $160**

(FRONT) (BACK)

CMD-21

❑ **CMD-21. Skelly Flight Patrol Brass Spinner Medal,**
1940. Spinner disk pictures Captain Midnight, Patsy Donovan, Chuck Ramsey, propeller design. - **$12 $20 $40**

CMD-22

CMD-23

❑ **CMD-22. "Mexican Jumping Beans" Paper Bag,**
1940. Skelly Oil Co. For premium game utilizing jumping beans.
Bag Only - **$115 $225 $350**
Bag With 3 Beans - **$200 $400 $600**

❑ **CMD-23. "Mexican Ringo-Jumpo" Game Sheet,**
1940. Skelly Oil Co. For jumping bean game. -
$125 $250 $500

CMD-24

❑ **CMD-24. "Captain Midnight's Flight Patrol Reporter" Vol. 1 #6 Newspaper,**
1940. Skelly Oil Co. Last issue. - **$30 $90 $165**

(ENLARGED VIEW)

CMD-25

❑ **CMD-25. Skelly Oil "Flight Patrol" Airline Map,**
1940. Scarce. 11x17" opened. -
$150 $385 $700

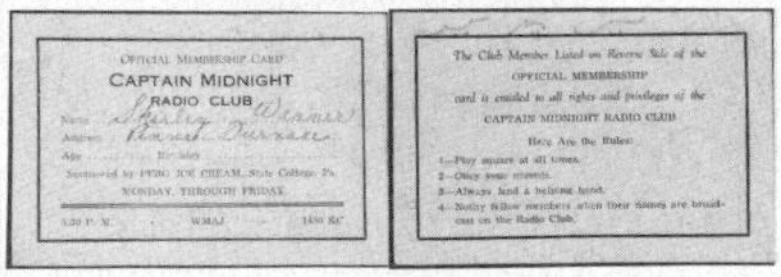

CMD-26

❑ **CMD-26. "Captain Midnight Radio Club" Member Card,**
c. 1940. Pero Ice Cream. Gray card printed in black on both sides for club hosted by WMAJ, State College, Pa. - **$90 $175 $300**

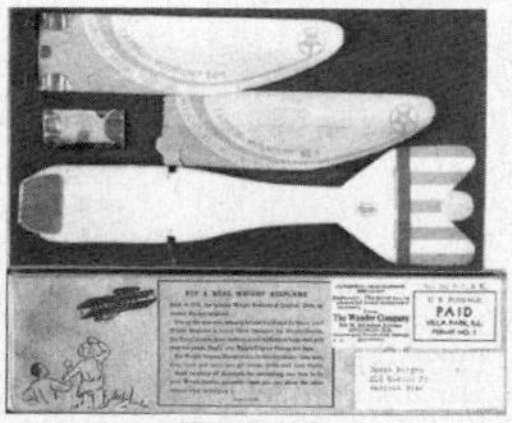

CMD-27

CMD-28

❑ **CMD-27. "Wright Airplane" Balsa/Paper Assembly Kit With Box ,**
1941. Scarce. Wings inscribed "Captain Midnight SS-1" and "Wright Aerial Torpedo".
Near Mint Boxed - **$525**
Assembled - **$125 $225 $350**

❑ **CMD-28. Mystery Dial Code-O-Graph Brass Decoder,**
1941. First Captain Midnight decoder. -
$45 $90 $175

CMD-29

❑ **CMD-29. "Detect-O-Scope",**
1941. Cardboard tube holds metal piece to judge altitudes. Also see item CMD-33.
Near Mint Boxed With Instructions -
$375
Complete Scope Only - **$60 $125 $250**

CMD-30

❑ **CMD-30. Club Manual With Member Papers,**
1941. With card and parents letter.
Complete Near Mint - **$325**
Manual Only - **$75 $150 $250**

CMD-31

❑ **CMD-31. American Flag Loyalty Pin With Paper,**
1941. Patriotic text paper held in tube on pin reverse.
Badge - **$35 $90 $150**
Paper - **$50 $100 $200**

CMD-32

❑ **CMD-32. "Flight Commander" Handbook,**
1941. - **$85 $250 $425**

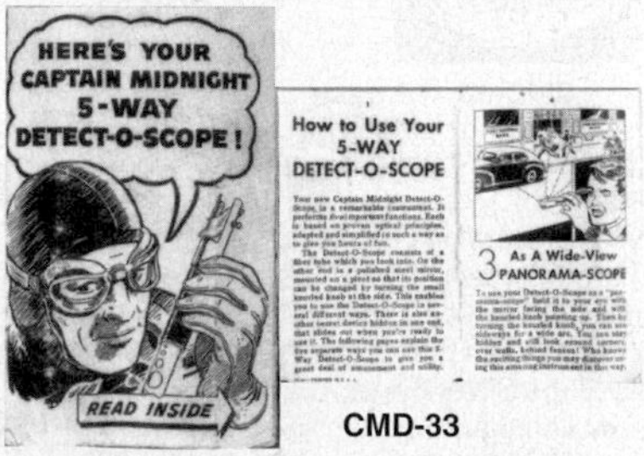

CMD-33

❑ **CMD-33. "Detect-O-Scope" Instruction Leaflet,**
1941. Came with CMD-29. - **$40 $95 $175**

CMD-34

CMD-35

❑ **CMD-34. Whirlwind Whistling Brass Ring,**
1941. No Captain Midnight markings. -
$100 $300 $850

❑ **CMD-35. "Whirlwind Whistling Ring" Instruction Sheet,**
1941. - **$100 $150 $300**

CMD-36

CMD-37

❑ **CMD-36. Flight Commander Brass Decoder Ring,**
1941. Inner side has "Captain Midnight Super Code 3". -**$125 $250 $600**

❑ **CMD-37. "Super Book Of Comics" Comic Book #3,**
1941. Various sponsors. - **$24 $72 $300**

CMD-38

CMD-39

❑ CMD-38. "Pilot's Badge" With Order Sheet,
1941. Brass wings badge. In 1933, National Chicle Company offered wings of the same design but finished in silver as a Sky Birds Chewing Gum premium available for 50 wrappers.
Sky Birds Silver Finish - **$50 $125 $250**
Capt. Midnight Gold Finish - **$150 $350 $1000**
Capt. Midnight Coupon - **$60 $125 $250**

❑ CMD-39. Pilot's Badge "Award Of Merit" Certificate,
1941. - **$90 $175 $350**

CMD-40

❑ CMD-40. Captain Midnight And Joyce Salt & Pepper Set,
c. 1941. Pair of 2.75" tall painted plaster figural shakers finished largely in yellow outfits. - **$50 $100 $175**

CMD-41

CMD-42

❑ CMD-41. Club Manual,
1942. - **$75 $165 $285**

❑ CMD-42. Manual Insert,
1942. Paper sheet. Owner was instructed to "Tear Out and Destroy After Reading!" Explains how instructions to use "Master Code 6" are to fool outsiders and to actually use "Master Code 2." Loose Insert - **$20 $40 $75**

CMD-43

❑ CMD-43. "Flight Commander" Club Manual,
1942. Leaflet including "Official Commission" certification panel. - **$100 $225 $425**

CMD-44

❑ CMD-44. Movie Serial Blotter,
1942. 4x9" promo card for 15-chapter Columbia serial. Text includes offer of member card for "Saturday Morning 10:30 A.M. Kiddie Club." - **$85 $175 $275**

CMD-45

CMD-46

CMD-47

❑ CMD-45. Photomatic Decoder Brass Badge,
1942. Original glossy black and white photo usually missing or replaced as club manual instructed owner to insert a photo of themselves. Manufactured in 1941, prior to Pearl Harbor attack, and used in 1942, 1943 and 1944.
With Original Photo - **$75 $150 $300**
Without Original Photo - **$35 $65 $130**

❑ CMD-46. Flight Commander Flying Cross Medal,
1942. Promoted in manual as "24-Karat Gold Finished."- **$50 $100 $200**

❑ CMD-47. Mystic Eye Detector Look-In Brass Ring,
1942. Brass eagle cover over viewer mirror, issued by Captain Midnight, Radio Orphan Annie, The Lone Ranger. - **$45 $90 $175**

CMD-48

CMD-49

❑ CMD-48. Sliding Secret Compartment Brass Ring,
1942. Also offered as Kix Pilot's Ring in 1945. - **$70 $135 $265**

❑ CMD-49. Marine Corps Insignia Brass Ring,
1942. - **$125 $300 $600**

CMD-50

❑ CMD-50. "Magic Blackout Lite-Ups" Kit With Envelope,
1942. Near Mint In Mailer - **$600**
Illustrated Folder Only - **$75 $150 $275**

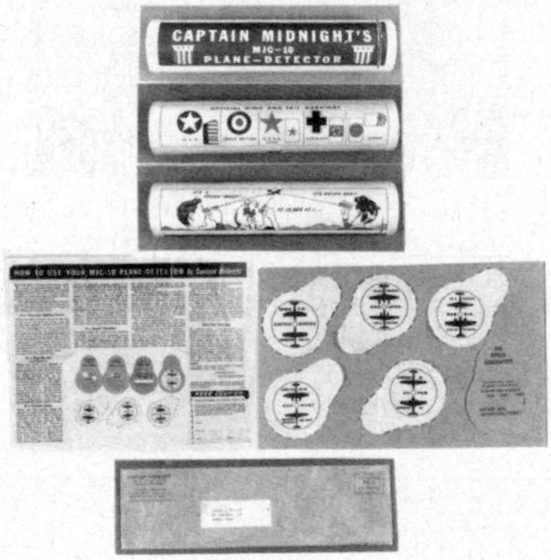

CMD-51

❑ CMD-51. MJC-10 Plane-Detector Set,
1942. Rare. Tube with seven disk inserts and 12 airplane silhouettes.
Complete - **$200 $600 $1200**
Tube Only - **$50 $200 $400**

CMD-52

❑ **CMD-52. "Joyce Of The Secret Squadron" Hardback Book,**
1942. Store item by Whitman. A Captain Midnight Adventure with Joyce Ryan
With Dust Jacket - **$15 $30 $70**
No Dust Jacket - **$8 $15 $25**

CMD-53

CMD-54

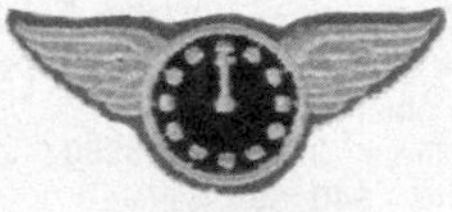

CMD-55

❑ **CMD-53. First Issue Comic Book,**
1942. Store item from Fawcett Publications September 30, 1942. - **$300 $900 $5000**

❑ **CMD-54. Newspaper Comic Strip Introduction Page,**
1942. Full page ad from Chicago Sun edition of Sunday, July 5. - **$35 $70 $165**

❑ **CMD-55. Shoulder Insignia 3-1/2" Wide Fabric Patch,**
1943. - **$65 $145 $250**

CMD-56

❑ **CMD-56. "Captain Midnight and the Moon Woman" Better Little Book #1452,**
1943. - **$25 $75 $175**

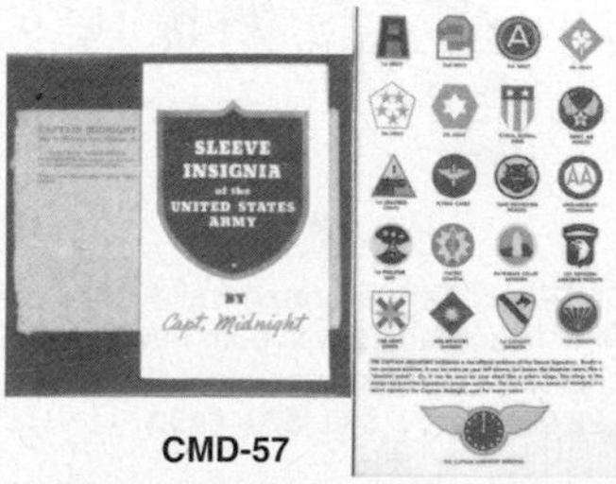

CMD-57

❑ **CMD-57. Army "Sleeve Insignia" Folder With Envelope,**
1943. Came with Captain Midnight insignia.
Folder - **$65 $135 $240**
Envelope - **$10 $30 $60**

CMD-58

❑ **CMD-58. "Captain Midnight" Boxed Puzzle,**
1943. From "Favorite Funnies" series of comic strip characters by Jaymar, assembling to full color Captain Midnight panel-style story. - **$75 $150 $275**

CMD-59

❑ **CMD-59. "Blue Feature News" With Captain Midnight,**
1943. Blue Network Co. 10.5x15.5" one-sided newspaper format sheet Vol. 2 #7 New York issue for March 22. Captain Midnight is featured by photo and text in addition to other popular radio programs of the era. - **$35 $75 $125**

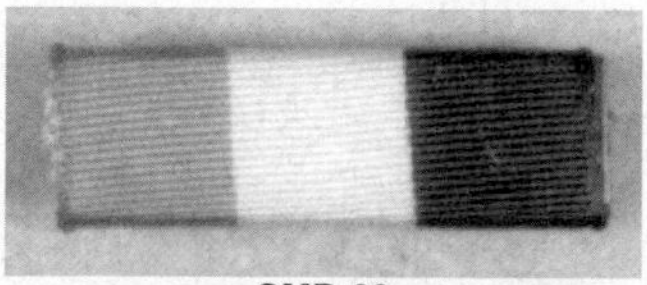

CMD-60

❑ **CMD-60. Distinguished Service Ribbon,**
1944. - **$85 $190 $335**

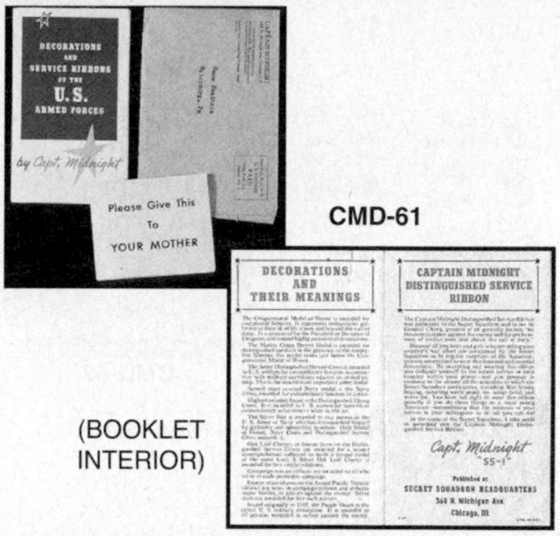

CMD-61

(BOOKLET INTERIOR)

❑ **CMD-61. Service Ribbon Booklet,**
1944. Radio premium.
Booklet - **$70 $145 $260**
Mailer - **$10 $30 $60**
Mother's Letter - **$5 $10 $20**

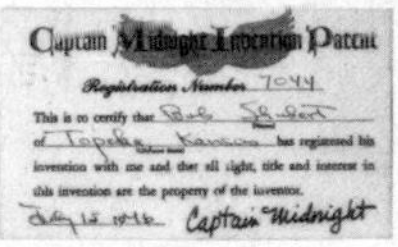

CMD-62

CMD-63

❑ **CMD-62. "Invention Patent" Acknowledgement Postcard,**
1944. Fawcett comic book premium. Assigns registration number for unknown invention by youthful fan. - **$75 $135 $265**

❑ **CMD-63. Club Manual,**
1945. - **$50 $115 $250**

CMD-64

CMD-65

CMD-66

❑ **CMD-64. Magni-Magic Decoder Metal Badge,**
1945. Produced in Fall 1944, stamped from sheet steel and overcoated in "gold" paint. Production was limited and demand exceeded supply. - **$60 $135 $225**

❑ **CMD-65. Mirro-Flash Code-O-Graph Brass Decoder,**
1946. - **$40 $100 $200**

❑ **CMD-66. Mystic Sun God Ring,**
1946. - **$200 $400 $800**

CMD-67

CMD-68

❑ **CMD-67. Mystic Sun-God Ring Leaflet,**
1946. - **$80 $150 $300**

❑ **CMD-68. Club Manual,**
1946. - **$60 $115 $240**

CMD-69

❑ **CMD-69. "Captain Midnight and Sheik Jomak Khan" Better Little Book #1402,**
1946. - **$24 $72 $165**

CMD-70

❑ **CMD-70. "Shake Up Game,"**
1947. Four page folder. Came with Ovaltine Mug 3.25x4". - **$100 $200 $400**

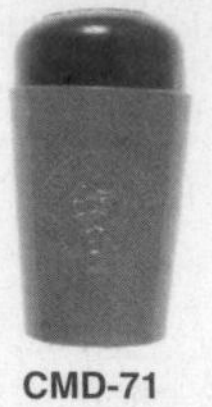

CMD-71

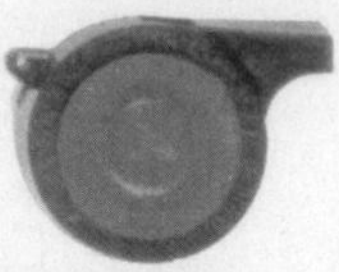

CMD-72

❑ **CMD-71. Shake-Up Mug,**
1947. Portrait on orange plastic with blue lid. A variation is known, perhaps a manufacturing test or error, with a blue top on a creamy white cup.
Orange Version - **$40 $85 $175**
White Version - **$175 $350 $700**

❑ **CMD-72. Whistling Code-O-Graph Plastic Decoder,**
1947. Whistle with movable code wheel. -
$45 $80 $140

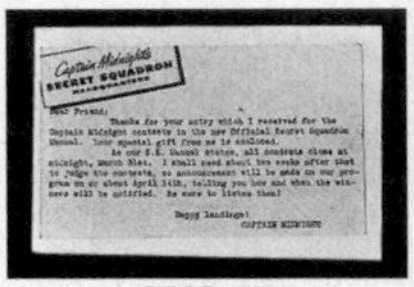

CMD-73

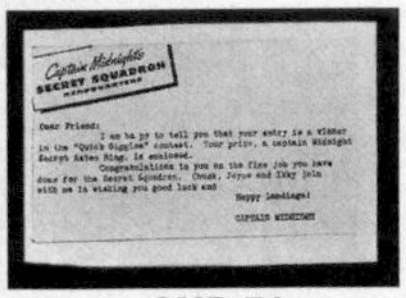

CMD-74

❑ **CMD-73. Contest Entry Acknowledgement,**
1947. Thank you card to entrant of contest closing March 31 with winners to be announced on radio program on or about April 14. -
$25 $75 $150

❑ **CMD-74. "Quick Giggles" Contest Winner Notification,**
1947. Winner's notice including prize "Secret Aztec Ring" (Mystic Sun God Ring). -
$25 $75 $150

CMD-75

❑ **CMD-75. Manual,**
1947. First of smaller format. - **$65 $130 $200**

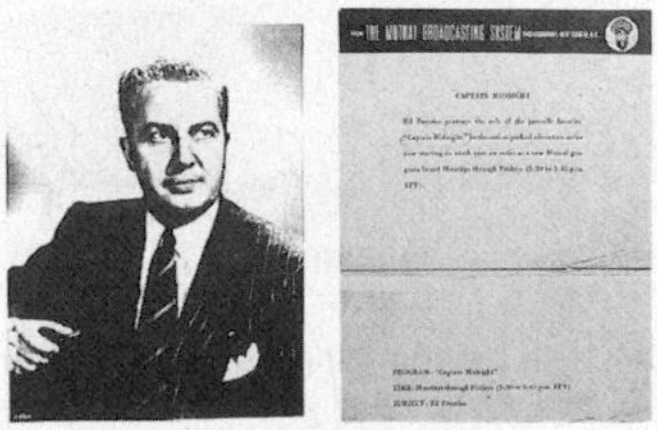

CMD-76

❑ **CMD-76. Ed Prentiss Publicity Photo,**
1947. The Mutual Broadcasting System. Glossy 8x10" with back label noting "Ninth Year On Radio" now "As A New Mutual Program." -
$40 $90 $150

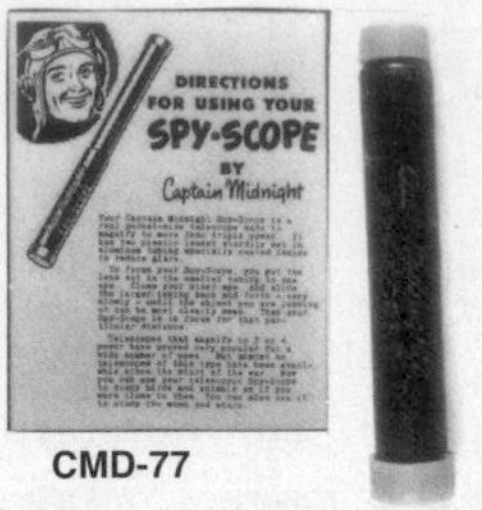

CMD-77

CMD-78

CMD-79

❑ **CMD-77. "Spy-Scope" With Instructions,**
1947. Black aluminum small telescope in two varieties of plastic rims.
Rare Blue Rims - **$75 $175 $350**
Orange Rims - **$40 $85 $175**
Instructions - **$30 $45 $90**

❑ **CMD-78. Mirro-Magic Brass/Plastic Decoder,**
1948. Red plastic reverse usually warped and often missing. - **$90 $175 $275**

❑ **CMD-79. Initial Printing Ring,**
1948. Brass ring with personalized single initial designated by orderer. - **$110 $225 $450**

CMD-80

❑ **CMD-80. Manual,**
1948 - **$70 $140 $215**

CMD-81

❑ **CMD-81. "Tattoo Transfers" Kit,**
c. 1948. "Pack No. 8" with both Fawcett and Wander Co. (Ovaltine) copyright. Two sheets with 22 transfers. - **$30 $70 $150**

CMD-82

❑ **CMD-82. Iron-On Transfer With Mailer Envelope,**
1949. Scarce. Cellophane transfer on tissue sheet with reverse lettering for application to fabric.
Envelope - **$15 $35 $65**
Transfer - **$40 $90 $185**

CMD-83

❑ **CMD-83. Club Manual,**
1949. - **$50 $140 $275**

CMD-85

CMD-84

❑ **CMD-84. Key-O-Matic Code-O-Graph Brass Decoder,**
1949. Without key. - **$45 $85 $185**

❑ **CMD-85. Key-O-Matic Code-O-Graph Brass Key,**
1949. Used with decoder to set letter and number combinations. - **$100 $200 $300**

CMD-86

❑ **CMD-86. Three-Sheet,**
1940s. Scarce. Columbia Pictures serial, 41" by 81". - **$2500 $5500 $7750**

CMD-87

CMD-88

❑ **CMD-87. "Captain Midnight" Litho. Button,**
1940s. Scarce. Issuer unknown. Pictures him at radio microphone, no identification other than his name. - **$400 $800 $1200**

❑ **CMD-88. Plaster Figure,**
1940s. Store item from series of characters (76 known). Issued between 1941-1947 in white plaster to be painted.
Captain Midnight - **$50 $100 $150**
Most Others- **$5 $10 $15**

CMD-89

❑ **CMD-89. "Hot Ovaltine Mug" Leaflet And Related Papers,**
1953. Three pieces included in the box which held the 1953 plastic mug.
Mug Brochure - **$25 $45 $85**
"Mother" Folder - **$5 $10 $20**
"Caution" Slip - **$3 $5 $10**

CMD-90

❑ **CMD 90. Plastic Mug With Decal,**
1953. - **$20 $40 $75**

CMD-91

❑ **CMD-91. Ovaltine Sales Staff Multi-Function Pocketknife,**
c. 1953. Approx. 3" long with red grips.
- **$100 $200 $400**

CMD-92

❑ **CMD-92. Membership Card,**
1955-56. - **$40 $75 $140**

CMD-93

❑ **CMD-93. Manual,**
1955-56. Scarce. - **$60 $200 $350**

CMD-94

❑ **CMD-94. Flight Commander Kit,**
1955-56. Envelope - **$10 $20 $30**
Certificate - **$85 $135 $275**
Handbook - **$125 $225 $450**

CMD-95

CMD-96

CMD-97

❑ **CMD-95. "SQ" Plane Puzzle Decoder Plastic Badge,**
1955-56. Near Mint Decoder With Mailer, Letter And Cardboard Holder- **$600**
Decoder Only - **$125 $250 $400**

❑ **CMD-96. "SQ" Cloth Peel-Off Patch,**
1955-56. Unused - **$10 $25 $50**

❑ **CMD-97. Mailer and Letter,**
1955. Mailer and cardboard insert for 1955 decoder. Letter descibes the rocket power of Ovaltine and its benefits.
Letter - **$25 $50 $100**
Mailer - **$25 $50 $100**

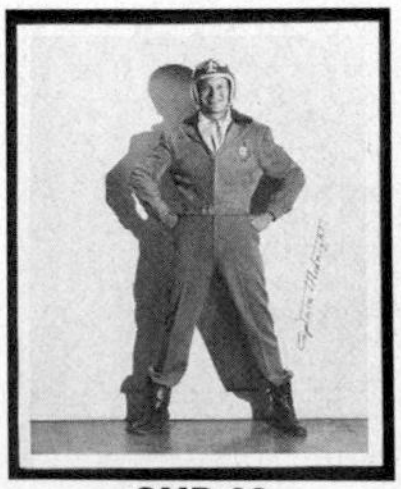

CMD-98

CMD-99

❑ **CMD-98. Photo,**
1955. Scarce. TV promotion premium. - **$75 $175 $300**

❑ **CMD-99. Richard Webb Photo,**
c. 1955. Issuer unknown. 4x4-1/2" photo. No inscriptions. - **$30 $60 $110**

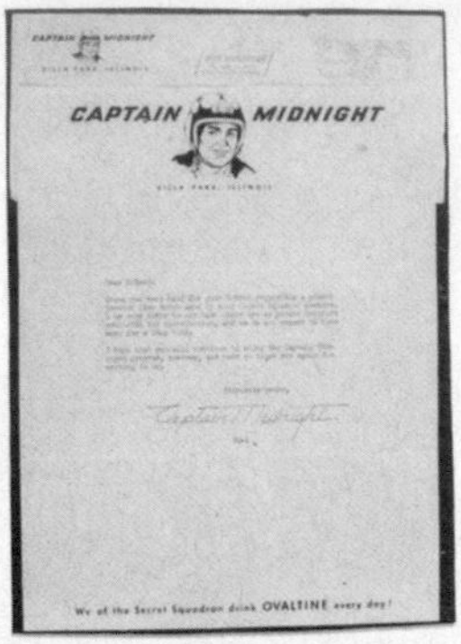

CMD-100

❑ **CMD-100. Ovaltine Premium Letter Of Apology With Envelope,**
1956. Explains "pocket locators" are no longer available. Envelope **- $10 $20 $30**
Letter - **$60 $125 $235**

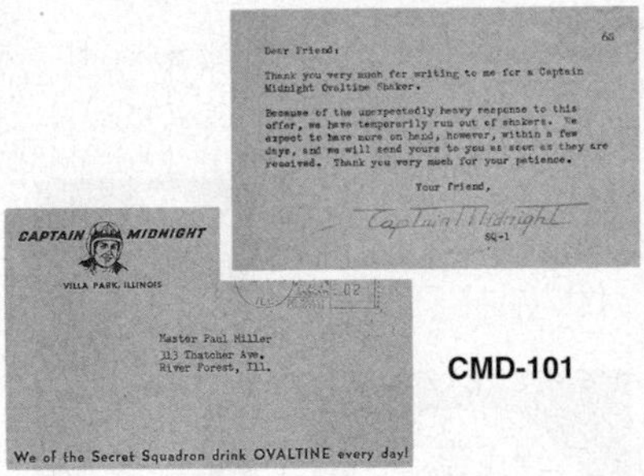

CMD-101

❑ **CMD-101. Postcard Notice,**
1957. Rare. Notice that Ovaltine ran out of shakers and will send when new shipments arrive. - **$50 $100 $165**

CMD-102

❑ **CMD-102. "Secret Squadron" Membership Kit,**
1957.
Complete With Envelope - **$150 $350 $700**
Club Manual - **$60 $150 $250**
Member Card - **$30 $50 $75**
Silver Dart Decoder - **$75 $175 $350**

CMD-103

CMD-104

❑ **CMD-103. Peel-Off Cloth Patch,**
1957. Unused - **$10 $20 $45**

❑ **CMD-104. Silver Dart "SQ" Jet Plane Decoder Plastic Badge,**
1957. - **$75 $175 $350**

CMD-105

CMD-106

❑ **CMD-105. Flight Commander Signet Ring,**
1957. Silvered plastic depicting jet plane inscribed "SQFC". - **$275 $600 $1250**

❑ **CMD-106. Plastic Shake-Up Mug,**
1957. - **$30 $60 $100**

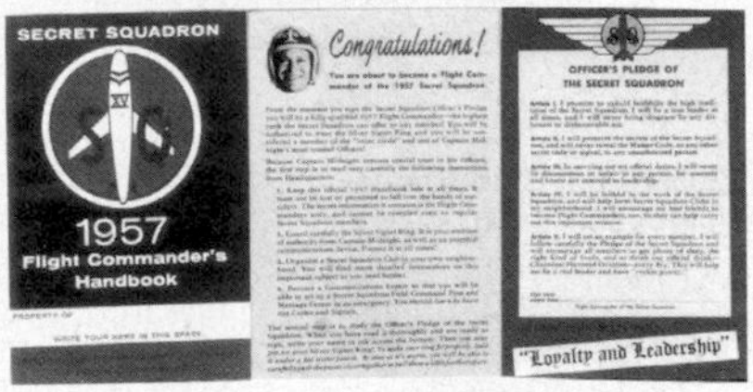

CMD-107

❑ **CMD-107. "Flight Commander's Handbook",**
1957. - **$125 $250 $475**

CMD-108

❑ **CMD-108. Flight Commander Commission Reproduction Certificate,**
c. 1970. Longines Symphonette Society. Accompanied vinyl records re-issue of radio programs. - **$10 $18 $30**

CMD-109

CMD-110

❑ **CMD-109. Flexible Record With Sleeve,**
c. 1970. Longines Symphonette Society. Set of eight radio show program recordings.
Each - **$3 $5 $8**

❑ **CMD-110. Punch-Out Decoder,**
c. 1970. Longines Symphonette Society.
Unpunched - **$10 $15 $25**

CMD-111

❑ **CMD-111. Record,**
1972. Ovaltine premium with sleeve. - **$15 $25 $50**

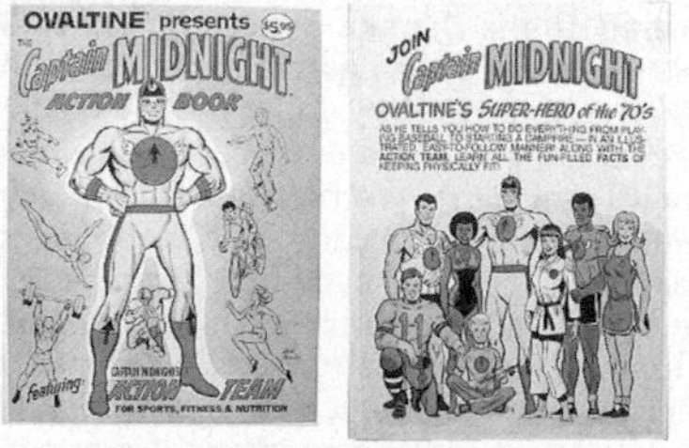

CMD-112

❑ **CMD-112. Ovaltine Action Book,**
1977. Ovaltine Products Inc. Published by Marvel Comics Group about 8x10-1/2" with 128 pages. Includes offers for cash and Ovaltine labels of two Captain Midnight records, an Orphan Annie record and an Ovaltine collector's mug showing a Swiss village. - **$35 $70 $125**

CMD-113

❑ **CMD-113. Captain Midnight Record,**
1977. Contains four adventures from the radio show. - **$15 $25 $50**

CMD-114

❑ **CMD-114. "Secret Squadron Watch" Promo Kit,**
1988. Ovaltine store promotion. - **$20 $35 $70**

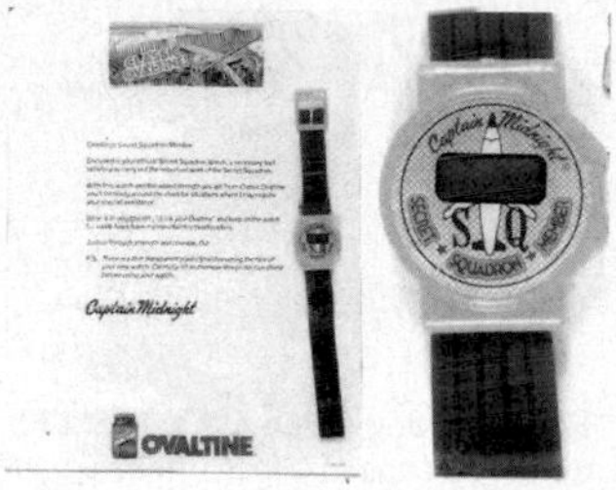

CMD-115

❑ **CMD-115. Cover Letter And Watch,**
1987. Offered for Ovaltine 30th anniversary year of 1988. Letter - **$10 $12 $25**
Watch- **$20 $50 $100**

CMD-116

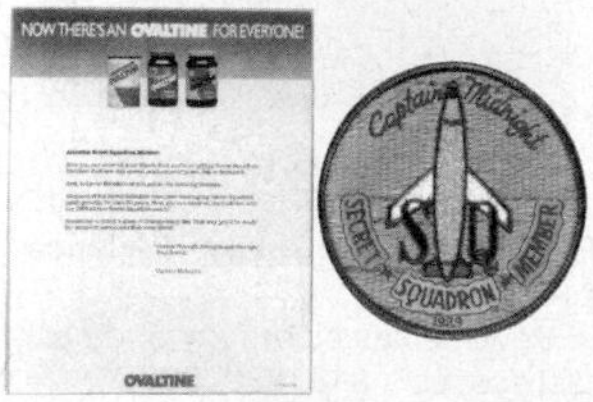

CMD-117

❑ **CMD-116. Cover Letter And T-Shirt,**
1988. Ovaltine 30th Anniversary Premium.
Letter - **$6 $12 $18**
T-Shirt- **$8 $20 $40**

❑ **CMD-117. Cover Letter And Patch,**
1989. Ovaltine offer from preceding 30th anniversary year of 1988. Letter - **$4 $8 $15**
Patch - **$8 $18 $35**

Captain Tim Healy

Kids interested in collecting postage stamps in the 1930s and 1940s could tune in their radios to the Tim Healy programs. From 1934 to 1945 under a variety of names – *Stamp Club, Ivory Stamp Club, Captain Tim's Adventures, Calling All Stamp Collectors* and *Captain Tim Healy's Adventure Stories* – and sponsored by Ivory soap or Kellogg's Pep cereal, real-life explorer and world traveler Tim Healy described the romance of stamps and encouraged kids to become collectors. The few premiums offered were, naturally, stamp-related.

CTH-1

CTH-2

❑ **CTH-1. Ivory Soap Stamp Club Album With Letter And Envelope,**
1934. Cover Letter - **$10 $20 $40**
Album - **$12 $25 $40**

❑ **CTH-2. Member's Stamp-Shaped Brass Pin,**
1934. Ivory Soap.
Red Background - **$10 $20 $35**
Black Background - **$20 $50 $125**

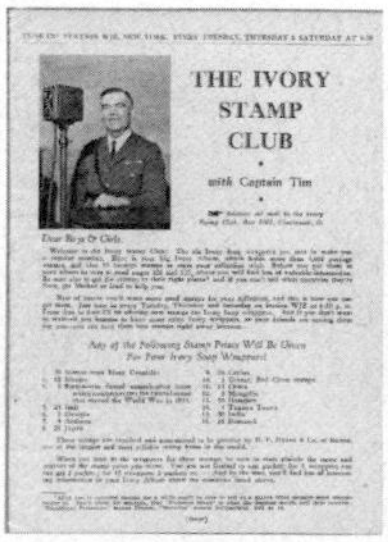

CTH-3

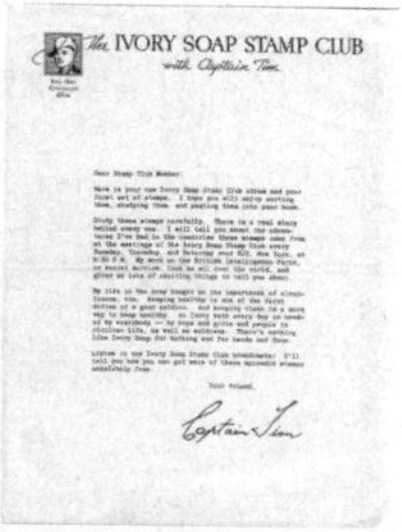

CTH-4

❑ **CTH-3. "Ivory Stamp Club" Ad,**
1934. - **$10 $20 $40**

❑ **CTH-4. "Ivory Stamp Club" Letter,**
1934. - **$10 $20 $40**

CTH-5

❑ CTH-5. Packet of Stamps,
1934. Offered on WJZ radio Tuesdays, Thursdays and Saturdays - 16 stamps for 4 Ivory Soap wrappers. Stamps were guaranteed by a Boston firm to be genuine. Stamps were displayed in albums also offered on the show. Each packet - **$15 $30 $60**

CTH-6

❑ CTH-6. "Ivory Stamp Club" Folder,
1934. Ivory Soap. Closed 4x6" sheet that opens to four panels printed in color on both sides to illustrate 68-page stamp album offered by Captain Tim Healy. - **$12 $25 $45**

CTH-7

CTH-8

❑ CTH-7. Stamp Club Book,
1934. Ivory Soap. Features pictures of Stamps of the World.- **$20 $35 $70**
Mailer - **$5 $10 $15**

❑ CTH-8. Ivory Stamp Club Album With Envelope,
c. 1935. Ivory Soap. - **$12 $28 $45**

CTH-9

CTH-10

❑ CTH-9. "Spies I Have Known" Booklet,
1936. Ivory Soap. Photo-illustrated stories about famous spies known by Captain Tim Healy. - **$20 $35 $70**

❑ CTH-10. Autographed Captain Tim Healy Photo,
c. 1938. Ivory Soap. - **$18 $30 $65**

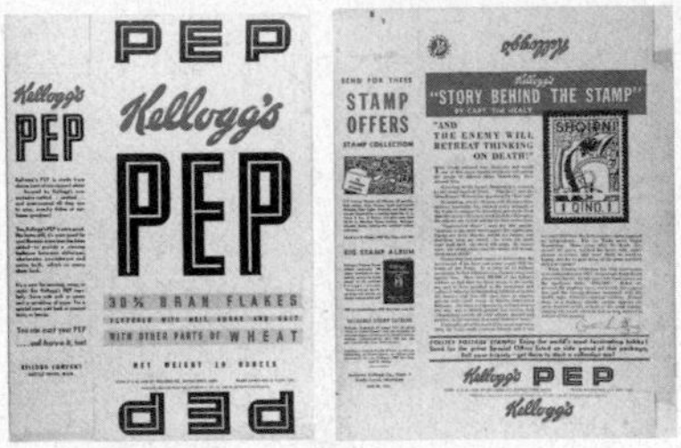

CTH-11

❑ CTH-11. Kellogg's Pep Cereal Box Flat,
1938. 10 oz. box has Captain Tim Healy stamp offer and story about stamps, the usual focus of the radio show. - **$40 $75 $175**

CTH-12

❑ CTH-12. "Capt. Tim Healy" Dixie Ice Cream Picture,
c. 1939. Reverse has biography and radio broadcast scenes. - **$18 $30 $60**

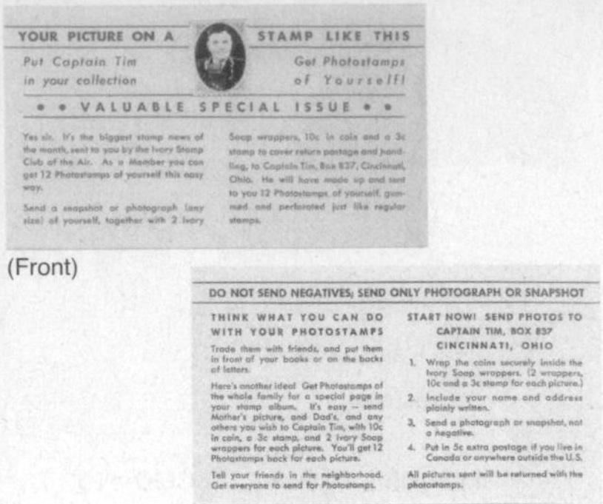

(Front)

CTH-13 (Back)

❑ CTH-13. "Captain Tim Photostamp" Card,
1930s. Ivory Stamp Club. 3-1/4x5-1/2" card with photo stamp of Captain Tim telling club members how to receive set of 12 "Photostamps" picturing themselves. Laminated stamp shows him at the microphone. Ivory Soap sponsored this promotion. Two wrappers, 10¢ and a 3¢ stamp were sent with your photo to get 12 photo stamps. - **$50 $100 $165**

CTH-14

❑ CTH-14. Dixie Ice Cream Picture,
c. 1940. - **$20 $35 $70**

Captain Video

Captain Video **was television's first venture into the solar system, beating Buck Rogers by a year. Created by Larry Menkin, the show premiered on the Dumont network in June 1949 with Richard Coogan as the super cop, a role taken over in 1951 by Al Hodge (1912-1979). The series, one of the most popular children's shows of its time, was notoriously low-budget, with props made of cardboard or household items, but it featured such futuristic devices as an Opticon Scillometer, a Radio Scillograph, an Atomic Rifle, a Discatron and a Cosmic Ray Vibrator. Sponsors such as Post cereals and Power House candy bars offered many premiums--rings, a plastic ray gun, a Captain Video helmet, a Rite-O-Lite flashlight and Luma-Glo card for writing secret messages. The series ended its network run in 1955, went local in New York City in 1956 and finally dissolved in 1957. The Captain appeared in comic books in 1949-1951 and a 15-episode chapter play with Judd Holdren in the title role was released by Columbia Pictures in 1951.**

CVD-1

CVD-2

❑ **CVD-1. Picture Ring,**
c. 1950. Power House candy bars. Brass holding plastic dome over black/white photo of Richard Coogan holding ray gun. -
$100 $185 $350

❑ **CVD-2. "Picture Ring" Instruction Leaflet,**
c. 1950. Power House candy bars. -
$45 $100 $200

CVD-3

❑ **CVD-3. Captain Video #1 Comic Book,**
1951. Fawcett Publications. - **$107 $321 $1500**

CVD-4

❑ **CVD-4. "Captain Video" Original Art Prototype Sign,**
1951. 14x21" for proposed premium tie-in campaign between Post's Raisin Bran and local theaters for 1951 Columbia Pictures Captain Video serial. Gordon Gold Archives. Unique. - **$850**

CVD-5

❑ **CVD-5. Post Toasties "Flying Saucer Ring" Set,**
1951. Base in brass or silver luster, saucers of metal or plastic, non-glow or glow-in-dark.
Near Mint Boxed - **$900**
Ring And Two Saucers - **$225 $475 $775**

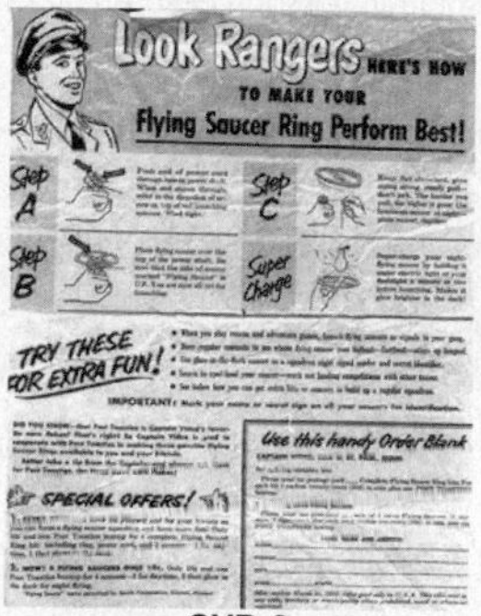

CVD-6

❑ **CVD-6. "Flying Saucer Ring" Instruction Sheet,**
1951. Post Toasties. Includes order coupon for additional rings with expiration date March 31, 1952. - **$90 $175 $260**

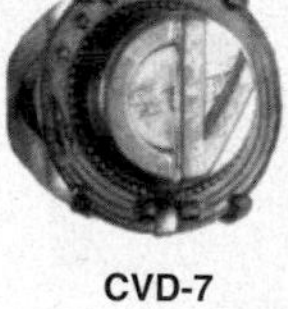

CVD-7

CVD-8

❑ **CVD-7. "CV" Secret Seal Brass Ring,**
1951. Two-piece top is designed to emboss in paper "CV" initials, but top cover frequently snapped off. Rim pictures tiny rocketship and four stars. Complete - **$125 $250 $600**
Missing Top - **$35 $65 $125**

❑ **CVD-8. "Secret Seal Ring" Leaflet And Card,**
1951. Power House candy bar. Instructions plus identification card. - **$115 $250 $375**

CVD-9

❑ **CVD-9. "Flying Saucer Ring" Instruction Sheet,**
1951. Power House Candy Bar. Different design than Post Toasties version. - **$50 $100 $200**

CVD-10

❑ **CVD-10. "Captain Video" Spaceship Set,**
1951. Lido Toy Product. Sets #2101 and #2102 were produced, containing different spaceships and accessories. Great packaging graphics! -
$160 $300 $600

CVD-11

❑ **CVD-11. Original Art Prototype Movie Theater Sign,**
1951. Prepared for proposed premium tie-in campaign between Post's Raisin Bran and local theaters for the 1951 Columbia Pictures Captain Video serial. Gordon Gold Archives.
Unique. - **$825**

CVD-12

❑ **CVD-12. Cast Photo,**
1951. Cast photo, 5-1/2" x 6-7/8". Rare.
- **$110 $200 $300**

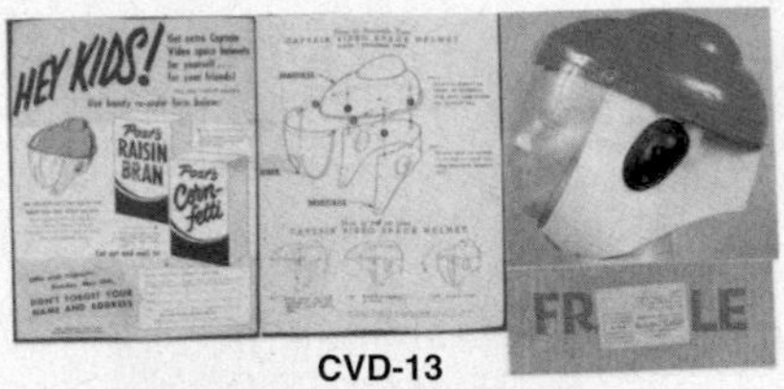

CVD-13

❑ **CVD-13. "Official Captain Video Space Helmet" Boxed Premium,**
c. 1951. Post's Raisin Bran. Fragile thin plastic. Premium version, see next item.
Near Mint Boxed with Insert Flier **- $675**

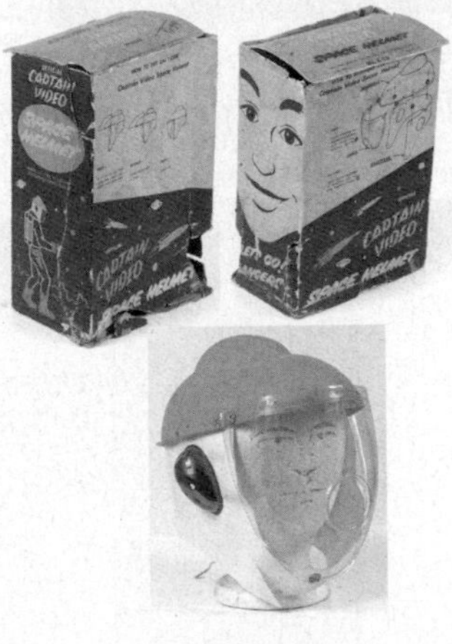

CVD-14

❑ **CVD-14. "Official Captain Video Space Helmet,"**
c. 1951. Box is 7.5x11x4.5" deep and contains three-piece helmet. There were two versions made, one a premium and one sold in stores. This is store version. Helmet is made out of thin fragile plastic. Front face shield can swing up to further reveal face. Store Box - **$60 $115 $225**
Helmet - **$60 $115 $225**

CVD-15

❑ **CVD-15. Original Art Prototype For Newspaper Ad,**
c. 1951. Post's Raisin Bran Cereal. 11x16" colorful original art titled "Join Captain Video's Ranger's Club And Get A Complete Membership Kit." Gordon Gold Archives. Unique. - **$850**

CVD-16 CVD-17

❑ **CVD-16. "Captain Video" Ink Signed Photo,**
c. 1951. Black and white 5-1/2x6-1/2". -
$40 $85 $185

❑ **CVD-17. Cast Photo,**
c. 1951. Facsimile signatures of Al Hodge and Don Hastings. - **$30 $50 $125**

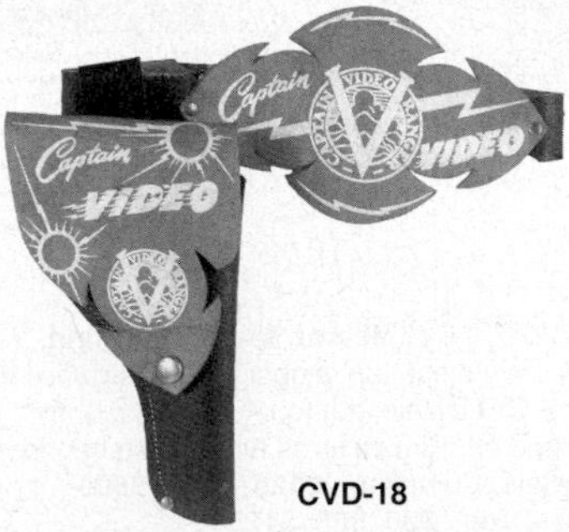

CVD-18

❑ **CVD-18. "Captain Video Ranger" Holster,**
c. 1951. Painted leather holster 5.25x9.25" and belt has 5x8.25" buckle section. Buckle has a 2.5" "Captain Video Ranger" logo and holster has 1-7/8" logo of same design.
- **$175 $350 $650**

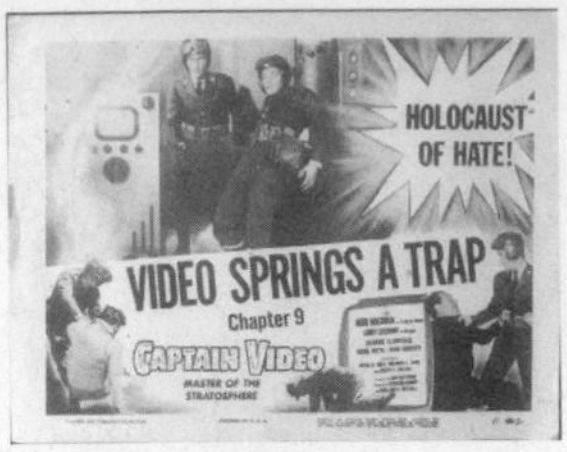

CVD-19

❑ **CVD-19. Lobby Card,**
1952. 11x14" for Chapter 9 "Video Springs A Trap" from 15-chapter serial by Columbia Pictures.
Each Picturing Captain Video - **$60 $145 $290**
Each Without Captain Video - **$30 $55 $85**

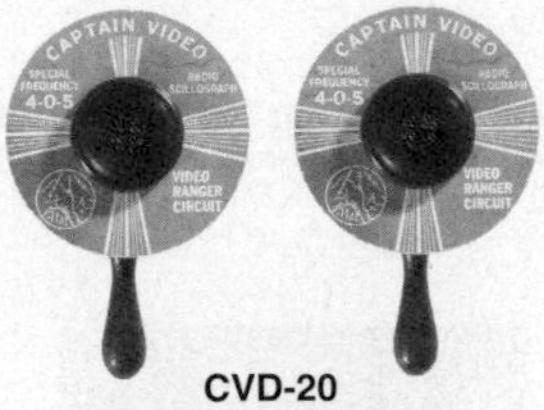

CVD-20

CVD-21

❑ **CVD-20. Radio Scillograph Set,**
1952. TV premium advertised in comics. Rare.
- **$125 $250 $500**

❑ **CVD-21. "Ranger" Cardboard Badge,**
1952. Badge came with pin on back. Came with Radio Scillograph set advertised in comics. TV premium. - **$85 $140 $250**

CVD-22

❑ **CVD-22. Mock-Up Test Photos For Proposed Premium,**
c. 1952. Issuer unknown. Pair of 4x5" black and white photos to test concept of including child's photo with Captain Video in rocketship cockpit. Only two examples we've seen.
Each Near Mint - **$350**

CVD-23

❑ **CVD-23. Captain Video Space Man,**
1953. Post's Raisin Bran. Hard plastic set of 12. Each - **$10 $20 $35**

CVD-24

❑ **CVD-24. "Secret Ray Gun",**
1950s. Power House candy bars. Includes instruction sheet and "Luma-Glo" card. Instruction sheet also seen with gun, titled as "Rite-O-Lite."
Complete - **$50 $100 $225**
Gun Only - **$25 $40 $90**

CVD-25

❑ **CVD-25. "Captain Video" Suspenders,**
1950s. Store item. - **$40 $70 $125**

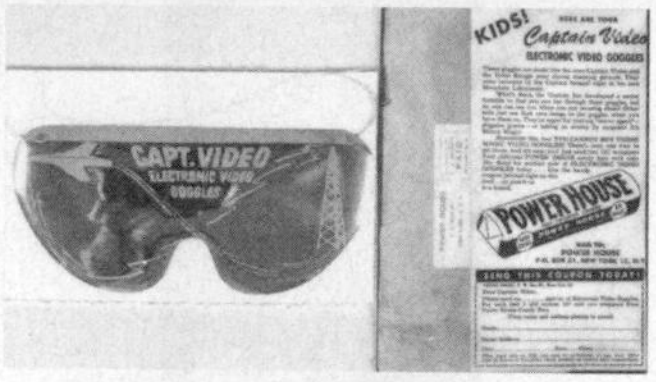

CVD-26

CVD-27

❑ **CVD-26. "Electronic Video Goggles" With Envelope,**
1950s. Power House candy bars.
In Envelope - **$125 $175 $400**
Loose - **$100 $185 $300**

❑ **CVD-27. "Video Ranger" Club Member Card,**
1950s. Scarce. Probable Post's Cereals. - **$60 $150 $250**

CVD-28

CVD-29

❑ **CVD-28. Purity Bread Litho. Tin Tab,**
1950s. - **$20 $40 $85**

❑ **CVD-29. Mysto-Coder Brass Decoder With Clip Fastener,**
1950s. Front has red plastic removable dome over Captain Video photo, back has two plastic code wheels. - **$100 $250 $500**

CVD-30

❑ **CVD-30. Plastic Rocket Ring/Pendant With Keychain,**
1950s. Rocketship includes glow portrait of Captain Video, magnifying glass and whistle.
Ring - **$250 $400 $800**
Instructions - **$75 $150 $250**

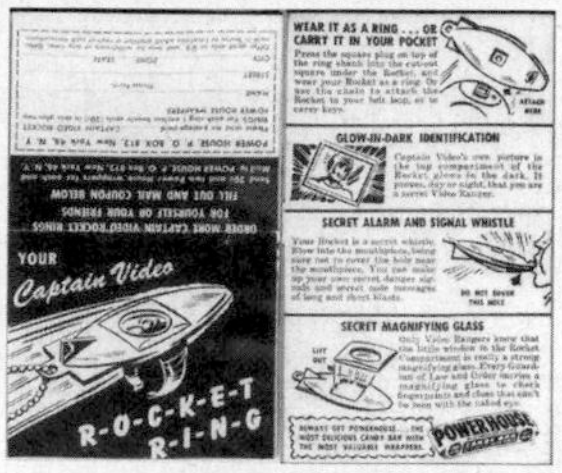

CVD-31

❑ **CVD-31. "Rocket Ring" Instruction Sheet,**
1950s. Scarce. Power House candy bars. - **$75 $150 $250**

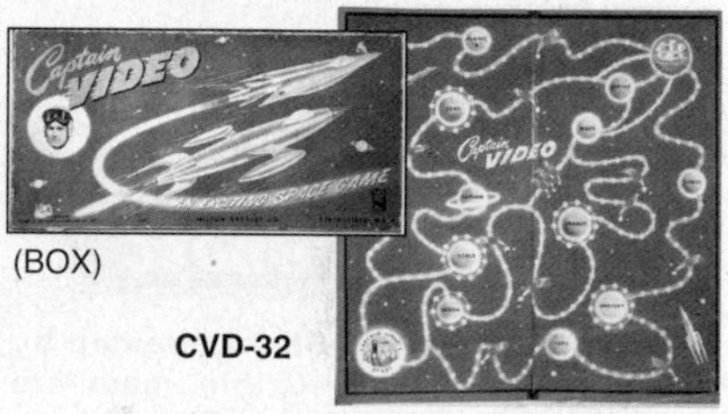

(BOX)

CVD-32

(GAME BOARD)

❑ **CVD-32. "Captain Video" Space Game,**
1950s. Scarce. Milton Bradley product.
Complete - **$210 $435 $650**
Board Only - **$60 $115 $165**

CVD-33

❑ **CVD-33. "Sunbeam Video Ranger" Club Button,**
1950s. 1-1/8" litho printed in black and white photo and red text on cream background. - **$115 $230 $350**

Casey, Crime Photographer

Flashgun Casey, Press Photographer, Crime Photographer--under whatever name, "the ace cameraman who covers the crime news of a great city" for the *Morning Express* was first broadcast on CBS in 1943. With Staats Cotsworth as the crusading crime fighter, the program ran until 1950, then was revived from 1953 to 1955. Sponsors included the Anchor Hocking Glass Co., Toni Home Permanents and Philip Morris cigarettes. A television adaptation for CBS (1951-1952) featured Richard Carlyle, then Darren McGavin, in the title role. A brief run of comic books appeared in 1949-1950.

CCP-1

❑ CCP-1. Photo Of Cast,
1940s. - **$40 $75 $135**

Casper the Friendly Ghost

Casper, The Friendly Ghost, created by Seymour Reit and Joe Oriolo, made his debut in animated cartoons in 1945 and has grown over the years into a merchandising giant through films, comic books, and television series. Between 1950 and 1959 Paramount/Famous Studios produced 62 *Casper* cartoons telling the simple story of the ghost who just wanted to make friends, not scare people. ("A g-g-ghost!") Casper made his first television appearance in 1959 on ABC in *Matty's Funday Funnies*, sponsored by Mattel toys. Other series followed in 1963, 1969, and *1979 (Casper and the Angels*, NBC). Two NBC specials, *Casper's Halloween* and *Casper's First Christmas*, also aired in 1979. The cartoons have been in syndication since 1963. A $50 million *Casper* film produced by Steven Spielberg was released in the summer of 1995, with a direct-to-video sequel that recently followed. Cast members include Good Witch Wendy, Spooky, The Ghostly Trio and Nightmare.

Casper made his first comic book appearance in 1949, then started again in 1950, and again in 1953, this time from Harvey Comics, which has also produced a wide variety of spin-off comic books and magazines. Harvey also acquired the television rights from Famous/Paramount in 1958. The merchandising of Casper has been extensive, including everything from costumes to candy dispensers to jewelry, records, toys, etc. Casper has also been an official recruiter for the Boy Scouts of America, and in 1972 he flew to the moon (painted on the side of Apollo 16).

CSP-1

❑ CSP-1. Casper Painted And Glazed Ceramic Bank,
c. 1960. American Bisque Co. 3x5x8" tall with accents to face and coin in his hand. Back of base reads "USA." Vertical coin slot at back of head. - **$65 $125 $275**

CSP-2

CSP-3

❑ CSP-2. Sliding Tile Puzzle On Card,
c. 1961. Store item by Roalex Co. Plastic puzzle for forming images of Casper, Katnip, Baby Huey, Little Audrey. On Card - **$35 $75 $135**
Loose - **$15 $30 $50**

❑ CSP-3. Talking Doll Made Of Terrycloth Fabric With Plastic Face,
1962. Store item by Mattel. 16" tall.
Talking - **$75 $125 $200**
Not Talking - **$25 $50 $75**

CSP-4

❑ CSP-4. Diecut Cardboard Standee,
c. 1963. ABC-TV. Colorful 20x20" picturing "Stars Of The New Casper Cartoon Show." - **$125 $250 $550**

CSP-5

❑ CSP-5. Vinyl Lunch Box,
1966. Store item by Thermos. - **$95 $225 $400**

CSP-6

❑ CSP-6. Casper Flicker Rings,
1960s. Vending machine issue. Believed set of two with one ring showing him peeking from left edge and then as full figure with name below in green and the second showing him flying through space and then walking to the right. Both on silver luster plastic bases.
Each - **$12 $25 $55**

CSP-7 CSP-8

❑ CSP-7. "Casper" Soaky Bottle,
1960s. Colgate-Palmolive Co. store item. Hard plastic container for liquid soap. - **$12 $30 $75**

❑ CSP-8. "Wendy" Soaky Bottle,
1960s. Colgate-Palmolive Co. store item. Hard plastic container for liquid soap. - **$12 $30 $75**

CSP-9

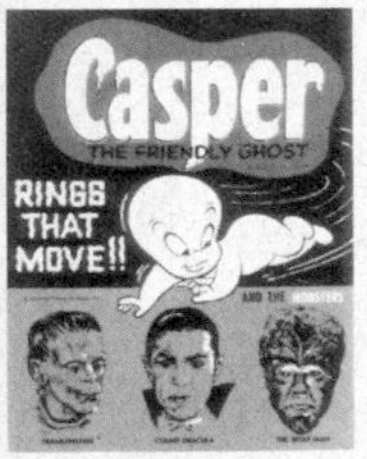

CSP-10

❑ CSP-9. "Casper's Ghostland Trick Or Treat" 12x12" Store Sign,
1960s. Thin plastic with Harvey Famous Cartoons copyright. - **$20 $40 $75**

❑ CSP-10. Vending Machine Display Paper,
1960s. Depicts Casper and shows three monsters appearing on flicker rings. - **$35 $55 $100**

CSP-11

❑ **CSP-11. Roll-Over Tank Wind-Up,**
1960s. Line Mar. Tin toy featuring Casper but also picturing other Harvey cartoon characters as passengers. Box - **$75 $125 $250**
Toy - **$100 $225 $350**

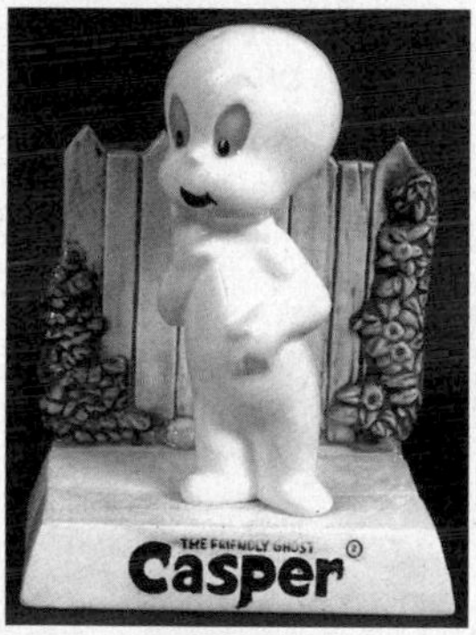

CSP-12

❑ **CSP-12. Figural Envelope Holder,**
1960s. 7" tall ceramic including background fence slotted for envelopes. - **$60 $125 $185**

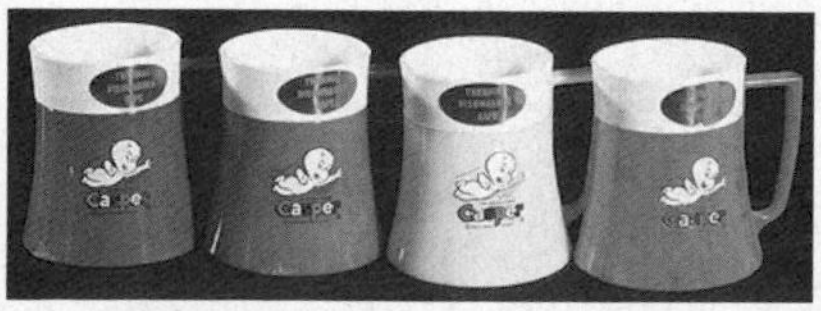

CSP-13

❑ **CSP-13. Mugs**
1971. In blue, red, yellow, and green colors. Each - **$12 $20 $50**

CSP-14

CSP-15

❑ **CSP-14. "Casper Day BSA Cub Scouts Equipment Center" 3" Cello. Button,**
1975. - **$8 $15 $35**

❑ **CSP-15. Cub Scouts Recruitment Litho. Button,**
1976. Boy Scouts of America (BSA). Harvey Comics copyright. - **$10 $15 $30**

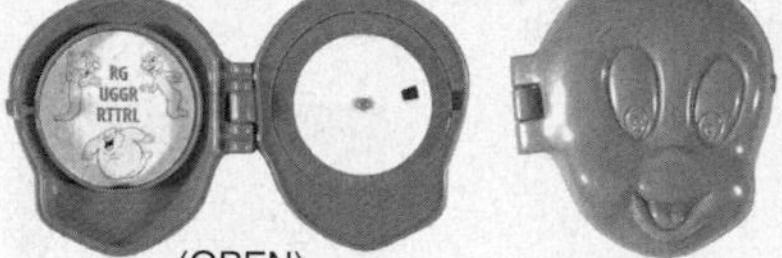

(OPEN) (CLOSED)

CSP-16

❑ **CSP-16. Plastic Decoder (Blue),**
1997. Boston Chicken premium. - **$6 $12 $35**

Cereal Boxes

See entries by name of company, program and character.

Chandu, the Magician

Chandu was actually Frank Chandler, an American secret agent who used ancient occult powers he learned from a Hindu yogi to combat evil. Created by Harry Earnshaw and Vera Oldham, the 15-minute program originated on Los Angeles radio station KHJ in 1932 and ran on Mutual until 1936, sponsored in the west by White King soap and in the east by Beech-Nut products. The series was revived in 1948, based on the original scripts, with White King again as sponsor. It had a final run as a half-hour weekly show on the ABC network in 1949-1950. Fox released a feature film in 1932 with Edmund Lowe as Chandu and Bela Lugosi as the villain Roxor. The serial *The Return of Chandu* was released in 1934 which re-cast Lugosi as Chandu. *Chandu on the Magic Island* was released in 1935 with Lugosi as Chandu.

CHA-1

❑ **CHA-1. "Chandu Book Of Magic,"**
1932. Rio Grande Oil Co. Twelve-page booklet of illustrated tricks plus sponsor ad on back cover. - **$45 $90 $185**

CHA-2

CHA-3

❑ **CHA-2. "The Return Of Chandu" Movie Serial Pressbook,**
1934. Principal Distributing Corp. -
$225 $375 $750

❑ **CHA-3. "The Return Of Chandu" 27x41" Movie Serial Poster,**
1934. Principal Distributing Corp. -
$250 $400 $800

CHA-4

❑ CHA-4. "Chandu The Magician" Softcover Little Big Book Movie Edition,
1935. Saalfield. #1323 based on film "The Return Of Chandu, The Magician" starring Bela Lugosi. Also published as Saalfield hardcover #1093. Softcover - **$16 $48 $115**
Hardcover - **$15 $45 $105**

CHA-5

❑ CHA-5. "Chandu Beech-Nut's King Of Magic" Flyer,
1930s. Glossy paper flyer is 11x18.5" and features two black and white images of Chandu, one peering into a crystal ball and the other casting a magic spell. Text also mentions the scheduled time of the program in major cities including Schenectady, Pittsburgh, Cleveland, Detroit and Chicago. - **$65 $125 $275**

CHA-6

❑ CHA-6. Radio Cast Members Photo Card,
1930s. Black and white 4.5x6.5" card with facsimile signatures of both real names and radio program names of the four major individuals. - **$60 $110 $200**

CHA-7

CHA-8

❑ CHA-7. Fan Photo,
1930s. Pictures four unidentified cast members.- **$70 $140 $225**

❑ CHA-8. Radio Listing Folder,
1930s. White King Soap. Contents include listing of stations in Central and Western United States carrying Chandu broadcasts. - **$80 $150 $285**

CHA-9

CHA-10

❑ CHA-9. "Beech-Nut's King Of Magic" Leaflet,
1930s. Contents include radio cast photo, magic trick offer. -**$30 $55 $100**

❑ CHA-10. Magic Slate,
1930s. Ernst Kerr Co., Detroit department store radio sponsor on WJR. Comes with wood stylus marker. - **$125 $300 $500**

CHA-11

❑ CHA-11. Paper Mask,
1930s. Possible Beech-Nut Gum. Probable give-away. - **$70 $150 $275**

CHA-12

CHA-13

❑ CHA-12. Chandu Club Cello Button,
1930s. - **$125 $250 $500**

❑ CHA-13. "Chandu Magicians Club" Cello. Member Button,
1930s. - **$60 $150 $300**

CHA-14

CHA-15

❑ CHA-14. "Beech-Nut Holiday Trick" Greeting Postcard,
1930s. Back lists radio cast members with holiday message. - **$30 $60 $125**

❑ CHA-15. Beech-Nut Galloping Coin Trick,
1930s. Boxed Set - **$35 $75 $150**

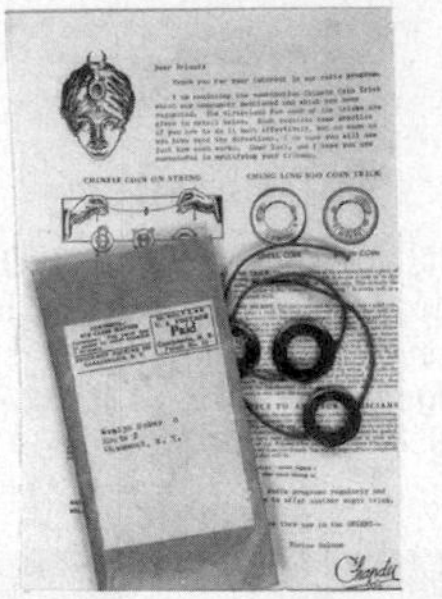

CHA-16

❑ CHA-16. "Chinese Coin On String" Trick With Mailer Envelope,
1930s. Beech-Nut Gum. - **$35 $75 $150**

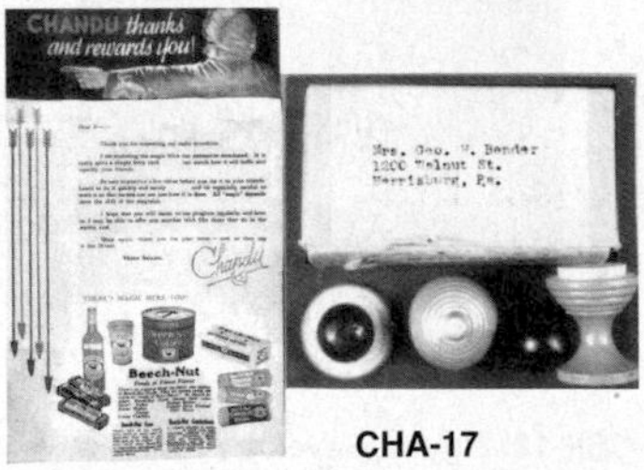

CHA-17

❑ CHA-17. "Chandu Ball And Base" Boxed Trick,
1930s. Beech-Nut Gum. With letter and instruction leaflet. - **$35 $75 $150**

CHA-18

CHA-19

❑ **CHA-18. Photo - Gayne Whitman in Costume,**
1930s. Beech-Nut Gum. - **$45 $90 $165**

❑ **CHA-19. Photo - Gayne Whitman in Business Suit,**
1930s. Beech-Nut Gum. - **$45 $90 $165**

CHA-20

CHA-21

❑ **CHA-20. "Betty Lou Regent" Portrait Print,**
1930s. Probably Beech-Nut Gum. 8-1/2x11" textured paper black and white photo also identifying Betty Webb as the portrayer. - **$30 $60 $120**

❑ **CHA-21. "Bob Regent" Portrait Print,**
1930s. Probably Beech-Nut Gum. 8-1/2x11" textured paper black and white photo also identifying Bob T. Bixby as the portrayer. - **$30 $60 $120**

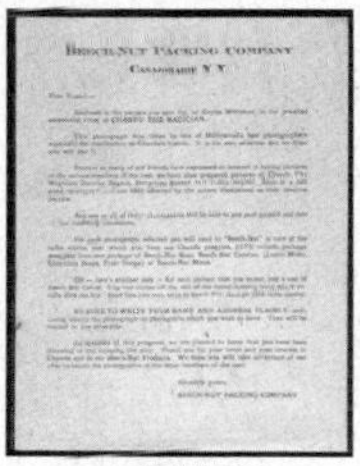
CHA-22

CHA-23

❑ **CHA-22. Letter,**
1930s. For costume photo. With color photos of products on back. - **$15 $30 $60**

❑ **CHA-23. Letter,**
1930s. For Bobby Regent photo. With color photos of products on back. - **$15 $30 $60**

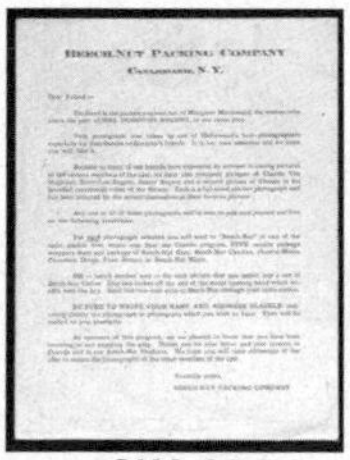
CHA-24

CHA-25

❑ **CHA-24. Letter,**
1930s. For Mrs.Bobby Regent photo. With color photos of products on back. - **$15 $30 $60**

❑ **CHA-25. Radio Broadcasts Guide 11x21" Cardboard Sign,**
1930s. Beech-Nut Gum. - **$175 $350 $750**

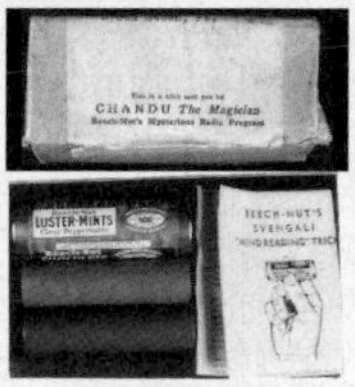
CHA-26

CHA-27

❑ **CHA-26. "Svengali Mind Reading Trick",**
1930s. Beech-Nut Gum. Boxed - **$35 $70 $150**

❑ **CHA-27. "The Great Beech-Nut Buddha Money Mystery" Packet,**
1930s. Magic trick based on Chandu radio series. -**$30 $60 $110**

CHA-28

CHA-29

❑ **CHA-28. "Hypnotized Silver Sphere" Trick With Box And Order Sheet,**
1930s. Beech-Nut Gum. - **$30 $60 $110**

❑ **CHA-29. "Chandu White King Of Magic" Boxed Trick Set,**
1930s. White King Soap.
Complete - **$125 $275 $500**

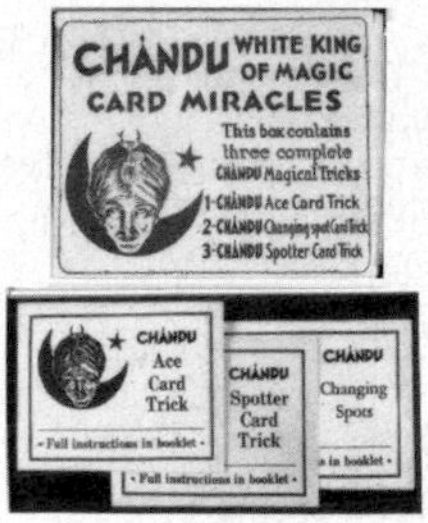

CHA-30

❑ **CHA-30. "Card Miracles" Boxed Set,**
1930s. White King Soap. - **$40 $65 $125**

CHA-31

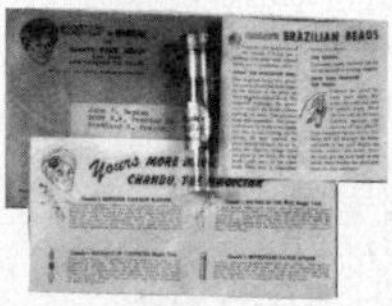

CHA-32

❑ **CHA-31. "Assyrian Money Changer" Trick With Mailer Envelope,**
1930s. White King Soap. With instruction card, wooden block, two metal bands for holding penny. - **$40 $75 $125**

❑ **CHA-32. "Brazilian Beads" Trick With Mailer Envelope,**
1930s. White King Soap. Comes with instructions, glass vial containing beads and cork. - **$40 $75 $125**

Charles Lindbergh

Charles Augustus Lindbergh (1902-1974), Midwestern farm boy, barnstorming stunt flier and airmail pilot, flew into history on May 21, 1927, when he completed the first nonstop solo flight across the Atlantic in his monoplane Spirit of St. Louis. America's Lone Eagle--Lucky, Plucky Lindy--became an instant international hero, with banner headlines, medals, awards, receptions, banquets, and a ticker tape parade up Broadway in New York City. Souvenirs and commemorative memorabilia followed in great profusion. James Stewart starred in the 1957 biographical movie *The Spirit of St. Louis.* The plane was built by Ryan Aircraft in San Diego near the site of what is now San Diego's airport, appropriately named Lindbergh Field.

To commemorate the 75th anniversary of Lindbergh's flight, his grandson, Erik Lindbergh, took off from San Diego on April 14, 2002, duplicating the cross-country and cross-Atlantic flight of his grandfather. His modern plane, named the New Spirit of St. Louis, cost $289,000 and cruised at 184 mph compared to the original plane, which was built for $10,580 and cruised at 108 mph.

CLD-1

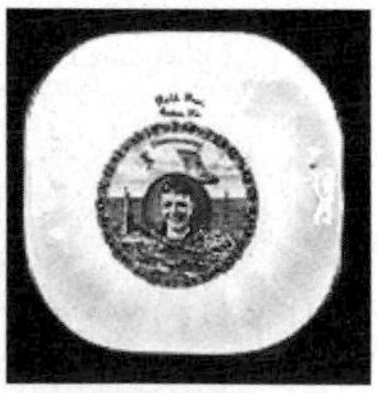
CLD-2

❑ **CLD-1. "Welcome Lindy" Cello. Button,**
1927. Depicts and names his aircraft "Spirit Of St. Louis." - **$40 $125 $250**

❑ **CLD-2. Transatlantic Flight Commemorative Plate,**
1927. Store item. 8-1/2x8-1/2" limoges china plate by "Golden Glow" process of somewhat irridescent quality on outer margin around full color Lindbergh portrait. Pictured example has imprint for local sponsor. - **$30 $55 $110**

CLD-3

CLD-4

❑ **CLD-3. "Lindy" Sheet Music,**
1927. - **$30 $50 $100**

❑ **CLD-4. Spirit Of St. Louis Pin,**
1927. Brass pin on card - **$75 $150 $300**

CLD-5

❑ **CLD-5. "Lindbergh-Merrick Reception Committee" Badge,**
1927. Badge is 4" tall. Text on ribbon continues "Cleveland Aug. 1st, 1927." Image on medallion reads "Commemorating Cleveland's Welcome To Col. Charles A. Lindbergh" with image of him and Myron T. Herrick in front of Spirit of St. Louis. Back of medal has image of "Seal Of The City Of Cleveland." - **$70 $165 $250**

CLD-6

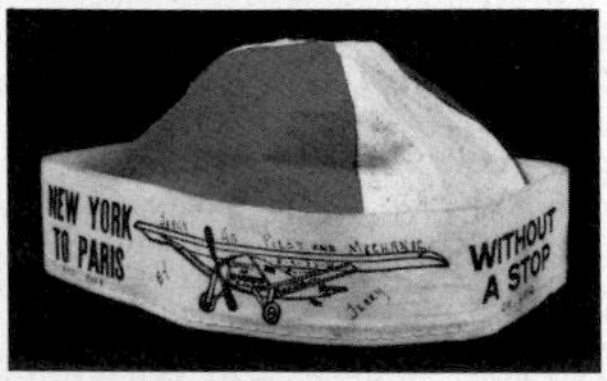

CLD-7

❑ **CLD-6. Flight School 13x15" Poster,**
1927. U.S. Army Flying Schools. Recruiting poster with Lindbergh tributes concluding "The Army Trained Him." - **$50 $100 $200**

❑ **CLD-7. Flight Celebration Cap,**
1927. Fabric over cardboard headband holding fabric crown. Pictured example has stamped name of local sponsor on headband rear. - **$40 $80 $150**

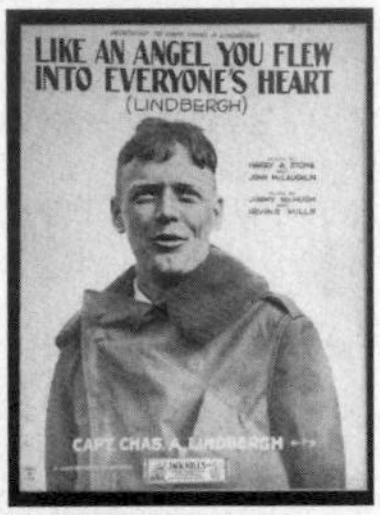

CLD-8

❑ **CLD-8. Song Sheet,**
1927. "Like An Angel You Flew Into Everyone's Heart, " a song dedicated to Capt. Lindbergh. - **$40 $80 $125**

CLD-9

CLD-10

❑ **CLD-9. "Our Hero" Cello. Button,**
1927. Red, white and blue rim surrounds black and white photo, 1-1/4". - **$35 $65 $135**

❑ **CLD-10. Transatlantic Flight Commemorative Glass,**
1927. White opaque glass with red illustrations. - **$25 $50 $100**

CLD-11

❑ **CLD-11. "Welcome Home" Felt Pennant,**
1927. 8x26". - **$60 $125 $250**

CLD-12

CLD-13

❑ **CLD-12. Commemorative Ring,**
1927. New York to Paris. - **$65 $135 $250**

❑ **CLD-13. "The Lone Eagle" Lindbergh/Bulova Endorsement Plaque,**
c. 1927. Bulova watches. 9x12" walnut wood plaque with mounted metal photo portrait plate including endorsement statement for sponsor plus facsimile Lindbergh signature. - **$100 $200 $400**

CLD-14

CLD-15

❑ **CLD-14. "Welcome Home Lindy" Pinback With Ribbon,**
1927. - **$50 $85 $175**

❑ **CLD-15. Medal With Ribbon,**
1927. Scarce. - **$140 $210 $375**

CLD-16

CLD-17

❑ **CLD-16. Lindbergh Pinback,**
1927. - **$75 $165 $300**

❑ **CLD-17. Lindbergh Souvenir Pin,**
1927. Rhinestones on white metal. - **$35 $80 $135**

CLD-18

CLD-19

❑ **CLD-18. Lindbergh Medal,**
1927. Bronze medal is 2-3/4" in diameter. Two diffferent versions exist, with small or large wording around edge. - **$65 $125 $250**

❑ **CLD-19. Lindbergh Medal,**
1927. Bronze medal is 2-3/4" in diameter. - **$90 $175 $350**

CLD-20

CLD-21

❑ **CLD-20. Lindbergh Button,**
1927. Three diffferent versions of enamel color combinations exist, with wording around edge. Each - **$60 $135 $200**

❑ **CLD-21. "We" in The Bulletin Button,**
1927. - **$30 $65 $125**

CLD-22

CLD-23

❑ **CLD-22. "Welcome Our Lindy" Litho. Button,**
1927. - **$90 $200 $400**

❑ **CLD-23. "Slim Lindy" Litho. Button,**
1927. - **$60 $110 $225**

CLD-25

CLD-24

CLD-26

❑ **CLD-24. "Plucky Lindbergh" Pinback With Ribbon Hanger ,**
1927. - **$30 $60 $125**

❑ **CLD-25. Col. Lindbergh & Mother Button,**
1927. - **$30 $55 $100**

❑ **CLD-26. Boston American Club Button,**
1927. - **$20 $40 $75**

CLD-27

CLD-28

❑ **CLD-27. "The Lone Eagle" Button,**
1927. - **$50 $100 $200**

❑ **CLD-28. "The Conqueror" Button,**
1927. - **$80 $150 $250**

CLD-29

CLD-30

❑ **CLD-29. "Capt. Charles A. Lindbergh-New York To Paris" Button,**
1927. 1.75" red/white/blue cello and one of the very best graphic designs for May 21 flight success. - **$100 $200 $400**

❑ **CLD-30. Lindbergh Print in Original Frame,**
1927. - **$75 $135 $200**

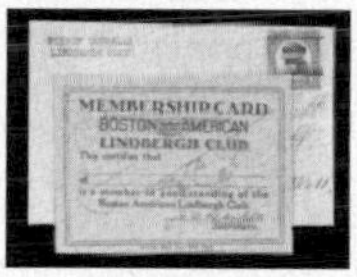

CLD-31

❑ **CLD-31. "Boston American Lindbergh Club" Member Card With Mailer,**
c. 1927. Sponsored by Boston Evening American newspaper. Mailer - **$10 $20 $35**
Card - **$30 $60 $100**

CLD-32

❑ **CLD-32. "Lindbergh Flight Commemorative Cigar Box Labels,**
c. 1927. Photo shows lid label and one end panel only. Lid Label - **$12 $20 $35**
End Panel Label - **$6 $12 $18**

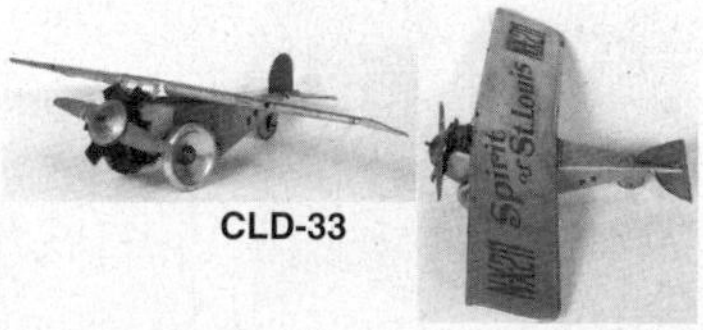

CLD-33

❑ **CLD-33. "Spirit Of St. Louis" Tin Airplane Wind-Up,**
c. 1927. 3" tall by 9" long by 13" wing span replica of Lindbergh's aircraft by unidentified maker. Winding action causes forward movement while propeller spins. - **$235 $500 $1000**

CLD-34

CLD-35

❑ **CLD-34. "Our National Hero Col. Lindbergh" China Ashtray,**
c. 1927. Full color portrait on glazed pastel yellow. - **$25 $55 $110**

❑ **CLD-35. "Mystery Picture" Card,**
c. 1927. Majestic Radio, "Mighty Monarch Of The Air." 3-1/2x5-1/2" black and white optical illusion card with instructions for causing Lindbergh image to enlarge, disappear, reappear. - **$15 $30 $60**

CLD-36

CLD-37

❑ **CLD-36. "We" Lindbergh & Plane Fan,**
c. 1927. 11.25" tall diecut cardboard printed in five colors with text poem titled "WE," also the title of his flight autobiography book. - **$25 $50 $100**

❑ **CLD-37. "We" Cello Button,**
1928. Includes title of his book, published after historic flight. - **$90 $160 $325**

CLD-38

❑ **CLD-38. Metal Bust Bank,**
1928. Gold colored. Rare. - **$125 $250 $475**

CLD-39

CLD-40

❑ CLD-39. Lindbergh High School Tribute Album,
1928. Little Falls High School, Little Falls, Minnesota. Tribute photo folio by his high school alma mater with 24 pages including numerous youth photos in addition to those from his adult flying career. - **$185 $350 $600**

❑ CLD-40. "Two Great Flyers" Cello. Button,
c. 1928. Flexible Flyer Sleds. - **$20 $35 $60**

CLD-41

❑ CLD-41. "Lindy Bread" Bullet Pencil Holder,
c. 1928. - **$35 $80 $150**

CLD-42

❑ CLD-42. "Lindy Bread" Wrapper,
c. 1928. Cottage Bakery, Springfield, Ohio. 10-1/2x15" waxed glassine loaf wrapper. Photo shows entire wrapper and detail from it. - **$40 $100 $175**

CLD-43

CLD-44

❑ CLD-43. Parachute Product Endorsement Photo,
c. 1928. Irvin Air Chutes. 8x10" black and white with product inscription on margin "He has saved his life on four different occasions by using Irvin Air Chutes." - **$25 $45 $80**

❑ CLD-44. "His Story in Pictures" Book,
1929. 320 pages by Francis Trevelyan Miller. Elaborate and well-documented book about one of America's greatest heroes. With dust jacket. - **$35 $70 $150**

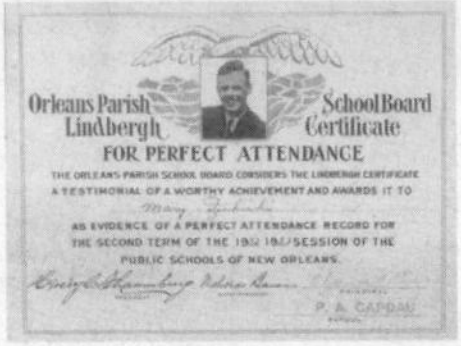

CLD-45

❑ CLD-45. "Lindbergh Certificate For Perfect Attendance,"
1932. Certificate is 8.25x11" reading "Orleans Parish School Board/Lindbergh Certificate For Perfect Attendance..." Has 1.75x2" black/white picture of Lindbergh at center. - **$40 $85 $135**

CLD-46

❑ CLD-46. Premium Map 31-1/2"x 42",
1935. Heinz 57. Map of famous aviator flights. Shows 25 famous pilots and 25 different planes. Photos could be cut out and used as cards. - **$90 $200 $375**

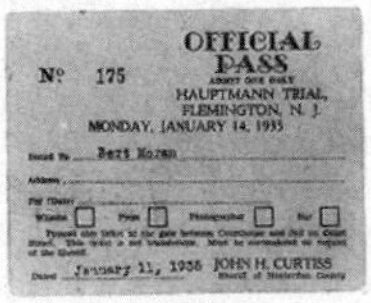

CLD-47

❑ CLD-47. Hauptmann Trial Official Pass,
1935. Single day authorization pass for January 14 day of trial for accused Lindbergh baby kidnapper and slayer Richard Bruno Hauptmann. - **$300 $600 $1000**

CLD-48

❑ CLD-48. Hauptmann Trial "Press" Badge,
1935. About 2" diameter celluloid button showing Lindbergh's young child. Attached ribbon has gold text on green. Limited distribution. Rare. - **$1000 $2000 $3000**

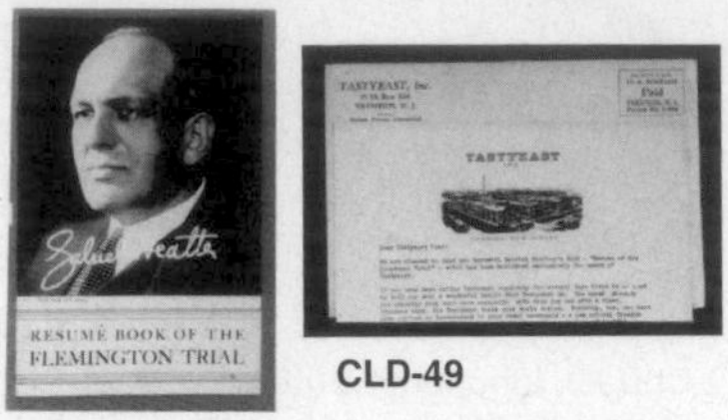

CLD-49

❑ CLD-49. Lindbergh Infant Kidnapping Murder Trial Summary,
c. 1936. Tastyeast, Inc. Cover letter and 24-page photo and text booklet summarizing evidence and trial of accused kidnapper and slayer. Contents include editorial by newscaster Gabriel Heatter.
Near Mint Complete with Mailer - **$250**
Booklet Only - **$40 $75 $150**
Letter Only - **$15 $30 $50**

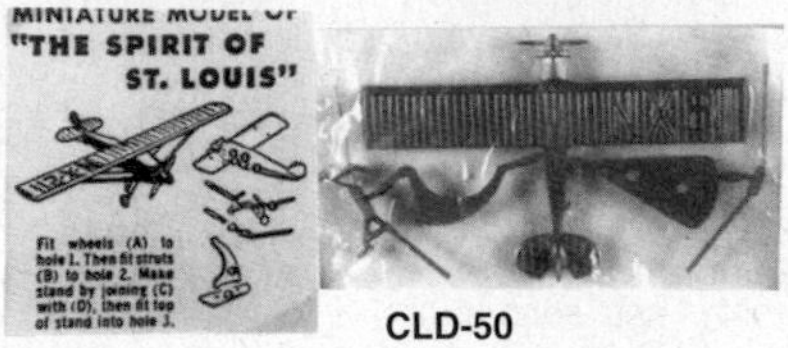

CLD-50

❑ CLD-50. "The Spirit Of St. Louis" Miniature Model,
c. 1956. Kellogg's. Cellophane pack holding assembly parts for 2x3" replica aircraft.
Cereal Box With Offer - **$60 $100 $200**
Model Kit - **$25 $50 $75**

CLD-51

❑ CLD-51. "Spirit of St. Louis" Lobby Card,
1957. For Warner Bros.' Lindbergh movie, starring Jimmy Stewart. Each - **$12 $30 $65**

Charlie Chan

Author Earl Derr Biggers (1884-1933) read about real life Chinese detective Chang Apana working in Honolulu and created Charlie Chan, writing *House Without A Key* in 1925. He published six Chan novels between 1925 and 1932 with Sgt. Chan becoming Inspector Chan by the end of the series. Chan lived on Punchbowl Hill with his wife and 12 children: five sons and seven daughters, including his Number One Son.

Besides the novels, Charlie Chan's greatest success would be in feature films. Most notably Warner Oland (1879-1938) played Chan in 16 films between 1931 and 1938; Sidney Toler (1874-1947) played Chan in 21 films between 1938 and 1947; and Roland Winters (1904-1989) played Chan in six films between 1947 and 1949. Keye Luke (1904-1991) was the most popular Number One Son, playing the role from 1935-1938.

Alfred Andriola drew the *Charlie Chan* comic strip from 1938 to 1942. The character was on the radio on four different networks between 1932 and 1940, played first by Walter Connally, then Ed Begley. Hanna-Barbera produced 15 *The Amazing Chan And The Chan Clan* cartoons in 1972 with former Number One Son Keye Luke providing Chan's voice. "Inscrutable!"

CCH-1

❑ **CCH-1. "The Black Camel" Charlie Chan Mystery Hardcover,**
1929. Curtis Publishing Co. 5x7.5" with 320 pages. Written by Earl Derr Biggers. With Dust Jacket - **$50 $100 $200**

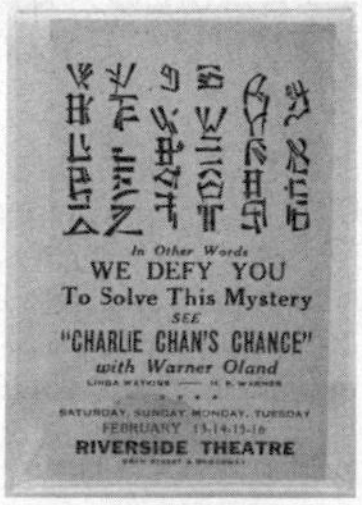

CCH-2

❑ **CCH-2. "Charlie Chan's Chance" Movie Premium Card,**
1931. Fox movie premium printed on unstable paper. This movie marked Warner Oland's 2nd appearance as Charlie Chan. -
$55 $110 $250

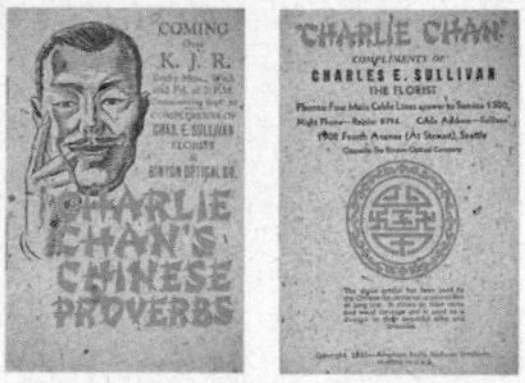

CCH-3

❑ **CCH-3. "Charlie Chan's Chinese Proverbs" Booklet,**
1935. American Radio Features Syndicate, with imprint of Seattle florist on the example pictured. 4x6" beautifully designed with 12 pages and stating "Coming Over K.J.R. Commencing Sept. 30." - **$65 $135 $250**

CCH-4

❑ **CCH-4. "Charlie Chan" Advertising Sticker With Envelope,**
1938. E.H. Karl & Co. 4x9.5" envelope with 1.75x2" advertising sticker on lower left featuring Charlie Chan with Van Camp's as sponsor of the radio program. - **$25 $50 $100**

CCH-5

❑ **CCH-5. "Charlie Chan" Card Game,**
1939. Whitman Publishing Co. 5x6.5" boxed card game includes 35 game cards and 1 instruction card. - **$50 $100 $200**

CCH-6

❑ **CCH-6. "Charlie Chan" Skull Cap,**
1930s. Van Camp's Chili Sauce. 7" diameter with white lettering on black fabric accented by red felt-covered button on top. -
$85 $175 $350

CCH-7

❑ **CCH-7. "Charlie Chan Mystery Midget" Premium Offer Original Art For Store Display,**
c. 1940. Prototype for Stokely's Tomato Juice. 12x19" stiff cardboard with tempera paint advertising "Mystery Midget 24 Inches High Including Complete Playlet And Instructions." Gordon Gold Archives. Unique - **$1000**

CCH-8

❑ **CCH-8. "Flip-O-Vision Presents Charlie Chan" Flip Book,**
1949. Topps. 1.25x2" stiff paper flip book with stiff paper pages with actual black and white photos from a set of 50 different titles. These were issued in unassembled form, the perforated sheets were to be separated and assembled by means of a rubber band at bottom. From film *Sky Dragon* and features Chan studying an envelope with magnifying glass. - **$25 $50 $100**

CCH-9

❑ **CCH-9. Charlie Chan Pair Of Better Little Books,**
1940s. Whitman Publishing Co. Whitman No. 1424 (1942) "Inspector Charlie Chan-Villainy On The High Seas" with flip book feature. Whitman No. 1459 (1940) "Charlie Chan Solves A New Mystery." Each - **$15 $45 $100**

Charlie Chaplin

Charles Spencer Chaplin (1889-1977) was born in London and spent most of his early years in homes and institutions. By 1898 he was working on stage, moved to the U.S.A. in 1912 after touring the vaudeville circuit with the Karno Troupe, and in 1913 he signed a contract to make comic movies with Mack Sennett's Keystone Studios. The next year, in *Kid Auto Races at Venice*, Chaplin unveiled his screen persona as "The Little Tramp" in baggy pants, floppy shoes, bowler hat and bamboo cane--a role he was to play in more than 70 films and one that brought him international acclaim as a true comic genius. Chaplin took The Tramp from Keystone to Essanay in 1915, to Mutual in 1916, and to First National in 1917. In 1919 he helped form United Artists with Douglas Fairbanks and Mary Pickford so he could produce and distribute his films independently. From *The Tramp* in 1915 to *Limelight* in 1952, Chaplin's fame and box-office appeal continued to grow.

The Tramp was adapted in a newspaper comic strip, *Charlie Chaplin's Comic Capers*, with art by E.C. Segar who would gain fame in 1929 with the creation of Popeye, for the *Chicago Record-Herald* and national syndication in 1915-1917, and *Baggy Pants*, an animated cartoon, aired on NBC in 1977-1978, but the humor and pathos of Chaplin's character proved impossible to capture in either medium.

In the late 1940s and 1950s Chaplin was wrongfully accused of "Communist leanings" by the American Legion and other right-wing organizations. He moved to Switzerland, returning only in 1972 to receive a special Academy Award. He was knighted in 1975, and his Little Tramp remains to this day the universal embodiment of the eventual triumph of the individual. He passed away Christmas Day 1977.

CPN-1

CPN-2

❑ **CPN-1. "Chas. Chaplin" Statuette,**
1915. Includes wire cane. Store item. -
$65 $110 $225

❑ **CPN-2. "Chas. Chaplin" Statuette,**
1915. 9" tall painted plaster figurine with underside token insert "Sold By Mark Hampton Co. Inc." with New York City address and copyright year. - **$65 $110 $225**

CPN-3

CPN-4

❑ **CPN-3. Early Water Shooting White Metal Novelty,**
c. 1915. 1-3/4" tall figure has tiny hole at waist with small metal tube on reverse originally affixed to a rubber tube and squeeze ball. The rubber disintegrated over time. - **$30 $50 $80**

❑ **CPN-4. Charlie Chaplin Composition/Cloth Doll,**
c. 1915. Scarce. Store item by Louis Amberg & Son. - **$175 $375 $750**

CPN-5

❑ **CPN-5. "Charlie Chaplin In Easy Street" Movie Book,**
1917. Contents include 32 sepia pages, each picturing photo plus cartoon drawing describing scene from Van Bueren Corp. film. Original copyright date was renewed in 1922. -
$45 $85 $165

CPN-6

❑ **CPN-6. "Charlie Chaplin's Comic Capers" Book,**
1917. Store item published by M. A. Donohue & Co. Softcover 9-1/2x16" with 16 black and white pages reprinting daily comic strips. -
$165 $525 $1200

CPN-7

❑ **CPN-7. "Charlie Chaplin in The Movies" Book,**
1917. Store item published by M. A. Donohue & Co. Softcover 9-1/2x16" with 16 black and white pages reprinting daily comic strips. -
$165 $525 $1200

CPN-8

CPN-9

❑ **CPN-8. Portrait Stickpin In Brass,**
c. 1917. - **$20 $30 $60**

❑ **CPN-9. "The Kid" Handbill,**
1920. Paper sheet for silent film starring Chaplin and "The Wonder Boy" Jackie Coogan in his first role. - **$18 $30 $60**

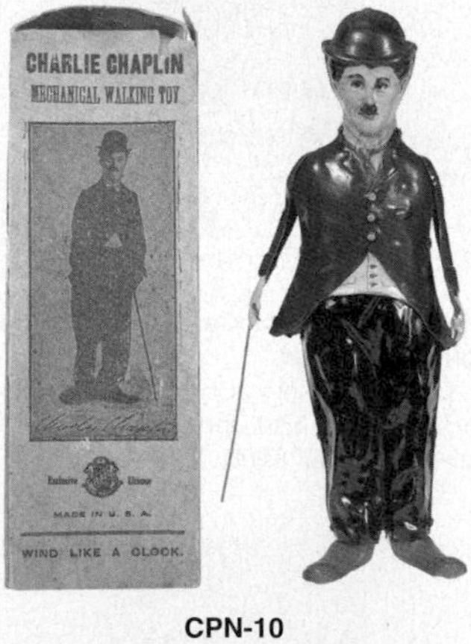

CPN-10

❑ **CPN-10. "Charlie Chaplin Mechanical Walking Toy" Wind-Up With Box,**
c. 1920. Toy is 2.5x3x8.5" tall with built-in key and comes in box that features Chaplin photo and facsimile signature on the lid. Box marked "B&R Exclusive License/Made In U.S.A."
Box - **$225 $450 $700**
Toy - **$300 $600 $1200**

CPN-11

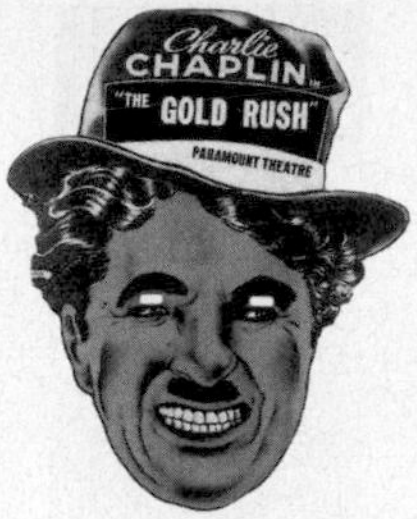

CPN-12

❑ **CPN-11. Early Portrait Button,**
c. 1920. 7/8" black and white, one of the earliest buttons to picture him. - **$45 $85 $185**

❑ **CPN-12. "The Gold Rush" Movie Promotion Mask,**
1924. Diecut stiff paper for silent film release. - **$75 $185 $400**

CPN-13

❑ **CPN-13. "Gold Rush Movie Medal,**
1925. 1-1/4" brass promoting screening in Hartford, Conn. - **$10 $20 $35**

CPN-14

CPN-15

❑ **CPN-14. "The Gold Rush" Movie Program,**
1925. From world premiere at Grauman's Egyptian Theater, Hollywood for dramatic comedy written, directed and starring Chaplin. - **$50 $100 $200**

❑ **CPN-15. Chaplin Image Party Favor,**
1920s. Store item. 7-1/2" crepe paper and confetti table marker with 3" figure of him formed by glossy paper and fabric. - **$20 $50 $80**

CPN-16

CPN-17

❑ **CPN-16. Charlie Chaplin Candy Container Bank,**
1920s. Store item. Glass plus metal lid. - **$95 $185 $350**

❑ **CPN-17. Charlie Chaplin Cello. Button,**
1920s. Sampeck Suits. - **$20 $40 $75**

CPN-18

CPN-19

❑ **CPN-18. Condiment Jar,**
1920s. Glazed ceramic jar and lid. #4628 stamped on underside, probably of European or Japanese origin. - **$65 $150 $275**

❑ **CPN-19. Mask,**
1920s. Made in England. Possible premium. - **$30 $60 $100**

CPN-20

CPN-21

❑ **CPN-20. Cardboard 9" Puppet With Mailer and Instructions,**
1920s. Made in England. Possible premium.
Puppet - **$35 $65 $100**
Mailer - **$15 $25 $40**
Instructions - **$8 $15 $25**

❑ **CPN-21. Painted Bisque German Figurine,**
c. 1933. 5" tall from series including Harold Lloyd and Tom Mix. Germany marking plus faint number, perhaps 3509 (same as Tom Mix version) or 3809. - **$75 $175 $325**

CPN-22

❑ **CPN-22. Movie Promo,**
1934. National Theatre Premium. 16 pages, shows coming attraction. - **$15 $30 $50**

CPN-23

CPN-24

❑ **CPN-23. "Modern Times" Movie Button,**
1936. 7/8" blue on orange. - **$18 $35 $70**

❑ **CPN-24. "The Great Dictator" Movie Promotion Mask,**
1940. Diecut stiff paper for United Artists film release. This mask was used as a promotion for Chaplin's films during the 1920s-1940s. For each new film, the title was displayed on the hat. - **$75 $185 $400**

CPN-25

❑ **CPN-25. Chaplin Litho Tin Mechanical Toy,**
1950s. Toy is 4.5" tall with "Made In England" on his cane. Pulling string tips his hat.
- $50 $85 $135

CPN-26

CPN-27

❑ **CPN-26. Charlie Chaplin Hat-Tipper Figure,**
1960s. Store item. Italian-made, hard plastic upper torso with flexible fabric over spring base. **- $45 $90 $160**

❑ **CPN-27. Charlie Chaplin Figural Ashtray,**
1970s. Store item by Lego, Japan. High gloss finish hollow ceramic. **- $30 $60 $100**

CPN-28

❑ **CPN-28. "Silent Star" Ornament in Box,**
1997. **- $28**

Charlie McCarthy

Edgar Bergen (1903-1978) and Charlie McCarthy accomplished the seemingly impossible--a successful ventriloquist act on radio. Charlie was carved from a block of pine by Illinois carpenter Theodore Mack. After years of knocking around vaudeville, Bergen and Charlie broke into radio with a guest appearance on Rudy Vallee's show in 1936. They were an instant hit and five months later they were stars on the Chase & Sanborn Hour. Week after week Charlie feuded with W. C. Fields and flirted with Dorothy Lamour and America loved him. Bergen received an honorary Oscar made of wood in 1938 for his creation of Charlie. Their film appearances include *The Goldwyn Follies (1938); You Can't Cheat an Honest Man (1939); and Charlie McCarthy Detective (1939).* Another dummy, Mortimer Snerd, was added in 1939 and Effie Klinker joined the crew in 1944 but Charlie ruled supreme. Chase & Sanborn's sponsorship ended in 1948 and other sponsors (Coca-Cola, Hudnut, Kraft cheese) carried the show until it ended in 1956. Charlie made an early TV appearance on the *Hour Glass* variety show in 1946 and, along with Bergen, hosted *Do You Trust Your Wife?* in 1956-1957 and *Who Do You Trust?* on daytime TV from 1957-1963. A comic strip had a brief run in the late 1930s and comic books were published in the late 1940s and early 1950s.

CHE-1

❑ **CHE-1. Animated Lap Doll Newspaper Ad,**
1937. Chase & Sanborn Coffee. Full page color ad for diecut cardboard 20" tall figure with movable eyes and mouth plus scored lines to form seated position. Doll was available by mail for four coffee bag fronts. Small corner box promotes radio program Sunday nights on NBC Red Network. **- $20 $40 $65**

CHE-2

CHE-3

❑ **CHE-2. "Chase & Sanborn Radio News" Newsletter,**
c. 1937. **- $35 $75 $135**

❑ **CHE-3. "Adventure Pops" Cardboard Folder,**
1938. Held six lollipops by E. Rosen Co. From a set of five. Each **- $40 $80 $150**

CHE-4

CHE-5

❑ **CHE-4. "Radio Party" Game,**
1938. Chase & Sanborn Coffee. Includes spinner and 21 figures. Complete **- $20 $40 $80**

❑ **CHE-5. Animated Alarm Clock,**
1938. Store item by Gilbert. **- $400 $900 $1800**

CHE-6

❑ **CHE-6. "Charlie McCarthy" Tin Walker Windup,**
1938. Marx Toys. 2.5x2.75" by 8.5" tall. Name on front of hat. Marx toys logo on back of tuxedo. **- $225 $450 $725**

CHE-7

❑ **CHE-7. Wind-Up Litho. Tin Car,**
1938. Store item by Marx. **- $225 $450 $900**

CHE-8

❑ CHE-8. "Edgar Bergen's Charlie McCarthy Meets Walt Disney's Snow White" Book,
1938. Whitman 9.5x11.5" softcover with full color front and back, 24 bw pages. -
$65 $135 $215

CHE-9

❑ CHE-9. "Charlie McCarthy Valentine Pops" Lollipop Holder/Valentine Card,
1938. Held six lollipops by E. Rosen Company from a set of five. Each - **$40 $80 $150**

CHE-10

❑ CHE-10. Flying Hats Game,
1938. Contains 4 games of chance and skill. -
$35 $70 $140

CHE-11 CHE-12

❑ CHE-11. "The Adventures Of Charlie McCarthy And Edgar Bergen" Fast Action Book,
1938. 4x5-3/8" in BLB format. - **$24 $72 $170**

❑ CHE-12. Photo,
1938. Philadelphia Record newspaper premium. -
$12 $22 $35

CHE-13 CHE-14

❑ CHE-13. Effanbee Doll "Edgar Bergen's Charlie McCarthy" Cello. Button,
c. 1938. For "An Effanbee Play-Product". -
$35 $80 $140

❑ CHE-14. "Charlie McCarthy" Wooden Figure With Rope Arms,
c. 1938. Store item. 5-1/4" tall. -
$65 $135 $265

CHE-15 CHE-16

❑ CHE-15. Cardboard Figure,
c. 1938. Chase & Sanborn Coffee. -
$40 $100 $200

❑ CHE-16. Mortimer Snerd Cardboard Figure,
c. 1938. Chase & Sanborn Coffee. -
$50 $140 $265

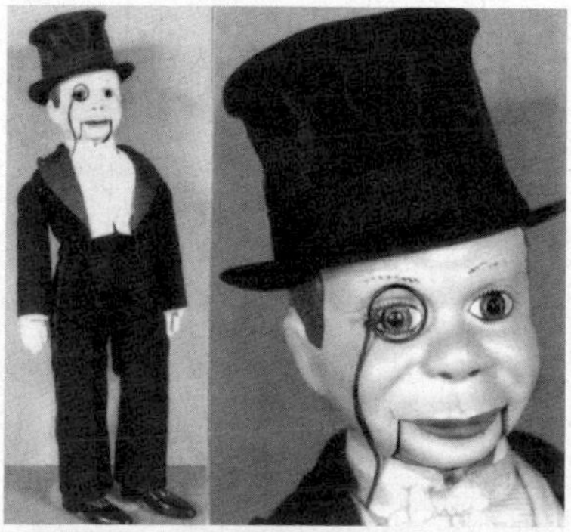

CHE-17

❑ CHE-17. Ventriloquist Doll In Tuxedo,
c. 1938. Store item believed to be Effanbee. -
$235 $475 $950

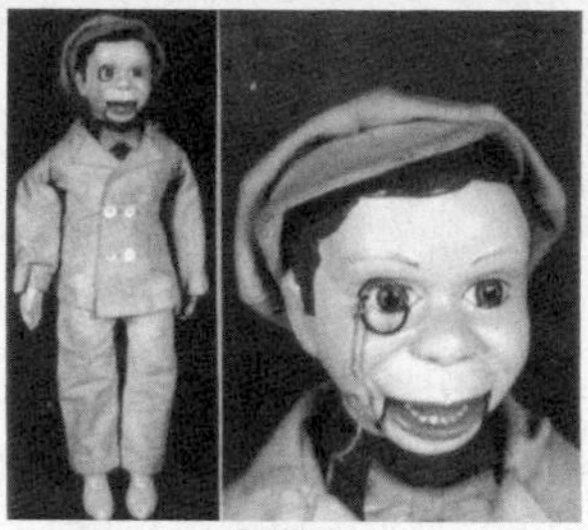

CHE-18

❑ CHE-18. Ventriloquist Doll Detective Outfit,
c. 1938. Store item believed to be Effanbee. -
$235 $475 $950

CHE-19

❑ CHE-19. "Majestic's Charlie McCarthy" Radio Boxed,
c. 1938. Illustrated box holding 7" wide hard plastic deco styling electrical radio plus related papers from maker Majestic.
Box - **$225 $450 $900**
Radio - **$575 $1150 $2300**

CHE-20

❑ CHE-20. "Radio Guide" Magazines With McCarthy Covers,
1938-1939. Issues for July 9, 1938 and February 25, 1939. Each - **$12 $20 $40**

CHE-21

❑ CHE-21. "Meet My Friend Mortimer Snerd" Tin Litho Wind-Up Toy,
1939. Marx Toys. - **$115 $250 $500**

CHE-22

❑ **CHE-22. "Charlie McCarthy And Mortimer Snerd Coupe" Boxed Wind-Up Toy,**
1939. Marx. 4.5x16.5x6.5" deep nicely illustrated box contains 16" long vehicle. Body of car has great design featuring different geometric patterns. Toy travels forward until the front bumper strikes an object and this causes the vehicle to reverse its direction, this time until the rear bumper is struck, all the while the heads spin. Box - **$300 $600 $1200**
Toy - **$1100 $2250 $3500**

CHE-23

CHE-24

❑ **CHE-23. "Speaking For Myself On Life And Love" Book,**
1939. Chase & Sanborn Coffee. - **$15 $30 $65**

❑ **CHE-24. Painted Plastic Portrait Pin,**
c. 1939. - **$15 $30 $50**

CHE-25

❑ **CHE-25. "Edgar Bergen's Mortimer Snerd Ideal Flexy Doll,"**
c. 1939. 12-1/2" tall composition.
Doll - **$125 $350 $750**
Tag - **$25 $50 $85**

CHE-26

❑ **CHE-26. Figural Soap In Diecut Box,**
c. 1939. Store item by Kerk Guild Inc., N.Y. 5-1/4" tall figure with small color accents.
Near Mint Boxed - **$135**
Soap Only - **$25 $50 $75**

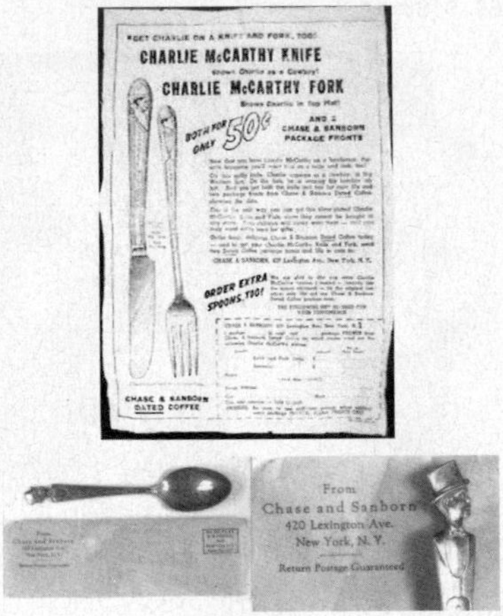

CHE-27

❑ **CHE-27. Silver Plate Spoon With Mailer,**
c. 1939. Mailer Only - **$20 $30 $50**
Standard Tuxedo Design Spoon - **$6 $12 $20**
Order Form For Knife and Fork - **$30 $60 $90**

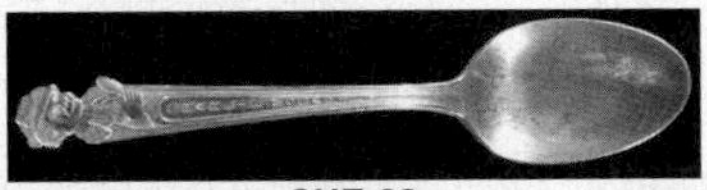

CHE-28

❑ **CHE-28. Detective Outfit Design Spoon,**
c. 1939. - **$10 $20 $40**

CHE-29

❑ **CHE-29. Silver Plate Knife And Fork,**
c. 1939. Each - **$18 $35 $60**

CHE-30

CHE-31

❑ **CHE-30. Carnival Statue,**
1930s. Yellow. - **$30 $60 $120**

❑ **CHE-31. "Charlie McCarthy" Figural Catalin Pencil Sharpener,**
1930s. 1.75" tall. - **$35 $75 $125**

CHE-32

CHE-33

❑ **CHE-32. "Goldwyn Follies Club" Cello. Button,**
1930s. Metro-Goldwyn-Mayer. - **$20 $40 $75**

❑ **CHE-33. "Gold-Plated Ring" Coupon Sheet,**
1940. Scarce. Clipping from can wrapper of Chase & Sanborn Coffee offering ring for 10 cents plus the clipping. - **$12 $25 $50**

CHE-34

CHE-35

❑ **CHE-34. Portrait Ring Newspaper Ad,**
1940. Chase & Sanborn Coffee. Black and white ad for adjustable ring offered by mail for 10 cents and one coffee label until offer expiration October 31. - **$12 $25 $40**

❑ **CHE-35. Bust Portrait Brass Ring,**
1940. Chase and Sanborn coffee. - **$125 $200 $400**

CHE-36

CHE-37

❑ **CHE-36. Bergen/McCarthy Glass,**
c. 1940. - **$25 $60 $100**

❑ **CHE-37. Composition Bank,**
c. 1940. Store item. - **$65 $150 $300**

CHE-38

❑ **CHE-38. Contest Card,**
1944. - **$25 $40 $80**

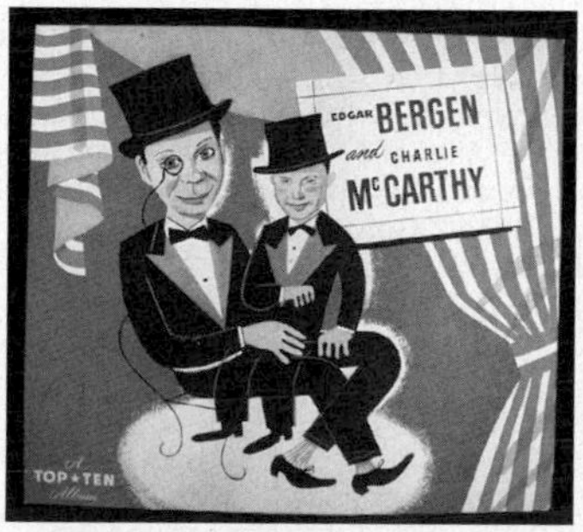

CHE-39

❑ **CHE-39. Record Album,**
1947. Contains four 78 RPM records. Inside are write-ups about the radio show. - **$35 $90 $175**

Charlie the Tuna

Charlie is the out-of-luck character created by Tom Rogers (1918-2005) for Star-Kist Foods in 1961. Charlie's ambition was to impress Star-Kist (and viewers) with his demonstrations of esthetic "good taste," inevitably rejected by "Sorry, Charlie. Star-Kist doesn't want tuna with good taste. Star-Kist wants tuna that tastes good" by voice actor Herschel Bernardi (1923-1986). Despite--or because of--his loser image, Charlie became a winner in premium popularity.

CTU-1

CTU 2

❑ **CTU-1. Talking Cloth Doll,**
1969. - **$25 $50 $100**

❑ **CTU-2. Metal Alarm Clock,**
1969. - **$30 $70 $140**

CTU-3

CTU-4

❑ **CTU-3. "Charlie For President" Litho. Button,**
1960s. - **$18 $35 $60**

❑ **CTU-4. Charlie The Tuna Predecessor Premium,**
1960s. Sponsored by Star-Kist. Mailer with inflatable 24x40" "Loona The Star-Kist Tuna" swim toy. Mailer - **$8 $15 $25**
Toy - **$20 $40 $65**

CTU-5

CTU-6

❑ **CTU-5. Plastic Radio,**
1970. Battery operated, base often missing.
Complete - **$45 $75 $125**
No Base - **$18 $35 $50**

❑ **CTU-6. Watch With Mailer & Paper,**
1971. Sponsored by Star-Kist Foods.
Mailer And Paper - **$8 $15 $25**
Watch - **$30 $60 $90**

CTU-7

CTU-8

❑ **CTU-7. Plastic Figural Camera,**
1971. - **$30 $65 $125**

❑ **CTU-8. Oval Bathroom Scale,**
1972. - **$25 $55 $110**

CTU-9

CTU-10

❑ **CTU-9. Charlie The Tuna Electric Clock,**
1972. Star-Kist Foods. 4x4x4" plastic cube with color paper images on all inner panels. - **$40 $80 $150**

❑ **CTU-10. Metal Wristwatch,**
1973. - **$25 $45 $80**

CTU-11

❑ **CTU-11. Mug,**
1977. - **$8 $18 $35**

CTU-12

CTU-13

❑ **CTU-12. Charlie The Tuna Ceramic Premium Bank,**
1980. Bank is 9.25" tall with light and dark blue full figure of smiling Charlie surrounded by stacks of silver accent "coins" with text in black on one "In Star-Kist We Trust" plus art image of Charlie. Figure and coins sit atop green and white base having Star-Kist name in red on front plus white text "Bank On Good Taste."
- **$30 $55 $95**

❑ **CTU-13. "25th Anniversary" Wristwatch,**
1986. Authorized Star-Kist limited edition metal case watch accompanied by paper slips for Charlie the Tuna history and other mail premiums. Near Mint Boxed - **$75**
Watch Only - **$25 $40 $60**

CTU-14

❑ **CTU-14. "Charlie The Tuna" Telephone,**
1987. Star-Kist Foods premium found in some quantity in late 1990s . Near Mint Boxed **- $60**

Cheerios Misc.

Cheerios ready-to-eat oat cereal was introduced by General Mills as Cheerioats in 1941. The name changed to Cheerios in 1945 and has remained a perennial favorite with kids and adults ever since. Over the years the Cheerios box has carried cutout toys and promotions for a wide variety of merchandisers, notably the Lone Ranger, Wyatt Earp, Superman, the Muppets, Bugs Bunny, Snoopy and Peanuts, Star Trek, Star Wars and Mickey Mouse. Disney comic books and 3-D glasses were featured giveaways in the 1940s and 1950s. Cheerios mascots include Cheeri O'Leary introduced in 1942 and the Cheerios Kid and Sue introduced in 1953. The items in this section are primarily a selection of Cheerios non-character premiums.

CEE-1

CEE-2

❑ **CEE-1. "Hall Of Fun/Groucho Marx" 3-D Picture,**
c. 1942. Assembled from box back. Set of eight.
Box Panel Or Assembled - **$30 $50 $75**

❑ **CEE-2. "Hall Of Fun/Joe E. Brown" 3-D Picture,**
c. 1942. Assembled from box back. Set of eight.
Box Panel Or Assembled - **$30 $50 $75**

CEE-3

❑ **CEE-3. "Cheerios Hall Of Fun" Box Back 3-D Pictures,**
1940s. Famous comedians include Jack Oakie, Hugh Herbert, Jerry Colonna, Joe E. Brown, Mischa Auer, Groucho Marx, and two others.
Each Complete Panel **- $30 $50 $75**

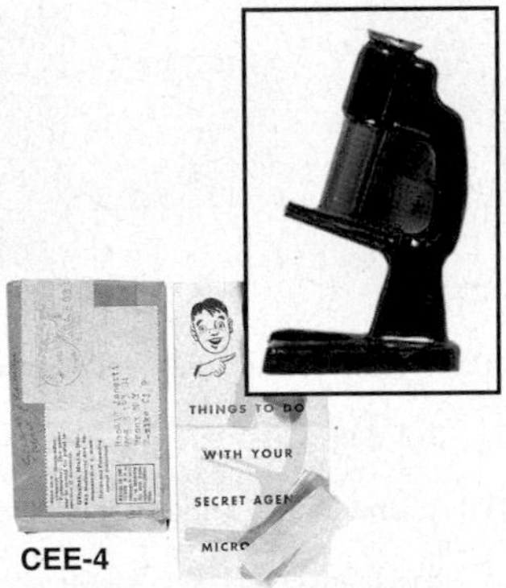

CEE-4

❑ **CEE-4. Secret Agent Microscope,**
1950. Secret Agent black microscope with six slides. Eight page instruction booklet and mailer. - **$35 $65 $120**

CEE-5

❑ **CEE-5. "Confederate Currency" Album With Envelope,**
1954. Reproductions of Confederate money. - **$45 $90 $175**

CEE-6

❑ **CEE-6. "Confederate Money" Box,**
1954. Front panel pictures one of nine different designs of replica currency bills of Confederate States of America issued individually as box insert. Complete Box - **$50 $125 $250**

CEE-7

❑ **CEE-7. "American Airlines Air Travel Game" Box Panel With Game Sheet,**
1955. Game designed by Milton Bradley.
Back Panel **- $10 $20 $40**
Game Sheet **- $12 $25 $45**

CEE-8

❑ **CEE-8. "Cheerios Airport Missile Control Center" Box Flat,**
1958. From a series of five different boxes with side panel offer of 39 piece set including missile launchers and airplanes as well as a "Full Color Layout Sheet." Gordon Gold Archives.
Each Near Mint Flat - **$160**
Each Used Complete - **$30 $60 $100**

CEE-9

❑ **CEE-9. "'Rocky' The Walking Horse" Cereal Box Flat,**
1950s. Canadian offer of small plastic ramp walker toy packaged in the box with cut-outs on back for "Rocky's Ranch." Gordon Gold Archives. Near Mint Flat - **$150**
Used Complete - **$30 $60 $100**

CEE-10

❑ **CEE-10. 3D Wiggle Picture Display,**
1950s. Cheerios Cereal. Thin plastic badge pictures Cheerio Kid. Center of circus tent design is open to hold one of six different Disney character flasher pictures. Offered as a set.
Badge Only - **$20 $45 $85**
Each Flasher - **$12 $20 $30**

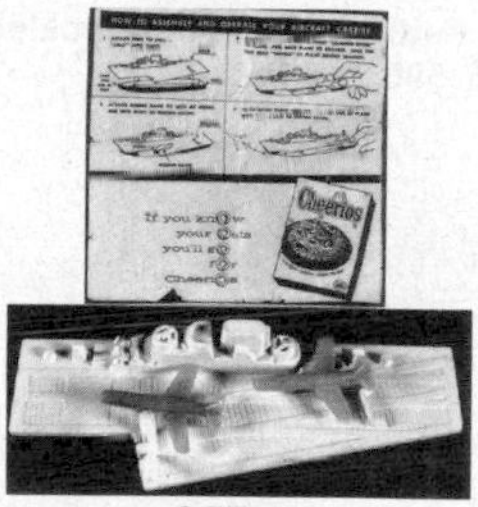

CEE-11

❑ **CEE-11. Aircraft Carrier And Planes Plastic Toy With Instructions And Box,**
1960s. Planes are launched by rubber band.
Near Mint In Mailer - **$150**

CEE-12

❑ **CEE-12. "Cheerios World War II Fighters" Cereal Box,**
1960s. Box is flattened to 11x16" full color complete with all flaps intact. Inset ad on front of box plus full back panel advertise send-away cutout airplane models. This box features Bell P-39 Airacobra and Stormovik IL-2 which were available by sending in order blank on one side of box plus 10 cents. Back panel also lists eight other airplanes available on various packages of General Mills cereal. Gordon Gold Archives.
Used Complete - **$25 $50 $80**

CEE-13

❑ **CEE-13. "Cape Cheerios Rocket Base" Box Panel Set,**
1960s. Completed by parts from five box backs.
Uncut Backs Each - **$18 $35 $60**

CEE-14

❑ **CEE-14. "Cape Cheerios Rocket Base",**
c. 1960s. Premium by Marx.
Complete Boxed - **$40 $70 $135**

CEE-15

❑ **CEE-15. "Cheerios Kids Snack Time Dispenser",**
2001. Eat your cereal from the back of his head. Cool! - **$6**

Cheyenne

Loosely based on the 1947 movie *Cheyenne*, the ABC-TV series ran between September 20, 1955 and September 13, 1963. The series alternated bi-weekly with other shows; which led to a total of 107 episodes.

Cheyenne **was television's first hour long series. The basic plot had frontiersman Cheyenne Bodie, capably played by Clint Walker, roaming the west righting wrongs and meeting single women along the way. Produced by Roy Huggins and William Orr, writers included Bert Arthur. The popular theme song was by William Lava and Stanley Jones.**

The series was hugely successful and won the Golden Globe Award in 1957. Dell Comics published twenty comic books with full color photo covers based on the show between 1956 and 1961.

CHY-1

❑ **CHY-1. "Cheyenne" From TV Cowboys Button Set,**
1957. Green Duck. 7/8" litho button in browntone on blue background. Reverse text is "Clint Walker Warner Bros. Star." - **$12 $25 $50**

CHY-2

❑ **CHY-2. "Cheyenne/Three Puzzles" Set,**
1957. Milton Bradley. 9-3/8x12.25x1.5" deep box holds 3 puzzles with color illustrations. Set #4705-1. - **$30 $60 $100**

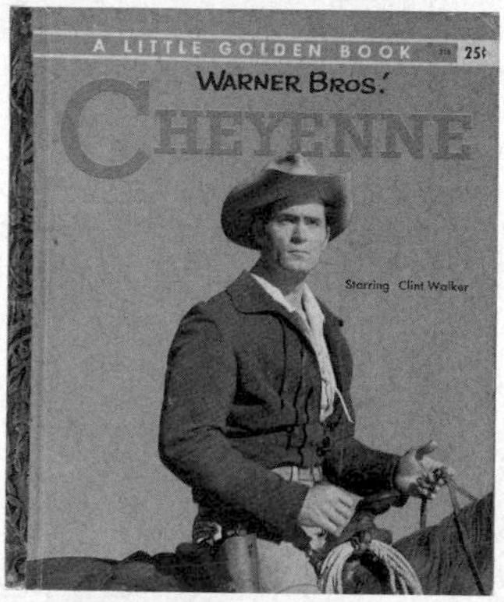

CHY-3

❑ **CHY-3. "Cheyenne Starring Clint Walker" Little Golden Book,**
1958. 6.75x8" with 24 pages. First printing. - **$10 $20 $60**

CHY-4

❑ **CHY-4. "Cheyenne Game",**
1958. Milton Bradley. 9-5/8x19x1-5/8" deep box holds colorful game board with action scenes plus spinner, game pieces including four multi-clored plastic guns and catalogue folder. - **$35 $70 $150**

CHY-5

❑ **CHY-5. "Cheyenne Three Puzzles",**
1959. Milton Bradley. 9.5x12.5x1.25" deep box holds three 9x12" puzzles. - **$25 $50 $85**

CHY-6

CHY-7

❑ **CHY-6. TV Guide with "Cheyenne" Cover,**
1959. Features Clint Walker. - **$12 $25 $60**

❑ **CHY-7. "Cheyenne" Pinback,**
c. 1959. Australian. Very colorful. - **$20 $40 $65**

CHY-8

❑ **CHY-8. Clint Walker And James Arness In Schwinn Bicycle Promo Folder,**
1950s. 5.75x8-7.8" opens to 17.75x23". Includes Dick Powell, June Allyson and Terry Moore. - **$25 $50 $90**

Chick Carter

Like father, like son, for detective work done. Nick Carter, a sleuth of considerable prominence to readers of early dime novels, pulp magazines and hardbound novels of the 1930s, adopted a son in his image--at least for purposes of radio and movie serial producers. The elder Carter, by name, was avoided for reasons unknown in broadcast and screen versions. *Chick Carter, Boy Detective,* with Lyle Talbot (1902-1996) as Chick, began as a radio drama on the Mutual network July 5, 1943 and ran until July 6, 1945. *Chick Carter, Detective*, a 1946 Columbia Pictures 15-episode serial, dropped all pretense that Chick was a youngster. Chick was an instant adult, portrayed by Lyle Talbot, a veteran actor of gangster and crime movie roles.

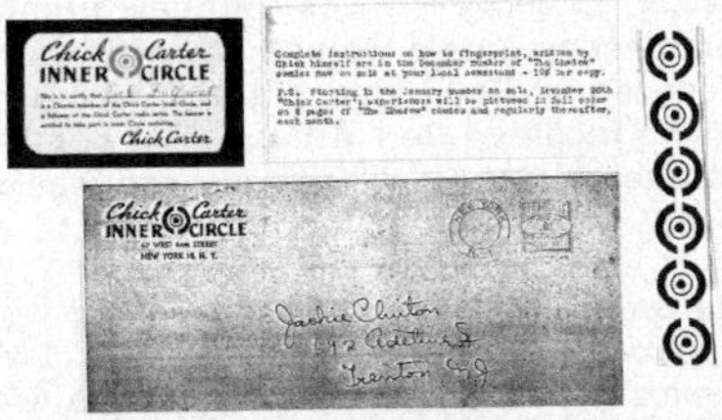

CCK-1

❑ **CCK-1. Chick Carter Club Kit,**
1944. Envelope - **$40 $85 $135**
Club Card - **$50 $100 $200**
"The Shadow" Comic Promo Insert - **$25 $50 $85**
Club Logo Stickers Each - **$1 $2 $5**

CCK-2

❑ **CCK-2. Radio Club Promo Booklet,**
1945. - **$35 $90 $185**

CCK-3

❑ **CCK-3. Club Kit Folder,**
1945. - **$50 $135 $240**

CCK-4

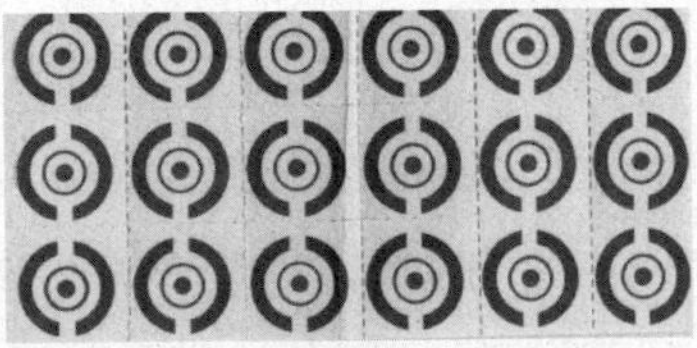

CCK-5

❑ **CCK-4. Club Kit Card,**
1945. Rare. - **$40 $75 $150**

❑ **CCK-5. Set of 24 Inner Circle Logo Stickers,**
1945. Each Sticker - **$1 $2 $5**

China Clipper

In spite of the early 1930s Depression years, air travel demand continued almost unabated. The enterprising Pan American Airways offered a challenge based on need: a transport aircraft capable of 2,500 mile non-stop flight to span the Pacific which signaled the beginning of Trans-Pacific air mail. Aircraft makers responded quickly. On November 22, 1935 the first of the romantically-named "China Clipper" flights began to the Orient. The selected aircraft, one by Martin and one by Boeing, were masterpieces of huge payload capacity, incredible size and magnificent interior elegance for crew and passengers. So remarkable was this advance in aviation technology, a 1936 movie starring Pat O'Brien detailed the account of the initial flight that compared in public stature to Lindbergh's earlier solo flight of the Atlantic. The "China Clipper" mystique and adulation resulted in several tribute premiums issued by Quaker Oats. The last China Clipper crashed in Trinidad on January 8, 1945.

CLP-1

CLP-2

❑ **CLP-1. China Clipper Brass Ring,**
1936. Quaker Puffed Wheat and Rice. -
$50 $100 $200

❑ **CLP-2. China Clipper 2" Brass Bar Pin,**
1936. Quaker Puffed Wheat and Rice. -
$20 $50 $90

CLP-3

CLP-4

❑ **CLP-3. Boys Life Magazine - Feature And Picture On Cover,**
1936. China Clipper pictures on cover with story about Pan-American Clippers. - **$18 $30 $60**

❑ **CLP-4. "Flying the Sky Clipper" Big Little Book #1108,**
1936. - **$10 $30 $68**

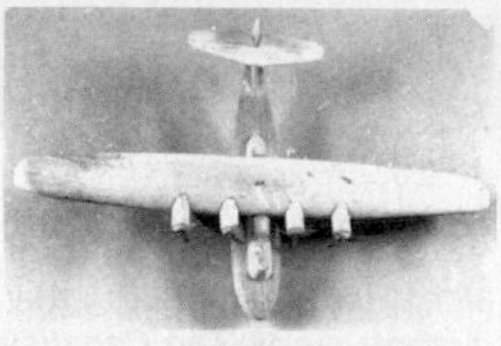

CLP-5

❑ **CLP-5. Quaker "China Clipper" Balsa Model,**
1936. Quaker Puffed Wheat and Rice. 12" wing span. Assembled - **$35 $90 $185**

CLP-6

CLP-7

❑ **CLP-6. Pilot's Cap,**
1936. Quaker Puffed Wheat/Puffed Rice. White twill with gilt braid, brass buttons, black bill, metal airplane ornament. - **$125 $250 $500**

❑ **CLP-7. Girl's Bracelet,**
1936. Quaker Puffed Wheat/Puffed Rice. Gold luster metal with personalized single initial on wing design. - **$60 $140 $290**

CLP-8

❑ **CLP-8. Standee 10x14",**
1939. Rare. Kraft Malted Milk. Promo for China Clipper model plane - **$150 $300 $600**

CLP-9

❑ **CLP-9. China Clipper Promo Wraparound Label for National Dairy Malted Milk,**
1939. Shows pictures of China Clipper model plane. Gordon Gold Archives. -
$35 $75 $160

CLP-10

❑ **CLP-10. Free China Clipper Model Store Sign,**
1939. Kraft Malted Milk. 18x24-1/2" full color sign with same image printed on each side. Has lightly scored top margin allowing it to be hung over a string so either side can be viewed. Advertises "Giant 22" Model." Gordon Gold Archives. - **$150 $300 $600**

CLP-11

❑ **CLP-11. Poster,**
1939. Rare. 32x44". Beautiful colorful poster for grocery stores which shows how to get free photos and models of the China Clipper.-
$175 $400 $800

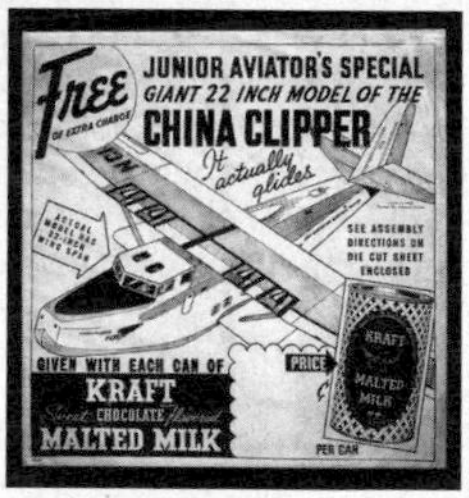

CLP-12

❑ **CLP-12. Model Mailer,**
1939. Kraft Malted Milk. - **$40 $75 $150**

CLP-13

❑ **CLP-13. "Giant Model Of The Famous China Clipper" Cardboard Punch-Out Folder,**
1939. Pan-American Airways. Folder opens to 11x30". - **$65 $150 $300**

CLP-14

❑ **CLP-14. "Kellogg's Model Airplanes" Punchout Book,**
1930s. Book is 10x14.5" with stiff paper cover and four inside pages. Contains 12 full color airplane model punchouts plus "Kellogg's Airport" and accessory pieces. Planes include "Douglas Transport, Vault Corsair, China Clipper, Martin Bomber, G-B Racer," others. As part of the punchout book, there are plain playing pieces and a die. From the Gordon Gold Archives.
Unpunched - **$50 $125 $185**

The Cinnamon Bear

Created by Glanville Heisch and first aired in 1937, *The Cinnamon Bear* was a syndicated children's Christmas tale broadcast five times a week between Thanksgiving and Christmas. In 26 chapters it followed the adventures of Judy and Jimmy Barton and Paddy O'Cinnamon as they travel through Maybe Land in search of their stolen Silver Star. They cross the Root Beer Ocean and come face-to-face with the Wintergreen Witch and Captain Taffy the Pirate. The show was sponsored by department stores, principally Wieboldt's of Chicago, and ran annually for many years.

CIN-1

CIN-2

CIN-3

❑ **CIN-1. Wieboldt's Litho. Tin Tab,**
1940s. Rare. - **$100 $300 $600**

❑ **CIN-2. Foil Silver Star Picturing Paddy,**
c. 1940s. - **$65 $135 $265**

❑ **CIN-3. "TV Club" Litho. Button With Cardboard Bear Attachment,**
1950s. Wieboldt's department store. -
$45 $90 $175

The Cisco Kid

The beloved bandito and his sidekick Pancho were created by William Sidney Porter (1862-1910) writing under the name O. Henry in a short story, *The Caballero's Way*, in the early 1900s and have lived a long entertainment life. They appeared in several silent movies and in 23 sound features between 1929 and 1950, starring either Warner Baxter (who won an Oscar for *In Old Arizona* in 1929), Cesar Romero, Duncan Renaldo (1904-1980) or Gilbert Roland. A radio series aired on Mutual from 1942 to 1956 and a popular television version with Renaldo and Leo Carrillo (1880-1961) was syndicated between 1950 and 1956. Over 150 half-hour episodes were filmed by ZIV Television--in color, though at the time TV could broadcast only in black and white. Comic books appeared in the 1940s and 1950s and a daily comic strip ran from 1951 to 1968 beautifully drawn by Jose Luis Salinas (1908-1985). Most premiums date from the successful broadcast period of the 1950s. A 1994 telefilm brought Cisco and Pancho back to TV audiences in the forms of Jimmy Smits and Cheech Marin, respectively. "Oh, Pancho! Ooooh, Ceesco!"

CIS-1

CIS-2

❑ **CIS-1. "Safety Club Member" Cello. Button,**
c. 1948. - **$25 $45 $95**

❑ **CIS-2. "I'm A Cisco Kid Fan!" Cello. Button,**
1949. ZIV Co. Radio Productions. Issued to show sponsors for promotional purposes. -
$10 $20 $40

CIS-3

❑ **CIS-3. Cisco Kid Radio Photo,**
1949. Radio premium photo with letter. -
$55 $110 $175

CIS-4

❑ **CIS-4. Merchandising Portfolio,**
1949. ZIV Co. Radio Productions . Contains over 25 promotional items such as bw photos, sample ads, source list for premiums.
Complete - **$300 $600 $1200**

CIS-5

❑ **CIS-5. Pancho Radio Photo,**
1949. Radio premium photo with letter.
Rare. - **$55 $110 $175**

(FRONT)

(BACK)

CIS-6

❑ **CIS-6. Cisco Kid Paper Mask,**
1949. Various sponsors. Pictured example for Cisco Kid cookies, Cisco Kid sweet buns by Schofer's Bakery. - **$18 $30 $60**

CIS-7

CIS-8

❑ **CIS-7. Pancho Paper Mask,**
1949. Various bakeries. - **$18 $30 $60**

❑ **CIS-8. "Wrigley's Cisco Kid Club" Cello. Button,**
c. 1949. Wrigley's Gum, Canadian issue. - **$45 $90 $165**

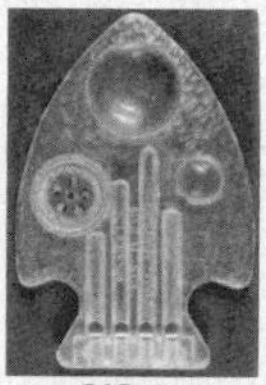
CIS-9

CIS-10

❑ **CIS-9. "Wrigley's Cisco Kid Signal Arrowhead",**
c. 1949. Available for 25¢ and two Wrigley's Spearmint gum wrappers.
Premium - **$75 $150 $350**
Wrigley's Mailer From Toronto And Order Form - **$150 $300 $350**

❑ **CIS-10. "Cisco Kid" Aluminum Saddle Ring,**
1950. Name in raised letters on saddle seat. - **$125 $275 $550**

CIS-11

❑ **CIS-11. Cisco Kid Humming Lariat,**
1950. Eddy's Bread. Cardboard rectangle with string and streamer roll of crepe paper to "Execute The Thrilling Rope Tricks Done By The Famous Cisco Kid". - **$30 $75 $150**

CIS-12

❑ **CIS-12. Paper Sign,**
1950. Cisco Kid paper sign advertises the 1st coloring book and Four Color Comics #292, also known a s The Cisco Kid #1. - **$75 $200 $300**

CIS-13

CIS-14

❑ **CIS-13. Triple "S" Club Litho. Button,**
1950. - **$12 $25 $50**

❑ **CIS-14. Kern's Bread "Triple S Club" Clothing Transfer,**
1950. Tissue paper with reverse image to be applied by warm iron on fabric. - **$20 $50 $75**

CIS-15

CIS-16

❑ **CIS-15. Kern's Bread Postcard,**
1950. - **$15 $28 $55**

❑ **CIS-16. Glass,**
c. 1950. Probably held dairy product. Seen in lime green/black or yellow/brown.
Each - **$30 $70 $135**

CIS-17

❑ **CIS-17. Secret Compartment Photo Ring,**
c. 1950. Rare. Brass bands holding plastic compartment with brass lid over bw picture. - **$2500 $7250 $13,000**

CIS-18

❑ **CIS-18. "Cisco Kid" Ring,**
c. 1950. Silvered brass. Name appears on each band. - **$75 $160 $310**

CIS-19

❑ **CIS-19. Freihofer's Bread Labels,**
c. 1950. From a set. Each - **$10 $20 $30**

CIS-20

CIS-21

CIS-22

❑ **CIS-20. Cello. Button,**
c. 1950. Possibly for rodeo appearance. - **$40 $90 $175**

❑ **CIS-21. "Cisco Kid On TV-Radio" Litho. Tin Tab,**
c. 1950. Various sponsors. Various hat colors. - **$15 $30 $50**

❑ **CIS-22. TV-Radio Pancho Litho. Tab,**
c. 1950. Various sponsors. Various hat colors. - **$15 $30 $50**

CIS-23

❑ **CIS-23. "Arden Milk" Black Fabric Bandanna,**
c. 1950. Opens to 16x16". - **$30 $60 $115**

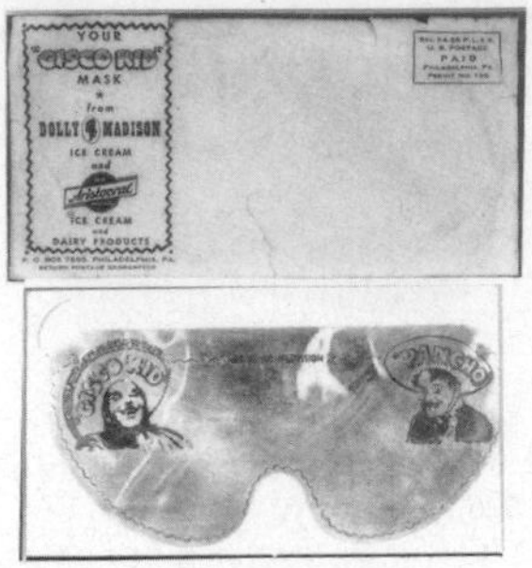

CIS-24

❑ **CIS-24. Thin Plastic Reflective Mask With Envelope,**
c. 1950. Scarce. Dolly Madison Ice Cream.
In Envelope - **$85 $175 $300**
Loose - **$35 $85 $150**

CIS-25

❑ **CIS-25. Comic Strip Announcement Portfolio,**
1951. Nine picture prints and three comic strip prints with art by Jose Luis Salinas. Issued by King Features Syndicate. **- $200 $400 $800**

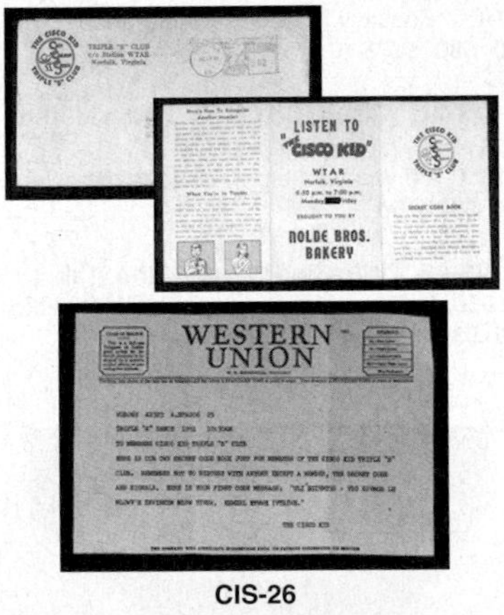

CIS-26

❑ **CIS-26. "Triple 'S' Club" Papers With Envelope,**
1951. Imprinted for Nolde Bros. Bakery and WTAR Radio, Norfolk, Virginia. Contents are replica "Western Union" transmittal telegram plus Code Book leaflet.
Near Mint In Envelope - **$150**
Folder - **$25 $40 $75**
Telegram - **$25 $40 $75**

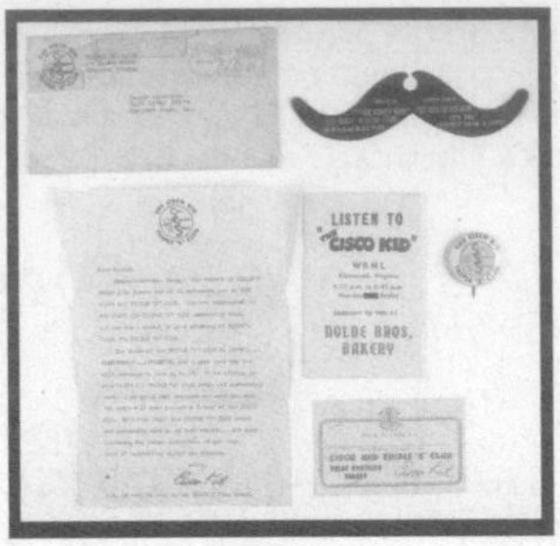

CIS-27

❑ **CIS-27. The Cisco Kid Triple "S" Club Members Pack,**
1951. Lot of six items. First is 3.5x6.5" envelope. Cisco Kid return address with WRNL Richmond 13, VA. Second is 4.75x9" double-fold secret code book. Next is 2.5x4" membership card with facsimile signature "Cisco Kid." Also includes 2x6" black paper mustache with ad for Cisco's radio show and 5.5x8.5" welcome letter. Last is 1-3/8" litho club button.
Complete Kit - **$75 $150 $225**

CIS-28

CIS-29

❑ **CIS-28. Bread Label Folder,**
1952. Freihofer's Bread. Holds 36 different bread labels. **- $75 $150 $300**

❑ **CIS-29. Pancho Photo,**
1952. Butter-Nut Bread. Shows Pancho and horse Loco. Promotes radio and TV show. - **$12 $25 $40**

CIS-30

CIS-31

❑ **CIS-30. Portrait Photo,**
1952. Butter-Nut Bread. - **$12 $25 $40**

❑ **CIS-31. Cisco Photo,**
1952. Butter-Nut Bread. Shows Cisco riding Diablo. Promotes radio and TV show. - **$12 $25 $40**

CIS-32

❑ **CIS-32. Paper Masks Set,**
1953. Tip-Top Bread. Each - **$18 $30 $60**

CIS-33

❑ **CIS-33. Tip-Top Bread Puzzle,**
1953. With Envelope - **$25 $60 $110**
Puzzle Only - **$15 $30 $60**

CIS-34

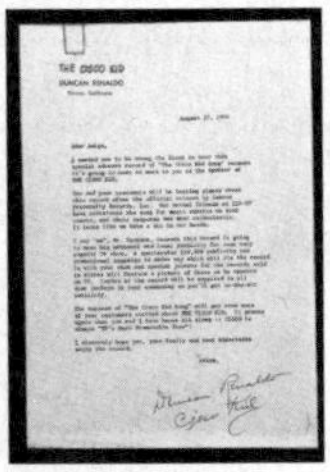

CIS-35

❑ **CIS-34. Record With Sleeve,**
1956. - **$25 $50 $125**

❑ **CIS-35. Letter For Record Promotion,**
1956. - **$25 $50 $125**

CIS-36

❑ **CIS-36. "Cisco Kid Ranchers Club" Member Kit,**
1956. Probable various breads. Includes two certificates, manual, application, "Cattle Brand" card. Complete - **$100 $225 $400**

CIS-37

❑ **CIS-37. "Cisco Kid Ranchers Club" Kit,**
1956. Issued locally by Leatherwood Dairy, Bluefield, West Virginia. Mailer - **$8 $12 $20**
Photo - **$12 $25 $40**
Button - **$10 $25 $50**
Certificate - **$30 $60 $110**

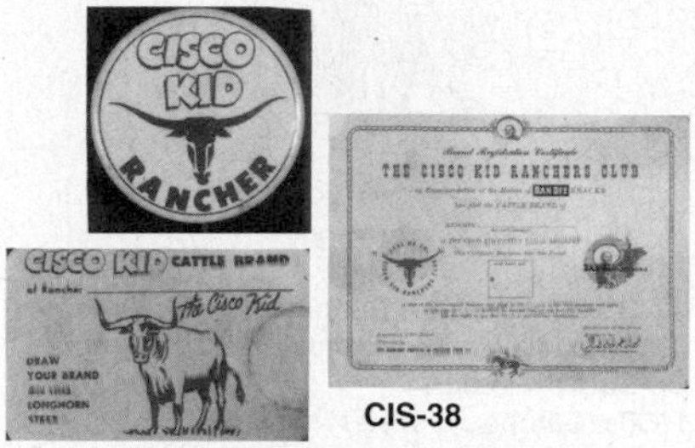

CIS-38

❑ **CIS-38. "Cisco Kid Ranchers Club" Kit,**
1956. Dan-Dee Pretzel And Potato Chip Co.
Certificate - **$30 $60 $110**
Card - **$12 $25 $40**
Button - **$10 $25 $50**
Letter - **$20 $45 $85**

CIS-39

❑ **CIS-39. "Ranchers Club" Card,**
1956. Pro-tek-tiv' Shoes. - **$20 $35 $75**

CIS-40

❑ **CIS-40. Honorary Citizenship Certificate,**
1956. Premium. - **$35 $75 $125**

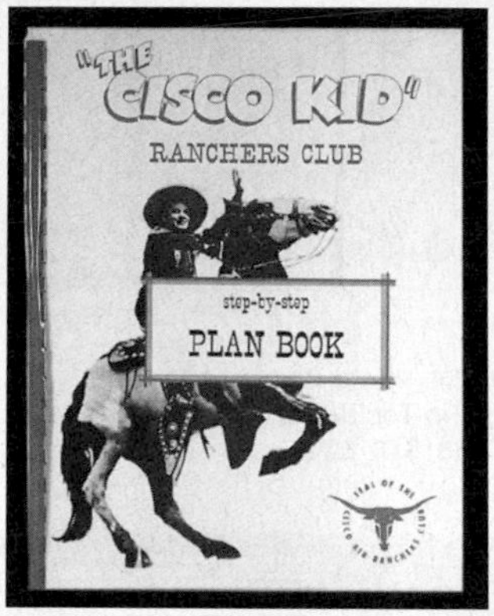

CIS-41

❑ **CIS-41. Ranchers Club Plan Book,**
1956. 28 pgs. including front and back covers. - **$135 $300 $500**

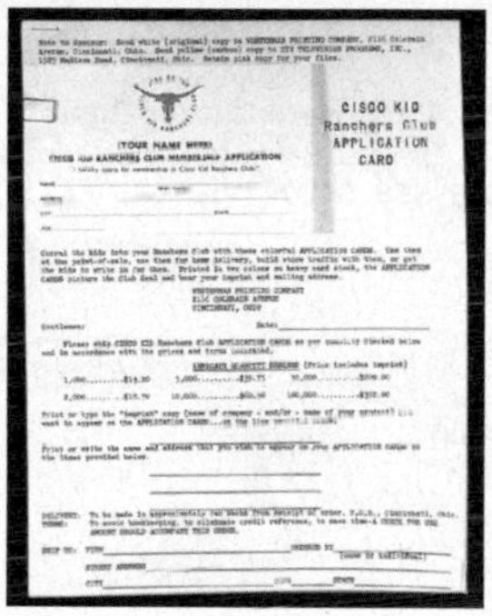

CIS-42

❑ **CIS-42. Ranchers Club Membership Application,**
1956. 3 pgs. of order blanks.
Each - **$30 $55 $90**

CIS-43

❑ **CIS-43. "Cisco Kid" Writing Tablet,**
1957. Scarce. Put out when show was cancelled. - **$30 $60 $115**

CIS-44

❑ **CIS-44. Range War Manual,**
1957. With cardboard back cover. Has two applications with pictures of game, one letter example and eight pages explaining game rules and distribution information. - **$135 $285 $525**

CIS-45

❑ **CIS-45. Range War Game With Punch-Outs,**
1957. Rare. Show was cancelled shortly after release of this game. Few were produced. - **$600 $1100 $1850**

CIS-46

CIS-47

❑ **CIS-46. Store Poster,**
1950s. Nolde's Bread and possibly others. 17x21" black on yellow. - **$50 $90 $175**

❑ **CIS-47. "Cisco Kid" Salesman's Sample Combination Comb And Shoe Horn ,**
1950s. 5-1/2" long ivory hard plastic reading "The Cisco Kid On Television/Sponsor's Imprint Here." - **$30 $75 $140**

CIS-48

CIS-49

❑ CIS-48. Plastic Tumbler,
1950s. Leatherwood Dairy. - **$25 $50 $110**

❑ CIS-49. Glass Bowl,
1950s. Dairy product container. - **$12 $18 $30**

CIS-50

CIS-51

❑ CIS-50. Photo,
1950s. Farm Crest Bakery. - **$20 $40 $85**

❑ CIS-51. Tip-Top Labels,
1950s. Tip-Top Bread. Bread labels were cut in shape of star to fit folder. Each - **$15 $30 $60**

CIS-52

❑ CIS-52. Tip-Top Bread Labels,
1950s. At least 28 in set. Each - **$15 $25 $40**

CIS-53

❑ CIS-53. Tip-Top Bread Folder,
1950s. Tip-Top Bread. Eight pages. Holds 16 star bread labels. Large photo inside of Cisco holding gun. Bread labels tell story of Bolders & Bullet when completed. - **$50 $100 $200**

CIS-54

❑ CIS-54. Photo Cards,
1950s. Tip-Top Bread but various sponsors. Each - **$8 $18 $30**

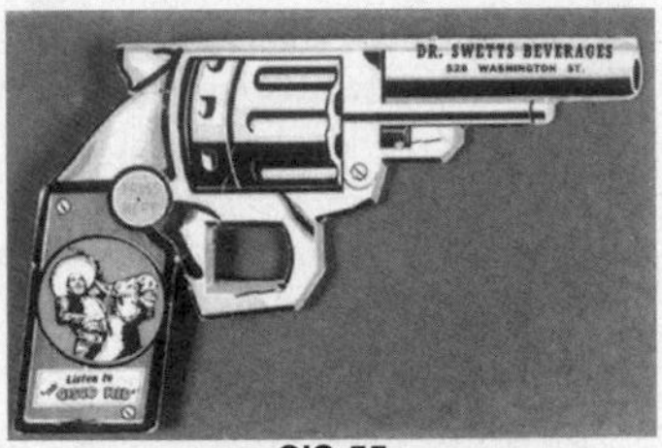

CIS-55

❑ CIS-55. Cardboard Clicker Gun,
1950s. Dr. Swetts beverages but various sponsors. - **$25 $50 $100**

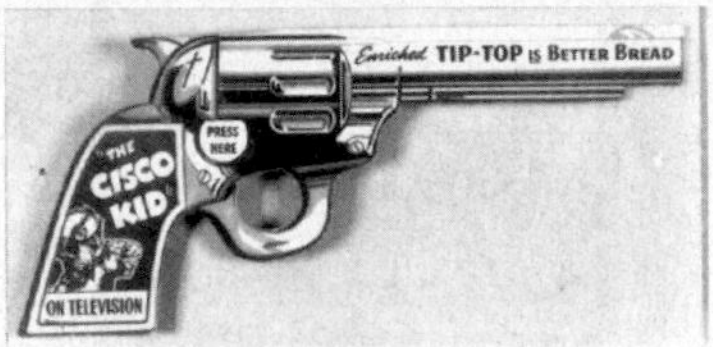

CIS-56

❑ CIS-56. Cardboard Clicker Gun,
1950s. Tip-Top Bread. - **$20 $40 $85**

CIS-57

CIS-58

❑ CIS-57. "Cisco Kid's Choice Tip Top Bread" Bread Labels,
1950s. Black and white center star design on white with red accents. Label back says "48 Pictures In All." Each **- $15 $25 $40**

❑ CIS-58. Milk Bottle,
1950s. Harrisburg (Pa.) Dairies. Company name plus "WTPA Channel 71" every Wednesday 6 P.M. **- $50 $85 $150**

CIS-59

❑ CIS-59. TV "Sponsor's Name" 10x18" Cardboard Sample Store Sign,
1950s. - **$85 $200 $300**

CIS-60

❑ CIS-60. "Duncan Renaldo The TV Cisco Kid And His Horse Diablo In Person Round Up Show" Poster,
1950s. Cardboard poster measures 14x22" with unprinted area at top for promoters to fill in dates and locations. - **$75 $165 $275**

CIS-61

❑ CIS-61. "Meet Duncan Rinaldo, 'The Cisco Kid'" Personal Appearance Poster,
1950s. Poster is 17x21". Text includes "At The Norfolk Municiple Arena In Person From 2 to 5 PM/Shake Hands With Cisco Himself/Get A Free 8x10" Autographed Picture Of Cisco/ Discover Cisco's Secret." - **$60 $125 $200**

CIS-62

❑ CIS-62. "The Cisco Kid" Radio/Bread Sign,
1950s. 11x14". Text is "Listen To 'The Cisco Kid' Adventure/Romance/Excitement/WTSV 5:30 PM Tues. And Thurs./Brought To You By Normand's Country Style Bread."
- **$40 $70 $125**

CIS-63

CIS-64

❑ CIS-63. "Cisco Kid 3-D Comics" Flip Lapel Pin,
1950s. Cardboard disk is 2.5" reading "I've Got 'It' Ask Me!" on one side and "Cisco Kid 3-D Comics" on the other. Original safety pin and string attached. When string is pulled, disk would flip up to read "Cisco Kid" side.
- **$20 $45 $90**

❑ CIS-64. Shopping Mall Photo,
1950s. Printed for "Thruway Plaza," likely various mall sponsors. - **$18 $30 $60**

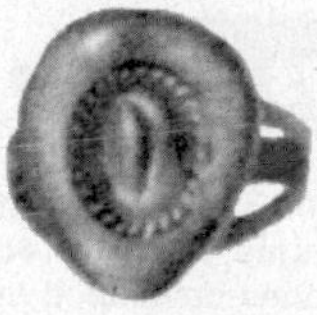
CIS-65

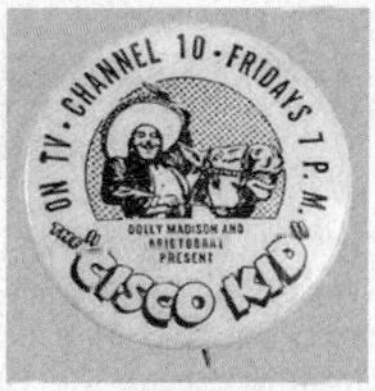

CIS-66

❑ CIS-65. "Cisco Kid" Silvered Brass Hat Ring,
1950s. Name on brim. - **$115 $325 $550**
Without Name - **$10 $20 $30**

❑ CIS-66. "TV Channel 10" Member Cello. Button,
1950s. Dolly Madison and Aristocrat. Comes with beige or green background.
Either - **$20 $40 $85**

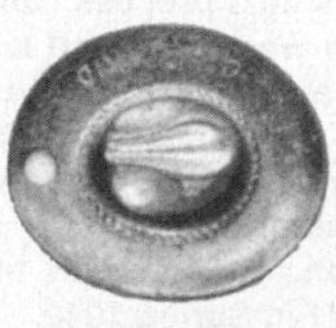
CIS-67

CIS-68

❑ CIS-67. "Cisco Kid" Silvered Brass Keychain Fob,
1950s. Store item stamped "Japan". -
$18 $30 $50

❑ CIS-68. Cisco Kid Inspired Doll,
1950s. Probably unlicensed. - **$80 $165 $275**

CIS-69

❑ CIS-69. "Cisco Kid" Advertising Press Book,
1950s. Has info on Duncan Renaldo's sessions as a performer at fairs, stadiums and auditoriums. Has 13" full figure photo of Cisco printed on press book. - **$75 $165 $325**

CIS-70

❑ CIS-70. Farm Fresh Moanalua Milk Button,
1950s. Litho likely from Hawaii. -
$75 $175 $325

CIS-71

CIS-72

❑ CIS-71. "Cisco Kid And Diablo" English Biscuit Tin,
1950s. Huntley & Palmer's Biscuits, London. Litho tin 5" diameter. Lid has color photo image of Cisco on rearing Diablo. - **$50 $85 $175**

❑ CIS-72. "Cisco & Pancho In '84" Video Release Promotional Cello. Button,
1984. Blair Entertainment. 3-1/2" full color button used when TV programs became available on video. - **$18 $35 $75**

Clara Bow

Billed as the "hottest jazz baby in films" by producer B.P. Schulberg in 1925, Clara Bow (1905-1965) appeared in some 58 films between 1922 and 1933. Clara was living in New York City when she won *Motion Picture* magazine's *Fame And Fortune* contest in 1921, leading to a part in the 1922 film *Beyond The Rainbow.* She became a major star by 1925 with *The Plastic Age* which co-starred Donald Keith. The film also had Clark Gable and Carole Lombard in minor roles.

The sexy redhead with big brown eyes and pouty lips was dubbed the "It" girl by Elinor Glyn who wrote a book with the same title which became a major motion picture in 1927. Bow starred in, and Glyn co-wrote the film which co-starred Antonio Moreno. The World War I epic *Wings,* directed by William Wellman was perhaps Clara's most famous film. Co-starring Buddy Rogers, Richard Arlen and Gary Cooper, the 1927 movie won Hollywood's first Academy Award for best picture. Clara's heavy Brooklyn accent led to a decline in her popularity with the advent of talking movies. She married cowboy star Rex Bell in 1932 and completely retired from films in 1933 to be a wife and mother.

CLA-1

❑ CLA-1. "Wings" Aviation Movie Program And Sheet Music,
1927. Program is 9x12" in full color with 16 pages. Sheet music is 9x12" with full color front cover. Bow starred with Richard Arlen, Gary Cooper, Charles "Buddy" Rogers. Program -
$20 $35 $75
Music - **$10 $20 $40**

CLA-2

❑ **CLA-2. "How I Broke Into The Movies By 60 Famous Movie Stars" Hardcover,**
1930. Copyright 1930 Hal C. Herman printed by Everett Sanders 8x10.75" hardcover with 124 pages. Pages have full page photo of star on left and biography at right plus facsimile autograph at bottom. Includes Bow, Chaplin, Garbo, Jolson, Chaney, Mix and others. - **$50 $100 $200**

CLA-3

❑ **CLA-3. Clara Bow - Greta Garbo Theater Window Card Pair,**
1931 Paramount Publix Corp. Each card is 13.75x22". Each - **$50 $100 $150**

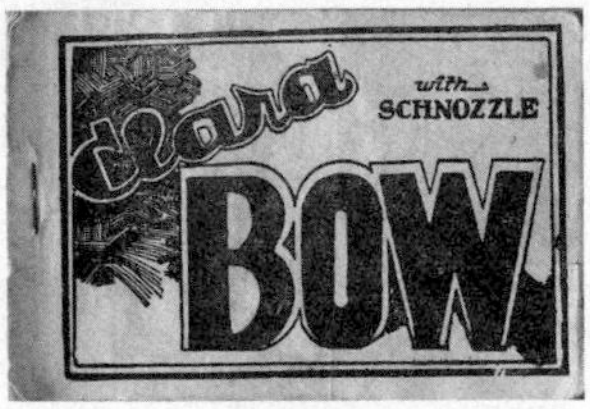

CLA-4

❑ **CLA-4. "Clara Bow With Schnozzle" 8 Pager,**
1930s. 2.75x4-1/8" with yellow covers and blue text containing eight sheets with x-rated story printed on front side. Early issue. - **$25 $50 $100**

Clara, Lu 'n' Em

This low-key comedy about three gossipy housewives was created by three Northwestern University coeds to amuse their sorority sisters. After graduation they took it to Chicago radio station WGN, which ran it locally in 1930-1931 and then as an evening program on NBC until 1932 when it became the nation's first daytime soap opera. The sponsor was Colgate. The program ran until 1936 and was revived for a short run on CBS in 1942 for Pillsbury flour. The three women were played by Louise Starkey, Isobel Carothers and Helen King.

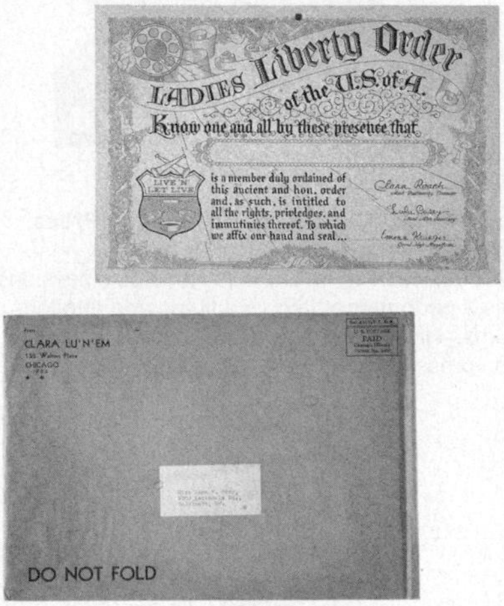

CLN-1

❑ **CLN-1. Certificate and Mailer,**
1932. Radio premium. Beautiful cardboard membership certificate for Ladies Liberty Order.
Certificate - **$35 $75 $150**
Mailer - **$12 $25 $40**

CLN-2 CLN-3

❑ **CLN-2. Cast Member Photo,**
1932. Fan photo 5x7" black and white with facsimile first name signature of each. - **$18 $30 $55**

❑ **CLN-3. Newspaper,**
1932. Radio premium. The Ladies Clarion Blast - Vol. #1. - **$30 $75 $125**

CLN-4

CLN-4. "Clara, Lu' n' Em" Radio Show Promotion Page,
1932. Featured in Ladies' Home Journal - **$5 $15 $20**

CLN-5

CLN-5. "Clara, Lu' n' Em" Puzzle,
c. 1933. Colgate. Envelope - **$8 $15 $30**
Puzzle - **$25 $55 $110**

Clowns

Clowns have been with us since ancient Greece. The clown costume with ruffled neck, hat and oversized shoes developed in England during the 1600s. Court jesters also played the part of the zany fool. Italian street theater in the 1700s gave birth to harlequin characters with patchwork costumes and Pierrot became one of the first clown types to use whiteface make-up. In 1768, in London, Philip Astley presented a show using a clown, leading to Charles Hughes founding the Royal Circus in 1782. Daniel Rice, considered the first white-faced American clown, made his first circus appearance in 1840. The five Ringling brothers began their circus in the 1870s and combined with Barnum and Bailey in 1907.

Max Fleischer brought animation to new heights with his *Out Of The Inkwell* cartoons and Koko the Clown. Using a process called rotoscoping, live action was combined with animation to film Max's brother Dave dressed as Koko. The series ran from 1919 to 1929. The most famous clown in comic books is The Joker, created by Bob Kane art assistant Jerry Robinson. He made his first appearance in *Batman* #1 in Spring 1940.

Clowning around continues to prove popular to worldwide cultures, enriching many lives.

CLO-1

❑ CLO-1. Omaha Exposition Button,
1899. Whitehead & Hoag Co. Rare 1.75" button. Backpaper advertises "The Western Trust And Investment Co." - **$150 $300 $600**

CLO-2

CLO-3

❑ CLO-2. Clown Promotes Carnival Button,
c. 1904. Pulver. 1.25" button. - **$8 $15 $30**

❑ CLO-3. Large Clown With Parasol Wind-Up,
1930s. 4x6x10.5" tall celluloid with built-in key. Made in Japan paper sticker. - **$75 $150 $300**

CLO-4

❑ CLO-4. Rabbit Clown Wind-Up,
1930s. 2.5x13x8" tall celluloid. Made in Japan. Rabbit revolves as two balls rotate with ringing bells. - **$40 $85 $150**

CLO-5

❑ CLO-5. Clown On Donkey Wind-Up,
1930s. 1.5x5x5.5" tall tin litho marked "SG/Made In Germany" has built-in key. - **$100 $200 $350**

CLO-6

CLO-7

❑ CLO-6. Circus Clown Monkey Bank,
1930s. J. Chein & Co. Tin litho toy with bulbous roly-poly body is 4" diameter and 5.75" tall. - **$125 $250 $400**

❑ CLO-7. Rare Texas "Circus Fans Association" Button,
1930s. St. Louis Button Co. 2-1/8" button. - **$20 $40 $100**

CLO-8

❑ CLO-8. Circus Theme "Daily Dime Bank",
c. 1930s. 2.5x2.5x.75" deep tin litho. This is the "orange hat" version. Also comes in a "red hat" version. - **$40 $85 $135**

CLO-9

❑ CLO-9. Mechanical Clown Bank,
c. 1930s. 1.5x3x4.25" tall tin litho marked "British Made." Tongue serves as coin tray. - **$65 $125 $200**

CLO-10

❑ CLO-10. "Ringling Bros. And Barnum & Bailey" Circus Poster With Lou Jacobs,
c. 1945. 81x122" poster in two parts, billboard size. - **$200 $400 $700**

CLO-11

❑ CLO-11. "Emmett Kelly's Willie The Clown" Large Doll,
1950s. Baby Barry Toy. Doll is 5x13x20" tall with molded vinyl head, plastic eyes, rooted life-like hair, stuffed body and vinyl hands. Clothing includes felt jacket, vest and pants; cloth shirt and tie with wooden clothespin tie bar and vinyl suspenders. - **$50 $100 $150**

CLO-12

❑ CLO-12. Clown Mechanical Bank,
1950s. Chein. 2.5" diameter by 5" tall litho tin bank with moveable tongue and trap under base. - **$20 $40 $75**

CLO-13

CLO-14

❑ CLO-13. Clown Rider Wind-Up Motorcycle,
1950s. Mettoy Co., England. 3x7.5x4.75" tall tin litho toy with built-in key. Clown's separate head is painted cast metal. - **$200 $500 $900**

❑ CLO-14. Clown With Donkey Wind-Up,
1950s. 1.5x7x5" tall celluloid toy with key. - **$75 $150 $250**

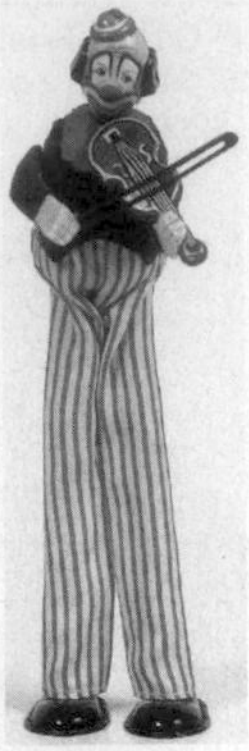

CLO-15 CLO-16

❑ **CLO-15. Roller Skating Clown Wind-Up By T.P.S.,**
1950s. About 6" tall. Tin litho with built-in key. Made in Japan. - **$100 $200 $300**

❑ **CLO-16. Happy The Violinist Clown Wind-Up,**
1950s. T.P.S. Tin litho toy. - **$50 $100 $200**

CLO-17

❑ **CLO-17. Child Clown Circus Promoter Wind-Up,**
1950s. Nikko. 2.5x4x6" tall tin litho toy with built-in key. Made in Japan. - **$25 $50 $100**

CLO-18 CLO-19

❑ **CLO-18. Clown On Unicycle Wind-Up,**
1950s. T.P.S. 2x2.5x5.5" tall tin litho toy with built-in key. Made in Japan. - **$50 $100 $200**

❑ **CLO-19. Joe The Xylophone Player Clown Wind-Up,**
1950s. T.P.S. 4x4x5" tall tin litho toy with built-in key. This toy came in two varieties and this is the "small hands" variety. - **$50 $100 $200**

CLO-20

❑ **CLO-20. Clown Juggler With Monkey Wind-Up,**
1950s. T.P.S. 2x3x9.5" tall tin litho toy with built-in key. - **$100 $200 $400**

CLO-21

❑ **CLO-21. "Clown Jalopy Cycle",**
1960s. T.P.S. 2.5x9x6" tall tin litho toy with box. Made in Japan. Box - **$100 $200 $300**
Toy - **$100 $200 $300**

Clyde Beatty

Clyde Beatty (1903-1965), world-famous wild animal trapper and trainer, played himself in two chapter plays: *The Lost Jungle* for Mascot in 1934 and *Darkest Africa* for Republic in 1936. In both he defeats hostile forces, human and animal, and wins the girl. His *Clyde Beatty Show* on radio, on the other hand, was said to dramatize actual incidents from his life in the wild and at his circus. The program was syndicated in the late 1940s and ran on the Mutual network from 1950 to 1952, sponsored by Kellogg's cereal. Scattered comic book appearances included a 1937 giveaway by Malto-Meal and a 1956 giveaway by Richfield Oil.

CLY-1

CLY-2

❑ **CLY-1. "Lions And Tigers With The Sensational Dare-Devil Clyde Beatty" Big Little Book,**
1934. Whitman #653. - **$14 $42 $95**

❑ **CLY-2. Jungle Animal Brass Link Charm Bracelet,**
1935. Scarce. Quaker Wheat Crackels. Unmarked Clyde Beatty premium. -
$115 $250 $500

CLY-3

❑ **CLY-3. Gold-Plated Lion Head Ring,**
1935. Quaker Wheat Crackels. Ring has adjustable bands with large open-mouth lion head on the top with lion displaying four large fangs. There are no jewels in the eyes or mouth. Ring was also issued in a jeweled version but we've seen no paperwork identifying such rings as Clyde Beatty premiums. -
$475 $950 $1800

CLY-4

❑ **CLY-4. "Clyde Beatty & His Wild Animal Act" Punch-Out Album,**
1935. Scarce. Quaker Wheat Crackels. Made by Fold-A-Way Toys.
Unpunched - **$100 $275 $500**

CLY-5

❑ **CLY-5. Quaker Oats Circus Book,**
1935. Inside front offers punch-out animal act, lion head ring, jungle bracelet, bullwhip. - **$30 $60 $125**

CLY-6

CLY-7

❑ **CLY-6. "Cole Bros. Circus" Cello. Button,**
1930s. - **$12 $25 $50**

❑ **CLY-7. Circus Souvenir Cello. Button,**
1930s. - **$18 $35 $70**

CLY-8

❑ **CLY-8. "Clyde Beatty Circus Fire Dept.,"**
1930s. This button is 2.25" with various fire emblems at the center. Maker's name on curl "L.A. Stamp Stat. Co." - **$30 $60 $100**

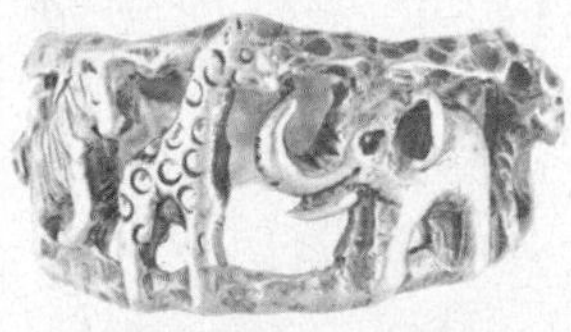

CLY-9

❑ **CLY-9. Clyde Beatty Jungle Ring In Sterling,**
c. 1940. Well-made single band stamped "925" on interior surface. Likely used as a circus souvenir. Well-detailed, die-cut animals shown are hippo, zebra, girafe, elephant and tiger. - **$115 $225 $460**

CLY-10

❑ **CLY-10. "Hingees" Punch-Out Kit In Envelope,**
1945. Store item. Unused - **$35 $60 $110**

CLY-11

❑ **CLY-11. "Richfield Presents Clyde Beatty's African Jungle Book,"**
1956. Issued by Richfield Oil. 16 pages. Has Disneyland back cover ad. - **$10 $30 $90**

CLY-12

❑ **CLY-12. "Clyde Beatty Circus" Program With Cisco Kid,**
1956. Season tour 18-page souvenir including photo article on performer Duncan Renaldo as Cisco Kid. - **$15 $25 $50**

Coca-Cola

Since the mid-1890s, Coca-Cola has distributed premiums in staggering numbers and almost every conceivable material and variety. What started as a patent medicine tonic soon evolved into a soda fountain or bottled drink sold in more than 160 countries globally. Coca-Cola premiums never lack for distinct self-advertising but over the years have frequently been related to war, entertainment and comic characters, sports, toy trucks, educational materials and much more. Hundreds of items intended originally as only convenience items to stores and customers now swell the ranks of advertising collectibles. Illustrator Haddon Sundblom (1899-1976) first painted what has become known as the Coca-Cola Santa in 1931. When his first model, Lou Prentice, passed away Sundblom used himself as the model. Sundblom and fellow artist Archie Lee designed the Sprite Boy in the 1940s. The hit song *I'd Like To Buy The World A Coke,"* written by Billy Davis, Roger Cook and Bill Backer and released on February 12, 1971 was updated in 2005 to appeal to the modern generation. The quantity of Coca-Cola premiums issued in the past century have resulted in several reference books devoted solely to this output.

COC-1

COC-2

❑ **COC-1. Cello. Note Pad,**
1902. Front cover has full color portrait, back has art illustrating sales growth 1886-1901. - **$200 $425 $850**

❑ **COC-2. "Drink Coca-Cola" Mirror,**
1907. Mirror is 2.75" tall. Tiny text on bottom edge "From The Painting Copyright 1906 By Wolf & Co. Phila." along with name of maker Bastian. Bottom curl edge offers a duplicate mirror by sending 5 (cents) postage to the company. - **$200 $400 $750**

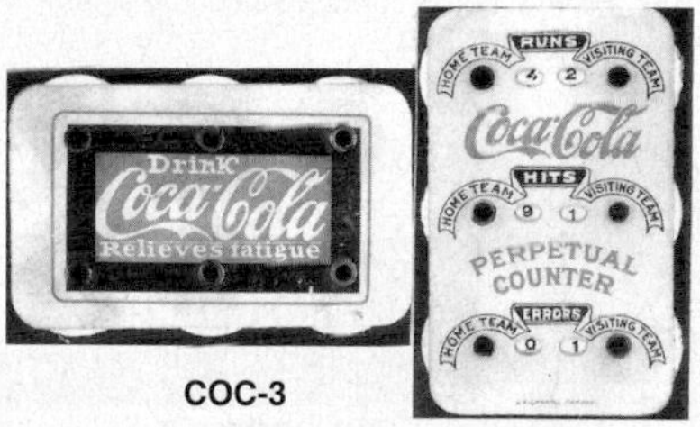

COC-3

❑ **COC-3. Cardboard Baseball Score Counter,**
c. 1907. - **$75 $150 $250**

COC-4

COC-5

❑ **COC-4. Cello. Pocket Mirror,**
1909. Illustration by Hamilton King. - **$150 $250 $500**

❑ **COC-5. "Drink Coca-Cola 5 (cents)" Mirror,**
1914. Mirror is 2.75" tall. - **$175 $350 $675**

COC-6

❑ **COC-6. Cello. Pocket Mirror,**
1917. Pictures World War I era girl. -
$150 $250 $500

COC-7

❑ **COC-7. "Toonerville Refreshment Palace" Leaflet,**
1931. From a series for distribution by salesman. - **$25 $40 $80**

COC-9

COC-8

❑ **COC-8. Coca-Cola Tin Thermometer,**
c. 1935. 7x16" litho tin. - **$90 $165 $300**

❑ **COC-9. "Horse Race Game,"**
c. 1930s. Milton Bradley. - **$90 $175 $325**

COC-10

COC-11

❑ **COC-10. Cleveland Press "Big Wheels Club" Cello. Button,**
1930s. - **$18 $30 $50**

❑ **COC-11. Rare "Kiddies Club" Button,**
1930s. Graphic 1.5" with white and yellow text on red, green rim. Likely c.1934.
- $115 $235 $400

COC-12

❑ **COC-12. Warplane 13x15" Cardboard Sign,**
1943. From series bordered in white and gold.
Each - **$35 $65 $100**

COC-13

❑ **COC-13. "Know Your War Planes" Booklet,**
1943. Coca-Cola. - **$25 $55 $100**

COC-14

❑ **COC-14. Warplane Cards,**
1943. Set of 20. Set - **$65 $125 $250**

COC-15

❑ **COC-15. Newspaper Ads For Premium Booklet "Know Your War Airplanes",**
1943. Our photos show three different ads, each featuring a different warplane.
Each - **$8 $15 $20**

COC-16

❑ **COC-16. Warplane 13x15" Cardboard Sign,**
1943. From series bordered in simulated wood.
Each - **$35 $65 $100**

COC-17

COC-18

❑ **COC-17. Felt Fabric Beanie,**
1940s. - **$25 $55 $110**

❑ **COC-18. "hi fi Club" Member Litho. Button,**
c. 1959. - **$12 $18 $30**

COC-19

❑ **COC-19. "Marx Coca-Cola Truck" Boxed,**
1950s. Truck is 4.5x12.5x5.25" tall. The truck has tin litho cab and pressed steel body. As part of the lithographed design, cab doors read "Drink Coca-Cola In Bottles." Comes with four hard plastic soda bottle cases.
Box - **$115 $225 $350**
Toy - **$125 $250 $400**

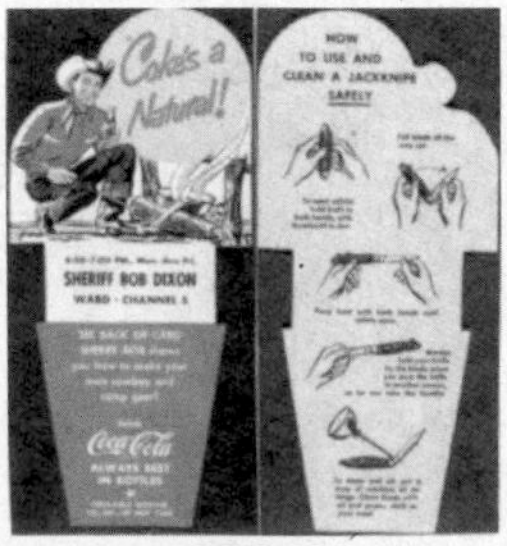

COC-20

❑ **COC-20. "Sheriff Bob Dixon" Insert,**
1950s. Promotes TV show on local station. - **$12 $25 $40**

COC-21

COC-22

❑ **COC-21. Celluloid 9" Wall Sign,**
1950s. - **$55 $110 $215**

❑ **COC-22. Plastic Cooler Replica,**
c. 1950s. 4x4x5" wide. - **$45 $90 $175**

COC-23

❑ **COC-23. "Coca-Cola" Australian Club Button,**
c. 1950s. 1.25" cello design of black and white bottle overprinted by red/green text then rimmed in green. For "Member Of The Bottlers Club." - **$25 $55 $100**

COC-24

❑ **COC-24. Diecut 5' Standee,**
1960s. - **$150 $325 $600**

COC-25

❑ **COC-25. Coca-Cola Dispenser And Bank,**
1960s. Store item by C&G Toys. Comes with two miniature mugs. Holds 6-1/2 ounces of soda. Near Mint Boxed - **$250**
Toy Only - **$50 $100 $150**

COC-26

❑ **COC-26. Red Vinyl Lunch Box,**
c. 1080. Issued with unmarked styrofoam lunch bottle. Made by Aladdin Industries.
Box - **$40 $75 $150**
Bottle - **$5 $10 $25**

COC-27

❑ **COC-27. "Bring Home the Classics" Poster Prize,**
1988. 17"x24". 2nd prize from Coca-Cola/Disney sweepstakes promotion. - **$50 $75 $175**

COC-28

COC-29

❑ **COC-28. Christmas Elf Cloth Doll,**
1980s. - **$18 $30 $50**

❑ **COC-29. Canadian 3" Cello. Endorsement Button,**
1980s. By Coca-Cola Ltd. of Canada picturing Bill Cosby. - **$8 $12 $20**

COC-30

❑ **COC-30. Coca-Cola International Bean Bag Standee Sign and Bean Bags,**
1999. There are 5 different signs for 5 sets of 10 bean bags. Series 2 sign shown here.
Each sign - **$10 $25 $50**

The 50 Bean Bags and the countries they represent:

❑ **Ardi The Aardvark**	**Nigeria**	**$10**
❑ **Badgey The Badger**	**Czech Rep.**	**$10**
❑ **Baltic The Reindeer**	**Sweden**	**$10**
❑ **Barris The Brown Bear**	**Russia**	**$15**
❑ **Barrot The Parrot**	**Brazil**	**$10**
❑ **Blubby The Pot Bellied Pig**	**Vietnam**	**$12**
❑ **Can Can The Pelican**	**Cuba**	**$10**
❑ **Clomp The Elephant**	**Kenya**	**$12**
❑ **Croon The Baboon**	**Pakistan**	**$10**
❑ **Crunch The Crocodile**	**Sudan**	**$12**
❑ **Curry The Tiger**	**India**	**$10**
❑ **Dover The Bulldog**	**England**	**$15**
❑ **Fannie The Fox**	**Germany**	**$10**
❑ **Gourmand The Moose**	**Canada**	**$10**
❑ **Heeta The Cheetah**	**Nambia**	**$10**
❑ **Hopps The Coki Frog**	**Puerto Rico**	**$12**
❑ **Howls The Wolf**	**Romania**	**$10**
❑ **Kelp The Kiwi**	**New Zealand**	**$10**
❑ **Key Key The Snow Monkey**	**Japan**	**$15**
❑ **Laffs The Llama**	**Bolivia**	**$10**
❑ **Locks The Rabbit**	**Scotland**	**$10**
❑ **Lors The Wild Boar**	**Italy**	**$10**
❑ **Masa The Lion**	**Mozambique**	**$12**
❑ **Masha The Ostrich**	**South Africa**	**$10**
❑ **Meeska The Hippo**	**Zambia**	**$12**
❑ **Nardie The St. Bernard**	**Switzerland**	**$15**
❑ **Neppy The Proboscis Monkey**	**Thailand**	**$10**
❑ **Oppy The Octopus**	**Greece**	**$12**
❑ **Orany The Orangutan**	**Singapore**	**$10**
❑ **Paco The Iguana**	**Mexico**	**$10**
❑ **Peng The Penguin**	**Chile**	**$10**
❑ **Pok The Peacock**	**Sri Lanka**	**$10**
❑ **Quala The Koala Bear**	**Australia**	**$20**
❑ **Ramel The Camel**	**Egypt**	**$12**
❑ **Reegle The Eagle**	**USA**	**$25**
❑ **Rhiny The Black Rhinoceros**	**Tanzania**	**$10**
❑ **Rif Raff The Giraffe**	**Somalia**	**$10**
❑ **Rilla The Gorilla**	**Rwanda**	**$12**
❑ **Salty The Sea Turtle**	**Bahamas**	**$12**
❑ **Streak The Jackal**	**Tunisia**	**$10**
❑ **Strudel The Poodle**	**France**	**$10**
❑ **Taps The Tapir**	**Venezuela**	**$10**
❑ **Toolu The Toucan**	**Honduras**	**$10**
❑ **Topus The Zebra**	**Nigeria**	**$10**
❑ **Toro The Bull**	**Spain**	**$12**
❑ **Vaca The Long Horned Cow**	**Argentina**	**$12**
❑ **Waks The Yak**	**Nepal**	**$10**
❑ **Waller The Walrus**	**Greenland**	**$10**
❑ **Woolsey The Sheep**	**Ireland**	**$10**
❑ **Zongshi The Panda Bear**	**China**	**$20**

Badgey

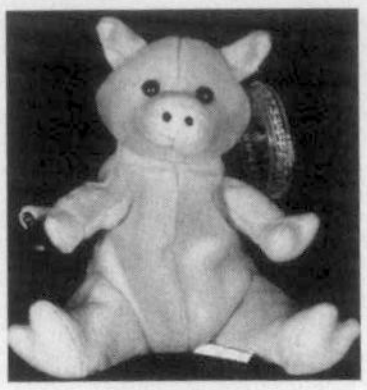

Blubby

Hopps

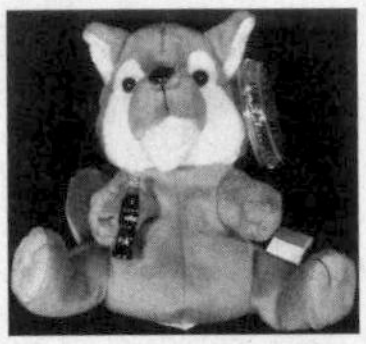

Howls

Key Key

Nardie

Quala

Reegle

Woolsy

Zongshi

Colonel Sanders

Harland Sanders (1890-1980) was operating a service station in Corbin, Kentucky when he began cooking chicken for hungry travelers in his back room Sanders Café in 1930. Governor Ruby Laffoon made him a Kentucky Colonel in 1935 and his establishment was listed in the 1939 Duncan Hines *Adventures In Good Eating* directory. Developing his "Secret Recipe" of 11 herbs and spices, Sanders went on the road selling Kentucky Fried Chicken restaurant franchises in 1955. By 1965 there were more than 600 outlets. Dave Thomas, founder of Wendy's hamburger chain, was a Kentucky Fried Chicken district manager at one point in his career.

Sanders appeared in numerous commercials throughout his career and was on *What's My Line?* in 1963 as well as two episodes of *Rowan & Martin's Laugh-In* in 1968. His company went public in 1966, was acquired by Pepsi Co. in 1986 and is now owned by Yum! Brands, Inc. with some 32,500 outlets in more than 100 countries in conjunction with Taco Bell.

A great rags to riches story based on "finger lickin' good" chicken.

COL-1

❑ **COL-1. "Col. Sanders" Banks,**
1962/1977. First bank is 10" tall hard vinyl with 1962 copyright and Canadian marking. Second is 7.75" tall with 1977 copyright. Both made by Margardt Co., Los Angeles.
1962 Version - **$12 $25 $50**
1977 Version - **$10 $20 $30**

COL-2

COL-3

❑ **COL-2. Colonel Sanders Composition Bobbing Head,**
1960s. - **$50 $125 $250**

❑ **COL-3. Colonel Sanders/Kentucky Fried Chicken Night Light,**
1976. 7" tall bisque-like figure on wooden base with on/off switch on cord. - **$30 $65 $125**

COL-4

COL-5

❑ **COL-4. Colonel Sanders 100 Club Award,**
1970s. Quality Service Club Award, approx. 4" in diameter. - **$35 $70 $125**

❑ **COL-5. Colonel Sanders "Kentucky Fried Chicken" Figural Bank,**
1991. 7" tall with 4x4.5" made of pliable vinyl. Back of base reads "Colonel Sanders Copyright KFC-J 1991." Issued only for Asian market. - **$50 $100 $150**

COL-6

COL-7

❑ **COL-6. Kentucky Fried Chicken/Colonel Sanders Cookie Jar,**
1998. KFC copyright. 15.5" tall limited edition. Inside lid marked "12/250 Wolfe Studio."
Near Mint - **$200**

❑ **COL-7. Colonel Sanders Wacky Wobbler Figure,**
2001. - **$25**

Comic Character Misc.

Comic strip characters, particularly prior to World War II and the following early years of television, could almost be considered "family" to readers. No surprise, then, that advertisers sensed that premiums based on such familiar and well-loved characters would boost sales. Historically, the Yellow Kid and Buster Brown led the way. These and 73 others of intense popularity are listed in *Hake's Guide To Comic Character Collectibles* published in 1993, as well as other pages of this book. This section is devoted to comic characters that may have a large number of associated collectibles but relatively few offered as actual premiums.

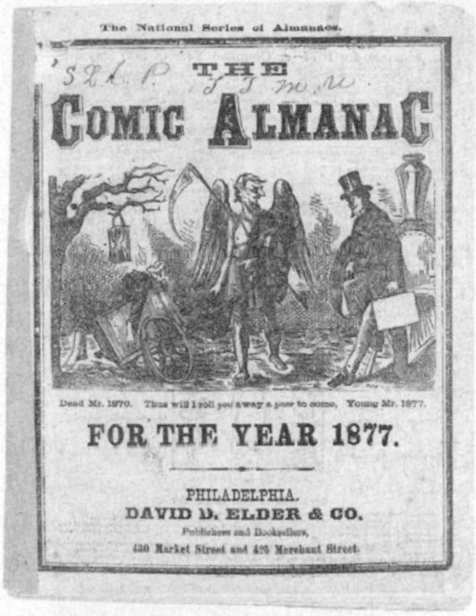

COM-1

❑ **COM-1. The Comic Almanac,**
1877. David D. Elder & Co.- **$50 $100 $175**

COM-2

❑ **COM-2. Comic "Library" Books.**
"New York Five Cent Library #87" Book, June 30, 1894. Rare. High grade copies are rarely found. Comic paper. - **$40 $85 $165**

"Comic Library #136" Softcover, April 10, 1896. Rare. Soft cover comic with staples. Comic paper. - **$90 $175 $325**

COM-3

❑ **COM-3. "Palmer Cox's Queer People" Book,**
1890s. Rare. Donohue and Co., Chicago. Illustrates many famous fairy tales with Brownie-like characters.- **$125 $275 $550**

COM-4

❑ **COM-4. "Punch" Pitcher,**
1890s. With ornate pewter lid. Pink background. Rare. - **$350 $675 $1350**

COM-5

COM-6

❑ **COM-5. "Punch's Book of Comical Pictures and Stories" Hardcover Book,**
c. 1890s. Rare. Published by Hurst & Co., New York. - **$125 $250 $500**

❑ **COM-6. "Sleeping Beauty" Hardcover Book,**
c. 1900. Published by Hurst & Co., New York. - **$60 $140 $250**

COM-7

❑ **COM-7. "Pore Lil Mose His Letters To His Mammy" Comic Strip Reprint Book,**
1902. Published by Grand Union Tea Company, copyright New York Herald.
Good - **$1500**
Fine - **$5500**

COM-8

❑ **COM-8. "Little Sammy Sneeze" Book,**
1905. Rare. By Winsor McCay. Rarely found better than very good.
Good - **$1700**
Fine - **$5000**

COM-9

❑ **COM-9. "Funny Folk Calendar" With Buster Brown, Little Nemo And Others,**
1905. Large 23x32" one-sided slick paper sheet issued as a special insert for the "New York Herald" Christmas 1905 with classic specialty art done by 11 different artists. Comic strips by Gustave Verbeck; Buster Brown and Tige by R.F. Outcault; Little Sammy Sneeze, Hungry Henrietta and Little Nemo by Winsor McKay; Happy Bear by R.F. Outcault and a fantasy elephant by Walter Crane. - **$1200 $2400 $3600**

COM-10

❑ **COM-10. "Buffalo Bill Stories" Magazines,**
1908. Street & Smith magazines. April 15, 1908 & June 6, 1908 shown. Each - **$40 $100 $200**

COM-11

COM-12

❑ COM-11. Tad Dorgan "Tad's Joke Book",
1911. New York Sunday American. 10x12" Sunday supplement with 16 pgs. - **$30 $60 $110**

❑ COM-12. T. E. Powers "The Little Hatchet Joke Book",
c. 1911. New York Sunday American. 10x12" Sunday supplement with 16 pgs. - **$30 $60 $110**

COM-13

COM-14

❑ COM-13. T. E. Powers "Joy & Gloom Joke Book",
c. 1911. New York Sunday American. 10x12" Sunday supplement with 16 pgs. - **$30 $60 $110**

❑ COM-14. Gus Mager "The Monkey Joke Book",
1912. New York Sunday American. 10x12" Sunday supplement with 16 pgs. - **$30 $60 $115**

COM-15

COM-16

❑ COM-15. Jimmy Swinnerton "Swinnerton's Joke Book",
1912. New York Sunday American. 10x12" Sunday supplement with 16 pgs. - **$30 $60 $110**

❑ COM-16. T. E. Powers "Married Life Joke-Book",
1912. New York Sunday American. 10x12" Sunday supplement with 16 pgs. - **$30 $60 $110**

(FRONT) COM-17 (BACK)

❑ COM-17. Pamphlet,
1922. Philadelphia Bulletin. 12 page premium."Jerry Muskrat Wins Respect." Harrison Cady art. - **$30 $55 $85**

COM-18

❑ COM-18. "Boob McNutt" Boxed Wind-Up,
1925. Ferdinand Strauss Corp. Tin litho toy with built-in key is 3x3x8.75" tall and comes in illustrated box. Box features Rube Goldberg art.
Box - **$250 $475 $800**
Toy - **$300 $600 $1200**

COM-19

❑ COM-19. "All The Funny Folks" King Features Syndicate Comic Character Hardback Book,
1926. Promoted through Sunday comic sections and published by The World Today Inc. 9-1/2x 11-3/4" hardbound with 112-page story of choice color specialty art by Louis Biederman, noted KFS staff artist. Theme of story is horse race with Barney Google on Spark Plug and Jiggs on Maud the Mule. Scarce in top condition. - **$150 $400 $700**

COM-20

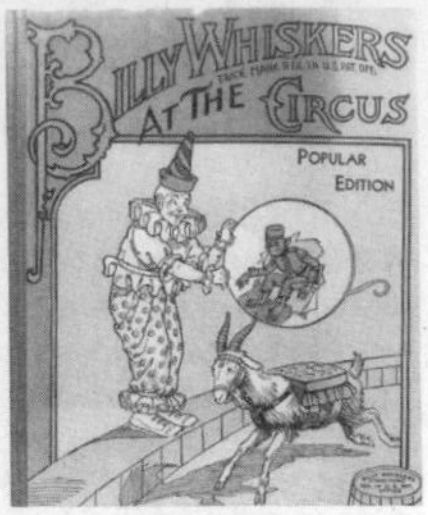

COM-21

❑ COM-20. "Ella Cinders" Song Sheet,
1927. Featured strip in comic newspapers. Scarce - **$35 $60 $115**

❑ COM-21. "Billy Whiskers at the Circus" Book,
1928. Published by Saalfield. 147 pages. - **$45 $85 $300**

COM-22

❑ COM-22. Little Jimmy Writing Tablet,
1920s. Scarce. - **$20 $50 $125**

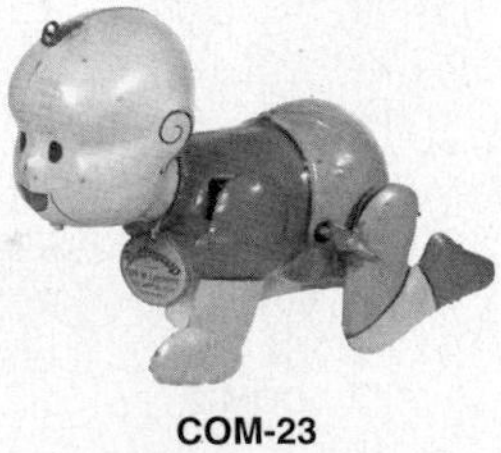

COM-23

❑ COM-23. Toots & Casper "Buttercup" Wind-Up,
1920s. Painted tin toy is 3x7.5x4.75" tall with built-in key. Attached around neck is original 1" diameter cardboard tag with tin rim and is marked."Germany" along with character's name and J. Murphy copyright.
Toy - **$225 $475 $900**
Tag - **$50 $100 $150**

COM-24

❑ **COM-24. "Buttercup And Spare Ribs" Tin Mechanical Pull Toy By Nifty,**
1920s. Toy is 3.5x7.5x5.5" tall. "Nifty" logo is on front of toy. Side has images of Buttercup and Spare Ribs. Mechanical action when toy is pulled. Spare Ribs raises and lowers head, Buttercup raises and lowers broom. Characters are two-piece embossed tin. - **$275 $550 $900**

COM-25

❑ **COM-25. Oscar Hitt's "Hi-Way Henry" Wind-Up Toy,**
1920s. Tin litho toy is 4x10.5x8.25" with built-in key and marked "Made In Germany."
- **$2200 $4500 $7000**

COM-26

❑ **COM-26. "16 Pages Of Color Comics Every Sunday" Promo Sign,**
1920s. 11x14" cardboard picturing 16 representative comic strip characters appearing in Boston Sunday Advertiser. - **$150 $300 $625**

Conductor Mouse

Violinist Mouse with Marquee

Fiddler Mouse without Marquee

COM-27

❑ **COM-27. Marx Merrymakers Band,**
1931. Came in three versions. Two were without marquees: one with a fiddler mouse sitting on top of the piano and one with a conductor mouse on top. The third version has a marquee and a violin mouse.
Each version - **$750 $1650 $2750**

COM-28

❑ **COM-28. "Houdini's BLB of Magic",**
1933. Issued as Whitman #715 and without number as Cocomalt and American Oil Co. premiums. Each - **$15 $45 $105**

COM-29

COM-30

❑ **COM-29. "Funnies on Parade" #1,**
1933. Scarce. Probably the 1st regular format comic book. Proctor & Gamble giveaway. -
$1100 $3000 $15,000

❑ **COM-30. "Century of Comics" #1,**
1933. Scarce. 100 pages. Probably the third comic book. Wheatena/Malt-O-Milk and others used as giveaway. Good - **$3670**
Fine - **$11,000** Very Fine - **$25,000**

COM-31

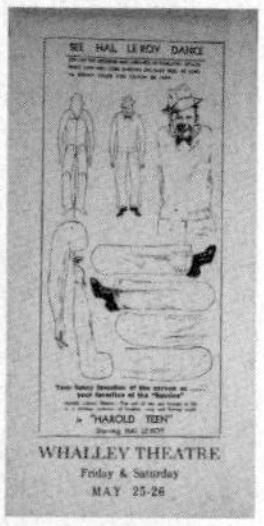

COM-32

❑ **COM-31. "Big Little Mother Goose" Book,**
1934. BLB #725. 576 pages. One of the top 3 rarest BLBs.
Hardcover - **$231 $693 $1850**
Softcover - **$169 $507 $1350**

❑ **COM-32. Harold Teen Movie Premium,**
1934. Pieces were cut out to make a dangle puppet. - **$35 $85 $165**

COM-33

❑ **COM-33. Sears, Roebuck "Funny Paper Puppets" Punch-Out Sheet,**
1935. Also seen with Marshall Field & Co. imprint. Unpunched - **$100 $300 $600**

COM-34

❑ **COM-34. "Popular Comics" Store Sign,**
1936. 8x10.5" cardboard printed as replica front cover of issue #9 from October. Featured characters are from Rinky Dinks and six other characters are pictured on left margin. -
$100 $200 $425

COM-35

❑ **COM-35. "Big Top Comic Circus" Original Art Prototype Punch-Out Book ,**
c. 1936. Similar to Orphan Annie punch-out circus book but also includes other Chicago Tribune comic strip characters. Gordon Gold archives. Unique**. - $1000**

COM-36

❑ **COM-36. "Feature Funnies" First Issue Store Sign,**
1937. 11x14" cardboard inset by replica cover for first issue comic book in October. Joe Palooka is featured and a total of four other comic book characters are pictured on left margin. - **$475 $950 $1900**

COM-37

❑ **COM-37. Red Falcon Adventures,**
1937. Rare. 8 page comic premium, Seal Right Ice Cream.
Issue #1 - **$125 $300 $575**
Issues #2-#5 - **$75 $190 $400**
Issues #6-#10 - **$65 $175 $325**
Issues #11-#50 - **$35 $125 $225**

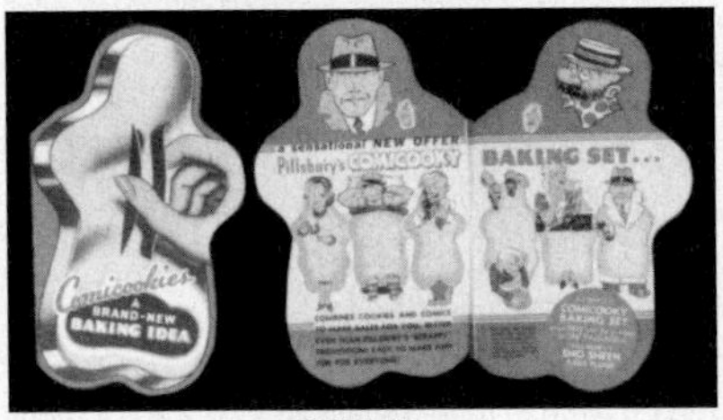

COM-38

❑ **COM-38. Comicookie Die-cut Promo Booklet,**
1937. - **$65 $135 $275**

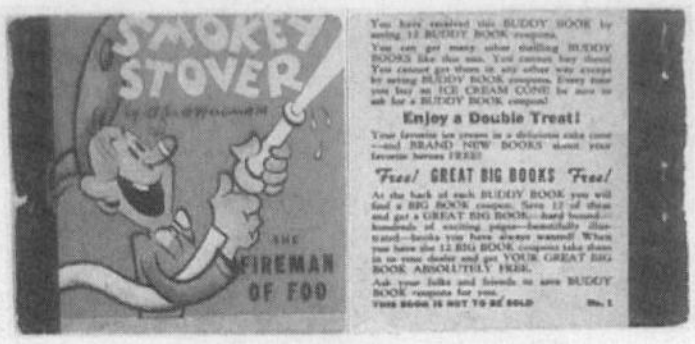

COM-39

❑ **COM-39. "Smokey Stover" Ice Cream Premium Buddy Book,**
1938. Whitman Publishing Co. used by various sponsors as giveaway. This example is marked #1 in the series and was obtained for 12 ice cream cone coupons. - **$37 $111 $260**

COM-40

❑ **COM-40. Federal Agent Fingerprint Outfit,**
1938. Gold Medal toy. - **$60 $145 $250**

COM-41

❑ **COM-41. Harold Teen Dummy Punchout 11x20",**
1938. Rare. Malt-O-Meal Cereal premium. -
$225 $375 $800

COM-42

COM-43

COM-44

❑ **COM-42. Harold Teen Bat-O-Ball,**
1938. Morton Salt premium. - **$18 $35 $70**

❑ **COM-43. Lillums Bat-O-Ball,**
1938. Morton Salt premium. - **$18 $35 $70**

❑ **COM-44. Shadow Bat-O-Ball,**
1938. Morton Salt premium. - **$18 $35 $70**

COM-45

❑ **COM-45. "Tip Top Comics" Store Sign,**
1938. 11x14" cardboard inset by replica front cover of issue #25 for May. Featured are Katzenjammers and left margin pictures three other comic book characters. - **$75 $150 $300**

COM-46

❑ **COM-46. "Comics On Parade" Store Sign,**
1938. 10.5x14" cardboard inset by replica cover of issue #3 for June. Tarzan is featured as parade leader for about 15 other comic book characters. - **$260 $625 $1250**

COM-47

❑ **COM-47. Early Comic Book Promo Button,**
c. 1938. Button is 7/8" with gold text on blue "A Comics On Parade Booster." Backpaper reads "Simon Co. N.Y.C." The design of this button is very similar to another comic book promotional button for Tip Top Comics. The title started April, 1938 and the button likely dates from very close to that time period. - **$115 $235 $350**

COM-48

❑ **COM-48. "Motion Picture Funnies Weekly" #1,**
1939. Rare. Origin & 1st printed appearance of The Sub-Mariner by Bill Everett. Reprinted in Marvel Comics #1.
Good - **$4400**
Fine - **$11,000**
Very Fine/Near Mint - **$29,000**

COM-49

❑ **COM-49. "Merry Christmas From Sears Toyland" Comic Book,**
1939. Scarce. Features Chicago Tribune Syndicate characters. - **$110 $330 $1600**

COM-50

❑ **COM-50. "Rang-A-Tang" Club Button,**
1939. Character from Blue Ribbon Comics. - **$160 $325 $600**

COM-51

❑ **COM-51. "Gasoline Alley" Ceramic Bowl,**
1930s. Very colorful. - **$100 $200 $350**

COM-52

❑ **COM-52. "Punch" Ceramic Pitcher,**
1930s. - **$100 $235 $475**

COM-53

❑ **COM-53. Dial Typewriter,**
1930s. Early tin toy typewriter by Marx. Boxed. - **$60 $135 $225**

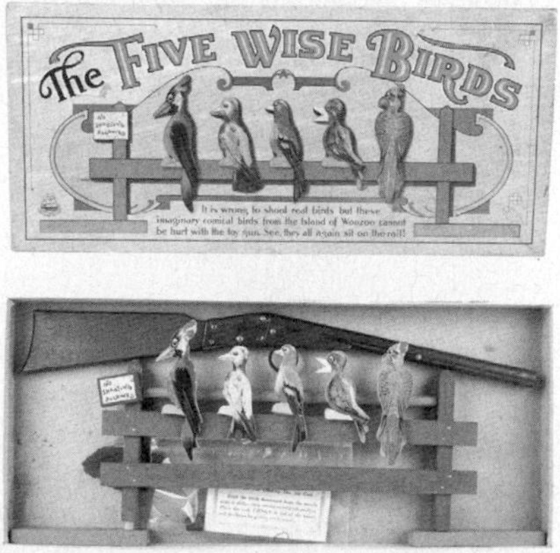

COM-54

❑ **COM-54. "The Five Wise Birds" Shooting Game,**
1930s. The birds came from "The Island of Woozoo". Box includes toy gun, bird targets, and directions. - **$80 $160 $275**

COM-55

COM-56

❑ **COM-55. Junior G-Man Badge,**
1930s. Large bronze color shield premium. - **$35 $70 $130**

❑ **COM-56. "Ella Cinders Spinner",**
1930s. United Feature Syndicate. Cello. over metal disk that has underside center bump for spinning. - **$75 $160 $300**

COM-57

COM-58

❑ **COM-57. Sky Pilot Pin Brass Wings,**
1930s. - **$15 $40 $80**

❑ **COM-58. Aviation Department Boy Flight Commander Brass Badge,**
1930s. - **$25 $50 $100**

COM-59

❑ **COM-59. "All Star Comics" Boxed Playing Card Game,**
1930s. Store item. 35 full color cards including Krazy Kat. - **$65 $130 $240**

COM-60

❑ **COM-60. Sky Rangers Wings,**
1930s. For childrens' club - **$20 $50 $95**

COM-61

❑ **COM-61. Embossed Blocks,**
1930s. Boxed set of wood blocks from the Embossing Company. - **$40 $70 $125**

COM-62

COM-63

COM-64

❑ **COM-62, 63, 64. Herby, Moon Mullins and Smitty Cloth Dolls,**
1930s. Starched fabric from set believed issued by unknown cereal sponsor. Back view of Herby illustrates artist's facsimile signature on each. Also known in set are Kayo, Little Orphan Annie and Sandy.
Annie - **$75 $150 $250**
Sandy - **$50 $85 $175**
Others - **$40 $80 $150**

COM-65

COM-66

❑ **COM-65. Eagle Shield Pin,**
1930s. For airplane children's club.- **$25 $50 $75**

❑ **COM-66. Boy Chief of Police Brass Badge,**
1930s. - **$25 $50 $100**

COM-67

COM-68

❑ **COM-67. Fire Department Boy Chief Brass Badge,**
1930s. - **$25 $50 $100**

❑ **COM-68. Junior Sheriff Brass Badge,**
1930s. - **$18 $30 $65**

COM-69

COM-70

❑ **COM-69. Ranger Pinback,**
1930s. For I-Spy show.- **$10 $15 $25**

❑ **COM-70. "Winds" Junior Police Children's Club Pinback,**
1930s. Probably a bread sponsor. - **$30 $50 $85**

COM-71

COM-72

❑ **COM-71. Sam Gold Comic Character Promotion Circular,**
c. 1940. Black and white 8-1/2x11" designed by Sam Gold for Alfred Loewenthal, President, Famous Artists Syndicate to encourage product advertisers to license the use of syndicate characters including Dick Tracy, Little Orphan Annie, Terry & The Pirates, Captain Midnight and 15 others listed on the sheet. - **$35 $75 $150**

❑ **COM-72. Great Comics Victory Club Pinback,**
1941. Comic book premium. Features the Great Zarro. - **$400 $850 $1500**

COM-73

❑ **COM-73. Sparkler Comics Ad Sign,**
1941. Promo sign for Sparkies cereal featuring the Sparkler Comics #1 cover. - **$450 $1000 $2000**

COM-74

❑ **COM-74. "True Comics" Ad,**
1941. - **$60 $100 $150**

COM-75

❑ COM-75. World War II Promotion Civil Defense Book,
1942. Features Flash Gordon, Phantom, Blondie & others. "Eat Right To Work And Win." - **$39 $117 $485**

COM-76

❑ COM-76. "Santa's Christmas Comic Variety Show" Book,
1943. Sears, Roebuck & Co. Features Dick Tracy, Orphan Annie, Terry and the Pirates, many others. - **$54 $162 $785**

COM-77

❑ COM-77. Captain Ben Dix Member Card,
1943. Entitled child to receive copy of a premium comic book. Scarce. - **$30 $70 $100**

COM-78

❑ COM-78. "Pete the Tramp" Hardback,
1944. With dust jacket - **$40 $95 $180**
Book only - **$20 $40 $80**

COM-79

❑ COM-79. "Magic Is Fun" Book,
1946. #1 issue with feature on Houdini. Includes photos and a pin-up picture of Houdini (1874-1926) - **$20 $40 $90**

COM-80

❑ COM-80. "Pigtails Club" Button,
c. 1946. Yellow/black cello for comic that began in January, later to become girls' fashion magazine sponsored by Parents Magazine Institute. - **$10 $20 $40**

COM-81

❑ COM-81. "Sears 1947 Back-To-School Giveaway Plan" Promo Folder,
1947. Promotion offers comic character bookmarks, bookplates, pencil holder. Gordon Gold Archives. - **$175 $350 $700**

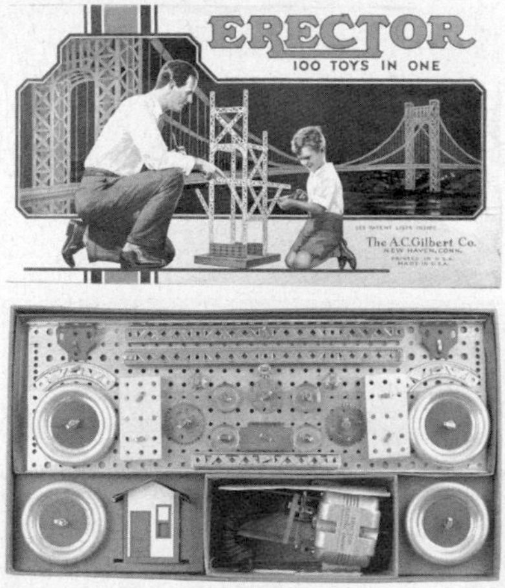

COM-82

❑ COM-82. Erector Set in Box,
1948. From A.C. Gilbert Co. - **$225 $425 $850**

COM-83

COM-84

❑ COM-83. Joe Palooka Matchbook,
1948. - **$10 $20 $50**

❑ COM-84. "America's Most Famous Characters" Christmas Cards Set Boxed,
c. 1948. News Syndicate Co./Famous Artists Syndicate. 9.5x12" boxed set of 16 different comic character greeting cards, each character pictured again in full color box lid design. Complete - **$75 $200 $400**

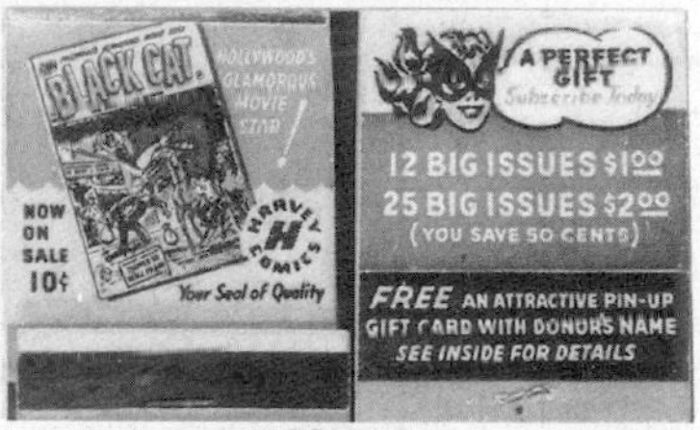

COM-85

❑ COM-85. "Black Cat" Comic Book Ad Matchbook,
1940s. Harvey Comics. - **$20 $45 $90**

COM-86

❑ COM-86. Royal Northwest Mounted Police Brass Badge,
1940s. Scarce. - **$50 $90 $175**

COM-87

❑ **COM-87. "America's Greatest Comics" Newspaper Promo Sign,**
1940s. Chicago Herald-American. 10.5x14" cardboard picturing representatives Blondie, Dagwood, Alexander, Donald Duck, Mickey Mouse, Popeye, Maggie and Jiggs. - **$100 $225 $450**

COM-88

❑ **COM-88. Junior Viewmaster With Box,**
1940s. Working - **$60 $125 $200**

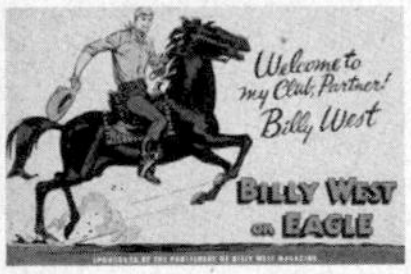

COM-90

COM-89

❑ **COM-89. "C99 Ranch Gang" Code Book,**
1940s. Eight pages with decoder. Sponsor unknown. Rare. - **$40 $75 $150**

❑ **COM-90. Billy West Promo Card,**
1950. Scarce. - **$40 $80 $150**

COM-91

❑ **COM-91. Children's Puzzles,**
1950. Two jigsaw puzzles featured elves.
Each puzzle - **$8 $15 $25**
Box - **$15 $25 $40**

COM-92

❑ **COM-92. "Sad Sack" Porcelain Salt & Pepper Figurines,**
c. 1950. First is 1.5" diameter by 3.5" tall Sad Sack in green uniform. Second is 1.5" diameter by 3.75" tall wearing Army khakis. Bottom of each reads "George Baker H-496." Each hs foil label reading "Norcrest Japan."
Set - **$65 $135 $250**

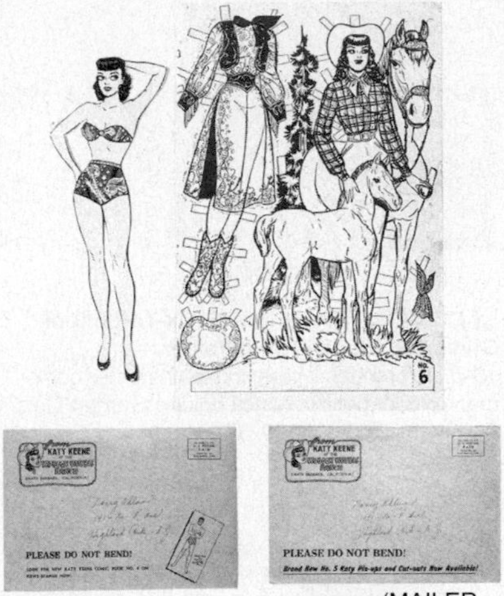

(MAILER FOR #4) COM-93 (MAILER FOR #5)

❑ **COM-93. Katy Keene Paper Dolls & Mailer,**
1951. Comic premiums for Katy Keene #4 & #5.
Each - **$65 $100 $175**

COM-94

❑ **COM-94. Metro Sunday Promo,**
1951. Rare. Features 29 comic characters from Metro Sunday newspapers. - **$275 $575 $1200**

COM-95

❑ **COM-95. Funny Paper Hour Card,**
1954. Denver Post. Birthday card premium. Many characters including Dick Tracy. Rare. - **$25 $60 $100**

COM-96

❑ **COM-96. Sparky's Fire Dept. Inspector Silvered Brass Badge,**
1950s. Scarce. - **$25 $55 $90**

COM-97

❑ **COM-97. Snuffy Smith Adult-Sized Over The Head-Style Costume,**
1960. Store item by Collegeville. 25" wide by 50" tall. Very graphic. Near Mint Carded - **$400**
Uncarded - **$90 $185 $300**

COM-98

❑ **COM-98. Cardboard Ad Sign,**
1960s. Promotes The Funnies in the Nashville Tennessean. - **$65 $115 $215**

COM-99

❑ **COM-99. Comic Character Reading Magnifier In Case,**
c. 1960s. 7" x 1-3/4" vinyl magnifier holder. - **$25 $50 $90**

COM-100

❑ **COM-100. Tasmanian Devil Plush Doll,**
1971. Scarce early figure. With original tags. - **$25 $70 $130**

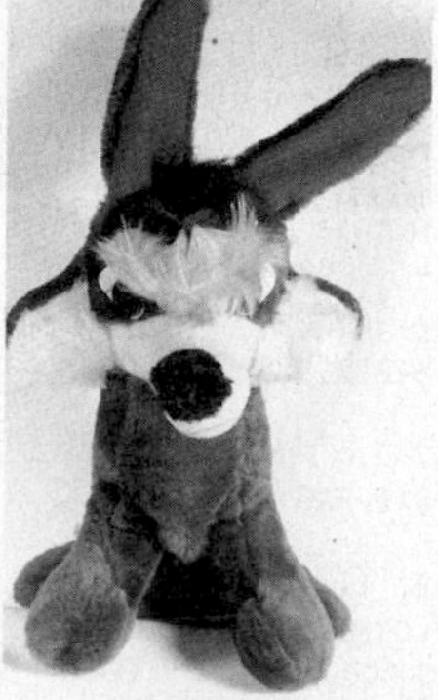

COM-101

❑ **COM-101. Wile E. Coyote Plush Doll,**
1978. 14" tall. - **$20 $40 $75**

COM-102

COM-103

❑ **COM-102. "Opus" Plush Doll,**
1982. 8 1/2" tall. From the newspaper strip "Bloom County." When sold, some of the proceeds went to the Greenpeace Foundation. Figure with tag - **$60**

❑ **COM-103. "Zippy" (The Pinhead) Doll,**
1984. Marth-My-Dear, Oakland, California. 16" tall stuffed cloth likeness of comic panel philosopher created by Bill Griffith. - **$25 $50 $110**

COM-104

❑ **COM-104. "Ella Cinders" Doll,**
1988. 17-1/4" high. Boxed. By Horsman. - **$140**

COM-105

❑ **COM-105. "The Tick" Neckerchief,**
1990s. - **$3 $6 $12**

COM-106

❑ **COM-106. Wile E. Coyote and Road Runner Bronze Sculpture,**
1990. Hand painted, 25" long. Limited edition. Warner Bros. exclusive product sold through their catalog. - **$2500**

COM-107

❑ **COM-107. Mt. Yosemite Sculpture,**
1991. Ron Lee's clever presentation of the four presidents and Yosemite Sam. - **$400**

COM-108

❑ **COM-108. Taz "No Pain No Gain" Figurine,**
1992. Warner Bros. copyright. Figure and base are 12" tall. Only 950 were made, and they sold out in 60 days. - **$325**

COM-109

❑ **COM-109. Pepe Le Pew and Penelope Sculpture,**
1992. Warner Brothers Store exclusive figures by Ron Lee. - **$175**

COM-110

❑ **COM-110. "Capt. Scarlet" Candy Wrapper,**
1993. For premium car. - **$4 $8 $15**

COM-111

❑ **COM-111. "Capt. Scarlet" Car,**
1993. Premium and Instructions With Box - **$30 $60 $100**

COM-112

❑ **COM-112. "Spawn The Game" Boardgame,**
1994. Over 110 total pieces. Spawn has made a successful leap to TV and movies.
Complete - **$65**

COM-113

❑ **COM-113. "Fone Bone" Resin Figure,**
1994. Dark Horse product, limited to 3,000. Map is a separate piece. In box - **$120**

COM-114

❑ **COM-114. Carl Barks Pocket Watch,**
1994. Gifted Images product. Watch features a Barks self portrait. Limited edition of 65. - **$400**

COM-115

❑ **COM-115. "Grendel" Resin Statue,**
1994. Character by Matt Wagner. Sculpted by Randy Bowen. Boxed - **$395**
1999 2nd Edition Boxed - **$220**

COM-116

COM-117

COM-118

❑ **COM-116. "Cerebus" Drinking Glass Mug,**
1994. - **$6 $12 $18**

❑ **COM-117. Taz Pin on Card,**
1995. - **$8 $15 $25**

❑ **COM-118. "Lady Death" Statue,**
1995. Resin on wood base. Limited to 3,200. Miniature version released in 2000. - **$375**

COM-119

❑ **COM-119. Carl Barks "The Barkster" Commemorative Figure,**
1995. Painted resin figure by Randy Bowen. Only 10 produced. - **$1750**

COM-120

❑ **COM-120. "The Maxx" Bust,**
1996. From MTV Networks. Limited to 2,500. Boxed - **$160**

COM-121

❑ **COM-121. Carl Barks Treasury Bill,**
1997. City of Ducksburg paper $100 dollar bill featuring Carl Barks and his autograph. - **$75**

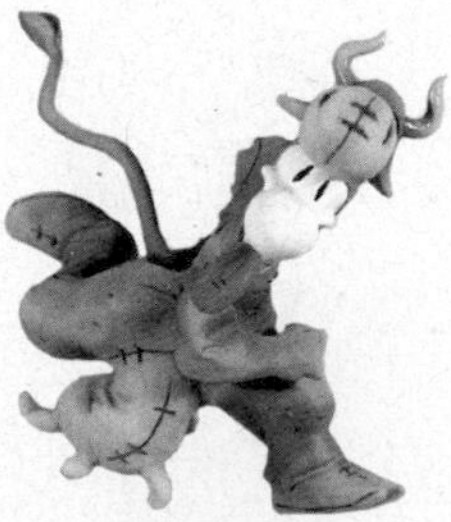

COM-122

❑ **COM-122. "Smiley Bone" Resin Figure,**
1997. Graphitti Designs product. Limited edition of 2,500. In box - **$100**

COM-123

❑ **COM-123. "Father Time" Dragster,**
1998. Limited edition of 15,000. On card - **$25**

COM-124 COM-125

❑ **COM-124. Alvin Singing Bean Bag,**
1998. Gund product. - **$3 $6 $18**

❑ **COM-125. Alvin Singing Bean Bag,**
1999. Gemme product. - **$3 $6 $18**

COM-126 COM-127

❑ **COM-126. Simon Singing Bean Bag,**
1998. Gund product. - **$3 $6 $18**

❑ **COM-127. Simon Singing Bean Bag,**
1999. Gemme product. - **$3 $6 $18**

COM-128 COM-129

❑ **COM-128. Theodore Singing Bean Bag,**
1998. Gund product. - **$3 $6 $18**

❑ **COM-129. Theodore Singing Bean Bag,**
1999. Gemme product. - **$3 $6 $18**

COM-130

COM-131

❑ **COM-130. "Tweety" Leprechaun Bean Bag,**
1999. With tag. - **$22**

❑ **COM-131. "Tweety" Skeleton Bean Bag,**
1999. With tag. - **$22**

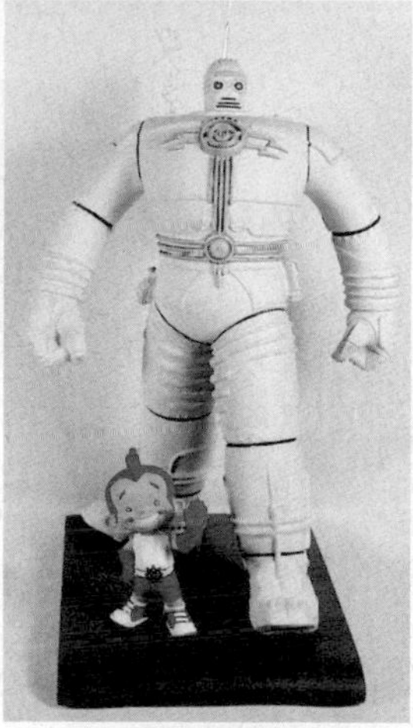

COM-132

❑ **COM-132. "Big Guy and Rusty the Boy Robot" Statue,**
1999. Produced by Dark Horse. Limited to 1,500. Sculpted by Kent Melton. - **$160**

COM-133

COM-134

❑ **COM-133. Danger Girl Action Figure,**
1999. Abby Chase with accessories on card. - **$20**

❑ **COM-134. Danger Girl Action Figure,**
1999. Natalia Kassle w/accessories on card. - **$20**

COM-135

COM-136

❑ **COM-135. Danger Girl Action Figure,**
1999. Sydney Savage w/accessories on card. - **$20**

❑ **COM-136. Danger Girl Action Figure,**
1999. Major Maxim w/accessories on card. - **$20**

COM-137

❑ **COM-137. "Cowboy Droopy" Resin Figure,**
1999. On his trusty horse. - **$150**

COM-139

COM-140

❑ **COM-139. "Flaming Carrot" Action Figure,**
1990s. On card. - **$12**

❑ **COM-140. "Marvin the Martian" Yo-Yo,**
1990s. Glows in the dark. - **$15**

COM-141

COM-142

❑ **COM-141. "Badrock" Action Figure,**
1990s. Deluxe ed. Spawn on card. - **$25**

❑ **COM-142. "Violator" Action Figure,**
1990s. With special edition comic book. - **$20**

COM-143

COM-144

❑ **COM-143. "Madman" Lunch Box,**
2000. Mike Allred artwork. - **$35**

❑ **COM-144. "Cy-Gor 2" Action Figure,**
2000. 12" figure boxed. - **$30**

COM-145

❑ **COM-145. Bone 10th Anniversary Figure,**
2001. PVC figure came with purchase of 10th Ann. Special Edition comic. Boxed - **$25**

COM-146

COM-147

❑ **COM-146. "Hot Stuff" Wacky Wobbler,**
2001. In box. - **$25**

❑ **COM-147. "Richie Rich" Wacky Wobbler,**
2001. In box. - **$25**

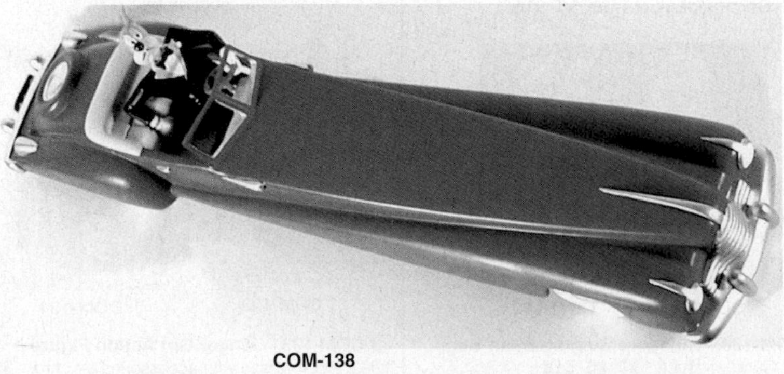

COM-138

❑ **COM-138. "Driving Wolfie" Resin Figure,**
1999. Tex Avery character. In box. - **$100**

COM-148

❑ **COM-148. Baby Huey Teeny Weeny Mini-Maquette,**
2003. Electric Tiki Designs. Design by Tracy Mark Lee. - **$75**

COM-149

COM-150

❑ **COM-149. Little Dot Teeny Weeny Mini-Maquette,**
2003. Regular edition with red dress. Electric Tiki Designs. Designed by Tracy Mark Lee and sculpted by Bruce Lau. A limited run of 500. - **$60**

❑ **COM-150. Little Dot Teeny Weeny Mini-Maquette Variant,**
2003. Variant edition with blue dress. Electric Tiki Designs. A limited run of 50 exclusively available at Comicon International San Diego 2003 and WizardWorld Chicago 2003. - **$90**

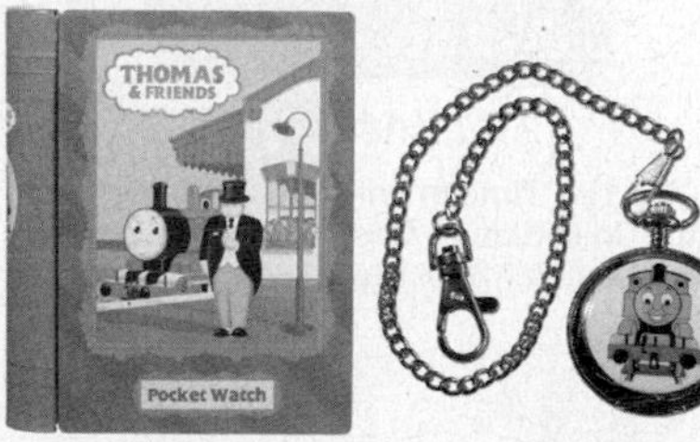

COM-151

❑ **COM-151. Thomas Pocket Watch,**
2003. Comes in tin box. - **$20**

Counter-Spy

Washington calling David Harding, Counter-Spy! In 1942, with the nation at war, the call was answered. One of radio's long-running adventure series, *Counter-Spy* aired on ABC, NBC or Mutual from 1942 to 1957. With Don MacLaughlin as the ace agent, Counter-Spy fought Axis enemies during the war and other security threats once the war was won. Sponsors over the years included Mail Pouch chewing tobacco, Schutter Candies, Pepsi-Cola and Gulf Oil.

COU-1

❑ **COU-1. Pepsi-Cola 8x19" Paper Store Sign,**
1949. - **$75 $135 $225**

COU-2

❑ **COU-2. Large Outdoor Sign,**
1949. Pepsi-Cola. 40x60" starched white fabric with red and blue printing advertising show on ABC radio station WJZ. - **$100 $200 $400**

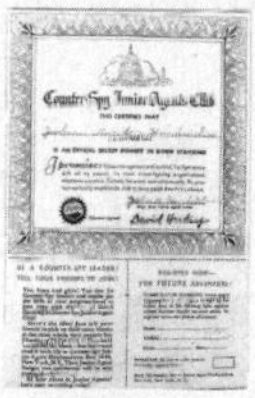
COU-3

COU-4

❑ **COU-3. Club Member Certificate,**
1949. Scarce. Pepsi-Cola. For "Counter-Spy Junior Agents Club". - **$30 $75 $140**

❑ **COU-4. Junior Agent Glow-In-Dark Brass Badge,**
1949. Pepsi-Cola. Centered by plastic lens over bw glow portrait. - **$40 $75 $165**

COU-5

❑ **COU-5. Matchbook,**
1940s. Old Nick candy bars. - **$15 $35 $75**

COU-6

❑ **COU-6. "Junior Counter-Spy" Activity Booklet,**
1951. Gulf Oil. Story pages feature David Harding, Counterspy. - **$15 $35 $75**

Cracker Jack

This blend of popcorn, peanuts and molasses candy has been a best-selling snack food for about 100 years. F. W. Rueckheim, a German immigrant, had opened a small popcorn stand in Chicago in 1872. He sold the first version of his candy combination at the 1893 Columbian Exposition; the product proved to be popular, but the kernels stuck together. By 1896 the company had found not only a process to keep the kernels separate, but also a name--cracker jack was a new slang term for excellent or superior, and F. W. promptly trademarked it for his sweet.

By 1899 Cracker Jack was being packaged in a waxed-sealed box to keep it fresh, by 1902 it was listed in the Sears catalogue and in 1908 it became part of sports Americana in the song *Take Me Out to the Ball Game.* A happy customer is said to have contributed the company slogan, The More You Eat, The More You Want. In 1910 the company started inserting coupons in the packages to be traded in for prizes and two years later the coupons were replaced by the prizes themselves.

Since 1912 every package has contained a toy surprise inside. Sailor Jack, modeled after F. W.'s grandson, appeared in advertisements in 1916 with his dog Bingo and made it onto the box in 1919. The company was sold to Borden in 1972 and then to Frito Lay in 1997. Today Cracker Jack, still with a toy in every box, is marketed worldwide.

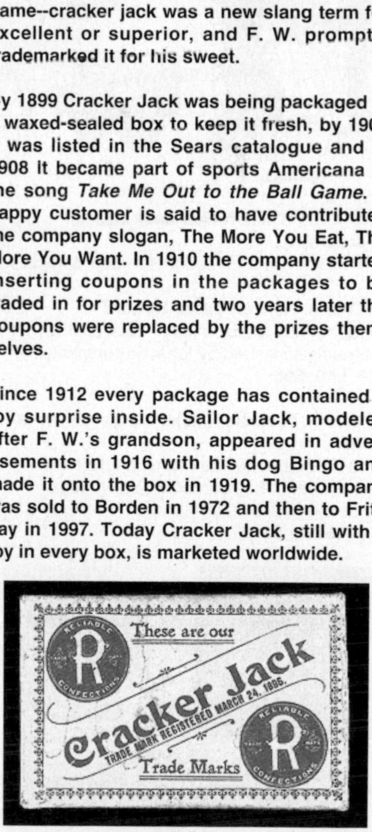

CRJ-1

❑ **CRJ-1. Early Sample Box,**
c. 1896. 1x1-3/4x2-3/4" long sample container for "Reliable Confections" by "F. W. Rueckheim & Bro.," Chicago. Trademark registration date is March 24, 1896 and precedes the added "Eckstein" partnership designation of 1902. - **$150 $350 $700**

CRJ-2

❑ **CRJ-2. Original Maker's Business Card,**
1890s. 3x4-7/8" rwb for "F. W. Rueckheim & Bro. Manufacturing Confectioners" plus Chicago address. - **$35 $85 $135**

CRJ-3

CRJ-4

CRJ-5

❑ **CRJ-3. "The Cracker Jack Bears" Postcard,**
1907. Example from set of 16. - **$20 $40 $75**

❑ **CRJ-4. Portrait Cello. Button,**
c. 1908. With "Cracker Jack" back paper. One of a series also issued by tobacco companies. - **$30 $50 $90**

❑ **CRJ-5. "Cracker Jack" Wagon In White Metal,**
c. 1910. Scarce. Metal has gold luster and wagon interior has cardboard insert floor. Horse's legs are usually broken. - **$100 $175 $350**

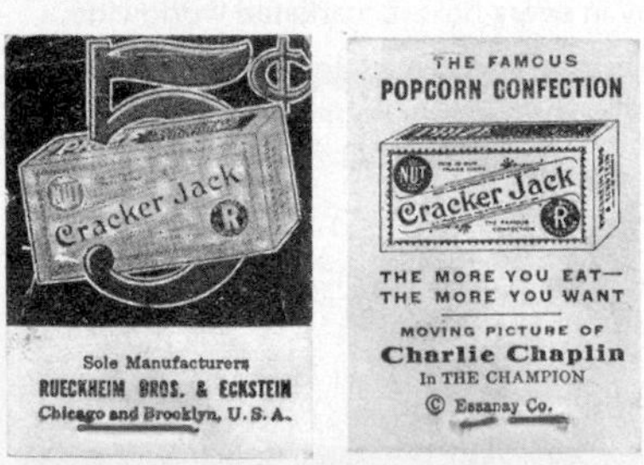

CRJ-6

❑ **CRJ-6. Cracker Jack Flip Book With Chaplin,**
1915. Book is 1.25x1.75" and has text "Cracker Jack Sole Manufacturers" and the names of the firms in Chicago and Brooklyn. Back cover has "Famous Popcorn Confection The More You Eat The More You Want Moving Picture Of Charlie Chaplin In The Champion." - **$50 $100 $150**

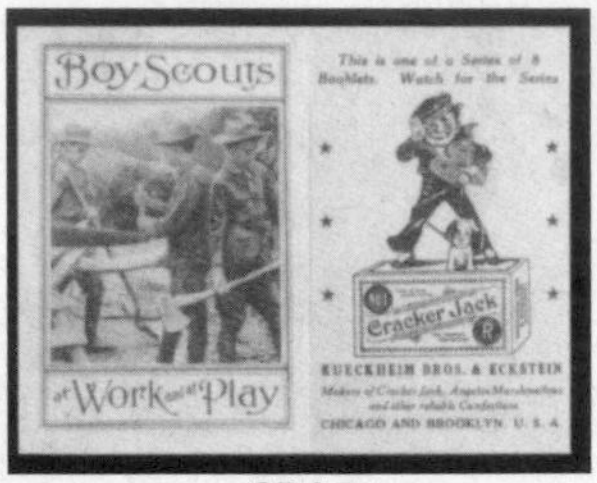

CRJ-7

❑ **CRJ-7. "Boy Scouts At Work And At Play" Booklet,**
c. 1923. 2-1/2x3-1/2" with 12 pages. Reverse reads "Series Of 8 Booklets."
Each - **$135 $225 $350**

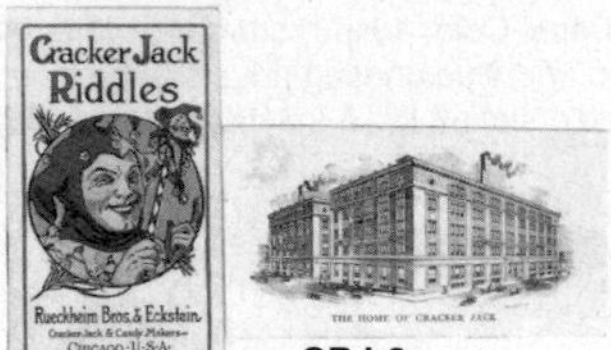

CRJ-8

❑ **CRJ-8. "Cracker Jack Riddles" Booklet,**
c. 1920s. - **$40 $75 $150**

CRJ-9

CRJ-10

❑ **CRJ-9. "Cracker Jack Drawing Book",**
c. 1920s. - **$25 $50 $100**

❑ **CRJ-10. Miniature Litho. Tin Wagon,**
c. 1920s. - **$40 $85 $175**

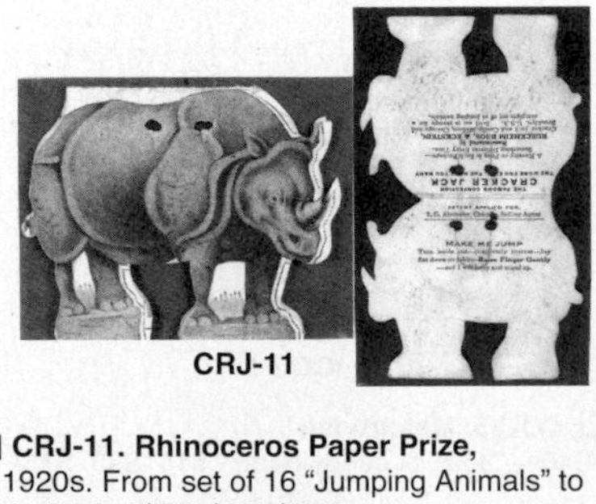

CRJ-11

❑ **CRJ-11. Rhinoceros Paper Prize,**
c. 1920s. From set of 16 "Jumping Animals" to fold. Each - **$45 $90 $165**

CRJ-12

❑ **CRJ-12. "Cracker Jack/The Famous Confection" Top,**
c. 1920s. Silver finish with incised lettering and slightly thicker metal than later versions. - **$50 $100 $165**

CRJ-13

❑ **CRJ-13. Cardboard String Toy,**
c. 1920s. - **$35 $75 $135**

CRJ-14

❑ **CRJ-14. Chicago World's Fair Miniature Booklet,**
1933. Ten pictures. - **$50 $110 $215**

CRJ-15

❑ **CRJ-15. "Tune In With Cracker Jack" Litho. Tin Miniature Desk Radio Replica,**
1930s. Scarce. - **$80 $165 $300**

CRJ-16

CRJ-17

❑ **CRJ-16. Queen Of Spades Litho. Tin Whistle,**
1930s. About 1-3/4" tall unmarked except "Japan." - **$50 $100 $200**

❑ **CRJ-17. Andy Gump Miniature Bisque Figure,**
1930s. 2-1/8" tall unmarked except for "FAS" (Famous Artists Syndicate) copyright and "Japan" on reverse. Similar Cracker Jack give-aways include: Chester Gump, Herby, Kayo, Little Orphan Annie, Sandy, Smitty.
Each - **$30 $55 $85**

CRJ-18 CRJ-19

❑ **CRJ-18. Litho. Tin Spinner Top,**
1930s. Red, white and blue with thin wooden dowel at center. - **$20 $40 $75**

❑ **CRJ-19. "Ambulance" Litho. Tin Miniature,**
1930s. About 1-1/2" long with Red Cross symbol on each side. - **$50 $100 $200**

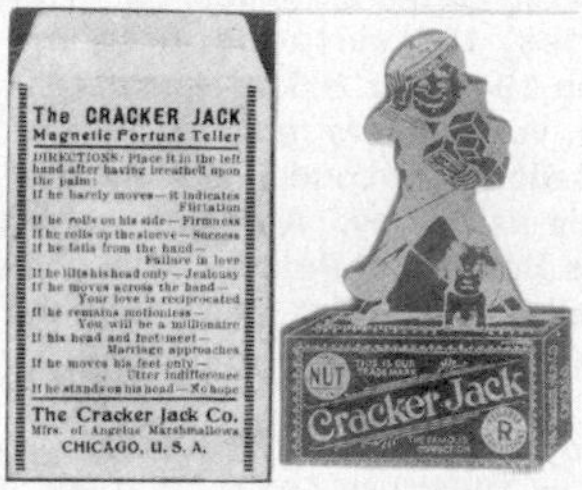

CRJ-20

CRJ-21 CRJ-22

❑ **CRJ-20. "Magnetic Fortune Teller" With Envelope,**
1930s. Gold printing on thin cellophane of various solid colors. - **$30 $50 $95**

❑ **CRJ-21. Litho. Tin Top,**
1930s. - **$18 $35 $65**

❑ **CRJ-22. Litho. Tin Top,**
1930s. - **$18 $35 $65**

CRJ-23 CRJ-24

❑ **CRJ-23. Toy Cart,**
1930s. Litho. tin with wood shaft. -
$12 $25 $40

❑ **CRJ-24. Beanie,**
1930s. Rare. Wool Beanie with bell on spring. -
$60 $125 $235

CRJ-25 CRJ-26 CRJ-27

❑ **CRJ-25. Tin Litho. Pocketwatch Replica,**
1930s. - **$25 $55 $110**

❑ **CRJ-26. Aluminum Snapper,**
1930s. - **$12 $28 $45**

❑ **CRJ-27. Tin Litho. Standup,**
1930s. From a set of 10: Chester, Harold Teen, Herby, Kayo, Moon Mullins, Orphan Annie, Perry, Skeezix, Smitty, Uncle Walt.
Each - **$40 $85 $150**

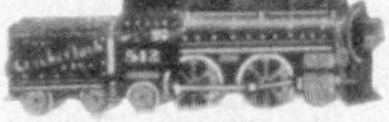

CRJ-28 CRJ-29

❑ **CRJ-28. "The Cracker Jack Line" Litho. Tin Train Engine,**
1930s. - **$55 $115 $225**

❑ **CRJ-29. Litho. Tin Delivery Truck,**
1930s. - **$45 $95 $165**

CRJ-30

❑ **CRJ-30. "Free Comic Valentine" 9x26" Paper Store Sign,**
1930s. Pictures examples from believed set of 25 given individually by purchase of individual boxes. - **$100 $200 $400**

CRJ-31 CRJ-32

❑ **CRJ-31. "Cracker Jack Shows" Tin Circus Wagon,**
1930s. Depicts caged lion on each side. -
$50 $100 $175

❑ **CRJ-32. Diecut Paper Frog,**
1930s. - **$30 $60 $100**

CRJ-33 CRJ-34 CRJ-35

❑ **CRJ-33. Tin Miniature Book Bank,**
1930s. - **$60 $100 $200**

❑ **CRJ-34. Tin Bank,**
1930s. Brass luster. - **$30 $60 $90**

❑ **CRJ-35. Litho. Tin Diecut Bookmark,**
1930s. One of scarcer in series. - **$18 $30 $60**

CRJ-36 CRJ-37

❑ **CRJ-36. Litho. Tin Fortune Wheel,**
1930s. Reveals fortune words by revolving upper disk to spell name of fortune-seeker. -
$30 $60 $100

❑ **CRJ-37. Paper Fortune Wheel,**
1930s. Similar design and function to litho. tin version. - **$20 $35 $65**

CRJ-38

❑ **CRJ-38. "Coney Island" Miniature Jigsaw Puzzle,**
1930s. Assembled 2.5x5.75" diecut stiff paper choice color puzzle picturing amusement rides including boy and girl holding Cracker Jack box while riding roller coaster. - **$35 $65 $135**

CRJ-39

CRJ-40

❑ **CRJ-39. "Cracker Jack Air Corps" Dark Metal Wings,**
1930s. Lapel stud reverse. - **$15 $30 $65**

❑ **CRJ-40. Oval Litho. Tin American Flag Stand-Ups,**
1940-1949. Unfolded 2-1/4" tall red, white and blue unmarked with Cracker Jack name but distributed by them and made by Cosmo Manufacturing Company. Primary titles of four examples issued in the 1940s read "Long May It Wave!, God Bless America, Stars And Stripes Forever!, The Flag Of Freedom."
Each - **$12 $25 $40**

CRJ-41

❑ **CRJ-41. "Razz Zooka" Paper Whistle Toy,**
1949. Cloudcrest Creations. - **$15 $30 $50**

CRJ-42

CRJ-43

❑ **CRJ-42. "Cracker Jack" Transfer Sheet Set,**
1940s. 25 in set. - **$60 $135 $225**

❑ **CRJ-43. "Midget Auto Race" Paper Prize,**
1940s. - **$18 $30 $45**

CRJ-44

❑ **CRJ-44. Slide Cards,**
1964. Gordon Gold Archives. Set of 27 full color 1.25 x 1.75" cards that change image viewed through one or two small openings activated by tab in rear. Set - **$100 $200 $400**

CRJ-45

❑ **CRJ-45 Box Insert Papers,**
c. 1965. Set of 20. Each is 4-1/4x6". Gordon Gold Archives. Near Mint Set - **$300**
Each - **$4 $8 $20**

CRJ-46

CRJ-47

❑ **CRJ-46 Cracker Jack Tin Wastebasket,**
1980s. - **$10 $25 $65**

❑ **CRJ-47. Baseball Card Sheet 8x11",**
1991. Uncut 36 card sheet with miniature replicas of Topps Gum "40 Years Of Baseball" cards. Uncut - **$35 $60 $100**

CRJ-48

❑ **CRJ-48. "Cracker Jack" Wacky Wobbler,**
2001. With box. - **$35**

Crusader Rabbit

Alex Anderson, nephew of Terrytoons animation studio pioneer Paul Terry, created the concept and characters. He approached old friend Jay Ward (1920-1989) who was a real estate broker at the time and they formed Television Arts Productions (T.A.P.) in 1948 in Berkeley, California. *Crusader Rabbit* was done in black and white utilizing limited animation similar to a comic strip format. The cast included Crusader as a Don Quixote type, Ragland "Rags" Tiger and villain Dudley Nightshade.

Recognized as the first made for TV animated series, 195 cartoons aired on NBC between 1949 and 1952. Narrated by Roy Whaley, voice actors included Lucille Bliss as Crusader, Vern Louden as Rags and Russ Coughlin as Dudley. A notable early sponsor was Bell Brand Potato Chips owned by Glen Bell who would go on to found the Taco Bell chain.

***Dell Comics* released *Four Color* comic books in 1956 and 1957. In 1957, Shull Bonsell's Capital Enterprises contracted to animate 260 color *Crusader Rabbit* cartoons but the series had limited success. It's conceivable that if Anderson and Ward hadn't formed their partnership, Anderson would have stayed at Terrytoons and the world would have never seen *Rocky And Bullwinkle* from Jay Ward Productions.**

CRR-1

❑ **CRR-1. "Crusader Rabbit" Pre-Production Concept Art,**
c. 1950. Original animation paper done in blue and red pencil has been double-matted to 9.75x11". Same Or Similar Near Mint - **$300**

CRR-2

CRR-3

❑ **CRR-2. "Crusader Rabbit Three Funny Picture Puzzles",**
1956. 9.5x11-7/8x1.25" deep box. - **$60 $120 $185**

❑ **CRR-3. "The Adventure Of Crusader Rabbit Presented By Friskies Dog Food" Season Ticket,**
c. 1959. KNBH-TV Station. 2x5" ticket for L.A./Hollywood area TV Station. Back has sponsor ad for canned dog food. - **$25 $50 $110**

CRR-4

❑ **CRR-4. "Crusader Rabbit Ring Toss" Diecut Game,**
1950s. Classic Ent. Inc., U.S.A. 9.75" tall cardboard piece fits into 3" wood block mounted on 4" wide thin cardboard designed like a shield. Comes with two 4" diameter cardboard rings. Copyright T.A.P. - **$50 $100 $175**

CRR-5

❑ **CRR-5. "Crusader Rabbit" Set Of Premium Cards,**
1950s. Bell Brand Chips. Set of 12 cards each 2-3/8x3.5" with T.A.P. copyright. Bell Brand logo on back along with 4-line poem. Pictured are: Crusader Rabbit, Rags the Tiger, Garfield Groundhog, Dudley Nightshade, Bilious Green, Arson and Sterno, S. Crow, Captain Huckleberry, Captain Jolly Roger, Al Catraz, Seymour the Dinosaur, Sam Quentin. Set - **$400 $1200 $2400**

CRR-6

❑ **CRR-6. "Crusader Rabbit Fun Kit",**
1950s. T.A.P. 14x25x1.5" deep box contains parts for an assortment of tricks. - **$50 $100 $175**

CRR-7

CRR-8

❑ **CRR-7. "Crusader Rabbit Slate 'N' Chalk Set",**
c. 1950s. Rosebud Art Co. 11.5x17x1.5" deep box holds chalkboard, chalk, paint tabs, crayons, eraser, unpunched stencils. - **$100 $200 $350**

❑ **CRR-8. "Crusader Rabbit Club" Member's Cello. Button,**
1950s. Celluloid 1-1/4" - **$35 $85 $165**
Litho. 1-1/8" - **$25 $75 $150**

CRR-9

❑ **CRR-9. "Crusader Rabbit" Storybook/ Coloring Books,**
c. 1960. Whitman Publishing. Book is "Crusader Rabbit In Bubble Trouble." Two coloring books are 8x10.5". Each - **$5 $10 $20**

Dan Dunn

Detective Dan began in 1933, and after the first issue sold poorly, the title was changed. Norman Marsh created this popular comic strip, now called *Dan Dunn, Secret Operative 48*, for the Publishers' Syndicate. Offered as a low-cost alternative to *Dick Tracy*, the strip ran daily and Sunday for 10 years, appearing in as many as 135 newspapers. The hard-boiled Dunn, along with his sidekick Irwin Higgs, his dog Wolf, and an orphan girl named Babs, fought urban crime and such arch-fiends as Wu Fang and Eviloff. At the height of its popularity in the 1930s the strip was reprinted in *Big Little Books* and in several comic books. Two issues of *Dan Dunn*, a dime novel pulp, were published in 1936, and a radio version of *Dan Dunn, Secret Operative 48* was syndicated in 1937.

DUN-1

DUN-2

DUN-3

❑ **DUN-1. Detective Dan Button,**
1933. Rare. First comic book character club premium. The club was canceled after the first issue of *Detective Dan* failed. -
$450 $1000 $1650

❑ **DUN-2. "Dan Dunn Secret Operative 48 Crime Never Pays" Big Little Book,**
1934. Whitman #1116. **- $12 $36 $85**

❑ **DUN-3. "Dan Dunn Detective Magazine" First Issue,** 1936. Vol. 1 #1 monthly issue for September. - **$150 $300 $600**

DUN-4

❑ **DUN-4. "Dan Dunn On the Trail of The Counterfeiters" Big Little Book #1125,**
1936. 432 pages. Art by Norman Marsh. -
$12 $36 $85

DUN-5

❑ **DUN-5. Comic Strip Reprint Variation Book,**
1937. Whitman. #1010 titled "Dan Dunn Secret Operative 48 And The Gangsters' Frame-Up" in 5.5x7-3/8" format with nickel original price on front cover in addition to red back cover. -
$41 $123 $290

DUN-6

❑ **DUN-6. Comic Strip Reprint Variation Book,**
1937. Whitman. #1010 titled "Dan Dunn Secret Operative 48 And The Gangsters' Frame-Up" in 5.75x7-3/8" format without original price marking on front cover in addition to back cover in black rather than red. - **$41 $123 $290**

DUN-7

❑ **DUN-7. "Dan Dunn On the Trail of Wu-Fang" Big Little Book #1454,**
1938. - **$15 $45 $105**

DUN-8

DUN-9

❑ **DUN-8. "Dan Dunn/Secret Operative 48 And The Counterfeiter Ring" Booklet,**
1938. From "Buddy Book" ice cream cone series printed by Whitman. Also seen as give-away from Stern & Co. with "Merry Christmas" on back cover. 132 pages in Big Little Book format with page art reprinted from comic strips. -
$36 $108 $250

❑ **DUN-9. "Dan Dunn Plays A Lone Hand" Whitman Penny Book,**
1938. - **$10 $30 $62**

DUN-10

DUN-11

❑ **DUN-10."Dan Dunn Secret Operative 48" Penny Book,**
1938. Published by Whitman**. - $10 $30 $62**

❑ **DUN-11. "Dan Dunn Secret Operative 48 And The Zeppelin Of Doom" Fast -Action Book,**
1938. Dell Publishing. 3-7/8x5-1/4" format**. -**
$30 $90 $210

DUN-12

❑ DUN-12. "Dan Dunn Meets Chang Loo" Pan Am Gasoline Premium Book,
1938. Whitman. 3.5x3.75" softcover copyright by Whitman based on comic strip by Norman March. Contents are 64 pages comprised of story art frame on each left hand page and story text on facing page. Sponsor is Pan-Am gasoline and motor oils and back cover repeats full color front cover as a Pan-Am ad.
- **$26 $78 $180**

DUN-13 DUN-14

❑ DUN-13. "Dan Dunn Junior Operative" Cello. Button, 1930s. - **$100 $225 $500**

❑ DUN-14. Dan Dunn "I'm Operative 48" Cello. Button,
1930s. Philadelphia Evening Ledger Comics. From colorful series depicting Ledger comic strip characters. - **$60 $125 $200**

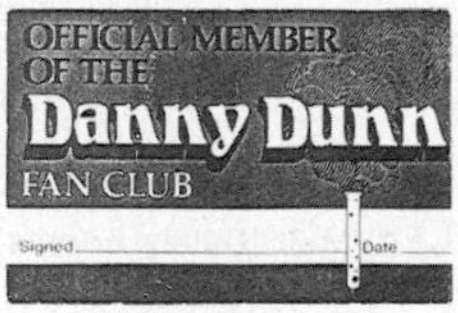

DUN-15 DUN-16

❑ DUN-15. "Dan Dunn Detective Corps/Secret Operative 48" Badge,
1930s. Probably a newspaper promotion item. Silvered tin shield with embossed lettering. - **$25 $50 $100**

❑ DUN-16. Fan Club Membership Card,
c. 1980s. Issuer unknown. Unknown if Dan Dunn item or perhaps local radio/TV personality club card. - **$6 $12 $25**
Pinback - **$10 $20 $35**

Daniel Boone

Dan'l Boone (1734-1820), legendary Kentucky frontiersman, hunter, farmer and wilderness scout, was brought to life by 20th Century-Fox in a successful adventure series on CBS-TV from 1964 to 1970. The show starred Fess Parker, who a decade earlier had found fame playing Davy Crockett on the *Disneyland* series. The stories were centered on Boone's Kentucky settlement days, his expeditions and his struggles with the Indians. Other featured actors included Patricia Blair, Ed Ames, Albert Salmi and Roosevelt Grier. Merchandised items are usually copyrighted by 20th Century-Fox TV. An hour-long animated TV special sponsored by Kenner toys premiered on CBS in 1981 with Richard Crenna as the voice of Boone.

DNL-1

DNL-2

❑ DNL-1. Picture,
1963. Cut-out premium found on back of Frosted Flakes box. - **$15 $30 $60**

❑ DNL-2. Fess Parker As Daniel Boone 5" Hard Plastic Doll,
1964. American Tradition Co. Store item. Accessories of fur hat, plastic rifle and strap with bag and powder horn. -
$40 $75 $165

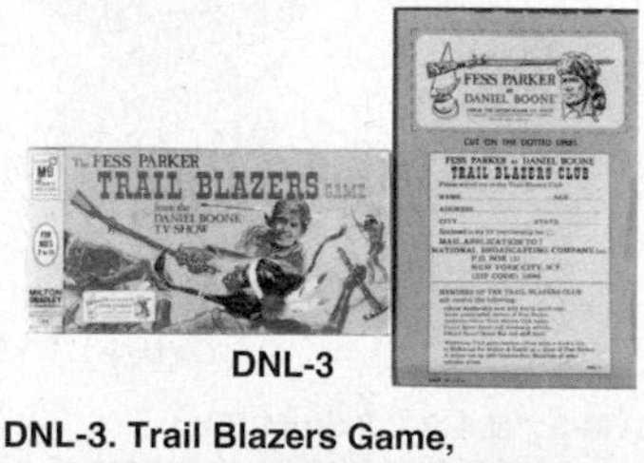

DNL-3

❑ DNL-3. Trail Blazers Game,
1964. N.B.C. tie-in with Milton Bradley. Includes Trail Blazers Club application. - **$25 $50 $110**

DNL-4

❑ DNL-4. Vinyl Zippered Pencil Case,
1964. Fess Parker/Daniel Boone Trail Blazers Club. Includes NBC premium leaflet offering wallet, ring binder, kaboodle kit, etc. -
$15 $30 $60

DNL-5 DNL-6

❑ DNL-5. "Fess Parker As Daniel Boone" Vinyl Wallet,
1964. N.B.C. Holds miniature magic slate and four photos from TV series. - **$25 $50 $85**

❑ DNL-6. "Official Daniel Boone Fess Parker Woodland Whistle",
1964. Autolite. Boxed - **$25 $50 $85**

DNL-7

❑ DNL-7. "Fess Parker As Daniel Boone" Coonskin Cap,
1964. Store item by American Tradition Co. -
$18 $30 $60

DNL-8

❑ DNL-8. "Trail Blazer" Cello Button,
1964. 2-1/8" black on cream promoting CBS-TV show. - **$15 $30 $60**

DNL-9

❑ DNL-9. "Daniel Boone" Boxed Card Game,
1965. Store item by Ed-U-Cards. Boxed Complete - **$10 $18 $35**

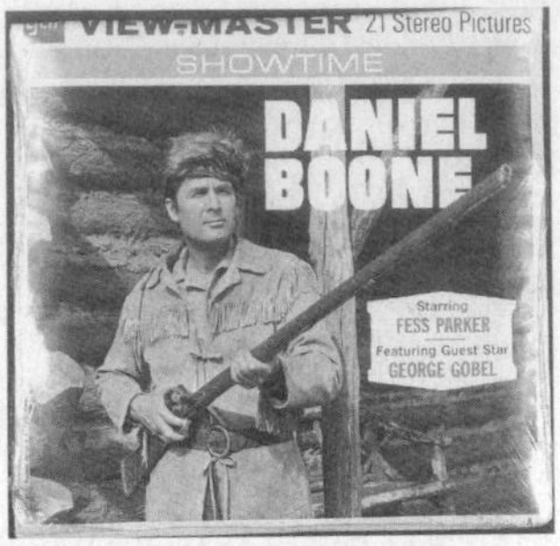

DNL-10

❑ **DNL-10. "Daniel Boone Starring Fess Parker" Sealed View-Master Pack,**
1965. Three reel pack measures 4.25x4.5" with color photo on front of Parker in costume as Boone holding long rifle standing in front of log cabin. Packet #B479. - **$12 $25 $50**

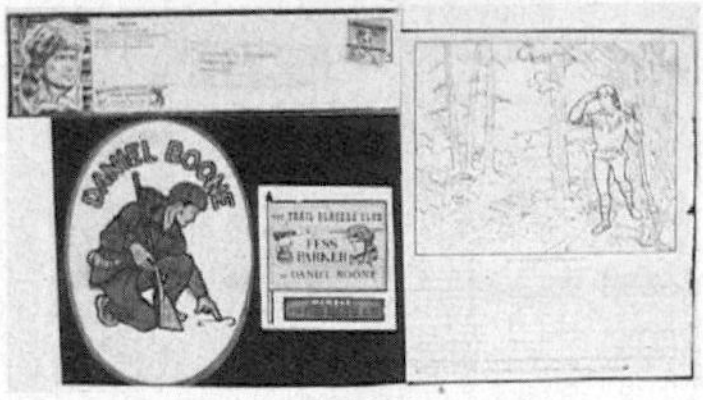

DNL-11

❑ **DNL-11. "Trail Blazers Club" Box With Contents,**
1965. American Tradition Co. Mailer contains fabric patch, water transfer decal, puzzle contest entry sheet requiring proof of purchase of store products by American Tradition Co.
Near Mint Boxed - **$125**
Patch - **$10 $20 $40**
Decal - **$6 $12 $30**
Form - **$6 $12 $30**

DNL-12

DNL-13

❑ **DNL-12. Fess Parker As Daniel Boone On "Fort Madison, Iowa" Rodeo Cello. Button,**
1966. 2-3/16" from a series issued annually. - **$25 $50 $75**

❑ **DNL-13. "TV Channels" Cover Article,**
1969. Weekly issue for July 6 of schedule guide supplement to Baltimore News American. - **$8 $15 $30**

Davey Adams, Son of the Sea

Details on this pre-World War II radio drama starring Franklin Adams are scarce but the program offered listeners membership in the DASC, the Davey Adams Shipmates Club, along with such premiums as a siren ring, a secret compartment members badge and a manual showing sailor knots and marine codes. Lava soap was the sponsor of this short-lived 1939 series.

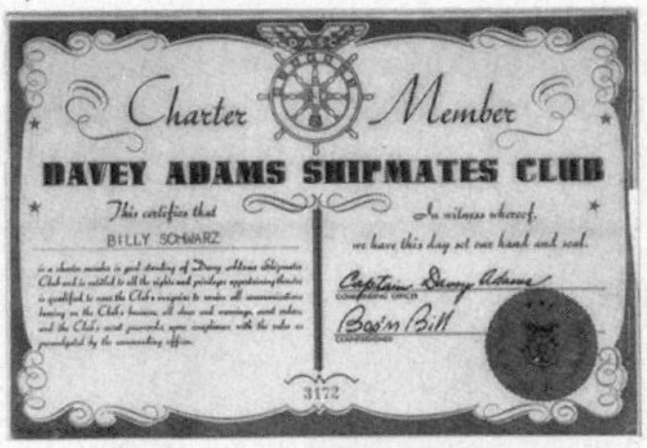

DVM-1

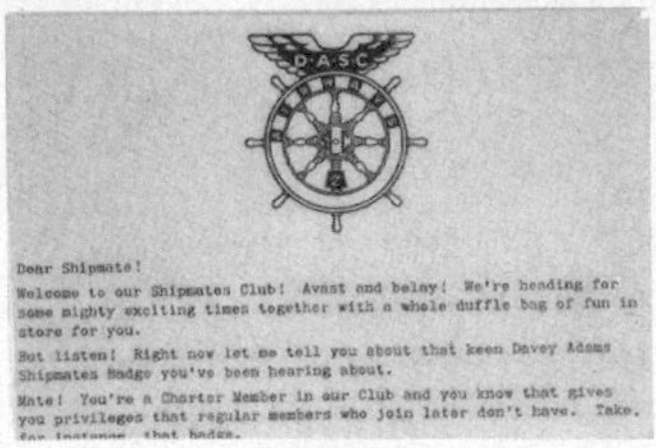

DVM-2

❑ **DVM-1. Club Charter Member Certificate,**
1939. Scarce. Lava soap. - **$45 $100 $185**

❑ **DVM-2. Club Letter,**
1939. Lava soap. Offers Secret Compartment Shipmate's Badge. - **$20 $35 $65**

DVM-3 DVM-4

❑ **DVM-3. "D.A.S.C." Siren Ring,**
1939. Scarce. Initials for "Davey Adams Shipmates Club." -**$225 $450 $750**

❑ **DVM-4. Shipmates Club Brass Decoder Badge,**
1939. Lava Soap. Decoder wheel front, back has secret compartment. - **$85 $165 $350**

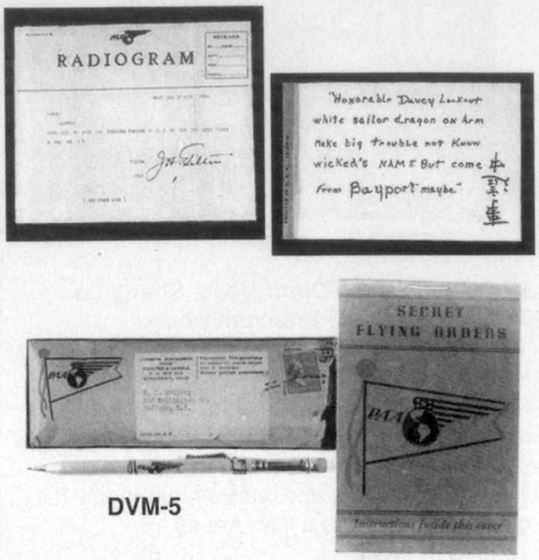

DVM-5

❑ **DVM-5. "Davey Adams Shipmates" Club Kit With Pencil,**
c. 1939. Pan American Airways. Mailing envelope containing Radiogram bulletin, Secret Flying Orders booklet, mechanical pencil with secret compartment, all identified by sponsor name. Near Mint Complete - **$600**
Pencil - **$75 $150 $250**
Each Paper Item - **$35 $70 $115**

DVM-6

❑ **DVM-6. "Davey Adams" Secret Message Tablet,**
1939. Lava Soap. 2.25x5.25". Front cover title is "Secret Clues And Messages For Davey Adams Shipmates" and includes "DASC" ship's wheel design for the Davey Adams Shipmates Club. Used in conjunction with club's secret compartment decoder badge. Instructions note you were to write messages on the tablet's tissue paper sheets and fold and slip into secret compartment on badge. First page has example message "Davey Adams Beware! Snake Is Laying For you. Hipi Will Try Double Cross You Look Out A Friend." - **$35 $65 $125**

Davy Crockett

Frontier scout, Indian fighter, bear killer, congressman, statesman, martyred at the Alamo--Davy Crockett (1786-1836) was a natural for television. Five fictionalized episodes from his life were broadcast on the *Disneyland* series on ABC in 1954 and 1955, starring Fess Parker in a coonskin cap and carrying his trusty rifle Old Betsy. Parker became an instant star, Crockett became an idol to an estimated 40 million viewers. Buddy Ebsen (1908-2003) co-starred as Davy's friend George Russel. *The Ballad Of Davy Crockett* written by Tom Blackburn and George Bruns landed on the *Hit Parade* and a merchandising mania swept the country. Some 500 products were licensed by Disney--toys, games, rifles, books, lunch boxes, costumes, coonskin caps--and unlicensed merchandise capitalizing on the craze followed in great profusion. Disney re-edited the films and released them to theaters as *Davy Crockett, King of the Wild Frontier* in 1955 and *Davy Crockett and the River Pirates* in 1956 and the original episodes were rebroadcast a half-dozen times over the next 20 years. An animated TV special sponsored by Kenner toys aired on CBS in 1976. NBC-TV aired *The New Adventures of Davy Crockett* starring Tim Dunigan in 1988-1989. Billy Bob Thornton played Davy in the 2004 feature film *The Alamo* reprising the role John Wayne played in the 1960 version.

DVY-1

❑ **DVY-1. "Davy Crockett's Boy Hunter" Book,**
1908. Store item. 5x7" paperback pulp published by Arthur Westbrook Company, Cleveland. #11 from series of 100 western titles. - **$25 $50 $100**

DVY-2

❑ **DVY-2. Canadian Lunch Box,**
1955. Store item by Kruger Mfg. Co. Ltd. - **$225 $500 $1000**

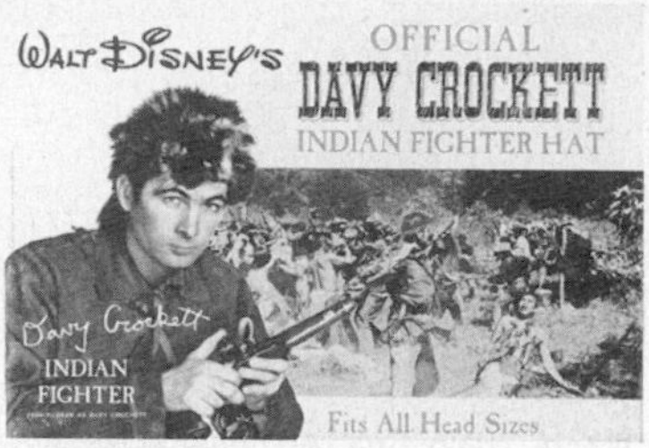

DVY-3

❑ **DVY-3. "Indian Fighter Hat" Box,**
1955. Weathermac Corp. store item. See next item. Box only - **$75 $150 $300**

DVY-4

❑ **DVY-4. "Indian Fighter Hat",**
1955. Weathermac Corp. Illustrated Fess Parker coonskin cap designed for all head sizes and formed from actual fur. Has cardboard portrait disk stapled on front. See previous item.
Hat only - **$90 $175 $300**

DVY-5

❑ **DVY-5. Davy Crockett Watch in Box,**
1954. With plastic gunpowder horn. Musical piece on top of horn that makes it blow is sometimes missing. Also has rawhide string that attaches to each end of the horn.
Complete - **$650**

DVY-6

❑ **DVY-6. "Davy Crockett King Of The Wild Frontier" TV Tray,**
1955. Store item, Disney Productions. 12-1/2x17". - **$60 $125 $200**

(ENLARGED VIEW)

DVY-7

❑ **DVY-7. "Frontier Action Ring" On Card,**
1955. Karo Syrup. Plastic ring holds flicker portrait.
Card - **$75 $150 $300**
Ring - **$35 $65 $125**

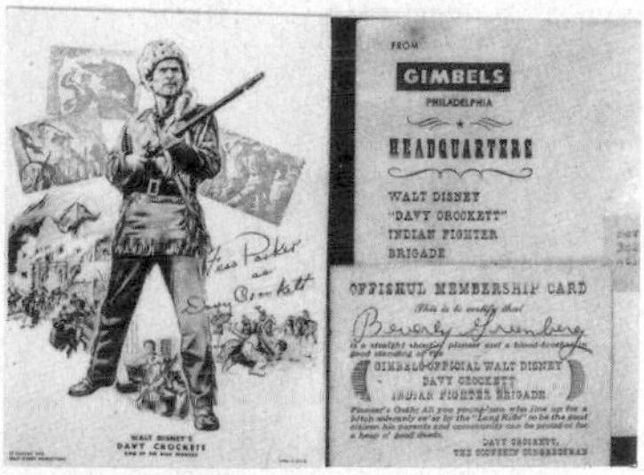

DVY-8

❑ **DVY-8. Gimbel's Club Kit In Mailer Envelope,**
1955. Gimbel's department store. Disney authorized contents include photo and member card.
Near Mint In Mailer - **$150**
Photo - **$20 $40 $70**
Card - **$15 $30 $60**

DVY-9

❑ **DVY-9. Frosted Glass,**
c. 1955. Farmers Dairy Milk Ice Cream. - **$12 $20 $35**

DVY-10

DVY-11

❑ **DVY-10. "Davy Crockett In The Raid At Piney Creek" Comic,**
1955. American Motors give-away. - **$8 $24 $60**

❑ **DVY-11. "Yaller Yaller Gold" Song Sheet,**
1955. Featured in TV's "Davy Crockett and Mike Fink" production. - **$18 $35 $70**

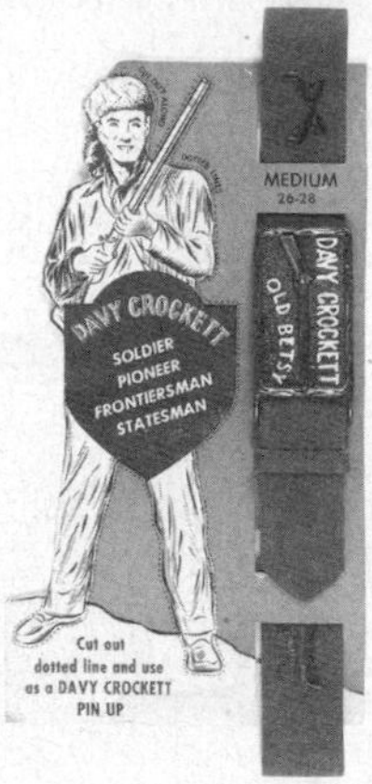

DVY-12

❑ **DVY-12. "Davy Crockett" Leather Belt With Metal Buckle,**
c. 1955. Diecut cardboard measures 6.5"x11.75" as full standing figure of Davy. Metal cast buckle has rifle. Four metal embossed accents are attached to belt. Accents are two each of Conestoga wagon and crossed hand guns.
Card - **$15 $30 $50**
Belt - **$15 $30 $50**

DVY-13

❑ **DVY-13. Plastic Bank,**
c. 1955. Various local sponsors. - **$18 $35 $60**

DVY-14

❑ **DVY-14. "Davy Crockett" Figural Metal Clock And Motion Light,**
c. 1955. Figure is 6x8x10" tall with gold luster and motion light showing Indians circling through woods. Scene is repeated on back. "Davy Crockett" below panel opening. Electric clock is 3.5" with 3.25" dial. - **$225 $450 $750**

DVY-15

❑ **DVY-15. Cloverbloom Box With Magic Viewer,**
c. 1955. Armour Co. Premium for "Cloverbloom '99' Oleomargarine." Eight different viewers with four 3-D scenes issued. Gordon Gold Archives.
Box - **$30 $65 $150**
Each Viewer - **$12 $18 $35**

DVY-16

❑ **DVY-16. Honey Grahams Box,**
c. 1955. Promotes Davy Crockett free cloth patches. All 12 pictured on back of box. - **$75 $150 $300**

DVY-17

❑ **DVY-17. "Free Cloth Patches" Store Display,**
c. 1955. Flavor Kist Honey Grahams. 17x20-1/2" thick diecut cardboard designed as back panel of a store display bin. Gordon Gold Archives. - **$175 $350 $700**

DVY-18

❑ **DVY-18. "Free Cloth Patches" Shelf Hanger Sign,**
c. 1955. Flavor Kist Honey Grahams. 5-1/2x10-1/4". Gordon Gold Archives. - **$100 $200 $350**

DVY-19

❑ **DVY-19. Davy Crockett Cloth Patches Set,**
c. 1955. Flavor Kist Honey Grahams. Set of 12 in five different shapes, each about 3x3". Reverse has paper covering over adhesive back. Gordon Gold Archives.
Each - **$15 $30 $60**

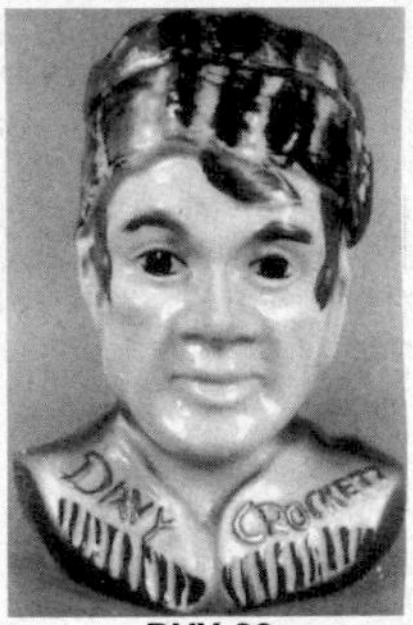

DVY-20 DVY-21

❑ **DVY-20. Ceramic Cookie Jar,**
c. 1955. Regal China. Store item. - **$100 $200 $300**

❑ **DVY-21. "Davy Crockett Hero Of The Alamo" Gold Finish White Metal Badge,**
c. 1955. "Tootsietoy" name appears on reverse. - **$50 $100 $200**

DVY-22

❑ **DVY-22. "Candies And Toy" Box,**
c. 1955. Super Novelty Candy Co. with Disney copyright. Cut-out cards on box back.
Uncut Box - **$35 $90 $160**

DVY-23

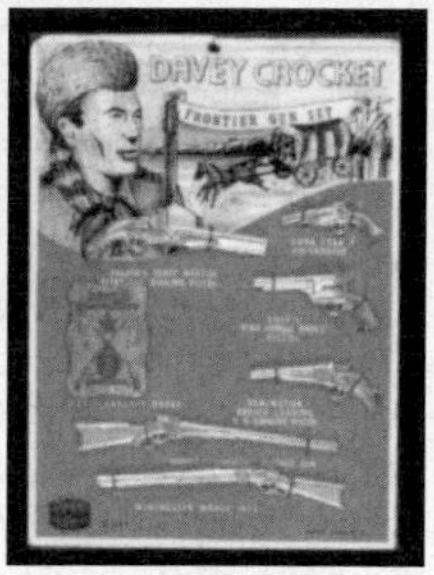

DVY-24

❑ **DVY-23. Pocketknives With Fess Parker,**
c. 1955. Store items by Imperial. Three varieties. 2-1/4" With Hatchet - **$40 $85 $145**
2-1/4" Single Blade - **$30 $65 $125**
3-1/2" Three Blades - **$30 $65 $125**

❑ **DVY-24. "Davey Crocket" Frontier Gun Set On Store Card,**
c. 1955. Store item by John Henry Products. - **$50 $115 $250**

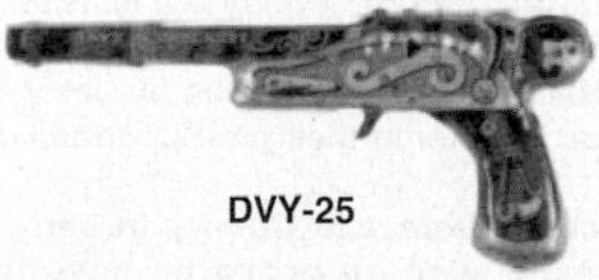

DVY-25

❑ **DVY-25. "Davy Crockett" Clicker Gun,**
c. 1955. Store item by Marx Toys. - **$85 $165 $300**

DVY-26

❑ **DVY-26. "Davy Crockett-Frontier Scout" Australian Button,**
c. 1955. 1.75" black/white/gray. - **$55 $110 $175**

DVY-27

❑ **DVY-27. "Davy Crockett Kills A Bear" Button,**
c. 1955. Tracy's. Multicolor also inscribed for sponsor. Maker is Philadelphia Badge Co. - **$40 $65 $135**

DVY-28

❑ **DVY-28. "Davy Crockett At The Alamo" Button,**
c. 1955. Tracy's. 1.25" multicolor. Maker is Philadelphia Badge Co. - **$40 $65 $135**

DVY-29

❑ **DVY-29. "Liberty Theatre Now/Davy Crockett Indian Scout" Button,**
c. 1955. 1.25" movie theater promo in blue/black on cream background. - **$20 $40 $85**

DVY-30 DVY-31

❑ **DVY-30. "Davidson's Davy Crockett Club" Button,**
c. 1955. 1.5" cello dark red or brown on white. Either - **$40 $75 $125**

❑ **DVY-31. "Walt Disney's Official" Australian Button,**
c. 1956. 1.75" black and white "Fess Parker" portrait on warm gray background. - **$75 $165 $325**

DVY-32

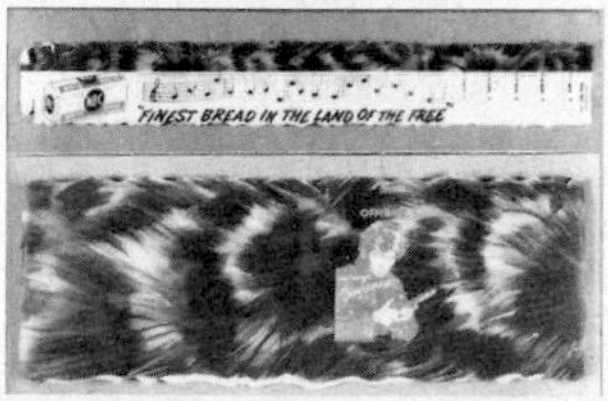

DVY-33

❑ **DVY-32. "Frontier Bread" Waxed Paper Bread Wrapper,**
1950s. - **$20 $40 $65**

❑ **DVY-33. Coonskin Cap Punch-Out Sheet,**
1950s. Nabisco. With simulated fur design. Unused With Tail - **$20 $40 $75**

DVY-34

❑ **DVY-34. "Davy Crockett Cookies" Box,**
1950s. Federal Sweets & Biscuit Co. - **$35 $75 $165**

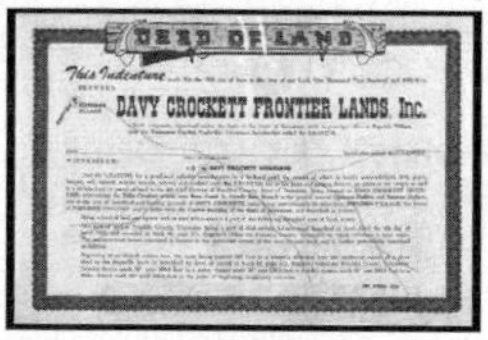

DVY-35

DVY-36

❑ **DVY-35. Deed of Land,**
1950s. Scarce. - **$30 $75 $135**

❑ **DVY-36. "Jackson Daily News Fan Club" 2-1/4" Cello. Button,**
1950s. - **$35 $75 $150**

DVY-37

❑ **DVY-37. Cardboard Money Saver,**
1950s. Various sponsors. - **$20 $35 $70**

DVY-38

DVY-39

❑ **DVY-38. "Davy Crockett Frontier Club" Cello. Button,**
1950s. - **$25 $40 $85**

❑ **DVY-39. "Big Yank Frontiersman" Litho. Button,**
1950s. Clothing company. - **$15 $30 $60**

DVY-40

DVY-41

❑ **DVY-40. "Pfeifers Davy Crockett Fan Club" Litho. Button,**
1950s. - **$30 $60 $115**

❑ **DVY-41. "King Of The Wild Frontier" Cello. Button,**
1950s. Disney authorized. - **$18 $40 $75**

DVY-42

DVY-43

❑ **DVY-42. "Frontiersman" Litho. Button,**
1950s. Disney authorized. - **$15 $35 $75**

❑ **DVY-43. "Walt Disney's Davy Crockett" Metal Compass Ring,**
1950s. Peter Pan Peanut Butter. -
$75 $150 $275

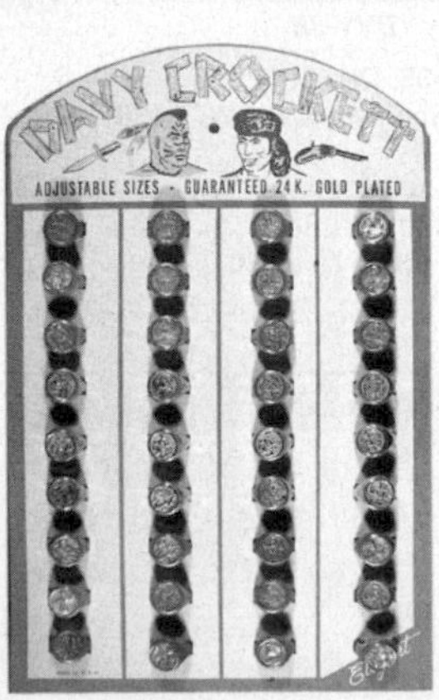

DVY-44

❑ **DVY-44. Davy Crockett Card with Rings,**
1950s. Card holds 36 rings, 24K gold plated.
Complete - **$1000**
Each gold ring - **$25**
Similar ring in silver - **$30**

DVY-45

❑ **DVY-45. "Davy Crockett Indian Scout Badge" On Store Card,**
1950s. Card - **$15 $30 $50**
Badge - **$10 $20 $30**

DVY-46

DVY-47

DVY-48

❑ **DVY-46. "Frontier Club" Litho. Tab,**
1950s. - **$15 $30 $45**

❑ **DVY-47. Fess Parker/Crockett English Metal Badge,**
1950s. Store item by "DCMT Ltd." of England. Silver finish, red lettering, black/white insert photo. - **$20 $50 $85**

❑ **DVY-48. Composition Bobbing Head,**
1950s. Store item. - **$85 $150 $300**

DVY-49

❑ **DVY-49. Play Suit in Box,**
1950s. - **$175 $350 $675**

DVY-50

❑ **DVY-50. Leatherette Jacket,**
1950s. Store bought. TV merchandise. -
$75 $250 $450

DC Comics

Former pulp magazine writer and army cavalry officer Major Malcolm Wheeler Nicholson published the first issue of *New Fun* (subsequent issues became *More Fun*) in 1935. Tabloid size with a full color cover and 32 black and white pages, it was the first comic book with original material in a Sunday comic page format. Although he wasn't making any money, the Major added *New Comics* (later to become *Adventure Comics* late in 1935). Most notable is that these two titles featured art by Walt Kelly as well as stories by Jerry Siegel and Joe Shuster in their pre-Superman days.

Next came *Detective Comics* in early 1937. The Major was so broke by now he was forced to take a partner, his printer. The new company was called Detective Comics, Inc. or DC Comics. Nicholson left soon afterwards. The new owners decided to add another title, *Action Comics*. Editor Vincent Sullivan was looking for new material when he saw samples of Superman by co-workers Siegel and Shuster. He decided to use the character. *Action Comics* #1 debuted in June 1938 and the comic book world was changed forever.

Sullivan also edited *Detective Comics* and after he suggested artist Bob Kane come up with something, Batman debuted in issue #27 in 1939. Within one year editor Vincent Sullivan oversaw the beginnings of the two greatest comic book characters to ever see print. These characters are covered in their own sections while this section touches on additional DC characters.

The addition of their own toy imprint, DC Direct, has greatly enhanced the number of character toys DC has generated and increased the number of characters represented in statues, action figures, plush toys and props. This trend can be expected to continue. Their toys are generally only available in comic book specialty shops.

See the DC characters which are part of the 1966 Super Hero Club button set in the Marvel Comics section.

DCM-1

❑ **DCM-1. Advertising Flyer for Boy Commandos #1,**
1942. Sign is 11 1/2" high, 8 1/2" wide. Also pictures other DC comics from that year. Rare. - **$225 $400 $800**

DCM-2

❑ **DCM-2. DC Publication Promo**
1942. Features top selling comics that are among the first 25 in newsstand sales. Note they refer to them as magazines and not comic books. - **$150 $300 $600**

DCM-3

❑ **DCM-3. "Boy Commandos" Transfers Pack,**
1948. DC Comics copyright. Store packet of transfer pictures based on comic book military cartoon characters. - **$65 $150 $300**

DCM-4

❑ **DCM-4. Flyer for The National Jamboree for Boy Scouts,**
1950. Features Superman, Batman and Robin. Also promotes DC's line of comics. - **$150 $300 $600**

DCM-5

❑ **DCM-5. Sugar and Spike Thank You Card,**
1950s. DC Comics editor thank you card with Sheldon Mayer facsimile signature. - **$30 $65 $100**

DCM-6

❑ **DCM-6. "DC" Promotional Glass,**
1950s. This is a 5-5/8" glass and there is a similar 6-3/4" glass with slightly different character designs. Characters on this example are Superman, Batman, Mutt, Wonder Woman, Tomahawk, The Crow (from Fox and The Crow), Judy (from A Date With Judy). Larger version features illustration of The Flash in place of Mutt.
Each version - **$60 $125 $225**

DCM-7

❑ **DCM-7. "Blackhawk" Comic Promo Card,**
1964. Oversized postcard dated June 17 picturing characters on one side. Mailing side features large Superman-DC Comics emblem. - **$30 $50 $85**

DCM-8

❑ **DCM-8. Advertising Poster for 48-Page Issues,**
1971. Shows Superman and Batman. - **$15 $30 $60**

DCM-9

❑ DCM-9. Promotional 3 1/2"x 8" Sticker,
1975. Shows Superman and Batman. -
$25 $40 $75

DCM-10

❑ DCM-10. Display Box and Mini-Comics,
1981. The display box holds 8 packs, each containing a secret origin comic and candy. Origins include Superman, Batman, Hawkman, Flash, Aquaman, Wonder Woman, Green Arrow, and the Justice League.
Box - **$15 $40 $80**
Each Comic with Candy - **$3 $5 $10**

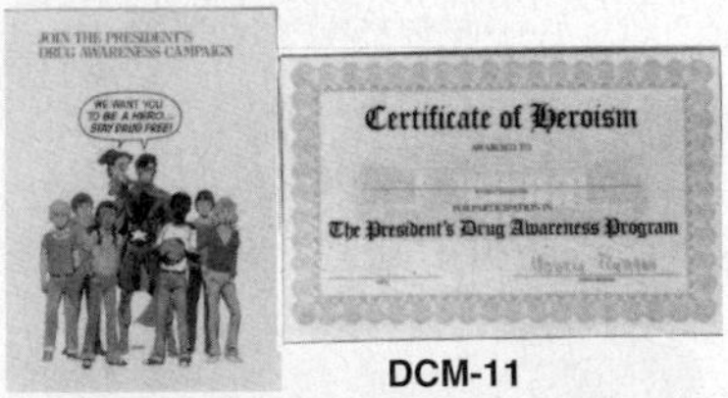

DCM-11

❑ DCM-11. "DC/Keebler President's Drug Awareness Campaign" Kit,
1983. Various paper items including those with facsimile endorsement signature of Nancy Reagan. Complete - **$10 $20 $35**

DCM-12

DCM-13

❑ DCM-12. Super Powers Metal Lunch Box,
1983. Aladdin Industries, Inc. Features Superman, Batman and Wonder Woman. -
$30 $60 $150

❑ DCM-13. "Justice League Of America" Collectors Series Plate,
1980s. China plate 8.5" in diameter from set of six "DC Super Heroes" series by The International Museum, McAllen, Texas. Features art of the team's lineup consisting of Superman, Batman, Wonder Woman, Aquaman, Flash, Green Lantern, Hawkman & Red Tornado. Rimmed in gold. Reverse in black and white has image of first Justice League of America comic from 1960 plus plate series information including individual number and firing master initials.
Each - **$12 $25 $50**

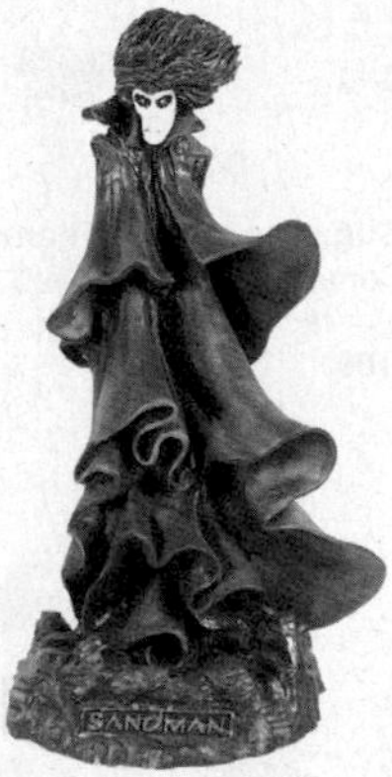

DCM-14

❑ DCM-14. "The Sandman" Statue,
1991. Graphitti Designs. Limited to 1,800. Based on designs from artist Kelley Jones. Miniature version released in 1998.
Boxed - **$825**

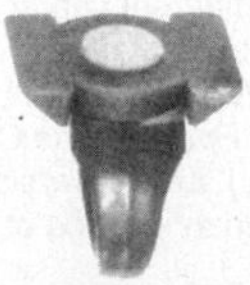

DCM-15

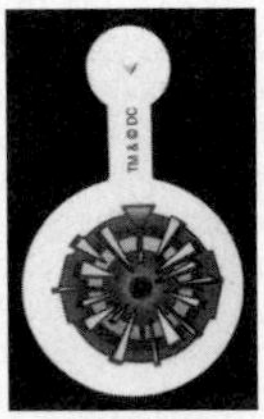

DCM-16

❑ DCM-15. Green Lantern Glow-In-Dark Plastic Ring,
1992. - **$5 $10 $15**

❑ DCM-16. Zero Hour Litho. Tin Tab,
1994. From mini series.
Unbent - **$2 $4 $6**

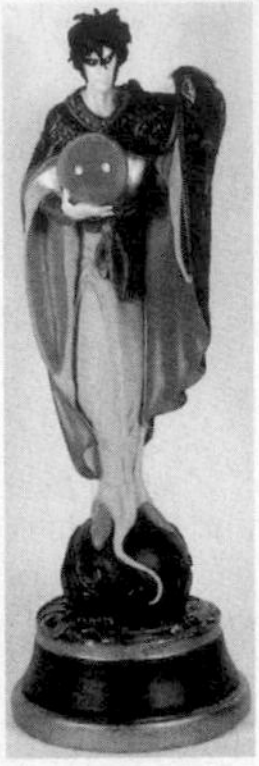

DCM-17

DCM-18

DCM-19

❑ DCM-17. "The Sandman Arabian Nights" Statue,
1994. Graphitti Designs. Limited to 7,200. Based on character designs in Sandman #50 from artist P. Craig Russell.
Boxed - **$240**

❑ DCM-18. Justice League Of America Litho. Button,
1997. - **$2 $4 $6**

❑ DCM-19. "U.S." (Uncle Sam) Comics Cello. Promo Button,
1997. DC/Vertigo mini series. - **$2 $4 $6**

DCM-20

DCM-21

❑ DCM-20. Modern Age Green Lantern Resin Statue of Kyle Rayner,
1997. Limited to 2,200. 13" tall including base. The base of this figure and the 2 other Green Lanterns fit together. All 3 sculpted by William Paquet. Figure with box - **$250**

❑ DCM-21. Green Lantern 5" Figure,
1998. Limited to 2,500. - **$90**

DCM-22

❑ DCM-22. Silver Age Green Lantern Resin Statue of Hal Jordan,
1998. Limited to 2,500. 12" tall including base. Figure with box - **$225**

DCM-23

❑ DCM-23. Golden Age Green Lantern Resin Statue of Alan Scott,
1999. Limited to 2,000. 13" tall including base. Figure with box - **$250**

DCM-24

❑ DCM-24. "Super Heroes" Die Cast Metal Figures in Box,
1998. Warner Bros. Store exclusive. Features Supergirl, Superman, Green Lantern, Captain Marvel and Batman. Set sold out quickly and is hard to find on the secondary market. - **$85**

DCM-25

DCM-26

❑ DCM-25. Green Lantern Bean Bag Figure,
1998. Warner Bros. Store exclusive. - **$10**

❑ DCM-26. Aquaman Bean Bag Figure,
1999. Warner Bros. Store exclusive. - **$10**

DCM-27

DCM-28

❑ DCM-27. Supergirl Bean Bag Figure,
1999. Animated series version. Warner Bros. Store exclusive. - **$10**

❑ DCM-28. Supergirl Resin Statue,
2000. Limited to 2,000. 12" tall including base. Figure with box - **$225**

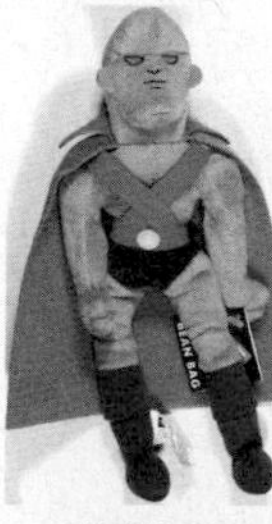

DCM-29

DCM-30

❑ DCM-29. Martian Manhunter Bean Bag Figure,
2000. Warner Bros. Store exclusive. - **$10**

❑ DCM-30. "Legion of Super-Heroes" PVC Set,
2000. From DC Direct. 7 figures in box shaped like the Legion's clubhouse. - **$55**

DCM-31

DCM-32

❑ DCM-31. Silver Age Green Lantern Figure with Ring on Card,
2000. - **$25**

❑ DCM-32. Plastic Man Figure on Card,
2000. Variant version - **$40**

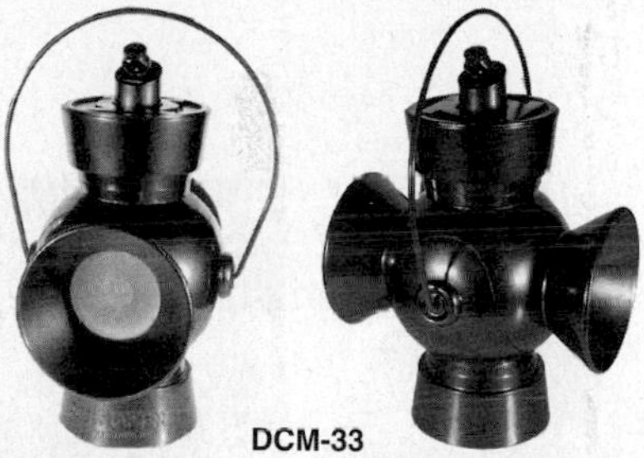

DCM-33

❑ DCM-33. Green Lantern Power Battery Prop with Ring and Box,
2000. Limited to 2,200. 11 3/4" tall and 9 3/4" wide. Lights up when ring touches it. - **$475**

DCM-34

❑ DCM-34. "The New Teen Titans" PVC Set,
2000. From DC Direct. 7 figures in box. - **$50**

DCM-35

❑ DCM-35. Sgt. Rock Resin Statue,
2000. Only 750 produced. Figure has removable helmet. Boxed with signed print by longtime Sgt. Rock artist Joe Kubert. - **$240**

DCM-36

DCM-37

❑ **DCM-36. Plastic Man Watch,**
2000. On card. - **$60**

❑ **DCM-37. Green Lantern PVC Set,**
2000. Seven figure set in box - **$50**

DCM-38

DCM-39

❑ **DCM-38. Golden Age Green Lantern Bust with Removable Power Ring,**
2001. Limited to 2,500. - **$120**

❑ **DCM-39. Sinestro Action Figure on Card,**
2001. Comes with yellow power ring. - **$25**

DCM-40

❑ **DCM-40. Hal Jordan Green Lantern Bust with Removable Power Ring,**
2001. Limited to 2,500. - **$125**

DCM-41

❑ **DCM-41. Hawkman Statue,**
2001. Limited edition of 1,350. DC Direct product came with signed print by Joe Kubert. With box - **$225**

DCM-42

❑ **DCM-42. Aquaman Water Globe,**
2001. Limited edition of 2,000. With box - **$90**

DCM-43

❑ **DCM-43. Green Arrow Resin Statue,**
2002. Limited edition of 2,200. Designed by Matt Wagner. With box - **$250**

DCM-44

❑ **DCM-44. Spectre Statue,**
2002. DC Direct. Sculpted by William Paquet. Limited edition of 1200. - **$235**

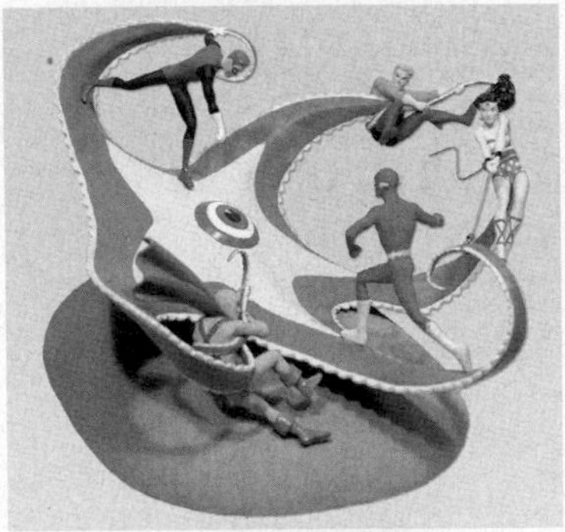

DCM-45

❑ **DCM-45. JLA *Brave & the Bold* #28 Statue,**
2002. DC Direct. Sculpted by Jon G. Mathews. Limited edition of 1200. - **$300**

Death Valley Days

One of the earliest radio dramas, *Death Valley Days* premiered on NBC in 1930. The stories of miners and homesteaders in the California desert, told by a character called the Old Ranger, were based on actual happenings and the show earned a reputation for historical accuracy. The program moved to CBS in 1941 and evolved into *Death Valley Sheriff* and then *The Sheriff* in 1945 when it aired on ABC. It ended its long radio life in 1951, sponsored from the beginning by 20 Mule Team Borax and Boraxo soap products. A syndicated television adaptation ran for 558 episodes, from 1952 to 1975, with Ronald Reagan, Robert Taylor, Dale Robertson or Merle Haggard playing the Old Ranger. The series has been rerun under a variety of titles.

DTH-1

DTH-2

❑ **DTH-1. "Radio Stars" Leaflet,**
1930. Pictures John White, Old Ranger, Virginia Gardiner. - **$15 $25 $40**

❑ **DTH-2. "Death Valley Days" Storybook,**
1931. - **$10 $20 $40**

DTH-3

DTH-4

❑ **DTH-3. "Old Ranger's Yarns Of Death Valley" Magazine,**
1933. - **$12 $25 $50**

❑ **DTH-4. "Hauling 20 Mule Team Borax Out Of Death Valley" Puzzle,**
1933. - **$18 $35 $85**

DTH-5

❑ **DTH-5. "Picture Sheet" Newspaper Style Folder Promoting Radio Show,**
1933. - **$15 $35 $75**

DTH-6

DTH-7

❑ **DTH-6. "Death Valley Days" Charles Marshall Song Book,**
1934. - **$8 $18 $35**

❑ **DTH-7. "Cowboy Songs As Sung By John White...",**
1934. - **$8 $18 $35**

DTH-8

❑ **DTH-8. "Death Valley Tales" Storybook,**
1934. - **$8 $18 $35**

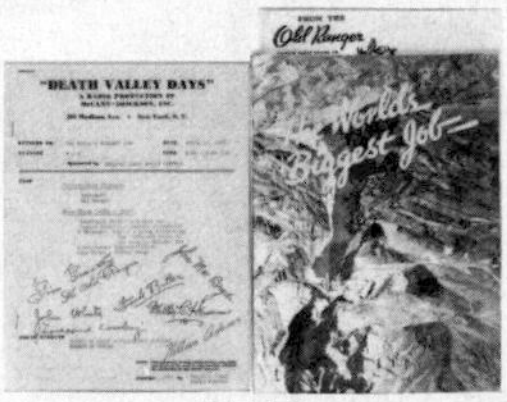

DTH-9

❑ **DTH-9. "The World's Biggest Job" Radio Broadcast Script With Cover Folder And Envelope,**
1935. For April 11 episode about construction of Boulder Dam. - **$15 $30 $65**

DTH-10

❑ **DTH-10. "High Spots Of Death Valley Days" Vol. 1 #1 Booklet With Envelope,**
1939. Includes six previous broadcast stories plus radio script for May 19, 1939 episode.
Booklet - **$12 $25 $50**
Envelope - **$5 $12 $20**

DTH-11

❑ **DTH-11. Old Ranger Seed Packets With Mailer,**
1939. Pacific Coast Borax Co.
Each - **$20 $40 $75**
Mailer - **$25 $50 $85**

DTH-12

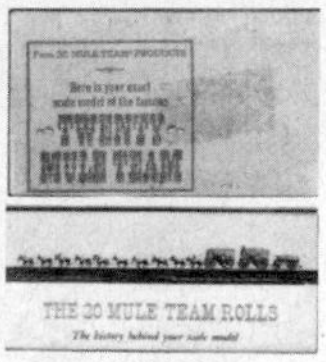

DTH-13

❑ **DTH-12. "Old Ranger" Fan Postcard,**
1930s. Pacific Coast Borax Co. Text for weekly broadcasts on NBC Blue Network in East and Red Network in West with back text for "Death Valley Days" program title. - **$15 $30 $50**

❑ **DTH-13. "20 Mule Team" Model Kit,**
1950s. Borax. Issued for many years from the 1950s through 1970s. Packaged in one or two boxes. Near Mint In Box - **$40**

DTH-14

❑ **DTH-14. Reagan Cover And Article In TV Week,**
1965. Issue is 8x11" with 20 pages. May 29-June 4, 1965 Chicago Tribune TV Week. Article titled "Ronald Reagan Signs For Death Valley Days 13th Year On Television." - **$8 $18 $30**

Dell Comics

Dell Publishing Company founder George Delacorte started in the comic book business in 1929 with *The Funnies*, a 24-page weekly tabloid with eight pages in color, all original features and a ten cent price. 36 issues appeared, then Delacorte tried a few black and white titles in the early 1930s. Late in 1935 he introduced *Popular Comics*, the first Sunday comic page reprint title to compete with *Famous Funnies*. This proved successful enough for Delacorte to begin *The Funnies*, using the title a second time, the summer of 1936. Both titles used original material in conjunction with reprints. Next came *The Comics* in March 1937. The Four Color series began in 1939. Delacorte really began rolling in 1940 as Dell published *Walt Disney's Comics and Stories*, followed by *Looney Tunes and Merrie Melodies* in 1941 and original stories featuring Captain Midnight and Andy Panda in *The Funnies* of 1942. *Four Color* #9 (the first Donald Duck comic with original story and art) appeared in 1942. Carl Barks, Walt Kelly, *Marge's Little Lulu, The Lone Ranger, Roy Rogers, Gene Autry, Tarzan* and a host of others appeared in comics with the Dell logo. Many paper premiums to promote comic book subscriptions are listed in this book under sections for specific characters.

DEL-1

❑ **DEL-1. Dell Characters 8x10" Color Print,**
1950. - **$70 $145 $275**

DEL-2

❑ **DEL-2. Comic Book Rack 6x15" Litho. Tin Sign,**
c. 1950. Display attachment picturing 13 Dell Comics characters. - **$135 $300 $550**

DEL-3

❑ **DEL-3. "KE" Plastic Puzzle Game,**
1952. Played by pegs with "Secret Formula" instruction sheet.
Complete Puzzle Only - **$25 $55 $110**

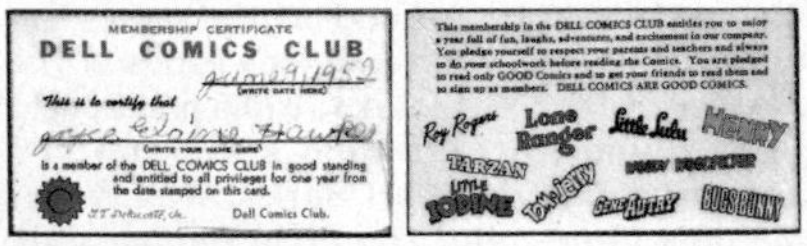

DEL-4

❑ **DEL-4. Club Membership Card,**
1952. - **$15 $30 $75**

DEL-5

❑ **DEL-5. Dell Comic Club Promo & Club Card,**
1953. Scarce. Barks cover.
Folder - **$50 $150 $300**
Card - **$30 $60 $125**

DEL-6

DEL-7

❑ **DEL-6. "Walt Disney Comics And Stories" Christmas Gift Subscription Certificate,**
1950s. - **$30 $85 $150**

❑ **DEL-7. "Official Dell Comics Club/Member" Aluminum Cased Lincoln Penny,**
1950s. Pictured example has 1953 penny, rim inscription "Keep Me And You Will Have Good Luck". - **$10 $20 $30**

DEL-8

❑ **DEL-8. "Official Dell Comics Club Member" Pen,**
1950s. Pen is 5.5" long hard plastic with metal pocket clip centered by .5" diameter "Dell" title. Full inscription is on pen barrel.
- **$60 $140 $275**

Dennis the Menace

Mischief-maker supreme, Dennis the Menace made his first appearance as a daily cartoon panel in 1951 and as a Sunday page the following year. Based on cartoonist Hank Ketcham's (1920-2001) own son, Dennis, trailed by his dog Ruff, has been harassing his suburban neighborhood ever since. Frequent victims include his parents, Henry and Alice Mitchell and their neighbor, cantankerous George Wilson. The strip has been a consistent winner, so much so that the title itself has entered the lexicon. Many paperback and hardcover reprints have been published and the first of many Dennis comic books appeared in 1953. A prime-time television series starring Jay North as Dennis ran on CBS from 1959 to 1963 and was rerun on NBC from 1963 to 1965. Most merchandised items are related to the comic strip; those based on the TV series are usually copyrighted by Screen Gems Inc. The panel appears in 1,000 newspapers worldwide, ably carried on by Marcus Hamilton and Ron Ferdinand.

DNS-1

❑ **DNS-1. "Dennis The Menace On Safety" Booklet,**
1956. National Safety Council. - **$10 $18 $35**

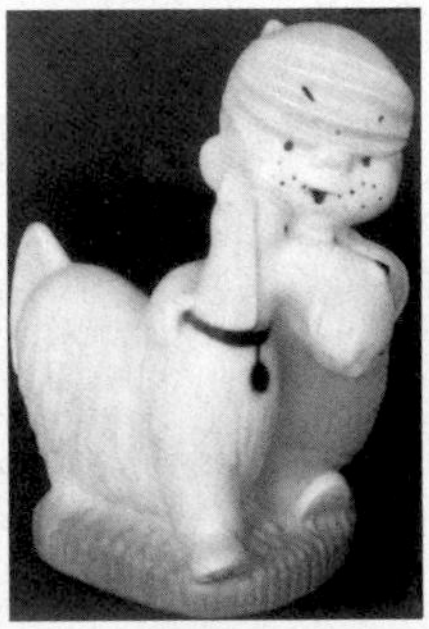

DNS-2

❑ **DNS-2. Dennis And Ruff Figural Vinyl Light,**
1950s. 7" tall molded and colorful likeness that glows from inner bulb. - **$35 $65 $125**

DNS-3

❑ **DNS-3. "Dennis The Menace Takes A Poke At Poison",**
1961. Food and Drug Administration.
Original 1961 Edition - **$2 $6 $12**
Later Reprints - **$1 $3 $7**

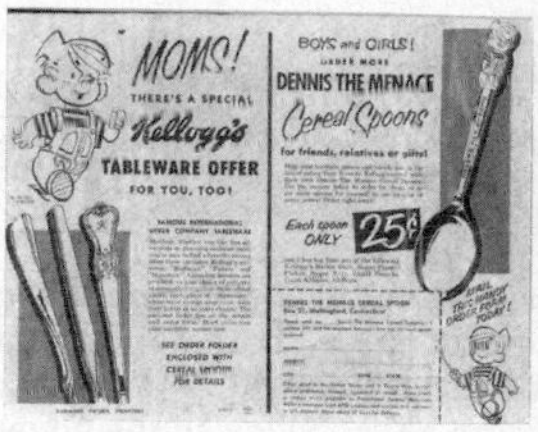

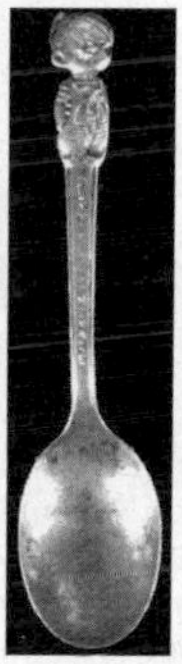

DNS-4

❑ **DNS-4. Spoon Ad Paper With Silver Plate Spoon,**
1961. Kellogg's Rice Krispies. Ad - **$5 $10 $15**
Spoon - **$6 $12 $25**

DNS-5

❑ **DNS-5. Spoon Offer Kellogg's Sugar Pops Cereal Box,**
1961. - **$75 $150 $275**

DNS-6

DNS-7

❑ **DNS-6. Silver Luster Metal Pin,**
c. 1962. Probable Kellogg's premium. 1-1/2" tall. - **$8 $15 $30**

❑ **DNS-7. Three-Reel View-Master Pack With Story Booklet,**
1967. - **$10 $18 $30**

DNS-8

❑ **DNS-8. 'Dennis The Menace" Plaster Lamp,**
1967. Base is 5.25" diameter and lamp is 12" tall to top of socket. Back of drum reads "1967 Hall Syndicate Inc." - **$65 $135 $200**

DNS-9

❑ **DNS-9. "Cast Your Ballot" Litho. Button,**
1968. Sears. - **$18 $30 $60**

DNS-10

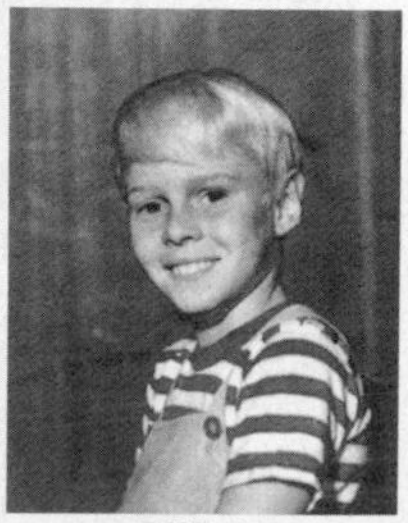

DNS-11

❑ **DNS-10. Cloth And Vinyl Hand Puppet,**
1960s. Store item. - **$20 $40 $65**

❑ **DNS-11. Fan Photo,**
1960s. - **$10 $18 $30**

DNS-12

DNS-13

❑ **DNS-12. "..And Away We Go!" Comic Book,**
1970. Caladryl medication. - **$1 $4 $10**

❑ **DNS-13. Joey From Dennis The Menace 2-1/4" Cello. Ad Button,**
1972. Dairy Queen. - **$15 $25 $40**

DNS-14

DNS-15

❑ **DNS-14. Dennis The Menace Plastic Assembly Ring,**
1970s. Dairy Queen. From same series as next three items picturing characters from "Ketcham" copyright comic strip. Parts separate for ring assembly.
Near Mint Unfolded On Tree - **$65**
Assembled - **$12 $25 $40**

❑ **DNS-15. Joey From Dennis The Menace Plastic Assembly Ring,**
1970s. Dairy Queen. Near Mint Unfolded On Tree - **$65**
Assembled - **$12 $25 $40**

DNS-16

DNS-17

❑ **DNS-16. Margaret From Dennis The Menace Plastic Assembly Ring,**
1970s. Dairy Queen.
Near Mint Unfolded On Tree - **$65**
Assembled - **$12 $25 $40**

❑ **DNS-17. Ruff From Dennis The Menace Plastic Assembly Ring,**
1970s. Dairy Queen. Near Mint Unfolded On Tree - **$65**
Assembled - **$12 $25 $40**

DNS-18

DNS-19

❑ **DNS-18. Dennis Doll with Tag,**
1987. 9 1/4" tall. - **$20 $40 $70**

❑ **DNS-19. Joey Doll with Tag,**
1987. 9 1/4" tall. - **$15 $30 $55**

Deputy Dawg

Created by Larz Bourne, *Deputy Dawg* was the first Terrytoons character to have his own syndicated show. Beginning in October 1960, CBS aired 102 cartoons. The show was set in rural Mississippi and the cast included Muskie the Muskrat, Ty Coon and Vincent Van Gopher. Dayton Allen and Lionel Wilson provided the voices. Directors included George Gordon, Dave Tendlar and Ralph Bakshi. In 1971, the show began re-runs on NBC Saturday mornings.

***Dell* published *Four Color* comic books #1238 and #1299 in 1961 and 1962.**

DEP-1

❑ **DEP-1. "Deputy Dawg" Pencil Case,**
1961. Hassenfeld Bros. Inc. 4.75x10-1/8x2" deep pencil case with insert for pencils and slide-out tray. - **$20 $40 $75**

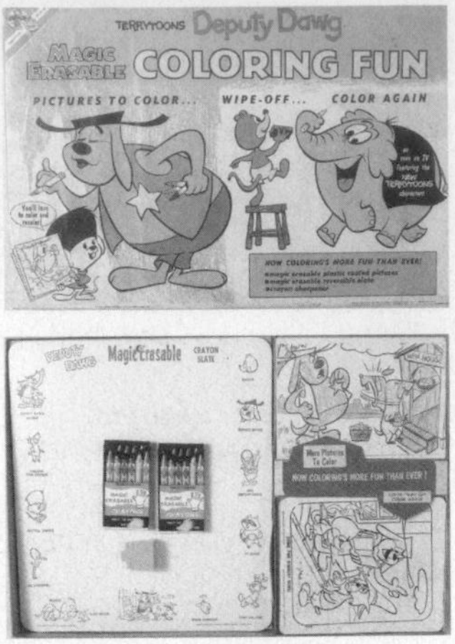

DEP-2

❑ **DEP-2. "Deputy Dawg Magic Erasable Coloring Fun" Set,**
1961. Transogram. 13-7/8x20-3/8x2" deep box with insert holding "Magic Erasable Crayon Slate," three 6.25x7.75" cards to color, two folders with scenes to color, red plastic sharpener designed like house with chimney and two boxes of "Magic Erasable" crayons. - **$30 $65 $125**

DEP-3

❑ **DEP-3. "Deputy Dawg" Vinyl Lunchbox,**
1964. American Thermos Products Co. Cream with black outline design on front. - **$100 $200 $400**

DEP-4

❑ **DEP-4. "Deputy Dawg" Variant Vinyl Lunchbox,**
1964. American Thermos Products Co. Tan with red outlines on images. Does not have "The American Thermos Products Co." text at bottom by hinge. - **$100 $200 $400**

DEP-5

DEP-6

❑ **DEP-5. "Deputy Dawg" Soaky Figure,**
1966. Colgate-Palmolive. 9.5" tall with plastic head and vinyl body. - **$8 $15 $30**

❑ **DEP-6. "Deputy Dawg" Puppet,**
1960s. 9.5" tall with soft vinyl head and cloth body with silk-screened body image. Comes with vacuform plastic hat with chin strap. - **$100 $200 $325**

Detectives Black and Blue

***Adventures of Detectives Black and Blue*, an early syndicated comedy crime show from Los Angeles radio station KHJ, aired from 1932 to 1934. The series followed the adventures of a pair of shipping clerks/amateur sleuths named Jim Black and Frank Blue in their bumbling attempts at criminology. "Detec-a-tives Black and Blue, good men tried and true."**

DTC-1

❑ **DTC-1. "Detectives Black And Blue" Premium Photo,**
c. 1932. Sepia tone photo is 4.75x7".
- $20 $40 $75

DTC-2

❑ **DTC-2. Fabric Double-Billed Detective Cap,**
c. 1932. Iodent toothpaste. Front bill names radio show and sponsor. **- $65 $160 $350**

DTC-3 **DTC-4**

❑ **DTC-3. "Detectives Black & Blue/Iodent Toothpaste" Brass Badge,**
c. 1932. **- $20 $50 $100**

❑ **DTC-4. "Detectives Black & Blue/Folger's Coffee" Brass Badge,**
c. 1932. **- $20 $50 $100**

Devil Dogs of the Air

The combination early in 1935 of a Warner Brothers real life U.S. Marine Flying Corps action adventure movie *Devil Dogs of the Air* and James Cagney in the starring role was quickly seized by Quaker Oats as a likely basis for premiums. A March 3, 1935 Sunday newspaper ad by Quaker offered Devil Dog ring, emblem badge and model airplane kit premiums based specifically on the movie plus closely related premiums of aviator goggles and leatherette flying helmet. Quaker Oats was thoroughly identified as Cagney's favorite cereal and the premium offer expiration date was May 15, 1935.

DVL-1

❑ **DVL-1. Quaker Oats Cardboard Sign,**
1935. Rare. Displays the premiums and pictures James Cagney. Less than 5 known.
- $850 $1700 $3000

DVL-2

❑ **DVL-2. Premiums Offer Sheet,**
1935. Scarce. Regular paper, color. -
$65 $140 $260

DVL-3

❑ **DVL-3. Quaker Cereals "Man's Wings/How To Fly" Booklet,**
1935. Scarce. Includes photo strip with James Cagney plus flight instruction pages. Has a 1931 copyright by Reilly & Lee Co. **- $45 $115 $200**

DVL-4

❑ **DVL-4. Quaker Oats Premium Order Blank,**
1935. **- $20 $45 $90**

DVL-5

DVL-6

❑ **DVL-5. "Devil Dogs" Brass Badge,**
1935. Quaker Cereals premium. - **$25 $50 $100**

❑ **DVL-6. "Military Order Of Devil Dogs" Brass Identification Tag,**
c. 1935. Probably Quaker Cereals premium. - **$30 $75 $150**

DVL-7

DVL-8

❑ **DVL-7. Brass Ring,**
1935. Quaker Cereals premium. Gold-plated with initial. - **$25 $75 $150**

❑ **DVL-8. Promo Card,**
1935. - **$100 $200 $300**

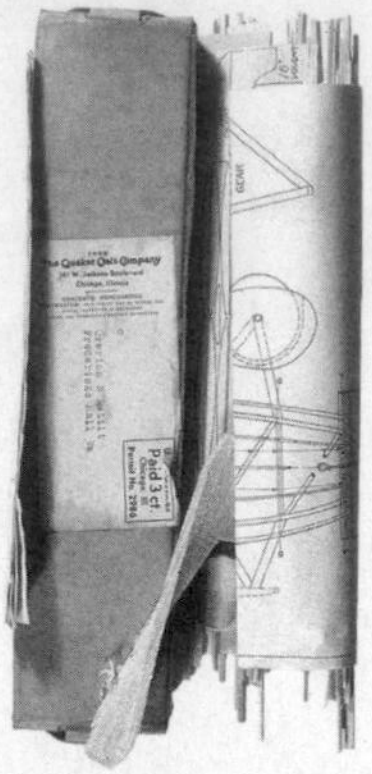

DVL-9

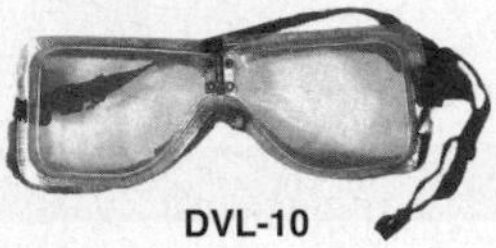

DVL-10

❑ **DVL-9. Plane Model With Mailer and Instructions,**
1935. Quaker Oats premium plane. - **$25 $75 $175**
Mailer - **$20 $40 $60**
Instructions - **$20 $40 $60**

❑ **DVL-10. Plane Goggles,**
1935. Quaker Oats premium. Rare. - **$40 $85 $165**

Dick Daring's Adventures

Merrill Fugit played Dick Daring and Donald Briggs was Coach Greatguy in this 15-minute afternoon adventure series that had a brief run in 1933 on the NBC Blue network. Quaker Oats sponsored the show and offered merchandised and generic premiums in exchange for boxtops.

DDA-1

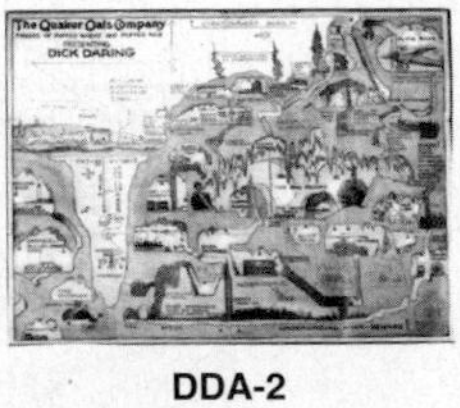

DDA-2

❑ **DDA-1. "Bag Of Tricks" Book,**
1933. Quaker Oats. - **$15 $30 $75**

❑ **DDA-2. Quaker Underground Cavern Headquarters Map, Matching Puzzle,**
c. 1933. Paper map and cardboard puzzle with identical design. Each - **$55 $150 $275**

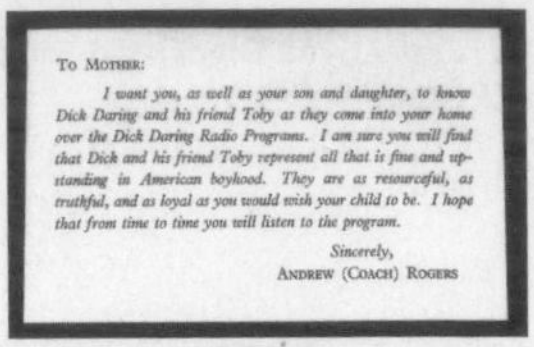

To Mother:

I want you, as well as your son and daughter, to know Dick Daring and his friend Toby as they come into your home over the Dick Daring Radio Programs. I am sure you will find that Dick and his friend Toby represent all that is fine and upstanding in American boyhood. They are as resourceful, as truthful, and as loyal as you would wish your child to be. I hope that from time to time you will listen to the program.

Sincerely,
Andrew (Coach) Rogers

DDA-3

❑ **DDA-3. "Coach" Rogers Card "To Mother",**
c. 1933. Promotes "Dick Daring Radio Programs" starring him and his friend Toby. - **$8 $15 $30**

DDA-4

DDA-5

❑ **DDA-4. Quaker Jigsaw Puzzle,**
c. 1933. Puzzle scene of headquarters beneath city. - **$55 $150 $275**

❑ **DDA-5. "New Bag Of Tricks" Book,**
1934. Quaker Oats. - **$15 $30 $75**

Dick Steel, Boy Reporter

Fresh from his role as Dick Daring, Merrill Fugit moved on to portray boy reporter Dick Steel in another 15-minute adventure series aired on NBC in 1934. The Educator Biscuit company was the sponsor and premiums included membership badges, booklets revealing secrets of police reporting and how to start a newspaper and such detective paraphernalia as a false mustache, invisible ink and handcuffs.

DST-1

DST-2

❑ **DST-1. "Secrets Of Police Reporting" Manual,**
1934. Scarce. Educator Hammered Wheat Thinsies. - **$50 $125 $210**

❑ **DST-2. "Neighborhood News" Vol. 1 #1 Newspaper,**
Feb. 15, 1934. Newspaper - **$50 $125 $225**
Envelope Mailer - **$8 $15 $25**

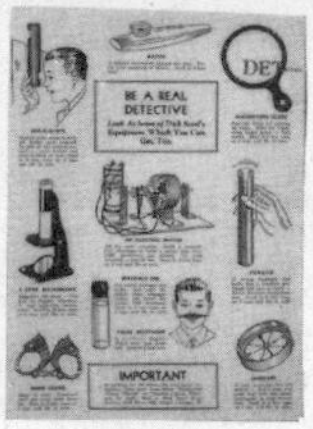

DST-3

❑ **DST-3. Premium Order Sheet,**
1934. Hammered Wheat Thinsies and Toasted Cheese Thins. Ten premiums offered. - **$20 $40 $75**

DST-4

DST-5

DST-6

❑ **DST-4. "Chief Editor" Silvered Metal Badge,**
1934. Rare. Awarded to "Reporter" advancing in rank. - **$50 $150 $300**

❑ **DST-5. "Reporter" Badge only,**
1934. - **$15 $30 $60**

❑ **DST-6. "Dick Steel News Service/Special Police Reporter" Brass Badge,**
1934. Design includes radio front, lightning bolts, portrait, eagle. - **$45 $90 $175**

DST-7

❑ **DST-7. Radio Cast Photo,**
1934. Shown entering United Airlines airplane. - **$20 $40 $80**

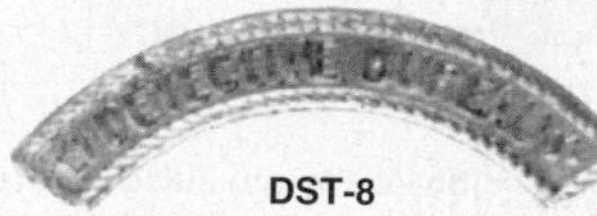

DST-8

❑ **DST-8. "Detective Bureau" Curved Brass Badge,**
1934. Rare. Awarded to "Special Police Reporter" as advancement in rank. Ownership of original badge was required. Kids collected three Wheat Thinsies labels and three names from friends, and sent them in with a form to receive this badge. - **$40 $80 $135**

DST-9

DST-10

❑ **DST-9. Dick Steel Whistle,**
1934. Scarce. - **$20 $75 $125**

❑ **DST-10. Press Card,**
1934. Rare. Membership card for Radio Reporters Club. - **$55 $110 $175**

DST-11

❑ **DST-11. News Service Pamphlet,**
1934. Hammered Wheat Thinsies. Four page premium "How to publish your own newspaper." - **$30 $50 $75**

Dick Tracy

October 4, 1931 saw the birth of *Dick Tracy* in the Sunday Chicago Tribune. Eight days later the first daily strip appeared. So began Chester Gould's (1900-1985) continuing saga of crime and violence that has produced a collection of appropriately named rogues and villains from Boris Arson to the Brow, Pruneface to Littleface, Flattop to the Mole, Gravel Gertie and B.O. Plenty and many others. Teamed with Tracy were his sidekicks Pat Patton and Sam Catchem and his enduring fiancee Tess Trueheart who he married on Christmas Eve 1949. Beginning the tradition of boy sidekicks, Junior first appeared September 8, 1932. Tracy became his guardian on August 9, 1933. The birth of Sparkle Plenty on May 30, 1947 led to one of the most merchandised dolls in comic product history.

Despite the fanciful characters, the strip has been recognized for its realism and attention to details of police procedure and crime prevention. Tracy's popularity spread out into other media as well. Radio series ran on the CBS, Mutual and NBC networks from 1935 to 1939 sponsored by Sterling Products and Quaker cereals. The majority of early premiums came from Quaker in 1938-39. The show was revived on ABC from 1943 to 1948 sponsored by Tootsie Rolls candy.

Four 15-episode chapter plays with Ralph Byrd as Tracy were released between 1937 and 1941, followed by four full-length films between 1945 and 1947, and ultimately the 1990 Disney blockbuster with Warren Beatty, Madonna as Breathless Mahoney and Al Pacino as Big Boy Caprice. A live-action television series with Ralph Byrd again in the title role ran for a season (1950-1951) on ABC and was syndicated throughout the 1950s, and 130 five-minute animated comic cartoons were released in the 1960s. Tracy cartoons were also reprised as segments of *Archie's TV Funnies* (1971-1973) on CBS.

The fearless crimefighter's first comic book appearance of many was in 1936 in *Popular Comics* #1. *The Celebrated Cases of Dick Tracy*, a hardbound anthology, was published in 1970. There have been countless Dick Tracy premiums over the years. The strip is currently drawn by former Gould assistant Dick Locher, who won a Pulitzer Prize for editorial cartooning in 1983; the same year he became the Tracy artist. Columnist and Washington correspondent Michael Kilian is the writer.

DCY-1

❑ **DCY-1. Paper Mask,**
1933. Text on back tab reads "Free with one package of Handi-Tape." Published by Einson-Freeman Co. - **$100 $200 $425**

DCY-2

❑ **DCY-2. "Dick Tracy" Book,**
1933. Cupples & Leon. 7x8.5" hardover titled "How Dick Tracy And Dick Tracy Jr. Caught The Racketeers." This is Book No. 2, a continuation of the "Stooge Viller" book. Features daily strip reprints. Has 88 pages in black and white.
Book only - **$94 $376 $750**
With Jacket - **$118 $472 $900**

DCY-3

DCY-4

❑ **DCY-3. "Dick Tracy And Dick Tracy, Jr." Book,**
1933. Perkins Products Co. - **$71 $213 $495**

❑ **DCY-4. "Comic Section" Promotion Poster,**
c. 1933. Sunday News, N.Y.C. 10x16" in full color. Early and rare. - **$300 $600 $1000**

DCY-5

DCY-6

❑ **DCY-5. "Dick Tracy/Junior" Cello. Button,**
c. 1933. Unknown sponsor but made by Parisian Novelty Co. - **$125 $250 $500**

❑ **DCY-6. Belt Attachment With Link Chain And Loop,**
1934. Scarce. Dated and inscribed "Dick Tracy Detective Agency." - **$100 $200 $350**

DCY-7

❑ **DCY-7. "Dick Tracy And The Stolen Bonds" Big Little Book,**
1934. Whitman #1105. - **$24 $72 $170**

DCY-8

DCY-9

❑ **DCY-8. "Big Thrill" Chewing Gum Booklets,**
1934. Goudey Gum Co. Set Of Six, Each - **$30 $65 $130**

❑ **DCY-9. Dick Tracy Playing Card Game,**
1934. - **$35 $75 $150**

DCY-10

❑ **DCY-10. "The Adventures Of Dick Tracy" BBB,**
1934. Whitman. Big Big Book #4055. - **$96 $288 $680**

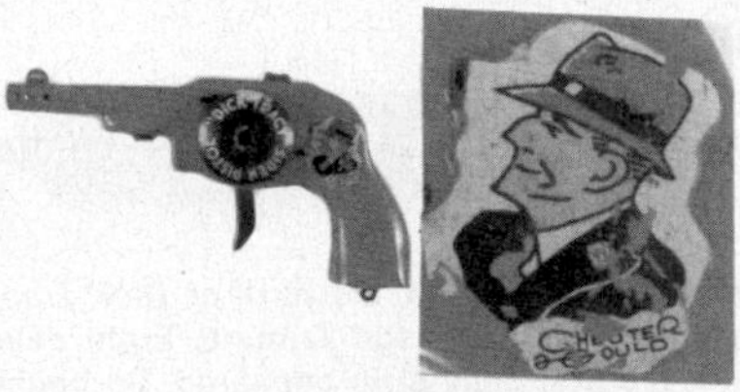

DCY-11

❑ **DCY-11. "Dick Tracy Siren Pistol,"**
c. 1934. Store item by Marx Toys. 8-1/2" long metal. - **$100 $200 $375**

DCY-12

❑ **DCY-12. Paint Book,**
1935. Whitman #665. 11x14" softcover 96 pages of full page pictures for coloring. - **$75 $175 $400**

DCY-13

❑ **DCY-13. "The 'Pop-Up' Dick Tracy 'Capture Of Boris Arson'",**
1935. Store item by Blue Ribbon Press. Contains three pop-ups. - **$150 $400 $750**

DCY-14

DCY-15

❑ **DCY-14. "Dick Tracy on the Trail of Larceny Lu" Big Little Book #1170,**
1935. - **$19 $57 $135**

❑ **DCY-15. "Dick Tracy and the Racketeer Gang" Big Little Book #1112,**
1936. - **$19 $57 $135**

DCY-16

DCY-17

❑ **DCY-16. "Libby's Tomato Juice" Poster,**
1936. 15-1/4x23-1/4". Gordon Gold Archives. - **$325 $675 $1350**

❑ **DCY-17. "Dick Tracy In Smashing The Famon Racket" Booklet,**
1936. 3.5x3.5" softcover Whitman #11 from "Buddy Book" series offered as ice cream cone premiums. Story is 126 pages illustrated on every other page. - **$63 $189 $445**

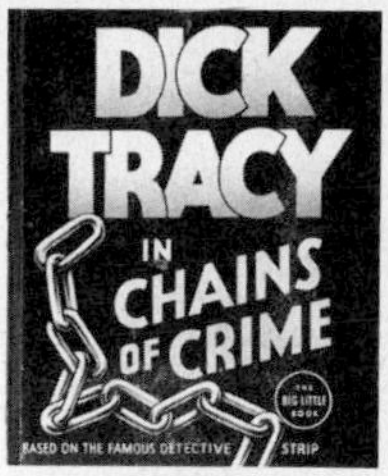

DCY-18

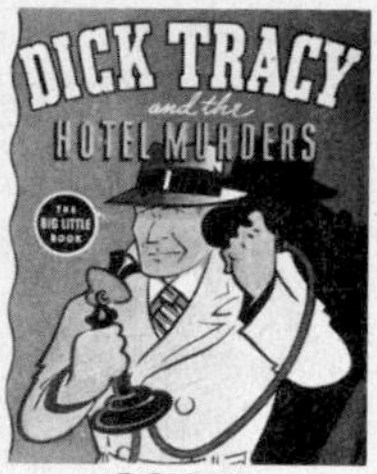

DCY-19

❑ DCY-18. "Dick Tracy in Chains of Crime" Big Little Book #1185,
1936. 432 pages. - **$21 $63 $145**

❑ DCY-19. "Dick Tracy and the Hotel Murders" Big Little Book #1420,
1937. - **$21 $63 $145**

DCY-20

❑ DCY-20. "Dick Tracy Detective Game,"
1937. Store item by Whitman. - **$50 $110 $235**

DCY-21

❑ DCY-21. "Comicooky Baking Set" Premium Offer Poster,
1937. 14x21" issued by Pillsbury's Sno Sheen cake flour. Gordon Gold Archives. -
$115 $275 $550

DCY-22

DCY-23

❑ DCY-22. "Dick Tracy and the Spider Gang" Big Little Book #1446,
1937. Story of the movie serial. -
$26 $78 $185

❑ DCY-23. "Diamond Theatre Dick Tracy Club" Cello. Badge,
c. 1937. - **$50 $100 $200**

DCY-24

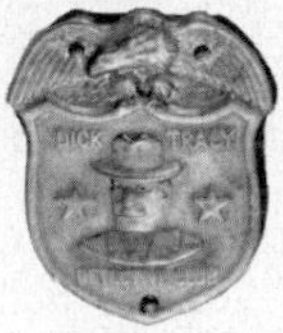

DCY-25

❑ DCY-24. "Dick Tracy Detective Club" Brass Shield Badge,
c. 1937. Reverse has leather cover slotted to wear on belt. - **$50 $90 $175**

❑ DCY-25. "Dick Tracy Detective Club" Brass Shield Badge,
c. 1937. Reverse has leather coin pouch with snap shut flap.- **$40 $80 $140**

DCY-26

❑ DCY-26. One Sheet Movie Poster,
1937. For "The Spider Strikes," Chapter 1 of the Republic Pictures serial "Dick Tracy" starring Ralph Byrd. - **$1250 $2500 $4000**

DCY-27

❑ DCY-27. "See Dick Tracy At Loew's" Badge,
c. 1937. 1-3/8" tall brass in two shades of luster printed by five-digit serial number. Issued for Republic Pictures film version. -
$80 $160 $275

DCY-28

DCY-29

DCY30

❑ DCY-28. Club Manual,
1938. - **$40 $80 $135**

❑ DCY-29. "Secret Service Patrol" Litho. Club Button,
1938. Quaker Cereals. - **$15 $25 $60**

❑ DCY-30. "Secret Service Patrol" Cello. Button,
1938. Rare celluloid version for Canadian membership. - **$40 $75 $135**

DCY-31

❑ DCY-31. Quaker Two-Sided Sign,
1938. Rare. Shows the 1938 premiums. -
$285 $550 $1100

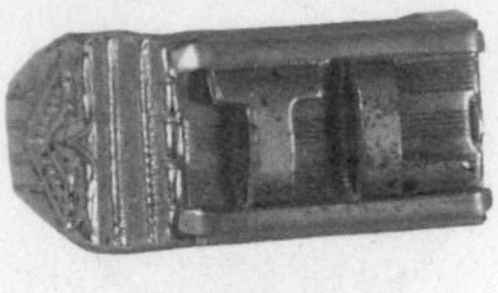

DCY-32

❑ **DCY-32. Quaker "Monogram" Ring,**
1938. No Tracy inscriptions, personalized initials in brass luster designated by orderer. Base issued in either brass or silver luster. Sent in Tracy mailer. - **$175 $325 $550**

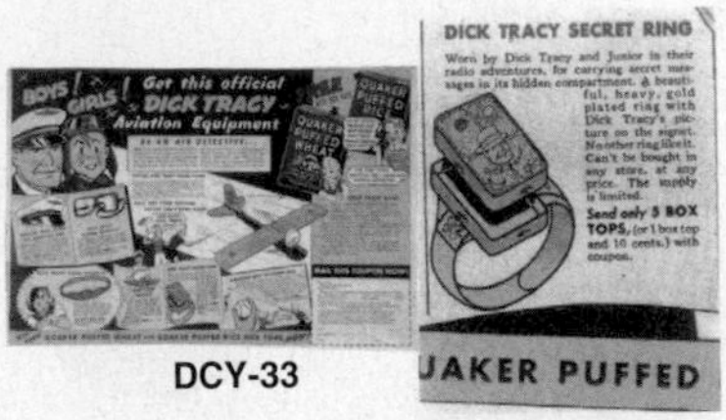

DCY-33

(ENLARGED VIEW)

❑ **DCY-33. Newspaper Premium Ad,**
1938. Quaker Cereals. - **$8 $15 $35**

DCY-34

❑ **DCY-34. "Secret Service Patrol Promotion Certificate",**
1938. Quaker Cereals. Add $25 for each applied promotion foil sticker.
Without Stickers - **$20 $40 $75**

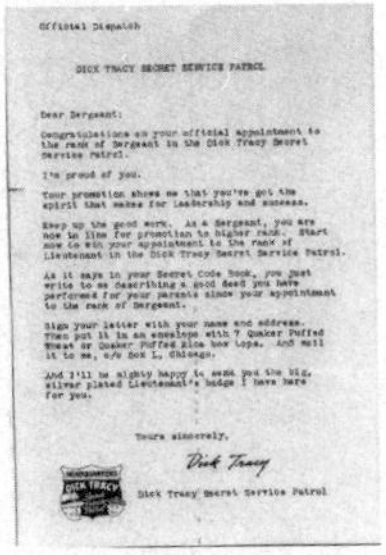

DCY-35 DCY-36

❑ **DCY-35. Sergeant 2-3/4" Tall Brass Badge,**
1938. - **$40 $75 $165**

❑ **DCY-36. Sergeant Promotion Letter,**
1938. Congratulatory letter also listing qualification for next rank of Lieutenant. - **$20 $45 $100**

DCY-37 DCY-38

❑ **DCY-37. Lieutenant Silvered Brass Badge,**
1938. - **$50 $125 $250**

❑ **DCY-38. "Captain" 2-1/2" Brass Rank Badge,**
1938. - **$60 $145 $300**

DCY-39

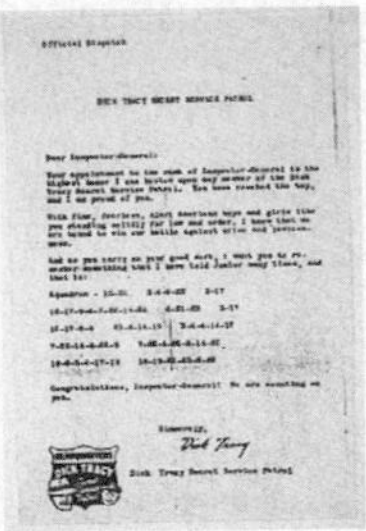

DCY-40

❑ **DCY-39. "Inspector General" 2-1/2" Brass Badge,**
1938. Scarce. - **$175 $350 $750**

❑ **DCY-40. "Inspector-General" Rank Notification Letter,**
1938. 5x7-1/2" "Official Dispatch" notifying recipient this appointment is "The Highest Honor I Can Bestow Upon Any Member Of The Dick Tracy Secret Service Patrol. You Have Reached The Top And I Am Proud Of You." -
$50 $100 $200

DCY-41

❑ **DCY-41. Secret Service Secret Compartment Brass Ring,**
1938. -**$50 $125 $225**

DCY-42

❑ **DCY-42. "Dick Tracy Air Detective" Brass Wings Badge,**
1938. - **$35 $65 $125**

DCY-43

DCY-44

❑ **DCY-43. Patrol Leader Brass Bar,**
1938. Rare. Awarded after "Inspector General" rank. - **$200 $400 $750**

❑ **DCY-44. Lucky Bangle Brass Bracelet,**
1938. Scarce. Charms of Tracy, Junior and four-leaf clover. - **$75 $150 $300**

DCY-45

❑ **DCY-45. Dick Tracy Penny Books,**
1938. Whitman. Each - **$10 $30 $68**

DCY-46

❑ **DCY-46. Rocket Gyro X-3 with Mailer,**
1938. Rare. - **$115 $275 $550**

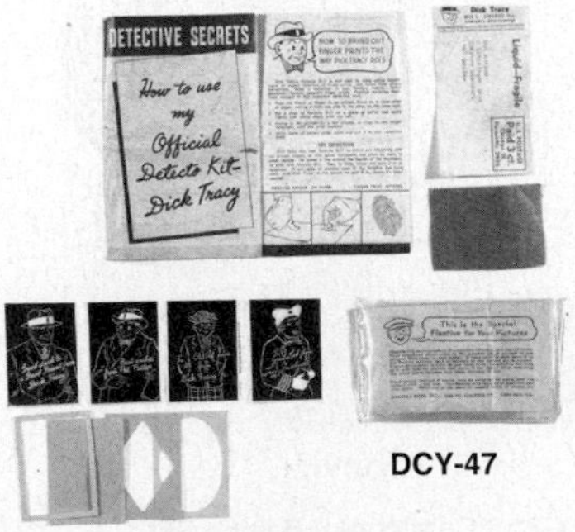

DCY-47

❑ **DCY-47. Official Detecto Kit,**
1938. Scarce. Quaker Cereals. Includes mailer, bottle of "Q-11 Secret Formula", four negative-like black photos and instructions.
Complete - **$100 $250 $450**

DCY-48

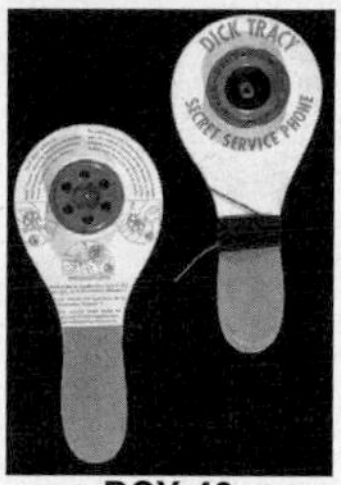

DCY-49

❑ **DCY-48. "Dick Tracy Air Detective" Brass Wing Bracelet,**
1938. Scarce. Top of bracelet opens to place on wrist. - **$75 $200 $425**

❑ **DCY-49. Secret Service Cardboard And Metal Phones,**
1938. Scarce. Quaker Cereals.
Pair - **$75 $200 $350**

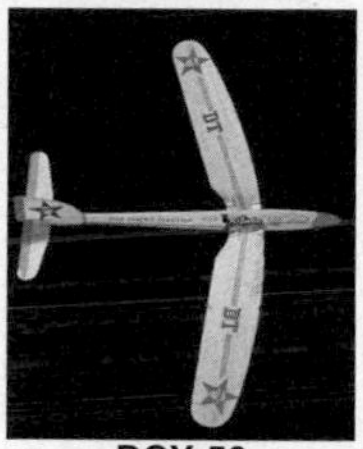

DCY-50

DCY-51

❑ **DCY-50. Dick Tracy Flagship Balsa Wood Plane,**
1938. Scarce. - **$125 $275 $525**

❑ **DCY-51. "Dick Tracy Returns" Movie Serial Promo Photo,**
1938. Republic. About 8x10" black and white. - **$40 $85 $190**

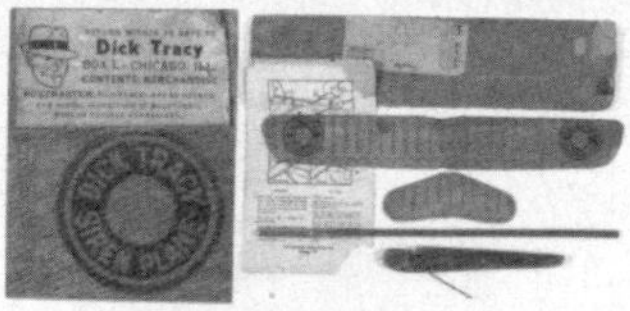

DCY-52

❑ **DCY-52. "Dick Tracy Siren Plane" Assembly Parts With Mailer,**
1938. Issued by Quaker Cereals.
Mailer - **$35 $60 $100**
Plane - **$125 $275 $525**

DCY-53

DCY-54

❑ **DCY-53. "Dick Tracy Returns" Movie Serial Handbill,**
1938. Republic Pictures. - **$25 $50 $100**

❑ **DCY-54. "Dick Tracy Detective" Large Silver Luster Badge,**
c. 1938. Inscribed "The Vindicator," a Youngstown, Ohio newspaper . - **$70 $150 $275**

DCY-55

DCY-56

❑ **DCY-55. "Secret Code Book Revised Edition",**
1939. Quaker Puffed Wheat & Puffed Rice. - **$45 $90 $150**

❑ **DCY-56. Quaker Radio Play Script,**
1939. "Dick Tracy And The Invisible Man" first of two booklets. - **$37 $111 $260**

DCY-57

DCY-58

❑ **DCY-57. Quaker "Dick Tracy's Ghost Ship" Booklet,**
1939. By Whitman with actual radio broadcast script. - **$37 $111 $260**

❑ **DCY-58. "Dick Tracy Returns" Better Little Book #1495,**
1939. Based on the Republic Movie Serial. Chester Gould art. - **$21 $63 $145**

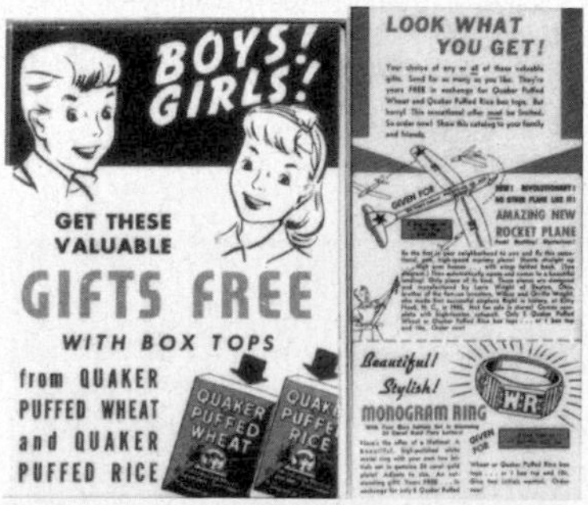

DCY-59

❑ **DCY-59. Quaker Fold-Out Premium Sheet,**
1939. Pictures 11 premiums including Tracy Flag Ship Rocket Plane, Pocket Flashlight, Radio Adventures Booklet, Siren Code Pencil. - **$40 $80 $160**

DCY-60

❑ **DCY-60. Quaker "Secret Detective Methods And Magic Tricks" Booklet,**
1939. Picture example shows both covers. - **$40 $80 $160**

DCY-61

DCY-62

❑ **DCY-61. "Dick Tracy Secret Service" 3" Pen Light,**
1939. Metal tube and plastic end cap. Seen with green, red or black tube. Silver Tracy portrait on black is Canadian version. Yellow Tracy portrait on black and black portrait on green or red are U.S. versions. Each - **$35 $75 $150**

❑ **DCY-62. "Dick Tracy Junior Secret Service" Brass Attachment,**
1939. Originally attached by cord to Dick Tracy pen light. - **$20 $40 $85**

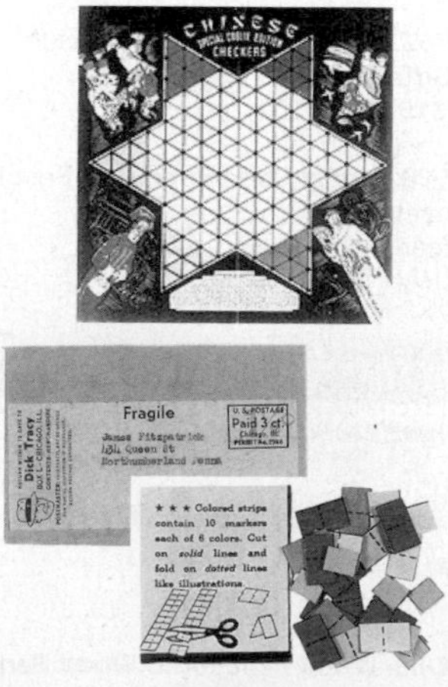

DCY-63

❑ **DCY-63. Chinese Checkers Game,**
1939. No Dick Tracy or Quaker identification on game but comes in envelope with Tracy pictured on mailing label. 13x13" cardboard playing board plus paper marker pieces.
Complete In Envelope - **$50 $100 $200**
Game Only - **$25 $50 $100**

(CLOSE-UP OF BADGE)

DCY-64

❑ **DCY-64. Dick Tracy Aviation/Hostess Cap With Brass Badge,**
1939. Quaker premium 10.25" long fabric cap. Brass badge is 2.25" long, embossed with an image of an airplane and the text "Dick Tracy Air Detective." - **$150 $300 $600**

DCY-65

DCY-66

❑ **DCY-65. "Member" Brass Badge,**
1939. - **$20 $40 $80**

❑ **DCY-66. "Second Year Member" Brass Badge,**
1939. - **$25 $50 $100**

DCY-67

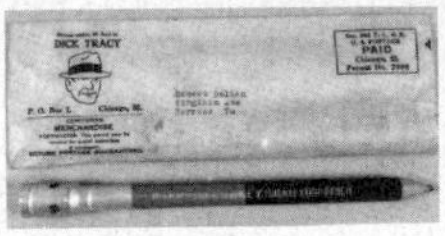

DCY-68

❑ **DCY-67. "Dick Tracy Secret Service Patrol/Girls Division" Brass Badge,**
1939. - **$15 $25 $50**

❑ **DCY-68. Signal Code Siren Cap Pencil With Envelope,**
1939. Near Mint In Mailer - **$225**
Pencil Only - **$50 $100 $150**

DCY-69

❑ **DCY-69. Wood Pencil And Wood Pen,**
c. 1939. Each - **$30 $55 $110**

DCY-70

❑ **DCY-70. "Girls Dick Tracy Club" Silvered Brass Chain Link Bracelet,**
c. 1939. Shield has red enamel accents (shown without bands). - **$60 $125 $240**

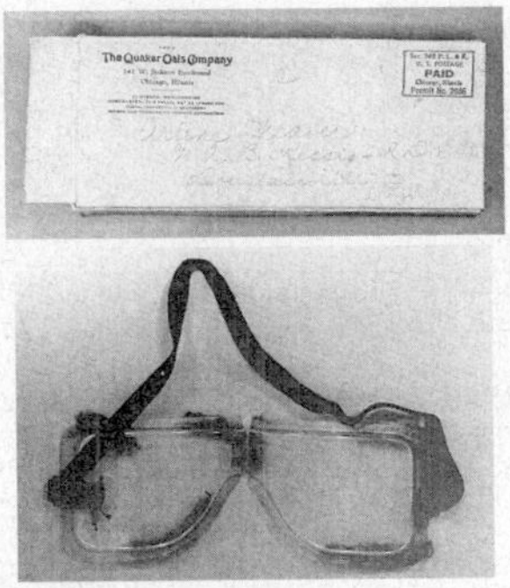

DCY-71

❑ **DCY-71. Goggles With Mailer Box,**
c. 1939. Clear plastic goggles with elastic headband in Quaker Oats mailer box.
Boxed - **$50 $100 $200**

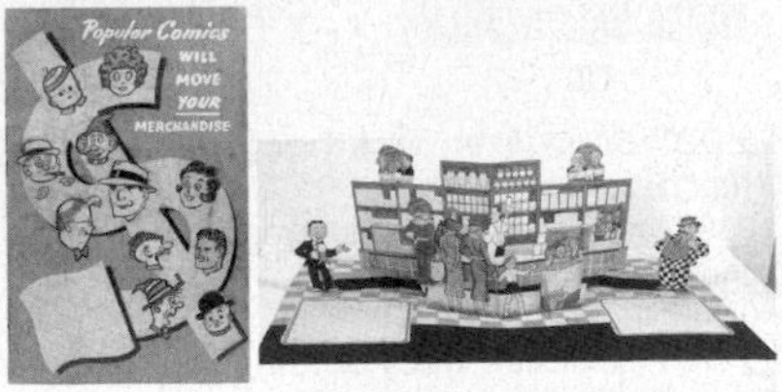

DCY-72

❑ **DCY-72. "Popular Comics" 3-D Pop-Up Folder Original Art Prototype,**
1930s. Art board folder opening to 11x17" pop-up display of Tracy characters and about 15 other popular comic strip characters in grocery store interior venue. Display is constructed of stiff paper with art in ink, watercolor. Gordon Gold Archives. Unique. - **$1000**

DCY-73

❑ **DCY-73. "Electric Casting Outfit,"**
1930s. Store item by Allied Mfg. Co. -
$225 $550 $1150

DCY-74

❑ **DCY-74. "The Ace Of Sleuths" Candy Store Sign,**
1930s. Walter H. Johnson Co., Chicago. 8-1/4x19" red, white and blue sign referring to caramel candy bars. Gordon Gold Archives. -
$675 $1350 $2500

DCY-75

DCY-76

❑ **DCY-75. Caramels Waxed Wrapper,**
1930s. Store item by Walter H. Johnson Candy Co., Chicago. 6x7" with red and blue design. -
$75 $125 $185

❑ **DCY-76. "Dick Tracy Caramels" Wrapper For Cardboard Box,**
1930s. Store item by Walter H. Johnson Co., Chicago. 12-1/4x19" wrapper from box which held 100 caramel candy bars. Gordon Gold Archives. - **$575 $1150 $1900**

DCY-77

❑ **DCY-77. Picture Card,**
1930s. Retailer incentive candy premium. Retailers received a few of these cards at the bottom of display boxes containing smaller individually wrapped cards with caramel candies. The larger premium cards could be distributed to favorite customers. 6x8" full color. -
$65 $150 $300

DCY-78

DCY-79

❑ **DCY-78. Diecut Paper Mask,**
1930s. Imprinted for Philadelphia Inquirer. Published by Einson-Freeman Co. -
$75 $150 $300

❑ **DCY-79. "Dick Tracy/Detective" Metal Lapel Stud,**
1930s. Unknown sponsor. Brass finish over white metal version. - **$15 $25 $60**

DCY-80

❑ **DCY-80. Detective Set,**
1930s. Store item. Two sizes: 7 x 12-1/2", no number on lid; 9-1/2 x 15" with #119 on lid, same contents. Includes tin badge.
Small - **$75 $135 $250**
Large - **$100 $175 $300**

DCY-81

DCY-82

DCY-83

❑ **DCY-81. "Detective" Cello. Button Facing Left, No Gun,**
1930s. Back paper advertises comic strip in "The Chicago Tribune" or sometimes with name of New York City newspaper. - **$30 $50 $115**

❑ **DCY-82. "Detective" Cello. Button Facing Left With Gun,**
1930s. Promoted newspaper comic strip with various newspapers indicated on back paper. -
$25 $45 $80

❑ **DCY-83. "Detective" Cello. Button Facing Forward,**
1930s. Chicago Tribune back paper. Promotes comic strip appearing in that newspaper. -
$25 $45 $80

DCY-84

❑ **DCY-84. Genung's Store Advertising Cello. Button With Dick Tracy/Little Orphan Annie,**
1930s. Rare. Considered one of the rarest and most desirable comic character buttons. -
$300 $750 $1500

DCY-85

DCY-86

❑ **DCY-85. "Dick Tracy/A Republic Picture" Enameled Brass Shield Badge,**
1930s. - **$30 $65 $115**

❑ **DCY-86. "Detective/Dick Tracy Club/Sun Papers" Silvered Embossed Tin Badge,**
1930s. Probably Baltimore newspaper. -
$30 $70 $165

DCY-87

DCY-88

❑ **DCY-87. "Boy's Police Automatic" Cardboard Noisemaker Gun,**
1930s. Philadelphia Inquirer. - **$25 $50 $85**

❑ **DCY-88. "Cleveland News Dick Tracy Club" Brass Badge,**
1930s. - **$25 $50 $100**

DCY-89

DCY-90

❑ **DCY-89. Pocketknife,**
1930s. Celluloid grips on steel made by Imperial Co. - **$60 $140 $275**

❑ **DCY-90. "Dick Tracy and the Phantom Ship" Better Little Book #1434,**
1940. - **$21 $63 $145**

DCY-91

❑ **DCY-91. "Family Fun Book",**
1940. Tip-Top Bread radio premium. 14 pages with no super-heroes inside. - **$46 $138 $650**

DCY-92

❑ **DCY-92. Plaster Figures,**
c. 1941. Store item. From a set of at least 76 characters which we believe started as early as 1941 and still appeared in catalogues as late as 1951. Catalogue carries name Professional Art Products, but we believe the maker was Plasto Mfg. Co. of Chicago. Sold unpainted. Unpainted or nicely painted examples.
Tracy - **$15 $40 $100**
Tess - **$12 $30 $60**

DCY-93

DCY-94

❑ **DCY-93. "Dick Tracy Detective Club" Enameled Brass Diecut Tab,**
1942. - **$30 $65 $115**

❑ **DCY-94. Junior Dick Tracy Crime Detection Folio Offer Sign,**
c. 1942. Miller Bros. Hat Co. 11x14" stiff cardboard easel sign offering premium for purchase of hat. Gordon Gold Archives. -
$175 $350 $700

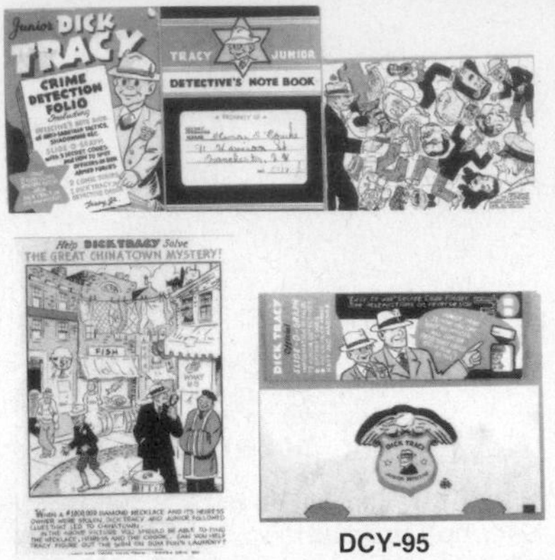

DCY-95

❑ DCY-95. "Junior Dick Tracy Crime Detection Folio",
c. 1942. Includes detective's notebook, jigsaw puzzle, cardboard code finder, etc.
Complete - **$110 $200 $400**

DCY-96

DCY-97

❑ DCY-96. Christmas Giveaway Promotion To Toy Department Managers,
1943. Sears. 8-1/2x11" black and white flyer promoting use of giveaway comic. Gordon Gold Archives. - **$50 $100 $160**

❑ DCY-97. Promotional Flyer To "Mr. Store Manager",
1943. Sears. 8-1/2x11" black and white with Dick Tracy stating he is "Mystified" why manager has not yet ordered Christmas comic giveaway comic. Gordon Gold Archives. -
$65 $135 $190

DCY-98

DCY-99

❑ DCY-98. Hardback Book with Dust Jacket,
1943. Whitman Publishing Co. - **$12 $25 $50**

❑ DCY-99. Tip-Top Bread Cardboard Noisemaker Gun,
1944. Urges radio broadcast listenership. -
$25 $50 $100

DCY-100

❑ DCY-100. Junior Detective Kit Newspaper Advertisement,
1944. Tootsie V-M Chocolate Drink Mix. -
$12 $18 $30

DCY-101

❑ DCY-101. Junior Detective Kit,
1944. Tootsie V-M Chocolate Drink Mix and Miller Bros. Hat Co. Includes manual, decoder, membership card, suspect sheets, ruler, line-up chart, badge. Two manual varieties: Type 1 includes anti-Japanese propaganda, Type 2 eliminates this and has different mailer.
Type 1 Near Mint Complete - **$700**
Type 2 Near Mint Complete - **$525**

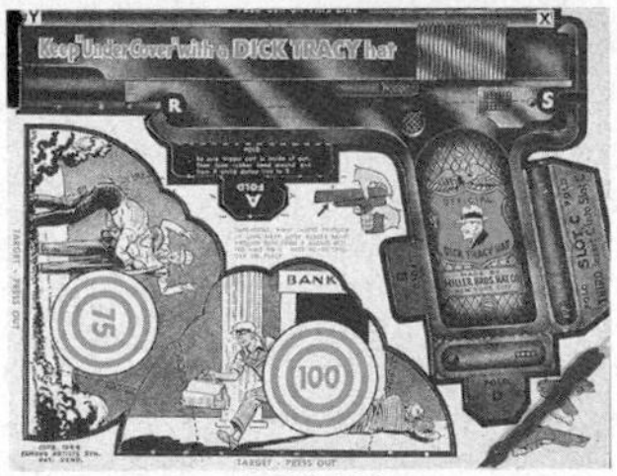

DCY-102

❑ DCY-102. Cardboard Rubber Band Pistol,
1944. Miller Brothers Hats.
Unpunched - **$60 $115 $235**

DCY-103

DCY-104

❑ DCY-103. "Dick Tracy's G Men" Cardboard Blotter/Ruler Card,
1945. Local theaters for 15-week movie serial. -
$40 $90 $200

❑ DCY-104. "Dick Tracy And The Wreath Kidnapping Case" Better Little Book,
1945. Whitman #1482. - **$18 $54 $125**

DCY-105

(Enlarged view of puzzle)

❑ DCY-105. Dick Tracy Jigsaw Puzzle in Box,
1946. - **$50 $110 $225**

DCY-106

❑ DCY-106. Color Portrait,
1946. Pillsbury Farina. 7x10". Cost was 10 cents plus box top and included Orphan Annie, Skeezix, Harold Teen, Shadow, Andy Gump, Winnie Winkle, Smitty. Each - **$35 $70 $135**

DCY-107

DCY-108

❑ **DCY-107. "Dick Tracy and Yogee Yamma" Big Little Book #1412,**
1946. Chester Gould art. - **$19 $57 $135**

❑ **DCY-108. "Dick Tracy and the Mad Killer" Big Little Book #1436,**
1947. - **$16 $48 $115**

DCY-109

❑ **DCY-109. "Flare-Top" Ice Cream Cone Sign,**
1947. Full color about 18x24". Gordon Gold archives. - **$100 $200 $400**

DCY-110

❑ **DCY-110. Dick Tracy Projector and Film Boxed,**
1947. Deluxe set of film and new style of projector. Box is rare with red insert that displays different art than the earlier Acme movie boxes. - **$250 $500 $750**

DCY-111

❑ **DCY-111. Dick Tracy Watch in Box with Insert,**
1948. Chester Gould art.
Watch - **$80 $175 $375**
Box - **$225 $450 $750**

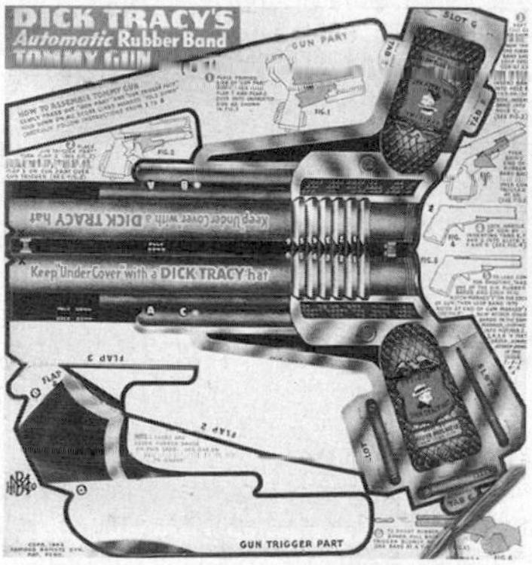

DCY-112

❑ **DCY-112. Cardboard Tommy Gun,**
1949. Rare. Miller Brothers Hats. From the Gordon Gold Archives.
Unpunched - **$115 $230 $400**

DCY-113

❑ **DCY-113. "Dick Tracy Squad Car" With Battery Operated Light,**
1949. Marx. 4.25x11.25x3.75" tall with friction mechanism. - **$85 $175 $350**

DCY-114

❑ **DCY-114. "Dick Tracy Siren Squad Car With Electric Flashing Light" In Box,**
1949. Box is 4-7/8x11.25x3-7/8" deep with illustrations on four sides. 4-1/8x11.25x3.75" tall tin wind-up squad car. Lithographed tin shows Tracy and other characters seated in car. Doors have Tracy image and name in shield shape.
Box - **$225 $450 $750**
Toy - **$225 $450 $750**

DCY-115

❑ **DCY-115. "Dick Tracy and The Tiger Lilly Gang" Big Little Book #1460,**
1949. - **$16 $48 $115**

DCY-116

❑ **DCY-116. Tracy Villain "Influence" Eyes On Card,**
c. 1948. Store item by Mac Novelty Co.
Carded **- $35 $75 $150**

DCY-117

❑ **DCY-117. "Straight From The Shoulder" Anti-Crime Booklet,**
c. 1949. Crime Prevention Council of Illinois. Chester Gould art, printed in Illinois Penitentiary. - **$35 $75 $165**

DCY-118

❑ **DCY-118. Dick Tracy Projector and Film Boxed,**
1940s. Projector is red and black. Acme product. - **$100 $250 $400**

DCY-119

❑ **DCY-119. Dick Tracy Candy Box,**
1940s. Cartoon strips on back of box. - **$50 $165 $300**

DCY-120

DCY-121

❑ **DCY-120. "Hatfull O' Fun!" Game Book,**
1940s. Miller Brothers Hats. - **$15 $45 $190**

❑ **DCY-121. "Dick Tracy Jr./Detective Agency" Silvered Brass Tie Clip,**
1940s. Store item. - **$45 $75 $150**

DCY-122

DCY-123

❑ **DCY-122. Kit Die-Cut Cardboard Sign,**
1940s. Miller Bros. Hat Corp. Dick Tracy Hat promo shows pieces of Junior Detective kit. Also seen as 11x16-1/2" thin paper sign in same red, black and white colors.
Cardboard Sign - **$250 $575 $1150**
Paper Sign - **$125 $250 $550**

❑ **DCY-123. "Dick Tracy Braces" Box,**
1940s. Store item by Strum & Schenberg Inc. Held 12. - **$125 $250 $400**

DCY-124

DCY-125

❑ **DCY-124. Hat Box,**
1940s. Store item by Miller Bros. Hat Corp. Brown box with large red, white and blue label. - **$165 $350 $600**

❑ **DCY-125. Cardboard Original Art Prototype Mask,**
c. 1940s. 11" tall by 13" wide with accordion-like paper ears. Reverse notation "Made For Sam Gold. Neuman Rudolph Litho. Co. 844 W. Jackson, Chicago." From archive of former Gold employee. Unique. - **$700**

DCY-126

❑ **DCY-126. Sparkle Plenty Plaster Bank,**
1940s. Store item by Jayess Co. - **$165 $360 $725**

DCY-127

DCY-128

❑ **DCY-127. "Dick Tracy Hat" Store Window Ad Card With Mailer,**
1940s. Miller Bros. Hat Co. 12x15-1/2" tan envelope holds 11x14" yellow, red, black and white sign offering free ring with hat purchase. - **$100 $200 $325**

❑ **DCY-128. "Dick Tracy" Enameled Brass Hat Ring,**
1940s. Miller Brothers Hat Corp. - **$60 $125 $225**

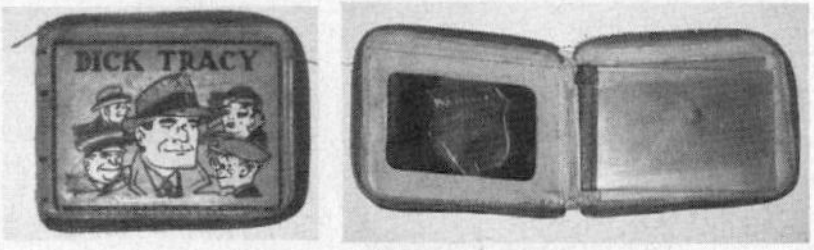

DCY-129

❑ **DCY-129. Wallet With Foil Shield,**
c. 1940s. Store item. Leather wallet with color portraits containing gold foil shield inscribed "Dick Tracy Badge/Junior Detective First Grade." Wallet **- $50 $100 $200**
Foil Badge - **$50 $100 $200**

DCY-130

(Enlarged view of gun decal)

DCY-131

❑ **DCY-130. Dick Tracy Rapid-Fire Tommy Gun,**
1940s. Advertised in Sunday comic pages for $3.79 from Parker Johns, Chicago. 20" all metal gun is gray with brown stock featuring full color Tracy decal on one side. Gun was issued with canvas shoulder strap (missing in our photo) and a brass "Dick Tracy Detective Club" shield badge. - **$200 $450 $850**

❑ **DCY-131. "Detective Club" Brass Shield Badge,**
1940s. Issued with the Dick Tracy Tommy Gun and used for many other licensed promotions as well. - **$20 $40 $80**

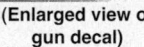

DCY-132

DCY-133

❑ DCY-132. "Dick Tracy Hatfull O' Fun!" Book Offer Sign,
1940s. Miller Bros. Hat Co. 11x14" easel sign offering activity book for purchase of hat. Gordon Gold Archives. - **$165 $300 $625**

❑ DCY-133. "Dick Tracy" and "Junior" Salt and Pepper Shakers,
1940s. Plaster shakers are a store item from a series of different characters. - **$25 $40 $85**

DCY-134

❑ DCY-134. "Dick Tracy Detective De-Coder And Clue Finder" Prototype Original Art,
c. 1950. 3x12" decoder bar with 3-1/4" tall sliding thin cardboard sleeve. Gordon Gold Archives. Unique. **- $1300**

DCY-135

DCY-136

❑ DCY-135. Chester Gould Personal Christmas Card,
c. 1950. 6x9-1/2" stiff paper picturing and naming 10 characters. - **$35 $65 $125**

❑ DCY-136. "Dick Tracy Crimestopper" Tin Shield Badge,
c. 1950. Lettering in black and red. - **$40 $85 $175**

DCY-137

❑ DCY-137. Dick Tracy Full Color Original Art Prototype Book Created By Sam Gold For Tip Top Bread,
c. 1950. 8x10-3/4" with 24 pages of color original art. Gordon Gold Archives. Unique**. - $1500**

DCY-138

DCY-139

❑ DCY-138. "Sunday Post-Gazette" 3" Cello. Button,
c. 1950. - **$50 $100 $200**

❑ DCY-139. Dick Tracy And B.O. Plenty Knife,
c. 1950. Store item includes whistle, magnifier and grips that glow in the dark. Grips usually cracked by rivet. - **$40 $85 $165**

DCY-140

❑ DCY-140. "Dick Tracy" Fully Three-Dimensional Plaster Lamp,
1951. Store item by Plasto Mfg. Co., Chicago. Sold unpainted to be painted by purchaser, Tracy stands 9" tall and with the shade, which has two identical images of Sparkle Plenty on the reverse, the total height is 16".
Base Only - **$300 $600 $1200**
Shade Only - **$300 $600 $1200**

DCY-141

❑ DCY-141. "Bonny Braids" Mini-Figure On Card,
1951. Charmore Co. 3x5" color illustrated card centered by miniature plastic figure about 1" tall.
Carded - **$30 $60 $100**
Loose - **$12 $25 $35**

DCY-142

DCY-143

❑ DCY-142. Dick Tracy Wrist Watch with Box,
1951. Produced by New Haven Corp.
Watch - **$115 $225 $450**
Box - **$125 $250 $500**

❑ DCY-143. "Dick Tracy TV Detective Club" Member Certificate,
1952. © Chicago Tribune. - **$25 $40 $75**

DCY-144

❑ DCY-144. Dick Tracy Movie Serial Re-Release Poster,
1952. Re-issue of 1941 Republic serial originally titled "Dick Tracy Vs. Crime Inc." -
$50 $100 $200

DCY-145

(FRONT VIEW)

❑ **DCY-145. Dick Tracy Police Station with Car in Original Box,**
1952. Original Box - **$100 $200 $400**
Police Station and Squad Car - **$175 $350 $700**

DCY-146

❑ **DCY-146. Cardboard Flip Badge,**
1952. Ward's Tip-Top Bread. - **$35 $75 $160**

DCY-147

❑ **DCY-147. Coco-Wheats Iron-On Transfers Set With Mailer Envelope,**
1956. Inner envelope holding two transfer sheets picturing Tracy friends and villains.
Mailer - **$12 $18 $30**
Illustrated Envelope With Two Sheets - **$35 $75 $135**

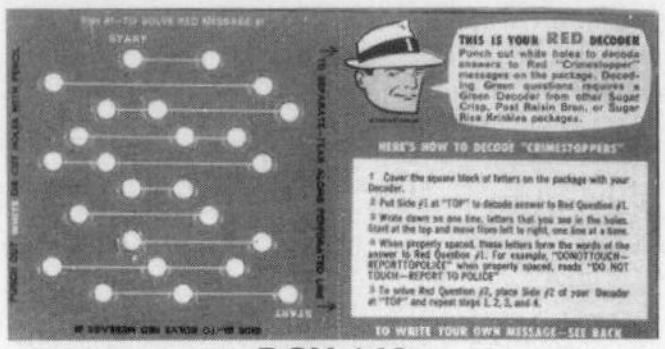

DCY-148

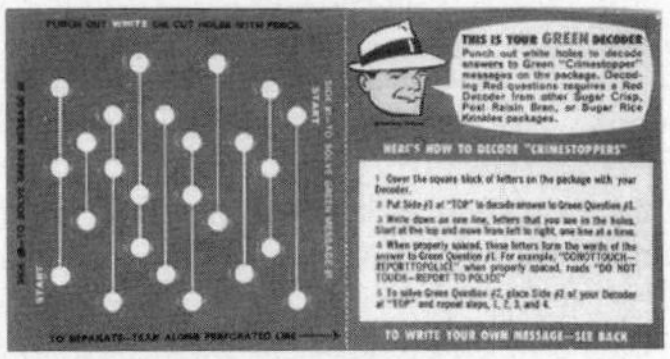

DCY-149

❑ **DCY-148. Post's Cereals "Red" Decoder Card,**
1957. To decode answers to red "Crimestopper" messages on cereal box. - **$18 $30 $65**

❑ **DCY-149. Post's Cereals "Green" Decoder Card,**
1957. Decodes green "Crimestopper" messages on cereal box. - **$18 $30 $65**

DCY-150

❑ **DCY-150. "Dick Tracy Squad Car" With Tracy And Sam Catchem Plastic Figures,**
1950s. Marx Toys. 20" long tin litho friction with battery operated light.
Near Mint With Figures - **$600**
No Figures - **$100 $200 $400**

DCY-151

DCY-152

❑ **DCY-151. Detective Club 2-1/4" Tall Fabric Sticker Patch,**
c. 1950s. - **$40 $85 $160**

❑ **DCY-152. Cracker Jack Giveaway,**
c. 1950s. From a series of comic characters, each 1-5/8" made of thin plastic with high relief portrait. Additional Tracy characters were also issued. Each - **$12 $25 $45**

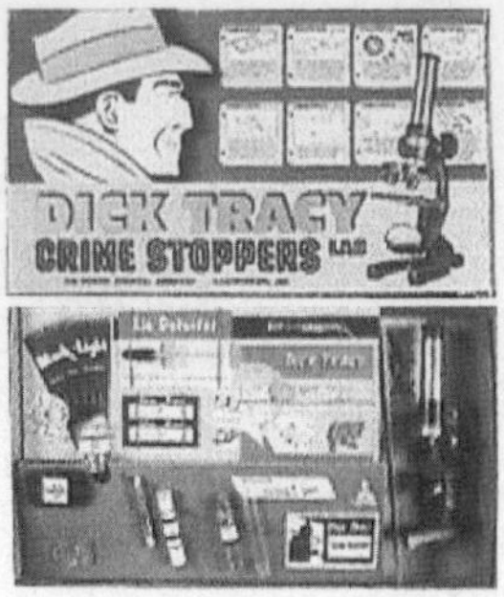

DCY-153

❑ **DCY-153. "Dick Tracy Crime Stoppers Lab" Boxed Set,**
1950s. Store item by Porter Chemical Co., Hagerstown, Md. 12x19x3" deep set designated "No. 3" on lid panels. Holds wide variety of equipment and chemicals used in crime detection. Scarce. - **$400 $900 $1750**

DCY-154

❑ **DCY-154. "Dick Tracy's Bonnie Braids" Realistic Creeping Action Wind- Up Doll Boxed,**
1950s. Marx. 6.5x8.5x12" box has color illustrations on all sides of cartoon characters and the wind-up doll. 5x10x8" tall plastic wind-up doll is dressed in red and white cloth outfit, life-like hair in ribbons. Box - **$100 $200 $400**
Toy - **$75 $135 $250**

DCY-155

DCY-156

❑ **DCY-155. "Dick Tracy Crime Stoppers" Litho. Tin Tab,**
1950s. Rare. Sponsored by Mercury Records. - **$75 $150 $250**

❑ **DCY-156. "Dick Tracy Detective Club" Brass Suspender Gripper,**
1950s. Slotted gripper from set of store bought elastic suspenders. - **$18 $30 $75**

DCY-157

❑ **DCY-157. "Dick Tracy Punch-Out Costume with Mask,"**
1950s. Includes instructions. Shirt/jacket piece was worn like a tunic. Complete - **$175**

DCY-158 DCY-159

❑ **DCY-158. "Crime Stoppers" Enameled Brass Suspender Gripper,**
c. 1950s. From set of elastic fabric suspenders, store item. - **$12 $25 $65**

❑ **DCY-159. "Dick Tracy/Crimestopper" Silvered Metal Badge,**
1961. Came with next item. - **$8 $15 $25**

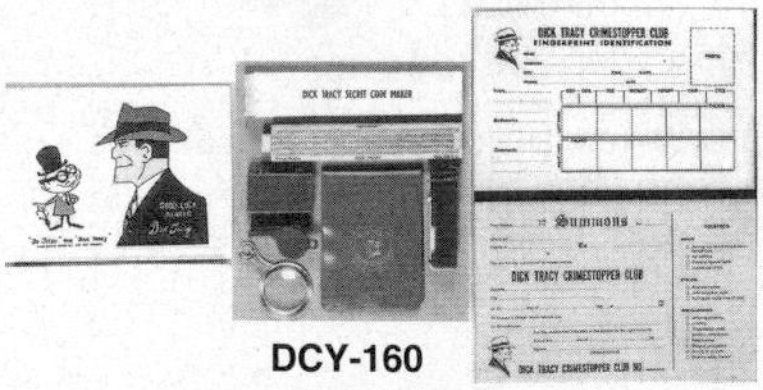

DCY-160

❑ **DCY-160. Crimestopper Club Kit,**
1961. Sponsor unknown. Many contents including badge (see previous item). Fairly common due to warehouse find in the 1980s.
Near Mint Boxed - **$55**

DCY-161

❑ **DCY-161. Sweepstakes Contest Packet,**
1962. Procter & Gamble. Includes leaflet, instruction sheet, store purchase coupons. - **$35 $65 $100**

DCY-162 DCY-163

❑ **DCY-162. Soaky Bottle,**
1965. Colgate-Palmolive. - **$15 $35 $75**

❑ **DCY-163. "WGN-TV" Crimestopper Litho. Tin Tab,**
1960s. Chicago TV station. - **$18 $35 $85**

DCY-164

❑ **DCY-164. Dick Tracy Space Coupe Model,**
1968. Aurora model kit in box. - **$65 $125 $250**

DCY-165

❑ **DCY-165. Tracy Villains Stationery Sample Kit,**
c. 1971. Boise Cascade Paper Group. Six 11x14" posters, stationery sheets and envelope. - **$25 $45 $85**

DCY-166

❑ **DCY-166. Dick Tracy Cap Gun on Card,**
1973. NM Carded - **$175**

DCY-167

❑ **DCY-167. Dick Tracy Teaser Poster,**
1990. A double sided advance one sheet poster for Buena Vista Pictures. - **$40**

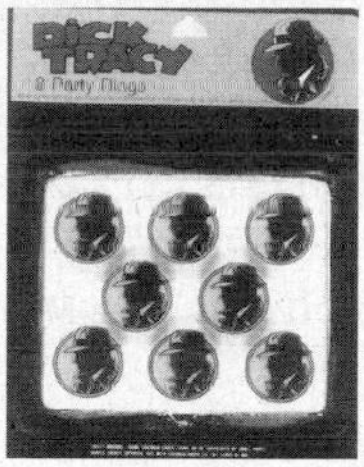

DCY-168 DCY-169

❑ **DCY-168. Dick Tracy/Detective Badge On Card,**
1990. Store item. Carded - **$12**
Loose - **$3 $6 $8**

❑ **DCY-169. "Dick Tracy Party Rings" On Card,**
1990. Total of eight. Store Item.
Carded Set - **$20**
Each Ring - **$1 $2 $3**

DCY-170

❑ **DCY-170. Comic Book Giveaway,**
1990. Gladstone published Dick Tracy Rogues Gallery book made for bakeries. Sixteen pages, featuring Blank, Flattop, Brow, Pruneface and other villains. - **$1 $4 $10**

DCY-171

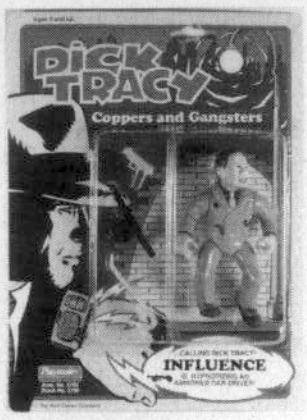

DCY-172

❑ DCY-171. Dick Tracy Movie Figure on Card,
1990. - **$20**

❑ DCY-172. Influence Figure on Card,
1990. - **$15**

DCY-173

DCY-174

❑ DCY-173. Lips Manlis Figure on Card,
1990. - **$15**

❑ DCY-174. Mumbles Figure on Card,
1990. - **$15**

DCY-175

DCY-176

❑ DCY-175. Pruneface Figure on Card,
1990. - **$15**

❑ DCY-176. The Rodent Figure on Card,
1990. - **$15**

DCY-177

DCY-178

❑ DCY-177. Shoulders Figure on Card,
1990. - **$15**

❑ DCY-178. Clip-On Magnet on Card,
1990. Features Steve the Tramp. - **$2 $4 $15**

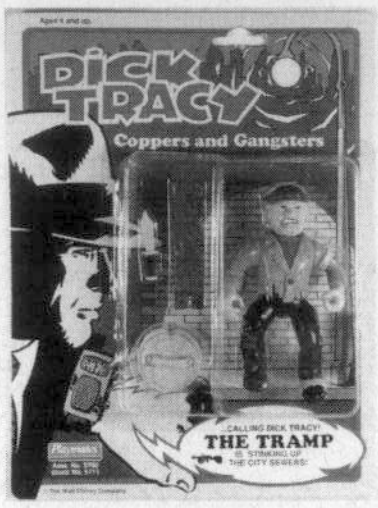

DCY-179

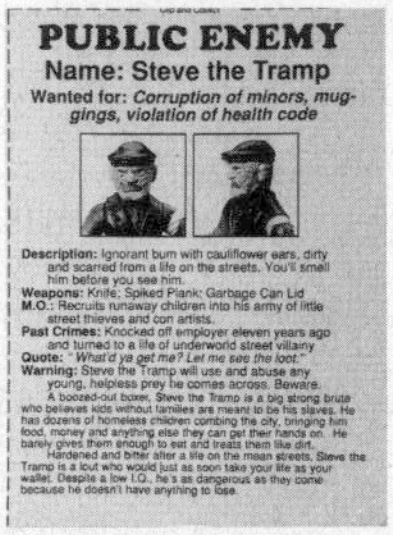

PUBLIC ENEMY
Name: Steve the Tramp
Wanted for: *Corruption of minors, muggings, violation of health code*

Description: Ignorant bum with cauliflower ears, dirty and scarred from a life on the streets. You'll smell him before you see him.
Weapons: Knife; Spiked Plank; Garbage Can Lid
M.O.: Recruits runaway children into his army of little street thieves and con artists.
Past Crimes: Knocked off employer eleven years ago and turned to a life of underworld street villainy
Quote: *"What'd ya get me? Let me see the loot."*
Warning: Steve the Tramp will use and abuse any young, helpless prey he comes across. Beware.

A boozed-out boxer, Steve the Tramp is a big strong brute who believes kids without families are meant to be his slaves. He has dozens of homeless children combing the city, bringing him food, money and anything else they can get their hands on. He barely gives them enough to eat and treats them like dirt.

Hardened and bitter after a life on the mean streets, Steve the Tramp is a lout who would just as soon take your life as your wallet. Despite a low I.Q., he's as dangerous as they come because he doesn't have anything to lose.

❑ DCY-179. The Tramp Figure on Card,
1990. When this Steve the Tramp Figure appeared, associations and support groups for the homeless complained, convincing Disney to conduct a well-publicized recall of this product. The content of his rap sheet raises the question, "What was the Disney brass thinking?" - **$25**

DCY-180

❑ DCY-180. Cap'n Crunch Crunch Berries Cereal Box with Door Hanger Promo,
1990. Premium door hanger came inside 19 oz. value pack box. - **$6 $12 $30**

DCY-181

❑ DCY-181. Dick Tracy Opening Night Ticket T-Shirt,
1990. Shirt was used as a ticket for the film on June 15, 1990. - **$30**

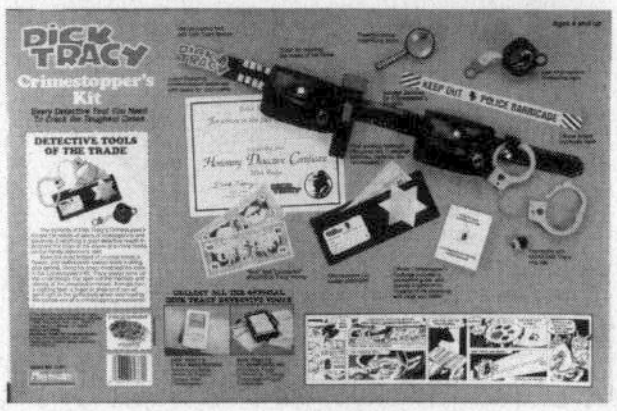

DCY-182

❑ DCY-182. Dick Tracy Crimestopper's Kit,
1990. Everything a kid needs to stop crime. The Kit's designers benefitted from using many Dick Tracy items from previous sets for inspiration. Includes a secret-compartment ring.
Boxed - **$30 $70 $140**
Ring Only - **$12 $25 $60**

DCY-183

❑ DCY-183. Dick Tracy and Breathless Mahoney Movie Dolls with Tags,
1990. Dick Tracy is 10" tall, Breathless 9 1/2".
Set - **$40**

DCY-184

DCY-185

❑ DCY-184. Movie Promo Pinback,
1990. - **$2 $4 $10**

❑ DCY-185. Movie Promo Neckerchief,
1990. - **$5 $15 $35**

Dionne Quintuplets

Their names were Annette, Cecile, Emilie, Marie and Yvonne and their combined weight at birth was less than 10 pounds. They were born on May 28, 1934, in Callander, Ontario. They were the Dionne quintuplets and they created an international sensation as the first documented set of quints to survive beyond a few days. Tourists and entrepreneurs flocked to see them, they were made wards of the government to protect them from exploitation, it was said, and a promotional and merchandising bonanza was born. The Quints appeared in three films between 1936 and 1938 with Jean Hersholt as Dr. Allan Roy Dafoe, the country doctor who delivered and cared for them and they earned fees in exchange for lending their names and images to promote a wide range of products, from soup to margarine to Karo syrup. Marketers took full advantage of the age of these charming little girls. Palmolive beauty soap, for example, offered adult purchasers a Dionne quintuplets cutout book--especially for the children. Disney got into the action with *Pluto's Quin-Puplets* in 1937. Their promotional appeal continued into their early teen years. CBS produced a made for television movie in 1994; and in 1998 Yvonne, Cecile and Annette were awarded $4 million dollars in compensation by the Ontario government. Emilie and Marie died in 1954 and 1970 respectively, and Yvonne died in 2001.

DIO-1

❑ **DIO-1. Quaker 15x32" Paper Store Poster,**
1935. Photo portrait set offer. - **$75 $150 $300**

DIO-2

❑ **DIO-2. Ink Blotter,**
1935. Various sponsors. - **$12 $22 $45**

DIO-3

❑ **DIO-3. Cardboard Fan,**
1935. Various advertisers. - **$12 $22 $35**

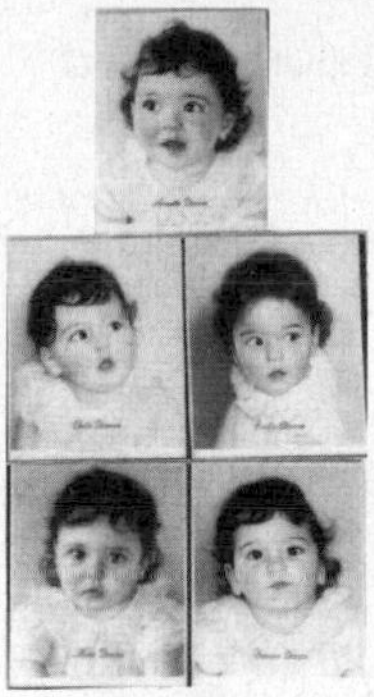

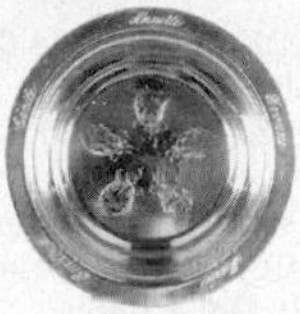

DIO-5

DIO-4

DIO-6

❑ **DIO-4. Quaker Cereals Color Photo Portrait Set,**
1935. - **$25 $50 $100**

❑ **DIO-5. Chrome Finish Metal Cereal Bowl,**
1935. Quaker Oats. - **$10 $30 $50**

❑ **DIO-6. China Mug,**
c. 1935. Probable store item. - **$30 $65 $115**

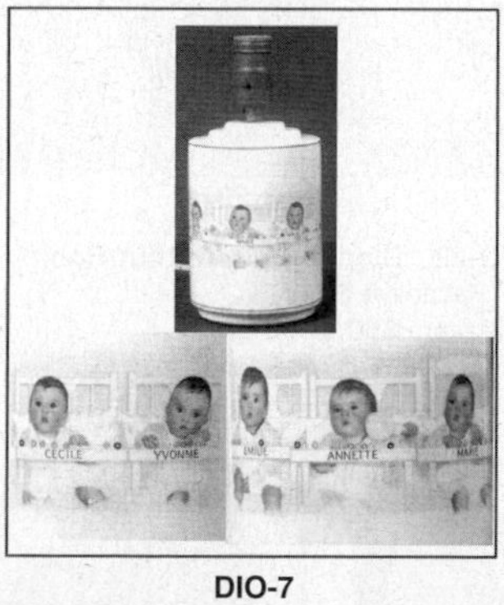

DIO-7

❑ **DIO-7. Dionnes Lamp,**
c. 1935. Ceramic lamp is 4.5" wide by 9" tall and features tinted images of the quintuplets in their high chairs with names written across front of chair. - **$115 $235 $360**

DIO-8

❑ **DIO-8. Three Piece China Set,**
c. 1935. Store item, no maker's mark. Emile on mug, Marie on bowl, others on plate.
Set - **$75 $165 $270**

DIO-9

❑ **DIO-9. Large 11-1/2" Platter,**
c. 1935. Printed with maple leaf design, their names, place and date of birth, "Niagara Falls." Underside marked "Photo Copyright N.E.A."
$85 $165 $285

DIO-10

❑ **DIO-10. "Quintland",**
c. 1935. Canadian published visit souvenir in mailer cover. - **$10 $35 $55**

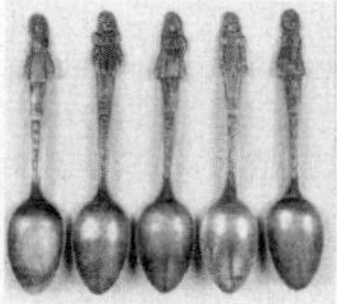

DIO-12

DIO-11

❑ **DIO-11. Silver Plate Spoons,**
c. 1935. Probably Quaker Cereals. Set of five.
Each - **$8 $15 $30**
Instructions and Box - **$40 $70 $125**

❑ **DIO-12. "Dionne Pops" Display Box,**
1936. Vitamin Candy Co. - **$60 $125 $250**

DIO-13

❑ **DIO-13. "Dionne Quins" Quaker Contest Sign,**
1936. 10-1/2x13" diecut cardboard. - **$70 $130 $265**

DIO-14

❑ **DIO-14. "Cut-Out Book" Offer Display,**
1936. Palmolive Soap. Cardboard combination of soap bar bin attached to front of 17x19" book cover display card. - **$175 $350 $750**

DIO-15

DIO-16

❑ **DIO-15. Portrait Fan,**
1936. Various advertisers. - **$10 $25 $40**

❑ **DIO-16. Cardboard Fan,**
1936. Various advertisers. - **$8 $20 $30**

DIO-17

❑ **DIO-17. "Country Doctor" Movie Herald,**
1936. 6x9" paper folder for 20th Century-Fox film starring Jean Hersholt as Dr. Allan Roy Dafoe. - **$12 $25 $40**

DIO-18

❑ **DIO-18. Ink Blotter Pad,**
c. 1936. Various advertisers. Clear plastic cover. - **$20 $40 $80**

DIO-19

DIO-20

❑ **DIO-19. Dionne Quintuplet Bread 3-1/2" Cello. Button,**
c. 1936. - **$30 $60 $125**

❑ **DIO-20. "Quintuplet Bread" Paper Hanger,**
c. 1936. Schulz Baking Co. Went on door knob. - **$30 $60 $100**

DIO-21

❑ **DIO-21. Shirley Temple/Dionnes 9x12" Store Card,**
1937. Modern Screen magazine. - **$65 $150 $300**

DIO-22

❑ **DIO-22. "Dionne Quin Cutout Book",**
1937. Palmolive Soap.
With Mailer - **$50 $100 $175**
No Mailer - **$35 $75 $125**

DIO-23

DIO-24

❑ **DIO-23. The Country Doctor Booklet,**
1937. Lysol. Radio premium. 32 page story about the Dionne Quintuplets. - **$25 $50 $75**

❑ **DIO-24. Cardboard Wall Calendar,**
1938. Published by Brown & Bigelow with local imprints. - **$12 $25 $40**

DIO-25

❑ **DIO-25. Movie Promo Photo,**
1938. For "The Dionne Quintuplets - Five of a Kind" movie. - **$20 $40 $65**

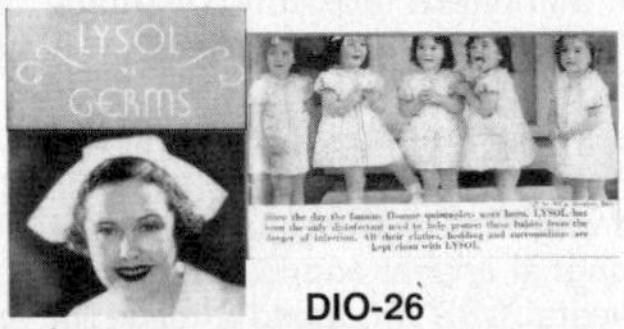

DIO-26

DIO-27

❑ **DIO-26. "Lysol Vs. Germs" Booklet,**
1938. Lehn & Fink Products. - **$15 $30 $45**

❑ **DIO-27. "Souvenir Of Callander" China Tray,**
c. 1938. Birthplace souvenir. - **$35 $80 $150**

DIO-28

❑ **DIO-28. Dionne Quintuplets Wood Pin,**
c. 1938. Birthplace souvenir. - **$35 $70 $140**

DIO-29

❑ DIO-29. Dexterity Puzzle,
1930s. Store item made by Bar Zim Toy Mfg. Co. Unauthorized but based on the Dionnes with caption "Place The Quintuplets In The Carriage." - **$25 $50 $100**

DIO-30

❑ DIO-30. "Let's Play House" Paperdoll Book Set,
1940. Merrill Publishing Co. Books are numbered 1-5 for each Quint.
Uncut Each - **$55 $100 $165**

DIO-31

❑ DIO-31. "Baby Ruth" Candy Box,
1941. Curtiss Candy Co. 8x11-1/2x2" deep display box which held individual bars. - **$65 $135 $275**

DIO-32

❑ DIO-32. "Queens Of The Kitchen" Calendar,
1946. Various sponsors. 8-3/4x11" with tipped-on 5x7-1/4" color print of painting by Andrew Loomis. Pictures them when 12 years old, one of the last calendars in the series. - **$15 $30 $60**

Disney Characters Misc.

Disneyana Convention

Disneyland

See Ted Hake's *Official® Price Guide to Disney Collectibles*, Second Edition, formatted identically to this book but in full color evaluating over 9,000 Disney company and character collectibles from 1924 through 2006.

Dixie Ice Cream

The disposable paper drinking cup, called the Health Kup, had been around for 15 years when the Individual Drinking Cup Company changed its name to the Dixie Cup in 1919 and began offering ice cream franchises in Cleveland in 1923. Dixie Cup has since become part of the lexicon. Lithographed photographs printed on the underside of the cup lids helped sell the five-cent ice cream. The first were a set of 24 animals featured on the *Dixie Circus* radio program (Blue network, 1929-1930, and CBS, 1930-1931 and 1934). In 1931 a set of U.S. President lids were issued and the nature series came out in 1932. In the early 1930s a set of 24 MGM movie stars followed, with an offer of enlarged photographs in exchange for a number of lids. A "Defend America" lid series in the early 1940s featured pictures of tanks and battleships, also available as enlarged full color pictures in exchange for lids. Roy Rogers and Wild Bill Elliott were on 12 different lids. In 1952, 24 baseball lids were introduced; and in 1953, 18 baseball lids in 3-D were introduced. The company continued offering lids and picture sets through 1954.

DIX-1

❑ DIX-1. Early Waxed Cardboard Lid,
c. 1920. Scarce. Patent date of 1918. Lid reads "This Lunch Box Dixie Made By The Individual Drinking Cup Co., Inc." - **$20 $35 $75**

DIX-2

❑ DIX-2. Circus Punch-Out Set,
1929. Stage and cut-outs in Series A patterned after Dixie Circus radio show. Art by illustrator Dan Smith.
Series A Stage - **$40 $85 $175**
Mailer - **$12 $25 $50**
Three sheets (B,C,D) consist of 5 figures for each series. Each Sheet - **$20 $35 $60**

DIX-3

DIX-4

❑ DIX-3. "Animal Heroes Of Dixie's Circus Radio Stories" Lids,
1929. Waxed cardboard set of 24 numbered cup lids, each 2-1/4" diameter.
Each - **$5 $10 $20**

❑ DIX-4. First Series Movie Star Dixie Lids,
1933. From set of 24 with M-G-M stars only.
Each **$10 $18 $30**

DIX-5

❑ DIX-5. "Portraits" 12x17" Cardboard Store Sign,
c. 1935. Easel sign picturing example of Barbara Stanwyck from "Annie Oakley" 1935 movie. - **$115 $250 $450**

DIX-6

❑ DIX-6. Dixie Lid Album,
1935. Breyers Ice Cream. 6x7" stiff paper which unfolds to 18" long with diecut slots to hold 15 lids which could then be exchanged for larger full color picture. - **$30 $65 $125**

DIX-7

❑ DIX-7. "Hoodsie Dixies" Store sign,
1930s. Paper sign is 6x20" reading "Hoodsie Dixies Now Ready New Set Of Free Movie Star Portraits In Colors/Begin Saving Ice Cream Dixie Lids Today. Ask In This Store For An Album." - **$60 $100 $175**

DIX-8

❑ DIX-8. "Movie Stars Ice Cream Dixie Lids" 6x18" Paper Sign,
c. 1930s. - **$90 $225 $450**

DIX-9

❑ DIX-9. "Defend America" Dixie Picture Covers,
1941. Front and back covers are 8x10" and inside back cover lists the 24 pictures in the series. Pair - **$15 $30 $65**

DIX-10

❑ DIX-10. "America's Fighting Forces" Dixie Pictures,
c. 1942. Four examples from set.
Each - **$12 $18 $35**

DIX-11

❑ DIX-11. "United Nations At War" Dixie Pictures,
c. 1944. Four examples from set.
Each - **$12 $18 $35**

DIX-12

❑ DIX-12. "United Nations At War" Lid Set,
c. 1944. Set of 24. Each - **$10 $16 $25**

DIX-13

❑ DIX-13. "Movie & Cowboy Stars" Dixie Lids Album,
1947. Velvet Ice Cream. Stiff paper fold-out opening to 18" width including two panels slotted for lids. Back cover lists star pictures from 1947 set. - **$25 $50 $75**

DIX-14

❑ DIX-14. "William 'Bill' Elliott" Dixie Picture,
1948. - **$10 $25 $50**

DIX-15

❑ DIX-15. Covers For Celebrity Dixie Pictures,
c. 1950. Titled "My Picture Book Of Movie, Cowboy And TV Stars" with front and back cover size of 8x10". Pair - **$25 $40 $85**

Dizzy Dean

Baseball's Jerome Herman Dean or Jay Hanna Dean (1911-1974), known to all as "Dizzy," was an outstanding pitcher for the St. Louis Cardinals from 1932 to 1937; and then for the Chicago Cubs (1938-1941) and St. Louis Browns in 1947. He was named the National League's Most Valuable Player in 1934, when his win-loss record of 30-7 helped carry the Cardinals to the World Championship. In 1952 his life story was the basis of the movie *Pride of St. Louis* starring Dan Dailey and he was elected to the Baseball Hall of Fame in 1953. Dean did the radio broadcasts of St. Louis games from 1941 to 1949, where his grammar proved to be as challenging as his pitching--"he slud into third!" In 1948 Dean did a dozen weekly shows on NBC radio for Johnson Wax. His *Dizzy Dean Winners*, sponsored by Post cereals in the 1930s and promoted in Sunday comic sections, offered pins, rings and other premiums to young fans.

DZY-1

❑ DZY-1. Dizzy Dean Watch with Box,
1933. Watch has either metal band or leather strap. Comes in colorful box. Rare.
Near Mint Boxed - **$3500**
Watch Only - **$400 $850 $1500**

DZY-2

DZY-3

❑ DZY-2. Dizzy Dean Watch Newspaper Ad,
1933. From the Everbrite Watch Company. Leather strip band is shown. Even in 1933, you could still get time payments. - **$45**

❑ DZY-3. Photo Baseball Card,
1933. Tattoo Orbit. - **$90 $155 $375**

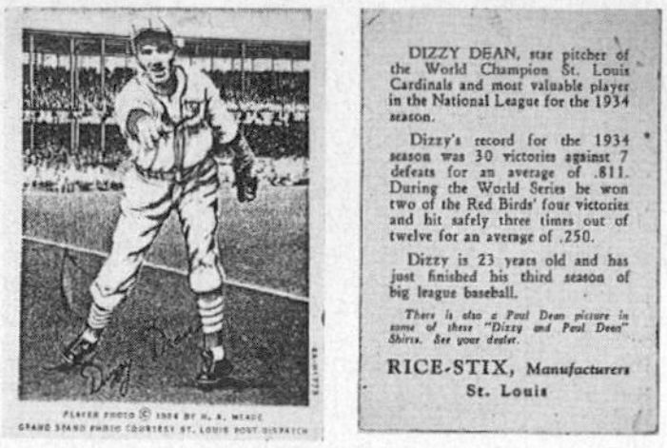

DZY-4

❑ DZY-4. Premium Photo Card,
1934. Rice-Stix, St. Louis. This and a matching Paul Dean picture were included with "Some Of These 'Dizzy And Paul Dean' Shirts." Cards are 2-1/4x3-1/4" in red and white.
Dizzy - **$200 $400 $1200**
Paul - **$125 $250 $750**
Note: Professionally graded cards in holders bring higher prices. These prices are for cards not professionally graded.

DZY-5

DZY-6

❑ DZY-5. Sepiatone Facsimile Autographed Portrait,
1935. - **$65 $175 $350**

❑ DZY-6. Grape-Nuts Booklet,
1935. - **$35 $75 $150**

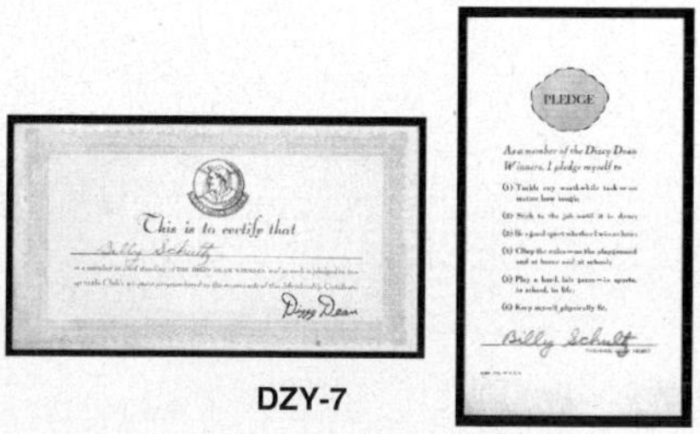

DZY-7

❑ DZY-7. "Dizzy Dean Winners" Club Certificate,
1935. Post Cereals. Both front and back pictured. This sample belonged to the Mayor of Cleveland, Tenn., Billy Schultz from his childhood. - **$40 $75 $150**

DZY-8

❑ DZY-8. Dizzy Dean Premium Folder,
1935. Grape Nuts premium. 12 pages of pictures, 36 premiums. Rare. - **$85 $190 $350**

DZY-9

❑ DZY-9. Post's "Dizzy Dean Winners" Brass Club Badge,
1935. Figural baseball with profile portrait. - **$10 $20 $40**

DZY-10

DZY-11

DZY-12

❑ DZY-10. Post's "Dizzy Dean Winners" Brass Bat Figural Pin,
1935. - **$15 $40 $80**

❑ DZY-11. "Win With Dizzy Dean" Brass Ring,
1935. Raised portrait and other baseball symbols. - **$80 $165 $325**

❑ DZY-12. "Dizzy Dean Winners" Brass Baseball Charm,
1935. - **$30 $65 $125**

DZY-13

DZY-14

❑ **DZY-13. "Dizzy Dean-Good Luck" Brass Token,**
1935. Portrait in horseshoe, back has short inspirational sports text. - **$25 $50 $100**

❑ **DZY-14. Post's "Dizzy Dean Winners" Brass Ring,**
1936. - **$75 $175 $300**

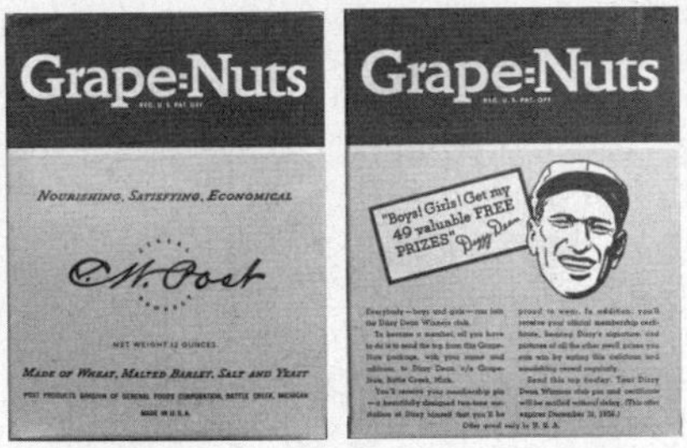

DZY-15

❑ **DZY-15. Grape Nuts Cereal Box,**
1936. Featuring Dizzy Dean. Promo on back for Winners Club premium. - **$325 $650 $1250**

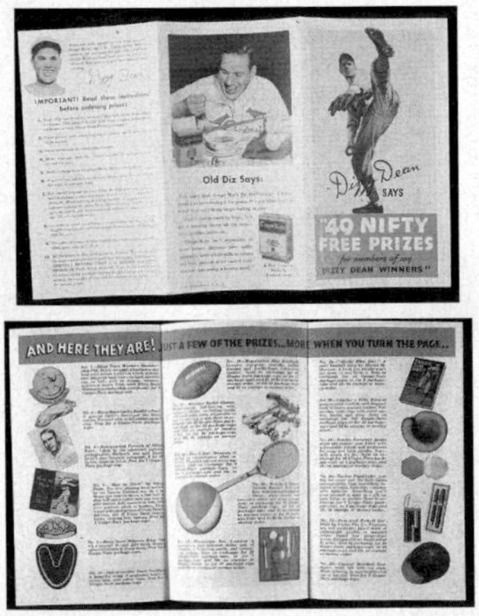

DZY-16

❑ **DZY-16. "Dizzy Dean Winners" Premium Leaflet,**
1936. Grape-Nuts. Pictures "49 nifty free prizes." - **$35 $75 $150**

DZY-17

DZY-18

❑ **DZY-17. "Dizzy Dean Helmet" Leaflet,**
1930s. Store item. Folder including "His Life Story" as supplement to safari-like pith helmet purchase. - **$25 $45 $85**

❑ **DZY-18. Cello. Button with Small Pennant,**
1939. 1.75" with Chicago Cubs pennant attached. With Pennant - **$30 $45 $75**
Without Pennant - **$15 $30 $50**

DZY-19

❑ **DZY-19. Dizzy Dean Real Photo Button,**
1930s. Light sepia-tone on cream with crystal clear photo of Dean smiling. St. Louis Button Co. backpaper. - **$500 $1000 $2000**

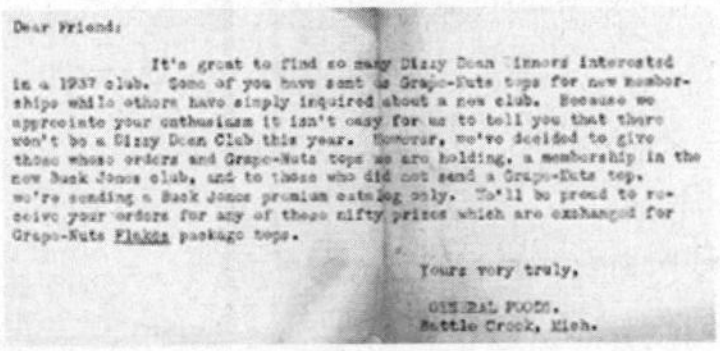

Dear Friend:

It's great to find so many Dizzy Dean Winners interested in a 1937 club. Some of you have sent us Grape-Nuts tops for new memberships while others have simply inquired about a new club. Because we appreciate your enthusiasm it isn't easy for us to tell you that there won't be a Dizzy Dean Club this year. However, we've decided to give those whose orders and Grape-Nuts tops we are holding, a membership in the new Buck Jones club, and to those who did not send a Grape-Nuts top, we're sending a Buck Jones premium catalog only. We'll be proud to receive your orders for any of these nifty prizes which are exchanged for Grape-Nuts Flakes package tops.

Yours very truly,

GENERAL FOODS.
Battle Creek, Mich.

DZY-20

❑ **DZY-20. "Dizzy Dean Club" Cancellation Letter,**
1937. Sent to those who sent in a Grape-Nuts box top. A membership in the new Buck Jones Club was given in place of the Dizzy Dean Club. - **$20 $35 $65**

Doc Savage

Doc Savage was the superhero of popular pulp magazine stories by Lester Dent and others, published by Street & Smith. He appeared in 181 pulp novels between March 1933 and 1949. He made his first comic appearance in *Shadow Comics* #1 of March 1940. Two months later he had his own comic book, which lasted only until October 1943, but he continued to show up occasionally in *Shadow Comics* until 1949. There were brief excursions into radio in 1934-1935 and 1942-1943, Warner Brothers made a film--*Doc Savage, Man of Bronze*--starring Ron Ely in 1975 and there have been comic book revivals into the 1990s, but nothing equaled the success of the original pulps. Fans who joined the Doc Savage Club and followed the membership code could obtain badges and other premiums.

DOC-1

DOC-2

❑ **DOC-1. "The Man Of Bronze" Hardcover Book,**
1933. Store item from Street & Smith Co. Ideal Library Series. - **$65 $150 $325**

❑ **DOC-2. "Quest Of The Spider" Hardcover Book,**
1933. Store item from Street & Smith Co. Ideal Library Series. - **$65 $150 $325**

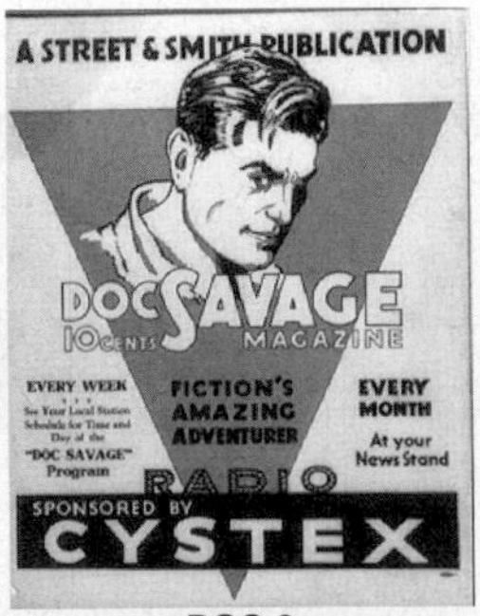

DOC-3

❑ **DOC-3. "Doc Savage Magazine" 11x14" Cardboard Window Poster,**
1930s. Scarce. Promotes "Doc Savage Radio Program Sponsored By Cystex". - **$325 $875 $1350**

DOC-4

DOC-5

DOC-6

❑ DOC-4. Pulp Magazine Ad Sticker,
1930s. - **$45 $90 $190**

❑ DOC-5. Pulp Subscriber Portrait,
1930s. Doc Savage Magazine. Color print of painting by Walter M. Baumhofer especially for magazine. - **$125 $225 $450**

❑ DOC-6. Pulp Subscriber Portrait,
1930s. Scarce. Doc Savage Magazine. Print of painting believed by Walter M. Baumhofer especially for magazine. - **$125 $225 $450**

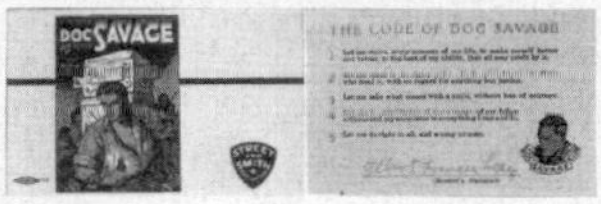

DOC-7

❑ DOC-7. "The Code Of Doc Savage" Wallet Card,
1930s. Street & Smith Publishing Co. - **$100 $225 $400**

DOC-8

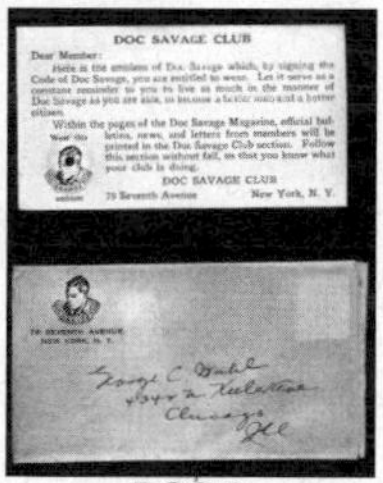

DOC-9

❑ DOC-8. "Doc Savage Club" Member's Bronze Lapel Stud,
1930s. - **$85 $165 $300**

❑ DOC-9. Lapel Stud Card With Envelope,
1930s. Pair - **$300 $600 $1200**

DOC-10

DOC-11

❑ DOC-10. "Doc Savage Award" Bronze Medallion,
1930s. Rare. Less than 10 known. Doc Savage pulp magazine. Inscribed "Service-Loyalty-Integrity" below portrait. - **$750 $2250 $4500**

❑ DOC-11. Application For Doc Savage Award,
1930s. Scarce. - **$150 $300 $600**

DOC-12

❑ DOC-12. "Doc Savage Club/Member" Rubber On Wood Stamp Block,
1930s. Photo example includes image of ink stamped picture. - **$225 $500 $900**

DOC-13

DOC-14

❑ DOC-13. "Doc Savage" Pulp,
1941. Pulp is 6-5/8x9.25" Vol. 18 #4 from Dec. Has nice cover by Clarke showing Doc Savage and criminal wrestling in midair with parachute collapsing above him and ice flow below. Has 114 black and white pages including book-length novel by Kenneth Robeson. Same Or Similar Vintage - **$25 $50 $110**

❑ DOC-14. Movie Card,
1975. Warner Bros. - **$10 $15 $30**

DOC-15

❑ DOC-15. "Doc Savage" Hardbacks,
1975. Published by Golden Press. Set of six. Each - **$5 $10 $18**

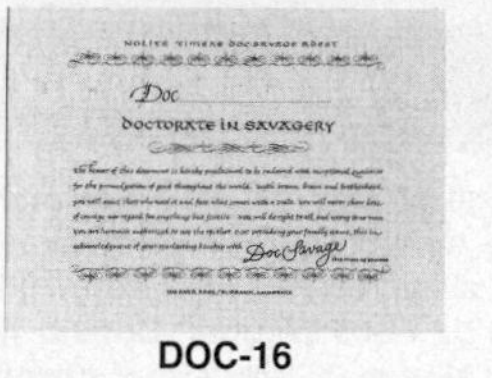

DOC-16

❑ DOC-16. Commemorative Certificate,
1975. Warner Bros. From "The Man Of Bronze" film kit. - **$10 $25 $55**

DOC-17

❑ DOC-17. "Doc Savage/Brotherhood Of Bronze" Fan Club Kit,
1975. Issued by comic artist Jim Steranko. Contents consist of Bulletin #1 (#2 and #3 followed), membership card, button.
Near Mint Complete - **$125**
Each Piece - **$10 $15 $30**

DOC-18

DOC-19

❑ DOC-18. First Issue Magazine,
1975. Store item. 8x11" with 76 pages. Volume 1 #1, August. - **$6 $12 $20**

❑ DOC-19. Boxed Jigsaw Puzzle,
1975. Store item by Whitman. 8-1/4x10" box holds parts for 14x18" puzzle. - **$8 $15 $40**

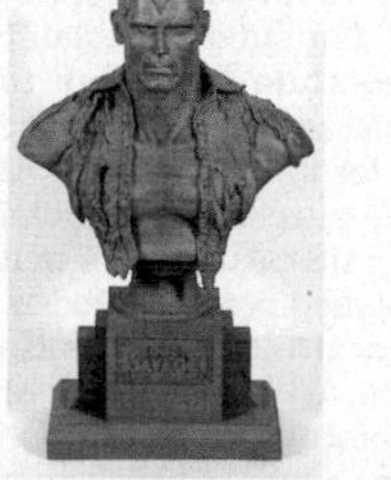
DOC-20

❑ DOC-20. Doc Savage Bust,
1991. By Graphitti Designs, limited to 543. Bronze in color, 9 1/4" tall. Difficult to find on the secondary market. - **$875**

Doctor Who

The original *Doctor Who* was the longest-running science-fiction television series in history, airing on the BBC from 1963 to 1989. Created by Cecil Webber, Donald Wilson and Sydney Newman, the show chronicled the adventures of a Time Lord from the planet Gallifrey who stole a time machine called a TARDIS (Time And Relative Dimension In Space) and left to explore the universe. The Doctor was capable of "regenerating" when near death, allowing the production to replace the lead actor when necessary. Seven actors played the Doctor regularly before the show's cancellation in 1989: William Hartnell, Patrick Troughton, Jon Pertwee, Tom Baker, Peter Davison, Colin Baker, and Sylvester McCoy.

Stories were aired in serialized form, with several half-hour episodes comprising a complete adventure. The second story, titled "The Daleks," introduced the Doctor's most popular adversaries and made the series a hit. Two feature films starring Peter Cushing as a human "Dr. Who" were released in the mid-'60s. Starting in the mid-'70s, the series was syndicated in the US largely through PBS stations. A 1996 TV-movie co-produced by the BBC and Universal aired on the Fox network, starring Paul McGann as the Eighth Doctor. New prose, audio and comic book adventures insured the continuation of the Doctor's travels well beyond his 40th anniversary in 2003. In September of that year, the BBC announced that a new television series of *Doctor Who* would debut on BBC1 in 2005.

The first new series of *Doctor Who*, starring Christopher Eccleston as the Ninth Doctor and Billie Piper as his companion, Rose, was an instant worldwide hit in the UK, Canada, and Australia as well as other countries, continuing the Doctor's adventures from the original series while offering far more polished and updated production values. Eccleston left the show after completing the first 13-episode series. David Tennant was cast as the Tenth Doctor and debuted in a 1-hour 2005 Christmas special. He began his first 13-episode series as the Doctor in Spring 2006 and is expected to remain with the series for the foreseeable future. The last piece of the puzzle for American fans fell into place when US-based cable network, The Sci Fi Channel, acquired the Eccleston episodes and began airing the new *Doctor Who* in March 2006. With the return of *Doctor Who* as a cornerstone of the British pop culture experience, a whole new generation of kids can now cower behind their sofas at the arrival of the Daleks or the Cybermen, secure in the knowledge that the Doctor will soon be there to save the day.

Classic series toys are licensed to Product Enterprise Ltd. New series toys are licensed to Character Options, and there is a plethora of other new and classic merchandise as well. *Doctor Who* is copyright the BBC. "Fantastic!"

DWH-1

❑ **DWH-1. "Dr. Who Dalek" British Bank,**
1965. Box is 2-5/8x3.5x4.25" with a 4" plastic bank in the shape of the mysterious robot from the "Dr. Who" TV show. Cowan Day de Groot Ltd., BBC TV. Comes with appendages for Dalek. Box - **$30 $65 $100**
Bank - **$30 $65 $100**

(CEREAL BOX)

(BADGES)

DWH-2

(POSTER)

DWH-3

❑ **DWH-2. Kellogg's Sugar Smacks Badges,**
1971. Cereal offered 6 different celluloid badges. Sample box with promotional artwork (which continued to run after the end of the offer) and advertisement also shown. Boxes came in 'standard' and 'mini' sizes.
Each Badge - **$12 $18 $30**
Unopened Small Box - **$115 $165 $310**
Unopened Large Box - **$145 $290 $400**

❑ **DWH-3. Radio Times 10th Anniversary Special,**
1973. Features photos, interviews, and story synopses. Beware of recent 'facsimile' editions released in 2003, which look identical and bear no distinct outside markings to distinguish them from the 1973 originals. Some photos on the interior pages are different, however. -
$45 $90 $175

DWH-4

❑ **DWH-4. Weetabix Cards,**
1975. Cereal offered 6 different sets of 2 cards each for use as playing pieces with board game on back of box. There were two Weetabix sets offered in 1975 and 1977.
SET 1 (1975)
Each Unpressed Figure - **$28**
Complete Figures - **$50**
Each Box-Back - **$22**
Unopened Box - **$90**

SET 2 (1977)
Each Unpressed Figure - **$22**
Complete Figures - **$40**
Each Box-Back - **$12**
Unopened Box - **$70**

DWH-5

DWH-6

❑ DWH-5. Ty-Phoo Tea Cards,
1976. Offered with tea bags, accompanied by poster and book of comic book reprints.
12 cards in set.
Each Card - **$3 $5 $7**
Book - **$18 $30 $60**
Poster - **$45 $70 $135**
Opened Box - **$50**
Unopened Box - **$120**

❑ DWH-6. Promotional Poster,
1977. Produced for Crosse & Blackwell baked beans. - **$50 $85 $150**

DWH-7

DWH-8

❑ DWH-7. Doctor Who Weekly #1,
October 17, 1979. Marvel Comics. Newsprint magazine featured articles, interviews, and an ongoing comic strip starring the current Doctor and a variety of companions, many of whom were original to the strip. The magazine has undergone substantial design improvements, and is still published continuously by Panini under the title Doctor Who Magazine.
With Free Gift - **$22**
Without Free Gift - **$17**

❑ DWH-8. "Terry Nation's Dalek 1979 Annual,"
1979. UK hardcover. - **$20 $30 $65**

DWH-9

❑ DWH-9. Radio Times 20th Anniversary Special,
1983. Features photos, an original story, and a pull-out poster. Also available in a United States edition from Starlog. - **$12 $30 $50**

DWH-10

❑ DWH-10. Dalek Model Kit,
1984. Sevans Models.
Complete and Unassembled in Box - **$95**

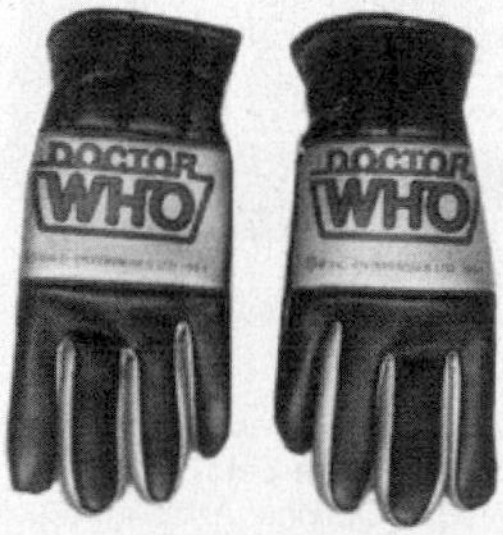

DWH-11

❑ DWH-11. Doctor Who Gloves,
1985. PeshawearUK Ltd. Available in a variety of sizes in black and silver with the neon logo on the back of the hand. - **$12 $25 $50**

DWH-12

❑ DWH-12. Golden Wonder Snacks Comic Book Giveaway,
1986. Snack packages offered reprint comic books and also advertised 1987 Doctor Who calendar. Sample packages and comic shown.
Unopened Packets - **$15**
Opened Packets - **$8**
Each Comic - **$4**

DWH-13

❑ DWH-13. Doctor Who Slippers,
1989. Mothercare. A matching pair of pajamas were also produced. - **$20 $40 $80**

DWH-14

❑ DWH-14. Bally Pinball Machine,
1991. Bally Midway. Features a second playing field activated by game play, a built-in video monitor for additional play, and specially recorded material by Seventh Doctor Sylvester McCoy. A number of plastic promotional disks were released for use at game locations and are also sought-after collectibles. - **$5000**

DWH-15

DWH-16

DWH-17

❑ DWH-15. Weapons Gunner Dalek Figure,
2000. Product Enterprise Ltd. In box on card. One of an extensive series of Dalek Rolykins, based on a 1960s line of Dalek ball-bearing toys. Now discontinued. - **$30**

❑ DWH-16. Promo Pen,
2000. - **$6**

❑ DWH-17. Dalek Figure on Card,
2000. Dapol. Dalek figures were mass produced in a variety of color schemes, but this crystal plastic version was limited to 2,000.
Crystal figure (shown) - **$50**
Colored figures Each - **$22**

DWH-18

❑ DWH-18. Limited Edition Chrome Weapons Gunner Dalek Figure,
2003. Product Enterprise Ltd. in conjunction with Telos Publishing Ltd. In box on card and numbered as one in a limited series of 600. These figuers, a variant of the regular Gunner Dalek Rolykin, were offered as premiums with the purchase of a copy of the second edition of the *Doctor Who* merchandise guide, *Howe's Transcendental Toybox*. - **$65**

DWH-19

❑ DWH-19. Limited Edition Remote Control Talking Davros Figure,
2005. Product Enterprise Ltd. in conjunction with SciFiCollector.co.uk. In display box with remote control. Limited to a run of 10,000 pieces. - **$110**

DWH-20

❑ DWH-20. Slitheen and Ninth Doctor Walktie Talkie Figure Set,
2005. Character Options. Articulated action figures of the Ninth Doctor and a Slitheen alien that also double as walkie talkies with the addition of 4 "AAA" batteries each. - **$33**

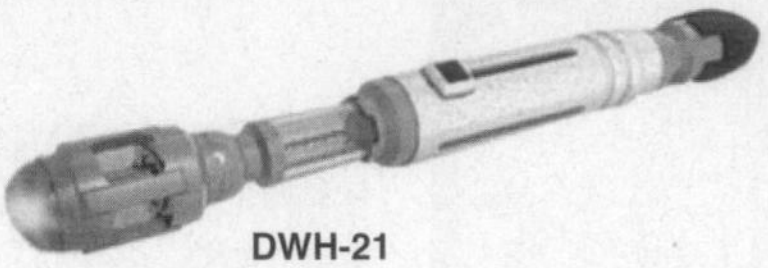
DWH-21

❑ DWH-21. Sonic Screwdriver,
2005. Character Options.Replica of the Ninth Doctor's sonic screwdriver with two sound effect variations, an extendable lighted end, and an interchangeable UV/standard ink pen on the other end. Comes in a display box with a 30-page code book. - **$25**

DWH-22

❑ DWH-22. Radio Control Dalek,
2005. Character Options. 12" tall new series style Dalek with remote control. Speaks seven phrases and blast sound, flashing lights and eye, head and eye movement, poseable arms and rotating center section. - **$65**

DWH-23

❑ DWH-23. Radio Control Dalek with Claw Arm,
2005. Character Options. UK Toys 'R' US exclusive. - **$100**

Don Winslow of the Navy

Don Winslow was conceived by Lt. Commander Frank V. Martinek (1895-1971) in the early 1930s as the hero of a series of novels written to promote navy recruiting. A Bell Syndicate comic strip, also originally written by Martinek and drawn by Leon Beroth and Carl Hammond, premiered in March 1934 and ran until July 1955. Winslow made his comic book debut in *Popular Comics* #1 of February 1936 and appeared in various Dell and Fawcett comics, among others, into the 1950s. Don Terry starred in two chapter plays, *Don Winslow of the Navy* in 1942 and *Don Winslow of the Coast Guard* in 1943, both of which were released to television in 1949. Winslow, along with his pal Lt. Red Pennington and his girlfriend Mercedes Colby, also fought the forces of evil on the radio from 1937 to 1943. His Squadron of Peace first did battle with the international Scorpia spy network, then turned its attention to the Axis menace of World War II. The series originated on WMAQ in Chicago and was aired on the NBC Blue network from 1937 to 1939 sponsored by Kellogg's cereals and Iodent toothpaste, and on ABC in 1942-1943 sponsored by Post cereals and Red Goose shoes.

DON-1

DON-2

❑ **DON-1. Secret Code Book,**
1935. 20 page premium from Metropolitan newspaper. - **$40 $100 $300**

❑ **DON-2. "Lieutenant Commander Don Winslow U.S.N." Big Little Book,**
1935. Whitman #1107. - **$18 $54 $125**

DON-3

DON-4

❑ **DON-3. "Don Winslow U.S. Navy" Penny Book,**
1938. Published by Whitman. - **$10 $30 $62**

❑ **DON-4. "Squadron Of Peace" Brass Ring,**
1938. Kellogg's. Each ring serially numbered. See DON-7. - **$250 $500 $1200**

DON-5

DON-6

❑ **DON-5. "Don Winslow Periscope" Countertop Display,**
1939. Kellogg's Wheat Krispies. Diecut cardboard 5x13x17" tall holding example periscope plus order coupons tablet.
With Periscope - **$290 $600 $975**
Without Periscope - **$175 $350 $625**

❑ **DON-6. Periscope Order Coupon,**
1939. Kellogg's Wheat Krispies. - **$18 $30 $65**

DON-7

❑ **DON-7. Guide Book,**
1939. Iodent Toothpaste. This booklet (folded) and the serially-numbered membership ring came in the mailer which has typed notation "Ring" on the label.
Mailer - **$30 $60 $115**
Booklet - **$85 $165 $310**

DON-8

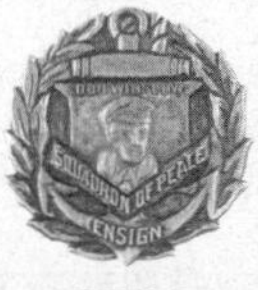

DON-9

DON-10

❑ **DON-8. "Squadron Of Peace" Member Card,**
1939. Kellogg's Wheat Krispies. - **$40 $70 $150**

❑ **DON-9. "Ensign/Squadron Of Peace" Silvered Brass Badge,**
1939. Kellogg's. - **$18 $30 $60**

❑ **DON-10. "Lt. Commander/Squadron Of Peace" Silvered Brass Badge,**
1939. Kellogg's. Scarce. Highest rank of series.- **$200 $400 $800**

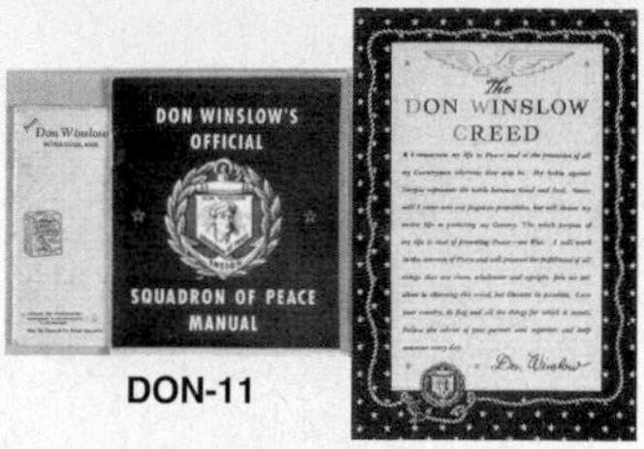

DON-11

❑ **DON-11. Club Manual And Creed,**
1939. Kellogg's. Near Mint In Mailer - **$300**
Manual - **$35 $75 $165**
Creed - **$20 $35 $80**

DON-12

❑ **DON-12. Kellogg's Cardboard Periscope,**
1939. Scarce. Slanted mirrors in each end. See DON-5. - **$115 $250 $350**

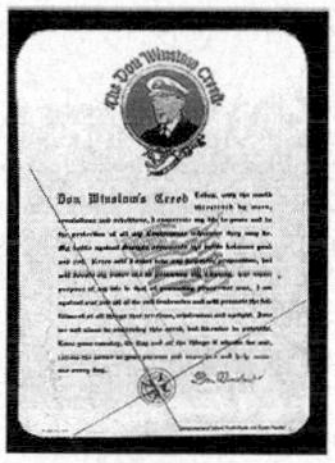

DON-13

DON-14

❑ **DON-13. "The Don Winslow Creed" Certificate,**
c. 1939. Iodent toothpaste and tooth powder. 9x12" parchment-like paper. - **$70 $150 $300**

❑ **DON-14. Honor Coin,**
c. 1939. Kellogg's. Center has spinner disk, back inscription is "Take Me For Luck". - **$25 $50 $100**

(FRONT) DON-15 (BACK)

❑ **DON-15. Pocket Watch,**
c. 1939. Store item by New Haven. Reverse has colorful decal portrait. Rare. - **$750 $1750 $3500**

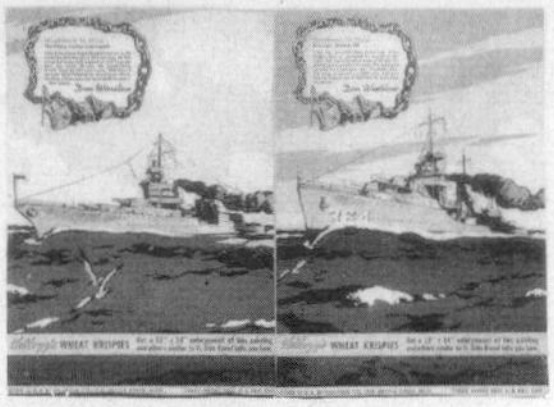

DON-16

DON-16. "Guardians Of Peace" Cereal Box Backs,
c. 1939. Kellogg's Wheat Krispies.
Each Back - **$12 $20 $40**

DON-17

DON-17. "Don Winslow's Secret And Private Code" Paper Sheet,
c. 1939. Includes Creed and decipher instructions. - **$30 $55 $110**

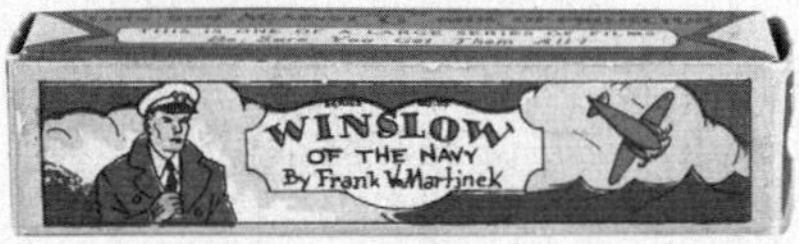

DON-18

DON-18. Movie Jecktor Film in Colorful Box,
1930s. - **$25 $50 $100**

DON-19

DON-19. "League For Defense" Kit,
1940. Fleer's Dubble Bubble Gum. Envelope containing Navy booklet, member card, additional "Signed" card. Kit originally included club member's pin-back button. See next item.
Complete Except Button - **$200 $450 $850**

DON-20

DON-20. "League For Defense" Kit With Autograph Card,
1940. Fleer's Dubble Bubble Gum. Includes pencil autograph of "Don And Red" on card with Navy text plus member card.
Autographed Card Only - **$40 $100 $150**

DON-21

DON-21. "Scorpia's Scrambled Code" Cardboard Sheet and Photo With Mailer Envelope,
1940. Scarce. Fleer's Dubble Bubble Gum. Explains code system with secret message to be deciphered. Mailer - **$15 $40 $80**
Code Sheet - **$40 $80 $140**
Winslow and Red Pennington Photo -
$40 $80 $140

DON-22

DON-23

DON-22. "Group Leader" Cello. Button,
1940. Scarce. Fleer's Dubble Bubble Gum. Radio club premium for League For Defense. -
$100 $200 $350

DON-23. Premium Photo,
c. 1940. Duquesne Baking Co. Black and white 5x7" with blue inscription. - **$40 $75 $150**

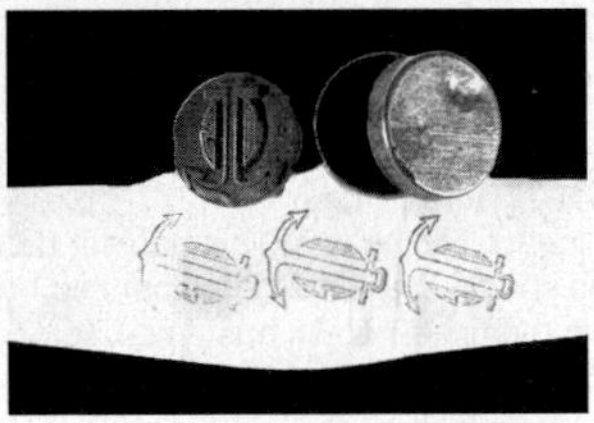

DON-24

DON-24. Identification Stamp Miniature Kit,
c. 1940. 1" tin container holding ink pad and rubber stamp personalized by initials designated by orderer with anchor design. - **$65 $135 $265**

DON-25

DON-25. "Don Winslow Of The Navy" Movie Poster,
1941. One-sheet is 27x41" for Universal Picture serial that starred Don Terry as Winslow. This was for Chapter 11 titled "Caught In The Caverns." - **$115 $235 $375**

DON-26

DON-26. Catapult Bomber,
1942. Scarce. Post Toasties. - **$125 $275 $550**

DON-27

DON-27. Golden Torpedo Decoder,
1942. Rare. Post Toasties. Came in two pieces, with wood top, cardboard side and metal fin. One of the toughest premiums to find. -
$600 $1650 $2750

(FRONT)

DON-28 (BACK)

DON-28. Undercover Deputy Certificate With Instructions,
1942. Scarce. Post Toasties. Goes with Golden Torpedo Decoder. - **$150 $300 $600**

DON-29

DON-30

DON-29. "Don Winslow Navy Intelligence Ace" Big Little Book #1418,
1942. 432 pages. Flip pictures. - **$16 $48 $115**

DON-30. "Don Winslow Red Goose Shoes" Portrait Picture,
c. 1942. 8-1/2x11" black and white. The only Red Goose premium known for the show. -
$90 $175 $350

DON-31

❑ **DON-31. "Don Winslow Of The Navy" Lobby Card Chapter 7 Group,**
1943. Lot of five 11x14" for original release of 13-chapter Universal serial.
Title Card - **$20 $40 $65**
Each Scene Card - **$10 $20 $35**

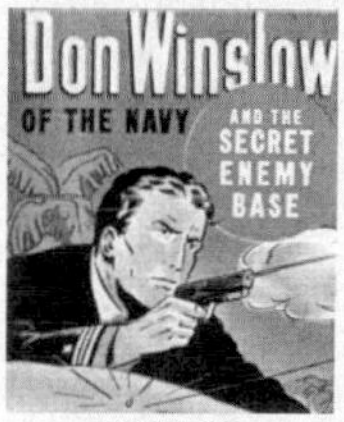

DON-32

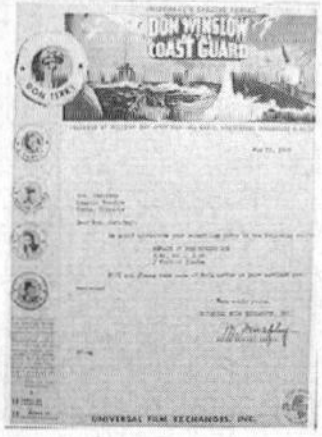

DON-33

❑ **DON-32. "Don Winslow Of The Navy And The Secret Enemy Base" Better Little Book,**
1943. Whitman #1453. - **$16 $48 $115**

❑ **DON-33. "Don Winslow Of The Coast Guard" Serial Letterhead,**
1943. Universal Film Exchanges, Inc. Colorful illustrations on 8-1/2x11" sheet. - **$35 $75 $150**

DON-34

DON-35

❑ **DON-34. "Flare-Top" Ice Cream Cone Store Sign,**
1947. Full color about 18x24". Gordon Gold archives. - **$75 $150 $325**

❑ **DON-35. Don Winslow & Red Pennington Plaster Salt & Pepper Set,**
1940s. Store item. From series of character sets. - **$25 $50 $90**

DON-36

DON-37

❑ **DON-36. Coco-Wheats "Tattoo Transfers" With Mailer Envelope,**
1956. Transfer sheets picture 22 characters.
Mailer - **$12 $20 $35**
Illustrated Inner Envelope With Two Sheets - **$30 $65 $125**

❑ **DON-37. Secret Code Booklet with Shirt/Box,**
1950s. Set - **$100 $175 $350**

Donald Duck

See Ted Hake's *Official® Price Guide to Disney Collectibles*, Second Edition, formatted identically to this book but in full color evaluating over 9,000 Disney company and character collectibles from 1924 through 2006.

Dorothy Hart, Sunbrite Jr. Nurse Corps

***Junior Nurse Corps* was broadcast on CBS radio in 1936-1937 and on the Blue network in 1937-1938. The series, sponsored by Sunbrite cleanser and Quick Arrow soap flakes, both products of Swift and Company, centered on the activities of teen nursing student Dorothy Hart and her Aunt Jane. The program was aimed at an audience of teenage girls, focusing on the nurse's life and the importance of knowing first aid, as well as on historical events. There were many premiums offered in exchange for Sunbrite and Quick Arrow labels; most of the premiums were nursing-oriented.**

DOR-1

DOR-2

❑ **DOR-1. Nurse Pin Back,**
1937. Radio premium. Different photo in center. This photo variety is scarcer than next example. - **$25 $45 $90**

❑ **DOR-2. Cello. Club Button,**
1937. - **$18 $35 $60**

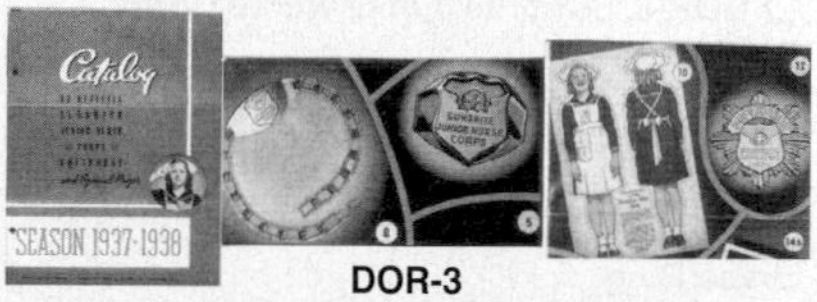

DOR-3

❑ **DOR-3. Club Premium Catalogue Fold-Out Sheet,**
1937. For 1937-1938 season. - **$40 $110 $165**

DOR-4

DOR-5

❑ **DOR-4. Club Newspaper,**
September 1937. - **$18 $35 $80**

❑ **DOR-5. Indian Princess Sa-ca-ja-wea Photo,**
1937. Radio cast member. - **$10 $25 $40**

DOR-6

❑ **DOR-6. Sa-ca-ja-wea Radio Premium,**
1937. Shows examples of Indian sign language throughout the 8 page booklet. Scarce. - **$40 $85 $160**

DOR-7

❑ **DOR-7. Cast Member Photo,**
1937. - **$15 $40 $80**

DOR-8

DOR-9

❑ **DOR-8. Sunbrite Junior Nurse Corps Card,**
1937. Rare. Membership card for radio show. - **$30 $75 $150**

❑ **DOR-9. "Sunbrite Junior Nurse Corps" Brass Ring,**
1937. - **$90 $275 $500**

DOR-10

DOR-11

DOR-12

❑ **DOR-10. "Sunbrite Junior Nurse Corps" Brass Badge,**
1937. - **$30 $40 $80**

❑ **DOR-11. "Graduate" Rank Brass Badge,**
1937. - **$35 $75 $150**

❑ **DOR-12. "Supervisor" Highest Rank Brass Badge,** 1937. - **$60 $125 $250**

DOR-13

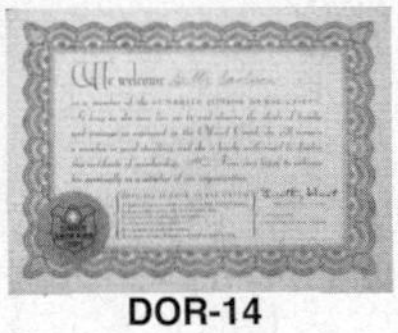

DOR-14

❑ **DOR-13. Radio Program/Premiums Promo Card,**
1937. Cardboard ink blotter including imprint for radio stations WHK, Cleveland and WLW, Cincinnati. - **$10 $18 $35**

❑ **DOR-14. Membership Certificate,**
c. 1937. Design in green and tan with black text and gold seal on 8-1/2x11" sheet. Has text of Nurse's Creed. - **$30 $60 $100**

DOR-15

DOR-16

❑ **DOR-15. "Sunbrite Junior Nurse Corps" Silvered Brass Bracelet,**
1937. - **$30 $85 $160**

❑ **DOR-16. "Sunbrite Junior Nurse Corps" Sewing Kit,**
c. 1937. Thimble tops 2" tall case holding threads and pins. - **$15 $35 $60**

Dr. Kildare

Created by author Frederick Faust (1892-1944) under the pen name Max Brand, the popular movie and TV series was loosely based on Faust's friend Dr. George Fish. The first film *Interns Can't Take Money* in 1937 starred Joel McRea as James Kildare and co-starred Barbara Stanwyck as Janet Haley. Lew Ayres took over the title role in 1938. Co-starring Lionel Barrymore as Dr. Gillespie, *Young Dr. Kildare* was released October 14, 1938 with Paramount releasing nine more titles up to 1942 with the popular acting team.

MGM ran a radio series starring Ayres and Barrymore *The Story Of Dr. Kildare* in 1949-1950 followed by syndication.

The NBC network broadcast five seasons of the TV series; 190 episodes between September 28, 1961 and April 5, 1966. Richard Chamberlain starred as Kildare with Raymond Massey as Dr. Gillespie. The basic plot had Kildare with his charming bedside manner working toward residency under Gillespie. Writers included Theodore Apstein and William Bast. Directors included Jack Arnold and Earl Bellamy. The 1962 theme song written by Hal Winn and Jerry Goldsmith and sung by Richard Chamberlain reached #10 on the pop charts. *Dell Comics* released nine comic books between 1962 and 1966 with color photo covers and Ken Bald drew the *Dr. Kildare* comic strip from 1962 to 1983. Is there a doctor in the house?

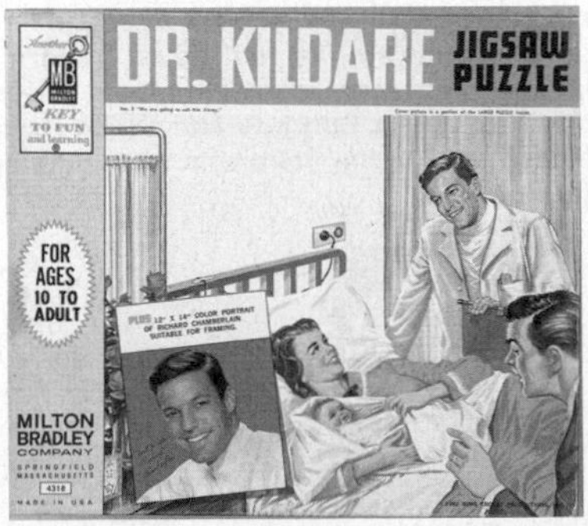

DRK-1

❑ **DRK-1. "Dr. Kildare Jigsaw Puzzle" With Portrait Insert,**
1962. Bing Crosby Productions Inc. 10x11x2" deep box contains Milton Bradley puzzle from a numbered series. Assembled puzzle is 14x24". Also includes 12x14" "Color Portrait Of Richard Chamberlain Suitable For Framing" in generic cardboard tube. - **$12 $25 $40**

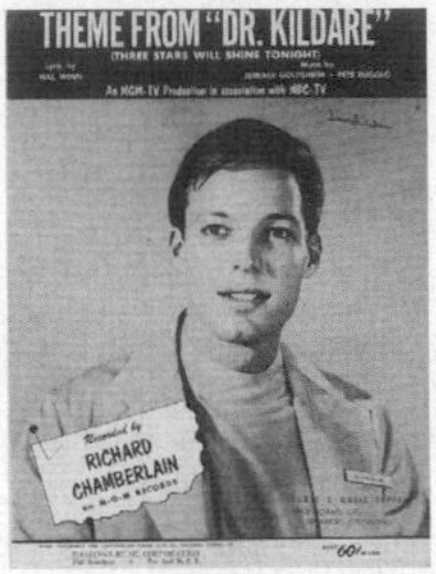

DRK-2

❑ **DRK-2. "Theme From Dr. Kildare" Sheet Music,**
1962. M-G-M Inc. 9x12" with four pages. - **$5 $12 $25**

DRK-3

❑ **DRK-3. "Dr. Kildare I Like Richard" Button,**
c. 1962. 2.25" high quality portrait button. - **$7 $15 $25**

DRK-4

❑ **DRK-4. "Dr. Kildare" Composition Bobbing Head,**
1960s. - **$45 $85 $165**

Dr. Seuss

Theodor Seuss Geisel (1904-1991), creator of verbally complex fantasies that have enchanted millions of children throughout the world for over 50 years, was born and raised in Springfield, Massachusetts, graduated from Dartmouth in 1925, and was soon contributing humor to magazines such as *Liberty* and *Judge*. After some success illustrating the "Quick Henry, the Flit!" insecticide ads; advertising art for Standard Oil for 15 years; and the comic strip *Henjji* in 1935, Geisel published the first of his nearly 50 books in 1937. Among the best-known: *Horton Hatches the Egg* (1940), *How the Grinch Stole Christmas* (1957), *The Cat in the Hat* (1957), *Yertle the Turtle* (1958), *Green Eggs and Ham* (1960) and *The Lorax* (1971). Television cartoon adaptations of some of the titles premiered on CBS or ABC between 1966 and 1994, winning Peabody and Emmy awards. Geisel also won Academy Awards for two documentary films (*Hitler Lives* in 1946 and *Design for Death* in 1947) and for his animated short *Gerald McBoing Boing* in 1951. Gerald also had a brief run in a series of comic books published by Dell in 1952-1953. *How The Grinch Stole Christmas* was released as a live action feature film starring Jim Carrey in 2000. Jim Carrey returns in 2008 as the voice of Horton in a CGI-animated feature film *Horton Hears a Who!*, also starring Steve Carell as the voice of the Mayor of Who-ville.

DSU-1

DSU-2

❑ **DSU-1. "Flit Cartoons" Booklet,**
1929. Stanco Inc. 24-page booklet of Seuss art single cartoon panels illustrating use of "Flit" insecticide spray. - **$115 $230 $375**

❑ **DSU-2. "Secrets Of The Deep Or The Perfect Yachtsman" Booklet,**
1935. Essomarine Oils & Greases. 36 pages including 18 character cartoons by Dr. Seuss. - **$125 $250 $400**

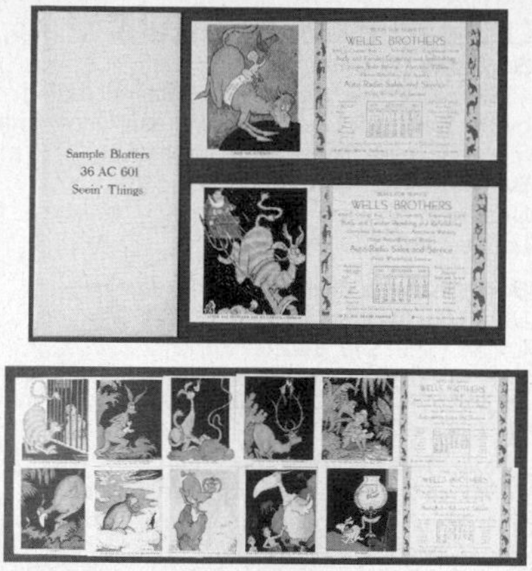

DSU-3

❑ **DSU-3. Early Dr. Seuss Salesman Sample Blotter Set,**
1936. Set of twelve, 3.75x8.5" each. Comes with 4x9" envelope with text reading "Sample Blotters/Seein'Things." Glossy paper samples do not have actual blotter backs.
Set - **$275 $550 $1100**

DSU-4

❑ **DSU-4. "Moto Monster" Puzzle With Envelope,**
1930s. Essolube motor oil. 11-1/2x17" envelope and assembled 150-piece jigsaw puzzle picturing various named motoring villain monsters "Foiled By Essolube" use.
Near Mint With Envelope - **$275**
Puzzle Only - **$60 $125 $200**

DSU-5

❑ **DSU-5. "Seuss Navy Muzzlepuss Official Seal" Metal Ashtray,**
c. 1940. 5.5" dia. tray completed by 3.75" tall figure wearing Admiral hat. Likely produced for Esso but unmarked. - **$275 $550 $1100**

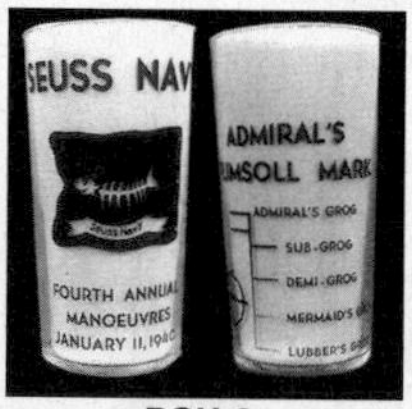

DSU-6

DSU-7

❑ **DSU-6. "Seuss Navy" "Fourth Annual Manoeuvres" Glass Tumbler,**
1940. Drinking glass designed for naval event gauged for minimum beverage consumption of Lubber to maximum consumption of Admiral. - **$50 $150 $275**

❑ **DSU-7. "Seuss Navy Fifth Annual Manocuvres" Glass,**
1941. Red and blue image and text including "1941 Snag Tooth Annie's/Raincheck Alaska." - **$50 $150 $275**

DSU-8

❑ **DSU-8. World War II Paper Poster,**
1943. U.S. Government Printing Office. Unsigned but Dr. Seuss art 8x32" anti-patriotic "Squander Bug" character for promotion of more War Bond purchases. - **$150 $300 $535**

DSU-9

❑ **DSU-9. Esso "Meet Gus!" Cello. Button,**
1940s. Esso/Standard Oil. Back paper has "Happy Motoring!" slogan plus logo.
With Back Paper - **$25 $50 $100**
Without Back Paper - **$15 $25 $50**

DSU-10

DSU-11

❑ DSU-10. Beer Serving Tray With Dr. Seuss Art,
c. 1940s. Narragansett Lager & Ale. Full color with 12" diameter and 1-3/8" tall rim. - **$50 $150 $265**

❑ DSU-11. "Seuss Navy" Glass Tumbler,
1940s. Esso products. Beverage glass with consumption gauge markings monitored by "Official When-Hen." - **$25 $50 $90**

DSU-12

❑ DSU-12. "Gerald McBoing Boing Told By The Great Gildersleeve" Dr. Seuss Record With Sleeve,
1950. Capitol Album CAS-304. Superflex Children's Series #5154. - **$100 $250 $450**

DSU-13

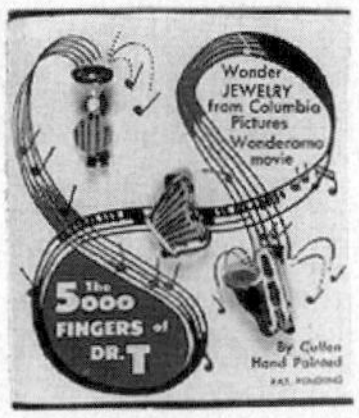

DSU-14

❑ DSU-13. "The 5000 Fingers Of Dr. T" Hair Barrettes On Card,
1953. Store item based on characters created by Dr. Seuss for Columbia Pictures Wonderama movie of same title. Two versions exist.
Barrettes with gold luster
Near Mint On Card - **$115**
Loose - **$20 $40 $60**

Barrettes with silver luster
Near Mint On Card - **$115**
Loose - **$20 $40 $60**

❑ DSU-14. "The 5000 Fingers Of Dr. T" Pins On Card,
1953. Figural miniature pins of horn, harp and trombone based on Dr. Seuss creations from Columbia Pict. Wonderama movie of same title.
Near Mint On Card - **$115**
Loose - **$20 $40 $60**

DSU-15

❑ DSU-15. Dr. Seuss Zoo Revell Model Sets,
1954. Group of four 1.75x7x10" boxes. Includes "Roscoe, Tingo The Noodle Topped Stroodle, Norval the Bashful Blinket and Gowdy the Dowdy Grackle."
Each Boxed Complete - **$100 $200 $350**

DSU-16

❑ DSU-16. "Chief Gansett" Beer Coaster,
c. 1950s. Narragansett Lager & Ale, Rhode Island. 4-1/4" diameter cardboard disk featuring sponsor character art by Seuss. - **$8 $15 $30**

DSU-17

❑ DSU-17. Puzzle,
1964. Premium with 18 characters pictured. - **$20 $30 $60**

DSU-18

❑ DSU-18. Book,
1968. Crest Toothpaste premium. 56 page story of "Horton Hatches the Egg". - **$20 $40 $70**

DSU-19

❑ DSU-19. Original Concept Drawing,
1960s. Hand colored pen and ink drawing of "The Cat in the Hat" by Maurice Noble for 1960s TV special about the Cat wearing different hats.- **$1750**

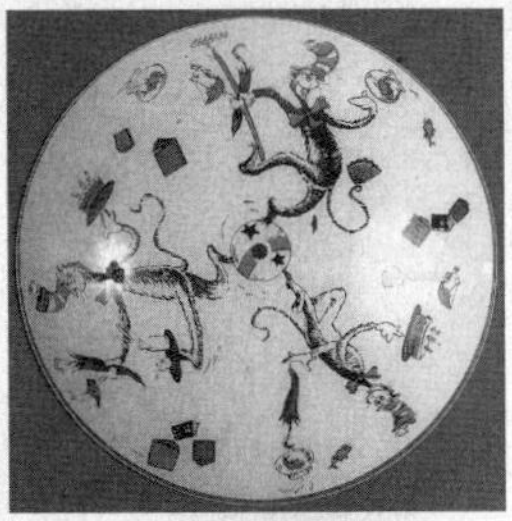
DSU-20

❑ DSU-20. Cat In The Hat Ceiling Shade,
1960s. 14.5" dia. domed glass picturing him in various activities. - **$50 $85 $175**

DSU-21

DSU-22

❑ **DSU-21. Large Litho. Tin Tab,**
1970. 2" diameter red on white reading "See Dr. Seuss 'Horton Hears A Who' On CBS-TV March 19." - **$10 $20 $50**

❑ **DSU-22. "The World Of Dr. Seuss" Vinyl Lunch Box,**
1970. Store item by Aladdin. - **$100 $200 $400**

DSU-23

❑ **DSU-23. "The World Of Dr. Seuss" Lunch Box With Bottle,**
1970. Store item by Aladdin Industries. Steel box and plastic bottle. Box - **$50 $125 $250**
Bottle - **$20 $40 $60**

DSU-24

❑ **DSU-24. "The Cat In The Hat" Boxed Plush Hand Puppet,**
1975. 20-1/2" tall store item by Douglas Co. Cuddle Toys. Near Mint Boxed - **$275**
Puppet Only - **$50 $110 $185**

DSU-25

❑ **DSU-25. "Sam I Am" Boxed Plush Hand Puppet,**
1975. 18" tall store item by Douglas Co. Cuddle Toys. Near Mint Boxed - **$275**
Puppet Only - **$50 $110 $185**

DSU-26

DSU-27

❑ **DSU-26. Cat In The Hat Alarm Clock,**
1978. Store item. Metal case and alarm bells, wind-up. - **$60 $115 $225**

❑ **DSU-27. Seuss Character Litho. Button,**
c. 1970s. Probable various stores for Christmas promotion of Dr. Seuss copyright items. - **$18 $35 $80**

DSU-28

DSU-29

❑ **DSU-28. Cat In The Hat 30th Birthday 2-1/2" Cello. Button,**
1987. - **$10 $20 $35**

❑ **DSU-29. "Cat In The Hat" 2-1/2x2-1/2" Cello. Button,**
1995. Macy's department store. For promotional use by store employee. - **$10 $25 $50**

DSU-30

❑ **DSU-30. Kix Cereal Box with Book Offer,**
1997. Celebrates 40 years of "The Cat in the Hat" with a mail-in offer. - **$5 $8 $15**

DSU-31

DSU-32

❑ **DSU-31. Cat In The Hat Yo-Yo,**
1999. Promotes Universal Studios Theme Park. On card - **$6 $12 $22**

❑ **DSU-32. Dr. Seuss Fish Yo-Yo,**
1999. Promotes Universal Studios Theme Park. On card - **$6 $12 $22**

(Two views of the item)

DSU-33

❑ **DSU-33. "Cat In The Hat" in Car Bisque Figure,**
1999. TM Dr. Seuss Enterprises. Universal Studios, Islands of Adventure exclusive.- **$40**

DSU-34

DSU-35

❑ **DSU-34. "Cat In The Hat" Bean Figure,**
1999. Seuss Landing set. With tag. - **$22**

❑ **DSU-35. "Sam I Am" Bean Figure,**
1999. Seuss Landing set. With tag. - **$18**

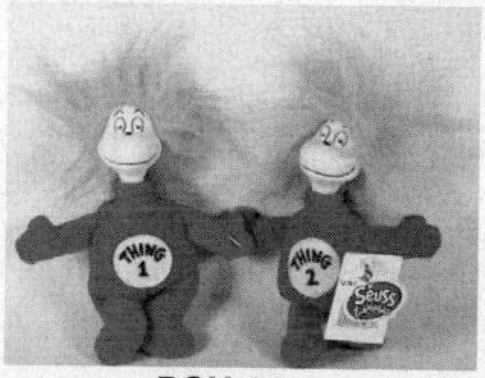

DSU-36

❑ **DSU-36. "Thing #1" and "Thing #2" Bean Figures,**
1999. Seuss Landing set. With tag.
Set of 2 - **$25**

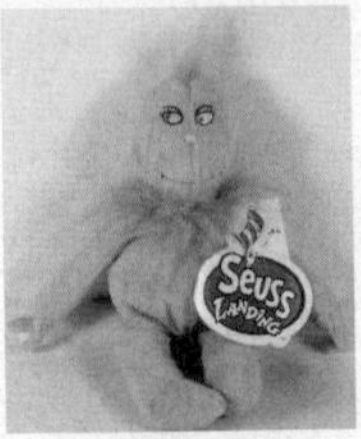
DSU-37

DSU-38

❑ **DSU-37. "The Grinch" Bean Figure,**
1999. Seuss Landing set. With tag. - **$22**

❑ **DSU-38. "Yertle the Turtle" Bean Figure,**
1999. Seuss Landing set. With tag. - **$18**

DSU-39

❑ **DSU-39. The Grinch Resin Figure,**
1990s. With tag. - **$65**

DSU-40

DSU-41

❑ **DSU-40. Talking "Grinch" Doll,**
2000. 19" tall in box. - **$15 $25 $45**

❑ **DSU-41. "Cindy Lou Who" Doll,**
2000. From the movie; has Whobilation Hair. 17" tall in box. - **$10 $20 $40**

DSU-42

DSU-43

❑ **DSU-42. "Grinch" Walkie Talkies,**
2000. On card. - **$35**

❑ **DSU-43. "Grinch" Wacky Wobbler,**
2000. Resembles animated Grinch. - **$25**

DSU-44

DSU-45

❑ **DSU-44. "Grinch" Lunch Box,**
2000. - **$18**

❑ **DSU-45. "Whoville-opoly" Board Game,**
2000. From the Grinch movie. Boxed. - **$35**

DSU-46

❑ **DSU-46. "Cat in the Hat" Tin Drum in Box,**
2003. - **$25**

DSU-47

DSU-48

❑ **DSU-47. "Cat in the Hat" Kaleidoscopes on Card,**
2003. - **$6**

❑ **DSU-48. "Cat in the Hat" Push Puppet,**
2004. Tube holds candy fish. - **$6**

Dragnet

Created by Jack Webb (1920-1982), the show first aired on NBC radio June 3, 1949 and ran until February 26, 1957. The cast included Webb as Sgt. Joe Friday and Barton Yarborough as Sgt. Ben Romero. Based on actual L.A.P.D. cases, the series premiered on TV December 16, 1951 and ran until August 23, 1959. Ben Alexander (1911-1969) became officer Frank Smith in episode three after Barton Yarborough passed away. The series was also syndicated under the *Badge 714* title. The show, with classic theme music by Mike Post, won four Emmy awards. A spin-off series produced and directed by Jack Webb aired on NBC from January 12, 1967 until April 16, 1970 which co-starred Harry Morgan as officer Bill Gannon. *The New Dragnet* aired on TV in 1989 and ABC produced *Dragnet* for two seasons beginning in 2003.

Warner Bros. produced a feature film in 1954 directed by and starring Jack Webb. Universal produced a 1987 feature film spoof starring Dan Aykroyd and Tom Hanks.

Parodies of the show included Stan Freberg's 1953 classic record *St. George And The Dragonet* voiced by Daws Butler and June Foray; and Harvey Kurtzman and Will Elder's *Dragged Net!* in 1953 in *MAD* comic book #3.

Dum-Dee-Dum-Dum. "All we want are the facts ma'am!"

DRA-1

DRA-2

❑ **DRA-1. "TV Guide" 8x11" Vending Rack Insert Card,**
c. 1952. Design based on Sgt. Joe Friday of Dragnet police TV series. - **$30 $60 $110**

❑ **DRA-2. Jack Webb "Dragnet" Sponsor Endorsement Sign,**
c. 1952. Fatima Cigarettes. Diecut cardboard countertop sign 16x16" with easel back. - **$75 $175 $300**

DRA-3

❑ DRA-3. "Dragnet" Sheet Music,
1953. Schumann Music Co. 9x12" with bluetone photo cover. - **$5 $10 $20**

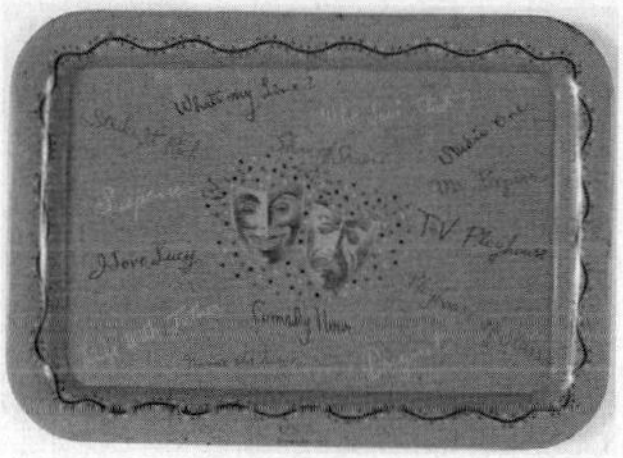
DRA-4

❑ DRA-4. Early TV Tray With Lucy/Dragnet,
1953. 12.25x17.5x1" deep tin litho tray. Issued in several color varieties. Names 14 TV shows. - **$20 $40 $75**

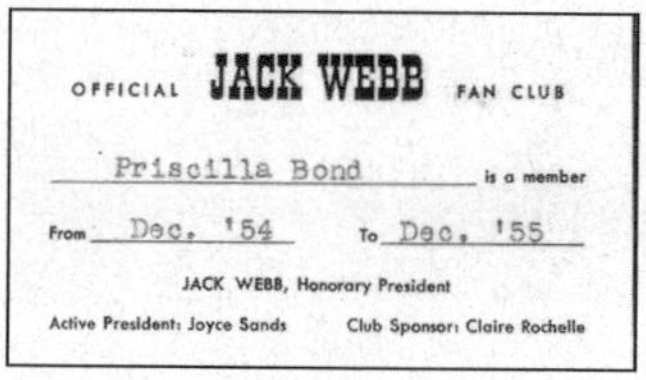
OFFICIAL JACK WEBB FAN CLUB
Priscilla Bond is a member
From Dec. '54 To Dec. '55
JACK WEBB, Honorary President
Active President: Joyce Sands Club Sponsor: Claire Rochelle

DRA-5

❑ DRA-5. "Jack Webb Fan Club" Membership Card,
1954. For star of Dragnet TV series. - **$10 $15 $25**

DRA-6

❑ DRA-6. "Ideal's Dragnet Talking Police Car" Boxed,
1954. Sherry TV Inc. 5.75x14.5x6" tall box with Jack Webb die-cut image contains 14" long plastic car. Includes removable plastic dome, flashlight, removable phone on dashboard, two pistols, camera, Tommy gun, riot gun, swivel chair and table with map, binoculars, two rifles and talking device in trunk activated by manual crank. Includes instruction sheet. - **$100 $200 $400**

DRA-7

❑ DRA-7. "Dragnet" Time Magazine Promotional Sign,
1954. 10.25x13.5" cardboard sign. Text inspired by Webb's famous phrase "Just the facts." - **$50 $100 $165**

DRA-8

❑ DRA-8. "Dragnet Badge 714 Puzzle" Game,
1955. Sherry TV Inc. 5.5x7x1" deep box holds 5x6.25x.5" deep hard plastic playing board and pair of plastic markers meant to represent Sgt. Joe Friday and a fugitive. - **$15 $30 $60**

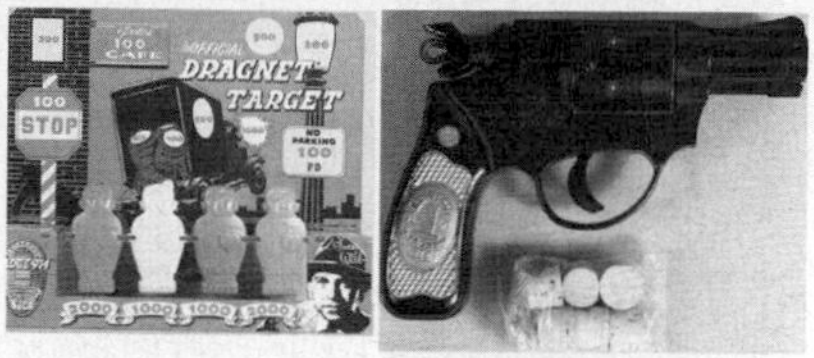

DRA-9

❑ DRA-9. "Official Dragnet Target" Complete Set,
1955. Sherry TV Inc. Tin litho target is 11x13x2" deep tall with four figural hard plastic targets attached on front. Wire easel attachment on reverse. Comes with 6" long hard plastic gun and cellophane pack of six corks. "714" badge logo on gun's grips. - **$35 $65 $125**

DRA-10

❑ DRA-10. "Dragnet Official Double Duty Rain Coat" Tag,
c. 1955. Sherry TV Inc. 2.5x3.25" two-sided glossy stiff paper tag. Reverse includes company information and has illustration of Joe Friday's badge. - **$20 $40 $65**

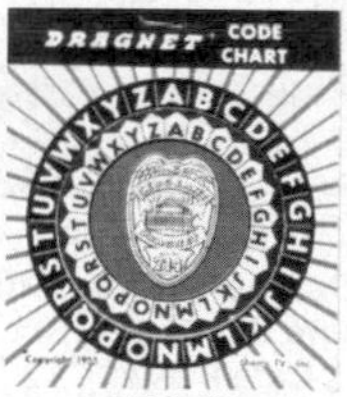

DRA-11

❑ DRA-11. "Dragnet Code Chart" Cardboard Decoder,
1955. Sponsor unknown. - **$15 $30 $55**

DRA-12

❑ DRA-12. "Dragnet" Cap Gun,
1955. Smoking gun in a decorative open box. Jack Webb picture on box. Has cut out I.D. card on back. Near Mint Boxed - **$225**
Loose - **$35 $75 $110**

DRA-14

DRA-13

❑ **DRA-13. "Dragnet" Water Gun with Refill Container,**
1955. Harder to find than regular gun. Jack Webb picture on box. Has cut out I.D. card on back. Near Mint Boxed - **$250**
Loose - **$40 $80 $125**

❑ **DRA-14. "Dragnet 714 Club" Metal Badge, Card and Case,**
1955. Store item. - **$20 $35 $75**

DRA-15

❑ **DRA-15. "Dragnet Whistle" 20x20" Cardboard Store Sign,**
1955. Kellogg's Corn Flakes.
Sign - **$75 $150 $275**
Whistle - **$1 $3 $5**

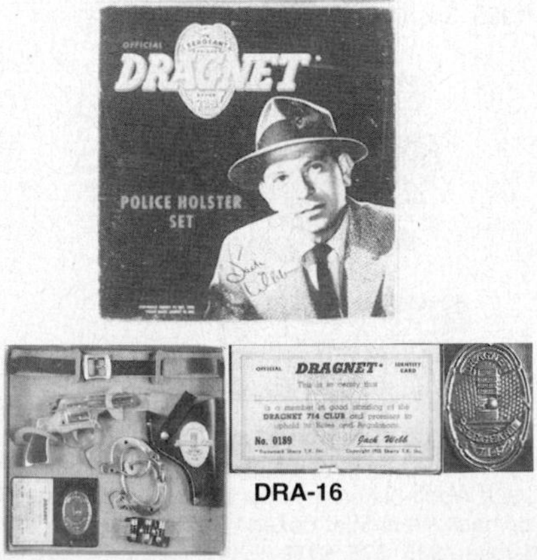

DRA-16

❑ **DRA-16. "Dragnet Police Holster Set" Boxed,**
1959. Carnell Mfg. Co. Set of cap gun, leather belt and holster, bullet belt attachment with three silver plastic bullets, metal handcuffs, vinyl wallet, tin "714" badge, Dragnet I.D. card with Jack Webb facsimile signature. -
$150 $300 $600

Dudley Do-Right

The misadventures of the noble Mountie Dudley Do-Right began life as a segment of *The Bullwinkle Show* in 1961. Created by Jay Ward (1920-1989), the dedicated lawman appeared on his own in *The Dudley Do-Right Show*, which premiered on ABC in 1969 and started in syndication the following year. *Dudley Do-Right* comic books were published in 1970-1971. A 1999 movie was released featuring Brendan Fraser and Sarah Jessica Parker.

Square-jawed and bone-headed, the ever-chivalrous Dudley pursued his arch-enemy, Snidely K. Whiplash (voiced by Hans Conreid), in one melodramatic tale after another. His romantic interest in Nell, his boss's daughter, was not returned; she preferred his horse, Horse. Items are usually copyrighted P.A.T.-Ward Productions.

DUD-1

❑ **DUD-1. Dudley Do-Right Lunchbox,**
1962. Universal. 3.5x6.5x9". Same image on front and back. - **$225 $450 $875**

DUD-2

DUD-3

❑ **DUD-2. Dudley Do-Right Figural Rubber Magnet,**
1960s. By "Magnetic Novelties" with "Ward" copyright. - **$6 $12 $18**

❑ **DUD-3. "Dudley Do-Right" Stuffed Fabric Pillow,**
1960s. - **$25 $40 $75**

DUD-4

DUD-5

❑ **DUD-4. T-Shirt,**
1970. Charlton Comics. - **$45 $90 $175**

❑ **DUD-5. Sweatshirt,**
1970. Charlton Comics. - **$60 $120 $200**

DUD-6

DUD-7

❑ **DUD-6. Dudley Do-Right Plastic Ring,**
1970. Charlton Comics. From membership kit. - **$20 $40 $80**

❑ **DUD-7. Portrait Wristwatch,**
c. 1971. Battery watch inscribed "Buren 17 Jewels" with Jay Ward Productions copyright. - **$90 $225 $350**

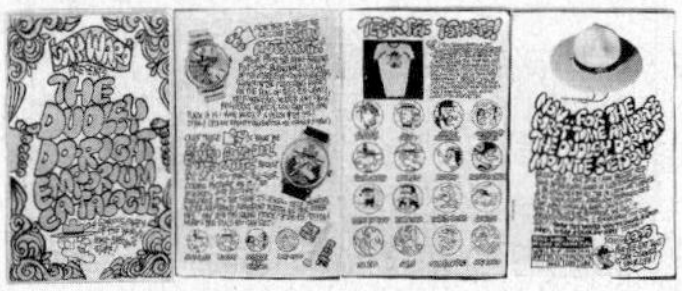

DUD-8

❑ **DUD-8. "Dudley Do-Right Emporium Catalogue,"**
1972. Jay Ward Productions. 24-page illustrated and priced listing of dozens of Ward character items including the Dudley Do-Right Mountie Stetson hat. - **$40 $85 $165**

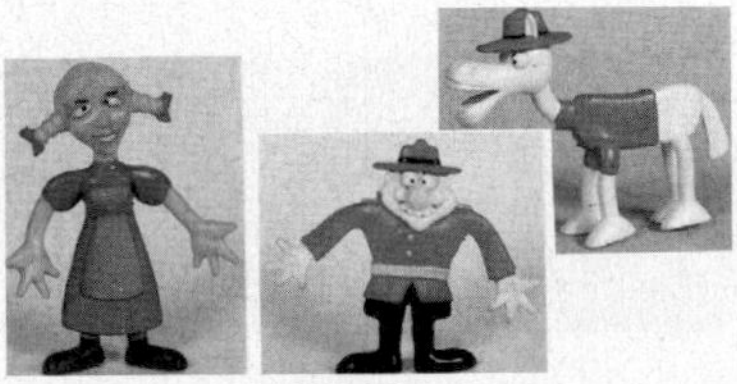

DUD-9

❑ **DUD-9. Limited Distribution Bendee Figures,**
1972. Store items sold on cards by Wham-O. Others in series had national distribution. These three are scarce. Carded Nell - **$75 $150 $250**
Carded Inspector Fenwick - **$100 $200 $300**
Carded Horse - **$75 $150 $250**

DUD-10

DUD-11

DUD-12

❑ **DUD-10. Vinyl Lunch Box,**
1972. Store item by Ardee Industries. -
$225 $600 $1100

❑ **DUD-11. "Snidely Whiplash" Cello. Button,**
c. 1972. P.A.T.-Ward copyright. - **$10 $20 $45**

❑ **DUD-12. "Nell" Cello. Button,**
c. 1972. P.A.T.-Ward copyright. - **$10 $20 $45**

DUD-13

DUD-14

❑ **DUD-13. "Pepsi Collector Series" Glass Tumblers,**
1973. Pepsi-Cola.
Each - **$8 $15 $25**

❑ **DUD-14. Dudley Do-Right Dakin Figure,**
1976. R. Dakin & Company. Store item. 6-3/4" tall. - **$15 $30 $45**

DUD-15

DUD-16

❑ **DUD-15. Patch On Card,**
1970s. - **$12 $25 $55**

❑ **DUD-16. "Dining With Dudley Do-Right" Plate, Soup, Cereal Bowl, Tumbler Boxed Set,**
c. 1980. Store item by Libbey.
Near Mint Boxed - **$90**
Each Loose - **$8 $15 $20**

DUD-17

DUD-18

❑ **DUD-17. "Deputy Mountie" Plastic Badge,**
1980s. Bullwinkle's Restaurant. 2-3/4" tall plastic badge in two shades of gold with title and his hat and collar in red. - **$15 $30 $60**

❑ **DUD-18. "Bendee" Figure On Card,**
1985. Store item. Flexible figure on blister card by Jesco Products. Carded - **$15 $30 $65**
Loose - **$12 $22 $35**

Duffy's Tavern

"Where the elite meet to eat," ***Duffy's Tavern*** **was the radio creation of actor/director Ed Gardner in 1940. Gardner played Archie, the manager and with Abe Burrows did most of the writing. Shirley Booth originated the role of Miss Duffy, daughter of the never-present proprietor. The program was a 30-minute comedy variety with show-business guests dropping by each week for banter with Archie. It premiered on CBS in March 1941, went to the Blue network in 1942, to NBC in 1944 and was last heard in 1951. Sponsors included Schick, Sanka, Ipana toothpaste and Blatz beer. A 1945 Paramount film with many Hollywood stars playing themselves was essentially a reprise of the radio show. CBS syndicated a series of 26 TV shows in 1954.**

DUF-1

❑ **DUF-1. "Duffy's First Reader By Archie" Booklet,**
1943. Bristol-Myers Co. - **$25 $40 $75**

DUF-2

DUF-3

❑ **DUF-2. Song Book,**
1944. Possible premium. Six pages. -
$25 $65 $110

❑ **DUF-3. "Etiket By Archie" Cover Article,**
1944. June issue of "Tune In" national radio magazine including three-page photo article by Ed Gardner, Archie of Duffy's Tavern. -
$10 $20 $35

DUF-4

❑ **DUF-4. "Ed (Archie) Gardner" Record Album,**
1947. Monitor, an appliance maker. Set of four 78 rpm records of actual broadcasts. Inside are write-ups about the radio show. -
$35 $80 $160

DUF-5

DUF-6

❑ **DUF-5. Ceramic Mug,**
1948. Probably a cast member item. -
$70 $125 $200

❑ **DUF-6. Ed Gardner As Archie Fan Photo,**
1940s. - **$10 $25 $50**

DUF-7

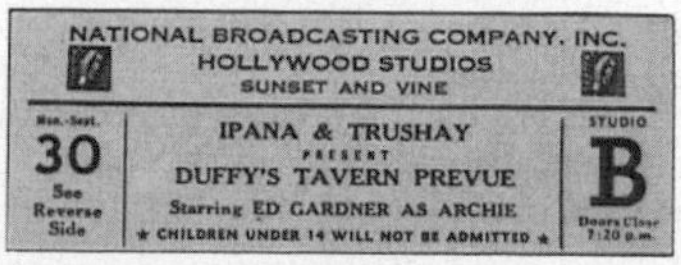
NATIONAL BROADCASTING COMPANY, INC.
HOLLYWOOD STUDIOS
SUNSET AND VINE
30
See Reverse Side
IPANA & TRUSHAY
PRESENT
DUFFY'S TAVERN PREVUE
Starring ED GARDNER AS ARCHIE
★ CHILDREN UNDER 14 WILL NOT BE ADMITTED ★
STUDIO
B

DUF-8

❑ **DUF-7. "Meet 'Archie' Thursday Night" Cello. Button,**
1940s. Promotion for Duffy's Tavern radio show. - **$15 $30 $60**

❑ **DUF-8. "Duffy's Tavern Preview" Radio Show Ticket,**
1940s. 1-1/2x4" ticket for NBC Hollywood Studios. - **$20 $40 $80**

Dukes of Hazzard

Created by Gy Waldron, the original TV series ran seven seasons on CBS between January 26, 1979 and February 8, 1985. The basic plot had the Duke family in fictional Hazzard County, Georgia fighting the corrupt sheriff and county commissioner. The cast included the Duke family cousins: John Schneider as Bo, Tom Wopat as Luke and Catherine Bach as Daisy. Denver Pyle was Uncle Jesse, Sorrell Booke was Boss Hogg and James Best was Sheriff Coltrane. A 1969 Dodge Charger, The General Lee, was used by the Dukes for racing and boot legging. Waylon Jennings wrote and performed the *Good Ol' Boys* theme song and also narrated the show. The cast re-united for reunion movies in 1997 and 2000.

Warner Bros. premiered *The Dukes Of Hazzard* feature film July 27, 2005 at Camp Pendelton, California. The cast included Johnny Knoxville as Luke, Sean William Scott as Bo, and Jessica Simpson as Daisy. Burt Reynolds played Boss Hogg and Willie Nelson was Uncle Jesse. ABC introduced the *Dukes Of Hazzard The Beginning* TV movie in 2007. The cast included Jonathan Bennett, Randy Wayne, April Scott and Willie Nelson.

Catherine Bach of the original series is credited with bringing short shorts back in fashion. Her "Daisy Dukes" are in the Smithsonian.

DKH-1

❑ **DKH-1. "Dukes Of Hazzard Annual" English Hardcover,**
1979. Warner Bros. 7.75x11.25" published by Grandreams Ltd. has 64 pages with comic book-style. - **$8 $15 $30**

DKH-2

❑ **DKH-2. "General" 1969 Dodge Charger Battery Car,**
1970s. Box holds 10" long tin litho car modeled after the General Lee. Car works with bump-and-go action. - **$25 $50 $115**

DKH-3

❑ **DKH-3. "The Dukes Of Hazzard Radio-Controlled General Lee Car",**
1980. Warner Bros. 7x12x7" tall box contains battery operated set by Pro Cision. Includes 8" hard plastic car with orange plastic remote control unit. - **$25 $50 $85**

DKH-4

❑ **DKH-4. "The Dukes Of Hazzard" Metal Lunchbox With Thermos,**
1980. Aladdin Industries Inc. Embossed metal box with plastic thermos. Box - **$15 $35 $85**
Bottle - **$5 $15 $30**

DKH-5

❑ **DKH-5. "The Dukes Of Hazzard General Lee Car" By Ertl,**
1981. Warner Bros. Inc. 5x10x5" tall box contains 1/25-scale, 8" long die-cast metal and plastic car designed like the General Lee. - **$25 $50 $85**

DKH-6

❑ **DKH-6. "The Dukes Of Hazzard Daisy Jeep" By Ertl,**
1981. Warner Bros. Inc. 5x8.5x5" tall box holds die-cast metal and plastic replica of vehicle from show in 1/25 scale. - **$25 $50 $85**

DKH-7

❑ **DKH-7. "The Dukes Of Hazzard/Daisy's Jeep" Mego Set,**
1981. Warner Bros. 4.25x7.5x4.25" deep box contains 3.75" tall action figure of Daisy Duke and 6.5" plastic replica of her jeep. - **$12 $25 $50**

DKH-8

❑ **DKH-8. "General Lee" 1:18 Scale Car,**
2001. From the show "The Dukes of Hazzard." Die cast metal 1969 Charger in box. - **$40**

Dumbo

See Ted Hake's *Official® Price Guide to Disney Collectibles*, Second Edition, formatted identically to this book but in full color evaluating over 9,000 Disney company and character collectibles from 1924 through 2006.

The Eagle

The first appearance of this patriotic hero was in issue #1 of *Science Comics* in February 1940. He then showed up in issue #8 of *Weird Comics*; in four issues of his own book, *The Eagle*, in 1941-1942; and in a second *Eagle* series of two issues in early 1945. The 1941-1942 membership club for fans was known as American Eagle Defenders.

EAG-1

❑ **EAG-1. Member's Cello. Button,**
1942. Scarce. - **$200 $600 $1200**

Ed Wynn

Ed Wynn (1886-1966) came to radio after a long career as a headliner in vaudeville and on Broadway. He was reluctant to try radio but he successfully made the transition from the visual comedy of his stage character, *The Perfect Fool*, to his radio persona, *The Fire Chief*, sponsored by Texaco "Fire Chief" gasoline, on NBC from 1932 to 1935. A feature film, *The Chief* was released in 1933. Wynn had several other radio shows in the 1930s and a brief run on *Happy Island* in 1944-1945 for Borden's milk, did comedy variety shows on television in 1949-1950 and 1958-1959 and appeared in a number of dramatic roles on television in the 1950s and 1960s.

EDW-1

❑ **EDW-1. Texaco Fire Chief Cardboard Mask,**
c. 1933. - **$60 $125 $250**

EDW-2

EDW-3

❑ **EDW-2. "The Chief" Movie Cello. Button,**
1933. Metro-Goldwyn-Mayer Pictures. -
$35 $75 $150

❑ **EDW-3. Ed Wynn Board Game,**
1934. Game has box with accessories and board. - **$100 $250 $400**

EDW-4

❑ **EDW-4. Fire Chief Ed. Wynn BLB-Style Book,**
1934. Goldsmith. 132 pages. - **$12 $36 $78**

EDW-5

❑ **EDW-5. Wood Jointed Figure,**
c. 1935. Store item. - **$40 $75 $160**

EDW-6

❑ **EDW-6. "The Grab Bag" Movie Promotion,**
1930s. Cloth bag holding 10 paper figures based on movie "The Perfect Fool". -
$60 $115 $200

EDW-7

❑ **EDW-7. Ed Wynn "Fire Chief" Wood Pull Toy,**
1930s. Toy is 3-1/8" long red wood wagon with rolling wheels. Has "Fire Chief" black text on each side plus 2-7/8" tall seated wood figure with fleshtone head wearing red helmet with black star on front and black facial accents, black arms, red hands that move up and down. In Texaco-style red wood. Likely by Fun-E-Flex.
- **$65 $135 $250**

EDW-8

EDW-9

❑ **EDW-8. "All Star Radio Show-Plymouth Radio Broadcast" Folder,**
1930s. Plymouth Motors. - **$15 $25 $45**

❑ **EDW-9. "Ed Wynn Nut Crunch" Candy Box,**
1930s. Store item by Quaker City Chocolate and Confectionary Co. of Philadelphia. 8-3/4x11x2" deep red, white and blue box for countertop display. - **$125 $250 $400**

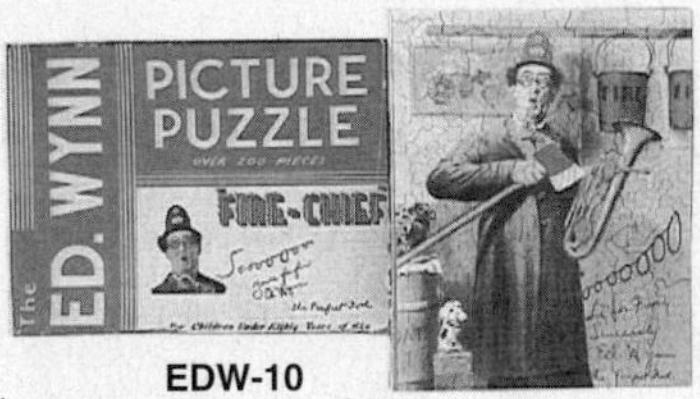

EDW-10

❑ **EDW-10. "Fire-Chief" Boxed Puzzle,**
1930s. Store item by Viking Mfg. Co., Boston. Assembles to 11x14-1/2" and includes facsimile autograph and nickname designation "The Perfect Fool." Boxed - **$25 $50 $100**

Eddie Cantor

Over a span of more than 50 years in show business, Eddie Cantor (1892-1964) went from singing waiter to radio superstar. Cantor juggled, sang, played in blackface in vaudeville and on the stage, made movies, hosted television series and toured Europe, but it was on the radio in the 1930s that the banjo-eyed comic achieved his greatest success. He premiered on the comedy-variety *Chase & Sanborn Hour* on NBC in September 1931 and during the next 20 years in various shows, mainly on NBC, he had a succession of major sponsors: Pebeco toothpaste (1935-1936), Texaco gasoline (1936-1938), Camel cigarettes (1938-1939), Sal Hepatica laxative (1940-1946), Pabst beer (1946-1949) and Philip Morris cigarettes (1951-1952). The manic comic often joked about his wife, Ida, and their five daughters, introduced many young performers and featured such accented characters as the Mad Russian and Parkyakarkas. On television he hosted *The Colgate Comedy Hour* (NBC, 1950-1954) and the *Eddie Cantor Comedy Theatre* (syndicated, 1954-1955).

EDD-1

❑ **EDD-1. "I'd Love to Call You My Sweetheart" Song Sheet,**
1926. - **$12 $25 $45**

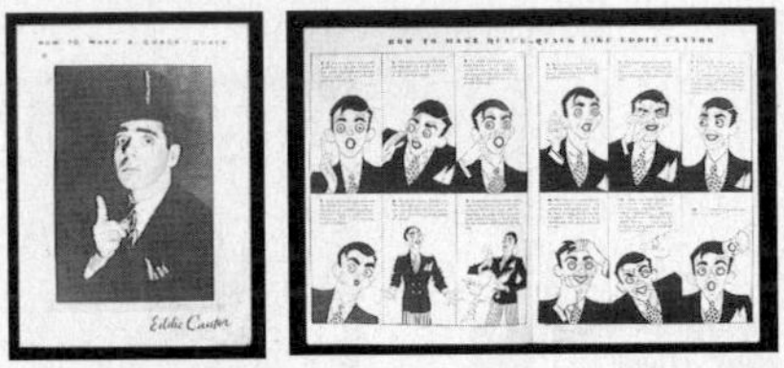

EDD-2

❑ **EDD-2. "How To Make Quack-Quack" Folder,**
1932. Standard Brands Inc. 9-1/4x12-1/4" folded single sheet with cartoon-style centerfold and text on back of "Dr. Cantor Examines Uncle Sam" radio sketch "For Which Chase & Sanborn Have Had The Greatest Number Of Requests." - **$12 $25 $50**

EDD-3

❑ **EDD-3. "Radio Stars And Stations" Booklet,**
1933. RCA Radiotron Co. Inc. 6x8" with 36 pages picturing many stars of the era. - **$18 $30 $60**

EDD-4

❑ **EDD-4. "Eddie Cantor's Picture Book",**
1933. Chase & Sanborn Coffee. - **$18 $30 $60**

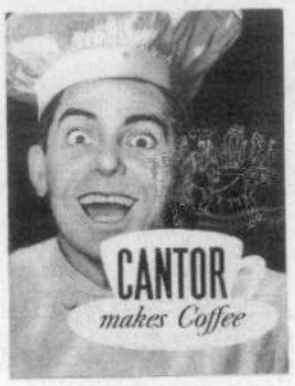

EDD-5

EDD-6

❑ **EDD-5. Folder,**
1934. Chase and Sanborn radio premium. Includes 8 page foldout- **$10 $25 $50**

❑ **EDD-6. Ink Blotter,**
1934. Various advertisers. - **$8 $18 $35**

EDD-7

EDD-8

❑ **EDD-7. Calendar Postcard,**
1934. Various advertisers. - **$8 $18 $35**

❑ **EDD-8. "Eddie Cantor Magic Club" Enameled Brass Club Badge,**
1935. Pebeco toothpaste. - **$15 $40 $90**

EDD-9

EDD-10

❑ **EDD-9. Magic Club Book And Trick,**
1935. Pebeco Milk of Magnesia. Trick includes 12 cards and two instruction sheets.
Book - **$20 $40 $80**
Trick Packet - **$10 $25 $50**

❑ **EDD-10. Pebeco Toothpaste 12x19" Paper Store Sign,**
1936. - **$60 $125 $200**

EDD-11

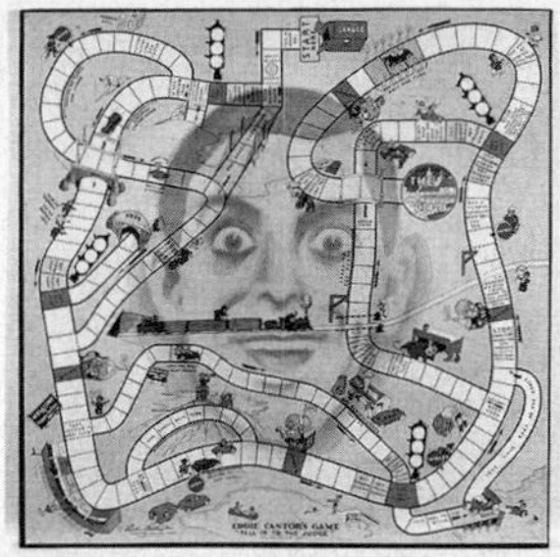

(Game board)

❑ EDD-11. "Tell It To the Judge" Game,
c. 1936. Came with board, instructions and various cards and pieces.
Complete - **$60 $115 $225**
Board only (scarce) **- $35 $70 $135**

EDD-12

EDD-13

❑ EDD-12. Jokes Booklet,
1936. Pebeco Toothpaste. - **$15 $40 $80**

❑ EDD-13. Photo,
1937. Philadelphia Record newspaper premium. - **$5 $12 $20**

EDD-14

❑ EDD-14. Rubber Figure With Tag And Wooden Base,
c. 1939. 7" tall molded and painted soft rubber figure positioned on walnut base. Figure has cardboard string tag with photo and facsmile signature plus reverse has company information for apparent maker A. Ponnock, Philadelphia.
Complete With Tag - **$450 $900 $1350**

EDD-15

❑ EDD-15. "Eddie Cantor" Appearance Button,
1939. Button is 4" in diameter with portrait photo and text "Welcome Back To Brooklyn Eddie Cantor In Person/Loew's Metropolitan West Thurs. Oct. 19." Marked on rim curl "Philadelphia Badge Company." - **$40 $80 $150**

EDD-16

EDD-17

❑ EDD-16. Magic Trick With Bag,
1930s. Pebeco Toothpaste Club premium. Includes 13 cardboard pieces. - **$30 $60 $110**

❑ EDD-17. "Tune In" Magazine With Cover Article,
1944. Monthly issue for August of "National Radio Magazine" including three-page article written by him and accompanied by photos. - **$8 $15 $25**

EDD-18

❑ EDD-18. Calendar Card,
1946. Pabst Blue Ribbon Beer. - **$12 $22 $35**

EDD-19

❑ EDD-19. "Eddie Cantor" Record Album,
1947. Set of 4 78rpm records. - **$25 $45 $90**

EDD-20

❑ EDD-20. "Eddie Cantor For President" Litho. Button,
1948. - **$12 $25 $50**

EDD-21

❑ EDD-21. "Eddie Cantor/Welch's Autographed Photo,
1940s. 8x10" glossy black and white printed "Here's Wishing You Health, Welch's And Happiness-Eddie Cantor." Reverse has inked autograph. Autographed - **$25 $50 $100**
Without Autograph - **$10 $20 $30**

EDD-22

❑ EDD-22. "The Eddie Cantor Comedy Theater" Clip,
1955. Salesman's sample. 2x3" plastic. - **$12 $25 $40**

Ellery Queen

Sophisticated detective and mystery writer Ellery Queen was the hero of a number of popular novels written by Frederic Dannay (1905-1982) and Manfred B. Lee (1905-1971) beginning in 1929. He had several incarnations on radio, beginning with Hugh Marlowe in *The Adventures of Ellery Queen* on CBS in 1939 and ending on ABC in 1948. Sponsors included Gulf Oil, Bromo-Seltzer and Anacin. The *Ellery Queen Mystery Magazine* began in

1941 and continues to this day. Live-action TV series appeared on DuMont and ABC from 1950 to 1952 and on NBC 1958-1959 and 1975-1976. Queen's first comic book appearance was in *Crackajack Funnies* #23 in May 1940 and he had his own book in the late 1940s and early 1950s. A number of second-feature Ellery Queen films were released between 1935 and 1952, most starring Ralph Bellamy or William Gargan as the gentleman detective. A TV series lasted only one season (1975-1976) with Jim Hutton in the lead role and David Wayne as Inspector Richard Queen.

ELL-1

ELL-2

❑ ELL-1. "Ellery Queen Club Member" Cello. Button,
c. 1939. - **$55 $150 $275**

❑ ELL-2. "The Adventure Of The Last Man Club" BLB,
1940. Store item. Whitman #1406. -
$14 $42 $95

ELL-3

ELL-4

❑ ELL-3. "Ellery Queen And The Murder Ring" Movie Poster,
1941. One-sheet is 27x41" for original release of Columbia film starring Ralph Belamy as Queen. Art includes six ace of spade cards at center with images of six suspects and below this are a pair of hands holding a pill bottle that contains a skull. Top shows Queen and Nikki Porter with text "Watch Radio And Fiction's Ace Amateur Sleuth Run Rings Around A Murder Ring." -
$100 $200 $300

❑ ELL-4. "Adventure Of The Murdered Millionaire" Better Little Book,
1942. Store item by Whitman #1472. - **$14 $42 $95**

Elmer Fudd

Loosely based on *Looney Tunes And Merrie Melodies* Warner Bros. cartoon director Tex Avery's Egghead character circa 1937, Elmer's name appeared on a vehicle in Avery's *A Feud There Was* in 1938. He appeared in *Dangerous Dan McFoo* in 1939, voiced by Arthur Bryan who would be the voice of Elmer until 1959. Elmer's first major appearance came while hunting "wabbits" in *Elmer's Candid Camera.* Directed by Chuck Jones, the 1940 cartoon had a wise-cracking rabbit who would evolve into Bugs Bunny; a match made in cartoon heaven.

Elmer's other animated highlights include playing the conductor in Bob Clampett's 1943 *Corny Concerto* and as a hunter in Chuck Jones' 1957 *What's Opera Doc?* which parodied Wagner's *Ring Cycle.* Elmer's last major cartoon was Friz Freleng's *What's My Lion?* in 1961, but he appeared in *Who Framed Roger Rabbit?* in 1988; *Tiny Toon Adventures* in 1990; and *Space Jam,* the 1996 feature combining in live action Michael Jordan and Warner Bros. animated characters.

Elmer appeared in Dell *Looney Tunes And Merrie Melodies* comic books from 1940 on as well as several *Elmer Fudd* titles between 1953 and 1962. "Wascawwy Wabbit....Heh, Heh, Heh, Heh."

ELM-1

❑ ELM-1. "Elmer" Fudd Figural Metal Planter,
c. 1947. W.B.C. 3x5.75x5-3/8" tall with "Elmer" in low relief text on front. - **$50 $100 $175**

ELM-2

❑ ELM-2. Elmer Fudd Figural Metal Bank,
c. 1947. W.B.C. 4.75" tall figure with "Elmer" name on front. - **$60 $120 $200**

ELM-3

❑ ELM-3. Elmer Fudd Glazed Ceramic Shaw Figure Seated,
1940s. 3-7/8" tall figure with "Elmer-Shaw & Co. Los Angeles" sticker on underside. - **$12 $25 $50**

ELM-4

❑ ELM-4. Elmer Fudd Glazed Ceramic Figural Vase By Shaw,
1940s. 3.75" diameter by 6.25" tall. - **$15 $30 $60**

ELM-5

❑ **ELM-5. "Elmer Fudd" Rubber Toy,**
1950s. Warner Bros. 2" tall rubber figure on 2" diameter plastic base. Metal crank under base turns figure to make Elmer tip his hat. - **$40 $80 $150**

ELM-6

❑ **ELM-6. Elmer Fudd Ceramic Figure,**
1975. Warner Bros. 4" tall. - **$5 $10 $20**

ELM-7

❑ **ELM-7. Cheney Hunting Accident Satirical Button By Brian Campbell,**
2006. 2.25" limited edition button with artist's name and designation "36/50" on front. Mint As Issued - **$85**

Elsie the Cow

In the late 1930s the Borden Company ran a series of advertisements for its milk featuring a herd of cartoon cows. One, dubbed Elsie, became a star at the 1939 New York World's Fair when visitors to the Borden exhibit insisted on knowing which of the cows there was Elsie. Elsie married Elmer, and their daughter Beulah was at the 1940 NYWF. Borden put Elsie to work during World War II touring the country to sell war bonds and promote its milk. Contests to name Elsie's calf Beauregard in 1947 and twins Larabee and Lobelia in 1957 brought overwhelming public responses. Elsie is still appearing in Borden advertising and in bovine appearances around the country. Merchandising has included giveaway comic books, fun activity books and a wide variety of glass and ceramic items related to food and drink such as bowls, glasses and mugs.

ELS-1

ELS-2

❑ **ELS-1. Brass 2-1/4" Badge,**
c. 1939. Likely issued during 1939 New York World's Fair. - **$35 $75 $135**

❑ **ELS-2. Mechanical Card,**
1940. 2x3-1/2" with action of Elsie opening and closing her eyes while her lower jaw moves back and forth. Reverse notes her appearance in RKO movie title "Little Men." - **$30 $60 $115**

ELS-3

❑ **ELS-3. Elsie Dexterity Game,**
1941. Borden. 3-1/2" tall. - **$35 $65 $135**

ELS-4

❑ **ELS-4. Wood Pull Toy,**
1944. Store item by Wood Commodities Corp.
Boxed - **$125 $250 $500**
Loose - **$85 $150 $300**

ELS-5

ELS-6

❑ **ELS-5. Store Display Poster,**
1945. 30x45". - **$50 $100 $200**

❑ **ELS-6. Elsie And Baby China Lamp,**
c. 1947. Store item. - **$85 $175 $300**

ELS-7

❑ **ELS-7. "Borden's Cheese Comic Picture Book,"**
1940s. Sixteen-page booklet of single page Elsie cartoons related to use of various Borden cheese products. - **$40 $85 $175**

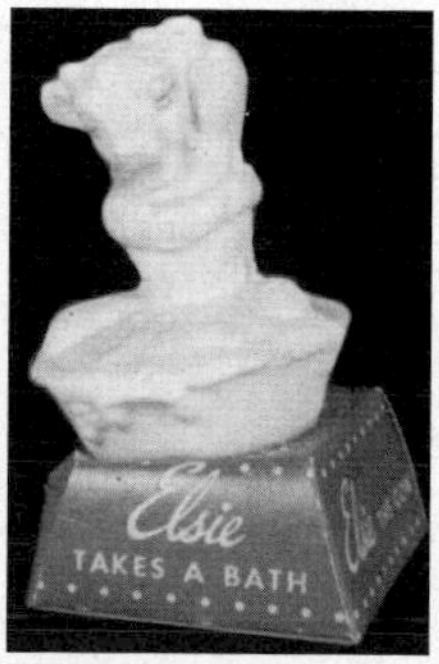

ELS-8

❑ **ELS-8. "Elsie Takes A Bath" Soap Figure,**
1940s. Store item by Lightfoot. 3" tall. - **$40 $80 $135**

ELS-9

❑ **ELS-9. Elsie Ceramic Mug,**
1940s. Scarce variation with full figure. -
$30 $60 $100

ELS-10 ELS-11

❑ **ELS-10. "Elsie" Ceramic Mug,**
1940s. - **$25 $50 $85**

❑ **ELS-11. "Beulah" Ceramic Mug,**
1940s. - **$25 $50 $85**

ELS-12

❑ **ELS-12. "Beauregard" Ceramic Mug,**
1940s. - **$25 $50 $85**

(BEULAH)

(BEAUREGARD)

(ELMER)

(ELSIE)

ELS-13

❑ **ELS-13. Elsie Large Ceramic Bowl,**
1940s. Features images of Elsie, Elmer, Beulah, and Beauregard. - **$100 $225 $450**

ELS-14

ELS-15

❑ **ELS-14. "Borden's" Glass Tumbler,**
1940s. - **$20 $35 $60**

❑ **ELS-15. Elsie Compo Store Display Figure,**
1940s. 10" tall. - **$200 $400 $800**

ELS-16

❑ **ELS-16. "Elmer" Boxed China Mug,**
1950. Box Only - **$35 $60 $115**
Mug Only - **$25 $50 $85**

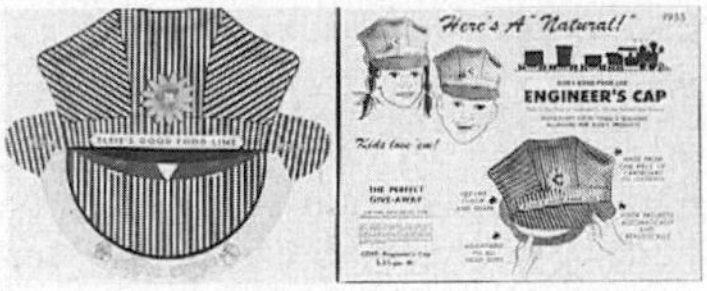

ELS-17

❑ **ELS-17. "Elsie's Good Food Line" Railroad Engineer Punch-Out Hat,**
1955. Blue and white 10x11-1/2" unpunched. Gordon Gold archives.
Hat Unpunched - **$35 $60 $120**
Order Sheet - **$12 $25 $35**

ELS-18

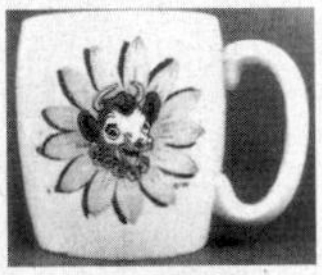

ELS-19

❑ **ELS-18. Activity Booklet,**
1957. 100th birthday fun book, 20 pages. -
$25 $55 $125

❑ **ELS-19. Elsie Ceramic Mug,**
1950s. - **$20 $35 $70**

ELS-20

❑ **ELS-20. Elsie Carded Whistle and Litho. Tab,**
1950s. Borden Co. 4-1/2" card with advertising items. - **$30 $60 $100**

ELS-21

❑ **ELS-21. Figural Squeak Toy,**
c. 1950. Toy is 5" tall and made of pliable rubber. Back of head reads "Copyright The Borden Co." - **$65 $125 $250**

ELS-22

❑ **ELS-22. Figural Cast Metal Bank,**
1950s. Master Caster Mfg. Co. 7" tall.
- **$100 $175 $350**

ELS-23

❑ **ELS-23. Large Aluminum Litho. Store Sign,**
1950s. 24" diameter. - **$125 $250 $500**

ELS-24

ELS-25

❑ **ELS-24. Elsie Vinyl and Cloth Doll,**
1950s. 22" tall. - **$75 $125 $250**

❑ **ELS-25. Beauregard Baby Rattle,**
1950s. Irwin. 6-1/2" tall. - **$65 $110 $165**

ELS-26

ELS-27

❑ **ELS-26. Fabric Uniform Patch,**
1950s. Large 7" diameter. - **$10 $30 $60**

❑ **ELS-27. Elsie And Elmer Serving Set,**
1950s. Hard plastic by F&F Mold Co.
Each - **$25 $60 $125**

ELS-28

ELS-29

❑ **ELS-28. Elsie Diecut Sign,**
1950s. - **$100 $225 $450**

❑ **ELS-29. Plush Doll With Rubber Head,**
1950s. 15" tall. - **$40 $85 $175**

ELS-30

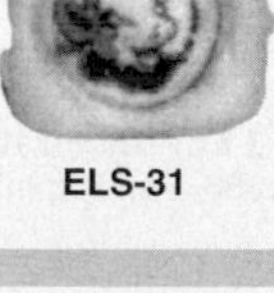

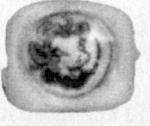

ELS-31

❑ **ELS-30. "Elsie's Fun Book",**
1950s. - **$14 $42 $150**

❑ **ELS-31. Plastic Ring,**
1950s. - **$8 $12 $30**

ELS-32

❑ **ELS-32. "A Trip Through Space" Booklet,**
1950s. - **$14 $42 $150**

ELS-33

❑ **ELS-33. Ceramic Cookie Jar,**
1950s. - **$125 $250 $475**

ELS-34

❑ **ELS-34. Elsie Milk Cap,**
1950s. Unused milk cap featuring Elsie the Cow. - **$20**

ELS-35

❑ **ELS-35. Ice Cream Stick in Wrapper,**
1950s. Featuring Elsie the Cow. - **$10**

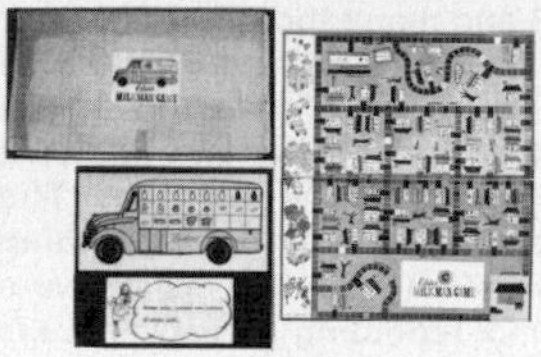

ELS-36

ELS-37

❑ **ELS-36. "Elsie's Milkman Game",**
1963. - **$35 $65 $125**

❑ **ELS-37. "Elsie The Borden Cow" Litho. Button,**
1960s. - **$8 $15 $30**

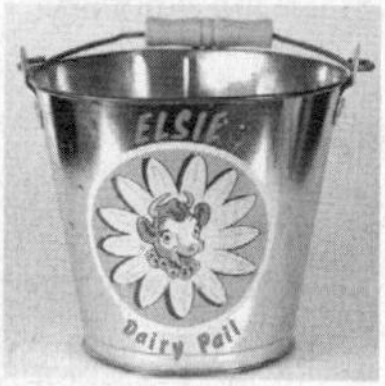

ELS-38

❑ **ELS-38. Elsie Tin Pail,**
1960s. Ohio Art, 5-1/2" tall. - **$50 $75 $150**

ELS-39

❑ **ELS-39. Figural Night Light,**
1960s. 8" tall vinyl head glows when illuminated. - **$135 $275 $500**

Elvis Presley

Elvis Presley (1935-1977) was born in a two-room house in Tupelo, Mississippi. He died in his Memphis, Tennessee mansion with an estate valued at more than $30 million. In his lifetime--and since his death--the rock 'n' roll legend spawned a merchandising cornucopia that has yet to subside. Elvis' recording career began with the release of "That's All Right Mama/Blue Moon Of Kentucky" on the Sun label in July 1954. Scotty Moore played lead guitar on many early records and was also Elvis' first manager; Bill Black played bass. The trio was billed as "Elvis Presley and the Blue Moon Boys" in early appearances. The national mania exploded in 1956 when Presley appeared on *The Ed Sullivan Show* and items from that period generate great collector interest. Elvis was

drafted in 1958 and many thought his career was over but he came home in 1960 to a prime time TV special with Frank Sinatra. He starred in 33 successful films, and has sold over one billion records worldwide. The 1993 Elvis postage stamp is the top-selling commemorative of all time; 500 million were printed. A re-mix recording of *A Little Less Conversation* released in 2002 stayed at #1 in England for three weeks. The King lives on: in addition to frequent Elvis sightings at shopping malls and county fairs, Elvis Presley Enterprises continues to license countless memorial and commemorative items. *TV Guide*, in its January 1-7 2000 issue, named Elvis "The Entertainer of the Century."...thank you very much. Elvis has obviously not left the building!

ELV-1

ELV-2

❑ **ELV-1. Fan Photo,**
c. 1955. 5x7" glossy bw with facsimile signature, a personal giveaway by him at his home on Audubon Street in Memphis in addition to other forms of distribution. - **$50 $125 $250**

❑ **ELV-2. "Elvis Presley Complimentary Fan Club Membership Card",**
1956. Fan club headquarters in Madison, Tenn. Includes facsimile Elvis signature as "Honorary President." - **$35 $70 $125**

ELV-3

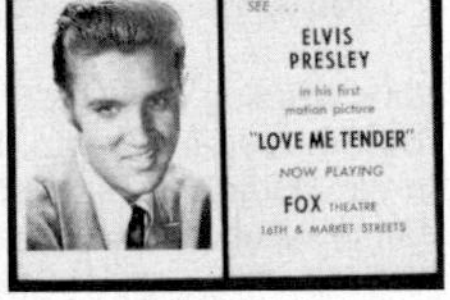

ELV-4

❑ **ELV-3. Elvis Gum Card Set,**
1956. Bubbles Inc./Elvis Presley Enterprises. Set of 66. Each - **$4 $8 $15**

❑ **ELV-4. "Elvis Presley/Love Me Tender" Movie Theater Giveaway Wallet Card,**
1956. Various theaters. 2-1/8x3-1/4". - **$40 $80 $150**

ELV-5

ELV-6

❑ **ELV-5. "R.C.A. Records" National Fan Club Button,**
1956. Black on pink.
Litho. Variety - **$50 $75 $150**
Scarcer Cello. Variety - **$75 $150 $250**

❑ **ELV-6. Color Photo 3" Cello. Button,**
1956. Vendor Item. - **$35 $70 $135**

ELV-7

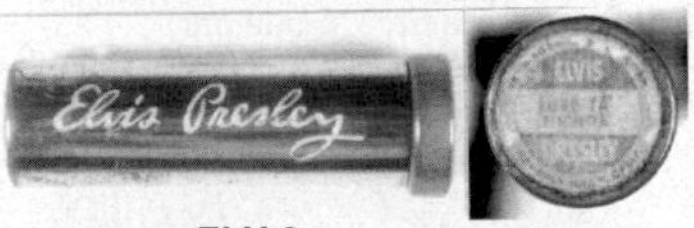

ELV-8

❑ **ELV-7. "TV Guide", September 8,**
1956. Issue has first part of three-part article. - **$75 $150 $300**

❑ **ELV-8. Brass Lipstick Tube,**
1956. Store item by Teen-Ager Lipstick Corp. Available in six colors. - **$75 $185 $400**

ELV-9

❑ **ELV-9. Five Buttons From Scarce Set,**
1956. Each is 7/8" litho with "1956 E.P.E." on curl. Issued in several different color combinations by Green Duck Co.
Each With Elvis Picture - **$20 $50 $80**
Each With Text Only - **$15 $30 $50**

ELV-10

ELV-11

❑ **ELV-10. Jeans Tag,**
1956. Elvis Presley Enterprises store item. - **$40 $90 $175**

❑ **ELV-11. Song Title T-Shirt,**
1956. Store item. Elvis Presley Enterprises copyright. -**$95 $250 $425**

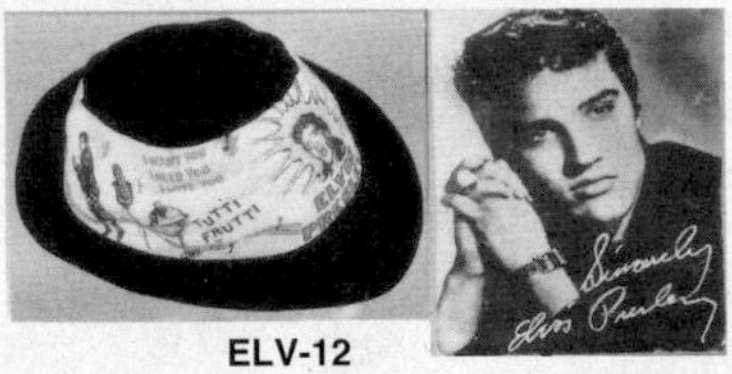

ELV-12

❑ **ELV-12. Fabric Hat,**
1956. Store item by Magnet Hat & Cap Corp.
With Tag - **$60 $125 $250**
No Tag - **$40 $80 $150**

ELV-13

ELV-14

❑ **ELV-13. Song Titles Handkerchief,**
1956. Elvis Presley Enterprises. Includes song titles Hound Dog, Mystery Train, Blue Moon, Tutti Frutti. 13x13-1/2". - **$115 $275 $550**

❑ **ELV-14. Glass Tumbler,**
1956. Store item. Copyright Elvis Presley Enterprises. - **$65 $125 $250**

ELV-15

ELV-16

❑ **ELV-15. Metal Charm Bracelet,**
1956. Store item. Elvis Presley Enterprises copyright. - **$40 $85 $165**

❑ **ELV-16. Plastic Picture Frame Charm,**
1956. Vending machine item. - **$10 $25 $50**

ELV-17

ELV-18

❑ **ELV-17. "Elvis Presley For President" Litho. Tin Tab,**
1956. - **$30 $50 $85**

❑ **ELV-18. "Love Me Tender" Litho. Button,**
1956. Elvis Presley Enterprises. From set of 10 with pictures, record titles or slogans.
Each - **$12 $25 $40**

ELV-19

❑ **ELV-19. Gold Record Litho. Button,**
1956. Known with seven different record titles.
Each - **$20 $35 $65**

ELV-20

❑ **ELV-20. "Love Me Tender" Paper Photo,**
1956. Theater hand-out. - **$15 $30 $60**

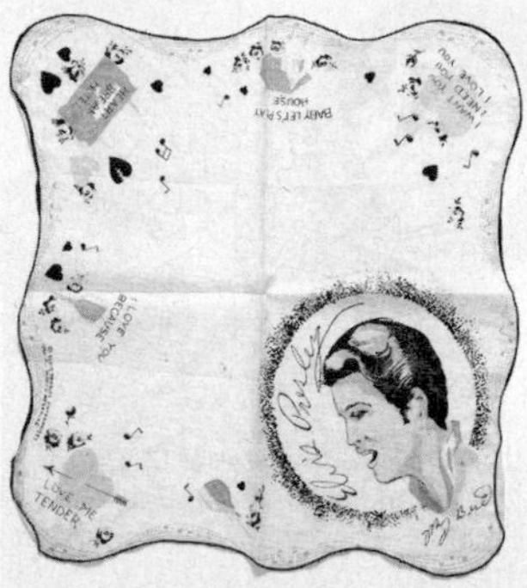

ELV-21

❑ **ELV-21. "Elvis Presley" Handkerchief,**
1956. Elvis Presley Enterprises. 12x13" cotton, one of three different produced. -
$115 $275 $550

ELV-22

❑ **ELV-22. "I Like/Hate Elvis" Buttons,**
1956. Each is 3-1/2" diameter, similar design also made as 1.75" size. Large - **$20 $40 $80**
Small - **$15 $30 $60**

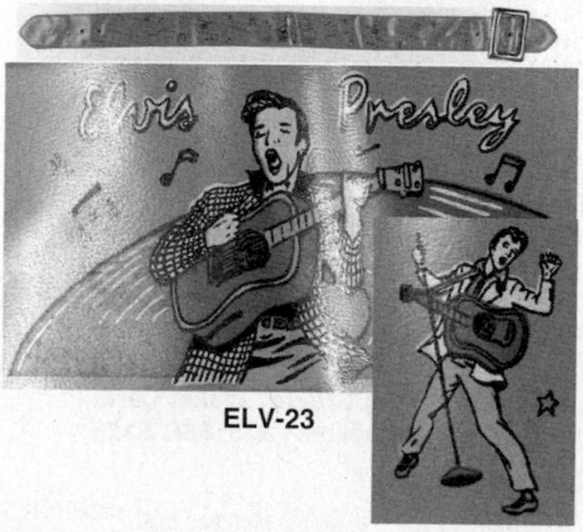

ELV-23

❑ **ELV-23. "Elvis Presley" Belt,**
1956. Vinyl belt 2" wide by 31" long with gold-tone metal buckle. Belt pictorial design is three different images of Elvis, musical notes, four different song titles. Copyright by Elvis Presley Enterprises. - **$125 $250 $500**

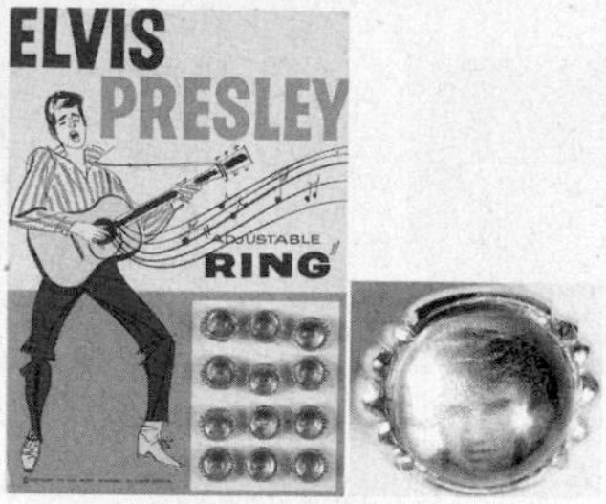

ELV-24

❑ **ELV-24. "Adjustable Ring" Complete Store Display,**
1956. 7x10" cardboard countertop standee holding complete original quantity of 12 rings copyright Elvis Presley Enterprises. Rings are identical brass luster expansion bands topped by full color photo portrait under acrylic dome. Full Card Near Mint - **$5500**
Each Ring - **$100 $250 $400**

ELV-25

❑ **ELV-25. "Elvis Presley" Two-Ring Zippered Binder,**
1956. Penn State Inc., Elvis Presley Enterprises. 11x14x1.25" deep vinyl-covered cardboard. Binder came in color variations and this is the blue version. - **$250 $500 $800**

ELV-26

❑ **ELV-26. "Elvis Presley" Canadian Gum Card Wrapper,**
1956. Elvis Presley Enterprises Inc. 5.5x6". Left margin is marked "In Canada Made And Distributed By O-Pee-Chee/For Bubbles Inc."
- **$75 $165 $300**

ELV-27

❏ **ELV-27. "Elvis Presley" Framed Pictures,**
1956. Plastic frame is 7x9x.5" deep with 4.5x6.5" opening around glossy photo.
Each - **$115 $235 $400**

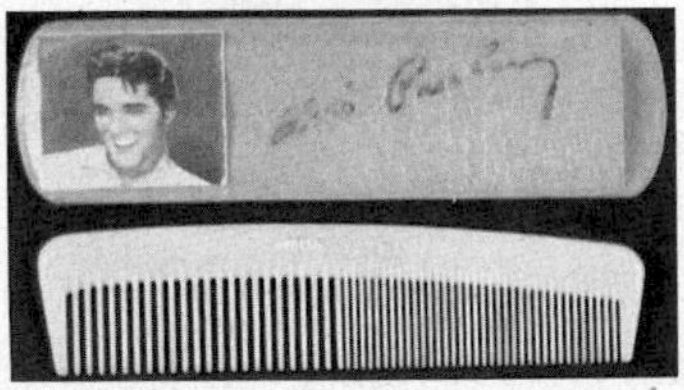

ELV-28

❏ **ELV-28. "Elvis Presley" Comb And Case,**
c. 1956. Store item. 5-1/2" long plastic case has color photo of Elvis and facsimile signature. Case holds a generic plastic "Dupont" comb. -
$100 $200 $400

ELV-29

❏ **ELV-29. "Elvis Presley Photo Folio",**
1957. Elvis Presley Enterprises. From concert tour. - **$30 $65 $135**

ELV-30

ELV-31

❏ **ELV-30. Fabric And Paper 6" Badge,**
c. 1957. Pleated fabric border around paper disk portrait, possibly designed for movie usher use.-
$45 $100 $200

❏ **ELV-31. RCA Promotional Photo,**
1958. 8x10" glossy black and white. -
$40 $75 $150

ELV-32

❏ **ELV-32. Christmas Card,**
1958. Red, green and white 5-1/2x8-1/2" including inset photo of Colonel Parker as Santa. -
$25 $50 $85

ELV-33

ELV-34

❏ **ELV-33. Elvis In Army Uniform 4" Cello. Button,**
c. 1958. No markings other than "U.S. Army" patch pictured above left pocket and part of "Presley" name patch visible above right pocket.
Rare. - **$100 $300 $600**

❏ **ELV-34. "King Creole" Wallet Card,**
1958. Movie promotion. - **$35 $65 $125**

ELV-35

❏ **ELV-35. Christmas Postcard,**
1959. - **$25 $45 $90**

ELV-36

❏ **ELV-36. "Elvis Presley" Record Player,**
1950s. RCA Victor. 12x12x7" tall wood case with thin paper covering. Elvis identification is facsimile signature on top front edge. Issued as manual Model 7-EP-45, as well as automatic Model 7-EP-2, which has 4 speeds.
Manual - **$300 $600 $1200**
Automatic - **$275 $500 $1000**

ELV-37

❏ **ELV-37. "Welcome Back Elvis" Button,**
1960. Vendor button by Emress Specialty Co. 3-1/2" issued for Elvis' return from the Army.
- $50 $100 $200

ELV-38

❏ **ELV-38. "G.I. Blues" Paper Army Hat,**
1960. Advertises movie and record album. -
$35 $75 $150

ELV-39

❏ **ELV-39. I.D. Bracelet,**
c. 1960. 5/8" wide chromed metal expansion band centered by 1.75" long hinged cover opening to inner black and white photo of Elvis. Hong Kong but no other markings. -
$40 $80 $160

ELV-40

❑ **ELV-40. "Blue Hawaii" Movie Promotion Lei,**
1961. Tissue paper lei with 5" cardboard disk. - **$40 $80 $175**

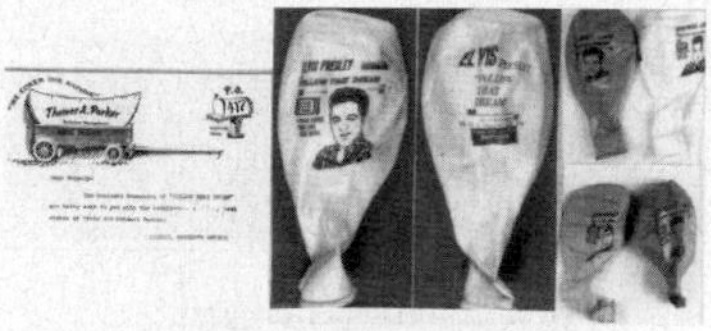

ELV-41

❑ **ELV-41. "Follow That Dream" Movie Balloons With Promotion Letter,**
1962. Rubber balloons with cover form letter from Thomas A. Parker, Elvis' manager.
Letter - **$20 $30 $60**
Each Balloon - **$10 $20 $30**

ELV-42 ELV-43

❑ **ELV-42. Movie Coloring Contest Sheet,**
1962. Paramount Pictures for local stores. Promotion for "Girls! Girls! Girls!" movie. - **$25 $50 $100**

❑ **ELV-43. Girls! Girls! Girls! Album Insert,**
1963. - **$20 $40 $75**

ELV-44 ELV-45

❑ **ELV-44. Fan Club Booklet,**
1967. - **$20 $40 $75**

❑ **ELV-45. "Elvis' Gold Car On Tour" RCA Postcard,**
1960s. - **$20 $40 $75**

ELV-46

❑ **ELV-46. "Elvis Presley" Embossed Tin Stickpin Badge,**
1960s. English issue from series featuring U.S. popular singers, probable premium from WOW Gum. - **$50 $100 $200**

ELV-47

❑ **ELV-47. Photo Cube Bank,**
1960s. Store item. 3-1/2" cube of hard plastic has removable circular disk panels on the sides and these hold color portraits of Elvis, John Wayne, two females models or actresses. - **$35 $75 $150**

ELV-48 ELV-49

❑ **ELV-48. "Something From Elvis' Wardrobe For You" Fabric Swatch In Envelope,**
1971. RCA Records. 3-1/2x5-1/2" window envelope holds 2x3" piece of fabric, sometimes a solid single color or sometimes with colorful pattern. - **$50 $100 $200**

❑ **ELV-49. Elvis Concert Program,**
1977. Souvenir Folio Concert Edition, Volume 6. Boxcar Enterprises. - **$12 $25 $50**

ELV-50

❑ **ELV-50. Post-Death Elvis Concert Ticket,**
1977. Unused ticket for concert to be held August 17, 1977 at Cumberland County Civic Center, Portland, Maine. Elvis died the previous day. - **$35 $75 $150**

ELV-51 ELV-52

❑ **ELV-51. "Elvis in Gold Suit" Doll in Box,**
1984. Includes guitar and microphone. - **$15 $35 $65**

❑ **ELV-52. "Elvis in Jumpsuit" Doll in Box,**
1984. Includes guitar and microphone. - **$15 $35 $65**

ELV-53

❑ **ELV-53. "Elvis' Lisa Marie" Airplane Pen,**
c. 1990. Plastic ballpoint with liquid in upper barrel around image of Elvis' jet plane that moves when pen is tilted. Other images include him and gates of Graceland. Possible souvenir from Graceland. - **$30 $55 $90**

ELV-54

❑ **ELV-54. "Teen Idol" Doll,**
1993. Hasbro. 11 1/2" doll in box. - **$60**

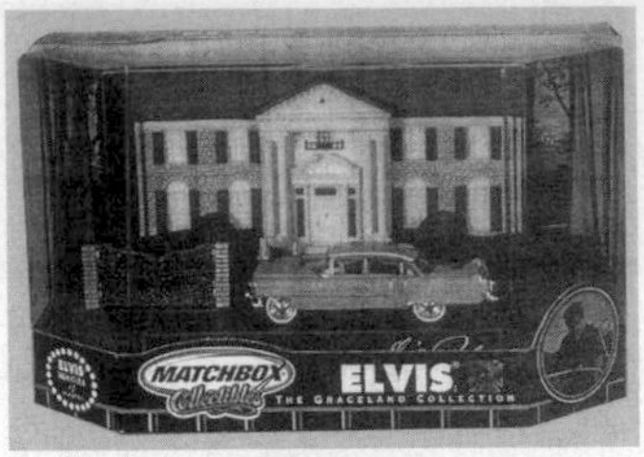

ELV-55

❑ **ELV-55. Matchbox Graceland Collection,**
2001. Vehicle #1 from the set of five. - **$20**

ELV-56

❑ **ELV-56. 25th Anniversary Standee,**
2002. 6' tall. - **$120**

Emergency!

Based on California's first paramedic program which began in 1969, the series aired on NBC from January 22, 1972 – September 3, 1977. There was a two hour pilot movie, 132 one hour shows and four two hour sequel movies. Created by Jack Webb, who also produced and directed, the series was set in Station 51 with a crew of six, including two firefighter/paramedics. The cast included: Robert Fuller as Dr. Kelly Brackett, Bobby Troup as Dr. Joe Early, Julie London as RN Dixie McCall, Randolph Mantooth as firefighter John Gage and Kevin Tighe as firefighter Roy Desoto. The fictional Station 51 is actually fire Station #127 in Carson, California and the fictional Rampart Emergency Hospital is actually Harbor UCLA Medical Center in Torrance, California. The series was titled *Emergency One!* in syndication. Charlton released four comic books based on the show in 1976, with art by John Byrne and Joe Staton. "We're on our way Rampart."

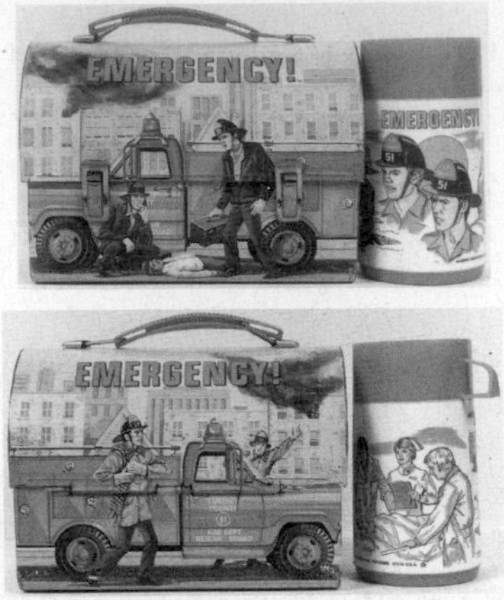

EME-1

❑ **EME-1. "Emergency" Lunch Box With Thermos,**
1973. Aladdin. 7x9x4.5" domed metal lunch box with 6.5" tall plastic thermos.
Box - **$35 $85 $200**
Bottle - **$12 $25 $50**

EME-2

❑ **EME-2. "The Emergency Game",**
1974. Milton Bradley. 9.5x16x1.5" deep box contains color photos from the show, gameboard, small three-dimensional hard plastic fire truck pieces and hospital/emergency cards. - **$10 $20 $40**

EME-3

❑ **EME-3. "Emergency!" Fireman's Helmet,**
1975. Placo Toys. 9.5x11.5x4.5" tall plastic play helmet. Color photo sticker on front pictures DeSoto and Gage. - **$8 $15 $30**

EME-4

❑ **EME-4. "Emergency" Puzzles,**
1975. American Publishing Co. Pair of puzzles in 5.5" tall, 4" diameter canisters. Assembled size is 11x17". Titles are "Hook and Ladder" and "The Pumper." Each - **$5 $10 $20**

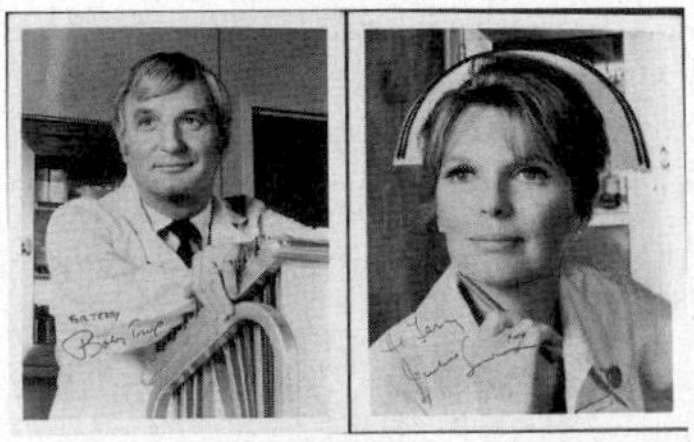

EME-5

❑ **EME-5. Emergency Cast Members Autographed Photos,**
c. 1970s. Pair of 8x10" glossy black and white photos. Bobby Troup as Dr. Joe Early and Julie London as nurse Dixie McCall. Each Near Mint - **$35**

E.T.

Steven Spielberg's *E.T. The Extra-Terrestrial* opened in mid-1982 and was soon being touted as the most popular movie in Hollywood history. Written by Melissa Mathison, the film is an endearing tale of a 10-year-old boy who befriends an alien creature stranded on earth, the film starred Henry Thomas, Dee Wallace, and Drew Barrymore. The phenomenal success of the movie was matched by a merchandising explosion. Universal City Studios licensed some 50 companies to produce E.T. products, including stuffed dolls (Kamar International), vitamins (Squibb), E.T. cereal (General Mills), trading cards and stickers (Topps), a tie-in promotion with Reese's Pieces (Hershey), and a flood of such items as video games (Atari), T-shirts, ice cream, candy, posters, pins, bed sheets, calendars, an animated alarm clock, a "power" tricycle from Coleco, and countless toys. A profusion of knock-offs and unlicensed items also appeared. An official E.T. Fan Club offered an "E.T. Speaks" record along with a photo, poster, newsletter, membership card and certificate. The film's 20th anniversary was marked by a March 2002 re-release in theaters, with new footage and improved special effects added to the classic. To date, the film has grossed over three quarters of a billion dollars.

ETT-1

❑ **ETT-1. "Reese's Pieces" 29x33" Cardboard Display Sign,**
1982. Reese Candy Co. Large diecut image of E.T. eating Reese's Pieces plus text for T-shirt and poster mail premiums. - **$40 $75 $150**

ETT-2

❑ **ETT-2. "E.T. Party Set,"**
1982. Store item by Shilton-Globe Inc. Contains 30 pieces. Near Mint Boxed - **$65**

ETT-3

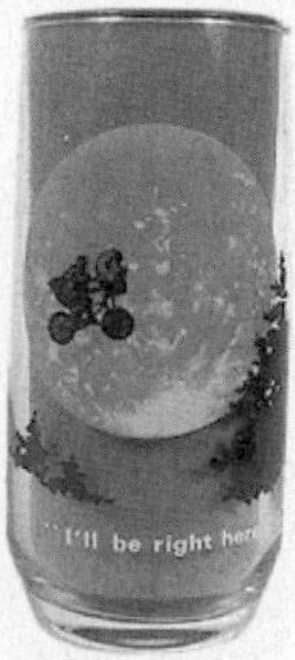

ETT-4

❑ **ETT-3. "E.T. Card Set,"**
1982. Topps Gum. Set of 87, each with different film scene. Near Mint Set - **$35**

❑ **ETT-4. "E.T." 6" Glass Tumbler,**
1982. Imprinted for Army & Air Force Exchange Service. Illustration "I'll be right here" from series of four copyright by Universal City Studios. - **$5 $10 $20**

ETT-5

❑ **ETT-5. "E.T." Phone Book,**
1982. For phoning home. - **$6 $12 $30**

ETT-6

❑ **ETT-6. Lunch Box With Bottle,**
1982. Store item by Aladdin Industries Inc.
Box - **$20 $45 $125**
Bottle - **$8 $15 $30**

ETT-7

ETT-8

❑ **ETT-7. "E.T." Glass Tumblers,**
1982. Pizza Hut. From set of four.
Each - **$3 $6 $15**

❑ **ETT-8. Wristwatch,**
1982. Store item by Nelsonic. Metal case with vinyl straps. - **$25 $60 $135**

ETT-9

❑ **ETT-9. Figural Plastic Ring With Box,**
1982. Store item by Naum Bros. Plastic head on adjustable metal band. Boxed - **$35**
Ring Only - **$10 $15 $22**

ETT-10

❑ **ETT-10. Figural Plastic Clock,**
1982. - **$35 $65 $150**

ETT-11

❑ **ETT-11. "E.T. The Extra-Terrestial Rider,"**
1983. Coleco. Large 15x20x6.5" deep box contains molded plastic child's riding toy meant to be Elliott's bicycle with basket attachment that has figure of E.T. peeking out from under a blanket. Toy "Makes A Clicking Sound When Ridden." Box - **$20 $40 $85**
Toy - **$20 $40 $85**

ETT-12

❑ **ETT-12. "E.T. Talking Phone" Toy Boxed,**
1983. Hasbro. 10" tall plastic toy phone designed to announce six messages "In E.T.'s Own Voice." In colorfully illustrated box.
Near Mint Boxed - **$75**
Loose - **$10 $20 $40**

ETT-13

❑ **ETT-13. "E.T." 20x28" Video Cassette Display Sign,**
1988. Pepsi-Cola sponsorship. Molded thin plastic for MCA Home Video Inc. designed for attachment to a light box or hung in window to enhance 3-D effect. - **$25 $40 $75**

ETT-14

❑ **ETT-14. Video Release Promo Items,**
1988. MCA Home Video. First item is 8-1/2x15x2" deep oversized cardboard display box designed like a video cassette box. Second item is 26x39" glossy poster. Both pieces include Pepsi-Cola ad for a rebate on the video. Each - **$6 $12 $25**

ETT-15

ETT-16

❑ **ETT-15. Walkie Talkies on Card,**
2002. - **$28**

❑ **ETT-16. Pez Pispenser on Card,**
2002. NM - **$6**

ETT-17

❑ **ETT-17. "E.T." Mini-Collectibles Figure Set,**
2003. Collectible figures housed in an "Opening Spaceship Display". - **$18**

Evel Knievel

The famed daredevil motorcycle stunt rider was born Robert Knievel Jr., October 17, 1938 in Butte, Montana. In the 1950s, he worked as a drill operator and then joined the Army and became a pole vaulter. By the early 1960s, he was an insurance salesman and also operated a Honda motorbike dealership. Impressed by the crowds at Joie Chitwood thrill shows featuring cars, he decided to start a motorcycle thrill show. Bob Blair, a Norton cycle dealer, sponsored him and gave him the pseudonym Evel. His first public event was January 3, 1966 at the National Date Festival in Indio, California. He began jumping cars and found that the more he crashed and got injured, the more publicity he received. On December 31, 1967 he jumped the fountains at Caesar's Palace. His fame led to A.J. Foyt making him part of his pit crew at the 1970 Indianapolis 500 race.

In 1971, 100,000 tickets were sold for back-to-back jumps in the Houston Astrodome and later that year Fanfare Films released *The Evel Knievel Story* movie starring George Hamilton. His most famous jump was over the Snake River Canyon in an X-2 Skycycle designed by NASA engineer Robert Truax. The date was September 8, 1974 but the chute deployed early and the jump failed. He played himself in the 1977 Warner Bros. film *Viva Knievel!* and made his last jump in 1996. He passed away on November 30, 2007. Amassing some 35 broken bones and 14 surgeries during his career, it was an interesting life and son Robbie, equally injury prone, carries on the family tradition and claims the title of America's most well-known daredevil.

EVK-1

❑ **EVK-1. Evel Knievel "Snake River Canyon" Set Of Souvenir Badges,**
1974. Set of three badges, each 2.5" issued for jump Sept. 8, 1974. Each - **$5 $12 $25**

EVK-2

EVK-3

❑ **EVK-2. "Evel Knievel" Gum Card Set,** 1974. Topps. Set consists of 60 cards, each 2.5x3.5". Card fronts have photos, backs have illustration plus text. Set - **$50 $100 $175**

❑ **EVK-3. "Evel Knievel" Curtains,** 1974. Each curtain is 22" across top and has length of 34". Made from fabric bolt. Same Or Similar - **$20 $35 $60**

EVK-4

❑ **EVK-4. "Evel Knievel Pennant Flag",** 1974. Fleet Mfg. Co. 8.5x17.5" display card contains 6" vinyl pennant. Near Mint Sealed Display Card - **$40**
Loose Pennant - **$5 $10 $20**

EVK-5

❑ **EVK-5. "Evel Knievel" Large Model Kit,** 1974. Addar. 12.25x18.25x3.75" deep box contains Evel figure, Harley Davidson replica, car body, ramp, flags, base, decals and instructions. Also comes with 8x10" black and white photo with facsimile signature. - **$20 $40 $85**

EVK-6

EVK-7

❑ **EVK-6. "Evel Knievel Stunt & Crash Car",** 1975. Ideal. 9x17x5" deep box contains "Energizer, Stunt And Crash Car, Figure." - **$100 $200 $400**

❑ **EVK-7. "Evel Knievel Racing Set",** 1975. Ideal. 10.5x10.5" blister card contains 7" poseable figure, tools, toolbox, gas can, grease gun, etc. Carded - **$20 $40 $85**

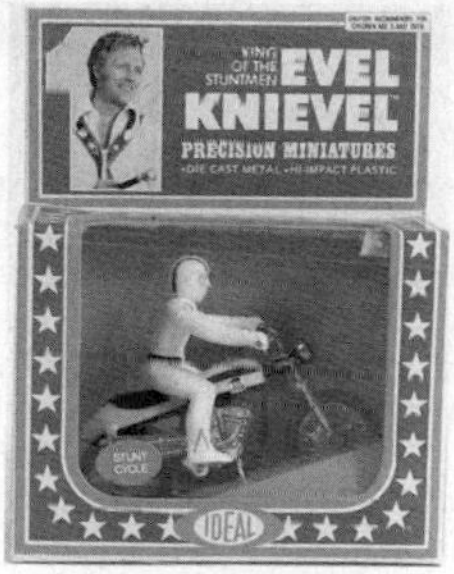

EVK-8

❑ **EVK-8. "Evel Knievel Stunt Cycle",** 1976. Ideal. 2x5x6" tall box contains 3.25" long die cast metal and plastic replica from "Precision Miniatures." Comes with three-dimensional figure of Evel. From series of six. - **$10 $20 $40**

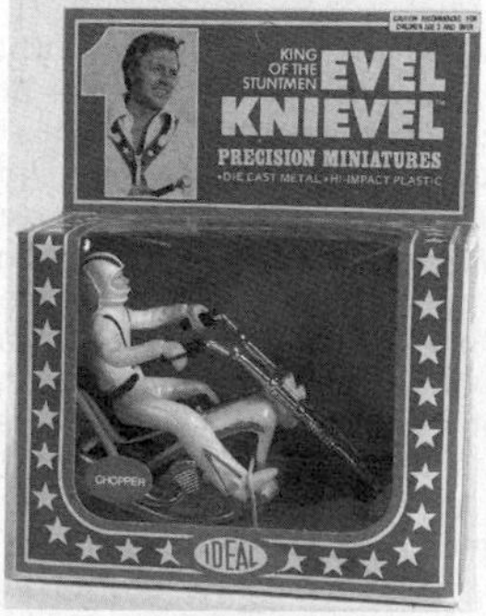

EVK-9

❑ **EVK-9. "Evel Knievel Chopper",** 1976. Ideal. 2x5x6" tall box contains die-cast metal and plastic chopper approximately 3.5" long. Includes three-dimensional figure of Evel. - **$10 $20 $40**

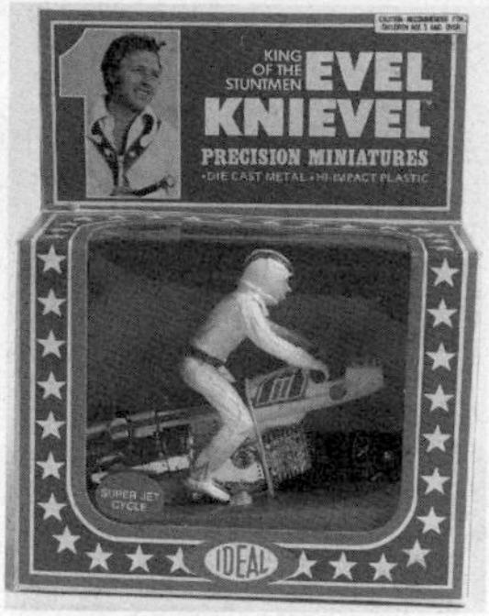

EVK-10

❑ **EVK-10. "Evel Knievel Super Jet Cycle",** 1976. Ideal. 2x5x6" tall displays box contains approximately 3.25" long die cast metal and plastic replica of Super Jet Cycle with large silver exhaust jets. Includes three-dimensional figure of Evel. - **$10 $20 $40**

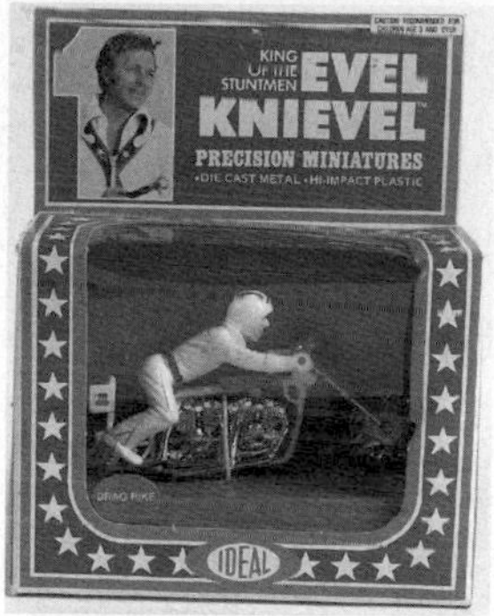

EVK-11

❑ **EVK-11. "Evel Knievel Drag Bike",** 1976. Ideal. 2x5x6" tall display box contains 3.25" long die cast metal and plastic replica of drag bike. Includes three dimensional figure of Evel. - **$10 $20 $40**

EVK-12

❑ **EVK-12. "Evel Knievel Funny Car",** 1976. Ideal. 2.5x5x4.75" tall box contains 4.25" long die cast metal and plastic replica from "Precision Miniatures." From set of six. Includes three-dimensional figure of Evel. - **$10 $20 $40**

EVK-13

❑ **EVK-13. "Evel Knievel Dragster",**
1976. Ideal. 2.5x5x4.75" tall box contains 4.25" long die cast metal and plastic replica from series of six. - **$10 $20 $40**

EVK-14

❑ **EVK-14. "Evel Knievel Funny Car",**
1976. Ideal. 7.5x15.5x8" deep box contains gyro-powered Funny Car and Energizer. - **$75 $150 $260**

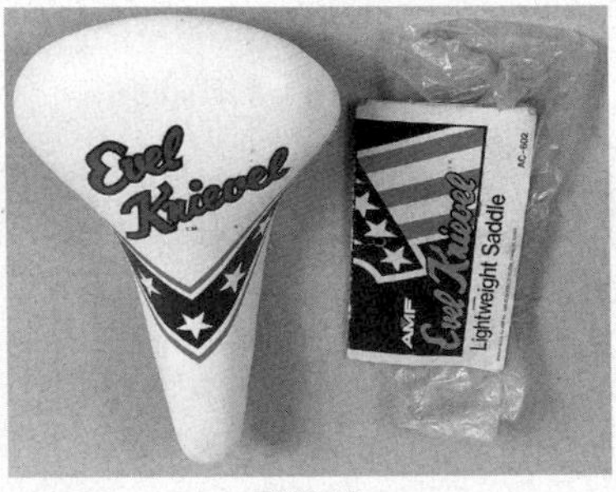

EVK-15

❑ **EVK-15. "Evel Knievel Lightweight Saddle",**
1970s. AMF. 7x11x2.5" deep vinyl bicycle seat with metal undeside and mounting bracket. Original display bag with two-sided header card.
Bag/Card - **$5 $15 $30**
Seat - **$10 $20 $45**

EVK-16

❑ **EVK-16. "Evel Knievel" X-2 Replica,**
1998. Johnny Lightning replica of the X-2 rocket with bonus snapshot picture. On card - **$20**

Fawcett Comics

Fawcett Publications began in 1919 with *Capt. Billy's Whiz Bang*, a digest-sized somewhat bawdy magazine. The mix of girlie photos, stories, and cartoons (later Donald Duck artist Carl Barks being a regular contributor) was successful enough that Fawcett would expand into a major magazine publisher in the 1930s. Titles included *True Confessions*, *Motion Picture*, and *Mechanix Illustrated*.

Late in 1939 Roscoe Fawcett announced the company's entry into the comic book field with *Whiz Comics*, dated February 1940. Captain Marvel was the lead feature, ably drawn by C.C. Beck and his assistants Pete Costanza and Kurt Schaffenberger. The success of Captain Marvel spawned a number of well-drawn spin-offs including Captain Marvel Jr. by Mac Raboy, Mary Marvel by Marc Swayze and Hoppy the Marvel Bunny by Chad Grothkopf.

By 1943 Fawcett was also publishing *Captain Midnight, Bulletman, Spy Smasher*, and *Don Winslow*. In the later 1940s the line was expanded to westerns (including *Hopalong Cassidy, Tom Mix Western*, and *Gabby Hayes Western*) as well as romance, humor, sports, horror, and science fiction titles. Fawcett had become a major comic book publisher, with a yearly circulation of 50 million copies in the mid 1940s which grew to over 70 million by 1949. A 1941 DC Comics lawsuit alleging Captain Marvel was an imitation of Superman was settled in DC's favor in 1953. This, combined with lost sales due to the popularity of TV, brought an end to the Fawcett comic book empire. They reentered the field with *Dennis the Menace* in 1958 and published that title until 1980. Fawcett was purchased by the Ballantine Books division of Random House in 1982.

FAW-1

❑ **FAW-1. "American Alphabet" Song Book,**
1944. Patriotism song pages with cover art of Hoppy the Marvel Bunny and other Fawcett characters. - **$25 $60 $125**

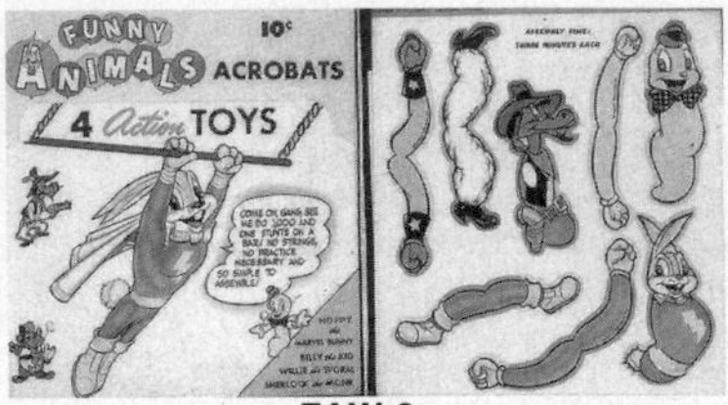

FAW-2

❑ **FAW-2. "Funny Animals Acrobats" Punch-Out,**
c. 1944. Store item and probable club issue. Unpunched - **$50 $85 $160**

FAW-3

FAW-4

❑ **FAW-3. "Tippy Toy" Punch-Out Sheet With Envelope,**
1945. Store item and club premium. For assembly of 3-D rocker toy featuring Hoppy the Marvel Bunny and Millie Bunny. Unused - **$25 $50 $75**

❑ **FAW-4. "Comic Stamps" Perforated Sheet,**
c. 1945. Pictures 24 Fawcett comic book characters. - **$90 $175 $300**

FAW-5

FAW-6

❑ **FAW-5. Captain Marvel Club Offer Sheet,**
c. 1945. Offers 18 action toys, games, puzzles, etc. for Captain Marvel and other Fawcett characters. 8-1/2x11" black on yellow printed both sides. - **$15 $30 $60**

❑ **FAW-6. "Funny Animals Coloring Book",**
1946. Store item by Abbott Publishing Co. Features Hoppy the Marvel Bunny and other Fawcett characters. - **$35 $60 $125**

FAW-7

❑ **FAW-7. "Funny Animal Paint Books" With Box,**
c. 1946. Store item by Abbott Publishing Co. Set of six including Hoppy the Marvel Bunny and five other Fawcett animals.
Box - **$55 $110 $175**
Hoppy Book - **$15 $30 $75**
Others Each - **$8 $15 $25**

FAW-8

❑ **FAW-8. Bulletman Child's T-Shirt,**
1947. Child-sized t-shirt by Fawcett Publications Inc. Shirt features "Bulletman the Flying Detective" and Bulletgirl flying above the countryside. - **$175 $350 $700**

FAW-9

❑ **FAW-9. Coco-Wheats "Tattoo Transfers" Kit With Mailer Envelope,**
1956. Transfer sheets picture 22 Fawcett characters. Mailer - **$15 $25 $40**
Illustrated Inner Envelope With Two Sheets - **$30 $60 $100**

Felix the Cat

Felix has been called one of the great creations of comic art...a supercat...an animation superstar...the Charlie Chaplin of cartoon characters. Alienated, alone, a heroic and resourceful battler against fate, Felix was created by cartoonists Otto Messmer(1892-1983) and Pat Sullivan (1885-1933) shortly after World War I. His first animated appearance came in 1919 and by the mid-1920s he was an international star, most notably in England. Along with Messmer, the animation staff included Bill Nolan and Al Eugster. Sullivan was quick to license the character and many early merchandised items were produced. A Sunday comic strip from King Features Syndicate debuted in August 1923 and a daily strip followed in May 1927. Jack Boyle assisted Messmer on the daily strip. Felix became the first cartoon character to be broadcast when station W2XBS New York Channel #1 transmitted an image of him as a three-dimensional paper mache figure in 1928. Comic book appearances began in the 1930s and Felix has had his own books from the 1940s into the 1990s. Hundreds of the silent shorts were distributed to television in 1953 by Pathe Films. New color episodes, produced for television by the Joe Oriolo Studios, appeared in 1960. Felix now had a magic bag of tricks to rely on in place of his talented and multifunctional tail.

FLX-1

❑ **FLX-1. Schoenhut First Version Wood Jointed Doll,**
1924. Large 8" tall. Label under foot "Felix Copyright 1922, 1924 By Pat Sullivan Pat. Applied For." Most versions have label "Pat June 23, 1925." Nose on first version extends 1/2", second version only 1/4".
First Version - **$350 $575 $1100**
Second Version - **$225 $400 $750**
Box - **$250 $500 $800**

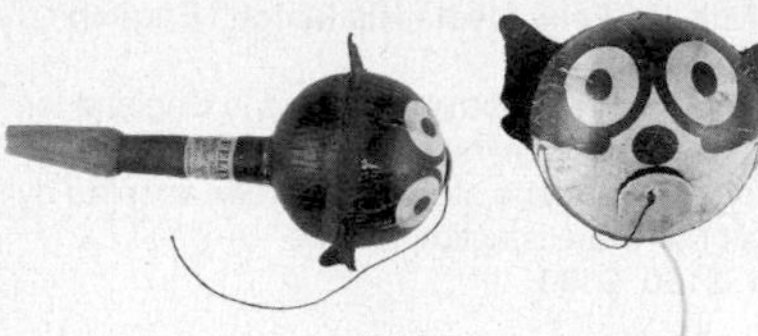

FLX-2

❑ **FLX-2. "Felix" The Cat Figural Horn,**
1924. Horn is 4.5" long. 1.75" diameter round head with paper ears. Label reads "Felix Copyright 1922, 1924 By Pat Sullivan." Germany. Wood and paper mache.
- **$75 $150 $300**

FLX-3

FLX-4

❑ **FLX-3. "Felix The Cat" Ceramic Plate,**
1925. 7" diameter. German. - **$125 $300 $475**

❑ **FLX-4. German Ceramic Bowl,**
c. 1925. 7.25" diameter copyright Pat Sullivan naming maker Rudolstadt on underside. - **$120 $260 $450**

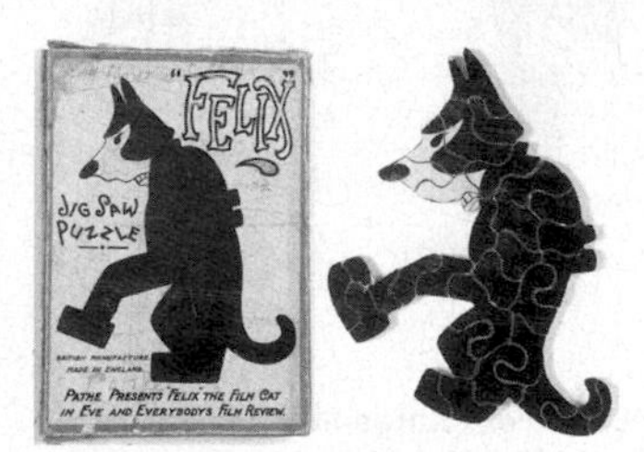

FLX-5

❑ **FLX-5. English Boxed Puzzle,**
c. 1925. Illustrated box inscribed "Pathe Presents Felix The Film Cat In Eve And Everybody's Film Review" holding 7.5" tall figure jigsaw puzzle repeating box lid image. - **$115 $225 $350**

FLX-6

FLX-7

❑ **FLX-6. "Felix Meets His Match" English Cartoon Booklet,**
c. 1925. Sportex clothing. Printed in England for distribution with clothing items locally and abroad. Eight-page story about Felix adopted by a tailor to dissatisfaction of both. -
$65 $150 $300

❑ **FLX-7. Sunday Page Comic Strip Reprint Book,**
1927. McLoughlin Bros. 48-page black/white and color comic strips from 1926-1927. -
$200 $800 $1550

FLX-8

❑ **FLX-8. "Felix" Plaster Figure On Base,**
1920s. Store item. 1-1/2x3x3-1/2" tall figure in classic pose. - **$175 $375 $700**

FLX-9

FLX-10

❑ **FLX-9. Felix Large Size Japanese Celluloid Figure,**
1920s. Store item. 3-1/2" tall. - **$40 $80 $165**

❑ **FLX-10. "Felix" Wood-Jointed Doll,**
1920s. Store item by Schoenhut. 4" tall. -
$60 $135 $215

FLX-11

❑ **FLX-11. English Cream Toffee Candy Tin,**
1920s. Scarce. Store item. -
$450 $1300 $2500

FLX-12

❑ **FLX-12. Spanish Candy Company Premium Card Set,**
1920s. San Fernando Chocolate, Barcelona, Spain. Full color set of 15 numbered cards comprise "Series C." Artist's name "Bofarull" appears on lower right corner.
Set - **$60 $100 $200**

FLX-13

FLX-14

❑ **FLX-13. Felix Stickpin,**
1920s. Stickpin is 1-1/8" and has .75" image of Felix on paper inside metal frame.
- $35 $65 $125

❑ **FLX-14. Buck-Toothed Felix Enamel Pin,**
1920s. Pin is 1" tall. English issue.
- $45 $85 $150

FLX-15

FLX-16

❑ **FLX-15. Felix Film Magazine English Enamel Pin,**
1920s. Pin is 1.5" and back reads "Pathe Presents Felix The Cat In Eye And Everybody's Film Review Made In England." Image of Felix with tennis racquet in one paw. - **$40 $75 $125**

❑ **FLX-16. Worried Felix Early Enamel Pin,**
1920s. Pin is 1" tall marked on back "Felix Made In England." - **$45 $85 $150**

FLX-17

❑ **FLX-17. German Wind-Up Car With Felix The Cat Hood Ornament,**
1920s. Tin litho open touring car is 3x6x3" tall with built-in key. Unmarked with exception of license plate reading "KBN 3042." Has driver depicted holding onto steering wheel, back seat has pair of slots where a passenger figure was once attached. The nicest feature of the car is 1" tall figural Felix the Cat hood ornament.
Complete - **$1150 $2750 $5500**

FLX-18

FLX-19

❑ **FLX-18. Felix Figural Pitcher,**
c. 1920s. China pitcher has 3.4" base and is 6" tall with high glaze. Felix name appears in large .5" tall letters on front. Bottom is marked "Made In CSR/Fabrique En CSR." Believed to be of French origin. - **$75 $135 $260**

❑ **FLX-19. Felix Celluloid Figural Tape Measure,**
c. 1920s. Item is 2" tall and made of heavy celluloid. Unmarked. - **$85 $165 $300**

FLX-20

❑ **FLX-20. "Good Old Felix Style!" Dexterity Puzzle,**
c. 1930. Puzzle is 2.25" with image of spinning Felix. Under the glass cover is a three dimensional aluminum mouse and object is to get it within a small opening formed by a black metal compartment. - **$40 $85 $150**

FLX-21

FLX-22

❏ **FLX-21. Hand Puppet,**
c. 1930. Store item. 9-1/2" tall plush fabric by Steiff. With Ear Button - **$325 $725 $1500**
Button Removed - **$225 $450 $900**

❏ **FLX-22. "Felix" Tin Litho Sparking Toy,**
c. 1930. Store item. Pat Sullivan copyright. - **$125 $300 $600**

FLX-23

❏ **FLX-23. "Felix The Cat" Golfing Pillow Cover,**
c. 1930. Store item by Vogue Needlecraft #198. - **$50 $100 $175**

FLX-24

❏ **FLX-24. Comic Strip Reprint Book,**
1931. McLoughlin #260. Cardboard covers 24-page book of full color strips printed four panels to a page. Panels are dated 1926 but we've seen this book with and without cover date of 1931. - **$79 $316 $900**

FLX-25

❏ **FLX-25. "Felix The Cat" BLB,**
1936. Whitman. #1129 with story art by Messmer. - **$30 $90 $210**

FLX-26

❏ **FLX-26 "Felix/12th & Grand Chevrolet Dealer/Los Angeles" Felt Patch,**
1930s. Patch is 5.5" tall. - **$60 $125 $200**

FLX-27

❏ **FLX-27. German Shuco Jointed Stuffed Doll,**
1930s. 10" tall velveteen fabric-covered doll with jointed shoulders, head, tail.
- **$200 $400 $600**

FLX-28

❏ **FLX-28. "Katz Kitten Klub" Member Card,**
1930s. Orange/black printed on both sides by club information and originally pinned by club button pictured at upper front corner. See FLX-29. - **$40 $75 $150**

FLX-29

FLX-30

❏ **FLX-29. "Katz Kitten Klub" Cello. Button,**
1930s.Type of business unknown, but member card printed with "Al Katz, General Meower." Felix image not identified as such. See FLX-28. -
$40 $80 $175

❏ **FLX-30. Tin Pull Toy,**
1930s. Store item by Nifty Toys. -
$250 $500 $1000

FLX-31

FLX-32

❏ **FLX-31. "Evening Ledger Comics" Cello. Button,**
1930s. Philadelphia newspaper. From set of 14 various characters. - **$60 $175 $350**

❏ **FLX-32. Felix Clicker,**
1930s. From Germany. Several in set. -
$35 $60 $140

FLX-33

FLX-34

❏ **FLX-33. "Herald & Examiner" Litho. Button,**
1930s. Chicago newspaper. From "30 Comics" series featuring various characters. -
$10 $20 $40

❏ **FLX-34. "Warner Bros. State" Theater Cello. Button,**
1930s. Obvious Felix image although "Krazy Kat Klub" designation. - **$45 $115 $250**

FLX-35

❏ **FLX-35. Occupational Shield Brass Badge,**
1930s. Known examples are "Aviation Dept.", "Fire Dept." and "Police Dept." Scarce.
Each - **$200 $400 $800**

FLX-36

❏ **FLX-36. "Felix The Cat Candies And Toy" Empty Box With Messmer Art,**
1952. Store item. Card on front punches out. -
$40 $85 $175

FLX-37

❑ **FLX-37. Felix Board Game Set,**
1956. Includes a box, 1 die, a board, and 6 punch out markers. - **$31 $60 $125**

FLX-38

❑ **FLX-38. "Felix The Cat" Litho. Button,**
1950s. From set of various King Features Syndicate characters. - **$10 $20 $30**

FLX-39

❑ **FLX-39. "Felix The Cat Candy And Toy" Product Box,**
1960. Phoenix Candy Co. - **$40 $85 $175**

FLX-40 FLX-41

❑ **FLX-40. Soaky Toy,**
1965. Colgate-Palmolive. Came in two colors - black and blue. Toy shown is blue version.
Black Variety - **$15 $25 $60**
Blue Variety - **$10 $20 $50**

❑ **FLX-41. Felix Plush Doll,**
1982. 23" tall with tag. - **$12 $40 $80**

FLX-42 FLX-43

❑ **FLX-42. Plush Doll,**
1982. 3" tall. Made in Korea. Hard to find. - **$10 $25 $35**

❑ **FLX-43. Felix Ceramic Bank,**
1980s. By Applause. 7 1/4" tall. - **$15 $35 $80**

FLX-44 FLX-45

❑ **FLX-44. Felix Beanie,**
1999. Beanie with tag. Heart on chest. - **$20**

❑ **FLX-45. Trophy Figure,**
1990s. Plastic figure with trophy stand that has revolving titles for Felix. Wendy's Premium. - **$12**

FLX-46 FLX-47

❑ **FLX-46. Felix Premium,**
1990s. From Wendy's Restaurants. Felix figure with a plastic fish in ball which you can catch when you turn Felix upside down. - **$4 $10 $28**

❑ **FLX-47. Felix Wacky Wobbler,**
2000. - **$20**

FLX-48

❑ **FLX-48. Felix Lunchbox,**
2003. - **$22**

Fibber McGee and Molly

Jim and Marian Jordan were veterans of small-time vaudeville before they ventured into radio comedy in Chicago, first as *The O'Henry Twins* in 1924, then as *The Smith Family* in 1925, as *The Air Scouts* in 1927 and in *Smackout* from 1931 to 1935. Finally along with writer Don Quinn, they created *Fibber McGee and Molly* for Johnson's Wax. The show premiered on the NBC Blue network in April 1935 and developed into one of the most popular radio comedies of all time.

From their home at 79 Wistful Vista, McGee, the blundering windbag, and Molly, his long-suffering, forgiving wife, presided over one domestic disaster after another. Listeners waited each week for Fibber to open his closet door, whereupon the stacked contents would crash to the floor. The show featured a number of regular supporting characters: their neighbor Gildersleeve, Beulah the maid, henpecked Wallace Wimple, the Old Timer, Mayor La Trivia and Myrt, the telephone operator whose voice was never heard.

After Johnson's Wax dropped the show in 1950, Pet milk sponsored it until 1952, then Reynolds Aluminum until 1953, when the half-hour format was replaced by a 15-minute weekday series that ran until 1957. There was a comic book in 1949, the Jordans made some movies in the 1940s and a television series had a brief run on NBC in 1959-1960, but nothing equaled the McGee success on radio.

FIB-1

❑ **FIB-1. Cast Photo,**
c. 1935. Shown at "NBC" microphone. - **$20 $40 $80**

FIB-2

FIB-3

❑ **FIB-2. Fibber Cello. Spinner Top On Wood Peg,**
1936. Scarce. Johnson's Wax Polishes. - **$50 $100 $150**

❑ **FIB-3. Molly Cello. Spinner Top With Wood Peg,**
1936. Scarce. Johnson's Wax Polishes. - **$50 $100 $150**

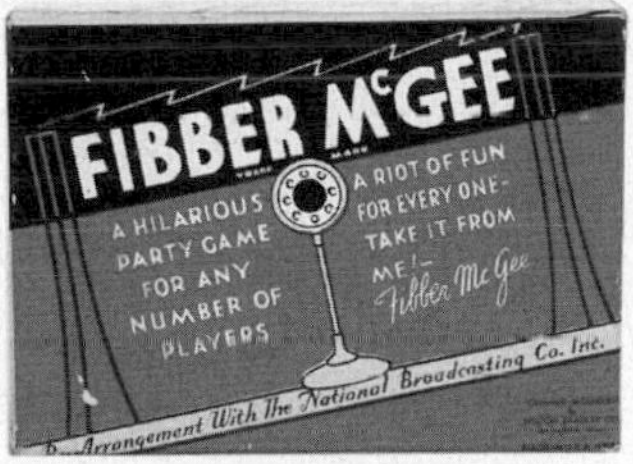

FIB-4

❑ **FIB-4. Party Game in Box,**
1936. NBC tie-in. - **$40 $75 $150**

FIB-5

❑ **FIB-5. "Fibber McGee/Johnson's Wax" Store Standee,**
1937. 15x20" diecut cardboard display with easel back. Front edge of wheelbarrow advertises NBC radio program. - **$100 $200 $400**

FIB-6

❑ **FIB-6. "Johnson Glo-Coat Floor Polish" 8x14" Cardboard Display Sign ,**
1937. - **$100 $200 $400**

FIB-7

FIB-8

❑ **FIB-7. Cardboard 9x15" Store Display Sign,**
c. 1937. Designed for holding sample can of Johnson's Wax. - **$90 $175 $350**

❑ **FIB-8. Cardboard 11x16" Store Display Sign,**
c. 1937. Designed for holding sample can of Johnson's Wax. - **$75 $150 $300**

FIB-9

FIB-10

❑ **FIB-9. Johnson Products 11x15" Countertop Sign,**
c. 1937. Johnson's auto wax and cleaner. Diecut cardboard with easel back. - **$75 $150 $300**

❑ **FIB-10. Countertop Display Sign,**
1930s. Johnson's Wax Polishes. Full color 13x20". - **$100 $200 $400**

FIB-11

❑ **FIB-11. Johnson's Wax Store Display Large Sign,**
1930s. Large 20x28" cardboard display with cardboard easel on reverse features choice art of Fibber buried under the contents of a closet which have fallen on and around him including a picture frame over his head. He says "Gotta Clean Up This Closet One Of These Days, Molly" and she is shown kneeling and collecting various Johnson Wax products. Bottom reads "Now's A Good Time To Pick Up Some Johnson's Wax Polishes." - **$125 $250 $500**

FIB-12

❑ **FIB-12. Cast Photo,**
1930s. - **$18 $35 $70**

FIB-13

FIB-14

❑ **FIB-13. Cardboard Advertising Blotter,**
1930s. Prudential Insurance. - **$18 $35 $70**

❑ **FIB-14. Fan Photo,**
c. 1940s. - **$15 $30 $60**

FIB-15

❑ **FIB-15. Record Album ,**
1947. Four 78 rpm rcords. - **$50 $100 $160**

FIB-16

❑ **FIB-16. "Fibber McGee And Molly" Record Set,**
c. 1940s. Store item. 10-1/4x12" cardboard album holds set of three 78 rpm records on the Capitol label. Mentions "Their First Appearance On Discs." - **$30 $60 $90**

The Flapper

The August 26, 1920 ratification of the 19th amendment to the Constitution gave women the right to vote, freeing them from corsets in the process. With their new found independence and jazz age music, young women danced the Charleston, Shimmy and Black Bottom; put on make-up (sometimes in public!); wore skirts just above the knees with rayon stockings attached to garter belts; drank liquor; smoked and attended "petting parties" surrounded by art deco stylizations.

The nationwide party was fueled by authors F. Scott Fitzgerald's *The Great Gatsby* and Anita Loos' *Gentlemen Prefer Blondes*, both published in 1925. Noted silver screen flapper types included Clara Bow, Joan Crawford, Louise Brooks and Colleen Moore along with animated short subject star Betty Boop. John Held's *LIFE* magazine cartoon covers epitomized the flapper, while Flapper Fanny and Dixie Dugan frolicked in newspaper funny pages. Blondie was a flapper in the early days of her comic strip before settling into family life with Dagwood.

The Great Depression, heralded by the October 24, 1929 Black Friday crash on Wall Street, combined with a conservative religious revival, led to the demise of the flapper in the early 1930s.

FPR-1

❑ **FPR-1. "Checkers Confection" Clicker Prize,**
1920s. 1.75" litho tin disk. Reads "Of All The Toys, That Make A Noise, The Kids Like Best This Snapper - While Checkers Sweet, Is Best To Eat, For Pa-Ma-Kid Or Flapper." - **$20 $40 $90**

FPR-2

❑ **FPR-2. "Omar Pearls" Mirror,**
1920s. Bastian Bros. 2.75" tall mirror. - **$100 $200 $400**

FPR-3

❑ **FPR-3. "Whoopie Car" Marx Wind-Up,**
1930s. 3x7x5.75" tall tin litho toy with built-in key in box. Toy has driver in raccoon coat, hat and bow tie and on the back are a pair of matching die-cut tin flapper girls. Box - **$125 $250 $600**
Car - **$100 $200 $500**

FPR-4

❑ **FPR-4. "Maverick/Roaring 20s America's Favorite Programs" Candy Box,**
c. 1961. Peter Paul Candy. 6.25x11x2.5" box with lid illustrations of Maverick and a "Roaring 20s" flapper. Held "Almond Joy" candy bars. - **$25 $50 $100**

The Flash

The fastest man alive, a superhero of the Golden Age of comic books, made his first appearance in *Flash Comics* #1 of January 1940 with art by Harry Lampert (1916-2004) and story by Gardner Fox (1911-1986). The book was discontinued in 1949 after 104 issues and was revived with issue #105 in March 1959. The speedster also appeared in *All-Flash* comics from 1941 to 1948 and showed up in early issues of *All-Star Comics* and *Comic Cavalcade* and in various DC Comics collections. He was revived in *Showcase* #4 of October 1956, with a new costume and a new secret identity with art by Carmine Infantino and story by Gardner Fox. Among the colorful villains confronted by The Flash were The Fiddler and his magic Stradivarius, Mirror Master and Captain Cold, each with special evil powers. The Scarlet Speedster had his own live-action TV series on CBS during the 1990-91 season, and he appeared in Cartoon Network's animated *Justice League Unlimited* series. A 1946 giveaway comic book was distributed taped to boxes of Wheaties and a comics club offered a membership card and button as premiums.

FLA-1

FLA-2

❑ **FLA-1. "The Flash/Fastest Man Alive" Litho. Button,**
1942. Rare. Flash Comics. Sent to everyone submitting a reader survey coupon printed in All-Flash #6 (July, 1942). The first thousand respondents also received a free copy of All-Flash #7. - **$500 $1500 $3000**

❑ **FLA-2. "Flash Comics" Wheaties Purchase Comic Book,**
1946. As taped to two-box purchase, highest grade is fine. Good - **$350**
Fine - **$1600**

FLA-3

❑ **FLA-3. Flash Trading Cards,**
1980s. - **$40**

FLA-4

FLA-5

❑ **FLA-4. Modern Age Flash Resin Statue,**
1995. Limited to 2,870. Boxed - **$275**

❑ **FLA-5. Flash Keepsake Ornament in Box,**
1998. From Hallmark. - **$22**

FLA-6

FLA-7

❑ **FLA-6. Flash 5" Figure,**
1998. Limited to 2,500 - **$115**

❑ **FLA-7. Golden Age Flash Resin Statue,**
1998. Limited to 1,600. Hard to find on secondary market. Boxed - **$125**

FLA-8

FLA-9

❑ **FLA-8. Barry Allen Flash Ring,**
1999. Replica of ring in which the Flash's costume was compressed and stored. Cast in pewter and plated in 24-karat gold and metallic finish. Limited to 1,100. - **$175**

❑ **FLA-9. Flash Bean Bag Figure,**
1999. Warner Bros. Store exclusive. - **$10**

FLA-10

❑ **FLA-10. Flash Seven-Piece PVC Set,**
2000. DC Direct. - **$48**

FLA-11

❑ **FLA-11. Flash and Kid Flash Action Figure Set,**
2001. DC Direct. Set includes a miniature Cosmic Treadmill and a Flash ring with a secret costume compartment. - **$60**

FLA-12

❑ **FLA-12. Justice League Animated Maquette,**
2002. DC Direct. 8-5/8" tall. Limited edition of 4,500. Sculpted by Karen Palinko. - **$125**

Flash Gordon

Flash Gordon first blasted into space in January 1934 in a Sunday comic strip created by Alex Raymond (1909-1956) for King Features. Since then, along with his companions Dale Arden and Dr. Zarkov, Flash has done violent battle with Ming the Merciless on the planet Mongo and with an assortment of interplanetary menaces in every possible medium. The Sunday strip, an immediate success, generated many comic book appearances--the first in *King Comics* #1 of April 1936; a radio series on the Mutual network in 1935-1936; an original novel published in 1936; three chapter plays for Universal starring Buster Crabbe (1907-1983), between 1936 and 1940; a daily comic strip that ran from 1940 to 1944 and was revived in 1951; a syndicated live-action television series in 1953-1954 starring Steve Holland; hardback reprints of early strips in 1967 and 1971; a Filmation animated cartoon for NBC in 1979-1980 and a lavish Technicolor movie in 1980. Mac Raboy (1914-1967) was the artist on the Sunday page from 1948 into the mid-1960s; Paul Norris did some nice work on the Dell comic book in the late 1940s as did Al Williamson and Reed Crandall in the late 1960s for King Comics. "Steady, Dale!"

FGR-1

❑ **FGR-1. Home Foundry Casting Set,**
1934. Store item by Home Foundry Mfg. Co. Inc. 9x16x2" deep beautifully designed box holds instruction book/catalogue along with a two-part mold and equipment needed to produce lead figures.
Complete Set - **$500 $1200 $2400**
Instruction Book Only - **$25 $50 $100**

FGR-2 FGR-3

❑ **FGR-2. "Flash Gordon" Litho. Button,**
1934. From set of seven showing various King Features Syndicate characters. - **$30 $70 $150**

❑ **FGR-3. "Dale Arden" Litho. Button,**
1934. From set of seven showing various King Features Syndicate characters. - **$30 $70 $150**

FGR-4 FGR-5

❑ **FGR-4. "Flash Gordon on the Planet Mongo" Big Little Book #1110,**
1934. - **$45 $135 $315**

❑ **FGR-5. "Flash Gordon and the Monsters of Mongo" Big Little Book #1166,**
1934. - **$38 $114 $265**

FGR-6

❑ **FGR-6. "Flash Gordon and the Tournaments of Mongo" Big Little Book #1171,**
1935. - **$39 $117 $275**

FGR-7 FGR-8

❑ **FGR-7. "Chicago Herald And Examiner" Club Litho. Button,**
c. 1935. The first Flash Gordon club button, 1-1/8" litho. - **$75 $150 $300**

❑ **FGR-8. Buster Crabbe Dixie Ice Cream Lid,**
1936. - **$20 $35 $75**

FGR-9

❑ **FGR-9. "Flash Gordon Strange Adventure Magazine" Vol. 1 #1,**
1936. - **$275 $650 $1300**

FGR-10

❑ **FGR-10. Movie Serial Club Member Card,**
1936. Scarce. Buster Crabbe pictured as Flash Gordon. - **$250 $750 $1500**

FGR-11

❑ **FGR-11. "Flash Gordon Vs. The Emperor Of Mongo" Book #6833,**
1936. 4x5" hardcover otherwise similar format to Fast-Action Book. - **$71 $213 $500**

FGR-12

❑ **FGR-12. "Flash Gordon/Buster Crabbe Movie Club" Cello. Button,**
1936. 1.25". - **$500 $1200 $2000**

FGR-13 FGR-14

❑ **FGR-13. "Buster Crabbe" Dixie Ice Cream Picture,**
c. 1936. He is pictured as Flash Gordon from "New Universal Serial" described on reverse. - **$60 $140 $275**

❑ **FGR-14. "Buster Crabbe" Dixie Ice Cream Picture,**
c. 1936. He is pictured as Flash Gordon from "New Universal Serial" described on reverse. - **$45 $125 $250**

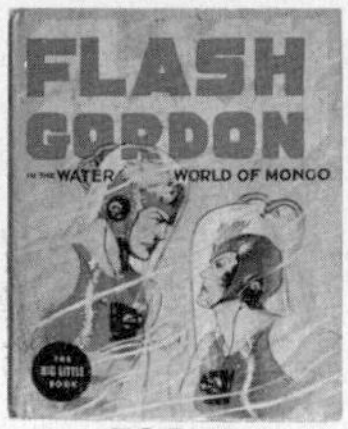

FGR-15

FGR-16

❑ **FGR-15. "Flash Gordon in the Water World Of Mongo" Big Little Book #1407,**
1937. By Alex Raymond. - **$35 $107 $245**

❑ **FGR-16. "Flash Gordon and the Witch Queen Of Mongo" Big Little Book #1190,**
1937. By Alex Raymond. - **$39 $117 $275**

FGR-17

❑ **FGR-17. "Flash Gordon's Trip to Mars" One Sheet Poster,**
1938. Universal Pictures serial stars Buster Crabbe. This duotone poster is for Chapter 4 of the 15 part serial. - **$2150 $4250 $6500**

FGR-18

FGR-19

❑ **FGR-18. "Flash Gordon Adventure Club" 1.25" Cello. Button,**
1938. Rare. Universal Pictures. For 12-chapter movie serial "Flash Gordon Conquers The Universe" starring Buster Crabbe and Carol Hughes, both pictured. - **$375 $850 $1850**

❑ **FGR-19. Movie Serial Australian Button,**
1938. Black and cream real photo with no dot pattern surrounded by creamtone blending from gray to solid black at outer rim. Inscription is "Flash Gordon-Trip To Mars-Buster Crabbe." Rare. - **$325 $650 $1300**

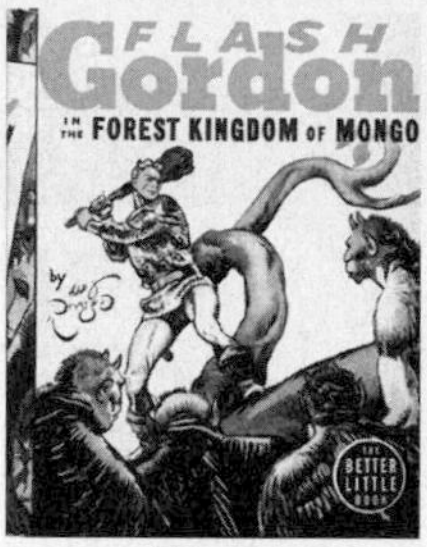

FGR-20

❑ **FGR-20. "Flash Gordon in the Forest Kingdom of Mongo" Better Little Book #1492,**
1938. - **$41 $123 $290**

FGR-21

❑ **FGR-21. "Flash Gordon and the Perils of Mongo" Better Little Book #1423,**
1940. - **$30 $90 $210**

FGR-22

❑ **FGR-22. Feature Book No. 25,**
1941. Art by Austin Briggs, noted American illustrator who drew the daily newspaper series. - **$121 $363 $1750**

FGR-23

FGR-24

❑ **FGR-23. "Flash Gordon and the Tyrant of Mongo" Better Little Book #1484,**
1941. - **$32 $96 $225**

❑ **FGR-24. "Flash Gordon in The Ice World of Mongo" Better Little Book #1443,**
1942. - **$32 $96 $225**

FGR-25

FGR-26

❑ **FGR-25. "World Battle Fronts" World War II Folder Map,**
1943. Macy's department store "Flash Gordon Headquarters". Map opens to 20x27" sheet picturing global areas on both sides. -
$40 $75 $150

❑ **FGR-26. "Flash Gordon and the Power Men of Mongo" Better Little Book #1469,**
1943. - **$32 $96 $225**

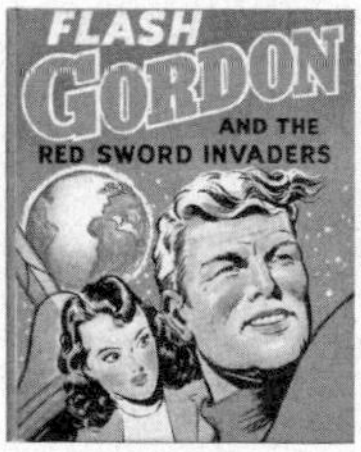

FGR-27

FGR-28

❑ **FGR-27. "Flash Gordon and the Red Sword Invaders" Better Little Book #1479,**
1945. - **$31 $93 $220**

❑ **FGR-28. "Flash Gordon in the Jungles of Mongo" Better Little Book #1424,**
1947. - **$22 $66 $155**

FGR-29

FGR-30

❑ **FGR-29. "Flash Gordon and the Fiery Desert of Mongo" Better Little Book #1447,**
1948. - **$22 $66 $155**

❑ **FGR-30. "S.F. Call-Bulletin" Cardboard Disk,**
c. 1940s. San Francisco newspaper. From series of contest disks, match number to win prize. - **$20 $40 $90**

FGR-31

❑ **FGR-31. Flash Gordon Spanish BTLB,**
1940s. Edition #1183 printed in Buenos Aires with all text in Spanish although identical to American edition Better Little Book #1469 copyright 1943 titled "Flash Gordon And The Power Men Of Mongo." - **$115 $225 $450**

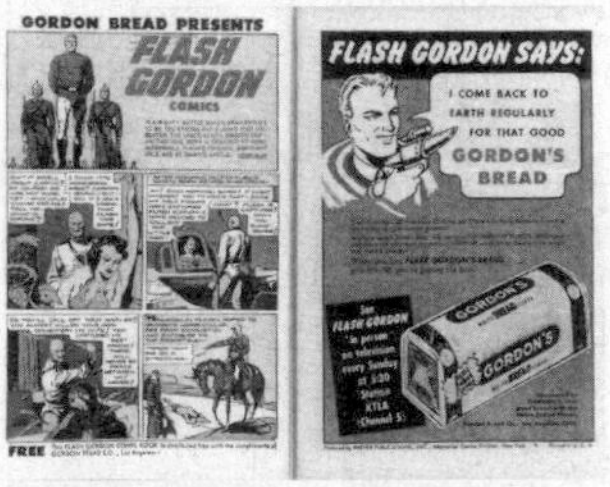

FGR-32

❑ **FGR-32. "Flash Gordon Comics",**
1951. Gordon Bread Give-Away. Two issues of strip reprints. Each - **$2 $6 $18**

FGR-33

❑ **FGR-33. Inlaid Puzzle,**
1952. Paper Sleeve - **$35 $75 $150**
Puzzle Only - **$35 $75 $150**

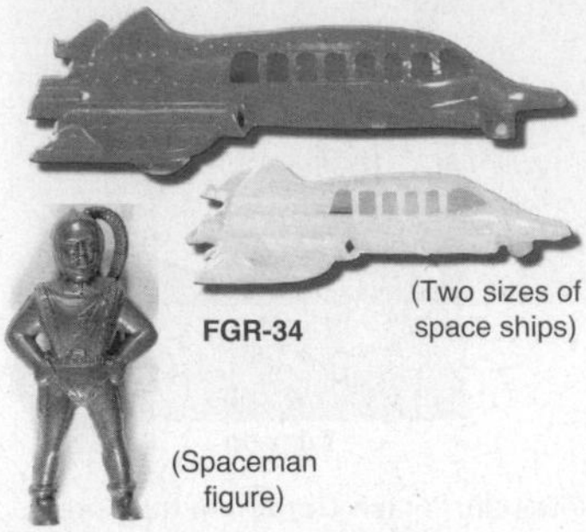

FGR-34 (Two sizes of space ships) (Spaceman figure)

❑ **FGR-34. Solar Commando Set,**
1952. Made by Premier. Set includes 2 space rockets (3 1/4" long) and 3 spaceman figures on card. Complete - **$500**
Space rockets (3 1/4") each - **$15 $30 $75**
Spaceman figures each - **$8 $20 $40**

Flash Gordon Space Rockets were also issued in different sizes on a separate card - 5 total.
Each 6 1/2" Rocket - **$50 $100 $170**
Each 4 3/4" Rocket - **$30 $60 $110**
Each 3 1/4" Rocket - **$15 $30 $75**

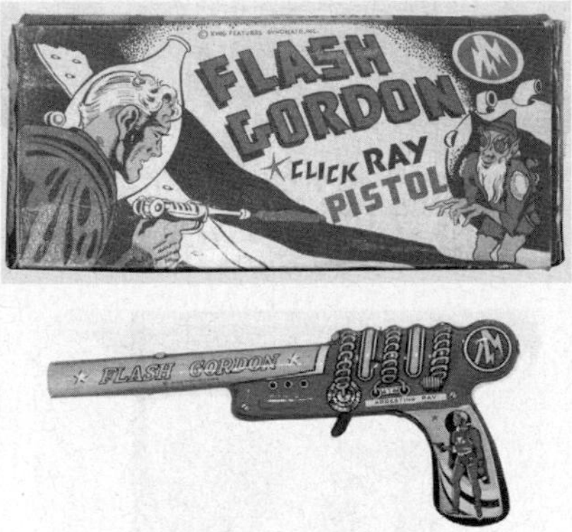

FGR-35

❑ **FGR-35. Flash Gordon Clicker Tin Gun With Box,**
1952. Gun - **$175 $350 $700**
Box - **$200 $400 $600**
Complete - **$375 $750 $1300**

FGR-36

❑ **FGR-36. "March Of Comics No. 133" Booklet,**
1955. Poll-Parrot Shoes. From series by K.K. Publications. - **$11 $33 $105**

FGR-37

FGR-38

❑ **FGR-37. "Flash Gordon and the Baby Animals" Wonder Book,**
1955. - **$18 $30 $65**

❑ **FGR-38. "Puck" 10x10" Paper Store Sign,**
1950s. Puck The Comic Weekly and Sunday Comics. From series for drugstore use picturing various King Features characters. -
$50 $100 $200

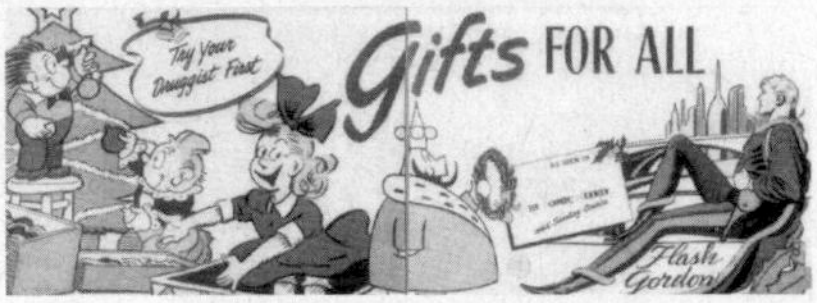

FGR-39

❑ **FGR-39. "Puck" 15x40" Large Paper Store Sign,**
1950s. Puck The Comic Weekly and Sunday Comics. For drugstore use picturing King Features characters. - **$75 $150 $300**

FGR-40

FGR-41

❑ **FGR-40. Litho. Button,**
1950s. 7/8" litho. from series picturing King Features Syndicate characters. Comes in several different color variations. - **$15 $30 $60**

❑ **FGR-41. Litho. Button,**
1950s. Issuer unknown but from a set of at least 30, each marked only by a tiny copyright symbol. 7/8" full color. - **$20 $40 $85**

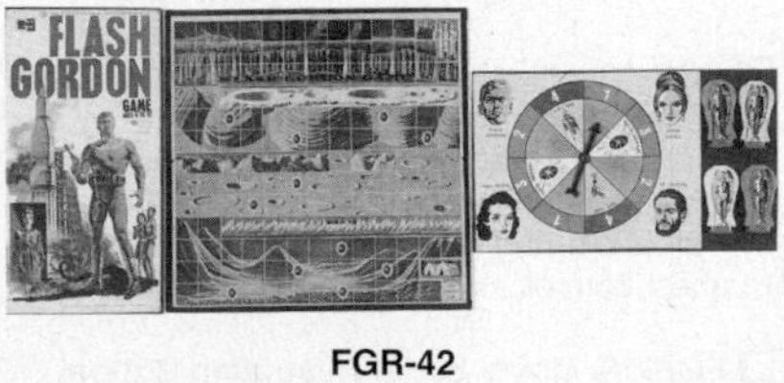

FGR-42

❑ **FGR-42. Board Game,**
1965. T. Cohn. Boxed graphic and colorful playing board and assortment of other game parts and figures. - **$75 $135 $250**

FGR-43

❑ **FGR-43. Dale Arden Litho. Button,**
1960s. From set of King Features characters marked only by copyright symbol. -
$20 $40 $75

FGR-44

❑ **FGR-44. Flash Gordon Boxed Watch,**
1971. Precision Time. 4.75x9.75x.5" deep box contains watch. Dial measures 1.25" diameter and features Flash Gordon with name and futuristic city in background. Insert features colorful art showing Flash and ally looking at watches as rocketships fire ahead amidst explosion with Flash Gordon name and KFS copyright. Watch band is leatherette with suede overlay.
Box - **$50 $100 $225**
Watch - **$100 $200 $350**

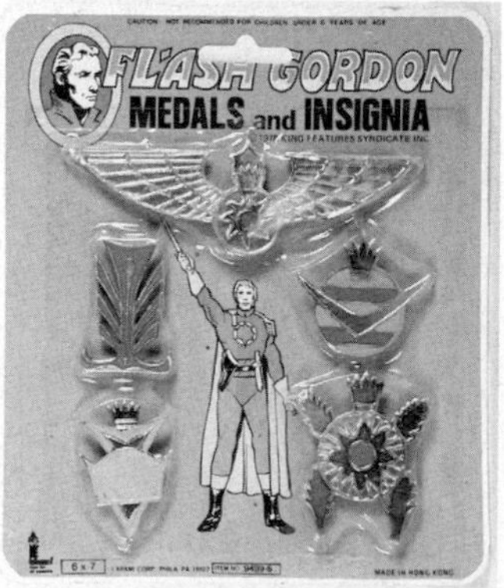

FGR-45

❑ **FGR-45. Medals and Insignia Pack,**
1978. Four medals and one insignia on card. -
$25 $50 $80

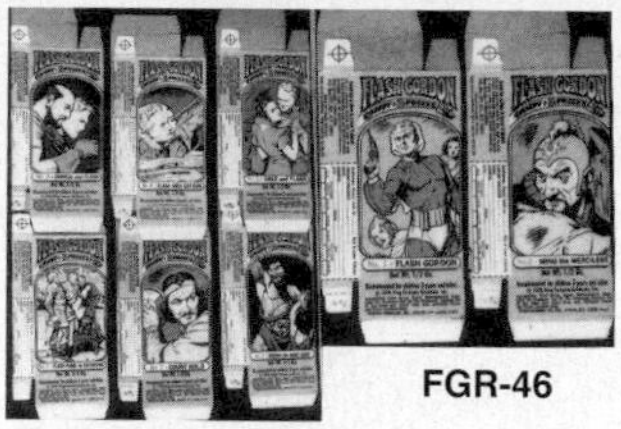

FGR-46

❑ **FGR-46. Candy Boxes,**
1978. Phoenix Candy Co. Set of eight.
Each - **$8 $15 $30**

FGR-47

❑ **FGR-47. "Flash Gordon" Pocket Watch By Bradley,**
1979. Watch has copyright date and "King Features Syndicate Inc." in tiny text along the bottom edge. The watch was from a very short-lived production run. - **$100 $250 $400**

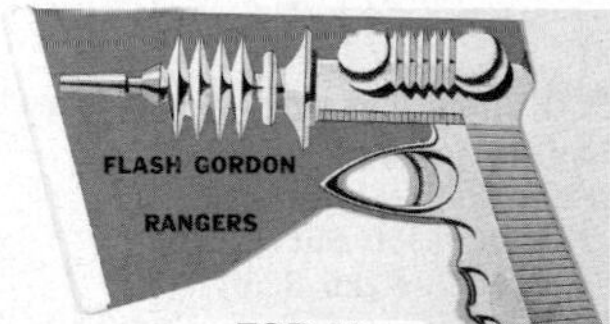

FGR-48

❑ **FGR-48. Flash Gordon Rangers Pop Gun,**
1970s.- **$25 $50 $75**

FGR-49

FGR-50

FGR-51

❑ **FGR-49. Ming the Merciless Figure on Card,**
1996. From the animated series. - **$15**

❑ **FGR-50. General Lynch Figure on Card,**
1996. From the animated series. - **$18**

❑ **FGR-51. Kobalt the Mercenary Figure on Card,**
1996. From the animated series. - **$15**

FGR-52

❑ **FGR-52. Ming's Jaws of Death Throne in Box,**
1996. From the animated series. Ming sold separately. - **$20**

FGR-53

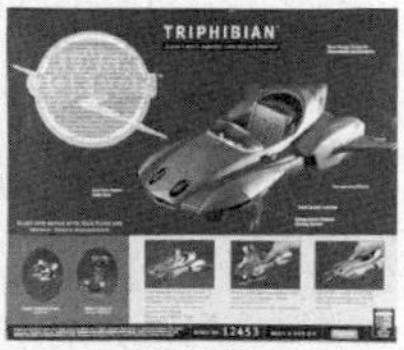

FGR-54

❑ **FGR-53. Flash Gordon Rebel Airbike in Box,**
1996. From the animated series. - **$20**

❑ **FGR-54. Flash Gordon Triphibian in Box,**
1996. Playmates. Multi purpose vehicle. - **$35**

FGR-55

❑ **FGR-55. Flash Gordon Lunch Box,**
2001. - **$35**

FGR-56

❑ **FGR-56. Flash Gordon and Ming the Merciless Mini-Busts Boxed Set,**
2003. Bowen Designs. Inspired by Alex Raymond art. Mint Set in Box- **$125**

The Flintstones

Hanna-Barbera's Flintstones started life as the first adult prime-time television cartoon, went on to become the longest running such animated series in TV history (until *The Simpsons* came along) and spawned numerous reruns, specials, spinoffs and adaptations--as well as a merchandising bonanza. *The Flintstones* premiered on ABC in September 1960 and ran uninterrupted for six years, was rebroadcast on NBC Saturday mornings from 1967 to 1970 and has been around in one form or another ever since. A major film starring John Goodman was released in 1994. Another movie with a different cast, *Viva Rock Vegas*, was released in 2000. The most recent animated feature, this time from the Cartoon Network, was titled *The Flintstones: On the Rocks* and debuted in 2001. The co-directors were Chris Savino and David Smith, with the characters based on the original designs of Ed Benedict.

Fred and Wilma Flintstone and their friends Barney and Betty Rubble are a prehistoric parody of the Kramdens and Nortons of *The Honeymooners,* complete with marital bickering, get-rich-quick schemes, bowling nights out and lodge membership. Voice actors Alan Reed (1907-1977) and Henry Corden (1920-2005) provided Fred's voice. As added attractions, Dino, their pet dinosaur, was joined in 1963 by a baby daughter, Pebbles and by the Rubbles' adopted son, Bamm-Bamm. Gene Hazelton (1919-2005) is credited with the creation of Pebbles and Bamm-Bamm and was also the main writer and artist on the Flintstones comic strip from the early 1960s until 1988. The kids spun off on their own show in 1971.

Comic book appearances began in 1961 and continued into the 1990s. The characters have been merchandised extensively, with several thousand tie-in items licensed. Post's Pebbles cereal and Flintstones chewable vitamins were promotional successes. "Yabba dabba doo!"

FLN-1

❑ **FLN-1. Fred Flintstone Large Vinyl Figure,**
1960. Stands 12" tall with head that turns left and right. - **$20 $40 $100**

FLN-2

❑ **FLN-2. "Flintstone Flivver" Friction Toy,**
1962. Marx Toys. Litho tin prehistoric steam roller except Fred's vinyl head under canopy. - **$100 $200 $400**

FLN-3

❑ **FLN-3. "Welch's Fruit Drinks" Store Sign,**
1962. Full color 11x14". - **$65 $125 $250**

FLN-4

❑ **FLN-4. "Fred Flintstone Racing Kart" Plastic Friction Toy,**
1962. Store item by Marx.
Boxed - **$200 $350 $650**
Toy Only - **$115 $225 $350**

FLN-5

❑ **FLN-5. "Flintstone Pals On Dino" Litho. Tin Wind-Up Toy,**
1962. Store item by Marx. Available with either Fred or Barney riding. Each is 8-1/2" long.
Box - **$100 $200 $300**
Toy - **$125 $250 $350**

FLN-6

❑ **FLN-6. "Fred Flintstone On Dino" Battery Operated Toy,**
1962. Store item by Marx. Large vinyl and metal toy about 20" long with Dino covered in purple plush fabric very subject to color fading. Toy performs many functions specified on the box side panels. Toy Only - **$225 $500 $1100**
Box Only - **$250 $550 $1200**

FLN-7

❑ **FLN-7. Fred Flintstone Tricycle With Box,**
1962. Marx. Tricycle - **$75 $150 $300**
Box - **$100 $200 $300**
Complete - **$175 $350 $600**

FLN-8

❑ **FLN-8. Wilma Line Mar Wind-Up,**
1962. Store item by Marx Toys. Cello figure on litho tin tricycle with bell. Box - **$100 $200 $300**
Toy - **$75 $150 $300**

FLN-9

❑ **FLN-9. "Fred Flintstone's Bedrock Band" Battery Toy Boxed,**
1962. 9" tall litho tin and vinyl single musical figure by "Alps." Box - **$75 $150 $300**
Toy - **$125 $250 $500**

FLN-10

❑ **FLN-10. "Stone Age Candy" Boxes,**
1962. Store item. Each - **$6 $12 $18**

FLN-11

❑ **FLN-11. Wilma Flintstone Car With Box,**
1962. Marx. Car - **$50 $100 $200**
Box - **$50 $100 $200**

FLN-12

❑ **FLN-12. Betty Rubble Tin Friction Car,**
1962. Marx. 3.5" tall with vinyl head.
Car - **$50 $100 $200**
Box - **$50 $100 $200**

FLN-13

❑ **FLN-13. Pebbles On Dino Ramp Walker,**
c. 1963. Plastic store item by Marx Toys. - **$35 $75 $135**

FLN-14

❑ **FLN-14. "March Of Comics" #243,**
1963. Various retail sponsors. - **$8 $24 $70**

FLN-15

❑ **FLN-15. "Pebbles-Wilma Pull Toy" In Plastic,**
1963. Store item by Transogram. 9" long by 10" tall. Toy - **$100 $200 $300**
Box - **$100 $200 $300**

FLN-16

FLN-17

❑ **FLN-16. 1964-1965 New York World's Fair Comic Book,**
1964. Officially licensed souvenir published by JW Books With Hanna-Barbera copyright. - **$5 $15 $75**

❑ **FLN-17. Dino Litho. Button,**
1960s. Hanna-Barbera copyright. From 1960s Flintstone character set. - **$12 $25 $40**

FLN-18

❑ **FLN-18. Flintstone Bedrock Express Wind-Up Train,**
1960s. Marx. 2x12.75" long by 2.25" tall. Lithographed in blue stone-like pattern, tin train depicts all the various Flintstone characters looking out of the windows. - **$75 $150 $275**

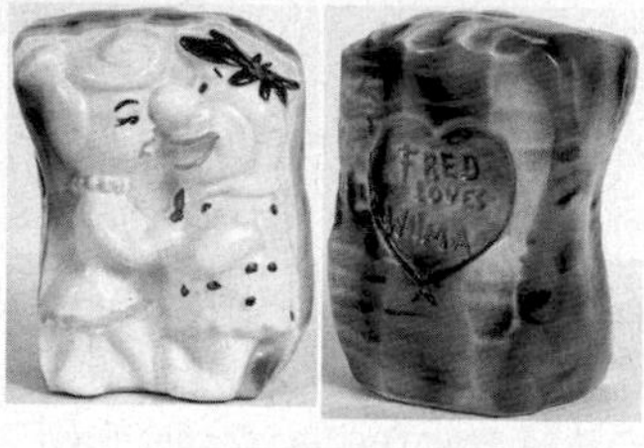

FLN-19

❑ **FLN-19. "Fred Loves Wilma" Ceramic Figural Bank,**
1960s. 8.25" tall front has raised figure image, reverse has their names incised within heart design. - **$50 $90 $175**

FLN-20

FLN-21

❑ **FLN-20. "History Of Bedrock" 23x28" Poster,**
1970. Miles Laboratories. - **$35 $65 $125**

❑ **FLN-21. Flintstone Jewelry Display With 36 Character Rings,**
1972. Store item by Cartoon Celebrities Inc.
Complete - **$175 $275 $425**
Each Ring - **$4 $6 $10**

FLN-22

❑ **FLN-22. Cocoa Pebbles Box Flat And Premium,**
1972. Issued by Post. 13x17" flat. Example of three different "bird" kite premiums. Gordon Gold Archives. Near Mint Flat **- $300**
Each Near Mint Bagged Premium **- $15**

FLN-23

FLN-24

❑ **FLN-23. Flintstone Land/Sea Vehicle,**
c. 1972. Probable Post's Fruity Pebbles.
Unassembled In Cellophane Wrapper - **$30**
Assembled - **$5 $10 $25**

❑ **FLN-24. Fred On Dino Digger Toy,**
c. 1972. Pebbles Cereal. Plastic mechanical action toy. - **$8 $15 $30**

FLN-25

FLN-26

❑ **FLN-25. Fred Flintstone "Powell Valves" Pencil Eraser,**
1972. Wm. Powell Co. - **$15 $30 $50**

❑ **FLN-26. Vending Machine Litho. Button Set,**
1973. Set of 12, various color combinations.
Each - **$5 $8 $20**

FLN-27

❑ **FLN-27. Litho. Buttons,**
1973. Store item. Set of 10. Each - **$8 $15 $25**

FLN-28

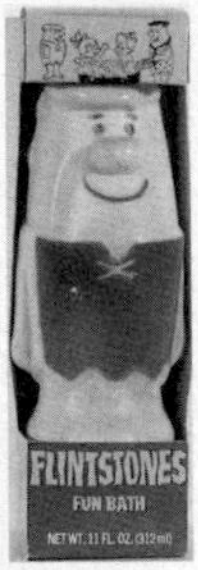

FLN-29

❑ **FLN-28. "Flint Cycle 16" Large Boxed Riding Toy,**
1974. Store item by AMF. Box - **$20 $40 $65**
Cycle - **$50 $85 $150**

❑ **FLN-29. Barney Fun Bath Bottle in Box,**
1977. Boxed - **$10 $25 $50**

FLN-30

❑ **FLN-30. "Flintstick" Plastic/Metal Miniature Cigarette Lighter,**
1970s. Flintstones Multiple Vitamins. -
$55 $110 $165

FLN-31

❑ **FLN-31. Flintstones Brand Multiple Vitamins Plastic Mugs,**
1970s. Each - **$5 $8 $15**

FLN-32

FLN-33

❑ **FLN-32. Vending Machine Header Card,**
1970s. Includes generic rings, generic Dino figure and rubber Flintstones figures.
Complete - **$100**

❑ **FLN-33. Fruit Drinks Litho. Tab,**
c. 1970s. Yabba Dabba Dew. - **$8 $12 $20**

FLN-34

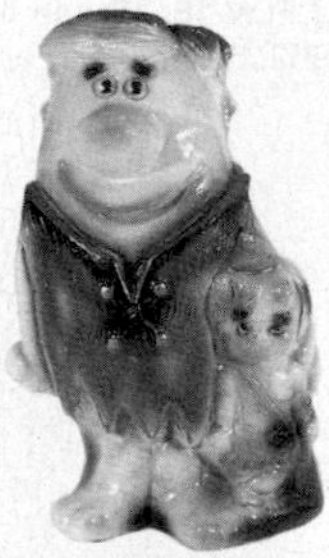
FLN-35

❑ **FLN-34. Fred Flintstone Bank Statue**
1993. 13" tall carnival statue. - **$30 $60 $125**

❑ **FLN-35. Barney Rubble Bank Statue**
1993. 12.5" tall carnival statue. - **$30 $60 $125**

FLN-36

❑ **FLN-36. "Post" Plastic Cereal Box Banks,**
1984. Cocoa Pebbles and Fruity Pebbles.
Each - **$10 $15 $30**

FLN-37

❑ **FLN-37. Fred & Barney Ceramic Figurines,**
1990. Post Cereals. Boxed - **$15 $30 $60**
Loose Pair - **$5 $15 $30**

FLN-38

❑ **FLN-38. Fruity Pebbles 17 oz. Cereal Box with Bendable Toys,**
1991. Post Cereals. Fred, Barney or Dino figures were packaged in the top of the box.
Each - **$10 $15 $30**

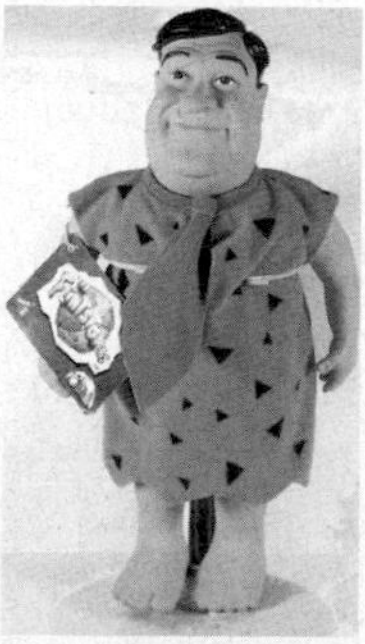

FLN-39

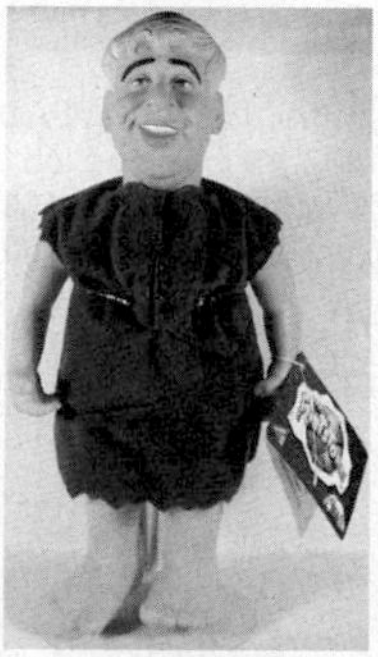

FLN-40

❑ **FLN-39. Fred Flintstone Movie Doll,**
1993. Dakin product. 13" tall with the likeness of actor John Goodman. - **$6 $18 $35**

❑ **FLN-40. Barney Rubble Movie Doll,**
1993. Dakin product. 12" tall with the likeness of actor Rick Moranis. - **$6 $18 $35**

(Lunch box) FLN-41 (Box)

❑ **FLN-41. Flintstones Barney Boxed Watch Set,**
1993. From Fossil. Watch and Barney pin come in a metal lunchbox picturing Fred and Barney.
Complete - **$400**

(Lunch box) FLN-42 (Box)

❑ **FLN-42. Flintstones Fred Boxed Watch Set,**
1993. From Fossil. Watch with 2 tags and Fred pin come in a metal lunchbox picturing Fred.
Complete - **$400**

FLN-43

FLN-44

❑ **FLN-43. Flintstones Movie Badge,**
1994. Giveaway badge. - **$4 $8 $15**

❑ **FLN-44. Replica Racing Car,**
1997. Features Flintstones on the car. - **$15**

FLN-45

❑ **FLN-45. Dino Bean Bag Figure,**
1998. Released a year before the other Flintstones Bean Bag figures. - **$25**

FLN-46

FLN-47

❑ **FLN-46. Fred Flintstone Bean Bag Figure,**
1999. With tag. - **$10**

❑ **FLN-47. Barney Rubble Bean Bag Figure,**
1999. With tag. - **$10**

FLN-48

❑ **FLN-48. Barney Rubble's Car on Card,**
1990s. Johnny Lightning series. - **$12**

Flip The Frog

Ub Iwerks (1901-1971), Walt Disney's original partner, struck out on his own in 1930. Erstwhile Disney distributor Pat Powers arranged to finance Iwerks' studio, perceiving the animator to be Disney's secret weapon. Iwerks' new star character, Flip the Frog, had debuted in embryo in a Disney cartoon—*Night* (1930)—but only now did he get his name.

Fiddlesticks (1930), featuring Flip in a vaudeville show, set the tone for Iwerks shorts to come. Flip mugs memorably at the viewer; musical sequences are expertly animated and blue humor is cheerfully deployed. Problematically for a pilot short, however, *Fiddlesticks*' storytelling was meandering and slow—and so it was, too, in the Flip cartoons that followed.

The drawback didn't hinder Flip at first. Released by Powers' own Celebrity Pictures, early releases were successful, leading MGM to buy distribution rights. The cartoons' characterization and plotting improved: Flip became a self-conscious, likeable loser in a racy urban environment.

Nevertheless, sound stories continued to be undermined on screen by slow pacing, soft gag impact and a meandering feel. Eventually, this took its toll on the series. In late 1933, Flip cartoons ceased production.

Flip merchandise peaked in 1932 and included dolls, books, figurines, and tin toys. Some items picture Flip's early costars: girlfriends Flap the Frog and Clarisse Cat, Flip's unnamed dog, and Orace the mule (a thinly veiled copy of Iwerks' Disney creation, Horace Horsecollar). Additional costars, the ragamuffin Kid and ditzy Spinster, seem not to have been merchandised.

Flip evolved over his four years on the screen, transforming from a goggle-eyed toad into a cuddly, anthropomorphic figure more closely resembling a humanized duck. Modern-day revivals of the character, some sanctioned by the Iwerks estate, tend to use the later model.

It should be noted that Clarisse Cat was retroactively named (in the 1990s); her name should not appear on any authentic 1930s item.

FLP-1

FLP-2

❑ **FLP-1. "Flip The Frog" Doll By Deans Rag Book Co.,**
c. 1930. Doll is 2.75x6x8.5" tall. Velveteen stuffed body with wire inserts in arms and legs for posing, checkered fabric bow tie, google eyes with felt eyelid accents. Underside of each foot has strong and distinct markings including company name, registration number and "Flip The Frog." - **$300 $600 $1200**

❑ **FLP-2. Flip The Frog Egg Timer,**
c. 1930. Glazed ceramic is 3.75" tall to the tip of the timer unit. Back of base has incised registration number and word "Foreign."
- **$100 $225 $350**

FLP-3

FLP-4

❑ **FLP-3. "Flip The Frog" Celluloid Figure With Movable Arms,**
1930s. Figure is 6.5" tall marked on the back "Flip The Frog" along with copyright and "Made In Japan." - **$250 $500 $850**

❑ **FLP-4. "Flip The Frog" Bisque,**
1930s. 5" tall. Reverse has faint incised copyright and name "Flip The Frog." Underside is marked "Made In Japan." - **$75 $150 $250**

FLP-5

❑ **FLP-5. Flip The Frog Musician Bisques,**
1930s. Pair, each 3.5" tall marked "Made In Japan." Also known with clarinet.
Each - **$50 $100 $200**

Flying Aces Club

One of the many 1930s aviation-themed clubs inspired in part by the accomplishment of Charles Lindbergh. There were 179 issues of the pulp *Flying Aces Magazine* published between September 1928 and November 1943. Most premiums carry the initials "FAC."

FAC-1

FAC-2

❑ **FAC-1. Club Membership Card,**
1932. Logo of wings only, no propeller. -
$25 $60 $100

❑ **FAC-2. Gold Cadet Wings,**
1932. - **$30 $60 $100**

FAC-3

FAC-4

❑ **FAC-3. Silver Pilot Wings,**
1932. - **$30 $60 $100**

❑ **FAC-4. "Pilot/FAC" Wings Badge,**
1932. Propeller on top of wings.
Silver version. - **$15 $25 $50**
Gold version - **$30 $60 $100**

FAC-5

FAC-6

❑ **FAC-5. "Cadet/FAC" Wings Rank Badge,**
1932. Propeller on top of wings.
Silver version. - **$15 $30 $50**
Gold version - **$30 $60 $100**

❑ **FAC-6. "Ace/FAC" Star Badge,**
1932. Scarce. - **$50 $100 $200**

FAC-7

FAC-8

❑ **FAC-7. "Flying Aces" Silvered Brass Bracelet,**
1932. Link bands with top plate in wing and propeller design. - **$60 $125 $250**

❑ **FAC-8. Club Membership Card,**
1932. Logo of wings mounted by propeller. -
$20 $50 $85

FAC-9

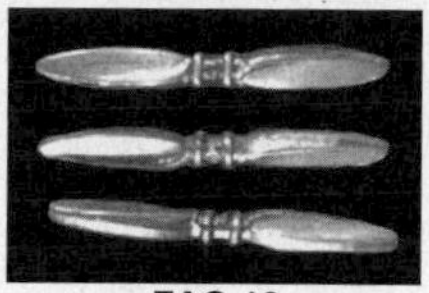

FAC-10

❑ **FAC-9. "F.A.C. Distinguished Service Medal" Brass Medal With Ribbon ,**
1932. Rare. Back inscription "Awarded By Flying Aces Club". - **$100 $175 $350**

❑ **FAC-10. FAC Propeller Pins,**
1932. Rare. For placement on "Service Medal" ribbon.
Each - **$15 $40 $75**

FAC-11

FAC-12

❑ **FAC-11. "FAC" Stitched Fabric Wings Patch,**
1932. Scarce. Flying Aces magazine. -
$30 $80 $150

❑ **FAC-12. "Flying Aces" Large Cloth Patch,**
1930s. Flying Aces Magazine. 1-7/8x4-1/4" long with nice design of red, white and blue plus large gold wings all against white background. -
$35 $85 $175

The Flying Family

This children's adventure program aired briefly on NBC in 1932-1933. The program dramatized the true-life story of Colonel George Hutchinson, his wife Blanche, and their daughters Kathryn and Janet. Accompanied by Sunshine, their lion cub mascot, the flying family found adventure in all parts of the country. Cocomalt sponsored the series, and young listeners could obtain their Flight Commander wings by drinking Cocomalt for at least 30 days and mailing in a statement witnessed and signed by a parent. A follow-up show, *The Flying Hutchinsons,* sponsored by Pepsi ran briefly in 1939 as the family attempted an around the world trip which had to be abandoned due to the outbreak of war in Europe.

FLY-1

❑ **FLY-1. Puzzle, Flight Commander Folder And Envelope,**
1932. Complete - **$25 $40 $75**

FLY-2

FLY-3

❑ **FLY-2. "Flight Commander/Flying Cubs" Brass Wings Rank Badge,**
1932. Highest rank depicting tiger head. -
$30 $50 $100

❑ **FLY-3. "Flying Cubs" Brass Wings Badge,**
1932. Depicts tiger head. - **$25 $45 $80**

FLY-4

FLY-5

❑ **FLY-4. Family Picture Wheaties Box Back,**
c. 1932. - **$10 $20 $30**

❑ **FLY-5. Family Adventures Map,**
c. 1932. Cocomalt. Pictures various global regions plus listing of air times on NBC radio stations. - **$60 $125 $250**

FLY-6

❑ **FLY-6. "Cub" Silvered Brass Lapel Stud,**
c. 1932. Association with this program is uncertain. - **$10 $30 $60**

Foodini

They started out in 1948 as the bumbling villains of the *Lucky Pup* series on CBS but Foodini and his dimwit accomplice Pinhead eventually took over the show and by 1951 were starring in their own series, *Foodini the Great,* on ABC which lasted until 1954 in syndication. Four issues of *The Great Foodini* comic book came out in 1950, and four issues of *Pinhead and Foodini* came out in 1951.The hand puppets, created by Hope and Morey Bunin(1911-1997), were fated never to accomplish their swindling schemes, defeated by the Pup's pal Jolo the clown as well as by their own ineptitude. Sponsors of the two series (1948-1951) included Ipana toothpaste, Good and Plenty candy, Sundial shoes and Bristol-Myers. Licensed items are normally copyrighted R. P. Cox.

FOO-1

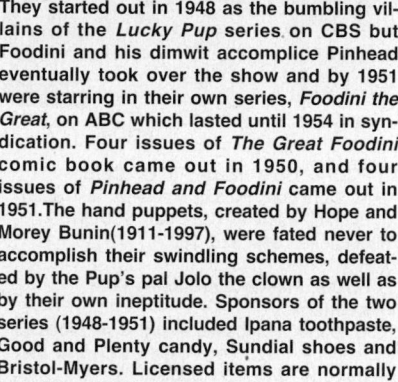

❑ **FOO-1. Paper Portraits,**
c. 1948. Scarce. CBS-TV. Set of four: Doris Brown with Lucky Pup, Foodini, Pinhead, Jolo.
Each - **$25 $40 $80**

FOO-2

❑ **FOO-2. Foodini Record In Sleeve,**
1949. 45 rpm titled "Foodini's Trip To The Moon." - **$25 $60 $125**

FOO-3

❑ **FOO-3. Foodini Characters Child Belt,**
1949. Leather belt inscribed "The Great Foodini" and "Bunin Puppets" featuring four repeated scenes of Foodini as magician plus Pinhead and Jolo. - **$50 $100 $175**

FOO-4

FOO-5

❑ **FOO-4. "Jolo" Metal Pin On Card,**
1949. Store item. Pins or bracelets, also seen for Foodini. Each Carded - **$25 $50 $100**
Each Loose - **$10 $25 $50**

❑ **FOO-5. Plastic Microscope With Instructions,**
1950. Ipana Toothpaste. Includes six slides for microscope. Instruction Folder - **$25 $45 $90**
Microscope - **$15 $30 $50**
Slides Each - **$1 $3 $5**

FOO-6

❑ **FOO-6. Birthday Card,**
1950. Store item by The Daline. Eight in a series for 1st-8th birthdays.
Each - **$20 $40 $75**

FOO-7

❑ **FOO-7. "Foodini T.V. Director" Chair,**
1950. Folding wood frame and canvas panels chair opening to 12x18x22" tall. -
$50 $125 $235

FOO-8

❑ **FOO-8. Cardboard Mask,**
c. 1950. Scarce. Punch-out from Magic Kit.
- $50 $150 $250

FOO-9

❑ **FOO-9. Foodini Fabric Scarf,**
c. 1950. Ipana Toothpaste. 19" long dark brown fabric with large gold illustration on each end picturing "Foodini And Pinhead" and "Smiley And Jolo." Front of Smiley's costume is inscribed "Ipana." Example shown has simulated brown leather slide accented by brass rivets and faceted emerald green stone but we're not certain this was actually part of the original item. - **$45 $90 $200**

FOO-10

❑ **FOO-10. "The Great Foodini Magic Set,"**
1951. 10.5x17.75x1.5" deep box contains complete set by Pressman Toy Corp. Box insert is designed like a stage and complete with a cellophane window. Set includes 3.5x4.5" illustrated instruction folder which explains all eight magic tricks. - **$165 $350 $600**

FOO-11 FOO-12

❑ **FOO-11. "Foodini" As Magician Dexterity Puzzle,**
1951. Plastic over tin frame puzzle. -
$30 $65 $140

❑ **FOO-12. "Jolo" Juggling Dexterity Puzzle,**
1951. Plastic over tin frame puzzle. -
$30 $65 $140

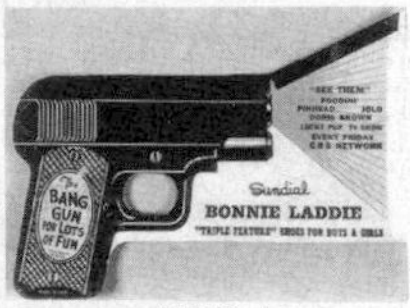

FOO-13 FOO-14

❑ **FOO-13. "Pinhead" Dexterity Puzzle,**
1951. Plastic over tin frame puzzle. -
$30 $65 $140

❑ **FOO-14. Cardboard Pop Gun,**
c. 1951. Sundial Bonnie Laddie Shoes. -
$25 $65 $130

FOO-15

❑ **FOO-15. Foodini & Friends Pop-Up Toy,**
c. 1951. Litho tin canister 5" tall pictures Foodini and Pinhead gazing at crystal ball within TV screen to see Jolo. TV set has "Pull Magic Knob" to release and pop up plastic 3-D figure of Jolo from waist up. - **$60 $150 $300**

FOO-16

❑ **FOO-16. "Foodini's Magic Glo-Mask,"**
c. 1951. Sundial Shoes. 10.5x12" diecut stiff paper face accented by glow-in-dark features. Reverse names sponsor and mentions Foodini appearance on "Lucky Pup" TV show. -
$75 $150 $300

FOO-17

❑ **FOO-17. "Sundial 'Lucky Pup' Jigsaw Puzzle,"**
c. 1951. Envelope is 9x12.5" from Sundial Shoes with 8.75x10.75" puzzle.
Envelope - **$20 $30 $50**
Puzzle - **$30 $60 $120**

FOO-18

❑ **FOO-18. "Television Studio" Cardboard Kit With Mailer,**
c. 1951. Sundial Bonnie Laddie Shoes. Includes stage, figures and accessories.
Near Mint In Mailer - **$400**

Foxy Grandpa

Cartoonist Carl E. Schultze (1866-1939) created his *Foxy Grandpa* comic strip for the Sunday New York Herald in 1900. The strip, which showed Grandpa consistently outwitting a pair of young tormentors, was an instant success with readers, but its popularity waned over the years. It moved to the New York American & Journal in 1902, then to the New York Press, where it ran until 1918. A series of nature tales, *Foxy Grandpa's Stories*, ran in newspapers during the 1920s. Cardboard cover reprints of the strip were published in the early years and a musical comedy based on the strip opened on Broadway in 1902. Schultze typically signed his drawings "Bunny," with an appropriate sketch. The American Mutoscope And Biograph Company released a series of live-action shorts in 1902. In 1937 Charles Biro did single gag pages for comic book publisher Harry Chesler in an attempt to bring new life to the character.

FOX-1

FOX-2

❑ **FOX-1. Comic Strip Introduction Button,**
1900. 1.75" multicolor cello promo for debut in Sunday New York Herald, possibly the first pinback for Foxy Grandpa. - **$65 $125 $250**

❑ **FOX-2. Foxy Grandpa Bisque Figure,**
c. 1900. Hollow bisque figure is 8" tall. Depicts Foxy seated with hands on legs. No markings. -
$50 $100 $150

FOX-3

FOX-4

❑ **FOX-3. Comic Strip Announcement 15x20" Paper Poster,**
1902. New York Sunday Journal. -
$150 $300 $650

❑ **FOX-4. "Foxy Grandpa's Grocery Store" Cut-Out Supplement,**
1902. New York American & Journal newspaper. Uncut - **$40 $75 $125**

FOX-5

❑ **FOX-5. Judge Magazine with Foxy Grandpa Cover,**
1902. Cover only - **$50 $100 $150**
Complete - **$100 $150 $200**

FOX-6

❑ **FOX-6. Foxy Grandpa See-Saw Cut-Out Supplement,**
1902. New York Herald newspaper. -
$40 $75 $125

FOX-7

FOX-8

❑ **FOX-7. "Six Months In New York" Cello. Button,**
1902. For theater version based on comic strip.-
$20 $35 $70

❑ **FOX-8. "Foxy Grandpa" Cello. Button,**
c. 1902. Hearst's Chicago American. Promotes start of comic strip by that newspaper. -
$20 $35 $70

FOX-9

❑ **FOX-9. Foxy Grandpa Song Sheet,**
c. 1902. Scarce. Newspaper supplement. -
$30 $60 $140

FOX-10

FOX-11

❑ **FOX-10. Foxy Grandpa Song Sheet,**
c. 1902. Scarce. Newspaper supplement. - **$30 $60 $140**

❑ **FOX-11. "Foxy Grandpa/Chicago American" Diecut White Metal Stickpin,**
c. 1902. Lightly tinted, depicts him and both boys. - **$30 $50 $100**

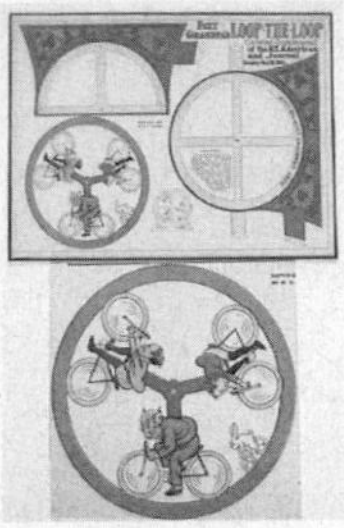

FOX-12

FOX-13

❑ **FOX-12. Foxy Grandpa's "Loop-The-Loop" Sunday Comic Cut-Out Supplement,**
1903. New York American and Journal. 10x14" stiff paper issued Sunday, May 10.
Uncut - **$40 $75 $125**

❑ **FOX-13. "Foxy Grandpa Second Year Of The Musical Comedy" Diecut Cello. Figure,**
1903. 2-1/2" tall full color thin cello. figure by Whitehead & Hoag Co. - **$35 $65 $125**

FOX-14

FOX-15

❑ **FOX-14. "Foxy Grandpa 2nd Year" Button,**
1903. 1.5" cello multicolor for theater production. - **$20 $45 $85**

❑ **FOX-15. "Foxy Grandpa 2nd Year" Button,**
1903. 1.5" cello multicolor for theater production. - **$20 $45 $85**

FOX-16

❑ **FOX-16. Sunday Newspaper Comics Reprint Book,**
1905. Store item by M. A. Donohue & Co., Chicago. One of a series of books by various publishers published between 1901 and 1916 with at least 18 known. For specific years, see the *Overstreet Comic Book Price Guide.*
Good Range - **$57-$313**
Fine Range - **$200-$1100**

FOX-17

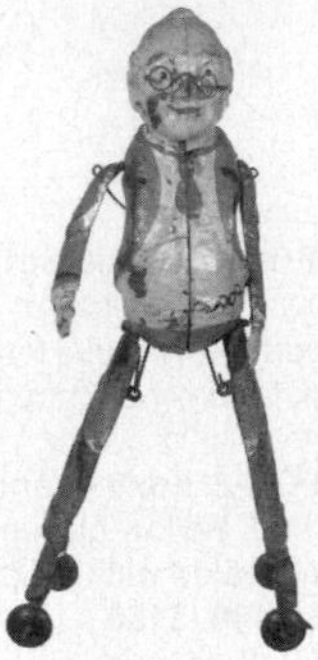

FOX-18

❑ **FOX-17. Foxy Grandpa Stuffed Cloth Doll,**
1905. - **$75 $165 $275**

❑ **FOX-18. Foxy Grandpa German Tin Wind-Up Toy,**
c. 1905. Painted tin toy is 2.5x3x8" tall. Unmarked but German made. Toy has separate attached eyeglasses. Attached to feet are axles, each with pair of wheels. Toy has built-in key. He opens and closes his legs, moving forward. - **$500 $1000 $2000**

FOX-19

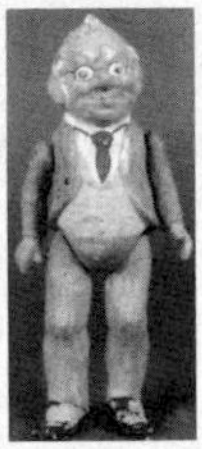

FOX-20

❑ **FOX-19. Bisque Figure,**
c. 1905. Store item. - **$65 $150 $250**

❑ **FOX-20. Composition Figure,**
c. 1905. Store item. Jointed arms and legs. - **$60 $125 $225**

FOX-21

FOX-22

❑ **FOX-21. Flocked Composition Candy Container,**
c. 1905. Store item. - **$100 $200 $400**

❑ **FOX-22. Foxy Grandpa And The Boys Stickpin,**
c. 1905. About 1-1/2" tall in silver luster white metal. - **$12 $25 $50**

FOX-23

❑ **FOX-23. Figural Bisque Humidor,**
c. 1905. Unmarked but probably German. Our photo example is missing lid.
No Lid - **$75 $135 $200**
Near Mint With Lid - **$300**

FOX-24

❑ **FOX-24. Postcard,**
1906. Boston Sunday American premium. Has heat-applied tattoo transfer on front. - **$8 $15 $25**

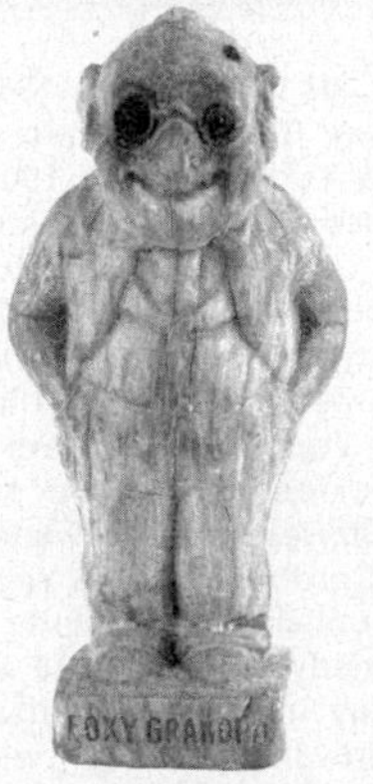

FOX-25

❑ **FOX-25. Foxy Grandpa Soap Figure,**
1900s. Rare. - **$150 $250 $400**

FOX-26

❑ **FOX-26. Foxy & Kids Antic Plate,**
1900s. 9.5" diameter full color china with amateur artist's depiction of bowling activity. - **$35 $75 $150**

FOX-27

❑ **FOX-27. Foxy Grandpa Antic Plate,**
1900s. 9.5" diameter. Brightly colored illustration of Grandpa bowling while two boys look on. Back has Hallmark and text "R. Briggs Co. Boston." - **$35 $75 $150**

FOX-28

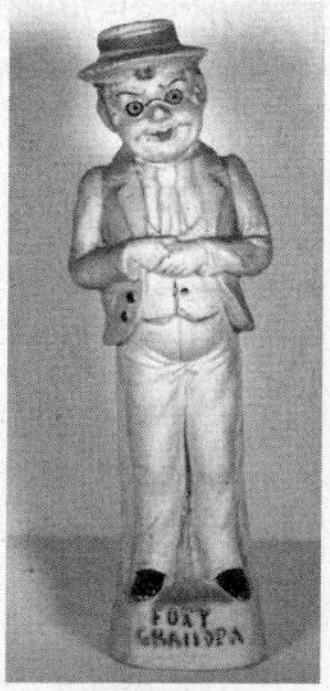

FOX-29

❑ **FOX-28. Bisque Figure,**
1900s. - **$75 $200 $300**

❑ **FOX-29. Bisque Figure,**
1920s. - **$65 $125 $250**

Frank Buck

Animal hunter and trapper Frank Buck (1884-1950) achieved international fame after World War I as a jungle explorer whose claim that he never intentionally harmed a wild animal led to his motto "Bring 'Em Back Alive." Buck went around the world more than a dozen times collecting animals, giving lectures, making movies and writing magazine articles and books, and at one point owned the world's largest private zoo in Massapequa, New York. He appeared as himself in two brief radio series: on NBC in 1932 sponsored by A. C. Gilbert toys and on the Blue network in 1934 sponsored by Pepsodent toothpaste. Buck and his animals were featured at the 1934 Century of Progress Exposition in Chicago and the 1939-1940 New York World's Fair. Items inscribed "Jungle Camp" are from the earlier exposition; those inscribed "Jungle Land" or "Jungleland" are from his 1939 exhibit. A 1932 documentary film followed him through the Malay jungles as he collected various animals and Buck played an adventurer in Columbia Pictures' first chapter play, *Jungle Menace*, in 1937. A Sunday comic page, *Frank Buck Presents Ted Towers Animal Master* with art by Glenn Cravath, Ed Stevenson and others ran from 1934 to 1939. CBS-TV aired a *Bring 'Em Back Alive* fiction series in 1982-1983 starring Bruce Boxleitner as the legendary hunter.

FRB-1

FRB-2

❑ **FRB-1. "Bring 'Em Back Alive" Book,**
1930. By Frank Buck. Published by Simon and Schuster.
Book - **$25 $50 $75**
Near Mint With Dust Jacket - **$175**

❑ **FRB-2. A.C. Gilbert Christmas Ad Photo,**
1932. Frank Buck inscription "I Hope You Get An Erector Set For Christmas". - **$20 $40 $80**

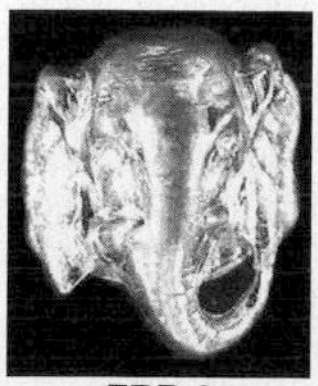

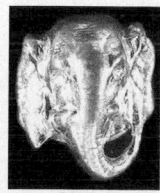

FRB-3

FRB-4

❑ **FRB-3. Movie Ring,**
1932. Silver luster with adjustable bands made by Uncas and issued to promote 1932 movie "Bring 'Em Back Alive."
Standard Version - **$150 $300 $500**
"Sterling" Version - **$200 $400 $600**

❑ **FRB-4. "Bring 'Em Back Alive" Button,**
c. 1932. 1-3/4" likely issued to promote the movie of this title. - **$35 $75 $150**

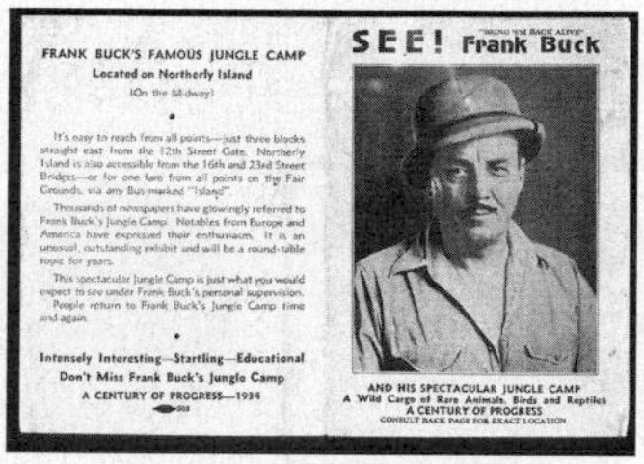

FRB-5

❑ **FRB-5. Chicago World's Fair Brochure,**
1934. Four pages. Promotes Jungleland exhibit. - **$25 $45 $75**

FRB-6

❑ **FRB-6. "Capturing Wild Elephants!" Book,**
1934. 28 page book, 12"x9". Merrill Publishing Co. - **$35 $70 $200**

FRB-7

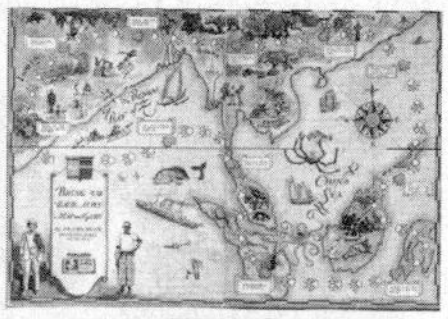

FRB-8

❑ **FRB-7. "Frank Buck's Jungle Camp" Cello. Button,**
1934. From exhibit at Chicago World's Fair. - **$25 $45 $90**

❑ **FRB-8. "Bring 'Em Back Alive" Map And Game 14x22",**
1934. Two versions: premium from "Scott's Emulsion" or store item by "Funland Books & Games". - **$100 $200 $400**

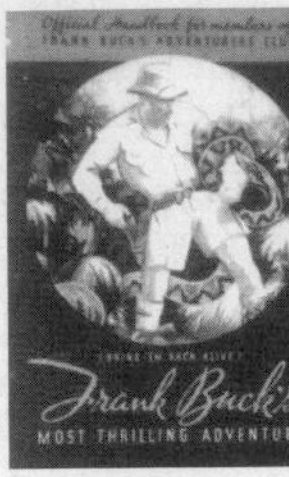

FRB-9

❑ **FRB-9. Club Manual,**
1934. Pepsodent toothpaste. - **$45 $110 $190**

FRB-10

FRB-11

❑ **FRB-10. Mailer,**
1934. For Club manual. Rare. - **$35 $85 $150**

❑ **FRB-11. "Frank Buck" Brass Lucky Piece,**
1934. Pepsodent toothpaste. Back pictures leopard head with inscription "Tidak Hilang Berani". Copy of Hindu hunter's charm carried by Ali, Frank Buck's Number 1 Boy. - **$30 $100 $150**

FRB-12

FRB-13

❑ **FRB-12. "A Century Of Progress" Chicago World's Fair Litho. Button,**
1934. From exhibit, dated for second year of fair. - **$40 $85 $175**

❑ **FRB-13. "Adventurers Club-Member" Brass Button,**
1934. Pepsodent toothpaste. - **$8 $15 $30**

FRB-14

FRB-15

❑ **FRB-14. Film Supplement,**
1934. Sixteen page premium. Promotes the film "Wild Cargo." - **$30 $60 $100**

❑ **FRB-15. "Adventurers Club" Fabric Neckerchief,**
1934. Pepsodent toothpaste. - **$50 $95 $185**

FRB-16

❑ **FRB-16. "Frank Buck Adventure Club" Lariat,**
1934. Rope loop totaling 116" length with metal slide fastener for loop size adjustment. One end has wood handle inscribed by club title. Mail premium obtained for five complete cartons from any Pepsodent product. - **$50 $100 $160**

FRB-17

❑ **FRB-17. "Young American News Weekly,"**
1935. Weekly issue with 16 pages. - **$20 $40 $75**

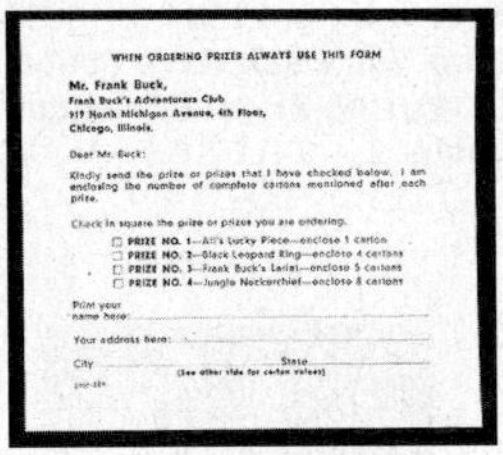
WHEN ORDERING PRIZES ALWAYS USE THIS FORM

Mr. Frank Buck,
Frank Buck's Adventurers Club
919 North Michigan Avenue, 4th Floor,
Chicago, Illinois.

Dear Mr. Buck:

Kindly send the prize or prizes that I have checked below. I am enclosing the number of complete cartons mentioned after each prize.

Check in square the prize or prizes you are ordering.

☐ PRIZE NO. 1—Ali's Lucky Piece—enclose 1 carton
☐ PRIZE NO. 2—Black Leopard Ring—enclose 4 cartons
☐ PRIZE NO. 3—Frank Buck's Lariat—enclose 5 cartons
☐ PRIZE NO. 4—Jungle Neckerchief—enclose 8 cartons

Print your name here: ____________

Your address here: ____________

City ____________ State ____________

(See other side for carton values)

FRB-18

FRB-19

❑ **FRB-18. Prize Checklist,**
1935. Pepsodent prize list. - **$12 $25 $40**

❑ **FRB-19. "Frank Buck Club" Cello. Button,**
1936. - **$50 $115 $235**

FRB-20

❑ **FRB-20. "Frank Buck's Adventure Club" Ring,**
1938. Issued with very thin muted silver luster finish. Air and wear quickly caused loss of silver flashing, leaving the base with a muted bronze finish. Scarce; rare in Near Mint.
Silver Luster Near Mint - **$1500**
Bronze Luster - **$200 $400 $750**

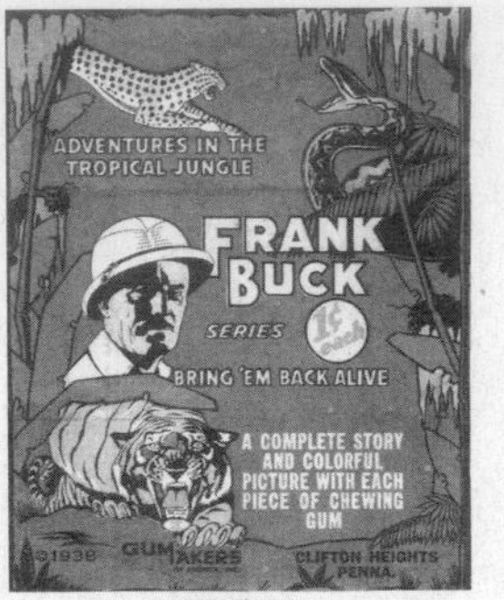

FRB-21

❑ **FRB-21. "Frank Buck Series Bring 'Em Back Alive" Wrapper,**
1938. Gum Makers of America. 5.25x6.5" waxed paper wrapper for earlier card series than the Topps issue. - **$200 $400 $600**

FRB-22

❑ **FRB-22. "Frank Buck's Jungleland" New York World's Fair Badge,**
1939. Brass die-cut badge 1-5/8" tall with two shades of luster and lettering and star border in red or blue. Reads in full "New York World's Fair Frank Buck's Jungleland." - **$135 $275 $500**

FRB-23

❑ **FRB-23. "Frank Buck's Jungleland" New York World's Fair Card,**
1939. Briefly described his exhibit in the amusement area. - **$12 $25 $50**

(CLOSE-UP)

FRB-24

❑ **FRB-24. "Jungle Camp" Metal Letter Opener/Bookmark,**
1939. From exhibit at New York World's Fair. - **$25 $65 $150**

FRB-25

FRB-26

❑ **FRB-25. "Bring 'Em Back Alive" Ivory Initial Ring,**
1939. Ivory Soap. Brass with personalized initial ivory-colored insert. - **$85 $200 $450**

❑ **FRB-26. "Frank Buck's Jungleland" New York World's Fair Brass Ring,**
1939. Rare. Tiny "NYWF" initials rather than traditional Frank Buck's Adventurers Club inscription. - **$550 $1600 $2750**

FRB-27

❑ **FRB-27. "New York World's Fair/Frank Buck's Jungleland" Leather Pennant,**
1939. 14-1/4" long. - **$75 $175 $300**

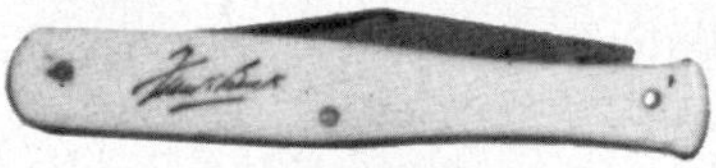

FRB-28

❑ **FRB-28. Cello./Steel Pocketknife,**
1939. Ivory Soap. White grips with facsimile signature on one. - **$65 $150 $275**

FRB-29

❑ **FRB-29. Pennant,**
1939. New York World's Fair Jungleland exhibit pennant. Scarce. - **$75 $175 $300**

FRB-30

FRB-31

FRB-32

❑ **FRB-30. World's Fair Promo,**
1939. New York World's Fair brochure. Eight pages. - **$25 $45 $75**

❑ **FRB-31. Coin,**
1939. Jungleland premium with hole for chain. New York World's Fair Coin. Scarce. - **$35 $70 $135**

❑ **FRB-32. New York World's Fair Exhibit Cello. Button,**
1939. Black and white 1-1/4". - **$30 $60 $125**

FRB-33

FRB-34

❑ **FRB-33. Buckhorn Rifle Manual,**
1930s. Twelve page premium. Shows Frank testing the gun, as well as various photos of the gun. - **$15 $25 $60**

❑ **FRB-34. Postcard,**
1930s. Premium for exhibition in New York - **$15 $30 $60**

FRB-35

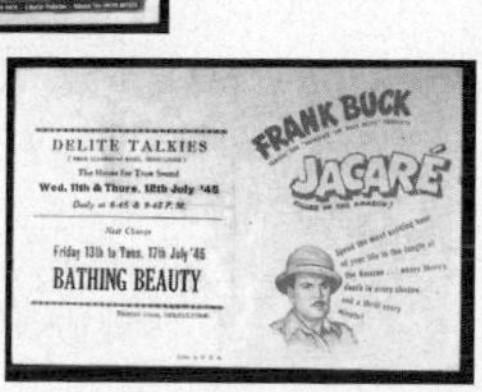

(Back view)

❑ **FRB-35. "Jacaré" Movie Promo,**
1942. United Artists film. - **$20 $50 $75**

FRB-36

FRB-37

❑ **FRB-36. "Frank Buck Explorer's Sun Watch",**
1949. Jack Armstrong/Wheaties. - **$20 $35 $75**

❑ **FRB-37. Wheaties Caribbean Cruise Contest And Sun Watch Leaflets,**
1949. Contest Sheet - **$8 $18 $35**
Sun Watch Order Form - **$6 $12 $18**

FRB-38

❑ **FRB-38. "Frank Buck Explorer's Sun Watch" Instruction Leaflet,**
1949. Wheaties. Folder opening to four panels w/instructions printed on both sides. - **$20 $30 $60**

Frank Merriwell

Dime novels, the forerunner of pulp magazines, became popular in the 1880s. Colorful covers highlighted text stories embellished with daring deeds and the triumph of good over evil. Writer Gilbert Patten (1866-1945), under various pseudonyms, had been doing stories for several years when approached by the large publishing company Street & Smith to come up with a character for their new magazine *Tip Top Library*. Using "Frank" for frankness, "Merri" for happy disposition and "Well" for good health, he came up with Frank Merriwell.

Written under the pen name Burt L. Standish, Frank's first adventure was published on April 18, 1896. Author Patten imbued Frank Merriwell with a Yale education, a sharp mind, physical fitness, an honest demeanor and a penchant for hard work. Merriwell became an inspiration to boys and girls nationwide. He was not only a role model, but an imaginary friend they could trust. Patten went on to author 208 Frank Merriwell books, which sold over 100 million copies. A 12-part serial *The Adventures of*

Frank Merriwell *(italic)* **starring Donald Briggs and Jean Rogers, was released by Universal in 1936.**

Merriwell's adventures remained popular well in the 1940s in a comic strip, a Big Little Book title, and a radio program with Lawson Zerbe in the title role. Frank Merriwell's adventures and personality set the tone for one of radio's most popular characters, the next "All-American Boy," Jack Armstrong.

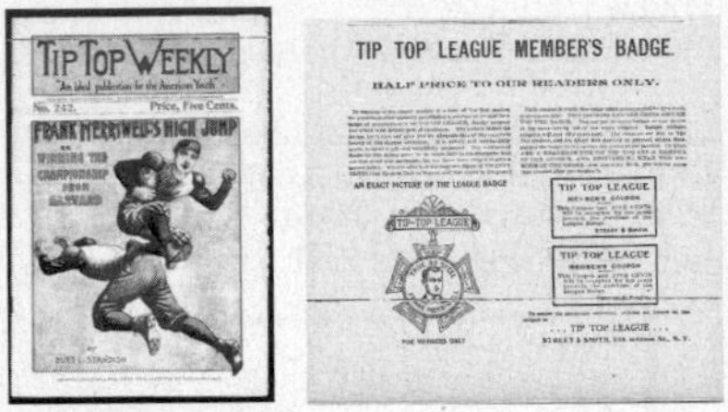

FRM-1

❑ **FRM-1. Tip Top Weekly #242,**
1900. Frank Merriwell's Tip Top League Badge pictured with application for 1st premium badge.- **$25 $50 $100**

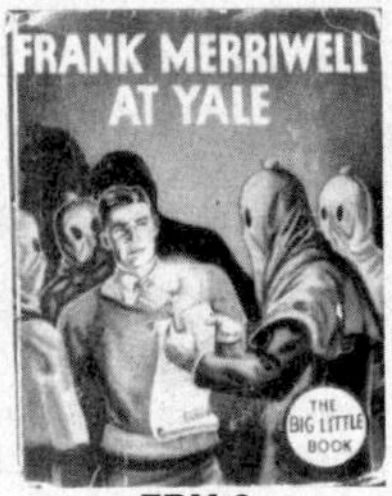

FRM-2 FRM-3

❑ **FRM-2. Frank Merriwell Tip Top League Brass Badge,**
1900. Tip Top Magazine premium. First character badge. Offered for 20¢ or a dime and two coupons from Tip Top Weekly. - **$175 $375 $850**

❑ **FRM-3. "Frank Merriwell At Yale" BLB,**
1935. Store item. Whitman #1121. - **$10 $30 $68**

FRM-4 FRM-5

❑ **FRM-4. "Club Member/Follow The Adventures Of Frank Merriwell" Cello . Button,**
1936. Scarce. Universal Pictures. For 12-chapter movie serial "The Adventures Of Frank Merriwell". - **$50 $125 $225**

❑ **FRM-5. "Follow Frank Merriwell" Cello. Button,**
1930s. Also reads "Daily In The Washington Herald." 1-1/4" blue and red on white from a scarce series of comic characters issued by this newspaper. - **$40 $100 $200**

Frank Sinatra

Francis Albert Sinatra (1915-1998), affectionately referred to as The Voice, Old Blue Eyes and Chairman of the Board during various stages of his career first came to the public's attention as a member of The Hoboken Four singing *Shine* on *Major Bowes Amateur Hour* radio show in 1935. On March 18, 1939 he released his first record *Our Love*, joined the Harry James Orchestra as a vocalist in June 1939, then Tommy Dorsey's band in 1940. Sinatra had his first hit record with *I'll Never Smile Again* in the summer of 1940. He made his first film appearance in *Las Vegas Nights* in the fall of 1940 and was voted top male singer in *Billboard* and *Downbeat* magazine polls in May, 1941.

Sinatra starred in or hosted various radio shows on NBC and CBS between 1943 and 1955, then moved to ABC-TV with various shows and specials from 1957 into the 1960s including a 1960 special welcoming Elvis Presley home from the Army. Sinatra made his Las Vegas debut at the Desert Inn in September 1951, and played a major role in the desegregation of Nevada hotels and casinos in the 1960s with his Rat Pack pals Sammy Davis Jr., Dean Martin, Joey Bishop and Peter Lawford. Sinatra retired in 1971, came back in 1973 and performed until February 25, 1995. He appeared in some 45 films, winning five Academy Awards and two Golden Globes. He has sold 250 million records worldwide, won 11 Grammy Awards and has three stars on the Hollywood Walk of Fame. On May 23, 1985 he was awarded the Presidential Medal of Freedom. The skinny kid from Hoboken did it his way.

FRS-1

❑ **FRS-1. "My Hero Frank Sinatra" Button,**
c. 1942. 1.25" diameter. - **$12 $25 $60**

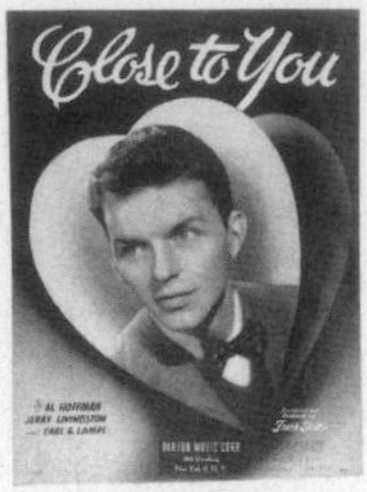

FRS-2

❑ **FRS-2. Frank Sinatra Song Sheet,**
1943. Features song "Close To You" and Sinatra photo on cover. - **$18 $35 $60**

FRS-3

❑ **FRS-3. "Lucky Strike Presents Your Hit Parade Starring Frank Sinatra" Cardboard Fan,**
1943. Scarce. Lucky Strike cigarettes. 12" tall diecut tobacco leaf replica inscribed on back "A Fan For My Fans-Frank Sinatra". - **$50 $100 $200**

FRS-4 FRS-5

❑ **FRS-4. Frank Sinatra "Old Gold Cigarettes" Advertising Sign,**
c. 1945. 5.5x10.75" thin cardboard sign advertising CBS musical radio show sponsored by Old Gold Cigarettes. - **$200 $400 $700**

❑ **FRS-5. Sinatra On 1947 High School Graduation Button,**
1947. 2.75" diameter button issued for "Jan '47" graduating class from "Bok" vocational high school in the Philadelphia area. It was a tradition of Philadelphia high schools to produce a graduating class button featuring some well-known personality or comic character. - **$25 $50 $100**

FRS-6

FRS-7

❑ **FRS-6. Frank Sinatra Vending Machine Card,**
1940s. Pictured in front of an NBC mike. Not common. - **$10 $20 $40**

❑ **FRS-7. "My Ideal Frank Sinatra" Button,**
1940s. 1.25" diameter. - **$10 $20 $45**

FRS-8

❑ **FRS-8. Frank Sinatra Figural Celebrity Mug,**
c. 1940s. Barclay. 6.5" wide by 5.75" tall painted and glazed ceramic mug. Stamped "Hollywood Mugs By Barclay" on bottom with artist name "Doya." - **$200 $400 $600**

FRS-9

❑ **FRS-9. "Frank Sinatra Fan Club" Card**
1940s. - **$35 $65 $125**

FRS-10

❑ **FRS-10. "Frank Sinatra" Bracelet,**
1940s. 6" metal link style centered by insert photo on heart-shaped charm incised "Faithfully Frank Sinatra." - **$65 $135 $200**

FRS-11

❑ **FRS-11. "Copacabana" Announcement Folder For Frank Sinatra,**
c. 1952. Folded size is 5.5x7" and opens to 7x11". Front illustration is of Copa Girls. Opens once to reveal portrait photo of Frank Sinatra with text "The Copacabana Proudly Presents Frank Sinatra Accompanied By Skitch Henderson In Our Gay Spring Review With Larry Storch, Fred & Sledge, Russ Emory, Lorna Lynn, Patricia Adair And A Ravishingly Lovely New Array Of De-Lovely Delectable Copa Girls." Folder opens again to reveal detailed text on the club noting its 10th year. - **$65 $135 $190**

FRS-12

❑ **FRS-12. "From Here To Eternity" Lobby Card Set,**
1953. Columbia Pictures. Set of eight 11x14" lobby cards. Set - **$200 $400 $600**

FRS-13

❑ **FRS-13. "Frank Sinatra" Record Store Sign,**
1950s. Capitol Records. 13-1/4x19" with black and white photo on yellow stiff paper. - **$60 $125 $185**

FRS-14

❑ **FRS-14. Frank Sinatra Leroy Neiman Print,**
1994. Leroy Neiman. 20x24" colorful print with Sinatra facsimile signature at bottom left. - **$12 $25 $50**

Freakies

Created by Jackie End, Ralston Purina Company introduced Freakies cereal--crunchy, sugary puffs--in 1971, along with a gang of seven creatures also called Freakies. The creatures, ugly little characters covered with bumps, were named Boss Moss, Cowmumble, Gargle, Goody-Goody, Grumble, Hamhose, and Snorkledorf. In-package premiums included PVC Freakies, stickers, holograms, and a set of rubber air bulb-powered vinyl race cars. The cereal was an initial success but failed to win repeat customers and lasted until 1977. An attempt to revive Freakies as Space Surfers in 1987 also failed.

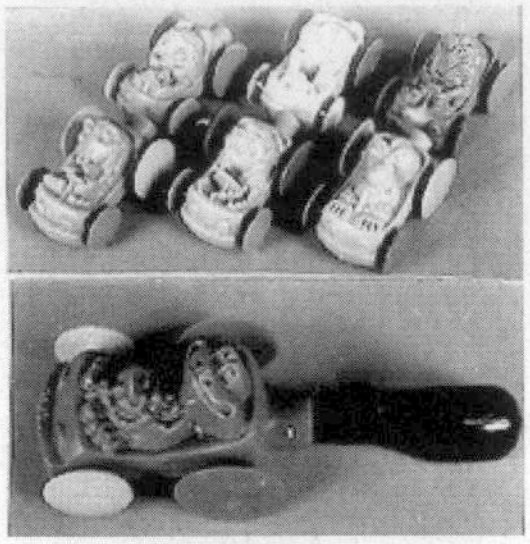

FRK-1

❑ **FRK-1. "Freakie Car" Set Of Seven Vinyl Racers,**
1974. Each is 2-1/2" long plus rubber air bulb to launch car. Top edge of front bumper names each as "Boss Moss, Goody Goody, Hamhose, Cowmumble, Snorkledorf, Gargle, Grumble."
Near Mint Boxed With Instructions - **$160**
Each With Air Bulb - **$12 $18 $35**

FRK-2

❑ **FRK-2. Fabric Iron-On Patches,**
1975. Pictured are Gargle, Cowmumble, Hamhose from probable set of seven.
Each - **$10 $18 $30**

FRK-3

FRK-4

FRK-5

❑ **FRK-3. Boss Moss Freakies Plastic Ring,**
1970s. Ralston Cereal. Orange plastic with 1-1/2" tall figure on top accented in black. -
$85 $165 $330

❑ **FRK-4. Freakies Rubber Magnet,**
1970s. At least five different characters seen in a small version about 1" to 1-1/2" and a larger version about 1-1/2" to 2". Each - **$3 $6 $12**

❑ **FRK-5. Freakies Vinyl Figures,**
1970s. At least seven different in various single colors, each about 1-1/2" to 2".
Each - **$4 $8 $15**

FRK-6

❑ **FRK-6. Freakies Boats,**
1970s. Soft plastic figures of Hamhose, Cowmumble, Grumble, each designed to hold balloon to propel in water by air loss after inflation. Each - **$8 $15 $30**

FRK-7

❑ **FRK-7. Freakies Cereal Box,**
1987. - **$20 $60 $125**

Fred Allen

Fred Allen (1894-1956) was a vaudeville juggler and standup comic who became one of the legendary radio comedians of the 1930s and 1940s. From his first show on CBS in 1932 to his last on NBC in 1949, hardly a week went by without a Fred Allen program of one sort or another. Allen wrote his own material and his "feud" with Jack Benny was a successful running gag from 1936 to 1949. They appeared in two films together: *Love Thy Neighbor* in 1940 and *It's In The Bag* in 1945. Also memorable was Allen's Alley, a mythical street he developed in 1942, inhabited by Mrs. Nussbaum, Titus Moody, Ajax Cassidy and Senator Claghorn. Sponsors over the years included Linit bath oil, Hellmann's mayonnaise, Sal Hepatica, Ipana toothpaste, Texaco gasoline, Tenderleaf tea and Ford automobiles. Allen made a number of television appearances in the 1950s on comedy and quiz shows most notably *What's My Line* from 1954 to 1956, but his biting wit and literate humor were better suited to radio.

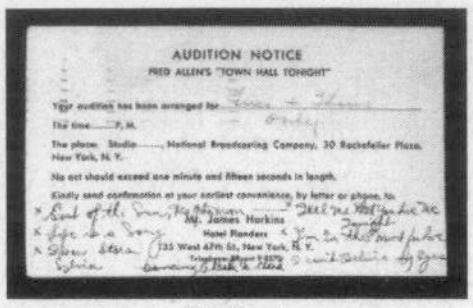

AUDITION NOTICE
FRED ALLEN'S "TOWN HALL TONIGHT"

Your audition has been arranged for ______
The time ______ P. M.
The place: Studio ______, National Broadcasting Company, 30 Rockefeller Plaza, New York, N. Y.
No act should exceed one minute and fifteen seconds in length.
Kindly send confirmation at your earliest convenience, by letter or phone, to
Mr. James Harkins
Hotel Flanders
135 West 47th St., New York, N. Y.

FRD-1

FRD-2

FRD-3

❑ **FRD-1. Fred Allen's "Town Hall Tonight" Audition Notice Postcard,**
1935. Notification to entertainer hopeful granting radio audition at NBC Studios, New York. -
$10 $15 $30

❑ **FRD-2. "Town Hall Tonight" Fan Postcard,**
1937. Radio show title on back. - **$12 $20 $40**

❑ **FRD-3. Fred Allen & Portland Hoffa Fan Photo,**
c. 1937. Ipana toothpaste and Salhepatica Stomach Relief. Back names "Town Hall Tonight" radio show. - **$12 $20 $40**

Friends of the Phantom

Between 1933 and 1953 Richard Curtis Van Loan--alias the Phantom--solved crimes in the pages of 170 issues of the pulp magazine *Phantom Detective.* Created by D.L. Champion writing under the name Robert Wallace, the Phantom was a genius of disguise and a physical marvel. During the 1930s, readers who joined his crime-fighting club would receive a Friends of the Phantom badge.

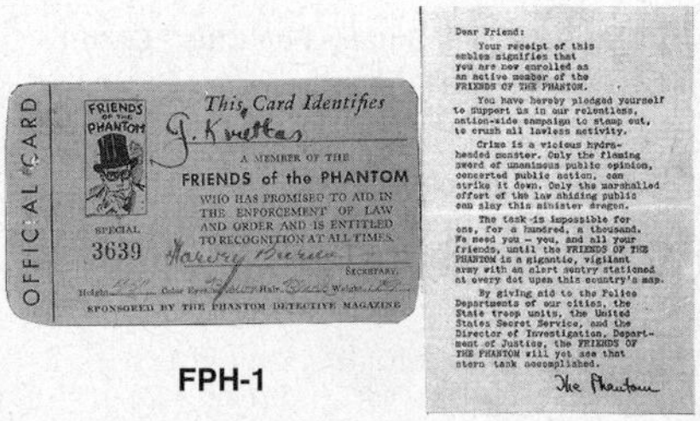

OFFICIAL CARD
FRIENDS OF THE PHANTOM
This Card Identifies
A MEMBER OF THE
FRIENDS of the PHANTOM
WHO HAS PROMISED TO AID IN THE ENFORCEMENT OF LAW AND ORDER AND IS ENTITLED TO RECOGNITION AT ALL TIMES.
SPECIAL
3639
SECRETARY.
Height ______ Color Eyes ______ Hair ______ Weight ______
SPONSORED BY THE PHANTOM DETECTIVE MAGAZINE

Dear Friend:

Your receipt of this emblem signifies that you are now enrolled as an active member of the FRIENDS OF THE PHANTOM.

You have hereby pledged yourself to support us in our relentless, nation-wide campaign to stamp out, to crush all lawless activity.

Crime is a vicious hydra-headed monster. Only the flaming sword of unanimous public opinion, concerted public action, can strike it down. Only the marshalled effort of the law abiding public can slay this sinister dragon.

The task is impossible for one, for a hundred, a thousand. We need you – you, and all your friends, until the FRIENDS OF THE PHANTOM is a gigantic, vigilant army with an alert sentry stationed at every dot upon this country's map.

By giving aid to the Police Departments of our cities, the State troop units, the United States Secret Service, and the Director of Investigation, Department of Justice, the FRIENDS OF THE PHANTOM will yet see that stern task accomplished.

The Phantom

FPH-1

❑ **FPH-1. "Friends Of The Phantom" Letter And Membership Card,**
1930s. Phantom Detective magazine.
Card - **$75 $150 $300**
Letter - **$50 $110 $185**

FPH-2

❑ **FPH-2. "Friends Of The Phantom" Brass Shield Badge,**
1930s. Phantom Detective magazine. Phantom depicted in mask and top hat. - **$65 $125 $250**

Fu Manchu

Master scientist and brilliant prince of evil, Fu Manchu was created by novelist Sax Rohmer (1883-1959) in 1913. He appeared in a series of silent films in the 1920s and in talkies from 1929 to 1980 played by Warner Oland, Boris Karloff, Henry Brandon, Christopher Lee or Peter Sellers. His stories were serialized in *Colliers* magazine from the mid-teens into the early 1930s with wonderful illustrations by J.C. Coll and John R. Flanagan. The evil oriental, who was either avenging the death of his wife and son or out to conquer or destroy the world, starred in several radio serials: on *The Collier Hour*, sponsored by Collier's magazine, on the Blue network in 1927; on CBS in 1932-1933 sponsored by Campana Balm and in *The Shadow of Fu Manchu*, a syndicated 1939-1940 serial. A syndicated television series had a brief run in 1956.

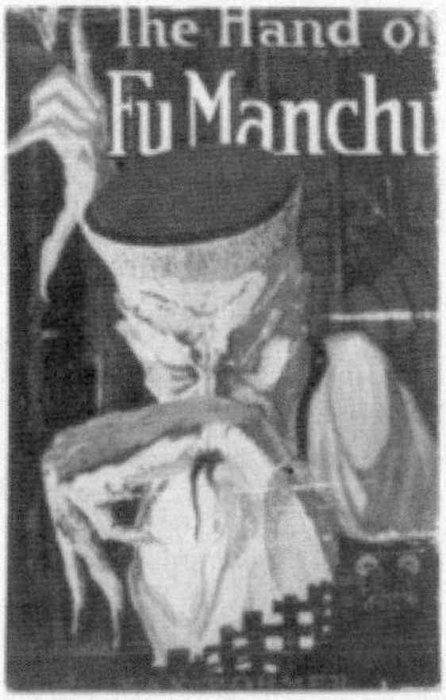

FUM-1

❑ **FUM-1. "The Hand Of Fu Manchu" Hardback With Dust Jacket,**
1917. Published by A. L. Burt Co. With Jacket - **$40 $65 $150**

FUM-2

❑ **FUM-2. "The Return Of Dr. Fu-Manchu" Hard Bound Novel With Dust Jacket,**
c. 1930. Book is 5x7.5" with 344 pages. Published by A.L. Burt Co. copyright 1916 Robert M. McBride And Co. Printed in conjunction with 1930 film "The Return Of Dr. Fu-Manchu" starring Warner Oland. The book has several black and white plate illustrations from film. Jacket - **$50 $150 $300**
Book - **$25 $50 $100**

FUM-3

❑ **FUM-3. "The Mask Of Fu Manchu" Hardcover Book,**
1932. Published by A. L. Burt Co. with art by J. R. Flanagan. - **$20 $40 $75**

FUM-4

FUM-5

❑ **FUM-4. Paper Mask,**
1932. Rare. Various theaters. - **$100 $225 $500**

❑ **FUM-5. "Mask Of Fu Manchu" Movie Herald,**
1932. Folder for M-G-M movie starring Boris Karloff in title role. - **$30 $60 $100**

FUM-6

FUM-7

❑ **FUM-6. "Shadow Of Fu Manchu" Radio Promo Matchbook Cover,**
1939. - **$20 $40 $80**

❑ **FUM-7. "The Shadow Of Fu Manchu" Radio Serial Cello. Button,**
1939. - **$30 $60 $125**

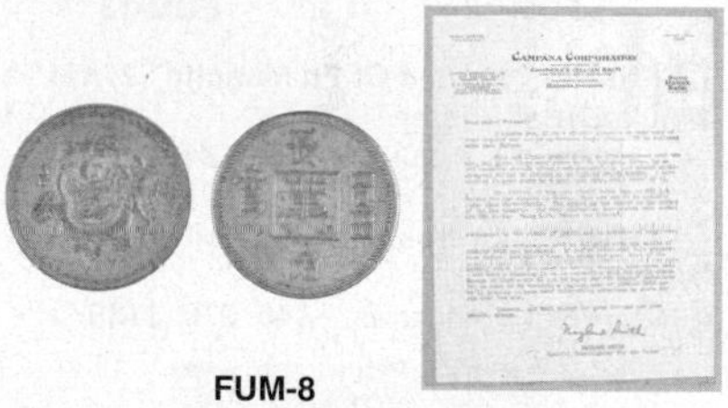

FUM-8

❑ **FUM-8. Fu Manchu Chinese Coin And Letter,**
c. 1939. Premium from Compana Italian Balm. 8.5x11" letter from Nayland Smith Special Investigator for the Crown discussing a Chinese lucky piece that is included. Letter comments on Dr. Fu Manchu saving his life. 1.25" Chinese Lucky piece brass coin is double-sided with a large dragon on obverse and reverse has Chinese symbols. Coin - **$25 $50 $100**
Letter - **$30 $65 $115**

FUM-9

FUM-10

FUM-11

❑ **FUM-9. "Shadow Of Fu Manchu" Keys Trick With Envelope,**
c. 1939. Dodge Motors Co. "Mystic Keys" dexterity trick of two interlocking 2" metal keys in envelope imprinted for WFBR Radio, Baltimore. Envelope - **$50 $100 $150**
Key Set - **$30 $60 $100**

❑ **FUM-10. "Drums Of Fu Manchu" Movie Serial Cello. Button,**
1940. Scarce. - **$50 $100 $250**

❑ **FUM-11. "Drums Of Fu Manchu" 41x77" Three-Sheet Poster,**
1940. Republic Pictures. 15-chapter movie serial. - **$200 $450 $900**

FUM-12

FUM-13

❑ **FUM-12. "Drums Of Fu Manchu" 27x41" Movie Serial Poster,**
1940. Republic Pictures. - **$200 $450 $850**

❑ **FUM-13. "Drums Of Fu Manchu" 14x22" Window Card,**
1940. Republic Pictures. - **$40 $70 $135**

FUM-14

❑ **FUM-14. Six-Sheet Poster,**
1940. Republic Pictures. Issued in folded size of 11x15" but assembles to 80x80". -
$350 $750 $1500

Fury

Fury was a black stallion and the star attraction on NBC-TV's Saturday morning lineup from 1955 to 1966. Fury's real name was Beaut (1943-1972); trained by Ralph McCutcheon, he also appeared in the feature films *Black Beauty* (1946), *Giant* (1956) and *Wild is the Wind* (1957). His human co-stars in this extremely popular series were Bobby Diamond as a young orphan and Peter Graves as the rancher who adopted the boy and gave him the horse as a means of teaching him responsibility. The show received a number of awards from various civic and service groups for its non-violent handling of problems of right and wrong. Post cereals was an early sponsor but merchandising was not extensive. Items are normally copyrighted Vision Productions Inc., Television Programs of America Inc. or Independent Television Corp. The show has been syndicated under the title *Brave Stallion.* Dell published a series of *Fury* comic books between 1957 and 1962.

FUR-1

❑ **FUR-1. Cast Member Photo,**
c. 1955. Glossy black and white with facsimile signatures of Bobby Diamond, Peter Graves, William Fawcett, Ann Robinson. - **$15 $25 $50**

FUR-2

❑ **FUR-2. "Fury Cowboy Neckerchief" Kit With Envelope,**
c. 1955. Mail premium of fabric bandanna, metal clasp, color photo. Near Mint In Mailer - **$175**
Photo - **$10 $20 $40**
Bandanna - **$8 $15 $25**
Clasp - **$20 $45 $100**

FUR-3

❑ **FUR-3. "Fury's Western Roundup" Party Kit,**
c. 1955. Borden Co. Extensive paper items including eight punch-out sheets.
Unused - **$25 $50 $100**

FUR-4

❑ **FUR-4. "Fury" Whitman Frame Tray Puzzle,**
c. 1955. Tray is 11-3/8x14-3/8" with color photo of Bobby Diamond and two other young boys sitting on bareback of Fury who is twirling lasso. Whitman #4420. Copyright Independent Television Corp. - **$20 $40 $80**

FUR-5

FUR-6

❑ **FUR-5. "Fury And The Lone Pine Mystery" Book,**
1957. Whitman #1537. - **$6 $12 $28**

❑ **FUR-6. "Fury And The Mystery At Trappers Hole" Book,**
1959. Whitman #1557. - **$6 $12 $28**

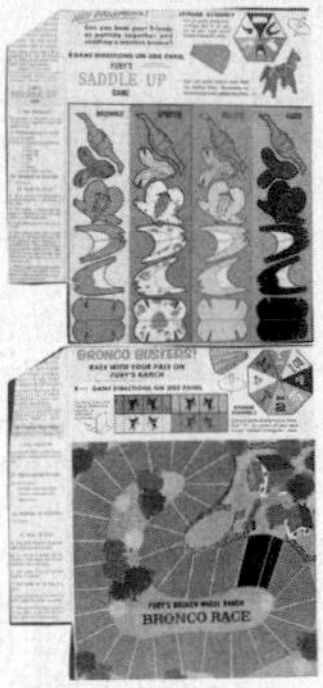

FUR-7

FUR-8

❑ **FUR-7. Fury Cereal Box Panels,**
1959. Two Post's Raisin Bran box panel clippings titled "Fury's Saddle-Up Game" and "Fury's Broken Wheel Ranch Bronco Race."
Each Box Back - **$12 $25 $40**
Each Complete Box - **$60 $125 $265**

❑ **FUR-8. "Dell TV Adventure" Comic Book,**
1960. Issue #1080 for February-April. -
$6 $18 $90

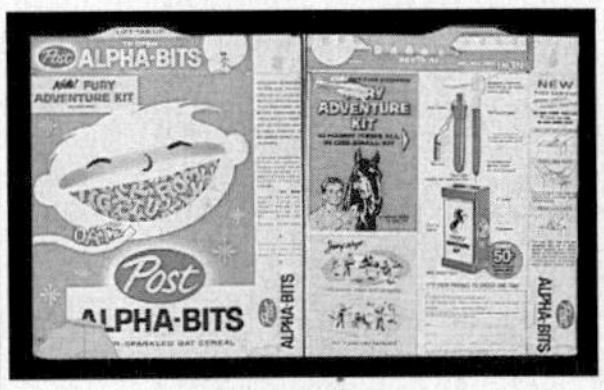

FUR-9

FUR-10

❑ **FUR-9. Cereal Box Offering Fury Adventure Kit,**
1960. Post Alpha-Bits.
Used Complete - **$65 $135 $285**

❑ **FUR-10. "Fury Adventure Kit",**
1960. Post Alpha-Bits. Multi-purpose plastic including weather indicator, flashlight, whistle, pen and miniature writing tablet. -
$50 $100 $175

Gabby Hayes

George "Gabby" Hayes (1885-1969) acted in a traveling repertory company and played burlesque and vaudeville before he went to Hollywood for a film career that spanned more than 30 years. Known as Windy, then Gabby, the whiskered, ornery, toothless geezer played sidekick to Hopalong Cassidy, Roy Rogers, Gene Autry, Bill Elliott, Randolph Scott and John Wayne in well over 100 Westerns. Hayes was a regular on radio's *Roy Rogers Show* in the 1940s and had his own program on the Mutual network in 1951-1952, sponsored by Quaker cereals. Adventure and "Gabby Hayes Western" comic books appeared between 1948 and 1957. On television, two separate series--both called *The Gabby Hayes Show*--ran concurrently. One was a weekly educational program about episodes in American history (NBC 1950-1951), the other a fictional series of tall tales and Western film clips (NBC 1950-1954 and ABC 1956). Sponsors were Quaker cereals and Peter Paul candy.

GAB-1

GAB-2

❑ **GAB-1. Gabby Hayes Arcade Card,**
Early 1940s. Photo is from his early movie era. Note that Gabby is not wearing his prospector's hat. - **$5 $10 $25**

❑ **GAB-2. Dixie Picture,**
c. 1942. Thinner paper than typical Dixie picture. - **$60 $125 $215**

GAB-3

❑ **GAB-3. "George 'Gabby' Hayes" Portrait Button,**
c. 1946. Button is 1.25" from series of western stars and this is from the series with small copyright symbol on the background. - **$20 $40 $80**

GAB-4

GAB-5

❑ **GAB-4. "George 'Gabby' Hayes" Dixie Ice Cream Picture,**
1947. - **$75 $175 $375**

❑ **GAB-5. "George 'Gabby' Hayes" Cello. Button,**
c. 1948. - **$25 $50 $100**

GAB-6

❑ **GAB-6. Fantasy Tales Storybook-Record Album,**
c. 1950. RCA Victor Little Nipper Series. - **$25 $50 $100**

GAB-7

❑ **GAB-7. Hand Puppet,**
c. 1950. Store item. 9" tall. - **$60 $115 $185**

GAB-8

GAB-9

❑ **GAB-8. Record Album With Story,**
c. 1950. Store item from RCA Victor "Little Nipper" series. 10x10" paper folder holding single 78 rpm record "Allee Bamee And The Forty Horse Thieves." - **$25 $50 $100**

❑ **GAB-9. School Tablet,**
c. 1950. Store item. 5-1/2x9" with color cover. - **$15 $25 $50**

GAB-10

❑ **GAB-10 "George 'Gabby' Hayes" Button,**
c. 1950. 1.25" black and white scarce version. - **$40 $85 $175**

GAB-11

❑ **GAB-11. Prospector's Hat 16x21" Paper Store Sign,**
1951. Quaker Cereals. - **$100 $225 $450**

GAB-12

❑ **GAB-12. Prospector's Black Felt Hat,**
1951. Quaker Cereals. - **$30 $90 $200**

GAB-13

❑ **GAB-13. Quaker Cereal Comic Booklets With Mailing Envelopes,**
1951. Set of five.
Each Book Or Mailer - **$10 $30 $90**

GAB-14

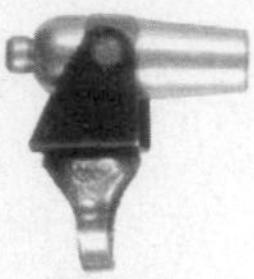

GAB-15

❑ GAB-14. Mother's Oats Container,
1951. Offers set of 5 Gabby Hayes comic books. - **$50 $100 $185**

❑ GAB-15. Quaker Cannon Ring,
1951. Puffed Wheat & Puffed Rice. Large ring with brass base and spring-loaded barrel in either brass or aluminum. - **$110 $225 $375**

GAB-16

❑ GAB-16. "Shooting Cannon Ring" Instruction Sheet,
1951. Quaker Cereals. Opposite side offers Miniature Western Gun Collection. - **$40 $80 $150**

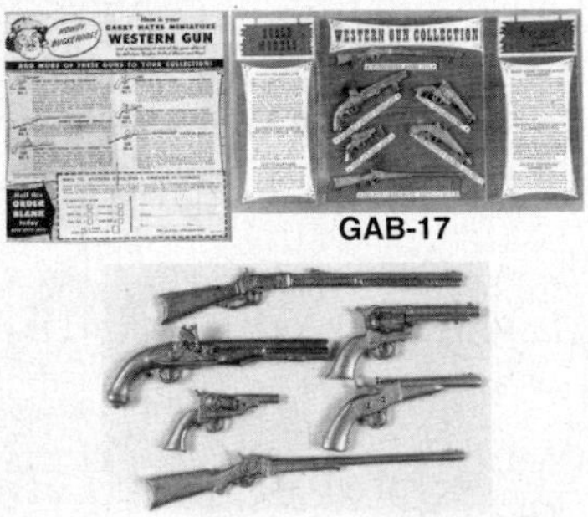

GAB-17

❑ GAB-17. "Gabby Hayes Miniature Western Gun Collection",
1951. Quaker Cereals. Set of six: Buffalo Rifle, Colt Revolver, Flintlock Dueling Pistol, "Peacemaker" Pistol, Remington Breech-Loader Rifle, Winchester 1873 Rifle.
Gun Set - **$30 $60 $150**
Display Folder - **$30 $75 $150**
Order Sheet - **$15 $30 $50**

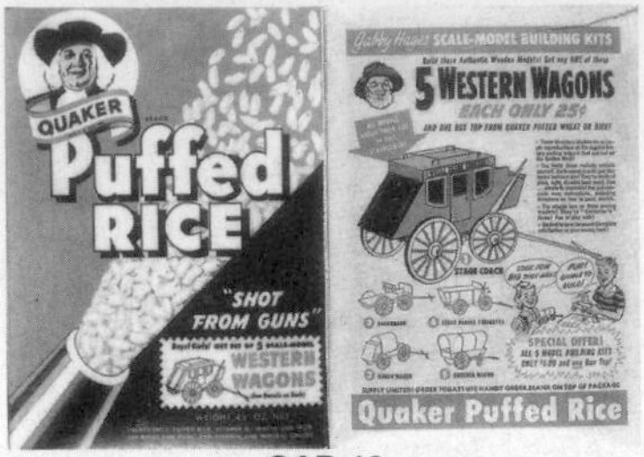

GAB-18

❑ GAB-18. Quaker "Five Western Wagons" Cereal Box,
1952. Quaker Puffed Rice.
Complete Box - **$75 $200 $400**

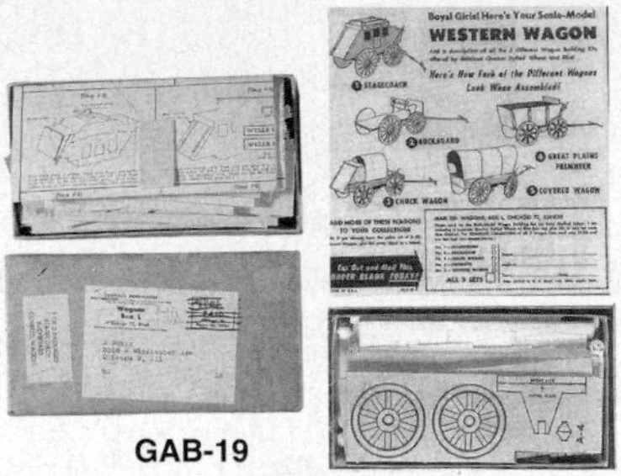

GAB-19

❑ GAB-19. Gabby Hayes Western Wagon Kits,
1952. Quaker Cereals. Five different kits: Buckboard, Chuck Wagon, Covered Wagon, Great Plains Freighter, Wells Fargo Stagecoach. Each Boxed - **$20 $50 $80**

GAB-20

❑ GAB-20. "Tall Tales For Little Folks" Mechanical Book,
1954. Inside front cover has diecut head and pair of boots that swing into position to create a 17" tall figure. Pages fold to give Gabby different outfits. Published by Samuel Lowe Co. - **$15 $35 $75**

GAB-21

❑ GAB-21. Movie Viewer Set,
1952. Quaker Cereals. Filmstrip with five titles, instruction slip, mailer. Near Mint Boxed - **$300**

GAB-22

❑ GAB-22. Quaker "Pocket-Sized Movie Viewer" Newspaper Ad,
1952. - **$8 $12 $25**

GAB-23

❑ GAB-23. Gabby Hayes Metal Automobiles,
1952. Quaker Cereals. Set of five.
Near Mint Boxed - **$240**
Each - **$5 $15 $35**
Instructions - **$15 $25 $35**

GAB-24

❑ GAB-24. Quaker "Clipper Ship in a Bottle" Cereal Box,
1950s. Quaker Puffed Wheat.
Complete Box - **$75 $200 $400**

GAB-25

❑ **GAB-25. Gabby Hayes Portrait Ring,**
1950s. Silver luster plastic base has clear plastic panel on the top over a closeup black and white paper photo of him. Ring is of the vending machine issue style. - **$40 $80 $150**

GAB-26

❑ **GAB-26. "Gabby Hayes Cottontail" Wooden Riding Horse,**
1950s. 10x22" tall by 30" long painted rocker horse toy accented by white yarn tail attached at seat rear. Front side of neck pictures and names Gabby while Cottontail name is also on neck and each rocker. - **$125 $235 $450**

Gang Busters

Marching against the underworld, proving each week that crime does not pay, *Gang Busters* was based on case files of the FBI and local police and proved so popular that it ran on network radio for 21 years. The program was created by Phillips H. Lord (1902-1975). The show premiered on CBS in 1936 sponsored by Palmolive. Succeeding sponsors including Cue magazine (1939-1940), Sloan's liniment (1940-1945), Waterman pens (1945-1948), Tide soap (1948), Grape-Nuts cereal (1949-1954) and Wrigley's gum (1954-1955). The show was last aired in 1957. Descriptions of actual criminals, broadcast at the end of each program, apparently resulted in the capture of hundreds of fugitives. Kent Taylor and Robert Armstrong starred in a 1942 movie serial with 13 chapters. Hosted by movie actor Chester Morris, a television series with the same format had a nine-month run on NBC in 1952. *Gang Busters* comic books were published from 1938 to 1959.

GNG-1

GNG-2

❑ **GNG-1. "Phillips H. Lord's Gang Busters" Badge,**
c. 1935. Brass luster on embossed tin. - **$85 $165 $350**

❑ **GNG-2. "Gang Busters" Badge,**
c. 1935. Beautifully designed 7/8" tall die-cut shield-shaped badge with eagle at center plus pair of crossed police batons. Reads "Gang Busters Fight Crime." - **$60 $115 $175**

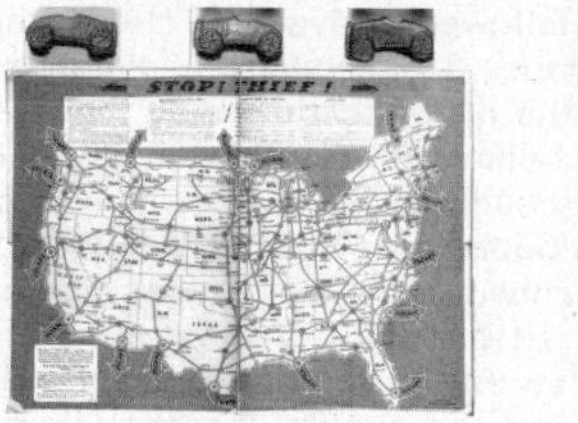

GNG-3

GNG-4

❑ **GNG-3. "Stop Thief" 22x30" Paper Game Board Map,**
1937. Palmolive. Came with nine metal cars.
Game - **$40 $90 $175**
Each Car - **$8 $12 $25**

❑ **GNG-4. Tie,**
1937. Scarce. - **$65 $150 $250**

GNG-5

GNG-6

GNG-7

❑ **GNG-5. Member's Badge,**
c. 1937. Comes with or without blue stars around edge. - **$25 $60 $125**

❑ **GNG-6. "Green's Gang Busters Crime Crusaders" Enameled Brass Badge,**
c. 1937. "Phillips H. Lord's" copyright. - **$50 $100 $175**

❑ **GNG-7. Enameled Belt Buckle,**
c. 1937. Rare. - **$65 $150 $250**

GNG-8

❑ **GNG-8. Cap Gun on Card,**
1938. Rare. Gun Only - **$200 $400 $675**
Complete - **$250 $500 $875**

GNG-9

GNG-10

❑ **GNG-9. "Gang Busters" Game,**
1938. Store item by Lynco Inc. -
$125 $275 $550

❑ **GNG-10. "Gang Busters Step In" Better Little Book,**
1939. Whitman #1433. Based on radio program.
- **$12 $36 $85**

GNG-11

❑ **GNG-11. Whitman Boxed Board Game,**
1939. Store item. - **$70 $125 $200**

GNG-12

❑ **GNG-12. "Gang Busters" Wind-Up Machine Gun,**
1930s. Store item by Marx. 23" long litho. tin with hand grip, missing from our photo example. Each side reads "Gang Busters/Crusade Against Crime." - **$175 $450 $900**

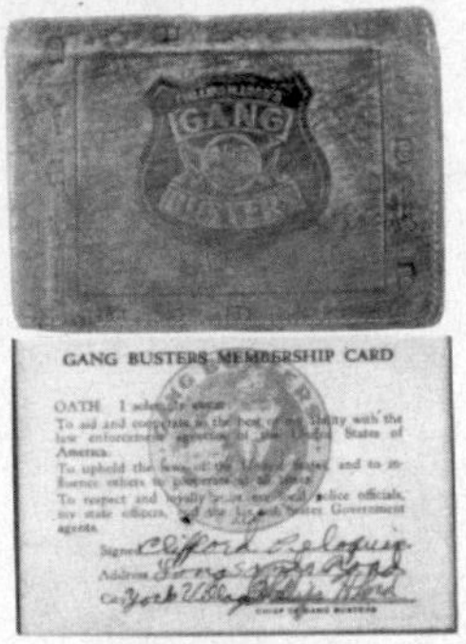

GNG-13

❑ **GNG-13. "Gang Busters" Wallet With Member Card,**
1930s. Store item. Wallet - **$35 $70 $150**
Card - **$30 $65 $125**

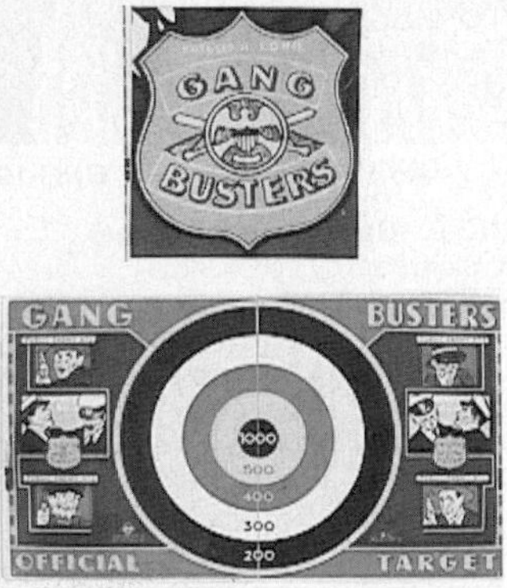

GNG-14

❑ **GNG-14. "Gang Busters" Litho. Tin Target,**
1940. Store item by Marx Toys with copyright of Phillips H. Lord. 16x27" full color litho. over rigid cardboard features "Public Enemy" pictorial targets designed to fall backwards when struck. - **$90 $185 $350**

Garfield

Thank goodness for Garfield creator Jim Davis' short attention span. If he hadn't gotten bored with a little-known Garfield predecessor, Gnorm the Gnat, our favorite loafing, lasagna-lifting feline may never have come to be. In 1978, Davis did get around to trying out a non-insect comic strip star and the most famous cat ever to pounce on the funny pages was the remarkable result. What started out as a small-scale endeavor on Davis' part (He hoped for publication in 100 papers, 300 max.) has now become an incredible quarter-century empire. All of Garfield's animated primetime television specials have been nominated for Emmys, and four have won: Garfield on the Town (1983), Garfield in the Rough (1984); Garfield's Halloween Adventure (1985) and Garfield's Babes & Bullets (1989). Jim Davis also bears the distinction of being the only author ever to have seven books on The New York Times bestseller list at once. Eleven of his Garfield books have made it to the top of the distinguished list, a near-impossible feat for comic strip books. Today, Garfield appears in an astounding 2,750 papers. He also has a not-too-shabby merchandising line, worth the overweight cat's girth in billions.

GAR-1

❑ **GAR-1. Garfield Die-Cut Display with Lapel Pins,**
1978. Display - **$25 $50 $75**
Each pin - **$2 $3 $4**

GAR-2

❑ **GAR-2. Garfield Animation Cel Signed By Bill Melendez,**
1983. Cel is 8x11". Near Mint Signed Same Or Similar - **$150**
Near Mint Unsigned Same Or Similar - **$120**

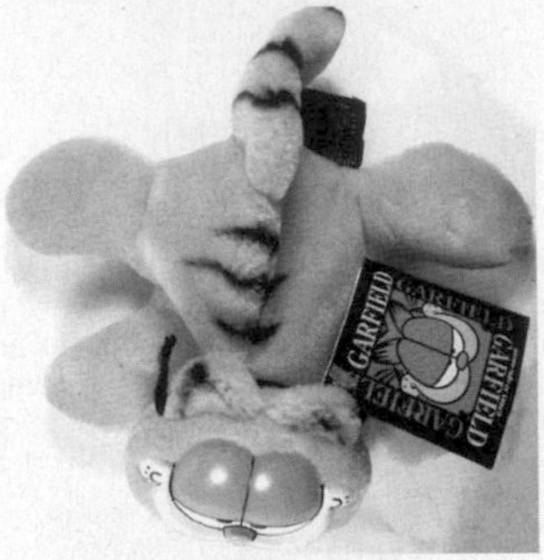

GAR-3

❑ **GAR-3. "Garfield" Bean Bag,**
1999. - **$12**

GAR-4

GAR-5

❑ **GAR-4. Garfield Figure with Watch,**
1990s. Limited Edition. Glass globe covers items. Complete - **$150**

❑ **GAR-5. Garfield Glass Bank,**
1990s. - **$35**

GAR-6

❑ **GAR-6. Talking Gumball Machine,**
1990s. Boxed. - **$110**

GAR-7

❑ **GAR-7. Garfield Playing Cards in Collector Tin,**
2001. Contains two decks of cards. Boxed - **$12**

GAR-8

❑ **GAR-8. "Garfield's Globe" Boxed,**
2001. - **$85**

GAR-9

❑ **GAR-9. "Garfield at 25" Hardcover Book,**
2002. Easton Press. Leather-bound, limited, signed edition of Ballantine Books release - **$110**

GAR-10

❑ **GAR-10. "Season's Eatings" Hardcover Book,**
2003. Easton Press. Leather-bound, limited, signed edition of Ballantine Books release - **$115**

GAR-11 GAR-12

❑ **GAR-11. Garfield Bobber Figure,**
2003. - **$22**

❑ **GAR-12. Garfield Bobber Figure,**
2003. - **$22**

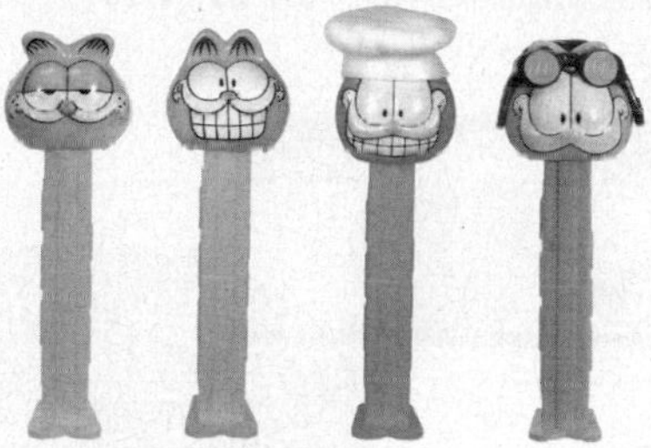

GAR-13

❑ **GAR-13. Garfield Pez Holders,**
2000-2004. - **$3**

Gene Autry

America's popular singing cowboy, Autry (1907-1998) was born on a small ranch in Texas and grew up in Oklahoma, where he worked as a railroad telegraph operator and began his career singing and composing. Local performances as a yodeling cowboy led to national radio spots on the *National Barn Dance* and *National Farm and Home Hour* programs in the 1930s. Autry began recording cowboy songs in 1929 and had phenomenal success both as a composer and as a singer. His first hit *That Silver Haired Daddy of Mine*, released in 1931, has sold over one million copies. He moved to Hollywood in 1934 and a year later starred in *Phantom Empire*, a 12-episode chapter play for Mascot. Over the years Autry was to write more than 250 songs and act in more than 100 Westerns. His recordings of *Here Comes Peter Cottontail* (1950) and *Here Comes Santa Claus* (1947) have each sold more than two million records. *Rudolph the Red-Nosed Reindeer* (1949) is the second best selling record of all time with sales over 30 million.

***Gene Autry's Melody Ranch*, a program of Western songs and stories told around a campfire, premiered on CBS radio in 1940 and ran continually until 1956, interrupted only by Autry's service in the Army Air Corps from 1942 to 1945. The program, sponsored by Wrigley's gum, featured bearded sidekick Pat Buttram for comic relief, along with a variety of musical groups.**

On television, also sponsored by Wrigley's gum, *The Gene Autry Show* aired on CBS from 1950 to 1956. Filmed at his 125-acre Melody Ranch and produced by his Flying A Productions company, the program put Autry back in the saddle again each week to do battle with assorted villains. Riding his wonder horse Champion and accompanied by saddle-partner Buttram, Autry set a consistently high moral tone for his young fans. A spinoff series, *The Adventures of Champion*, which ran for a season (1955-1956) on CBS, featured young Barry Curtis and his dog Rebel along with the hero horse.

A *Gene Autry* Sunday comic strip from General Features Syndicate was begun in 1940 and revived from 1952 to 1955, and Autry comic books from Dell and Fawcett--including giveaways from Pillsbury (1947) and Quaker Oats (1950)--appeared from 1941 through the 1950s. Autry and Champion made countless personal appearances at fairs, parades, Wild West shows, and rodeos, and Flying A Productions did extensive merchandising of Autry-related items ranging from 10-cent club membership cards to complete buckskin outfits.

In the 1950s Autry began a career in business that mirrored his show-business success. He invested in oil and real estate, bought a radio-TV chain and the California Angels baseball team, served as chairman of the Cowboy Hall of Fame and opened the Museum of the American West in Los Angeles in November, 1988.

GAU-1

GAU-2

❑ **GAU-1. Movie Serial Club Member Button,**
1935. Rare. Name of club formed by kids in Mascot serial The Phantom Empire. - **$250 $500 $1000**

❑ **GAU-2. "Red River Valley" Song Sheet,**
1935. - **$20 $40 $65**

GAU-3

❑ **GAU-3. The Phantom Empire Song Sheet,**
1935. Features the song "Uncle Noah's Ark." Gene Autry starred in this movie classic. **- $75 $150 $300**

GAU-4

❑ **GAU-4. "Gene Autry In Comin' Round The Mountain" Movie Poster,**
1936. Poster is 27x41". **- $125 $250 $500**

GAU-5

GAU-6

❑ **GAU-5. "Gene Autry in Public Cowboy #1" Big Little Book #1433,**
1937. Autry's 1st BLB. Has photo cover and movie scenes. **- $34 $102 $235**

❑ **GAU-6. Wheaties Box Back,**
c. 1937. For Republic Picture "The Big Show" released late 1936. **- $12 $25 $50**

GAU-7

GAU-8

❑ **GAU-7. "Gene Autry's Deluxe Edition Of Famous Original Cowboy Songs & Mountain Ballads" Song Folio,**
1938. **- $10 $20 $40**

❑ **GAU-8. "Gene Autry In Law Of The Range" Better Little Book,**
1939. Whitman #1483. **- $17 $51 $120**

GAU-9

❑ **GAU-9. Bandit Trail Game Featuring Gene Autry,**
1939. Game is 2x10x19.25" boxed. Large black/white photo of Gene on box top and on 18.5x18.5" gameboard. The Canton Hardware Company, Canton, Ohio. Four painted cast iron markers in shape of horse and riders. Also cast markers of kneeling cowboys. Game spinner is also cast metal. Comes with playing cards and instructions. **- $300 $700 $1000**

GAU-10

GAU-11

❑ **GAU-10. "South of the Border" Song Sheet,**
1939. **- $12 $25 $40**

❑ **GAU-11. Photo,**
1930s. Radio premium shows Gene Autry in a business suit. **- $20 $40 $60**

GAU-12

GAU-13

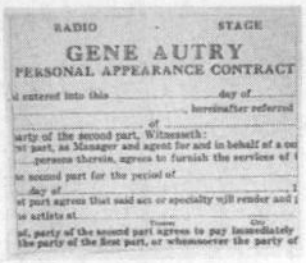

GAU-14

❑ **GAU-12. Photo,**
1930s. Radio premium shows Gene Autry playing guitar with foot on bench next to toy dog. **- $25 $50 $80**

❑ **GAU-13. Composition Statue,**
1930s. Rare. Store item. **- $250 $600 $1200**

❑ **GAU-14. Personal Appearance Contract,**
1930s. Republic Studios, North Hollywood. 8-1/2x14" legal document printed in black on canary paper. Our photo shows detail from upper 3-1/2" of contract front page.
Signed **- $125 $225 $400**
Unsigned **- $35 $65 $100**

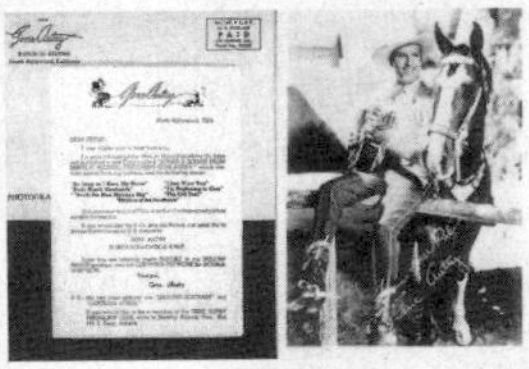

GAU-15

GAU-16

❑ **GAU-15. Fan Photo With Insert Sheet,**
1940. Republic Studio. Near Mint In Mailer **- $45**
Photo Only **- $8 $12 $20**

❑ **GAU-16. Rodeo Handbill,**
c. 1940. World Championship Rodeo, Boston Garden. **- $35 $65 $100**

GAU-17

❑ **GAU-17. "Gene Autry The Screen Singing Cowboy In Person" Poster,**
c. 1940. Issued for Clovis, New Mexico appearance. 14x22". **- $75 $150 $300**

GAU-18

GAU-19

GAU-20

❑ **GAU-18. Cello. Button,**
c. 1940. 1-3/4" crisp black and white. - **$20 $40 $75**

❑ **GAU-19. "Boston Garden Rodeo" Litho. Button,**
c. 1940. Single event issue. - **$50 $100 $200**

❑ **GAU-20. "Gene Autry" Friendship Ring,**
1941. Brass and silvered brass varieties issued by American Specialty Co. of Lancaster, PA for selling seed packs or Christmas cards. An aluminum variety with gold lustre on portrait is c. 1950, issuer unknown.
Brass or Silvered Brass - **$50 $90 $175**
Aluminum - **$90 $150 $300**

GAU-21

❑ **GAU-21. "Cowboy Punch-Out Book",**
1941. The 2nd Gene Autry punch-out book. From Merrill Publishing Co. Has 5 pages of cardboard punch-outs. Odd sized 13 1/4" x 13". Rare. **- $150 $325 $525**

GAU-22

❑ **GAU-22. "Gene Autry 'Ridin On A Rainbow' Movie Poster,"**
1941. 27x41". - **$150 $300 $600**

GAU-23

❑ **GAU-23. "Movie Western" Pulp Featuring Gene Autry Cover And Roy Rogers Story,**
1941. Pulp is 7x10" with 116 pages. Published bi-monthly by Albing Publications. Vol. 1, No. 1 from July. - **$165 $275 $550**

GAU-24

❑ **GAU-24. "Gene Autry's Flying A Ranch Rodeo" Program With Performance Insert Folder,**
1942. 16 pages with four-page insert for New Haven, Connecticut performance.
Program **- $25 $40 $85**
Insert **- $10 $18 $30**

GAU-25

GAU-26

❑ **GAU-25. "Gene Autry and the Hawk of the Hills" Big Little Book #1493,**
1942. Flip pictures. - **$17 $51 $120**

❑ **GAU-26. "Gene Autry and the Raiders of the Range" Big Little Book #1409,**
1946. - **$14 $42 $95**

GAU-27

GAU-28

❑ **GAU-27. "Gene Autry and the Mystery of Paint Rock Canyon" Big Little Book #1425,**
1947. - **$14 $42 $95**

❑ **GAU-28. "Adventure Comics And Play-Fun Book",**
1947. Pillsbury Pancake Mix. - **$37 $111 $460**

GAU-29

❑ **GAU-29. "Gene Autry Adventure Comics And Play-Fun Book" Store Poster,**
1947. Pillsbury Pancake Mix. 9-1/2x26-1/2" full color showing premium activity book. Gordon Gold Archives. - **$100 $200 $400**

GAU-30

❑ **GAU-30. Pancake Mix Full Color Box Wrapper,**
1947. Pillsbury Pancake Mix. 3-1/2x18" segmented cardboard strip picturing the comic and play-fun book "Packed Between These Packages." Scarcer than the premium itself. - **$45 $90 $185**

GAU-31

❑ **GAU-31. Gene Autry Watch Box Set,**
1948. Comes with stand-up insert and instructions. Scarce. Watch - **$100 $225 $450**
Box - **$250 $500 $1000**

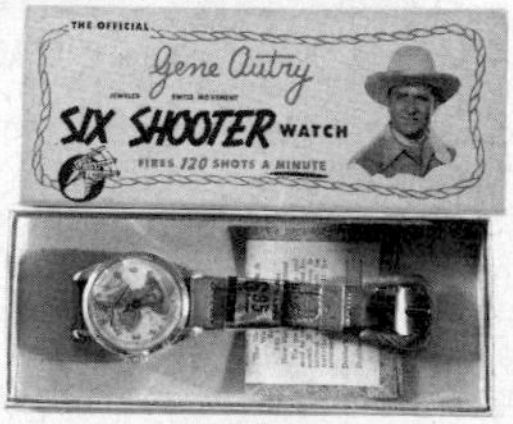

GAU-32

❑ **GAU-32. Gene Autry "Six Shooter" Watch Box Set,**
1948. New Haven Watch Co. Comes in box with instructions. Watch - **$90 $200 $400**
Box - **$200 $400 $800**

GAU-33

GAU-34

❑ **GAU-33. Clothing Manufacturer Photo And Cover Note,**
1948. J. M. Wood Mfg. Co., maker of Autry shirts and jeans. Set - **$30 $60 $90**

❑ **GAU-34. "Gene Autry and the Land Grab Mystery" Big Little Book #1439,**
1948. - **$13 $39 $90**

GAU-35

GAU-36

❑ **GAU-35. Gene Autry Dixie Ice Cream Picture,**
1948. - **$25 $65 $130**

❑ **GAU-36. Gene Autry/Lone Ranger Plastic Ring,**
c. 1948. Dell Comics. U.S. flag pictured under plastic dome, offered for comic book subscription for each character. - **$50 $100 $165**

GAU-37

GAU-38

❑ **GAU-37. "Gene Autry/Champ Crackshot Cowboy" Metal Badge,**
c. 1948. Store item by Daniel Smilo & Sons, New York City. Hanger bar has "Deputy" inscription, linked pendant includes words "Valor/Honor Merit." Also issued with oval hangar bar reading "Expert Sharpshooter" around a target design.
Each Medal - **$150 $300 $600**
Card - **$75 $150 $400**

❑ **GAU-38. "Gene Autry and the Red Bandit's Ghost" Big Little Book #1461,**
1949. - **$12 $36 $85**

GAU-39

❑ **GAU-39. Dell Publishing Co. Picture Strip,**
1949. Folder strip of five color photos. - **$30 $55 $110**

GAU-40

❑ **GAU-40. "Gene Autry" Toy Drum Set,**
c. 1949. Base drum is 5.5x20" tall colorful lithographed tin with large paper drum head of Gene Autry. Made by Colmor. Attached to both sides of drum are 6" diameter smaller drums. Also attached to top is 5" diameter red tin symbol. - **$200 $400 $700**

GAU-41

❑ **GAU-41. "Columbia Records" Listing Card,**
1940s. Black and white photo with facsimile signature, reverse lists album and individual record titles. - **$12 $25 $50**

GAU-42

GAU-43

❑ **GAU-42. Official Club Badge Cello. Button,**
1940s. - **$25 $45 $85**

❑ **GAU-43. "Republic's Singing Western Star" Cello. Button,**
1940s. - **$65 $140 $290**

GAU-44

GAU-45

❑ **GAU-44. Store Owner's 10x12" Cardboard Sign,**
1940s. Wrigley Doublemint Gum. Signifies sponsorship of "Doublemint Melody Ranch" radio show. - **$50 $100 $175**

❑ **GAU-45. "March Of Comics" #25,**
1940s. Various sponsors. - **$21 $63 $260**

GAU-46

GAU-47

GAU-48

❑ **GAU-46. Cello. Button,**
1940s. Probably a rodeo souvenir. - **$18 $30 $65**

❑ **GAU-47. Portrait Ring,**
1940s. Brass frame holds black and white photo under clear plastic cover. - **$40 $85 $175**

❑ **GAU-48. "Minneapolis Aquatennial Rodeo" Cello. Button,**
1940s. Souvenir button. - **$85 $175 $325**

GAU-49

❑ **GAU-49. Real Photo Australian Button,**
1940s. Black and white without dot pattern. - **$30 $60 $90**

GAU-50

❑ **GAU-50. "Expert Sharpshooter" Autry Award Medal,**
1940s. Brass badge inscribed by award title on hanger bar also centered by target design. Brass pendant pictures Gene on Champion surrounded by "Valor-Honor-Merit" and "Gene Autry Champ Crackshot Cowboy."
Medal - **$150 $300 $600**
Card - **$75 $150 $400**

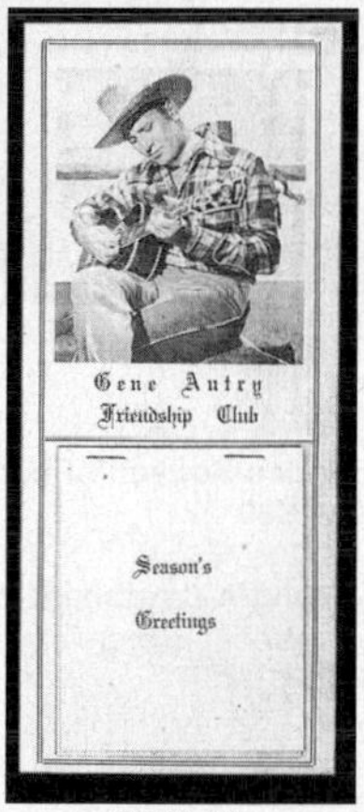

GAU-51

❑ **GAU-51. "Friendship Club" Calendar,**
1950. 4x9" featuring photo above 12-month calendar tablet under "Season's Greetings" cover page. - **$25 $50 $75**

GAU-52

❑ **GAU-52. Gene Autry Stencil Book,**
1950. - **$40 $80 $165**

GAU-53

❑ **GAU-53. Gene Autry's Melody Ranch Cut-Out Dolls,**
1950. Book is 10.5x13" with 12 pages. Back cover has punch-out cowboys and ladies. Front cover has punch-out of Gene. - **$65 $120 $190**

GAU-54

❑ **GAU-54. Quaker Comic Booklets,**
1950. Puffed Wheat/Rice box inserts. Set of five. Each - **$14 $42 $160**

GAU-55

❑ **GAU-55. Three-Dimensional Ceramic Figure On Horseshoe-Shaped Base,**
c. 1950. Store item. 8-1/4" tall beautifully colored figure with his facsimile signature on the base. Seen with underside of base either blank or ink stamped Wilfred Enterprises Holywood, Calif. Same company likely made Bob Hope and Bing Crosby items BOB-11. - **$200 $400 $800**

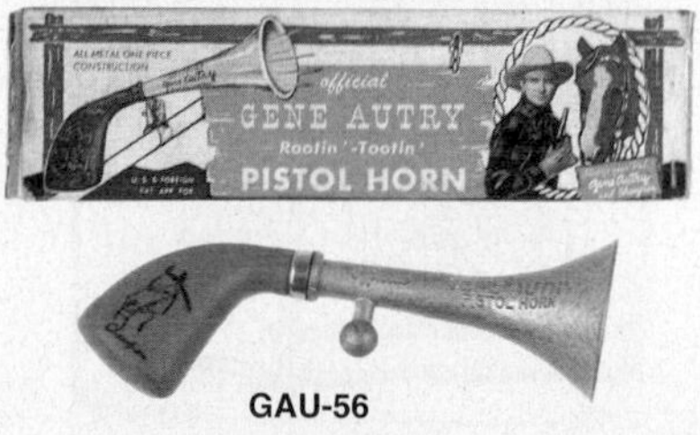

GAU-56

❑ **GAU-56. "Gene Autry Rootin' Tootin' Pistol Horn" Boxed,**
c. 1950. Clarion Metal Products. 2x2x7.5" box with two illustrations of Gene and "Always Your Pal Gene Autry And Champion." Box holds metal horn with rubber bulb handle. Comes with three-piece mounting bracket.
Box - **$50 $100 $160**
Horn - **$50 $100 $160**

GAU-57

❑ **GAU-57. "Jaegers Butter-Nut Bread" Button,**
c. 1950. Litho by scarce sponsor. -
$25 $50 $75

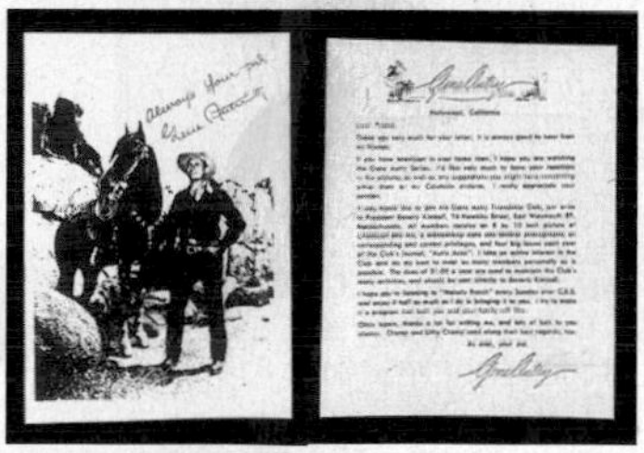

GAU-58

❑ **GAU-58. Fan Letter With Photo,**
c. 1950. Letter includes references to Columbia Pictures, Melody Ranch radio program, fan club address. Photo has facsimile signature.
Letter - **$8 $15 $25**
Photo - **$12 $18 $30**

GAU-59

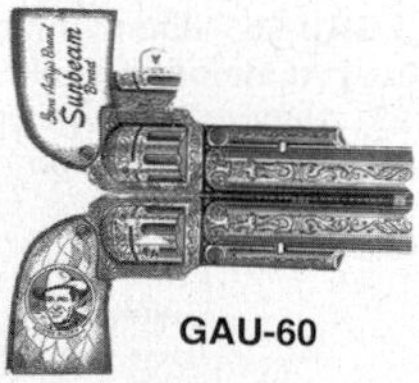

GAU-60

❑ **GAU-59. "Sunbeam Bread" Color Photo,**
c. 1950. - **$18 $30 $50**

❑ **GAU-60. "Sunbeam Bread" Cardboard Gun,**
c. 1950. - **$30 $45 $90**

GAU-61

GAU-62

GAU-63

❑ GAU-61. Sunbeam Bread Litho. Button,
c. 1950. 1-3/8" size, also as 1-1/4" cello.
Each - **$10 $20 $30**

❑ GAU-62. Sunbeam Bread "Gene Autry Show" 3-1/2" Cello. Button,
c. 1950. - **$75 $125 $250**

❑ GAU-63. Plastic Ring,
c. 1950. Store item. Gold finish with inset paper photo. - **$12 $18 $30**

GAU-64

❑ GAU-64. March of Comics #78,
1951. This Gene Autry issue is the last sized like a regular comic book. - **$15 $45 $180**

GAU-65

❑ GAU-65. "Jimmy And Jane Visit Gene Autry At Melody Ranch" Paperdoll Book,
1951. Published by Whitman.
Uncut **- $60 $115 $185**

GAU-66

❑ GAU-66. "Gene Autry/Melody Ranch" Lunch Box,
1954. Store item by Universal.
Box - **$300 $600 $1350**
Bottle - **$100 $200 $300**

GAU-67

GAU-68

❑ GAU-67. "March Of Comics No. 120",
1954. Poll-Parrot Shoes. - **$11 $22 $105**

❑ GAU-68. "Hit Show" Live Performance 14x22" Cardboard Poster,
1955. - **$100 $200 $400**

GAU-69

❑ GAU-69. Gene Autry Guitar With Case And Song Book,
c. 1955. Emenee Musical Toys. Cardboard guitar case is 4" deep by 33" long with printed alligator skin exterior with name on outside. Case holds 31" long plastic four-string guitar. Body has Gene Autry name and images with western motif in high relief on body. Top of neck reads ""Emenee/Gene Autry Cowboy Guitar." Comes with 16-page "Songbook For Gene Autry Cowboy Guitar" with Gene's picture and 12-page illustrated catalogue.
Box - **$50 $100 $225**
Booklet - **$10 $25 $50**
Guitar - **$50 $100 $225**
Complete Near Mint - **$500**

GAU-70

❑ GAU-70. Wallet With Inset Photo,
c. 1956. Store item. Wallet front has black and white Autry photo under clear window cover. - **$35 $75 $175**

GAU-71

❑ GAU-71. Pair Of Litho. Buttons,
1957. Probable vending machine issue. 7/8" with browntone photo on various single-color backgrounds. From a larger set depicting western TV stars, probably totaling 14 different.
Autry Or Champion Each - **$12 $25 $60**

GAU-72

GAU-73

❑ GAU-72. Rodeo Souvenir Photo,
1957. - **$8 $15 $30**

❑ GAU-73. Flying A Cardboard Wrist Cuffs,
1950s. Scarce. Probable premium. - **$50 $175 $325**

GAU-74

❑ GAU-74. Horseshoe Nail Ring On Card,
1950s. Store item. Complete - **$275**
Ring Only - **$25 $50 $100**

GAU-75

❑ **GAU-75. "Gene Autry Official Ranch Outfit,"**
1950s. Leslie-Henry Co. Inc. 11.75x11.75x1.75" deep box contains "500" set which consists of matched pair of 9" cap guns made of cast metal with plastic horse head grips. Marked on each side with "Gene Autry" name and image on rearing horse. Holster is black leather with heavy sculptured metal fronts featuring raised flower and vine-like design. Top of each holster is silk-screened with Gene Autry name and "Flying A Ranch" logo. Has metal belt buckle with embossed steer head.
Box - **$125 $250 $500**
Gun Set - **$250 $500 $800**

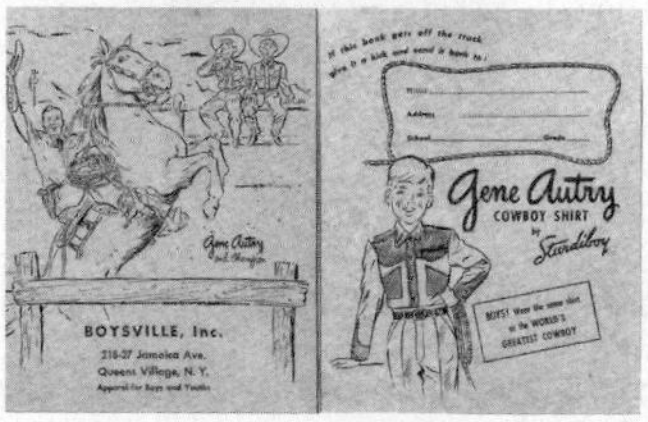

GAU-76

❑ **GAU-76. School Tablet,**
1950s. Clothing stores. - **$18 $30 $60**

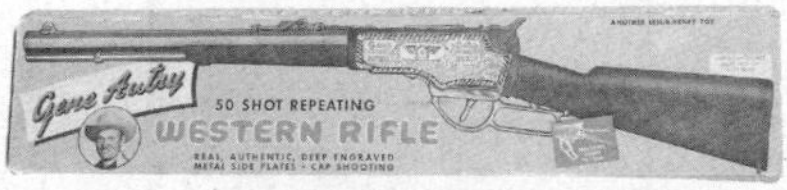

GAU-77

❑ **GAU-77. "Gene Autry 50 Shot Repeating Western Rifle" Cap Rifle In Box,**
1950s. Box is 2x5.5x27" long. Repeated illustrations and text on both sides. Leslie-Henry toy. Side of rifle reads "Gene Autry Flying A Ranch." Brown marbled plastic giving simulated wood appearance. Box - **$200 $400 $600**
Rifle - **$250 $500 $1000**

GAU-78

❑ **GAU-78. Gene Autry Cowboy Boots Boxed,**
1950s. Box is 3.75x9.5x11" and holds 9" tall leather cowboy boots with name on interior straps, name and image impressed on bottom of soles. Box - **$60 $125 $250**
Boots - **$50 $100 $200**

GAU-79

❑ **GAU-79. "Gene Autry" Child's Rubber Boots Boxed,**
1950s. Box measures 4.5x9x13.5" and reads "One Pair/Four-Buckle Dress/Brown/11" but not identified as Gene Autry. Boots are 3.5x8.5x9.5" tall, each with 2x2.5" color illustration with name below in script "Gene Autry."
Box (without Gene Autry name) - **$15 $30 $50**
Boots - **$40 $75 $150**

GAU-80

GAU-81

❑ **GAU-80. Plastic Ring With Photo,**
1950s. Store item, from card of rings featuring various personalities. Plastic cover over photo. - **$18 $35 $70**

❑ **GAU-81. "Adventure Story Trail Map",**
1950s. Stroehmann's Bread. Large folder to hold 16 color photo bread end labels telling story of "Gene Autry And The Black Hat Gang!". Folder - **$40 $75 $165**
Each Mounted Label - **$5 $10 $15**

GAU-82

GAU-83

❑ **GAU-82. Bread Labels,**
1950s. Various bread companies. Numbered photos in at least five different series.
Each - **$6 $12 $20**

❑ **GAU-83 Publicity Photo,**
1950s. Columbia Records. - **$8 $15 $30**

GAU-84

❑ **GAU-84. Rain Boots Merchandise Card,**
1950s. Servus Rubber Co. - **$12 $25 $40**

GAU-85

GAU-86

❑ **GAU-85. English Fan Club Badge On Card,**
1950s. Gene Autry Comics, Silvered tin with insert photo. Near Mint On Card - **$275**
Loose - **$50 $85 $175**

❑ **GAU-86. "Gene Autry & Champion" Cello. Button,**
1950s. Star design in gold or silver. - **$15 $30 $65**

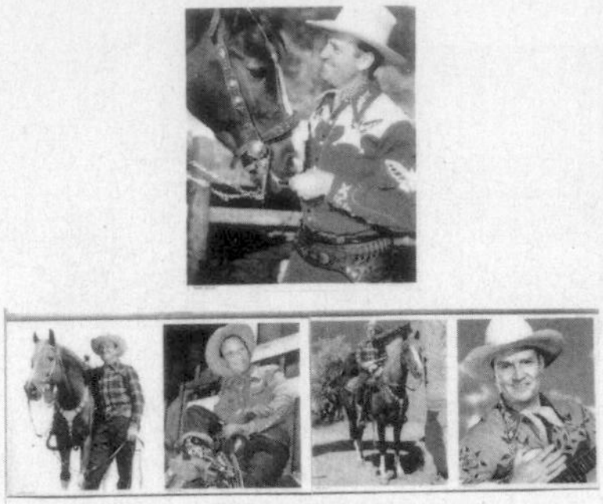

GAU-87

❑ **GAU-87. Dell Picture Strip,**
1950s. Unfolds with five photos. - **$30 $60 $100**

GAU-88

GAU-89

❑ **GAU-88. Litho. Tin Club Tab,**
1950s. - **$20 $50 $100**

❑ **GAU-89. Second Variety Litho. Tin Club Tab,**
1950s. Same image as other version but design is of five-pointed star. 1-5/8" diameter in black and white with two shades of blue. - **$35 $65 $125**

GAU-90

GAU-91

❑ **GAU-90. Flying A Symbol Brass Wings Badge,**
1950s. - **$20 $50 $100**

❑ **GAU-91. Ranch Symbol Cigarette Lighter,**
1950s. Promotional item by Penguin. Chrome metal with plastic wrapper, other side has "Melody Ranch". - **$45 $90 $175**

GAU-92

GAU-93

❑ **GAU-92. Store Clerk's Or Bread Delivery Man's Cello. Badge,**
1950s. Stroehmann Bread. 2-1/4" with celluloid covering a paper bread loaf end label from their series meant to be collected and mounted in paper album. About five different seen.
Each - **$35 $85 $165**

❑ **GAU-93. Photo,**
1950s. Black & white premium photo of him playing guitar. - **$10 $20 $30**

GAU-94

GAU-95

❑ **GAU-94. Photo,**
1950s. Radio premium for radio show featuring Doublemints Melody Ranch on CBS. - **$25 $50 $100**

❑ **GAU-95. "Gene Autry Deputy Sheriff",**
1950s. Issuer unknown. Large embossed brass badge. - **$200 $400 $800**

GAU-96

❑ **GAU-96. "Western Story Round-Up And Picture Map" Album,**
1950s. Sunbeam Bread. Paper folder for mounting 16 numbered bread loaf end pictures.
Album - **$50 $90 $175**
Each Mounted Label - **$5 $10 $15**

GAU-97

GAU-98

❑ **GAU-97. Gene Autry Small Photo Button,**
1950s. British Commonwealth. 1-1/4". Black on yellow with red accents on vest and bandanna. - **$40 $85 $175**

❑ **GAU-98. Gene Autry Large Photo Button,**
1950s. US version. 1-3/4". Black and white photo, sometimes with red tint on various colored backgrounds.
Yellow Background - **$15 $30 $45**
Blue Background - **$30 $60 $100**
Purple Background - **$35 $70 $135**

GAU-99

❑ **GAU-99. "Gene Autry Trail" Boy Scout Related Ribbon Badge,**
1950s. Silver luster metal pendant includes text "Character Counts"plus arrowhead symbol. Other details include profile image of man's head wearing hat, Autry's Flying A Symbol. - **$80 $165 $275**

GAU-100

❑ **GAU-100. "Trail Book" Boy Scout Folder,**
1962. Gene Autry Trail And Camp (Festus, Missouri). Four-page folder offering camping, hiking, Scout advancement activities accompanied by club medallion badge.
Brochure - **$15 $30 $60**

General Mills Misc.

This mammoth food and related products company, born and still based in Minneapolis, was a mid-1920s pioneer in national radio advertising via a powerful transmitter provided jointly by an immediate preceding company, Washburn Crosby Co. and other business interests in the Minneapolis-St. Paul Twin Cities area. The first three programs--*Betty Crocker, The Wheaties Quartet, The Gold Medal Fast Freight*--were of homemaker nature and offered a few premiums in like style. The premium heyday for youngsters, however, began in the early 1930s through the *Skippy and His Pals* program based on the Percy Crosby comic strip. Skippy was followed in 1933 by *Jack Armstrong, The All-American Boy*. Both offered premiums by sponsor Wheaties, a very popular Depression era cereal that continues to the present. General Mills through the years has offered hundreds of premiums for purchase of food products, principally breakfast cereals. In 1949, Adelaide Hawley Cumming became television's original Betty Crocker, billed as "America's First Lady of Food." Various General Mills brands are represented in this section while Cheerios, Wheaties and major characters they sponsored are covered in separate sections.

GEN-1

❑ **GEN-1. "Gen'l Mills/Five Star Hour" Plaster Figurine,**
c. 1938. Rare. Probably issued to retailers, base lists six radio programs. - **$275 $625 $1050**

GEN-2

❑ **GEN-2. Hedy Lamarr Key Pin And Photo,**
1946. Kix Cereal. Key - **$30 $60 $100**
Photo - **$12 $25 $50**

GEN-3

❑ **GEN-3. Kix Plastic Planes,**
1946. 22 planes in set. Booklet - **$25 $75 $165**
Each Plane - **$12 $25 $40**

GEN-4

❑ **GEN-4. Kix Cereal Box with Cut-outs,**
1948. Baldy the Regal Eagle cut-outs on back. 12 boxes in the series. **$60 $115 $200**

GEN-5

❑ **GEN-5. "General Mills Map Of The Old West" 20x28",**
c. 1940s. - **$50 $90 $175**

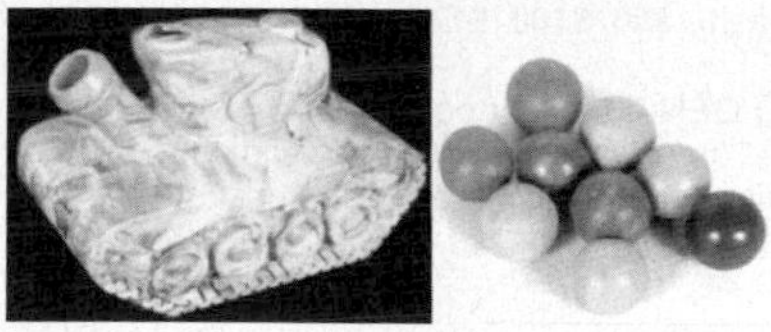
GEN-6

❑ **GEN-6. "10 Shooter Tank" With Mailer,**
c. 1956. 3-1/2" tall General Mills premium. Came with ten colored wood balls which fire from gun barrel as tank is pushed. 3x5x3-1/2" tall. - **$35 $65 $125**

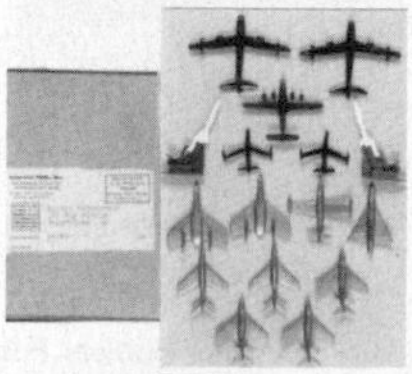
GEN-7

❑ **GEN-7. General Mills Airplanes/Missile Launchers,**
1950s. At least eight different planes in various colors and missile launchers. Each - **$3 $8 $15**

GEN-8

GEN-9

❑ **GEN-8. Toytimer,**
1950s. Stop watch with mailer. - **$30 $50 $80**

❑ **GEN-9. Tex-Son Cowhand Badge,**
1950s. General Mills premium. - **$65 $135 $275**

GEN-10

GEN-11

❑ **GEN-10. "Twinkles And Sanford's Boat" Book,**
1962. Whitman hardcover issued by General Mills. - **$12 $25 $50**

❑ **GEN-11. Franken Berry 2-3/4" Tall Figural Plastic Pencil Sharpener,**
1960s. - **$10 $18 $35**

GEN-12

❑ **GEN-12. "Henny Youngman's Pocket Jester,"**
1960s. Item is 2" diameter by .75" thick hard plastic designed like a tape measure. Comes in original but plain cardboard box. "Created By Alexander Rose." Contains 5' long fabric tape, when fully extended, with jokes printed on each side. Top has sticker with his portrait and a violin plus title "Henny Youngman's Pocket Jester." Reverse sticker pictures a box of "Joey Chips" by General Mills. Generic Mailer - **$1 $3 $5**
Tape - **$8 $18 $35**

GEN-13

❑ **GEN-13. "General Mills Cocoa Puffs Bobbing Cuckoo Bird" Box Flat With Premium,**
c. 1970. Gordon Gold Archives.
Near Mint Flat - **$425**
Used Complete - **$50 $125 $200**
Cuckoo Bird - **$8 $12 $25**

GEN-14

❑ **GEN-14. Cereal Box With "Monster Eraser" Offer,**
1972. Set of six consisting of Boo Berry, Count Chocula, Franken Berry, bat, owl and skull/crossbones. Gordon Gold archives.
Used Complete Box - **$125 $250 $400**
Each Eraser - **$5 $12 $25**

GEN-15

GEN-16

❑ **GEN-15. "Franken Berry" Vinyl Doll With Box,**
1975. Near Mint Boxed - **$225**
Loose - **$40 $75 $125**

❑ **GEN-16. "Count Chocula" Vinyl Doll With Box,**
1975. Near Mint Boxed - **$160**
Loose - **$25 $40 $80**

GEN-17

GEN-18

❑ **GEN-17. "Fruit Brute" Vinyl Squeeze Doll,**
1975. Near Mint Boxed - **$160**
Loose - **$25 $40 $80**

❑ **GEN-18. "Boo Berry" Vinyl Squeeze Doll,**
1975. Near Mint Boxed - **$175**
Loose - **$25 $40 $85**

GEN-19

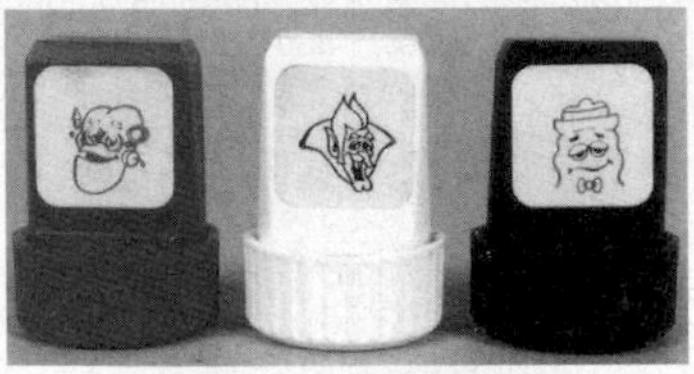
GEN-20

❑ **GEN-19. Secret Compartment Plastic Ring Set,**
1976. Four rings with Hasbro name in four colors depicting Franken Berry, Boo Berry, Count Chocula, Fruit Brute.
Each - **$50 $100 $175**

❑ **GEN-20. "Stampos" Printing Kit,**
1970s. Ink stampers with portraits of Franken Berry, Count Chocula, Boo Berry.
Each - **$20 $40 $80**

GEN-21

❑ **GEN-21. Big Monster Flicker Rings,**
1970s. Five of six shown: two feature the Count and Franken Berry, two feature the Count only, two feature Franken Berry only.
Each - **$35 $75 $150**

GEN-22

❑ **GEN-22. Count Chocula Original Art Prototype Ring,**
1970s. Made for presentation to General Mills. Hard plastic base like the six box insert flicker rings with a full color original art insert on the top. Gordon Gold archives. Unique - **$800**

GEN-23

❑ **GEN-23. Cereal Box With "Pop Rocket" Offer And Premium,**
1970s. Rockets came in three colors and consisted of base, center stage and nose cone. Gordon Gold Archives.
Near Mint Flat - **$600**
Used Complete - **$100 $200 $350**
Rocket - **$10 $20 $30**

GEN-24

❑ **GEN-24. "Count Chocula Monster Action Ring" Offer Cereal Box,**
1970s. Gordon Gold Archives.
Near Mint Flat - **$650**
Used Complete - **$125 $250 $400**

GEN-25

❑ **GEN-25. "Franken Berry Monster Action Ring" Offer Box Flat,**
1970s. Gordon Gold Archives.
Near Mint Flat - **$650**
Used Complete - **$125 $250 $400**

GEN-26

GEN-27

❑ **GEN-26. Count Chocula Vinyl Flat Figure,**
1970s. Finished image front and back, molded small base. - **$8 $15 $25**

❑ **GEN-27. Franken Berry Vinyl Flat Figure,**
1970s. Finished image front and back, molded small base. - **$8 $15 $25**

GEN-28

❑ **GEN-28. Count Chocula Toothbrush Holder,**
1970s. 3" tall soft plastic with raised portrait design looped on back to hold toothbrush. - **$12 $25 $45**

GEN-29

❑ **GEN-29. Monster Cereal Characters Wristwatch,**
1970s. 1-1/8" metal case holding clear plastic over animated wheel picturing Franken Berry, Count Chocula, Boo Berry. Portrait wheel spins as background image of haunted mansion darkens and lightens between black and gray. Designed as General Mills premium but never put into mass production. - **$225 $450 $875**

GEN-30

❑ **GEN-30. Character Card Games,**
1981. Two sets of cards featuring Lucky Charms, Cocoa Puffs, Trix, Franken Berry, Count Chocula, Boo Berry. Complete With Mailer - **$15 $25 $55**

GEN-31

❑ **GEN-31. "Raiders Of The Lost Ark" Packaged Action Figures,**
1982. Set of "Indiana Jones Four Pack" of him, Toht, Cairo Swordsman, Marian Ravenwood. Near Mint Complete - **$240**

GEN-32

❑ **GEN-32. "Count Chocula" Cereal Box And Disguise Stickers,**
1987. Box art depicts necklace on Dracula's neck with design similar to Star of David. Box was quickly redesigned. Box - **$45 $115 $225**
Stickers - **$5 $15 $30**

GEN-33

❑ **GEN-33. "Count Chocula" Cereal Box,**
1987. Box art altered to remove Dracula's necklace that resembled Star of David. - **$30 $80 $190**

GEN-34

❑ **GEN-34. Franken Berry Cereal Box With Spooky Shape Maker Offer,**
1987. Three different to emboss paper with images of Franken Berry, Count Chocula, Fruity Yummy Mummy. Box - **$20 $40 $80**
Each Shape Maker - **$5 $10 $20**

GEN-35

❑ **GEN-35. Fruity Yummy Mummy Cereal Box,**
1987. Packaging introduces the character and the cereal to the public while back panel introduces the new character to the established monsters. - **$75 $150 $300**

GEN-36

❑ **GEN-36. Boo Berry Cereal Box With Monster Poster And Crayons Offer,**
1988. Last premium issued for monster cereals. Crayons shaped like monsters in their correct colors. Box - **$20 $40 $85**
Poster And Crayons - **$20 $35 $60**

GEN-37

❑ **GEN-37. Franken Berry Mask,**
1980s. Thin shell plastic with high relief design. - **$10 $25 $100**

GEN-38

❑ **GEN-38. Count Chocula Die-cast Car,**
2000. Team Lightning metal Road Rod. **- $10**

GEN-39 GEN-40

❑ **GEN-39. Count Chocula Wacky Wobbler,**
2001. **- $20**

❑ **GEN-40. Franken Berry Wacky Wobbler,**
2001. **- $30**

Get Smart

Created by Mel Brooks and Buck Henry and produced by Paramount, the spoof of James Bond and spy films ran on CBS and NBC-TV between September 18, 1965 and May 15, 1970; 138 episodes and five seasons. The premise has the secret agents of "CONTROL" battling the forces of "KAOS" who want to rule the world. The main cast included Don Adams (1923-2005) as Agent 86, Barbara Feldon as Agent 99 and Edward Platt as the Chief. Don Adams won an Emmy award three years in a row between 1967 and 1969.

Universal released a feature film *The Nude Bomb* (aka *The Return Of Maxwell Smart*) in 1980 starring Adams and Sylvia Kristel. In 1989, ABC-TV ran the *Get Smart Again!* movie written and produced by Leonard Stern starring Don Adams, Barbara Feldon and Bernie Kopell. Fox-TV aired a short lived series of seven shows in 1995 with Adams and Feldon reprising their characters. Andy Dick played their bumbling son. In 2008, Steve Carell will bring *Get Smart* into the 21st century.

Dell published eight comic books between June 1966 and September 1967. All have Don Adams photo covers. "Would you believe?"

GET-1

❑ **GET-1. "Get Smart The Exploding Time Bomb Game,"**
1965. Store item by Ideal**. - $45 $90 $200**

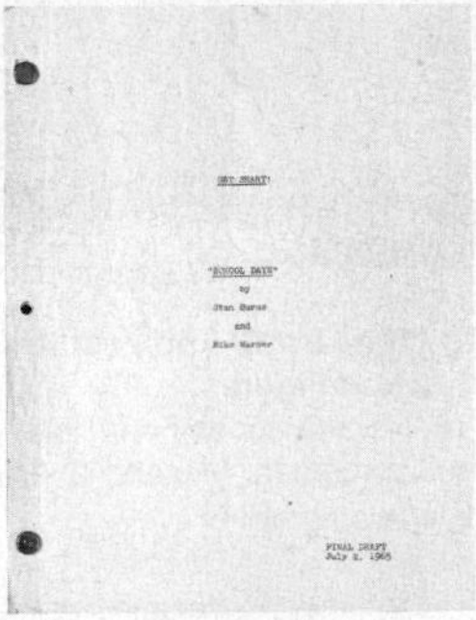

GET-2

❑ **GET-2. "Get Smart" Original TV Show Script,**
1965. 8.5x11" personal copy of Bob Simpson who worked the sound boom on the production set. Titled "School Days." 33 pages. Same Or Similar **- $20 $40 $65**

GET-3

GET-4

❑ **GET-3. "Get Smart" Limited Issue Promo Button,**
1966. 3.5" in diameter. Only 250 made to promote Portland, Maine TV station. **- $15 $30 $65**

❑ **GET-4. Get Smart Thermos,**
1966. King-Seeley Thermos Co. 6.5" tall with full color wrap-around design. **- $20 $40 $90**

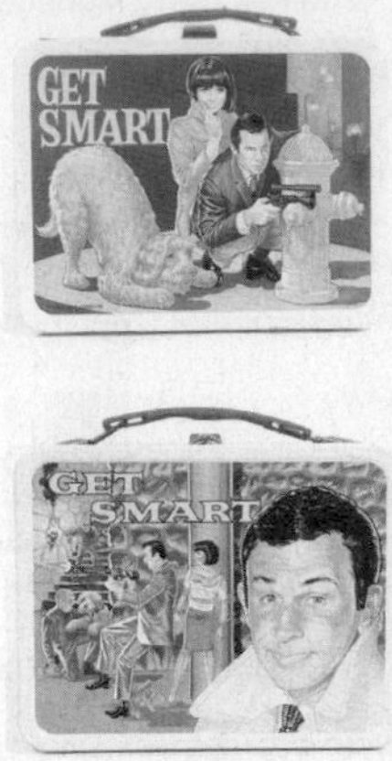

GET-5

❑ **GET-5. "Get Smart" Lunch Box,**
1966. King Seeley Thermos Co. 6.75x8.75x4" deep metal lunch box. **- $60 $125 $200**

GET-6

❑ **GET-6. "Get Smart" Gum Card Wrapper And Cards,**
1966. Topps. 6x6.5" waxed paper wrapper and cards each 2.25x2.5" in a set of 66. Cards have photo fronts and were issued in two-card panels. Wrapper **- $8 $15 $30**
Each Card **- $1 $2 $4**

GET-7

❑ **GET-7. "Get Smart Secret Agent 86 Pen-Radio" Boxed Set,**
1966. Multiple Toy Makers. Boxed set contains earplug attachment and 5.5" pen radio receiver and contact clip. **- $75 $150 $250**

GET-8

❑ **GET-8. "Get Smart Secret Agent 99 Spy Purse" Boxed,**
1966. 8.5x11.5x2" deep box designed with diecut topper for store display showing Don Adams and Barbara Feldon. - **$50 $100 $215**

GET-9 GET-10

❑ **GET-9. "Agent 86 - I'm A Smartie" Button,**
1980. 3" in diamotor. Promotional item for "The Smart Bomb" movie starring Don Adams. - **$20 $40 $85**

❑ **GET-10. Maxwell Smart Says "Buy A Datsun" Button,**
1980s. 2-1/8". - **$10 $20 $40**

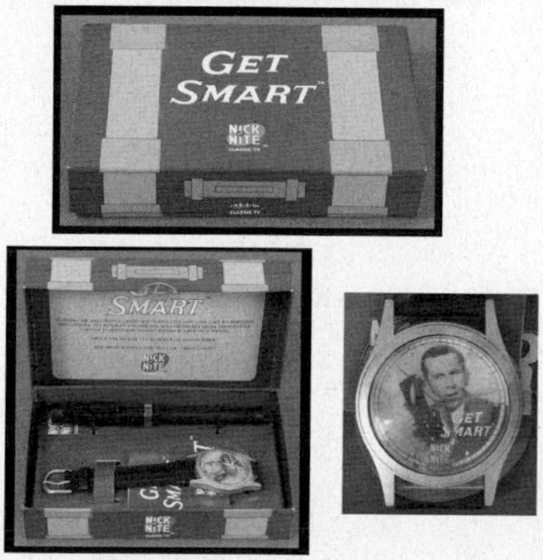

GET-11

❑ **GET-11. "Get Smart Nick At Nite" Limited Edition Boxed Watch,**
1994. 4x6x1" deep box designed like an attache case contains watch/pen set. Metal watch case is 1.25" in diameter with pewter finish. Reverse has incised number "2539." Pen is 5" long black hard plastic with spring-loaded firing mechanism. Has warranty and instruction papers. From an edition of only 10,000 sold exclusively through the TV channel. Mint As Issued - **$165**

G.I. Joe

Hasbro's Creative Director of Product Development Don Levine was approached by independent toy designer Stanley Weston in March of 1962. Weston was selling merchandising rights to the TV show *"The Lieutenant,"* based on a Marine, and thought Hasbro would be interested in doing combat action figures for boys similar in design to what the Mattel Co. was doing with Barbie figures for girls. Levine and the people at Hasbro decided to go with a more universal appeal, basing the name on a 1945 Robert Mitchum war movie *The Story of G.I. Joe*. Hasbro claimed the trademark and christened the new product GI Joe.

Test marketing began in New York stores in August, 1964 and the figures sold out in one week. By early fall the figures were selling out nationwide. The GI Joe Club started in December and soon had 150,000 members. 1965 saw the introduction of a black action soldier into the line of American Army, Air Force, Navy and Marine figures.

Action Soldiers of the World debuted in 1966, offering soldiers from six countries. In 1969 GI Joe's hard core military image was softened to an "Adventurer" concept which would expand the merchandising even further. 1975 saw the introduction of the 11-1/2" Atomic Man.

The oil shortage of 1976 halted production due to lack of petroleum used in manufacturing the figures. In 1982 Joe was re-introduced in a new 3-3/4" size. In 1991 Hasbro brought out the first original 12-inch action figure since 1976, Master Sergeant Duke, based on the *GI Joe, A Real American Hero* cartoon series. The same title was used for a 1982-1994 comic book series published by Marvel Comics. All 155 issues were written by Larry Hama and illustrated by some of the foremost comic book artists, including Todd McFarlane (*Spawn*).

Paramount Pictures has announced a release date of August 7, 2009 for an upcoming live-action feature length film based on the 1980s GI Joe action figures. The current cast members signed for the film include Sienna Miller, Ray Park, Adewale Akinnuoye-Agbaje, Said Taghmaoui, Rachel Nichols, Channing Tatum, Dennis Quaid, and Arnold Vosloo. Since 1964 the success of GI Joe has continued to help fuel the sales of millions of the ever-popular figures, vehicles, and gear associated with the toy line.

GIJ-1

❑ **GIJ-1. "GI Joe Action Soldier" Boxed,**
1964. Store item by Hasbro.
Near Mint Boxed - **$600**
Used Complete - **$50 $95 $185**

GIJ-2 GIJ-3

❑ **GIJ-2. GI Joe Sailor Action Figure With Shore Patrol Uniform,**
1964. Hasbro #7612. Near Mint Boxed - **$1800**
Loose Complete - **$250 $500 $800**

❑ **GIJ-3. "GI Joe" Action Sailor Deep Sea Diver Set,**
1965. Store item by Hasbro #7620.
Boxed - **$500 $1000 $1800**
Loose Complete - **$200 $400 $750**

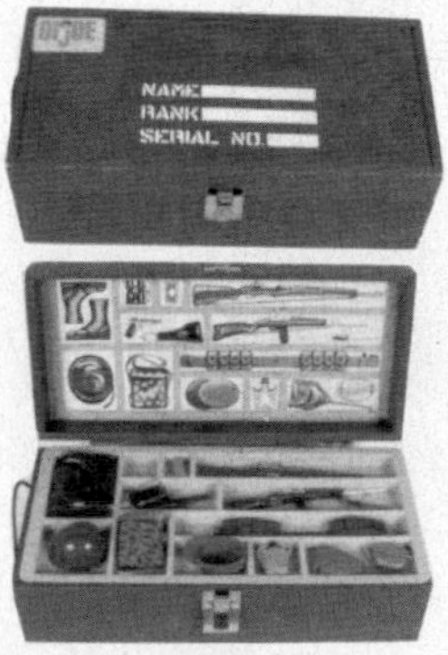

GIJ-4

❑ **GIJ-4. Footlocker With Equipment,**
1965. Store item by Hasbro.
Near Mint Complete - **$225**
Without Accessories - **$12 $25 $45**

GIJ-5

GIJ-6

❑ **GIJ-5. "Command Post News" Newspaper. Vol. 1 #1,**
April, 1965. - **$30 $50 $100**

❑ **GIJ-6. "Command Post News" #4,**
April, 1966. - **$10 $20 $40**

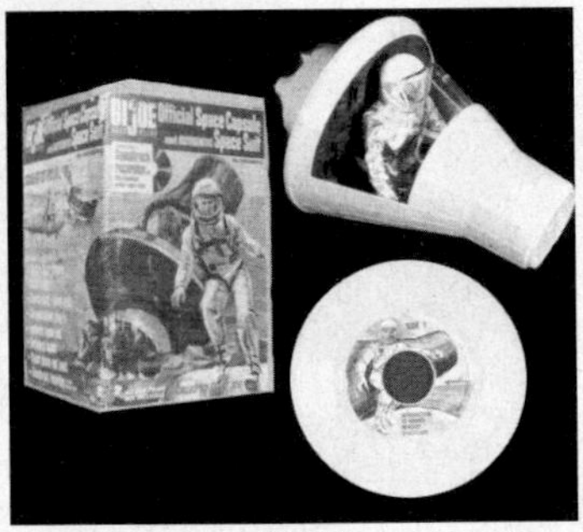

GIJ-7

❑ **GIJ-7. "GI Joe Space Capsule And Space Suit" Boxed Set,**
1966. Store item by Hasbro. Contents include 45 rpm record, stickers and instruction sheet. Small "handles" inside cockpit often snapped off. Boxed **- $300 $600 $1200**

GIJ-8

❑ **GIJ-8. Russian Infantryman Boxed Figure,**
1966. From Hasbro "Action Soldiers Of The World Series." Near Mint Boxed - **$1200**
Loose - **$100 $250 $500**

GIJ-9

GIJ-10

❑ **GIJ-9. Japanese Imperial Soldier Action Figure,**
1966. Store item by Hasbro #8201.
Near Mint Boxed - **$1500**
Loose - **$200 $400 $750**

❑ **GIJ-10. "GI Joe At The Battle Of The Bulge" Record Album,**
1967. Store item by United Artists Records Inc. Certainly inspired by GI Joe but no Hasbro reference. - **$15 $30 $60**

GIJ-11

❑ **GIJ-11. "GI Joe Action Pilot Crash Crew Fire Truck",**
1967. Store item by Hasbro.
Near Mint Boxed - **$3250**
Loose Complete - **$300 $600 $1200**

GIJ-12

GIJ-13

❑ **GIJ-12. Catalogue,**
1967. Came only with the 1967 series of talking GI Joe figures. - **$15 $25 $50**

❑ **GIJ-13. "Command Post Yearbook",**
1967. - **$35 $65 $125**

GIJ-14

❑ **GIJ-14. "Talking GI Joe Astronaut",**
1969. Store item by Hasbro.
Near Mint Boxed - **$1000**
Loose Complete - **$85 $175 $350**

GIJ-15

❑ **GIJ-15. GI Joe Adventurer Action Figure,**
1969. Store item by Hasbro.
Near Mint Boxed - **$1350**
Loose - **$125 $275 $475**

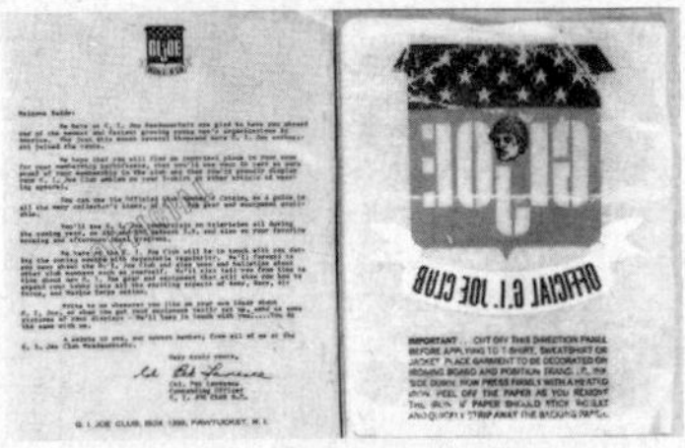

GIJ-16

❑ **GIJ-16. GI Joe Letter With Transfer,**
1960s. Letter - **$8 $12 $20**
Transfer - **$10 $20 $30**

GIJ-17

❑ **GIJ-17. "Combat Soldier" Pencil Case,**
1960s. Store item by Hasbro. 5-1/2x9" brown vinyl with zipper. - **$15 $25 $50**

GIJ-21

❑ **GIJ-21. "Search For The Stolen Idol" Boxed,**
1971. Store item by Hasbro #7418.
Near Mint Boxed - **$400**
Used Complete - **$50 $85 $150**

GIJ-25 GIJ-26

❑ **GIJ-25. "Breaker" Figure on Card,**
1982. 3-3/4" tall. On card. - **$50 $125 $250**

❑ **GIJ-26. "Cobra Officer" Figure on Card,**
1982. On card. - **$75 $225 $350**

GIJ-18 GIJ-19

❑ **GIJ-18. "GI Joe Land Adventurer" Action Figure,**
1970. Store item by Hasbro #7401.
Near Mint Boxed - **$200**
Complete Unboxed - **$20 $50 $75**

❑ **GIJ-19. "GI Joe Sea Adventurer" Boxed,**
1970. Store item by Hasbro #7402.
Near Mint Boxed - **$300**
Used Complete - **$30 $60 $100**

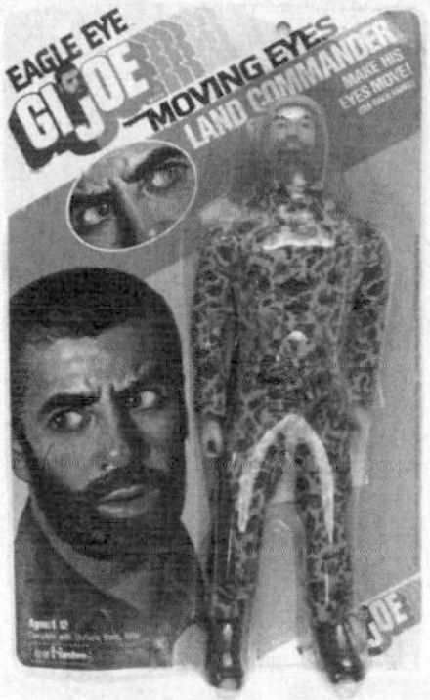

GIJ-22

❑ **GIJ-22. "Eagle Eye GI Joe With Moving Eyes" Carded Figure,**
1976. Hasbro Industries #7276. 12" figure on 8.75x14" card. Flocked and bearded figure comes with camouflage outfit, rifle and instruction sheet. Features moving eyes that consumer could try out via die-cut hole in back and lever on back of Joe's head. Near Mint Carded - **$200**
Loose - **$30 $60 $100**

GIJ-27 GIJ-28

❑ **GIJ-27. "Cobra Soldier" Figure on Card,**
1982. On card. - **$75 $225 $350**

❑ **GIJ-28. "Flash" Figure on Card,**
1982. On card. - **$50 $125 $250**

GIJ-20

❑ **GIJ-20. "GI Joe Sea Adventurer-The Shark's Surprise" Playset,**
1970. Hasbro #7442. 4x14.75x20.5" boxed playset contains GI Joe Sea Adventurer, aqua sled, three-piece scuba suit, swim fins, face mask, oxygen tanks, spear gun, shark, treasure chest, treasure coins, comic book, instruction sheet. Near Mint Boxed - **$700**
Used Complete - **$75 $150 $250**

GIJ-23 GIJ-24

❑ **GIJ-23. Super Joe Commander With Power Vest Ring,**
1970s. Store item by Hasbro. Color photo under acrylic on non-adjustable brass base. Six to eight in set. Each - **$6 $12 $30**

❑ **GIJ-24. Cello. Button,**
c. 1970s. Probably Hasbro promotional button. - **$30 $60 $90**

GIJ-29 GIJ-30

❑ **GIJ-29. "Grunt" Figure on Card,**
1982. On card. - **$50 $125 $225**

❑ **GIJ-30. "Rock 'N' Roll" Figure on Card,**
1982. On card. - **$75 $150 $300**

GIJ-31

GIJ-32

❑ **GIJ-31. "Scarlett" Figure on Card,**
1982. On card. - **$150 $325 $600**

❑ **GIJ-32. "Short-Fuse" Figure on Card,**
1982. On card. - **$50 $125 $250**

GIJ-33

(CLOSE-UP OF FIGURE)

❑ **GIJ-33. "Snake Eyes" Figure on Card,**
1982. On card. - **$250 $500 $1000**

GIJ-34

GIJ-35

❑ **GIJ-34. "Stalker" Figure on Card,**
1982. On card. - **$75 $150 $300**

❑ **GIJ-35. "Zap" Figure on Card,**
1982. On card. - **$75 $150 $300**

GIJ-36

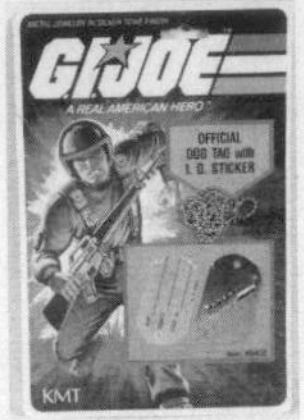

GIJ-37

❑ **GIJ-36. Official Commando Medal and Bar Pin,**
1982. On card. - **$20 $40 $70**

❑ **GIJ-37. Official Dog Tag with I.D. Sticker,**
1982. On card. - **$10 $20 $50**

GIJ-38

GIJ-39

❑ **GIJ-38. Official I.D. Bracelet,**
1982. On card. - **$10 $20 $50**

❑ **GIJ-39. Official Key Ring with Dog Tag and Bullet Charm,**
1982. On card. - **$15 $25 $50**

GIJ-40

GIJ-41

❑ **GIJ-40. Official Machine Gunner Medal and Sergeant Stripes Pin,**
1982. On card. - **$10 $20 $50**

❑ **GIJ-41. Official Ranger-Medal and Ranger Bar Pin,**
1982. On card. - **$25 $35 $80**

GIJ-42

GIJ-43

❑ **GIJ-42. Official G.I. Joe Ring and Bar Pin,**
1982. On card. - **$25 $40 $80**

❑ **GIJ-43. Official G. I. Joe Whistle,**
1982. On card. - **$10 $20 $50**

GIJ-44

GIJ-45

❑ **GIJ-44. "GI Joe Shuttle Crew" Plastic Ring,**
1980s. Image of space shuttle high above world globe. - **$6 $10 $15**

❑ **GIJ-45. "Cryo-Freeze Sgt. Savage" Figure on Card,**
1994. From Hasbro's Sgt. Savage series. With energy pack squirt ring on card. - **$35**

GIJ-46

GIJ-47

❑ **GIJ-46. "Urban Attack Dynamite" Figure on Card,**
1994. From the Sgt. Savage series. With decoder ring on card. - **$35**

❑ **GIJ-47. "Jet-Pack General Blitz" Figure on Card,**
1994. From the Sgt. Savage series. With working compass ring on card. - **$35**

GIJ-48

❑ **GIJ-48. G.I. Joe Action Astronaut Masterpiece Edition,**
1996. Limited edition from FAO Schwarz. Includes book and reproduction of a G.I. Joe astronaut doll. Boxed - **$200**

GIJ-49

GIJ-50

❑ **GIJ-49. Teddy Roosevelt G.I. Joe in Box,**
1999. 12" tall. From the G.I. Joe Classic Collection, commemorating 35 years. Set includes gun, flag and pin. Boxed - **$40**

❑ **GIJ-50. Resin Statue,**
1990s. 13 1/2" tall. Limited to 400. - **$200**

GIJ-51

❑ **GIJ-51. Blackhawk Figure With Outfits in Display Box,**
2003. Limited to 2000. GI Joe product. - **$265**

GIJ-52

GIJ-53

❑ **GIJ-52. Sgt. Rock Figure ,**
2003. Limited to 2000. GI Joe product. - **$185**

❑ **GIJ-53. Sgt. Rock Normandy Accessory Set in Display Box,**
2003. GI Joe product. - **$38**

The Goldbergs

***The Goldbergs*, the first memorable Jewish radio comedy, was the brainchild of Gertrude Berg, who wrote, produced, directed, and starred as Molly, the benevolent matriarch of a working-class family in the Bronx. With husband Jake, children Sammy and Rosalie, and Uncle David, Molly was a fixture on the NBC, CBS, or Mutual networks from 1929 to 1945 and again in 1949-1950. Sponsors included Pepsodent (1931-1934), Colgate (1936), Oxydol (1937-1945), and General Foods (1949-1950). Originally titled *The Rise of the Goldbergs*, the show became *The Goldbergs* in 1936. In 1939 the show moved from its Bronx locale to Laştonbury, Connecticut. Noted Golden Age comic book artist Irwin Hasen produced a Goldbergs comic strip in 1944-45. A successful television series aired from 1949 to 1954, a Broadway play (*Molly and Me*) was produced in 1948, and a movie (*Molly*) was released in 1951. "Yoo-Hoo, Mrs. Bloom!"**

GLD-1

❑ **GLD-1. Goldbergs Puzzle,**
1932. Pepsodent Co. 8x10" full color jigsaw puzzle. - **$25 $45 $95**

GLD-2

GLD-3

❑ **GLD-2. Molly Goldberg Fan Photo,**
1930s. - **$10 $20 $40**

❑ **GLD-3. Gertrude Berg 11x14" Frame Tray Jigsaw Puzzle,**
1952. Store item by Jaymar. - **$25 $45 $95**

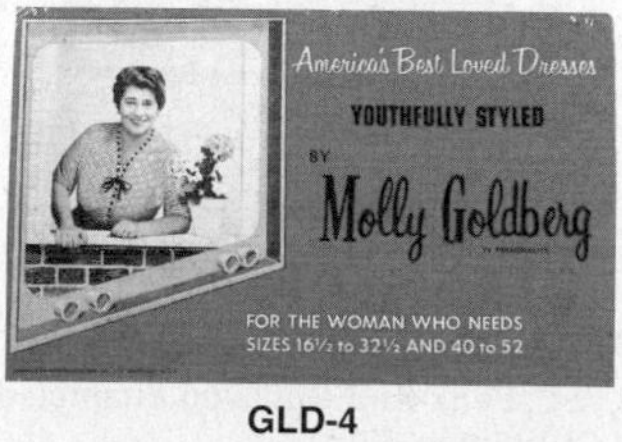

GLD-4

❑ **GLD-4. Molly Goldberg Store Sign,**
1954. - **$40 $90 $175**

Golliwog

British author Florence Upton (1873-1922) created Golliwogg (note spelling), "the blackest gnome," for an 1895 children's book, *The Adventures of Two Dutch Dolls and a Golliwogg*. Though initially described as a "horrid sight," the black-skinned, black-haired figure quickly proved himself gallant and heroic. He was also a hit with young readers; so much so that when *Two Dutch Dolls* spawned a series of sequels, Golliwogg became the lead character.

With stardom came controversy. The Golliwogg's visual design was inspired by an American-made black minstrel doll that Upton had owned as a child. Like then-popular stereotypical caricatures of blacks, the Golliwogg sported large eyes, larger lips, frizzy hair, and garish "dandy" clothing.

Upton seemingly meant no offense by her use of the image; while "Golly" may have physically resembled an ethnic caricature, the gnome's behavior was smart, brave, and in no way demeaning. Unfortunately, Upton did not copyright her creation, and the other toy and children's book creators who appropriated it generally depicted it in a less positive light.

These later golliwogs—the final "g" dropped from the name around 1910—were often portrayed as villains or layabouts. Their racial identity was made crudely explicit. The racial slur "wog," common at the time, may not have derived directly from golliwogs, but tended to be associated with them in the public eye.

Golliwogs vanished from American pop culture after World War II, but remained a British nursery staple into the 1990s. This is not to call the English insensitive; toymakers and advertisers—most notably the Robertson's preserves company—tried to purge the characters' derogatory elements. Nevertheless, the gnomes' visual association with stereotype seems ultimately to have been unshakeable. Today, golliwogs survive mainly as figures of grown-up nostalgia.

GLW-1

❑ **GLW-1. "The Golliwogg's Bicycle Club" Book,**
1896. Art by Florence K. Upton and words by Bertha Upton, Florence's mother.
- **$475 $1000 $1650**

GLW-2

GLW-3

❑ **GLW-2. "The Golliwogg's Desert Island" Book,**
1906. By Florence K. and Bertha Upton. 64 pages of color. - **$350 $825 $1350**

❑ **GLW-3. "Golliwogg In The African Jungle" Book,**
1909. Art by Florence K. Upton and words by Bertha Upton, Florence's mother.
- **$625 $1250 $2400**

GLW-4

❑ **GLW-4. Early Golliwog Glazed Ceramic Cup,**
c. 1910. - **$75 $125 $175**

GLW-5

❑ **GLW-5. Perfume Bottle,**
1920s. Various sizes. This example about 3" tall. Near Mint, Unopened - **$400**

GLW-6

❑ **GLW-6. Perfume Bottle,**
1920s. From Paris, France. Bottle with original sticker. Near Mint, Unopened - **$750**

GLW-7

❑ **GLW-7. Felix And Golliwog Enameled Metal Christmas Sign,**
c. 1920s. Sign is 14x19". Australian.
- **$550 $1150 $2250**

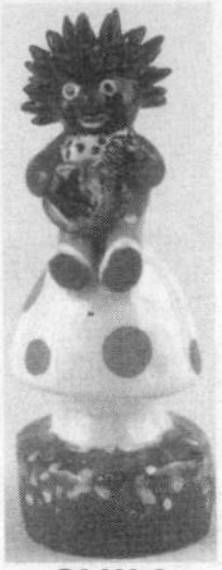

GLW-8 GLW-9

❑ **GLW-8. Golliwog Felt Stuffed Doll,**
1930s. Rare. - **$175 $350 $650**

❑ **GLW-9. Golliwog Figure on Mushroom,**
1930s. Used for cooking. - **$115 $225 $400**

GLW-10 GLW-11

❑ **GLW-10. Golly 3-3/4" Sitting Figure,**
1930s. Used for cooking. - **$85 $165 $325**

❑ **GLW-11. Golly 4-3/4" Kneeling Figure,**
1930s. Used for cooking. - **$115 $200 $375**

GLW-12

❑ **GLW-12. Child's Glazed Ceramic Plate,**
1930s. - **$75 $150 $250**

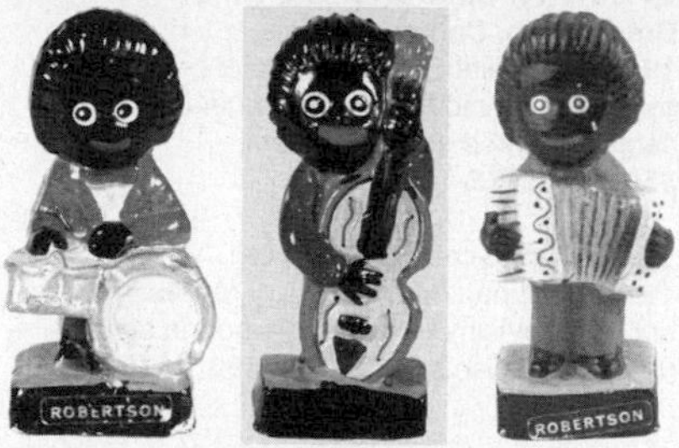

GLW-13

❑ **GLW-13. Robertson Figures,**
1940s. Promotes preserves (jelly) company. Each - **$25 $50 $100**

GLW-14

❑ **GLW-14. Golliwog Soccer Player Figures,**
1940s. Robertson's Jams. Each - **$25 $50 $100**

GLW-15

❑ **GLW-15. Golliwog Counter-top Display,**
1950s. Robertson's Jams. About 2.5 feet tall hollow composition with interior bulb that illuminates product jar resting in cut-out area of left arm. **- $600 $1200 $2500**

GLW-16

❑ **GLW-16. Cardboard Diecut Store Sign,**
1950s. Roberts Preserves. Great Britain. 28" tall. - **$250 $500 $1000**

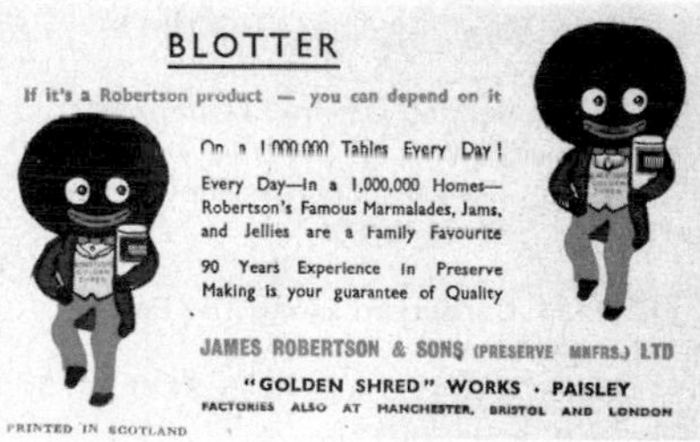

GLW-17

❑ **GLW-17. Robertson & Sons Blotter,**
1950s. Promotes preserves (jelly) company. **- $25 $40 $60**

GLW-18

GLW-19

❑ **GLW-18. Golliwog "Golden Shred" Enamel Pin,**
c. 1960s. 1-5/16" tall colorful enamel on brass English pin. - **$8 $12 $20**

❑ **GLW-19. Golliwog With Guitar Enamel Pin,**
c. 1960s. 1-5/16" tall colored enamel. English issue. - **$8 $12 $20**

Gone With The Wind

One of the most popular films of all time, *Gone with the Wind* premiered in Atlanta, Georgia, on December 15, 1939, won 10 Academy Awards, including the first Oscar for a black actor, Hattie McDaniel as Best Supporting Actress. The film remains a perennial smash in theaters, on television, and in video rentals. This Civil War saga, based on Margaret Mitchell's 1936 Pulitzer Prize winning novel, starred Clark Gable, Vivien Leigh, an all-star cast including future TV "Superman" George Reeves - and the burning of Atlanta. Merchandising, including portrait dolls, collector plates, and porcelain figurines, continues to this day. Frankly Scarlett, GWTW collectors do give a damn!

GON-1

❑ **GON-1. Book Publishing House Summary Booklet,**
1936. Macmillan Co. - **$50 $100 $200**

GON-2

GON-3

❑ **GON-2. Pre-Movie Sheet Music,**
1937. Store item by Irving Berlin Inc. and Selznick International Pictures Inc. 9x12" captioned "Based Upon Margaret Mitchell's Novel, And The Forthcoming Greatest Of All Motion Pictures Gone With The Wind." - **$25 $50 $100**

❑ **GON-3. "Gone With The Wind" Souvenir Program,**
1939. Large numbers sold and saved so condition is critical to higher value. **- $35 $75 $150**

GON-4

❑ GON-4. "Gone With The Wind" Large Framed Publicity Portrait Group,
1940. Group of four 18x19" portraits with simulated three dimensional frames of cardboard. Portraits show Vivien Leigh, Clark Gable, Leslie Howard and Olivia de Havilland. Each portrait labeled with actor's name and character's name as well as film title below portrait. Examples shown are custom-framed.
Leigh and Gable Each - **$165 $325 $500**
Howard and de Havilland Each - **$135 $265 $375**

(FRONT) GON-5 (BACK)

❑ GON-5. Paper Doll Book,
1940. Merrill Publshing Co. 10.75" x 13" book has 8 pages of costumes for the 2 punch-out dolls on the cover and 3 on the back cover.
- **$130 $250 $550**

GON-6

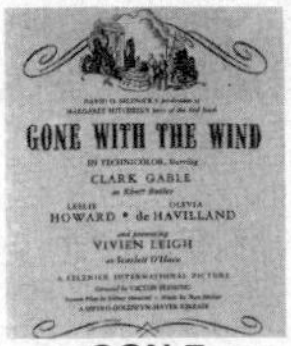

GON-7

❑ GON-6. "Gone With The Wind" Curtain Fabric,
1940. Example shown is 34x51". Similar Size Near Mint - **$325**

❑ GON-7. Movie Theater Herald,
1940. Various theaters. - **$20 $35 $75**

GON-8

GON-9

❑ GON-8. "Scarlett O'Hara" Handkerchief,
1940. Store item. Sheer fabric with design image repeated on all four quadrants. -
$50 $100 $200

❑ GON-9. "Scarlett O'Hara Perfume" Novelty Container,
1940. Store item. - **$65 $110 $225**

GON-10

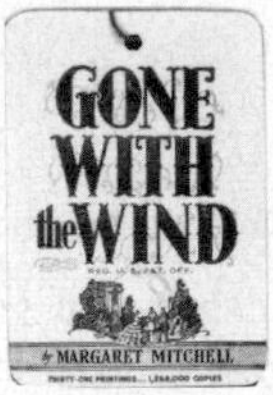

GON-11

❑ GON-10. Scarlett O'Hara "Yesteryear" Perfume Glass Vial,
1940. Babs Creations. Figure image within vertical dome. - **$75 $175 $350**

❑ GON-11. Cardboard String Tag From Clothing Dress,
1940. Mae Delli's Originals. - **$45 $110 $175**

GON-12

GON-13

❑ GON-12. Brass Heart-Shaped Jewelry Pin,
1940. Store item. - **$75 $160 $325**

❑ GON-13. "Gone With The Wind" Brass Charm Locket Designed In Book Image,
1940. Opens to hold two miniature pictures. -
$65 $125 $275

GON-14

GON-15

❑ GON-14. Gone With The Wind Brass/Cello. Cameo Brooch,
1940. Lux Toilet Soap. Replica of brooch worn by Scarlett in movie, offered originally for 15 cents and three soap wrappers. -
$50 $90 $175

❑ GON-15. Scarlett's Brooch,
1940. Lux Soap. Movie jewelry replica in brass accented by simulated pearls around single simulated turquoise stone. - **$50 $90 $175**

GON-16

GON-17

❑ GON-16. Cookbook,
1940. Pebeco Toothpaste premium. -
$40 $75 $150

❑ GON-17. Cookbook Store Display From Pebeco Toothpaste,
1940. Scarce. - **$125 $200 $400**

GON-18

GON-19

❑ GON-18. "I've Seen Gone With The Wind" Cello. Button,
1940. Rare. - **$65 $165 $300**

❑ GON-19. "Clark Gable/Gone With The Wind" Cigarette Series Card,
c. 1940. Turf Cigarettes. Card #34 from series of 50 "Famous Film Stars" with photo head on illustrated body. - **$10 $20 $40**

GON-20

GON-21

❑ **GON-20. "Tara's Theme" Sheet Music,**
1941. Store item by Remick Music Corp. 9x12" with browntone illustration. Also seen with 1954 copyright date. First Printing - **$20 $40 $80**
Later Printing - **$8 $15 $30**

❑ **GON-21. Gone With The Wind Spanish Herald Sheet,**
1940s. 3-1/2x5-1/2" full color with Spanish text on reverse. - **$15 $30 $50**

GON-22

❑ **GON-22. Re-release Promo Poster,**
1998. 20" x 13". Promotes re-release of the movie in its original technicolor and with digital sound. - **$8 $15 $30**

Gorgeous George

Born George Wagner, Gorgeous George (1914-1963) invented his flamboyant alter ego persona in the early 1940s. In 1947, the new medium of television was the perfect outlet for the theatrics of professional wrestling. Billing himself as the Human Orchid, George's valet would spray the ring with perfume as George, with dyed long blonde hair curled and pinned with gold plated bobby pins, began his long entrance to the mat. George was the villain people loved to hate. He packed arenas and was credited with selling millions of TV sets to home viewers.

George starred in the 1949 Universal feature film *Alias The Champ* and won the AWA World Championship by defeating Chief Don Eagle May 26, 1950. He later lost the title to Lou Thesz. In one match, he bet a haircut on the outcome and wound up having his golden locks sheared off in the ring.

Gorgeous George not only influenced other wrestlers like Nature Boy Buddy Rogers, Dr. Jerry Graham and Ric Flair but was also an inspiration to Liberace, Little Richard and Muhammad Ali. Tycoon Donald Trump even used the haircut bet during a professional wrestling match in 2007 but still has his pompadour as of this writing.

GOR-1

❑ **GOR-1. "Gorgeous George For President" Button,**
1956. 1" in diameter with no backpaper as issued. - **$15 $30 $60**

GOR-2

❑ **GOR-2. Exhibit Card Machine Insert Wrestlers,**
1950s. Insert is 8x12" and measures 11x14" with mat. Black and white glossy paper with photos and facsimile signatures of Ruffy Silverstein, Gorgeous George and Farmer Don Martin. - **$60 $125 $225**

GOR-3

❑ **GOR-3. Multi-Artist Concert Poster,**
1965. 22x28" poster on card stock for November 2, 1965 concert in Chattanooga, TN with Gorgeous George as "MC" along with Bill Murry. - **$200 $400 $650**

The Great Gildersleeve

Throckmorton P. Gildersleeve started life as a character on the *Fibber McGee and Molly* radio series in the 1930s. Created and played by actor Harold Peary (1908-1985), Gildy was a pompous windbag who was spun off successfully to his own program on NBC in 1941. He was a small-town water commissioner, but the show centered on his life as the bachelor uncle of Leroy and Marjorie and his romantic encounters as the town's most prominent eligible man. Willard Waterman stepped into the role in 1950, and the program ran until 1958. Kraft Foods was the sponsor. There was a brief television series in 1955. RKO released four feature films: *The Great Gildersleeve* (1942); *Gildersleeve on Broadway* (1943); *Gildersleeve's Bad Day* (1943); *Gildersleeve's Ghost* (1944).

GIL-1

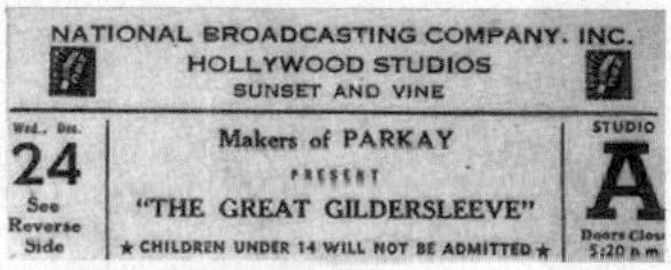

GIL-2

GIL-3

❑ **GIL-1. Kraft Foods Litho. Tin 2-1/4" Jar Lid,**
1946. - **$20 $30 $60**

❑ **GIL-2. Radio Show Studio Audience Ticket,**
1947. Parkay margarine. Pictured example for December 24 Christmas Eve broadcast. - **$15 $25 $60**

❑ **GIL-3. Great Gildersleeve Record w/Sleeve,**
1940s. Radio premium. Titled "Name My Song Contest" part 1& 2. - **$30 $50 $110**

Green Giant

The Green Giant was born in 1925 as the trademark for a new variety of peas by the Minnesota Valley Canning Company. The original illustration of a giant wrapped in fur, created to satisfy trademark requirements, was redesigned 10 years later into the character we now recognize--a smiling green giant clothed in leaves. A novelty record by the Kingsmen, "The Jolly Green Giant" soared to number four on the pop charts in 1965. Little Sprout was added in the early 1970s, and the company has merchandised both characters.

GNT-1

❑ **GNT-1. 20th Anniversary Birthday Record With Envelope,**
1949. In Mailer - **$15 $30 $55**
No Mailer - **$5 $15 $30**

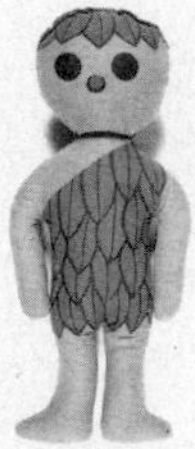
GNT-2

GNT-3

❑ **GNT-2. Earliest Cloth Doll,**
1966. - **$10 $20 $50**

❑ **GNT-3. "Footprint Rug" In Mailer,**
1967. Issued both as "Left Foot" and "Right Foot" versions, each about 22" wide by 42" long mailed in a 24" long green plastic sleeve.
Near Mint In Mailer - **$50**
Loose - **$10 $15 $25**

GNT-4

❑ **GNT-4. Campaign Kit,**
1968. Voter card, litho. badge, sticker, 26x38" poster.
Set - **$20 $35 $75**

GNT-5

GNT-6

❑ **GNT-5. Little Sprout Cloth Doll,**
c. 1970. - **$5 $12 $25**

❑ **GNT-6. "Speakin' Sprout" Talking Cloth Doll,**
1971. Contains battery operated tape recorder. - **$25 $50 $80**

GNT-7

GNT-8

❑ **GNT-7. "Little Sprout" Sleeping Bag With Mailer,**
1977. Mail order premium. **- $15 $30 $60**

❑ **GNT-8. Little Sprout Vinyl Doll,**
1970s. - **$10 $20 $45**

GNT-9

❑ **GNT-9. Little Green "Sprout Touch Lamp,"**
1985. Lamp is 7.5" diameter by 15" tall. Figure of Sprout is plastic, yellow 'balloons' glow when lit. Has 'touch' switch mechanism.
- **$30 $60 $100**

GNT-10

❑ **GNT-10. "Little Sprout Radio" With Box,**
1980s. Hard plastic battery operated figural radio 9-1/2" tall. Near Mint Boxed - **$100**
Loose - **$15 $25 $50**

The Green Hornet

Opening with the music to "Flight of the Bumblebee," and accompanied by his faithful valet Kato, the Green Hornet matched wits with the underworld on the radio from 1936 to 1952, first on WXYZ in Detroit, then on the Mutual network in 1938, on NBC in 1939, on the ABC Blue network in 1940, and finally back on Mutual in 1952. Sponsors included General Mills in 1948 and Orange Crush in 1952. Under his mask the Hornet was Britt Reid, crusading newspaper publisher and grand-nephew of the Lone Ranger, and his crime-fighting exploits in the big city resembled those of his relative in the West. (Both shows were created by George W. Trendle and written largely by Fran Striker.) Also featured was Miss Case, secretary and love interest, along with Black Beauty, the Hornet's supercharged limousine, and his non-lethal gas gun. Kato, originally Japanese, became a Filipino after Pearl Harbor.

Two Green Hornet chapter plays were released by Universal in 1940, with Gordon Jones as Britt Reid and Keye Luke as Kato, and a souped-up television series aired for a season (1966-1967) on ABC, with Van Williams in the title role and Bruce Lee as Kato. Comic books appeared more or less regularly from 1940 to 1949, followed by a one-shot in 1953, three issues in 1966-1967 timed to coincide with the television series, and a revival in 1989.

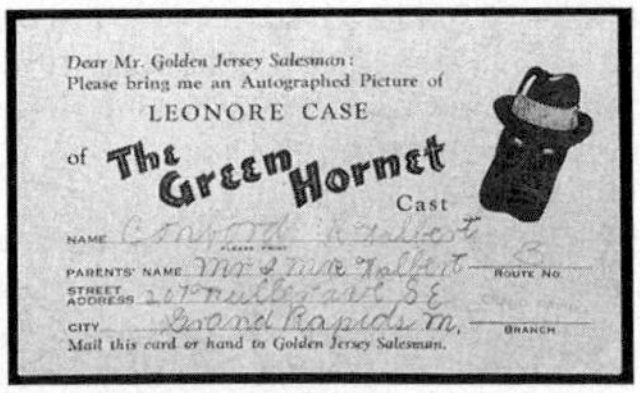

GRN-1

❑ **GRN-1. Postcard,**
1936. Golden Jersey Milk. Radio premium- **$125 $300 $600**

GRN-2

❑ **GRN-2. Radio Fan Club Photo,**
1938. Golden Jersey Milk. Pictures Britt Reid (Al Hodge) as Green Hornet with back ad text. - **$75 $250 $500**

GRN-3

GRN-4

❑ **GRN-3. Radio Fan Club Photo,**
1938. Golden Jersey Milk. Pictures Miss Case (Lee Allman) with back ad text, from G-J-M Club photo series of several cast members. - **$60 $175 $275**

❑ **GRN-4. "Kato" Portrait Photo,**
1938. Golden Jersey Milk. - **$75 $200 $300**

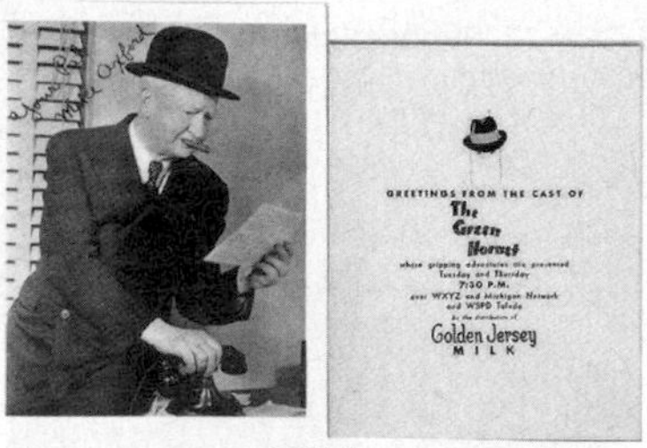

GRN-5

❑ **GRN-5. "Mike Oxford" Portrait Photo,**
1938. Golden Jersey Milk. - **$60 $175 $275**

GRN-6

❑ **GRN-6. Membership Card,**
1938. Golden Jersey Milk. - **$100 $275 $450**

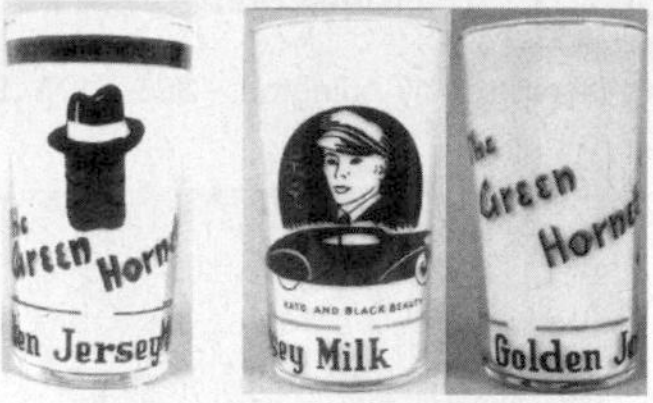

GRN-7

GRN-8

❑ **GRN-7. "Golden Jersey Milk" Premium Glasses,**
c. 1938. Set of four, each 4.75" tall. Pictured are "The Green Hornet" and "Kato And Black Beauty." Also in set is "Leonore Case," Green Hornet glass - **$100 $300 $450**
Others, each - **$125 $325 $500**

❑ **GRN-8. Mike Oxford Premium Glass,**
c. 1938. Golden Jersey Milk. 4.75" tall. - **$125 $325 $500**

GRN-9

GRN-10

❑ **GRN-9. Radio Show Postcard,**
1939. - **$100 $200 $400**

❑ **GRN-10. "The Green Hornet Strikes" Better Little Book,**
1940. Whitman #1453. - **$45 $135 $315**

GRN-11 GRN-12 GRN-13

❑ **GRN-11. "The Green Hornet Adventure Club" Cello. Button,**
1940. Rare. Universal Pictures. For 13-chapter movie serial. - **$100 $225 $450**

❑ **GRN-12. "The Green Hornet Strikes Again" Movie Serial Cello. Button,**
1940. Rare. Universal Serial/Adventure Club. For 13-chapter serial. - **$175 $400 $800**

❑ **GRN-13. "Green Hornet Loyalty Club" Cello. Button,**
c. 1940. - **$200 $300 $600**

GRN-14

GRN-15

❑ **GRN-14. "The Green Hornet Returns" Better Little Book #1496,**
1941. 432 pgs. Flip pictures. - **$45 $135 $315**

❑ **GRN-15. "The Green Hornet Cracks Down" Better Little Book,**
1942. Whitman #1480. - **$41 $123 $290**

GRN-16

GRN-17

❑ **GRN-16. Speed Comics/Green Hornet Comics News Vendor's Apron,**
c. 1945. Includes text "Nationally Distributed By Publisher's Distributing Corporation." Black and red type on tan fabric featuring three pockets for change. - **$300 $600 $1200**

❑ **GRN-17. Secret Compartment Glow-In-Dark Ring,**
1947. General Mills. Brass with hinged lid over glow plastic compartment. - **$300 $600 $1200**

GRN-18

GRN-19

❑ **GRN-18. "Green Hornet Night Signaling Ring" Enclosure Slip,**
c. 1947. Betty Crocker Cereal Tray offer. Instructions are on one side, order coupon for additional rings on reverse. - **$115 $175 $350**

❑ **GRN-19. "Newspaper Reporter" Recruitment Letter,**
1940s. Union Biscuit Co. Offers reporter's kit described in full over radio broadcasts on KWK, St. Louis. - **$75 $165 $350**

GRN-20

GRN-21

❑ **GRN-20. Vernors Plastic "Trick Or Treat Bag",**
1966. Vernors Ginger Ale. - **$25 $45 $90**

❑ **GRN-21. "Agent" 4" Litho. Button,**
1966. Store item. - **$15 $30 $60**

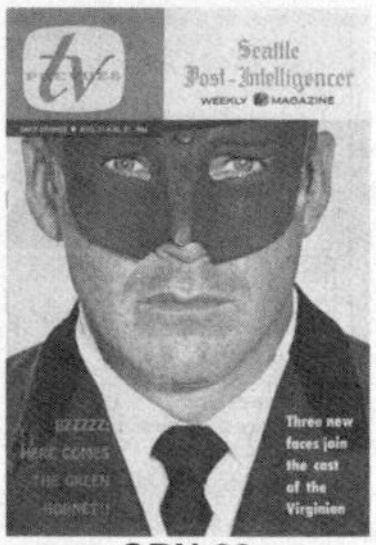

GRN-22

❑ **GRN-22. Regional "TV Prevues" Weekly Magazine,**
1966. 7.25" x 10.25" from Seattle for Aug. 21-27. - **$12 $25 $50**

GRN-23

❑ **GRN-23. "The Green Hornet" Hat With Mask,**
1966. Store item by Arlington. - **$85 $175 $300**

GRN-24

❑ **GRN-24. "The Green Hornet Oil Painting" Set,**
1966. Greenway Productions Inc. 1.25x14.25x21.5" made by Hasbro. Set includes unusual sculptured green plastic frame, 12x16" canvas, 10 oil paint capsules and a brush. Insert art features Green Hornet with Black Beauty in background. Paint-by-number canvas has same image as insert along with large hornet insect image. - **$225 $450 $850**

GRN-25

GRN-26

❑ **GRN-25. "The Green Hornet/Kato" Glass,**
1966. Probable food product container. - **$75 $150 $250**

❑ **GRN-26. TV Promo Postcard,**
1966. - **$25 $50 $75**

GRN-27

GRN-28

❑ **GRN-27. Pennant 28-1/2",**
1966. Promotes TV show. - **$40 $90 $175**

❑ **GRN-28. Green Hornet Character Plastic Flicker Rings,**
1966. Set of 12, each with double image when tilted.
Silver Base Each - **$12 $25 $50**
Blue Base Each - **$8 $15 $30**

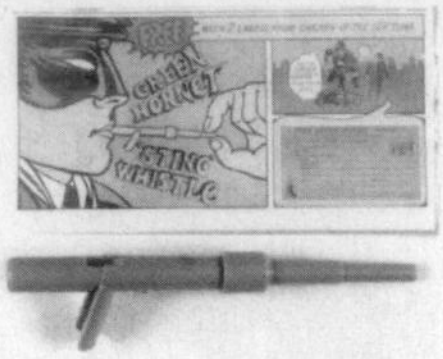

GRN-29

GRN-30

❑ **GRN-29. Green Hornet Sting Whistle,**
1966. Scarce. Chicken Of The Sea Tuna (Required Two Labels). Two-piece plastic slide whistle with small name mark on handle.
Newspaper Ad - **$25 $50 $100**
Whistle - **$150 $350 $750**

❑ **GRN-30. Battery Operated "Signal Ray",**
1966. Store item by Colorforms. Display card is 10x11". Display With Toy - **$350 $700 $1350**

GRN-31

GRN-32

❑ **GRN-31. Litho. Buttons,**
1966. Vending machine set of nine. Two color styles, with or without yellow.
Each - **$8 $15 $30**

❑ **GRN-32. Rubber Figural Ring,**
1966. Vending machine issue. - **$6 $8 $15**

GRN-33

GRN-34

GRN-35

❑ **GRN-33. 3-1/2" Cello. Button,**
c. 1966. Store item by Button World Mfg. - **$15 $30 $60**

❑ **GRN-34. "The Green Hornet" Drinking Glass,**
1966. Probable food product container. - **$85 $165 $275**

❑ **GRN-35. Green Hornet Pez Dispenser,**
c. 1966. Several hat variations, grey & brown hats worth more. - **$75 $150 $300**

GRN-36

❑ GRN-36. "Black Beauty" Car Boxed,
1966. Store item by Corgi. 5-1/2" long die cast metal featuring missile-firing grille and trunk with spinner-firing mechanism. Issued with four orange saucers and four missiles plus instruction paper. Near Mint Boxed - **$700**
Car With At Least One Saucer And One Missile - **$85 $175 $350**

GRN-37

❑ GRN-37. "The Green Hornet Wallets" Store Display,
1966. Store item by Standard Plastic Products Inc. 22" tall stiff cardboard countertop display with header card holding 12 wallets.
Near Mint Complete - **$2000**
Single Wallet - **$35 $65 $125**

GRN-38

GRN-39

❑ GRN-38. "The Green Hornet" Charm Bracelet,
1966. Store item. Card - **$15 $25 $50**
Bracelet - **$25 $45 $90**

❑ GRN-39. "The Green Hornet Quick Switch Game,"
1966. Milton Bradley. - **$60 $150 $300**

GRN-40

GRN-41

❑ GRN-40. "The Green Hornet Ring,"
1966. Vari-Vue. Flicker ring with silver base and full color flicker. Packaged **$175 $350 $600**

❑ GRN-41. Hand Puppet,
1966. Store item by Ideal. Photo example is missing hat. Complete - **$115 $225 $350**
Without Hat - **$60 $100 $150**

GRN-42

❑ GRN-42. "Green Hornet Bike Badge" Burry's Cookies Premium,
1966. Badge is 6x6.5" with 3" diameter flicker/flasher made of vacuform plastic that features image of Black Beauty car, Green Hornet and Kato and came in a 6.5x10" mailer that included a 4.25x5.5" instruction sheet.
Each Mailer/Instructions - **$25 $50 $80**
Badge - **$125 $250 $500**

GRN-43

❑ GRN-43. Pin-Ball Bagatelle,
1966. Hasbro. 10.5x16" hard plastic cover over cardboard playing surface illustrated by Green Hornet action scenes. Marble game toy is operated by mechanical flippers. - **$125 $250 $500**

GRN-44

❑ GRN-44. Flicker Picture Ruler On Card,
1967. 4.5x7" blister card holding six-inch ruler by Vari-Vue that alternates image when tilted for total of six detail image changes.
Near Mint Carded - **$350**
Ruler Only - **$60 $125 $225**

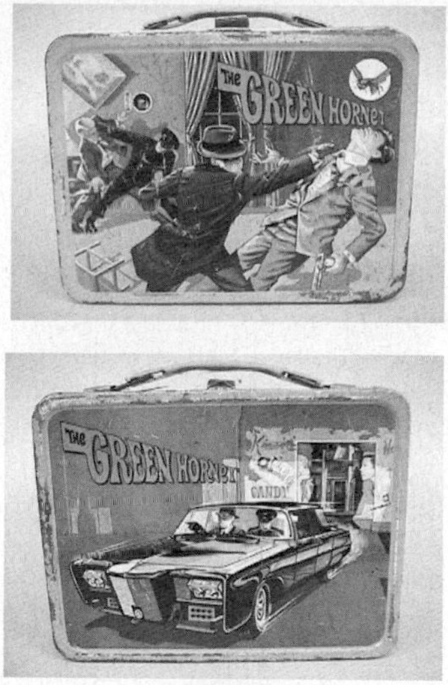

GRN-45

❑ GRN-45. Metal Lunch Box,
1967. Store item by King-Seeley. -
$150 $350 $850

GRN-46

❑ GRN-46. Lunch Box Metal Bottle,
1967. Store item by King-Seeley Thermos Co. Came with matching lunch box. -
$75 $200 $400

GRN-47

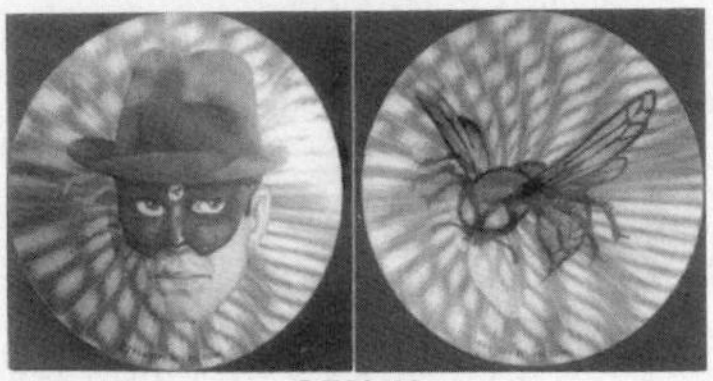

GRN-48

❑ **GRN-47. Flicker Button 3",**
1967. Store item. - **$12 $30 $75**

❑ **GRN-48. Flicker Disk 7",**
1967. Store item. - **$25 $50 $100**

GRN-49

❑ **GRN-49. "The Green Hornet/American Motors" Record,**
1973. Mark 56 Records. - **$40 $80 $135**

GRN-50

❑ **GRN-50. "Bruce Lee/The Green Hornet" Movie Poster,**
1977. 27x41" for 20th Century Fox film. - **$85 $165 $350**

GRN-51

GRN-52

❑ **GRN-51. "Green Hornet" Record,**
1977. With sleeve. Plays two complete radio programs from 1943. - **$65**

❑ **GRN-52. Green Hornet Large Rubber Ring,**
1970s. Vending machine issue. Thin band of green rubber attached to matching 2x2-1/4" hornet image. - **$10 $18 $30**

GRN-53

❑ **GRN-53. Green Hornet TV Syndication Promotion Kit,**
1990. 20th Century Fox Television. 8.5x12" kit consists of six slides, five 8x10" glossy photos in a glassine envelope, double-sided page with Green Hornet art on front and half-page of black/white photo with brief synopsis of series, fact sheet, comic strip-like folder titled "Kick The Competition In The %&^*)(*," double-sided promo sheet featuring Bruce Lee in action on front and brief synopsis on back, Green Hornet episode guide and storylines booklet, Green Hornet music cue sheets booklet.
- **$175 $350 $600**

GRN-54

GRN-55

❑ **GRN-54. "Green Hornet" Die-cast Car,**
2000. Team Lightning metal Road Rod. - **$8**

❑ **GRN-55. "Black Beauty" Die-cast Car,**
2001. Johnny Lightning metal model. - **$8**

The Green Lama

Created by Ken Crossen under the pseudonym Richard Foster, the Green Lama first appeared in the *Double Detective* pulp in April 1940. His first comic book appearance was in *Prize Comics #7*, December 1940. He then appeared in his own book for eight issues from 1944 to 1946 with superb art by Mac Raboy. For a dime readers could join the *Green Lama Club* and receive a membership card, the key to the Lama's secret code, and an Escapo folding trick that showed victory over Fascist rats. The character was revived on CBS radio for the summer of 1949 as a New York-based crime fighter with special powers acquired after 10 years of study in a Tibet monastery.

(INSTRUCTIONS)

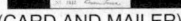

(CARD AND MAILER)

(VARIATION 2)

GLM-1

❑ **GLM-1. Club Kit,**
1945. Victory Game.
Club Card - **$100 $250 $500**
Mailer - **$50 $85 $175**
Escape Trick with Instructions, Two Variations, Each - **$125 $250 $500**

GLM-2

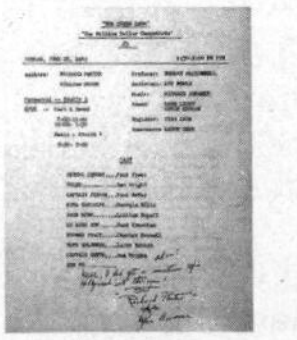

GLM-3

❑ **GLM-2. Code Letter,**
1940s. M.L.J. Magazines. Came with kit. "Green Lama Code Chart" with instructions concluding by translated "Buy Bonds" message. -
$125 $275 $600

❑ **GLM-3. Radio Episode Script,**
1949. For June 26 broadcast "Million Dollar Chopsticks". - **$75 $150 $300**

Gulliver's Travels

Jonathan Swift's masterpiece, published in 1726 and amended in 1735, has retained its satirical thrust and fairy-tale aura for almost three centuries. The voyages of Lemuel Gulliver to Lilliput, Brobdingnag, and the land of the Yahoos continue to enchant readers and viewers to this day. In addition to the many print editions of the classic, the tales have been adapted in various media, including: a full-length animated film by the Fleischer studios (1939); a Japanese animated feature that sent Gulliver into outer space (1966); a part live-action British film with Richard Harris (1977); *The 3 Worlds of Gulliver* (British, 1960); a Hanna-Barbera animated series, *The Adventures of Gulliver* (ABC, 1968-1970); a Hanna-Barbera feature for CBS, sponsored by Kenner toys (1979); Saban's *Gulliver's Travels*, syndicated in 1992; a Classic Comics edition first published in 1943; and Dell Comics editions in 1956 and again in 1965-1966. Ted Danson starred in a filmed version on NBC-television in 1996. Even the BBC tried its hand with a four-part adaptation for radio. A 3-D Imax film is in production.

GLL-1

❑ **GLL-1. "Gulliver's Travels" Booklet,**
1939. Macy's department store. - **$30 $65 $150**

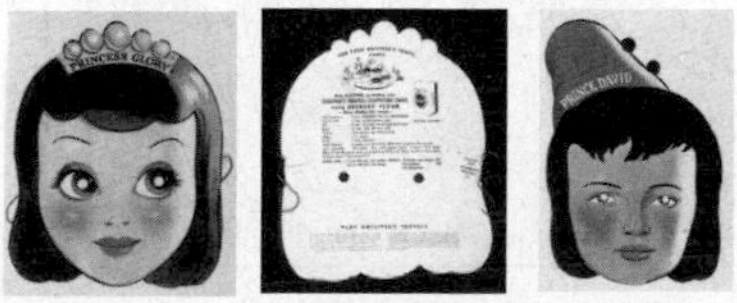

(BACK OF MASK)

GLL-2

❑ **GLL-2. Character Masks,**
1939. Hecker's Flour. Diecut stiff paper full color masks of Princess Glory, Prince David, King Bombo, Snitch, Gabby.
Each - **$20 $50 $100**

GLL-3

❑ **GLL-3. "Gulliver's Travels" Tin Litho. Spinning Top,**
1939. Store item. 5" diameter by 4-3/4" tall with red wood handle on rod at center. -
$65 $175 $275

GLL-4

GLL-5

❑ **GLL-4. Gulliver's Travels "Prince David" Lamp With Shade,**
1939. Lamp base is 4.25x4.25" and 12.5" tall to top of bulb socket. Painted plaster. Back of bse reads "1939 Paramount Pic Inc/Mfd. Exclusively By Ivon Bear Inc." Comes with 8" diameter tapering to 5" diameter paper shade standing 5.75" tall. Features large image of Gulliver and small images of Snitch, Gabby, King Bomba and King Little. Lamp - **$100 $175 $300**
Shade - **$125 $225 $400**

❑ **GLL-5. Gulliver's Travels "Gabby" Lamp,**
1939. Base is 2.5x4.5" and 11" tall to top of bulb socket. Painted plaster. Back of base reads "1939 Paramount Pic Inc/Mfd. Exclusively By Ivon Bear Inc." - **$100 $175 $300**

GLL-6

GLL-7

❑ **GLL-6. Boxed English Card Deck,**
1939. Store item copyright Paramount Pictures Inc., England. Set of 44 playing cards picturing various film scenes in color. - **$40 $75 $150**

❑ **GLL-7. Cereal Bowl,**
1939. White glass picturing characters from Fleischer animated film around perimeter. -
$20 $40 $80

GLL-8

GLL-9

❑ **GLL-8. "Gulliver" Glass Tumbler,**
1939. Probably distributed as dairy product container. Reverse has descriptive verse. -
$10 $20 $35

❑ **GLL-9. "King Little" Glass Tumbler,**
1939. Probably distributed as dairy product container. Reverse has descriptive verse. -
$10 $20 $35

GLL-10

GLL-11

❑ **GLL-10. "Snoop" Glass Tumbler,**
1939. Probably distributed as dairy product container. Reverse has descriptive verse. -
$10 $20 $35

❑ **GLL-11. "Snitch" Glass Tumbler,**
1939. Probably distributed as dairy product container. Reverse has descriptive verse. -
$10 $20 $35

GLL-12

❑ **GLL-12. Child's China Cup,**
1939. Pictures Gabby, Snitch and bird character from Fleischer animated cartoon movie. - **$25 $50 $100**

GLL-13

GLL-14

❑ **GLL-13. Gabby, Princess Glory And Prince David Glazed Ceramic Cup,**
1939. Store item by Hammersley & Co., England. - **$40 $75 $150**

❑ **GLL-14. China Pitcher,**
1939. Store item by Hammersley & Co., England. Pictures two scenes and five characters. - **$65 $150 $250**

GLL-15

❑ **GLL-15. Glazed Ceramic Creamer,**
1939. Store item. 3-1/2" tall. Hammersley & Co., England. - **$65 $150 $250**

GLL-16

GLL-17

❑ **GLL-16. "Gulliver's Travels" Saalfield Book,**
1939. #1172, similar to Whitman Big Little Book. - **$18 $54 $125**

❑ **GLL-17. "Gulliver's Travels" Flip Movie Booklet With Four Scenes,**
1939. Issued by Kitchen Kleanzer. 2-1/2x4-7/8". - **$55 $110 $165**

GLL-18

❑ **GLL-18. "Paperdoll Cut-Outs Of Gulliver's Travels" Book,**
1939. 10.75x15.5" Saalfield book picturing characters on each cover over contents of six doll sheets. - **$80 $165 $350**

GLL-19

❑ **GLL-19. Diecut Mechanical Valentines,**
1939. Pair of full color mechanical action cards featuring Gulliver and King Little.
Each - **$20 $40 $75**

Gumby

Art Clokey began experimenting with stop motion clay animation in the early 1950s, producing the film *Gumbasia* at USC film school in 1955. Sam Engel of 20th Century Fox enjoyed the film and formed a partnership with Clokey, leading to the creation of Gumby. The character made his first appearance as a test in a 1956 Howdy Doody show and proved popular enough that NBC gave him his own show. Hosted by Pinky Lee, the series began in 1957. Twenty-two twelve minute shows were produced, then these were recycled into 44 six minute episodes in the 1960s. The cast included Gumby, Pokey the Horse, Nopey the Dog and their enemies the Blockheads.

Gumby went into semi-retirement in the late 1960s but was revived by Eddie Murphy in the early 1980s when Murphy portrayed him as a cigar smoking, somewhat disenchanted, character on *Saturday Night Live.* Ninety-nine new Gumby shows were syndicated by Lorimar in 1987-1988 and Clokey Productions released *Gumby: The Movie,* a ninety minute feature film in 1995.

Comico released two comic books: *Gumby's Summer Fun Special* in 1987 and *Gumby's Winter Fun Special* in 1988. Both have art by Art Adams. Wildcard Ink. began a new comic book series in 2007, written by Bob Burden and illustrated by Rick Geary.

Gumby, after being molded and shaped into a pop culture icon over the last fifty plus years, has achieved iconic status.

GUM-1

❑ **GUM-1. "Gumby's Adventure Costumes" Sign and Packaged Outfits,**
1965. Lakeside Industries. 6x20" glossy paper sign. Four original 6x9" cards, three holding Gumby action costumes and one for Pokey.
Sign - **$10 $20 $35**
Each Carded Costume - **$3 $5 $10**

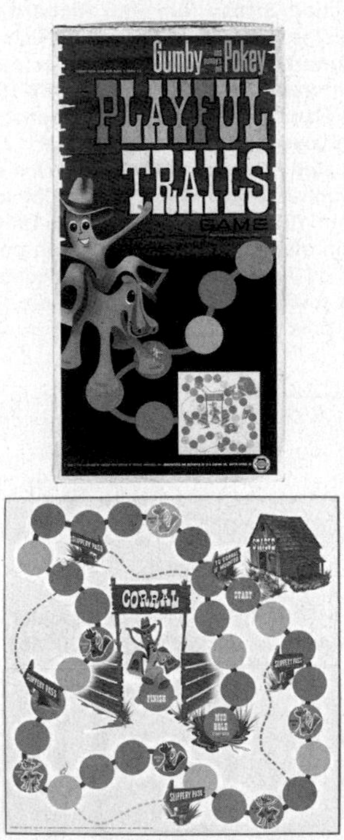

GUM-2

❑ **GUM-2. "Gumby And Pokey Playful Trails Game",**
1968. Lakeside Industries. 9.5x18.5x1.25" deep box contains 18" square gameboard, playing cards and four pairs of Gumby/Pokey figural markers. - **$15 $30 $65**

GUM-3

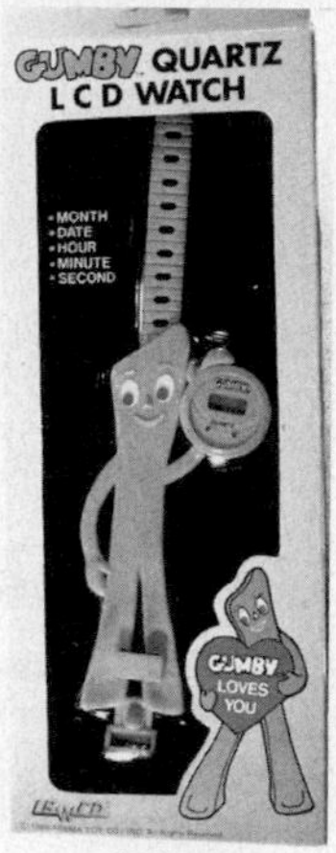

GUM-4

❑ **GUM-3. Gumby Flexible Plastic Ring,**
1960s. - **$5 $10 $15**

❑ **GUM-4. "Gumby" Quartz Watch with Box,**
1985. In colorful box with insert. - **$25 $45 $100**

GUM-5

❑ **GUM-5. "Gumby In '88!" Presidential Campaign Button,**
1988. 2-7/16" TV industry promotional. - **$5 $10 $20**

GUM-6

❑ **GUM-6. Gumby Ceramic Bank,**
1996. Made in Taiwan. - **$65**

GUM-7

❑ **GUM-7. "Gumby For President",**
1990s. Family Home Entertainment Co. Issued as a 3" button and a 3" mirror used as video store promotional. Each - **$4 $8 $15**

The Gumps

***The Gumps*, one of the most popular comic strips of the 1920s, was created by Sidney Smith (1887-1935) for the *Chicago Tribune*. The story of Andy and Min, son Chester, and rich Uncle Bim began as a daily strip in 1917 and as a Sunday feature in 1919, and lasted until 1959, some 24 years after Smith was killed in an automobile accident. Gus Edson was the main artist. Andy Gump ran for Congress in 1922 and for President in 1924. Comic book reprints appeared from 1918 into the 1940s, and a radio series based on the strip and sponsored by Pebeco toothpaste was aired on CBS from 1934 to 1937. The popularity of the Gumps is reflected by the large variety of licensed items - toys, games, books, buttons, etc. "Oh Min!"**

GMP-1

❑ **GMP-1. "Andy Gump For Congress" Cello. Button,**
1922. Various newspapers. - **$10 $20 $30**

GMP-2

❑ **GMP-2. "Andy Gump" Pictorial Sheet Music,**
1923. Store item. Words and music for novelty song illustrated by 15 characters from comic strip by Sidney Smith. - **$20 $35 $75**

GMP-3

❑ **GMP-3. Andy Gump "Read My Book" Pocket Mirror,**
1924. 2.25" cello multicolor promoting "His Life Story" book retailed at $1 during his 1924 candidacy for U.S. President. - **$60 $125 $225**

GMP-4

GMP-5

❑ **GMP-4. "Andy Gump For President" Cello. Button,**
c. 1924. Wonder Milk, various other food products. - **$20 $40 $80**

❑ **GMP-5. "Andy Gump For President" 2" Cello. Button,**
c. 1924. Good Humor Ice Cream Suckers. - **$50 $125 $250**

GMP-6

❑ **GMP-6. "The Sunshine Twins" Book,**
1925. Sunshine Andy Gump Biscuits by Loose-Wiles Biscuit Co. Pictured example is designated fourth edition. - **$35 $65 $125**

GMP-7

❑ **GMP-7. "Andrew Gump For President" Record On Original Card,**
1920s. Card is 5x6.5" and holds 4.75" record. Image of Andy at podium with text "He Wears No Man's Collar/100% For The People/Andrew Gump For President." - **$40 $85 $150**

GMP-8

❑ **GMP-8. Andy Gump Roadster By Arcade Mfg. Co.**
1920s. Toy is 4x7x6" tall cast iron including the separate figure of Andy holding steering wheel, wheels are nickel plated as is the "348" license plate. This version does not have a crank attached below the grille. On this version Andy wears green suit and hat and this color matches the hubs. - **$650 $1500 $2500**

GMP-9

❑ **GMP-9. "The Gumps At The Seashore" Boxed Game,**
c. 1930. Milton Bradley store item #4520. - **$75 $150 $300**

GMP-10

❑ **GMP-10. "Chester Gump At Silver Creek Ranch" Whitman Premium Book,**
1933. Sundial Shoes and others. Similar to a Big Little Book but 4x5-5/8" format and only 48 pages plus covers. - **$24 $72 $165**

GMP-11

GMP-12

❑ **GMP-11. "Chester Gump Finds Hidden Treasure" Premium Whitman Book,**
1934. Perkins Products (Korlix Pudding). Seen both with and without the Perkins name on the back cover. 48 pages plus covers. - **$24 $72 $165**

❑ **GMP-12. "Chester Gump And His Friends" Booklet,**
1934. Tarzan Ice Cream Cups. #5 from series of various character titles. - **$26 $78 $180**

GMP-13

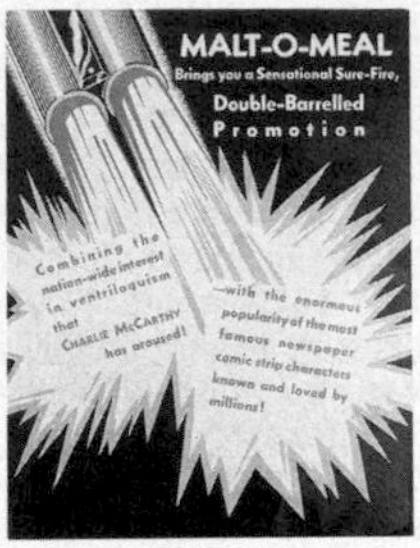

GMP-14

❑ **GMP-13. "The Gumps In Radio Land" Booklet,**
1937. Pebeco toothpaste. - **$21 $63 $145**

❑ **GMP-14. Malt-O-Meal Cereal Premium Folder,**
1938. Four pages of pictures of Andy Gump, Harold Teen, Herby, and cardboard Dummys. - **$35 $70 $165**

GMP-15

❑ **GMP-15. "Andy Gump" Die Cut Sign 14x16",**
1938. Rare. Probably unique. Gordon Gold Archives. Malt-O-Meal promotional sign (standee.) Tells how to get comic character dummies. - **$550 $1350 $2750**

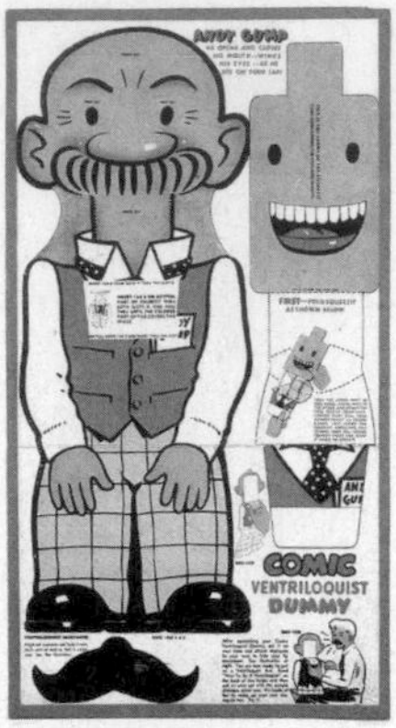

GMP-16

GMP-17

❑ **GMP-16. "Andy Gump" Dummy Punchout 11x20",**
1938. Rare. Malt-O-Meal Cereal premium. - **$165 $325 $750**

❑ **GMP-17. "Andy Gump" Wood Jointed Doll,**
1930s. Store item. - **$50 $85 $175**

GMP-18

GMP-19

❑ **GMP-18. "Investigator/Gump Charities/Use Solder Seal" Cello. Button,**
1930s. - **$20 $40 $75**

❑ **GMP-19. "The Gumps/Friendly Refreshment" Metal Cap For Soda Bottle,**
1930s. Bon-Ton Beverages, Chicago. - **$15 $25 $50**

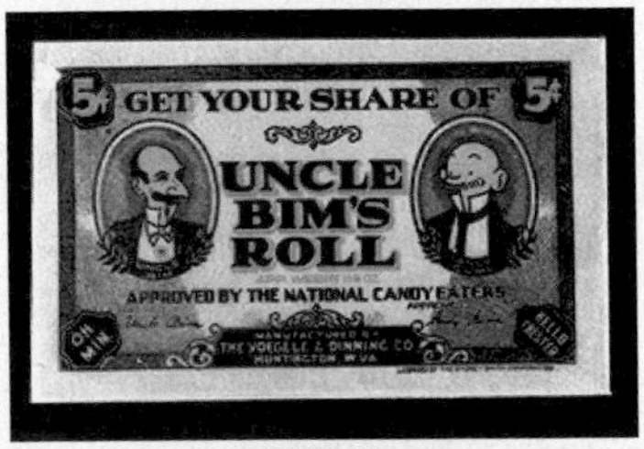

GMP-20

❑ **GMP-20. "Uncle Bim's Roll" Candy Wrapper,**
1930s. Voegele & Dinning Co. Waxed paper and design of currency money. - **$35 $75 $125**

Gunsmoke

Dodge City, Kansas, in the 1880s was the site of this adult Western that starred William Conrad (1920-1994) on CBS radio from 1952-1961. The CBS-TV version lasted twenty years from 1955-1975, making it the longest running western in TV history. Starring James Arness as Matt Dillon, other continuing characters included the saloon keeper Miss Kitty (Amanda Blake), old Doc Adams (Milburn Stone), and the Marshal's deputy Chester (Dennis Weaver), replaced by Festus (Ken Curtis) in 1964. Radio sponsors included Post Toasties (1953), Chesterfield cigarettes (1954), and Liggett & Myers (1954-1957). L & M cigarettes was also a television sponsor. Related comic books appeared from the 1950s to 1970, and two Gunsmoke movies starring James Arness were released in 1987 and 1990. Items usually carry a copyright of CBS Television Enterprises or Columbia Broadcasting System. The TV show continues in syndication worldwide.

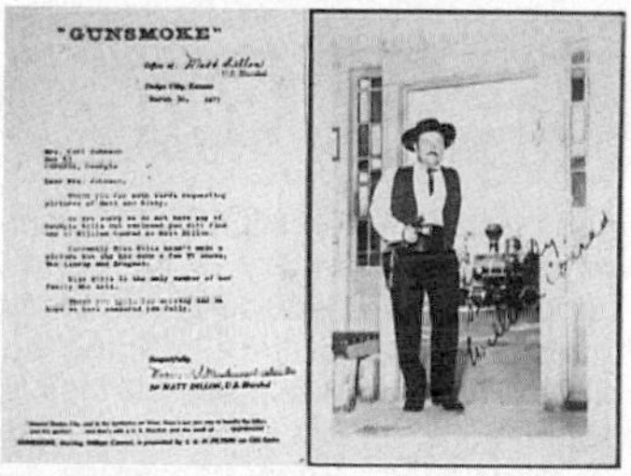

GUN-1

❑ GUN-1. Radio Fan Letter With William Conrad Signed Photo,
c. 1952. "L&M Filters on CBS Radio." 7-1/4x10-1/2" "Gunsmoke" letterhead sheet thanks fan for requesting "Pictures Of Matt And Kitty." Comes with 3-1/2x5-1/2" glossy black and white real photo autographed postcard.
Letter - **$35 $70 $135**
Photo - **$35 $70 $135**

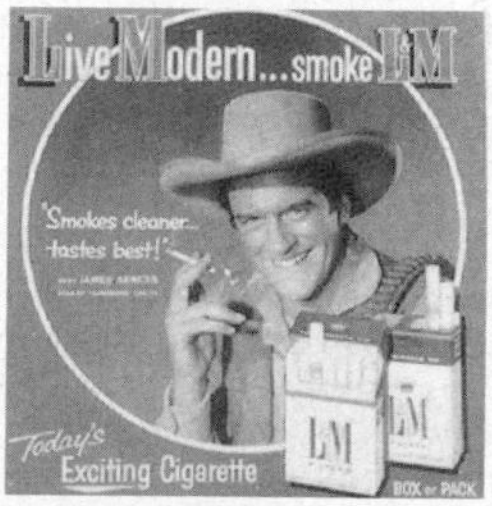

GUN-2

❑ GUN-2. "L&M Cigarettes" 21x22" Cardboard Store Sign,
c. 1954. Liggett & Meyers. - **$60 $125 $250**

GUN-3

❑ GUN-3. L&M Cigarettes Cast Card,
c. 1954. - **$12 $25 $50**

GUN-4

GUN-5

❑ GUN-4. Matt Dillon And Miss Kitty 21x21" Cigarette Sign,
c. 1954. L&M Cigarettes of Liggett & Myers Tobacco Co. Stiff cardboard with full color photos. - **$65 $135 $275**

❑ GUN-5. Big Little Book - TV Series,
1958. Hard to find without cracks in the spine. Cover is laminated, which splits when opened repeatedly. One in a series of 6. - **$10 $20 $65**

GUN-6

❑ GUN-6. Boxed Board Game,
1958. Store item by Lowell Toy Corp. Has playing board along with four cardboard stand-up stockade structures. - **$40 $80 $175**

GUN-7

GUN-8

GUN-9

❑ GUN-7. Matt Dillon Diecut Cardboard Standee,
c. 1958. L&M Cigarettes. 8-1/2x25" tall with easel back. - **$150 $300 $600**

❑ GUN-8. "James Arness Fan Club" Cello. Button,
c. 1958. - **$25 $50 $100**

❑ GUN-9. Packaged 3-1/2" Cello. Button,
1959. Store item. From series of "Top Western T.V. Stars" packaged in cellophane bag with header card.
Near Mint Bagged - **$135**
Button Only - **$30 $60 $115**

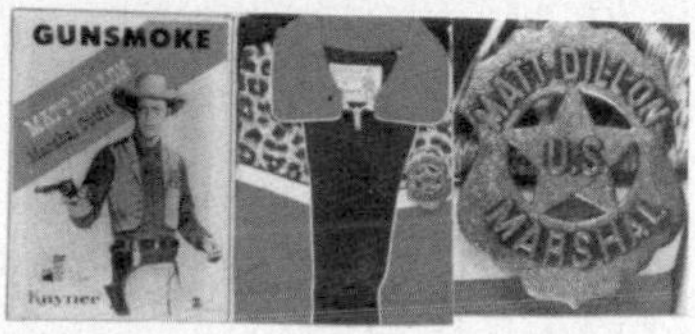

GUN-10

❑ GUN-10. "Matt Dillon-U.S. Marshal" Outfit,
1959. Store item by Kaynee. Boxed - **$65 $135 $250**

GUN-11

GUN-12

❑ GUN-11. "Matt Dillon/U.S. Marshal" Metal Badge,
1959. Store item. On Card - **$20 $30 $60**
Loose - **$10 $20 $30**

❑ GUN-12. "U.S. Marshal" Metal Badge,
1959. Store item. Badge version omits "Matt Dillon" name. On Card - **$20 $30 $60**
Loose - **$10 $20 $30**

GUN-13

❑ GUN-13. Double "L" Error First Lunch Box,
1959. Aladdin Industries. Metal box first version noted for erroneous spelling of word "Marshall" rather than correct single letter ending. Rare version quickly replaced by correct version.
Error Version - **$300 $600 $1200**
Correct Version - **$65 $150 $300**
Bottle - **$20 $50 $100**

GUN-14

❑ **GUN-14. "Gunsmoke" Glass,**
1950s. 5.5" tall weighted bottom tumbler printed in black text and gold art related to show characters and Dodge City. - **$65 $125 $225**

GUN-15

❑ **GUN-15. Personal Appearance Souvenir Folder With Photo,**
c. 1960. - **$25 $40 $85**

GUN-16

GUN-17

❑ **GUN-16. "All Star Dairies" Litho. Button,**
c. 1960. - **$12 $25 $45**

❑ **GUN-17. "Gunsmoke" Lunch Box,**
1962. Store item by Aladdin Industries. - **$85 $200 $400**

GUN-18

❑ **GUN-18. TV Show Commemorative Promotional Pocket Watch Encased As Paperweight,**
1968. Clear lucite block 2-3/4x4-1/2x3/4" thick holds actual pocket watch and fob depicting CBS-TV logo plus text "Gunsmoke Starts Its 13th Year September 11 New Day Monday New Time 7:30 PM." Watch hands point to 7:30. - **$100 $200 $400**

GUN-19

❑ **GUN-19. "Gunsmoke Target Game" In Original Packaging,**
1960s. Box is 1.25x16x22" with text "Double Barrel Dart Gun - Shoots Two Darts...One Or Two At A Time - Exclusive 'Spring Back' Action Target...Resets Automatically." Made by Park Plastic Co. Boxed - **$175 $350 $650**

GUN-20

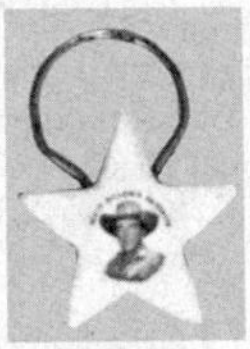

GUN-21

❑ **GUN-20. Metal Cuff Links With B&W Photo Inserts,**
1960s. Issuer unknown. Set - **$50 $100 $150**

❑ **GUN-21. "Matt Dillon's Favorite" Key Ring,**
1960s. Reverse of plastic star reads "Sanders Dairy/All Star". - **$30 $55 $115**

GUN-22

❑ **GUN-22. Matt Dillon Figure,**
1960s. Hartland Plastics. Full sized replica figure of Gunsmoke star in illustrated box.
Complete Figure - **$50 $125 $225**
Box - **$100 $200 $400**

GUN-23

❑ **GUN-23. TV Publicity Stills,**
c. 1972. CBS-TV. 8x10" high gloss black and white photos of cast members. Each - **$5 $8 $15**

GUN-24

❑ **GUN-24. "Gunsmoke" Three-Reel View-Master Set With Color Story Booklet,**
1972. Complete - **$15 $30 $45**

Happy Days

Created by Garry Marshall, ABC-TV aired 255 episodes between January 15, 1974 and July 12, 1984. Set in the 1958-1962 era, the basic plot had high school kids hanging out at Arnold's Drive-In and focused on their trials and tribulations against a comedic backdrop. The cast included: Henry Winkler as Arthur "The Fonz" Fonzarelli, motorcycle jacket wearing hood type; the Cunningham family: Ron Howard as Richie, Erin Moran as Joanie, Tom Bosley as Dad Howard, Marion Ross as Mom Marion. Richie's friends included Anson Williams as Potsie and Donny Most as Ralph Malph. Scott Baio as Chachi joined the cast in 1977.

In the September 20, 1977 episode, a rather preposterous scenario had Fonzie "jumping the shark" on water skis, and pop culture had a new term for the sure sign that a TV show had sadly passed its peak...and then that point was driven home again in 1980 when Ted McGinley joined the cast.

Spin off series *Laverne And Shirley* starring Penny Marshall and Cindy Williams aired on ABC from 1976 to 1983. Season five of *Happy Days* introduced Robin Williams as the Mork from Ork character, leading to the *Mork And Mindy* series co-starring Pam Dawber which ran on ABC from 1978-1982. Hanna-Barbera produced the animated series *Fonz And The Happy Days Gang* between 1980 and 1982. Gold Key published six Happy Days comic books between 1979 and 1980. "Heeeey......Sit on it!"

HPD-1

❑ **HPD-1. "Happy Days Playset",**
1976. The Toy Factory. 10x13x1" deep box contains die-cut cardboard pieces of Happy Days characters, Arnold's Drive-In, juke box, Fonzie's motorcycle and cars plus plastic stands. - **$10 $20 $40**

HPD-2

HPD-3

❑ **HPD-2. "Fordzie" Campaign Button,**
1976. 3.5" button for Gerald Ford inspired by Fonzie. - **$10 $20 $40**

❑ **HPD-3. "Official Happy Days Fonzie" Necklace,**
1976. Paramount Pictures Corp. 1.5x1/8" thick heavy brass pendant with 24" chain. - **$6 $12 $25**

HPD-4

❑ **HPD-4. "Happy Days - The Fonz!" Bedspread,**
1970s. 5'1"x8'3.5" with images of Happy Days characters, Arnold's drive-in and several catch phrases. - **$10 $20 $40**

HPD-5

❑ **HPD-5. "Happy Days" Cast-Signed Photo,**
1970s. 8x10" glossy photo signed by Erin Moran, Don Most, Henry Winkler, Tom Bosley, Anson Williams, Marion Ross and Ron Howard. Same Or Similar Near Mint - **$450**

HPD-6

❑ **HPD-6. "Happy Days" Cast-Signed Photo,**
1970s. 7x9" signed photo. Same signatures as previous item. Same Or Similar Near Mint - **$450**

Happy Hooligan

Happy Hooligan, the ever-innocent optimist, was created by Frederick Opper (1857-1937) for the Hearst Sunday comics in 1900 and continued, under a variety of titles, until 1932. The strip, considered a major classic comic, also involved Happy's pet dog Flip and his brothers Gloomy Gus and Lord Montmorency in a series of ill-fated adventures. His three little nephews, complete with little tin cans on their heads, look and act like turn of the last century versions of Donald Duck's three nephews. Happy, with his tin-can hat, and Gus, with his battered top hat, were immensely popular characters, appearing early on in stage plays, silent films and animated cartoons, sheet music, and reprints of the strips in book form.

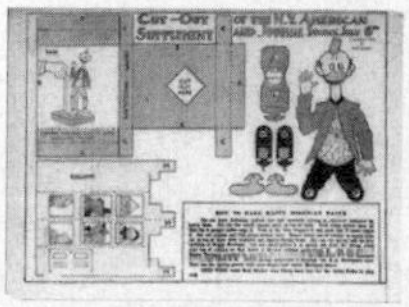

HAP-1

HAP-2

❑ **HAP-1. "How To Make Happy Hooligan Dance" Cut-Out Supplement,**
1902. New York American & Journal newspaper. Uncut - **$50 $85 $150**

❑ **HAP-2. Postcard,**
1904. United States Card premium. Shows Happy facing left. Says "You have seen my face before 'Guess where". - **$10 $20 $30**

HAP-3

HAP-4

❑ **HAP-3. Valentine Postcard,**
1904. Shows Happy fishing. - **$10 $20 $30**

❑ **HAP-4. Valentine Postcard,**
1904. Shows Happy looking straight ahead. - **$10 $20 $30**

HAP-5

HAP-6

❑ **HAP-5. Bisque Match Holder,**
c. 1905. Probably German. 8-3/8" tall. - **$75 $150 $300**

❑ **HAP-6. "Shoemakers Fair" Cello. Button,**
1905. Figure back view although frontal head for slogan "Are You Goin' Or Comin'?" - **$25 $50 $100**

HAP-7

HAP-8

❑ **HAP-7. Happy Hooligan Song Sheet,**
c. 1905. Rare. Newspaper supplement. - **$30 $60 $125**

❑ **HAP-8. Figural White Metal Stickpin,**
c. 1905. Detailed image finished in black. - **$20 $35 $75**

HAP-9

❑ **HAP-9. Embossed Mechanical Valentine,**
1906. Rafael Tuck & Son, Germany. 13.5" tall from series including Buster Brown and Mama Katzenjammer with Hans and Fritz.
- $65 $135 $225

HAP-10

HAP-11

❑ **HAP-10. Mechanical Postcard,**
1906. New York Sunday American & Journal newspaper. Shows picture of cops pulling Hooligan & others out of water. Card folds out to give a 3-D look. **- $15 $30 $60**

❑ **HAP-11. Postcard,**
1906. American Journal Examiner. Shows Happy watching the Moon. **- $10 $15 $25**

HAP-12

HAP-13

❑ **HAP-12. Postcard,**
1906. Boston Sunday American newspaper premium. **- $10 $15 $30**

❑ **HAP-13. Postcard,**
1906. Boston Sunday American newspaper premium. Egyptian police catch Happy & friend trying to steal the Sphinx. **- $10 $15 $30**

HAP-14

HAP-15

❑ **HAP-14. Painted Figural Clock,**
c. 1910. 10" tall. **- $900 $1750 $2750**

❑ **HAP-15. Happy Hooligan Majolica Cookie Jar,**
c. 1910. Two-piece jar measures 3.75x3.75x9.75" and is colorful with high gloss glaze. Bottom is numbered "8674."
- $135 $275 $550

HAP-16

HAP-17

❑ **HAP-16. Composition Figure,**
c. 1910. Store item. Jointed arms and legs. -
$60 $100 $200

❑ **HAP-17. Papier Mache Roly-Poly,**
c. 1910. Store item. **- $175 $325 $600**

HAP-18

❑ **HAP-18. Painted Bisque Figure,**
c. 1910. 8-1/2" tall. Made in Germany with #8232 on the reverse. **- $50 $150 $250**

HAP-19

❑ **HAP-19. Happy Hooligan Bank,**
c. 1910. Austrian ceramic bank. -
$50 $100 $150

HAP-20

HAP-21

❑ **HAP-20. Happy Hooligan Figural White Metal Stickpin,**
c. 1910. **- $20 $30 $60**

❑ **HAP-21. "F. Oppers Joke Book,"**
1911. New York Sunday American. 10x12" Sunday supplement with 16 pages of Frederick Opper cartoons including Happy Hooligan, Alphonse and Gaston, And Her Name Was Maud. **- $25 $50 $100**

HAP-22

❑ **HAP-22. Cello. Button,**
c. 1915. **- $15 $30 $60**

HAP-23

❑ **HAP-23. "Happy Hooligan Game" With Die-Cut Figures,**
1925. Milton Bradley. Cardboard 10x14". Reverse of lid has directions. Set consists of eight die-cut figures. Each is 2-3/8" wide, height ranges from 4" to 8.5". Each printed figure attached to heavy cardboard backing and .5" square piece of wood attached to bottom back. Bottom of each character has "Copyright 1925 By Int'l Feature Services Inc." Each character has name identified on their clothing. Included are "Happy/ Gloomy Gus/Mr. Dough/ Montmorency/The Cop/Boitram/Foidinand/ Hoiman." Box - **$50 $125 $200**
Eight Figures - **$65 $160 $240**

HAP-24

HAP-25

❑ **HAP-24. Seated Bisque Nodder Figure,**
1920s. Store item. Head moves left and right. Among the earliest character nodders. - **$125 $250 $500**

❑ **HAP-25. Glazed Majolica Toothpick Holder,**
1920s. Number 2828 on bottom. 4-1/2" by 4". - **$80 $150 $250**

HAP-26

❑ **HAP-26. Glazed Majolica Candy Container,**
1920s. Number 11388 on bottom. 5" by 5". - **$100 $200 $300**

HAP-27

❑ **HAP-27. "The Story of Happy Hooligan" Feature Book #281,**
1932. 9 1/2" x 12". GD - **$57** FN - **$228** VF- **$400**

HAP-28

❑ **HAP-28. Hooligan On Donkey Mechanical Toy,**
1930s. P. R. Italy. 6.5" tall celluloid and cloth figure activated by depressing top to cause donkey head and tail to move up and down. - **$60 $125 $200**

Have Gun, Will Travel

Created by Sam Rolfe and Herb Meadow, CBS aired 226 episodes between September 14, 1957 and September 21, 1963. Richard Boone (1917-1981) starred as Paladin, a white suited intellectual resident of San Francisco's Hotel Carlton whose alter ego was a grim black suited gunfighter for hire. Co-stars included Kam Tong as Kim "Hey Boy" Chan and Hal Needham as the bartender. Sam Rolfe and Herb Meadow wrote some 210 episodes and directors included Richard Boone, Andrew McLaglen and Gene Roddenberry. The theme song was written and sung by Johnny Western. Boone and Rolfe co-wrote the song.

The popular series spawned a radio show which aired on CBS from November 23, 1958 to November 22, 1960 starring John Dehner as Paladin.

Dell published 14 comic books between August 1958 and September 1962 with Richard Boone photo covers.

Paladin's business card with its stylized horsehead reads simply "Have Gun – Will Travel – Wire Paladin San Francisco."

HGW-1

❑ **HGW-1. "TV's Paladin Motor Trend" Magazine Article,**
1958. 8-3/8x10-7/8" issue for May, 1958 with 82 pages including two-page article "Have Car Will Travel" showing Richard Boone and his car. - **$8 $15 $30**

HGW-2

❑ **HGW-2. "Have Gun Will Travel/Paladin Fan Club" Vinyl Card Holder,**
1958. 2.5x4" black vinyl with clear vinyl window holding photo of Richard Boone as Paladin with facsimile signature. One pocket holds "Paladin Fan Club" member card and other pocket contains six black and white Paladin business cards. Complete With One Or More Business Cards - **$30 $60 $125**

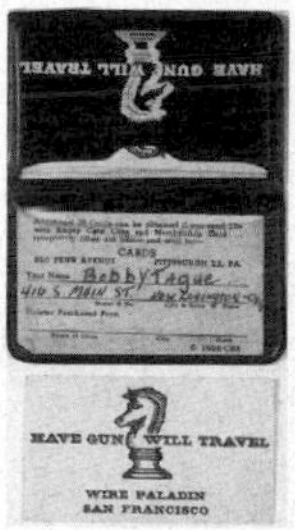

HGW-3

❑ **HGW-3. "Have Gun Will Travel/Paladin Fan Club" Vinyl Card Holder Variety Without Photo,**
1958. CBS. 2.5x4" contains 16 business cards plus yellow membership card. Complete With One Or More Business Cards - **$25 $50 $100**

HGW-4

❑ **HGW-4. "Paladin" Halloween Costume In Box,**
1958. Ben Cooper. 8.5x11.25x3.5" deep box holds molded plastic mask, black pants and shirt with white logo, plastic pouch with 2 Paladin business cards, vinyl belt with metal buckle. - **$125 $200 $350**

HGW-5

❑ **HGW-5. "Have Gun Will Travel" Boxed Game,**
1959. Parker Bros. 9-3/8x19x1.25" deep box contains 18.5" square gameboard, red and white die-cut cardboard hand gun spinner, cards, wooden "bullet" playing pieces and four painted cast metal cowboys on horseback playing pieces. - **$20 $40 $100**

HGW-6

❑ **HGW-6. "Rinso Blue" Detergent Box Containing Paladin Trading Card,**
1959. Store item. Box is 8-3/4" tall in yellow, red, white and blue. See next item.
Near Mint Sealed - **$725**
Open - **$135 $250 $400**

HGW-7

❑ **HGW-7. Paladin Trading Card,**
1959. Rinso Blue. 2-1/4x3-5/8" black and white card which was in the product box. Unknown number in set but highest number card we know of is #22. See previous item.
Each - **$20 $40 $65**

HGW-8

❑ **HGW-8. Paladin Chess Piece Logo Pin,**
1950s. 2" tall white metal pin. - **$12 $25 $50**

HGW-9

HGW-10

❑ **HGW-9. "Have Gun Will Travel" Promo Glasses,**
1950s. Filmaster Productions Inc. Two 5.5" tall glasses, first showing famous Paladin business card and "CBS" eye logo. Second shows TV/movie themes, etc. and electric "waves" (not Paladin related) from Consolidated Film Industries. Paladin - **$30 $65 $150**
Non-Paladin - **$10 $20 $40**

❑ **HGW-10. "Paladin/Have Gun Will Travel" Lunch Box,**
1960. Aladdin. 6.75x8x3.75" deep metal lunch box. - **$125 $250 $500**

HGW-11

❑ **HGW-11. "Have Gun Will Travel" Thermos,**
1960. Aladdin. 6.5" tall with wrap-around art. - **$30 $60 $135**

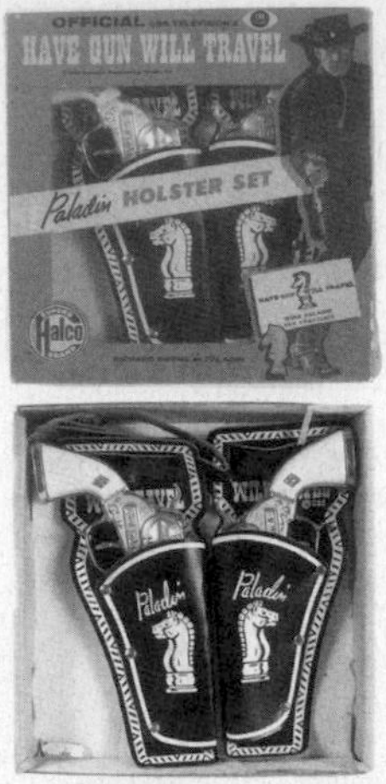

HGW-12

❑ **HGW-12. "Official Have Gun Will Travel/Paladin" Holster In Box,**
1960. Columbia Broadcasting Systems Inc. 10.25x10.25x1.5" deep box with two 1.25x4.25x7.5" cast metal cap guns with simulated bone handles designed to take roll caps. Holster consists of 9.75" painted cardboard pockets attached to 28" belt with silver luster metal buckle. - **$500 $1500 $2500**

HGW-13

❑ **HGW-13. "Official Paladin Kit" Hat Purchase Premium,**
c. 1960. Arlington Hat Co. 2-1/2x4-1/4" black and white envelope was attached to hat and holds 4" wide fake mustache and four "Have Gun Will Travel" business cards.
Complete - **$35 $90 $175**

HGW-14

HGW-15

❑ **HGW-14. "Have Gun Will Travel" Ring,**
1960s. Issuer unknown, may have come with costume or cap gun set. Version with silver plastic base and white plastic top with gold design. - **$30 $60 $100**

❑ **HGW-15. "Have Gun Will Travel" Ring,**
1960s. Same as previous item but version with top piece in black plastic. - **$25 $50 $90**

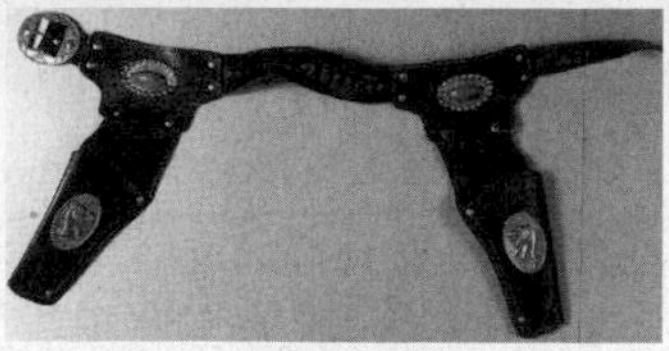

HGW-16

❑ **HGW-16. Paladin Style Leather Double Holster,**
1960s. 31" long black leather with silver luster oval metal accents. - **$65 $125 $200**

HGW-17

❑ **HGW-17. "Have Gun Will Travel" Boxed Limited Edition Plate,**
1991. CBS, Inc. 10x10.5x2.25" deep box holds 8.5" diameter plate rimmed in gold with underside numbered 3725A. Near Mint - **$50**

Helen Trent

***The Romance of Helen Trent* reigned as the melodramatic queen of the daytime soap operas for over a quarter of a century on CBS radio from 1933 to 1960. Helen, remaining single and 35 through the years, was noble, pure, and pursued by dozens of suitors, most of whom came to a violent end. Three actresses played Helen over the years: Virginia Clark, Betty Ruth Smith and Julie Stevens. Sponsors included American Home Products, Affiliated Products, Whitehall Drugs, Pharmaco, Spry, Breeze, and Scott Waldorf tissue.**

HLN-1

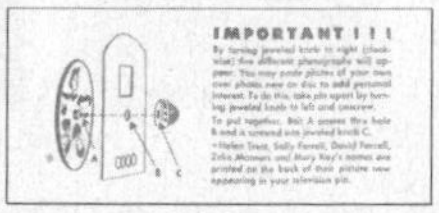

HLN-2

❑ **HLN-1. Radio Replica Mechanical Brass Badge,**
1949. Five identified cast members are pictured in sequence through diecut opening by rear disk wheel. - **$25 $65 $125**

❑ **HLN-2. "Helen Trent" Mechanical Badge Instruction Sheet,**
1949. Instruction sheet is 2.25x5.5".
- **$12 $25 $40**

HLN-3

❑ **HLN-3. Silvered Brass Medallion,**
1949. Kolynos dental product. Design motifs on both sides including Sphinx, pyramids, other abstract symbols. - **$10 $20 $35**

Henry

Cartoonist Carl Anderson (1865-1948) worked for Hearst and Pulitzer newspapers and for *Puck, Judge* and other magazines. In the early 1930s, at age 67, he came up with the idea for a bald young boy in a t-shirt who doesn't speak. Henry first appeared as a panel cartoon in the March 19, 1932 *Saturday Evening Post.* The character proved popular and became a daily comic strip December 17, 1934 and a Sunday page on March 10, 1935. He also appeared in the Fleischer Studios animated cartoon *Betty Boop With Henry The Funniest Living American* in 1935. The comic strip featured Henrietta as his girlfriend. John Liney took over the daily strip in 1942 and worked on it until 1979. Don Trachte (1915-2005) began working on the Sunday page in the 1930s and continued until 1993. Jack Tippit and Dick Hodgins are the most recent artists.

Mute Henry finally spoke in his 1940s comic book series. Dell released Four Color #122 in 1946 and Four Color #155 in 1947, following with a regular Henry series which ran until 1961. John Liney handled most of the art chores.

Don Trachte was in the news in 2006. Back in 1960, he paid friend Norman Rockwell $900 for the painting *Breaking Home Ties.* The painting was later loaned to the Rockwell Museum. When Trachte passed away his sons found a secret closet in his home. He had retained the original and loaned the museum a copy. His sons then sold the original for $15.4 million in 2006.

HEN-1

❑ **HEN-1. "Henry & Henrietta Travelers" Wind-Up,**
1934. 7.25" tall wind-up by Kuramochi & Co., Japan. - **$800 $1600 $2800**

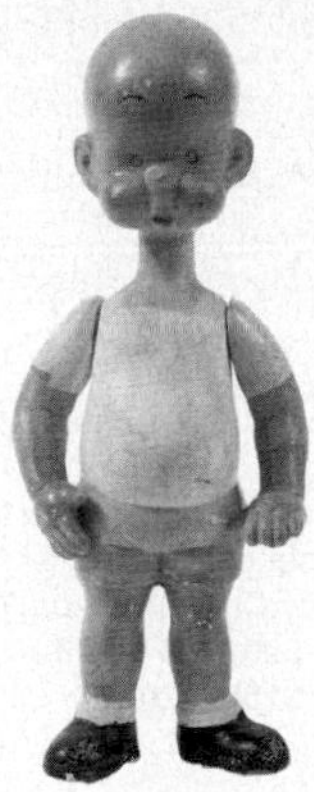

HEN-2

❑ **HEN-2. "Henry" Painted Bisque Figure,**
1934. 6.5" tall with movable arms. Made in Japan. Back reads "Henry/Copyright 1934/Carl P. Anderson." - **$50 $100 $200**

HEN-3

❑ **HEN-3. "Henry" Large Format Cigarette Card Set,**
1935. J. Wix & Sons Ltd. 4x5.75" cards with color illustrations by Carl Anderson on the fronts while backs have promotional text for cigarette company. Set of 25. Set - **$75 $150 $300**

HEN-4

❑ **HEN-4. "Henry" Complete Cigarette Card Album,**
c. 1936. J. Wix & Sons Ltd. 7.25x10" album contains complete set of 50 cards for Kensitas Cigarettes. Art by Carl Anderson. Cards are 2.5x3". Album - **$20 $40 $100**
Card Set - **$50 $100 $200**

HEN-5

❑ **HEN-5. "Henry" Boxed Bisque Figures,**
1930s. 3.5x5.25x1.25" deep box holds four 3.5" tall bisque Henry figures. Box reads "Copyright Carl Anderson/Geo. Borgfeldt Corporation/Made In Japan." Box - **$50 $100 $200**
Each Bisque - **$15 $30 $60**

HEN-6

❑ **HEN-6. Carl Anderson "Henry" Original Art,**
c. 1942. Curtis Publishing Co. 13.75x14.5" illustration board has pen and ink/ink wash drawing of Henry. Signed in left-hand corner by Carl Anderson. Fine. Same Or Similar - **$300**

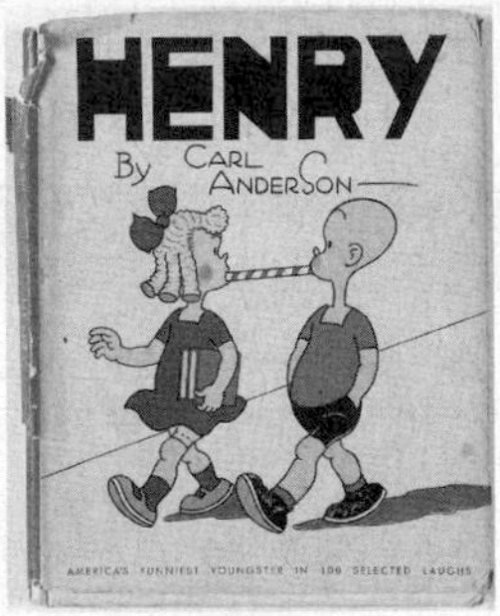

HEN-7

❑ **HEN-7. "Henry By Carl Anderson" Hardbound Book With Dust Jacket,**
1945. KFS. 5-5/8x7.25" with 120 pages. Color cover. Contains four-panel black and white cartoons. Jacket - **$15 $30 $60**
Book - **$10 $20 $40**

HEN-8

❑ **HEN-8. Henry Limited Issue Christmas Cards By Cartoonists,**
1950s. King Features. Lot of 5, with art by cartoonists associated with the strip, Liney and Trachtes. Each Card - **$5 $10 $25**

The Hermit's Cave

Produced at Los Angeles radio station KMPC, this syndicated horror show aired from 1940 to 1944, offering ghost stories, weird stories, and mayhem and murders galore. Scary sound effects and the voice of Mel Johnson as the old hermit distinguished these weekly tales of carnage. Olga Coal was the sponsor.

HER-1

❑ **HER-1. Cast Pictures,**
1940s. Scarce. Each - **$25 $50 $85**

HER-2

HER-3

❑ **HER-2. Promo Brochure,**
1940s. - **$50 $100 $300**

❑ **HER-3. Letter,**
1940s. - **$35 $65 $125**

HER-4

❑ **HER-4. Radio Show Promotion Mailer,**
1940s. Olga Coal of Carter Coal Company. Printed photos include "The Hermit With His Whiskers On." - **$75 $150 $300**

Highway Patrol

Broderick Crawford (1911-1986) played the gruff, fast talking head of the Highway Patrol, set in a large western state. Produced on a low budget by Frederic Ziv of Ziv TV, the show had 156 episodes between October, 1955 and 1959. Narrated by Art Gilmore, co-stars included William Boyett and Roy Bourgois. Clint Eastwood had an occasional bit part. Writers included Jack Rock, Don Brinkley and Gene Roddenberry. Directors included Jack Herzberg and Eddie Davis. The theme *March Of The Highway Patrol* was written by David Rose.

The show used "quick cuts" due to its low budget but was television's highest rated syndicated show by 1956. This was due in part to Broderick Crawford's rapid fire portrayal of Dan Matthews. Crawford, whose first film was MGM's 1937 feature *Woman Chases Man*, won an Oscar playing Willie Stark in *All The Kings Men* in 1949 and was well known to TV audiences by the time *Highway Patrol* aired. The later TV series *CHiPs* had an episode with Crawford playing himself in 1977. "Ten Four! Call for the coroner!"

HWP-1

❑ **HWP-1. "Highway Patrol Chief",**
1950s. 2-1/8" large heavy white metal badge in high relief design with silver luster. Most likely came with boxed gun and holster set for show starring Broderick Crawford. - **$15 $30 $75**

HWP-2

❑ **HWP-2. "Highway Patrol Chief Dan Mathews" Holster And Belt,**
1950s. Leather holster with 26" long belt and separate attached shoulder strap. Has metal clip with attached 2" long hard plastic whistle. Holster has "Highway Patrol" badge design and belt has "Chief" badge and name "Dan Mathews." - **$15 $30 $75**

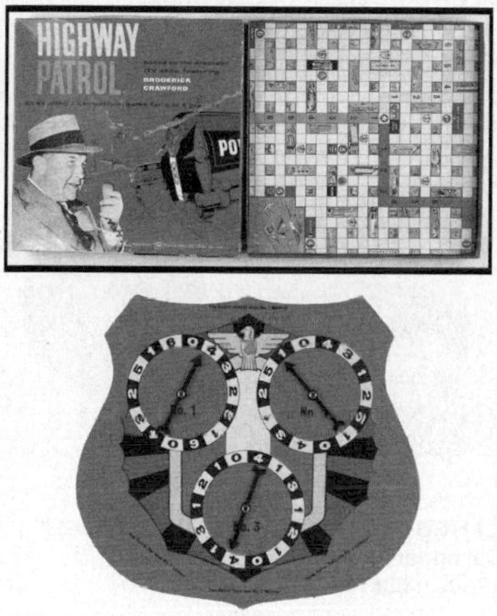

HWP-3

❑ **HWP-3. "Highway Patrol" English Game,**
1950s. Bell Ltd. 14x14x1.5" deep box with insert tray that serves as gameboard with three separate spinners on die-cut badge and 4.5x4.75" instruction booklet, 4 plastic cars, 2 packs of cards, 6 counters and 4 roadblock squares. - **$50 $100 $165**

HWP-4

❑ **HWP-4. "Watch Highway Patrol" Ballentine Beer Badge,**
1950s. P. Ballantine & Sons Newark, New Jersey. 3.25" convex plastic badge with bar pin. Center and each star point has Ballentine symbol. Bold center text "Watch Highway Patrol Starring Broderick Crawford." - **$20 $40 $85**

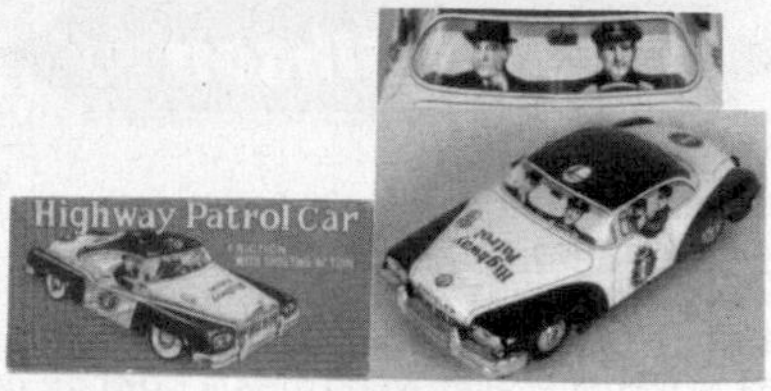

HWP-5

❑ **HWP-5. "Highway Patrol" Boxed Friction Toy,**
1950s. Store item by MS, Japan. 4x8-1/2x2-1/2" tall. Box - **$25 $50 $125**
Car - **$50 $85 $175**

Hobby Lobby

From 1937 to 1949 on various networks this popular half-hour program highlighted listeners' unusual hobbies, everything from collecting elephant hairs to talking backwards. Dave Elman created the show, and each week a celebrity guest would show up to "lobby his hobby." Sponsors over the years included Hudson cars, Jell-O, Fels-Naptha soap, Colgate, and Anchor-Hocking glass. A television version with Cliff Arquette (Charley Weaver) as host was broadcast on ABC in 1959-60.

HOB-1

HOB-2

❑ **HOB-1. Promotional Ad,**
c. 1940s. Rare. - **$30 $65 $125**

❑ **HOB-2. "Hobby Lobby" Rocking Horse Charm,**
c. 1940s. - **$20 $40 $60**

HOB-3

❑ **HOB-3. Merry Christmas And A Happy New Year Card,**
1940s. Fels-Naptha Soap Chips. 5x7-1/2" red, black and white card with inscription of "Dave Elman." - **$10 $20 $40**

Hoot Gibson

Edmund R. Gibson (1892-1962), known as Hoot because as a boy he liked to hunt owls, was born in Nebraska and learned to rope and ride on his father's ranch. He left home as a teenager and worked as a cowboy on the trail and in Wild West shows before arriving in Hollywood in 1910. Gibson was a skilled rider; he won the all around championship at the Pendelton, Oregon Western Roundup as well as World Championship Roper at the Calgary Stampede in 1912. His first minor film role was in 1911, but he became a star in the 1920s, ultimately appearing in well over 200 silent and talking movies. Gibson's popularity in the late 1920s was second only to Tom Mix. He retired in 1944, then had a few cameo film roles and a brief run as the host of a local television show in Los Angeles. Hoot Gibson comic books appeared in 1950.

HGB-1

HGB-2

❑ HGB-1. "Rope Spinning" Instruction Folder,
1929. Came with Hoot Gibson Rodeo Ropes by Mordt Co., Chicago. - **$25 $40 $75**

❑ HGB-2. Exhibit Cards,
1920s. Vending machine cards by Exhibit Supply Co. Copyright year or movie titles from late 1920s.
Each - **$8 $12 $20**

HGB-3

HGB-4

❑ HGB-3. Dixie Ice Cream Picture,
1936. Title on reverse is "Frontier Justice." - **$25 $50 $125**

❑ HGB-4. Dixie Ice Cream Picture,
c. 1936. Reverse has four scenes from "Frontier Justice." - **$25 $50 $125**

HGB-5

HGB-6

❑ HGB-5. Cello. Button,
1930s. Black and white 1-3/4". - **$40 $100 $200**

❑ HGB-6. "Hoot Gibson" Button,
1930s. From movie star set. 13/16" litho. - **$10 $20 $40**

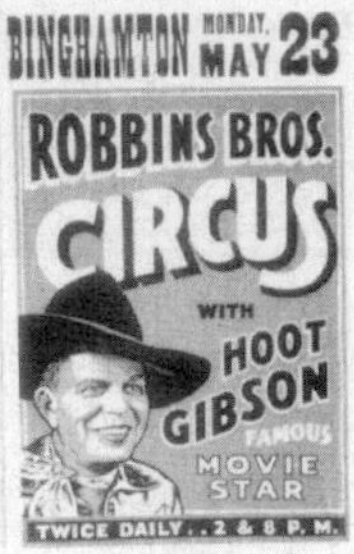

HGB-7

HGB-8

❑ HGB-7. "Robbins Bros. Circus" 14x22" Cardboard Poster,
1930s. - **$85 $200 $300**

❑ HGB-8. Movie Felt Patch,
1930s. - **$30 $75 $150**

HGB-9

HGB-10

HGB-11

❑ HGB-9. Cello. Button,
1930s. Probably circus souvenir. - **$50 $125 $250**

❑ HGB-10. Litho. Button From Movie Star Set,
1930s. - **$10 $20 $30**

❑ HGB-11. "Ideal Moving Pictures" Flip Booklet,
1930s. Flip sequence pictures Gibson lassoing two fistfighters. - **$40 $75 $150**

Hop Harrigan

Created by artist Jon Blummer, America's ace of the airways, Hop Harrigan made his debut in *All-American Comics* #1 in 1939, complete with Flying Club wings, patch, and other membership paraphernalia. On the ABC and Mutual radio networks from 1942 to 1948, Hop and his mechanical pal Tank Tinker conquered the Axis powers during the war years and fought assorted American villains once the war ended. The program was locally sponsored for much of its run; network sponsors included Grape-Nuts Flakes (1944-1946) and Lever Brothers (1947-1948). Columbia Pictures released a 15-episode Hop Harrigan chapter play starring William Bakewell in 1946.

HPH-1

❑ HPH-1. "Hop Harrigan All American Flying Club" Wings Badge,
1940. Copper Luster - **$45 $90 $175**
Silver Luster (Scarcer Variety) - **$75 $150 $275**

HPH-2

❑ HPH-2. Certificate of Membership,
1940. All American Comics premium- **$100 $200 $325**

HPH-3

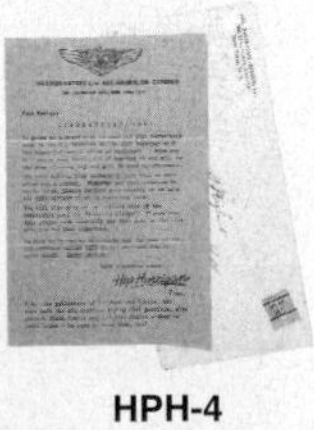

HPH-4

❑ HPH-3. Photo,
1940. All American Comics. DC premium - **$85 $175 $300**

❑ HPH-4. Letter and Mailer For Badge,
1940. All American Comics premium.
Letter - **$55 $110 $165**
Mailer - **$50 $60 $90**

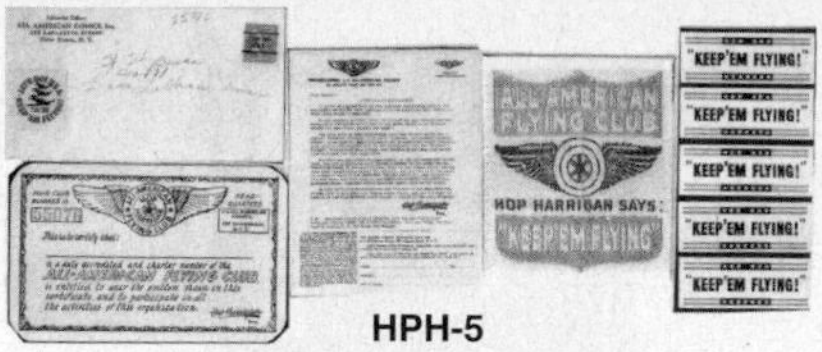

HPH-5

❑ **HPH-5. "All-American Flying Club" Kit.**
c. 1942. Membership letter, card, stickers, fabric patch. Near Mint In Mailer - **$350**
Patch - **$30 $75 $150**
Card - **$20 $50 $100**

HPH-6

❑ **HPH-6. Club Fabric Patch,**
c. 1942. - **$30 $75 $150**

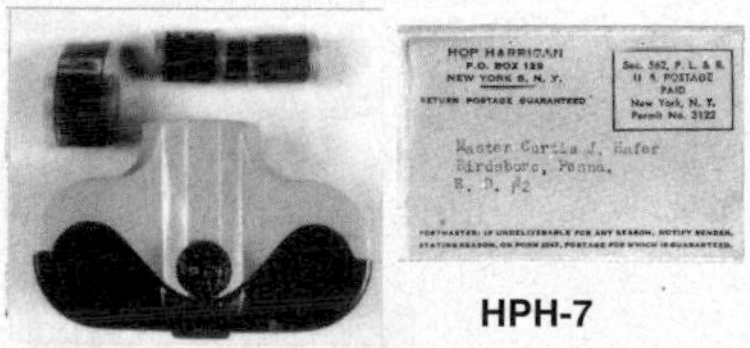

HPH-7

❑ **HPH-7. Plastic Movie Viewer With Films,**
c. 1942. Includes three films.
Near Mint Boxed - **$275**
Viewer And Films - **$50 $110 $190**

HPH-8 HPH-9

❑ **HPH-8. Jolly Junketeers Badge,**
1942. Jolly Junketeers Flying Club. Canada. - **$25 $50 $85**

❑ **HPH-9. Patch,**
1942. "Keep 'Em Flying" American Observation Corps patch. Rare. - **$60 $150 $300**

HPH-10

❑ **HPH-10. Grapenuts Flakes Sign 13x18",**
1944. Rare. Promotes radio show and shows Para-plane offer. - **$125 $275 $600**

HPH-11

❑ **HPH-11. "Para-Plane With Parachutists" 15x16" Diecut Cardboard Store Sign,**
1944. Rare. Grape-Nuts Flakes. Sign is three-dimensional and has open center to display cereal box. Sign - **$400 $900 $1850**

HPH-12

❑ **HPH-12. Superfortress Grape Nuts Flakes Sign,**
1944. Scarce. - **$125 $235 $450**

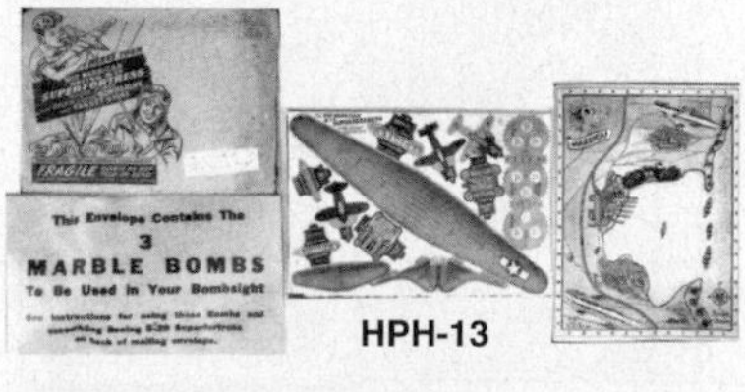

HPH-13

❑ **HPH-13. "Boeing B-29 Superfortress Model Plane And Target Game",**
1944. Scarce. Grape-Nuts Flakes. Includes target, two punch-out sheets, marbles. Complete - **$150 $350 $650**

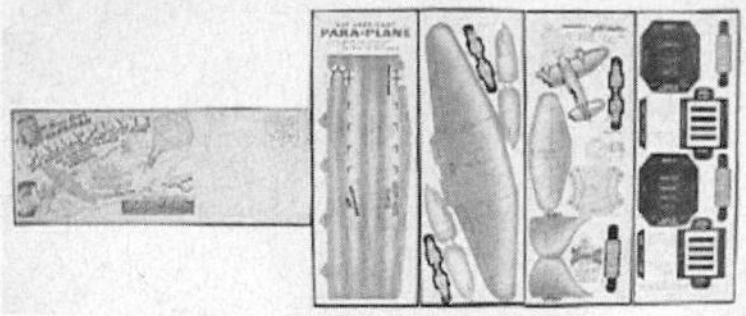

HPH-14

❑ **HPH-14. Hop Harrigan Para-Plane Punch-Out Premium,**
1944. Grape-Nuts Flakes. Consists of four punch-out sheets to form plane along with pair of "Code Signal Blinkers." An additional sheet forms the "Launching Tube" plus color sheet for "Rescue Helicopter." Comes with small wooden launching stick and red rayon fabric as parachute. Gordon Gold Archives.
Complete In Mailer - **$150 $350 $650**

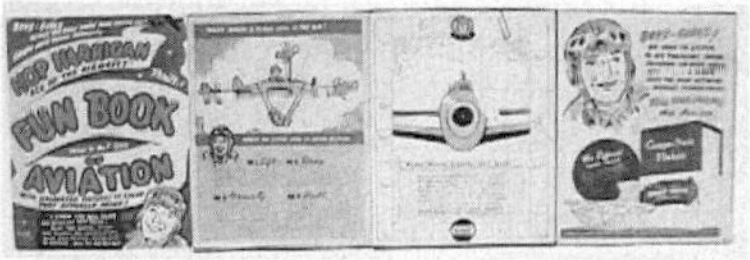

HPH-15

❑ **HPH-15. "Fun Book Of Aviation" Original Art Prototype,**
1944. Prepared for Grape-Nuts Flakes but not produced. Twenty-eight pages of original art featuring various activities. Gordon Gold Archives. Unique - **$1000**

HPH-16

❑ **HPH-16. "Hop Harrigan" Autographed Postcard Premium,**
1945. Black and white photo postcard is 5.5x7". Front has Hop Harrigan facsimile signature. Lower left edge has autograph of Albert Aley who portrayed Hop Harrigan on the radio. Reverse has printed note from Hop Harrigan thanking people for interest in the radio program. Autographed - **$60 $125 $200**
Unsigned - **$20 $40 $75**

HPH-17

❑ **HPH-17. Three-Sheet Movie Serial Poster,**
1946. Paper poster in two panels assembling to 41x81" for original release of 15-chapter Columbia serial starring William Blakewell in title role and "America's Ace Of The Airways." - **$200 $350 $750**

Hopalong Cassidy

William Boyd (1898-1972) was born in Ohio, grew up in Oklahoma, and worked at odd jobs before he went to Hollywood in 1919 to look for work in the movies. By the mid-1920s he had become a major star of silent films. Boyd made his first cowboy movie in 1931, and his first as Hopalong Cassidy in 1935. (The original Cassidy character came from the pulp stories and novels of C.E. Mulford (1883-1956) beginning with Bar 20 in *Outing* magazine in 1907, illustrated by Frank Schoonover). Dressed in black, with silver spurs and saddle, riding his white stallion Topper, with Andy Clyde or Gabby Hayes as sidekick, Hoppy battled outlaws in a series of movies among the most successful "B" Westerns ever made. Boyd became completely identified with the noble cowboy, and by the time he retired in 1959 he had made more than 100 theatrical and television Cassidy films.

Boyd bought the rights to the Hoppy character in 1948 and released edited versions of the films for syndication to Los Angeles television station KTLA, where they ran from 1948 to 1950. Barbara Ann bread and Wonder bread were sponsors. In 1950 the programs were leased to NBC, with General Foods as sponsor. *The Hopalong Cassidy Show*--the first major television Western series--was a sensation, airing on more than 60 stations and ranking consistently among the top three programs in the country. After two years a new series of half-hour made-for-TV films ran until 1954, with Edgar Buchanan in the sidekick role.

The television success spawned a radio series (1950-1952) on the Mutual and CBS networks, also sponsored by General Foods, and a comic strip drawn by Dan Spiegle that ran in more than 150 newspapers until 1955. Millions of Hoppy comic books appeared from 1943 through the 1950s, including give-aways by White Tower in 1946, Grape-Nuts Flakes in 1950, and several by Bond bread in 1951.

Hoppy's immense popularity with his young audience around the nation also generated an unprecedented merchandising cornucopia. Hundreds of endorsements and licensed products flooded the land, from roller skates to bicycles, watches, pocket knives, toy guns, cowboy outfits, pajamas, peanut butter, candy bars, cottage cheese, bread, cereal, cookies, milk, toothpaste, savings banks, wallpaper--even hair oil became part of the Hopalong Cassidy legend. William Boyd licensed over 2,000 Hoppy character products.

HOP-1

❑ **HOP-1. "Bill Boyd" Dixie Ice Cream Picture,**
c. 1935. First in a series of five. 11" photo with movie info on back, highlighting films "Call of the Prairie", and "The Eagle's Brood". Text says to watch for 3 other films: "Bar 20 Rides Again", "Bar 23", and "Call of the Prairie". Scarce. - **$75 $150 $300**

HOP-2

❑ **HOP-2. Dixie Ice Cream Picture,**
1938. - **$50 $100 $200**

HOP-3

❑ **HOP-3. "Bill Boyd" Dixie Ice Cream Picture,**
c. 1938. - **$50 $100 $200**

HOP-4

HOP-5

❑ **HOP-4. "Bill Boyd" Dixie Ice Cream Picture,**
1939. Reverse scenes from movie "Silver On The Sage." - **$50 $100 $200**

❑ **HOP-5. Dixie Lid,**
c. 1939. - **$12 $25 $40**

HOP-6

HOP-7

❑ **HOP-6. Dixie Lid,**
1939. Includes Paramount movie title "Silver On The Stage." - **$10 $20 $35**

❑ **HOP-7. Premium Offer Store Sign,**
1940. 6-1/2x25" paper sign printed full color horizontally on front and black and white vertically on reverse. Both sides feature rubber band gun and second premium offered is "Linda Ware" standup paperdoll. Gordon Gold Archives. - **$125 $275 $550**

HOP-8

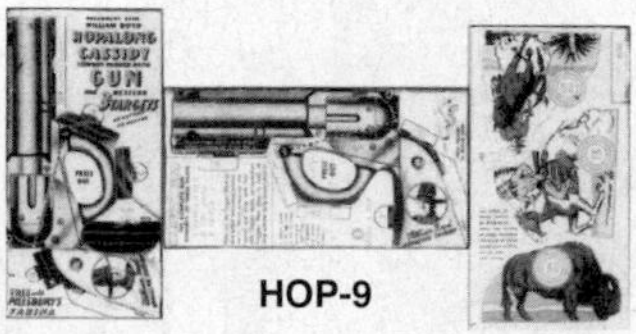

HOP-9

❑ **HOP-8. Pillsbury's Promotional 12x24" Sign,**
1940. Scarce. Advertises punch-out gun and targets. - **$200 $400 $800**

❑ **HOP-9. Punch-Out Gun And Targets Sheet,**
1940. Pillsbury's Farina. Boyd/Hoppy identified as "Paramount" star. Unpunched -
$75 $150 $300

HOP-10

HOP-11

❑ **HOP-10. Postcard,**
1941.Chrysler Plymouth premium shows Hoppy in suit in front of car. Ads for cars on back. -
$20 $45 $80

❑ **HOP-11. "Bill Boyd/For Democracy 100%" Cello. Button,**
c. 1942. Rare. From patriotism series picturing various cowboys. - **$300 $600 $1200**

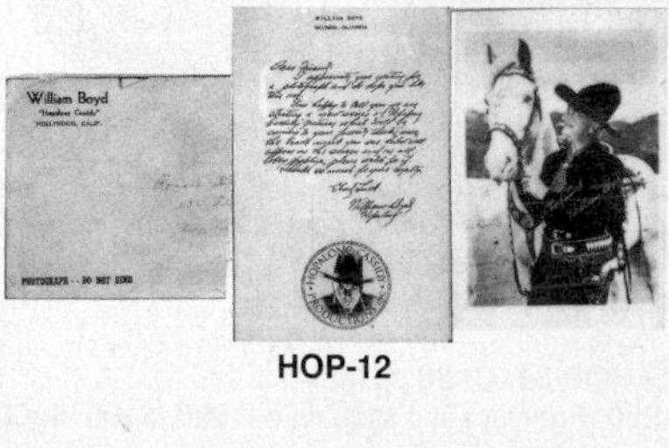

HOP-12

❑ **HOP-12. Fan Club Form Letter With Envelope,**
1946. Hopalong Cassidy Productions. Promotes new film series, photo on folder reverse.
With Envelope - **$70 $150 $250**
No Envelope - **$60 $125 $225**

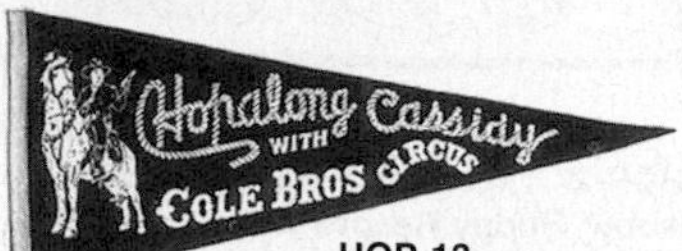

HOP-13

❑ **HOP-13. Cole Bros. Circus Pennant,**
c. 1948. - **$30 $60 $120**

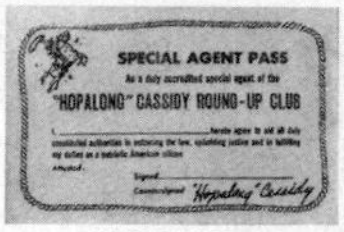

HOP-14

HOP-15

❑ **HOP-14. Round-Up Club "Special Agent Pass" Card,**
c. 1948. Probable movie theater give-away. -
$20 $35 $70

❑ **HOP-15. Card,**
1948.Special Agents pass. - **$20 $40 $80**

HOP-16

HOP-17

❑ **HOP-16. Barclay Knitwear Co. Photo,**
1949. Given with sweater purchase. -
$15 $25 $50

❑ **HOP-17. "Hopalong Cassidy Official Bar 20 T-V Chair",**
1949. Store item and Big Top Peanut Butter premium. Wood and canvas folding chair that opens to 16x16x22" tall. - **$215 $435 $750**

HOP-18

❑ **HOP-18. Butter-Nut Bread "Troopers News" Vol. 1 #1,**
1949. First issue of periodic newsletter. -
$75 $150 $300

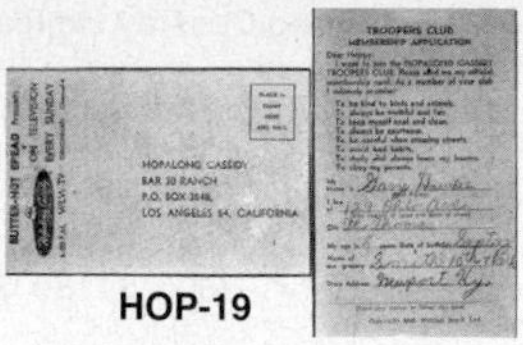

HOP-19

❑ **HOP-19. "Trooper's Club" Application Card,**
1949. Various sponsors. - **$18 $30 $60**

HOP-20

❑ **HOP-20. "Hopalong Cassidy And The Big Ranch" Record Album,**
1949. Capitol Records. Album cover is five action scenes printed in four colors. -
$40 $60 $125

HOP-21

HOP-22

❑ **HOP-21. Troopers Club Card,**
1949. Barbara Ann Bread premium. Brown on yellow background with secret code on back. -
$25 $60 $120

❑ **HOP-22. Photo,**
1940s. Rare. Early Bill Boyd movie premium with frame. - **$25 $50 $80**

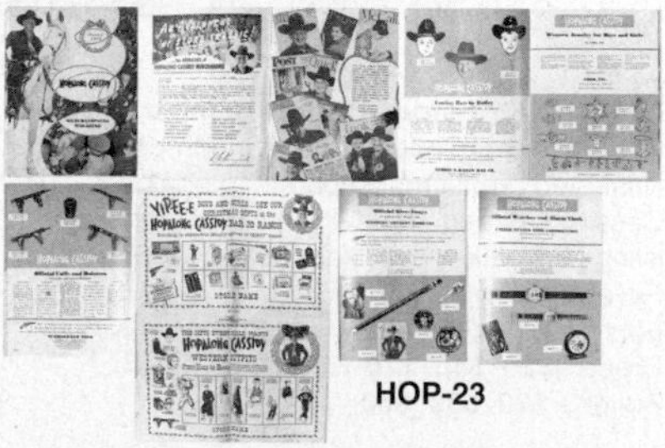

HOP-23

❑ **HOP-23. "Hopalong Cassidy Holidays" Merchandising Magazine,**
1950. 9x12" for retailers with 68 pages plus large fold-out insert, all related to pictures, descriptions and prices of Hoppy merchandise for Christmas season. A classic of the character merchandising industry. - **$600 $1150 $1850**

HOP-24

❑ **HOP-24. "Hoppy TV Show" Sign,**
c. 1950. Bond Bread. - **$125 $275 $550**

HOP-25

❑ **HOP-25. "Hopalong Cassidy/Drink Milk" Promo Glass,**
c. 1950. - **$60 $125 $250**

HOP-26

❑ **HOP-26. "Dairylea" Club Member Kit,**
c. 1950. Six-page folder including three pages of illustrated premiums, separate "Hopalong Cassidy's Creed" sheet listing 10 rules for good living plus yellow and black litho "Hoppy's Favorite Dairylea" button.
Folder - **$25 $50 $85**
Creed - **$20 $40 $70**
Button - **$20 $30 $60**

HOP-27

❑ **HOP-27. "America's Most Beloved Cowboy" Hoppy Record With Picture Sleeve,**
c. 1950. Capitol Records. #30128 in black and white paper sleeve picturing him front and back. Song titles are "Hoppy's Good Luck Coin" and "The Legend Of Phantom Scout Pass." - **$30 $60 $120**

HOP-28

❑ **HOP-28. "Hopalong Cassidy Club" Australian Real Photo Button,**
c. 1950. 1" black and white cello photo without dot pattern. - **$85 $150 $265**

HOP-29

❑ **HOP-29. "Hopalong Cassidy Rides Again" Newspaper Comic Strip Promo S ign,**
c. 1950. Albany Times Union. 11x21" cardboard subtitled "The Knickerbocker News." - **$85 $175 $325**

HOP-30

❑ **HOP-30. "Post's Raisin Bran" Trading Cards Store Poster,**
c. 1950. 13x26" paper offering single "Wild West Trading Card" packaged in individual cereal boxes. Gordon Gold Archives. - **$300 $600 $1200**

HOP-31

❑ **HOP-31. Hoppy & Pals Plaster Figure Paint Set Boxed,**
c. 1950. Laurel Ann Arts. Illustrated box and trio set of 7.5" tall Hoppy, Lucky, California. Figures are accompanied by paint containers, brush.
Complete Unused - **$350 $700 $1200**
Complete Painted - **$250 $500 $800**

HOP-32

❑ **HOP-32. "Barbara Ann Bread" Store Sign,**
c. 1950. 6.75x13.75" cardboard. - **$100 $200 $400**

HOP-33

HOP-34

❑ **HOP-33. Adult Hat,**
1950. Scarce. Premium and store item. Has white picture band and photo button. - **$125 $300 $600**

❑ **HOP-34. Child's Hat,**
1950. Premium and store item. - **$90 $195 $400**

HOP-35

❑ **HOP-35. Savings Club Brochure,**
1950. Worcester County Institution for Savings and others. Three-fold brochure, we show both sides open. - **$35 $65 $110**

HOP-36

❑ **HOP-36. "Hoppy" Arcade Photo Card,**
1950. - **$5 $10 $25**

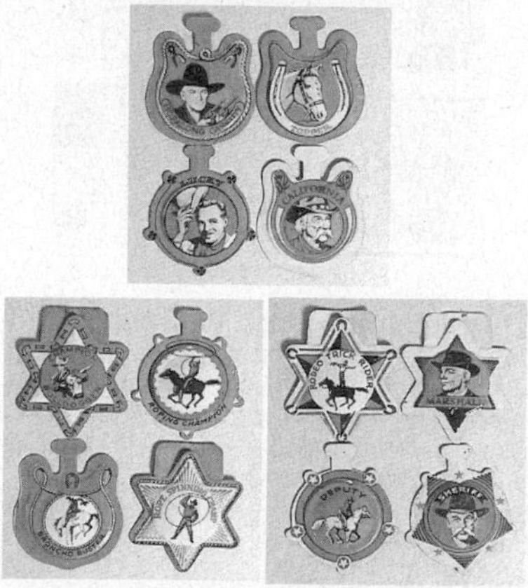

HOP-37

❑ **HOP-37. "Burry's Hopalong Cassidy Cookies" Litho. Tin Tabs,**
1950. 2" tall with 12 in set titled Hopalong Cassidy, Topper, Lucky, California, Champion Bulldogger, Rodeo Champion, Bronco Buster, Rope Spinning Champ, Rodeo Trick Rider, Marshal, Deputy, Sheriff. Reverse of each shows "Hoppy's Secret Code" with various symbols matching letters of the alphabet. Scarce. Each - **$30 $55 $115**

HOP-38

HOP-39

HOP-40

❑ **HOP-38. "Capitol Records" Premium Photo,**
c. 1950. Dealer's giveaway. 8x10" black and white. - **$20 $40 $80**

❑ **HOP-39. "Hopalong/Topper" Silver Luster White Metal Pin,**
c. 1950. Store item. 1-1/2" diameter. - **$30 $65 $100**

❑ **HOP-40. "Hopalong Cassidy" Silver Luster White Metal Pin,**
c. 1950. Store item. 1-1/8" tall. - **$20 $35 $70**

HOP-41

❑ **HOP-41. "Hopalong Cassidy And Smokey Bear" Radio Spots Brochure,**
c. 1950. Cooperative Forest Fire Prevention Campaign. 8x10-1/2" black and white 12-page folder captioned "Radio Platter #12." Contains scripts of various lengths with dialogue for announcer, Hoppy and Smokey. - **$40 $75 $150**

HOP-42

HOP-43

❑ **HOP-42. "Hoppy" Silver Luster Bracelet With Figural Charm,**
c. 1950. Store item. Charm is 1-1/4" tall. - **$25 $50 $100**

❑ **HOP-43. Employee's Large Litho. Tin Button,**
c. 1950. Used by Bond Bread delivery men and/or store clerks. Large 4" button with bw photo on red and black background. - **$125 $325 $650**

HOP-44

❑ **HOP-44. "Hopalong Cassidy Cookies" Box,**
1950. Burry Biscuit Corp. 12x16" waxed cardboard with back panel "Trading Post" ad as well as text for "Hopalong Cassidy's Creed For American Boys And Girls." Side panel pictures insert premiums set of 12 litho. tin badges. Gordon Gold Archives. Near Mint Flat - **$1650**
Used Complete - **$250 $500 $1000**

HOP-45

HOP-46

❑ **HOP-45. Canadian Newspaper Cello. Button,**
c. 1950. Toronto Star. 1-1/4" white on dark blue. - **$125 $250 $425**

❑ **HOP-46. "Hopalong Cassidy In The Mirror" Cello. Button,**
c. 1950. Probably issued with names of various newspapers. - **$35 $85 $150**

HOP-47

❑ **HOP-47. Watch Paper Sign 6x24",**
1950. Scarce. US Time. - **$125 $300 $600**

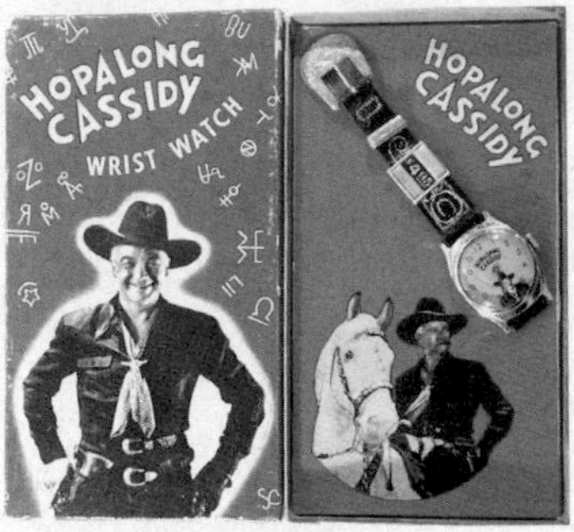

HOP-48

❑ **HOP-48. Wrist Watch with Insert in Box,**
1950. Complete - **$200 $400 $850**
Watch only - **$20 $40 $75**

HOP-49

HOP-50

❑ **HOP-49. Bond Bread Loaf End Labels,**
1950. Photo style pictures, unnumbered series. Each - **$3 $6 $12**

❑ **HOP-50. Bond Bread Loaf End Labels,**
1950. Numbered with perforation around illustration, 16 in set (#17-32). Each - **$3 $6 $12**

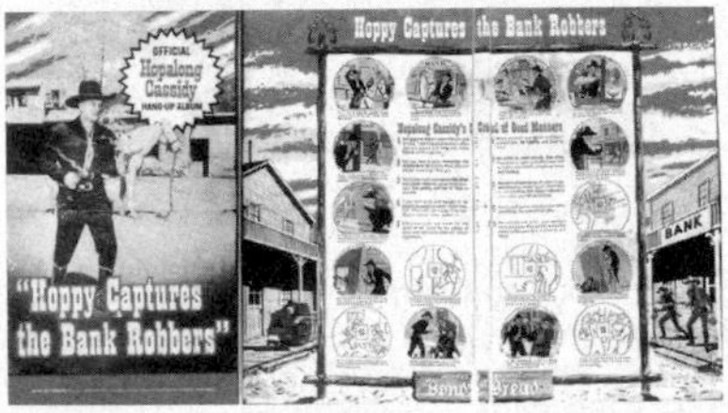

HOP-51

❑ **HOP-51. Bond Bread "Hang-Up Album",**
1950. Folder wall poster for bread loaf end pictures for story "Hoppy Captures The Bank Robbers." Unused - **$30 $75 $160**

HOP-52

HOP-53

❑ **HOP-52. Wrist Watch on Saddle Display in Box,**
1950. Boxed - **$675**
Watch only - **$20 $40 $75**

❑ **HOP-53. "Timex" 16" Painted Latex Store Display,**
1950. Rare. Timex Watches. English made. - **$1500 $3000 $7000**

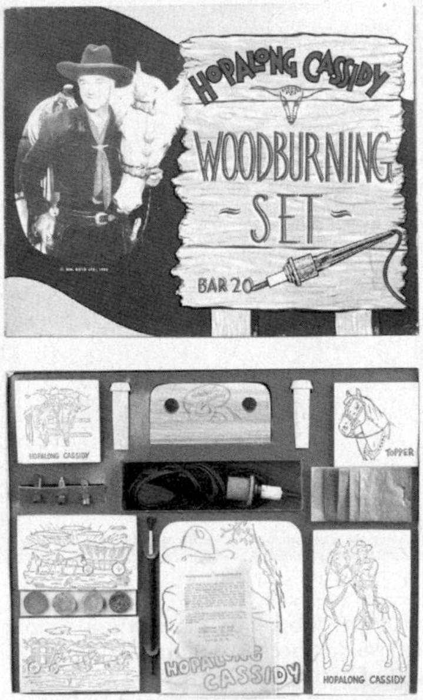

HOP-54

❑ **HOP-54. Woodburning Set in Box,**
1950. - **$75 $150 $300**

HOP-55

HOP-56

❑ **HOP-55. Bond Bread Label Flyer 6x9",**
1950. - **$40 $75 $125**

❑ **HOP-56. Metal Pocketwatch,**
1950. Store item by US Time.
Black Case - **$225 $475 $900**
Cream Case (Rare) - **$250 $500 $1000**

HOP-57

❑ **HOP-57. "Bond Bread" Store Hanger Sign 6x7",**
1950. - **$125 $250 $400**

HOP-58

❑ **HOP-58. Savings Club Thrift Kit,**
1950. Advertised in comic book and sponsored by various banks. Includes certificate, cover letter, color photo, postcard, folder showing club ranks. Near Mint In Mailer - **$300**
Certificate - **$30 $60 $100**
Letter - **$10 $20 $30**
Photo - **$5 $10 $15**
Postcard - **$5 $12 $20**
Folder - **$25 $50 $75**

HOP-59

❑ **HOP-59. Savings Club Membership Card,**
1950. Various sponsor banks. - **$40 $65 $100**

HOP-60

❑ HOP-60. Savings Club Postcard,
1950. Various sponsoring banks. -
$20 $30 $60

HOP-61

HOP-62

❑ HOP-61. Plastic Bank,
1950. Store item and Hopalong Cassidy Savings Club give-away.
Gold Plastic - **$25 $50 $100**
White Plastic - **$100 $200 $450**
Green - **$60 $135 $375**
Yellow - **$60 $135 $375**
Red - **$60 $135 $375**
Blue - **$85 $200 $450**

❑ HOP-62. Bank Teller's 3" Button,
1950. Litho Tin - **$10 $20 $40**
Celluloid - **$20 $40 $80**

HOP-63

HOP-64

HOP-65

❑ HOP-63. Saving Rodeo "Tenderfoot" Canadian Version Litho. Button,
1950. Various Canadian banks. Smaller size than U.S. versions, first five ranks are 1-1/8" litho. while Straw Boss and Foreman versions are 1-3/8". - **$20 $50 $80**

❑ HOP-64. Saving Rodeo "Tenderfoot" Litho. Button,
1950. Various banks. Awarded for saving $2.00. - **$15 $30 $60**

❑ HOP-65. Saving Rodeo "Wrangler" Litho. Button,
1950. Various banks. Awarded for saving $10.00. - **$12 $20 $30**

HOP-66

HOP-67

HOP-68

❑ HOP-66. Saving Rodeo "Bulldogger" Litho. Button,
1950. Various banks. Awarded for saving $25.00. - **$15 $25 $35**

❑ HOP-67. Saving Rodeo "Bronc Buster" Litho. Button,
1950. Various banks. Awarded for saving $50.00. - **$20 $35 $50**

❑ HOP-68. Saving Rodeo "Trail Boss" Litho. Button,
1950. Fifth highest of 7 ranks. - **$25 $50 $85**

HOP-69

HOP-70

❑ HOP-69. Saving Rodeo "Straw Boss" 2-1/4" Litho. Button,
1950. Scarce. Honor circle rating awarded for saving $250.00, also Canadian issue in smaller cello. version. - **$75 $175 $300**

❑ HOP-70. Saving Rodeo"Foreman" 2-1/4" Litho. Button,
1950. Scarce. Highest rank Honor Circle rating awarded for saving $500, also Canadian issue in smaller cello. version. - **$75 $200 $350**

HOP-71

❑ HOP-71. Western Badges Box Wrapper,
1950. Post's Raisin Bran. 11x17-1/2" picturing set of 12 litho. tin tabs. Near Mint Flat - **$1000**
Used Complete - **$200 $400 $600**

HOP-72

❑ HOP-72. Punch-Out Figure Sheet,
c. 1950. Issuer unknown. Full color 7x7" sheet for forming Hoppy figure seated on Topper. Gordon Gold Archives.
Unpunched - **$65 $120 $200**

HOP-73

HOP-74

❑ HOP-73. "Hopalong Cassidy's Western Magazine" First Issue,
1950. Vol. 1 #1 quarterly pulp magazine. - **$75 $225 $400**

❑ HOP-74. Candy Bar Wrapper,
1950. Foil paper with mail offer for "Hopalong Cassidy Cowboy Neckerchief With Stone Set Metal Steerhead Loop" expiring June 30. See HOP-212. - **$40 $100 $175**

HOP-75

HOP-76

HOP-77

❑ HOP-75. "Timex Watches" Cello. Button,
1950. English made. - **$65 $125 $250**

❑ HOP-76. Newspaper Strip Promotion Cello. Button,
c. 1950. Sun-Telegram. - **$25 $65 $125**

❑ HOP-77. Milk Bottle Cap,
c. 1950. Jo-Mar Milk. Foil paper with inner card-board liner. - **$15 $30 $60**

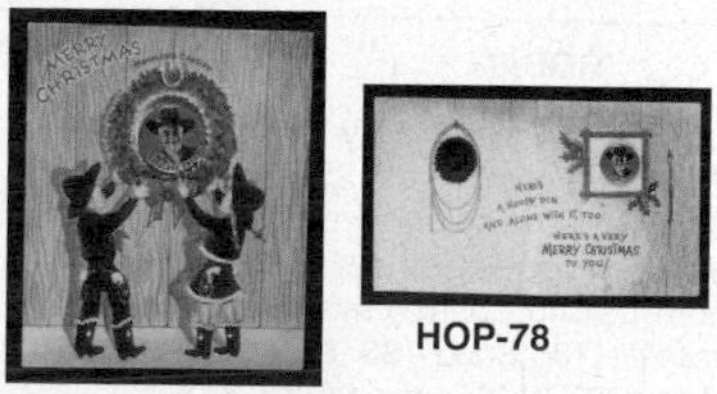

HOP-78

❑ HOP-78. Christmas Card With Cello. Button,
1950. Store item. Folder card from authorized greeting card series by Buzza Cardozo, Hollywood. Inside button is visible through diecut opening on front cover.
With Button - **$30 $60 $115**
Card Only - **$20 $35 $70**

HOP-79

HOP-80

❑ **HOP-79. Christmas Card,**
1950. - **$25 $60 $120**

❑ **HOP-80. Die Cut Christmas Card,**
1950. Features Schmidt cap gun on front and inside card. - **$25 $60 $120**

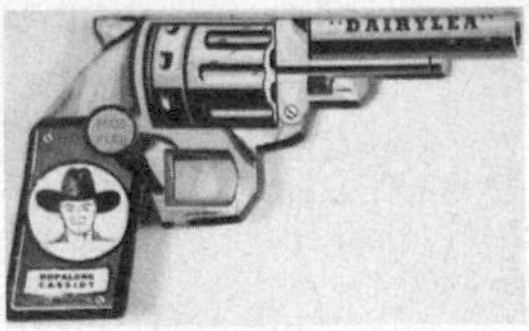

HOP-81

❑ **HOP-81. Cardboard Clicker Pistol,**
c. 1950. "Dairylea" and others. 7" long in blue, black and white. - **$40 $75 $125**

HOP-82

❑ **HOP-82. "Hoppy's Favorite Bond Bread" Shelf Sign,**
c. 1950. 6x9-1/2" slick paper in black, white and red. - **$30 $70 $125**

HOP-83

HOP-84

❑ **HOP-83. Card Set By Topps Gum Co.,**
1950. Store item. Set of 230 numbered cards done in various color combinations according to numbered sub-sets showing scenes from various Hopalong Cassidy movies.
Cards #1-186 Each - **$3 $5 $10**
Cards #187-230 Each - **$4 $7 $15**

❑ **HOP-84. Metallic Foil Card By Topps Gum Co.,**
1950. Store item. For each of the eight sub-sets in the Topps set of 230 cards, one "Header" card was produced with a metallic foil image. These eight cards were un-numbered.
Each - **$60 $100 $200**

HOP-85

HOP-86

❑ **HOP-85. Australian Candy Tin,**
c. 1950. Bester's Sweets Ltd., Melbourne. Litho. tin box and lid with color portrait. Side panels list eight rules of "Hopalong Cassidy's Troopers Creed For Boys And Girls." - **$125 $250 $500**

❑ **HOP-86. "Hopalong Cassidy" Large Doll,**
c. 1950. Store item and promotional award from Chicago Sun-Times news paper. 22" tall stuffed cloth and plush fabric body with thin vinyl boy image face with felt hat holding title headband. - **$300 $600 $1200**

HOP-87

❑ **HOP-87. "Buzza Cardozo Greeting Cards" 15x27" Store Sign,**
1950. Diecut cardboard for officially licensed Hoppy greeting card series. -
$750 $1500 $2500

HOP-88

HOP-89

❑ **HOP-88. "Hoppy's Favorite" Litho. Button,**
1950. Issued with names of various sponsors.
Each - **$15 $35 $60**

❑ **HOP-89. Postcard,**
1950.Beautiful color card of Hoppy with hands on gun. Bill Boyd write up on back. Says he started in films in 1919. - **$25 $50 $75**

HOP-90

❑ **HOP-90. Crayon Set In Box,**
1950. Crayons- 42 small, 28 large- with stencils and Hoppy pad. Promoted in Life Magazine. -
$125 $275 $550

HOP-91

❑ **HOP-91. Premium Catalogue With Order Form,**
1950. Big Top Peanut Butter. - **$65 $125 $250**

HOP-92

HOP-93

❑ **HOP-92. Metal Binoculars,**
1950. Store item and Big Top Peanut Butter premium. - **$35 $85 $200**

❑ **HOP-93. Boxed Camera,**
1950. Store item and Big Top Peanut Butter premium. Boxed - **$100 $150 $250**
Loose - **$40 $80 $150**

HOP-94

HOP-95

❑ **HOP-94. Silvered Brass Identification Bracelet,**
1950. Big Top Peanut Butter. Center plate edges have "Hopalong Cassidy-XX Ranch", center is designed for engraving owner's name. - **$50 $100 $150**

❑ **HOP-95. Silvered Brass Hair Barrette,**
1950. Store item and Big Top Peanut Butter premium. - **$20 $35 $65**

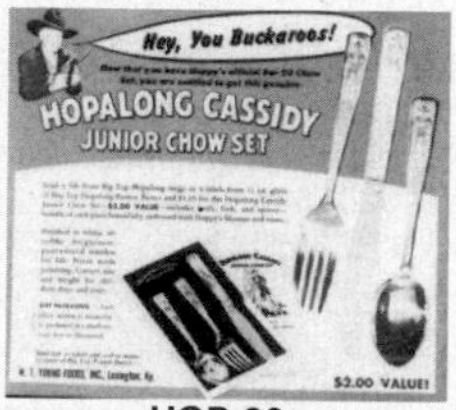

HOP-96

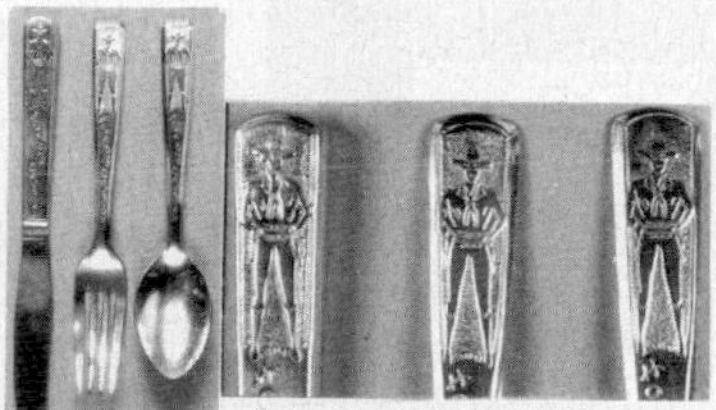

(ENLARGED VIEW)
HOP-97

❑ **HOP-96. "Junior Chow Set" Ad Sheet,**
1950. Big Top Peanut Butter. - **$25 $45 $70**

❑ **HOP-97. Stainless Steel Table Utensils,**
1950. Store item and Big Top Peanut Butter premium. Each - **$10 $20 $40**
Box With Insert - **$55 $110 $175**

HOP-98

❑ **HOP-98. "Bar 20 Chow Set" Boxed Glassware,**
1950. Store item and Big Top Peanut Butter premium. Set for "Gun Totin' Buckaroos".
Near Mint Boxed - **$450**
Each - **$30 $50 $90**

HOP-99

HOP-100

❑ **HOP-99. Plastic Wrist Compass,**
1950. Store item also used as Big Top Peanut Butter and Popsicle premium. - **$25 $50 $85**

❑ **HOP-100. Glass Mugs,**
1950. Big Top Peanut Butter. Set of four in black, green, blue, red on white.
Each - **$8 $15 $30**

HOP-101

HOP-102

HOP-103

❑ **HOP-101. Metal Thermos,**
1950. Store item by Aladdin Industries and Big Top Peanut Butter premium. - **$25 $75 $160**

❑ **HOP-102. Metal Lunch Box,**
1950. Store item by Aladdin Industries and Big Top Peanut Butter premium. Rectangular decal. - **$85 $175 $500**

❑ **HOP-103. Metal Lunch Box,**
1950. Store item by Aladdin Industries. Cloud-shaped decal. - **$75 $150 $450**

HOP-104

❑ **HOP-104. Wallet With Coin & Papers,**
1950. Store item and Big Top Peanut Butter premium. Complete - **$75 $150 $250**
Coin Only - **$8 $12 $20**

HOP-105

HOP-106

❑ **HOP-105. "Hopalong Cassidy Picture Card Gum" Waxed Paper Wrapper,**
1950. Topps Chewing Gum. Wrappers come with white, green or yellow backgrounds.
Each - **$25 $55 $120**

❑ **HOP-106. Candy Bag,**
1950. Topps Candy Division. - **$25 $50 $90**

HOP-107

HOP-108

❑ **HOP-107. Litho. Tin Potato Chips Can,**
1950. Kuehmann Foods Inc. - **$85 $215 $450**

❑ **HOP-108. Grape-Nuts Flakes Comic Book,**
1950. - **$14 $42 $160**

HOP-109

❑ **HOP-109. Boxed Drinking Straws,**
1950. Various pictures on reverse.
Complete - **$50 $80 $160**

HOP-110

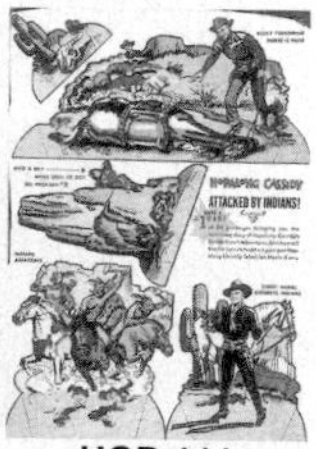

HOP-111

❑ **HOP-110. "Good Luck From Hoppy" Aluminum Medal,**
1950. Earliest version with Hoppy image on each side was produced in 1948 for a Hoppy rodeo in Hawaii. The 1950 version for inclusion with wallets by Pioneer has a four-leaf clover within a horseshoe on the reverse. A heavy pewter-like version is a reproduction.
Rodeo Version - **$12 $25 $50**
Wallet Style - **$8 $12 $20**

❑ **HOP-111. Burry's Cookies Cut-Out Box Panel,**
1950. #1 panel from 24 different packages with "The Continued Story Of Hopalong Cassidy's Bar-20 Ranch Adventures".
Each Uncut Panel - **$20 $50 $80**

HOP-112

❑ HOP-112. "Hair Trainer" 8x22" Paper Poster With Picture,
1950. Poster - **$125 $250 $500**
Picture - **$8 $15 $25**

HOP-115

HOP-113 HOP-114

❑ HOP-113. Vinyl Pocketknife Loop,
1950. Store item. - **$25 $50 $100**

❑ HOP-114. Pocketknife,
1950. Store item by Hammer Brand. - **$30 $75 $150**

❑ HOP-115. Cardboard Noisemaker Gun,
1950. Capitol Records. - **$30 $75 $150**

HOP-116

❑ HOP-116. Die-cut Birthday Card,
1950. - **$25 $50 $120**

HOP-117 HOP-118

❑ HOP-117. "Hopalong Cassidy and Lucky at Copper Gulch" Television Book,
1950. - **$40 $80 $160**

❑ HOP-118. "Hopalong Cassidy and Lucky at the 'Double X' Ranch" Book,
1950. With 2 pop-ups. - **$45 $90 $180**

HOP-119

❑ HOP-119. Bond Bread Promotional Sign,
1950. Promotes the 32 Hoppy pictures on Bond Bread labels. Rare. - **$275 $600 $1200**

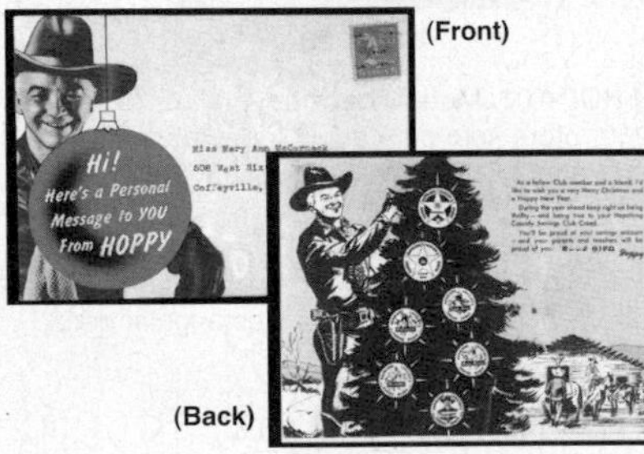

(Front)

(Back)

HOP-120

❑ HOP-120. Christmas Post Card,
1950. Promotes the Hopalong Cassidy Savings Club. Pinbacks are on other side of card. Rare. - **$85 $175 $350**

HOP-121

❑ HOP-121. Hoppy "Clover Lake Ice Cream" Canister,
c. 1950. 6-1/2" tall. - **$40 $70 $150**

HOP-122

❑ HOP-122."Hopalong Cassidy's Favorite Ice Cream" Quart Container,
c. 1950. 6" tall issued by O'Fallon Quality Dairy and others. - **$20 $45 $85**

HOP-123

❑ HOP-123. "Hopalong Cassidy Lends A Helping Hand" Pop-Up Book,
1950. A Bonnie Book from John Martin's House, published by Doubleday. - **$20 $35 $85**

HOP-124

❑ HOP-124. "Hopalong-Aid" Drink Packet,
1950. Bol Mfg. Co. 3-1/2x5". - **$35 $75 $150**

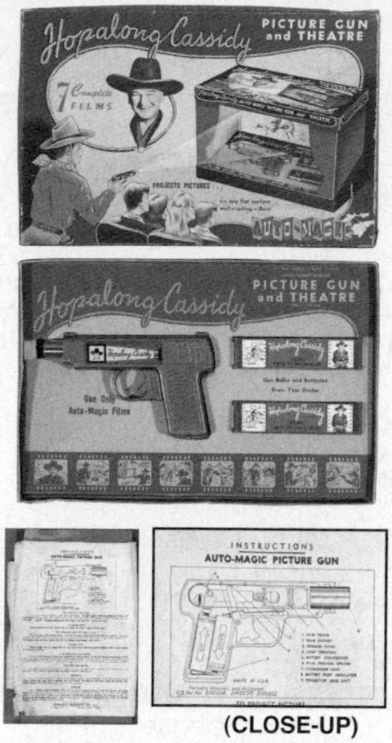

(CLOSE-UP)

HOP-125

❑ **HOP-125. Hopalong Cassidy Picture Gun and Theatre,**
1950. Theatre in box with 7 complete films and instructions. Complete - **$200 $400 $650**

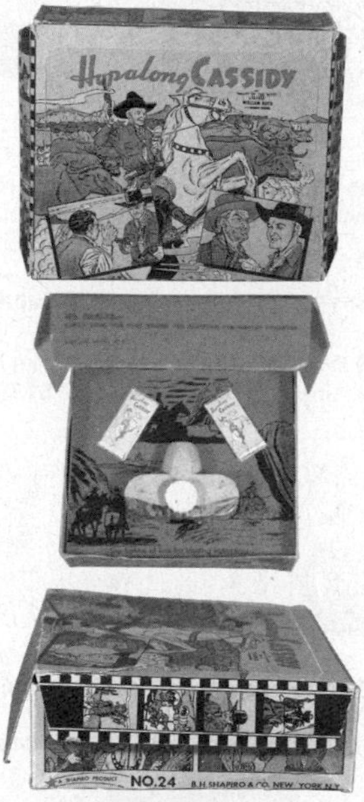

HOP-126

❑ **HOP-126. Hopalong Cassidy Film With Projector Boxed,**
1950. Projector is yellow and purple. Features movie "Heart of the West." Rare.
Complete - **$250 $500 $800**
Box and Insert Separate - **$200 $400 $600**

HOP-127

❑ **HOP-127. Full Color Bread Loaf End Label,**
1950. Sponsored by Mary Jane Bread. - **$25 $60 $100**

HOP-128

❑ **HOP-128. Camera With Box,**
1950. Box - **$40 $85 $175**
Camera - **$35 $75 $150**

HOP-129

❑ **HOP-129. Life Magazine With Hoppy Cover Article,**
1950. June 12 issue. - **$15 $30 $75**

HOP-130

❑ **HOP-130."Hopalong Cassidy Potato Chips" Bag,**
1950. Kuehmann Foods. - **$12 $25 $40**

HOP-131

❑ **HOP-131. Photo Images Child's Shirt,**
c. 1950. Store item by "The Little Champ Of Hollywood." Eight different repeating Hoppy photos in black and white plus inscriptions in red lettering. - **$115 $250 $400**

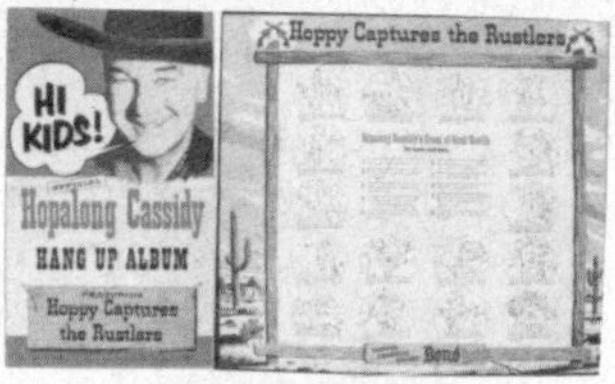

HOP-132

❑ **HOP-132. "Official Hopalong Cassidy Hang-Up Album" Bread Label Display Folder,**
1950. Issued by Bond Bread. Holds 16 different bread end labels. - **$35 $85 $175**

HOP-133

❑ **HOP-133. Hard Plastic Figures,**
1950. Store item by Ideal Corp.
Boxed - **$95 $175 $375**
Loose - **$40 $75 $175**

HOP-134

HOP-135

❑ **HOP-134. "Hopalong Cassidy Bikes And Skates" Ad Card,**
1950. Rollfast Co. - **$25 $60 $125**

❑ **HOP-135. "Hopalong Cassidy In The Daily News" 2" Cello. Button From NYC,**
1950. New York - **$20 $45 $75**
Other Cities - **$25 $50 $90**

HOP-136

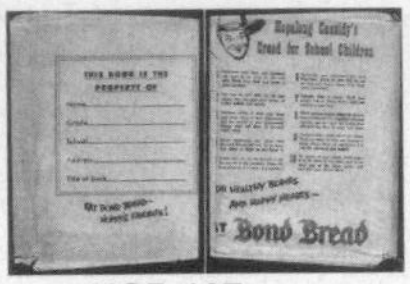

HOP-137

❑ HOP-136. New York Daily News 10x13" Cardboard Poster,
1950. Announces start of daily comic strip. - **$125 $250 $400**

❑ HOP-137. Bond Bread Book Cover,
c. 1950. - **$15 $25 $50**

HOP-138

❑ HOP-138. Hoppy and Topper Die Cut Christmas Card with Envelope,
1950. Various sponsors. - **$20 $60 $120**

HOP-139

HOP-140

HOP-141

❑ HOP-139. Hopalong Cassidy Western Badge,
1950. Post's Raisin Bran. From set of 12 including titles: Hopalong Cassidy, Calamity Jane, General Custer, Wild Bill Hickok, Rodeo Trick Rider, Sheriff, Ranch Boss, Bull Dogging Champ, Annie Oakley, Chief Sitting Bull, Roping Champ, Indian Scout. Also seen is "Ranger" with same border as Hopalong Cassidy but without "Post's Raisin Bran" on reverse.
Hopalong Cassidy or "Ranger" Tab - **$12 $25 $60**
Others Each - **$5 $12 $25**

❑ HOP-140. Radio Show 9x11" Handbill,
c. 1950. Grape-Nuts Flakes. Probable grocery bag insert. - **$50 $85 $175**

❑ HOP-141. "Strawberry Preserves" Glass,
c. 1950. Ladies Choice Foods.
With Label - **$45 $90 $175**

HOP-142

HOP-143

❑ HOP-142. "Hoppy's Favorite" Bond Bread Cards,
c. 1950. Some fronts advertise bread loaf seals. Reverse caption "Ways Of The West." Unnumbered, set of 16.
Each - **$6 $12 $20**

❑ HOP-143. Bond Bread Postcard,
c. 1950. - **$8 $15 $30**

HOP-144

HOP-145

❑ HOP-144. Bond Bread Book Cover,
c. 1950. - **$15 $25 $50**

❑ HOP-145. "Ranch House Race" Game,
c. 1950. Stroehmann's Sunbeam Bread. - **$50 $100 $175**

HOP-146

HOP-147

❑ HOP-146. TV Show "Special Guest" 11x16" Cardboard Store Sign,
c. 1950. Wonder Bread. - **$60 $150 $275**

❑ HOP-147. Dairylea Milk 13x20" Paper Store Poster,
c. 1950. Various dairies. - **$50 $125 $200**

HOP-148

❑ HOP-148. Dairylea Ice Cream Carton,
c. 1950. Offers neckerchief and t-shirt. - **$45 $85 $175**

HOP-149

HOP-150

❑ HOP-149. "Dairylea Milk" Glass Inscribed "Do As Hoppy And Miss Dairylea Do/Drink Dairylea Milk",
c. 1950. - **$75 $150 $300**

❑ HOP-150. "1 Cent Play Money" Cardboard Milk Bottle Cap,
c. 1950. - **$10 $15 $25**

HOP-151

❑ HOP-151. Product Box And Premium Order Coupon,
c. 1950. Scarce. Honey Roll Sugar Cones.
Box - **$225 $375 $750**
Coupon - **$20 $40 $85**

HOP-152

HOP-153

❑ HOP-152. Waxed Cardboard Ice Cream "Hoppy Cup",
c. 1950. - **$15 $30 $75**

❑ HOP-153. Miniature Plastic TV With Hoppy Film,
c. 1950. Hole on side for key chain, film has four color pictures of Hoppy. - **$35 $75 $135**

HOP-154

❑ HOP-154. "Bob Atcher's Meadow Gold Song" TV Show Music Folder,
c. 1950. Meadow Gold Butter. - **$20 $40 $75**

HOP-155

HOP-156

❑ **HOP-155. "All-Star Milk" Pint Glass Bottle,**
c. 1950. Local imprint for "McClellan's". -
$30 $65 $100

❑ **HOP-156. Blue Image Vinyl Tumbler,**
c. 1950. Cloverlake Cottage Cheese.
With Lid - **$30 $70 $125**
No Lid - **$20 $40 $70**

(FRONT) HOP-157 (BACK)

❑ **HOP-157. Dinner Milk Glass,**
1950. Three different in set.
Each - **$20 $40 $60**

(RED & BLACK FRONT)

HOP-158

❑ **HOP-158. Hoppy Milk Glass Set,**
1950. Black design on white with red accents.
Four glasses in set with different backs.
Breakfast - **$50 $100 $250**
Lunch - **$50 $100 $250**
Dinner - **$50 $100 $250**
Snack - **$75 $150 $400**

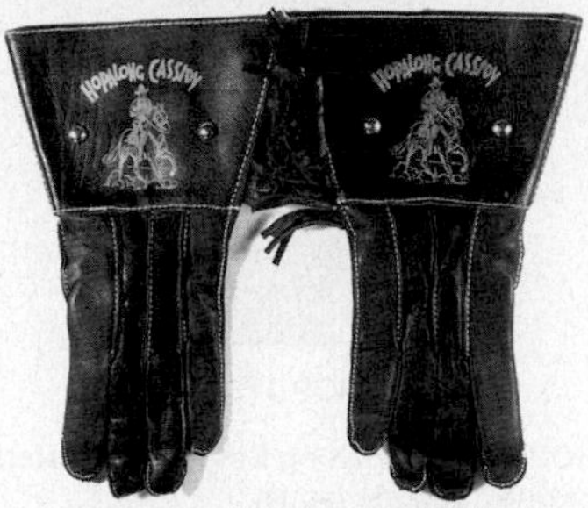

HOP-159

❑ **HOP-159. "Hopalong Cassidy" Black Leather Gloves,**
1950. Hard to find in high grade. White lettering rubs off easily. Pair - **$125 $250 $450**

HOP-160 HOP-161 HOP-162

❑ **HOP-160. Popsicle "Hopalong Cassidy" Silvered Tin Badge,**
c. 1950. Various sponsors. Sold carded in stores. - **$20 $40 $75**

❑ **HOP-161. "HC" Silvered Metal Portrait Ring,**
c. 1950. Popsicle and various sponsors. -
$20 $40 $60

❑ **HOP-162. "Hopalong Cassidy Bar 20" Vectograph Brass Clip,**
c. 1950. Hopalong Cassidy Ice Cream Bar and others. Plastic mechanical insert reveals Hoppy picture, although image almost always gone. Used as belt or pocket clip.
No Image - **$15 $40 $75**
NM With Image - **$350**

HOP-163

❑ **HOP-163. "Dudin'-Up Kit",**
c. 1950. Fuller Brush Co. Hair treatment set with two trading cards on box back.
Complete - **$150 $300 $600**

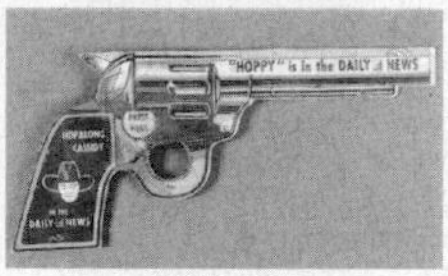

HOP-164 HOP-165

❑ **HOP-164. "Daily News" Cardboard Clicker Gun,**
c. 1950. Various sponsors. - **$40 $70 $150**

❑ **HOP-165. Color Photo,**
c. 1950. Came with gun to project filmstrips. -
$18 $30 $60

HOP-166 HOP-167 HOP-168

❑ **HOP-166. "Hopalong Cassidy/Sheriff" Cello. Button,**
c. 1950. From Arizona radio station. For Mutual Network broadcasts. - **$50 $100 $200**

❑ **HOP-167. Double Sponsor Cello. Button,**
c. 1950. Filene's department store, Boston and Loew's State Theater. Dark red/black featuring Hoppy portrait. - **$125 $275 $500**

❑ **HOP-168. Encased Penny With Coded Message,**
1951. Reads "Member Hopalong Cassidy Savings Club/Security-First National Bank." Coded message and good luck symbols on rim. Code was printed on member's club card. -
$25 $75 $150

HOP-169

❑ **HOP-169. "Hopalong Cassidy" Jacket,**
1950. Bell Company. - **$135 $325 $675**

HOP-170

❑ **HOP-170. "Hopalong Cassidy" Pants,**
1950. Bell Company. - **$100 $300 $600**

HOP-171

❑ **HOP-171. "Hoppy, Topper And Me" Sheet Music,**
1951. Back cover ad for "Hopalong Cassidy Musical Roundup" song folio. - **$30 $60 $115**

HOP-172

❑ **HOP-172. "Blue Moon on the Silver Sage" Sheet Music,**
1951. - **$15 $25 $50**

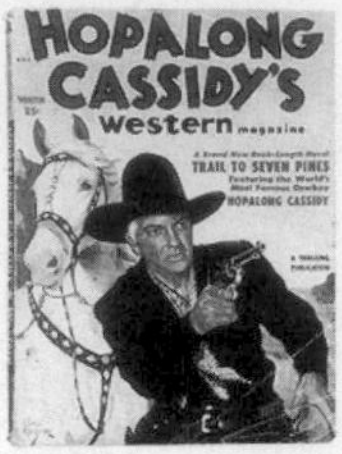

HOP-173

❑ **HOP-173. "Hopalong Cassidy's Western Magazine" Second Issue,**
1951. Vol. 1 #2 quarterly pulp magazine. Believed to be final issue. - **$90 $175 $450**

HOP-174

HOP-175

❑ **HOP-174. Wild West Trading Cards,**
1951. Post Cereals. Set of 36.
Each - **$8 $12 $30**

❑ **HOP-175. Bond Bread "The Strange Legacy" Comic Booklet,**
1951. 3-1/2x7" format. Titles also in series "The Mad Bomber" and "Meets The Brend Brothers, Bandits." Each - **$10 $30 $100**

HOP-176

❑ **HOP-176. Waxed Box Wrapper Promoting "Wild West Trading Cards",**
1951. Gordon Gold Archives.
Used Complete - **$300 $600 $1200**

HOP-177

HOP-178

❑ **HOP-177. "Trading Cards" Store Sign,**
1951. Post Cereals. 13x26" full color promoting set of 36 cards. Gordon Gold Archives. - **$300 $600 $1200**

❑ **HOP-178. "Trading Cards" Oversized Envelope For Promotion Materials,**
1951. Post Cereals. Likely held promotional posters for store use. Gordon Gold Archives. - **$250 $525 $1000**

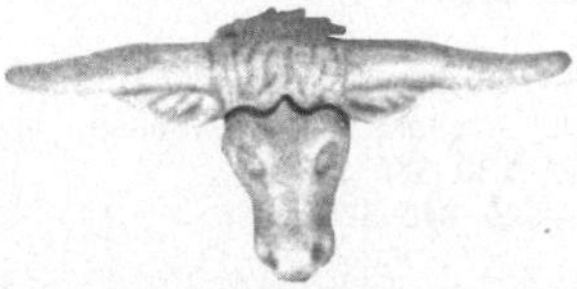

HOP-179

❑ **HOP-179. Concho/Branding Iron,**
c. 1951. Post's Grape-Nuts Flakes. Plastic steer head with tie slide loop on back, used as ring or tie clip. Front has steer head cover over "HC" initials for printing paper. See next item. - **$75 $150 $250**

HOP-180

❑ **HOP-180. Concho/Branding Iron Instruction Leaflet,**
c. 1951. Post's Grape-Nuts Flakes. See HOP-176. - **$35 $60 $110**

HOP-181

❑ **HOP-181. "Western Badges" 9x20" Paper Sign,**
1952. Shows set of 12 litho. tin tabs, but Hoppy is not pictured. Possibly the star design picturing a "Ranger" was never produced, or if it was, a "Hopalong Cassidy" image was soon substituted and produced using the identical border design of a horse head, four pistols and arrowhead. When the set with Hoppy was issued, the reverses were marked "Post's Raisin Bran," but the Post's name does not appear on this sign. - **$65 $125 $250**

HOP-182

HOP-183

❑ HOP-182. Hat/Compass Ring,
1952. Post cereal, Meadow Gold dairy, possibly others. Brass bands, removable metal hat over plastic magnetic compass. - **$100 $200 $300**

❑ HOP-183. Hoppy Savings Club "Honor Member" Litho. Button,
1952. Rare. Highest ranking award for early 1950s youthful bank savings program. Club folder from 1950 (HOP-58) does not show this button, which is the final in series. It was awarded for recruitment of one new savings account member. For three new accounts, the Honor Member wallet was awarded. Rarest of all in series. See HOP-184. - **$85 $175 $350**

HOP-184

❑ HOP-184. "Savings Club Honor Member" Diecut Promo Folder For Bank Premium Wallet,
1952. Various banks. 3-3/8x4-1/8" four-section diecut paper folder in shape of wallet. Back cover illustrates "Honor Member" button and invites club membership. Wallet depicted is the high quality metal-covered example although we've never seen one inscribed with slogan "Honor Member Savings Club" as depicted in this artwork. Item is diecut in a parallelogram shape. See HOP-183. - **$150 $300 $600**

HOP-185

❑ HOP-185. 12-Pictures Calendar,
1952. Surgeon's Orthopedic Supplies (S.O.S.). 6x12" paper hanger calendar with different Hoppy photo for each month. Issued by various sponsors. - **$85 $165 $350**

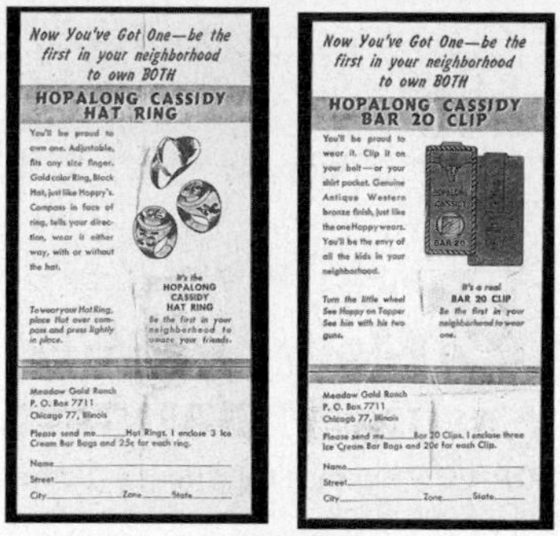

HOP-186

❑ HOP-186. Hat Ring & "Bar 20 Clip" Order Card,
c. 1952. Meadow Gold Ranch Ice Cream Bars. 3x7" card printed on one side by ring offer and reverse by clip offer. Each was available for three ice cream bar bags plus 25 cents and 20 cents respectively. - **$25 $45 $90**

HOP-187

❑ HOP-187. "Hopalong's Cowboy Calendar",
1953. Issued with various sponsorship imprints. 6x11-1/2" with metal strip holding 12 monthly pages. Pages are in sepia hues with orange tint. Each page back features item of western lore followed by "Hoppy Says" advice to youngsters and "Hoppy's Corral" segment devoted to western history. - **$85 $165 $350**

HOP-188

❑ HOP-188. "Crispo Cake Cone Co." Dealer Price Sheet,
1953. 8-1/2x11" red, white and blue sheet showing eight product boxes, two of which are marketed as "Hopalong Cassidy's Favorite Brand." - **$15 $30 $50**

HOP-189

❑ HOP-189. "Hopalong Cassidy" Metal Lunchbox With Thermos,
1954. Aladdin Industries Inc. Thermos has bright yellow lid. Lunchbox - **$200 $400 $1200**
Bottle - **$50 $125 $300**

HOP-190

❑ HOP-190. English Song Sheet,
c. 1954. Scarce. - **$50 $100 $150**

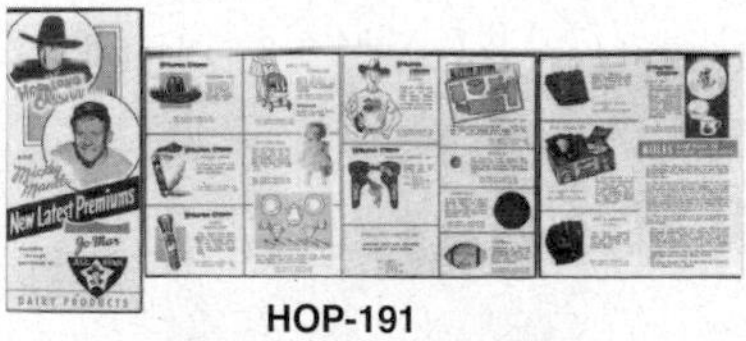

HOP-191

❑ HOP-191. All-Star Dairy Products Folder,
c. 1956. Pictured premiums include those for Hoppy as well as baseball stars Mickey Mantle and Stan Musial. - **$45 $90 $165**

HOP-192 HOP-193

❑ HOP-192. Autographed Photo,
1950s. Pictured holding supplement to Philadelphia Sunday Bulletin. - **$75 $150 $225**

❑ HOP-193. Secretarial Autographed Photo,
1950s. Signed by secretary or similar representative. - **$15 $30 $60**

HOP-194 HOP-195

❑ **HOP-194. Hopalong Cassidy 20 1/2" Doll,**
1950s. Has removable hat, metal star badge, removable belt with metal buckle inscribed with "Hopalong Cassidy." Has metal gun and holster, and a scarf with metal cowhead tie holder. - **$525 $1100 $1850**

❑ **HOP-195. Hopalong Cassidy Solid Core Carnival Statue,**
1950s. The second-most rare and valuable character carnival piece. Rare in any condition. - **$150 $400 $800**

HOP-196

❑ **HOP-196. Savings Club Pamphlet,**
1950s. "A New Plan" promotes Hoppy Savings Club Accounts with various promotional aids. Rare. - **$65 $125 $250**

HOP-197

HOP-198

❑ **HOP-197. "Hoppy's Bunkhouse Clothes Corral" Wood Rack,**
1950s. Northland Milk. - **$85 $165 $300**

❑ **HOP-198. Melville Milk 11x42" Cardboard Store Sign,**
1950s. Various dairies. Simulated wood grain. - **$85 $165 $300**

HOP-200

HOP-199 HOP-201

❑ **HOP-199. Photo Postcard,**
1950s. Shows Hoppy from the waist up in cowboy outfit. - **$15 $25 $40**

❑ **HOP-200. Pin Back,**
1950s. Scarce. Harmony Farms Dairies. - **$15 $35 $60**

❑ **HOP-201. Pin Back,**
1950s. Scarce. Med-O Pure Dairy. - **$15 $35 $60**

HOP-202

❑ **HOP-202. "Hopalong Cassidy's Favorite Grape Juice" Full Bottle,**
1950s. Store item by Betsy Ross California Pure Grape Juice. 8" tall. - **$60 $125 $250**

HOP-203 HOP-204

❑ **HOP-203. Pin Back,**
1950s. Promotes strip in the Detroit News. Uncommon. - **$35 $60 $90**

❑ **HOP-204. Paper Mask in Realistic Color,**
1950s. Gordon Gold Archives - **$100 $300 $550**

HOP-205

❑ **HOP-205. "Hopalong Cassidy Fan Club" English Black And White Photo Postcards,**
1950s. Each - **$10 $20 $40**

HOP-206

❑ **HOP-206. Premium Poster For Hoppy Bread Label Pictures,**
c. 1950s. Stroehmann's Sunbeam Bread. 11-1/2x14-3/8" Sunday comic strip-style format with 12-panel story "Stagecoach Robbery" with white silhouette areas for placement of numbered Hoppy images cut from bread loaf end labels. - **$125 $250 $400**

HOP-207

❑ **HOP-207. Picture Card Gum Box,**
1950s. Store item by Topps Chewing Gum. Held individual packs of six cards. - **$175 $350 $700**

HOP-208

HOP-209

❑ **HOP-208. Portrait Photo,**
1950s. Various sponsors. - **$15 $30 $60**

❑ **HOP-209. Restaurant Ad Postcard,**
1950s. Sherman Skipalong Club, Hotel Sherman, Chicago. Also pictures manager "Skipalong Tattler". - **$25 $40 $75**

HOP-210

HOP-211

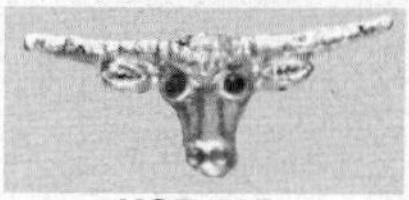

HOP-212

❑ **HOP-210. Quart Milk Carton,**
1950s. Various sponsors. - **$40 $75 $150**

❑ **HOP-211. Western Series Glass,**
1950s. Probably held food product. At least four in the set. - **$25 $50 $100**

❑ **HOP-212. "Hopalong Cassidy" Silvered Metal Kerchief Slide,**
1950s. Steer head has rhinestone eyes, his name is across the horns. See HOP-74. - **$15 $30 $60**

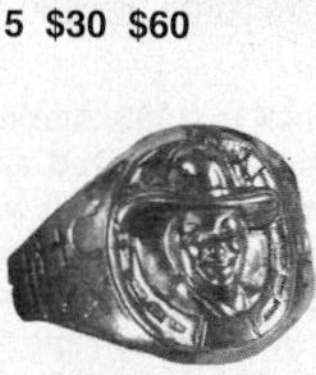

HOP-213

HOP-214

❑ **HOP-213. Sterling Silver Ring,**
1950s. Portrait framed by horseshoe, non-adjustable band. - **$90 $175 $350**

❑ **HOP-214. "Hopalong Cassidy Bar 20 Ranch" 2" Silvered Metal Badge,**
1950s. English made store item with "Sheriff" under inset b&w photo. - **$35 $60 $90**

HOP-215

❑ **HOP-215. Milk Promo Sign,**
1950s. Die Cut Bust sign was used to promote milk products. - **$85 $175 $350**

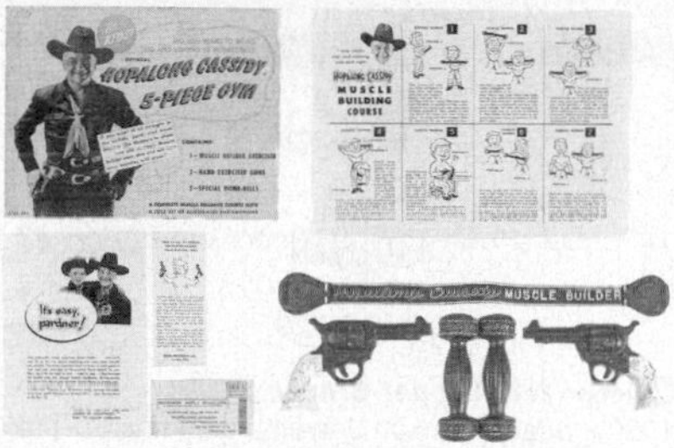

HOP-216

❑ **HOP-216. "Official Hopalong Cassidy 5-Piece Gym" Complete In Original Box,**
1950s. Dyer Products Co., Canton, Ohio. Box is 9.5x12.25x2" deep. Facsimile signature to right of Hoppy image reads "Good Luck From Hoppy" Wm. Boyd. Includes 1x20" long rubber belt with horseshoe-style ends, 1.75" diameter by 6" long rubber dumbbell, two 7.5" rubber pistols, 2.5x7" "Muscle Building Course," instructions and 2.75x5" business reply envelope. - **$550 $1100 $1750**

HOP-217

❑ **HOP-217. "Hoppy's Favorite/Royal Crest All Star Dairy Products" Store Display Clock,**
1950s. Clock is 15" diameter by 4" deep. Has image of Hoppy in star and "Wm. Boyd" on inner domed clock face. Sticker on back reads "The Sign Of Quality AP/Advertising Products Cincinnati Ohio." - **$650 $1750 $3000**

HOP-218

❑ **HOP-218. The Official Hopalong Cassidy Western Series Metal Figures Boxed,**
1950s. Timpo Toys - England. 1.5x3.5x15" long box holds seven 2.5" tall painted metal figures. Set includes Hoppy, Lucky, California, Sheriff, cowboy and two bandits.
Boxed Set - **$600 $1200 $1850**

HOP-219

HOP-220

❑ **HOP-219. Hopalong Cassidy Milk Glass Variety,**
1950s. Blue design on white. Rare. - **$100 $200 $350**

❑ **HOP-220. Hopalong Cassidy Plastic Tumbler,**
1950s. Black image on yellow plastic. Scarce. - **$50 $100 $200**

HOP-221

HOP-222

❑ **HOP-221. Hopalong Cassidy Jelly Jar Glass,**
1950s. Black design on clear glass. Rare. - **$100 $225 $375**

❑ **HOP-222. Hopalong Cassidy Lasso Glass,**
1950s. Black design on white with red text. - **$75 $150 $300**

HOP-223 HOP-224

❑ **HOP-223. Hopalong Cassidy Endorsed Product Glass,**
1950s. Black design on clear glass. Fluted base. Scarce. - **$75 $150 $300**

❑ **HOP-224. Hopalong Cassidy and Topper Glass,**
1950s. Red image on clear glass. Scarce. - **$75 $150 $300**

HOP-225

❑ **HOP-225. "Hoppy's Favorite" Endorsed Product Glass,**
1950s. Red design on clear glass. Ribbed base. Rare. - **$125 $250 $400**

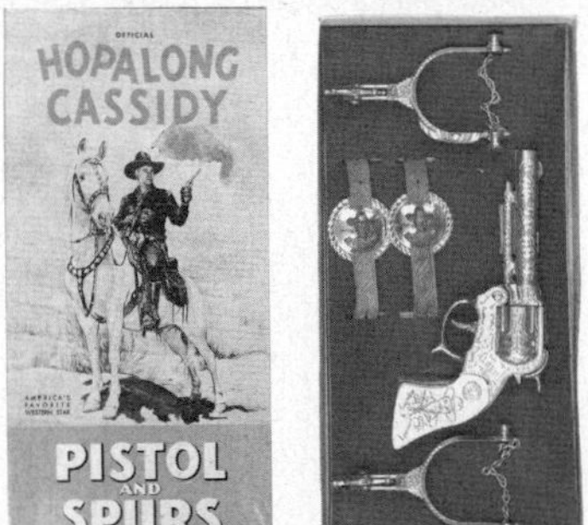

HOP-226

❑ **HOP-226. "Hopalong Cassidy Pistol And Spurs" Boxed Set,**
1950s. Wyandotte. 7.25x15x2" deep box contains 8.5" cast metal cap gun with plastic grips that have incised image of Hoppy along with his name. "Hopalong" also appears in raised lettering on gun along with ornate design. Spurs are die cast metal with chains and separate leather straps each with tooled design and 2" diameter die-cast metal concho with relief image of Hoppy. Boxed Set - **$300 $600 $1200**

HOP-227

❑ **HOP-227. Newspaper Ad Proof with Western Badge Offer,**
1950s. From the Gordon Gold Archives. - **$20 $40 $75**

HOP-228

HOP-229

❑ **HOP-228. Topper Bracelet,**
1950s. Scarce. Anson Jewelry, gold finish. - **$30 $60 $150**

❑ **HOP-229. Bar 20 Bracelet,**
1950s. Rare. Anson Jewelry, gold finish. - **$40 $80 $190**

HOP-230

❑ **HOP-230. "People and Places" Magazine,**
1950s. Scarce. Car premium. - **$30 $60 $125**

HOP-231

❑ **HOP-231. Poster,**
1980s. Promotes tapes of old films. - **$10 $20 $30**

HOP-232

❑ **HOP-232. Bar 20 Ranch Badge,**
1995. Store item, sold as party badges in blister-packs. Badge comes in gold and silver chrome on plastic. Gold - **$4 $8 $15**
Silver - **$5 $10 $20**

Howdy Doody

It aired on NBC-TV from 1947 to 1960, starting out as *The Puppet Playhouse*, created and hosted by Buffalo Bob Smith (1917-1998). It was one of television's all-time successes, winner of the first Peabody award, attracting millions of devoted young viewers and responsible for millions of dollars in licensed merchandise. It was *Howdy Doody Time*, a combination of fantasy, music, films, and slapstick played out by puppets and humans in front of a screaming studio audience of 40 kids for more than 2,300 performances. Puppeteer Frank Parris was the designer of the first Howdy puppet used on the show. Eddie Kean wrote and co-produced over 2,000 scripts and wrote over 100 songs including *It's Howdy Doody Time*. Former Disney animator Milt Neil designed many of the toys.

Howdy, with voice supplied by Buffalo Bob, consorted with a long list of characters, including Clarabell the clown (played originally by Bob Keeshan); Mr. Bluster, the mayor of Doodyville; Flub-A-Dub, a fantastic animal crossbreed; Dilly-Dally, a big-eared carpenter; Indian Princess Summerfall-Winterspring; and many others. The original Howdy puppet was replaced with a new design in 1948.

Among the program's many sponsors: Wonder Bread, Colgate tooth powder, Ovaltine, Poll-Parrot shoes, Mars candy, Tootsie Rolls, Welch's grape juice, Marx and Ideal toys, Kellogg's and Nabisco cereals, and Royal pudding. Character licensees were barely able to meet the huge demand for toys, dolls, lunch boxes, clothes, marionettes, wristwatches, mugs, piggy banks, figurines, records, T-shirts, even a musical rocking chair. Items were copyrighted Bob Smith (1948-1951), Kagran Corp. (1951-1959), or NBC (1960 on).

A Sunday *Howdy Doody* comic strip drawn by Chad Grothkopf appeared from 1950 to 1953, and Dell published comic books from 1950 to 1957. A radio version of the show aired on NBC from 1952 to 1958, and the TV series was revived briefly on NBC in 1976, but, sadly, it was no longer *Howdy Doody Time.*

HOW-1

❑ HOW-1. Photo Doody,
Late 1940s. First advertising piece to sell for more than $100,000. This marionette was the third Howdy Doody to be created, and was used strictly for promotional purposes, It is virtually identical to the Howdy Doody we remember except for the lack of strings (to allow for easier use in photo shoots). Sold at Leland's 1997 auction for **$113,431**

HOW-2

HOW-3

❑ HOW-2. "I'm For Howdy Doody" Cello. Button,
1948. First item and premium offered March 23, 1948 as part of Howdy Doody for President campaign. Five stations carried the show and the offer was made seven times. NBC was astonished by 60,000 requests. Colgate, Continental Baking, Ovaltine and Mars candy quickly signed as sponsors. - **$45 $90 $185**

❑ HOW-3. "The Billboard" Magazine With Cover Photo,
November 27, 1948. Early item from second year of Howdy show. - **$35 $60 $125**

HOW-4

❑ HOW-4."Hobby Reporter-Yankee Enterprise" Booklet With Review Article,
1949. 6x9" issue for July-August. -
$50 $100 $200

HOW-5

❑ HOW-5. Howdy Doody Newspaper #1,
1950. Poll-Parrot. Rare. - **$100 $200 $450**

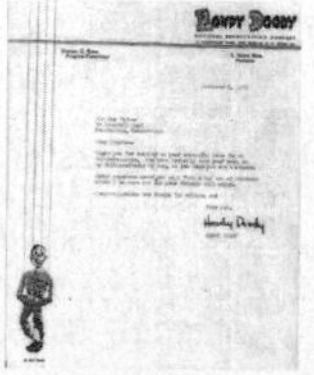

HOW-6

HOW-7

❑ HOW-6. Thank-You Letter,
1950. Rare. Recipient awarded box of Snickers for poem selected from a contest. -
$90 $165 $325

❑ HOW-7. Poll-Parrot Coloring Book,
c. 1950. - **$45 $100 $225**

HOW-8

HOW-9

HOW-10

❑ HOW-8. Wood Jointed Doll,
c. 1950. Store item. Includes leather belt and fabric bandanna. - **$175 $400 $750**

❑ HOW-9. Ovaltine Plastic Mug With Decal,
c. 1950. - **$20 $50 $100**

❑ HOW-10. Ovaltine Plastic Shake-Up Mug,
c. 1950. - **$35 $75 $160**

HOW-11

❑ HOW-11. "It's Howdy Doody Time" Button,
c. 1950. 1-3/8" white on red litho copyright "Bob Smith" between 1948-1951 when items carried his copyright. - **$45 $100 $190**

HOW-12

HOW-13

❑ HOW-12. Cardboard Store Sign,
c. 1950. Colgate Dental Cream.
Large (About 24") Size - **$300 $600 $1200**
Small (About 6") Size - **$35 $75 $150**

❑ HOW-13. "Magic Trading Card" 14x21" Proof Sheet,
1951. Issued individually in boxes of Burry's Howdy Doody Cookies. Backs read "Howdy Doody Frozen Treats."
Uncut - **$150 $375 $750**
Each Card - **$10 $20 $30**

HOW-14

❑ **HOW-14. "Santa Visits Howdy Doody's House" Coloring Booklet,**
1951. 16 pages. Usually has store imprint. - **$35 $65 $150**

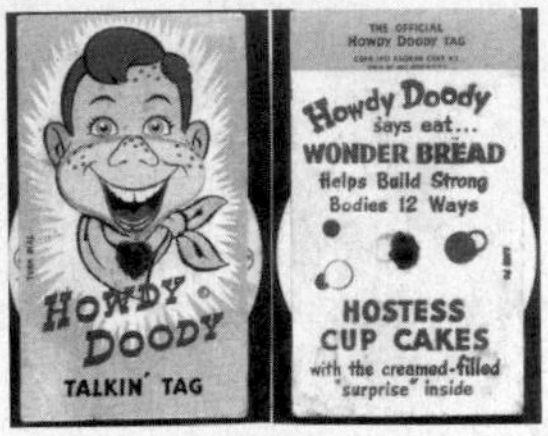

HOW-15

HOW-16

❑ **HOW-15. "Howdy Doody Talkin' Tag",**
1951. Wonder Bread/Hostess Cupcakes. Disk turns to form four mouth expressions. - **$35 $70 $125**

❑ **HOW-16. "Poll Parrot's" Comic Book #4,**
1951. Issues #2-#4. Each - **$15 $45 $185**

HOW-17

❑ **HOW-17. "Howdy Doody Marionette,"**
c. 1951. Peter Puppet Playthings Inc. 3x5.5x16" box marked "Bob Smith/Designed by Raye Copeland/Manufactured by Peter Puppet Playthings Inc. Made In U.S.A." 16" tall wood/composition/cloth figure of Howdy, with movable mouth. Box - **$75 $150 $300**
Marionette - **$65 $135 $275**

HOW-18

❑ **HOW-18. Howdy Doody's Sister Heidi Doody Marionette,**
c. 1951. Marionette is 14" tall with painted composition head, hands and legs. Plastic eyes and yarn hair and cloth outfit. Name printed on front of dress in cross stitch type pattern.
- $300 $600 $1200

HOW-19

❑ **HOW-19. Howdy & Friends "Crayon Set" Boxed,**
c. 1951. Milton Bradley. Set of 16 different colored crayons, full color paper sheet picturing three characters, additional black and white three-panel fold-out sheet picturing various characters. - **$115 $225 $450**

HOW-20

❑ **HOW-20. "Doody Bubble Bath" Canister With Contents,**
c. 1951. Shamprel Co. 6" tall cardboard cylinder with full color paper label picturing Howdy and four other major characters. - **$60 $125 $175**

HOW-21

❑ **HOW-21. "Howdy Doody And His Friends Bubble Pipe" Display,**
c. 1951. Lido Toy Co. 10.25x16.5" display card holding original 12 hard plastic figural soap bubble pipes, each about 4.25" long in single solid color. Near Mint Complete - **$850**

HOW-22

❑ **HOW-22. Store Clerk Paper Cap,**
c. 1951. Wonder Bread. - **$25 $55 $100**

HOW-23

❑ **HOW-23. "Circus Album" 5-1/2x8" Ad Sheet,**
c. 1951. Wonder Bread. - **$50 $100 $185**

HOW-24

HOW-25

❑ **HOW-24. "American History" Bread Label Album,**
c. 1951. Wonder Bread. Holds 19 label cut-outs depicting Howdy Doody characters in historial situations such as "Landing Of The Pilgrims."
Album Only - **$20 $40 $80**
Each Uncut Label - **$15 $25 $50**
Each Cut Label - **$5 $10 $20**

❑ **HOW-25. Puppet Show Punch-out Book,**
1952. Book is 14 3/4" tall. Includes heavy cardboard punch-outs of Howdy, Clarabell, Mr. Bluster, Flub a Dub, Dilly Dally and the Inspector. - **$85 $175 $375**

HOW-26

❑ **HOW-26. T.V.-Merrimat Paper Place Mat,**
1952. Store item. Placematters, Inc. - **$30 $60 $110**

HOW-27

❑ **HOW-27. Rice Krispies Cereal Box,**
1952. 9 1/2 oz box. Crossover promotion for Wild Bill Hickok Show. Side panel has ad for Snap, Crackle, and Pop face rings premiums. - **$200 $400 $800**

HOW-28

(Side of box)

❑ **HOW-28. Fifth Avenue Candy Box,**
1952. Rare. - **$200 $325 $550**

HOW-29

HOW-30

❑ **HOW-29. T.V.-Merrimat Plastic Place Mat,**
1952. Store item. Placematters, Inc. - **$35 $75 $150**

❑ **HOW-30. "Howdy Doody For President" Cello. Button,**
1952. Wonder Bread. - **$45 $95 $190**

HOW-31

❑ **HOW-31. "It's Howdy Doody Time" Record Album,**
1952. RCA Victor. 10x10" sleeve with full color art holding record featuring Howdy and Bob Smith. - **$25 $50 $100**

(BOTTOM OF BOTTLE)

HOW-32

HOW-33

❑ **HOW-32. Welch's Grape Juice Glass Bottle,**
1952. Various character portraits embossed on bottom. Each - **$15 $30 $60**

❑ **HOW-33. Welch's Grape Juice Tin Cap From Bottle,**
1952. - **$8 $15 $30**

HOW-34

HOW-35

❑ **HOW-34. Welch's Cookbook,**
1952. Welch's Grape Juice. - **$25 $60 $100**

❑ **HOW-35. "Campaign Cap",**
c. 1952. Poll-Parrot Shoes. Paper punch-out assembled by slots and tabs.
Unpunched - **$45 $90 $215**
Assembled - **$35 $75 $150**

HOW-36

❑ **HOW-36. Sipping Straws Box And Premium Card,**
c. 1952. Colonial Paper Products. Cards are 2x2-3/4" from a set of 42 different picturing the image in color on the front while reverse has same image in black and white to be colored. Box offers both Howdy Doody Straw Holder as well as card set as mail-in premiums.
Box With Contents - **$45 $90 $200**
Each Of 42 Cards - **$12 $18 $35**

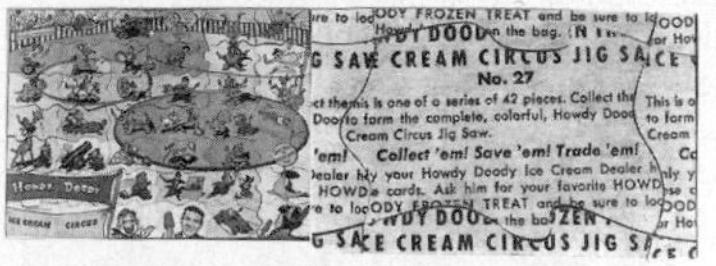

HOW-37

❑ **HOW-37. "Howdy Doody Ice Cream Circus" Puzzle,**
c. 1952. Howdy Doody Frozen Treat products. 10-1/2x14" jigsaw puzzle comprised of 42 numbered pieces obtained individually by product purchase. Complete - **$150 $300 $600**

HOW-38

❑ HOW-38. "Cut-Out Masks" Store Sign,
c. 1953. Issued by Kellogg's. 14-1/2x20-1/2". -
$125 $225 $450

HOW-39 HOW-40

❑ HOW-39. Kellogg's "Free Cut-Out Masks" 15x20" Paper Store Sign,
1953. Corn Flakes and Rice Krispies. Offers masks on box rear panels. - **$45 $90 $175**

❑ HOW-40. Kellogg's Howdy Doody Oversized Sample Mask,
1953. Diecut 12x15" paper promotion for masks offered on back panels of Corn Flakes and Rice Krispies boxes.
Howdy Doody - **$115 $175 $300**
Pirate, Witch Or Devil - **$35 $60 $90**

HOW-41

❑ HOW-41. Kellogg's "Free Cut-Out Masks" 15x20" Paper Store Sign,
1953. Corn Flakes and Rice Krispies. Advertises pirate mask from series on box back panels.
Howdy Doody - **$115 $190 $350**
Pirate, Witch Or Devil - **$35 $60 $90**

HOW-42

❑ HOW-42. Kellogg's Rice Krispies Flat,
1953. Box (9 1/2 oz.) features Howdy on front and large mask of Howdy on back. -
$400 $800 $1600

HOW-43

❑ HOW-43. Kellogg's Rice Krispies Flat,
1953. Canadian issued. Offers free masks on back (the Princess pictured). - **$150 $300 $700**

HOW-44

❑ HOW-44. Kellogg's Rice Krispies Box Panel Masks,
1953. One of a set: Howdy, Clarabell, Dilly Dally, The Princess.
Each Uncut Box Back - **$15 $30 $60**

HOW-45

❑ HOW-45. Welch's Grape Juice 3" Tin Lid From Glass Jelly Jar,
1953. - **$10 $20 $30**

HOW-46

❑ HOW-46. Welch's Grape Jelly Glasses,
1953. Six designs, various colors, character faces on bottom. Each - **$8 $15 $25**

HOW-47

❑ HOW-47. "Doodyville" Cardboard Houses,
1953. Welch's Grape Juice. Set of eight.
Each Unused - **$30 $60 $125**
Each Assembled - **$15 $35 $75**

HOW-48 HOW-49

❑ HOW-48. "Coloring Comics" Sheet #1,
1953. Blue Bonnet Margarine. From numbered series of box inserts. Each - **$10 $18 $35**

❑ HOW-49. "Snap-A-Wink" Target,
1953. Poll-Parrot Shoes. - **$45 $85 $150**

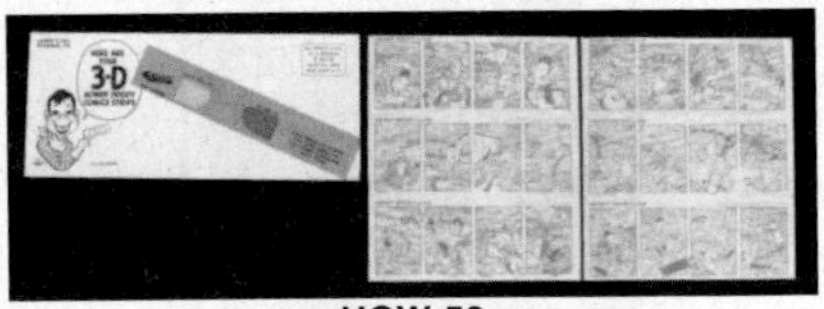

HOW-50

❑ HOW-50. Luden's Cough Drops 3-D Comics,
1953. With Mailer. - **$125 $250 $500**

HOW-51

❑ HOW-51. "It's Howdy Doody Time" Boxed Princess Summerfallwinterspring Doll,
c. 1953. Box is 2.25x5x9.5" and holds 7.5" tall plastic Indian princess doll by Virga. Sleep eyes. Complete with tag. Box - **$50 $100 $165**
Doll - **$50 $100 $165**

HOW-52

❑ HOW-52. "Howdy Doody Television Show" Cardboard Standee,
c. 1953. Standee is 12.5x19.5" die-cut. Howdy holds 4.5x7" sign reading "Howdy Doody NBC-TV Saturday Morning." - **$850 $1750 $2500**

HOW-53

❑ HOW-53. "Comic Circus Animals" Picture Toy,
1954. Poll-Parrot Shoes. - **$45 $90 $175**

HOW-54

❑ HOW-54. Cast and Staff Photo,
1954. Photo was taken in the famous "Peanut Gallery" for Christmas 1954. This 13.5" x 10.5" photo was displayed in Buffalo Bob's North Carolina family room until his death. - **$550**

HOW-55

❑ HOW-55. "Big Prize Doodle List" Sheet,
1954. Howdy Doody Ice Cream Club. Premium listing for 1954-1955. - **$15 $25 $50**

HOW-56

HOW-57

❑ HOW-56. Wrist Watch with Die-Cut Display Box,
1954. Display box had a mylar-like clear top which is usually damaged or missing. Instructions are included.
Near Mint Boxed - **$1750**
Box Only - **$300 $600 $1250**
Watch Only - **$125 $250 $500**

❑ HOW-57. TV Guide,
1954. Weekly issue for June 25 with cover photo and related article. - **$50 $110 $225**

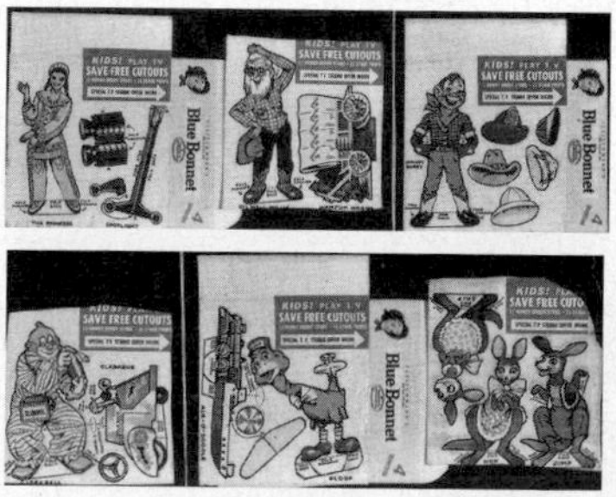

HOW-58

❑ HOW-58. Blue Bonnet Margarine Box Panels,
1954. Waxed cardboard set of 12 for "Play TV" stage offered separately as mail premium.
Each Uncut Panel - **$20 $35 $70**

HOW-59

❑ HOW-59. "Howdy Doody TV Studio" Punch-Out Premium,
1954. Blue Bonnet Margarine. Mailer holds 8-1/2x11" four-page instructions and six stiff paper 11x18" punch-out sheets to set up TV studio with Peanut Gallery and broadcasting accessories. Characters were depicted on product box panels as a set of 12 cut-outs. -
$250 $500 $1000

HOW-60

❑ HOW-60. Howdy Doody Characters Play Money/Coupon,
1954. Ogilvie Flour Mills Co., Canada. Play money in at least eight denominations and picturing at least eight characters. When one million dollars was collected, a BSA bicycle was awarded. Each - **$5 $10 $20**

HOW-61

❑ HOW-61. Merchandise Manual,
1954. Rare. - **$150 $375 $775**
1955. Rare. Has been reproduced.
- **$125 $325 $675**

HOW-62

HOW-63

❑ **HOW-62. Kellogg's Rice Krispies Box,**
1955. Features free Dangle-Dandies as a premium. - **$175 $350 $650**

❑ **HOW-63. Plastic Puppets on Card,**
1955. Figures have movable mouths which you can use by pressing lever on back.
Set with Card - **$100 $200 $300**

HOW-64

HOW-65

❑ **HOW-64. Ice Cream Cup Lid,**
1955. Doughnut Corp. of America. Lid and 25 cents used to order "Howdy Doody Magic Talking Pin." - **$20 $40 $75**

❑ **HOW-65. Jumble Joy Book,**
1955. Scarce. Poll Parrot shoe premium. 16 pages in color. - **$50 $110 $175**

HOW-66

❑ **HOW-66. "Howdy Doody" And Clarabell Line Mar Wind-Up Toy,**
c. 1955. This 1950s toy is not to be confused with larger Howdy Doody piano toy by Unique Art that features Buffalo Bob Smith playing the piano. On this toy Clarabell sits at the piano and Howdy stands next to him. Toy is 4x5x5.75" tall tin litho. Front of piano has large lettering "Howdy Doody." Full figure Clarabell is seated and 4.25" tall Howdy. - **$750 $1600 $2500**

HOW-67

❑ **HOW-67. Tin Litho. Trapeze Toy,**
c. 1955. Store item made by Arnold of West Germany, imported by Novelty Toy Associates. 4x9x16" tall frame holding 9-1/2" tall figure of Howdy with composition head and cloth clothes. When vertical rod is pushed down, figure spins on horizontal bar. - **$175 $375 $650**

HOW-68

HOW-69

❑ **HOW-68. "Clarabell Dangle-Dandy" Box Back,**
c. 1955. Kellogg's. One of a series.
Uncut Each - **$25 $55 $100**
Assembled Each - **$15 $30 $75**

❑ **HOW-69. "Twin-Pop" 7x14" Paper Store Sign,**
1956. - **$40 $90 $165**

HOW-70

HOW-71

HOW-72

❑ **HOW-70. Litho. Tab,**
c. 1956. Ten tabs were collected for free "Twin Pop Or Fudge Bar". - **$20 $50 $100**

❑ **HOW-71. Ice Cream Waxed Cardboard Cup,**
c. 1956. - **$20 $35 $75**

❑ **HOW-72. Packaged Wood Ice Cream Spoon,**
c. 1956. - **$10 $20 $30**

HOW-73

❑ **HOW-73. "Fudge Bar" Waxed Paper Bag,**
c. 1956. Offers talking pin and ice cream club membership. - **$10 $20 $30**

HOW-74

❑ **HOW-74. "Fudge Bar" Store Sign,**
c. 1956. Doughnut Corp. of America. 9x12" glossy paper with text "Save All Howdy Doody Bags For Swell Prizes." - **$60 $140 $275**

HOW-75

❑ **HOW-75. "Howdy Doody Smile Ballot",**
1957. 4x6" ballot to select best smile from among 10 competitors. - **$30 $50 $75**

HOW-76 HOW-77

❑ **HOW-76. "Jackpot Of Fun" Comic Book,**
1957. DCA Food Industries. - **$20 $40 $90**

❑ **HOW-77. Ceramic Piggy Bank,**
1950s. Store item. - **$135 $275 $600**

HOW-78

❑ **HOW-78. TV Set Instructions,**
1950s. Rare. Colgate premium. - **$45 $90 $150**

HOW-79

❑ **HOW-79. Four-Sided Mask,**
1950s. Philco TV. Scarce. Clarabell, Howdy, Gabby and Tom Corbett featured. -
$50 $125 $250

HOW-80

❑ **HOW-80. Clarabelle Marionette,**
1950s. Marionette has a cardboard simulated squeak box. Note: End panel of the box specifies the particular character.
Marionette - **$100 $250 $400**
Box - **$100 $200 $350**

HOW-81

❑ **HOW-81. Dilly Dally Marionette,**
1950s. Peter Puppet Playthings Inc. 5.5x14x13.5" deep box contains 14.5" tall marionette with attached cardboard hand control. Marionette has painted composition head, hands and feet. Body is wood covered by fabric outfit. Complete with separate plastic glasses attached to head by staples. Marionette - **$125 $275 $550**
Box - **$100 $200 $350**

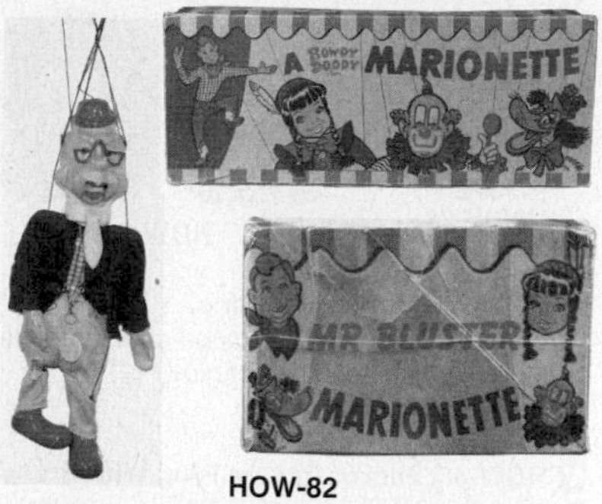

HOW-82

❑ **HOW-82. Mr. Bluster Marionette,**
1950s. Marionette has plastic glasses and a plastic pocket watch. Note: End panel of the box specifies the particular character.
Marionette - **$125 $275 $550**
Box - **$100 $200 $350**

HOW-83

❑ **HOW-83. SummerFall-WinterSpring Marionette,**
1950s. Marionette has necklace of chain links and seasonal symbols on plastic disks. Note: End panel of the box specifies the particular character. Marionette - **$125 $275 $550**
Box - **$100 $200 $350**

HOW-84

❑ **HOW-84. Flub-A-Dub Marionette,**
1950s. Scarce. Marionette - **$150 $300 $600**
Box - **$200 $350 $450**

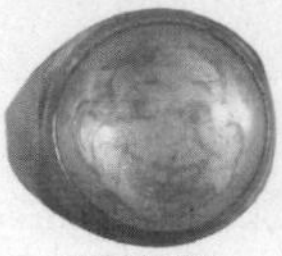

HOW-85

HOW-86

❑ **HOW-85. Photo Glow Ring,**
1950s. Ring name implies image glows in dark but all examples seen do not glow. -
$65 $125 $250

❑ **HOW-86. Flicker Picture Ring With Brass Base,**
1950s. Portrait of Howdy alternates with image of Poll Parrot on a perch. - **$50 $75 $145**

HOW-87

❑ **HOW-87. Official Ice Cream Club "Fun And Prizes" Premium Catalogue,**
1950s. Catalogue directs points and money to Premium Associates Inc ., N.Y.C. 4x5" booklet includes club song and pictures eight premiums. -
$45 $90 $165

HOW-88

❑ **HOW-88. Dilly Dally Pennant,**
1950s. Felt pennant measures 4" long.
- **$8 $15 $30**

HOW-89

❑ **HOW-89. Large Glazed Ceramic Bust Bank,**
1950s. Store item. - **$150 $250 $500**

HOW-90

❑ **HOW-90. "Howdy Doody Climber" Store Poster,**
1950s. Welch's Frozen Grape Juice. 11x14" offering toy for 10 cents plus can top. Gordon Gold archives. - **$135 $275 $500**

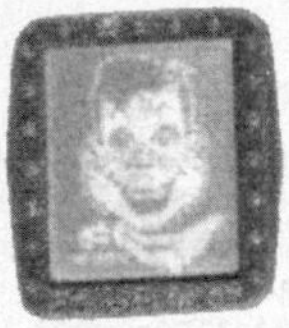

HOW-91

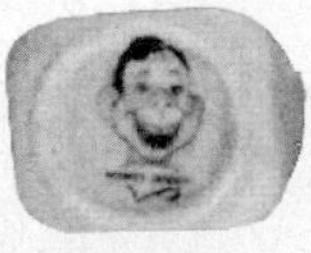

HOW-92

HOW-93

❑ **HOW-91. Poll-Parrot TV Plastic Ring With Flicker Picture,**
1950s. Frame image of TV screen, image alternates between Howdy and parrot. -
$50 $100 $150

❑ **HOW-92. Plastic Ring With Paper Insert Picture,**
1950s. - **$60 $125 $200**

❑ **HOW-93. "Poll-Parrot" Plastic Ring,**
1950s. Raised portrait. - **$15 $25 $50**

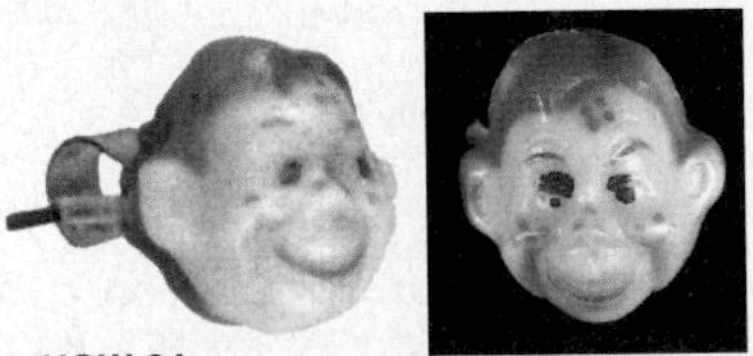

HOW-94 **(2 views of the ring)**

❑ **HOW-94. Illuminated Head Ring,**
1950s. Palmolive Soap. Brass bands holding plastic head lighted by bulb and battery. -
$100 $200 $400

HOW-95

HOW-96

❑ **HOW-95. Clarabell Face/Hat Ring,**
1950s. Rare. Less than five known. Original paint on face is very unstable and chips easily. Only one known in NM. - **$750 $1500 $3300**

❑ **HOW-96. Clarabell's Horn Ring,**
1950s. Scarce. Brass bands picture Clarabell and Howdy, top has aluminum horn that works by blowing. - **$115 $225 $450**

HOW-97

❑ **HOW-97. Sailor Style Hat,**
1950s. Store item. - **$15 $30 $65**

HOW-98

❑ **HOW-98. "Poll-Parrot's Howdy Doody Photo Album",**
1950s. Includes four blank pages to mount four photos. Complete - **$85 $175 $300**

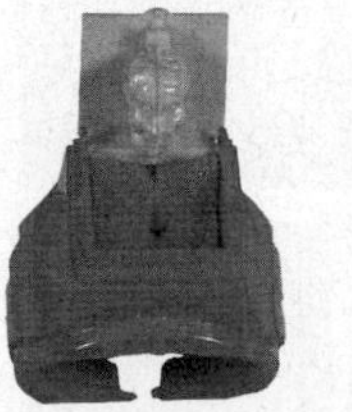

HOW-99

HOW-100

❑ **HOW-99. Jack-In-The-Box Plastic Ring,**
1950s. Poll-Parrot Shoes. Lid lifts, revealing miniature 3-D plastic Howdy head. Ring exists in two varieties, red ring base with yellow top and yellow ring base with red top.
- **$150 $250 $500**

❑ **HOW-100. "Sunday Post-Dispatch" Litho. Button,**
1950s. Issued for newspaper comic strip. -
$60 $135 $200

HOW-101

HOW-102

HOW-103

❑ **HOW-101. Newspaper Comic Strip Litho. Button,**
1950s. - **$50 $100 $200**

❑ **HOW-102. "Howdy Doody Safety Club/CBC" Cello. Button,**
1950s. Canadian Broadcasting Company Canadian issue by Toronto maker. - **$35 $75 $125**

❑ **HOW-103. Jointed Cardboard Puppet,**
1950s. Wonder Bread. 13" tall. - **$20 $50 $100**

HOW-104

❑ **HOW-104. Tuk-A-Tab Mask,**
1950s. Poll-Parrot. Masks of Howdy and Clarabell.
Each Unpunched - **$25 $50 $100**

HOW-105 HOW-106

❑ **HOW-105. Jointed Cardboard Puppet,**
1950s. Wonder Bread. 7-1/2" tall. - **$20 $50 $100**

❑ **HOW-106. Princess Cardboard Jointed Puppet,**
1950s. Wonder Bread. 7-1/2" tall. - **$20 $50 $100**

HOW-107

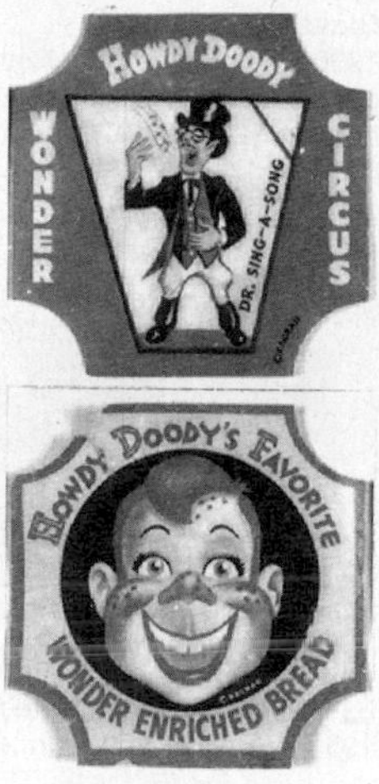

HOW-108

❑ **HOW-107. Howdy Doody Periscope,**
1950s. Rare. Wonder Bread. - **$300 $675 $1200**

❑ **HOW-108. Bread Labels,**
1950s. Wonder Bread. From two different sets.
Each - **$12 $20 $35**

HOW-109

❑ **HOW-109. "Wonder-Land Game" Sheet,**
1950s. Wonder Bread. With spinner and 16 spaces for cut-outs from bread end labels.
Unused - **$40 $85 $175**
Complete - **$150 $300 $550**

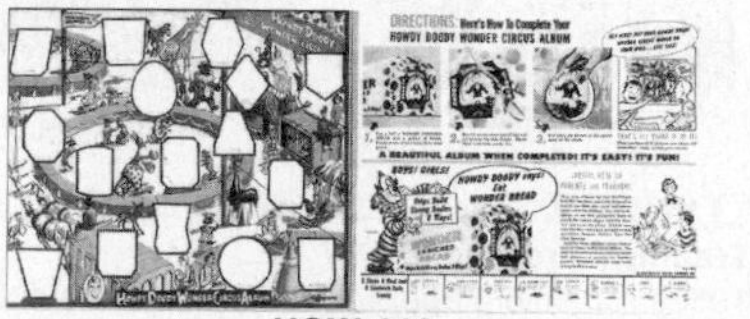

HOW-110

❑ **HOW-110. "Wonder Bread Circus Album" Label Sheet,**
1950s. Unused - **$40 $85 $175**
Complete - **$150 $300 $550**

HOW-111

❑ **HOW-111. "Wonder Bread Balloon Parade" Label Sheet,**
1950s. Unused - **$40 $85 $175**
Complete - **$150 $300 $550**

HOW-112

❑ **HOW-112. Christmas Cards,**
1950s. Mars Candy. Set of 8 with 8 blank envelopes. Each - **$10 $15 $30**

HOW-113

HOW-114

❑ **HOW-113. "Howdy Doody's Favorite Doughnuts" Cellophane Package,**
1950s. Tom Thumb. - **$30 $60 $125**

❑ **HOW-114. "Wonder Bread Zoomascope",**
1950s. Opens to 3-1/2x51". - **$60 $125 $250**

HOW-115

HOW-116

❑ **HOW-115. Cardboard Disk Flipper Badge,**
1950s. Wonder Bread. Disk flips by pulling string to complete phrase "The Princess Says...Eat Wonder Bread". From set picturing various Howdy Doody characters.
Each - **$10 $20 $40**

❑ **HOW-116. "Hostess" Cupcake Package Tag,**
1950s. Continental Baking Co. - **$50 $75 $135**

HOW-117

HOW-118

❑ **HOW-117. "Mason Candy Words To The 'Howdy Doody' Song" Sheet,**
1950s. - **$20 $40 $75**

❑ **HOW-118. "Howdy Doody Animated Puppet" Punch-Out With Envelope,**
1950s. Three Musketeers/Mars candy bars.
Near Mint In Mailer - **$215**

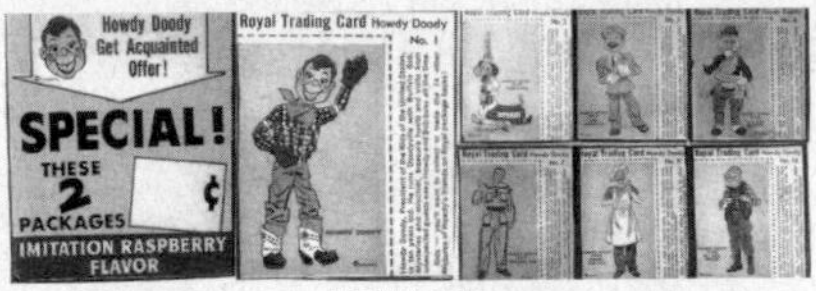

HOW-119

❑ **HOW-119. "Royal Trading Card",**
1950s. Royal Pudding. Set of 16. Text on each card refers to "14 other pictures" but a sixteenth card designated on the card as "No. 16" exists. It pictures "Captain Scuttlebutt."
Each Complete Box - **$20 $45 $90**
Each Cut Card - **$10 $15 $35**

HOW-120

HOW-121

❑ **HOW-120. "Clarabell Animated Puppet" Punch-Out With Envelope,**
1950s. Mars Coconut Bar.
Near Mint In Mailer - **$215**

❑ **HOW-121. "E-Z DO Junior Space Saver" 2-1/4" Tin Tab,**
1950s. - **$35 $85 $175**

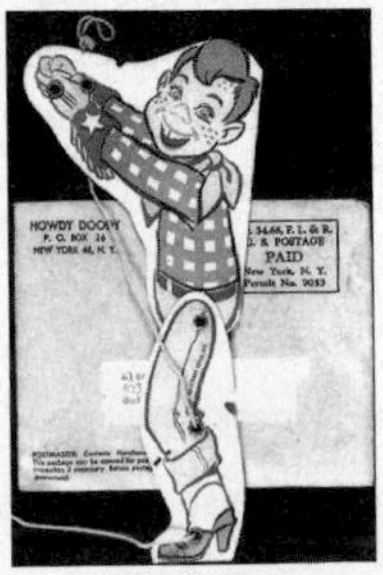
HOW-122

HOW-123

❑ **HOW-122. "Howdy Doody Climber" Cardboard Figure,**
1950s. Luden's Wild Cherry Cough Drops, Welch's Grape Juice and probably others.
Near Mint In Mailer - **$100**
Loose - **$10 $30 $60**

❑ **HOW-123. Princess Face Mask With Glassine Envelope,**
1950s. Royal Desserts. Issued for additional characters. With Envelope - **$20 $65 $125**
Loose - **$20 $35 $75**

HOW-124

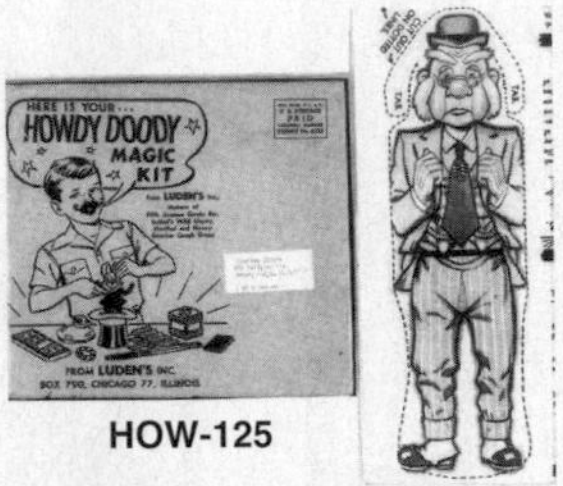

HOW-125

❑ **HOW-124. Silver Plate Spoon,**
1950s. Sponsor unknown. - **$10 $20 $40**

❑ **HOW-125. "Magic Kit" With Envelope,**
1950s. Luden's, makers of Fifth Avenue candy bar. Tricks on punch-out sheets.
Near Mint In Mailer - **$225**

HOW-126

❑ **HOW-126. Four-Sided Mask,**
1950s. Philco TV depicting Howdy, Gabby Hayes and National/American League baseball players to promote World Series on Philco TV. - **$75 $150 $300**

HOW-127

HOW-128

❑ **HOW-127. "Howdy Doody Napkins" Trading Card Sheet,**
1950s. Colonial Paper Products Co. At least two different sheets. Each Uncut - **$35 $75 $135**

❑ **HOW-128. "Princess Summerfall Winterspring" Photo,**
1950s. Pictures Judy Tyler. - **$30 $60 $120**

HOW-129

HOW-130

❑ **HOW-129. Hat,**
1950s. Store bought. - **$25 $50 $100**

❑ **HOW-130. Large Postcard,**
1950s. - **$40 $85 $150**

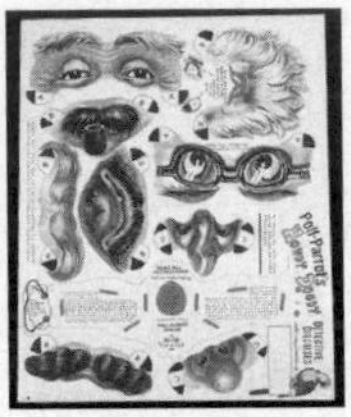
HOW-131

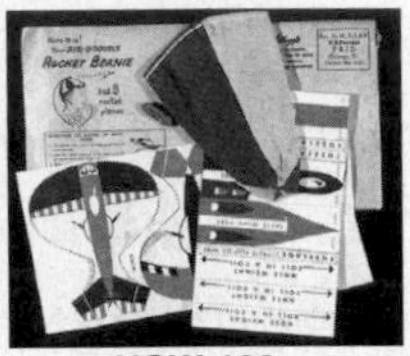
HOW-132

❑ **HOW-131. Detective Disguise Punch-Out Sheet,**
1950s. Poll-Parrot Shoes - **$40 $80 $150**

❑ **HOW-132. Air-O-Doodle Rocket Beanie with Mailer,**
1950s. Rare. Kellogg's Rice Krispies premium. - **$100 $200 $300**

HOW-133

HOW-134

❑ **HOW-133. "Frosty Snow Spray" Can With Howdy Doody,**
1950s. Has offer "20 Free Stencils With Purchase Of This Can." **- $15 $35 $60**

❑ **HOW-134. "Howdy Doody Cookie-Go-Round" Canister,**
1950s. Store item by Luse Mfg. Co. 7" diameter by 7-1/2" tall. **- $100 $200 $425**

HOW-135

❑ **HOW-135. Salt & Pepper Set With Box,**
1950s. Store item by Doodlings Inc. Each is 3" tall plastic. Box - **$35 $85 $175**
Set UnBoxed - **$35 $75 $150**

HOW-136

❑ **HOW-136."Clarabell Double Doody Bar" Sign,**
1950s. Issued by Doughnut Corp. of America. 8-1/2x22". - **$100 $200 $400**

HOW-137

❑ **HOW-137. Howdy Doody And Santa Claus Christmas Light,**
1950s. Store item by Royal Electric Co. 10-1/4x14" Vaccu-Form thin plastic. - **$100 $200 $400**

HOW-138

❑ **HOW-138. "Howdy Doody Puppet-Show" Stage With Puppets,**
1950s. Peter Puppet Playthings. Toy comes in original box designed to convert into 18" wide stage for six vinyl puppets, each about 10" tall. Puppets are Howdy, Flub-A-Dub, Clarabell, Princess, Mr. Bluster, Dilly Dally.
Stage - **$300 $600 $1200**
Each Puppet - **$35 $65 $115**

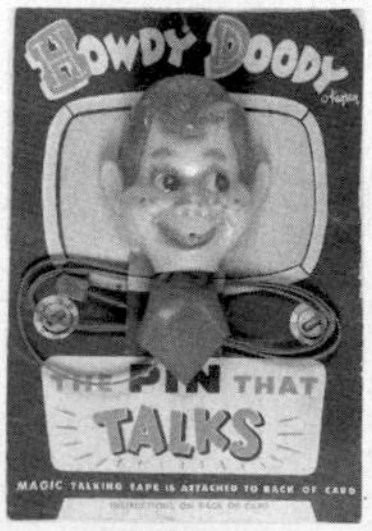

HOW-139

❑ **HOW-139. Howdy "Pin That Talks" On Card,**
1950s. 4x5.5" TV set replica display card holding 3-D plastic head except flat back with bar pin fastener. Toy speaks by "Magic Talking Tape" slotted through the card.
Near Mint Carded - **$400**
Pin And Talking Tape - **$50 $100 $200**

HOW-140

❑ **HOW-140. Promo Cereal Box,**
1960. Nabisco. Wheat Honeys box originally contained one of 8 rings.
Complete - **$225 $450 $750**

HOW-141

❑ **HOW-141. Set Of Eight Flicker Rings,**
1960. Nabisco. Color images on gray plastic bases issued one per box. Each - **$10 $20 $40**

HOW-142

HOW-143

❑ **HOW-142. "Revival Show" Local Cello. Button,**
1971. Towson State College. Single day issue for May 5 event. - **$10 $20 $40**

❑ **HOW-143. "Howdy Doody For President" Litho. Tin Tab,**
c. 1976. National Broadcasting Corp. - **$10 $20 $30**

HOW-144

HOW-145

❑ **HOW-144. Buffalo Bob Smith "Tootsieroll" Personal Appearance Costume Patch,**
1970s. From personal collection of Bob Smith. - **$10 $25 $50**

❑ **HOW-145. "A 40-Year Celebration" 3" Cello. Button,**
1987. National Broadcasting Co. - **$15 $30 $60**

HOW-146

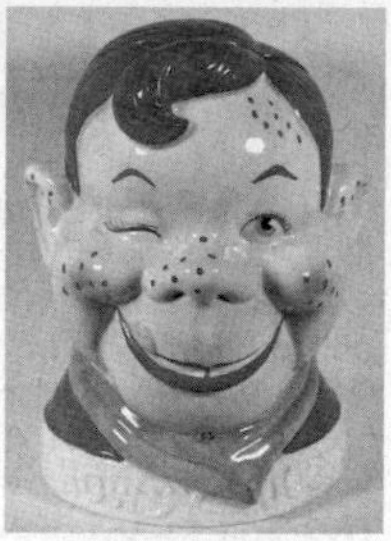

HOW-147

❑ **HOW-146. 40th Anniversary Watch With Box,**
1987. Store item with copyrights of NBC and King Features Syndicate.
Near Mint Boxed - **$125**
Watch Only - **$15 $30 $60**

❑ **HOW-147. Howdy Doody Cookie Jar,**
1980s. Made by Vandau. Produced in Japan. Very limited production. - **$650**

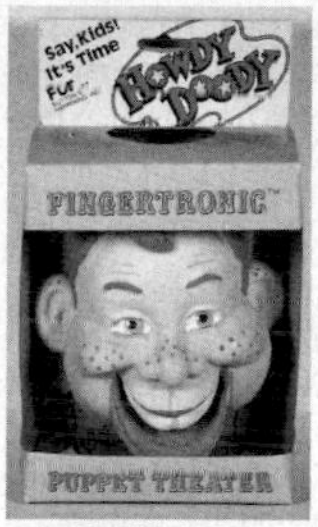

HOW-148

HOW-149

❑ **HOW-148. Howdy Doody Finger Puppet in Box,**
1980s. - **$20 $40 $80**

❑ **HOW-149. Christmas Ornaments,**
1998. Clarabell, Howdy and Buffalo Bob.
Set - **$65**

HOW-150

❑ **HOW-150. Lunch Box,**
2000. - **$40**

Howie Wing

Howie Wing, A Saga Of Aviation was a 15-minute children's serial sponsored by Kellogg's cereal. Written by WWI ace Captain Wilfred Gibbs Moore (co-author of *The Air Adventures of Jimmie Allen*), the show was broadcast from Chicago during its first season. The actor portraying Howie is unknown. This first season was a limited run, heard in the Western United States and Canada. Premiering in early 1938, *Howie Wing* was initially broadcast Monday through Thursday. By the time its second season rolled around in October 1938, the show had gone to 5 days per week, was picked up on CBS, moved from Chicago to New York, and was heard coast to coast in both the US and Canada. A little later, the show also aired in Australia, via transcription. Kellogg's was the sponsor of all broadcasts and issued premiums in each country.

The second season show, broadcast from New York over CBS, starred film actor William Janney as Howie. Movie actress Barbara Weeks shared the role of Howie's girlfriend, Donna Cavendish, with Mary Parker during the New York season. Audrey McGrath played Donna during the first (Chicago) season. Also affiliated with the show were some famous pilots: air mail pilot James (Jack) H. Knight was the "Commanding Officer" of Kellogg's *Howie Wing Cadet Aviation Corps* and offered greeting to young members in the North American club handbooks. In the Australian handbook, WWI aviator Robert McKenzie was the featured "Chief Pilot."

Research indicates there was a shortened third season, but it was broadcast in Canada only. The premiums Canadian Lakes Map and the Mystery Message Decoder relate to these final episodes which aired following the death of the author Captain Willfred Moore who died of a heart attack July 14, 1939.

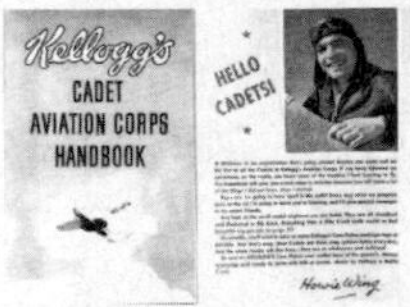

HWN-1

HWN-2

❑ **HWN-1. "Kellogg's Cadet Aviation Corps" Club Manual,**
1938. - **$25 $60 $115**

❑ **HWN-2. Mailer For Manual,**
1938. - **$10 $20 $30**

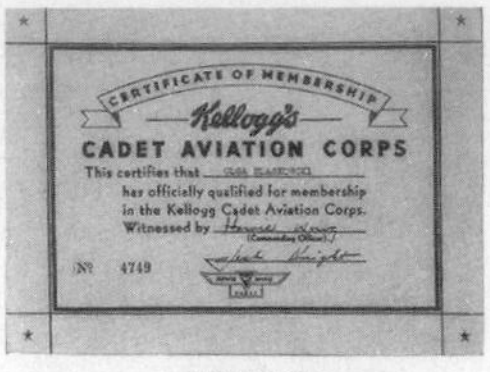

HWN-3

HWN-4

❑ **HWN-3. "Kellogg's Cadet Aviation Corps" Club Member Certificate,**
1938. - **$15 $30 $60**

❑ **HWN-4. Premium Order Sheet,**
c. 1938. Offers Cadet Aviation Corp. button, Flying Guide and Pilot Test Card. - **$25 $50 $75**

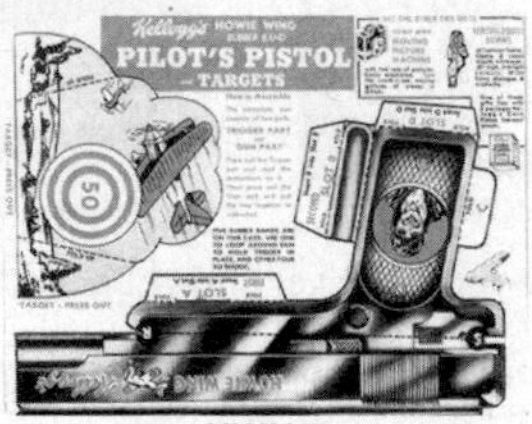

HWN-5

❑ **HWN-5. "Kellogg's Rubber Band Pilot's Pistol And Targets",**
c. 1938. Unpunched - **$60 $140 $275**

HWN-6

❑ **HWN-6. "Kellogg's Moving Picture Machine",**
c. 1938. Unpunched - **$85 $165 $330**

HWN-7

❑ **HWN-7. Group Of Canadian Premiums,**
c. 1938. The Kellogg Co. of Canada. Group consists of: 8-1/2x10-3/4" "Howie Wing's Aviation Album," 8-1/2x10" folder with "Fellow Cadet" letter which folds out to chart of "Important Parts Of An Airplane...," 8-1/2x11" salesman's folder to grocery store owners which opens to a color store sign, 2-3/4x4-3/4" ad promoting radio program and "Planes Of All Nations" cereal boxes, 3-1/2x5-1/2" "Pilot Test Card." Gordon Gold Archives. Album - **$85 $165 $300**
Cadet Folder - **$20 $35 $75**
Salesman Folder/Sign - **$85 $175 $325**
"Listen" Flyer - **$12 $20 $45**
Pilot Card - **$12 $20 $45**

HWN-8

❑ **HWN-8. Cadet Aviation Corps News,**
c. 1938. - **$25 $50 $75**

HWN-9

❑ HWN-9. "Howie Wing's Adventures On The Canadian Lakes" Map,
1939. Kellogg's of Canada. 11x16" opened. - **$150 $325 $600**

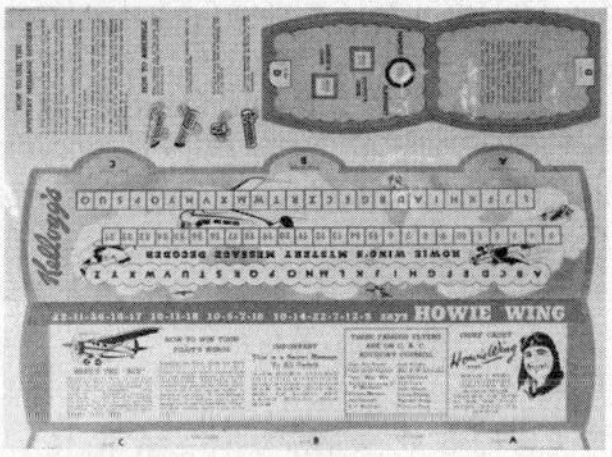

(DECODER)

(MAILER)

HWN-10

❑ HWN-10. "Howie Wing Mystery Message Decoder" Punch-Out,
1939. Kellogg's marked "Printed In Canada." Rare 9-1/2x13" mailer has image and text in orange. Rare punch-out decoder sheet has airplane illustrations and Howie Wing portrait. Gordon Gold Archives. Mailer - **$15 $30 $75**
Punch-Out - **$75 $150 $300**

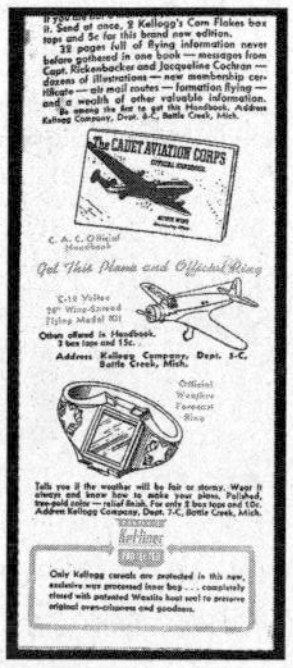

HWN-11

❑ HWN-11. Kellogg's Corn Flakes Box - 8 oz.,
1939. Cereal box features Wings Over America. Vultee V-12 plane pictured. Premium offer of ring, plane model kit, and handbook pictured on side of box. Complete - **$140 $280 $525**

HWN-12

HWN-13

❑ HWN-12. Kellogg's Corn Flakes Box Back,
1939. Wings Over America series. Brewster F2A-1 plane pictured. Premium offer for membership kit pictured on side of box. - **$20 $30 $55**

❑ HWN-13. Kellogg's Corn Flakes Box -13 oz.,
1939. Wings Over America series. Curtiss SBC-40 plane pictured. Premium offer for club material on side of box. Shows badge at top. Complete - **$140 $280 $525**

HWN-14

❑ HWN-14. "Official Handbook",
1939. Kellogg's. Mailer - **$12 $18 $35**
Handbook - **$30 $60 $120**

HWN-15

HWN-16

❑ HWN-15. "Howie Wing/Cadet Aviation Corps" Club Membership Card,
1939. Kellogg's. - **$15 $35 $75**

❑ HWN-16. Australian Club Member's Aluminum Wings Pin,
1930s. Kellogg's in Australia. 1-5/8" long aluminum with red shield. - **$25 $55 $110**

HWN-17

HWN-18

❑ HWN-17. Ventriloquist Dummy Cardboard Fold-Out,
1930s. Kellogg's premium. - **$115 $275 $500**

❑ HWN-18. Instructions For Dummy,
1930s. Kellogg's premium. - **$12 $20 $40**

HWN-19

HWN-20

HWN-21

❑ HWN-19. "Howie Wing/Kellogg's" Holed Aluminum Coin,
1930s. - **$10 $15 $25**

❑ HWN-20. "Howie Wing Cadet" Silvered/Enameled Brass Badge,
1930s. - **$10 $20 $30**

❑ HWN-21. "Pilot CAC" Aluminum Wings Badge,
1930s. For Australian members of Howie Wing Cadet Aviation Corps. - **$25 $55 $110**

HWN-22

HWN-23

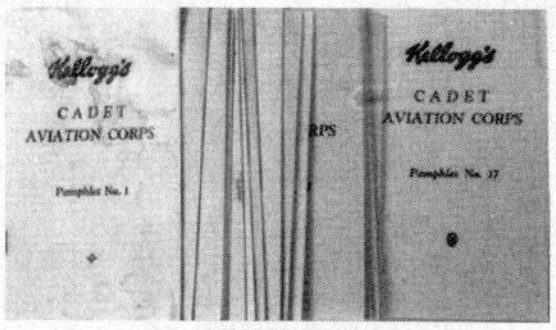

HWN-24

❑ HWN-22. Weather Forecast Ring,
1930s. Brass bands with metal clip holding slip of litmus paper. - **$100 $225 $450**

❑ HWN-23. "Cadet" Cello. Button,
1930s. Distributed to Canadian members. - **$15 $30 $50**

❑ HWN-24. "Kellogg's Cadet Aviation Corps" Pamphlet Set,
1930s. Set of 17. Each - **$8 $12 $25**

H.R. Pufnstuf

Produced by Sid and Marty Krofft, this Saturday morning children's television series, which used both live actors and puppets, aired on NBC from 1969 to 1971 and was repeated on ABC from 1972 to 1974. The program told, with songs and dances, the adventures of young Jimmy and his golden talking flute Freddie as they try to escape the clutches of the wicked Witchiepoo on Living Island, a community led by friendly dragon H.R. Pufnstuf, played by Van Snowden and voiced by Lennie Weinrib who also wrote many of the episodes. A movie version was released by Paramount in 1970, and comic books appeared from 1970 to 1972.

HPF-1

❑ HPF-1. Peel-Off Patch,
1969. Probably a Kellogg's premium and the eight we show are probably a set.
Each Unused On Card - **$12 $18 $30**

HPF-2

❑ HPF-2. Soundtrack Record Album and Photo,
1970. Kellogg's. With Mailer - **$40 $100 $175**
No Mailer - **$25 $75 $115**

HPF-3

❑ HPF-3. "H.R. Pufnstuf Hand Puppets" Cereal Box,
1970. Kellogg's Apple Jacks. Offers series of rare premium puppets that were available for $1 plus two "Puppet Stamps" from Kellogg's cereal boxes. See HPF-9. Gordon Gold Archives. Complete - **$250 $500 $775**

HPF-4

❑ HPF-4. Fun Rings And Flute Premium Offer Cereal Box,
1970. Back panel offers set of seven plastic character rings and side panel offers "Freddy The Flute" premium for 50 cents and one box top. Gordon Gold Archives.
Near Mint Flat - **$800**
Used Complete - **$200 $400 $600**

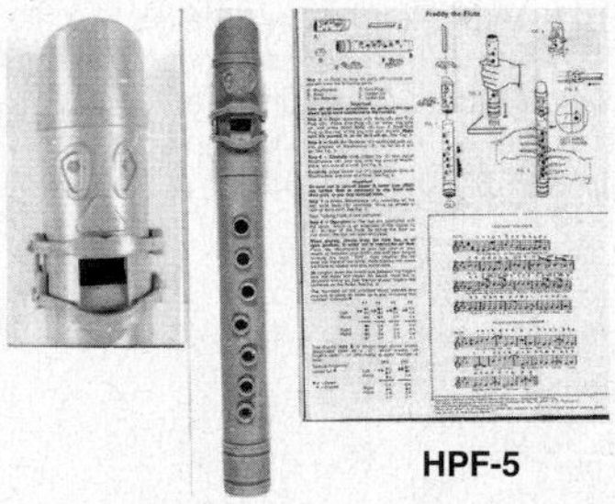

HPF-5

HPF-5. "Freddie The Flute" Musical Toy With Instructions,
1970. Kellogg's. Flute - **$150 $325 $550**
Instruction Sheet - **$30 $60 $100**

HPF-6

❑ HPF-6. Cereal Box With Pennants Offer,
1970. The vinyl pennants were printed two per sheet with a total of eight character illustrations. Gordon Gold Archives.
Used Complete - **$150 $300 $500**

HPF-7

HPF-8

❑ HPF-7. "Pufnstuf" Translucent Plastic Ring,
1970. Copyright Sid & Marty Krofft Prod. Inc. Slightly raised character image from seven different versions also picturing Witchipoo, Cling and Clang, Jimmy and Freddie, Orson, two unknown. Each - **$40 $60 $90**

❑ HPF-8. "Witchipoo" Translucent Plastic Ring,
1970. Copyright Sid & Marty Krofft Prod. Inc. From series of seven different also picturing Pufnstuf, Cling and Clang, Jimmy and Freddie, Orson, two unknown.
Each - **$40 $60 $90**

HPF-9

❑ HPF-9. H.R. Pufnstuf Premium Hand Puppet Set,
1970. Typically 5" to 6" wide by 9" to 10" tall. Made from felt and yarn, fleece-like material. These premium puppets were available individually for $1 plus two "Puppet Stamps" from Kellogg's cereal boxes. Set includes Pufnstuf, Witchiepoo, Kling, Klang, Ludicrous the Lion.
Each - **$100 $200 $400**

HPF-10

HPF-11

HPF-12

❑ HPF-10. H.R. Pufnstuf Vinyl Hand Puppet,
1970. Store item by Remco. - **$25 $50 $100**

❑ HPF-11. Jimmy Vinyl Hand Puppet,
1970. Store item by Remco. - **$25 $50 $100**

❑ HPF-12. Cling Or Clang Vinyl Hand Puppet,
1970. Store item by Remco. - **$25 $50 $100**

HPF-13

HPF-14

❑ **HPF-13. Witchiepoo Doll,**
1970. My Toy Inc. 23" tall cloth stuffed doll with vinyl head, hands, shoes, hat. -
$100 $200 $400

❑ **HPF-14. Lunch Box,**
1970. Aladdin Industries. Embossed metal with color illustrations on all panels.
Box - **$65 $150 $400**
Bottle - **$20 $40 $80**

HPF-15

HPF-16

❑ **HPF-15. H.R. Pufnstuf Mayor Bean Figure,**
1999. - **$10**

❑ **HPF-16. "Pufnstuf" Signed Poster Reprint,**
1999. 11x17" reprint of 1970 one-sheet movie poster used for autographing purposes and signed by Marty Krofft and Jack Wild.
Near Mint - **$80**

HPF-17

❑ **HPF-17. Marty Krofft Signed "Blast" Program,**
1990s. For Sid & Marty Krofft theater production. Near Mint Signed by Krofft - **$40**
Unsigned - **$8 $12 $20**

Huckleberry Hound

***Huckleberry Hound*, the first animated cartoon to win an Emmy, was Hanna-Barbera's first major television hit and the source of hundreds of licensed products. The syndicated series, sponsored by Kellogg's cereals, aired from 1958 to 1962 and was watched by millions of viewers all over the world. Huck was a noble-hearted bloodhound who remained untroubled no matter what misfortunes plagued him. Other cartoon segments on the show: Pixie and Dixie, a pair of carefree mice who tormented the affable tomcat Mr. Jinks ("I hate those meeces to pieces!"); Yogi Bear, who debuted on the show and went on to his own major series in 1961; and Hokey Wolf, a Sgt. Bilko-like con artist whose pal was Ding-a-Ling, a fox. Noted voice actor Charles Dawson "Daws" Butler (1916-1988) did the voices for: Huck, Yogi, Mr. Jinks, Dixie Mouse and Hokey Wolf. *Huckleberry Hound* comic books appeared from 1959 into the 1970s.**

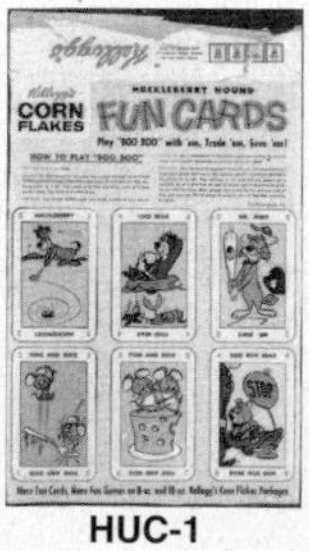

HUC-1

HUC-2

❑ **HUC-1. "Fun Cards" Box Back,**
1959. Kellogg's Corn Flakes. Back Panel Only -
$10 $20 $40

❑ **HUC-2. Plush Doll With Vinyl Face,**
1960. Store item by Knickerbocker and Kellogg's premium. - **$30 $60 $135**

HUC-3

❑ **HUC-3. "Huck Hound Club" Kit,**
1960. Kellogg's. Includes letter, member card, two color pictures, club button, Breakfast Score Card (not shown). Complete - **$75 $150 $250**

HUC-4

HUC-5

❑ **HUC-4. "Huckleberry Hound For President" 3" Litho. Button,**
1960. - **$35 $65 $125**

❑ **HUC-5. "The Great Kellogg's TV Show" Record Album,**
c. 1960. - **$12 $25 $50**

HUC-6

HUC-7

❑ **HUC-6. "Huckleberry Hound" Glazed Ceramic Figure,**
1960. Store item by Ideas Inc., Des Moines, Iowa. 5-3/4" tall. - **$20 $40 $70**

❑ **HUC-7. Plastic Bank,**
c. 1960. Store item by Knickerbocker. -
$15 $25 $40

HUC-8

HUC-9

❑ **HUC-8. "Huck Hound Club" Enameled Brass Ring,**
c. 1960. Kellogg's. - **$15 $30 $60**

❑ **HUC-9. "Huck Hound Club" Brass Ring Copyrighted,**
1961. Kellogg's. Variety without enamel paint accents. - **$20 $50 $80**

HUC-10

❑ **HUC-10. "Huckleberry Go-Mobile" Friction Toy Boxed,**
1961. Line Mar. Colorfully illustrated box holding 7.5" long litho tin and vinyl racer friction toy.
Near Mint Boxed - **$450**
Toy Only - **$80 $175 $325**

HUC-11

❑ **HUC-11. Club Card,**
1962. Scarce. Certified member as a "Top-Dog" in the club. - **$20 $40 $80**

HUC-12

❑ **HUC-12. "Huckleberry Car" Vinyl And Litho. Tin Friction Car,**
1962. Store item by Marx.
Box - **$40 $75 $150**
Car - **$65 $125 $235**

HUC-13

HUC-14

❑ **HUC-13. Litho. Tin Wind-Up Toy,**
1962. Store item by Line Mar. 4" tall. - **$65 $150 $300**

❑ **HUC-14. March Of Comics,**
1962. Used as giveaway by various stores. Issue #235. - **$7 $21 $50**

HUC-15

HUC-16

❑ **HUC-15. Vinyl/Plastic Figural Lamp,**
1962. 12" tall store item by Arch Lamp Mfg. Corp. - **$40 $85 $175**

❑ **HUC-16. Hanna-Barbera Cartoon Character Waste Can,**
c. 1962. 12-1/2" tall metal. - **$65 $135 $275**

HUC-17

❑ **HUC-17. "Huckleberry Hound Viewmarx" Boxed Micro-Viewer,**
1963. Marx Toys. Box is 1.5x3x2.75" tall. Red box with yellow accent color has die-cut window designed like stage curtain which reveals colorful 2.5" tall plastic circus wagon which is film viewer. Boxed - **$10 $20 $40**

HUC-18

HUC-19

❑ **HUC-18. "Kellogg's Special K" 17x41" Cardboard Hanger String Sign,**
1960s. - **$85 $150 $300**

❑ **HUC-19. Huck Hound/Mr. Jinks Plastic Flicker Ring,**
1960s. Kellogg's Cereal. Believed to be set of six. - **$60 $150 $250**

HUC-20

❑ **HUC-20. Cereal Box Plastic Figures,**
1960s. Kellogg's OK Cereal. Miniatures of Huck Hound, Pixie and Dixie, Mr. Jinks, Yogi Bear, Boo Boo Bear, Tony the Tiger.
Each - **$6 $12 $20**

Hula Girl

Dating back centuries, the hula was performed by men and women in the Hawaiian Islands to honor gods and chieftains. Dance, gestures and chanting simulate nature including ocean waves, bird flight and palm tree fronds blowing in island breezes. Stories are told without words. Female performers originally wore floral leis, knee length grass skirts, anklets made of whale bones or animal teeth and not much else. Christian missionaries visiting in the 1800s found such attire lewd and tried to ban the hula and get more clothes on the populace, but fortunately the hula became part of popular culture and survives today.

Sheet music, postcards and magazines like *National Geographic* promoted early 20th century island life. Hollywood films included Gilda Gray in *Aloma Of The South Seas* and Clara Bow in *Hula* in 1927, as well as *Betty Boop's Bamboo Isle* in 1932. The Wham-O slingshot company, founded in 1948 by Richard Knerr and Arthur Melin, introduced the Hula hoop in 1958 and sold some 20 million for $1.98 each within six months. The Elvis Presley 1973 *Aloha From Hawaii* special was broadcast live by satellite to a worldwide audience. Bobbing head hula girls adorn many dashboards today, symbolizing the spirit of fun and good humor based on the aloha in all of us.

HUL-1

❑ **HUL-1. 1939 New York World's Fair Bromo Seltzer Flip Book,**
1939. Bromo Seltzer. 1-7/8x2.5" cartoon flip book. Front side story of man finding pain relief with endorsement of golf champion Gene Sazaren. Reverse "movie" has cartoon hula dancer. - **$15 $30 $75**

HUL-2

❑ **HUL-2. Rittgers Hula Girl Ashtray,**
1943. L.L. Rittgers. 7.75" tall topless hula girl with 2.5" diameter ashtray. - **$150 $300 $500**

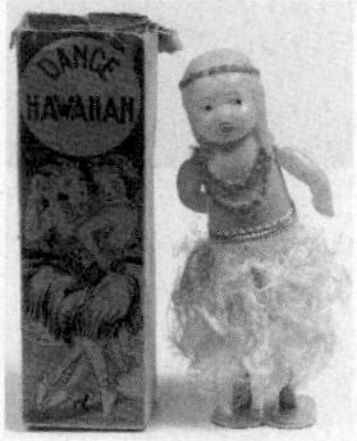

HUL-3

HUL-4

❑ **HUL-3. "Dance Hawaiian" Boxed Wind-Up,**
1940s. 2x6.5x2" deep box contains 6.25" toy marked "Made In Occupied Japan." Toy has celluloid upper body, legs and feet are painted tin with string fabric "grass skirt." When wound with matching painted yellow key, toy shakes rapidly as if hula dancing. Box - **$40 $75 $150**
Toy - **$20 $40 $90**

❑ **HUL-4. Boxed Rubber Hula Girl,**
1940s. 1.5x3x8.25" tall box contains 7.25" tall soft rubber figure of topless woman with string hula skirt. Original box shown has added satin-like cloth inlay for display. Box - **$10 $20 $40**
Toy - **$15 $25 $60**

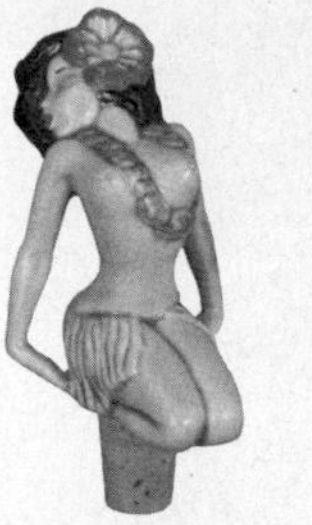

HUL-5

HUL-6

❑ **HUL-5. Topless Hula Girl Bottle Stopper,**
1940s. 4.25" tall painted and glazed figurine with over-the-glaze accents. Cork in bottom. Marked "Dorothy Kindell" a Laguna Beach, California artist. - **$50 $100 $200**

❑ **HUL-6. Topless Tropics-Inspired Pin-Up Statue,**
c. 1940s. 9.5" tall plaster figure of bare-breasted woman in sarong on tropical plant-covered base. - **$50 $100 $175**

HUL-7

❑ **HUL-7. "Hula Hoop" Sheet Music With Steve Allen,**
1958. First is 9x12" for song "Hula Hoop" with Steve Allen photo. Second is 5x6.75" for song "My Hula Hoop." Each - **$5 $15 $25**

HUL-8

❑ **HUL-8. Large Hawaiian Hula Dancer Celluloid Wind-Up,**
1950s. 2.5x3.5x8.5" tall with built-in key. Made in Japan. Upper body in celluloid while legs and feet are painted tin under fabric string "grass skirt." When wound, figure shakes rapidly as if hula dancing. - **$30 $75 $125**

Humpty Dumpty

Humpty Dumpty is a nursery rhyme character portrayed as an anthropomorphic egg but his origin is uncertain. In 1648, the name was used for a powerful cannon used in the siege of Colchester during the English Civil War. The cannon was mounted on the tower of St. Mary's at the Wall Church. When enemy cannons destroyed the tower, the cannon tumbled to the ground and was smashed beyond repair.

Artists of note portraying Humpty include: John Tenniel in *Through The Looking Glass* by Lewis Carroll in 1871 and by Maxfield Parrish in *Oz* creator L. Frank Baum's first major book *Mother Goose In Prose* in 1897.

One of his more interesting influences was the 1968 presidential campaign. Richard Nixon's campaign put out the slogan "Dump the Hump" against vice-president Hubert Humphrey who eventually lost the election.

Whatever Humpty Dumpty's origins may be, he's certainly one of popular culture's earliest icons.

HUM-1

❑ **HUM-1. Humpty Dumpty Promotional Chapbook For "Sea Foam" Baking Powder,**
1877. Gantz, Jones & Co. 4 x 3-1/2" Victorian Age comic. Has 10¢ on the cover but used as a giveaway. Promotes Gantz Sea Foam Baking Powder using an early app. of a costumed character dressed as Humpty Dumpty. Possibly the 1st costumed character that flies in a comic book story. - **$50 $100 $350**

HUM-2

❑ **HUM-2. "Schoenhut's Toy Humpty Dumpty Circus" Catalogue And Price List,**
1928. Schoenhut. 7x10", 50-page catalogue and accompanying 7x10", 16-page price list. Illustrates most products made by Schoenhut.
Catalogue - **$50 $100 $200**
Price List - **$25 $50 $100**

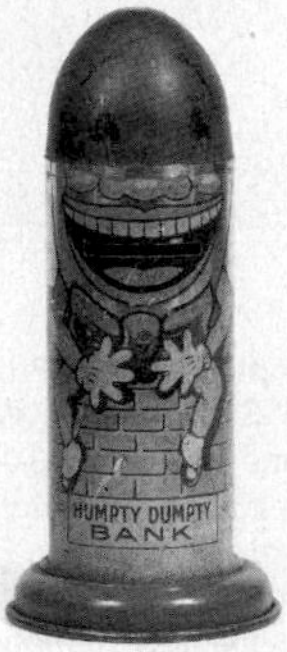

HUM-3

❑ **HUM-3. "Humpty Dumpty Bank",**
1930s. Tin litho bank has 2.5" diameter base and height of 5". Marked "Made In U.S.A." Underside has trap. - **$50 $100 $175**

HUM-4

❑ **HUM-4. Non-Disney Alice In Wonderland Top,**
1950s. Tin litho top is 9.5" in diameter and 7" tall to top of wooden handle. Marked "Colmor/Made In U.S.A." Has images of Alice, Mad Hatter, White Rabbit and Humpty Dumpty. - **$50 $100 $150**

HUM-5

❑ **HUM-5. Humpty Dumpty Bobbing Head Planter,**
1950s. Dixon. 4x4x6.5" tall painted ceramic. Made in Japan. Base depicts toy soldiers on all 4 sides and on one corner Humpty Dumpty sits with arms and legs extended. Hollow spring-mounted head bobs when tapped. - **$12 $25 $50**

HUM-6

❑ **HUM-6. Anti-Hubert Humphrey Humpty Dumpty Cartoon Button,**
1968. 2.5" diameter campaign button. - **$5 $15 $30**

I Dream of Jeannie

Created by Sidney Sheldon (1917-2007) NBC aired 139 episodes of the series between September 18, 1965 and September 1, 1970. The first 30 episodes were originally filmed in black and white. The basic plot had an astronaut finding a beautiful genie in a bottle after his space capsule landed on a desert island. The show was set in Cocoa Beach, Florida and the cast included Barbara Eden as Jeannie, Larry Hagman as Air Force Major Anthony "Tony" Nelson and Bill Daily as Roger Healey. Writers included Sidney Sheldon, Arnold Howitt and Bill Daily. Directors included Gene Nelson. Hugo Montenegro wrote the theme.

Censors allowed Jeannie and Tony to live in the same house with Barbara Eden wearing a sexy harem costume but took exception to her exposed navel. Hanna-Barbera produced a 1973 cartoon series with *Jeannie* portrayed as a red headed teenager. Voice talent included Mark Hamill, Julie McWhorter and Joe Besser. NBC aired the reunion movies *I Dream Of Jeannie: 15 Years Later* in 1985 and *I Still Dream Of Jeannie* in 1991. Dell published two comic books with full color photo covers in 1965-1966. Barbara Eden's costume is in the Smithsonian and the image of Barbara wearing it is in a lot of collectors' minds.

IDJ-1

❑ **IDJ-1. "I Dream Of Jeannie Game",**
1965. Milton Bradley. 9.5x19x1.5" deep box holds 15.75x18.5" gameboard with large image of Jeannie appearing from her bottle, die-cut cardboard figure of Jeannie with stand and 28 cardboard "Magic Disks." - **$25 $50 $100**

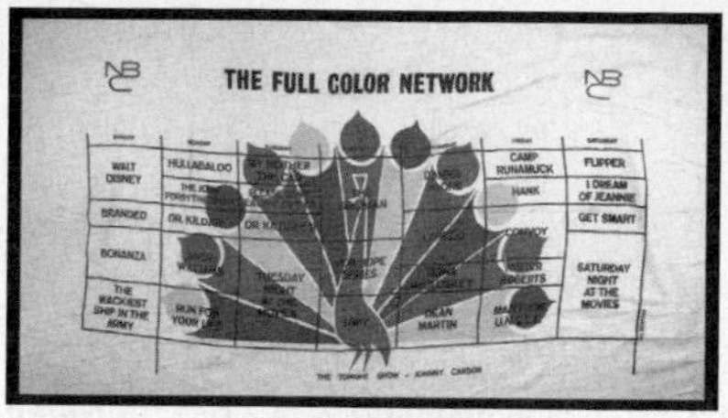

IDJ-2

❑ **IDJ-2. NBC Programming Beach Towel,**
c. 1965. Beach towel is 35x63" with NBC's peacock symbol. Towel is broken up into columns depicting days of the week with listings for shows: Walt Disney, Bonanza, My Mother The Car, I Spy, Mr. Roberts, Man From U.N.C.L.E., Flipper, I Dream Of Jeannie, Get Smart and others. - **$50 $100 $200**

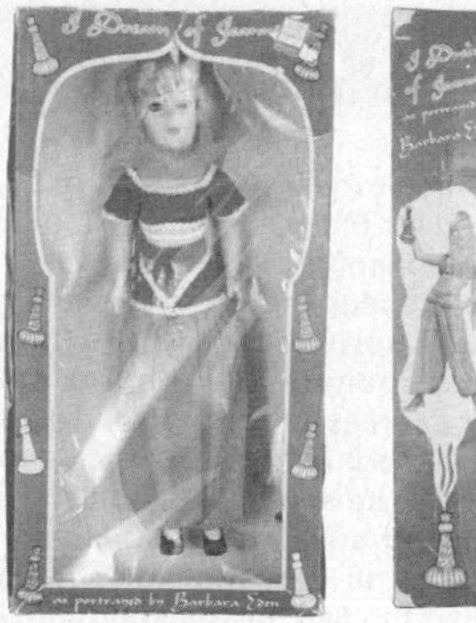

IDJ-3

❑ **IDJ-3. "I Dream Of Jeannie" Boxed Doll,**
1966. Libby. Box is 11.5x22.25x4" deep and contains 20" doll with hollow hard plastic body, vinyl arms, head with rooted life-like hair and sleep eyes. Doll was issued in several slightly different outfits. This outfit has velvet-like and sheer see-through materials with white trim and black shoes. Box - **$100 $200 $400**
Doll - **$75 $150 $300**

IDJ-4

❑ **IDJ-4. "I Dream Of Jeannie Dreamy Fashions",**
1967. Screen Gems. Four 6.5x9x.5" deep colorful display boxes each containing a different outfit for use with doll by Remco. There were 36 sets available. Each - **$5 $10 $20**

IDJ-5

❑ **IDJ-5. "I Dream Of Jeannie" Rare Large Button,**
1960s. Button is 6" diameter and features Larry Hagman and Barbara Eden. Easel back. - **$30 $65 $125**

IDJ-6

IDJ-7

❑ **IDJ-6. "I Dream Of Jeannie" Doll,**
1977. Store item by Remco. 6-1/2" tall version.
Boxed - **$65 $125 $200**
Loose - **$40 $100 $150**

❑ **IDJ-7. "I Dream of Jeannie" Matchbox Car on Card,**
1999. - **$10**

IDJ-8

❑ **IDJ-8. "I Dream Of Jeannie" Barbara Eden Autographed Lunch Box,**
2000. CPT Holdings Inc. 7x8x4" deep metal dome lunch box by Vandor. Front has show logo, pair of eyes and 4 Jeannie cartoons. Back has large cartoon image of jeannie with two bottle illustrations, one having smoke coming out. Barbara Eden has signed in this smoke "bubble" in blue sharpie pen - "Barbara Eden 'Jeannie'." Signed in person at 2002 Hollywood collector's show. Near Mint Same Or Similar - **$200**

Inner Sanctum

The memorable squeaking door and the sinister voice of "Raymond, your host" introduced the macabre *Inner Sanctum* mysteries on radio from 1941 to 1952, first on the Blue network, then on CBS (1943-1950), and ABC. The morbid anthology featured such film veterans as Boris Karloff, Peter Lorre, and Claude Raines in ghostly tales of murder and mayhem. Raymond Edward Johnson hosted the show until 1945 when Paul McGrath took over. The show was created, produced and directed by Himan Brown. Sponsors included Carter's Little Liver Pills (1941-1943), Colgate-Palmolive shaving cream (1943-1944), Lipton tea and soup (1945), Bromo-Seltzer (1946-1950), and Mars candy (1950-1951). A number of second-feature Inner Sanctum movies were made in the 1940s by Universal, most starring Lon Chaney Jr.

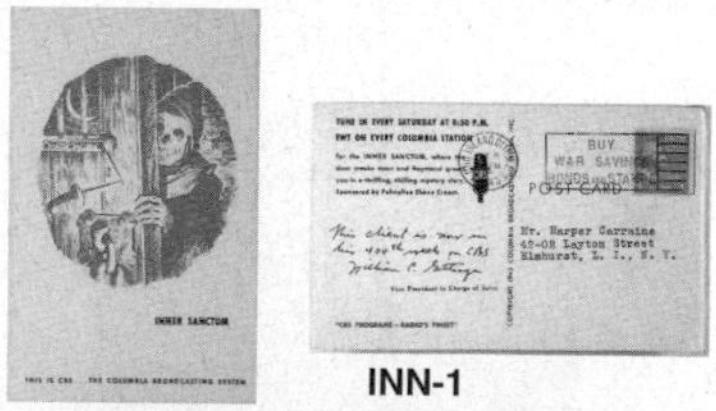

INN-1

❑ **INN-1. Promotional Postcard,**
1943. Rare. Sponsored by Palmolive Shave Cream. - **$135 $250 $500**

INN-2

❑ INN-2. Cardboard Ink Blotter,
1945. Scarce. Lipton tea and soup. -
$40 $80 $160

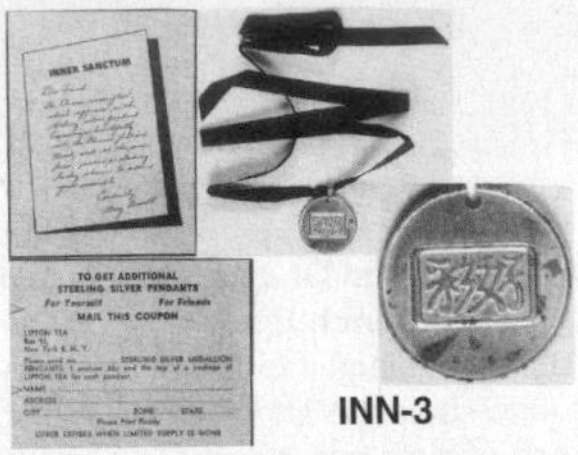

INN-3

❑ INN-3. "Inner Sanctum" Silver Pendant With Card,
c. 1945. Lipton Tea. Folder card opens to facsimile note on Inner Sanctum letterhead describing pendant and offering additional pendants. Pendant itself is 1" silvered Chinese inscription with "Sterling" marking although likely referring to plating luster only.
Card - **$50 $100 $200**
Pendant - **$75 $150 $300**

INN-4

❑ INN-4. "Inner Sanctum" Lobby Card,
1948. Card is 11x14" for 1948 M.R.S. Pictures film starring Charles Russell and Mary Beth Hughes. Card also mentions both the radio program and the best selling book. This is #7 in the set. - **$15 $30 $50**

INN-5

❑ INN-5. Advertising Cello. Button With Radio Show Title Tie-In,
1940s. Inner Sanctum Wallets. 2-1/8" issued in several different color combinations to promote wallets. We are uncertain if they were also sponsors of the show. - **$10 $20 $35**

Inspector Post

General Foods created Post's Junior Detective Corps in 1932-1933 to promote its line of cereals. The club was advertised in Sunday newspaper comic sections and on the cereal boxes, offering its young members manuals edited by Inspector General Post and badges for detective ranks up to the level of Captain.

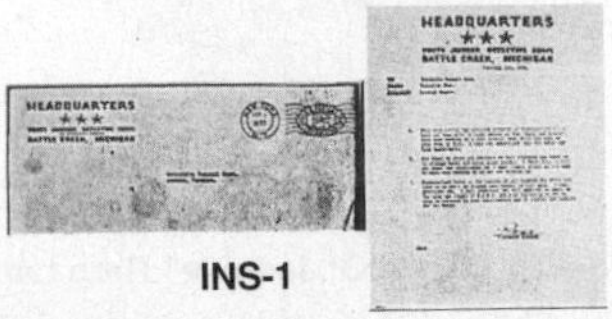

INS-1

❑ INS-1. Club Letter With Envelope,
1933. Text urges current club member to "Recruit New Members For The Corps."
Envelope - **$6 $12 $20**
Letter - **$10 $25 $50**

INS-2

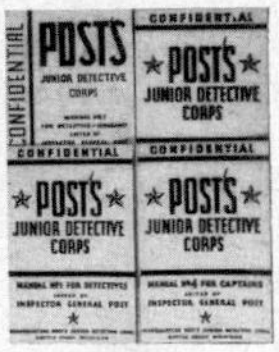

INS-3

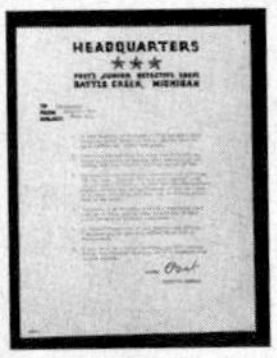

INS-4

❑ INS-2. "Inspector Post's Case Book" Manual,
1933. Post Toasties. Includes 10 mysteries solved by answers on back. - **$20 $45 $90**

❑ INS-3. Junior Detective Corps" Club Manuals,
1933. Set of four. Each - **$15 $40 $80**

❑ INS-4. Headquarters To Lieutenants Letter,
1933. Announces lowering of requirements to advance from Sergeant to Lieutenant. -
$15 $25 $50

INS-5

INS-6

❑ INS-5. "Detective/Post's J.D.C." Silvered Tin Badge,
1933. - **$15 $30 $50**

❑ INS-6. "Detective Sergeant/Post's J.D.C." Brass Rank Badge,
1933. - **$15 $30 $50**

INS-7

INS-8

❑ INS-7. "Lieutenant Post's J.D.C." Silvered Brass Rank Badge ,
1933. Most examples are glossy all silver luster. Also issued in matte silver luster with red text.
Glossy Silver - **$15 $35 $60**
Matte Silver - **$25 $50 $90**

❑ INS-8. "Captain/Post's J.D.C." Brass Rank Badge,
1933. Scarce. - **$30 $60 $100**

Jack Armstrong

Created by Robert Hardy Andrews, Jack Armstrong hit the air in July 1933 and ruled the late-afternoon airwaves until 1951, one of the most popular and longest-running radio adventure series ever--and, thanks to Wheaties' sponsorship, one of the most bountiful sources of premiums. Jack started as a sports hero at Hudson High School, but within a year he and cousins Billy and Betty were seeking adventure with Uncle Jim in exotic spots all over the world. They were still waving the flag for Hudson High, but the intrepid four were tackling Tibet, searching out the elephants' graveyard in darkest Africa, recovering sunken uranium in the Sulu Sea, always looking for something lost or stolen or buried.

Jack Armstrong premiums were frequently linked to the program's story line--a Hike-O-Meter just like the one Jack used to measure how far he'd walked, a torpedo flashlight or explorer telescope, a signaling mirror or secret whistle ring to send messages, a bombsight, a bracelet just like Betty's, and, of course, club memberships. During World War II listeners were urged to buy war bonds, collect scrap, and write letters to servicemen, and to stay strong by eating their Wheaties. In 1950 the program was renamed *Armstrong of the SBI* and Jack, Billy, and Betty began working for the Scientific Bureau of Investigation. The series went off the air in 1951.

Jack Armstrong comic strips and a series of 13 comic books were published from 1947 to 1949, all drawn by Bob Schoenke. Also in 1947, Columbia Pictures released a 15-episode chapter play starring John Hart.

JAC-1

❑ JAC-1. Wheaties Box With 1st Premium Offer On Back,
1933. Rare. Offers hand exercise grips.
Complete - **$300 $750 $1250**

JAC-2

JAC-3

❑ JAC-2. "Johnny (Tarzan) Weissmuller" Photo,
1933. Rare. One of earliest Jack Armstrong Wheaties premiums. - **$75 $225 $400**

❑ JAC-3. Wheaties Babe Ruth "How To Hit A Home Run" Flip Booklet,
1933. Scarce. Photo pages in sequence of batting stance, complete swing, follow-through. - **$175 $400 $750**

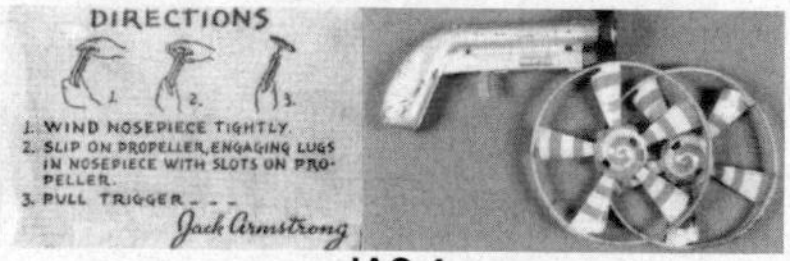

JAC-4

❑ JAC-4. "Shooting Plane" With Directions And Mailer,
1933. Made by Daisy Mfg. Co. Metal gun and two spinner wheels. Near Mint Boxed - **$400**
Gun - **$50 $75 $150**
Each Spinner - **$20 $40 $75**

JAC-5

❑ JAC-5. "Wee-Gyro" Flying Ship, Instruction Paper,
1934. Sheet came with a balsa model similar to autogyro. - **$25 $75 $150**

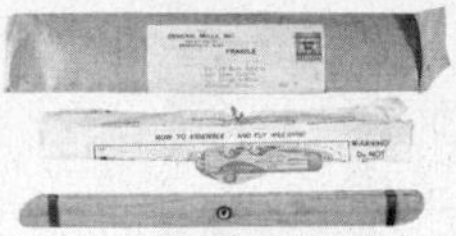

JAC-6

JAC-7

❑ JAC-6. Jack Armstrong Wee-Gyro,
1934. General Mills Cereal premium. Includes Wee gyro, mailer, and instructions.
Gyro - **$110 $225 $350**
Mailer - **$20 $40 $75**
Instructions - **$25 $75 $150**

❑ JAC-7. All American Team Photo,
1934. Radio premium. - **$10 $20 $30**

JAC-8

JAC-9

JAC-10

❑ JAC-8. Armstrong On Horse Blackster Photo,
1934. - **$10 $20 $35**

❑ JAC-9. Jack Armstrong Photo,
1934. Radio premium. - **$10 $20 $35**

❑ JAC-10. Betty Fairfield Photo,
1934. Radio premium. - **$10 $20 $35**

JAC-11

JAC-12

❑ JAC-11. Box Back Panel,
1935. - **$15 $35 $70**

❑ JAC-12. Box Back Panel,
1935. - **$25 $50 $100**

JAC-13

JAC-14

❑ JAC-13. Betty Fairfield Box Back Panel,
1935. - **$15 $35 $70**

❑ JAC-14. Betty Fairfield Box Back Panel,
1935. - **$15 $35 $70**

JAC-15

JAC-16

❑ JAC-15. Box Back Panel,
1935. - **$20 $40 $80**

❑ JAC-16. Stamp Collecting Items,
1935. Includes booklet and pamphlets about stamp collecting with offer of oriental stamps.
Each - **$15 $25 $50**

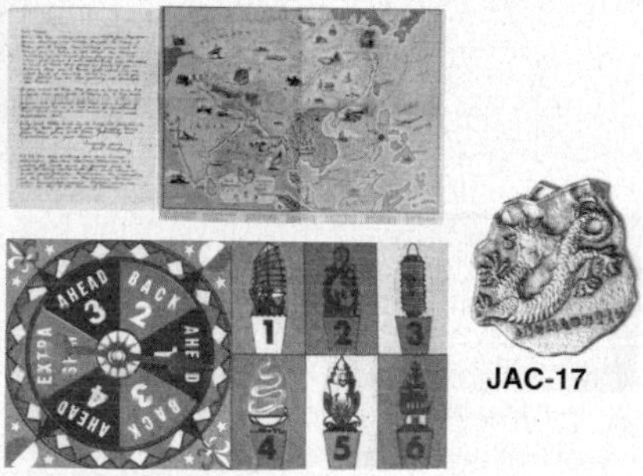

JAC-17

❑ JAC-17. "Jack Armstrong's Chart Game/Adventures With The Dragon Talisman" Map Game,
1936. The talisman inscription translated is: "China - The Key To The Door Of The Room Is Very Precious."
Map Game Only - **$75 $175 $300**
Spinner and Game Markers (4) - **$10 $20 $40**
Dragon Talisman - **$20 $50 $100**

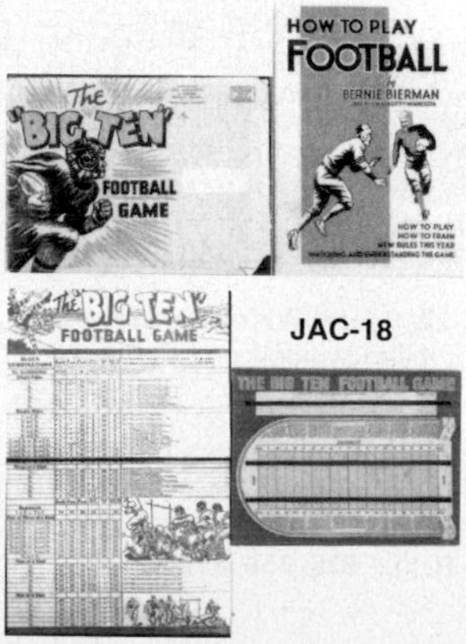

JAC-18

❑ **JAC-18. "Big Ten Football Game",**
1936. Near Mint In Mailer - **$250**
Board Only - **$20 $40 $65**
Booklet Only - **$15 $30 $45**

JAC-19

❑ **JAC-19. "Jack Armstrong's Mystery Eye" Book,**
1936. Cupples & Leon Co. - **$15 $30 $60**

JAC-20

JAC-21

❑ **JAC-20. Milk Glass Bowl,**
1937. - **$10 $25 $50**

❑ **JAC-21. Movie Viewer With Filmstrip,**
1937. Film title is "Graveyard Of Elephants".
Box - **$15 $30 $60**
Viewer And Film - **$60 $125 $200**

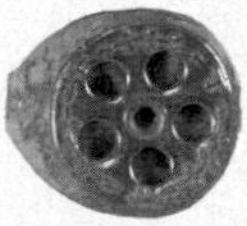

JAC-22

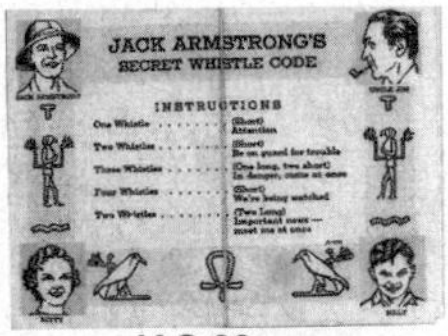

JAC-23

❑ **JAC-22. Secret Whistling Brass Ring,**
1937. Egyptian symbols on sides. -
$40 $75 $150

❑ **JAC-23. "Secret Whistle Code" Instruction Sheet,**
1937. Paper (not cardboard). For Egyptian Whistle Ring. - **$25 $50 $100**

JAC-24

❑ **JAC-24. "Treasure Hunt" Instruction Booklet,**
1938. Came with Hike-O-Meter pedometer. -
$20 $30 $60

JAC-25 JAC-26

❑ **JAC-25. "Baseball Centennial" Brass Ring,**
1938. Offered as Jack Armstrong premium by General Mills Wheaties and Corn Kix from 7/27/38-10/28/38. Company recorded 46,501 responses. Manufacturer's remainder offered by Quaker Puffed Rice in 1939. - **$250 $500 $900**

❑ **JAC-26. "Hike-O-Meter" Aluminum Pedometer,**
1938. Blue painted rim. - **$20 $40 $75**

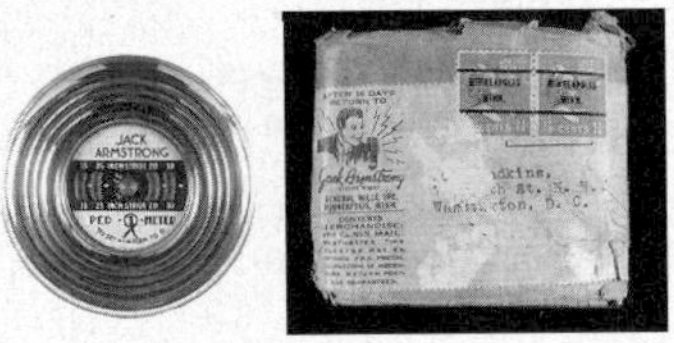

JAC-27

❑ **JAC-27. "Jack Armstrong Ped-O-Meter" Variety With Mailer,**
c. 1938. 2-5/8" dia. scarce version metal pedometer in chrome finish case rather than traditional blue rim plus title variation from traditional "Hike-O-Meter" title.
Near Mint In Mailer - **$160**
Ped-O-Meter Only - **$30 $50 $115**

JAC-28

JAC-29

❑ **JAC-28. Explorer Telescope,**
1938. Cardboard tube with metal caps holding glass lenses. - **$10 $25 $50**

❑ **JAC-29. Heliograph And Distance Finder,**
1938. Scarce. Brass multi-function premium for land and water measurements, message sender, secret compartment, Morse Code. Scarce test premium. - **$350 $850 $1750**

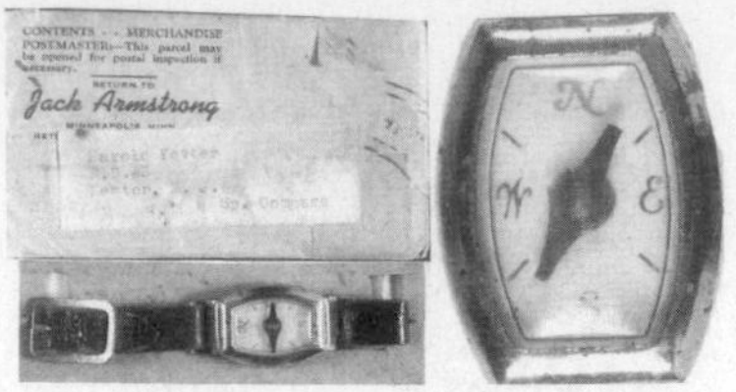

JAC-30

❑ **JAC-30. Test Premium Compass With Mailer,**
1938. Wheaties. Mailer envelope and compass documented in General Mills Archives as only 3,017 distributed between June 2 and December 12. Compass has brass case and 8" leather wrist strap. Reverse pictures three constellations of galaxy. Mailer - **$50 $100 $150**
Compass - **$100 $200 $350**

JAC-31

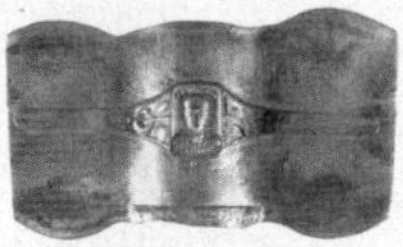

JAC-32

❑ **JAC-31. "Lie Detektor" Metal Answer Box,**
c. 1938. Supposed first version of "Magic Answer Box" quickly redesigned because parents objected to children telling lies. -
$100 $200 $400

❑ **JAC-32. All American Boy Ring Lead Proof,**
1939. Unique - **$3000**

JAC-33

❑ **JAC-33. "Adventures Of Jack Armstrong" Box Backs,**
1938. Wheaties. Set of six.
Each Back Panel - **$20 $35 $70**

JAC-34

JAC-35

❑ **JAC-34. Decoder Lead Proof,**
1939. Designed by Orin Armstrong for Robbins Company. Never produced. Unique - **$2750**

❑ **JAC-35. Pedometer,**
1939. Version with unpainted aluminum rim. See JAC-40. - **$20 $30 $60**

JAC-36

❑ **JAC-36. "Jack Armstrong" Original Art Prototype Book,**
c. 1939. 8-1/4x10-1/2" with four pages of art in lead and colored pencil for proposed 52-page book. Gordon Gold archives. Unique. - **$650**

JAC-37

❑ **JAC-37. "Jack Armstrong And The Mystery Of The Iron Key" Better Little Book,**
1939. Whitman #1432. - **$12 $36 $78**

JAC-38

JAC-39

❑ **JAC-38. Torpedo Flashlight Set,**
1939. Set of three in red, blue, or black cardboard barrels with metal nose and rear cap.
Blue - **$15 $25 $50**
Red - **$15 $30 $60**
Black - **$20 $35 $70**

❑ **JAC-39. Ad for the Torpedo Flashlight Wheaties Premium,**
1939. - **$10 $20 $45**

JAC-40

❑ **JAC-40. Serial - "Return To Mars,"**
1939. American Boy Magazine which features ad for Jack Armstrong promoting Wheaties and serial adventure "Return To Mars." Also shown is inside front cover featuring Armstrong ad. - **$18 $35 $70**

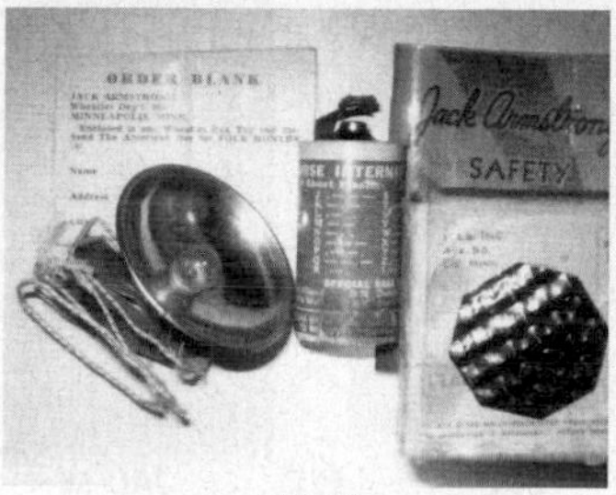

JAC-41

❑ **JAC-41. Bicycle Safety Kit,**
1939. Wheaties premium of instruction folder, 2" light with bulb and red plastic cover, metal clamp, metal battery switch, and battery to insert in red cardboard tube printed with "Morse International Code."
Complete - **$115 $225 $350**

JAC-42

JAC-43

❑ **JAC-42. Gold Rim Pedometer,**
c. 1939. Similar to JAC-34 but outer rim has bright gold luster and the word "Official" appears above the name "Jack Armstrong." In addition the center dial is red on cream rather than red, black and white. Scarce. - **$85 $175 $300**

❑ **JAC-43. Windfair W. J. A. C. Club Lead Proof,**
1930s. Unique. - **$1900**

JAC-44

❑ **JAC-44. "Pilot's Physical Fitness Test" Original Art Prototype,**
1930s. 10.75x17.25" art board with watercolor and tempera artwork and hand-lettered text for likely Sunday comic section ad for "Jack Armstrong Air Cadet" Wheaties offering. Gordon Gold Archives. Unique. - **$800**

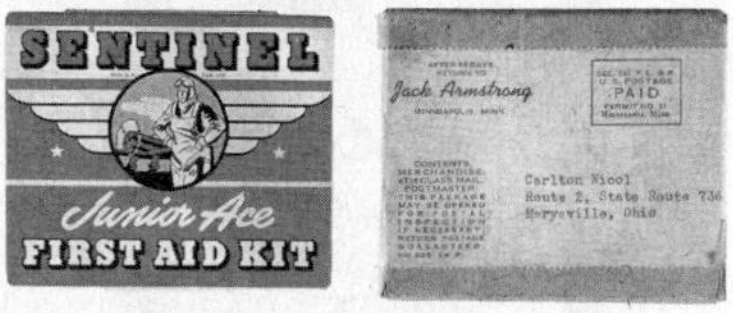

JAC-45

❑ **JAC-45. Sentinel Junior Ace First Aid Kit Complete with Mailer ,**
1930s. Complete With Mailer and Contents - **$100 $300 $400**
Tin Box Only - **$30 $60 $100**

JAC-46

❑ **JAC-46. Wheaties "Stampo" Game With Mailer Envelope,**
1930s. Two sheets to be cut and four leaflets for game devised by H. E. Harris Co., domestic and foreign postage stamps dealer of Boston. Uncut In Mailer - **$65 $125 $250**

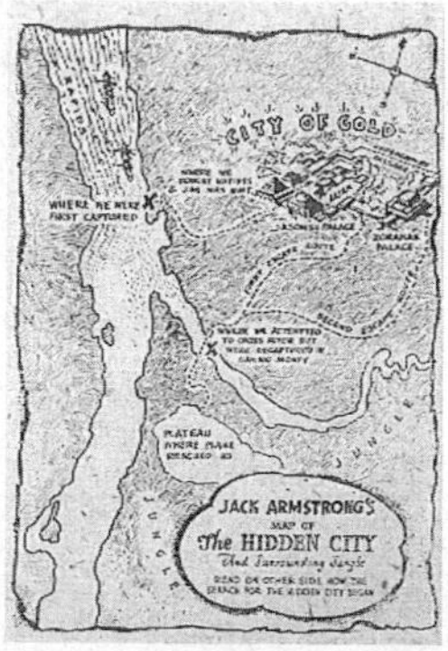

JAC-47

❑ **JAC-47. Map Of The Hidden City And Surrounding Jungle,**
1930s. 4x5-1/4" black on tan paper with perforated top edge. Reverse has story and lists several west coast radio stations. Probably the first Jack Armstrong overseas trip (to South America) because the reverse mentions he won a scholarship to make the trip. Rare. - **$275 $500 $900**

JAC-48

❑ **JAC-48. Fan Card,**
1930s. "To My Friend" is imprinted followed by personalized inked first name of recipient above facsimile signature. - **$35 $75 $150**

JAC-49

JAC-50

❑ **JAC-49. "Lieutenant/Listening Squad" Brass Whistle Badge,**
1940. Scarce. Test premium, small quantity distributed. - **$150 $300 $750**

❑ **JAC-50. Lieutenant/Listening Squad Whistle Lead Proof,**
1940. Unique - **$1650**

JAC-51

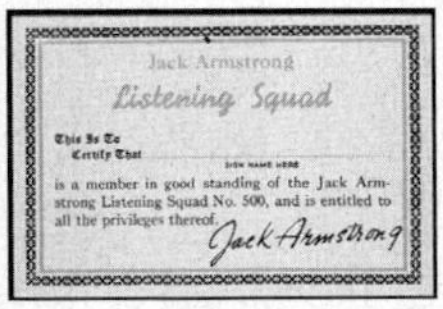

JAC-52

❑ **JAC-51. Sky Ranger Plane,**
1940. - **$150 $300 $650**

❑ **JAC-52. Listening Squad Membership Card,**
1940. Rare. Test premium. - **$150 $300 $500**

JAC-53

❑ **JAC-53. "Jack Armstrong Magic Answer Box",**
1940. Complete Boxed - **$100 $200 $300**
Answer Box Only - **$35 $60 $100**

JAC-54

JAC-55

❑ **JAC-54. "Captain/Listening Squad" Sample Brass Whistle Badge,**
1940. Rare. Test premium, even scarcer than Lieutenant version. - **$300 $1000 $2000**

❑ **JAC-55. Captain/Listening Squad Whistle Lead Proof,**
1940. Unique - **$2500**

JAC-56

❑ **JAC-56. "Dragon's Eye Ring" Instructions/Order Blank Sheet,**
1940. Order coupon for additional rings expired January 2, 1941. - **$40 $85 $175**

JAC-57

JAC-58

❑ **JAC-57. Dragon's Eye Ring With Instruction Paper,**
1940. White glow plastic ring topped by dark green stone. Yellow instruction sheet (shown folded) has expiration date of July 1, 1941.
Ring - **$150 $300 $600**
Paper - **$40 $85 $175**

❑ **JAC-58. "Sound Effects Kit" and Instruction Sheet,**
1941. "Spy Hunt" mystery script utilizing sound effects.
Complete - **$150 $250 $500**

JAC-59

❑ **JAC-59. Betty's Luminous Gardenia Bracelet,**
1941. Rare. Glows in the dark. -
$85 $175 $400

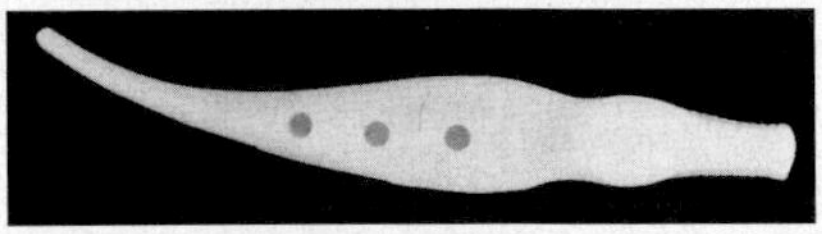

JAC-60

❑ **JAC-60. Crocodile Glow in the Dark Plastic Whistle,**
1941. Rare. Test premium offered over only two Minnesota radio stations. General Mills recorded only 809 requests, and today only four are known. - **$1250 $3500 $5000**

JAC-61

JAC-62

❑ **JAC-61. "Write A Fighter Corps" Kit,**
1942. Includes manual, stencils (6), star sticker sheets (6), insignia patches (6).
Near Mint In Mailer - **$225**
Manual Only - **$25 $50 $80**

❑ **JAC-62. Press Release Photo Picturing Wood Bombsight,**
1942. Mutual Broadcasting System. Pictures radio cast members Uncle Jim and Jack Armstrong holding Wheaties premium. -
$40 $75 $150

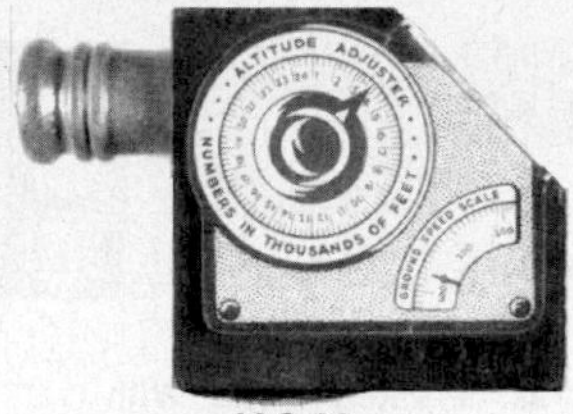

JAC-63

❑ **JAC-63. Wheaties Secret Bombsight,**
1942. Wood/litho. paper bomb release holding three wooden bombs.
Bombsight Only - **$85 $200 $400**
Each Bomb - **$25 $50 $75**

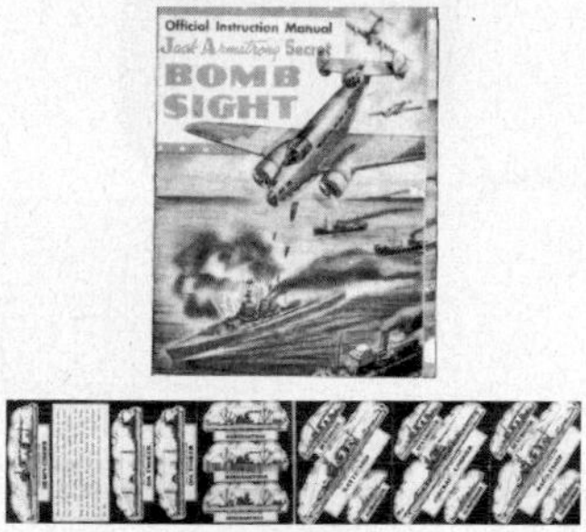

JAC-64

❑ **JAC-64. "Secret Bomb Sight Instruction Manual",**
1942. Scarce. Includes cut-out ships for use with bomb sight. Uncut - **$65 $140 $275**

JAC-65 JAC-66

❑ **JAC-65. "Future Champions Of America" Club Manual,**
1943. - **$25 $50 $100**

❑ **JAC-66. "Future Champions Of America" Fabric Patch,**
1943. - **$8 $15 $25**

JAC-67

❑ **JAC-67. Model Planes 16x36" Paper Store Sign,**
1944. - **$150 $300 $600**

JAC-68

❑ **JAC-68. Wheaties Tru-Flite Warplane Paper Model Kit With Envelope,**
1944. Seven sets (A-G), each with two cut-out airplanes and instructions. Each Uncut Set In Mailer - **$30 $70 $125**

JAC-69 JAC-70

❑ **JAC-69. Tru-Flite News Vol. 1 #1 Newspaper,**
Sept. 1944. - **$20 $40 $80**

❑ **JAC-70. Tru-Flite News Vol. 1 #2 Newspaper,**
Oct. 1944. - **$15 $30 $70**

JAC-71

❑ **JAC-71. "Cub Pilot Corps" Contest Newspaper With I.D. Tag And Envelope,**
1945. Includes newspaper #3 and metal "G.I. Identification Tag". Near Mint In Mailer- **$300**
Newspaper - **$15 $35 $70**
Tag - **$50 $100 $175**

JAC-72

❑ **JAC-72. Jack Armstrong Sign,**
1945. Scarce. 17x22" sign promotes radio show and advertises joining Cub Pilots Corps. Talks about contest and how to get Piper Cub Pre-Flight Kit. Sponsored by Wheaties. -
$165 $325 $600

JAC-73

❑ **JAC-73. Pre-Flight Training Kit,**
1945. Mailer holds "How To Fly" booklet, "Cub Pilot Corps. News" first issue newspaper, three-fold punch-out "Trainer" with short cardboard dowel "stick," and sheet of club logo transfers.
Complete Near Mint in Mailer - **$675**
Booklet - **$25 $50 $75**
Newspaper - **$20 $40 $80**
Punch-Out With Stick - **$125 $225 $350**
Transfers - **$10 $20 $30**

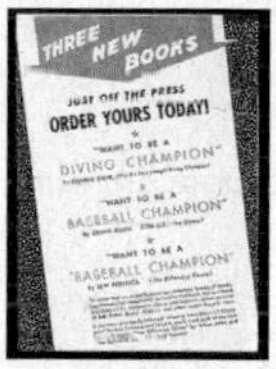

JAC-74 JAC-75

❑ **JAC-74. Announcement,**
1945. Announces 3 new books available for order from Library of Sports Books. -
$10 $20 $40

❑ **JAC-75. Book 1,**
1945. Wheaties. Library of Sports book premium. -
$18 $35 $75

JAC-76 JAC-77

❑ **JAC-76. Book 2 - Type 1 (Offense),**
1945. Wheaties. Library of Sports book premium. Features Bucky Walters, Bob Feller, Joe Cronin, the late Lou Gehrig and others. -
$35 $65 $135

❑ **JAC-77. Book 2 - Type 2 (Defense),**
1946. Wheaties. Library of Sports book premium. Cover and interior are different than 1945 edition. Also features Bucky Walters, Bob Feller, Joe Cronin, the late Lou Gehrig and others. -
$35 $65 $135

JAC-78 JAC-79

❑ **JAC-78. Book 3,**
1945. Wheaties. Library of Sports book premium. - **$20 $40 $85**

❑ **JAC-79. Book 4,**
1945. Wheaties. Library of Sports book premium. - **$20 $40 $85**

JAC-80 JAC-81

❑ **JAC-80. Book 5,**
1945. Wheaties. Library of Sports book premium. - **$20 $40 $85**

❑ **JAC-81. Book 6,**
1945. Wheaties. Library of Sports book premium. - **$20 $40 $85**

JAC-82 JAC-83

❑ **JAC-82. Book 7,**
1945. Wheaties. Library of Sports book premium. - **$20 $40 $85**

❑ **JAC-83. Book 8,**
1945. Wheaties. Library of Sports book premium. - **$20 $40 $85**

JAC-84 JAC-85

❑ **JAC-84. Book 10,**
1945. Wheaties. Library of Sports book premium. - **$20 $40 $85**

❑ **JAC-85. Book 11,**
1945. Wheaties. Library of Sports book premium. - **$20 $40 $85**

JAC-86 JAC-87

❑ **JAC-86. Book 12,**
1945. Wheaties. Library of Sports book premium. - **$20 $40 $85**

❑ **JAC-87. Book14,**
1945. Wheaties. Library of Sports book premium. - **$20 $40 $85**

JAC-88 JAC-89

❑ **JAC-88. Book 15,**
1945. Wheaties. Library of Sports book premium. Features Marty Marion, Johnny Mize, Mel Ott, Lou Boudreau and others. - **$35 $65 $135**

❑ **JAC-89. Book 16,**
1945. Wheaties. Library of Sports book premium. - **$20 $40 $85**

JAC-90

❑ **JAC-90. Library Of Sports Mailer,**
1945. General Mills. - **$20 $30 $60**

JAC-91

❑ **JAC-91. "Cub Pilot Corps" Dog Tag,**
1945. Silvered metal incised by member's address then designated "Official Member General Mills Cub Pilot Corps." - **$50 $100 $175**

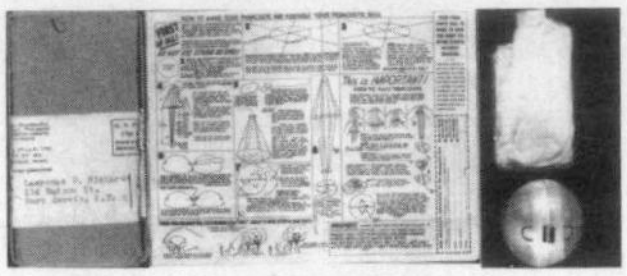

JAC-92

❑ **JAC-92. "Parachute Ball" With Instructions And Mailer,**
1946. Aluminum ball with paper parachute. Near Mint Boxed - **$375**
Ball And Parachute Only - **$65 $125 $250**

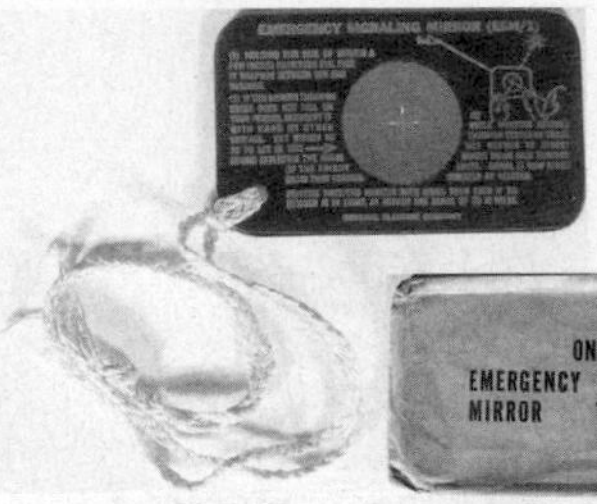

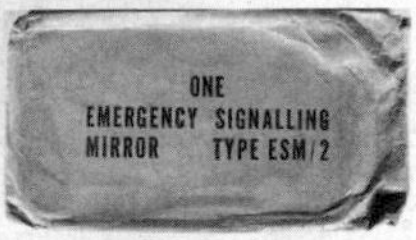

JAC-93 (Mailer)

❑ **JAC-93. Navy Emergency Signaling Mirror,**
1947. General Mills Premium. With braided cord. Obtained for 25¢ and 1 box top. - **$80 $140 $250**

JAC-94

❑ **JAC-94. Jack Armstrong Movie Serial Campaign Book,**
1947. 11x16" glossy pressbook with 4 pages promoting Jack Armstrong Columbia serial. Front cover shows May 1947 Parents Magazine cover that gives Jack Armstrong critical praise. Interior two-page spread features numerous illustrations of Jack Armstrong club cards, advertisements and photos from contests. - **$75 $150 $300**

JAC-95

❑ **JAC-95. Press Book for Movie Serial,**
1947. - **$65 $135 $225**

JAC-96

JAC-97

❑ **JAC-96. Jack Armstrong #1 Comic,**
1947. Odd size. - **$43 $129 $600**

❑ **JAC-97. "Explorer's Sun Watch" With Glow-In-Dark Dial,**
1948. Version without "Frank Buck" name with insert compass and movable pointer. Also offered by "Rocky" Lane, sponsored by Carnation Malted Milk, in 1951. - **$25 $40 $75**

JAC-98

JAC-99

❑ **JAC-98. Armstrong & Betty Fairfield Photo Cards,**
c. 1940s. Each - **$35 $70 $140**

❑ **JAC-99. Pictorial Pedometer,**
1940s. Metal with lt. green rim picturing six golfers. - **$70 $135 $275**

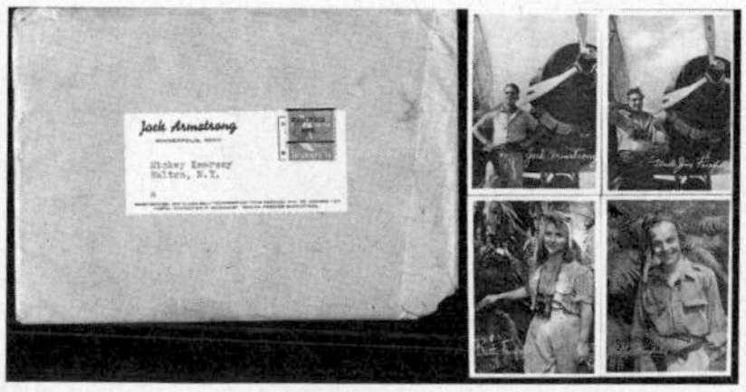

JAC-100

❑ **JAC-100. Photo Set With Mailer Envelope,**
c. 1940s. Four 5x7" glossy bw photos picturing Jack, Uncle Jim, Billy, Betty, each with facsimile signature. Mailer - **$25 $45 $110**

JAC-101

❑ **JAC-101. Jack & Fairfields Photo Set,**
1940s. Four black and white photos with facsimile signatures Jack Armstrong, Uncle Jim Fairfield, Betty Fairfield, Billy Fairfield. Examples shown have added notebook ring holes.
Each - **$30 $60 $85**

JAC-102

❑ **JAC-102. Record,**
1973. Wheaties. Volume One with sleeve. - **$15 $25 $50**

Jack Benny

Jack Benny, born as Benjamin Kubelsky (1894-1974), started in show business at the age of eight as a combination usher and violinist in a theater in Waukegan, Illinois. Thirty years later, when his program debuted on radio, he was a major star of stage and vaudeville. For 23 years on radio (1932-1955) and for 15 years on television (1950-1965) Benny was a Sunday night comic institution. His long-running feud with Fred Allen, his penny-pinching, his blue eyes, his ancient Maxwell car, his vault in the basement, his violin, his age--always 39--became part of the country's pop culture. Also featured over the years were his wife Mary Livingston, Rochester the valet, Don Wilson, Dennis Day, Phil Harris, Mel Blanc, and a host of others. The theme song was *Love in Bloom*. Long-term radio sponsors were Jell-O (1934-1942) and Lucky Strike cigarettes (1944-1955); others included Canada Dry ginger ale (1932-1933), Chevrolet (1933-1934), General Tire (1934), and Grape-Nuts Flakes (1942-1944). Benny also appeared on numerous other television shows and appeared in 30 movies between 1930 and 1972.

JBE-1

JBE-2

❑ **JBE-1. Fan Photo,**
c. 1934. Jell-O. - **$12 $25 $40**

❑ **JBE-2. Jell-O Recipe Book,**
1937. Inside covers have Jack Benny and Mary Livingston comic strips. - **$15 $30 $60**

JBE-4

JBE-3

❑ **JBE-3. Photo,**
1937. Philadelphia Record newspaper premium. - **$8 $15 $25**

❑ **JBE-4. "Benny Buck" Movie Theater Play Money,**
1939. Local theaters. For film "Buck Benny Rides Again" picturing supporting stars Ellen Drew and Andy Devine on back. - **$15 $30 $45**

JBE-5

JBE-6

❑ **JBE-5. Dixie Ice Cream Picture,**
1930s. - **$15 $30 $50**

❑ **JBE-6. "Grape-Nuts Flakes" Endorsement Box,** c. 1942. Back panel pictures him with balloon statement "Take It From Benny They're Better Than Any!" - **$55 $100 $200**

JBE-7

❑ **JBE-7. Radio Show Program,**
c. 1944. Lucky Strike cigarettes. - **$20 $40 $80**

JBE-8

❑ **JBE-8. "The Jack Benny Album" Record Set,**
1947. Set #2 from a numbered series of seven different featuring radio programs on the Top Ten Records label. Has four 78 rpm records, each featuring actual radio broadcast. -
$20 $50 $85

JBE-9

❑ **JBE-9. Jack Benny And Wife Mary Livingston Premium Photo,**
1940s. Photo is 4.75x7" nice quality, slightly textured glossy paper in black and white. Includes facsimile signatures at lower left.
- **$12 $25 $40**

JBE-10

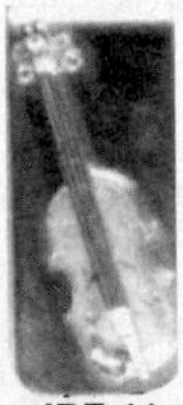
JBE-11

JBE-12

❑ **JBE-10. "Rochester" Fan Photo,**
c. 1940s. Store item, probable sample from dime store picture frame. Pictured is Jack Benny's long-time valet on radio show, played by Eddie Anderson. - **$15 $30 $55**

❑ **JBE-11. "Friars Luncheon/Jack Benny" Gold Luster Metal Money Clip,**
c. 1950s. Dinner event souvenir. Raised design of his violin. - **$18 $30 $60**

❑ **JBE-12. Plaster Statue,**
c. 1979. Store item by Esco Products. 16-1/2" tall from series of personality statues. -
$25 $45 $90

Jack Paar

Jack Paar (1918-2004) had various stints on radio and early TV but his first early success was hosting the NBC radio show *The $64 Dollar Question* in 1951-52. He also had a brief career in films, including a small part in *Love Nest* with Marilyn Monroe in 1951. He went on to host TV game shows including *Up To Paar* in 1952 and *Bank On The Stars* in 1953. Paar's quick wit and comedic timing led to taking over as host of the *Tonight Show* from Steve Allen in July, 1957, where he reigned as king of the late night airwaves until March 29, 1962. Compelling conversation, combined with Paar's emotional and sentimental nature delighted viewers. Cliff "Charley Weaver" Arquette read letters from Mama, Richard Nixon played the piano and comedians were born including: Woody Allen, Jonathan Winters, Bill Cosby, Bob Newhart and Carol Burnett. Stimulating conversation was held with John Kennedy, Robert Kennedy and Albert Schweitzer. He talked to Castro and was present when the Berlin Wall was built.

***The Jack Paar* January 3, 1964 NBC prime-time show had film of the Beatles and early in 1968 he hosted a telethon for D.C. Children's Village in Washington, D.C. The highlight was a quintet composed of Robert Kennedy, Ted Kennedy, Perry Como, Andy Williams and Eddie Fisher. In the late 1960s, he produced documentaries on the people and culture of Europe and the Far East.**

Jack Paar set a high standard for excellence as the father of late night TV. "I kid you not."

JKP-1

❑ **JKP-1. Jack Paar 12" Cardboard Standee,**
1950s. Schrafft's. - **$65 $100 $175**

JKP-2

JKP-3

❑ **JKP-2. Jack Paar Beech-Nut Gum Container,**
1950s. Held small free sample boxes. -
$30 $60 $100

❑ **JKP-3. "Welcome Back Jack" Paar Button,**
1960. 3.5" diameter button with black and white photo of Paar. Reverse has ink stamp of maker "Emress Specialty Co." Issued for his return to The Tonight Show, after he and NBC worked out issues regarding censorship that had led to his walking off the live broadcast a month earlier. - **$12 $25 $50**

JKP-4

❑ **JKP-4. "Jack Paar Advertises Mirro Aluminum" Button,**
c. 1960. 2.5" cello button with bar pin on reverse. - **$20 $40 $60**

The Jack Pearl Show

A veteran comic of vaudeville and burlesque, Jack Pearl (1895-1982) brought his dialect character Baron Munchausen to radio in 1932. When straight man Cliff Hall expressed doubts about one of the Baron's tall tales, the inevitable response, "Vas you dere, Sharlie?" brought down the house. Sponsors of *The Jack Pearl Show* included Chrysler (1932), Lucky Strike cigarettes (1932-1933), Royal gelatin (1934), Frigidaire (1935), and Raleigh and Kool cigarettes (1936-1937). Comeback attempts in 1942 and 1948 were not successful.

JPL-1

❑ **JPL-1. "Baron Munchausen" Map Of Radioland 19x24",**
c. 1932. Scarce. - **$150 $300 $650**

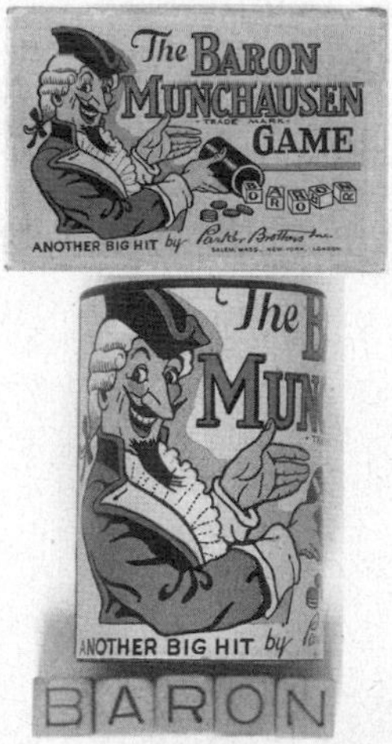

JPL-2

❑ **JPL-2. "The Baron Munchausen Game,"**
1933. Parker Brothers. 3.5x5x2" deep box. Game obviously produced due to the popularity of the Jack Pearl radio program of 1932. Box features illustrations of Baron on all sides including two panels depicting him catching a giant fish. Game has 3" tall dice cup, 5 specialty wood dice and green cardboard chips. Dice cup has paper label with same illustration as lid. Object of game was to spell "Baron." Comes with instruction sheet. - **$30 $65 $125**

JPL-3

❑ **JPL-3. "Jack Pearl As Dectective Baron Munchausen" Book,**
1934. Store item published by Goldsmith Co. with endorsement of Juvenile Educators League. - **$12 $36 $78**

Jack Westaway Undersea Adventure Club

Membership in Jack Westaway's U.S.A.C. entitled young fans of the 1930s to wear the club badge (shaped like a diving helmet) and to a member's identification card that spelled out the club rules--including, whenever possible, eating a breakfast of Malt-O-Meal hot puffed wheat and puffed rice cereal.

JWS-1

(FRONT)

JWS-2

(BACK)

❑ **JWS-1. "Under Sea Adventure Club News" Vol. 1 #1 Newspaper With Envelope,**
1930s. Malt-O-Meal. Newspaper - **$25 $50 $110**
Mailer - **$5 $10 $15**

❑ **JWS-2. Club Membership Card,**
1930s. Malt-O-Meal. - **$30 $60 $125**

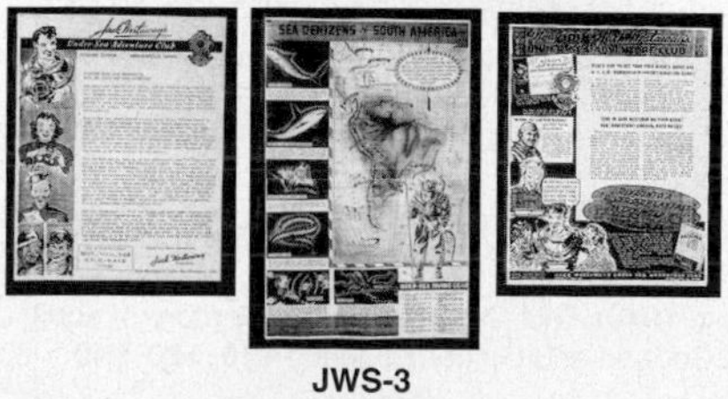

JWS-3

❑ **JWS-3. Member Recruitment Brochure,**
1930s. Malt-O-Meal. Cover features letter from Jack Westaway, center depicts "Sea Denizens of South America" with map and back cover tells how to order diver's badge and membership card. - **$40 $80 $175**

JWS-4

JWS-5

❑ **JWS-4. Shark's Tooth Story Letter,**
1930s. Malt-O-Meal. Front describes shark's tooth premium with coupon for a friend. Reverse recruits new member with coupon for diver's badge and membership card. - **$18 $30 $60**

❑ **JWS-5. "Jack Westaway Under The Sea/U.S.A.C." Brass Diver's Helmet Badge,**
1930s. - **$15 $30 $70**

Jackie Coogan

Jackie Coogan (1914-1984) is recognized as the movies' first major child star. He first appeared on screen in the 1917 feature *Skinner's Baby*, then in the 1919 short *A Day's Pleasure*. He became a major star with the February 6, 1921 First National feature *The Kid*. Charlie Chaplin wrote, produced, directed and starred in the film story of Chaplin's tramp character rescuing the orphaned Coogan. Other notable Coogan films of the 1920s and 1930s include: *Peck's Bad Boy* 1921, *Circus Days* as Toby Tyler in 1923, Tom Sawyer 1930, Huckleberry Finn 1931. He was married to Betty Grable from 1937 to 1939 and they both appeared in the 1939 feature *Million Dollar Legs*. In 1935, Coogan was due to receive what he thought would be four million dollars for his work as a child actor. He had to take his mother and stepfather to court, and only received $126,000. The unjust treatment led to passage of the Child Actors Bill, known as the Coogan act. He served in the Army in WWII, then returned to acting in films and the new medium of television.

Fame once again came to Jackie Coogan in the form of *The Addams Family* TV show. Based on the macabre *New Yorker* cartoons of Charles Addams, the series aired from September 18, 1964 until April 8, 1966. Coogan played Uncle Fester Frump in 35 episodes. He wore a fur coat, was bald and sadistic and capable of conducting electricity. He was the voice of the same character in the spin-off Hanna-Barbera cartoon series in 1973-1974. His last film was *The Escape Artist* in 1982.

JKC-1

❑ **JKC-1. Jackie Coogan As The Kid Celluloid Figure,**
1921. 5.5" tall figure in outfit like he wore in the movie "The Kid" which was Charlie Chaplin's first self-produced and directed feature. - **$25 $50 $125**

JKC-2

❑ **JKC-2. "Jackie Coogan" Metal Pair,**
1921. 3.5" tall painted metal place card holder with thin metal stand for card at feet. 3.25" tall matchbox/match holder. Metal figure of Coogan on top with nameplate.
Card Holder - **$20 $40 $65**
Match Holder - **$25 $50 $75**

JKC-3

❑ **JKC-3. Jackie Coogan "The Kid" Pencil Boxes And Figurine,**
1921. Two 2x7.75x.75" hinged tin litho pencil boxes. Green box has 1.75" "Boston Confectionary" sticker at bottom and is marked "Beautebox/Canco." Blue box is marked "Wallace Pencil Co./USA" at bottom. 7.5" tall painted chalk figure reads "Jackie Coogan/The Kid." Each Box - **$20 $40 $75**
Figure - **$25 $50 $100**

JKC-4

JKC-5

❑ **JKC-4. "Jackie Coogan In 'Circus Days'" First Toby Tyler Movie Button,**
1923. A.W. Patrick, Maker Adelaide. 1.25" Australian promotional button for silent movie. - **$20 $35 $65**

❑ **JKC-5. "Jackie Coogan Club" Cello. Button,**
1920s. - **$15 $40 $80**

JKC-6

❑ **JKC-6. Jackie Coogan Notes,**
1930s. 12 Note paper sheets and envelopes.
Each Note with Envelope - **$25**
Box - **$35 $70 $150**

JKC-7

❑ **JKC-7. "Jackie Coogan In The Kid Grows Up" 8-Pager,**
c. 1940s. 3x4-3/8" x-rated 8-page story of adult Coogan and Ginger Rogers. - **$10 $20 $40**

Jackie Gleason

Born Herbert John "Jackie" Gleason (1916-1987), the Great One excelled as a comedian, actor, composer and conductor. Gleason worked in carnivals and sideshows in the late 1930s. By the early 1940s he had minor roles in feature films, including *Navy Blues* with Ann Sheridan in 1941 and *All Through The Night* with Humphrey Bogart in 1942. He went on to work in nightclubs. His popularity led to the starring role on the Dumont TV show *The Life Of Riley* playing aircraft worker Chester A. Riley. The show aired from October 4, 1949 through March 28, 1950 and won TV's first Emmy Award for best film made for TV. Gleason also hosted *The Cavalcade of Stars* variety show from 1949 to 1952. A comedy sketch, *The Honeymooners* first aired on the October 6, 1951 show. He played Ralph Kramden, bus driver, and Art Carney played sewer worker Ed Norton. *The Jackie Gleason Show* originally aired October 1, 1955 through September 22, 1956 and included 39 episodes of *The Honeymooners*. Still in syndication today, Audrey Meadows played Ralph's wife Alice and Joyce Randolph played Norton's wife Trixie. Gleason also produced the Dorsey Brothers *Stage Show* which featured young Elvis Presley in his first TV performance on January 28, 1956.

Later films included *The Hustler* as Minnesota Fats in 1961, *Gigot* (which he also wrote) in 1962, *Papa's Delicate Condition* in 1963 and two *Smokey And The Bandit* films as Sheriff Buford T. Justice (1980 and 1983). He released 20 instrumental record albums on the Capitol label between 1953 and 1969. "How sweet it is!"

JKG-1

❑ **JKG-1. Jackie Gleason Photo Card,**
1940s. NBC TV premium. - **$25 $50 $75**

JKG-2

❑ JKG-2. Rare Jackie Gleason Glass,
1955. VIP Corp. 5.5" tall with weighted bottom and wrap-around design of Gleason characters. - **$50 $125 $225**

JKG-3

JKG-4

❑ JKG-3. "Jackie Gleason Plays Romantic Jazz" Record,
1955. Capitol. 12.25x12.25" cardboard album cover contains 33-1/3 rpm record in "Capitol" inner sleeve. - **$5 $15 $30**

❑ JKG-4. "Jackie Gleason Bus Driver's Outfit" Boxed Set,
1955. Empire Plastic Corp. 10x15x3.25" deep box contains thin vinyl bus driver's cap, money changer, ticket puncher, bus transfers, plastic coins. - **$150 $300 $600**

JKG-5

❑ JKG-5. "Story Stage Starring Jackie Gleason And His TV Troupe" Boxed Punchout Dolls And Stage,
1955. VIP Corp. 12.25x18.25x1.75" deep box contains 13 punchout dolls, 2 stage sets, stage curtain, 8 costume changes, players' scripts, studio tickets, "Magic Magnet Character Animator." - **$175 $325 $550**

JKG-6

❑ JKG-6. "Jackie Gleason The Bus Driver" Button,
1955. VIP Corp. 1.25" button that was sold off store cards. - **$10 $20 $40**

JKG-7

❑ JKG-7. TV Repair Shop Sign Featuring Jackie Gleason,
1950s. 11.75x15.75" cardboard sign with small die-cut hole as made for hanging. Reverse has stenciled name of TV repair shop. - **$35 $65 $125**

JKG-8

JKG-9

❑ JKG-8. "Jackie Gleason Fan Club" Litho. Button,
1950s. - **$20 $40 $80**

❑ JKG-9. "And Away We Go! With Jackie Gleason" 10" Vinyl Record,
1950s. Capitol. 33-1/3 rpm vinyl record in 10x10" sleeve with illustration of Jackie Gleason as "The Poor Soul." - **$25 $50 $100**

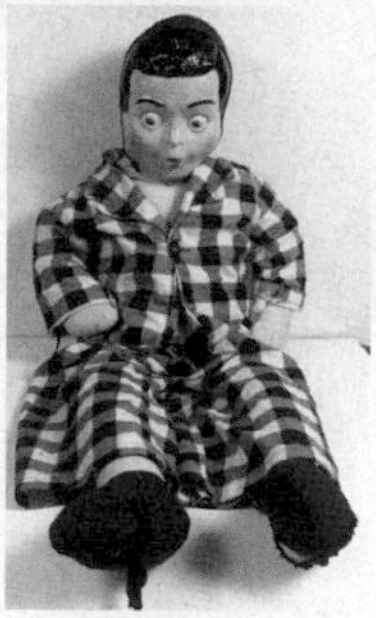

JKG-10

❑ JKG-10. Jackie Gleason Large Dancing Doll,
1950s. 6x14x38" tall doll with stuffed body and dressed in checkered jacket and pants, both having plastic buttons and suspenders. Front of head is molded plastic. Both feet and one hand have elastic straps, while other hand is without strap as made and was intended to just be held when "dancing" with doll. - **$60 $125 $200**

JKG-11

❑ JKG-11. "Jackie Gleason American Cancer Society" Poster,
1950s. 18" glossy paper poster featuring photo of Gleason with text "Jackie Gleason Says...Put Up A Buck To Fight Cancer." - **$50 $100 $160**

JKG-12

❑ JKG-12. Jackie Gleason Golf Watch,
1980. Timex. 3-3/8x4x2" deep snap case contains watch with 1.25" diameter dial. Watch was for the "1980 Jackie Gleason Inverrary Classic." Only 125 made. - **$65 $125 $250**

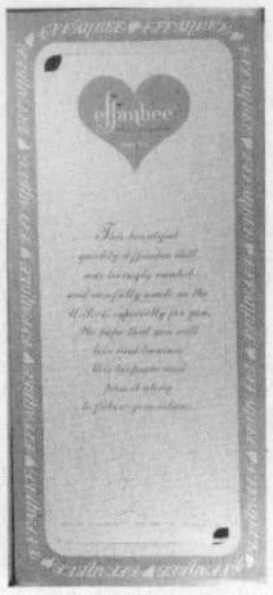

JKG-13 (SAME BOX FOR BOTH DOLLS) JKG-14

❑ **JKG-13. "Honeymooners" Jackie Gleason as Ralph Kramden Doll with Box,**
1986. From Effanbee. Boxed with 2 tags- **$225**

❑ **JKG-14. "Honeymooners" Art Carney as Ed Norton Doll with Box,**
1986. From Effanbee. Boxed with 2 tags- **$225**

Jackie Robinson

Born in Cairo, Georgia, John Roosevelt (Jackie) Robinson is well-remembered by baseball fans as the first black athlete admitted to Major League play in 1947. Fewer recall that he was previously a three-sport star at UCLA from 1939 to 1941, a US army lieutenant in WWII from 1942 to 1944, and a star shortstop and batter for the Kansas City Monarchs of the Negro League in 1945.

Robinson was selected personally as a Major League hopeful by Branch Rickey, venerable owner of the Brooklyn Dodgers. Rickey insisted that his candidate not only be a promising athlete but an individual of courage to withstand the expected insults and other abuse that might result from being the first black man in a white man's game. Robinson was signed to a 1946 contract with the Montreal farm club of the Dodgers and demonstrated his baseball ability through the batting championship that year for Montreal as well as the International League. Still, his Major League acceptance faced an obstacle–a 15-1 negative vote by club owners that was overridden by the single vote of Baseball Commissioner A.B. (Happy) Chandler.

Robinson thus became a Brooklyn Dodger in 1947, earning Rookie of the Year by talent alone, as well as the grudging admiration of players and fans alike. His subsequent career only added to his accomplishments as a fielder, batter, baserunner (National League's Most Valuable Player of 1949) and contributor to National League championships by Brooklyn in 1947, 1949, 1952, 1953, 1955 and 1956. Principally he is known as the pioneer who opened the Major Leagues to many other black players hitherto restricted to "their" leagues.

Robinson starred as himself in the 1950 film biography, The Jackie Robinson Story. After the 1956 season, at age 37, he was traded to the New York Giants but chose retirement instead. He was inducted into Baseball's Hall of Fame in 1962.

As a baseball retiree, Robinson continued as a highly-regarded spokesman for the NAACP and the YMCA in addition to business successes. Robinson suffered his second heart attack in 1972 at his Stamford, Connecticut home and died at age 53.

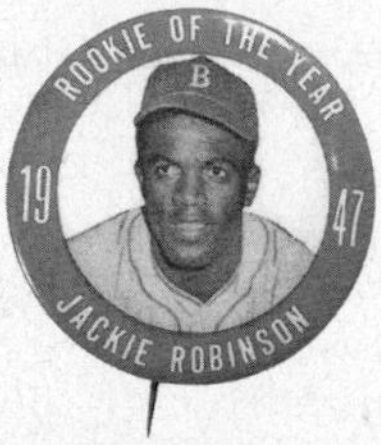

JKR-1

❑ **JKR-1. Rookie of the Year Pinback,**
1947. - **$55 $120 $175**

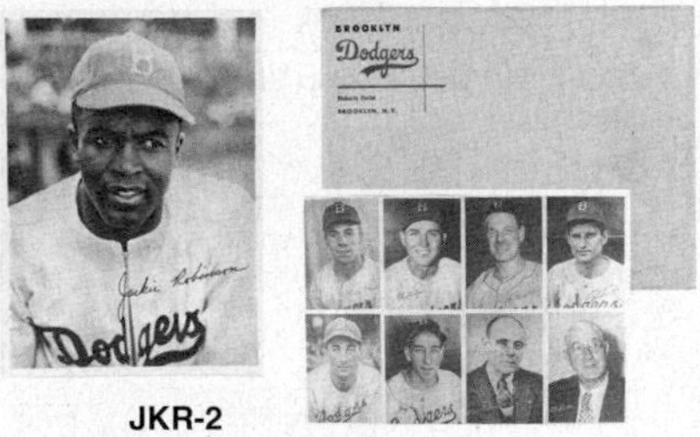

JKR-2

❑ **JKR-2. Brooklyn Dodgers Complete Picture Pack With Envelope,**
1948. Set consists of 26 black and white photos, each 6.5x9" with facsimile signatures in 7x10.75" original envelope.
Set In Envelope - **$60 $125 $225**

JKR-3

❑ **JKR-3. "Slugger At The Bat" Record Album,**
1949. Two 78 rpm records featuring voices of Brooklyn Dodgers Pee Wee Reese and Jackie Robinson. Columbia Records. - **$60 $125 $250**

JKR-4

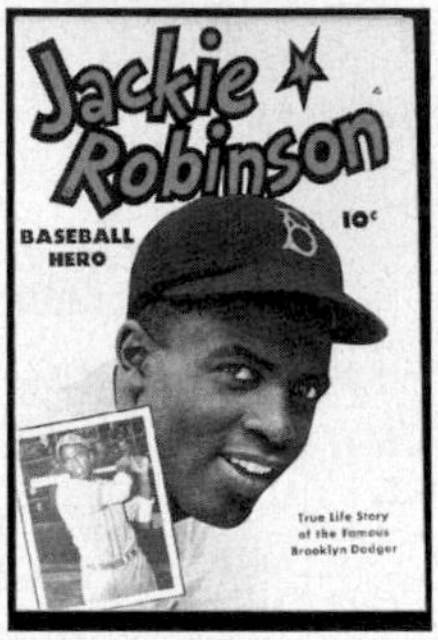

JKR-5

❑ **JKR-4. "Jackie Robinson" Button With Attachments,**
c. 1949. 1.75" cello centered by black and white photo on upper blue background. Attached are red/white/blue striped fabric ribbons plus keychain holding miniature gold baseball and bat. - **$65 $150 $300**

❑ **JKR-5. Jackie Robinson Baseball Hero Comic Book #1,**
1950. Fawcett Publications. Has photo cover and life story presented inside. Hard to find in high grade. - **$55 $165 $800**

JKR-6

❑ **JKR-6. Dime Bank,**
1950. Sold at stores and through ads in comic books. - **$165 $350 $550**

JKR-7

❑ **JKR-7. Dime Bank Variety,**
1950. Kalm Mfg. Co. 5/8" thick by 2.5x2.5". Images on two edges show action play. Third edge has "Jackie Robinson" facsimile signature. Top has notation "Insert Dime Here" by slot. Back has panel that reads "Press Down at $5." - **$175 $375 $600**

JKR-8

❑ **JKR-8. Metal Bust Bank,**
1950. Rare. Offered as a premium in Jackie Robinson comic books. Original is very detailed and has black color on face and arms over a bronze color for the rest of the bust. - **$350 $700 $1200**

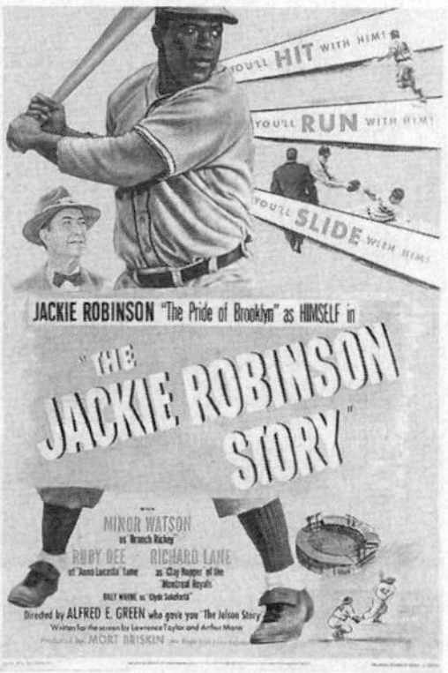

JKR-9

❑ **JKR-9. "The Jackie Robinson Story" Movie Poster,**
1950. Scarce. 41"x 61". One of the great baseball posters of the time. - **$650 $1300 $2250**

JKR-10

JKR-11

❑ **JKR-10. Life Magazine,**
1950. May 8 issue subtitled "Star Ball Player Stars In A Movie." **$20 $35 $75**

❑ **JKR-11. Cane With Plastic Handle,**
c. 1950. Store or vendor's item. 31-1/2" tall with 3-1/4" hard plastic hand grip inscribed "Jackie." **$200 $350 $650**

JKR-12

❑ **JKR-12. Doll with Box and Accessories,**
c. 1950. Allied-Brand Doll Mfg. Co. Uniformed doll comes with wooden bat and pocket baseball game in box. Box - **$300 $800 $1350**
Doll - **$480 $1300 $2500**
Tag - **$40 $75 $100**
Bat - **$30 $75 $150**
Pocket Baseball Game - **$150 $300 $600**
Complete - **$1000 $2500 $4800**

JKR-13

❑ **JKR-13. Calendar Sample Photo,**
c. 1950. Full color 7-1/2x9-1/2" with 2x2" sticker upper right for unnamed publisher listing costs for using the photo on calendars. - **$40 $75 $150**

JKR-14

❑ **JKR-14. Quick Magazine,**
1952. October 6 issue subtitled "The World Series: Does The Best Team Win?" - **$15 $30 $60**

JKR-15

❑ **JKR-15. Hoak-Robinson Topps Double Header Card,**
1955. From Topps Gum card set of folders designed with both player images sharing the same lower leg and foot artwork. - **$60 $115 $300**

JKR-16

❑ **JKR-16. "Jackie Robinson" Figural Candy Container Cover,**
1950s. Plastic store item by Petitto Studio. - **$65 $140 $280**

JKR-17

JKR-18

❑ **JKR-17. "Team For Rockefeller" Endorsement Paper,**
c. 1962. 3-1/8" diecut to be made into a button.
Paper Unfinished - **$50 $100 $150**
Paper Finished Into Button - **$75 $125 $200**

❑ **JKR-18. "The Jackie Robinson Story" Hardback Book,**
1963. 254 page book with a 5 page photo gallery. - **$12 $25 $50**

JKR-19

❑ **JKR-19. Commemorative Coin,**
1997. $1 Silver and $5 gold coins, uncirculated and proofs. Official coins struck at the U.S. Mint to commemorate the 50th anniversary of Robinson's arrival in the Majors.
$1 Silver uncirculated - **$85**
$1 Silver proof - **$70**
$5 Gold uncirculated - **$3200**
$5 Gold proof - **$800**

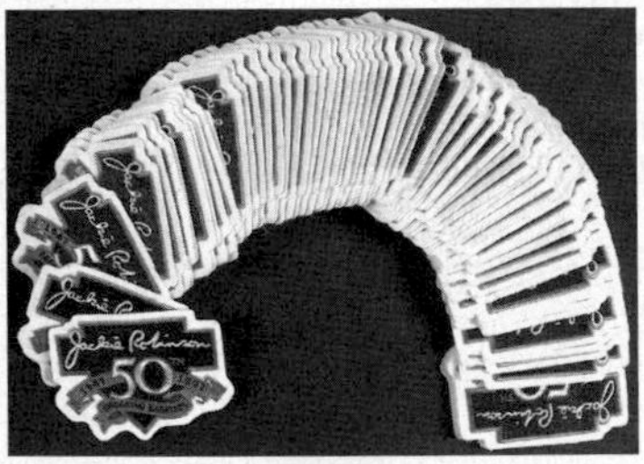

JKR-20

❑ **JKR-20. Jackie Robinson 50th Anniversary Patches,**
1997. Pictured is lot of 70 original and official 3x4" fabric patches sewn on each major league player's uniform that year to commemorative his 1947 "Breaking Barriers" as Black player into major league baseball. Each - **$8 $15 $30**

James Bond

English novelist Ian Fleming (1908-1964) created James Bond, the fabled Agent 007 of the British secret service, in a series of thrillers beginning with *Casino Royale* in 1953 and continuing until his death. But it was the film versions of the novels, starting with *Dr. No* in 1963, that made Bond an international hero. Sean Connery first embodied the cool but deadly Bond for millions of fans around the world. Licensed to kill, carrying a Baretta or Walther PPK, drinking his martinis shaken not stirred, and enjoying success with the ladies, Bond has defeated a string of unlikely villains in the most exotic of settings. Connery and Roger Moore each played Bond in seven films. Others who played the smooth commander: David Niven in the 1967 spoof (with Peter Sellers playing his replacement as James Bond and Woody Allen playing his evil nephew, Jimmy), *Casino Royale*; George Lazenby in *On Her Majesty's Secret Service* (1969); Timothy Dalton in *The Living Daylights* (1987) and *Licence to Kill* (1989); and Pierce Brosnan in *Goldeneye* (1995), *Tomorrow Never Dies* (1997), *The World is Not Enough* (1999), and *Die Another Day* (2002). Daniel Craig was cast as Bond for a serious remake of *Casino Royale*, released in November 2006. He'll return in *Quantum of Solace,* due for a November 2008 release. Agent 007 has also entered the world of high tech video games. *Everything Or Nothing*, with Brosnan voicing the Bond role, and Connery reprised his role as 007 in the video game version of *From Russia With Love*.

Bond comic books appeared in the 1980s and 1990s, and the novels were adapted as a comic strip for the *London Daily Express* from 1957 into the 1960s. *James Bond Jr.*, a syndicated half-hour television cartoon, aired in 1991-1993. Merchandising of Bond items has been extensive, with most toys of the 1960s era produced by Gilbert and Corgi.

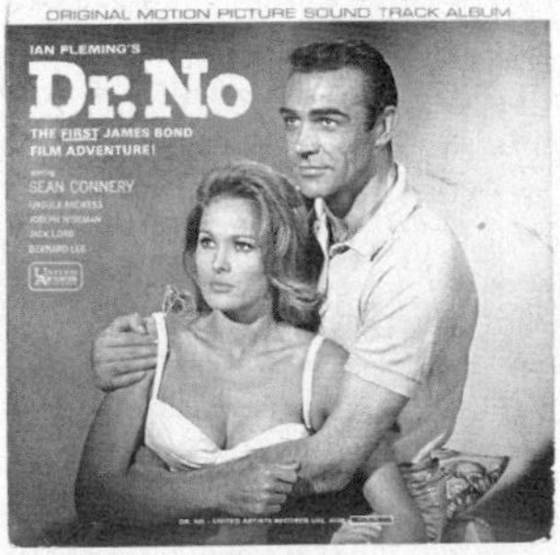

JBD-1

❑ **JBD-1. "Dr. No" Sound Track Album,**
1962. - **$75 $125 $185**

JBD-2

JBD-3

❑ **JBD-2. "Agent 007" 3-1/2" Cello. Button,**
1964. Design includes image of woman painted gold from Goldfinger movie. - **$30 $50 $100**

❑ **JBD-3. Dell "James Bond 007" Magazine,**
1964. - **$25 $40 $90**

JBD-4

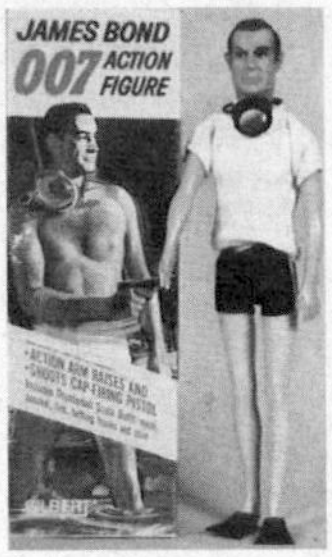

JBD-5

❑ **JBD-4. "Special Agent 007" Badge,**
1965. On card. - **$55 $85 $185**

❑ **JBD-5. "James Bond Action Figure" Boxed,**
1965. Store item by Gilbert. 12-1/2" tall with complete accessories of shirt, shorts, fins, mask, snorkel, small metal cap-firing gun with holster in envelope plus instruction sheet.
Near Mint Boxed - **$450**
Complete Unboxed - **$65 $150 $275**

JBD-6

❑ **JBD-6. Odd Job Action Figure,**
1965. Store item by Gilbert. 10-1/4" tall in karate outfit plus black belt, elastic headband and with plastic derby. Near Mint Boxed - **$550**
Unboxed Complete - **$100 $200 $350**

JBD-7

❑ **JBD-7. Action Toys Display Sign,**
1965. Gilbert. 6x19-1/2" stiff cardboard sign originally held in a wire display rack. -
$90 $200 $400

JBD-8 JBD-9

❑ **JBD-8. "James Bond Secret Agent 007 Odd Job Action Puppet" On Card,**
1965. Gilbert. 12" tall soft vinyl puppet with 9" arm span and a 4" diameter vacuform plastic derby. Figure is attached with wire twists to a 9.75x15.75" unpunched cardboard.
Near Mint on Card - **$1200**
Loose - **$150 $300 $600**

❑ **JBD-9. Gum Card Set,**
1965. Set of 66 issued by Philadelphia Chewing Gum Co. Set - **$65 $135 $260**

JBD-10

❑ **JBD-10. "James Bond Secret Agent 007 Marksmanship Range Target Set,"**
1965. Multiple Products. 14.25x17.5x3.25" deep cellophane-wrapped frame with insert. Set includes 4.75x9.5" long shooting pistol, scope, silencer, three swing targets and harmless bullets. Gun and scope both have "007 Gun" logo and grip of pistol has initials "JB."
Boxed - **$450 $875 $1750**

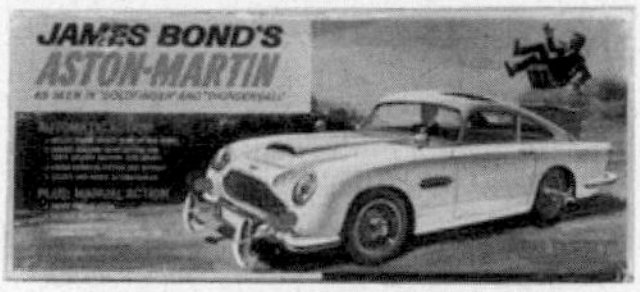

JBD-11

❑ **JBD-11. "James Bond's Aston-Martin" Toy Car With Box,**
1965. Store item by Gilbert Co. Battery operated metal replica including design feature that ejects passenger in addition to other mechanical features. Near Mint Boxed - **$1000**
Loose - **$200 $400 $750**

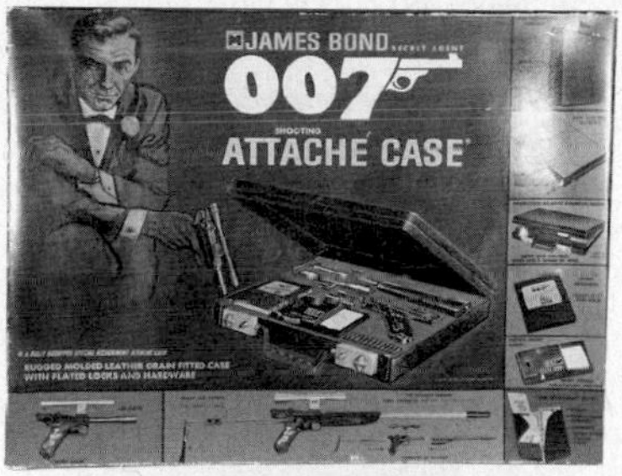

(Original box)

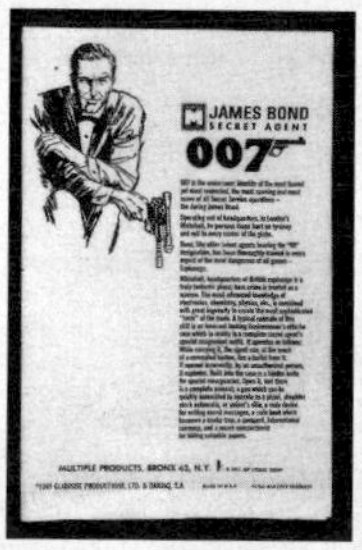

(front view)

JBD-12

(side view)

❑ **JBD-12. "James Bond Secret Agent 007 Attaché Case,"**
1965. Store item by Multiple Products. Black plastic case holding gun and attachments, black flexible plastic dagger (frequently missing), code and decoder items, wallet with passport, business cards, play money. Case itself has trick-firing mechanism. Case Only - **$300 $600 $1200**
With original rare box, add **$500 $1000 $1500**
NM Complete - **$2700**

JBD-13

❑ **JBD-13. "James Bond 007 Spy Tricks" Magic Set,**
1965. Gilbert. 13.75x20.25x2.25" deep box designed like briefcase includes James Bond's Secret Pistol, Third Degree Disk Trick, Secret Key Detector, Odd Job Hat Trick, Magic Spy Tag, Amazing Chain Escape, Double Agent Trick, The Vanishing Key, 007 Lie Detector and The Magic Money Converter.
Boxed - **$400 $800 $1200**

JBD-14

❑ **JBD-14. "James Bond Secret Agent 007 Secret 7 Rifle And Pistol" Set,**
1965. Box is 14x22x2" deep by Multiple Toy Makers. Set is composed of "The Complete Arsenal": Rifle Barrel, Silencer, Rifle Stock, Bullets, Pistol, "Super" Scope And Calling Cards." Set could be used as "Pistol Only, Automated Pistol With Scope, Shoulder Stock Automated Pistol, "Secret 7" Rifle." "Fires Harmless Bullets Automatically. Assembles In Seconds." Complete Boxed - **$350 $700 $1350**

JBD-15

❑ **JBD-15. "Goldfinger James Bond" 100 Shot Cap Pistol with Silencer,**
1965. Gun With Silencer - **$75 $150 $300**
Box - **$65 $125 $200**
Complete - **$140 $275 $500**

JBD-16

❑ **JBD-16. "James Bond Road Race" Boxed,**
1965. Sears, Roebuck & Co. Exclusive. Large 12x18x26" box containing elaborate slot car race course and accessories by A. C. Gilbert Co. Accessories include Aston Martin and Mustang slot cars as packaged.
Boxed Complete - **$500 $1000 $2000**

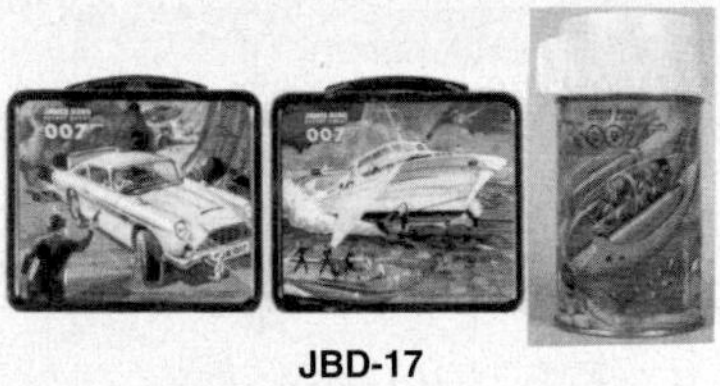

JBD-17

❑ **JBD-17."James Bond" Lunch Box,**
1966. Store item by Aladdin.
Box - **$150 $300 $750**
Bottle - **$85 $150 $250**

JBD-18

❑ **JBD-18. Fabric Banner,**
1966. 15x25" white cotton printed by portrait and action scenes in combination of black/red/yellow/blue. Copyright Glidrose Productions. -
$50 $100 $200

JBD-19

❑ **JBD-19. James Bond Spy Watch,**
1968. Made by Gilbert. Comes in display box with instructions.
Boxed - **$200 $375 $650**

JBD-20

❑ **JBD-20. "James Bond Thunderball" Gum Card Set,**
1966. Second set issued by Philadelpha Chewing Gum Co. Set of 66.
Set - **$75 $160 $325**

JBD-21

❑ **JBD-21. Spanish Weapon Set,**
1960s. Large 14x21x2" box containing set by "Lemssa" although nearly identical to U.S. set by Gilbert consisting of plastic and metal 8" pistol with rifle barrel extension, silencer, scope with cover, shoulder stock, packet of projectiles. - **$85 $175 $350**

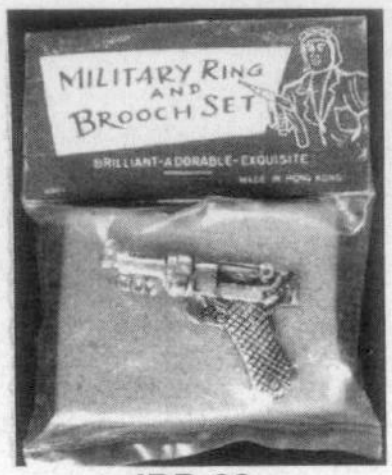

JBD-22 JBD-23

❑ **JBD-22. Sean Connery Fan Photo,**
1960s. - **$10 $20 $40**

❑ **JBD-23. "007" Replica Pistol Ring in Package,**
1960s. Store item, unauthorized. Gold luster or aluminum.
Packaged - **$10 $20 $30**
Loose - **$5 $15 $20**

JBD-25

JBD-24

JBD-26

❑ **JBD-24. James Bond Plastic Snow Dome,**
1960s. Store item. - **$60 $165 $315**

❑ **JBD-25. James Bond "Agent 007 Espionage" Litho. Button,**
1960s. Vending machine issue. - **$5 $10 $15**

❑ **JBD-26. James Bond "Goldfinger's Death Derby" Litho. Button,**
1960s. Vending machine issue. - **$5 $10 $15**

JBD-27 JBD-28 JBD-29

❑ **JBD-27. James Bond "Laser Beam/ Goldfinger's Ray Machine" Litho. Button,**
1960s. Vending machine issue. - **$5 $10 $15**

❑ **JBD-28. James Bond "Calling Agent 007" Litho. Button,**
1960s. Vending machine issue. - **$5 $10 $15**

❑ **JBD-29. James Bond "Agent 007" Plastic Ring,**
1960s. Vending machine issue. - **$20 $40 $80**

JBD-30 JBD-31

❑ **JBD-30. "007" Plastic Ring,**
1960s. Vending machine item depicting shield symbol. From set of five. Each - **$18 $30 $60**

❑ **JBD-31. "007" Plastic Ring,**
1960s. Vending machine item depicting face silhouette. From set of five. Each - **$18 $30 $60**

JBD-32 JBD-33

❑ **JBD-32. "007" Plastic Ring,**
1960s. Vending machine item picturing car. From set of five. Each - **$18 $30 $60**

❑ **JBD-33. "007" Plastic Flicker Ring,**
1960s. Vending machine issue from set of 12. Images are James Bond portrait and "007" numeral partially formed by image of pistol as the third numeral.
Each Silver Base - **$15 $30 $55**
Each Blue Base - **$5 $15 $30**

JBD-34 JBD-35 JBD-36

❑ **JBD-34. "007 Coming Soon!" 3" Cello. Button,**
1960s. Probably worn by movie theater employees. - **$18 $35 $70**

❑ **JBD-35. "James Bond's Brew/007 Special Blend" 2-1/2" Cello. Button,**
1960s. For apparently unauthorized beverage. - **$15 $30 $50**

❑ **JBD-36. "Agent 0007" Bond-Inspired 3" Cello. Ad Button,**
1960s. "Wilton Vise Squad" issue picturing example bench vise. - **$15 $30 $50**

JBD-37

❑ **JBD-37. "Moonraker View-Master" Store Display,**
1979. 13-1/2x17" diecut. - **$25 $50 $100**

JBD-38

❑ **JBD-38. Official James Bond 007 Secret Agent Complete Spy Set,**
1970s. Set by Coibel is 14x14x1.75" deep. Set includes 6.5" long metal 45 automatic cap-firing gun, silencer, caps, shoulder holster, exploding pen with Union Jack decal, James Bond badge and "Her Majesties Secret Service Secret Agent Identification" wallet.
Boxed Set - **$60 $125 $175**

JBD-39

JBD-40

❑ **JBD-39. Movie Promotion Cello. English Buttons,**
1981. Eon Productions Ltd. For release of movie "For Your Eyes Only." Each - **$5 $10 $20**

❑ **JBD-40. "Michelin Dealers' 007 Sweepstakes" 3-1/2" Cello. Button,**
1985. Michelin tires. Art pictures Roger Moore as James Bond posed beside Michelin Man. - **$15 $30 $50**

JBD-41 JBD-42

❑ **JBD-41. James Bond Action Episode Game,**
1985. The Man With the Golden Gun.
Boxed - **$55**

❑ **JBD-42. James Bond Action Episode Game,**
1985. You Only Live Twice. Boxed - **$55**

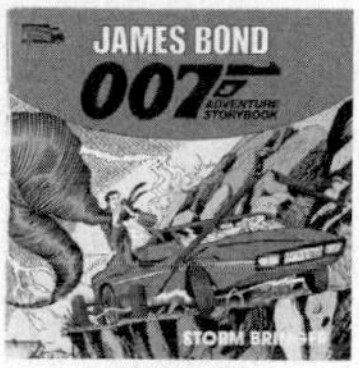

JBD-43 JBD-44

❑ **JBD-43. James Bond Adventure Storybook,**
1985. Blackclaw's Doomsday Plot. - **$8 $18 $30**

❑ **JBD-44. James Bond Adventure Storybook,**
1985. Storm Bringer. - **$8 $18 $30**

JBD-45 JBD-46

❑ **JBD-45. Movie Car Replica on Card,**
1998. Johnny Lightning series - For Your Eyes Only. - **$15**

❑ **JBD-46. Movie Car Replica on Card,**
1998. Johnny Lightning series - Goldeneye. - **$15**

JBD-47 JBD-48

❑ **JBD-47. Movie Car Replica on Card,**
1998. Johnny Lightning series - Goldfinger. - **$15**

❑ **JBD-48. Movie Car Replica on Card,**
1998. Johnny Lightning series - On Her Majesty's Secret Service. - **$15**

JBD-49

JBD-50

❑ **JBD-49. Movie Car Replica on Card,**
1998. Johnny Lightning series - The Living Daylights. - **$15**

❑ **JBD-50. Movie Car Replica on Card,**
1998. Johnny Lightning series - The Spy Who Loved Me. - **$15**

JBD-51

JBD-52

❑ **JBD-51. Movie Car Replica on Card,**
1998. Johnny Lightning series - Ford Mustang from Thunderball. - **$10**

❑ **JBD-52. Movie Car Replica on Card,**
1998. Johnny Lightning series - Aston Martin from Goldfinger. - **$10**

James Dean

The untimely and tragic death of this young actor (1931-1955) evoked an international outpouring of anguish and disbelief by his fandom. While he appeared in several TV dramas, he is most remembered for three feature films: *Rebel Without A Cause* (1955); *East of Eden* (1955); and *Giant* (1956). His brief acting career epitomized the moody, brooding, casual restlessness of young adulthood. Due to this brevity, related memorabilia from the 1950s is scarce. A few buttons were produced before his death but the most frequently encountered 1950s item is a memorial brass medalet offered by *Modern Screen Magazine* in October 1956.

JDN-1

❑ **JDN-1. "Rebel Without A Cause" Insert Poster,**
1955. Poster is 14x36" - **$350 $750 $1500**

JDN-2

JDN-3

❑ **JDN-2. "James Dean's" Denim Jeans,**
1955. Store item by J.S.B. Adult sized, likened to those worn in his movies Rebel Without a Cause, East of Eden, Giant. With Tag - **$50 $100 $200**

❑ **JDN-3. Cello. 3-1/2" Photo Button,**
1955. Store item. Issued before his death. - **$25 $50 $100**

JDN-4

❑ **JDN-4. Premium Color Photo,**
1955. 8 x 10" color photo printed on unstable thin paper. Promotes "Rebel Without a Cause" movie. These were passed out at drive-in theaters. - **$25 $45 $90**

JDN-5

❑ **JDN-5. Printing Plate for First Promo Button,**
1955. - **$150**

JDN-6 **JDN-7** **JDN-8**

❑ **JDN-6. Cello. 3-1/2" Button,**
c. 1955. Store item. Issued before his death. - **$30 $60 $115**

❑ **JDN-7. Color Portrait 2-1/2" Cello. Button,**
c. 1955. Photo with facsimile signature. - **$25 $40 $80**

❑ **JDN-8. "James Dean" Hanky,**
c. 1955. Store item totally unmarked but seems to be of the 1955-1956 era. 11x11-1/2" sheer fabric with color portrait of him in red shirt against blue background. - **$35 $75 $150**

JDN-9

❑ **JDN-9. Commemorative Brass Necklace Medallion,**
c. 1955. "Modern Screen" magazine. Inscription "In Memory Of James Dean 1931-1955". - **$5 $15 $30**

JDN-10

❑ **JDN-10. Cello Button,**
c. 1955. 2.5" color photo on green background issued prior to death. - **$25 $40 $80**

JDN-11

❑ **JDN-11. "This Then Is Texas" Song Sheet,**
1956. From "Giant" movie, Dean's last. -
$20 $40 $60

JDN-12

JDN-13

❑ **JDN-12. Commemorative China Plate,**
c. 1956. Store item. - **$40 $60 $125**

❑ **JDN-13. "I, James Dean" Paperback Biography,**
1957. Store item published by Popular Library. First published biography after his death. -
$8 $15 $40

JDN-14

❑ **JDN-14. James Dean And Tony Perkins Magazine Cut-Out Record,**
1957. Record was bound into an issue of "Hear, The Voice Of Hollywood" magazine. Label is inscribed "Rainbo Records." 7" diameter stiff cardboard. Gordon Gold archives.
Magazine Complete - **$35 $75 $150**
Record Only - **$15 $30 $60**

JDN-15

❑ **JDN-15. "James Dean's Jeans!" Card With Sample,**
1983. 4x6" card with blister pack square that "Actually Contains A Piece Of Jimmy's Clothing." - **$30 $60 $100**

(Box)

(Certificate Booklet)

JDN-16

❑ **JDN-16. James Dean Doll with Tag in Box,**
1985. By Elegante Dolls. 17 3/4" tall doll has uncanny likeness of Dean. Hard to find.
Boxed - **$675**

JDN-17

JDN-17. "Rebel Without a Cause" Movie Alarm Clock,
1991. Turner product. - **$15 $30 $65**

JDN-18

JDN-19

JDN-18. 100 Piece Photo Puzzle,
1995. 8x10". Boxed - **$4 $8 $15**

JDN-19. James Dean Ornament,
1990s. Carlton ornament in box. - **$20**

JDN-20

JDN-20. "1949 Mercury Coupe" Model Car,
2000. Limited edition die-cast metal car. - **$50**

The Jetsons

Hanna-Barbera Studios had great success with the stone age Flintstones primetime animated series and decided to try something new. *The Jetsons* was set 100 years hence in the ultra futuristic, sky high Orbit City. The original series ran on ABC between September 23, 1962 and March 3, 1963 with a total of 24 episodes. The family lived in Skypad Apartments and the show utilized a multitude of sophisticated gadgets. Voice actors included: George O'Hanlon as George Jetson, Penny Singleton as wife and mother Jane, Daws Butler as Son Elroy, Janet Waldo as daughter Judy, Don Messick as Astro the dog, Jean Vander Pyl as the maid Rosie the robot and Mel Blanc as George's boss Cosmo Spacely.

A new series of cartoons came out between 1985 and 1987. Two TV movies were released: *The Jetsons Meet The Flintstones* in 1987 and *Rockin' with Judy Jetson* in 1988. Universal released *Jetsons: The Movie* animated feature film July 6, 1990.

The Jetsons had quite a career in comic books, with publishers including: Gold Key #1-36 January 1963-October 1970, Charlton #1-20 November 1970-December 1973, Harvey Vol 2 #1-5 September 1992-November 1993, Archie #1-17 September 1995-August 1996 and DC *The Flintstones and the Jetsons* #1-21 August 1997-April 1999.

The August 1, 2004 issue of *TV Guide* lists George Jetson fourth in a list of the 25 greatest sci-fi legends.

JET-1

❑ **JET-1. "The Jetsons" Die-cut Magic Slate,**
1962. Watkins-Strathmore Co. 8.5x13.5" die-cut thin cardboard slate with stylus. - **$15 $30 $60**

JET-2

JET-3

❑ **JET-2. "The Jetsons Fun Pad" Boxed Game,**
1963. Milton Bradley. 10.75x14x1.5" deep box contains white plastic dome with three colored vinyl pads and die-cut orange plastic fun pad base, 18 blue plastic figural space cars with Jetson family inside each. - **$50 $100 $200**

❑ **JET-3. "The Jetsons Out Of This World Game",**
1963. Transogram. 10x19.25x2" deep box holds 19x19" gameboard, instructions, punch-out figures, playing pieces and dice. - **$50 $100 $175**

JET-4

❑ **JET-4. George Jetson Marx Wind-Up,**
1963. 4" tall litho tin likeness figure that moves up and down and hops when wound. -
$85 $185 $325

JET-5

❑ **JET-5. "The Jetsons Spaceball" Pinball Game In Box,**
1960s. Marx. 10.5x22.5x1" deep box holds plastic and tin pinball machine.
Box - **$50 $100 $200**
Game - **$100 $200 $300**

JET-6

❑ **JET-6. Jetsons Ramp Walkers,**
1960s. Marx. 3" tall ramp walkers, one with Rosie and Astro and one with Astro and George. Each - **$25 $50 $100**

JET-7

❑ **JET-7. Elroy Jetson Pull Toy,**
1960s. Marked "Elroy" but no other markings. Plastic. 11" long by 12" tall. - **$90 $175 $300**

JET-8

❑ **JET-8. "The Jetsons Mini Puzzle" In Box,**
c. 1960s. 5-3/8x7-3/8x1.5" deep blue box contains puzzle showing George with mechanical arm dumping his automated meal on his head at the table. - **$5 $12 $20**

JET-9

❑ **JET-9. "The Jetsons" Button Lot,**
1983. Button-Up Co. Lot of 26 from set of 27, each 1.5" diameter showing various Jetsons characters in different activities. Each - **$1 $2 $3**

JET-10

❑ **JET-10. "The Jetsons" Boxed Game,**
1985. Milton Bradley. 8x15x1.25" deep box contains game including new member Orbitty. - **$10 $18 $35**

JET-11

❑ **JET-11. "The Jetsons" Watch and Pin in Small Tin Lunch Box,**
1993. Fossil product. Limited edition watch pictures the family. Pin shows Astro the dog.
Near Mint as Issued - **$300**

JET-12

JET-13

JET-14

❑ **JET-12. "Astro" Bean Bag,**
1998. With tag.Came out 1 year earlier than the rest of the Jetsons figures. - **$25**

❑ **JET-13. "George Jetson" Bean Bag,**
1999. With tag. - **$15**

❑ **JET-14. "Jane Jetson" Bean Bag,**
1999. With tag. - **$15**

JET-15

JET-16

JET-17

❑ **JET-15. "Elroy Jetson" Bean Bag,**
1999. With tag. - **$15**

❑ **JET-16. "Judy Jetson" Bean Bag,**
1999. With tag. - **$15**

❑ **JET-17. The Jetsons "Rosie" Bean Bag,**
1999. Warner Bros. copyright. 8 1/2" tall. - **$20**

JET-18

❑ **JET-18. "The Jetsons" Car Set,**
2001. Five pack set of die cast cars in box. Each family member is featured on a car. - **$30**

Jimmie Allen

Created by Robert M. Burtt and Wilfred G. Moore, *The Air Adventures of Jimmie Allen* thrilled its young radio listeners from 1933 to 1947. Jimmie was a 16-year-old messenger at the Kansas City airport, taught to fly by veteran pilot Speed Robertson. Together they courted danger, searched for lost treasure, and competed in international air races. The series was syndicated, sponsored initially by the Skelly Oil company in the Midwest, then by Richfield Oil on the West Coast and by bakeries and many other companies eager to share in the show's large audience.

Premiums were an integral part of the program from the beginning, starting with a free jigsaw puzzle offer during the third week of broadcasting and available only at Skelly gas stations. The *Jimmie Allen Flying Club* and the *Weather-Bird Flying Club* attracted thousands of applicants, all of whom received membership cards, wings, emblems, patches, flight charts, and personal letters from Jimmie. Members could pick up weekly flying lessons and model airplane kits at their local gas stations.

Other promotional items followed in great profusion: photo albums, stamp albums, road maps, whistles, ID bracelets, model planes, Flying Cadet wings. Since sponsors were free to design and mark their own premiums, many varieties were produced. Jimmie Allen Air Races were held throughout the Midwest, with thousands of fans gathering to watch the young contestants piloting their model planes. John Frank played Jimmie through 1943; Jack Schlicter took over in 1946.

Paramount Pictures released a Jimmie Allen movie, *The Sky Parade*, in 1936. Transcriptions of the original broadcasts were re-released in 1942-1943.

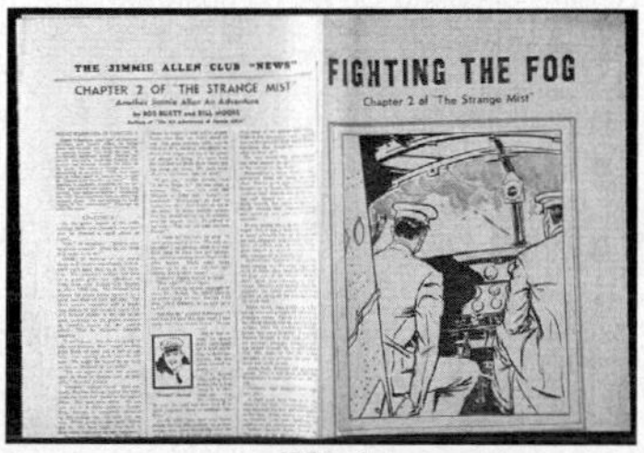

JMA-1

❑ **JMA-1. Club News Chapter 2 - "The Strange Mist",**
May 1933. Richfield Oil Co. Radio premium. At least six in series. Each - **$25 $50 $100**

JMA-2

❑ **JMA-2. Air Races Sterling Silver Wings Badge,**
1934. Skelly. 1-1/2" long marked on reverse "Sterling." Awarded only to participants. - **$150 $250 $450**

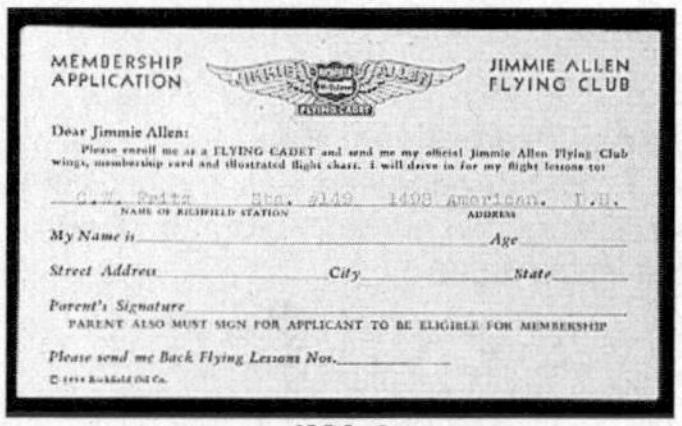

JMA-3

❑ **JMA-3. Membership Application Postcard,**
1934. Richfield Oil Co. - **$10 $20 $40**

JMA-4

❑ **JMA-4. Flying Club Promo Letter,**
1934. Letter for acceptance into Flying Club. Also promotes silver wing premium badge. Butter-Nut Bread sponsor. Brown background on letter. - **$50 $85 $135**

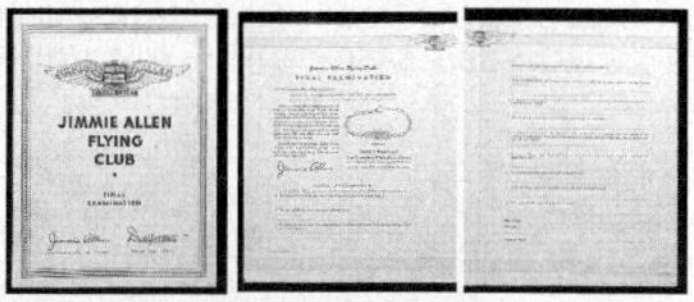

JMA-5

❑ **JMA-5. "Final Examination" Folder,**
1934. Richfield Oil Co. 8-1/2x11" folder in white, blue and yellow picturing "Pilot's Wristlet" to be sent when question and answer form is received by Jimmie Allen. - **$18 $35 $70**

JMA-6

❑ **JMA-6. Promotional Map,**
1934. Promotes Hi Speed Gas and his flight to China featured on his radio program. Rare.
- $225 $375 $600

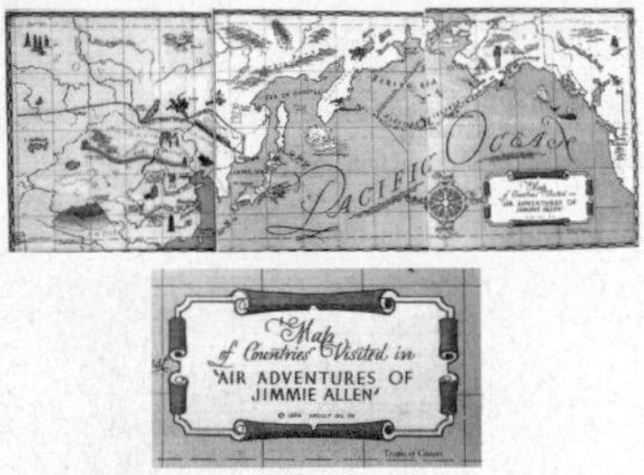

JMA-7

❑ **JMA-7. "Map Of Countries Visited In 'Air Adventures Of Jimmie Allen ' 11x25",**
1934. Skelly Oil Co. - **$90 $225 $425**

JMA-8

❑ **JMA-8. Contest Certificate,**
1934. Sponsored by Pacific Coast Newspapers. Rare. - **$150 $300 $450**

JMA-9

❑ **JMA-9. Skelly Oil Holiday Newsletter,**
1934. - **$25 $45 $80**

JMA-10

JMA-11

❑ **JMA-10. "Flight Lesson" Sheet,**
1934. Various sponsors. Five lessons in set.
Each - **$5 $10 $20**

❑ **JMA-11. "Merry Christmas" Photo,**
1934. Skelly Oil Co. - **$10 $20 $40**

JMA-12

❑ **JMA-12. Radio Listener Letter With Photos,**
1934. Skelly Oil Co. Letter thanks listener for name of gasoline dealer not handling Skelly products. Photos are Allen and Speed Robertson. Letter - **$20 $35 $70**
Each Photo - **$10 $20 $40**

JMA-13

❑ **JMA-13. Advertising Plaque,**
1934. High quality plaque is 4.5" x 13" with relief design and gold color. Used in Richfield Hi-Octane Gas and Oil Ad campaign. Rare.
- $175 $350 $700

JMA-14

JMA-15

❑ **JMA-14. Richfield Flight Wings,**
1934. - **$18 $30 $70**

❑ **JMA-15. Richfield I.D. Bracelet,**
1934. - **$15 $50 $90**

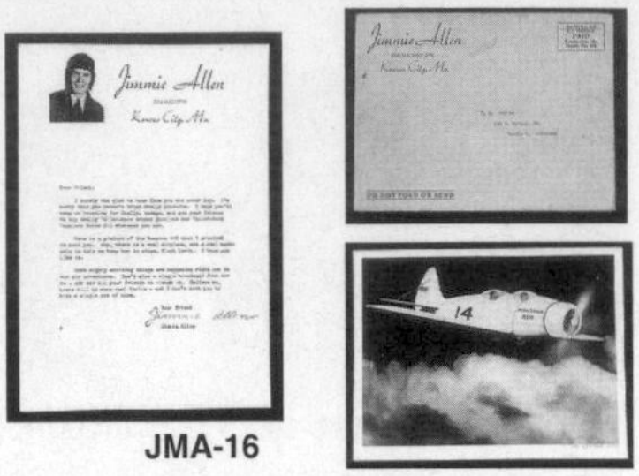

JMA-16

❑ **JMA-16. Radio Listener Letter With Picture And Mailer,**
1934. Skelly Oil Co. Letter urges trial of Skelly products, picture is "Monsoon 800" aircraft.
Near Mint In Mailer - **$200**
Letter Only - **$20 $35 $70**
Picture Only - **$20 $40 $80**

JMA-17

JMA-18

❑ **JMA-17. "What's On The Air" Pacific Coast Schedule Book,**
1934. Richfield Oil Co. - **$15 $30 $75**

❑ **JMA-18. Skelly "Jimmie Allen Flying Cadet" Brass Airplane Badge,**
1934. - **$18 $30 $70**

JMA-19

❑ **JMA-19. "She Sure Is A Honey-" Premium Photo,**
c. 1934. Richfield Oil Company of California. Shows Jimmie flying "Monsoon 800." -
$18 $35 $70

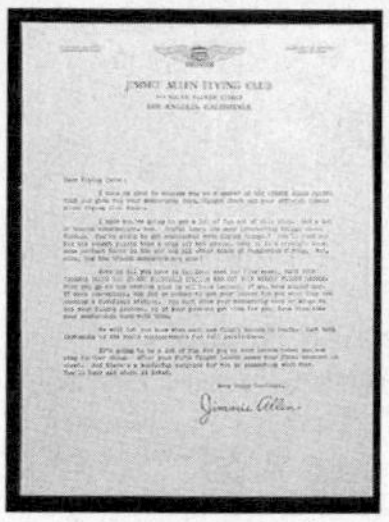

JMA-20

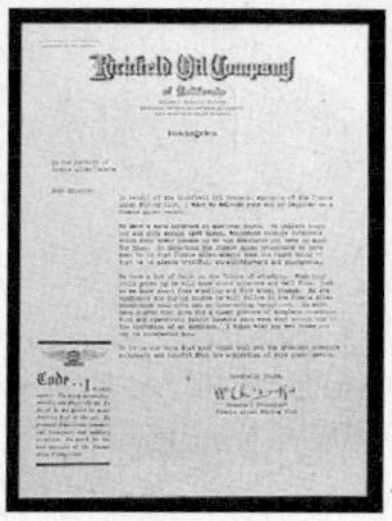

JMA-21

❑ **JMA-20. New Member Welcome Letter,**
c. 1934. Richfield Oil Co. Came with membership card, flight chart and wings. -
$18 $35 $70

❑ **JMA-21. Welcome Letter To New Member's Parents,**
c. 1934. Richfield Oil Company of California. 8-1/2x11" black and white letter to new cadet's parents. - **$18 $35 $70**

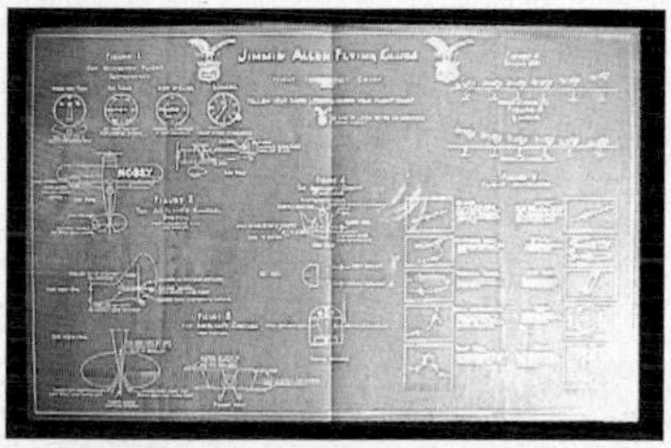

JMA-22

❑ **JMA-22. Flight Chart,**
c. 1934. Richfield Oil Co. 11x17" folder printed on one side white on blue like a blueprint. Used to follow the lessons heard over radio. -
$15 $30 $50

JMA-23

❑ **JMA-23. Diecut Window Sticker,**
c. 1934. Richfield Oil Co. 2-1/2x5-1/2". -
$40 $80 $150

JMA-24

❑ **JMA-24. "B-A Flying Cadet" Canadian Flight Wings Pin,**
c. 1934. British-American Oil. Embossed Brass. -
$30 $70 $150

JMA-25

❑ **JMA-25. Skelly Club Membership Card,**
c. 1934. - **$15 $40 $80**

JMA-26

JMA-27

❑ **JMA-26. Skelly "Jimmie Allen Flying Cadet" Bronze Luster Brass Wings Badge,**
c. 1934. - **$18 $30 $60**

❑ **JMA-27. "Jimmie Allen/Skelly Flying Cadet" Brass Wings Badge,**
c. 1934. - **$35 $75 $145**

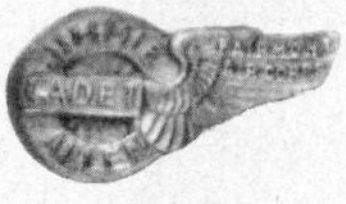

JMA-29

JMA-28

❑ **JMA-28. "Jimmie Allen Cadet/Fairmont Air Corps" Brass Wings Badge,**
c. 1934. - **$70 $160 $300**

❑ **JMA-29. "B-A Flying Cadet" Canadian Flight Wings,**
c. 1934. British-American Oil. Red on silvered metal. - **$50 $100 $180**

JMA-30

❑ **JMA-30. Membership Card,**
c. 1934. Richfield Oil Co. - **$15 $30 $60**

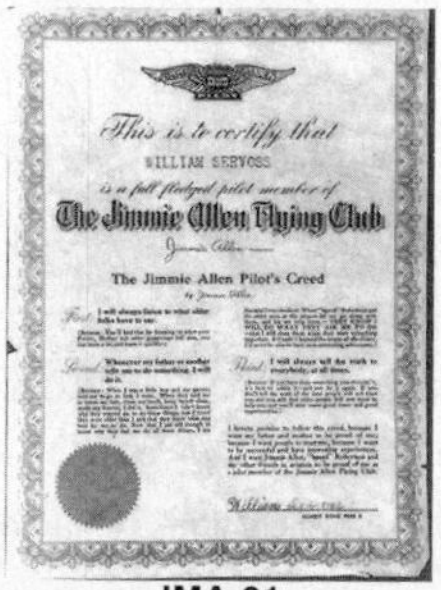

JMA-31

❑ **JMA-31. Club Creed Certificate,**
c. 1934. Richfield Oil. - **$20 $45 $85**

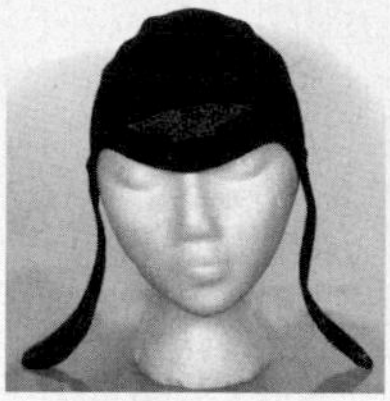

JMA-32

❑ **JMA-32. Jimmie Allen Aviator's Hat,**
c. 1934. Rare. - **$80 $175 $350**

JMA-33

❑ **JMA-33. Postcard,**
c. 1934. Log Cabin Bread. - **$15 $35 $75**

JMA-34

JMA-35

❑ **JMA-34. "Jimmie Allen Flying Cadet/Log Cabin" Brass Wings Badge,**
c. 1934. Log Cabin Syrup. - **$30 $60 $115**

❑ **JMA-35. "Speed Robertson" Photo Card,**
c. 1934. Hi-Speed Gasoline of Hickok Oil Corp. Pictured is comrade aviator of Jimmie Allen. -
$18 $30 $60

JMA-36

❑ **JMA-36. Jimmie Allen Glossy Promo Photo,**
1935. Scarce. - **$35 $60 $120**

JMA-37

❑ JMA-37. Richfield Oil Travel Map,
1935. Paper folder that opens to 18x24" map of California with panel ad for Jimmie Allen radio show. - **$15 $40 $80**

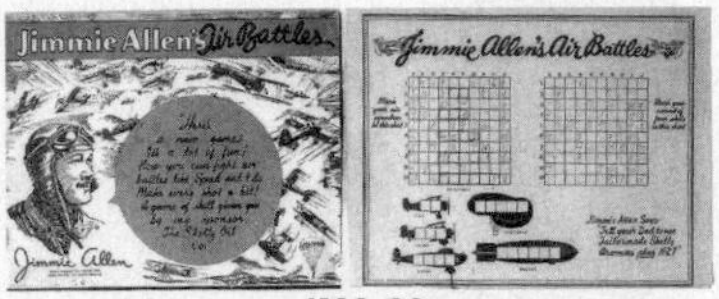

JMA-38

❑ JMA-38. Skelly "Jimmie Allen's Air Battles" Booklet,
1935. Contents include game pages plus comic strips. - **$35 $75 $140**

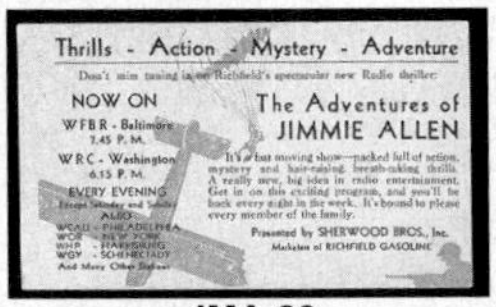

JMA-39

JMA-40

❑ JMA-39. Postcard,
1935. Richfield Oil Co. Radio premium. - **$18 $35 $60**

❑ JMA-40. Road Map,
1935. Skelly Oil Co. Map of U.S. and Kansas. - **$15 $40 $80**

JMA-41

JMA-42

❑ JMA-41. "Jimmie Allen Air Races" Silvered Brass Bracelet,
1935. Skelly Oil. - **$75 $200 $350**

❑ JMA-42. Kansas City Air Races Enameled Bracelet,
1935. Rare. Skelly Oil. - **$150 $300 $625**

JMA-43

❑ JMA-43. "Jimmie Allen Club News,"
1935. Sponsored by Richfield Oil. Numbered set of 11 with serialized "The Strange Mist" story. Each - **$15 $25 $50**

JMA-44

❑ JMA-44. Air Adventures Map,
1935. Hickok Oil. 11x17" sheet printed two sides including featured side "Map Of Countries Visited In Air Adventures Of Jimmie Allen." Reverse side is letter from him to "Flying Cadets About His Adventures Across The Pacific To The Orient." This side is totally different from the otherwise similar Skelly Oil version of one year earlier. - **$115 $230 $400**

JMA-45

❑ JMA-45. "Jimmie Allen" Canadian Sponsor Photo,
c. 1935. 6x7.5" black and white unmarked for specific Canadian sponsor but probably British-American Gasoline. - **$20 $35 $70**

JMA-46

JMA-47

❑ JMA-46. "Jimmie Allen Air Races" Sterling Silver Bracelet With Silvered Brass Chain,
c. 1935. Skelly Oil. - **$60 $150 $300**

❑ JMA-47. "Jimmie Allen/Pilot" Silvered Brass Bracelet,
c. 1935. Skelly Oil. - **$60 $150 $300**

JMA-48

❑ JMA-48. Browntone Photos,
1936. Skelly Oil Co. Numbered set of six. Each - **$8 $12 $25**

JMA-49

JMA-50

❑ JMA-49. Club Card,
1936. Scarce. Skelly Oil Co. Membership card with pledge on back. Blue trim, plane on left. - **$15 $30 $60**

❑ JMA-50. "Jimmie Allen in the Air Mail Robbery" Big Little Book #1143,
1936. - **$10 $30 $68**

JMA-51

JMA-52

❑ JMA-51. "Flying Club Stamp Album",
1936. Richfield Oil Co.
Near Mint With Stamps - **$200**
Album Only - **$25 $55 $100**

❑ JMA-52. Richfield Gasoline Cardboard Ink Blotter,
1936. - **$15 $35 $60**

JMA-53

JMA-54

❑ JMA-53. "Official Jimmie Allen Secret Signal" Brass Whistle,
1936. - **$55 $100 $180**

❑ JMA-54. "Jimmie Allen Air Races" Silvered Brass Pin,
1936. Skelly Oil. - **$75 $175 $300**

JMA-55

JMA-56

❑ JMA-55. Movie Cast Photo,
1936. For movie "The Sky Parade" picturing Jimmie Allen, Grant Withers, Katherine DeMille, Kent Taylor. - **$18 $30 $60**

❑ JMA-56. "Jimmie Allen In The Sky Parade" Movie Herald,
1936. 6x9" issued by Paramount. - **$20 $40 $80**

JMA-57

❑ JMA-57. Jimmie Allen "The Sky Parade Lobby Card,"
1936. Paramount Productions Picture. 11x14" release. Main image is photo of Jimmie Allen. - **$30 $60 $90**

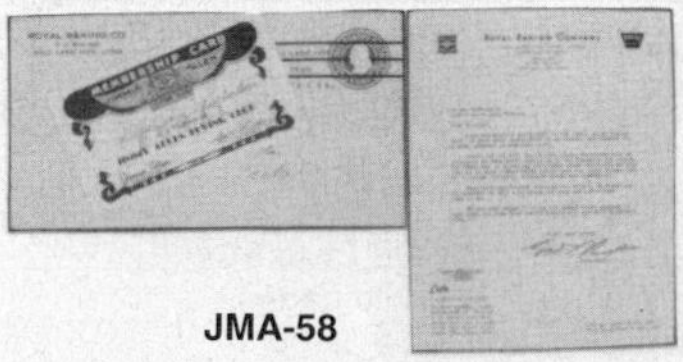
JMA-58

❑ JMA-58. "Jimmie Allen Flying Club" Letter/Membership Card,
1937. Issued by Royal Baking Powder.
Mailer - **$8 $12 $20**
Card - **$15 $30 $60**
Letter - **$12 $25 $40**

(CLOSE-UP)

JMA-59

❑ JMA-59. "Jimmie Allen" Air Races First Place Award,
c. 1937. Josten Trophy. 10.5x15" award for Jimmie Allen Air Races First Place Junior Flight Award Mankato, Minnesota. Has small metal maker's plate on reverse of award and front features large metal relief image with Skelly Oil logo. Same Or Similar - **$225 $450 $700**

JMA-60

❑ JMA-60. "Flying B-A Cadet" Certificate,
1939. British-American Oil. Canadian certificate received with Squadron Commander Badge. - **$45 $90 $190**

JMA-61

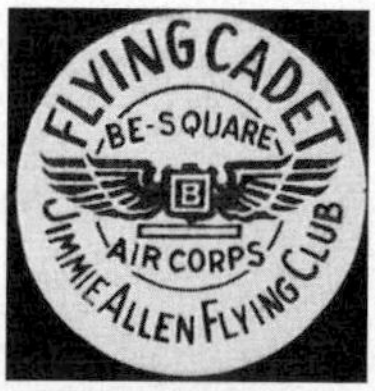

JMA-62

❑ JMA-61. "Squadron Commander" Canadian Brass Badge,
1939. British-American Oil. - **$125 $275 $550**

❑ JMA-62. "Flying Cadet Be-Square Air Corps" Felt Patch,
1930s. Sponsor unknown. 3" diameter white felt with design in blue. - **$100 $200 $300**

JMA-63

❑ JMA-63. "Jimmie Allen Thunderbolt" Flying Model,
1930s. Model is 3x18.5" with white and blue printing on red cardboard box. Includes instruction sheet. - **$75 $150 $250**

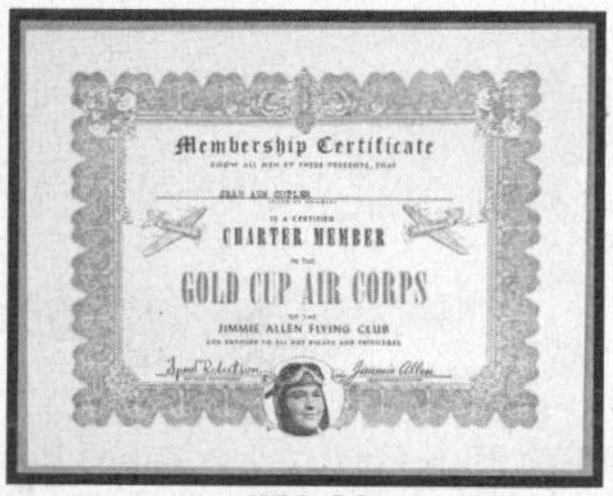

JMA-64

❑ JMA-64. "Jimmie Allen Gold Cup Air Corps Charter Membership Certificate,"
1930s. Paper certificate is 7x9" for Charter Member in the Gold Cup Air Corps of the Jimmie Allen Flying Club. Certificate features a photo of Jimmie Allen and facsimile signatures of "Speed" Robertson Advising Commander and Jimmie Allen Commander-In-Chief. - **$45 $90 $190**

JMA-65

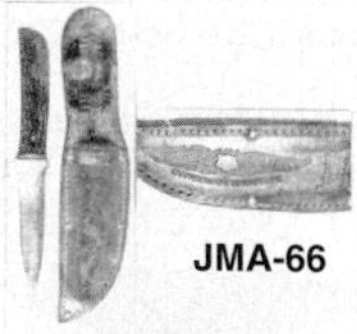
JMA-66

JMA-67

❑ JMA-65. "Jimmie Allen" Bone Handle Pocketknife,
1930s. Sponsor unknown. Grip has silvered metal club symbol. - **$75 $150 $300**

❑ JMA-66. "Official Outing Knife" With Sheath,
1930s. Sponsor unknown. - **$100 $200 $350**

❑ JMA-67. "Jimmie Allen Model Builder Merit Award" Brass Badge,
1930s. Scarce. Richfield Oil. Also designated "Richfield Hi-Octane Flying Cadet". - **$100 $200 $350**

JMA-68

JMA-69

❑ **JMA-68. Club Membership Card,**
1930s. - **$15 $30 $65**

❑ **JMA-69. Flying Club Membership Card,**
1930s. Skelly Oil Co. Blue trim on white with airplanes circling border. - **$25 $50 $80**

JMA-70

JMA-71

❑ **JMA-70. Blue Flash Brass Wings Badge,**
1930s. Blue Flash. Says "Jimmie Allen Flying Cadet". - **$40 $80 $140**

❑ **JMA-71. Certified Flying Cadet Brass Wings Badge,**
1930s. - **$45 $90 $170**

JMA-72

JMA-73

❑ **JMA-72. Cleo Cola Brass Wings Badge,**
1930s. Cleo Cola. - **$20 $45 $80**

❑ **JMA-73. Colonial Brass Wings Badge,**
1930s. Colonial. - **$15 $35 $60**

JMA-74

JMA-75

❑ **JMA-74. Duplex Brass Wings Badge,**
1930s. Duplex. - **$15 $35 $60**

❑ **JMA-75. Fair-Maid Brass Wings Badge,**
1930s. Fair-Maid. - **$25 $50 $100**

JMA-76

JMA-77

❑ **JMA-76. Rain-Bo Brass Wings Badge,**
1930s. Rain-Bo. - **$25 $50 $100**

❑ **JMA-77. Richfield Brass Wings Badge,**
1930s. Richfield. - **$15 $35 $50**

JMA-78

JMA-79

❑ **JMA-78. Richfield Silver Wings Badge,**
1930s. Richfield. - **$40 $80 $160**

❑ **JMA-79. Sawyer Brass Wings Badge,**
1930s. Sawyer. - **$40 $80 $160**

JMA-80

JMA-81

❑ **JMA-80. Skelly Gold Wings Badge,**
1930s. Skelly Oil. - **$35 $75 $135**

❑ **JMA-81. Town Talk Bread Brass Wings Badge,**
1930s. Town Talk Bread. - **$40 $80 $160**

JMA-82

JMA-83

❑ **JMA-82. Weatherbird Brass Wings Badge,**
1930s. Weatherbird Shoes. - **$25 $50 $100**

❑ **JMA-83. "Jimmie Allen Hi-Speed Flying Cadet" Brass Wings Badge,**
1930s. - **$15 $30 $50**

JMA-84

JMA-85

❑ **JMA-84. Die-Cut Window Sticker,**
1930s. Hi-Speed Gasoline. - **$45 $85 $165**

❑ **JMA-85. Hi-Speed Photo Card,**
1930s. Hickok Oil Co. - **$18 $30 $60**

JMA-86

❑ **JMA-86. "Certificate In Aviation",**
1930s. Republic (Oil) Air Corps. Awarded for completion of advanced aviation course. - **$55 $110 $200**

JMA-87

❑ **JMA-87. "Jimmie Allen/Republic Pilot" Brass Wings Badge,**
1930s. - **$45 $90 $170**

JMA-88

JMA-89

❑ **JMA-88. Cloth "Mail Pouch",**
1930s. Cleo Cola. For saving bottle caps. - **$35 $75 $150**

❑ **JMA-89. Club Membership Card,**
1930s. Hi-Speed Gasoline. - **$12 $30 $60**

JMA-90

❑ **JMA-90. Flying Club Aviation Lesson Newspapers,**
1930s. Republic Motor Oil. Map inside lesson #1. Each - **$15 $30 $60**

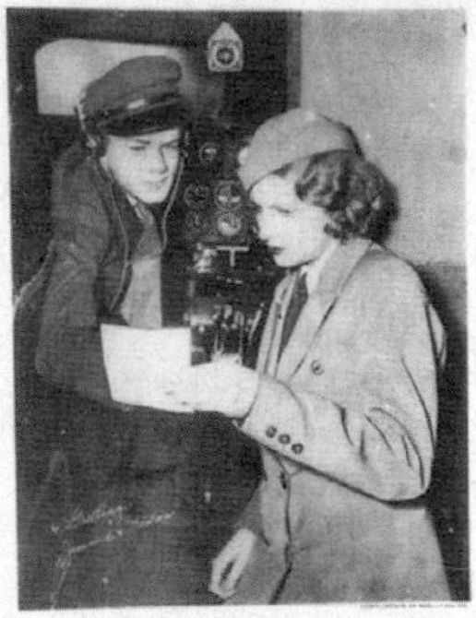
JMA-91

❑ **JMA-91. Jimmie & Barbara Photo,**
1930s. Skelly Oil. - **$15 $30 $60**

JMA-92

❑ **JMA-92. Skelly Oil Club Album,**
1930s. Booklet of photo pages.
Album Only - **$25 $50 $100**
Each Photo Page - **$8 $12 $25**

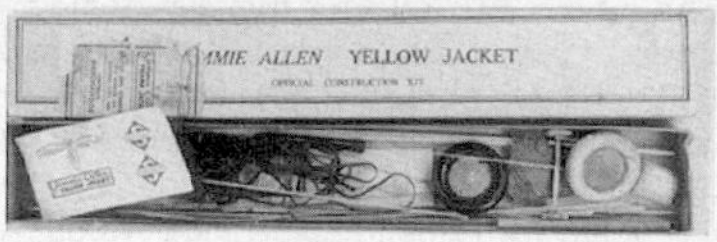

JMA-93

❑ **JMA-93. "Yellow Jacket" Model Airplane Construction Kit,**
1930s. Skelly Oil. Balsa parts with instructions and insignia cut-outs. - **$75 $125 $240**

(Plane parts)

(Labels)

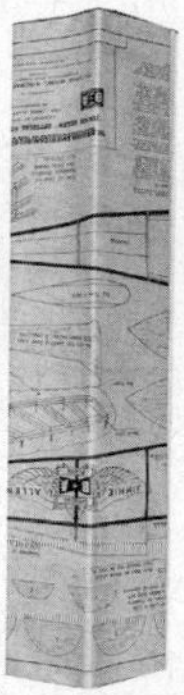

(Instructions)

(Box)

JMA-94

❑ **JMA-94. Official "Contest" Model Kit,**
1930s. B-A plane. Scarce. - **$75 $125 $240**

JMA-95

JMA-96

❑ **JMA-95. "Thunderbolt" Model Airplane Construction Kit,**
1930s. Skelly Oil. Balsa parts with instruction sheet and insignia cut-outs. - **$75 $125 $240**

❑ **JMA-96. "J.A. Air Cadets" Cello. Button,**
1930s. Canadian issue. - **$50 $100 $200**

JMA-97

JMA-98

❑ **JMA-97. Flying Club Membership Card,**
1930s. Skelly Oil Co. Brown trim on white. Propeller at top & bottom on front. - **$25 $50 $80**

❑ **JMA-98. Coin,**
1930s. Bond Bread premium. - **$60 $115 $225**

JMA-99

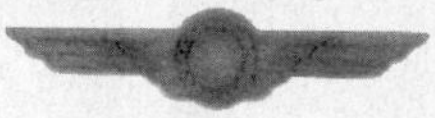

JMA-100

❑ **JMA-99. "J.A. Air Cadets" Brass Ring,**
1930s. Rare. Canadian issue. - **$200 $450 $850**

❑ **JMA-100. "J.A. Air Cadets" Brass Wings Badge,**
1930s. Canadian issue. - **$40 $80 $165**

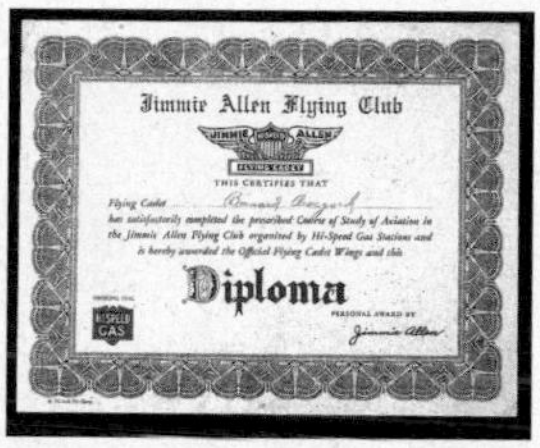

JMA-101

❑ **JMA-101. Diploma,**
1930s. Hi-Speed Gasoline. - **$40 $80 $160**

JMA-102

❑ **JMA-102. Season's Greetings Card,**
1930s. Richfield Oil Co. - **$35 $80 $175**

JMA-103

❑ **JMA-103. Flight Lesson #1-6 Lessons,**
1930s. Weather Bird Shoes.
Each - **$25 $55 $90**

JMA-104

JMA-105

❑ **JMA-104. Flight Lesson #4,**
1930s. Colonial Bread. - **$15 $30 $60**

❑ **JMA-105. Membership Card,**
1930s. Weather Bird Shoes. - **$25 $60 $115**

JMA-106

❑ **JMA-106. Membership Certificate,**
1930s. Weather Bird Shoes. - **$40 $80 $160**

JMA-107

❑ **JMA-107. Air Corps Patch,**
1930s. Weather Bird Shoes. Rare. White design on red background. - **$100 $200 $300**

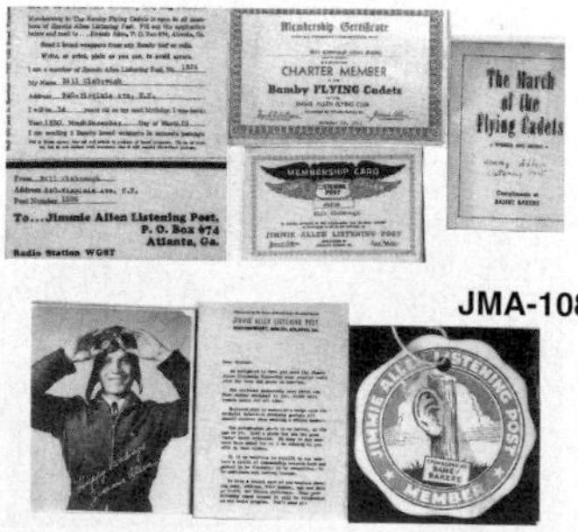

JMA-108

❑ **JMA-108. "Jimmie Allen Listening Post" Member Kit,**
1944. Re-broadcast of shows sponsored by Bamby Bread, Atlanta, Georgia. Includes cover letter, photo, member card, charter, song sheet, application, "Listening Post" tag.
Each Item - **$10 $20 $40**

Jimmie Mattern

An actual aviator in the early 1930s era of personal and mechanical endurance flying, Mattern is best remembered for his June 3 to August 3, 1933 solo flight around the world begun in his "Century of Progress" single engine aircraft (crashed en route) and finished by other borrowed planes. Premiums were typically aviation theme booklets and photo albums by sponsor Pure Oil.

JMT-1

❑ JMT-1. "Jimmie Mattern" Postcards,
c. 1934. Pure Oil Co. Two different, each 3.5x5.5". One features closeup portrait while the other has inset portrait and "The Pure Oil Company" plane, both have facsimile signature. Reverses include list of his world records of 1931-1933 and text promotion for "Diary Of Jimmie Mattern" radio program and Pure Oil Co.
Each - **$12 $25 $40**

JMT-2

❑ JMT-2. "The Diary Of Jimmie Mattern" Paper Folder,
1935. Pure Oil Co. "Diary Sheet" insert pages issued separately, probably weekly.
Folder Only - **$20 $35 $65**
Each Insert Page - **$5 $10 $15**

JMT-3

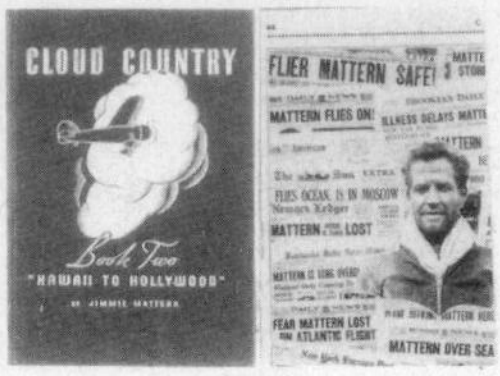

JMT-4

❑ JMT-3. "Book One 'Cloud Country/Wings Of Youth'",
1936. Pure Oil Co. hardcover. - **$5 $15 $35**

❑ JMT-4. "Book 2 'Hawaii To Hollywood'",
1936. Pure Oil Co. Hardcover. - **$5 $15 $35**

JMT-5

JMT-6

❑ JMT-5. "Air-E-Racer" Figural Rubber Eraser,
c. 1936. Pure Oil Co., also marked "Tiolene Motor Oil". - **$20 $40 $80**

❑ JMT-6. Aerial Navigation Device With Mattern Logo,
1930s. 7.5" tall aluminum hinged pointers designed to measure aeronautical degrees in addition to features for Morse Code, conversions between the two temperature standards, kilometers to miles. Unnamed sponsor but likely Pure Oil. - **$35 $70 $125**

Jimmy Durante

At the age of 17 Jimmy Durante (1893-1980) was playing piano in a Coney Island beer garden. By his mid-thirties, after years in vaudeville and burlesque, he was playing Broadway and making movies. Most notably, *Jumbo* on Broadway and as a fight promoter in the 1934 feature film *Joe Palooka* where he introduced his trademark song *Inka Dinka Doo.* In 1943, when he and Garry Moore appeared together on NBC in the *Camel Comedy Caravan,* Durante was on the road to national stardom. With his joyful mangling of the language, his legendary nose which earned him the nickname "The Schnoz," his mythical friends Umbriago and Mrs. Calabash, Durante charmed his radio audience for seven years, first for Camel cigarettes (1943-1945), then for Rexall drugs (1945-1948), then again for Camel (1948-1950). A couple of Durante comic books appeared in the late 1940s, and from 1950 to 1957 Durante was a regular on television for such sponsors as Buick, Colgate, and Texaco. "Good Night Mrs. Calabash, Wherever You Are!"

JIM-1

JIM-2

❑ JIM-1. "Schnozzle Durante/Vice-President" Cello. Button,
1932. Paramount Pictures. Based on movie "Phantom President" that year. - **$25 $55 $100**

❑ JIM-2. Song Book - Inka Dinka Doo,
1933. Store bought. - **$20 $40 $65**

JIM-3

❑ JIM-3. "Palooka" Movie Premium,
1934. Die-cut book marker. - **$75 $175 $300**

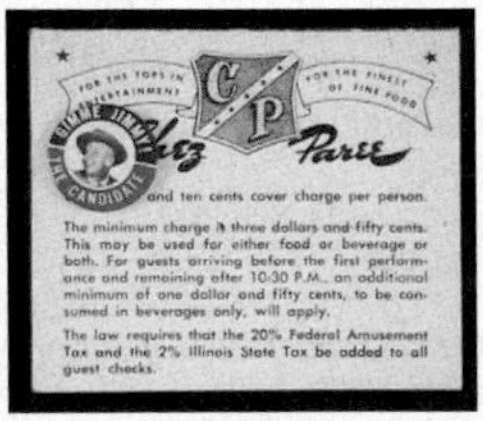

JIM-4

JIM-5

❑ JIM-4. Cello. Button With Restaurant Card,
1948. Chez Paree, Chicago. 1-1/4" button reads "Gimme Jimmy! The Candidate." Card from where he performed has no Durante reference but discusses cover charges per person.
Button - **$10 $20 $30**
Card - **$5 $10 $15**

❑ JIM-5. "My Friend Umbriago" Litho. Button,
1940s. Durante holds hand puppet. -
$15 $25 $50

JIM-6

❑ **JIM-6. Jimmy Durante Figural Celebrity Mug,**
1940s. Figural painted and glazed ceramic mug is 4x6.5x5.5" tall. Durante's likeness is caricature and features the odd use of his prominent nose (which has been enlarge some) as a handle. From celebrity series with bottom stamped "Hollywood Mugs By Barclay."
- **$125 $250 $450**

JIM-7

JIM-8

❑ **JIM-7. "The Great Rupert" Movie Poster,**
1950. Pathe Industries. 27x41". - **$30 $60 $125**

❑ **JIM-8. "The Candidate" Book,**
1952. Simon & Schuster. - **$12 $18 $35**

JIM-9

❑ **JIM-9. Humor Book Promo Button,**
1952. Button is 3.5" and also comes in two smaller sizes, but this is likely a clerk's button and much rarer. - **$30 $45 $90**

JIM-10

JIM-11

❑ **JIM-10. "Gimme Jimmy! The Candidate" Button,**
1952. Issued with booklet of same title. Issued as 1.25" cello. and 1-1/8" litho.
Cello. - **$10 $20 $35**
Litho. - **$10 $15 $25**

❑ **JIM-11. Rubber/Fabric Hand Puppet,**
1950s. Store item. - **$15 $25 $ 60**

JIM-12

JIM-13

❑ **JIM-12. "Children's Fund" Metal Portrait Pin On Card,**
1950s. - **$8 $15 $30**

❑ **JIM-13. Portrait Pen,**
c. 1950s. Plastic and metal ballpoint with miniature bronze luster metal portrait attached on pocket clip. - **$10 $20 $35**

(FRONT) JIM-14 (BACK)

❑ **JIM-14. Corn Flakes Box With Testimonial From Durante,**
1965. Gary Lewis and the Playboys record offer on side of box. Complete - **$45 $90 $200**

Jimmy Neutron

Jimmy Neutron isn't just a boy genius. He's also a TV and film star and an Academy Award nominee. Creators John A. Davis and Keith Alcorn first featured him in a 1995 40-minute short called *Runaway Rocket Boy*. At the time, his name was Johnny Quasar. By the time writer Steve Oedekerk (*Ace Ventura: Pet Detective*) got involved, Davis founded DNA productions with Alcorn, where the motley three polished and developed the short into a feature, tentatively titled *The Adventures of Johnny Quasar*. They first pitched the idea to Nickelodeon execs in 1997 and were greenlighted for a series pilot in the 1999 season. The series, *The Adventures of Jimmy Neutron*, garnered an immediate fanbase. Kids and adults alike joined in to follow the exploits of Jimmy, his brilliant dog Goddard, his dumpy, loyal best friend Carl Wheezer, his brainy mom, Judy and not-so-brainy dad, Hugh. By 2001, the space-dwelling prodigy made his way to the big screen in *Jimmy Neutron: Boy Genius*. Made popular by its retro-futuristic 3-D computer animation, *The Adventures of Jimmy Neutron* is sure to be a fan favorite for years to come.

JNT-1

JNT-2

❑ **JNT-1. 2003 16-Month Calendar,**
2003. - **$12**

❑ **JNT-2. 2003 16-Month Calendar,**
2003. - **$12**

JNT-3

❑ **JNT-3. Jet To Lunch Pack,**
2003. Insulated lunch pack- **$22**

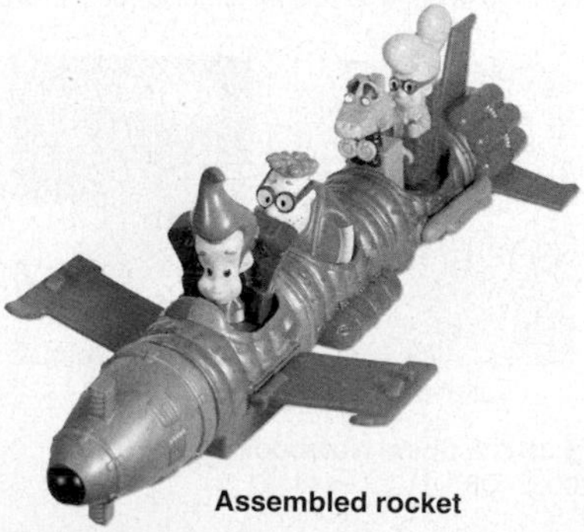

Assembled rocket

JNT-4

JNT-5

JNT-6

JNT-7

❑ **JNT-4. Joy Ride Jimmy,**
2003. Burger King toy which links with other parts to form a rocket. - **$4**

❑ **JNT-5. Carl's Swamp Buggy,**
2003. Burger King toy. - **$4**

❑ **JNT-6. Gotta Dash Goddard,**
2003. Burger King toy. - **$4**

❑ **JNT-7. Cindy's Rocket Booster,**
2003. Burger King toy. - **$4**

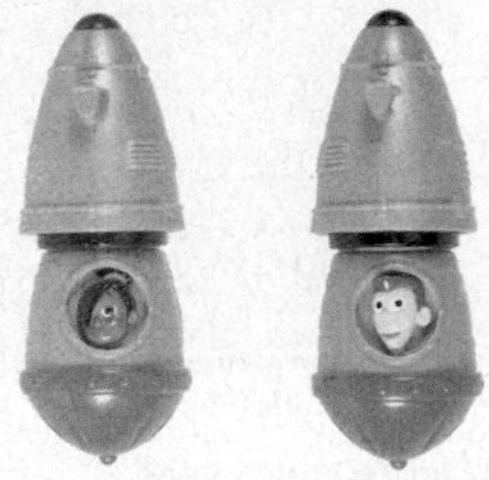

(FRONT) (BACK)

JNT-8

❑ **JNT-8. Libby's and Sheen's Sonic Spinner,**
2003. Nose cone for the assembled rocket.- **$10**

JNT-9

JNT-10

❑ **JNT-9. Spiral Notebook,**
2003. - **$6**

❑ **JNT-10. Spiral Notebook,**
2003. - **$6**

JNT-11

JNT-12

❑ **JNT-11. Toon Pop,**
2003. Lollipop with a Toon inside. - **$4**

❑ **JNT-12. Mini Holiday Ornament Set,**
2003. 5 piece set. - **$12**

JNT-13

JNT-14

❑ **JNT-13. Holiday Ornament,**
2003. Jimmy on ice skates. - **$12**

❑ **JNT-14. Holiday Ornament,**
2003. JImmy and Goddard. - **$12**

JNT-15

JNT-16

❑ **JNT-15. Reward Certificates and Decals,**
2003. - **$6**

❑ **JNT-16. Stickers Sheet,**
2003. - **$3**

JNT-17

JNT-18

❑ **JNT-17. Neutronic Writers Pencils,**
2003. - **$5**

❑ **JNT-18. Fruit Snacks Box,**
2003. Nabisco. - **$3**

JNT-19

❑ **JNT-19. Cap'n Crunch's Choco Donuts Cereal Box,**
2003. - **$6**

JNT-20

❑ **JNT-20. Cap'n Crunch's Neutron Berries Cereal Box,**
2003. - **$6**

JNT-21

JNT-22

❑ **JNT-21. Snack Wrapper,**
2003. Nabisco. - **25¢**

❑ **JNT-22. Snack Wrapper,**
2003. Nabisco. - **25¢**

JNT-23

JNT-24

❑ **JNT-23. Writing Pad,**
2003. - **$5**

❑ **JNT-24. Writing Pad,**
2003. - **$5**

JNT-25

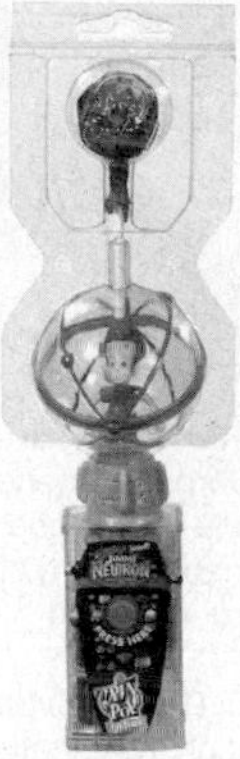
JNT-26

JNT-27

❑ **JNT-25. Cool Topz Bottle,**
2003. Orbit Orange Drink. - **$4**

❑ **JNT-26. Spin Pop,**
2003. Lollipop with Jimmy figure. - **$6**

❑ **JNT-27. Spin Pop,**
2003. Lollipop with Jimmy and Goddard. - **$6**

JNT-28

JNT-29

❑ **JNT-28. Skateboard,**
2003. - **$40**

❑ **JNT-29. Boys Briefs,**
2003. Fruit of the Loom 3-pack. - **$5**

JNT-30

❑ **JNT-30. Vitamins,**
2003. CentrumKids. - **$5**

JNT-31

JNT-32

❑ **JNT-31. Standee on Card,**
2003. - **$7**

❑ **JNT-32. Pinata With Toy,**
2003. - **$30**

JNT-33

❑ **JNT-33. Party Plates,**
2003. - **$5**

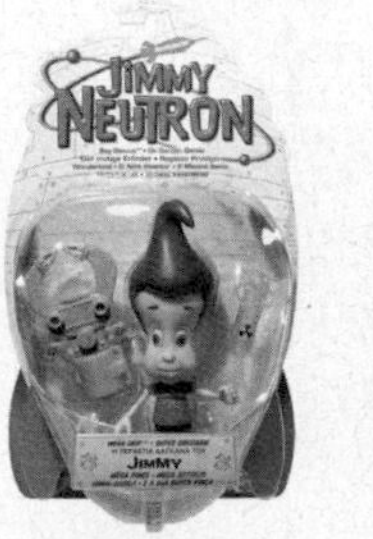
JNT-34

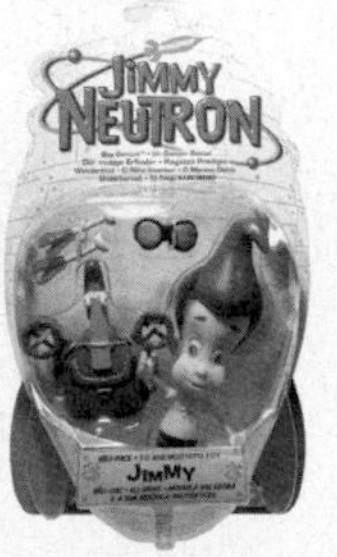
JNT-35

❑ **JNT-34. Mega Grip Figure on Rocket Card,**
2003. - **$20**

❑ **JNT-35. Heli-Pack Figure on Rocket Card,**
2003. - **$20**

JNT-36

JNT-37

JNT-38

❑ **JNT-36. Gripper Grabber Goddard Toy,**
2003. - **$6**

❑ **JNT-37. Nick Toy,**
2003. With skateboard. - **$20**

❑ **JNT-38. Yokian King Toy,**
2003. - **$5**

Joe E. Brown

Show-business veteran Joe E. Brown (1892-1973), noted for the contortions of his big mouth, started out as a circus acrobat at the age of 10, was a featured comedian in burlesque and vaudeville in his mid-twenties, graduated to musical comedies, and started making movies in 1927. He made dozens of films, with memorable roles in *You Said a Mouthful* (1932), *Alibi Ike* (1935), and *Some Like It Hot* (1959). Quaker Oats issued the *Joe E. Brown Bike Club* premiums in 1934. In 1936, Post cereal sponsored the *Joe E. Brown Club* through newspapers and packaging offers. On radio, the *Joe E. Brown Show*, a musical variety program, ran for a season (1938-1939) on CBS, sponsored by Post Toasties cereal. He was also a baseball fan and was part owner of the Kansas City Blues minor league team and provided TV commentary for the 1950s Yankees games.

JOE-1

❑ **JOE-1. 1932 Los Angeles Olympics And Movie Star Playing Cards,**
1932. Complete standard deck with Joe E. Brown joker. Face cards show two movie stars on each including Douglas Fairbanks and Loretta Young. Text on box is "Xth Olympiad Los Angeles 1932 Playing Cards/Olympic And Movie Star Souvenir." - **$80 $160 $275**

JOE-2

JOE-3

❑ JOE-2. Theatre Promo Baseball Glove,
1933. Movie premium from baseball film "Elmer the Great." Lettering is printed on card shaped like a padded glove. Scarce. - **$55 $110 $175**

❑ JOE-3. Theatre Promo Card,
1933. 8 1/2" tall movie premium of Joe E. Brown, starring in the film "Son of a Sailor." - **$50 $100 $225**

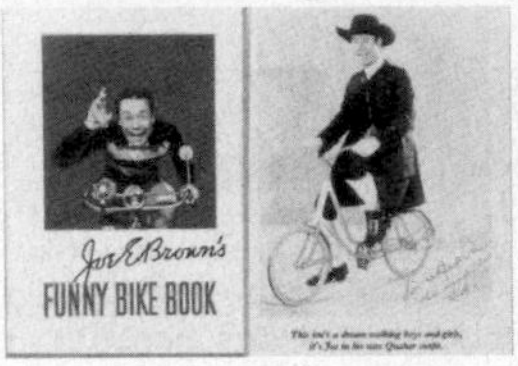

JOE-4

JOE-5

❑ JOE-4. "Joe E. Brown's Funny Bike Book",
1934. Quaker Oats. - **$10 $30 $60**

❑ JOE-5. "Member/Joe E. Brown Bike Club" Cello. Button,
1934. Quaker Oats. - **$5 $15 $30**

JOE-6

❑ JOE-6. Bicycle Contest 15x20" Store Sign,
1934. Quaker Oats. Diecut cardboard display also picturing Joe E. Brown Bike Club button and book plus advertises his new film "6-Day Bike Rider." - **$125 $275 $500**

JOE-7

JOE-8

❑ JOE-7. Club Member Brass Badge With Three Award Bars,
1936. Grape-Nuts Flakes. Bars in different colors individually marked by 1, 2, or 3 stars denoting club ranks of Sergeant, Lieutenant, or Captain.
Portrait Badge Only - **$5 $15 $25**
For Each Bar Add - **$5 $15 $30**

❑ JOE-8. Brass Club Member Ring,
1936. Grape-Nuts Flakes. Features small portrait. - **$60 $140 $250**

JOE-9

JOE-10

❑ JOE-9. Premium Folder Sheet,
1936. Grape-Nuts Flakes. Offers about 30 premiums with expiration date December 31. - **$12 $22 $45**

❑ JOE-10. Radio Fan Photo,
c. 1936. Probable Grape-Nuts Flakes. - **$8 $15 $25**

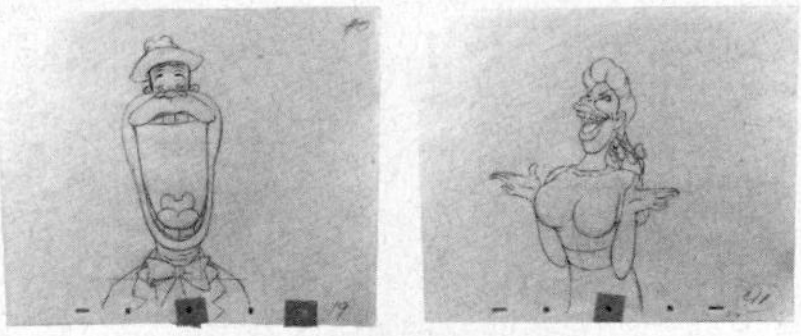

JOE-11

❑ JOE-11. Pencil Drawings for Movie Short,
1939. For Donald Duck animated short "The Autograph Hound." Joe E. Brown and Martha Raye have a dance scene in this Disney short. Each same or similar - **$360**

JOE-12

❑ JOE-12. Fan Photo,
1930s. Issuer unknown although possibly issued by Quaker Cereals. 8x10" browntone. - **$8 $12 $30**

JOE-13

JOE-14

❑ JOE-13. "Smiler's Club" Cello. Button,
1930s. - **$25 $50 $85**

❑ JOE-14. "Smiler's Club" Button,
1930s. For Senior Members. - **$75 $150 $300**

JOE-15

JOE-16

❑ JOE-15. "You Said A Mouthful" Booklet,
1944. Doughnut Corp. of America with local dealer imprint. Contents include World War II tour photos plus mention of radio quiz show "Stop Or Go". - **$10 $20 $40**

❑ JOE-16. Joe E. Brown Event Button,
1949. For celebration in Holgate, Ohio hometown. - **$18 $35 $65**

JOE-17

❑ JOE-17. Joe E. Brown "How To Play Baseball" Record Album,
1940s. Store item by RCA Victor. - **$20 $30 $75**

Joe Louis

Joe Louis (1914-1981) was born Joseph Louis Barrow in Alabama but made Detroit his home for many years. Louis won the world heavyweight championship by knocking out James J. Braddock in 1937 and successfully defended the title 24 times in 12 years. Known as the "Brown Bomber," he won 68 of his 71 bouts, 54 by knockouts during a time when many fights lasted 15 rounds. He was elected to the Boxing Hall of

Fame in 1954. Louis enlisted in the U.S. Army in 1942 and gave many exhibition bouts for troops around the world. He retired undefeated as champion in 1949, then returned to the ring the following year, without success. Louis is buried in Arlington Cemetery. Noted sports writer Jimmy Cannon wrote "Louis was a credit to his race...the human race."

JLO-1

❑ **JLO-1. Joe Louis/Max Baer Fight Souvenir Menu,**
1935. Menu is 5.25x8.5". Text reads "Washington Times Baer-Louis Fight Special To Yankee Stadium New York/September 24, 1935 Via Baltimore & Ohio Railroad Souvenir Menu." Inside has dinner menu in center with top reading "On Board The Washington Times Baer Louis Special." - **$75 $150 $265**

JLO-2

JLO-3

❑ **JLO-2. "Braddock Or Louis" Puzzle In Envelope,**
1937. Green River Whiskey. Novelty cardboard puzzle based on upcoming June 22 bout between champion James J. Braddock and contender Joe Louis. Assembled puzzle is about 2-1/2x4" consisting of four pieces to form image pictured on envelope. - **$50 $85 $175**

❑ **JLO-3. "Louis-Schmeling Fight" 14x22" Tavern Poster,**
1938. Martin's Scotch Whiskey. Cardboard sign promoting radio listenership of return bout between Joe Louis and Max Schmeling of Germany with cartoon art by O. Soglow. - **$60 $125 $250**

JLO-4

JLO-5

❑ **JLO-4. Joe Louis "Heavyweight Sensation" Cello. Button,**
c. 1938. Sponsored by Valmor Products Co., Chicago. - **$75 $150 $300**

❑ **JLO-5. "Joe Louis Good Luck Club" Litho. Button,**
c. 1938. Bottom rim design includes tiny four-leaf clover symbol. - **$60 $125 $250**

JLO-6

JLO-7

❑ **JLO-6. Real Photo Stickpin,**
1930s. Probable store item. 1" tall with black and white photo mounted on yellow celluloid. Reverse reads "Photo Pin Co. Chicago." - **$35 $75 $135**

❑ **JLO-7. "Joe Louis" Portrait Ring,**
1930s. Probable store item. Silvered brass non-adjustable with overlapping boxing gloves on each side. - **$150 $325 $700**

JLO-8

JLO-9

❑ **JLO-8. "Be Lucky With Joe Louis" Button,**
1930s. Button is 7/8" litho. - **$50 $100 $200**

❑ **JLO-9. "Joe Louis World's Heavyweight Champion" Cello Button,**
1930s. - **$50 $100 $200**

JLO-10

JLO-11

JLO-12

❑ **JLO-10. Premium Photo,**
1930s. Tie-in with premium ring giveaway. See JLO-15 & 16. - **$30 $60 $125**

❑ **JLO-11. "Joe And Me For Willkie" Cello. Button,**
1940. Endorsement attributed to Joe Louis for U.S. Presidential candidate Wendell L. Willkie. - **$15 $30 $75**

❑ **JLO-12. Joe Louis Endorses Willkie Button,**
1940. Button is 1.25" with presidential campaign slogan "Joe And I Want Willkie." - **$175 $375 $800**

JLO-13

JLO-14

❑ **JLO-13. "The Brown Bomber" Figural Painted Chalk Ashtray,**
1940s. Ashtray is 3.5x4x12" with "The Brown Bomber" on front of base. 2" diameter recessed area by foot acts as ashtray. A matching figure was produced as a lamp. - **$200 $400 $675**

❑ **JLO-14. "Joe Louis" Facsimile Signature And Boxing Stance Portrait Ring,**
1940s. Probable store item. Non-adjustable heavy metal ring has base in silver finish while oval top plate comes in either silver or brass finish. Ring sides show overlapping boxing gloves. On the inner surface of the band, originals have sharply incised arrow design running horizontally through a letter "U", the trademark of the maker Uncas. On all silver finish reproductions, the Uncas trademark is crudely hand-engraved and not deeply incised.
Silver Top - **$300 $600 $1200**
Brass Top - **$325 $650 $1300**

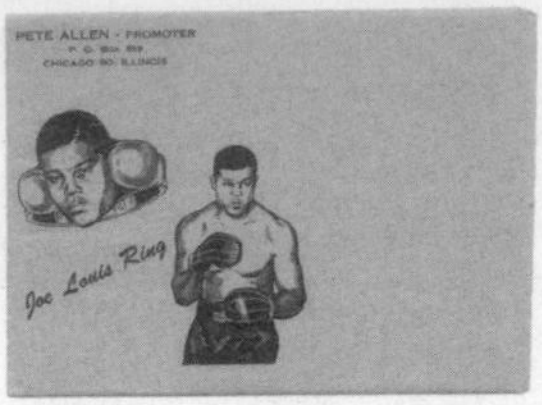
JLO-15

❑ JLO-15. Joe Louis Ring Envelope,
1940s. Features images of Joe Louis and Louis face ring. Included premium photo with envelope (see JLO-10). - **$75 $175 $350**

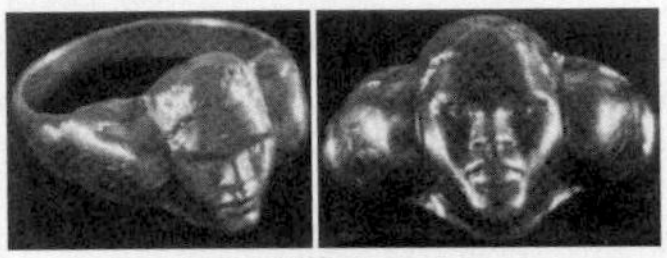
JLO-16

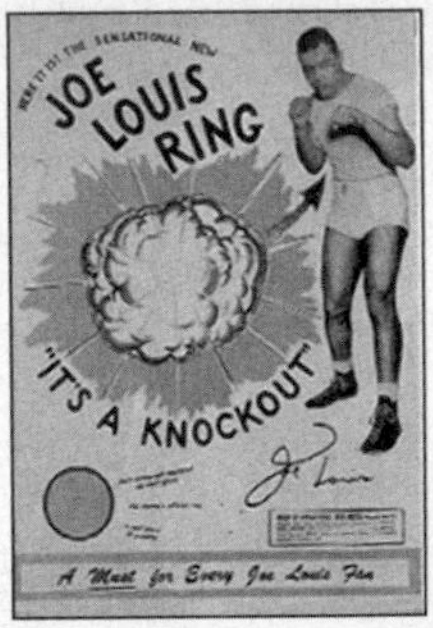

JLO-17

❑ JLO-16. "Joe Louis" Ring,
1940s. Features Louis' face next to two boxing gloves with signature. Rare - less than 10 known. Silver color, non-adjustable. - **$1100 $2200 $3750**

❑ JLO-17. "Joe Louis" Ring Promo Sign,
1940s. See JLO-15. - **$90 $160 $300**

JLO-18

JLO-19

JLO-20

❑ JLO-18. "Joe Louis Punch" Cello. Button,
1940s. For soda beverage product also inscribed "It's A Knockout." - **$35 $70 $140**

❑ JLO-19. "Joe Louis Punch" Soda Bottle Tin Cap,
1940s. For carbonated beverage. - **$25 $40 $75**

❑ JLO-20. "Joe Louis Punch" Soda Bottle,
1940s. All American Drinks Corp. Reverse slogan is "It's A Knockout." - **$35 $65 $110**

JLO-21

❑ JLO-21. "Mrs. Joe Louis" Lucky Strike Cigarettes Poster,
1940s. 21x22" glossy paper endorsement photo identified "Rose Morgan (Mrs. Joe Louis)." - **$70 $140 $250**

JLO-22

❑ JLO-22. Biography Movietone Movie Promo Sheet,
1953. 6x10.75" black and white herald sheet titled "Roar Of The Crowd" picturing him as victorious boxer in ring. - **$10 $20 $40**

JLO-23

❑ JLO-23. "Joe Louis" Memoriam Badge,
1981. 3-1/2" sold by vendors. - **$5 $15 $25**

Joe Palooka

Ham Fisher (1901-1955) created the *Joe Palooka* comic strip, the most successful sports strip of all time. It started small, appearing in a handful of papers in 1928, but a decade later the strip was running in hundreds of papers. Joe was sweet, innocent, clean-cut, and given to uttering clichés about home, mother, and fair play. He was also a top boxer, winning the World Heavyweight Championship in 1931. Al Capp was an assistant on the strip in 1933 doing a hillbilly sequence. He left in 1934 to do *Li'l Abner*, leading to a life-long feud with Fisher. *Joe Palooka* was hugely popular in its day, and he's featured prominently on the covers of early comic strip reprints like *Funnies on Parade* and *Famous Funnies* comic books. Joe joined the army in 1940 and married his longtime girlfriend Ann Howe in 1949--two events that generated great reader interest and sent circulation soaring. Other characters included the Palooka's daughter Joan and Joe's sidekicks Humphrey Pennyworth and (mute) Little Max. The strip outlived Fisher, surviving until 1984.

A *Joe Palooka* radio series aired on CBS in 1932, sponsored by Heinz, with Ted Bergman as Joe. *Palooka*, a feature film based on the strip, was released in 1934 with Stu Erwin as Joe and Jimmy Durante as his manager Knobby Walsh. Ten more live-action feature films starring Joe Kirkwood were released between 1946 and 1951. Two series of comic books were published, the first in 1942-1944, the second in 1945-1961. A live-action television series, *The Joe Palooka Story*, with Joe Kirkwood as Joe, was syndicated in 1952.

JPA-1

JPA-2

❑ JPA-1. "Joe Palooka" Wood Jointed Doll,
1930s. Store item. - **$40 $80 $165**

❑ JPA-2. Anti-V.D. World War II Poster,
1943. U.S. Government Printing Office. 14x20" designed like Sunday comic page with story warning that "Liquor An' Dames Don't Mix!" - **$60 $135 $275**

JPA-3

❑ JPA-3. "Joe Palooka Lunch Kit",
1948. Store item by Continental Can. 5x7x4" tall full color tin litho. box with handles. - **$50 $90 $175**

JPA-4

❑ **JPA-4. "Joe Palooka" Characters Glass,**
c. 1948. Clear glass tumbler with color images of him, Knobby, Ann, Humphrey, Little Max. - **$75 $150 $300**

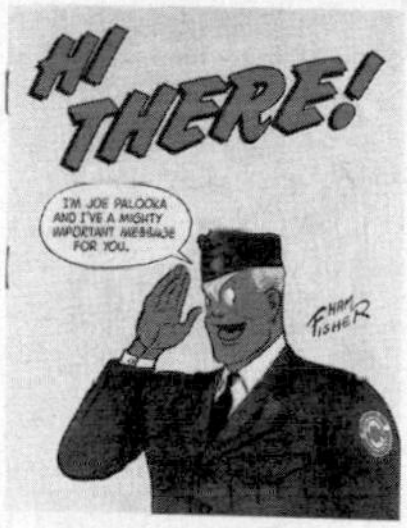

JPA-5

JPA-6

❑ **JPA-5. Red Cross Cartoon Booklet,**
1949. Softcover 12-page color booklet featuring Joe explaining work of American Red Cross. - **$9 $27 $80**

❑ **JPA-6. "Joe Palooka Championship Belt" Metal Buckle,**
1940s. Store item by Ham Fisher Belt Rite Leather Goods.
Buckle - **$30 $60 $90**
With Belt - **$45 $110 $225**

JPA-7

JPA-8

❑ **JPA-7. Joe Palooka "Tangle Comics" Cello. Button,**
1940s. Philadelphia Sunday Bulletin. - **$20 $35 $80**

❑ **JPA-8. Color Portrait Litho. Button,**
1940s. Reverse says "Manufactured Under Exclusive Rights By President's Novelty & Jewelry Co." - **$30 $60 $135**

JPA-9

JPA-10

❑ **JPA-9. "Joe Palooka Cap" Litho. Button,**
1940s. Sponsor not indicated. Pictures Joe as he appeared in early years of comic strip. - **$20 $40 $80**

❑ **JPA-10. Newspaper Strip Cello. Button,**
1940s. Philadelphia Bulletin. - **$25 $55 $125**

JPA-11

JPA-12

❑ **JPA-11. "Hi!-Humphrey" Cello. Button For Doll,**
1940s. Ideal Novelty & Toy Co. for character doll of Palooka sidekick Humphrey Pennyworth. - **$25 $55 $125**

❑ **JPA-12. Club Medal,**
1940s. New York Daily Mirror. Aluminum with portrait front and horseshoe/boxing glove design on reverse. - **$15 $25 $50**

JPA-13

❑ **JPA-13. Joe Palooka Candy Box,**
1940s. Boxing lesson card on back. - **$125 $250 $500**

JPA-14

❑ **JPA-14. Humphrey Doll,**
1940s. Came with removable (and usually missing) tag, pin back and apron. Made by Ideal. Rare when complete. - **$300 $600 $1350**

JPA-15

❑ **JPA-15. "Meet The Champ!" Comic Strip Introduction Sign,**
c. 1950. 11x17" cardboard introducing Joe Palooka as a daily strip in Albany Times-Union subtitled "Knickerbocker News." - **$70 $135 $275**

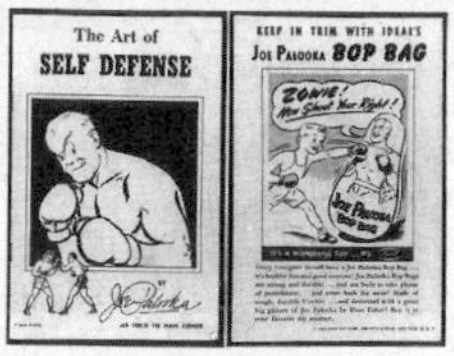

JPA-16

❑ **JPA-16. "The Art Of Self Defense" Booklet,**
1952. Store item by Ideal Toy Corp. Came with "Bop Bag" punching toy. - **$10 $25 $50**

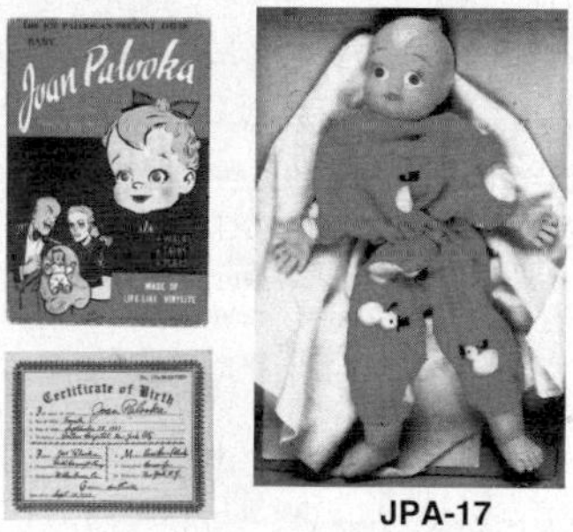

JPA-17

❑ **JPA-17. "Joan Palooka" Boxed Doll/Hand Puppet,**
c. 1952. Store item by National Mask & Puppet Corp. Replica doll of Joe and Ann's daughter plus flannel blanket, paper birth certificate and instruction sheet. Near Mint Boxed - **$200**
Doll - **$30 $60 $100**
Certificate - **$12 $20 $35**

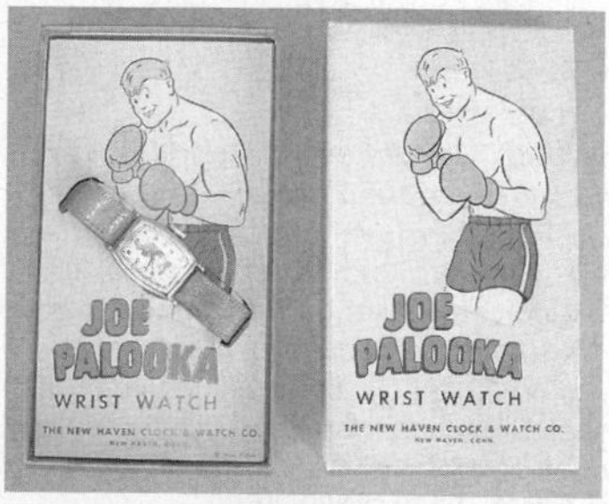

JPA-18

❑ **JPA-18. Joe Palooka Wrist Watch in Colorful Box,**
1950s. Scarce. Box - **$300 $600 $1200**
Watch - **$100 $250 $500**

JPA-19

❑ **JPA-19. "Little Max's Lunch" Boxed Plastic Bank,**
1950s. Store item by Comics Novelty Candy Corp. 4-1/2" tall. Box **- $20 $35 $70**
Bank **- $15 $30 $60**

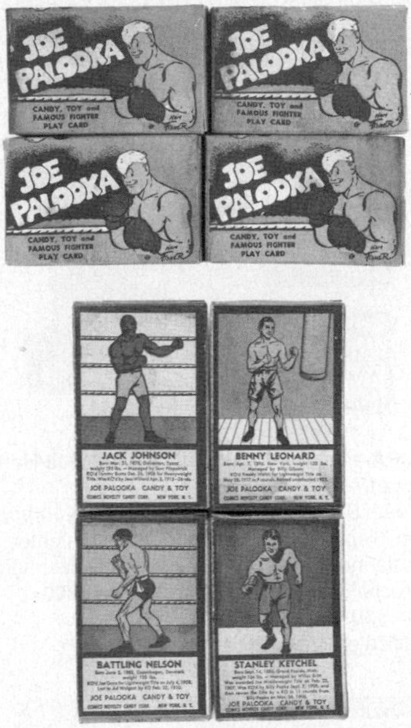

JPA-20

❑ **JPA-20. "Joe Palooka" Candy Boxes Featuring "Famous Fighter" Cards,**
1950s. Four 2.5x4x1" deep boxes issued by Comics Novelty Candy Corp. Each box features Joe Palooka as boxer on top and two side panels. Perforated back panel is boxing card. Boxers on these four are Jack Johnson, Stanley Ketchel, Benny Leonard, Battling Nelson. Includes boxer bio/stats.
Each Intact - **$150 $300 $600**

Joe Penner

"Wanna buy a duck?" Perhaps no other comedian is so well remembered for such a single phrase as Joe Penner (1905-1941). Penner's trademark prop, of course, from vaudeville days into radio and 1930s to early 1940s films, was the inevitable live duck carried in a basket. The 1930s Warner Bros. cartoon character Egghead, who would evolve into Elmer Fudd, was based on Penner. His wacky repartee style ended with his death in 1941 at the early age of 37 years with his duck remaining unbought.

JOP-1

❑ **JOP-1. "Wise Quacks" Fan Newsletter Vol. 1 #4,**
November 1934. - **$15 $30 $50**

JOP-2

❑ **JOP-2. "Marx Joe Penner And His Duck Goo-Goo" Boxed Wind-Up,**
1934. Tin litho toy is 4x4.5x8" tall with built-in key and comes in nicely illustrated box with inscription "Want To Buy A Duck Sincerely Joe Penner." Toy depicts Penner in detailed suit and has separate hat and cigar. In one hand he holds a basket containing three ducks while his other hand rests on the back of his duck "Goo-Goo." Box - **$125 $275 $600**
Toy - **$150 $300 $650**

JOP-3

JOP-4

❑ **JOP-3. "Stay As Sweet As You Are" Sheet Music,**
1934. From Penner's movie "College Rhythm". - **$15 $30 $45**

❑ **JOP-4. "Don't Never Do-o-o That" Sheet Music,**
1934. Six pages of words and music for novelty song subtitled "You Nasty Man" featuring cover art of Penner and his duck. - **$15 $30 $45**

JOP-5

❑ **JOP-5. "Joe Penner's Duck Farm" Book,**
1935. Goldsmith. 5x5.25" from "Radio Star Series" similar to Big Little Book format with Penner and ducks story illustrated by Henry Vallely. - **$12 $36 $78**

JOP-6

JOP-7

❑ **JOP-6. "Cocomalt Big Book Of Comics",**
1938. Featuring Joe Penner, various comic characters. - **$214 $642 $3100**

❑ **JOP-7. Premium Photo with Autograph,**
1938. - **$175**

JOP-9

JOP-8

JOP-10

❑ **JOP-8. Photo Promo,**
1934. 5"x7" photo from Penner's movie "I'm From the City". - **$10 $20 $30**

❑ **JOP-9. "Raisin Bread/Radio Special" Cello. Button,**
1930s. Unknown bakery or bakeries. From series listing various types of breads or rolls. - **$5 $15 $30**

❑ **JOP-10. "I'm A Joe Penner Quacker" Cello. Button,**
1930s. - **$12 $25 $50**

JOP-11

JOP-12

JOP-13

❑ **JOP-11. "Joe Penner/Goo-Goo" Duck Doll,**
1930s. 11.5" tall cloth stuffed doll wearing sash inscribed by Penner's traditional question "Wanna Buy A Duck?" - **$50 $95 $175**

❑ **JOE-12. First Issue "Joe Penner Songs" Folio,**
1941. - **$15 $30 $60**

❑ **JOE-13. Photo/Dexterity Game Brass Ring,**
c. 1940s. Scarce. - **$325 $650 $1200**

John Wayne

Born Marion Morrison in Iowa, John Wayne (1907-1979) was to grow from a football player at the University of Southern California to become one of the legendary giants of American film. After bit parts in silent films in the 1920s, he played the lead in *The Big Trail* (1930) and three chapter plays for Mascot Pictures (1932-1933). He achieved stardom with his role as the Ringo Kid in John Ford's *Stagecoach* in 1939. Wayne was to appear in more than 250 films over half a century, the most memorable directed by Ford or Howard Hawks, and most of them westerns. He won an Academy Award for *True Grit* (1969). The Duke, who came to symbolize the rugged courage of the American West, was one of the greatest box office attractions of all time. He was awarded a Congressional Medal of Freedom posthumously.

***John Wayne Adventure Comics* was published from 1949 to 1955 with art by Frank Frazetta and Al Williamson in the earlier issues. Wayne made scattered appearances in other comic book series between 1948 and 1967, mostly associated with his movie roles, and in one of a set of six pocket-size giveaways from Oxydol-Dreft in 1950. Commemorative items appear to this day.**

JWA-1

JWA-2

❑ **JWA-1. "Raoul Walsh's The Big Trail" Cello. Button,** 1930. Contest or club member promotion for movie of John Wayne's first starring role. - **$75 $150 $275**

❑ **JWA-2. Dixie Ice Cream Picture,**
1936. Four scenes on reverse from "King Of The Pecos." - **$50 $125 $225**

JWA-3

JWA-4

❑ **JWA-3. "John Wayne King Of The Pecos" Dixie Lid,**
1936. - **$10 $18 $40**

❑ **JWA-4. "John Wayne In 'Flying Tigers'" Look Magazine,**
1942. Magazine is 10.5x13.5" with 74 pages for October 6, 1942. Four pages on John Wayne movie. - **$20 $45 $90**

JWA-5

❑ **JWA-5. "The Song of the Seabees" Song Sheet,**
1944. Republic Pictures. From the movie "The Fighting Seabees."- **$15 $30 $60**

JWA-6

JWA-7

❑ **JWA-6. "The Fighting Seabees" Movie Postcard,**
1944. Republic Pictures. - **$12 $20 $40**

❑ **JWA-7. Ring With Photo Under Plastic,**
1940s. Store item. From series of movie star rings with black and white photo on brass base with adjustable bands. - **$30 $65 $135**

JWA-8

JWA-9

❑ **JWA-8. John Wayne Cello. Button,**
1940s. Black and white photo on blue background. - **$20 $40 $75**

❑ **JWA-9. "John Wayne/The Cowboy Troubleshooter" Comic Booklet,**
1950. Procter & Gamble wrappers or boxtops from Dreft, Oxydol or Ivory Soap. - **$15 $45 $185**

JWA-10

JWA-11

❑ **JWA-10. John Wayne Photo Charm,**
c. 1950. Vending machine item. Red plastic frame with black and white glossy photo. - **$5 $10 $20**

❑ **JWA-11. John Wayne Photo Charm,**
c. 1950. Vending machine item. Silver plastic frame with black and white glossy photo. - **$8 $12 $25**

JWA-12

JWA-13

❑ **JWA-12. John Wayne Photo Ring,**
c. 1950. Silvered plastic base with inset glossy black and white paper photo. - **$15 $30 $60**

❑ **JWA-13. John Wayne Photo Charm,**
c. 1950. Vending machine item. White plastic frame with glossy black and white photo. Example shown missing top edge loop. - **$8 $12 $25**

JWA-14

JWA-15

❑ **JWA-14. John Wayne Coloring Book,**
1951. Saalfield Publishers. Book is 10.75x14" with 16 pages. - **$25 $50 $110**

❑ **JWA-15. Dixie Ice Cream Picture,**
c. 1952. Reverse has scenes from famous movies and promo text for "The Quiet Man." - **$50 $100 $175**

JWA-16

❑ **JWA-16. "The Searchers" 11x14" Cardboard Sign For Book Store,**
c. 1956. Popular Library. Announces release of paperback novel by Alan Lemay "soon to be a great motion picture starring John Wayne." - **$45 $100 $200**

JWA-17

❑ **JWA-17. "She Wore A Yellow Ribbon" Lobby Card,**
1959. RKO Radio Pictures. 11x14" from set of eight. Title Card - **$70 $135 $250**
Other Cards With Wayne - **$35 $65 $115**

JWA-18

❑ **JWA-18. Transfer Picture Sheet,**
1950s. Store item. 4-1/2x5-1/2" paper with full color reverse image portrait for application to fabric. - **$12 $25 $50**

JWA-19

JWA-20

❑ **JWA-19. Leather Billfold,**
c. 1950s. Store item. Zippered wallet with color portrait on front. - **$85 $175 $350**

❑ **JWA-20. John Wayne And Ronald Reagan Cello. Button,**
c. 1968. Rim curl names "Big Little Store" of San Francisco. - **$20 $40 $80**

JWA-21

❑ **JWA-21. "McQ" Movie Mug,**
1974. Ceramic mug belived given to cast members of the film starring him as modern-day detective policeman. 3-1/2" tall with facsimile signature. - **$15 $25 $50**

JWA-22

JWA-23

❑ **JWA-22. John Wayne Life-Sized Poster,**
c. 1976. 26.5x76" black and white photo of him rolling cigarette. - **$20 $40 $75**

❑ **JWA-23. Commemorative 3-1/2" Cello. Button,**
1979. - **$5 $10 $20**

JWA-24

❑ **JWA-24. Boxed Rifle Cartridges,**
1970s. Winchester. Each 32-40 cartridge has tiny "Duke" designation on firing cap.
Boxed - **$15 $30 $75**

JWA-25

JWA-26

❑ **JWA-25. Plaster Statue,**
c. 1979. Store item by Esco. 18-1/2" tall from a series of personality statues. - **$35 $75 $135**

❑ **JWA-26. Boxed Commemorative Doll,**
1982. Store item by Effanbee Doll Corp. 18" vinyl in fabric cavalry outfit from limited "Legend Series." Near Mint Boxed - **$250**
Loose - **$35 $60 $125**

JWA-27

❑ **JWA-27. "Pick It Up Pilgrim" Replica Car,**
1999. Die cast replica at 1:64 scale. Features John Wayne on car and packaging. Issue #43. - **$20**

JWA-28

❑ **JWA-28. John Wayne Bust Cookie Jar,**
2005. Vandor, licensed by Wayne Enterprises. Limited Edition of 3,600. Sculpted by Roger Sun Studios. - **$70**

Jonny Quest

***Jonny Quest*, a prime-time animated adventure series from the Hanna-Barbera studios, premiered on ABC in 1964 and aired for a year. The series was repeated on Saturday mornings on CBS (1967-1970), on ABC (1970-1972), and on NBC, first as part of the *Godzilla Power Hour* (1978), then on its own (1979-1981). Created by comic book artist Doug Wildey, Jonny and his scientist father traveled to exotic places in their supersonic plane, fought mythical beasts, confronted unsolved mysteries, and triumphed over danger wherever they found it.**

JNY-1

❑ **JNY-1. ABC TV Promo Photo With Text Information,**
1964. Black and white glossy promoting particular show "Calcutta Adventure" from October 23, 1964. - **$35 $70 $135**

JNY-2

❑ **JNY-2. "Jonny Quest Game,"**
1964. Box is 10x19.5x2" deep containing board game manufactured by Transogram and copyright Hannah-Barbera Productions Inc. Game includes 19x19" game board with character images in each corner and island with boat-coarse in center. Includes two spinners, 24 gun pieces, 12 rafts and two pier cards. Comes with instruction sheet. - **$150 $300 $550**

JNY-3

❑ **JNY-3. Boxed Card Game,**
1965. Store item by Milton Bradley. - **$25 $50 $115**

JNY-4

❑ **JNY-4. Original Cover Art for TV Edition Book,**
1965. Art is 12 1/2" x 17", acrylic on illustration board. Book was published in Great Britain. - **$1000**

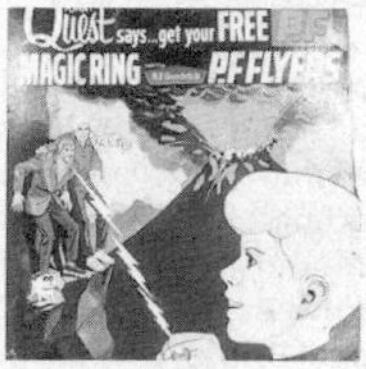

JNY-5

JNY-6

❑ **JNY-5. "Magic Ring" 21x22" Cardboard Store Sign,**
1960s. P.F. footwear of B.F. Goodrich. Shows gold plastic decoder ring (Pictured in Rings, Miscellaneous section). - **$75 $150 $300**

❑ **JNY-6. Large Plastic Ring,**
1996. Issuer unknown. Blue plastic base has large oval top with color label. - **$6 $12 $20**

Julia

Diahann Carroll received a Metropolitan Opera scholarship to study at the New York High School of Music and Art at age ten. By the early 1950s, she had become a nightclub singer and actress. In 1954 alone, she appeared on Broadway in Truman Capote's *House of Flowers* and in the feature film *Carman Jones*. Her career continued on a high note, leading to the TV series *Julia* establishing her as the first African American woman to have her own show. *Julia* aired on NBC from September 17, 1968 until February 9, 1971. Carroll played widowed nurse Julia Baker living with her young son. Cast members included Lloyd Nolan (1902-1989) as Dr. Morton C. Hegley, Marc Copage as Julia's son Corey and Fred Williamson as Steve Bruce. Directors included Don Ameche and Luther James. Writers included Arthur Alsberg and Harry Dolan. Carroll won the 1969 Golden Globe Award for Best Actress. The series had 86 episodes.

Diahann Carroll's multi-faceted career continues today, playing Jane Burke on *Grey's Anatomy*.

JUL-1

❑ **JUL-1. "Diahann Carroll As Julia" Boxed Doll,**
1968. Mattel. 5.5x12.25x2.25" deep box holds 11.5" tall doll with bendable legs, "Twist 'N Turn Waist," and real eyelashes. - **$50 $150 $250**

JUL-2

❑ **JUL-2. "Julia Colorforms Dress-Up Kit",**
1969. 20th Century Fox Film Corp. 8x12.5x1" deep box contains 4.5x9" glossy cardboard board with full color photo of Julia in her slip. Comes with two sheets of die-cut vinyl outfits and instruction folder. - **$20 $50 $140**

JUL-3

❑ **JUL-3. "Julia" View-Master Set,**
1969. 20th Century Fox Film Corp. 4.5x4.5" sealed envelope contains set of three reels and story booklet. - **$10 $20 $40**

JUL-4

❑ JUL-4. "Julia" Lunch Box With Thermos,
1969. King-Seeley Thermos Co. 7x9x4" deep metal lunch box with color illustrations. 6.5" tall metal thermos with color illustrations and green cup. Box - **$50 $100 $250**
Thermos - **$15 $30 $60**

JUL-5

❑ JUL-5. "Julia Paperdolls" Boxed Set,
1970. 20th Century Fox Film Corp. 11x14.5x1" deep box contains a 10.5x14" full color cardboard sheet with punch-out dolls of Julia, Corey, Marie and Earl J. Waggedorn and a large 20x42" full color glossy paper sheet with outfits and accessories. - **$15 $30 $65**

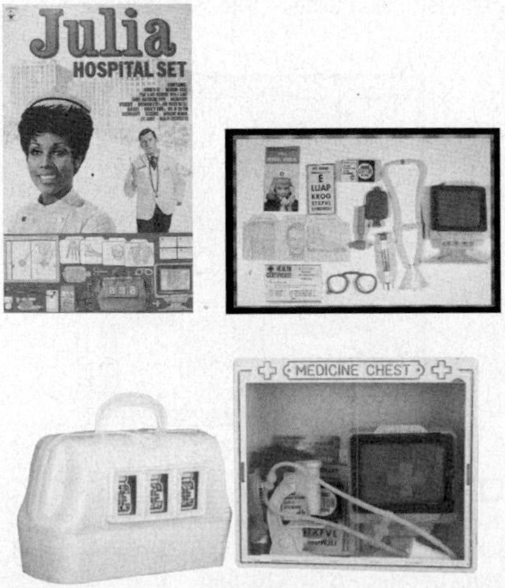

JUL-6

❑ JUL-6. "Julia Hospital Set",
1970. Transogram. 10.25x16.25x4" deep box holds "Nurses Kit, Medicine Chest, Play X-Ray Machine With Four X-Rays, Candy Dispensing Hypo, Microscope, Otoscope, Thermometer, Hot Water Bottle, Glasses, Nurses Ring, Box of Cotton, Stethoscope, Medicine Manual, Eye Chart and Health Certificates. - **$50 $100 $175**

Junior Birdmen of America

Hearst newspapers sponsored this club for young aviation enthusiasts in the 1920s and 1930s, offering membership cards and manuals along with pins and patches. Club activities included flying model airplanes, with medals awarded to contest winners. The club motto was "Today Pilots of Models, Tomorrow Model Pilots." At one point the club had 645,000 members.

JRB-1

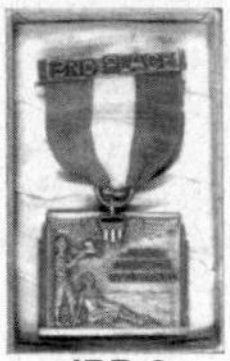

JRB-2

❑ JRB-1. Champion Award Medal In Presentation Box,
1934. Rare. Near Mint Boxed - **$350**
Unboxed - **$35 $100 $250**

❑ JRB-2. Second Place Award Medal In Presentation Box,
1934. Scarce. Near Mint Boxed - **$250**
Unboxed - **$35 $75 $150**

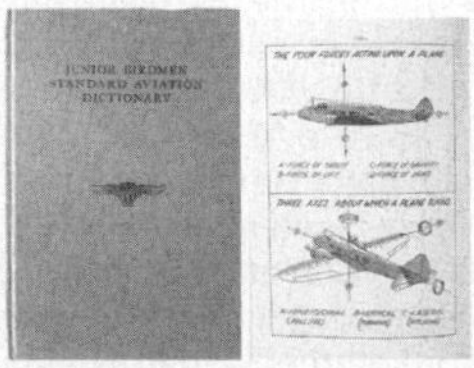

JRB-3

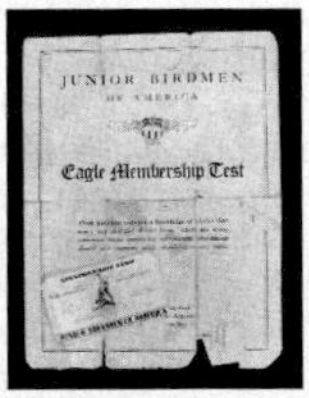

JRB-4

❑ JRB-3. "Junior Birdmen Of America" Handbooks And Dictionary,
1935. Each handbook is 6x9" from "Junior Birdmen Library Series." From a numbered series and these are #5-9, each with black/blue cover with different art relating to specific handbook, contents are black/white with 24-32 pages. The "Standard Aviation Dictionary" is a hardcover with 40 pages. Extensive dictionary includes charts, diagrams and illustrations, definitions of aviation words, terms and phrases.
Each Handbook - **$5 $10 $20**
Dictionary - **$12 $25 $40**

❑ JRB-4. "Eagle Membership Test" Brochure And Membership Card,
1938. Brochure - **$15 $30 $60**
Card - **$15 $30 $60**

JRB-5

❑ JRB-5. "Flight Squadron Plan" Folder,
1930s. Contents include depiction of rank insignia pins for Commander, Captain, Eagle. - **$15 $30 $60**

JRB-6

JRB-7

❑ JRB-6. Club Manual,
1930s. Folder explains how to form a squadron and advance in rank. - **$15 $30 $60**

❑ JRB-7. Hearst Newspapers Club Card,
1930s. For various newspapers of Hearst Syndicate with facsimile signature of George Hearst, National Commander. - **$20 $45 $80**

JRB-8

❑ JRB-8. "Field Day" Felt Fabric Pennant,
1930s. 22" long. - **$40 $110 $185**

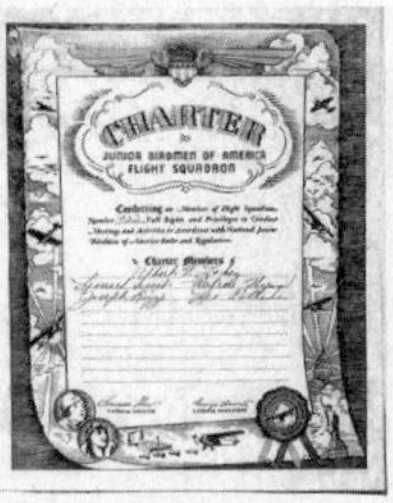

JRB-9

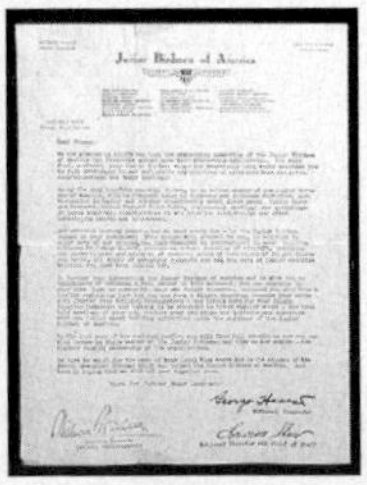

JRB-10

❑ **JRB-9. Hearst Newspapers "Flight Squadron" Charter Certificate,**
1930s. For various newspapers of Hearst Syndicate with facsimile signature of George Hearst, National Commander. - **$35 $65 $125**

❑ **JRB-10. Membership Approval Letter,**
1930s. Lists 22 different "Hearst Newspapers." Came with wings and membership card. - **$10 $18 $35**

JRB-11

JRB-12

❑ **JRB-11. Membership Card,**
1930s. Shows boy and girl on front. - **$25 $50 $100**

❑ **JRB-12. Rule Book,**
1930s. Also lists newspapers where Junior Birdmen column appears. - **$25 $50 $80**

JRB-13

❑ **JRB-13. Felt Fabric Emblem,**
1930s. Large 2-1/2x8" size. - **$45 $135 $235**

JRB-14

JRB-15

❑ **JRB-14. "Jr. Birdmen Of America" Enameled Brass Wings Badge,**
1930s. - **$15 $30 $50**

❑ **JRB-15. "Eagle" Enameled Brass Wings Badge With Rank Bar,**
1930s. Scarce. - **$35 $100 $200**

Justice Society of America

The first time superheroes ever got together and formed a team was when The Justice Society of America debuted in the pages of *All-Star Comics* #3, published in the Fall of 1940. This collection of heroes, including at various times the Flash, Green Lantern, the Spectre, Wonder Woman, Hawkman, Hourman, Doctor Mid-Nite, Sandman and many others, set the stage for every super group that was to follow. Readers thrilled to the exploits of this first team until 1951, when trends led *All-Star* to change to *All-Star Western* with #58. The title would be revived in the '70s with old and new members, but it would not be until August 1999 that the JSA would receive its own title. Many interesting things happened in the meantime for Justice Society collectors and historians, though. Not the least of these was the creation of the Junior Justice Society of America.

The Junior Justice Society debuted in an ad in *All-Star Comics* #14, the December 1942 issue. Like many other clubs for young comic book readers, a membership kit was offered for a nominal charge, in this case 15¢. For their money, members received a welcome letter from Wonder Woman, a silver-plated membership badge (later replaced by a cloth sew-on patch), a cardboard decoder, a four-page War Bond comic entitled *The Minute Man Answers the Call*, with art by Sheldon Moldoff, and a four-color membership certificate. Though it has been theorized elsewhere that there were only four variations on this kit over the life of the Junior Justice Society, there were actually five distinct kits (see article elsewhere in this edition). The JJSA kits, including their mailers, have become among the most prized collectibles of this type.

The resurgence of superhero comics in the late '50s and early '60s owed a tremendous debt to their predecessors, particularly the Justice Society. Their spiritual successors, the Justice League of America, became their modern day counterparts and engaged with them in many cross-reality team-ups.

The modern incarnation of the JSA has established the team and its characters as contemporaries of the JLA and continues to open the world of the classic characters to new readers through DC's Archives series of hardcover collections and through DC Direct's line of JSA toys including PVCs and action figures.

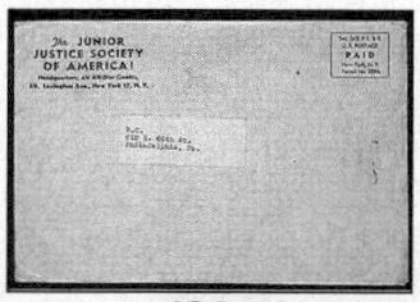
JSA-1

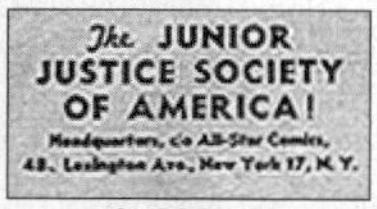

(CLOSE-UP)

JSA-2

(CLOSE-UP)

JSA-3

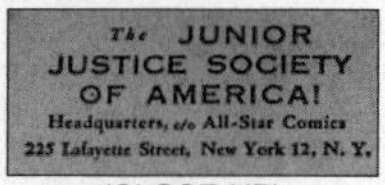

(CLOSE-UP)

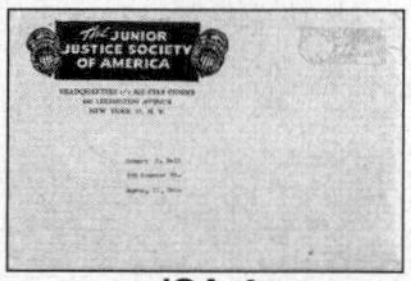
JSA-4

(CLOSE-UP)

❑ **JSA-1. Club Kit Envelope,**
1942. - **$45 $90 $175**

❑ **JSA-2. 1943-1944 Club Kit Envelope,**
1943-44. - **$35 $70 $145**

❑ **JSA-3. 1945 Club Kit Envelope,**
1945. Scarce. - **$70 $135 $210**

❑ **JSA-4. Club Kit Envelope,**
1948. - **$45 $90 $175**

JSA-5

❑ **JSA-5. Solid Brass Badge,**
1942. Rare. In-house prototype with tie-tac fastener. The back of the badge is flat, unlike the later silver models. - **$850 $1850 $3700**

JSA-6

(CLOSE-UP)

❑ **JSA-6. Silver Finish Club Badge,**
1942. Large letter style only offered for two months. This version has a tie-tac fastener. See JSA-7 for pin version. - **$250 $600 $1200**

JSA-7

(CLOSE-UP)

❑ **JSA-7. Silver Finish Club Badge,**
1942. Large letter style only offered for two months. This version has a pin fastener. See JSA-6 for tie-tac version. - **$250 $600 $1200**

JSA-8

(TWO VERSIONS OF THE BACK)

JSA-8
(CLOSE-UP)

❑ **JSA-8. Silver Finish Club Badge,**
1948. Small letter style. Badge also existed with variation of pin on back running across. -
$215 $475 $950

JSA-9

(1942-44)

These similar looking patches can be distinguished by the differences in the stitching behind the shield. The red stitching stays within the circle on the 1942-44 patch.

JSA-10

(1945)

❑ **JSA-9. Club Member Fabric Patch,**
1942-44. Replaced large letter badge because of metal shortage. - **$200 $550 $1000**

❑ **JSA-10. Club Member Fabric Patch,**
1945. Scarce. Similar to 1942-44 patch but shield is 1/2" larger. - **$275 $650 $1200**

JSA-11

❑ **JSA-11. Club Kit Decoder,**
1942-1944. - **$115 $225 $400**

JSA-12

(CLOSE-UPS)

❑ **JSA-12. Club Kit Decoder,**
1945. Note different names in window. Rare. -
$250 $500 $750

JSA-13

❑ **JSA-13. Club Kit Decoder,**
1948. Black rectangle design. -
$125 $275 $500

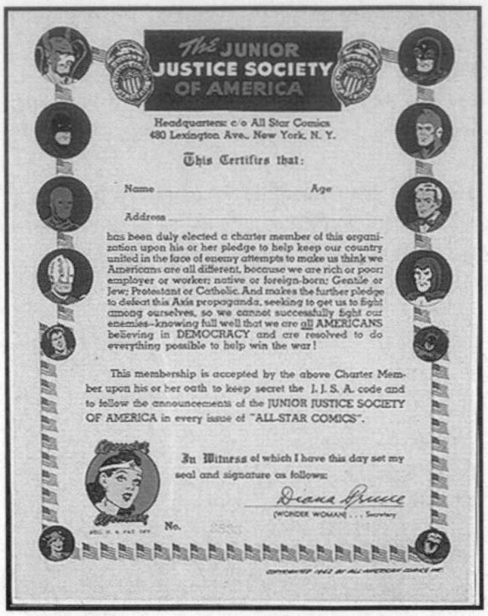

The JUNIOR JUSTICE SOCIETY OF AMERICA

Headquarters: c/o All Star Comics
480 Lexington Ave., New York, N. Y.

This Certifies that:

Name ________ Age ____

Address ________

has been duly elected a charter member of this organization upon his or her pledge to help keep our country united in the face of enemy attempts to make us think we Americans are all different, because we are rich or poor; employer or worker; native or foreign-born; Gentile or Jew; Protestant or Catholic. And makes the further pledge to defeat this Axis propaganda, seeking to get us to fight among ourselves, so we cannot successfully fight our enemies—knowing full well that we are all AMERICANS believing in DEMOCRACY and are resolved to do everything possible to help win the war!

This membership is accepted by the above Charter Member upon his or her oath to keep secret the J. J. S. A. code and to follow the announcements of the JUNIOR JUSTICE SOCIETY OF AMERICA in every issue of "ALL-STAR COMICS".

In Witness of which I have this day set my seal and signature as follows:

Diana Prince
(WONDER WOMAN) . . . Secretary

No.

JSA-14

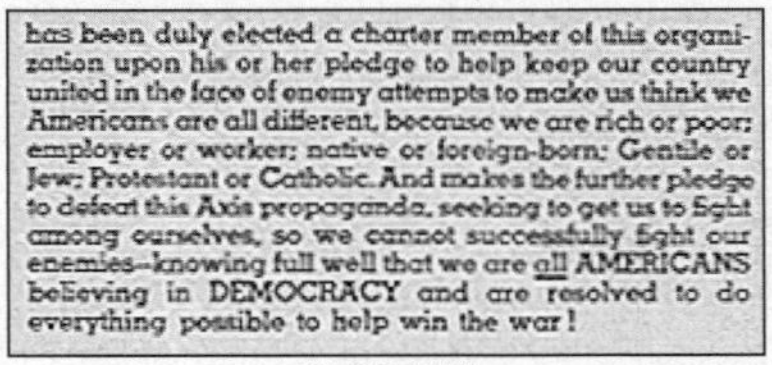

has been duly elected a charter member of this organization upon his or her pledge to help keep our country united in the face of enemy attempts to make us think we Americans are all different, because we are rich or poor; employer or worker; native or foreign-born; Gentile or Jew; Protestant or Catholic. And makes the further pledge to defeat this Axis propaganda, seeking to get us to fight among ourselves, so we cannot successfully fight our enemies—knowing full well that we are all AMERICANS believing in DEMOCRACY and are resolved to do everything possible to help win the war!

(CLOSE-UP)

❑ **JSA-14. Club Kit Certificate,**
1942. First certificate. - **$150 $375 $600**

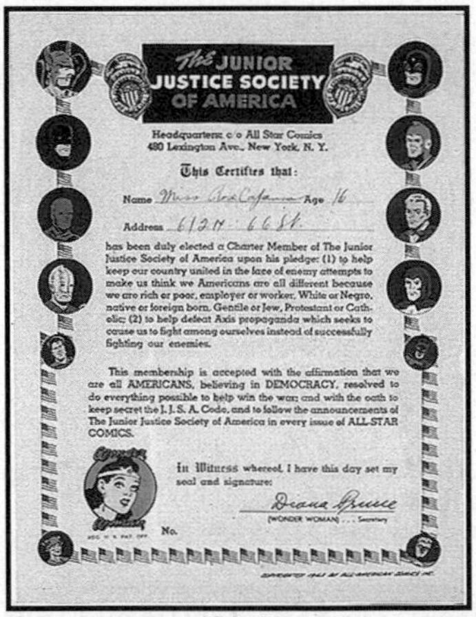

The JUNIOR JUSTICE SOCIETY OF AMERICA

Headquarters: c/o All Star Comics
480 Lexington Ave., New York, N. Y.

This Certifies that:

Name ________ Age ____

Address ________

has been duly elected a Charter Member of The Junior Justice Society of America upon his pledge: (1) to help keep our country united in the face of enemy attempts to make us think we Americans are all different because we are rich or poor, employer or worker, White or Negro, native or foreign born, Gentile or Jew, Protestant or Catholic; (2) to help defeat Axis propaganda which seeks to cause us to fight among ourselves instead of successfully fighting our enemies.

This membership is accepted with the affirmation that we are all AMERICANS, believing in DEMOCRACY, resolved to do everything possible to help win the war; and with the oath to keep secret the J. J. S. A. Code, and to follow the announcements of The Junior Justice Society of America in every issue of ALL-STAR COMICS.

In Witness whereof, I have this day set my seal and signature:

Diana Prince
(WONDER WOMAN) . . . Secretary

No.

JSA-15

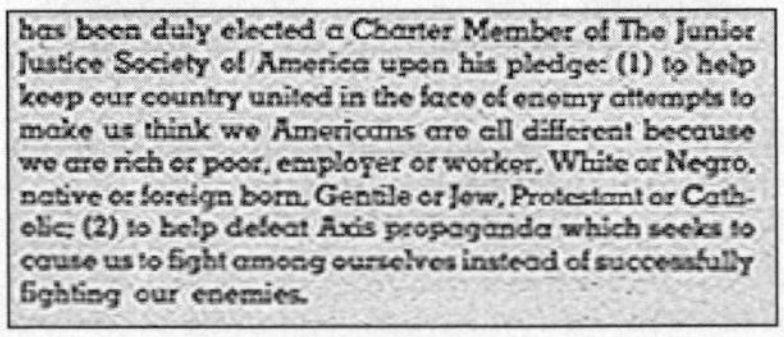

has been duly elected a Charter Member of The Junior Justice Society of America upon his pledge: (1) to help keep our country united in the face of enemy attempts to make us think we Americans are all different because we are rich or poor, employer or worker, White or Negro, native or foreign born, Gentile or Jew, Protestant or Catholic; (2) to help defeat Axis propaganda which seeks to cause us to fight among ourselves instead of successfully fighting our enemies.

(CLOSE-UP)

❑ **JSA-15. Club Kit Certificate,**
1942-44. - **$125 $325 $525**

JSA-16

This membership is accepted with the affirmation that we are all AMERICANS, believing in DEMOCRACY, resolved to do everything possible to help win the war; and with the oath to keep secret the J. J. S. A. Code, and to follow the announcements of The Junior Justice Society of America in every issue of ALL-STAR COMICS.

❑ **JSA-16. 1945 Club Kit Certificate,**
1945. Rare certificate with 225 Lafayette St. address at top. Note Wildcat photo is added. The Axis reference was deleted because Germany had already surrendered on May 7th. Japan had not, so the reference to war remained. Rare. - **$250 $550 $1000**

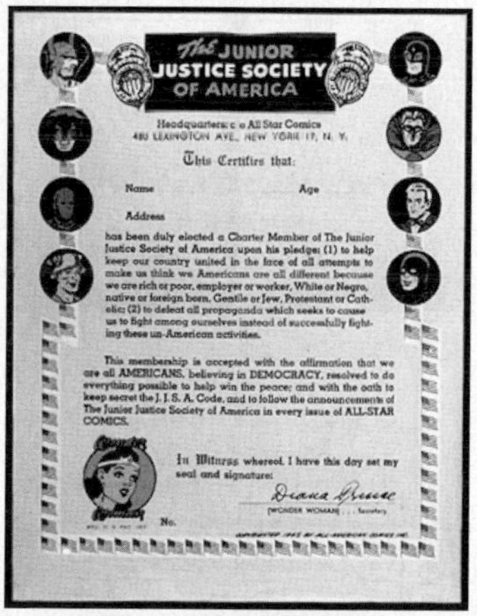

JSA-17

This membership is accepted with the affirmation that we are all AMERICANS, believing in DEMOCRACY, resolved to do everything possible to help win the peace; and with the oath to keep secret the J. J. S. A. Code, and to follow the announcements of The Junior Justice Society of America in every issue of ALL-STAR COMICS.

(CLOSE-UP)

❑ **JSA-17. 1945 Club Kit Certificate,**
1945. Address is now 480 Lexington Ave. Text refers to "win the peace" following the surrender of Japan on August 14th. General MacArthur and U.S. troops had been put in charge of keeping peace in Japan. With the war over, the club was discontinued in Dec. 1945.
Rare. - **$275 $650 $1100**

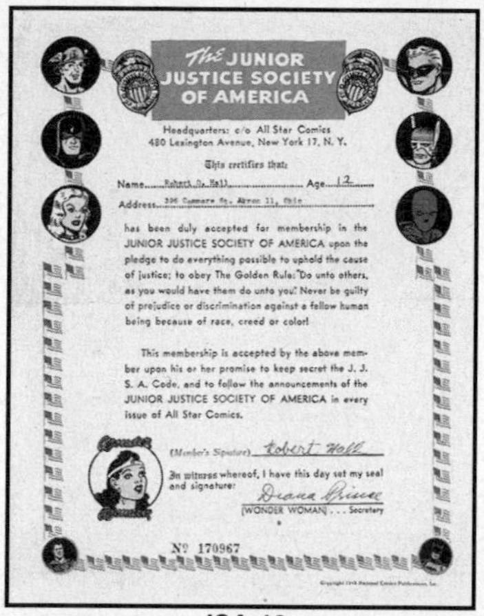

JSA-18

This membership is accepted by the above member upon his or her promise to keep secret the J. J. S. A. Code, and to follow the announcements of the JUNIOR JUSTICE SOCIETY OF AMERICA in every issue of All Star Comics.

(CLOSE-UP)

❑ **JSA 18. Club Kit Certificate,**
1948. Club kit was offered again in comics in late 1947. Earliest kit documented from this release was early 1948. The same materials were used up until 1951. Note Black Canary & Atom pictured. - **$150 $375 $600**

JSA-19 JSA-20

❑ **JSA-19. Club Kit Brochure,**
1942. - **$40 $60 $120**

❑ **JSA-20. Club Kit Brochure,**
1945. Newly printed for 1945. Rare. Brochure has different layout, a different font and the star on the cover is smaller. - **$80 $150 $250**

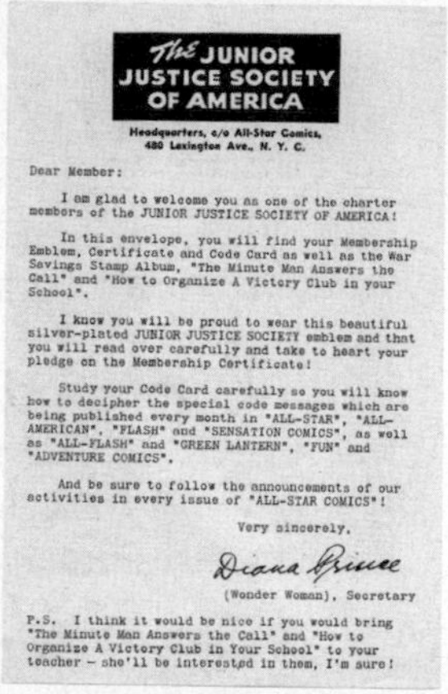

The JUNIOR JUSTICE SOCIETY OF AMERICA
Headquarters, c/o All-Star Comics, 480 Lexington Ave., N. Y. C.

Dear Member:

I am glad to welcome you as one of the charter members of the JUNIOR JUSTICE SOCIETY OF AMERICA!

In this envelope, you will find your Membership Emblem, Certificate and Code Card as well as the War Savings Stamp Album, "The Minute Man Answers the Call" and "How to Organize A Victory Club in your School".

I know you will be proud to wear this beautiful silver-plated JUNIOR JUSTICE SOCIETY emblem and that you will read over carefully and take to heart your pledge on the Membership Certificate!

Study your Code Card carefully so you will know how to decipher the special code messages which are being published every month in "ALL-STAR", "ALL-AMERICAN", "FLASH" and "SENSATION COMICS", as well as "ALL-FLASH" and "GREEN LANTERN", "FUN" and "ADVENTURE COMICS".

And be sure to follow the announcements of our activities in every issue of "ALL-STAR COMICS"!

Very sincerely,

Diana Prince

(Wonder Woman), Secretary

P.S. I think it would be nice if you would bring "The Minute Man Answers the Call" and "How to Organize A Victory Club in Your School" to your teacher - she'll be interested in them, I'm sure!

JSA-21

I know you will be proud to wear this beautiful silver-plated JUNIOR JUSTICE SOCIETY emblem and that you will read over carefully and take to heart your pledge on the Membership Certificate!

(CLOSE-UP)

❑ **JSA-21. 1942 Club Kit Member Letter,**
1942. This letter which lists the silver-plated emblem badge was only sent out for 2 months. The patch replaced the badge, noted in the following version. Rare. - **$75 $150 $250**

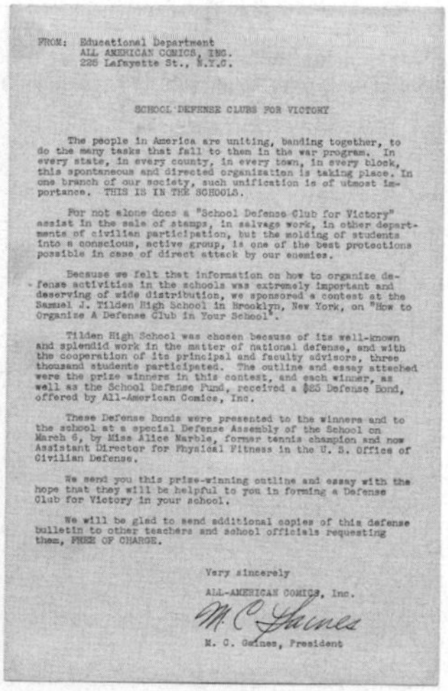

FROM: Educational Department
ALL AMERICAN COMICS, INC.
225 Lafayette St., N.Y.C.

SCHOOL DEFENSE CLUBS FOR VICTORY

The people in America are uniting, banding together, to do the many tasks that fall to them in the war program. In every state, in every county, in every town, in every block, this spontaneous and directed organization is taking place. In one branch of our society, such unification is of utmost importance. THIS IS IN THE SCHOOLS.

For not alone does a "School Defense Club for Victory" assist in the sale of stamps, in salvage work, in other departments of civilian participation, but the molding of students into a conscious, active group, is one of the best protections possible in case of direct attack by our enemies.

Because we felt that information on how to organize defense activities in the schools was extremely important and deserving of wide distribution, we sponsored a contest at the Samuel J. Tilden High School in Brooklyn, New York, on "How to Organize A Defense Club in Your School".

Tilden High School was chosen because of its well-known and splendid work in the matter of national defense, and with the cooperation of its principal and faculty advisors, three thousand students participated. The outline and essay attached were the prize winners in this contest, and each winner, as well as the School Defense Fund, received a $25 Defense Bond, offered by All-American Comics, Inc.

These Defense Bonds were presented to the winners and to the school at a special Defense Assembly of the School on March 6, by Miss Alice Marble, former tennis champion and now Assistant Director for Physical Fitness in the U. S. Office of Civilian Defense.

We send you this prize-winning outline and essay with the hope that they will be helpful to you in forming a Defense Club for Victory in your school.

We will be glad to send additional copies of this defense bulletin to other teachers and school officials requesting them, FREE OF CHARGE.

Very sincerely

ALL-AMERICAN COMICS, Inc.

M C Gaines

M. C. Gaines, President

JSA-22

❑ **JSA-22. School Defense Club for Victory Letter,**
1942. Offered $25 Defense Bond to essay winners. Facsimile signature of M.C. Gaines. - **$60 $125 $175**

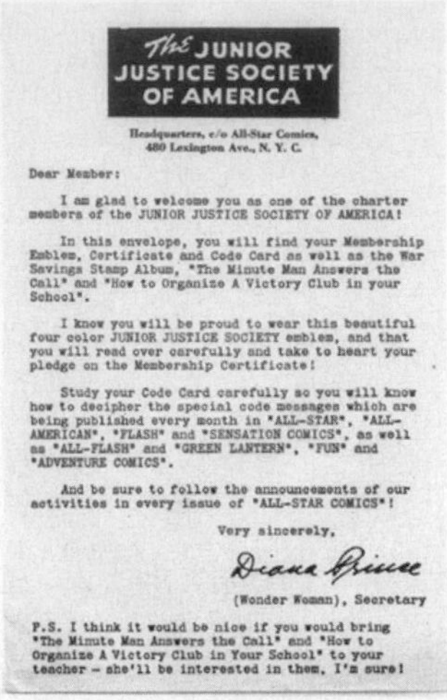

The JUNIOR JUSTICE SOCIETY OF AMERICA

Headquarters, c/o All-Star Comics,
480 Lexington Ave., N. Y. C.

Dear Member:

I am glad to welcome you as one of the charter members of the JUNIOR JUSTICE SOCIETY OF AMERICA!

In this envelope, you will find your Membership Emblem, Certificate and Code Card as well as the War Savings Stamp Album, "The Minute Man Answers the Call" and "How to Organize A Victory Club in your School".

I know you will be proud to wear this beautiful four color JUNIOR JUSTICE SOCIETY emblem, and that you will read over carefully and take to heart your pledge on the Membership Certificate!

Study your Code Card carefully so you will know how to decipher the special code messages which are being published every month in "ALL-STAR", "ALL-AMERICAN", "FLASH" and "SENSATION COMICS", as well as "ALL-FLASH" and "GREEN LANTERN", "FUN" and "ADVENTURE COMICS".

And be sure to follow the announcements of our activities in every issue of "ALL-STAR COMICS"!

Very sincerely,

Diana Prince

(Wonder Woman), Secretary

P.S. I think it would be nice if you would bring "The Minute Man Answers the Call" and "How to Organize A Victory Club in Your School" to your teacher - she'll be interested in them, I'm sure!

JSA-23

I know you will be proud to wear this beautiful four color JUNIOR JUSTICE SOCIETY emblem, and that you will read over carefully and take to heart your pledge on the Membership Certificate!

(CLOSE-UP)

❑ JSA-23. Club Kit Member Letter,
1943-44. This later version lists the four color embroidered patch. - **$60 $125 $175**

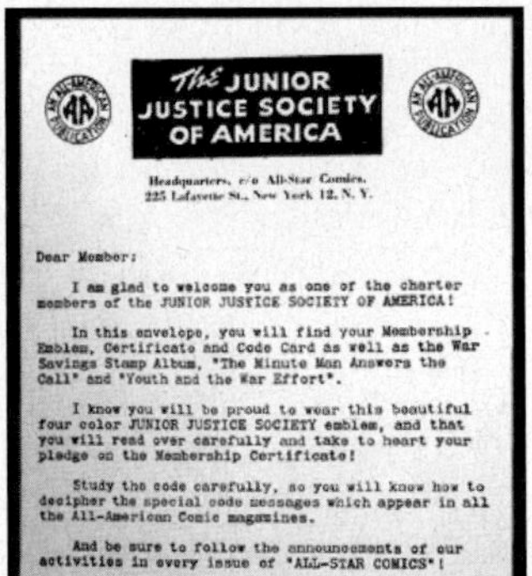

The JUNIOR JUSTICE SOCIETY OF AMERICA

Headquarters, c/o All-Star Comics,
225 Lafayette St., New York 12, N. Y.

Dear Member:

I am glad to welcome you as one of the charter members of the JUNIOR JUSTICE SOCIETY OF AMERICA!

In this envelope, you will find your Membership Emblem, Certificate and Code Card as well as the War Savings Stamp Album, "The Minute Man Answers the Call" and "Youth and the War Effort".

I know you will be proud to wear this beautiful four color JUNIOR JUSTICE SOCIETY emblem, and that you will read over carefully and take to heart your pledge on the Membership Certificate!

Study the code carefully, so you will know how to decipher the special code messages which appear in all the All-American Comic magazines.

And be sure to follow the announcements of our activities in every issue of "ALL-STAR COMICS"!

Very sincerely,

Diana Prince

(Wonder Woman), Secretary

P.S. I think it would be nice if you would bring "The Minute Man Answers the Call" to your teacher - she'll be interested in it, I'm sure!

JSA-24

❑ JSA-24. Club Kit Letter,
1945. Welcome letter for members has "An All-American Publication" stamps in top corners, a feature unique to this version. Rare. - **$100 $200 $375**

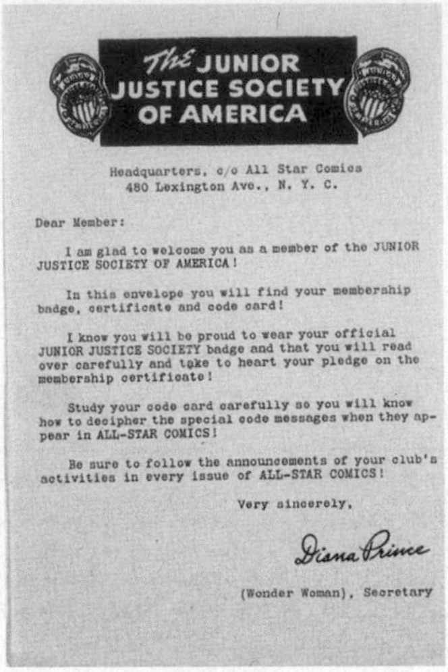

The JUNIOR JUSTICE SOCIETY OF AMERICA

Headquarters, c/o All Star Comics
480 Lexington Ave., N. Y. C.

Dear Member:

I am glad to welcome you as a member of the JUNIOR JUSTICE SOCIETY OF AMERICA!

In this envelope you will find your membership badge, certificate and code card!

I know you will be proud to wear your official JUNIOR JUSTICE SOCIETY badge and that you will read over carefully and take to heart your pledge on the membership certificate!

Study your code card carefully so you will know how to decipher the special code messages when they appear in ALL-STAR COMICS!

Be sure to follow the announcements of your club's activities in every issue of ALL-STAR COMICS!

Very sincerely,

Diana Prince

(Wonder Woman), Secretary

JSA-25

❑ JSA-25. Club Kit Letter,
1948. - **$80 $150 $225**

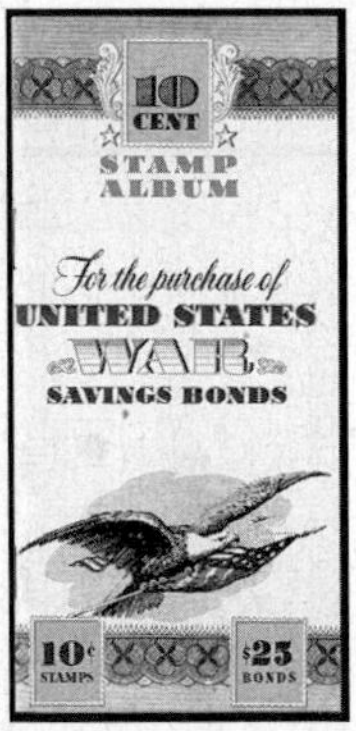

JSA-26

JSA-27

❑ JSA-26. Stamp Album,
1942-44. U.S. War Savings Bonds pamphlet which came with kits during 1942-44. - **$12 $25 $50**

❑ JSA-27. Defense Stamp Album,
1945. Savings bonds promotional pamphlet that only came with the 1945 Kit. - **$25 $50 $110**

(Enlarged panel from back cover of 1942 issue)

JSA-28

❑ JSA-28. "The Minute Man Answers the Call" Comic,
1942. EC comic included in 1942-44 club kits. - **$21 $63 $260**

(Enlarged panel from back cover of 1945 issue)

JSA-29

❑ JSA-29. "The Minute Man Answers the Call" Comic,
1945. Newer version with references to 1945. Rare. - **$21 $63 $260**

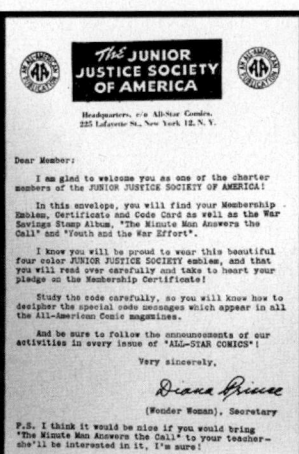

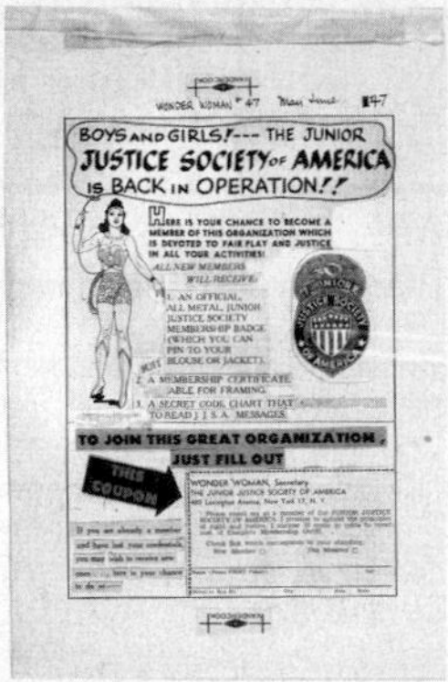

JSA-30

❑ **JSA-30. Comic Book Ad for Club,**
1947. Original art. Unique. - **$700**

JSA-31

❑ **JSA-31. JSA Badge with Plastic Case,**
2000. - **$33**

JSA-32

❑ **JSA-32. Justice Society of America Series 2 PVC Set,**
2000. DC Direct product in box. 7 figures. - **$50**

JSA-33

❑ **JSA-33. Justice Society of America Bookends,**
2001. DC Direct product. Hand painted cold-cast porcelain figures. Limited edition of 1,000. Boxed - **$375**

Kate Smith

Kate Smith (1907-1986) had a brief stage career on Broadway before she moved to radio and became a beloved American institution. Guided throughout by her partner and friend Ted Collins, she broadcast continually from 1931 to 1959, mainly on CBS. Known as the Songbird of the South, she was a large woman, with voice and personality to match. She made her opening theme, *When the Moon Comes Over the Mountain*, practically her own, and for a time she had exclusive rights to Irving Berlin's *God Bless America* which she introduced in 1938. Audiences loved her, and sponsors followed: La Palina cigars (1931-1933), Hudson cars (1934-1935), Philip Morris (1947-1951), and Reader's Digest (1958-1959). During World War II her patriotic efforts sold millions of dollars in war bonds. On television, she had an afternoon show (1950-1954) and two evening variety programs, in 1951-1952 on NBC and in 1960 on CBS.

KAT-1

KAT-2

❑ **KAT-1. "Crying Myself to Sleep" Song Sheet,**
1930. Features her hit song. - **$15 $30 $55**

❑ **KAT-2. Fan Photo,**
c. 1931. La Palina Cigars. - **$10 $20 $40**

KAT-3

KAT-4

❑ **KAT-3. "Kate Smith La Palina Club" Litho. Button,**
c. 1931. La Palina cigars. - **$15 $30 $60**

❑ **KAT-4. "Philadelphia A & P Party" 2-1/2" Cello. Button,**
1935. Great Atlantic & Pacific Tea Co. (grocery chain). Single day issue for November 4. - **$25 $40 $85**

KAT-5

KAT-6

❑ **KAT-5. "There's a Goldmine in the Sky" Song Sheet,**
1937. - **$10 $25 $40**

❑ **KAT-6. Photo,**
1937. Philadelphia Record newspaper premium. - **$10 $25 $45**

KAT-7

KAT-8

❑ **KAT-7. Recipe Folder - Christmas,**
1937. CBS. Radio premium. - **$15 $35 $60**

❑ **KAT-8. Recipe Folder - New Years,**
1938. CBS. Radio premium. - **$15 $35 $60**

KAT-9

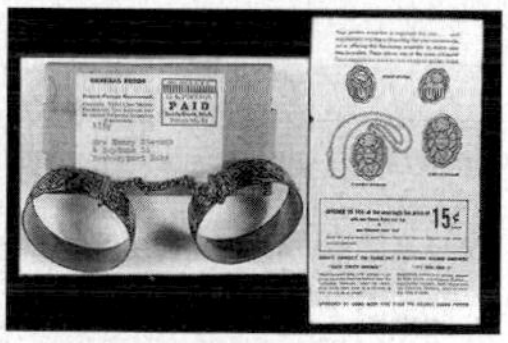

KAT-10

❑ **KAT-9. CBS Radio Card,**
1930s. - **$10 $20 $40**

❑ **KAT-10. Bracelets With Mailer And "Kate Smith Speaks" Reference,**
1940. Swan's Down Cake Flour and Calumet Baking Powder. Brass bracelets with enclosure slip naming Kate Smith program plus another sponsored daytime program "My Son And I." Near Mint Boxed - **$75**

KAT-11

KAT-12

❑ **KAT-11. "Violins Were Playing" Song Sheet,**
1943. - **$10 $15 $30**

❑ **KAT-12. Recipe Book - 16 pages,**
1945. Swans Down. Radio premium. - **$20 $40 $70**

KAT-13

❑ **KAT-13. Arcade Radio Card,**
1940s. - **$5 $10 $20**

Katzenjammer Kids

Considered by some to be the first true comic strip, *The Katzenjammer Kids* premiered in December 1897 in the *New York Journal.* The hell-raising kids, patterned after the similar 19th century story favorites Max and Moritz (see their section) created by Wilhelm Busch (1832-1908), were introduced to Americans by Rudolph Dirks (1877-1968) as Hans and Fritz. Their debut has been called the single most important event in the history of the comic strip. Hans and Fritz, and their long-suffering Mamma, were joined by der Captain in 1902 and by der Inspector in 1905. As the result of a legal battle, Harold Knerr (1882-1949) took over the strip in 1914, while Dirks started a new strip, *The Captain and the Kids*, for the *New York World.* A stage adaptation appeared in 1903, and over the years the strips have been reprinted frequently in comic books. Both strips had their own comic books from the 1930s to the 1950s. Animated cartoon versions were directed by Gregory LaCava in 1916-1918 and by Friz Freleng for MGM in 1938-1939, and the Kids appeared on television in *MGM Cartoons* (ABC, 1960) and *The Fabulous Funnies* (NBC, 1978-1979). *The Katzenjammer Kids* is the oldest comic strip still in syndication, Hy Eisman draws the strip today.

KAZ-1

❑ **KAZ-1. "The Katzenjammer Kids' Rocking Horse" Early Newspaper Premi um Cut-Out Toy,**
1903. 10x14" stiff paper from Hearst Sunday newspaper. - **$30 $65 $135**

KAZ-2

❑ **KAZ-2. "The Katzies" Comic Strip Folder,**
1904. King Features copyright but no sponsor indicated. 2x3" folder that opens to 13-panel story. - **$20 $35 $60**

KAZ-3 KAZ-4

❑ **KAZ-3. Mama Spanking The Boys White Metal Stickpin,**
c. 1905. About 1-1/2" tall hand-colored with translucent reddish color wash. - **$18 $30 $60**

❑ **KAZ-4. Katzenjammers Heat Image Cartoon Postcard,**
1906. American Journal Examiner. Hidden image appears when heat is applied. - **$6 $12 $20**

KAZ-5 KAZ-6

❑ **KAZ-5. Katzenjammers Heat Image Postcard,**
1906. Hidden image appears when heat is applied. - **$6 $12 $20**

❑ **KAZ-6. Katzenjammer Heat Image Postcard,**
1906. Hidden image appears when heat is applied. - **$6 $12 $20**

KAZ-7

❑ **KAZ-7. Embossed Mechanical Valentine,**
c. 1906. Rafael Tuck & Son, Germany. 9" tall from series including Buster Brown and Happy Hooligan. - **$60 $125 $250**

KAZ-8 KAZ-9

❑ **KAZ-8. Captain And The Kids Postcard,**
1907. Hearst's Boston Sunday American Newspaper Premium. Includes water color paint to paint comic. - **$20 $50 $100**

❑ **KAZ-9. "The Komical Katzenjammers By R. Dirks" Reprint Book,**
1908. Book is 10x15.5" with 60 pages and consists of six-panel color comic strips printed on one side. Back page is titled "Stokes' Comic Juveniles" with names of reprint publications. GD - **$150** FN - **$450** VF - **$800**

KAZ-10

❑ **KAZ-10. Captain And The Kids Bell Ringer Toy,**
c. 1910. Gong Bell Toy Co. 2.5x8.5x5" tall cast iron with cast metal wheels.
- $2750 $5500 $8750

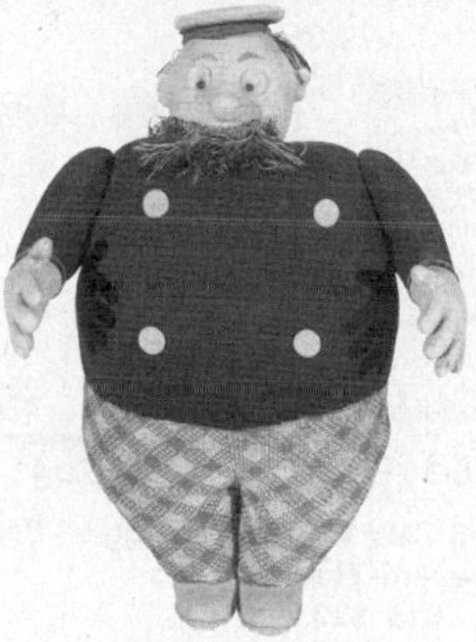

KAZ-11

❑ **KAZ-11. The Captain Doll,**
c. 1910. 15" tall. Felt and cloth doll. Made in Germany by Steiff. Arms and head swivel.
- $800 $2200 $4400

KAZ-12

❑ **KAZ-12. "Jungle Joke Book" With R. Dirks Cover,**
1912. New York Sunday American. 10x12" Sunday supplement with cover cartoon by Katzenjammer artist Rudolph Dirks and 16 pages by various contemporary cartoonists.
- $25 $45 $90

KAZ-13

❑ **KAZ-13. Hot Air Balloon Picture Puzzle,**
c. 1915. Newspaper Feature Service. 4x4-1/2" cardboard jigsaw with eight interlocking pieces. - **$18 $35 $70**

KAZ-14

❑ **KAZ-14. Mama Katzenjammer Tea Cozy,**
c. 1915. 14-1/2" tall. Felt and cloth doll. Made in Germany by Steiff. Arms and head swivel.
- $600 $1500 $3000

KAZ-15

❑ **KAZ-15. Mama Katzenjammer & Kids Candy Container,**
c. 1915. 6-1/2" tall. Molded composition. One-piece with removable Mama head. Made in Germany. - **$1000 $2500 $5000**

KAZ-16

❑ **KAZ-16. Postcard Promo,**
1917. Promotes New York Examiner Sunday edition. - **$55 $110 $200**

KAZ-17

KAZ-18

❑ **KAZ-17. Mama And Kids Figurine,**
c. 1920. Store item. German made, hand-painted hollow bisque group figure. - **$100 $200 $400**

❑ **KAZ-18. Hans German Bisque Figure,**
c. 1920. 3" tall. Fritz also likely produced. Each **- $80 $175 $325**

KAZ-19

❑ **KAZ-19. Comic Strip Reprint Book #2,**
1929. Store Item by Saalfield Publishing Co. inscribed #193. 10x13-3/4" with color covers and 24 black & white pages.
GD **- $58** FN **- $204** VF **- $350**

KAZ-20

KAZ-21

❑ **KAZ-20. Hans And Fritz Mechanical Cardboard Figures,**
c. 1920s. No markings. 11-1/2" tall.
Each - **$20 $40 $60**

❑ **KAZ-21. "Comicaps" Bottle Caps,**
c. 1935. Golden Rod Beer. 1" diameter full color litho. tin. Each - **$12 $20 $35**

KAZ-22

KAZ-23

❑ **KAZ-22. Premium Spinner,**
1930s. Celluloid spinner with metal reverse measures 1.25" and reads "United Feature Captain And Kids Spinner." Metal back has words "Good Luck" with wishbone, horseshoe, four-leaf clover and rabbit's foot. No maker name. - **$125 $250 $400**

❑ **KAZ-23. "The Katzenjammer Kids" Fast Action Book,**
1942. Store item by Dell Publishing Company. #14 in series. - **$21 $63 $145**

KAZ-24

❑ **KAZ-24. Multi-Products Figures,**
1944. Store items. Painted wood composition.
Captain - **$35 $70 $165**
Hans - **$20 $45 $100**
Fritz - **$20 $45 $100**

KAZ-25

KAZ-26

❑ **KAZ-25. "Hingees" Punch-Out Kit With Envelope,**
1945. Store item. Contains two sheets of punch-out body parts for assembly into 3-D figures of major characters.
Unpunched In Envelope - **$25 $45 $90**

❑ **KAZ-26. Katzenjammer Character Litho. Buttons,**
1946. Kellogg's Pep. From box insert set picturing total of 86 comic characters.
Each - **$5 $15 $25**

Kellogg's Cereal Misc.

Dr. John Harvey Kellogg (1852-1945) was at the center of a vegetarian health-food craze in Battle Creek, Michigan, in the late 19th century. The experimental kitchen at his Battle Creek Sanitarium created a number of meat substitutes for his patients, including Protose, Nuttose, Nuttolene, Granola, and Caramel Coffee. With his brother, W.K. Kellogg, he devised a wheat flake cereal in 1894 and, four years later, a variety made from corn, which he sold by mail as Sanitas Corn Flakes.

W.K. Kellogg struck out on his own in 1903, adding flavorings to the cereal, naming it Kellogg's Toasted Corn Flakes, and promoting it heavily with advertising and free samples. The cereal became, and remains, a breakfast staple in millions of homes. Over the years the company has used a variety of promotional symbols, starting with the Sweetheart of the Corn in 1907. With new cereals came the need for new personalities: Snap, Crackle, and Pop in 1933 to promote Kellogg's Rice Krispies, Tony the Tiger in 1953 for Kellogg's Sugar Frosted Flakes, and Toucan Sam in 1964.

Kellogg's sponsored many programs such as *Tom Corbett, Howdy Doody, Superman,* and *Huckleberry Hound* but the items in this section focus on characters specifically created for Kellogg's advertising and a sampling of the many non-character premiums they offered over the years. See separate sections devoted to Snap, Crackle, and Pop, as well as Tony the Tiger.

KEL-1

❑ **KEL-1. "Kellogg's Funny Jungleland Moving-Pictures" Booklet,**
1909. Among the earliest premium booklets (3-1/2x4-3/4") but re-issued in 6x8" and available for many years.
Earliest Version - **$30 $60 $135**
Later Version - **$15 $25 $60**

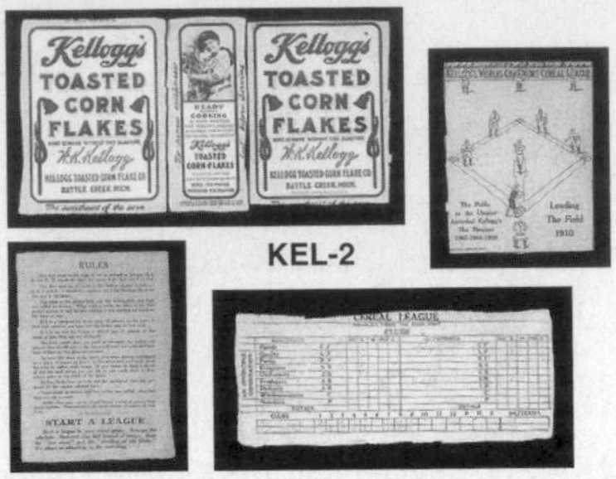

KEL-2

❑ **KEL-2. "Cereal League" Baseball Game Box Panels,**
1910. Three panels from same box of Kellogg's Toasted Corn Flakes, possibly the earliest cereal box game.
Complete Box - **$200 $400 $750**
As Shown - **$100 $200 $300**

KEL-3

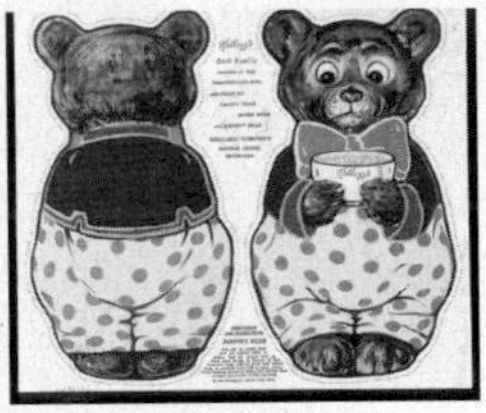

KEL-4

❑ **KEL-3. "My Visit To Kellogg's" Factory Visit Souvenir Book,**
c. 1924. - **$15 $22 $45**

❑ **KEL-4. Johnny Bear Uncut,**
1925. Kellogg's Corn Flakes premium. Goldilocks & The Three Bears cloth series. - **$40 $70 $135**

KEL-5

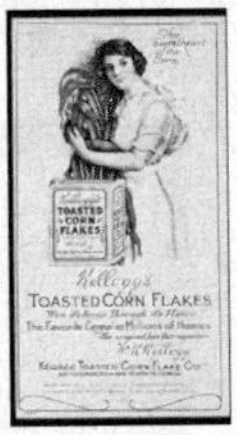

KEL-6

❑ **KEL-5. "Kellogg's Toasted Corn Flakes" Cello. Button,**
c. 1920s. - **$10 $25 $50**

❑ **KEL-6. Corn Flakes Blotter,**
1920s. Art deco blotter. Premium. - **$8 $15 $30**

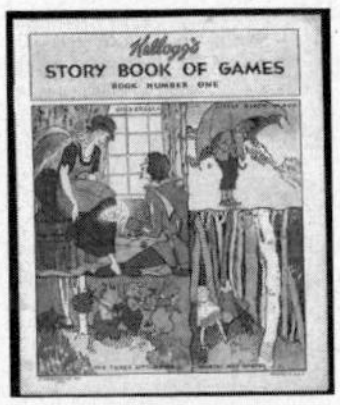

KEL-7

KEL-8

❑ KEL-7. Stamp Games #1,
1931. 12 page book of fairy tales and games. Includes spinner and paper chips. -
$25 $45 $85

❑ KEL-8. Stamp Games #3,
1931. 12 page book of fairy tales and games. Includes spinner and paper chips. -
$25 $45 $85

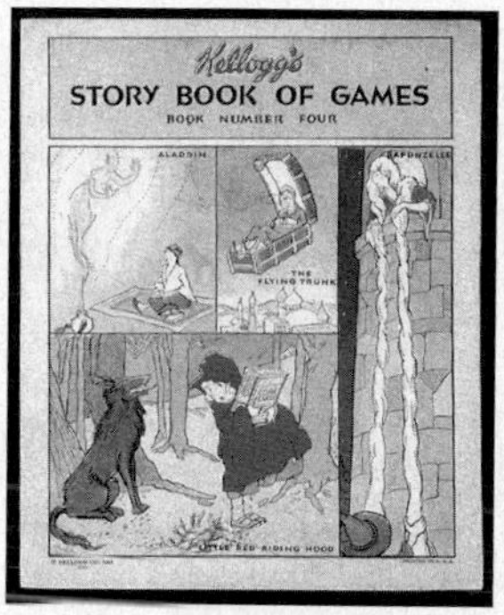

KEL-9

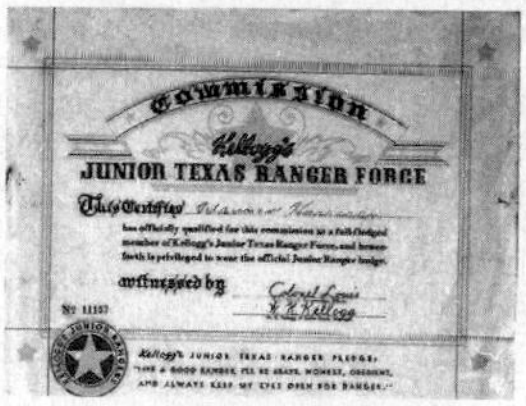

KEL-10

❑ KEL-9. Stamp Games #4,
1931. 12 page book of fairy tales and games. Includes spinner and paper chips. -
$25 $45 $85

❑ KEL-10. "Junior Texas Ranger Force" Member Certificate,
1933. Facsimile signatures of commanding officer Colonel Louis and W. K. Kellogg. -
$25 $55 $110

KEL-11

❑ KEL-11. Diet Book,
1933. All Bran premium. 33 pages. "Keep On The Sunny Side Of Life." - **$10 $20 $30**

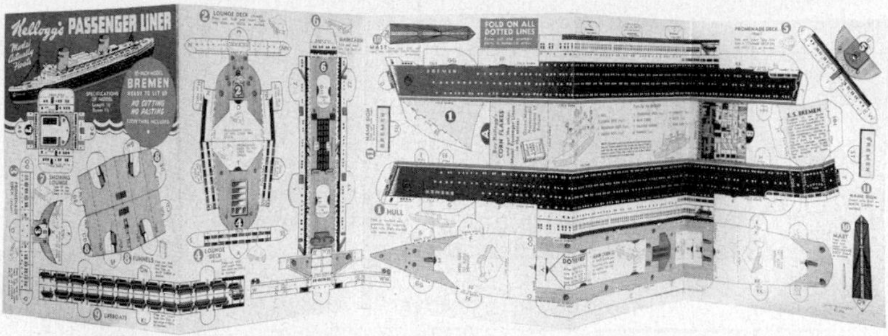

(FOLDOUT OF BREMEN SHIP)

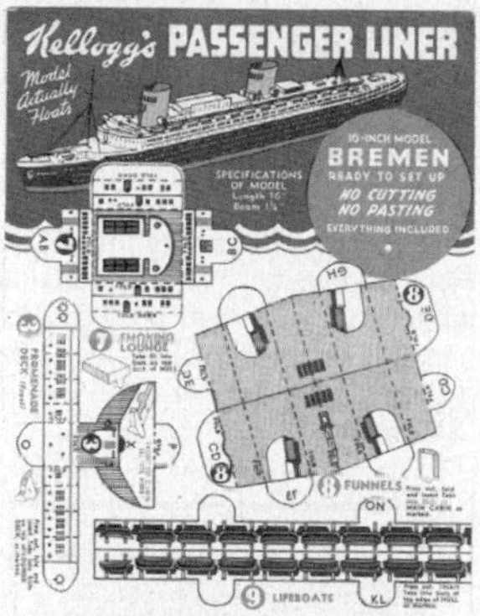

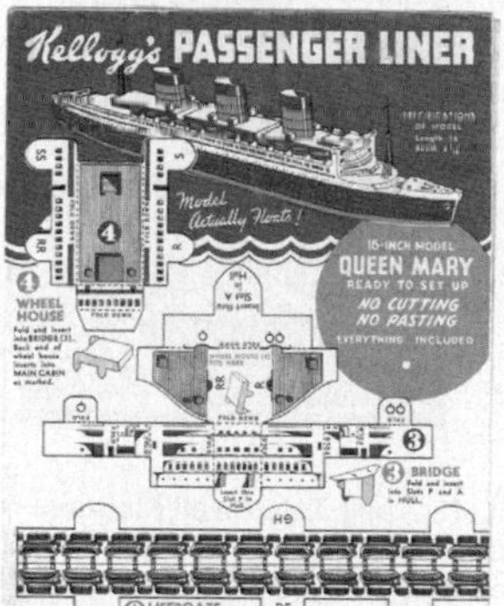

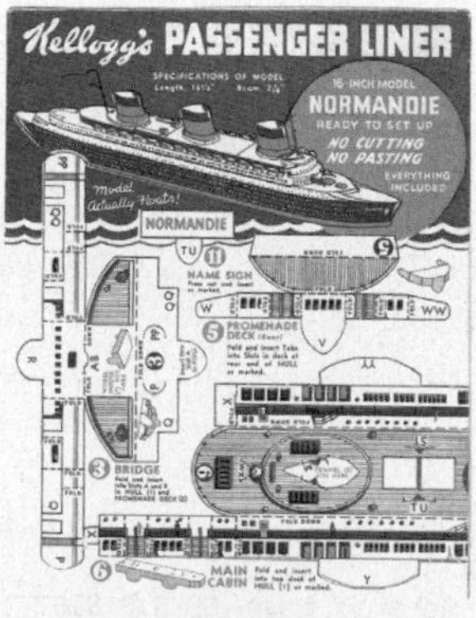

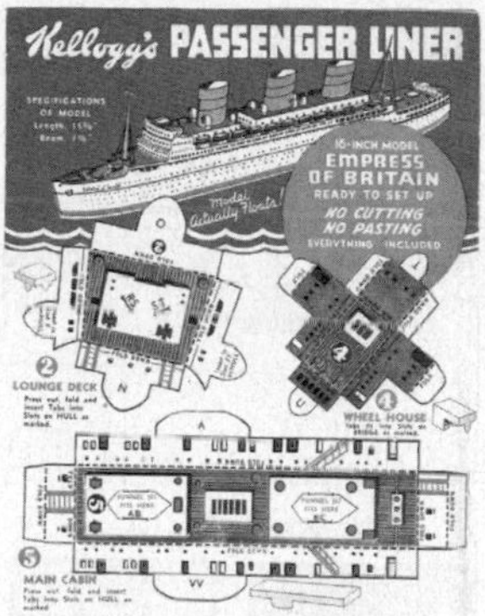

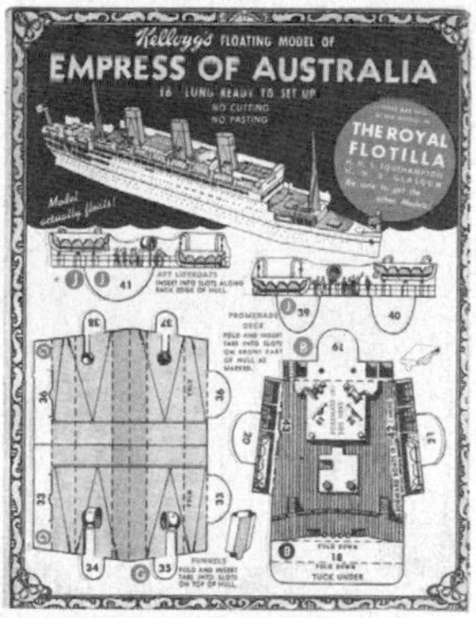

KEL-12

❑ KEL-12. Kellogg's Passenger Liner Series Premium Booklets,
1935. Rare, elaborate punchout booklets unfold to 8-1/2" x 32-1/2", for creating 16" long floating models. The ships are: Bremen, Queen Mary, Normandie, Empress of Britain and Empress of Austalia. Must be unpunched for NM price. Gordon Gold Archives.
Each - **$165 $275 $550**

KEL-13

❏ **KEL-13. Corn Flakes Box Backs,**
1935. Features Kellogg's adventure stories on back. Tells plane stories about famous aviators like Admiral Byrd, Floyd Bennett, Cy Armstrong, Jack Traywick, and others.
Titles: Parachutes; Desperation and Science; Old Jonah
(1936 on); The Flying Dog; Bennett's Last Flight; Do-X The Flying Giant; Army Acrobatics; Mountain Mystery; An Unsung Hero; A Matter of Routine; The Red Dash Warning; Mid-AirTransfer; Night Wings.
Each - **$10 $25 $50**

KEL-14

❏ **KEL-14. "Junior Texas Ranger" Club Kit,**
1936. Five paper items: Two premium folders, card that held badge, survey postcard, leaflet promoting Mother Goose stories by Kellogg's Singing Lady plus mailer.
Each - **$10 $25 $50**

KEL-15

❏ **KEL-15. Fairy Tales Wall Plaques Premium Sign 12x18",**
1930s. Rare. Designed by Vernon Grant, picturing six plaques. Sign - **$225 $450 $750**
Each Plaque - **$25 $50 $110**

KEL-16

❏ **KEL-16. "Vernon Grant Kellogg Town Kut-Outs,"**
1930s. Set of six. Each - **$6 $12 $25**

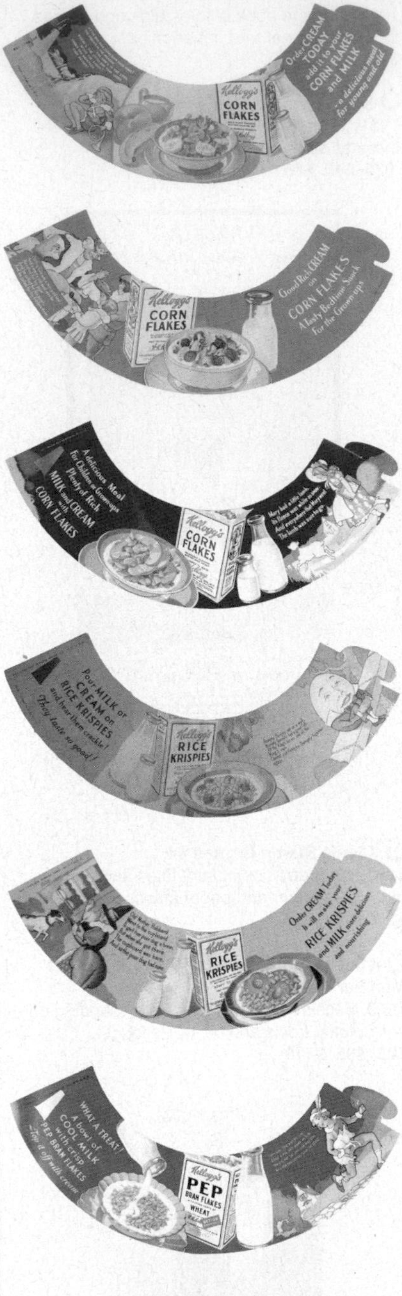

KEL-17

❏ **KEL-17. Promotional Milk Collars,**
1930s. Colorful advertising promos, each 10" long by 2-1/2" wide. Promote famous fairy tales with art by Vernon Grant. "Mary Had a Little Lamb," "Old King Cole," "Little Boy Blue," "Humpty Dumpty," "Old Mother Hubbard" and "Tom Tom the Piper's Son."
Each - **$25 $50 $100**

KEL-18

❑ **KEL-18. "Kellogg's 8 Model Planes" Store Display,**
1930s. 15x15x7" deep diecut cardboard. Gordon Gold Archives. - **$225 $550 $1000**

KEL-19

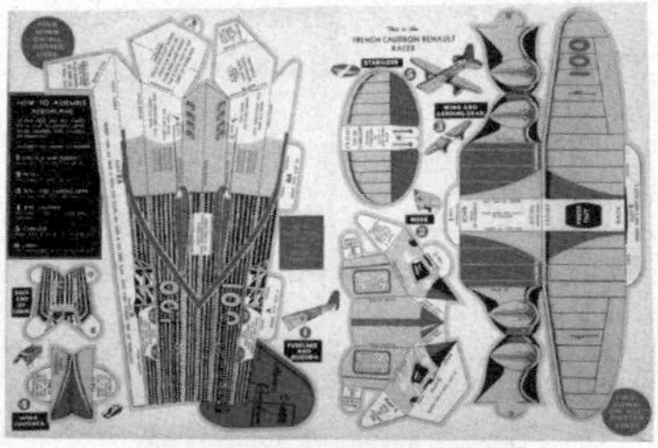

KEL-20

❑ **KEL-19. Die Cut Aeroplane Sign,**
1930s. Rare. Die cut standee promotes Corn Flakes and free planes. - **$200 $500 $850**

❑ **KEL-20. Premium Plane 13-1/2x20",**
1930s. Rare. Features Avion Cauldron cut-out plane. - **$50 $110 $210**

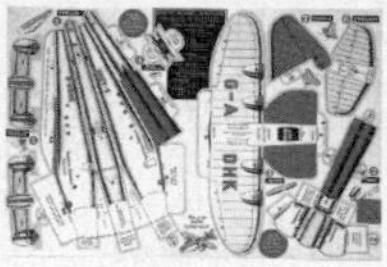

KEL-21

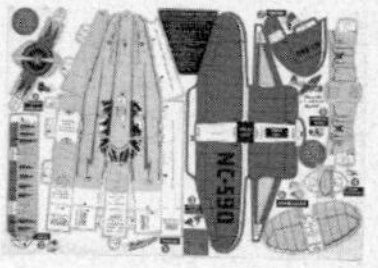

KEL-22

❑ **KEL-21. Premium Plane 13-1/2x20",**
1930s. Rare. Features Empire Flying Boat cut-out plane. - **$50 $110 $210**

❑ **KEL-22. Premium Plane 13-1/2x20",**
1930s. Rare. Features U.S. Stinson Reliant cut-out plane. - **$50 $110 $210**

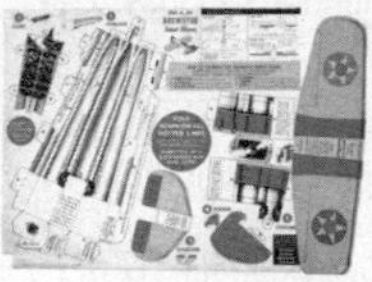

KEL-23

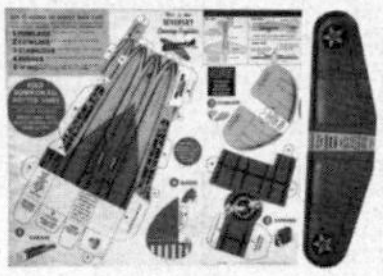

KEL-24

❑ **KEL-23. Premium Plane 13-1/2x20",**
1930s. Rare. Features Brewster Scout Plane cut-out. - **$50 $110 $210**

❑ **KEL-24. Premium Plane 13-1/2x20",**
1930s. Rare. Features Seversky Convoy Fighter Plane cut-out. - **$50 $110 $210**

KEL-25

❑ **KEL-25. "Kellogg's Planes Of All Nations" Store Sign,**
1930s. Kellogg's All-Wheat. 18x25" in red, white, blue and yellow. Depicts the initial series of six designs on back panels of cereal boxes. Gordon Gold Archives. - **$65 $165 $350**

KEL-26

KEL-27

❑ **KEL-26. Baseball Hat with Mailer,**
1930s. - **$25 $50 $100**

❑ **KEL-27. Beamy Beanie with Mailer,**
1942. Scarce. - **$35 $85 $135**

KEL-28

❑ **KEL-28. "Kellogg's Pep Model Warplanes" 16x43" Advertising Poster,**
c. 1942. Scarce. - **$150 $400 $750**

KEL-29

❑ **KEL-29. "Kellogg's Pep Model Plane Kit" Store Sign,**
c. 1942. 10-1/2x14" stiff cardboard in red, green and white. Gordon Gold Archives. - **$75 $175 $375**

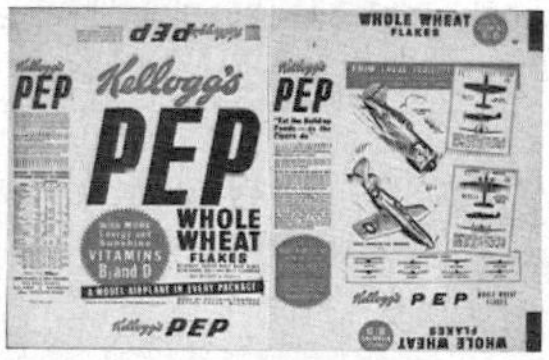

KEL-30

❑ **KEL-30. Cereal Box Flat Featuring Model Airplanes,**
c. 1942. 12x17-1/2" cardboard flat promotes punch-out planes and has pair of cut-out "Plane Spotter Cards." Gordon Gold Archives.
Near Mint Flat - **$375**
Used Complete - **$50 $125 $250**

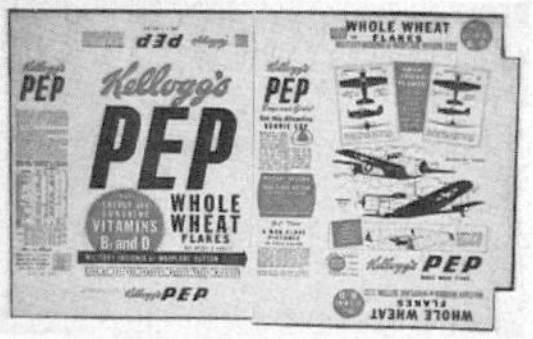

KEL-31

❑ **KEL-31. Cereal Box Flat,**
c. 1942. Front offers military insignia and warplane buttons. Side panel offers "Beanie Cap" and a set of six "Warplane Pictures." Back panel has cards #41 and #42 from series of at least 42 different. Gordon Gold Archives.
Near Mint Flat - **$375**
Used Complete - **$50 $125 $250**

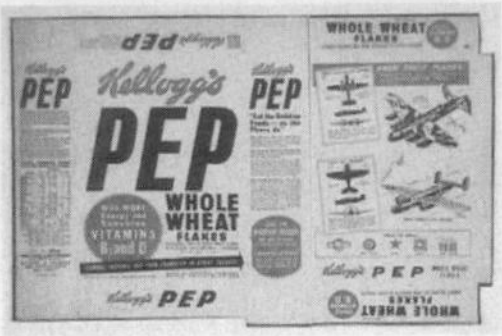

KEL-32

❑ KEL-32. Cereal Box Flat,
c. 1942. Promotes "Combat Insignia Hot Iron Transfers" included in each box while back panel has cards #3 and #4 from series of at least 42 different. Gordon Gold Archives.
Near Mint Flat - **$375**
Used Complete - **$50 $125 $250**

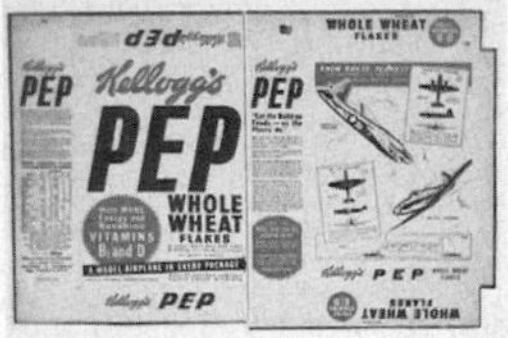

KEL-33

❑ KEL-33. Cereal Box Flat,
c. 1942. Front promotes series of color model warplane punch-outs while reverse has cut-out airplane cards #17 and #18 from a series of at least 42 different. Gordon Gold Archives.
Near Mint Flat - **$375**
Used Complete - **$50 $125 $250**

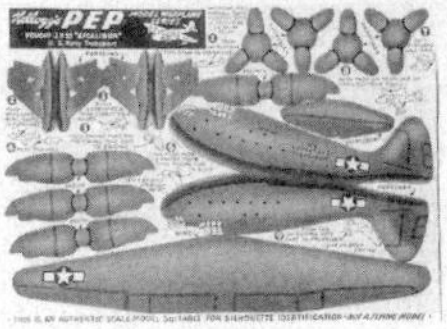

KEL-34

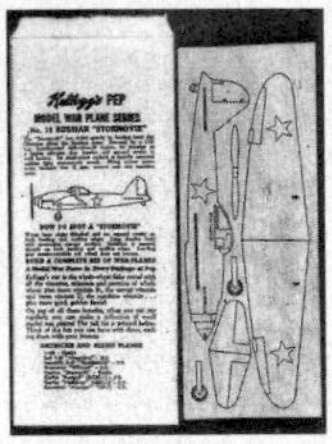

KEL-35

❑ KEL-34. "Kellogg's Pep Model Warplane" Punch-Out,
c. 1942. Set of 28 as follows:
Series "A":
❑ A1 - Vought SB2U "Vindicator" U.S. Dive Bomber
❑ A2 - Boulton Paul "Defiant" British Night Fighter
❑ A3 - Lockheed P-38 "Lightning" U.S. Fighter
❑ A4 - Sikorsky VS-300 U.S. Helicopter
❑ A5 - Douglas A-20C or A-20 "Havoc" U.S. Attack Bomber
❑ A6 - Grumman F6F "Hellcat" U.S. Fighter
❑ A7 - North American B-25 "Mitchell" U.S. Attack Bomber.
Series "B":
❑ B1 - Westland "Whirlwind" British Fighter
❑ B2 - YAK-4 Russian Fighter/Bomber
❑ B3 - Douglas A-24 "Dauntless" U.S. Dive Bomber
❑ B4 - Curtiss P-40F "Warhawk" U.S. Fighter
❑ B5 - Short "Sunderland" British Patrol Bomber
❑ B6 - Vought JR2S "Excalibur" U.S. Navy Transport
❑ B7 - Consolidated Vultee B-24 "Liberator" U.S. Heavy Bomber
Series "C":
❑ C1 - Boeing B-17E "Flying Fortress" U.S. Heavy Bomber
❑ C2 - De Havilland "Mosquito" British Medium Bomber
❑ C3 - Grumman F4F "Wildcat" U.S. Navy Fighter
❑ C4 - Republic P-47 "Thunderbolt" U.S. Fighter
❑ C5 - Doulgas A-17A U.S. Attack Bomber
❑ C6 - "Mosca" Russian Fighter
❑ C7 - Supermarine "Spitfire" British Fighter
Series "D":
❑ D1 - Lockheed C-69 "Constellation" U.S. Transport Plane
❑ D2 - Curtiss SB2C-1C "Helldiver" U.S. Dive Bomber
❑ D3 - Douglas C-54 "Skymaster" U.S. Transport
❑ D4 - Handley-Page "Hampden" British Bomber
❑ D5 - Avro "Lancaster" British Heavy Bomber
❑ D6 - Lockheed B-34 "Ventura" U.S. Bomber
❑ D7 - I-18 Russian Fighter
Each Unpunched - **$10 $30 $60**

❑ KEL-35. "Pep Model Warplane" Balsa Sheet In Envelope,
c. 1942. Numbered series, some envelopes mention Superman radio show. Believed to be a set of 21. Each In Envelope - **$15 $35 $70**

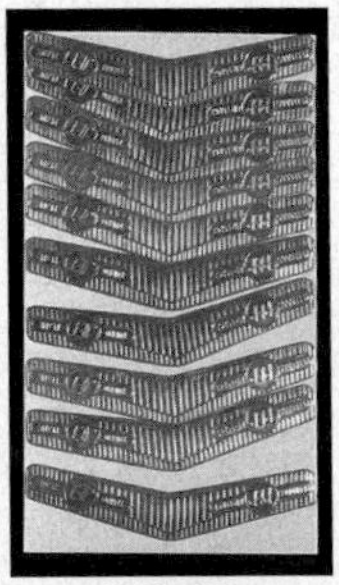

KEL-36

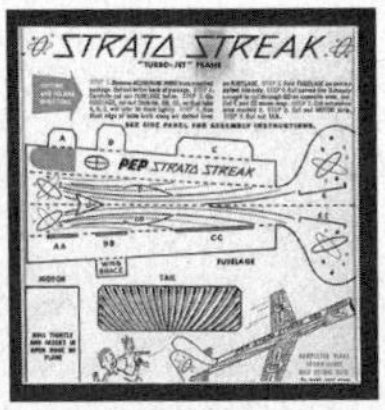

KEL-37

❑ KEL-36. Pep Aluminum Wings,
1943. Each Pep box contained an aluminum wing for turbo jet cut-out planes on back. Ten wings pictured for the ten plane set shown.
Each - **$5 $10 $20**

❑ KEL-37. Pep Cereal Back For Turbo Jet Plane Cut-Outs,
1943. Strato Streak cut-out plane. - **$10 $25 $50**

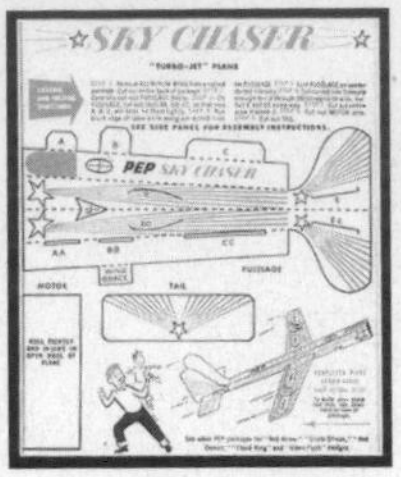

KEL-38

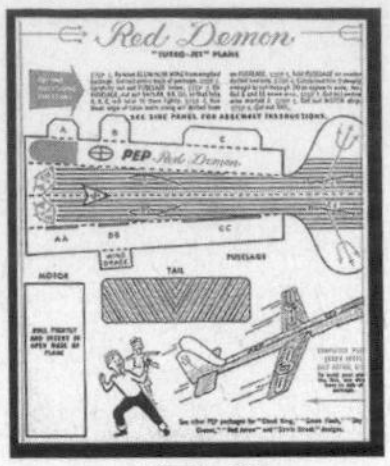

KEL-39

❑ KEL-38. Pep Cereal Back For Turbo Jet Plane Cut-Outs,
1943. Sky Chaser cut-out plane. - **$10 $25 $50**

❑ KEL-39. Pep Cereal Back For Turbo Jet Plane Cut-Outs,
1943. Red Demon cut-out plane. - **$10 $25 $50**

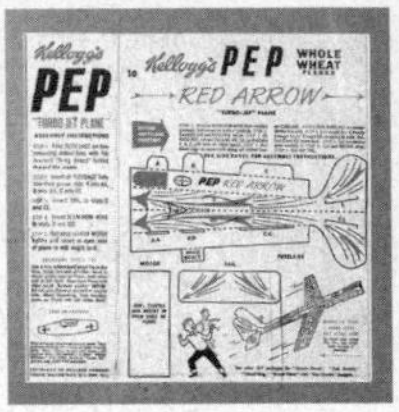

KEL-40

KEL-41

❑ KEL-40. Pep Cereal Back For Turbo Jet Plane Cut-Outs,
1943. Red Arrow cut-out plane. - **$10 $25 $50**

❑ KEL-41. Pep Cereal Back For Turbo Jet Plane Cut-Outs,
1943. Cloud King cut-out plane. - **$10 $25 $50**

KEL-42

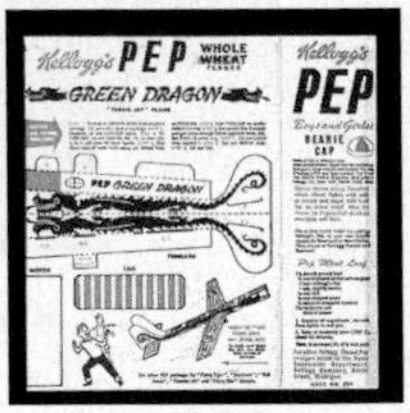

KEL-43

❑ KEL-42. Pep Cereal Back For Turbo Jet Plane Cut-Outs,
1943. Green Flash cut-out plane. -
$10 $25 $50

❑ KEL-43. Pep Cereal Back For Turbo Jet Plane Cut-Outs,
1943. Green Danger cut-out plane. -
$10 $25 $50

KEL-44

❏ **KEL-44. Pep Cereal Back For Turbo Jet Plane Cut-Outs,**
1943. Thunder-Jet cut-out plane. - **$10 $25 $50**

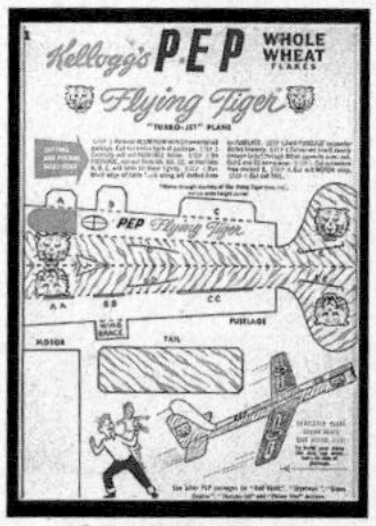

KEL-45

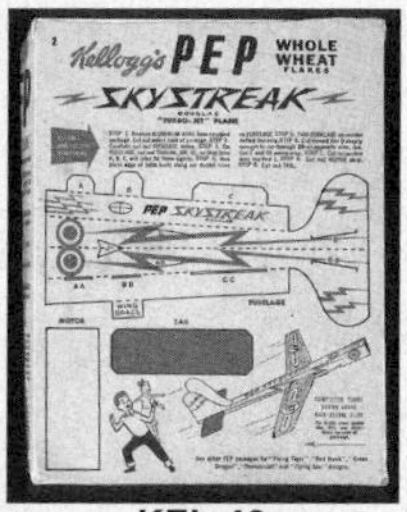

KEL-46

❏ **KEL-45. Pep Cereal Back For Turbo Jet Plane Cut-Outs,**
1943. Flying Tiger cut-out plane. - **$10 $25 $50**

❏ **KEL-46. Pep Cereal Box,**
1943. Promotes Turbo Jet Plane program. Each box shows cut-out. Sky Streak plane pictured. Complete Box - **$60 $135 $275**

KEL-47

❏ **KEL-47. "Pep Military Insignia Buttons" 16x44" Paper Store Banner,**
1943. Scarce. Reverse offers beanie cap as mail premium for pinning box insert insignia and aircraft litho. buttons. - **$250 $575 $1200**

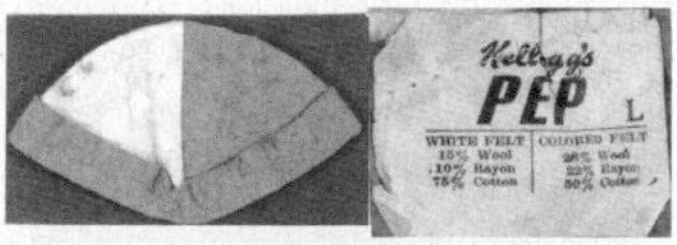

KEL-48

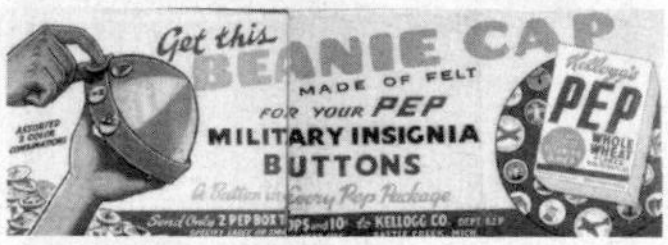

KEL-49

❏ **KEL-48. "Kellogg's Pep" Felt Beanie,**
1943. Orange and white.
With Tag - **$30 $70 $150**
Missing Tag - **$15 $25 $60**

❏ **KEL-49. Pep Beany/Military Insignia Buttons 16x44" Paper Store Poster,**
1943. Scarce. - **$200 $400 $800**

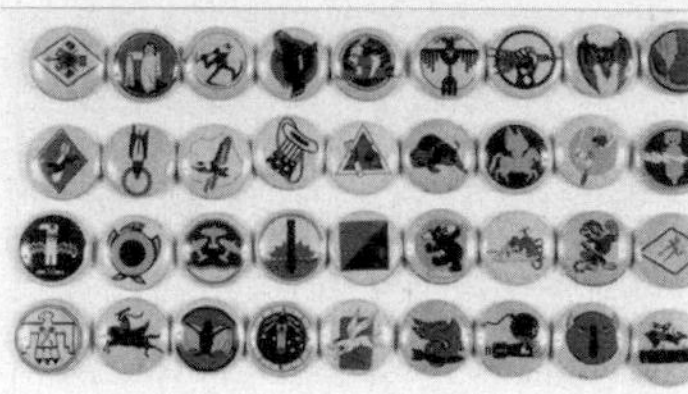
KEL-50

❏ **KEL-50. Pep Military Insignia Litho. Buttons,**
1943. Set of 36 issued in two parts. First 18 insignia plus four airplanes in green (see next item) were 1943 followed about July 1945 by second group of eighteen insignia and four airplanes in brown. Paint very susceptible to aging and wear, most examples grade fine or worse. Gordon Gold, who joined his father Sam Gold in the premium business after World War II, relates that for the Kellogg's button sets, the FDA required and approved ink type and glossy coating lower in hardness but less toxic in case children chewed and consumed the inks from the button. Each - **$5 $10 $22**

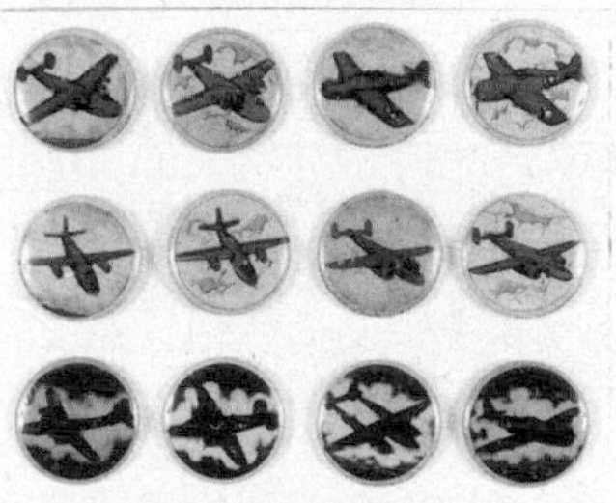
KEL-51

❏ **KEL-51. Pep Airplane Litho. Buttons,**
1943. Set of 12 issued in two parts. Four planes in green from 1943 followed in 1945 by four planes in brown with photo-style artwork and same four planes in brown with hand illustrated style artwork. Paint very susceptible to wear. Each - **$35 $70 $140**

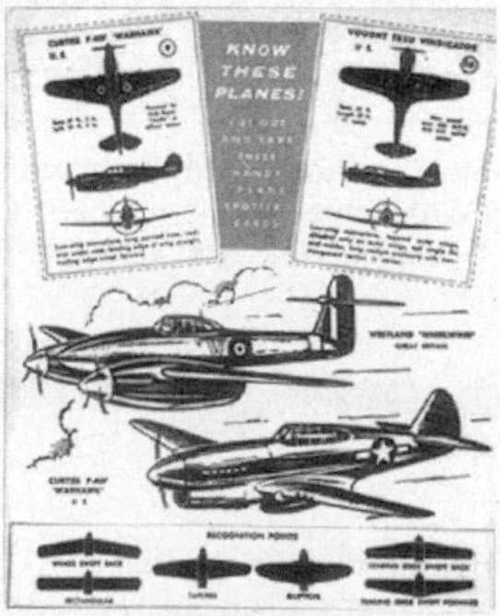

KEL-52

❏ **KEL-52. Pep "Plane Spotter" Box Card,**
c. 1944. Two cards on each back, at least 42 cards in set. Uncut Back - **$12 $18 $35**

KEL-53

❏ **KEL-53. Pep Large Diecut Cardboard Sign,**
1945. 38" x 26". Features Pep buttons and boy wearing Pep beanie. Three known. - **$1250 $3500 $5500**

KEL-54

❏ **KEL-54. Pep Large Promo Letter Picturing Sign,**
1945. Letter to grocer explaining the value of the comic button program. Shows picture of the rare sign. Gold Archives. - **$225 $375 $750**

KEL-55

❑ KEL-55. Pep Comic Character Litho. Button Set,
1945. Complete set of 86. Issued in 1945-46 sealed in paper or cellophane packet inside specially marked boxes of Kellogg's Pep cereal. There were 5 sets each of 18 buttons, but Superman was included in each set, so the result is 86 different buttons.
Near Mint Set of 86 - **$2000**
Most Characters - **$8 $15 $25**
Felix - **$10 $20 $40**
Phantom - **$25 $50 $85**

KEL-56

❑ KEL-56. Comic Character Error Litho. Button,
1945. Manufacturing error caused by running the litho. tin sheet with images printed on both sides facing the wrong direction as it passed through the stamping machine. Reverse of this button has perfect color image of "Uncle Bim." Typically an error of this nature would have been discarded but somehow this example survived. Similar Examples - **$125 $250 $500**

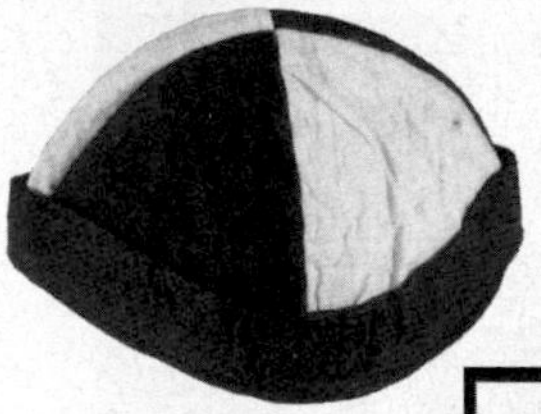

KEL-57

KEL-58

❑ KEL-57. Pep Beanie,
1945. Black and white.
With Tag - **$35 $75 $175**
Missing Tag - **$20 $40 $85**

❑ KEL-58. "Metal Pin-On Comic Buttons" Ad,
c. 1945. Comic book page ad for Kellogg's Pep box insert buttons although indicating complete set of 18 as opposed to eventual final set of 86. - **$5 $10 $15**

KEL-59

❑ KEL-59. Kellogg's Pep Comic Button Store Sign,
c. 1945. 16x22" paper store sign features large image of Kellogg's Pep cereal box, beanie and 12 Pep comic character buttons. Image of the Superman button is seen on the front of the cereal box. - **$325 $675 $1350**

KEL-60

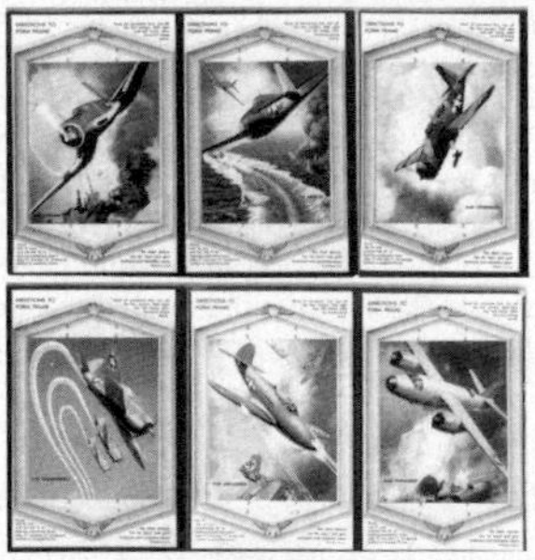

❑ KEL-60. Pep Punch-Out Warplane Pictures With Envelope,
c. 1945. Set of six. Near Mint In Mailer - **$450**

KEL-61

❑ KEL-61. Sundial Wristwatch,
c. 1945. Totally unmarked but believed offered 9/24/45 on Superman radio program for two box tops of Kellogg's Pep and 10 cents. Sundial is 1.25" aluminum with movable pointer on leather straps. - **$30 $65 $125**

KEL-62

❑ KEL-62. "Kellogg's Walky Talky" Punch-Out,
c. 1945. Near Mint In Mailer - **$425**
Complete Assembled Pair - **$50 $125 $200**
Promotional Sign (Not Shown) -
$125 $275 $425

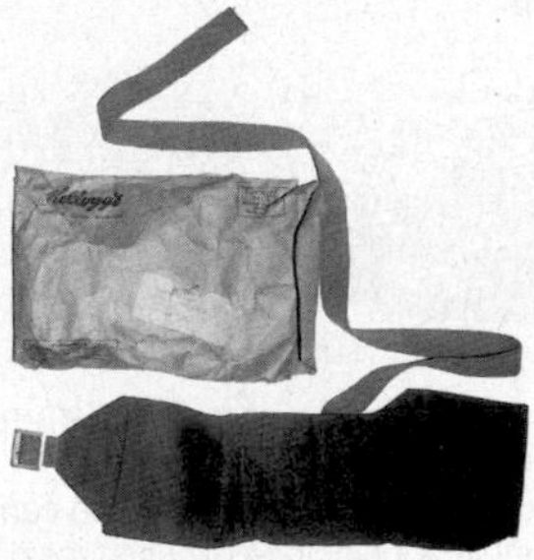

KEL-63

❑ KEL-63. Money Belt (Army Issue) With Envelope,
c. 1946. Fabric military-style belt, advertised on Superman radio program, with mailer.
Belt And Mailer - **$35 $65 $135**

KEL-64

❑ KEL-64. "Kellogg's Pep Real Photos" 16x20" Paper Sign,
1947. Pictures example movie and sports stars miniature photos offered individually as box inserts. - **$100 $200 $400**

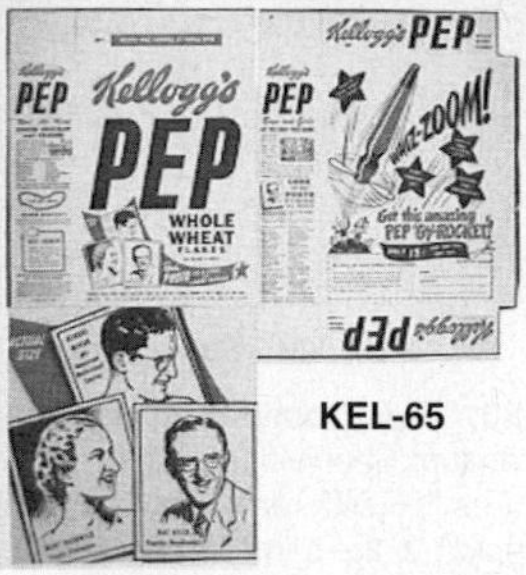

KEL-65

❑ KEL-65. "Real Photo" And "Gy-Rocket" Cereal Box Flat,
1947. Front panel promotes series of 66 photos with offer for a photo album. Reverse has offer for "Pep Gy-Rocket." Gordon Gold Archives.
Near Mint Flat - **$300**
Used Complete - **$45 $90 $175**

KEL-66

❑ KEL-66. Pep Comic Character Buttons Ad Sheet,
1947. Canadian issue. - **$75 $150 $300**

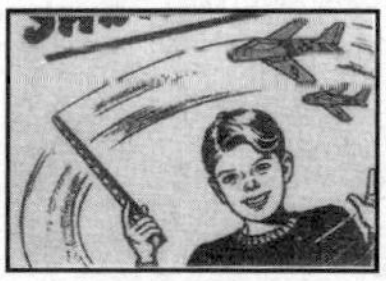
(CLOSE-UP)

KEL-67

❑ KEL-67. "Flight Control Sabre Jet Plane",
c. 1948. Unused In Mailer - **$30 $60 $135**

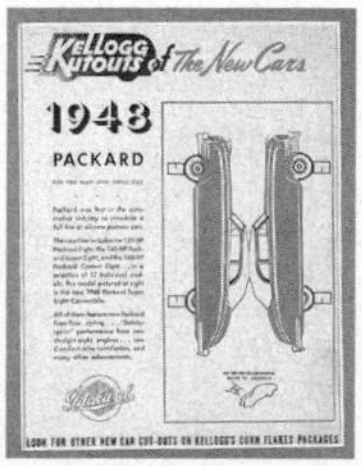

KEL-68

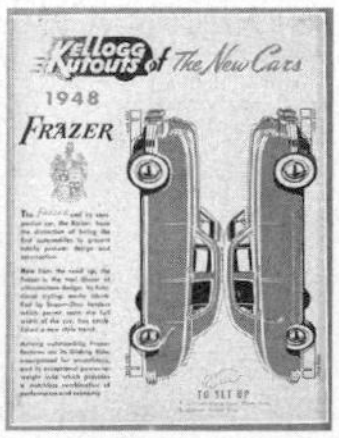

KEL-69

❑ KEL-68. Auto Cut-Outs,
1948. Corn Flakes box back shows cut-out of 1948 Packard. - **$25 $40 $65**

❑ KEL-69. Auto Cut-Outs,
1948. Corn Flakes box back shows cut-out of 1948 Frazer. - **$25 $40 $65**

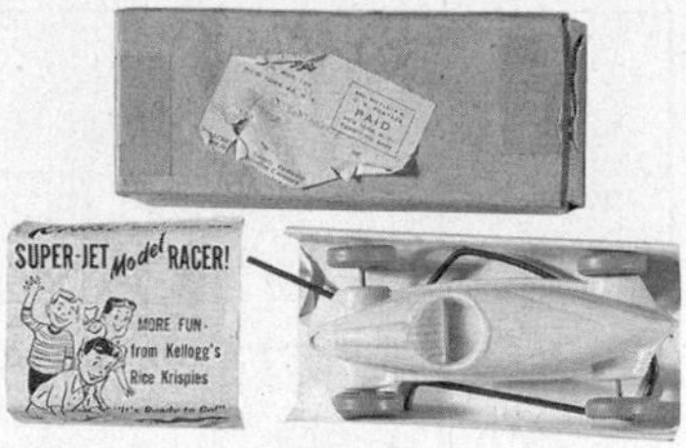

KEL-70

❑ KEL-70. Super Jet Racer
1949. Rare. Yellow racer with red wheels, instructions, spring, mailer, and Rice Krispies ad. Complete - **$60 $115 $240**

KEL-72

KEL-71

KEL-73

❑ KEL-71. Presidents Album,
1949. Kellogg's Premium. 36 page stamp album. - **$10 $20 $40**

❑ KEL-72. Presidents Album Mailer,
1949. Kellogg's Premium. - **$5 $12 $20**

❑ KEL-73. Presidents Album - The Stamps,
1949. Kellogg's Premium. 32 different large stamps (cereal box contained 1 stamp).
Each - **$2 $4 $6**

KEL-74

❑ KEL-74. "Warship Transfer" Cereal Box Flat,
c. 1940s. Transfers came one per box. Back panel illustrates "L.S.T./Landing Ship, Tank" plus four "U.S. Navy Specialty Insignia" with panel marked "#9 Of A Series." Gordon Gold Archives. Near Mint Flat - **$250**
Used Complete - **$35 $65 $125**

KEL-75

❑ KEL-75. Punch-Out Airport in Mailer,
1940s. - **$40 $100 $200**

KEL-76

❑ KEL-76. Kellogg's Pep "Photo Album",
1940s. 10 pages for mounting miniature premium photos of sports and entertainment stars.
Near Mint With Mailer - **$200**
Album Only - **$40 $65 $125**

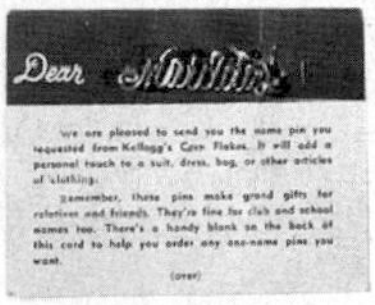

KEL-77

KEL-78

❑ KEL-77. Pin Premium On Card,
1940s. Metal name pin premium for 2 Corn Flakes box tops and 10¢. - **$20 $40 $65**

❑ KEL-78. Pennant,
1940s. Cereal premium, 17" long. - **$35 $70 $150**

KEL-79

❑ KEL-79. College Prom Photo Sign,
1940s. Pep On The Air - N.B.C. Blue Network. - **$20 $40 $75**

KEL-80

❑ **KEL-80. "Stagecoach" Toy With Mailer And Coupon,**
1950. Sugar Frosted Flakes, Sugar Smacks, Sugar Pops. 7" long replica plastic toy with order coupon in mailer carton. Near Mint Box - **$110**
Stagecoach - **$15 $30 $60**

KEL-81

❑ **KEL-81. Box Flat And Ad Proof For Picture Ring Premiums,**
1950. Cereal box promotes set of 16 plastic rings with domed inserts which were inserted one per box. Ad proof is 10x15" picturing example Wanda Hendricks ring. Gordon Gold Archives. Near Mint Flat - **$350**
Used Complete - **$50 $100 $225**
Ad Proof - **$10 $20 $50**

KEL-82

❑ **KEL-82. "Kellogg's Pep" Box With "Magno-Power '50 Ford" Ring Ads,**
1950. Complete Box - **$100 $200 $375**

KEL-83

KEL-84

❑ **KEL-83. Sugar Smacks Flat,**
1951. Soldier premium offer. Maxie the seal on front. - **$50 $200 $325**

❑ **KEL-84. Soldiers in Mailer,**
1951. 12 total. Complete - **$35 $100 $200**

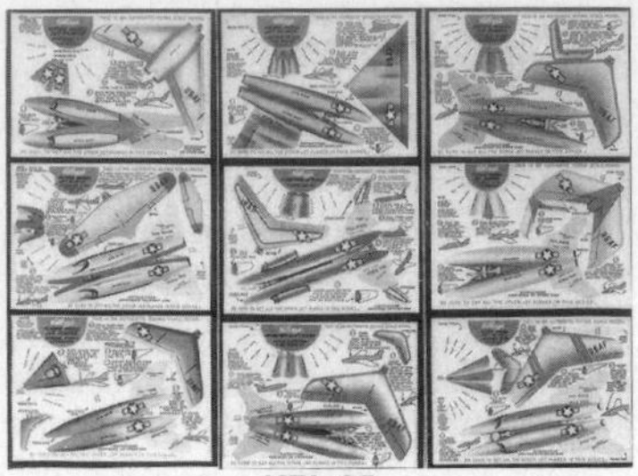

KEL-85

❑ **KEL-85. "Flying Model Jet Planes" Punch-Outs,**
1951. Ten in the set: Convair the Flying Triangle, Douglas Sky Rocket, Lockheed Fighter, Lockheed Shooting Star, Martin XB-51, North American Saber Jet, Northrop Flying Laboratory, Republic Interceptor, Republic Thunderjet (2 different). Unpunched Each - **$12 $18 $35**

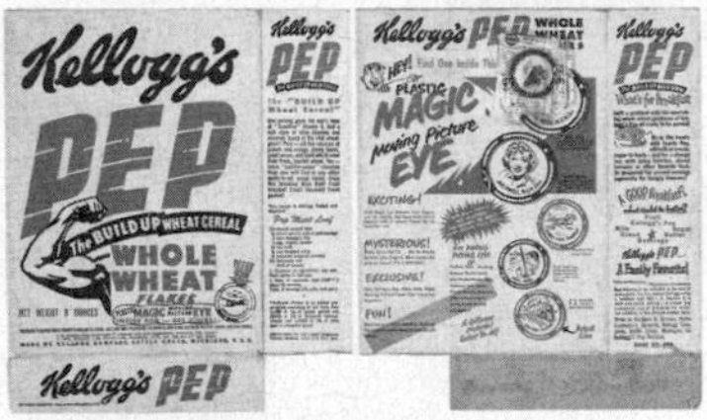

KEL-86

❑ **KEL-86. "Kellogg's Pep Magic Moving Picture Eye" Cereal Box,**
1951. Box pictures example premiums, each 1.25" diameter packaged one per cereal box. Gordon Gold Archives.
Used Complete - **$100 $200 $375**

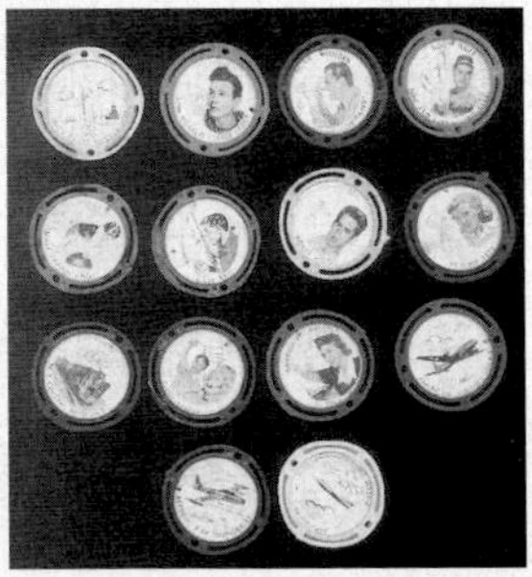

KEL-87

❑ **KEL-87. Magic Moving Picture Eye Probable Set,**
1951. Kellogg's Pep. Plastic rimmed flicker disks originally advertised as set of 16 including Gene Kelly and Jane Powell. These two have not been seen and later ads replaced these two by William Holden and Bob Hope.
Each Corbett (2 Varieties) Bob Hope, Clyde Beatty, Bobby Riggs, Mark Trail's Dog Andy - **$10 $20 $35**
Other Eight Each - **$5 $10 $15**

KEL-88

❑ **KEL-88. "Free Comic Buttons" Store Sign,**
1952. Premium Specialties, Chicago, Ill. 9x20" sign pictures "18 Different Comics" buttons identical in design to the same characters in the Kellogg's Pep set of 86. However, this was a later offering unrelated to the Kellogg's promotion. Sign has blank area for sponsor's imprint. Gordon Gold Archives. - **$100 $200 $350**

KEL-89

❑ **KEL-89. Sugar Frosted Flake Insignia Box Back,**
1953. Armed Forces shoulder patch insignia. Box back with patch premium offer.
Each Patch - **$5 $10 $20**
Box Back - **$20 $35 $70**

KEL-90

❑ **KEL-90. Corn Flakes Cereal Box Flat,**
1953. Promotes Demon Dan mask on back of box. - **$35 $100 $250**

KEL-91

❑ **KEL-91. Rice Krispies Cereal Box Flat,**
1953. Canadian issued. Promotes free Atom Sub inside box. - **$60 $140 $300**

KEL-92

KEL-93

KEL-94

❑ **KEL-92. Baking Soda Frogman 3-1/2" Size,**
1954. Obstacles Scout. Depicts scuba diver holding knife. Various colors. - **$10 $30 $65**

❑ **KEL-93. Baking Soda Frogman 3-1/2" Size,**
1954. Demolitions Expert. Depicts diver holding mine. Various colors. - **$10 $30 $65**

❑ **KEL-94. Baking Soda Frogman 3-1/2" Size,**
1954. Torch Man. Depicts diver holding cutting torch. Various colors. - **$10 $30 $65**

KEL-95

❑ **KEL-95. U.S. Army Swamp Glider,**
1955. Sugar Frosted Flakes premium. Includes glider, instructions, and box. - **$40 $85 $175**

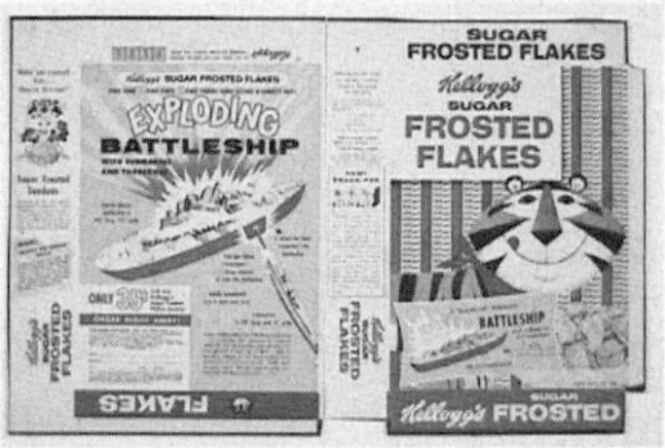

KEL-96

❑ **KEL-96. "Exploding Battleship" Cereal Box Flat,**
1958. Premium consisted of hard plastic battleship and submarine with torpedos. Gordon Gold Archives. Near Mint Flat - **$275**
Used Complete - **$40 $85 $150**

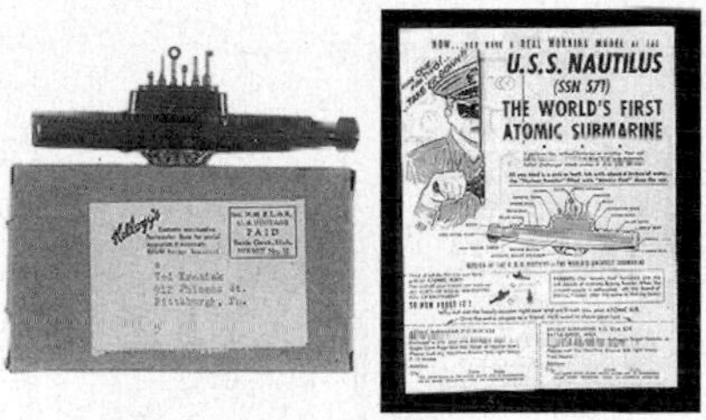

KEL-97

❑ **KEL-97. U.S.S. Nautilus Submarine Toy With Mailer,** 1950s. Sugar Smacks or Sugar Corn Pops. 4-1/2" toy powered by "Atomic Fuel" of baking powder. Pictured instruction sheet is earliest version. See KEL-112.
Near Mint Boxed - **$250**
Nautilus Only - **$10 $30 $75**

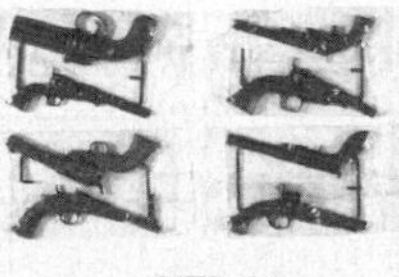

KEL-98

KEL-99

❑ **KEL-98. "Famous Guns of History" Sets,**
1950s. Pep Wheat Flakes premium. 8 different, 2 to a set. Each Set - **$10 $20 $40**

❑ **KEL-99. "Famous Guns of History" Box Back,**
1950s. Famous guns of history pictured. - **$12 $25 $40**

KEL-100

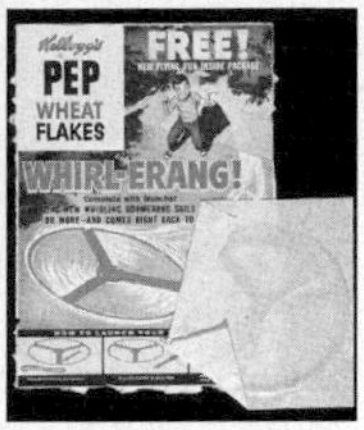

KEL-101

❑ **KEL-100. Jumbly Jungle Book with Mailer,**
1950s. - **$20 $30 $50**

❑ **KEL-101. Pep Whirl-Erang,**
1950s. Scarce. Discontinued because children were injured. - **$20 $35 $60**
Box Back with Ad - **$60**

KEL-102

❑ **KEL-102. "Kellogg's Motorcycle" Boxed Premium,**
1950s. Two-piece hard plastic premium is 1.5x4x3" tall and comes in mailing box with instruction sheet. Cycle is designed with removable rider figure. Has crank on one side, back has gear shift lever. Working and travels forward when wound. Mailer - **$10 $20 $35**
Instructions - **$10 $20 $40**
Rider & Cycle - **$100 $200 $300**

KEL-103

❑ **KEL-103. Men Of The Wild West Cereal Box Back Panels,**
1963. Kellogg's. Set of 12: Cody, Custer, Carson, Bowie, Boone, "Yellowstone" Kelly, Houston, Sutter, Fremont, Slaughter, "Portugee" Phillips. Used Complete Box - **$40 $85 $150**
Each Cut Back - **$8 $12 $25**

KEL-104

❑ **KEL-104. Famous Indians Cereal Box Backs,**
c. 1963. No date or company name appears on the back panel cut-outs but these seem closely related to the Kellogg's "Men Of The Wild West" set. Probably set of 12. We have seen: Corn Planter, King Philip, Little Turtle, Logan, Osceola, Pontiac, Tecumseh.
Used Complete Box - **$40 $85 $150**
Each Cut Back - **$8 $12 $25**

KEL-105

❑ **KEL-105. "Kellogg's Corn Flakes" Box Flat Featuring Cessna 150 Flying Model,**
1965. Kellogg's. 10.25x14.25" unused flat. Front panel has inset ad for "Cessna 150 Scale Flying Model." Back panel features illustration of boy playing with the Cessna 150 model.
Near Mint Flat - **$115**
Used Complete - **$15 $30 $60**

KEL-106

❑ **KEL-106. "Corvette" Battery Operated Plastic Model Car,**
1965. Made by Ideal, issued by Kellogg's. 4-1/2" long. Near Mint Boxed **- $175**

KEL-107

❑ **KEL-107. Old West Trail Booklet,**
1968. Kellogg's premium. 16 pages history of the Old West.- **$15 $30 $50**

KEL-109

❑ **KEL-109. Postcard,**
1960s. Postcard features many cartoon and cereal characters like Yogi Bear and Tony the Tiger. - **$8 $15 $30**

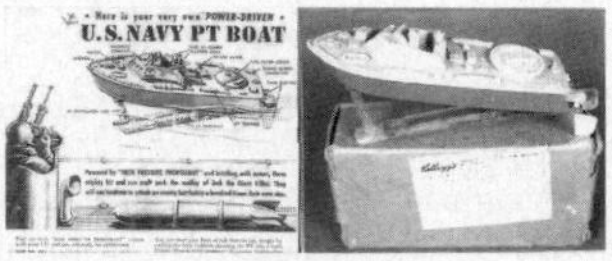

KEL-110

❑ **KEL-110. "U.S. Navy PT Boat",**
1960s. Includes boat, jet race way, package of propellant and instruction sheet.
Near Mint Boxed - **$200**
Boat Only - **$20 $35 $75**

KEL-111

❑ **KEL-111. Cereal Box With "Pin-Me-Ups" Back,**
1960s. Set of eight featuring Hanna-Barbera characters. Complete Box - **$30 $65 $135**

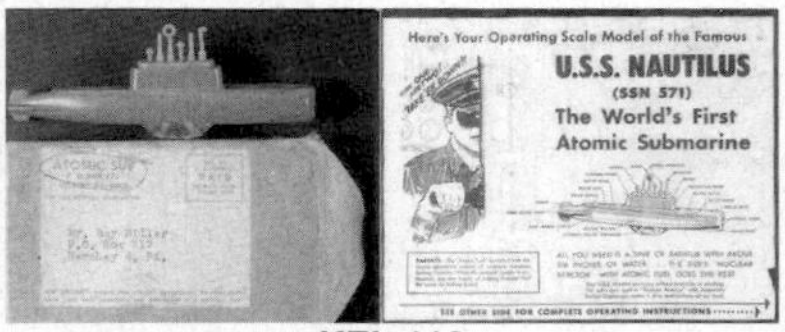

KEL-112

❑ **KEL-112. "U.S.S. Nautilus" Plastic Atomic Sub,**
1960s. Later issue than KEL-97 with different box label and small differences on instructions.
Near Mint In Box - **$200**
Sub Only - **$10 $30 $65**

KEL-113

❑ **KEL-113. Sugar Pops 12 oz. Cereal Box Flat with Yo-yo Offer,**
1970. Offers free yo-yo in box.
Box - **$35 $60 $125**
Yo-yo - **$3 $6 $12**

KEL-114 KEL-115

❑ **KEL-114. "Dig 'Em" Metal Wind-Up Alarm Clock,**
1979. - **$15 $35 $65**

❑ **KEL-115. "Toucan Sam" Plastic Secret Decoder,**
1983. Movable disk code wheel. Comes in different colors - **$5 $12 $20**

KEL-117

❑ **KEL-117. Plastic Cereal Bowl Premiums,**
1995. Four bowls feature Corny, Rice Krispies' Snap, Crackle and Pop, Tony and Toucan Sam. Each bowl - **$20**

Ken Maynard

An all-around sagebrush hero, cowboy actor Maynard (1895-1973) was first an accomplished trick rider and rodeo championship rider. Pre-movie years included performances at King Ranch, Texas; Buffalo Bill's Wild West Show, Ringling Bros. Wild West Show, Tex Rickard's World's Champion Cowboy competition (first place in 1920). He was introduced into silent movies by Tom Mix and best remembered for his First National films of the mid-1920s and following decade, also featuring his talented horse Tarzan. He is credited by many as the first to introduce song to the western movie. His 1938-1948 years were mostly a return to live performances and he continued to draw audiences even into his fifties.

KEN-1

KEN-2

KEN-3

❑ **KEN-1. "First National Films" Studio Matchbook,**
1929. Reverse lists six film titles from that year. - **$15 $25 $50**

❑ **KEN-2. "Ken Maynard Club/First National Pictures" Cello. Button,**
c. 1929. - **$15 $35 $75**

❑ **KEN-3. Paper Mask,**
1933. Einson-Freeman movie promo. - **$60 $135 $300**

KEN-4

KEN-5

❑ **KEN-4. Dixie Ice Cream Picture,**
1934. Title on reverse is "In Old Santa Fe." - **$20 $40 $80**

❑ **KEN-5. Dixie Ice Cream Picture,**
1934. Reverse pictures scenes from serial "Mystery Mountain." - **$20 $40 $70**

KEN-6

❑ **KEN-6. "Gun Justice Featuring Ken Maynard" Big Little Book,**
1934. Whitman #776. Issued as hardcover and softcover. Each - **$19 $57 $135**

KEN-7

❑ **KEN-7. "Wheels Of Destiny Featuring Ken Maynard" Book,**
1934. Engel-Van Wiseman Five Star Library Book #5. Movie edition. - **$19 $57 $135**

KEN-8

❑ **KEN-8. "Strawberry Roan" Movie Edition Book,**
1934. Saalfield. #1090 based on Universal film of same title. Hard or soft cover - **$12 $36 $85**

KEN-9

❑ **KEN-9. "Ken Maynard in Western Justice" Big Little Book #1430,**
1938. - **$12 $36 $78**

KEN-10

KEN-11

❑ **KEN-10. "Ken Maynard" Penny Book,**
1938. Store item by Whitman. - **$9 $27 $57**

❑ **KEN-11. "Ken Maynard & Tarzan" Pinback,**
1930s. Large 1-3/4" with yellow background. Scarce. - **$25 $50 $75**

KEN-12

❑ **KEN-12. "Tales From The Diamond K Starring Ken Maynard" Record,**
1930s. Record is 8" in diameter, 78-rpm on red vinyl. For 1930s radio program. Images in center show Maynard and his horse Tarzan. **- $25 $50 $75**

KEN-13

KEN-14

❑ **KEN-13. Movie Photo Card,**
1930s. Color card. Scarce. - **$15 $25 $50**
Black and white card - **$5 $10 $20**

❑ **KEN-14. "Round Up/Buckaroo Club" Card,**
1930s. Various radio stations. - **$15 $30 $80**

KEN-15

❑ **KEN-15. "Ken Maynard Western Star First Nat'l" Cigar Band,**
c. 1930s. Gold foil with black and white photo. - **$10 $20 $40**

KEN-16

KEN-17

❑ **KEN-16. Portrait Cello. Button,**
1930s. Probably circus souvenir. -
$45 $85 $175

❑ **KEN-17. "Cole Bros. Circus" Cello. Button,**
1930s. - **$60 $125 $185**

KEN-18

KEN-19

KEN-20

❑ **KEN-18. "Ken Maynard's Wild West And Indian Congress" Performance Ticket,**
1930s. Printed identically on both sides including small title for Diamond K Ranch. -
$15 $30 $50

❑ **KEN-19. "Ken Maynard's Wild West Circus And Indian Congress" Contract Agreement Pass,**
1930s. Paper perforated into billing contract on left for right to post advertising, entitling free admission pass on right.
Complete - **$25 $45 $90**

❑ **KEN-20. Movie Press Book,**
1940. Colony Pictures Inc. 12x18" glossy eight-page exploitation manual. - **$25 $50 $100**

KEN-21

❑ **KEN-21. Portrait Button,**
1940s. 1.75" black/white on yellow from rodeo or other personal appearance. - **$25 $50 $85**

Kewpie

Illustrator Rose O'Neill (1874-1944) worked for *Puck, Woman's Home Companion* and other magazines in the 1890s and early 1900s. Her first Kewpie illustrations were published in *Ladies' Home Journal* in December 1909. Based on Cupid, the Kewpie was a cherubic child with small wings, a little tuft of hair and a heartwarming smile. O'Neill's Kewpie quickly became a hit with the public, leading to *The Kewpies, Their Book* in 1911. O'Neill obtained the first patent for a three dimensional Kewpie doll in 1913 and George Borgfeldt began producing bisque dolls made in Germany at the same time. Early Kewpies were unclothed but would soon be available in various costumes with figures made of celluloid, composition, chalk and plaster. A Kewpie musical was performed in 1919 at the Amsterdam Theater in New York City and Rose O'Neill did full color ads for Jell-O as the Kewpies appeared on numerous items in a merchandising tidal wave lasting until the early 1930s.

A Sunday newspaper comic strip page ran in 1917-1918, and again from 1935 to 1937. Noted creator of *The Spirit* comic book, Will Eisner, published a *Kewpies* comic in 1949. Hickman High School in Columbia, Missouri adopted the Kewpie as their mascot in WWI and students refer to themselves as Kewpies today. The International Rose O'Neill Club currently has over 500 members. The O'Neill family estate near Branson, Missouri, obtained by homesteading in 1893, has been fully restored and is open to the public. Bonniebrook is located at 485 Rose O'Neill Road in Walnut Shade, Missouri. The Kewpies' motto is "Keep Smiling."

KEW-1

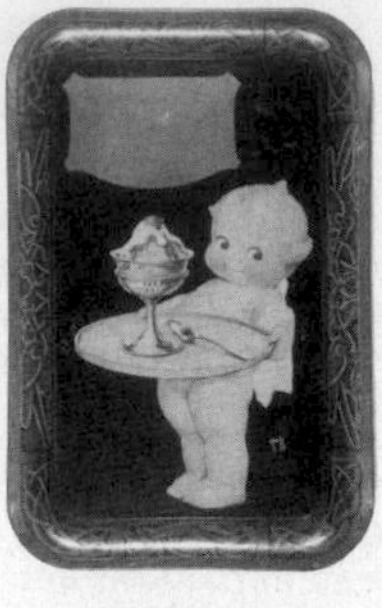

KEW-2

❑ **KEW-1. Kewpie Early Composition Doll,**
1913. 8.5" tall composition with elastic jointed arm sockets, July 22, 1913 patent label on underside, and "Kewpie" heart sticker on chest.
- **$100 $200 $400**

❑ **KEW-2. Rose O'Neill Kewpie Ice Cream Tray,**
1915. Parker-Brawner & Rose O'Neill.
11.5x17.5" litho tin. - **$400 $800 $1500**

KEW-3

❑ **KEW-3. "Kewpie" Sterling Silver Ring,**
c. 1920s. Store item. Depicts single Kewpie with raised hands and kicking one foot. -
$85 $150 $250

KEW-4

❑ **KEW-4. Kewpies "Velvet Kind" Ice Cream Tray,**
1920s. Parker-Brawner Co. 13.5x13.5x1" deep litho tin server with Rose O'Neill copyright. Printed for Tennessee maker. - **$100 $200 $400**

KEW-5

❑ **KEW-5. "The Kewpies By Rose O'Neill" Sunday Comic Strip Original Art,**
1936. 16.75x25.5" thin art board has 11 panels with India ink art. Has Rose O'Neill paper copyright sticker at bottom of 10th panel. Signed in ink at bottom of ninth panel with unusual O'Neill signature designed as legs with feet. Same Or Similar - **$500 $1000 $1500**

KEW-6

❑ **KEW-6. Kewpie-Like Large Carnival Statue Bank,**
1940s. 4.5x5x12.5" tall painted plaster with dark sparkle accents on shirt and flower in hair. Wings on back. Unpunched coin slot. - **$15 $30 $50**

KEW-7

❑ **KEW-7. "The Kewpies" Die-cut Cut-out and Punch-out Book,**
1963. Saalfield. 10.75x14" with stiff paper punch-out covers containing six colorful one-sided sheets of clothes. - **$8 $15 $30**

Kilroy Was Here

A true folk legend, the Kilroy character with bald head and long nose peering from behind a wall is synonymous with the World War II American G.I. The hand-scrawled slogan appeared on all types of munitions and supplies in the U.S., and overseas on tents and latrines and virtually anywhere a soldier was going to or returning from.

The most commonly accepted story of Kilroy's origin is based on welding inspector James Kilroy. In WWII he was working at the Bethlehem Steel Company shipyard in Quincy, Mass. He would write his name as an approval for completed work on the inside of ships' hulls, at the end of lines of rivets, etc. The American Transit Association had a contest at the end of the war to find the real Kilroy. James Kilroy won and was awarded a full-sized real trolley car which he put in the yard for his kids to use as a playhouse. The graphic likeness of Kilroy may be traced back to English cartoonist George Chatterton who did a drawing similar to Kilroy for the character Mr. Chad.

One of the more interesting vintage collectibles is a statuette of a young pregnant woman with the "Kilroy Was Here" slogan. This was an early product of Hartland Plastics, later famous in the 1950s and 1960s for their plastic replica figures of major league baseball players and TV western stars.

The phrase continues in use by soldiers and the public today and is in competition to become a USPS stamp in 2008. Kilroy is still here!

KIL-1

❑ **KIL-1. World War II Character "Kilroy" On Radio Station Card,**
1947. 2.25x2.75" stiff die-cut card cut so that upper half will fold leaving "Kilroy Was Here" image along fence top. Front copyright is "Harry S. Goodman N.Y.C., N.Y. 1947." - **$5 $15 $25**

KIL-2

❑ **KIL-2. "Genius At Work Silence!/Kilroy Was Here!" Glazed Ceramic Salt & Pepper Set,**
1940s. Each is about 1.5x3x2.5" tall depicting Kilroy figure draping nose and hands over triangular base. - **$15 $30 $60**

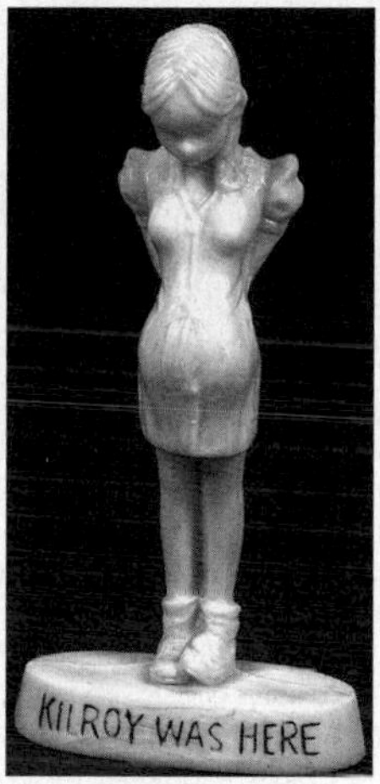

KIL-3

❑ **KIL-3. "Kilroy Was Here" Pregnant Girl Hartland Figure,**
1940s. 3-5/8" tall ivory color plastic figure with black text on base. Ivory - **$12 $25 $50**
Other Colors - **$25 $50 $100**

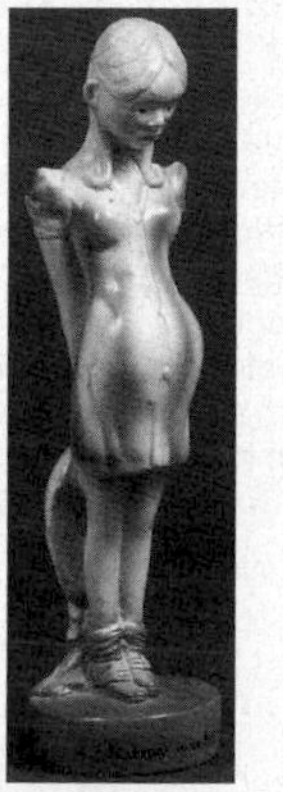

KIL-4

❑ **KIL-4. "Kilroy Was Here" Chalk Figure,**
1940s. 2.5" diameter base with incised black text. 9.5" tall painted chalk figure with painted accents. - **$50 $100 $200**

KIL-5

❑ **KIL-5. United Nations Satirical "Kilroy Was Here" Badge,**
1940s. 1.5" diamond-shaped thin celluloid sheet with original string. - **$15 $30 $60**

KIL-6

❑ **KIL-6. "Smoo Pix/Kilroy Is Here" Figural Plastic Cocktail Picks With Box,**
1950s. Edward Don & Co. 8x8x3" deep box contains 270 opaque plastic picks in various colors based on popular World War II character. Each is 2" tall. - **$12 $25 $50**

King Features Misc.

King Features Syndicate, the country's largest newspaper comic-strip syndicator, has been the agency of such legendary giants as Popeye, Flash Gordon, Felix the Cat, Krazy Kat, Beetle Bailey, Henry, Skippy, Betty Boop, Barney Google, and dozens of other major comic characters. Originally titled Newspaper Feature Service as organized in 1913 by Moses Koenigsberg under William Randolph Hearst's direction, in 1915 King Features became the sales agent for all the combined Hearst Newspapers syndicate operations. Over the years it has issued a number of items promoting various combinations of its comic characters.

KIN-1

KIN-2

❑ **KIN-1. "Polar Lark" Metal Paperweight,**
1926. 10 King Features character heads form North Pole in homage to Commander Byrd's flight over pole. - **$175 $350 $675**

❑ **KIN-2. King Features Syndicate Ink Blotter,**
1928. Blotter is 4x9". Characters include Barney Google, Blondie, Felix, Katzenjammer Kids, Krazy Kat and many others. Text reads "Moving Just Across The Street To No. 2 Columbus Circle July 31st, 1928/King Features Syndicate, Inc./International Features Service, Inc./Newspaper Feature Service, Inc./Premiere Syndicate, Inc./Star Adcraft Service."
- $85 $175 $300

KIN-3

❑ **KIN-3. The Comic Club Stamps,**
1934. Wrigley's Gum. 18 stamps on sheet. - **$70 $150 $225**

KIN-4

❑ **KIN-4. Christmas Card Folder To Media Customers,**
1935. Authorized Hallmark Card publication with 24 full color pages featuring prominent King Features comic strip characters illustrating story theme "T'was The Night Before Christmas." - **$200 $350 $600**

KIN-5

❑ **KIN-5. King Features Syndicate Character Cloth Panel,**
1938. 12-3/4x16-7/8" premium offered as "Comic Flag." Issued by KFS via comic book ad. - **$100 $200 $400**

KIN-6

KIN-7

❑ **KIN-6. "Sunday Examiner" Newspaper Contest Litho. Button,**
1930s. Part of a set of various characters. - **$15 $35 $70**

❑ **KIN-7. "King Features Syndicate Blue Book,"**
1943. 11x15-1/2" with 80 slick pages of sample comic strips in black/white and full color. Limited distribution to newspaper editors. -
$115 $225 $375

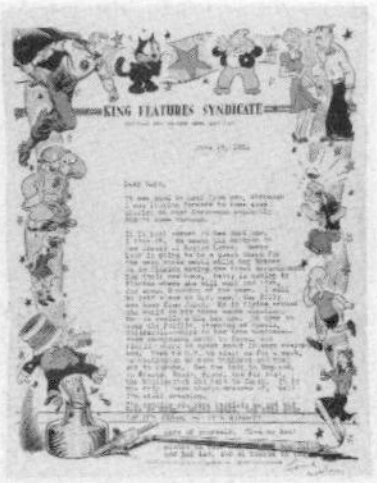

KIN-8

❑ **KIN-8. "King Features Syndicate" Colorful Stationery With Characters,**
1944. Characters include Felix, Katzenjammer Kids, Blondie and Dagwood, Popeye, Henry, Jiggs, Annie Rooney, Barney Google, Super Hero that carries rifle, wears cape and has skull and crossbones insignia on chest. Stationery is copyright 1944. Typed letter signed is personal correspondence from employee written in 1951.
- $100 $200 $300

KIN-9

❑ **KIN-9. "A Christmas Carol Holiday Greetings" Book With Slipcase,**
1946. Christmas theme hardcover with 160 pages picturing on the endpapers virtually all King Features comic strip characters. Slipcase and book cover have identical illustration.
With Slipcase - **$75 $150 $250**
No Slipcase - **$50 $100 $150**

KIN-10

❑ **KIN-10. "Blue Book",**
1946 and other years before and after. King Features Syndicate. Sent annually to newspaper editors with black and white as well as beautiful color sample pages of the comic strips and features available to local newspapers. This Example - **$115 $225 $375**

KIN-11

❑ **KIN-11. "King Features Syndicate Famous Artists & Writers" Book,**
1949. Biographies of those represented by K.F.S. - **$200 $400 $800**

KIN-12

❑ **KIN-12. "King Features Syndlcate Blue Book,"**
1949. 9-1/2x12" spiral-bound with 140 black and white and color pages. Limited distribution to newspaper comic page editors. -
$110 $215 $335

KIN-13

❑ **KIN-13. "Sing With King At Christmas" Book,**
1949. Pictures numerous Christmas carols sung by various syndicate characters. -
$50 $100 $175

(FRONT)

(BACK)

KIN-14

❑ **KIN-14. "Prince Valiant" Promotional,**
c. 1940s. King Features Syndicate. 11x17" stiff paper promo. Front features castle with separate die-cut drawbridge that folds open to reveal a 7" tall die-cut, pop-out figure of Prince Valiant. Art on the back of the piece depicts different castle view with banner that includes name F.J. Nicht and address for King Features Syndicate. Below is die-cut slot which probably held a form or envelope to be returned to King Features Syndicate. - **$500 $1500 $3000**

KIN-15

❑ **KIN-15. "Popular Comics" Boxed Christmas Cards,**
1951. Set of 16. - **$50 $100 $200**

KIN-16

❑ **KIN-16. "Merry Christmas From King Features Syndicate" Music Box Book With Character Fold-Out,**
1953. 3-3/4x5-1/2x1" thick with card on back that folds out to 39-1/2" with characters. Limited distribution. - **$60 $135 $185**

KIN-17

❑ **KIN-17. Merry Christmas/Happy New Year Comic Strip Character Table Cover With Mailer,**
1954. Mailer is 10x15" and holds folded 8-1/4x13-1/2" textured paper tablecloth which opens to 4-1/2' times 6'. Pictures many of the Syndicate's characters including Prince Valiant, The Phantom, Donald Duck, Popeye, Flash Gordon, others. Mailer - **$20 $30 $60**
Tablecloth - **$60 $135 $275**

KIN-18

❑ **KIN-18. "Comic Strip Cartoon Charm Set" Boxed,**
1954. 6.25x8.5" boxed set of 10 King Features miniature character charms plus tiny accent chains and small packet of "Jewelry Materials." - **$40 $80 $150**

KIN-19

❑ **KIN-19. Character Promo Pen/Pencil Holder,**
c. 1955. 2-3/4" diameter by 3-1/2" tall plastic. Limited issue. - **$20 $40 $80**

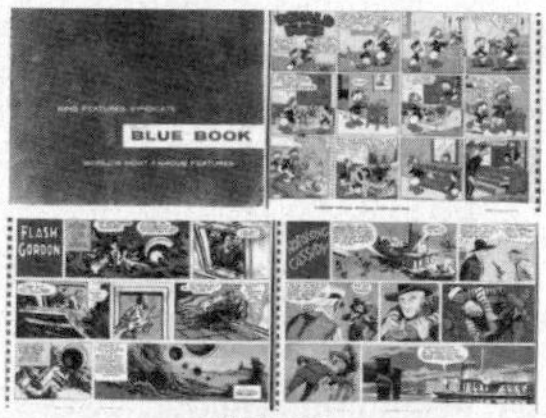

KIN-20

❑ **KIN-20. "King Features Syndicate Blue Book",**
1955. Full color sample pages of strips represented by K.F.S. - **$75 $150 $275**

KIN-21

❏ KIN-21. Plastic Ornament Set Showing 12 Characters,
c. 1950s. Boxed - **$60 $135 $250**

KIN-22

❏ KIN-22. Comic Strip Character Lighter,
1950s. Bowers "Storm Master." Metal case cigarette lighter picturing total of eight characters on both sides. Probably an executive or salesman giveaway. - $**100 $200 $400**

KIN-23

❏ KIN-23. "Christmas Greetings" Comic Strip Characters Candle,
1950s. 4.25" dia. by 3.5" tall wax candle featuring colorful depiction around perimeter of character(s) from 11 different comic strips involved in Christmas scenes. Limited KFS distribution, mainly to newspaper editors. - **$30 $60 $90**

KIN-24 KIN-25

❏ KIN-24. Glass Ashtray,
1950s. Pictures 14 comic strip characters. - **$20 $35 $70**

❏ KIN-25. Plastic Pen Holder,
1964. - **$30 $50 $100**

KIN-26

❏ KIN-26. "World's Greatest Comics" Promo Book,
1980. 8.5x11" spiral-bound 24-page full color limited distributed edition featuring major character(s) from all KFS strips. - **$115 $225 $350**

KIN-27

❏ KIN-27. Character Promo Letter Opener,
1981. 1x8-1/8" silvered metal with characters on handle. Limited issue. **- $12 $25 $50**

KISS

In 1971, Gene Simmons and Paul Stanley gave birth to a modern rock legend by playing their first show as Wicked Lester. In August of 1973, after a name change and the addition of new personnel, Kiss took the stage at the Grand Ballroom of the Diplomat Hotel in New York, shortly resulting in a record deal. Gene Simmons (bass player), Paul Stanley (guitarist), Ace Frehley (guitarist), and Peter Criss (drummer) had transformed themselves into The Demon, Starchild, Space Ace, and The Cat, respectively, through makeup. By mixing a hard rock edge with glam rock theatrics, Kiss took the world by storm as evidenced by their legion of followers, known as The Kiss Army. The group spawned best selling albums, action figures, a made-for-TV movie (*Kiss Meets the Phantom of the Park*–1978), a comic book, and scores of other merchandise.

In 1983, the group shed its makeup, and in the following years shuffled the lineup around mainstays Simmons and Stanley. In 1996, an appearance of the original Kiss in full makeup highlighted the Grammy Awards. The subsequent reunion tour was a huge success. Once again back on top, they launched new merchandise like best-selling action figures from McFarlane Toys, and a comic line, entertaining thousands of fans who only wanted to "rock 'n' roll all night and party every day."

KIS-1

❏ KIS-1. "Rock And Roll Over" Promo Button,
1976. 3" dia. full color classic art that appeared on album cover. - **$15 $30 $60**

(INSIDE)

KIS-2

❏ KIS-2. "Kiss On Tour" Program,
1976. Boutwell Enterprises Inc. 11x16.75" with eight double-sided pages and two inserts. Inserts are for "A Special Iron-On For All KISS Fans" transfer that is 6.5x10". It reads "KISS." Second insert is for membership to the "KISS Army." Complete With Inserts - **$12 $25 $50**

KIS-3 KIS-4

❏ KIS-3. Kiss Bracelet,
1977. Aucoin. Gold with red logo on Love Gun display card. - **$12 $20 $35**

❏ KIS-4. "Kiss Guitar",
1977. Store item by Carnival Toys Inc. 11-1/2x30-1/2x3-1/2" deep box contains 29" long hard plastic guitar with photo label on front of body. Packaging includes instruction book.
Near Mint Boxed - **$950**
Guitar Only - **$165 $350 $600**

KIS-5 KIS-6

❏ KIS-5. "Kiss Destroyer" Autographed Album,
1976. Issued by Casablanca. Signed in gold ink. Similar Examples **- $85 $175 $350**

❏ KIS-6. "Kiss Custom Chevy Van" Model Kit,
1977. AMT. Unbuilt **- $30 $50 $90**

KIS-7

❑ **KIS-7. "Kiss Rockstics,"**
1978. Store item by Aucoin.
Each Unused Card - **$10 $20 $40**

KIS-8

❑ **KIS-8. "Kiss" Large Litho. Tin Waste Can,**
1978. Store item by P&K Products Co. Inc. 10" diameter by 19-1/2" tall. - **$75 $150 $300**

KIS-9

❑ **KIS-9. "Kiss" Jacket,**
1978. Store item by Rockrollium Corp. Brightly colored jacket made of thin fiberglass material. Originally packaged in plain plastic bag. - **$15 $30 $60**

KIS-10

❑ **KIS-10. "Kiss On Tour Game",**
1978. Store item by American Publishing Corp.
Near Mint Sealed - **$110**
Open Complete - **$20 $30 $45**

KIS-11

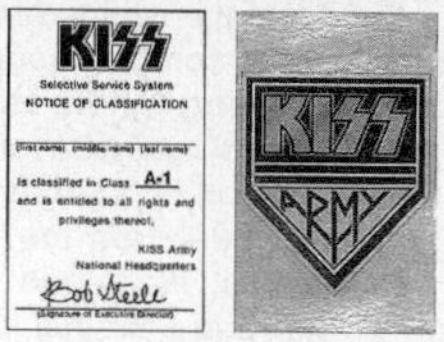

KIS-12

❑ **KIS-11. "Kiss Dynasty" Press Kit,**
1979. Issued by Casablanca Records. - **$10 $20 $45**

❑ **KIS-12. Kiss Army Selective Service Notification,**
1970s. - **$10 $15 $30**

KIS-13

KIS-14

❑ **KIS-13. Colorform Set,**
1970s. Colorforms. - **$50 $75 $150**

❑ **KIS-14. "Destroyer" Puzzle,**
1970s. By Casse-tete. - **$25 $40 $60**

KIS-15

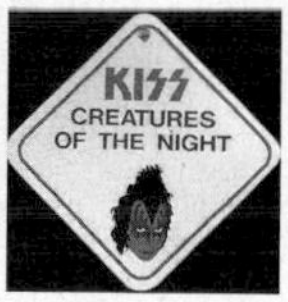

KIS-16

❑ **KIS-15. Kiss Make-Up Kit,**
1970s. By Remco. First issue. - **$85 $160 $265**

❑ **KIS-16. Window Sign,**
1970s. Blue Gene face. Creatures of the Night. - **$4 $8 $15**

KIS-17

❑ **KIS-17. View-Master Special Subjects Series,**
1970s. 21 3-D pictures on 3 reels in photo envelope. - **$12 $20 $30**

KIS-18

KIS-19

❑ **KIS-18. Rub 'N' Play Magic Transfer Set,**
1970s. 8 stand-up play figures by Colorforms. - **$60 $115 $200**

❑ **KIS-19. Kiss Signature Necklace,**
1970s. One of four featuring Ace, Gene, Paul, and Peter. Ace Frehely version pictured. Each - **$35 $65 $100**

KIS-20

KIS-21

❑ **KIS-20. Kiss Promo Card,**
1970s. 4x5" card says "Compliments of Kiss." - **$10 $20 $30**

❑ **KIS-21. "Kiss Meets the Phantom of the Park" Video,**
1986. World Vision Home Video. Tape of a 1978 Hanna Barbera production in association with Kiss/Aucoin Productions. 96 minute made-for-TV movie also starred Anthony Zerbe, Carmine Caridi, and Deborah Ryan. - **$55**

KIS-22

KIS-23

KIS-24

KIS-25

❑ **KIS-22. Kiss Toy Car - Paul Stanley,**
1996. Johnny Lightning Car Series - **$16**

❑ **KIS-23. Kiss Toy Car - Gene Simmons,**
1996. Johnny Lightning Car Series - **$16**

❑ **KIS-24. Kiss Toy Car - Ace Frehley,**
1996. Johnny Lightning Car Series - **$16**

❑ **KIS-25. Kiss Toy Car - Peter Criss,**
1996. Johnny Lightning Car Series - **$16**

KIS-26

❑ **KIS-26. Kiss Rings,**
1997. Three different plastic rings with a filigree metal base. Gene, Paul and the group.
Each - **$8 $18 $40**

KIS-27

KIS-28

❑ **KIS-27. Kiss Christmas Ornaments,**
1997. Two different. Each - **$18**

❑ **KIS-28. Standee Promo for Neon Telephone,**
1998. 14 1/2" sign. - **$25 $40 $85**

KIS-29

KIS-29. Kiss Bean Bag Collection,
1999. First edition, limited to 25,000, with art deco open box - **$130**

Krazy Kat and Ignatz

George Herriman (1880-1944), creator of the comic strip *Krazy Kat*, has been ranked with Chaplin as one of the giants of American popular art. The strip, which began as a minor part of a daily strip called *The Dingbat Family* in the *New York Journal* in 1910, came into its own in 1913, and a Sunday page debuted in 1916. For the next 28 years the complex saga of Krazy Kat, the brick-throwing Ignatz Mouse, and Offissa Pupp unfolded against ever-changing backgrounds of Coconino County, Arizona. Animated cartoons based on the strip were produced in the teens, 1920s and 1930s and later as part of the King Features Trilogy and Screen Gems Theatrical Cartoon Package. Dell published a series of *Krazy Kat* comic books in the 1950s. The strip was retired upon Herriman's death.

KRA-1

KRA-2

❑ **KRA-1. "Krazy Kat" Stuffed Doll,**
c. 1915. Store item by Averill Co.
Black - **$300 $600 $1200**
Purple - **$400 $750 $1500**

❑ **KRA-2. "Don't Be A Krazy Kat" Cello. Button,**
c. 1915. Cigarette purchase give-away. Art by character creator George Herriman. - **$25 $45 $95**

KRA-3

❑ **KRA-3. "Krazy Kat" Pin on Card,**
1927. Krazy votes "Yes" for the repeal of the Prohibition Act. Rare. - **$45 $90 $140**

KRA-4

KRA-5

❑ **KRA-4. "Cats Pajamas" Enamel On Brass Pin,**
c. 1920s. - **$50 $100 $150**

❑ **KRA-5. "Krazy Kat Kiddies Klub" Member Card,**
c. 1920s. Art is unsigned, issuer is unknown. - **$125 $275 $500**

KRA-6

❑ **KRA-6. "Whoopee" Enamel On Brass Figure Pin,**
c. 1920s. Blue/black accented dancing figure in cowboy outfit including gun belt. - **$75 $150 $250**

KRA-7

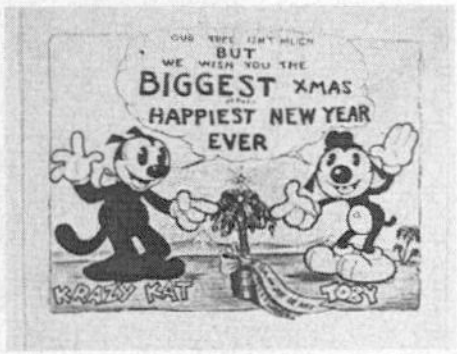

KRA-8

❑ **KRA-7. "Ignatz" Flexible Figure,**
c. 1930. Store item. Composition/wood/wire by Cameo Doll Co. - **$150 $300 $600**
Box - **$150 $300 $600**

❑ **KRA-8. Animator Joe DeNat's Personal Christmas Card,**
1930. 5x7" also depicts cartoon character "Toby." - **$60 $125 $250**

KRA-9

❑ **KRA-9. "Ignatz Mouse" Squeaking Pull Toy,**
1932. Chein. 9" tall metal and wood tricycle toy that produces squeak sound and foot pedals action when pulled by string. - **$500 $1000 $1750**

KRA-10

❑ **KRA-10. "Krazy Kat" Wood Jointed Doll.**
1932. Chein. 7" tall detailed by leather ears and felt bow on back shoulders. -
$425 $850 $1500

KRA-11

❑ **KRA-11. "Popeye/Krazy Kat/Ignatz Mouse/ Comic Toys By J. Chein & Co." Fold-Out Illustrated Price List,**
1932. List is 8.5x11" and unfolds to 17x22". Toys shown are Popeye Heavy Hitter, Popeye Sparkler, Popeye wood jointed figure, Popeye Shadow Boxer, Popeye pliable rubber funny face, Popeye the Swab, Popeye Bag Puncher, Popeye the Drummer, Squeaky Ignatz Cycle Rider, Krazy Kat Sparkler. - **$200 $400 $600**

KRA-12

❑ **KRA-12. "All Star Comics" Boxed Playing Card Game,**
1934. Store item by Whitman. Card characters also include those from "Just Kids" and "Captain And Kids" comic strips. - **$65 $125 $225**

KRA-13 KRA-14

❑ **KRA-13. "Archy Does His Part" Book With Art By Krazy Kat Creator Herriman,**
1935. Hardback published by Doubleday.
With Dust Jacket - **$65 $150 $250**

❑ **KRA-14. "Krazy Kat" Wood Jointed Doll,**
1930s. Store item. No maker's name. Example shown possibly missing a hat. 5-3/4" tall. -
$125 $275 $500

KRA-15

❑ **KRA-15. "Krazy Kat" Necktie,**
1930s. Fabric tie is 3x40" long with bright image of Krazy Kat. Back of tie reads "International Feature Service Inc. 50." - **$40 $75 $150**

KRA-16 KRA-17

❑ **KRA-16. Krazy Kat Enameled Brass Figural Pin,**
1930s. Accents are four enamel colors and tiny rhinestone eyes. - **$20 $40 $65**

❑ **KRA-17. Krazy Kat Enameled Brass Figure Pin,**
1930s. Sign inscription is "If You Can Read This You're Too Darn Close." - **$20 $40 $65**

KRA-18 KRA-19

❑ **KRA-18. "Krazy Kat/New York Evening Journal" Cello. Button,**
1930s. From series of newspaper contest buttons, match number to win prize. - **$20 $50 $115**

❑ **KRA-19. "Krazy Kat/New York Evening Journal" Cello. Button,**
1930s. From series of newspaper contest buttons, match number to win prize. - **$15 $40 $75**

KRA-20 KRA-21

❑ **KRA-20. "Ignatz Mouse/New York Evening Journal" Cello. Button,**
1930s. From series of newspaper contest buttons, match number to win prize. - **$15 $40 $80**

❑ **KRA-21. "Kiddies Krazy Kat" Cello. Button,**
c. 1930s. State Theatre. 7/8" black on cream with red image of Krazy Kat. - **$60 $125 $250**

KRA-22

❑ **KRA-22. Krazy Kat Calendar,**
1999. - **$2 $8 $25**

Kukla, Fran and Ollie

Puppeteer Burr Tillstrom (1917-1985) created Kukla, a chronic worrier, and Ollie, a one-tooth dragon, in Chicago in the late 1930s. Along with singer-actress Fran Allison (1908-1989), the Kuklapolitans were to produce one of early television's most beloved long-running successes, first as *Junior Jamboree* on WBKB (1947-1948), then as *Kukla, Fran & Ollie* on NBC (1948-1954), on ABC (1954-1957), again on NBC (1961-1962), on public television (1970-1971), and in syndication (1975-1976). Sponsors included RCA Victor, Sealtest, Ford and Pontiac automobiles, National Biscuit, Life magazine, Procter & Gamble, and Miles Laboratories. Promotional items are normally copyrighted Burr Tillstrom. A radio version aired on NBC in 1952-1953. Ted Drake (1907-2000) was responsible for the art used on the show and on merchandise.

KUK-1

❑ **KUK-1. "Kuklapolitan Courier" Newsletter With Envelope,**
1949. One of series sent to fans.
With Envelope - **$25 $75 $125**
Without Envelope - **$10 $35 $80**

KUK-2

❑ **KUK-2. Fan Postcard,**
1950. Announces August 8 starting day for third season of TV show. - **$20 $35 $80**

KUK-3

❑ **KUK-3. "Kuklapolitan Courier Year Book",**
1951. - **$25 $50 $140**

KUK-4 **KUK-5**

❑ **KUK-4. Kukla, Fran & Ollie Pre-National TV Program,**
1951. 5.25x8.5" pre-national program for the Chicago area. TV Forecast from 10/13/51.
- $25 $50 $100

❑ **KUK-5. Songs Record Album,**
1951. RCA Victor. 10x10" full color sleeve holding single record from Little Nipper Series. - **$25 $50 $80**

KUK-6 **KUK-7**

❑ **KUK-6. "TV Forecast" Cover Article,**
1953. - **$25 $50 $100**

❑ **KUK-7. "TV Guide" Cover Article,**
1953. Weekly issue for October 30 with two-page Kukla, Fran & Ollie article titled "Beulah Witch's Halloween." - **$25 $50 $100**

KUK-8 **KUK-9**

❑ **KUK-8. Tru-Vue Film Card,**
1953. Store item. Scenes of a wild west show. - **$8 $15 $30**

❑ **KUK-9. Vinyl On Cardboard Postcard Record,**
c. 1957. Curtiss Candy Co. Several versions. - **$15 $30 $60**

KUK-10

❑ **KUK-10. Kukla And Ollie Masks,**
1950s. Store items. Molded thin plastic. Each **- $15 $30 $60**

KUK-11

❑ **KUK-11. "Kukla And Ollie Doddly Dolly" Boxed Set,**
1950s. Store item by H. Davis Toy Corp. 12x18x2" deep box contains yarn and fabric pieces for doll construction.
Unused - **$30 $75 $150**

KUK-12

❑ **KUK-12. Curtiss Candy Co. Vinyl Cardboard Record,**
1950s. - **$15 $40 $90**

(KUKLA) (OLLIE)

KUK-13

❑ **KUK-13. Spoon Set Of Two,**
1950s. Rare. - **$75 $150 $300**

KUK-14

❑ **KUK-14. "Kukla And Ollie" Store Banner,**
1950s. 21x34" fabric on metal hanging rod. - **$125 $250 $400**

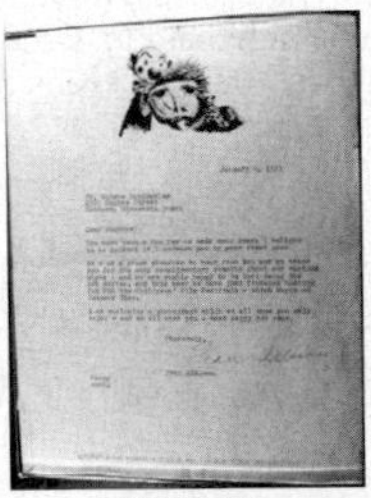

KUK-15

❑ **KUK-15. Personal Autographed Letter,**
1971. From Fran Allison on Kukla and Ollie stationery. - **$200**

Lash LaRue

Alfred LaRue (1917-1996) began acting using his real name in two Hollywood musicals in 1944. In 1945, he was hired to play Eddie Dean's partner the Cheyenne Kid in *Song of Old Wyoming*, released October 12 by Producers Releasing Corporation (PRC). LaRue had to learn how to use a bullwhip. He became an expert and began starring in his own "B" westerns wearing an all-black outfit in 1947. His first feature film, *Law of the Lash* was released February 28, 1947. A close resemblance to Humphrey Bogart and co-stars Al "Fuzzy" St. John and LaRue's horse Black Diamond helped keep LaRue starring on the western big screen until 1952. His 18-foot-long bullwhip was often used to rip six-guns from hands of bad guys. He would go on to some acting on television including episodes of *Judge Roy Bean* and *The Life And Legend Of Wyatt Earp.* LaRue played Ranger Girard in the 1985 B-movie *The Dark Power* and had a part in the 1986 TV adaptation of *Stagecoach* which starred Willie Nelson and Johnny Cash. Fawcett released 46 *Lash LaRue Western* comics between the summer of 1949 and January 1954 with photo covers. Charlton picked up the series with issue #47 and continued until June 1961 with #84 as the last issue. AC published two more issues in 1990.

Lash LaRue made many new friends with collectors from numerous personal appearances at western film conventions throughout his last 20 years.

LLR-1

❑ **LLR-1. Al "Lash" LaRue Dixie Picture,**
1947. - **$25 $60 $115**

LLR-2

❑ **LLR-2. "Lash LaRue" Button,**
1940s. 1.25" celluloid button with black and white photo. - **$30 $60 $125**

LLR-3

❑ **LLR-3. Lash LaRue Personal Whip With Signed And Inscribed Photos,**
1950s. Leather whip is 9' long with 8" wooden handle. These two photos were signed in the 1980s. 8x10" glossy with red inked inscription and 3.5" long signature. 8x9.25" glossy with inked inscription and 3" signature. Whip Used But Undamaged - **$1000**
Each Photo - **$10 $20 $40**

LLR-4

❑ **LLR-4. "Lash LaRue" Autographed Photo,**
c. 1983. 8x10" black and white glossy photo signed "To Joe Best Wishes Lash LaRue." Bottom margin has printed "Lash LaRue Public Relations" plus address in Ft. Walton Beach, Florida. - **$10 $20 $40**

Lassie

The story of the courageous, intelligent collie first appeared in Erick Knight's 1938 short story and 1940 best-selling novel *Lassie Come Home*--the start of an odyssey that was to continue for some 35 years: the 1943 MGM movie starring Roddy McDowall, followed by a half-dozen sequels over eight years; the radio serial sponsored by Red Heart dog food on ABC (1947-1948) and NBC (1948-1950); three decades of comic books beginning in 1949; and ultimately the CBS television saga, from 1954 to 1971, followed by three years of syndication under various titles (1972-1975), all sponsored by Campbell's soup. Originally trained by Rudd Weatherwax (1907-1985) Lassie was actually a male collie named Pal. Lassie's human companions were played by Tommy Rettig (1954-1957) and Jon Provost (1957-1964), and by Robert Bray (1964-1969) as an adventurous forest ranger. *Lassie's Rescue Rangers*, an animated series, ran on ABC from 1973 to 1975. The 50th anniversary of the original movie was celebrated in 1994 with the release of a new movie (*Lassie*), a TV program, a new book (*Lassie: A Dog's Life*), and numerous deals for spinoff products. Items bear the copyright of Wrather Corp., Rankin & Bass Productions, or Jack Wrather Productions.

LAS-1 LAS-2

❑ **LAS-1. Color Premium Picture - Red Heart, Large,**
1949. Scarce. - **$20 $50 $85**

❑ **LAS-2. Comic Book Premium - Red Heart,**
1949. Scarce. - **$32 $96 $400**

LAS-3

❑ **LAS-3. "Courage Of Lassie" Australian Button,**
1940s. Black and white real photo without dot pattern. - **$20 $35 $60**

LAS-4

❑ **LAS-4. "M-G-M's Lassie" First Issue Comic Book,**
1950. Published by Dell. - **$15 $45 $285**

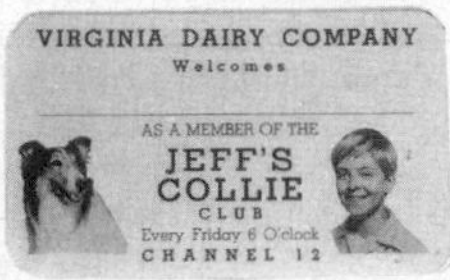

LAS-5

LAS-6

❑ **LAS-5. "Jeff's Collie Club" Member Card,**
c. 1954. Virginia Dairy Co., probable others. No direct Lassie reference but obviously based on early version of TV series. - **$15 $35 $70**

❑ **LAS-6. Lassie Friendship Silvered Brass Ring,**
c. 1955. Campbell Soup Company. Initial "L" on each side with high relief portrait on top. - **$30 $55 $110**

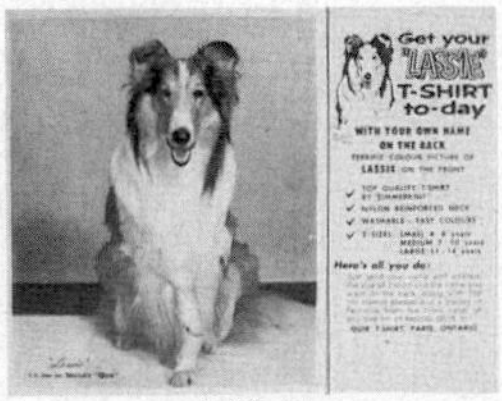

LAS-7

❑ **LAS-7. "'Lassie' T-Shirt" Offer And Photo,**
1956. Nestle's Quik. 8x10" full color photo with reverse ad for T-shirt available "With Your Own Name On The Back." - **$10 $20 $50**

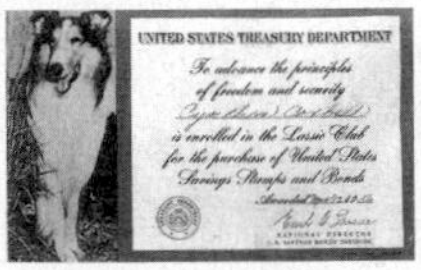

LAS-8

LAS-9

❑ **LAS-8. "Lassie Club" Savings Bond Certificate,**
c. 1956. - **$25 $50 $75**

❑ **LAS-9. Postcard,**
1956. Thank you postcard for entering contest. - **$10 $25 $40**

LAS-10

❑ **LAS-10. Fan Christmas Card,**
c. 1957. 5x12" stiff paper scored at center for intended use as folder although unfolded. Front is color photo of Timmy (Jon Provost), Lassie and Uncle Petrie. - **$10 $20 $35**

LAS-11

❑ **LAS-11. "Tim Magazine For Boys" Issues With Lassie,**
1957-1958. Each has cover article featuring Tommy Rettig as youthful star of Lassie TV series. Issues are for September 1957 and November 1958 with imprint for local Tim store. Each - **$8 $18 $40**

LAS-12

❑ **LAS-12. "Lassie & Timmie Plastic Palette Coloring Set,"**
c. 1958. Store item by Standard Toykraft. **- $35 $65 $135**

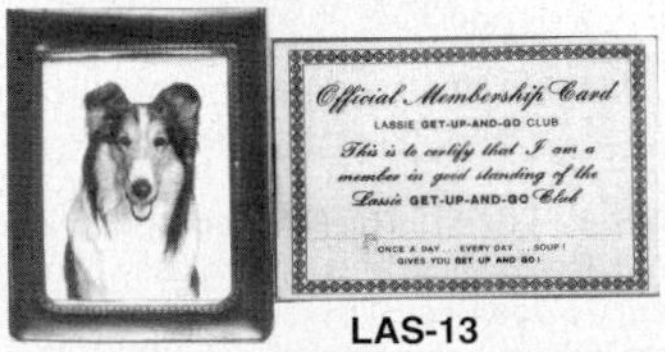

LAS-13

❑ **LAS-13. Wallet With Membership Card,**
1959. Campbell's Soups. Card reads "Lassie-Get-Up-And-Go Club". - **$15 $25 $75**

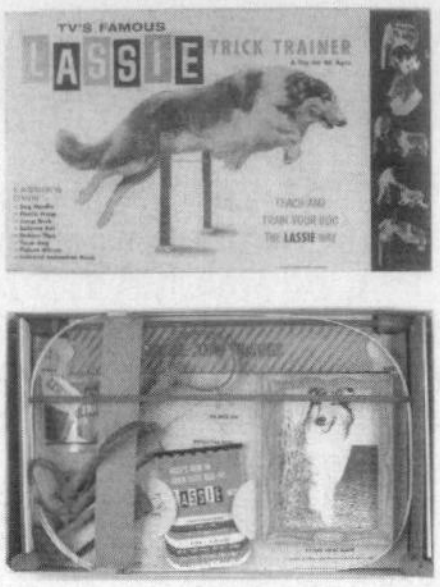

LAS-14

❑ **LAS-14. "Lassie Trick Trainer" Dog Training Kit,**
1950s. Box is 13x21x2.5" deep manufactured by Geo. E. Mousley Inc. and copyright Robert Maxwell Associates. Set includes: dog hurdle, plastic hoop, jump stick, balance bar, rubber pipe, treat bag, picture album and instruciton booklet. Set also comes with six double-sided 6.55x8" black and white photos. Complete Boxed - **$55 $110 $175**

LAS-15

❑ **LAS-15. Western Series Card,**
1950s. Card #4 - **$10 $20 $35**

LAS-16

LAS-17

❑ **LAS-16. "Have You Voted For Lassie?" Cello. Button,**
1950s. 1-3/4" size. - **$15 $25 $50**

❑ **LAS-17. "I Voted For Lassie" Cello. Button,**
1950s. 1" version. - **$10 $15 $25**

LAS-18

❑ **LAS-18. "Lassie Forest Ranger" Vinyl Wallet With Contents,**
1964. Campbell's Soups. Includes white metal badge and Lassie photo.
Complete - **$30 $65 $115**

LAS-19

❑ **LAS-19. "Forest Ranger Handbook",**
1967. Authored by "Corey Stuart And Lassie." - **$10 $20 $40**

LAS-20

LAS-21

❑ **LAS-20. "Lassie" Watch,**
1968. Store item by Bradley. - **$20 $40 $75**

❑ **LAS-21. "Lassie Gold Award For Meritorious Action" Brass Medal,**
1960s. Champion Valley Farms, Inc. 1" with areas on reverse where dog's name and owner's name can be engraved along with text reading "For Giving Meaning To The Tradition That 'Man's Best Friend Is His Dog.'" - **$30 $75 $135**

LAS-22

LAS-23

❑ **LAS-22. TV Patch,**
1960s. - **$25 $50 $110**

❑ **LAS-23. Lassie/Corey Stuart TV Photo,**
1960s. - **$20 $40 $60**

LAS-24

❑ **LAS-24. Fan Card,**
1960s. Recipe Brand Dinners. Back has facsimile paw print of Lassie and signature of trainer Rudd Weatherwax. - **$10 $20 $35**

LAS-25

❑ **LAS-25. Lassie Action Figure Boxed,**
1976. Gabriel Industries. Vinyl and hard plastic 2.5x10x6" tall likeness with movable head, legs and tail. Box - **$25 $50 $100**
Figure - **$25 $50 $100**

LAS-26

❑ **LAS-26. "A Friend Of Lassie" Brass Dog Tag,**
c. 1970s. Probable dog food sponsor. Back identification inscription to be completed by dog owner. - **$10 $20 $35**

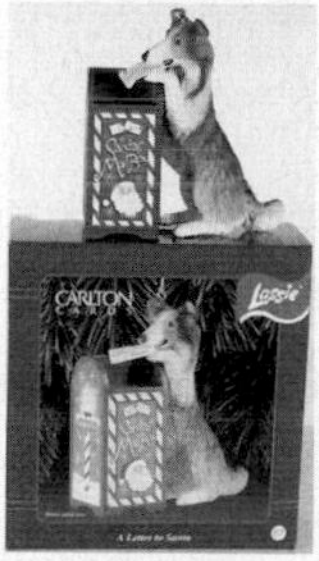

LAS-27

LAS-28

❑ **LAS-27. Christmas Ornament,**
1999. From Carlton Cards. Boxed. - **$25**

❑ **LAS-28. Christmas Ornament,**
1990s. From Carlton Cards. Boxed. - **$35**

Laugh-In

***Rowan & Martin's Laugh-In* was the psychedelic concoction of Dan Rowan and Dick Martin, a classic comic team of straight man and foil. The program, which aired on NBC television from 1968 to 1973 was a free-wheeling, frenetic mix of sight gags, low humor, and political satire. Among the supporting cast: Goldie Hawn, Lily Tomlin, Henry Gibson, Arte Johnson, Ruth Buzzi, Joanne Worley and Judy Carne. Catch phrases from the show such as "You bet your bippy," "Look that up in your *Funk & Wagnall's*," and "Sock it to me," became part of the nation's vocabulary. *Laugh-In* was the No. 1 television show during its first two seasons, winning numerous awards. A dozen issues of *Laugh-In Magazine* were published in 1968-1969. While running for president, Richard Nixon appeared on the show September 16, 1968 asking "Sock It To Me?" Verrry interesting!**

LAU-1

LAU-2

❑ **LAU-1. "Laugh-In Magazine" First Issue,**
1968. Laufer Publishing Co. Vol. 1 #1 for October. - **$15 $25 $40**

❑ **LAU-2. "Laugh-In" Gum Pack Box,**
1968. Topps Gum. Box Only - **$30 $60 $125**

LAU-3

LAU-4

LAU-5

LAU-6

❑ **LAU-3. Laugh-In Flicker Ring,**
1968. Store item made by L. M. Becker Co., Appleton, Wisconsin. This and the next 11 rings comprise a set of 12. Images are slogan "Here Comes The Judge" and photo of Pigmeat Markham. - **$12 $20 $40**

❑ **LAU-4. Laugh-In Flicker Ring,**
1968. Images are Henry Gibson as Indian and Priest. - **$12 $20 $40**

❑ **LAU-5. Laugh-In "Beauty/Beast" Flicker Ring,**
1968. Images are Dan Rowan and Ruth Buzzi. - **$12 $20 $40**

❑ **LAU-6. Laugh-In Joke Flicker Ring,**
1968. Text images are "If Minnehaha Married Don Ho/She'd Be Minne Ha Ha Ho." - **$12 $20 $40**

LAU-7

LAU-8

LAU-9

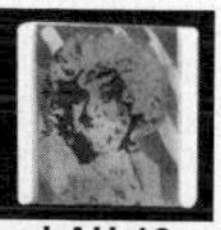
LAU-10

❑ **LAU-7. Laugh-In Phrase Flicker Ring,**
1968. Images are text "Flying Fickle Finger Of Fate Award" to winged hand featuring pointed index finger. - **$12 $20 $40**

❑ **LAU-8. Laugh-In Flicker Ring,**
1968. Alternate image is Dan Rowan and Dick Martin. - **$12 $20 $40**

❑ **LAU-9. Laugh-In Goldie Hawn Flicker Ring,**
1968. Images are close-up of her in black hat and as bikini dancer. - **$12 $20 $40**

❑ **LAU-10. Laugh-In Ruth Buzzi Flicker Ring,**
1968. Images are close-up of her in hair net and another in wig. - **$12 $20 $40**

LAU-11

LAU-12

LAU-13

LAU-14

❑ **LAU-11. Laugh-In "Good Night, Dick" Flicker Ring,**
1968. Images are Dan Rowan to Dick Martin with caption "Who's Dick?" - **$12 $20 $40**

❑ **LAU-12. Laugh-In Judy Carne Flicker Ring,**
1968. Images are "Sock It To Me" text to photo of her in striped sweater. - **$12 $20 $40**

❑ **LAU-13. Laugh-In Joanne Worley Flicker Ring,**
1968. Images are photo of her screaming to another with sad face. - **$12 $20 $40**

❑ **LAU-14. Laugh-In Arte Johnson Flicker Ring,**
1968. Images are "Verry Innteresting" slogan picturing him as German soldier to slogan "But Stupid" picturing him in different style German helmet. - **$12 $20 $40**

LAU-15

❑ **LAU-15. Laugh-In Flicker Rings,**
1968. Vending machine issue. Photo shows 15 from set of 16 by Vari-Vue. Rings show the show stars and classic slogans on psychedelic-colored backgrounds.
Each On Original Base - **$15 $22 $45**
Each On "China" Base - **$6 $12 $20**

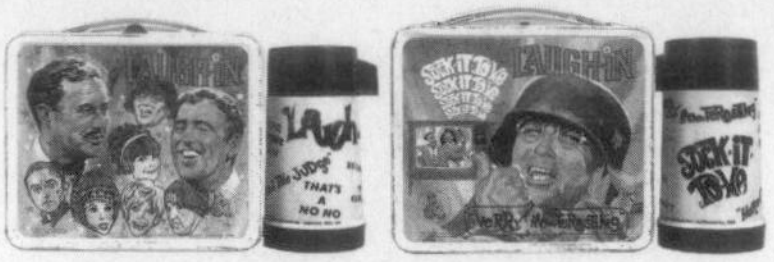
LAU-16

❑ **LAU-16. "Laugh-In" Lunch Box With Thermos,**
1968. Aladdin Industries. Metal embossed box and plastic bottle. Box - **$60 $100 $200**
Bottle - **$25 $50 $75**

LAU-17

LAU-18

❑ **LAU-17. "Laugh-In View-Master" Set,**
1968. - **$10 $20 $40**

❑ **LAU-18. "Laugh-In" Paperdoll Book,**
1969. Saalfield Publishing Co.
Unpunched - **$12 $20 $40**

LAU-19

❑ **LAU-19. Laugh-In "Flying Fickle Finger Of Fate" Award,**
1969. George Schlatter/Friendly Productions And Romart Inc. 6x7" hollow metal award on a 2.25x2-7/8x3" wooden base. Award is of hand with pointing index finger that has wings on the side. This was an actual award given weekly by hosts Dan Rowan and Dick Martin for the dumbest news item of the week on the NBC TV show "Rowan Martin's Laugh-In" that ran from January 1968 through May 1973. Also known as the "Rigid Digit, Winged Weinie, Wonderful Wiggler, Friendly Phalenge, Nifty Knuckle."
- **$300 $600 $1000**

LAU-20

LAU-21

❑ **LAU-20. "Rowan And Martin's Laugh-In" Book,**
1969. Store item by World Publishing Co. Hardcover 160-page assortment of photos, fold-outs, sayings and jokes. - **$10 $20 $40**

❑ **LAU-21. "Laugh-In" 17x26" Fabric Banner,**
1970. Copyright by George Schlatter-Ed Friendly Productions and Romart Inc. -
$20 $35 $70

LAU-22

❑ **LAU-22. "Here Come The Judge" Pendants,**
c. 1970. Store items. Cast metal in silver or gold finish featuring one of the popular humor slogans from the show. Each - **$8 $12 $30**

LAU-23

LAU-24

❑ **LAU-23. "Rowan & Martin Laugh-In" Cello. Button,**
c. 1970. For "Westbury Music Fair" related appearance or event. - **$6 $12 $18**

❑ **LAU-24. Laugh-In Vending Machine Display,**
c. 1970. Paper insert on styrofoam with two plastic rings with Laugh-In slogans, other generic rings and novelties. - **$20 $50 $80**

LAU-25

❑ **LAU-25. Lily Tomlin "Edith Ann For President" Button,**
c. 1972. 2.5" black and white depicting her holding rag doll while seated in giant rocking chair. Unmarked but based on her Laugh-In character portrayal. - **$50 $100 $150**

Laurel and Hardy

Stan Laurel (1890-1965), the British-born thin one, and Oliver Hardy (1892-1957), the pompous fat one, teamed in 1926 to become one of the screen's finest comedy teams. In silent two-reelers, and in feature films between 1929 and 1950, the slapstick misadventures of Laurel, scratching his head, and Hardy, fiddling with his tie, found them in "one fine mess" after another, 106 films in total. Stan Laurel wrote the scripts and sometimes directed the films. Hal Roach Studios musical director Marvin Hatley (1905-1986) wrote the theme song *The Cuckoo Song.* A British comic strip ran in *Film Fun* (1930-1942), and *Laurel and Hardy Comics* appeared in the U.S. from 1949 to 1956 and in 1962-1963. Vintage films were edited and cut for syndication to television in 1948 and ran locally for over three decades. Five-minute animated episodes based on the films, co-produced by Hanna-Barbera and Larry Harmon, were syndicated to television in 1966 with limited success. Merchandising in the 1960s and 1970s was extensive, with the pair used to promote a wide variety of products--toys, dolls, games, coloring books, watches, spray deodorants--and film clips used in television commercials in the 1970s. Items associated with the animated cartoons are usually copyrighted either by the co-producers or by Wolper Productions Inc.

L&H-1

L&H-2

L&H-3

❑ **L&H-1. Laurel & Hardy "Old Gold Cigarettes" 31x42" Cardboard Sign,**
1934. - **$500 $1000 $2000**

❑ **L&H-2. Laurel And Hardy Metal Figures,**
1930s. Store item by Mignot of France, maker of lead soldier toys. Paint and detailing on front and back of each figure standing on small base. Pair - **$30 $60 $85**

❑ **L&H-3. Derby Hats Enameled Metal Pin,**
1930s. English made without markings. - **$20 $40 $75**

L&H-4

L&H-5

❑ **L&H-4. Figural Caricature Ceramic,**
1930s. Store item made in Japan with reverse open compartment for use as pencil holder or planter . - **$45 $90 $165**

❑ **L&H-5. Salt And Pepper Set,**
1930s. China figural pair by Beswick of England. - **$90 $165 $300**

L&H-6

❑ **L&H-6. "Mickey Mouse With The Movie Stars" Gum Card,**
1930s. Gum, Inc. Card #120 from series featuring Mickey and various stars. - **$75 $150 $325**

L&H-7

❑ **L&H-7. Diecut Cardboard Mechanical Figure,**
1930s. 9.25" tall mechanical that raises heads and arms as if tipping their hats. Lower left has Spanish inscription. - **$55 $110 $175**

L&H-8

❑ **L&H-8. Laurel And Hardy "Saps At Sea" Lobby Card,**
1940. Card is 11x14". - **$125 $250 $350**

L&H-9

❑ **L&H-9. "The Big Noise" Movie Poster,**
1944. One sheet poster from the 20th Century Fox Pictures film. - **$325 $775 $1300**

L&H-10

L&H-11

❑ **L&H-10. "Join The Laurel And Hardy Laff Club!" 3-1/2" Button,**
1960s. Larry Harmon's Pictures Corp. - **$15 $25 $55**

❑ **L&H-11. Donuts 9x13" Diecut Cardboard Store Signs,**
1960s. Various users. Depict Laurel and Hardy. Each - **$40 $70 $140**

L&H-12

❑ **L&H-12. Jack In The Box Cardboard, Vinyl And Fabric Toy,**
1960s. Store item by Larry Harmon Pictures Corp. 3-1/2" square by 4" tall with pop-up figure of Laurel. - **$25 $50 $100**

L&H-13

❑ **L&H-13. Ceramic Figural Salt & Pepper Set,**
1960s. 4" tall pair. Japan. - **$40 $75 $150**

L&H-14

L&H-15

❑ **L&H-14. Esco Products Large Statuettes,**
1971. Set of 17" tall painted solid plaster figures colorfully painted. Each - **$35 $55 $125**

❑ **L&H-15. Stan Laurel Figural Bank,**
1972. 13-1/2" tall store item by Play Pal Plastics. - **$15 $30 $50**

L&H-16

❑ **L&H-16. Figure Set By Dakin,**
c. 1974. Store items by R. Dakin Co. Painted hard plastic figures with movable arms, soft vinyl movable heads, fabric jackets. Each is about 8". Each - **$18 $35 $70**

L&H-17

❑ **L&H-17. Pair Of Figural Steins,**
1970s. Each - **$25 $50 $100**

L&H-18

❑ **L&H-18. Bisque Figurine Set,**
1970s. Each is 6-1/2" tall on 2-1/2x3" base. Each - **$12 $25 $40**

L&H-19

❑ **L&H-19. "Laurel & Hardy '25T Roadster" Model,**
1970s. Store item by AMT.
Near Mint Boxed - **$60**
Complete Assembled - **$15 $30 $50**

L&H-20

L&H-21

L&H-22

❑ **L&H-20. Oliver Hardy "TV Pals" Plastic Candy Dispenser,**
1970s. - **$35 $70 $150**

❑ **L&H-21. "Ask Me About My Partner" 2-1/4" Cello. Button,**
c. 1980s. Ziyad Printers. - **$4 $10 $18**

❑ **L&H-22. "Together We're A Team" 2-1/2" Cello. Button,**
c. 1980s. Ziyad Printers. - **$4 $10 $18**

L&H-23

❑ **L&H-23. Keystone Cops Resin Figures,**
1999. Fully painted 6" figures. Limited edition of 5,000 sets based on their 1930's movie "Midnight Patrol." Set - **$125**

Leave It To Beaver

Set in the fictional town of Mayfield, this half-hour family situation comedy aired on CBS from October 4, 1957 to July 16, 1958 and on ABC from October 2, 1958 until September 12, 1963 for a total of 234 episodes. The story line was based on the Cleaver family with emphasis on the adventures and mis-adventures of two brothers. The cast included: Jerry Mathers as Theodore "Beaver" Cleaver, Tony Dow as older brother Wally, Hugh Beaumont (1909-1982) as father Ward, Barbara Billingsley as mother June, Ken Osmond as the smart aleck wise guy friend of Wally, Eddie Haskell, Rusty Stevens as Beaver's friend Larry Mondello and Stephen Talbot as Beaver's friend Gilbert Bates. As the series progressed, Beaver went from the 2nd grade to high school and Wally went from the 8th grade to captain of the high school football team. Joe Connelly and Bob Mosher created the show and wrote many episodes. Hugh Beaumont is credited with writing and directing the final episode titled *The Family Scrapbook.*

CBS aired the reunion movie *Still The Beaver* in 1983 which led to the *New Leave It To Beaver* series which ran on TBS from 1985 to 1989. The 1997 Universal feature film *Leave It To Beaver* starred Cameron Finley as the Beaver, Erik Von Detten as Wally, Christopher McDonald as Ward and Janine Turner as June.

Dell published *Four Color Comic* #912 in June 1958, followed by five more issues in 1962. All have photo covers. "Jeez Beav, you're really gonna get it when Dad gets home!"

LBV-1

❑ **LBV-1. "Leave It To Beaver" Golden Record,**
1958. Gomalco Productions Inc. 6.5x7.5" full color paper sleeve contains 78-rpm record on yellow vinyl featuring show's theme music. - **$15 $30 $60**

LBV-2

❑ **LBV-2. "I'm An Eager Beaver And A U.S. Keds Kid" 3" Cello. Button,**
c. 1958. - **$50 $125 $225**

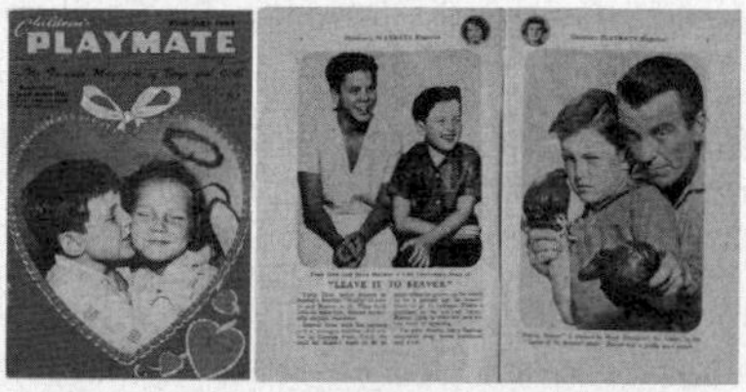

LBV-3

❑ **LBV-3. "Children's Playmate" With Leave It To Beaver,**
1959. 6x9" Volume 30, #9 with 60 pages. Features two-page article on Leave It To Beaver. - **$10 $20 $40**

LBV-4

❑ **LBV-4. "Leave It To Beaver GE Flash Bulbs" Store Display,**
c. 1959. 8.75x9.25x9.75" tall display base with 9.5x16" die-cut display topper featuring Jerry Mathers as Beaver. - **$100 $200 $400**

LBV-5

❑ **LBV-5. "Leave It To Beaver" Buttons,**
1983. Button-Up Co. 1.5" diameter group of 20 buttons from unknown total in set with black and white photos. One button features show title and all others are photos of cast members. Each - **$1 $3 $5**

LBV-6

❑ **LBV-6. "Eddie For President" Spoof Campaign Button,**
1984. Button-Up Co. 1.75" button showing Eddie Haskell from "Leave It To Beaver." - **$8 $15 $30**

Liberace

Walter Valentino Liberace (1919-1987) received a scholarship to the Wisconsin College of Music and debuted at age 14 as a soloist with the Chicago Symphony. By 1940, he was the intermission pianist in the Persian room of New York City's Plaza Hotel. He played a honky-tonk pianist in the 1950 Shelley Winters feature film *South Sea Sinner*. Billing himself as Liberace, his TV show began on NBC on July 1, 1952, was syndicated nationally from 1953 to 1956, then ran on ABC in 1958-1959, earning him two Emmy Awards along the way. Noted for extravagant costumes, a candelabra on the piano and a self-deprecating sense of humor, *Ripley's Believe It Or Not* called him the fastest piano player in the world in 1953 noting that he played 6,000 notes in two minutes. He opened at the Las Vegas Riviera Hotel in 1955 and quickly became the highest paid entertainer in the city's history at $50,000 a week. He sold two million records in 1953 alone and had 160 fan clubs with over a quarter million members. He starred in the 1955 Warner Brothers feature film *Sincerely Yours* with Dorothy Malone.

In 1966, Liberace appeared on the *Batman* TV show playing the dual role of pianist Chandell and his crooked twin brother Harry. In real life, his brother George played the violin and was his business partner. In the mid 1980s, Liberace sold out 56 straight shows at Radio City Music Hall.

The Liberace Museum opened in Las Vegas April 15, 1979 and the Liberace Foundation has awarded over five million dollars in grants to date.

Liberace paved the way for Little Richard, Elton John and other extravagant entertainers.

LIB-1

❑ **LIB-1. "Liberace" Signed Christmas Card,**
1953. 4x4" card and original mailing envelope which has Liberace's Hollywood address ink stamped on reverse flap. Card is marked "A Gibson Card" and inside has bold signature and inscription "Your Christmas Remembrance Was Very Thoughtful. Thank You. Liberace." Liberace also added a small piano drawing. Same Or Similar - **$25 $50 $100**

LIB-2

❑ **LIB-2. "Liberace" Gold Luster Metal Link Charm Bracelet,**
c. 1956. Store item. Miniature framed photo plus charms depicting hands on keyboard, grand piano, candelabra, piano lid. - **$20 $40 $75**

LIB-3

❑ **LIB-3. Liberace Autographed Photo,**
1984. 8x10" glossy photo signed in felt tip pen "To Fannie, Love, Liberace 1984." Same Or Similar - **$50 $100 $150**

Lightning Jim

U.S. Marshal Lightning Jim Whipple was the hero of a Western adventure radio series broadcast on the West Coast beginning in 1939 and syndicated in the 1950s. Meadow Gold dairy products sponsored the program. Membership in Lightning Jim's Special Reserve entitled the young listener to wear the Meadow Gold Round-Up Badge. Whitey Larsen served as Jim's sidekick and deputy.

LGH-1

LGH-2

❑ **LGH-1. "Lightning" Jim Big Little Book #1441,**
1940. 432 pages. Based on the radio show. - **$12 $42 $78**

❑ **LGH-2. Special Reserve Pinback,**
1940. Sponsored by Meadow Gold Dairy. Children would send in their photo which would be paired with Jim's on the pinback. Very rare in high grade. - **$60 $150 $300**

LGH-3

❑ **LGH-3. "Lightning Jim Blackout Kit,"**
1942. Kix Cereal. Includes patch, "Pledge To The Flag" text, headband, four blank sheets of glow fabric, leaflet. **- $125 $300 $600**

LGH-4

❑ **LGH-4. "Meadow Gold Round-Up" Photo,**
1940s. - **$10 $20 $45**

LGH-5

LGH-6

❑ **LGH-5. Membership Card,**
1940s. Scarce. - **$25 $55 $120**

❑ **LGH-6. Membership Brass Badge,**
1940s. Scarce. - **$30 $75 $145**

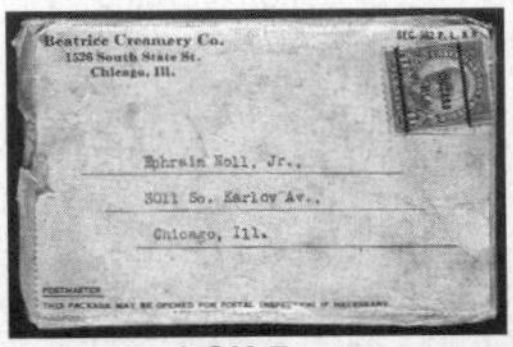

LGH-7

LGH-8

❑ **LGH-7. Mailer,**
1940s. Scarce. - **$10 $20 $50**

❑ **LGH-8. Drinking Glass,**
1940s. Rare. - **$40 $100 $210**

LGH-9

❑ **LGH-9. "Round-Up" Radio Broadcast Ad Paper,**
1940s. Meadow Gold Dairies. 3x5-1/2" imprinted for WMBC Radio, Columbus, Mississippi with text including names of Marshal "Lightning" Jim Whipple and his Deputy Whitey Larsen. - **$15 $25 $55**

LGH-10

LGH-11

❑ **LGH-10. "Lightning Jim Posse" Litho. Tin Tab,**
1950s. Sponsor is NuGrape Soda. Other inscriptions are "Learning-Justice-Power." - **$25 $45 $85**

❑ **LGH-11. Canadian Club Cello. Button,**
c. 1950s. Red image and blue text on white background, 1-1/4". - **$50 $90 $185**

Li'l Abner

Al Capp (1909-1979) created *Li'l Abner* for United Feature as a daily comic strip in 1934 and as a Sunday page in 1935. Capp was an early assistant to artist Ham Fisher on the *Joe Palooka* comic strip where he "ghosted" a hillbilly sequence in 1933 before leaving, leading to a life-long feud with Fisher. Along with the handsome hillbilly from Dogpatch has come a string of unforgettable characters: Daisy Mae, Mammy and Pappy Yokum, Marryin' Sam, Sadie Hawkins, Sir Cecil and Lady Cesspool, Hairless Joe, Lonesome Polecat, Fearless Fosdick, the bountiful Shmoos, the Kigmys, Kickapoo Joy Juice, and many others. Comic books appeared from the 1930s into the 1950s. A *Li'l Abner* radio show on NBC in 1939-1940 featured John Hodiak as Abner; Granville Owen played Abner and Buster Keaton played Lonesome Polecat in a 1940 feature film; a brief run of five animated shorts was released in 1944-1945; a musical comedy ran on Broadway for almost 700 performances in 1956-1957; and a Paramount film was released in 1959. Notable art assistants on the strip included Frank Frazetta from 1954 to 1959 and Creig Flessel in the early 1960s. The marriage of Daisy Mae and Abner in 1952 made front page news, including the cover of *LIFE*. A theme park, Dogpatch USA, operated in Arkansas from 1967 to 1993.

LIL-1

LIL-2

❑ **LIL-1. "Li'l Abner in New York" Big Little Book #1198,**
1936. 432 pages by Al Capp. 1st Abner book. - **$19 $57 $135**

❑ **LIL-2. "Tip Top Comics" 11x14" Store Sign,**
c. 1938. - **$85 $175 $300**

LIL-3

LIL-4

❑ **LIL-3. "Li'l Abner Among The Millionaires" Better Little Book,**
1939. Whitman #1401. - **$19 $57 $135**

❑ **LIL-4. "Buy War Stamps" 14x18" Poster,**
c. 1944. U.S. Government. - **$75 $200 $350**

LIL-5

LIL-6

❑ **LIL-5. Li'l Abner And His Dogpatch Band Wind-Up,**
1946. By Unique Art Mfg. Co. Advertised in 1946 Playthings magazine as the first post-war metal wind-up toy. - **$225 $450 $900**

❑ **LIL-6. Li'l Abner Beanie with Tag,**
1948. Store item. - **$35 $70 $150**

LIL-7

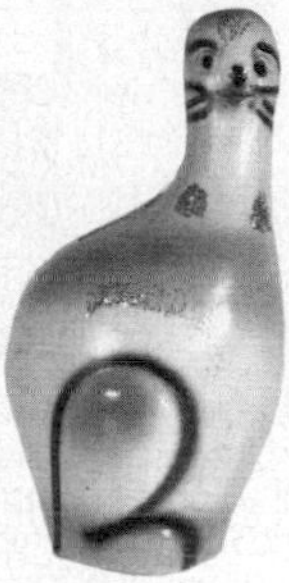

LIL-8

❑ **LIL-7. Shmoo Paddle Ball,**
1948. - **$50 $100 $200**

❑ **LIL-8. Shmoo Carnival Bank,**
1948. Rare. - **$300 $700 $1250**

LIL-9

❑ **LIL-9. "Shmoos Fruit Flavored Hard Candies" Box And Card,**
1948. United Feature Syndicate. 1x2.5x3.5" cardboard box. Comes with 2x3" fortune card.
Box - **$65 $140 $290**
Each Card - **$18 $35 $60**

LIL-10

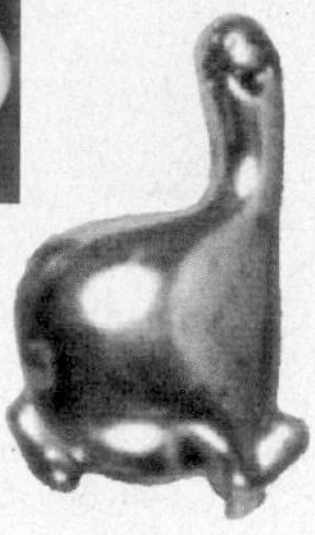

LIL-11

❑ **LIL-10. Shmoo Plastic Wall Clock,**
c. 1948. Store item by Lux Clock Co.
Near Mint Boxed - **$600**
Loose - **$90 $165 $350**

❑ **LIL-11. High Relief Brass Badge,**
c. 1948. - **$20 $35 $60**

(Box) **LIL-12** (Bag)

❑ **LIL-12. "Shmoo" Utility Bag,**
1948-49. Has small printed Shmoos on bag and large Shmoo figure on top of bag.
Box - **$75 $150 $300**
Bag - **$150 $300 $600**

LIL-13

❑ **LIL-13. "I Kicked A Kigmy" Button,**
c. 1948. Black on cream cello. - **$35 $75 $165**

LIL-14

LIL-15

❑ **LIL-14. "Daisy Mae Needs You!" Cello. Button,**
c. 1948. Red, black and white 1-1/2". -
$35 $75 $165

❑ **LIL-15. "Shmoo Club Member" Litho. Button,**
c. 1948. - **$30 $60 $90**

LIL-16

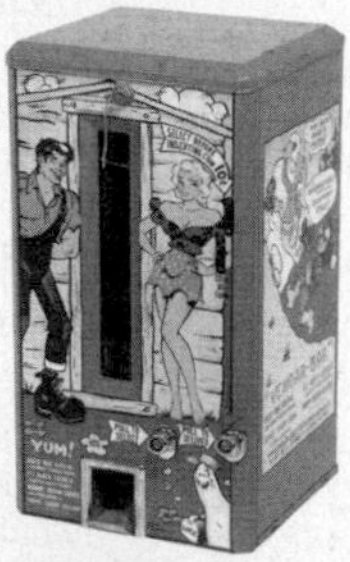

LIL-17

❑ **LIL-16. "Li'l Abner Braces" On Card,**
1949. Full color portrait card holding set of youthful elastic suspenders. - **$40 $75 $150**

❑ **LIL-17. Vending Machine,**
1949. 12-1/2" x 22-1/2" x 11-1/2". -
$325 $675 $1300

LIL-18

LIL-19

❑ **LIL-18. Shmoo Soap in Box,**
1949. In black and white box. Unused. - **$250**

❑ **LIL-19. "Good Luck Shmoo" Coin,**
1949. Li'l Abner on back. - **$50 $100 $150**

LIL-20

❑ **LIL-20. Shmoo Bank on Card,**
1949. Yellow version. Scarce - **$70 $135 $250**
White version - **$35 $70 $125**
Lt. blue and dark blue versions. Scarce -
$60 $125 $185

LIL-21

❑ **LIL-21. Shmoo Pocketbook,**
1949. Children's vinyl pocketbook with strap. Rare. - **$175 $350 $700**

LIL-22

LIL-23

❑ **LIL-22. Shmoos Savings Bond Certificate,**
1949. - **$40 $70 $165**

❑ **LIL-23. Shmoo "Snow Week" Cello. Button,**
1949. University of Minnesota. Rim curl has 1948 copyright. - **$50 $110 $235**

LIL-24

❑ **LIL-24. "Shmoo Tumbler" Boxed Set Of Eight Glasses,**
1949. Fronts show Li'l Abner characters while reverses depict Shmoos in various outfits and activities. Probable dairy product container somehow offered for purchase as boxed full set.
Box - **$50 $100 $200**
Each Glass - **$5 $15 $25**

LIL-25

LIL-26

LIL-27

❑ **LIL-25. Shmoo Club 2-1/4" Litho. Tab,**
1949. Sealtest ice cream. - **$10 $20 $35**

❑ **LIL-26. Shmoo Club 2-1/4" Litho. Tab,**
1949. Sealtest ice cream. - **$10 $20 $35**

❑ **LIL-27. Shmoo Club 2-1/4" Litho. Tab,**
1949. Sealtest ice cream. - **$10 $20 $35**

LIL-28

LIL-29

❑ **LIL-28. Shmoo Club 2-1/4" Litho. Tab,**
1949. Sealtest ice cream. - **$10 $20 $35**

❑ **LIL-29. Shmoo 2" Pinback,**
1949. - **$40 $85 $175**

LIL-30

❑ **LIL-30. "Shmoo" Birthday Card,**
1949. - **$25 $50 $75**

LIL-31

❑ **LIL-31. "Shmoo" Counter Card,**
1949. Advertises magnet set of Shmoos. - **$125 $250 $400**

LIL-32

❑ **LIL-32. Shmoo Figural Plaster Pin,**
c. 1949. - **$45 $100 $165**

LIL-33

❑ **LIL-33. Shmoo Character Litho. Buttons,**
c. 1949. United Feature Syndicate copyrights. Pictured examples from series of about 12 are Captain Kidd, Sailor, Joe. Each - **$10 $18 $30**

LIL-34

❑ **LIL-34. "Shmoo Whistle Pencil Box,"**
c. 1949. Store item by Dixon. 10-3/4" long. - **$60 $145 $275**

LIL-35

❑ **LIL-35. Figural Pencil Sharpener,**
c. 1949. Probable store item. 2-1/8" tall yellow plastic. - **$50 $85 $175**

(Figures inside)

LIL-36

❑ **LIL-36. Pet Shmoo 6 in 1 Figure,**
1940s. Large Shmoo figure contains 5 small Shmoo figures inside. Has plastic food products for "feeding" your Shmoo. On display card. Card and plastic food are both rare.
Shmoo 6 in 1 figure - **$125 $250 $500**
Card with food - **$175 $350 $700**

LIL-37

❑ **LIL-37. Decal Sheet With Envelope,**
1940s. Orange-Crush. - **$12 $25 $55**

LIL-38

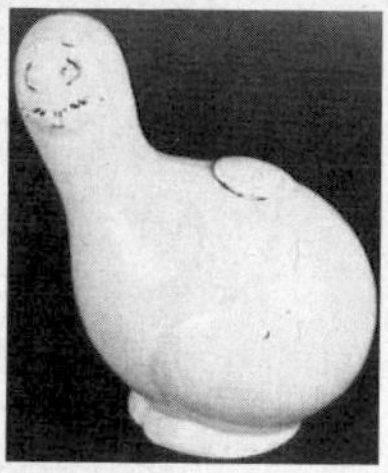

LIL-39

❑ **LIL-38. "Fearless Fosdick" Plaster Figure,**
1940s. 7-1/2" tall hand-painted figure atop base which has his name incised on front and copyright of "UFS" (United Feature Syndicate) on reverse. Figure was apparently sold unpainted.
Near Mint Unpainted - **$525**
Painted - **$125 $250 $450**

❑ **LIL-39. Figural Ceramic Air Freshener Container,**
1940s. 5-1/2" tall pale green with color facial accents. Has rubber cap on back which pulls up to reveal air freshener. - **$55 $85 $175**

LIL-40

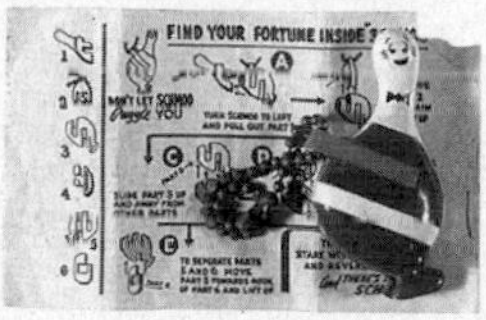

LIL-41

❑ **LIL-40. "Tangle Comics" Cello. Button,**
1940s. Philadelphia Sunday Bulletin. - **$20 $45 $80**

❑ **LIL-41. Shmoo Figure Puzzle,**
1940s. Red, white, and green puzzle with instructions. - **$25 $50 $100**

LIL-42

LIL-43

❑ **LIL-42. Shmoo Ad,**
1940s. - **$5 $10 $20**

❑ **LIL-43. Shmoo Ad,**
1940s. Shows 8 different glasses. - **$5 $10 $20**
Each Glass - **$5 $15 $25**

LIL-44

LIL-45

❑ **LIL-44. Boy Shmoo Bottle,**
1940s. Blue bottle. - **$55 $110 $185**

❑ **LIL-45. Girl Shmoo Bottle,**
1940s. Pink bottle. Rarer than the boy model. - **$80 $135 $225**

LIL-46

❑ **LIL-46. "Al Capp's Sensational Comic Character Kigmy" Boxed Marble Game,**
1950. Store item by Milton Bradley. - **$165 $350 $750**

LIL-47

❑ **LIL-47. "Li'l Abner's Spoof Game" Boxed,**
1950. Milton Bradley store item. Game of 40 cards picturing total of 10 different character designs. - **$75 $150 $300**

LIL-48

LIL-49

❑ **LIL-48. "Shmoo Lucky Rings" 12x13" Cardboard Store Display Sign,**
c. 1950. Store item by Jarco Metal Products.
Empty Card - **$115 $225 $475**
Brass Ring - **$40 $65 $125**

❑ **LIL-49. "Li'l Abner" Cello. Button,**
c. 1950. - **$15 $30 $60**

LIL-50

❑ **LIL-50. "The Shmoo Sings" 78 RPM Record In Picture Sleeve,**
c. 1950. Allegro Junior. In 10x10" paper sleeve illustrated front and back by Shmoos and other Li'l Abner characters. - **$75 $160 $250**

LIL-51

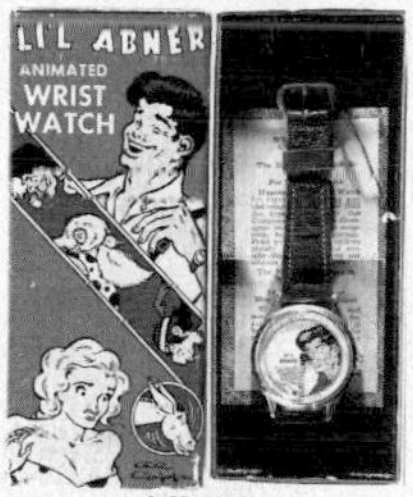

LIL-52

❑ **LIL-51. "Shmoo Girls" Felt Patch,**
c. 1950. 5x8" diecut fabric. - **$30 $65 $125**

❑ **LIL-52. L'il Abner Wrist Watch,**
1951. With flag second hand. In box with instructions. Box - **$200 $300 $600**
Watch - **$100 $225 $450**

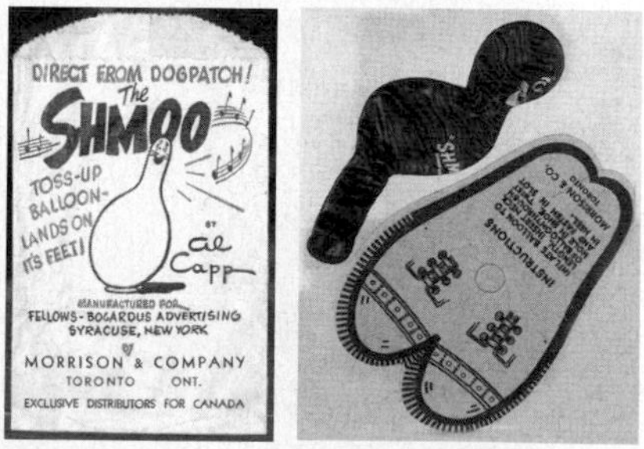

LIL-53

❑ **LIL-53. Shmoo Balloon With Cardboard Shoes and Wrapper,**
1952. Canadian version.
Complete With Wrapper - **$30 $60 $115**

LIL-54

❑ **LIL-54. "Can O Coins" Cylinder Bank,**
1953. 2.5" diameter by 4.75" tall litho tin canister picturing Li'l Abner, Daisy Mae, four other characters. - **$35 $65 $135**

LIL-55

❑ **LIL-55. Metal Store Display Rack,**
1954. Wildroot Cream-Oil. All metal about four feet tall with red, black and white display sign. - **$185 $400 $650**

LIL-56

❑ **LIL-56. "Fearless Fosdick" Product Sticker,**
1954. Wildroot Cream-Oil Hair Dressing. 3x7" probable design for store window display. - **$25 $50 $85**

LIL-57

❑ **LIL-57. "Picture Week" Magazine With Capp Characters Cover Article,**
1955. Weekly issue for December 6 with full color cover art of Daisy Mae and Bald Iggle. - **$10 $20 $45**

LIL-58

❑ **LIL-58. "Namely You" Song Sheet,**
1956. From the theater show. The cast list includes pre-fame Julie Newmar and Tina Louise. - **$12 $25 $40**

LIL-59

LIL-60

❑ **LIL-59. Civil Defense Comic Book,**
1956. Features Civil Defense comic figure created by Al Capp. - **$10 $30 $90**

❑ **LIL-60. Li'l Abner Jointed Vinyl Doll,**
1950s. By Baby Barry. Daisy Mae, Mammy and Pappy Yokum also produced.
Each - **$65 $135 $250**

LIL-61

❑ **LIL-61. Fearless Fosdick 15x36" Standee,**
1950s. Scarce. Wildroot Hair Tonic. Five pieces attached to box. - **$650 $1250 $2000**

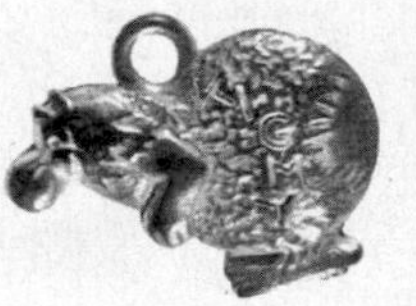

LIL-62

LIL-63

❑ **LIL-62. Kigmy Plastic Charm,**
1950s. Scarce. - **$30 $60 $90**

❑ **LIL-63. Dogpatch Mug,**
1974. Li'l Abner and Daisy Mae pictured. Scarce. - **$50 $100 $150**

(BOX LID)

(PUZZLE IMAGE)

LIL-64

❑ **LIL-64. 100 Piece Jumbo Floor Puzzle,**
1990. Features scene recreated from the 1948 debut of the Shmoos. Hardest of the four different puzzles to find. 17" x 22" puzzle.
Boxed - **$25 $40 $80**

LIL-65

❑ **LIL-65. 100 Piece Jumbo Floor Puzzle,**
1990. 17" x 22" puzzle features "Sadie Hawkins Day" race. Boxed - **$15 $25 $40**

LIL-66

❑ **LIL-66. 100 Piece Jumbo Floor Puzzle,**
1990. 17" x 22" puzzle features L'il Abner and family. Boxed - **$10 $20 $30**

LIL-67

LIL-68

❑ **LIL-67. 100 Piece Jumbo Floor Puzzle,**
1990. 17" x 22" puzzle features L'il Abner and family adn 3 shmoos. Boxed - **$15 $25 $40**

❑ **LIL-68. Shmoo Pin,**
1997. From Kitchen Sink. - **$5**

Little Black Sambo

Written by Helen Bannerman (1892-1946), a Scottish author and illustrator living in India, *Little Black Sambo* was first published in London in 1899. The story line has Sambo losing his clothes to hungry tigers who wind up chasing each other so fast around a tree that they turn into butter. Sambo gets his clothes back, takes the butter home and has a pancake feast with his mother Black Mumbo and father Black Jumbo. Sambo consumes 169 pancakes, certainly breaking any record for pancake eating in a children's Victorian-age book.

The book was not copyrighted and was first published in the U.S. by Frederick A. Stokes in 1900. Oz creator L. Frank Baum wrote the introduction for the 1905 Reilly and Britton edition and many different artists have illustrated the story over the years.

Billy Marriner and Otis Wood created the *Sambo And His Funny Noises* Sunday comic page in 1905 which animation pioneer Pat Sullivan drew between 1912 and 1914. Disney pioneer animators Ub Iwerks and Al Eugster did a Sambo *Comicolor* cartoon for P.A. Powers in 1935. The Sambo's restaurant chain had a motif based on the story with 1,200 sites in 47 states.

Helen Bannerman set the Sambo story in India but the pop culture icon has been controversial due to his racially-stereotyped art image over the years.

LBS-1

❑ **LBS-1. The "Pop-Up Little Black Sambo" Midget Hardcover,**
1934. Blue Ribbon Press. 3-7/8x5" book with 60 black and white pages and one color pop-up. - **$150 $300 $600**

LBS-2

❑ **LBS-2. "Little Black Sambo The Little Color Classics" Book,**
1938. 5.25x6.75" with 60 pages. Inside has 13 color plates. - **$20 $40 $80**

LBS-3

❑ **LBS-3. "If You Like Chocolate Malted Milk Drink Sambo" Tin Sign With Black Bellhop,**
1930s. Senn Products Corp. 13.75x19.5" sign with smiling black bellhop holding tray which has bottle of "Sambo" and glass. Additional text on bottom says "Refreshing/Pure/Nourishing." - **$100 $200 $400**

LBS-4

❑ **LBS-4. "Sambo Target" Wyandott Toys Tin Game,**
1930s. All Metal Products Co. 14x23.5" tin target with easel wire back. Cardboard Sleeve - **$10 $25 $50**
Target - **$35 $65 $125**

LBS-5

❑ **LBS-5. "Camera Chief" Stereoscope Coin-Op Machine,**
1950s. 12.5" long by 8.5" high steel with protruding plastic eyepiece. Penny-operated machine to view three dimensional cards. Titles available included Ringling's Circus Day, Mother Goose, Black Sambo and several others.
Machine - **$50 $100 $200**
Each Film Card - **$5 $10 $20**

The Little King

Cartoonist Otto Soglow (1900-1975) had his first cartoon published in 1919 and worked for numerous publications through the 1920s including *The New York World* and magazines of the day like *LIFE, Judge,* and *Collier's.* His crisp, clean style would lead to the *New Yorker* magazine where the Little King first appeared in 1931. Newspaper mogul William Randolph Hearst saw the character and Soglow got a contract with King Features Syndicate.

The Little King made his Sunday funny page debut September 9, 1934. Sentinel Louie ran as the topper strip and both characters were in pantomime with Soglow utilizing sight gags and slapstick humor. Sentinel Louie was a guard at a palace and the Little King ruled an unnamed monarchy with a childlike sense of fun. Both characters appeared in their own animated cartoons, released by the Van Buren Studio in 1933 and 1934. The Little King also appeared as a co-star in a 1937 Betty Boop cartoon.

Otto Soglow continued contributing gag cartoons to magazines, illustrated several books and did advertising campaign art for clients including Tydol Oil Co., Pepsi and Nabisco Shredded Wheat. The Rum and Maple Tobacco Company produced Little King cigarettes in 1953.

The Little King Sunday page was reprinted in David McKay's *King Comics* from 1936 into the 1940s and he finally spoke in three issues of Four Color Comics in the 1950s.

LKG-1

❑ **LKG-1. "The Little King" Restaurant Ashtray,**
1934. King Features Syndicate. 4.5" wide by 1" deep glass ashtray with black and white art. Text reads "The Little King Where A Sandwich Is A Complete Meal." - **$50 $100 $150**

LKG-2

❑ **LKG-2. Rare Little King Button From Philadelphia,**
1936. 1.25" button issued by West Philadelphia high school graduating "Class of Feb, '46." Area schools had tradition of designing a comic character button for the graduating class. - **$20 $40 $80**

LKG-3

❑ **LKG-3. "The Little King" Boxed Size Variety Jaymar Wood Roller Figures,**
1939. King Features Syndicate.
2.25x2.25x3.75" tall box with Little King figure on all four sides holds 4" tall figure and 1-7/8x1-7/8x3-3/8" tall box holds 3-5/8" tall figure. Figures are painted wood with wheel spool on underside with string wrapped around it which goes through head to be pulled allowing figure to roll. Each Box - **$20 $40 $75**
Each Figure - **$20 $40 $75**

LKG-4

❑ **LKG-4. Little King Glass Tumbler,**
1930s. 3x3.25" tall. - **$40 $85 $165**

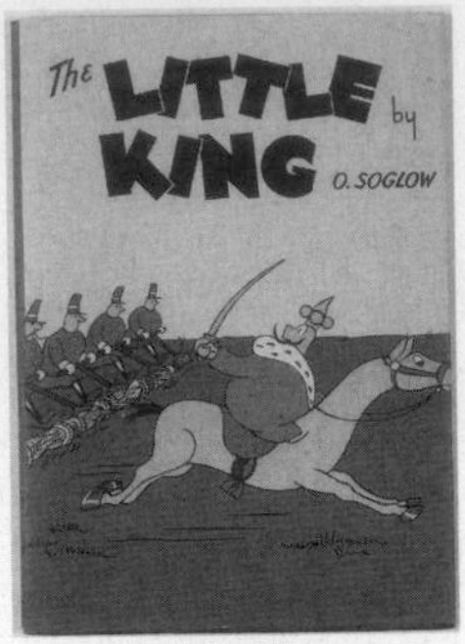

LKG-5

❑ **LKG-5. "The Little King" Storybook With Dust Jacket,**
1945. John Martins House. 7.5x11" hardcover with 32 color pages. Jacket - **$15 $30 $75**
Book - **$15 $30 $75**

LKG-6

❑ **LKG-6. Little King Ramp Walker,**
1963. Marx. 3" tall hard plastic. - **$20 $40 $75**

Little Lulu

Mischievous Little Lulu Moppet, the brainchild of Marjorie Henderson Buell (Marge) (1904-1993), started life as a single-panel cartoon in the *Saturday Evening Post* in 1935. She began her comic book career as a one-shot in 1945 and as a regular series in 1948, scripted by John Stanley and drawn by Irving Tripp. A newspaper strip drawn by Roger Armstrong in the early years ran from 1951 to 1967, and from 1944 to 1960 Lulu was featured in advertising campaigns for Kleenex tissues. She also appeared, along with boyfriend Tubby Tompkins and little Alvin, in an animated cartoon series from Paramount Pictures in 1944-1948. The series was syndicated on television in 1956, and other series were produced in the 1970s. A short-lived animated series with Tracey Ullman as the voice of Little Lulu debuted on HBO in 1995. Friends of Lulu, an organization in Marge's honor, supports comic books for women and female comic book creators.

LUL-1

LUL-2

❑ **LUL-1. "Little Lulu on Parade" Book,**
1941. Hardback book shows Marge art printed from "Saturday Evening Post" cartoons. - **$40 $85 $175**

❑ **LUL-2. "Little Lulu" Sheet Music,**
1943. 9x12" naming her "Featured In Paramount's Little Lulu Cartoons Produced By Famous Studios." - **$35 $80 $160**

LUL-3

LUL-4

❑ **LUL-3. Original Color Art,**
1944. Used for "Saturday Evening Post". - **$1500**

❑ **LUL-4. "Little Lulu" Vinyl Doll By Earle Pullan,**
1944. Doll is 14" tall. Original outfit with 2x3" tag. "Little Lulu Made In Canada By Earle Pullan Co. Ltd. Toronto/Exclusive Licensed Manufacturers."
Doll - **$125 $300 $600**
Tag - **$25 $50 $100**

LUL-5

❑ **LUL-5. "Marge's Little Lulu Adventure Game,"**
1945. Milton Bradley. 10x16x1.75" deep box. Comes with 16 round, flat playing pieces on original punch-out boards, game cards, dice, four wooden playing pieces. - **$65 $125 $225**

LUL-6

❑ **LUL-6. "Little Lulu, Alvin And Tubby" Better Little Book,**
1947. Whitman #1429. - **$28 $84 $195**

LUL-7

❑ **LUL-7. "Little Lulu" Scarf,**
1948. Scarf is 23.5x23.5" with bright illustrations of Lulu with name on all four margins. Notation in corner is printed "Marge/Copr. 1948, Marjory H. Buell." - **$50 $85 $160**

LUL-8

❑ **LUL-8. Crayons Set Boxed,**
1948. Milton Bradley. Boxed full set of eight crayons, each in paper wrapper picturing Lulu, Tubby and dog. - **$20 $45 $90**

LUL-9

LUL-10

❑ **LUL-9. Stuffed Doll,**
1940s. Store item with label reading "Handmade By Hazel." 17" tall with yarn hair.
- **$125 $300 $600**

❑ **LUL-10. "Little Lulu's Hard Candies" Box,**
c. 1940s. 1.75" cardboard square printed in four colors plus Buell copyright. - **$30 $50 $100**

LUL-11

❑ **LUL-11. "Little Lulu/Baldy" Glass,**
1951. Dairy product container from set of six. - **$25 $50 $85**

LUL-12

LUL-13

❑ **LUL-12. "Tubby Tom And Flipper" Glass,**
1951. Dairy product container, from set of six. - **$25 $50 $85**

❑ **LUL-13. Annie And Mops Glass,**
1951. Dairy product container, from set of six. - **$25 $50 $85**

LUL-14

LUL-15

❑ **LUL-14. Wilbur Van Snobbe and Nick Glass,**
1951. Dairy product container from set of six. - **$25 $50 $85**

❑ **LUL-15. Gloria And Tipper Glass,**
1951. Dairy product container from set of six.- **$25 $50 $85**

LUL-16

❑ **LUL-16. Paint Book,**
1951. Kleenex. - **$25 $50 $100**

LUL-17 LUL-18

❑ **LUL-17. Little Lulu Mask,**
1952. Kleenex. - **$25 $45 $70**

❑ **LUL-18. Tubby Mask,**
1952. Kleenex. - **$30 $60 $85**

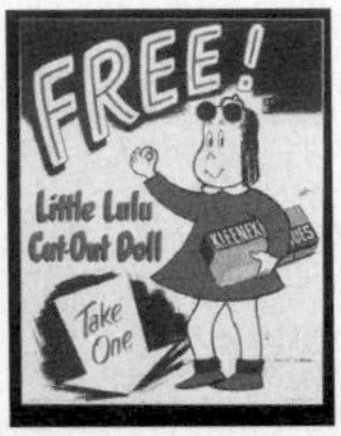

LUL-19 LUL-20

❑ **LUL-19. Kleenex Cut-Out Doll 11x14" Cardboard Store Sign,**
1952. - **$45 $90 $150**

❑ **LUL-20. March of Comics Booklet,**
1964. Various retail stores. - **$10 $30 $95**

LUL-21 LUL-22

❑ **LUL-21. Little Lulu Ceramic Figurine,**
1974. Western Publishing copyright on back of figure. - **$25 $75 $150**

❑ **LUL-22. Tubby Ceramic Figurine,**
1974. Western Publishing copyright on back of figure. - **$25 $75 $150**

LUL-23

❑ **LUL-23. Little Lulu Comic Cover Recreation Art by John Stanley,**
1977-1989. Painting shown is 15 1/2" x 12 1/2". Stanley painted approximately 15 covers during the period of 1977-1989. Years later he was offered high prices to do more paintings for other collections, but he declined. His paintings have brought $5,000 - $10,000 in recent years. However, they are in collections now and none are for sale as of the publication of this book.

LUL-25

LUL-24

❑ **LUL-24. Promo Glass,**
1982. 6-1/2" tall issued by Kleenex. - **$15 $25 $50**

❑ **LUL-25. Little Lulu Rubber Bank,**
1990s. - **$5 $15 $40**

LUL-26

❑ **LUL-26. Little Lulu Toon Tumbler,**
2005. PopFun Merchandising. Two versions. Glass tumblers with logos for Pepsi and the Baltimore Comic-Con.
Clear glass, edition of 450. - **$30**
Frosted glass, edition of 175. - **$75**

Little Nemo

Winsor McCay (1869-1934), widely considered the greatest of the comic strip artists, created his masterpiece, *Little Nemo in Slumberland,* out of dreams and visions, exploring the unconscious with grace and fairy-tale beauty through the dazzling nocturnal voyages of his little hero. The cast included: Flip, The Princess, King Morpheus, Dr. Pill and The Imp.The strip ran in the *New York Herald* from 1905 to 1911 and from 1924 to 1927. From 1911 to 1914 the adventures appeared as *The Land of Wonderful Dreams* in the Hearst newspapers. A musical with a score by Victor Herbert was produced in 1908, and in 1911 McCay started a parallel career in film cartoons with the release of a hand-colored version of *Nemo.* Scattered reprints of the strips were published from 1905 to 2005.

LNE-1

LNE-2

❑ **LNE-1. "Little Nemo" Bicycle Nameplate,**
c. 1905. Bicycle maker is Baker, Murray & Imbrie Inc., N.Y. 2x2-1/2" aluminum with accents in black, silver and orange. -
$60 $125 $200

❑ **LNE-2. "Little Nemo A Fairy Tale" Sheet Music,**
1906. Store item by Graul Publishing Company, Detroit, Mich. 10-1/4x13-1/4" mostly in blue and white with red accent. Covers hold a loose center sheet. - **$35 $75 $150**

LNE-3

❑ **LNE-3. "Little Nemo In Slumberland" First Comic Strip Reprint Book,**
1906. Store item by Duffield & Co. 11x16" with 58 pages of Winsor McCay strips printed one side to a page. Good - **$1200** Fine - **$4500**

LNE-4

❑ **LNE-4. Little Nemo Postcard,**
1906. New York Herald Co. published by Tuck. From numbered set of about 12. Scarce. Each - **$15 $25 $60**

LNE-5

❑ **LNE-5. "Little Nemo And His Bear" Sheet Music With Mention Of Wizard Of Oz,**
1907. Published by Jerome Remick & Co. Subtitled "Successfully Interpolated In The Wizard Of Oz." Cover also says "After Winsor McCay" with artist name appearing to be "Detakacs." **- $35 $75 $175**

LNE-6

❑ **LNE-6. "Wake Up Little Nemo" Game,**
1908. Milton Bradley. 9x9x.75" deep box. Box bottom is colorful and graphic gameboard with directions. Image includes Nemo, Flip and Imp. In-house Milton Bradley art, not by Winsor McKay. Comes with 2x3" spinner.
- $200 $400 $750

LNE-7

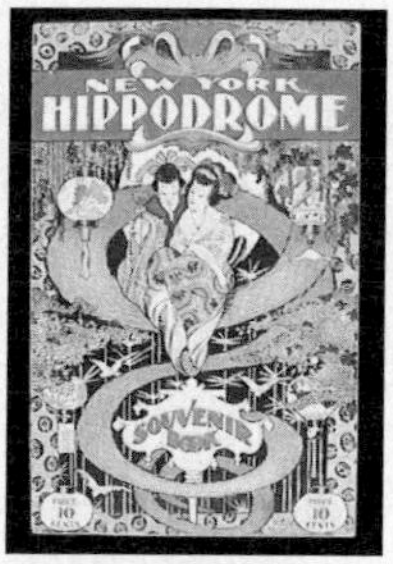

LNE-8

❑ **LNE-7. "Won't You Be My Playmate" Sheet Music,**
1908. New York Herald Co. Words and music for song by Victor Herbert from "Little Nemo" stage play. From series of various song titles. Each **- $40 $95 $200**

❑ **LNE-8. "New York Hippodrome Souvenir Book",**
1909. Unrelated to Little Nemo but 8x12" booklet has ornate color cover with art by Winsor McCay. Theatrical play was titled "A Trip To Japan." **- $75 $135 $200**

LNE-9

❑ **LNE-9. Dr. Pill Figural Bisque Toothbrush Holder,**
c. 1910. Store item. 5-1/4" tall holding bag with his name incised in his right hand while left hand rests atop hollow compartment for toothbrush. Made in Germany with #8317 on reverse. -
$750 $1750 $3500

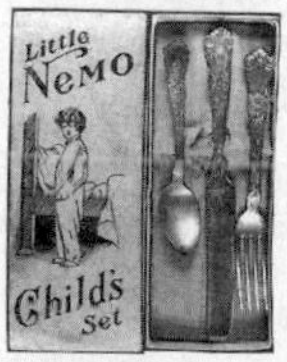

LNE-10

LNE-11

❑ **LNE-10. "Little Nemo Child's Set" Boxed Place Setting,**
c. 1910. Silver plate metal knife, fork and spoon with matching generic handle design. Box art is not attributed to Nemo creator Winsor McCay. Boxed **- $75 $175 $350**

❑ **LNE-11. "Little Nemo" Brass Clothing Buttons,**
c. 1910. 1/2" diameter with profile bust relief image of him. Each **- $15 $25 $50**

LNE-12

LNE-13

❑ **LNE-12. Flip Of Little Nemo Bobbing Head Figure,**
c. 1910. 6-1/2" tall painted composition with spring-mounted head on wooden rod neck. -
$135 $275 $675

❑ **LNE-13. Bell Ringer Metal Toy,**
c. 1910. Pull or push toy on turning wheels causing ringing of bell chimes by figures of Nemo and Flip. **- $450 $1000 $2000**

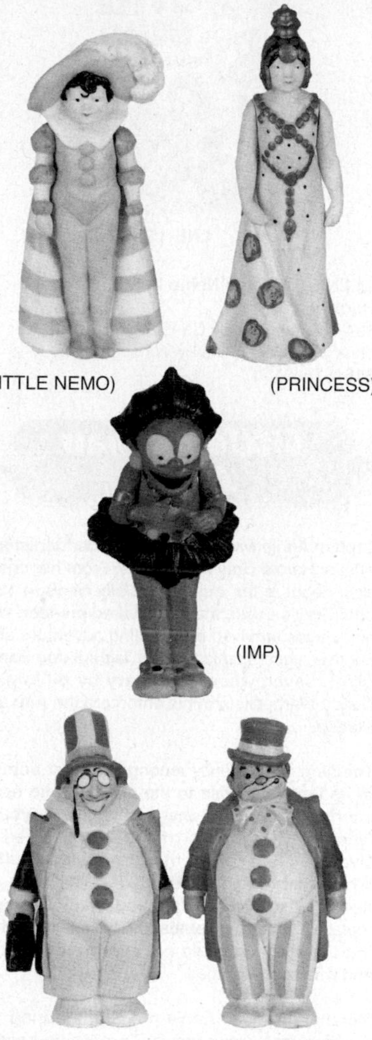

(LITTLE NEMO) (PRINCESS)

(IMP)

(DR. PILL) (FLIP)

LNE-14

❑ **LNE-14. "Little Nemo" Bisque Figure Set,**
1914. Complete set of 5 bisque figurines with movable arms made in Germany and distributed by Strobel and Wilken Co. of New York and Chicago. Featured in "Playthings" trade publication in May 1914. In the set: Little Nemo (4-7/8"), Princess (5.25"), Flip (4.5"), Doctor Pill (4-5/8") and Imp (5"). Flip shown has tiny shallow indent at mouth that at one time held a small cigar. These are the rarest character bisques.
Little Nemo **- $1750 $3000 $5000**
Princess **- $2000 $4000 $6000**
Imp **- $1500 $2500 $4000**
Dr. Pill **- $1500 $2500 $4000**
Flip **- $1500 $2500 $4000**

LNE-15

❑ **LNE-15. "Little Nemo In Slumberland" Book,**
1941. Rand McNally Co. 5.5x6.75" stiff cover book with illustrations by Winsor McCay. -
$35 $75 $150

Little Orphan Annie

Orphan Annie was the life work of cartoonist/storyteller Harold Gray (1894-1968). From her comic strip debut in the *New York Daily News* in 1924 until Gray's death, the curly-haired pre-teen with blank eyes survived one thrilling adventure after another, accompanied by her faithful dog Sandy (Arf!), saved when necessary by billionaire Daddy Warbucks and his enforcers the Asp and Punjab.

The strip, consistently among the most popular of its time, gave rise to the classic radio serial starring Shirley Bell that captivated its young fans on NBC from 1931 to 1942, sponsored by Ovaltine (1931-1940), then by Quaker Puffed Wheat and Rice Sparkies (1941-1942). With the new sponsor, Annie's pal Joe Corntassel was replaced by heroic combat pilot Captain Sparks, but the program could not survive the change and was soon dropped.

Merchandising of Annie premiums during the Ovaltine years was extensive, producing a seemingly endless stream of mugs, masks, decoders, games, books, pins, dolls, toys, dishes, rings, photos, whistles, and membership gear for *Radio Orphan Annie's Secret Society*. Premiums during the Puffed Wheat years included membership in the Secret Guard and the Safety Guard, along with aviation-related items.

A string of artists and writers continued the Annie comic strip after Gray's death, most notably Leonard Starr who did the strip from 1979 until 2000. Comic books, hardcover reprints of the newspaper strips, and giveaway books proliferated from 1926 through the 1940s.

Movies added to the legend: the 1932 *Little Orphan Annie* from RKO starring Mitzi Green, the 1938 Paramount film starring Ann Gillis and the 1982 *Annie* from Columbia Pictures starring Andrea McArdle, the latter based on the successful 1977 Broadway musical.

LAN-1

❑ **LAN-1. "Little Orphan Annie" Sheet Music,**
1925. Wyrick Music Publishers. Folder of words and music with front cover full color character picture plus inset bluetone photo of Harold Gray. -
$75 $160 $350

LAN-2

LAN-3

❑ **LAN-2. "Little Orphan Annie/Her Story By Harold Gray" Convention Booklet,**
1927. Chicago Tribune Newspaper Syndicate. 32 pages of "Her Adventures To Date" given away at convention of American Newspapers Publishers Association. - **$125 $275 $550**

❑ **LAN-3. "Some Swell Sweater" Cello. Button,**
1928. Given with sweater purchase. -
$25 $50 $100

LAN-4

❑ **LAN-4. "Little Orphan Annie" Storybook,**
1928. 4x5-1/2" paperback with 48 pages. Published by Whitman. **- $36 $108 $250**

LAN-5

LAN-6

❑ **LAN-5. Song Sheet Giveaway,**
1928. Scarce. Chicago Tribune. -
$55 $110 $225

❑ **LAN-6. "Some Swell Sweater" Cello. Button,**
1928. Given with sweater purchase. -
$35 $85 $175

LAN-7

LAN-8

❑ **LAN-7. Pictorial Plaque,**
c. 1928. Early store item. 7.25x9.5" painted plaster scene formed in stages of raised relief and depicting Annie, her doll Emily Marie, Sandy, two squirrels. Made in Japan. -
$100 $250 $500

❑ **LAN-8. Little Orphan Annie Early Rare Button,**
c. 1928. Button is 1-3/8" striking silver on dark metallic blue litho by Geraghty, Chicago. Possibly the earliest as well as rarest Annie button. - **$650 $1300 $2750**

LAN-9

❑ **LAN-9. "Little Orphan Annie Game,"**
c. 1930. Store item by Milton Bradley. -
$50 $125 $275

LAN-10

❑ **LAN-10. "Little Orphan Annie" Jumping Rope Toy,**
1931. Marx. 1.5x3.25x5.25" tall tin windup with removable key. Back of shoe reads "Harold Gray." Box - **$150 $300 $600**
Toy - **$300 $600 $1000**

LAN-11

LAN-12

❑ **LAN-11. "Little Orphan Annie Candy Bar" Ad,**
1931. Monthly issue for September of "The Northwestern Confectioner" trade magazine for candy makers and retailers with cover art introducing new candy bar by Shotwell Mfg. Co., Chicago. - **$60 $110 $225**

❑ **LAN-12. "Little Orphan Annie" Candy Bar Wrapper,**
1931. Waxed paper cover for product of Shotwell Mfg. Co. also offering Orphan Annie doll and coloring book as mail premiums. - **$75 $175 $350**

LAN-13

❑ **LAN-13. "Mitzie Green's Art Needlework Outfit" Set,**
1931. Store item by Standard Solophone Mfg. Co. She is titled "Paramount's Child Star, Appearing In Tom Sawyer And Skippy." A year later she starred in the Little Orphan Annie movie. Box is 13-1/2x18" holding fabrics, needles, snaps, scissors, thimble, embroidery hoops and a 7" tall jointed bisque doll. - **$100 $200 $400**

LAN-14

❑ **LAN-14. "Little Orphan Annie's Song" Sheet Music,**
1931. Probably 1st Ovaltine Annie premium.
Near Mint in Mailer - **$125**
Music Only - **$15 $25 $60**

(CLOSE-UP OF BUTTON ART)

LAN-15

❑ **LAN-15. Annie & Joe "Voters Button" Sheet,**
1931. 10.25x16.75" one-sided glossy paper for voting contest between preference for each character's Ovaltine recipe. Entrants were sent picture button reflecting character chosen and each button is pictured beside voting coupon to be clipped. Coupon Clipped - **$100 $250 $400**
Complete - **$200 $500 $800**

LAN-16 LAN-17

❑ **LAN-16. "Orphan Annie" Cello. Button,**
1931. Scarce. Known as Voter's Button issued as companion pair with Joe Corntassel version, awarded respectively for vote preferring Ovaltine with ice or Ovaltine with ice cream. - **$150 $250 $500**

❑ **LAN-17. "Joe Corntassel" Cello. Button,**
1931. Known as Voter's Button with companion Orphan Annie button issued respectively for voters preferring Ovaltine with ice cream or simply ice. - **$100 $200 $400**

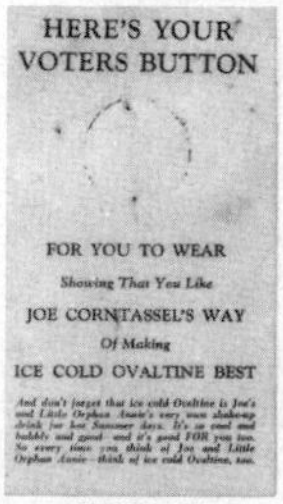

LAN-18 LAN-19

❑ **LAN-18. Joe Corntassel "Voters Button" Card,**
1931. Also issued for Annie.
Each - **$75 $150 $300**

❑ **LAN-19. Beetleware Shake-Up Mug,**
1931. - **$30 $60 $135**

LAN-20

❑ **LAN-20. "Shake-Up Game" Instruction Folder,**
1931. Came with Shake-Up mug. - **$30 $60 $100**

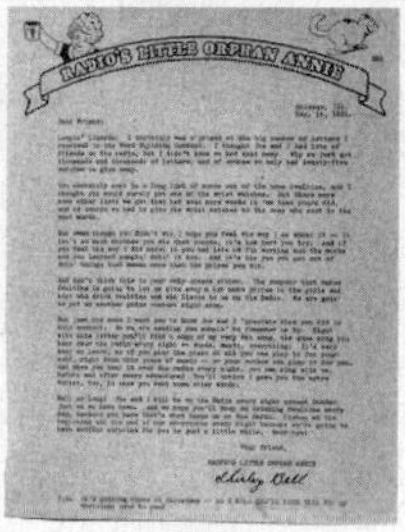

LAN-21

❑ **LAN-21. "Word Building Contest" Acknowledgement Letter,**
1931. Response to entrant in contest to see how many different words can be made from single word Ovaltine plus Christmas greeting from Shirley Bell, ROA portrayer. Dated Dec. 14, 1931. "P.S." reads "It's getting close to Christmas -- so I hope you'll take this as my Christmas card to you!" - **$35 $65 $125**

LAN-22

❑ **LAN-22. RKO Film Promo,**
1932. Scarce. 4-page promo with Mitzi Green. - **$85 $175 $300**

LAN-23 LAN-24

❑ **LAN-23 Ceramic Mug,**
1932. - **$25 $45 $90**

❑ **LAN-24 "Mitzi Green As Little Orphan Annie" Movie Photo,**
1932. Imprinted for local theaters. -
$25 $60 $115

LAN-25

❑ **LAN-25. Sun Picture Negative And Envelope,**
1932. RKO Radio Pictures probable giveaway. 2-1/4x3-1/4" with scenes from movie starring Mitzi Green. - **$12 $25 $60**

LAN-26

LAN-27

❑ **LAN-26 "Shirley Bell" Radio Show Photo,**
1932. Pictured is Radio Orphan Annie portrayer. -
$20 $50 $85

❑ **LAN-27. "Joe Corntassel/Allan Baruck" Radio Show Photo,**
1932. - **$15 $40 $75**

LAN-28

❑ **LAN-28. "Little Orphan Annie" Figure,**
c. 1932. Figure is 1.25x1.5" at bottom by 7.5" tall. Printed paper belt reads "Little Orphan Annie" on front and back reads "Harold Gray." Molded into back and on paper label on foot reads "Made In Japan." - **$90 $185 $350**

LAN-29

❑ **LAN-29. "Tucker County Fair" Jigsaw Puzzle With Mailer Box,**
1933. Near Mint In Mailer - **$165**
Loose - **$30 $60 $100**

LAN-30

LAN-31

❑ **LAN-30. Paper Face Mask,**
1933. - **$30 $70 $125**

❑ **LAN-31. Beetleware Plastic Cup,**
1933. - **$20 $35 $70**

LAN-32

❑ **LAN-32. "Treasure Hunt" Game With Paper Boats,**
1933. Includes cut-out card with four sailboats. Brown & yellow cover variations.
Set - **$60 $125 $250**
Board Only - **$20 $30 $75**
Mailer Only - **$20 $40 $60**

LAN-33

❑ **LAN-33. Ovaltine Cup Rare Color Variety,**
1933. Decal is identical to the standard 1933 issue but the Beetleware material is bright orange rather than standard cream color. Perhaps used briefly when supply of standard cups was temporarily exhausted. -
$225 $450 $900

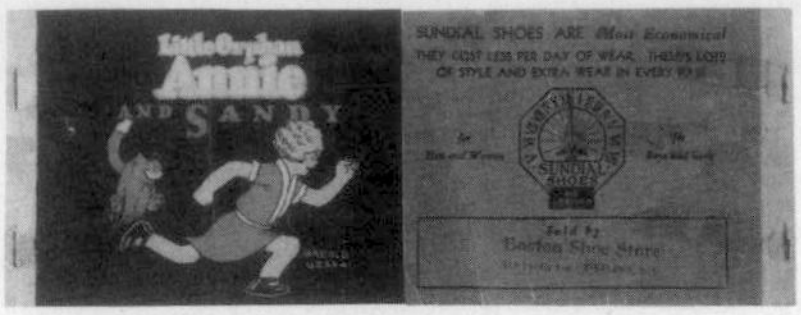

LAN-34

❑ **LAN-34. "Little Orphan Annie And Sandy" Booklet,**
1933. Sundial Shoes. 4x5.5" horizontal format Whitman book with 48 pages. Each left page is story text and each facing page is additional text plus story art. - **$36 $108 $250**

LAN-35

❑ **LAN-35. "Little Orphan Annie Embroidery Set,"**
c. 1933. Store item by J. Pressman Company. -
$100 $225 $375

LAN-36

❑ **LAN-36. Biscuit Box,**
c. 1933. Store item by Loose Wiles Biscuit Co. -
$150 $300 $500

LAN-37

LAN-38

❑ **LAN-37. Little Orphan Annie And Sandy Toothbrush Holder,**
c. 1933. Store item. Japan painted hollow bisque marked "S1565." - **$40 $85 $175**

❑ **LAN-38. "Little Orphan Annie Hair Brush,"**
c. 1933. Store item. - **$70 $150 $250**

LAN-39

LAN-40

❑ **LAN-39. "Secret Society" Manual,**
1934. - **$25 $50 $100**

❑ **LAN-40. Secret Society Bronze Badge,**
1934. - **$10 $15 $25**

LAN-41

❑ **LAN-41. Adventure Books & Contest Winner Sheet,**
1934. One side lists winners of "Shake-Up Naming Contest". - **$20 $45 $75**

LAN-42

❑ **LAN-42. Bandanna Ring Slide Offer Sheet,**
1934. "Face" ring also used as bandanna holder. - **$25 $50 $95**

LAN-43

LAN-44

❑ **LAN-43. "Flying W" Bandanna,**
1934. - **$30 $70 $135**

❑ **LAN-44. "Flying W" Bandanna Explanation Card,**
1934. Explains the 26 brands pictured on bandanna. - **$30 $60 $120**

LAN-45

LAN-46

❑ **LAN-45. Annie Portrait Ring and Bandanna Slide,**
1934. Ring - **$15 $30 $75**
"Secret Seals" Instruction Folder - **$100 $200 $300**

❑ **LAN-46. "Identification Bureau" Bracelet With Mailer Envelope,**
1934. Silver finish, personalized with initial.
Near Mint In Mailer - **$200**
Bracelet Only - **$20 $50 $75**

LAN-47

LAN-48

❑ **LAN-47. Silver Star Club Badge,**
1934. Silvered brass. - **$15 $30 $50**

❑ **LAN-48. "Silver Star Member" Manual,**
1934. Near Mint In Mailer - **$135**
Loose - **$30 $60 $90**

LAN-49

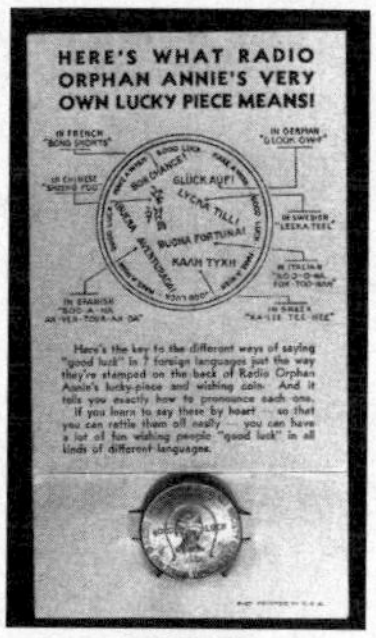

LAN-50

❑ **LAN-49. "Good Luck" Brass Medal,**
1934. Includes "Ovaltine 3 Times A Day" with back "Good Luck" in several languages. - **$10 $20 $40**

❑ **LAN-50. Pronunciation Card For "Good Luck" Medal,**
1934. Offers correct phonetic pronunciation for each of the seven foreign language "Good Luck" inscriptions on medal reverse.
Slotted to hold medal. - **$25 $55 $115**

LAN-51

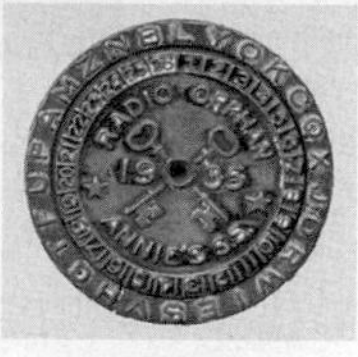

LAN-52

❑ **LAN-51. Club Manual,**
1935. - **$30 $65 $125**

❑ **LAN-52. Brass Decoder,**
1935. Silver flashing often worn off outer rim. - **$15 $30 $100**

LAN-53

❑ **LAN-53. Premium Catalogue Folder With Envelope,**
1935. Opens to 4x22" with May 15 expiration date, envelope has NRA symbol of Depression era.
Near Mint In Mailer - **$450**
Folder - **$85 $175 $350**

LAN-54

❑ **LAN-54. Annie Lucky Chip With Mailer,**
1935. Newspaper premium.
Chip - **$20 $40 $75**
Mailer - **$20 $40 $75**

LAN-55

❑ **LAN-55. Magic Transfers and Instruction Sheet,**
1935 Scarce. - **$30 $80 $165**

LAN-56

LAN-57

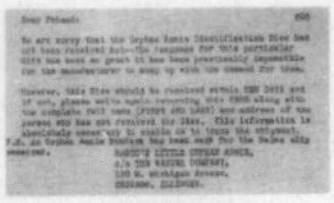

LAN-58

❑ **LAN-56. Beetleware Cup,**
1935. Green circle background. - **$20 $45 $90**

❑ **LAN-57. Beetleware Plastic Shake-Up Mug,**
1935. Orange lid. Shows Annie from waist up. - **$25 $60 $125**

❑ **LAN-58. Ovaltine Apology Postcard,**
1935. Form message for delay in shipment of Orphan Annie Identification Disk postmarked January 5. - **$25 $60 $90**

LAN-59

LAN-60

❑ **LAN-59. "Little Orphan Annie and the Ghost Gang" Big Little Book #1154,**
1935. - **$18 $54 $125**

❑ **LAN-60. "Little Orphan Annie and Punjab the Wizard" Big Little Book #1162,**
1935. - **$18 $54 $125**

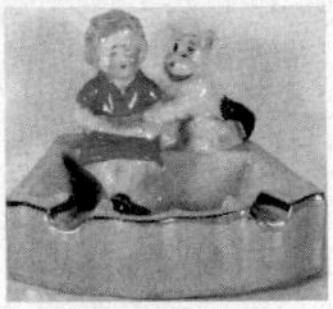

LAN-61

❑ **LAN-61. Little Orphan Annie with Sandy Ashtray,**
Mid 1930s. One in a series of comic character ashtrays produced in Japan in the mid 1930s. - **$45 $90 $225**

LAN-62

LAN-63

❑ **LAN-62. Club Manual,**
1936. - **$20 $45 $95**

❑ **LAN-63. Secret Compartment Brass Decoder,**
1936. - **$12 $25 $65**

LAN-64

LAN-65

❑ **LAN-64. Dog-Naming Contest Notice,**
1936. Thank you notice for entering contest to name Bob Bond's new dog. - **$15 $30 $65**

❑ **LAN-65. "Book About Dogs",**
1936. Contents include Annie characters in various activities plus photo descriptions of various dog breeds. - **$18 $35 $75**

LAN-66

❑ **LAN-66. "Silver Star Member" Secrets Ring with Folder,**
1936. Ring has silvered brass design of crossed keys over star. Folder shows ring on cover.
Ring- **$60 $125 $200**
Folder - **$35 $70 $125**

LAN-67

❑ **LAN-67. "Birthday Ring" With Folder And Envelope,**
1936. Birthstones in various colors. Offer appeared October, 1935.
Near Mint In Mailer - **$625**
Ring - **$115 $250 $500**
Folder - **$30 $50 $75**

LAN-68

❑ **LAN-68. "Welcome To Simmons Corners" 19x24" Paper Map,**
1936. - **$35 $75 $150**

LAN-69

❑ **LAN-69. "Little Orphan Annie And The Big Town Gunmen" Comic Strip Reprint Book,**
1936. Published by Whitman. 5-1/2x7-1/2" format. - **$14 $42 $95**

LAN-70

LAN-71

❑ **LAN-70. "Little Orphan Annie Circus" Punch-Out Book,**
1936. Six pages including more than 30 punch-outs. Unpunched - **$165 $325 $650**

❑ **LAN-71. Glassips Package In Mailer,**
1936. Rare. Contents are cellophane drinking straws. - **$100 $300 $600**

LAN-72

❑ **LAN-72. Club Manual with Mailer and Silver Star Ring Order Form,**
1937. Manual - **$25 $45 $90**
Other Items each - **$8 $12 $25**

LAN-73

❑ **LAN-73. Sunburst Brass Decoder Badge,**
1937. - **$15 $30 $85**

LAN-74

❑ **LAN-74. "Big Little Kit" With Crayons,**
1937. Store item. Box holds 192 paper sheets. -
$150 $300 $625

LAN-75

LAN-76

❑ **LAN-75. Silver Star Member Secret Message Ring,**
1937. Silvered brass with coded message to be decoded by that year's decoder. -
$60 $125 $250

❑ **LAN-76. Rummy Cards,**
1937. - In a colorful box. - **$35 $85 $190**

LAN-77

❑ **LAN-77. Two Initial Signet Brass Ring,**
1937. Ring was customized with recipient's initials. Ring - **$15 $30 $75**
Instruction Sheet - **$65 $150 $300**

LAN-78

❑ **LAN-78. "Talking Stationery",**
1937. Diecut paper mouths open and close, came with 12 letter sheets and envelopes.
Folder Only - **$60 $125 $200**
Each Sheet With Envelope - **$5 $10 $20**

LAN-79

❑ **LAN-79. "Silver Star Members" Ring Folder,**
1937. Opens to three panels printed both sides. Folder - **$60 $125 $200**
Mailer - **$10 $20 $30**

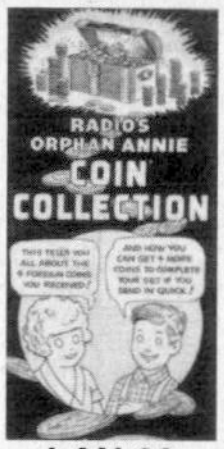

LAN-80 LAN-81

❑ **LAN-80. Foreign "Coin Collection" Folder,**
1937. - **$20 $45 $85**

❑ **LAN-81. Club Manual,**
1938. - **$25 $60 $120**

LAN-82 LAN-83

❑ **LAN-82. "Little Orphan Annie Saves Sandy" Penny Book,**
1938. Published by Whitman. - **$10 $30 $62**

❑ **LAN-83. "Little Orphan Annie Gets Into Trouble" Booklet,**
1938. J. C. Penney Co. - **$10 $30 $62**

LAN-84

LAN-85

❑ **LAN-84. Telematic Brass Decoder Badge,**
1938. - **$25 $60 $120**

❑ **LAN-85. Silver Star Manual,**
1938. - **$90 $200 $425**

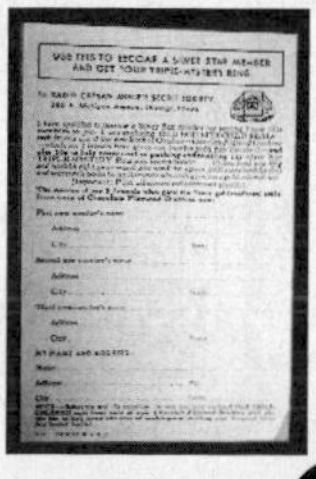

LAN-86

❑ **LAN-86. Silver Star Triple Mystery Secret Compartment Ring,**
1938. Silvered brass with removable cap covering member's serial number.
Ring - **$250 $550 $1200**
Order Form - **$15 $25 $40**

LAN-87

LAN-88

❑ **LAN-87. Miracle Compass Sun-Watch,**
1938. - **$30 $60 $135**

❑ **LAN-88. School Brass Badge,**
1938. Customized with two initials. -
$20 $45 $85

LAN-89

❑ **LAN-89. "Snow White And The Seven Dwarfs Cut-Out Book" With Envelope ,**
1938. Scarce. Ovaltine as Radio Orphan Annie premium, also store item. Published by Whitman with six punch-out sheets. See LAN-95.
Near Mint In Mailer - **$750**
No Mailer, Unpunched - **$150 $300 $600**

LAN-90

LAN-91

❑ **LAN-90. Beetleware Shake-Up Mug,**
1938. Light blue with orange top, dancing scene. - **$40 $75 $150**

❑ **LAN-91. Beetleware Plastic Shake-Up Mug,**
1938. Brown mug with orange lid. Newspaper ad states "Free To Boys and Girls Who Try New Chocolate Flavored Ovaltime" with expiration date of July 19, 1938. - **$40 $85 $155**

LAN-92

LAN-93

❑ **LAN-92. Silver Plated Foto-Frame,**
1938. Scarce. Metal base inscribed on front "To My Best Friend". - **$115 $275 $450**

❑ **LAN-93. Ann Gillis Photo,**
c. 1938. Little Orphan Annie radio portrayer of late 1930s. - **$30 $60 $90**

LAN-94

❑ **LAN-94. "Shado-ettes" Mechanical Paper Portraits,**
1938. Set of six. Sandy, Annie, Warbucks, Joe Corntassel, Mr. Silo, Mrs. Silo.
Near Mint In Mailer - **$325**
Each Assembled - **$10 $20 $40**

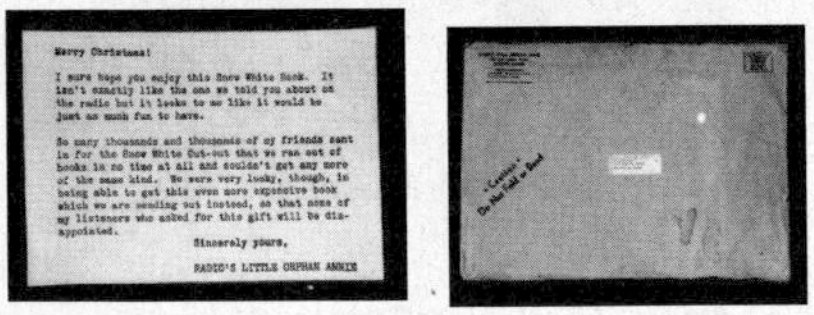

LAN-95

❑ **LAN-95 "Snow White And The Seven Dwarfs Paperdolls" Book With Envelope And Replacement Notice Slip,**
1938. Ovaltine Orphan Annie premium letter reads "even more expensive book" with full color cover sent as replacement due to depleted supply of lesser quality book originally offered as Christmas premium. Originally offered version had blue and yellow cover. Enclosed replacement slip explains details. Doll book is copyright Walt Disney Enterprises, 1938. See LAN-89.
Christmas Insert - **$30 $60 $135**
Unpunched Book - **$325 $775 $1550**
Mailer - **$50 $100 $150**

LAN-96

❑ **LAN-96. Contest Winners/Shado-Ettes Paper,**
1938. Folder sheet opening to 19x24" printed both sides. Listed are prize winners in "Island-Naming" contest plus panel illustration of Shado-Ettes special prize gift. - **$30 $50 $90**

LAN-97 LAN-98

❑ **LAN-97. "Little Orphan Annie And The Ancient Treasure Of Am" Better Little Book,**
1939. Whitman #1468. - **$12 $36 $78**

❑ **LAN-98. "Little Orphan Annie And The Ancient Treasure Of Am" Better Little Book,**
1939. Whitman #1414. - **$15 $45 $105**

LAN-99 LAN-100

❑ **LAN-99. Manual with Mailer,**
1939. Manual - **$25 $50 $100**
Mailer - **$8 $15 $30**

❑ **LAN-100. Mysto-Matic Brass Decoder Badge,**
1939. - **$15 $30 $85**

LAN-101 LAN-102

❑ **LAN-101. "Goofy Gazette" First Issue,**
1939. Ovaltine. Vol. 1 #1 issue of eight-page newspaper including information on two contests closing June 15. - **$40 $80 $175**
Mailer - **$20 $35 $50**

❑ **LAN-102. Greater Boston Community Fund Campaign 13x22" Cardboard Poster,**
1939. Orphan Annie and Sandy art by Harold Gray. - **$50 $115 $225**

LAN-103

LAN-104

❑ **LAN-103. Code Captain Secret Compartment Badge,**
1939. Silvered finish. Sometimes found with link chain on back to fasten to that year's decoder badge. - **$35 $80 $160**

❑ **LAN-104. "Code Captain Secrets" Folder,**
1939. - **$60 $125 $250**

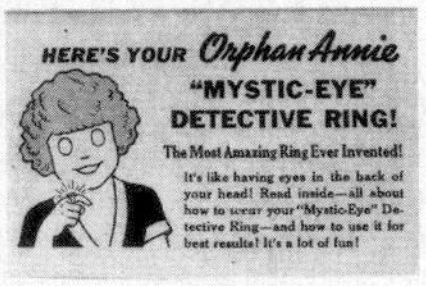

LAN-105 LAN-106

❑ **LAN-105. Mystic-Eye Detective (Look-Around) Ring,**
1939. Brass ring with American eagle cover cap over look-in mirror. Also issued for Captain Midnight and The Lone Ranger. -
$65 $135 $250

❑ **LAN-106. "Mystic-Eye Detective Ring" Instruction Sheet,**
1939. - **$100 $200 $300**

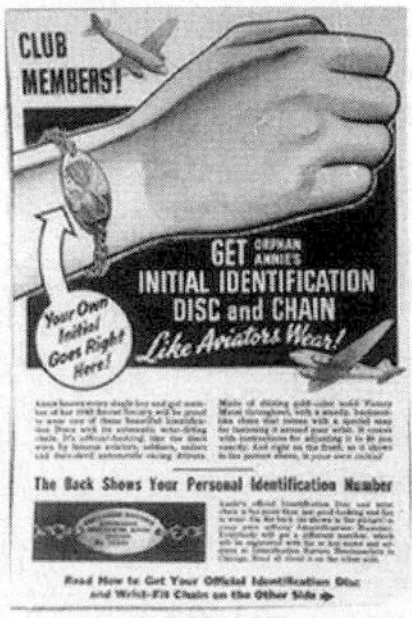

LAN-107

❑ **LAN-107. "Initial Identification Disc And Chain" Order Sheet,**
1939. Back explains how Identification Bureau works above order coupon. Brass finish. -
$20 $50 $80

LAN-108

❑ **LAN-108. Identification Bracelet,**
1939. Brass version with American flag in bow design, personalized by single initial designated by orderer. - **$35 $65 $140**

LAN-109

❑ **LAN-109. "Goofy Gazette" Newspaper #3 With Envelope,**
1939. Last of three issues.
Newspaper - **$35 $60 $115**
Mailer - **$20 $35 $50**

LAN-110

❑ **LAN-110. "Goofy Circus" Punch-Out Kit With Mailer Envelope,**
1939. Mailer - **$25 $65 $100**
Unpunched - **$215 $375 $775**

LAN-111

❑ **LAN-111. Greater Boston's 1939 Community Fund Campaign,**
1939. 7-1/2x10" with 16 pages featuring cover art by Harold Gray. - **$35 $60 $110**

LAN-112

❑ **LAN-112. "Easter Egg Dress-Ups" Sheet,**
1939. Swift & Co. 3.5x10.5" paper perforated pieces for decorating eggs. Decoration sheet has gummed reverse. Uncut - **$70 $145 $300**

LAN-113

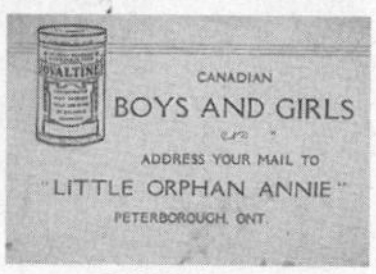

LAN-114

❑ **LAN-113. Rare Color Variety Shake-Up Mug,**
1939. Same decal design as the 1939 brown mug and the 1940 green mug but this has a light blue cup covered by a reddish orange lid. Only a few examples known. - **$125 $300 $600**

❑ **LAN-114. Canadian Ovaltine Premium Insert Card,**
1930s. A. Wander Limited. 3x4-1/4" red on white providing "Canadian Boys And Girls" with address for letters. - **$12 $25 $50**

LAN-115

❑ **LAN-115. Doll Offer Sheet To Dealers,**
1930s. Ralph A. Freundlich Inc. Self-mailer opening to 8x21" printed on both sides offering composition 12" tall Annie doll and matching 7" tall Sandy doll. - **$65 $125 $200**

LAN-116

LAN-117

❑ **LAN-116. Little Orphan Annie Oilcloth Doll,**
1930s. Starched fabric from set believed issued by unknown cereal sponsor. Also in set are: Herby, Kayo, Moon Mullins, Smitty (see COM-62-64), and Sandy (see next item). - **$85 $165 $275**

❑ **LAN-117. Sandy Oilcloth Doll,**
1930s. See previous item. - **$50 $85 $175**

LAN-118

❑ **LAN-118. Little Orphan Annie And Sandy Wind-Up With Box,**
1930s. Kuramochi, Japan. Annie is 6.75" tall and Sandy is 2.75". Both are celluloid attached to painted tin platform bases with wheels. Base has built-in key for windup. Sandy's head bobs up and down and toy travels in a circle.
Box - **$125 $250 $500**
Toy - **$200 $400 $800**

LAN-119

❑ **LAN-119. "Little Orphan Annie" Boxed Bisque Set,**
1930s. George Borgfeldt Corporation. Four painted bisque figures in 1x3.75x5" paper-covered cardboard box. Annie and Daddy Warbucks are 3.5" tall marked on back "Made In Japan/Famous Artist Syndicate." Sandy and radio are 1.5" tall. Box - **$50 $100 $200**
Bisque Set - **$50 $100 $200**

LAN-120

❑ **LAN-120. "Sandy" Boxed Mechanical Toy,**
1930s. Marx. 5x8.5x7.5" tall box holds 4x8x4.75" tall tin litho toy designed like "Sandy's Doghouse." Front has perforated door to be punched out. Other three sides of doghouse feature images of Annie. Toy depicts Sandy wearing dog collar with his name, has pair of rubber ears and holds a wood ball between his front paws. Tail is pressed down to activate the inner mechanism and then it launches forward.
Dog House - **$90 $185 $375**
Toy - **$75 $150 $300**

LAN-121

LAN-122

❑ **LAN-121 Cello. Button,**
1930s. Cunningham Ice Cream. - **$70 $150 $275**

❑ **LAN-122. Heart's Desire Dress Clip,**
1930s. Ovaltine. Offered as Orphan Annie unmarked premium with her name on order form of "Costume Jewelry Gifts" Ovaltine folder. Also issued by radio show "Girl Alone/Patricia Roberts" on a pink card. See LAN-125. - **$50 $125 $235**

LAN-123

LAN-124

❑ **LAN-123. "Pittsburgh Post-Gazette" Newspaper Contest Cello. Button,**
1930s. Part of a set showing other characters in the newspaper. - **$30 $55 $115**

❑ **LAN-124. "Funy Frostys Club" Cello. Button,**
1930s. Two styles: "Member" in straight or curved type. - **$75 $175 $325**

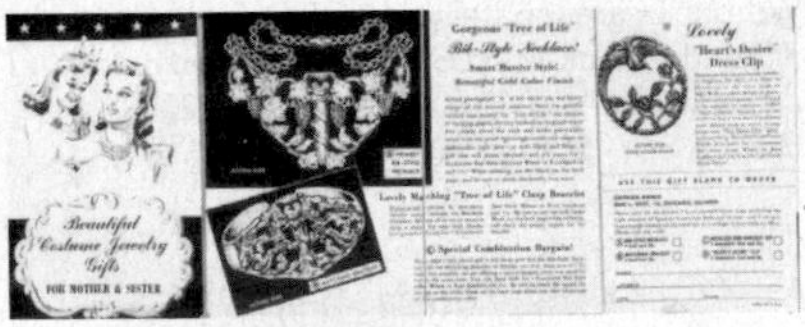
LAN-125

❑ **LAN-125. "Beautiful Costume Jewelry Gifts" Folder,**
1930s. Annie name on order coupon. See LAN-122. - **$50 $125 $185**

LAN-126

❑ **LAN-126. Annie and Sandy Soap in Box,**
1930s. Box - **$10 $20 $30**
Annie - **$25 $50 $100**
Sandy - **$15 $30 $60**

LAN-127

LAN-128

❑ **LAN-127. "Funy Frostys" Waxed Paper Wrapper,**
1930s. Funy Frostys Ice Cream. Bottom has cardboard finger hole card for holding ice confection bar. - **$25 $50 $100**

❑ **LAN-128. "Sunshine Biscuits" Box,**
1930s. Loose-Wiles Biscuit Co. - **$150 $300 $500**

LAN-129

LAN-130

❑ **LAN-129. "Los Angeles Evening Express" Cello. Button,**
1930s. From set of newspaper characters, match number to win prize. - **$30 $60 $125**

❑ **LAN-130. Bisque Toothbrush Holder,**
1930s. Store item. - **$85 $135 $250**

LAN-131

❑ **LAN-131. Club Manual,**
1940. - **$55 $95 $175**

LAN-132

LAN-133

❑ **LAN-132. Speed-O-Matic Brass Decoder Badge,**
1940. - **$30 $60 $135**

❑ **LAN-133. Beetleware Plastic Shake-Up Mug,**
1940. Green with red lid. - **$40 $90 $175**

LAN-134

LAN-135

LAN-136

❑ **LAN-134. Shake-Up Mug Leaflet,**
1940. Came with green mug. - **$35 $75 $135**

❑ **LAN-135. Sandy 3-Way Dog Whistle,**
1940. 3-1/4" brass tube whistle that extends to 5-1/4" length. - **$20 $35 $80**

❑ **LAN-136. "3 Way Mystery Dog-Whistle" Instruction Leaflet,**
1940. - **$30 $55 $100**

LAN-137

❑ **LAN-137. "Code Captain Secrets" Folder With Mailer,**
1940. Red, white and blue small paper folder that opens to 6-1/2x9-1/2". Describes club secrets including use of Code Captain Belt.
Mailer - **$15 $25 $40**
Folder - **$75 $185 $350**

LAN-138

LAN-139

LAN-140

❑ **LAN-138. Metal Puzzle,**
1940. Four metal ball puzzle tin. Store bought. - **$40 $95 $175**

❑ **LAN-139. "Code Captain" Brass Buckle With Fabric Belt,**
1940. Complete - **$85 $150 $250**
Buckle Only - **$45 $80 $150**

❑ **LAN-140. Card,**
1940. Card premium from the radio show. "How to Become a Code Captain." - **$30 $60 $100**

LAN-141

❑ **LAN-141. Watch with Box and Insert,**
1941. Watch was promoted as girls' watch. Also has a price tag and cardboard New Haven seal. Complete - **$250 $500 $1000**

LAN-142

LAN-143

❑ **LAN-142. "Slidomatic Radio Decoder",**
1941. Quaker Cereals. Cardboard slide with instructions on back. - **$40 $95 $175**

❑ **LAN-143. "Safety Guard" Application Blank for Captain's Commission,**
1941. Quaker Cereals. Also see item LAN-159. - **$12 $25 $50**

LAN-144

❑ **LAN-144. Quaker Rice Sparkies Shipping Carton,**
c. 1941. 11x16x25" long corrugated cardboard box originally holding 24 boxes of cereal plus 12 comic books. - **$85 $175 $300**

LAN-145

LAN-146

❑ **LAN-145. Secret Guard Double-Sided Sign,**
1941. Gordon Gold Archives. - **$550 $1100 $2000**

❑ **LAN-146. Club Manual,**
1941. Quaker Cereals. - **$60 $125 $235**

LAN-147

LAN-148

❑ **LAN-147. Secret Guard Mysto-Snapper,**
1941. Quaker Cereals. Litho. tin clicker. - **$20 $35 $100**

❑ **LAN-148. "Captain's Secrets" Folder Manual,**
1941. Quaker Sparkies. - **$75 $200 $400**

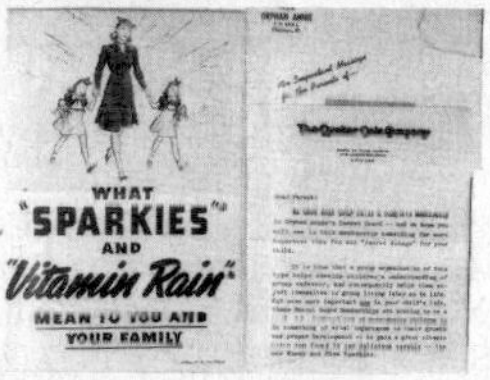

LAN-149

❑ **LAN-149. Secret Guard Member Letter With Quaker Cereal Leaflet,**
1941. Both explain "Vitamin Rain" additives to Quaker cereals. Each - **$15 $30 $65**

LAN-150

❑ **LAN-150. "The Adventures Of Little Orphan Annie" Comic Book,**
1941. Quaker Puffed Wheat & Rice Sparkies. "...Kidnappers/Magic Morro..." stories. - **$16 $48 $200**

LAN-151

❑ **LAN-151. "Captain Sparks Airplane Cockpit" Cardboard Assembly Kit,**
1941. Quaker Cereals. 6x27" assembled with him pictured at center.
Unassembled - **$165 $335 $650**
Assembled - **$100 $225 $350**

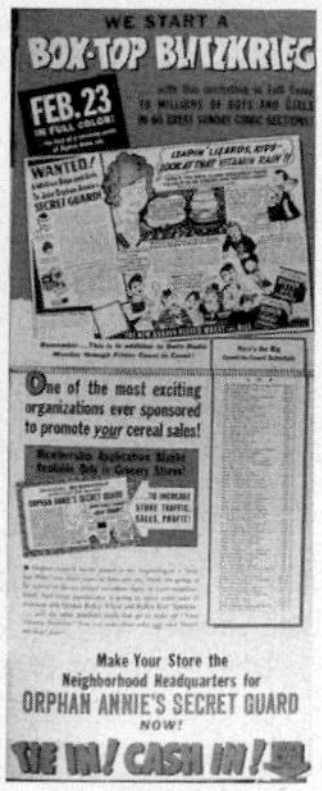

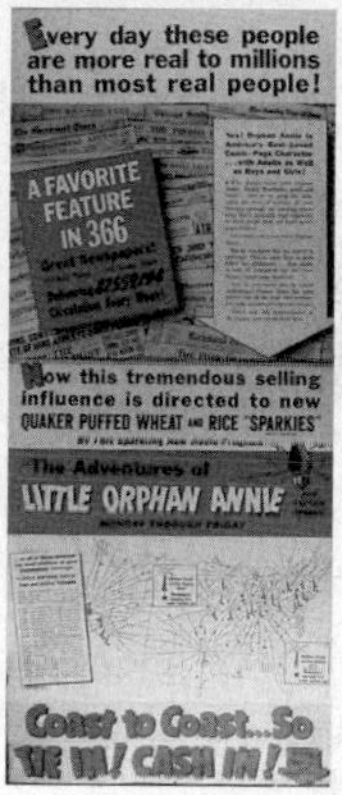

(Back of booklet)

(Front of booklet)

LAN-152

❑ **LAN-152. Secret Guard 8 Page Promotional Booklet,**
1941. Large booklet displays all the info for the Secret Guard Club. The sponsor was Quaker Puffed Wheat Sparkies. This campaign was designed to tie "Little Orphan Annie" to the War effort. Captain Sparks was also created to help. Unfortunately, it didn't work and the show was cancelled in 1942. The premiums produced in 1941 and 1942 are very hard to find. Gordon Gold Archives. - **$450 $900 $1950**

LAN-153

LAN-154

❑ LAN-153. Secret Guard Wood Handle Rubber Stamp With Mailer,
1941. Rare. Quaker Cereals.
Stamp Only - **$165 $350 $700**
Mailer - **$65 $135 $300**

❑ LAN-154. Brass Slide Dog Whistle,
1941. Scarce. Quaker Cereals. End has Orphan Annie head. - **$50 $100 $200**

LAN-155

LAN-156

❑ LAN-155. "The Adventures Of Little Orphan Annie" Comic Book,
1941. Quaker Puffed Wheat & Rice Sparkies. "...Rescue/Magic Morro..." stories. -
$16 $48 $200

❑ LAN-156. Quaker "How To Fly" Manual,
1941. Came with Airplane Pilot Training Cockpit.
- $30 $75 $135

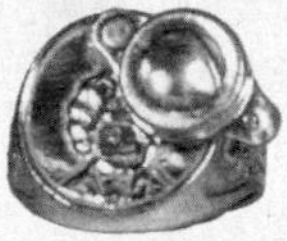

LAN-157

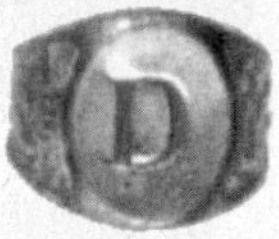

LAN-158

❑ LAN-157. Secret Guard Magnifying Ring,
1941. Quaker Cereals. Offered briefly in 1941 with 8/31/41 expiration date "before Orphan Annie comes back on the air next Fall". -
$500 $1100 $2250

❑ LAN-158. "SG" Secret Guard Brass Ring,
1941. Scarce. Quaker Cereals. Also inscribed "Bravery/Health/Justice" and personalized with initial. - **$525 $1150 $2750**

LAN-159

LAN-160

❑ LAN-159. "SG/Captain" Glow-In-Dark Plastic Badge,
1941. Quaker Cereals. Also see item LAN-143. -
$75 $175 $300

❑ LAN-160. "S.G." Secret Guard 3" Metal Flashlight,
1941. Scarce. Quaker Cereals. -
$100 $200 $375

LAN-161

❑ LAN-161. "Little Orphan Annie Scribbler" Canadian Booklet,
1941. Quaker Puffed Wheat And Puffed Rice. Canadian issue. - **$40 $85 $175**

LAN-162

❑ LAN-162. Captain Sparks Box Cut-Outs,
c. 1941. Quaker Sparkies cereal. From "Home Defense Series" set of 12.
Each Panel Cut-Out - **$10 $20 $30**

LAN-163

❑ LAN-163. "The Adventures Of Little Orphan Annie" Comic Book Offer Store Sign,
1941. Quaker Puffed Rice 'Sparkies.' 12-3/4x19" red, black and white. Gordon Gold Archives. -
$325 $650 $1250

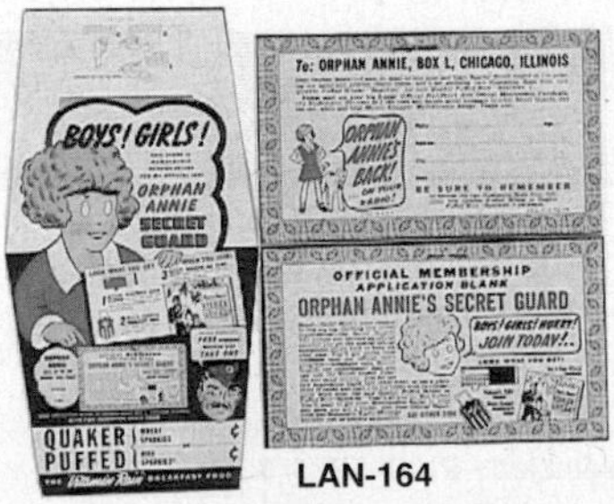

LAN-164

❑ LAN-164. Secret Guard Store Display Sign With Application Blanks,
1941. Flattened 11-1/2x23-1/2" diecut display designed to fold at mid-point. Lower center has area for tablet of application coupons. Pictured are handbook and both 1941 paper decoder and tin clicker member's badge. Gordon Gold Archives. Display - **$500 $1000 $2000**
Single Coupon - **$12 $25 $50**

LAN-165

❑ LAN-165. "Captain Sparks' Airplane Pilot Training Cockpit" Paper Sign ,
1941. Full color 13x21" sign. Gordon Gold Archives. - **$225 $450 $900**

LAN-166

❑ LAN-166. Airplane Cockpit Offer Diecut Display Sign,
1941. Flattened size of 14x25-1/2" designed to fold into dimensional display with holder for order blank coupons. Gordon Gold Archives. -
$200 $400 $800

LAN-167

❑ LAN-167. "Sparkies 2-Way Aviation Drive!" Dealer's Promo,
c. 1941. Probable trade magazine advertising pages promoting cereal boxes with "Authentic U.S. Plane Pictures From Backs Of Sparkies Boxes." - **$30 $50 $100**

LAN-168

❑ **LAN-168. "Little Orphan Annie's Adventures In Fun-Land" Prototype Premium Activity Book,**
c. 1941. Prepared for Quaker Puffed Wheat Sparkies. 6x9" full color all original art prototype design for 16-page activity book. Gordon Gold Archives. Unique - **$1500**

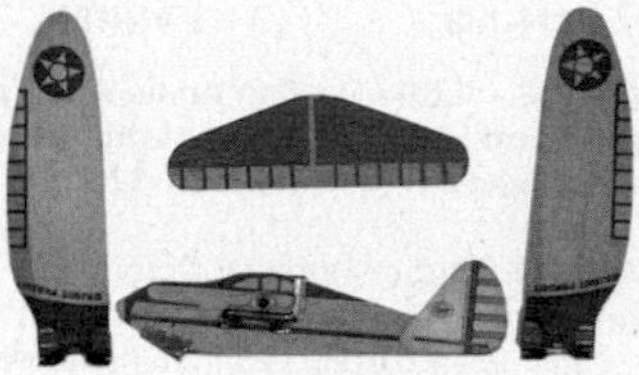

LAN-169

❑ **LAN-169. "Wright Pursuit" Balsa Plane,**
1941. Offered as giveaway pictured in Radio Orphan Annie comics. Shown in comic with "SG" on wings. The two letters on wing pictured appear to be rough design overlays and used for promo as only. Probably used as a Capt. Midnight giveaway as well. - **$50 $100 $200**

LAN-170

❑ **LAN-170. "ROA Cadet" Pendant,**
c. 1941. Possibly a Quaker premium used in Canada. Marked "Sterling" on reverse. Two designs. Each - **$75 $200 $350**

LAN-171

❑ **LAN-171. "Little Orphan Annie And The Haunted Mansion" Better Little Book,**
1941. Whitman #1482. - **$15 $45 $105**

LAN-172

❑ **LAN-172. "Cap't Spark's Gliding Model Airplanes" Original Art Prototype Sign,**
c. 1941. 13x19" art sheet overlaid by tracing paper original art in combination of crayon, colored pencil for proposed Quaker toy. Gordon Gold Archives. Unique. - **$550**

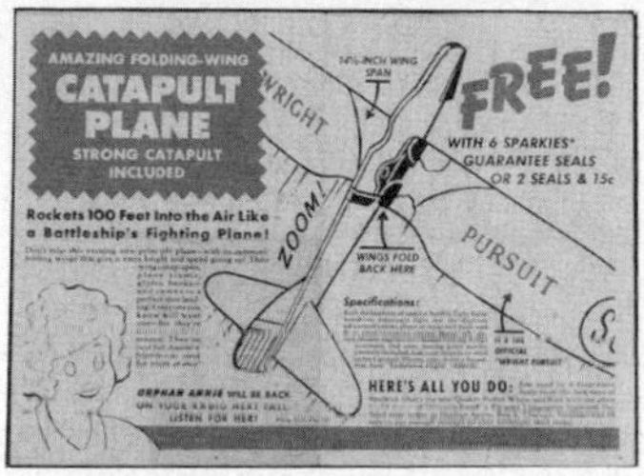

LAN-173

❑ **LAN-173. "Folding-Wing Catapult Plane" Offer Sheet,**
c. 1941. 6.25x8.5" paper picturing and describing "Wright Pursuit" balsa wood airplane fired by rubber band. Pictured example includes partial "SG" Safety Guard emblem on one wing tip. - **$30 $75 $135**

LAN-174

❑ **LAN-174. Orphan Annie "Captain's Secrets" Manual With Commission,**
1942. Quaker Cereal. Red/white/blue 4.5x7" folder that accompanied Captain's Magic Glow Bird badge. Folder opens to 8.5x11" including 1942 Safety Guard Captain's Commission certificate, Secret Master Code Key text and "New 1942 Captain's Password." - **$125 $250 $500**

LAN-175

❑ **LAN-175. "Junior Commandos" Premium Comic Book,**
1942. Published by K.K. Publications, Inc., with back ad "Big Shoe Store." 16 pages reprinting strips from 9/7/42 to 10/10/42. -
$28 $84 $350

(CLOSE-UP OF DECODER)

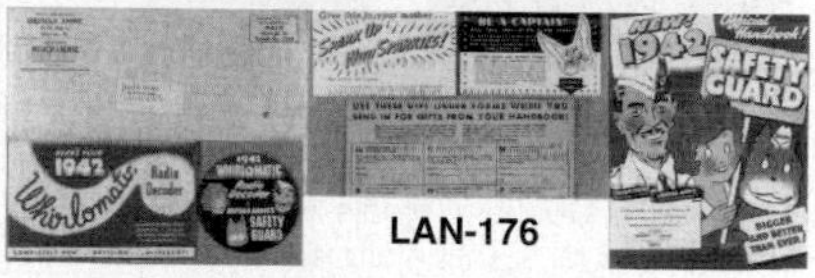

LAN-176

❑ **LAN-176. "Safety Guard" Membership Kit,**
1942. Quaker Cereals. Included tin whistle not shown (see item LAN-178).
Set Near Mint - **$635**
Decoder - **$50 $100 $165**
Whistle - **$20 $40 $85**
Handbook - **$60 $150 $325**

LAN-177

LAN-178

❑ **LAN-177 "Safety Guard" Captain Application Blank,**
1942. Quaker Cereals. Also see item LAN-183. -
$10 $20 $40

❑ **LAN-178. "Safety Guard" Tri-Tone Signaler Badge,**
1942. Quaker Cereals. Litho. tin whistle from member's kit (see item LAN-176). -
$20 $40 $85

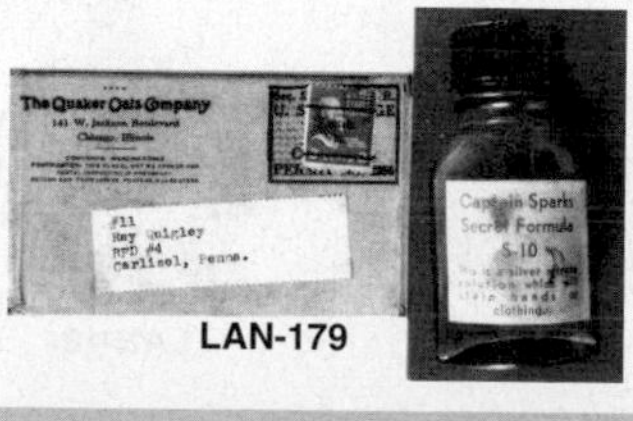

LAN-179

❑ **LAN-179. Quaker "Detector-Kit" With Mailer Box,**
1942. Many items for photo printing, "Captain Sparks Secret Formula S-10" on bottle label. Boxed - **$100 $150 $300**

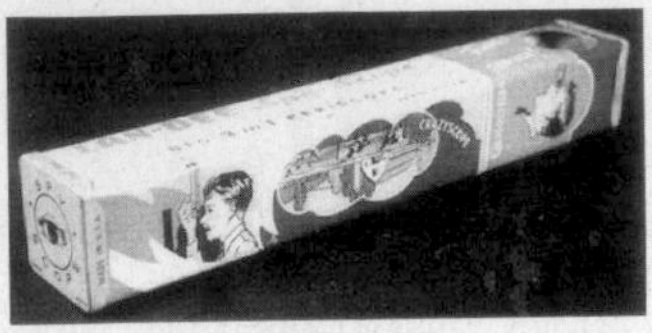

LAN-180

❑ **LAN-180. "3 In 1 Periscope",**
1942. Scarce. Quaker Cereals. No Annie name but offered in 1942 Safety Guard handbook. - **$110 $240 $500**

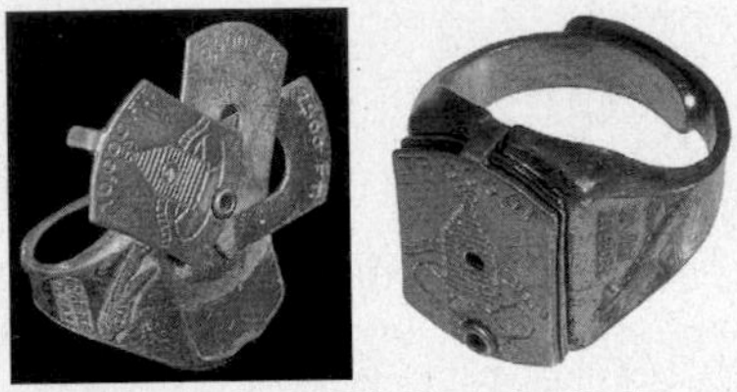

(OPEN) **LAN-181** (CLOSED)

❑ **LAN-181. Altascope Ring,**
1942. Rare. Quaker Cereals. Several moveable brass plates for sighting airplanes and estimating their altitudes. Nine known: two in good grade, three in very good, none in fine, two in very fine, one in excellent and one in near mint.
Good - **$4000**
Fine - **$6000**
Very Fine - **$8500**
Excellent - **$12,000**
Near Mint - **$22,500**

LAN-182

❑ **LAN-182."Little Orphan Annie And Her Junior Commandos" Better Little Book,**
1942. Whitman #1457. - **$12 $36 $78**

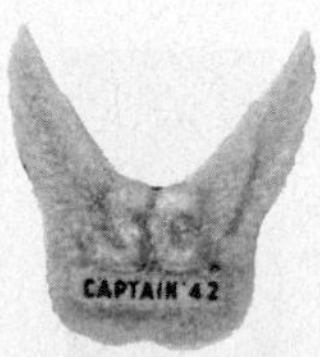

LAN-183

LAN-184

❑ **LAN-183. "SG Captain" Safety Guard Magic Glow Bird Badge,**
1942. Rare. Quaker Cereals. Also see item LAN-173. - **$150 $300 $600**

❑ **LAN-184. "SG Captain" Glow-In-Dark Canadian Club Brass Badge,**
1942. Rare. Quaker Cereals. Design includes Canadian maple leaf symbol. - **$350 $700 $1500**

LAN-185

❑ **LAN-185. "Super Book Of Comics-Little Orphan Annie",**
c. 1943. Pan-Am gasoline. Book #7 from numbered series featuring various characters. - **$11 $33 $115**

LAN-186

❑ **LAN-186. "Junior Commandos" Coloring Book,**
1943. McLaughlin Co. 11x15" including a few inside pictures of Annie wearing her "Junior Commando" armband. - **$40 $85 $190**

LAN-187

❑ **LAN-187. Harold Gray Personal Christmas Card,**
1945. Choice color front cover art. Limited issue. - **$40 $85 $150**

LAN-188

LAN-189

❑ **LAN-188. "Little Orphan Annie And The Underground Hide-Out" Better Little Book,**
1945. Whitman #1461. - **$12 $36 $78**

❑ **LAN-189. "Super-Book Of Comics Featuring Little Orphan Annie",**
1946. Omar Bread. Book #23 from numbered series featuring various characters. - **$8 $24 $60**

LAN-190

LAN-191

❑ **LAN-190. Quaker Puffed Wheat Comic Book,**
1947. - **$4 $12 $25**

❑ **LAN-191. "Little Orphan Annie and the Gooneyville Mystery" Better Little Book,**
1947. #1435. - **$12 $36 $85**

LAN-192

❑ **LAN-192. "Little Orphan Annie And The Secret Of The Well" Better Little Book,**
1947. Whitman #1417. - **$12 $36 $78**

LAN-193

❑ **LAN-193. "Flare-Top" Ice Cream Cone Sign,**
1947. Full color about 18x24". Gordon Gold Archives. - **$65 $165 $350**

LAN-194

LAN-195

❑ **LAN-194. Newspaper Comics Advertising Cello. Button,**
c. 1948. 1-1/4" light blue and maroon from small series of comic characters promoting "Rotocomic" Sunday section. - **$90 $175 $350**

❑ **LAN-195. Cracker Jack Giveaway,**
c. 1950s. From a comic character series of 1-5/8" diameter made of thin plastic with high relief portrait. An Orphan Annie and Daddy Warbucks are also known. Each - **$12 $25 $40**

LAN-196

LAN-197

❑ **LAN-196. "Orphan Annie's Parents Smoked" Litho. Tin Tab,**
1968. "Truth About Smoking" group. - **$10 $20 $40**

❑ **LAN-197. Original Radio Broadcast Record Album,**
1972. Product of Mark 56 Records. "Ovaltine Presents..." unabridged radio broadcasts (with commercials.) Back of record jacket shows many premiums. - **$80**

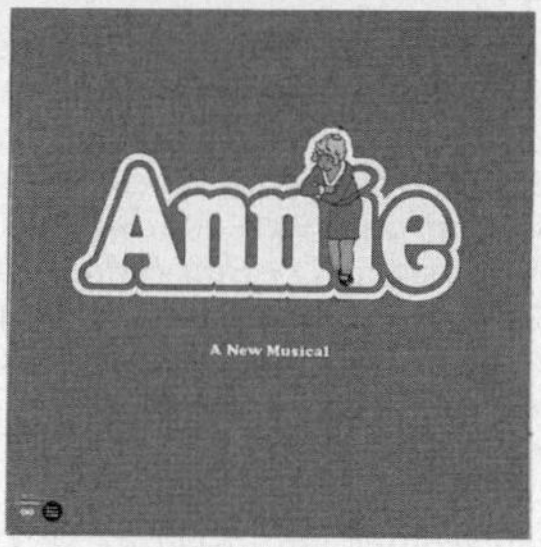

LAN-198

❑ **LAN-198. Soundtrack Album for Musical,**
1977. CBS Records. Stars Dorothy Loudon as Annie. Has fold-out of 14 scenes that are explained in detail. - **$35**

LAN-199

LAN-200

❑ **LAN-199. Plastic Cup,**
1980. Ovaltine. - **$18 $30 $50**

❑ **LAN-200. Ceramic Anniversary Mug,**
1981. Ovaltine. - **$10 $20 $45**

LAN-201

❑ **LAN-201. Revival Era Lunch Box With Bottle,**
1981. Soft vinyl store item by Adi.
Box - **$25 $45 $75**
Generic Bottle - **$5 $10 $15**

LAN-202

❑ **LAN-202. Annie Motion Lamp,**
1982. Lamp fixture with shade. - **$50 $115 $200**

LAN-203

LAN-204

❑ **LAN-203. Movie Plastic Shake-Up Mug,**
1982. Ovaltine. - **$15 $30 $60**

❑ **LAN-204. Plastic 50-Year Anniversary Shake-Up Mug,**
1982. Ovaltine. - **$15 $30 $60**

LAN-205

LAN-206

❑ **LAN-205. "Annie" Cloth Doll With Order Form,**
1982. Ivory, Zest, Camay soaps and others. Offered April 15 to September 30.
Doll - **$10 $18 $35**
Order Form - **$3 $6 $12**

❑ **LAN-206. "In Person At Kennedy Center" Litho. Button,**
1980s. Related to stage play. Scarce - **$15 $30 $50**

LAN-207

❑ **LAN-207. Annie and Sandy Doll Set,**
2000. Madame Alexander product. Comes with locket and two toys. - **$85**

Little Pinkies

A series of product insert buttons made by Whitehead & Hoag around 1896 featured cartoon drawings of Little Pinkies in various guises. Including varieties, the set totals 21: The Actor, The Bad Boy, The Ball Player (with and without a period), the Boot Black, Boy Orator, The Clown, The Colonel, The Drum Major, The Dude, The Dunce, The Fireman, Greenie, Just Landed, The Letter Carrier, The News Boy, The Policeman, The Sailor, The Soldier (with sabre or with toy sword), and Uncle Sam. The buttons are usually found with back papers for American Pepsin gum, sometimes for Old Gold cigarettes or Whitehead & Hoag. Nothing else is known about Little Pinkies. They seem to be the briefly popular creation of an unknown Whitehead & Hoag staff artist, possibly inspired by Palmer Cox's Brownie characters.

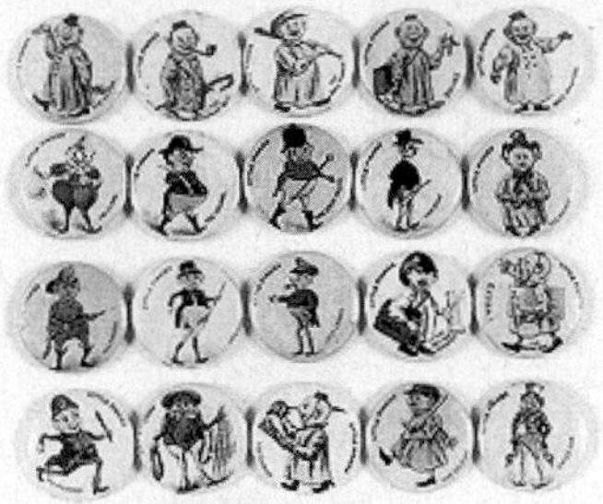

LPS-1

❑ **LPS-1. Little Pinkies Button Set,**
1896. American Pepsin Gum or less frequently Old Gold Cigarettes.
Near Mint Set - **$800**
Each - **$10 $15 $25**

Little Red Riding Hood

The folklore tale of the red-cloaked girl on her way to Grandma's house and her encounter with a wolf dates back centuries in various forms. French author Charles Perrault (1628-1703) wrote the basic story in his *Tales of Mother Goose Anthology* published in 1697, but the wolf survives after eating both Grandma and Red Riding Hood. The Brothers Grimm (Jacob 1785-1863 and William 1786-1859) 1857 version titled *Little Red Cap* is the most accepted version. A hunter kills the wolf and rescues Red. The classic tale has been in print ever since.

Walt Disney's first cartoon was *Little Red Riding Hood*, released in 1922, featuring a human wolf, and issued as the first of his *Laugh-O-Grams* series. Directed by Rudy Ising, Walt himself did much of the art. Legendary animator Fred "Tex" Avery (1908-1980) devoted four screwball cartoons to the character *Little Red Walking Hood* 1937, *The Bear's Tale* 1940, *Red Hot Riding Hood* 1943 and *Little Rural Riding Hood* 1949. Sam Samudio's group Sam the Sham and the Pharaos released *Li'l Red Riding Hood* on the MGM label September 10, 1966. The record soared to number one on the Cashbox charts and number two on the Billboard charts.

The 1996 feature film *Freeway* twisted the basic plot and had Reese Witherspoon lured to a trailer park by sadistic killer Bob Wolverton, played by Keifer Sutherland. Keep your doors locked on the way to Grandma's kiddies!

LRH-1

❑ **LRH-1. "Fairy Stories For Tiny Folk" The Little Big Book,**
1928. 4x5.25" book with 224 pages of text and art. McLaughlin #18282213 copyright 1928/1934. - **$15 $30 $65**

LRH-2

LRH-3

❑ **LRH-2. "Little Red Riding Hood And The Big Bad Wolf" Book,**
1934. 7.75x10" cardboard cover with 32 stiff paper pages. Printed in England. - **$50 $100 $200**

❑ **LRH-3. "Three Little Pigs" With Little Red Riding Hood Sand Pail,**
1934. Ohio Art. 5.25" diameter by 5.5" tall tin litho pail with attached carrying handle and pedestal base. - **$200 $400 $600**

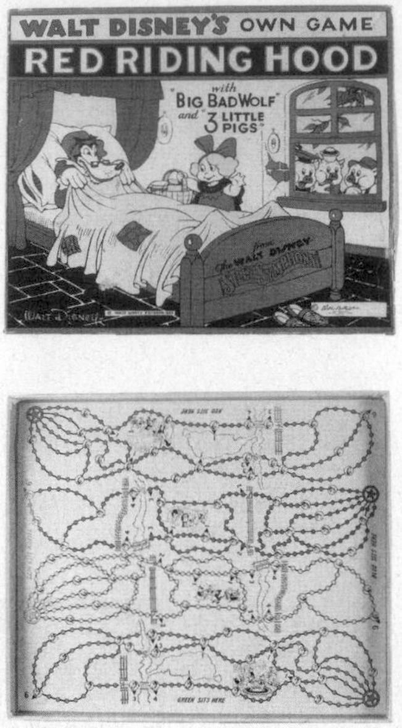

LRH-4

❑ **LRH-4. "Red Riding Hood With Big Bad Wolf And Three Little Pigs" Game,**
c. 1934. Parker Bros. 13x15.5x1" deep box contains instruction folder, generic spinner, wax paper bag with 4 wooden markers. Bottom of box is gameboard. - **$50 $100 $200**

LRH-5

❑ **LRH-5. "Mother Goose Characters Christmas Tree Lamps" Figural Lights Boxed Set,**
c. 1935. 5-3/8x6.75x1.5" deep box with colorful lid art showing Mother Goose surrounded by characters. Hand-painted glass bulbs range in size from 2.5" to 3" tall. Made in Japan. Characters are: Old King Cole, Three Men In A Tub, Old Woman In A Shoe, Queen Of Hearts, Little Boy Blue, Red Riding Hood, Peter Piper, Humpty Dumpty. - **$100 $200 $300**

LRH-6

❑ **LRH-6. "Children's Motion Picture TV",**
1977. Nasta Industries Inc. 5x6.25x2" deep box contains 3.5" long hard plastic TV set replica. Comes with six different full color cardboard pictures which are inserted into the back and when knob is turned it distorts the picture so it appears as if it is moving. Comes with six pictures for Cinderella, Red Riding Hood, Snow White. - **$8 $15 $25**

The Lone Ranger

The legend of the Lone Ranger was born on Detroit radio station WXYZ in January 1933, the product of station owner George W. Trendle and writer Fran Striker. The program was a success from the start, and within a year was also being heard on WGN in Chicago and WOR in New York--in effect forming the nucleus of the new Mutual network. By 1937, "Hi-Yo Silver!" was echoing nationwide. Initially sustained by the station, the program was sponsored by Silver Cup bread starting in November 1933. Bond bread took over as sponsor in 1939 except in the Southeast states, where Merita bread retained its franchise. General Mills became the sponsor in 1941, tying the masked rider to such cereals as Kix and Wheaties until the radio series went off the air in 1955. Cheerios sponsored rebroadcasts until 1956, ending some 23 years and over 3,000 episodes of Western radio thrills and adventure.

Jack Deeds was the first actor to play the Lone Ranger, but only for the first six broadcasts. George Stenius, later a movie producer under the name George Seaton, assumed the role for the next three months. When Stenius quit, WXYZ station manager Brace Beemer took over the role for a few months, but then he left to open an advertising agency. Finally, in May 1933, Earl Graser became the Lone Ranger voice and he continued the role until his death in 1941. At this point, Brace Beemer was recruited to return to the role. He played the part from 1941 to 1955 and became the voice most closely associated with the character.

On television, the Lone Ranger rode for more than 30 years on the networks and in syndication. The series, sponsored by General Mills (and Merita bread), premiered on ABC in 1949 and aired in prime time until 1957. Reruns were shown on all three networks: CBS (1953-1960 and 1966-1969), ABC (1957-1961 and 1965), and NBC (1960-1961). Syndication began in 1961. Clayton Moore (1914-1999) played the lead for most of the series (John Hart covered the years 1952-1954) and Jay Silverheels (1919-1980), a Mohawk Indian, was Tonto, his faithful companion.

Republic Pictures released two 15-episode chapter plays; *The Lone Ranger* (1938), with Lee Powell as the lead, and *The Lone Ranger Rides Again* (1939), with Robert Livingston. Wrather Productions made three full-length films, *The Lone Ranger* (1955) and *The Lone Ranger and the Lost City of Gold* (1958), both with Clayton Moore and Jay Silverheels, and *The Legend of the Lone Ranger* (1981), with Klinton Spilsbury and Michael Horse.

A Saturday morning animated Lone Ranger series aired on CBS from 1966 to 1969, with the Ranger and Tonto battling mad scientists as well as conventional Western villains. The animated defenders of law and order surfaced again on CBS in 1980-1981 as part of *The Tarzan/Lone Ranger Adventure Hour*.

A Sunday comic strip distributed by King Features appeared from 1938 to 1971 and was revived from 1981 to 1984--one of the longest running of the Western strips. Charles Flanders took over the strip from Ed Kresse in 1939 and continued as the main daily and Sunday artist until the mid-1960s. Comic books, including giveaways, novels, coloring books, photo albums, and scrapbooks appeared in great numbers from the 1940s on. Artist Tom Gill did most of the interior story art for the comic books in the 1950s-60s; Don Spaulding painted some of the classic 1950s covers. Younger incarnations of the Lone Ranger and Tonto failed to make a go of it in a WB television pilot aired in 2002. A new comic book incarnation of the masked man started in 2006 from Dynamite Entertainment.

It would be hard to overestimate the number of items licensed and merchandised in the name of the Lone Ranger, especially during the years the program ruled the air on radio and television. Items may be copyrighted by Lone Ranger Inc., Lone Ranger Television Inc., or, starting in 1954, Wrather Corp.

LON-1

LON-2

❑ **LON-1. Photo,**
1933. First premium photo for the Lone Ranger Show. Shows Lone Ranger on Silver with head tilted down. Michigan Radio Network printed on left and signed bottom right. -
$350 $750 $1500

❑ **LON-2. Photo On Horse,**
1934. Early Silvercup radio premium. -
$35 $65 $135

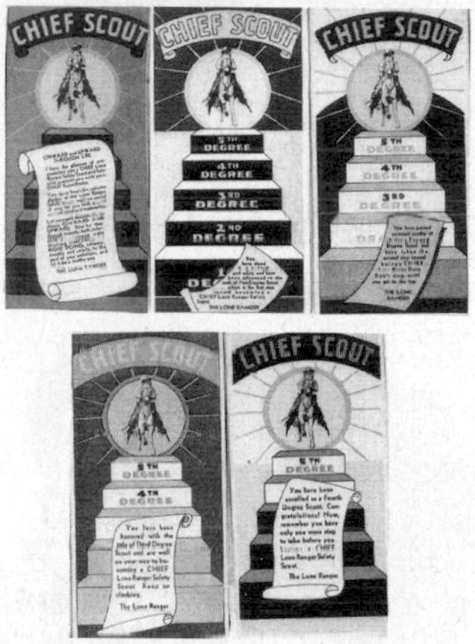

LON-3

❑ **LON-3. Silvercup Bread "Chief Scout" Qualification Cards Set,**
1934. Scarce. Fifth card (shown first) came with "Chief Scout" brass badge, others denoted "Degree" rank advancements to the badge.
1st - **$30 $80 $150**
2nd - **$30 $80 $150**
3rd - **$40 $90 $190**
4th - **$50 $100 $225**
5th - **$60 $150 $350**

LON-4

❑ **LON-4. Radio Sponsorship Brochure Opens To 19x25",**
c. 1934. Silvercup Bread. - **$125 $250 $500**

LON-5

❑ **LON-5. Silvercup Bread Safety Club Folder,**
c. 1934. - **$50 $125 $250**

LON-6

LON-7

❑ **LON-6. Silvercup Bread "Chief Scout" Enameled Brass Badge,**
1934. Also inscribed "Lone Ranger Safety Scout/Silvercup". - **$50 $100 $225**

❑ **LON-7. "Oke Tonto" Photo Card,**
1934. Various bread company radio sponsors. - **$20 $45 $90**

LON-8

LON-9

❑ **LON-8. Safety Scout Member's Badge,**
1934. Silvercup Bread. - **$10 $20 $50**

❑ **LON-9. Safety Scout Badge Mailer,**
1934. Silvercup Safety Scout premium. Rare.- **$50 $75 $150**

LON-10

❑ **LON-10. Scout Badge Offer Card With Pledge,**
1934. Silvercup Bread radio premium.- **$35 $80 $160**

LON-11

❑ **LON-11. Campfire Photo,**
1935. Tonto and Lone Ranger at campfire with horses in background. - **$40 $90 $200**

LON-12

LON-13

❑ **LON-12. "The Lone Ranger and His Horse Silver" Big Little Book #1181,**
1935. - **$26 $78 $180**

❑ **LON-13. "The Lone Ranger" Composition Figure By Dollcraft,**
c. 1935. Figure is 2x4.5" wide at ankles by 10.5" tall without 1.25" tall removable hat. Back embossed with "Dollcraft." Complete with hat, mask, neckerchief, horseshoe-shaped labels on chaps reading "Hi-Yo Silver/The Lone Ranger." - **$600 $1300 $2000**

LON-14

❑ **LON-14. Silvercup Bread Picture,**
1936. - **$18 $35 $75**

LON-15

❑ **LON-15. "How The Lone Ranger Captured Silver" Booklet,**
1936. Silvercup Bread. - **$60 $180 $400**

LON-16

❑ **LON-16. "Lone Ranger Target Game",**
1936. Morton's Salt. Punch-out cardboard parts include gun and six targets.
Near Mint Unpunched - **$450**
Loose - **$115 $225 $325**

LON-17

LON-18

❑ **LON-17. Cobakco Bread Story Booklet,**
c. 1936. "How The Lone Ranger Captured Silver" seven-page story collected over seven weeks. - **$70 $200 $450**

❑ **LON-18. "The Lone Ranger" Hardcover With Dust Jacket Correctly Crediting Author Gaylord Du Bois,**
1936. Grosset & Dunlap. 220-page novel credited to Du Bois, prolific and famous popular fiction writer, on later editions Fran Striker is given credit with no reference to Du Bois.
Example With Jacket - **$200 $375 $700**

LON-19

LON-20

❑ **LON-19. "The Lone Ranger and the Vanishing Herd" Big Little Book #1196,**
1936. - **$21 $63 $150**

❑ **LON-20. "The Lone Ranger and the Secret Killer" Big Little Book #1431,**
1937. H. Anderson art. 432 pages. - **$21 $63 $150**

LON-21

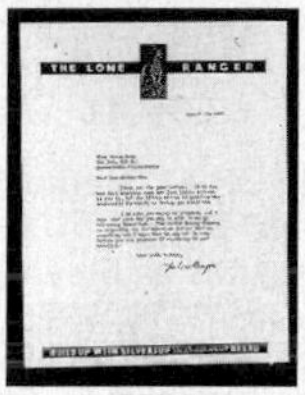

LON-22

❑ **LON-21. "The Lone Ranger Magazine" Vol. 1 #1,**
1937. Trojan Publishing Corp., Chicago. - **$275 $550 $1200**

❑ **LON-22. Silvercup Lone Ranger Personalized Letter,**
1937. Silvercup Bread. Response from Gordon Baking Co. to youngster who adopted kitten and wished Lone Ranger to know of it.
Same or similar - **$35 $75 $150**

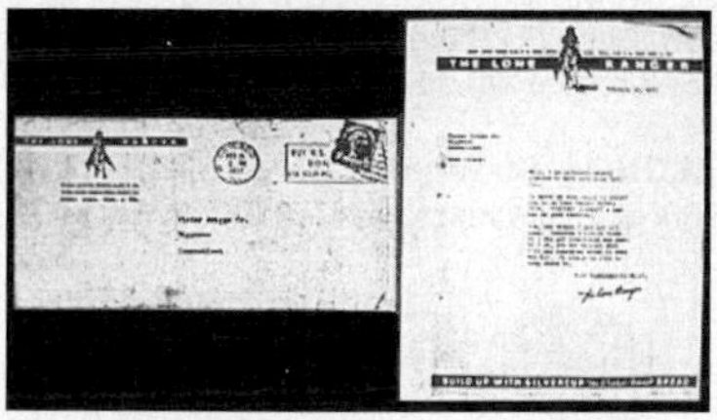

LON-23

❑ **LON-23. Silvercup Letter Noting Badge Supply Exhausted,**
1937. Letter assures new member that he is enrolled but states "Now, The Badges I Had Are All Gone. Sometime A Little Later On I May Get Some Brand New Ones. If I Do, You Can Be Sure That I'll Say Something About It Over The Air. So Always Be Sure To Keep Tuned In."
Letter - **$35 $75 $150**
Envelope - **$15 $25 $40**

LON-24

❑ **LON-24. "Lone Ranger News" Vol. 1 No. 1 Newspaper,**
1937. Weber's Bread. 11-1/2x17" four-page newspaper with black and red accents on newsprint. Contains seven black and white photos of "Frontier Scenes And People Familiar To The Lone Ranger." - **$125 $250 $500**

LON-25

❑ **LON-25. "The Lone Ranger" Republic Serial Poster,**
1938. For a 15 episode serial.
Chapter 1 Stock Sheet - **$1500 $3000 $5000**
Chapter 2 15 each - **$600 $1200 $1850**

LON-26

❑ **LON-26. Fatal Treasure Serial Card,**
1938. Blue & white title card for Chapter 8. These cards are very rare. - **$225 $450 $750**

LON-27

❑ **LON-27. "The Lone Ranger" Cover On Radio Guide Magazine,**
1938. Vol. 7 #48 issue for September 17, 1938. - **$30 $60 $115**

LON-28

❑ **LON-28. Plastic Case Radio By Pilot,**
1938. Radio is 9x14x7" deep. Dial shows him holding lasso and riding Silver against blue background with white caption "Hi-Yo Silver" and title "The Lone Ranger." Two Varieties.
White Case (shown) - **$500 $1000 $1650**
Brown Case - **$250 $500 $1150**

LON-29

❑ **LON-29. Sunday Newspaper Historic Debut Poster,**
1938. Newspaper page 16.5x21.5" from the Sun., Sept. 11, 1938 issue of the Sunday Chicago Herald and Examiner. The image is titled at top "The Lone Ranger-Masked Idol Of Millions." The block of promotional text below makes the gala announcement that the Lone Ranger has come to America's Sunday comic pages. - **$265 $525 $800**

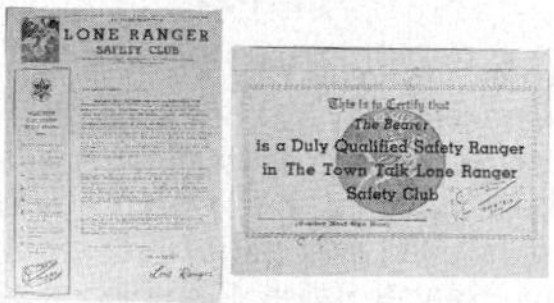

LON-30

❑ **LON-30. Club Membership Admission Letter And Card,**
1938. Town Talk Bread. Letter - **$35 $65 $125**
Card - **$20 $40 $85**

LON-31

❑ **LON-31. Membership Card,**
1938. Brown's Bread. Uncommon card with three illustrations. - **$35 $70 $145**

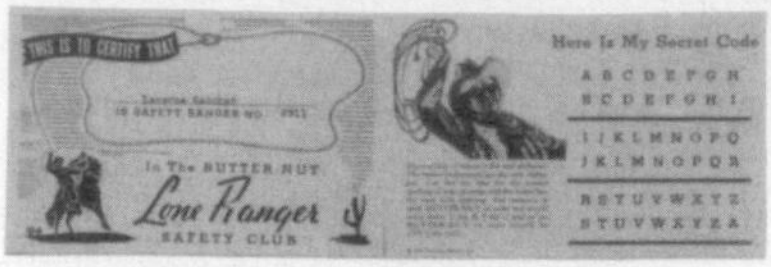

LON-32

❏ **LON-32. "Butter-Nut Safety Club" Card,**
1938. 3-1/4x5" has individual Safety Ranger number. Card back has secret code. - **$40 $85 $190**

LON-33

❏ **LON-33. "Wear This Mask And Look Like The Lone Ranger,"**
1938. Issued by Schulze Butter-Nut Bread, Dolly Madison Cakes. Diecut stiff paper with list of five mid-west radio stations and Lone Ranger show times on reverse. - **$70 $145 $275**

LON-34

❏ **LON-34. First Aid Kit,**
1938. American White Cross Labs Inc. Lithographed tin box, issued in at least two sizes, holding various basic medical supplies. The box included a 24-page "First Aid Guide" with Lone Ranger Safety Club Pledge and 10 Safety Rules.
Box With Contents Except Manual - **$30 $50 $115**
Box Empty - **$15 $30 $60**

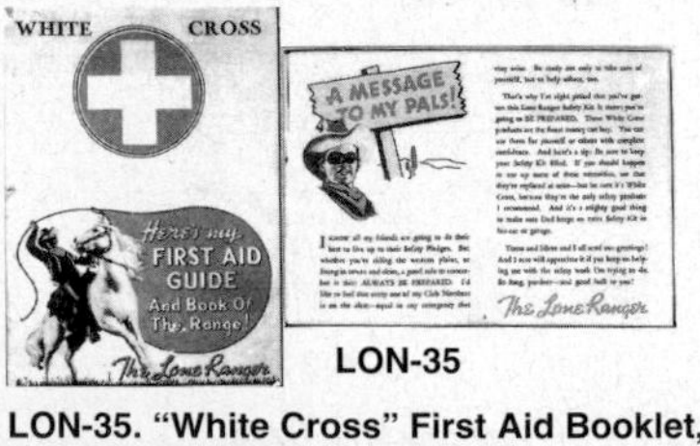

LON-35

❏ **LON-35. "White Cross" First Aid Booklet,**
1938. - **$35 $85 $165**

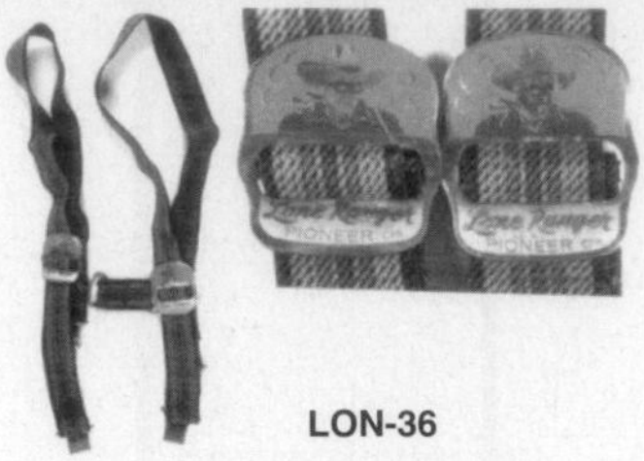

LON-36

❏ **LON-36. "Lone Ranger" Suspenders With Adjustible Brass Slides,**
1938. Store item by Pioneer. - **$100 $185 $350**

LON-37

❏ **LON-37. "V-Bev Lone Ranger News" First Issue,**
1938. V-Bev soda beverage. - **$80 $175 $350**

LON-38

❏ **LON-38. Safety Club Membership Card,**
1938. Cobakco Bread. Back has code alphabet. - **$100 $200 $300**

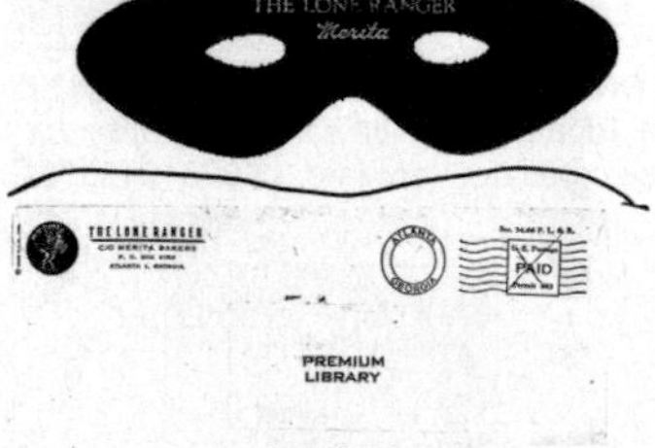

LON-39

❏ **LON-39. "Merita" Bread Mask With Mailer,**
1938. Made of oilcloth-like material.
Mask - **$40 $85 $175**
Mailer - **$15 $30 $50**

LON-40

❏ **LON-40. "The Lone Ranger Merita" Mask with Copyright Date,**
1938. Made of starched muslin. Note that fabric covers nose, unlike cut-out on oil cloth-like variety, This example came in mailer (not shown) postmarked 1942. Mask - **$40 $85 $175**
Mailer - **$15 $30 $50**

LON-41 LON-42

❏ **LON-41. Merita "Lone Ranger Salesmen's Club" Badge,**
1938. Merita Bread. White enamel and silvered brass. - **$175 $375 $750**

❏ **LON-42. Republic Serial Club Brass Badge,**
1938. Republic Pictures. Badges are serially numbered. - **$40 $75 $135**

LON-43

LON-44

❏ **LON-43. Movie Discount Card,**
1938. Republic Pictures. Admits child for 5 cents to Saturday matinee. - **$50 $90 $175**

❏ **LON-44. Strong Box Bank,**
1938. Sun Life Insurance. - **$100 $250 $450**

LON-45 LON-46

❏ **LON-45. Bat-O-Ball,**
1938. Scarce. Pure Oil premium. WOR Radio. - **$50 $125 $250**

❏ **LON-46. Bond Bread Promo,**
1938. Scarce. WOR Radio. - **$70 $135 $300**

LON-47

LON-48

❑ **LON-47. Glass,**
1938. - **$20 $50 $100**

❑ **LON-48. Republic Serial Promo,**
1938. Scarce. 15 episodes. - **$50 $150 $300**

LON-49

❑ **LON-49. Detroit Sunday Times Comic Strip Announcement,**
1938. Strip began September 11. -
$45 $85 $150

LON-50

❑ **LON-50. Sign for Lone Ranger Gun Offer,**
1938. Gordon Gold Archives. -
$275 $550 $1100

LON-51

❑ **LON-51. Lone Ranger Game in Box,**
1938. Includes 5 metal "Lone Ranger on horse" playing pieces, game board, instructions, 12 silver discs, 4 red discs, 2 spinning indicators, an insert and the game box.
Complete - **$75 $160 $350**

LON-52

LON-53

❑ **LON-52. Composition/Cloth Doll With Fabric Outfit,**
1938. Store item as well as premium. 16" tall.
Lone Ranger - **$550 $1300 $2500**
Matching Tonto - **$425 $1050 $2100**

❑ **LON-53. Lone Ranger Doll with Tag,**
1938. 16" tall. Comes with neckerchief, badge, gun and holster, belt, removable vest, hat, mask, shirt and pants. Used as a premium for Lone Ranger ice cream cones.
- **$550 $1300 $2500**

LON-54

❑ **LON-54. Star Badge Used On Large Composition Doll,**
1938. Rare. Dollcraft Novelty Doll Co.
- **$60 $135 $275**

LON-55

❑ **LON-55. "Lee Powell/Original Motion Picture" Cello. Button,**
1938. Scarce. Republic Pictures. 1.75".
- **$125 $300 $500**

LON-56

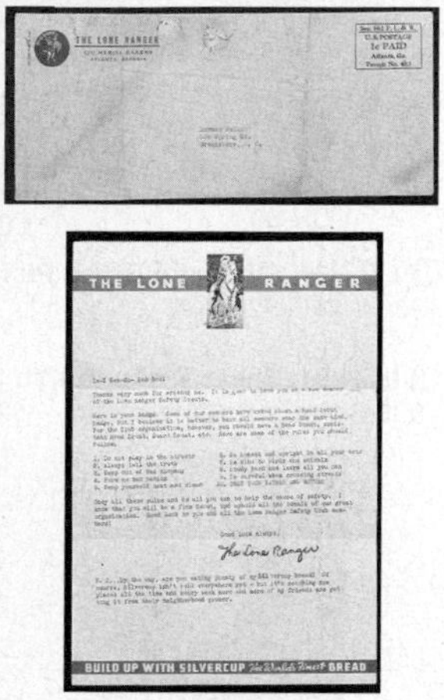

LON-57

❑ **LON-56. Radio WOR Promo,**
1938. - **$35 $65 $125**

❑ **LON-57. Safety Scouts Letter,**
1938. Silvercup Bread premium.
Mailer - **$25 $50 $75**
Letter - **$30 $65 $110**

LON-58

LON-59

❑ **LON-58. Certificate/Pledge,**
1938. Safety Club Bread premium. -
$50 $150 $300

❑ **LON-59. Tin Litho. Wind-Up,**
1938. Store item by Marx Toys.
"Silver" In White - **$100 $250 $500**
"Silver" In Silver - **$150 $400 $600**
Box - **$125 $200 $350**

LON-60

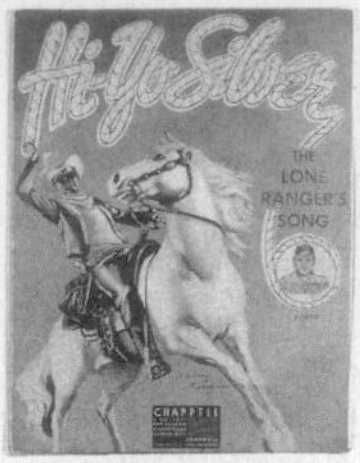

LON-61

❑ **LON-60. Silvercup Bread Picture,**
1938. - **$10 $20 $45**

❑ **LON-61. Sheet Music - Hi Yo Silver**
1938.Six pages. Store bought. - **$25 $65 $135**

LON-62

❑ **LON-62. Wright Bread Picture,**
1938. - **$25 $55 $110**

LON-63

LON-64

❑ **LON-63. Cellophane Picture Sheet,**
1938. Blue Ribbon Bread. Probably for window display.- **$50 $150 $300**

❑ **LON-64. High Gloss Photo,**
1938. Shown on horse with name at bottom right. Blank back. - **$30 $55 $110**

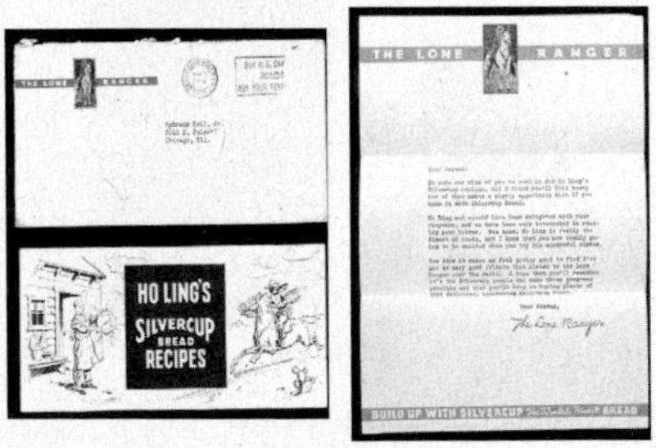

LON-65

❑ **LON-65. Ho-Ling Recipes Pamphlet and Letter,**
1938. Silvercup Bread. Mailer also shown.
Pamphlet - **$30 $75 $150**
Letter - **$30 $65 $110**
Mailer - **$20 $40 $60**

LON-66

❑ **LON-66. "Lone Ranger Safety Club" Membership Card,**
1938. Merita Bread. - **$25 $55 $100**

(CARD #1 WITHOUT MASK)

(CARD #1 WITH MASK)

LON-67

❑ **LON-67. Gum Wrappers Mail Picture,**
1938. Scarce. Lone Ranger Bubble Gum. Card #1 of five collected by sending wrappers. 8x10" size. Card #1 came with and without mask on Lone Ranger's face.
Card Without Mask - **$250 $375 $750**
Others - **$125 $225 $400**

LON-68

LON-69

LON-70

❑ **LON-68. Bond Bread 9x13" Paper Poster,**
1938. Scarce. Announces local radio broadcast times on WABY and WOR. - **$70 $135 $300**

❑ **LON-69. "Bond Bread Lone Ranger Safety Club" Enameled Brass Star Badge,**
1938. - **$18 $35 $70**

❑ **LON-70. "Lone Ranger Cones" Matchbook,**
1938. - **$10 $20 $50**

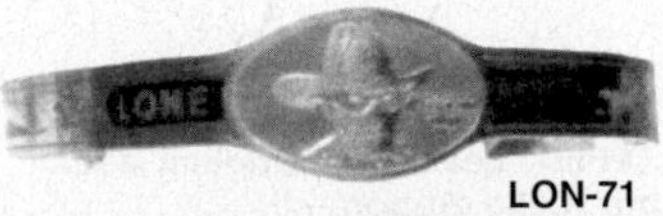

LON-71

❑ **LON-71. Lone Ranger Ice Cream Cones Enameled/Silvered Metal Picture Bracelet,**
1938. Rare. - **$400 $800 $1500**

LON-72

LON-73

❑ **LON-72. Tonto Lucky Ring,**
1938. Rare. Lone Ranger Ice Cream Cones. Green plastic to simulate onyx with paper portrait, also issued for Lone Ranger.
Tonto - **$1250 $2500 $5000**
Lone Ranger - **$1450 $2750 $6250**

❑ **LON-73. Felt Beanie,**
1938. Lone Ranger Ice Cream Cones. Seen in blue with red trim and red with blue trim. Rare. - **$100 $250 $550**

LON-74

❑ **LON-74. "Lone Ranger/Hi-Yo Silver" Brass Good Luck Medal,**
1938. Reverse design and inscription "Silver's Lucky Horseshoe". Sent in Detroit station WXYZ mailer with medal in red,white and blue stiff card.
Near Mint Complete - **$240**
Card Only - **$35 $65 $135**
Medal Only - **$15 $25 $50**

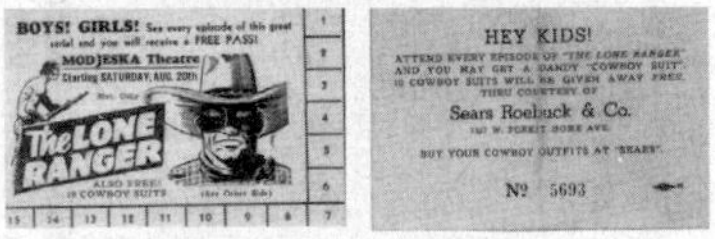

LON-75

❑ **LON-75. Movie Serial Ticket With Sears Offer,**
1938. Scarce. Ticket for 15-episode serial, reverse promotes cowboy suits at Sears, Roebuck. - **$125 $300 $600**

LON-76

❑ **LON-76. "Lone Ranger News" Second Issue Newspaper,**
1938. Butter-Nut Bread. 11.5x16" four-page publication dated July 1938. Contents include "Lone Ranger Safety Club Charter" certificate. - **$115 $225 $450**

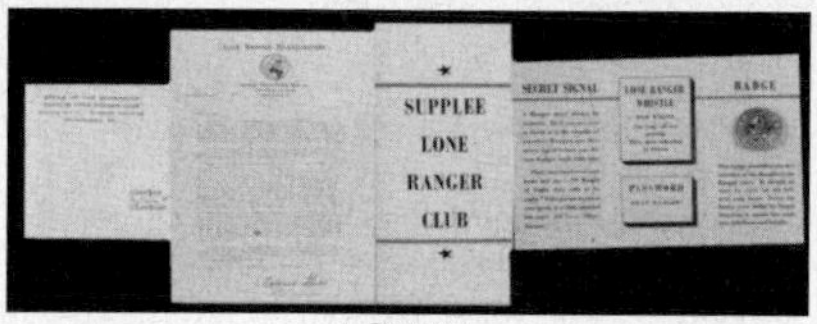

LON-77

❑ **LON-77. "Supplee" Club Member's Kit,**
c. 1938. Supplee-Wills-Jones Milk Co. Envelope has return address of "Office Of The Commander-Supplee Lone Ranger Club-Station WFIL." The folder is 3x6" and opens to 6x9" including secret signal, Lone Ranger whistle, password. The 8-1/2x11" letter is signed by "Colonel Bill, Commander Of Supplee Rangers."
Near Mint In Mailer **- $425**
Mailer **- $10 $15 $25**
Folder **- $35 $60 $125**
Letter **- $25 $50 $75**
Badge (see LON-100) **- $60 $125 $250**

LON-78

LON-79

❑ **LON-78. Silvercup Bread Photo,**
c. 1938. - **$30 $60 $120**

❑ **LON-79. Book Cover,**
c. 1938. Blue design on brown paper. Promotes Safety Club and program on "Mutual-Don Lee Stations." - **$35 $65 $125**

LON-80

LON-81

❑ **LON-80. Gately's Enameled Brass Star Badge,**
c. 1938. Gately's Bread. - **$35 $75 $150**

❑ **LON-81. Master Bread Enameled Brass Star Badge,**
c. 1938. - **$35 $75 $150**

LON-82

LON-83

LON-84

❑ **LON-82. "Dr. West's Tooth Paste" Cello. Club Button,**
c. 1938. 7/8" size. - **$45 $100 $200**

❑ **LON-83. Cobakco Bread "Your Friend Tonto" Picture Card,**
c. 1938. - **$30 $60 $120**

❑ **LON-84. Cobakco Bread Picture Card,**
c. 1938. - **$35 $65 $130**

LON-85

LON-86

❑ **LON-85. "Friend Of The Lone Ranger" Photo Card,**
c. 1938. Cobakco Bread. Pictured is "Your Friend, U.S. Marshal" from radio series. - **$35 $65 $130**

❑ **LON-86. Cobakco Bread "Chuck Livingston" Picture Card,**
c. 1938. Pictures "Outlaw On Lone Ranger Dramas". - **$35 $65 $130**

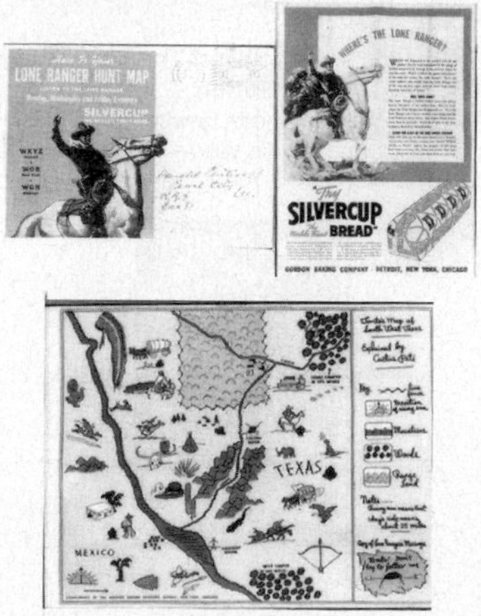

LON-87

❑ **LON-87. Silvercup Bread 13x17" "Lone Ranger Hunt Map" With Envelope,**
c. 1938. With Envelope **- $85 $225 $400**
Map Only **- $60 $140 $275**

LON-88

LON-89

❑ **LON-88. "Cobakco Safety Club" Enameled Brass Badge,**
c. 1938. Cobakco Bread. - **$30 $75 $135**

❑ **LON-89. 7up Personalized Picture,**
c. 1938. Black/white print personalized in white ink "To" recipient's first name. - **$30 $60 $120**

LON-90

LON-91

❑ **LON-90. Merita Bread Photo,**
c. 1938. - **$35 $75 $150**

❑ **LON-91. Merita Enameled Brass Star Badge,**
c. 1938. Merita Bread. - **$25 $70 $125**

LON-92

❑ **LON-92. Postcard,**
c. 1938. Eddy's Bread. Reverse has club information. - **$30 $60 $120**

LON-93

LON-94

❑ **LON-93. Cramer's Enameled Brass Star Badge,**
c. 1938. Cramer's Bread. - **$35 $85 $175**

❑ **LON-94. Franz Enameled Brass Star Badge,**
c. 1938. Franz' Bread. - **$30 $65 $145**

LON-95

❑ **LON-95. "Silver's Lucky Horseshoe" Sterling Silver Good Luck Piece,**
c. 1938. Merita Bread. 1-3/16" marked "Sterling" on side edge. Scarcer than similar versions described as "Solid Bronze." - **$35 $75 $125**

LON-96

❑ **LON-96. Safety Club Member's Button,**
c. 1938. Black and white on bright yellow 1-1/2" probably from bread company sponsor, possibly Merita. - **$50 $125 $250**

LON-97

❑ **LON-97. "Silver's Lucky Horseshoe" Enameled Brass Badge,**
c. 1938. Smaller 1-1/8" size. - **$20 $40 $85**
Same design but lower panel reading "The May Co." - **$50 $100 $220**

LON-98

LON-99

❑ **LON-98. "Silver's Lucky Horseshoe" Enameled Brass Badge,**
c. 1938. Larger 1-3/8" size. - **$25 $45 $95**

❑ **LON-99. "WFIL/Daily News Safety Club" Cello. Button,**
c. 1938. Philadelphia radio station. 1.25". - **$70 $150 $300**

LON-100

LON-101

❑ **LON-100. "Supplee Lone Ranger Club" Enameled Brass Badge,**
c. 1938. See LON-77. - **$60 $125 $250**

❑ **LON-101. "The Lone Ranger Radio Station" Cello. Button,**
c. 1938. WCSC, Charleston, South Carolina. 1-1/2". - **$45 $100 $200**

LON-102

LON-103

LON-104

❑ **LON-102. Rath's Enameled Brass Star Badge,**
c. 1938. Rath's Bread. - **$35 $85 $175**

❑ **LON-103. Bestyett Enameled Brass Star Badge,**
c. 1938. Bestyett Bread. - **$35 $85 $175**

❑ **LON-104. A. B. Poe Enameled Brass Star Badge,**
c. 1938. Poe Bread. - **$35 $85 $175**

LON-105

LON-106

❑ **LON-105. "Sunday Herald And Examiner" Litho. Button,**
c. 1938. - **$10 $20 $40**

❑ **LON-106. "Hi-Yo, Silver! The Lone Ranger Every Week" Cello. Button,**
c. 1938. Boston American newspaper and others. 1" black and red on yellow. - **$30 $85 $160**

LON-107

❑ **LON-107. "Kilpatrick's Safety Ranger" Club Postcard,**
c. 1938. Kilpatrick Bread. Black and white illustration card with safety club and sponsor text on reverse. Also known for sponsor "Eddy's Bread." - **$75 $150 $300**

LON-108

❑ **LON-108. "Lone Ranger Club" Movie Button,**
c. 1938. Republic Studios. 1.25" cello centered in black/white rimmed in red for "A Republic Western." - **$60 $150 $275**

LON-109

❑ **LON-109. Bond Bread Safety Poster,**
1939. 16.25x21.25" paper with school safety text plus promo line for radio program on station WOR (New York). - **$250 $500 $1000**

LON-110

❑ **LON-110. Sailor-Type Cloth Hat,**
1939. Issuer unknown. Fabric hat featuring brim front portrait illustration and Hi-Yo Silver! inscription in combination of white on gray/green. - **$40 $75 $150**

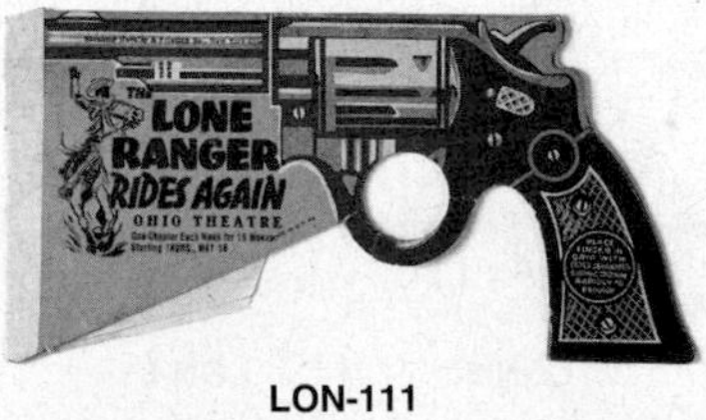

LON-111

❑ **LON-111. "The Lone Ranger Rides Again" Movie Theater Pop Gun,**
1939. 3.5x6.75" diecut stiff paper promo printed for local theater movie showing. Gun produces popping sound when vigorously flicked. - **$140 $275 $400**

LON-112

LON-113

❑ **LON-112. "Republic Picture" Horseshoe Enameled Brass Badge,**
1939. - **$40 $75 $150**

❑ **LON-113. "Lone Ranger Cones" Paper Wrapper,**
1939. Offers comic book, bracelet, Lone Ranger Ring, Tonto Ring with October 31, 1940 expiration date. - **$20 $50 $75**

LON-114

❑ **LON-114. "Lone Ranger Safety Sentinel" Brass Badge,**
1939. Miami Maid Bread. - **$65 $165 $350**

LON-115

❑ **LON-115. "Lone Ranger Special" Cap Pistol Box,**
1939. Store item by Kilgore. - **$125 $250 $500**

LON-116

❑ **LON-116. "Ice Cream Cone Coupons" Envelope To Merchant,**
1939. Lone Ranger Cones. Originally held 100 mail coupons expiring Jan. 1, 1940.
Envelope Only - **$35 $75 $135**
Each Coupon - **$10 $20 $30**

LON-117

❑ **LON-117. "The Lone Ranger Comic Book No. 1",**
1939. Rare. Lone Ranger Ice Cream Cones.
GD - **$914** FN - **$2742** VF - **$6400**

LON-118

❑ **LON-118. Large Feature Comic,**
1939. Whitman #715. - **$145 $435 $2100**

LON-119

❑ **LON-119. "Lone Ranger Ice Cream Cones" Dealer Sheet,**
1939. Reprinted ad from November issue of ice cream trade magazine for upcoming promotion in 1940. - **$45 $85 $150**

LON-120

LON-121

❑ **LON-120. Safety Club Letter,**
1939. Weber Bread premium. - **$75 $125 $200**

❑ **LON-121. Post Card,**
1939. Weber Bread. Back of postcard is an order form for 2 book covers.- **$25 $50 $80**

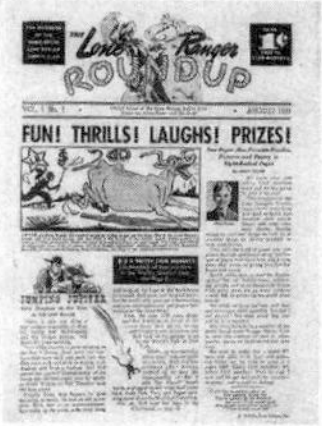

LON-122

❑ **LON-122. Bond Bread Safety Club "Lone Ranger Roundup" Vol. 1 #1 Newspaper,**
August 1939. Rare. Six issues, one every two months through Vol. 2 #3, June 1940.
First Issue - **$115 $225 $350**
Other Issues - **$60 $135 $215**

LON-123

❑ **LON-123. Creed Postcard And Mailer,**
1939. Weber Bread premium. Postcard is used to join club.- **$60 $100 $145**

LON-124

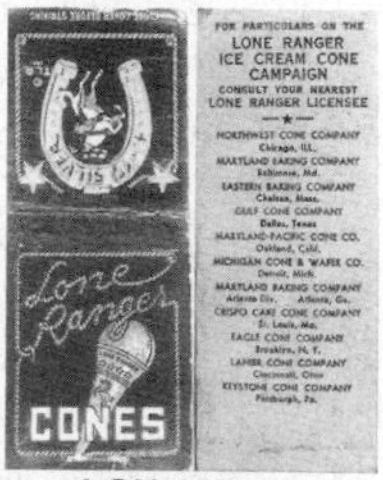

LON-125

❑ **LON-124. "Lone Ranger Cake Cones" Matchbook,**
1939. - **$10 $20 $50**

❑ **LON-125. "Lone Ranger Cones" Matchbook Cover,**
1939. Inscribed "Lone Ranger Ice Cream Cone Campaign." - **$10 $20 $50**

LON-126

❑ **LON-126. Photo,**
1939. Rare. Premium from New York World's Fair. Sponsored by Gimbel's Lone Ranger Show. - **$25 $50 $100**

LON-127

LON-128

❑ **LON-127. World's Fair Bond Bread Premium,**
1939. Rolled penny. - **$55 $125 $250**

❑ **LON-128. "Lone Ranger Secret Code" Cardboard Decoder,**
1939. Dr. West's Toothpaste. Came boxed with two bottles of "Invisible Writing Ink" and "Ink Developer" plus cotton swab.
Complete Boxed - **$125 $250 $500**
Decoder Only - **$75 $150 $300**

LON-129 LON-130

❑ **LON-129. Membership Card,**
1939. Dr. West's Toothpaste. Came with club newsletter. - **$60 $120 $240**

❑ **LON-130. Membership Certificate,**
1939. Dr. West's Toothpaste. Came with club newsletter. - **$75 $175 $350**

LON-131

❑ **LON-131. Dr. West's Lone Ranger News,**
1939. Dr. West's Toothpaste. Vol.1 #1 newsletter with 8 pages. Back cover offers Secret Writing Set that includes cardboard "Official Lone Ranger Automatic Decoder." (See LON-128). - **$125 $250 $550**

LON-132

❑ **LON-132. Weber's Bread Club Manual,**
1939. - **$75 $175 $350**

LON-133

❑ **LON-133. Calendar,**
1939. Cobakco Bread. - **$115 $235 $450**

LON-134

LON-135

❑ **LON-134. Merita Safety Club Radio Card,**
1939. Merita Bakers. Card sent by WBT Radio, Charlotte, North Carolina. Code translates: "Be Sure To Obey My Ten Safety Rules Always And Remember That You Help To Make My Great Safety Drive Possible By Eating Merita Bread And Cakes. So Be Sure To Ask Mother To Always Buy Merita Products!" - **$135 $275 $550**

❑ **LON-135. Silver Club Bronze Pin,**
1939. Butter-Nut Bread. Rare. - **$125 $265 $475**

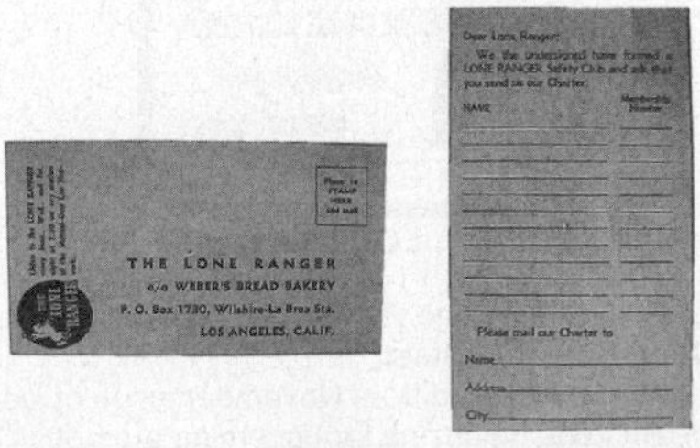

LON-136

❑ **LON-136. Request For Club Charter Card,**
1939. Weber's Bread/Lone Ranger Safety Club. Black on red with spaces to list 12 members with their membership number to acquire a charter certificate. - **$20 $50 $80**

LON-137

❑ **LON-137. "Lone Ranger Makeup Kit" On Card,**
1939. A premium comprised of theatrical make-up by "Miners." - **$75 $150 $350**

LON-138

❑ **LON-138. Club Member's Kit,**
1939. Weber's Lone Ranger Safety Club.
Mailer - **$10 $20 $40**
Member Registration Letter - **$30 $65 $100**
Brass Badge - **$30 $60 $90**
Member Card With Code - **$30 $60 $90**

LON-139

❑ **LON-139. Fabric Patch,**
1939. Probable club premium. 2-3/4" yellow and white on blue. - **$75 $125 $300**

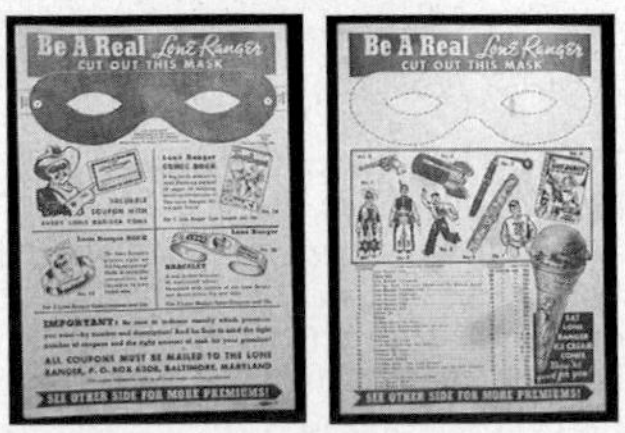

LON-140

❑ **LON-140. Lone Ranger Ice Cream Cones Premium Information Sheet,**
1939. 6x8-1/2" two-sided sheet in black and white which includes cut-out mask and list of 26 premiums along with combinations of coupons and cash needed to order. - **$100 $200 $375**

LON-141

❑ **LON-141. Horlick's Malted Milk Picture,**
1939. "Over Station WGN-Chicago". H.J. Ward did the original painting used for this premium in 1937. - **$25 $65 $125**

LON-142 LON-143

❑ **LON-142. Roundup Paper,**
1939. Bond Bread. Vol. 1 #2. 8 pages.- **$60 $135 $215**

❑ **LON-143. Roundup Paper,**
1939. Bond Bread. Vol. 1 #3. 8 pages.- **$60 $135 $215**

LON-144

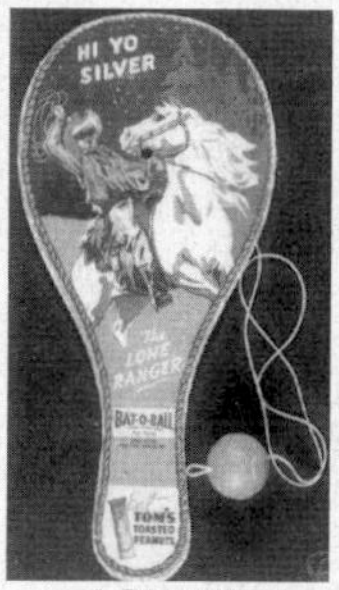

LON-145

❑ **LON-144. Leather Watch Fob Holster With Miniature Gun,**
1939. Came with some issues of New Haven pocketwatches. - **$35 $50 $150**

❑ **LON-145. "Bat-O-Ball" Toy,**
1939. Scarce. Tom's Toasted Peanuts. Cardboard paddle with rubber band and ball.
With Ball - **$60 $135 $260**
No Ball - **$50 $125 $250**

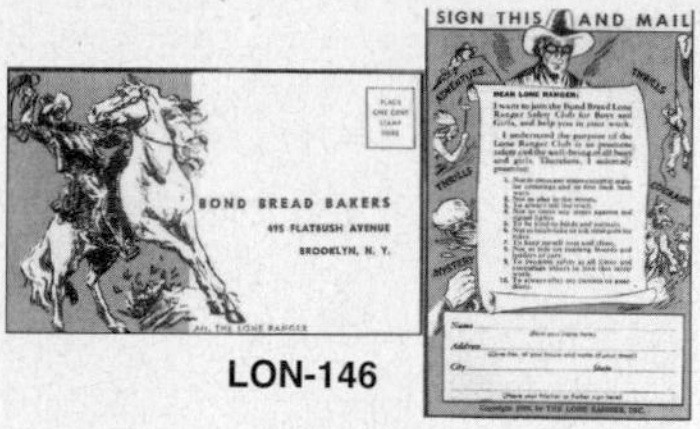

LON-146

❑ **LON-146. "Safety Club" Application Postcard,**
1939. Bond Bread. - **$15 $35 $65**

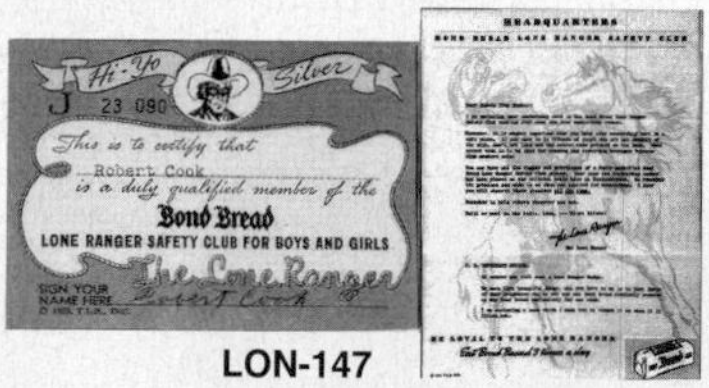

LON-147

❑ **LON-147. "Bond Bread Safety Club" Letter And Membership Card,**
1939. Card - **$20 $45 $100**
Letter - **$35 $65 $145**

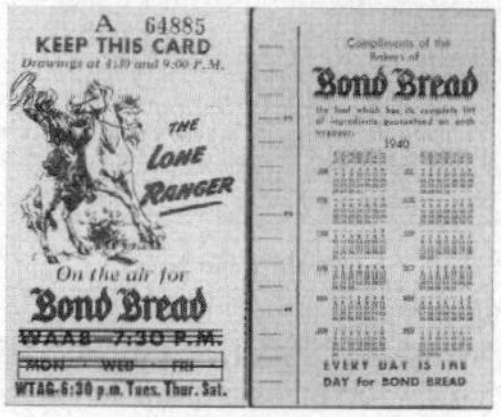

LON-148

❑ **LON-148. Bond Bread Contest Card Stub,**
1939. - **$40 $85 $195**

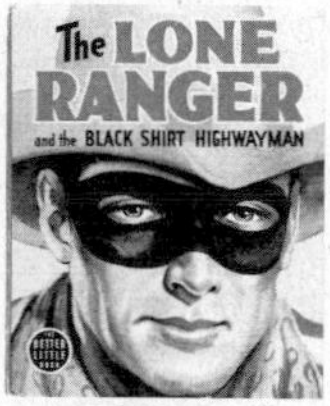

LON-149 LON-150

❑ **LON-149. May Co. Activity Booklet,**
1939. May department store. Christmas issue. - **$50 $150 $350**

❑ **LON-150. "The Lone Ranger and the Black Shirt Highwayman" Better Little Book #1450,**
1939. - **$20 $60 $140**

LON-151

❑ **LON-151. "Lapel Watch" Boxed Pocketwatch,**
1939. Store item by New Haven Time Co. as well as premium. Two different decal designs.
Near Mint Boxed - **$1600**
Watch Only - **$250 $450 $800**
Box Only - **$200 $400 $800**

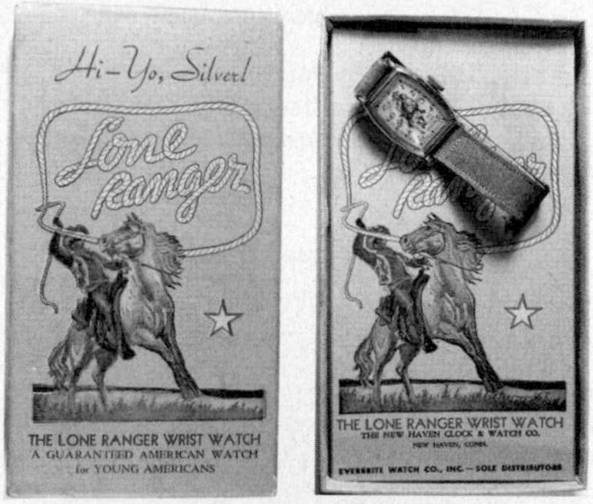

LON-152

❑ **LON-152. Lone Ranger Wrist Watch,**
1939. Watch in colorful box with scarce stand-up display insert.
Watch with Box - **$350 $800 $1600**
Watch Only - **$100 $300 $600**
Box with Insert Only - **$250 $500 $1000**

LON-153

❑ **LON-153 Pony Contest 11x14" Cardboard Poster,**
c. 1939. Cobakco Bread. - **$60 $145 $300**

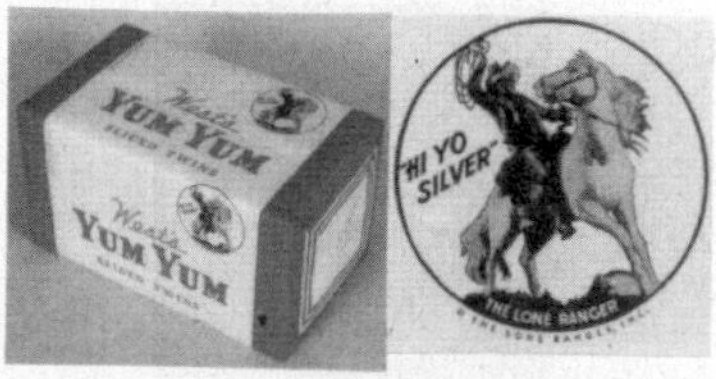

LON-154

❑ **LON-154. "West's" Bread Wrapper,**
c. 1939. Sponsored by West's Yum Yum Sliced Twins. - **$45 $85 $175**

LON-155

❑ LON-155. Fabric Patch,
c. 1939. 3.5" diameter red/black/white possibly from Lone Ranger clothing or costume. - **$30 $60 $110**

LON-156

❑ LON-156. Calendar Top,
c. 1939. Merita Bread. Our photo shows 14x15" top while lower portion held calendar and pad of club applications. The Tonto image depicts Chief Thundercloud of the 1938-39 movie serials. Complete - **$450 $1000 $2250**

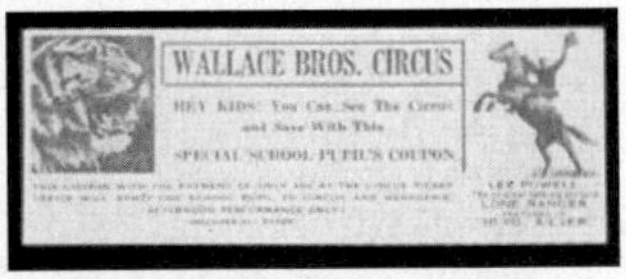

LON-157

❑ LON-157. "Special School Pupil's Coupon",
c. 1939. Wallace Bros. Circus. Used with 20 cents for admission with captioned redtone image on right "Lee Powell/The Original Talking Picture Lone Ranger Featured In Hi-Yo Silver." - **$60 $135 $225**

LON-158

❑ LON-158. "The Lone Ranger Comic Daily And Sunday Examiner" Cello. Button,
c. 1939. Examiner newspaper. 1-1/4" with red lettering and blue and white image on white. - **$175 $375 $850**

(CLOSE-UP OF 1939 VERSION TEXT)

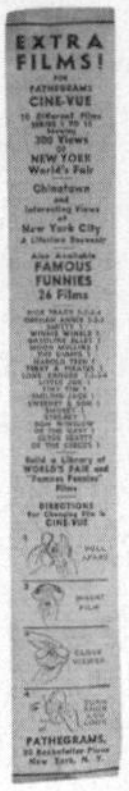

LON-159

❑ LON-159. Lone Ranger Pathegrams Movies with Viewer in Box,
1939. Viewer is multi-colored with a black removable panel. Lid of box has a white square with text only found on this 1939 version. Box insert is blue and holds film. Side of box has "Pathegrams" and a rooster logo with a 1939 copyright date. The company sold production rights to Acme Products in late 1939. Very rare. Complete - **$300 $600 $1200**

LON-160

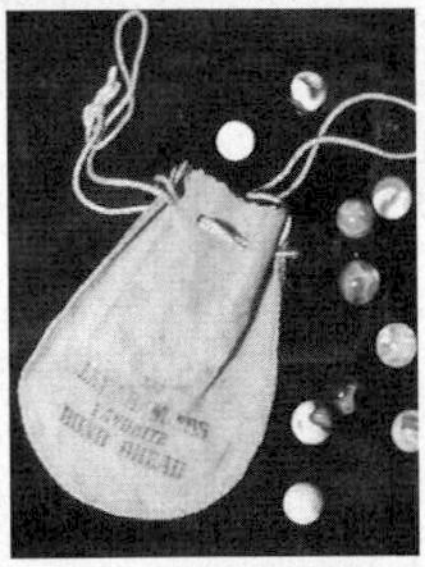

LON-161

❑ LON-160. Bond Bread Color Cellophane Picture Sheet,
c. 1939. 6x9" probably for window display. - **$50 $150 $300**

❑ LON-161. "The Lone Ranger's Favorite Bond Bread" Leather Pouch For Marbles,
1930s. Bond Bread. 5" tall with cord drawstring. Pouch Only - **$100 $225 $400**

LON-162

LON-163

❑ LON-162. Lone Ranger Carnival Statue,
1930s. Used as a bookend. Flat back. Scarce. - **$50 $100 $200**

❑ LON-163. Lone Ranger Carnival Statue,
1930s. Various designs used from 1930s into 1940s. - **$40 $75 $150**

(CLOSE-UP OF 1940 VERSION TEXT)

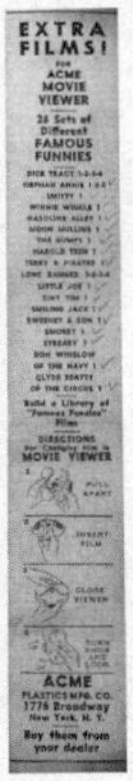

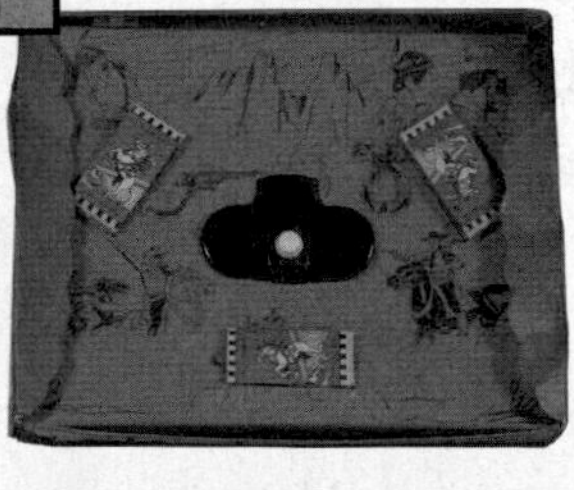

LON-164

❑ LON-164. Lone Ranger Acme Movies with Viewer in Box,
1940. Unlike the 1939 Pathegrams version, viewer is all black, lid of box has a white square with updated text, box insert is red and holds film boxes with different art than 1939. Side of box has "An Acme Product" and a 1940 copyright date. Complete - **$200 $375 $550**
"Extra Film" Advertisement Insert - **$10 $25 $40**

LON-165

❑ **LON-165. Bond Bread 8x12" Cardboard Store Sign,**
1940. Scarce. - **$140 $300 $600**

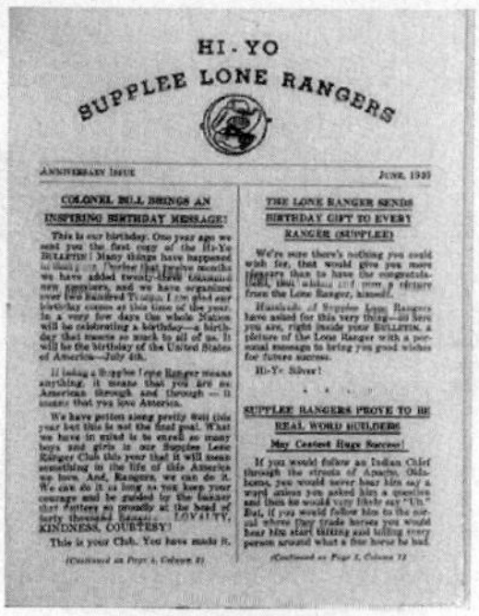

LON-166

LON-167

❑ **LON-166. "Hi-Yo Supplee Lone Rangers" Newsletter,**
1940. Supplee Milk. First anniversary issue. - **$35 $70 $165**

❑ **LON-167. "Orange Pops" 6x12" Cardboard Store Sign,**
1940. Scarce. - **$150 $400 $750**

LON-168

❑ **LON-168. "Cloverine Salve" Premium Catalogue With Watch Ads,**
c. 1940. - **$18 $35 $70**

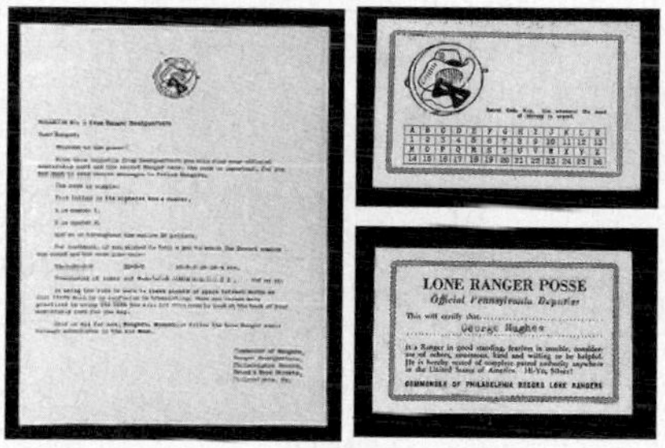

LON-169

❑ **LON-169. "Lone Ranger Posse" Club Papers,**
c. 1940. Philadelphia Record. Letter and membership card for comic strip promotion.
Letter - **$25 $60 $125**
Card - **$35 $75 $150**

LON-170

❑ **LON-170. Bond Bread Wrapper,**
1940. - **$30 $60 $125**

(CLOSE-UP OF HANDLE END)

LON-171

❑ **LON-171. Lone Ranger Spoon,**
1940. Rare. Has "The Lone Ranger Hi Yo Silver" engraved on handle. - **$100 $175 $300**

LON-172

❑ **LON-172. Merita "The Life Of Tonto" Story Chapter,**
1940. Merita Bread of American Bakeries Co. 11-chapter newspaper ad/feature jointly sponsored by various radio stations. Pictured example is Chapter 10 co-sponsored by WDBJ, Roanoke, Virginia. Each - **$40 $75 $150**

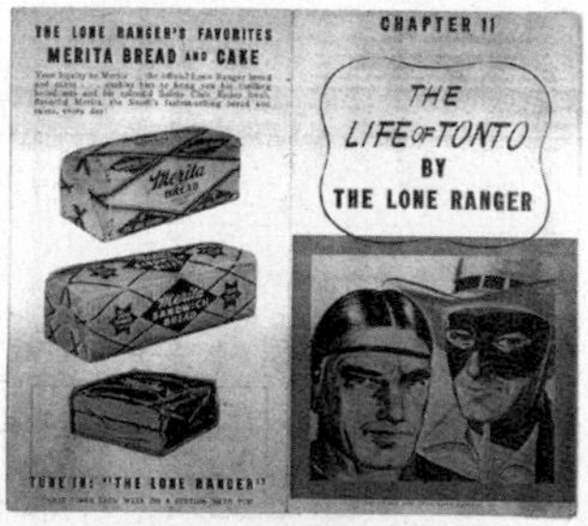

LON-173

❑ **LON-173. Merita "The Life Of Tonto" Story Folder,**
1940. Merita Bread. Set of 11 folders, about 4x7" (shown open). Same story text as version with photos but this version features cover illustration and no photo. Each - **$35 $70 $125**

Picture of Lone Ranger Picture of Silver

LON-174

❑ **LON-174. Lone Ranger Prototype Secret Compartment Ring,**
1940. Rare Orin Armstrong designed ring has pictures of the Lone Ranger and Silver inside. The design was later modified by the Robbins Company and offered with smaller pictures and a sliding top in 1942. - **$1250 $2500 $5000**

(FRONT COVER) (BACK COVER)

LON-175

❑ **LON-175. Punch-Out Book,**
1940. Rare. - **$400 $1200 $2500**

LON-176

❑ **LON-176. Roundup Paper,**
1940. Bond Bread. Vol. 2 #3. 8 pages.-
$60 $135 $215

LON-177

❑ **LON-177. Merita Bread Club Calendar With Member Application Papers,**
1940. 13x26" cardboard wall calendar completed by glued cardboard box near center as made for holding quantity of application slips to obtain membership card and key to secret code. Application includes 10-point safety club pledge. - **$650 $1350 $2250**

LON-178

❑ **LON-178. Color Photo,**
c. 1940. Bond Bread. - **$15 $25 $60**

LON-179

LON-180

❑ **LON-179. "Lone Ranger Cones" Paper Wrapper,**
c. 1940. Offers same premiums as 1939 wrapper without expiration date. - **$20 $50 $75**

❑ **LON-180. Australian Lone Ranger Club Badge,**
c. 1940. This silvered brass six-pointed star badge is rather small but very distinctly detailed including tiny image of Lone Ranger on rearing Silver at top above inscription "Allan & Stark Lone Ranger Safety Club." Reverse has large stamped-in serial numbe "2389" above tiny company logo image and text "Amor Brisbane."
- **$115 $225 $450**

LON-181

❑ **LON-181. Kix Cereal "Name Silver's Son" 16x20" Contest Poster,**
1941. Rarest of all the contest posters. Less than 5 known. - **$1500 $3000 $5000**

LON-182

❑ **LON-182. Photo With Insert And Envelope,**
1941. Came with insert announcing Kix as new radio sponsor. H.J. Ward did the original painting used for this premium in 1937.
Complete - **$40 $80 $175**
Photo Only - **$15 $25 $60**

LON-183

❑ **LON-183. "National Defenders Secret Portfolio" Manual,**
1941. See "Whistling Jim" version in Premiums Misc. section. - **$85 $200 $350**
Mailer - **$20 $40 $75**

LON-184

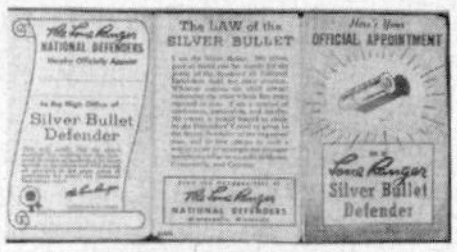

LON-185

❑ **LON-184. Glow-In-Dark Brooch 3" Plastic Pin,**
1941. General Mills. Offered in the Lone Ranger National Defenders Portfolio from Kix cereal as "something for mother" along with matching earrings. Also offered on soap operas sponsored by General Mills and in the southeastern states as a Whistling Jim premium. Not associated with Jack Armstrong as previously believed.
Brooch - **$50 $100 $150**
Earring Set - **$60 $125 $185**

❑ **LON-185. "Silver Bullet Defender" Leaflet With 45-Caliber Silver Bullet,**
1941. Contains silver ore.
Bullet - **$20 $50 $100**
Folder - **$45 $85 $160**

LON-186

❑ **LON-186. Kix Luminous Blackout Plastic Belt,**
1941. Near Mint Boxed With Insert Folder - **$250**
Belt Only - **$50 $75 $150**

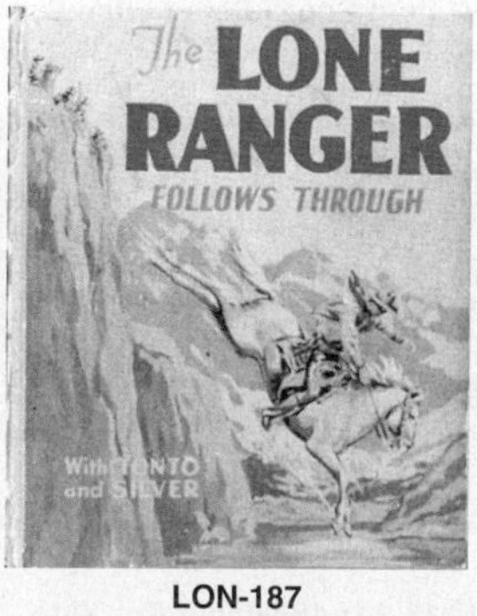

LON-187

❑ **LON-187. "The Lone Ranger Follows Through" Better Little Book,**
1941. Whitman #1468. - **$19 $57 $135**

LON-188

❑ **LON-188. National Defenders Danger-Warning Siren,**
1941. Scarce. Came with carrying cord. Offered as bounce back premium with Gardenia Brooch. - **$165 $425 $850**
Tube Mailer - **$30 $60 $125**

LON-189

❑ **LON-189. "Danger-Warning Siren" Offer Ad,**
1941. Kix Cereal. Sunday comics one-half page color ad offering premium as part of Lone Ranger National Defenders Club kit. - **$20 $35 $80**

LON-190

LON-191

❑ **LON-190. National Defenders Look-Around Brass Ring,**
1941. No inscription but offered in Lone Ranger promium advertisements. Also issued for Captain Midnight and Radio Orphan Annie. - **$65 $135 $250**

❑ **LON-191. Safety Club Card,**
1941. Rare. Felber Biscuit Co. Shows Silver, Lone Ranger, and Tonto on front.Secret code on back. - **$65 $135 $200**

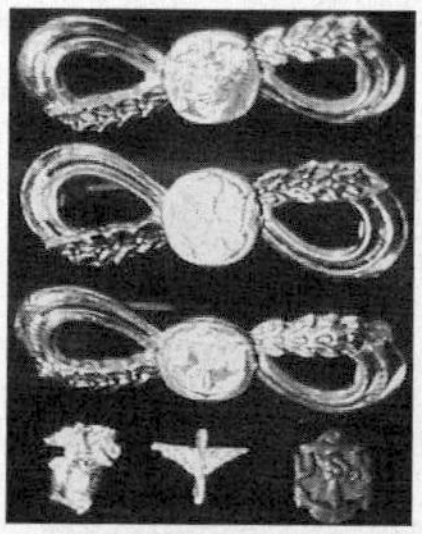

LON-192

❑ **LON-192. Military Sweetheart Pins,**
1941. General Mills, Korn Kix. Set of three large and three small brass luster pins depicting insignias of service branches. Verified by Evie Wilson, former General Mills archivist.
Near Mint In Original Case - **$500**

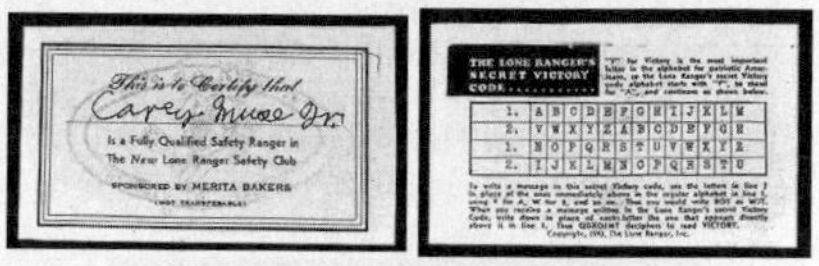

LON-193

❑ **LON-193. Merita Safety Club Card,**
1941 Merita Bakers. - **$20 $50 $80**

LON-194

LON-195

❑ **LON-194. Brass Lucky Piece "From WXYZ Detroit",**
1941. Radio station where The Lone Ranger originated. Same design as the 1938 brass version but this piece has silvered finish plus incised WXYZ message within the design of Silver's horseshoe. - **$50 $100 $150**

❑ **LON-195."The Lone Ranger Rides Again",**
1941. Feature Book No. 24 - **$86 $258 $1250**

LON-196

LON-197

❑ **LON-196. Lone Ranger Contest Prize Award Poster,**
c. 1941. Awarded by Kix cereal as prize from contest to 'name Silver's son.' 22-1/2x31" in gray, black and white. H.J. Ward did the original painting used for this premium in 1937. - **$200 $400 $800**

❑ **LON-197. "The Lone Ranger" Cello. Button,**
c. 1941. Possibly Merita Bread Safety Club. - **$50 $125 $200**

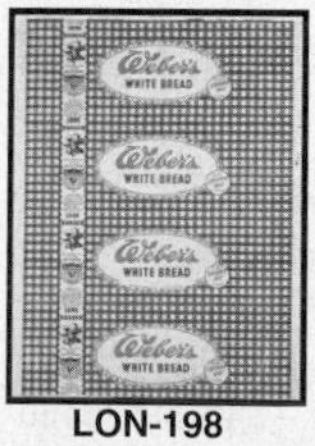

LON-198

LON-199

❑ **LON-198. Victory Bread Wrapper,**
1942. Weber's White Bread. - **$30 $65 $125**

❑ **LON-199. Sailor Hat,**
1942. Blue on white. - **$50 $75 $150**

LON-200

❑ **LON-200. Victory Corps Club Promo,**
1942. - **$100 $250 $500**

LON-201 **LON-202**

❑ **LON-201. Bread Loaf Wrapper,**
1942. Merita Bread. Small diamond designs between the company name diamonds say "Hi-Yo Silver/Lone Ranger." - **$25 $55 $110**

❑ **LON-202. "Lone Ranger Victory Corps" Brass Tab,**
1942. - **$15 $30 $65**

LON-203

❑ **LON-203. Military Hat with Metal Button,**
1942. Rare. - **$150 $350 $650**

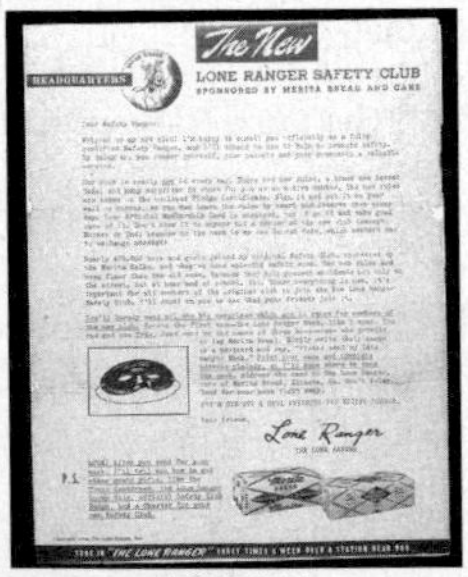

LON-204

❑ **LON-204. Safety Club Letter,**
1942. Merita Bread premium. - **$40 $90 $150**

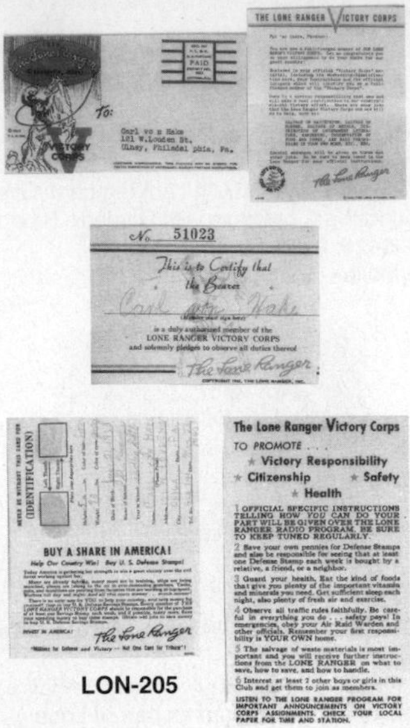

LON-205

❑ **LON-205. "Victory Corps" Membership Kit,**
1942. Cheerios/Kix. Includes cover letter with membership/I.D. folder plus brass tab (see item LON-202). Envelope - **$30 $50 $100**
Letter - **$30 $85 $135**
Member Card Folder - **$30 $85 $135**

LON-206 **LON-207**

❑ **LON-206. "Lone Ranger VC" Victory Corps Cello. Button,**
1942. - **$35 $70 $150**

❑ **LON-207. Kix Army Air Corps Ring,**
1942. Interior ring photos of Lone Ranger and Silver often missing.
Ring Complete - **$150 $300 $600**
Ring; No Photos - **$50 $100 $200**

LON-208

❑ **LON-208. Secret Compartment Ring Instruction Paper,**
1942. Leaflet opens to four panels with other Lone Ranger radio and club notes. - **$65 $135 $225**

LON-209

❑ **LON-209. Marine Corps Brass Ring,**
1942. Two inside photos of Lone Ranger and Silver often missing.
Complete - **$150 $300 $600**
No Photos - **$50 $100 $200**

LON-210 **LON-211**

❑ **LON-210. Army Insignia Secret Compartment Brass Ring,**
1942. Two inside photos of Lone Ranger and Silver often missing.
Complete - **$150 $300 $600**
No Photos - **$50 $100 $200**

❑ **LON-211. "USN" Navy Photo Ring,**
1942. Brass, two inside photos of Lone Ranger and Silver often missing.
Complete - **$150 $300 $600**
No Photos - **$50 $100 $200**

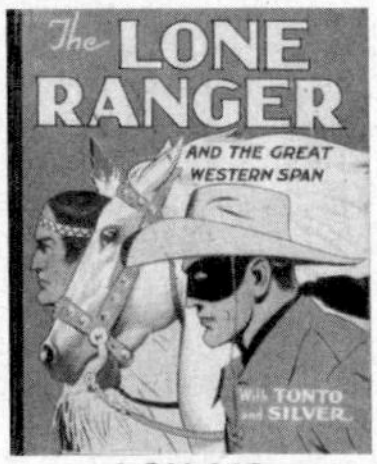

LON-212

❑ **LON-212. "The Lone Ranger And The Great Western Span" Better Little Book,**
1942. Whitman #1477. - **$17 $51 $120**

LON-213

❑ **LON-213. Kix "Blackout Kit" With Envelope,**
1942. Contents include luminous paper items.
Near Mint In Mailer - **$375**

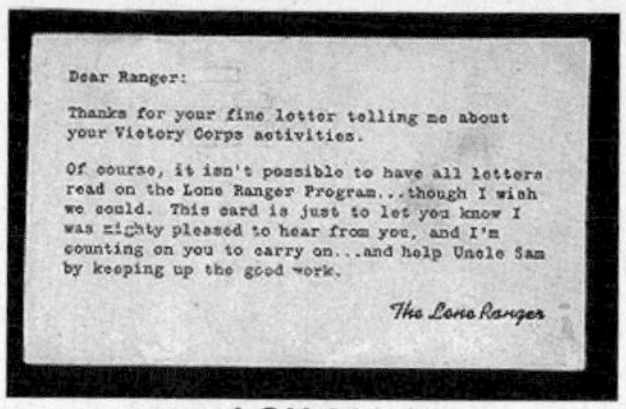
Dear Ranger:

Thanks for your fine letter telling me about your Victory Corps activities.

Of course, it isn't possible to have all letters read on the Lone Ranger Program...though I wish we could. This card is just to let you know I was mighty pleased to hear from you, and I'm counting on you to carry on...and help Uncle Sam by keeping up the good work.

The Lone Ranger

LON-214

❑ **LON-214. "Victory Corps" Postcard To Member,**
1942. Acknowledgement to "Dear Ranger" thanking member for letter describing Victory Corps activities. Pictured example has reverse August 5 postmark from Minneapolis. - **$30 $60 $100**

LON-215

❑ **LON-215. Lone Ranger Safety Club Merita Headdress With Letter,**
1942. Premium includes 4x9.5" envelope, 8x10.5" letter that mentions Tonto headdress enclosed and pictures "Lucky Coin." Included is 14" long felt headdress.
Envelope - **$10 $20 $30**
Letter - **$30 $60 $100**
Headdress - **$55 $110 $175**

LON-216

❑ **LON-216. Merita Bread Standee,**
1942. 10x17-1/2" diecut cardboard shown framed with Merita Club Member's Application.
Standee - **$675 $1350 $2700**
Application - **$25 $50 $75**

LON-217

LON-218

❑ **LON-217. Lone Ranger Safety Club Calendar And Membership Application Pad Holder,**
1942. Merita Bread. 17x25". Boy shown wearing Lone Ranger Merita Bread Brass Club Badge. Example shown without application and calendar pads.
Complete - **$750 $1500 $2250**
Without Pads - **$500 $1000 $1500**

❑ **LON-218. Meteorite Ring,**
1942. Scarce. Kix bounce back offer with Lone Ranger military rings April, 1942. Company recorded 85 requests. Brass with plastic dome over tiny "meteorite" granules. Following General Mills (Kix) offer, also offered briefly by Kellogg's Corn Flakes or Pep as Gold Ore ring for seven package tops and 5¢.
- **$600 $1450 $3350**

LON-219

❑ **LON-219. "V" Toy Gun,**
c. 1942. 7" composition play gun with "Lone Ranger" name on right side and "V" letter symbol on both sides, symbolizing Lone Ranger Victory Corps. - **$100 $225 $400**

LON-220

❑ **LON-220. Merita Safety Club Card,**
1943. Merita Bakers. - **$20 $50 $80**

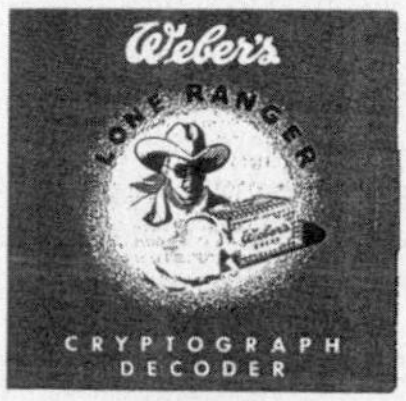

LON-221

❑ **LON-221. Weber's Decoder Folder,**
1943. Rare. - **$100 $175 $325**

LON-222

❑ **LON-222. Lone Ranger And Tonto Color Prints,**
1943. Merita Bread. Each about 9x11" with artist's name Sheffield. Each - **$75 $125 $250**

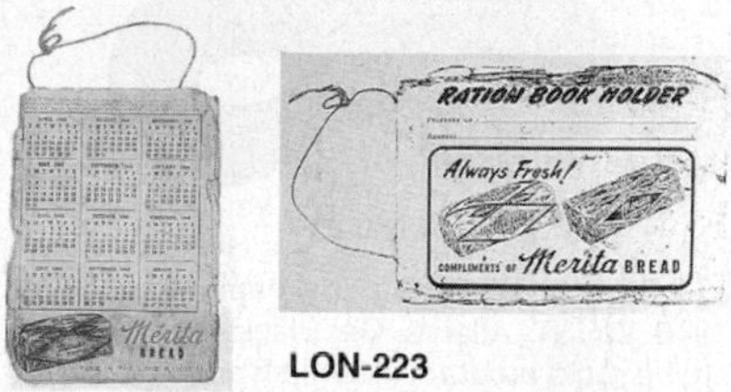

LON-223

❑ **LON-223. World War II Ration Book Holder,**
1943. Merita Bread. 4-1/2x6" inscribed "Tune In The Lone Ranger." - **$40 $80 $165**

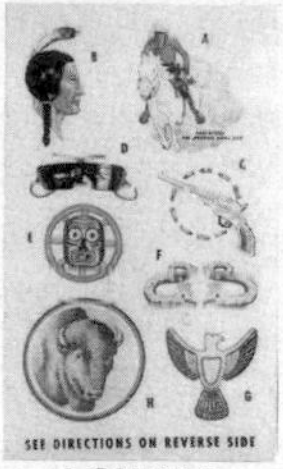

LON-224

❑ **LON-224. Kix Decal Sheet,**
1944. Set #5 sheet from series with water transfer decals of Lone Ranger and other western subjects. - **$20 $40 $80**

LON-225

❑ **LON-225. "War Album Of Victory Battles" With Mailer Envelope,**
1945. General Mills. No Lone Ranger mention but offered on radio show, came with battle scene stamps.
Mailer - **$15 $30 $50**
Complete Album - **$40 $80 $150**
Album No Stamps - **$15 $30 $50**

LON-226

❑ **LON-226. "Kix Airbase" 27x27" Play Sheet Map With Envelope,**
1945. No Lone Ranger inscription but offered on his show. Used with 32 warplane cut-outs from four Kix cereal boxes.
Envelope - **$25 $75 $150**
Airbase - **$50 $100 $200**

LON-227

❑ **LON-227. Radio Station Paper Mask,**
1945. WGST, Atlanta, Ga. Black thin cardboard urging radio program listenership. - **$35 $65 $135**

LON-228

❑ **LON-228. Movie Theatre Card With Reverse Cut-Out Mask,**
1945. Stanley Theatre, Jersey City, N.J. Example likely from series printed for various individual theaters. Movie showing days of week document to 1945. Uncut - **$50 $100 $200**
Cut - **$10 $20 $50**

LON-229

❑ **LON-229. "Merita" Bread Loaf Label,**
c. 1945. Full color. Each - **$25 $50 $140**

LON-230

❑ **LON-230. Cereal Box With "Kix Atomic Bomb Ring" Offer,**
1946. Box has 1946 copyright of General Mills but company archive records indicate ring distribution began January 19, 1947. Gordon Gold Archives. Used Complete - **$475 $850 $1750**

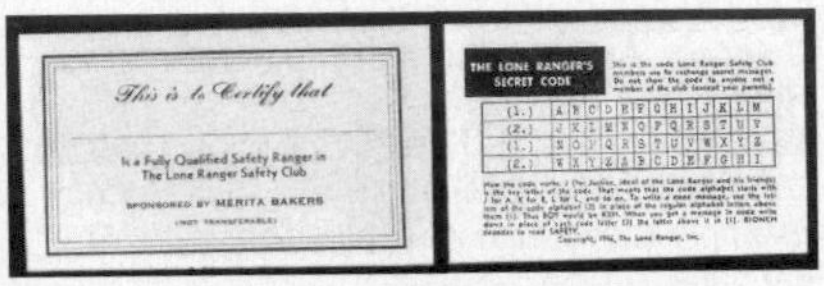

LON-231

❑ **LON-231. Merita Safety Club Card,**
1946. Merita Bakers. - **$15 $40 $70**

LON-232

❑ **LON-232. Lone Ranger Safety Club Calendar And Membership Application Pad Holder,**
1946. Merita Bread. 16-1/2x25-1/2" cardboard. Example shown without application and calendar pads. Complete - **$800 $1600 $3000**
Without Pads - **$600 $1100 $2000**

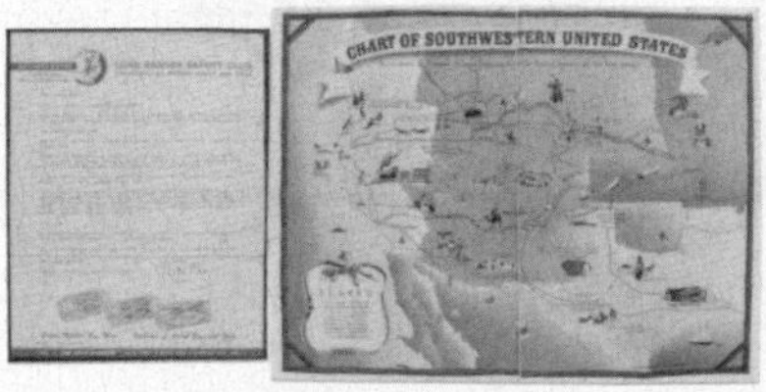

LON-233

❑ **LON-233. Merita Club Letter With Tonto Map And Envelope,**
1946. Merita Bakers. Map opens to 17x22" titled "Chart Of Southwestern United States."
Mailer - **$10 $20 $40**
Letter - **$30 $60 $120**
Chart - **$275 $625 $1150**

LON-234

❑ **LON-234. "The Lone Ranger and the Silver Bullets" Big Little Book #1498,**
1946. - **$17 $51 $120**

LON-235

LON-236

❑ **LON-235. Weather Forecasting Ring,**
1946. Brass with clear lucite cover over small litmus paper. - **$35 $75 $150**

❑ **LON-236. Merita Bread Portrait Picture,**
1946. Artist signature appears to be Frederic Myer. Also issued as a calendar.
Picture - **$100 $250 $525**

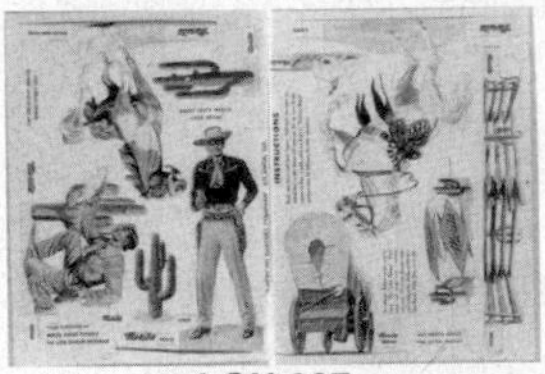
LON-237

LON-238

❑ **LON-237. Punch-Out Sheet,**
1947. American Bakeries Co. - **$50 $125 $250**

❑ **LON-238. "Lone Ranger .45" Secret Compartment Bullet,**
1947. Aluminum with removable cap. - **$20 $40 $75**

LON-239

LON-240

❑ **LON-239. "Atomic Bomb Ring" Newspaper Ad,**
1947. Kix Cereal. 10x14" clipping from Sunday newspaper comic section. - **$25 $50 $100**

❑ **LON-240. Atomic Bomb Ring,**
1947. Kix cereal. Brass with plastic bomb cap. A Kix cereal box dated 1946 with Atomic Bomb ring offer is known. However, most distribution began January 1947. - **$50 $125 $250**

LON-241

❑ **LON-241. Lone Ranger Deluxe Movie Viewer With Film,**
1947. Large box updated with new graphics. Box is extremely fragile with many perforated areas - probably the reason this item is so rare. Complete - **$250 $500 $750**

LON-242

❑ **LON-242. Lone Ranger Acme Movies with Viewer in Box,**
1948. Box is similar to the 1940 version, but viewer is black and red, box insert is yellow and holds film boxes using a different font than 1940 version. Side of box has "An Acme Product" and a 1948 copyright date. Complete - **$100 $250 $400**

LON-243

LON-244

❑ **LON-243. Six-Gun Ring,**
1948. Brass with plastic gun holding flint. - **$60 $130 $260**

❑ **LON-244. "Lone Ranger 6-Shooter Ring" 17x22" Store Poster,**
1948. - **$75 $140 $275**

LON-245

❑ **LON-245. Merita Bread Safety Club Calendar,**
1948. Rare. 16"x24". With calendar tablet pages and club application forms. - **$800 $1600 $3000**

(MAP) (BUILDING SECTION)

LON-246

❑ **LON-246. "Lone Ranger Frontier Town" Punch-Outs And Maps,**
1948. Four separate maps and four separate unpunched Building sections.
Each Unpunched Section With Mailer - **$300**
Complete Punched Section - **$200**
Each Map - **$60 $100 $200**

LON-247

❑ **LON-247. Merita Bread Safety Club Large Color Picture,**
1948. Smaller version of 1948 calendar, but without the calendar pages and application forms. Sent to new member. - **$135 $275 $575**

LON-248

LON-249

❑ **LON-248. Tonto Set Of Two Metal Bracelets,**
1948. Scarce. No character name on the bracelets, each has Indian symbols. Complete With Mailer - **$100 $200 $400**

❑ **LON-249. Flashlight Ring,**
1948. Brass with lightbulb and battery. - **$25 $50 $120**

LON-250

❑ **LON-250. "Flashlight Ring" Instruction Sheet,**
1948. Cheerios. Reverse includes "Good Deed Order Blank" for friend. - **$25 $50 $75**

LON-251

LON-252

❑ **LON-251. Cheerios Aluminum Pedometer With Fabric Strap,**
1948. Near Mint Boxed - **$85**
Loose - **$15 $30 $50**

❑ **LON-252. Lone Ranger/Gene Autry Flag Ring,**
c. 1948. Dell Comics. Plastic with dome over flag image, for one-year subscription to comic book for either. - **$50 $100 $175**

LON-253

❑ **LON-253. Merita Safety Club Card,**
1948. Merita Bakers. Dark blue or dark green variations. Either - **$15 $40 $70**

LON-254

❑ **LON-254. Christmas Card To Dell Comic Subscriber,**
1948. Photos show front and back of card.
Card - **$125 $250 $400**
Envelope - **$20 $40 $60**

LON-255

❑ **LON-255. "Lone Ranger Frontier Town" Newspaper Ad,**
1948. Cheerios. 10x14" clipping from Sunday newspaper comic section. - **$15 $30 $60**

LON-256

❑ **LON-256. "Frontier Town" Cheerios Box,**
1948. Set of nine.
Complete Box Each - **$165 $375 $750**
Each Back Panel Used to Complete Lone Ranger Town - **$18 $35 $75**

LON-257

❑ **LON-257. "Movie Film Ring" Instruction Sheet,**
1949. Cheerios. Reverse has order blank and description of Marine Corps film. - **$20 $40 $80**

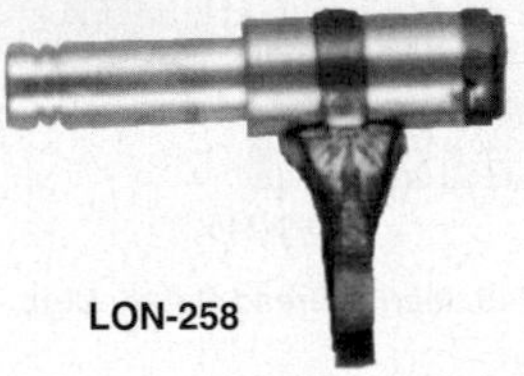

LON-258

❑ **LON-258. Lone Ranger Movie Film Ring,**
1949. Brass bands with aluminum viewing tube, came with 25-frame 8mm color filmstrip titled "U.S. Marines". Ring - **$25 $50 $125**
Film - **$50 $85 $150**

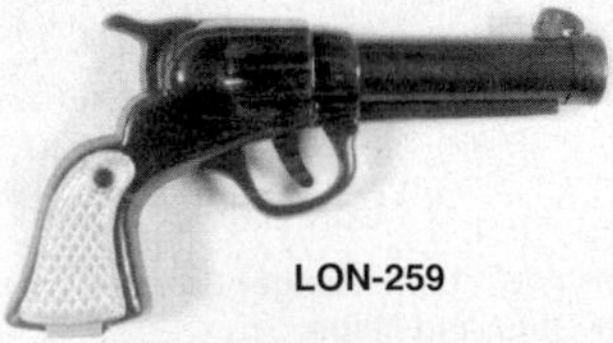

LON-259

❑ **LON-259. Flashlight Gun With Secret Compartment Handle and Lenses,**
1949. Battery operated with clear, red and green lenses. - **$65 $150 $235**

LON-260

❑ **LON-260. General Mills Outfit,**
1949. Rare. Includes shirt, mask, neckerchief, cardboard tag with official seal.
Set - **$275 $600 $1200**

LON-261

❑ **LON-261. Merita Bread Calendar,**
1949. Calendar is 8x15" with illustration in color at top and caption "Tonto, Dan Reid And The Lone Ranger." Below image reads in large letters "Merita 'Tender-Blended' Bread." Bottom notation reads "Every Day Obey The Rules Of The Lone Ranger Safety Club."
- **$300 $700 $1200**

LON-262

❑ **LON-262. Dan Reid With Lone Ranger And Tonto Color Picture,**
1949. Merita Bread. About 10x11".
- **$200 $400 $800**

LON-263

LON-264

❑ **LON-263. Cheerios "Deputy Secret Folder",**
1949. - **$18 $35 $70**

❑ **LON-264. "Lone Ranger Deputy" 2" Brass Badge With Secret Compartment,**
1949. - **$25 $50 $100**

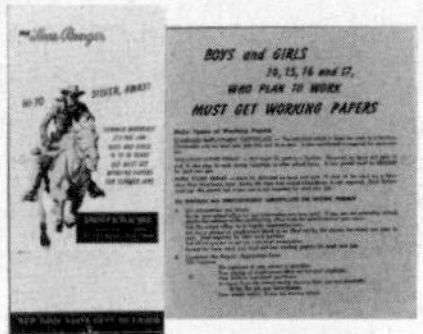

LON-266

LON-265

LON-267

❑ **LON-265. "Lone Ranger" Waxed Paper Bread Loaf Liner,**
1940s. Harris-Boyer Bakeries. - **$30 $65 $125**

❑ **LON-266. Child Labor Law Folder,**
1940s. New York State Department of Labor. Lone Ranger endorsement for labor laws affecting boys and girls aged 14-17. - **$35 $70 $135**

❑ **LON-267. Buchan's Bread Cello. Button,**
c. 1940s. 12 known in 7/8" size, various Lone Ranger slogans. Each - **$15 $30 $60**

LON-268 LON-269 LON-270

❑ **LON-268. Lone Ranger "Member" Star Button,**
1940s. Issued for "Buchan's (Bread) Lone Ranger Community Safety Club." -
$30 $100 $150

❑ **LON-269. Lone Ranger "Captain" Star Button,**
1940s. - **$40 $125 $200**

❑ **LON-270. Lone Ranger "Deputy" Star Button,**
1940s. - **$40 $125 $200**

LON-271

LON-272

❑ **LON-271. Color Photo Card,**
1940s. Madison Square Garden promo (#A6181 at bottom.).Shows Lone Ranger riding horse. -
$25 $50 $75

❑ **LON-272. Silver Bullet Offer,**
1940s. Kix Cereal. Explains how to order a silver bullet for 15¢ and 1 box top. - **$15 $30 $55**

LON-273

❑ **LON-273. "The Lone Ranger Rides Again!" Cardboard Punch-Out Figure Set,**
1940s. Store item by DeJournette Mfg. Co., Atlanta. Consists of stiff cardboard punch-outs of unknown total quantity but including 5" tall Lone Ranger and Tonto plus 7-1/2" tall rearing horse, fence rails and small accessories such as gun, knife, dog, teepee, etc.
Complete - **$100 $250 $550**

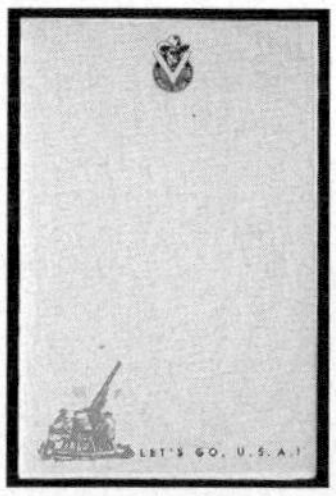

LON-274

LON-275

❑ **LON-274. Note Paper,**
1940s (pre-1945). Rare. Test program for Victory Corps note paper. Shows 3 men firing cannon on left and says "Let's Go U.S.A." Put out during WWII. Each - **$40 $90 $165**

❑ **LON-275. Lone Ranger Official Hat,**
1940s. Lone Ranger name stamped on inside. -
$70 $135 $275

LON-276

❑ **LON-276. "The Lone Ranger" Fabric Mask,**
c. 1940s. Issuer unknown. Possibly a movie theater giveaway or from a western costume set. -
$20 $40 $80

LON-277

❑ **LON-277. Lone Ranger Calendar,**
1940s. Merita Bread. 16x28". Example shown without pad. Bread wrapper design includes children wearing masks and Indian headbands.
Complete - **$800 $1600 $3000**
Without Pad - **$600 $1100 $1600**

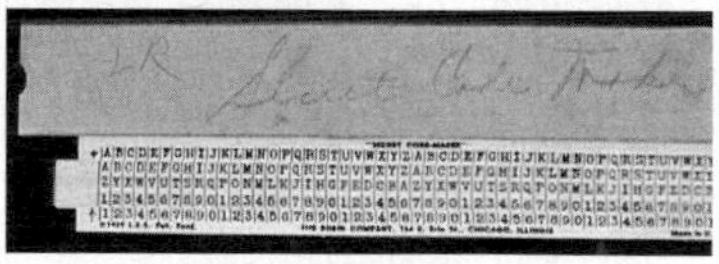

LON-278

❑ **LON-278. "Secret Code-Maker" Wooden Coding Device,**
1940s. General Mills. Item is marked "The Robin Company" Chicago with 1939 copyright. It does not carry the Lone Ranger name but its use was verified by Evie Wilson, former General Mills archivist. Also available as non-The Lone Ranger item. - **$40 $75 $140**

LON-279

❑ **LON-279. Pocketknife,**
1940s. Store item with grips in black, red or white. - **$35 $75 $135**

LON-280

❑ **LON-280. Gum Wrapper,**
1940s. Bowman Gum. 4.5x6" waxed paper. - **$250 $500 $1000**

LON-281

❑ **LON-281. "The Lone Ranger Chewing Gum" Paper Band,**
1940s. Gum Inc. 3x3" paper band that encircled five individual gum packs.
- $1000 $2000 $3000

LON-282

LON-283

LON-284

❑ **LON-282. Seal Print Face Ring,**
1940s. Unmarked believed Lone Ranger premium tin ring designed to press face image into soft material. - **$50 $150 $300**

❑ **LON-283. "Lone Ranger Lucky Piece" Silvered Brass 17th Anniversary Key Ring Fob Medal,**
1950. Cheerios. - **$20 $30 $60**

❑ **LON-284. Merita Bread Safety Club 8x15" Cardboard Wall Calendar,**
1950. Scarce. - **$200 $400 $800**

LON-285

❑ **LON-285. Shelf Hanger Or Topper,**
1950. Merita Bread. 8x18" in full color. - **$300 $600 $1200**

LON-286

LON-287

❑ **LON-286. Bandanna Order Blank,**
1950. General Mills.- **$10 $15 $30**

❑ **LON-287. Fabric Bandanna,**
1950. Offered by Betty Crocker Soups. - **$25 $60 $120**

LON-288

LON-289

❑ **LON-288. Lone Ranger Calendar,**
1950. Merita Bread 16x28". Example shown without pad. Complete - **$600 $1200 $2200**
Without Pad - **$500 $900 $1400**

❑ **LON-289. Photo Card,**
1950. TV premium.- **$10 $20 $40**

LON-290

❑ **LON-290. Lone Ranger Original Art Prototype Book Created By Sam Gold For Morton Salt,**
c. 1950. "The Lone Ranger Western And Fun Book" with 48 pages of original art. Gordon Gold Archives. Unique. **- $1650**

LON-291

LON-292

❑ **LON-291. "Lone Ranger" Foil On White Metal Badge,**
c. 1950. Badge is 1-5/8" tall with 1-1/8" blue and red on silver foil center inset which is surrounded by small raised accent lines on the surrounding white metal. - **$100 $200 $300**

❑ **LON-292. "Sheriff Lone Ranger" Foil On Metal Star,**
c. 1950. Badge is 2-3/8" tall in white metal with raised center circle holding metallic foil insert.
- $75 $150 $250

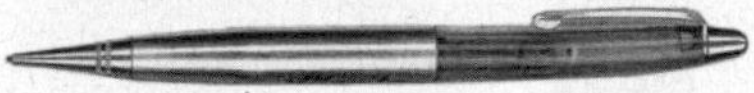

LON-293

❑ **LON-293. "Merita Bread Cake" Floaty Mechanical Pencil,**
c. 1950. Brass barrel has text in red. Full figure Lone Ranger in blue outfit floats in chamber. Possibly a salesman's promotional giveaway. - **$50 $125 $250**

LON-294

❑ **LON-294. "The Lone Ranger" Wristwatch,**
1951. Store item, no maker specified. - **$115 $225 $450**

LON-295

❑ **LON-295. Picture Strip Premium,**
1951. Subscription premium by Dell Publishing Co. 6-3/4x8-1/4" slick paper opens to 33-1/2" wide with five picture panels. **- $50 $80 $175**

LON-296

LON-297

❑ **LON-296. Cheerios Contest Postcard,**
1951. Back text for coloring contest. - **$12 $25 $45**

❑ **LON-297. Cheerios Crayon Offer Box Back,**
1951. #1 from set of four. - **$12 $25 $40**

LON-298

❑ **LON-298. Cheerios Crayon Offer Box Backs,**
1951. #2 and #4 shown, from set of four offering free crayon set for crayoned box picture sent to General Mills. - **$12 $25 $40**

LON-299

❑ **LON-299. Cheerios Saddle Ring With Filmstrip, Paper And Box,**
1951. Near Mint Boxed - **$350**
Ring Only - **$60 $100 $150**
Film Only - **$20 $40 $60**
Instructions - **$25 $50 $100**

LON-300

❑ **LON-300. Calendar With Slot To Hold Club Application Blanks,**
1951. Merita Bread. Full color about 15x16" with additional text on reverse. With Or Without Application Blanks - **$600 $1200 $1800**

LON-301

❑ **LON-301. Cheerios Paper Mask,**
c. 1951. Back text "See The Lone Ranger And Silver In Person At Minneapolis Aquatennial". - **$40 $85 $175**

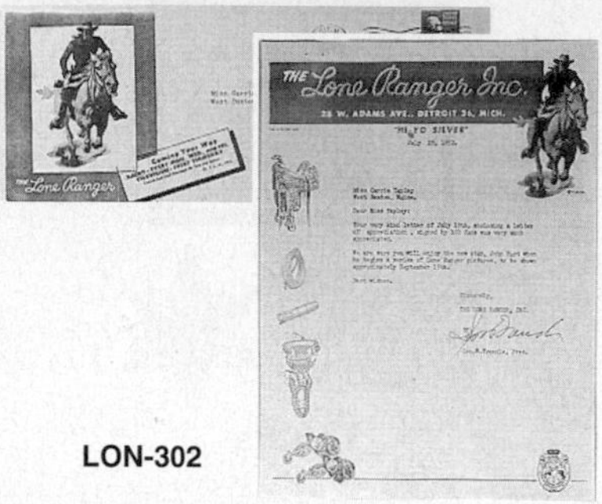

LON-302

❑ **LON-302. Fan Response Envelope With Letter Signed By "Geo. W. Trendle ",**
1952. Trendle acknowledges a letter of appreciation signed by 100 fans and says "We Are Sure You Will Enjoy The New Star, John Hart..."
Envelope - **$35 $75 $150**
Letter - **$100 $165 $300**

LON-303

❑ **LON-303. Safety Club Calendar,**
1953. Merita Bread Co. 8x14" paper wall calendar with color picture for entire 12 months. - **$200 $350 $700**

LON-304

❑ **LON-304. "The Lone Ranger" Lunch Box,**
1954. Adco Liberty. Red Border. - **$250 $600 $1300**
Blue Border - **$300 $700 $1500**

LON-305

❑ **LON-305. Cheerios Box With Comic Book Advertising,**
1954. - **$225 $400 $850**

LON-306

❑ **LON-306. "The Lone Ranger, His Mask And How He Met Tonto" Comic Booklet,**
1954. 16-page full color newsprint issued by Cheerios. - **$15 $45 $175**

LON-307

❑ **LON-307. "The Lone Ranger And The Story Of Silver" Comic,**
1954. Cheerios. - **$15 $45 $175**

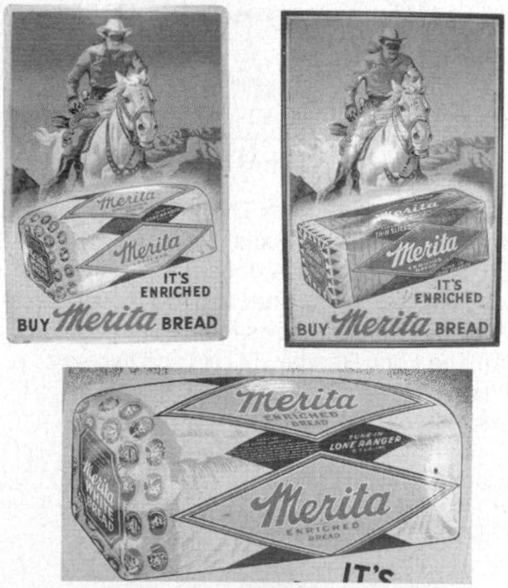

LON-308

❑ **LON-308. "Buy Merita Bread" Outdoor Metal Sign,**
1954. Includes text "A-M Sign Co. Lynchburg, Va." 23-7/8x35-7/8" with embossed details. Two varieties with several bread loaf design differences; but, most obviously, coded "1-54" sign has rounded loaf corners and sign coded "2-54" has squared loaf corners.
Each - **$1100 $2300 $4500**

LON-309

❑ **LON-309. Merita Bread Coloring Book,**
1955. - **$15 $30 $75**

LON-310

❑ **LON-310. "Lone Ranger Rapid-Fire Revolver" Cereal Box,**
1955. Premium offer was 12" long plastic revolver with accessories.
Complete - **$175 $300 $600**

LON-311

❑ **LON-311. "Ride With The Lone Ranger" Premium Game And Mailer,**
1955. Merita Bakers. Cardboard folder opens to 11x17" with built-in spinner and four small bread loaf-shaped punch-outs as markers. These are titled "The Lone Ranger, Tonto" and two say "Outlaw." Mailer - **$15 $25 $40**
Game - **$95 $190 $385**

LON-312

❑ **LON-312. Merita Bread Safety Club "Branding" Booklet,**
1956. Cattle branding explained by Lone Ranger. - **$35 $85 $185**

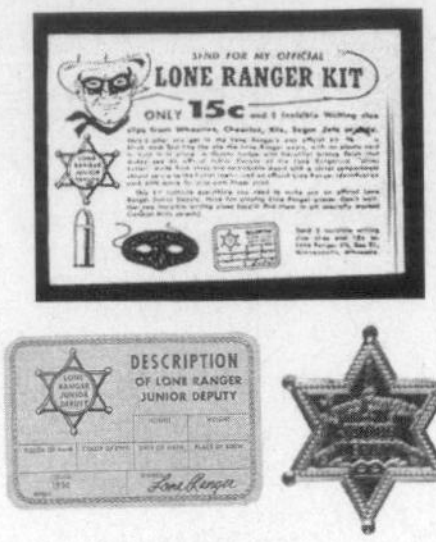

LON-313

❑ **LON-313. "Lone Ranger Junior Deputy" Kit,**
1956. Various General Mills cereals.
Copper luster tin star badge - **$20 $30 $70**
Identification Card - **$15 $25 $45**
Black Fabric Mask (unmarked) - **$5 $15 $25**
Bullet same or similar to 1947 issue - **$20 $40 $75**
Descriptive Coupon - **$10 $15 $25**

LON-314

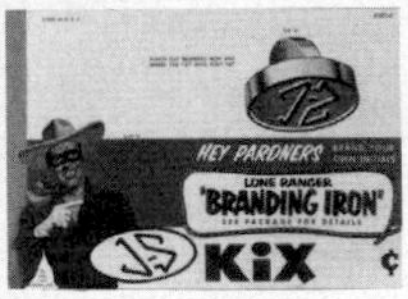

LON-315

❑ **LON-314. Trix "Tonto Belt" Sign,**
1956. Diecut 6x8" paper display sign. - **$30 $50 $75**
Belt with Mailer - **$35 $70 $160**

❑ **LON-315. Kix "Lone Ranger Branding Iron" Sign,**
1956. Diecut 6x8" paper display sign. - **$35 $55 $85**

LON-316

LON-317

❑ **LON-316. Wheaties "Lone Ranger Hike-O-Meter" Sign,**
1956. Diecut 6x8" paper display sign. - **$35 $55 $85**

❑ **LON-317. Sugar Jets "Lone Ranger Six-Shooter Ring" Sign,**
1956. Diecut 6x8" paper display sign. - **$35 $55 $85**

LON-318

❑ **LON-318. Merita Safety Club Card,**
1956. Merita Bakers. - **$10 $35 $70**

LON-319

❑ **LON-319. Cheerios "Lone Ranger Fun Kit" Sign,**
1956. Diecut 6x8" paper display sign. - **$40 $75 $150**

LON-320

❑ **LON-320. "Lone Ranger Ranch Fun Book",**
1956. Cheerios. - **$40 $85 $200**

LON-321

❑ **LON-321. Lone Ranger/Tonto/Lassie Pennant,**
c. 1956. 25.5" fabric pennant picturing all three. - **$60 $125 $200**

LON-322

❑ **LON-322. Lone Ranger With Guns 6' Standee,**
1957. Rare. General Mills. - **$800 $1600 $3600**

LON-323

❑ **LON-323. Wheaties Life-Sized Posters,**
1957. Set of two 25x75" paper posters.
Lone Ranger - **$80 $175 $340**
Tonto - **$80 $175 $340**

LON-324

❑ **LON-324. Life-Sized Uncut Poster Sheet (not separated),**
1957. Used in the lobby at General Mills headquarters. Unique **$2500**

LON-325

❑ **LON-325. Wheaties Box With Posters Offer,**
1957. Complete Box - **$225 $400 $850**
Box Back - **$30 $65 $125**

LON-326

❑ **LON-326. Litho. Button,**
1957. Probable vending machine issue. 7/8" with browntone photo on various single-color backgrounds. From a larger set of western TV stars, probably totaling 14 different. -
$25 $50 $100

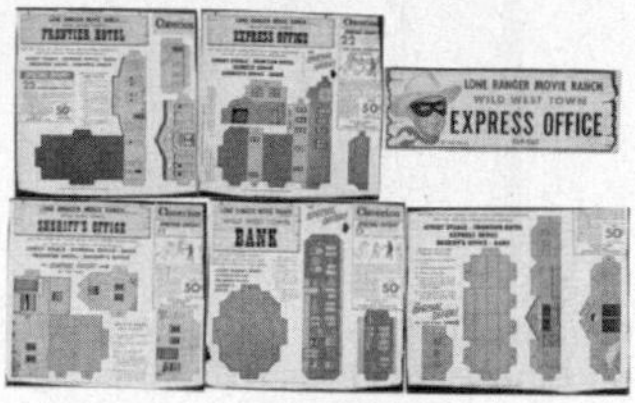

LON-327

❑ **LON-327. "Lone Ranger Movie Ranch Wild West Town" Box Panels,**
1957. Five in set.
Each Complete Box - **$100 $200 $400**
Each Uncut Back Panel - **$25 $45 $80**

LON-328

❑ **LON-328. Cheerios "Wild West Town" Figures With Sheet And Box,**
1957. Scarce. Set of 22 figures including Lone Ranger, Tonto, three horses, nine cowboys, eight Indians. Near Mint Complete - **$650**

LON-329

❑ **LON-329. Cheerios "Movie Ranch Wild West Town" Ad Sheet,**
1957. Box insert 3x4".
Sheet - **$15 $40 $65**

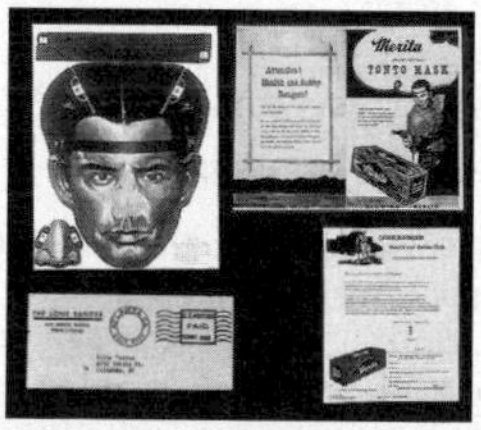

LON-330

❑ **LON-330. Merita "Tonto Mask" Kit,**
1957. Mailer with Lone Ranger Health And Safety Club letter including order form for Lone Ranger Growth Chart, punch-out face mask.
Near Mint In Mailer - **$425**
Letter - **$25 $50 $75**
Mask Unpunched - **$50 $100 $275**
Mask Assembled - **$35 $75 $150**

LON-331

❑ **LON-331. The Lone Ranger Large General Mills Standee,**
1957. 4x6' diecut with easel back. -
$700 $1350 $2750

LON-332 LON-333

❑ **LON-332. Photo Album,**
1957. General Mills, Nestle, Swift, and Merita Bread. Contains 12 black and white photos plus 2 front and back color photos. Has the history of the Lone Ranger and promotes the next year's 25th silver anniversary of his program. TV premium.- **$50 $100 $175**

❑ **LON-333. "T-Vue Time" Weekly Schedule Booklet,**
1957. Baltimore Sunday American. Issued for May 19 with front cover color photo and short article. - **$12 $25 $50**

LON-334

❑ **LON-334. Calendar Card,**
1958. Premium calendar. Shaped like a loaf of bread. - **$25 $50 $75**

LON-335

❑ **LON-335. Child's Stiff Cardboard Table ,**
c. 1958. - **$95 $175 $375**

LON-336

LON-337

❑ **LON-336. Merita Bread "Lone Ranger Peace Patrol" Aluminum Token,**
1959. Sponsored in conjunction with U.S. Treasury Department. Promotion for savings bonds. Front rim reads "Member Lone Ranger Peace Patrol." Reverse reads "Enjoy Merita Bread." - **$40 $85 $160**

❑ **LON-337. "Peace Patrol" Member Card,**
1959. U.S. Treasury Department. Encourages savings bond purchase, back has creed and pledge. - **$10 $20 $40**

LON-338

LON-339

❑ **LON-338. "Join The Peace Patrol" 11x14" Paper Poster,**
1959. U.S. Treasury Department. Encourages savings bond purchase. - **$90 $200 $450**

❑ **LON-339. Full Color 1-1/4" Cello. Button,**
1959. Unmarked but related to Treasury Department campaign to promote sales of U.S. Savings Bonds. - **$10 $20 $40**

LON-340

LON-341

❑ **LON-340. Litho. Button With B&W Photo On Lt. Blue,**
1959. Same design as full color 1-1/4" cello. button but rare 1-3/8" litho. - **$100 $250 $500**

❑ **LON-341. Deputy Chief Badge,**
1950s. Rare. Detail of paper also shown. Also issued by Kellogg's Rice Krispies as "Official Tim McCoy Badge." - **$150 $400 $700**

LON-342

❑ **LON-342. "The Lone Ranger Color Picture Cards" Ed-U-Cards Promo Card,**
1950s. 8-1/2x11" one-sided black and white sheet. - **$20 $35 $75**

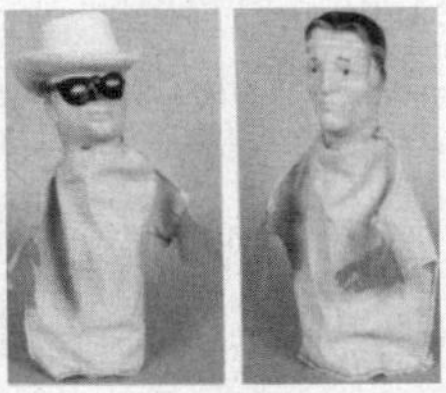

LON-343

❑ **LON-343. Lone Ranger And Tonto Hand Puppets,**
1950s. Store items. Each is 9" tall.
Each - **$30 $65 $125**

LON-344

LON-345

❑ **LON-344. "Merita Bread" Color Picture,**
1950s. - **$15 $30 $75**

❑ **LON-345. Merita Bread Aluminum Silver Bullet Pencil Sharpener,**
1950s. - **$20 $50 $85**

LON-346

❑ **LON-346. Dell Comics Picture Strip,**
1950s. Strip folio of five pictures. - **$40 $80 $160**

LON-347

❑ **LON-347. Smoking Click Plastic Pistol,**
1950s. Store item by Marx Toys.
Box - **$50 $100 $200**
Loose Pistol - **$75 $175 $350**

LON-348

❑ **LON-348. "Magic Lasso" With Brass Badge,**
1950s. Store item by Round-Up Products. Badge variety with pin has copyright notice found on front and additional red paint around shirt collar. Tab variety has no copyright and no color around neck area
Near Mint Boxed - **$1500**
Badge With Pin (about 20 reported examples) - **$125 $250 $500**
Badge With Tabs (3 reported examples) - **$250 $500 $1000**

LON-349

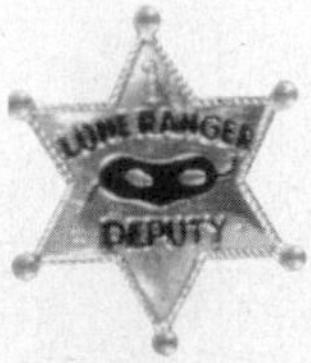

LON-350

❑ **LON-349. "Lone Ranger Deputy" 2-1/4" Silvered Metal Badge,**
1950s. Red and black painted versions. Store Item. Card with 12 Badges - **$575**
Each - **$10 $20 $35**

❑ **LON-350. "Lone Ranger Deputy" Gold Finish Metal Badge,**
1950s. Store item. - **$15 $25 $50**

LON-351

LON-352

❑ **LON-351. Litho. Tin Tab Star Badge,**
1950s. Pictures Clayton Moore. - **$30 $60 $100**

❑ **LON-352. Lone Ranger and Silver Figure,**
1950s. Earliest version. Lone Ranger with chaps on Silver Hartland figure. Has two guns, saddle and hat as accessories. - **$100 $185 $325**

LON-353

❑ **LON-353. Portrait Aluminum Ring,**
1950s. Packaged in Canadian containers of Nestle's Quik. Eye holes of mask have black accent paint and scarf has red accent paint. **- $50 $100 $200**

LON-354

❑ **LON-354. Canadian Color Photo Premium,**
1950s. Nestle's Quik. 9x10" with facsimile signature and "T.V. Star For Nestle's 'Quik' The 'Quick As A Wink' Chocolate Drink." - **$30 $60 $135**

LON-355

❑ **LON-355. Western Series T.V. Card,**
1950s. Card #109 - **$10 $20 $35**

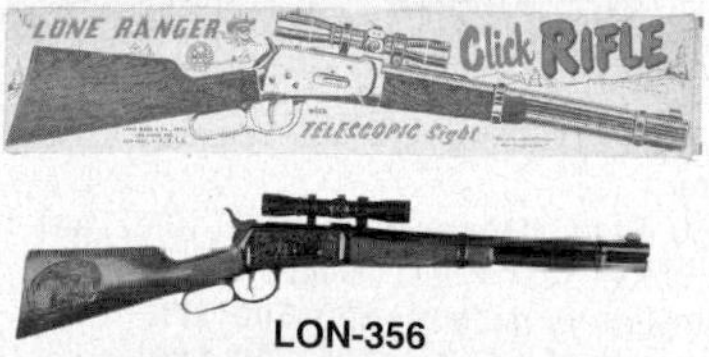

LON-356

❑ **LON-356. The Lone Ranger Click Rifle With Telescopic Sight,**
1950s. Marx. 1-1/8x5.25x25" deep box holds 23" long molded plastic rifle with metal spring-loaded click action. Simulated wood stock shows bear on one side, Native American on other with "The Lone Ranger" name in script with gold paint highlights. Box - **$60 $125 $250**
Rifle - **$50 $100 $200**

LON-357

LON-358

❑ **LON-357. Silver Bullet,**
1950s. Probably General Mills premium. 1-1/2" metal replica in silver finish with his name in cursive lettering on side. TLR Inc. copyright. - **$15 $30 $50**

❑ **LON-358. "The Dodge Boys" Silver Bullet,**
c. 1950s. Dodge Motors Corp. 1-1/2" silver luster metal bullet issued for TV sponsor. - **$20 $40 $60**

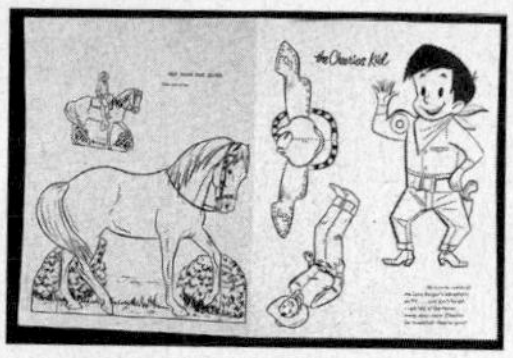
LON-359

❑ **LON-359. Coloring Book,**
1950s. Cheerios. Large two page premium featuring the Cheerios Kid and Tonto.- **$20 $40 $85**

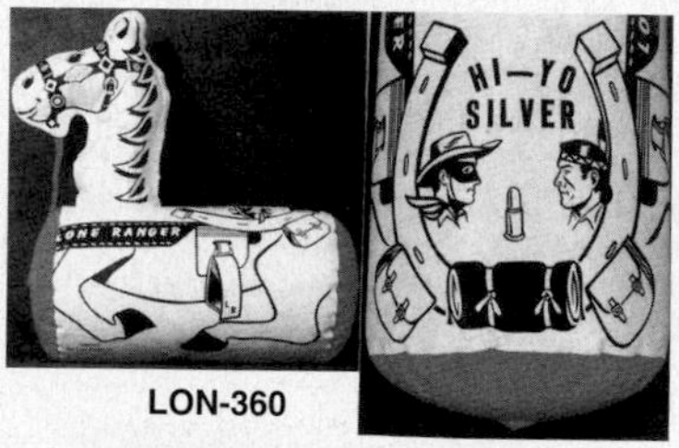

LON-360

❑ **LON-360. "Hi-Yo Silver" Inflatable Toy,**
1950s. Inflated 18" tall by 22" long vinyl swimming pool toy picturing and naming Lone Ranger and Tonto on saddle seat area. - **$75 $150 $275**

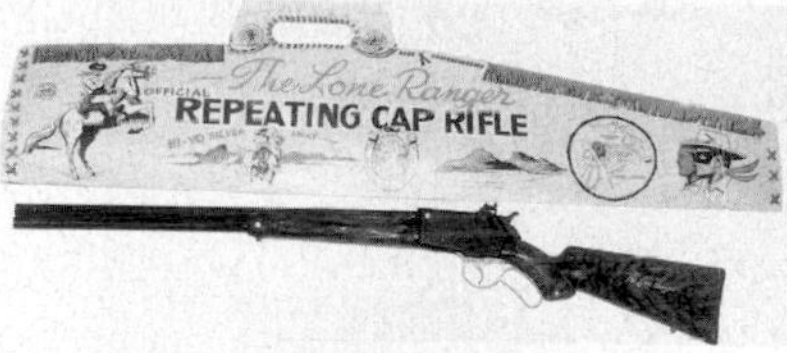

LON-361

❑ **LON-361. Repeating Cap Rifle With Carrying Case,**
1950s. Marx Toys. 34" long replica western rifle for roll caps. Case - **$115 $225 $475**
Rifle - **$100 $200 $425**

LON-362

❑ **LON-362. "27th Year" TV Networks Promotion Kit,**
1960-1961. Jack Wrather Productions. 9x12" with black and white image on red brochure holding extensive publicity and informational items issued for the 1960-1961 seasons on ABC-TV and NBC-TV. Includes Clayton Moore biography as Lone Ranger, TV fact sheet, Lone Ranger Creed, interview questions and more. - **$150 $300 $500**

LON-363

LON-364

❑ **LON-363. English Cookie Tin,**
1961. Huntley & Palmers Biscuits. - **$65 $150 $290**

❑ **LON-364. English Cookie Tin,**
1961. Huntley & Palmers Biscuits. Version pictures Tonto only. - **$65 $150 $290**

LON-365

LON-366

❑ **LON-365. "The Legend Of The Lone Ranger" Comic Book,**
1969. Chain restaurant promotion. Identifies him as "The Good Food Guy". - **$4 $12 $45**

❑ **LON-366. "The Good Food Guy" Cello. Button,**
1969. Chain restaurant promotion. - **$12 $25 $40**

LON-367

LON-368

❑ **LON-367. "The Dodge Boys" TV Sponsor Card,**
1960s. 9x11" counter card for agency of Dodge Motors Corp. Facsimile Clayton Moore signature. - **$15 $30 $50**

❑ **LON-368. Railway Express Advertising Silver Bullet,**
c. 1960s. 1-3/4" long silver luster plastic with removable end cap inscribed "Hi-Yo REA Awaaay." - **$5 $10 $15**

LON-369

❑ **LON-369. Record,**
1972. Coca Cola premium with sleeve. - **$15 $25 $60**

LON-370

❑ **LON-370. Record,**
1977. Record album contains two famous radio episodes. - **$15 $25 $60**

LON-371

❑ **LON-371. Lone Ranger & Tonto Poster Autographed,**
1977. 24x30" paper full color poster produced by Snuff Garrett, prominent record producer and owner of issuing company Nostalgia Merchant. Design includes central photo surrounded by six other photos and two covers of Dell comic books. Signatures are "Clayton Moore" and "Jay Silverheels" within center oval. Near Mint - **$1250**

LON-372

LON-373

❑ **LON-372. Autographed Clayton Moore Photograph,**
1977. Lynn Wilson's Convenient Fun Food. Design includes Lone Ranger Creed.
Signed - **$35 $75 $150**
Unsigned - **$8 $15 $30**

❑ **LON-373. Amoco Gas Station "Ride With Silver" 44x70" Vinyl Sign,**
1970s. "Amoco Silver" lead-free gasoline. - **$65 $135 $275**

LON-374

❑ **LON-374. "The Lone Ranger Wants You" Poster,**
1970s. Issued by The Lone Ranger Family Restaurant. 17-1/2x21-1/2" tan paper. - **$20 $40 $90**

LON-375

❑ **LON-375. "Lone Ranger Silver Bullet Award" Button With Ribbons,**
1970s. Button is 2.5" with two 4" ribbons attached. - **$35 $75 $135**

LON-376

❑ **LON-376. "Lone Ranger Deputy Kit",**
1980. Cheerios. Contains Deputy certificate, "Legend" story folder, punch-out mask, 2-1/2" plastic Deputy badge and 17x22" color poster.
Complete - **$10 $20 $40**

LON-377

❑ **LON-377. Cheerios Box "Deputy Kit" Offer,**
1980. Promotion ran on identical 10 oz. and 15 oz. boxes. Box size is listed on the bottom.
Complete 10 oz. box - **$20 $40 $75**
Complete 15 oz. box - **$25 $50 $90**

LON-378

❑ **LON-378. "Legend of the Lone Ranger" Gun and Holster Set in Display Box,**
1980. Gabriel product. 6 piece set includes 2 guns, 2 holsters, a belt and a mask. Hard to believe this movie is already 25 years old.- **$50 $100 $185**

LON-379

LON-380

❑ **LON-379. Movie Press Kit,**
1981. Contains saddle bag mailer with 14 photos & script. - **$25 $65 $125**

❑ **LON-380. Movie Lone Ranger Rocking Book,**
1981. Lone Ranger on front cover, Tonto on back cover. - **$10 $20 $35**

(NECKERCHIEF)

(LUNCH BOX) **LON-381**

(BOX)

❑ **LON-381. Lone Ranger Watch Box Set,**
1994. Watch has vintage dial. It comes in a metal lunchbox with insert which pictures Clayton Moore as the Lone Ranger. Each box also contained a large neckerchief as a premium. The limited edition watch set sold out quickly and is hard to find on the secondary market. Complete - **$250**

LON-382

LON-383

❑ **LON-382. Lone Ranger 9 3/4" Bobbing Head Figure,**
1996. - **$80**

❑ **LON-383. Tonto 9 3/4" Bobbing Head Figure,**
1996. - **$80**

LON-384

❑ **LON-384. Hallmark Christmas Ornament,**
1997. Shaped like a Lone Ranger lunchbox. - **$45**

LON-385

❑ **LON-385. Porcelain Container,**
1999. Hinged container with a wooden "Silver bullet" inside. Golden Books product. - **$28**

(3 VIEWS OF THE RING)

(POUCH)

(MEMBERSHIP CARD)

(BOX)

LON-386

❑ **LON-386. Secret Compartment Ring Set,**
2000. Ring comes in box with pouch and membership card. Complete - **$40**

LON-387

❑ **LON-387. Cheerios Then and Now Set,**
2001. 60th Anniversary set includes a 1941 design Cheerios box, a 2001 box and a retro lunch box. Complete near mint - **$50**

LON-388

❑ **LON-388. Cookie Jar With Box,**
2003. - **$75**

Lone Wolf Tribe

Wrigley's gum sponsored this children's program on CBS in 1932-1933. The series offered dramatized versions of the American Indian way of life, told by Chief Wolf Paw to the tribe members "with the voice that flies (radio)." Listeners could obtain premiums by sending in "wampum" (Wrigley's wrappers). Most premiums were marked with the imprint of a wolf paw. The club ring, sterling silver and non-adjustable, is considered the earliest issued premium ring. Based on factual history, the Lone Wolf Tribe of Cherokee Indians organized in 1992 in Northern Indiana.

LWF-1

LWF-2

❑ **LWF-1. Wrigley's Chewing Gum Samples Folder,**
1932. Held three sticks of gum, reverse lists radio times and offers Lone Wolf Tribe Book.
With Gum - **$55 $120 $240**
Folder Only - **$25 $40 $85**

❑ **LWF-2. Club Manual,**
1932. Wrigley Gum. - **$20 $50 $100**

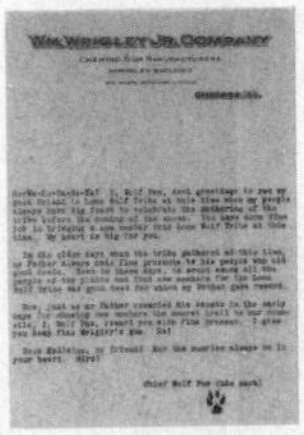

LWF-3

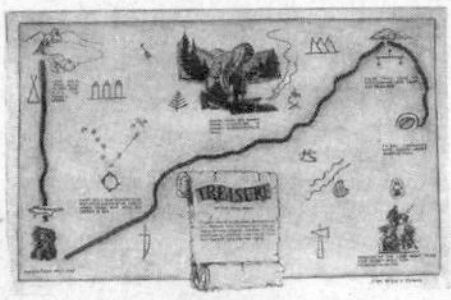

LWF-4

❑ **LWF-3. New Member Letter,**
1932. Wrigley Gum. - **$18 $30 $65**

❑ **LWF-4. "Treasure Of The Lone Wolf" 11x17" Paper Map,**
1932. Scarce. Wrigley Gum. - **$115 $250 $500**

LWF-5

❑ **LWF-5. "Lone Wolf Tribe Tom-Tom" Leather And Thin Rubber Drum With Beater Stick,**
1932. Rare. Wrigley's Gum.
Box - **$30 $60 $100**
Drum & Beater - **$40 $95 $185**

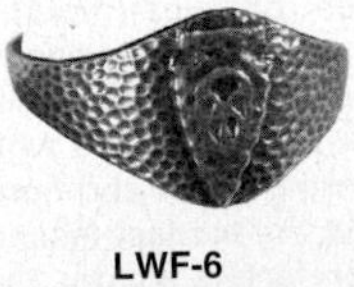

LWF-6

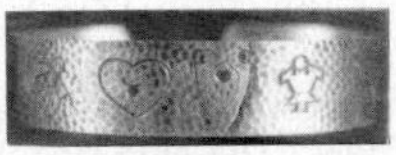

LWF-7

❑ **LWF-6. Chief Wolf Paw Sterling Ring,**
1932. Wrigley's Gum. Considered the first radio premium ring. - **$75 $160 $350**

❑ **LWF-7. Tribe Bracelet,**
1932. Wrigley Gum. Silvered metal expansion bracelet with tribal code symbols. -
$100 $175 $375

LWF-8

❑ **LWF-8. Arrowhead Silvered Brass Member's Badge,**
1932. Card - **$30 $60 $90**
Badge - **$10 $20 $40**

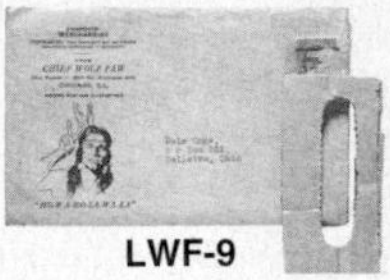

LWF-9

LWF-10

❑ **LWF-9. Lone Wolf Arrowhead Pin Mailer,**
1932. Wrigley's Gum. - **$30 $60 $110**

❑ **LWF-10. Lone Wolf Letter (Goes With Pin),**
1932. Wrigley's Gum. - **$15 $30 $60**

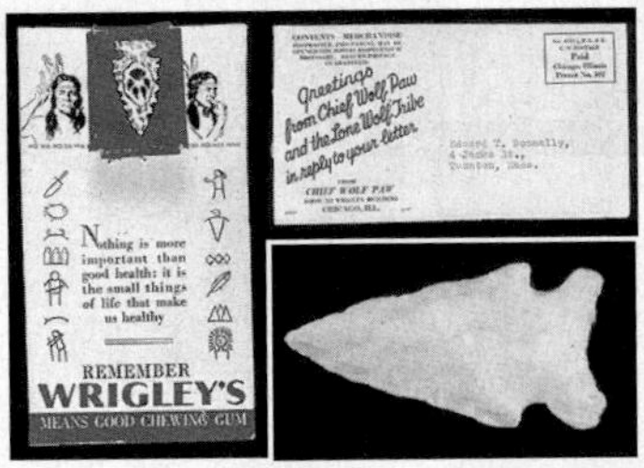

LWF-11

❑ **LWF-11. Chief Wolf Paw/Lone Wolf Tribe Arrowhead With Mailer Card,**
1932. Wrigley's Gum. Stone arrowhead held in flap pocket of 3x5-1/2" mailer card.
Arrowhead With Mailer - **$45 $90 $175**

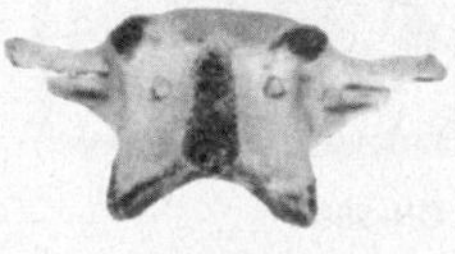

LWF-12

LWF-13

❑ **LWF-12. Cow Head Tie Holder,**
1932. Actual bone tie slide from "Vertebra Of A Range Animal". - **$20 $40 $70**

❑ **LWF-13. "Sitting Bull" Picture,**
1932. Lone Wolf Tribe premium with back text "How Sitting Bull Got His Name". -
$30 $60 $110

LWF-14

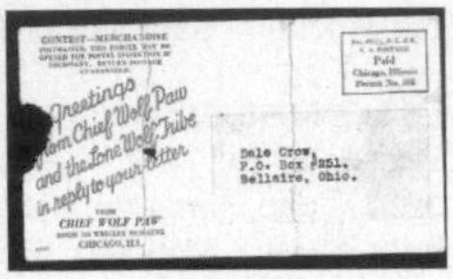

LWF-15

❑ **LWF-14. Tribe Necklace,**
1932. Scarce. - **$100 $250 $375**

❑ **LWF-15. Lone Wolf Tribe Postcard,**
1932. Wrigley's Gum. - **$20 $40 $70**

LWF-16

LWF-17

❑ **LWF-16. Chief Wolf Paw Arrowhead Fob,**
1932. Wrigley Gum. Thin silvered brass picturing paw and arrow designs. - **$35 $75 $135**

❑ **LWF-17. Lone Wolf Silvered Brass Pin,**
1932. Thunderbird broach. - **$30 $60 $120**

LWF-18

LWF-19

❑ **LWF-18. Lone Wolf Closing Mailer,**
1933. Wrigley's Gum. - **$20 $40 $60**

❑ **LWF-19. Lone Wolf Tribe Trading Post Closing Folder,**
1933. Wrigley's Gum. Includes "Farewell Message." Four page folder with 3 sticks of gum. - **$100 $300 $600**

LWF-20

❑ **LWF-20. Lone Wolf Arrowhead Chain,**
1933. Unmarked - Hunt Buffalo sign. -
$20 $30 $75

LWF-21

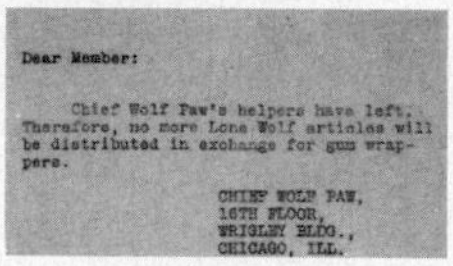
Dear Member:

Chief Wolf Paw's helpers have left. Therefore, no more Lone Wolf articles will be distributed in exchange for gum wrappers.

CHIEF WOLF PAW,
16TH FLOOR,
WRIGLEY BLDG.,
CHICAGO, ILL.

LWF-22

❑ **LWF-21. Lone Wolf Pin,**
1933. Unmarked - Horse symbol for journey. -
$20 $30 $75

❑ **LWF-22. Out Of Business Paper,**
1933. Wrigley Gum. Paper reads "Dear Member: Chief Wolf Paw's Helpers Have Left. Therefore, No More Lone Wolf Articles Will Be Distributed In Exchange For Gum Wrappers." -
$30 $65 $135

Lost In Space

"Never fear, Smith is here!" This cult sci-fi TV series, created by Irwin Allen for 20th Century Fox Television and aired on CBS from 1965-1968, ran up against another memorable science fiction show with its own following--something called *Star Trek*. It was *Lost in Space* that was the first-run success, though, and to this day its three seasons remain popular in syndication and on the Sci-Fi Channel. Following the exploits of the intrepid Robinson family--Professor John Robinson, wife Maureen, daughters Judy and Penny, son Will, their pilot Major Don West, their Robot...called "Robot," and a stock villain stowaway known as Dr. Smith originally sent to sabotage the ship--the series was a campy hit that mixed cheap special effects, excessive over-acting, and a wild sense of fun to produce a show enjoyed by both children and adults. The cast included: Guy Williams, June Lockhart, Marta Kristen, Angela Cartwright, Bill Mumy, Mark Goddard and Jonathan Harris.

Originally sent from Earth to colonize the nearby star system of Alpha Centauri, the family finds themselves encountering a bizarre collection of aliens thanks to the bumbling malevolence of Dr. Smith, who often attempts to exploit opportunities to return home at the expense of the family's safety. *Lost in Space* has now enjoyed a resurgence of popularity thanks to several anniversary celebrations, including a Sci-Fi Channel tribute aired on October 16th, 1997 (the date on which the Robinson's spacecraft, the Jupiter II, was supposedly launched) as well as the 1998 New Line feature film of the same name, starring William Hurt, Mimi Rogers, and Gary Oldman taking over for Jonathan Harris as Dr. Smith. Most items are copyright 20th Century Fox. "Oh the pain, the pain!"

LIS-1

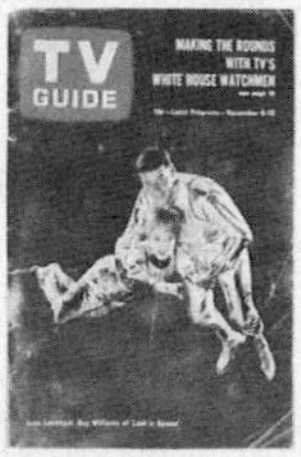

LIS-2

❑ **LIS-1. "March Of Comics" Booklet #352,**
1964. Various sponsors. "Space Family Robinson/Lost In Space" story. - **$8 $24 $125**

❑ **LIS-2. TV Guide Weekly Issue,**
1965. Volume 13 #45 for week of November 6.
Without Mailing Label - **$20 $40 $75**
With Mailing Label - **$15 $30 $50**

LIS-3

❑ **LIS-3. "Lost In Space Game" Boxed,**
1965. Milton Bradley. Game featuring space scene playing board picturing Cyclops monster. -
$25 $50 $80

LIS-4

❑ **LIS-4. "Lost In Space" Model Kit,**
1966. Store item by Aurora.
Near Mint Boxed - **$1000**
Complete Assembled - **$100 $225 $350**

LIS-5

❑ **LIS-5. "Lost In Space" Remco Helmet,**
1966. Box is 9x11x9" deep and contains 9" tall plastic helmet. The box labels this as "Helmet & Gun Set." Box - **$50 $100 $200**
Helmet - **$25 $50 $100**
Gun (Shown On Label) - **$50 $100 $200**

LIS-6

❑ **LIS-6. "Lost In Space" Battery Operated Robot,**
1966. Store item by Remco.
Boxed - **$250 $600 $900**
Loose - **$200 $400 $600**

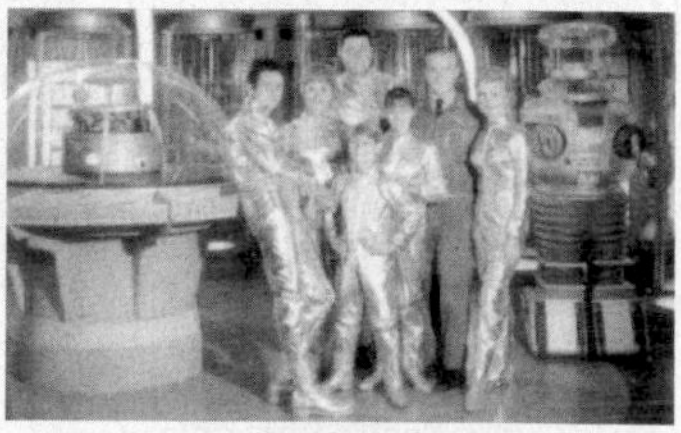

LIS-7

❑ **LIS-7. "Lost In Space" Cast Photo,**
c. 1966. CBS-TV fan card. - **$20 $40 $75**

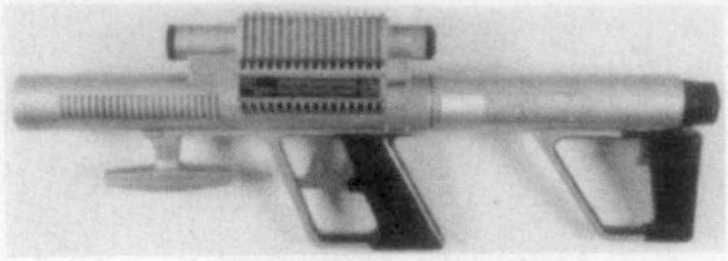

LIS-8

❑ LIS-8. Roto Jet Gun,
c. 1966. Mattel. Two main pieces transform to weapons. Came with two saucers and whistle attachment. Rare.
Near Mint In Store Box - **$3500**
Near Mint In Sears' Mail Order Plain Box - **$2750**
Gun and Parts - **$600 $1200 $1800**

LIS-9

❑ LIS-9. Elaborate Press Kit,
1967. 9-1/2x12" folder holds publicity materials for the third season. Primary contents are five glossy 8x10" photos and 35 fact sheets, cover letter has facsimile signature of Irwin Allen. - **$135 $300 $500**

LIS-10

❑ LIS-10. Lost in Space Metal Lunch Box With Thermos,
1967. King Seeley Thermos. - **$200 $500 $900**

LIS-11

❑ LIS-11. View-Master Reel Set,
1967. Three stereo color photo reels with story booklet in 4.5" square envelope. - **$25 $50 $100**

LIS-12

❑ LIS-12. "The Robot From Lost In Space",
1968. Store item by Aurora.
Near Mint Boxed - **$800**
Complete Assembled - **$115 $225 $450**

LIS-13

❑ LIS-13. "Lost In Space" Battery Operated Robot,
1977. Store item by Ahi.
Boxed - **$100 $250 $400**
Loose - **$65 $150 $200**

LIS-14

❑ LIS-14. "Lost In Space" Robot YM-3,
1985. 16" talking figure in box by Masudaya.
Boxed - **$200**

LIS-15

❑ LIS-15. Lost in Space 10" Talking Environmental Robot B-9,
1997. Trendmasters, Inc. and Newline Productions. 10" tall Robot with two recorded sayings (delivered by the original Robot voice, Dick Tufeld): "Danger, Danger Will Robinson!" and "My sensors indicate an intruder is present." Comes with removable laser pistol, retractable arms, light-up dome and pull-back tread action. - **$55**

LIS-16 LIS-17

❑ LIS-16. Lost in Space 7" Robot B-9,
1997. Trendmasters, Inc. and Newline Productions. 7" tall Robot with two recorded sayings. - **$33**

❑ LIS-17. Lost in Space Flashlight on Card,
1997. - **$25**

LIS-18 LIS-19

❑ LIS-18. Battle Ravaged Robot in Box,
1997. 8" tall movie Robot. - **$28**

❑ LIS-19. Motorized Robot,
1997. 10" figure with remote control hacker deck. Box is approx. 13" wide. - **$38**

LIS-21

LIS-20

❑ **LIS-20. The Robot Model Kit in Box,**
1998. - **$28**

❑ **LIS-21. Movie Premium Pinback,**
1998. Large. - **$30**

LIS-22

❑ **LIS-22. Frosted Cheerios Cereal Box with Action Figure Offer,**
1998. Movie action figures pictured on back of box. - **$6 $12 $25**

Lucille Ball

Lucille Ball (1911-1989) developed the character of the wacky housewife on radio in *My Favorite Husband*, which ran for three years (1948-1951) on CBS, sponsored by General Foods. But it was on CBS television that she became a comic star, first on *I Love Lucy* (1951-1957). The show, an instant hit, also featured Lucy's husband, Desi Arnaz, as bandleader Ricky Ricardo, and Vivian Vance and William Frawley as neighbors Ethel and Fred Mertz. The birth of little Ricky on the show in 1953--on the same night Lucille Ball was actually giving birth--was a major national event. A radio adaptation aired briefly in 1952, sponsored by Philip Morris cigarettes. Other television shows on CBS followed: *The Lucille Ball-Desi Arnaz Show* (1957-1959), *The Lucy Show* (1962-1968), *Here's Lucy* (1968-1974), and *Life With Lucy* on ABC in 1986. She received an Emmy Award as Best Comedy Actress for 1955, 1966 and 1967. Syndicated reruns are still being widely broadcast to this day.

Ball began her career as a model and showgirl and became the Chesterfield Cigarette Girl in 1933. Her first screen appearance was in Eddie Cantor's musical *Roman Scandals* in 1933. She met Cuban band leader Desi Arnaz in 1940 while they were filming *Too Many Girls* and married later that year. By the end of the 1940s she had appeared in over 60 films. Comic book versions of the television series include *I Love Lucy Comics* (1954-1962), *The Lucy Show* (1963-1964), and *I Love Lucy* (1990-1991). Licensed items are usually copyrighted Lucille Ball and Desi Arnaz or Desilu, the name of their production studio.

LUC-1 LUC-2

❑ **LUC-1. Dixie Ice Cream Picture,**
c. 1940. - **$25 $45 $90**

❑ **LUC-2. Footwear 12x17" Countertop Display Sign,**
c. 1949. Summerettes Shoes by Ball-Band. Cardboard easel back with replica ad from Life magazine. - **$110 $225 $375**

LUC-3

❑ **LUC-3. "The Fuller Brush Girl" Movie Insert,**
1950. Starring Lucille Ball. - **$75 $150 $300**

LUC-4

❑ **LUC-4. "The Fuller Brush Girl" Window Card,**
1950. 14x22" cardboard for original release of Columbia Pictures comedy starring Lucy and Eddie Albert. Top margin names local theater as designed. - **$45 $85 $150**

LUC-5

❑ **LUC-5. "I Love Lucy" 3-D Picture Storybook,**
1953. Store item by 3 Dimension Publications Inc. 24-page photo magazine includes four pages printed in process for viewing by "Foto Magic 3-D Spex" eyeglasses.
With Glasses - **$100 $225 $350**
Without Glasses - **$75 $175 $275**

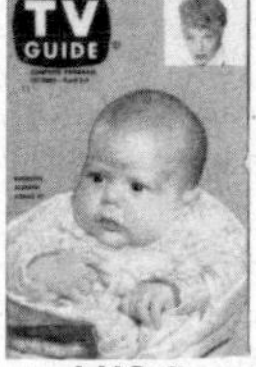

LUC-6 LUC-7

❑ **LUC-6. "TV Guide" Vol. 1 #1,**
April 3, 1953. First national issue with cover article "Lucy's Fifty Million Dollar Baby".
With label - **$200 $500 $1000**
No label - **$300 $750 $1600**

❑ **LUC-7 "TV Guide" Cover Article,**
1953. Weekly issue for July 17 with three-page article on Lucy and Desi movie "The Long-Long Trailer." - **$35 $65 $140**

LUC-8

❑ **LUC-8. "I Love Lucy - There's A Brand New Baby (At Our House)" Sheet Music,**
1953. Music is 9x12" with four pages. Published by Barton Music Corp. after the birth of Lucille Ball & Desi Arnaz's son. - **$50 $100 $150**

LUC-9

❑ **LUC-9. Lucille Ball And Desi Arnaz Dixie Picture,**
1953. 8.5x10" from set of stars. Reverse pictures 4 action scenes from "I Love Lucy."
- **$50 $100 $200**

LUC-10

❑ **LUC-10. "I Love Lucy-Desi Jr." Collapsible Baby Carriage,**
1953. Carriage is 17x27x11.5" tall when collapsed and 17x31x30.5" when set up and has metal frame with hard rubber wheels. Body is covered with leatherette-like material. Bonnet is collapsible. Each side of carriage has image of little girl pushing carriage at front and back has large "Ricky Jr." emblazoned at middle of carriage. - **$175 $350 $600**

LUC-11

LUC-12

❑ **LUC-11. "Philip Morris 1953 Football Schedule" Booklet,**
1953. Philip Morris Cigarettes. 3-3/4x6-1/2" booklet with 40 pages. Lucy is pictured on both the front cover and inside back cover. -
$25 $50 $80

❑ **LUC-12. Lucy & Desi Ad Postcard,**
1955. Pontiac Motors. - **$18 $30 $50**

LUC-13

LUC-14

❑ **LUC-13. "Pocket Encyclopedia Of Alaska" With Lucy/Desi Cover,**
1959. Westinghouse Corp. TV show sponsor folder opening to 20x25" featuring map and text about newly-admitted 49th state. - **$15 $30 $45**

❑ **LUC-14. "I Love Lucy" Cigarette Sponsor Display Card,** 1950s. Philip Morris Cigarettes. Cardboard hinge card for countertop or merchandise use with color photo lower half geared to Father's Day cigarette gifts. - **$85 $165 $350**

LUC-15

LUC-16

❑ **LUC-15. "Desi's Conga Drum",**
1950s. Store item by A&A American Metal Toy Co. Came with wooden beater. -
$300 $600 $1200

❑ **LUC-16. "'I Love Lucy' Cupid" Boxed Squeeze Toy,**
1950s. Store item by Peter Puppet Playthings Inc. 9" tall colorful window box holds 7-1/2" tall molded soft rubber Cupid figure which squeaks. Side panel reads "Watch The Philip Morris 'I Love Lucy' Show On CBS."
Near Mint Boxed - **$650**
Doll Only - **$75 $150 $300**

LUC-17

LUC-18

❑ **LUC-17. "I Love Lucy" Doll With Apron,**
1950s. Store item. - **$225 $500 $1000**

❑ **LUC-18. "How To Adjust And Service Your TV Set" Book,**
1950s. Store item by Popular Science Publishing Co. Inc. 6-1/2x9-1/4" with 160 pages. Lucy and Desi on cover but not in contents. -
$25 $45 $75

LUC-19

LUC-20

❑ **LUC-19. "Lucille Ball Star-Cal" Pair Of Packaged Decals,**
1950s. Store item by The Meyercord Co. From a series picturing TV and movie personalities. Each - **$8 $15 $30**

❑ **LUC-20. "Lucy's Notebook",**
1950s. Philip Morris cigarettes. 40-page recipe booklet with Lucy/Desi photos. - **$25 $45 $75**

LUC-21

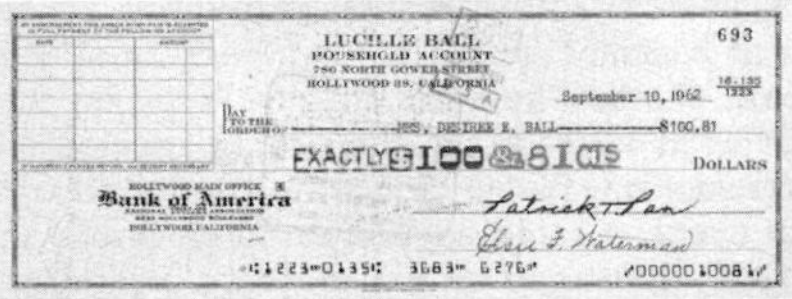

LUC-22

❑ **LUC-21. "Wildcat" Broadway Production 3" Cello. Button,**
c. 1961. For "Musical Smash Hit" at Alvin Theater. - **$22 $45 $70**

❑ **LUC-22. Check,**
1962. From Lucille Ball's household account, made out to her mother. - **$50 $100 $150**

LUC-23

LUC-24

❑ **LUC-23. "Lucy Day" New York World's Fair 3-1/2" Cello. Button,**
1964. Macy's department store. Single day issue for August 31. - **$50 $100 $185**

❑ **LUC-24. "Lucy Day" New York World's Fair 3-1/2" Cello. Button,**
1964. Single day issue for August 31 event designated for "Press" representative. -
$50 $100 $185

LUC-25

❑ **LUC-25. "Salesman's Opportunity Magazine" With Lucy Cover Article,**
1968. Trade publication has one-page article titled "Women Are Winners In Sales." -
$12 $25 $50

LUC-26

❑ **LUC-26. "Home Painting And Color Guide,"**
1960s. Issued by Dupont. - **$10 $25 $50**

LUC-27

❑ **LUC-27. "Lucy" China Bust Bank,**
1998. - **$55**

Lum and Abner

For 22 years on various radio networks and for a long list of sponsors, Lum Edwards and Abner Peabody ran the Jot 'Em Down Store in the mythical town of Pine Ridge, Arkansas. The show was conceived by Chester Lauck (1902-1980) and Norris Goff (1906-1978), boyhood friends in rural Arkansas who played not only the title roles but also most of the other characters in a continuing mixture of dialect comedy and rustic soap opera. The program premiered on Hot Springs station KTHS in 1931 and soon moved to Chicago and went national. Sponsors included Quaker Oats (1931), Ford automobiles (1933), Horlick's malted milk (1934-1938), Postum (1938-1940), Alka-Seltzer (1941-1948), and Frigidaire (1948-1949). The final broadcast was in 1954. Six feature films were released between 1940 and 1946. (In 1936, in honor of the show, the town of Waters, Arkansas, officially changed its name to Pine Ridge).

LUM-1

LUM-2

❑ **LUM-1. Horlick's Drink Mixer With Letter,**
1933. 6-1/2" tall glass and aluminum malted milk drink mixer prize with letter informing a contest winner. Letter - **$8 $18 $35**
Mixer - **$35 $75 $170**

❑ **LUM-2. "Pine Ridge News" Vol. 1 #1 Newspaper, November**
1933. Ford Motor Co. - **$25 $50 $85**

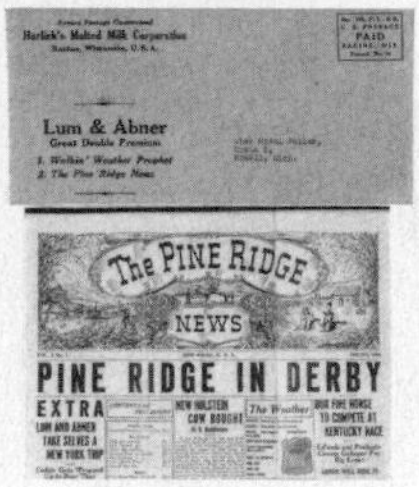

LUM-3

LUM-4

❑ **LUM-3. "The Pine Ridge News" Newspaper With Envelope,**
1936, Spring. Horlick's Malted Milk.
Near Mint In Mailer- **$80**
Loose - **$20 $35 $60**

❑ **LUM-4. "Lum And Abner's Almanac",**
1936. Horlick's Malted Milk. - **$10 $20 $45**

LUM-5

LUM-6

❑ **LUM-5. Lum Edwards For President Cello. Button,**
1936. Horlick's Malted Milk. - **$12 $25 $40**

❑ **LUM-6. "Walkin' Weather Prophet" Brass Badge,**
1936. Horlick's Malted Milk. Litmus paper insert changes color with humidity but almost always inactive due to age. - **$20 $50 $100**

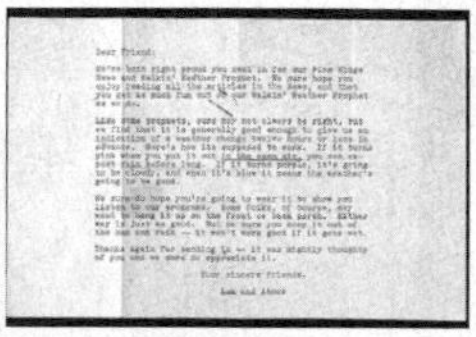

LUM-7

LUM-8

❑ **LUM-7. Letter,**
1936. Premium letter explains how the Weather Prophet Badge works.- **$15 $25 $40**

❑ **LUM-8. Glass Shake-Up Decanter With Aluminum Lid,**
c. 1936. For preparing Horlick's Malted Milk. Lid has pouring spout. - **$40 $90 $200**

LUM-9

LUM-10

❑ **LUM-9. "Family Almanac",**
1937. Horlick's Malted Milk. - **$10 $25 $40**

❑ **LUM-10. "Lum And Abner's Family Almanac",**
1938. Horlick's Malted Milk. - **$10 $25 $40**

LUM-11

❑ **LUM-11. Postcard,**
1938. Shows Lum and Abner in and out of costume. Bottom card says "Mena, Arkansas Home of Lum and Abner." - **$18 $35 $70**

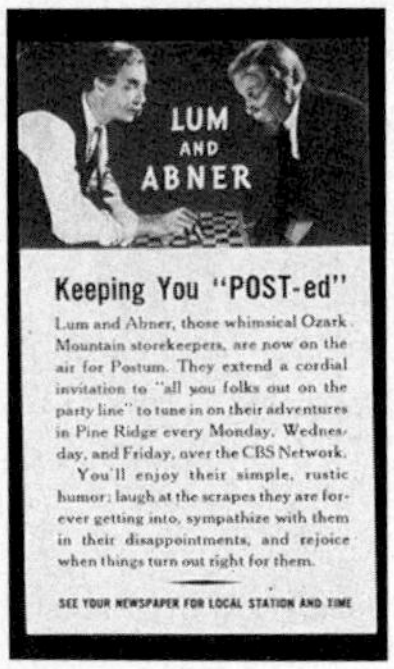

LUM-12

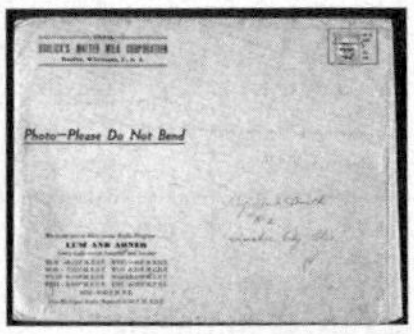

LUM-13

❑ **LUM-12. Promo,**
1930s. Postum Cereal. Promotes radio show.- **$12 $20 $35**

❑ **LUM-13. Mailer For Photo,**
1930s. Horlick's Malted Milk. - **$10 $20 $30**

LUM-14

LUM-15

❑ **LUM-14. Tour Book,**
1930s. Ten page premium. Gives a tour of the town. - **$25 $45 $75**

❑ **LUM-15. Fan Photo,**
1930s. 8x10" glossy b&w showing the characters in and out of costume and with facsimile signatures. - **$12 $25 $50**

LUM-16

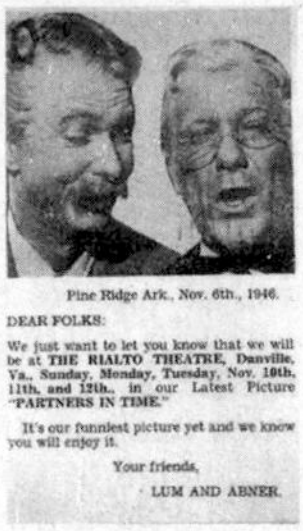

LUM-17

❑ **LUM-16. Fan Photo,**
1930s. Inset photo of radio portrayers Chester Lauck and Norris Goff. - **$20 $35 $60**

❑ **LUM-17. Movie Postcard,**
1946. Various theaters. Announces upcoming movie "Partners In Time". - **$10 $20 $40**

LUM-18

❑ **LUM-18. Photo Card of Actors,**
1940s. Photo of radio portrayers Chester Lauck and Norris Goff without the usual character make-up. - **$10 $20 $40**

Ma Perkins

Beginning in 1933, Oxydol's own Ma Perkins solved her neighbors' problems and dished out her homespun philosophy from her lumber yard in Rushville Center for a total of 27 years. The program, created by Frank and Anne Hummert, first heard on Cincinnati radio station WLW, went national on NBC four months after its debut. From 1942 to 1948 it was broadcast on both the NBC and CBS networks, and from 1948 until it went off the air in 1960 it aired exclusively on CBS. Virginia Payne (1910-1977) played the part of the widowed Ma for the entire run of over 7,000 episodes, and Procter & Gamble's Oxydol was the long-term sponsor.

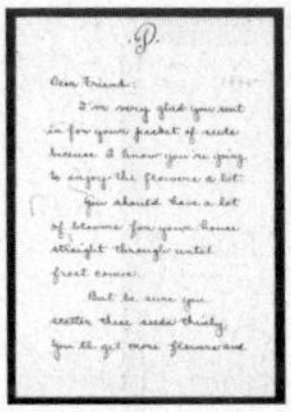

MPK-1

MPK-2

❑ **MPK-1. Garden Planner,**
1935. Oxydol. 3 pages. Letter came with flower seeds. Radio premium. - **$15 $30 $50**

❑ **MPK-2. Seeds and Mailer,**
1935. Oxydol.Cultivation instructions on packets. Radio premium. Seeds - **$5 $10 $25**
Mailer - **$5 $10 $25**

MPK-3

MPK-4

❑ **MPK-3. Oxydol Fan Photo,**
1930s. - **$12 $25 $45**

❑ **MPK-4. "Ma Perkins-Your Radio Friend" Photo,**
1930s. Oxydol. - **$8 $20 $33**

MPK-5

❑ **MPK-5. Seed Packs,**
1946. Oxydol. Zinnia, Morning Glory, Gourds and Sweet Alyssum. Each - **$10 $20 $35**

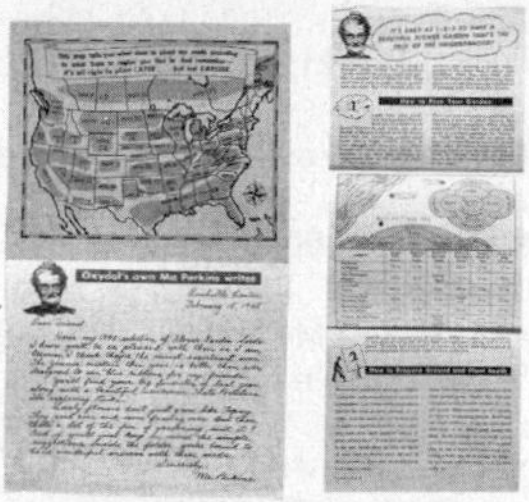
MPK-6

❑ **MPK-6. Garden Planner,**
1948. Oxydol. 6 pages. - **$15 $30 $50**

MAD Magazine

What started as an irreverent little comic book in August 1952 has grown into what was once the nation's leading humor magazine. Early issues, edited by Harvey Kurtzman (1924-1993), satirized popular comic strips with features such as *Little Orphan Melvin* and *Batboy and Rubin*. The brilliant art staff included: Will Elder, Wally Wood, Jack Davis, John Severin and Kurtzman himself who also wrote most of the stories. With issue #24 in 1955 publisher Bill Gaines changed the format from comic book to magazine. Alfred E. Neuman, a cartoon rendering of a 19th century icon, made his debut on the cover of issue #21 and has become the magazine's (What--Me Worry?) trademark. Annual issues of *More Trash from MAD* and *The Worst from MAD* appeared from 1958 to 1969, *MAD Follies* from 1963 to 1969, and *MAD Specials* from 1970 on. Licensed merchandise includes clothing, food products, games, trading cards, and greeting cards. *MAD TV*, a late-night comedy show, debuted on the Fox television network in October 1995. In 1997 *MAD* underwent an extensive editorial makeover with the addition of many new artists and writers. *Tales Calculated To Drive You MAD*, a limited series from DC Comics (now the publisher of *MAD*) reprinting *MAD*'s first 23 full-color issues in magazine format, ran for eight issues from 1997 to 1999. Hoohah!

MAD-1

MAD-2

❑ **MAD-1. "Comfort Soap" Cello. Button,**
c. 1901. Very strong early character resemblance to later Alfred E. Neuman. - **$300 $600 $1500**

❑ **MAD-2. "me worry?" Alfred E. Neuman-Like Relief Metal Wall Hanging,**
1927. Sculptured plaque is 3.25x6x1" deep of cast aluminum with gold lustrous finish. Just above caption are small incised images of summer themes including swimming at fishing hole, camping in sunset, fishing, dog chasing bird. Text on back A.E. Mitchell Art Co. Los Angeles, Calif. - **$60 $125 $225**

MAD-3

❑ **MAD-3. Pre-MAD Magazine Sign,**
1920s. Embossed tin sign is 6x13" advertising "Exquisite Cherry Sparkle" soda. Sign is by The Crown Cork & Seal Co. - **$150 $300 $600**

MAD-4

MAD-5

❑ **MAD-4. Birthday Card,**
1930s. - **$50 $125 $250**

❑ **MAD-5. Anti-FDR/Pre-Neuman Postcard,**
c. 1940. Black and white grinning caricature image of young lad bearing striking resemblance to Alfred E. Neuman of later decades MAD Magazine. Caption is "Sure-I'm For Roosevelt" and reverse offers additional cards to those opposed to FDR's third term. - **$10 $20 $40**

MAD-6

❑ **MAD-6. "Me Worry?" Cello. Button,**
1941. "Superior" unknown sponsor. - **$150 $350 $750**

MAD-7

❑ **MAD-7. Get Well Card,**
1940s. - **$40 $80 $175**

MAD-8

MAD-9

❑ **MAD-8. "In Hollywood-Me Worry?" Postcard,**
1940s. Glossy black and white picturing character resembling later years Alfred E. Neuman of MAD Magazine. - **$15 $30 $60**

❑ **MAD-9. Robert Taft Presidential Hopeful Campaign Button,**
1952. 4" diameter with attached ribbon reading "Circus Saints And Sinners Jan. 25, 1952." Also issued without ribbon depicts character adopted a few years later as icon for MAD Magazine. With Or Without Ribbon - **$100 $200 $400**

MAD-10

Failure to carry this card at all times will result...
This is to certify that
is a life member in good standing of
THE NATIONAL E.C. FAN-ADDICT CLUB
and is therefore entitled, upon presentation of this card, to purchase any ten cent E.C. magazine for the special membership newsstand price of 10c.
20443
Melvin
If you find this card, kindly drop it...

❏ **MAD-10. "Mad Member EC Fan-Addict Club" Patch, Card And Bronze Badge,**
1953. Part of membership kit. Re-issue patch includes copyright symbol.
Original Patch - **$75 $200 $450**
Reissue Patch - **$25 $50 $75**
Card - **$65 $125 $250**
Badge - **$100 $250 $550**

(The Crypt-Keeper)

(The Vault-Keeper)

(The Old Witch)

MAD-11

❏ **MAD-11. "EC Fan-Addict Club" Kit Photographs,**
Early 1950s. Part of membership kit. Photos are posed by Johnny Craig.
Each - **$40 $80 $150**

MAD-12

❏ **MAD-12. "I Read MAD" T-Shirt,**
1958. Made by Champknit and first offered for sale on inside back cover of issue #39, May 1958. Reportedly three to four thousand were sold and now quite scarce. - **$150 $300 $900**

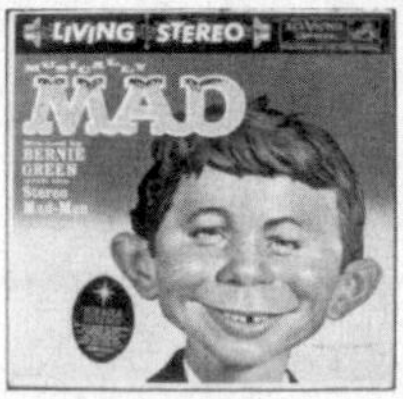

MAD-13

❏ **MAD-13. "Musically Mad" LP Album,**
1959. Issued by RCA. Monaural - **$12 $25 $50**
Stereo - **$18 $30 $60**

MAD-14

❏ **MAD-14. "Me-Worry?" Plaster Bust,**
1950s. Moseley Products. 4-5/8" tall likeness of Alfred E. Neuman although possibly issued before MAD Magazine adopted the character. - **$100 $200 $400**

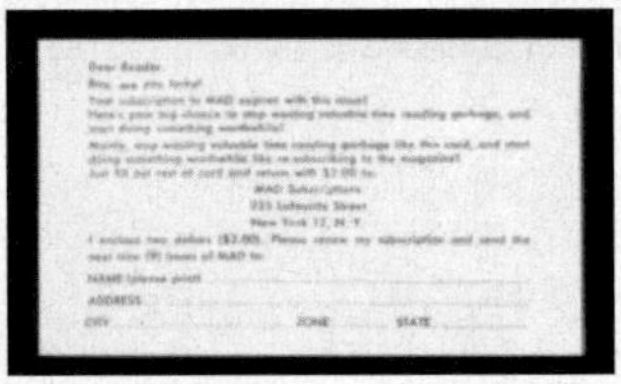
MAD-15

❏ **MAD-15. Subscription Card,**
1950s. - **$15 $25 $40**

MAD-16

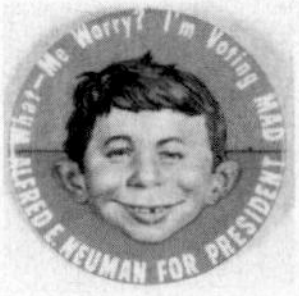

MAD-17

MAD-18

❏ **MAD-16. Figurine,**
1960. Glazed base with unglazed white bust to be painted by recipient.
Small 3-3/4" Size - **$75 $125 $150**
Medium 4-1/4" Size - **$100 $150 $200**
Large 5-1/2" Size - **$125 $250 $400**

❏ **MAD-17. "For President" 2-1/2" Cello. Button,**
1960. - **$30 $60 $100**

❏ **MAD-18. "What Me Worry" Adult-Sized Over The Head-Style Costume,**
1960. Collegeville. 25" wide by 50" tall.
Near Mint Carded - **$1600**
Uncarded - **$325 $650 $1200**

MAD-19

❏ **MAD-19. "Me Worry??" Composition Bust Figure,**
c. 1960. Unlicensed. With Tag - **$90 $175 $350**
No Tag - **$60 $140 $300**

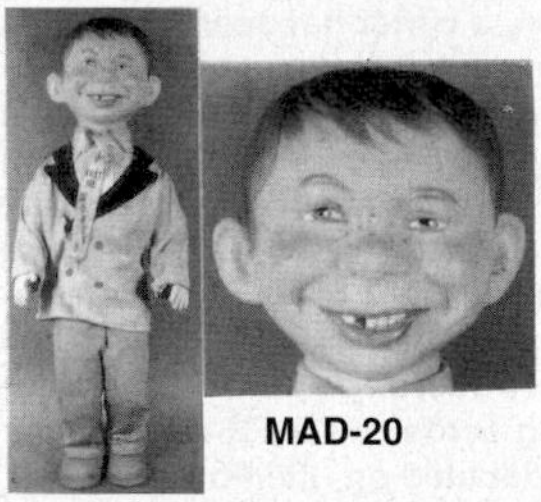
MAD-20

❏ **MAD-20. "What Me Worry?" Doll,**
1961. Unlicensed store item by Baby Barry. - **$500 $1250 $2250**

MAD-21

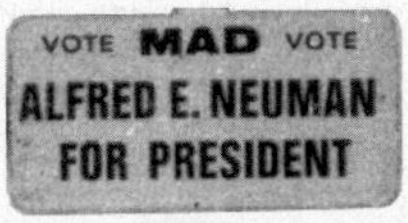

MAD-22

❏ **MAD-21 "For President" 2-1/2" Cello. Button,**
1964. - **$25 $45 $95**

❏ **MAD-22. "Alfred E. Neuman For President" Litho. Tin Tab,**
1964. - **$10 $15 $25**

MAD-23

MAD-24

❑ **MAD-23. "Alfred E. Neuman" Aurora Plastic Hobby Model Kit,**
1965. Store item. Boxed And Unbuilt - **$400**

❑ **MAD-24. "Me Worry?" Unauthorized Painted Bisque Bust,**
1960s. Nicely hand-painted bust is 4.5" tall. Several different 1960s unauthorized busts were produced with this being the nicest quality and image. - **$100 $200 $400**

MAD-25

❑ **MAD-25. "What-Me Worry? I Read MAD!" Premium Picture,**
1960s. Full color 7x9".
Mailer - **$10 $15 $30**
Picture - **$20 $35 $65**

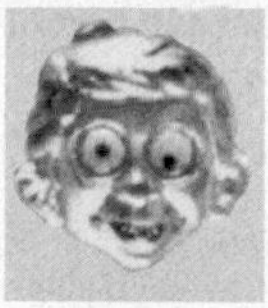

MAD-26

MAD-27

❑ **MAD-26. Alfred E. Neuman Plastic Portrait Pin,**
c. 1960s. Store item. Vending machine issue, unlicensed, marked "Hong Kong". - **$15 $30 $50**

❑ **MAD-27. "What Me Worry?" Dark Gold Luster Metal Necklace Pendant,**
c. 1960s. Store item. Depicts Alfred E. Neuman riding bomb. Also issued as silver luster pin.
Each - **$45 $90 $175**

MAD-28

❑ **MAD-28. "Mad" Plastic Bookend Set,**
1970s. Issued in shrink wrap with five Mad paperbacks. Produced either in gold plastic with blue printing or red plastic with gold printing.
Set Without Books - **$18 $35 $75**

MAD-29

MAD-30

❑ **MAD-29. "Up the Academy" Movie Promotion 3" Cello Button,**
1980. Warner Brothers. MAD Magazine name was removed from the film after initial release but some versions now restore the full title and opening and closing cameo by a live-action Alfred E. Neuman. - **$10 $15 $25**

❑ **MAD-30. Official MAD 35th Anniversary Edition" Watch On Card,**
1987. Store item from E.C. Publications. Back of packaging shows three design varieties.
Near Mint Carded - **$35**

MAD-31

❑ **MAD-31. William Gaines Autographed Photo,**
1988. Black and white photo of MAD Magazine and EC Comics publisher measures 3x4.75" and is signed "For Dave. Enjoy! Bill Gaines." Photo features bushy-bearded, long haired, bespectacled Gaines chuckling in front of a black background. Back of photo has text "Bill Gaines 1988 MAD Magazine."
Same Or Similar - **$25 $60 $100**

MAD-32

❑ **MAD-32. Magazine Subscription Promotion Buttons,**
1980s. E. C. Publishing Inc. Set of 24 cello. 1" pin-backs reproducing art from MAD Magazine covers 1950s-1980s. The set was used as a promotion for individuals who had subscribed to the magazine for 3 years. Each subscriber only received 3 pins. Many collectors did not know there were more than 3 styles. Rare to find in complete sets.
Complete set - **$250 $400 $600**
Each - **$10 $15 $25**

MAD-33

❑ **MAD-33. "What, Me Worry?" Pinback,**
1996. Alfred E. Neuman pictured. - **$2 $4 $6**

MAD-34

MAD-35

❑ **MAD-34. Alfred E. Neuman Bobbing Head Figure,**
1999. With tag. - **$8 $12 $30**

❑ **MAD-35. Alfred E. Neuman Resin Statue,**
1990s. Limited to 900. Warner Bros. store exclusive. Boxed. - **$175**
During 1999, a second edition of the figure was produced. This version was slightly smaller and the "What--me worry?" slogan was printed using a different font and then pasted onto the base.
1999 Edition - **$80**

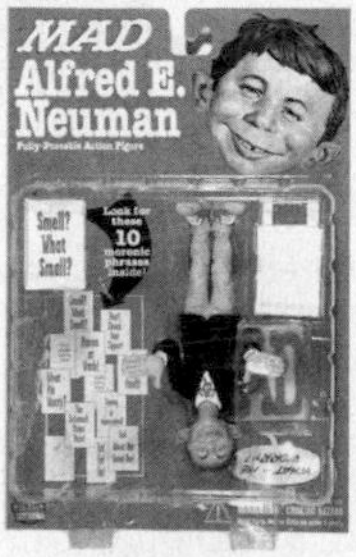

MAD-36

❑ **MAD-36. Poseable Action Figure,**
2000. On card - **$33**

MAD-37

(BOX)

❑ **MAD-37. "Alfred E. Neuman" Cookie Jar,**
2001. With box. - **$70**

MAD-38 MAD-39

❑ **MAD-38. Alfred E. Neuman as Batman Poseable Action Figure,**
2001. On card - **$22**

❑ **MAD-39. Alfred E. Neuman as Superman Poseable Action Figure,**
2001. On card - **$22**

Mae West

Born Mary Jane West, Mae West (1893-1980) started in vaudeville in 1905 at age 12. Noted for bawdy double entendres, West wrote and starred in several Broadway plays. She received major publicity when she was charged with obscenity during the 1926-1927 run of *Sex* and served eight days of a ten day jail sentence. Her 1928 play *Diamond Lil* was a major success.

West co-starred in the 1932 Paramount feature film *Night After Night* with George Raft and Constance Cummings. She moved into the Ravenswood apartments near the studio and lived there the rest of her life. She co-starred with Cary Grant in two 1933 Paramount features. *She Done Him Wrong* introduced her famous line "Why don't you come up sometime and see me," which was changed to "Why don't you come up and see me sometime" in *I'm No Angel*. Other notable films include: Universal's 1940 *My Little Chickadee* with W.C. Fields and screenplay written by West and Fields; 20th Century Fox's 1970 *Myra Breckinridge* based on the novel by Gore Vidal, recognized as a cult classic and contender for worst film of all time; and *Sextette* co-starring George Raft, released when West was 85. She had a Las Vegas stage show in the 1950s and her autobiography *Goodness Had Nothing To Do With It* was published in 1959. World War II soldiers referred to their life preserver vests as Mae Wests, perhaps in homage to another Mae West film quote "Is that a gun in your pocket, or are you just glad to see me?"

MAE-1

❑ **MAE-1. Mae West 1912 And 1934 Sheet Music Pair,**
1912. First is 10.75x13.5" titled "Good Night, Nurse". Six pages copyright 1912 Jerome Remick, N.Y. Second is 9x12-1/8" titled "My Old Flame" copyright 1934 Famous Music Corp.
First - **$10 $20 $40**
Second - **$5 $15 $25**

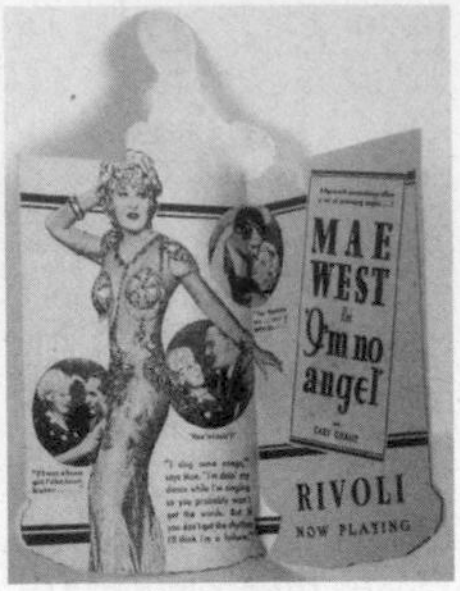

(COVER) (OPEN)

MAE-2

❑ **MAE-2. "I'm No Angel" Die-Cut Herald,**
1933. Rare. Paramount giveaway for movie starring the one and only Mae West. Standee card opens to display ad for the film. Cary Grant also starred. - **$100 $225 $450**

MAE-3

❑ **MAE-3. "Mae West" 17x30" Cardboard Store Sign,**
1934. Old Gold cigarettes. Text includes "Goin' To Town" movie title. - **$500 $1000 $2000**

MAE-4

❑ **MAE-4. Mae West-Inspired China Ashtray,**
c. 1934. Store item. - **$50 $100 $200**

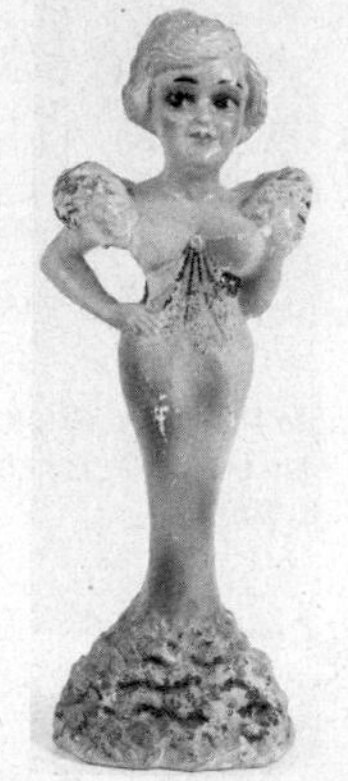

MAE-5

❑ **MAE-5. Mae West Painted Chalkware Figure By Rainwater,**
1936. 3.25x10.5x3" deep painted chalkware with sparkle accents. Includes 1936 copyright and name William D. "Bill" Rainwater. - **$100 $200 $300**

MAE-6

MAE-7

❑ **MAE-6. "Lou Gehrig Goes West For A Vacation!" 8-pager,**
1930s. 2-5/8x4" x-rated story including Lefty Grove and Mae West. - **$30 $65 $150**

❑ **MAE-7. Large Format 16-Pager Including Popeye Titled "Around The World With Mae West",**
1930s. 3.75x6" x-rated story of Mae West's sexual adventures. Well drawn. - **$50 $100 $200**

MAE-8

❑ **MAE-8. First Seen Mae West Button,**
1930s. Western Badge. 1.25" with backpaper. - **$15 $30 $75**

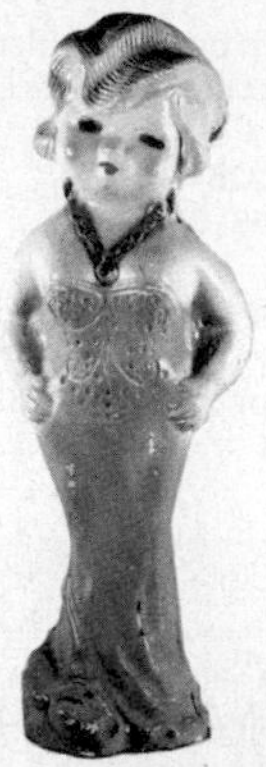

MAE-9

❑ **MAE-9. Mae West Carnival Doll,**
1930s. 14" tall painted chalkware. - **$50 $125 $250**

MAE-10

MAE-11

❑ **MAE-10. "My Little Chickadee" With Mae West And W.C. Fields Lobby Card Set,**
1940. Universal. Set of eight 11x14" lobby cards, five cards feature both West and Fields, two feature just West and one features just Fields. Set - **$600 $1400 $2400**

❑ **MAE-11. Signed Mae West Photo,**
1960s. Glossy 8x10" photo inscribed "To Richard Best Wishes Mae West." - **$20 $45 $75**

MAE-12

❑ **MAE-12. "The Sin-Sational Mae West" Autographed Poster,**
1978. Nostalgia Merchant. 24x30" poster signed in black ink at bottom "Sin-Cerely Mae West." - **$50 $100 $225**

MAE-13

❑ **MAE-13. Mae West Doll From Effanbee Legend Series,**
1982. 4.75x10-1/8x20" tall die-cut box with clear cellophane window contains 18" tall vinyl doll wearing black dress, feather boa, feather-accented hat, rhinestone choker. Includes letter insert from Effanbee and hang tag. Produced for only one year. Near Mint Boxed - **$100**

Major Bowes Original Amateur Hour

Edward Bowes (1874-1946), a major in U.S. Army intelligence in World War I and a show-business veteran, introduced his amateur hour on New York radio station WHN in 1934. The following year, sponsored by Chase & Sanborn coffee, it aired on the NBC network, and from 1936 to 1946, sponsored by Chrysler automobiles, it was a Thursday night institution on CBS. 'Round and 'round she goes, and where she stops nobody knows--so went the wheel of fortune, each week drawing thousands of amateur performers looking for the big break. One of the most notable acts to audition was the *Hoboken Four* in 1935, featuring Frank Sinatra. For most, it was a dream that didn't come true.

MJB-1

MJB-2

❑ **MJB-1. First Fan Newsletter #1,**
1935. Chase & Sanborn Coffee. - **$25 $40 $75**

❑ **MJB-2. Second Fan Newsletter #2,**
1935. Chase & Sanborn Coffee. - **$20 $35 $60**

MJB-3

❑ **MJB-3. Fan Photo,**
1936. Chrysler Corp. Radio show title on back. - **$12 $18 $35**

MJB-4

MJB-5

❑ **MJB-4. "Major Bowes Amateur Parade" Photo Newsletter,**
June 1937. Chrysler Corp. - **$15 $30 $45**

❑ **MJB-5. Gong Alarm Clock,**
1930s. Made by Ingersoll. - **$100 $200 $400**

MJB-6

MJB-7

❑ **MJB-6. Home Broadcasting Microphone With Box,**
1930s. Store item by Pilgrim Electric Corp. Metal actual working device for household radio set.
Boxed - **$125 $325 $450**
Loose - **$75 $185 $300**

❑ **MJB-7. Major Bowes Gong With Hammer Clasp,**
1930s. Prize from radio show. Sterling Silver. - **$75 $135 $250**

MJB-8

❑ **MJB-8. "Capitol Theatre Family" Fan Photo Card,**
1930s. Pictures Capitol Radio orchestra of radio broadcasts. - **$8 $15 $25**

MJB-9

❑ **MJB-9. Fan Postcards,**
1930s. Each - **$8 $15 $25**

Major Jet

A mid-1950s character created to promote Sugar Jets cereal of General Mills, Major Jet was an otherwise unidentified individual although always appearing in his jet-age flight helmet snappily accented by voltage bolt symbols centered by a "J" symbol denoting speed. His resemblance to an established comic strip jetting hero of the era, Milton Caniff's *Steve Canyon*, may have been more than coincidental. Actor Roger Pace portrayed Major Jet in TV commercials. His motto, "Jet Up And Go With Sugar Jets," accompanied premium offer--notably a mail premium Rocket-Glider kit of styrofoam and plastic but "made for high, jet-speed flying." The Rocket-Glider was offered by a May 1, 1955 Sunday comic section ad "while supplies last" and probably by cereal box as well.

MAJ-1

❑ **MAJ-1. Magic Paint Set Booklet,**
1954. Sugar Jets cereal. #1 from set of three.
Each - **$10 $20 $40**

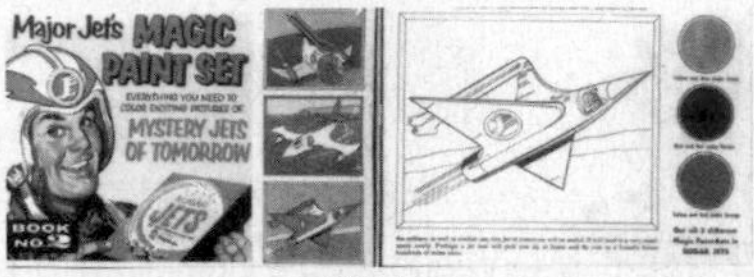

MAJ-2

❑ **MAJ-2. "Magic Paint Set" Book #2,**
1954. Sugar Jets cereal. From set of three.
Each - **$10 $20 $40**

MAJ-3

❑ **MAJ-3."Magic Paint Set" Book No. 3,**
1954. Sugar Jets Cereal. From set of three. - **$10 $20 $40**

MAJ-4

MAJ-5

❑ **MAJ-4. Sugar Jets "Filmo Vision" Box Back,**
1954. Cut-out parts for assembly of spaceship viewer for watching two cut-out films. Uncut Back - **$12 $22 $45**

❑ **MAJ-5. Rocket-Glider With Launcher,**
1955. Sugar Jets cereal.
Near Mint Boxed - **$70**
Loose - **$15 $30 $45**

MAJ-6

❑ **MAJ-6. Sugar Jets Cereal Box with Decoder,**
1955. On the front of the box is a Major Jet decoder which could be punched out and used to solve puzzles and comics on back. Rare.
Uncut Box with Decoder - **$85 $175 $325**

Man From U.N.C.L.E.

An admitted intentional television spoof of James Bond movies, (Bond creator Ian Fleming drafted the original outline of the series) *The Man From U.N.C.L.E.* was first telecast on September 22, 1964, continuing weekly on NBC until the death-gasp final episode on January 15, 1968. During those three and a half years, the U.N.C.L.E. (United Network Command for Law and Enforcement) team battled the persistent ne'er-do-well plots of the international crime syndicate known as THRUSH. U.N.C.L.E. was headed by Alexander Waverly (Leo G. Carroll), whose singular function was to hand out assignments and follow them up from the security of his secret office somewhere in New York City.

Assignments were doled out to agents Napoleon Solo (Robert Vaughn) and Ilya Kuryakin (David McCallum). Episodes were generally titled "The [specific name] Affair." Agent Solo was a borrowed name from the Bond movie *Goldfinger*. Solo and Kuryakin defeated THRUSH efforts through ingenuity, exotic weaponry and gadgets, and often with the aid of ordinary citizens.

The hour-long show spawned a one season spin-off series, *The Girl From U.N.C.L.E.* (September 13, 1966-August 29, 1967), starring Stefanie Powers in the title role of April Dancer. Her efforts were also directed by Mr. Waverly, but sans Solo and Kuryakin. The original U.N.C.L.E. series managed to make it into the Nielsen Top 20 only once, during its second season, but maintained a cadre of viewers to the end. The end was possibly due in part to NBC's numerous changes in evenings and time slots throughout the run of the series.

Vaughn and McCallum reunited for a 1983 made-for-TV movie, *The Return of the Man From U.N.C.L.E.*, on CBS. The movie also featured an amusing cameo by one-time James Bond, George Lazenby.

***The Man From U.N.C.L.E.* generated a surprising quantity of merchandise in comparison to other shows of higher-rated viewership in that era. *The Girl From U.N.C.L.E.* generated less due to its brevity.**

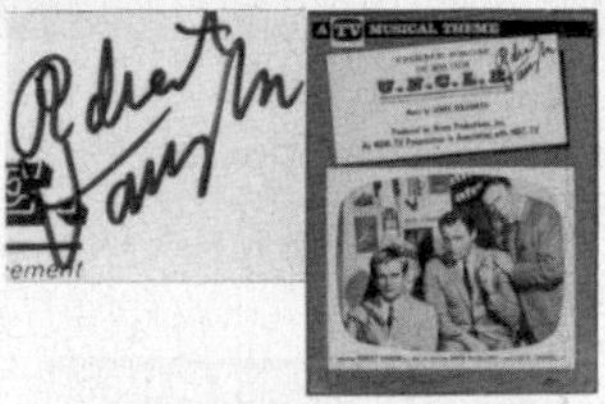

MFU-1

❑ **MFU-1. "Theme From The Man From U.N.C.L.E." Autographed Sheet Music ,**
1964. Hastings Music Corp. M-G-M. Signed by Robert Vaughan. Near Mint Autographed - **$100**
Unsigned - **$15 $25 $50**

MFU-2

❑ **MFU-2. "The Man From U.N.C.L.E. Card Game,"**
1965. Milton Bradley. - **$18 $35 $90**

MFU-3

❑ **MFU-3. Man From U.N.C.L.E. Membership Kit,**
1965. Premium, sponsor unknown.
Instructions - **$10 $20 $30**
Card - **$15 $30 $60**
Photo - **$20 $40 $90**

MFU-5

MFU-4

❑ **MFU-4. Man From U.N.C.L.E. Illya Kuryakin Action Figure**
1965. Stands 12 1/4" tall with metal gun, metal gun holder, paper badge, club card and instructions. Near Mint Boxed - **$500**

❑ **MFU-5. Man From U.N.C.L.E. Plastic Badge,**
1965. Store item that came with various sets by Ideal Toy Corp. - **$10 $20 $40**

MFU-6

❑ **MFU-6. "The Man From U.N.C.L.E. Spy Magic Tricks" Boxed Set,**
1965. Gilbert, M-G-M Inc. 12.5x18.5x2.25" deep box. Box insert contains a variety of objects, mostly hard plastic, for a total of eight tricks.
- $125 $250 $450

MFU-7

❑ **MFU-7. Napoleon Solo Gun in Box,**
1965. Boxed with instructions. Box is rare. -
$750 $1500 $2750

MFU-8

❑ MFU-8. "The Man From U.N.C.L.E. Illya Kuryakin Gunset" By Ideal,
1965. Open-faced box is 13.75x20x2" deep and contains 12" long gun with "Cap Storage Compartment And Clip Loading Magazine." Set also comes with U.N.C.L.E. identification wallet and ID card. Gun has U.N.C.L.E. sticker logo at cap storage compartment.
Complete Boxed - **$350 $700 $1350**

MFU-9

❑ MFU-9. "The Man From U.N.C.L.E." Badge On Card,
1965. Store item by Lone Star, England.
Near Mint Carded **- $115**
Badge Only **- $12 $25 $45**

(DISPLAY BOX)

(CARD BOX)

(BACK OF CARD BOX)

MFU-10

❑ MFU-10. "The Man From U.N.C.L.E. Playing Cards" Display Box With Deck,
1965. Store item by Ed-U-Cards. Display box is scarce. Box **- $50 $100 $200**
Boxed deck of cards **- $40 $60 $165**

MFU-11

❑ MFU-11. "The Man From U.N.C.L.E." Board Game,
1965. Ideal Toy Corporation. Rare in high grade. - **$40 $120 $480**

MFU-12

❑ MFU-12. "The Man From U.N.C.L.E." Credentials and Secret Message Sender,
1965. On card. - **$75 $135 $250**

MFU-13

MFU-14

❑ MFU-13. "Napoleon Solo" 3-1/2" Cello. Button,
1965. Store item. From "The Man From U.N.C.L.E." Also issued for Illya.
Each **- $15 $30 $60**

❑ MFU-14. "The Men From U.N.C.L.E." 6" Cello. Button,
1966. **- $100 $200 $300**

MFU-15

MFU-16

❑ MFU-15. "The Girl From U.N.C.L.E." English Gum Card Wrapper,
1966. Store item by A. & B.C. Chewing Gum Ltd. - **$12 $25 $50**

❑ MFU-16. "U.N.C.L.E. Secret Agent" Wristwatch,
1966. Store item by Bradley. - **$85 $160 $300**

MFU-17

❑ MFU-17. "The Man From U.N.C.L.E. Husky Extra" Die Cast Replica Car,
1966. Carded - **$50 $100 $200**

MFU-18

MFU-19

❑ MFU-18. "The Man From U.N.C.L.E. Sweet Cigarettes" Candy Box,
1966. English issue by Cadet Sweets. - **$60 $115 $175**

❑ MFU-19. "The Man From U.N.C.L.E. Magazine" First Issue,
1966. 144 pages. First Issue **- $20 $40 $65**
Other Issues **- $5 $10 $20**

MFU-20

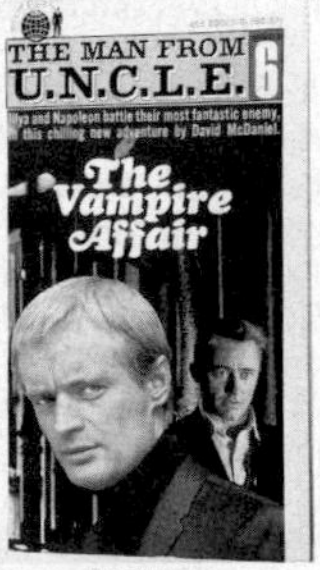

MFU-21

❑ MFU-20. "The Copenhagen Affair" Man From U.N.C.L.E. Paperback Book #3,
1966. Ace Books. **- $5 $10 $20**

❑ MFU-21. "The Vampire Affair" Man From U.N.C.L.E. Paperback Book #6,
1966. Ace Books. **- $5 $10 $20**

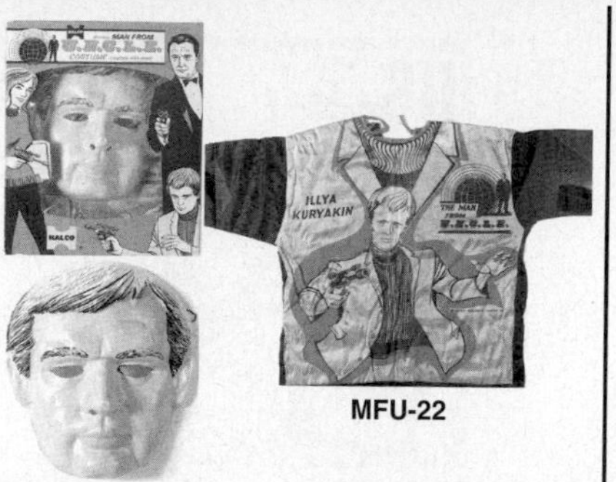

MFU-22

❑ **MFU-22. Ilya Kuryakin Costume Boxed,**
c. 1966. Halco copyright M-G-M. Thin plastic mask and rayon outfit. - **$50 $100 $200**

MFU-23

MFU-24

❑ **MFU-23. "The Monster Wheel Affair" Man From U.N.C.L.E. Paperback Book #8,**
1967. - **$5 $10 $20**

❑ **MFU-24. "The Affair of the Gunrunners' Gold" Man From U.N.C.L.E. Hardcover Book,**
1967. 212 pages. - **$10 $20 $30**

Mandrake the Magician

Created by writer Lee Falk (1911-1999) and artist Phil Davis, Mandrake debuted as a daily comic strip in 1934 and as a Sunday page in 1935. Distributed by King Features, the adventures of the top-hatted magician with supernatural and hypnotic powers was an immediate success. Assisted by his faithful companion Lothar, an African king with enormous strength, and Princess Narda, Mandrake triumphed over earthly enemies and extraterrestrial invaders. He made his first comic book appearance in *King Comics* #1 in 1936 and has appeared in numerous collections in the decades since. Columbia Pictures released a 12-episode chapter play in 1939 with Warren Hull as Mandrake, and a syndicated radio series aired on the Mutual network from 1940 to 1942 starring Edward Johnson. A pilot made-for-TV movie was broadcast in 1979. Mandrake also appeared as part of the cast of the 1986 syndicated cartoon series *The Defenders Of The Earth* which lasted one season with 66 episodes.

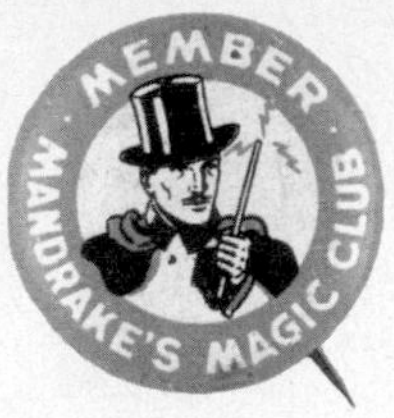

MAN-1

MAN-2

❑ **MAN-1. "Member Mandrake's Magic Club" Litho. Button,**
1934. - **$50 $135 $275**

❑ **MAN-2. "Mandrake Magicians' Club/Taystee Bread" Enameled Brass Pin,**
1934. - **$30 $125 $225**

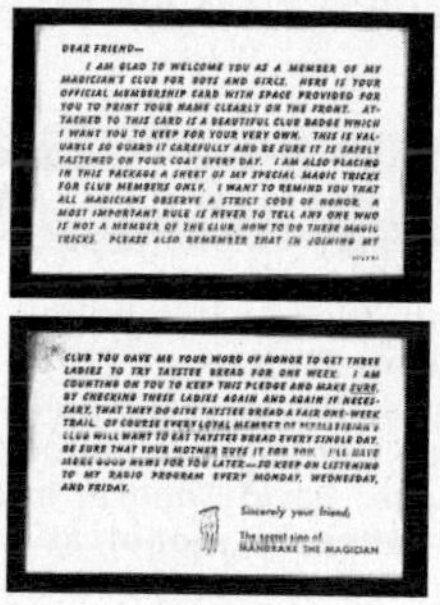
DEAR FRIEND—

I AM GLAD TO WELCOME YOU AS A MEMBER OF MY MAGICIAN'S CLUB FOR BOYS AND GIRLS. HERE IS YOUR OFFICIAL MEMBERSHIP CARD WITH SPACE PROVIDED FOR YOU TO PRINT YOUR NAME CLEARLY ON THE FRONT. ATTACHED TO THIS CARD IS A BEAUTIFUL CLUB BADGE WHICH I WANT YOU TO KEEP FOR YOUR VERY OWN. THIS IS VALUABLE SO GUARD IT CAREFULLY AND BE SURE IT IS SAFELY FASTENED ON YOUR COAT EVERY DAY. I AM ALSO PLACING IN THIS PACKAGE A SHEET OF MY SPECIAL MAGIC TRICKS FOR CLUB MEMBERS ONLY. I WANT TO REMIND YOU THAT ALL MAGICIANS OBSERVE A STRICT CODE OF HONOR. A MOST IMPORTANT RULE IS NEVER TO TELL ANY ONE WHO IS NOT A MEMBER OF THE CLUB, HOW TO DO THESE MAGIC TRICKS. PLEASE ALSO REMEMBER THAT IN JOINING MY

CLUB YOU GAVE ME YOUR WORD OF HONOR TO GET THREE LADIES TO TRY TAYSTEE BREAD FOR ONE WEEK. I AM COUNTING ON YOU TO KEEP THIS PLEDGE AND MAKE SURE, BY CHECKING THESE LADIES AGAIN AND AGAIN IF NECESSARY, THAT THEY DO GIVE TAYSTEE BREAD A FAIR ONE-WEEK TRAIL. OF COURSE EVERY LOYAL MEMBER OF [illegible] CLUB WILL WANT TO EAT TAYSTEE BREAD EVERY SINGLE DAY. BE SURE THAT YOUR MOTHER BUYS IT FOR YOU. I'LL HAVE MORE GOOD NEWS FOR YOU LATER—SO KEEP ON LISTENING TO MY RADIO PROGRAM EVERY MONDAY, WEDNESDAY, AND FRIDAY.

Sincerely your friend,
The secret sign of
MANDRAKE THE MAGICIAN

MAN-3

❑ **MAN-3. Club Kit Card,**
1934. Taystee Bread. Accompanied membership card and enameled brass member's pin. - **$35 $75 $135**

MAN-4

MAN-5

❑ **MAN-4. "Mandrake the Magician" Big Little Book #1167,**
1935. - **$22 $66 $155**

❑ **MAN-5. "Mandrake the Magician and the Midnight Monster" Better Little Book #1431,**
1939. - **$15 $45 $105**

MAN-6

❑ **MAN-6. Christmas Card,**
1939. King Features Syndicate. From portfolio featuring various syndicate characters. - **$15 $30 $60**

MAN-7

MAN-8

❑ **MAN-7. "New Magic Tricks" Sheet,**
c. 1940. Taystee Bread and WOR (New York City). Sheet has earlier 1934 King Features copyright. - **$30 $60 $110**

❑ **MAN-8. "Mandrake the Magician Mighty Solver of Mysteries" Better Little Book #1454,**
1941. 432 pages. - **$15 $45 $105**

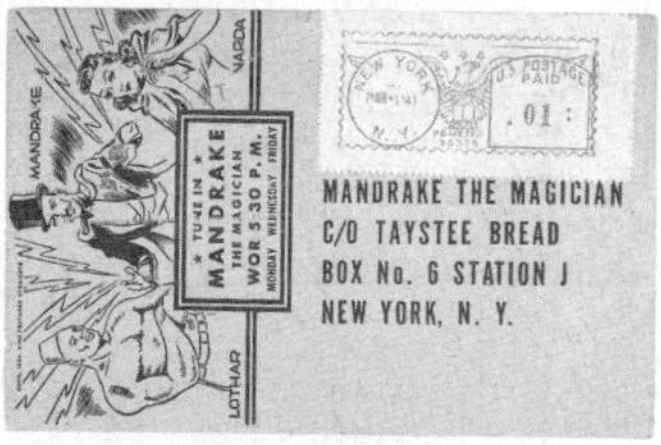

MAN-9

❑ **MAN-9. Mandrake Club Application Card,**
1941. Mailing card is 3.5x5.5". Front promotes program on radio "WOR" NYC. Top back printed text reads "Dear Mandrake I Would Like To Be A Member Of Your Mandrake Magicians Club So I Can Obtain The Club Pin And Learn How To Do Magic Tricks." - **$60 $125 $250**

MAN-10

❑ **MAN-10. "Mandrake The Magician And The Flame Pearls" Better Little Book,**
1946. Whitman #1418. - **$14 $42 $95**

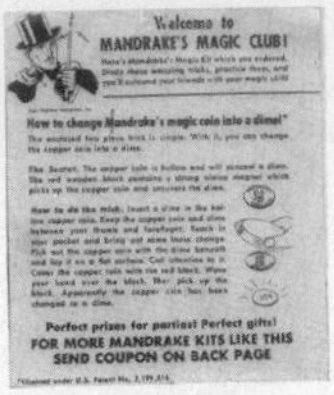

MAN-11

❑ **MAN-11. Magic Kit Leaflet,**
1948. Suchard Chocolate Bars. Offers trick premiums with expiration date of January 31, 1949. - **$20 $30 $60**

MAN-12

❑ **MAN-12. Exhibit Card,**
1949. Arcade vending card copyright by King Features. - **$5 $10 $15**

MAN-13

❑ **MAN-13. Magic Kit,**
1952. Transogram issue that came in at least four different box sizes. - **$50 $125 $200**

MAN-14

MAN-15

❑ **MAN-14. Plastic Gumball Charm,**
c. 1950s. Store item. Clear plastic with insert paper picture, from vending machine series. Second character on reverse. - **$10 $15 $25**

❑ **MAN-15. Boxed Game,**
1966. Store item by Transogram. - **$35 $75 $160**

MAJ-16

MAN-17

❑ **MAN-16. Mandrake Publisher's Response Card,**
1967. King Comics. 3-1/2x5-1/2" card with color portrait on front and blue text on back thanking writer for ideas and suggestions. -
$12 $25 $45

❑ **MAN-17. Sponge,**
c. 1960s. Store item. - **$8 $15 $25**

Marilyn Monroe

The iconic blonde bombshell was born Norma Jeane Mortenson (1926-1962) and later baptized Norma Jeane Baker. She was discovered working in an aircraft plant by photographer David Conover in June, 1945 and worked as a model at Blue Book Modeling Agency into the late 1940s. Her first magazine cover was the January, 1946 issue of *Douglas Airview*, an in-house publication of Douglas Aircraft.

Marilyn signed her first movie studio contract August 26, 1946 with *20th Century Fox* and first appeared on the silver screen in 1947 with a small part in *The Shocking Miss Pilgrim* which starred Betty Grable. She adopted her mother's family name of Monroe. By 1950 Marilyn was on her way to stardom with positive reviews for *The Asphalt Jungle* and *All About Eve.* Notable films include: 1953 *Gentlemen Prefer Blondes* with Jane Russell; 1955 *The Seven Year Itch* with Marilyn on a subway grate with skirt waist high; 1959 *Some Like It Hot* with Jack Lemmon and Tony Curtis; and her last film *The Misfits* in 1961 with Clark Gable.

Marilyn was on the cover of the first issue of *Playboy* in 1953 and also it's first nude centerfold, based on the classic Tom Kelley *Golden Dreams* photo. She was married to baseball legend Joe DiMaggio for nine months in the mid-1950s and noted playwright Arthur Miller from 1956 to 1961. Marilyn shocked and delighted the crowd at JFK's 45th birthday party May 19, 1962 when she seductively sang "Happy Birthday, Mr. President" in a skin tight gown. That gown sold for $1.2 million dollars at a 1999 auction. Marilyn smoldered on the screen and continues to be a hot collectible worldwide.

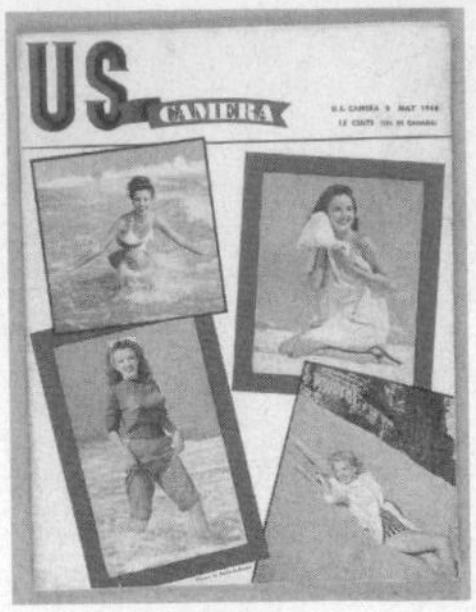

MMR-1

❑ **MMR-1. "US Camera" Magazine With Early Marilyn Monroe,**
1946. U.S. Camera Publishing Corp. 10.5x13.5" with 72 pages. Marilyn is featured in only 1 of 4 photos on cover. Photo by Andre de Dienes. -
$75 $175 $300

MMR-2

❑ **MMR-2. "Laff" Magazine With Early Marilyn Monroe Cover,**
1946. Magazine is 10.5x13.5" with 32 pages. Published by Volitant Publishing Company in August 1946. Magazine features cover photo only of a young Marilyn Monroe, when she was going by the name Norma Jean. The magazine, however, misunderstood and has her labeled as Jean Norman. - **$175 $325 $650**

MMR-3

❑ **MMR-3. "Foto Parade" Vol. 1 #1 Magazine Featuring Marilyn Monroe,**
1949. Foto Parade Inc. 10.25x13" with 52 pages. Features large color photo of Marilyn and two-page article titled "Meet Marilyn Monroe - And A New Picture Magazine." - **$50 $125 $200**

MMR-4

❑ **MMR-4. "Glance" Magazine With Monroe,** May 1950. Features Marilyn Monroe by her original married name, Norma Jean Dougherty. - **$75 $140 $250**

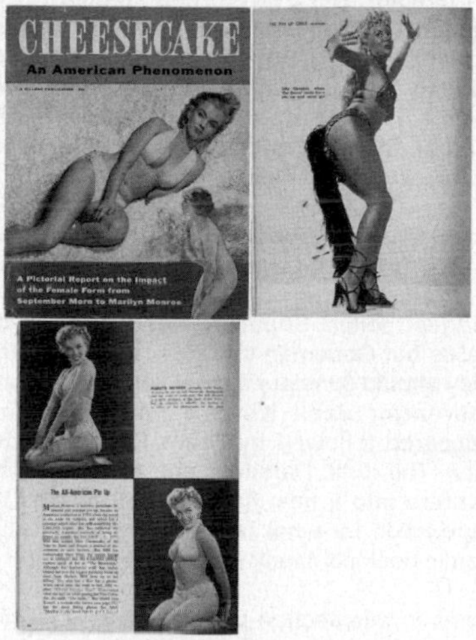

MMR-5

❑ **MMR-5. "Cheesecake An American Phenomenom" With Marilyn Monroe Cover,**
1953. Hillman Periodicals Inc. 8-3/x10.75" magazine with 112 pages having numerous photos of "sexy" women including Marilyn. - **$20 $40 $75**

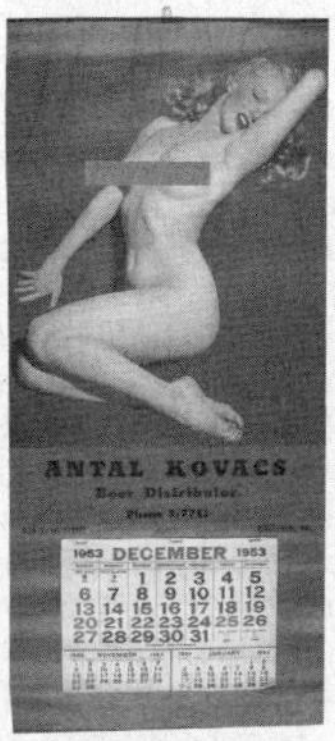

MMR-6

❑ **MMR-6. Marilyn Monroe "Golden Dreams" Nude Calendar,**
1953. 14.5x33.5" with 14.5x19.5" image of Marilyn. - **$50 $100 $200**

MMR-7

❑ **MMR-7. Marilyn Monroe Movie Postcard,**
1953. For movie "Niagara." - **$25 $65 $140**

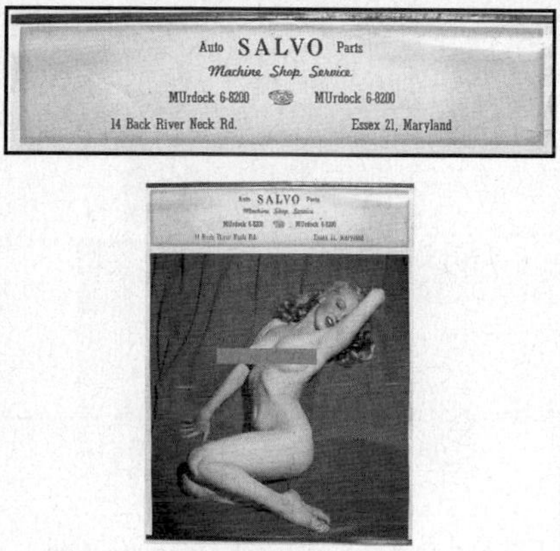

MMR-8

❑ **MMR-8. Marilyn Monroe Nude Calendar,**
1954. 12x16-1/8" calendar with 11x5x12.75" classic nude photo of Marilyn. - **$50 $100 $150**

MMR-9

❑ **MMR-9. Desk Calendar With Marilyn Monroe Pages,**
1954. 5x5" aluminum panel stapled by 12-month calendar including at least two but unidentified Marilyn poses. - **$75 $175 $375**

MMR-10

MMR-11

❑ **MMR-10. Calendar With Marilyn Monroe Pages,**
1954. 8.25x12" with 8 full color pages, including two of Marilyn. - **$25 $50 $100**

❑ **MMR-11. Marilyn Monroe "The Seven Year Itch" Title Card,**
1955. 20th Century Fox. 11x14" lobby card. - **$50 $125 $200**

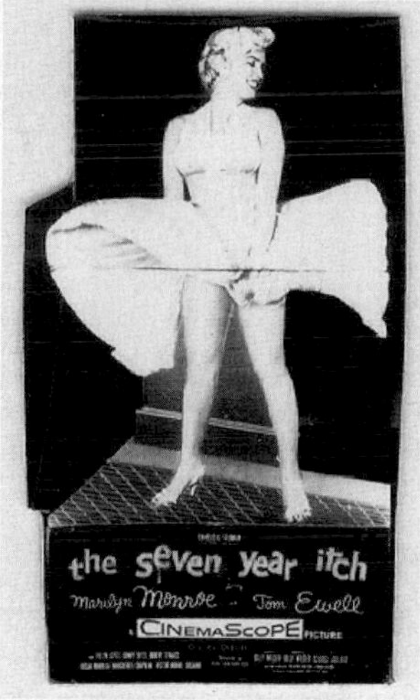

MMR-12

❑ **MMR-12. "The Seven Year Itch" 39x80" Theater Lobby Standee,**
1955. - **$1500 $3000 $6000**

MMR-13

❑ **MMR-13. "Some Like It Hot Marilyn Monroe Sings!" Soundtrack Record Album,**
1959. United Artists Records. 12.25x12.25" album. Back cover has 10 inset photos of Marilyn. - **$15 $30 $60**

MMR-14

❑ **MMR-14. "Marilyn Monroe" Boxed Double Card Deck,**
1950s. 3-3/8x8.5x7/8" deep velvet-flocked cardboard box contains two card decks with her two most famous nude photos taken by photographer Tom Kelley. - **$50 $100 $200**

MMR-15

❑ **MMR-15. Large Marilyn Monroe Calendar By Earl Moran,**
1950s. Brown & Bigelow. 16x33" calendar titled "Maid In Baltimore." Marilyn image is 11x20". - **$100 $200 $400**

MMR-16

❑ **MMR-16. Picture Frame With Marilyn Monroe Original Insert Picture,**
1950s. 8x10" with easel back holds color-tinted photo of young Marilyn as presented for sale in five and dime stores. - **$15 $30 $65**

MMR-17

❑ **MMR-17. Marilyn Monroe Pocket Mirror,**
1950s. Store item. Full color paper photo with cello. rim. - **$40 $75 $150**

MMR-18

❑ **MMR-18. "Avant Garde" Magazine With Marilyn Monroe Serigraphic Prints,**
1968. 10.75x11.25" with stiff paper covers has 72 pages. Contains six full color stiff paper sheets in day-glo colors with photos incorporated with art in section titled "The Marilyn Monroe Trip" By Bert Stern. - **$10 $25 $50**

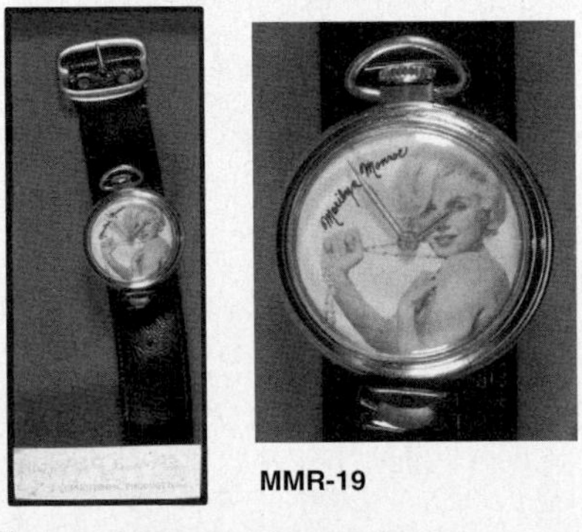

MMR-19

❑ **MMR-19. "Marilyn Monroe" Boxed Combination Watch/Pocket Watch,**
1970s. Photorific Products Inc. 3.75x10" window box contains 2" diameter pocket watch which could also be used as a wrist watch on 9" leather band. Dial has photo of Marilyn from last photo shoot she did before her death.
Box - **$25 $50 $100**
Watch - **$200 $400 $600**

Marvel Comics

Marvel began in 1939 with a firm known as Timely Publications operated by Martin Goodman who began publishing pulp magazines in 1932. Science fiction, western, crime and horror were steady sellers and Goodman became very astute at publishing and distribution. Superman had created quite a splash in 1938 and Goodman took notice. Funnies Inc. was a comic book shop, a business with artists, writers and editors who would produce comic books for others to publish. Their art director, Bill Everett, had created Prince Namor, The Sub-Mariner for another title and co-worker Carl Burgos came up with the Human Torch. Both characters made their debut in Goodman's *Marvel Comics* #1, October 1939. Martin Goodman was in the comic book business.

Joe Simon was Goodman's first editor and he and fellow artist Jack Kirby came up with *Captain America Comics*, the company's biggest seller. Super heroes waned in the 1950s but Goodman told Editor Stan Lee that they should consider a revival in 1961. Shortly thereafter Jack Kirby's Fantastic Four appeared followed by Steve Ditko's Spider-Man, The Hulk, Daredevil and others. A risky venture into a new field in 1939 formed the foundation for what is today the best selling comic book company in the world.

Items in this section promote Marvel Comics in general and a variety of their superhero characters. Captain America, Spider-Man and the X-Men are in separate sections. Following the successes of the three *Spider-Man* and three *X-Men* motion pictures and the build-up surrounding *Iron Man*, *Incredible Hulk* and other feature films, it can be expected that both the general Marvel category and the specific categories of their more notable heroes will continue to grow.

Please note the "Super Hero Club" set of 3.5" buttons includes D.C. characters (those buttons numbered on the front rim as 13 through 16) as well as Marvel characters. This set was produced in 1966 by Button World Manufacturing of Brooklyn, N.Y. Buttons numbered 1, 2, 11, 12 and above 16 are unknown. For Marvel characters there are variant designs for buttons numbered 4, 6, 8 and 9, but there are no known variations to the header card design that sealed the button into its clear plastic bag. Some numbered designs are common, some are scarce and some are scarce when bagged but common when loose. The 4 variants are all scarce. These factors are reflected in the evaluations.

MAR-1

MAR-2

❑ **MAR-1. Newspaper Ad for 1st Issue of Marvel Comics,**
1939. Ka-Zar gets top billing in this ad for Marvel Comics #1. Notice it was called a magazine at the time. - **$175**

❑ **MAR-2. "Marvel Action Rings" Vending Machine Display Card,**
1966. Promotes set of 12 flicker rings and features Jack Kirby signed art. - **$45 $90 $150**

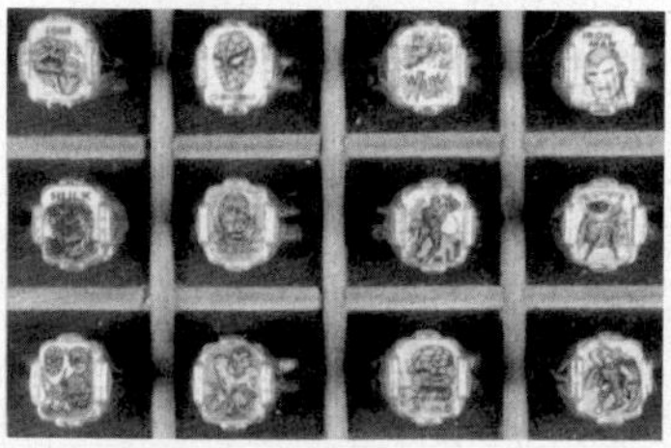
MAR-3

❑ **MAR-3. Vending Machine Flicker Rings,**
1966. Set of 12.
Each Silver or Gold Base - **$15 $25 $50**
Each Blue Base - **$8 $12 $25**

MAR-4

MAR-5

❑ **MAR-4. Marvel Pennant Iron Man,**
1966. 6 1/2" sold through comic books. - **$25 $50 $75**

❑ **MAR-5. Marvel Pennant Thor,**
1966. 6 1/2" sold through comic book. - **$25 $50 $75**

MAR-6

MAR-7

MAR-8

❑ **MAR-6. "Captain America" 3.5" Cello. Button,**
1966. Button World Mfg. Co. #3 in numbered series. Near Mint Bagged - **$75**
Loose - **$10 $20 $35**

❑ **MAR-7. "Dare Devil" 3.5" Cello. Button,**
1966, Button World Mfg. Co. #4 in numbered series. Near Mint Bagged - **$60**
Loose - **$10 $20 $35**

❑ **MAR-8. "Daredevil" 3.5" Cello. Button,**
1966. Button World Mfg. Co. #4 variant in numbered series. Differs from standard design primarily by showing full figure. Also includes words "Man Without Fear."
Near Mint Bagged - **$200**
Loose - **$25 $50 $100**

MAR-9

MAR-10

❑ **MAR-9. "The Incredible Hulk" 3.5" Cello. Button,**
1966. Button World Mfg. Co. #5 in numbered series. Near Mint Bagged - **$90**
Loose - **$12 $22 $45**

❑ **MAR-10. "Hulk" 3.5" Cello. Button,**
1966. Button World Mfg. Co. #5 variant in numbered series. Differs from standard design with this image having clenched fists and being of early 1960s style. This variant seems to be the scarcest of all designs.
Near Mint Bagged - **$350**
Loose - **$65 $135 $275**

MAR-11

MAR-12

❑ **MAR-11. "The Amazing Spider Man" 3.5" Cello. Button,**
1966. Button World Mfg. Co. #6 in numbered series. Near Mint Bagged - **$175**
Loose - **$20 $40 $75**

❑ **MAR-12. "The Amazing Spider-Man" 3.5" Cello. Button,**
1966. Button World Mfg. Co. #6 variant in numbered series. Differs from standard design by showing full figure with web design on black background. On this variant, his name is hyphenated. Near Mint Bagged - **$375**
Loose - **$75 $150 $300**

MAR-13

MAR-14

MAR-15

❑ **MAR-13. "The Invincible Iron Man" 3.5" Cello. Button,**
1966. Button World Mfg. Co. #7 in numbered series. Near Mint Bagged - **$135**
Loose - **$10 $20 $40**

❑ **MAR-14. "Prince Namor Sub-Mariner" 3.5" Cello. Button,**
1966. Button World Mfg. Co. #8 in numbered series. Near Mint Bagged - **$150**
Loose - **$15 $35 $65**

❑ **MAR-15. "Sub-Mariner" 3.5" Cello. Button,**
1966. Button World Mfg. Co. #8 variant in numbered series. Differs from standard design by showing full figure in swimming pose. The name "Prince Namor" does not appear.
Near Mint Bagged - **$225**
Loose - **$30 $60 $125**

MAR-16

MAR-17

MAR-18

❑ **MAR-16. "The Mighty Thor" 3.5" Cello. Button,**
1966. Button World Mfg. Co. #9 in numbered series. Near Mint Bagged - **$75**
Loose - **$10 $20 $40**

❑ **MAR-17. "Thor" 3.5" Cello. Button,**
1966. Button World Mfg. Co. #9 variant in numbered series. Differs from standard design by showing full figure and his name is simply "Thor."
Near Mint Bagged - **$150**
Loose - **$20 $40 $75**

❑ **MAR-18. "The Avengers." 3.5" Cello. Button,**
1966. Button World Mfg. Co. #10 in numbered series.
Near Mint Bagged - **$225**
Loose - **$30 $60 $125**

MAR-19

MAR-20

❑ **MAR-19. "Green Lantern." 3.5" Cello. Button,**
1966. Button World Mfg. Co. #13 in numbered series. Near Mint Bagged - **$175**
Loose - **$10 $25 $50**

❑ **MAR-20. "Wonder Woman." 3.5" Cello. Button,**
1966. Button World Mfg. Co. #14 in numbered series. Near Mint Bagged - **$150**
Loose - **$22 $45 $85**

MAR-21

MAR-22

❑ **MAR-21. "Aquaman." 3.5" Cello. Button,**
1966. Button World Mfg. Co. #15 in numbered series. Near Mint Bagged - **$225**
Loose - **$20 $40 $75**

❑ **MAR-22. "Hawkman." 3.5" Cello. Button,**
1966. Button World Mfg. Co. #16 in numbered series. Near Mint Bagged - **$115**
Loose - **$12 $25 $50**

MAR-23

❑ **MAR-23. "Merry Marvel Marching Society" Newsletter,**
1966. In addition to membership kit, member's received this mailing with first issue of "Merry Marvel Messenger" and a sheet for subscribing to various titles plus merchandise offers.
Mailer - **$10 $20 $30**
Newsletter - **$30 $60 $100**
Order Sheet - **$10 $20 $30**

MAR-24

❑ **MAR-24. "Mini-Books" Vending Machine Insert Paper,**
1966. Advertises tiny 1" tall, 48 page books for Captain America, Incredible Hulk, Millie the Model, Sgt. Fury, Spider-Man, Thor.
Insert Paper - **$15 $30 $60**
Each Book - **$8 $15 $40**

MAR-25

❑ **MAR-25. "Merry Marvel Marching Society" Membership Kit,**
1967. Envelope with letter, card, record, etc.
Complete Near Mint - **$400**
Each Paper Piece - **$15 $30 $90**
Record - **$10 $40 $90**

MAR-26

❑ **MAR-26. Marvel 'Bull Pen' Button Proofs,**
1967. Four 1.5" diameter black and white button proofs from set of five featuring popular slang phrases used by Marvel bullpen in comic publications. Proofs were then produced in final different two color combinations. Marshall Levin Collection. Each Proof As Made - **$40**

MAR-27

MAR-28

❑ **MAR-27. "Make Mine Marvel" 3-1/2" Cello. Button,**
1967. Issued with Marvel Marching Society club kit. - **$20 $40 $80**

❑ **MAR-28. Club Member 3" Cello. Button,**
1967. - **$10 $25 $60**

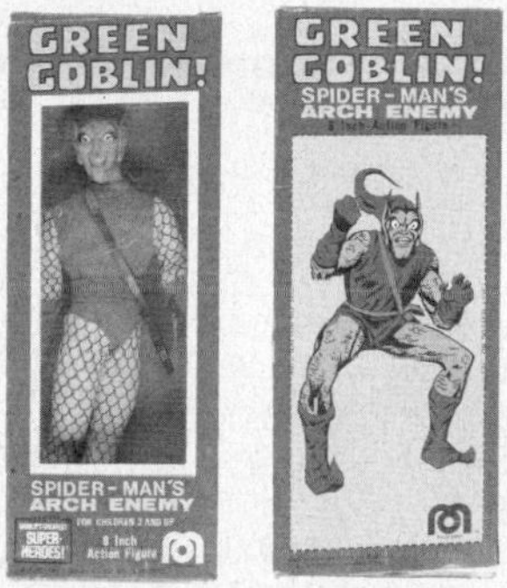

MAR-29

❑ **MAR-29. Green Goblin Boxed Mego Action Figure,**
1974. Vinyl figure is 8" tall in a one-piece stretch fabric outfit. Manufactured by Mego copyright Marvel Comics Group. Complete with boots and satchel. Box has nice cut out card featuring large image of the Green Goblin.
Boxed - **$200 $250 $350**

MAR-30

❑ **MAR-30. The Falcon Boxed Mego Action Figure,**
1974. Poseable vinyl figure 8" tall. Box has cut out card featuring large image of the Falcon on back. Boxed - **$150 $200 $300**

MAR-31

❑ **MAR-31. "Convention '75" 3" Cello. Button,**
1975. - **$25 $45 $85**

MAR-32

❑ **MAR-32. "Marvel Comics Convention" Shopping Bag,**
1975. 13x16" plastic bag with drawstring top given away at comic book collectors convention. - **$4 $8 $18**

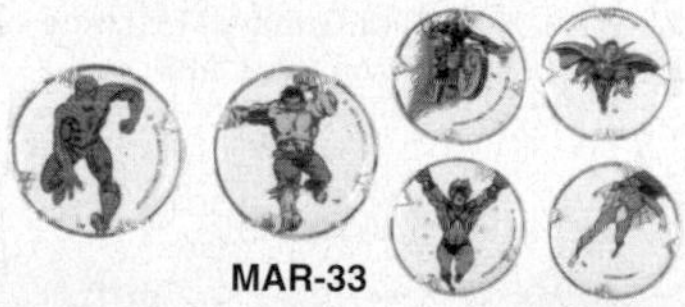

MAR-33

❑ **MAR-33. Marvel Super Heroes Ring Set,**
1977. Store or vending machine issue. Set of six. Each - **$3 $6 $10**

MAR-34

❑ **MAR-34. "7Eleven Marvel Comics Cup,"**
1977. Six cups, each 4-3/4" tall white plastic. Includes The Amazing Spider-Man, Captain America and The Falcon, The Mighty Thor, The Silver Surfer, Dr. Strange, The Incredible Hulk. Each - **$3 $6 $10**

MAR-35

❑ **MAR-35. The Incredible Hulk Game with The Fantastic Four,**
1978. Milton Bradley. - **$15 $30 $75**

MAR-36

❑ **MAR-36. Hulk/Spider-Man Mini Car City Playset,**
1979. Tara Toy Corp. Large vinyl carrying case holding extensive set including character punch-out figures, plastic "Change Machine" and other accessories for use with die cast cars such as Hot Wheels, Corgi, Matchbox.
Near Mint Complete - **$80**

MAR-37

❑ **MAR-37. "Incredible Hulk Is Here!" Newspaper Daily Strip Debut Sign,**
1970s. 10.5x15.75" cardboard for start of strip in Albany Times-Union. - **$40 $75 $150**

MAR-38

MAR-39

❑ **MAR-38. Cello. Button,**
1970s. 2" red and black on white. - **$10 $20 $40**

❑ **MAR-39. Hulk Cloth Cover Football,**
1981. Marvel Comics Group. Mostly green with red and black highlights. - **$15 $35 $60**

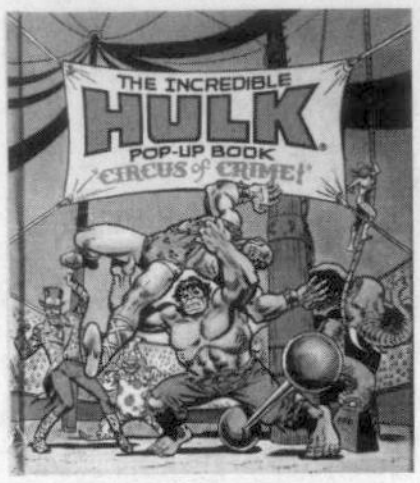

MAR-40

MAR-41

❑ MAR-40. Hulk Pop-Up Book,
1982. Hulk vs. Ringmaster. - **$10 $20 $38**

❑ MAR-41. "Secret Wars" Decoder,
1984. Secret messages set and hero shields. - **$20 $40 $65**

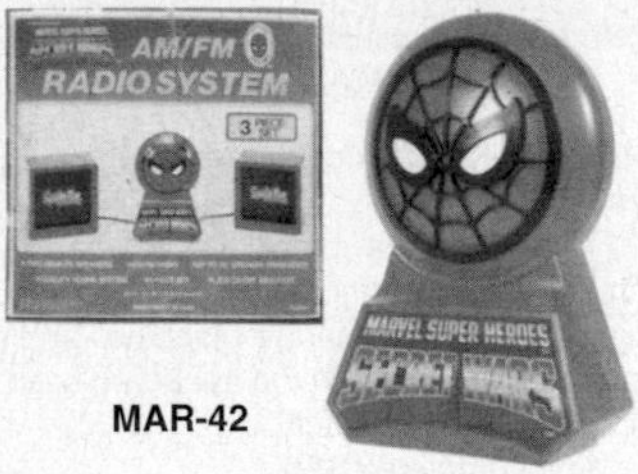

MAR-42

❑ MAR-42. "Marvel Super Heroes Secret Wars/Spider-Man" Radio System,
1984. Three piece "Power Tronic" system by Nasta. Boxed - **$30 $60 $95**
Radio Only - **$15 $25 $40**

MAR-43

❑ MAR-43. "Avengers" Collector's Pin Set,
1989. Six different on card. - **$45**

MAR-44

MAR-45

❑ MAR-44. "Disc Shooter Target Set,"
1990. - **$6 $18 $35**

❑ MAR-45. "Soft Darts Target Set,"
1990. - **$6 $18 $35**

MAR-46

MAR-47

❑ MAR-46. "Ball Blaster,"
1990. - **$6 $18 $35**

❑ MAR-47. "Sparkling Gun,"
1991. - **$8 $20 $40**

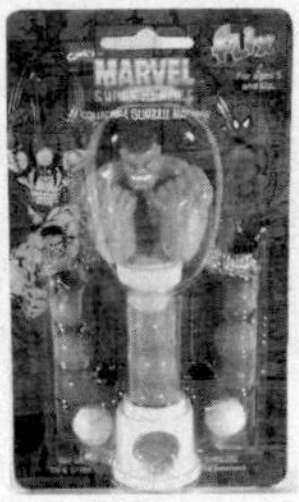

MAR-48

MAR-49

❑ MAR-48. "Flying Props" Toy Gun,
1991. - **$8 $20 $40**

❑ MAR-49. Hulk Mini-Gumball Machine,
1996. Has bust figure on top. - **$10**

MAR-50

MAR-51

❑ MAR-50. "Daredevil" Resin Statue,
1998. Limited to 2,000. Sculpted by Randy Bowen. 14" tall including base. Miniature versions were released in 2001.
Yellow costume version - **$450**
Red costume version - **$275**

❑ MAR-51. "Thor" Resin Statue,
1999. Limited to 5,000. Sculpted by Randy Bowen. A miniature version was released in 2001. Boxed - **$425**

MAR-52

❑ MAR-52. Avengers #1 Cover Figures Box Set,
1999. Box contains six figures from the cover of the Avengers #1 comic, as well as flying ants. - **$33**

MAR-53

MAR-54

❑ MAR-53. Hulk Lunch Box,
1999. Circular format. One in a series of 3 different Marvel Lunch Boxes. - **$4 $12 $28**

❑ MAR-54. Wonder Man Action Figure,
1999. Comes with Avengers Ring. Figure lights up when you press his belt buckle. Animated Avengers series was cancelled after only a few airings, so these figures are hard to find on the secondary market. - **$22**

MAR-55

MAR-56

❑ MAR-55. "Mole Man" Bust,
1999. From Bowen Designs. - **$90**

❑ MAR-56. "Scarlet Witch" Bust,
1999. From Bowen Designs.
Limited to 5,000. - **$55**

MAR-57

❑ MAR-57. "The Punisher" Collector's Pin Set,
1990s. Six different on card. - **$30**

MAR-58 MAR-59

❑ MAR-58. "Hawkeye" Bust,
2000. From Bowen Designs.
Limited to 5,000. - **$45**

❑ MAR-59. "The Vision" Bust,
2000. From Bowen Designs.
Limited to 5,000. - **$55**

MAR-60 MAR-61

❑ MAR-60. "Iron Man" Statue,
2000. Sculpted by Randy Bowen in two versions: gold color and grey color. Pose and base are identical for both versions. Limited to 2,000 in gold and 4,000 in grey. Gold Color Version - **$160**
Grey Color Version - **$140**

❑ MAR-61. "The Thing" Statue,
2000. Sculpted by Randy Bowen. Bases of the Fantastic Four statues are interlocking.
Limited to 4,000. - **$275**

MAR-62

❑ MAR-62. "Dr. Doom" Statue,
2000. Sculpted by Randy Bowen.
Limited to 5,000. - **$325**

MAR-63 MAR-64

❑ MAR-63. "Black Widow" Statue,
2001. Sculpted by Randy Bowen.
Limited to 4,000. - **$165**

❑ MAR-64. "The Invisible Woman" Statue,
2001. Sculpted by Randy Bowen.
Painted version, limited to 4,000, shown. - **$175**

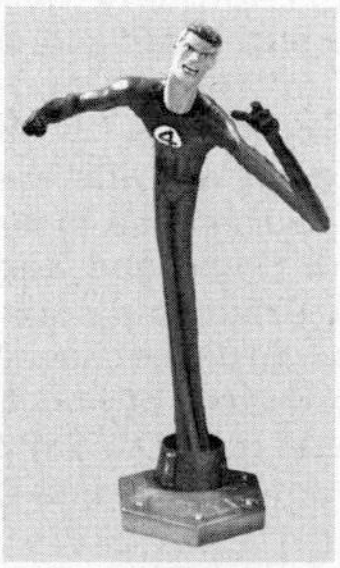
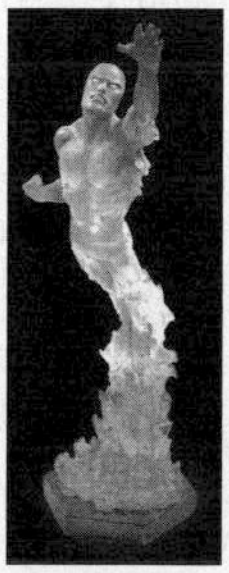

MAR-65 MAR-66

❑ MAR-65. "Mr. Fantastic" Statue,
2001. Sculpted by Randy Bowen.
Limited to 4,000. - **$175**

❑ MAR-66. "The Human Torch" Statue,
2001. Sculpted by Randy Bowen.
Limited to 4,000. - **$175**

(With beard)

(Clean shaven)

MAR-67

❑ MAR-67. Thor "Change-O Head" Statue,
2001. Has the basic body sculpt of the 1999 Randy Bowen figure. Statue has 2 interchangeable heads, one bearded and one shaven. Some costume details are different, and the rock base is a darker grey. Limited to 2,500. - **$225**

MAR-68 MAR-69

❑ MAR-68. "Silver Surfer" Chrome Edition Mini-Bust,
2002. Bowen Designs. Available exclusively at the WizardWorld Chicago 2002 convention.
Limited edition of 500. - **$725**

❑ MAR-69. "Nick Fury" Steath Version Mini-Bust,
2002. Bowen Designs.
Limited edition of 4000. - **$60**

(CLASSIC) MAR-70 (RETRO)

❑ MAR-70. "Iron Man" Mini-Statue Set,
2002. Bowen Designs. The Classic and Retro statues were only available as a set.
Limited edition of 5000. Statue set - **$90**

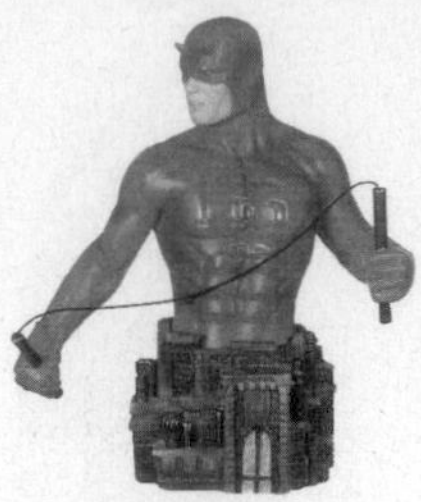

MAR-71 MAR-72

❑ **MAR-71. "Black Widow II" Bust,**
2003. Marvel Universe series from Diamond Select. Limited to 4,000. - **$50**

❑ **MAR-72. "Daredevil" Bust,**
2003. Marvel Universe series from Diamond Select. Limited to 5,000. - **$50**

MAR-73 MAR-74

❑ **MAR-73. "Thing" Mini-Bust,**
2003. Bowen Designs. - **$55**

❑ **MAR-74. "Doctor Doom" Bust,**
2003. Marvel Universe series from Diamond Select. Limited to 5,000. - **$50**

MAR-75

❑ **MAR-75. "The Incredible Hulk" Statue,**
2003. Diamond Select Toys. From the Marvel Milestones series and based on the artwork of Dale Keown. Limited edition of 2,500. - **$275**

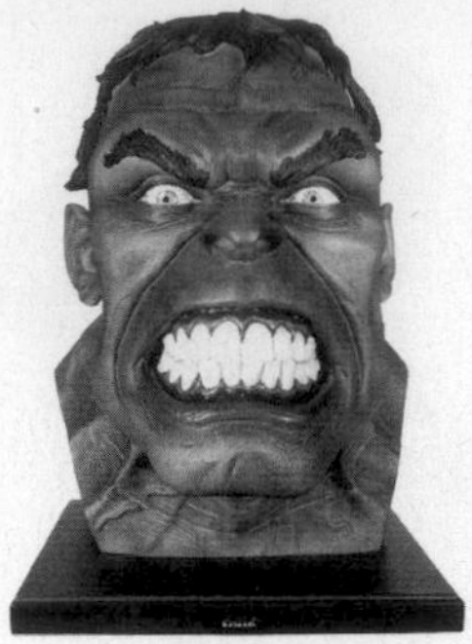

MAR-76

❑ **MAR-76. "The Incredible Hulk" Life-Size Head Bust,**
2003. Dynamic Forces. - **$400**

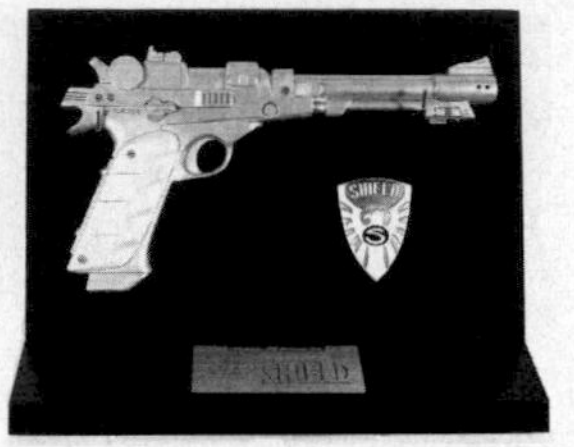

MAR-77

❑ **MAR-77. "Nick Fury, Agent of S.H.I.E.L.D." Needle Gun and Badge Prop Set,**
2003. Factory X. Limited edition of 1,515. - **$150**

The Marx Brothers

Born to Minnie and Sam Marrix (anglicized to Marx), The Marx Brothers included: Chico (Leonard) 1887-1961, Harpo (Adolph Arthur) 1888-1964, Groucho (Julius) 1890-1977, Gummo (Milton) 1892-1977 and Zeppo (Herbert) 1901-1979. Groucho debuted as a singer in vaudeville in 1905, joined by Gummo in 1907 and Harpo in 1908. By 1912, they had become a comedy act with Harpo as a mute harp player. Gummo left to serve in World War One and Chico and Zeppo joined the act. Under Groucho's creative direction, with Chico as business manager, they began playing Broadway. They became stars during the 1924-1925 run of *I'll Say She Is*, written by Will B. Johnstone and Tom Johnstone.

Noted playwright George S. Kaufman (1989-1961) collaborated with composer Irving Berlin (1888-1989) and the brothers on *The Cocoanuts* in 1925-1926 and with Morrie Ryskind and Harry Ruby on *Animal Crackers* in 1928-1929. Both were huge hits on Broadway, leading to a film contract with Paramount. *Cocoanuts* was released in 1929 and *Animal Crackers* was released in 1930. The films introduced Margaret Dumont (1882-1965) as a wealthy high society widow wooed and insulted by Groucho. *Monkey Business* came out in 1931, followed by *Horse Feathers* in 1932 and *Duck Soup* in 1933. Zeppo left to become an agent. The three Marx Brothers with Groucho, Chico and Harpo would go on to more films including: *A Night At The Opera* in 1935, *A Day At The Races* in 1937, *Room Service* in 1938 and *At The Circus* in 1939.

Groucho's fame continued as host of the popular game show *You Bet Your Life*. Created by John Guedel, the show first aired on NBC radio in 1947, then on TV from October 5, 1950 to June 29, 1961. "Say the secret word."

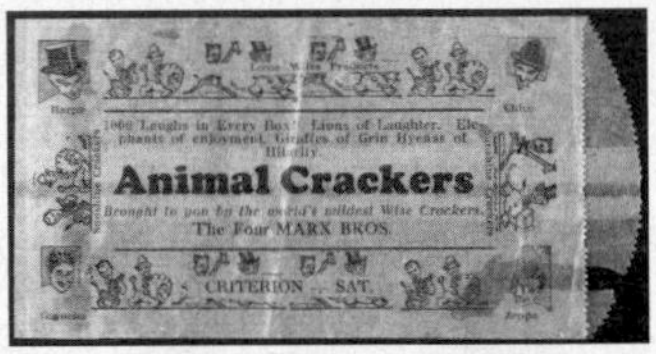

MRX-1

❑ **MRX-1. "Animal Crackers" Marx Brothers Theater Giveaway Glassine Envelope,**
1930. Loose-Wiles Biscuit Co. 2.75x5.5" bag given away at theaters for showing of Animal Crackers movie. Bag contained animal crackers and has images of the four Marx Brothers. - **$125 $250 $400**

MRX-2

❑ **MRX-2. "Animal Crackers" Marx Brothers Herald,**
1930. 7x8.5" with four pages. - **$100 $200 $300**

MRX-3

❑ **MRX-3. "Horse Feathers" Sheet Music,**
1932. Music for "Ev'ryone Says 'I Love You' " from the Marx Brothers movie. Features Paramount Pictures promo on cover. - **$30 $60 $125**

MRX-4

❑ **MRX-4. Marx Brothers "Lydia, The Tattooed Lady" Sheet Music From At The Circus,**
1939. Leo Feist Inc. 9x12" music with 12 pages. - **$75 $150 $300**

MRX-5

MRX-6

MRX-7

❑ **MRX-5. "Groucho Marx" Bisque Figure,**
1930s. 5.5" tall. - **$200 $400 $650**

❑ **MRX-6. "Chico Marx" Bisque Figure,**
1930s. 5.5" tall figure **$100 $200 $425**

❑ **MRX-7. "Harpo Marx" Bisque Figure**
c. 1930s. 5.5" tall figure. Made in Japan. - **$100 $200 $425**

MRX-8

❑ **MRX-8. Marx Brothers "If It's You" Sheet Music From "The Big Store",**
1941. Leo Feist Inc. 9x12" with six pages. - **$35 $75 $150**

MRX-9

❑ **MRX-9. Marx Brothers "A Night In Casablanca" Linen-Mounted One- Sheet Poster,**
1946. 27x41" for the film billed as "The Howl Raiser of 1946!" - **$250 $500 $1000**

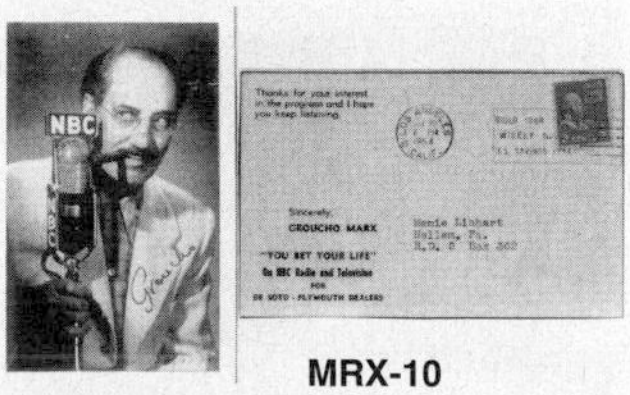

MRX-10

❑ **MRX-10. "Groucho Marx" Fan Postcard,**
1954. Back ad for "You Bet Your Life" NBC-TV show. - **$30 $50 $90**

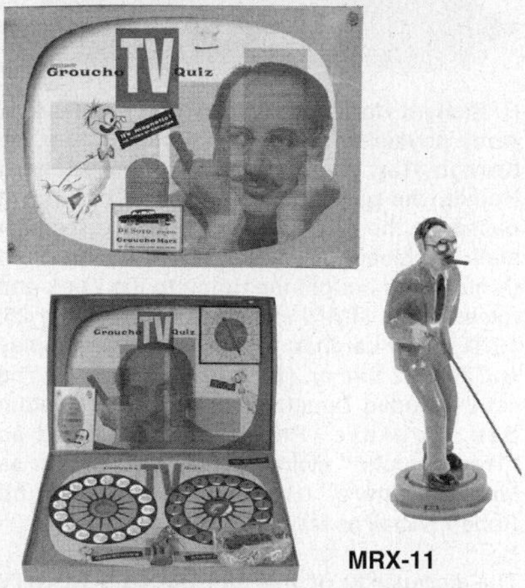

MRX-11

❑ **MRX-11. "Groucho TV Quiz" Game,**
1950s. Pressmen Toy Corp. 13.25x18.25x2" deep box contains complete game consisting of game cards, fake money, cigar, eyebrows and mustache and plastic glasses, 4" tall plastic figure of Groucho with cigar and metal cane. Lid has spinner and 3.5x5.5" instruction booklet. - **$100 $200 $450**

MRX-12

MRX-13

❑ **MRX-12. Marx Brothers "Love Happy" Rare Puppet Trio,**
1950s. National Mask And Puppet. Set of three puppets measuring 11" tall for Groucho, Chico and Harpo. Heads are molded in dark brown rubber. Cloth bodies and felt hands. Set - **$200 $400 $600**

❑ **MRX-13. Groucho Marx Doll,**
1950s. National Mask And Puppet. 17" tall wtih pliable rubber head and painted features, stuffed cloth body and felt hands and feet. - **$350 $750 $1200**

MRX-14

❑ **MRX-14. Marx Brothers Figurines,**
1970s. Store items by Royal Crown. 6-1/2" to 7" tall hollow bisque. Each - **$12 $25 $50**

M*A*S*H

H. Richard Hornberger (1924-1997) was a U.S. Army physician at a field hospital during the Korean War. Using the pen name Richard Hooker, he published the 1968 *MASH* novel based on the hi-jinks of the wartime medical staff at a Mobile Army Surgical Hospital. 20th Century Fox bought the rights to the book and released the *M*A*S*H* feature film January 25, 1970. Ring Lardner, Jr. wrote the screenplay and Robert Altman (1925-2006) directed. The cast included Donald Sutherland as Captain Ben "Hawkeye" Pierce, Elliott Gould as "Trapper John" McIntyre, Sally Kellerman as Major Margaret "Hot Lips" Houlihan and Robert Duvall as Major Frank Burns.

The popularity of the film led to a CBS-TV series. 251 episodes ran over 11 seasons between September 17, 1972 and February 28, 1983. The noted cast included: Alan Alda as Hawkeye, Wayne Rogers as Trapper John, Loretta Swit as Hot Lips, Larry Linville as Frank Burns and Jamie Farr as cross-dresser Max Klinger. The final episode became the most watched show in television history.

MSH-1

❑ **MSH-1. "M*A*S*H Field Hospital Playset",** 1974. Multiple Toy Makers. 9.5x14x1.75" deep box contains die-cut cardboard field hospital, soft plastic helicopter, jeep, medics and base personnel with accessories. Figures each 2" tall, jeep is 4.5" long and helicopter is 9" long. - **$50 $100 $200**

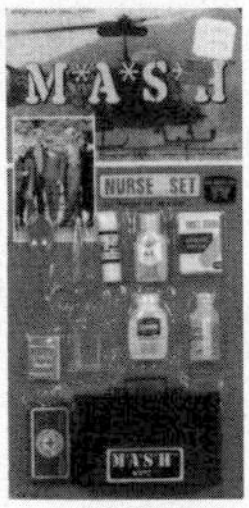

MSH-2

MSH-3

❑ **MSH-2. "M*A*S*H Nurse Set",** 1981. Ja-Ru. 6x12" blister card contains miniature set of 3.5" long soft plastic case with M*A*S*H logo sticker, plastic and cardboard accessories of cup, spoon, scissors, Band-Aids, aspirin, Pepto-Bismol, cough syrup, etc. Carded - **$5 $15 $25**

❑ **MSH-3. "M*A*S*H Puzzles",** 1981. Milton Bradley. Two boxes, each 8.5x12.5x1.5" deep by Milton Bradley, each containing a puzzle with full color scene from the show. Each - **$5 $10 $15**

MSH-4

❑ **MSH-4. "M*A*S*H" Action Figures,** 1982. Tri-Star International. Six 6x9" blister cards each containing a 3.75" poseable figure. Each - **$5 $10 $15**

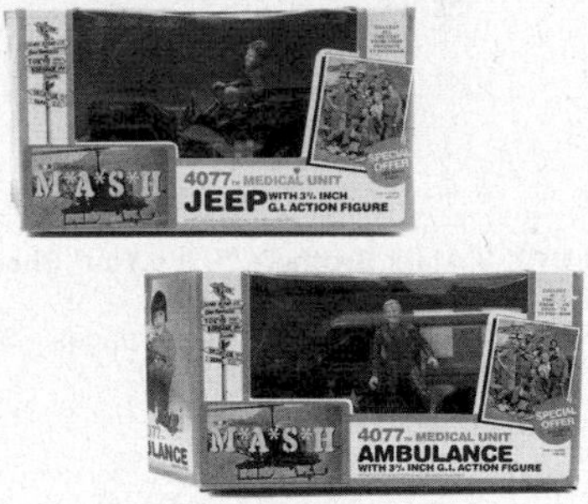

MSH-5

❑ **MSH-5. "M*A*S*H" Boxed Vehicle Pair,** 1982. Tri-Star International. Two vehicles in 5.5x9.25x5" deep boxes, one holding "4077 Ambulance" and the other "4077 Jeep". Each also comes with 3.75" action figure. Each - **$10 $20 $30**

MSH-6

❑ **MSH-6. M*A*S*H Photo Buttons,** 1983. Button-Up Co. 15 buttons, each 1.5" in diameter from set of unknown total. - **$1 $2 $3**

MSH-7

❑ **MSH-7. "M*A*S*H 4077th" Glass,** 1983. TCFFC. 5.5" tall glass with flared top. - **$5 $10 $20**

Masters of the Universe

In 1981, the Mattel toy company launched a new toy line titled The Masters of The Universe. The toy line featured a muscular sword wielding character named He-Man who along with his friends protected their home of Eternia from the evil Skeletor and his legion of villains. He-Man also had a secret identity, Prince Adam, whose father King Randor ruled Eternia. The characters were an instant success and Mattel decided to capitalize on their popularity by hiring the animation studio, Filmation, to produce a cartoon based on the toy line. The show made its debut in 1983 also sparking controversy as the cartoon was viewed by some as a half hour advertisement for the toy line. However, the show also featured positive public service messages during the program. This portion of the program included a social or moral lesson for the show's viewers and was hosted by a small magician named Orko who supplied comic relief to the program.

DC Comics was quick to jump on the Masters of The Universe bandwagon in 1982. *DC Comics Presents* #47 teamed Superman with He-Man to battle Skeletor. In 1986, Marvel Comics released the *Masters of the Universe* comic books under their Star Comics imprint aimed at younger readers.

Cannon Films released a live action film in 1987 titled *Masters of the Universe* starring Dolph Lundgren as He-Man and Frank Langella as Skeletor. While the film was based on the familiar characters it received lackluster response from fans of the toys and cartoon. Many fans felt that the movie strayed from the history of the characters and storylines.

Over the years a number of new animated programs, toys, and comic books have attempted to bring back the Masters of the Universe line. While all were successful on various levels, none have ever been able to match the original success of the early release of Masters of the Universe. The popularity of the characters continue today with numerous products, toys, comics, and merchandise still offering both new and old fans alike an opportunity to enjoy these classic 1980s characters. In 2009, *He-Man and the Masters of the Universe* is due to grace the silver screen, produced by Joel Silver.

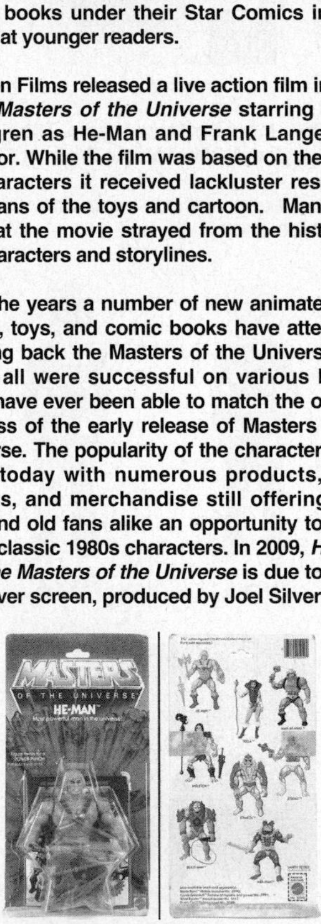

MAS-1

❑ **MAS-1. "He-Man" Figure on Card,**
1982. On card. Eight figures shown on card back. - **$75 $150 $300**

MAS-2

❑ **MAS-2. "Teela" Figure on Card,**
1982. On card. - **$50 $125 $250**

MAS-3 MAS-4

❑ **MAS-3. "Beast Man" Figure on Card,**
1982. On card. - **$50 $125 $250**

❑ **MAS-4. "Man-At-Arms" Figure on Card,**
1982. On card. - **$50 $125 $250**

MAS-5 MAS-6

❑ **MAS-5. "Mer-Man" Figure on Card,**
1982. On card. - **$50 $125 $250**

❑ **MAS-6. "Skeletor" Figure on Card,**
1982. On card. - **$75 $150 $300**

Maverick

Created by Roy Huggins (1914-2002) the Warner Brothers series ran on ABC-TV from August 22, 1957 until July 8, 1962. James Garner starred as Bret Maverick, joined early in the series by Jack Kelly (1927-1992) as brother Bart. They played anti-hero gambling poker players who used their wits and humor, resorting to fighting and gunplay as a last resort. Garner left the series in 1960 and Roger Moore joined the cast as cousin Beau in 1960-61. Robert Colbert played brother Brent in two episodes in 1961-62. The theme song was written by David Buttolah and Paul Webster.

Garner and Kelly reprised their roles as Bret and Bart for the 1978 TV movie *The New Maverick* which led to James Garner starring in *Bret Maverick*, a short-lived NBC-TV series in 1981-82.

Warner Brothers released the *Maverick* feature film May 20, 1994. Directed by Richard Donner, Mel Gibson starred as Bret. Jodie Foster played gambler Annabelle Bransford and James Garner played Marshal Zane Cooper.

Dell published 19 Four Color Comic Books with photo covers between April, 1958 and June, 1962. Anyone want to cut the cards?

MAV-1

❑ **MAV-1. Standing Gunfighter Bret Maverick Hartland,**
1958. 7.5" tall figure with movable arms. Figure has gun but example shown is missing hat. Complete - **$65 $125 $200**

MAV-2

❑ **MAV-2. "Bret Maverick" Hartland Gunfighter Box,**
1958. 2x3.25x9.25" tall box with cellophane window. - **$75 $150 $250**

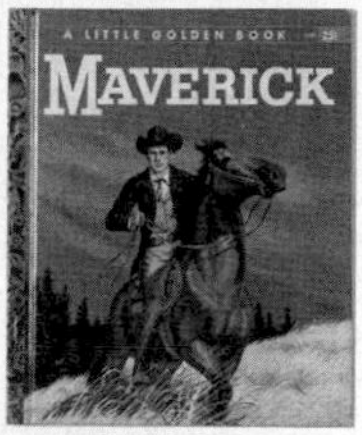

MAV-3 MAV-4

❑ **MAV-3. "Maverick Cap-Shooting Derringer" In Original Packaging,**
1958. Warner Bros. 5x6.25" store card holds gun and holster in sealed blister pack. - **$100 $200 $400**

❑ **MAV-4. "Maverick A Little Golden Book",**
1959. 6.75x8" with 24 pages. No. 354. First printing. - **$10 $20 $50**

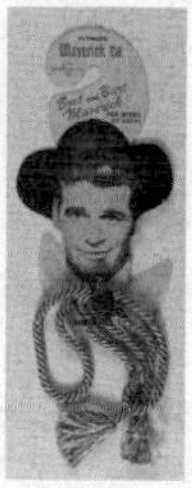

MAV-5 MAV-6

❑ **MAV-5. "Authentic Maverick Tie/Bret And Bart Maverick For Sport Or Dress" On Original Card,**
1959. Warner Bros. 4x7" die-cut cardboard with instructions. Metal clasp in center of bolo-type tie in shape of cowboy boot with spur. Carded - **$50 $100 $200**

❑ **MAV-6. "Bret And Bart Maverick/ Authentic Maverick Tie For Sport Or Dress",**
1959. Warner Bros. 4x7" die-cut cardboard with attached clip-on, bolo-type tie. Metal clasp at center is in the shape of a stagecoach. - **$40 $80 $175**

MAV-7

❑ **MAV-7. "Maverick" Book,**
1959. Whitman #1566; 5 1/2" x 7 3/4". Based on the Warner Bros. TV show. James Garner as Maverick pictured on the cover. 286 pages. TV Edition. - **$10 $20 $50**

MAV-8

MAV-9

❑ **MAV-8. "Maverick" Leather Belt And Buckle By Keystone Bros. San Francisco,**
c. 1959. 1.5x31" leather belt with 2.25x4" cast metal buckle that reads "Maverick." - **$20 $40 $85**

❑ **MAV-9. "Maverick Starring James Garner" Packaged Toy Handcuffs And Badge,**
c. 1959. 6x10" plastic bag with header card "A 20th Century Toy" holds display card, handcuffs and white metal badge with photo of Maverick playing cards. Packaged - **$50 $100 $200**
Badge Only - **$30 $60 $125**

MAV-10

❑ **MAV-10. Western TV Stars "Acme Boots" Christmas Tree Standee,**
c. 1960. 9x35" tall die-cut cardboard tree has six circular pictures of TV stars as ornaments. Shown are James Garner "Maverick"/Jack Kelly "Maverick"/Will Hutchins "Sugar Foot"/Wade Preston "Colt .45"/John Russell "Lawman"/ Peter Brown "Lawman." - **$150 $300 $600**

MAV-11

❑ **MAV-11. James Garner As Bret Maverick Signed Photo,**
c. 1970s. 8x10" glossy photo with bold 3" signature. - **$20 $40 $80**

Max und Moritz

Wilhelm Busch's (1832-1908) immortal 1865 tale of two trouble-making brats was a primordial comic strip: though it featured rhymed narration, not voice balloons, its sequential drawings in color told much of the story by themselves. Over seven chapters, Max and Moritz play seven destructive pranks. They kill Widow Bolte's chickens, then steal the roasting birds from her hearth. They trick Tailor Bock into falling in the river, then blast Teacher Lampel with a pipeful of gunpowder. They fill their uncle Fritz's bed with ladybugs. They raid a bakery and escape captivity at the baker's hands. Finally, they slit a farmer's grain sacks—but are caught and milled by the farmer, transforming them into goose feed.

Busch cut his teeth creating *Max und Moritz*-like picture stories for the children's magazine *Münchener Bilderbogen*, but *Moritz* itself debuted in book form, a first for Busch. Braun und Schneider, a Munich publisher, marketed the book to great success. Strong sales continued for decades; indeed, the book remains a part of children's lives in modern-day Germany.

***Max und Moritz* was the first German children's property to be licensed in other media. A stage musical appeared in 1878; tactile merchandise followed in the late 1890s. Spin-offs during Busch's lifetime included dolls, food products, and—in 1902—even a licensed restaurant. The author's death slowed none of this activity down. In 1921, a play money set showed how Max and Moritz survived their apparent death; to this day, animated films and other products feature the characters' "new" adventures.**

Today, Max and Moritz are little-known outside Germany, but this was not always the case. English editions appeared as early as 1871, and the characters' popularity led to overseas marketing efforts. In 1897, William Randolph Hearst licensed Max, Moritz and their entourage for use in an American comic strip; though duly called *Max und Moritz* in Hearst's German language newspapers, the feature became better known stateside under its English title—*The Katzenjammer Kids*. Initially drawn by Rudolph Dirks in an imitation of Busch's style, *Kids* found its own "look" by 1902, at which point new characters entered the strip and its resemblances to *Max und Moritz* slowly disappeared.

(Max) (Moritz)

MAX-1

❑ **MAX-1. Max And Moritz Nodder/Mirror,**
c. 1900. Cast metal nodder/mirror measuring 1x1.75x2.75" tall with hand-painted figures of Max and Moritz sitting on bench with Moritz's head on a thin metal rod allowing it to nod. Has 2" diameter metal cased mirror attached. Germany. - **$100 $200 $400**

MAX-2

❑ **MAX-2. "Moritz" Dexterity Puzzle,**
c. 1900. 1-1/8" diameter with glass cover over compartment with three beads to place in recesses of color image. - **$40 $75 $150**

MAX-3

MAX-3 (continued)

❑ **MAX-3. Max And Maurice Boxed Card Game,**
1905. Rare. By McLoughlin Bros., New York. Box is .75" x 4.5" x 6.25" holding complete deck of twenty-four 2-7/8" x 3-7/8" full color illustrated game cards made of sturdy cardboard with black backs. Instructions in bottom of box. Similar to Yellow Kid card set in material used.
Each Card - **$10 $20 $35**
Box with Separate Instructions - **$75 $150 $250**
Complete - **$325 $650 $1150**

MAX-4

❑ **MAX-4. Max Glazed Ceramic Toothbrush Holder,**
c. 1920. Beautifully colored 3-7/8" tall with reverse compartment for one toothbrush.
- **$115 $265 $550**

(Max) (Moritz)

MAX-5

❑ **MAX-5. Ceramic Figures,**
1920s. Rare. Each - **$85 $150 $275**

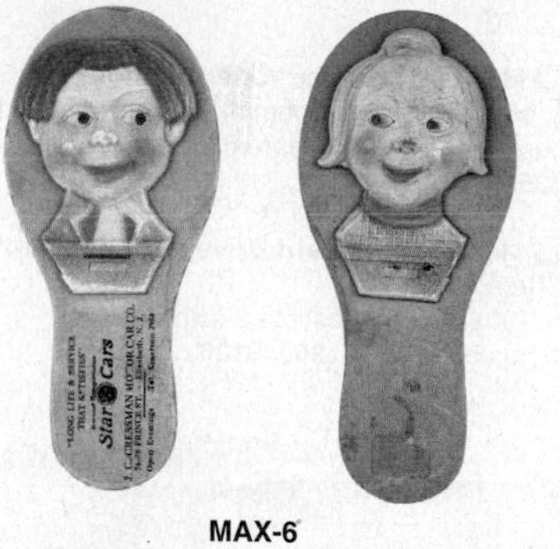

MAX-6

❑ **MAX-6. Max/Moritz "Star Cards" Advertising Noisemaker,**
1920s. Paddle-shaped heavy cardboard is 3x6.5" and holds two embossed heavy paper faces of Max & Moritz. Handle of Max side reads "Long Life & Service That Satisfies/Lost Cost Transportation/Star Cars" with name of car dealer. - **$20 $40 $85**

McDonald's

What began as a simple hamburger joint in southern California has become an international symbol of American initiative and drive. At last count there were more than 18,000 McDonald's fast-food restaurants in some 89 countries--the busiest of all in Pushkin Square, Moscow. It all started in 1937 when the McDonald brothers, Maurice and Richard, opened a small stand near Pasadena. Two years later they opened a second spot, fine-tuning their fast-food philosophy in a building with two yellow arches poking through the roof. A character called Speedee, with a hamburger for a head, courted drive-in customers atop another arch offering 15-cent hamburgers. Franchising the successful operation began in 1954, and Ray Kroc (1902-1984) opened his first franchise in 1955 in Des Plaines, Illinois. Now a

museum, artifacts include the "Multimixer" milkshake machine Ray Kroc had been distributing when he first met the McDonald brothers. Six years later, with more than 200 stores licensed, Kroc bought out the entire operation. Speedee was retired in 1962 and replaced by the Ronald McDonald character in 1963. Other characters--Big Mac, the Hamburglar, Grimace, Mayor McCheese, Captain Crook, and the Professor--were introduced in the 1970s. Toys, games, premiums, licensed products, and promotional items continue to proliferate.

McD-1

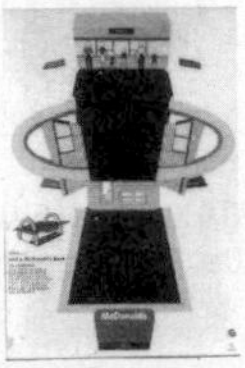
McD-2

❑ McD-1. "Speedee" Litho. Button,
c. 1955. Pictures trademark character used from beginnings until his retirement c. 1962. - **$35 $70 $140**

❑ McD-2. Cardboard Drive-In Punch-Out Sheet,
c. 1962. Assembles into a coin bank. Unpunched - **$30 $60 $130**

McD-3

❑ McD-3. "Archy McDonald's Club" Member Button,
1964. 1.5" red on cream with early symbol character face in pale yellow. - **$40 $75 $160**

McD-4

McD-5

❑ McD-4. "Let's Go To McDonald's" Plastic/Tin Palm Puzzle,
1964. Pictured is "Archy" serving character. - **$25 $50 $90**

❑ McD-5. "Let's Eat Out!" Storybook,
1965. Issued for 10th anniversary, stiff covers. - **$35 $75 $150**

McD-6

McD-7

❑ McD-6. Philadelphia Area TV Show Cast Photo,
1965. Pictures Gene London, Sally Starr, Lorenzo, Capt. Philadelphia, Bill Webber, Ronald McDonald, Happy the Clown, Rex Morgan. - **$20 $35 $75**

❑ McD-7. "Ronald McDonald Goes To The Moon" Coloring Book,
1967. Story and art about his victorious race to the moon against rival Mr. Muscle to establish a McDonald's restaurant there. - **$35 $65 $130**

McD-8

❑ McD-8. McDonald's Hamburger School Graduation Ring,
c. 1968. Non-adjustable stainless steel by Balfour. "M" logo on top, one side "M" logo above field with three cows, other side shows restaurant above initials "QSC." - **$40 $75 $135**

McD-9

McD-10

❑ McD-9. Premium Game Sheet,
1960s. Folded sheet 9x12" opens to 17-1/2x24" with nine numbered figures of Ronald to be cut out and used as game played blindfolded. Uncut - **$40 $70 $140**

❑ McD-10. Ronald McDonald Christmas Record,
1960s. Song "The Night Before Christmas" on both sides of 45 rpm record. - **$18 $30 $45**

McD-11

❑ McD-11. Model Kit,
c. late 1960s. Store item made by Life-Like Products (H.O. scale). - **$65 $150 $250**

McD-12

❑ McD-12. Ronald McDonald Face Portrait First Ring Set,
1971. Six yellow plastic figural portrait rings differing by color ring bases producing different color in the diecut eye holes. Given out by Ronald actors. Each - **$5 $10 $15**

McD-13

❑ McD-13. "McDonaldland" Remco Playset,
1976. Large 7x16x30" box containing elaborate railroad toy set including wind-up train, railroad track sections, McDonald's restaurant with accessories, much more.
Near Mint Boxed - **$300**

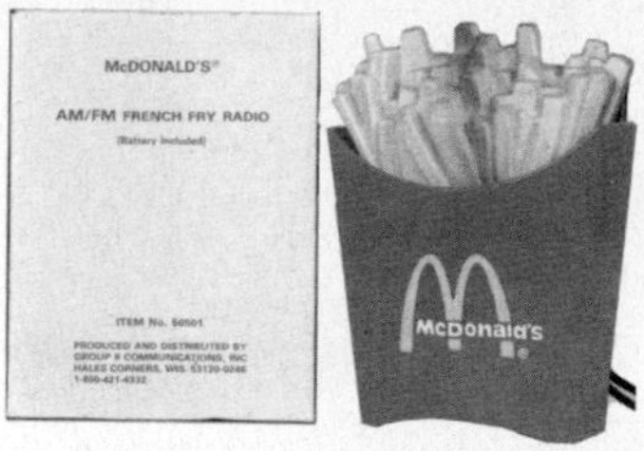

McD-14

❑ **McD-14. "McDonald's French Fry Radio,"**
1977. Near Mint Working **- $50**

McD-15

McD-16

❑ **McD-15. Captain Crook Bubble Boat,**
1979. Vacuum form plastic punch-out 2-1/2x2-1/2" toy that runs on baking powder. Near Mint Unassembled **- $80**
Assembled **- $10 $25 $50**

❑ **McD-16. Ronald Cloth Doll,**
1970s. First 1971 version designed with black zipper pull. Later 1970s versions have zipper design without pull.
First Style **- $10 $20 $40**
Later Style **- $6 $12 $20**

McD-17

❑ **McD-17. Ronald McDonald Bop Toy,**
1970s. 13" tall soft vinyl inflatable figure on 4-1/2" diameter base. **- $10 $20 $40**

McD-18

McD-19

❑ **McD-18. "Big Mac" Radio,**
1970s. Red plastic replica of hamburger carton 4x4x2-1/2" deep. **- $15 $25 $45**

❑ **McD-19. Ronald Wristwatch,**
1970s. **- $25 $55 $110**

McD-20

McD-21

❑ **McD-20. Ronald Litho. Tin Tab,**
1970s. **$3 $8 $15**

❑ **McD-21. Mayor McCheese Litho. Tin Tab,**
1970s. **- $3 $8 $15**

McD-22

McD-23

❑ **McD-22. Employee Doll,**
1970s. Jointed vinyl 11" doll in brown uniform. **- $30 $50 $75**

❑ **McD-23. Ronald McDonald Doll,**
1970s. With zip-up uniform. **- $15 $35 $65**

McD-24

❑ **McD-24. "Ronald McDonald's Travel Fun" Booklet,**
1970s. Twelve pages of quizzes, riddles, pencil games, etc. Back cover has menu picture ad. **- $8 $15 $30**

McD-25

McD-26

McD-27

❑ **McD-25. Employees Glasses Promotion 3-1/2" Cello. Button,**
c. 1970s. McDonald's and Coca-Cola Canadian issue. **- $10 $15 $25**

❑ **McD-26. Captain Crook Orange Vinyl Ring,**
c. 1980. **- $6 $10 $15**

❑ **McD-27. Big Mac Yellow Vinyl Ring,**
c. 1980. **- $6 $10 $15**

McD-28

McD-29

❑ **McD-28. Grimace Purple Vinyl Ring,**
c. 1980. **- $6 $10 $15**

❑ **McD-29. "Ronald McDonald" Alarm Clock,**
c. 1983. 6" tall metal. **- $40 $75 $150**

McD-30

McD-31

❑ **McD-30. Hamburglar Plastic Siren Whistle,**
1986. **- $6 $8 $12**

❑ **McD-31. Manager's Promotional Hamburgler Clock,**
1980s. 9x12". **- $50 $90 $160**

Mechanical Banks

Mechanical banks, created as an entertaining way to teach children to save, date back to the early 1800s. The definition of mechanical bank is a toy savings device that has a mechanism which moves and receives a coin. While the earliest versions were made primarily out of wood, the first cast iron mechanical bank was the Hall's Excelsior made by J. & E. Stevens of Cromwell, Connecticut in 1869.

Other large producers of cast iron banks include Shepard Hardware Co. of Buffalo, New York, and Kyser & Rex Co. of Philadelphia, Pennsylvania. Numerous other American and European firms also created banks. In addition to early wood and subsequent cast iron creations, banks were also manufactured in tin, aluminum, and lead. There are well over 500 documented antique mechanical banks that were produced prior to World War II. Mechanical banks are known to be in high demand, with a sustained period of interest and record prices realized. Listed below are some great examples of mechanical banks readily found in the marketplace.

The prices are broken down by percentage of paint remaining. The three breaks would be at 25% paint, 75% paint, and 97% paint. It is extremely rare to find any bank with more than 97% original paint and would justify a price at least twice that of the 97% price.

MEC-1

❑ **MEC-1. Hall's Excelsior,**
Patent 1869. Made by J. & E. Stevens Company. Pull the string with the bead attached to the right of the door. This causes the monkey to rise. Place a coin on the desk and the weight of the coin causes the monkey to drop down, closing the top and the coin is deposited into the bank. - **$150 $350 $1400**

MEC-2

❑ **MEC-2. Horse Race,**
Patent 1871. Made by J. & E. Stevens Company. Pull the string with the bead attached to lock the mechanism into place. Steady the two horses next to the star on the inner base and drop a coin into the slot. The horses will race around the track. One or the other will be the winner. - **$800 $7000 $30,000**

MEC-3

❑ **MEC-3. Magic Bank,**
Patent 1873. Made by J. & E. Stevens Company. Pull door open to reveal a cashier with tray. Place a coin on the tray, press lever and the door flips closed and deposits the coin. There is a slot on the roof which will accept larger coins. No action occurs when this slot is used. - **$350 $2200 $6500**

MEC-4

❑ **MEC-4. Tammany**
Patent 1873. Made by J. & E. Stevens Company. Place a coin in the figure's right hand and the weight of the coin causes the hand to lower and deposit the coin into the pocket of the figure. - **$150 $450 $1800**

MEC-5

❑ **MEC-5. Creedmore Bank,**
Patent 1877. Made by J. & E. Stevens Company. Pull back the metal "V" on the gun, the man's head will tilt forward. Place a coin in "V" and press the man's foot. He shoots the coin into the tree and the head raises up.
- **$200 $600 $1800**

MEC-6

❑ **MEC-6. Hall's Liliput,**
Patent 1877. Made by J. & E. Stevens Company. Place a coin in the hands of the figure and the weight of the coin turns the figure to the left depositing it into the bank.
- **$200 $700 $3000**

MEC-7

❑ **MEC-7. I Always Did 'Spise A Mule – Jockey,**
Patent 1879. Made by J. & E. Stevens Company. Place a coin the jockey's mouth. Press the lever and the mule kicks forward, the jockey falls over the mule's head and the coin is deposited into the base. - **$150 $650 $2200**

MEC-8

❑ **MEC-8. Bull Dog Bank,**
Patent 1880. Made by J. & E. Stevens Company. Place a coin on the dog's nose. Push the tail down. This causes the head to recede into the bank. The mouth snaps open and the lower jaw drops down. The coin rest rises up and the coin slides forward and drops into the open mouth. - **$400 $1100 $4000**

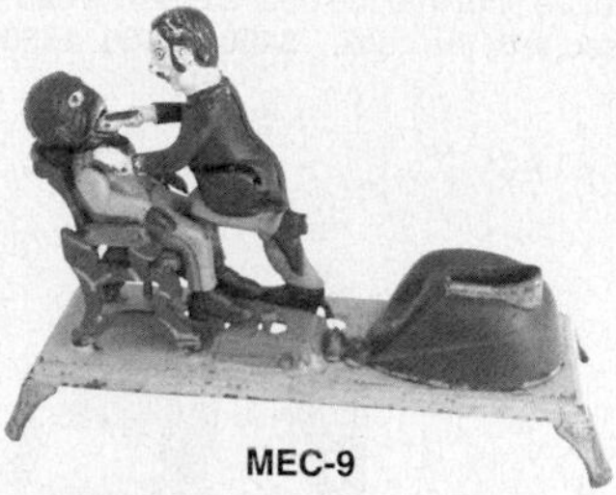

MEC-9

❑ **MEC-9. Dentist,**
Patent 1880. Made by J. & E. Stevens Company. Place a coin in the left pocket of the dentist and press lever located at the feet of the figures. The dentist extracts a tooth and falls backwards against the gas bag and the coin drops into the bank. At the same time the patient falls backwards in the chair, throwing his arms up. - **$2200 $8500 $25,000**

MEC-10

❑ **MEC-10. Freedman's Bank,**
Patent 1880. Made by Jerome B. Secor. Begin by winding the spring in the rear of the bank. Place a coin on the table by the figure's left hand and press the lever. This causes him to turn his head from side to side as he scoops the coin into the slot on top of the table. Simultaneously, he raises his right hand to his face and thumbs his nose, moving each finger independently. He then lowers and shakes his head. - **$35,000 $175,000 $350,000**

MEC-11

❑ **MEC-11. Mule Entering Barn**
Patent 1880. Made by J. & E. Stevens Company. Lock the mule into position and put a coin behind his hind legs. Push the lever forward, he kicks his hind legs up and the coin flips into the barn. Simultaneously, he swings forward as the dog springs forward. -
$200 $850 $2800

MEC-12

MEC-13

❑ **MEC-12. Owl Turns Head**
Patent 1880. Made by J. & E. Stevens Company. Insert a coin on the branch and press the lever. This causes the owl to turn his head and the coin is deposited into the bank.
- **$200 $650 $1800**

❑ **MEC-13. Cat & Mouse,**
Patent 1881. Made by J. & E. Stevens Company. The mouse must be locked into position. Place a coin on the platform in front of the mouse and press the lever. The mouse disappears and the kitten appears holding the mouse on the ball. The coin is deposited into the bank by lever action. - **$600 $3800 $12,000**

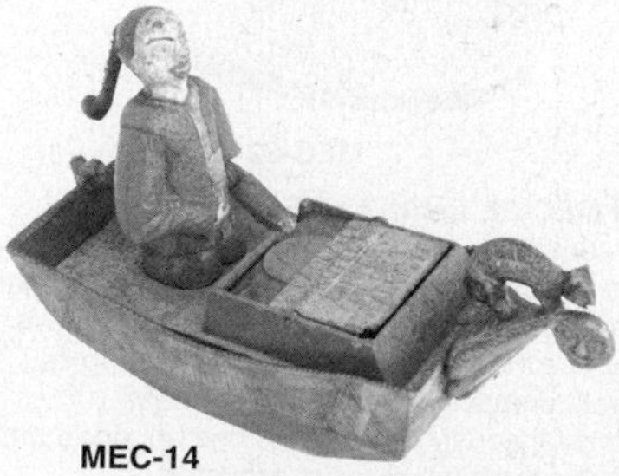

MEC-14

❑ **MEC-14. Chinaman In Boat,**
Patent 1881. Made by Charles A. Bailey. Place a coin in the front of the Chinaman and press his queue. He raises his left arm and flips the table top over. The coin is deposited into the bank and the table now has a rat on a platter with a knife and fork beside it. When the queue is released the weight of the arm flips the table top back to its original position.
- **$8000 $35,000 $85,000**

MEC-15

❑ **MEC-15. Confectionery Bank,**
Patent date 1881. Made by Kyser & Rex. The first step is to load the bank with candy, which is inserted in a compartment at the back of the bank. Place a coin in the slot and press the button. The figure slides over to receive the candy and as the coin disappears into the bank a bell rings. - **$3500 $18,000 $38,000**

MEC-16

❑ **MEC-16. Organ Bank**
Patent 1881. Made by Kyser & Rex. Place a coin on the tray which is raised to position by turning the crank on the left side of the bank. In doing so the monkey lowers the tray and the coin slides forward into the organ. He tips his hat. As the action takes place the cat and dog revolve. Bells ring inside the bank as the action takes place. - **$250 $850 $2800**

MEC-17

❑ **MEC-17. Elephant And Three Clowns,**
Patent 1882. Made by J. & E. Stevens Company. Set coin in rings held by clown on right, pull ball on left. The elephant's trunk moves down and knocks the coin into the slot. The clown rider turns at the waist during the action. - **$350 $1600 $5500**

MEC-18

❑ **MEC-18. Humpty Dumpty,**
Patent 1882. Made by Shepard Hardware Company. Place a coin in the right hand and press the lever located behind the left shoulder. The tongue falls back and the eyes roll up as the hand deposits the coin into his mouth. -
$300 $1000 $9000

MEC-19

❑ **MEC-19. Paddy And The Pig**
Patent 1882. Made by J. & E. Stevens Company. Place a coin on the pig's snout and press the lever at the back. This causes Paddy's eyes to roll back, his mouth to open and he sticks out his tongue. Simultaneously, the pig's front legs kick the coin onto Paddy's tongue and it is deposited into the bank.
- $400 $3000 $9000

MEC-20

❑ **MEC-20. Two Frogs**
Patent 1882. Made by J. & E. Stevens Company. Place a coin on the plate located on the stomach of the small frog and press the lever. This causes the smaller frog to kick the coin into the mouth of the large frog. -
$600 $2400 $7500

MEC-21

❑ **MEC-21. Cabin Bank,**
Patent 1883. Made by J. & E. Stevens Company. The coin is placed on the roof, just above the door. Pull the handle on the broom, on the right side of the cabin, and the figure will flip up and his feet kick the coin into the bank. -
$200 $800 $2500

MEC-22

❑ **MEC-22. Eagle And Eaglets,**
Patent 1883. Made by J. & E. Stevens Company. Place a coin in the mouth of the large eagle and press the lever under the tail. This causes the eagle to tilt forward lowering its beak, dropping the coin into the nest. Simultaneously, the eaglets rise up, open their beaks and the bellows is activated.
- $400 $1200 $3000

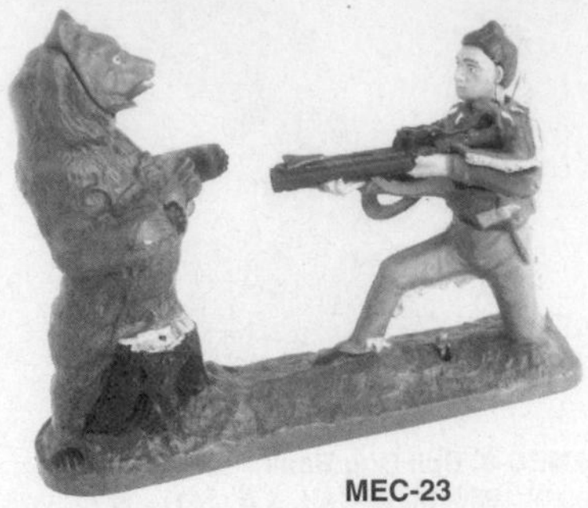

MEC-23

❑ **MEC-23. Indian Shooting Bear,**
Patent 1883. Made by J. & E. Stevens Company. Pull the trigger of the gun back into a locked position. The head of the Indian drops forward as though taking aim. Place a coin on the gun and press the lever which causes the coin to be shot into the bear's chest. A cap can be used with the bank. - **$400 $1600 $6500**

MEC-24

MEC-25

❑ **MEC-24. Lion And Two Monkeys,**
Patent 1883. Made by Kyser & Rex. Place a coin in the large monkey's right hand and press the provided lever. The arm lowers dropping the coin into the lion's mouth. Simultaneously, the baby monkey moves upward onto the large monkey's back. - **$400 $1800 $6000**

❑ **MEC-25. Mammy And Child**
Patent 1884. Made by Kyser & Rex. Place a coin in the slot of mammy's apron and press lever (left side of bank). Mammy lowers the spoon, her head dips and the baby's legs rise and coin goes into the bank. The slot will take coins up to a half dollar. A nickel can be deposited in the baby's mouth. The lever must be activated to deposit the coins. Many of the tin spoons have been broken attempting to adjust them so a coin will fall into the baby's mouth. Even though the patent shows the coin on the spoon, the operation described above is suggested. - **$2000 $9000 $18,000**

MEC-26

❑ **MEC-26. Punch And Judy**
Patent 1884. Made by Shepard Hardware Company. There are 2 levers on the bank. Pull out the top lever to set the figures. Place a coin on the tray, press the lower lever and Judy turns back to deposit the coin. Simultaneously, Punch tries to hit her with his stick.
- $500 $2800 $7500

MEC-27

❑ **MEC-27. Trick Pony**
Patent 1885. Made by Shepard Hardware Company. Place a coin in the mouth of the pony and pull the lever. A lid on the trough opens to allow the coin to be deposited.
- $400 $3000 $7000

MEC-28

❑ **MEC-28. Speaking Dog**
Patent 1885. Made by J. & E. Stevens Company. Place a coin on the girl's tray and press the lever in front of the dog. The girl's arm moves and the coin falls from the tray and is deposited into the bank. Simultaneously, the dog's mouth opens and closes and his tail wags.
- $400 $2400 $6000

MEC-29

❑ **MEC-29. Bread Winners Bank,**
Patent date 1886. Made by J. & E. Stevens Company. Raise the hammer held by Labor and place a coin in the club held by Rascal. There is a small lever located on the back of Labor and when it is held down the hammer strikes the club. This causes the Rascal to flip up and the coin is deposited into the loaf of bread.
- $3000 $18,000 $45,000

MEC-30

MEC-31

❑ **MEC-30. Stump Speaker**
Patent 1886. Made by Shepard Hardware Company. Place a coin in the figure's right hand and press the lever. He closes his mouth and lowers the coin into the carpetbag. Release the lever and the mouth continues to move up and down. **- $650 $3400 $8500**

❑ **MEC-31. Uncle Sam**
Patent 1886. Made by Shepard Hardware Company. Place a coin in Uncle Sam's hand. Press the lever at the rear of the bank. This lowers the arm and the coin drops into the carpetbag. As the lever is released the coin drops into the bank and Uncle Sam's mouth and beard move in a realistic talking fashion.
- $600 $4500 $15,000

MEC-32

❑ **MEC-32. Mason Bank**
Patent 1887. Made by Shepard Hardware Company. Place a coin on the hod and press the lever located on the right. This causes the hod carrier to lean forward and the coin falls into the brick wall. Simultaneously, The bricklayer raises his arms to receive the coin.
- $450 $4500 $12,000

MEC-33

❑ **MEC-33. Trick Dog - 6 Part Base**
Patent date 1888. Place a coin in the dog's mouth and press the lever located in the end plate. The dog goes through the hoop and stops over the barrel, depositing the coin.
- $250 $1200 $3500

MEC-34

❑ **MEC-34. Bad Accident,**
Patent date 1888. Made by J. & E. Stevens Company. Place the coin between shoes of the driver. A two-part lever beside the cat-tail plant is then pressed together. The boy darts from behind the plant and turns facing the front. Simultaneously, the donkey rears back and causes the cart to flip back. The coin slides into the slot in the cart and is deposited. Upon releasing the lever the boy automatically returns to his hidden position. The cart must then be reset. **- $600 $3000 $8000**

MEC-35

❑ **MEC-35. Boy On Trapeze,**
Patent date 1888. Made by Barton Smith Company. Place a coin on the top of the boy's head. The weight of the coin causes the boy to revolve. One cent will give one revolution, a nickel will give two, a quarter gives three, and a clad half dollar gives four. A silver half dollar gives six revolutions. - **$400 $3000 $8500**

MEC-36

❑ **MEC-36. Butting Buffalo,**
Patent date 1888. Made by Kyser & Rex. The coin is placed on top of the tree trunk. When the lever is pressed the buffalo raises his head and butts the boy. The boy moves up the trunk. The raccoon on the top of the trunk moves down into the tree and the coin is pushed into the bank. - **$800 $6000 $20,000**

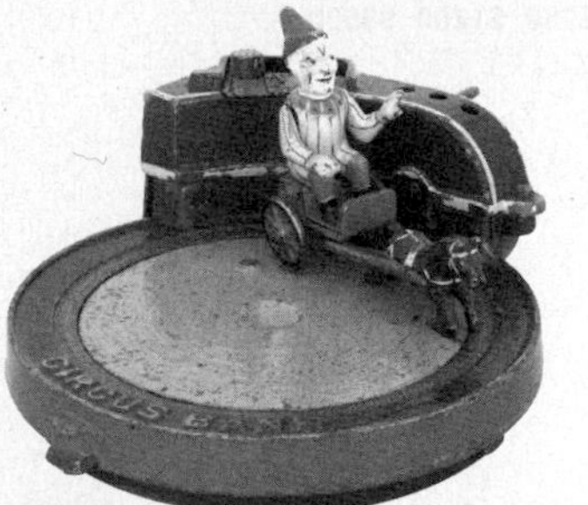

MEC-37

❑ **MEC-37. Circus Bank,**
Patent 1888. Made by Shepard Hardware Company. To operate the bank you turn the crank and position the clown and his cart at the rear of the bank. A coin is placed in the position on the raised platform. The crank is then turned which will move the clown in the cart around the circle. The pony goes up and down as it pulls the cart. When the clown nears the platform he raises his arm and it pushes the coin into the bank as he goes by. - **$2800 $15,000 $40,000**

MEC-38

❑ **MEC-38. Darkey And Watermelon,**
Patent 1888. Made by J. & E. Stevens Company. Place the coin in the football and pull the darkey's right leg back until it locks. This causes the figure to lean forward. Press the lever on the darkey's back and he kicks the football. It ends its flight above the watermelon and the coin drops into the bank. At the same time the figure returns to its upright position. - **$30,000 $100,000 $250,000**

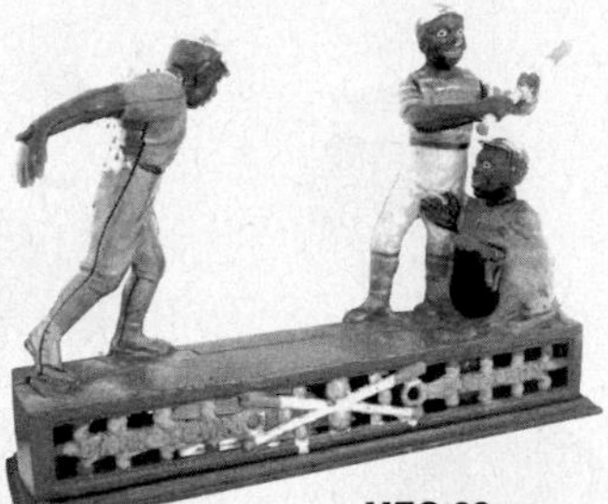

MEC-39

❑ **MEC-39. Darktown Battery,**
Patent 1888. Made by J. & E. Stevens Company. Pull the pitcher's arm back into position, his head lowers and moves forward as the players snap into position. Place a coin in his right hand and press the lever which is located by the tree stump. The pitcher throws the coin and his head raises up. The batter raises his bat and turns his head from right to left and the catcher moves his head forward and his left hand moves toward his body, as though catching the coin. The lower front section of the catcher moves inward so the coin can enter his body and drop into the bank. - **$600 $3500 $12,000**

MEC-40

❑ **MEC-40. Jonah And The Whale – Pedestal,**
Patent 1888. Made by J. & E. Stevens Company. Pull back the rod located behind the tail to lock the bank into position. Place a coin in the small boat shaped holder located by the whale's tail and press the lever. It shoots forward and deposits the coin into the bank. Simultaneously, the whale opens its mouth and Jonah's head and shoulders emerge. Also, the whale's tail flips up during the action. - **$20,000 $100,000 $250,000**

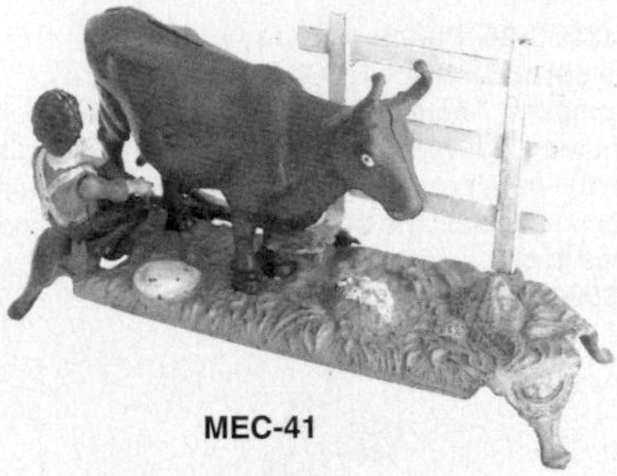

MEC-41

❑ **MEC-41. Milking Cow**
Patent 1888. Made by J. & E. Stevens Company. Place a coin in the slot on the back of the cow and press the flower-shaped lever to deposit. At the same time the cow kicks its right leg, swings its tail and the boy falls over backwards. Simultaneously, his arms elevate, dumping the bucket onto his face. - **$1800 $8500 $22,000**

MEC-42

❑ **MEC-42. Merry-Go-Round**
Patent 1889. Made by Kyser & Rex. Place a coin in the slot. Turn the crank and the man pivots and raises the stick in his hand. The coin slot becomes operational and the coin is automatically deposited. Simultaneously, the animals suspended from the canopy revolve and the bells chime. - **$3000 $20,000 $65,000**

MEC-43

❑ **MEC-43. Santa Claus**
Patent 1889. Made by Shepard Hardware Company. Place a coin in the right palm of Santa and press the lever located behind his foot. He then lowers the coin into the chimney. **- $650 $3800 $9000**

MEC-44

❑ **MEC-44. Girl Skipping Rope,**
Patent 1890. Made by J. & E. Stevens Company. Insert a coin in the squirrel's paws. Wind the mechanism once. (The keywind is just above the squirrel.) Press the lever which is located between the girl and the mechanism. The rope revolves, the girl moves up and down, as her legs move in conjunction with the winding mechanism. She realistically turns her head side-to-side. The coin is automatically deposited. The bank should average 14 revolutions. **- $8000 $25,000 $75,000**

MEC-45

❑ **MEC-45. Clown On Globe,**
Patent 1890. Made by J. & E. Stevens Company. Lock the clown into sitting position and push up the lever. It will snap into place and releases a plate to partially cover the coin slot so the coin does not drop into the bank. Revolve the clown clockwise one revolution and place a coin in the slot. push the lever down and the clown will spin counter-clockwise, the plate covering the coin slot releases and the coin drops into the bank. Reset the bank, push the lever in the back of the globe and the clown will stand on his head and spin around with the globe. **- $600 $2800 $7500**

MEC-46

❑ **MEC-46. Jonah And The Whale,**
Patent 1890. Made by Shepard Hardware Company. Place a coin on the back of Jonah and press the lever located at the rear of the boat. This causes Jonah to turn toward the whale's mouth, allowing the coin to fall in and be deposited into the bank. The weight of the coin causes the whale's mouth to flap. **- $400 $3000 $10,000**

MEC-47

❑ **MEC-47. Leap Frog,**
Patent 1891. Made by Shepard Hardware Company. Place the figure of the standing boy behind the boy in the stooping position. Insert a coin in the slot and move the lever to the side. This causes the boy in the standing position to leap over the other boy and push a lever on the tree. This releases the coin, allowing it to be deposited into the bank. **- $400 $3000 $8000**

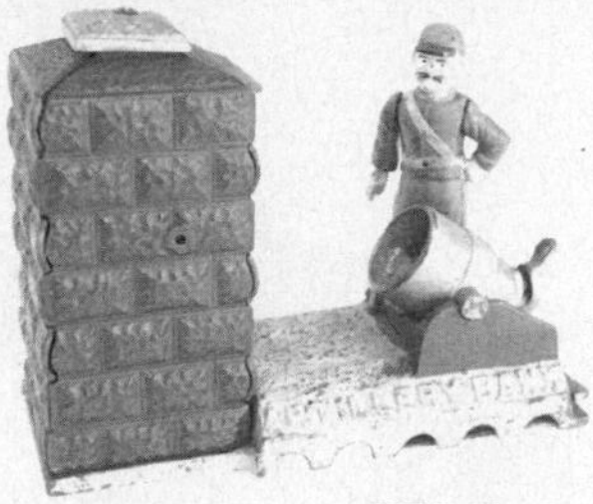

MEC-48

❑ **MEC-48. Artillery,**
Patent date 1892. Made by J. & E. Stevens Company. Pull the hammer down on the mortar. This will move the right arm of the soldier into the horizontal position. Place a coin in the barrel of the mortar. Press the lever located by the letter ""K"" and the soldier's arm will drop signaling the firing of the mortar. The hammer snaps up and strikes the coin propelling it into the opening of the building. Paper caps may be used to add sound to the action. **- $600 $3000 $8000**

MEC-49

❑ **MEC-49. William Tell**
Patent 1896. Made by J. & E. Stevens Company. Pull the coin launcher back until it is locked into position. The figure lowers his head as if aiming. The boy's arms must be pulled down so the apple appears on top of his head. Place a coin on the rifle and press the shooter's right foot. The coin is fired into the castle knocking the apple off the boy's head, as he raises his arms. It strikes a gong when it enters the castle. A percussion cap may be used.
- $250 $800 $3000

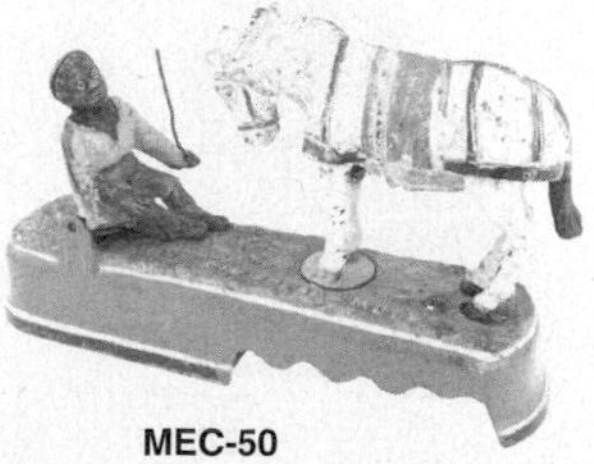

MEC-50

❑ **MEC-50. I Always Did 'Spise A Mule - Bench,**
Patent 1897. Made by J. & E. Stevens Company. Insert a coin and press the lever. Donkey spins around and kicks the boy over backwards and the coin is deposited into the base. **- $300 $1200 $4000**

MEC-51

❑ MEC-51. Chief Big Moon,
Patent 1899. Made by J. & E. Stevens Company. Place a coin in the slot just to the front of the fish's tail. When the lever is operated the large frog springs from under the lake towards the fish. The squaw lifts the fish up and away from the frog. The coin is automatically deposited into the bank. - **$500 $2500 $6000**

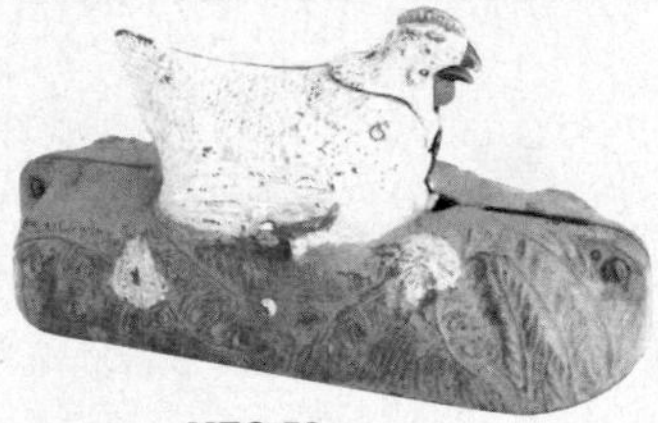

MEC-52

❑ MEC-52. Hen And Chick,
Patent 1901. Made by J. & E. Stevens Company. Place a coin in the slot in the base. Move the lever backwards, the hen begins to cluck and peck with her head. Simultaneously, the little chick springs forward from under the hen and pecks the coin into the bank. There is an internal bellows which makes the ""clucking"" sound. - **$450 $3800 $12,000**

MEC-53

❑ MEC-53. Magician Bank,
Patent 1901. Made by J. & E. Stevens Company. Place a coin on the table and press the lever on the steps. This causes the magician to lower his hat over the coin and move his head up and down. Release the lever, he returns to original position and the coin disappears into the bank. - **$500 $4000 $15,000**

MEC-54

❑ MEC-54. Calamity,
Patent 1905. Made by J. & E. Stevens Company. The players must be pulled into position. The coin is then placed in the slot, it remains there until the action takes place. When the lever is pressed the two ""tacklers"" swing in front of the ball carrier, who moves to avoid them. He tilts forward causing their heads to touch. The coin drops into the bank.
- **$2500 $18,000 $40,000**

MEC-55

❑ MEC-55. Mama Katzenjammer,
Patent 1905. Made by Kenton Hardware Company. Place a coin in the slot behind mama's back. As the coin is pushed in her eyes roll back and the coin is deposited into the bank.
- **$1500 $12,000 $50,000**

MEC-56

❑ MEC-56. Boy Robbing Bird's Nest,
Patent 1906. Place a coin in the slot on the limb, just below the boy. The coin will stick out slightly. The lever is below the bird on the left and when it is pressed down it releases the limb with the boy on it. The limb falls against the tree trunk and pushes the coin into the bank. The bank is reset by pulling the limb into position.
- **$800 $3500 $10,000**

MEC-57

❑ MEC-57. Teddy And The Bear
Patent 1907. Made by J. & E. Stevens Company. Cock the gun by sliding the piece back into position. Push the bear into the tree stump and close the cover. Lay a coin on the barrel of the gun and press the lever. His head lowers as if taking aim. The coin shoots into the stump and the bear pops up. A percussion cap can be used in the gun. - **$300 $1200 $5500**

MEC-58

❑ MEC-58. Boy Scout Camp,
Patent date 1912. Made by J. & E. Stevens Company. Place a coin in the slot located in the tree just above the tent. The coin stays into position until the lever, which is located below the owl, is depressed. The coin then falls into the bank and the Boy Scout with the flag raises it above his head. When the lever is released the flag returns to the lowered position.
- **$800 $4000 $14,000**

MEC-59

❑ **MEC-59. Monkey Bank**
Patent 1925. Made by Hubley Mfg. Company. Place a coin in the monkey's mouth and press the lever. He springs forward depositing the coin into the organ. - **$100 $350 $900**

MEC-60

❑ **MEC-60. Mickey Mouse (Tin)**
Made by Saalheimer & Strauss. Germany. 1930 - 1936. The verse printed on the back says, "If you only pull my ear you will see my tongue appear. Place a coin upon my tongue. Save your money while you're young."
- **$5,000 $12,000 $28,000**

Mego Superheroes

In 1972, New York based toy manufacturer Mego Corporation was approached by toy designer Stan Weston about licensing characters from DC, Marvel and ERB Inc to create action figures utilizing the 8" body of Mego's then in production Action Jackson toy line.

The first four World's Greatest Superheroes consisted of Superman, Batman, Robin and Aquaman which were an immediate runaway hit during their tests at Long Island's Korvette's stores. The line was quickly expanded to include new heroes and catapulted Mego from being a background player to one of the top ten toy companies of the 1970s.

From 1974 to 1976, the line was expanded to include vehicles, play sets and new characters such as the Super Foes, Teen Titans, Super Gals and the Fantastic Four.

After 1976, the line began to shrink as no new characters were offered and Mego began to trim figures from the assortment. While the World's Greatest Superheroes remained in production until Mego's demise in 1982, the assortment had then dwindled to the six most popular characters.

For the first four characters, Mego utilized a windowless solid box which was problematic due to children damaging them on the store shelves. Later releases were in window boxes which allowed the child to see the figure.

While Mego went on to have success with properties such as Star Trek, The Micronauts and Planet of the Apes, the Superheroes remain their most fondly remembered line today.

MEG-1

MEG-2

❑ **MEG-1. Superman Action Figure in Windowless Box,**
1972. From the initial release in the windowless box. - **$1000 $1500 $2500**

❑ **MEG-2. Aquaman Action Figure in Windowless Box,**
1972. From the initial release in the windowless box. - **$1000 $1500 $2500**

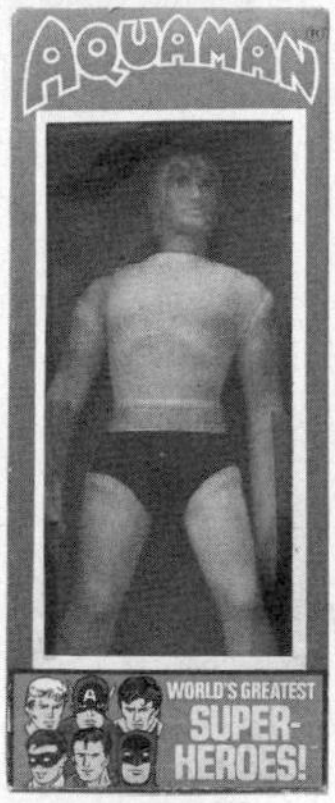

MEG-3

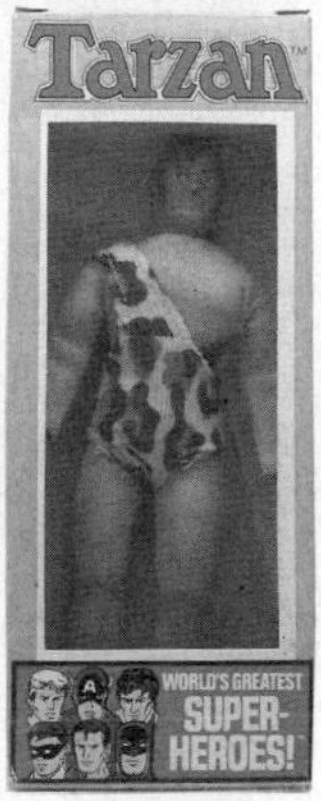

MEG-4

❑ **MEG-3. Aquaman Action Figure in Window Box,**
1973. From the later release in the window box.
- **$200 $250 $400**

❑ **MEG-4. Tarzan Action Figure in Window Box,**
1973. - **$200 $250 $400**

MEG-5

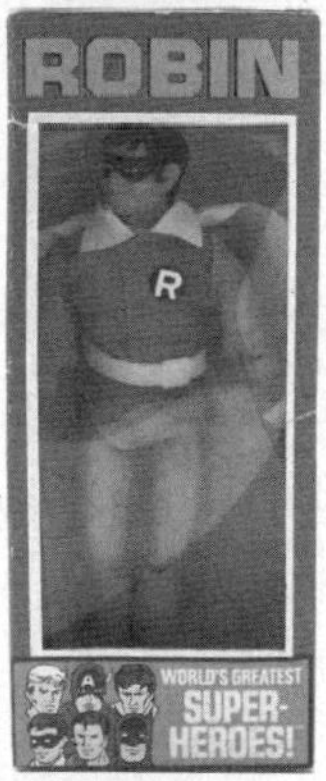

MEG-6

❑ **MEG-5. Batman Action Figure in Window Box,**
1973. Version shown has painted-on cowl. A version with a removable cowl also exists.
Painted Cowl Version - **$200 $250 $400**
Removable Cowl Version - **$250 $575 $800**

❑ **MEG-6. Robin Action Figure in Window Box,**
1973. Version shown has painted-on mask. A version with a removable mask also exists.
Painted Mask Version - **$125 $200 $300**
Removable Mask Version - **$600 $900 $1200**

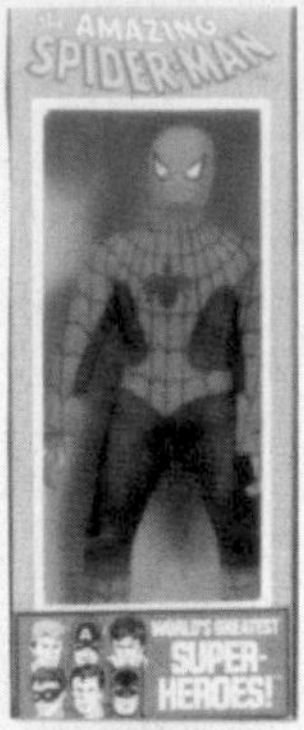

MEG-7

MEG-8

❑ **MEG-7. The Amazing Spider-Man Action Figure in Window Box,**
1973. - **$150 $250 $350**

❑ **MEG-8. Captain America Action Figure in Window Box,**
1973. - **$200 $275 $400**

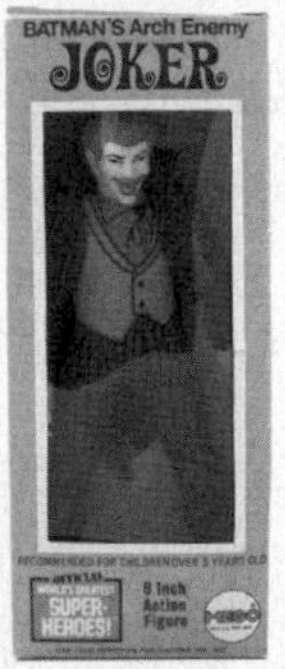

MEG-9

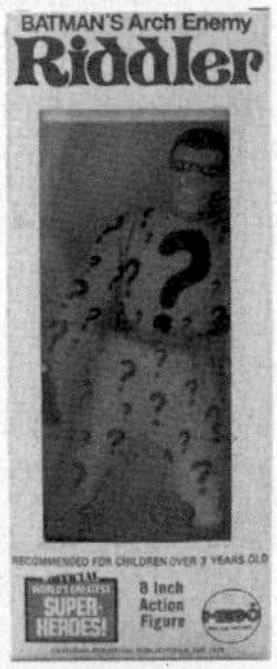

MEG-10

❑ **MEG-9. Joker Action Figure in Window Box,**
1973. - **$150 $200 $300**

❑ **MEG-10. Riddler Action Figure in Window Box,**
1973. - **$200 $300 $400**

MEG-11

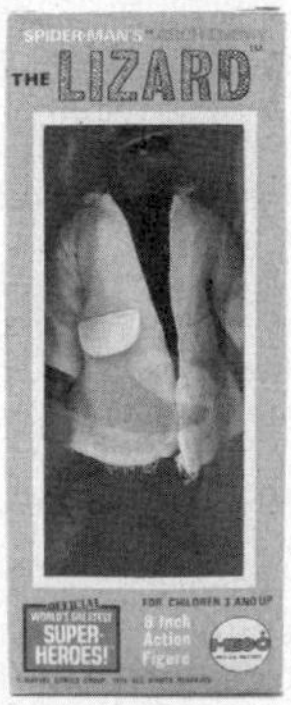

MEG-12

❑ **MEG-11. Green Goblin Action Figure in Window Box,**
1974. Vinyl figure is in a one-piece stretch fabric outfit. Complete with boots and satchel.
- **$200 $250 $350**

❑ **MEG-12. The Lizard Action Figure in Window Box,**
1974. - **$200 $250 $350**

MEG-13 (BOX BACK)

❑ **MEG-13. The Falcon Action Figure in Window Box,**
1974. - **$150 $200 $300**

MEG-14

❑ **MEG-14. "Batman Mobile Bat Lab" Boxed Vehicle Set,**
1975. Store item by Mego. Large 8x14x7" tall hard plastic vehicle. Near Mint Boxed - **$800**
Used Complete - **$85 $150 $250**

MEG-15

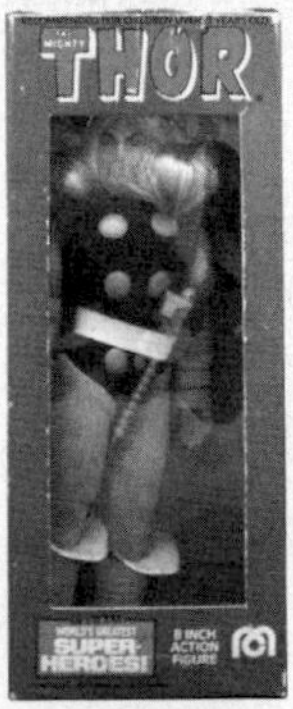

MEG-16

❑ **MEG-15. Human Torch Action Figure in Window Box,**
1975. - **$150 $200 $250**

❑ **MEG-16. Thor Action Figure in Window Box,**
1975. - **$250 $300 $400**

Melvin Purvis

The story of FBI agent Melvin Purvis (1903-1960) is a mixture of fact and legend. Purvis, a South Carolina lawyer, joined the FBI in 1927 and chased minor criminals in Texas and Oklahoma, eventually ending up in the Bureau's Chicago office. In 1934, with the help of a "woman in red," Purvis and other agents ambushed and killed the notorious John Dillinger as he left the Biograph movie theater in Chicago. Three months later Purvis, again acting on a tip, led a raid on an Ohio farm that ended in the killing of Pretty Boy Floyd. Purvis left the FBI in 1935, wrote a book about his experiences, and worked in law and broadcasting. In 1960, in poor health, he committed suicide. Purvis captured more public enemies than any other agent in FBI history, a record which still stands today.

As the embodiment of law and order and the implacable enemy of criminals, Purvis was heavily promoted in the 1930s by Post cereals in newspapers, on cereal boxes, and in magazine advertising. His *Junior G-Man Corps* and *Law and Order Patrol* enlisted kids by the thousands with a profusion of premiums--a variety of badges, ID cards, rings, flashlights, knives, fingerprint kits, manuals, pen and pencil sets, even separate badges for members of the Girls Division. Dale Robertson played Purvis in a 1974 television movie.

MLV-1

❑ **MLV-1. Premium Photo,**
1936. Rare. - **$50 $100 $225**

MLV-2

❑ **MLV-2. "Melvin Purvis Secret Operator Fingerprint Set",**
1936. Made by New York Toy & Game Co. Used as a premium by various sponsors and was also likely a store item. Back cover of booklet offers "G-Men Club" membership in club sponsored by G-Men pulp magazine.
Version With Purvis Name - **$50 $125 $250**
Without Purvis Name - **$30 $60 $125**

MLV-3

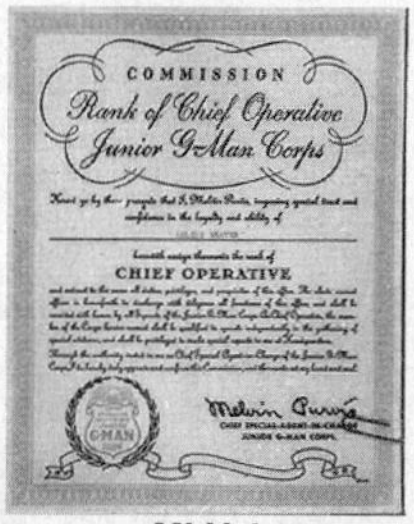

MLV-4

❑ **MLV-3. Club Manual Of Instructions,**
1936. - **$20 $35 $75**

❑ **MLV-4. Junior G-Man Corps "Chief Operative" Certificate,**
1936. - **$75 $150 $350**

MLV-5

MLV-6

❑ **MLV-5. Premium Folder,**
1936. - **$20 $45 $85**

❑ **MLV-6. "Junior G-Man Corps" Brass Badge,**
1936. - **$15 $30 $60**

MLV-7

MLV-8

MLV-9

❑ **MLV-7. "Roving Operative" Brass Badge,**
1936. - **$20 $45 $120**

❑ **MLV-8. "Chief Operative" Brass Shield Badge,**
1936. - **$20 $45 $120**

❑ **MLV-9. "Girls Division" Brass Club Badge,**
1936. - **$15 $40 $80**

MLV-10

MLV-11

❑ **MLV-10. "Melvin Purvis Junior G-Man Corps" Brass Ring,**
1936. - **$30 $60 $125**

❑ **MLV-11. "Special Agent" Metal Flashlight Gun,**
1936. Battery operated. - **$85 $175 $350**

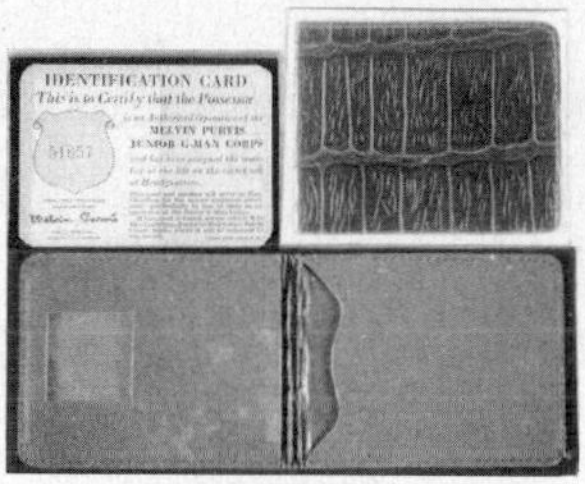

MLV-12

❑ **MLV-12. "Junior G-Man Corps" Member Card In Leather Wallet,**
1936. Wallet - **$30 $75 $160**
Card - **$20 $40 $75**

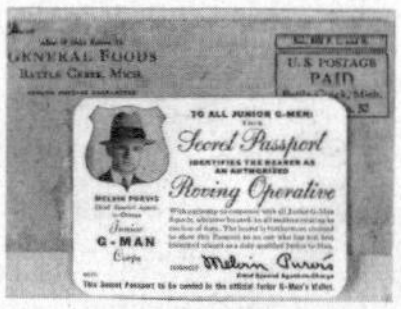

MLV-13

MLV-14

❑ **MLV-13. "Junior G-Men Secret Passport",**
1936. Envelope - **$10 $20 $30**
Card - **$40 $80 $135**

❑ **MLV-14. Junior G-Men Fingerprint Set With Mailer Envelope,**
1936. Cardboard folder containing fingerprint powder, ink pad, instruction booklet.
Mailer - **$10 $20 $30**
Set - **$40 $115 $225**

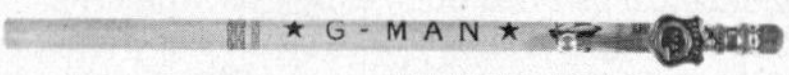

MLV-15

❑ **MLV-15. Wood Pencil With "G-Man" Metal Clip,**
c. 1936. Scarce. No Purvis markings.
Pencil - **$20 $50 $75**
Clip - **$20 $50 $75**

MLV-16

MLV-17

❑ **MLV-16. "G-Men" Brass Watch Fob,**
c. 1936. Unmarked for Purvis but pictured in his premium catalogues. Came with unmarked dark brown leather strap.
Fob Only - **$25 $50 $90**
With Correct Strap - **$50 $100 $250**

❑ **MLV-17. Club Manual,**
1937. Pictures 33 premiums. - **$15 $30 $75**

MLV-18

❑ **MLV-18. "Certificate of Appointment" with Mailer,**
1937. Rank of Captain. Rare. - **$125 $250 $500**

MLV-19

MLV-20

❑ **MLV-19. Premium Catalogue Folder Sheet,**
1937. Pictures 12 premiums. - **$20 $45 $85**

❑ **MLV-20. Scarab Ring,**
1937. Scarab in green. Also issued for Captain Frank Hawks. - **$300 $650 $1200**

MLV-21

MLV-22

❑ **MLV-21. Secret Operator/Law & Order Patrol Brass Ring,**
1937. - **$40 $75 $150**

❑ **MLV-22. "Secret Operator" Brass Badge,**
1937. - **$20 $40 $100**

MLV-23 MLV-24

❑ **MLV-23. "Lieutenant" Brass Rank Badge,**
1937. - **$20 $40 $110**

❑ **MLV-24. "Captain" Brass Rank Badge,**
1937. - **$25 $50 $120**

MLV-25

❑ **MLV-25. "Secret Operator/Girls Division" Brass Badge,**
1937. - **$20 $60 $150**

MLV-26

MLV-27

❑ **MLV-26. "Secret Operator" Grained Leather Wallet,**
1937. Inside has two slot pockets and small note pad. - **$45 $90 $185**

❑ **MLV-27. Prize Folder,**
1937. Junior G-Man premium folder. 4 pages. - **$25 $50 $90**

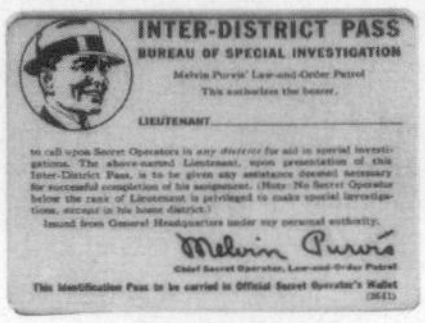

MLV-28

❑ **MLV-28. "Inter-District Pass" Club Card,**
1937. - **$30 $65 $125**

MLV-29

(CAP ON)

(CAP OFF)

MLV-30

❑ **MLV-29. "Melvin Purvis Official Secret Operator Pencil",**
1937. Scarce. 5-1/2" bakelite mechanical pencil with inscription plus portrait. - **$100 $200 $400**

❑ **MLV-30. "Melvin Purvis Official Secret Operator Combination" Bakelite Pen/Mechanical Pencil,**
1937. Rare. - **$125 $250 $500**

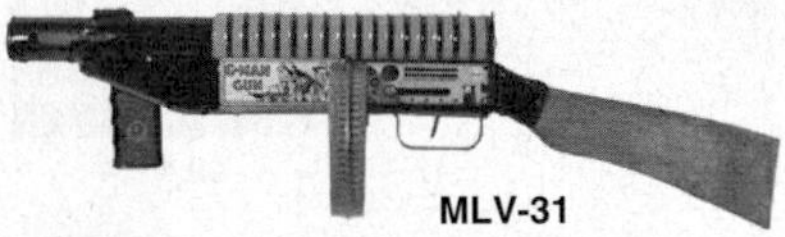

MLV-31

(Front view)

(Gun box)

❑ **MLV-31. "G-Man Squad" Gun,**
1937. Rare premium offered in the 1937 Junior G-Man Corps Prize Booklet by Post Toasties. You had to send in 69 Post Toasties box tops, or 36 Post Toasties box tops plus 50¢ in stamps or money order. Gun is 23" long and made of tin with a wood handle. Metal finish is red, yellow and black. This item was the hardest premium to get in all the offers presented by Melvin Purvis Chief Special Agent in charge. Made by Louis Marx & Co. Also sold in stores.
Gun - **$200 $400 $800**
Box for Gun - **$75 $125 $175**

MLV-32

MLV-33

❑ **MLV-32. "Secret Operator" Pocketknife,**
1937. Steel with cello. grips. Pictured in premium catalogue for Secret Operators. - **$65 $150 $350**

❑ **MLV-33. G-Man Tin Whistle,**
1930s. No Purvis markings. - **$20 $50 $100**

Mickey Mantle

Oklahoma-born Mickey Mantle (1931-1995) joined the New York Yankees in 1951 and soon succeeded Joe DiMaggio in center field. A powerful switch-hitter, Mantle hit 536 home runs in his 18 seasons with the team. The Mick won the Triple Crown in 1956, was voted the American League's Most Valuable Player in 1956, 1957, and 1962, and played in every All-Star game between 1951 and 1968, when he retired. He was elected to the Baseball Hall of Fame in 1974. With Mantle on the team, the Yankees won 12 pennants and seven world championships. He holds world series records for home runs (18), R.B.I. (40), runs (42), walks (43), extra base hits (26) and total bases (123). One of the most popular athletes of his time, Mantle slugged his way into the hearts of sports fans everywhere.

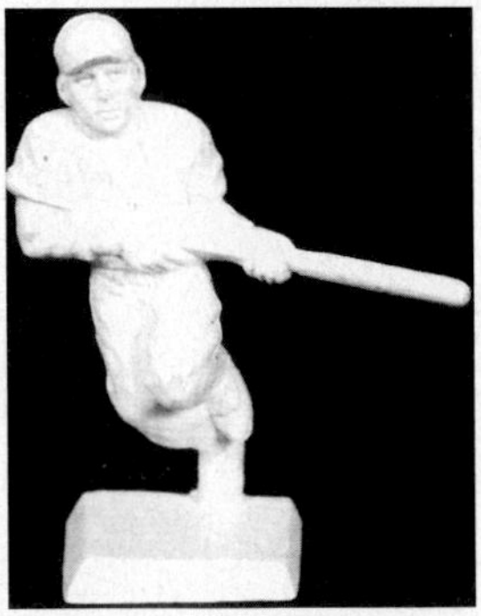

MKM-1

❑ **MKM-1. "Mickey Mantle" Statuette,**
c. 1955. Dairy Queen. 2-1/8" tall white hard plastic figurine on 1" square base inscribed by his name. From set of various major league baseball players. - **$70 $150 $250**

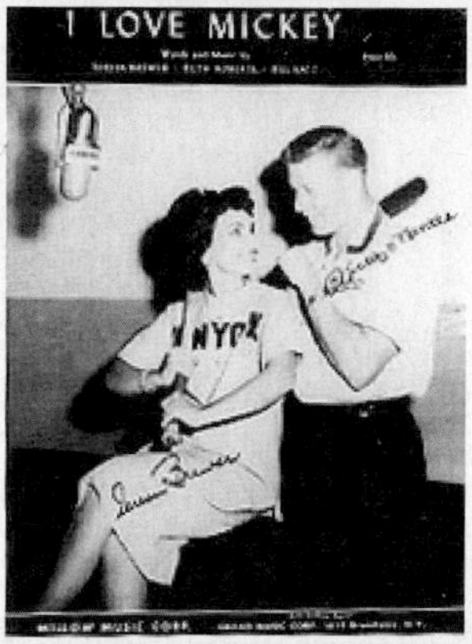

MKM-2

❑ MKM-2. "I Love Mickey" Sheet Music,
1956. Words and music for fan song popularized by songstress Teresa Brewer. - **$20 $40 $85**

MKM-3

❑ MKM-3. "I Love Mickey" Cello. Button,
1956. Promotion for tribute song to Mickey Mantle inspired and sung by songstress Teresa Brewer. - **$50 $95 $175**

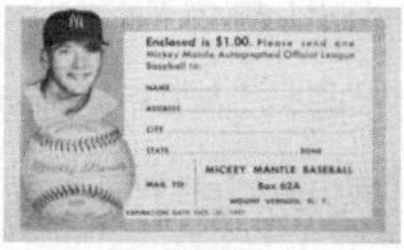

MKM-4

MKM-5

❑ MKM-4. Baseball Offer Coupon,
1957. Issuer unknown. 3x4-3/4" black and white coupon offering "Autographed Official League Ball" for $1.00. - **$25 $45 $80**

❑ MKM-5. Mickey Mantle Hartland Statue,
c. 1958. Figure is 8" tall with plastic bat. With Original Bat - **$75 $150 $250**
No Bat - **$45 $115 $200**

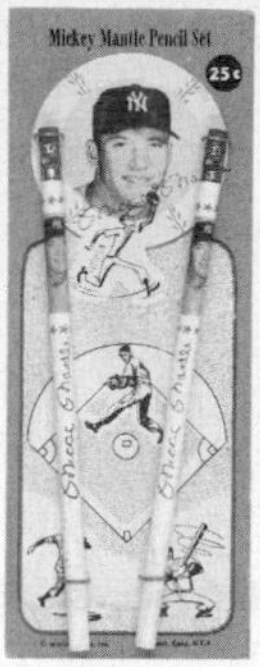

MKM-6

MKM-7

❑ MKM-6. "Mickey Mantle Pencil Set,"
c. 1958. Card is 3.5x9.25" and holds two 7.5" pencils. Bottom text reads "World Pencils Inc./Bridgeport, Conn. U.S.A." Identical 7" pencils have black and white photo with facsimile signature surrounded by red stars.
Carded - **$30 $60 $125**

❑ MKM-7. "Boys' Life" Cover Article,
1959. Monthly issue for August with color photos cover for article "Star Of The Stadium" with 11 more photos. - **$12 $25 $75**

MKM-8

❑ MKM-8. Pale Blue Background 3-1/2" Button,
1950s. Vendor button sold at stadiums. - **$25 $50 $85**

MKM-9

MKM-10

❑ MKM-9. "Mickey Mantle" Cello. Button,
1950s. Stadium souvenir with fabric ribbon and plastic charms. - **$65 $125 $250**

❑ MKM-10. Mickey Mantle Cello. Button,
1950s. Youthful photo image with attachments of fabric ribbon plus plastic charms on keychain. - **$100 $200 $300**

MKM-11

❑ MKM-11. "Yoo-Hoo" Beverage Can,
c. 1950s. Litho. metal 5-1/2" tall showing images on bottle caps of Yankees Skowron, Mantle, Berra, Kubek, Ford. - **$35 $75 $150**

MKM-12

❑ MKM-12. Paper Decal,
1950s. Issuer unknown. 3-1/2x4" full color positive image of Mantle as right-hand batter.
Unused - **$15 $30 $60**

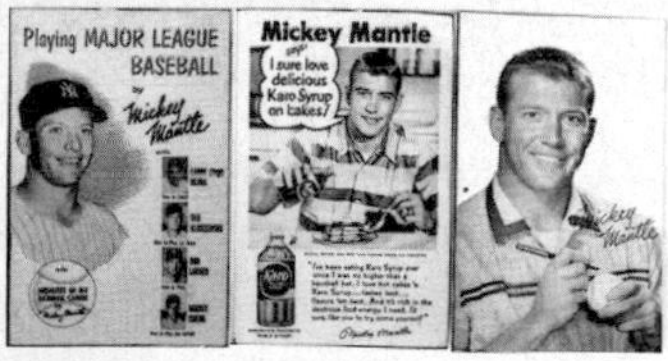

MKM-13

❑ MKM-13. "Playing Major League Baseball" Booklet,
1950s. Karo Syrup. 6x9" with 32 pages including baseball tips attributed to Mickey Mantle plus similar tips from various other major league stars. - **$30 $60 $100**

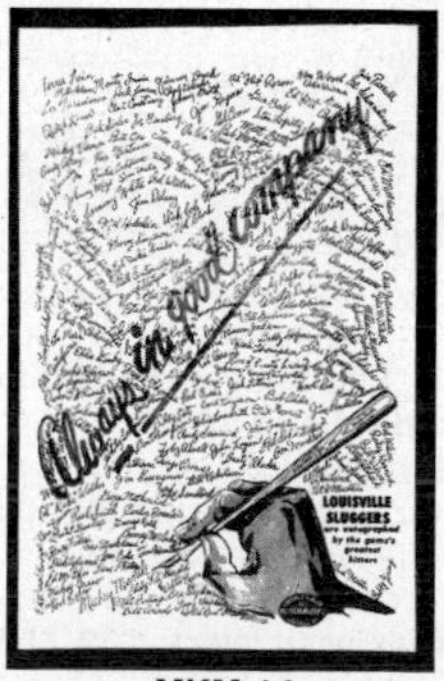

MKM-14

❑ **MKM-14. "Louisville Sluggers" 11x17" Paper Sign With Mantle And Others,**
1950s. Hillerich & Bradsby Co. Poster by bat maker company with facsimile signatures of dozens of well-known batters featuring "Mickey Mantle" signature on depicted baseball bat writing pen. - **$25 $45 $90**

MKM-15

❑ **MKM-15. Autographed Photo of Mantle, Pee Wee Reese and Duke Snider,**
1950s. Photo is 16 x 20". Mantle's signature is 5" long. - **$1650**

MKM-16

❑ **MKM-16. New York Yankees "World Champions" Photo Pennant,**
c. 1961. 28-1/2" wide. - **$35 $85 $175**

MKM-17

❑ **MKM-17. "Life" Magazine With Post Cereals Card Ad And Insert,**
1962. Weekly issue for April 13 with full page ad for cereal box cards plus example bound insert card picturing Mantle on one side and Roger Maris on other side.
Magazine With Insert Intact - **$30 $65 $125**

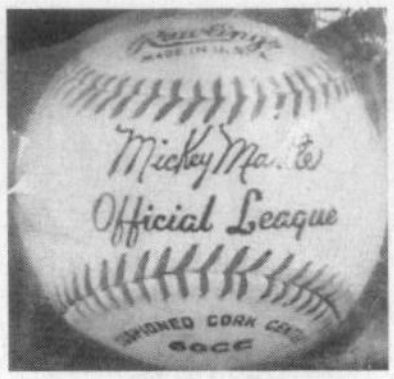

MKM-18

MKM-19

❑ **MKM-18. Mickey Mantle Official League Rawlings Baseball,**
1962. Premium from Campbell's Beans and possibly Rawlings Sporting Goods.
- **$15 $25 $60**

❑ **MKM-19. Baseball Tips Folder,**
1962. Paper sheet opening to 5.5x11" printed on both sides by playing tips. - **$10 $20 $35**

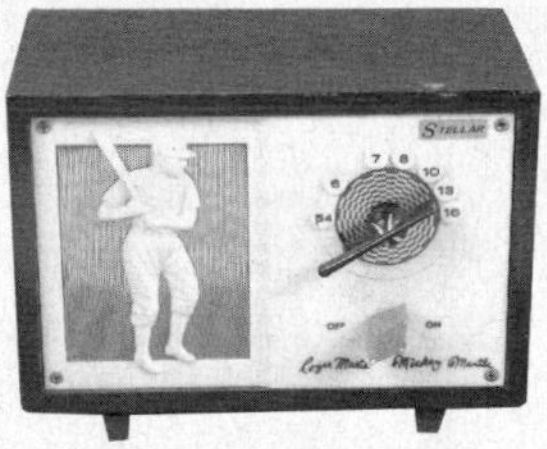

MKM-20

❑ **MKM-20. Roger Maris/Mickey Mantle Baseball Theme Radio,**
c. 1962. Radio is 4x5.25x7" with wood case. Molded plastic front has high relief image of batter over speaker panel. Tuning dial is in the shape of a ball and bat. Volume knob is diamond-shaped. Mantle and Maris facsimile signatures appear at bottom of volume control. Made by Stellar. - **$425 $750 $1500**

MKM-21

MKM-22

❑ **MKM-21 "Mickey Mantle" 3" Cello. Button,**
c. 1962. Full color photo with facsimile signature, image is 1955 Dormand postcard photo. - **$25 $45 $85**

❑ **MKM-22. Closeup Photo,**
1963. Phillies cigars. 6-1/2x9" black and white with facsimile signature. - **$15 $35 $75**

MKM-23

❑ **MKM-23. Life Magazine Cover Story,**
1965. Weekly issue for July 30 with front cover color photo for inside article "Last Innings Of Greatness." - **$15 $25 $55**

MKM-24

❑ **MKM-24. "Mantle And Mays Baseballs" Store Card,**
1967. Transogram. 9.5" wide cardboard display pack holding three vinyl baseballs. -
$60 $135 $225

MKM-25

MKM-26

❑ **MKM-25. "The Baseball Life of Mickey Mantle" Paperback,**
1969. First printing. 176 pages. - **$20 $35 $65**

❑ **MKM-26. "All Star" Wristwatch With Mantle, Others,**
1960s. Store item. Dial face has facsimile signatures of Mickey Mantle, Roger Maris, Willie Mays. Watch - **$75 $135 $250**
Box (Rare) - **$400 $800 $1200**

MKM-27

MKM-28

❑ **MKM-27. Mickey Mantle Guest Appearance Cello. Button,**
1982. For local mall visit in his retirement years. - **$8 $12 $30**

❑ **MKM-28. Mickey Mantle Personal Appearance Cello. Button,**
1982. For local mall visit in his retirement years. - **$8 $12 $30**

MKM-29

❑ **MKM-29. "Mickey Mantle" Hartland Statue With Box,**
1988. From 25th anniversary commemorative series. Near Mint Boxed - **$125**

MKM-30

❑ **MKM-30. "Mickey Mantle" Comic Book,**
1991. Magnum Comics. Features his life story. - **$5**

Mickey Mouse

See Ted Hake's *Official® Price Guide to Disney Collectibles*, Second Edition, formatted identically to this book but in full color evaluating over 9,000 Disney company and character collectibles from 1924 through 2006.

Mighty Mouse

The rodent equivalent of Superman, Captain Marvel and other humanoid cloaked flying heroes, Mighty Mouse was probably the best-known Terrytoons character and certainly one of the most prolific in animated episodes. Originally dubbed Supermouse in his first cartoon *The Mouse of Tomorrow* by Paul Terry in 1942, the battler of villainous cats was renamed Mighty Mouse in 1944. He starred in about 80 television episodes between 1955 and 1967, frequently saving girlfriend Pearl Pureheart from her perils with the villain cat "Oil Can Harry." In addition to animated adventures, Mighty Mouse starred also in numerous comic books by various publishers, including Gold Key and Dell, from the mid-1940s into the early 1990s. Animator Ralph Bakshi created a new series *Mighty Mouse: The New Adventures* which aired on CBS in 1987-1988 and was re-run on *Fox Kids* in 1992.

MGH-1

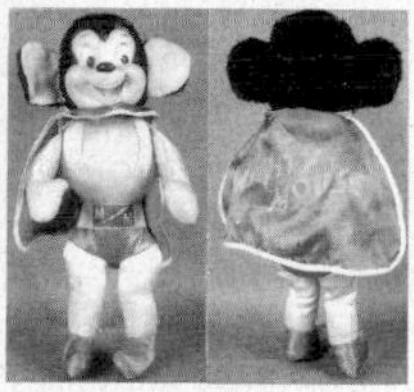

MGH-2

❑ **MGH-1. Mighty Mouse 12" Stuffed Oilcloth Doll,**
1942. Rare. Rubber head, star designs on cape. - **$400 $850 $1500**

❑ **MGH-2. Vinyl/Plush/Fabric Doll,**
c. 1950. Store item by Ideal Toys. Tag inscriptions include "CBS". - **$125 $275 $550**

MGH-3

❑ **MGH-3. "Mighty Mouse In Toyland" Record Album,**
1952. Peter Pan Records. 10x10" full color sleeve holding record musical story copyright by Terrytoons. - **$12 $30 $60**

MGH-4

❑ **MGH-4. "Three Dimension Comics" Comic Book With 3-D Glasses,**
1953. Second printing, came with glasses. First printing says "World's First!" on cover.
First Printing - **$28 $84 $350**
Second Printing - **$20 $60 $250**

MGH-5

❑ **MGH-5. Post Cereals "Merry-Pack" Punch-Outs With Envelope,**
1956. Post Treat-Pak and Post Alpha-Bits. Consists of three sheets to form about 20 items. Unpunched - **$50 $100 $150**

MGH-6

❑ **MGH-6. "Mighty Mouse" Tennis Shoes In Original Box,**
1956. Shoe box is 4x10.25x3.5" tall with images of "CBS Television's Mighty Mouse" on all sides including bottom. Box text includes "Washable/Arch Cushion/Canvas Footwear." Inside heel is black and white image of Mighty Mouse with yellow background and text below reading "CBS Television's Mighty Mouse Full Cushion/Arch Cushion." Comes with 2x2.5" fold-over die-cut tag. Inside tag lists features of the shoe and maker name "Randolph Mfg. Co. Randolph, Mass." Box - **$60 $125 $250**
Shoes - **$60 $125 $250**

MGH-7

❑ **MGH-7. Club Member Paper Wallet,**
1956. Part of previous punch-out set. -
$5 $10 $15

MGH-8

❑ **MGH-8. Cereal Box Wrapper With "Magic Mystery Picture" Offer,**
1957. Gordon Gold Archives.
Used Complete - **$65 $165 $325**

MGH-9

❑ **MGH-9. "Post Cereals Mighty Mouse Mystery Color Picture" Cards,**
1957. Set of six. Water makes invisible character appear. Unused Set - **$40 $60 $90**
Used Set - **$20 $40 $60**

MGH-10

❑ **MGH-10. Mighty Mouse/Heckle & Jeckle Board Game,**
1957. 12x12" boxed Milton Bradley game including game board picturing them plus Tom Terrific and Oilcan Harry. - **$40 $80 $165**

MGH-11

❑ **MGH-11. Cereal Box With Cut-Out,**
c. 1957. Post Sugar Crisp. Back panel printed for cutting and assembly of action scene toy from set of four.
Uncut - **$75 $150 $250**

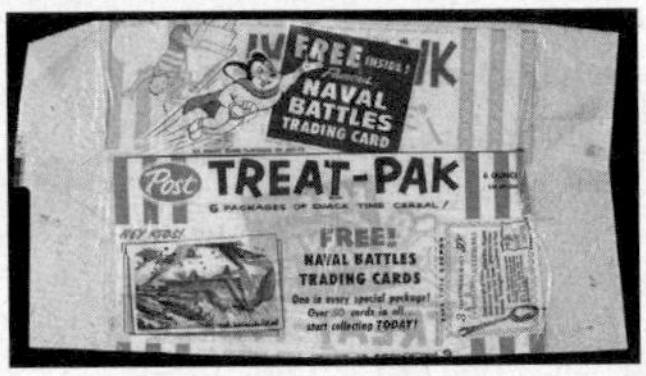

MGH-12

❑ **MGH-12. Cereal Pack Wrapper,**
1950s. Post. Advertises Naval Battles Trading Card. Back panel printed for cutting and assembly of action scene toy from set of four.
Uncut - **$55 $110 $160**

MGH-13

❑ **MGH-13. Terrytoons Store Hankies,**
1950s. Store item. Mighty Mouse opens display. Six hankies with all the Terrytoons characters featured. - **$70 $140 $280**

MGH-14

MGH-15

❑ **MGH-14. Rubber Squeaker Figure,**
1950s. Store item. Comes with red felt cape. -
$35 $80 $165

❑ **MGH-15. Original Comic Book Cover Art,**
1950s. 20" x 13". - **$2250**

MGH-16

MGH-17

MGH-18

❑ **MGH-16. Terrytoons Fabric Scarf,**
1950s. Store item. - **$25 $40 $80**

❑ **MGH-17. "Mighty Mouse In Toyland" Record,**
1960. Store item by Peter Pan Records. -
$15 $25 $50

❑ **MGH-18. Soaky Toy,**
1965. 10" tall. - **$15 $30 $60**

MGH-19

MGH-20

❑ **MGH-19. Vinyl/Cloth Hand Puppet,**
1960s. 9" tall. - **$20 $30 $60**

❑ **MGH-20. "Terrytoons" Characters Cereal Bowl,**
1977. Store item by Deka Plastic Inc., N.J. 5-1/2" diameter with many characters shown in color. - **$10 $20 $35**

MGH-21

MGH-22

❑ **MGH-21. Plush Doll,**
1981. 10" tall with tag. Hard to find. Beanie-like. Figure with tag - **$100**

❑ **MGH-22. Christmas Ornament in Box,**
1998. - **$22**

MGH-23

❑ **MGH-23. Tin Lunch Box,**
2001. - **$22**

MGH-24

❑ **MGH-24. Figure on Base with Box,**
2003. Limited Edition of 750. Figure and base are 6-1/2" tall. - **$25 $50 $100**

Milton Berle

Born Mendel Berlinger, Milton Berle (1908-2002) began his show business career as a child actor in silent films with the *Perils of Pauline* in 1914 which starred Pearl White. Berle made his stage debut at age 12 in the 1920 production of *Florodora* which became a success on Broadway. He appeared in vaudeville and was the first comedian to appear on television in a 1929 experimental broadcast.

Various stints on the radio led to NBC's *The Milton Berle Show* which aired March 11, 1947 to April 13, 1948 followed by the highly successful *Texaco Star Theater* which aired September 22, 1948 until June 15, 1949. The TV version began in 1948 and made Berle a household name, earning him an Emmy and the nickname "Mr. Television" in the process. The series became *The Buick-Berle Show* in 1953, then simply *The Milton Berle Show* from 1954 to 1956. Young Elvis Presley appeared on the April 3 and June 5, 1956 shows including a slow motion performance of *Hound Dog* replete with pelvic gyrations which outraged censors.

Notable Berle films include: *Leave Them Laughing* 1949, *Let's Make Love* with Marilyn Monroe 1960, *It's A Mad, Mad, Mad, Mad World* 1963, *Broadway Danny Rose* 1984, and *Driving Me Crazy* 1991. He played Louie The Lilac on the 1960s *Batman* TV series.

Milton Berle hosted the first charity TV telethon in 1949 and co-founded the L.A. Friar's Club the same year. *The Guinness Book Of World Records* credits him with the greatest number of charity performances by an entertainer. Fellow comedians referred to Berle as the "Thief of Bad Gags."

MBL-1

❑ **MBL-1. "Milton Berle's Jumbo Fun Book",**
1940. Pre-TV era. - **$15 $20 $40**

MBL-2

❑ **MBL-2. "Milton Berle" ABC Radio Sign,**
1940s. - **$375 $550 $1100**

MBL-3

MBL-4

❑ **MBL-3. Milton Berle Windup Car,**
1950s. By Marx. 9" long tin with plastic hat. This toy is version with red hat, wheels are black/brown.
Box - **$50 $100 $200**
Toy - **$75 $150 $250**

❑ **MBL-4. Milton Berle Windup Car,**
1950s. By Marx. 9" long tin with plastic hat. This toy is version with tan hat, red/yellow wheels.
Box - **$50 $100 $200**
Toy - **$85 $175 $300**

MBL-5

❑ **MBL-5. "The Milton Berle Make-Up Club",**
1950s. 1.75" button. - **$50 $100 $200**

Miss America

The pageant began as a two-day beauty contest in Atlantic City on September 7, 1921. Margaret Gorman of Washington, D.C. was the first Miss America.

Other notable winners include: 1943 Jean Bartel of Los Angeles who sold more Series E war bonds than anyone else in the USA; 1945 Bess Myerson of New York City, the first Jewish Miss America; 1955 Lee Ann Meriweather of San Francisco, who went on to play Catwoman in the 1966 movie spun off from the *Batman* TV series; 1984 Vanessa Williams of Milwood, New York the first African American Miss America; 1994 Heather Whitestone of Birmingham, Alabama, the first woman with a disability to win the competition (she was deaf.)

The pageant was hosted by Bert Parks (1914-1992) on TV from 1955 to 1980. He introduced the theme song *There She Is, Miss America* written by Bernie Wayne on the first televised show.

Marvel published two issues of *Miss America Comics* in 1944. The title became *Miss America Magazine* in November, 1944 and ran 93 issues, ending in November, 1958.

MSA-1

❑ **MSA-1. Inter-City Beauty Pageant 1926 Contestant Framed Photo,**
1926. 11.75x43" frame contains 9.75x41" sepia photo labeled "Inter-City Beauties - Atlantic City 1926 No. 6.P. Copyright 1926 - Atlantic Photo Service 1235 Boardwalk - Atlantic City, N.J." Includes woman in center wearing sash reading "Miss America 1925." - **$100 $200 $400**

MSA-2

❑ **MSA-2. "Lucky Strike Cigarettes" Bridge Hand Game,**
1930s. American Tobacco Co. 4x5-1/2" paper insert from package of "Lucky Strike Fifties" from series of 50 numbered hands to test Bridge playing skill. Fronts have full color glamour pose by model titled "Miss America" although likely not associated with the pageant. - **$5 $10 $20**

MSA-3

❑ **MSA-3. Philco Corp. War Effort "Miss America" Poster,**
1943. 12x18" white sheet centered by 9x13.25" black and white art. Art is "Drawn For Philco By John Maxwell" from series commissioned by Philco utilizing various artists. - **$25 $50 $85**

MSA-4

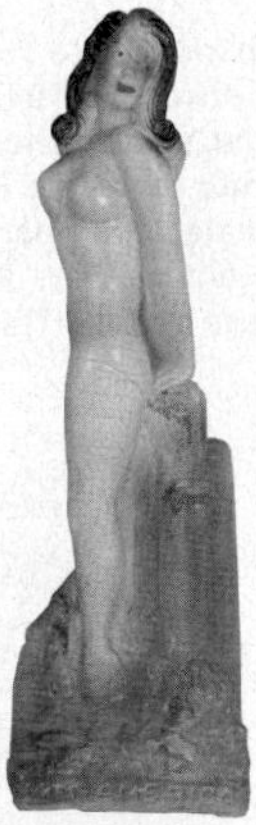

MSA-5

❑ **MSA-4. Miss America Magazine #2 November,**
1944. Miss America Pub. First appearance of Patsy Walker comic strip. - **$100 $400 $1600**

❑ **MSA-5. "Miss America" Pin-Up Girl Plaster Statue,**
1940s. 15.25" tall statue with sparkle accents, - **$35 $65 $135**

MSA-6

❑ **MSA-6. "Miss America" Paperdoll Set,**
1974. Whitman. 5x14-1/2x1.5"deep boxed set includes 10" tall die-cut cardboard stand-up doll with plastic slotted base, glossy paper folder sheet containing 29 pieces of punch-out clothing. - **$5 $15 $25**

MSA-7

❑ **MSA-7. Vanessa Williams 1984 Miss America Commemorative Corn Flakes Box,**
1984. These boxes hit the stores just before the scandal surfaced that cost her the crown. She has since moved on to become a successful actress and singer. - **$45 $125 $210**

Mister Softee

Sales of soft ice cream dispensed from a spigot blossomed in the 1950s, not only from ice cream trucks playing *Turkey in the Straw* over loudspeakers in urban areas but also from drive-in retail outlets. Thousands of these outlets were opened on the nation's highways by such retail chains as Dairy Queen, Tastee Freeze, and Carvel. By the end of the decade hard ice cream was making a comeback, but the soft ice cream chains had established themselves as a continuing roadside fixture. Dairy Queen issued a few premiums (see Dennis the Menace rings), but Mister Softee was the leader, and issued premiums through the "Mister Softee Club," probably established in the late 1950s.

MSF-1

❑ **MSF-1. Club Items With Sign,**
1960s. Kit Near Mint Complete - **$95**
Plastic Ring - **$5 $10 $20**
Membership Card - **$5 $10 $20**
Litho. Button - **$5 $10 $20**
Cloth Patch - **$5 $10 $20**
Iron-On Transfer Order Form - **$2 $5 $10**

MSF-2

MSF-3

❑ **MSF-2. "Mister Softee" Enameled Brass Keychain Tag,**
c. 1960s. - **$10 $25 $40**

❑ **MSF-3. "I Like Mister Softee" Logo Figure Plastic Flicker Ring,** 1960s. Mister Softee cones, shakes, sundaes. - **$25 $40 $75**

MSF-4

❑ **MSF-4. "Adventures Of Captain Chapel" Space Cards,**
1960s. Mister Softee. Cards 1-10 are numbered, following cards are unnumbered from unknown set total. Each - **$2 $3 $6**

MSF-5

❑ **MSF-5. Portrait Litho Tin Yo-Yo,**
1960s. 1" dia. by 5/8" thick printed on each side by red image and name on white. - **$8 $15 $30**

The Monkees

Four "insane" boys--actors Mickey Dolenz (formerly Mickey Braddock of the TV series *Circus Boy*) and Davy Jones, and musicians Peter Tork and Mike Nesmith--picked from hundreds of hopefuls who answered an audition call, comprised the Monkees, a fictional rock group that nevertheless enjoyed considerable success on records and on network television. The show, inspired stylistically by the Beatles' 1964 film *A Hard Day's Night*, featured surrealistic camera work and comic or melodramatic story lines. The series ran on the three television networks, originally on NBC (1966-1968), and repeated on CBS (1969-1972) and ABC (1972-1973). *Monkees* comic books appeared from 1967 to 1969. Merchandising was extensive, and a custom-built Monkeemobile was created for appearances at automobile shows and shopping centers. After years of obscurity, a resurgence of popularity in Japan and a re-airing of the original television episodes on MTV in 1985 and 1986 sparked a 20th anniversary reunion that produced multiple live performances (a handful including Nesmith, now a successful video production entrepeneur) and a new album in 1987. In 1996, Mike reformed the group yet again to film a special 30th anniversay "episode" of the series and record another new album, and VH-1 produced a TV-movie about the history of the band in the summer of 2000. Items are usually copyrighted by Raybert Productions or Screen Gems. "Now crayon I can say!"

MON-1

❑ **MON-1. "Monkees Record Tote,"**
1966. Tote is 7.5x8" vinyl-covered cardboard with latch on front, plastic carrying handle at top. By Mattel marked "Made In Canada," Copyright Raybert Productions Inc.
- **$100 $200 $300**

MON-2

MON-3

❑ **MON-2. Playing Cards,**
1966. 52 card deck with 40 action pictures. - **$50 $85 $170**

❑ **MON-3. Celluloid 3-1/2" Button,**
1966. Vendor item. - **$30 $65 $125**

MON-4

MON-5

❑ **MON-4. "Official Monkees Fan" Cello. Button,**
1966. Raybert Productions. - **$30 $65 $125**

❑ **MON-5. First Gum Card Set,**
1966. Store item by Donruss Co. Set of 44 with sepia photo fronts and full color photo puzzle backs. Near Mint Set - **$185**

MON-6

MON-7

❑ **MON-6. "Series A" Card Set,**
1966. Store item by Donruss Co. Forty-four cards in set with color photo fronts and color photo puzzle backs. Near Mint Set - **$185**

❑ **MON-7. "Series B" Gum Card Set,**
1966. Store item by Donruss Co. Forty-four cards in set with color photo fronts and color photo puzzle backs with Monkee Questions and Answers. Near Mint Set - **$185**

MON-8

❑ **MON-8. Punch-Out Model Book,**
1966. Large size 10x14.25" English book by Young World Productions Ltd. with four inside punch-outs of the four Monkees plus 12 coloring pages featuring them. - **$50 $90 $175**

MON-9

❑ **MON-9. "Series C" Gum Card Set,**
1967. Store item by Donruss Co. Set of 44 with color photo fronts and color backs with photo puzzles and text. Near Mint Set - **$185**

MON-10

❑ **MON-10. Gum Card Display Box,**
1967. Store item by Donruss Co. Box held packs of "Series C" cards. - **$75 $175 $300**

MON-11

❑ **MON-11. "Monkees Husky Extra Monkeemobile" On Card,**
1967. Display card is 4x4" and contains 3" long detailed die-cast metal and plastic replica copyright Raybert Productions Inc. Card is variety with original stock number "1004" crossed off as printed with addition of new number above this "1204." Carded - **$75 $150 $275**
Car Only - **$25 $50 $100**

MON-12

❑ **MON-12. Monkees Bracelet On Store Card,**
1967. Near Mint Carded - **$100**
Bracelet Only - **$15 $25 $50**

MON-13

❑ **MON-13. Fan Club Postcard,**
1967. - **$8 $15 $30**

MON-14

❑ **MON-14. Tour Sign 29x22",**
1967. Promotional sign for performance at the Cow Palace in San Francisco. -
$225 $400 $850

MON-15

MON-16

❑ **MON-15. Official Fan Club Button,**
1967. Litho. 2-1/4". - **$10 $20 $40**

❑ **MON-16. Monkees Litho. Button,**
1967. Vending machine issue set of six. Four with single portraits, two with group portraits.
Each - **$5 $10 $15**

MON-17

❑ **MON-17. Kellogg's Flicker Rings,**
1967. Set of 12 silvered plastic with insert alternating picture of individual for group.
Each - **$10 $25 $50**

MON-18

❑ **MON-18. "Monkee Coins",**
1967. Kellogg's. Set of 12 color photos in yellow plastic frames. Canadian issue with reverse text in English and French. Each - **$10 $20 $30**

MON-19

❑ **MON-19. Photo Flip Booklets,**
1967. Store item. Set of 16. Each - **$10 $20 $50**

MON-20

MON-21

❑ **MON-20. "Talking Hand Puppet" Boxed,**
1967. Store item by Mattel, Inc.
Near Mint Boxed Talking - **$800**
Unboxed Talking - **$115 $225 $500**
Unboxed Not Talking - **$65 $135 $275**

❑ **MON-21. "Monkee-Mobile" Tin Friction Car,**
c. 1967. Store item, Japanese made. Has battery operated singing mechanism.
Box - **$135 $275 $500**
Car - **$135 $275 $500**

MON-22

MON-23

❑ **MON-22. Unopened Third Series Gum Card Pack,**
1967. Donruss. - **$15 $30 $60**

❑ **MON-23. Program,**
1967. 12x12" published by Raybert Prod. Inc. - **$15 $30 $65**

MON-24

❑ **MON-24. "Monkees Flip Movies" Display Box,**
1967. 5-1/4" long x 7-1/4" wide x 1" deep box only without contents. - **$100 $200 $350**

MON-25

❑ **MON-25. Monkeemobile Corgi Large Replica Boxed,**
c. 1967. 5" long die cast metal and plastic precise replica including all four Monkee figures.
Near Mint Boxed - **$600**
Car With Four Figures - **$100 $175 $300**

MON-26

MON-27

❑ **MON-26. Mike Nesmith Hanger,**
1967. Black and white diecut cardboard photo clothing hanger on plastic hook. From set featuring each of the individual Monkees.
Each - **$50 $100 $200**

❑ **MON-27. "Monkees" Cereal Box Cut-Out Record,**
c. 1970. Kellogg's. Series of four box backs.
Each - **$5 $10 $20**

MON-28

MON-29

❑ **MON-28. "Monkees" Summer Tour Program,**
1987. - **$15 $30 $60**

❑ **MON-29. Monkee Mobile Die Cast Car,**
2002. - **$30**

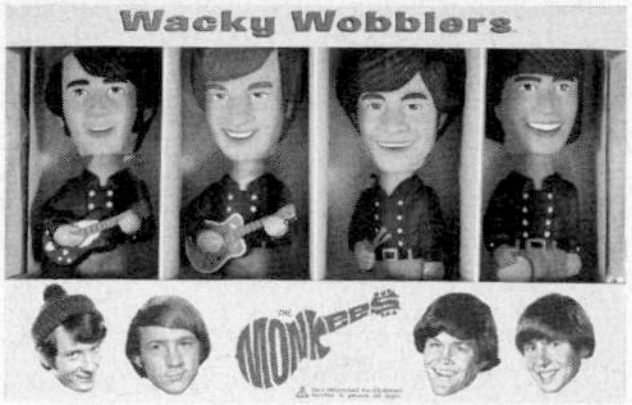

MON-30

❑ **MON-30. "Monkees" Wacky Wobblers,**
2002. - **$40**

Monsters Misc.

The monster and horror genre had its origins in late 18th and early 19th century British gothic novels. Theatrical adaptations, however, with their lighting and stage machinery, served as the inspiration and model for filmmakers, not the books themselves. In silent films, America and Europe took different approaches. European films suggested darker possibilities with *Das Cabinet des Dr. Caligari* (1919, German), which shows cinema's ability to transcend photographic realism, and *Nosferatu* (1921, German), which emphasized the sexual aspect of Bram Stoker's Dracula. Universal Studios led the way in the US with emphasis on fast-paced action and macabre chills and dominated the genre in the 1930s (more on their influence can be seen in the section devoted specifically to Universal Studios monster memorabilia).

Later in the 1930s, other studios like RKO added to the spectacle. *King Kong* (1933) made a mighty ape into a symbol of subversive power. RKO also produced a new version of *The Hunchback of Notre Dame* (1939) with Charles Laughton, which restored some of the complexity removed from the Lon Chaney version produced by Universal in 1923.

The genre declined in the 1940s and most films were routine and uninspired. By the late 1950s there was a rebirth, but these "modern" horror films were far removed from the innocent films of the '30s. Director Terence Fisher (Hammer Studios) led the way in Britain with his reinterpretation of the Frankenstein and Dracula stories. Fisher's *The Curse of Frankenstein* (1957) caused a protest about its sensuality. Fisher emphasized the Baron's character more than the creature's and used subtle characterizations and dramatic timing. He also made excellent use of color (this was the first British monster film in color). In *Horror of Dracula* (1958), Fisher created a film of subtle realism, with atmosphere and rhythm.

Beginning in the late 1950s, local television stations introduced "horror hosts" to spice up the telecasts of monster and horror movies. On the west coast, Maila Nurmi, a model and aspiring actress, went to a Hollywood costume ball dressed as a Charles Addams cartoon character which was at the time unnamed but now known as Morticia Addams. Los Angeles producer Hunt Stromberg, Jr. was struck by her macabre appearance and hired her as Vampira to host a Saturday night horror movie show on KBS-TV. Her popularity led to *Life* magazine coverage, guest appearances on TV shows and several films, including Ed Wood's cult classic Plan 9 From Outer Space. On the east coast, Philadelphia got its chills from Roland, played by John Zacherle, who later moved to haunt New York City as Zacherley.

On the publishing front, in 1958 Forrest J. Ackerman began to chronicle monster and horror history in *Famous Monsters of Filmland*. Warren Publishing Company introduced *Creepy* in 1964 and *Eerie* in 1965, which both featured the work of many excellent artists. Warren's *Vampirella* made her debut in September 1969 and to this day, she remains one of the premiere "Bad Girls" of the comic book world and a major success story with current comic books published by Harris Comics.

This section features an assortment of the monster items distinct from the Universal monsters, which are covered in their own section.

MNS-1

❑ **MNS-1. King Kong Herald,**
1933. Tri-fold, die-cut herald for the 1933 release of the classic big monster tale. 5x7" four-panel herald opens to 16".
- **$300 $600 $1000**

(COMPLETED PUZZLE)

(MAILER) MNS-2

❑ **MNS-2. "King Kong" Jig Saw Puzzle,**
1933. With mailer. RKO Radio Picture Product. 21-3/4" high x 10-1/2" wide. Rare. -
$750 $1500 $3000

MNS-3

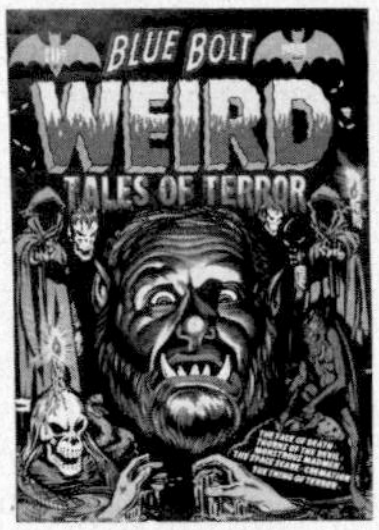

MNS-4

❑ **MNS-3. King Kong Slogan Button,**
1930s. Black/white/red cello inscribed "What Is The 8th Wonder Of The World/I Know/Ask Me!" Possible movie promo for original release in 1933 or for later 1930s or after re-release. -
$60 $135 $275

❑ **MNS-4. Cover Press Proof,**
1951. For Blue Bolt Weird Tales of Terror #111. Art by L.B. Cole. Blank on back side. - **$350**

MNS-5

❑ **MNS-5. "Charles Addams' Nightcrawlers" Hardcover With Dust Jacket,**
1957. Various titles. Non-first editions typically -
$15 $35 $75

MNS-6

❑ **MNS-6. "Monster Times" First Fanzine,**
1961. Single two-sided sheet Vol. 1 #1 issue from January-March by Science-Fiction Times. -
$65 $125 $200

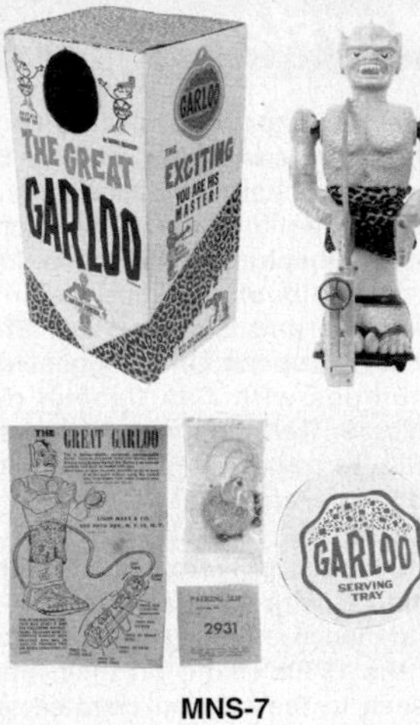

MNS-7

❑ **MNS-7. "The Great Garloo" Boxed Battery Operated Toy,**
1961. Marx. 11x13x24" tall cardboard box contains 22" tall hard plastic toy with attached remote control battery unit. Toy features great design, Garloo wears a fabric loincloth. Remote controls three separate functions. Comes with 5.5x8" instruction folder. Garloo's plastic necklace comes sealed in bag. Inludes box punch-out 5x5" diameter cardboard "Garloo Serving Tray." Box - **$125 $250 $500**
Toy - **$200 $400 $600**

MNS-8

❑ **MNS-8. "The Great Son Of Garloo" Boxed Windup,**
c. 1961. Marx Toys. 2.5x3x5.75" tall with built-in key. Nicely designed box in matching style to large battery operated Garloo toy. Toy was produced in two versions, one with litho tin body and the other with hard plastic body. This is the latter. Legs are painted metal. Has separate "Son Of Garloo" plastic medallion with plastic link chain. Box - **$60 $115 $225**
Toy (Metal Body) - **$125 $235 $450**
Toy (Plastic Body) - **$100 $200 $400**

MNS-9

MNS-10

❑ **MNS-9. "Monster Mash" 45 RPM Record,**
1962. Store item on Garpax Records label. Black and white paper sleeve holds record by Bobby "Boris" Pickett and The Crypt-Kickers. -
$25 $50 $90

❑ **MNS-10. The Hunchback Of Notre Dame Model Kit,**
1963. Store item by Aurora.
Near Mint Boxed - **$400**
Built No Box - **$20 $40 $80**

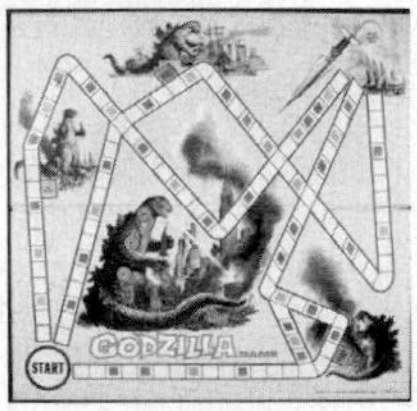

MNS-11

❑ **MNS-11. "Godzilla Game" By Ideal,**
1963. WMC. 18.5x19" board has images of Godzilla attacking various aspects of city. Perforated spinner and game pieces.
- **$100 $200 $300**

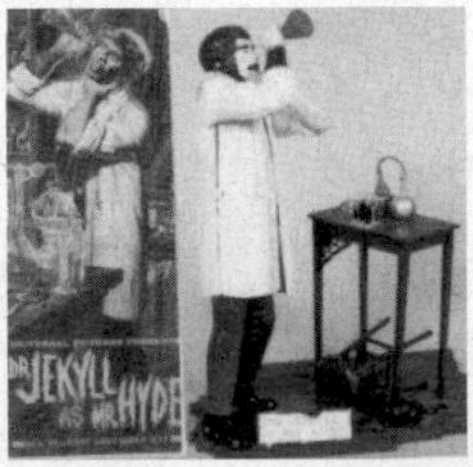

MNS-12

❑ **MNS-12. "Dr. Jekyll As Mr. Hyde" Model Kit,**
1964. Aurora. Near Mint Boxed - **$450**
Built No Box - **$20 $40 $75**

MNS-13

❑ **MNS-13. Godzilla Model Kit,**
1964. Store item by Aurora.
Near Mint Boxed - **$700**
Built No Box - **$65 $125 $250**

MNS-14

❑ **MNS-14. Aurora "The Witch" Model Kit,**
1965. Store item by Aurora.
Near Mint Boxod **$350**
Built No Box - **$25 $50 $75**

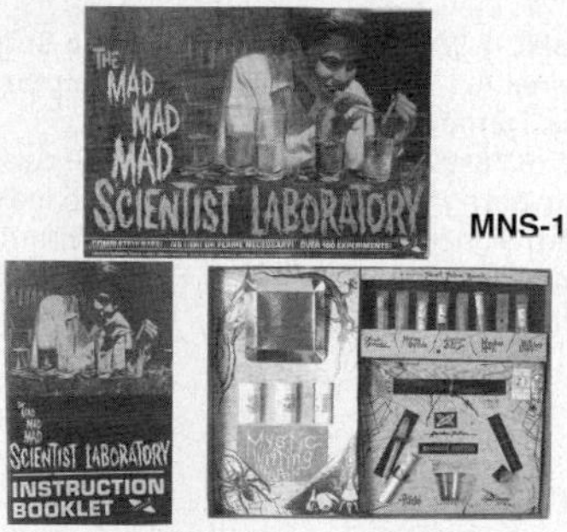

MNS-15

❑ **MNS-15. "Mad Mad Mad Scientist Laboratory" Boxed Set,**
1965. Homelab Division of Physio-Chem Corp. Large 13.5x18.5x2" deep box contains very elaborate assortment of materials and equipment plus instructions for developing ghoulish projects while learning about actual chemistry. - **$1100 $2150 $4000**

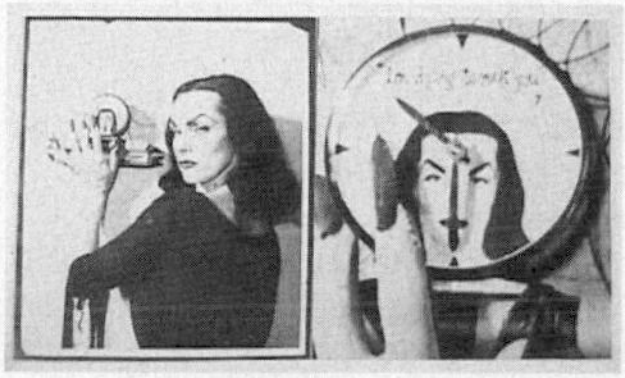
MNS-16

❑ **MNS-16. Vampira Publicity Photo,**
1960s. Depicts her holding time bomb with her portrait plus text "I'm Dying To Meet You/Saturdays 10:30 On 7." - **$40 $75 $140**

MNS-17

❑ **MNS-17. King Kong Figure With Woman,**
1960s. 3" tall unmarked but issued by Palmer Plastics. - **$40 $75 $165**

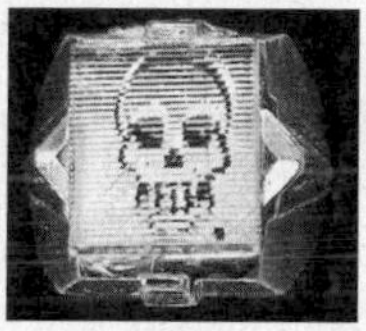
MNS-18

❑ **MNS-18. Famous Monsters Magazine Flicker Ring,**
1960s. From set of five with flicker images that change from positive to negative. Set was advertised in the magazine. Silver luster plastic base. Each - **$20 $45 $75**

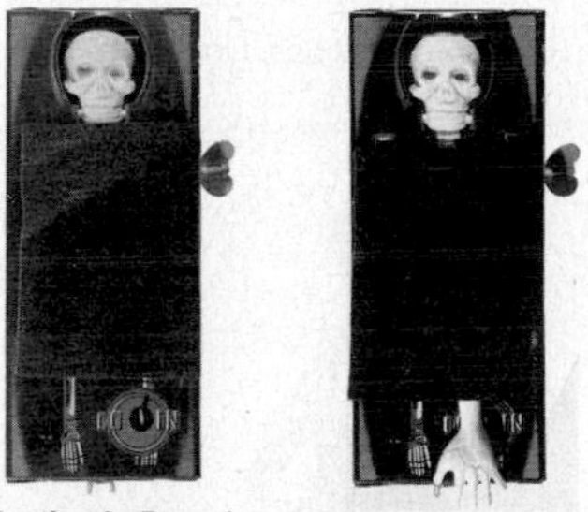
(Resting in Peace) **(Grabbing the Coin)**
MNS-19

❑ **MNS-19. Skeleton Wind-up Bank,**
1960s. Hand reaches out and grabs coin, pushing it into the tin box. - **$20 $40 $70**

MNS-20

MNS-21

❑ **MNS-20. "Vampirella Fan Club" Member's Button,**
1972. Warren Publishing Co. Membership cost was $2 and recipient received button and membership card. Button is full color 2-1/2". - **$40 $75 $150**

❑ **MNS-21. Magazine Fan Club Card,**
1972. Warren Pub. Co. Black and white on bright yellow. - **$30 $55 $100**

MNS-22

❑ **MNS-22. "Vampirella Giant Poster Puzzle" Boxed,**
1974. Store item by IPL. 9-1/4x13-1/2" box holds puzzle 15x21" assembled. - **$30 $55 $100**

MNS-23

MNS-24

❑ **MNS-23. "King Kong Colorforms Panorama Playset,"**
1976. Store item. - **$25 $55 $110**

❑ **MNS-24. Large Godzilla Figure,**
1977. 19" tall plastic figure by Mattel. Features spring-loaded fist that flies off. - **$40 $85 $170**

MNS-25

❑ **MNS-25. Vampirella Statue,**
1993. Graphitti Designs. Limited edition of 350. Boxed - **$725**

MNS-26

❑ **MNS-26. Mecha-Ghidora Figure,**
1994. From Godzilla series. In box - **$28**

MNS-27

❑ **MNS-27. Hot Wheels "Rodzilla",**
1999. Collectors' edition. - **$10**

MNS-28

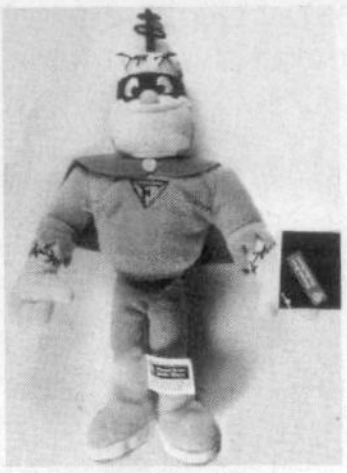

MNS-29

❑ **MNS-28. Comic Book Fan Club Member's Cello. Button,**
1999. Harris Publications. 1-3/4" full color. - **$4 $6 $22**

❑ **MNS-29. Frankenstein Jr. Bean Bag,**
1999. Figure with tag. - **$15**

MNS-30

MNS-31

❑ **MNS-30. Comic Book Fan Club Member's Cello. Button,**
1990s. Harris Publications. 1" red, fleshtone, black and white. - **$4 $6 $22**

❑ **MNS-31. Comic Book Fan Club Member's Card,**
1990s. Harris Publications. Done in black and white. - **$4 $6 $22**

MNS-32

❑ **MNS-32. "Godzilla" Statue,**
2001. 12" tall polyester resin statue. Fully painted with deluxe base. Limited edition of 1,000. Sculpted by Yukifusa Shibata. - **$150**

Moon Mullins

Created by Frank Willard (1893-1958) the Moon Mullins comic strip first appeared June 19, 1923. The cast included kid brother Kayo, Mamie the cook and her lazy husband Willie. Moon moved into Emmy Schmatz's boarding house in 1924. She married Lord Plushbottom in 1933 and became Lady Plushbottom. A topper strip, *Kitty Higgins*, appeared with the Sunday page for many years.

Ferd Johnson (1905-1996) began as Willard's art assistant in 1924 and was soon drawing the entire strip for golfing fan Willard. He officially took the strip over in 1958 and continued the strip until its demise in 1991.

Dell published four different Four Color Comics between 1941 and 1945 and Michel Publishing/St. John issued eight *Moon Mullins* comic books between 1947 and 1949.

MML-1

❑ **MML-1. Moon Mullins Daily Comic Strip Original Art With Moon Boxing Champion Gene Tunney,**
1925. 8.75x22.5" mat has 5-7/8x19-7/8" opening revealing four-panel black and white India ink art. Signed in ink by artist-creator Willard at bottom of last panel. Same Or Similar - **$250 $500 $1000**

MML-2

❑ **MML-2. "Moon Mullins" Sunday Page Large Original Art With Three Main Characters,**
1930. 17-7/8x23.5" art board has 16.5x22" black and white India ink area with logo and 11 panels. Art is signed at bottom of last panel by creator Willard in ink. - **$200 $400 $800**

MML-3

❑ MML-3. "Moon Mullins Big Book" Platinum Age Comic Book,
1930. Cupples & Leon. 10x10.25" with 140 pages. Book - **$100 $250 $500**
Dust Jacket - **$85 $325 $550**

MML-4

❑ MML-4. "Kayo And Moon Mullins-'Way Down South" Booklet,
1934. Lemix & Corlix Desserts. Book #7 from Whitman series. - **$29 $87 $200**

MML-5

❑ MML-5. "Funny Pop" Mechanical Game with Orphan Annie/Dick Tracy/ Moon Mullins And Kayo,
1936. Allied Manufacturing Company Chicago. 12x14.5x2" deep box lid fits over mechanical cardboard game. Includes pop-up figures of Dick Tracy, Smitty, Herby, Kayo, Orphan Annie and four red painted wooden balls. - **$150 $300 $500**

MML-6

❑ MML-6. Moon Mullins Dummy Punchout 11x20",
1938. Pure Oil premium. - **$175 $325 $650**

MML-7

❑ MML-7. "Kayo And Moon Mullins And The One Man Gang" Better Little Book,
1939. Whitman #1415. - **$12 $36 $78**

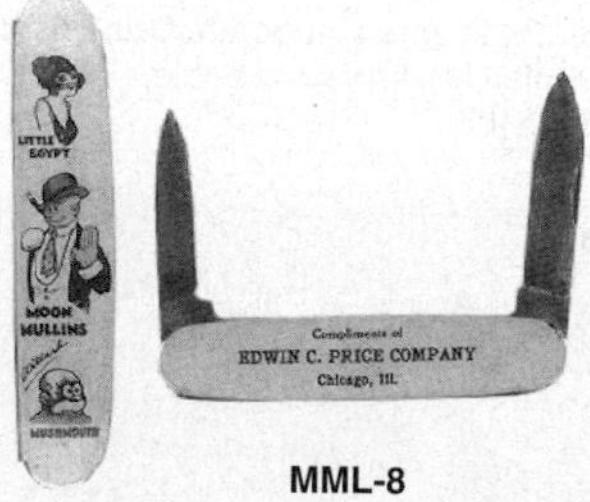

MML-8

❑ MML-8. "Moon Mullins" Pocketknife,
1930s. Imprinted for local sponsor. Cello. grip also pictures comic strip sidebar characters Little Egypt and Mushmouth. - **$75 $150 $325**

MML-9

❑ MML-9. "Moon Mullins" Original Art Premium Prototype Display,
1930s. Designed for Ivory Soap. 12-1/8x21-1/2". Gordon Gold Archives. Unique. - **$600**

MML-10

❑ MML-10. Moon Mullins And Kayo Pair Of Jointed Wood Dolls,
1930s. Store item by Jaymar. 5-1/2" and 4" tall respectively. Moon - **$45 $75 $150**
Kayo - **$60 $110 $185**

MML-11

(FRONT) (BACK)
MML-12

❑ MML-11. Moon Mullins And Kayo Glazed Ceramic Figural Perfume Bottles ,
1930s. Store item, unmarked but likely German-made. Moon is 8-1/4" tall with cigar in mouth and Kayo is 5-3/8" tall. Each - **$75 $150 $265**

❑ MML-12. Cloth Doll,
1930s. Starched fabric from set believed issued by unknown cereal sponsor. Artist's facsimile signature on reverse. Six known.
Kayo, Moon Mullins, Herbie, Smitty Each - **$40 $80 $150**
Little Orphan Annie - **$75 $150 $250**
Sandy - **$50 $85 $175**

MML-13 MML-14 MML-15

❑ **MML-13. Club Member Cello. Button,**
1930s. Kayo Chocolate. - **$12 $25 $50**

❑ **MML-14. "Kayo Comics Club" Litho. Button,**
1930s. San Francisco Chronicle newspaper. - **$35 $65 $125**

❑ **MML-15. "Park Theater Kayo Club" Cello. Button,**
1930s. - **$35 $65 $125**

MML-16

❑ **MML-16. "Kayo/The Real Chocolate Malted Drink" Jigsaw Puzzle,**
1930s. - **$50 $100 $175**

MML-17

❑ **MML-17. Moon Mullins & Kayo Tin Wind-Up Handcar,**
1930s. Boxed. Toy - **$175 $400 $750**
Box - **$100 $250 $500**
Complete - **$275 $650 $1250**

(BOTTOM VIEW SHOWING DICE)

MML-18

❑ **MML-18. Statue with Dice Salesman's Premium,**
1930s. - **$200 $400 $900**

MML-19

❑ **MML-19. Moon Mullins "Order Of The Fish" Litho. Button,**
1930s. No sponsor but probably a newspaper issue. - **$12 $25 $50**

MML-20 MML-21

❑ **MML-20. "Drink Kayo Chocolate" Transfer Picture,**
1940s. Kayo Chocolate Drink. Image is reversed in unused condition. - **$25 $45 $90**

❑ **MML-21. Promo Chocolate Drink Sign,**
1940s. Holed for display on bottle. - **$40 $80 $175**

MML-22

❑ **MML-22. "Kayo" Soft Drink Embossed Tin Sign,**
1940s. Sign is 14x27". Text at bottom right edge reads "Donaldson Art Sign Co Cov., KY." Six holes at margins as made. - **$115 $225 $350**

MML-24

MML-23

❑ **MML-23. Decal - Transfer Picture,**
1940s. Promotes chocolate drink. - **$20 $40 $80**

❑ **MML-24. Yellow Mug,**
1940s. Mug pictures Kayo and promotes Kayo Hot Chocolate. - **$25 $50 $100**

Movie Misc.

The first known moving pictures on a public screen were shown at Koster and Bial's Music Hall in New York City April 23, 1896. The program included films of two blonde girls performing an umbrella dance, a comic boxing exhibition and a view of surf breaking on a beach. Movies remained only a novelty until shortly after the turn of the century. 1903 released two pioneer efforts, *The Passion Play* and *The Great Train Robbery* and movies as mass entertainment were born.

The 1920s added dimensions of sound plus color experimentation; full-length features were soon followed by the popular episode serial or "chapter play" that remained popular to the mid-1950s. Premiums followed individual stars of universal acclaim such as Charlie Chaplin, Our Gang and Shirley Temple.

Movies also produced souvenirs of non-premium original purpose, e.g., heralds and programs, lobby cards, posters and the like that since have matured to status paralleling premiums. Some classic films produced a greater selection of premiums in addition to the standard theater fare. These included *Gone With The Wind*, Disney creations from the early 1930s Mickey Mouse to the 1990s *Dick Tracy* version, other animated cartoons and the most popular of the adventure hero serials.

Movie premiums after the advent of television were very limited for a time but recent years have seen frequent tie-ins between movies aimed at family audiences and fast food restaurants.

MOV-1

❑ MOV-1. "Miss Florence Lawrence/Van's Bio." Button,
c. 1909. 1" black and white cello of actress originally known as the 'Biograph Girl' noted as the first starlet to be publicly known by her given name. She appeared in D. W. Griffith's first films at Biograph. - **$65 $120 $185**

MOV-2

❑ MOV-2. Movie Serial Early Give-Away,
1914. Key is 2-1/8" long die-cut brass issued for serial "The Master Key." - **$25 $45 $85**

MOV-3 MOV-4

❑ MOV-3. Movie Serial Promotional Button,
1916. Universal. 7/8" naming stars Grace Cunard and Francis Ford. - **$12 $22 $40**

❑ MOV-4. "Detective/The Purple Mask" Diecut Tin Star Badge Premium,
1916. Universal. 2" tall, the earliest non-button movie serial giveaway designed to be worn that we have seen. - **$35 $65 $135**

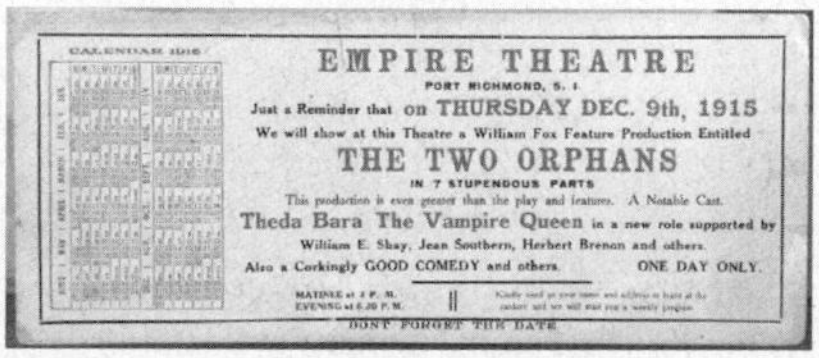

MOV-5

❑ MOV-5. Calendar Blotter,
1916. Featuring silent film star Theda Bara, "The Vampire Queen." Rare. - **$75 $150 $275**

MOV-6 MOV-7

❑ MOV-6. "Civilization" Press Book,
1916. Rare. 24 pages plus front and back covers. Includes 12 photo pages. Covers are color, insides are black & white. - **$100 $225 $450**

❑ MOV-7. "Oh Helen!" Song Sheet,
1918. Song is dedicated to Roscoe "Fatty" Arbuckle. - **$20 $40 $65**

(COVER)

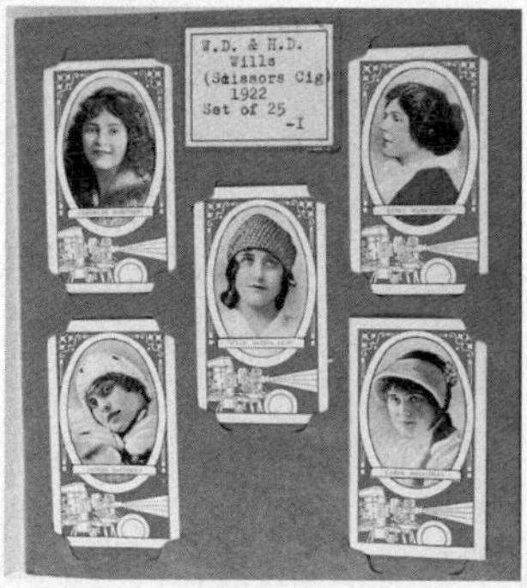

MOV-8

❑ MOV-8. Silent Film Picture Card Album
1922. Scissors Cigarettes premium. Shows notable stars like Ethel Barrymore, Pearl White, Mary Minter, Lucille Taft and 21 others.
Each Card - **$7**
Album - **$20 $30 $70**

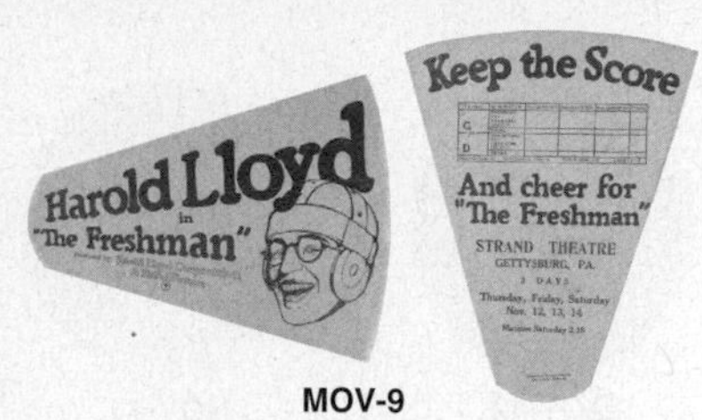

MOV-9

❑ MOV-9. Harold Lloyd In "The Freshman" Megaphone Promotional Theatre Handout,
1925. Handout is 9x11.75" cardboard megaphone printed to promote the Harold Lloyd film. Lloyd is pictured on front side of megaphone wearing football helmet. Printed for the Strand Theatre in Gettysburg, Pennsylvania by the Advertising Novelty Mfg. Co. - **$45 $85 $135**

MOV-10

❑ MOV-10. "Wings" Hardcover Book,
1927. Feature story was based on the Paramount Pictures film "Wings." Starring Gary Cooper and Clara Bow, the film won the first Academy Award for Best Picture.
Book - **$50 $85 $175**
With Dust Jacket - **$75 $135 $250**

MOV-11

❑ MOV-11. "The Flying Fool" Music Book,
1929. Book has 19 instrument song sheets with a wraparound cover (38 printed pages total.) Movie stars William Boyd. - **$50 $125 $250**

MOV-12

MOV-13

❑ MOV-12. "The Ace of Scotland Yard" Club Button,
1929. Billed as the 1st talking serial (10 chapters.) From Universal Pictures, starring Crawford Kent and Florence Allen. Rare. **- $50 $75 $150**

❑ MOV-13. "The Ace" Historic Serial Cello Button,
1929. For movie publicized by Universal Studios as their first "Talking Serial" including sound effects, dialogue, synchronized music score. Also imprinted for local movie house, probably San Francisco. - **$50 $75 $150**

MOV-14

❑ MOV-14. Cardboard Fan,
1920s. Promotes silent film stars with Rodolph Valentino pictured in center. Various products are advertised on the back. **- $75 $200 $300**

MOV-15

❑ MOV-15. Roscoe "Fatty" Arbuckle Cello. Button,
1920s. Button is 1.25". Issued to promote men's suits. Also issued showing Charles Chaplin, Douglas Fairbanks and William S. Hart. **- $20 $35 $70**

MOV-16

❑ MOV-16. Harold Lloyd Novelties,
1920s. 2.25" diameter dexterity puzzle with silver luster tin rim holding glass cover over portrait of Lloyd. Manufactured in Spain. Object of game was to get black tin eyeglasses with yellow celluloid lenses to properly attach to Lloyd's face. Second item is Harold Lloyd bisque smoking novelty about 3" tall. Bisque has open area on right shoulder to rest cigarette and back has small 1/16" holes to allow smoke to escape creating strange visual effect. Made in Germany.
Dexterity **- $25 $50 $80**
Bisque **- $65 $135 $225**

MOV-17

❑ MOV-17. Harold Lloyd German Wind-Up Carnival Bumper Car,
1920s. Tin litho toy measures 3.5x4x5.25" tall with built-in key. Marked "Made In Germany."
- $2250 $4500 $7000

MOV-18

❑ MOV-18. Harold Lloyd Mechanical Bank,
1920s. Tin litho toy is 2x3x5.25" tall. Unmarked but German made. To operate the bank, a lever on the left top side is depressed. This causes his eyes to roll and mouth opens and he sticks out his tongue. A coin is placed on the tongue and on releasing the lever all parts return automatically to position as coin is stored inside the bank. **- $1650 $3750 $6250**

MOV-19

❑ MOV-19. Movie Star Album,
1920s. Cover has 54 pictures of silent film stars arranged like a fan. Book holds cards of stars like Theda Bara (the first major woman sex symbol in "The Vamp"), Ruth Roland, Douglas Fairbanks, Roscoe "Fatty" Arbuckle and others.
Album **- $45 $85 $165**
Theda Bara "The Vamp" card **- $25 $50 $85**
Arbuckle or Fairbanks cards **- $15 $35 $60**
Other cards **- $3 $5 $10**

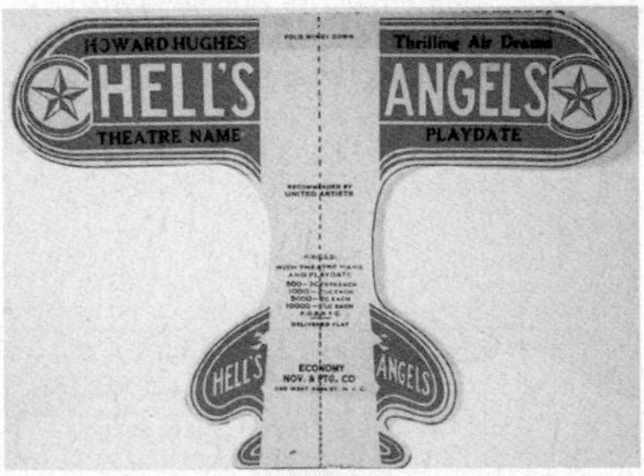

MOV-20

❑ MOV-20. "Hell's Angels" Movie Promo,
1930. Very rare promo airplane premium which was passed out at the movie. "Hell's Angels," produced by Howard Hughes for United Artists, was the breakthrough movie for platinum-tressed star Jean Harlow -
$200 $375 $750

MOV-21

❑ MOV-21. The Indians Are Coming! Serial Promotional Headdress,
1930. Headdress is 30" wide by 16" tall for the first all-talking Universal serial which starred Col. Tim McCoy. - **$75 $150 $250**

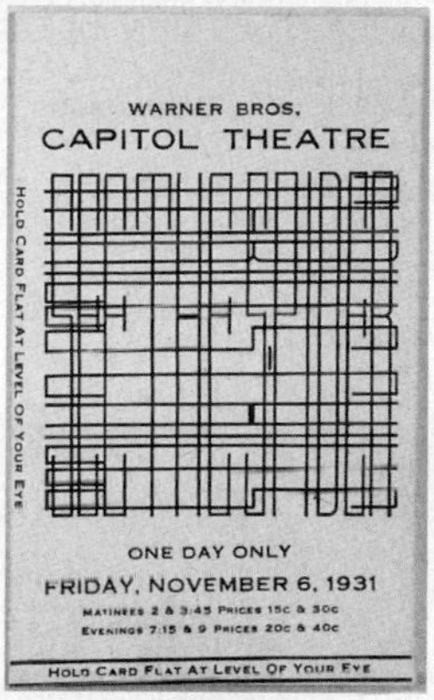

MOV-22

❑ MOV-22. Promo Card for "The Spider",
1931. Warner Brothers Theater premium for a Fox feature starring Edmund Lowe. When the card is held flat at eye-level, the design reads "See the Spider." How about those prices to get in the movies: Evenings 20¢ & 40¢. - **$40 $85 $160**

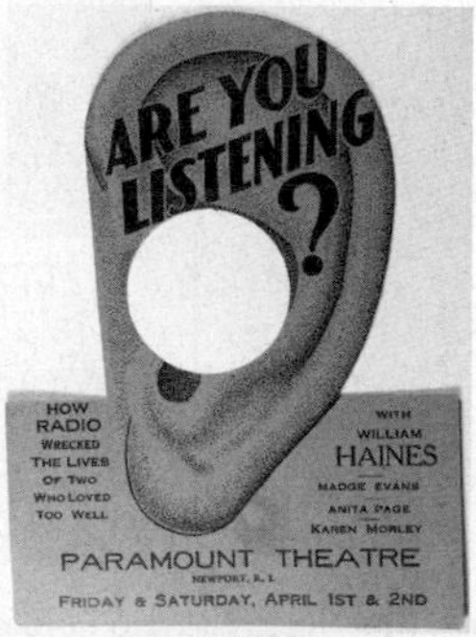

MOV-23

❑ MOV-23. "Are You Listening?" Promo,
1932. Premium for MGM film starring William Haines. - **$35 $65 $135**

MOV-24

MOV-25

❑ MOV-24. "Movie Crazy" Mechanical Sign,
1932. Premium for Paramount film starring Harold Lloyd. When Lloyd's hand is moved to the right, the title of the film slowly disappears. Picture claims to be for kids as old as 60. - **$85 $225 $350**

❑ MOV-25. "Winner Take All" Promo,
1932. Very Rare. Great Warner Brothers movie starring James Cagney. Item pictured was a boxing glove shaped premium. - **$100 $250 $450**

MOV-26

MOV-27

❑ MOV-26. "'Freaks' Metro-Goldwyn-Mayer's Amazing Picture" Cello. Button,
1932. Scarce. Movie was quickly withdrawn from distribution. - **$300 $800 $1600**

❑ MOV-27. "Tom Tyler/Clancy Of The Mounted" Movie Club Cello. Button,
1933. Universal Pictures. For 12-chapter serial. - **$75 $200 $335**

MOV-28

MOV-29

❑ MOV-28. "Silver Dollar" Movie Premium,
1933. Rare. Classic premium from 1st National Pictures. Ironically the silver dollar depicted is dated 1933, although there were no real silver dollars minted in 1933. - **$85 $175 $350**

❑ MOV-29. "Meet The Baron" Movie Membership Certificate,
1933. Rare. "Meet The Baron" starred Jimmy Durante. Certificate bestowed membership in the Baron Munchausen Club. - **$80 $150 $200**

MOV-30

❑ MOV-30. "Captured" Premium Puzzle,
1933. Warner Bros.premium puzzle for Douglas Fairbanks, Jr. classic film. - **$40 $80 $125**

MOV-31

❑ MOV-31. "Button Gum" Wrapper,
c. 1933. Store item, no company specified on wrapper. Buttons in these sets are often credited to Cracker Jack, who possibly used them, but it seems this product is the original source. Wrapper states "Start A Collection Of 500 Buttons." Set titles are: Presidents, Ball Players, Movie Stars, Generals, Soldiers, Animals, Indians, Scouts, Birds, World's Fair. We've seen examples from all sets except World's Fair. Wrapper - **$65 $185 $350**

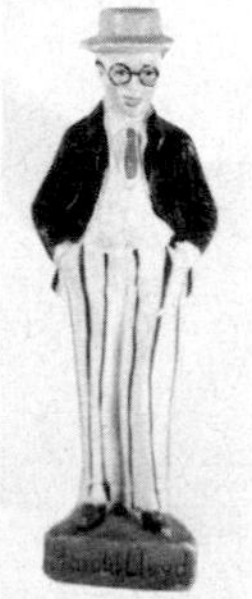

MOV-32

❑ MOV-32. "Harold Lloyd" Painted Bisque German Figurine,
c. 1933. 5" tall marked by name on base front plus back marking for Germany plus number 3511. See examples from same series for Charlie Chaplin and Tom Mix. - **$100 $200 $400**

(COVER) (INSIDE)

MOV-33

❑ **MOV-33. "20 Million Sweethearts" Movie Premium,**
1934. Movie starred Dick Powell and Ginger Rogers. - **$30 $60 $115**

MOV-34

❑ **MOV-34. Claudette Colbert Old Gold Cigarette Store Sign,**
1934. Old Gold Cigarettes. 36.5x41.5" store sign advertisign Old Gold Cigarettes "America's Smoothest Cigarette." Top fatures a testimonial from her "The Mildness And Throat-Ease Of Old Gold Won Me" with her name below. Ad tag line and pack of cigarettes runs at bottom of sign. - **$350 $675 $1200**

MOV-35

❑ **MOV-35. "Viva Villa" Movie Promo,**
1934. Wallace Beery art on cut out hat for MGM movie promo. 10 3/4" x 17". Rare. - **$100 $225 $375**

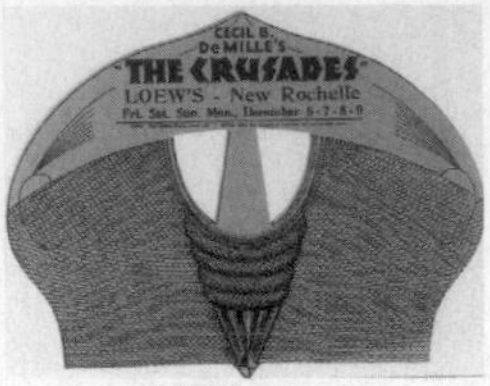

MOV-36

MOV-37

❑ **MOV-36. "The Crusades" Movie Mask,**
1935. Rare premium. 10x13". - **$50 $150 $300**

❑ **MOV-37. "Mutiny on the Bounty" Promo,**
1935. For MGM movie that won the Academy Award for best picture. This premium was used to hang on the doors of the parked cars of the-ater patrons. Very rare. - **$125 $250 $500**

MOV-38

❑ **MOV-38. Hollywood Snapshots,**
1935. Booklet with actual photos of stars inside. Photos taken by an editor of the L.A. Evening Herald. - **$40 $90 $160**

MOV-39

❑ **MOV-39. Frankie Darro Stamp Album,**
1935. Tootsie Roll. Movie Club premium. Holds 24 stamps. - **$40 $90 $185**

MOV-40

❑ **MOV-40. Frankie Darro Stamps,**
1935. Large premium stamp given at each movie. Each - **$10 $20 $40**

MOV-41

MOV-42

MOV-43

❑ **MOV-41. "Gangster's Boy" BLB #1402,**
1936. Starring Jackie Cooper. - **$14 $42 $95**

❑ **MOV-42. "Bullets or Ballots" Promo,**
1936. Warner Bros. premium for Edward G. Robinson movie. Humphrey Bogart receives billing in the small print at bottom. Premium is bullet-shaped of course. - **$85 $185 $350**

❑ **MOV-43. "Captains Courageous" Bookmarker,**
1937. Die-cut premium for the MGM movie star-ring Spencer Tracy. He won a best actor Oscar for his role. - **$75 $175 $325**

MOV-44

❑ **MOV-44. "Boy of the Streets" Blotter,**
1937. Scarce. Jackie Cooper photo on premium '37 calendar, ruler and blotter. - **$30 $60 $140**

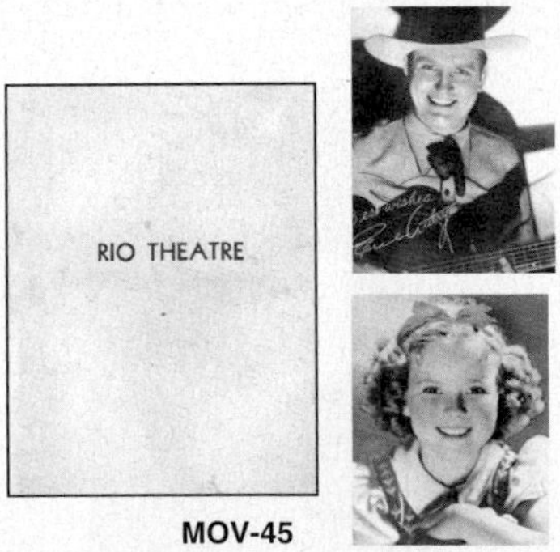

MOV-45

❑ **MOV-45. Rio Theatre Photo Folder,**
1938. Theatre premium. 16 photos (folder & two photos shown). Photos - **$8 $15 $20**
Folder - **$10 $20 $40**

MOV-46

MOV-47

❑ **MOV-46. Judy Garland Photo Promo,**
1938. 5"x7" photo for "Love Finds Andy Hardy". - **$10 $20 $40**

❑ **MOV-47. Wallace Beery Photo Promo,**
1938. 5"x7" photo for "Stablemates". - **$10 $20 $35**

MOV-48

❑ **MOV-48. Wallace Beery Photo,**
1930s. Autographed. - **$250**

MOV-49

❑ **MOV-49. Pencil Drawing of Wallace Beery For Animated Film,**
1938. Beery is "Little Boy Blue" for the film "Mother Goose Goes to Hollywood." - **$375**

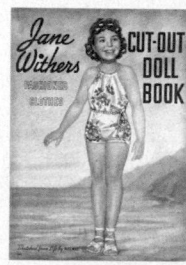

MOV-50

❑ **MOV-50. Jane Withers Cut-Out Doll Book,**
1938. 14-1/4" x 10-1/2". - **$85 $175 $325**

MOV-51

❑ **MOV-51. "Motion Picture Funnies Weekly" Comic Book,**
1939. Rare. Origin & 1st printed appearance of The Sub-Mariner by Bill Everett. Reprinted in Marvel Comics #1.
Good - **$4400**
Fine - **$11,000**
Very Fine/Near Mint - **$29,000**

MOV-52

MOV-53

❑ **MOV-52. Mickey Rooney and Judy Garland Fan Club Button,**
1939. Rare. Button is 1.25", black print on bright yellow. - **$65 $150 $265**

❑ **MOV-53. "The Black Falcon Of The Flying G-Men" Game,**
1939. Store item by Ruckelshaus Game Corp. Based on Columbia Pictures movie serial. - **$250 $500 $1000**

MOV-54

MOV-55

❑ **MOV-54. "Blackmail" Movie Promo,**
1939. Glasses-shaped promo for MGM movie starring Edward G. Robinson. - **$75 $165 $285**

❑ **MOV-55. "Daredevils of the Red Circle" Promo Badge,**
1939. Silver cardboard movie premium badge outlined in red. Given to kids who attended the Republic Serial "Daredevils of the Red Circle" starring Herman Brix. Rare. - **$75 $165 $285**

MOV-56

❑ **MOV-56. "John Mack Brown's Oregon Trail Club" Button,**
1939. Premium for Universal serial release. - **$60 $150 $250**

MOV-57

❑ **MOV-57. Movie Stars Button Set,**
1930s. Used as Cracker Jack prizes and distributed with gum in a wrapper titled "Button Gum." Set of 25 litho 13/16" buttons, printed largely in soluable blue ink on white picturing and naming actor or actress.
Near Mint Set - **$750**
Each - **$8 $15 $30**

MOV-58

MOV-59

❑ **MOV-58. Rudy Vallee Club Button,**
1930s. 7/8" black/white cello for "Va-Ka-Shun Klub" plus imprint for Brooklyn Paramount Theater. - **$20 $40 $80**

❑ **MOV-59. Campaign Movie Button,**
1930s. For campaign to change Sunday Blue laws. Scarce.
7/8" size - **$15 $30 $50**
3-1/2" size - **$30 $60 $100**

MOV-60

❑ **MOV-60. Junior Cagney Club Litho. Buttons,**
1930s. Theater patrons collected set of 11, each with single letter of James Cagney name, to gain free admission. Each - **$10 $20 $40**

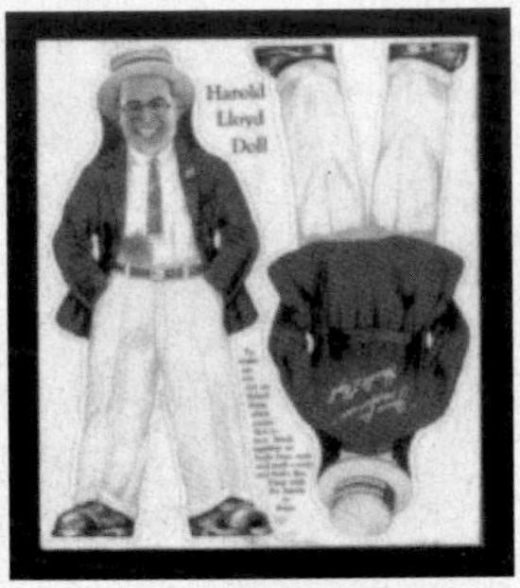

MOV-61

❑ **MOV-61. "Harold Lloyd Doll" Fabric Pattern,**
1930s. Fabric to form 12-1/2" tall doll. Uncut - **$50 $110 $215**

MOV-62

❑ **MOV-62. Park Drive Album Series 1,**
1930s. Cigarette premium from England. Album for 48 cards. U.S. stars.
Album Only - **$12 $25 $40**

MOV-63

❑ **MOV-63. Park Drive Album Cards For Series 1 & 2 - Spencer,**
1930s. Cigarette premium from England. 96 total cards. Each Card - **$2 $4 $7**

MOV-64

❑ **MOV-64. Park Drive Album Series 2,**
1930s. Cigarette premium from England. Album for 48 cards. Each card - **$2 $4 $7**

MOV-65

MOV-66

❑ **MOV-65. Churchman's Card Album,**
1930s. Cigarette premium from England. Holds 50 cards. Album Only - **$12 $25 $40**

❑ **MOV-66. Churchman's Card Album - The Cards,**
1930s. Famous U.S. movie stars on cards.
Each Card - **$2 $4 $7**

MOV-67

❑ **MOV-67. Film Star Album,**
1930s. Cigarette premium from England. Holds cards for 53 stars from U.S. movies.
Album Only - **$15 $30 $50**

MOV-68

❑ **MOV-68. Film Star Album Cards,**
1930s. Cigarette premium from England. 53 different colorful cards. 3rd series.
Each Card - **$2 $4 $7**

MOV-69 MOV-70

❑ **MOV-69. "The Terrytooners Music And Fun Club" Cello. Button,**
1930s. Pictures Farmer Alfalfa and Little Wilbur. - **$35 $70 $160**

❑ **MOV-70. "George O'Brien Outdoor Club" Cello. Button,**
1930s. - **$20 $45 $100**

MOV-71

MOV-72

❑ **MOV-71. Wallace Beery Movie Pinback,**
1930s. One in a series of different stars. - **$10 $25 $50**

❑ **MOV-72. Bobby Breen Pinback on Card**
1930s. Promotes movie contest.
Button - **$5 $15 $25**
Card - **$15 $30 $50**

MOV-73

❑ **MOV-73. Sabu Doll With "Thief Of Bagdad" Litho. Button,**
1940. Store item, maker unknown. Jointed composition doll 14" tall with fabric outfit and 1" black and white litho. button reading "Sabu Club/Sabu In 'The Thief Of Bagdad.'"
Doll - **$135 $275 $550**
Button - **$15 $30 $50**

MOV-74

❑ MOV-74. "Sonja Henie" Paper Doll Book,
1940. Book is 10.75x13" with eight single-sided pages, with one punch-out doll on front and two on back. Two dolls are designed with skates and several outfits are skating-themed. No. 3492 Merrill Publishing Co. - **$65 $125 $200**

MOV-75

MOV-76

❑ MOV-75. "Flight Command" Premium,
1940. Has small silver plane attached to promo card. Movie starred Robert Taylor. -
$75 $140 $250

❑ MOV-76. "Sky Raiders" Club Button,
1941. Promotes 12-chapter serial by Universal starring Donald Woods and Billy Halop. -
$30 $85 $175

MOV-77

MOV-78

❑ MOV-77. "Keep 'Em Flying" Button,
1941. 7/8" blue and white for their famous movie. - **$15 $30 $65**

❑ MOV-78. "The Bad Man" Promo,
1941. 7" movie premium of Wallace Beery starring in "The Bad Man." Rare. - **$40 $90 $190**

MOV-79

❑ MOV-79. Movie Star Premium Cards,
1941. From J.C. Penney department stores. Each - **$2 $5 $10**
Lucille Ball, Clark Gable, John Wayne, Roy Rogers and Gene Autry each - **$8 $15 $30**

MOV-80

❑ MOV-80. "Citizen Kane" Program,
1941. Souvenir of RKO Radio Pictures classic film directed by and starring Orson Welles. -
$70 $140 $260

MOV-81

❑ MOV-81. Citizen Kane "Souvenir Of Xanadu" Card Deck,
c. 1941. Playing cards with box art picturing seaside mansion Xanadu of William Randolph Hearst, the pattern for 1941 Orson Welles film "Citizen Kane." - **$115 $250 $450**

MOV-82

MOV-83

❑ MOV-82. "Perils Of Nyoka" 27x41" Movie Serial Poster,
1942. Republic Pictures. Poster is for Chapter 1. -
$225 $450 $900

❑ MOV-83. "Perils Of Nyoka" 27x41" Movie Serial Poster,
1942. Republic Pictures. Same art for Chapters 2-15. Each - **$125 $275 $450**

MOV-84

❑ MOV-84. "As Time Goes By" Song Sheet,
1943. Features song from "Casablanca," starring Humphrey Bogart and Ingrid Bergman. - **$20 $35 $75**

MOV-85

MOV-86

❑ MOV-85. Cardboard Stand-Up,
1943. Two piece 6x9" promo from "The Outlaw" starring Jane Russell. - **$100 $200 $400**

❑ MOV-86. "Secret Service In Darkest Africa" 27x41" Movie Serial Poster,
1943. Republic Pictures. - **$60 $125 $225**

MOV-87

❑ MOV-87. "International Reno Browne Fan Club" Newsletter And Membership Card,
c. 1946. Issued by Canadian headquarters.
Near Mint In Mailer - **$90**
Newsletter - **$10 $15 $35**
Card - **$10 $15 $35**

(ENLARGED VIEW OF HOPPY STAMP)

MOV-88

❑ MOV-88. Hollywood Star Stamps,
1947. Set Q - 12 stamps on uncut sheet in mailer. Eleven Stamps - **$10 $25 $40**
Hoppy Stamp - **$10 $20 $40**

MOV-89 MOV-90

❑ MOV-89. Hollywood Star Stamps,
1947. Set Y - 12 stamps on uncut sheet in mailer. - **$10 $25 $40**

❑ MOV-90. Hollywood Star Stamps,
1947. Set H - 12 stamps on uncut sheet in mailer. - **$10 $25 $40**

MOV-91

❑ MOV-91. Betty Grable Movie Promo,
1947. Chunky Candy Premium. Ten pages of highlights of stars. - **$40 $80 $150**

MOV-92

MOV-93

❑ MOV-92. "The Black Widow" 27x41" Movie Serial Poster,
1947. Republic Pictures. - **$150 $300 $600**

❑ MOV-93. "The Sea Hound Club" Movie Serial Card,
1947. For admission to 15-episode Columbia Pictures serial starring Buster Crabbe. - **$75 $175 $350**

MOV-94

❑ MOV-94. "King of the Rocket Men" Movie Serial 1 Sheet Poster,
1949. Republic Pictures. - **$550 $1100 $2500**

MOV-95

❑ **MOV-95. "Mighty Joe Young" Movie 3 Sheet Poster,**
1949. Promotes the classic RKO Pictures movie starring Terry Moore and Ben Johnson.
- $550 $1100 $2500

MOV-96

❑ **MOV-96. Martin & Lewis Fan Club Member Card And Cello. Button,**
1949. Card - **$15 $40 $90**
Button - **$15 $45 $80**

MOV-97

❑ **MOV-97. "The Adventures of Alan Ladd #1" Comic Book,**
1949. DC Comics. Shows highlights from his movie "Chicago Deadline." **- $81 $243 $1175**

MOV-98

MOV-99

❑ **MOV-98. Kirk Douglas Movie Photo,**
1940s. With frame. **- $15 $25 $50**

❑ **MOV-99. James Stewart Movie Photo,**
1940s. With frame. **- $15 $25 $50**

MOV-100

❑ **MOV-100. Susan Hayward Puzzle,**
1940s. Esquire Magazine premium includes puzzle and mailer. **- $25 $60 $135**

MOV-101

MOV-102

❑ **MOV-101. Claudette Colbert Photo,**
1940s. With original frame. **- $20 $40 $80**

❑ **MOV-102. "Reno Browne/Queen Of The Westerns" Cello. Button,**
1940s. **- $25 $50 $100**

MOV-103

❑ **MOV-103. Brass Luster Bracelet,**
1940s. Store item. Facsimile signatures in black of 13 stars including Bing Crosby, Nelson Eddie, Clark Gable, Tyrone Power and Spencer Tracy. **- $25 $50 $100**

MOV-104

MOV-105

❑ **MOV-104. Humphrey Bogart Then and Now Movie Card,**
1940s. Color tint. From set of stars by Exhibit Supply Co. for vending machines. **- $6 $12 $30**

❑ **MOV-105. George Raft Movie Arcade Card,**
1940s. **- $5 $10 $25**

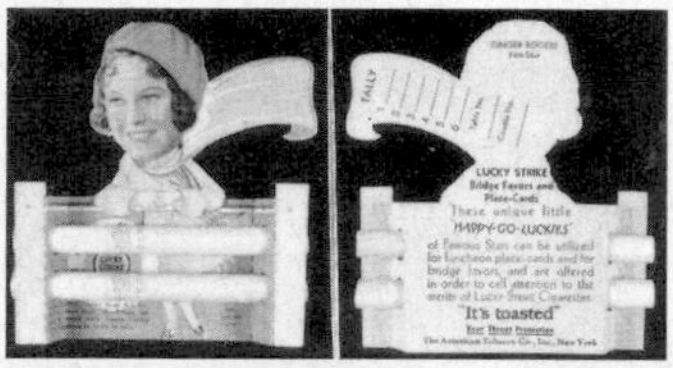

MOV-106

❑ **MOV-106. "Ginger Rogers" Cigarette Ad Paper Standup,**
1940s. Lucky Strike Cigarettes. Lunch place card holder also designed to hold two cigarettes, one of a series. **- $12 $25 $40**

MOV-107

❑ **MOV-107. "Little Women" Movie Premium Plastic Jewel Box with Mailer,**
1940s. Scarce. **- $40 $100 $175**

MOV-108

❑ **MOV-108. Elizabeth Taylor Lapel-Pin Perfume Atomizer,**
1950. Ralston. Near Mint Boxed **- $200**
Pin Only **- $20 $40 $80**

MOV-109

MOV-110

❑ **MOV-109. Esther Williams Coloring Book,**
1950. - **$20 $60 $175**

❑ **MOV-110. MGM Star Esther Williams Cut-Out Doll Book,**
1950. With "look thru" window. Has 2 dolls and 19 cut-out outfits. - **$75 $125 $225**

MOV-111

MOV-112

❑ **MOV-111. Betty Grable Coloring Book,**
1951. - **$20 $60 $175**

❑ **MOV-112. Betty Grable Paper Doll Book,**
1951. Paper dolls with outfits. - **$50 $110 $200**

MOV-113

❑ **MOV-113. "The Day The Earth Stood Still" 5' Standee,**
1951. Rare. - **$6000 $15,000 $22,500**

MOV-114

❑ **MOV-114. "Quo Vadis" Boxed Movie Figure Set,**
1951. Johillco. 9x11.5x2.5" deep box contains complete and unused set by John Hill Co., England. Ten piece metal figure set based on the 1951 film that starred Robert Taylor and Deborah Kerr. Set consists of six Roman gladiators, chariot with charioteer, lion and leopard. Boxed - **$325 $650 $1300**

MOV-115

❑ **MOV-115. Martin & Lewis 21x22" Cardboard Sign,**
1951. Chesterfield cigarettes. - **$100 $200 $450**

MOV-116

❑ **MOV-116. "Abbott & Costello Meet Frankenstein" Movie Showing Promo,**
1951. 4x6.5" diecut orange/black thin cardboard of Halloween cat although printed for Friday, July 13 midnight show documenting to 1951 although movie earlier release year was 1948. Local movie house offered "Every 13th Person Admitted Free." - **$55 $110 $175**

MOV-117

MOV-118

❑ **MOV-117. "Jungle Drums Of Africa" Republic Serial, 27x41",**
1952. Starred Clayton Moore. - **$40 $85 $160**

❑ **MOV-118. "Radar Men From The Moon" 27x41" Movie Serial Poster,**
1952. Republic Pictures. - **$175 $325 $675**
Three Sheet - **$600 $1200 $2250**

MOV-119

MOV-120

❑ **MOV-119. Ann Blyth Coloring Book,**
1952. Universal Studios Movie Star large squarebound coloring book - **$30 $60 $125**

❑ **MOV-120. Ann Blyth Paper Doll Book,**
1952. Paper dolls with outfits. - **$35 $70 $140**

MOV-121

MOV-122

❑ **MOV-121. Betty Grable Paper Doll Book,**
1953. Has "look thru" window. - **$50 $110 $235**

❑ **MOV-122. Esther Williams Cutouts and Coloring Book,**
1953. Large size book. - **$50 $100 $175**

MOV-123

❑ MOV-123. "The War of the Worlds" Poster,
1953. Original 1 sheet for the Paramount Pictures movie starring Gene Barry.
- **$825 $1650 $3250**

MOV-124

❑ MOV-124. "The War of the Worlds" Movie Premium from Spain,
1953. Has info on back with movie theater listings. Scarce. - **$85 $165 $300**

MOV-125

❑ MOV-125. "Buster Crabbe Western Club" Photo Card And Button,
1953. Black and white photo card with facsimile autograph plus litho. "Official Badge" pin-back button. Card - **$10 $20 $40**
Button - **$25 $75 $150**

MOV-126

MOV-127

❑ MOV-126. Janet Leigh Cutouts and Coloring Book,
1953. Large size book. - **$50 $100 $175**

❑ MOV-127. Jane Russell Paper Doll Book,
1955. Paper dolls with outfits. Photo cover. - **$60 $125 $250**

MOV-128

MOV-129

❑ MOV-128. Doris Day Doll and Her Wardrobe of Magic Stay-On Clothes,
1957. - **$50 $110 $225**

❑ MOV-129. Dean Martin and Jerry Lewis Trade Card,
1950s. Not common. - **$10 $20 $40**

MOV-130

MOV-131

❑ MOV-130. Martin & Lewis Ceramic Salt & Pepper Set,
1950s. Store item by Napco Ceramic Japan. - **$135 $250 $500**

❑ MOV-131. Jerry Lewis Watch,
1950s. Store item. - **$65 $150 $265**

MOV-132

❑ MOV-132. Sunbeam Bread Movie Star Loaf End Labels,
1950s. Each - **$10 $18 $40**

MOV-133

MOV-134

❑ MOV-133. Rock Hudson Fan Club Cello. Button,
1950s. Black and white real photo button without dot pattern, 1-1/4". - **$20 $35 $70**

❑ MOV-134. "Walkie-Talkie Set" Offer Folder,
1950s. Campbell's tomato products. Promotional folder for distributors or retailers featuring endorsements of Abbott & Costello, Howdy Doody TV shows. - **$20 $40 $60**

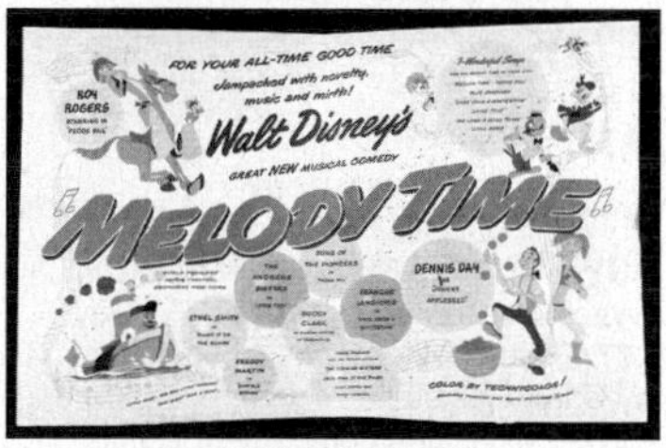

MOV-135

❑ MOV-135. "Melody Time" Promotional Brochure (Disney),
1950s. - **$35 $75 $150**

MOV-136

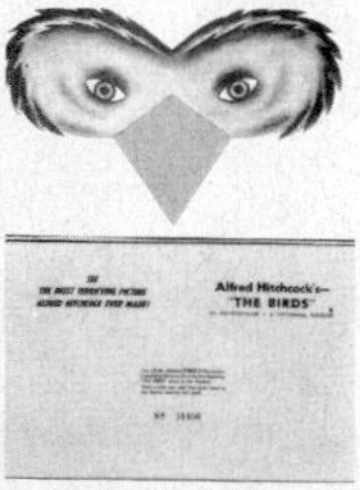

MOV-137

❑ **MOV-136. "Sal Mineo Fan Club" Button,**
1950s. - **$15 $30 $65**

❑ **MOV-137. "Alfred Hitchcock's The Birds" Movie Theater Mask,**
1963. - **$20 $40 $75**

MOV-138

MOV-139

❑ **MOV-138. "Tom Thumb" Standee,**
1960s. - **$45 $90 $175**

❑ **MOV-139. "Billy Jack For President" Pin,**
1976. 2 1/4" diameter. Black print on white. - **$15 $30 $60**

MOV-140

❑ **MOV-140. "The Stars Of Republic Pictures" 24x30" Autographed Poster,**
c. 1977. Paper poster from limited edition printing by Snuff Garrett,prominent record producer and owner of issuing company Nostalgia Merchant. Poster is signed by 28 prominent western film stars of Republic Studios. - **$150 $300 $800**

MOV-141

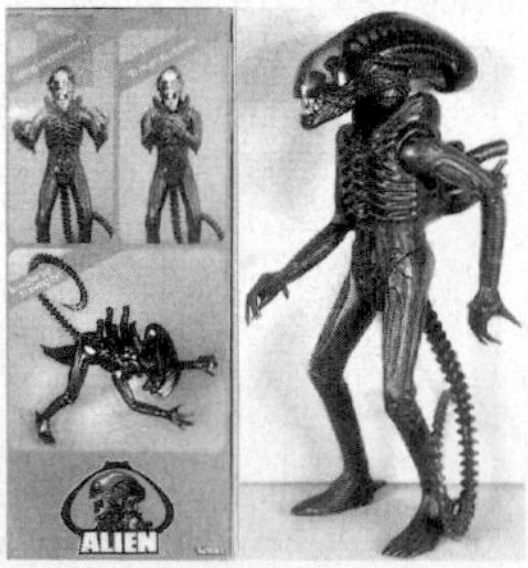

MOV-142

❑ **MOV-141. "Lou Costello" Plaster Statue,**
1979. 16 1/2" tall by Esco. - **$30 $60 $110**

❑ **MOV-142. "Alien" Poseable Plastic Figure,**
1979. Store item by Kenner. Came with poster in box. Often missing fangs from mouth.
Near Mint Boxed - **$700**
Figure Only - **$115 $225 $350**

MOV-143

❑ **MOV-143. "The Stars Of Columbia Pictures" 24x30" Autographed Poster,**
c. 1981. Paper poster from limited edition printing by Snuff Garrett, prominent record producer and owner of issuing company Nostalgia Merchant. Poster is signed by 18 prominent stars of western or dramatic movies by Columbia Studios. - **$100 $200 $450**

MOV-144

❑ **MOV-144. Robby the Robot Figure,**
1984. With instructions and box.
Complete - **$375**

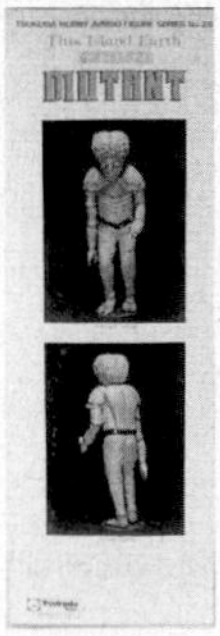

MOV-145

MOV-146

❑ **MOV-145. "This Island Earth" Metaluna Mutant Figure,**
1984. Tsukuda Model. Doll in box.
Complete - **$400**

❑ **MOV-146. "Gremlins" Stripe Figure,**
1984. 14" poseable figure in box. Boxed - **$120**

MOV-147

❑ **MOV-147. "Alien" Figure,**
1984. Tsukuda Model. Doll in box.
Complete - **$325**

MOV-148

MOV-149

❑ **MOV-148. Back To The Future Dream Truck,**
c. 1985. Toyota. 4-3/4" long black plastic truck with movie title on hood in red and yellow. Toy is battery operated and comes in mailing box with the name of the premium as part of the return address. Box - **$2 $5 $8**
Truck - **$8 $15 $22**

❑ **MOV-149. "Over the Top" Movie Figure,**
1986. 17" tall poseable figure of Lincoln Hawks, played by Sylvester Stallone.
Boxed - **$25 $55 $135**

MOV-150

MOV-151

❑ **MOV-150. "Ghostbusters Ectomobile" Die-Cast Vehicle,**
1988. Carded offer with two film rolls from Fuji Film. Carded - **$40 $75 $145**
Loose - **$10 $20 $30**

❑ **MOV-151. "Beetlejuice" Talking Figure,**
1989. Produced by Kenner. 12" talking figure. Head spins. Figure in original box - **$115**

MOV-152

❑ **MOV-152. "The Maltese Falcon" 50th Anniversary Figure,**
1991. Limited edition of 1250. The 4 1/4" figure celebrates the 50th anniversary of the 1941 film starring Humphrey Bogart. Very heavy. Copyright Warner Bros. - **$375**

MOV-153

MOV-154

❑ **MOV-153. "Rocketeer Thrill Club" Badge,**
1991. This hard-to-find badge was issued to promote the Disney film starring Billy Campbell and Jennifer Connelly. The Rocketeer character was created by Dave Stevens and first appeared in Starslayer #2 comic book in 1982. - **$25 $50 $75**

❑ **MOV-154. "Rocketeer" Watch,**
1991. Limited edition of 1,500. Giveaway to promote the movie. Shows the Rocketeer flying over Los Angeles. No box was made. - **$175**

MOV-155

❑ **MOV-155. "Gort" Figure,**
1992. Limited edition boxed figure from the movie "The Day The Earth Stood Still." This was sculptor Randy Bowen's 3rd figure. Some assembly required. Two sets of arms were included. Box is scarce. Box - **$110**
Figure with extra set of arms - **$300**

MOV-156

MOV-157

❑ **MOV-156. "Jurassic Park" Lunch Box,**
1993. Includes a thermos. - **$25 $50 $80**

❑ **MOV-157. "Back To The Future/Hill Valley High" Class Ring,**
1994. Universal Studios. Six rings in set with red, green or blue birthstones and done in gold or silver finishes. Each Near Mint - **$28**

MOV-158

MOV-159

❑ **MOV-158. "Waterworld" Watch,**
1995. Universal Studios premium tie-in for the video release. Nice wooden display box with map insert.
Boxed - **$50 $75 $150**

❑ **MOV-159. "Independence Day" Patch,**
1996. Premium notes "Restricted Access" to "Area 51." - **$160**

MOV-160

MOV-161

❑ **MOV-160. "Mars Attacks" Martian Supreme Commander Figure,**
1996. 11 3/4" tall figure talks and lights up. In display box. - **$5 $10 $33**

❑ **MOV-161. "Mars Attacks" Supreme Martian Ambassador Figure,**
1996. Figure talks. - **$5 $10 $33**

MOV-162

MOV-163

❑ **MOV-162. "Mars Attacks" Martian Brain Disintegrator Gun,**
1996. In green display box. - **$10 $20 $65**

❑ **MOV-163. "Mars Attacks" Martian Brain Disintegrator Gun,**
1996. In blue display box. - **$12 $25 $70**

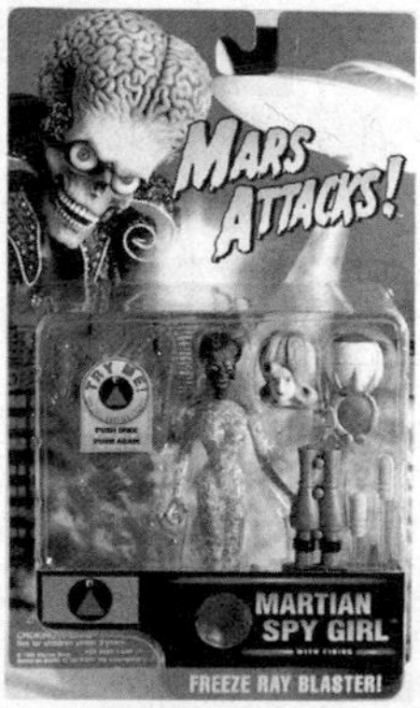

MOV-164

MOV-164. "Mars Attacks" Martian Spy Girl Figure,
1996. Two versions exist.
❑ Green gun version laughs and says "Mars will rule." - **$30 $50 $85**
❑ Red gun version is scarcer. It laughs and says "Trust me." - **$35 $65 $125**

(FRONT OF BOX)

(BACK OF BOX)

(3 DOLLS SHOWN INSIDE BOX)

MOV-165

❑ **MOV-165. "James and the Giant Peach" Doll Set in Box,**
1996. Three dolls in the set. - **$70**

MOV-166

MOV-167

❑ **MOV-166. "Jack Frost" Snowman Bean Bag,**
1999. Distributed exclusively at Warner Bros stores. Promotes the movie which starred Michael Keaton. - **$25**

❑ **MOV-167. "Quack Nicholson" Bean Bag,**
1998. Infamous Meanies Series with tag. - **$8**

MOV-168

MOV-169

MOV-170

MOV-171

❑ **MOV-168. "Antz" Z Action Figure on Card,**
1999. From the computer animated film. Character was voiced by Woody Allen. - **$15**

❑ **MOV-169. "Antz" Princess Bala Action Figure on Card,**
1999. Bala was voiced by Sharon Stone. - **$12**

❑ **MOV-170. "Antz" Colonel Cutter Action Figure on Card,**
1999. Reconnaissance pilot. Character was voiced by Christopher Walken. - **$12**

❑ **MOV-171. "Antz" General Mandible Action Figure on Card,**
1999. Military leader of the colony. Character was voiced by Gene Hackman. - **$12**

MOV-172

MOV-173

❑ **MOV-172. "Austin Powers" Movie Car,**
1999. Replica of the "Shaguar." Johnny Lightning series on card. - **$22**

❑ **MOV-173. "The King and I" Promo Whistle**
1999. Premium whistle offered with video tape of animated movie. - **$5**

MOV-174

MOV-175

❑ **MOV-174. "The Iron Giant" Bean Bag,**
1999. Warner Bros. store exclusive. - **$18**

❑ **MOV-175. "The Iron Giant" 11" Figure,**
1999. With small Hogarth figure. - **$48**

MOV-176

❑ **MOV-176. "The Iron Giant" 20" Figure,**
1999. With small Hogarth figure. Unlike the 11" version, this has a remote control. Highly sought after and hard to find. Boxed - **$90**

MOV-177

MOV-178

❑ **MOV-177. "Nightmare Before Christmas" "Zero the Dog" Bean Bag,**
1999. With tag. First bean bag offered from the set. Hardest to find of the group. Sold at Disney Parks and Stores. - **$28**

❑ **MOV-178. "Nightmare Before Christmas" "Jack Skellington" Bean Bag,**
1999. With tag. - **$12**

MOV-179

MOV-180

❑ **MOV-179. "Nightmare Before Christmas" 11" "Sally" Bean Bag,**
1999. With tag. - **$28**

❑ **MOV-180. "Nightmare Before Christmas" "Mayor" Bean Bag,**
1999. With tag. - **$22**

MOV-181

MOV-182

❑ **MOV-181. "Nightmare Before Christmas" "Oogie Boogie" Bean Bag,**
1999. With tag. - **$18**

❑ **MOV-182. "Nightmare Before Christmas" "Santa" Bean Bag,**
1999. With tag. - **$18**

MOV-183

MOV-184

MOV-185

❑ MOV-183. "Nightmare Before Christmas" 8" "Lock" Bean Bag,
1999. With tag. Voiced in movie by Paul Reubens. - **$18**

❑ MOV-184. "Nightmare Before Christmas" 8" "Shock" Bean Bag,
1999. With tag. - **$18**

❑ MOV-185. "Nightmare Before Christmas" 8" "Barrel" Bean Bag,
1999. With tag. - **$22**

MOV-186

❑ MOV-186. "The Rocketeer" Resin Statue,
1999. Sculpted by Kent Melton. 1,000 produced. There are also 50 bronze editions created a few years earlier. The resin version comes with a colorful box, but the bronze version does not.
Resin - **$180**
Bronze - **$2600**

MOV-187

MOV-188

❑ MOV-187. "Puppet Master" Totem Figure,
1999. Previews exclusive. Has silver helmet mask and black body with cape. Stand is green with blue diamond on top. Scarcer of 2. - **$22**

❑ MOV-188. "Puppet Master" Totem Figure,
1999. Previews exclusive. Has gold helmet mask and brown body; no cape. Stand is red with orange diamond on top. - **$18**

MOV-189

MOV-190

❑ MOV-189. "Puppet Master" Jester Figure,
1999. Previews exclusive on card. Has purple hat and shirt, and green pants. - **$33**

❑ MOV-190. "Puppet Master" Pinhead Figure,
1999. Previews exclusive. Two versions. Gold Edition shown with gold shirt. - **$28**

MOV-191

MOV-192

❑ MOV-191. "Puppet Master" Torch Figure,
1999. Previews exclusive on card. Has dark green coat and green pants. - **$33**

❑ MOV-192. "Puppet Master" Tunneler Figure,
1999. Figure on card. - **$22**

MOV-193

MOV-194

❑ MOV-193. "King Kong" Model Kit,
2000. Aurora. Boxed - **$22**

❑ MOV-194. "Ymir" Resin Statue ,
2000. From the 1957 movie "20 Million Miles to Earth." 12" tall and fully painted. Sculpted by Hirokazu Tokugawa. Limited to 1,000. - **$125**

MOV-195

MOV-196

❑ MOV-195. "Kali" Resin Statue,
2000. From the movie "The Golden Voyage of Sinbad." 12" tall and fully painted with deluxe base. Limited to 1,000. - **$150**

❑ MOV-196. "Minotaur" Resin Statue,
2000. A Ray Harryhausen product from the movie "Sinbad and the Eye of the Tiger." Limited to 1,000. - **$125**

MOV-197

MOV-198

❑ MOV-197. "Cyclops" Resin Statue ,
2000. From the 1958 movie "7th Voyage of Sinbad." 12" tall and fully painted. Sculpted by Ryu Ohyama. Limited to 1,000. - **$180**

❑ MOV-198. "Talos" Statue,
2000. 16 1/2" high. From Sinbad movie. Limited to 1,000. Boxed - **$140**

MOV-199

MOV-200

❑ MOV-199. "Dinosaur" Movie Lunch Box,
2000. With Thermos and tag. Features Aladar from the Disney film. - **$20**

❑ MOV-200. "The Crow" Lunch Box,
2001. With Thermos. - **$35**

MOV-201

❑ MOV-201. "Beetlejuice" Lunch Box,
2001. With Thermos. - **$45**

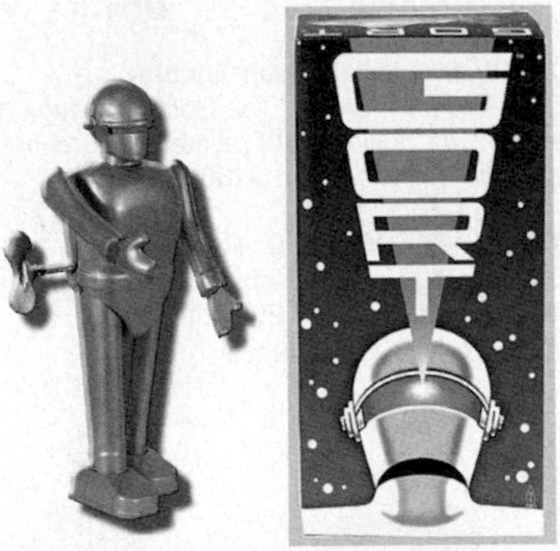

MOV-202 (BOX)

❑ MOV-202. "Gort" Wind-Up Toy,
2001. 8-1/2" tall. In box. - **$28**

(Masks)

MOV-203

❑ MOV-203. "Monsters, Inc. Masks and More!" Book,
2001. Has 4 masks, game board and monster playing pieces. - **$5**

MOV-204

❑ MOV-204. "Harry Potter" Tin Lunch Box,
2001. - **$25**

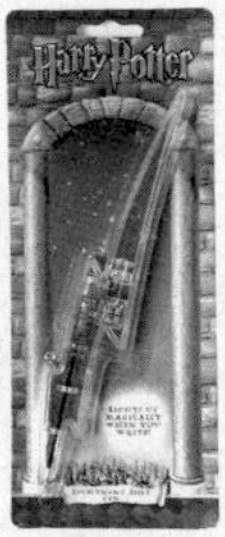

MOV-205

MOV-206

❑ MOV-205. "Harry Potter" Lightning Bolt Pen,
2001. On card. Lights up when used. - **$6**

❑ MOV-206. "Harry Potter" Broom Pen,
2001. On card. - **$6**

MOV-207

❑ MOV-207. "Lord of the Rings" Movie Posters,
2001. The four posters were giveaways from Toys R Us. Each NM - **$12**

MOV-208

❑ MOV-208. "Finding Nemo" Aquarium Gang Set,
2003. Eight figures and accessories. NM - **$12**

MOV-209

❑ MOV-209. "Finding Nemo" View-Master,
2003. Viewer and 3 reels. NM - **$25**

Mr. Magoo

Near-sighted, stubborn, crotchety Mr. Magoo created by John Hubley (1914-1977) first stumbled into view in 1949 in the UPA animated cartoon *Ragtime Bear*, and over the next 10 years he starred in more than 50 theatrical cartoons. *When Magoo Flew* (1953) and *Mr. Magoo's Puddle Jumper* (1956) both won Academy Awards. He went to television on Los Angeles station KTTV in 1960 and to prime-time network television on NBC in *The Famous Adventures of Mr. Magoo* in 1964-1965. Other televised specials followed, and in 1977-1979 the old-timer reappeared in *What's New, Mister Magoo?* on CBS. A theatrical film, *1001 Arabian Nights*, was released by UPA in 1959. Jim Backus (1913-1989) was the voice of Magoo from the beginning. Comic books appeared between 1953 and 1965. General Electric has featured Mr. Magoo in various promotions, and Magoo films have been made for the National Heart Association, Timex, General Foods, Rheingold beer, Ideal toys, Dell Publishing, Colgate-Palmolive, and other advertisers. A 1997 Disney feature film starred Leslie Nielsen as Magoo.

MGO-1

❑ **MGO-1. "Mr. Magoo At The Circus" Target Game Boxed,**
1957. Knickerbocker Toys. Set of cardboard stand-up target figures, pair of plastic pistols with rubber tipped darts. - **$45 $85 $150**

MGO-2

❑ **MGO-2. Mr. Magoo Figural Vinyl Squeak Toy,**
1958. Toy is 4x7x12" tall. Arms, legs, head move. Photo example is missing cane. Bottom of foot reads "1958 U.P.A. Pictures Inc." Complete - **$200 $400 $800**

MGO-3

MGO-4

❑ **MGO-3. Figural Metal Badge,**
1960. GE Lightbulbs. On Card - **$15 $25 $60**
Badge Only - **$8 $15 $30**

❑ **MGO-4. General Electric Flicker Plastic Keychain Tag,**
1961. - **$15 $25 $50**

MGO-5

❑ **MGO-5. "The Official Mr. Magoo Battery Operated Car By Hubley",**
1961. Store item. Detailed litho. tin car with vinyl figure of Mr. Magoo and fabric roof.
Box - **$75 $125 $250**
Car - **$125 $275 $500**

MGO-6

MGO-7

❑ **MGO-6. Vinyl/Cloth Doll,**
1962. Store item. - **$60 $125 $250**

❑ **MGO-7. Hand Puppet,**
1962. Store item. Soft vinyl head with fabric body. - **$20 $40 $90**

MGO-8

❑ **MGO-8. Board Game,**
1964. Standard Toykraft. Game accessories include "Magnifying Glasses" red opaque plastic sheet. - **$25 $50 $100**

MGO-9

❑ **MGO-9. "Mr. Magoo Tattoo Gum" Box Insert,**
1967. Store item by Fleer. 4-1/4x5-1/2" diecut. - **$12 $25 $50**

MGO-10

❑ **MGO-10. Boxed Double Deck Set Of Playing Cards,**
1960s. General Electric produced by Brown & Bigelow. - **$12 $25 $50**

MGO-11

MGO-12

❑ **MGO-11. Glass Ashtray,**
1960s. General Electric. - **$15 $25 $50**

❑ **MGO-12. Plastic Ring Kit,**
1960s. Store item. Comes with attachment heads of Magoo, Waldo or Charlie.
Near Mint Bagged - **$35**
Each Complete Ring - **$10 $15 $25**

MGO-13

❑ **MGO-13. "Big Pop Birthday Bash" Party Kit,**
1960s. GE/Hershey's numerous paper items of circus theme. Near Mint In Mailer - **$150**

MGO-14

❑ **MGO-14. Fabric Store Sign,**
1960s. General Electric. 15x25" white fabric with art in red and black. - **$50 $100 $200**

Mr. Peanut

The corporate symbol for the Planters Nut and Chocolate Company founded by Amedeo Obici in 1906 was the inspiration of a 13-year-old schoolboy, Antonio Gentile, in a 1916 company-sponsored contest. Decked out in top hat, monocle, and cane, Mr. Peanut has been promoting the products of this Suffolk, Virginia, company ever since. The design has been refined from the original figure, first in 1927 and again in 1962. Mr. Peanut has appeared in the form of a wide variety of promotional items, from lamps to salt and pepper sets, peanut dishes, banks, buttons, pins, bookmarks, figures and dolls of wood, plastic, bisque, and cloth, silverware, cigarette lighters, and mechanical pencils, as well as in a series of children's story and paint books first published in 1928 and available from the company in exchange for product wrappers.

MRP-1

❑ **MRP-1. "The Planters Peanut Salted Peanuts" Tin Measuring Cup,**
c. 1910. Cup is 1.75" diameter by 2.75" tall. Text on side reads 1-45/100 Ounce Net In Full For 5 Cents." Has image of "Mr. Peanut" on side. Cup came in peanut jar. - **$135 $250 $400**

MRP-2

❑ **MRP-2. "Mr. Peanut Book No. 1" Canadian Version Coloring Book,**
c. 1928. Pictured example shows cover and sample coloring page. - **$40 $75 $175**

MRP-3

MRP-4

MRP-5

❑ **MRP-3. New York World's Fair Cardboard Bookmark,**
1939. - **$15 $25 $50**

❑ **MRP-4. Laminated Wooden Pin As Santa,**
c. 1939. - **$35 $65 $135**

❑ **MRP-5. Laminated Wood Pin,**
c. 1939. - **$20 $45 $85**

MRP-6

MRP-7

❑ **MRP-6. Wood Jointed Figure,**
1930s. Frequently missing his cane. - **$125 $275 $500**

❑ **MRP-7. Bisque Ashtray,**
1930s. - **$40 $80 $160**

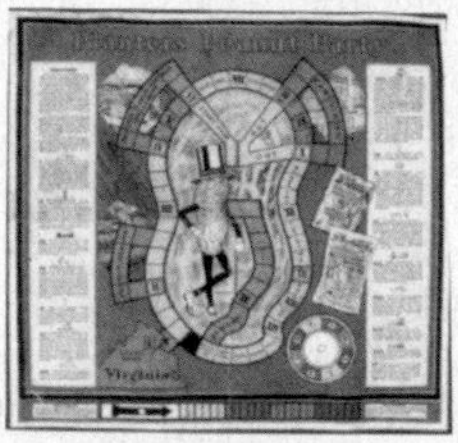
MRP-8

MRP-9

❑ **MRP-8. "Planters Peanut Party" Game Sheet,**
1930s. 9x9-1/4" paper opens to 17-1/2x18-1/2". - **$45 $90 $185**

❑ **MRP-9. New York World's Fair Wood Figure Pin,**
1940. Dated on Trylon either 1939 or 1940. Each - **$40 $75 $150**

MRP-10

MRP-11

❑ **MRP-10. "Spooky Picture" Optical Illusion Card,**
c. 1940. Believed insert for Planter's Jumbo Block Bar. - **$18 $35 $60**

❑ **MRP-11. "The People's Choice" Litho. Button,**
c. 1940. - **$15 $30 $60**

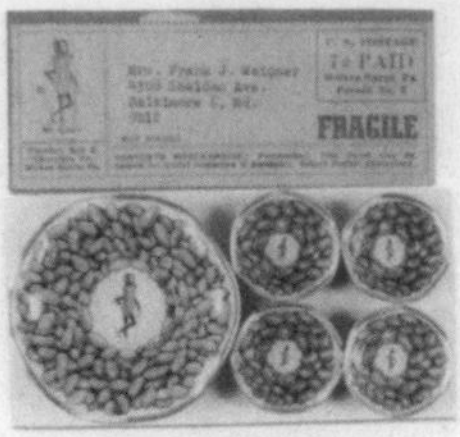

MRP-12

MRP-13

❑ **MRP-12. Metal Serving Dish Set With Mailer,**
1940s. Distributed into 1950s.
Mailer (Rare) - **$20 $40 $75**
Five Piece Dish Set (Common) - **$20 $40 $75**

❑ **MRP-13. Paperweight Figure,**
c. 1940s. 7" tall painted metal figural weight with inscription on rear base "Compliments Planters Nut & Chocolate Co." - **$250 $500 $1000**

MRP-14

MRP-15

❑ **MRP-14. "The Personal Story Of Mr. Peanut" Anniversary Comic Book,**
1956. Full color 7x10" with 16 pages. Back cover offers mail premiums of mechanical pencil, nut spoon, figural bank, drinking cup, presidents paint book. - **$35 $60 $125**

❑ **MRP-15. 50th Anniversary Metal Tray,**
1956. - **$20 $40 $80**

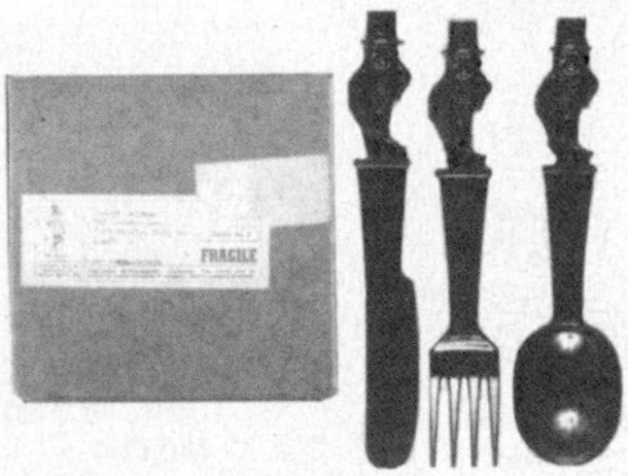

MRP-16

❑ **MRP-16. Knife/Fork/Spoon Sets With Mailer,**
1959. Nine plastic sets. Mailer - **$5 $10 $15**
Utensils - **$20 $40 $60**

MRP-17

❑ **MRP-17. "Mister Peanut Cocktail Glasses" Boxed Set of 8,**
1950s. Boxed **- $75 $135 $285**

MRP-18

MRP-19

❑ **MRP-18. Mr. Peanut Chopper With Mailer,**
1950s. Mailer **- $10 $20 $30**
Chopper **- $12 $25 $50**

❑ **MRP-19. Composition Bobbing Body Figure,**
1960s. **- $75 $150 $250**

MRP-20

❑ **MRP-20. "Mr. Peanut Vendor Bank" Boxed,**
1960s. Plastic figural bank is 5x5x7.5" tall and comes with one-half pound vacuum can of Planters Peanuts. Bank is pictured on each box side with text including "Fresh Refills Available Everywhere/Made By The Geo. S. Scott Mfg. Co./Wallingford, Conn., U.S.A."
Box **- $35 $65 $125**
Bank **- $110 $225 $325**

MRP-21

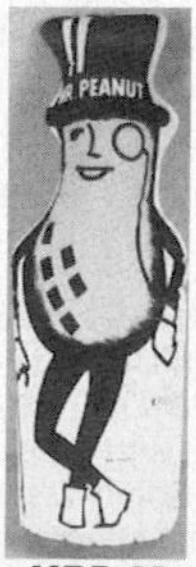
MRP-22

❑ **MRP-21. Mr. Peanut Metal Ring,**
1960s. Gold luster with raised image of him. - **$10 $20 $40**

❑ **MRP-22. Vinyl Inflatable Figure,**
1970s. Image on each side. When inflated has 8" bottom diameter and stands 26" tall. **- $15 $30 $50**

MRP-23

MRP-24

❑ **MRP-23. Fabric Cosmetic Bag,**
c. 1970s. Yellow and black images on blue denim. **- $10 $20 $40**

❑ **MRP-24. Mr. Peanut Silver Coin,**
1991. Limited edition 1 oz. coin came in box with certificate. Boxed **- $50**

MRP-25

MRP-26

❑ **MRP-25. Peanut Butter Maker,**
1996. Boxed. **- $60**

❑ **MRP-26. Stuffed Doll,**
1997. Modeled after the 1960's version of the character. **- $10 $25 $50**

MRP-27

MRP-28

❑ **MRP-27. Hand on Monocle Cookie Jar,**
1998. Nabisco premium from mail order offer. 10 1/4" tall. Black hat scuffs and chips easily. - **$30 $65 $140**

❑ **MRP-28. Beanie with Planters Tag,**
1999. **- $10 $15 $22**

MRP-29

MRP-30

❑ **MRP-29. Key Chain on Card,**
1990s. **- $6**

❑ **MRP-30. Vending Machine,**
1999. Boxed. **- $45**

MRP-31

❑ **MRP-31. Wall Clock,**
1990s. Modern quartz wall clock. TM Nabisco. 9 1/2 x 9 1/2" in box with instructions. **- $60**

Mr. Zip

The U.S. Post Office inaugurated its system of ZIP Codes (Zone Improvement Program) on July 1, 1963, to help speed delivery of increasing volumes of mail. A wide-eyed, cheerful character, Mr. ZIP was created to help popularize the program. He zipped along in advertising and at postal conventions between 1963 and July 1986, when he was officially retired.

MRZ-1

❑ **MRZ-1. "Meet Mr. Zip" Post Office Diecut Wood Display,**
c. 1963. 12" wide by 10.25" tall picturing him running while "U.S. Mail" bag is over shoulder. - **$75 $175 $350**

MRZ-2

MRZ-3

❑ **MRZ-2. Service Introduction 32x56" Paper Poster,**
1963. Large Mr. ZIP image on post office department poster issued in May. -
$50 $100 $175

❑ **MRZ-3. "Zip Code" Game,**
1964. Store item by Lakeside Toys. Game is based on actual post office and zip code operations. - **$35 $75 $150**

MRZ-4

❑ **MRZ-4. "Mr. Zip" U.S. Mail Truck With Mail Bags,**
1969. Plastic 7.5" tall three-wheeled pull toy with moving head. Toy whistle is attached to the end of red and white string. Comes with 3 cloth mail bags and pre-printed address cards with addresses including Santa Claus/teddy bear/Daddy/Wizard of Oz/Easter Bunny/My Valentine, etc. Also comes with tri-fold explanation of postal zip codes.
Complete Near Mint - **$250**
Toy Only - **$35 $60 $100**

MRZ-5

MRZ-6

MRZ-7

❑ **MRZ-5. "Mr. ZIP" Cello. Button,**
1960s. U.S. Postal Service. - **$6 $12 $25**

❑ **MRZ-6. "Use Zip Code" Cello. Button,**
1960s. U.S. Postal Service. - **$6 $12 $25**

❑ **MRZ-7. "Mr. ZIP" Figure Pin,**
1960s. U.S. Postal Service. Gold luster figure image in salute pose with "US Mail" pouch over one shoulder. - **$10 $20 $50**

MRZ-8

MRZ-9

❑ **MRZ-8. Mail Box Bank,**
1960s. Store item. 6" tall litho. tin replica of mail drop box with coin savings chart on back panel. -
$20 $35 $70

❑ **MRZ-9. "Zip Code System" First Day Commemorative Cover,**
1974. Probably a 10th anniversary issue postmarked January 4 from Washington, D.C. -
$10 $20 $30

Muhammad Ali

He was born Cassius Clay in Louisville, Ky., in 1942, began amateur boxing at age 12, and burst into boxing prominence in 1960, when he won the Amateur Athletic Union light-heavyweight title, the National Golden Gloves heavyweight title, and an Olympic gold medal as a light-heavyweight. Then he turned professional, and four years later defeated Sonny Liston to win the world heavyweight championship. Clay changed his name to Muhammad Ali and embraced the Muslim religion. In 1967 he refused induction into the army as a conscientious objector and was stripped of his title and banned from boxing. In 1971 his refusal was upheld in a unanimous decision of the Supreme Court. Ali regained his title in 1974, knocking out George Foreman in "The Rumble in the Jungle" in Zaire, then lost it in 1978 to Leon Spinks, and won it back from Spinks seven months later. Ali retired in 1979, then returned to the ring and lost bouts in 1980 and 1981, after which he again retired. Personal trainer and friend Drew Bundini Brown helped Ali with his prose including "Float Like A Butterfly, Sting Like A Bee." Ali's professional record is 61 fights. He won 56, 37 by knockout, and lost five.

Always a popular and beloved champion, Ali lent his name and image to a variety of commercial products, including shoe polish, potato chips, cookies, barbecue sauce, candy bars, cologne, shaving cream, Knockout shampoo, roach traps, dolls and games. He played himself in a 1977 biographical movie, *The Greatest*, and provided his voice for the 1977 NBC-television animated series, *I Am the Greatest: The Adventures of Muhammad Ali*. In 1996, Ali lit the torch at the summer Olympics in Atlanta. Also, a 1997 documentary, *When We Were Kings*, about Ali's "Rumble in the Jungle" with Foreman, has garnered many awards and much critical praise. A biographical feature film, *Ali*, featuring Will Smith in the title role, opened strong in late 2001 but did not possess Ali's stamina at the box office. "Rumble Young Man, Rumble!"

MUH-1

❑ **MUH-1. Cassius Clay "The Champ Sings!" Record,**
c. 1962. 7x7" sleeve holding 45 rpm record sung by him of song titles "Stand By Me" and "I Am The Greatest." - **$45 $90 $175**

MUH-2

❑ **MUH-2. "Referee" Christmas Magazine With Cassius Clay,**
1963. December 28 issue of boxing fan magazine with front cover photo and upcoming fight vs. Sonny Liston prediction text prior to Clay's name change to Muhammad Ali. -
$50 $100 $200

MUH-3

❑ **MUH-3. "The Ring" Boxing Magazine Issues With Cassius Clay Covers,**
1964-1966. Each - **$12 $20 $40**

MUH-4

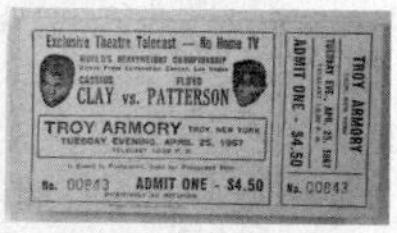

MUH-5

❑ **MUH-4. "Cassius Clay" Button,**
c. 1965. 1.75" black and white cello picturing and naming him prior to his name change to Muhammad Ali. - **$85 $175 $350**

❑ **MUH-5. Cassius Clay vs. Floyd Patterson Theatre Telecast Ticket,**
Apr. 25, 1967. Complete ticket. - **$15 $30 $60**

MUH-6

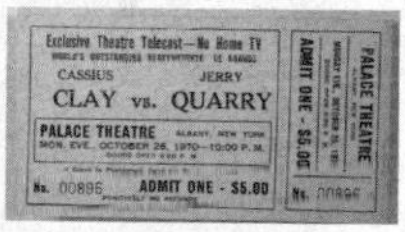

MUH-7

❑ **MUH-6. "People's Champ-Ali" Cello Button,**
c. 1968. 3" black and white picturing him as youthful boxer. - **$35 $65 $135**

❑ **MUH-7. Cassius Clay vs. Jerry Quarry Theatre Telecast Ticket,**
Oct. 26, 1970. Complete ticket. - **$12 $20 $40**

MUH-8

MUH-9

❑ **MUH-8. Cassius Clay vs. Bonavena Theatre Telecast Ticket,**
Dec. 7, 1970. Complete ticket. - **$6 $12 $35**

❑ **MUH-9. Ali-Joe Frazier Championship Fight Pennant,**
1971. 8x21" felt fabric for undated but March 8 bout at Madison Square Garden. -
$35 $65 $125

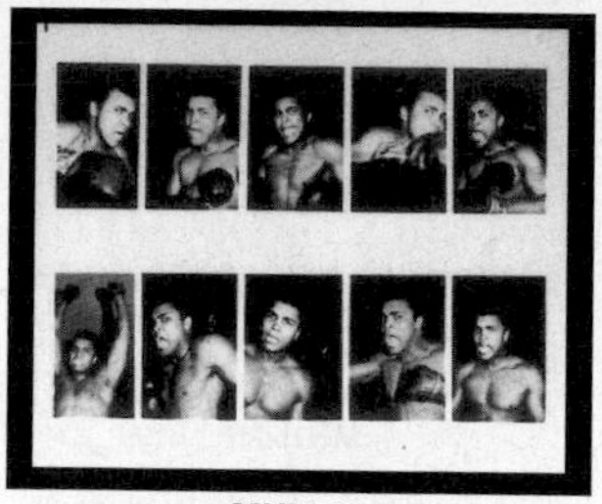
MUH-10

❑ **MUH-10. Ali-Jimmy Ellis Fight Promotion Photo,**
1971. 8x10" black and white print of 10 Ali facial expressions and contortions with inscriptions including upcoming July 26 closed circuit telecast bout from Houston Astrodome. -
$20 $40 $60

MUH-11

❑ **MUH-11. Ali-Frazier Fight Promo Button,**
1971. 1.75" black and white cello for March 8 heavyweight bout at Madison Square Garden between Joe Frazier and Ali. - **$75 $165 $275**

MUH-12

MUH-13

❑ **MUH-12. Ali-Joe Frazier 14x22" Fight Poster,**
1974. For closed circuit telecast of January 28 "Super Fight II" bout. - **$85 $175 $400**

❑ **MUH-13. Mr. Toothdecay Pinback,**
1974. 4" pin promotes St. John's toothpaste. -
$65 $150 $300

MUH-14

MUH-15

❑ **MUH-14. Ali-George Foreman Championship Fight Pennant,**
1974. 8-1/2x27" felt fabric for October 29 bout in Zaire, Africa. - **$40 $75 $150**

❑ **MUH-15. Foreman vs. Ali Theatre Telecast Ticket,**
Sept. 24, 1974. Complete ticket. - **$20 $35 $85**

MUH-16

❑ **MUH-16. "A Thrilla In Manila" Pennant,**
1975. 12" wide. - **$35 $70 $125**

MUH-17

❑ **MUH-17. "Thrilla In Manila Ali-Frazier" Full Color Fight Poster,**
1975. Poster is 14x22". Art by Leroy Neiman. Not one of the modern repros which are a different size, this is an original. Text includes "The Saga Of Our Lifetime/Philippeans 1975/Tues., Sept. 30" with space below where local venues were supposed to fill in their address. Bottom notations "No Home TV/A Presentation Of Don King Products Inc./No Radio." - **$100 $200 $300**

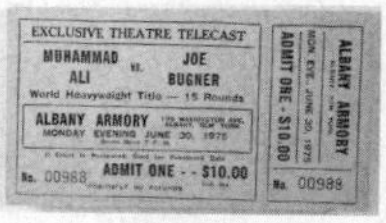

MUH-18

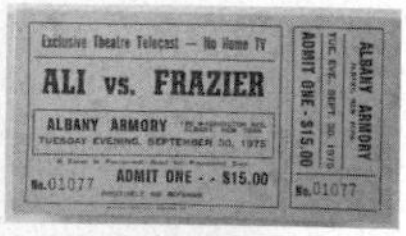

MUH-19

❑ **MUH-18. Ali vs. Joe Bugner Theatre Telecast Ticket,**
June 30, 1975. Complete ticket. - **$10 $15 $30**

❑ **MUH-19. Ali vs. Frazier Theatre Telecast Ticket,**
Sept. 30, 1975. Complete ticket. - **$20 $40 $85**

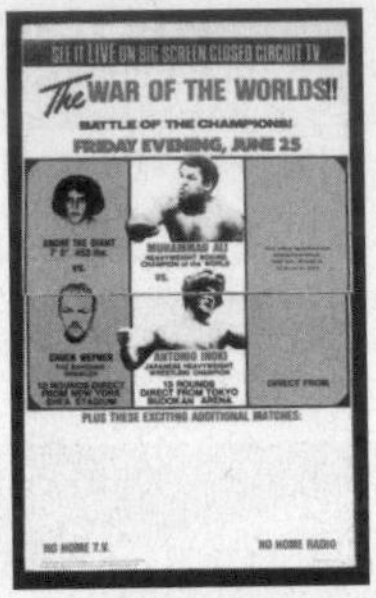

MUH-20

❑ MUH-20. Ali vs. Inoki Exhibition Match 14x23" Paper Poster,
June 25, 1976. For closed circuit TV 15-round specialty match between him and Antonio Inoki, Japanese heavyweight wrestling champion, televised from Tokyo. - **$60 $125 $200**

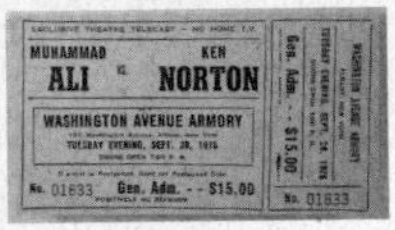

MUH-21 MUH-22

❑ MUH-21. Ali vs. Inoki Exhibition Match Theatre Telecast Ticket,
June 25, 1976. Complete ticket. - **$10 $15 $30**

❑ MUH-22. Ali vs. Ken Norton Theatre Telecast Ticket,
Sept. 28, 1976. Complete ticket. - **$12 $20 $40**

MUH-23

❑ MUH-23. Ali-Norton Fight Poster,
1976. 14-1/2x23" for closed circuit TV viewing of fight at Yankee Stadium September 28. -
$70 $150 $250

MUH-24

❑ MUH-24. "Boxing Ring" Mego Toy Boxed,
1976. Herbert Muhammad Enterprises. Mechanical plastic figures of Ali and opponent resembling Ken Norton operated by squeeze triggers. In 3.25x15.25x15.5" box.
Boxed - **$135 $265 $425**

MUH-25

❑ MUH-25. "Ali Bom-Ba-Ye!" Record,
1977. 12" 45 rpm record on Arista label. -
$20 $40 $65

MUH-26

❑ MUH-26. Boxed Costume By Collegeville,
1977. Thin molded plastic mask with fabric costume including chest inscription "I Am The Greatest." Near Mint Boxed - **$175**
Complete No Box - **$25 $50 $100**

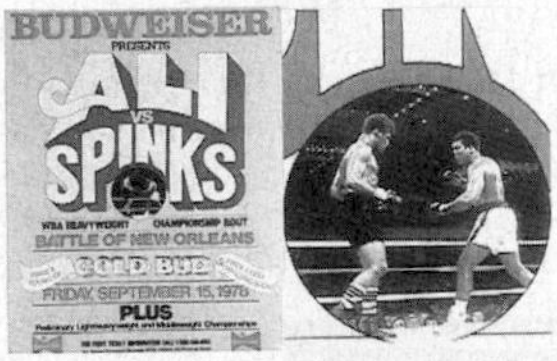

MUH-27

❑ MUH-27. Ali-Spinks Fight Poster,
1978. Budweiser beer. 21x28" high gloss tavern poster promoting fight in New Orleans September 15, 1978. - **$70 $150 $250**

MUH-28 MUH-29

❑ MUH-28. Ali/Charity Event 3" Cello. Button,
1979. Promotion for exhibition match between him and "The Urban Fighter" Mayor Tommie Smith of Jersey City, New Jersey. -
$40 $80 $160

❑ MUH-29. Ali/Charity Event 3-1/2" Cello. Button,
1979. For same event as preceding item also picturing New Jersey Governor Byrne and apparent Ali unnamed body guard to prevent thrashing by Mayor Smith. - **$20 $40 $80**

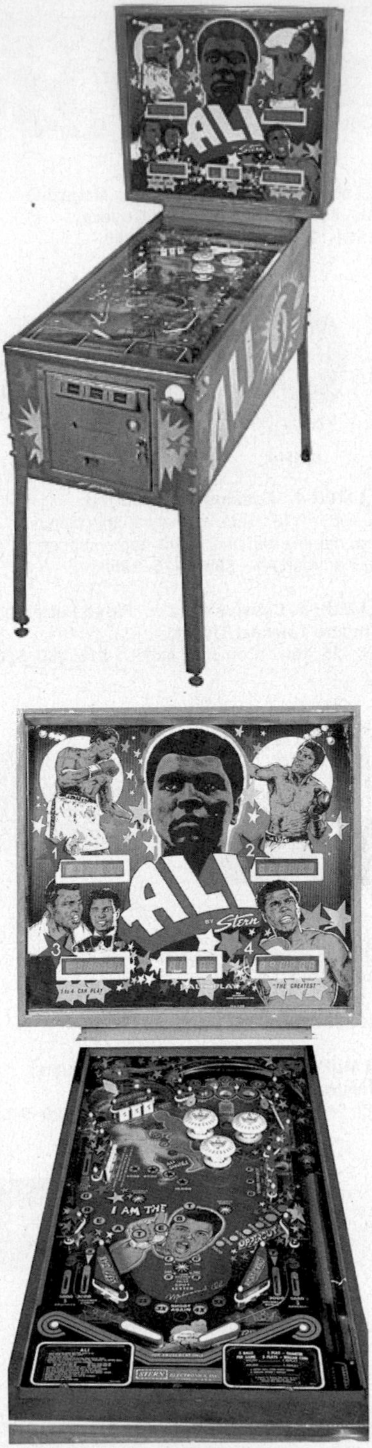

MUH-30

❑ MUH-30. Ali Pinball Machine,
1970s. By Stern Company. One sold at auction in 2004 for $2,363. - **$1000 $2000 $3000**

MUH-31

❑ **MUH-31. Ali Civil Rights Button,**
1970s. Button is 3.5" reading "Ali Is An Equal Opportunity Employer." Made by N.G. Slater Corp. - **$60 $115 $230**

MUH-32

❑ **MUH-32. Ali "He's The Greatest" Tin Tab,**
1970s. Issued for Ali's endorsement of Richard Hatcher, Mayor, Gary, Indiana. Marshall Levin Collection. - **$30 $60 $125**

MUH-33

MUH-34

❑ **MUH-33. "Muhammad Ali" Belt Buckle,**
c. 1970s. Everlast boxing equipment. Bronze luster finish on thick metal with image and inscriptions in raised relief. - **$20 $45 $90**

❑ **MUH-34. Ali-Larry Holmes Championship Fight 4" Cello. Button,**
1980. For employee of hosting Caesar's Palace, Las Vegas prior to October 2 match. - **$15 $25 $55**

MUH-35

❑ **MUH-35. Ali and Frazer Signed Lithograph,**
1983. Limited to 300. Also signed by reknowned sports artist Don Lewis. - **$1850**

MUH-36

MUH-37

MUH-38

❑ **MUH-36. Promotional Standee,**
1992. Promotes "His Life and Times" book by Thomas Hauser. - **$125 $250 $400**

❑ **MUH-37. Starting Lineup Figure on Card,**
1998. - **$25**

❑ **MUH-38. Starting Lineup Figure on Card,**
1998. - **$20**

MUH-39

MUH-40

❑ **MUH-39. Starting Lineup "Timeless Legend" Figure in Box,**
1998. - **$60**

❑ **MUH-40. Starting Lineup Figure in Box,**
1999. - **$40**

MUH-41

❑ **MUH-41. Wheaties Box,**
1999. - **$5 $10 $20**

Multi-Products

Multi-Products, Inc. existed in Chicago from the 1940s to at least 1959. While their products are well known, the company history is a mystery. Their Disney merchandise 1940-41 catalogue ads state: Division of Protectoseal Company of America, Inc. Protectoseal began in the 1920s when R.J. Anschicks created a mine safety device known as a "flash arrester." Today the company produces many products to minimize fire loss and provide employee safety.

Multi-Products' extensive 1940 Pinocchio line included character figures in three different sizes along with Pinocchio characters bookends, lamps, wall plaques, pen holders and brush holders. See the Pinocchio section in Ted Hake's *Official® Price Guide to Disney Collectibles* for some of these items.

Multi-Products' 1945 series of non-Disney comic characters was for many years credited in error to Syroco (The Syracuse Ornamental Company), another firm specializing in molded woodfiber products. This erroneous attribution occurred because the 24 figures in the series carry only a King Features Syndicate copyright and no manufacturer's name.

In 2003, Hake's Americana auctioned a figure of Hans, which was in a rarely seen box stating "Produced by Multi-Products, Inc., Chicago 8, Illinois under license from King Features Syndicate Inc., Copyright 1945." Of the 24 characters in the series, these 14 are pictured on the box: Alexander, Blondie, Captain Katzenjammer, Cookie, Dagwood, Fritz, Hans, Jiggs, Maggie, Olive Oyl, Popeye, Prince Valiant, The Phantom and Wimpy. Seven of the previous characters plus the following five were also used as premiums by Pillsbury Farina Cereal: Annie Rooney, Archie, Barney Google, Little King and Tim Tyler. (See item MUL-26 for full list). The other five known figures are Casper, Flash Gordon, Rosie, Tillie and Toots. While the figures carry a 1944 King Features copyright, both the Multi-Products box and the Pillsbury offer specify a 1945 date, and it seems this later date is the likely date of issue. Given the total large number of these figures that have survived, the rarity of the box is surprising.

Other Multi-Product items include the 1943 Captain Marvel rare premium produced for Fawcett Publications and a rather diverse group of figures created to serve as Community Chest and United Fund volunteer awards during the late 1940s and 1950s. See the Syroco section in this book for similar items.

(VARIOUS VIEWS OF THE BOX)

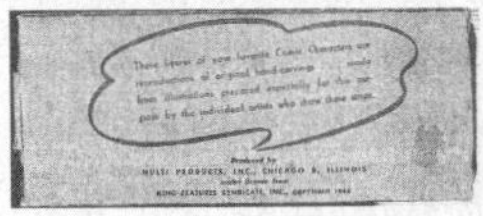

MUL-1

❑ **MUL-1. "Your Favorite Comic Character" Box,**
1945. 2x2x6" cardboard box illustrated on all panels by total of 14 composition wood figures often referred to as Syroco figures but this series was not made by that company. - **$60 $125 $200**

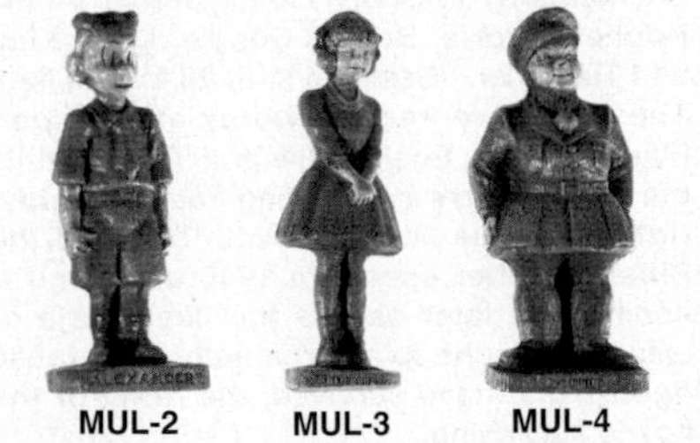

MUL-2 MUL-3 MUL-4

❑ **MUL-2. Alexander Syroco Figure,**
1945. This and the following 23 figures comprise a set of 24 King Features Syndicate characters, all from 1944. - **$30 $60 $110**

❑ **MUL-3. Annie Rooney,**
1945. - **$30 $100 $160**

❑ **MUL-4. Archie In Uniform,**
1945. - **$30 $100 $165**

MUL-5 MUL-6 MUL-7 MUL-8

❑ **MUL-5. Barney Google In Navy Uniform,**
1945. - **$25 $75 $125**

❑ **MUL-6. Blondie,**
1945. Issued with dress in either red or blue. Scarce. - **$60 $150 $450**

❑ **MUL-7. Captain,**
1945. - **$30 $100 $150**

❑ **MUL-8. Casper,**
1945. - **$20 $85 $135**

MUL-9 MUL-10 MUL-11 MUL-12

❑ **MUL-9. Cookie,**
1945. - **$20 $40 $100**

❑ **MUL-10. Dagwood,**
1945. - **$30 $100 $150**

❑ **MUL-11. Flash Gordon,**
1945. Scarce. - **$200 $400 $1000**

❑ **MUL-12. Fritz,**
1945. - **$25 $75 $125**

MUL-13 MUL-14 MUL-15

❑ **MUL-13. Hans,**
1945. - **$25 $75 $125**

❑ **MUL-14. Jiggs,**
1945. - **$40 $85 $135**

❑ **MUL-15. Little King,**
1945. - **$40 $150 $275**

MUL-16 MUL-17 MUL-18

❑ **MUL-16. Maggie,**
1945. Scarce. - **$125 $200 $450**

❑ **MUL-17. Rosie,**
1945. Rare. - **$250 $600 $1200**

❑ **MUL-18. Olive Oyl,**
1945. - **$125 $200 $425**

MUL-19 MUL-20 MUL-21

❑ **MUL-19. Phantom,**
1945. Scarce. A Cream of Wheat premium available for 10¢.
Brown Costume - **$300 $800 $1800**
Purple Costume - **$250 $600 $1350**

❑ **MUL-20. Popeye,**
1945. - **$50 $120 $200**

❑ **MUL-21. Prince Valiant,**
1945. - **$75 $200 $475**

MUL-22 MUL-23 MUL-24 MUL-25

❑ **MUL-22. Tillie In Uniform,**
1945. Scarce. - **$200 $400 $800**

❑ **MUL-23. Tim Tyler In Navy Uniform,**
1945. - **$20 $75 $125**

❑ **MUL-24. Toots,**
1945. Scarce. - **$200 $400 $800**

❑ **MUL-25. Wimpy,**
1945. - **$40 $80 $150**

MUL-26

❑ **MUL-26. Comic Character Statuettes Ad,**
1945. Pillsbury Farina Cereal. Sunday comic section ad offering figures of Dagwood, Cookie, Alexander, Blondie, Popeye, Wimpy, Tim Tyler, Archie, Jiggs, Little King, Annie Rooney, Barney Google. - **$40 $80 $160**

The Munsters

Created by Alan Burns and Chris Hayward and produced by Joe Connelly and Bob Mosher, the spooky sitcom aired on CBS-TV from September 24, 1964 until September 1, 1966. Jack Marshall wrote the theme song. The basic premise had the Munster family, including two vampires, a Frankenstein monster look-a-like, a young werewolf son and a beautiful blonde daughter, living in a neighborhood and acting like they were no different than their suburban neighbors.

The cast included: Yvonne DeCarlo (1922-2007) as Lily, Fred Gwynne (1926-1993) as Herman, Al Lewis (1923-2006) as Grandpa, Butch Patrick as Eddie and Beverley Owen as Marilyn for the first 13 episodes and Pat Priest as Marilyn for episodes 14 on. Family pets included: Spot, a fire-breathing dragon, Igor the bat and Kittycat who roars like a lion. George Barris customized two cars for the show: The Munster Koach, a hot rod built on a 1923 Model T Ford chassis and Drag-U-La, a dragster built with a real coffin.

Spin-off TV shows and films included: *The Munsters Today* 1988-1991 series, *Munster, Go Home* 1966, *The Munsters' Revenge* 1981, *Here Come The Munsters* 1995 and the *Munsters Scary Little Christmas* 1996.

Gold Key published 16 comic books between January, 1965 and January, 1968 with photo covers and TV Comics! published four issues of *The Munsters* in 1997.

MUN-1

❑ **MUN-1. "The Munsters" Aurora Model Kit,**
1964. Kit No. 804-198. Contains parts, instruction sheet and accent sticker sheet. - **$150 $300 $500**

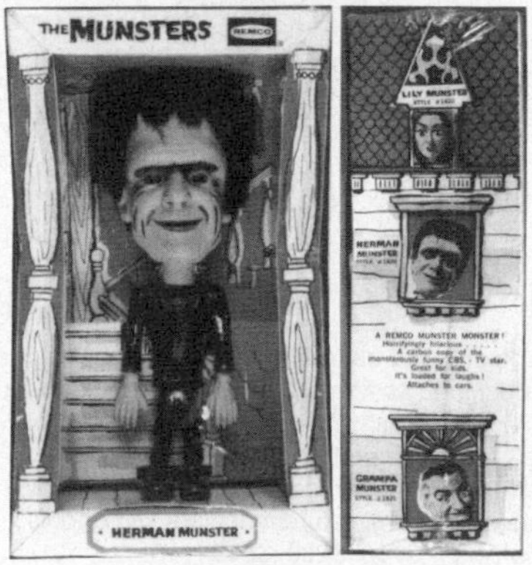

MUN-2

❑ **MUN-2. "Remco Herman Munster" Boxed Figure,**
1964. Kayro-Vue Productions. 4.75x7.75x2.5" deep box contains 6" tall hard plastic figure with soft vinyl head and life-like rooted hair. Near Mint Sealed - **$1500**
Box Unsealed - **$150 $300 $600**
Figure - **$125 $250 $500**

MUN-3

❑ **MUN-3. "Marilyn Munster Of The Munsters" Rare Boxed Japanese Doll,**
1964. 3.25x12.5x2.25" deep brown cardboard box contains 11" tall poseable hollow soft plastic and vinyl doll with rooted life-like hair and vinyl dress, headband and shoes. Made in Japan.
Box - **$20 $40 $75**
Doll - **$50 $100 $200**

MUN-4

❑ **MUN-4. "The Munsters Picnic Game",**
1964. Hasbro. 9.5x19x1.5" deep box holds 15.5x18.5" gameboard, 8x10" sheet of game cards, die-cut cardboard playing pieces for Herman, Lily, Eddie and Grandpa with wooden bases and spinner. Near Mint Unused - **$1500**
Used - **$300 $600 $1200**

MUN-5

❑ **MUN-5. "The Munsters Masquerade Party Game",**
1964. Hasbro. 9.5x19x1.5 deep box holds 15.5x18.5" gameboard, four 3" tall cardboard markers of Herman, Lily, Grandpa and Eddie with wooden holders, playing cards and spinner mounted in box insert.
Near Mint Unused - **$1500**
Used - **$300 $600 $1200**

MUN-6

❑ **MUN-6. "The Munsters Theatre" Gum Card Box,**
1964. Leaf Gum. - **$75 $125 $200**

MUN-7

❑ **MUN-7. "Munsters" Gum Card Set,**
1964. Leaf. Set of 72 cards, each 2-3/8x3.5" with photo front and joke backs. Set - **$150 $300 $500**

MUN-8

❑ **MUN-8. "Munsters Castex 5" Boxed Casting Molds Set,**
1964. Emenee. Large 13.5x21x3.5" deep box containing set of five vinyl molds to produce plaster statues 5.5" tall or less of Herman, Grandpa, Lily, Marilyn, Eddie. Molds are accompanied by necessary tools, supplies, instructions. - **$125 $225 $350**

MUN-9

❑ **MUN-9. "The Munsters" Metal Lunch Box With Thermos,**
1965 King-Seeley Thermos Co. Lunch box with 6.5" tall metal thermos with plastic lid.
Box - **$75 $150 $300**
Bottle - **$35 $75 $150**

MUN-10

❑ **MUN-10. Mini-Monster/Munster Doll,**
1965. Ideal Toy Corp. 8.75" tall vinyl movable parts doll with outfit. From series of four originally designed as Munster dolls but remarketed as "Mini-Monsters" following show cancellation. Doll has wolf head corresponding to doll that Eddie Munster carried around and has accessories of two miniature monsters and ghouls booklets. - **$100 $200 $300**

MUN-11

❑ **MUN-11. "The Munsters Frame Tray Puzzle",**
1965. Whitman. 11.5x14.5" puzzle. - **$100 $200 $300**

MUN-12

❑ **MUN-12. "The Munsters" CBS Publicity Still,**
c. 1965. 7x9" glossy photo of Fred Gwynne and Pat Priest with attached "CBS Photo Division Press Information" sheet. - **$75 $150 $250**

MUN-13

❑ **MUN-13. Munsters Flicker Picture Rings,**
c. 1966. Vending machine issue. Set of four plastic rings in either silver or blue base.
Silver Base Each - **$40 $65 $100**
Blue Base Each - **$20 $40 $60**

MUN-14

❑ **MUN-14. "Lily Munster" Yvonne DeCarlo Signed Photo,**
c. 1990s. 8x10" color photo signed in black felt tip pen. - **$50 $100 $200**

MUN-15

MUN-16

❑ **MUN-15. "Herman Munster" Bobbing Head Figure,**
1998. In motorcyclist outfit. - **$90**

❑ **MUN-16. "Grandpa" Bobbing Head Figure,**
1998. From Munsters TV show. - **$90**

The Muppets

Jim Henson (1936-1990) introduced his Muppets on local television in Washington, D.C. in 1955, with *Sam and Friends*, a five minute show that aired twice nightly on WRC-TV until 1961. The creatures (the name is a combination of marionette and puppet) found use in commercials and gained national exposure in periodic guest appearances on a number of variety shows.

They debuted as regulars in 1969 on *Sesame Street*, the phenomenally successful children's television series, where Big Bird, Oscar the Grouch, Bert and Ernie, and the Cookie Monster have enchanted millions. *The Muppet Show* (syndicated, 1976-1981) was hosted by Kermit the Frog, who managed to avoid the persistent romantic advances of the divine Miss Piggy. The show garnered three Emmys. In 1975-1976, during the first season of *Saturday Night Live*, Jim Henson's creations—The Scred (lizard-like muppets that became the prototypes for the characters featured in the 1982 film *The Dark Crystal*)—appeared alongside the Not Ready For Prime Time Players. *Muppet Babies*, the animated series sponsored by Campbell soups and Sears, premiered on CBS in 1984 and went on to win numerous Emmy awards.

New Muppet characters were introduced on *Fraggle Rock* (cable, 1983). The creatures also made movies: *The Muppet Movie* (1979), *The Great Muppet Caper* (1981), *The Muppets Take Manhattan* (1984), and *Muppet Treasure Island* (1996). *Muppet-VIsion 3D* opened in 1991 at Walt Disney World's Disney/MGM Studios Theme Park. Kermit and pals also returned to TV, but less successfully than before. Jim Henson died on May 16, 1990. Despite the passing of this gifted man, his legacy lives on--Henson's son Brian continues to guide the Muppets through a variety of all-new adventures. Merchandising of the Muppet characters has become a multi-million-dollar industry.

MUP-1

❑ **MUP-1. TV Guide Magazine Australian Edition With Jim Henson/Muppets Sesame Street Premiere Cover,**
1971. Item is 5.5x8.5" with 36 pages. Published for the week of Jan. 3-9. - **$15 $25 $40**

MUP-2

❑ **MUP-2. "The Muppet Show" Lunch Box With Bottle,**
1978. Store item by King-Seeley Co. Metal box and plastic bottle. Box - **$30 $50 $125**
Bottle - **$8 $15 $30**

MUP-3

❑ **MUP-3. Kermit The Frog Figural Container,**
1978. Store item. Ceramic holder and lid by Sigma. - **$25 $60 $135**

MUP-4 **MUP-5**

❑ **MUP-4. Fan Club Litho. Button,**
1978. 2-1/4" with color design on black. - **$10 $18 $30**

❑ **MUP-5. Miss Piggy Wristwatch,**
1979. Store item. By Picco with Henson Associates Inc. copyright. - **$15 $30 $75**

MUP-6 **MUP-7**

❑ **MUP-6. Fozzie Bear Enameled Brass Figure Pin,**
1970s. Satchel inscription is "Jaycee Kids." - **$8 $15 $30**

❑ **MUP-7. Kermit Frog Enamel Brass Figure Pin,**
1970s. Local sponsor is "NJ Jaycees." - **$8 $15 $30**

MUP-8 **MUP-9**

❑ **MUP-8. Miss Piggy Ceramic Mug,**
1970s. Store item by Sigma. - **$10 $20 $30**

❑ **MUP-9. Kermit The Frog Ceramic Mug,**
1970s. Store item by Sigma. - **$5 $15 $30**

MUP-11

MUP-10

❑ **MUP-10. Miss Piggy Ceramic Figural Bank,**
1970s. Store item by Sigma. - **$20 $40 $80**

❑ **MUP-11. Toy Promotion Litho. Button,**
c. 1970s. 2-1/4" inscribed "Bulletin Board Games." - **$12 $25 $40**

MUP-12

❑ **MUP-12. Muppets For President Pin-Back Buttons,**
1980. Store item. Each is 3-1/2" diameter with full color photo under acetate.
Each - **$8 $15 $30**

MUP-13

❑ **MUP-13. "The Great Muppet Caper" Glass Tumblers,**
1981. McDonald's. From set of four.
Each - **$3 $6 $10**

MUP-14

❑ **MUP-14. Kermit The Frog Telephone,**
1983. Store item by American Telecommunications Corp. copyright Henson Associates Inc. Hard plastic actual function telephone 8x8x11". - **$50 $125 $250**

MUP-15

MUP-16

❑ **MUP-15. "Miss Piggy's Calendar Of Calendars" 2-1/4" Cello. Promo Button,**
1983. Alfred A. Knopf Publishing Co. with Henson Associates copyright. - **$10 $18 $35**

❑ **MUP-16. "National Children's Dental Health Month" Litho. Button,**
1985. 2-1/4" with color portrait. - **$8 $18 $40**

Music Misc.

Great vocalists, instrumentalists or instruments do not necessarily great premiums make. Vocalists, other than Elvis and the Beatles, have created little furor in premiums throughout the years, other than a small flurry of pin-back buttons picturing crooner stars of the 1940s-1950s. Rock music groups beginning in the 1960s have inspired some very attractively designed buttons, although mainly of retail nature. Music instruments and premiums seldom mingle. Possibly a kazoo here, a harmonica there and--by considerable leeway - bird calls, sirens, etc. Still, music in its broadest sense has produced a modest assortment of premiums such as songbooks, records and novelty items.

MUS-1

❑ **MUS-1. Rudy Vallée Song Sheet,**
1929. Features his song "I'm Just A Vagabond Lover." - **$10 $20 $33**

MUS-2

MUS-3

❑ **MUS-2. "Four Aces" Cello. Button,**
1940s. Philadelphia Fan Club. - **$10 $20 $45**

❑ **MUS-3. Tony Bennett "Bennett Tones Fan Club" Litho. Button,**
1940s. - **$15 $30 $60**

MUS-4

MUS-5

❑ **MUS-4. "Guy Lombardo" Record Brush,**
1940s. Decca Records. - **$15 $25 $50**

❑ **MUS-5. "Bing Crosby" Record Brush,**
1940s. Decca Records. - **$15 $25 $50**

MUS-6

MUS-7

❑ **MUS-6. "Woody Herman's Sweetwind" Litho. Advertising Button,**
1940s. Pioneer Musical Inst. Co. 1-5/8" black and white includes his endorsement signature. - **$20 $35 $70**

❑ **MUS-7. "Rock-Ola Leads Again!" Button,**
c. 1950. 3" diameter. - **$20 $35 $70**

MUS-8

❑ **MUS-8. Pat Boone Standee,**
1953. 2-1/2 ft. tall. - **$150 $350 $775**

MUS-9

❑ **MUS-9. Rosemary Clooney Paper Doll Book,**
1954. No. 2566:25 published by Lowe. 11x14" book with six single-sided pages with costume and black/white images of the famous singer. Front cover features punch-out doll which has had thicker cardboard cut-out glued on top of doll, as made. Uncut - **$50 $90 $175**

MUS-10

❑ **MUS-10. Bill Haley and his Comets Program,**
1956. 32 pages & cover features photos and songs. - **$50 $90 $150**

MUS-11

❑ **MUS-11. The "Chirping" Crickets (with Buddy Holly) Album ,**
1957. Brunswick Records. Their first album. Textured cover. - **$150 $250 $450**

MUS-12

❑ **MUS-12. "That'll Be the Day" Song Sheet,**
1957. Song by Buddy Holly and the Crickets. - **$40 $85 $160**

MUS-13

MUS-14

❑ **MUS-13. "Eddie Cochran Fan Club" Pinback,**
1957. Rare. - **$50 $100 $200**

❑ **MUS-14. "Witch Doctor" Song Sheet,**
1958. From the hit record. - **$15 $35 $55**

MUS-15

MUS-16

❑ **MUS-15. "Chipmunks" Wallet,**
1959. Vinyl. - **$15 $25 $50**

❑ **MUS-16. "Chipmunks" Song Tote,**
1959. By Monarch Music Co. Vinyl holder for 10 records, with a separate record index. - **$25 $50 $100**

MUS-17 (Reverse side)

❑ **MUS-17. "Chipmunks" 45 Record,**
1959. With 2-sided sleeve.
Record - **$6 $12 $20**
Sleeve - **$12 $18 $30**

MUS-18

MUS-19

MUS-20

❑ **MUS-18. "Pat Boone/4th Anniversary" Litho. Button,**
1959. Dot Records. - **$5 $10 $15**

❑ **MUS-19. "Pat Boone Fan" Litho. Button,**
c. 1959. - **$10 $18 $30**

❑ **MUS-20. "Spike Jones" Pair Of Souvenir Programs,**
1950s. Each has 16 pages issued by RCA. Each - **$18 $30 $60**

MUS-21

❑ **MUS-21. Pat Boone Brass Luster Jewelry Pin With Charms,**
1950s. Store item. 1" diameter frame has black and white photo under celluloid. - **$20 $40 $75**

MUS-22

❑ **MUS-22. "Picture Patches",**
1950s. Store item. Probable set of eight. Includes Ricky Nelson, Dave Nelson, Bobby Darin, Frankie Avalon, Tommy Sands, Jimmie Rodgers, Fabian. Each Packaged - **$8 $15 $25**

MUS-23

MUS-24

❑ **MUS-23. Fabian And Frankie Avalon 3-1/2" Cello. Buttons,**
1950s. Store item. Matching designs, possibly issued for others. Each - **$20 $35 $75**

❑ **MUS-24. "Everly Brothers Fan Club" Litho. Button,**
1950s. - **$18 $30 $60**

MUS-25

MUS-26

❑ **MUS-25. "Bill Haley And His Comets Fan Club" Cello. Button,**
1950s. - **$40 $85 $175**

❑ **MUS-26. Tony Bennett Fan Club 2" Cello. Button,**
1950s. - **$12 $25 $45**

MUS-27

❑ **MUS-27. Pat Boone Song Sheet,**
1950s. Features his hit "Love Letters in the Sand." - **$15 $30 $45**

MUS-28

❑ **MUS-28. "Fabian" "Chancellor" Record Button,**
1950s. Button is 3.5" and has text "Unique Boutique, N.Y.C." and "Distributed By Am-Par Record Corp" on curl. - **$25 $45 $70**

MUS-29

❑ **MUS-29. 'Teen Magazine,**
Jan. 1960. Features Alvin on cover with a story on David Seville, as well as other recoding stars like Fabian, Frankie Avalon, Bobby Darin, Nancy Sinatra and others. - **$10 $20 $40**

MUS-30

MUS-31

❑ **MUS-30. "The Alan Freed Show" Ticket,**
1960. For Carnegie Music Hall concert. - **$90**

❑ **MUS-31. "Beach Boys In Concert" Early Program,**
1965. 16 pages. - **$50 $130 $250**

MUS-32

MUS-33

❑ **MUS-32. "Animals Fan Club" Button,**
c. 1965. Button is 3.5" in diameter featuring band photo. - **$25 $45 $80**

❑ **MUS-33. "Sam The Sham And The Pharaos" Large Button,**
c. 1965. Button is 4" diameter litho with portrait photos of band members in their trademark Pharaoh attire. - **$60 $125 $200**

MUS-34

MUS-35

❑ **MUS-34. "Herman's Hermits" 3-1/2" Cello. Button,**
c. 1965. Store item. - **$15 $25 $40**

❑ **MUS-35. "The Rolling Stones" 3-1/2" Cello. Button,**
c. 1966. Probably sold at concerts. "N.G. Slater Corp." on the curl. Originals in black and white. Fakes are known in other colors. - **$35 $65 $140**

MUS-36

MUS-37

❑ **MUS-36. "Freddie and the Dreamers" Photo Button,**
c. 1966. Known for single "I'm Telling You Now." - **$25 $45 $80**

❑ **MUS-37. "The Supremes Official Fan" 2-1/2" Cello. Button,**
1968. - **$20 $40 $80**

MUS-38

MUS-39

❑ **MUS-38. "Rascals" Button,**
c. 1968. Button is 3" diameter with band photo including member's names "Gene, Eddie, Dino, Felix." Rim curl marked "N.G. Slater Corp."
- **$30 $50 $85**

❑ **MUS-39. "Woodstock" Celebration Litho. Button,**
1969. Issued for 1970 live-action movie filmed during four-day concert. - **$10 $15 $25**

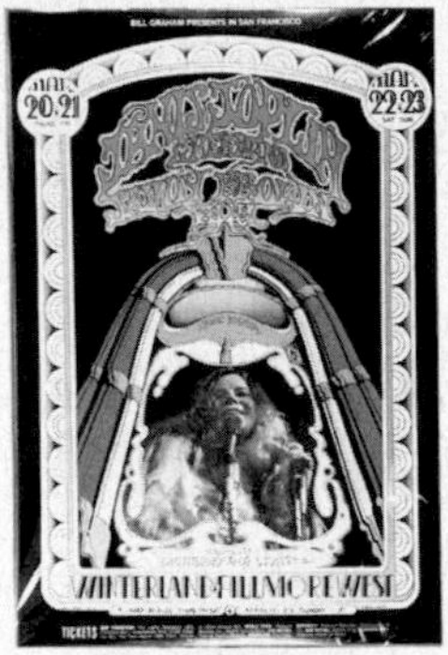

MUS-40

❑ **MUS-40. Janis Joplin Concert Poster,**
1969. First Printing (14-1/8 x 21") - **$150 $300 $450**
Second Printing (14-1/4 x 20-7/8") - **$50 $100 $200**

MUS-41

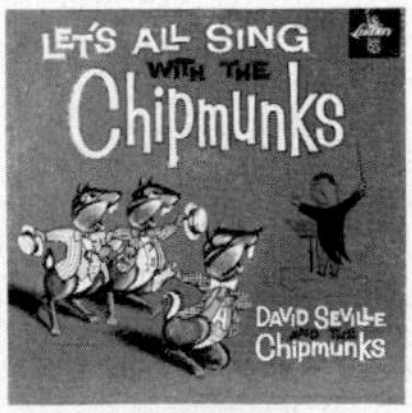

MUS-42

❑ **MUS-41. Frank Zappa Photo Button,**
c. 1969. 3". - **$35 $65 $120**

❑ **MUS-42. "Chipmunks" Album,**
1960s. Bright copper colored 33 1/3 rpm Hi-Fi record. - **$20 $40 $60**

MUS-43

❑ **MUS-43. "The Rolling Stones" Pennant,**
1960s. Black felt pennant is 12x29.5" with red felt border. White silk screened text.
- **$45 $90 $165**

MUS-44

❑ **MUS-44. "Honey West" Soundtrack Album,**
1960s. Soundtrack album for TV show. -
$15 $30 $60

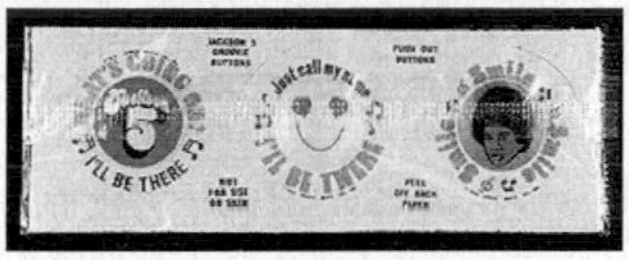

MUS-45

❑ **MUS-45. Jackson 5 Groovie Push-Out Buttons,**
1970. Frosted Rice Krinkles. Strip of three 1-1/2" thin vacuum form sticker buttons. Set of 9 different titles. Each Near Mint Strip - **$15**
Each Used Button - **$2 $4 $6**

MUS-47

MUS-46

❑ **MUS-46. Fleetwood Mac Concert Poster,**
1977. For Oakland Stadium. - **$50 $100 $200**

❑ **MUS-47. David Bowie Pinback,**
1978. Promotes Madison Square Garden concerts. - **$10 $20 $30**

MUS-48

❑ **MUS-48. "The Who" Back Stage Pass Button Set,**
1979. Each is 1-1/2" diameter.
Each **- $10 $20 $40**

MUS-50

MUS-49

❑ **MUS-49. "The Police" Concert Badge,**
1979. 1st version has gold heads on silver background. 2nd version has solid gold color.
Each version - **$15 $25 $50**

❑ **MUS-50. "Bee Gees" Promo Button,**
1970s. 2 1/2" button is from the pre-"Saturday Night Fever" period. - **$15 $25 $50**

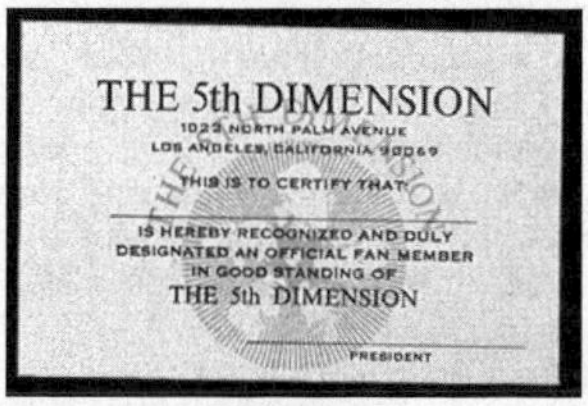

MUS-51

❑ **MUS-51. 5th Dimension Club Card,**
1970s. Card for official fan member. -
$10 $15 $35

MUS-52

❑ **MUS-52. "Elton John" Ecology 3" Cello. Button,**
1980. Also inscribed "Central Park-Keep It Green." Issued for 9/13/80 concert on The Great Lawn. Audience estimated at 400,000. Button is scarce. - **$20 $35 $75**

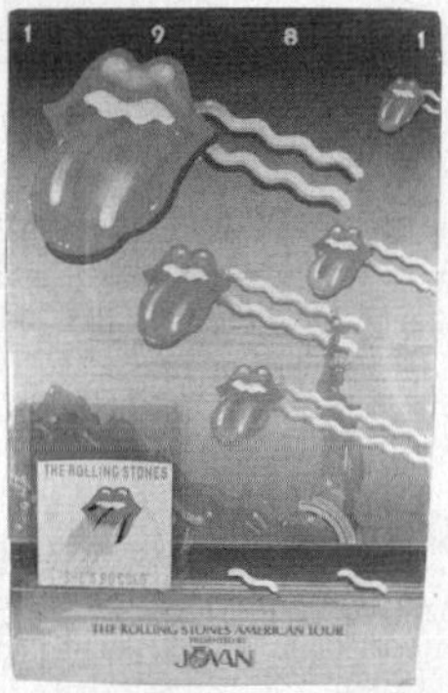

MUS-53

❑ **MUS-53. Rolling Stones Tour Poster,**
1981. One-sheet poster with record.
Poster - **$50 $75 $160**
Record - **$20 $35 $60**

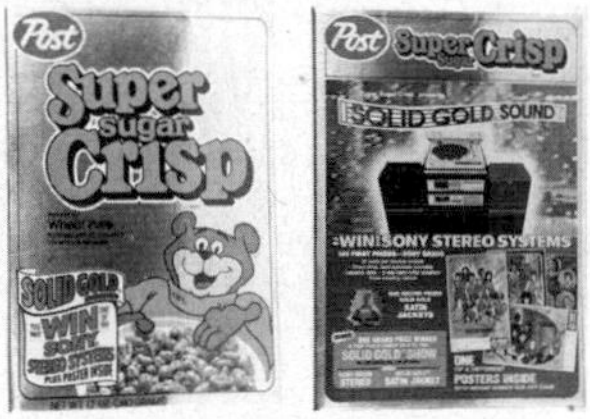

MUS-54

❑ **MUS-54. Solid Gold Dancers Promo on Super Sugar Crisp Cereal Box,**
1984. Box offers poster premiums for the Solid Gold Dancers, featured on their popular TV show "The Solid Gold Show." - **$20 $50 $100**
Each Poster - **$22**

MUS-55

MUS-56

❑ **MUS-55. "David Bowie" Moonlight Concert Pin,**
1985. Red, white and blue background with black color on outfit. - **$10 $20 $55**

❑ **MUS-56. "Cyndi Lauper" Promo Pin,**
1980s. Very ornate. - **$10 $20 $55**

MUS-57

MUS-58

❑ **MUS-57. "Freddie Mercury" Badge,**
1991. Commemorates lead singer of Queen. Badge has pin on back. - **$25 $50 $110**

❑ **MUS-58. Pink Floyd Promo Sign,**
1994. - **$45**

MUS-59

MUS-60

❑ **MUS-59. "Mick Jaguar" Bean Bag,**
1998. Famous Meanies series with tag. - **$12**

❑ **MUS-60. Beach Boys Die-cast Car,**
1999. Racing Champions, Inc. Limited edition. On card. - **$15**

MUS-61

MUS-62

❑ **MUS-61. Janis Joplin Lunch Box,**
2000. - **$25**

❑ **MUS-62. Janis Joplin Figure on Card,**
2000. McFarlane Toys. - **$25**

MUS-63

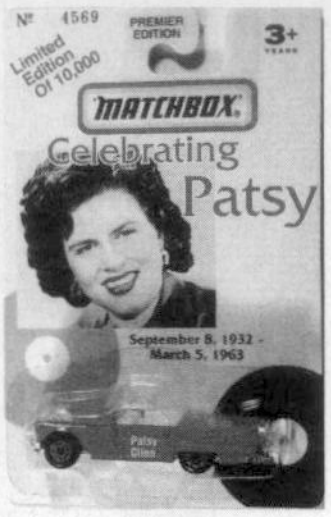

MUS-64

❑ **MUS-63. 'N Sync Button Set,**
2000. Set of 5 on card. - **$5**

❑ **MUS-64. Patsy Cline Matchbox Car,**
2001. Limited edition on card. - **$15**

MUS-65

❑ **MUS-65. Buddy Holly Bobblehead Figure,**
2003. Boxed. - **$25**

Mutt and Jeff

***Mutt and Jeff*, the first continually published six-day-a-week comic strip, was to become one of the best known, funniest, and most popular strips in America. Created by Harry Conway "Bud" Fisher (1885-1954), it started as a horseracing cartoon called *A. Mutt* in the *San Francisco Chronicle* in 1907. Jeff showed up the following year but it wasn't until 1916 that the strip was titled *Mutt and Jeff*. A Sunday color strip was added in 1918. There were many early collections of reprints starting around 1910, hardback books, and comic books into the 1960s. A series of *Mutt and Jeff* musicals toured the country from about 1911 to 1915, and from 1918 to 1923 Bud Fisher Productions turned out animated cartoons, typically at a pace of one a week. Art assistants included Ed Mack and Ken Kling but Al Smith (1902-1986) worked the longest, 1932-1980. The strip was retired in 1982.**

MUT-1

MUT-2

❑ **MUT-1. Postcard,**
1910. New York American newspaper premium. - **$25 $50 $80**

❑ **MUT-2. Mutt and Jeff #1 Hardcover Book,**
1910. 5 3/4" x 15 1/2". Shows photo of Bud Fisher on title page. Scarce in high grade. Reprints cartoon strips published prior to 1910.
GD - **$71** FN - **$286** VF - **$500**

MUT-3

❑ **MUT-3. Mutt and Jeff #2 Hardcover Book,**
1911. 5 3/4" x 15 1/2". Notice cover has been changed and title modified. Reprints cartoon strips published prior to 1911.
GD - **$71** FN - **$286** VF - **$500**

MUT-4

❑ **MUT-4. Stage Show Cardboard Ink Blotter,**
1912. - **$20 $40 $75**

MUT-5

❑ **MUT-5. "Mutt And Jeff In Mexico" Cardboard Blotter,**
c. 1912. For musical comedy stage production. - **$20 $40 $75**

MUT-6

❑ **MUT-6. Hand-Painted Composition Figural Nodders,**
c. 1912. Set of 4.25" tall figures on wooden base, probably German. Each - **$60 $125 $250**

MUT-7

❑ **MUT-7. "Mutt And Jeff In Panama" Song Album,**
1913. 20 pages, 10-1/4" x 13" book. Scarce. - **$20 $40 $90**

MUT-8

❑ **MUT-8. "Mutt And Jeff In College" Cardboard Blotter,**
c. 1913. For musical comedy stage production. - **$20 $40 $75**

MUT-9

MUT-10

❑ **MUT-9. Mutt And Jeff Brass Stickpins,**
c. 1915. Issuer Unknown. Each - **$12 $25 $40**

❑ **MUT-10. Cast Iron Bank,**
c. 1915. Store item. - **$100 $200 $375**

MUT-11

MUT-12

❑ **MUT-11. "Join The Evening Telegraph" Cello. Button,**
c. 1915. Promotion for strip beginning and "Mutt & Jeff Club". - **$35 $75 $125**

❑ **MUT-12. "Cut That Stuff" Cartoon Litho. Button,**
c. 1916. Various cigarette sponsors. Example from set featuring art by Bud Fisher and other cartoonists. Paint easily worn.
Fisher Cartoons - **$8 $15 $35**
Other Artists - **$5 $10 $20**

MUT-13

❑ **MUT-13. German Bisques,**
c. 1920. Mutt is 3-1/8", Jeff is 3".
Each - **$50 $85 $160**

MUT-14

❑ **MUT-14. Mutt And Jeff Jointed Figures,**
c. 1921. Buco, Switzerland. Mutt is 8" and Jeff is 6.25" tall with composition head, hands, shoes with ball jointed body parts. See Peter Rabbit by same company. Each - **$225 $450 $700**

(CRAYON BOX)

MUT-15

❑ **MUT-15. Cupples And Leon Book Seven Boxed With Crayons As Set,**
1924. Store item. 10-1/4x12-1/4x1/2" deep box titled "Crayon Drawing Book." Interior holds book of strip reprints from 1920 along with six crayons. Apparently an effort to sell books from previous years. Boxed Set - **$150 $300 $850**

MUT-16

❑ **MUT-16. Mutt and Jeff Big Book,**
1926. By Bud Fisher. 144 pages.
Hardcover - GD - **$114** FN - **$456** VF - **$800**
With Dust Jacket - GD - **$193** FN - **$772**
VF - **$1350**

MUT-17

❑ **MUT-17. "Mutt And Jeff Play Croquet" Dexterity Puzzle,**
1928. Tin and glass 2-1/2x4" skill game by Herbert Special Mfg. Co., Chicago with instructions on underside. - **$80 $140 $225**

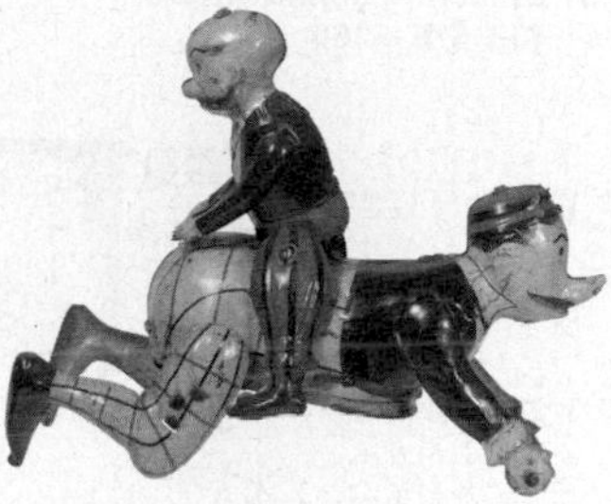

MUT-18

❑ **MUT-18. Mutt And Jeff German Wind-Up Toy,**
1920s. Tin litho toy is 2.5x6.5x5.75" with built-in key and marked with company initials "SG" as well as "Made In Germany." Mutt is depicted on his hands and knees while Jeff sits backward on his back with hands resting on Mutt's rear end. Mutt hops about causing Jeff to bounce around on his back. - **$850 $1650 $3300**

MUT-19

❑ **MUT-19. Bronze Statue of Jeff,**
1920s. 5 3/4" - Premium /Award. -
$65 $135 $250

MUT-20

MUT-21

❑ **MUT-20. Mutt Celluloid Figure,**
1920s. - **$35 $75 $150**

❑ **MUT-21. Jeff Celluloid Figure,**
1920s. - **$35 $75 $150**

MUT-22

MUT-23

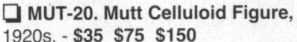

❑ **MUT-22. "Meet Us At Forest Park" Cello. Button,**
c. 1920s. - **$30 $55 $120**

❑ **MUT-23. "I Am Mister Mutt/I Am Little Jeff" Pair Of Gas Station Premium Paper Masks,**
1933. Shell Oil Company. Each - **$25 $45 $90**

MUT-24

❑ **MUT-24. "Mutt And Jeff" Big Little Book,**
1936. Whitman #1113. - **$24 $72 $165**

MUT-25

MUT-26

❑ **MUT-25. "Buffalo Evening News" Cello. Button,**
1930s. From series of newspaper contest buttons, match number to win prize. - **$20 $35 $75**

❑ **MUT-26. "Tangle Comics" Cello. Button,**
1940s. Philadelphia Sunday Bulletin. -
$25 $45 $85

MUT-27

❑ **MUT-27. Jeff And Mutt Adult-Sized Over The Head-Style Costume,**
1960. Store item by Collegeville. 25" wide by 50" tall. Each Near Mint Carded - **$350**
Each Uncarded - **$75 $150 $225**

Nabisco Misc.

The giant National Biscuit Company was formed in 1898 by the merger of a number of smaller companies and independent bakers. The following year its sales totaled 70% of all the crackers and cookies sold in America. Adolphus Green, company chairman, set about to create a new product and a national brand. He named it the Uneeda biscuit, developed a carton (In-er-Seal) to keep it fresh, chose a picture of a boy wrapped in rain gear as a symbol, and invested heavily in advertising. In 1900 the company sold 100 million boxes of Uneeda biscuits. Then quickly came Oysterettes, Zu Zu ginger snaps, Fig Newtons, sugar wafers, and Barnum's Animal Crackers. Oreo, the best selling cookie in the USA, was introduced in 1912. Nabisco, always a heavy advertiser, issued a number of promotional items over the years and has sponsored such children's television classics as *The Adventures of Rin-Tin-Tin, Jabberwocky, Kukla, Fran & Ollie*, and *Sky King*. In the mid-1980s the company was acquired by R.J. Reynolds and became part of RJR Nabisco.

NAB-1

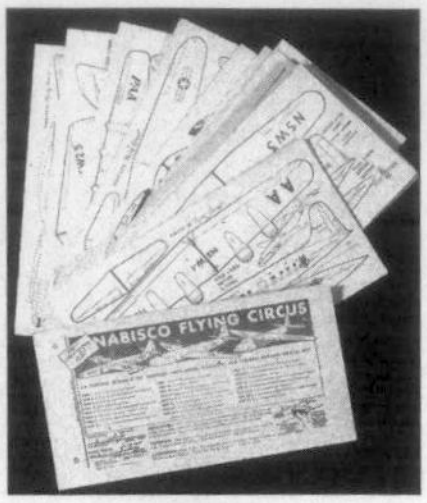

NAB-2

❑ **NAB-1. Golden Anniversary Pinback,**
1948. Metallic gold with child icon which promoted the company. Scarce. - **$10 $20 $35**

❑ **NAB-2. Flying Circus Cards,**
1948. Shredded Wheat premium. Card set of 25 model planes and 12 card set of index and preparation of flight. Since cards were made of cardboard, they were to be cut out and assembled into planes and used like gliders. Cards were obtained in cereal boxes. The 12 card set tells how to fold, cut, and assemble the 25 card set of planes. Each - **$4 $8 $12**

NAB-3

NAB-4

❑ **NAB-3. Arthur Godfrey 6 1/2" Standee,**
1940s. Cardboard standee promoting his radio show for Nabisco. Scarce. - **$60 $100 $200**

❑ **NAB-4. Picture Story Album,**
1940s. Seven card set of classic fairy tales found in boxes of Shredded Wheat. Cards were used as a coloring book. Each - **$2 $4 $8**

NAB-5

NAB-6

❑ **NAB-5. Picture Story Album,**
1940s. 28 card set of boys and girls of all nations Each card tells the story of children in each foreign country. Each - **$2 $4 $8**

❑ **NAB-6. Toytown Cards,**
1940s. Rare. Shredded Wheat premiums. 36 card set which when assembled makes a toytown. Includes cut-outs of buildings like firehouses, stores, bank, church, general store, ice cream parlor and gas station. Also includes bus, car, trees, and of all things, an antique store. Yes, collecting was very popular in the 1940s. Each - **$4 $8 $12**

NAB-7

❑ **NAB-7. Box Promoting Jungle Beasts In 3-D,**
c. 1950. Complete - **$40 $65 $150**

NAB-8

❑ **NAB-8. "Nabisco Wheat Honeys/Prehistoric Beasts" Cereal Box,**
1957. Eight in set issued as companion to set of 10 dinosaurs. Gordon Gold Archives.
Complete Box **- $150 $275 $500**

NAB-9

❑ **NAB-9. Plastic Dinosaurs With Guide Folder And Box,**
1957. Near Mint In Mailer - **$300**

NAB-10

❑ **NAB-10. Wheat Honeys Store Promotional Box Replica Kit With Plastic Dinosaurs,**
1957. Stiff cardboard box with hinged cover and interior compartments. Set of 10.
Box Only - **$100 $225 $400**
Each Figure - **$6 $12 $20**

NAB-11

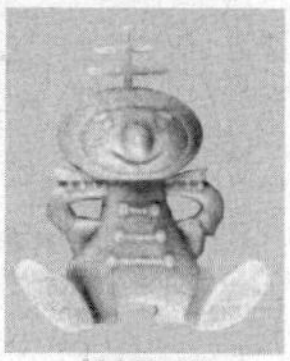
NAB-12

❑ **NAB-11. "Munchy The Spoonman" Pillow,**
1958. 3x9-1/2x15" stuffed fabric figure. -
$85 $165 $350

❑ **NAB-12. "Munchy" Vinyl Attachment For Spoon Handle,**
1959. One of three Nabisco Spoon Men. Three rows of buttons. - **$20 $35 $65**

NAB-13

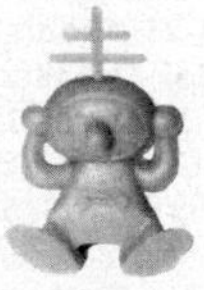
NAB-14

❑ **NAB-13. "Crunchy" Vinyl Attachment For Spoon Handle,**
1959. Two rows of buttons. - **$20 $35 $65**

❑ **NAB-14. "Spoon Size" Vinyl Attachment for Spoon Handle,**
1959. One row of buttons and smaller size than Munchy and Crunchy. - **$30 $50 $75**

NAB-15.

❑ **NAB-15. "Rocket Man" Paper Mask,**
1950s. - **$25 $50 $90**

NAB-16

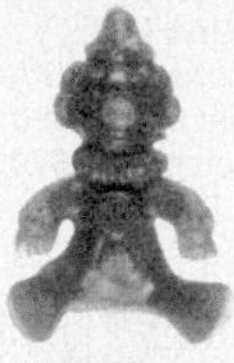
NAB-17

❑ **NAB-16. Buffalo Bee Breakfast Buddy,**
1961. Vinyl figure designed to perch on edge of cereal bowl. - **$5 $12 $20**

❑ **NAB-17. Jolly Clown Breakfast Buddy,**
1961. Vinyl figure designed to perch on edge of cereal bowl. - **$5 $12 $20**

NAB-18

NAB-18. Defenders Of America Cards,
1950s. Shredded Wheat. 24 cards in the set. 8 of the 24 are Rocket cards. 7 pictured. Full color.
Eight Rocket cards. Each - **$6 $12 $25**
Other sixteen cards. Each - **$4 $8 $15**

(FRONT) NAB-19 (BACK)

❑ **NAB-19. "Shredded Wheat" Cereal Box with Promo for 3-D Cut-outs on Back,**
1950s. The Spoonmen appear on front. - **$100 $200 $360**

NAB-20

❑ **NAB-20. Buffalo Bee Breakfast Buddy Cereal Box Flat,**
1961. Gordon Gold Archives.
Near Mint Flat - **$320**
Used Complete - **$70 $140 $260**

NAB-21

❑ **NAB-21. "Speedy Spaceman" Cereal Box Flat,**
1961. Back panel promotes 1-3/4" tall figure packaged in box. Came with a balloon to propel the toy. A matching toy called "Racing Robot" was packaged in Wheat Honeys cereal boxes.
Each Near Mint Flat - **$275**
Each Used Complete - **$50 $100 $160**

NAB-22

❑ **NAB-22. "Jolly Clown Breakfast Buddy" Cereal Box,**
1961. Gordon Gold Archives.
Near Mint Flat - **$320**
Used Complete - **$70 $140 $260**

NAB-23

❑ **NAB-23. "Comic Patch!" Cereal Box,**
1963. Four in set, inserted one per box: Little Orphan Annie, Smilin' Jack, Smitty, Smokey Stover. Gordon Gold Archives.
Used Complete - **$60 $120 $225**

NAB-24

❑ **NAB-24. Cereal Box With Dinosaur Figures Offer,**
1966. Promotes set of 12 "Kooky Spooky" figures packaged one per box. Gordon Gold Archives. Used Complete - **$90 $185 $350**

NAB-25

NAB-26

❑ **NAB-25. Football Premium Offers Box,**
1967. Nabisco Shredded Wheat. Gordon Gold Archives. Complete - **$35 $60 $135**

❑ **NAB-26. "Nabisco Wheat Honeys Jungle Pals" Box Flat With Premium Figure Set,**
1967. Figures are 3" long or tall in solid soft plastic. Gordon Gold Archives.
Near Mint Flat - **$350**
Used Complete - **$60 $115 $225**
Jungle Pals Each - **$5 $12 $20**

NAB-27

❑ **NAB-27. "Nabisco Brands" Award Statuette,**
1982. Statue is 9.5" tall bronze accent plaster on 3.4x5" black wood base. Depicts figure of youngster in rain slicker carrying product package in trademark character from early years, engraved brass inscription plate on base front is "Kroger Sav-On/1982 $1000,000/Nabisco Brands." - **$45 $80 $150**

Nancy and Sluggo

Nancy, a stubby little girl with a perpetual hair arrangement resembling black steel wool held by a white bow, was created in 1933 by cartoonist Ernie Bushmiller (1905-1982), originally as a niece and periodic visitor to her aunt, the established Fritzi Ritz. By the late 1930s, niece and aunt had reversed their featured roles. *Fritzi Ritz* became a Sunday page and *Nancy* got her own daily strip. Nancy's equally-stubby platonic boyfriend & sidekick, Sluggo, came into her life and the pair remains an inseparable cartoon strip duo to this day. Guy and Brad Gilchrist produce the strip today.

NAN-1

NAN-2

❑ **NAN-1. "Fritzi Ritz Spinner",**
1930s. United Feature Syndicate. Cello. over metal disk that has underside center bump for spinning. - **$65 $150 $300**

❑ **NAN-2. "Journal-Transcript Funnies Club" Litho. Button,**
c. 1930s. From set of various characters, also has radio call letters for station in Peoria, Illinois. - **$35 $70 $135**

NAN-3

❑ **NAN-3. "Nancy Has Fun" All Picture Comics,**
1944. Whitman #1487. - **$12 $36 $85**

NAN-4

❑ **NAN-4. "Nancy And Sluggo" BTLB,**
1946. Store item. Whitman Better Little Book #1400. - **$12 $36 $85**

NAN-5

❑ **NAN-5. Nancy and Sluggo 7-1/2" Hard Plastic Dolls,**
c. 1948. Sold in box reading "Designed by Marcie" made by A&H Doll Manufacturing Corp. Also offered as Post Grape-Nuts Flakes premiums. Store box - **$100 $200 $300**
Each doll - **$200 $500 $1000**

NAN-6

❑ **NAN-6. "Comic Capers Club" 2-1/8" Cello. Button,**
1940s. Sun-Times (newspaper). One of the rarest and most desirable comic character buttons. - **$825 $2250 $3750**

NAN-7

❑ **NAN-7. Stuffed Cloth Doll,**
1940s. Store item. 14" tall. - **$115 $230 $475**

NAN-8

❑ **NAN-8. "Metropolitan Group Comics Calendar For 1954" with Nancy And Others,**
1954. Calendar is 5x8.75" overall. 5x7.25" cover page with notation at bottom "1953 Metropolitan Sunday Newspapers Inc." Calendar consists of 12 glossy 5x6.75" pages with comic characters representing each month of the year.
- **$65 $135 $240**

NAN-9

NAN-10

❑ **NAN-9. Nancy Rubber/Vinyl Doll,**
1954. Store item by S&P Doll and Toy Co.
Near Mint Boxed - **$700**
Loose - **$100 $200 $400**

❑ **NAN-10. Sluggo Rubber/Vinyl Doll,**
1954. Store item by S&P Doll and Toy Co.
Near Mint Boxed - **$700**
Loose - **$100 $200 $400**

NAN-11

❑ **NAN-11. Punch-Out Paperdoll Book,**
1974. Store item by Whitman. 10x12-7/8" with 16 pages. Unpunched - **$12 $25 $45**

New Fun Comics

Former pulp magazine writer and cavalry officer Major Malcolm Wheeler-Nicholson came up with the idea of a comic book containing all original material in late 1934. The 10x15" tabloid size magazine *New Fun*, with color covers and black and white interiors, appeared on newstands with a cover date of February 1935. Pages were laid out in a Sunday comic page format with continuing stories, humor pages, text stories and games. Beginning with issue #7, the title became *More Fun*. The magazine added more color and adapted to the standard comic book size and format by 1936. Historically, *More Fun* not only was one of the first comic books with original material but also the first to publish work by Walt Kelly of later *Pogo* fame and Siegel and Shuster of *Superman* fame. *New Fun* formed the cornerstone of the DC Comics publishing empire. The title ran through issue #127 dated November-December 1947.

NEW-1

❑ **NEW-1. "Fun Club" Cello. Button,**
1935. Rare. - **$200 $400 $800**

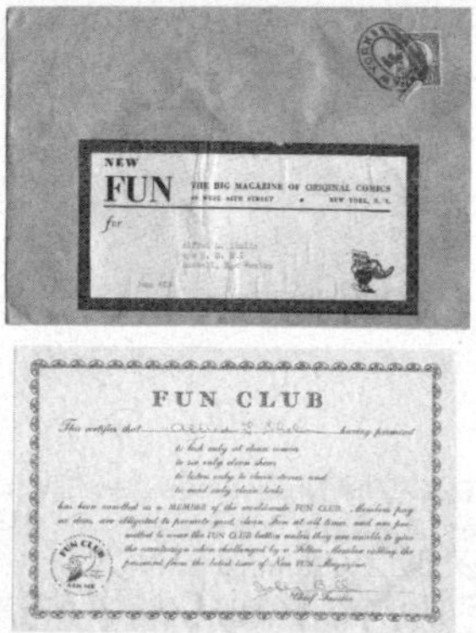

NEW-2

❑ **NEW-2. "Fun Club" Member Certificate With Envelope,**
c. 1935. Accompanied club button.
Mailer - **$150 $300 $600**
Certificate - **$500 $1500 $3000**

The Newlyweds

Created by George McManus (1884-1954), *The Newlyweds* first appeared in Joseph Pulitzer's *New York World* newspaper April 10, 1904. The lovely Gibson girl-like Mrs. Newlywed had a baby boy in 1907, making the strip one of the first in history with a family theme. Commonly known as Snookums, the baby was spoiled to the extreme to the delight of readers. A touring musical comedy began in 1908 and continued into the teens. Cartoonist McManus moved to William Randolph Hearst's *New York Journal* September 1, 1912 where the strip ran as *Their Only Child* until January 30, 1916. Noted animator Emile Cohl (1857-1938) produced a series of cartoons with limited animation in 1913. The strip would have run longer but the success of McManus's *Bringing Up Father* was too much of a workload.

Snookums was brought back as a topper strip to *Bringing Up Father* in 1941 and ran until 1956. "Da!"

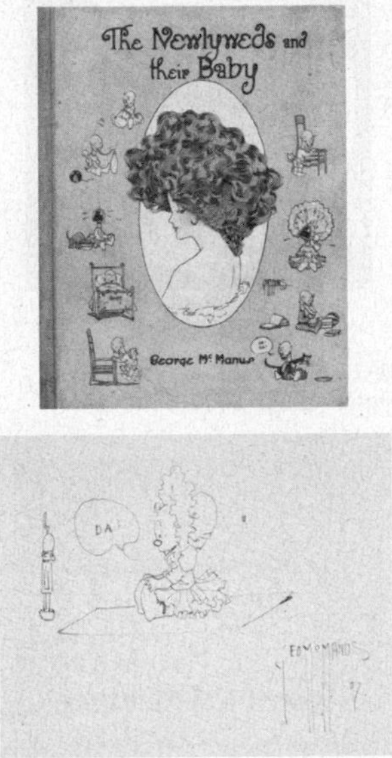

NWD-1

❑ **NWD-1. "The Newlyweds And Their Baby" Platinum Age Comic Book With McManus Original Sketch Signed,**
1907. Saalfield Publishing Co. 10x13" hardcover with 52 pages. McManus has hand-drawn a sketch of Baby Snookums with toy soldier and word bubble reading "Da!" Has signature with "07" added in purple ink. Good - **$250**
Fine - **$900**

NWD-2

❑ **NWD-2. The Newlyweds Snookums Hand-Painted China Plate,**
c. 1910. 7.5" diameter. Back marked "Crosby." - **$40 $75 $125**

NWD-3

❑ **NWD-3. "Snookums" Ceramic Figures,**
1910. Came in two sizes.
Large 4" - **$75 $210 $350**
Small 3" - **$60 $180 $275**

NWD-4

❑ **NWD-4. Snookums German Wind-Up Toy With Customized Box,**
c. 1913. Painted toy is 3x3.5x6.5" with built-in key depicting Snookums from the George McManus newspaper comic strip "Their Only Child" which was originally titled "The Newlyweds." Tiny hole in each hand indicates figure likely held an object. Plain original box, but example shown has namesake comic strip panels glued on. Box - **$25 $50 $100**
Toy Complete - **$500 $1000 $2000**

NWD-5

❑ **NWD-5. "Snookums" Bisque Figure,**
c. 1915. Schafer-Veder. 5" tall. - **$75 $225 $400**

NWD-6

❑ **NWD-6. "Snookums" Cello. Button On Card,**
1927. Universal Exchange (Movie Publicity Agency). Pictured is toddler star of comedy based on "Newlyweds And Their Baby" comic strip. Button maker is Philadelphia Badge Co.
Complete - **$50 $100 $225**
Button Only - **$30 $70 $140**

Newspaper Clubs

During the 1930s, newspapers reached out to younger readers by means of loosely organized clubs, usually associated with comic strip characters featured in their pages. Pinback buttons were a favored means of promotion; some papers offered buttons with a variety of different characters, while syndicated characters appeared with imprints from dozens of newspapers. Often the buttons were serially numbered for use in prize-winning contests designed to boost circulation.

NES-1

NES-2

❑ **NES-1. Grit Newspaper Club Early Button,**
c. 1912. Button is 1.25" with Whitehead & Hoag backpaper. Reads "Grit's Golden Rule Club Do Unto Others As You Would Have Others Do Unto You." - **$15 $25 $60**

❑ **NES-2. S. F. Chronicle Kiddies Club Button,**
c. 1915. Button is 1.25" with Brunt backpaper. - **$10 $20 $35**

NES-3

NES-4

❑ **NES-3. Comic Strips Promotion Postcard,**
1929. Imprinted for Buffalo Courier-Express. For member of "Jolly Junior Sunshine Club" birthday greeting featuring group image of characters. - **$20 $40 $75**

❑ **NES-4. "Bud Billiken Club" Cello. Button,**
c. 1920s. Chicago Defender. - **$8 $15 $25**

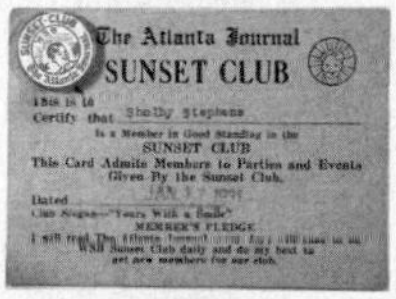

NES-5

(CLOSE-UP OF PIN)

❑ **NES-5. "Sunset Club" Pinback and Card,**
1931. Pinback - **$20 $40 $60**
Card - **$15 $35 $50**

NES-6

NES-7

❑ **NES-6. "The World War" Big Little Book #779,**
1934. Shows newspaper photos of WW1. - **$10 $30 $62**

❑ **NES-7. "Times Junior Pilot" Pinback,**
1930s. - **$20 $40 $60**

NES-8

(CLOSE-UP OF PIN)

❑ **NES-8. "Our Club" Pinback on Membership Card,**
1930s. A great example of one of the early children's clubs promoting the Milwaukee Journal.
Pinback - **$15 $25 $40**
Club Card - **$15 $30 $55**

NES-9

NES-10

NES-11

❑ **NES-9. Evening Ledger Comics "Relentless Rudolph" Cello. Button,**
1930s. Philadelphia Evening Ledger. From colorful series in 1-1/4" size with Evening Ledger promotional back paper. - **$30 $85 $175**

❑ **NES-10. Evening Ledger Comics "Connie" Cello. Button,**
1930s. Philadelphia Evening Ledger. - **$20 $50 $100**

❑ **NES-11. Evening Ledger Comics "Harold Teen" Cello. Button,**
1930s. Philadelphia Evening Ledger. - **$25 $60 $125**

NES-12

NES-13

NES-14

❑ **NES-12. Evening Ledger Comics "Bobby Thatcher" Cello. Button,**
1930s. Philadelphia Evening Ledger. - **$20 $50 $100**

❑ **NES-13. Evening Ledger Comics "Babe Bunting" Cello. Button,**
1930s. Philadelphia Evening Ledger. - **$15 $50 $75**

❑ **NES-14. Evening Ledger Comics "Smitty" Cello. Button,**
1930s. Philadelphia Evening Ledger. - **$20 $60 $100**

NES-15

NES-16

❑ **NES-15. "Just Kids Safety Club" Cello. Buttons,**
1930s. Imprinted for at least 48 different newspapers. Set includes 11 characters in 18 picture variations. Pictured examples are "Mush" and "Marjory." Each - **$12 $20 $40**

❑ **NES-16. Bronco Bill Litho. Button,**
1930s. Example is imprinted for media of Peoria, Illinois. From set of at least 15 different characters. - **$20 $40 $80**

Nick Carter, Master Detective

Nick Carter, created by John Coryell (1848-1924), hero of hundreds of dime novels, began life in 1886 in the pages of Street & Smith's *New York Weekly*. The stories, signed by "Nicholas Carter," were mostly written by Frederick Van Rensselaer (1862-1922). Following decades of pulp magazine appearances, the master detective came to the Mutual radio network in 1943 and was broadcast until 1955. Lon Clark played the master sleuth in the 700+ episodes. The series spawned a spin-off series *Chick Carter Boy Detective.* Sponsors included Lin-X Home Brighteners (1944-1945), Cudahy meats (1946-1951), and Old Dutch cleanser (1946-1952). Walter Pidgeon played Carter in a 1939 MGM movie. *The Nick Carter Club* was a 1930s Street & Smith promotion.

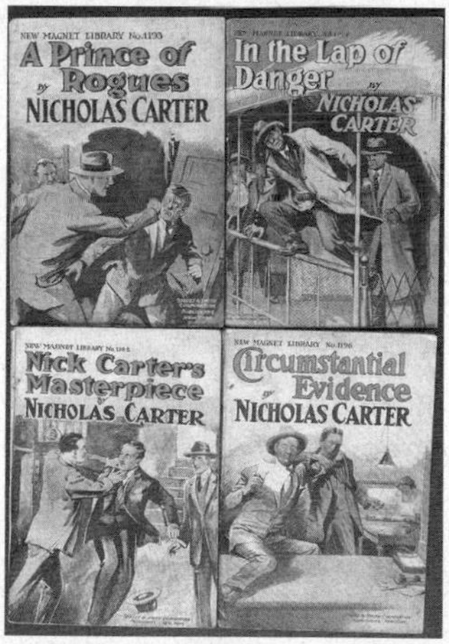

NCK-1

❑ **NCK-1. Nicholas Carter Digest-Sized Pulps,**
1902. Street & Smith Publishing Corp. Four examples 5x7" with 224 pages. Each cover features two men fighting with one startled onlooker. "New Magnet Library" numberings are: 1192 "Nick Carter's Masterpiece," 1193 "A Prince Of Rogues," 1194 "In The Lap Of Danger," 1196 "Circumstantial Evidence." Published between 1902-1905. Each - **$15 $30 $65**

NCK-2 NCK-3

❑ **NCK-2. "Nick Carter Magazine" Store Window 10x13" Ad Card,**
1933. Pictures cover of May issue. -
$75 $150 $300

❑ **NCK-3. "Nick Carter Magazine" Pulp Vol. 1 #3,**
May 1933. Published by Street & Smith. -
$25 $50 $120

NCK-4

❑ **NCK-4. "Nick Carter Fingerprint Set",**
1934. Store item by New York Toy & Game Co. Includes "Nick Carter 999 Club" instruction book with Street & Smith club enrollment form.
Complete - **$50 $100 $200**
Book Only - **$20 $40 $85**

NCK-5 NCK-6

❑ **NCK-5. Club Members Shield,**
c. 1934. Silver luster metal 1-1/16" tall. Issued with pin on reverse or with threaded post and screw-on cap to wear as a stud.
Pinback - **$60 $120 $180**
Stud - **$75 $150 $210**

❑ **NCK-6. Club Card,**
c. 1934. Nick Carter Magazine. Came with badge. - **$35 $85 $150**

NCK-7

❑ **NCK-7. Club Member's Rubber Stamp,**
c. 1934. Street & Smith Publications. Wood handle with rubber stamp about 1x1.5". Rare.
- $75 $150 $250

NCK-8

❑ **NCK-8. "Nick Carter Magazine" Gummed Envelope Sticker,**
1930s. Street & Smith Publications. -
$25 $50 $100

NCK-9

❑ **NCK-9. "Mutual" Radio Program Sign,**
c. 1945. WFBR, Baltimore, Maryland. Photos of stars from Nick Carter, Bulldog Drummond, Sherlock Holmes. 10-1/2x27-1/2". -
$125 $200 $400

Og, Son of Fire

The prehistoric adventures of Og and his companions--Ru, Nada and Big Tooth--were broadcast for a year (1934-1935) on CBS radio, sponsored by Libby. Alfred Brown played the primeval hero of the series, written by Irving Crump (1887-1979), the author of the original Og stories. Og first appeared in the December, 1921 issue of *Boy's Life* magazine; in 1922 Dodd, Mead & Co. published the first book. *Og - Son of Og*; a final sequel was published in 1965.

OGS-1

❑ **OGS-1. "Adventures Of Og, Son Of Fire" 15x20" Map,**
1935. Rare. Libby. - **$200 $400 $800**

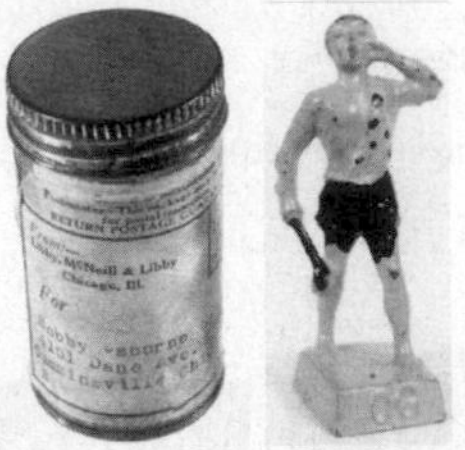

OGS-2 OGS-3

❑ **OGS-2. "Og" 2-1/4" Painted Metal Figure,**
c. 1935. Marked under base "Made For Libby's Milk By Lincoln Logs USA." Six figures in set. For each mailing canister with metal lid add $20-40-60. Figure - **$45 $85 $175**

❑ **OGS-3. "Ru" Metal Figure,**
c. 1935. Part of Og set. - **$40 $75 $160**

OGS-4 OGS-5

❑ **OGS-4. "Nada" Metal Figure,**
c. 1935. Part of Og set. - **$40 $75 $160**

❑ **OGS-5. "Big Tooth" Metal Figure,**
c. 1935. Part of Og set. Bow often broken.
- $50 $110 $220

OGS-6

OGS-7

❑ **OGS-6. "Three Horn" Metal Figure,**
c. 1935. Part of Og set. - **$60 $150 $250**

❑ **OGS-7. "Rex" Metal Figure,**
c. 1935. Part of Og set. - **$55 $125 $230**

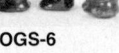

OGS-8

❑ **OGS-8. "Og Son of Fire" BLB #1115,**
1936. By Irving Crump. - **$15 $45 $105**

OGS-9

❑ **OGS-9. "Og, Son Of Fire" Adventure Game,**
1930s. Store item. Whitman game licensed by Stephen Slesinger Inc. "Based On The Famous Stories By Irving Crump" rather than radio premium by sponsor Libby Foods. - **$90 $225 $475**

Omar the Mystic

Also known as *Omar, Wizard of Persia*, this radio series ran for a year (1935-1936) on the Mutual radio network, sponsored by Taystee bread. M.H. Joachim played Omar, a mentor of Chandu the Magician.

OMR-1

❑ **OMR-1. "The Secrets Of Omar The Mystic" Book,**
1936. Scarce. Taystee Bread. - **$40 $70 $135**

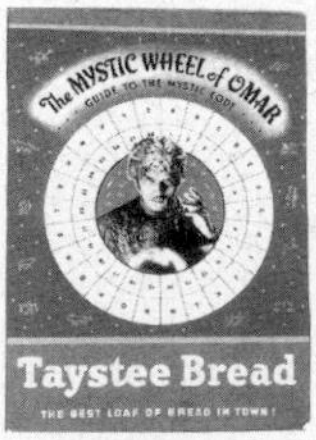

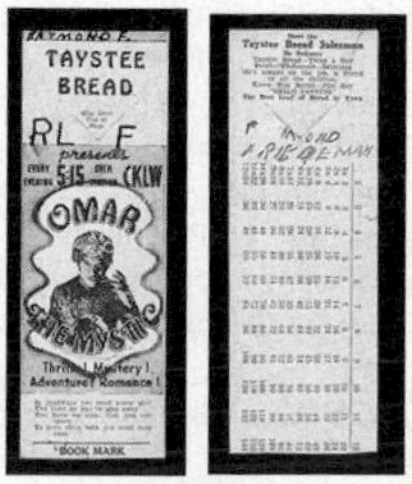

OMR-2 OMR-3

❑ **OMR-2. Taystee Bread Code Card,**
1936. Back has instructions for using "Mystic Wheel". - **$30 $60 $110**

❑ **OMR-3. Taystee Bread Code Bookmark,**
1936. Cardboard marker printed by code numerals on one side. - **$15 $35 $65**

OMR-4

❑ **OMR-4. "Chief Of Secret Ten/Chief Mystic" Higher Rank Member's Card,**
1936. Reverse lists "Duties Of A Chief Mystic." - **$35 $70 $135**

OMR-5

❑ **OMR-5. "Mystic Omar Club" Cello. Member Button,**
1936. Blue and white 1" oval. - **$30 $60 $125**

OMR-6

❑ **OMR-6. "Secret 10 Membership Card",**
1936. Taystee Bread. Reverse lists 10 rules dealing with safety, obedience, school studies and related moral principles under the "Agreement Of The Secret Ten." - **$30 $65 $120**

OMR-7

❑ **OMR-7. Bread Wrapper,**
1930s. - **$30 $45 $85**

One Man's Family

The saga of the Barbour family, written lovingly by Carlton E. Morse (1901-1993), was the longest running serial drama in the history of radio. The program debuted in 1932 on NBC's San Francisco station KGO and a year later went to the NBC network, where it continued until 1959; broadcasting a total of 3,256 episodes. The family tree series told the stories of Henry and Fanny Barbour, their five children (Paul, Hazel, the twins Claudia and Clifford, and Jack), and succeeding generations of Barbours as they lived and died, married, had children, and faced family crises against the backdrop of a changing world. Sponsors included Wesson Oil (1932-1933), Kentucky Winner tobacco (1933-1935), Royal gelatin (1935-1936), Tenderleaf tea (1936-1949), Miles Laboratories (1950-1954), and Toni Home Permanents (1954-1955). A television version ran on NBC prime time from 1949 to 1952 and as a daytime serial in 1954-1955.

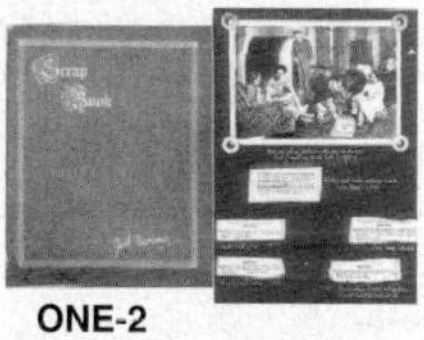

ONE-1 ONE-2

❑ **ONE-1. "One Man's Family History In Words And Pictures" Folder,**
1935. Standard Brands Foods. - **$15 $25 $50**

❑ **ONE-2. "Scrapbook" Yearbook,**
1936. Tenderleaf Tea. Published in graphic style of personally kept album. - **$12 $25 $45**

ONE-3 ONE-4

❑ **ONE-3. Teddy Barbour "Diary" Book,**
1937. Standard Brands Foods. Family events in simulated handwriting. - **$10 $20 $40**

❑ **ONE-4. "One Man's Family" Book,**
1938. Titled "Looks at Life." Has cast photos. Radio premium. - **$15 $25 $50**

ONE-5

ONE-6

❑ **ONE-5. Fanny Barbour "Memory Book",**
1940. Standard Brands Foods. Family photos, notes, etc. in simulated scrapbook form. - **$12 $25 $45**

❑ **ONE-6. "I Believe In America" Album,**
1941. Standard Brands Foods. Style of family scrapbook heavily emphasizing early war years. - **$25 $40 $80**

ONE-7

ONE-8

❑ **ONE-7. Barbour Family Scrapbook,**
1946. Standard Brands Foods. Format of simulated family photos, news clippings, telegrams, etc. - **$15 $30 $60**

❑ **ONE-8. "One Man's Family" Broadcast Highlights Record Album,**
c. 1947. Store item. Vol. 1 hardcover album of three 78 rpm records of selected excerpts from episodes between 1940-1946 on NBC Radio sponsored by Standard Brands Inc. - **$20 $40 $60**

ONE-9

❑ **ONE-9. TV Cast Photo,**
c. 1949. - **$10 $20 $40**

ONE-10

ONE-11

❑ **ONE-10. "Barbour Family Album",**
1951. Miles Laboratories. - **$15 $25 $50**

❑ **ONE-11. "Mother Barbour's Favorite Recipes" Booklet,**
c. 1951. Miles Laboratories. 20th anniversary souvenir picturing cast members over the years. - **$15 $25 $50**

Open Road For Boys

The Open Road for Boys, a popular magazine published monthly from October 1925 to 1950, organized The Open Road Pioneers Club in 1927 for boys and young men who loved the outdoor life and were willing to live up to the ideals of the old pioneers: courage, self-reliance, honesty, determination, endurance, progress, and meeting obstacles squarely. For 35¢ (in coins or stamps) sent to Deep-River Jim, members received a pin, certificate, and sweater emblem. The Club boasted over 3,000 chapters and lasted well into the 1950s.

OPN-1

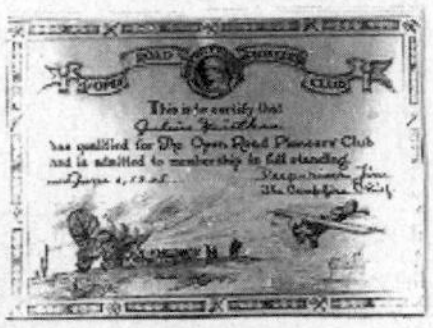

OPN-2

❑ **OPN-1. Open Road For Boys Magazine,**
1934. Has write-up for club & application for pin - **$12 $20 $40**

❑ **OPN-2. "Open Road Pioneers Club" Certificate,**
1935. - **$15 $30 $60**

OPN-3

OPN-4

❑ **OPN-3. Club Particulars Folder,**
c. 1938. Black and white 4-3/8x6-7/8" folder which opens to five panels 6-7/8x21-3/4". Details club aims and discusses various ranks which in order are Trailsman, Woodsman, Hunter, Explorer, Member of the Inner Circle. Text claims 85,000 registered boys and men as members. - **$12 $25 $50**

❑ **OPN-4. "Open Road Pioneers" Cello. Button,**
1930s. - **$5 $10 $20**

OPN-5

OPN-6

❑ **OPN-5. "Open Road Pioneers" Brass Badge,**
1930s. - **$10 $20 $40**

❑ **OPN-6. "Open Road Pioneers" 4-1/2" Fabric Patch,**
1930s. - **$30 $55 $110**

OPN-7

❑ **OPN-7. Leader's Certificate,**
1954. Different wording than member's certificate and "Deep-river Jim" no longer titled as "The Campfire Chief." - **$20 $40 $85**

Operator #5

America's Undercover Ace, handsome young Jimmy Christopher, fought spies and foreign agents from 1934 until the outbreak of World War II in 1939 as Secret Service Operator #5 in the pages of the pulp magazine of the same name. Written by Frederick Davis, his task, month after month, was to save the United States from destruction. A 1934 offer of a replica Operator #5 skull ring must have been short-lived as the ring is quite scarce.

OPR-1

OPR-2

❑ **OPR-1. Enameled Silvered Metal Club Ring,**
1934. Rare. Operator 5 Magazine. Came in the same box as The Spider ring (see SPD-2 for photo). Silvering easily worn off. Twelve reported known: three in Good grade, three in Very Good, one in Fine, one in Very Fine, one in Excellent, two in Near Mint, and one in Mint.
Good - **$2500**
Fine - **$6000**
Very Fine - **$10,000**
Near Mint - **$16,000**
Box - **$175 $350 $750**

❑ **OPR-2. "Secret Service Operator #5" Pulp Magazine,**
June-July 1936. Published by Popular Publications. - **$45 $90 $200**

Oswald, the Lucky Rabbit

Between May, 1927 and August, 1928, Disney's animation studio produced 26 films featuring a slick, enthusiastic rabbit named Oswald. He was Disney's first featured cartoon character that had been developed specifically for a starring role. The series' financial backer was film producer Charles Mintz and the shorts were released by Universal.

With each Oswald cartoon Disney made, the quality of the animation took a leap forward. But it did come at a price. Within a year, production costs became troublesome. Disney visited Mintz to apply for a higher per-film budget. To the great amazement of Disney, Mintz instead told him that he was to cut production costs by twenty percent. Mintz also pointed out that Universal owned the character of Oswald. Should Disney not accept the budget cut, Mintz could produce the series without him. In preparation for this possibility, Mintz had already contracted with many of Disney's staffers behind Disney's back.

Disney made the decision to separate from Oswald; on the train trip home from his meeting with Mintz, he created Mickey Mouse.

As for Oswald himself, Universal eventually reassigned control of the character to former Bray studio animator Walter Lantz. Lantz's studio made more than a hundred Oswald shorts, but took the ill-advised decision to make the character's design cuter and simplify his formerly mischievous personality. By the late 1930s, Oswald had lost his ability to function in complex cartoons. In 1943, he made his final starring appearance on-screen.

This was not the end for the character, however. In 1942, when Lantz characters became the stars of Dell Publishing's *New Funnies* comic book, Oswald immediately began to feature in stories of his own. Through the 1960s, the rabbit regularly appeared in Lantz comics titles, but by the 1970s he pretty much vanished from sight. The character made a comeback in Japan, though, thanks to new merchandise and reruns of his original cartoons on Japan's Cartoon Network.

In February 2006, The Walt Disney Company acquired Oswald from NBC – Universal in a unique trade that involved sportscaster Al Michaels and various broadcasting rights for sporting events, so it seems likely that this character will receive increased attention in coming years.

OSW-1

OSW-2

❑ **OSW-1. "Universal Weekly" With Oswald,** 1927. Volume 25, #20 with 40 pages is 8x10.5". Limited distribution to movie theater exhibitors.- **$40 $80 $135**

❑ **OSW-2. "Universal Weekly" With Oswald,** 1927. Volume 26, #2 with 40 pages is 8x10.5". - **$40 $80 $135**

OSW-3

❑ **OSW-3. "Universal Weekly" With Oswald,** 1927. Volume 26, #13 with 40 pages is 8x10.5". - **$35 $75 $125**

OSW-4

❑ **OSW-4. "Universal Weekly" With Oswald,** 1927. Volume 26, #16 with 40 pages is 8.5x10.5". - **$35 $75 $125**

OSW-5

OSW-6

❑ **OSW-5 "Universal Weekly" With Oswald,** 1927. Volume 26, #17 with 40 pages is 8x10.5". - **$60 $115 $175**

❑ **OSW-6. "Universal Weekly" With Oswald,** 1927. Volume 26, #18 with 40 pages is 8x10.5". - **$40 $75 $125**

OSW-7

❑ **OSW-7. Earliest Known Disney-Related Button Reads "Oswald The Lucky Rabbit",** 1927. Universal Exchange (Movie Publicity Agency). 7/8" celluloid. Pictured is animated cartoon character in Disney art. - **$1000 $2000 $4000**

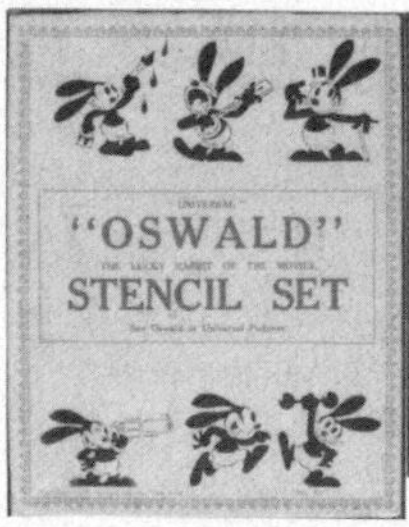

OSW-8

❑ **OSW-8. "Universal Oswald," The Lucky Rabbit Of The Movies Stencil Set,** 1928. Universal Toy & Novelty Co. N.Y. One of the very earliest items of Disney character merchandise and possibly the earliest Disney-related "toy." Complete set comes in 6.5x8.5x.75" deep box with six different images of Oswald which are identical to the set of six stencils included with this set. Stencils are each 4.5x5.5" on stiff cardboard and come with set of six glossy paper sheets. - **$175 $350 $650**

OSW-9

OSW-10

❑ **OSW-9. "Oswald" Celluloid Crib Toy,**
c. 1928. "Oswald Copr. Universal Pictures/An Irwin Product." 6.75" tall with celluloid body, wood ball hands and feet, felt ears. Attached to top of head is string loop for hanging. **- $100 $200 $300**

❑ **OSW-10. Early "Oswald" Doll,**
c. 1928. Universal Pictures Corp. 2.5x6.5x14.5" tall stuffed felt doll. **- $200 $400 $800**

OSW-12

OSW-11

❑ **OSW-11. Early "Oswald" Color Variety Doll,**
c. 1928. "Oswald Copyrighted Universal Pictures Corp./An Irwin Product." 2.5x6.5x14.5" tall stuffed felt doll with additional terrycloth material on front lower half of body. Face has printed design as well as a separate felt nose. The other pictured example has body entirely in red felt whereas this body is primarily orange with red felt ears. **- $175 $350 $700**

❑ **OSW-12. "Oswald" Windup Doll,**
c. 1928. Doll is 5x8x16.5" tall and has built-in key and stitched to the shirt is fabric ribbon which serves as his belt and reads "Oswald/Copyrighted Universal Picture Corp." Has velveteen face while rest of fabric-covered body is cloth and felt. Has leatherette shoes with strings. When wound, rocks back and forth as it slowly moves itself forward. **- $325 $650 $1200**

OSW-13

❑ **OSW-13. Oswald The Lucky Rabbit Doll By Dean's Rag Book Co.,**
1931. 2.5x3x7.5" tall doll. Has velveteen stuffed body with five fingered felt hands, glass eyes and string whiskers attached at nose. Attached to the doll and apparently as issued is a backpack held in place by string around neck and ribbon belt. **- $300 $600 $1200**

OSW-15

OSW-14

❑ **OSW-14. "Oswald The Lucky Rabbit" Large Size Doll By Dean's Rag Book Co.,**
c. 1931. England. 5x7x20.5" tall to the tips of his ears. Doll has stuffed velveteen body with felt ears, glass eyes and nose, round "cotton tail." Printed facial features include Dean's trademark toothy grin. The head is movable. Small lettering on one side of head reads "Oswald The Lucky Rabbit" while on opposite side text includes registration number. Underside of each foot has company mark and "Oswald" name. **- $1650 $3250 $5500**

❑ **OSW-15. Oswald Enamel On Brass Pin,**
1930s. Store item. About 1" tall with ears and pants in coppertone enamel and other areas in green enamel. **- $100 $200 $300**

Our Gang

Between 1922 and 1944 the Hal Roach Studios and MGM produced 221 *Our Gang* comedies. The short films, one- or two-reelers, were immensely successful, with the little rascals--Alfalfa, Baby Jean, Buckwheat, Butch, Darla Hood, Farina, Jackie, Mickey, Spanky, Stymie, Waldo and their dogs Pete the Pup, Pal, and Von--joyfully getting into and out of mischief, playing hooky, putting on musicals, and generally doing no harm and having lots of fun. Their first and only vintage feature film, *General Spanky* was released in 1936. The films were syndicated on television as *The Little Rascals* (1955-1965), as *Our Gang Comedies* (1956-1965), and as *Mischief Makers* (1960-1970). *The Little Rascals* series was re-edited and televised again in the 1970s. A prime-time animated cartoon, *The Little Rascals Christmas Show*, aired on NBC in 1979. *Our Gang* comic books were published in the 1940s with art by Walt Kelly. A feature film, *The Little Rascals*, was released in 1994.

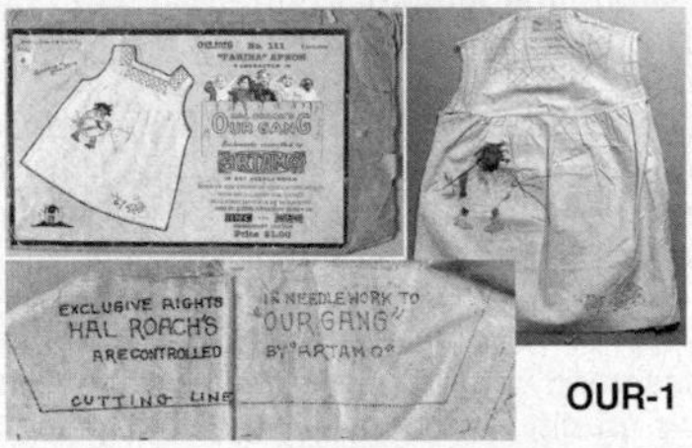

OUR-1

❑ **OUR-1. "Our Gang-Farina" Cloth Apron With Store Bag,**
c. 1925. 7.5x12" store bag holding apron unfolding to 20x24" and picturing Farina activity. Bag label pictures him plus color photo of five members of Our Gang. **- $125 $225 $450**

OUR-2

❑ **OUR-2. Lobby Card,**
1926. For "The Fourth Alarm." **- $85 $210 $325**

OUR-3

OUR-4

❑ **OUR-3. "Pete" With Child Photo,**
c. 1920s. Child's souvenir of Steel Pier, Atlantic City. - **$20 $35 $75**

❑ **OUR-4. Cardboard Ad Blotter,**
1920s. Various sponsors. - **$15 $40 $80**

OUR-5

OUR-6

❑ **OUR-5. Joe Cobb China Mug,**
1920s. Store item by Sebring Pottery Co. - **$75 $150 $300**

❑ **OUR-6. Scooter Lowry China Mug,**
1920s. Store item by Sebring Pottery Co. - **$75 $150 $300**

OUR-7

❑ **OUR-7. "Jay Smith" Portrait Dish,**
1920s. The Seabring Pottery Co., probably used as movie theater premium. 5-1/4" diameter by 1" deep with color portrait. One of the scarcer pieces in a series picturing various Our Gang stars. - **$70 $135 $250**

OUR-8

❑ **OUR-8. Composition Book and Three Tablets,**
1920s. Sizes from 5.5x9" to 6.75x8.5". Composition book has photo of Harry Spear. Back cover has Our Gang cast photo with Spot the Dog. First tablet features Farina. Second tablet features photo of Wheezer holding stuffed dog and horn. Third tablet features cast photo of Our Gang on front cover.
Composition Book - **$40 $70 $135**
Each Tablet - **$30 $60 $110**

OUR-9

OUR-10

❑ **OUR-9. "Hal Roach's Rascals" Photo,**
1920s. - **$20 $40 $80**

❑ **OUR-10. "Majestic Electric Radio" Cardboard Ink Blotter,**
1920s. - **$25 $45 $90**

OUR-11

❑ **OUR-11. Bisque Figure Set Boxed,**
1930. 5x9.25x1.25" graphic design box of 10 painted bisque figures authorized by Hal Roach Studios. Near Mint Boxed - **$1250**
Each Figure - **$60 $100 $210**

OUR-12

❑ **OUR-12. Rubber Stamps Set,**
1930. Nifty/Geo. Borgfeldt Co. 5x10" boxed set of eight character stamps from cast of "Our Gang Of Movie Fame" copyright Hal Roach Studios. - **$60 $125 $225**

OUR-13

❑ **OUR-13. Figure Mold Play Kit,**
1931. Store item by Gem Clay Forming Co. for Louis Wolf Co. Eight hollow plaster figures for painting plus backdrop panel.
Near Mint Boxed - **$875**
Each Painted Figure - **$15 $30 $60**

OUR-14

❑ **OUR-14. "Our Gang" Bab-O Premium Punchout Dolls,**
c. 1931. Bab-O Cleanser. 12.25x18.25" sheet with punchout dolls for nine Our Gang characters - Farina (2), Echo, Wheezer, Jackie Cooper, Chubby, Pete (the pup), Stymie and Mary Ann Jackson. Each character is holding or using "Bab-O." Also includes cut-outs of bathtub and sink as well as four cans of Bab-O.
Unpunched - **$90 $175 $300**

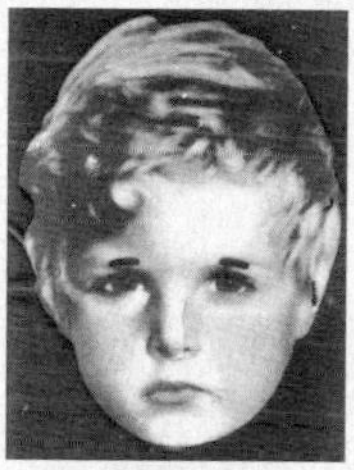
OUR-15

OUR-16

❑ **OUR-15. Dickie Moore Mask,**
c. 1932. U.S. Caramel Co. One of a set. - **$20 $40 $85**

❑ **OUR-16. "Pete" Cello. Button,**
c. 1932. From "Member Spanky Safety Club" series with Hal Roach copyright. - **$50 $100 $200**

OUR-17

OUR-18

OUR-19

❑ **OUR-17. "Buckwheat" Cello. Button,**
c. 1932. From "Member Spanky Safety Club" series with Hal Roach copyright. - **$60 $135 $275**

❑ **OUR-18. "Alfalfa" Cello. Button,**
c. 1932. From "Member Spanky Safety Club" series with Hal Roach copyright. - **$40 $115 $190**

❑ **OUR-19. "Darla Hood" Cello. Button,**
c. 1932. From "Member Spanky Safety Club" series with Hal Roach copyright. - **$35 $90 $160**

OUR-20

OUR-21

❑ **OUR-20 Puzzle,**
1932. McKesson's Milk of Magnesia. -
$50 $85 $170

❑ **OUR-21. Puzzle Mailer,**
1932. McKesson's Milk of Magnesia. -
$15 $30 $60

OUR-22

❑ **OUR-22. Fan Photo,**
1934. Hal Roach Studios. - **$15 $25 $55**

OUR-23

❑ **OUR-23. Portraits Candy Box,**
1935. Novel Package Corp. 2x3.25x1" deep box featuring Spanky lid. Underside pictures him plus Harold, Alfalfa, Darla, Buckwheat, Scottie, Baby Patsy, Pete. - **$225 $450 $750**

OUR-24

❑ **OUR-24. Our Gang Candy Box,**
1935. Large size 6" x 3-3/4". Novel Package Corp. Front features photo of Spanky while additional group photo on back pictures him with Harold, Alfalfa, Darla, Buckwheat, Scotty, Baby Pasty and Pete. "Our Gang" logo is repeated on all side panels. Bottom and flap serves as a coupon and three of these were to be sent in with 10 cents to receive "An Album With Photos Of Our Gang." - **$300 $600 $1100**

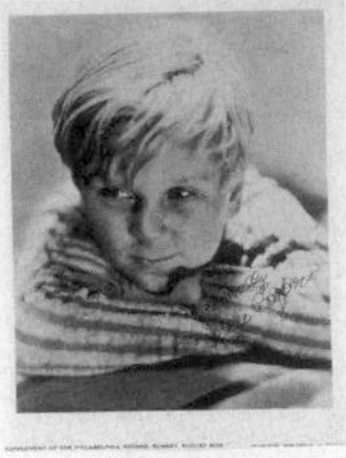

OUR-25

OUR-26

❑ **OUR-25. Jackie Cooper Photo,**
1936. Philadelphia Record newspaper premium. -
$10 $18 $35

❑ **OUR-26. Fan Photo,**
1937. Hal Roach Studios. - **$15 $25 $55**

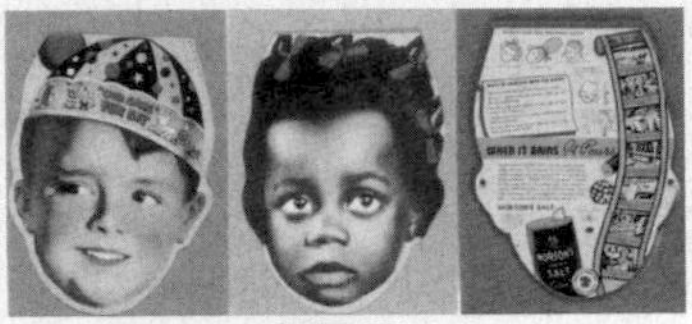

OUR-27

❑ **OUR-27. "Fun Kit" Diecut Booklet,**
1937. Morton's Salt. Features colored mask-like photos, activity pages, rules for their "Eagles Club". - **$100 $225 $375**

OUR-28

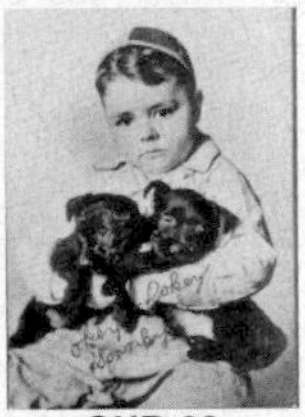

OUR-29

❑ **OUR-28. "Our Gang Painting Book",**
1937. Sears, Roebuck. Copyright by Hal Roach Studios. - **$45 $90 $175**

❑ **OUR-29. Spanky Fan Photo,**
c. 1937. Hal Roach Studios. - **$12 $25 $50**

OUR-30

❑ **OUR-30. "Our Gang" Pencil Box,**
1930s. Textured red cardboard. Eagle Pencil Co. - **$35 $70 $145**

OUR-31

OUR-32

OUR-33

❑ **OUR-31. "Spanky" Pencil Sharpener,**
1930s. 1-3/16" red catalin plastic. -
$50 $100 $175

❑ **OUR-32. "Scottie" Pencil Sharpener,**
1930s. 1-3/16" green catalin plastic. -
$50 $100 $175

❑ **OUR-33. "Pete" Pencil Sharpener,**
1930s. 1-3/16" red catalin plastic. -
$80 $160 $275

OUR-34

OUR-35

❑ **OUR-34. Endorsement Poster For Boat Motors,**
1938. Evinrude-Elto Outboard Motors. 20x26" black and white with red borders. -
$90 $175 $350

❑ **OUR-35. Our Gang Calendar,**
1939. Taystee bread. Cardboard sheet issued monthly. Each - **$40 $85 $160**

OUR-36

OUR-37

❑ **OUR-36. Litho Advertising Button,**
1930s. Sunfreze. 3/4" blue and white litho. Comes with and without sponsor's name. Each - **$10 $20 $40**

❑ **OUR-37. Movie Photo Including "Buster Brown",**
1930s. Probable premium. Shows kids and dog in boxing ring with caption "Buster Brown, Skinny, Tige & Kids." - **$25 $50 $80**

OUR-38

❑ **OUR-38. Our Gang Comedy Blatz Gum,**
1930s. Each Card - **$18 $30 $65**

OUR-39

OUR-40

❑ **OUR-39. "Contestant" Cello. Button,**
1930s. Probable theater or newspaper contest. - **$30 $60 $120**

❑ **OUR-40. "Our Gang Club" Cello. Button,**
1930s. Superba Theatre by Chicago button maker. Matinee inscription plus "Watch For Your Color". - **$25 $50 $100**

OUR-41

❑ **OUR-41. Our Gang Character Ad Standup,**
1930s. 3" tall with grooved wooden base holding die-cut colorful cardboard picturing both front and back view of "Joe Cobb" with Pete the dog. Advertises "Felin's Ham." - **$20 $40 $75**

OUR-42

OUR-43

OUR-44

❑ **OUR-42. "Safety First" Cello. Button,**
1930s. Probable Our Gang member club button, rim curl copyright "Hal Roach Studios". - **$12 $25 $50**

❑ **OUR-43. "King Carl 'Alfalfa' Switzer" 2-1/2" Cello. Button,**
1930s. National Ice Cream Week. His name is followed by "Of Hal Roach's Our Gang-A MGM Release". - **$75 $150 $300**

❑ **OUR-44. "Spanky's Safety Patrol" 14x28" Sample Wall Calendar,**
1943. - **$60 $120 $200**

OUR-45

❑ **OUR-45. Bisque Nodders,**
1930s. German made store item. Set of six as shown: Pete, Chubby Chaney, Wheezer, Jackie Cooper, Farina, Mary Ann Jackson.
Each - **$75 $150 $275**

OUR-46

OUR-47

❑ **OUR-46. "Our Gang Adventures" Big Little Book #1456,**
1948. - **$12 $36 $78**

❑ **OUR-47. "The Little Rascals' Club" Member Card,**
c. 1955. WHUM-TV Channel 61. - **$20 $45 $85**

OUR-48

❑ **OUR-48. "Spanky" Felt Beanie,**
c. 1955. Beanie is 9.5" diameter by 5" tall. One of the four panels that make up the beanie has image of an older Spanky wearing beanie with "Spanky" text on it and text "Spanky" below picture. - **$55 $110 $165**

Ovaltine Misc.

Ovaltine was created in 1904 by Swiss physician Dr. George Wander as a flavored milk additive, and the original combination of malt, eggs, vitamins, and minerals is still in use in Europe. The Wander Company brought Ovaltine to the United States in 1905, using the same mix of ingredients except for the addition of sugar. Ovaltine found wide use as a tasty health food for children and adults. (The Red Cross shipped Ovaltine to Allied prisoner-of-war camps as a nutritional supplement during both World Wars.) The Sandoz Pharmaceutical Company acquired the Wander Company in 1967 and Ovaltine is now sold in "chocolate malt" (introduced in the 1960s) and "rich chocolate" (introduced in the 1980s) flavors, as well as the "original malt" version. In addition to the many premiums the company issued as the sponsor of such classic radio programs as *Radio Orphan Annie* and *Captain Midnight*, Ovaltine has produced promotional items not related to specific programs.

OVL-1

❑ **OVL-1. "Lecture On Nutrition And Digestion By The Wonder Robot" Booklet,**
1934. Issued at Century of Progress Hall of Science. - **$50 $90 $185**

OVL-2

❑ **OVL-2. "Betty The Nail Biter" Sunday Comics Ad,**
1936. One-half page with coupon for Orphan Annie cup with green background decal. Text promotes Ovaltine as cure for nervousness. - **$8 $12 $25**

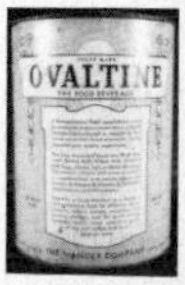

OVL-3

OVL-4

OVL-5

❑ **OVL-3. Litho. Tin Canister,**
1939. 9" tall "Hospital Size". - **$25 $40 $80**

❑ **OVL-4. Glass Shaker with Mixer,**
1930s. - **$30 $55 $110**

❑ **OVL-5. English "Delicious Ovaltine" China Mug,**
1930s. - **$20 $35 $65**

OVL-6

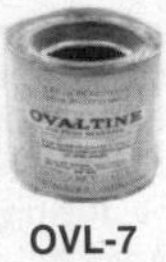

OVL-7

OVL-8

❑ **OVL-6. English "Delicious Ovaltine" China Mug Designed Without Handle,**
1930s. - **$25 $40 $75**

❑ **OVL-7. Sample Size Tin Container,**
1930s. Miniature 2-1/4" diameter by 2" tall. With Lid - **$20 $40 $80**

❑ **OVL-8. "School Size" Sample Tin Container,**
1930s. English issue miniature 1-1/2" diameter by 1-3/4" tall. Pictures Johnnie, Winnie, Elsie. Complete - **$30 $50 $90**
Opened - **$20 $35 $65**

OVL-9

OVL-10

❑ **OVL-9. Plastic Mug,**
1940s. Sandy Strong. - **$25 $55 $110**

❑ **OVL-10. "Ding Dong School" Plastic Mug,**
1950s. Decal pictures "Miss Frances," the teacher on 1952-1956 TV educational series. - **$35 $65 $125**

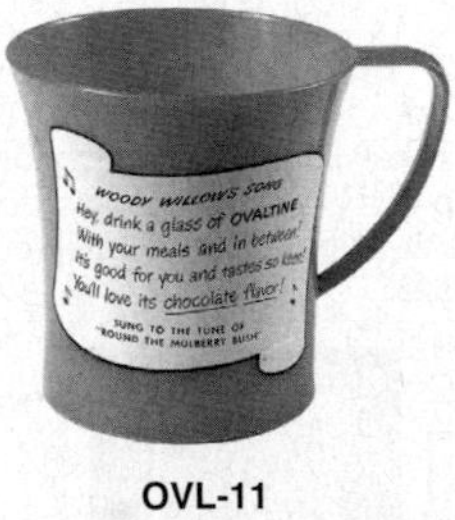

OVL-11

❑ **OVL-11. "Woody Willow's Song" Plastic Cup,**
1950s. 3" with song verse promoting Ovaltine use to tune of 'Round The Mulberry Bush.' - **$25 $55 $110**

OVL-12

❑ **OVL-12. Canadian "Ovaltine Trading Cards",**
1960s. Made by Canada Decalcomania Co. Ltd. Distributed on Ovaltine jars with 12 in the set. Each - **$8 $15 $25**

OVL-13

OVL-14

❑ **OVL-13. "Ovaltine Shaker Cup,"**
1970s. Cup is 6.25" tall premium white soft plastic with text in red/brown and matching brown soft plastic lid. - **$15 $25 $40**

❑ **OVL-14. Ovaltine Secret Decoder Ring,**
2000. - **$35**

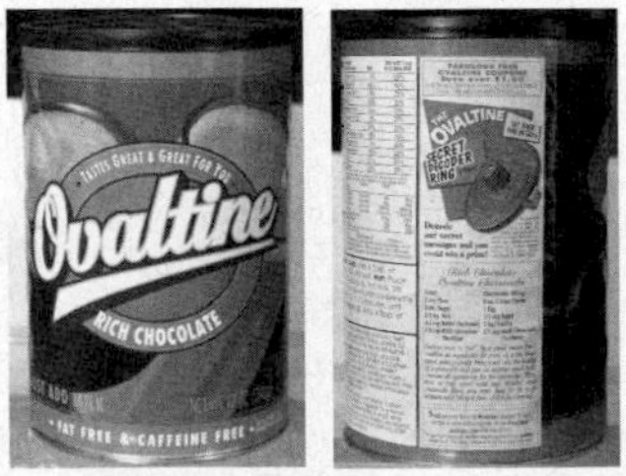

OVL-15

❑ **OVL-15. Ovaltine Can With Coupon,**
2000. Coupon on back of can for Secret Decoder Ring (OVL-14). - **$28**

Ozzie and Harriet

Ozzie Nelson, born Oswald George Nelson (1906-1975) began in show business with his own orchestra in 1930. Harriet Hilliard (1909-1994) joined Ozzie as a singer in 1932. Venues like the Glen Island Casino led to their headlining the *Baker's Broadcast* radio show with hosts including Joe Penner and cartoonists Robert Ripley and Feg Murray. They joined the cast of the Red Skelton radio show from 1941 to 1944.

***Ozzie and Harriet* premiered on CBS radio October 8, 1944 and ran until Jun 18, 1954. The TV series debuted on ABC and ran October 10, 1952 until September 3, 1966. The show was a classic family situation comedy with sons David and Ricky (1940-1985) playing themselves with Ozzie producing, writing and directing. Co-stars included: Don Defore as Thorny, Lyle Talbot as Joe Randolph, Mary Jane Crist as Clara Randolph, Parley Baer as Darby and Skip Young as Wally.**

The show proved to be a perfect promotional outlet for son Ricky. He first sang on the April 10, 1957 episode *Ricky The Drummer,* performing Fats Domino's *I'm Walkin'.* He had 30 top 40 hits between 1957 and 1962, second only in popularity to Elvis Presley at the time. Rick also appeared in feature films, most notably *Rio Bravo* with John Wayne and Dean Martin in 1959 and *The Wackiest Ship In The Army* with Jack Lemmon in 1960.

DC published five issues of *The Adventures Of Ozzie And Harriet* comics in 1949-1950.

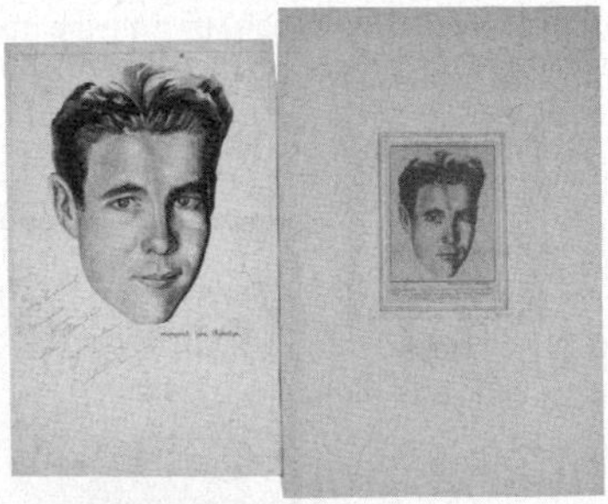

OZH-1

❑ **OZH-1. Ozzie Nelson Signed Original Art,**
1937. 9-7/8x16" artboard with image of Ozzie by Margaret Jane Thornton signed "Every Best Wish To Margaret Jane Thornton From Ozzie Nelson And Harriet Hilliard." Very Fine, Same Or Similar - **$150**

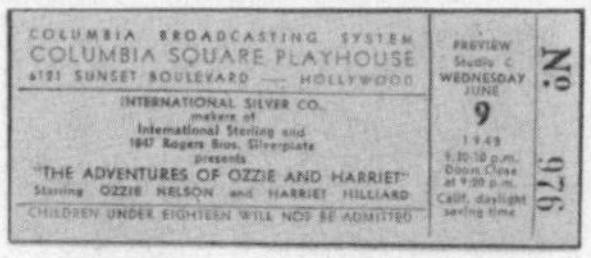

OZH-2

❑ **OZH-2. "The Adventures Of Ozzie And Harriet" Radio Program Ticket,**
1948. - **$12 $25 $65**

OZH-4

OZH-3

❑ **OZH-3. "The Adventures Of Ozzie And Harriet" Fan Photo,**
c. 1953. H. J. Heinz Co. Nelson family photo including sons David and Ricky for show newly sponsored by Heinz over ABC network. - **$15 $30 $50**

❑ **OZH-4. Nelson Family Fan Photo,**
c. 1956. Pictures Ozzie, Harriet, Ricky, David with facsimile signatures. - **$12 $25 $45**

OZH-5

❑ **OZH-5. "The Adventures Of Ozzie & Harriet" Candy Box,**
c. 1958. Almond Joy candy bars of Peter Paul Candies. TV sponsorship also indicated for "Maverick" series. - **$35 $60 $90**

OZH-6

❑ **OZH-6. Radio Station Sign With Ozzie & Harriet And Others,**
c. 1950s. 11x28" cardboard sign from WFBR, Baltimore radio station. - **$40 $85 $175**

Peanuts

Probably the most successful comic strip of all time, Charles Schulz's (1922-2000) *Peanuts* appeared for a couple of years as *Li'l Folks* in the St. Paul *Pioneer Press* before it was syndicated under its new name by United Feature in 1950. The antics of Charlie Brown, the strip's unlikely hero, Snoopy the wonder dog, Lucy van Pelt, Linus, Schroeder, and Pigpen have become part of American culture. There have been numerous reprint books, feature-length animated films, prime-time television specials, a musical comedy, and extensive merchandising and licensing of the major characters. Creator Charles Schulz died in his sleep on February 12, 2000; the next day his final Sunday page appeared in newspapers around the world. He was one of a very few cartoonists who never had an assistant, and *Peanuts* strips appearing in newspapers today are reprints. The Charles M. Schulz Museum and Research Center opened in Santa Rosa, CA. on August 17, 2002. Items are usually copyrighted Charles M. Schulz or United Feature Syndicate. Copyright dates on items relate to character designs and are usually unrelated to the date an item was issued.

PEA-1

PEA-2

❑ **PEA-1. College Football Homecoming 2-1/4" Litho. Button,**
1960. Minnesota Star and Sunday Tribune. For University of Minnesota vs. University of Illinois game with rim curl authorizations by Peanuts and United Feature Syndicate. - **$25 $50 $80**

❑ **PEA-2. Daily Comic Strip Introduction 11x28" Promotion Card,**
c. 1960. United Feature Syndicate. Imprinted for (New York) Daily News. - **$85 $175 $300**

PEA-3

❑ **PEA-3. "Peanuts" Child's Concert Wooden Piano,**
1962. Store item by Ely Mellow-Tone Chime Pianos. 18x18x11" tall black on white. - **$85 $175 $350**

PEA-4

PEA-5

❑ **PEA-4. Charlie Brown 7 1/2" Vinyl Doll,**
1966. With removable hat, shirt and pants. Produced by Pocket Dolls in Hong Kong. - **$20 $45 $90**

❑ **PEA-5. Charlie Brown's Reflections,**
1967. By Charles M. Schulz. Hallmark Product. 52 pages. - **$12 $25 $50**

PEA-6

❑ **PEA-6. Pre-School Child's Eye Exam Promotion Booklet,**
1967. Imprinted for Detroit Department of Health. Eight pages of comic strips illustrating vision information by members of Peanuts gang. - **$15 $35 $75**

PEA-7

❑ **PEA-7. "Have Lunch With Snoopy" Dome Top Metal Lunch With Thermos,**
1968. Store item by Thermos.
Box - **$50 $100 $200**
Bottle - **$10 $25 $50**

PEA-8

❏ PEA-8. Snoopy WWI Aviator Figural Music Box,
1968. Wood/composition by Anri. Plays It's A Long Way To Tipperary. - **$65 $125 $225**

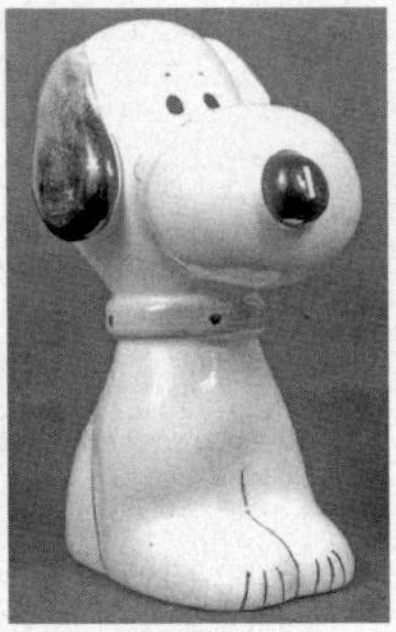

PEA-9 PEA-10

❏ PEA-9. Charlie Brown Glazed Pottery Figural Bank,
1968. Bank is 2.5x3.5x7" tall. Notations on bottom read "Quagrifogilio Florence/Hand-Painted In Italy/United Feature Syndicate Inc., 1968." - **$85 $175 $300**

❏ PEA-10. Snoopy Glazed Pottery Figural Bank,
1968. Bank is 2.75x4.75x6.5" tall. Bottom has two circular notations "Quagrifgilio-Florence Hand-Paipnted In Italy/United Feature Syndicate Inc., 1968." - **$85 $175 $300**

PEA-11

❏ PEA-11. "Snoopy For President" Button,
1968. Button is 2.5". Edge curl has "Copyright 1966 United Feature Syndicates." - **$30 $60 $110**

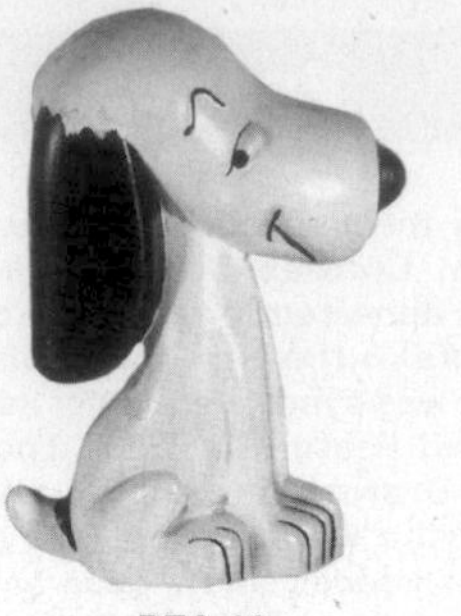

PEA-12

❏ PEA-12. Snoopy Ceramic Figure,
1968. Scarce. - **$65 $135 $200**

PEA-13

❏ PEA-13. Parade Drum With Box,
c. 1968. J. Chein & Co. Tin snare drum with wooden drumsticks plus carrying cord.
Box - **$25 $50 $100**
Drum - **$115 $225 $375**

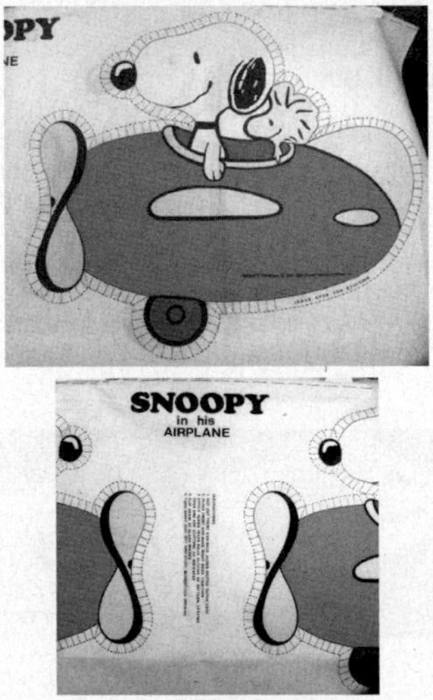

PEA-14

❏ PEA-14 "Snoopy in his Plane" Cloth Doll,
1968. Large. - **$50 $90 $160**

PEA-15

PEA-16

❏ PEA-15. Charlie Brown Ceramic Figure,
1968. 9" tall. - **$70 $150 $235**

❏ PEA-16. "I'm On The Moon" Cello. Button,
1969. Store item made by Simon Simple. 1-3/4" red, white and blue issued to commemorate moon landing. One of the nicest and most popular Snoopy buttons. - **$50 $100 $200**

PEA-17

❏ PEA-17. Peanuts Vinyl Figure Set,
1960s. Believed set of seven, charactes stand 7" to 9.5" tall. Included are Charlie Brown, Snoopy, Lucy, Linus, Sally, Schroeder, Pig Pen. Each has text reading "United Feature Syndicate." Each - **$30 $60 $115**

PEA-18 PEA-19

❏ PEA-18. Charlie Brown Composition Bobbing Head,
1960s. Store item. Other characters also issued. - **$60 $140 $250**

❏ PEA-19. Lucy Composition Bobbing Head,
1960s. Store item, other characters also issued. - **$60 $140 $250**

PEA-20

PEA-21

❑ **PEA-20 Pig Pen Composition Bobbing Head,**
1960s. Most valuable of the series and hardest to find. - **$90 $225 $475**

❑ **PEA-21. Charlie Brown Enameled Metal Necklace Charm,**
1960s. Store item. United Feature Syndicate copyright. From character series. -
$30 $60 $110

PEA-22

PEA-23

❑ **PEA-22. "Get Newsday For Peanuts" Button,**
1960s. Newspaper promo for comic strip readership. - **$20 $45 $85**

❑ **PEA-23. Lucy "Be A Know-It-All" Newspaper Promo Button,**
1960s. The News. 2.25" black/white/red. -
$25 $50 $100

PEA-24

PEA-25

PEA-26

❑ **PEA-24. Plastic Clip-On Badge,**
1970. Millbrook Bread. Five or more characters in set. Carded - **$10 $18 $30**
Loose - **$5 $8 $15**

❑ **PEA-25. "Snoopy's Spotters Club" 2" Litho. Tab,**
c. 1970. Millbrook Bread. - **$8 $15 $25**

❑ **PEA-26. Litho. Tab,**
c. 1970. Restaurant issue. - **$5 $10 $15**

PEA-27

PEA-28

❑ **PEA-27. "Peanuts Patches",**
1971. Interstate Brands. Set of five with envelope and order coupon.
Set With Mailer - **$25 $45 $90**

❑ **PEA-28. "Colonial Capers Cartoon Comics" 2-1/2" Cello. Button,**
1971. Probable newspaper issue. -
$15 $25 $40

PEA-29

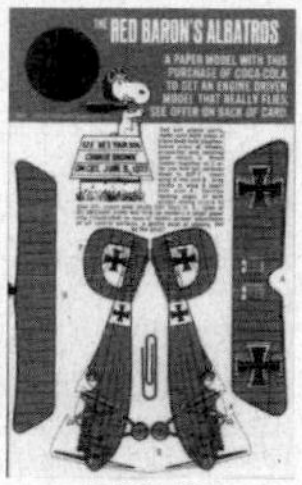

PEA-30

❑ **PEA-29. "It's The Great Pumpkin" Promo Button,**
1971. Promotes October 23 CBS TV program. 3". - **$35 $65 $135**

❑ **PEA-30. "Red Baron's Albatross" Punch-Out,**
1973. Coca-Cola. - **$30 $55 $95**

PEA-31

PEA-32

❑ **PEA-31. "Happy Birthday, America!" Cello. Button,**
1976. Bicentennial issue. - **$12 $18 $35**

❑ **PEA-32. Original Daily Comic Strip Art With Snoopy And Woodstock,**
1977. 7-1/2x29-1/2" black and white india ink art with four panels.
Similar Age With Snoopy - **$2000 $4000 $6500**

PEA-33

❑ **PEA-33. Linus Candle Figure,**
1970s. Hallmark. - **$20 $40 $95**

PEA-34

PEA-35

❑ **PEA-34. "Peanuts" Metal Lunch Box With Thermos,**
1980. Store item by Thermos.
Box - **$25 $50 $100**
Bottle - **$10 $20 $30**

❑ **PEA-35. "Snoopy and the Gang" Top**
1980s. Very colorful. - **$30 $50 $90**

PEA-36

PEA-37

❑ **PEA-36. Snoopy Bean Bag**
1998. With two tags. - **$28**

❑ **PEA-37. Snoopy as Frankenstein Stuffed Toy,**
1999. Halloween premium for Whitman's chocolates. - **$12**

PEA-38

❑ **PEA-38. Charles Schulz Final "Peanuts" Sunday Comic Strip,**
2000. Historic, and undoubtedly saved by many fans. Near Mint - **$7**

PEA-39

PEA-40

❑ **PEA-39. Snoopy Standee,** 2000. United Feature Synd. Unusual die-cut standee which promotes the return of products after Charles Schulz's passing. - **$20 $40 $90**

❑ **PEA-40. Charlie Brown Ornament,** 2000. In box. - **$22**

PEA-41

❑ **PEA-41. Snoopy Ceramic Figure,** 2000. Made in Indonesia. - **$45**

PEA-42

❑ **PEA-42. Snoopy #1 Ace Pewter Figure,** 2000. Hallmark product in box. - **$50**

PEA-43

❑ **PEA-43. Peanuts Christmas Figures,** 2001. - **$30**

PEA-44

PEA-45

❑ **PEA-44. Snoopy Candy Container,** 2001. Plastic doghouse holds candy. Roof comes in blue, green or yellow. Each - **$10**

❑ **PEA-45. Playing Cards with Tin Box,** 2001. Two decks of cards in a collectors tin. In box. - **$18**

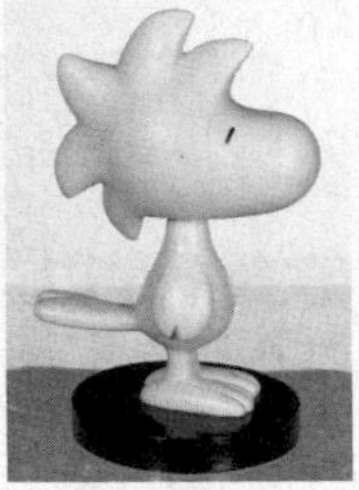

PEA-46

PEA-47

❑ **PEA-46. Woodstock Bobbing Head Figure,** 2003. - **$22**

❑ **PEA-47. Pigpen Bobbing Head Figure,** 2003. - **$22**

PEA-48

❑ **PEA-48. Schroeder Bobbing Head Figure,** 2003. - **$22**

PEA-49

❑ **PEA-49. Halloween Display,** 2005. Danbury Mint. - **$85**

PEA-50

❑ **PEA-50. Christmas Display,** 2005. Danbury Mint. - **$85**

PEA-51

❑ **PEA-51. Valentine's Day Display,** 2006. Danbury Mint. - **$85**

Pee-wee Herman

Comedian and actor Paul Reubens grew up in Sarasota, Florida, the winter home of the Ringling Brothers and Barnum and Bailey Circus. After graduation, he moved to Hollywood and joined the Groundlings comedy troupe. Along with Groundlings member Phil Hartman (1948-1998) he developed the funny but geeky man-child alter ego of Pee-wee Herman in 1978, inspired by the fun of the circus and the slapstick comedy of the 1950s kids TV show hosted by Pinky Lee.

The live *Pee-wee Herman Show* ran five months at the Roxy Theater, leading to an HBO-TV special which made Pee-wee a star in 1981. Numerous appearances on the *David Letterman Show*, concert tours, including sold-out performances at Carnegie Hall, were followed by the August 1, 1985 feature film *Pee-wee's Big Adventure*. Directed by Tim Burton, the basic plot has Pee-wee searching for his stolen bike. The CBS-TV series *Pee-wee's Playhouse* aired from 1986 to 1991. Talking furniture and flowers joined a cast including George McGrath as Globey, Lynne Marie Stewart as Miss Yvonne, Laurence Fishbourne as Cowboy Curtis and Alison Mork as talking chair Chairry. The feature film *Big Top Pee-wee* was released June 27, 1988 with Pee-wee playing a farmer when a big storm causes a circus to be set up on his land. Co-Stars included Penelope Ann Miller as Winnie and Kris Kristofferson as Mace. In June 2007 Paul Reubens made his first

appearance in character as Pee-wee in 16 years at Spike TV's Guy Choice Awards. "I know you are, but what am I?

PWH-1

❑ **PWH-1. "Pee-wee Herman" Action Figure,**
1980. Matchbox. 6.5x10" blister card contains 5.75" tall poseable figure. Sealed - **$5 $10 $20**

PWH-2

❑ **PWH-2. "Pee-wee's Playhouse" Playset,**
1988. Matchbox. 12x27x7.5" deep box contains set to be used with Pee-wee Herman action figures. Comes with Pee-wee's scooter, Floory, Clockey, Mr. Window, Dancing Flowers, etc. - **$30 $60 $125**

PWH-3

❑ **PWH-3. "Pee-wee Herman" Limited Edition Large Doll Boxed With Certificate,**
1989. J. C. Penney by Herman Toys. Exclusive edition of 2000 or less. 40" tall doll of cloth stuffed body and hard vinyl head, hands and shoes. Accompanied by 8x10" certificate of authenticity in white cardboard box marked "Limited Edition" within larger shipping box that has matching edition number. Near Mint - **$250**

PWH-4

❑ **PWH-4. "Pee-wee Herman" Bobbing Head Doll,**
2000. - **$22**

Pep Boys

Three pals opened an auto supply store in Philadelphia in 1921. Founded by Emanuel "Manny" Rosenfeld, Maurice "Moe" Strauss and Graham "Jack" Jackson, the store prospered and eventually grew into a chain of operations in the Eastern states, watched over through the years by the smiling cartoon faces of the founders. The company currently has 595 stores in 36 states with headquarters still in Philadelphia.

PEP-1

❑ **PEP-1. U.S. Sesquicentennial Exposition 6x8" Decal,** 1926. Pep Auto Supply Co. copyright. Full color patriotic art water transfer decal with "Pep Boys" glassine envelope. Decal reverse inscription includes "All Over Philadelphia And Camden."
Near Mint With Envelope - **$135**
Loose - **$20 $40 $80**

PEA-2

❑ **PEP-2. Early Catalogue,**
c. 1926. 4-1/2x6-3/4" catalogue of 68 pages captioned "All Over Philadelphia And Camden!" - **$35 $70 $115**

PEP-3

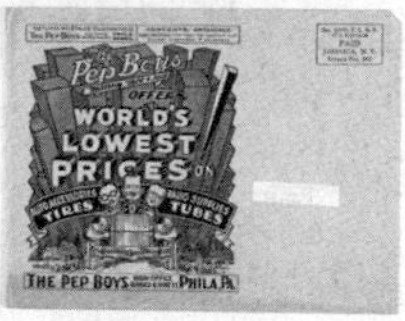

PEP-4

❑ **PEP-3. Catalog,**
1930. 72 pages and front and back cover. - **$30 $60 $90**

❑ **PEP-4. Mailer For Catalog,**
1930. - **$10 $20 $40**

PEP-5

PEP-6

❑ **PEP-5. Catalog,**
1931. 96 pages and front and back cover. - **$30 $60 $90**

❑ **PEP-6. "Pep Boys Dawn Patrol" Postcard,**
1933. Response to listener over WIP Radio w/facsimile signature of announcer Fred Wood. - **$40 $75 $150**

PEP-7

PEP-8

❑ **PEP-7. Catalogue,**
1938. - **$25 $55 $85**

❑ **PEP-8. Catalogue,**
1939. - **$25 $55 $85**

PEP-9

PEP-10

❑ **PEP-9. Patch,**
1930s. Red outline with yellow background premium patch. - **$15 $35 $75**

❑ **PEP-10. Brass Match Cover Holder,**
1940s.Brass match holder which has opening for Pep Boy logo at bottom. - **$30 $60 $90**

PEP-11

❑ **PEP-11. "The Pep Boys" Christmas Bonus Check Unused,**
1940s. Check is 3.25x9.25" with notation at top right reading "To The Philadelphia National Bank/Philadelphia, Penna." Colorful graphics of Santa sack with Manny, Moe and Jack riding out of sack in car. Blank reverse.
- **$15 $30 $60**

PEP-12

PEP-13

❑ **PEP-12. Matches,**
1940s. No name printed at bottom. -
$8 $12 $25

❑ **PEP-13. Matches,**
1940s. "Pep Boys" printed at bottom. -
$8 $12 $25

PEP-14

PEP-15

❑ **PEP-14. Boxed Playing Cards,**
1940s. - **$60 $125 $200**

❑ **PEP-15. Catalogue,**
1954. Store premium. - **$20 $40 $65**

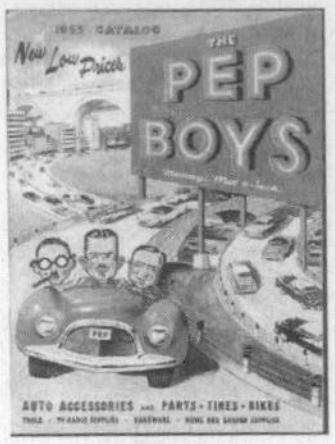

PEP-16

PEP-17

❑ **PEP-16. Catalogue,**
1955. Store premium. - **$20 $40 $65**

❑ **PEP-17. Plastic Cigarette Holder,**
c. 1950s. - **$35 $65 $125**

Pete Rice

Pistol Pete Rice was the sheriff of Buzzard Gap, Arizona, in a series of Street and Smith pulp westerns. A total of 32 issues written by Ben Conlon under the name Austin Gridley, *Pete Rice Western Adventures* appeared from November 1933 to June 1936. For a dime, readers could get a *Pete Rice Club* deputy badge and a members' pledge card.

PTR-1

❑ **PTR-1. "Pete Rice" Gummed Paper Envelope Sticker,**
c. 1934. Street & Smith Co., publishers of Pete Rice pulp magazine. - **$15 $30 $60**

PTR-2

❑ **PTR-2. Deputy Club Metal Badge,**
c. 1934. Badge - **$20 $40 $90**
Envelope - **$10 $15 $30**

PTR-3

❑ **PTR-3. "Wild West Weekly" Pulps With "Pete Rice" Stories,**
1938. Two issues: August 27, 1938 issue is 6-7/8x9-7/8" with 130 black/white pages having cover painting by Saunders. Contents include "The Cougar's Claws" Pete Rice story by Austin Gridley. Jan. 21, 1939 issue is 7x9.75" with 130 black/white pages. Front cover art by Scott. Contains Pete Rice story "Terror In Sunup Valley" by Austin Gridley. Each Of Similar Vintage - **$15 $25 $50**

Peter Pan

See Ted Hake's *Official® Price Guide to Disney Collectibles*, Second Edition, formatted identically to this book but in full color evaluating over 9,000 Disney company and character collectibles from 1924 through 2006.

Peter Rabbit

First to use the Peter Rabbit name was British artist and author Beatrix Potter. She was born in London in 1866. As a teenager, she often vacationed with her wealthy parents in the Lake District of England. She loved drawing her pets and wildlife and a friend, the Vicar Hardwicke Rawnsley, encouraged a serious pursuit of her artistic talent. Her first book "*The Tale of Peter Rabbit*" was originally in letter form to children of a friend. The Vicar urged her on and she self-published it in 1902. The story was immediately a success and by 1903 sales exceeded 50,000 copies.

A few years later in America, Thornton Burgess began writing stories as letters for his young son. The son apparently believed all rabbits should be named "Peter" and the father complied. Burgess published "Old Mother West Wind" in 1910. The book told adventure stories, featuring many different animals, one of which was titled "Peter Rabbit Plays A Joke." Subsequent "West Wind" titles were quickly published and in 1912 Burgess began his long collaboration with illustrator Harrison Cady.

Starting in 1920, Cady adapted the Burgess characters for publication as the Peter Rabbit Sunday comic strip in the *New York Tribune*. The strip, however, soon became more Cady than Burgess, featuring an essentially new rabbit family and slap-stick humor. Comic book reprints appeared in the 1940s and 1950s. The strip ceased publication in 1956.

Today, the Potter rabbit is generally known as Peter Rabbit while the Burgess rabbit is known as Peter Cottontail.

PET-1

❑ **PET-1. Celluloid Flip On Stickpin,**
c. 1915. Columbia Records. - **$60 $135 $200**

PET-2

❑ **PET-2. "Quaddy Note Paper" Box,**
1916. Store item. Stationery box copyright by Harrison Cady. - **$45 $95 $185**

PET-3 PET-4

❑ **PET-3. "Peter Rabbit Puts On Airs" Miniature Pamphlet,**
1922. Newspaper premium with Harrison Cady art. - **$35 $65 $100**

❑ **PET-4. "How Peter Rabbit Went to Sea" Miniature Hardback Book,**
1920s. From a series of hardbacks. Scarce. - **$75 $125 $215**

PET-5

❑ **PET-5. Peter Rabbit Jointed Figure,**
1920s. Buco of Switzerland. 2x3x7.5" tall figure has ball-jointed neck, arms and legs and finely detailed hand-painted face. Wears felt clothing over padded body with buttons on shirt and jacket. This company also produced similar figures for Mutt and Jeff. - **$350 $750 $1250**

PET-6

PET-7

❑ **PET-6. Peter Rabbit Child's Sterling Silver Ring,**
1920s. Miniature figure image in clothing outfit. - **$75 $165 $350**

❑ **PET-7. Peter Rabbit "Bedtime Stories Club" Cello. Button,**
1920s. Newspaper sponsor name specified. - **$40 $80 $150**

PET-8 PET-9

❑ **PET-8. Peter Rabbit "Bedtime Stories Club" Cello. Button,**
1920s. Newspaper sponsor unspecified. - **$30 $65 $110**

❑ **PET-9. Newspaper Club Cello. Button,**
1920s. - **$40 $80 $150**

PET-10

❑ **PET-10. "Peter Rabbit" Tin Canister,**
1920s. Store item. 4" dia. by 2" tall can and lid, both with full color Peter Rabbit family art. - **$60 $110 $235**

PET-11 PET-12

❑ **PET-11. "Peter Rabbit Club" Cello Button,**
1920s. This example from Peoria Journal. Also seen without white panel and with name of the Utica Observer and also the Los Angeles Examiner. - **$25 $50 $100**

❑ **PET-12. "Peter Rabbit Club" Cello. Button,**
1920s. Sponsor "Wisconsin News." - **$60 $125 $250**

PET-13

❑ **PET-13. Paint Book,**
1937. Store item. Whitman book with 36 pages of Harrison Cady art in comic strip panel format. - **$35 $70 $150**

PET-14

❑ **PET-14. "Peter Rabbit" Toothbrush Holder,**
1930s. Holder is 2x2x5" tall, high glaze china. Back reads "Japan." - **$60 $125 $175**

Pez

This peppermint candy originated in Austria in 1927. Edward Haas, the inventor, shortened the German word for peppermint, *pfefferminz*, to Pez. Sales were slow until the company, Pez Candy Inc., entered the United States in 1952 targeting the children's market with a figural head on the dispenser and a cherry flavored candy. Collectors are now willing to spend four-figure amounts for a rare example. In 1987 feet were added to the dispenser base. In addition to the classic dispensers featuring cartoon figures, animals, superheroes, and Disney characters, PEZ watches, jewelry, keychains, and clip-ons have been produced. Most dispensers are priced as Fine or Near Mint.

PEZ-1

❑ **PEZ-1. Litho. Tin Clicker,**
c. 1955. - **$160 $325 $525**

PEZ-2

❑ **PEZ-2. Space Gun Display Sign,**
1956. Scarce. Cardboard sign that held the 6 candy-shooting guns. - **$200 $500 $800**

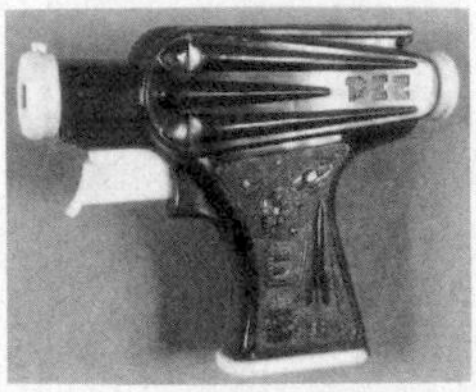

PEZ-3

PEZ-4

❑ **PEZ-3. Space Gun,**
1950s. Candy shooter gun came in red, yellow, blue, green and black. - **$200 $400 $750**

❑ **PEZ-4. Witch "Pez" Dispenser,**
1950s. Dispenser is 4.25" tall marked "Made In Austria." Detailed witch head and one side of body has raised image of witch flying on a broom. - **$100 $200 $325**

PEZ-5

❑ **PEZ-5. Litho. Tin Yo-Yo,**
1950s. - **$100 $200 $375**

PEZ-6 (ENLARGED VIEW)

❑ **PEZ-6. Tin Rotating Store Rack,**
1950s. 16" tall. - **$300 $600 $1150**

PEZ-7

PEZ-8

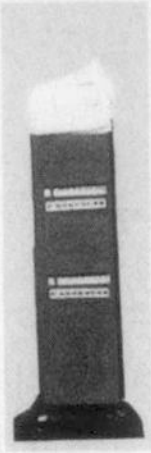

PEZ-9

PEZ-10

❑ **PEZ-7. Space Trooper Pez,**
1950s. Blue - **$275-$350**
Red - **$325-$450**
Yellow - **$375-$475**

❑ **PEZ-8. Popeye Pez,**
1950s. Blue stem. - **$200-$300**

❑ **PEZ-9. Pez Arithmetic,**
1962. Blue - **$650-$900**
Red or green - **$900-$1250**

❑ **PEZ-10. Pez Lions Club,**
1962. With 1962 stem - **$3000-$4000**
With generic stem - **$1900-$2400**

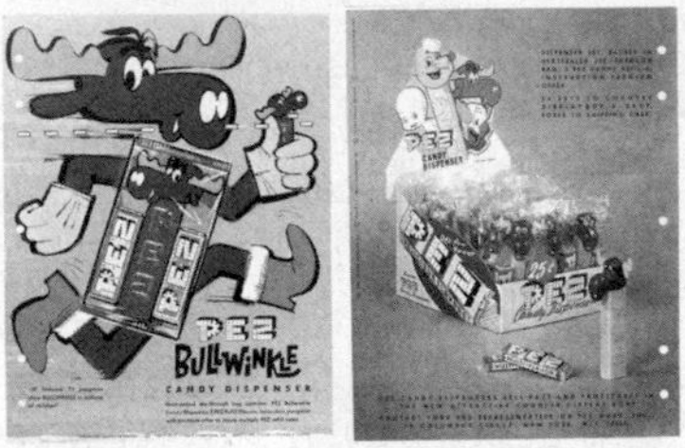

PEZ-11

❑ **PEZ-11. "Pez Bullwinkle" Retailer's Sales Sheet,**
1964. Single two-sided glossy paper sheet is 8.5x11". Left margin has ring binder holes as issued. Reverse is photo of multi-character display box containing complete amount of 24 identical Bullwinkle Pez dispensers. The die-cut display also has images of Popeye, Casper the Ghost and Bozo. - **$65 $125 $225**

PEZ-12

PEZ-13

PEZ-14

❑ **PEZ-12. Green Creature Pez,**
1965. - **$450-$550**

❑ **PEZ-13. Football Player Pez Dispenser,**
c. 1965. Version with tape strip on helmet rather than plastic strip. - **$75 $150 $225**

❑ **PEZ-14. Peter Pan Pez Dispenser,**
1968. - **$100 $200 $300**

PEZ-15

PEZ-16

PEZ-17

❑ **PEZ-15. Go-Pez,**
1968. Flesh - **$325-$450**
Black - **$525-$850**

❑ **PEZ-16. Tin Clicker,**
c. 1960s. - **$10 $15 $25**

❑ **PEZ-17. Tinker Bell Pez,**
1960s. Pink stem. - **$150-$250**

PEZ-18

❑ **PEZ-18. Bullwinkle Sealed Pez Dispenser,**
1960s. Yellow stem variety. Sealed in cellophane with two orange candy packs and insert paper. NM sealed - **$750**

PEZ-19

❑ **PEZ-19. Pez Candy Shooter Gun,**
1960s. Pez dispenser is 5.5" long hard plastic. Actually fires Pez candy. Red - **$75 $150 $275**
Black - **$100 $225 $375**
Blue - **$135 $275 $450**

PEZ-20

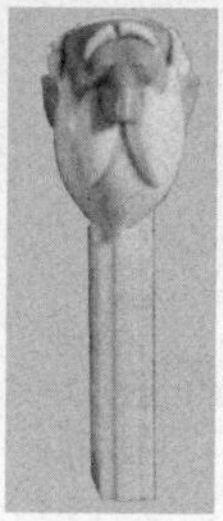

PEZ-21

PEZ-22

❑ **PEZ-20. Asterix Pez,**
1960s. Rare. Usually missing parts - **$1350-$1750**

❑ **PEZ-21. Müeslix Pez,**
1960s. Rare. - **$1700-$2100**

❑ **PEZ-22. Obelix Pez,**
1960s. Rare. - **$1500-$1900**

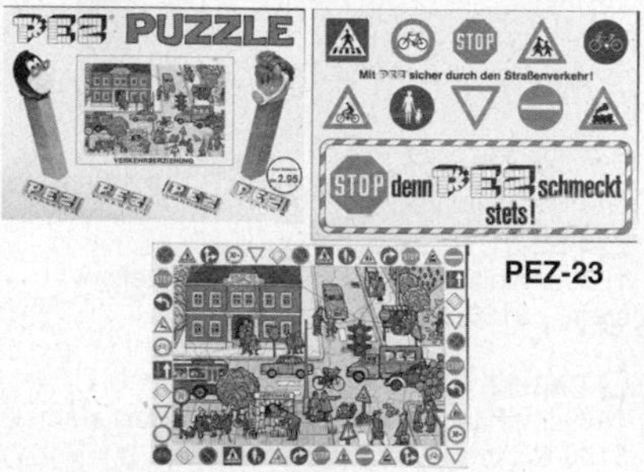

PEZ-23

❑ **PEZ-23. Austrian Puzzle,**
1960s. 8.25x11.75" illustrated cardboard folder holding full color Pez scenes jigsaw puzzle. Unpunched - **$25 $50 $75**

PEZ-24

❑ **PEZ-24. Disney Pez Dispenser Display Card,**
1970. Card fits into the back of a display box. - **$30 $50 $85**

PEZ-25

❑ **PEZ-25. Promotional Pocket Knife,**
c. 1970. 2-3/4" long with vinyl over metal case depicting Pez logo, the word "International" and stylized globe. - **$25 $50 $135**

PEZ-26

PEZ-27 PEZ-28

❑ **PEZ-26. Pez Alpine,**
1972. - **$1900-$2400**

❑ **PEZ-27. Mary Poppins Pez,**
1972. - **$900-$1300**

❑ **PEZ-28. Spare Froh Pez,**
1972. - **$1650-$1850**

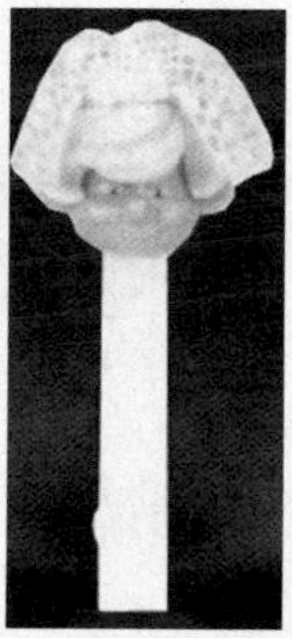

PEZ-29

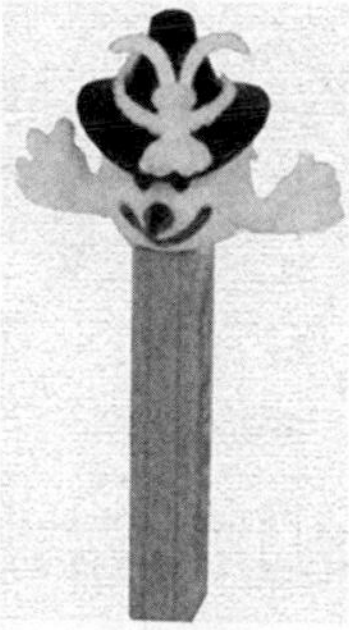

PEZ-30

❑ **PEZ-29. Pez Bride,**
1975. Red Hair - **$1550-$1850**
Brown Hair - **$1650-$2050**
Blonde Hair - **$1750-$2250**

❑ **PEZ-30. Olympic Snowman,**
1976. - **$625-$725**

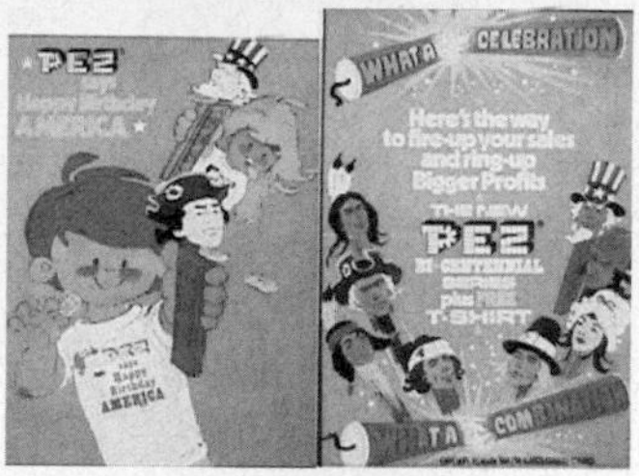

PEZ-31

❑ **PEZ-31. Retailer's Sales Promotion Folder,**
1976. 8-1/2x11" promoting line of bicentennial dispensers. - **$30 $60 $120**

PEZ-32

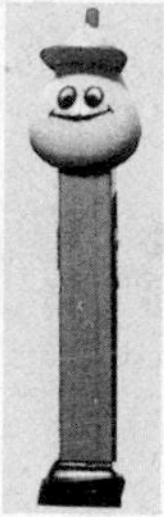

PEZ-33

PEZ-34

PEZ-35

❑ **PEZ-32. Batman Soft Head Dispenser,**
1978. From series of super hero dispensers with vinyl rather than hard plastic heads. - **$65 $150 $300**

❑ **PEZ-33. Pez Pear,**
1979. - **$1000-$1350**

❑ **PEZ-34. Pez Pineapple,**
1979. - **$2650-$3200**

❑ **PEZ-35. Orange Pez,**
1970s. Orange head with green stem and leaves. - **$125-$300**

PEZ-36

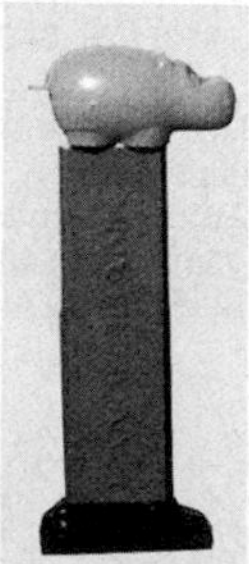

PEZ-37

❑ **PEZ-36. Popeye Pez,**
1970s. Light blue stem. - **$80-$120**

❑ **PEZ-37. Pez Hippo,**
1970s. - **$1200-$1500**

PEZ-38

❑ **PEZ-38. Make-A-Face on Card,**
1970s. German version. One of the most sought-after Pez dispensers.
Loose complete - **$2500-$2900**
Mint on card-USA Card - **$3750-$4350**
Mint on card-Foreign Card - **$3550-$4050**

PEZ-39 PEZ-40 PEZ-41 PEZ-42

❑ **PEZ-39. Miniature Duck Plastic Dispenser Stick Pin,**
1970s. Premium. - **$10 $20 $35**

❑ **PEZ-40. Donald Duck Miniature Plastic Dispenser Replica On Brass Stickpin,**
1970s. From European made Disney character series. - **$10 $25 $40**

❑ **PEZ-41. Bambi Miniature Plastic Dispenser Replica On Brass Stickpin,**
1970s. From European made Disney character series. - **$10 $25 $40**

❑ **PEZ-42. Pluto Miniature Plastic Dispenser On Brass Stickpin,**
1970s. From European made Disney character series. - **$10 $25 $40**

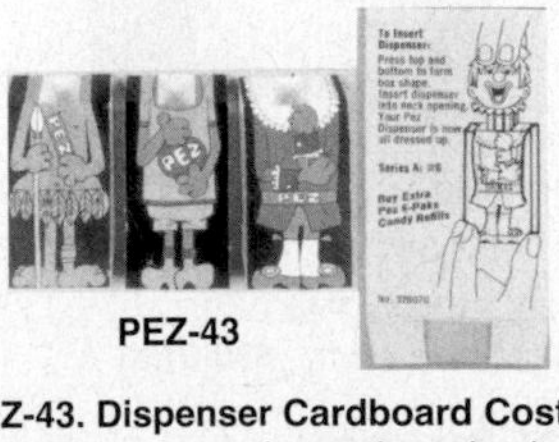

PEZ-43

❑ **PEZ-43. Dispenser Cardboard Costumes,**
c. 1970s Three examples and one back panel from 12 in series "A". Each - **$15 $25 $40**

PEZ-44

❑ **PEZ-44. Insert Paper,**
1970s. Paper slip illustrating different dispensers plus reverse ad for Golden Glow candy dispenser and Pez Costume Fun Books. - **$20 $30 $60**

PEZ-45

❑ **PEZ-45. Pez Flag,**
1970s. 5.5x9" glossy paper on 15-1/2" wood rod. - **$10 $20 $40**

PEZ-46

❑ **PEZ-46. "Pez Premium Club" Paper,**
1970s. - **$20 $30 $65**

PEZ-47

PEZ-48

PEZ-49

❑ **PEZ-47. Spider-Man Cardboard Mask,**
1970s. - **$20 $30 $65**

❑ **PEZ-48. Hulk Cardboard Mask,**
1970s. - **$20 $30 $65**

❑ **PEZ-49. Silver Coin,**
Late 1970s. Pez premium coin given to employees. Came in small red case attached to illustrated folder.
Coin only - **$115-$175**
Complete - **$150 $250 $500**

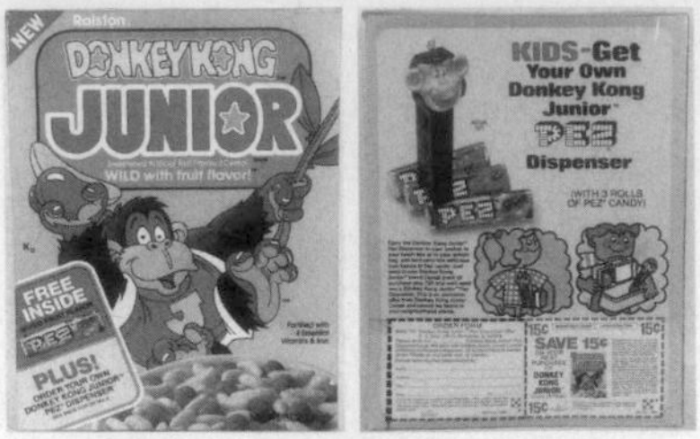

PEZ-50

❑ **PEZ-50. Donkey Kong Jr. Cereal Box with Pez Promo,**
1984. Has promotion and order form for Donkey Kong Jr. Pez Dispenser.
Complete - **$135 $275 $450**
With coupon missing - **$100 $175 $300**

PEZ-51 PEZ-52 PEZ-53

❑ **PEZ-51. Scarewolf Pez,**
1980s. White and orange head with yellow stem. - **$150-$200**

❑ **PEZ-52. Spook Pez,**
1980s. White and grey head with yellow stem. - **$150-$200**

❑ **PEZ-53. Vamp Pez,**
1980s. White head and blue stem. - **$150-$200**

PEZ-54 PEZ-55 PEZ-56

❑ **PEZ-54. Zombie Pez,**
1980s. Red and black head with orange stem. - **$150-$200**

❑ **PEZ-55. Diabolic Pez,**
1980s. Orange head and dark green stem. - **$150-$200**

❑ **PEZ-56. Air Spirit Pez,**
1980s. Red head and blue stem. - **$150-$200**

PEZ-57

❑ PEZ-57. Pez Promo Decal,
1980s. 8 1/2" tall and 12" wide. Shows Donald and Mickey Pez holders. - **$40**

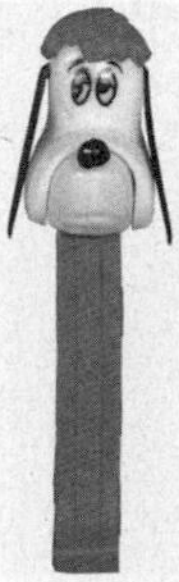

PEZ-58

PEZ-59

PEZ-60

❑ PEZ-58. Droopy Type 1 Pez,
1980s. Light blue stem. - **$10-$30**

❑ PEZ-59. "Müeslix" Pez Dispenser,
1997. On card. - **$30**

❑ PEZ-60. "Roman" Pez Dispenser,
1997. On card. - **$30**

PEZ-61

PEZ-62

❑ PEZ-61. Collectors Watch,
1998. Limited edition watch has an eyeball held by a black hand. In box - **$35**

❑ PEZ-62. Crystal Pumpkin Head Pez Dispenser,
1999. From the Crystal Animals set. Head is blue-tinted. On card. - **$25**

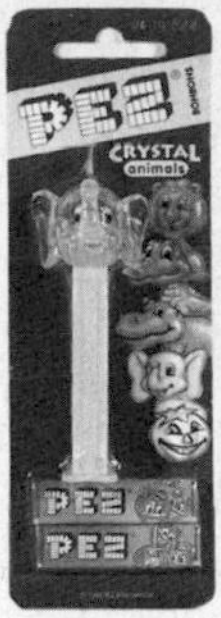

PEZ-63

PEZ-64

❑ PEZ-63. Crystal Elephant Head Pez Dispenser,
1999. Head is yellow-tinted. On blue card. - **$35**

❑ PEZ-64. Crystal Hippo Head Pez Dispenser,
1999. Head is blue-tinted. On blue card. - **$35**

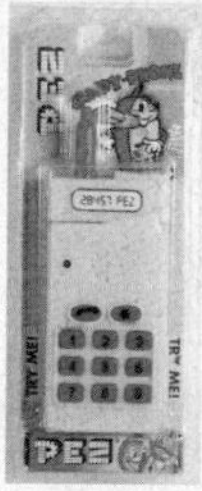

PEZ-65

PEZ-66

PEZ-67

❑ PEZ-65. Candy Phone on Card,
1999. Came in several colors - yellow, green, blue, red and others. - **$15**

❑ PEZ-66. Marvin the Martian Candy Hander,
1999. On card. - **$5 $10 $25**

❑ PEZ-67. Wile E. Coyote Candy Hander,
1999. On card. - **$5 $10 $25**

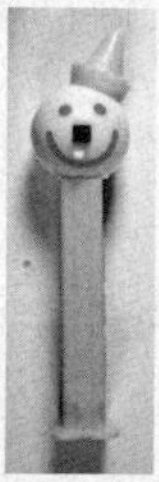

PEZ-68

PEZ-69

PEZ-70

❑ PEZ-68. Jack In The Box Premium,
1999. Comes in yellow, red and blue. Each - **$12**

❑ PEZ-69. Johnny Lightning Car on Card,
1999. One-time promotion run. - **$50**

❑ PEZ-70. Tweety With Baseball Hat,
1999. Dispenser. - **$3**

PEZ-71

PEZ-72

❑ PEZ-71. Wolverine Pez on Card,
1990s. Comes in yellow or black stem. - **$3**

❑ PEZ-72. Pez Playworld,
1990s. Set with dispenser, candy, outfit and pencils on card. - **$45**

PEZ-73

❑ PEZ-73. Pezmania Electronic Dispenser,
1990s. NM - **$50**

PEZ-74

PEZ-75

❑ PEZ-74. "Gyro Gearloose' Pez Dispenser,
2000. On blue card. - **$10**

❑ PEZ-75. "Webby" Pez Dispenser,
2000. On blue card. - **$12**

PEZ-76

PEZ-77

❑ **PEZ-76. Eyewear Case,**
2000. Exclusive by A&A Optical in Dallas. - **$35**

❑ **PEZ-77. Eyewear Case,**
2000. Exclusive by A&A Optical in Dallas. - **$35**

PEZ-78

PEZ-79

❑ **PEZ-78. Valentine's Dispenser,**
2000. Heart is printed with "Happy Valentine's Day." Comes in red or pink. - **$8**

❑ **PEZ-79. Rocket Pen Candy Dispenser,**
2000. It lights, it writes and has a secret compartment. Comes in 6 different colors. - **$6**

PEZ-80

❑ **PEZ-80. Pez Card Game in Box,**
2000. Premiere edition. - **$12**

PEZ-81

❑ **PEZ-81. Bride & Groom Wacky Wobblers,**
2000. Limited to 5,000 sets. In colorful box - **$50**

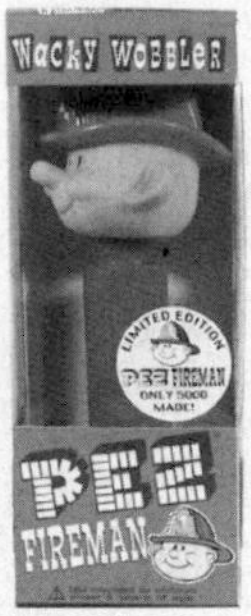

PEZ-82 PEZ-83

❑ **PEZ-82. "Pez Policeman" Wacky Wobbler,**
2000. Limited to 5,000. In box - **$35**

❑ **PEZ-83. "Pez Fireman" Wacky Wobbler,**
2000. Limited to 5,000. In box - **$35**

PEZ-84

❑ **PEZ-84. General Mills Cereal Boxes with Mini-Pez on Box,**
2001. For Cocoa Puffs, Honey Nut Cheerios, Lucky Charms, and Trix. Each - **$35**

PEZ-85

❑ **PEZ-85. Smiley Face Pez Dispenser,**
2001. On card. - **$5**

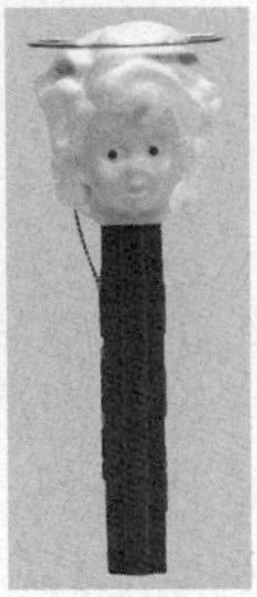

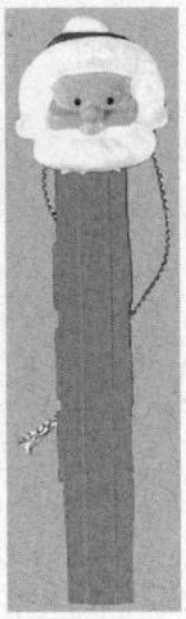

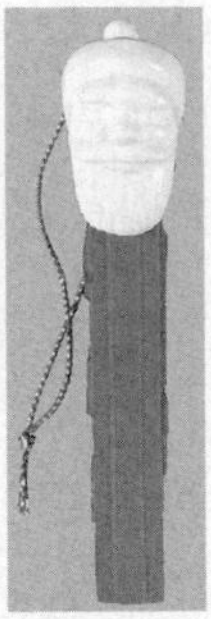

PEZ-86 PEZ-87 PEZ-88

❑ **PEZ-86. Pez "Angel" Christmas Ornament,**
2001. Boxed - **$25**

❑ **PEZ-87. Pez "Santa" Christmas Ornament,**
2001. Boxed - **$25**

❑ **PEZ-88. Pez "Old Style Santa" Christmas Ornament,**
2001. All white face. Boxed - **$25**

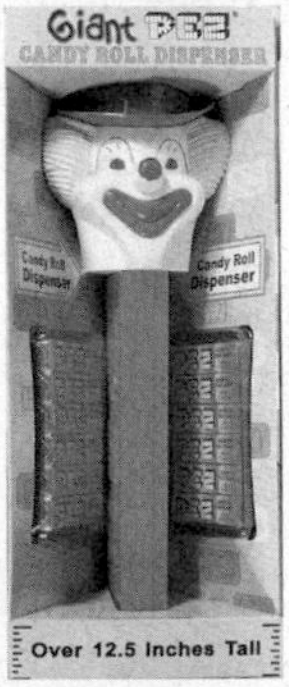

PEZ-89 PEZ-90

❑ **PEZ-89. "Giant Pez" Candy Roll Dispenser,**
2001. 12-1/2" tall in box. - **$30**

❑ **PEZ-90. "Fuzzy Friends" Dispenser,**
2001. With candy. 4 different. Each - **$6**

PEZ-91

PEZ-92

❑ **PEZ-91. "Johnny Lightning" Pez Bus,**
2002. Celebrates 50 years of Pez Candy Inc. - **$35**

❑ **PEZ-92. "Johnny Lightning" Pez Holiday Truck,**
2002. Celebrates 50 years of Pez Candy Inc. - **$35**

PEZ-93

PEZ-94

❑ **PEZ-93. 50th Anniversary "Golden Glow" Dispenser on Stand,**
2002. Limited. NM - **$55**

❑ **PEZ-94. "Pez Pirate" Wacky Wobbler,**
2000s. Limited to 5,000. NM In box - **$85**

PEZ-95

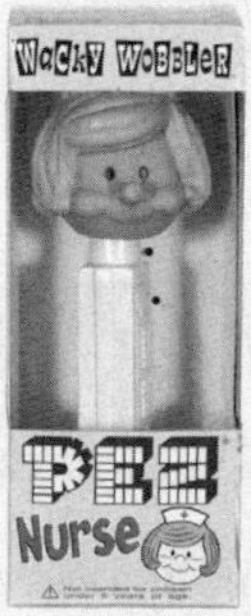

PEZ-96

❑ **PEZ-95. "Pez Doctor" Wacky Wobbler,**
2000s. Limited to 5,000. NM In box - **$30**

❑ **PEZ-96. "Pez Doctor" Wacky Wobbler,**
2000s. Limited to 5,000. NM In box - **$30**

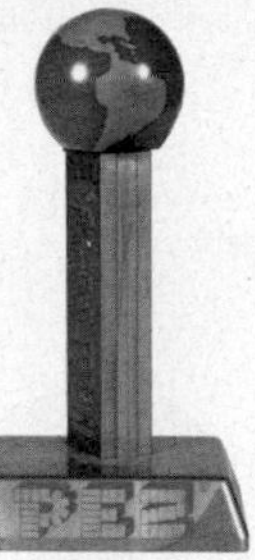

PEZ-97

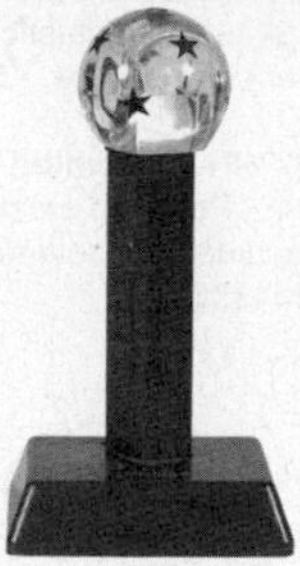

PEZ-98

❑ **PEZ-97. Earth Pez,**
2000s. First Pez on base for Planet Series. - **$35**

❑ **PEZ-98. Mystical Crystal Ball Pez On Base,**
2000s. Has blue stars on ball. Limited edition of 2,000. - **$35**

The Phantom

The legendary ghost-who-walks was created by writer Lee Falk (1912-1999) and artist Ray Moore as a daily comic strip for King Features in 1936. A Sunday page was added in 1939. Wilson McCoy took over the dailies and Sundays in 1949 and continued as artist until 1961 when Sy Barry took the reins. Barry retired in 1994. Paul Ryan draws the daily strip today. Aided by Guran, the leader of the Bandar pygmies, and by his wolf Devil, the masked crime fighter with the sign of the skull has been battling evil and pursuing his fiancee Diana Palmer in comic strips in the U.S. and overseas ever since. Comic book reprints were first published in 1939, with new material added starting in 1951. A 15-episode chapter play starring Tom Tyler was released by Columbia Pictures in 1943. In 1996, Paramount Pictures released a big screen version of *The Phantom* staring Billy Zane. Despite an average box office showing, the film received favorable word of mouth from fans and has received good ratings on cable TV.

PHN-1

❑ **PHN-1. "The Phantom And The Sign Of The Skull" Better Little Book,**
1939. Whitman #1474. - **$26 $78 $185**

PHN-2

PHN-3

❑ **PHN-2. Vending Machine Display Sign,**
1930s. Criss Cross Machines, manufactured by Calex Mfg. Co., Amityville, NY. Red on light yellow 10-1/2 x 14". Cards were used as Amoco gasoline give-aways but also sold via vending machines. Sign shows 5 Phantom cards. - **$350 $600 $1100**

❑ **PHN-3. Amoco Gas Station Premium Card,**
1930s. The earliest of all Phantom trading cards. On light cardboard, these 3"x3" black and white cards each depicted a different comic panel from the original Lee Falk/Ray Moore story from 1936. The reverse had an ink-stamped logo. Each - **$60 $110 $165**

PHN-4

❑ **PHN-4. "The Phantom And Desert Justice" Better Little Book,**
1941. Whitman #1421. - **$25 $75 $175**

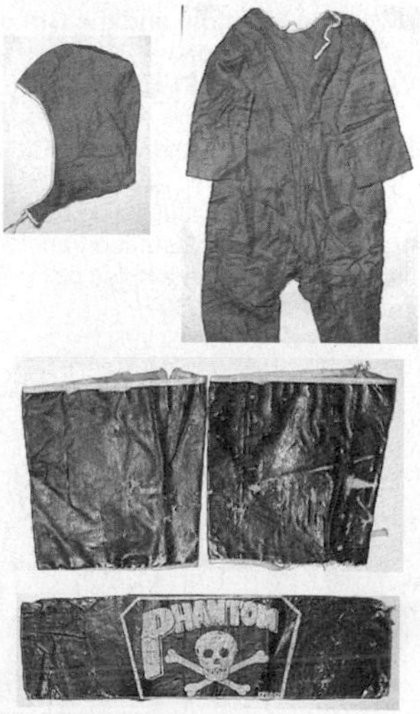

PHN-5

❑ **PHN-5. "Phantom" Child's Costume,**
1942. Store item with initials of "King Features Syndicate," a copyright symbol and a date of "42" on the waistband. Waistband is 5x25-1/2" with white illustration on black oilcloth. Photo shows black oilcloth leg cuffs. Matching wrist cuffs with a white stripe were also provided. The two fabric pieces are in deep purple and consist of a head covering along with a pull-on one-piece bodysuit. Came with a generic molded black fabric mask. As Illustrated - **$550 $1175 $1850**

PHN-6

❑ **PHN-6. One-Sheet Spanish Poster,**
1943. To coincide with the release of the Tom Tyler serial. - **$275 $450 $900**

PHN-7

PHN-8

❑ **PHN-7. "The Phantom and the Girl of Mystery" Big Little Book,**
1947. Whitman #1416. - **$19 $57 $130**

❑ **PHN-8. Comic Strip Characters Tattoo Pack,**
c. 1948. Classic Comics, published by Gilberton Co. Store item packet of 20 tattoo transfers with The Phantom and other examples pictured on envelope. - **$75 $150 $250**

PHN-9

PHN-10

❑ **PHN-9. Portrait Ring,**
c. 1948. Gold plastic bands with clear cover over color picture. - **$75 $115 $165**

❑ **PHN-10. Exhibit Card,**
1949. Postcard stock and size. Vending machine item sold for one penny. - **$20 $35 $60**

PHN-11

PHN-12

❑ **PHN-11. "The Phantom's Club Member" Australian Cello. Button,**
1940s. Scarce. - **$75 $175 $350**

❑ **PHN-12. "S.F. Call-Bulletin" Cardboard Disk,**
1940s. San Francisco newspaper. From series of contest disks, match number to win prize. - **$20 $40 $75**

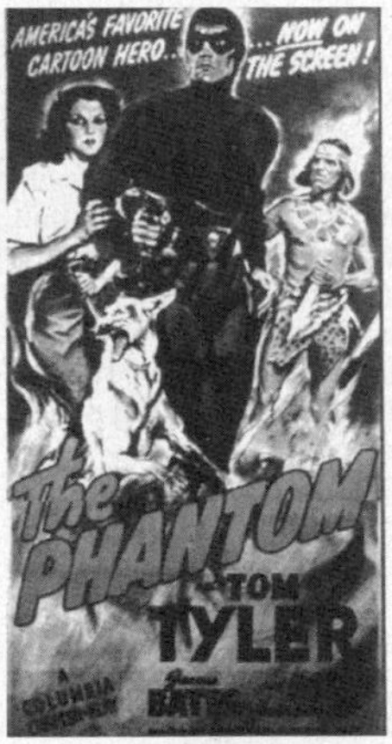

PHN-13

PHN-14

❑ **PHN-13. Three-Sheet,**
1940s. Columbia Pictures. 80" by 40". - **$2500 $4750 $8000**

❑ **PHN-14. Radio Show Billboard Poster,**
1940s. Produced in cooperation for the intended Phantom radio show to be heard on WEBR/Canada. One of two. - **$400 $750 $1500**

PHN-15

PHN-16

❑ **PHN-15. Australian Brass Stickpin,**
1953. Comic book premium. Embossed skull symbol with red eye accents. - **$65 $140 $250**

❑ **PHN-16. China Portrait Mug,**
1950s. Store item. - **$45 $85 $175**

PHN-17

PHN-18

PHN-19

❑ **PHN-17. Litho. Tab,**
1950s. - **$25 $65 $150**

❑ **PHN-18. "The Phantom" Litho. Button,**
1950s. From set of various King Features Syndicate characters. - **$15 $30 $65**

❑ **PHN-19. Plastic Frame Picture Charm,**
1950s. Store item. Gumball vending machine issue. - **$10 $20 $40**

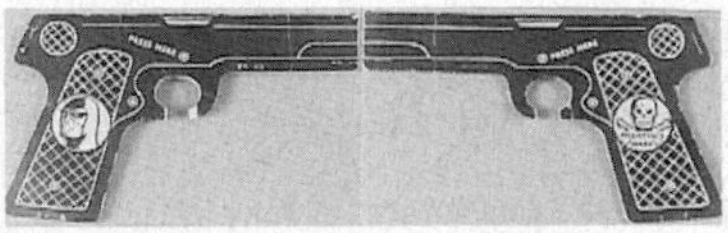
PHN-20

❑ **PHN-20. Australian Issue Cardboard Premium Gun,**
1950s. Possibly a comic book premium. Contains metal clicker. One grip has Phantom portrait while other has skull and crossbones captioned "Phantom's Mark." - **$60 $125 $225**

PHN-21

❑ **PHN-21. Litho. Buttons,**
1950s. Issuer unknown but from series of at least 30 different marked only with small copyright symbol. Each is 7/8" full color.
Phantom - **$30 $75 $150**
Phantom's Fiancee Diana Palmer - **$15 $30 $50**
Phantom's Wolf Dog, Devil - **$10 $15 $30**

PHN-22

❑ PHN-22. Board Game With Plastic Skull Ring,
1966. Store item by Transogram.
Near Mint Boxed With Ring - **$375**
Ring Only - **$60 $125 $200**

PHN-23

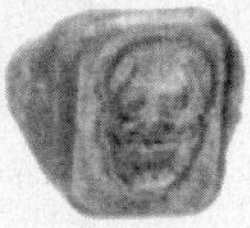
PHN-24

PHN-25

❑ PHN-23. Comic Book Fan Reply Card,
1967. King Features Syndicate. Color postcard with reverse message from King Comics thanking recipient for ideas and suggestions. - **$25 $60 $125**

❑ PHN-24. Australian Ink Stamp Ring,
1960s. Rubber with raised skull symbol as ink stamp, "Phantom" name on ring band. - **$200 $400 $800**

❑ PHN-25. Australian Brass Ring,
1960s. Depicts raised skull symbol with red eye sockets. - **$200 $400 $650**

PHN-26

PHN-27

❑ PHN-26. Sticker,
1975. King Features. - **$15 $30 $60**

❑ PHN-27. Soda Cardboard Display,
c. 1980. Swedish. Two-sided, for the promotion of carbonated lemon drink. - **$300 $600 $1250**

PHN-28

PHN-29

❑ PHN-28. Soda Lemon Drink Bottle,
c. 1980. Swedish store item. Phantom pictured in blue garb. - **$20 $40 $75**

❑ PHN-29. The Phantom Graphic Australian Button,
1980s. Button is 2-1/8" with KFS copyright. - **$25 $45 $80**

PHN-30

❑ PHN-30. Phantom "Bengali" Map,
c. 1980. Swedish. Premium folded into Swedish comic book. - **$50 $100 $150**

PHN-31

❑ PHN-31. Figure with Two Rings on Card,
1995. Great graphics on blister card. - **$60**

PHN-32

PHN-33

❑ PHN-32. Movie Badge,
1996. Given away at premiere. - **$3 $6 $12**

❑ PHN-33. Movie Badge,
1996. Given away at premiere. - **$3 $6 $12**

PHN-34

PHN-35

❑ PHN-34. Slurpee Cardboard Promo Sign,
1996. 7-11 store promo for free ring. - **$50**

❑ PHN-35. Popcorn Bag,
1996. Promo theater bag. - **$2 $4 $6**

PHN-36

❑ PHN-36. Premium Ring And Tattoo Transfer Set,
1996. Movie theater giveaway as well as 7-Eleven stores and Best Buy stores. Ring is heavy silver luster metal and set of five transfers are on 2x2" sheets. Ring - **$5 $10 $15**
Transfer Set - **$6 $12 $20**

PHN-37

PHN-38

❑ **PHN-37. Milk Promo 18" x 12" Poster,**
1996. Given away at theaters. - **$10 $15 $35**

❑ **PHN-38. Promo Movie Box,**
1996. Sponsored by Blockbuster Video and Visa. Has 6"x9" Phantom envelope showing him riding a horse. Has coupons inside; one with the Phantom on it. - **$28**

PHN-39

❑ **PHN-39. Phantom Mini-Bust,**
2003. Bowen Designs. - **$60**

Phantom Pilot Patrol

Langendorf baked goods sponsored this regionally broadcast radio adventure series on the West Coast in the 1930s which featured Howard Duff (1913-1990) in his first starring role. We picture the items comprising the club membership kit. The club was headed by "Dennis O'Hara or Sparks - the operator of the radio station at the base of the Sierra Mountain."

PLT-1

PLT-2

❑ **PLT-1. Black Enamel On Brass Member's Badge,**
1930s. - **$15 $35 $90**

❑ **PLT-2. Enrollment Card,**
1930s. 3-1/2x5-1/2" as shown with enrollment coupon removed from bottom edge. Reverse lists premiums. With Coupon - **$30 $50 $95**
Without Coupon - **$20 $35 $65**

PLT-3

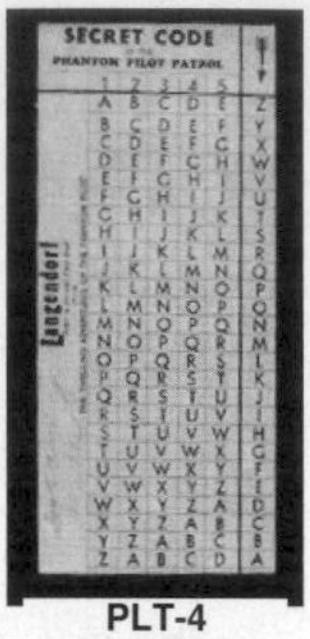

PLT-4

❑ **PLT-3. Official Orders Folder,**
1930s. Four pages, 8-1/2x11". Includes "A Personal Message From The Chief" (The Phantom Pilot), club secrets and instructions for decoding secret messages sent via radio. - **$35 $70 $125**

❑ **PLT-4. "Secret Code" Card,**
1930s. The "Chief" or club members began messages with "Langendorf" and a 3 digit number. The second digit specified which of the five columns shown on this card was the correct master code to use. 4x9-1/4" black on orange. - **$40 $80 $140**

Pillsbury

The Pillsbury Company was formed in 1869 when 27-year-old Charles Alfred Pillsbury bought a flour mill in Minneapolis and set about improving the milling process and producing a finer flour. Pillsbury's Best XXXX, a conversion of the historic bakers' XXX symbol for premium bread, was adopted as a company trademark in 1872. The Pillsbury Doughboy, created by animator Hal Mason, was introduced in television commercials in 1965, voiced by Paul Frees (1920-1986) and named Poppin' Fresh in 1971. He was soon joined by Poppie Fresh, and the two characters have been successfully merchandised as corporate symbols.

In 1964, Pillsbury introduced the Funny Face products, a sugar-free drink mix for children. There were six flavors originally. The line went national in 1965 and more flavors were added throughout the 1970s. The brand faded in the late 1970s with stiff competition from market leader Kool-Aid. Pillsbury sold the line in 1980 to Brady Enterprises. The new owners test marketed Chug A Lug Chocolate in 1983 and offered the final plastic cup premium. Limited distribution makes this the scarcest of the nine cups in the Funny Face series. In 2004 J.M. Smucker acquired the company.

PLS-1

❑ **PLS-1. Pillsbury Products Ad Statuettes,**
1930s. Each is 3-1/4" tall diecut wood.
Each - **$12 $25 $50**

PLS-2

❑ **PLS-2. "Injun Orange" Unopened Drink Mix Pack,**
c. 1964. Store product depicts one of the six original characters whose name was later changed to Jolly Olly Orange.
Near Mint Sealed - **$300**
Open Pack - **$65 $125 $225**

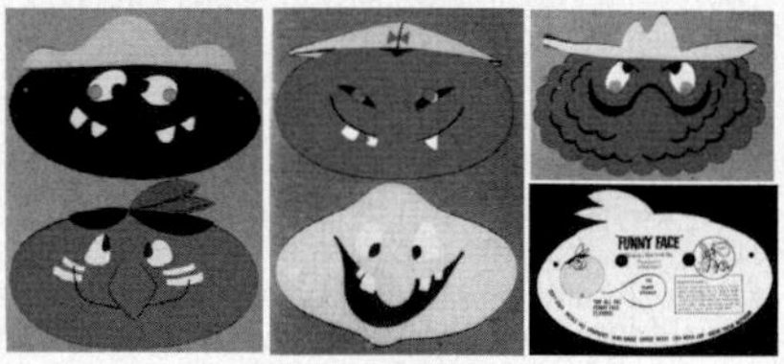

PLS-3

❑ **PLS-3. Funny Face Masks,**
c. 1964. Set of six diecut paper images of Freckle-Face Strawberry, Goofy Grape, Loud-Mouth Lime, Rootin' Tootin' Raspberry, Chinese Cherry, Injun Orange. Latter two were subsequently renamed Choo Choo Cherry and Jolly Olly Orange. Each - **$100 $200 $300**

PLS-4

❑ **PLS-4. Funny Face Finger Puppets,**
c. 1964. 2x4" plastic sheeting set of six: Chinese Cherry, Goofy Grape, Loud-Mouth Lime, Injun Orange, Rootin' Tootin' Raspberry and Freckle Face Strawberry. Each - **$65 $165 $325**

PLS-5

❑ **PLS-5. "Funny Face Fun Book",**
1965. Full color 5x7" self-mailer booklet with 20 pages of games, puzzles, jokes, rhymes, etc. - **$40 $80 $185**

PLS-6

❑ **PLS-6. Funny Face Contest Prize Wristwatch,**
1965. A standard design "Lord Nelson" wristwatch with goldtone case and matching expansion band has on the inside of the crystal a 1-1/2" disk with image of Goofy Grape. 10,000 were produced and used as prizes. Gordon Gold Archives. - **$150 $375 $700**

PLS-7 PLS-8

❑ **PLS-7. Litho. Tin Tab,**
1965. 1-1/2" showing character in purple with yellow hat. - **$15 $30 $45**

❑ **PLS-8. "How Freckle Face Strawberry Got His Freckles" Book,**
1965. - **$25 $40 $85**

PLS-9

❑ **PLS-9. Goofy Grape Unopened Packet,**
1965. Unopened purple paper packet is 3.25x4.25". - **$65 $125 $225**

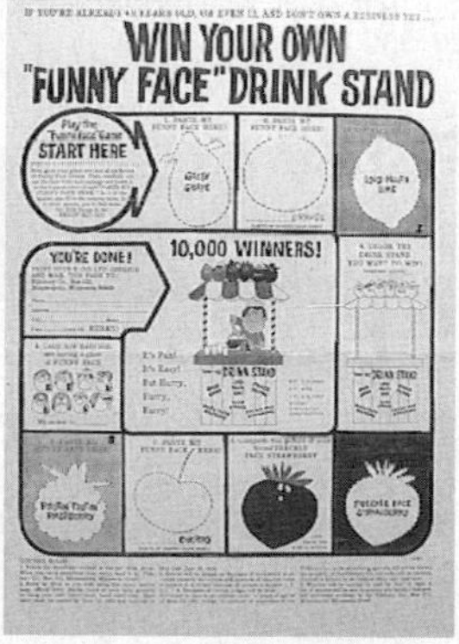

PLS-10

❑ **PLS-10. Entry Sheet For Drink Stand Contest,**
1965. Large 11x14" contest order form noting closing date of June 30, 1965. Ten thousand drink stands were awarded. - **$20 $50 $85**

PLS-11

❑ **PLS-11. "Funny Face Drink Stand" Miniature 3-D Premium Art Prototype ,**
c. 1965. Designed for Pillsbury. 1-1/2x3x6-1/2" tall. Gordon Gold Archives. Unique. - **$3500**

PLS-12

❑ **PLS-12. Drink Stand Contest Prize,**
1965. Stand was shipped in a flat carton but when assembled was three feet wide, five feet three inches high, one foot four inches deep. Made of sturdy cardboard.
Near Mint Boxed - **$3500**
Unboxed - **$750 $1500 $2500**

PLS-13

❑ **PLS-13. "Funny Face" Contest Papers,**
1966-1967. First two photos are front and back of 5-1/2x8-1/2" coloring contest sheet. This has 1967 expiration date. Prizes included Matt Mason Deluxe Space Action Set and Twist-N Turn Barbie with house. Third image is of 14-1/4x21-1/2" Sunday comic section with picture to be colored and submitted. Expiration date of 1966. Grand prize was a giant "Funny Face Funhouse." Contest Sheet - **$20 $40 $60**
Newspaper Page - **$5 $10 $15**

PLS-14

❑ **PLS-14. "Funny Face/Tart N' Tangy" Large Store Display,**
1967. Diecut thin cardboard trio of parts assembling to finished size 34x49" promoting series of three new drink mixes featuring aviation characters to join the previous seven traditional Funny Face characters. -
$1150 $2250 $3800

PLS-15

PLS-16

❑ **PLS-15. "Crash Orange" Book,**
1967. - **$30 $60 $100**

❑ **PLS-16. Funny Face Mugs,**
1969. Nine in set. Chug A Lug Chocolate introduced in 1983. First Eight Each - **$10 $20 $35**
Chug A Lug - **$15 $25 $50**

PLS-17

❑ **PLS-17. "Funny Face" Powder Unopened Packs,**
c. 1969. Two 3.5x4.25" envelopes for "Goofy Grape" and "Jolly Olly Orange" copyright Pillsbury but imprinted "Compliments Of Your Union 76 Dealer." Back of each pack has same pictorial offer for the six different Funny Face mugs with offer expiration date of 1970.
Near Mint Unopened Each - **$25 $50 $75**
Opened Each - **$10 $20 $30**

PLS-18

❑ **PLS-18. Poppin' Fresh Salt & Pepper Set With Mailer,**
1970. Ceramic shakers issued by Pillsbury.
Mailer - **$2 $4 $10**
Set - **$8 $16 $30**

PLS-19

PLS-20

❑ **PLS-19. Choo Choo Cherry Cloth Pillow Doll,**
1970. Pillsbury Co. - **$20 $40 $85**

❑ **PLS-20. Lefty Lemon Cloth Pillow Doll,**
1970. Grape and Strawberry also issued.
Each - **$20 $40 $85**

PLS-21

❑ **PLS-21. Funny Face Plastic Walkers,**
1971. Set of four, each with plastic weight.
Each - **$20 $30 $50**

PLS-22

PLS-23

❑ **PLS-22. "Poppin' Fresh Doughboy",**
c. 1971. Full figure color label on plastic can holding vinyl figure. - **$20 $40 $80**

❑ **PLS-23. "Poppin' Fresh Doughboy",**
c. 1971. Closeup portrait label on plastic can holding vinyl figure. - **$20 $40 $80**

PLS-24

PLS-25

❑ **PLS-24. "Poppin' Fresh" & "Poppie" Plastic Salt & Pepper Shakers,**
1974. - **$15 $20 $35**

❑ **PLS-25. "Poppin' Fresh" Vinyl Playhouse,**
1974. Complete with four figures. -
$60 $110 $175

PLS-26

PLS-27

❑ **PLS-26. Goofy Grape Plastic Pitcher,**
1974. Pillsbury Co. Two versions: Single face or face on each side of pitcher. - **$30 $60 $110**

❑ **PLS-27. "Lefty Lemonade" Funny Face Iron-On Fabric Patch,**
1975. - **$10 $20 $40**

PLS-28

PLS-29

❑ **PLS-28. "Pillsbury" Cloth Doll,**
c. 1970s. - **$8 $12 $30**

❑ **PLS-29. "Goofy Grape Sings" Record,**
1970s. - **$20 $35 $75**

The Pink Panther

This slinky, bulgy-eyed pantomime creature first appeared in the opening credits of the 1964 live-action feature film of the same title starring actors David Niven and Peter Sellers, directed by Blake Edwards. The catchy animated antics, abetted by Henry Mancini theme music, prompted a spin-off single cartoon short that evolved into a career of other performances in theaters, TV cartoons and comic books. Creators were animators DePatie-Freleng Enterprises, more precisely David DePatie and veteran Warner Bros. animator Friz Freleng. Their short *The Pink Phink* won a 1964 Oscar. Early adventures typically pitted Pink Panther against his traditional inept, dim-witted foil Inspector Clouseau. Later animations added other characters and the 1985 *Pink Panther And Sons* (Pinky, Panky, Punkin) TV series was produced in association with Hanna-Barbera Studios. MGM released a new film *The Pink Panther,* starring Steve Martin in 2006.

PNK-1

PNK-2

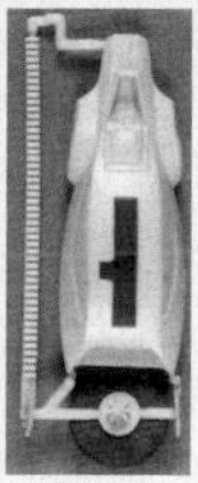

PNK-3

❑ **PNK-1. Inspector Clouseau 3" Cello. Button,**
c. 1965. Issued following original 1964 Pink Panther film starring Peter Sellers as Clouseau. - **$12 $20 $40**

❑ **PNK-2. Jointed Figure,**
1971. Store item by R. Dakin. 8" tall. - **$12 $25 $50**

❑ **PNK-3. RPX Race Car,**
1973. Pink Panther Cereal. Styled after George Barris car. - **$30 $55 $95**

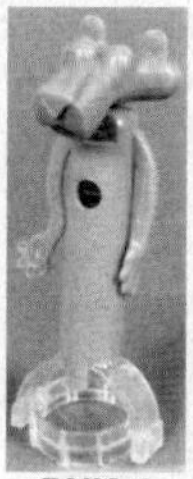

PNK-4

PNK-5

❑ **PNK-4. 5-1 Spy Kit,**
1973. Pink Panther Cereal. - **$50 $75 $150**

❑ **PNK-5. Pink Panther Advertising Button Pair,**
1978. Each is 3" with stylized "S" company logo. Each - **$5 $10 $15**

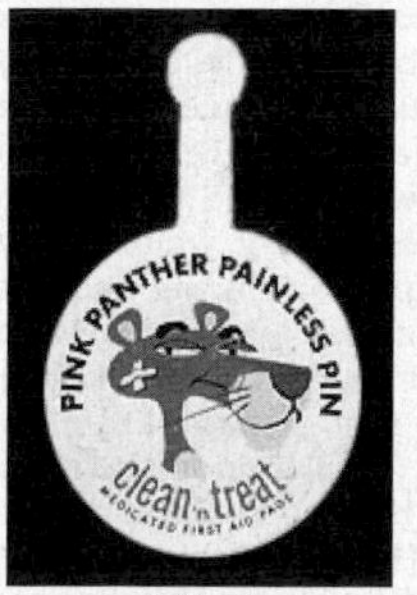

PNK-6

❑ **PNK-6. "Pink Panther Painless Pin" Litho. Tin Tab,**
1970s. Issued by Clean 'N Treat Medicated First Aid Pads. One of a series.
Each - **$5 $10 $18**

PNK-7

PNK-8

❑ **PNK-7. The Pink Panther In Swimsuit Animation Cel,**
1970s. Hand-inked.
Near Mint Similar Examples - **$125**

❑ **PNK-8. "One Man Band" Battery Toy With Box,**
c. 1980. Store item by Illco Toys. Plush/vinyl/metal action movement toy.
Boxed - **$40 $75 $145**
Loose - **$25 $50 $90**

PNK-9

❑ **PNK-9. Figural Ceramic Bowl,**
c. 1980. Store item by Royal Orleans. 7" diameter featuring 4.25" rim figure. - **$15 $30 $60**

PNK-10

❑ **PNK-10. "The Pink Panther/The Inspector" Wind-up Plastic Figures On Store Cards,**
1981. Store items by Bandai.
Each Near Mint Carded - **$38**

PNK-11

PNK-12

❑ **PNK-11. Ceramic Figural Mug,**
1981. Store item by Royal Orleans. 4-1/4" tall. - **$8 $15 $30**

❑ **PNK-12. Albertson's 3-1/2" Cello. Button,**
1984. - **$5 $10 $20**

Pinky Lee

Pincus Leff (1907-1993) began his career as a baggy pants comedian in vaudeville and burlesque. His popularity led to a brief film career, most notably a part in the 1943 feature *Lady of Burlesque* based on *The G-String Murders* novel by stripper Gypsy Rose Lee (1911-1970). The film starred Barbara Stanwyck and Michael O'Shea. Pinky would go on to host a 1950 TV variety show, then appear in a 15-minute musical TV sitcom *Those Two* from 1951 to 1953 with co-star Vivian Blaine.

The *Pinky Lee Show* for children aired on NBC from January 4, 1954 to June 1956. The frenetic host with a lisp and checkered suit was joined by youthful singers Molly Bee and Robert Shore. The show was successful, due to the host's high energy, pratfalls and wild stunts. Pinky collapsed live on the air during a Fall 1955 broadcast, shocking young viewers. Rumored to have had a heart attack, later reports placed the blame on a serious asthma or sinus condition. In 1957, Pinky hosted the NBC Saturday morning Gumby show but future success was moderate at best. He hosted a few game shows and worked the burlesque and dinner theater circuit. In the mid-1960s KABC aired a new *Pinky Lee Show* which only lasted a few months.

Atlas Comics published five issues of *The Adventures Of Pinky Lee* July-December, 1955. "Goodbye, Toodle-oo To You!"

PKL-1

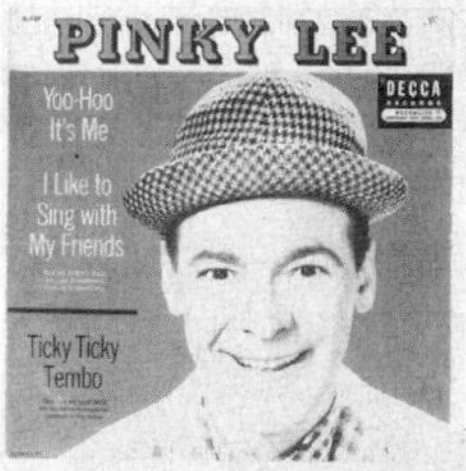

PKL-2

❑ **PKL-1. Pinky Lee Figure,**
c. 1950. The Stern Toy Co. 8.5" tall soft vinyl figure designed so that when his stomach is squeezed, his head pops off. - **$20 $40 $75**

❑ **PKL-2. "Pinky Lee" Record Album,**
1954. Decca Records. Single record of children's songs in 10x10.5" sleeve featuring black/white photo portrait. - **$20 $40 $65**

PKL-3

PKL-4

❑ **PKL-3. "Pinky Lee" View-Master Reel,**
1955. Single reel issue in 3.5x3.5" envelope marked "750 Pinky Lee's Seven Days." - **$5 $10 $20**

❑ **PKL-4. Pinky Lee Peg-O-Bank,**
1955. Banner Plastics Corp. 1.5x4x4.75" tall plastic bank has two slots at top sides with bagatelle-like structure so coins bounce from peg to peg until landing in deposit area. - **$25 $50 $100**

PKL-5

❑ **PKL-5. "Pinky Lee Dancing Clothes Rack",**
1955. Peg-Pal Creations. 12x19x1.25" deep box contains clothes rack made to look like Pinky Lee. Legs are jointed and swing. Came with three metal hooks with colored wooden balls to be inserted into hanger. - **$20 $40 $85**

PKL-6

❑ **PKL-6. "Pinky Lee Mask" Premium,**
1950s. Fun Face Mfger./Circus Candies Inc. 6.5x8.75" stiff die-cut paper mask. Gatefold design with front half featuring Pinky Lee and back half has large "Weather-Bird Shoes" logo. Originally issued with "Midgee Size Tootsie Rolls" in four die-cut openings on mask front. - **$15 $30 $60**

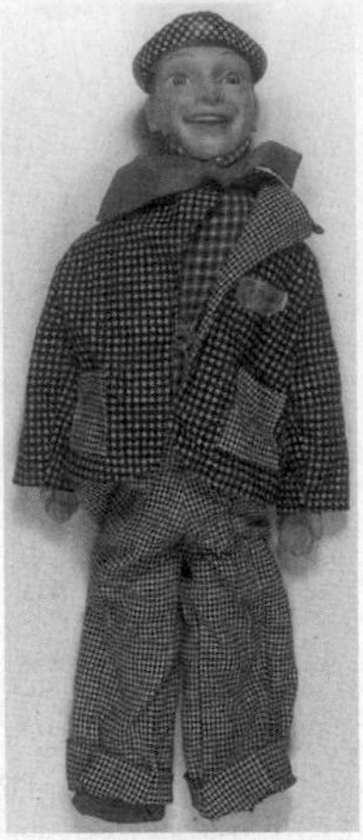

PKL-7

❑ **PKL-7. "Pinky Lee" Doll,**
1950s. 4x7x24" tall stuffed doll with fabric outfit, soft vinyl head with plastic eyes and composition head. Back of neck is marked "A Juro Celebrity Product." Dressed in jacket with "Pinky Lee NBC TV" tag, pants, plaid shirt, silk bow tie. Photo example is missing shoes. Connected to doll are a pair of strings with plastic pull rings to move arms and legs. - **$25 $50 $100**

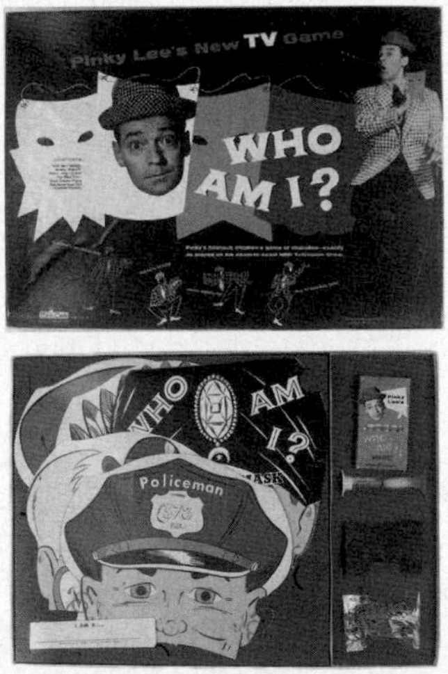

PKL-8

❑ **PKL-8. Pinky Lee "Who Am I?" Boxed Mask Game,**
1950s. Ed-U-Cards. 13.25x18.25x1.5" deep box holds 8 "Who Am I?" masks, 2 mystery "Wipe-Off" masks, a Pinky Lee mask, hourglass timer, magic crayons, wiping pad, directions, bag of rubber bands, I.D. slips and re-usable score card on inside of lid. - **$20 $40 $100**

PKL-9

❑ **PKL-9. "Pinky Lee Party Pack",**
1950s. Includes booklet, place mats, napkins, party hats, cardboard figures, "Pin The Hat On Pinky" poster with paper hats.
Near Mint In Envelope - **$135**

Pinocchio

See Ted Hake's *Official® Price Guide to Disney Collectibles*, Second Edition, formatted identically to this book but in full color evaluating over 9,000 Disney company and character collectibles from 1924 through 2006.

Planet of the Apes

First released in 1968, the intensely popular sci-fi film *Planet of the Apes*, starring Charlton Heston, Roddy McDowall, and Kim Hunter, is appreciated by science fiction and pop culture fans worldwide, with Heston's hammy dialogue still quoted and parodied to this day. Heston's Colonel Taylor is a hapless astronaut who crash-lands on a planet ruled by talking apes, only to discover that it is in fact the Earth of the far future. The simple morality play with a *Twilight Zone*-like twist (no surprise, since it was scripted from the original Pierre Boulle novel by Rod Serling) also featured some heavy-handed political commentary, which would become a regular ingredient in the sequels: *Beneath the Planet of the Apes* (1970), with Heston in only a brief appearance at the beginning and end of the film, *Escape From the Planet of the Apes* (1971), *Conquest of the Planet of the Apes* (1972), and *Battle for the Planet of the Apes* (1973). All but *Beneath* featured Roddy McDowall as chimpanzee scientist Cornelius, and later Cornelius' son Caesar, the leader of the new ape civilization.

Thinly-veiled protests against the Vietnam war and racial tensions at home gave the films a political identity unusual for "sci-fi" films of the time. A short-lived TV series also

starring McDowall as another chimpanzee named Galen aired in 1974, and a cartoon spin-off, *Return to the Planet of the Apes*, lasted one season as well. Today, the original movies and TV show are frequently aired on cable TV, contributing to strong collector interest and an attempt by the studio to jumpstart a new franchise. In 2001, 20th Century Fox and Director Tim Burton released a new version of *Planet of the Apes* to mixed reviews and some box office success. The film was accompanied by a significant amount of hype and licensing. Also in 2001, the superb *Behind the Planet of the Apes* documentary, was released. A DVD set featuring all of the films, the TV series, the cartoon series, the documentary and bonus material was released in March 2006. Most items are copyright 20th Century Fox.

PLA-1

❑ **PLA-1. Planet of the Apes Novel,**
1968. By Pierre Boulle. This edition was released with a photo cover to promote the film. - **$10 $18 $40**

PLA-2

❑ **PLA-2. Movie Poster,**
1968. 27x41" issued by 20th Century Fox. - **$200 $400 $750**

PLA-3

❑ **PLA-3. Original Soundtrack Album,**
1968. Inside shows scenes from the film and features some of the cast. - **$15 $30 $75**

PLA-4

PLA-5

❑ **PLA-4. Colorforms Adventure Set,**
1960s. Full color box with plastic clinging figures and coated color backgrounds. - **$20 $40 $90**

❑ **PLA-5. "Battle for the Planet of the Apes" Novelization,**
1973. Award Books. Written by David Gerrold, the book is one of several novelizing the five films in the series (see also PLA-1). - **$6 $10 $15**

PLA-6

PLA-7

❑ **PLA-6. Planet of the Apes Coloring Book,**
1974. Authorized edition by Artcraft. One of several coloring and activity books. - **$10 $20 $40**

❑ **PLA-7. Planet of the Apes Press Book,**
1974. 14x8-1/2" U.S. press book. In 1974, all 5 films in the series were released on a marathon bill. Press books were supplied to theaters with ads, stories, photos, and mock newspaper front pages. Unclipped - **$20 $35 $75**

PLA-8

❑ **PLA-8. "Planet Of The Apes" Game,**
1974. Store item By Milton Bradley. - **$15 $30 $70**

PLA-9

❑ **PLA-9. "Candy & Two Prizes" Box,**
c. 1974. Store item by Phoenix Candy Co. Inc. 2-1/2x5x1" deep box #3 from a series of 8. - **$18 $30 $60**

PLA-10

❑ **PLA-10. "Planet Of The Apes Playset,"**
1974. Store item by Multiple Toymakers. - **$100 $200 $350**

PLA-11

❑ **PLA-11. Playset,**
c. 1974. Store item by Multiple Toymakers, box text includes "Sears" and this was likely an exclusive to them. Contains four 2-1/2" Ape figures, five generic Army men, Army man with jeep, two horses, bridge, pair of trees that bridge attaches to plus bridge assembly instructions. Near Mint Boxed - **$175**
Used Complete - **$30 $60 $100**

PLA-12

❑ **PLA-12. "Planet Of The Apes Village Playset,"**
c. 1974. Mego. Large boxed set including numerous accessories and featuring cardboard headquarters opening to 3' length for use with 8" action figures sold separately.
Boxed - **$115 $225 $385**

PLA-13

❏ **PLA-13. Planet Of The Apes Zaius Mego Action Figure,**
1974. Apjak Productions Inc. 8" tall poseable figure has complete two-piece fabric outfit and boots on 8.25x9" unpunched blister card.
NM Carded - **$125**
Loose - **$15 $25 $50**

PLA-14

PLA-15

❏ **PLA-14. Planet of the Apes Magazine,**
1974. Volume 1 #9 shown. Published by Magazine Managment Co.
Volume 1 #1- **$8 $15 $40**
Later issues in Near Mint **- $10-$20**

❏ **PLA-15. Planet of the Apes Toy Rings,**
1975. Stan Toy Co., England. Scarce. 5 rings in set: Dr. Zaius, Galen, Zira, Urko, and Cornelius or Caesar. Galen and Dr. Zaius rings shown. Came in gold, silver, green or black on iodized aluminum base. Similar rings were made in Japan in recent years. Each - **$60 $135 $240**

PLA-16

❏ **PLA-16. "Planet Of The Apes Periscope,"**
1976. Apjac Productions Inc. 19" long cardboard tube with mirror mechanism at top and bottom to be used as a periscope. Tube includes art images of Dr. Zaius and two scenes.
- **$30 $60 $90**

PLA-17

PLA-18

❏ **PLA-17. Cornelius Figure Boxed,**
1998. 12" doll for the 30th Anniversary. - **$30**

❏ **PLA-18. Dr. Zaius Figure Boxed,**
1998. 12" doll for the 30th Anniversary. - **$30**

PLA-19

PLA-20

❏ **PLA-19. General Ursus Figure Boxed,**
1998. 12" doll for the 30th Anniversary. - **$35**

❏ **PLA-20. Gorilla Soldier Figure,**
2000. Collectors' Edition in circular box. - **$35**

PLA-21

❏ **PLA-21. Medicom Kubrick Set A,**
2000. First in a series of six 'Kubrick' playsets from Medicom based on the classic film series. Contains Lawgiver, Cornelius, Zira and Dr. Zaius figures. Boxed - **$45**

PLA-22

❏ **PLA-22. Medicom Kubrick Set B,**
2000. From Medicom. Contains General Ursus, two soldier apes and a horse. Boxed - **$45**

PLA-23

❏ **PLA-23. Medicom Kubrick Set C,**
2000. From Medicom. Contains Taylor, Nova, a horse, and the Statue of Liberty. Boxed - **$45**

PLA-24

❏ **PLA-24. Medicom Kubrick Set D,**
2000. From Medicom. Contains General Urko, a soldier ape, a horse, and a jail cart. Boxed - **$45**

PLA-25

❏ **PLA-25. Medicom Kubrick Set E,**
2000. From Medicom. Contains Caesar, a slave ape, General Aldo, and a bridge set piece. Boxed - **$45**

PLA-26

❑ **PLA-26. Medicom Kubrick Set F,**
2000. From Medicom. Contains Zira, Cornelius and Milo in spacesuits with variant helmet heads, and Taylor's spaceship. Boxed - **$45**

PLA-27

❑ **PLA-27. Medicom Kubrick Set G,**
2000. From Medicom. Contains soldier ape with jail cage, Taylor and Lucius. Boxed - **$45**

PLA-28

❑ **PLA-28. Medicom Kubrick Set H,**
2000. From Medicom. Contains Brent, two mutants, and a subway station set piece. Boxed - **$45**

PLA-29

❑ **PLA-29. Movie Lunch Box and Thermos,**
2001. Limited to 5,000. This features photos from the Tim Burton movie. - **$35**

Punchouts

Background

PLA-30

❑ **PLA-30. "Pop Out People" Punchouts,**
2001. Cardboard punchouts of movie photos with background. - **$5**

Pogo

Walt Kelly (1913-1973) chose the Okefenokee Swamp as home for his characters making their debut in *Animal Comics*, which ran briefly in the early 1940s. The strip then ran in the *New York Star* in 1940 and moved to the *New York Post* and syndication in 1949. Pogo the wise possum and his contrary pal Albert the alligator thrived for more than 25 years, dealing with the eccentricities of a cast of characters that included such creatures as Howland Owl, Churchy la Femme the turtle, Beauregard the retired veteran bloodhound, Porky Pine, and P.T. Bridgeport the scheming bear. George Ward was Walt Kelly's main art assistant from 1948 on. Comic books appeared in the 1940s and 1950s and Simon & Schuster published more than 30 Pogo books between 1951 and 1976. An animated cartoon by Kelly and noted animator Chuck Jones (1912-2002) aired on NBC in 1969 and an animated "claymation" film was produced by Warner Brothers in 1980, starring the voices of Skip Hinnant, Vincent Price and Jonathan Winters. The strip itself was discontinued in 1975, but enjoyed a brief revival in the late 1980s. Ohio State University in Columbus Ohio has an extensive collection of Kelly's papers.

POG-1

❑ **POG-1. "The Little Fir Tree" Storybook,**
1942. W. T. Grant Co. Christmas giveaway with color cover and eight pages of bw unsigned Walt Kelly art. - **$100 $300 $1300**

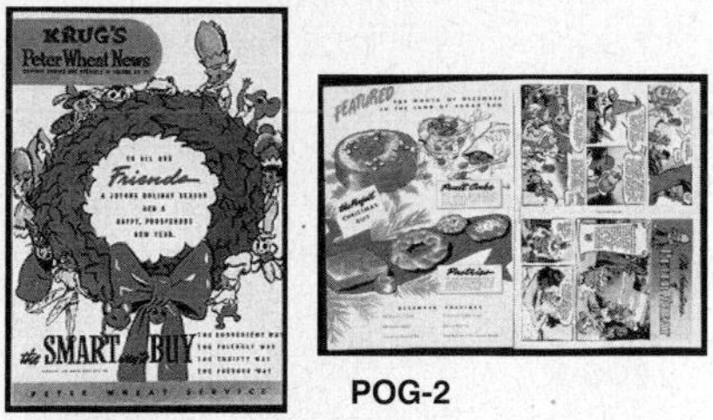

POG-2

❑ **POG-2. "Peter Wheat News" Comic Book With Kelly Art,**
1949. Peter Wheat Bread, Bakers Associates Inc. Issue #21 including cover and three pages of art by Walt Kelly, Pogo creator. -
$8 $24 $60

POG-3

❑ **POG-3. "Peter Wheat" Coloring Book With Kelly Art,**
1951. Peter Wheat Bread, Bakers Associates Inc. Sixteen pages including art examples by Walt Kelly, Pogo creator. - **$40 $85 $175**

POG-4

❑ **POG-4. "Peter Wheat" Cut-Out Circus,**
1951. Bakers Assoc. Designed by Walt Kelly.
Near Mint Uncut - **$350**
Cut - **$40 $100 $200**

POG-5

❑ **POG-5. "The Glob" Walt Kelly Hardcover With Dust Jacket,**
1952. With Jacket - **$20 $40 $95**

POG-6

POG-7

❑ **POG-6. "I Go Pogo" Litho. Button,**
1952. 7/8" version, similar button issued for 1956. - **$10 $15 $25**

❑ **POG-7. "Pogo Parade" Comic Book Promo Sign,**
1953. 9.75x13" stiff paper announcement for 98-page Dell comic. - **$65 $165 $300**

POG-8

❑ **POG-8. Pogomobile Kit,**
1954. Store item published by Simon and Schuster. Cardboard assembly parts for ceiling mobile. Near Mint In Envelope - **$300**

POG-9

POG-10

❑ **POG-9. 4" Diameter Litho. Button,**
1956. Probably sent by Post-Hall Syndicate to newspapers carrying the strip. - **$35 $90 $175**

❑ **POG-10. "I Go Pogo" Litho. Button,**
1956. 7/8" version. - **$5 $10 $20**

POG-11

❑ **POG-11. Walt Kelly Christmas Card,**
1958. His own personal issue.
Unsigned. - **$35 $75 $140**

POG-12

❑ **POG-12. Walt Kelly Christmas Card,**
1960. His own personal issue.
Unsigned - **$35 $75 $140**

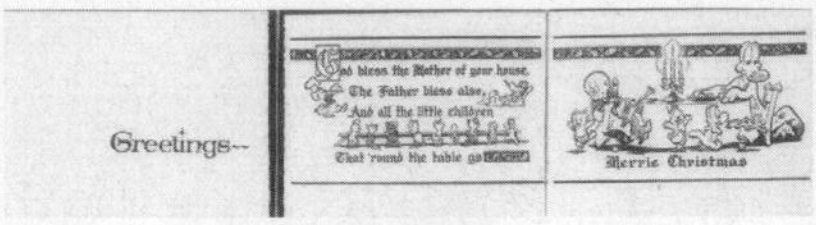

POG-13

❑ **POG-13. Walt Kelly Christmas Card,**
1961. His own personal issue.
Unsigned - **$35 $75 $140**

POG-14

❑ **POG-14. "Pogo Primer For Parents TV Division" Government Booklet,**
1961. U.S. Dept. of Health, Education and Welfare. 8x10" with 24 pages and theme of parents loving their children rather than letting television do that. - **$35 $65 $140**

POG-15

POG-16

❑ **POG-15. Advertising Cello. Button,**
1964. Crest Paperback Books. 1-1/4" black on yellow promoting 35 cents "Pogo For President" book. - **$50 $100 $175**

❑ **POG-16. Cello. Button,**
1968. One of 30 known designs with Walt Kelly facsimile signature on each. - **$25 $50 $95**

POG-17

POG-18

❑ **POG-17. Vinyl Figures,**
1968. Poynter Products, distributed exclusively by Montgomery Ward. Includes Beauregard, Albert, Churchy, Howland, Hepzibah, Pogo. Often missing are Pogo's hat and flowers, Howland's glasses, Beauregard's hat and cane, and Albert's cigar. Each - **$50 $100 $175**

❑ **POG-18. Okefenokee City Council Family Birthday Certificate,**
1969. Issuer unknown but has Walt Kelly copyright. 7-1/2x11-1/2" parchment-type paper with facsimile "Pogo" signature as "Curator Okefenokee Memorial Swamp." -
$60 $115 $175

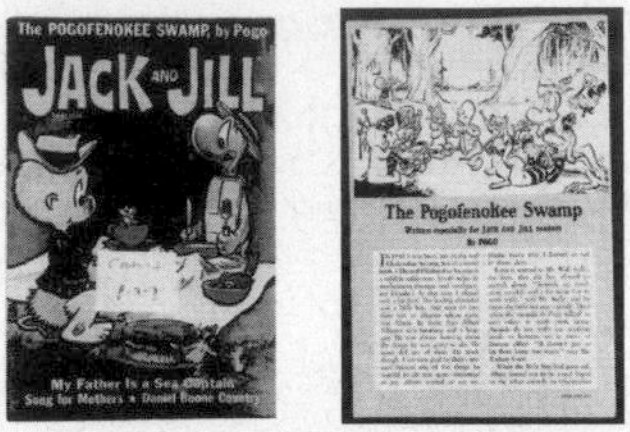

POG-19

❑ **POG-19. "Jack And Jill" Magazine With Cover Article,**
1969. Monthly issue of child's magazine for May with specialty cover art related to four-page historic article about Pogo plus promotion for NBC-TV Pogo cartoon. - **$10 $20 $50**

POG-20

❑ **POG-20. Vinyl Figures,**
1969. Procter & Gamble. Six in set: Pogo, Beauregard Hound, Churchy La Femme, Howland Owl, Albert Alligator, Porky Pine.
Each - **$5 $10 $25**

POG-21

❑ **POG-21. Pogo Characters Plastic Mug Set,**
1969. Procter & Gamble. Set of six: Pogo, Albert, Churchy, Porky Pine, Howland, Beauregard. Each - **$5 $10 $25**

POG-22

❑ **POG-22. "Sunday Newsday" 2-1/2" Cello. Button,**
1972. Long Island newspaper promotion. Further inscribed "Try It/You'll Like It". -
$25 $50 $100

POG-23

POG-24

❑ **POG-23. Pogo Character Christmas Card,**
1975. Simon And Schuster. - **$15 $25 $50**

❑ **POG-24. "Vote Pogo For President" Campaign Poster,**
1979. Estate Of Walt Kelly. 14x22" red, white and blue slick paper. - **$10 $20 $40**

Pokémon

Pokémon was created from a video game in Japan. In 1996, Nintendo took the Japanese game and developed Pocket Monsters, a Game Boy product. When it was introduced in 1998 in the U.S., it was marketed as Pokémon. In 1999, Wizards of the Coast issued a trading card game which was an instant success. To date there are over 250 Pokémon characters. Where it will end, one can only guess. The characters have an angular futuristic look to them which adds to their appeal. The classic old marketing scheme is at work here. Television shows, movies, videos, books, cards and of course an endless array of toys promote the series. The marketing staff has done a great job of packaging the toys as well. Listed below is a sampling of some of the products and their suggested values.

POK-1

POK-2

❑ **POK-1. Pikachu Figure Yo-Yo in Card,**
1999. Tiger Electronics. - **$8 $15 $20**

❑ **POK-2. Pikachu Talking Calculator,**
1999. In open front box. - **$38**

POK-3

POK-4

❑ **POK-3. 5 Pencil Set on Card,**
1999. - **$7**

❑ **POK-4. Cap'n Crunch Cereal Box with Pocket Camera Offer,**
1999. - **$12**

POK-5

POK-6

❑ **POK-5. Meowth Key Chain,**
1999. Part of a series. - **$2 $4 $10**

❑ **POK-6. Meowth Rubber Figure,**
1999. - **$5 $10 $20**

POK-7

❑ **POK-7. Poliwhirl Beanie-type Hat,**
1999. With tag. - **$15**

POK-8

POK-9

❑ **POK-8. Puzzle Featuring Meowth,**
1999. - **$2 $4 $10**

❑ **POK-9. Crayons,**
1999. Set of 16 crayons. Rose Art. - **$5**

POK-10

❑ **POK-10. Candy Dispenser on Card,**
1999. Set of 6. Each - **$9**

POK-11

POK-12

❑ **POK-11. Pikachu Digital Ring Watch,**
1999. With Bonus Band. - **$18**

❑ **POK-12. Jigglypuff Digital Ring Watch,**
1999. With Bonus Band. - **$18**

POK-13

POK-14

❑ **POK-13. Gold Plated Trading Card,**
1999. Burger King premium - **$2 $4 $8**

❑ **POK-14. Trading Card Game Box,**
1999. - **$25**

POK-15

POK-16

❑ **POK-15. Trainers Figure with Poké Ball,**
1999. With Battle Disc. On card. - **$12**

❑ **POK-16. Water Toy on Card,**
1999. - **$10**

POK-17

POK-18

❑ **POK-17. Poké Ball,**
1999. Also called a Voltorb or Electrode. - **$3**

❑ **POK-18. Toy Holder,**
1999. - **$3**

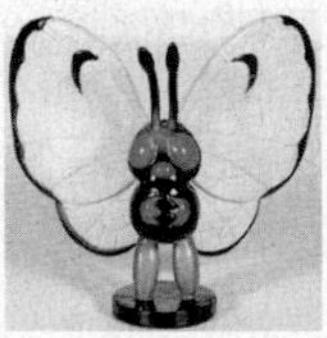
POK-19

POK-20

❑ **POK-19. Butterfree (Batafuly) Figure,**
1999. - **$6**

❑ **POK-20. Figures,**
1999. Misty, Poliwrath (Nyolobon) and Ash.
Each - **$6**

Various Pokémon Figures (and their Japanese Names)
$6 Each

Pikachu (Pickachuu) | Golem (Golonya) | Rattata (Kolatta) | Alakazam (Fuudin)

Ponyta (Bonita) | Togepi (Togepee) | Spearow (Onisuzume) | Beedrill (Supier)

Venonat (Konpan) | Wartotortle (Kameeru) | Weezing (Matadogasu) | Ekans (Ahbo)

Scyther (Sutolaiku) | Omastar (Omster) | Clefable (Pikucy) | Venomoth (Molufon)

Vaporeon (Shawazu) | Arbok (Ahbock) | Tangela (Monjala) | Lapras (Lapulasu)

Venusaur (Fushigibana) | Abra (Keshy) | Gyarados (Gyalodosu) | Rhydon (Saidon)

POK-21

POK-22

❑ **POK-21. Marble Case with 8 Marbles,**
1999. 8 sets (Raichu shown). Each - **$18**

❑ **POK-22. Marble Pouch with 10 Marbles,**
1999. 8 sets in both Series 1&2 (Golem shown).
Each - **$18**

Poll-Parrot Shoes

Paul Parrot, owner of the Parrot Shoe Company, decided to christen his products Poll-Parrot Shoes in 1925. Extensive use of advertising and appropriate giveaways for boy and girl customers--carrying the parrot trademark--were successful marketing tools for the company's shoes and replacement parts. From 1947 to 1950 the company sponsored the *Howdy Doody* program on NBC television, resulting in a number of paper premiums and rings linking the puppet and the parrot.

POL-1

POL-2

POL-3

❑ **POL-1. Litho. Tin Spinner Top With Wood Peg,**
c. 1920s. - **$15 $22 $55**

❑ **POL-2. Litho. Tin Top with Wood Peg,**
1930s. - **$12 $20 $45**

❑ **POL-3. Litho. Tin Disk Spinner,**
1930s. - **$18 $30 $60**

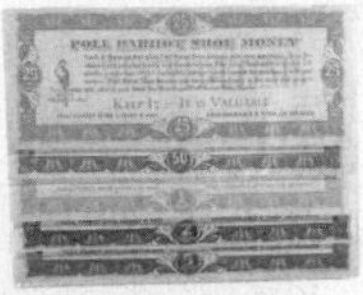

POL-4

POL-5

❑ **POL-4. Bracelet,**
1930s. - **$30 $60 $90**

❑ **POL-5. "Poll Parrot Shoe Money",**
1930s. Various denominations and colors.
10¢, 25¢ and 50¢ shoe money - **$3 $5 $10**
$1 and $2 shoe money - **$4 $6 $12**
$5 shoe money bill - **$5 $10 $15**

(2 views of the whistle)

POL-6

❑ **POL-6. "Poll Parrot Tin Whistle",**
1930s. - **$12 $25 $55**

POL-7

❑ **POL-7. "Poll-Parrot Shoes" Wooden Pull Toy,**
1930s. Toy is 4" tall. Back reads "Geo. Ursin 4113 W North Ave." - **$40 $75 $150**

POL-8

POL-9

POL-10

❑ **POL-8. "Pre-Tested Poll-Parrot Shoes" Litho. Button,** 1930s. - **$8 $15 $30**

❑ **POL-9. Litho. Tin Whistle,**
1930s. - **$15 $30 $55**

❑ **POL-10. Litho. Tin Clicker,**
1930s. - **$10 $15 $30**

POL-11

POL-12

❑ **POL-11. "The Cruise Of The Poll-Parrot" Radio Show Paper,** 1930s. Store hand-out clip imprinted for WSVA Radio, Harrisonburg, Virginia, also offering shoe purchase premium of magnetic compass. - **$8 $15 $25**

❑ **POL-12. "U KUZU" Tin Kazoo,**
1930s. - **$25 $50 $100**

POL-13

❑ **POL-13. Baseball Game,**
1944. Premium includes cardboard baseball game with spinner, mailer, wooden pegs, holder, and scoreboards. Also promotes the War Bond drive. - **$75 $165 $275**

POL-14

❑ **POL-14. "Uncle Sam" Paper Over Tin Bank,**
c. 1945. - **$30 $60 $115**

POL-15

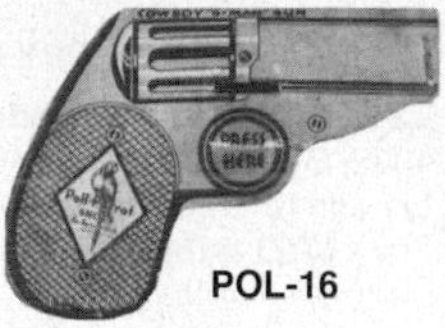

POL-16

❑ **POL-15. "Poll-Parrot Shoes" Solid Plaster Display Figure,**
c. 1940s. Inscription on front base. 6x7x11-1/2" tall. - **$90 $185 $300**

❑ **POL-16. "Cowboy 'G-Man' Gun" Cardboard Premium,**
c. 1940s. 4-1/2" long blue and gray with tin clicker mounted inside. - **$15 $35 $65**

POL-17

POL-18

❑ **POL-17. "G-Man" Premium Pop Gun,**
1940s. - **$10 $30 $50**

❑ **POL-18. Die-cut Standee,**
1950s. 10 1/2" tall. - **$30 $65 $130**

POL-19

POL-20

POL-21

❑ **POL-19. Flying Parrot Plastic Flicker Ring,**
1950s. - **$25 $50 $75**

❑ **POL-20. "Poll-Parrot Shoes" Symbol Brass Ring,**
c. 1950s. - **$20 $35 $60**

❑ **POL-21. "Poll-Parrot Shoes" Symbol Aluminum Ring,**
c. 1950s. - **$20 $35 $60**

Popeye

Popeye was introduced to the world in E.C. Segar's (1894-1938) *Thimble Theatre* comic strip in 1929 and within a year was the strip's most popular character. The strip, begun in 1919, featured the characters Olive Oyl, Harold Hamgravy and Castor Oyl in the first ten years. The adventures of the spinach-chomping sailor, Olive Oyl, the hamburger-mooching Wimpy, Jeep, Swee'pea, and a host of other characters proved to be a phenomenal success. Comic book reprints appeared as early as 1931, and in 1933 the Fleischer Studios released the first of what would eventually add up to more than 450 animated cartoon shorts for theaters and television. A *Popeye* radio series aired on NBC and CBS from 1935 to 1938, sponsored by Wheatena (1935-1937) and Popsicle (1938) with Detmar Poppen as Popeye until Floyd Buckley took over in 1937. Early cartoon shorts were syndicated on television starting in 1956, new films were added in 1961, plus a further series from Hanna-Barbera on CBS in 1978. Robin Williams and Shelley Duvall starred in the 1980 Paramount film. The Popeye characters have been merchandised extensively since the 1930s. Hy Eisman draws the comic strip today.

PPY-1

❑ **PPY-1. Character Painted Cast Iron Figurines,**
c. 1929. Store items. Each - **$90 $215 $400**

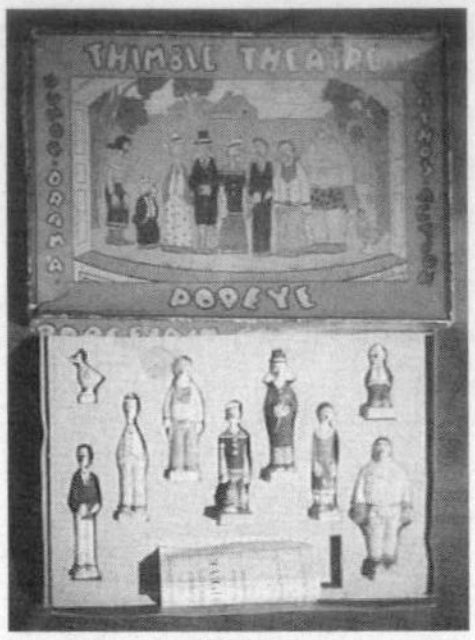

PPY-2

❑ **PPY-2. "Thimble Theatre" Character Set To Paint,**
c. 1930. Copyrighted 1929 but issued in 1930s. Store item by Davidson Porcelain Co., Ohio. Early set predating Wimpy. Figures are 2" to 5" tall and came unpainted with watercolor pad and brush. Characters are: Popeye, Olive Oyl, Ham Gravy, Caster Oyl, Professor Kilph, Glint Gore, Jack Snork, Tinearo, Whiffle Hen.
Boxed Unpainted - **$500 $1000 $1750**
Boxed Painted - **$300 $600 $1200**
Loose Figures Unpainted Or Nice Paint
Each - **$15 $30 $60**

PPY-3

PPY-4

❑ **PPY-3. Popeye Paper Face Mask,**
c. 1930. Einson-Freeman Co. Exceptionally large 9x11" diecut full color. - **$45 $90 $175**

❑ **PPY-4. Parrot Cages Wind-Up Toy,**
1932. Store item by Marx Toys. 7-1/2" tall tin litho. **- $150 $400 $800**

PPY-5

❑ **PPY-5. "Popeye & Baggage" Tin Wind-Up With Box,**
1932. Marx. 3x8.25x8.5" box holds 2x8.5x8" tall lithographed tin wind-up with built-in key. Side of wheelbarrow reads "Popeye Express."
Box - **$300 $650 $1300**
Toy - **$300 $600 $1200**

PPY-6

❑ **PPY-6. "Popeye Shadow Boxer" Wind-Up,**
1932. By Chein. 7.25" box holds 7" tall tin litho toy with KFS copyright. Box - **$200 $400 $700**
Toy - **$750 $1500 $2500**

PPY-7

❑ **PPY-7. "Popeye Drummer" Wind-Up,**
1932. By Chein. 7.25" box holds 7" tall toy copyright King Features Syndicate.
Box - **$200 $400 $700**
Toy - **$750 $1500 $2500**

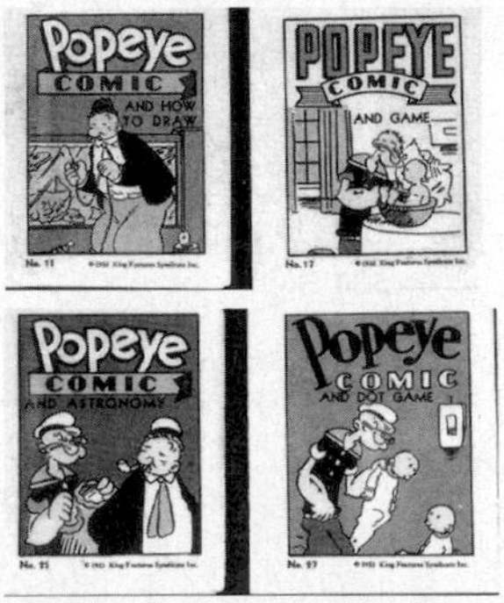

PPY-8

❑ **PPY-8. "Popeye Comic" Gum Folders,**
1933. Tattoo Gum by Orbit Gum Co. From numbered set. Each - **$15 $35 $85**

PPY-9

PPY-10

❑ **PPY-9. Popeye Musical Pipe Display Card With Pipes,**
1934. Store item by Northwestern Products. Full color card 11x17" originally holding one dozen metal and cardboard kazoos. Theater managers also gave away pipes to members of the Popeye Clubs.
Display Card Only - **$300 $600 $1150**
Each Pipe - **$20 $50 $85**

❑ **PPY-10. Sheet Music For Cartoon "Popeye The Sailor",**
1934. Six pages. Store bought. - **$20 $40 $90**

PPY-11

❑ **PPY-11. Large Sign,**
1935. Promotes Magic Transfer picture premiums. IGA Rolled Oats sponsor. -
$300 $600 $1200

PPY-12

❑ **PPY-12. "Popeye Boat Fleet" Boxed Set,**
1935. Store item by Transogram. Contents are four numbered plastic sailboats depicting Popeye on each sail. - **$300 $600 $1000**

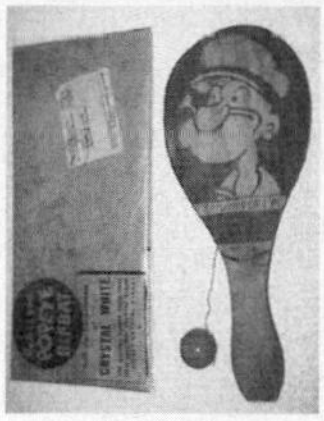

PPY-13

PPY-14

❑ **PPY-13. "Popeye Bifbat" With Mailer,**
c. 1935. Crystal White Soap and others. With Mailer - **$65 $130 $200**

❑ **PPY-14. Octagon Products Free Popeye Bifbat Cardboard Display,**
1935. Colgate Palmolive/Peet Co. 29-1/2" tall in red, black and white. - **$450 $900 $1750**

PPY-15

❑ **PPY-15. Popeye Pocketwatch And Box Dated,**
1935. New Haven Clock Company. Box is 2.25x2.75x.75" deep. Top reads "Popeye Watch" with creator's name "Segar" along lower edge. Has die-cut cardboard insert reading "Popeye Watch Nickel Finish." Watch is in pentagonal case with rounded corners. Dial pictures many characters from the strip. Popeye's die-cut arms and hands with pointing fingers tell the time while below his spread legs is second wheel showing Wimpy chasing a hamburger.
Box - **$1000 $2000 $3000**
Watch - **$600 $1200 $2000**

PPY-16

❑ **PPY-16. "Popeye Speed Boat" Large Wind-Up Toy By The Hoge Mfg. Co.,**
1935. Hoge also produced a Popeye row boat toy and as rare as that toy is, this speed boat is even rarer. 5x15x7.25" tall with body of boat in heavy tin with enameled paint, top of boat is mostly tin litho as is the separate Popeye figure who is depicted from the waist up holding the steering wheel. On the front right side of boat is a .5x1.25" decal reading "Popeye Speed Boat No. 400" along with company name and King Features Syndicate Inc., 1935.
- **$5000 $10,000 $15,000**

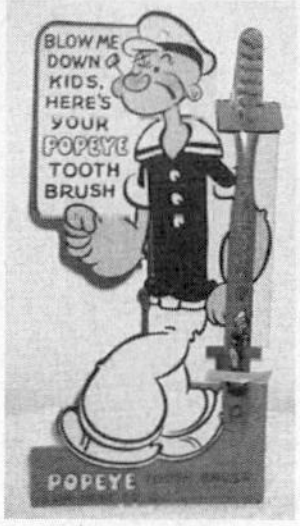

PPY-17

PPY-18

❑ **PPY-17. Tooth Brush On Card,**
1935. Store item by Lor-Dent Co., N.Y.C. Brush has Popeye decal and card is fleshtone, red, white and blue. Brush - **$40 $85 $175**
Card - **$100 $225 $350**

❑ **PPY-18. Pipe Toss Game,**
1935. Store item by Rosebud Art Co. Also used as Popsicle premium. - **$40 $80 $150**

PPY-19

❑ **PPY-19. "Popeye Magic Transfer Pictures" Store Sign With Premium,**
1935. IGA Rolled Oats. Store poster 10x21-1/2" along with 3-1/4" square decal sheet. Gordon Gold Archives. Sign - **$200 $400 $650**
Transfer Sheet - **$10 $30 $60**

PPY-20

❑ **PPY-20. Popeye & Olive Oyl On Roof Wind-Up,**
c. 1935. Marx Toys. 9.5" tall. Winding causes Popeye to dance and Olive to rock side to side as simulated accordion player. -
$650 $1500 $2500

PPY-21

PPY-22

❑ **PPY-21. "Penney's 'Back To School Days' With Popeye" Cello. Button,**
1935. J. C. Penney Co. - **$10 $20 $35**

❑ **PPY-22. Jeep Largest Size Jointed Composition Figure,**
1936. Cameo Doll Co. Store item sold in several sizes. The largest size is 13" tall. Other versions are 6", 7" and 8" tall. All are typically found with serious composition crazing.
Largest Unrestored - **$350 $1100 $2200**
Largest Expertly Restored - **$1350**
Others Expertly Restored - **$1000**
Others Unrestored - **$250 $650 $1200**

PPY-23

PPY-24

❑ **PPY-23. Popeye/Wimpy Glass Tumbler,**
1936. Although copyrighted 1929, part of dairy product set of 8 picturing one character on each side. - **$35 $85 $140**

❑ **PPY-24. Popeye/Jeep Glass Tumbler,**
1936. From same set as previous item, but with 1936 copyright. - **$50 $100 $160**

PPY-25

❑ **PPY-25. "Goon" Glass Tumbler,**
1936. From set that held dairy product.
- **$65 $150 $300**

PPY-26

❑ PPY-26. "Popeye Thimble Theater Puppet Show" Punch-Out Book,
1936. Pleasure Books. Large 10.5x15.5" book #130 comprised of six cardboard punch sheets for stage, outdoor scene backdrop, eight character puppets. Gordon Gold Archives. - **$300 $600 $1350**

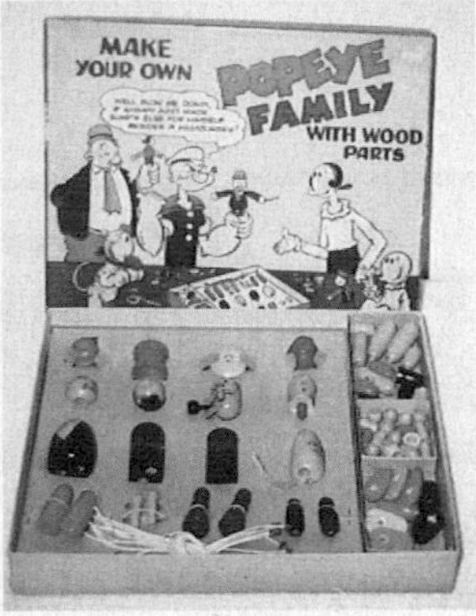

PPY-27

❑ PPY-27. "Make Your Own Popeye Family With Wood Parts" Boxed Set,
1936. Store item by Jaymar. Holds wooden parts and elastic cords to make figures of Popeye, Olive, Wimpy and Jeep.
Complete - **$500 $1250 $2250**

PPY-28

❑ PPY-28. "Ask Popeye's Lucky Jeep" Fortune Toy,
c. 1936. Store item by Northwestern Products. Cardboard with wood handle.
Box Only - **$100 $200 $350**
Toy Only - **$100 $200 $350**

PPY-29

❑ PPY-29. "Popeye Cut-Outs" Premium Folder,
1936. Popeye Fly Swatter. 2-1/2x6" stiff folder opens to 6x10". Apparent first issue as text refers to another "Group No. 2 Of The Popeye Family." Uncut - **$40 $85 $175**

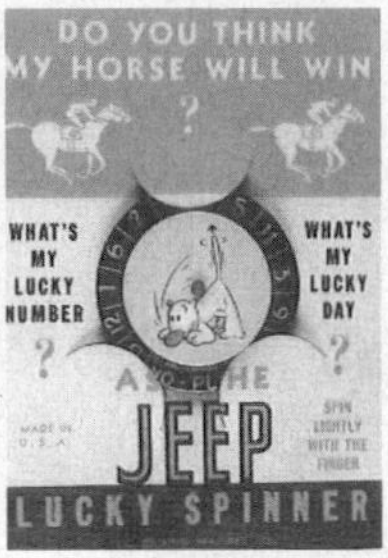

PPY-30 PPY-31

❑ PPY-30. "Ask The Jeep Lucky Spinner" On Store Card,
1936. Store item. 3x4" card holds 1-1/2" plastic disk with a second 1" plastic disk depicting Jeep sniffing the gound with his tail in the air accented by a tiny arrow which will point at one of the numerals 1-12 when spun.
Card - **$50 $150 $250**
Spinner - **$100 $225 $400**

❑ PPY-31. "Popeye The Sailor Man" 9x13" Cardboard Book Sign,
c. 1937. Grosset & Dunlap. - **$300 $600 $1200**

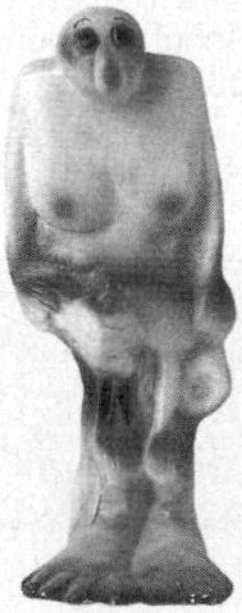

PPY-33

PPY-32

❑ PPY-32. "Alice the Goon" Carnival Figure,
1937. Figure is holding a knife. Rare. - **$250 $600 $1200**

❑ PPY-33. "Popeye And The Jeep" Big Little Book,
1937. Whitman #1405. - **$22 $66 $155**

PPY-34

❑ PPY-34. "Popeye In Quest Of His Poopdeck Pappy" Big Little Book,
1937. Whitman #1450. - **$22 $66 $155**

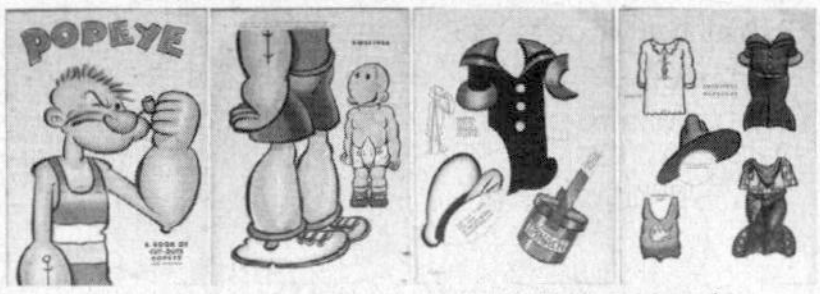

PPY-35

❑ PPY-35. Huge Punch-Out Book,
1937. Whitman. 13.25x18.25" stiff paper cover book of six full color pages of assembly parts for Popeye and Swee'pea plus outfits for them. - **$350 $900 $1750**

PPY-36 (CLOSE-UP OF SEAL)

❑ PPY-36. "State Theatre Popeye Club" Membership Certificate,
1938. Paper document for theater in Kingsport, Tennessee with affixed foil paper seal. Local particulars are inked including member name and August 27 effective date of membership. - **$40 $85 $175**

PPY-37 PPY-38

❑ **PPY-37. Popsicle-Fudgsicle-Creamsicle 13x18" Cardboard Store Sign,**
1938. Scarce. Pictures premiums and announces Popeye "On The Radio After May 1st". - **$400 $950 $2000**

❑ **PPY-38. "Popeye All Pictures Comics,**
1939. Big Little Book #1406. - **$20 $60 $175**

PPY-39

❑ **PPY-39. "Popeye And The Deep Sea Mystery" Better Little Book,**
1939. Whitman #1499. - **$19 $57 $135**

PPY-41

PPY-40

❑ **PPY-40. Newsstand Apron,**
1930s. News-Sentinel. Red and white on dark blue fabric. - **$175 $300 $550**

❑ **PPY-41. "Popeye Navy/Admiral" Brass Badge,**
1930s. Store item. 1-1/2" tall in two shades of brass luster with red and black details. - **$100 $300 $600**

PPY-42

❑ **PPY-42. "Blow-Me-Down Handkerchiefs!" Boxed,**
1930s. Store item. Beautiful color box holds three hankies done in three colors on white.
Box Only - **$75 $150 $300**
Each Hanky - **$20 $40 $75**

PPY-43 PPY-44

❑ **PPY-43. Newsstand Vendor's Apron,**
1930s. Chicago American. Black and white on orange fabric with pockets for change. - **$200 $350 $650**

❑ **PPY-44. Bisque Toothbrush Holder,**
1930s. Store item. Has moveable arm. - **$100 $225 $450**

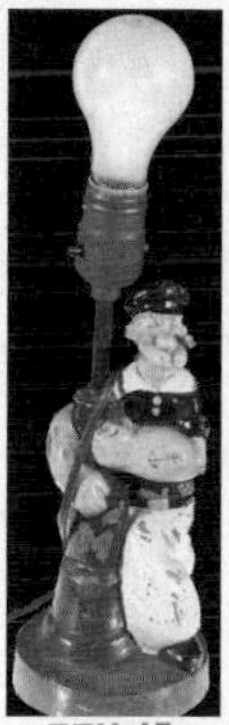

PPY-45 PPY-46

❑ **PPY-45. Painted White Metal Lamp With Pipe,**
1930s. Store item. - **$150 $300 $600**

❑ **PPY-46. Poll-Parrot Shoes Photo Ad Card,**
c. 1930s. Probable unauthorized use of Popeye character by local store owner. - **$20 $40 $65**

PPY-47

❑ **PPY-47. Enameled Metal Pin,**
1930s. Wheatena cereal. Set of three: Popeye, Olive Oyl, Wimpy. Each On Card (Two Varieties) - **$75 $150 $260**
Popeye Pin - **$20 $50 $90**
Olive Pin - **$30 $70 $110**
Wimpy Pin - **$30 $70 $110**

PPY-48

❑ **PPY-48. Theatre Club Card And Cello. Button,**
1930s. Various theaters.
Button - **$10 $20 $35**
Card - **$30 $65 $135**

PPY-51

PPY-49 PPY-50

❑ **PPY-49. Olive Oyl Enamel On Silvered Brass Pin,**
1930s. Wheatena cereal.
On Card - **$75 $150 $260**
Pin Only - **$30 $70 $110**

❑ **PPY-50. Jeep Enamel On Brass Pin,**
1930s. Apparent store item, similar to Wheatena giveaways and used as premium by Popsicle. Also comes with figure surrounded by a silvered brass horseshoe. - **$75 $150 $300**

❑ **PPY-51. Wimpy Color Picture Silvered Brass Ring,**
1930s. - **$75 $135 $225**

PPY-52

❑ **PPY-52. "New York Evening Journal" Club Card,**
1930s. - **$30 $65 $135**

PPY-53

❑ **PPY-53. "The Popeye Line Of Hats & Caps" Store Carton,**
c. 1930s. Unidentified clothing maker. 16x19x24" long carton with lid. - **$200 $400 $800**

PPY-54

PPY-55

PPY-56

❑ **PPY-54. "I Yam Strong For King Comics" Cello. Button,**
1930s. One of earliest buttons to advertise comic books. - **$25 $60 $100**

❑ **PPY-55. "Sunday Examiner" Litho. Button,**
1930s. From "50 Comics" set of various newspaper characters, match number to win prize. - **$25 $50 $80**

❑ **PPY-56. "S. F. Examiner" Litho. Button,**
1930s. San Francisco newspaper. From set of various characters, match number to win prize. - **$30 $60 $110**

PPY-57

PPY-58

PPY-59

❑ **PPY-57. "Keep This Button" Cello. Button,**
1930s. Los Angeles Evening Herald & Express. Promotes cash prizes for contest. - **$20 $30 $60**

❑ **PPY-58. "New York Evening Journal" Button,**
1930s. Promotes Popeye strip. - **$15 $25 $50**

❑ **PPY-59. "Evening Ledger Comics" Button,**
1930s. - **$75 $150 $275**

PPY-60

❑ **PPY-60. "Popeye Bag Puncher" Wind-Up,**
1930s. J. Chien & Co. 9" tall tin with celluloid punching bag. Box - **$1250 $2500 $5000**
Toy - **$2000 $4000 $7500**

PPY-61

❑ **PPY-61. "Popeye Heavy Hitter" Litho. Tin Wind-Up,**
1930s. J. Chien & Co. 11.5" tall.
Box - **$2000 $4000 $6000**
Toy - **$2500 $5000 $8500**

PPY-62

❑ **PPY-62. Jeep Plaster Carnival Statue,**
1930s. Figure is 8.5" tall with thick rope tail. - **$1000 $2000 $3000**

PPY-63

PPY-65

PPY-64

❑ **PPY-63. "Popeye is in The News Bee" Pin,**
1930s. Promotes strip. - **$40 $80 $175**

❑ **PPY-64. Journal Pinback,**
1930s. Scarce. Promotes strip. - **$25 $50 $100**

❑ **PPY-65. Popeye Cello Wind-Up With Moving Head,**
1930s. 8.5" tall figure featuring up and down head movement as vibrations cause toy to move about. - **$225 $450 $900**

PPY-66

❑ **PPY-66. Popeye Characters Alarm Clock,**
1930s. New Haven Clock Co. 3.75" diameter metal case, perimeter and back have Popeye character images. Dial face pictures Popeye and his two diecut tin arms point to the time. - **$900 $1750 $3500**

PPY-67

❑ **PPY-67. Popeye Soap Figure in Boat,**
1930s. In original box. - **$100 $225 $450**

PPY-68

❑ **PPY-68. "Popeye The Pilot" Airplane Wind-Up Toy,**
1940. Tin litho store item by Marx. - **$375 $850 $1800**

PPY-69

❑ **PPY-69. "Popeye And Caster Oyl The Detective" Better Little Book,**
1941. Whitman #1497. - **$19 $57 $135**

PPY-70

PPY-71

❑ PPY-70. Coca-Cola Postcards With Wrapper,
1942. Set of four.
Near Mint With Wrapper - **$135**
Each Card - **$5 $10 $20**

❑ PPY-71. "Buy War Stamps" 14x18" Poster,
c. 1944. U.S. Government. - **$100 $200 $400**

PPY-72

❑ PPY-72. Popeye & Friends "Hingees" Kit,
1945. Store item by Martin P. King & Son.
Unpunched - **$30 $65 $135**

PPY-73

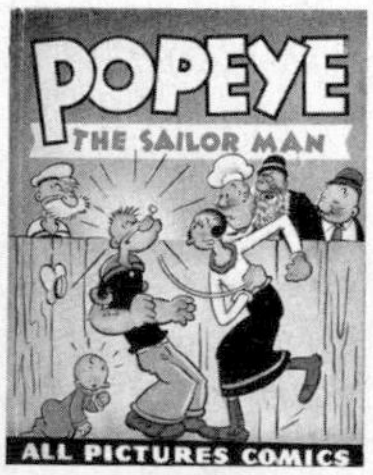

PPY-74

❑ PPY-73. "Popeye The Spinach Eater" Book,
1945. Big Little Book #1480. - **$15 $45 $105**

❑ PPY-74. "All Pictures Comics" Book,
1947. #1422. - **$15 $45 $105**

PPY-75

❑ PPY-75. Australian Popeye Club Badge,
1949. - **$75 $125 $250**

PPY-76

❑ PPY-76. Comic Book Ad for Popeye Club Badge,
1949. Australian Popeye Club.- **$20 $30 $50**

PPY-77

❑ PPY-77. Comic Book Colouring Contest Ad for Popeye Club Badge,
1949. Australian Popeye Club. - **$15 $25 $40**

(enlarged view of puzzle)

PPY-78

❑ PPY-78. Popeye Puzzle and Box,
1949. - **$60 $125 $210**

PPY-79

PPY-80

❑ PPY-79. "Popeye and Queen Olive Oyl",
1949. Big Little Book #1458. - **$15 $45 $105**

❑ PPY-80. Popcorn Bank,
1949. Van Camp premium. 20 oz.popcorn can which converts into bank. - **$20 $50 $85**

PPY-81

❑ PPY-81. Ruler,
1940s. 7 inch ruler. Came with pencil box. Store bought. - **$10 $25 $50**

PPY-82

❑ PPY-82. Popeye Sailor's Cap,
1940s. Probable premium. - **$100 $200 $400**

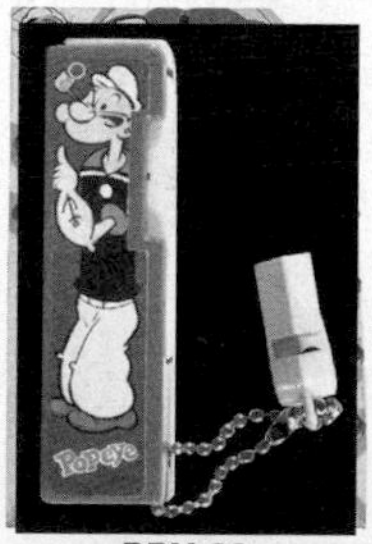

PPY-83

PPY-84

❑ PPY-83. Popeye Flashlight and Whistle,
1940s. Came on display of 12 Magic Nite Glo flashlights with whistles.
Display Card (Not Shown) - **$100 $200 $400**
Each Glow In Dark Flashlight - **$20 $50 $85**

❑ PPY-84. "Sunshine Popeye Cookies" Cardboard Tab,
c. 1940s. - **$30 $70 $125**

PPY-85

❑ **PPY-85. "Popeye Bubble 'N Clean" Soap Box With Turtle Offer,**
c. 1950. Woolfoam Corp.
Complete Box - **$65 $130 $200**

PPY-86

❑ **PPY-86. Christmas Store Display,**
1952. King Features Syndicate. Pair of full color cardboard diecuts. Pair - **$150 $250 $500**

PPY-87

PPY-88

❑ **PPY-87. Popeye Tin Bank,**
1956. Holds $5.00 worth of dimes. King Features copyright. - **$35 $75 $150**

❑ **PPY-88. "The Sailor Man" Golden Record In Sleeve,**
1957. Plastic record in 7x7.5" color portrait sleeve. - **$10 $15 $30**

PPY-89

PPY-90

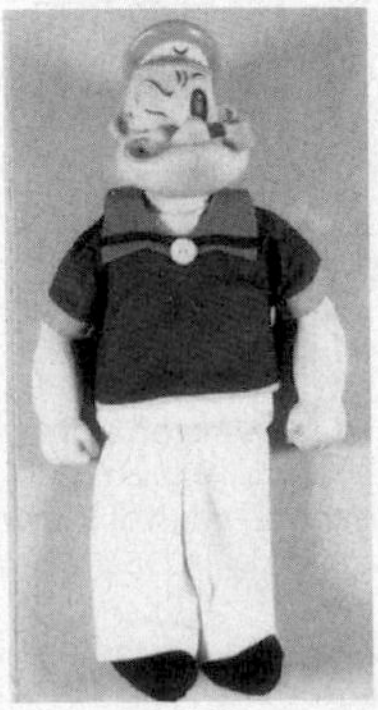

PPY-91

❑ **PPY-89. "Popeye: The First Fifty Years" 2-1/4" Cello. Button,**
1959. Workman Publishing Co. For book promotion with King Feautures copyright. -
$8 $12 $25

❑ **PPY-90. Popeye Cello. Button,**
1950s. Comes in 3-1/2" size and scarcer 1-3/4" size. Larger Size - **$15 $30 $60**
Smaller Size - **$25 $50 $80**

❑ **PPY-91. Cloth/Vinyl Doll,**
1950s. Store item by Gund Mfg. Co. -
$65 $125 $200

PPY-92

❑ **PPY-92. Popeye Sports Roadster Friction Car,**
1950s. Store item by Linemar. Tin with vinyl head. Popeye's car is known in yellow while a matching car for Olive, with simulated hair long ponytail, is known in red or yellow.
Boxed Popeye - **$600 $1200 $2000**
Boxed Olive - **$500 $1000 $1750**

PPY-93

❑ **PPY-93. "Line Mar Battery Operated Popeye And Olive Oyl Tank" Boxed Toy,**
1950s. This is considered to be the rarest of all Popeye toys with only three known in the hobby. The box is 5x8.5x5" deep. The tin litho toy is 4x11x5" tall. Box - **$1000 $3000 $5000**
Toy - **$5000 $10,000 $15,000**

PPY-94

❑ **PPY-94. "Popeye The Basketball Player" Boxed Mechanical Toy By Line Mar,**
1950s. Box is 3x3.25x9". Instructions printed on box side "After Winding Lift The Ball And Then Drop Into Popeye's Hands." 2.5x3.5x9" tall toy with 5" tall Popeye figure standing below basketball hoop that has Popeye and Wimpy pictured on back board. Box - **$300 $600 $1200**
Toy - **$300 $600 $1200**

PPY-95

❑ **PPY-95. "Wooden Popeye" Pull Toy,**
1950s. Store item by Linemar. About 10" tall designed to roll flat on the floor with parts including "Spinach" can which revolve.
Boxed - **$250 $500 $800**

PPY-96

❑ **PPY-96. "Pop Up Olive Oyl With Squeaker" Push Action Toy,**
1950s. Store item by Linemar. Made of cloth with composition head and shoes. A matching Popeye was made.
Each Boxed - **$550 $1100 $1800**

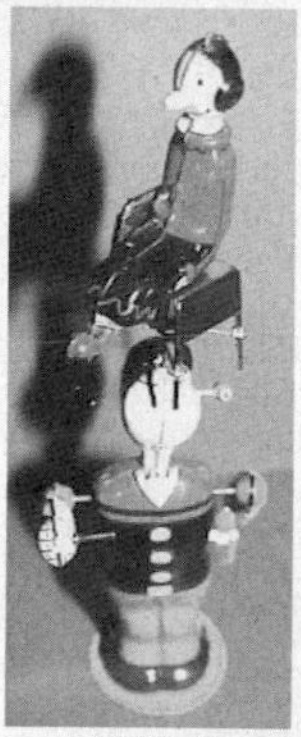

PPY-97

PPY-98

❑ **PPY-97. "Juggling Popeye And Olive Oyl" Wind-Up,**
1950s. Store item by Linemar. 9" tall with action of Popeye hitting Olive's chair with a metal rod which causes the chair to spin.
Boxed - **$1300 $2750 $4000**

❑ **PPY-98. "Popeye Lantern" Tin And Glass Light,**
1950s. Store item by Line Mar.
Boxed - **$150 $400 $750**

PPY-99

❑ **PPY-99. Tricycle Wind-Up Toy,**
1950s. Line Mar. 4-1/2" tall tin litho. - **$300 $600 $1200**

PPY-100

❑ **PPY-100. Popeye And Eugene The Jeep Canadian Glass,**
1950s. Issuer unknown. 4-3/4" tall. #5 from rare Canadian series under King Features Syndicate copyright. - **$25 $50 $75**

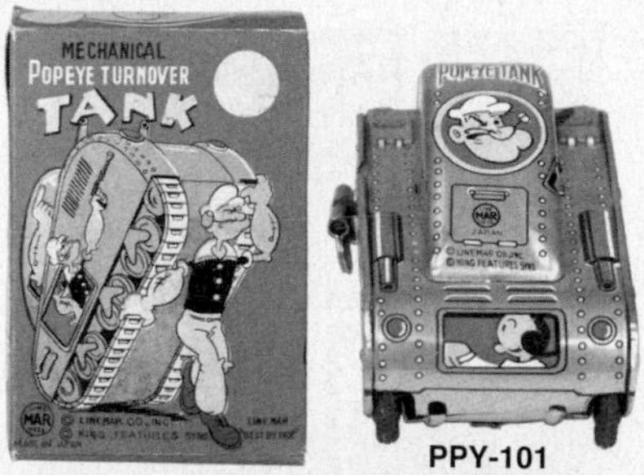

PPY-101

❑ **PPY-101. "Popeye Tank" Wind-Up,**
1950s. Linemar. 4" long litho tin toy picturing other Popeye characters as well. Winding causes his diecut figure on underside to lift the tank which does not then flip over as designed.
Toy - **$200 $400 $800**
Box - **$225 $450 $750**
Complete - **$425 $850 $1550**

PPY-102

❑ **PPY-102. Popeye Tin Roller Skater With Box,**
1950s. Linemar. Toy - **$225 $450 $675**
Box - **$250 $400 $600**
Complete- **$475 $850 $1275**

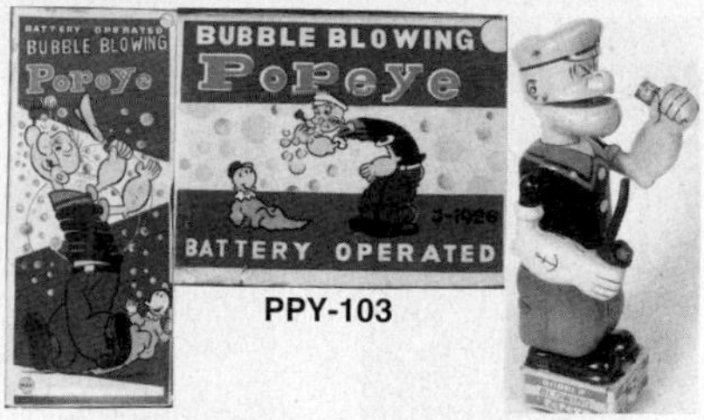

PPY-103

❑ **PPY-103. "Bubble Blowing Popeye" Battery Toy Boxed,**
1950s. Linemar. Illustrated box holding 12" tall litho tin figure toy on square base. Toy blows soap bubbles through tiny ring that dips into reservoir while a red bulb lights in the bowl of his pipe as the arms move alternately to raise and lower the pipe and spinach can held in opposite hand. Box - **$150 $300 $600**
Toy - **$200 $500 $1000**

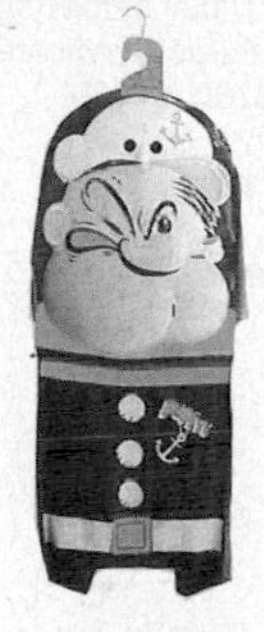

PPY-104

PPY-105

❑ **PPY-104. Popeye Adult-Sized Over The Head-Style Costume,**
1960. Collegeville. 25" wide by 50" tall.
Near Mint Carded - **$375**
Uncarded - **$85 $175 $300**

❑ **PPY-105. Gasoline Pump Metal Sign,**
1960s. Crown Gas. Full color image on white. - **$125 $225 $450**

PPY-106

❑ **PPY-106. "Wooden Popeye" Figure,**
1960s. Store item by Line Mar.
Boxed - **$200 $400 $800**

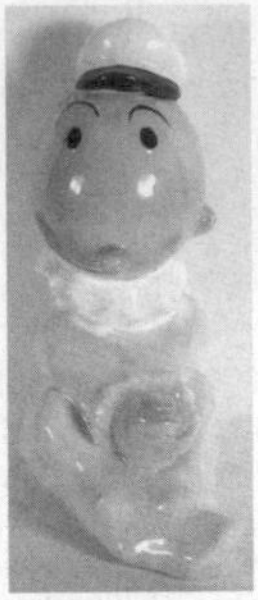

PPY-108

PPY-107

❑ **PPY-107. Popeye Carpet Store Standee With Carpet,**
1970s. Bigelow Carpet. Diecut store display with seven feet tall Popeye holding actual carpet with many panels showing King Features Syndicate characters. Complete - **$350 $750 $1400**
Rug Alone - **$200 $450 $800**
Standee Alone - **$150 $300 $600**

❑ **PPY-108. Swee' Pea Ceramic Figure,**
1980. 6" tall. - **$40 $85 $185**

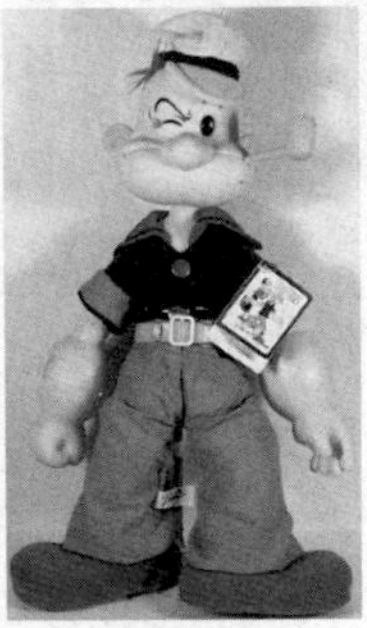

PPY-109 PPY-110

❑ **PPY-109. Popeye Doll with Tag,**
1985. 18 1/2" tall. King Features copyright. - **$25 $50 $150**

❑ **PPY-110. Olive Oyl Doll with Tag,**
1985. 18" tall. - **$25 $40 $125**

PPY-111 PPY-112

❑ **PPY-111. Brutus Doll with Tag,**
1985. 22" tall. King Features copyright. - **$20 $40 $125**

❑ **PPY-112. Poopdeck Pappy Doll with Tag,**
1985. 18" tall. - **$20 $55 $150**

PPY-113

❑ **PPY-113. "Crew Club" 16-Page Comic Booklets,**
1989. Instant Quaker Oatmeal. Photo shows set of 4 different plus one back. Each - **$1 $4 $10**

PPY-114

❑ **PPY-114. Popeye Tin Wastebasket,**
1985. Features Popeye and Olive on one side and a litho of the entire cast on the other. - **$12 $25 $70**

PPY-115 PPY-116

❑ **PPY-115. Popeye Limited Edition Figure,**
1999. 8" tall resin. Made in France. Sculpted by Leblon-Delienne. Only 999 made. - **$135**

❑ **PPY-116. Olive Oyl Limited Edition Figure,**
1999. 7 1/2" tall resin. Made in France. Sculpted by Leblon-Delienne. Only 999 made. - **$135**

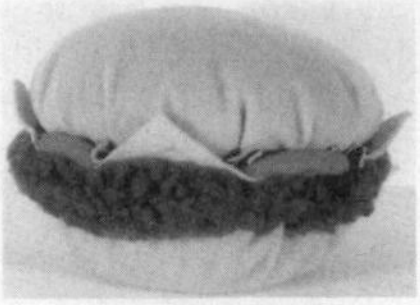

PPY-118

PPY-117

❑ **PPY-117. Swee' Pea Limited Edition Figure,**
1999. 4 1/2" tall resin. Made in France. Sculpted by Leblon-Delienne. Only 999 made. - **$75**

❑ **PPY-118. Wimpy Burger Bean Bag with Tag,**
1999. Exclusive from Universal Studios Island of Adventure Theme Park. - **$20**

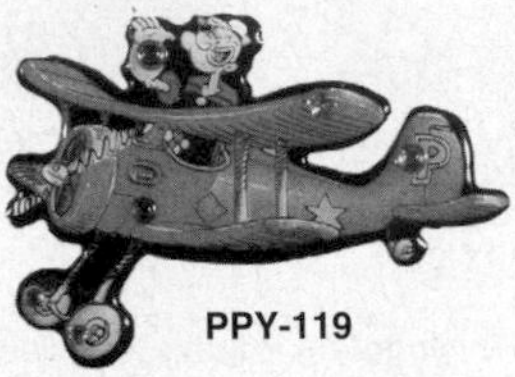

PPY-119

❑ **PPY-119. Popeye Bronze Pin,**
1999. Very decorative. - **$55**

PPY-120 PPY-121

❑ **PPY-120. Popeye Bean Figure Set,**
2000. Sold at CVS Pharmacy. Limited set includes Popeye, Olive, Bluto, Swee'pea, Wimpy, and the Jeep.
Set of figures with tags - **$60**
Box - **$60**

❑ **PPY-121. "Popeye" Wacky Wobbler,**
2001. In box. - **$22**

PPY-122 PPY-123

❑ **PPY-122. Popeye Doll in Box,**
2001. Toys "R' Us exclusive. 14" tall. Boxed - **$28**

❑ **PPY-123. Popeye Maquette Figure,**
2001. Limited to 1,000. - **$100**

PPY-124

PPY-125

❑ **PPY-124. Bluto Maquette Figure,**
2001. Limited to 1,000. - **$100**

❑ **PPY-125. Olive Oyl Maquette Figure,**
2001. Limited to 1,000. - **$100**

Popsicle

Add some flavor and coloring to water, freeze it around a pair of flat sticks, and the result is a Popsicle, a popular alternative to ice cream promoted as a frozen drink on-a-stick. Frank Epperson created the confection, originally named "Epsicle," applying for a patent in 1923. He sold the rights to the Joe Lowe Company in 1925. In addition to flavored ice, the producers created Popsicle Pete, a comic book character that started on a long run in *All-American Comics* in 1939. *The Popsicle Pete Fun Book* (1947) and *Adventure Book* (1948) contained stories, games, and cut-outs, and the company sponsored two short-lived television variety shows: *The Popsicle Parade of Stars* on CBS in 1950 and *Popsicle Five-Star Comedy* on ABC in 1957. See additional early Popsicle premiums in the Buck Rogers section. Good Humor owns the Popsicle brand today, and orange continues to be the favorite flavor.

PSC-1

PSC-2

❑ **PSC-1. Uncle Don Club Card Popsicle Premium,**
1932. Rare. - **$50 $100 $150**

❑ **PSC-2. "Popsicle" Premium Sheet,**
1937. - **$15 $25 $50**

PSC-3

PSC-4

❑ **PSC-3. Store Sign Showing Premiums,**
c. 1937. Orange, black and white sheet 12-3/8x19-1/4". Only character premium shown is "Bob Burns Bazooka." - **$40 $80 $140**

❑ **PSC-4. Sign,**
1930s.Very early die-cut cardboard sign for Popsicle when they were offered one stick for 5¢. Young girl promoter was later replaced by Popsicle Pete. Superb color. - **$135 $275 $600**

PSC-5

PSC-6

❑ **PSC-5. "Jo-Lo Creamsicles" Waxed Paper Bag,**
1930s. Popsicles with Joe Lowe Corp. copyright for various local retailers. Bags were saved for gifts. - **$10 $15 $30**

❑ **PSC-6. "Adventurer's Popsicle Club" Litho. Button,**
1930s. - **$15 $35 $70**

PSC-7

❑ **PSC-7. Popsicle Sign,**
1930s. - **$75 $150 $250**

PSC-8

PSC-9

❑ **PSC-8. Popsicle Pete Cheerio Bag,**
1941. Cheerio bags were used as coupons to get gifts. - **$10 $15 $30**

❑ **PSC-9. Popsicle Pete Gift News,**
1941. 8 page flyer for gifts. Popsicle Pete pictured upper left. - **$30 $45 $90**

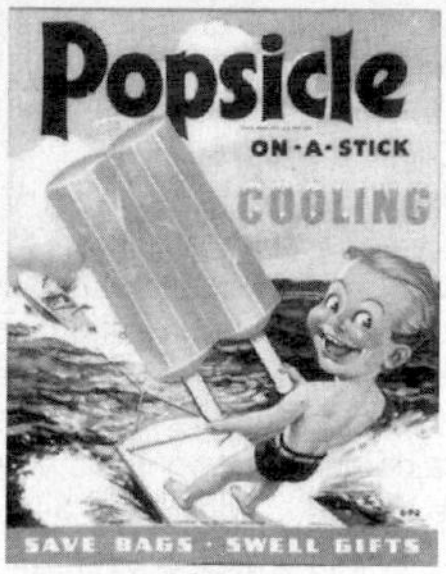

PSC-10

❑ **PSC-10. Paper Store Sign 11x14",**
1946. - **$50 $100 $200**

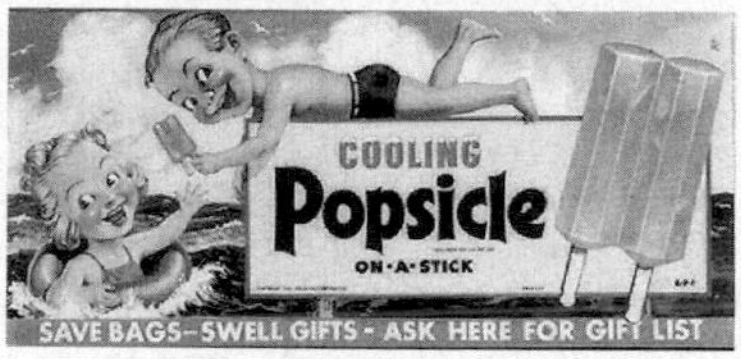

PSC-11

❑ **PSC-11. Paper Store Sign 9x19",**
1946. - **$50 $100 $200**

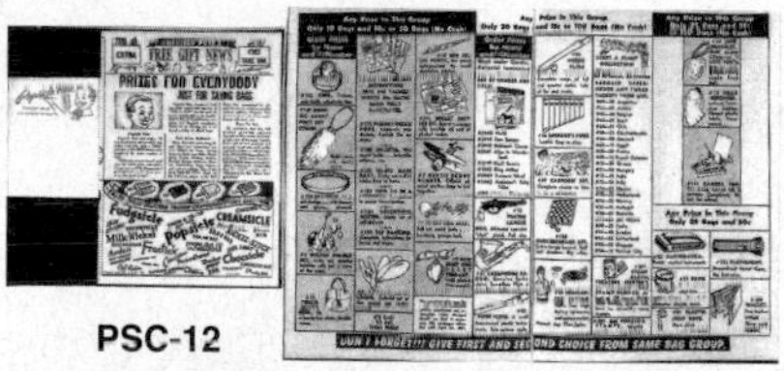

PSC-12

❑ **PSC-12. "Popsicle Pete Free Gift News",**
1947. - **$20 $40 $75**

PSC-13

PSC-14

❑ **PSC-13. "Giant Gift List" Catalogue,**
1949. - **$30 $50 $85**

❑ **PSC-14. "Popsicle Pete Jo-Lo-Fone",**
1940s. Assembled Pair - **$25 $50 $100**

PSC-15

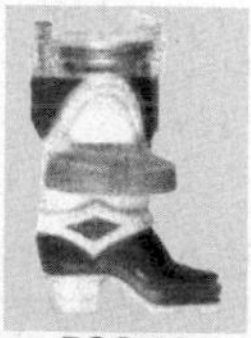

PSC-16

❑ **PSC-15. Popsicle Pete's "Mystery Box With Mystery Prize",**
c. 1940s. Held prize and stick good for free Popsicle. Complete - **$150**
Empty - **$35 $70 $125**

❑ **PSC-16. Cowboy Boot Plastic Ring,**
1951. Popsicle. Top has magnifier lens, compass, secret compartment. Boot holds "Cowboy Ring Secret Code" symbols paper. Also offered by Bazooka Joe and shown in his premium catalog as late as 1966. Complete - **$40 $85 $150**
Without Code Paper - **$25 $65 $100**

PSC-17

PSC-18

❑ **PSC-17. Popsicle Pete Gift List,**
1952. Paper sheet opening to 11x15" printed on both sides including illustration of 34 premium offers for 1952-1953 years. - **$18 $30 $60**

❑ **PSC-18. "Giant Gift List" Sheet,**
1953. For 1953-1954 premium offers. - **$18 $30 $60**

PSC-19

❑ **PSC-19. Store Sign,**
1953. Issued by Joe Lowe Corp. 8x20". - **$30 $75 $140**

(DETAIL)

PSC-20

❑ **PSC-20. "Popsicle Music Maker Truck,"**
1954. Store item by Mattel. 5" tall hard plastic. - **$65 $150 $275**

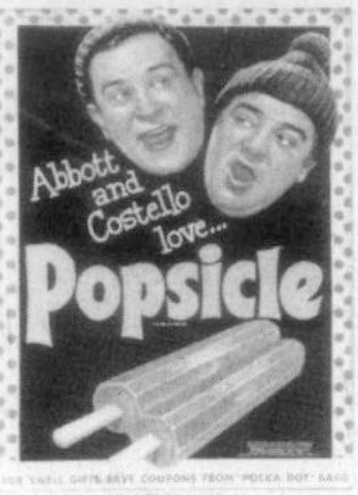

PSC-21

PSC-22

❑ **PSC-21. Abbott And Costello Paper Sign,**
1954. 11x15". Superb color. - **$100 $200 $400**

❑ **PSC-22. "Giant Gift List" Sheet,**
1954. For 1954-1955 premium offers. - **$18 $30 $60**

PSC-23

PSC-24

❑ **PSC-23. "5 Star Comedy Party" 8x15" Paper Poster,**
1957. For short-lived May-July ABC-TV program. - **$75 $135 $275**

❑ **PSC-24. "Popsicle Gift List" Catalogue,**
1958. Eight-page color booklet picturing more than 40 premiums offered 1958-1959 for various coupon quantities. - **$18 $35 $60**

PSC-25

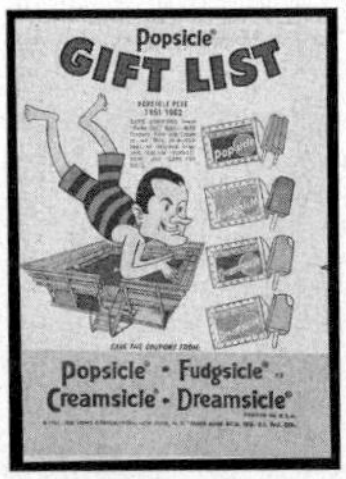

PSC-26

❑ **PSC-25. Popsicle Gift List,**
1959. 1959-1960 list of prizes. 8 pages. Children riding train on front. - **$18 $35 $60**

❑ **PSC-26. Popsicle Gift List,**
1961. 8 page premium. Has Bob Hope on the front and promotes his new film inside. - **$18 $35 $60**

PSC-27

❑ **PSC-27. "Popsicle Space-Shots" Store Sign,**
1964. Joe Lowe Corp. 7.5x13" glossy stiff paper. Advertises rocket-shaped Popsicle treats with text at bottom "Different, Exciting, Space Shapes On-A-Stick." Six different Popsicles are pictured flying through space toward the moon plus image of boy and girl wearing space helmets holding Popsicles. - **$80 $150 $275**

PSC-28

❑ **PSC-28. "Popsicle 50th Anniversary" Promotional Paperweight,**
1973. Solid marble with enameled brass attachments on top. - **$15 $25 $50**

Pop-Up Books

What many collectors consider the most beautiful and imaginative children's books of the 1930s were produced by Pleasure Books Inc. of Chicago under the imprint "A Blue Ribbon Press Book." The word "Pop-Up" served as their registered trademark. Sam Gold, who created and produced *The Mickey Mouse Waddle Book* and *The Wizard of Oz Waddle Book* for Blue Ribbon Books, was also involved in the creative efforts, character licensing and marketing plan for the "Pop-Up" series. Most books in the series featured a licensed character, but a few were also done for nursery rhyme characters such as Mother Goose and Little Red Riding Hood.

PUP-1

❑ **PUP-1. "Mickey Mouse In King Arthur's Court With 'Pop-Up' Illustrations",**
1933. Store item by Blue Ribbon Books. Contains four pop-ups. Originally issued with dust jacket.
Dust Jacket Only - **$100 $250 $500**
Book Only - **$250 $525 $1500**

PUP-2

❑ **PUP-2. "Jack the Giant Killer" Book,**
1933. Blue Ribbon Books, Inc. Illustrated by Harold B. Lentz. - **$85 $225 $650**

PUP-3

❑ **PUP-3. "The 'Pop-Up' Silly Symphonies" Book With Dust Jacket,**
1933. Store item by Blue Ribbon Books. Story titles are "Babes In The Woods" and "King Neptune." Contains four pop-ups.
Dust Jacket - **$75 $175 $325**
Book - **$175 $350 $950**

PUP-4

❑ **PUP-4. "The Pop-Up Minnie Mouse" Book,**
1933. Store item by Blue Ribbon Books, Inc. Contains three pop-ups. - **$125 $350 $900**

PUP-5

❑ **PUP-5. "The Pop-Up Mickey Mouse" Book,**
1933. Store item by Blue Ribbon Books. Includes three pop-ups. - **$125 $350 $900**

PUP-6

❑ **PUP-6. "The Pop-Up Mother Goose" Hardcover Book,**
1933. Blue Ribbon Books Inc. Has four full color diecut pop-ups. - **$75 $200 $625**

PUP-7

❑ **PUP-7. "The 'Pop-Up' Popeye In Among The White Savages" Book,**
1934. Store item by Blue Ribbon Press. Small 4x5" format with single center pop-up. - **$175 $400 $1000**

PUP-8

❑ **PUP-8. "The Wizard Of Oz Waddle Book",**
1934. Store item by Blue Ribbon Books. Not a pop-up but contains instructions and separate loose punch-out sheets for forming the characters Dorothy, Toto, Tin Man, Scarecrow, Lion and Wizard who when assembled walk down a cardboard ramp.
Dust Jacket Only - **$100 $200 $400**
Book Only - **$75 $150 $300**
Each Assembled Waddle - **$200 $400 $650**
Each Unpunched Waddle - **$500 $1100 $1800**
Near Mint Complete - **$11,500**

PUP-9

❑ **PUP-9. "The 'Pop-Up' Buck Rogers In A Dangerous Mission" Book,**
1934. Blue Ribbon Press. Small 4x5" format with a single center pop-up. - **$250 $650 $1750**

PUP-10

❑ **PUP-10. "The 'Pop-Up' Mickey Mouse In Ye Olden Days" Book,**
1934. Store item by Blue Ribbon Press. Small 4x5" format with single center pop-up. - **$150 $400 $1200**

PUP-11

❑ PUP-11. "Little Red Riding Hood" Pop-Up Book,
1934. Store item by Blue Ribbon Press. Contains three pop-ups. - **$65 $175 $475**

PUP-12

❑ PUP-12. "Mickey Mouse Waddle Book",
1934. Store item by Blue Ribbon Books. Not a pop-up but rear of book has instruction sheets and separate punch-out sheets for assembling characters of Mickey, Minnie, Pluto and Tanglefoot who when assembled will walk down a cardboard ramp.
Cover Slip Band - **$150 $350 $700**
Dust Jacket Only - **$100 $300 $600**
Book Only - **$100 $250 $500**
Each Assembled Waddle - **$300 $600 $1000**
Each Unpunched Waddle - **$500 $1200 $4000**
Ramp - **$300 $600 $1200**
Near Mint Complete - **$19,000**

PUP-13

❑ PUP-13. Goldilocks And Three Bears Pop-Up Book,
1934. Blue Ribbon Press. Twenty pages including three diecut pop-ups. - **$50 $150 $400**

PUP-14

❑ PUP-14. "The Tale Of Peter Rabbit With Pop-Up Picture" Book,
1934. Blue Ribbon Books, Inc. Has single pop-up. - **$125 $250 $700**

PUP-15

❑ PUP-15. "The 'Pop-Up' Terry And The Pirates" Book,
1935. Store item by Blue Ribbon Press. Contains three pop-ups. - **$125 $350 $850**

PUP-16

PUP-17

❑ PUP-16. "The 'Pop-Up' Little Orphan Annie And Jumbo The Circus Elephant" Book,
1935. Blue Ribbon Press. Contains three pop-ups. - **$150 $450 $1200**

❑ PUP-17. "Popeye With The Hag Of The Seven Seas" Pop-Up Book,
1935. Store item by Blue Ribbon Press. Contains three pop-ups. - **$125 $350 $1100**

PUP-18

❑ PUP-18. "Tim Tyler In The Jungle" Pop-Up Book,
1935. Store item by Blue Ribbon Press, Pleasure Books Inc. Twenty pages including three double-page color pop-ups. - **$125 $250 $700**

PUP-19

❑ PUP-19. "Flash Gordon Tournament Of Death" Pop-Up Book,
1935. Store item by Blue Ribbon Press. Contains three pop-ups. - **$250 $750 $1850**

PUP-20

❑ PUP-20. "The 'Pop-Up' Buck Rogers" Book,
1935. Store item by Blue Ribbon Press. 8x9" with three pop-ups. Subtitled "Strange Adventures In The Spider-Ship." Reprinted in 1994 by Applewood Books, 8x9-1/2". -
Original - **$250 $750 $1850**
Reprint - **$5 $10 $15**

PUP-21

❑ PUP-21. "The New Adventures Of Tarzan 'Pop-Up'" Book,
1935. Store item by Blue Ribbon Press. 8x9-1/4" with three pop-ups. - **$175 $500 $1400**

PUP-22

❑ PUP-22. "The Pop-Up Dick Tracy Capture Of Boris Arson" Hardcover,
1935. Book is 8x9.25" by Blue Ribbon Press, Pleasure Books Inc. There are three pop-ups.
- $150 $450 $1200

PUP-23

❑ PUP-23. Buck Rogers In The 25th Century,
1980. Store item by Random House. 6-3/4x9-1/4". Also published in Spanish by Editorial Norma. Each - **$8 $20 $50**

Porky Pig

Porky Pig, one of the star cartoon characters created by the Warner Brothers studio in the 1930s, made his screen debut in 1935 and had his first feature role the following year. From then until the mid-1960s the stuttering little porker appeared in more than 100 cartoon shorts, frequently paired with Daffy Duck, Sylvester the cat, or his girlfriend Petunia. Porky was originally designed by Bob Clampett and his first cartoon was directed by Friz Freleng. He went on to greater fame and laughs when animator Tex Avery joined the staff in 1936. Porky went through several early design changes, and from 1937 on was given voice by Mel Blanc. Porky made his comic book debut in issue #1 of *Looney Tunes & Merrie Melodies* in 1941, had his own book by 1943, and over the years has appeared in numerous special issues and as a guest star in other Warner character books. On television the *Porky Pig Show* aired on ABC from 1964 to 1967 and *Porky Pig and His Friends* was syndicated to local stations starting in 1971. "Tha- Tha- That's All Folks!"

PRK-1

PRK-2

❑ **PRK-1. Bisque Bank,**
c. 1936. Store Item - **$45 $115 $200**

❑ **PRK-2. Coloring Book,**
1938. Store item by Saalfield Publishing Co. Probably first Porky coloring book. Sixteen pages of art by Ralph Wolfe involving Porky and Petunia in various activities. - **$65 $150 $300**

PRK-3

❑ **PRK-3. "Porky Pig Of Looney Tunes" Stationery Folder,**
1938. Store item by Mitchell Publishing Co. Very early appearance of Daffy and Elmer on a Warner Bros. merchandised item. - **$50 $85 $175**

PRK-4

❑ **PRK-4. "Porky Pig" Boxed Wind-Up Toy,**
1939. Marx. Tin litho toy with built-in key is 3x5x8.5" tall and comes in nicely illustrated box.
Box - **$225 $450 $750**
Toy - **$350 $750 $1500**

PRK-6

PRK-5

❑ **PRK-5. Early Linen-Like Book With First Daffy Duck Appearance,**
1930s. Store item. 9-3/4x12-1/2" with 12 linen-like textured pages. Porky goes on a duck hunt and runs into a wacky duck who later evolves into Daffy in Warner cartoons, although he is unnamed here. - **$74 $222 $1075**

❑ **PRK-6. "Porky's Book Of Tricks" Activity Booklet,**
1942. K. K. Publications. - **$48 $144 $675**

PRK-7

PRK-8

❑ **PRK-7. All Pictures Comics #1408,**
1942. Reprints Four Color Comics #16 and Famous Gang Book of Comics. - **$15 $45 $105**

❑ **PRK-8. "Porky" Figural White Metal Bank,**
1947. Store item. From a series of banks, plant holders, and bookends. Series includes Porky Pig, Bugs Bunny, Elmer, Daffy Duck, Sniffles, Beaky. Each - **$65 $150 $250**

PRK-9

❑ **PRK-9. Porky Pig Wrist Watch,**
1949. Rare.
Watch with box. - **$200 $750 $1300**
Watch Only. - **$90 $200 $450**

PRK-10

❑ **PRK-10. "Petunia" Wood Jointed Doll,**
1940s. Store item. - **$60 $135 $260**

PRK-11

❑ **PRK-11. "Daffy/Porky/Petunia/Gabby" Child's Hanky,**
1940s. Brightly colored hanky measures 9.25x9.25". - **$20 $35 $65**

PRK-12

❑ **PRK-12. Warner Bros. Character Place Mats,**
c. 1940s. Probable store item. "Rhyme-A-Day Series" set of seven. Each - **$30 $75 $135**

PRK-13

❑ **PRK-13. Dell Comic Pictures,**
1940s. Version in top hat with Warner Bros. copyright, second version Leon Schlesinger copyright. Each - **$20 $40 $80**

PRK-14

❑ **PRK-14. "Looney Tunes" Porky & Petunia Pig Card With Bow,**
1940s. 5.5" square store card holding fabric hair bow and attachment hair pin. - **$30 $65 $125**

PRK-15

❑ **PRK-15. "Galloping Pals" Porky & Petunia Pull Toy Boxed,**
1940s. 7.5" tall wooden toy with litho paper labels by Brice Toy & Novelty Inc. Box art also pictures Bugs Bunny and Elmer Fudd toys.
Box - **$100 $200 $400**
Toy - **$350 $700 $1500**

PRK-16

❑ **PRK-16. "March Of Comics" #175,**
1958. Various sponsors. - **$4 $12 $24**

PRK-17

❑ **PRK-17. "Porky's Lunch Wagon" Dome Lunch Box With Matching Thermos,**
1959. Thermos. Box - **$125 $275 $600**
Bottle - **$35 $75 $150**

PRK-18

PRK-19

❑ **PRK-18. Porky Pig Adult-Sized Over The Head-Style Costume,**
1960. Store item by Collegeville. 25" wide by 50" tall. Near Mint Carded - **$375**
Uncarded - **$80 $160 $275**

❑ **PRK-19. Porky Pig Glazed Ceramic Figure,**
1975. Warner Bros. Inc., Japan. - **$5 $15 $30**

PRK-20

❑ **PRK-20. Porky and Petunia Salt & Pepper Shakers,**
1998. Warner Bros. Store exclusive. - **$38**

PRK-21

❑ **PRK-21. Model Car Kit,**
1999. In box. - **$22**

Post Cereals Misc.

Charles W. Post (1854-1914), a patient at Dr. John Kellogg's Battle Creek Sanitarium, was introduced to the benefits of a vegetarian diet in 1891. His enthusiasm for Kellogg's Caramel Coffee led him to develop his own formula and by 1895 he was marketing Postum Cereal Food Drink, a coffee substitute that "Makes Red Blood." Within two years he had created Grape-Nuts, a cold breakfast cereal that was also promoted as a health food. Post advertised his products as if they were medicines under the theme "There's a Reason." The company flourished, expanded, and took the name of General Foods in the late 1920s.

PST-1

❑ **PST-1. "Post Toasties Movie Book" Folder,**
1920s. - **$20 $40 $80**

PST-2

❑ **PST-2. Classic Celebrity Photo Sign,**
1936. Rare 18" x42" sign. Features Jack Benny, Dizzy Dean, Joe E. Brown, Capt. Frank Hawks and Melvin Purvis. Benny was promoting Jello products and later in 1942 promoted Post cereals. The others were all bigger than life stars, and each had a children's club sponsored by Post cereals. Note - Melvin Purvis is holding the membership badge for his club. -
$150 $350 $700

PST-3

❑ **PST-3. Smiley Burnette Dixie Color Photo,**
1942. - **$18 $35 $65**

PST-4

❑ **PST-4. "Free Comic Rings" Store Sign,**
1948. 15-1/4x20" full color sign promoting set of 12 rings packaged one per box. Gordon Gold Archives. - **$175 $400 $800**

PST-5

❑ **PST-5. Cereal Box With "Comic Rings" Offer,**
1948. Gordon Gold Archives.
Complete - **$225 $400 $850**

PST-6

❑ **PST-6. Comic Rings Store Shelf Display,**
1948. Post's Raisin Bran. Cardboard assembly display for litho. tin ring box inserts. Twelve character rings are identified. -
$150 $350 $700

PST-7

❑ **PST-7. Andy Gump Litho. Tin Ring,**
1948. This and the next 11 rings are from the 1948 Post Raisin Bran set. The Near Mint price is for unbent examples with no rust. -
$10 $25 $65

PST-8

❑ **PST-8. Dick Tracy Litho. Tin Ring,**
1948. - **$25 $65 $150**

PST-9

❑ **PST-9. Harold Teen Litho. Tin Ring,**
1948. - **$10 $25 $65**

PST-10

❑ **PST-10. Herby Litho. Tin Ring,**
1948. - **$10 $25 $65**

PST-11

❑ **PST-11. Lillums Litho. Tin Ring,**
1948. - **$10 $25 $65**

PST-12

❑ **PST-12. Orphan Annie Litho. Tin Ring,**
1948. - **$25 $65 $150**

PST-13

❑ **PST-13. Perry Winkle Litho. Tin Ring,**
1948. - **$10 $25 $65**

PST-14

❑ **PST-14. Skeezix Litho. Tin Ring,**
1948. - **$10 $25 $65**

PST-15

❑ **PST-15. Smilin' Jack Litho. Tin Ring,**
1948. - **$15 $40 $80**

PST-16

❑ **PST-16. Smitty Litho. Tin Ring,**
1948. - **$10 $25 $65**

PST-17

❑ **PST-17. Smokey Stover Litho. Tin Ring,**
1948. - **$10 $25 $65**

PST-18

❑ **PST-18. Winnie Winkle Litho. Tin Ring,**
1948. - **$10 $25 $65**

PST-19

❑ **PST-19. Alexander Litho. Tin Ring,**
1949. This and the next 23 rings are from the 1949 Post Toasties set. The Near Mint price is for unbent examples with no rust. - **$10 $25 $65**

PST-20

❑ **PST-20. Blondie Litho. Tin Ring,**
1949. - **$10 $25 $65**

PST-21

❑ **PST-21. Captain Litho. Tin Ring,**
1949. - **$10 $25 $65**

PST-22

❑ **PST-22. Casper Litho. Tin Ring,**
1949. - **$10 $25 $65**

PST-23

❑ **PST-23. Dagwood Litho. Tin Ring,**
1949. - **$15 $35 $75**

PST-24

❑ **PST-24. Felix The Cat Litho. Tin Ring,**
1949. - **$25 $80 $185**

PST-25

❑ **PST-25. Flash Gordon Litho. Tin Ring,**
1949. - **$35 $100 $210**

PST-26

❑ **PST-26. Fritz Litho. Tin Ring,**
1949. - **$10 $25 $65**

PST-27

❑ **PST-27. Hans Litho. Tin Ring,**
1949. - **$10 $25 $65**

PST-28

❑ **PST-28. Henry Litho. Tin Ring,**
1949. - **$10 $25 $65**

PST-29

❑ **PST-29. Inspector Litho. Tin Ring,**
1949. - **$10 $25 $65**

PST-30

❑ **PST-30. Jiggs Litho. Tin Ring,**
1949. - **$10 $25 $65**

PST-31

❑ **PST-31. Little King Litho. Tin Ring,**
1949. - **$15 $40 $80**

PST-32

❑ **PST-32. Mac Litho. Tin Ring,**
1949. - **$10 $25 $65**

PST-33

❑ **PST-33. Maggie Litho. Tin Ring,**
1949. - **$10 $25 $65**

PST-34

❑ **PST-34. Mama Litho. Tin Ring,**
1949. - **$10 $25 $65**

PST-35

❑ **PST-35. Olive Oyl Litho. Tin Ring,**
1949. - **$15 $40 $75**

PST-36

❑ **PST-36. The Phantom Litho. Tin Ring,**
1949. - **$35 $100 $210**

PST-37

❑ **PST-37. Popeye Litho. Tin Ring,**
1949. - **$20 $70 $150**

PST-38

❑ **PST-38. Snuffy Smith Litho. Tin Ring,**
1949. - **$15 $40 $75**

PST-39

❑ **PST-39. Swee' Pea Litho. Tin Ring,**
1949. - **$15 $40 $75**

PST-40

❑ **PST-40. Tillie The Toiler Litho. Tin Ring,**
1949. - **$10 $25 $65**

PST-41

❑ **PST-41. Toots Litho. Tin Ring,**
1949. - **$10 $25 $65**

PST-42

❑ **PST-42. Wimpy Litho. Tin Ring,**
1949. - **$15 $40 $75**

PST-43

❑ PST-43. "Turbo Jet Pilot" 3-1/2" Plastic Badge,
1949. Center has built-in siren whistle. - **$15 $30 $75**

PST-44

❑ PST-44. Air Speed Indicator,
1940s. Premium for bike with mailer.
Device - **$20 $45 $85**
Mailer - **$10 $20 $40**

PST-45

❑ PST-45. "Free Comic Rings" Store Sign,
1952. Premium Specialties, Chicago, Ill. 9x20" sign reads "12 Different Rings In The Series" and designs are the same as the rings used in the 1948 Post Raisin Bran set. However, this was a later use of the same rings unrelated to the Post promotion. Sign has blank area for sponsor's imprint. Gordon Gold Archives. - **$135 $275 $450**

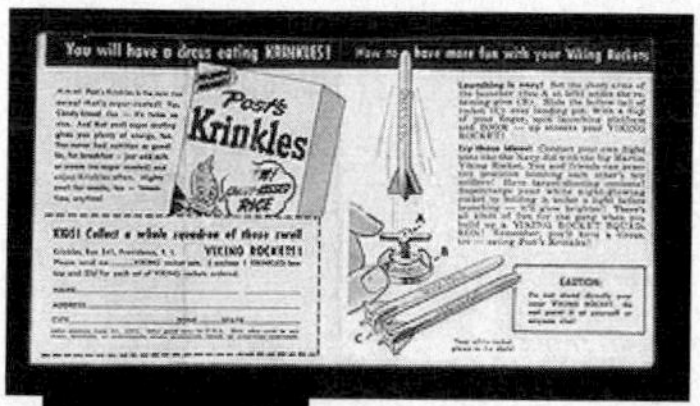

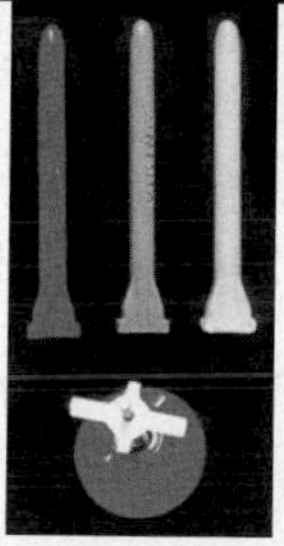

PST-46

PST-47

❑ PST-46. "Viking Rockets" Toy With Instructions And Mailer,
1952. Post's Krinkles. Set of plastic spring launcher and three 2-3/4" plastic rockets.
Near Mint Boxed - **$275**
Launcher and Three Rockets - **$40 $80 $160**

❑ PST-47. Sugar Crisp Order Form for Puppets (Handy, Dandy, Candy),
1953. Post Cereal. - **$12 $25 $50**

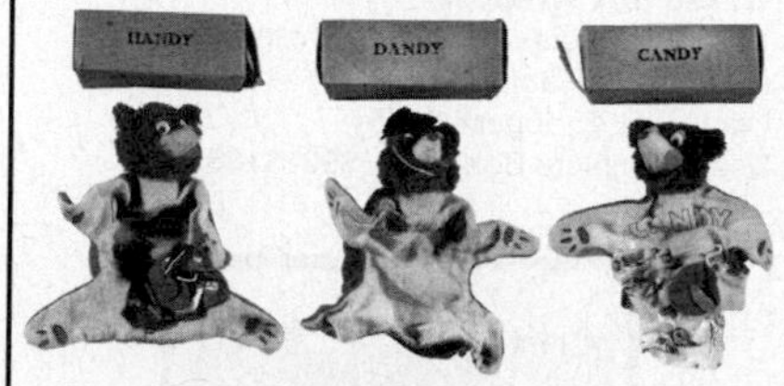

PST-48

❑ PST-48. Sugar Crisp Puppets,
1953. Post Cereal. With accesories add $30 each. - **$25 $50 $100**

PST-49

❑ PST-49. Grape-Nuts Flakes Cars,
1954. Plastic cars of models, Ford County Sedans, Ford Tudors, Ford Crown Victorias. Various colors: red, dark blue, turquoise, yellow, and brown. 8 cars pictured.
Each - **$8 $15 $25**

PST-50

❑ PST-50. Sugar Crisp Bears Mug & Bowl Set,
1954. With instructions & mailer. Blue & Pink. Post Cereal. - **$50 $85 $175**

PST-51

❑ PST-51. Railroad Tin Signs,
1954. 28 different tin signs of railroad companies logos and mailer.
Near Mint Complete - **$450**
Each - **$5 $10 $15**

PST-52 PST-53

❑ PST-52. Plastic Cars,
1955. Eight different colors and models.
Each - **$8 $15 $25**

❑ PST-53. Sugar Crisp Tractor Trailers,
1955. Grey and orange color pictured. Freuhauf written on top of trailers. Each - **$10 $15 $30**

PST-54

❑ PST-54. Leo Durocher Baseball Book Sugar Crisp Premium Store Display,
1955. Cardboard display is 20x31" designed to sit on top of carton of cereal boxes. Die-cut design including Leo's hand where a copy of the book was to be placed for display over top of the cover design printed on the sign.
- **$125 $250 $450**

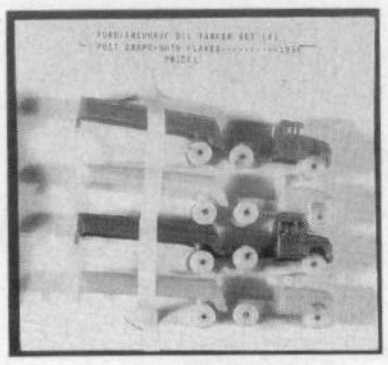

PST-55

PST-56

❏ PST-55. Grape-Nuts Flakes Plastic Tanker Set,
1956. Ford/Freuhauf Oil. Set contained a red, yellow, orange, and grey tanker.
Each - **$10 $15 $30**

❏ PST-56. Rocket Racer,
1950s. Scarce. Orange battery powered plastic rocket racer. With mailer and instructions. - **$50 $90 $175**

PST-57

PST-58

❏ PST-57. Post Race Car Premium (Speed Town) with Mailer,
1950s. - **$30 $70 $125**

❏ PST-58. Railroad Fun Book - Sugar Crisp,
1950s. 36 page premium which promotes trains. - **$10 $35 $60**

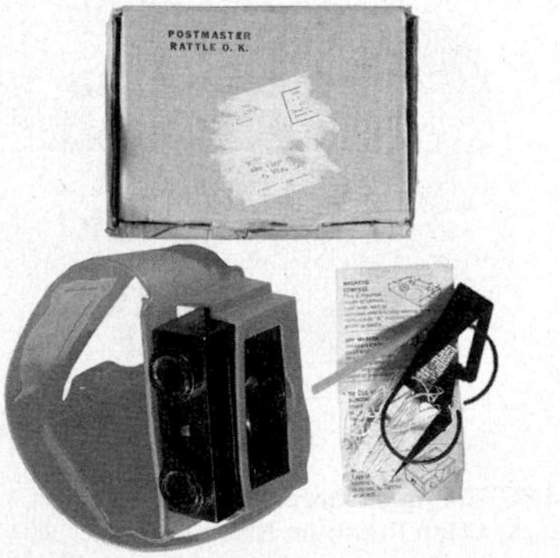

PST-59

❏ PST-59. Spy Master Belt Set,
1950s. Includes command belt which lights up, with camera, signal mirror, magnifying glass, sundial, compass, a measure with glasses and plastic mustache. With mailer and instructions. - **$50 $90 $175**

PST-60

❏ PST-60. "Sugar Crisp Bear Jacket Patch" Waxed Box Wrapper,
1950s. Promotes three different in box premiums. Gordon Gold Archives.
Uncut Flat Wrapper - **$275**
Used Complete Box - **$50 $90 $185**

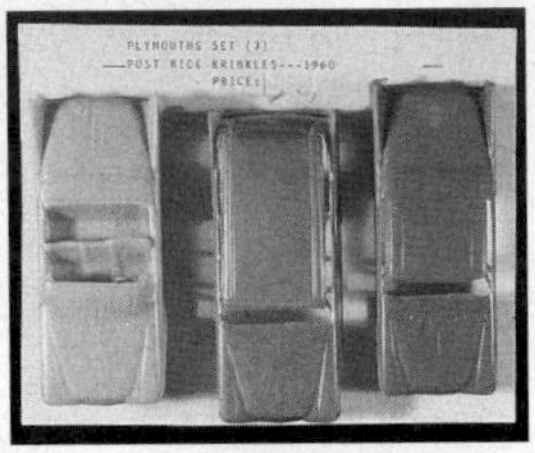

PST-61

❏ PST-61. Plymouth Plastic Cars,
1960. Post Rice Krinkles. Red, blue, and turquoise colors. Features convertible, hard top, and station wagon. Each - **$10 $20 $30**

PST-62

❏ PST-62. Post Rice Krinkles Box With Baseball Trading Cards,
1962. Back has five cards to cut out from total set of 200. Gordon Gold Archives.
Near Mint Flat - **$350**
Used Complete - **$65 $135 $275**

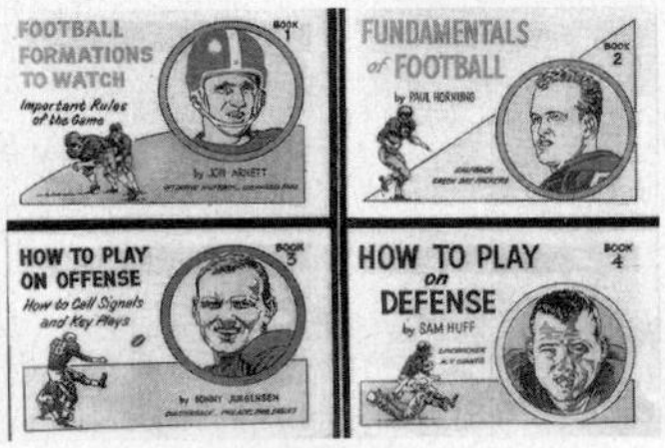

PST-63

❏ PST-63. Football Booklet Set,
1962. Each - **$5 $10 $20**

PST-64

❏ PST-64. "3-Dimensional Jet Fighter" Cereal Box,
1963. Numbered back panels of unknown total.
Near Mint Flat - **$250**
Used Complete - **$25 $45 $110**

PST-65

❏ PST-65. Cereal Box with Football Trading Card on Back,
c. 1963. 7 cards from a set of 200 on each back.
Used Complete - **$65 $135 $275**

PST-66

❏ PST-66. "Linus The Lion Fun Book" With Play Scene Card,
1964. Near Mint In Mailer - **$135**
Book Only - **$20 $40 $90**

PST-67

❏ PST-67. "Post's Crispy Critters Linus The Lion Card Game" Cereal Box ,
c. 1963. Gordon Gold Archives.
Near Mint Flat - **$400**
Used Complete - **$55 $135 $250**

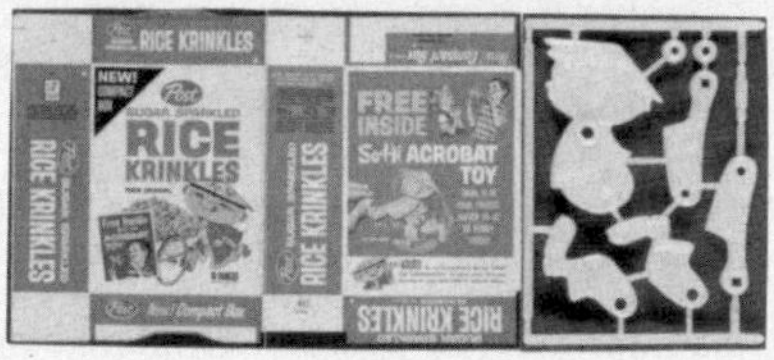

PST-68

❑ **PST-68. "Post Sugar Sparkled Rice Krinkles So-Hi Acrobat Toy" Box Flat With Premium,**
c. 1965. Gordon Gold Archives.
Near Mint Flat - **$350**
Used Complete - **$50 $125 $200**
So-Hi Premium - **$8 $12 $25**

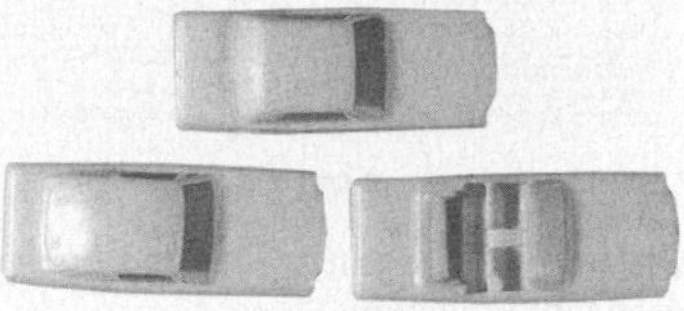

PST-69

❑ **PST-69. Plastic Cars,**
1966. Ford Mustang, Ford hardtop, fastback and convertible. All yellow. Each - **$10 $20 $30**

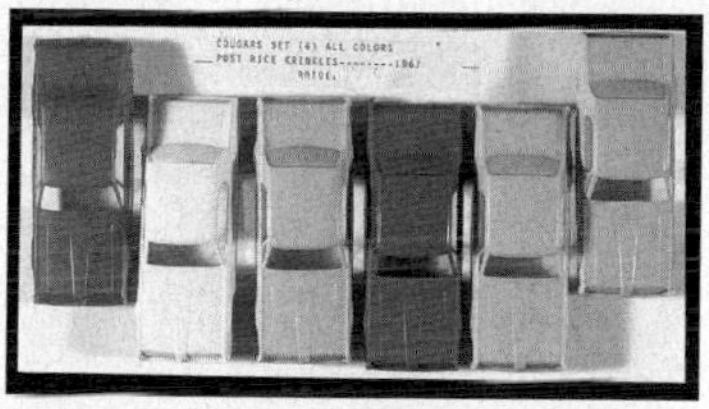

PST-70

❑ **PST-70. Rice Krinkles Plastic Cars,**
1967. Premium cars. Mercury Cougar. Green, dark blue, light blue, brown, red, and yellow. Each - **$10 $20 $30**

PST-71

❑ **PST-71. "Linus The Lion Fun Book" Cereal Box Flat,**
1967. Post Crispy Critters cereal.
Near Mint Flat - **$400**
Used Complete - **$55 $135 $250**

PST-72

❑ **PST-72. "Post Grape-Nuts Flakes" Box Flats With Porky Pig And Bugs Bunny Masks,**
1960s. Post Grape-Nut Flakes. 13.5x10.5" unused pair of flats. Front has small inset ad with image of Bugs Bunny and mentions "Free Mask On Back Panel Offer." Back panel features uncut mask of Porky Pig and instructions for constructing the mask. Second box flat has Bugs Bunny mask on back panel.
Each Near Mint Flat - **$150**
Each Used Complete - **$30 $60 $90**

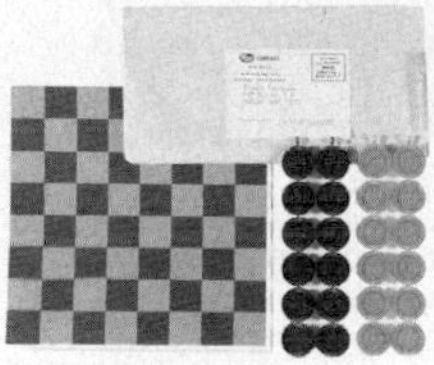

PST-73

PST-74

❑ **PST-73. Checkers Game and Mailer,**
1960s. Premium. Complete- **$10 $25 $50**

❑ **PST-74. 3-D Poster (Honeycomb Cereal),**
1970s. Kirby art. Premium with 3-D glasses. - **$15 $20 $50**

Pot O' Gold

A thinly-disguised lottery radio show hosted by Horace Heidt and sponsored by Tums from 1939-1941 on NBC, although briefly revived for one season by ABC in 1946. A "Wheel of Fortune" was spun three times during each broadcast to determine: (1) a telephone directory from a random city, (2) a page from it, and (3) a specific home telephone number from that page. The number, then called by Heidt, rewarded the answerer $1,000 by Western Union. Obviously people listened in hopes of being selected, probably with no concept of the millions-to-one odds against it. The wheel selections were interspersed by musical entertainment by Heidt's Musical Knights. The show left the air as a result of a ruling by the Federal Communications Commission. The show was the inspiration for the *Pot O' Gold* feature film released in 1941 starring James Stewart and Paulette Goddard.

PGL-1

❑ **PGL-1. Matchbook Cover,**
1939. Promotes radio program and shows broadcast times. - **$30 $60 $100**

PGL-2

PGL-3

❑ **PGL-2. "Pot O' Gold" Game,**
1939. Store item. Large 13x20" box reading "America's Newest Radio Game Craze As Played Over NBC Network". - **$60 $125 $200**

❑ **PGL-3. "Tums Pot-O-Gold" 3" Metal Pocket Flashlight,**
c. 1939. Inscription continues "With Horace Heidt On Your Radio Thursday Night". - **$50 $100 $215**

PGL-4

❑ **PGL-4. Facsimile Money,**
c. 1939. Lists NBC show times and states "1,000 Or More Dollars Given Away." 2x4-1/2". - **$12 $25 $50**

PGL-5

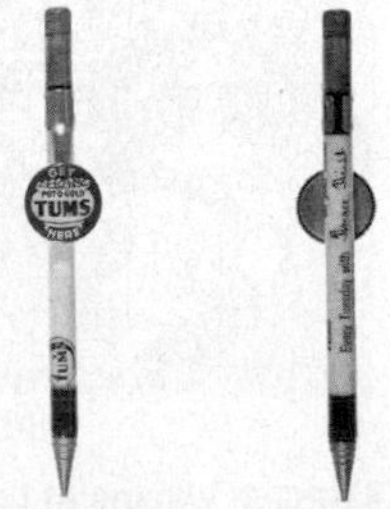

(FRONT) (BACK)

PGL-6

❑ **PGL-5. Tums Metal Container With Show Logo,**
c. 1939. Rare. Logo wears easily and is usually chipped. - **$20 $40 $200**

❑ **PGL-6. Metal Pencil With Logo On Attached Cello. Pencil Clip,**
c. 1939. - **$25 $50 $110**

Powerpuff Girls

The Powerpuff Girls, created by Craig McCracken, debuted on the Cartoon Network in 1998 and quickly gained a following among young and old alike. The series focused on the slightly skewed exploits of diminutive superheroines Bubbles, Blossom, and Buttercup as they defended Townsville with the help of their mentor, Professor Utonium. The series also mixed pop culture references and the sort of visual humor familiar from other sophisticated cartoon series like The Simpsons with cute character design and explosive action. An irreverent series suitable for all ages, The Powerpuff Girls has proliferated into a wide variety of merchandise, from videos and toys to fashion accessories. Most items are copyright the Cartoon Network. An animated feature film written and directed by Craig McCracken was released in 2002.

PPG-1

PPG-2

❑ **PPG-1. Pinback,**
2000. Colorful. - **$2 $4 $7**

❑ **PPG-2. Perfume Rings,**
2000. Four rings on card. - **$26**

PPG-3

❑ **PPG-3. Villains At Large Game,**
2000. Has 73 cards, 4 pawns with stands. - **$38**

PPG-4

(Back enlarged)

❑ **PPG-4. Promo Decal Set,**
2000. Promotes the Rhino Records release of songs inspired by the show. Set - **$4**

PPG-5

❑ **PPG-5. Kellogg's Pop-Tarts Box,**
2001. Limited edition. - **$1 $2 $4**

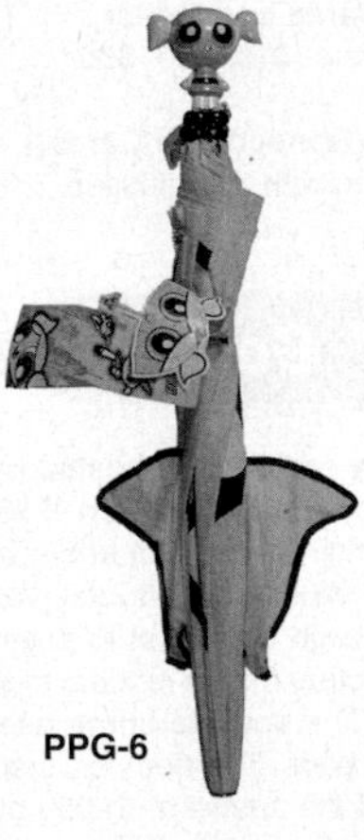

PPG-6

PPG-7

PPG-8

❑ **PPG-6. Umbrella with Tags,**
2001. - **$20**

❑ **PPG-7. Bandages,**
2001. Box of 25 bandages from Kidz Health. - **$5**

❑ **PPG-8. Pop-Up Book,**
2001. A 12 page Pop-Up adventure. - **$16**

Premiums Misc.

This brief category features interesting premiums which don't fit elsewhere. They are included because collectors are likely to encounter them or because of interesting graphics or subject matter. If readers have information about those items listed without an identifying sponsor, the author would appreciate receiving information about them.

PRM-1

❑ **PRM-1. "Buffalo Bill Gun" 19th Century Personality Premium,**
1887. Farm and Fireside Newspaper. Advertisement offers 35-1/2" long wooden rifle with cast iron trigger. Text reads "Given As A Premium For 3 Subscribers To This Paper." Photo courtesy Jim Wojtowicz from his book Buffalo Bill Collectors Guide published by Collector Books. Gun - **$1000 $1500 $3500**

PRM-2

❑ **PRM-2. "Mother Hubbard" Drawing Book,**
1905. Fleischmann premium. Scarce. - **$40 $80 $160**

PRM-3

PRM-4

❑ **PRM-3. "Eskimo Pie" Premiums Poster,**
1935. 22x28" cardboard and depicting Tracy wristwatch and penlight, Mickey Mouse wrist and pocket watches plus many generic premiums. Also issued as a flyer with coupon on bottom. Poster - **$125 $250 $450**
Flyer Intact - **$30 $60 $100**

❑ **PRM-4. "Tip Top Comics Booster" Cello. Button,**
c. 1936. Dark blue on bright gold 7/8" coinciding very closely to their first publications beginning April 1936. Button maker's back paper reads "Simon Co. 373-Fourth Ave. N.Y.C." - **$110 $265 $450**

PRM-5

❑ **PRM-5. "Junior G-Men Of America Manual" And Pledge Card,**
1936. Manual is 4x5-3/8" with 32 pages. Cover text includes "Courtesy Of Fischer Baking Co., Newark, N.J." Inside cover has image of Jr. G-Man Badge and text "Jr. G-Men Of America/The Largest Junior Police Organization In The World." Comes with 4.25x5.25" pledge card titled "Junior G-Men Of America Pledge."
Manual - **$100 $200 $300**
Card - **$25 $50 $100**

PRM-6

❑ **PRM-6. Flying Model Airplanes Blueprint And Instruction Book,**
c. 1936. Curtiss Candy. 10x16" with 24 pages for construction of six different models and two pages picturing premiums. - **$60 $125 $240**

PRM-7

❑ **PRM-7. "Dari-Dan Volunteers" Official Silver Luster Star Badge With Mailer Insert,**
1937. Dari-Rich Chocolate Flavored Drink. Badge came with 11x17" folder promoting membership in "Detective Corps" and picturing "G-Man" supplies of ring, tie clasp, lapel button, watch fob, secret writing outfit, Jiu Jitsu book, Detectoscope and the badge we illustrate.
Mailer - **$8 $12 $25**
Badge - **$25 $55 $110**
Folder - **$25 $50 $90**

PRM-8

❑ **PRM-8. "Young Explorer's Club" Brass Shield Badge,**
1930s. Sponsor unknown. Two shades of brass luster with black accents. - **$20 $40 $85**

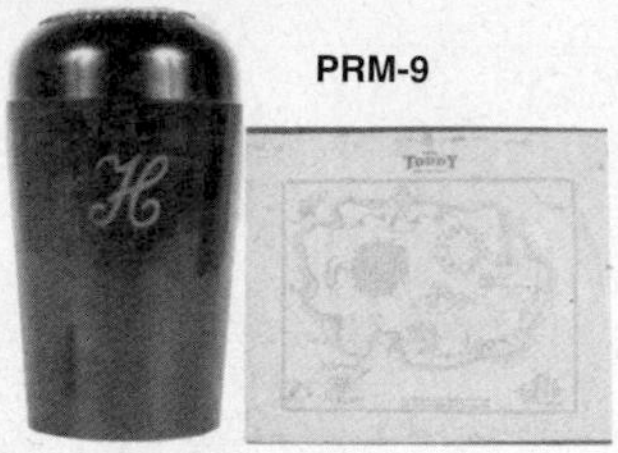

PRM-9

❑ **PRM-9. "Toddy" Shake-Up Mug And Map,**
1930s. Mug is 4-1/2" tall, map is 8-1/4x11-3/4". Issued by drink mix company.
Mug - **$10 $25 $50**
Map - **$25 $55 $110**

PRM-10

❑ **PRM-10. "Rang-A-Tang The Wonder Dog" Button,**
1930s. Character from Blue Ribbon Comics. - **$150 $300 $550**

PRM-11

PRM-12

❑ **PRM-11. "Wings Of America" Club Wings Badge,**
1940. Wings Comics. About 1-1/2" long with red panel on chrome finish. Our photo illustrates the wings on an application for the club which appeared in comic books from late 1940 through at least March 1942. - **$125 $250 $375**

❑ **PRM-12. "Junior Flying Legion" Brass Wings Member's Badge,**
1940. United Feature Comic Group. About 2-1/2" long in brass. Our photo shows club application from inside back cover of Tarzan Single Series #20. Described as "A Great Nationwide Aviation Club..." - **$65 $135 $225**

PRM-13

PRM-14

❏ PRM-13. "Whistling Jim's National Defenders Secret Portfolio",
1941. General Mills. Similar to The Lone Ranger item in the same format but this has eight pages compared to 12. Used in states where General Mills did not have the rights to The Lone Ranger. - **$100 $225 $400**

❏ PRM-14. "Sea Raiders Destroyer Club" Movie Serial Cello. Button,
1941. 1-1/4" black and green. Cast members included Huntz Hall and Billy Halop. -
$65 $175 $265

PRM-15

❏ PRM-15. "Junior G-Men Of The Air" Movie Serial Brass Wings,
1942. Universal. 2" long in brass luster with blue lettering and red, white and blue star design. -
$75 $150 $250

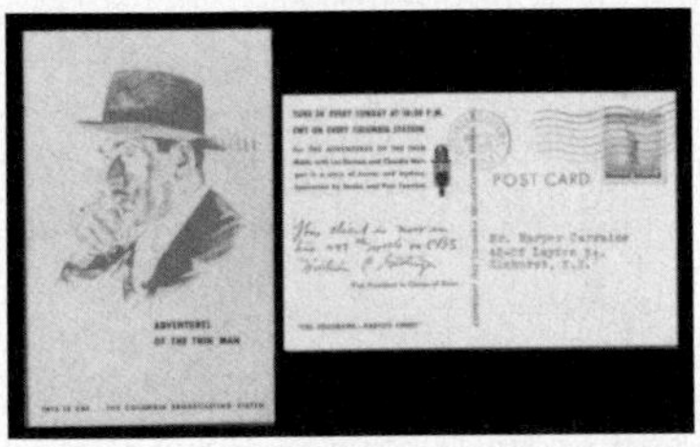

PRM-16

❏ PRM-16. "The Adventures Of The Thin Man" Fan Postcard,
1943. Sponsored by Sanka and Post Toasties. -
$40 $80 $165

PRM-17

❏ PRM-17. "Ato McBomb" Cello. Button,
c. 1940s. Issuer unknown and we can find no references to this character. 1-1/4" beautifully designed button in black, red, yellow and flesh-tone. - **$100 $200 $375**

PRM-18

PRM-19

❏ PRM-18. "Cowboy G-Men" Fan Card,
1952. Issued by "Taystee Enriched Bread" for syndicated TV show. - **$25 $50 $85**

❏ PRM-19. "3 In 1 Gift" Punch-Out Assembly Kit,
1953. Sponsored by Nash Motors. 15-1/2x16-1/2" with parts to assemble show room, service area, three 1953 Nash cars and five early vintage Nash cars. Unpunched - **$100 $200 $350**

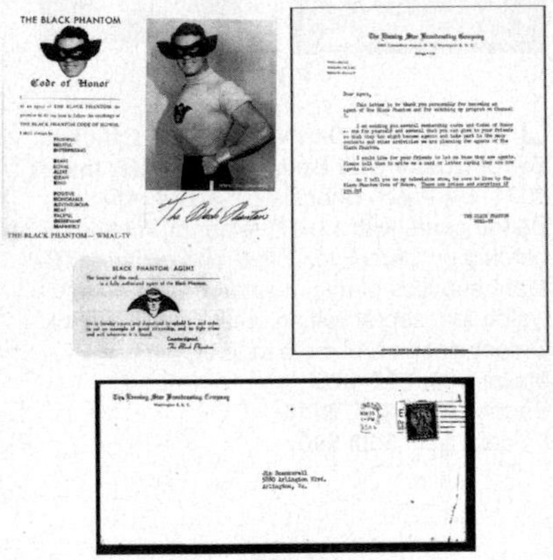

PRM-20

❏ PRM-20. "The Black Phantom" TV Club Member's Kit,
1954. The Evening Star Broadcasting Company. Issued by Washington, D.C. station WMAL-TV for local area show hosted by station personality who aired old movies. At first, membership cards were addressed on reverse and mailed separately. Later, membership card issued as part of three-piece club kit with cover letter.
Envelope - **$8 $12 $20**
Cover Letter - **$15 $20 $40**
Portrait Card - **$20 $30 $60**
Code Of Honor Card - **$20 $30 $60**
Member Card - **$20 $30 $60**

PRM-21

❏ PRM-21. "Junior Forest Fire Fighting Warden" Brass Badge,
1950s. Possibly Kellogg's Pep, issued as a Mark Trail radio premium. 2-3/4" tall also reading "Jackie Davis Chief Warden/Protect Our Trees." - **$25 $50 $100**

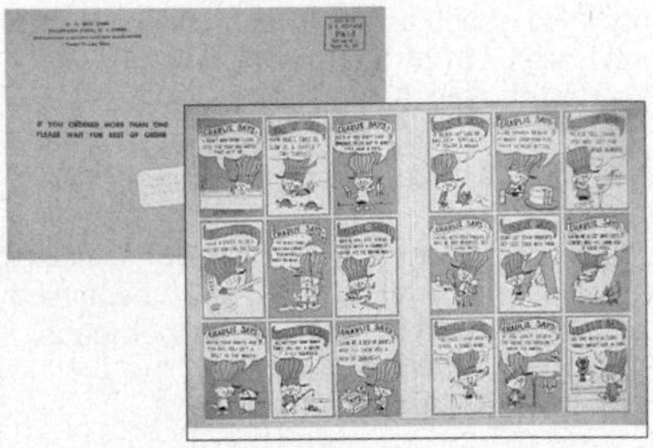

PRM-22

❏ PRM-22. Choo-Choo Charlie Sticker Sheet,
c. 1970s. Good & Plenty. 7-1/2x10-1/2" sheet sent folded with 18 black, white and pink peel-off stickers. Mailer - **$2 $4 $10**
Sheet - **$10 $20 $40**

Pretty Kitty Kelly

The story of a young Irish immigrant girl who arrived in New York with amnesia, no friends and charged with murder, aired on CBS radio from 1937 to 1940. Kitty managed to make friends and had a number of spirited adventures during her three-year run. Continental Baking Company's Wonder bread and Hostess cupcakes were sponsors. The song *Pretty Kitty Kelly* by Harry Pease and Ed Nelson was released in 1920 which likely was the inspiration for the title of the radio show.

PKK-1

PKK-2

❑ **PKK-1. "Pretty Kitty Kelly" 12x17-1/2" Paper Store Sign,**
c. 1937. Wonder Bread. - **$25 $50 $100**

❑ **PKK-2. "Pretty Kitty Kelly Balloon" 11x15" Paper Store Sign,**
c. 1937. Wonder Bread. - **$15 $30 $45**

PKK-3

❑ **PKK-3. "Kitty Kelly" Enameled Brass "Perfume Pin" On Card,**
c. 1937. Wonder Bread.
Complete - **$25 $50 $100**
Pin Only - **$15 $30 $75**

PKK-4

PKK-5

❑ **PKK-4. Cello. Button,**
c. 1937. Columbia Broadcasting System. - **$4 $8 $12**

❑ **PKK-5. Store Sign,**
c. 1937. Wonder Bread and Hostess Cake. 11x16-1/2" in black, white and red. - **$15 $35 $50**

Prince Valiant

Harold R. Foster (1892-1982) illustrated numerous magazines in the 1920s and early 1930s. Inspired by the Brandywine school of artists, including Howard Pyle and N.C. Wyeth, he first drew the Tarzan daily comic strip January 7, 1929. Continuing on with magazine work, Foster was signed by United Feature to do the Tarzan Sunday page. He drew the Sunday from September 27, 1931 until May 2, 1937.

William Randolph Hearst of King Features Syndicate gave Foster the opportunity to create his own strip. Based on the legends of Camelot and King Arthur, *Prince Valiant In The Days Of King Arthur* began on February 13, 1937. Recognized as one of the most beautifully drawn comic strips in history, highlights include: 1938 Val gets his Singing Sword; 1940 Val is knighted by King Arthur; 1946 Val marries Aleta; 1947 first child Arn is born. The National Cartoonist's Society awarded Foster its Reuben Award in 1957 and the Gold Key Award in 1971. Foster would continue on Val until May 16, 1971. John Cullen Murphy (1919-2004) did the strip from 1971 until March 2004. Gary Gianni draws the Sunday page today with Mark Schultz as writer.

20th Century Fox released a Prince Valiant feature film in 1954 with Robert Wagner as Val and Janet Leigh as Aleta. *The Legend of Prince Valiant* animated series aired on the Family Channel from 1991 to 1993.

David McKay/Dell published four different Four Color Comics between 1941 and 1958 and Marvel published four comics in 1994-1995.

PRV-1

❑ **PRV-1. Hal Foster Signed "Prince Valiant" Sunday Page Panel Original Art,**
c. 1930s. 8.25x11.25" pen and India ink illustration inscribed "To Miss Harriet Meyer With Best Wishes Hal Foster." Same Or Similar - **$1000**

PRV-2

❑ **PRV-2. "Prince Valiant" Multi-Products Figure,**
1944. King Features Syndicate. 5" tall wood composition painted figure. - **$100 $200 $400**

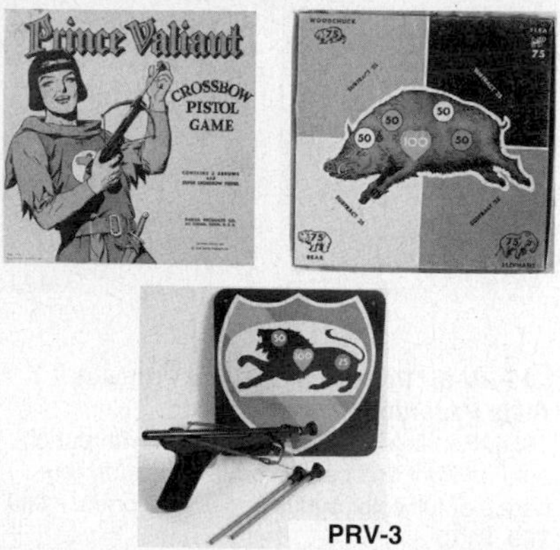

PRV-3

❑ **PRV-3. "Prince Valiant Crossbow Pistol Game",**
1948. Parva Products Co. 10.25x10.25x1" deep box contains 9" hard plastic pistol with detachable wire and elastic crossbow unit, 3 arrows with wood shaft and suction cup end. Underside of box is designed as wild boar target. Has second separate target panel that is 9.75" square on thick cardboard. - **$25 $50 $100**

PRV-4

❑ **PRV-4. "Prince Valiant" Rare Promotional,**
1940s. King Features Syndicate. 11x17" stiff paper used to promote newspaper comic strip to newspaper comic page editors. Front has castle with drawbridge and back depicts different castle. Includes 7" pop-up figure of Prince Valiant in battle stance. - **$500 $1000 $2000**

PRV-5

❑ **PRV-5. Prince Valiant Dime Bank,**
1940s. Issued with either blue or gray uniform. Each - **$65 $125 $250**

PRV-6

❑ **PRV-6. "Prince Valiant And Princess Aleta Paperdolls",**
1954. Saalfield. 10.75x12.75" book with punch-outs on front and back. Contents include four pages of full color outfits and accessories. - **$30 $60 $110**

PRV-7

PRV-8

❑ **PRV-7. "Prince Valiant Coloring Book",**
1954. Saalfield. 11x14" coloring book with 16 pages. - **$15 $30 $75**

❑ **PRV-8. "Prince Valiant" Candy Box,**
1954. Leader Novelty Candy Co. Inc. 3x5x1" deep box. Side panel has coupon for Prince Valiant t-shirt costing fifty cents and two coupons. - **$75 $150 $250**

PRV-9

❑ **PRV-9. "Prince Valiant" Shield,**
1950s. Mattel. 12" diameter litho tin shield with pair of vinyl handle straps attached to reverse. **- $12 $25 $50**

Pulp Magazine Misc.

Pictured is sampling of 1930s to 1940s membership cards. "Pulps" derived the name from inexpensive paper used for publication of fantasy and adventure magazines produced at low cost; very few pulps made the leap to producing a badge, ring or other premiums.

PUL-1

❑ **PUL-1. "Black Mask" Pulp With Maltese Falcon And First Appearance of Sam Spade,**
1929. Issue for September including first installment of Maltese Falcon story by Dashiell Hammett, later to become classic movie starring Humphrey Bogart plus first pulp appearance of Sam Spade. Possibly the only issue to have Maltese Falcon title printed on cover. - **$350 $725 $1500**

Join Trail's End
The Club of Friendly Folk

TRAIL'S END MEMBERSHIP COUPON
I am a regular reader of RANCH ROMANCES.
I want to become a member of Trail's End Club.
(Miss)
(Mrs.)
(Mr.)
Address..........
City..........
State..........
This coupon makes you a member of America's greatest outdoor club.
Ten cents brings you the lovely "Trail's End" pin.
You must be a member to secure the pin.
Please print your name and address plainly.

PUL-2

PUL-3

❑ **PUL-2. "Trail's End" Membership Coupon,**
1935. "Ranch Romance" pulp premium.
- $15 $25 $45

❑ **PUL-3. "Ranch Romance" Club Pin,**
1935. "Trail's End" premium. Rare. - **$100 $175 $350**

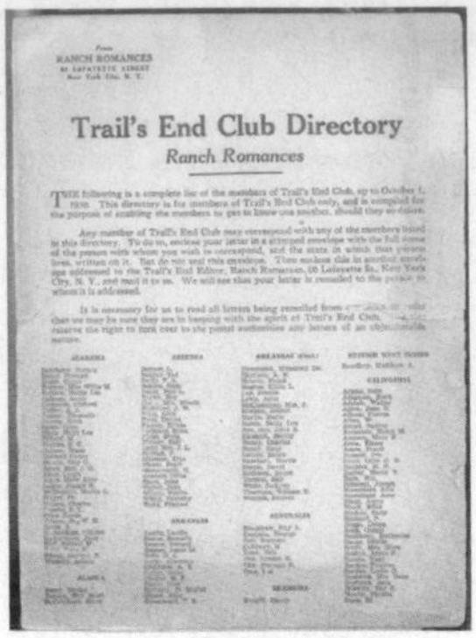
RANCH ROMANCES

Trail's End Club Directory
Ranch Romances

PUL-4

❑ **PUL-4. "Trail's End" Club Directory,**
1935. This directory listed all members world-wide for correspondence. - **$40 $85 $150**

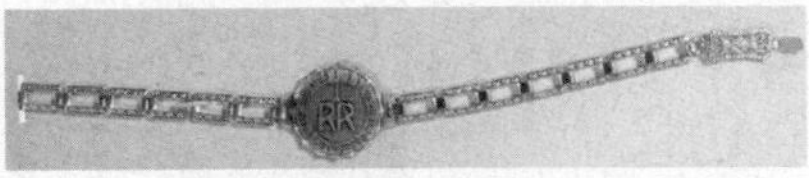

PUL-5

❑ **PUL-5. "Ranch Romance" Club Bracelet,**
1935. Trail's End Club premium. Rare. - **$125 $185 $400**

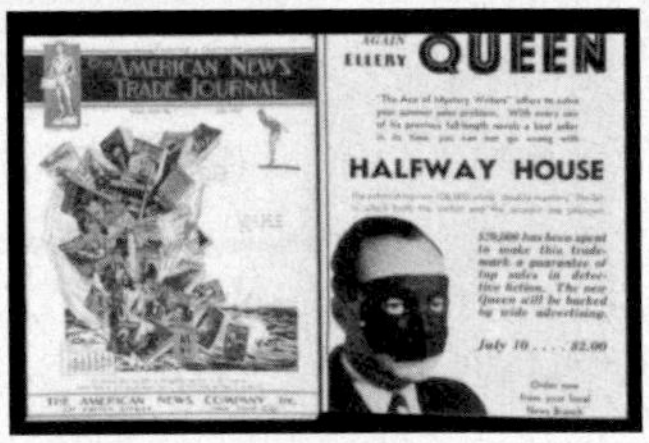

PUL-6

❑ **PUL-6. "The American News Trade Journal" Industry Magazine With Pulp Scene Cover,**
1936. Issue for July. - **$15 $30 $60**

PUL-7 PUL-8

❑ **PUL-7. "The Witch's Tales" First Issue,**
1936. Vol. 1 #1 for November based on popular radio program. - **$150 $375 $750**

❑ **PUL-8. "Thrilling Wonder Stories" Store Sign,**
c. 1938. 11x14" cardboard inset by full color front cover art. - **$100 $200 $300**

PUL-9

❑ **PUL-9. "Boys' Magazine Detective Club" Badge,**
1930s. Has metal tab on back. First of a series of premiums from the popular pulp magazine. Rare. - **$250 $500 $750**

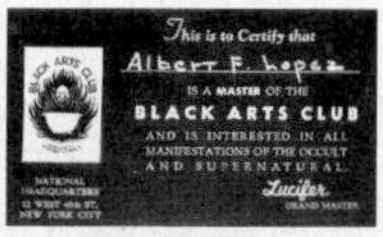

PUL-10 PUL-11

❑ **PUL-10. "Weird Tales Club" Member Card,**
1930s. - **$135 $300 $650**

❑ **PUL-11. "Black Arts Club" Member Card,**
1930s. - **$50 $125 $275**

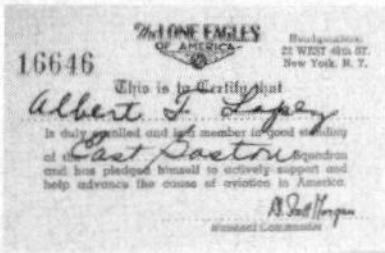

PUL-12 PUL-13

❑ **PUL-12. "The Futuremen" Club Card,**
1930s. Captain Future magazine. -
$50 $125 $275

❑ **PUL-13. "The Lone Eagles Of America" Member Card,**
1930s. Lone Eagle magazine. Back has club Ten Commandments. See ADV-30 & ADV-31. - **$40 $115 $240**

PUL-14

❑ **PUL-14. "Air Adventures" Pulp Magazine Premium, Badge,**
1930s. - **$80 $165 $325**

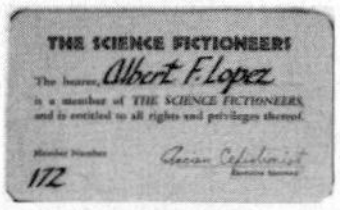

PUL-15 PUL-16

❑ **PUL-15. "Science Fiction League" Club Card With Metal Lapel Stud,**
1930s. Thrilling Wonder Stories magazine.
Card - **$60 $125 $250**
Lapel Stud - **$45 $90 $200**

❑ **PUL-16. "The Science Fictioneers" Club Card,**
1930s. Facsimile signature of executive secretary "Ascien Cefictionist". - **$60 $125 $250**

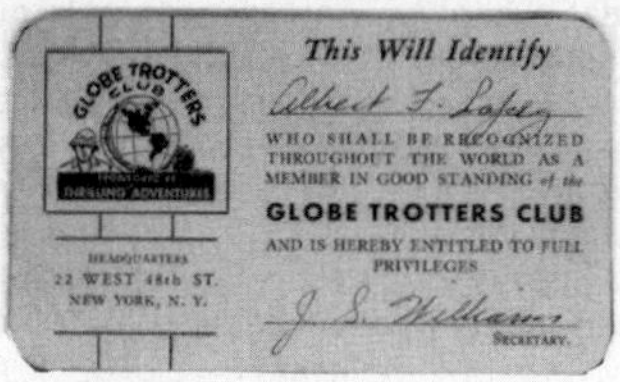

PUL-17

❑ **PUL-17. "Globe Trotters Club" Member Card,**
1930s. Thrilling Adventures magazine. -
$60 $125 $250

PUL-18 PUL-19

❑ **PUL-18. "Breezy Stories" Store Window Card,**
1930s. C. H. Young Publishing Co., N.Y. 11x14". - **$75 $150 $300**

❑ **PUL-19. Carl Claudy Science Fiction Books Store Window Ad Card,**
1930s. 11x14" stiff paper advertising "New Thrilling Astounding Books by the Jules Verne Of Today." - **$75 $135 $275**

PUL-20 PUL-21

❑ **PUL-20. Street & Smith Publications Advertising Sign,**
1930s. Thin cardboard sign 11x14". Text reads "If It's A Street & Smith Magazine It's The Best Of It's Kind." - **$60 $120 $200**

❑ **PUL-21. Clues-A Street & Smith Publication Advertising Sign,**
1930s. Thin cardboard sign is 11x14". Text reads "Action! Vivid! Exciting" and shows three scenes, one of man bound to chair with noose around neck, man stabbing unsuspecting victim and stick-up. - **$60 $120 $200**

PUL-22 PUL-23

❑ **PUL-22. Street & Smith Western Story Magazine Advertising Sign,**
1930s. Thin cardboard sign is 11x14". "The Best Of The West Surging Stirring Stories Of Plain And Trail." - **$60 $120 $200**

❑ **PUL-23. Street & Smith Western Story Magazine Advertising Sign,**
1930s. Thin cardboard sign is 11x14". Text block reads "Big Clean Stories Of The Outdoor West." - **$60 $120 $200**

Purple People Eater

For six weeks in 1958 this novelty tune featuring a one-eyed, one-horned creature was the No. 1 record on the charts in America. The song was written and recorded by Sheb Wooley (1921-2003), a Western band leader with an MGM recording contract. Wooley also had an acting career, appearing in some 50 movies (he was the killer Ben Miller in *High Noon*) and on television as Pat Nolan in *Rawhide* (CBS, 1959-1965) and in the cast of *Hee Haw* (CBS, 1969) for which he also wrote the theme song. A feature film based on the song was released in 1988 starring Ned Beatty and Shelley Winters with guest appearances by Sheb Wooley, Chubby Checker and Little Richard.

PUR-1 PUR-2

❑ **PUR-1. Stuffed Fabric Figure,**
1958. Store item copyright by Cordial Music Co. Features include jiggle eyeball in single eye. -
$40 $80 $160

❑ **PUR-2. Plastic Figure,**
1950s. Store item by J. H. Miller Mfg. Co. 5" tall. -
$75 $150 $300

PUR-3

❑ **PUR-3. Plastic Hat On Store Card,**
1950s. Store item by Spec-Toy-Ulars, Inc. Thin shell plastic purple hat designed with single eye on front plus markings "One-Eyed, One-Horned Purple People Eater." Came with pair of plastic horns that represented ears and attached to hat by adhesive strip.
Card - **$20 $40 $75**
Hat Only - **$15 $30 $60**
Each Horn - **$15 $20 $40**

PUR-4

PUR-5

❑ **PUR-4. "I'm A Purple People Eater" Litho. Button,**
1950s. Probably a vending machine issue. - **$8 $15 $25**

❑ **PUR-5. Cello. 3-1/2" Button,**
1950s. Store item. Purple and white art. - **$15 $30 $60**

PUR-6

PUR-7

❑ **PUR-6. "I'm A Purple People Eater" Cello Button,**
1950s. 3.5" purple/white. - **$12 $25 $50**

❑ **PUR-7. Singing and Dancing Plush Doll,**
1999. In box. Doll plays the original 1950s song and dances. - **$40**

Quaker Cereals Misc.

The Quaker Oats Company got its start in 1877 when an oatmeal processor named Henry D. Seymour opened his Quaker Mills Company in Ravenna, Ohio, and registered a likeness of a somber Quaker as his trademark. The company was sold in 1879 and by 1890 was part of the giant American Cereal Company. With the Quaker as the symbol of its principal product, the company sold its rolled oats in cardboard boxes rather than in bulk, making it one of the first packaged foods. Heavy advertising and promotion--including cross-country trains distributing free samples--made Quaker Oats a national success. The company entered the cold cereal market with Puffed Wheat and Puffed Rice, "shot from guns." The Quaker logo was revised in 1945 and further modernized in 1971. This section shows Quaker premiums not associated with the many major characters they sponsored over the years. The company merged with Pepsico in 2001.

QKR-1

QKR-2

❑ **QKR-1. Trade Card,**
1883. Shows Quaker cereal assembly line. - **$15 $25 $50**

❑ **QKR-2. "Quaker Rolled White Oats" Cello. Button,**
c. 1905. - **$15 $30 $60**

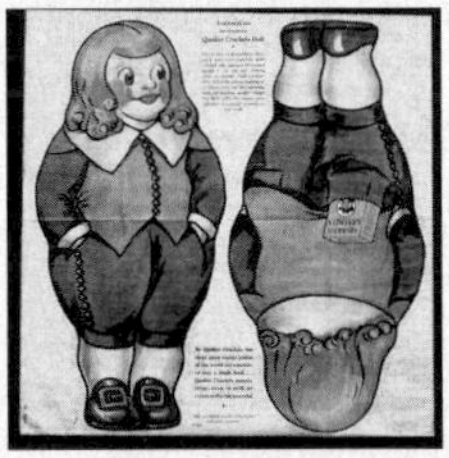

QKR-3

QKR-4

❑ **QKR-3. Quaker Oats Doll,**
1930. Rare. Cloth uncut mascot doll for Quaker Crackels Cereal. - **$75 $200 $300**
Assembled Doll - **$40 $85 $150**

❑ **QKR-4. "Phil Cook/The Quakerman" With Doll Photo,**
c. 1930. Quaker Crackels. Black and white photo of radio show host at NBC microphone while displaying 'Crackels Boy' assembled stuffed fabric cut-out premium doll.
Photo - **$10 $25 $50**

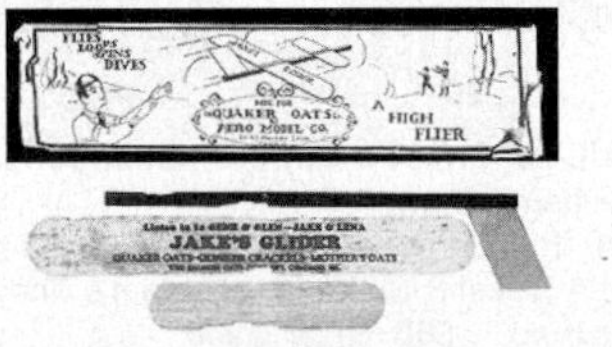

QKR-5

❑ **QKR-5. "Jake's Glider" Kit With Envelope,**
c. 1931. Quaker Oats/Quaker Crackels/Mother's Oats. Instructions envelope holding balsa assembly parts for 12x12" glider toy propelled by rubber band. Offered on "Quaker Early Birds" NBC radio program that began December 29, 1930. Envelope Only - **$10 $25 $45**
Glider Only - **$20 $40 $70**

QKR-6

QKR-7

❑ **QKR-6. Muffets Biscuits Humming Rocket Premium Sign 12x15",**
1930s. - **$75 $135 $250**

❑ **QKR-7. Muffets Biscuits Humming Rocket,**
1930s. - **$20 $40 $80**

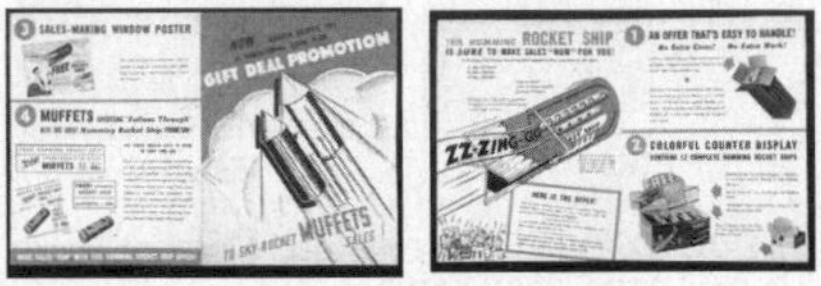

QKR-8

❑ **QKR-8. Humming Rocket Ship Promo Manual,**
1930s. - **$35 $70 $125**

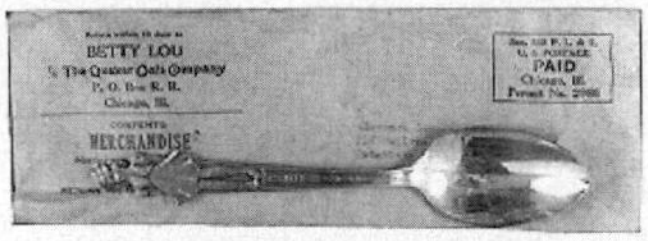

QKR-9

❑ **QKR-9. "Betty Lou" Silver Plate Spoon With Mailer,**
1930s. Quaker Oats. Handle tip is figural depiction of young girl in polka dot dress.
With Mailer - **$10 $20 $30**
Spoon Only - **$5 $10 $15**

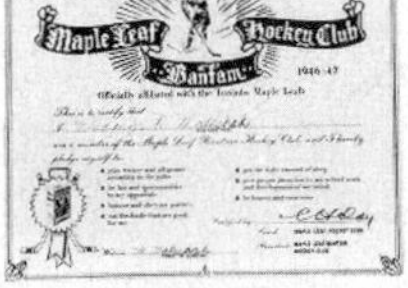

QKR-10

QKR-11

❑ **QKR-10. "Maple Leaf Bantam Hockey Club" Certificate,**
1946. Canadian youth pledge certificate for club affiliated to professional Toronto Maple Leafs 1946-1947 season. - **$30 $50 $85**

❑ **QKR-11. "Veronica Lake" Litho. Button,**
1948. Quaker Puffed Wheat & Rice. From set of 20 movie stars, each including studio name in inscription. Lake and Reagan - **$10 $20 $35**
Others - **$5 $10 $15**

QKR-12

❑ **QKR-12. Movie Star Button Cereal Box,**
1948. Side panel shows 20 buttons in set distributed one per box. Each button is 13/16" tin litho. Gordon Gold Archives.
Used Complete - **$75 $175 $350**

QKR-13 QKR-14

❑ **QKR-13. Lizabeth Scott Litho. Button,**
c. 1948. Similar to photographic set of 20 distributed in America by Quaker Puffed Wheat & Rice but this is Canadian version with line drawings and back inscription "Quaker Puffed Wheat And Rice Sparkies." Eleven different known, all marked "A PARAMOUNT STAR".
Each - **$10 $20 $35**

❑ **QKR-14. Plastic Mug,**
c. 1950. - **$10 $20 $35**

QKR-15

❑ **QKR-15. "Space Flight To The Moon" Cereal Box**
1953. Quaker Puffed Rice. Last of a series of eight. Complete Box - **$75 $175 $350**

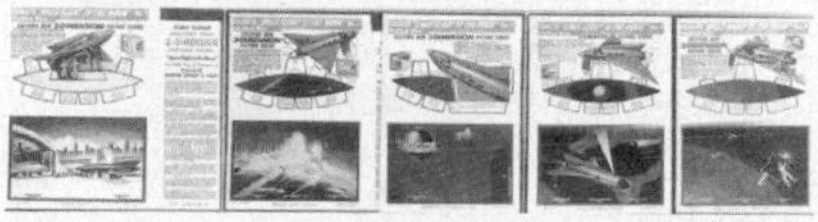

QKR-16

❑ **QKR-16. "Space Flight To The Moon" Box Backs #1-5,**
1953. Quaker Puffed Rice. From set of eight.
Each Complete Box - **$75 $175 $350**
Each Uncut Back - **$15 $30 $60**

QKR-17

❑ **QKR-17. Indian Picture Cards (18) & Mailer,**
1950s. Set - **$60 $120 $240**
Mailer - **$10 $20 $40**

QKR-18

❑ **QKR-18. "Quaker Stamps Of The Golden West Album" With Envelope,**
1950s. Mailer - **$5 $10 $20**
Album - **$12 $25 $45**

QKR-19

❑ **QKR-19. "Quaker Pack-O-Ten Cereals" Indian-Theme Cereal Box Storage Tray,**
1950s. Flattened cardboard tray is 7x16" and originally contained 12 individual cereal boxes. Advertises series of five different "Indian Headbands" that were included one per package as well as a set of 18 "Braves Of Indian Nations" trading cards that were available for ten cents and cut-out order blank included as part of the tray. From Gordon Gold Archives.
- **$50 $85 $150**

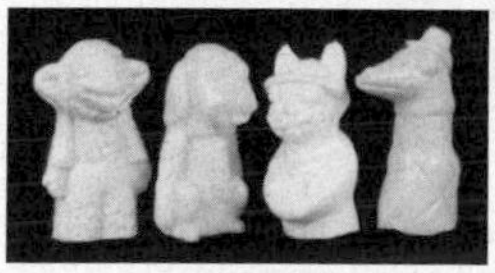

QKR-20

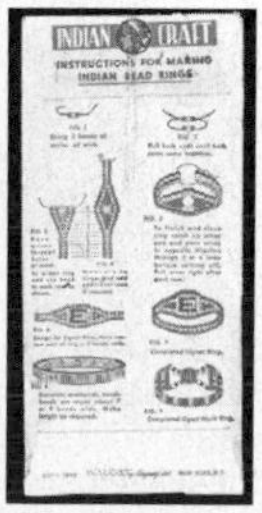

QKR-21

❑ **QKR-20. Shari Lewis Character Finger Puppets,**
1962. Quaker Oats. Each - **$4 $8 $15**

❑ **QKR-21. Indian Bead Rings Unassembled With Mailer,**
1962. Frosty-O's cereal premium. Rare. -
$60 $115 $175

Quick Draw McGraw

The animated show with the bumbling horse sheriff and his quick-witted Mexican burro deputy Baba Looey was the third cartoon series released by Hanna-Barbera Studios. The show was syndicated by Screen Gems from September 29, 1959 until 1962, then re-run on CBS from September 28, 1963 until September 3, 1966. Some segments featured Quick Draw as El Kabong, a send-up of "Zorro," using his guitar kabonger to capture outlaws. Other show segments included Augie Doggie and Doggie Daddy, a sitcom with a young dog idolizing his not too bright dad and Snooper and Blabber, a cat and mouse detective team. Voice actors included Daws Butler, Don Messick and Doug Young. The Quick Draw theme song was written by Hoyt Curtin along with Bill Hanna and Joe Barbera.

Dell/Gold Key published 15 comics between 1959 and 1969 and Charlton published eight comics between November 1970 and January 1972. "Now Hoooold On Thar, Baba Looey!"

QDM-1

❑ **QDM-1. "Quick Draw McGraw Moving Battery Operated Target",**
1960. Knickerbocker Toys. 10.25x12.5x3.5" deep box comes with 9" long plastic/spring-loaded gun, two rubber-tipped darts, 5x10x13" tall plastic/cardboard battery operated moving target. Top of target is die-cut cardboard illustration of Quick Draw McGraw and Baba Looey.
Box - **$25 $50 $75**
Toy - **$35 $65 $125**

QDM-2

QDM-3

❑ **QDM-2. "Quick Draw McGraw" Purex Soap Figural Banks Color Varieties,**
1960. Knickerbocker Toys. Pair of figures each 9.5" tall hard vinyl with plastic head and coin slot at top of hat. Each - **$8 $15 $30**

❑ **QDM-3. "Quick Draw McGraw Play Book",**
1960. Whitman. 10x14" with six blank back punch-out pages. - **$20 $40 $85**

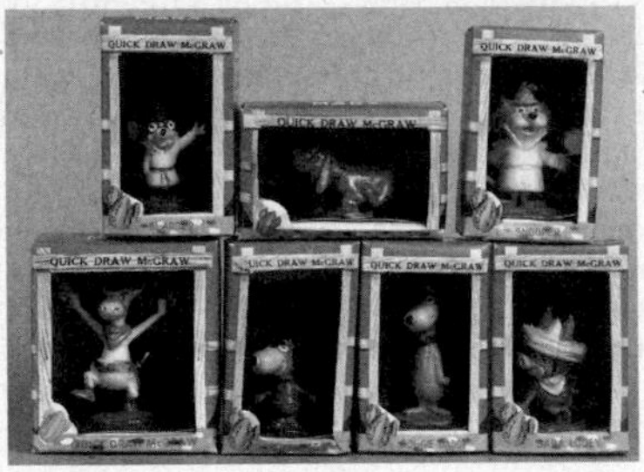

QDM-4

❑ **QDM-4. "Quick Draw McGraw" Boxed TV Tinykins Set,**
1961. Marx. Set of seven die-cut boxes, each 2.25" tall with die-cut windows revealing hand-painted characters Blabber, Snuffles, Snooper, Quick Draw McGraw, Augie Doggie, Doggie Daddy, Baba Looey. Each - **$5 $10 $20**

QDM-5

❑ **QDM-5. "Baba Looey Featuring Quick Draw McGraw" Punch-Out Book,**
1961. Golden Press. 7.25x13" with 12 full color pages printed on one side. - **$15 $30 $75**

QDM-6

❑ **QDM-6. Cereal Box Featuring Quick Draw McGraw,**
1963. Sugar Smacks 9 oz. box has Magic Aquarium offer on back. - **$165 $400 $800**

QDM-7

QDM-8

❑ **QDM-7. "Quick Draw McGraw" Button,**
1960s. 1.25" diameter button, English issue. - **$8 $15 $30**

❑ **QDM-8. "Quick Draw McGraw" Glazed Ceramic Figure,**
c. 1960s. Ideas Inc. 7" tall ceramic figure with "Ideas Inc. #611" red and gold foil sticker on underside. - **$30 $60 $125**

QDM-9

❑ **QDM-9. "Hold On Thar" Quickdraw McGraw and Baba Louie Lamp,**
1996. With shade. Limited edition. Many of these lamps were damaged in transit and destroyed. - **$85 $175 $335**

Quisp and Quake

Quaker Oats Company introduced a pair of competing new cereals in 1965--Quisp, for quazy energy, and earthquake-powered Quake. The Quisp character was a propeller-headed pink alien who promoted "the biggest selling cereal from Saturn to Alpha Centauri," and Quake was a spelunking superhero in a hard hat and logging boots who could swim through bedrock. Initial promotions included battery-operated helmets as premiums for grocers. Though the two cereals were virtually identical, Quake was dropped in the early 1970s, while Quisp still survives in selected areas.

QSP-1

❑ **QSP-1. "Quake Explorer's Kit,"**
1965. Quaker Oats. Boxed mail premium of plastic play parts, paper maps and diagrams. Includes hammer, 4 color plastic rocks, Geiger counter, magnifying glass, tweezers and stand, goggles with mirrors, exploration maps, instructions and mailer. Near Mint Boxed - **$285**

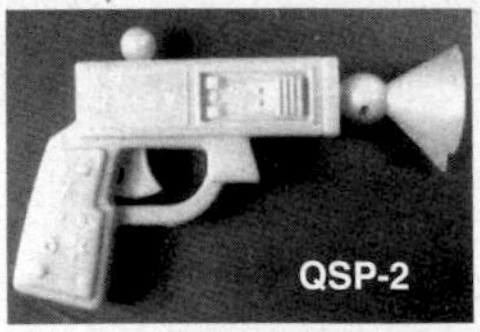

QSP-2

❑ **QSP-2. "Cosmiclouder" Smoke Gun,**
1965. Plastic inscribed "Quisp" on each side. - **$125 $250 $500**

QSP-3

❑ **QSP-3. "Quispmobile" Offer Cereal Box,**
1965. Three-dimensional plastic flying saucer was packaged one per box. Back panel features four cut-out "United Monsters Of Outer Space Targets." Gordon Gold Archives.
Used Complete - **$375 $850 $1500**

QSP-4

❑ **QSP-4. Quake "Mini-Movie Viewer" Offer Cereal Box,**
1965. In box premium was small plastic viewer and back panel features one of four different cardboard filmstrips. Viewers came in three different colors. Gordon Gold Archives.
Used Complete - **$275 $500 $1000**

QSP-5

❑ **QSP-5. Quisp Cereal Box With "Mini-Movie Viewer" Offer,**
1965. Back panel pictures premium consisting of small figural plastic Quisp with attached viewing lens. Panel also has cut-out filmstrip from a series of four different. Gordon Gold Archives.
Used Complete - **$200 $400 $800**

QSP-6

❑ **QSP-6. "Adventures Of Quake And Quisp" Comic Book,**
1966. Three in series titled "Kite Tale," "Lava Come-Back," and "Plenty of Glutton."
Each - **$3 $9 $24**

QSP-7

❑ **QSP-7. "Quisp Flying Saucer" With Instruction Sheet,**
1966. Battery operated plastic toy.
Near Mint In Generic Box - **$400**
Saucer Only - **$85 $165 $300**

QSP-8

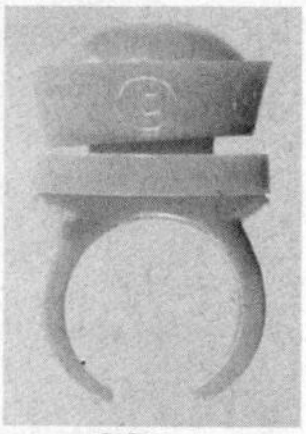

QSP-9

❑ **QSP-8. Quisp Friendship Figural Plastic Ring,**
1966. - **$125 $300 $600**

❑ **QSP-9. Quisp Space Disk Whistle Plastic Ring,**
1966. - **$75 $150 $275**

QSP-10

QSP-11

❑ **QSP-10. Quisp Meteorite Plastic Ring,**
1966. - **$75 $150 $275**

❑ **QSP-11. Quisp Space Gun Plastic Ring,**
1966. - **$75 $150 $275**

QSP-12

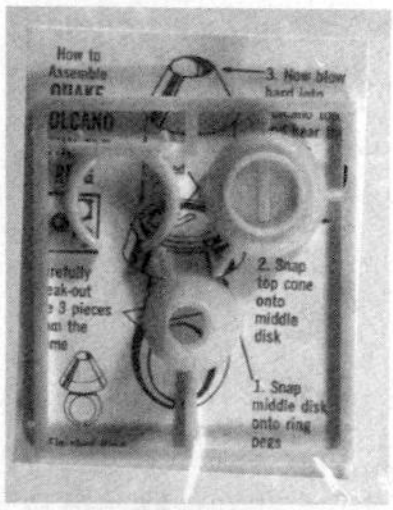

QSP-13

❑ **QSP-12. Quake Friendship Plastic Ring,**
1966. - **$100 $250 $475**

❑ **QSP-13. Quake Volcano Whistle Plastic Ring,**
1966. - **$75 $150 $250**

QSP-14

QSP-15

❑ **QSP-14. Quake World Globe Plastic Ring,**
1966. - **$75 $150 $275**

❑ **QSP-15. "Quake" Cavern Helmet,**
1967. Features include battery operated light bulb housing. - **$60 $125 $200**

QSP-16

QSP-17

❑ **QSP-16. Quisp Playmate Cloth Doll,**
1968. - **$50 $125 $250**

❑ **QSP-17. Quake Playmate Cloth Doll,**
1968. - **$40 $115 $225**

QSP-18

❑ **QSP-18. "Quisp Space Beanie",**
1968. Battery operated plastic with turning propeller. Working - **$65 $135 $250**

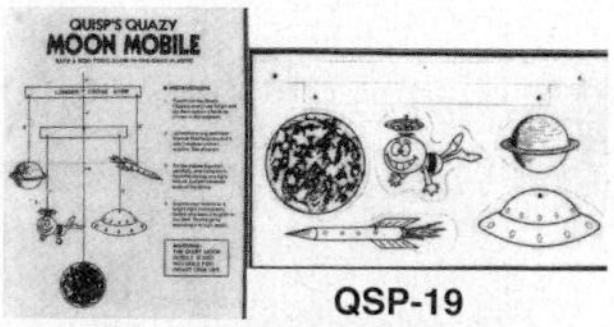

QSP-19

❑ **QSP-19. "Quazy Moon Mobile" Punch-Out Assembly Sheet,**
c. 1960s. Assembly parts glow in the dark.
Complete/Unpunched - **$55 $110 $165**

QSP-20

QSP-21

❑ **QSP-20. Quisp Gyro Trail Blazer,**
c. 1960s. - **$10 $20 $50**

❑ **QSP-21. Quisp Figural Composition Bank,**
c. 1970. 6-1/2" tall with rubber trap. -
$150 $300 $550

QSP-22

❑ **QSP-22. Quisp On Unicycle Toy,**
c. 1970. Issued by Quaker Oats. 2-1/2" tall.
Near Mint With Pull Cord - **$40**
Without Cord - **$5 $12 $20**

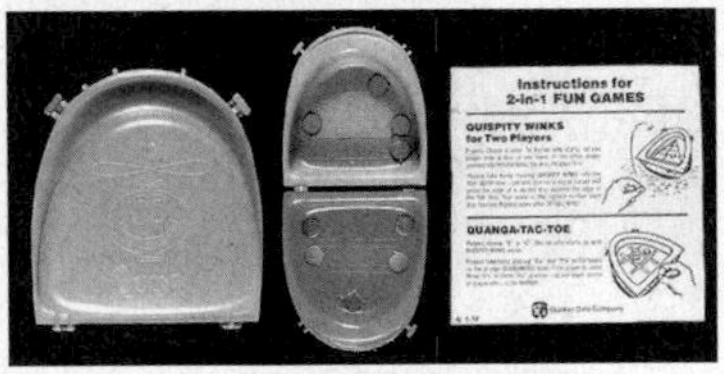

QSP-23

❑ **QSP-23. Quisp 2-In-1 Fun Bowl With Instructions,**
1972. Quaker Oats. Hinged plastic game bowl with four orange "X" and four blue "O" playing disks for game "Quispity Winks" or "Quanga-Tac-Toe." Near Mint Complete - **$235**
Bowl Only - **$25 $50 $100**

QSP-24

❑ **QSP-24. "Quake Super Spinner" Toy,**
1970s. Cellophane pack holds plastic disk ship and launcher with rubber band. Near Mint
Sealed - **$40**
Loose - **$5 $15 $25**

QSP-25

❑ **QSP-25. Cereal Box,**
1985. Two panels have "Space Trivia" game parts. Complete Box - **$15 $25 $40**

QSP-26

❑ **QSP-26. "Quisp" Wristwatch In Colorful Illustrated Tin,**
1997. Offered to promote the re-entry of the cereal in the markets of Milwaukee, Chicago, parts of New York and Pennsylvania. Required proof of purchase and $16.95. Offer expired 12/31/97 but was reoffered the following year, this time in a plain tin without any graphics.
Near Mint Boxed Illustrated Tin - **$70**
Near Mint Boxed Plain Tin - **$50**

QSP-27

❑ **QSP-27. Quisp Wacky Wobbler,**
2003. - **$20**

Quiz Kids

A panel of juvenile experts (from as young as 4 to as old as 16) answering questions submitted by listeners, the *Quiz Kids* had a successful 13-year run on network radio from 1940 to 1953. The program was heard initially on NBC, then on the Blue Network (1942-1946), and again on NBC (1946-1951)--sponsored throughout by Alka-Seltzer. For its final season it was sustained on CBS. The show was simulcast on television starting in 1949 and continued on NBC or CBS until 1953, sponsored by Alka-Seltzer (1949-1951) and Cat's Paws Soles (1952-1953). Show-business veteran Joe Kelly served as moderator and quizmaster. A brief television revival in 1956 was hosted by Clifton Fadiman.

QIZ-1

❑ **QIZ-1. "Quiz Kids" Game,**
1940. Store item by Parker Brothers. -
$25 $50 $85

QIZ-2

QIZ-3

❑ **QIZ-2. Red Book,**
1941. 32 page book of popular questions and answers from radio show. - **$25 $50 $100**

❑ **QIZ-3. Blue Book,**
1941. Blue cover. Popular questions and answers from radio show. - **$30 $60 $135**

QIZ-4

QIZ-5

❑ **QIZ-4. "Best Teacher Contest Certificate Of Honor",**
1947. Awarded to teachers nominated by their students. - **$25 $50 $100**

❑ **QIZ-5. Photo Postcard,**
c. 1949. Alka-Seltzer. - **$5 $10 $15**

QIZ-6

QIZ-7

❑ **QIZ-6. Photo Postcard,**
c. 1949. Alka-Seltzer. - **$5 $10 $15**

❑ **QIZ-7. "Ask How" Cello. Button,**
1940s. Scarce with this exact text. -
$35 $75 $160

QIZ-8

QIZ-9

QIZ-10

QIZ-11

❑ **QIZ-8. "Quiz Kids" Cello. Button,**
1940s. - **$10 $15 $30**

❑ **QIZ-9. "Quiz Kids" Cello. Button,**
1940s. Kaynee. - **$15 $25 $45**

❑ **QIZ-10. Tin Badge,**
1940s. - **$10 $20 $50**

❑ **QIZ-11. "Quiz Kids" Gold Finish Metal Figural Badge,**
1940s. Quiz Kid figure suspends miniature metal book that opens to pull-out paper listing questions and answers. - **$35 $75 $150**

Radio Misc.

Radio of the 1930s to early 1950s has little resemblance to the typical formats offered to today's listeners. Newspapers and other periodicals could be perused as time or leisure allowed but radio program timing was firm if "live" household entertainment was desired. There was little casual listening, no lengthy spans of similar format. Program nature differed distinctively from one time slot to the next and the intervening commercial breaks could be as creative as the program itself. The earliest and infrequently offered radio premiums were usually tailored to adult listeners. The early 1930s ushered in premiums for youngsters--ever mindful that mom or other adult was still necessary for product purchase--and the subsequent flourishing of club badges, manuals, secret devices, etc. is a matter of record. This section is a sampling of shows, some admittedly obscure, whose sponsors issued at least one imaginative premium.

RAD-1

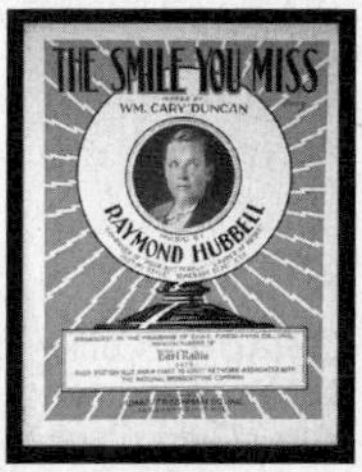

RAD-2

❑ **RAD-1. Real Folks Radio Show,**
1925. Vaseline Hair Tonic. Thompkins' Corner Enterprise newspaper premium. - **$20 $30 $60**

❑ **RAD-2. "The Smile You Miss" Song Sheet,**
1929. Music by Raymond Hubbell broadcast on WJZ radio station. Autograph in center of sheet.
Signed - **$20 $40 $75**
Unsigned - **$5 $10 $15**

RAD-3

❑ **RAD-3. Blue Network "Stories For Children" Book,**
1929. Saalfield Publishing Co. 7.5x9.75" hardcover "Collection Of Stories Which Are Favorites With Children Over The Radio" based on radio program created in 1927. -
$18 $30 $65

RAD-4

❑ **RAD-4. True Story Hour Book,**
1931. True Story hardcover. 196 pages. "Mary and Bob Radio Show" started in 1929. -
$25 $50 $80

RAD-5

RAD-6

❑ **RAD-5. Old Time Songs & Mountain Ballads,**
1931. WLW Radio premium. - **$10 $18 $35**

❑ **RAD-6. Radio Pictorial Log Book, 34 Pages,**
1932. Photos of stars and listing of radio stations. - **$20 $35 $70**

RAD-7

❑ **RAD-7. "Just Plain Bill" Puzzle With Mailer Envelope,**
1933. Koloynos toothpaste. Puzzle pictures the three major radio cast members.
Envelope - **$8 $15 $25**
Puzzle - **$15 $25 $40**

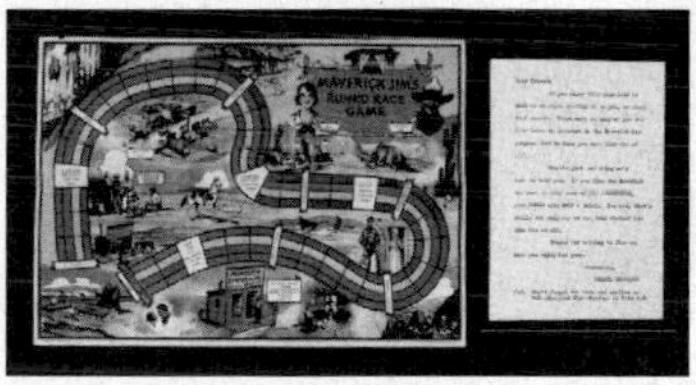

RAD-8

❑ **RAD-8. "Maverick Jim's Runko Race Game" With Letter,**
1934. Runkel Bros. Co. 14x20" full color map includes images of Maverick Jim, Amy, Sam, Aunt Sarah Hardy, Sackfull Wilkes. Map printer is Einson-Freeman Co. Letter urges listenership over WOR, New York City and sampling of new "Runko With Malt". Letter - **$8 $15 $25**
Game Sheet - **$30 $60 $125**

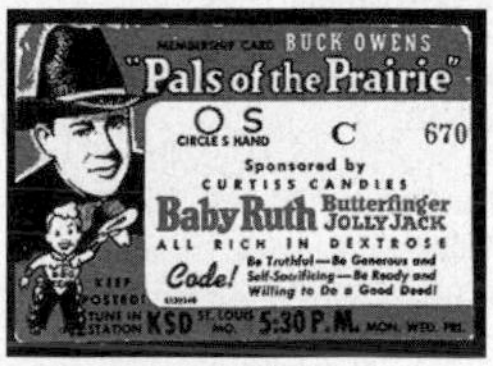

RAD-9

❑ **RAD-9. Buck Owens "Pals Of The Prairie" Membership Card,**
c. 1934. Curtiss Candies. Imprinted for KSD, St. Louis. - **$18 $35 $65**

RAD-10

❑ **RAD-10. Congo Bartlett's "Ethiopia" 21x29" Paper Map,**
1935. Karl's White Bread. - **$75 $150 $300**

RAD-11

RAD-12

❑ **RAD-11. Radio Explorers Club Kit,**
1935. American-Bosch radios. Contents of certificate and folder sheet that opens to 17x22" including picture of Captain James P. Barker, master mariner and club commander.
Folder - **$30 $50 $75**
Certificate Only - **$15 $25 $45**

❑ **RAD-12. "Radio Explorers Club" Metal Globe,**
c. 1935. American-Bosch, made by J. Chein Co. - **$35 $70 $125**

RAD-13

RAD-14

❑ **RAD-13. Calling W-1-X-Y-Z Better Little Book #1412,**
1936. Jimmy Kean and the Radio Spies.- **$11 $33 $72**

❑ **RAD-14. Happy Hollow Promo With Mailer,**
1936. Network feature. Flyer with recipes. - **$12 $25 $50**

RAD-15

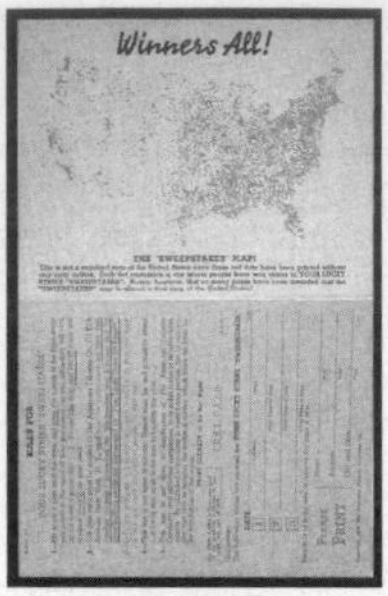

RAD-16

❑ **RAD-15. Lucky Strike Hit Parade Six Page Contest Flyer,**
1936. Radio premium which allowed you to pick hits for radio's Top 15 songs. Includes self addressed postcard still attached with 1¢ stamp. - **$35 $70 $125**

❑ **RAD-16. Lucky Strike Hit Parade Four Page Contest Flyer,**
1936. Radio contest flyer that was handed out with business reply card still attached. - **$25 $50 $100**

RAD-17

❑ **RAD-17. Monk And Sam Radio Show Kit,**
1936. Features photo, mailer, song book, and 1936 calendar called Monkalendar.
Complete - **$25 $50 $100**

RAD-18

❑ **RAD-18. Sara And Aggie's Cook Book,**
1936. 32 page radio premium from "The Tuttle Parlor Show." - **$10 $20 $45**

RAD-19

RAD-20

RAD-21

❑ **RAD-19. Mary Marlin Cast Photo Of David Post,**
1936. Kleenex. Radio premium from "The Story of Mary Marlin" show. - **$5 $10 $25**

❑ **RAD-20. Mary Marlin Cast Photo Of Joe Marlin,**
1936. Kleenex. Radio premium from "The Story of Mary Marlin" show. - **$5 $10 $25**

❑ **RAD-21. Mary Marlin Cast Photo Of Sally Gibbons,**
1936. Kleenex. Radio premium from "The Story of Mary Marlin" show. - **$5 $10 $25**

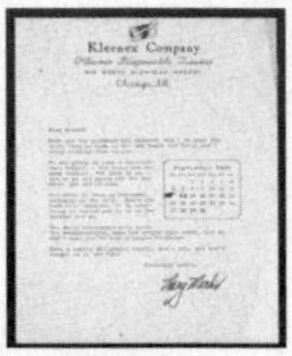

RAD-22

RAD-23

RAD-24

❑ **RAD-22. Mary Marlin Letter,**
1936. Kleenex. Talks about the cast pictures that were ordered. - **$10 $25 $40**

❑ **RAD-23. Mary Marlin Photo Of Actress Joan Gaine,**
1936. Kleenex. Radio premium from "The Story of Mary Marlin" show. - **$10 $25 $40**

❑ **RAD-24. Mary Marlin Photo Of Wedding,**
1936. Kleenex. - **$10 $25 $40**

RAD-25

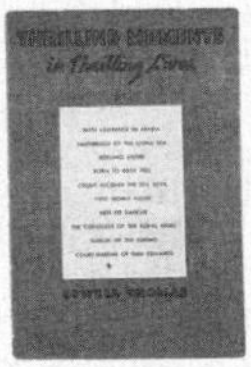

RAD-26

❑ **RAD-25. Mary Marlin Photo With Station Attachment,**
1936. Kleenex. Holds letter and 5 cast photos from "The Story of Mary Marlin" show. - **$25 $65 $135**

❑ **RAD-26. Thrilling Moments,**
1936. Sun Oil Co. Lowell Thomas - news voice on the air. - **$10 $20 $35**

RAD-27

RAD-28

❑ **RAD-27. Alka Seltzer Song Book,**
1937. 16 pages of songs featuring radio stars. - **$10 $20 $30**

❑ **RAD-28. Stars Of Radio Book,**
1937. 16 pages of stars like Kate Smith, Orphan Annie and others. - **$15 $30 $50**

RAD-29

RAD-30

❑ **RAD-29. Rudy Vallee Photo,**
1937. Philadephia Record newspaper premium. - **$10 $15 $25**

❑ **RAD-30. "The Woman In White" Photo Book,**
1938. Pillsbury Flour Co. 8 1/2x11-3/4" cast member and information promotion for hospital drama radio show beginning January 3 that year. - **$12 $25 $45**

RAD-31

❑ **RAD-31. "I Want A Divorce" Radio Show Game & Mailer,**
1938. Large colorful game with punch-outs and game spinner. Called S&W "Happy Marriage Game." - **$75 $150 $250**

RAD-32

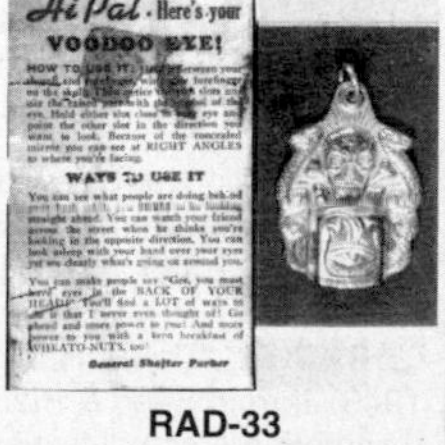

RAD-33

❑ **RAD-32. Roi-Tan Cigars Contest Novelty,**
1939. Miniature metal car with mounted litho. tin sign for contest offering 1939 Chevrolet daily prize with added inscription for Sophie Tucker CBS radio show. - **$75 $150 $300**

❑ **RAD-33. "Voodoo Eye" Metal Pendant With Envelope,**
1930s. Wheato-Nuts. Pendant designed as look-around device. Envelope - **$50 $100 $150**
Pendant - **$100 $250 $400**

RAD-34

RAD-35

❑ **RAD-34. Jolly Joe's *Secret Code* and Radio Club Book,**
1930s. Coco Wheat. Booklet for youth program utilizing partial code lettering. - **$15 $25 $50**

❑ **RAD-35. Promo Punchout Board,**
1930s. Promoted radio stations. Certain stations received more points than others. Prizes were offered when you reached high point totals. - **$30 $60 $120**

RAD-36

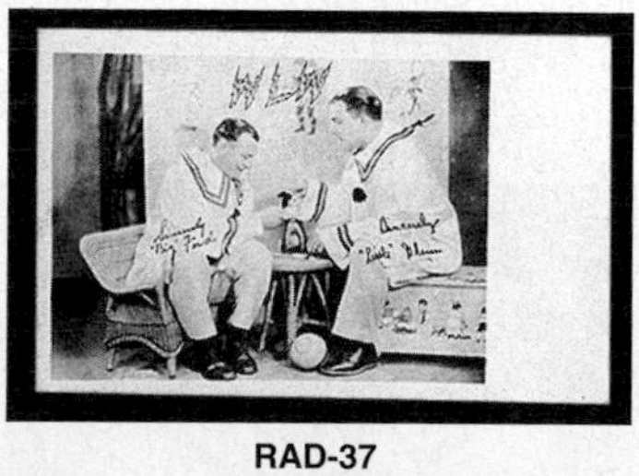

RAD-37

❑ **RAD-36. "Adventures Of Frank Farrell" Bronze Luster Metal Badge,**
1930s. Poll Parrot shoes. This was a series of 35 syndicated radio programs. Badge features torch, winged foot along with various pieces of sporting equipment. - **$15 $30 $70**
Cello. pinback with same design - **$25 $60 $110**

❑ **RAD-37. WLW Radio Photo Postcard Of Lullaby Boys,**
1930s. Big Ford & Little Glenn pictured. - **$5 $10 $20**

RAD-38

❑ **RAD-38. Rudy Vallée Jigsaw Puzzle,**
1930s. 200-piece puzzle in its original box. Store bought for 25¢. From a Radio Stars series. - **$40 $80 $145**

RAD-39

RAD-40

❑ **RAD-39. "Coco Wheats Radio Club" Brass Badge,**
1930s. About 1-1/4" tall depicting radio microphone. - **$20 $40 $80**

❑ **RAD-40. Radio Folks Brochure,**
1930s. Keystone Steel. Barn Dance Party, 16 pages, features George Gobel, Red Foley, and others. - **$10 $20 $40**

RAD-41

❑ **RAD-41. New Bachelor Cigar Cutter,**
1930s. Brass cutter premium for cigars. - **$20 $50 $85**

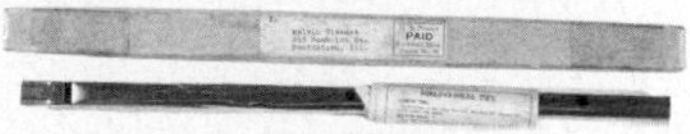

RAD-42

❑ **RAD-42. Fife Musical Instrument In Mailer,**
1930s. Symphony Hour sponsored by Malt O'Meal. Includes instructions and mailer. - **$50 $75 $125**

RAD-43

RAD-44

❑ RAD-43. Sohio Radio Puzzle,
1930s. Boxed puzzle from "In Dutch" radio show. Bought at gas station. - **$18 $35 $70**

❑ RAD-44. Rudy Vallee Photo,
1930s. Fleischmann's Yeast. Radio premium with story of life folder.
Complete - **$20 $40 $85**

RAD-45

❑ RAD-45. "Stoopnocracy" Stoopnagle & Budd Club Button,
1930s. Radio and later newspaper club evolving from radio personalities team in Buffalo. Club members were "Stoopnocrats" who either furnished ideas or things to be eliminated or furnished methods for eliminating them. -
$20 $30 $60

RAD-46

❑ RAD-46. "Radio Guide" Magazines Delivery Bag,
1930s. Fabric bag carrier for copies of "The National Weekly Of Programs And Personalities." - **$50 $85 $175**

RAD-47

❑ RAD-47. "Junior Police" Badge On Card,
1930s. Etched Products Corp. 3.5x5" card holding brass luster metal star badge with "808" designation. Card - **$25 $50 $100**
Badge - **$70 $160 $275**

RAD-48

❑ RAD-48. Uncle Bob Birthday Card,
1930s. Hydrox premium for "Curb is the Limit Radio Show." Shows Mr. & Mrs. Uncle Bob on front. - **$12 $20 $40**

RAD-49

❑ RAD-49. Radio Personalities and Radio Log,
1940. Celebrates 10 years of Philco Leadership. Has 144 photos of radio stars, 4 pages of radio logs and 2 pages of ads for radio products. Shows sponsor of each radio show. -
$30 $50 $85

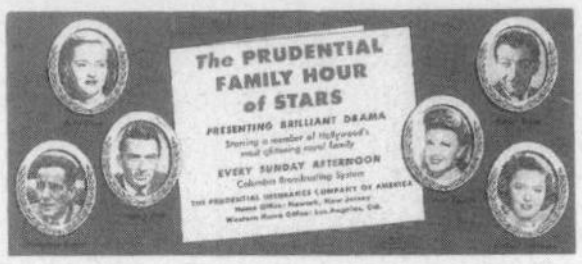

RAD-50

❑ RAD-50. Family Hour of Stars Blotter,
1940. Prudential. Radio premium from sponsor. -
$20 $40 $80

RAD-51

❑ RAD-51. Truth Or Consequences Brochure,
1940. Thirty-two pages. Radio show premium. -
$30 $60 $100

RAD-52

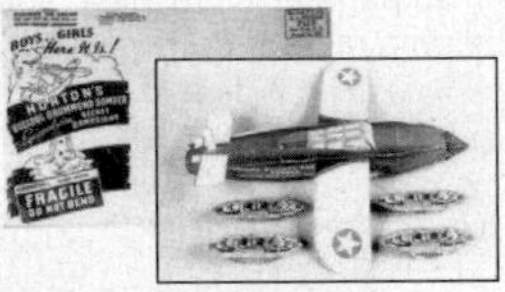

RAD-53

❑ RAD-52. "The Aldrich Family" Schedule Sheet,
c. 1940. Jell-O Puddings. Picture sheet of Ezra Stone as Henry Aldrich of NBC radio comedy series with listing on reverse of more than 75 stations coast to coast offering Thursday evening episode. - **$15 $25 $45**

❑ RAD-53. "Horton's Bulldog Drummond Bomber",
c. 1941. Cardboard punch-out that releases marble bombs onto four small battleships.
Near Mint In Mailer - **$500**
Used - **$100 $175 $300**

RAD-54

RAD-55

❑ RAD-54. "The Sea Hound" Paper Map,
1942. Blue Network. Pictures "Captain Silver's Sea Chart". - **$35 $75 $165**

❑ RAD-55. "David Harum" Seed Packets,
1943. Jermin Seed & Plant Co., Los Angeles. Contents are actual flower seeds "Packed For Season Of 1943". Each - **$5 $15 $30**

RAD-56

RAD-57

❑ RAD-56. WFBL Radio Stars Cook Book With Mailer,
1945. Featured Aunt Jenny, Lionel Barrymore, Milton Berle, Fanny Brice, Major Bowes, Burns & Allen, Danny Kaye, Frank Sinatra, and many others. - **$25 $40 $85**

❑ RAD-57. Big Brother Radio Kit with Mailer,
1945. KMBC radio, Kansas City, Kansas. -
$30 $55 $125

RAD-58

❑ RAD-58. Ruth Lyons Song Sheet,
1946. Contains "The Nu-Maid Song" and "The Birthday Song" from Ruth Lyons, the star of "Morning Matinee" radio program on WLW and WINS stations. Nu-Maid was a sponsor of the show. - **$10 $20 $40**

RAD-59

❑ RAD-59. "The Mel Blanc Show" Radio Program Ticket,
1946. Sponsored by Colgate. - **$15 $30 $60**

RAD-60

❑ RAD-60. "The Whistler" Blotter Card,
1947. Household Finance Corp. Cardboard ink blotter for weekly drama suspense detective program. Pictured examples are imprinted for WBBM Radio, Chicago. - **$50 $120 $240**
CKAC Radio, Montreal. - **$75 $180 $325**

RAD-61

❑ RAD-61. NBC "On The Air" Comic Book,
1947. National Broadcasting Co. Full color 16-page illustrated description of network operations. Photo example shows front cover and final frame of story. - **$24 $72 $300**

RAD-62

RAD-63

❑ RAD-62. Texaco Star Theater Sign,
1940s. 13x9-1/2" sign for ABC radio show featured famous stars. - **$65 $140 $200**

❑ RAD-63. "Cowboy Thrills Club" Premium Pinback,
1940s. Sponsored by Everybody's & Admiral radio products. Scarce. - **$40 $85 $175**

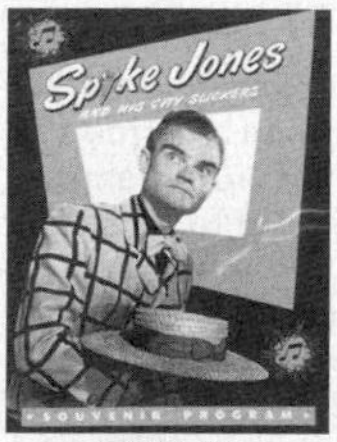

RAD-64

RAD-65

❑ RAD-64. Spike Jones Souvenir Program,
1949. 16 page program premium for RCA. -
$15 $25 $50

❑ RAD-65. "David Harum Handprint" Folder,
c. 1940s. Bab-o Cleanser. Cover pictures "Homeville" community and cast members, inside "Handprint" is apparent clue to ongoing serial mystery. - **$15 $25 $40**

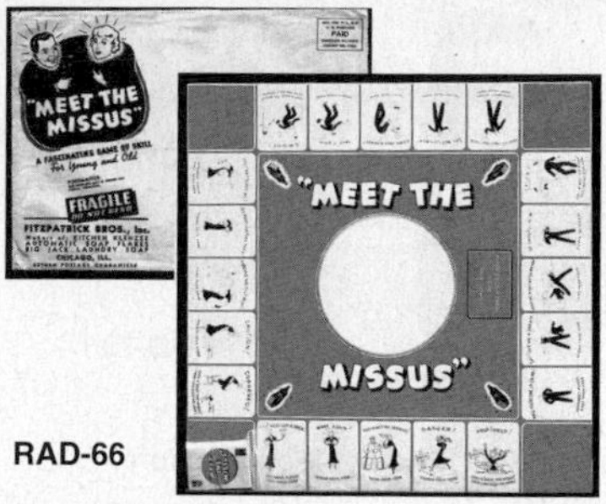

RAD-66

❑ RAD-66. "Meet The Missus" Radio Game & Mailer,
1940s. Automatic Soap Flakes. 48 cards and 19"x19" playing paper board with mailer. -
$65 $125 $250

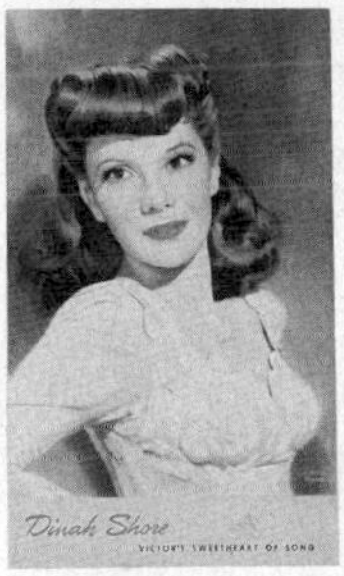

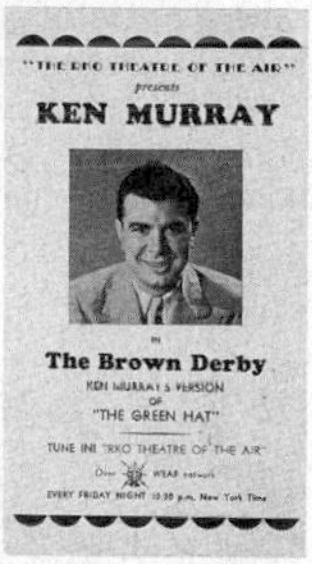

RAD-67 RAD-68

❑ RAD-67. Dinah Shore Postcard,
1940s. Promotes her RCA radio show "Up In Arms." - **$15 $30 $60**

❑ RAD-68. Ken Murray Promo - NBC Radio,
1940s. The Brown Derby. "RKO Theatre of the Air" program review. - **$15 $25 $45**

RAD-69

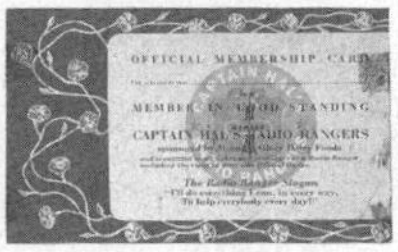

RAD-70

❑ RAD-69. Radio Syd & Suzie's Scrapbook,
1940s. Gas & Electric radio premium. Shows photo of cast. - **$10 $20 $40**

❑ RAD-70. Captain Hal's Membership Card,
1940s. Radio Rangers premium for radio show. -
$10 $20 $45

RAD-71

RAD-72

❑ **RAD-71. "Richard 'Red' Skelton" Postcard,**
1940s. 3.5x5.5" black/white photo card of him at NBC microphone. - **$15 $30 $50**

❑ **RAD-72. "Big John & Sparky,"**
1950s. Two buttons, one a 2.5" litho with covered metal back and bar pin reading "Official Member Big John & Sparky Club No. 1 KCA Walkers Spokane, Wash." Second is 1.25" showing character and reading "Marin-Dell's Sparky Club" and copyright on curl "Arthur Sampson Enterprises."
"Official" Button - **$15 $25 $50**
"Marin-Dell's" Button - **$5 $10 $20**

RAD-73

RAD-74

❑ **RAD-73. Big Jon Arthur & Sparkie Fan Card,**
1950s. American Broadcasting Corp. - **$25 $40 $75**

❑ **RAD-74. WOR Radio 25 Year Anniversary Gold Tie Tack,**
1950s. Gold Tie Tack with diamond set in radio mike. - **$200**

RAD-75

RAD-76

❑ **RAD-75. "War of the Worlds" Album,**
1950s. Radio broadcast of the invasion from Mars. Album and record. - **$35 $60 $100**

❑ **RAD-76. "When Radio Was King" Album,**
1972. Features big-name radio stars, entertainment highlights, and news reports. Premium from Reader's Digest. RCA Custom Record. - **$25 $50 $125**

RAD-77

RAD-78

❑ **RAD-77. "Radio Super Heroes At War" Album,**
1975. - **$20 $35 $75**

❑ **RAD-78. "Mallard Stern" Bean Bag,**
1998. Famous Meanies series with tag. - **$15**

Raggedy Ann

Cartoonist and illustrator Johnny Gruelle (1880-1938) worked for various publications, but his first major position was as assistant illustrator on the *Indianapolis Star* newspaper in 1903. In 1911, he created the *Mr. Twee Deedle* Sunday comic page for *The New York Herald* which ran until 1914. At home he was entertaining his daughter Marcella and drew a face on a doll for her. Based on Indiana poet James Whitcomb Riley's characters of Raggedy Man and Little Orphant Annie, he named the doll Raggedy Ann.

The doll was patented September 7, 1915 and Gruelle went to work on a children's book. P.F. Volland published *Raggedy Ann Stories* in 1918 and introduced her partner in *Raggedy Andy Stories* in 1920.

Ann also had a successful career in animation. Fleischer Studios released a cartoon in 1941, followed by three more from Famous Studios in 1947. 20th Century Fox released the 1977 feature *Raggedy Ann and Andy: A Musical Adventure* directed by Richard Williams with music by Joe Raposo. Chuck Jones (1912-2002) directed two TV specials: *The Great Santa Claus Caper* in 1978 and *The Pumpkin Who Couldn't Smile* in 1979. CBS-TV ran an animated series between 1988 and 1991.

Ann was voted into the National Toy Hall of Fame in 2002 and there is a Raggedy Ann and Andy museum in Johnny Gruelle's birthplace of Arcola, Illinois. Dell and Gold Key published numerous comic books between 1942 and 1973. Calico wears well with collectors.

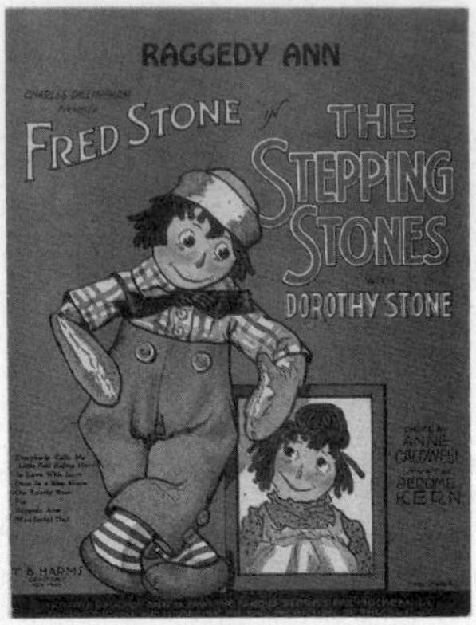

RAG-1

❑ **RAG-1. "Raggedy Ann" Sheet Music,**
1923. T.B. Harms Co., N.Y. 9x12" with six pages. Music by Jerome Kern. - **$12 $25 $50**

RAG-2

❑ **RAG-2. "Raggedy Ann's Sunny Songs" Record Album,**
1934. RCA Victor. Three records in album illustrated on front cover by her and Andy plus two gnomes. - **$60 $100 $190**

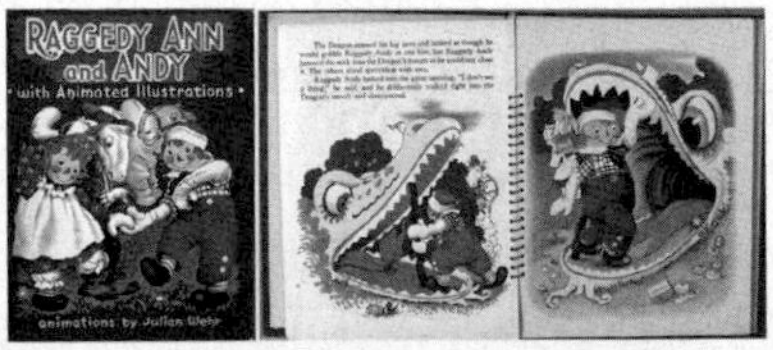

RAG-3

❑ **RAG-3. "Raggedy Ann And Andy" Die-cut Mechanical Storybook,**
1944. Saalfield Publishing Co. 6.75x8.75" hardcover with 24 full color pages, six of which have movable mechanical parts designed by Julian Wehr. - **$40 $80 $165**

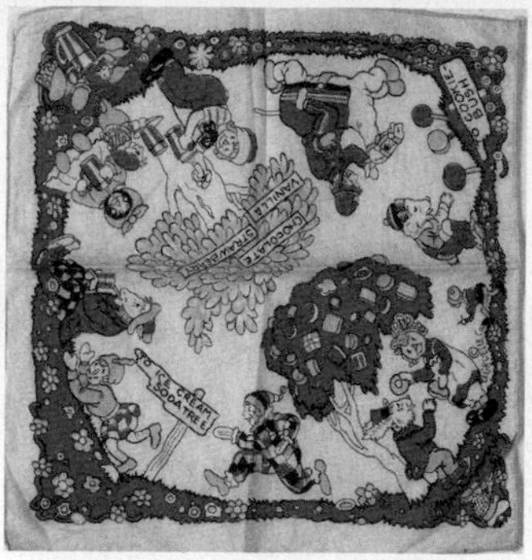

RAG-4

❑ **RAG-4. Raggedy Ann Character Hanky,**
c. 1940s. J. Gruelle Co. 7.5x8". - **$30 $65 $150**

RAG-5

❑ **RAG-5. Raggedy Ann And Andy Child's Bowl,**
c. 1940s. 7.75" diameter with raised rim. - **$20 $40 $85**

RAG-6

❑ **RAG-6. "Raggedy Ann And Andy" Boxed Metal Camper,**
c. 1960s. Buddy L. 5.5x6x11.5" long box con tains 11-3/8" long metal camper with plastic doors and inside camper bed. Comes with two plastic figures, each 3.5" tall, 4.75" long plastic boat, plastic dog. Box - **$15 $30 $60**
Camper - **$30 $60 $100**

RAG-7

❑ **RAG-7. Raggedy Ann And Andy Figural Night Light,**
c. 1960s. Nan San Ind. Inc. 3x5.5x5" tall vinyl light with switch on cord. - **$15 $30 $60**

RAG-8

❑ **RAG-8. Raggedy Ann and Andy Bean Dolls,**
1998. With tags. - **$40**

RAG-9

❑ **RAG-9. Raggedy Ann Doll in Box,**
2002. Special Edition commemorating the doll's original patent on September 7, 1915. - **$35**

Ramar of the Jungle

Actor Jon Hall (1915-1979) began his film career in the mid 1930s, becoming a star playing Terangi in the 1937 feature *The Hurricane*. Directed by John Ford, the film also made a star of Dorothy Lamour. Hall's success continued into the 1940s with a series of Technicolor films which co-starred Maria Montez (1912-1951).

The Ramar series was syndicated between October, 1952 and January, 1954 with a total of 52 episodes. Hall portrayed Dr. Tom Reynolds in the jungle, known as Ramar to the natives which translates to white medicine man. He's aided by co-star Ray Montgomery as Professor Ogden. Lippert Productions released four theatrical films, each comprised of three TV episodes, between 1953 and 1955 titled: *White Goddess, Eyes of the Jungle, Thunder Over Sangoland* and *Phantom of the Jungle.* I.T.C. issued seven TV movies compiled from the series in 1964.

Jon Hall's later credits in Hollywood include special effects for the noted 1972 environmental film *Survival of Spaceship Earth.*

Toby Press/Charlton published five *Ramar of the Jungle* comic books between 1954 and 1956.

RMJ-1

❑ **RMJ-1. Jon Hall Autographed Photo,**
1930s. 5x7" photo with 3.3" black fountain pen autograph. - **$10 $20 $40**

RMJ-2

❑ **RMJ-2. "Ramar Of The Jungle And The Blue Fire" Tru-Vue Film Card,**
1955. 3.75x5.5" card in envelope features photos from the show. - **$10 $20 $35**

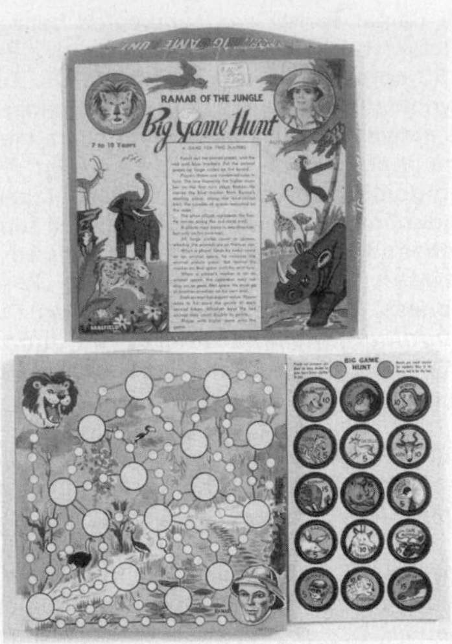

RMJ-3

❑ **RMJ-3. "Ramar Of The Jungle Big Game Hunt" Game,**
1957. Saalfield. 9.75x9.75x1.25" deep box contains unpunched card of animal point tokens. Box insert serves as gameboard. - **$20 $40 $85**

RMJ-4

RMJ-5

❑ **RMJ-4. Jon Hall Ramar Of Jungle Membership Card,**
1950s. Rare. Membership card for Safari Scouts. 2 cards attached with code and order form for badge and tattoos. - **$30 $60 $125**

❑ **RMJ-5. Jon Hall Ramar Safari Scout Pin,**
1950s. Yellow with red and brown lettering. - **$85 $165 $300**

RMJ-6

❑ **RMJ-6. "Ramar Of The Jungle Game",**
1950s. 12x16x1" deep box contains 15x15.5" gameboard, instruction sheet, 5x5" cardboard spinner, 2.5x4" membership card with instructions to fill out and mail membership card in for registration to include numbering, signing and its return along with club badge and jungle tattoos. **- $50 $100 $200**

RMJ-7

❑ **RMJ-7. "Ramar Of The Jungle Coloring Book",**
1966. Saalfield Publishing co. 10.75x14" with 16 pages. - **$12 $25 $50**

The Range Rider

An early 1950s television weekly series, *The Range Rider* starred Jock Mahoney (1919-1989) in the title role and Dick Jones as his youthful sidekick Dick West. The two wandered the West, apparently for the sole purpose of correcting local injustices. Both actors were accomplished stuntmen, a skill well displayed in each episode. The show was produced by Gene Autry's Flying A Productions and ran 1951-1953 on CBS-TV before syndication. Premiums were issued by bread companies in addition to non-premium coloring books and Dell comic books.

RAN-1

❑ **RAN-1. "Range Rider" Picture,**
c. 1951. Issued by local sponsor Bueter's Butter-Krust Bread, Hannibal, Missouri. Color paper photo. **- $20 $50 $90**

RAN-2

RAN-3

❑ **RAN-2. Langendorf Bread Photo,**
c. 1951. - **$15 $30 $60**

❑ **RAN-3. Sunbeam Bread "Range Rider's Brand" Cello. Button,**
c. 1951. Pictures Jock Mahoney. - **$20 $40 $80**

RAN-4

RAN-5

❑ **RAN-4. "The Range Rider" Aluminum Ring With Paper Tag,**
c. 1951. Tag names TV show title produced by Autry Flying A Productions.
Near Mint With Tag - **$325**
No Tag - **$60 $125 $200**

❑ **RAN-5. Michigan Bread Litho Button,**
c. 1952. 1-3/8" black and white portrait on red with black text. - **$18 $35 $65**

RAN-6

RAN-7

❑ **RAN-6. "Dick West/Jock Mahoney Range Rider/TV Guide Cowboy Album" Celluloid-Covered Wall Plaque,**
1953. Plaque is 6x9.25" from series of TV Guide promotional plaques sent to stations.
- $60 $125 $215

❑ **RAN-7. Cello. Button 2-1/4",**
1950s. Peter Pan Bread. - **$25 $75 $150**

RAN-8

❑ **RAN-8. "Range Rider" Pair Of Children's Cowboy Boots,**
1950s. Store item by Built-Wel Footwear. - **$55 $110 $175**

RAN-9

RAN-10

❑ **RAN-9. Bread Loaf End Paper,**
1950s. Issued by Langendorf Bread. Sepia photo on yellow background.
Each - **$10 $25 $50**

❑ **RAN-10. "Range Rider" Bread Label Sheet,**
1950s. Bueter's Butterkrust Bread. Opens to 11x17" to hold 16 labels. - **$50 $100 $185**

RAN-11

RAN-12

❑ **RAN-11. Philadelphia TV Program Promotion Card,**
1950s. Pictures Jock Mahoney, Sally Starr and Gene Autry. Back has an offer for Oldsmobile "Wild West Fun And Game Booklet". -
$12 $25 $50

❑ **RAN-12. "Range Rider's Brand" Cello. Button,**
1950s. No sponsor's names appear but there is space around the bottom rim for an imprint. 1-1/4" bw photo on dark red. - **$30 $60 $135**

RAN-13

RAN-14

❑ **RAN-13. ButterKrust Bread Label Folder,**
1950s. Opens to 11x17" for mounting 16 labels. -
$50 $100 $185

❑ **RAN-14. "The Range Rider And Dick West" Mini-Flashlight,**
1950s. Store item by Bantam Lite. Metal case with plastic cap plus vinyl carrying cord. -
$25 $50 $100

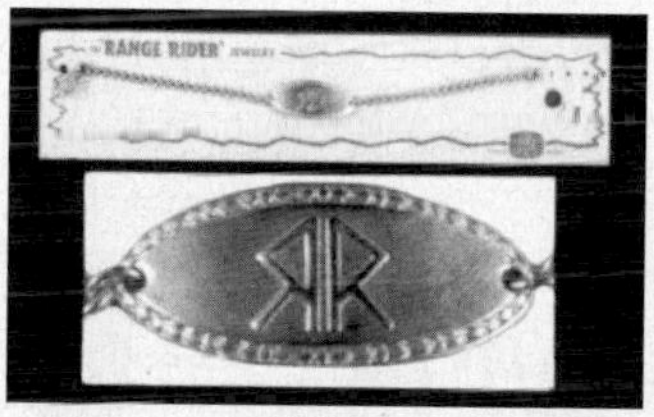

RAN-15

❑ **RAN-15. "Range Rider" Bracelet On Card,**
1950s. Store item. Carded - **$30 $65 $135**
Bracelet Only - **$20 $40 $80**

RAN-16

❑ **RAN-16. Member's Card,**
1950s. Peter Pan Peanut Butter. 2-1/2x3-3/4" lightly textured stiff brown paper identifying "Junior Range Rider" and with facsimile signature of "Dick West," the Range Rider's sidekick. -
$30 $75 $140

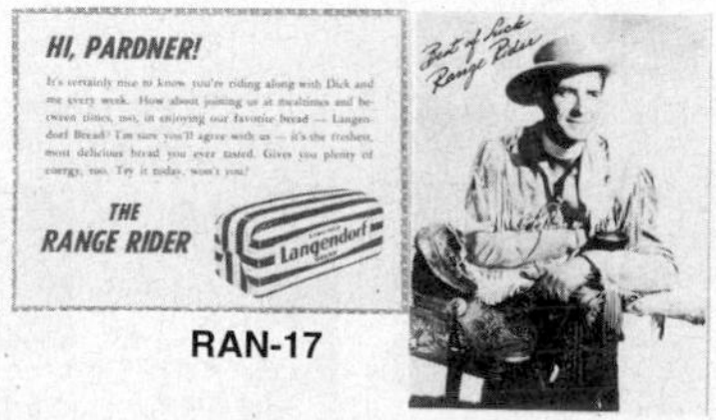

RAN-17

❑ **RAN-17. Range Rider/Jock Mahoney Picture,**
1950s. Langendorf Bread. Stiff paper black and white photo with reverse text for TV show and sponsor. - **$12 $25 $50**

Ranger Joe

Ranger Joe Honnies began in 1939, a creation of Jim Rex for the Philadelphia area. A new owner extended distribution throughout the east and south, operating as Ranger Joe, Inc. from Chester, Pennsylvania, a suburb southwest of Philadelphia. Despite this limited Western exposure, the cereal box depicted him as an authentic cowboy with horse; glassware premiums of "Ranch Mug" and cereal bowl repeated his image plus cowboy scenes. The other known Ranger Joe premium is a wood and cardboard gun designed for shooting rubber bands. Product and premiums were apparently tied into local telecasts of *Ranger Joe*, a 1951-1952 NBC-TV Saturday morning adventure show for youngsters.

Rice Honnies joined the original Wheat Honnies product in 1951 and both are considered among the forerunners of coated cereals. Nabisco bought the company in 1954 replacing Ranger Joe with Buffalo Bee, changing Honnies to Honeys and initiating national distribution.

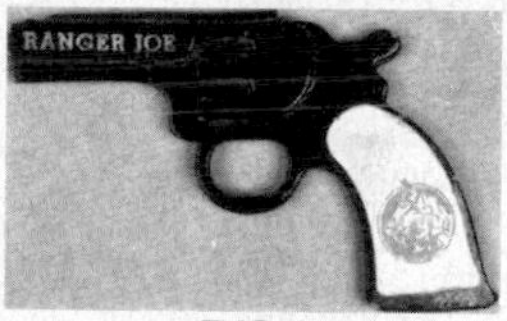

RJO-1

RJO-2

❑ **RJO-1. Rubber Band Cardboard Gun,**
c. 1940s. - **$75 $150 $300**

❑ **RJO-2. "Ranger Joe Safety Siren,"**
1951. Pink, white, red and black siren whistle is 2.5" long with large sticker label. - **$30 $60 $75**

RJO-3

❑ **RJO-3. Cereal Ad Poster,**
1951. 12x16-1/2" in navy blue. - **$35 $65 $85**

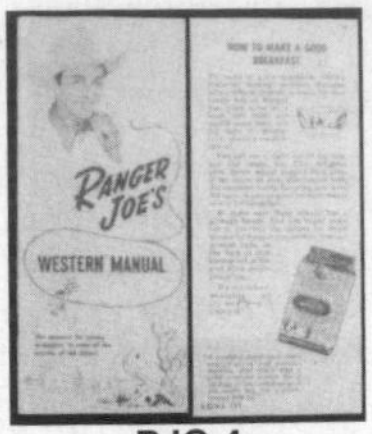

RJO-4

RJO-5

❑ **RJO-4. "Ranger Joe's Western Manual,"**
1951. Promotes "Ranger Joe Popped Wheat" product. - **$40 $70 $135**

❑ **RJO-5. Fan Card,**
c. 1951. - **$12 $25 $50**

RJO-6

RJO-7

❑ **RJO-6. Glass Cup,**
c. 1951. Blue & red. - **$8 $15 $30**

❑ **RJO-7. Glass Cereal Bowl,**
c. 1951. Blue & red. - **$10 $18 $35**

RJO-8

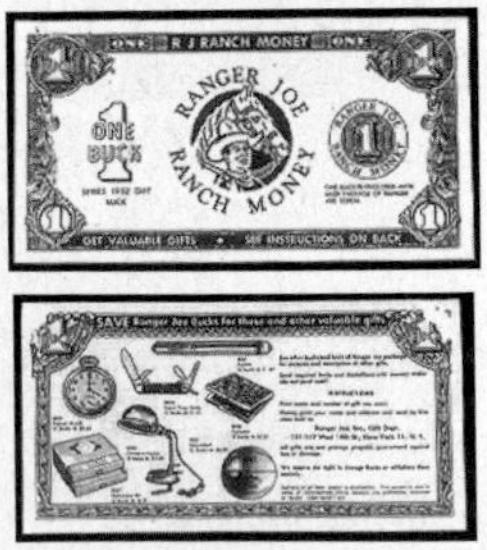

RJO-9

❑ **RJO-8. "Ranger Joe & Topaz" Patch,**
1951. - **$35 $75 $135**

❑ **RJO-9. "Ranger Joe Ranch Money" Premium Currency Bill,**
1952. Ranger Joe Cereal. Box insert to be accumulated for ordering premiums pictured on reverse. - **$8 $15 $30**

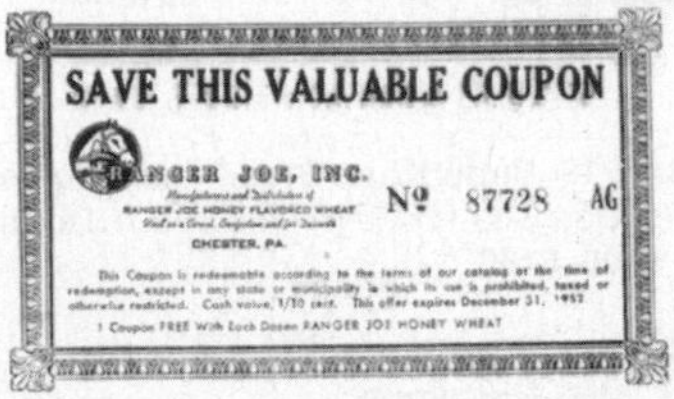

RJO-10

❑ **RJO-10. Free Gift Coupon,**
1952. - **$7 $15 $25**

RJO-11

❑ **RJO-11. Prototype Cereal Boxes,**
1954. Black & white prototype boxes for Wheat Honnies and Rice Honnies. Three different. Each - **$275**

RJO-12

❑ **RJO-12. Wheat Honnies Cereal Boxes,**
1954. Colorful boxes features Air field and plastic planes in each box. Two different shown. Each - **$165 $425 $700**

RJO-13

❑ **RJO-13. Ranger Joe Premium Planes,**
1954. Each plane is numbered on the wing. Five different: small yellow, small red, small green, large yellow and large blue with camouflage markings. Each Plane - **$15 $30 $65**

RCA and Nipper

Nipper (1884-1895) was a mixed bull/fox terrier owned by the brother of English illustrator Francis Barraud (1856-1924). Barraud first painted Nipper in September, 1895 listening to an Edison Bell cylinder phonograph, then modified the painting to have Nipper listening to a disc Gramophone. The art first appeared as a promotion in January, 1900, and the logo text *His Master's Voice* was first used on the British Gramophone company's letterhead in 1907. The painting and text were registered in 1910. The Victor Talking Machine Company took over Gramophone and the Radio Corporation of America (RCA) bought Victor in 1929.

A terrier puppy named Chipper joined Nipper in 1991 RCA TV commercials. A four ton Nipper figure can be seen on the roof of the Arnoff Moving Company building in Albany N. Y., put there in 1954 when the building was a regional operation of RCA.

The original Nipper painting by Barraud is on display at EMI Music's Gloucester, England headquarters.

RCA-1

❑ **RCA-1. RCA Nipper Two Charms,**
1930s. Red charm is 5/8" tall, white charm is 1" tall. Each - **$3 $6 $12**

RCA-2

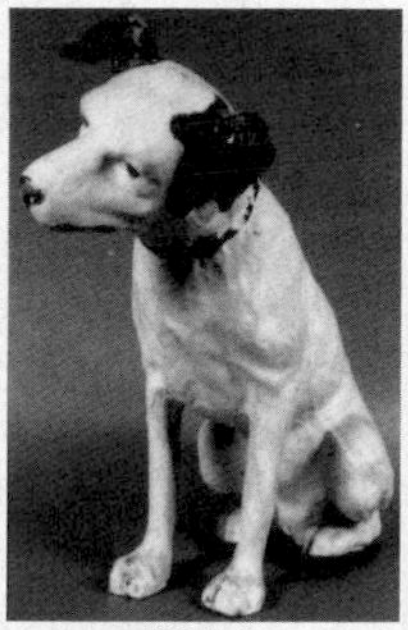

RCA-3

❑ **RCA-2. "RCA" Cardboard Fan,**
1930s. Radio Corp. of America. -
$30 $60 $85

❑ **RCA-3. Nipper Papier Mache Store Display,**
1930s. Victor Talking Machine Co. -
$225 $450 $700

RCA-4

❑ **RCA-4. RCA Nipper Salt & Pepper Shaker Set,**
1930s. By Lenox, 3" tall white china. -
$30 $60 $100

RCA-5

❑ **RCA-5. "RCA Victor Little Nipper" Cello. Button,**
c. 1948. "Club Member" designation for children's records series. - **$35 $60 $135**

RCA-6

❑ **RCA-6. "RCA" Victor Plastic Salt & Pepper Set,**
1950s. RCA Victor Corp. - **$40 $60 $110**

RCA-7

❑ **RCA-7. RCA Repair Truck With Box,**
1950s. By Marx. Truck - **$45 $110 $240**
Box - **$20 $50 $110**

RCA-8

❑ **RCA-8. "RCA-NBC" Battery Operated Mobile TV Truck,**
1950s. Yonezawa. 8" long tin litho truck with manually movable front wheels. Toy goes forward and reverse, cameraman revolves. - **$200 $400 $800**

Red Ryder

Artist Fred Harman (1902-1982) created the *Red Ryder* comic strip as a Sunday feature in 1938 and added a daily version the following year. The strip was loosely based on Harman's *Bronc Peeler* comic strip which had a brief run in the mid-1930s. The strip, which ran until the late 1960s, told the story of rancher Ryder and his Navajo ward Little Beaver as they ranged the West of the 1890s, battling bandits and rustlers and settling frontier quarrels. Comic book reprints first appeared in 1939 and continued through most of the 1950s, and more than 20 "B" Westerns from Hollywood chronicled the popular hero's adventures. Daisy introduced the Red Ryder BB gun in 1939 and has sold over nine million units. A radio series aired on the Mutual network--primarily on the West Coast--from early 1942 to 1949, sponsored by Langendorf bread and other bakeries. A television adaptation was syndicated in 1956. The Red Ryder character was used extensively for many years to promote Daisy air rifles.

RYD-1

❑ **RYD-1. Red Ryder Target Game with Box,**
1939. Store item. - **$90 $225 $450**

RYD-2

❑ **RYD-2. "Red Ryder And Little Beaver On Hoofs Of Thunder" Better Little Book,**
1939. Whitman #1400. - **$18 $54 $125**

RYD-3

❑ **RYD-3. "Daisy Air Rifles" Catalogue,**
1940. Near Mint In Mailer - **$450**
Loose - **$85 $175 $375**

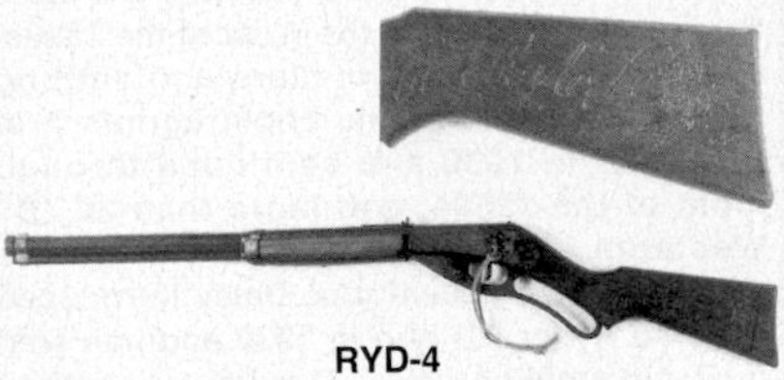
RYD-4

❑ **RYD-4. "Red Ryder" First Issue BB Rifle,**
c. 1940. 35.5" long Model 111-40 with cocking action, adjustable rear sight. Copper accent band on muzzle and stock were used for model produced only in 1940-1941. - **$125 $300 $600**

RYD-5

❑ **RYD-5. "Red Ryder And Western Border Guns" Better Little Book,**
1942. Whitman #1450. - **$17 $51 $120**

RYD-6 RYD-7

❑ **RYD-6. Victory Patrol Member Card,**
1943. Included in membership kit. Back has Red Ryder radio listings. - **$40 $75 $150**

❑ **RYD-7. Victory Patrol Magic V-Badge,**
1943. Scarce. Luminous cardboard badge. Ordered by sending coupon from membership kit. - **$75 $200 $425**

RYD-8

❑ **RYD-8. Membership Kit Promotion Sheet for Magic V-Badge,**
1943. Example shown has coupon to order and membership card trimmed off the bottom.
As Shown - **$30 $65 $125**

RYD-9

❑ **RYD-9. "Rodeomatic Radio Decoder",**
1943. Rare. Cut out and assembled from "Victory Patrol" kit.
Assembled - **$200 $400 $650**

RYD-10

❑ **RYD-10. Victory Patrol Membership Kit With Comic,**
1943. Langendorf Bread. Scarce. Includes cut-out "Rodeomatic" decoder, order coupon for "Magic V-Badge", cut-out membership card and membership certificate, comic book.
Complete - **$300 $900 $4400**

RYD-11

RYD-12

❑ **RYD-11. "Victory Patrol" Paper Store Signs,**
1944. Scarce. Langendorf Bread. Larger sign 7x15", smaller oval 4x5".
Picture Sign - **$100 $250 $400**
Oval Sign - **$30 $70 $140**

❑ **RYD-12. "Red Ryder Victory Patrol" Copper Luster Metal Badge,**
1944. - **$50 $110 $225**

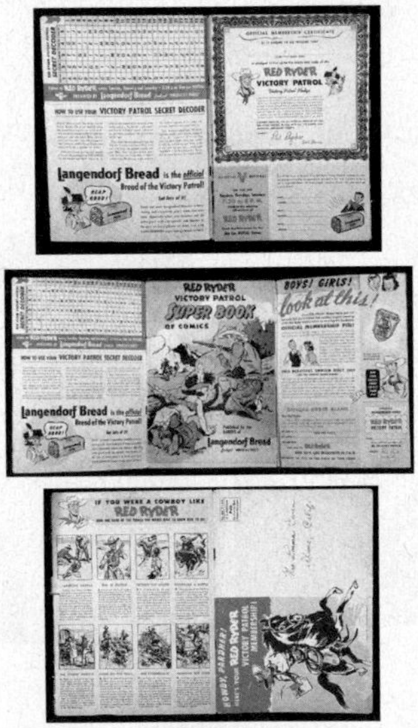

RYD-13

❑ **RYD-13. Victory Patrol Membership Kit With Comic,**
1944. Scarce. Includes membership card, map, comic book, code card and regular cards.
Complete - **$300 $900 $4400**

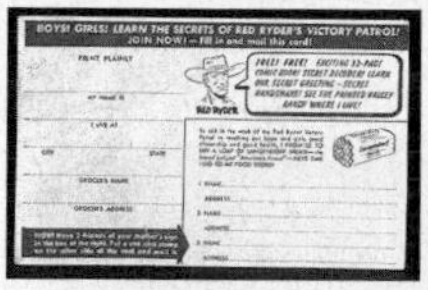

RYD-14

RYD-15

❑ RYD-14. Postcard,
1944. Langendorf Bread. Promotes Red Ryder Victory Patrol comic book and shows how to get other premiums. - **$25 $50 $100**

❑ RYD-15. "Bobby Blake/Little Beaver" Dixie Ice Cream Picture,
1945. - **$35 $65 $110**

RYD-16

RYD-17

❑ RYD-16. "War On The Range" BLB,
1945. Better Little Book #1473. - **$14 $42 $100**

❑ RYD-17. "Red Ryder and the Squaw-Tooth Rustlers" BLB,
1946. Big Little Book #1414. - **$14 $42 $100**

RYD-18

RYD-19

❑ RYD-18. "Red Ryder and Circus Luck" BLB,
1947. Big Little Book #1466. - **$13 $39 $90**

❑ RYD-19. "Red Ryder and the Rimrock Killer" BLB,
1948. Big Little Book #1443. - **$13 $39 $90**

RYD-20

RYD-21

❑ RYD-20. "Red Ryder and the Secret Canyon" BLB,
1948. Big Little Book #1454. Harman art. - **$13 $39 $90**

❑ RYD-21. Air Rifle Safety Litho. Button, c. 1948. Daisy Mfg. Co. Given with Red Ryder rifle and handbook. - **$10 $18 $35**

RYD-22

❑ RYD-22. "Daisy Handbook No. 2",
1948. - **$75 $200 $450**

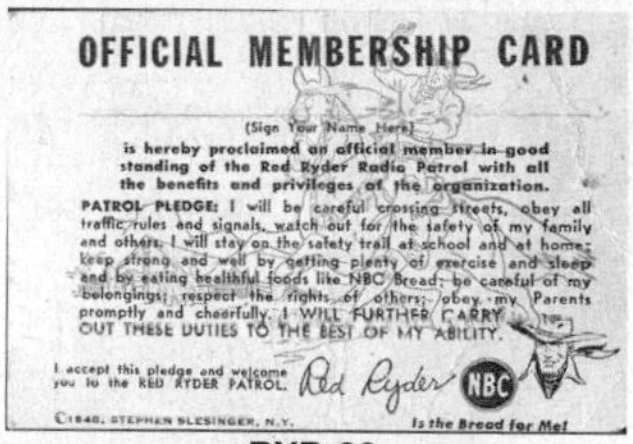

RYD-23

❑ RYD-23. "Red Ryder Radio Patrol" Member Card,
1948. NBC Bread. Accompanied member badge. See RYD-26. Card - **$30 $60 $150**
Badge - **$40 $80 $150**

RYD-24

❑ RYD-24. Red Ryder Hat,
1948. Red hat with yellow cloth band printed in red. One of the rarest of the cowboy character hats. - **$150 $300 $400**

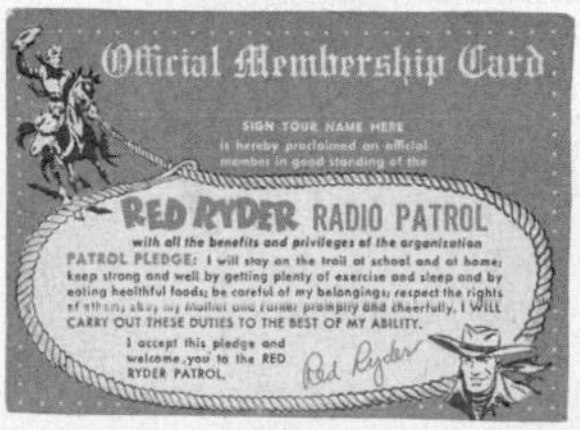

RYD-25

❑ RYD-25. Red Ryder Radio Patrol Membership Card,
c. 1948. Card is 2.75x3.75" printed on front with pledge for "Red Ryder Radio Patrol."
- **$50 $100 $160**

RYD-26

❑ RYD-26. "Red Ryder Radio Patrol" Badge,
c. 1948. NBC Bread. White metal accompanied by member card. See RYD-23. Badge - **$40 $80 $150**
Card - **$30 $60 $115**

RYD-27

❑ RYD-27. "Red Ryder Secret Pocket Billfold" Box,
1949. Box - **$30 $60 $115**
Wallet (Not Shown) - **$40 $80 $150**

RYD-28

❑ RYD-28. Pocketknife,
1940s. Store item by Camco USA. 3-1/2" long. Steel with plastic grips. - **$110 $225 $350**

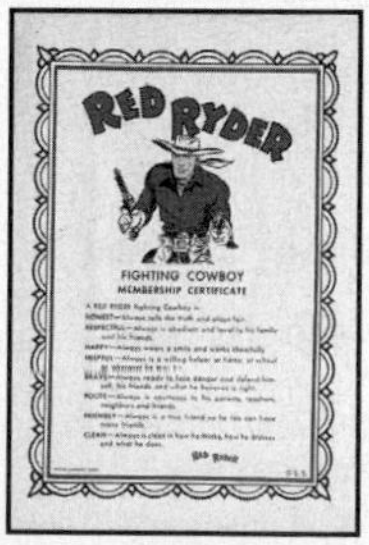

RYD-29

RYD-30

❑ **RYD-29. "Red Ryder Fighting Cowboy" Certificate,**
c. 1940s. Wells Lamont Corp., maker of Red Ryder gloves. Text details 10 qualities of character for youthful members. - **$50 $115 $250**

❑ **RYD-30. Salesman's Fiberboard Glove Case,**
1940s. Wells-Lamont Co. - **$125 $275 $500**

RYD-31

RYD-32

❑ **RYD-31. Radio Sponsor Handbill,**
1940s. N.B.C. Bread, probably others. Imprint includes local broadcast times. - **$40 $75 $150**

❑ **RYD-32. "Red Ryder" Cello. Button,**
1940s. - **$25 $55 $90**

RYD-33

RYD-34

RYD-35

❑ **RYD-33. "Little Beaver" Cello. Button,**
1940s. - **$18 $35 $70**

❑ **RYD-34. "Red Ryder Patrol" Silvered Metal Badge,**
1940s. - **$60 $115 $235**

❑ **RYD-35. "I Have Entered The Red Ryder Pony Contest" Litho. Button,**
1940s. - **$12 $20 $40**

RYD-36

RYD-37

RYD-38

❑ **RYD-36. Penney's "Red Ryder Lucky Coin",**
1940s. J. C. Penney Co. Brass, holed for key-chain. Back slogan "Penney's For Super Value". - **$10 $15 $30**

❑ **RYD-37. "Red Ryder Gloves" Silvered Tin Whistle,**
1940s. Wells-Lamont Co. - **$40 $80 $160**

❑ **RYD-38. "Red Ryder Gloves/Red Ryder Sheriff" Silvered Metal Star Badge,**
1940s. Probable Wells-Lamont Co. - **$125 $250 $425**

RYD-39

RYD-40

❑ **RYD-39. Red Ryder Tie,**
1940s. With cardboard slide. By Gold Seal.
Tie - **$25 $50 $100**
Paper Band - **$12 $25 $60**

❑ **RYD-40. Red Ryder/Little Beaver Fan Card,**
c. 1950. Fred Harman art. - **$18 $35 $65**

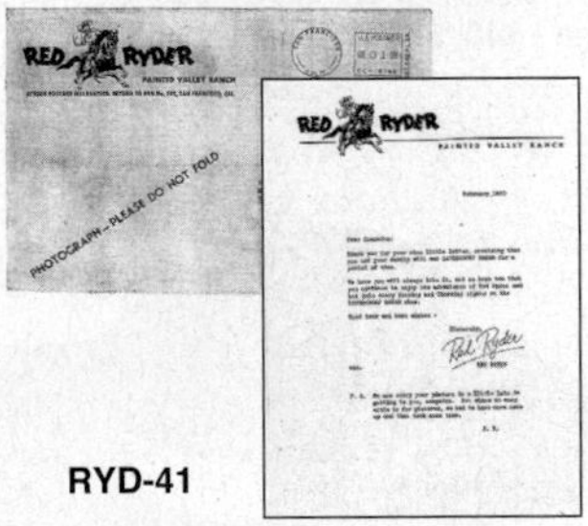

RYD-41

❑ **RYD-41. "Howdy Compadre" Photo and Letter,**
1950. Langendorf Bread. 5x7" photo with "Dear Compadre" letter as a thank-you for promising to eat Langendorf Bread.
Mailer - **$10 $20 $30**
Letter - **$20 $35 $70**
Photo - **$30 $60 $100**

RYD-42

❑ **RYD-42. "Little Beaver Buffalo Gun" Toy,**
c. 1950. Daisy Mfg. Co. 19" long. - **$75 $145 $300**

RYD-43

❑ **RYD-43. Red Ryder Gloves,**
1952. From the Wells-Lamont Company. - **$25 $75 $150**

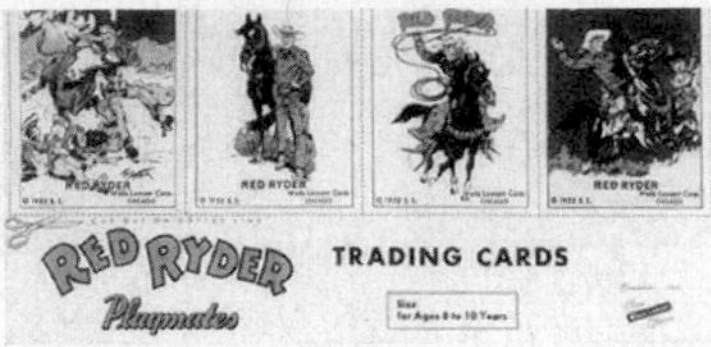

RYD-44

❑ **RYD-44. Trading Cards Sheet,**
1952. Wells-Lamont Corp.
Uncut. - **$25 $50 $100**

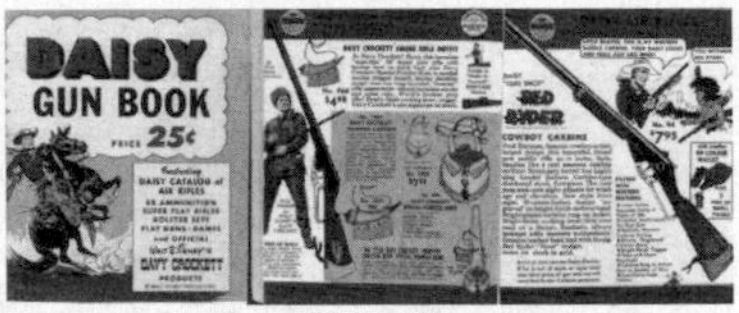

RYD-45

❑ **RYD-45. "Daisy Gun Book",**
1955. Daisy Mfg. Co. - **$50 $150 $300**

RYD-46

❑ **RYD-46. "Little Beaver's Complete 3 Game Set For Boys & Girls",**
1956. Store item by Red Ryder Enterprises. 6x11" box holds single board with three games plus accessories of six punch-out markers and pair of dice. - **$30 $50 $100**

RYD-47

RYD-48

❑ **RYD-47. "Good Luck/Red Ryder" Plastic Arrowhead Keychain Charm,**
1955. Daisy Mfg. Co. - **$25 $60 $150**

❑ **RYD-48. Contest Prize Figure Set,**
1956. One of 100 second place prizes in Wells Lamont contest for selling Red Ryder gloves. Plastic horse has "Red Ryder" name on each side of red saddle blanket and "Wells Lamont Co." on inner side of horse's rear leg. Indian also has company name on seat with design identical to Chief Thunderbird figure by Hartland Plastics Co. Includes accessories of war bonnet, tomahawk and knife.
Figure Complete - **$75 $150 $300**
Generic Mailing Box - **$20 $40 $75**

RYD-49

❑ **RYD-49. "Daisy Red Ryder BB Gun",**
1950s. - **$85 $190 $375**

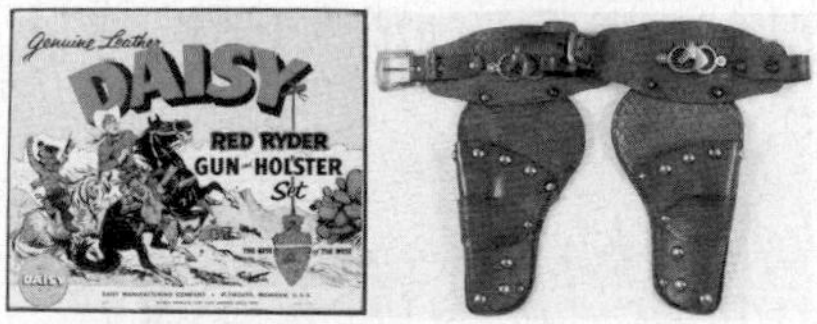

RYD-50

❑ **RYD-50. "Red Ryder Daisy" Holster Set Boxed,**
1950s. Illustrated box holding brown tooled leather double holster set #2531.
Box - **$125 $250 $400**
Holsters - **$125 $250 $400**

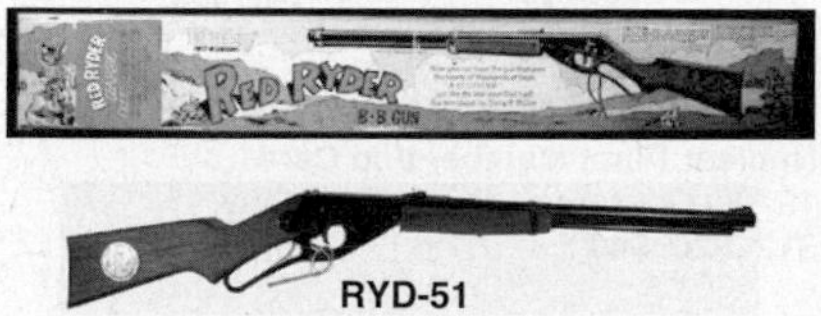

RYD-51

❑ **RYD-51. "Daisy Red Ryder Commemorative BB Gun with Box",**
1983. Gun has medal in the stock. Set includes reprint of the Red Ryder comic book's first issue. - **$350**

RYD-52

❑ **RYD-52. "Daisy Red Ryder Commemorative BB Gun with Box",**
2000. Model commemorates old issue of rifle. Has flat snub nose which is different than old model. New box design. - **$145**

Reddy Kilowatt

The friendly little fellow with a lightbulb for a nose and a lightning-bolt torso was created in 1926 by A.B. Collins of the Alabama Power Company. Designed to personify the electric power industry, Reddy was licensed freely to local power companies for promotional use, and his image has adorned a wide variety of items from ashtrays to soap, pinback buttons to comic books. A competing figure, Willie Wiredhand, was created in 1951 by the National Rural Electric Cooperative.

RKL-1

❑ **RKL-1. Counter Display Early Figure,**
c. 1935. 12" tall wood. - **$150 $275 $450**

RKL-2

RKL-3

❑ **RKL-2. Early Silvered Metal Badge With Red Accent,**
c. 1938. - **$50 $100 $160**

❑ **RKL-3. Glass Bubble Bank With Wood Base,**
c. 1940. 6" diameter glass dome holds diecut thick cardboard figure of Reddy. Base reads "Reddy Kilowatt Says: Bank On Electric Cooking To Save Your Money." - **$165 $350 $700**

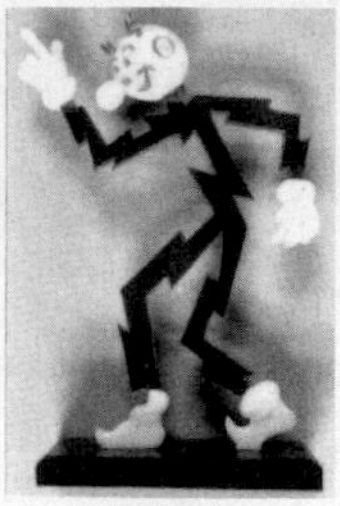
RKL-4

❑ **RKL-4. Translucent Plastic Figure,**
1940s. Earliest design style.
Pink - **$85 $150 $275**
1950s-60s design style.
Red - **$75 $125 $215**

RKL-5

RKL-6

❑ **RKL-5. Impressive Large Reddy Kilowatt Figural Floor Display,**
c. 1950. Display measures 53.75" tall overall. 45" tall x 27" wide large figure of Reddy Kilowatt. Constructed of.75" thick painted wood with paper mache hands, feet and head. Has 200 watt light bulb for a nose. Figure stands on a 8.75" tall, 22" diameter revolving base. Same Or Similar - **$1750 $3500 $6000**

❑ **RKL-6. "25th Anniversary Public Service" Cello. Button,**
1951. Public Service Co. of New Hampshire. - **$20 $40 $80**

RKL-7

❑ **RKL-7. "Your Favorite Pin-Up" Enameled Brass Pin On Card,**
1952. On Card - **$10 $15 $25**
Loose - **$3 $5 $12**

RKL-8

RKL-9

❑ **RKL-8. "Light's Diamond Jubilee" Cello. Button,**
1954. - **$20 $40 $75**

❑ **RKL-9. Cuff Links,**
c. 1950s. Color image under glass dome with brass frame and shaft. - **$30 $60 $120**

RKL-10

RKL-11

❑ **RKL-10. Fabric 8-1/2x11" Jacket Patch,**
1950s. Diecut flannel with stitched fabric image of Reddy Kilowatt as bowler. - **$40 $80 $150**

❑ **RKL-11. Cello. Button,**
c. 1950s. Canadian. - **$20 $50 $90**

RKL-12

❑ **RKL-12. Plastic Cookie Cutter With Card,**
c. 1950s. Boxed - **$15 $25 $45**
Loose - **$8 $18 $30**

RKL-13

❑ **RKL-13. "The Mighty Atom" Comic Book,**
1950s. Back cover may designate sponsoring electric utility company. - **$3 $9 $24**

RKL-14

RKL-15

❑ **RKL-14. "Sergeant Safety Deputy" Brass Badge,**
1950s. 2.5" tin star centered by Reddy wearing cowboy-style hat. - **$65 $135 $265**

❑ **RKL-15. Service Counter Figure,**
c. 1950s. 11" tall jigsawed wood figure in finished image both sides and wire spring clip on raised fingertip for holding card or leaflet. - **$125 $250 $500**

RKL-16

❑ **RKL-16. Figural Vinyl Bank,**
c. 1960. 3-1/2x5-1/2" tall by 6-1/2" wide 3-D image of him dashing through clouds with coin slot in rear, trap in bottom.
Near Mint With Both Plastic Lightning Bolt Head Accents - **$1200**
Missing Accents - **$165 $375 $600**

RKL-17

RKL-18

RKL-19

❑ **RKL-17. Glow-In-The-Dark Plastic Figure,**
1961. 1961 copyright on base. - **$75 $125 $215**

❑ **RKL-18. "Reddy" Composition Bobbing Head,**
1960s. - **$200 $400 $750**

❑ **RKL-19. Employee Bowling Trophy,**
1960s. Metal figure and award plate on wood base. - **$250 $500 $800**

RKL-20

❑ **RKL-20. Night Light,**
1960s. Relief image of Reddy with miniature light bulb nose. - **$25 $40 $80**

RKL-21

RKL-22

❑ **RKL-21. "Courteous Personal Attention To Every Customer" Litho. Button,**
1960s. - **$15 $25 $55**

❑ **RKL-22. Hard Plastic Electric Alarm Clock,**
1960s. Inscribed "Compliments of Philadelphia Light and Electric." - **$60 $125 $250**

RKL-23

❑ **RKL-23. Trophy-Style Statuette,**
c. 1960s. 3-D metal figure in action pose on 1.5" tall walnut wood base. Head, hands and feet are silver luster and body, arms and legs and other detail accents are gold and brass luster. - **$150 $285 $425**

RKL-24

RKL-26

RKL-25

❑ **RKL-24. "Inspectors Club Big Rock Point Nuclear Plant Membership Card",**
1970s. Consumers Power Company. - **$12 $20 $40**

❑ **RKL-25. "Mod Power" Litho. Tin Button,**
1970s. About 1-3/8" green and white on fuchsia background. - **$10 $20 $30**

❑ **RKL-26. Wacky Wobbler Figure,**
2000. Boxed. - **$60**

Reg'lar Fellers

Cartoonist Gene Byrnes (1889-1974) began his career as a sports cartoonist. By World War I he was doing a panel cartoon, *It's A Great Life If You Don't Weaken*, which was using kids regularly in the gags. Byrnes began the *Wide Awake Willie* Sunday page for the *New York Herald* in 1919 and by 1920 he had incorporated the gang of kids into *Reg'lar Fellers* as a daily and Sunday comic strip. The cast included: Jimmy Dugan, brothers Puddinhead and Pinhead Duffy, Angie Riley and Jimmy's dog Bullseye.

Noted Disney alumnus Ub Iwerks released *Happy Days*, based on *Reg'lar Fellers*, the last cartoon from his company in September, 1936.

Producers Releasing Corporation released a *Reg'lar Fellers* movie September 5, 1941. The notable cast included: Carl 'Alfalfa' Switzer, Dick Van Patten, Buddy Boles and Joyce Van Patten. NBC aired a summer radio show from June 8 to August 31, 1941.

Reg'lar Fellers ended in 1949 but the very prolific Gene Byrnes would go on to publish the book *A Complete Guide To Professional Cartooning* in 1950 with tips by top cartoonists including Hal Foster, Alex Raymond, Milton Caniff and Byrnes himself.

Reg'lar Fellers comic book appearances include the 1934 first issue of *Famous Funnies, Popular Comics* November, 1936 on, the first issue of *All-American Comics* in 1939, *Reg'lar Fellers Heroic Comics* #1-15, 1940-41 and *Reg'lar Fellers* #5 and #6, 1947-48.

RGF-1

❑ **RGF-1. "Jimmie Dugan And The Reg'lar Fellers" Reprint Book,**
1921. Cupples & Leon. 11x16" with 42 pages. - **$43 $171 $300**

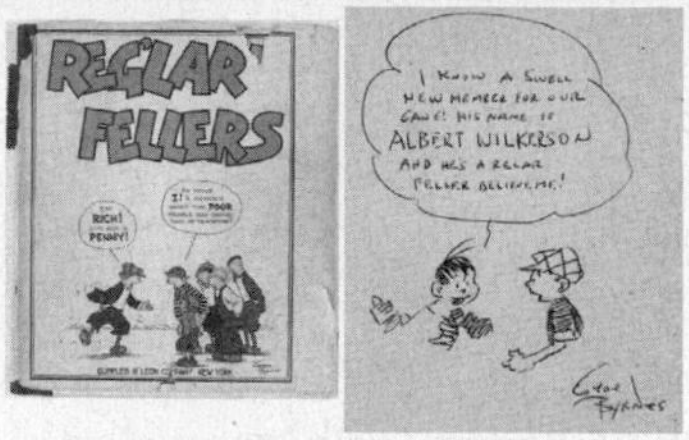

RGF-2

❑ **RGF-2. "Reg'lar Fellers" Autographed Book With Sketch And Dust Jacket,**
1930. Cupples & Leon. 7.5x8.75" hardcover with 88 pages of daily comic strips signed by artist-creator Gene Byrnes. Same Or Similar - **$100 $200 $300**

RGF-3

❑ **RGF-3. "Reg'lar Fellers" Boxed Paint Set,**
1932. American Toy Works, N.Y. 9.5x14-3/8x1.25" deep box has paint tablets glued in place, wooden paint brush, tin round palettes, 4 paper sheets, each 3.75x6.25". - **$20 $40 $85**

RGF-4

❑ **RGF-4. "Reg'lar Fellers Grand Piano" Toy,**
1933. 11x12x6" tall wooden piano with decal has 13 numbered keys. Marked on bottom "Made In Japan." - **$25 $50 $100**

RGF-5

❑ **RGF-5. "Reg'lar Fellers" BLB,**
1933. Whitman #754 or no number as Cocomalt premium. Each - **$12 $36 $87**

RGF-6

❑ **RGF-6. "Reg'lar Fellers" Pencil Box,**
1930s. Eagle Pencil Co. 6x10.75x1.25" deep box with metal snap. - **$15 $30 $60**

RGF-7

❑ **RGF-7. "Reg'lar Fellers Legion Of Honor" Litho. Button,**
1930s. Comic book premium. - **$25 $60 $125**

Renfrew of the Mounted

Inspector Douglas Renfrew of the Royal Canadian Mounties, the hero of a dozen adventure novels by Laurie York Erskine, came to CBS radio in 1936 with House Jamieson in the lead role, followed by Bud Collyer. Sponsored by Wonder bread for two years, the series then moved to the Blue network, where it was sustained until it went off the air in 1940. Renfrew movies, produced by Grand National Pictures and Monogram in the late 1930s and early 1940s starring Jim Newill, were edited into 30-minute tales for television syndication in 1953. While he lasted, the strong, silent Renfrew always got his man.

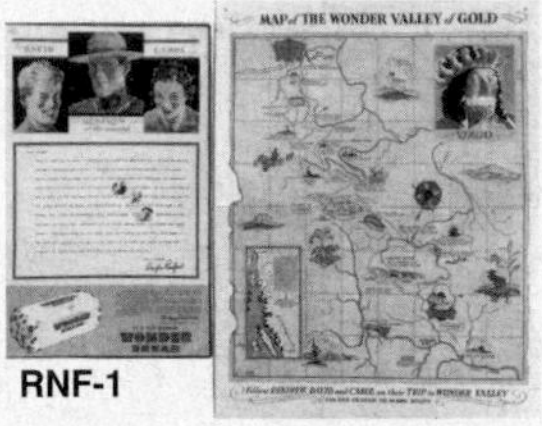

RNF-1

❑ **RNF-1. "Renfrew Of The Mounted" 17x22" Premium Map,**
1936. Wonder Bread. - **$45 $95 $200**

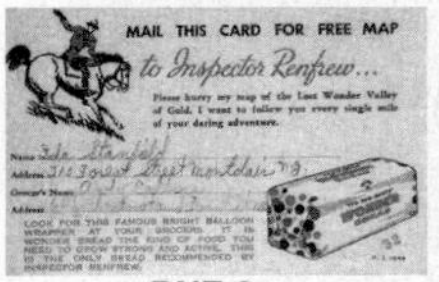

RNF-2

RNF-3

❑ **RNF-2. "Lost Wonder Valley Of Gold" Map Order Postcard,**
1936. Wonder Bread. Used to order previous item. - **$10 $20 $40**

❑ **RNF-3. "Around The Camp Fire With Carol And David" Leaflet,**
c. 1936. Wonder Bread. Illustrated magic tricks including "Tricks That Fooled Renfrew". - **$15 $30 $50**

RNF-4

❑ **RNF-4. Renfrew Sign 9 1/2 x 20",**
1936. Wonder Bread. Promotes radio show. - **$55 $135 $275**

RNF-5

❑ **RNF-5. Renfrew Radio Sponsor Folder,**
c. 1936. Wonder Bread. Four-page ad leaflet with mention on back for daily radio show. - **$10 $15 $30**

RNF-6

❑ **RNF-6. Fan Postcard,**
c. 1936. Wonder Bread. - **$25 $45 $80**

RNF-7

❑ **RNF-7. Renfrew Adventure Store Window Signs,**
c. 1936. Wonder Bread. Paper "Wanted" and "Missing" posters, each 11x17" from radio episode "The Sunken City Of The Arctic." Each - **$35 $70 $125**

RNF-8

❑ **RNF-8. Radio Program Debut Folder,**
c. 1936. Columbia Broadcasting System. Four-page leaflet previewing "Coming Thrills" plus mention of premium map and member badge. Card Only - **$40 $70 $115**

RNF-9

RNF-10

❑ **RNF-9. Wonder Bread Radio Show Paper Sign 10x17",**
c. 1936. - **$80 $160 $350**

❑ **RNF-10. "Renfrew Of The Mounted" Cello. Button,**
c. 1936. Wonder Bread. - **$5 $10 $15**

RNF-11

❑ **RNF-11. "Renfrew Of The Royal Mounted" Pressbook,**
1937. Large format 12x18" from Grand National Films Inc. Film starred Jimmy Newill as Renfrew. Eight pages including a single fold-out panel. - **$25 $45 $95**

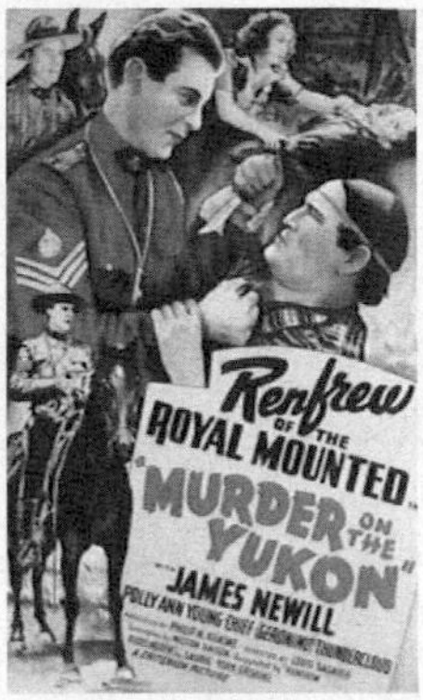

RNF-12

❑ **RNF-12. One-Sheet Movie Poster,**
1940. Criterion Pictures. 27x41" showing James Newill as Renfrew. - **$85 $145 $275**

The Rifleman

Created by Sam Peckinpah (1925-1984), who also wrote several episodes, the series was produced by Four Star Television and aired on ABC-TV from September 30, 1958 until April 8, 1963, 169 episodes over five seasons. The cast included Chuck Connors as rancher Lucas McCain, Johnny Crawford as son Mark and Paul Fix as Marshal Micah Torrance. The basic plot had Lucas and his trusty rapid firing Winchester Model 1892 rifle helping the Marshal save the town from outlaws and desperadoes while teaching his son lessons in morality in rural northern New Mexico in the 1880s.

Notable guest stars included Sammy Davis Jr., Dennis Hopper and James Coburn. Writers included Arthur Browne and Sam Clements. Directors included Joseph Lewis and Arnold Levin. Theme music was by Herschel Burke Gilbert.

Thanks to the series, Johnny Crawford had a successful recording career in the early 1960s with several pop hits on the Del-Fi record label.

Russian leader Leonid Breshnev allowed *The Rifleman* series to air during the Cold War and had a meeting with Chuck Connors at President Nixon's western White House in the early 1970s. Dell/Gold Key published 20 *Rifleman* comics between 1959 and 1964 with photo covers.

RIF-1

❑ **RIF-1. "The Rifleman Flip Special" Cap Rifle In Original Box,**
1958. Hubley. 8x33x2" deep box holds 32" metal and plastic rifle with caps.
Box - **$50 $100 $200**
Rifle - **$100 $200 $400**

RIF-2

❑ **RIF-2. "The Rifleman" Chuck Connors TV Adventure Book,**
1959. Whitman. 5.75x7.75" with 284 pages. - **$10 $20 $40**

RIF-3

❑ **RIF-3. "Rifleman" Frame Tray Puzzle,**
c. 1959. Whitman. 11-3/8x14-3/8" puzzle #4427. - **$12 $25 $50**

RIF-4

❑ **RIF-4. "The Rifleman" Lunchbox With Thermos,**
1960. Aladdin. 7x8x4" deep metal lunchbox with 6.5" metal thermos. Box - **$100 $200 $400**
Bottle - **$25 $50 $100**

Rin-Tin-Tin

The Wonder Dog was introduced to the world by Warner Brothers in 1923 and the talented German shepherd, an instant success, proved to be the studio's first major film star. There were a number of Rintys over the years, but the canine hero consistently battled villains and the elements, rescued those in danger, preserved his good name, turned into a noteworthy "actor"--and saved the studio from bankruptcy. Rinty starred in 19 films for Warner Brothers between 1923 and 1930, and went on to make a series of chapter plays for the Mascot studios.

On radio, *Rin-Tin-Tin* aired on the Blue network (1930-1933) and CBS (1933-1934), sponsored by Ken-L-Ration, and returned for a season on the Mutual network in 1955, sponsored by Milk Bone.

On television, Rinty joined young Corporal Rusty and the troopers of the 101st Cavalry, the Fighting Blue Devils, in maintaining law and order in the West of the 1880s. The cast included: Rinty trained by Lee Duncan, Lee Aaker as Rusty, Joe Sawyer as Sgt. Biff O'Hara, James Brown as Lt. Rip Masters and Rand Brooks as Cpl. Randy "Kit" Boone. The hit series, sponsored by the National Biscuit Company, aired in prime time on ABC from 1954 to 1959 and was the source of a wide variety of premiums and licensed products. Reruns were broadcast on ABC (1959 to 1961) and CBS (1962 to 1964), and sepia-tinted episodes were offered briefly for syndication in 1976. Comic books appeared during most of the 1950s and early 1960s.

RIN-1

❑ **RIN-1. Fan And Premium Photo,**
1927. 5x7" with text "Most Faithfully Rin-Tin-Tin/ Lee Duncan Master And Friend." Issued dated 1927 and again dated 1930 or 1931 with ink stamp of his radio show sponsor Ken-L-Ration on the reverse. - **$10 $20 $35**

RIN-2

❑ **RIN-2. "A Race For Life" Silent Movie Slide,**
1920s. 3.25x4" cardboard mount holding glass transparency picture of Rin-Tin-Tin featured in Warner Bros. movie. - **$15 $30 $60**

RIN-3

RIN-4

❑ **RIN-3. "King Of Canines" Button,**
c. 1930. 1-1/2" black and white with title applying to his fame rather than a movie title. - **$35 $75 $150**

❑ **RIN-4. Movie Promotional Button,**
1930. 7/8" brown on yellow. - **$20 $40 $80**

RIN-5

RIN-6

❑ **RIN-5. "The Lone Defender" Cello. Button,**
1930. 1-1/4" diameter. For Mascot Pictures 12-chapter movie serial. - **$30 $50 $135**

❑ **RIN-6. "The Lightning Warrior" Movie Serial Cello. Button,**
1931. Mascot Pictures. Comes in 7/8" or 1-1/4" sizes. - **$25 $45 $90**

RIN-7

RIN-8

❑ **RIN-7. Fan Club Pin-Back,**
1931. Warner Bros. 1-1/4" with color portrait plus diecut cardboard attachment forming his body. Complete - **$45 $85 $165**
Pin-Back Only, No Body - **$20 $40 $85**

❑ **RIN-8. "Rin-Tin-Tin In An All Talking Serial The Lightning Warrior" Movie Herald,**
1931. - **$20 $35 $70**

RIN-9

❑ **RIN-9. Invitation To Join Fan Club,**
1931. Flyer for button premium - **$30 $60 $100**

RIN-10

RIN-11

❑ **RIN-10. Photo With Mailer,**
1931. Fan Club movie premium. Photo of two dogs. - **$25 $40 $85**

❑ **RIN-11. "What Every Dog Should Know" Booklet,**
c. 1931. Ken-L-Ration. - **$25 $40 $85**

RIN-12

❑ **RIN-12. Rin Tin Tin Carnival Statue,**
1930s. Red base with name on bottom.
- **$85 $165 $265**

RIN-13

RIN-14

❑ **RIN-13. Advertising Litho. Button,**
1930s. Atwater Kent Radios. - **$40 $75 $125**

❑ **RIN-14. Rin Tin Tin III Postcard,**
1940s. Premium promotes Camp Haan Training Center. - **$15 $30 $60**

RIN-15

❑ **RIN-15. Club Membership Kit,**
1954. Nabisco. Includes fabric banner, membership card, white metal badge.
Complete Near Mint - **$450**
Banner - **$60 $100 $225**
Card - **$15 $35 $75**
Badge - **$20 $40 $90**

RIN-16

❑ **RIN-16. Shredded Wheat Box,**
1954. Nabisco. Shows Rin Tin Tin and Rusty on front. Back shows cast and promotes radio and TV show. - **$60 $125 $275**

RIN-17

❑ **RIN-17. Stereo Cards With Viewer,**
1954. Nabisco. Set of 24 cards.
Viewer - **$15 $30 $50**
Card Set - **$40 $60 $125**

RIN-18

❑ **RIN-18. Toy Dog Premium,**
1954. Nabisco. Premium plush and vinyl toy dog. 10" long. A 17" store bought version was released in 1959.
1954 Small Version Dog - **$50 $100 $250**

RIN-19

❑ **RIN-19. Magic Brass Ring,**
c. 1954. Nabisco. Portrait cover opens over two miniature felt pads. Came with magic pencil and chemically treated paper strips.
Complete Boxed - **$200 $350 $650**
Ring Only - **$60 $115 $235**
Magic Pencil Only - **$40 $110 $185**
Instructions Only - **$40 $75 $160**

RIN-20

RIN-21

❑ **RIN-20. Nabisco "Wonda-Scope",**
c. 1954. Components include compass, mirror, magnifying lenses. Dial marked "Rin-Tin-Tin". - **$20 $40 $85**

❑ **RIN-21. "Bugle Calls" Vinyl Cardboard Record,**
1955. Nabisco. Came with plastic bugle premium. - **$15 $25 $50**

RIN-22

❑ **RIN-22. Cereal Box With Plastic Rings Offer,**
1955. Gordon Gold Archives.
Used Complete - **$75 $165 $375**

RIN-23

❑ **RIN-23. "Rusty's Golden Bugle" Box With Bugle And Attachment,**
1955. Store item by Spec-Toy-Culars. Set Includes "Bugle Book" instructions.
Near Mint Complete - **$350**

RIN-24

RIN-25

❑ **RIN-24. Jack Knife Store Display Card,**
1955. - **$75 $135 $250**

❑ **RIN-25. Plastic On Steel Pocketknife,**
1955. Store item by Colonial. Two varieties: Either same photo on both grips or photo on one side and Morse Code chart on the opposite side (pictured). Each - **$40 $90 $185**

RIN-26

RIN-27

❑ **RIN-26. Nabisco Plastic Rings,**
1955. Set of 12: Cochise, Cpl. Boone, Fort Apache, Geronimo, Lt. Rip Masters, Major Swanson, Rin-Tin-Tin (front view), Rin-Tin-Tin (side view), Rinty & Rusty, Rusty, Rusty's Horse, and Sgt. Biff O'Hara.
Each - **$12 $18 $35**

❑ **RIN-27. Nabisco Cast Photo,**
c. 1955. - **$12 $25 $50**

RIN-28

❑ **RIN-28. Nabisco Cereal Promotion Folder,**
c. 1955. 9x12-3/4" folder opens to 18x23" printed largely in yellow, red, white and blue. Urges grocer participation in publicity program tied to Rin-Tin-Tin popularity. Shows example window poster and shelf card picturing the Rin-Tin-Tin plastic premium rings. Gordon Gold Archives. - **$75 $135 $250**

RIN-29

❑ **RIN-29. "Rusty" Boxed Costume,**
c. 1955. Store item by Ben Cooper.
Near Mint Boxed - **$190**
Mask And Costume Only - **$30 $60 $150**

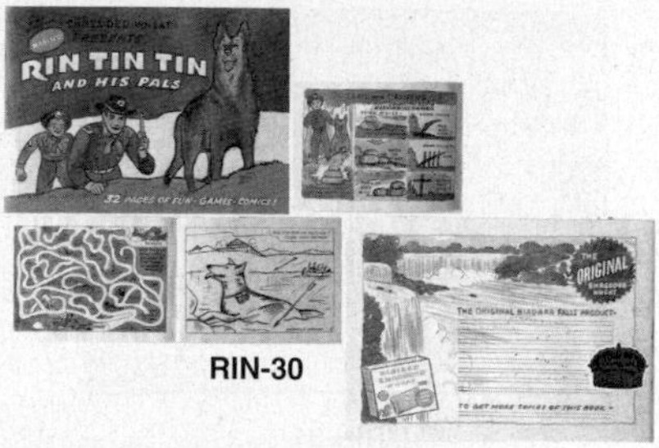

RIN-30

❑ **RIN-30. "Rin-Tin-Tin And His Pals" Original Art Prototype Nabisco Ac tivity Book,**
c. 1955. 5x7" completely hand-illustrated and colored 32-page booklet proposed as Nabisco Shredded Wheat premium. Gordon Gold Archives. Unique. - **$650**

RIN-31

RIN-32

❑ **RIN-31. English Postcard,**
c. 1955. - **$10 $20 $35**

❑ **RIN-32. "Rusty" Tin/Plastic Palm Puzzle,**
1956. From "Nabisco Juniors" set of 12: Army Wagon, Cochise, Conestoga Wagon, Fighting Blue Devils 101st Cavalry, Geronimo, Lt. Rip Masters, 101st Cavalry Trooper, Rinty & Rusty, RIn-Tin-Tin (close-up portrait), Rin-Tin-Tin (full body portrait), Rusty ("Go Rinty!"), and Sgt. Biff O'Hara. Each - **$8 $15 $30**

(BOARD)

RIN-33

❏ **RIN-33. "Adventures of RinTinTin" Game,**
1956. Transogram Product. Has colorful board and pieces. - **$60 $120 $175**

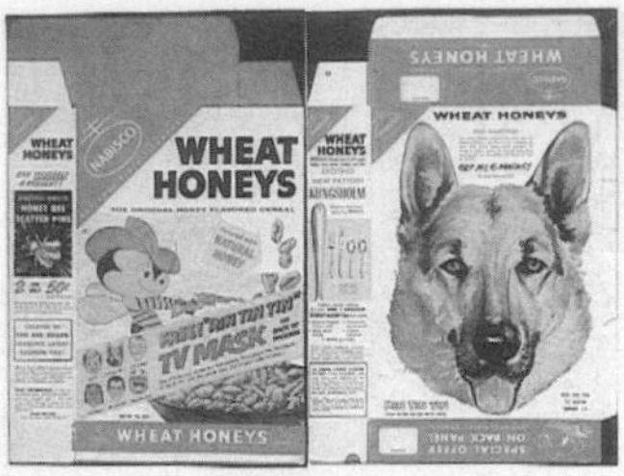

RIN-34

❏ **RIN-34. Cereal Box With Cut-Out Mask,**
1956. This is "Series 1" from a set of six to be cut from box back panels.
Each Used Complete Box - **$75 $150 $300**

RIN-35

❏ **RIN-35. "Rin Tin Tin And Rusty Fighting Blue Devils" Nabisco Cereal Premium T-Shirt,**
1956. Coach. Size "Small" measures 13" wide by 14.5" tall. Offered as a premium for 50-cents and one Nabisco Shredded Wheat box top. Scarce. - **$50 $100 $200**

RIN-36

❏ **RIN-36. Felt Cavalry Hat,**
1956. Nabisco. Fabric patch on brim front. - **$60 $135 $240**

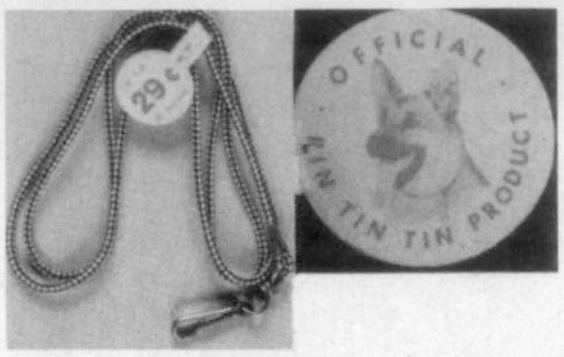

RIN-37

❏ **RIN-37. "Rin-Tin-Tin" Dog Leash,**
1956. Store item with tag. - **$18 $35 $70**

RIN-38

❏ **RIN-38. Sweatshirt With Box Insert Offer Card,**
1956. Heavy cotton with 6x9-1/2" image area. Card insert is green ink on gray cardboard offering shirt for one box top plus $1.
Shirt - **$75 $200 $350**
Card - **$4 $8 $15**

RIN-39

RIN-40

❏ **RIN-39. Club Member's Cello. Button,**
c. 1956. Dairy Fresh. 1-1/2" black on cream. - **$40 $85 $175**

❏ **RIN-40. Gun And Holster,**
1956. Nabisco. Includes gun and leather holster with belt and buckle. Belt - **$20 $40 $100**
Holster - **$30 $100 $200**
Gun - **$65 $150 $400**

RIN-41

❏ **RIN-41. Nabisco Box Insert Cards,**
1956. At least 12 different examples.
Each - **$4 $8 $15**

RIN-42

❏ **RIN-42. "Rin-Tin-Tin At Fort Apache" Playset,**
1956. Store item by Marx Toys.
Complete - **$200 $450 $950**

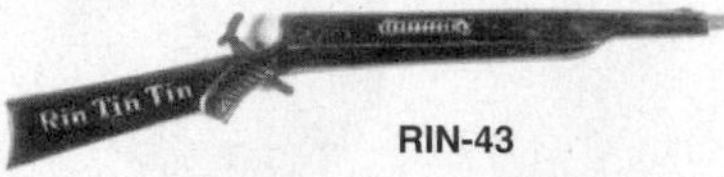

RIN-43

❏ **RIN-43. Cavalry Rifle Ballpoint Pen,**
1956. Nabisco. Near Mint with Flier In Mailer - **$165**
Rifle Pen Only - **$8 $15 $30**

(box front)

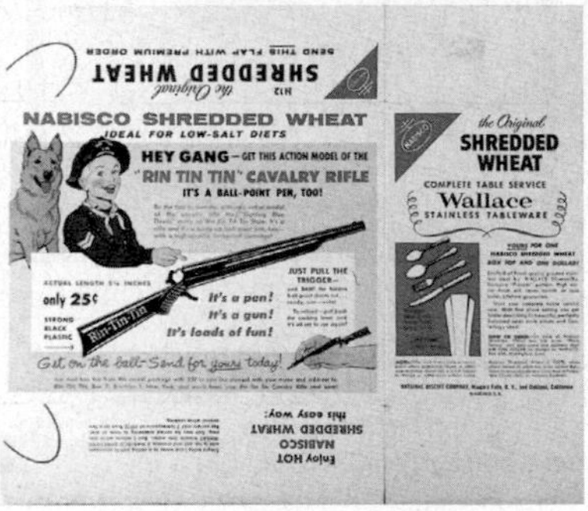

(back of box - enlarged)

RIN-44

❏ **RIN-44. Shredded Wheat Cereal 12 oz. Box Flat with Cavalry Rifle Ballpoint Pen Offer,**
1956. Nabisco. 12 oz. box. - **$75 $150 $300**

RIN-45

❑ **RIN-45. Shredded Wheat Cereal 6 oz. Box Flat with Cavalry Rifle Ballpoint Pen Offer,**
1956. Nabisco. 6 oz. box is much scarcer. Box is 7 1/2" high by 4 1/2" - **$110 $225 $425**

RIN-46

RIN-47

❑ **RIN-46. Plastic Mug,**
1956. - **$18 $35 $75**

❑ **RIN-47. Plastic Cup,**
1956. - **$15 $30 $65**

RIN-48

❑ **RIN-48. "Telegraph Key" Cereal Box Flat,**
1956. Plastic premium came in the package and back panel includes listing of proper clicks for 10 different messages. Gordon Gold Archives.
Near Mint Flat - **$350**
Used Complete - **$75 $150 $300**

RIN-49

RIN-50

❑ **RIN-49. Cast Member Photo,**
c. 1956. - **$12 $20 $40**

❑ **RIN-50. Color Litho. Button,**
1956. Sent to participants in Nabisco's 'Name The Puppy Contest.' - **$10 $20 $35**

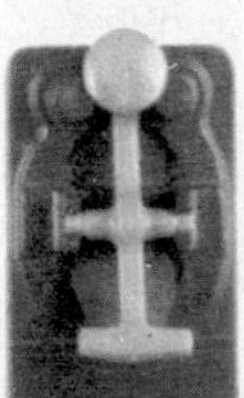
RIN-51

RIN-52

❑ **RIN-51. Miniature Plastic Telegraph Set,**
1956. Nabisco. Tapper key makes clicking sound. - **$10 $15 $30**

❑ **RIN-52. "101st Cavalry" Plastic Canteen With Strap,**
1957. Nabisco. - **$12 $25 $55**

RIN-53

❑ **RIN-53. Litho. Button,**
1957. Probable vending machine issue. 7/8" with browntone photo on various single-color backgrounds. From a larger set of western TV stars, probably totaling 14 different. -
$18 $35 $75

RIN-54

❑ **RIN-54. Cereal Box With Coloring Panel,**
c. 1958. Nabisco Shredded Wheat. -
$60 $125 $250

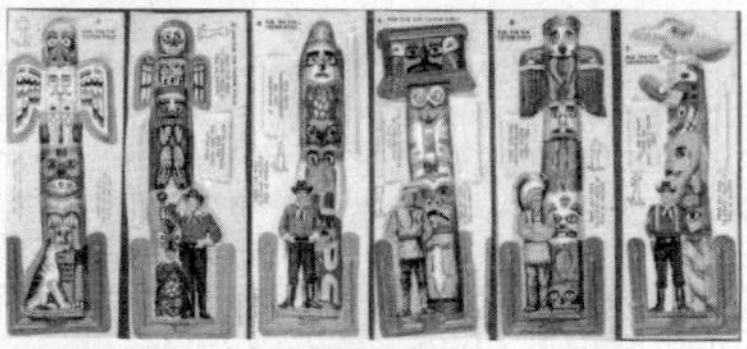
RIN-55

❑ **RIN-55. Totem Pole Plastic Punch-Outs,**
1958. Nabisco. Set of eight.
Each Unpunched - **$10 $20 $40**

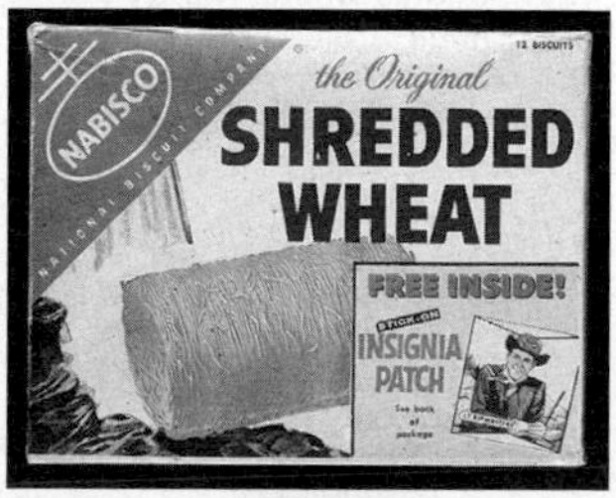

RIN-56

❑ **RIN-56. Shredded Wheat Box,**
1958. Nabisco. Lt. Rip Masters on front. Offers insignia patch. Back of box shows picture of all seven patches. - **$60 $125 $250**

RIN-57

❑ **RIN-57. Insignia Patch,**
1958. Nabisco, paper peel-off stickers. Set of seven: Cochise, Fort Apache, Lt. Rip Masters, Major Swanson, Rin Tin Tin, Rusty, and Sgt. O'Hara. Each Unused - **$8 $15 $30**

RIN-58

❑ **RIN-58. Plush And Vinyl Toy Dog with Tag,**
1959. Smile Novelty Co. Store bought item, about 17" long. Smaller (10") version was released in 1954 as a Nabisco premium.
1959 Large Version Dog - **$60 $125 $275**
Tag - **$18 $30 $60**

RIN-59

❑ **RIN-59. "Indian Totem Pole" Cereal Box,**
1958. Gordon Gold Archives.
Near Mint Flat - **$300**
Used Complete - **$60 $100 $250**

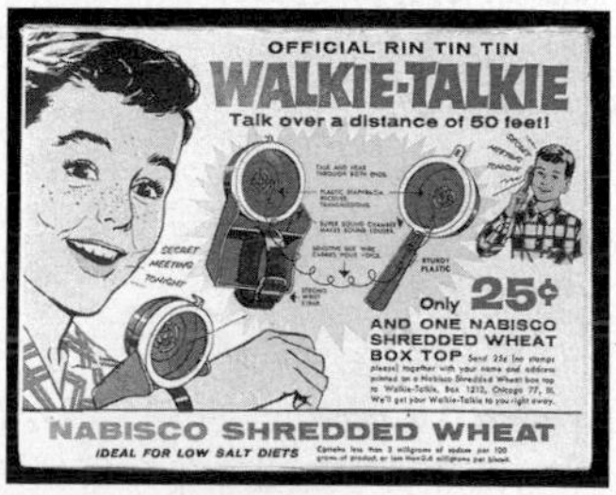

RIN-60

❑ **RIN-60. Cereal Box,**
1950s. Nabisco Shredded Wheat premium. Shows walkie talkie offer for 25¢ and box top. - **$70 $160 $300**

RIN-61

❑ **RIN-61. "Rin Tin Tin" Real Photo Button,**
1950s. 1.5" black and white cello photo without dot pattern, rare issue for the era. - **$45 $90 $175**

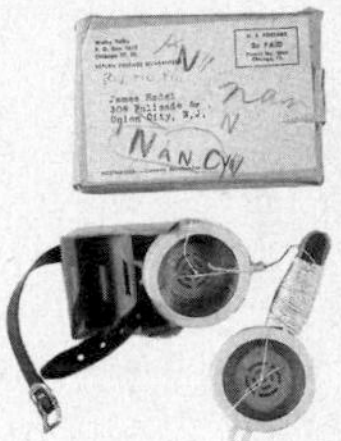

RIN-62

RIN-63

❑ **RIN-62. Walkie Talkies And Mailer,**
1950s. Nabisco Shredded Wheat premium. Also enclosed plastic belt for wrist to hold walkie-talkies - **$85 $165 $350**

❑ **RIN-63. Cast Photo,**
1950s. Movie premium. - **$30 $60 $90**

RIN-64

❑ **RIN-64. Cereal Box With Medal Ads,**
1960. Nabisco Wheat Honeys. Front and back panels picture and describe "Indian Wars Medal" and "Frontier Hero" medals offered as box inserts. - **$75 $150 $300**

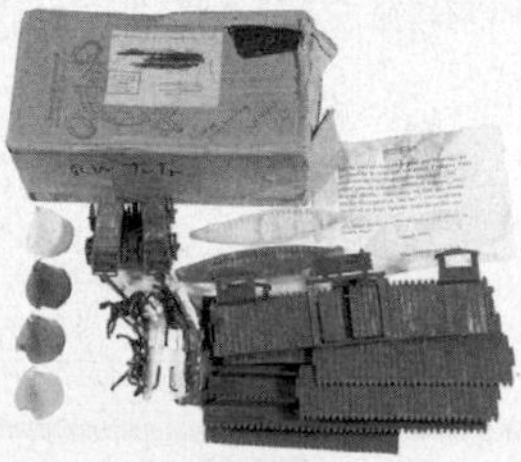

RIN-65

❑ **RIN-65. Fort Set,**
1960. Honeycomb Cereal premium. Plastic Ft. Apache with horses, wagons, teepees, canoes, instruction letter and box. Has printed name mistake at top on front of plastic fort. Says Fort Boone instead of Fort Apache. - **$100 $200 $350**

RIN-66

❑ **RIN-66. Rin-Tin-Tin Related Vacuum-Form Medals,**
c. 1960. Nabisco Rice Honeys and Wheat Honeys. Believed to have been offered while Nabisco sponsored the show but no reference to Rin-Tin-Tin on items or cereal box. Set of eight with four in "Indian Wars" series from Wheat Honeys, four in "Frontier Hero" series from Rice Honeys. Each - **$12 $25 $50**

Rings Misc.

Kids love to wear rings, and the sponsors of radio programs and their merchandisers, particularly cereal makers, learned that offering a ring related to their heroes was sure to bring in a flood of box tops. Hardly a radio character in the 1930s and 1940s could get through a season without a special ring premium offer. There were rings with secret compartments, glow-in-the-dark rings, flashlight rings, magnifying-glass rings, whistle rings, saddle rings, compass rings, magnet rings, rocket rings, decoder rings, baseball rings, movie rings, microscope rings, treasure rings, cannon rings, weather rings, and membership rings, along with rings bearing photos, faces, and logos. Collecting premium rings has become a specialty of its own. (For more information, refer to *The Overstreet Toy Ring Price Guide*, 3rd edition.)

RGS-1

❑ **RGS-1. "Rosalie Gimple" Brass Ring,**
1936. Rare. Pabst-ett cheese food. Depicts air hostess. - **$250 $650 $1200**

RGS-2

(Cereal Box) (Cover)
RGS-3

(Inside)

❑ **RGS-2. "Huskies Club" Brass Ring,**
1937. Post's Huskies Cereal. Top depicts discus thrower, bands picture various sports equipment. - **$150 $300 $600**

❑ **RGS-3. "Huskies Club" Brochure,**
1937. Post's Huskies Cereal. Lou Gehrig photo on cover. Inside displays prizes and athletes. - **$85 $135 $225**
Cereal Box - **$35 $65 $135**

RGS-4

RGS-5

❑ **RGS-4. "Murray-Go-Round" Brass Spinner Ring,**
1937. Fleischmann's Yeast for Arthur Murray Dance Studios. Disk pictures male dancer on one side, female on other. They appear to unite in dance when disk is spun. - **$30 $60 $120**

❑ **RGS-5. "Murray-Go-Round Ring" Folder,**
1937. Radio sponsor Fleischmann's Yeast. - **$20 $40 $65**

RGS-7 RGS-8

RGS-6

❑ **RGS-6. "Base Ball Centennial" Brass Ring,**
1939. Quaker Puffed Rice. Also offered in 1938 by General Mills as Jack Armstrong premium from July 27, 1938 to October 28, 1938 with company recording 46,501 responses. Quaker offered manufacturer's remainder in 1939. -
$250 $500 $1000

❑ **RGS-7. Chicago "Cubs" Gold Luster Metal Ring,**
1930s. Cubs name accented in blue, bands have baseball motifs. - **$60 $110 $200**

❑ **RGS-8. Lucky Sheik Brass Ring,**
1930s. Catalogue item from Johnson & Smith Novelty Co. Coiled snake design around Pharoh's head plus tiny accent stones. -
$75 $150 $300

RGS-9

❑ **RGS-9. "Majestic" Radio Company School Class Graduation Ring,**
1930s. Black bakelite-like substance inlaid by aluminum text and designs including "Majestic-The World In Your Home." Known in serveral different colors. - **$65 $165 $335**

RGS-10

❑ **RGS-10. "Walnetto's Tribe" Candy Premium Initial Ring,**
1930s. Brass with adjustable bands. Initial "L" on top has red accent. Club name is on each side with one side depicting a Thunderbird Indian symbol and the other an Indian-style drawing of a horse. A 1930s premium from the maker of chocolate and walnut candy still in production today. - **$200 $400 $600**

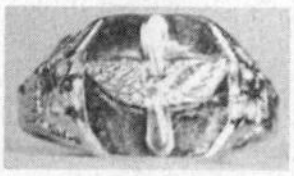

RGS-11 RGS-12 RGS-13

❑ **RGS-11. "Junior Broadcasters Club" Brass Ring,**
1930s. Top depicts radio microphone, bands depict radio transmission towers. -
$40 $75 $150

❑ **RGS-12. Kool-Aid "Treasure Hunt" Brass Ring,**
1940. - **$60 $125 $275**

❑ **RGS-13. Sky Birds Army Air Corps Ring,**
1941. Sky Birds Bubble Gum by Goudey. Brass insignia on silver luster base with adjustable bands. - **$30 $60 $135**

(closed) (open)

RGS-14

❑ **RGS-14. Viking Magnifying Ring,**
1941. Rare. Kellogg's All Rye Flakes. Brass with magnifying glass to view Prince "Valric Of The Vikings". Very limited distribution. -
$3000 $5000 $10,000

RGS-15

❑ **RGS-15. "Valric Of The Vikings" Premium Ring Advertisement,**
1941. Kellogg's. 10.75x15" advertisement from newpaper comic strip section that advertises the Valric of the Vikings Magnifying ring. The ring saw very limited distribution and this advertisement notes Los Angeles California address on the order form. - **$60 $125 $250**

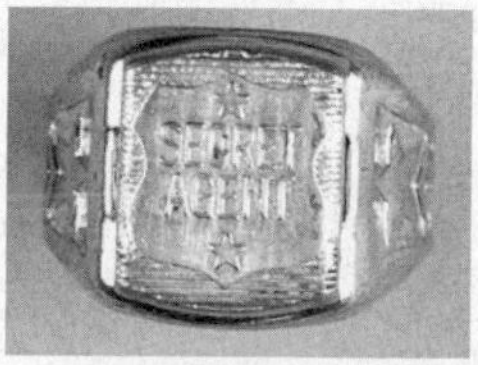

RGS-16

❑ **RGS-16. "Secret Agent" Look-Around Prototype Ring,**
c. 1941. This ring has the same base as the Orphan Annie Mystic Eye Ring and the Lone Ranger National Defenders Ring. Like those, this has a compartment on the top containing a mirror and the ring is used by looking into a small slot on the front edge and then whatever is at the far right can be seen on the interior mirror. Ring top reads "Secret Agent" with a pair of star accents. Just a few are known.
- **$500 $1000 $2500**

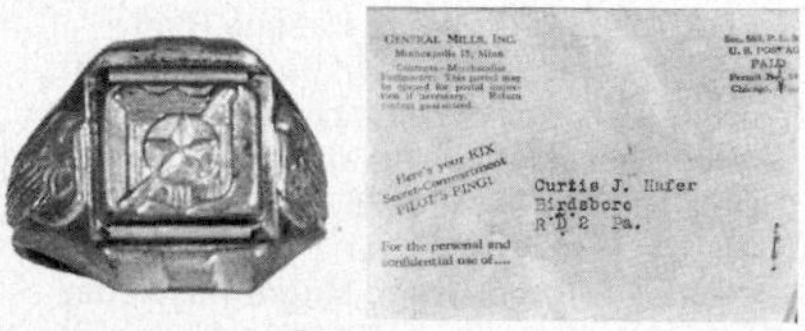

RGS-17

❑ **RGS-17. Kix Pilot's Ring,**
1945. Brass secret compartment ring with slide-off top. Also issued in 1942 as Capt. Midnight ring. See item CMD-48.
Envelope - **$15 $30 $70**
Ring - **$70 $135 $265**

RGS-18

❑ **RGS-18. Peter Paul Glow Ring,**
c. 1946. Premium ring from candy maker featuring plastic stone on top that both glows in the dark and is removable so that hollowed-out inside serves as a secret compartment. Ring is made quite similar to the Sky King Radar Ring but this ring has numerous good luck symbols on each side of the ring base. When the cover is slid off the top, a profile image of an elephant with his trunk above his head is revealed.
- **$225 $450 $1000**

RGS-19

❑ **RGS-19. "His Nibs Compass Ring" On Card,**
1947. Nabisco. Ring - **$20 $30 $70**
Card - **$25 $45 $75**

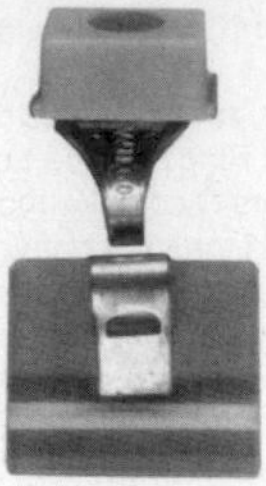
RGS-20

RGS-21

❑ RGS-20. Roger Wilco Rescue Ring,
1948. Power House Candy. Brass base with glow-in-dark plastic top which fits over brass whistle. Boxed near mint with Instructions - **$650**
Ring Complete - **$85 $175 $350**

❑ RGS-21. Roger Wilco Magni-Ray Brass Ring,
1948. Power House candy bar. Paper insert which glows in dark under hinged cover. - **$45 $90 $200**

RGS-22

❑ RGS-22. F-87 Super Jet Plane Ring.
1948. Kellogg's Corn Flakes. Black plastic plane on nickel-plated ring. Advertised on Superman radio program but no other association.
Ring - **$60 $135 $225**
Instructions - **$55 $110 $165**

RGS-23

RGS-24

❑ RGS-23. Jet Plane Ring,
1948. Kellogg's Pep. Brass bands, metal airplane shoots off ring by spring lever. Advertised on Superman radio program but no other association. - **$75 $150 $275**

❑ RGS-24. Fireball Twigg Explorer's Ring,
1948. Post Cereals. Brass bands hold glow-in-dark plastic sundial under clear plastic dome. Boxed near mint with Instructions - **$225**
Ring Only - **$30 $60 $125**

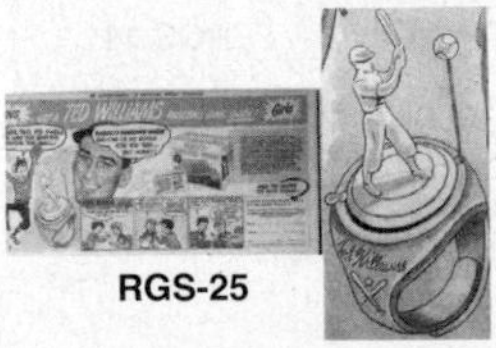

RGS-25

❑ RGS-25. "Ted Williams Baseball Ring" Newspaper Ad,
1948. Nabisco Shredded Wheat. - **$12 $25 $50**

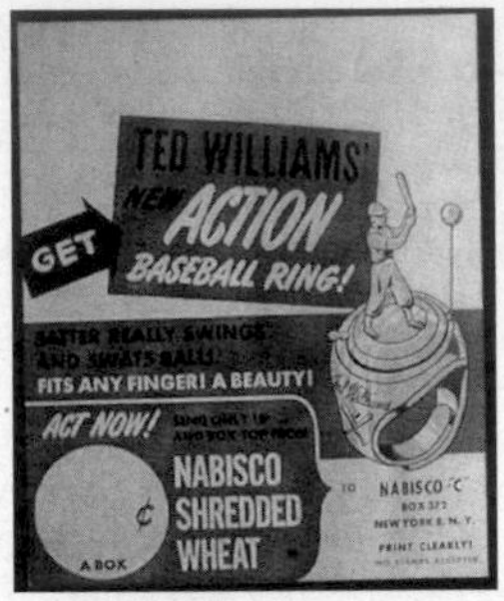

RGS-26

❑ RGS-26. "Ted Williams' Action Baseball Ring" Sign,
1948. 10-1/4x12". - **$175 $325 $650**

RGS-27

RGS-28

❑ RGS-27. "Ted Williams" Mechanical Ring,
1948. Nabisco. Plastic batter figure moves by spring in brass base. - **$200 $400 $800**

❑ RGS-28. "Andy Pafko" Baseball Scorer Brass Ring,
1949. Muffetts cereal. Named for Chicago Cubs star, top has three turning wheels for counting balls, outs, strikes. - **$60 $115 $210**

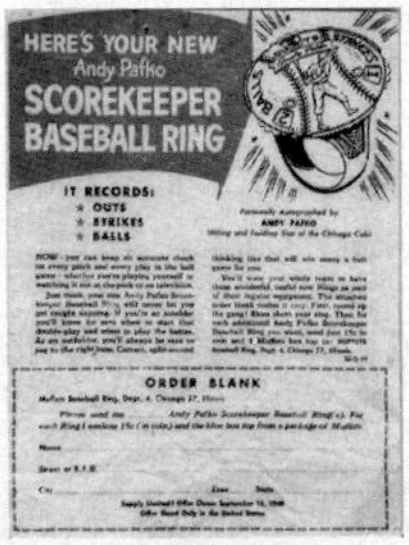

RGS-29

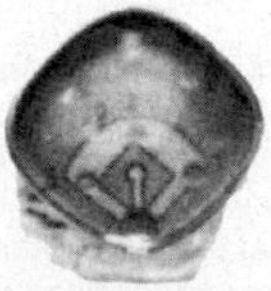
RGS-30

❑ RGS-29. "Scorekeeper Baseball Ring" Order Blank,
1949. Mechanical ring featuring Andy Pafko of Chicago Cubs. - **$25 $40 $80**

❑ RGS-30. Baseball Game Mechanical Ring,
1949. Kellogg's. Silvered metal capped by diamond-shaped plastic compartment with lever action for game of miniature palm puzzle nature. - **$50 $100 $225**

RGS-31

RGS-32

❑ RGS-31. Your Name Ring,
1949. Kellogg's Rice Krispies. Brass bands with good luck symbols hold plastic dome over paper with personalized first name designated by orderer. - **$15 $25 $50**

❑ RGS-32. Glow-In-Dark "Flying Tigers Rescue Ring",
c. 1949. Red or yellow plastic base with glow-in-dark top featuring secret compartment holding tiny brass whistle. - **$100 $200 $385**

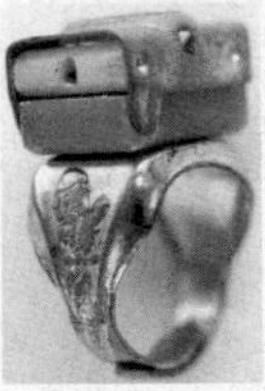
RGS-33

❑ RGS-33. "Super Puff Popcorn" Ring,
c. 1949. Other than text on brass base, virtually identical design to Sky King Magni-Glo writing ring comprised of brass ring base topped by brass and red plastic hinged in three sections that open to magnifying glass and glowing segment holding pen point. - **$100 $200 $350**

RGS-34

RGS-35

❑ RGS-34. "Flying Tiger Rescue Ring" Leaflet,
c. 1949. Power House candy bar. See RGS-32. - **$30 $60 $100**

❑ RGS-35. "Billy West Club" Silvered Brass Ring,
1940s. Depicts cowboy on horseback. - **$30 $70 $165**

RGS-36

RGS-37

RGS-38

❑ **RGS-36. Cap-Firing Brass Ring,**
1940s. Store item. Cover snaps down to fire single cap. On Card - **$75**
Loose - **$20 $30 $50**

❑ **RGS-37. Glow-In-Dark Whistle Ring,**
1940s. Rare. Probable candy sponsor. Very similar to Kix atom bomb ring but varies by glow white plastic cap, whistle element is aluminum. - **$800 $1750 $3500**

❑ **RGS-38. "Arthur Murray" Watch Ring,**
1940s. Brass bands pronged at top to hold actual miniature watch in brass case. - **$115 $225 $375**

RGS-39

RGS-40

RGS-41

❑ **RGS-39. Indian Chewing Gum Ring,**
1940s. Goudey Gum Co. Silver luster with adjustable bands. - **$30 $60 $135**

❑ **RGS-40. Basketball Action Brass Ring,**
1940s. Scarce. Holds back board with tiny hoop and chained basketball to throw through it. - **$125 $250 $500**

❑ **RGS-41. "Red Goose Shoes" Glow-In-Dark Secret Compartment Ring,**
1940s. Metal and plastic with swing-out disk over paper lapel in glow compartment. - **$125 $200 $350**

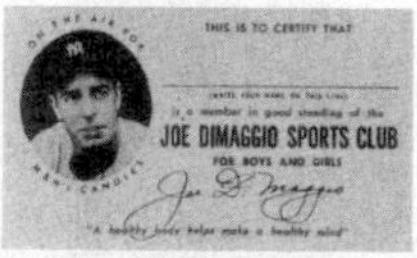

RGS-42

RGS-43

❑ **RGS-42. "Joe DiMaggio Sports Club" Member Card,**
1940s. M&M's Candies. Came with club ring. - **$55 $110 $225**

❑ **RGS-43. "Joe DiMaggio Sports Club" Brass Ring,**
1940s. Scarce. M & M's candies. Bands have club name and picture sports equipment. - **$200 $375 $800**

RGS-44
(closed) (open)

❑ **RGS-44. Knights Of Columbus Secret Compartment Glow-In-Dark Metal Ring,**
1940s. Rare. Same base as Green Hornet version except initials "GH" altered to "HG" (Holy Ghost). - **$1500 $3500 $6000**

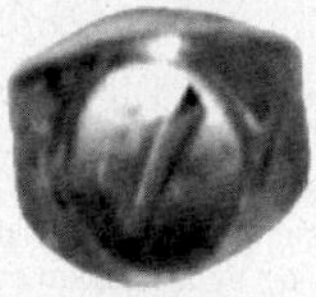
RGS-45

❑ **RGS-45. Skelly Oil Co. Red Checkmark Brass Ring,**
1940s. Top has stamped-in red enameled checkmark, possible Captain Midnight association but no documentation seen. - **$125 $250 $500**

RGS-46

RGS-47

❑ **RGS-46. "Magno-Power '50 Ford Mystery Control" Ring With Instruction Slip,**
1950. Kellogg's Pep. Magnetized plastic ring and car. Ring - **$75 $150 $300**
Instructions - **$25 $50 $100**

❑ **RGS-47. Sundial Brass Ring,**
c. 1950. Sundial Shoes. Top has plastic dome over sundial. - **$30 $50 $80**

RGS-48

RGS-49

❑ **RGS-48. Ralston Wheat Chex "Magic Pup" Ring,**
1951. Magnet ring moves pup's magnetized head.
Complete - **$30 $50 $80**

❑ **RGS-49. "Western Saddle Ring" Offer Ad,**
1951. Smith Brothers Cough Drops. Comic book ad for finely detailed replica saddle expansion ring. Ad - **$2 $4 $8**
Ring - **$15 $30 $60**

RGS-50

❑ **RGS-50. Rocket-To-The-Moon Ring,**
1951. Kix Cereal. Brass bands with plastic top for launching three glow-in-dark rockets.
Ring Only - **$65 $150 $300**
Each Rocket Near Mint - **$125**

RGS-51

❑ **RGS-51. "Rocket-To-The-Moon Ring" Instruction Sheet,**
1951. Kix Cereal. - **$50 $100 $150**

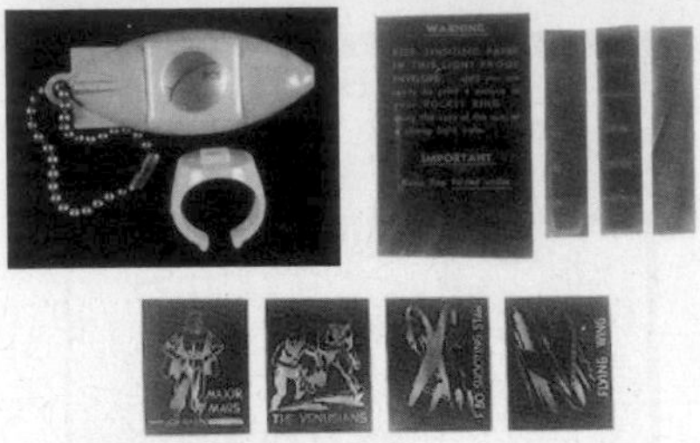

RGS-52

❑ **RGS-52. "Major Mars Rocket Ring" Kit,**
1952. Popsicle. Mailer holds plastic rocket with brass chain, ring base, instruction folder, strip with four negatives, envelope with 12 light-sensitive paper strips. A strip of four different negatives, 24 papers could be ordered separately.
Near Mint Complete - **$1200**
Rocket With Base - **$200 $400 $600**
Rocket Without Base - **$100 $200 $300**

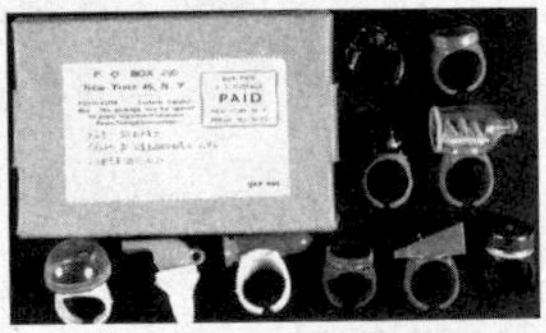

RGS-53

RGS-54

❑ **RGS-53. "Steve Donovan Western Marshal" Aluminum Ring,**
1955. Sponsor unknown. For syndicated western TV show. - **$75 $150 $250**

❑ **RGS-54. Quaker Cereals "Crazy Rings" Set,**
1957. Set of 10 plastic rings of assorted nature.
Near Mint In Mailer - **$275**
Each - **$10 $15 $20**

RGS-55

RGS-56

❑ **RGS-55. Bazooka Joe Initial Ring,**
1950s. Topps Chewing Gum. Gold luster metal expansion ring with personalized single initial. Issued as late as 1966. - **$35 $60 $115**

❑ **RGS-56. "Smile" Orange Flavor Drink Ring,**
1950s. Brass with adjustable bands. -
$20 $40 $75

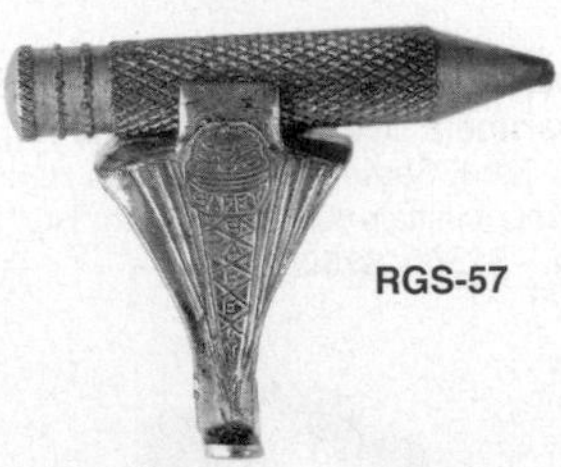

RGS-57

❑ **RGS-57. "SafeT" Ice Cream Cone Ballpoint Pen Ring,**
c. 1950s. Brass ring topped by clip holding 1.25" brass pen detailed by ice cream cone image on each side. - **$225 $450 $750**

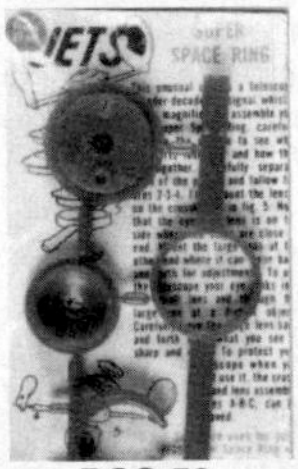

RGS-58

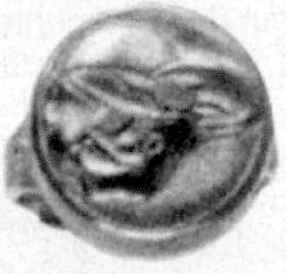

RGS-59

❑ **RGS-58. "Jets Super Space Ring",**
c. 1950s. Ball-Band. One of the few rings that actually decodes. Near Mint In Package - **$60**
Assembled - **$15 $25 $40**

❑ **RGS-59. Bazooka Joe Brass Initial Ink Stamp Ring,**
1962. Bazooka Joe Gum. Personalized by rubber stamp single initial designated by orderer. -
$60 $125 $225

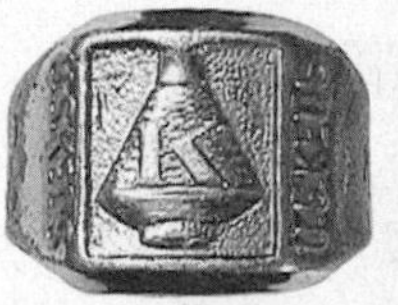

RGS-60

RGS-61

❑ **RGS-60. "U.S. Keds" Space Symbols Silvered Brass Ring,**
c. 1962. Keds footwear. Depicts "K" space capsule, band has atomic symbol. - **$45 $85 $165**

❑ **RGS-61. "Smokey Stover" Assembly Ring,**
1964. Sugar Jets Cereal and Cracker Jack. From plastic series including Kayo, Smilin' Jack, Terry and the Pirates, others.
Each Near Mint On Tree - **$125**
Each Assembled - **$20 $35 $65**

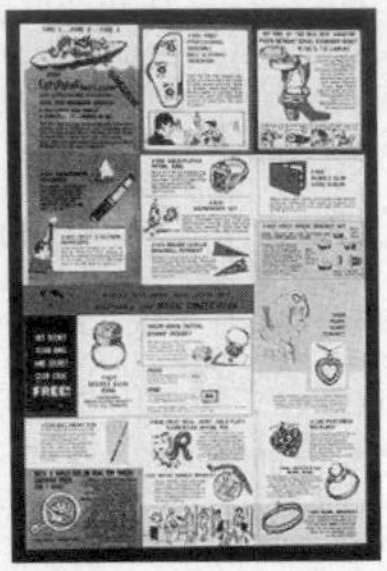

RGS-62

❑ **RGS-62. Bazooka Comics Premium Order Sheet,**
1966. Topps Chewing Gum. Paper folder opening to 9x14" picturing total of more than 30 items on both sides including Bazooka Joe Magic Circle Initial Stamp Club Ring, Gold-Plated Initial Ring and Cowboy Boot Ring. - **$20 $40 $75**

RGS-63

❑ **RGS-63. Old West Trail Club Kit,**
1968. Old West Trail Foundation. Includes map, member card, ring. Complete Near Mint - **$175**
Ring Only - **$30 $60 $125**

RGS-64

RGS-65

❑ **RGS-64. "Cousin Eerie" Brass Ring,**
1969. Warren Publishing Co., publisher of Eerie Comics. - **$20 $40 $85**

❑ **RGS-65. "Uncle Creepy" Gold Finish Metal Ring,**
1969. Warren Publishing Co., publisher of Eerie Comics. - **$60 $125 $265**

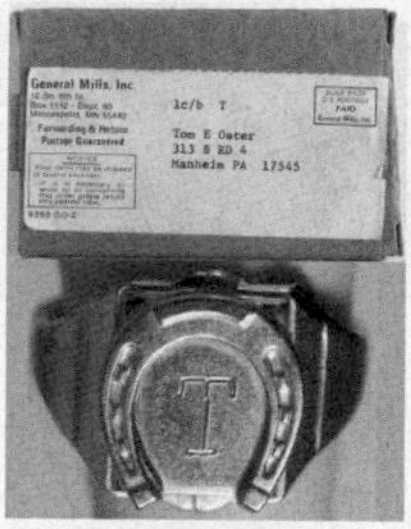

RGS-66

❑ **RGS-66. General Mills Good Luck Initial Ring,**
1960s. Mailing box is 2.75x4x.75" deep and contains metal ring with expansion bands. Ring has raised horseshoe design with the initial "T" at center. Mailer - **$15 $25 $40**
Ring - **$18 $35 $60**

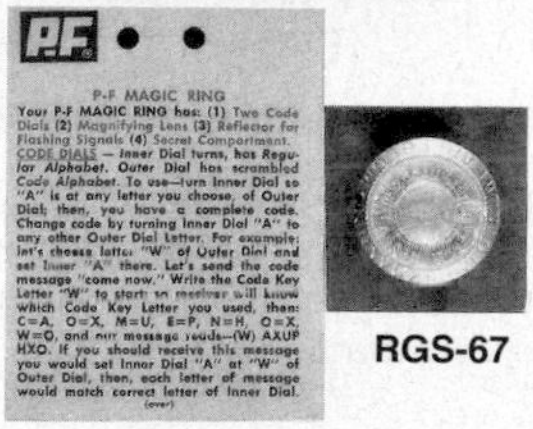

RGS-67

❑ **RGS-67. P.F. Magic Decoder Ring With Card,**
1960s. P.F. footwear. Also used as Jonny Quest premium. Gold plastic ring with several functions. Card - **$10 $20 $30**
Ring - **$25 $45 $75**

RGS-68

❑ **RGS-68. "Kolonel Keds Space Patrol" Decoder Card And Ring,**
1960s. Issued by U.S. Keds.
Card - **$18 $30 $65**
Ring - **$50 $100 $165**

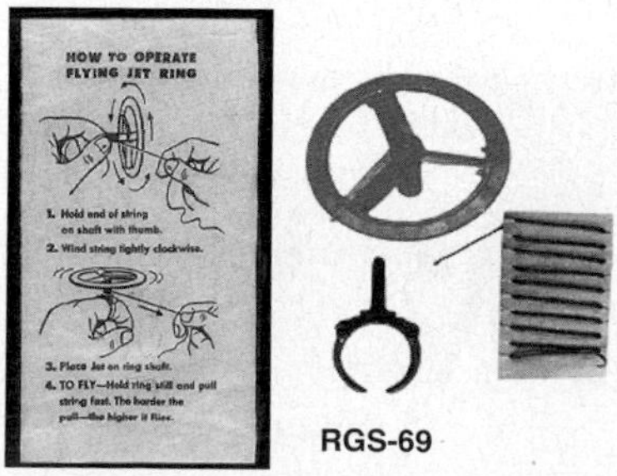

RGS-69

❑ **RGS-69. Flying Jet Ring With Envelope And Instructions,**
1960s. Cereal premium by unknown issuer.
Near Mint In Envelope - **$110**
Ring Only - **$20 $40 $75**

RGS-70

❑ **RGS-70. "Miss Dairylea" Plastic Ring,**
1960s. Dairylea Products. Domed plastic trademark girl image. - **$15 $30 $60**

RGS-71

RGS-72

❑ **RGS-71. Ralston "Chex's Agent" Decoder Ring,**
c. 1960s. Plastic base topped by two cardboard dials. - **$10 $18 $35**

❑ **RGS-72. Large Plastic Decoder Ring,**
c. 1970s. Station "WABX." Call letters of Detroit station. Mostly red and green plastic with large 2" diameter decoding wheel on top. - **$30 $60 $100**

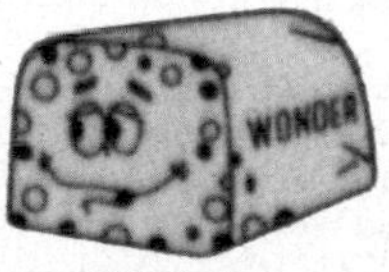

RGS-73

RGS-74

❑ **RGS-73. "Wonder" Bread Loaf Plastic Ring,**
c. 1970s. - **$8 $12 $20**

❑ **RGS-74. Tekno Comix Logo Secret Compartment Ring,**
1994. Silvery-gray metal. - **$8 $12 $20**

Ripley's Believe It or Not!

Robert L. Ripley's Believe It or Not! **started life as a newspaper cartoon for the *New York Globe* in 1919 and was ultimately syndicated in as many as 300 newspapers. The focus was on bizarre or freakish events and people and human oddities, all of which, Ripley (1893-1949) claimed, could be substantiated. In 1930 he took the show to radio, where it aired in various formats on NBC or CBS for 18 years. Sponsors included Colonial Oil, Esso, General Foods, Royal Crown Cola and Pall Mall cigarettes. A television version ran on NBC in 1949-1950, with other hosts after Ripley's death and resurfaced on CBS in 1982 with Jack Palance as host. Collections were published in book form around 1930 and as comic books in the 1960s. Twenty-seven museums are in operation in ten countries.**

RPY-1

❑ **RPY-1. "Disk-O-Knowledge" Cardboard Diecut Mechanical Wheel,**
1932. Oddities appear in diecut openings on both sides. - **$25 $45 $90**

RPY-2

❑ **RPY-2. "Electric Flash" Game,**
1933. Store item by Moccano Co. of America. Battery operated game flashes miniature light bulb for correct response to question of Ripley nature. - **$75 $200 $300**

RPY-3

❑ **RPY-3. "Odditorium" Exhibit Souvenir,**
1936. From Texas Centennial exposition. Booklet and 12 postcards. Set - **$40 $75 $150**

RPY-4

RPY-5

❑ **RPY-4. Oddities Fabric Bandanna,**
1930s. - **$15 $30 $60**

❑ **RPY-5. "Believe It Or Not/Ripley" Diecut Metal Miniature Charm,**
1930s. Post Huskies cereal. Known as "Hand of Fatima." Green antiqued copper finish.
- **$10 $20 $50**

RPY-6

❑ **RPY-6. Pair Of Hankies,**
1930s. Each is 5x7-1/4" in brown, green and white. Each - **$15 $30 $60**

RPY-7

❑ **RPY-7. Oddities Fold-Out Card,**
1940. Various local sponsors as Christmas premium. Opens to 13x19" sheet illustrated on both sides. - **$20 $40 $80**

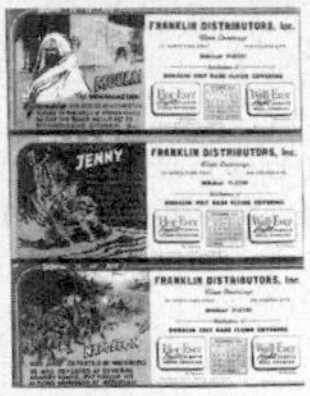

RPY-8

RPY-9

❑ **RPY-8. Cardboard Ink Blotters,**
1948. Various local sponsors. Examples from monthly series dated October, November, December. Each - **$10 $18 $30**

❑ **RPY-9. Stamp,**
1940s. Scarce. Royal Crown Cola radio premium. - **$25 $40 $75**

RPY-10

❑ **RPY-10. Card Set,**
1962. Set of 45 large size 3-1/4x5-1/4" cards issued by Dynamic Toy Inc. Set - **$30 $60 $100**

Robin Hood

The English folklore tale of the Earl of Locksley, Robin Hood, dates back to the 1400s. The archer and outlaw, intent on robbing from the rich and giving to the poor, is joined by his band of Merry Men including Friar Tuck, Will Scarlet and Little John in Sherwood Forest. Maid Marian is Robin's love interest.

Noted author and illustrator Howard Pyle's 1883 book *The Merry Adventures of Robin Hood* brought the legend up to date and is still in print today.

Notable feature films of the 20th century include: *Robin Hood*, 1922, released by United Artists starring Douglas Fairbanks, Enid Bennett, Wallace Beery; Warner Brothers 1938 *The Adventures of Robin Hood* with Errol Flynn, Basil Rathbone, Olivia DeHavilland; 1952 Disney *The Story of Robin Hood and His Merrie Men* with Richard Todd, Joan Rice and Peter Finch; 1973 Disney *Robin Hood* animated feature directed by Wolfgang Reitherman; and Warner Brothers 1991 *Robin Hood: Prince of Thieves* with Kevin Costner, Morgan Freeman, Mary Elizabeth Mastrantonio.

CBS-TV aired the live action series *The Adventures of Robin Hood* from September 26, 1955 until September 22, 1958. The cast included Richard Greene, Victor Wolf, Patricia Driscoll and Archie Duncan. BBC in England began a new live action series October 3, 2006.

Various publishers have issued comic books since 1944 including: Gilberton, Dell, Eclipse, ME, Quality and Western.

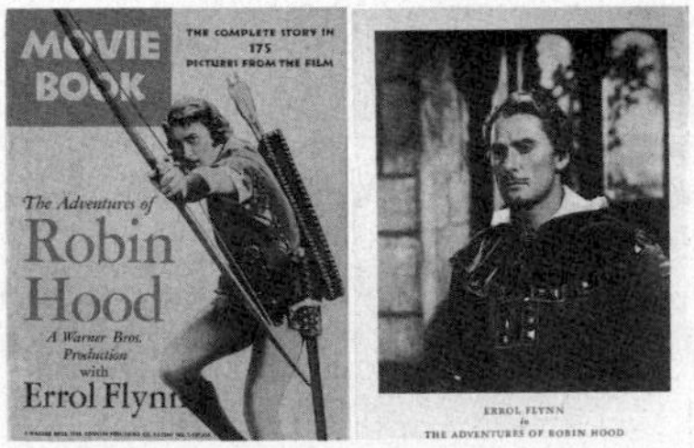

RBH-1

❑ **RBH-1. "The Adventures Of Robin Hood With Errol Flynn" Movie Book,**
1938. Conklin Publishing Co., N.Y. 8-3/8x10.75" book contains 32 slick paper pages with many captioned photos from the Warner Bros. film. - **$25 $50 $100**

RBH-2

❑ **RBH-2. "The Adventures Of Robin Hood Game",**
1938. Milton Bradley Co. 9.5x19x1.75" deep box 18.25x18.5" gameboard, 5.5x6.5" instruction sheet, 4 playing pieces, 36 yellow bags of gold cards, 36 character cards and dice. - **$40 $80 $150**

RBH-3

❑ **RBH-3. Errol Flynn "The Adventures Of Robin Hood" English Hardcover,**
1938. Ward, Lock & Co. Ltd. 7.5x9.75" with 128 pages and 16 full color plates. - **$65 $130 $225**

RBH-4

❑ **RBH-4. "Robin Hood Flour" Store Sign,**
1952. 9-1/2x17" promoting company's product and Disney movie. - **$35 $75 $150**

RBH-5

❑ RBH-5. Robin Hood Showing Richard Greene Button,
c. 1955. 1-5/8" button to promote "The Adventures Of Robin Hood." - **$25 $50 $100**

RBH-6

❑ RBH-6. "Robin Hood's Band Of Merry Men" Membership Card,
c. 1955. Johnson & Johnson. Front depicts Richard Greene and reverse has "Sherwood" pledge. - **$12 $25 $50**

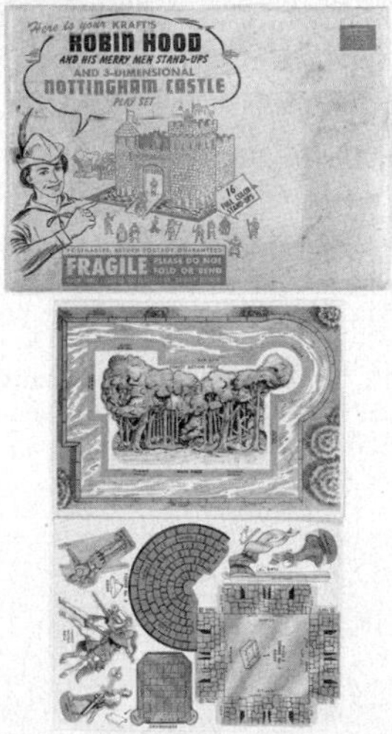

RBH-7

❑ RBH-7. "Kraft's Robin Hood Nottingham Castle Playset" Premium,
1956. Mailing envelope is 8x11" and contains complete punch-out premium set consisting of three 10.5x15" thick cardboard sheets holding 16 stand-up figures, detailed castle and "Forest Action Piece." Unpunched - **$60 $110 $165**

RBH-8

❑ RBH-8. "Robin Hood" Gum Card Set,
1957. Topps. Set of 60, each 2.5x3.5". Set - **$60 $120 $200**

RBH-9 RBH-10

❑ RBH-9. "Robin Hood And Maid Marian" Paperdoll Book,
1950s. Saalfield. 10-3/8x12.5" book contains four sheets printed on one side with fashions and accessories. - **$20 $40 $85**

❑ RBH-10. "Robin Hood Shoes For Boys And Girls" Store Display,
1950s. 2.5" deep by 9.5" wide by 17.5" tall figure with metal hook for wall display or can sit to be counter display. - **$100 $200 $400**

RBH-11

❑ RBH-11. Robin Hood Watch,
1950s. In open box with die-cut display. Mylar type top. Near Mint Boxed - **$750**
Watch only - **$50 $150 $300**

RBH-12

❑ RBH-12. Robin Hood Hat,
1950s. Store bought. - **$25 $55 $110**

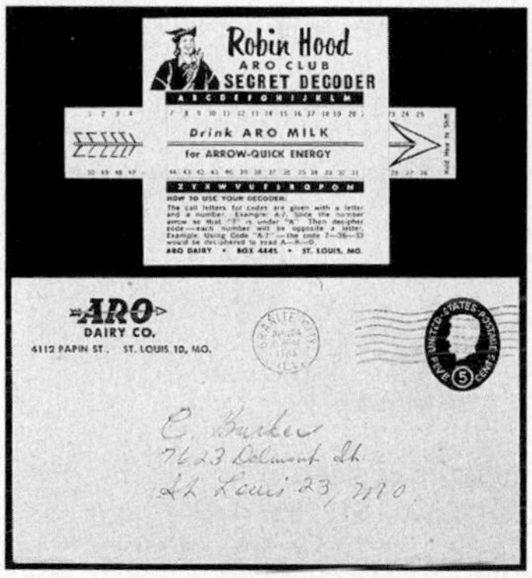

RBH-13

❑ RBH-13. Robin Hood Decoder and Mailer,
1963. ARO Milk premium. - **$35 $85 $175**

RBH-14

❑ RBH-14. Robin Hood Premium Figures,
1968. Kellogg's Sugar Smacks. About 2" tall plastic figures in various single colors with "Kellogg's" and character name under base. Set of 14 different. Each - **$8 $15 $30**

Rocky Jones, Space Ranger

This early television space opera was two years in preparation and survived only one season of 39 episodes before it was syndicated. The series premiered in December 1953 on KNXT in Los Angeles, in February 1954 on WNBT in New York, and late in 1954 on WBKB in Chicago. Richard Crane played Rocky, chief of a 21st century security patrol force charged with maintaining peace in the galaxies. Silvercup Bread was a sponsor, and Space Ranger toys, uniforms, and comic books were licensed to promote the series.

RKJ-1

❑ **RKJ-1. "Rocky Jones And The Space Pirates" Record,**
1953. 78 rpm issued by Columbia. - **$25 $45 $90**

RKJ-2

❑ **RKJ-2. Two Stills,**
c. 1954. Each - **$12 $25 $45**

RKJ-3

❑ **RKJ-3. Cast Photo,**
1954. TV still of key cast members. Scarce. - **$15 $35 $70**

RKJ-4

❑ **RKJ-4. Color Photo,**
c. 1954. Possible school tablet cover. - **$15 $30 $60**

RKJ-5

❑ **RKJ-5. "Official Space-Ranger" Metal Wings Pin On Card,**
c. 1954. Space Rangers Enterprises.
On Card - **$20 $40 $80**
Loose - **$10 $20 $30**

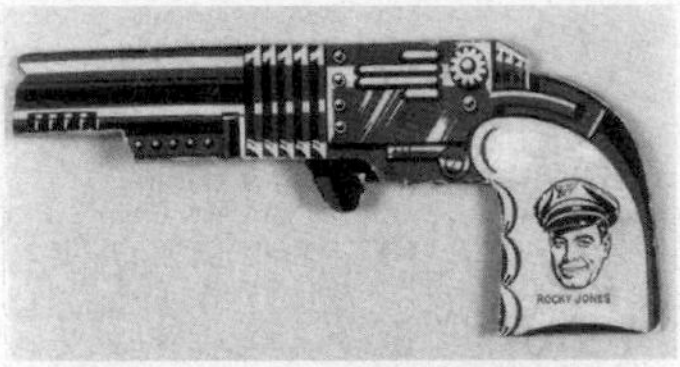

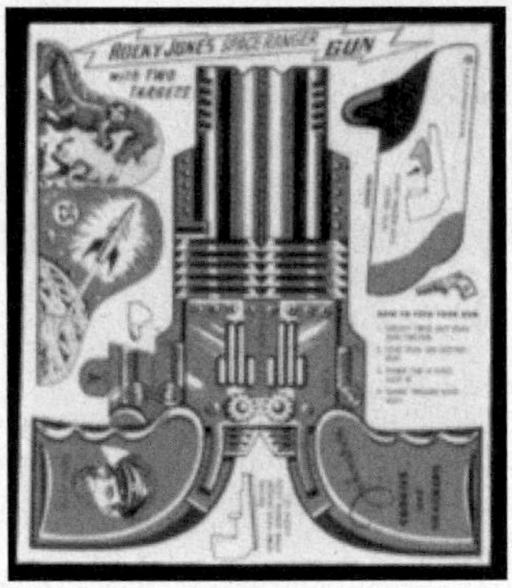

RKJ-6

❑ **RKJ-6. Cardboard Rubber Band Gun,**
c. 1954. Johnston Cookies And Crackers.
Near Mint Unpunched - **$200**
Punched - **$25 $50 $100**

RKJ-7

❑ **RKJ-7. "Rocky Jones, Space Ranger" Billfold,**
1954. Space Ranger secret code card & billfold with seal on right. - **$40 $75 $135**

RKJ-8

❑ **RKJ-8. Code Card,**
1954. Mickelberry's Meats. - **$40 $110 $175**

RKJ-9 RKJ-10

❑ **RKJ-9. "Johnston Cookies" Litho. Button,**
c. 1954. Litho is 1-3/8" and includes sponsor's name. - **$12 $25 $50**

❑ **RKJ-10. "Rocky Jones-Space Ranger" Cello. Button,**
c. 1954. Button is 1-1/4" - **$20 $40 $85**

RKJ-11 RKJ-12

❑ **RKJ-11. "Silvercup Bread" Litho. Button,**
c. 1954. Litho is 1-3/8" and includes sponsor's name. - **$12 $25 $50**

❑ **RKJ-12. "Roberts Milk" Litho. Button,**
c. 1954. Litho is 1-3/8" and includes sponsor's name. - **$20 $40 $85**

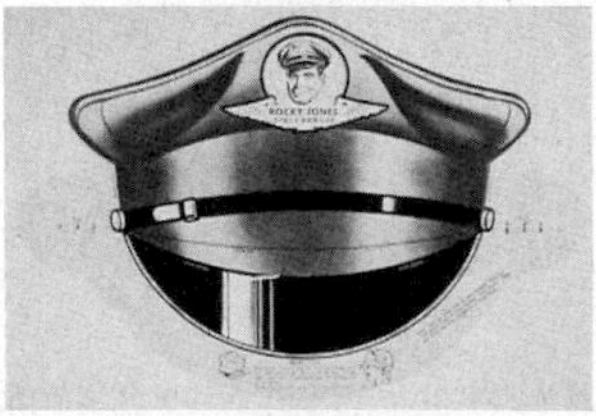

RKJ-13

❑ **RKJ-13. Punch-Out Hat Premium,**
c. 1954. Pied Piper Line, one of the bread companies sponsoring the show. 9x12-1/2" thin cardboard in blue, black and white. Gordon Gold Archives. Unpunched - **$45 $90 $200**

Rocky Lane

Harold Albershart (1909-1973), as Allan Rocky Lane, was a longtime actor in adventure films. He made dozens of "B" Westerns, Royal Mountie serials, and jungle epics for Republic Pictures between 1938 and 1961. Lane took over the film role of Red Ryder around 1944 and continued as a star for the studio into the 1950s. He also appeared in the last chapter of the last Republic western serial *Man With a Steel Whip*, released in 1954. *Rocky Lane* comic books were published between 1949 and 1959, and Lane was the television voice of Mr. Ed, the talking horse, from 1961 to 1965.

RLN-1

RLN-2

❑ **RLN-1. "Alan Rocky Lane And His Stallion Black Jack" Dixie Picture,**
c. 1950. - **$20 $35 $70**

❑ **RLN-2. "Alan Rocky Lane" Dixie Picture,**
c. 1950. - **$20 $35 $70**

RLN-3

RLN-4

RLN-5

❑ **RLN-3. Cello. Button,**
c. 1950. Three varieties: 1.25" black and white on orange - **$15 $25 $60**
1.25" black and white only - **$25 $35 $75**
1.75" black and white with "Member" at top - **$75 $125 $250**

❑ **RLN-4. "Allan 'Rocky' Lane" Cello. Button,**
c. 1950. Store item. - **$15 $25 $45**

❑ **RLN-5. "Rocky Lane Posse" Cello. Button,**
1950. Carnation Malted Milk. - **$60 $110 $225**

RLN-6

❑ **RLN-6. "Member 'Rocky' Lane Posse" Decal Club Patch,**
1950. Rare. Carnation Malted Milk.
Patch - **$100 $300 $450**
Mailer - **$25 $50 $100**

RLN-7

RLN-8

❑ **RLN-7. "Posse Shoulder Patch" Premium Offer Ad,**
1950. Carnation Malted Milk. Comic book page ad for clothing patch available until January 30, 1951. - **$5 $10 $15**

❑ **RLN-8. "Explorer's Sun Watch" Ad,**
1951. Carnation Malted Milk. Comic book page ad with product endorsement by "Rocky" Lane. - **$5 $10 $15**

RLN-9

RLN-10

❑ **RLN-9. Dixie Ice Cream Picture,**
c. 1952. - **$30 $55 $100**

❑ **RLN-10. "Thundering Caravans" Movie Poster,**
1952. Republic Pictures. 27x41". - **$40 $85 $150**

RLN-11

❑ **RLN-11. "Rocky Lane Western Comic" English Annual,**
1960. #4 in series by L. Miller & Co. Ltd. - **$20 $40 $85**

Rootie Kazootie

Who is the lad who makes you feel so glad? He was Rootie Kazootie, created by Steve Carlin, the little puppet hero who became a giant hit in children's television. The series, known initially as *The Rootie Tootie Club* when it debuted locally in New York in 1950, changed its name to *The Rootie Kazootie Club* and was broadcast nationally on NBC (1951-1952) and ABC (1952-1954). Other puppet characters were Polka Dottie, El Squeako Mouse, the villainous Poison Zoomack, and the pup Little Nipper, who became Gala Poochie when RCA dropped out as a sponsor. Todd Russell served as host, and Mr. Deetle Doodle, the silent policeman, was the only other human to appear. Sponsors, in addition to RCA, included Coca-Cola, Power House candy, and Silvercup bread. *Rootie Kazootie* comic books were published in the early 1950s.

ROO-1

ROO-2

❑ **ROO-1. "Rootie Kazootie Stars" Puppet Punch-Outs,**
c. 1952. Coca-Cola. Set of five. Each Unpunched - **$20 $35 $65**

❑ **ROO-2. "Rootie Kazootie Stars" Animated Punch-Outs,**
c. 1952. Coca-Cola. Set of five. Each Unpunched - **$20 $35 $65**

ROO-3

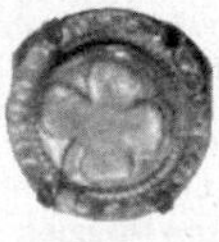
ROO-4

ROO-5

❑ **ROO-3. Club Member Litho. Button,**
c. 1952. Color (6 characters) or black/white (5 characters) versions. Each - **$12 $25 $55**

❑ **ROO-4. "Rootie Kazootie's Lucky Spot" Embossing Ring,**
c. 1952. Designed to emboss title and four-leaf clover image on paper. - **$165 $325 $750**

❑ **ROO-5. "Rootie Kazootie Rooter" Glow-In-Dark Plastic Disk,**
c. 1952. Back has pin fastener. - **$40 $75 $150**

ROO-6

❑ **ROO-6. "Rootie Kazootie Rooters Club" Membership Card,**
c. 1952. - **$30 $65 $100**

ROO-7

ROO-8

❑ **ROO-7. Flicker Ring,**
c. 1952. Premium issue probably from Power House Candy. - **$40 $85 $185**

❑ **ROO-8. "Rootie Kazootie Word Game,"**
1953. Store item by Ed-U-Cards. - **$12 $25 $45**

ROO-9 ROO-10

❑ **ROO-9. Hand Puppet,**
1950s. 9" tall. - **$50 $100 $165**

❑ **ROO-10. Hand Puppet,**
1950s. Store item. 10" tall with soft vinyl head and plain red fabric body. - **$50 $100 $165**

ROO-11

❑ **ROO-11. Picture Puzzles Set,**
1950s. Store item by E. E. Fairchild Corp. Three-puzzle set featuring Rootie, Polka Dottie, Gala Poochie. Boxed Set - **$35 $70 $150**

ROO-12

❑ **ROO-12. "Fix-A-Rootie Tool Box,"**
1950s. 6x14x3" deep metal box with character illustration lid. - **$70 $135 $200**

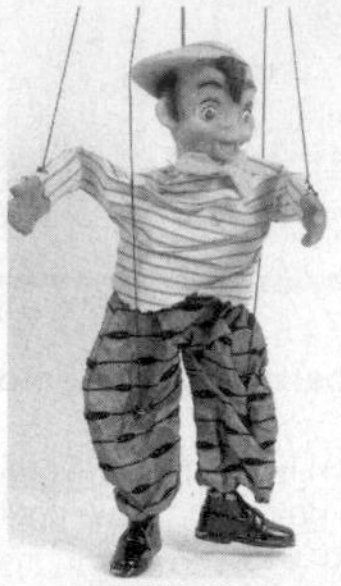
ROO-13

❑ **ROO-13. Rootie Kazootie Marionette,**
1950s. 13" tall vinyl, hard rubber, composition figure with fabric outfit parts suspended by wire and strings from wooden hand control unit. Copyright but no maker indicated.
- **$85 $150 $300**

ROO-14

❑ **ROO-14. "Polka Dottie" Child's Dress,**
1950s. 24" long pink cotton accented by red polka dots plus pocket cover image of her. - **$20 $40 $70**

ROO-15

❑ **ROO-15. "Rootie Kazootie Cut-Out Coloring Book,"**
1950s. Pocket Books Inc. 8.5x11" with 24 pages of pictures to be colored with cut-outs on inside front and back cover of a Magic Kazootie and Polka-Dot Baseball Bat and Treasure Box.
- **$25 $50 $85**

Roscoe Turner

A real-life aviator hero and successful aviation entrepeneur, Col. Roscoe Turner (1895-1970) was idolized in the 1930s much like cowboy fans adored Tom Mix. Turner was a barnstormer flyer and stunt performer of the 1920s following the start of his air career in the Balloon Service during World War I. He was the major test pilot for the DC-2 (Douglas Commercial) first passenger transport aircraft in 1934. In the latter 1930s, his frequent winning of the Thompson Trophy and Bendix Trophy for speed events at annual National Air Races enthralled a nation of speed fans. His enterprises included a passenger run from Los Angeles to Reno to Las Vegas and return, called by some the "Alimony Special" circuit due to frequent use by movie stars. Turner's popularity promoted premiums by several sponsors, notably Gilmore Oil, H. J. Heinz and Wonder Bread (see Sky Blazers). Probably his best remembered gimmick was for Gilmore Oil Co. An actual African lion--a Gilmore trademark lookalike--was acquired and flew with Turner throughout the United States, Canada and Mexico. Despite insistence by humane agencies that the lion be equipped with a parachute, Turner and his lion were welcomed everywhere until the lion died of old age and natural causes. Turner trained more than 3,300 pilots at his flight school in Indianapolis in WWII. The U.S. Air Force awarded him the Distinguished Flying Cross in 1952.

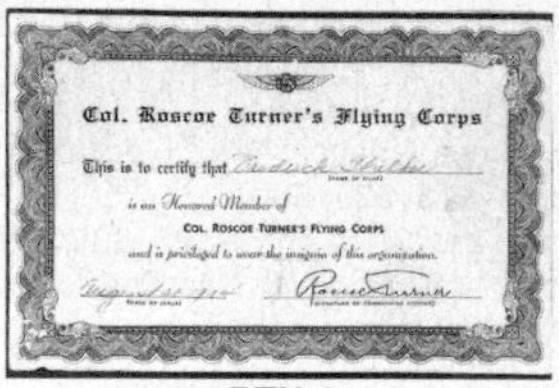

RTU-1

❑ **RTU-1. Flying Corps Certificate,**
1934. Heinz Rice Flakes. - **$25 $55 $100**

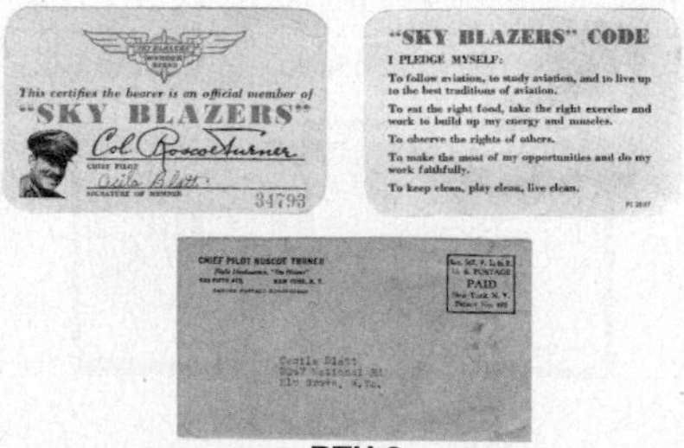

RTU-2

❑ **RTU-2. Membership Card with Mailer,**
c. 1934. Heinz Rice Flakes. - **$30 $75 $125**
Mailer - **$15 $30 $50**

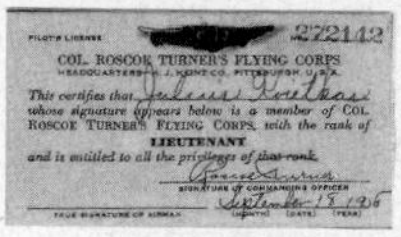

RTU-3

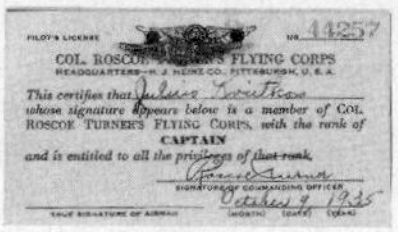

RTU-4

❑ **RTU-3. "Flying Corps" Bronze Wings Badge On Card,**
1934. Heinz Co. "Lieutenant" version.
Card - **$10 $25 $50**
Badge - **$10 $25 $45**

❑ **RTU-4. "Flying Corps" Silver Wings Badge On Card,**
1934. Heinz Co. "Captain" version.
Card - **$15 $30 $60**
Badge - **$15 $30 $50**

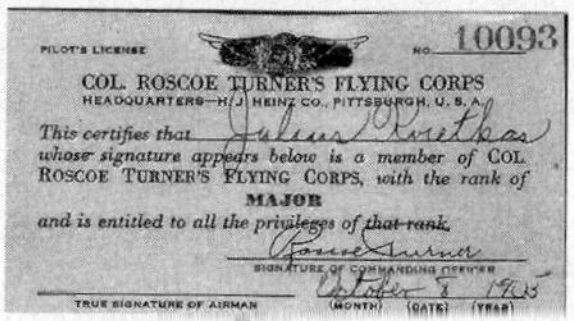

RTU-5

❑ **RTU-5. "Flying Corps" Gold Wings Badge On Card,**
1934. Heinz Co. "Major" version.
Card - **$20 $35 $70**
Badge - **$20 $35 $65**

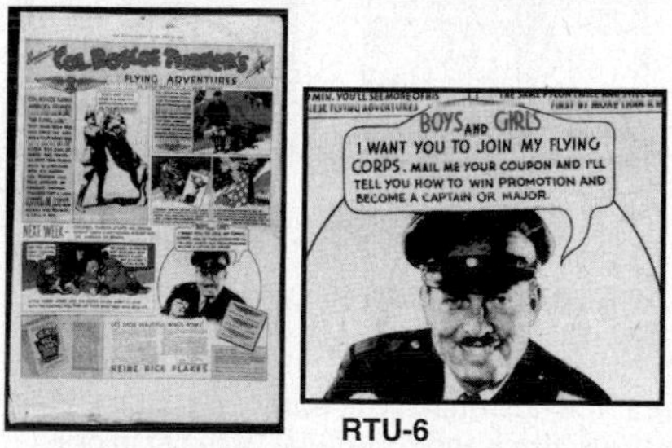

RTU-6

❑ **RTU-6. "Beginning Col. Roscoe Turner's Flying Adventures,"**
1934. Full page in May 27 Sunday comic section sponsored by H. J. Heinz Co. -
$15 $25 $50

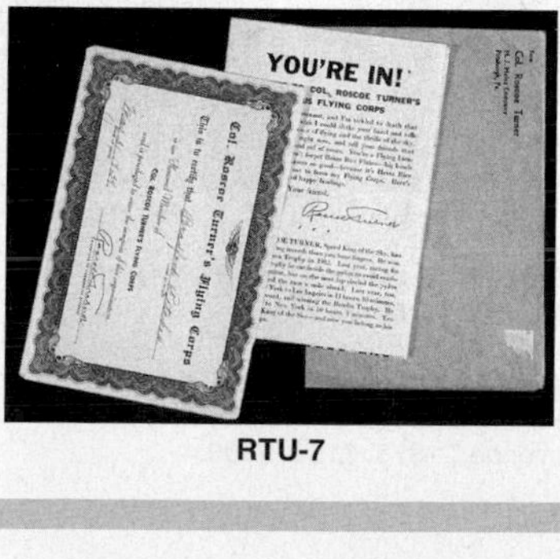

RTU-7

❑ **RTU-7. Certificate With Booklet and Mailer,**
1934. Mailer for Flying Corp Certificate.
Mailer - **$15 $30 $50**
Booklet - **$15 $30 $60**
Certificate - **$25 $55 $100**

RTU-8

❑ **RTU-8. Thompson Trophy Race "Winner" Color Print,**
1939. Thompson Products. 13-1/4x14-1/2" beautiful color print with art by Charles H. Hubbel surrounded by black border with photo inset of pilot below. Total number of prints in the set is unknown but Turner is pictured as winner of the 1934, 1938 and 1939 air races held in Cleveland.
Each Print Picturing Turner - **$20 $40 $75**

RTU-9

❑ **RTU-9. "Sky Blazers Airplane" Punch-Out Model,**
1939. 6x6.5" stiff paper punch sheet including ad for CBS radio program also titled "True Adventures Of Heroes Of The Air."
Punched - **$10 $20 $40**
Unpunched - **$35 $75 $125**

RTU-10

❑ **RTU-10. "Roscoe Turner Aeronautical Corp." Match Pack Cover/Postcard ,**
1930s. Flattened thin cardboard cover is 3x4.5" in red, white and blue with browntone photo of aviator at bottom and browntone photo of his building at Municipal Airport in Indianapolis at top. Reverse is printed in red for use as post-card with place for stamp, address and greeting.
- $12 $25 $50

RTU-11

RTU-12

❑ **RTU-11. "Roscoe Turner" Photo,**
1930s. Heinz Rice Flakes. - **$15 $30 $60**

❑ **RTU-12. "Col. Roscoe Turner" Cello. Button,**
1930s. For "Corinth Airport Dedication". -
$10 $20 $40

RTU-13

❑ **RTU-13. "I Want You To Join My Flying Corps" 20x23" Cardboard Store Sign,**
1930s. Heinz Rice Flakes. - **$150 $300 $500**

RTU-14

❑ **RTU-14. Roscoe Turner Photo,**
1940. 3.5x5.5" black and white glossy fan photo with facsimile autograph "To A Fellow Sky Blazer Sincerely Roscoe Turner." From kit distributed by sponsor Wonder Bread at New York's World's Fair - **$15 $25 $50**

Roy Rogers

Singing, movies, radio, records, comic books, comic strips, television, rodeos, personal appearances, merchandising--Roy Rogers (1911-1998) did it all, with style and huge success. Born Leonard Slye in Ohio in 1911, he started out organizing cowboy bands and singing in a hillbilly group, and made his first movies--in bit roles or as a member of the Sons of the Pioneers--as Slye or as Dick Weston in the mid-1930s.

His first film as Rogers was Republic Pictures' *Under Western Stars* (1938). He changed his name legally to Roy Rogers in 1942, and went on to make more than 80 Westerns for Republic, pursuing the Happy Trails to stardom as "King of the Cowboys," riding his palomino Trigger ("The Smartest Horse in the Movies") and accompanied by wife Dale Evans ("Queen of the West") on her steed Buttermilk. Evans died in 2001.

On radio, *The Roy Rogers Show* aired on the Mutual or NBC networks from 1944 to 1955, initially as a musical variety show with Dale, the Sons of the Pioneers, and a movie sidekick Gabby Hayes, later as a Western thriller with Pat Brady replacing Hayes. The show was sponsored by Goodyear Tire (1944-1945), Miles Laboratories (1946-1947), Quaker Oats and Mother's Oats (1948-1951), Post Sugar Crisp (1951-1953), and Dodge automobiles (1954-1955).

***Roy Rogers* comic books were first published in 1944 and continued well into the 1960s, and daily and Sunday strips syndicated by King Features appeared from 1949 to 1961.**

On television, *The Roy Rogers Show* was seen on NBC from 1951 to 1957, sponsored by Post cereals. The series was then syndicated for six years, sponsored by Nestle's from 1958 to 1964 and co-sponsored by Ideal Novelty & Toy Corp. from 1961 to 1964. Further syndication followed in 1976. The programs continued the successful mix of adventure, music, and comedy of the Rogers movies, with the usual cast, including Pat Brady and his trick jeep Nellybelle, and Bullet the Wonder Dog. *The Roy Rogers & Dale Evans Show,* a musical variety hour, had a brief run on ABC in 1962.

Merchandising of the Roy Rogers empire and sponsor premiums peaked during the radio and television years. At one point some 400 products were franchised by Roy Rogers Enterprises, earning millions for manufacturers and for the endorsers. A chain of family restaurants opened in the 1960s.

In 2003, the Roy Rogers–Dale Evans Museum opened at its new location in Branson, Missouri.

ROY-1

❑ **ROY-1. "The Sons Of The Pioneers" Photo Ad Card With Roy,**
c. 1934. Radio KQV, Pittsburgh, Pa. 8-1/4x11-1/4" stiff paper advertising daily noon radio program. Photo identifies Roy by his actual name "Len Slye." Photo captions on the item are both misplaced and in some cases spelled incorrectly. Actually pictured from left to right are Hugh Farr, Bob Nolan, Lloyd Perryman, Len Slye. Karl Farr is not pictured. - **$150 $300 $500**

ROY-2

❑ **ROY-2. Sons Of Pioneers Photo Card With Roy,**
1935. One of earliest items to picture Roy. Text on reverse. - **$90 $190 $375**

ROY-3

ROY-4

❑ **ROY-3. Dixie Ice Cream Picture,**
1938. - **$50 $85 $180**

❑ **ROY-4. "Broadway Journal" 12x16" Publicity Newspaper,**
1938. Republic Studios. "Special Roy Rogers Edition" for July 16 appearances in New York City. - **$125 $225 $400**

ROY-5

ROY-6

❑ **ROY-5. Movie Promo Picture with Frame,**
1938. Republic Pictures. From the movie "Shine On Harvest Moon" starring Roy Rogers and Gabby Hayes. - **$30 $60 $90**

❑ **ROY-6. "Republic's Singing Western Star" Cello. Button,**
c. 1938. Republic Studios. 1-1/4" with bluetone photo on dark beige background. Probably issued in conjunction with his first Republic film "Under Western Stars." - **$100 $200 $400**

ROY-7

❑ **ROY-7. Dale Evans Early Sheet Music,**
1939. Store item by Calumet Music Co. Front cover reads "Dale Evans Over W.B.B.M.-Chicago/Columbia Broadcasting System." - **$15 $25 $45**

ROY-8

ROY-9

❑ **ROY-8. Photo,**
1930s. Republic Pictures. Color photo of Roy. - **$20 $35 $70**

❑ **ROY-9. Button With Early Portrait,**
1930s. Black and white 1-1/4" with photo of young Roy smiling and wearing floral pattern shirt. - **$75 $150 $275**

ROY-10

ROY-11

❑ **ROY-10. Dixie Ice Cream Picture,**
1940. - **$50 $100 $210**

❑ **ROY-11. Dixie Ice Cream Picture,**
1942. Reverse has scenes from "Man From Cheyenne." - **$75 $150 $300**

ROY-12

❏ **ROY-12. Boston Garden Rodeo Program,**
1942. Souvenir for single November 9 appearance. Contents are 36 pages including two-page Roy photo article plus full page ad for his film "Heart Of The Golden West."
- $115 $225 $350

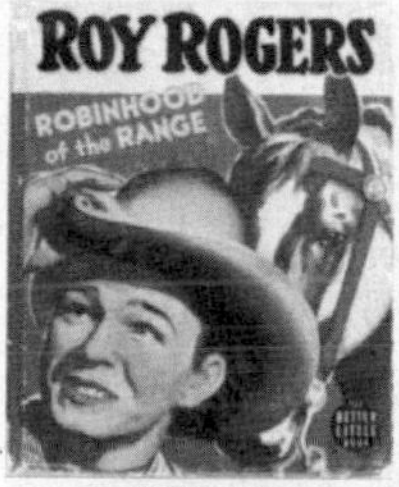

ROY-13

ROY-14

❏ **ROY-13. "Roy Rogers Robin Hood Of The Range" Better Little Book,**
1942. Whitman #1460. **- $19 $57 $130**

❏ **ROY-14. "Roy Rogers King Of The Cowboys" Dixie Lid,**
c. 1942. **- $10 $20 $40**

ROY-15

ROY-16

❏ **ROY-15. "For Democracy 100%" Cello Button,**
c. 1942. 1.25" from series believed used only in Reading, Pa. area to promote Freihofer Bread. Issued in black and white or blue and white. Each **- $225 $500 $1000**

❏ **ROY-16. Los Angeles Rodeo Souvenir Program,**
1944. **- $75 $200 $300**

ROY-17

❏ **ROY-17. "The Roy Rogers Show" Radio Announcement Brochure,**
c. 1944. Goodyear Tire & Rubber Co. Press kit folder promoting radio series on Mutual Broadcasting System including listing of 67 radio stations. Complete **- $125 $275 $450**

ROY-18

ROY-19

❏ **ROY-18. "Roy Rogers And Trigger" Dixie Ice Cream Picture,**
1945. **- $100 $200 $350**

❏ **ROY-19. "Dale Evans" Dixie Ice Cream Picture,**
1945. **- $50 $100 $200**

ROY-20

ROY-21

❏ **ROY-20. "Roy Rogers at Crossed Feathers Ranch" Big Little Book #1494,**
1945. **- $16 $48 $115**

❏ **ROY-21. "My Pal Trigger" 13x19" Contest Paper Poster,**
1946. Republic Pictures for local theaters. **-**
$125 $250 $500

ROY-22

❏ **ROY-22. "Roy Rogers And His Trick Lasso" Photo,**
1947. Store item packaged with trick lasso. **-**
$20 $40 $75

ROY-23

❏ **ROY-23. "Roy Rogers Trick Lasso",**
1947. Store item. Came with photo (see item ROY-22) and game book. Cellophane wrapper very fragile. Wrapper **- $15 $30 $75**
Lasso **- $10 $20 $40**
Game Book **- $40 $100 $200**

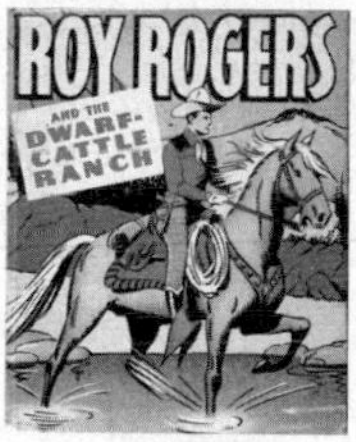

ROY-24

ROY-25

❏ **ROY-24. "Roy Rogers and the Dwarf-Cattle Ranch" Big Little Book #1421,**
1947. 352 pages. **- $16 $48 $115**

❏ **ROY-25. "Roy Rogers and the Deadly Treasure" Big Little Book #1437,**
1947. **- $16 $48 $115**

ROY-26

❏ **ROY-26. "World's Championship Rodeo" Program,**
c. 1947. 8-1/2x11" with 20 pages. **-**
$40 $80 $150

ROY-27

❑ **ROY-27. First Issue "Dale Evans Comics",**
1948. National Comics Publications. Issue #1 for September-October. - **$76 $228 $1100**

ROY-28

❑ **ROY-28. Quaker Oats Contest Store Poster,**
1948. 16x22" in full color announcing prizes for "Naming This Son Of Trigger" with grand prize of "Win A Vacation With Me In Hollywood." Gordon Gold Archives. - **$550 $1100 $1750**

ROY-29

ROY-30

❑ **ROY-29. "Roy Rogers and the Mystery of the Howling Mesa" Big Little Book #1448,**
1948. - **$16 $48 $115**

❑ **ROY-30. "Roy Rogers in Robbers' Roost" Big Little Book #1452,**
1948. - **$16 $48 $115**

ROY-31

❑ **ROY-31. "Roy Rogers And His World Championship Rodeo" Program,**
1948. - **$45 $85 $150**

ROY-32

❑ **ROY-32. Product Box With "Branding Iron" Ring Offer,**
1948. - **$35 $65 $125**

ROY-33

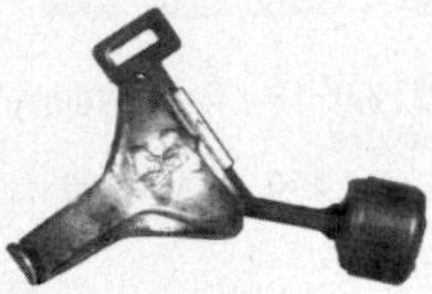
ROY-34

❑ **ROY-33. Dixie Ice Cream Picture,**
1948. - **$50 $85 $160**

❑ **ROY-34. Branding Iron/Initial Brass Ring With Black Cap,**
1948. Quaker Cereals. Plastic stamper under brass cover with ink pad was personalized with any requested initial. - **$50 $100 $200**

ROY-35

ROY-36

❑ **ROY-35. Contest Card,**
1948. Quaker Oats. - **$15 $30 $60**

❑ **ROY-36. Sterling Silver Saddle Ring,**
1948. Store item by W. G. Simpson Co., Phoenix, Az. Facsimile signature on saddle seat. - **$100 $200 $300**

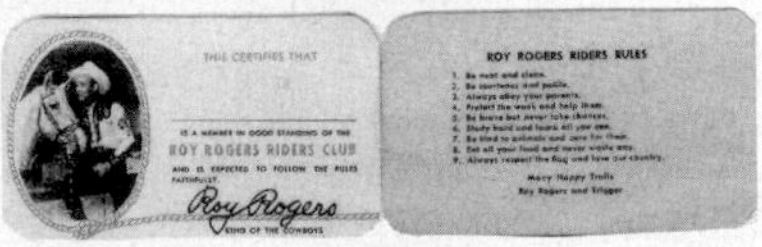

ROY-37

❑ **ROY-37. "Roy Rogers Riders Club" Membership Card,**
c. 1948. - **$25 $60 $100**

ROY-38

❑ **ROY-38. "Tattoo Transfers" Kit,**
c. 1948. Pack #7 with Fawcett Publications copyright, two sheets with 22 transfers. - **$30 $75 $160**

ROY-39

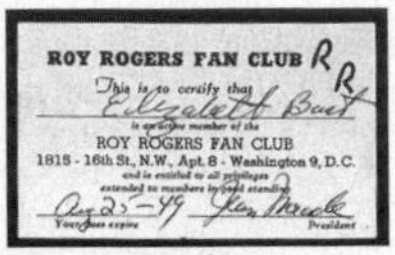

ROY-40

❑ **ROY-39. Quaker Contest Postcard,**
1949. - **$18 $35 $65**

❑ **ROY-40. Fan Club Membership Card,**
1949. Washington DC chapter. - **$12 $25 $50**

ROY-41

❑ **ROY-41. Microscope Ring/Saddle Ring Newspaper Ad,**
1949. Quaker Oats. - **$15 $30 $50**

ROY-42

❑ **ROY-42. "March Of Comics" #47,**
1949. Various sponsors. Pictured example for Sears merchandise. - **$19 $57 $240**

ROY-43

❑ **ROY-43. Quaker Contest Prize 19x26" Poster With Mailer,**
1949. Rare.
Near Mint With Label On Tube - **$1600**
Poster Only - **$300 $600 $1250**

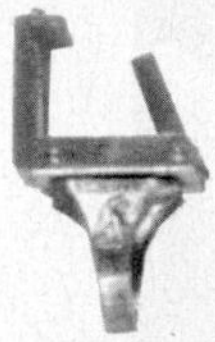

ROY-44

ROY-45

❑ **ROY-44. Quaker Microscope Ring,**
1949. - **$35 $65 $135**

❑ **ROY-45. Mother's Oats Container with Offer for Roy Rogers Microscope Ring,**
1949. Quaker Oats.
Large Container - **$50 $100 $175**
Small Container - **$35 $65 $125**

ROY-46

❑ **ROY-46. Dale Evans Wristwatch,**
1949. - **$125 $250 $500**

ROY-47

ROY-48

❑ **ROY-47. "Roy Rogers and the Mystery of the Lazy M" Big Little Book #1462,**
1949. - **$14 $42 $100**

❑ **ROY-48. "Roy Rogers And Trigger" Dixie Ice Cream Picture,**
c. 1949. Reverse has photo montage and titles of seven movies from 1947-1949 era. -
$100 $200 $300

ROY-49

❑ **ROY-49. "Roy Rogers Trick Lasso" Diecut Cardboard Mechanical Countertop Display,**
c. 1949. Knox-Reese Mfrs. 11.5x23" thick cardboard mounted to wood backing that holds electrical mechanism to turn lasso that is held in Roy's hand. 3.5" diameter plastic text with facsimile signature is attached at Roy's feet. Text reads "Anyone Can Spin The Roy Rogers Trick Lasso/Autographed Picture Free."
- **$500 $1500 $2500**

(MAILING LABEL)

ROY-50

❑ **ROY-50. "Roy Rogers Trick Lasso" Cardboard Standee,**
c. 1949. Counter display is 15x24" in original packaging. Has three-dimensional lasso attached at Roy's hands. Packaging has original mailing label with return address with illustration of Roy and reads "Roy Rogers Trick Lasso From Knox-Reese Mfrs. Philadelphia 31, Pa." Postmarked 1949. Mailer - **$50 $100 $200**
Display - **$500 $1500 $2500**

ROY-51

ROY-52

❑ **ROY-51. "Roy Rogers' Thrill Circus" Button,**
c. 1949. Blue on white for use by an "Official." -
$45 $100 $200

❑ **ROY-52. Real Photo Australian Button,**
1940s. Black and white photo without dot pattern. - **$30 $60 $100**

ROY-53

❑ **ROY-53. "Roy Rogers" Button,**
1940s. Button is 1.75" seldom-seen portrait button with pale blue bkg. - **$65 $150 $250**

ROY-54

ROY-55

❑ **ROY-54. Sterling Silver Ring By Uncas,**
1940s. Depicts Roy on Trigger facing left flanked by image on each band of six-shooter. -
$75 $150 $300

❑ **ROY-55. Sterling Silver Bracelet,**
c. 1940s. Link chain and 1.5" wide bar plate centered by mounted oval design of Roy on rearing Trigger. Underside of bar plate has "Sterling" marking by unidentified maker. -
$75 $150 $300

ROY-56

ROY-57

❑ **ROY-56. Portrait Pinback,**
1940s. 1-3/4" black & white pinback. Scarce. -
$40 $75 $150

❑ **ROY-57. Large Photo Portrait,**
1940s. 29-1/2x37" color photo on rigid cardboard. Likely for theater lobby or record store display. Marked only "Sign And Pictorial Local 230" at lower right. - **$150 $275 $500**

ROY-58

ROY-59

❑ **ROY-58. RCA Victor 18x24" Cardboard Store Sign,**
1940s. - **$250 $450 $850**

❑ **ROY-59. Fan Club Membership Card,**
1940s. - **$30 $60 $100**

ROY-60

ROY-61

❑ **ROY-60. Rodeo Souvenir Cello. Button,**
1940s. Various attachments. With Metal Boot - **$40 $75 $150**
With Miniature Iron Gun And Holster "Roy Rogers Championship Rodeo" - **$85 $175 $400**

❑ **ROY-61. Republic Studios Photo,**
1940s. - **$10 $25 $50**

ROY-62

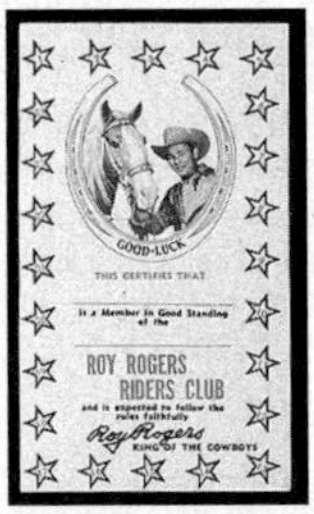

ROY-63

❑ **ROY-62. Republic Studios Photo,**
1940s. Includes facsimile signature. - **$20 $40 $70**

❑ **ROY-63. Riders Club Card,**
1940s. Scarce. Vertical card with 24 marked stars around card. - **$45 $90 $175**

ROY-64

ROY-65

❑ **ROY-64. Movie Card,**
1940s. Roy's picture on a King card, symbolizing his trademark "King of the Cowboys." - **$10 $20 $35**

❑ **ROY-65. Roy Rogers & Trigger Glove Set,**
1940s. Gloves have a red jewel and silver colored studs. - **$125 $250 $400**

ROY-66

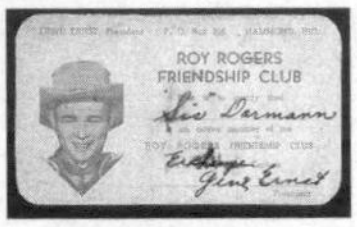

ROY-67

❑ **ROY-66. Postcard,**
1940s. Quaker Oats. Radio premium announcing free signed photo. - **$12 $25 $50**

❑ **ROY-67. Friendship Club Card,**
1940's. Hammond, Ind. Picture of Roy on left Red on white. - **$20 $50 $100**

ROY-68

ROY-69

❑ **ROY-68. Photo,**
1940s. Quaker Oats. Color photo of Roy on Trigger. - **$20 $40 $70**

❑ **ROY-69. Photo,**
1940s. Movie premium of Roy and the Sons of the Pioneers. - **$30 $50 $100**

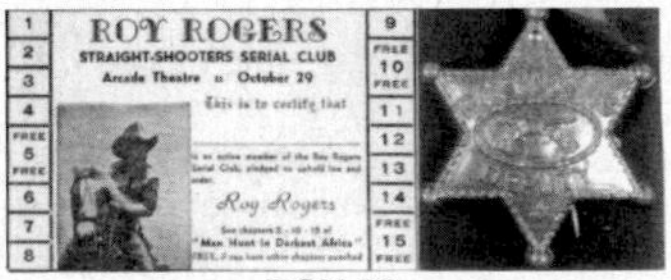

ROY-70

❑ **ROY-70. Movie Serial Club Card/Ticket With Metal Badge,**
1940s. Badge designated "Roy Rogers Deputy".
Card - **$30 $50 $100**
Badge - **$15 $30 $70**

ROY-71

ROY-72

❑ **ROY-71. "Roy Rogers" Sterling Silver Child's Ring,**
1940s. Store item. Image of Roy on rearing Trigger, bands have branding iron design. - **$75 $150 $300**

❑ **ROY-72. "Dale Evans Fan Club" Cello. Button,**
1940s. 1.75". - **$75 $150 $300**

ROY-73

❑ **ROY-73. Plastic Mug,**
1950. Quaker Oats. - **$15 $30 $75**

ROY-74

❑ **ROY-74. "Roy Rogers Riders Club" Member's Pack,**
1950. Package includes two cover letters, six cards, and 1-1/8" litho. button on card.
Near Mint In Mailer - **$450**
Each Card - **$12 $25 $50**
Loose Button - **$10 $18 $35**

ROY-75

❑ **ROY-75. Quaker Brass Badge With Sheet And Mailer,**
1950. Near Mint Boxed - **$225**
Badge Only - **$25 $50 $100**

ROY-76

ROY-77

❑ **ROY-76. "Souvenir Cup" 15x20" Paper Store Sign,**
1950. Quaker Oats. - **$150 $300 $600**

❑ **ROY-77. Quaker Canister With "Souvenir Cup" Offer,**
1950. - **$35 $65 $125**

ROY-78

ROY-79

❑ **ROY-78. "Roy Rogers Range Detective" New Better Little Book #715-10,**
1950. Whitman. 3-1/4x5-1/2" vertical format. - **$12 $36 $75**

❑ **ROY-79. Roy and Dale Cut Out Book**
1950. Large cut out of Trigger on back cover. - **$65 $150 $350**

ROY-80

❑ **ROY-80. "Sheriffs' Annual 'World's Championship Rodeo'" Program,**
1950. Sheriffs' Relief Assn. of Los Angeles County. Issued for single day event August 27, 1950. Inside back cover has Roy ad sponsored by Quaker Oats. - **$75 $150 $335**

ROY-81

ROY-82

❑ **ROY-81. "Roy Rogers" Vinyl Notebook,**
c. 1950. Store item. 10-1/2x13". - **$100 $250 $400**

❑ **ROY-82. "Roy Rogers Birthday Club" Button,**
c. 1950. Times Newspapers. Large 2-1/2" button in black and white and various shades of red. Rare. - **$125 $250 $450**

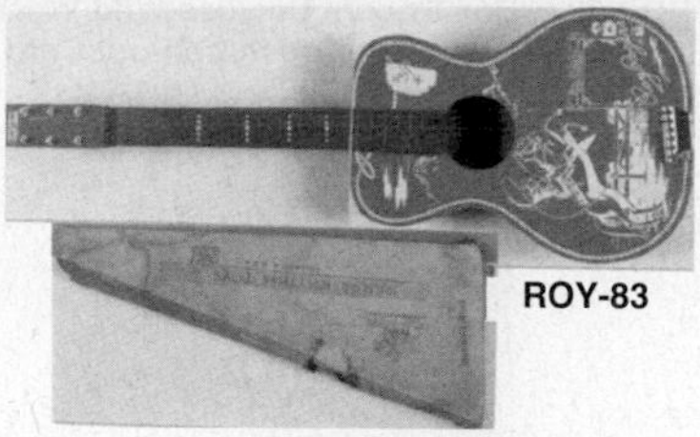

ROY-83

❑ **ROY-83. "Roy Rogers" Guitar With Carton,**
c. 1950. Store item by Range Rhythm Toys. 30" tall guitar. Box - **$35 $75 $125**
Guitar - **$45 $90 $175**

ROY-84

ROY-85

❑ **ROY-84. Record Album 12x12" Cardboard Store Sign,**
c. 1950. RCA Victor. - **$50 $100 $160**

❑ **ROY-85. "Roy Rogers And Trigger" Dixie Ice Cream Picture,**
c. 1950. Reverse has montage of five photos plus titles of four movies from 1949 or 1950. - **$100 $200 $300**

ROY-86

❑ **ROY-86. "Thrill Circus" Felt Pennant,**
c. 1950. - **$45 $85 $190**

ROY-87

ROY-88

❑ **ROY-87. "Roy Rogers & Trigger" Lamp With Shade,**
c. 1950. 8" tall figural plaster on 3-1/4x5" base.
Near Mint With Shade - **$550**
Lamp Only - **$75 $150 $300**

❑ **ROY-88. "Dale Evans" Lamp With Shade,**
c. 1950. 8" tall figural plaster on 3-1/4x5" base.
Near Mint With Shade - **$500**
Lamp Only - **$65 $140 $250**

ROY-89

ROY-90

❑ **ROY-89. Dixie Ice Cream Picture,**
1951. - **$60 $100 $175**

❑ **ROY-90. Wrist Watch With Deputy Badge,**
1951. Mini "Western belt"-type strap. In box with clear mylar top and instructions. - **$750**
Watch only - **$75 $150 $350**

ROY-91

❑ **ROY-91. Newspaper Strips Promo,**
1951. Rare. Large & colorful. - **$200 $350 $725**

ROY-92

ROY-93

❑ **ROY-92. Quaker "Roy Rogers Cookies" Box,**
1951. One side panel pictures his gun belt.
Complete - **$250 $500 $900**

❑ **ROY-93. Quaker "Roy Rogers Cookies" Newspaper Ad,**
1951. Offers Humming Lariat premium. - **$15 $35 $60**

ROY-94

❑ **ROY-94. Roy Rogers' Cookies "Crackin' Good" Paper Pop Gun,**
1951. - **$20 $40 $85**

ROY-95

❑ **ROY-95. Bubble Gum Album,**
1951. Designed to hold two sets of 24 cards for movies "In Old Amarillo" and "South Of Caliente." Album
Complete - **$60 $125 $250**
Album Empty - **$25 $50 $85**

ROY-96

ROY-97

❑ **ROY-96. Quaker Cereal Box Puzzle Panel,**
1951. Back Panel Uncut - **$20 $35 $75**

❑ **ROY-97. "March Of Comics" Sears Christmas Book #77,**
1951. - **$15 $45 $190**

ROY-98

❑ **ROY-98. "Sears Christmas Trading Cards,"**
1951. Sears Happi-Time Toy Town. 10x10-1/2" punch-out sheet with card of Roy, Dale and six with Christmas theme. Gordon Gold archives.
Near Mint Unpunched - **$275**
Roy Card Loose - **$10 $25 $50**
Dale Card Loose - **$8 $15 $35**
Others Loose - **$2 $5 $10**

ROY-99

❑ **ROY-99. "Roy Rogers Cookies Wild West Action Toy" Store Sign And Punch-out Card,**
1951. Sign is 13x16-3/4". Shown with 5-1/4x7" punch-out carton insert premium. Gordon Gold Archives. Sign - **$100 $250 $500**
Unpunched Premium - **$15 $30 $60**

ROY-100

❑ **ROY-100. "Roy Rogers Riders Club Comics",**
1952. From membership kit. - **$30 $90 $375**

ROY-101

ROY-102

❑ **ROY-101. Gun And Holster Premium Offer Sheet,**
1952. Post's Cereals. 6x7" red on white sheet for "Big Chrome Gun" and "Embossed Steer Hide Holster With Chrome Trappings And Bullets In Gun Belt." Expiration date of July 31. Inserted with Roy Rogers Riders Club Kit. - **$30 $60 $125**

❑ **ROY-102. Litho. Tin Tab,**
1952. Roy Rogers Riders Club. Came with club comic book. - **$20 $50 $100**

ROY-103

❑ **ROY-103. "Pop Out Card" Post's Box Wrapper,**
1952. Post's 40% Bran Flakes. Waxed paper wrapper offering set of 36 cards issued 1952-1955. Wrapper - **$175 $375 $825**

ROY-104

❑ **ROY-104. Pony Contest Entry Paper,**
1952. Post's Krinkles. For four consecutive weekly contests offering first prize pony each week plus other Roy merchandise prizes. - **$12 $25 $50**

ROY-105

ROY-106

❑ **ROY-105. "Trick Lasso Contestant" Transfer Sheet,**
1952. Issued for national lasso contest. - **$30 $60 $100**

❑ **ROY-106. Post Cereals Pop-Out Card #22,**
1952. From numbered set of 36 issued into 1955. Each Unpunched - **$8 $15 $30**
Each Punched - **$3 $6 $12**

ROY-107

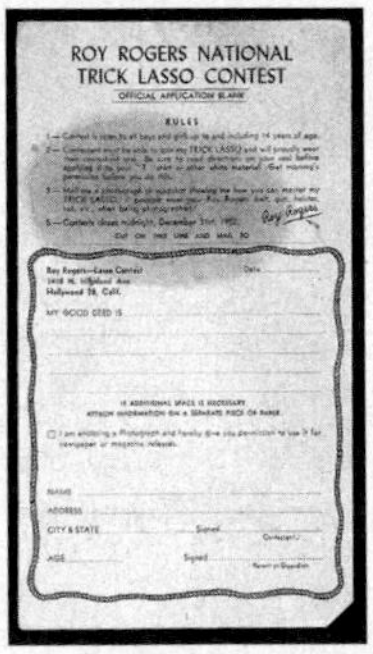

ROY-108

❑ **ROY-107. Grape Nuts Flakes Wrapper Flat,**
1952. Promotes pop-out cards. Gordon Gold Archives. - **$175 $375 $825**

❑ **ROY-108. Lasso Application,**
1952. National Trick Lasso contest application. - **$12 $25 $50**

ROY-109

❑ ROY-109. "Riders Club" Newspaper Ad,
1952. Post's Cereals. 14x22" full color Sunday comic section ad from May 25 offering club kit by mail of four items plus gun premium offer sheet. See following entries for comic book, gun premium offer sheet, tab badge.
Ad - **$15 $25 $40**
Member Card - **$20 $30 $50**
Color Photo - **$10 $20 $30**

ROY-110

❑ ROY-110. "Roy Rogers Comics" Christmas Subscription Notification Mailer,
c. 1952. Dell Publishing Co. 5x7" envelope containing full color illustrated folder card, paid subscription card, black and white photo of Roy and Trigger. Envelope - **$10 $20 $30**
Christmas Card - **$30 $60 $125**
Photo - **$20 $40 $75**
Subscription Card - **$10 $20 $30**

ROY-111

❑ ROY-111. "Roy Rogers/Post Cereals" Store Display Standee,
c. 1952. Very large 34.5x66" die-cut cardboard standee. Above Roy's right shoulder is circle bearing the text "Kids! Join The Roy Rogers Riders Club." - **$1250 $2500 $5000**

ROY-112

❑ ROY-112. Roy Rogers and Dale Evans Cut-Out Dolls Book
1953. With outfits. - **$65 $125 $275**

ROY-113

ROY-114

ROY-115

❑ ROY-113. Knife in Sheath with Compass,
1953. Knife handle shows Roy and Trigger. - **$80 $160 $350**

❑ ROY-114. "Western Ring" Post's Box Wrapper,
1953. Post's Raisin Bran. Waxed paper wrapper offering set of 12 litho. tin rings. Gordon Gold Archives. Wrapper - **$175 $375 $825**

❑ ROY-115. "Roy Rogers Western Medals" 17x24" Store Sign,
1953. Post's Raisin Bran. Diecut cardboard with easel back. Pictures six example litho. tin tabs from set of 27 offered as box inserts. Gordon Gold Archives. - **$350 $800 $1500**

(ENLARGED VIEW)

ROY-116

❑ ROY-116. "Post's Grape-Nuts Flakes" Store Window Display,
1953. 18x24" clear thin plastic with brightly colored inscriptions and box art featuring 3x4" Roy image. Top and bottom margins are banded by narrow peel-off adhesive strip for window mounting. Gordon Gold Archives. - **$100 $250 $600**

(AD)

ROY-117

❑ **ROY-117. Post Cereals "Roy Rogers Ranch" Set,**
1953. Twenty-three piece set with plastic figures of Roy, Dale, Pat, Trigger, Buttermilk and Bullet. Set also included metal Nellybelle jeep and cardboard punch-outs of ranch house, gate, trees and ranch animals.
Complete - **$135 $275 $485**

ROY-118

❑ **ROY-118. Post Cardboard Sign 13x18",**
1953. Scarce. Pictures all 12 Raisin Bran rings. Gordon Gold Archives. - **$250 $575 $1000**

ROY-119

❑ **ROY-119. "Bullet" Post's Raisin Bran Litho. Tin Ring,**
1953. This and the next 11 rings comprise a set of 12. The Near Mint price is for unbent examples with no rust. - **$10 $40 $120**

ROY-120

❑ **ROY-120. "Dale Evans" Post's Raisin Bran Litho. Tin Ring,**
1953. - **$10 $55 $135**

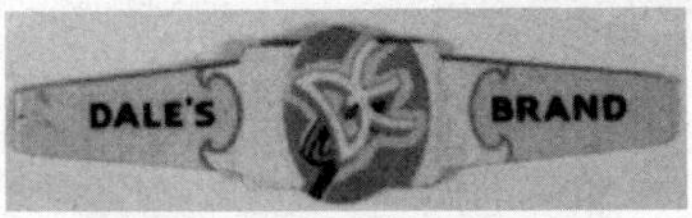

ROY-121

❑ **ROY-121. "Dale's Brand" Post's Raisin Bran Litho. Tin Ring,**
1953. - **$10 $30 $70**

ROY-122

❑ **ROY-122. "Deputy Sheriff" Post's Raisin Bran Litho. Tin Ring,**
1953. - **$10 $35 $75**

ROY-123

❑ **ROY-123. "Roy Rogers" Post's Raisin Bran Litho. Tin Ring,**
1953. - **$10 $55 $140**

ROY-124

❑ **ROY-124. "Roy's Boots" Post's Raisin Bran Litho. Tin Ring,**
1953. - **$10 $30 $70**

ROY-125

❑ **ROY-125. "Roy's Brand" Post's Raisin Bran Litho. Tin Ring,**
1953. - **$10 $30 $70**

ROY-126

❑ **ROY-126. "Roy's Gun" Post's Raisin Bran Litho. Tin Ring,**
1953. - **$10 $30 $70**

ROY-127

❑ **ROY-127. "Roy's Holster" Post's Raisin Bran Litho. Tin Ring,**
1953. - **$10 $30 $70**

ROY-128

❑ **ROY-128. "Roy's Saddle" Post's Raisin Bran Litho. Tin Ring,**
1953. - **$10 $30 $70**

ROY-129

❑ **ROY-129. "Sheriff" Post's Raisin Bran Litho. Tin Ring,**
1953. - **$10 $30 $70**

ROY-130

❑ **ROY-130. "Trigger" Post's Raisin Bran Litho. Tin Ring,**
1953. - **$10 $40 $120**

ROY-131

❑ **ROY-131. "Double R Bar Ranch" Cut-Outs,**
1953. Post Grape-Nuts Flakes. Canadian Box, three in set.
Each Complete Box - **$135 $275 $550**

ROY-132

❑ **ROY-132. Roy Rogers Western Medal Litho. Tin Tab,**
1953. Post's Raisin Bran, with cereal name on reverse, from set of 27. Also see 1955 Post's Sugar Krinkles set with blank back.
Each - **$10 $15 $30**

ROY-133

ROY-134

❑ **ROY-133. "King Of The Cowboys/Roy Rogers" Litho. Button,**
1953. Comes in 1-5/8" and 1-1/8" sizes. The 1-5/8" size comes with and without the Post's name on the reverse and was used as the "extra large" button in the U.S.A. along with fifteen 7/8" buttons to make a set of 16. The 1-1/8" button has not been seen with Post's name on the reverse but may have been used at a later time as the "extra large" button in both the U.S.A. and Canadian sets. Each - **$15 $30 $60**

❑ **ROY-134. "Queen Of The West/Dale Evans" Litho. Button,**
1953. Seen in 1-1/8" size only. Design matches ROY-119, but seen only with blank reverse. No documentation known indicates this is part of U.S.A. or Canadian set of 16 Post's buttons. - **$15 $30 $60**

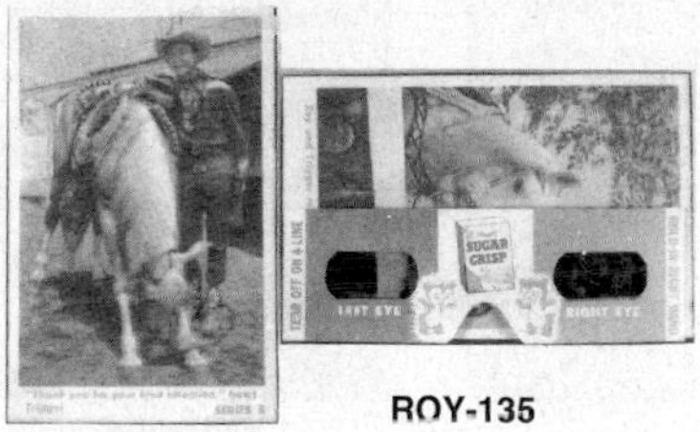

ROY-135

❑ **ROY-135. 3-D Photos,**
1953. Post's Sugar Crisp. Four photo folder with 3-D glasses, numbered series.
Intact - **$15 $25 $50**

ROY-136

❑ **ROY-136. Litho. Tin Button Set,**
1953. Post's Grape-Nuts Flakes and Rogers copyright text appears on reverse but also issued with blank reverses. Fifteen buttons are 7/8" and "extra large" portrait button inscribed "King of the Cowboys" in 1-5/8" or 1-1/8" size makes 16 in set. Each 7/8" - **$8 $12 $25**
"King of the Cowboys"-1-5/8" or 1-1/8" - **$15 $30 $60**

ROY-137

❑ **ROY-137. Canadian Litho. Tin Button Set,**
1953. Post's Canadian version of American set with different designs and smaller size. Fifteen small buttons are 3/4". The sixteenth button to complete the set is described as "extra large" and was likely the 1-1/8" version of the "King of the Cowboys" button pictured as ROY-133.
Each 3/4" - **$10 $20 $40**
Extra Large - **$15 $30 $60**

ROY-138

❑ **ROY-138. "March Of Comics" #105,**
1953. Various sponsors. Pictured example for Sears Christmas give-away. - **$11 $33 $105**

ROY-139

❑ **ROY-139. Roy Rogers Watch in Box,**
1953. With die-cut display. Box has a mylar top. Watch is the deluxe model with the metal band.
Boxed - **$850**
Watch only - **$65 $125 $250**

ROY-140

❑ **ROY-140. Dale Evans Watch in Box,**
1953. With die-cut display. Box has a mylar top. From Bradley Time Corp. Dale's watch is rarer than Roy's. Boxed - **$900**
Watch only - **$75 $135 $275**

ROY-141

❑ **ROY-141. "Western Medals" Store Sign,**
1953. Full color about 17x24". Roy pictured only on the example medal. Gordon Gold Archives. - **$225 $450 $700**

ROY-142

❑ **ROY-142. "Roy Rogers 3-D Pictures" Promotional Folder,**
1953. 8-1/2x11" full color stiff paper folder sent to grocery stores promoting 3-D pictures packaged with Post's Sugar Crisp cereal. Folder shows six of 48 photos and has attached envelope with 3-D glasses so store owner may view cards. Upper left has actual 3-D card glued in place while other images are replicas. Gordon Gold Archives. - **$200 $400 $750**

ROY-143

❑ **ROY-143. "3 Dimension Pictures" Offer On Waxed Wrapper Cereal Box,**
1953. Promotes set of 48 pictures. Each box held folder consisting of three-dimensional eyeglasses joined to a pair of picture cards with a separate picture on each side of the two cards. Gordon Gold Archives.
Used Complete - **$175 $375 $825**

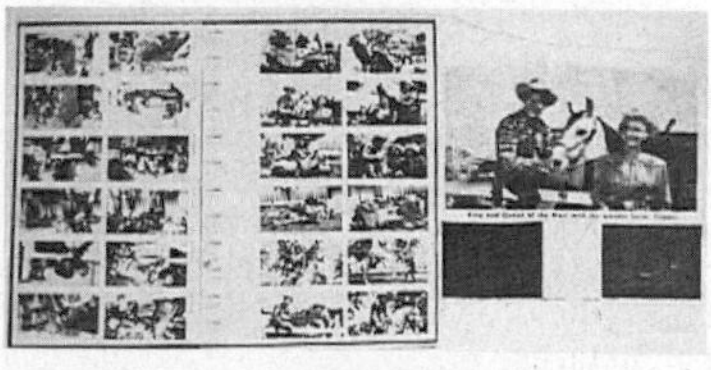
ROY-144

❑ **ROY-144. 3-D Premium Pictures Uncut Sheet With Viewer,**
1953. Post's Sugar Crisp. 16-1/2x21-1/2" single sheet showing 24 of the 48 different 3-D pictures. Gordon Gold Archives.
Sheet - **$200 $360 $725**
Glasses - **$10 $20 $30**

ROY-145

❑ **ROY-145. "Free! Roy Rogers Medals" Store Sign,**
1953. 8x9-1/8" diecut stiff paper designed like badge and holding actual litho. tin example "Roy Rogers." Gordon Gold Archives. - **$125 $325 $600**

ROY-146

❑ **ROY-146. "Free! Buttons" Store Poster,**
1953. 18x24" full color picturing all 15 litho. tin pin-backs packaged in Grape-Nuts Flakes. Gordon Gold Archives. - **$325 $675 $1250**

ROY-147

❑ **ROY-147. "King Of The Cowboys Roy Rogers Super Beanie" Complete Premium,**
1953. Mailer is 6x9" with red accent art with coupon on back to "Get The Entire Series Of 15 Roy Rogers Buttons." Green felt beanie is uninscribed. Button is full color 1-1/2" litho. Gordon Gold Archives.
Mailer And Beanie - **$100 $200 $400**
Button - **$15 $30 $60**

ROY-148

❑ **ROY-148. Cereal Box Wrapper With "Pin-On Button" Offer,**
1953. Includes offer for "Super Beanie! With Jumbo Roy Rogers Button" for 20 cents and one box top. Gordon Gold Archives.
Used Complete - **$325 $650 $1150**

ROY-149

❑ **ROY-149. Cereal Box Wrapper With "Western Medal" Offer,**
1953. Gordon Gold Archives.
Used Complete - **$175 $375 $825**

1953

1954-55

1955-56

ROY-150

❑ **ROY-150. Merchandise Manuals (all rare),**
1953 - **$250 $500 $1000**
1954-1955 - **$150 $425 $850**
1955-1956 - **$125 $375 $725**

ROY-151

❑ **ROY-151. Post Grape-Nut Flakes Box With Roy Billboard,**
c. 1953. - **$75 $150 $300**

ROY-152

❑ **ROY-152. Paint By Number Set,**
1954. Post's Sugar Crisp. Three sets, each with two pictures. Each - **$35 $75 $150**

ROY-153

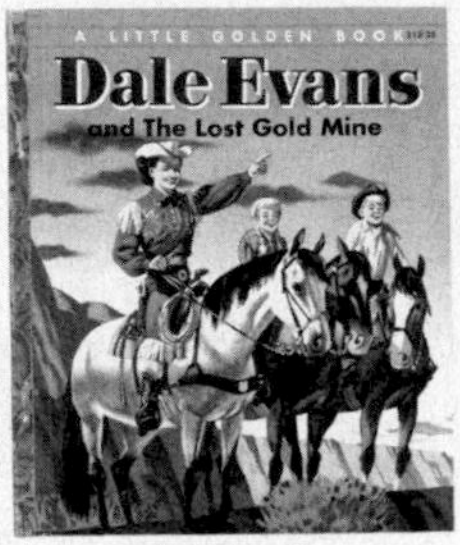

ROY-154

❑ **ROY-153. Wrist Watch For Boys,**
1954. Deluxe watch with metal elastic band. On die-cut card in box with grey cardboard slipcase.
Boxed - **$800**
Watch with Metal Band - **$65 $125 $250**

❑ **ROY-154. Dale Evans and the Lost Gold Mine" Golden Book,**
1954. - **$8 $20 $40**

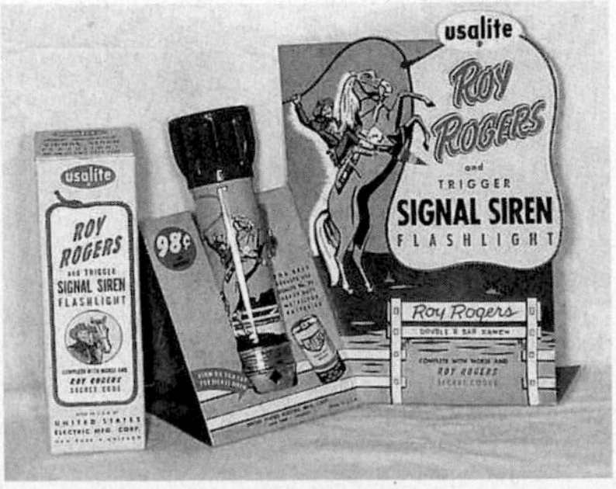

ROY-155

❑ **ROY-155. Roy Rogers and Trigger Counter Display With Signal Flashlight and Box,**
c. 1954. Display - **$150 $400 $700**
Flashlight and Box - **$50 $100 $200**
Flashlight - **$30 $65 $100**
Box - **$30 $65 $100**

ROY-156

❑ **ROY-156. "Roy Rogers Ranch Set" 21x22" Store Poster,**
1955. Post Cereals. Advertises the 18 piece all-cardboard set. - **$125 $250 $500**

ROY-157

❑ **ROY-157. "Roy Rogers Ranch" Cardboard Set,**
1955. Post Cereals. This 18 piece set was sent as a cardboard folder. - **$45 $80 $150**

ROY-158

❑ **ROY-158. Roy & Dale Golden Records Set With Mail Envelope,**
1955. Post's Sugar Crisp "Special Premium" offer not available at retail. Set of two.
Near Mint In Mailer - **$125**
Each Record - **$10 $20 $40**

ROY-159 (AD)

❑ **ROY-159. Dodge Motors Comic Booklet,**
1955. Ad story "Roy Rogers And The Man From Dodge City". - **$14 $42 $150**

ROY-160 **ROY-161**

❑ **ROY-160. March of Comics #136,**
1955. Various sponsors. - **$10 $30 $95**

❑ **ROY-161. "San Antonio World Championship Rodeo" Cello. Button,**
1955. Admittance serial number. - **$65 $110 $200**

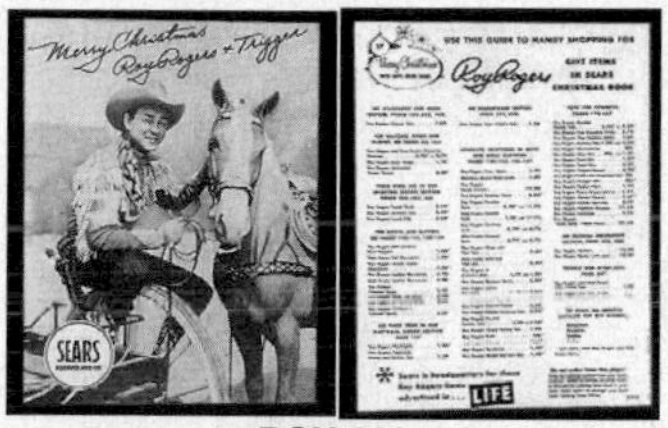

ROY-162

❑ **ROY-162. Roy/Sears Merchandise Handbill,**
c. 1955. Sears, Roebuck & Co. Single sheet with black and white photo plus listing on reverse of more than 60 Roy and/or Dale Evans gift items in Sears Christmas catalogue. - **$30 $60 $110**

ROY-163

❑ **ROY-163. Cereal Box Wrapper With "Ranch Set" Offer,**
1955. Waxed wrapper offering 18-piece set available for four box tops. Gordon Gold Archives. - **$200 $400 $850**

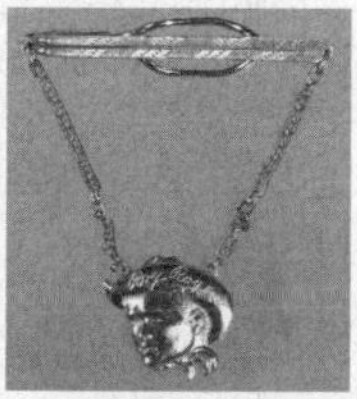

ROY-164

❑ **ROY-164. Roy Rogers Tie Clasp,**
1955. With metal die-cut portrait. Rare. - **$50 $125 $250**

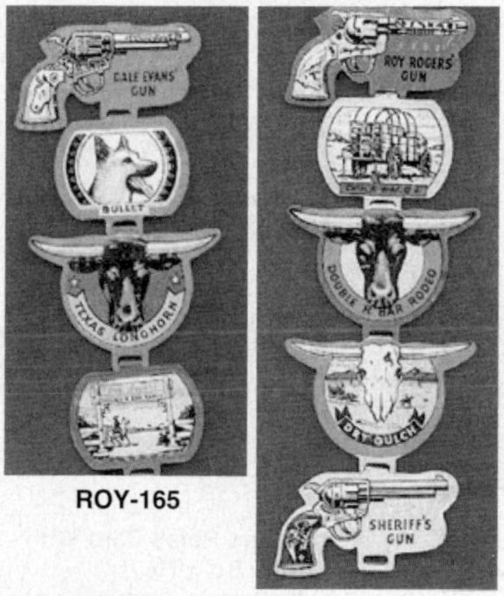

ROY-165

❑ **ROY-165. Blank Back Western Medals With Envelope,**
1955. Post's Sugar Krinkles. 3x5" envelope holding set of nine diecut tin tabs, offered as a set in that quantity or larger set of 27 either as box inserts or by mail order. Earlier 1953 set has Post's Raisin Bran marking on reverse.
Envelope - **$25 $50 $100**
Each Medal - **$10 $15 $30**

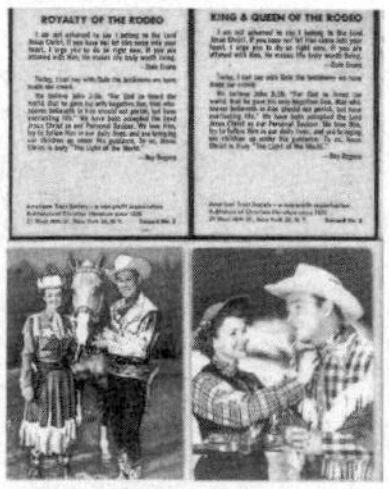

ROY-167

ROY-166

❑ **ROY-166. Sheathed Rubber Knife,**
1955. Knife has painted red handle. Sheath has imprint of Roy. Very hard to find in nice condition. - **$100 $250 $500**

❑ **ROY-167. "Tracard" Photo Cards #2-3,**
c. 1955. American Tract Society. Examples from Christian message set. Each - **$5 $10 $20**

ROY-168

❑ **ROY-168. "Roy Rogers Riders Club" Theater Exhibitor Kit,**
c. 1955. Includes two cover letters, packet of eight pages with club information, "Rogergram" 14x20" poster. Complete **- $150 $250 $400**

ROY-169

❑ **ROY-169. Roy Rogers Retail Card With "Western Blinkin' Blue Bolo Tie, "**
c. 1955. Store item by Putnam Products Company**. - $65 $140 $300**

ROY-170

ROY-171

❑ **ROY-170. "Roy Rogers Riders" Cello. Button,**
c. 1955. Scarce variety with imprint of local "Mt. Ephraim Theatre." - **$65 $125 $235**

❑ **ROY-171. Advertising Calendar,**
1956. Sundial Shoes. 10x17" stiff paper with tipped-on 8-1/2x10-1/2" full color glossy photo with facsimile signature. - **$40 $80 $175**

ROY-172

❑ **ROY-172. "March Of Comics" #146 Booklet,**
1956. Printed for Sears, Roebuck. - **$10 $30 $95**

ROY-173

ROY-174

❑ **ROY-173. Schwinn Bicycles Catalogue With Roy And Others,**
1956. Folder opening to 18x24" printed on both sides including endorsement photos by Roy Rogers, Bill Williams as TV's Kit Carson, Gail Davis as TV's Annie Oakley. - **$40 $80 $175**

❑ **ROY-174. Roy Rogers, Dale Evans and Dusty Cut Out Doll Book,**
1957. Photo cover. - **$60 $125 $250**

ROY-175

❑ **ROY-175. Post Cereal Puzzles,**
1957. Set of six. Each - **$8 $15 $25**

ROY-176

❑ **ROY-176. Jig Saw Puzzle Wax Wrapper Cereal Box,**
1957. Six puzzles in set, inserted one per box. Gordon Gold Archives.
Used Complete - **$125 $300 $575**

ROY-177

❑ **ROY-177. "Roy Rogers March Of Comics" #161,**
1957**. - $9 $27 $85**

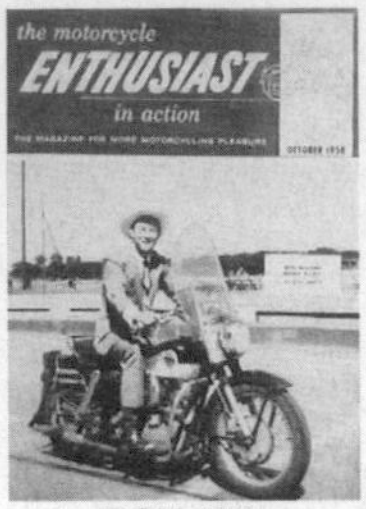

ROY-178

ROY-179

❑ **ROY-178. Harley-Davidson Motorcycle Monthly Magazine,**
1958. 9x12" with eight pages from October showing Roy on "Sportster" model at Wisconsin State Fairgrounds. - **$40 $80 $150**

❑ **ROY-179. "Guns" Magazine Monthly Issue,**
1958. 8-1/2x11" with 68 pages from August. - **$12 $25 $55**

ROY-180

❑ **ROY-180. "Roy Rogers Ranch Calendar",**
1959. Unmarked probably Nestle Quik. -
$65 $135 $225

ROY-181

❑ **ROY-181. Large Roy Rogers And Trigger Figural Store Display,**
1959. Sears. Wooden base 42" long holds 39.5" tall figure of Roy on rearing Trigger. Cast in plastic composite and hand-painted in oils. 5" length of right hoof is removable possibly done for shipping purposes. Roy is made as a separate figure but attached by metal fasteners on side as designed. Base - **$750 $1500 $2500**
Figure - **$2000 $4000 $8000**

ROY-182

❑ ROY-182. Merchandise Promotion Button,
1959. Black and white photo on red background 1-3/4" seen with various imprints but this example promoted sales of merchandise in a special department of the Sears stores. -
$35 $80 $135

ROY-183 ROY-184

❑ ROY-183. "Roy Rogers Stop Watch" Box,
1959. Store item by Bradley Time. -
$150 $300 $700

❑ ROY-184. "Roy Rogers & Trigger" Pocketwatch,
1959. Store item by Bradley. Also functions as a stopwatch. Beware of reproductions with color photocopy dial. - **$200 $400 $600**

ROY-185

❑ ROY-185. Lariat Flashlight On Store Display Card,
1950s. Bantamlite Inc.
Carded - **$100 $200 $400**
Light Only - **$35 $75 $150**

ROY-186

❑ ROY-186. Promo Folder with Premium Record,
1950s. Scarce. Sugar Crisp Cereal. -
$175 $300 $500

ROY-187

❑ ROY-187. "Double R Bar Ranch News" Club Newspaper,
1950s. Issued bi-monthly. - **$30 $60 $100**

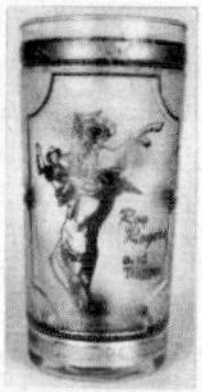

ROY-188 ROY-189

❑ ROY-188. "Roy Rogers Riders" Metal/Plastic Harmonica,
1950s. Store item by Harmonic Reed Corp. Also inscribed "King Of The Cowboys".
Boxed - **$40 $75 $145**
Loose - **$10 $20 $45**

❑ ROY-189. Frosted Glass Tumbler With Gold Image,
1950s. Probable store item. On old glass, Trigger's front legs overlap. On Roy Rogers Museum new glass, Trigger's front legs each show without overlap.
Old - **$35 $70 $145**
New - **$4 $6 $10**

ROY-190

❑ ROY-190. Western Clock,
1950s. Electric clock with metal lasso rope that revolves as clock runs. - **$85 $175 $350**

(AD)

ROY-191

❑ ROY-191. Trigger with Horseshoe Clock,
1950s. These were used as prizes and sometimes sold at stores generically.
- $75 $150 $300

ROY-192

❑ ROY-192. Flash Camera With Papers And Box,
1950s. Includes camera club card, press pass card.
Near Mint Boxed - **$450**
Unboxed With Flash - **$40 $75 $150**
Unboxed, No Flash - **$20 $50 $100**
Each Card - **$15 $30 $50**

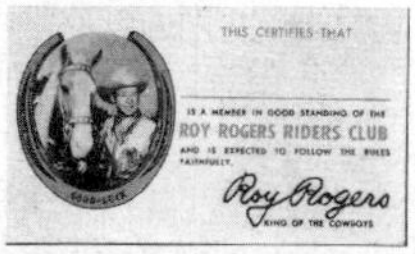

ROY-193 ROY-194

❑ ROY-193. "Riders Club" Membership Card,
1950s. Back has club rules. - **$15 $30 $60**

❑ ROY-194. "Roy Rogers Riders" Cello. Club Button,
1950s. - **$25 $50 $100**

ROY-195

ROY-196

ROY-197

❑ **ROY-195. Fan Club Response Card,**
1950s. Club Headquarters. Back includes offer for View-Master reels plus name of TV sponsor Post Cereals. - **$15 $30 $60**

❑ **ROY-196. Fan Club Response Card,**
1950s. Club Headquarters. Back includes ad for store item decals plus name of TV sponsor Post Cereals. - **$15 $30 $60**

❑ **ROY-197. English Candy Cigarette Box,**
1950s. - **$40 $75 $165**

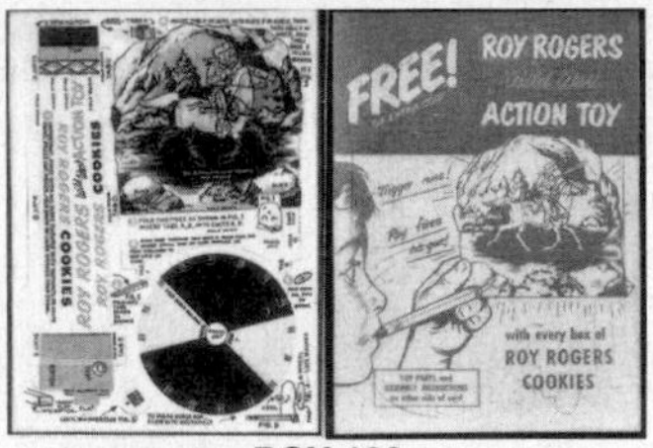

ROY-198

❑ **ROY-198. "Wild West Action Toy" Punch-Out Sheet,**
1950s. Roy Rogers Cookies.
Unpunched - **$15 $30 $60**

ROY-199

ROY-200

❑ **ROY-199. "Roy Rogers Riders Lucky Piece",**
1950s. 1" brass medalet holed as made for key fob with Roy pictured facing right. - **$8 $20 $30**

❑ **ROY-200. "Roy Rogers Riders Lucky Piece",**
1950s. 1-1/16" brass medalet holed as made for key fob w/Roy pictured facing straight ahead. - **$8 $20 $30**

ROY-201

ROY-202

❑ **ROY-201. "Roy Rogers Riders Lucky Piece",**
1950s. 1" brass medalet with Roy pictured looking upward and facing slightly left. - **$10 $20 $30**

❑ **ROY-202. "Roy Rogers Riders Lucky Piece",**
1950s. 1-3/16" brass medalet picturing Roy with broad smile facing left. - **$15 $25 $40**

ROY-203

ROY-204

❑ **ROY-203. "Roy Rogers Riders Lucky Piece",**
1950s. 1-1/8" white metal with copper luster medalet picturing Roy facing straight ahead. Design is in much higher relief than other medalets with same inscription. - **$12 $22 $35**

❑ **ROY-204. English Club Member's Cello. Button,**
1950s. 1-1/4" with b&w photo on white and bright yellow rim. - **$85 $150 $300**

ROY-205

ROY-206

❑ **ROY-205. Deputy Tin Star Badge,**
1950s. Issued by Post's, Popsicle, and probably others. Comes in copper, yellow brass, or silver finish. - **$10 $20 $40**

❑ **ROY-206. Glass,**
1950s. Probably held dairy product. - **$40 $80 $135**

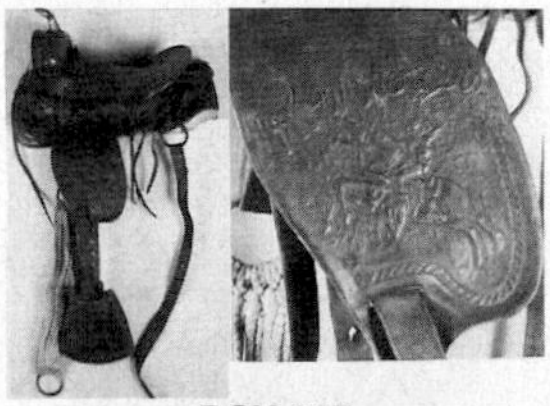

ROY-207

❑ **ROY-207. "Roy Rogers" Child's Leather Saddle,**
1950s. Store item. Well made brown leather western saddle with each side panel inscribed "Roy Rogers" in rope script above image of him on rearing Trigger. - **$400 $800 $1600**

ROY-208

❑ **ROY-208. Deputy Badge On Store Display Card,**
1950s. Post Cereals with seven varieties shown on card. 5x6-1/4" diecut stiff paper with actual example of copper finish badge mounted at center. Display - **$250 $500 $1000**
Badge Only - **$10 $20 $40**

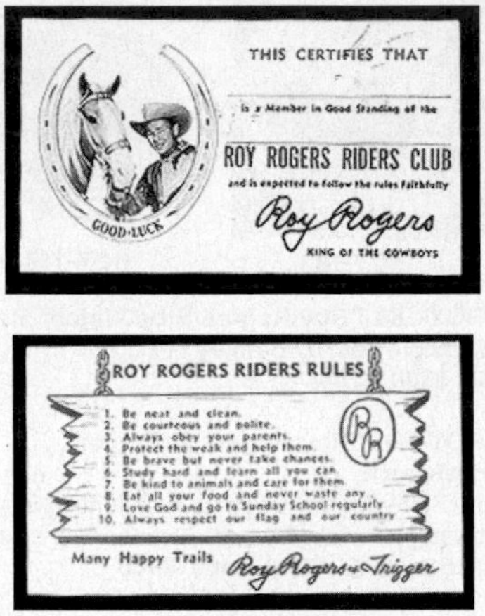

ROY-209

❑ **ROY-209. "Roy Rogers Riders Club" Membership Card,**
1950s. Version in red, white and blue front and black, blue and white reverse. - **$20 $40 $90**

ROY-210

ROY-211

❑ **ROY-210. "Roy Rogers Rodeo" 13x21" Cardboard Poster,**
1950s. - **$150 $300 $500**

❑ **ROY-211. "Roy Rogers Sweaters" Store Postcard,**
1950s. - **$12 $25 $50**

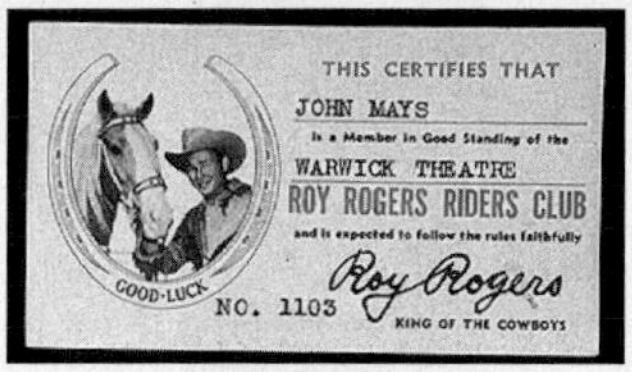

ROY-212

❑ **ROY-212. Riders Club Membership Card,**
1950s. Movie premium from Warwick Theater. - **$20 $40 $90**

ROY-213

❑ **ROY-213. "Roy Rogers Gun Puzzle" On Card,**
1950s. Store item by Plas-Trix Co.
Carded - **$40 $85 $150**

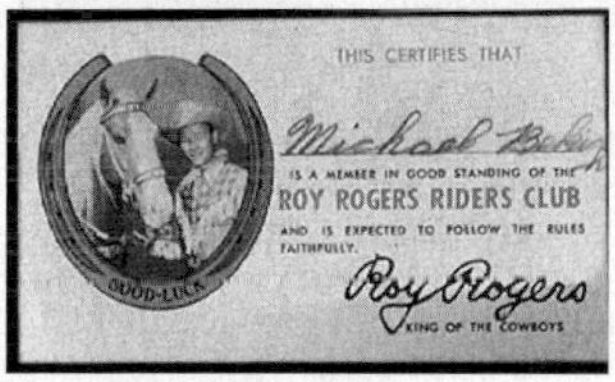

ROY-214

❑ **ROY-214. Riders Club Card,**
1950s. Yellow card. Movie premium. - **$20 $40 $90**

ROY-215

❑ **ROY-215. Photo,**
1950s. Movie premium. Black & white photo featuring Roy and Gabby Hayes. - **$12 $25 $50**

ROY-216

ROY-217

❑ **ROY-216. Photo,**
1950s. Movie premium. Black & white photo of Roy and his gun. - **$10 $20 $40**

❑ **ROY-217. Photo,**
1950s. Movie premium. Black & white photo of Roy with two Deputy Sheriffs. - **$10 $20 $40**

ROY-218

❑ **ROY-218. "Best Wishes Roy Rogers, Dale Evans & Trigger" Picture,**
1950s. Issued by Nestle's Quik. 8x9-1/2". - **$20 $35 $70**

ROY-219

❑ **ROY-219. Dell Comics Photo Strip Folder,**
1950s. - **$40 $75 $145**

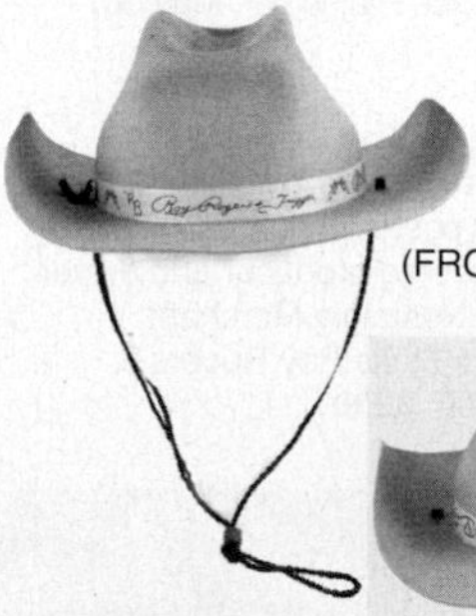

(FRONT)

(BACK)

ROY-220

❑ **ROY-220. Child's Cowboy Hat Boxed,**
1950s. 100% wool hat has band that says "Roy Rogers & Trigger" along with western symbols. Roy Brand is stamped inside hat.
Hat - **$100 $150 $300**
Box and insert only - **$25 $50 $75**

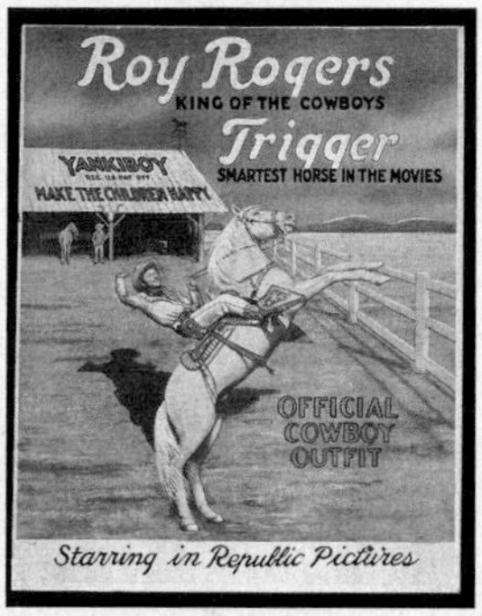

ROY-221

❑ **ROY-221. Official Cowboy Outfit In Box,**
1950s. Yankiboy. Shirt, cloth chaps, marked Roy and Trigger, gun, holster, lariat, and belt. Republic Pictures promoted on colorful box. - **$100 $250 $500**

ROY-222

❑ **ROY-222. Roy & Dale School Bag,**
1950s. 10x12.5" leather/vinyl satchel featuring front pocket color photo of Roy, Dale and Trigger. - **$150 $350 $700**

ROY-223

❑ **ROY-223. Roy On Trigger Rare Ceramic Figural By Beswick Of England,**
1950s. Figure has 3x4.75" base by 9" tall with 9.5" long Trigger. Finely detailed glazed ceramic figure> No inscription except bottom is marked "Beswick-England-1377." - **$350 $700 $1200**

ROY-224

❑ **ROY-224. "Nestle's Quik" Canister With Premium Offer,**
1960. Back offers 3-D plastic plaque set with expiration date June 30. - **$65 $150 $275**

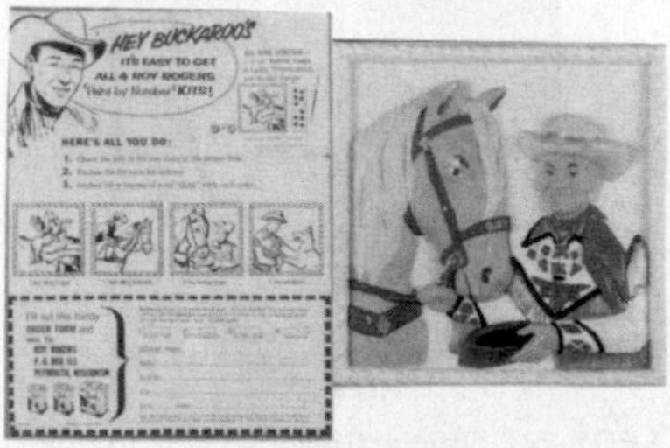

ROY-225

❑ **ROY-225. Roy Feeding Trigger Hand-Painted Relief Picture With Order Form,**
1960. 8-7/8x8-7/8" molded thin plastic issued by Nestle's Quik for 50 cents each and lid from can. Order Form **- $20 $40 $65**
Each Picture Unpainted Or Nicely Painted **- $75**

ROY-226

❑ **ROY-226. "Roy Rogers Chevy Show" Pair Of "NBC" Transcription Records,**
1960. Songs include Happy Trails.
Pair **- $65 $125 $250**

ROY-227

ROY-228

❑ **ROY-227. "Roy Rogers Ranch Calendar",**
1960. Nestle's Quik. - **$50 $125 $200**

❑ **ROY-228. "Roy Rogers Ranch Calendar",**
1961. Nestle's Quik. - **$50 $125 $200**

ROY-229

❑ **ROY-229. Nestle Candy Coupon,**
1961. - **$20 $40 $75**

ROY-230

ROY-231

❑ **ROY-230. Quick Shooter Hat in Box,**
1961. - **$100 $300 $550**
Hat Only - **$50 $125 $250**

❑ **ROY-231. Litho. Soda Can,**
c. 1960s. Continental Beverage Corp., La Jolla, California. - **$75 $150 $250**

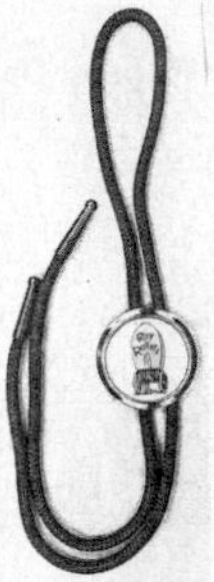
ROY-232

ROY-233

❑ **ROY-232. Bolo Tie,**
1970. Roy Rogers Restaurants. Given at opening of restaurant in Des Plains, Ill., May 30. - **$20 $30 $60**

❑ **ROY-233. "King Of The Cowboys" Autographed Poster,**
1977. 24x30" paper poster produced by Snuff Garrett, prominent record producer and owner of issuing company Nostalgia Merchant. Autograph is "Happy Trails Roy Rogers & Trigger." - **$100 $200 $300**

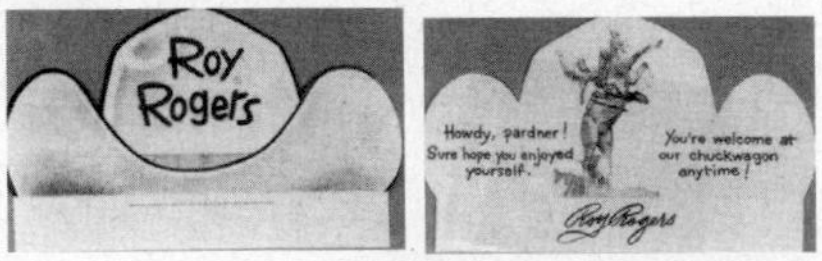

ROY-234

❑ **ROY-234. Paper Hat,**
c. 1970s. Roy Rogers Restaurants. -
$5 $10 $25

ROY-235

❑ **ROY-235. Life-Sized 75" Tall Cardboard Standee,**
c. 1980. Thousand Trails Campgrounds. -
$125 $275 $550

ROY-236

❑ **ROY-236. "Happy Trails" Roy & Dale Wristwatch Boxed,**
1985. Bradley. Styrene plastic display case holding watch featuring dial face art of Roy, Dale and Trigger. Loose - **$15 $25 $50**
Near Mint Boxed - **$100**

ROY-237

❑ **ROY-237. "Roy Rogers Family Restaurants" 2" Litho. Button,**
1980s. Various locations, pictured example from Maryland. - **$8 $12 $25**

(Gun)

ROY-238 (Box)

❑ **ROY-238. Daisy Limited Edition BB Gun,**
1995. With commemorative scarf and box with instructions. Only 2,500 produced. A medal with the edition number is embedded in the stock of the gun. Includes a certificate of authenticity. Complete - **$350**

ROY-239

❑ **ROY-239. Limited Edition Cookie Jar,**
1996. Edition of 2,500. - **$625**

ROY 240

ROY-241

❑ **ROY-240. "King of the Cowboys" Guitar,**
2000. Commemorates his life (1911-1998). - **$35**

❑ **ROY-241. Two Coin Proof Set,**
2000. From the Legends of the American West series. Authorized coins by the Republic of Liberia. Happy Trails coin was limited to 1,000. Set in box with certificate - **$85**

Rudolph the Red-Nosed Reindeer

Rudolph originated as a 1939 story created by Robert L. May for use by Montgomery Ward & Company. The company printed 2,400,000 copies to give away. The character achieved even greater recognition in 1949 when Johnny Marks wrote a song based on the story and the Gene Autry recording went off the charts. Over the years, in excess of ten million copies have sold, making it Autry's greatest hit.

DC Comics published thirteen comic books between 1950 and Winter 1962-63 with stories by Seymour Reit and art by Rube Gossman. A daily comic strip by Rube Grossman ran during the 1950-1951 Christmas season. Rudolph came to life first as a 1944 Max Fleischer animated cartoon and later as a 1964 "Dynamation" TV special produced by Rankin-Bass Productions and aired annually over twenty years, becoming one of the most popular holiday TV specials ever produced. In the last few years a restored print of the special with restored footage that was cut over the years has been aired several times.

Rankin-Bass' Rudolph went on to star in the television special *Rudolph's Shiny New Year* (1976) and the feature-length *Rudolph and Frosty's Christmas in July* (1979), with Ethel Merman offering her own unique rendition of Rudolph's theme song. Johnny Marks composed many additional songs for the various Rudolph productions, and a resurgence in the original special's popularity has led to a flood of new merchandise, from beanbag characters to Christmas tree ornaments, all in the Rankin-Bass style. A new animated film by another production company was released to video in recent years as well, but did not capture the level of attention and popularity that Rankin-Bass' version did.

RUD-1

❑ **RUD-1. Push-Out Puzzle Toy With Envelope,**
1940s. Montgomery Ward. Christmas greetings envelope holding card of punch-out assembly parts for standup figure. Exclusive issue for this department store chain with additional Rudolph items advertised on envelope back.
Unpunched With Envelope - **$25 $50 $100**
Assembled - **$15 $30 $60**

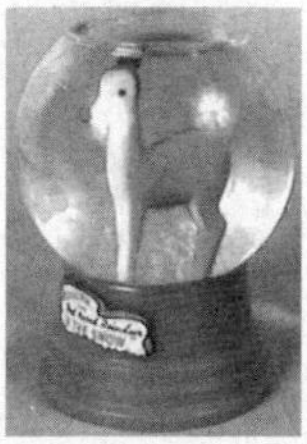
RUD-2

RUD-3

❑ **RUD-2. Snow Dome,**
c. 1950. Store item. Driss Co., Chicago. 4" tall on green plastic base with red and black name decal. - **$30 $60 $125**

❑ **RUD-3. Figural Plastic Light-Up Bank,**
c. 1950. Store item. 5-1/2" long. Inserted coin hits brass tab and should light the red bulb nose. - **$40 $80 $160**

RUD-4

❑ **RUD-4. "Rudolph's 32 Page Fun Book" Original Art Prototype,**
c. 1950. Presentation piece for Montgomery Ward stores. 8x10-1/2" with 32 pages of original art. Gordon Gold Archives. Unique - **$1250**

RUD-5

❑ **RUD-5. "Yearling" Litho. Tin Wind-Up Toy,**
c. 1950. Store item with box marked "Made In Occupied Japan" and toy marked "Made In Japan." 5-1/4" tall unlicensed but with red nose obviously inspired by Rudolph. Has leather ears.
Box - **$15 $30 $70**
Toy - **$25 $50 $100**

RUD-6

RUD-7

❑ **RUD-6. Classic Song Record By Gene Autry,**
1951. Store item by Columbia Records. 45 rpm with jacket. - **$10 $18 $40**

❑ **RUD-7. Classic Song Record By Gene Autry,**
1951. Store item by Columbia Records. 78 rpm with 10x10" jacket. - **$10 $18 $40**

RUD-8

❑ **RUD-8. "I Like Rudolph" Button,**
c. 1951. 1.25" probable Montgomery Ward issue copyright by Rudolph creator Robert May. Red design on yellow. - **$30 $55 $95**

RUD-9

❑ **RUD-9. "Rudolph The Red-Nosed Reindeer" Group,**
1950s. First is 3.5x4" card that holds 1.75" plastic figure of Rudolph with keychain. Second is 2.25" celluloid button with text "I Talked With Rudolph At Rollman's.' Third is 4" stainless steel fork with image of Rudolph's face and reads "Rudolph." Keychain Near Mint Carded - **$35**
Keychain Loose - **$8 $12 $20**
Button - **$8 $12 $20**
Fork - **$5 $10 $15**

RUD-10

❑ **RUD-10. Alvin And The Chipmunks 45 RPM Record,**
1961. Store item by Liberty. - **$8 $15 $35**

RUD-11

RUD-12

❑ **RUD-11. Plastic Mug With Flicker Eye,**
1960s. Store item. Eagle, U.S.A. 4-1/4" tall with brown and red art, black and white flicker eye. - **$15 $30 $60**

❑ **RUD-12. Rudolph Bean Figure,**
1998. 1st series. The set of 12 was available exclusively at CVS Pharmacies. - **$20**

RUD-13

RUD-14

❑ **RUD-13. Santa Claus Bean Figure,**
1998. 1st series. - **$20**

❑ **RUD-14. Clarice Bean Figure,**
1998. 1st series. Mouth is larger than 2nd series figure. - **$12**

RUD-15

RUD-16

RUD-17

❑ **RUD-15. Herbie Bean Figure,**
1998. 1st series. - **$10**

❑ **RUD-16. Sam the Snowman Bean Figure,**
1998. 1st series. - **$15**

❑ **RUD-17. Yukon Cornelius Bean Figure,**
1998. 1st series. No snowshoes, unlike 2nd series version. - **$12**

RUD-18

RUD-19

❑ **RUD-18. Misfit Train Bean Toy,**
1998. 1st series. From the Land of Misfit Toys.- **$12**

❑ **RUD-19. Misfit Doll Bean Figure,**
1998. 1st series. - **$12**

RUD-20

RUD-21

RUD-22

❑ **RUD-20. Spotted Elephant Bean Figure,**
1998. 1st series. - **$12**

❑ **RUD-21. King Moonracer Bean Figure,**
1998. 1st series. - **$12**

❑ **RUD-22. Charlie-in-the Box Bean Figure,**
1998. 1st series. - **$15**

RUD-23

RUD-24

❑ **RUD-23. Rudolph Bean Figure,**
1999. 2nd series. This 2nd set of 12 was also sold at CVS Pharmacies. - **$15**

❑ **RUD-24. Santa Bean Figure,**
1999. 2nd series. - **$10**

RUD-25

RUD-26

❑ **RUD-25. Clarice Bean Figure,**
1999. 2nd series. This Clarice has a smaller mouth than the 1st series figure. - **$12**

❑ **RUD-26. Reindeer Coach Comet Figure,**
1999. 2nd series. - **$10**

RUD-27

RUD-28

RUD-29

❑ **RUD-27. Boss Elf Bean Figure,**
1999. 2nd series. - **$10**

❑ **RUD-28. Tall Elf Bean Figure,**
1999. 2nd series. - **$10**

❑ **RUD-29. Sam the Snowman Bean Figure,**
1999. 2nd series. - **$12**

RUD-30

RUD-31

RUD-32

❑ **RUD-30. Yukon Cornelius Bean Figure,**
1999. 2nd series. This version has snowshoes unlike 1st series. - **$10**

❑ **RUD-31. Misfit Water Pistol Bean Figure,**
1999. 2nd series. - **$10**

❑ **RUD-32. Misfit Plane Bean Figure,**
1999. 2nd series. - **$10**

RUD-33

RUD-34

❑ **RUD-33. Frosty the Snowman Bean Figure,**
1999. Modeled after the cartoon character. Set of 4 figures sold at CVS. - **$12**

❑ **RUD-34. Karen Bean Figure,**
1999. Frosty series. - **$10**

RUD-35

RUD-36

❑ **RUD-35. Professor Hinkle Bean Figure,**
1999. Frosty series. - **$10**

❑ **RUD-36. Traffic Cop Bean Figure,**
1999. Frosty series. - **$10**

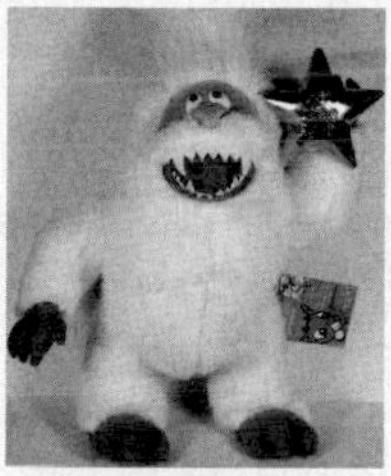
RUD-37

❑ **RUD-37. Abominable Snowman Bean Figure,**
1999. 16" tall. "Land of Misfit Toys" series. Released at the end of 1999 to celebrate New Year's 2000. Hard to find on the secondary market. - **$60**

RUD-38

❑ **RUD-38. Rudolph Lunch Box,**
2000. - **$25**

RUD-39

RUD-40

❑ **RUD-39. Altoids Tin Box,**
2003. Limited edition features the Abominable Snowman. - **$3**

❑ **RUD-40. Altoids Tin Box,**
2003. Limited edition features Heat Miser from "Year Without a Santa Claus." - **$3**

Rudolph Valentino

Born Rodolpho Gugliemi (1895-1926) in Italy, the family moved to the U.S. in 1913 and settled in New York City. Valentino worked as a waiter, then as a tango dancer. He moved to California and worked as a bit player in various film roles which led to a major part in *The Four Horsemen of the Apocalypse*. Metro Pictures released the feature March 6, 1921. Based on a novel by Vincente Ibanez with screenplay by June Mathis and direction by Rex Ingram, co-stars included Pomeroy Cannon, Josef Swickard and Bridgeta Clark.

Paramount released *The Sheik* October 31, 1921. Written by Edith Hall and directed by George Melford, co-stars included Agnes Ayres, Adolphe Menjou and Walter Long. The film was a box office smash, making Valentino a star and coining the slang term "sheik" for a man irresistible to women. The Tin Pan Alley song *Sheik of Araby* by Harry Smith and Francis Wheeler became a huge hit. Valentino followed that success with Paramount's *Blood and Sand* directed by Fred Niblo released August 5, 1922; United Artists *The Eagle* directed by Clarence Brown released November 8, 1925; and his last feature United Artists' *The Son of the Sheik* directed by George Fitzmaurice released September 3, 1926.

Rudolph Valentino died August 23, 1926 of complications from a perforated ulcer. Worldwide, young women mourned his passing, establishing Valentino historically as the silver screen's first major romantic leading man.

RDV-1

❑ **RDV-1. "Rudolph Valentino Monsieur Beaucaire" Color Movie Herald,**
1924. New Regent Theater, Harrisburg, Pa. 4.5x6" with four pages. - **$10 $25 $50**

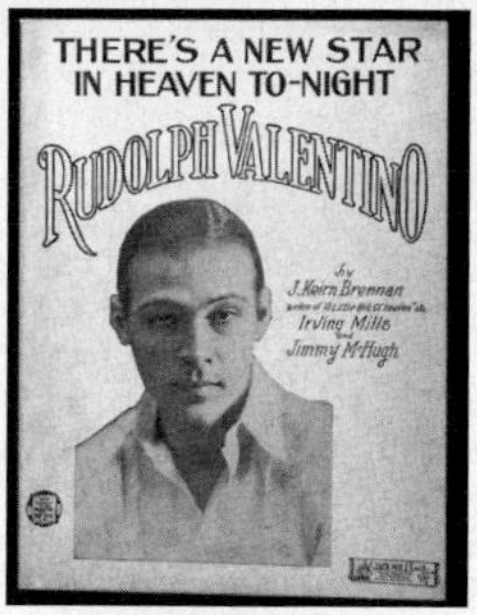

RDV-2

❑ **RDV-2. "There's A New Star In Heaven To-Night" Song Sheet,**
1925. Rudolph Valentino on cover. - **$20 $40 $65**

RDV-3

❑ **RDV-3. "The Son Of The Sheik" Rudolph Valentino Lobby Card,**
1926. 10.25x13.25" lobby card for the last film before his death in 1926. - **$150 $300 $600**

RDV-4

❑ **RDV-4. Rudolph Valentino Son Of The Sheik-Inspired Bust,**
1926. Leach Studios. 4x5x8" tall plaster bust with name inscribed on base. - **$200 $400 $600**

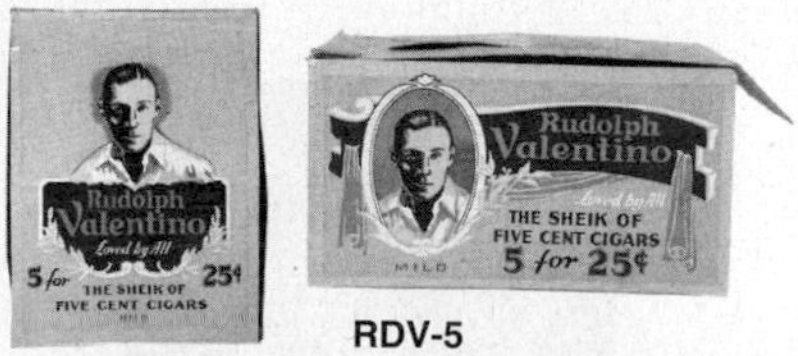

RDV-5

❑ **RDV-5. Rudolph Valentino Cigar Box,**
1920s. Cardboard. - **$50 $100 $275**

RDV-6

❑ **RDV-6. "Rudolph Valentino" Tin With Facsimile Signature,**
1920s. 7.5" diameter by 1.3/8" deep tin with art by Henry Clive. - **$30 $75 $150**

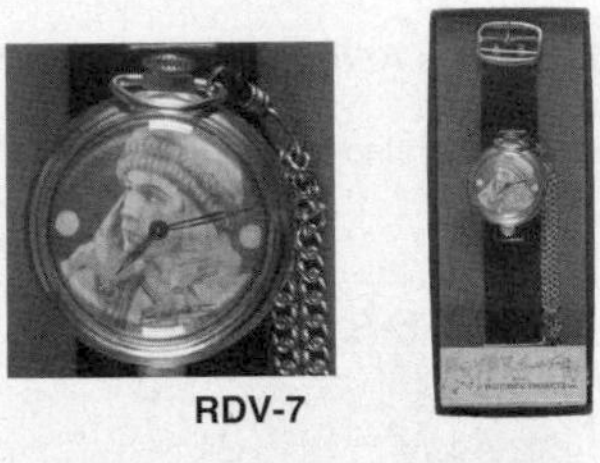

RDV-7

❑ **RDV-7. "Rudolph Valentino" Boxed Combination Watch/Pocket Watch,**
1970s. Photorific Products Inc. 3.75x10" window box contains 2" diameter watch. This version comes with chain so pocket watch could also be hung as a pendant. Box - **$25 $50 $100**
Watch - **$100 $200 $400**

Sally Starr

Sally Starr, born in Kansas City, Mo., in 1923, was singing on a CBS country radio show at the age of 12. She worked as a radio disc jockey, and in 1950 became hostess of *Popeye Theater* on Channel 6, WFIL, in Philadelphia. Dressed as a cowgirl and calling herself Our Gal Sal, she showed cartoons and *Three Stooges* shorts, read original stories, and chatted with show business visitors. The program became Philadelphia's highest rated children's show and ran until 1972. In the mid-1980s Sal made personal appearances in the tri-state area and in 1993 she was named Grand Marshal of the 84th Annual Baby Parade in Ocean City, New Jersey. She continued to be a weekly radio hostess until her retirement in September 2006, however a year later, she returned to spinning country records, something she continues to do at the outset of 2008.

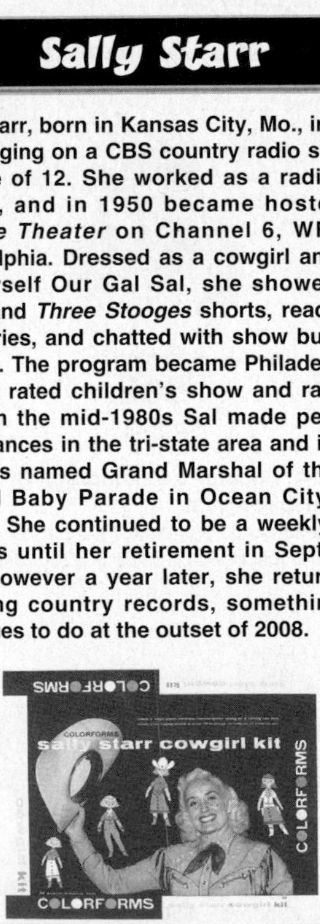

SAL-1

❑ **SAL-1. "Sally Starr Cowgirl Kit" Colorforms Company Archive Box Proof,**
1958. Proof measures 17x21.75".
- $20 $40 $65

SAL-2

SAL-3

❑ **SAL-2. Full Color 3-1/2" Cello. Button,**
1950s. - **$18 $30 $65**

❑ **SAL-3. "Sally Starr" Outfitted Doll,**
1950s. 10" tall vinyl doll with fabric cowgirl outfit patterned after actual performance outfit. -
$40 $85 $175

SAL-4

❑ **SAL-4. "Cowgirl Outfit" With Photo,**
1950s. Store item by Herman Iskin & Co. 8x10" photo accompanies youngster's denim and suede-like fabric colorful jacket and skirt.
Near Mint Boxed - **$200**
Photo Only - **$8 $15 $30**
Outfit Only - **$30 $50 $100**

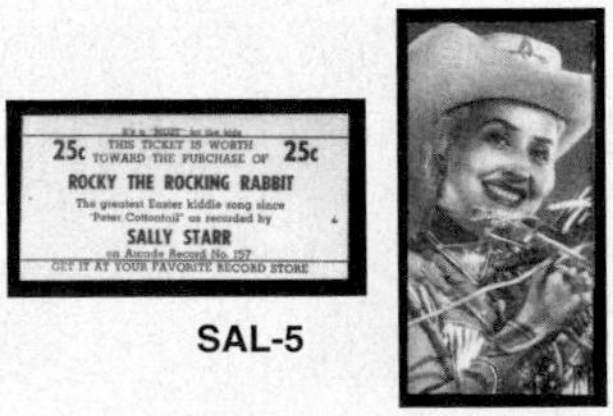

SAL-5

❑ **SAL-5. Performance Ticket With Record Offer,**
1950s. Photo ticket with reverse offer for child's Easter song record by her. - **$8 $12 $25**

SAL-6

❑ **SAL-6. Cowgirl Doll Outfit,**
1950s. Store item by Dandee Doll Mfg. Co. Scaled for 10-1/2" dolls. - **$30 $65 $135**

SAL-7

❑ **SAL-7. TV Show Photo,**
1950s. 5x7" issued by "Gold Square Trading Stamps." **$20 $35 $65**

SAL-8

❑ **SAL-8. "Sally Starr-Frontierland" Button,**
1950s. 1.75" cello black and white photo of popular Philadelphia area show hostess. -
$45 $85 $175

Santa Claus

The legend of Saint Nicholas, Father Christmas and Kris Kringle dates back to Europe centuries ago. The American version was inspired by the stories of Sinter Klaas brought to New York by the Dutch in the 17th century. Washington Irving's 1809 *History of New York* tells of Saint Nicholas' arrival on horseback. The Troy, New York *Sentinel* newspaper published *A Visit By Saint Nicholas* December 23, 1823. Written by Clement Moore (1779-1863) the poem has become a classic.

Noted political cartoonist Thomas Nast (1840-1902) brought the image of Santa

Claus to life in the pages of *Harper's Weekly* beginning January 3, 1863 and continuing into the 1880s.

On September 21, 1897 *The New York Sun* published a letter from eight year old Virginia O'Hanlon asking if there is a Santa Claus. Newsman Frank Church replied in the affirmative including "Yes, Virginia There Is A Santa Claus." In 1856, the post office department gave a town in Indiana the name Santa Claus. The town was featured in Ripley's *Believe It Or Not* in 1929. Curtiss Candy Company opened *Santa Claus Town* there in 1935 and what may have been the world's first theme park *Santa Claus Land* opened in 1946. Notable films include *Miracle On 34th Street* with Natalie Wood and Edmund Gwynn released May 2, 1947 and *Santa Claus: The Movie* with Dudley Moore and John Lithgow released November 27, 1985.

SNT-1

SNT-2

❑ **SNT-1. Santa Claus/Bellsnickel Early Figure,**
1900s. 3x3x10.5" tall German composition figure with pipe cleaner-type accent around hood and holding a feather tree. - **$200 $400 $650**

❑ **SNT-2. Santa Choice Color "Wishing" Button,**
1900s. 1.25" diameter. - **$50 $100 $200**

SNT-3

SNT-4

❑ **SNT-3. Rare Santa Upside Down In Chimney Button,**
1900s. Keystone Badge, Reading, Pa. 1.25" diameter button. - **$200 $400 $600**

❑ **SNT-4. "The Santa Claus Club" Button,**
c. 1900s. Whitehead & Hoag. 1.25" diameter. - **$200 $400 $800**

SNT-5

❑ **SNT-5. "Dear Old Santa Claus" Story-Coloring Book,**
1910. Charles E. Graham & Co./Newark, N.J. & N.Y. 10x12" book with 12 pages. - **$35 $75 $150**

SNT-6

❑ **SNT-6. Santa Claus Sleigh Cast Iron Toy,**
1910. Hubley. 16" long sleigh with removable Santa figure. Reindeer figures move up and down as toy is pulled. - **$400 $800 $2000**

SNT-7

SNT-8

❑ **SNT-7. "Christmas Greetings" Orhate Santa Claus Post Card,**
c. 1910. 3.5x5.5" glossy front with choice color. German. - **$15 $30 $60**

❑ **SNT-8. Santa Claus With Lantern Large Celluloid Figure,**
1930s. 5.75" tall figure. Underside has Japan paper label. - **$35 $65 $125**

SNT-9

❑ **SNT-9. Santa Claus Wind-Up Mechanical Celluloid Figure,**
c. 1930s. 7" tall in relief on front with flat back. Rubberband mechanism causes head to rock. - **$100 $200 $300**

SNT-10

❑ **SNT-10. "Santa Claus On Sled" Boxed Wind-Up,**
1940s. Mitsushima. 8" long tin sled with celluloid Santa and reindeer. When wound, sled moves forward and reindeer move up and down as bell rings. Made in Japan.
Box - **$14 $30 $60**
Toy - **$25 $50 $100**

SNT-11

SNT-12

❑ **SNT-11. Santa Claus "Recordiodisk" Unused Record,**
c. 1940s. 6.5" square record in envelope. Center reads "Recordiodisk/Wilcox/Gay Corp./Charlotte, Michigan." Record was used for personal message on both front and back. - **$8 $15 $25**

❑ **SNT-12. "Santa Claus Club" Rare Indiana Membership Button,**
c. 1940s. American Badge Co. 1.5" diameter. - **$100 $200 $350**

SNT-13

❑ **SNT-13. Rubber Squeaker Santa Claus In Original Box,**
c. 1950. Rempel Mfg. Co. Inc., Akron, Ohio. 4.5x9x11.5" box holds 11" tall figure of Santa with belt buckle having letters "SC." Box - **$15 $35 $60**
Santa - **$20 $40 $75**

SNT-14

❑ **SNT-14. Santa Claus On Tricycle Wind-Up,**
1950s. 2x4x3.75" tall with three dimensional celluloid figure of Santa attached to tin litho tricycle. Toy travels in circle and bell rings. Made in Japan. - **$25 $50 $85**

SNT-15

❑ **SNT-15. Santa Claus Ramp Walker,**
1950s. Marx. 3" tall hard plastic. - **$20 $40 $80**

SNT-16

❑ **SNT-16. "Merry Christmas Story And Coloring Book From Newberrys",**
1960. Promotional Publishing Co. 7.5x10.5" with 16 pages. Color glossy cover and color center spread with black and white pages. - **$8 $15 $25**

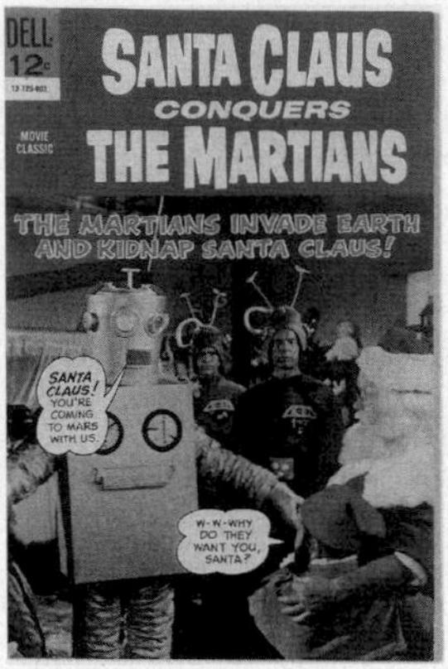

SNT-17

❑ **SNT-17. "Santa Claus Conquers The Martians" Movie Comic Book,**
1966. Embassy Pictures Corp. Published by Dell. 1964 Issue - **$10 $30 $140**
1966 Issue - **$8 $25 $100**
1966 Version With Golden Record - **$15 $40 $200**

SNT-18

❑ **SNT-18. "Battery Operated Santa Claus",**
1960s. 13" tall toy in box with cellophane window. Toy has fabric/plush-covered body with life-like beard and face is vinyl. Upper body rocks back and forth, head turns side to side as eyes light, arms move and he rings the bell. Box - **$15 $30 $60**
Toy - **$25 $50 $100**

Scooby-Doo

Created by Joe Ruby, Ken Spears and Iwao Takamoto for Hanna-Barbera, the cartoon series first aired on CBS-TV September 13, 1969. The basic plot line has Great Dane Scooby-Doo helping the Mystery, Inc. gang of young people track monster or ghost crooks and bring them to justice. The original voice cast included: Casey Kasem as Shaggy, Frank Welker as Fred, Nicole Jaffe as Velma and Stefanianna Christopherson as Daphne.

From 1972 to 1974 the show became the hour long *The New Scooby-Doo Movies.* The series moved to ABC with various title changes through the years: 1976-77 *The Scooby-Doo/Dynomutt Hour,* 1977-78 *Scooby's All-Star Laff-A-Lympics,* 1978-79 *Scooby's All-Stars.* Scooby's nephew joined the cast and the show became *Scooby-Doo And Scrappy-Doo.* In 1985-86 it was *The 13 Ghosts of Scooby-Doo,* and from 1988-1991 *A Pup Named Scooby-Doo.*

Between 1998 and 2007 Warner Brothers released one new direct-to-video movie a year. The WB Network aired *What's New, Scooby-Doo?* in 2002-2005 and *Shaggy & Scooby-Doo Get A Clue!* in September 2006.

Warner Brothers released the *Scooby-Doo* live action movie June 14, 2002 followed by a sequel *Scooby-Doo 2: Monsters Unleashed* in March, 2004. Both films were written by James Gunn and directed by Raja Gosnell with cast including Freddie Prinze Jr., Sarah Michelle Gellar and Matthew Lillard.

Gold Key, Charlton, Marvel, Harvey, Archie and DC have all published Scooby-Doo comics. "And I would've gotten away with it if not for you meddlin' kids and your dog!"

SCD-1

❑ **SCD-1. "Scooby-Doo" Pepsi Series Glass,**
1977. 3" diameter by 6.25" tall glass from set of six. - **$3 $6 $12**

SCD-2

❑ **SCD-2. "Hanna-Barbera's Scooby-Doo Cartoon Annual" Hardcover Book,**
1981. 7-1/8x10.25" with 76 pages published in Great Britain. - **$8 $15 $25**

SCD-3

❑ **SCD-3. Scooby-Doo And Shaggy Cel,**
1987. Hanna-Barbera Productions Inc. 10.5x14" cel with 3.25x6" image has matching 11x14" laser background. Near Mint Same Or Similar - **$65**

SCD-4

❑ **SCD-4. Scooby-Doo Character Litho Buttons,**
1997. Cartoon Network. Five 1" buttons. Each - **$1 $2 $3**

SCD-5

SCD-6

❑ **SCD-5. Scooby-Doo Race Car Replica,**
1997. Revell. - **$12**

❑ **SCD-6. "Scooby-Doo" Street Wheels,**
1999. 5 die cast cars in box. - **$25**

SCD-7

❑ **SCD-7. Scooby-Doo Bean Bag,**
1999. - **$15**

Scoop Ward

Laddie Seaman, alias Scoop Ward, narrated dramatizations of the news for his teenage audience in *News of Youth* on CBS radio from late 1935 to 1937. The program was sponsored by Ward's Soft Bun bread and Silver Queen pound cake.

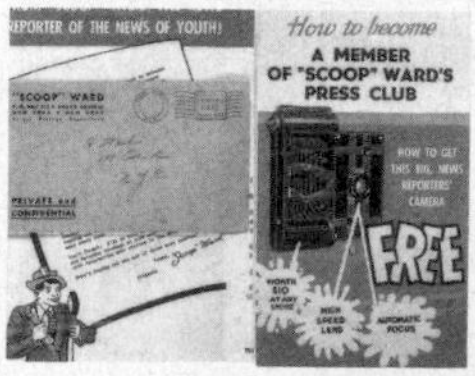

SCW-1

SCW-2

❑ **SCW-1. Club Newsletter With Envelope,**
1936. Ward's Bread and Silver Queen Pound Cake. Mailer - **$5 $10 $15**
Newsletter - **$15 $30 $80**

❑ **SCW-2. "Official Reporter" Brass Shield Badge,**
1936. Ward's Soft Bun Bread. - **$5 $10 $20**

SCW-3

❑ **SCW-3. Member Recruitment Brochure With Typewriter Offer,**
c. 1936. Ward's Bread/Silver Queen Pound Cake. - **$30 $65 $125**

Scrappy

Animation pioneer producer Charles Mintz (1896-1940) married Margaret Winkler in 1924 and through Winkler Productions gained control of Walt Disney's Oswald the Lucky Rabbit in 1928. In 1930, Mintz joined with Columbia Studios to get the backing on a new cartoon series featuring a young boy. The character and his friends were designed by animator Dick Huemer who wanted to depart from the Mickey Mouse genre. He gave his cast huge heads, small bodies and most surprisingly, in-depth personalities. Mischievous Scrappy was introduced in 1931, joined by his barely tolerated little brother Oopy, girlfriend Margy and terrier dog Yippy. Bobby Winkler supplied Scrappy's voice. Animators Dick Huemer, Sid Marcus and Art Davis had free rein and the cartoons grew more weird and wild as the years went on. Experimentation flourished and the mid-1930s Scrappy cartoons were the first in the industry to use moving backgrounds. After 75 cartoons, the series ended in 1941. Though never highly popular with the public, licenses of the character produced a moderate assortment of merchandise and a few premiums.

SCR-1

❑ **SCR-1. "Presenting Scrappy, Margy And Yippy" Boxed Soap Figures,**
1935. Kirk Guild Inc. 5x8.5x2.25" deep box holds three painted soap figures ranging in size from 2-5/8" to 3-3/8" tall. - **$50 $100 $175**

SCR-2

❑ **SCR-2. "Scrappy/Yippy/Margie" Drinking Glass,**
1935. 2-5/8" diameter by 4.75" tall. - **$20 $40 $60**

SCR-3

❑ **SCR-3. "Scrappy's Puppet Theater" Standee,**
1936. Has die-cut front to hold Pillsbury's puppet punchouts kit. - **$135 $325 $650**

SCR-4

❑ **SCR-4. "Scrappy's Animated Puppet Theater" Punch-Out Kit,**
1936. Pillsbury's Farina cereal. Unpunched - **$35 $85 $150**

SCR-5

SCR-6

❑ **SCR-5. Pillsbury's Farina Salesman's Presentation Book,**
1936. Pillsbury. Includes 27x41" poster for Scrappy cartoon from Columbia Pictures and 11x14" salesman's presentation to grocer book with 14 pages and numerous inserts for posters, handbills, brochures, etc. Gordon Gold Archives. Scrappy Poster - **$200 $400 $800**
Salesman's Book - **$250 $500 $1000**

❑ **SCR-6. "Scrappy" Metal Book Bank,**
1930s. Zell Prod. Co., N.Y. 1x3x3.5" tall. - **$25 $50 $100**

SCR-7

❑ **SCR-7. Largest "Scrappy Paint Set",**
1930s. 13x18x2" deep box contains small crayons with Scrappy wrappers, 18 paint tablets, 4 paint bottles, 2 tin water pans a paint brush and 5 pictures to color. - **$40 $80 $150**

SCR-8

❑ **SCR-8. Scrappy Rare Enamel On Silvered Brass Pin,**
1930s. 1-1/8" tall pin. - **$20 $40 $75**

SCR-9

❑ **SCR-9. Scrappy/Margy/Yippie Bisque Figures Boxed,**
1930s. 3.75x6x1.5" deep box holds bisque figures including Scrappy 3.5", Margie 4" and Yippie 1.75". - **$100 $200 $300**

SCR-10

SCR-11

❑ **SCR-10. Scrappy/Margy/Yippie/Doghouse Bisque Figures Boxed,**
1930s. 3.75x6x1.5" deep box contains four bisque figures for Scrappy 3.5", Margie 3.5", Yippie 1.75" and doghouse 2". - **$150 $260 $440**

❑ **SCR-11. "Scrappy" And Margy Bisque Figures In Box,**
1930s. 3.75x6.5x1.5" deep box holds .75x1x3.5" tall painted bisque figures. Made in Japan. - **$75 $150 $250**

SCR-12

❑ **SCR-12. "Scrappy" Celluloid Figure With Moving Arms And Head,**
1930s. 5.5" tall. - **$200 $400 $700**

Seckatary Hawkins

This children's program was developed from a comic strip and books of the same name by Robert F. Schulkers (1890-1972) in the early 1920s. Hawkins was the leader of a boys' club that spent its time helping to round up bad boys. The club's motto was "Fair and Square." The radio series, sponsored by Ralston Purina, was broadcast on NBC in 1932-1933. The club is still in existence today as the "Seckatary Hawkins Club."

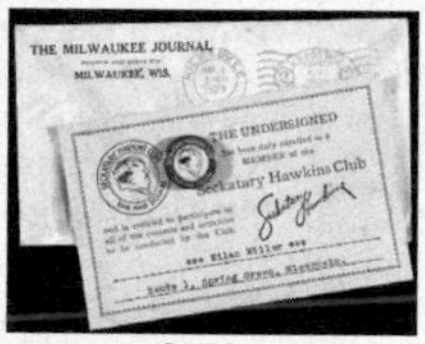

SKH-1

❑ **SKH-1. Club Kit,**
1929. With pin, card, and mailer.
Set - **$30 $60 $100**

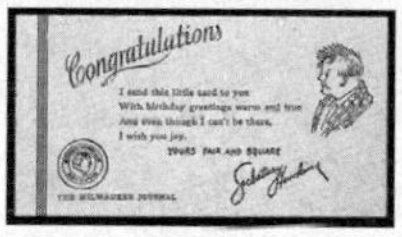

SKH-2

SKH-3

❑ **SKH-2. Birthday Card,**
1929. Newspaper premium from the Milwaukee Journal. - **$12 $25 $40**

❑ **SKH-3. Birthday Card Mailer,**
1929. Premium mailer for card. - **$5 $10 $20**

SKH-4

SKH-5

SKH-6

❑ **SKH-4. "Fair And Square" Member's Cello. Button,**
1932. 7/8" size. Red rim. - **$8 $12 $25**

❑ **SKH-5. "Fair And Square" Cello. Club Button,**
1932. 7/8" size. Blue rim. - **$5 $10 $18**

❑ **SKH-6. "Fair And Square" Litho. Club Button,**
1932. 3/4" size. - **$10 $15 $30**

SKH-7

SKH-8

SKH-9

❑ **SKH-7. "Fair And Square" Ralston Club Enameled Brass Spinner,**
1932. Spinner disk forms club slogan when spun. - **$20 $50 $80**

❑ **SKH-8. "Sunday Baltimore American" Cello. Club Button,**
c. 1932. - **$12 $25 $40**

❑ **SKH-9. Figure Of Hollow Pressed Cardboard,**
c. 1932. About 12" tall. - **$40 $80 $150**

SKH-10

SKH-11

❑ **SKH-10. The Ghost of Lake Tapako Book,**
1932. Ralston. - **$10 $35 $100**

❑ **SKH-11. Good Luck Fair and Square Coin,**
1960s. Scarce. - **$15 $30 $60**

Secret Agent X-9

Written by Dashiell Hammett and drawn by Alex Raymond, *Secret Agent X-9* was introduced by King Features in January 1934. X-9 is a loner who fights urban criminals by seeming to become part of their evil world. Hammett and Raymond went on to other things in 1935, and the strip was continued by an assortment of writers and artists, evolving in 1967 to *Secret Agent Corrigan.* Comic book reprints of the first eight months of the strip were published in 1934. There was a short-lived radio program, and Universal Pictures made two *Secret Agent X-9* chapter plays, one in 1937 starring Scott Kolk; the other, with Lloyd Bridges starring, in 1945.

SCX-1

❑ **SCX-1. Daily Comic Strip Book,**
1934. Store item. - **$83 $250 $650**

SCX-2

❑ **SCX-2. Secret Agent X-9 Original Comic Strip Art By Alex Raymond,**
1935. 7x27" three-panel comic strip art for publication September 19. Examples Of Similar Age And Content - **$500 $850 $1600**

SCX-3

SCX-4

❑ **SCX-3. Big Little Book #1144,**
1936. - **$15 $40 $125**

❑ **SCX-4. Movie Serial Cello. Button,**
1937. Universal. 1-1/4" red, black and white naming stars "Scott Kolk-Jean Rogers." - **$115 $225 $350**

SCX-5

SCX-6

❑ **SCX-5. Newspaper Sponsored Club Membership Card With Envelope,**
1930s. Envelope - **$10 $20 $30**
Card Only - **$20 $40 $80**

❑ **SCX-6. "Secret Agent X-9/Chicago Herald And Examiner" Silvered Metal Badge,**
1930s. Also seen with "Wisconsin News" imprint, "New York Journal" imprint and likely issued by additional newspapers.
- **$30 $60 $125**

SCX-7

SCX-8

❏ **SCX-7. Cello. Button,**
1940s. - **$20 $50 $110**

❏ **SCX-8. Water Gun On Card,**
1950s. Irwin. Store item. Billy club serves as water tank. - **$30 $60 $120**

SCX-9

❏ **SCX-9. Secret Agent X-9 Pair Of Original Daily Strips,**
1960. Art by Paul Norris, assistant to main artist Mel Graff.
Examples Of Similar Age And Content Each - **$15 $30 $60**

The Secret 3

Murray McLean starred in this serial detective drama sponsored by 3-Minute Oat Flakes and apparently broadcast only regionally in the 1930s. Premiums included a membership badge, a Confidential Code Book, and a variety of generic crime-fighting paraphernalia. The show's main characters were: Ben Potter, Chief of Detectives; Jack Williams, 1st Lieutenant; Mary Lou Davis, 2nd Lieutenant.

SCT-1

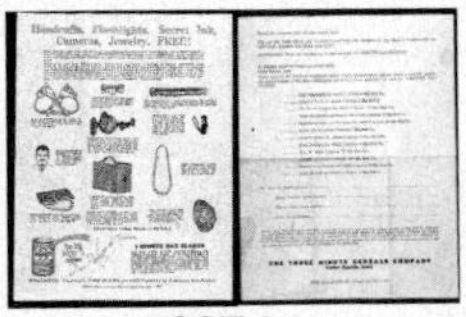

SCT-2

❏ **SCT-1. Silvered Brass Badge,**
1930s. Rare. - **$25 $50 $100**

❏ **SCT-2. Secret 3 Premium List,**
1930s. 3-Minute Oat Flakes Cereal premium. Shows color picture of 12 pieces of equipment on back. Front side lists premiums and how to get them. - **$20 $40 $80**

SCT-3

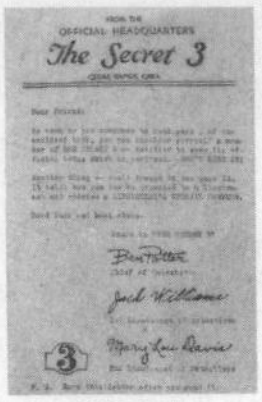

SCT-4

❏ **SCT-3. Club Member Code/Rule Book,**
1930s. Rare. 3-Minute Oat Flakes. Includes two pages of detective premiums. - **$35 $65 $125**

❏ **SCT-4. Club Headquarters Cover Letter,**
1930s. Scarce. P.S. notation on letter is "Burn this letter after you read it." - **$10 $35 $65**

SCT-5

❏ **SCT-5. "Lieutenant" Rank Pin,**
1930s. 3-Minute Oat Flakes premium.
1.25" wide. - **$30 $60 $100**

SCT-6

❏ **SCT-6. "Special Secret Code Book For Lieutenants Of The Secret 3,"**
1930s. 4x6" eight-page booklet accompanying Lieutenant badge and including secret signs, signals, requirements for "Captain Of Detectives" rank. - **$65 $125 $225**

Sergeant Preston of the Yukon

Under its original title, *Challenge of the Yukon*, this adventure series of the Royal Canadian Mounties during the gold-rush days of the 1890s was heard initially on Detroit radio station WXYZ from 1938 to 1947. Created by George W. Trendle and Fran Striker after their success with *The Lone Ranger* and *The Green Hornet*, the program centered on the crime-fighting exploits of Sgt. Frank Preston and his malamute partner Yukon King, "the swiftest and strongest lead dog of the Northwest." The series moved to the ABC network in 1947 and then to Mutual in 1950, where it remained until 1955. Quaker Puffed Wheat and Rice were the long-term sponsors. In 1951 the program changed its name officially to *Sergeant Preston of the Yukon*, although it was also popularly known as Yukon King, a reflection of the dog's central role in Preston's always getting his man.

On television, the series was broadcast on CBS from 1955 to 1958, sponsored by Quaker Oats and Mother's Oats. Richard Simmons (1913-2003) starred in the title role, riding his black stallion Rex and assisted, as always by Yukon King. Reruns were seen on NBC during the 1963-1964 season.

***Sergeant Preston* comic books were published between 1951 and 1959, including a set of four giveaways in two sizes from Quaker cereals in 1956. The cereal company also offered a great variety of other premiums, notably a 1955 in-package deed to a one-square-inch tract of land in the Yukon. "On King, On You Huskies..!"**

SGT-1

SGT-2

❏ **SGT-1. Autographed Photo,**
c. 1947. Believed to picture Paul Sutton radio voice of Sgt. Preston. - **$90 $175 $350**

❏ **SGT-2. Fan Photo,**
1947. - **$20 $40 $75**

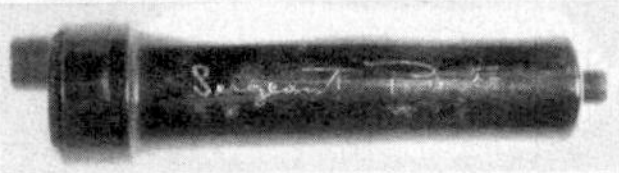

SGT-3

❏ **SGT-3. 2-Way Signal Flashlight,**
1949. Plastic disk produces red or green light. - **$30 $60 $140**

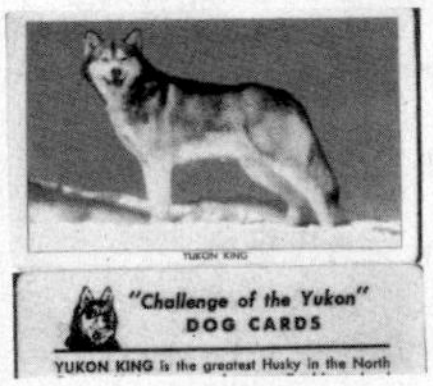

SGT-4

SGT-5

❏ **SGT-4. Dog Cards,**
1949. Set of 35. Each - **$2 $4 $8**

❏ **SGT-5. Club Photo,**
1949. Radio premium. - **$50 $75 $135**

SGT-6

❑ **SGT-6. "Sergeant Preston Gets His Man" Game,**
1949. Game board and playing pieces from Quaker cereal boxes.
Cut But Complete - **$20 $40 $80**
Complete Box - **$100 $200 $400**

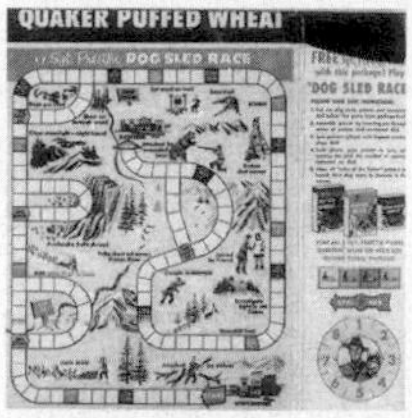

SGT-7

SGT-8

❑ **SGT-7. "Dog Sled Race" Quaker Box Back,**
1949. From series of three games offered.
Complete Box - **$100 $200 $400**
Uncut Box Back With Side Parts Panel - **$20 $40 $80**

❑ **SGT-8. "Great Yukon River Canoe Race" Quaker Box Back,**
1949. From series of three games offered.
Complete With Markers - **$20 $40 $80**

SGT-9

SGT-10

❑ **SGT-9. Sgt. Preston Autographed Photo,**
1949. 8x10" glossy signed with character name probably by Paul Sutton, one of the radio voices of Sgt. Preston. - **$75 $150 $275**

❑ **SGT-10. "Official Seal" Litho. Button,**
c. 1949. Rare.1-3/8" black and red on yellow background. Five known. - **$400 $1000 $2000**

SGT-11

SGT-12

❑ **SGT-11. Mountie Badge,**
1940s. Canada. No documentation as Sgt. Preston item. Came with Toy Clicker Gun Set. - **$25 $50 $100**

❑ **SGT-12. Rectangular Bar,**
1940s. Canada. No documentation as Sgt. Preston item. Came with Toy Clicker Gun Set. - **$25 $50 $100**

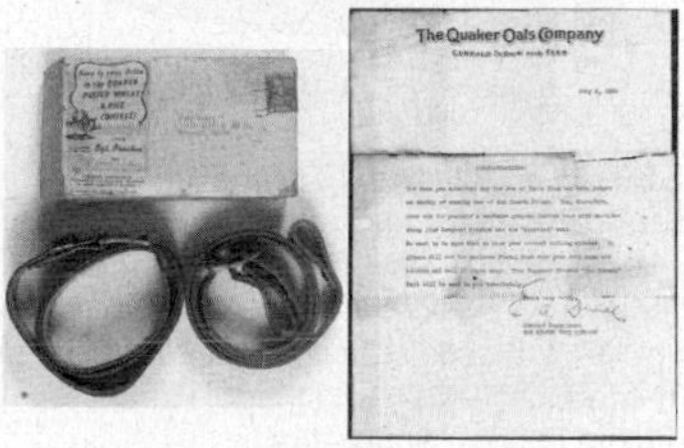

SGT-13

❑ **SGT-13. "Sgt. Preston" Rare Contest Prize,**
1950. First is 8.5x11" letter by the Quaker Oats Co. States recipient won one of the fourth prizes in the Son of Yukon King dog-naming contest. Mailing box label pictures Preston saying "Here Is Your Prize In The Quaker Puffed Wheat And Rice Contest." 32" belt has Preston name, image and dogsled. 30.5" shoulder strap has no images. Mailer - **$25 $50 $100**
Letter - **$25 $50 $100**
Belt & Strap - **$50 $100 $150**

SGT-14

❑ **SGT-14. "Yukon Trail" Quaker Puffed Wheat Box Back,**
1950. Set of eight.
Complete Box - **$100 $200 $400**
Each Uncut Box Back - **$25 $50 $85**

SGT-15

SGT-16

❑ **SGT-15. "Sergeant Preston Yukon Adventure Picture Cards",**
1950. Set of 36. Each - **$3 $6 $10**
Complete Set With Mailer - **$400**

❑ **SGT-16. Quaker Contest Entrant Acknowledgement Postcard,**
1950. - **$20 $35 $75**

SGT-17

SGT-18

❑ **SGT-17. Dog-Naming Contest 19x25-1/2" Award Poster,**
1950. Scarce. - **$200 $400 $800**

❑ **SGT-18. Mailing Tube For Dog-Naming Contest Award Poster,**
1950. Rare. - **$25 $75 $150**

SGT-19

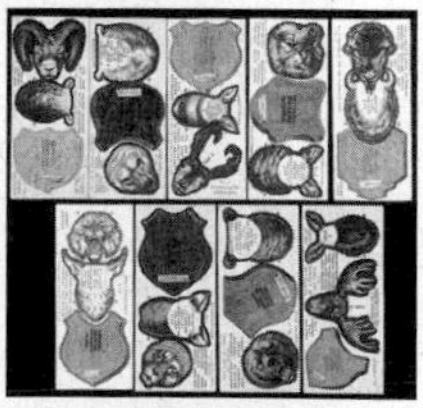
SGT-20

❑ **SGT-19. Award Poster Small Version,**
1950. About 8 x 10".- **$25 $50 $85**

❑ **SGT-20. Trophies,**
1950. 9 different punch-outs of animal heads.
Unpunched Each - **$8 $15 $30**

SGT-21

❑ **SGT-21. Cereal Box With "Yukon Adventure" Cards Offer,**
1950. Cards were issued two per box for set of 36. Gordon Gold Archives.
Used Complete - **$100 $200 $400**

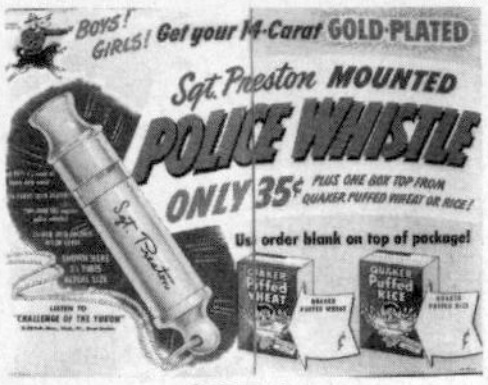

SGT-22

SGT-23

❑ **SGT-22. Police Whistle 17x22" Paper Store Sign,**
1950. - **$135 $300 $500**

❑ **SGT-23. Brass Whistle,**
1950. Facsimile signature on side. -
$20 $30 $60

SGT-24

SGT-25

❑ **SGT-24. Portrait Photo,**
c. 1950 Probably a Quaker premium. -
$20 $35 $75

❑ **SGT-25. "Quaker Camp Stove" With Folder,**
1952. Scarce. Metal items are firebox & cover, oven, tongs. Set - **$60 $150 $300**
Folder Only - **$30 $45 $75**

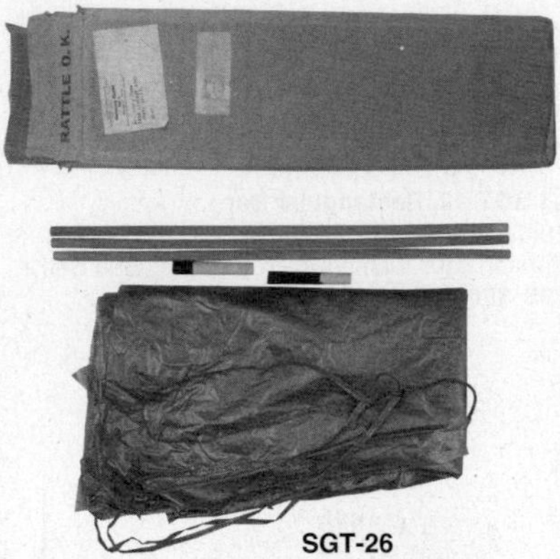

SGT-26

❑ **SGT-26. Prospector Tent With Mailer,**
1952. Considered the rarest of the produced premiums for Sgt. Preston. Offered by Quaker Puffed Wheat & Rice. Includes 3 wooden section poles, 2 plastic sheets, 4 metal stakes and a vinyl tent covering with strings. Rare.
Complete in box - **$600**

SGT-27

❑ **SGT-27. Trading Card/Records Offer Cereal Box,**
1952. Quaker Puffed Rice. Back panel offers record series including theme song from TV series. Complete Box - **$75 $150 $300**

SGT-28

❑ **SGT-28. "Electronic Ore Detector" With Instructions And Box,**
1952. Plastic battery operated detector, black variety. Near Mint Boxed - **$300**
Detector Only - **$50 $100 $200**

SGT-29

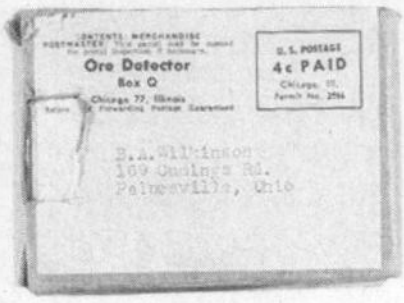

SGT-30

❑ **SGT-29. Electronic Ore Detector, Red Variety,**
1952. Near Mint Boxed - **$450**
Detector Only - **$100 $200 $375**

❑ **SGT-30. Ore Detector Mailer,**
1952. Quaker Puffed Wheat premium. -
$20 $40 $75

SGT-31

❑ **SGT-31. Wood Totem Poles,**
1952. Set of five. Named in order pictured left to right: Thunderbird, The Fight With the Land Otters, Burial Pole, Killer Whale, Sun and Raven. Near Mint Boxed - **$300**
Each Totem Loose - **$10 $25 $50**

SGT-32

SGT-33

❑ **SGT-32. Aluminum Pedometer,**
1952. - **$20 $40 $75**

❑ **SGT-33. "Sgt. Preston Trail Goggles" Quaker Cereal Box Cut-Out,**
1952. - Complete Box - **$100 $200 $300**
Cut-out - **$15 $25 $50**

SGT-34

SGT-35

❑ **SGT-34. "The Case That Made Preston A Sergeant" Decca Record #1,**
1952. - **$20 $40 $85**

❑ **SGT-35. "The Case Of The Indian Rebellion" Decca Record #3,**
1952. - **$20 $40 $85**

SGT-36

❑ **SGT-36. Picture To Color Cereal Box Panel,**
1952. From a series of three boxes with different "Action Pictures."
Back Panel Only - **$15 $30 $60**
Used Complete Box - **$75 $150 $300**

SGT-37

❑ **SGT-37. Cereal Box With Ore Detector Offer,**
1952. Gordon Gold Archives.
Used Complete - **$100 $200 $400**

SGT-38

SGT-39

❑ **SGT-38. "Distance Finder",**
1954. Metal and paper insert distance gauge. -
$20 $40 $60

❑ **SGT-39. Distance Finder Instructions,**
1955. Quaker Puffed Wheat premium. -
$25 $45 $75

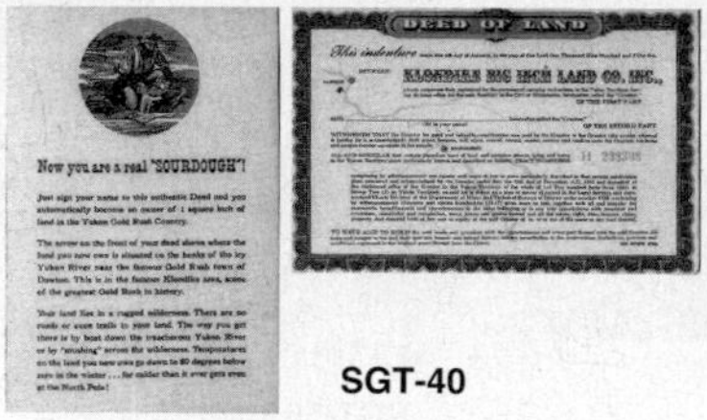

SGT-40

SGT-41

❑ **SGT-40. "Klondike Big Inch Land Deed" Certificate With Cover Sheet,**
1955. Deed - **$10 $15 $25**
Sheet - **$12 $25 $50**

❑ **SGT-41. Deed Mailer,**
1955. Radio premium. - **$60 $135 $225**

SGT-42

❑ **SGT-42. "Map Of Yukon Territory" 8x10",**
1955. Quaker Cereals box insert. -
$20 $40 $70

SGT-43

❑ **SGT-43. "Prospector's Pouch Order Blank",**
1955. - **$20 $35 $70**

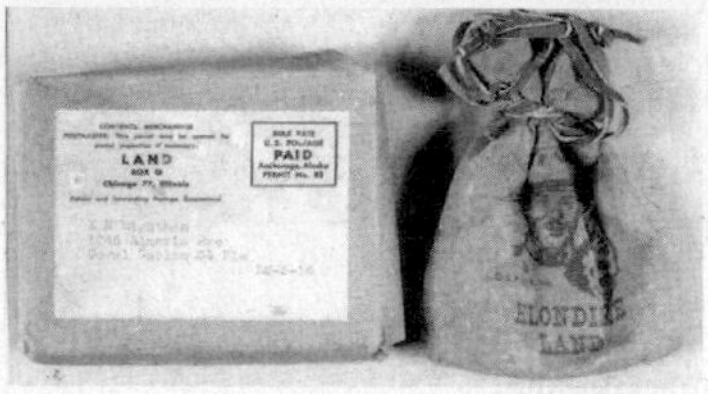
SGT-44

❑ **SGT-44. "Klondike Land" Pouch,**
1955.
Near Mint Boxed With Klondike Dirt Still In Pouch - **$350**
Pouch Only (pouch is generally cracked) -
$50 $100 $250

SGT-45

SGT-46

❑ **SGT-45. Order Form,**
1955. Order form for prospector's pouch & 1 oz. of Klondike land & deed to 1 square inch of gold rush land. - **$30 $60 $90**

❑ **SGT-46. Official Seal Cello. Button,**
1956. Full color 1-1/4". White rim. Scarce. -
$150 $300 $500

SGT-47

❑ **SGT-47. "How He Found Yukon King" Comic Booklet,**
1956. Quaker box insert. Set of four, each 5" or 7" long. - **$10 $30 $95**

SGT-48

❑ **SGT-48. "How Yukon King Saved Him From The Wolves" Comic Booklet,**
1956. Quaker box insert. Set of four, each 5" or 7" long. - **$10 $30 $95**

SGT-49

❑ **SGT-49. "How He Became A Mountie" Comic Booklet,**
1956. Quaker box insert. Set of four, each 5" or 7" long. - **$10 $30 $95**

SGT-50

❑ **SGT-50. "The Case That Made Him A Sergeant" Comic Booklet,**
1956. Quaker box insert. Set of four, each 5" or 7" long. - **$10 $30 $95**

SGT-51

SGT-52

❑ **SGT-51. Quaker Cereals T-Shirt,**
c. 1956. Scarce. Shirt - **$125 $250 $500**
Mailer - **$25 $50 $100**

❑ **SGT-52. Official Seal Tin Badge,**
c. 1956. Seen in copper, silver or brass luster, all rare. - **$125 $250 $500**

SGT-53

SGT-54

❑ **SGT-53. Official Seal White Metal Badge With Insert Paper Photo,**
c. 1956. Photo is yellow/black. - **$125 $250 $500**

❑ **SGT-54. Quaker Cereals Coloring Contest Letter And Photo,**
1957. Near Mint In Envelope - **$200**
Photo Only - **$30 $60 $110**

SGT-55

❑ **SGT-55. "Tim Magazine For Boys" With Sergeant Preston,**
1958. September issue with 16 pages including cover photo and two-page article with added photos. - **$18 $30 $65**

SGT-56

SGT-57

❑ **SGT-56. "Sergeant Preston 10-In-1 Trail Kit,"**
1958. 6" plastic pen/flashlight/sundial/compass/whistle including Sgt. Preston and King image on mouthpiece.
Box - **$15 $20 $40**
Instructions - **$20 $40 $75**
Device - **$50 $100 $200**

❑ **SGT-57. "Richard Simmons" Pencil Tablet,**
1950s. Store item. - **$20 $40 $75**

SGT-58

❑ **SGT-58. Sergeant Preston Pencil Tablet,**
1950s. Store item. - **$18 $35 $70**

SGT-59

❑ **SGT-59. "Sunday News TV Week" With Sgt. Preston,**
1960. TV listing supplement for week of July 24-30 featuring Richard Simmons as Preston on front cover and inside two-page article. - **$25 $50 $125**

Seth Parker

Seth Parker **was an early radio creation of Phillips H. Lord (1902-1975), who was later to create *Gang Busters* and other adventure programs. In contrast, Seth Parker, played by Phillips H. Lord, combined the story of a gentle, kindly Maine philosopher with lots of hymn singing, and it was immensely successful. Also known as *Sunday at Seth Parker* and *Sunday Evenings at Seth Parker*, the series was sustained on NBC from 1929 to 1933, and sponsored by Frigidaire as *Cruise of the Seth Parker* in 1933-1934. It later aired from 1935 to 1939, sponsored by Vick Chemical for its final three years. A feature film based on the show *Way Back Home* was released in 1932 starring Phillips Lord as Seth and a young Bette Davis in a supporting role.**

SET-1

❑ **SET-1. Schooner 11x15" Paper Print,**
c. 1934. Frigidaire Corp. Pictures world cruise ship used by Phillips H. Lord, creator and radio voice of Seth Parker. - **$15 $25 $45**

SET-2

SET-3

❏ **SET-2. "Aboard The Seth Parker" Booklet,**
1934. Frigidaire Corp. Includes drawings of the various rooms of global sailing boat. -
$5 $10 $20

❏ **SET-3. "Seth Parker's Two-Year Almanac And Party Book",**
1939. Vicks Chemical Co. Hardcover edition for 1939-1940. - **$5 $10 $20**

SET-4

SET-5

❏ **SET-4. "Seth Parker's Scrapbook",**
1930s. Collection of folksy, small-town humor and wisdom. - **$15 $25 $40**

❏ **SET-5. Cast Member Fan Photo,**
1930s. Pictures family in a parlor hymn sing. -
$10 $15 $25

Sgt. Bilko

Comedian Phil Silvers (1911-1985) worked in burlesque and vaudeville in the 1930s, then moved on to Hollywood as a character actor. In 1952, he became a star on Broadway, earning a Tony award for *Top Banana.*

The Phil Silvers Show*, originally titled *You'll Never Get Rich*, aired on CBS-TV from September, 1955 to September, 1959 with 143 episodes. Phil Silvers created the show with Nat Hiken (1914-1968), who also co-wrote and produced the series. Silvers played Sgt. Ernest E. Bilko, a scheming hustler with an underlying heart of gold who was head of the motor pool at fictional Fort Baxter, Kansas. Co-stars included: Paul Ford as Col. John Hall, Harvey Lembeck as Cpl. Rocco Barbella, Maurice Gosfield as Pvt. Duane Doberman. Guest stars included: Dick Van Dyke, Alan Alda, Mike Todd and Fred Gwynne. After ending its original run, the show went to NBC in re-runs as *Sgt. Bilko.

Steve Martin starred in the March 29, 1996 feature film *Sgt. Bilko.* Released by Imagine Entertainment, co-stars included: Dan Aykroyd, Phil Hartman and Glenne Headly.

National Periodical Publications released 18 *Sergeant Bilko* comics between May, 1957 and March, 1960 and 11 *Sgt. Bilko's Pvt. Doberman* comics between June, 1958 and February, 1960. "Hey......Hut Hut Hut!"

SBK-1

❏ **SBK-1.. Sgt. Bilko Cardboard Ad Fan,**
c. 1955. Amana Refrigeration. - **$15 $30 $75**

SBK-2

❏ **SBK-2. "Win A Sgt. Bilko Money Tree" Contest Folder,**
1957. Joy liquid dishwashing soap. Contest expired October 15. - **$12 $20 $40**

SBK-3

❏ **SBK-3. "Sgt. Bilko" English Game,**
1958. Bell (Toys & Games) Ltd. 14x14x1.5" deep box holds spinner, game cards, token money, markers and gameboard. - **$50 $100 $150**

SBK-4

❏ **SBK-4. "Sgt. Bilko" Coloring Book,**
1959. Treasure Books Inc. 8.25x10.75" with 64 pages. - **$20 $40 $75**

SBK-5

❏ **SBK-5. "Sergeant Bilko Holster Outfit" By Halco,**
1950s. J. Halpern Co. Set consists of 10" diameter officer's cap with band reading "Sergeant Bilko,", 9.5" long "USA/US Army" leather holster, 6.75" long metal cap-firing pistol, 29" long belt with metal buckle, and 3.5x5" fabric/elastic strap "Sgt. Bilko" armband.
Box - **$50 $100 $200**
Contents - **$50 $100 $200**

SBK-6

❏ **SBK-6. "Phil Silvers/Black Label Beer" Store Display,**
1950s. Carling Brewing Co. 18x22.5" cardboard display with easel frame on reverse with separate cardboard panel as it was designed to attach to a cardboard tube as part of a bin display. Also has separate arm and small pop-out panel on chest where a bottle of beer is to be attached as though he was holding it. - **$65 $135 $225**

SBK-7

❏ **SBK-7. United Jewish Appeal Tabs Lot Including Bilko,**
c. 1960. Three 2" tabs showing basketball players Dolph Schayes, Phil Silvers and Sam Levenson. Silvers - **$10 $20 $35**
Others - **$5 $10 $20**

SBK-8

❑ **SBK-8. "Sgt. Bilko" Sliding Tile Puzzle On Card,**
1960s. Roalex Co. 2.5x2.5" plastic puzzle with sliding tiles. Carded - **$50 $100 $150**
Loose - **$10 $20 $40**

The Shadow

The Shadow, alias Lamont Cranston, was born in the 1930s, both as a character in Street & Smith publications and by radio sponsor Blue Coal. Written by Walter B. Gibson under the pen name Maxwell Grant, the Shadow fought crime and clouded men's minds not only in the pulps and on the radio but also, along with the lovely Margot Lane, in the movies, in comic books, and in a comic strip.

The Shadow debuted as the announcer of the *Detective Story* radio program in 1930, which became *The Shadow* in 1932. The show aired on CBS, NBC, or Mutual from 1932 to 1954, and the programs were resurrected and syndicated in the 1960s and 1970s. There were a number of regional or national sponsors: Blue Coal for most of the years between 1932 and 1949, along with Perfect-O-Lite (1932), Goodrich tires (1938-1939), Grove Laboratories (1949-1950), the Army Air Force (1950-1951), Wildroot Cream Oil (1951-1953), Carey Salt Company, and Bromo Quinine cold tablets. Both Blue Coal (in 1941) and Carey Salt (in 1945) offered glow-in-the-dark premium rings, and *The Shadow Magazine* offered a club membership lapel emblem and other items.

A *Shadow* comic strip appeared in newspapers from 1938 to 1942 with art by Vern Greene, and comic books were published from 1940 to 1950 with art by Charles Coll, in 1964-1965 (with the Shadow as costumed superhero), and in 1973-1975 with well done stories by Dennis O'Neil and Michael Uslan and superb art by Michael Kaluta. The Shadow made a number of low-budget film appearances in the 1930s and 1940s, notably in a 15-episode chapter play from Columbia Pictures in 1940 with Victor Jory in the title role. In 1994 Alec Baldwin played the lead in a Universal film. "Who knows what evil lurks in the hearts of men?"

SHA-1

❑ **SHA-1. "The Shadow Laughs" Maxwell Grant Book,**
1931. Hardcover published by Street & Smith. - **$75 $150 $425**

SHA-2

❑ **SHA-2. "Eyes Of The Shadow" First Hardcover Novel,**
1931. Maxwell Grant story published by Street & Smith. A concluding page has text promo for "The Shadow Magazine" pulp. - **$75 $150 $425**

SHA-3 SHA-4

❑ **SHA-3. "Eyes Of The Shadow" 7x11" Ad Card,**
1931. For Maxwell Grant novel. -
$100 $225 $450

❑ **SHA-4. Perfect-O-Lite Radio Broadcast Promotion Folder,**
1932. For Perfect-O-Lite sales people. 11x17" folder that opens to 17x22" promoting new radio sponsorship over 29 stations of Columbia network. - **$125 $275 $550**

SHA-5

❑ **SHA-5. "The Shadow" Cover Photo On Radio Schedule Magazine,**
1932. Subscription publication by Radio Log Company, Boston, Mass. 5-1/4x8-1/4" with 36 pages for week of December 11. -
$135 $350 $700

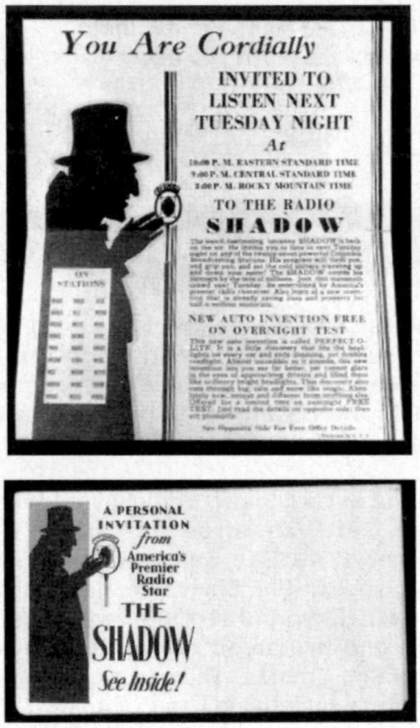

SHA-6

❑ **SHA-6. Radio Broadcasts Schedule Folder With Envelope,**
1932. Perfect-O-Lite (automotive accessory). Lists 27 stations in three time zones.
Envelope - **$35 $80 $150**
Folder - **$75 $225 $450**

SHA-7

❑ **SHA-7. Radio Broadcasts Trolley Insert Sign,**
1932. 17x33" placement poster for interior of trolley or other public transit car, New York City. Advertised is radio program on WEF/NBC Red Network every Wednesday evening at 8:00 PM in addition to "Radio Revue" program by same sponsor blue coal every Sunday at 5:30 PM on Columbia Network. Believed published in the Fall of 1932 as Shadow broadcasts moved to 8:30 PM in December that year. -
$750 $1500 $3000

SHA-8

❑ **SHA-8. "The Shadow" 11x14" Cardboard Window Poster,**
c. 1934. Blue Coal, Shadow magazine. Promotes Monday and Wednesday radio broadcasts on Columbia network. - **$750 $1800 $3500**

SHA-9

❑ **SHA-9. "The Shadow Strikes" Movie Pressbook,**
1937. Grand National Picture release. Film starred Rod LaRocque as The Shadow. Contents are black, white and purple tone. Cover text reads "The Master-Avenger Comes To The Screen In Mystery-Romance It Will Get You!" Center fold-out includes photo of cut-out one-sheet as well as a rare promo visor to be passed out at movie theaters. - **$85 $175 $350**

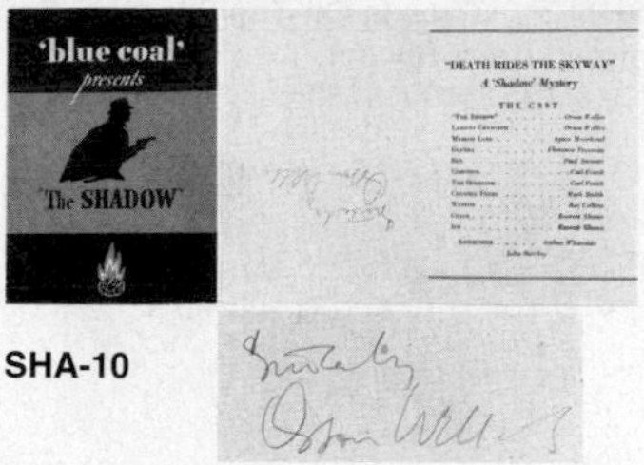

SHA-10

❑ **SHA-10. "The Shadow" Radio Program Folder Signed By Portrayer Welles,**
c. 1937. blue coal. Folder from 1937-1938 years when Orson Welles was voice of characters Shadow and Lamont Cranston. Inside panel lists cast members for episode "Death Rides The Skyway" including Agnes Moorehead as Margot Lane. Back cover is signed by Welles.
Unsigned - **$150 $300 $600**
Signed - **$500 $800 $1500**

SHA-11

SHA-12

❑ **SHA-11. Blue Coal Portrait Photo,**
1930s. Shows Frank Readick Jr., the second Shadow radio program narrator. -
$100 $200 $400

❑ **SHA-12. The Shadow Unmasked Pulp Magazine Photo,**
1930s. Image on thin matte finish cardboard. Later re-issued by Carey's Salt as glossy photo. See SHA-52. - **$300 $650 $1200**

SHA-13

❑ **SHA-13. "Shadow Is No More" Cello. Button,**
1930s. Rare. Reported one known.
- **$1250 $2500 $4000**

SHA-14

❑ **SHA-14. First Version "The Shadow Club" Lapel Stud,**
1930s. Street & Smith Publishers. 3/4" silvered brass with threaded prong and brass screw cap on reverse. Apparently used briefly before being re-designed. Differences between this and later design are: shape of the hat, a coat is worn with turned up collar (not a cape), his hair shows beneath the hat and the nose is more pronounced. We know of two examples, both with little silver flashing, which disappears over time.
- **$350 $800 $1600**

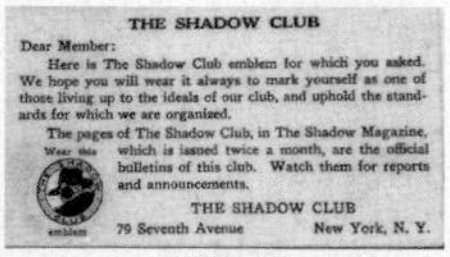

SHA-15

SHA-16

❑ **SHA-15. The Shadow Club Card,**
1930s. Street & Smith Publishers. Originally held Shadow lapel stud.
Card - **$175 $350 $600**
Mailer (Pictures The Shadow) - **$200 $375 $650**

❑ **SHA-16. "The Shadow Club" Silvered Brass Lapel Emblem,**
1930s. Lapel Stud - **$100 $200 $350**
Girl's Version With Pin - **$125 $300 $450**

SHA-17

❑ **SHA-17. "The Shadow" Rare Stationery Pack,**
1930s. Stationary pack is 5.25x8.25" cellophane sealed. Top of stationery paper features same image of The Shadow as the club label. The stationery set has a paper band that reads "The Shadow Knows" and also features a copyright from Shadow Magazine.
NM Sealed Pack - **$2250**

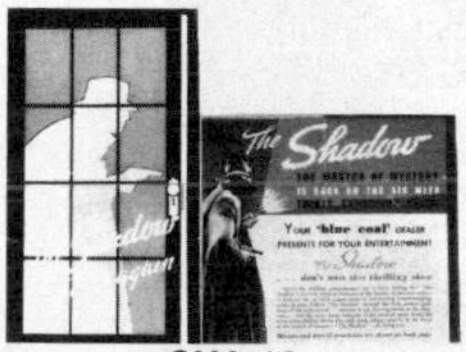

SHA-18

SHA-19

❑ **SHA-18. "The Shadow Strikes Again" Paper Folder,**
1930s. Blue Coal. Includes listing of radio stations and broadcast times. - **$100 $225 $425**

❑ **SHA-19. The Shadow Large Enamel Pin,**
1930s. After auctioning an example of this 2-1/8" tall black enamel on 1/16" thick brass pin we were told the pin was used by members of the Shadow radio cast. Rare. -
$250 $500 $1000

SHA-20

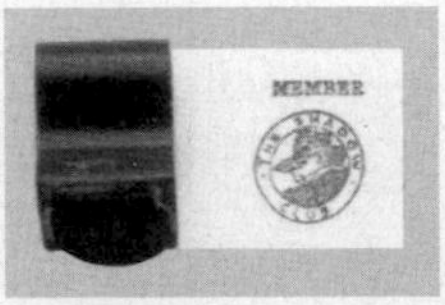

SHA-21

❑ **SHA-20. "The Shadow Hypno-Coin" Brass Medalet,**
1930s. About 1-1/4". Inscribed "Compliments Of Your Blue Coal Dealer." Rare. - **$150 $325 $650**

❑ **SHA-21. "Member/The Shadow Club" Rubber On Wood Stamp Block,**
1930s. Picture example includes ink stamp image from the block. Offered only from April 1, 1934 until the end of August 1934. -
$350 $700 $1400

SHA-22

SHA-23

❑ **SHA-22. "Thrilling Radio Program" Match Cover,**
1930s. Williams Coal Co. and others.
Near Mint Complete - **$125**
Used - **$25 $50 $75**

❑ **SHA-23. "Protect Your Home" Match Cover,**
1930s. Steward B. Rex and others.
Near Mint Unused - **$175**
Used - **$35 $65 $110**

SHA-24

❑ **SHA-24. "Tune In On-The Shadow" Paper Gummed Back Sticker,**
1930s. - **$35 $100 $150**

SHA-25

❑ **SHA-25. "The Shadow On The Air" Gummed Back Paper Sticker,**
1930s. - **$25 $50 $100**

SHA-26

SHA-27

❑ **SHA-26. "The Shadow Is Back On The Air" Paper Gummed Back Sticker,**
1930s. - **$40 $110 $175**

❑ **SHA-27. Pulp Magazine Ad Sticker,**
1930s. - **$75 $225 $350**

SHA-28

❑ **SHA-28. "The Shadow Magazine" Window Card,**
1930s. Smith & Street Publications. 11x14".
- **$300 $600 $1200**

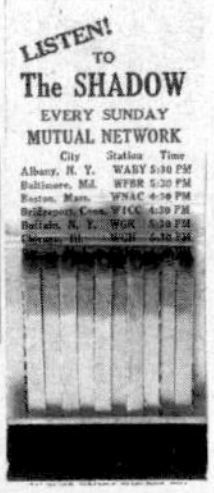

SHA-29

❑ **SHA-29. "The Shadow" Matchbook,**
1930s. Blue Coal urging listenership on radio every Sunday over Mutual Network.
Near Mint Unused - **$175**
Used - **$35 $65 $110**

SHA-30

❑ **SHA-30. "The Shadow-blue coal" Fabric Cape,**
1930s. 36" long glossy black cotton accented in blue with tie string at neck. -
$650 $1300 $2500

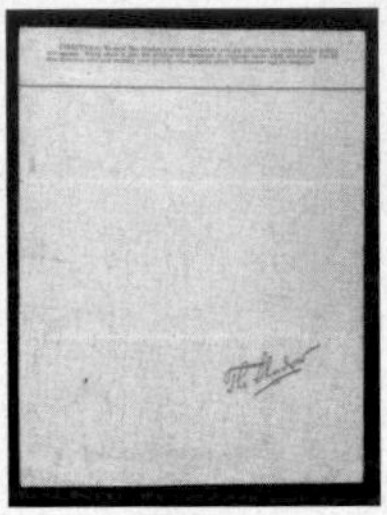

SHA-31

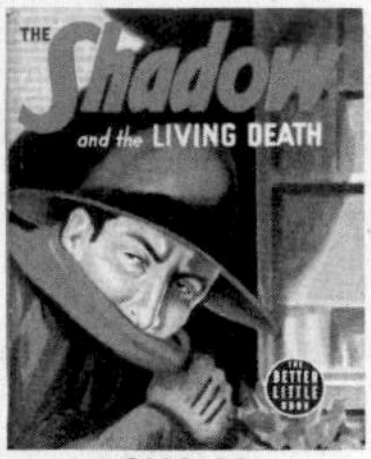

SHA-32

❑ **SHA-31. "The Shadow's Secret Message" Sheet,**
1930s. The Shadow pulp magazine. 8-1/2x11" yellow paper sheet treated to reveal message when dipped in water and then disappears when sheet is dry. Rare. - **$200 $400 $800**

❑ **SHA-32. "The Shadow and the Living Death" Better Little Book #1430,**
1940. - **$60 $180 $420**

SHA-33

❑ **SHA-33. "The Shadow" Movie Poster,**
c. 1940 Australian insert poster for 15-chapter Columbia serial. 13-1/2x30". Most likely for first Australian release. - **$75 $175 $350**

SHA-34

❑ **SHA-34. Boxed Board Game,**
1940. Store item by Toy Creations. -
$350 $750 $1650
Board Only - **$125 $250 $500**

SHA-35

❑ **SHA-35. "The Shadow" Brown Felt Fabric Hat,**
1940. Adult size, offered by The Shadow Magazine. - **$225 $400 $750**

SHA-36

❑ **SHA-36. "The Shadow Movie Club" Member's Cello. Button,**
1940. 7/8" black on green. One of three examples found wrapped in a paper in the desk of Walter B. Gibson as his estate was prepared for auction. Possibly produced as samples but never used to promote the club tie-in with the Columbia Pictures 1940s serial. -
$1250 $2500 $5500

SHA-37

❑ **SHA-37. Shadow Magazine Costume,**
c. 1940. Street & Smith Publishers. Consists of hat, mask and cape. Pocket of cape has image of the Shadow with text above "The Shadow Knows" and text below "The Shadow Magazine." Set - **$1000 $2000 $4000**

SHA-38

❑ **SHA-38. Blue Coal Ink Blotter,**
1940. - **$25 $50 $75**

SHA-39

❑ **SHA-39. "The Shadow And The Voice Of Murder" Paperback,**
1940. Published by Bantam with Street & Smith copyright. - **$275 $550 $1100**

SHA-40

❑ **SHA-40. Shadow/blue coal Canadian Blotter,**
1940. Blue Coal dealers of Canada. 3.5x6" promo for weekly radio broadcasts. -
$35 $75 $175

SHA-41

❑ **SHA-41. Blue Coal Ring,**
1941. Glows in the dark. - **$100 $225 $350**

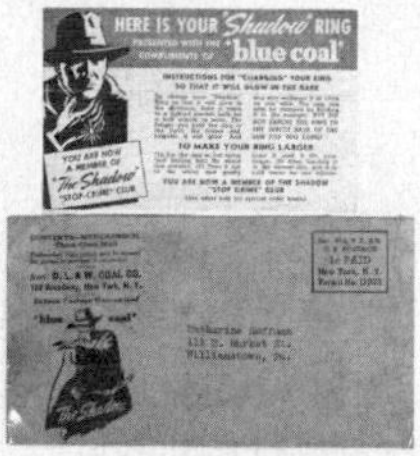

(US version)

(Canadian version)

SHA-42

❑ **SHA-42. "Blue Coal" Ring Instruction Sheet With Mailer Envelope,**
1941. Rare. Note differences in US and Canadian versions. Canadian version is blue with different text. US version is black and white. Same price for each version.
Envelope - **$300 $600 $900**
Instruction Sheet - **$300 $600 $900**

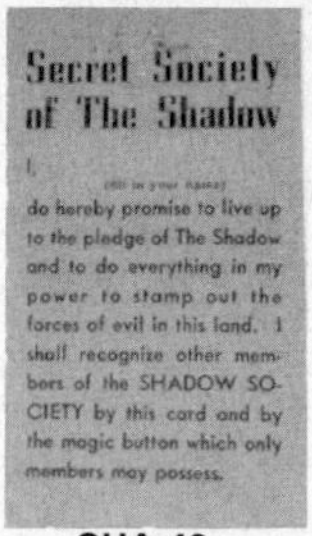

SHA-43

SHA-44

❑ **SHA-43. "Secret Society Of The Shadow" Club Card Sent With Magic Button,**
1942. Offered in May and July issues of *Shadow Comics* for ten cents. Pledge card originally holding glow-in-dark "Magic Button". -
$200 $400 $800

❑ **SHA-44. "The Shadow" Glow-In-Dark Cello. Magic Button,**
1942. Offered in May and July issues of *Shadow Comics*. Came with pledge card for price of ten cents. Rare not cracked or stained.
Cream background - **$250 $500 $2500**
Turquoise Blue bkg (1 seen) - **$300 $600 $2600**

SHA-45

❑ **SHA-45. Cardboard 11x16" Ad Wall Calendar,**
1942. Picture example shows calendar and corner detail from it. - **$250 $500 $1000**

SHA-46

❑ **SHA-46. "The Shadow and the Ghost Makers" Better Little Book #1495,**
1942. - **$60 $180 $420**

SHA-47

❑ **SHA-47. WOR Radio Broadcast Ticket,**
1944. 1.5x3.5" ticket for Sunday, February 6 broadcast from WOR Mutual Theatre, New York City. Entry times were limited 5:30 to 6:00 PM. Reverse notes complimentary use only. - **$75 $165 $300**

SHA-48

❑ **SHA-48. "The Shadow" Radio Club Button From Kansas,**
c. 1944. 1.75" with back paper design of St. Louis Button Co. first used in 1944. Button features profile with trademark hat. Text below reads "The Shadow Sundays-3:00 PM-KWHK Dial 1190." Text above profile reads "Cerotex Rock Wool Member Shadow Club." Text on rim reads "Guy P. Miller Insulation Co. 907 West 4th, Hutchinson, Kan." This company sponsored The Shadow radio show for only a few years. Rare. - **$1000 $2000 $3600**

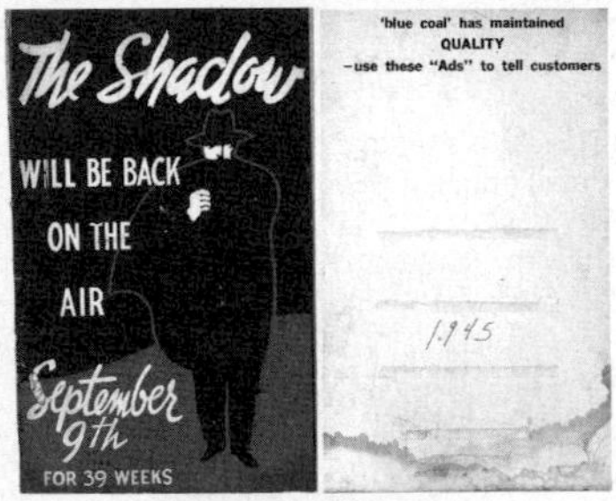

SHA-49

❑ **SHA-49. "The Shadow" Radio Return Sign,**
1945. blue coal. 11x17.5" glossy thin cardboard informing "The Shadow Will Be Back On The Air September 9th For 39 Weeks" under continued sponsorship of blue coal. - **$350 $750 $1500**

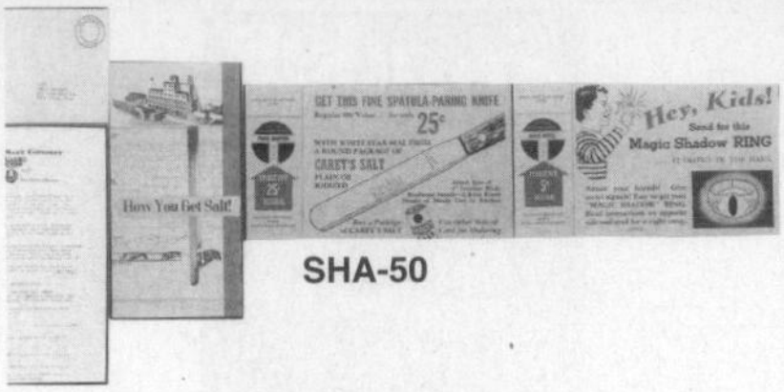

SHA-50

❑ **SHA-50. "Magic Shadow" Carey Salt Ring Mailer With Letter & Inserts,**
c. 1945. Business size mailer envelope holding 8.5x11" mimeographed letter of ring instructions, two insert coupons for additional ring and a spatula-paring knife, descriptive folder "How You Get Salt!"
Complete Except Ring - **$550 $1100 $2000**

SHA-51

SHA-52

❑ **SHA-51. Magic Ring,**
1945. Carey Salt. Black plastic stone, base glows in dark. - **$200 $400 $800**

❑ **SHA-52. The Shadow Unmasked Photo,**
1945. Rare. Carey's Salt. Illustrated in the sales portfolio used by company salesmen. 8x10 glossy photo. See earlier pulp magazine issue, SHA-12. - **$250 $500 $1000**

SHA-53

❑ **SHA-53. Dealer's Promotional Campaign Book,**
1945. Carey Salt. 10-1/2x16" spiral-bound covers plus 20 pages in red, white and blue including glued-in color covers of Shadow comics (Vol. 5 #8, September 1945) and The Shadow pulp magazine October 1945. About 75 produced and used by Carey Salt salesmen. - **$2750 $5500 $8000**

SHA-54

❑ **SHA-54. Mutual Network Radio Broadcast Ticket,**
1948. 1.5x3.5" admission to Sunday, October 3 broadcast in Mutual Longacre Theatre, New York City. Entry time was limited between 5:00 to 5:30 PM. Reverse notes complimentary use only. - **$65 $135 $275**

SHA-55

SHA-56

❑ **SHA-55. Blue Coal Sticker,**
1940s. - **$65 $135 $215**

❑ **SHA-56. Matchbook Cover,**
1940s. Inside cover has diecut hinged tab that lowers to expose jail cell view.
With Matches - **$50 $100 $200**
Empty - **$25 $50 $75**

SHA-57

❑ **SHA-57. Blotter,**
1940s. Blue Coal. - **$25 $50 $85**

SHA-58

❑ **SHA-58. Blotter,**
1940s. Blue Coal. - **$20 $40 $65**

SHA-59

❑ **SHA-59. Blotter,**
1940s. Blue Coal. - **$20 $40 $65**

SHA-60

❑ **SHA-60. Blotter,**
1940s. Blue Coal. - **$15 $35 $60**

SHA-61

❑ **SHA-61. Blotter,**
1940s. Blue Coal. Man shows 2 bags of coal on front. - **$25 $50 $85**

SHA-62

SHA-63

❑ **SHA-62. Blotter,**
1940s. Blue Coal. Man on right talks about the pleasures of a warm home. - **$25 $50 $85**

❑ **SHA-63. Full Figure Blotter,**
1940s. Scarce. Blue Coal. Promotes program "Every Sunday Afternoon." - **$60 $150 $235**

SHA-64

SHA-65

❑ **SHA-64. Blotter,**
1940s. Blue Coal. - **$25 $50 $90**

❑ **SHA-65. Blotter,**
1940s. Blue Coal. Colorful. - **$30 $60 $125**

SHA-66

SHA-67

❑ **SHA-66. Blotter,**
1940s. Blue Coal. Rare design. - **$65 $125 $250**

❑ **SHA-67. Canadian Ink Blotter,**
1940s. Various coal companies. Scarce. - **$55 $120 $240**

SHA-68

❑ **SHA-68. High Quality Glazed Ceramic Figure,**
c. 1940s. Store item with maker's mark under base of "K" with a crown above. Beautifully colored and designed 7" tall figurine depicting The Shadow in classic pose holding a dagger. - **$200 $400 $800**

SHA-69

❑ **SHA-69. "The Shadow" Boxed Costume,**
1973. Store item by Collegeville. Holds thin plastic mask with red fabric panel at lower half. Comes with black rayon cape with large silk screen design which includes his classic question "Who Knows..." Near Mint Boxed - **$225**
Complete Unboxed - **$40 $75 $150**

SHA-70

SHA-71

❑ **SHA-70. Shadow Radio Broadcast Album,**
1974. Plays original Shadow radio shows. - **$15 $25 $50**

❑ **SHA-71. Crime Fighter Copter,**
1976. Battery operated. In original box. - **$25 $75 $150**

SHA-72

❑ **SHA-72. "The Shadow" Crime Fighter Detection Belt,**
1976. Box is 8x14" and contains crime fighter detection belt with accessories including a cap gun, walkie talkie, handcuffs and whistle. Boxed - **$60 $125 $190**

SHA-73

❑ **SHA-73. Crime Fighter Super Jet,**
1976. In original package. NM Carded - **$100**
Loose - **$10 $20 $50**

SHA-74

❑ **SHA-74. "The Shadow Secret Society" Club Button,**
1970s. 2.25" multicolor member button for revival club created by comic book artist Jim Steranko. - **$30 $60 $110**

SHA-75

❑ **SHA-75. Pre-Release Promo Flyers,**
c. 1993. Universal. Pair of 8-1/2x11" glossy sheets. Each - **$3 $6 $12**

SHA-76

SHA-77

❑ **SHA-76. The Shadow Hologram Plastic Ring,**
1994. Coupon offer from Kenner Toys.
Ring - **$10 $20 $35**
Coupon - **$2 $3 $4**

❑ **SHA-77. Movie Giveaway Badge,**
1994. - **$2 $4 $10**

SHA-78

❑ **SHA-78. "The Shadow Club" Kit,**
1994. Promotes the movie. Includes pinback, photo, club card, mailer and newsletter.
Complete - **$85**

SHA-79

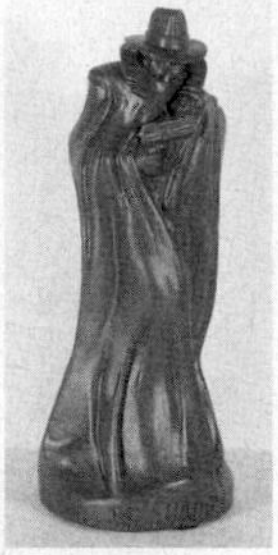

SHA-80

❑ **SHA-79. "The Shadow " 9" Bust,**
1994. Graphitti Designs. Limited to 2500, then reduced to 1500. - **$225**

❑ **SHA-80. "The Shadow " 6 1/2" Figurine,**
1994. Made from wood-like substance. Produced for promotion of the movie. Less than 125 made. Given out at Toy Fair.- **$275**

SHA-81

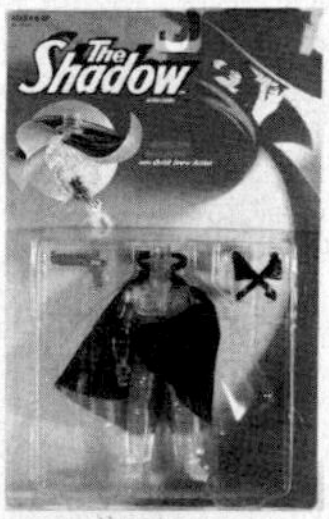

SHA-82

❑ **SHA-81. "The Shadow " Action Figure,**
1994. Lightning Draw. With Silver Heat 45s.
On card. - **$12**

❑ **SHA-82. "The Shadow " Action Figure,**
1994. Ambush Shadow with Quick Draw Action.
On card. - **$12**

SHA-83

SHA-84

❑ **SHA-83. "Transforming Lamont Cranston" Action Figure,**
1994. With snap-on armor. On card. - **$12**

❑ **SHA-84. "Ninja Shadow " Action Figure,**
1994. On card. - **$12**

SHA-85

SHA-86

❑ **SHA-85. Shiwan Khan Action Figure,**
1994. With Rapid Strike Chopping Action.
On card. - **$12**

❑ **SHA-86. Dr. MocQuino Action Figure,**
1994. On card. - **$12**

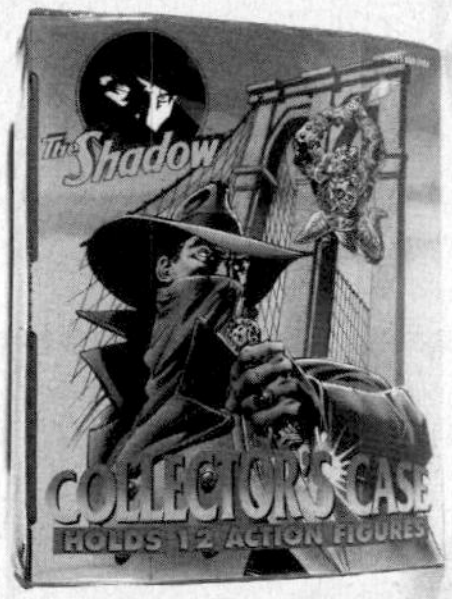

SHA-87

❑ **SHA-87. Action Figure Collector's Case,**
1994. - **$65**

(BOX FRONT) (BOX BACK)

SHA-88

❑ SHA-88. "The Shadow" Nightmist Cycle,
1994. Kenner. In original box. - **$10**

SHA-89

❑ SHA-89. "The Shadow" Mirage SX-100 Action Vehicle,
1994. Kenner. In original box. - **$25**

SHA-90

❑ SHA-90. "The Shadow" Thunder Cab Action Vehicle,
1994. Kenner. With firing cannons and side-swiping swords. In original box. - **$30**

(BOX FRONT)

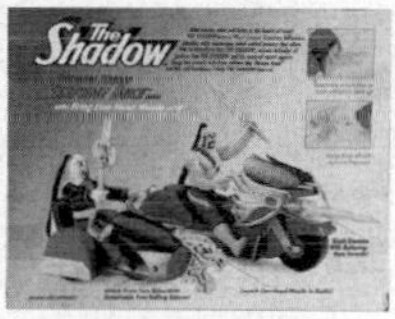

(BOX BACK)

SHA-91

❑ SHA-91. Shiwan Khan Serpent Bike,
1994. Kenner. In original box. - **$15**

SHA-92

❑ SHA-92. Electronic Video Game on Card,
1994. This is the hardest item to find on all the Shadow products produced to support the movie. - **$20 $50 $125**

SHA-93

❑ SHA-93. "The Shadow" Board Game,
1994. In original box. - **$85**

SHA-94

❑ SHA-94. Club Promo Button,
1994. 1.5" green/black/gray accented in white. Rim curl copyright for Advance Publishers, likely for publication at time of movie release. -
$5 $15 $30

Sheena

Sheena, Queen of the Jungle was the first female heroine to appear in comic books. Her first appearance in January 14, 1938 was drawn by Mort Meskin for weekly tabloid issues of *Wags* created for British and Australian markets by comic book pioneers Jerry Iger (1903-1990) and Will Eisner (1917-2005). Following the success of *Wags*, Iger and Eisner brought out *Jumbo* #1 in the USA in September, 1938. Sheena appeared in every issue until 1953 and was featured on the cover of 143 issues. She had her own comic from 1942 to 1952 with 18 issues published by Fiction House.

Irish McCalla, born Nellie McCalla (1928-2002) was a struggling artist from Nebraska who moved to Los Angeles in the late 1940s. To finance her art career she posed for cheesecake photos and modeled for noted pin-up artists Alberto Vargas and Fritz Willis. The statuesque beauty won the role of Sheena in the mid-1950s. Produced by Nassour Studios and Rodriguez Productions, 26 episodes were filmed in the jungles of Las Estacas, Mexico between December, 1955 and September 16, 1956 for syndication in the U.S. The popularity of the series led to an appearance on the June 5, 1956 *Milton Berle Show* along with newcomer Elvis Presley. McCalla continued with her art career, completing 1,000 paintings by the mid-1980s.

Hearst International released the feature film *Sheena: Queen of the Jungle* with Tanya Roberts August 17, 1984 and Columbia Tri-Star produced the *Sheena* TV series with Gena Lee Nolin in 2001-2002, with 35 episodes.

SHE-1

SHE-2

❑ SHE-1. Jumbo Comics #37,
1942. Fiction House Magazines. Issues #31-40.
- **$52 $156 $725**

❑ SHE-2. "Sheena-Queen Of The Jungle" Pulp First Issue,
1951. Fiction House Magazines. Volume 1, No. 1. First and only issue published for this title. -
$50 $125 $300

SHE-3

❑ SHE-3. "Eye" Digest,
1955. 5x7-1/8" April issue Vol. 5, #2 with 130 pages. Arlene Hunter on cover, photo article of Irish McCalla as Sheena and also on Tarzan movie set with Gordon Scott. - **$25 $50 $75**

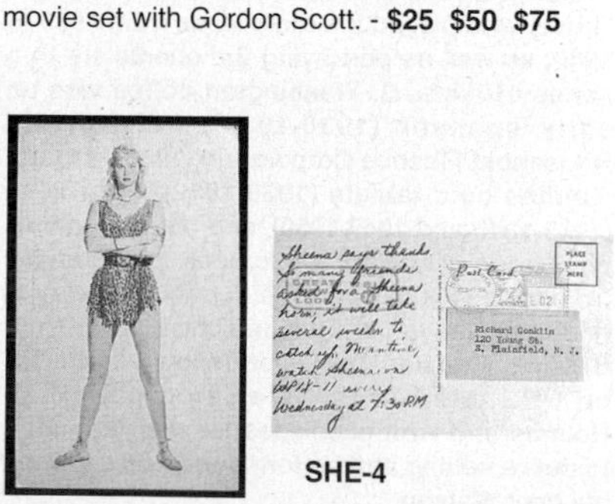

SHE-4

❑ SHE-4. Sheena Queen Of The Jungle Postcard,
1956. WPIX-TV, N.Y.C. Front is glossy B&W picturing Irish McCalla. Reverse message says "Demand Will Delay Delivery Of The Sheena Horn Several Weeks." - **$35 $75 $125**

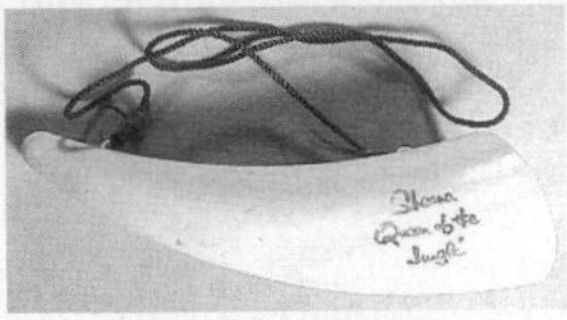

SHE-5

❑ SHE-5. "Sheena Queen Of The Jungle" Plastic Horn With Cord,
1956. WPIX-TV, N.Y.C. 8-1/2" long with green text on ivory plastic. - **$65 $135 $200**

SHE-6

❑ SHE-6. Irish McCalla Autographed Photo,
c. 1970s. 8x10" glossy photo signed "To Dick Enjoyed Talking With You Irish McCalla." Same Or Similar - **$15 $30 $50**

Sherlock Holmes

The world's most famous detective made his debut in 1887 in Arthur Conan Doyle's (1859-1930) story *A Study in Scarlet.* Since then millions of fans have followed the adventures of the brilliant Holmes and his trusted chronicler Dr. John Watson in books, on stage, on the radio, on television, and in numerous films as early as 1903. *The Adventures Of Sherlock Holmes* was serialized in *The Strand* magazine beginning in 1891. Holmes solved cases in radio series from 1930 to 1936 and from 1939 to 1950, on various networks, with different sponsors, and through multiple cast changes. Best remembered are Basil Rathbone and Nigel Bruce, who played the radio leads from 1939 to 1946, as well as portraying the characters in a series of films. G. Washington coffee was an early sponsor (1930-1935), followed by Household Finance Corporation (1936), Bromo-Quinine cold tablets (1939-1942), Petri wine (1943-1946 and 1949-1950), and others. Holmes also made scattered comic book appearances from the 1940s to the 1970s. A popular series of one-hour shows and feature-length films from Britain's Granada Television (shown in the US on PBS) starred the late Jeremy Brett as Holmes and won accolades for their attention to detail, setting and performance. "Elementary, my dear Watson."

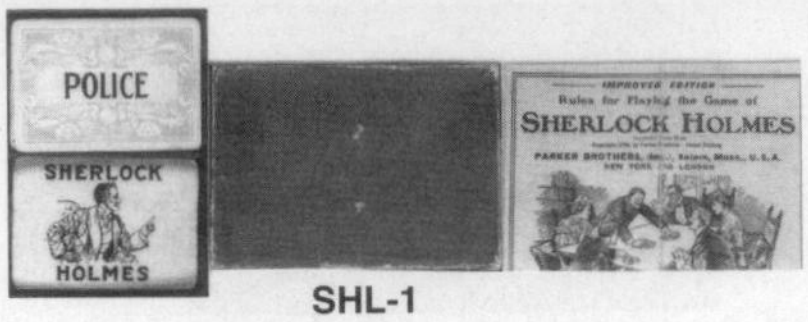

SHL-1

❑ SHL-1. Sherlock Holmes Game,
1904. Store item by Parker Brothers. -
$65 $135 $250

SHL-2

❑ SHL-2. Apparent Sherlock Holmes Newspaper Serialized Story Promotional,
c. 1919. Whitehead & Hoag. Large 4" heavy celluloid button. Front pictures man in derby hat and reads " $100 Reward For The Capture Of Mr. Raffles - See The Evening World." Button coincides with the first U.S. printing in 1919 of Arthur Conan Doyle's book The Doings Of Raffles Haw. If button does not relate directly to Holmes title, it may relate to Holmes-inspired writing of E.W. Hornung who achieved success by inverting Doyle's formulas and creating stories about the gentleman thief A.J. Raffles.
- **$50 $100 $175**

SHL-3

❑ SHL-3. Sherlock Holmes Map,
1930s. Rare. Household Finance. -
$750 $1500 $3000

SHL-4

❑ SHL-4. "Mutual" Radio "Thriller Dillers" Sign,
c. 1945. WFBR, Baltimore, Md. 10-1/2x27-1/2" orange, black and white cardboard sign with photos of stars from "Return Of Nick Carter, Adventures Of Bulldog Drummond, Sherlock Holmes." - **$150 $300 $500**

SHL-5

❑ SHL-5. "Sherlock Holmes' London" Prototype Map And Printed Example,
1955. Prepared for TV show's producer Motion Pictures for Television, Inc. 16-1/2x22". Gordon Gold Archives. Prototype Original Art - **$3500**
Printed Example - **$350 $750 $1500**

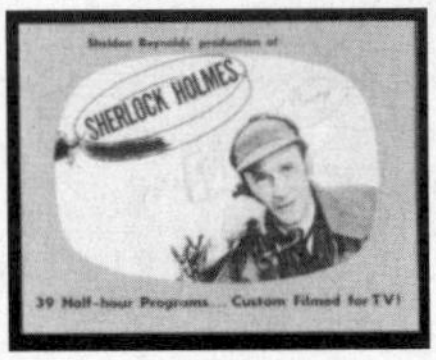

SHL-6

SHL-7

❑ SHL-6. Syndicated TV Show Promotional Folder,
1955. Motion Pictures for Television Inc. 8-1/2x11" with black and white photos and magazine article reprints. Gordon Gold Archives. -
$75 $150 $300

❑ SHL-7. "Baker Street" Stage Production Postcard,
c. 1970s. Broadway Theater, New York City. -
$15 $30 $70

SHL-8

❑ SHL-8. "Sherlock Holmes Game Of Mystery",
c. 1970s. English store item by Tri-Ang. Contains 16x16" board, clue cards, cardboard "Newspaper Clippings" folders and diecut playing pieces of Holmes, Dr. Watson and policeman. - **$35 $65 $135**

SHL-9

❑ **SHL-9. Record Set Boxed With Book,**
1970s. Murray Hill Records. Set of four 33-1/3 rpm records of "8 Original Radio Broadcasts" from years 1939-1940, 1945. Set is accompanied by 326-page book "The Complete Adventures And Memoirs Of Sherlock Holmes." -
$20 $35 $75

SHL-10

❑ **SHL-10. Sherlock Holmes, Jack The Ripper & Others English Figures,**
c. 1990. Lot of 15 painted lead pieces by Unicorn Miniatures, typically 2" tall. Depicted are variations of Holmes, Dr. Watson, Baker Street Irregulars, Patrolmen Bobbies, Jack the Ripper holding knife, distraught prostitute, slain prostitute.
Pair Holmes And Watson Near Mint - **$60**
Set Holmes And Irregulars (6) Near Mint - **$155**
Set Holmes And Ripper (7) - **$190**

Shield G-Man Club

Joe Higgins, alias the Shield, was one of the most popular comic book heroes of the 1940s, fighting to protect the American way of life with truth, justice, patriotism, and courage--and a costume that made him invulnerable. Well drawn by Irving Novick (1916-2004), The Shield was the first superhero to wear a patriotic costume. He debuted in *Pep Comics* #1 in 1940 and, despite some changes in character, lasted until *Pep* #65 in 1948. Between 1940 and 1944 he also appeared in *Shield-Wizard Comics*. The *Shield G-Man Club*, which offered pins and a membership card, had a short life before becoming the *Archie Club*.

SGM-1

SGM-2

❑ **SGM-1. Club Member Card,**
1940. Pep Comics, M.L.J. Magazines.
Card - **$100 $175 $400**
Mailer - **$20 $40 $75**

❑ **SGM-2. "Shield G-Man Club" Cello. Button (blue border),**
c. 1940. Rare. 1-3/4" version. -
$175 $350 $750

SGM-3

❑ **SGM-3. "The Shield" Cardboard Movie Projector,**
c. 1941. Shield Wizard Comics. Filmstrips cut from comic book page by reader to produce "film." Pictured example has replaced viewing tube. - **$250 $675 $1250**

(badge)

(button)

SGM-4

❑ **SGM-4. Club Member's Cello. Badge and Button In Two Sizes,**
c. 1943. Bar pin behind top folded edge. Also issued as 1-1/4" circular cello. button.
Badge - **$10 $20 $40**
Button (1.25" size) - **$75 $150 $250**
Button (1.5" size) Rare - **$200 $400 $800**

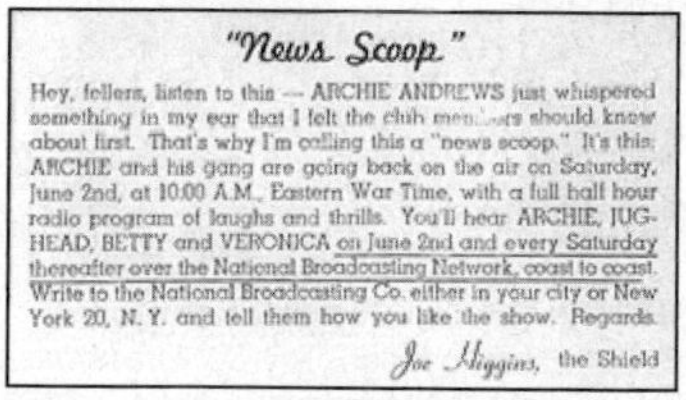

"News Scoop"

Hey, fellers, listen to this — ARCHIE ANDREWS just whispered something in my ear that I felt the club members should know about first. That's why I'm calling this a "news scoop." It's this: ARCHIE and his gang are going back on the air on Saturday, June 2nd, at 10:00 A.M., Eastern War Time, with a full half hour radio program of laughs and thrills. You'll hear ARCHIE, JUGHEAD, BETTY and VERONICA on June 2nd and every Saturday thereafter over the National Broadcasting Network, coast to coast. Write to the National Broadcasting Co. either in your city or New York 20, N. Y. and tell them how you like the show. Regards.

Joe Higgins, the Shield

SGM-5

❑ **SGM-5. The Shield "News Scoop" Postcard,**
c. 1945. Announcement of Archie Andrews and his gang returning to radio on Saturday, June 2, Eastern War Time with facsimile signature of Joe Higgins as The Shield. - **$50 $85 $175**

Shirley Temple

America's dimpled sweetheart, the world's darling, Shirley Temple was probably the most popular child prodigy actress ever to come out of Hollywood. Born in 1928, she sang, danced, and acted in 30 movies by the age of 13, was a top box-office star, and charmed the nation. Merchandising during the 1930s was extensive, including Shirley Temple dresses, hats, underwear, mugs, soap, and an estimated 1.5 million Shirley Temple dolls from Ideal Novelty & Toy Corp. She made further films as a teen and as an adult, but could not sustain her immense popularity. There were several short-lived ventures on CBS radio: *Shirley Temple Time* (1939), the *Shirley Temple Variety Show*, sponsored by Elgin watches (1941), and *Junior Miss* (1942). On television, *Shirley Temple's Story Book* was seen in 1958-1959 and *The Shirley Temple Show* aired in 1960-1961.

Married from 1945-49 to actor John Agar, she remarried in 1960, to TV executive Charles Black. In 1967, as Shirley Temple Black, she lost a primary race for a California Congressional seat, but was appointed as a U.S. representative to the United Nations. From 1974 to 1976, Black served as U.S. Ambassador to Ghana, then became Chief of Protocol. She then took the appointment of Ambassador to Czechoslovakia in 1989. She has also authored an autobiography, *Child Star*, in 1988.

SHR-1

SHR-2

❑ **SHR-1. Cello. Covered Pocket Mirror,**
1935. Curl has copyright date and "Fox Film Corp." - **$15 $25 $50**

❑ **SHR-2. Drawing Set With Coloring Book,**
1935. 10x13x1" deep boxed Saalfield kit. -
$125 $300 $500

SHR-3

❑ **SHR-3. Near Life-Size Plaster Bust,**
c. 1935. 12" tall realistic likeness finished in bronze luster with French maker marking on reverse. - **$100 $200 $400**

SHR-4

SHR-5

❑ **SHR-4. Patriotic Hair Bow,**
c. 1935. Store item. Her portrait on lustrous star at center. - **$85 $175 $300**

❑ **SHR-5. "Shirley Temple" Quaker Cereal Box,**
c. 1935. Complete - **$165 $325 $600**

SHR-6

❑ **SHR-6. Photo,**
1936. Philadelphia Record newspaper premium. - **$15 $25 $45**

SHR-7

SHR-8

❑ **SHR-7. Theater Club Cello. Button Scarcer Variety,**
1936. 1-1/4" black and white real photo button without dot pattern and made as a standard celluloid button rather than the other variety which uses a brass rim to hold the button parts into a single unit. - **$75 $135 $250**

❑ **SHR-8. Theatre Club Cello. Button,**
1936. Also inscribed for WFBR Radio, Baltimore. Beaded brass rim. Similar to SHR-7. - **$35 $100 $165**

SHR-9

SHR-10

❑ **SHR-9. "The American Girl" Scout Magazine With Doll Ad,**
1936. Doll offered as premium for four subscriptions. - **$8 $10 $25**

❑ **SHR-10. Cello. Button Off Doll,**
1936. Ideal Novelty and Toy Co. 1-1/4" with white border surrounding browntone photo. There are two versions in darker and lighter brown, both with orange accent on her hair ribbon but only the lighter version seems to also have orange accent on her dress strap. Original issues have metal plate covering the reverse holding a straight pin anchored at one side which snaps under a metal tab at the opposite side. Each Version - **$35 $75 $135**

SHR-11

❑ **SHR-11. Doll Contest Newspaper Advertisement,**
1936. - **$15 $30 $50**

SHR-12

SHR-13

❑ **SHR-12. 15" Tall Composition Doll,**
1936. Store item by Ideal Toy Co. Dress based on 1934 "Bright Eyes" movie costume. - **$250 $550 $1100**

❑ **SHR-13. Wheaties Box Back Panels,**
c. 1936. Set of 12. Promoted by at least five different half-page General Mills newspaper ads in the Sunday color comics section.
Each - **$12 $25 $50**

SHR-14

❑ **SHR-14. Shirley Temple Pair Of Painted Salt Figures,**
c. 1936 Store items. Much scarcer than white salt uncolored version.
Each Colored - **$35 $75 $140**
Each White - **$15 $30 $75**

SHR-15

SHR-16

❑ **SHR-15. Enameled Brass Figural Pin,**
c. 1936. Probable store item. - **$75 $150 $325**

❑ **SHR-16. "Shirley Temple's Pet/Rowdy" Enameled Brass Pin,**
c. 1936. Pictures her pet dog. Probably store item. - **$75 $160 $300**

SHR-17

SHR-18

❑ **SHR-17. "Chicago Times Shirley Temple Club" Litho. Button,**
c. 1936. - **$50 $100 $175**

❑ **SHR-18. Cello. Button Off Doll,**
c. 1936. Ideal Novelty And Toy Co. 1-1/4" with pink border. Many non-authentic doll button designs made in the 1970s-1990s exist. On original, reverse has metal plate holding a horizontal bar pin in fixed position. - **$30 $60 $100**

SHR-19

SHR-20

❑ **SHR-19. Shirley Temple "Dimples" Carnival Statue,**
1937. Statue is 3.75x5.75x16.5" tall painted plaster made by Carnival Art Statuary. Features her in costume from movie "Dimples" from 1936. Showcases her wearing three-piece suit including top hat and shirt with bow tie featuring dark sparkle accents. - **$175 $325 $600**

❑ **SHR-20. "Shirley Temple League" Enameled Brass English Pin,**
c. 1937. Sunday Referee newspaper. - **$35 $60 $100**

SHR-21

SHR-22

❑ **SHR-21. "Sweetheart" Australian Button,** c. 1937. Published for Kurri & Weston featuring real photo without dot pattern. - **$50 $100 $150**

❑ **SHR-22. "The Toy Trumpet" Song Sheet,** 1938. From her movie "Rebecca of Sunnybrook Farm." - **$10 $20 $50**

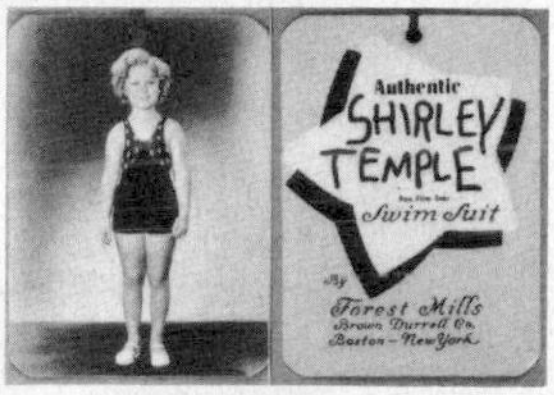

SHR-23

❑ **SHR-23. Swimsuit Cardboard String Tag,** 1930s. Forest Mills. Various photos. - **$20 $40 $80**

SHR-24

❑ **SHR-24. "Shirley Temple Wheaties Pitcher" Full Store Display,** 1930s. Wheaties. 3.25x16.75x17.25" box contains twelve 4.5" tall glass pitchers plus one additional display piece which fits into die-cut slot on box lid. Box states "Free! Shirley Temple Wheaties Pitcher For Your Breakfast Table! and has large portrait of Shirley on lid. Also used as premiums were a blue glass cereal bowl and a blue glass juice glass.
Complete - **$800 $1600 $2750**

SHR-25

❑ **SHR-25. Shirley Temple String Holder,** 1930s. Painted plaster string holder is 6x7x3" deep with recessed area in back to hold string ball. Hole at mouth, wire hanger at top are both as made. - **$100 $200 $400**

SHR-26

SHR-27

❑ **SHR-26. Portrait Picture Predominately In Pink,** 1930s. Probably store or theater give-away. - **$20 $40 $75**

❑ **SHR-27. "A Movie Of Me" Flip Book,** 1930s. Probably Wheaties Cereal. - **$75 $150 $275**

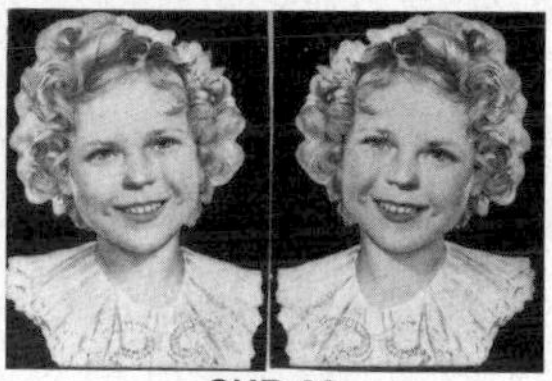

SHR-28

❑ **SHR-28. Diecut 12x16" Cardboard Hanger Sign For Theater Lobby,** 1930s. Color portrait each side. - **$85 $165 $325**

SHR-29

❑ **SHR-29. Enamel Charms Bracelet,** 1930s. Store item. 6" silver link bracelet holding two miniature Shirley portrait charms plus single elephant and pony charm. - **$100 $200 $325**

SHR-30

SHR-31

❑ **SHR-30. Child's Toy Ring,** 1930s. Narrow brass non-adjustable band for small finger topped by brass frame holding plastic cover over black and white real photo without dot pattern of her in apparent prayer pose. At least three different photo versions.
Each - **$50 $100 $200**

❑ **SHR-31. Carnival Doll,** 1930s. 18" tall painted chalkware on rounded base. - **$75 $150 $275**

SHR-32

SHR-33

❑ **SHR-32. Photo,** 1930s. Sealtest Milk. Promotes the movie "Just Around The Corner" on back of photo. - **$25 $50 $100**

❑ **SHR-33. Shirley Temple Box Of Books,** 1940. Saalfield Publishing. Six storybooks and two paperdoll books. Set - **$450 $800 $1500**

SHR-34

❑ **SHR-34. Shirley Temple Paper Dolls Book,**
1940. No. 1787 published by Saalfield Publishing Company. Measures 10x15.5". Shirley Temple is depicted as a butterfly on the front cover and some inside fashions include, merry-go-round dress, christmas tree dress, Little Boy Blue costume, Mother Goose costume, blue bird costume, ace of clubs costume, alarm clock costume, knitting bag costume and valentine costume. Uncut - **$75 $165 $275**

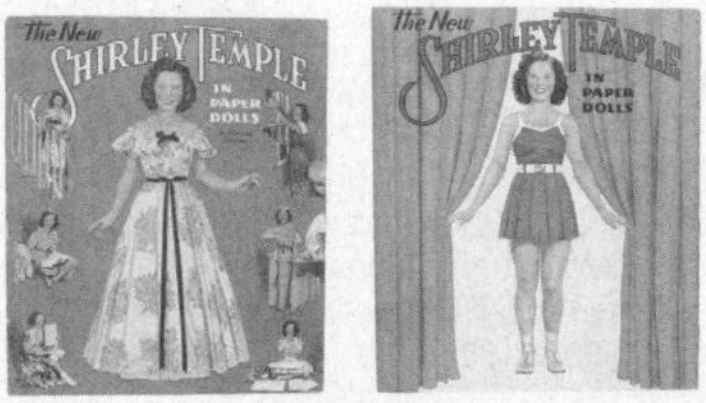

SHR-35

❑ **SHR-35. "The New Shirley Temple" Paper Doll Book,**
1942. Saalfield Book No. 2425 is 10.75x12.5". Front and back cover each have 10.5" tall punch-out cardboard doll image of Temple as a teenager. Contents are eight pages of uncut clothing. - **$60 $125 $200**

SHR-36

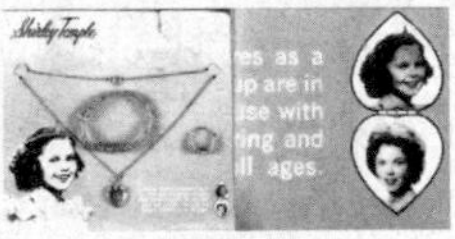

SHR-37

❑ **SHR-36. Cardboard Advertising Fan,**
1944. Royal Crown Cola. Inscribed for her 1944 movie "I'll Be Seeing You". - **$25 $50 $85**

❑ **SHR-37. "Picture Locket Jewelry" On Card,**
1940s. Store item. Heart-shaped symbol on ring, bracelet, locket. Set - **$75 $150 $250**

SHR-38

❑ **SHR-38. Ideal Doll Boxed,**
c. 1958. Ideal Toy Corp. 12" vinyl jointed doll with rooted hair plus outfit.
Near Mint Boxed - **$450**

SHR-39

SHR-40

❑ **SHR-39. Vendor Card,**
1950s. - **$10 $20 $40**

❑ **SHR-40. Photo Guide,**
1960. TV Guide from St. Louis Post Digest. 52 pages. - **$20 $40 $65**

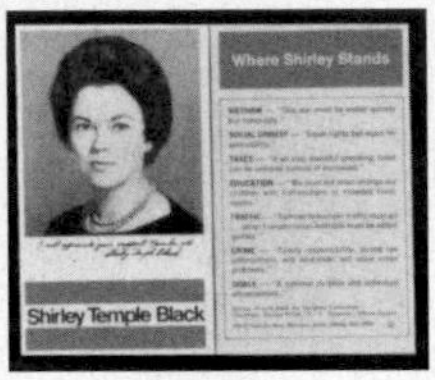

SHR-41

SHR-42

❑ **SHR-41. "Shirley Temple Black" Campaign Issues Position Card,**
1967. Issued for special election (November 14) Congressional campaign in California to fill 11th District seat in U.S. Congress. Shirley lost a December 12 run-off election to Paul McCloskey. - **$15 $30 $65**

❑ **SHR-42. "Shirley Temple" Boxed Doll,**
1973. Store item by Ideal. 16" tall jointed vinyl.
Near Mint Boxed - **$135**

Shock Gibson

***Speed Comics* began in October 1939 with the origin and first appearance of Shock Gibson in issue #1. Gibson was the cover feature and lead character of the first 15 issues. *Speed Comics* continued through issue #44 in 1947.**

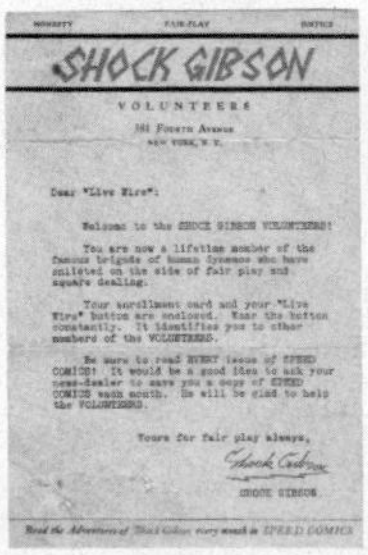

SHG-1

SHG-2

❑ **SHG-1. Shock Gibson Volunteers Club Letter,**
1939. - **$85 $125 $200**

❑ **SHG-2. Shock Gibson Volunteers Club Envelope,**
1939. - **$75 $100 $125**

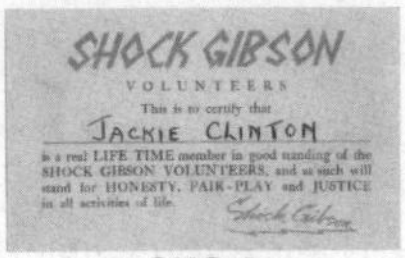

SHG-3

SHG-4

❑ **SHG-3. Volunteers Club Membership Card,**
1939. Brookwood Publishing/Speed Publishing.
- **$50 $150 $265**

❑ **SHG-4. Volunteers Club Cello. Button,**
c. 1939. - **$50 $125 $200**

SHG-5

❑ **SHG-5. Mask With Envelope,**
1940. Starched black linen generic mask in envelope from "Shock Gibson Volunteers" with New York City address.
With Envelope - **$65 $165 $250**

Shrek

In 1990, William Steig authored a children's book about a kind of gross, but ultimately sensitive green ogre, a lovely red-haired princess with sass and considerable kung-fu prowess, and a talking donkey named Donkey. Steig used his book to turn many of our culture's cherished fairy tale characters on their heads, including revised interpretations of Pinocchio, the Gingerbread Man, and the Three Little Pigs. The colorful picture-book, *Shrek*, enjoyed nominal success in young reading circles and classrooms. But, it would be another 11 years before the franchise experienced its greatest success – as a computer-animated feature film series.

The first film, *Shrek*, debuted in 2001 and starred Mike Myers as the voice of Shrek,

Cameron Diaz as Princess Fiona and Eddie Murphy as Donkey. The film grossed $42,347,760 in its opening weekend and boasted a total domestic gross of $267,665,011. The film's extreme popularity yielded tons of collectibles and toys including fast-food and snack toy tie-ins, watches, clothes, plush toys, snow gloves, lunch boxes and so much more.

Three years later, Dreamworks released *Shrek 2*, which picked up where the first film left off, with an ogre-faced Princess Fiona and Shrek as newlyweds. This sequel, featuring a scene-stealing Puss in Boots voiced by Antonio Banderas, far surpassed the original film in opening weekend ticket sales. In fact, *Shrek 2* became the second-largest three-day opening in US history with a gross of $108 million. It also holds the record as the highest grossing animated film of all time, with a total box office gross of $436 million domestically.

A third film, *Shrek The Third* was released in U.S. theaters on May 18, 2007.

SHK-1

SHK-2

❑ **SHK-1. "Shrek" Doll in Box,**
2001. - **$55**

❑ **SHK-2. "Shrek" Donkey Figure in Box,**
2001. Figure stands on base; has 6 sound phrases. - **$40**

SHK-3

❑ **SHK-3. Shrek Candy Gumball Machine,**
2001. - **$15 $35 $55**

SHK-4

❑ **SHK-4. Bandage Box,**
2003. - **$1 $2 $5**

SHK-5 SHK-6

❑ **SHK-5. Animated Shrek Bank in Box,**
2004. 17" tall figure sings and dances. - **$25**

❑ **SHK-6. Bubble Bath with Tag,**
2004. - **$2 $5 $10**

SHK-7

❑ **SHK-7. Large Die Cut Candy Promo Sign,**
2004. 15-1/2" tall, 16" wide. - **$15 $35 $65**

SHK-8

❑ **SHK-8. Dixie Cup Dispenser,**
2004. Shrek 2. - **$25**

(FRONT) SHK-9 (BACK)

❑ **SHK-9. Shrek 2 Dixie Cups,**
2004. 180 cups in box. - **$20**

SHK-10 SHK-11

❑ **SHK-10. Shrek 2 Candy Dispenser,**
2004. M&M Minis. - **$6**

❑ **SHK-11. Shrek 2 Candy Dispenser,**
2004. M&M Minis. From set of 6. - **$6**

(FRONT) SHK-12 (BACK)

❑ **SHK-12. Shrek 2 Fruit Gushers Box,**
2004. Each had one of four figurines inside.
Box - **$2 $4 $10**
Each Figurine - **$5**

SHK-13 SHK-14

❑ **SHK-13. Shrek 2 Frosted Sugar Cookies Box,**
2004. - **$2 $4 $10**

❑ **SHK-14. Soft Taco Dinner Kit with Cards,**
2004. Box has premium trading cards on back. - **$3 $6 $12**

SHK-15

❑ **SHK-15. 100 Piece Puzzle,**
2004. - **$5**

SHK-16

❑ **SHK-16. Play-Doh Root Canal Game,**
2004. - **$28**

SHK-17

SHK-18

❑ **SHK-17. Shrek 2 Pencil Set,**
2004. Eight pencils on card. - **$5**

❑ **SHK-18. Shrek 2 Party Favors,**
2004. Four rings on card. - **$5**

SHK-19

❑ **SHK-19. Shrek 2 Ogre Costume Kit,**
2004. - **$30**

SHK-20

SHK-21

❑ **SHK-20. Shrek 2 Napkin Pack,**
2004. Sixteen napkins in wrapper. - **$10**

❑ **SHK-21. Monopoly Junior Game,**
2004. - **$15**

SHK-22

❑ **SHK-22. Twisted Fairy Tale Game,**
2004. - **$15**

Silver Dollar Brady

Silver Dollar Brady was a character created to promote Seagram's alcohol. Hoppy, Roy and Gene refused to support projects that used alcohol or cigarettes as sponsors. As a result of this dilemma, these companies had to create their own cowboy heroes. Silver Dollar Brady is a classic example of using in-house characters for this type of advertising. The premium listed was designed to test whether or not you had too much to drink and were off on your own "happy trails."

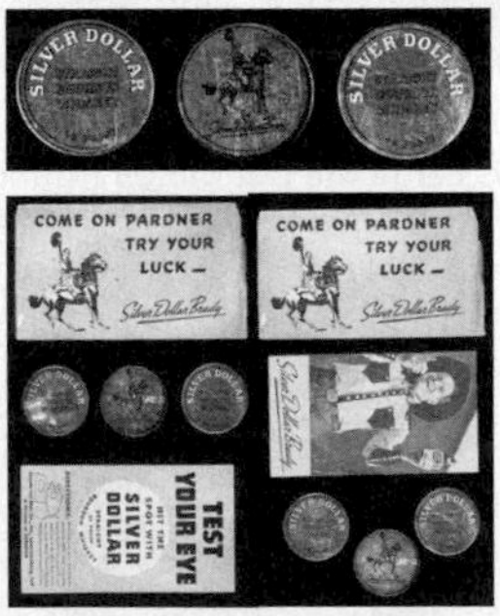

SIL-1

❑ **SIL-1. Test Your Eye Card,**
1940s. Includes three different thin metal silver dollar sized play coins with Brady pictured on obverse.
Mailer - **$25 $50 $100**
Card - **$25 $50 $75**
Each Play Dollar - **$25 $50 $75**

Silver Streak

Magazine publisher Arthur Bernhard entered the comic book market with _Silver Streak Comics_ #1 in December 1939. Jack Cole (1914-1958), later the creator of Plastic Man and a popular Playboy cartoonist, was brought in as artist/editor and drew the first Silver Streak story for issue #3, March 1940. Silver Streak became the second super-speed hero introduced that year, following the debut of The Flash just weeks earlier. The title is notable not only for Silver Streak but for the first appearance of Daredevil and the villainous Claw in issue #6. With issue #22 the title was changed to _Crime Does Not Pay_. Arthur Bernhard sold out to Lev Gleason shortly afterwards and Gleason continued to build a modest success based on the crime comics genre. See related entries in the Captain Battle section.

SLV-1

❑ **SLV-1. Photo,**
c. 1941. Rare. - **$200 $400 $750**

SLV-2

❑ **SLV-2. Award Card From "Daredevil And Crimebuster" With Facsimile Charles Biro Signature,**
1944. Daredevil Comics. Daredevil made his first appearance in Silver Streak #6. Has recipient's name written in ink. - **$500 $1000 $2000**

The Simpsons

In 1987, a series of 30-second animated shorts appeared on the new Fox network's *The Tracey Ullman Show*. Created by cartoonist Matt Groening, until then best known for his *Life in Hell* comic strip of 1980-1990, these short features would soon grow into a pop-culture phenomenon. On December 17, 1989, *The Simpsons* premiered with their own show on Fox as a half-hour Christmas special, soon followed by a regular series that debuted on January 14, 1990. After becoming Fox's #1 show for children under 17 and #4 for adults 18 to 34, and garnering critical praise and numerous awards including Emmys and a Peabody, *The Simpsons*, in February 1997, dethroned *The Flintstones* as the longest running animated series.

The Simpsons, like *The Flintstones*, concerns the exploits of a family: Homer—the dim-witted father; Marge—the loving wife and mother; Bart—the 10-year old trouble-making son; Lisa—the angst-ridden, intelligent sister; and Maggie—the toddler who communicates via pacifier. Also highlighted on the show are the citizens of Springfield, The Simpsons' hometown, plus guest appearances by a supporting cast of hundreds, voiced by many of Hollywood's top stars, including Dustin Hoffman, Kelsey Grammer, Michael Jackson, Mel Brooks, Leonard Nimoy, Meryl Streep, Mel Gibson, and many others.

Taking advantage of the popularity of his creations, Groening turned *The Simpsons* into a licensing empire, including comics, videos, CDs, and a string of best selling books. A long-awaited movie finally hit theaters on July 27, 2007, eventually earning a worldwide gross of $525 million. *The Simpsons* continue to be seen in syndication across the country in addition to new episodes airing on Fox. Most items are copyright Twentieth Century Fox or Matt Groening Productions. "D'oh!"

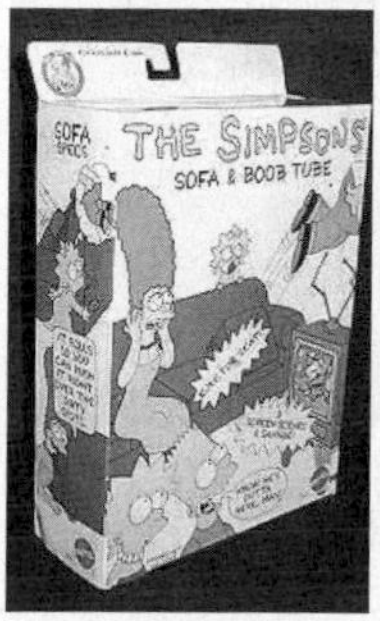

SIM-1

SIM-2

SIM-3

❑ **SIM-1. Simpsons Sofa and Boob Tube,**
1990. Mattel. Near Mint Boxed - **$90**

❑ **SIM-2. Bart Poseable Figure,**
1990. Mattel. Near Mint On Card - **$45**

❑ **SIM-3. Bartman Poseable Figure,**
1990. Mattel. Near Mint On Card - **$45**

SIM-4

❑ **SIM-4. Simpsons 3-D Chess Set,**
1991. Near Mint Boxed - **$30**

SIM-5

SIM-6

❑ **SIM-5. Simpsons Shampoo,**
1991. Cosrich. Each - **$10**

❑ **SIM-6. Anti-Dan Quayle Political Button,**
1992. 1-3/4" with black and white photo of Quayle against black background plus yellow cartoon of Bart. - **$5 $10 $20**

SIM-7

❑ **SIM-7. Roller Toys,**
1992. From UK Burger King. Each - **$5 $8**

SIM-8

❑ **SIM-8. Butterfinger Olympics Bronze Medal,**
1992. Butterfinger. Large 3" solid bronze medal limited to 5,000 which promoted the Summer Olympics. - **$50 $75 $100**

SIM-9

❑ **SIM-9. Presidential Campaign Satirical Button Featuring Krusty,**
1992. Colorful 3" button includes facsimile Matt Groening signature. - **$20 $40 $90**

SIM-10

❑ **SIM-10. Bongo Comics Promotional Badges,**
1993. Each - **$10**

SIM-11

SIM-12

❑ **SIM-11. Simpsons Series 1 Trading Cards,**
1993. Skybox. Metal storage container available by mail-order only. - **$20**

❑ **SIM-12. Simpsons 3-D Checker Set,**
1994. Near Mint Boxed - **$35**

SIM-13

❑ **SIM-13. Bongo Comics Promotional Badges,**
1994. Each - **$6**

SIM-14

❑ **SIM-14. Bongo Comics Promotional Badges,**
1995. Each - **$6**

SIM-15

❑ **SIM-15. Bongo Comics Promotional Badges,**
1996. Each - **$6**

SIM-16

❑ **SIM-16. "Puffa Pal" Asthma Inhaler Cover,**
1996. From Oddball in Australia. Lisa, Homer and Bart produced.
Each on unpunched card - **$20**
Each on punched card - **$10**

SIM-17

❑ **SIM-17. Simpsons Babies,**
1996. Mexican. Bart and Lisa. Made of Plaster of Paris standing 6" tall. Each - **$60**

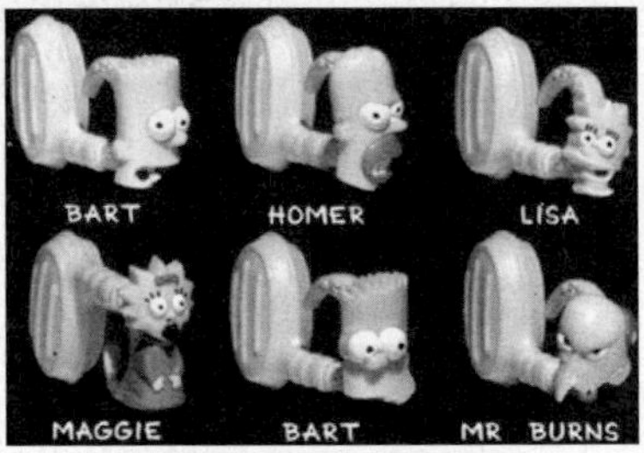

SIM-18

❑ **SIM-18. Squirt Rings,**
1997. United Kingdom Kellogg's Corn Pops premium. Bart (2 different versions), Homer, Lisa, Maggie, Mr. Burns. Total 6 different.
Near Mint Complete Wrapped Set - **$175**
Near Mint Complete Unwrapped Set - **$90**
Box - **$8 $12 $25**

SIM-19

❑ **SIM-19. Bongo Comics Promotional Badges,**
1997. Each - **$6**

SIM-20

❑ **SIM-20. Simpsons at the Beach Squirt Set,**
1998. Australian. 4 pieces. - **$25**

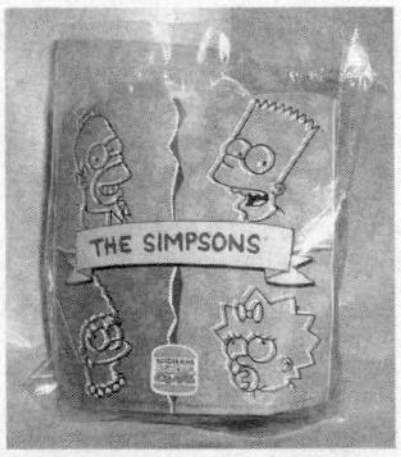

SIM-21

❑ **SIM-21. Burger King Figures,**
1998. From England. Marge, Homer, Bart and Maggie in Kid's Club bags or boxes.
Full set in bags - **$10**
Box - $3

SIM-22

❑ **SIM-22. Subway Giveaways,**
1998. Set of 4. Set - **$20**

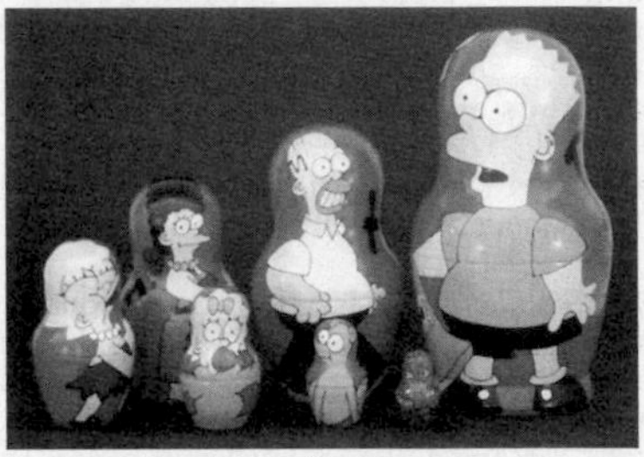

SIM-23

❑ **SIM-23. Russian Nesting Dolls,**
1999. 7 dolls in all. - **$65**

SIM-24 SIM-25

❑ **SIM-24. Apu Coffee Mug,**
1999. - **$15**

❑ **SIM-25. Moe Mug,**
1999. Beer stein. - **$15**

SIM-26

SIM-27

❑ **SIM-26. Prototype Ring,**
1999. - **$75**

❑ **SIM-27. Electronic LCD Game,**
1999. In plastic package. - **$30**

SIM-28

❑ **SIM-28. Ceramic Figures,**
1999. Feves from France. 1" tall ceramic figures typically baked into cakes as a surprise. Set of 9. Set - **$72**

SIM-29

❑ **SIM-29. Plush Animal Figures,**
1999. Plushes of the show's animal characters: Itchy, Scratchy, Snowball II, Santa's Little Helper, and Blinky the 3-Eyed Fish. 4"-6" tall. From Giftware International PLC. Before importation to the U.S., the manufacturer was made to obliterate the word "Beanie" from the tag.
Each with tag - **$15**
Each without tag - **$7**

SIM-30

❑ **SIM-30. Panini Figures,**
1999. Set of 8 from Panini of Italy. 1-1/2" tall hard plastic figures. Set - **$40**

SIM-31

❑ **SIM-31. Plastic Family Set,**
1990s. Kinder Egg Germany. 1" tall. Set - **$40**

SIM-32

❑ **SIM-32. Winchells Donuts Figures,**
1990s. Winchells Donuts. Bart and Homer with changeable word balloons in Spanish and English. Each Figure - **$12**

SIM-33

❑ **SIM-33. Lucky Dip Set and Cards,**
1990s. Australian. 8 pieces with 15 cards.
Eight Piece Set - **$60**
With Cards - **$80**

SIM-34

❑ **SIM-34. Gum Containers,**
1990s. Each - **$6**

SIM-35 SIM-36

❑ **SIM-35. Bart Figural Cookie Jar,**
1990s. Extinct Collectibles. Near Mint Boxed - **$125**

❑ **SIM-36. Homer Figural Cookie Jar,**
1990s. Extinct Collectibles. Near Mint Boxed - **$125**

SIM-37

❑ **SIM-37. Bart & Lisa Salt & Pepper Set,**
1990s. Extinct Collectibles. Bart & Lisa watching TV. 3 piece set. Near Mint Boxed - **$50**

SIM-38 SIM-39

❑ **SIM-38. Bart Simpson Pez,**
1990s. 5 different. Each - **$4**

❑ **SIM-39. Homer & Marge Salt & Pepper Set,**
1990s. Extinct Collectibles. Homer & Marge with Maggie on couch. Near Mint - **$55**

SIM-40

❑ **SIM-40. Burger King Giveaways,**
1990s. Each - **$3**
With Backgrounds, Each - **$15**

SIM-41

SIM-42

❑ **SIM-41. Simpsons Toy Display,**
1990s. Subway promotion with 4 toys.
Near Mint - **$75**

❑ **SIM-42. Bartman Watch,**
1990s. Nelsonic. Near Mint On Card - **$45**

SIM-43

❑ **SIM-43. Panini Figures,**
2000. Set of 12 from Panini of Italy. 3/4"-1" tall hard plastic figures. Set - **$50**
Bag - **$2**

SIM-44

❑ **SIM-44. Lounge-A-Rama Set,**
2000. Set of 4 figures plus the couch from Little Red Rooster restaurant of Australia. 2-1/2"-5" tall plastic figures. Came in decorative box.
Set with box - **$30**

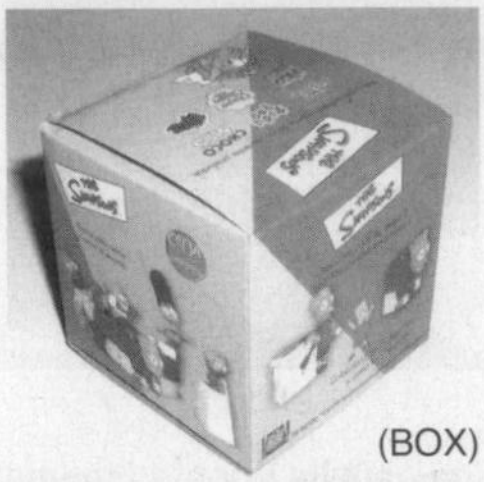

(BOX)

SIM-45

❑ **SIM-45. Dinner Table and Bar-B-Que Set,**
2000. 2 sets of 5 figures from Sabritas of Mexico. 1-1/2"-2" tall plastic figures. Came in decorative box.
10 figures bagged with box - **$50**
Set Unbagged - **$20**

SIM-46

❑ **SIM-46. "Radioactive Homer" Action Figure in Box,**
2000. A Toyfare magazine mail-order exclusive from the World of Springfield Interactive set. The figure glows in the dark. - **$150**

(PACKAGING)

(FIGURE WITH PLASTIC EGG FOUND IN CANDY)

SIM-47

❑ **SIM-47. Italian Candy Figure Set,**
2000. Set of 6 figures from Dolcerie Veneziane of Italy. Plastic figures came in plastic eggs found inside chocolate candy.
Set - **$40**

(COMIC BOOK)

(BAG)

SIM-48

❑ **SIM-48. Global Fanfest Figure Set,**
2000. From Burger King UK Global Fanfest Kid's Meal. Set of 10 soft plastic figures 5"-6" tall and a comic book in a decorative bag.
Each figure bagged with tag - **$5**
Each figure without bag or tag - **$3**
Carry bag - **$5**
Comic Book - **$3**

(FRONT)

(BACK)

SIM-49

❑ **SIM-49. "Get Duffed" Chocolates,**
2000. Can contains milk chocolates shaped like Duff Beer cans. From England.
Unopened - **$5 $10 $20**

SIM-50

❑ **SIM-50. Krusty the Clown Action Figure on Card,**
2000. From the World of Springfield Interactive set. - **$7**

SIM-51

❏ SIM-51. "The Simpsons" Color Glossy Photo Autographed By Creator Matt Groening And Voice Actors,
c. 2000. Photo is 8.5x10". Groening added 2x2" art image of Bart to left. Also signed by Nancy Cartwright (voice of Bart)/Julie Kavner (Marge)/ Yeardley Smith (Lisa). Same or Similar - **$450**

SIM-52

❏ SIM-52. Barney Christmas Ornament,
2001. In box. - **$5**

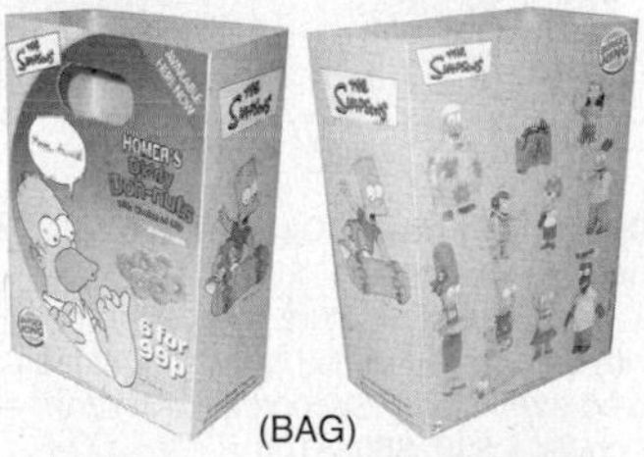

(BAG)

SIM-53

❏ SIM-53. Diddy Doh-nuts Figure Set,
2001. From Burger King UK Diddy Doh-nuts. Set of 11 soft plastic figures 5"-6" tall in a decorative box.
Each figure bagged with tag - **$5**
Mumu Homer bagged with tag - **$8**
Each figure without bag or tag - **$3**
Burger King box - **$5**

SIM-54

❏ SIM-54. "Pin Pal Burns" Action Figure in Box,
2001. A Toyfare magazine mail-order exclusive from the World of Springfield Interactive set. The episode "Team Homer" has Mr. Burns replacing star bowler Otto on the Pin Pals team, threatening the team's championship dreams with his poor athletic ability. - **$45**

PUNCHOUTS

SIM-55 (BACKGROUND)

❏ SIM-55. "Pop-Out People" Punchouts,
2001. Cardboard punchouts of characters with background. - **$3**

SIM-56

❏ SIM-56. "Woo-hoo!" Homer Sculpture,
2001. From the "Misadventures of Homer Sculpture Collection. The Hamilton Collection. In box - **$40**

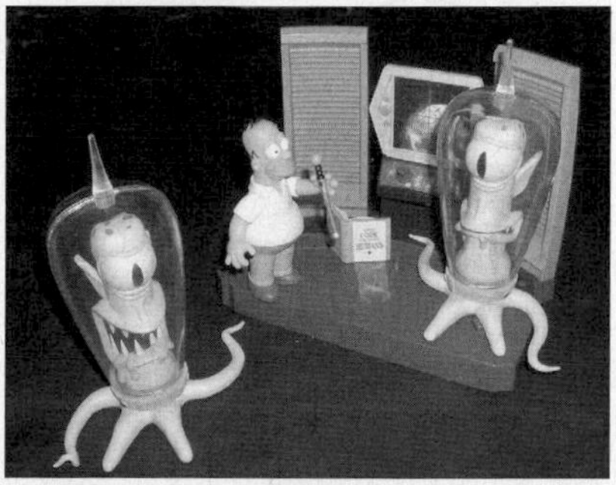

SIM-57

❏ SIM-57. "Treehouse of Horror II" Action Figure Set,
2001. Toys 'R' Us exclusive. Limited edition of 20,000 sets.
In box - **$90**

(ACTIVITY BOOK)

SIM-58

❏ SIM-58. "Spooky Light-Ups" Figure Set,
2001. Burger King Halloween. Set of 15 figures, 4" tall. Came with a 4-page Spooky Adventures 8-1/2"x 11" activity book.
Each figure in packaging - **$5**
Each figure loose - **$2**
Spooky Adventures activity book - **$5**

SIM-59

❑ **SIM-59. "Spooky Light-Ups" Promotional Poster,**
2001. Burger King Halloween. 26" x 39" paper poster. - **$30**

SIM-60

❑ **SIM-60. "Spooky Light-Ups" Promotional Poster,**
2001. Burger King Halloween. 19-1/2" x 19-1/2" cardboard poster. Some posters have a paste-over sticker changing the program air date from Oct. 30th to Nov. 6th. - **$15**

SIM-61

❑ **SIM-61. "Spooky Light-Ups" Window Cling,**
2001. Burger King Halloween. 17" x 24" plastic static window cling. Some have a paste-over sticker changing the program air date from Oct. 30th to Nov. 6th. - **$28**

SIM-62

❑ **SIM-62. PEZ Keychains,**
2002. Bart, Homer and Marge dispensers on a keychain with candy. Each NM - **$6**

SIM-63

❑ **SIM-63. Krusty-in-the-Box,**
2003. - **$28**

SIM-64

❑ **SIM-64. Simpsons Moe's Tavern Pool Game,**
2003. Rocket USA. Large wind-up tin toy. Boxed - **$40**

SIM-65

❑ **SIM-65. Simpsons Barney's Bowl-A-Rama Game,**
2003. Rocket USA. Large wind-up tin toy. Boxed - **$40**

Sinclair Oil

Harry F. Sinclair (1876-1956) founded the Sinclair Oil & Refining Corporation in 1916, and the company soon grew to become one of the nation's largest integrated oil companies. (Sinclair himself was caught up in the Teapot Dome oil-lease scandal and served a prison term in 1929 for contempt of the Senate.) The company started using dinosaurs in its advertising in 1930 to illustrate its theme that Sinclair oil was mellowed a hundred million years, and by 1931 had fixed on the brontosaurus as its symbol. Dino was put on signs and oil cans, the company sponsored dinosaur exhibits at the 1933 Century of Progress Exposition in Chicago and Dinoland at the 1964 New York World's Fair, funded dinosaur exploration, and in 1935 started giving out dinosaur stamps and albums at gas stations. Over the years Sinclair issued a number of dinosaur toys and other brontosaurus-oriented promotional items. In 1973 the company became part of the Atlantic Richfield Company, now ARCO.

SNC-1

❑ **SNC-1. "Big News" Chicago World's Fair Sinclair Newspaper,**
1933. 11x16" photo feature eight-page publication devoted largely to the dinosaurs exhibit. Pictured example is "Second Edition" front and back cover. - **$30 $60 $100**

SNC-2

❑ **SNC-2. Dinosaur Book,**
1934. Twelve pages in color describing and picturing six reptiles. - **$25 $45 $90**

SNC-3

❑ **SNC-3. Dinosaur Stamp Album,**
1935. Holds 24 stamps. Orange cover.
Complete - **$40 $85 $175**

SNC-4

❑ **SNC-4. Dinosaur Stamp Album No. 2,**
1938. Holds 24 stamps. Red cover.
Complete - **$40 $85 $175**

SNC-5

SNC-6

❑ **SNC-5. "Picture News" Issue,**
c. 1938. 11x16" monthly four-page news and human interest photo feature publication imprinted on top front and bottom rear page for local Sinclair dealer. - **$20 $35 $65**

❑ **SNC-6. Sinclair H-C Gasoline Button,**
1930s. Button is 1.75" with St. Louis Badge paper. - **$10 $25 $50**

SNC-7

❑ **SNC-7. Dinosaur Stamp Album,**
1959. Holds 12 stamps.
Complete - **$15 $25 $50**

SNC-8

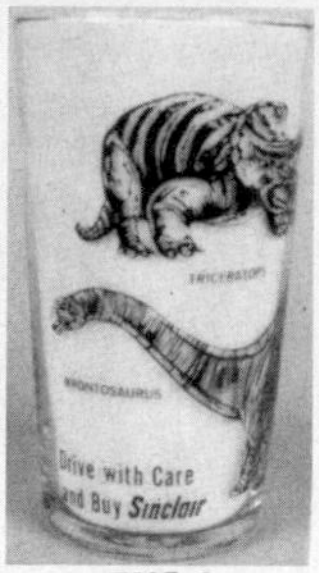

SNC-9

❑ **SNC-8. "Sinclair Power-X" Litho. Tin Bank,**
c. 1950s. 4" tall with gauge showing price per gallon of 33 cents. - **$35 $80 $150**

❑ **SNC-9. Dinosaurs Glass,**
1950s. 4-3/4" tall with images in green. -
$12 $25 $40

SNC-10

SNC-11

❑ **SNC-10. Coloring Book,**
1963. 8x10-3/4" with 32 pages including two which depict "Sinclair Dinoland" at 1964-65 New York World's Fair. - **$15 $25 $50**

❑ **SNC-11. "Dinoland" New York World's Fair Glass Tumbler,**
1964. Pictures symbolic twins at exhibit. -
$15 $25 $45

SNC-12

❑ **SNC-12. "Sinclair Dinoland" New York World's Fair Souvenir Booklet,**
1964. Twelve-page picture summary from life-sized dinosaur exhibit. Pictured are front and back cover. Offered flat by stations, or in sealed plastic bag holding several various colored dinosaur plastic small models. - **$10 $20 $35**

SNC-13

❑ **SNC-13. "Sinclair Dinoland" New York World's Fair Figure,**
1965. 9" long waxy-plastic molded dinosaur with inscriptions for Sinclair and the second year of the fair. From series of at least six different, 5" to 9" long, purchased via coin vending machine at the exhibit. Each - **$15 $30 $50**

SNC-14

❑ **SNC-14. Dinosaur Vinyl Bank,**
1960s. 9" long figure in green hard plastic unmarked but believed Sinclair issue. -
$10 $20 $30

SNC-15

SNC-16

❑ **SNC-15. Dinosaur Toy Pack,**
1960s. Six miniature plastic replica figures in cellophane packet naming each plus Sinclair Oil's logo. Near Mint Packaged - **$35**

❑ **SNC-16. "Drive With Care" Applique,**
c. 1960s. Molded thin shell plastic sign with peel-off adhesive strips on reverse. No Sinclair markings but obvious dinosaur symbol. -
$12 $25 $40

SNC-17

❑ **SNC-17. "Sinclair Dino" Inflatable Figure With** Instructions,
1960s. Came in plastic bag. Green vinyl figure inflates to 13.25" tall. - **$15 $25 $45**

SNC-18

❑ **SNC-18. Inflatable Dinosaur Toy/Hanger Display,**
c. 1970s. Made by Alvimar. 48" long. -
$15 $25 $45

The Singing Lady

Ireene Wicker was the Singing Lady, and for 13 years (1932-1945) she told fairy tales and sang to the nation's children on a highly popular network radio program called *The Singing Story Lady*. The show, loved by parents as well as children, won many major broadcasting awards, including a Peabody. Kellogg's cereals, the long-term sponsor, offered a number of premiums, mostly song and story booklets designed by whimsical illustrator Vernon Grant (1902-1990). *The Singing Lady* moved to ABC television (1948-1950) with a similar format, using puppets to illustrate fairy tales and historical sketches. In 1953-1954, with Kellogg's again sponsoring, the program returned as *Story Time*.

SNG-1

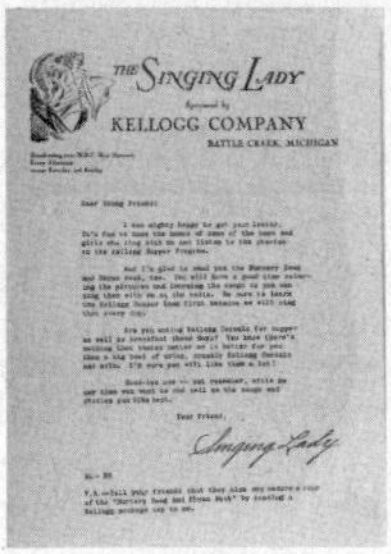

SNG-2

❑ **SNG-1. "Singing Lady Song Book",**
1931. Has coloring book pages. - **$20 $40 $70**

❑ **SNG-2. Singing Lady Promo Letter,**
1931. Kellogg's. Suggests you eat Kellogg's cereals for breakfast **and** supper. - **$12 $25 $50**

SNG-3

SNG-4

❑ **SNG-3. "Singing Lady Song Book",**
c. 1932. Art by Vernon Grant. - **$20 $40 $65**

❑ **SNG-4. Singing Lady Punchouts,**
1932. Kellogg's. Three cardboard pages of punchouts. Unpunched - **$35 $65 $140**

SNG-5

❑ **SNG-5. Kellogg's "Mother Goose" Booklet,**
1933. Cover art by Vernon Grant. - **$18 $35 $65**

SNG-6

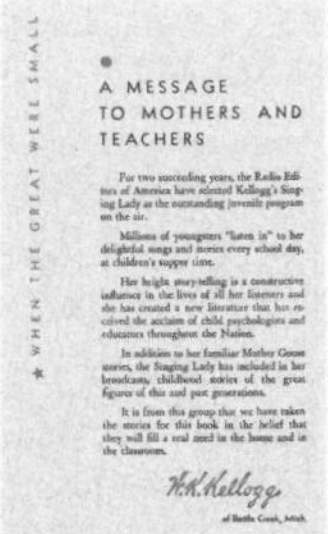

SNG-7

❑ **SNG-6. Singing Lady Booklet Titled "When The Great Were Small",**
1935. Kellogg's premium with mailer.
Booklet - **$35 $75 $150**
Mailer - **$8 $12 $25**

❑ **SNG-7. Singing Lady Promo Letter,**
1935. Kellogg's. - **$15 $30 $60**

SNG-8

SNG-9

❑ **SNG-8. "Mother Goose" Booklet,**
1935. Kellogg's Rice Krispies. Subtitled "Mother Goose As Told By Kellogg's Singing Lady" with artwork over 16 pages by Vernon Grant. - **$15 $30 $60**

❑ **SNG-9. Film Stories,**
1935. Kellogg's Rice Krispies. Promotes radio show. Has movie film cut-outs that can be played with by running through attached toy theatre. Features Mother Goose stories. - **$25 $50 $85**

SNG-10

❑ **SNG-10. Punch-Out Paper "Party Kit",**
1936. Near Mint With Mailer - **$225**
Book Only - **$40 $75 $165**

SNG-11

❑ **SNG-11. "Mother Goose Action Circus" Punch-Out Book With Mailer Envelope,**
1936. Six sheets of Vernon Grant illustrations.
Mailer - **$15 $30 $60**
Punch-Out Book - **$100 $275 $425**

SNG-12

SNG-13

❑ **SNG-12. "Kellogg's Rice Krispies" Box Flat With Vernon Grant Art,**
1937. Has ad for Singing Lady Mother Goose Action Circus Book. Near Mint Flat - **$190**
Used Complete - **$30 $65 $125**

❑ **SNG-13. "Ireene Wicker" Fan Postcard,**
1940. National Broadcasting Co. for her "Musical Stories" radio broadcasts on Blue Network. - **$15 $30 $50**

The Six Million Dollar Man

Based on a Martin Caidin novel, *Cyborg*, this TV series debuted as an ABC Movie of the Week March 7, 1973. As an ABC series it ran January 18, 1974 ending March 6, 1978. It followed the adventures of Steve Austin, a former test pilot and astronaut who is rebuilt ("better, stronger, faster") with the latest technology after a freak accident. He is given replacement limbs which heighten his strength, and a telescopic eye. As the series became a '70s phenomenon, the Bond-like missions of the early episodes gave way to more cartoonish, comic-book adventures, involving stock Arab terrorists, dangerous space probes, and in several memorable episodes, aliens from outer space and a huge robot Bigfoot. A wide variety of toys and action figures were available.

***The Bionic Woman*, a spin-off based on a story that aired on *The Six Million Dollar Man* in 1975, debuted in 1976 and ran until 1978. Lindsay Wagner played Jamie Sommers, Steve's on-and-off girlfriend, and another enhanced government agent working for OSI. When *The Bionic Woman* switched networks, Richard Anderson and Martin E. Brooks (who played Goldman and bionics scientist Rudy Wells) made history as the first actors to play the same characters simultaneously on two different networks. There have been three reunion TV-movies: *Return of the Six-Million Dollar Man and the Bionic Woman* (1987), *Bionic Showdown: The Six-Million Dollar Man and the Bionic Woman* (1989), featuring a young Sandra Bullock, and *Bionic Ever After?* (1994), in which Steve and Jamie were finally wed. Persistent rumors of new incarnations of this popular series continue to pop up, but nothing concrete has happened as of this writing. Most items are copyright Universal City Studios.**

SXM-1

❑ **SXM-1. Lunch Box,**
1974. Aladdin Industries, Inc.
Box - **$30 $65 $175**
Thermos - **$12 $25 $40**

SXM-2

❑ **SXM-2. Boxed Game,**
1975. Store item by Parker Brothers. - **$10 $20 $45**

SXM-3

❑ **SXM-3. "Six Million Dollar Man" Model Kits,**
1975. Three different 6.5x9x3.5" deep boxes from MPC/Fundimensions. Model titles are "Jaws Of Doom, Evil Rider, Fight For Survival." Each Unused Boxed - **$18 $35 $60**

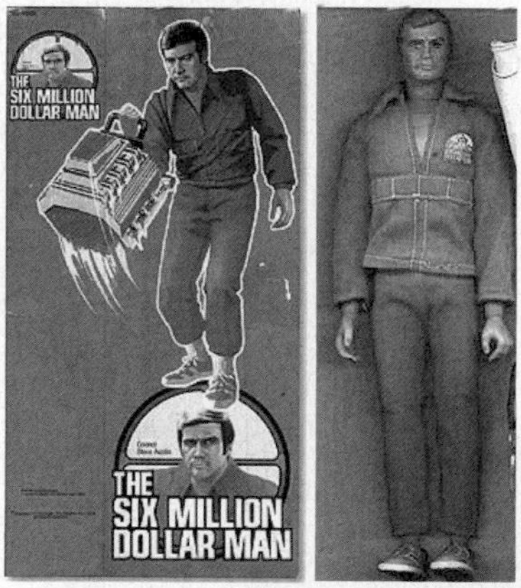

SXM-4

❑ **SXM-4. Six Million Dollar Man Action Figure,**
1975. 13" doll by Kenner. Figure was released in two versions. The first, with telescopic vision and bionic lifting arm with removable modules, came with an engine block. The second featured bionic gripping action and came with an orange I-beam. Box art for first version also shown. Boxed Each - **$40 $70 $145**

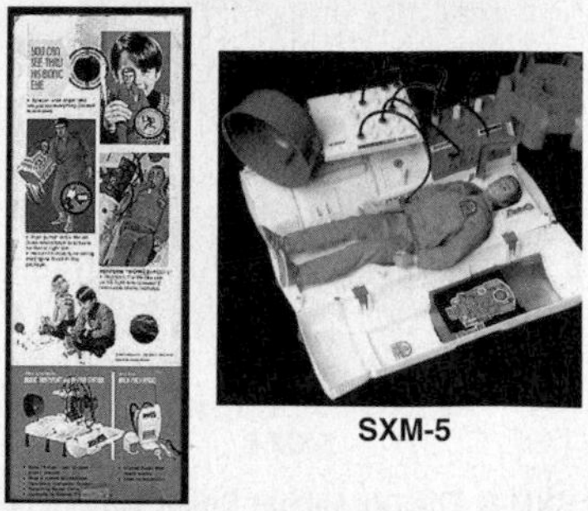

SXM-5

❑ **SXM-5. Bionic Transport and Repair Station,**
1975. Kenner. Side panel of box also shown. Boxed - **$25 $45 $80**

SXM-6

❑ **SXM-6. "The Bionic Woman Action Club Kit,"**
1975. Issued by Kenner. Jamie Sommers portrait, membership card and certificate. Complete **- $20 $45 $85**

SXM-7

❑ **SXM-7. Bionic Action Club Kit,**
1975. The kit included a mailing envelope (not pictured), a certificate, wallet card, logo sticker and portrait photo. A comic book ad with a coupon to join the club is also pictured. Complete Kit - **$25 $50 $95**

SXM-8

❑ SXM-8. The Six Million Dollar Man Record,
1975. Peter Pan Industries. Four stories, including "Birth of the Bionic Man," "The Iron Heart," "The Man From the Future," and "Bionic Berserker." - **$8 $15 $25**

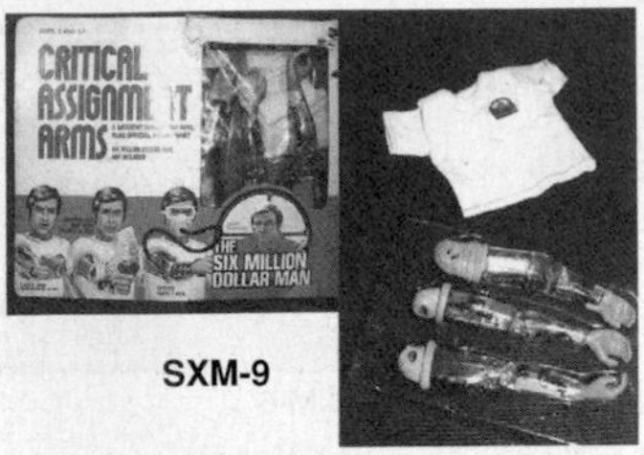

SXM-9

❑ SXM-9. Critical Assignment Arms,
1976. Accessories for the action figure. Set comes with three arms (laser, neutralizer, and oxygen supply) and a white T-shirt.
Boxed - **$20 $30 $65**

SXM-10 SXM-11

❑ SXM-10. "Maskatron Six Million Dollar Man's Enemy" Action Figure,
1976. Store item by Kenner. Figure is 13" tall.
Near Mint Boxed - **$150**
Loose Complete - **$15 $30 $75**

❑ SXM-11. Figural Bank,
1976. 10" tall hard vinyl depiction of Steve Austin in orange suit bursting through red brick wall above gray base. - **$10 $20 $40**

SXM-12

❑ SXM-12. "The Six Million Dollar Man Bionic Mission Vehicle,"
1977. Store item by Kenner.
Near Mint Boxed - **$50**
Loose Complete - **$10 $15 $25**

SXM-13

❑ SXM-13. "O.S.I. Headquarters" Boxed Set,
1977. Store item by Kenner.
Near Mint Boxed - **$100**
Loose Complete - **$15 $25 $50**

SXM-14

❑ SXM-14. "The Bionic Woman" Metal Lunchbox With Thermos,"
1977. Aladdin. Thermos is plastic.
Lunchbox - **$40 $100 $200**
Thermos - **$15 $30 $50**

SXM-15 SXM-16

❑ SXM-15. "6 Million Dollar Man Club" Cello. Button,
1977. - **$18 $30 $60**

❑ SXM-16. The Six Million Dollar Man Activity Book,
1977. Rand McNally & Co. - **$10 $15 $20**

SXM-17 SXM-18

❑ SXM-17. Book & Record Set,
1977. Peter Pan Industries. Includes "Birth of the Bionic Man" and "The Man From the Future." - **$5 $10 $20**

❑ SXM-18. "Hear 4 Exciting Christmas Adventures" Record,
1978. Peter Pan Industries. Includes "The Toymaker," "Christmas Lights," "The Kris Kringle Caper," and "Elves Revolt." - **$5 $10 $20**

SXM-19

❑ SXM-19. "The Six Million Dollar Man Venus Space Probe,"
1978. Scarcest accessory in the Kenner series.
Complete Boxed - **$150 $300 $600**

Skeezix

The central character of the meandering continuity comic strip *Gasoline Alley*, Skeezix was an exception to the traditional comic style in that he aged accordingly as the strip continued over the years. Skeezix was a doorstep infant foundling left by unknown parents in 1921. He served in World War II and returned to continue his small town, middle-class life so readily identifiable to mass readership. Skeezix was an adult and father in the 1960s but the vast majority of related premiums are from his 1930s happy childhood years with guardian Uncle Walt surrounded by the extensive assortment of relatives, friends and neighbors created by cartoonist Frank King (1883-1969). The strip is ably carried on today by Jim Scancarelli, who also frequently contributes new listings for the *Hake's Guide*.

SKX-1

❑ SKX-1. Diecut Cardboard Standee For Cartoon Film,
c. 1920. Capital Film Co. Inc., Chicago. About 7x7" full color. - **$135 $250 $500**

SKX-2

❑ **SKX-2. Uncle Walt And Skeezix Blotter,**
c. 1922. Various sponsor imprints. -
$20 $40 $75

SKX-3

SKX-4

❑ **SKX-3. Uncle Walt & Skeezix Oilcloth Dolls,**
c. 1923. Stuffed dolls finished by oilcloth front and back panels. Uncle Walt - **$75 $150 $300**
Skeezix - **$50 $100 $200**

❑ **SKX-4. Skeezix Pets & Friend Oilcloth Dolls,**
c. 1923. Three stuffed dolls finished by oilcloth front and back panels, each identified by character name. Puff The Cat - **$25 $50 $100**
Pal The Dog - **$25 $50 $100**
Jean - **$50 $75 $150**

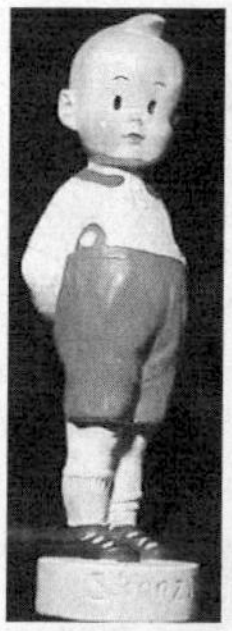

SKX-5

SKX-6

❑ **SKX-5. Large Plaster Statue,**
c. 1923. Store item by Live Long Toys, Chicago. 14-1/2" tall with realistic facial paint and red pants. - **$175 $350 $650**

❑ **SKX-6. "Handkerchiefs For Tiny Tots" Boxed Set,**
c. 1924. Store item. 6x6" box which held three.
Box - **$60 $135 $240**
Each Hanky - **$10 $20 $40**

SKX-7

❑ **SKX-7. "Skeezix" And "Pal" Pull Toy,**
c. 1924. Jigsawed and painted wooden toy by unidentified maker. - **$85 $165 $350**

SKX-8

SKX-9

❑ **SKX-8. "Party Invitations" Boxed,**
c. 1924. Store item. About a dozen full color in full color 4x6" box. Box - **$40 $75 $150**
Each Invitation - **$8 $15 $30**

❑ **SKX-9. Napkin Holder Boxed,**
c. 1926. Store item. 5x5" color box holding diecut flat wood figure of Pal the dog designed as napkin ring. Box - **$45 $85 $165**
Figure - **$40 $80 $150**

SKX-10

❑ **SKX-10. Toothbrush Holder Box,**
c. 1926. Full color 3x6-1/4".
Box Only - **$60 $125 $250**

SKX-11

❑ **SKX-11. Christmas Seals Poster,**
1930. Chicago Tuberculosis Institute and other TB Assn. chapters. 10.5x14" paper poster featuring Skeezix and Pal promoting sale of that year's fund-raising sticker seals.
- **$60 $125 $225**

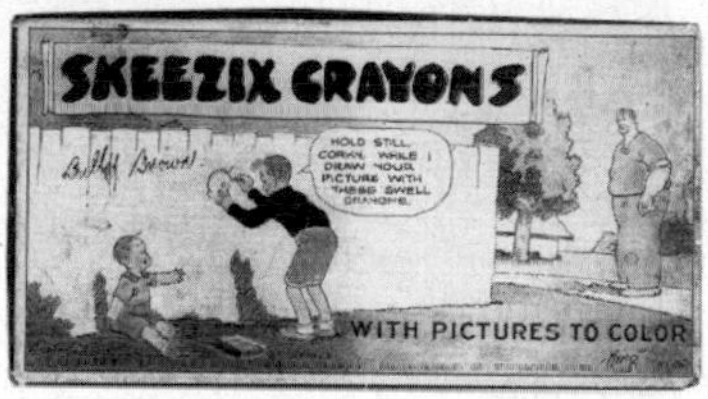

SKX-12

❑ **SKX-12. "Skeezix Crayons With Pictures To Color" Boxed Set,**
c. 1930. Store item by Milton Bradley. Art includes Corky, born in 1928. - **$35 $70 $140**

SKX-13

❑ **SKX-13. "Skeezix" Pocket Watch,**
c. 1930. Ingraham. 1-7/8" nickel-plated case surrounds dial with colorful full figure of "Skeezix" with name of character at lower left and name of strip creator "King" at lower right. Below is second wheel. - **$500 $1000 $1750**

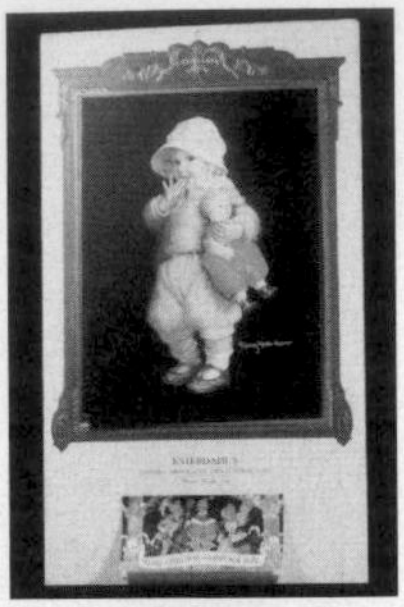

SKX-14

❑ **SKX-14. Toddler With Skeezix Doll Calendar,**
1932. 10x17" paper wall calendar featuring full color art of youngster grasping his Skeezix oil-cloth doll. Imprint for local sponsor is "Estherdahl's Lincoln Ambulance And Funeral Cars." Complete with 12-month calendar tablet and cover page. - **$40 $80 $150**

SKX-15

❑ **SKX-15. "Walt & Skeezix Gasoline Alley Game,"**
c. 1932. Store item by Milton Bradley Co. - **$50 $115 $225**

SKX-16

❑ **SKX-16. "The Skeezix Game,"**
c. 1936. Store item by Milton Bradley Co. - **$40 $90 $185**

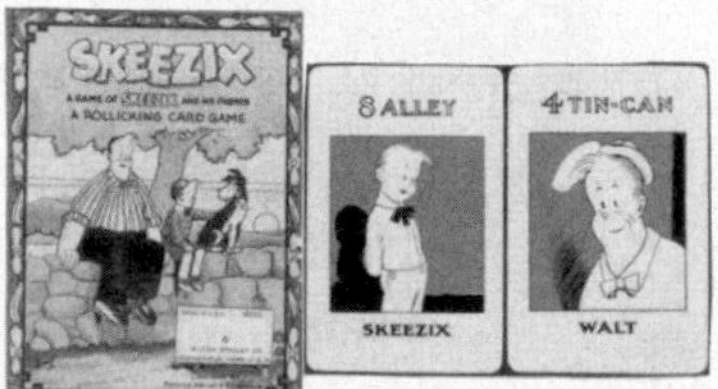

SKX-17

❑ **SKX-17. Card Game,**
1930s. Milton Bradley. Two varieties.
Boxed With Black, White, Red Cards - **$25 $50 $80**
Boxed With Full Color Cards - **$35 $65 $110**

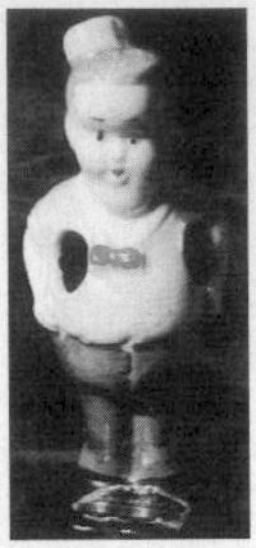

SKX-18

SKX-19

❑ **SKX-18. Uncle Walt Ceramic Toothbrush Holder,**
1930s. Store item. Full color 5-1/2" tall. - **$30 $85 $150**

❑ **SKX-19. "Skeezix At Military School" Premium Book,**
1930s. Pan-Am Gasoline. - **$25 $50 $200**

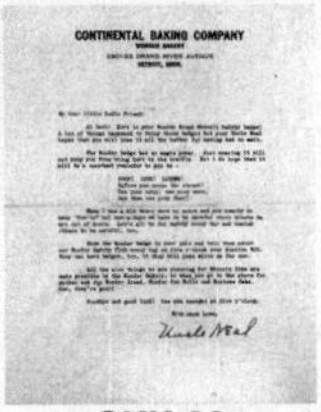

SKX-20

SKX-21

❑ **SKX-20. Club Letter,**
1930s. Wonder Bread. - **$20 $30 $60**

❑ **SKX-21. Skeezix Club Badge,**
1930s. Wonder Bread. Rare. - **$40 $80 $160**

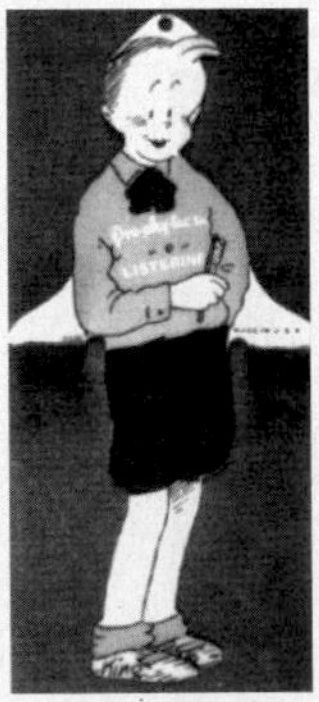

SKX-22

SKX-23

❑ **SKX-22. Litho. Tin Toothbrush Holder,**
1930s. Text on shirt promotes Pro-phy-lac-tic Listerine. - **$75 $165 $300**

❑ **SKX-23. Birthstone Design "I Wear Skeezix Shoes" 2-1/4" Cello. Pocket Mirror,**
1930s. - **$20 $40 $80**

SKX-24

❑ **SKX-24. Celluloid Spinning Top,**
1930s. Skeezix Shoes. - **$35 $75 $150**

SKX-25 SKX-26

❑ **SKX-25. Skeezix Clothes Cello. Button,**
1930s. Braverman's Children's Shop. 1-1/4" full color. - **$25 $50 $100**

❑ **SKX-26. Skeezix' Clothes Cello. Button,**
1930s. Joseph Spiess Company. Full color 1-1/4". - **$20 $40 $80**

SKX-27 SKX-28

❑ **SKX-27. "I Wear Skeezix Shoes" Cello. Button,**
1930s. Unidentified sponsor. Added slogan is "Outgrown Before Outworn." - **$20 $40 $80**

❑ **SKX-28. "I Like Skeezix Sweaters" Cello. Button,**
1930s. - **$15 $25 $50**

SKX-29

❑ **SKX-29. "Skeezix" Cello. Button,**
1930s. Scarce variety. - **$30 $60 $110**

SKX-30

SKX-31

❑ **SKX-30. "Skeezix Loves Red Cross Macaroni" Cello. Button,**
1930s. - **$20 $35 $75**

❑ **SKX-31. "Buffalo Evening News" Cello. Button,**
1930s. From series of newspaper contest buttons, match number to win prize. - **$15 $30 $60**

SKX-32

❑ **SKX-32. "Skeezix" All Pictures Comic,**
1941. On his own in the big city. -
$12 $36 $87

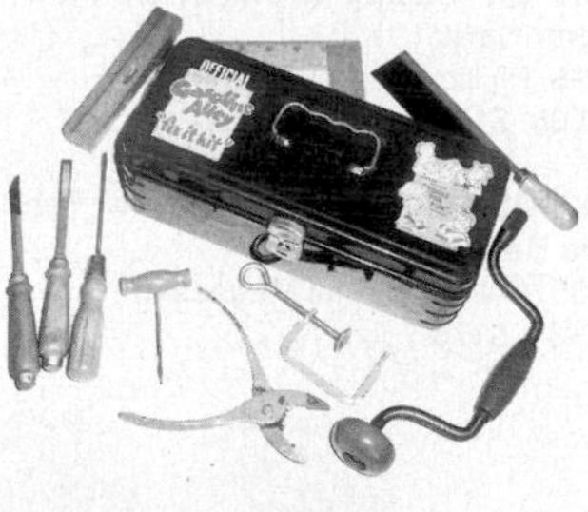
SKX-33

❑ **SKX-33. "Gasoline Alley" Tool Chest,**
c. 1948. Metal "Fix It Kit" hinged chest with lid image of Skeezix and three other family characters. Contents are generic tools.
Value For Box Only, Not Generic Tools -
$50 $90 $175

SKX-34

SKX-35

❑ **SKX-34. Clovia Doll Button,**
1949. About 2" diameter green and white. Character was "Born" May 15, 1949 and doll followed shortly after. - **$20 $40 $70**

❑ **SKX-35. "Skeezix Mask",**
1940s. Wheaties box panel.
Box Back Mask Uncut - **$15 $30 $50**
Cut Mask - **$5 $10 $15**

Skippy

Artist Percy Crosby (1891-1964) created the cartoon Skippy Skinner for the old *Life* humor magazine in the early 1920s and began syndicating the strip in 1925. Dressed in shorts, long jacket, and a checked hat, Skippy was the neighborhood pessimist, with a cynical view of the adult world, his humor shadowed by sadness and defeat. Even so, the strip was a popular one and ran until 1943, when Crosby became too ill to continue it. Comic book collections and illustrated Skippy novels appeared in the 1920s and 1930s, and there were two 1931 movies, *Skippy* and *Sooky*, both starring Jackie Cooper. A radio series aired on NBC (1932) and CBS (1932-1935), sponsored first by Wheaties (1932-1933), then by Phillips Magnesia toothpaste (1933-1935). Premiums included membership in *Skippy's Secret Service Society* and the *Skippy Mystic Circle Club*.

SKP-1

❑ **SKP-1. "Skippy" Handkerchief,**
1930. - **$12 $25 $50**

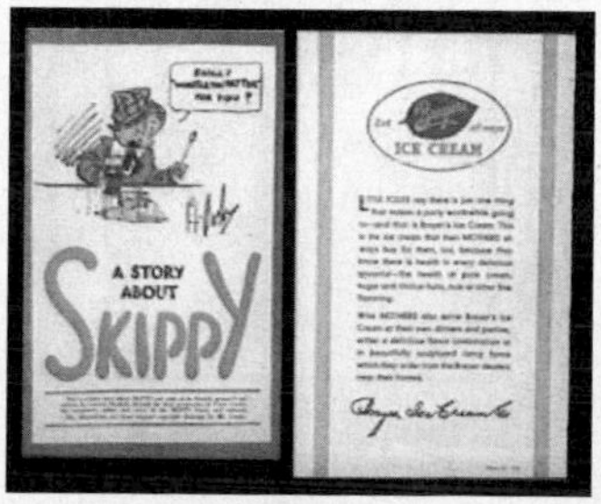

SKP-2

❑ **SKP-2. "A Story About Skippy" Booklet,**
c. 1930. Breyer's Ice Cream. 6x9-1/8" with 16 pages of specialty art by Crosby. -
$35 $75 $150

SKP-3

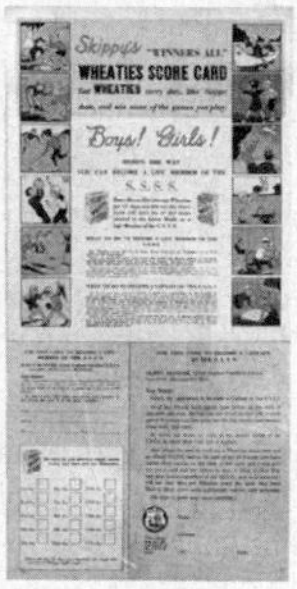

SKP-4

❑ **SKP-3. Skippy Plate - Boxed,**
1931. Large silver plate Skippy plate with price coupon. Store bought. Near Mint Boxed - **$400**
Plate Only - **$50 $100 $300**

❑ **SKP-4. Wheaties 9x18" Club Application and Information,**
1932. Rare with three perforated pieces intact.
Near Mint Intact - **$300**
Each Piece Loose - **$20 $40 $65**

SKP-5 SKP-6

❑ **SKP-5. Wheaties Ceramic Bowl (Sooky),**
1932. Rare. Same side view shown for both. Sooky pictured in bottom. - **$75 $135 $300**

❑ **SKP-6. Wheaties Ceramic Bowl (Skippy),**
1932. Rare. Skippy pictured in bottom. -
$50 $150 $250

SKP-7

SKP-8

❑ **SKP-7. Plastic Bowl,**
1932. Beetleware bowl premium from Wheaties. Comes in green and orange.
Each - **$15 $30 $50**

❑ **SKP-8. Wheaties Cello. Club Button,**
1932. Initialed for Skippy's Secret Service Society. - **$5 $10 $20**

SKP-9

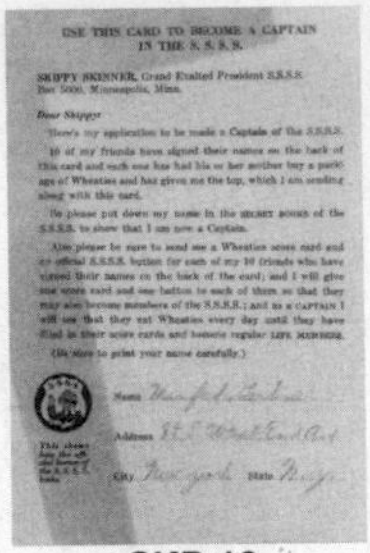

SKP-10

❑ SKP-9. Life Membership,
1932. Certificate for the Secret Service Society, plus 4 page secret code. - **$35 $65 $130**

❑ SKP-10. Captain Application Form,
1932. Wheaties. - **$8 $15 $30**

SKP-11

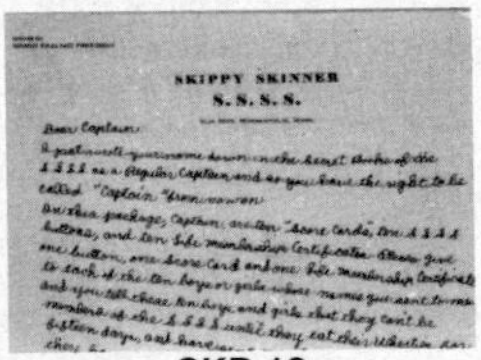

SKP-12

❑ SKP-11. Wheaties "Captain" Cello. Rank Button,
1932. For highest club rank. - **$30 $65 $100**

❑ SKP-12. Wheaties Skippy Letter,
1932. "Dear Captain" form letter in simulated Skippy handwriting certifying rank attained by eating Wheaties "According To The Regulations And Rules". - **$10 $20 $40**

SKP-13

SKP-14

❑ SKP-13. Wheaties "Captain's Commission" Certificate,
1932. Paper award for proven Wheaties consumption. - **$35 $75 $150**

❑ SKP-14. Wheaties "Skippy Racer Club" Cello. Button,
c. 1932. - **$25 $55 $110**

SKP-15

❑ SKP-15. Skippy Cards,
1933. Wheaties premium. Set of 12 different, 6 pictured. Each - **$10 $20 $40**

SKP-16

❑ SKP-16. Skippy "Jig Saw" Puzzle in Box,
1933. Set of 3. Each - **$20 $40 $60**
Box - **$75 $150 $225**

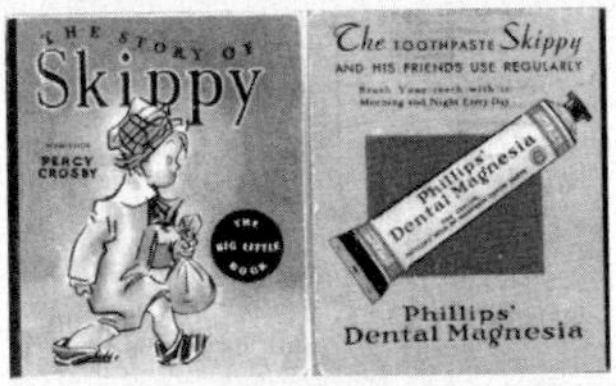

SKP-17

❑ SKP-17. "The Story Of Skippy" BLB,
1934. Phillips' Dental Magnesia Toothpaste. - **$12 $36 $87**

SKP-18

❑ SKP-18. "Skippy" Big Little Book,
1934. Whitman #761. - **$12 $36 $87**

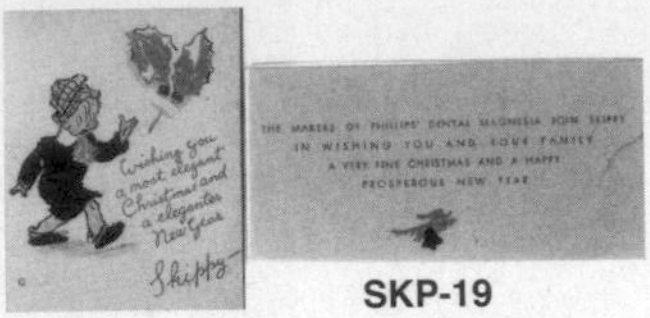
SKP-19

❑ SKP-19. Christmas Card,
c. 1935. Phillips Dental Magnesia. - **$20 $40 $75**

SKP-20

❑ SKP-20. Mystic Circle Club Folder,
c. 1935. Phillips Toothpaste. Folder opens to 16" length. - **$40 $75 $150**

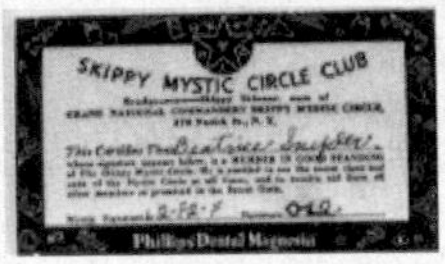

SKP-21

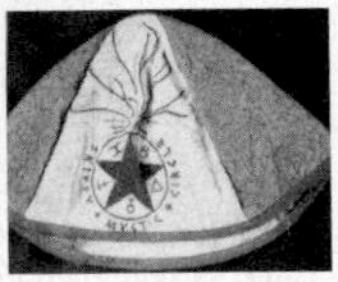
SKP-22

❑ SKP-21. "Skippy Mystic Circle Club" Member Card,
c. 1935. Phillips Dental Magnesia. - **$30 $60 $125**

❑ SKP-22. "Skippy Mystic Circle" Felt Fabric Beanie,
c. 1935. Phillips Dental Magnesia. - **$45 $90 $175**

SKP-23

❑ SKP-23. "Skippy Puritan Blouses" Promo. Button,
c. 1935. 1 1/4" diameter, orange background with black print. Parisian Novelty Company product, Chicago. - **$20 $40 $65**

SKP-24

SKP-25

SKP-26

❑ **SKP-24. "The Atlanta Georgian's Silver Anniversary" Litho. Button,**
1937. Named newspaper. From set of various characters. - **$45 $85 $175**

❑ **SKP-25. "Stories Of Interesting People Who Wear Glasses Booklet,**
1937. Manual for "Skippy Good Eyesight Brigade". - **$25 $50 $100**

❑ **SKP-26. Skippy Good Eyes Brigade Silvered Badge,**
1937. Scarce. - **$40 $85 $175**

SKP-27

❑ **SKP-27. "Skippy" Eyeglasses Case,**
1937. 2.25x4.5" hinged stiff case marked on lid by Skippy portrait, name and Crosby copyright. Inside sticker notes "This Case Contains A Pair Of Genuine 'Skippy' Glasses," probably related to Good Eyesight Brigade promotion.
Case Only - **$25 $50 $75**

SKP-28

❑ **SKP-28. "Washington Herald" Newspaper Button,**
1930s. 1.25" cello with character images in blue on cream plus text in red from comic character series by that newspaper. - **$40 $75 $150**

(Movable Arms)

(Green Base)

(Celluloid Figure)

SKP-29

❑ **SKP-29. Bisque and Celluloid Figures,**
1930s. Store item, several versions.
Movable Arms, No Base - **$40 $85 $150**
One Arm Moves, Green Base - **$35 $75 $125**
Celluloid Figure - **$75 $200 $400**

SKP-30

SKP-31

❑ **SKP-30. "Fire Siren" Whistle Toy,**
1930s. Wooden tube 1-3/8" long with black image on red background. - **$15 $30 $60**

❑ **SKP-31. Skippy Cello. Button From Effanbee Doll,**
1930s. - **$20 $40 $85**

SKP-32

❑ **SKP-32. Skippy/Westinghouse Mazda Lamps Die-Cut Cardboard Standee,**
1930s. Item is 19x25.5" cardboard with easel. - **$250 $500 $1000**

SKP-33

SKP-34

❑ **SKP-33. Skippy Mazda Lamps Sign,**
1930s. 15" by 26". - **$250 $500 $1000**

❑ **SKP-34. "Fro-Joy Ice Cream" 24x36" Cardboard Store Sign,**
1930s. - **$175 $350 $700**

SKP-35

SKP-36

❑ **SKP-35. Paper Mask,**
1930s. Socony Oil. From set of "Five Free Funny Faces". - **$20 $40 $75**

❑ **SKP-36. Fabric Patch,**
1930s. Probably Wheaties. Orange/blue/white stitched design. Scarce. - **$35 $75 $150**

SKP-37

SKP-38

SKP-39

❑ **SKP-37. Cello. Button,**
1930s. Includes artist's name "P. L. Crosby". - **$20 $40 $80**

❑ **SKP-38. "Saturday Chicago American" Litho. Button,**
1930s. From newspaper "16 Pages Of Comics" series of 10 known characters including two Skippy versions. - **$10 $20 $40**

❑ **SKP-39. "Sunday Examiner" Litho. Button,**
1930s. From "50 Comics" set of various newspaper characters, match number to win prize. - **$15 $30 $60**

The Sky Blazers

***The Sky Blazers*, a radio series that dramatized episodes in the history of aviation, aired on CBS for a season (1939-1940), sponsored by Wonder bread. The show was created by Phillips H. Lord and hosted and narrated by Colonel Roscoe Turner, an early aviation hero and holder of various speed records. Each show closed with Turner interviewing the subject of that night's episode. Two issues of a *Sky Blazers* comic book appeared in 1940.**

SBZ-1

❑ **SBZ-1. "Sky Blazers" Cardboard Tag,**
1939. One-sided tag is 3" diameter with design in red, white, blue and yellow. Probably a fan pull and has original string attached at top. Features front view of airplane and reads "Wonder Bread Sky Blazers/Radio's New Thrill Sensation/CBS Network Every Saturday."
- $25 $50 $75

SBZ-2

❑ **SBZ-2. Balsa Airplane In Tube,**
c. 1939. **- $60 $200 $300**

SBZ-3

❑ **SBZ-3. "'Sky Blazers' Wonder Bread" Brass Wings Pin,**
c. 1939. **- $20 $35 $80**

SBZ-4

❑ **SBZ-4. Paper Plane,**
1939. Wonder Bread premium. Issued as a 6 x 6.5" punch-out sheet.
Unpunched **- $35 $75 $125**
Punched **- $10 $20 $40**

SBZ-5

❑ **SBZ-5. "Sky Blazers" Badge,**
1940. Silvered brass with red enamel paint. **- $65 $135 $235**

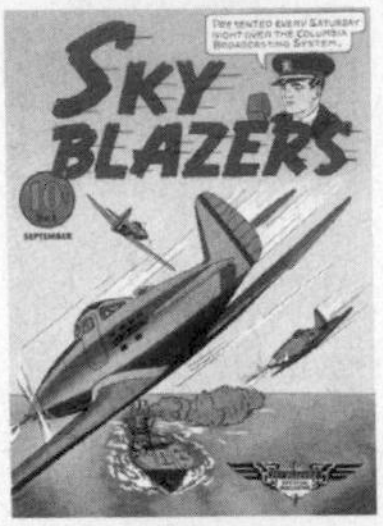

SBZ-6

SBZ-7

❑ **SBZ-6. Comic Book #1,**
Sept. 1940. **- $60 $180 $875**

❑ **SBZ-7. "Sky Blazers/Roscoe Turner" Photo,**
1940. Wonder Bread. From Sponsor Day Kit at New York World's Fair. **- $15 $25 $50**

SBZ-8

❑ **SBZ-8. Wonder Bread 8x12" Diecut Paper Sign,**
1940. Scarce. Promotes 7:00 P.M. CBS radio show. **- $50 $150 $300**

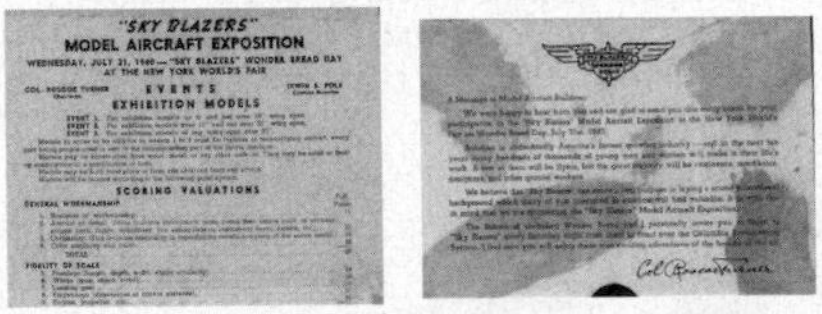

SBZ-9

❑ **SBZ-9. "Sky Blazers Model Aircraft Exposition/Roscoe Turner" Contest Registration Folder,**
1940. Wonder Bread. For Sponsor Day at New York World's Fair. **- $15 $30 $60**

SBZ-10

❑ **SBZ-10. "Sky Blazers/Roscoe Turner" Waxed Paper Bread Loaf Inserts,**
c. 1940. Wonder Bread. Each **- $15 $30 $60**

Sky Climbers

The Sky Climbers of America was an aviation-related club sponsored by boys' clothing stores around 1929. Members could qualify as Oiler, Mechanic, Pilot or Ace. The Flight Leader was reserved for the head of a club, like a Patrol Leader in Scouts. The "Chief" was the head of the sales department at the store. The symbol of the club was a youthful aviator type known as Pete Weet.

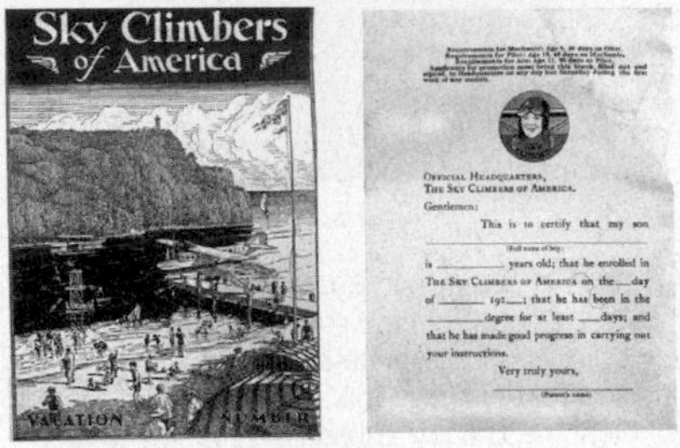

SCL-1

❑ **SCL-1. "Sky Climbers Of America" Club Manual,**
1929. **- $30 $75 $135**

SCL-2

SCL-3

❑ **SCL-2. Fabric Patch,**
1929. **- $30 $75 $135**

❑ **SCL-3. Club Member Card,**
1929. **- $30 $50 $100**

SCL-4

SCL-5

❑ **SCL-4. Club Water Transfer Paper Picture,**
1929. Rare. **- $45 $100 $185**

❑ **SCL-5. "The Sky Climbers" Cello. Button,**
1929. **- $15 $25 $55**

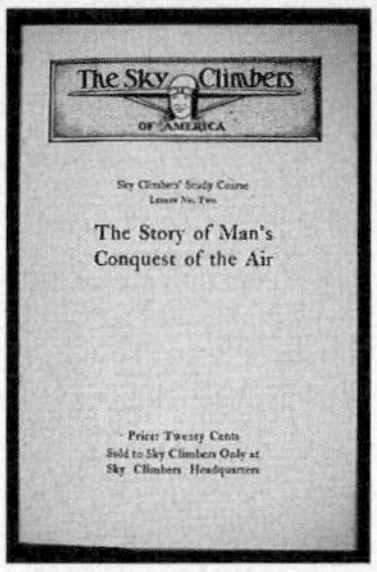

SCL-7

SCL-6

❑ **SCL-6. "Sky Climbers' Study Course Lesson No. Two" Booklet,**
1929. 5x7-1/2" booklet with 16 pages.
Each In Series - **$12 $20 $40**

❑ **SCL-7. "The Sky Climbers Of America" Secret Manual,**
c. 1929. 4-1/4x6" with 12 pages. -
$40 $80 $125

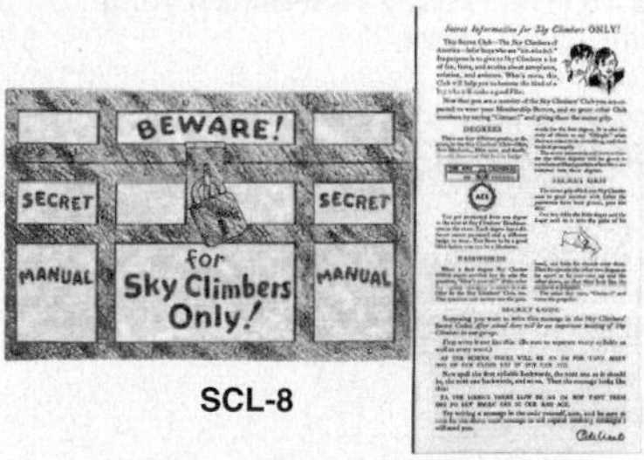

SCL-8

❑ **SCL-8. "Secret Manual For Sky Climbers Only!",**
c. 1930. - **$40 $80 $125**

SCL-9

SCL-10

❑ **SCL-9. "Pilot/The Sky Climbers Of America" Brass Bar And Pendant Badge,**
c. 1930. "Pilot" designation on pendant. The third degree in the club. - **$25 $60 $140**

❑ **SCL-10. "Ace/The Sky Climbers Of America" Brass Bar And Pendant Badge,**
c. 1930. "Ace" designation on pendant is for the rank above Pilot. - **$35 $75 $165**

SCL-11

❑ **SCL-11. "The Sky Climbers Of America/Flight Leader" Brass Award Bar Badge,**
c. 1930. The Flight Leader was the person who ran each local club, like a Patrol Leader in Scouts. Each Flight Leader was appointed. - **$60 $115 $185**

SCL-12

❑ **SCL-12. "Senior Flight Leader/The Sky Climbers Of America" Brass Award Bar Badge,**
c. 1930. Apparent title for an adult supervisor second only to store owner's rank of Chief Sky Climber. - **$70 $150 $200**

SCL-13

❑ **SCL-13. "Chief Sky Climber/The Sky Climbers Of America" Brass Bar and Pendant Badge,**
c. 1930. The Chief Sky Climber was the head of the clothing store that helped promote the club. - **$75 $175 $275**

SCL-14

❑ **SCL-14. Last Club Manual,**
c. 1930. - **$40 $80 $125**

Sky King

America's favorite flying cowboy, Sky King, created by Robert M. Burtt and Wilfred G. Moore, aired on ABC radio from 1946 to 1950 and on Mutual from 1950 to 1954, sponsored starting in 1947 by Peter Pan peanut butter. The series, which starred Earl Nightingale among others, centered on the crime-fighting exploits of rancher-pilot Schuyler King and his niece Penny and nephew Clipper. King's Flying Crown Ranch had an airstrip from which he and his young sidekicks flew off in his plane The Songbird to bring criminals to justice. The program made a successful transition to television as *Sky King Theater*, airing on NBC (1951-1952) and ABC (1952-1954), with Peter Pan again sponsoring. A new television series titled *Sky King* was syndicated from 1956 to 1958, then aired on CBS from 1959 to 1966, sponsored by Nabisco. Kirby Grant (1911-1985) played King and Gloria Winters was Penny. Both Peter Pan and Nabisco issued program-related premiums, usually copyrighted by Jack Chertok Productions.

SKY-1

SKY-2

❑ **SKY-1. Radar Signal Ring,**
1946. Top glows in dark. - **$75 $150 $300**

❑ **SKY-2. "Secret Signalscope" With Instructions,**
1947. Whistle/magnifier held in scope tube.
Near Mint In Mailer - **$250**
Scope - **$35 $75 $150**

SKY-3

❑ **SKY-3. Sky King Secret Compartment Belt Buckle,**
1948. Unique. Prototype was designed by Orin Armstrong for Robbins Co. With decoder symbols on back. Made in three pieces and highly prized by collectors because of its appearance and rarity. Product was never made for distribution. - **$8500**

SKY-4

❑ SKY-4. Mystery Picture Ring Newspaper Ad,
1948. Peter Pan Peanut Butter. Illustrated descriptions and enlarged view of actual ring offered by mail for 15 cents plus foil disk from peanut butter jar. - **$10 $20 $30**

SKY-5 SKY-6 SKY-7

❑ SKY-5. "Mystery Picture Ring" Instruction Sheet,
1948. - **$75 $150 $200**

❑ SKY-6. Mystery Picture Ring,
1948. Faint image on rectangular plastic sheet under gray plastic top has almost always disappeared. Complete No Image - **$125 $200 $300**
With Image And Ease of Visibility - **$300 $600 $1000**

❑ SKY-7. Magni-Glo Writing Ring,
1949. - **$25 $50 $135**

SKY-8

\❑ SKY-8. "Admiral Television" Store Sign,
c. 1948. 16x22" glossy paper two-sided hanger display featuring images of TV set, Sky King, Penny. Text includes "Get A Front Row Seat At Every Show." Half of sign is missing although not affecting Sky King completeness. Remaining half is known to feature spaceman with record player. Sky King Only - **$125 $235 $400**
Complete - **$150 $300 $600**

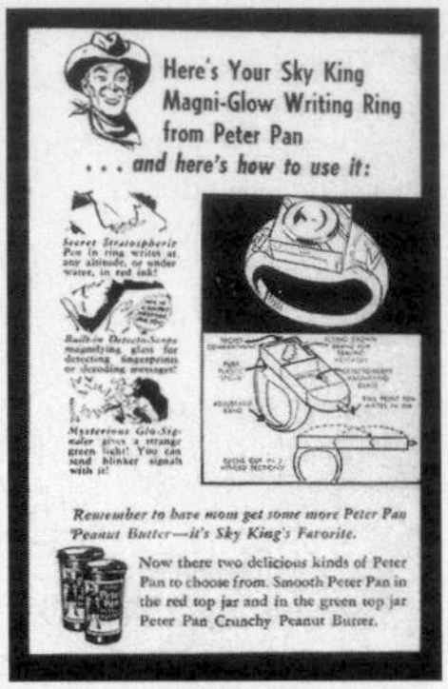

SKY-9

SKY-10

❑ SKY-9. "Magni-Glow Writing Ring" Instruction Paper,
1949. Peter Pan Peanut Butter. - **$60 $120 $175**

❑ SKY-10. Electronic Television Picture Ring,
1949. Brass and plastic, came with photo strip to be developed and cut showing Jim, Penny, Clipper, Martha. See SKY-12.
Ring Only - **$25 $50 $100**
Photo Set - **$50 $75 $150**

SKY-11

❑ SKY-11. "Spy-Detecto Writer",
1949. Elaborate premium that includes decoder. Comes in all brass or brass/aluminum versions.
Writer - **$55 $110 $190**
Instruction Sheet - **$50 $100 $150**

SKY-12

❑ SKY-12. "Electronic Television Picture Ring" Instruction Sheet,
1949. Peter Pan Peanut Butter. See SKY-10. - **$50 $100 $150**

SKY-13

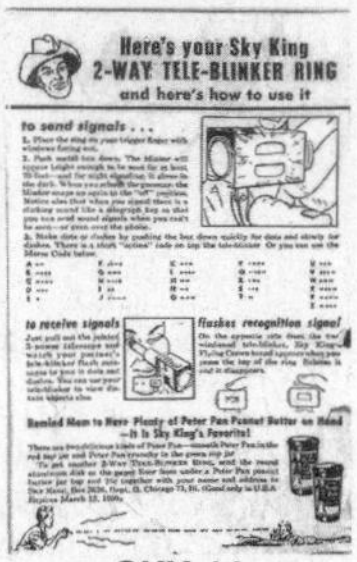

SKY-14

❑ SKY-13. Tele-Blinker Ring,
1949. Brass and other metals signal ring. When pressed, ring sides reveal cut-out panels with glow-in-dark inserts. - **$50 $100 $150**

❑ SKY-14. "2-Way Tele-Blinker Ring" Instruction Sheet,
1949. Peter Pan Peanut Butter. Sheet includes ring order coupon expiring March 13, 1950. - **$50 $100 $150**

SKY-15

❑ SKY-15. Navajo Treasure Ring Newspaper Ad,
1950. Peter Pan Peanut Butter. Illustrated description plus coupon for ordering ring plus a re-seal jar cap "For Mom." Offer expired July 31. - **$8 $15 $25**

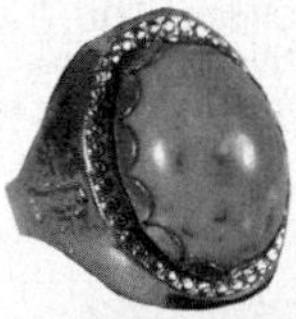

SKY-16 SKY-17

❑ SKY-16. Navajo Treasure Ring,
1950. - **$30 $60 $125**

❑ SKY-17. "Safety Is No Accident" Litho. Button,
c. 1950. - **$20 $40 $65**

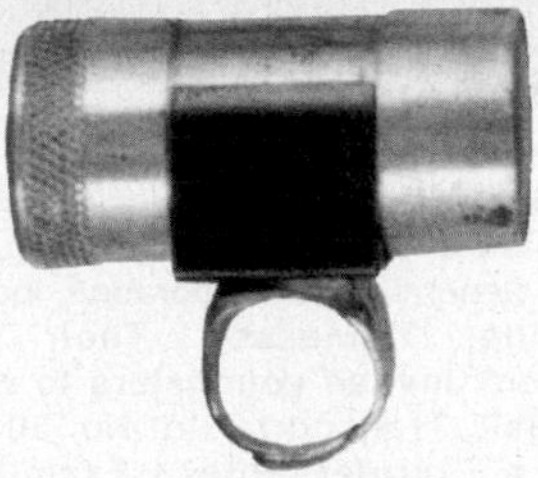

SKY-18

❑ **SKY-18. Kaleidoscope Prototype Ring,**
c. 1950. Large brass and other metals viewer ring developed in prototype design by Orin Armstrong but never actually offered as premium. Has multiple pictures of Sky King which change when you turn the top. Unique - **$17,500**

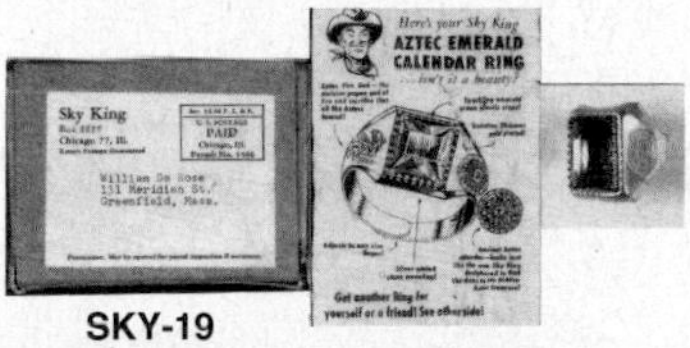

SKY-19

❑ **SKY-19. "Aztec Emerald Calendar Ring" With Instruction Sheet,**
1951. Mint Boxed With Instructions - **$1200**
Ring - **$200 $400 $800**
Instructions - **$150 $225 $300**

SKY-20

❑ **SKY-20. "Detecto-Microscope" With Accessories,**
1952. Cardboard stand and four specimens not shown, map glows in dark.
Near Mint Complete - **$500**
Plastic Tube Only - **$25 $50 $100**
Map - **$25 $50 $100**

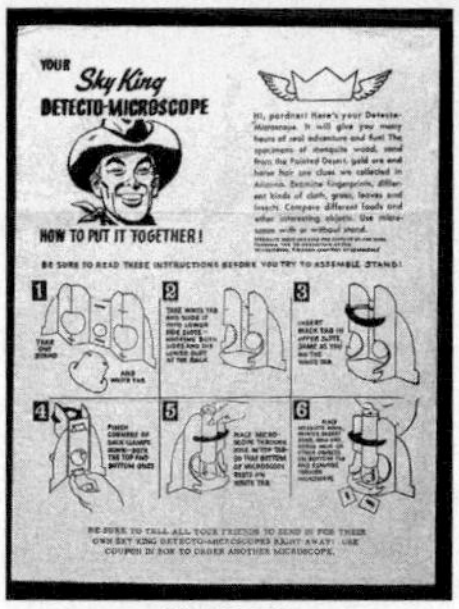

SKY-21

❑ **SKY-21. Detecto Instructions,**
1952. Six step instruction sheet for Detecto-Microscope. - **$25 $50 $100**

SKY-22

❑ **SKY-22. "Stamping Kit" Newspaper Ad,**
1953. - **$10 $20 $30**

SKY-24

SKY-23

❑ **SKY-23. "Stamping Kit" Order Blank,**
1953. - **$20 $35 $75**

❑ **SKY-24. Stamping Kit,**
1953. Tin container holding ink pad and personalized rubber stamp. Ink often rusts the tin. - **$20 $40 $85**

SKY-25

❑ **SKY-25. Figure Set,**
1956. Nabisco Wheat & Rice Honeys. Soft plastic in various colors. Sky King, Clipper, Penny, Sheriff, Songbird (plane), Yellow Fury (horse). Each - **$5 $10 $20**

SKY-26

SKY-27

❑ **SKY-26. Nabisco Fan Postcard,**
c. 1956. - **$12 $25 $50**

❑ **SKY-27. "TV Eye" Cover Article,**
1956. Weekly television supplement to June 24 newspaper with color cover photo plus one-page Sky King article including three other bw photos. - **$20 $40 $65**

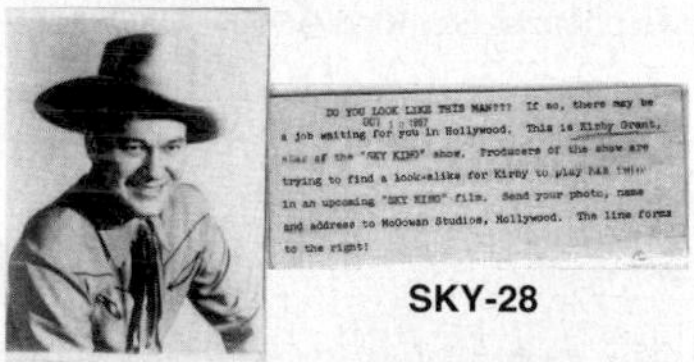

SKY-28

❑ **SKY-28. Kirby Grant Contest Photo,**
1957. McGowan Studios. Note on back about search for look-alike to play Kirby's twin in upcoming film. - **$20 $40 $80**

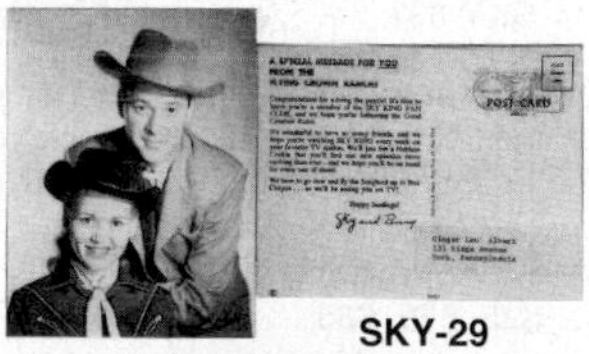

SKY-29

❑ **SKY-29. Fan Club Nabisco Contest Postcard,**
1959. Oversized 5-1/2x7" card. - **$25 $50 $100**

SKY-30

❑ **SKY-30. "Sky King Fan Club" Folder,**
1959. Nabisco. 3x5" closed but opens to five panels printed on both sides. Example shown is missing one panel. Includes membership card, good conduct rules, cut-out photos of Sky and Penny plus more. Came with litho. tin tab (SKY-31). Folder Complete - **$50 $85 $175**

SKY-31

❑ **SKY-31. Nabisco "Sky King Fan Club" Litho. Tin Tab Wings,**
1959. - **$30 $60 $100**

SKY-32

❑ **SKY-32. "Sky King" TV Promotion Sign,**
1959. Sponsored by Nabisco. 11"x28" sign shows photo of Sky King. - **$100 $200 $350**

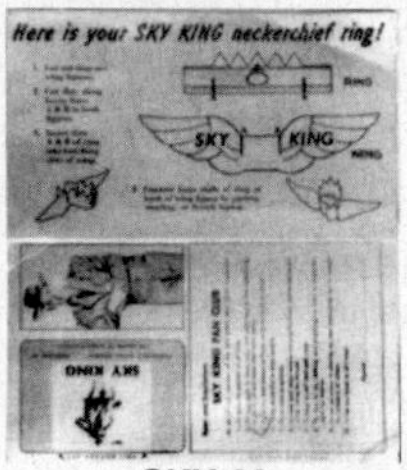

SKY-33

SKY-34

❑ **SKY-33. Nabisco Fan Club Member Kit,**
c. 1959. Includes cut-out Sky King neckerchief ring plus membership card. - **$45 $90 $200**

❑ **SKY-34. Autographed Photo,**
1950s. - **$25 $50 $85**

SKY-35

❑ **SKY-35. "Sky King And Penny" Autographed Photo,**
1950s. Issued by Zembo Shrine Circus. Signed in blue ink. Signed **- $35 $60 $100**
Unsigned **- $10 $25 $50**

SKY-36

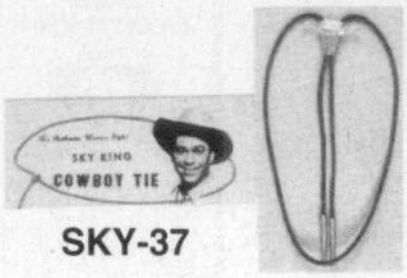

SKY-37

❑ **SKY-36. "Cook Out With Sky King" Recipe Folder,**
1950s. Nabisco. - **$30 $60 $100**

❑ **SKY-37. Cowboy Tie With Envelope,**
1950s. Near Mint In Mailer - **$150**
Tie Only - **$15 $30 $60**

SKY-39

❑ **SKY-38. "Runaway Train" Premium Comic Book,**
1964. Nabisco. 7x10" with 16 color pages. Reverse has ad for Sky King TV show. -
$6 $18 $90

❑ **SKY-39. Autographed Photo,**
c. 1965. Carson & Barnes Circus. 8x10" black and white. He was with the circus from 1965 to about 1971. Signed - **$25 $50 $85**
Unsigned - **$10 $25 $50**

SKY-40

❑ **SKY-40. "Sky King/Carson And Barnes" Circus Poster,**
c. 1965. Poster is 24x30" featuring a live appearance by Sky King. - **$100 $200 $350**

Skyriders

Skyriders was a 1930s aviation-themed club sponsored by Belle Meade Shoe Co., a division of General Shoe Corporation, located in Nashville, Tennessee. Their Pilot's Handbook invited youngsters to write to John Ball, Transport Pilot No. 20390, to obtain a Skyriders Pilot's Examination, which if passed secured the applicant a Skyriders Pilot's License. The club operated through much of the 1930s and was advertised in model airplane magazines of the era.

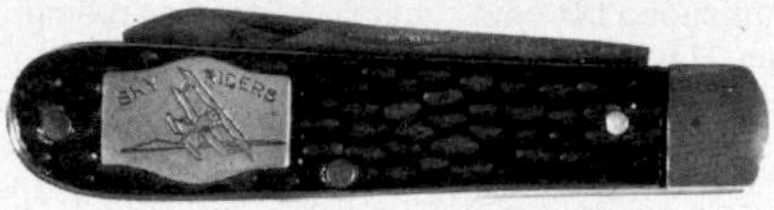

SRD-1

❑ **SRD-1. Club Knife,**
1930. Scarce. - **$60 $125 $225**

SRD-2

SRD-3

❑ **SRD-2. "Skyrider Pilot's Club/Certified Pilot" Cello. Button,**
1930s. - **$20 $40 $85**

❑ **SRD-3. "Sky Riders Club" Member Cello. Button,**
1930s. - **$20 $40 $80**

SRD-4

❑ **SRD-4. "Lieutenant/Member Skyriders Club" Brass Wings Badge,**
1930s. Bronze luster. - **$20 $35 $60**

SRD-5

SRD-6

❑ **SRD-5. "Captain/Member Skyriders Club" Brass Wings Badge,**
1930s. Dark gold luster. - **$25 $40 $75**

❑ **SRD-6. "Colonel/Member Skyriders Club" Brass Wings Badge,**
1930s. Bronze luster. - **$30 $50 $100**

SRD-7

SRD-8

❑ **SRD-7. "General" Brass Wings Badge,**
1930s. Highest rank club badge. -
$35 $60 $125

❑ **SRD-8. "Lieutenant" Litho. Tin Rank Badge,**
1930s. - **$15 $35 $70**

SRD-9

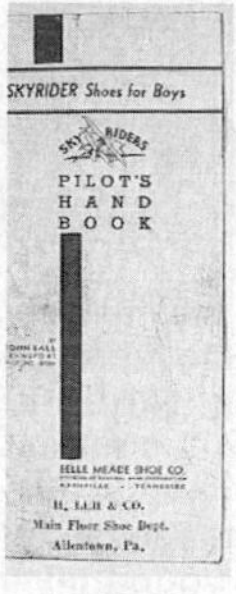

SRD-10

❑ **SRD-9. "Royal Order Of Sky Riders",**
1930s. 3/4" blue on cream member's button. -
$15 $30 $60

❑ **SRD-10. "Skyriders Pilot's Hand Book",**
1930s. Example issued by H. Leh & Co., Allentown, Pa. Details history of flight and encourages youngster to write for Skyriders Pilot's Examination which if passed, results in Skyriders Pilot's License. - **$20 $35 $65**

SRD-11

❑ **SRD-11. "Captain" Litho. Tin Rank Badge,**
1930s. - **$20 $40 $80**

SRD-12

❑ **SRD-12. Brass Wings Badge With Celluloid Bar,**
1930s. Brass reads "Member Sky Riders Club" with small rivet holding red, white and blue diecut celluloid award for advancement to "Lieutenant." - **$25 $45 $90**

Skyroads

This pioneer aviation comic strip was created in 1929 by two former World War I pilots, Dick Calkins (who gained fame with Buck Rogers) and Lester J. Maitland. The strip was distributed by the John F. Dille company. Zack Mosley, later creator of Smilin' Jack, and Russell Keaton, later creator of Flyin' Jenny, did the artwork, with Keaton taking over and signing the strip after 1933. The Skyroads Flying Club began in January 1930. Over the years the strip featured a variety of daredevil pilots dealing with many perils and romantic adventures. A children's club, the Flying Legion, offered readers metal badges for Pilot, Lieutenant, Captain, Major, Colonel, and Ace. Additional "intermediate ranks" of Aviation Mechanic, Stunt Flyer, and Combat Flyer were awarded, probably by letter, but not accompanied by metal badges. Reprints of the strip appeared in *Famous Funnies* comic books in the early 1940s and some early episodes were reprinted in a paperback in 1966. The strip ended in 1942.

SRO-1

SRO-2

❑ **SRO-1. Skyroads Big Little Book,**
1936. Whitman #1127. - **$11 $33 $72**

❑ **SRO-2. "Skyroads With Clipper Williams Of The Flying Legion" BTLB,**
1938. Store item. Whitman Better Little Book #1439. - **$12 $36 $78**

SRO-3

SRO-4

❑ **SRO-3. "Sky Roads" Cello. Button,**
1930s. Buffalo Evening News. From series of newspaper contest buttons, match number to win prize. - **$25 $45 $85**

❑ **SRO-4. "Hurricane Hawk Flying Club" Membership Card,**
1930s. Certifies "Aerial Machine Gunner" with Skyroads emblem. - **$30 $60 $90**

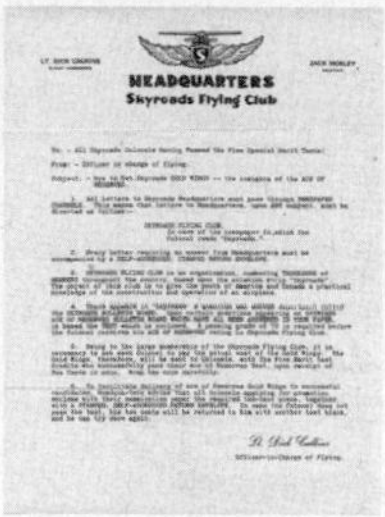

SRO-5

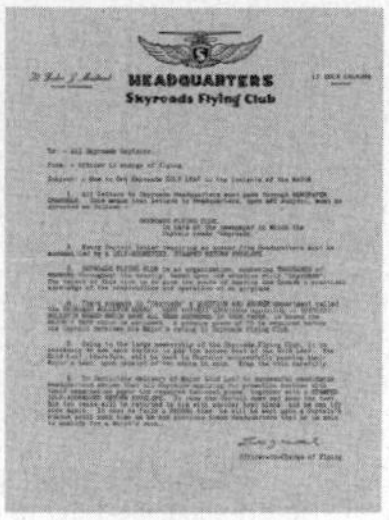

SRO-6

❑ **SRO-5. Skyroads "Gold Wings" Certificate,**
1930s. - **$10 $25 $50**

❑ **SRO-6. Skyroads "Gold Leaf" Certificate,**
1930s. - **$10 $25 $50**

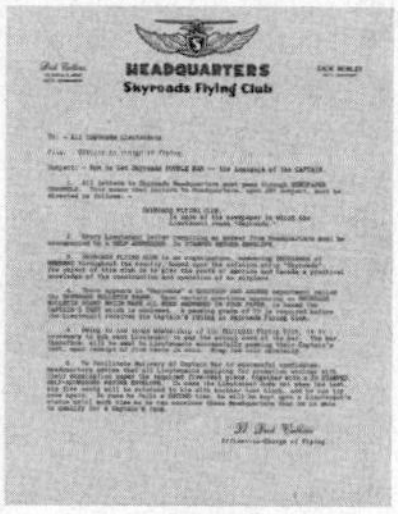

SRO-7

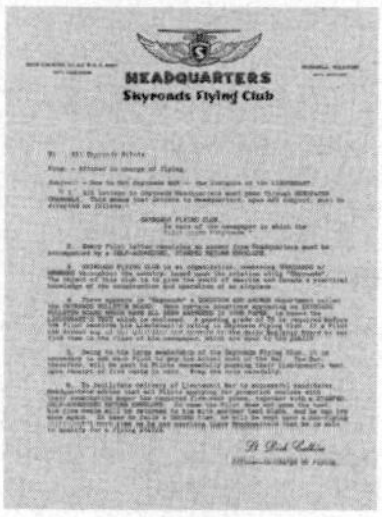

SRO-8

❑ **SRO-7. Skyroads "Captain Double Bar" Certificate,**
1930s. - **$10 $25 $50**

❑ **SRO-8. Skyroads "Lieutenant Bar" Certificate,**
1930s. - **$10 $25 $50**

SRO-9

❑ **SRO-9. "Skyroads Flying Club" Canadian Award Bars Badge,**
c. 1940. 1.5" tall metal link badge headed by wings hanger bar centered by Canadian maple leaf symbol. The three link segments are inscribed Victoria Times/Flight Lieutenant/Squadron Leader. - **$100 $200 $300**

SRO-10

❑ **SRO-10. "Skyroads Flying Club" Member Card,**
1941. Certified member to be "Flying Cadet." Club offered progressions in rank entitling member to officer pins pictured in next six examples. - **$35 $70 $110**

SRO-11

SRO-12

❑ **SRO-11. Skyroads Cadet Litho. Button,**
1941. - **$10 $30 $65**

❑ **SRO-12. Skyroads Cadet Litho. Button,**
1941. Has "Cleveland News" printed on bottom of pin. - **$15 $35 $75**

SRO-13

SRO-14

SRO-15

❑ **SRO-13. Skyroads Pilot Metal Wings Pin,**
1941. Silver luster. - **$20 $40 $90**

❑ **SRO-14. Skyroads Lieutenant Metal Bar Pin,**
1941. - **$20 $40 $90**

❑ **SRO-15. Skyroads Captain Metal Bar Pin,**
1941. Silver luster. - **$30 $60 $110**

SRO-16

SRO-17

❑ **SRO-16. Skyroads Major Oak Leaf Metal Pin,**
1941. Silver luster. - **$40 $75 $140**

❑ **SRO-17. Skyroads Colonel Metal Pin,**
1941. Highest rank eagle insignia. - **$50 $100 $200**

SRO-18

❑ **SRO-18. Skyroads Combat Plane Metal Pin,**
1941. Rare. - **$50 $100 $200**

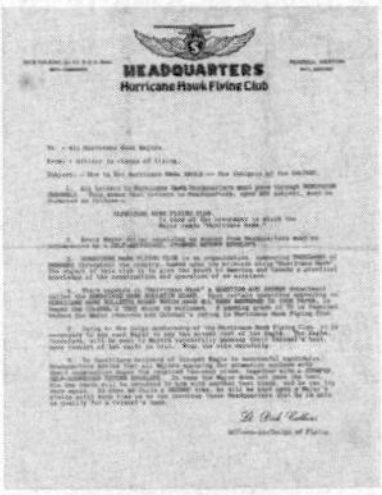

SRO-19

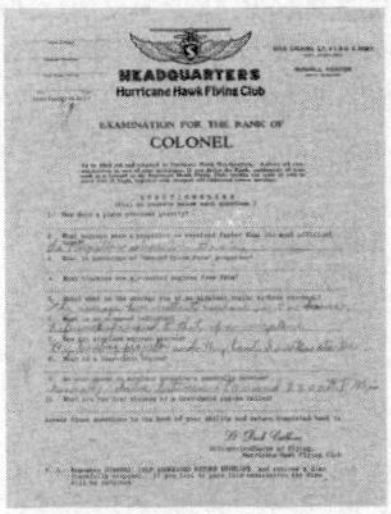

SRO-20

❑ **SRO-19. "Colonel" Hurricane Hawk's Eagle Instructions,**
1940s. - **$15 $30 $60**

❑ **SRO-20. "Colonel" Examination Sheet,**
1940s. A written test which had to be completed and sent with 10¢ and a self-addressed stamped envelope to get your promotion. - **$15 $30 $60**

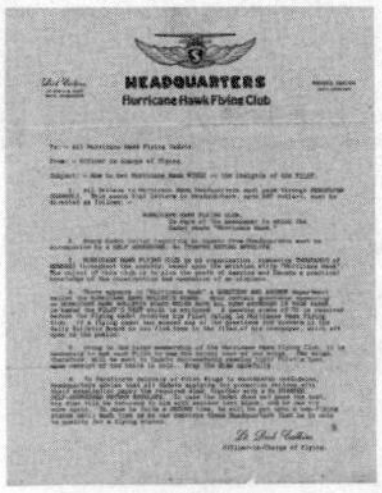

SRO-21

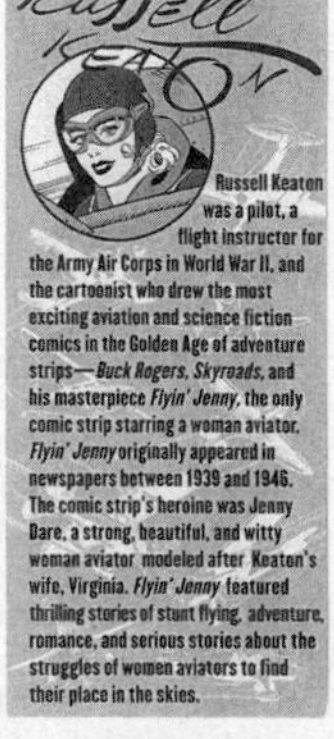

SRO-22

❑ **SRO-21. "Pilot" Hurricane Hawk's Wing Instructions,**
1940s. Club was set up to support the newspaper strip. Hurricane Hawk was one of the main stars of the Skyroads strip. - **$10 $25 $50**

❑ **SRO-22. Russell Keaton Bookmark,**
1995. Kitchen Sink Press. 3x7" colored cardboard issued to promote book "The Aviation Art Of Russell Keaton." Marker includes brief biography and summaries of his aviation comic strips Skyroads and Flyin' Jenny. - **$2 $4 $8**

Small Soldiers

The movie *Small Soldiers* hit the screen in 1998 to mixed reviews. The film had an interesting twist - the good guys, the Argonites, were the monsters and the soldiers, the Commando Elite ended up being the bad guys. The plot of the movie centered around two young inventors who were hired by a "hot shot" promoter to create "aggressive" toys quickly. In order to meet an impossible deadline, the inventors take a short-cut by purchasing computer chips from the government. What they didn't realize was that the chips gave the toys their own personalities and made them uncontrollable. The Commandos were programmed to destroy the Argonites, and they took their mission seriously. They developed weapons to destroy anyone in their path. The Argonites were programmed to lose, and their personalities were marked with low self-esteem. This drew the sympathies of the movie's audience. A set of the Argonites is delivered to a young boy, who instantly takes a liking to "Archer," the leader of the Argonites. The boy soon learns that Archer can talk and think on his own. Archer reveals that his wish is to help his fellow Argonites find a home where they can live safely in peace. The Commandos stand in the way, and a violent battle ensues. By the end, the Argonites have defeated the bad guys. Many film critics felt the violence of the film was too intense for children who were not accustomed to seeing their toys behave in such ways.

Since the video was released and the movie was shown on cable, *Small Soldiers* has gained a solid following. The toys that were produced for the film were of the highest quality and packaged well. Because of the mixed reviews, the box office numbers were disappointing and some of the toys were discounted at the stores. However, now that more people have seen the movie, the toys are gaining the interest of collectors.

SMA-1

SMA-2

❑ **SMA-1. "Talking Chip Hazard" 12" Figure,** 1998. In box. - **$100**

❑ **SMA-2. "Talking Archer" 12" Figure,** 1998. In colorful box. With punching action, electronic lights and sounds. Harder to find than Chip Hazard Talking Figure. - **$125**

SMA-3

❑ **SMA-3. "Archer" String Shooting Gun,** 1998. Includes can of string fluid in box. - **$40**

SMA-4

❑ **SMA-4. "Slam Fist" Figure in Box,** 1998. Giant with boulder-throwing fist. - **$35**

SMA-5

❑ **SMA-5. "Punch-It" With Firing Assault Cannon in Box,** 1998. - **$35**

SMA-6

SMA-7

SMA-8

❑ **SMA-6. "Archer" Pop Candy Figure,** 1998. - **$7**

❑ **SMA-7. "Chip Hazard" Pop Candy Figure,** 1998. - **$7**

❑ **SMA-8. "Archer" Figure on Card,** 1998. - **$18**

SMA-9

SMA-10

❑ **SMA-9. "Insaniac" Figure on Card,** 1998. - **$30**

❑ **SMA-10. "Freakenstein" Figure on Card,** 1998. - **$30**

SMA-11

SMA-12

❑ **SMA-11. "Witchdoctor Insaniac" Figure on Card,** 1998. - **$25**

❑ **SMA-12. "Archer's Battle Headquarters,"** 1998. With 3 Small Figures on Card. - **$8**

SMA-13

SMA-14

❑ **SMA-13. "Punch-It's Battle Headquarters,"** 1998. With 3 Small Figures on Card. - **$8**

❑ **SMA-14. "Chip Hazard's Battle Headquarters,"** 1998. With 3 Small Figures on Card. - **$8**

SMA-15

SMA-16

❑ **SMA-15. "Chip Hazard" Figure on Card,** 1998. Comes with Combat Blaster. - **$15**

❑ **SMA-16. "Electro-Charged Chip Hazard" Figure on Card,** 1998. Comes with Combat Blaster. - **$12**

SMA-17

SMA-18

❑ **SMA-17. "Battle Damage Chip Hazard" Figure on Card,** 1998. Comes with Blow-Apart Legs. - **$12**

❑ **SMA-18. "Brick Bazooka" Figure on Card,** 1998. - **$40**

SMA-19

SMA-20

❑ **SMA-19. "Battle Changing Kip" Figure on Card,**
1998. - **$40**

❑ **SMA-20. "Nick Nitro" Figure on Card,**
1998. With Launching Dual Missile Pack. - **$40**

SMA-21

SMA-22

❑ **SMA-21. "Action Car" on Card,**
1998. Promotes Shell Oil. - **$10 $20 $45**

❑ **SMA-22. War Games Activity Set,**
1998. - **$20**

SMA-23

SMA-24

❑ **SMA-23. "Chip Hazard" Squeeze Toy,**
1998. - **$1 $3 $15**
"Archer" Squeeze Toy - **$1 $3 $15**
"Slam Fist" Squeeze Toy - **$1 $3 $15**

❑ **SMA-24. "Archer" Burger King Figure,**
1998. With working bow and arrow. - **$2 $4 $8**

SMA-25

SMA-26

❑ **SMA-25. "Ocula" Burger King Figure,**
1998. - **$2 $4 $8**

❑ **SMA-26. "Witchdoctor Insaniac" Burger King Figure,**
1998. - **$2 $4 $8**

SMA-27

SMA-28

❑ **SMA-27. "Freakenstein" Burger King Figure,**
1998. Attacking and riding a soldier figure. - **$2 $4 $8**

❑ **SMA-28. "Punch-It" Burger King Figure,**
1998. - **$2 $4 $8**

SMA-29

SMA-30

❑ **SMA-29. "Chip Hazard" Burger King Figure,**
1998. - **$2 $4 $8**

❑ **SMA-30. Burger King Figure,**
1998. With binoculars. - **$2 $4 $8**

SMA-31

SMA-32

❑ **SMA-31. "Brick Bazooka" Burger King Figure,**
1998. On toaster vehicle. - **$2 $4 $8**

❑ **SMA-32. "Nick Nitro" Burger King Figure,**
1998. On wind-up motorcycle. - **$2 $4 $8**

SMA-33

❑ **SMA-33. Buzzsaw Tank in Box,**
1998. With Ocala figure. - **$35**

SMA-34

❑ **SMA-34. "Archer's Crossbow" in Box,**
1998. Space Shooter Target Game. - **$60**

SMA-35

❑ **SMA-35. "Archer" Radio Control Cycle,**
1998. - **$75**

SMA-36

❑ **SMA-36. Power Drill Cycle,**
1998. With Scratch-It figure. - **$5 $10 $40**

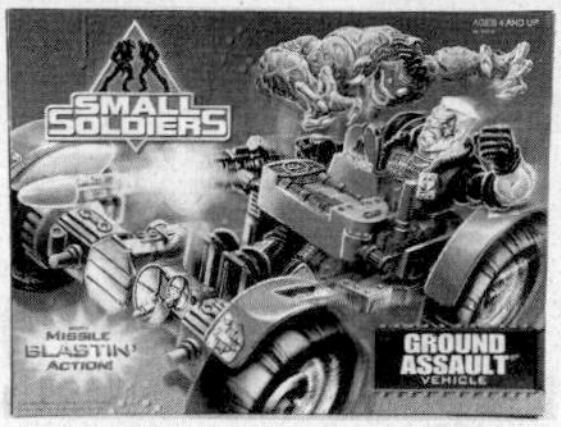

SMA-37

❑ **SMA-37. Ground Assault Vehicle,**
1998. With "Missile Blastin' Action." - **$40**

(FRONT)

(BACK)

SMA-38

❑ **SMA-38. "Attack Zones" Micro Playset,**
1998. With 4 action figures. - **$15**

(FRONT)

(BACK)

SMA-39

❑ **SMA-39. Big Battle Game,**
1998. With 12 action figures. - **$60**

(FRONT)

(BACK)

SMA-40

❑ **SMA-40. Globotech Battle Command Case,**
1998. With accessories. - **$30**

(FRONT)

(BACK)

SMA-41

❑ **SMA-41. Secret Decoder Activity Case,**
1998. With accessories. - **$35**

SMA-42 SMA-43

❑ **SMA-42. Hand To Hand Combat Game,**
1998. Electronic game on card. - **$10 $20 $60**

❑ **SMA-43. Colorforms Play Set,**
1998. With 23 colorforms. - **$18**

SMA-44 SMA-45

❑ **SMA-44. Color Chrome Valentines,**
1998. With 32 valentines and 48 stickers. - **$6**

❑ **SMA-45. Clear Treat Bags,**
1998. In wrapper. - **$6**

SMA-46

❑ **SMA-46. Fun Bags,**
1998. 15 bags in package. - **$3**

SMA-47 SMA-48

❑ **SMA-47. Color and Activity Book,**
1998. Series 2. Nick Nitro on cover. - **$5**

❑ **SMA-48. Color and Activity Book,**
1998. Series 2. Punch-It on cover. - **$5**

SMA-49 SMA-50

❑ **SMA-49. Sticker Book,**
1998. Series 3. Freakenstein on cover. - **$10**

❑ **SMA-50. Sticker Book,**
1998. Series 3. Brick Bazooka on cover. - **$10**

SMA-51 SMA-52

❑ **SMA-51. "Archer" Ringed Notebook,**
1998. - **$8**

❑ **SMA-52. "Slam Fist" Ringed Notebook,**
1998. - **$8**

SMA-53 SMA-54

❑ **SMA-53. "Archer" Study Kit,**
1998. - **$8**

❑ **SMA-54. Black Ink Pen Set,**
1998. Features picture of Archer and Chip. - **$5**

SMA-55

❑ **SMA-55. "Punch-It and Brick Bazooka" 60 Piece Puzzle,**
1998. - **$10**

SMA-56

❑ **SMA-56. "Slam Fist" 60 Piece Puzzle,**
1998. - **$15**

SMA-57

❑ **SMA-57. "Witchdoctor Insaniac" 60 Piece Puzzle,**
1998. - **$10**

SMA-58 SMA-59

❑ **SMA-58. Personal Tape Player,**
1998. Boxed - **$75**

❑ **SMA-59. "Small Soldiers" Pocket Pops,**
1998. Archer and Chip character busts on lollipop. Each - **$5**

SMA-60 SMA-61

❑ **SMA-60. "Small Soldiers" Wrist Watch,**
1998. With 5 interchangable lenses. - **$35**

❑ **SMA-61. "Small Soldiers" Wrist Watch,**
1998. With interchangable Archer and Chip dial tops. On card. - **$35**

SMA-62 SMA-63

❑ **SMA-62. "Small Soldiers" Archer Figure,**
1998. - **$12**

❑ **SMA-63. "Small Soldiers" Archer Party Ring,**
1998. - **$12**

SMA-64 SMA-65

❑ **SMA-64. "Small Soldiers" Chip Hazard Figure,**
1998. - **$12**

❑ **SMA-65. "Small Soldiers" Chip Hazard Party Ring,**
1998. - **$12**

Smiley Burnette

Lester Smiley Burnette (1911-1967), a bluegrass singer and comic, starred in one movie, Republic's *Call of the Rockies* in 1944, but in a floppy black hat and checkered shirt he provided comic relief as Frog Millhouse in a series of "B" Westerns with his pal Gene Autry. Burnette also appeared in a number of chapter plays in the 1930s, and he had his own syndicated radio show in 1950-1953. Smiley Burnette Western comic books were published in 1950.

SMY-1

SMY-2

❑ **SMY-1. Fan Club Photo,**
c. 1940s. Black and white image of him and horse "Black Eyed Nellie" with club pledge on bottom margin. - **$12 $25 $50**

❑ **SMY-2. "Frog" Autographed Photo,**
c. 1940s. Personally signed by nickname only. - **$15 $30 $65**

SMY-3

❑ **SMY-3. "Smiley Burnette" Dixie Ice Cream Pictures,** 1940s. Back of each includes text for 1940 or 1941 Gene Autry movie.
Each - **$15 $30 $60**

SMY-4

❑ **SMY-4. "Checkered Shirt Drive-In Sandwich Shops" Folder,**
1955. Self-mailer sheet opening to 11x16" printed on both sides by whimsey art and text seeking individual investors for franchise endorsed by Burnette. - **$15 $30 $60**

SMY-5

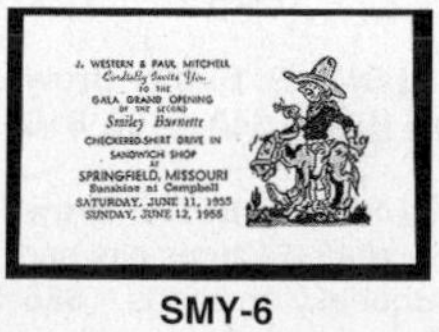

SMY-6

❑ **SMY-5. "Checkered Shirt Drive-In Sandwich Shops" Signed Letter,**
1955. Art letterhead stationery with typewritten information on shop investment venture franchise, personally signed "Smiley." - **$30 $50 $90**

❑ **SMY-6. "Checkered Shirt Drive-In Sandwich Shop" Invitation,**
1955. Card for grand opening of second shop endorsed franchise by Burnette. - **$5 $10 $20**

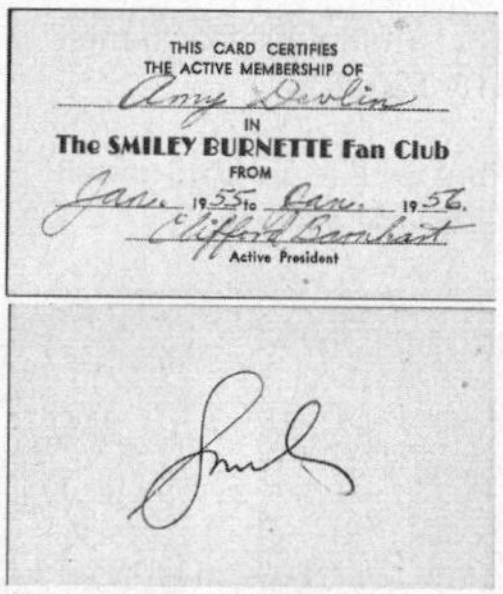

SMY-7

❑ **SMY-7. "The Smiley Burnette Fan Club" Autographed Membership Card,**
1955. Card is 2x3.5". Reverse has blue ballpoint pen signature "Smiley."
Autographed - **$15 $30 $50**
No Autograph - **$8 $15 $30**

SMY-8

❑ **SMY-8. Premium Mask Sheet,**
1957. Bardahl Motor Oil. 11x14" stiff paper with large black, white and fleshtone mask of "TV's Ole Frog." Upper right has small photo of him with Autry. - **$25 $45 $90**

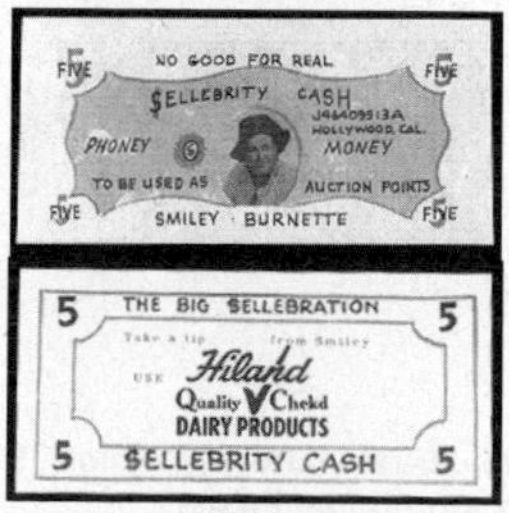

SMY-9

❑ **SMY-9. "$ellebrity Cash Phoney Money" Currency Bill,**
c. 1950s. Hiland Dairy Products. "Auction Points" paper bill picturing him on one side with his product endorsement on reverse. - **$8 $12 $25**

Smilin' Ed McConnell

Ed McConnell (1892-1954), singer and banjo picker, moved from vaudeville to local radio in 1922, then to the networks from 1932 to 1941, doing his musical variety shows for a number of sponsors. In 1944 McConnell teamed with Buster Brown shoes to create a children's program combining dramatic tales, music, and listeners' letters. Known variously as *Smilin' Ed's Buster Brown Gang, The Smilin' Ed McConnell Show, The Buster Brown Gang*, or *The Buster Brown Show*, the program aired on NBC radio until 1953 and in the meantime made a successful move to television in 1950, appearing on all three networks: NBC (1950-1951), CBS (1951-1953), and ABC (1953-1955). Former "Oz" Munchkin Jerry Maren played Buster Brown. The imaginary cast starred Froggy the Gremlin, along with Squeeky the Mouse, Midnight the Cat, and Old Grandie the Piano. Items are normally copyrighted J. Ed. McConnell. After McConnell's death, Andy Devine (1905-1977) took over and the show was renamed *Andy's Gang*. The show ran from 1955 to 1960.

SMI-1

SMI-2

❑ **SMI-1. Photo,**
1920s. Radio premium. - **$20 $30 $60**

❑ **SMI-2. "Smilin' Ed McConnell" Autographed Photo,**
1932. First year of CBS radio show. - **$35 $70 $140**

SMI-3

SMI-4

❑ **SMI-3. "Under His Wing" Theme Song Folder,**
1939. Taystee Bread. - **$20 $40 $80**

❑ **SMI-4. "Smilin' Ed McConnell/Bill Stewart" Fan Card,**
1930s. - **$10 $15 $35**

SMI-5

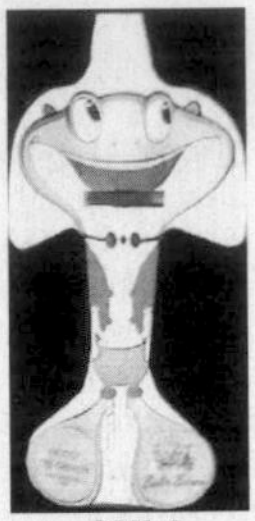

SMI-6

❑ **SMI-5. "Smilin' Ed McConnell" Advertising Calendar Card,**
1940. Taystee Bread, Purity Bakeries Service Corp. 12x17-1/2" color cardboard calendar from series issued on monthly basis. - **$50 $100 $175**

❑ **SMI-6. Buster Brown Shoe Store Premium Paper Glider,**
1946. 4" wide by 7" long diecut paper with smiling image of Froggy. Photo example may be missing a cardboard tube and small tip from top edge of item. - **$35 $75 $160**

SMI-7

SMI-8

❑ **SMI-7. Froggy Paper Mask,**
1946. - **$30 $65 $110**

❑ **SMI-8. "Froggy" Litho. Tin Tab,**
1946. From radio show. - **$15 $30 $50**

SMI-9 SMI-10 SMI-11

❑ **SMI-9. "Member Buster Brown Gang" Litho. Tin Tab,**
1946. From radio show. - **$12 $25 $40**

❑ **SMI-10. "Member Buster Brown Gang/Squeeky" Litho. Tin Tab,**
1946. From radio show. - **$10 $20 $35**

❑ **SMI-11. "Midnight" Litho. Tin Tab,**
1946. From radio show. - **$10 $20 $35**

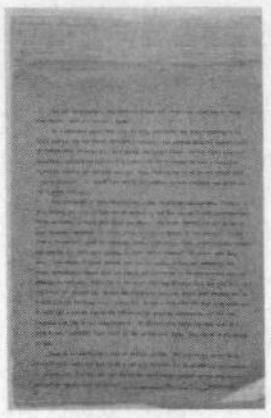

SMI-12

SMI-13

❑ **SMI-12. "Smilin' Ed McConnell" Letter**
1946. - **$10 $20 $30**

❑ **SMI-13. "Smilin' Ed McConnell" Picture**
1946. - **$12 $25 $45**

SMI-14

SMI-15

❑ **SMI-14. "Smilin' Ed McConnell" Picture**
1946. - **$12 $25 $45**

❑ **SMI-15. "Smilin' Ed McConnell" Picture**
1946. - **$12 $25 $45**

SMI-16

❑ **SMI-16. "Buster Brown Comics" Shoe Store Promomtional Poster,**
c. 1946. Poster is 17.75x24.75". Main image features stereotypical evil Asian man slicing barrel of machine gun off while two other characters jump back with surprise. Bottom third features ad for NBC radio program with microphone and smiling face of Smilin' Ed.
- **$85 $165 $350**

SMI-17

❑ **SMI-17. Squeeze Toy,**
1948. Store item by Rempel Mfg. Co.
Small 5" Size - **$75 $175 $350**
Large 9-1/2" Size - **$100 $250 $450**

SMI-18

❑ **SMI-18. "Smilin' Ed's Buster Brown Comics" #13,**
1948. Buster Brown Shoes. Issued between 1945 and 1959. First Issue - **$61 $183 $885**
Second Issue - **$18 $54 $225**
Others - (See *The Overstreet Comic Book Price Guide*)

SMI-19

SMI-20

❑ **SMI-19. Buster Brown Paddle Ball Game,**
c. 1948. - **$40 $100 $185**

❑ **SMI-20. Buster Brown Gang Brass Ring,**
c. 1948. Pictures him and Tige with Froggy and Squeeky on bands. - **$25 $50 $115**

SMI-21

❑ **SMI-21. "Buster Brown Gang" Card With Brass Badge,**
c. 1948. Card - **$20 $35 $60**
Badge - **$12 $25 $50**

SMI-22

❑ **SMI-22. "Smilin' Ed McConnell's Buster Brown Gang" Bandanna,**
c. 1948. - **$30 $60 $125**

SMI-23

SMI-24

❑ **SMI-23. "Buster Brown T.V. Theatre" Flicker Card,**
c. 1950. Screen area has movement image of Froggy jumping up and down. - **$20 $40 $85**

❑ **SMI-24. "Buster Brown Gang" Card With Litho. Button,**
1953. Card - **$20 $40 $75**
Button - **$10 $20 $30**

SMI-25

❑ **SMI-25. "Treasure Hunt Game" Shoe Box,**
c. 1950s. - **$25 $50 $100**

SMI-26

❑ **SMI-26. "Buster Brown Shoes" Periscope,**
1950s. 17" long cardboard and mirror lenses toy with design art including images of Smilin' Ed and various Buster Brown Gang members. -
$40 $100 $150

Smilin' Jack

Cartoonist Zack Mosley (1906-1993) began his career as an assistant to Dick Calkins on the *Buck Rogers* and *Skyroads* comic strips. Jack Martin first appeared October 1, 1933 in a Sunday page titled *On The Wing,* which became *Smilin' Jack* December 31, 1933. The daily strip began June 15, 1936. Mosley, an amateur aviator, set the strip in a small airport locale with Jack as a top aviator. Notable cast members over the years included: Jack's girlfriend Dixie Lee; Downwind Jaxon, who was so handsome his face couldn't be shown; Hawaiian friend Fat Stuff whose shirt buttons pop off and are eaten by a chicken; and villains The Claw, Toemain the Terrible, The Head and The Mongoose.

A radio show aired briefly between December, 1939 and August, 1940. Universal released a 13 chapter serial in 1943, written by Mosley and Morgan Cox. The cast included Tom Brown, Rose Hobart, Keye Luke and Eddie Barrier. Dell published 17 comics between 1940 and 1949. Mosley helped start the Civilian Air Patrol and logged over 3,000 hours at the controls of nine planes he owned.

The *Smilin Jack* strip ended on April 1, 1973 with the wedding of Jack Martin Jr. Collectors continue to fly high with memorabilia from the longest running aviation strip in comic strip history.

SMJ-1

❑ **SMJ-1. Top-Line Comic,**
1935. From a Whitman series similar to Big Little Books done in softcover with 164 pages. -
$16 $48 $110

SMJ-2

❑ **SMJ-2. "Smilin' Jack" 1936 Daily Comic Strip Art With Jack And Dixie In Love,**
1936. Chicago Tribune. 7x23" thin art board has 6.25x21" India ink image with three panels of Smilin' Jack and Dixie wearing aviator hats.
Same Or Similar - **$150 $300 $500**

SMJ-3

❑ **SMJ-3. Smilin' Jack Fan Photo,**
c. 1939. Has inked-in recipient's name and "Zack Mosley" autograph.
Signed - **$35 $75 $150**

SMJ-4

❑ **SMJ-4. Smilin' Jack Creator & Portrayer Photo,**
1939. 8x10" black and white of Zack Mosley and signed portrait board also held by Frank Readick, the Smilin' Jack radio voice over Mutual Broadcasting. - **$25 $35 $65**

SMJ-5

❑ **SMJ-5. "The Adventures Of Smilin' Jack" Movie Serial Lobby Card Set With Envelope,**
1942. Universal Pictures Co. Inc. Set of six 11x14" cards and plain brown paper envelope for Chapter 1 "The High Road To Doom." - **$75 $150 $300**

SMJ-6

❑ **SMJ-6. "The Adventures Of Smilin Jack" Movie Serial Poster,**
1942. Universal Studios. 27x41" poster for 13-chapter serial. This is for Chapter 1 "The High Road To Doom." - **$75 $150 $300**

SMJ-7

❑ **SMJ-7. "Smilin' Jack's Victory Bombers" Assembly/Play Game,**
c. 1943. Store item by Plane Facts, Inc. - **$125 $300 $600**

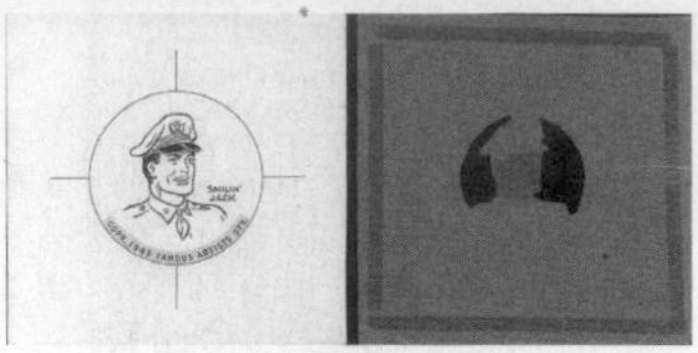

SMJ-8

❑ **SMJ-8. Smilin' Jack Pep Pin Original Art,**
c. 1944. 1.75x2" image on 5.75x5.75" sheet of thin white art board with separate 5.75" square sheet of translucent paper with blue/fleshtone colors which when placed over art provide the colors for the finished button. Gordon Gold Archives. Unique - **$300**

SMJ-9

❑ **SMJ-9. "Smilin' Jack And The Jungle Pipeline" Better Little Book,**
1940s. Whitman. Book No. 1419. - **$12 $36 $78**

SMJ-10

❑ **SMJ-10. "The Adventures Of Smilin' Jack" Strip Card Set,**
1940s. Complete set of 16 strips, each 2.5x25" long with eight cards per strip for a total card set of 128. - **$100 $200 $300**

Smitty

Cartoonist Walter Berndt (1899-1979) began as an office boy at *The New York Journal* doing odd jobs for legendary cartoonists including Winsor McCay, George Herriman and Thomas A. Dorgan. After several years of on the job training, Berndt approached the Chicago Tribune Syndicate with an idea. Berndt, the former office boy, would do a comic strip about an office boy. The first daily appeared November 27, 1922. The *Smitty* cast included: Augustus Smith, his boss Mr. Bailey, stenographer Ginnie, Mom, Dad and four-year-old brother Herby. The *Smitty* Sunday page began February 25, 1923 and the Herby topper strip began in 1930. Over the years, Smitty went from age 13 to married and 23.

Walter Berndt organized a weekly lunch with other cartoonists on Long Island in the late 1940s. Regular attendees including Creig Flessel, Bill Lignante, Frank Springer and Lee Ames made the group an official part of The National Cartoonists' Society in 1979. The Berndt Toast Gang still meets regularly.

Walter Berndt won the NCS' highest honor, the *Reuben Award*, as cartoonist of the year in 1969.

Dell published 13 Four Color *Smitty* comic books between 1940 and 1958.

SMT-1

❑ **SMT-1. "Smitty At The Ball Game" 1929 Strip Reprint Book Featuring Babe Ruth,**
1929. Cupples & Leon. 7x8.5" book with 88 pages. - **$57 $229 $450**

SMT-2

❑ **SMT-2. Smitty Characters Painted Bisque Nodders,**
1920s. Sizes range from 2" to 3.5" tall depicting Herby, Scraps, Mr. Bailey "The Boss." Each - **$30 $65 $100**

SMT-3

❑ **SMT-3. "Smitty The Flying Office Boy" Reprint Book,**
1930. Cupples & Leon. 6.75x8.5" with 88 pages. - **$31 $126 $250**

SMT-4

❑ **SMT-4. "Smitty Scooter" Wind-Up,**
1932. Marx Toys. 8" tall litho tin toy licensed by Famous Artists Syndicate. - **$775 $1600 $2600**

SMT-5

❑ **SMT-5. "Smitty Golden Gloves Tournament" BLB,**
1934. Whitman #745 also issued as Cocomalt Premium. Whitman #745 - **$14 $42 $95**
Cocomalt - **$15 $45 $105**

SMT-6

❑ **SMT-6. "Smitty" Cupples & Leon Softcover From The "Treasure Box Of Famous Comics" Set,**
1934. 6.75x8.5" with 32 pages from a boxed set of 5 titles. - **$43 $172 $300**

SMT-7

❑ **SMT-7. "Smitty In Going Native" Big Little Book,**
1938. Whitman. Book No. 1477. - **$10 $30 $67**

SMT-8

❑ **SMT-8. "Smitty Says" Rare Cap Ad Button,**
1930s. 1.25" diameter. - **$12 $25 $50**

SMT-9

❑ **SMT-9. "Smitty" and Family Ceramic Bowl,**
1930s. - **$85 $150 $275**

SMT-10

❑ **SMT-10. "Eat It All Cake Cup" Store Sign With Smitty,**
1947. Famous Artists Syndicate. 8x15.5" paper sign. Gordon Gold Archives. - **$50 $100 $200**

Smokey Bear

Smokey was created for a U.S. Forest Service poster in 1944 to warn of the dangers--and the threat to the country's wartime lumber supply--of forest fires. Since then the brown bear with the ranger hat has become the beloved symbol of the Forest Service and spokesbear for the nation's trees. Rudolph Wendelin (1910-2000) is the artist most recognized for "Smokey" images. Smokey has been given special trademark status, had his own zip code, appeared on a postage stamp in 1984, and in balloon form has floated in Macy's Thanksgiving Day Parade since 1968. "Remember--only you can prevent forest fires!" dates from 1947. In 1950 a four-pound black bear cub that survived a forest fire in New Mexico was given the name Smokey, nursed back to health, and sent to live at the National Zoo in Washington, D.C. That Smokey died in 1976 but he was promptly replaced to continue as a symbol of conservation. Steve Nelson and Jack Rollins wrote the *Smokey The Bear* song in 1952 but technically his name is correct as "Smokey Bear."

***The Smokey Bear Show*, a half-hour animated cartoon series, was broadcast on ABC from 1969 to 1971, stressing the importance of saving natural resources and protecting wildlife. Smokey comic books appeared from 1950 into the 1970s, and in 1994 a traveling exhibition and party on the Mall in Washington celebrated Smokey's golden anniversary.**

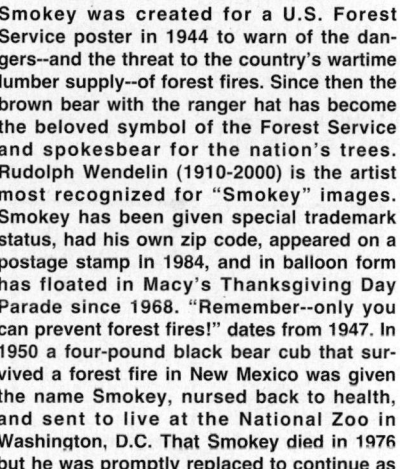

SMO-1

SMO-2

❑ **SMO-1. Smokey Bear Poster,**
c. 1947. 18-1/4x24-3/4". - **$45 $90 $195**

❑ **SMO-2. Slogan Litho. Button,**
c. 1950. - **$10 $15 $35**

SMO-3

SMO-4

❑ SMO-3. "Prevent Woods Fires" 12x14" Cardboard Sign,
1955. - **$35 $75 $150**

❑ SMO-4. Calendar,
1956. - **$10 $20 $40**

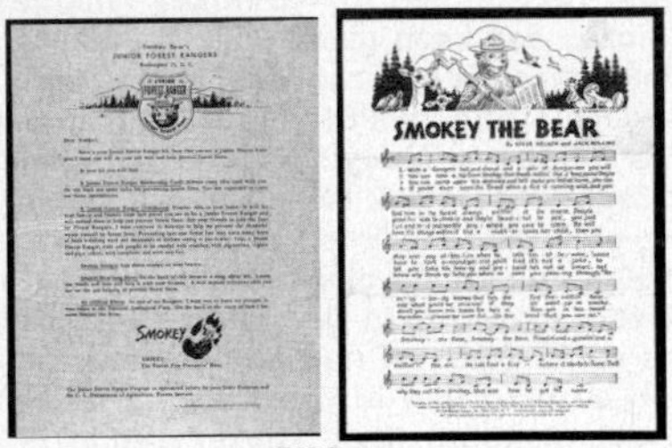

SMO-5

❑ SMO-5. Letter,
1957. Letter explains Kit, with song sheet on back - **$15 $35 $60**

SMO-6

SMO-7

❑ SMO-6. "Forest Fire Prevention" Award Certificate,
1950s. - **$20 $35 $70**

❑ SMO-7. Cloth Doll With Plastic Hat And Badge,
c. 1950s. Store item by Ideal Toy Corp. - **$30 $65 $115**

SMO-8

SMO-9

❑ SMO-8. Fabric Patch,
c. 1950s. - **$12 $25 $45**

❑ SMO-9. "Picnics Are Fun" Hanky,
1950s. Probable store item, no markings. Very colorful 8" square. - **$20 $30 $60**

SMO-10

SMO-11

❑ SMO-10. "Join Smokey Ranger Club" Litho. Tin Tab,
1950s. - **$15 $30 $70**

❑ SMO-11. Biographical Card,
1965. U.S. Department Of Agriculture-Forest Service. - **$8 $12 $25**

SMO-12

SMO-13

❑ SMO-12. "Soaky" Plastic Soap Bottle,
c. 1965. Colgate-Palmolive Co. - **$10 $20 $35**

❑ SMO-13. Ceramic Salt & Pepper Shakers,
1960s. Store item. - **$20 $40 $70**

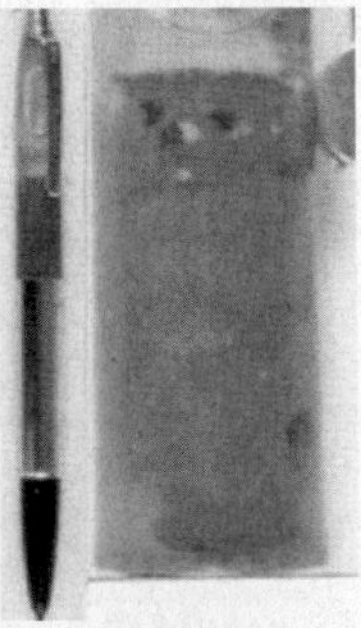
SMO-14

❑ SMO-14. "Sign Up With Smokey" Ballpoint Pen With Floating Figure,
1960s. USA otherwise unmarked. - **$25 $45 $85**

SMO-15

❑ SMO-15. Smokey The Bear Vinyl Lunchbox With Thermos,
1960s. King Seeley Thermos Co. 7x9x4" deep vinyl lunchbox with 6.5" tall metal thermos with plastic cup/cap. Both items have logo reading "Official Product Cooperative Forest Fire Prevention Program" with Smokey the Bear images in center. Box - **$100 $225 $400**
Bottle - **$25 $60 $110**

SMO-16

❑ SMO-16. Boxed Game,
1960s. Milton Bradley store item #4932. - **$20 $40 $85**

SMO-17

SMO-18

❑ SMO-17. Plastic Coin Bank,
1960s. Store item. 4" diameter in copper-colored plastic. - **$12 $25 $50**

❑ SMO-18. Fabric Patch,
1960s. U.S. Forest Service. 4" tall in shades of browns and greens on yellow background. - **$10 $20 $40**

SMO-19

❑ **SMO-19. "Smokey" Bear Ceramic Mug With Music Box,**
1960s. Mug is 3.75" diameter by 4" tall. Front of mug has image of Smokey wearing hat with name and text below "Use Fire Carefully." Base has wind-up music box that plays "Born Free" when mug is lifted. Inside bottom edge reads "Authorized By Forest Service, U.S.D.A."
- $30 $60 $90

SMO-20

SMO-21

❑ **SMO-20. Wristwatch,**
1960s. Store item. Boxed - **$60 $90 $150**
Loose - **$25 $40 $90**

❑ **SMO-21. Plastic Bank,**
1960s. Store item. - **$20 $40 $85**

SMO-22

SMO-23

❑ **SMO-22. Composition Bobbing Head,**
1960s. Store item. - **$75 $150 $250**
Wooden handle on shovel - **$100 $200 $325**

❑ **SMO-23. "Junior Forest Ranger/Prevent Forest Fires" Tin Badge,**
1960s. Either silver, brass or copper luster. -
$6 $12 $30

SMO-24

❑ **SMO-24. "Smokey's Reading Club" Litho. Button,** 1960s. Also says "Keep California Green & Golden." - **$15 $30 $65**

SMO-25

❑ **SMO-25. Whitman Punch-Out Book,**
1970. Back cover and six stiff paper pages printed on one side for Smokey Bear activity display. Unpunched - **$15 $25 $50**

SMO-26

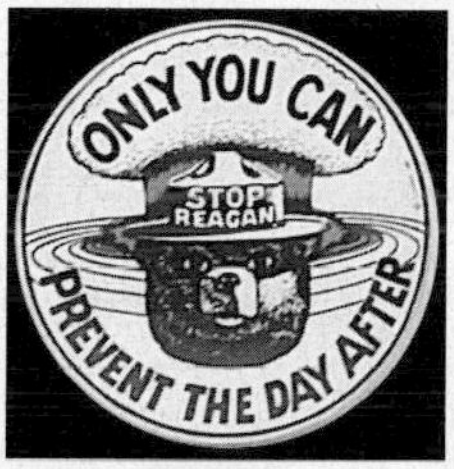

SMO-27

❑ **SMO-26. "March Of Comics #383",**
1973. Various Advertisers. - **$2 $6 $14**

❑ **SMO-27. Smokey Bear Anti-Reagan Button,**
1984. 2.25" cello picturing orange mushroom cloud overprinted by black and white image of Smokey wearing "Stop Reagan" hat. -
$30 $60 $165

SMO-28

SMO-29

❑ **SMO-28. Smokey Bear Book and Bear Set,**
1996. Plush doll and book in box. It's official, but Smokey's facial expression makes you wonder. -
$45

❑ **SMO-29. "Smokey" Ring,**
1990s. No sponsor. Silver luster finish thin embossed metal expansion ring with name inscription on hat. - **$2 $4 $6**

SMO-30

❑ **SMO-30. Smokey Bear Wacky Wobbler,**
2000. In box. - **$25**

Smurfs

Belgian cartoonist Pierre Culliford, known as Peyo (1928-1992) began his career drawing *Poussy*, a cat for *LeSoir* from 1949 to 1952. He went to work for *Le Journal de Spirou*, an illustrated children's weekly in 1952. The first *Smurf* appeared October 25, 1958 in a *Jonah and Peewit* story and the Smurfs got their own magazine series in 1959. The basic premise has the society of good hearted little blue people living in mushroom houses in Smurf Village. There are over 100 Smurfs, but the main cast includes: Papa, Jokey, Smurfette, Brainy, Hefty, Grouchy, Dreamy, Clumsy, Greedy, Handy, Vanity along with the evil Wizard Gargamel and his cat Azrael.

As the series became more popular, Peyo assumed a supervisory position, letting his son Thierry run the art studio and daughter Veronique handle the merchandising. Belgium released the animated feature *The Smurfs and the Magic Flute* in 1976, which came to the U.S. in 1984. Hanna-Barbera began *The Smurfs* cartoon show on NBC-TV September 12, 1981. The series lasted until August 25, 1990; nine seasons with 421 episodes. Directors included: Ray Patterson, Don Lusk and George Gordon. Voice actors included: Don Messick, Danny Goldman and June Foray. Music was by Hoyt Curtin and Paul DeKorte.

A Smurfs theme park was open in France from 1991 to 1998. Marvel published three comic books in 1982-1983 and many collections have been published in Europe. The skies are always blue in a Smurf collector's world.

SMF-1

❏ SMF-1. "Smurfs" Metal Lunch Box,
1980. King Seeley Thermos. 6.75x8.75x3-7/8" lunch box. Box - **$20 $40 $135**
Plastic Bottle (not shown) - **$5 $12 $25**

SMF-2

SMF-3

❏ SMF-2. "Smurfs Out of This World" Large Plush Doll,
1980. Wallace Berrie & Co. 20" tall doll. - **$8 $15 $25**

❏ SMF-3. "Smurf" Wood Board Frame Tray Puzzles In Store Packs,
1982. Wallace Berrie & Co. Group of five, each in 11.25x13.25" package containing 9.25x11.5" puzzle by Playskool. Each - **$1 $3 $6**

SMF-4

SMF-5

❏ SMF-4. "Smurf Glass" Promotion Button,
1982. Hardee's Restaurants. 3" litho worn by employees to promote first series, set of eight glasses. - **$6 $12 $20**

❏ SMF-5. "You're Invited To A Smurfday Party/Smurf Bank",
1982. 2x6" header card has clear plastic bag holding eight invitations and envelopes by Unique Industries Inc. Invitations are 3.25x5.5". Bank is 10.5" tall hard vinyl.
Invitations - **$3 $6 $10**
Bank - **$3 $6 $10**

SMF-6

❏ SMF-6. "Smurf" Boxed Game,
1988. Milton Bradley. 8x15x1.25" deep box. - **$5 $10 $15**

SMF-7

❏ SMF-7. Smurf-Berry Crunch Cereal Box with Campaign Button Ad and Buttons,
1984. Box - **$15 $30 $60**
Each Button - **$3 $8 $15**

SMF-8

❏ SMF-8. "Smurfs" Slogan Badges,
1980s. Group of twelve, each 2.25" in a variety of colors. Each - **$1 $2 $3**

SMF-9

❏ SMF-9. "Super Smurf!!" Boxed Lawn Mower/Basketball/Photographer Figures,
1980s. Schleich. Each box is 1.5x2.25x3.25" tall and holds hard vinyl figure with plastic accessory pieces. Each - **$1 $3 $5**

Snap, Crackle, Pop

The Kellogg Company introduced Snap, Crackle, and Pop in 1933 to personify the lively sounds made when a bowl of its Rice Krispies meets cold milk. Originally drawn in a whimsical Art Deco style by Vernon Grant (1902-1990), the cartoon trio has survived to this day on cereal boxes and in advertising, singing and dancing and crackling and popping for kids everywhere.

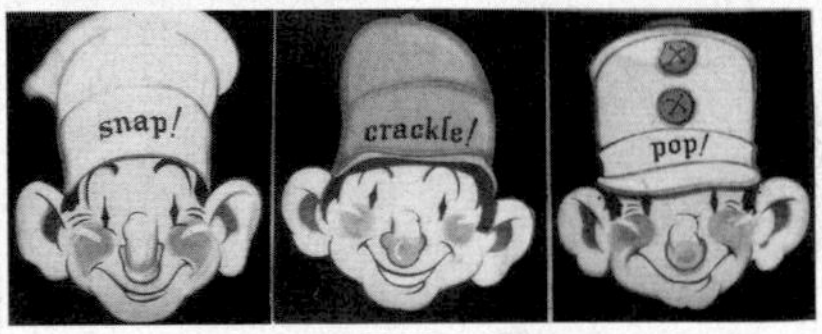

SNP-1

❏ SNP-1. Paper Masks,
1933. Kellogg's copyright with unsigned Vernon Grant art. Each - **$40 $80 $160**

SNP-2

❏ SNP-2. Booklet,
1933. Six pages of Vernon Grant art and combination picture game. - **$25 $50 $80**

SNP-3

❑ SNP-3. Comic,
1933. Vernon Grant art on 8 pages plus 2 pages of premiums for Singing Lady. - **$20 $35 $65**

SNP-4

❑ SNP-4. Blotter,
1930s. Vernon Grant art. - **$10 $20 $35**

SNP-5

❑ SNP-5. "Snap/Pop" China Salt & Pepper Shakers,
1930s. - **$15 $25 $50**

SNP-6 SNP-7

❑ SNP-6. Cloth Pattern Doll,
1947. Issued as late as 1954.
Uncut - **$25 $45 $90**
Mailer - **$10 $20 $40**

❑ SNP-7. Cloth Pattern Doll,
1947. Issued as late as 1954.
Uncut - **$25 $45 $90**
Mailer - **$10 $20 $40**

SNP-8 SNP-9

❑ SNP-8. Cloth Pattern Doll,
1947. Issued as late as 1954.
Uncut - **$25 $45 $90**
Mailer - **$10 $20 $40**

❑ SNP-9. Cloth Dolls Store Sign,
1947. 16x20". Gordon Gold Archives. - **$65 $125 $265**

SNP-10

❑ SNP-10. Rice Krispies Folder With Dolls Ad,
1947. 10.5x14" four-page issue picturing cloth dolls of Snap, Crackle and Pop plus a "Motor Bike Imitator" bicycle attachment. Gordon Gold Archives. - **$30 $60 $100**

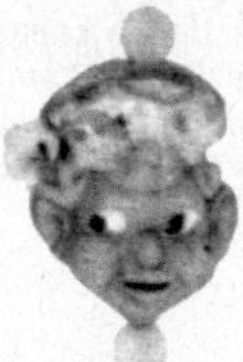

SNP-11 SNP-12 SNP-13

❑ SNP-11. "Snap" Face Ring,
1952. Brass bands holding soft rubber head that changes expressions by turning small knobs. - **$75 $175 $350**

❑ SNP-12. "Crackle" Face Ring,
1952. Brass bands holding soft rubber head that changes expressions by turning small knobs. - **$50 $100 $250**

❑ SNP-13. "Pop" Face Ring,
1952. Brass bands holding soft rubber head that changes expressions by turning small knobs. - **$100 $250 $500**

SNP-14

❑ SNP-14. "Pop" Rice Krispies Hand Puppet,
1950s. Kellogg's copyright on neck. From set of three. Each - **$25 $50 $85**

SNP-15

❑ SNP-15. Friendly Folk Wood & Fabric Figure Set,
1972. Frosted Mini-Wheats. Accent by simulated hair or fur. Each - **$5 $10 $15**

SNP-16

❑ SNP-16. Vinyl Figure Set,
1975. Each - **$15 $30 $65**

SNP-17

❑ SNP-17. "Kellugh Mice Krusties" Kellogg Parody Bank,
1970s. Bank is 2.25x3.25x5" tall painted composition designed like a cereal box and parody of Kellogg's Rice Krispies, obviously produced to capitalize on the popularity of Wacky Packages trading cards. Front has raised design including three mice modeled after Snap, Crackle and Pop in front of a large bowl of cereal. - **$20 $35 $65**

SNP-18

❑ **SNP-18. Glow Plastic Figures,**
c. 1980. Snap, Crackle, Pop, Tony, Tony Jr., Toucan Sam, Dig 'Em, Tusk (elephant). Each - **$3 $6 $9**

SNP-19

SNP-20

❑ **SNP-19. "Snap" Rubber Doll,**
1984. In box with mini comic. - **$20 $35 $60**

❑ **SNP-20. "Crackle" Rubber Doll,**
1984. In box with mini comic. - **$20 $35 $60**

SNP-21

SNP-22

❑ **SNP-21. "Pop" Rubber Doll,**
1984. In box with mini comic. - **$20 $35 $60**

❑ **SNP-22. "Pop" Bean Bag Figure,**
1997. With tag. - **$15**

SNP-23

SNP-24

❑ **SNP-23. "Snap" Bean Bag Figure,**
1997. With tag. - **$15**

❑ **SNP-24. "Crackle" Bean Bag Figure,**
1997. With tag. - **$15**

Snow White & the Seven Dwarfs

See Ted Hake's *Official® Price Guide to Disney Collectibles*, Second Edition, formatted identically to this book but in full color evaluating over 9,000 Disney company and character collectibles from 1924 through 2006.

Soupy Sales

Born Milton "Soupbone" Hines in North Carolina in 1926, Soupy Sales grew up to become television's long-term clown and master of wacky pie-in-your-face humor. Wearing a battered top hat and giant polka-dot bow tie, his slapstick shows combined corny jokes, puns, zany conversations with animal puppets such as White Fang and Black Tooth, and the inevitable cream pies. After local television outings in Detroit in 1953, *The Soupy Sales Show* went national on ABC in 1955, again in 1959-1961, and in 1962 sponsored by Jell-O, and to syndication in 1965. *The New Soupy Sales Show* was syndicated in 1979-1980. Sales also hosted game shows and teen dance programs and made countless guest appearances on a number of variety programs. In the 1960s he created a popular dance called The Mouse. *The Official Soupy Sales Comic Book* was published in 1965. Items are usually copyrighted Soupy Sales--W.M.C. (Weston Merchandising Corp.)

SOU-1

SOU-2

SOU-3

❑ **SOU-1. "Soupy Sales Society" 3-1/2" Cello. Button,**
1950s. - **$10 $20 $45**

❑ **SOU-2. "Soupy Sales Society Charter Member" 3-1/2" Cello. Button,**
1965. - **$5 $10 $20**

❑ **SOU-3. "SSS" 3-1/2" Cello. Button,**
1965. - **$8 $15 $30**

SOU-4

SOU-5

❑ **SOU-4. "Soupy Sez" 3-1/2" Cello. Button,**
1965. - **$18 $35 $70**

❑ **SOU-5. "Soupy Sales" 3" Litho. Button,**
1965. - **$15 $30 $50**

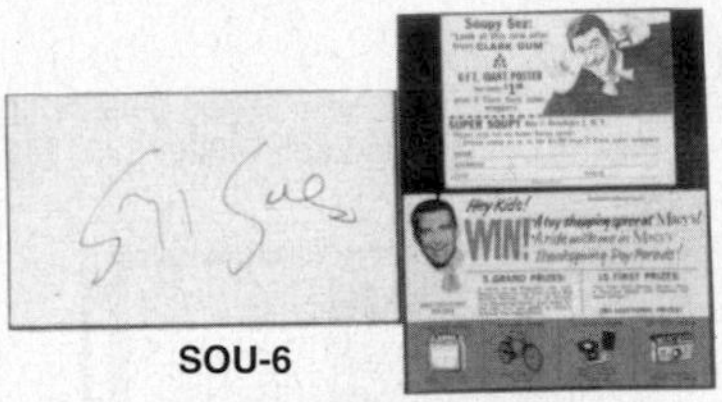

SOU-6

❑ **SOU-6. Autograph And Order Blanks,**
1965. Shown are: 3x5" signed index card, 3x4" order blank for 6' "Super Soupy" poster from Clark Gum and 3-1/4x5-1/4" "Burry's Soupy Sales Scooter-Pies Sweepstakes Entry Blank." Each - **$10 $18 $35**

SOU-7

❑ **SOU-7. Lunch Box,**
1965. King-Seeley Thermos Co. Vinyl box picturing him identically front and back plus additional action art of him on both sides. - **$100 $200 $400**

SOU-8

❑ **SOU-8. "Soupy Sales Our Hero" Remco-Like Boxed Doll,**
1965. Doll is 5.25" tall in 5x7.25x3" deep box manufactured by Sunshine Doll Co. Doll has soft vinyl body and head with realistic hair. Doll also has cloth bow tie. Designed to "Stick To Any Surface, Clip To Jackets And Notebooks."
Box - **$75 $150 $250**
Figure - **$75 $150 $250**

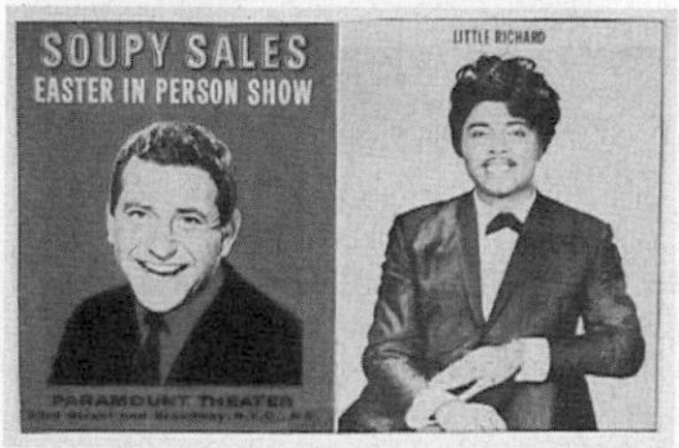

SOU-9

❑ **SOU-9. Souvenir Program,**
c. 1965. The Paramount Theater, New York. Sixteen pages with photos and text on Soupy and music performers that were in the show including Little Richard and The Hollies. -
$20 $35 $60

SOU-10

❑ **SOU-10. "Soupy Sales" Cylindrical Lamp,**
c. 1965. Lamp is 13.25" tall with 6" diameter base and a 5" cylindrical tube for a light. Lamp features large image and name of Soupy Sales with other names of characters "Blacktooth, Pookie, White Fang." Also has phrases associated with the show. - **$200 $400 $625**

SOU-11

❑ **SOU-11. "Op-Yop" Toy Promotion Store Sign,**
1968. Paper banner 11x34" for "Op-Yop Funtastic Spinning Toy" by Kramer Designs. -
$40 $75 $150

SOU-12

❑ **SOU-12. "Wallet-Size Photos" Display Box,**
1960s. Topps Gum. Countertop box originally holding gum/photo card packs.
Empty Box - **$55 $110 $175**

SOU-13

SOU-14

❑ **SOU-13. Miniature License Plate,**
1960s. Marx Toys of Grĉat Britain. 2-1/4x4" litho. tin possible prototype or probable limited issue example. - **$15 $30 $60**

❑ **SOU-14. Advertising Litho. Button,**
1960s. United Dairies. 1-5/16" with bluetone photo and lettering plus logo in red. -
$20 $40 $85

Space Misc.

The mysteries of the stars have always fascinated earth-bound humans, with poets and scientists alike dreaming of soaring into space and exploring the planets. In the 20th century, even before Yuri Gagarin's historic flight in 1961, there were Buck Rogers and Flash Gordon and Captain Video. These and other comic strip, film, and television heroes, along with toy manufacturers, accounted for countless space-oriented premiums and novelties--spaceships, rockets, exotic space guns, games, puzzles, and robots. In addition, many items have been issued to commemorate events in the ongoing official program of space exploration.

SPA-1

❑ **SPA-1. "The War Of The Worlds" Book,**
1938. Whitman. Softcover #711 published shortly after the radio broadcast that year about Martian invaders that was accepted literally by listeners and terrified the nation, particularly the east coast. 48 pages with illustrations. -
$75 $150 $350

SPA-2

SPA-3

❑ **SPA-2. "John Carter of Mars" BLB #1402,**
1940. - **$76 $228 $530**

❑ **SPA-3. "Strat-O-Flier" Kite,**
1951. Classic design. - **$30 $60 $100**

SPA-4

❑ **SPA-4. Archer First Series Spacemen Store Display Box,**
1952. Box is 8.5x11x3" deep containing 4" hard plastic figures. This box was a store display and has die-cut lid featuring Archer name and Archer spaceman image with rocket background. Box originally contained two dozen figures. This includes five different poses: walking, with guns drawn, holding machine controls, bugler and robot. Figures come in three metallic colors (purple, green, copper). Spacemen have removable helmets.
Box Only (Empty) - **$50 $100 $200**

SPA-5

❑ **SPA-5. Archer "Space Men",**
1952. Listed under a number of different names. Sold with or without clear plastic helmets. The figures were made in a number of different poses and colors.
Each 3-3/4" Space Man - **$8 $15 $30**
Each Helmet - **$10**

SPA-6

❑ **SPA-6. "Captain Space" Figures,**
1952. By Ajax. 3-1/4" tall. Sold with or without clear plastic helmets. The figures were made in a number of different poses and colors.
Each 3-1/4" Space Man - **$5 $10 $25**
With helmet add **$8**

SPA-7

❑ **SPA-7. The War Of The Worlds Playset,**
1953. Archer Plastics Inc. 12x26.5x4" deep box. Lid battle scene between "Mars Men" and US Military with civilians fleeing, buildings crumbling and flying saucer. Bottom panel depicts "Civil Defense Station" with Civil Defense workers and civilians. Original intent was to cut the box apart to create a diorama. Six plastic 3.75" Men of Mars, ten 2.5" tall GI's and 12 plastic accessory pieces, 6 weapons, 6 Astro-packs and a 10" long hard plastic friction truck with sound beam attachment. Boxed Complete (41 pieces) -
$1350 $2750 $5000

JUNIOR ROCKET RANGERS
This is to certify that Howard Larson
Rod Brown of the Rocket Rangers
is hereby declared to be a member in good standing
D.A. Swift
Commanding

SPA-8

❑ **SPA-8. Membership Card,**
1953. Issuer unknown. 2-1/2x4" gray card for CBS-TV program starring Cliff Robertson which aired from April 1953 to May 1954. Pledge printed on reverse. - **$20 $35 $75**

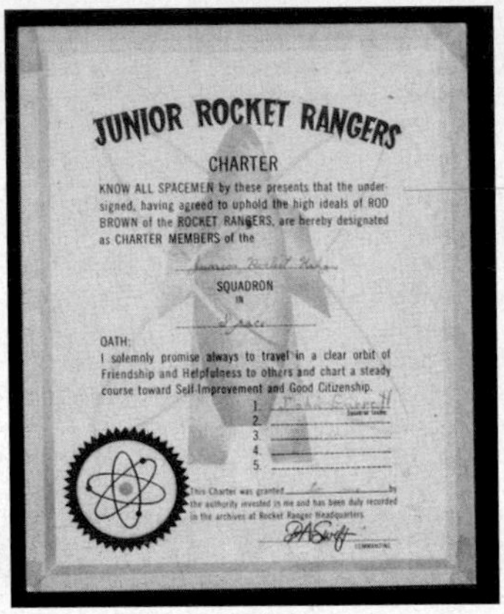
JUNIOR ROCKET RANGERS
CHARTER
KNOW ALL SPACEMEN by these presents that the undersigned, having agreed to uphold the high ideals of ROD BROWN of the ROCKET RANGERS, are hereby designated as CHARTER MEMBERS of the
SQUADRON
IN
OATH:
I solemnly promise always to travel in a clear orbit of Friendship and Helpfulness to others and chart a steady course toward Self-Improvement and Good Citizenship.
1.
2.
3.
4.
5.
This Charter was granted ______ by the authority invested in me and has been duly recorded in the archives at Rocket Ranger Headquarters.
D.A. Swift
COMMANDING

SPA-9

❑ **SPA-9. "Rocket Rangers Charter" Sheet,**
1953. 8.75x11" issue for 1953-1954 program "Rod Brown Of The Rocket Rangers." -
$30 $60 $100

SPA-10

❑ **SPA-10. "Rod Brown Of The Rocket Rangers" Record,**
1953. Columbia Playtime. 7x7.5" paper sleeve containing 78 rpm record. Titles are "Rocket Ranger March" and "Rocket Ranger Song." -
$25 $45 $85

SPA-11

❑ **SPA-11. "Rex Mars Planet Patrol Sparkling Space Tank" Boxed Wind-Up,**
c. 1953. Marx. 4x10x5" tall tin litho toy comes in box very nicely illustrated on all sides.
Box - **$150 $250 $500**
Toy - **$200 $400 $650**

SPA-12

❑ **SPA-12. "Starr Of Space" Record,**
c. 1953. Produced and recorded by Al Gannaway for Bill Brody Company. 7x7" sleeve holds 78 rpm record featuring original cast of 1953-1954 radio series. - **$20 $35 $70**

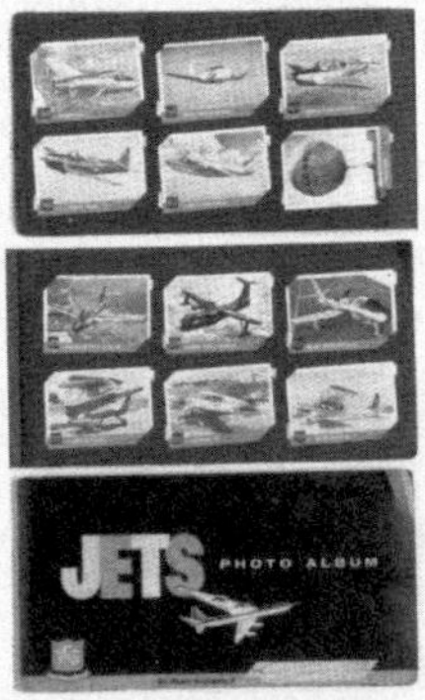

SPA-13

❑ **SPA-13. Topps "Jets" Cards and Albums,**
1956. A set of 240 cards was issued. They fit into 2 photo albums.
Photo Albums each - **$15 $30 $60**
Each card - **$2 $4 $10**

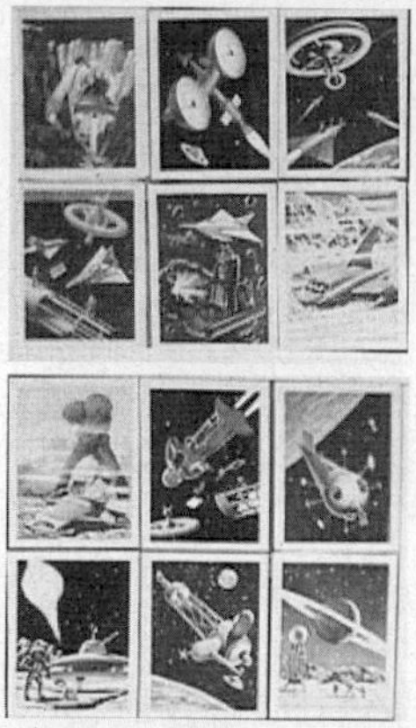

SPA-14

❑ **SPA-14. "Swift's Space Trading Card" Set,**
c. 1958. Swift's Premium Meats. Set of 12, each 2-1/4x3". Gordon Gold Archives.
Each - **$12 $25 $45**

SPA-15

❑ **SPA-15. Store Sign With Space Premiums Offer,**
c. 1958. Swift's Premium Meats. 21-1/2x30" paper sign promoting trading cards, celestial map, space guides and booklets. Sign was mailed in folded size of 8x11". Gordon Gold Archives. - **$200 $400 $700**

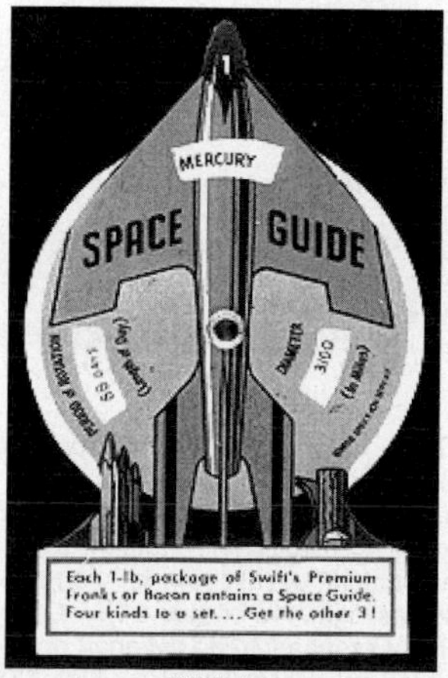

SPA-16

❑ **SPA-16. "Space Guide" Mechanical Card,**
1958. Swift's Premium franks and bacon. Diecut cardboard with revolving disks to provide planetary information. - **$15 $30 $60**

SPA-17

SPA-18

❑ **SPA-17. "Dan Dare" Cello. Button,**
1950s. English issue for popular space hero of comics and radio. - **$15 $25 $50**

❑ **SPA-18. "Dan Dare" Cello. Button,**
1950s. English issue depicting him in space helmet. - **$20 $30 $60**

SPA-19

❑ **SPA-19. Space Fantasy Scene Card,**
1950s. Bond Bread. 3-1/2x6-1/4" ink blotter. - **$5 $10 $25**

SPA-20

❑ **SPA-20. Space Viewer Picture Gun and Theatre,**
1950s. Has 7 films. - **$100 $200 $400**

SPA-21

❑ **SPA-21. Nabisco Shredded Wheat Box with Sound-Jet Space Ship Glider,**
1950s. Glider is pictured on back and found in cereal box. Complete - **$50 $100 $200**

SPA-22

❑ **SPA-22. "Space Helmet And Rocket Ray Gun" Paper Poster,**
1950s. General Electric refrigerators. Colorful 21x49" poster offer for space toys to youngsters bringing parents to "Roto-Cold" refrigerator demonstration. - **$135 $275 $500**

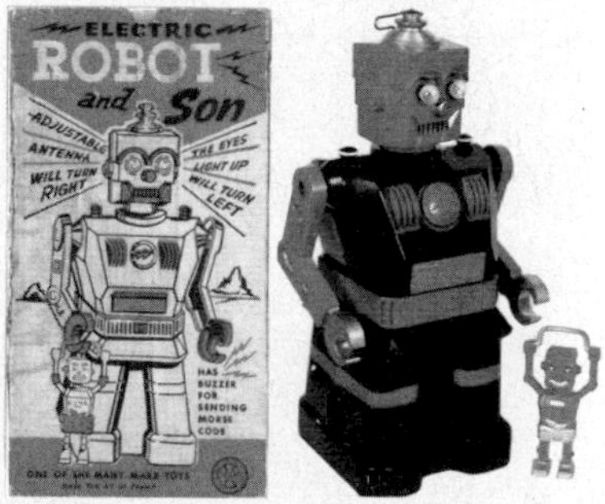

SPA-23

❑ **SPA-23. "Marx Electric Robot and Son" Battery Toy,**
1950s. Marx Toys. 16-1/2" tall box holds 14" tall red and black hard plastic robot and his matching 5" tall "son." Many functions. One of the classic '50s robot toys.
Box - **$125 $225 $450**
Toy - **$150 $250 $500**

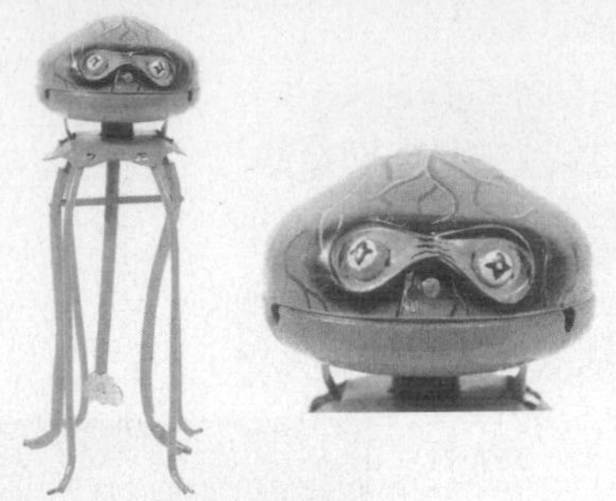

SPA-24

❑ SPA-24. Martian Rare Wind-up Toy,
1950s. Hishimo, Japan. 7" tall depicting head with exposed veins on six vinyl covered skinny wire legs. - **$1000 $3000 $5000**

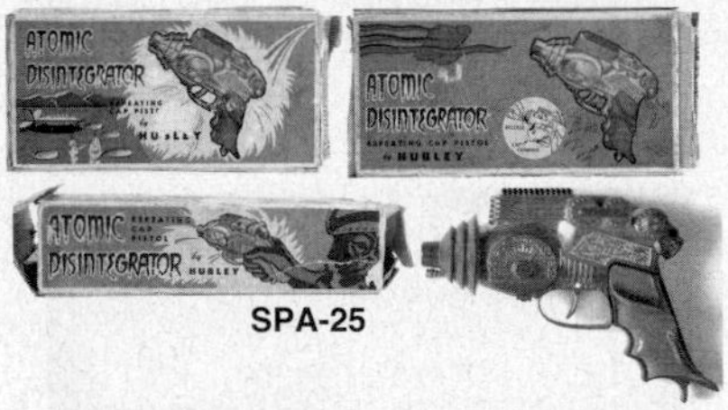

SPA-25

❑ SPA-25. "Automatic Disintegrator" Cap Pistol Boxed,
1950s. Hubley. 7.25" long cast metal repeating cap pistol with plastic grips in nicely illustrated box. Box - **$125 $250 $500**
Pistol - **$225 $450 $750**

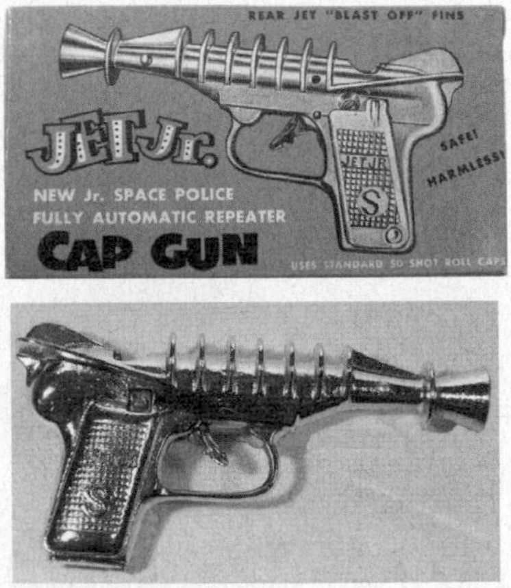

SPA-26

❑ SPA-26. "Jet Jr." Space Police Cap Gun with Box,
1950s. Gun - **$125 $225 $400**
Box - **$75 $125 $200**

SPA-27

❑ SPA-27. "Captain Meteor Holster Set With Cosmic Ray Gun,"
1950s. Carnel Manufacturing Co. 5.75x11x2" deep box contains 4.5x10.5" leather holster printed with space themes and Captain Meteor name. Includes 29.5" leather belt. Gun is made of pressed plastic and translucent plastic with metal spark shield. Box - **$75 $125 $200**
Gun - **$65 $125 $200**
Holster - **$85 $150 $250**

SPA-28

❑ SPA-28. "Space Patrol Walkie Talkie" In Display Box,
1950s. Boxed - **$75 $150 $300**

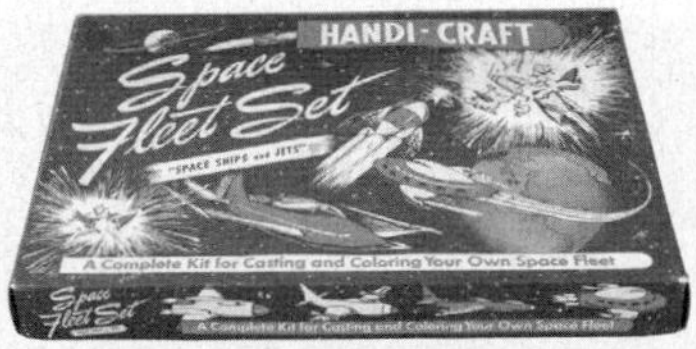

SPA-29

❑ SPA-29. Space Fleet Set Casting Set By Handi-Craft,
1950s. Handi-Craft. 12.25x17.5x2" deep box. Includes six hard plastic molds used to make casts of spaceships and planes. Also comes with tin of "Handi-Craft Casting Powder," brush, airplane parts and four paint discs.
- **$75 $150 $250**

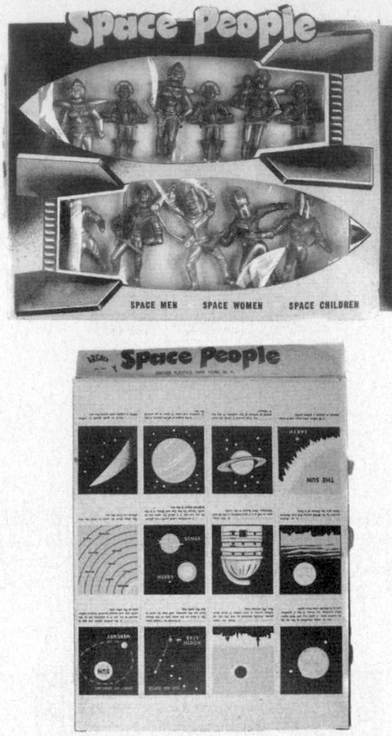

SPA-30

❑ SPA-30. Archer "Space People" Eleven Figure Boxed Set,
1950s. Box measures 11.25x13.5x1.5" and contains 11 hard plastic figures from 3" to 4" tall. Includes 3 spacewomen, one holding baby; 3 robots and 5 spacemen, 4 of which have helmets. Box has die-cut text at top and windows are designed to look like rockets. Back of box features 12 perforated 2.75x3.75" cards giving various facts on the solar system.
Box Only - **$75 $150 $300**
Each Figure - **$8 $15 $30**
Each Helmet - **$10**

SPA-31

❑ SPA-31. Captain Ray-O-Vac Rocketship Flashlight,
1950s. Box is 2x2x8.25" long containing 7.5" long metal flashlight with "Captain Ray-O-Vac; Leader Of Light" decal showing flying spaceman holding flashlight. His body is a Ray-O-Vac battery. Box was meant to be cut apart and re-assembled into rocketship. Box - **$50 $75 $150**
Flashlight - **$50 $75 $150**

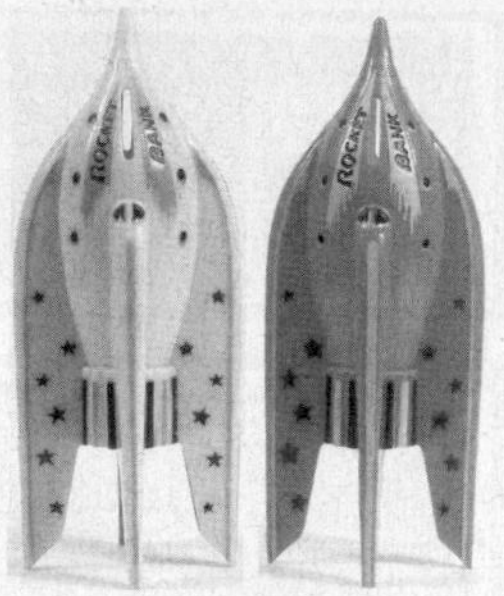

SPA-32

❑ **SPA-32. "Rocket Bank,"**
1950s. Bank is 3x3x9.75" tall, three-dimensional hard plastic in superb design. - **$90 $175 $300**

SPA-33

❑ **SPA-33. "Speedy Spaceman" Toy With Cereal Box,**
c. 1960. Nabisco Rice Honeys. Plastic figure activated by loss of air from attached balloon following inflation.
Box - **$75 $125 $200**
Toy - **$10 $20 $30**

SPA-34

❑ **SPA-34. "Mystery Gyro Space Ship in Box,**
1961. Louis Marx product was heavily promoted on television. Comes with parts and instructions.
Boxed - **$100 $250 $500**

SPA-35

❑ **SPA-35. "America's Astronauts-Men Of The Year" Trigate Button,**
1962. 3-1/2" cello. Scarce. - **$50 $100 $200**

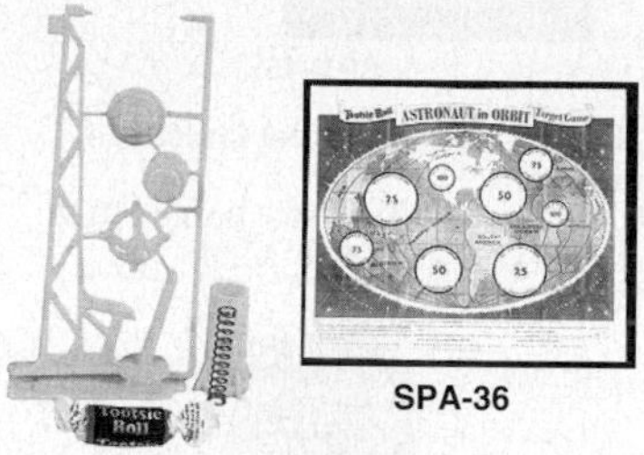

SPA-36

❑ **SPA-36. Astronaut In Orbit Target Game, Map And Parts,**
1963. Tootsie Roll. Plastic launcher assembly parts and 17x20" paper target map in mailer box.
Near Mint Boxed Unassembled - **$150**
Assembled With Target - **$30 $50 $80**

SPA-37

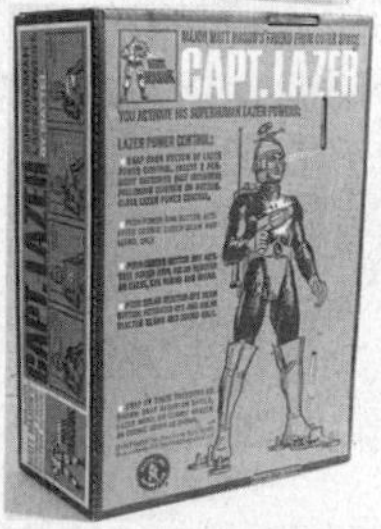

❑ **SPA-37. "Capt. Lazer" Action Figure Boxed,**
1967. Mattel. Major Matt Mason's Friend From Outer Space." Near Mint Boxed - **$350**
Loose Complete - **$65 $125 $200**

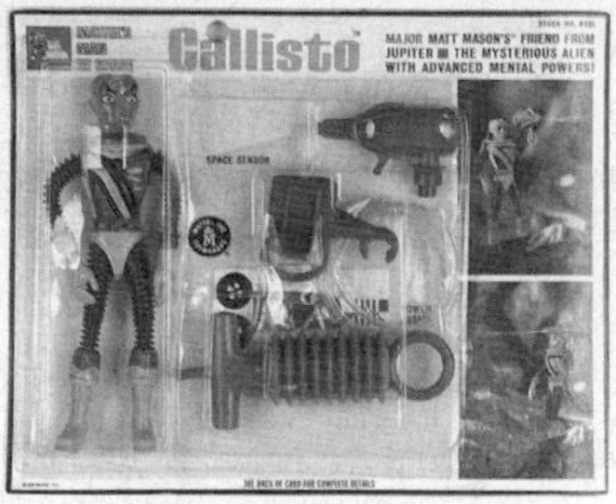

SPA-38

❑ **SPA-38. "Matt Mason/Callisto" Action Figure,**
1968. Mattel. 8.25x10.25" blister card contains 6.25" tall poseable figure and accessories. Figure comes with power pack accessory with space sensor designed to "Flick Out Sensor Line To Collect And Gather In Planet Samples For Analysis." Near Mint Carded - **$600**
Used Complete - **$85 $150 $300**

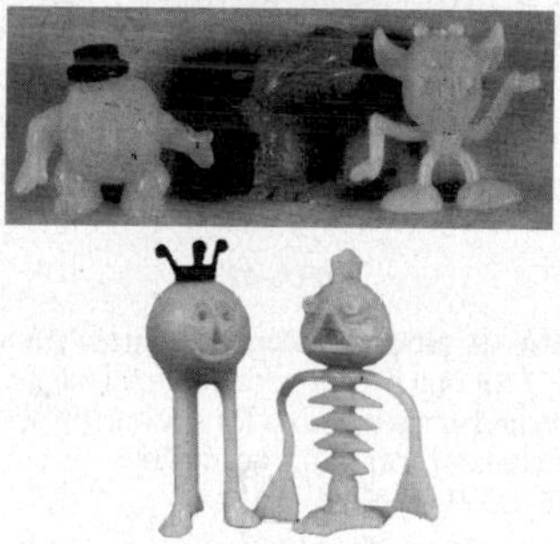

SPA-39

❑ **SPA-39. Crater Critters,**
1968. Kellogg's Apple Jacks. Designed by Rosenhain & Lipmann (R&L) of Australia. Pictured are five of the eight vinyl figures, each about 3/4" to 1-1/4" tall. Each - **$5 $10 $25**

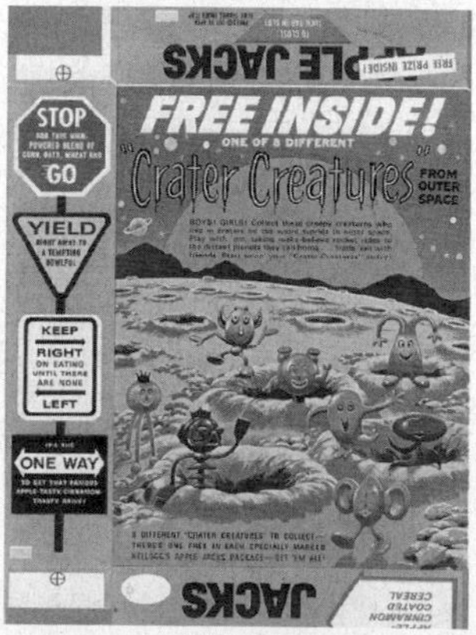

SPA-40

❑ **SPA-40. Cereal Box Flat With Crater Critters Ad,**
1968. Kellogg's Apple Jacks. - **$175 $350 $700**

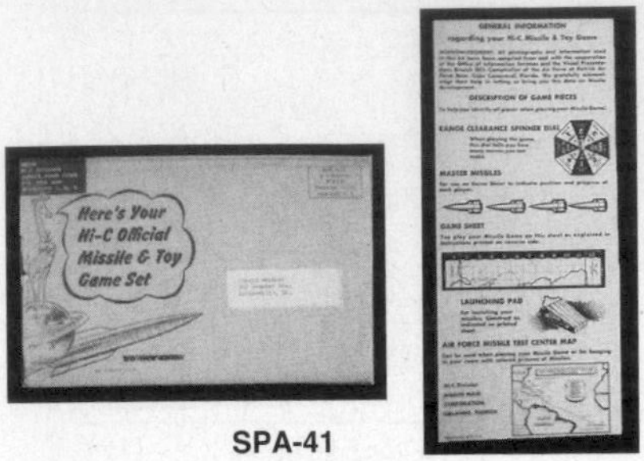

SPA-41

❑ **SPA-41. "Hi-C Official Missile & Toy Game Set",**
1969. Minute Maid. Consists of instruction sheet, 8-1/2x21" punch-out sheet, 4-1/2x21-1/2" game sheet picturing Cape Canaveral and target area ascension island, Cape Canaveral information booklet and 20x25" Air Force Missile Test Center Map. - **$35 $70 $125**

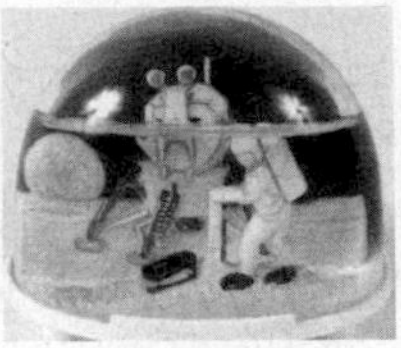

SPA-42

❑ **SPA-42. Moon Exploration Snow Dome,**
1969. 2.25" tall plastic dome holding miniature figures and white granules for snow flurry scene when shaken. West German maker.
- **$100 $250 $500**

SPA-43

❑ **SPA-43. "Bubble Beanie With Satellite Spire" Space Novelty,**
1960s. Store item by F. M. Crump & Co.
Near Mint Boxed - **$150**
Toy Only - **$25 $45 $85**

SPA-44

❑ **SPA-44. "Buitoni" Macaroni Box,**
1960s. Promotes their premium products "Space Men." Cut outs of Rocket and Space Men on back. - **$25 $75 $100**

SPA-45

❑ **SPA-45. Martian Figural Christmas Ornament,**
1960s. Store item. Near Mint Boxed - **$150**
Ornament Only - **$25 $50 $100**

SPA-46

❑ **SPA-46. "Captain Jet" Cello. Button,**
1960s. "Channel 2" sponsorship includes CBS-TV logo. - **$15 $25 $45**

SPA-47

❑ **SPA-47. "Space: 1999" Lunch Box With Thermos,**
1975. King-Seeley Thermos Co. 7x9x4" deep metal lunch box with color photos and illustrations. Came with thermos. Box - **$45 $90 $200**
Bottle - **$10 $20 $30**

SPA-48

❑ **SPA-48. "Space:1999 Eagle 1 Spaceship" Boxed,**
1976. Large 13x27x5" boxed Mattel set of detailed hard plastic spaceship "Over 2-1/2 Feet Long" plus scaled 3" tall figures of Commander Koenig, Dr. Russell, Professor Bergman.
Near Mint Complete - **$400**

SPA-49

❑ **SPA-49. "Billy Blastoff" Toys Booklet,**
1970s. Eldon Toys. Full color 16-page comic story booklet illustrating space, scuba and other toys in "Billy Blastoff" series. - **$5 $10 $20**

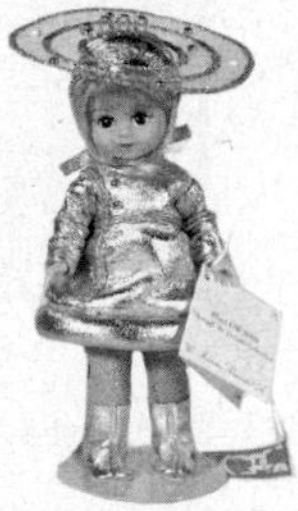

SPA-50 SPA-51

❑ **SPA-50. "Magic Stars" Cereal Box,**
1992. With watch premium. - **$5 $10 $30**

❑ **SPA-51. "Blast Off 2000" Doll,**
2000. Madame Alexander product 8" tall with 2 tags. Great example of space-themed collectible for the year 2000. Boxed - **$65**

SPA-52

❑ **SPA-52. "Robot 2000" with Box,**
2000. The Millennium Robot comes with blinking lights and a shooting gun behind its chest doors. - **$50**

Space Patrol

High adventure in the wild, vast reaches of space! Missions of daring in the name of interplanetary justice! Led by Commander Buzz Corry, the crew of the spaceship Terra policed the galaxies for the United Planets of the 30th century, traveling through time and battling crazed scientists, space pirates, and weird creatures.

Space Patrol, **created by Michael Moser was first broadcast locally on KECA-TV in Los Angeles in March 1950. Six months later it went national on the ABC television and radio networks, where it aired until 1955. Corry, played by Glen Denning and then Ed Kemmer, was accompanied by young Cadet Happy (Smokin' rockets!), played by Lyn Osborne, and lovely Carol Karlyle, played by Virginia Hewitt, as they triumphed over such villains as Mr. Proteus, Captain Dagger, the Space Spider, and the evil Black Falcon, alias Prince Baccarratti.**

The shows were sponsored by Ralston cereals (1951-1954) and Nestle foods (1954-1955), and dozens of program-related items were created for premium use and retail sales. Space suits, helmets, communicators, signal flashlights, a miniature spaceport, a rocket cockpit, Paralyzer Ray Gun, Cosmic Smoke Gun, trading cards, and club membership material were among the available merchandise.

Many licensed items were sold by the May Stores on the west coast, but national distribution was limited. In 1952-1953, a wide variety of merchandise could be purchased through catalog flier order blanks from "Space Headquarters" Hollywood, California. Two comic books were published in 1952 with painted covers by Norman Saunders and interior art by Bernie Krigstein. Then, in 1954 Ralston awarded a $30,000 replica of Buzz's spaceship to a nine-year-old contest winner Ricky Walker of Washington, Illinois, who submitted the name "Cesaria." The family sold the rocket around 1960 to a traveling carnival who in turn later sold it to a Quincy, Illinois couple that made it a mobile NASA museum. From there it spent years as an entrance display for an east coast construction company, and finally, ravaged by a lifetime outdoors it was scrapped about 1985. Items are normally copyrighted Mike Moser Enterprises.

SPC-1

❑ **SPC-1. Boxed Watch With Compass,**
1951. Store item by U.S. Time.
Box - **$200 $400 $800**
Compass - **$25 $50 $100**
Watch - **$50 $100 $150**

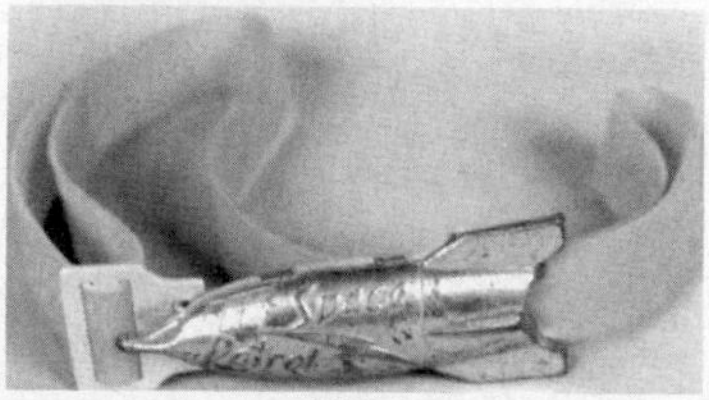
SPC-2

❑ **SPC-2. "Space Patrol" Metal Buckle On "Jet-Glow" Belt,**
1951. Decoder on back of buckle, belts usually no longer glow. Complete - **$75 $125 $250**
Buckle Only - **$40 $75 $175**

SPC-3

SPC-4

❑ **SPC-3. Membership Card,**
1952. - **$30 $90 $175**

❑ **SPC-4. Official Catalogue,**
1952. Shows 22 items priced for sale. - **$40 $85 $175**

SPC-5

❑ **SPC-5. Space Patrol Blood Boosters Booklet,**
1952. Ralston. Back cover reads "...Presented In Behalf Of The National Blood Program..." - **$75 $150 $350**

SPC-6

❑ **SPC-6. Wheat Chex Cereal Box - 12 oz.,**
1952. "Jet Glow" code belt and cosmic smoke gun pictured on back. Membership kit offer. Shows badge. - **$250 $500 $1000**

SPC-7

SPC-8

❑ **SPC-7. TV Forecast Issue,**
1952. Cadet Happy on cover and story about the Ralston Rocket. - **$50 $100 $150**

❑ **SPC-8. "TV Digest" With Cover Article,**
1952. Weekly issue for October 11 with two-page article including photos. - **$30 $75 $125**

SPC-9

❑ **SPC-9. Ralston Club Membership Kit,**
1952. Letter, handbook, photo, envelope.
Complete Near Mint - **$350**
Handbook - **$50 $75 $150**
Others, Each - **$12 $25 $50**

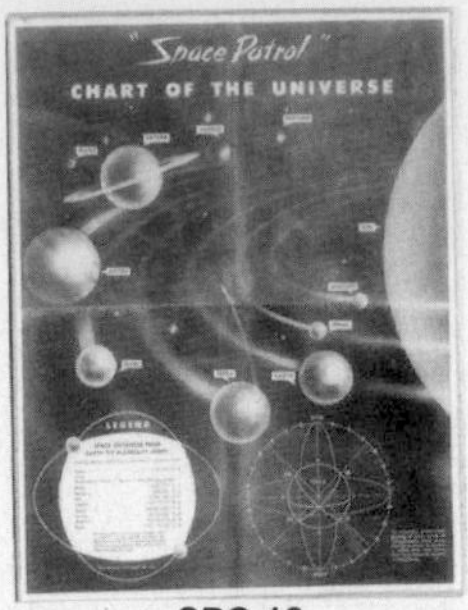

SPC-10

❑ **SPC-10. "Chart Of The Universe" 8x11",**
1952. - **$50 $100 $200**

SPC-11

❑ **SPC-11. "Space Patrol" Comic Book V.1 #1,**
1952. Back cover premium ad. -
$89 $267 $1285

SPC-12

❑ **SPC-12. "Space Patrol" Inlaid Puzzle,**
1952. With paper sleeve which went over the puzzle. Cast is pictured.
Sleeve - **$30 $60 $100**
Puzzle - **$40 $80 $125**

SPC-13

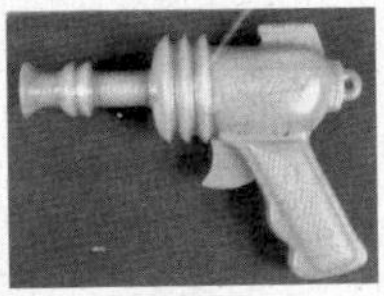

SPC-14

❑ **SPC-13. "Space Patrol" Vol. 1 #2 Comic Book,**
Oct.-Nov. 1952. Store item by Approved Comics. - **$65 $195 $935**

❑ **SPC-14. Cosmic Smoke Gun,**
1952. Smaller 4-1/2" size in red plastic. -
$65 $135 $250

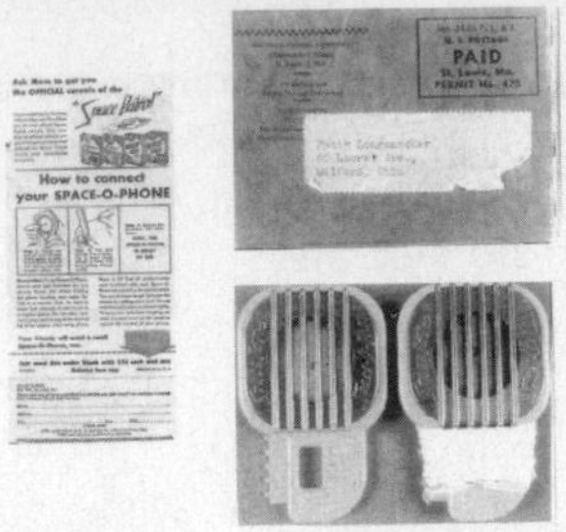

SPC-15

❑ **SPC-15. Space-O-Phone Set,**
1952. Boxed - **$50 $75 $165**
Phones Only - **$25 $50 $75**

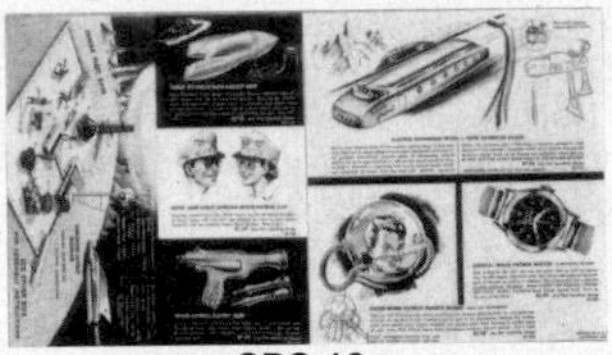

SPC-16

❑ **SPC-16. "Lunar Fleet Base" Instruction Sheet/Premium Catalogue,**
1952. - **$50 $150 $250**

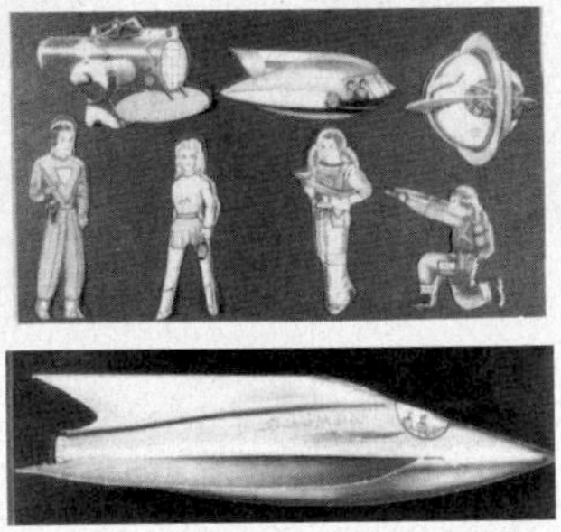

SPC-17

❑ **SPC-17. Ralston "Lunar Fleet Base",**
1952. Rare. Plastic parts shown, set also includes cardboard buildings, etc.
Near Mint In Mailer - **$3000**
Complete Used - **$375 $750 $1500**

SPC-18

❑ **SPC-18. Space Patrol Premium Offer Sheet,**
1952. Ralston Cereals. Instruction for Cosmic Smoke Gun plus offer of member insignia and kit. - **$20 $35 $60**

SPC-19

SPC-20

❑ **SPC-19. Plastic Badge,**
1952. Metallic red, blue, and silver finish. -
$100 $225 $375

❑ **SPC-20. Cosmic Glow Rocket Ring,**
1952. Unmarked Space Patrol premium plastic holding glow-in-dark powder in viewer. -
$250 $500 $1000

SPC-21

SPC-22

❑ **SPC-21. "Space Patrol Blood Boosters" Litho. Tin Tab,**
1952. - **$20 $40 $75**

❑ **SPC-22. "Outer Space Plastic Helmet",**
1952. Store item and also used as a contest prize. Includes inflatable vinyl piece that fits around neck.
Near Mint Boxed - **$1250**
Helmet Only - **$175 $350 $750**

SPC-23

❑ **SPC-23. Rice Chex Cardboard Hanging Mobile Store Display,**
1953. Scarce. Each part printed identically on both sides, largest part is 27" long. -
$600 $1350 $2250

SPC-24

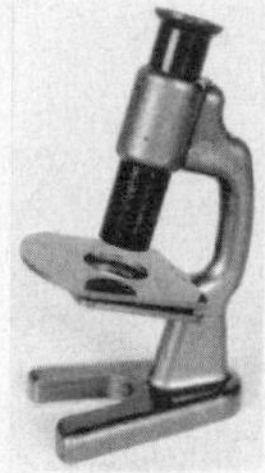

SPC-25

❑ SPC-24. "Magic Space Pictures" Five-Part Diecut Cardboard Store Ceiling Mobile,
1953. Scarce. Ralston Wheat Chex. Hanger display with 20" wide upper title part. -
$450 $1000 $2000

❑ SPC-25. Plastic Microscope,
1953. Came with plastic slides.
Complete - **$60 $100 $160**

SPC-29

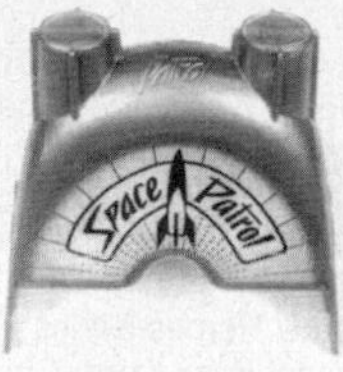

SPC-30

❑ SPC-29. Magic Space Picture,
1953. Set of 24. Each - **$20 $50 $100**

❑ SPC-30. Binoculars,
1953. Issued in both green or black plastic, used as Ralston premium and also available in stores. Each - **$60 $90 $165**

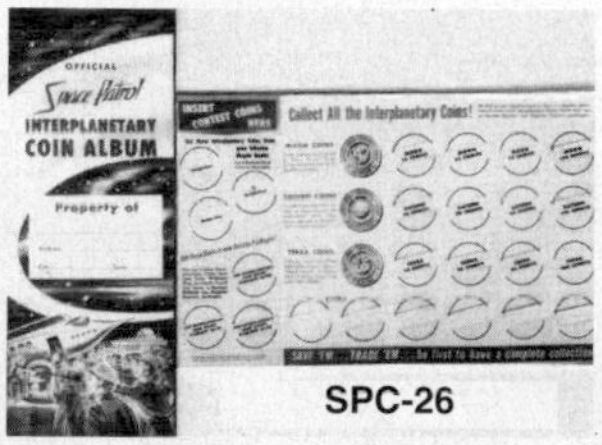

SPC-26

❑ SPC-26. "Interplanetary Coin Album",
1953. Schwinn Bicycles, others. Slotted for 24 coins plus supplemental Schwinn coins. -
$75 $175 $300

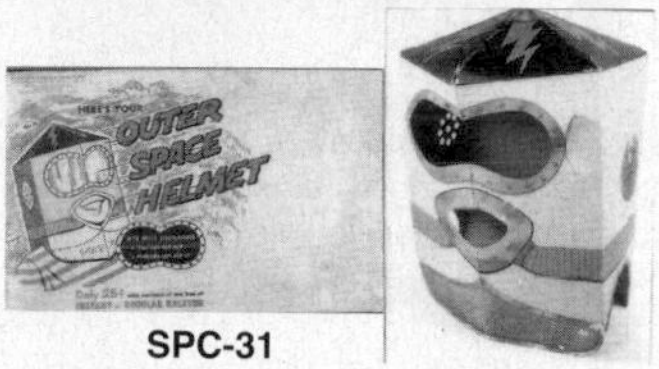

SPC-31

❑ SPC-31. Ralston Cardboard "Outer Space Helmet",
1953. Includes one-way viewing panel.
Near Mint With Mailer - **$250**
Complete Helmet - **$60 $100 $175**

SPC-27

SPC-28

❑ SPC-27. "Interplanetary Space Patrol Credits" Plastic Coin,
1953. Four denominations each for Moon, Saturn, Terra in gold, blue, black or silver (most common). 48 coins in full set. Gold coins have been seen in a bright gold and a darker gold, apparently the result of two distinct production runs. Silver - **$5 $12 $20**
Other Colors - **$8 $15 $25**

❑ SPC-28. "Terra V" Rocket Film Projector,
1953. Also known as the Project-O-Scope. Film is one long strip with four stories of six frames each. Projector - **$75 $200 $300**
Film - **$35 $90 $175**
Instructions - **$30 $60 $100**
Near Mint In Mailer - **$625**

SPC-32

❑ SPC-32. Wheat Chex Cereal Box - 12 oz.,
1953. Cadet Happy and magic space picture offer shown on front. Microscope kit offer on side. - **$250 $500 $1000**

SPC-33

❑ SPC-33. Christmas Catalogue Mailing Folder,
c. 1953. Shows 13 items priced for sale. -
$50 $110 $195

SPC-34

❑ SPC-34. "Ralston Rocket" Card,
c. 1953. - **$40 $90 $150**

SPC-35

❑ SPC-35. Ralston "Buzz Corry Color Book",
c. 1953. Example picture shows both covers. -
$30 $75 $135

SPC-36

❑ SPC-36. "Ralston Rocket? Ask Me" Space Patrol Button,
c. 1953. Ralston. 4" dia. cello over paper sheet message, likely from tour of Space Patrol rocket ship, and worn by store clerks where cereal products were sold. - **$40 $80 $175**

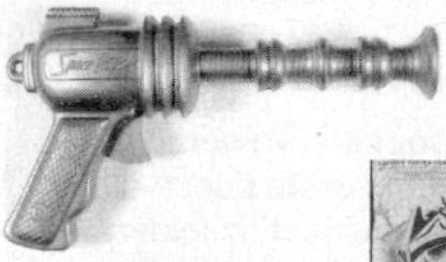

SPC-37

SPC-38

❑ SPC-37. Smoke Gun,
c. 1953. 6" green metallic. Came on card with smoke packets "Good For 10,000 Safe Shots".
Gun Only - **$85 $150 $300**
On Card - **$185 $250 $500**

❑ SPC-38. Man-From-Mars Totem Head,
1954. Includes silvered one-way plastic sheet for viewing.
In Envelope - **$40 $75 $175**
Assembled - **$25 $50 $100**

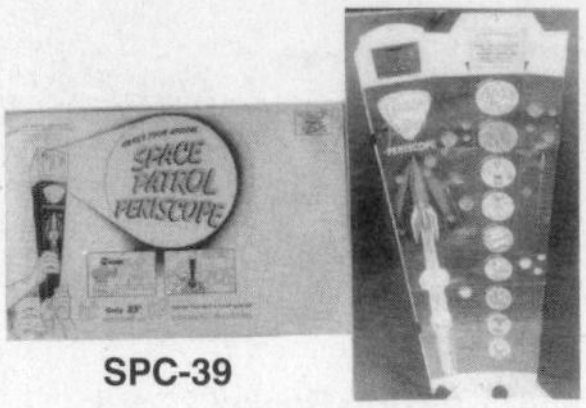

SPC-39

❑ SPC-39. Periscope Cardboard Assembly Kit In Mailer Envelope,
1954. Near Mint In Envelope - **$450**
Assembled - **$100 $200 $375**

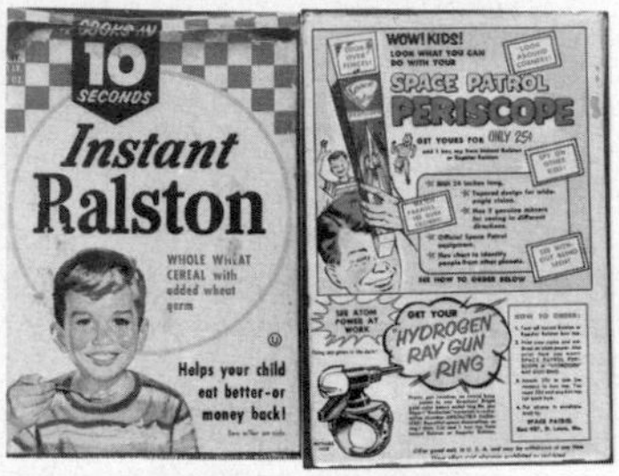

SPC-40

❑ SPC-40. "Instant Ralston Space Patrol" Cereal Box,
1954. 7.25" tall cardboard box in waxed paper wrapper. Back panel pictures periscope and hydrogen ray gun ring available as mail offers.
Complete - **$200 $400 $800**

SPC-41

❑ SPC-41. "Rocket Cockpit" Assembly Kit,
c. 1954. Nestle Foods. Elaborate punch-out cockpit assembly kit with instruction folder. Assembled size is 5x13x21" wide.
Unassembled - **$300 $700 $1200**
Assembled - **$150 $350 $700**
Instructions - **$20 $35 $60**
Mailer - **$20 $35 $60**

SPC-42

SPC-43

❑ SPC-42. Hydrogen Ray Gun Ring,
1954. - **$75 $175 $300**

❑ SPC-43. Ralston Trading Card,
1950s. Wheat and Rice Chex. One card insert per box, set of 40.
Star And Planets Series (13) - **$10 $25 $65**
Rockets, Jets And Weapons Series (14) - **$10 $25 $65**
Space Heroes Series (13) - **$15 $40 $90**
Except Buzz Corry-Cadet Happy Each - **$35 $75 $150**

SPC-44

❑ SPC-44. Cast Photos Folder,
1950s. Dr. Ross dog & cat food. Front cover has photo, back cover facsimile signatures. - **$75 $175 $400**

SPC-45

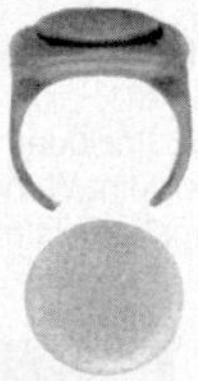

SPC-46

❑ SPC-45. Plastic Frame Character Charms,
1950s. Unsure if Ralston premium or vending machine issue. Each - **$12 $25 $50**

❑ SPC-46. "Space Patrol" Title Printer Plastic Ring,
1950s. Top has "Space Patrol" printed backwards for correct stamped image after inking from included tiny ink pad. Two versions exist with raised area of ring top being either perfectly circular or with slightly squared corners.
Each Complete -**$250 $500 $800**
Each Without Ink Pad - **$125 $200 $350**

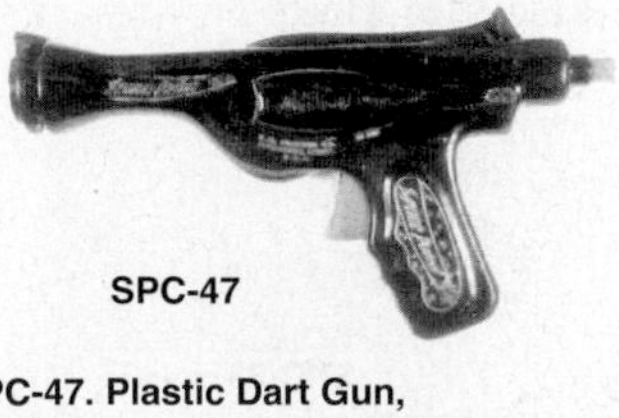

SPC-47

❑ SPC-47. Plastic Dart Gun,
1950s. Store item by U.S. Plastic Co. as well as premium. Came with two darts. Black plastic is store item; red plastic is premium but also known bagged with header card for store sales.
Complete With Darts - **$75 $150 $275**
Gun Only - **$50 $100 $225**

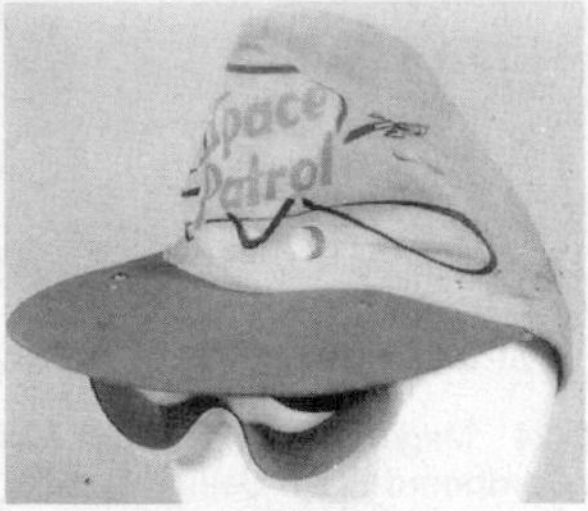

SPC-48

❑ SPC-48. Fabric "Cosmic Cap" With Fold Down Sunglasses,
1950s. Store item by Bailey of Hollywood. - **$175 $350 $650**

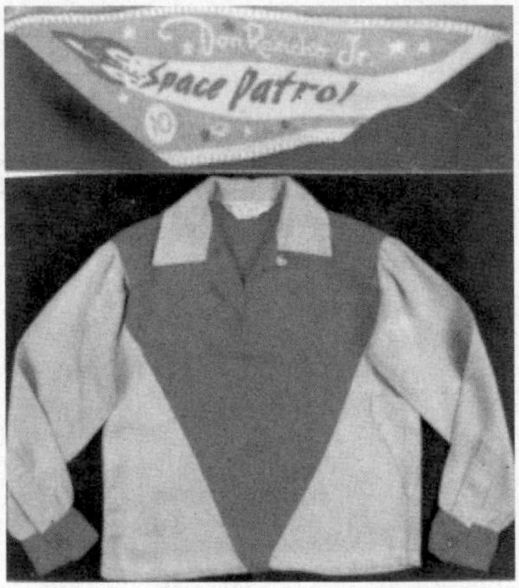

SPC-49

❑ SPC-49. "Space Patrol" Child's Shirt,
1950s. Store item. Gray with red accents issued by Don Rancho Jr. - **$125 $250 $500**

SPC-50

SPC-51

❑ SPC-50. "Space Patrol Napkins,"
1950s. Store item by Reed with 32 napkins.
Near Mint Sealed - **$50**

❑ SPC-51. "Space Patrol Party Plates,"
1950s. Store item by Reed. Set of eight.
Near Mint Sealed - **$50**

SPC-52

❑ SPC-52. "Giant Balloon" Mailing Envelope,
1950s. Ralston. 10 cents with Wheat or Rice Chex purchase. Balloon usually disintegrated.
Envelope Only (8-1/2x11") - **$50 $100 $150**

SPC-53

❑ SPC-53. Gun & Holster Set,
1950s. Holster has rare silver Space Patrol Cadet badge on top of flap. Blue telescope gun is unmarked & has whistle on butt of gun.
Holster With Badge - **$150 $325 $650**
Blue Gun **$15 $40 $75**

SPC-54

❑ SPC-54. "Space Patrol Cadet" Silvered Metal Badge,
1950s. Made in Japan.
Near Mint On Card - **$450**
Badge Only - **$75 $175 $300**

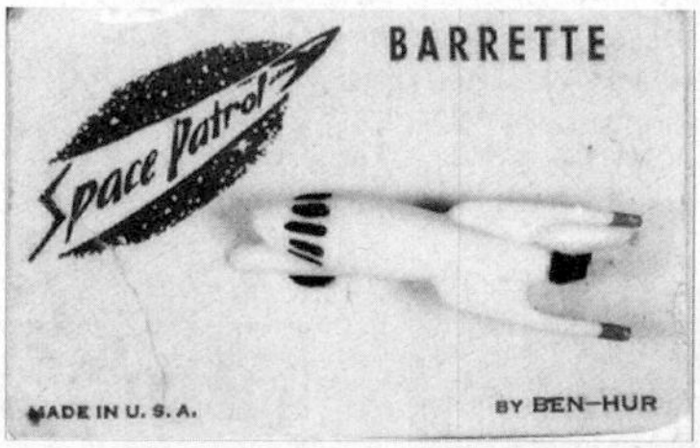

SPC-55

❑ SPC-55. Plastic Rocketship Barrette,
1950s. Store item by Ben-Hur.
On Card - **$40 $100 $160**

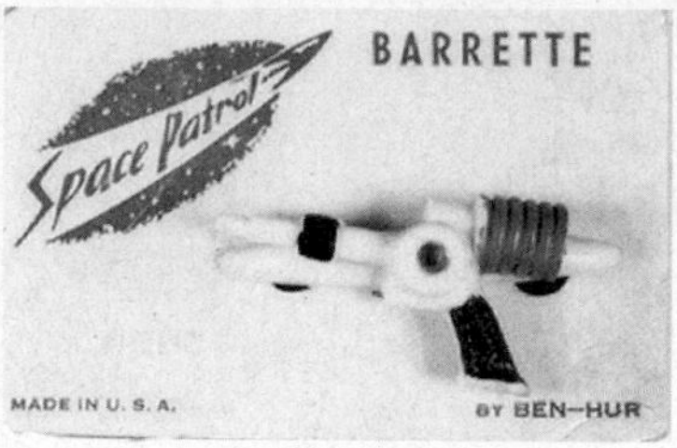

SPC-56

❑ SPC-56. Plastic Gun Barrette,
1950s. Store item by Ben-Hur.
On Card - **$40 $100 $160**

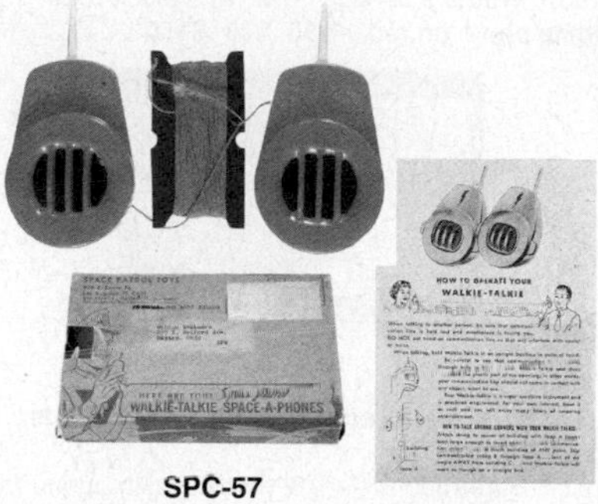

SPC-57

❑ SPC-57. Premium Walkie Talkies With Box & Instructions,
1950s. Scarce. Communication line with two plastic red walkie talkies. Rare Space Patrol premium box has Space graphics on back with Commander Cory on front.
Complete - **$150 $300 $600**

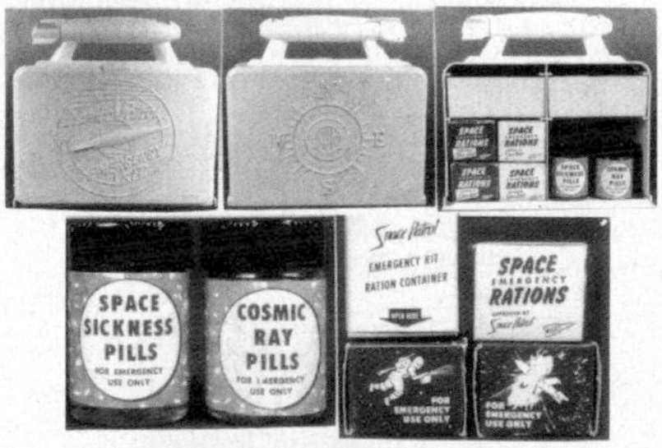

SPC-58

❑ SPC-58. Plastic "Emergency Kit",
1950s. Store item by Regis Space Toys. Handle contains flashlight.
Complete - **$450 $1050 $2000**
Kit Empty Except Insert Forming Compartments - **$150 $300 $600**
Graphic Packaged Box And Large Yellow Cardboard Insert That Fits In Box (not shown) - **$200 $400 $800**

SPC-59

❑ SPC-59. "Commander" Vinyl Rain Hat With Cardboard Tag,
1950s. Store item by Marketon Co. with license of Space Patrol Enterprises.
Hat - **$75 $165 $300**
Tag - **$40 $75 $150**

SPC-60

❑ SPC-60. "Official Space Patrol Atomic Pistol Flashlite,"
1950s. Marx Toys. 2-3/8x5.5x7.75" box contains 5.5x7.5" flashlight. Gun also came in red version, this is blue version. Comes with envelope containing "Auxiliary Red And Green Signal Lenses." Also includes 1.5x2.25" instruction sheet. Gun lights and produces a pinging sound when trigger is pulled. Near Mint Boxed - **$850**
Box - **$100 $200 $400**
Gun - **$150 $300 $450**

SPC-61

❑ SPC-61. "United Planets Treasury Department Top Secret Diplomatic Pouch" Set,
early 1950s. 11-1/2x11-1/2" portfolio holding Space Patrol stationery, United Planets currency bills, full color United Planets stamps, 16-page color stamp album, United Planets plastic coins and coin album.
Complete - **$75 $125 $250**

SPC-62

❑ **SPC-62. "Space Patrol" Helmet,**
1950s. Bailey of Hollywood, 9x11x5" tall sturdy pressed blue cardboard centered on front by Space Patrol name, rocketship, planets and stars design. - **$150 $275 $550**

Speed Gibson of the I.S.P.

Young Speed Gibson, at the age of 15, was an ace pilot and member of the International Secret Police in this radio adventure series that was syndicated briefly in 1937-1938. Speed, created by Virginia Cooke, along with his uncle, top agent Clint Barlow, and pilot Barney Dunlap, circled the globe in their ship The Flying Clipper on the trail of the criminal Octopus gang. "Suffering whang-doodles, Speed."

SGB-1

SGB-2

❑ **SGB-1. Speed Gibson Rare Sponsor Brass Badge,**
1937. Sweetheart Bread. 2". - **$30 $60 $130**

❑ **SGB-2. "Speed Gibson" Store Clerk's Rare Promotional Button,**
1937. 3" celluloid button with covered metal back and bar pin reads "Tune In Speed Gibson." Likely used by local store clerks whose companies sponsored the local radio broadcast. - **$50 $100 $150**

SGB-3

SGB-4

❑ **SGB-3. Code Book Manual,**
1937. Dreikorn's Orange Wrap Bread. Also seen with Stroehmann's Prize Winner Bread imprint. Includes membership card and oath to sign. - **$65 $150 $250**

❑ **SGB-4. Portrait Cello. Button,**
1937. Winter's Bread. 1-1/2" with black and white photo on red. - **$35 $75 $150**

SGB-5

❑ **SGB-5. Textured Cardboard Card Holder With Photo,**
1937. Buttercup Bread. 3-1/2x5" which opens to reveal storage pocket on right while left holds sepia photo with facsimile signature. Text inside reads "Property Of I.S.P. Operator Confidential Information." - **$50 $100 $215**

SGB-6

❑ **SGB-6. Adventure Map With Promotion Record And Envelope,**
1937. Peter Pan Bakery and others.
Map - **$100 $225 $450**
Promotion Record - **$15 $40 $75**
Envelope - **$5 $20 $30**

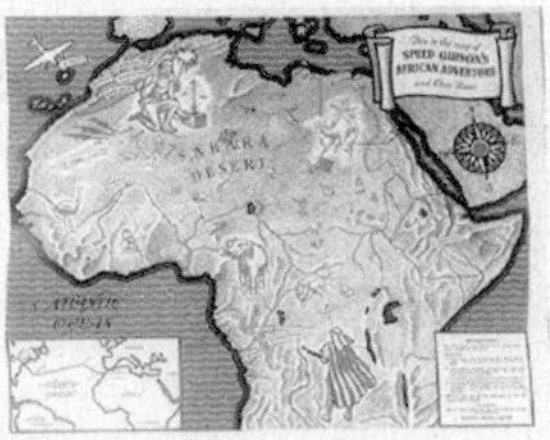

SGB-7

❑ **SGB-7. "African Adventure And Clue Hunt" Map,**
1937. Brown's Bread Ltd. (Canada). - **$150 $300 $600**

SGB-8

❑ **SGB-8. "Wings" Newspaper #1,**
1937. Cote's Master Loaf Bread. - **$40 $75 $150**

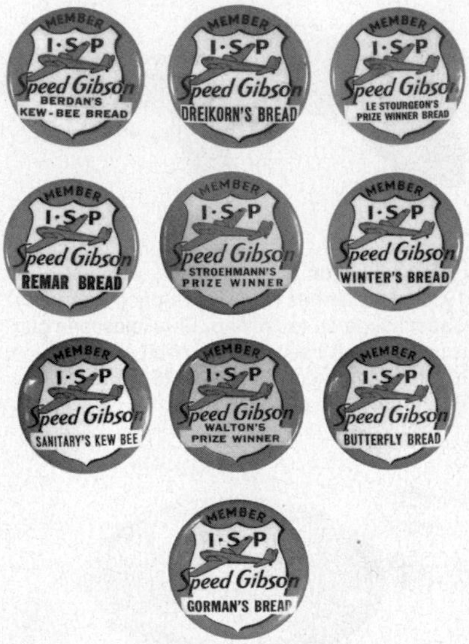

SGB-9

❑ **SGB-9. Bread "Prize Winner" Cello. Badges,**
1937. Various sponsors.
Berdan's Kew-Bee Bread (rare) - **$20 $40 $80**
Delorge's Prize Winner - **$15 $30 $60**
Dreikorn's Bread (scarce) - **$20 $40 $75**
Le Stourgeon's Bread - **$15 $30 $60**
Remar Bread - **$15 $30 $60**
Stroehmann's Bread - **$12 $25 $40**
Winter's Bread (scarce) - **$20 $40 $75**
Sanitary's Kew Bee (rare) - **$25 $50 $100**
Walton's (rare) - **$25 $50 $100**
Butterfly Bread (rare) - **$25 $50 $100**
Gorman's Bread (rare) - **$25 $50 $100**

SGB-10

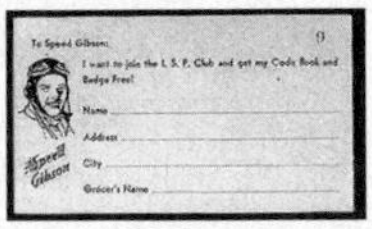

SGB-11

❑ SGB-10. "Speed Gibson's Bread" Store Sign,
1937. Paper poster 10x17" including club membership offer text plus local imprint for radio station. - **$75 $150 $275**

❑ SGB-11. I.S.P. Club Membership Application Postcard,
1937. Offers free Code Book and Badge for submission of grocer's name. - **$10 $20 $35**

SGB-12

❑ SGB-12. "Rocket-Gyro X-3" Balsa/Cardboard Flying Toy With Mailer,
1937. "Hikes" chocolate-coated wheat cereal. Assembled toy flown by rubber band.
Near Mint With Mailer - **$225**
Without Mailer - **$25 $75 $150**

SGB-13

SGB-14

❑ SGB-13. "Secret Police I.S.P." Litho. Club Member Button,
1937. - **$10 $25 $40**

❑ SGB-14. Member's Small Blue/Silvered Brass Button,
1937. Phil A. Halle. - **$25 $45 $80**

SGB-15

SGB-16

❑ SGB-15. Gorman's Bread "Speed Gibson Flying Police" Enameled Brass Badge,
1937. - **$25 $50 $100**

❑ SGB-16. "Speed Gibson/Secret Police I.S.P." Canadian Cello. Button,
1937. Made by Shaw Mfg. Co., Toronto. - **$30 $60 $90**

SGB-17

SGB-18

❑ SGB-17. Badge,
1937. Dreikorn's Bread. Flying Police Badge, shaped like a shield. - **$25 $50 $100**

❑ SGB-18. Badge,
1937. Promote's Cote's Master Loaf Bread. Rare. - **$50 $100 $165**

SGB-19

SGB-20

❑ SGB-19. Badge,
1937. Staudt's Bread. Rare. - **$75 $125 $185**

❑ SGB-20. Badge,
1937. Corps Member badge. Rare. - **$75 $125 $185**

SGB-21

❑ SGB-21. Badge,
1937. Dreikorn's Bread. Flying Police Badge with two stars on it. - **$85 $150 $200**

SGB-22

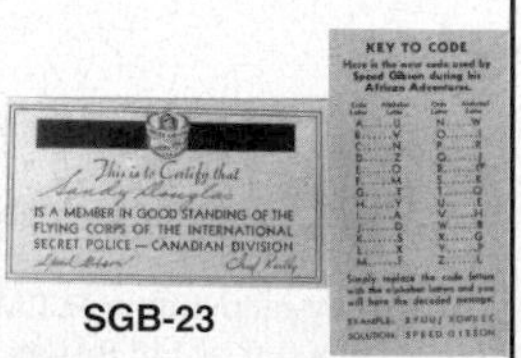

SGB-23

❑ SGB-22. "Speed Gibson Flying Corps I.S.P." Brass Badge,
1937. Pictures him in aviator helmet above airplane. - **$125 $250 $500**

❑ SGB-23. I.S.P. "Canadian Division" Club Card,
1937. Back has code used during Speed Gibson African adventures. - **$50 $100 $200**

SGB-24

❑ SGB-24. "Speed Gibson's Great Clue Hunt" Paper Sheet,
1938. Unidentified bread company. Pencil activity sheet for following radio broadcasts.
Rare. - **$125 $250 $500**

SGB-25

❑ SGB-25. Fan Postcard,
1938. Gorman's Bread. Browntone photo. - **$30 $60 $110**

Speedy Alka-Seltzer

Alka-Seltzer, an antacid/analgesic combination tablet, was first marketed in 1931 by Miles Laboratories of Elkhart, Indiana. From 1951 to 1964 product promotion featured a perky little fellow with a prominent forelock and a tablet for a hat. Originally called Sparky, Speedy evolved into a popular spokesfigure in television commercials and in promotional items issued by the manufacturer. Speedy was created by Robert Watkins and voiced by Richard Beals. Speedy is translated as Pron-Tito in Spanish.

SAS-1

SAS-2

❑ SAS-1. Bank 5-1/2" Rubber Figure,
1950s. Earliest version with word "Bank" below coin slot on top of hat, later version without word.
First Version - **$65 $200 $300**
Later Version - **$50 $175 $250**

❑ SAS-2. Variant of Bank 5-1/2" Figure,
1950s. Blonde haired variant of later version of SAS-1 figure. Scarce. - **$65 $200 $300**

SAS-3

SAS-4

❑ **SAS-3. Cardboard Store Display,**
1950s. About 12-15" tall. - **$100 $175 $300**

❑ **SAS-4. "Speedy Alka-Seltzer" Enameled Brass Figural Pin,**
c. 1950s. Back has threaded post fastener for lapel or button hole. - **$25 $50 $75**

SAS-5

❑ **SAS-5. "Pron-Tito" Spanish Translation Sign,**
1962. Cardboard 21x28" with full color art. - **$75 $150 $300**

SAS-6

SAS-7

❑ **SAS-6. Store Display 8" Vinyl Figure,**
1960s. - **$300 $600 $900**

❑ **SAS-7. "Pron-Tito" Spanish Litho. Tray,**
1960s. - **$85 $175 $325**

SAS-8

❑ **SAS-8. Speedy Alka Seltzer Inflatable Squeak Toy,**
1960s. Toy is 15" tall. - **$75 $150 $250**

SAS-9

❑ **SAS-9. Visor Cap,**
1960s. Diecut thin cardboard. - **$15 $25 $50**

SAS-10

SAS-11

❑ **SAS-10. Small Flicker Sheet,**
1960s. About 1-1/2" square with "Pron Tito" name on his hat. He holds magician's wand and when tilted, a glass of the product appears. - **$20 $45 $70**

❑ **SAS-11. Paper Cup,**
1977. Miles Laboratories. - **$20 $40 $75**

SAS-12

❑ **SAS-12. "Speedy Alka-Seltzer" Bean Bag,**
1999. With tag. - **$25**

The Spider

Created by pulp author R.T.M. Scott, the *Spider* pulp had a run of 118 issues between 1933 and 1944. The Spider was actually Richard Wentworth, a wealthy New York crime fighter who divided his time between battling master criminals and hiding his true identity from the police. In the 1933 tale *Spider Strikes* and in the pulps into the 1940s, Wentworth's symbol, the drawing of a red spider, marked the foreheads of his vanquished and deceased criminal opponents. The same symbol appears on the pulp magazine club ring. Warren Hull played the lead in the Columbia Serials *The Spider's Web* in 1938 and *The Spider Returns* in 1941.

SPD-1

❑ **SPD-1. Spider Enamel and Silver Luster Metal Ring,**
1934. First offered in "The Spider" pulp magazine #6, March 1934. Later used as 1941 "The Spider Returns" movie premium. The latest date of issue would be 1943, when the magazine ceased publication. The ring has a silver non-adjustable band, and examples prior to about 1940 are stamped on the inner band only with the maker's logo, an arrow through a letter "U" to represent "Uncas." Around 1940, because of increasing world conflict, the words "Made in USA" were also stamped on the inner band. An example with an adjustable band exists. The band matches the one found on a 1934 World's Fair premium ring by Uncas. Reported known: five in Good grade, ten in Very Good, five in Fine, five in Very Fine and three in Near Mint.
Good - **$500**
Fine - **$1500**
Very Fine - **$2000**
Near Mint - **$4000**

❑ An authorized modern reproduction exists in a limited edition run of 250 (originally sold for $55) with the spider image in red paint instead of red translucent enamel and a gold adjustable band.

Warning: A crude fake exists and can be identified by a visible seam running inside and on top of the ring.

SPD-2

❑ **SPD-2. The Spider Ring Box,**
1934. Small red cardboard ring box with removable lid that held the premium ring. This box was also used for the Operator #5 ring. (See OPR-1). - **$175 $350 $750**

SPD-3

❑ **SPD-3. Membership Card,**
1938. Columbia Pictures. Rare. First serial premium from "The Spider Web," based on "The Spider Magazine" stories. - **$300 $600 $1000**

SPD-4

❑ **SPD-4. Movie Theater Club Member Card,**
1938. Columbia Pictures. Rare. For 15-episode serial "The Spider Web" based on "The Spider Magazine" stories. - **$300 $600 $1000**

SPD-5

❑ **SPD-5. "The Spider's Web Movie Pennant,"**
1938. Rare. Columbia Pictures Corporation. 8.25x22" pennant features graphic image of a spider with web and logo in white printed on green felt. Pennant notes abbreviation "CPC" for Columbia Pictures Corporation on front.
- **$275 $550 $850**

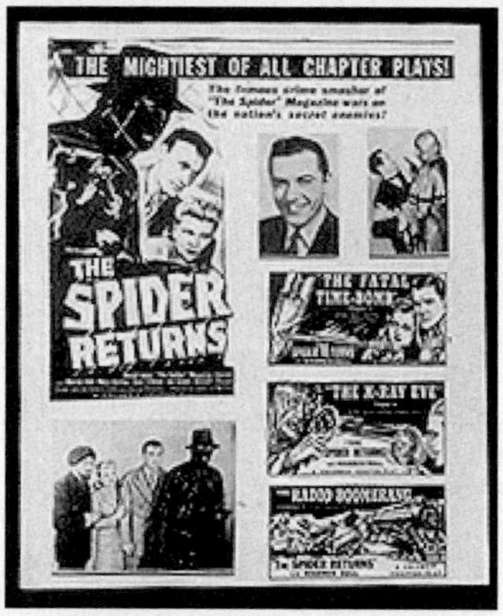

SPD-6

❑ **SPD-6. "The Spider Returns" Movie Serial 9x10-1/2" Handbill,**
1941. Columbia Pictures. - **$35 $65 $125**

SPD-7

SPD-8

❑ **SPD-7. "The Spider Returns" Movie Serial 9x12" Handbill,**
1941. Columbia Pictures for local theater imprint. - **$45 $85 $175**

❑ **SPD-8. "The Spider Returns" Movie Pressbook,**
1941. Columbia Pictures. Contents show ring, example of pulp cover, club card, mask. - **$150 $300 $600**

SPD-9

❑ **SPD-9. "The Spider Returns" Movie Serial Lobby Card,**
1941. Columbia Pictures. 11x14" card from set of eight for chapter play based on pulp magazine hero. Each - **$25 $50 $100**

SPD-10

❑ **SPD-10. Spider Ring Variety,**
c. 1941. Same as standard ring except no red enamel on spider image and bands are adjustable, not one piece. Interior has trademark of maker Uncas & "Made In U.S.A." Three examples known to us. - **$450 $1200 $2000**

(cap on)

(cap off)

(close-up of eraser)

SPD-11

❑ **SPD-11. Cello. Mechanical Pencil With "The Spider" Eraser,**
c. 1942. Rare. The Spider pulp magazine. End cap covers rubber eraser with image on top surface. Succeeded Spider ring as premium, produced in very limited quantity. - **$750 $1600 $3250**

Spider-Man

Writer Stan Lee and artist Steve Ditko created *Spider-Man* for the Marvel Comics Group in the 1960s and the superhero has been battling for justice ever since. *Spider-Man* debuted in *Amazing Fantasy* #15 in August 1962. Six months later he appeared in his own comic book, the start of a series that continues to this day. (A syndicated newspaper strip started publication in 1979.) Teenage Peter Parker, who acquired his superhuman powers after being bitten by a radioactive spider, takes on a variety of villains and criminals, all the while working as a photographer for the New York *Daily Bugle* and struggling with the problems of a typical 1962 adolescent. In recent years, Peter has taken on the added responsibility of marriage to his long-time girlfriend Mary Jane.

On television an animated *Spider-Man* series aired on ABC from 1967 to 1970, and *Spider-Man and His Amazing Friends* appeared on NBC in 1981. A 1977 live-action CBS special with Nicholas Hammond was followed by a brief prime-time series in 1978 and scattered repeats for a year. The character was also featured on *The Electric Company*, speaking only in word balloons visible on the screen. In 1995 Ralston Foods introduced Spider-Man sweetened rice cereal, complete with trading cards inside specially marked boxes. Fox television launched an animated version of the popular character in 1994 with Christopher Daniel Barnes voicing Peter Parker/Spider-Man. Like Fox's (now WB's) *Batman* series, the guest voices were supplied by a veritable who's who of Hollywood. Ed Asner played J. Jonah Jameson, Martin Landau voiced the Scorpion, Roscoe Lee Brown supplied the voice for the Kingpin, and Mark Hamill (*Batman*'s Joker) voiced Hobgoblin. *Spider-Man* ended its original run of episodes in February 1998. In the last few years, numerous Spider-toys have appeared, chiefly from Toy Biz.

In 2002, after years of anxious anticipation from fans, a feature film adaptation of the wall-crawler's adventures hit theaters in May. Starring Tobey Maguire as Peter Parker/Spider-Man, Kirsten Dunst as Mary Jane, and Willem Dafoe as Norman Osborn/The Green Goblin, the film was directed by Sam Raimi. The first big screen Spider-Man brought in more than $400 Million at the box office and had record sales on DVD. It was followed by a 13-part MTV animated series, and the second feature film *Spider-Man 2*, again starring Tobey Maguire and Kirsten Dunst, came out in 2004 winning an Oscar for best achievement in visual effects in 2005. A black costume appeared in *Amazing Spider-Man* #252, later becoming the costume of Spider-foe Venom. A new costume appeared first in *Amazing Spider-Man* #529. The film *Spider-Man 3*, released in 2007, featured a version of the black costume.

Merchandised items are usually copyrighted Marvel Comics.

SPM-1

❑ **SPM-1. Aurora Model Kit,**
1966. Near Mint Boxed - **$450**
Built - **$40 $85 $175**

SPM-2

SPM-3

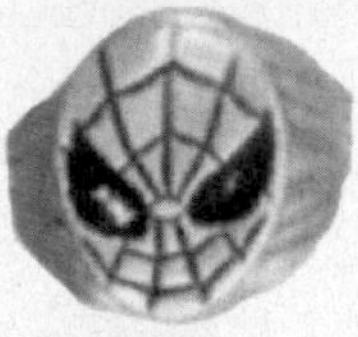

SPM-4

❑ **SPM-2. "The Amazing Spider-Man" 3-1/2" Cello. Button,**
1966. Store item. #6 from numbered series. For variant Spider-Man and other Marvel characters in the series, see the Marvel Comics section.
Near Mint Bagged - **$175**
Loose - **$20 $40 $75**

❑ **SPM-3. Litho. Metal Bicycle Attachment Plate,**
1967. Store item by Marx Toys. - **$15 $30 $65**

❑ **SPM-4. "Hong Kong" Vending Machine Aluminum Ring,**
1960s. - **$20 $35 $75**

SPM-5

SPM-6

❑ **SPM-5. "The Amazing Spider-Man" Boxed Action Figure,**
1972. Store item by Mego. 8" tall figure in window box. Type 2 body with vinyl cape. Box has eight characters on sides and six heads on bottom front. - **$150 $250 $350**

❑ **SPM-6. "The Amazing Spider-Man" Button Varieties,**
1975. Marvel Comics promotional button. Comes as 2" diameter celluloid or 7/8" litho.
Celluloid - **$10 $15 $30**
Litho. - **$3 $6 $12**

SPM-7

SPM-8

❑ **SPM-7. Spider-Man Vitamins Ring,**
1976. Hudson Pharmaceutical Co. -
$35 $60 $125

❑ **SPM-8. Spider-Man Talking View-Master Gift Pak,**
1976. Battery operated. Also features Captain America and Thor. Six reels included. -
$75 $150 $250

SPM-9

❑ **SPM-9. "Amazing Spider-Man" Newspaper Daily Strip Debut Sign,**
1977. 11x17" cardboard for January 3 start of strip "On The Dispatch Comic Page," believed Columbus, Ohio. - **$85 $150 $300**

SPM-10

SPM-11

❑ **SPM-10. Spidey Super Stories Record,**
1977. Peter Pan Records and Children's Television Workshop. Features Electric Company cast in "Spider-Man is Born" and 7 other stories. Narrated by Morgan Freeman. - **$4 $8 $12**

❑ **SPM-11. Plastic Magnetic Compass,**
1978. - **$8 $12 $25**

SPM-12

❑ SPM-12. "The Amazing Spider-Man Radio,"
1978. Marvel Comics Group. 4x4.25x5.75" box with hard plastic "AM Solid State Radio" in the shape of Spider-Man's head. Made by Amico, Inc. Box - **$50 $100 $150**
Radio - **$75 $150 $225**

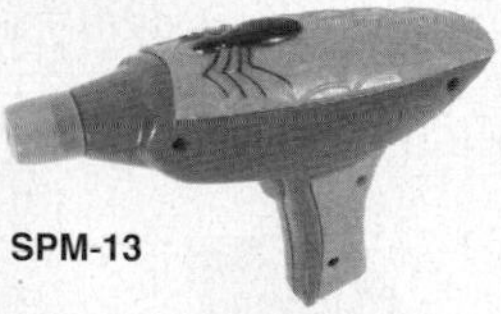

SPM-13

❑ SPM-13. "Spider-Man Sting Ray Gun,"
1978. Remco Toys Inc. 2.75x7.75x10.75" box contains 6x8" long Spider-Man themed gun. Gun is "Transistorized" with electronic sting sound and spider ray light. Has molded plastic top done in Spider-Man costume theme and raised "Spider-Ray" text on side of gun. Lights up to show "spider" and has instruction sheet.
Box - **$30 $60 $110**
Gun - **$35 $65 $135**

SPM-14

❑ SPM-14. Corgi Junior "Spider-Copter" Carded,
1978. 4x5.25" blister card holding 2.75" long die cast metal and plastic replica helicopter.
Near Mint On Card - **$30**

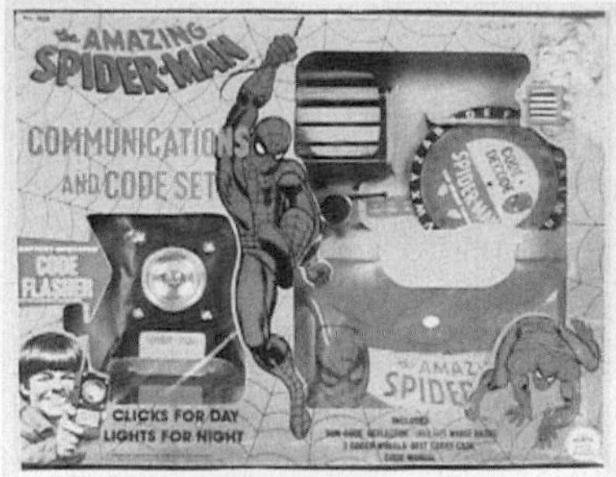

SPM-15

❑ SPM-15 "Communications And Code Set",
1978. Store item by HG Toys. Includes plastic battery operated Code Flasher and Sun Code Reflector, simulated wrist radio, vinyl belt carrying case and pair of cardboard code wheels with instruction card. Near Mint Complete - **$200**
Decoder Only - **$25 $50 $100**

SPM-16

SPM-17

❑ SPM-16. "Spider-Man" 2-1/4" Cello. Button,
1978. Store item by Rainbow Designs. - **$8 $12 $18**

❑ SPM-17. "Make Mine Marvel" Cello. Button,
c. 1970s. Marvel Comics promotion featuring Spider-Man image. - **$12 $25 $45**

SPM-18

❑ SPM-18. Newspaper Daily Strip Announcement Sign,
1970s. 10.75x17" cardboard sponsored by Democrat And Chronicle, Rochester, N.Y. - **$100 $175 $350**

SPM-19 SPM-20

❑ SPM-19. Newspaper Comic Strip Litho. Button,
1970s. Miami Herald. 1-5/8" red, white and blue. Limited distribution. - **$45 $85 $175**

❑ SPM-20. Advertising Button,
1984. 2" black on bright yellow. - **$12 $25 $35**

SPM-21

❑ SPM-21. Spider-Man Sunglasses,
1980s. On card. - **$40**

SPM-22

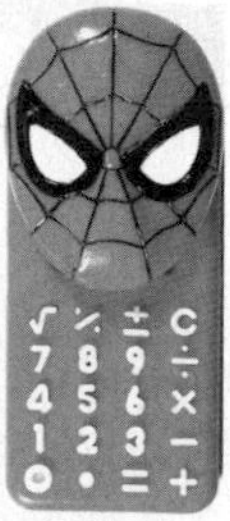

SPM-23

❑ SPM-22. Spider-Man Gold Ring,
1993. Edition of 12. - **$3500**
Silver version, edition of 50 - **$475**
Bronze version, edition of 50 - **$275**

❑ SPM-23. Spider-Man Calculator,
1995. 5" long. Copyright Marvel.- **$12 $25 $40**

SPM-24

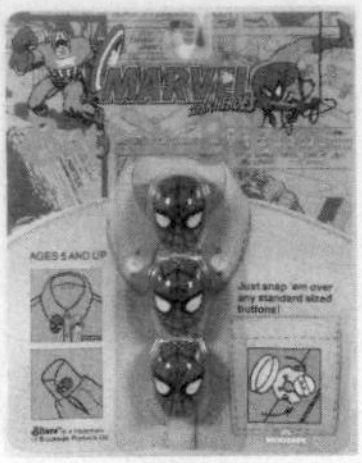

SPM-25

❑ **SPM-24. Dr. Strange Action Figure on Card,**
1996. From the Spider Wars set from the animated series. Comes with collector pin. - **$12**

❑ **SPM-25. Spider-Man Button Biters,**
1990s. On card. - **$5**

SPM-26

SPM-27

❑ **SPM-26. Spider-Man Cereal Box,**
1990s. Has offer of trading card in box. Five cards in the set. Box - **$20**
Each card - **$2**

❑ **SPM-27. Cookie Crisp Cereal Box,**
1990s. Has offer of trading card in box. Six cards in the set. Box - **$5**
Each card - **$1**

SPM-29

❑ **SPM-29. Spider Racer in Box,**
2000. 1/18 scale with remote and includes 5" multi-jointed Spider-Man figure. - **$40**

SPM-30

❑ **SPM-30. Spider-Man Face Silver Ring,**
2000. 3,000 made. Sterling silver. Boxed - **$125**

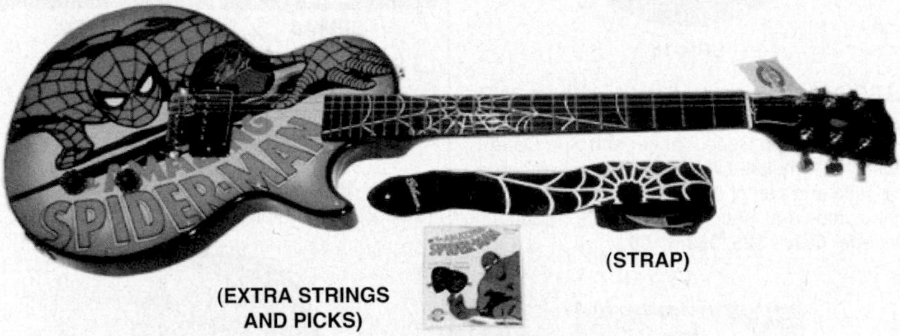

(STRAP)

(EXTRA STRINGS AND PICKS)

SPM-28

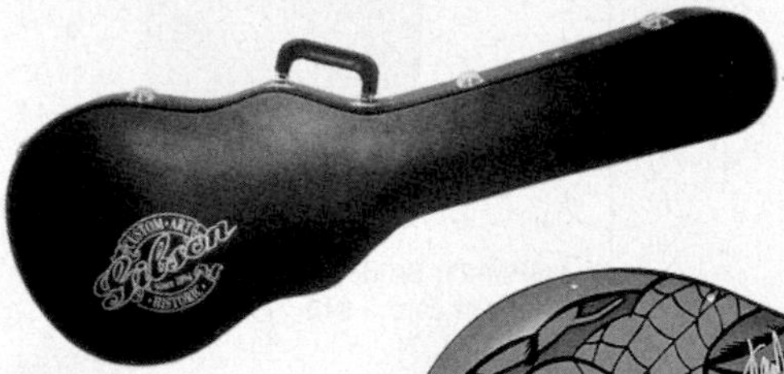

(CASE, SHOWN SMALLER IN RELATIVE SIZE)

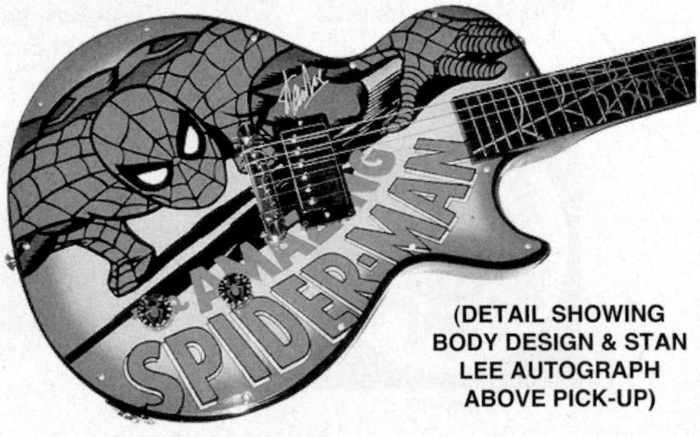

(DETAIL SHOWING BODY DESIGN & STAN LEE AUTOGRAPH ABOVE PICK-UP)

❑ **SPM-28. "Web-Slinger" Limited Edition Signed Gibson Electric Guitar**
2000. Released in a limited run of 150. The first 75 were signed on the body by Stan Lee, the last 75 by the designer, John Romita Sr. The guitar came in a hardshell case with blue velvet lining. The case also included a certificate of authenticity, a plastic envelope with extra strings and plastic picks all featuring unique Spider-Man design touches, and a fabric strap with a white webbing pattern. Near Mint in Case With All Contents - **$5000**

SPM-31

❑ **SPM-31. Spider-Man Mini-Bust in Box,**
2001. Randy Bowen product. Limited to 12,000. - **$40**

SPM-32

❑ **SPM-32. "Doctor Octupus" Mini-Bust,**
2001. Fully painted 5 1/2" tall bust sculpted by John Dennent. Limited to 6,000. Boxed - **$50**

SPM-33

❑ **SPM-33. "Rhino" Mini-Bust,**
2001. Fully painted 5 1/2" tall bust sculpted by Randy Bowen. Limited to 6,000. Boxed - **$50**

SPM-34

SPM-35

❑ **SPM-34. Peter Parker, The Amazing Spider-Man Mini-Bust in Box,**
2001. By Randy Bowen. Limited to 6,000. - **$50**

❑ **SPM-35. Green Goblin Mini-Bust in Box,**
2001. Limited to 10,000. - **$45**

SPM-36

❑ **SPM-36. "Spider-Man" Water Cannon With Box,**
2002. Produced to promote movie. Hard to find an undamaged box. - **$60**

SPM-37

❑ **SPM-37. "Spider-Man" Glass Tumblers,**
2006. PopFun Merchandising. Two versions. Glass tumblers with logos for Marvel and the New York Comic-Con.
Clear glass, edition of 1600. - **$12**
Frosted glass, edition of 1600. - **$12**

The Spirit

***The Spirit* was created by Will Eisner (1917-2005) in 1940 in the unusual form of a comic book insert to be included with the comic sections of Sunday newspapers. The feature, distributed by the Register and Tribune Syndicate, survived until 1952, accompanied by a daily strip from 1941 to 1944. *The Spirit*--actually Denny Colt, a Central City crime fighter in a meager eye mask--has become a strip classic. There have been numerous comic book reprints from the 1940s into the 1990s, and a TV series pilot was broadcast in 1987. A brand new comic book series, *The Spirit--The New Adventures*, debuted in 1998 from Kitchen Sink Press with creator Eisner supervising some of the most popular modern comic book professionals. The Eisner Award, begun in 1988 and presented annually at Comic-con International in San Diego, recognizes achievements in the field. In 2000 *DC* began reprinting all 645 stories in hardcover and full color. Ohio State University in Columbus, Ohio has an extensive collection of Will Eisner material. A feature film is in the pre-production stages with writer Jeph Loeb attached, and DC Comics debuted a new ongoing series in 2006.**

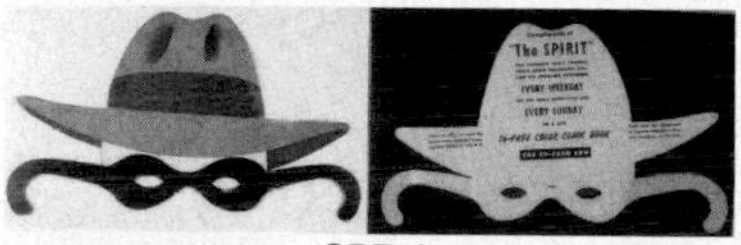

SPR-1

❑ **SPR-1. "Paper Mask",**
c. 1942. Various newspapers for daily strip and Sunday comic book supplement beginning June 1940. - **$125 $300 $600**

SPR-2

SPR-3

❑ **SPR-2. "Star Journal" Cello. Button,**
c. 1942. Various newspapers. For Sunday comic book supplement. - **$125 $225 $475**

❑ **SPR-3. "Minneapolis Morning Tribune" Cello. Button,**
c. 1942. Announcement for daily comic strip. - **$150 $250 $500**

SPR-4

❑ **SPR-4. "The Spirit" Example Of Weekly Newspaper Comic Insert,**
1940s. Various newspapers 1940-1952. Prices vary widely by issue date, artist, condition. Consult *The Overstreet Comic Book Price Guide.*

SPR-5

❑ **SPR-5. First Issue Comic Book Commemorative Poster,**
1966. 17.5x22.5" Harvey Comics promo paper poster with inset art of first issue "Spirit Giant Size Harvey Thriller." - **$40 $85 $190**

SPR-6

SPR-7

❑ **SPR-6. "The Spirit" Large Colorful Button,**
1982. Button is 2.25" with text on right side "Will Eisner Copyright 1982." - **$15 $30 $50**

❑ **SPR-7. "The Spirit" Resin Figure,**
2000. 11 3/4" high. Limited to 1,000.
With Box - **$225**

SPR-8

SPR-9

❑ **SPR-8. "The Spirit" Pinback Giveaway,**
2000. DC Comics promotion for the Spirit Archive reprint series by Will Eisner. - **$3**

❑ **SPR-9. Action Figure ,**
2001. From the Millennium Series. Comes with interchangeable head. - **$25**

SPR-10

❑ **SPR-10. "The Spirit" Lunch Box,**
2001. - **$20**

SpongeBob SquarePants

In 1999, Nickelodeon took a chance on an unknown sponge who lives in a pineapple under the sea. The absorbent and yellow guy was none other than the now-immortal SpongeBob Squarepants. The story of an incredibly optimistic sponge (the voice of Tom Kenny) who works as a fry cook in the local burger joint, The Krusty Krab, SpongeBob SquarePants appeals to audiences of all ages. With a lively and colorful cast, including SpongeBob's dimwitted best friend Patrick, his neighbor Squidward, Sandy, a wiry squirrel who makes her home in an underwater tree dome and Mr. Krabs, the curmudgeonly crustacean who owns The Krusty Krab, SpongeBob is sure to be around for years to come—and there'll most likely be no shortage of cast-based character toys. Creator Stephen Hillenburg may have had high hopes for his Bikini Bottom resident spokesponge, but it's safe to say that SpongeBob has exceeded his expectations. Nearly 100 companies are marketing SpongeBob collectibles and paraphernalia. He's been a sales mascot for macaroni and cheese, snack crackers, fruit snacks, watches, bedding, beach towels, paper towels, skateboards, juice boxes, Halloween costumes and much, much more.

SPO-1

SPO-2

❑ **SPO-1. Sponge Bob Squirt Toy,**
2000s. From Burger King Kids Meal. NM - **$5**

❑ **SPO-2. Button Set,**
2000s. Four buttons on card. NM - **$5**

SPO-3

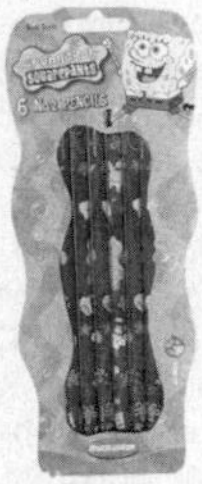

SPO-4

❑ **SPO-3. Cheese Nips Box,**
2000s. Nabisco. NM - **$3**

❑ **SPO-4. Pencil Pack,**
2000s. Six No. 2 pencils. NM - **$4**

SPO-5

SPO-6

❑ **SPO-5. Deep-Sea Trailer and Concept 1 Beetle,**
2000s. Matchbox. NM - **$12**

❑ **SPO-6. Alarm Clock,**
2000s. Figure sits above LED clock. NM - **$28**

SPO-7

❑ **SPO-7. CD Karaoke Machine,**
2000s. NM - **$80**

SPO-8

SPO-9

❑ **SPO-8. Valentine Hat Candy Buddy,**
2000s. NM - **$3**

❑ **SPO-9. Santa Hat Candy Buddy,**
2000s. NM - **$3**

SPO-10

SPO-11

❑ **SPO-10. Pirate Hat Candy Buddy,**
2000s. NM - **$3**

❑ **SPO-11. Sheriff Hat Candy Buddy,**
2000s. NM - **$3**

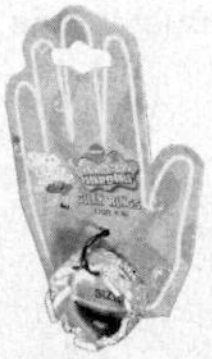

SPO-12

SPO-13

❑ **SPO-12. Silly Ring on Card,**
2000s. Epoxy ring on hand-shaped card. NM - **$12**

❑ **SPO-13. Silly Rings on Card,**
2000s. Epoxy rings featuring Sponge Bob and Sandy. Rings have adjustable bands. NM - **$12**

SPO-14

SPO-15

❑ **SPO-14. 100 Piece Puzzle,**
2000s. Shows SpongeBob blowing bubble rings. NM - **$5**

❑ **SPO-15. 100 Piece Puzzle,**
2000s. Shows SpongeBob flipping burgers at the Krusty Krab. NM - **$5**

SPO-16

SPO-17

SPO-18

❑ **SPO-16. Matchbox Vehicle Set,**
2000s. 5 die-cast cars and trucks. NM - **$10**

❑ **SPO-17. Great Smile Gift Set,**
2000s. Contains a 2 minute timer and 2 toothbrushes. NM - **$15**

❑ **SPO-18. Caramel Popcorn Tin,**
2000s. NM - **$5**

SPO-19

SPO-20

❑ **SPO-19. Cereal Box,**
2003. Kellogg's. NM - **$4**

❑ **SPO-20. Cheez-It Cracker Box,**
2003. NM - **$3**

SPO-21

SPO-22

❑ **SPO-21. Holiday Ornament,**
2003. NM In Box - **$5**

❑ **SPO-22. Plastic Drink Container,**
2004. NM - **$5**

Spy Smasher

Playboy Alan Armstrong took on the identity of *Spy Smasher* to battle America's domestic enemies for Fawcett Publications during World War II. The caped crusader made his debut in *Whiz Comics* #1 in 1940, had his own comic book from 1941 to 1943, made a brief appearance as *Crime Smasher* in 1948, and finally was allowed to expire in 1953. Republic Pictures released a 12-episode chapter play in 1942 starring Kane Richmond in a life-and-death struggle against Nazi agents. Like Captain Marvel, the Marvel Family and the rest of the Fawcett Characters, Spy Smasher is now the property of DC Comics. He resurfaced on the cover of *The Power of Shazam* #24 (1997).

SPY-1

SPY-2

❑ **SPY-1. Fawcett Picture,**
c. 1941. Title inscription "Hero Of Whiz Comics And Spy Smasher Comics". - **$125 $250 $400**

❑ **SPY-2. "I Am A Spy Smasher" Litho. Button,**
c. 1941. For comic book club member. - **$15 $25 $60**

SPY-3

SPY-4

❑ **SPY-3. "Spy Smasher" Argentine 27x41" Movie Serial Paper Poster,**
1942. - **$100 $200 $350**

❑ **SPY-4. "Spy Smasher" 27x41" Movie Serial Poster,**
1942. Republic Pictures. - **$275 $550 $1200**

SPY-5

❑ **SPY-5. Movie Three-Sheet,**
1942. Republic Pictures serial. Rare. - **$2500 $6500 $10,000**

SPY-6

❑ **SPY-6. "Spy Smasher" Lobby Cards,**
1942. Republic Pictures. Pair of 11x14" cards in greentone, one for Chapter 2 and the other for Chapter 11. Each - **$35 $65 $100**

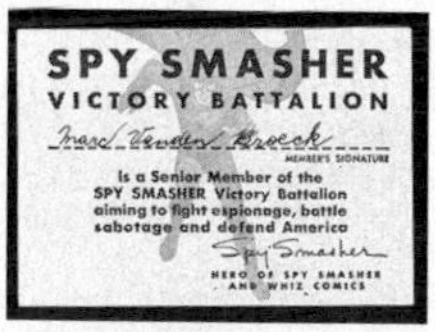

SPY-7

❑ **SPY-7. "Victory Batallion" Member Card,**
c. 1942. Fawcett Publications. - **$125 $250 $500**

Star Trek

The *Star Trek* phenomenon originated with the futuristic TV series created by Gene Roddenberry (1921-1991) that aired on NBC from 1966 to 1969, and has grown over the years into an international community of devoted fans, generating four additional TV series, eight movies, dozens of books, comic books, an animated cartoon, countless Trekkie conventions, and millions of dollars in licensed merchandise.

On television *Star Trek* was followed by *Star Trek: The Animated Series* (1973), *Star Trek:*

The Next Generation (1987), *Star Trek: Deep Space Nine* (1993), *Star Trek: Voyager* (1995), and *Enterprise* (2001). The first movie--*Star Trek-The Motion Picture* (1979)--was followed by *Star Trek II: The Wrath of Khan* (1982), *Star Trek III: The Search for Spock* (1984), *Star Trek IV: The Voyage Home* (1986), *Star Trek V: The Final Frontier* (1989), *Star Trek VI: The Undiscovered Country* (1991), *Star Trek: Generations* (1994), *Star Trek: First Contact* (1996), *Star Trek: Insurrection* (1998), and *Star Trek: Nemesis* (2003). Captain Kirk (William Shatner) has been succeeded by Captain Picard (Patrick Stewart), Captain Sisko (Avery Brooks), Captain Janeway (Kate Mulgrew), and Captain Archer (Scott Bakula). Spock (Leonard Nimoy) joins a new cast of actors portraying the original crew (including a young Spock as well) as the early adventures of the U.S.S. Enterprise come to the big screen in May 2009. Paramount Pictures holds the copyright.

STR-1

❑ **STR-1. TV Show Debut Poster,**
1966. 22x28" paper colorful design plus bottom margin text "Adventures In Space/William Shatner Stars/Thursday At 8:30 PM" plus local TV station logo. - **$375 $750 $1500**

STR-2

❑ **STR-2. "Star Trek Rapid-Fire Tracer Gun,"**
1967. Store item by Ray Plastic Inc.
Carded - **$15 $30 $75**

STR-3

❑ **STR-3. Game,**
1967. Store item by Ideal. - **$75 $150 $300**

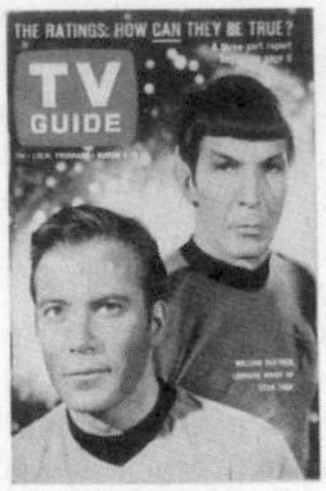

STR-4

STR-5

❑ **STR-4. "TV Guide" Weekly Issue,**
1967. Volume 15 #9 from March 4.
Without Mailing Label - **$20 $40 $85**
With Mailing Label - **$12 $30 $50**

❑ **STR-5. Pencil Tablet,**
c. 1967. Store item. 8x10" with glossy color cover. - **$15 $30 $60**

STR-6

❑ **STR-6. Domed Metal Lunch Box,**
1968. Store item by Aladdin. Came with lunch bottle not shown. Box - **$500 $1000 $2000**
Bottle - **$110 $215 $425**

STR-7

❑ **STR-7. "Star Trek View-Master" Set,**
1968. Complete With Booklet - **$18 $35 $70**

STR-8

❑ **STR-8. "Capt. Kirk" Mego Action Figure,**
1974. 8" tall poseable figure on blister card.
- **$20 $50 $75**

STR-9

❑ **STR-9. "Mr. Spock" Mego Action Figure,**
1974. 8" tall poseable figure on blister card.
- **$25 $50 $100**

STR-10

❑ **STR-10. "Dr. McCoy (Bones)" Mego Action Figure,**
1974. 8" tall poseable figure on blister card.
- **$25 $50 $100**

STR-11

❑ **STR-11. "Mr. Scott (Scottie)" Mego Action Figure,**
1974. 8" tall poseable figure on blister card.
- **$25 $50 $100**

STR-12

❑ **STR-12. "Klingon" Mego Action Figure,**
1974. 8" tall poseable figure on blister card.
- **$20 $50 $75**

STR-13

❑ **STR-13. Colorforms Adventure Set,**
1975. Store item. 8x12-1/2x1" deep box with thin diecut vinyl pieces for creating scenes. - **$15 $35 $70**

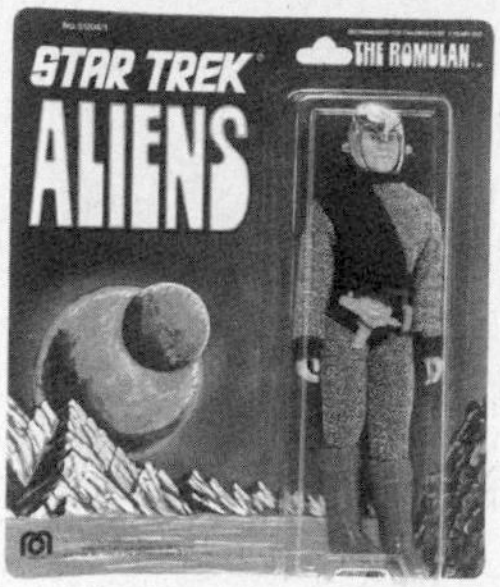

STR-14

❑ **STR-14. "Star Trek Aliens-The Romulan" Mego Action Figure,**
1976. Blister card is 8.5x9.25" and contains 8" tall poseable figure. Near Mint Carded - **$1450**

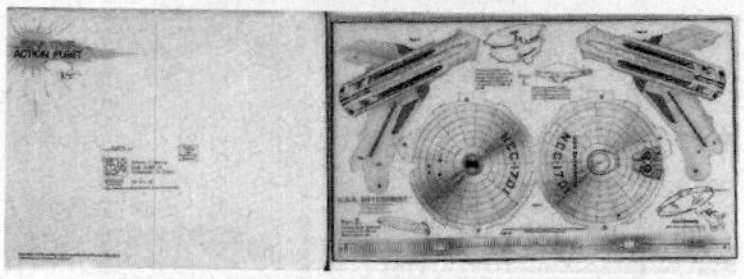

STR-15

❑ **STR-15. Action Fleet Punch-Out Mobile,**
1978. M&M/Mars Inc. Includes six punch-out sheets, instruction sheet, poster.
In Envelope - **$25 $45 $75**

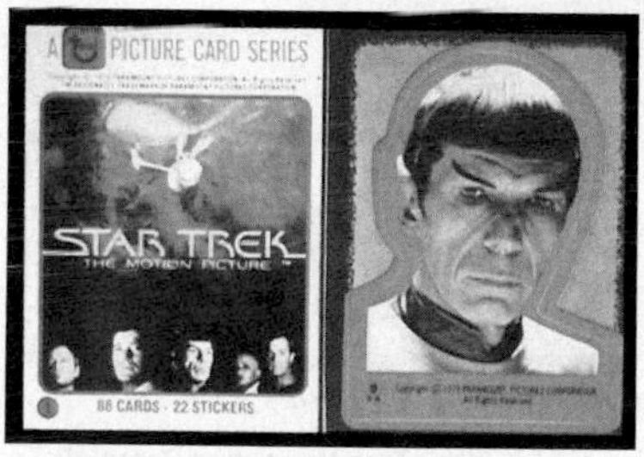

STR-16

❑ **STR-16. "Star Trek The Motion Picture" Card And Sticker Set,**
1979. Store item by Topps Gum. Set of 88 cards and 22 unused stickers.
Near Mint Complete - **$40**

STR-17

❑ **STR-17. "Star Trek The Motion Picture" Premium Card Set,**
1979. Same cards as in standard set of this title but only 33 and these were offered by various bread companies. This example has "Rainbo." Backs feature text and repeated cast photo, none with puzzle backs. Near Mint Set - **$35**

STR-18

❑ **STR-18. Star Trek USS Enterprise Dinky,**
1979. Paramount Pictures Corp. 7.75x10x4.25" deep box contains 9.25" long die-cast metal replica featuring disk-firing action and opening bay doors which release a shuttle. Hang tag features photos of Mr. Spock and Captain Kirk. Dinky No. 358. Box - **$25 $50 $75**
Toy - **$25 $50 $75**

STR-19

STR-20

❑ **STR-19. "The Bridge" McDonald's Meal Box,**
1979. Two versions: Reverse panel pictures Mr. Spock or Dr. McCoy. Unused/Flat - **$5 $12 $30**

❑ **STR-20. "Spacesuit" McDonald's Meal Box,**
1979. Unused/Flat - **$5 $12 $30**

STR-21

STR-22

❑ **STR-21. "Klingons" McDonald's Meal Box,**
1979. Unused/Flat - **$5 $12 $30**

❑ **STR-22. "Transporter" McDonald's Meal Box,**
1979. Unused Flat - **$5 $12 $30**

STR-23

STR-24

❑ **STR-23. "United Federation Of Planets" McDonald's Meal Box,**
1979. Unused/Flat - **$5 $12 $30**

❑ **STR-24. McDonald's Plastic Secret Compartment Ring,**
1979. Set of four: Kirk, Spock, U.S.S. Enterprise, insignia. Each - **$12 $25 $40**

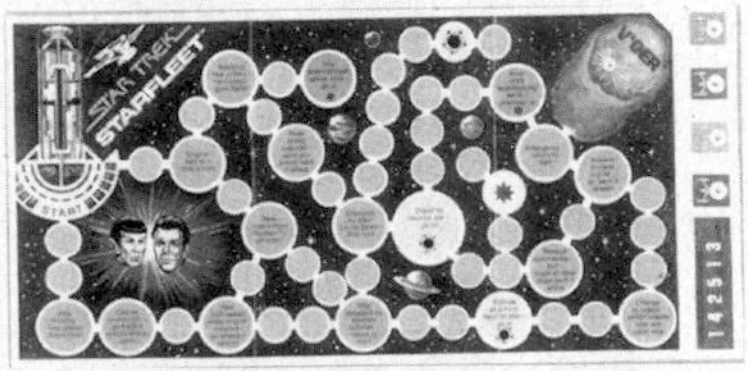

STR-25

❑ **STR-25. Star Fleet Game,**
1979. McDonald's. - **$5 $8 $15**

STR-26

❑ **STR-26. Matches,**
1979. Promo for *Star Trek-The Motion Picture.* Premium offer inside. - **$10 $15 $30**

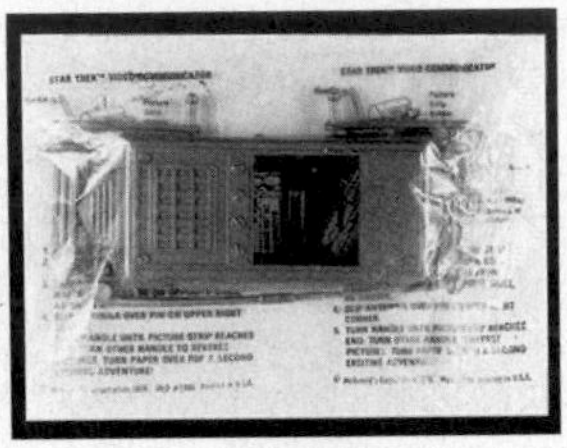

STR-27

❑ **STR-27. "Star Trek Video Communicator" Packaged Toy,**
1979. McDonald's Happy Meals. Unopened packet contains 4" plastic toy with full color picture strip from series of five.
Each Sealed - **$3 $6 $12**
Each Loose - **$1 $3 $6**

STR-28

❑ **STR-28. "Star Trek Navigation Bracelet" Toy,**
1979. McDonald's Happy Meals. Unopened packet containing 9" plastic bracelet plus sheet with color portrait stickers, paper scene strip for bracelet viewer. Sealed - **$3 $6 $12**
Loose - **$1 $3 $6**

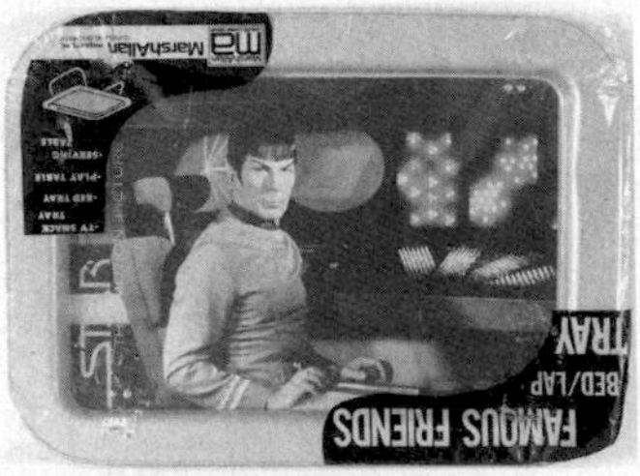

STR-29

❑ **STR-29. TV Tray Featuring Spock,**
1979. 12.5x17.5" metal tray with folding legs. - **$30 $60 $120**

STR-30

❑ **STR-30. Spoon Premium,**
1970s. - **$35 $45 $75**

STR-31

STR-32

❑ **STR-31. Twentieth Anniversary 3" Plastic Badge,**
1986. - **$5 $10 $20**

❑ **STR-32. Pocket Books 2-1/4" Tin Tab,**
1986. - **$10 $15 $30**

STR-33

❑ **STR-33. Cheerios Box With First Promotion For Star Trek The Next Generation,**
1987. Boxes contained six different sticker portraits to determine winners of 75,000 replicas of Enterprise (4" pale blue vinyl) by Galoob.
Box - **$40 $85 $185**
Each Sticker - **$5 $10 $25**
Replica - **$75 $150 $300**

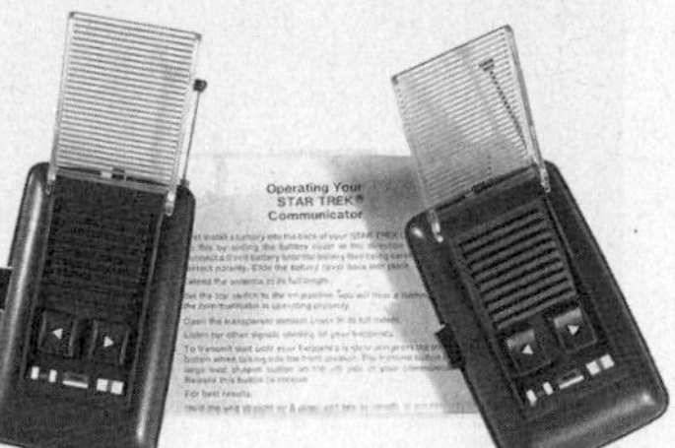

STR-34

❑ **STR-34. Walkie-Talkie Communicators,**
1989. P.J. McNerney & Associates. *Star Trek V* film tie-in offered by Procter & Gamble. Also came with instruction sheet. - **$40 $90 $175**

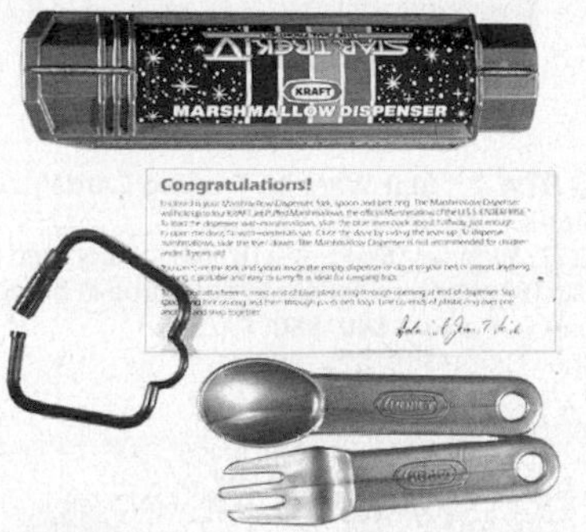

STR-35

❑ **STR-35. Marshmallow Dispenser and Utensils,**
1989. Kraft premium offered in conjunction with *Star Trek V.* Includes plastic dispenser, fork, spoon, and belt hook. Letter signed by "Admiral James T. Kirk" congratulates recipient. - **$20 $35 $90**

STR-36

❑ **STR-36. Sign,**
1991. Space exploration stamp promo. Also promotes *Star Trek VI.* - **$25 $50 $100**

STR-37

STR-38

❑ **STR-37. Deep Space 9 Figural Premium Ink Stamps,**
1993. Canadian issued by Nabisco Shreddies. Stamps are: Odo, Cardassian, Quark and Kira. Set - **$10 $18 $35**

❑ **STR-38. Movie Promo I.D. Pass,**
1997. - **$5 $10 $20**

STR-39

STR-40

❑ **STR-39. "Andorian" Bean Bag Alien,**
1998. With tag. - **$10**

❑ **STR-40. "Ferengi" Bean Bag Alien,**
1998. With tag. - **$10**

STR-41

STR-42

❑ **STR-41. "Gorn" Bean Bag Alien,**
1998. With tag. - **$10**

❑ **STR-42. "Mugato" Bean Bag Alien,**
1998. With tag. - **$15**

STR-43

STR-44

❑ **STR-43. "Romulan" Bean Bag Alien,**
1998. With tag. - **$10**

❑ **STR-44. "Targ" Bean Bag Alien,**
1998. Klingon pet. With tag. - **$10**

STR-45

❑ **STR-45. Star Trek Monopoly Game,**
2000. Limited Edition version. 8 pewter figures included. - **$60**

STR-46

❑ **STR-46. Movie Giveaway Badge,**
1998. - **$3 $6 $12**

Star Wars

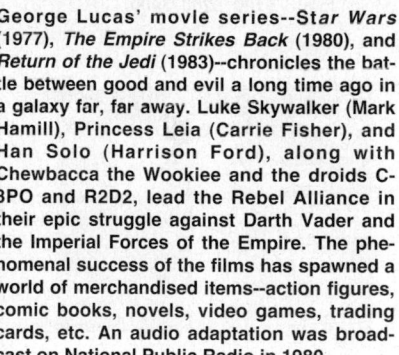

George Lucas' movie series--*Star Wars* (1977), *The Empire Strikes Back* (1980), and *Return of the Jedi* (1983)--chronicles the battle between good and evil a long time ago in a galaxy far, far away. Luke Skywalker (Mark Hamill), Princess Leia (Carrie Fisher), and Han Solo (Harrison Ford), along with Chewbacca the Wookiee and the droids C-3PO and R2D2, lead the Rebel Alliance in their epic struggle against Darth Vader and the Imperial Forces of the Empire. The phenomenal success of the films has spawned a world of merchandised items--action figures, comic books, novels, video games, trading cards, etc. An audio adaptation was broadcast on National Public Radio in 1980.

The movies were digitally remastered for home video in 1995, and enhanced versions of the films were re-released theatrically as "Special Editions" in 1997, with additional scenes and all-new special effects. These releases were the prelude to the first new Star Wars films in fifteen years--"Episode I" of the Star Wars saga debuted in May 1999 to huge box office success, with two sequels to follow (the original trilogy serves as Episodes IV-VI). *Star Wars – Episode I: The Phantom Menace* earned more than $430 Million at the U.S. box office, while *Star Wars – Episode II: Attack of the Clones* brought in more than $300 Million. The concluding episode of the first arc, *Star Wars: Episode III - Revenge of the Sith,* came out in 2005. A *Clone Wars* cartoon "micro series" has also proven popular.

STW-1

❑ STW-1. "Star Wars" Style "A" Original Poster,
1977. Twentieth Century Fox Film Corp. 27x41" one-sheet numbered 77-21-0 is a first printing of style A "Star Wars" poster. Posters were released both rolled and folded and printed on heavy paper stock. Soundtrack is mentioned but not the later edition that was produced for record stores. Poster has appropriate NSS exhibition notice, a sharp and clear GAU image and the 1977 copyright notice is correctly indented. Background shows C-3PO and R2-D2 in early design form. - **$100 $200 $400**

STW-2

❑ STW-2. Lucky Charms Box,
1977. General Mills. Offers four "Character Stick-ons". Complete - **$50 $75 $175**

STW-3

❑ STW-3. Cocoa Puffs Box,
1977. General Mills. Offers four "Robot" stick-ons. Complete - **$50 $75 $175**

STW-4

❑ STW-4. Trix Box,
1977. General Mills. Offers four "Creature" stick-ons. Complete - **$50 $75 $175**

STW-5

❑ STW-5. Cantina Adventure Set,
1977. Store item by Kenner. Sears Exclusive version with blue Snaggletooth figure.
- **$200 $400 $800**

STW-6

❑ STW-6. Boxed Ring Set,
1977. Store item. 20th Century Fox Film Corp. copyright depicting R2-D2, Darth Vader, C-3PO.
Near Mint Boxed Set - **$28**
Each - **$3 $5 $8**

STW-7

❑ STW-7. "Star Wars 16 Trading Cards" Signs,
1977. Wonder Bread. 12x16" poster sign and 5-1/2x18" shelf sign for cards packaged in bread loaves. Poster - **$40 $80 $175**
Shelf Card - **$10 $25 $50**

STW-8

STW-9

❑ STW-8. "Star Wars" First Series Card Set With Box,
1977. Store item by Topps. Cards #1-66 and stickers #1-11. Box - **$3 $5 $10**
Near Mint Cards And Sticker Set - **$25**

❑ STW-9. "Star Wars" Second Series Card Set,
1977. Store item by Topps. Cards are #67-132 and stickers are #12-22.
Box (Not Shown) - **$3 $5 $10**
Near Mint Cards And Sticker Set - **$25**

STW-10

STW-11

❑ **STW-10. "Star Wars" Third Series Card Set,**
1977. Store item by Topps. Cards are #133-198 and stickers are #23-33. Box - **$3 $5 $10**
Near Mint Cards And Sticker Set - **$25**

❑ **STW-11. "Star Wars" Fourth Series Card Set,**
1977. Store item by Topps. Cards are #199-264 and stickers are #33-44. Box - **$3 $5 $10**
Near Mint Cards And Sticker Set - **$25**

STW-12

STW-13

❑ **STW-12. "Star Wars" Fifth Series Card Set,**
1977. Store item by Topps. Cards are #265-330 and stickers are #45-55. Box - **$3 $5 $10**
Near Mint Cards And Sticker Set - **$20**

❑ **STW-13. C-3PO Model Kit,**
1977. Store item by MPC.
Near Mint Boxed - **$75**

STW-14

STW-15

❑ **STW-14. R2-D2 Model Kit,**
1977. Store item by MPC.
Near Mint Boxed - **$75**

❑ **STW-15. "Star Wars Gredo" Action Figure,**
1977. Store item by Kenner. Card is 21 back.
Carded - **$75 $150 $300**

STW-16

❑ **STW-16. Luke Skywalker Blonde Hair Action Figure,**
1977. By Kenner Toys. Card is 21 back - **$50 $125 $250**

STW-17

STW-18

❑ **STW-17. Luke Skywalker Large Action Figure,**
1978. Store item by Kenner. Poseable figure is 12" tall. Near Mint Boxed - **$400**
Loose Complete - **$75 $125 $250**

❑ **STW-18. Chewbacca Large Action Figure,**
1978. Store item by Kenner. 12" tall.
Near Mint Boxed - **$200**
Loose Complete - **$25 $50 $100**

STW-19

STW-20

❑ **STW-19. Princess Leia Organa Large Size Action Figure,**
1978. Store item by Kenner. Box holds 12" poseable figure. Near Mint Boxed - **$250**
Loose Complete - **$35 $70 $125**

❑ **STW-20. Darth Vader Large Action Figure,**
1978. Store item by Kenner. 15" tall poseable figure. Near Mint Boxed - **$600**
Loose - **$50 $150 $250**

STW-21

❑ **STW-21. "Star Wars R2-D2" Missile-Firing Japanese Figure,**
1978. Store item issued only in Japan by "Takara." 3" tall die cast metal and plastic figure with plastic sprue holding three missiles. Comes with sheet of accent stickers.
Near Mint Boxed - **$375**
Used Complete - **$75 $150 $275**

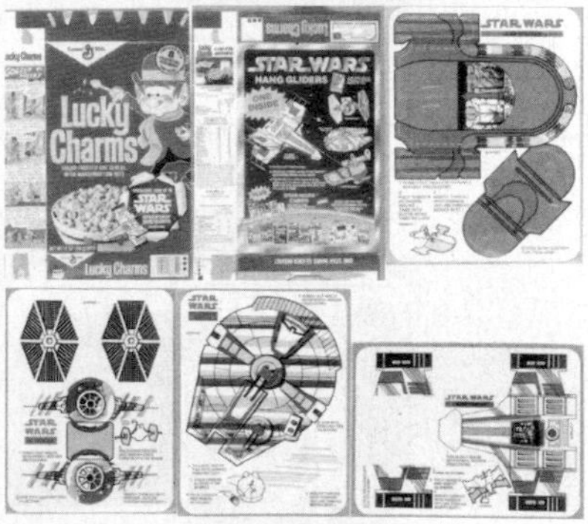

STW-22

❑ **STW-22. Lucky Charms Cereal Box With Hang Gliders Offer,**
1978. Boxes included four different punch-outs.
Complete Box - **$50 $75 $175**
Punch-Outs Each - **$10 $20 $50**

STW-23

❑ **STW-23. "Ben Kenobi" Figure On Card,**
1978. Card is 12 back. - **$200 $400 $800**

STW-24

❑ **STW-24. "C3PO" Figure On Card,**
1978. Card is 12 back. - **$125 $225 $400**

STW-25

❑ **STW-25. "Chewbacca" Figure On Card,**
1978. Card is 12 back. - **$125 $225 $400**

STW-26

❑ **STW-26. "Darth Vader" Figure On Card,**
1978. Card is 12 back. - **$275 $625 $900**

STW-27

❑ **STW-27. "Death Squad Commander" Figure On Card,**
1978. Card is 12 back. - **$110 $225 $350**

STW-28

❑ **STW-28. "Han Solo" Figure On Card,**
1978. Card is 12 back. - **$250 $500 $1000**

STW-29

STW-30

❑ **STW-29. "Jawa" Figure With Vinyl Cape On Card,**
1978. Card is 12 back. - **$1250 $2500 $5000**

❑ **STW-30. "Jawa" Figure With Cloth Cape On Card,**
1978. Card is 12 back. - **$75 $150 $300**

STW-31

❑ **STW-31. "Luke Skywalker" Figure On Card,**
1978. Card is 12 back. - **$275 $625 $900**

STW-32

❑ **STW-32. "Princess Leia" Figure On Card,**
1978. Card is 12 back. - **$200 $400 $800**

STW-33

❑ **STW-33. "R2D2" Figure On Card,**
1978. Card is 12 back. - **$125 $225 $400**

STW-34

❑ **STW-34. "Sand People" Figure On Card,**
1978. Card is 12 back. - **$125 $225 $400**

STW-35

❑ **STW-35. "Stormtrooper" Figure On Card,**
1978. Card is 12 back. - **$125 $225 $400**

STW-36

❑ STW-36. "Star Wars Weekly" Vol. 1 #1,
February 8, 1978. English edition by Marvel Comics International. - **$10 $30 $60**

STW-37

❑ STW-37. "Official Star Wars Fan Club" Button Set,
1978. 20th Century Fox. Set of 14, each 1-1/2", picturing 12 characters, George Lucas and title design. Set - **$30 $60 $180**

STW-38

❑ STW-38. Procter & Gamble 19x20" Paper Posters,
1978. Set of three. Set - **$15 $30 $60**

STW-39

❑ STW-39. Creature Cantina Action Playset,
1979. Store item by Kenner.
Near Mint Boxed - **$135**
Complete Unboxed - **$10 $20 $30**

STW-40

❑ STW-40. "Star Wars Radio Controlled Jawa Sand Crawler" Vehicle,
1979. Kenner. 9x17x7" box contains 16" long Jawa Sand Crawler with elevator, opening side panel and a radio control unit.
Near Mint Boxed - **$600**
Complete Unboxed - **$50 $100 $200**

STW-41 STW-42

❑ STW-41. Ben Kenobi Large Action Figure,
1979. 12" tall poseable figure store item by Kenner. Near Mint Boxed - **$350**
Loose Complete - **$115**

❑ STW-42. Boba Fett Large Action Figure,
1979. Store item by Kenner. 13" tall poseable figure. Near Mint Boxed - **$550**
Loose - **$50 $100 $200**

STW-43 STW-44

❑ STW-43. Jawa Large Action Figure,
1979. Store item by Kenner. 8" tall poseable figure. Near Mint Boxed - **$200**
Loose - **$15 $30 $60**

❑ STW-44. "Stormtrooper" Large Size Action Figure,
1979. Store item by Kenner. Figure is 12" tall.
Near Mint Boxed - **$275**
Loose - **$35 $65 $100**

STW-45

❑ STW-45. "Star Wars Action Figures" Store Display Sign,
1979. Kenner. 18.25x20.5" two-sided diecut stiff cardboard printed identically on each side including photos of the original "12" and "9 New" action figures for "Collect All 21" set. - **$150 $300 $500**

STW-46

❑ STW-46. "The Empire Strikes Back" Cards,
1980. Burger King. Set of 36.
Set - **$10 $20 $40**

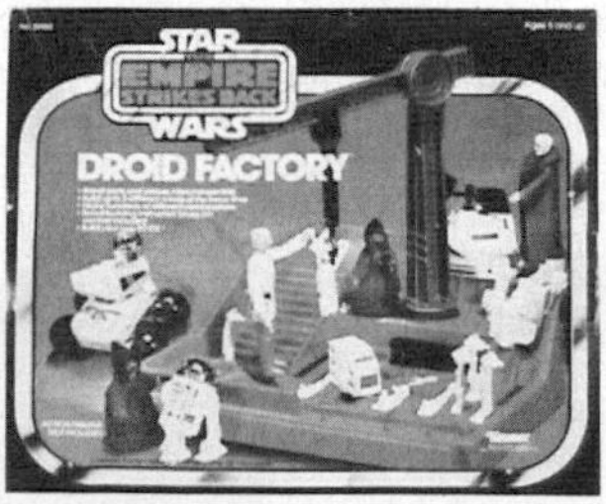

STW-47

❑ STW-47. Droid Factory,
1980. Store item by Kenner.
Near Mint Boxed - **$150**
Complete Unboxed - **$12 $25 $50**

STW-48

❑ **STW-48. Official Wrist Watch,**
1980. Store item by Bradley.
Near Mint Boxed - **$125**
Loose - **$15 $25 $50**

STW-49

STW-50

❑ **STW-49. Radio Promotion Cello. Button,**
1981. National Public Radio/KBPS. Lucasfilms copyright. - **$10 $20 $40**

❑ **STW-50. Record Tote,**
1982. Includes seal inside with index card. - **$12 $25 $50**

STW-51

❑ **STW-51. "3-D Electronic Quartz Clock",**
1982. Store item by Bradley.
Near Mint Boxed - **$135**
Loose - **$15 $25 $60**

STW-52

STW-53

❑ **STW-52. "Star Wars IG-88" Action Figure,**
1982. Kenner. "Empire Strikes Back" card is 48 back variety with front and back stickers advertising "Revenge Of The Jedi" Admiral Ackbar mail offer figure. Near Mint On Card - **$300**

❑ **STW-53. "Revenge Of The Jedi" Incorrect Movie Title Button,**
c. 1982. 20th-Century Fox. Red on black cello for original movie title changed prior to film release to "Return Of The Jedi." - **$10 $20 $30**

STW-54

❑ **STW-54. Ewok Combat Glider,**
1983. Store item by Kenner.
Near Mint Boxed - **$50**
Near Mint Loose - **$15**

STW-55

❑ **STW-55. "Return of the Jedi" Poster,**
1983. 17-1/2x22" premium promotional poster from Oral B Star Wars Toothbrush. Shows set of six at bottom with coupons. Poster With Coupons - **$15 $25 $65**
Without Coupons - **$5 $10 $20**

STW-56

STW-57

❑ **STW-56. Cookie Box,**
1983. Pepperidge Farms.
Complete - **$15 $25 $60**

❑ **STW-57. "Return of the Jedi" Soundtrack,**
1983. Original soundtrack with 16 page color souvenir photo book. Complete - **$35**

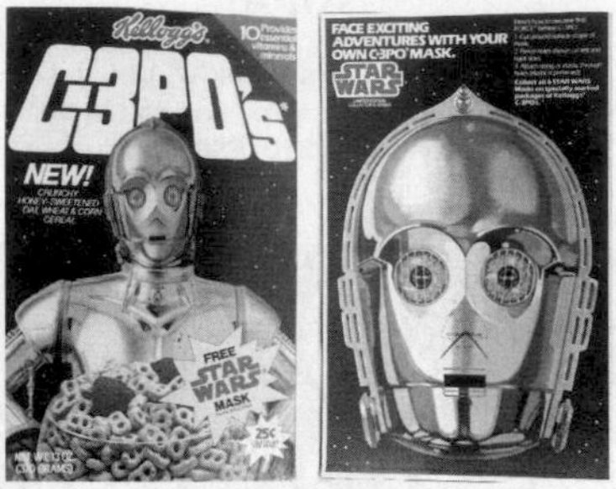

STW-58

❑ **STW-58. "C-3PO's" Cereal Box with Star Wars C-3PO Mask,**
1984. - **$15 $45 $80**

STW-59

❑ **STW-59. "C-3PO's" Cereal Box with Star Wars Luke Skywalker Mask,**
1984. - **$15 $45 $80**

STW-60

❑ **STW-60. "C-3PO's" Cereal Box with Star Wars Stormtrooper Mask,**
1984. - **$15 $45 $80**

STW-61

❑ **STW-61. "Sci-Fi Channel Star Wars" Limited Edition Watch,**
1992. Given to executives for the launch of the Sci-Fi Channel on 9/24/92 which premiered with the showing of Star Wars. Case reverse is marked "Manufactured By Fantasma."
Near Mint Boxed - **$250**

STW-62

❑ **STW-62. "Apple Jacks" Cereal Box with Star Wars Droids Comic Strip on Back,**
1995. Dark Horse Comics. - **$8 $12 $30**

STW-63

❑ **STW-63. "Froot Loops" Cereal Box with Star Wars Action Figure Offer on Back,**
1995. Han Solo as Stormtrooper. - **$8 $12 $30**

STW-64

❑ **STW-64. "Raisin Bran" Cereal Box with Star Wars Videos Rebate Offer on Back,**
1995. Original movie versions. - **$8 $12 $30**

STW-65

❑ **STW-65. "Star Wars" Pop-Up Book,**
1995. - **$8 $16 $30**

STW-66

❑ **STW-66. "Star Wars" Monopoly Game,**
1997. Limited colector's edition. - **$60**

STW-67

STW-68

❑ **STW-67. "C-3PO" Bean Figure with Tag,**
1997. Series 1. - **$25**

❑ **STW-68. "R2-D2" Bean Figure with Tag,**
1997. Series 1. - **$20**

STW-69

STW-70

❑ **STW-69. "Yoda" Bean Figure with Tag,**
1997. Series 1. - **$20**

❑ **STW-70. "Chewbacca" Bean Figure with Tag,**
1997. Series 1. Figure has brown belt. - **$25**

STW-71

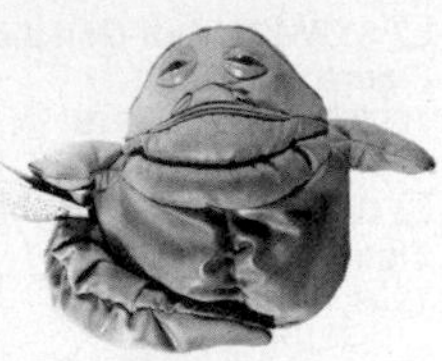

STW-72

❑ **STW-71. "Salacious Crumb" Bean Figure with Tag,**
1997. Series 1. - **$10**

❑ **STW-72. "Jabba the Hutt" Bean Figure with Tag,**
1997. Series 1. - **$15**

STW-73

STW-74

❑ **STW-73. "Jawa" Bean Figure with Tag,**
1997. Series 1. - **$15**

❑ **STW-74. "Wampa" Bean Figure with Tag,**
1997. Series 1. - **$15**

STW-75

STW-76

❑ **STW-75. "Wicket the Ewok" Bean Figure with Tag,**
1997. Series 1. - **$15**

❑ **STW-76. "D'An" Bean Figure with Tag,**
1998. Series 1. - **$12**

STW-77

STW-78

❑ **STW-77. "Qui-Gon Jinn" Episode 1 Bean Figure with Tag,**
1999. Series 2. - **$10**

❑ **STW-78. "Jar Jar Binks" Episode 1 Bean Figure with Tag,**
1999. Series 2. - **$10**

STW-79

STW-80

❑ **STW-79. "Obi-Wan Kenobi" Episode 1 Bean Figure with Tag,**
1999. Series 2. - **$10**

❑ **STW-80. "Darth Maul" Episode 1 Bean Figure with Tag,**
1999. Series 2. - **$10**

STW-81

STW-82

❑ **STW-81. "Padmé Naberrie" Episode 1 Bean Figure with Tag,**
1999. Series 2. - **$8**

❑ **STW-82. "Watto" Episode 1 Bean Figure with Tag,**
1999. Series 2. - **$10**

STW-83

❑ **STW-83. "Watto" Pepsi Standee,**
1999. Watto was a popular character in *Episode I*, making this standee eagerly sought when it appeared in grocery stores. Hard to find on the secondary market. - **$175**

STW-84

❑ **STW-84. Rebel Command Assault and Communications Set,**
2001. Includes laser guns, targets and walkie talkies. Boxed - **$120**

The Statue of Liberty

The people of France gave the statue to the people of the United States in recognition of their alliance in the Revolutionary War. Commissioned in 1876, America would build the base and France would build the statue for assembly here. Noted sculptor Frederic-Auguste Bartholdi (1834-1923) built the armature framework. The statue was completed in France July, 1884, arrived in New York Harbor June, 1885 and was dedicated by President Grover Cleveland on October 28, 1886 on Fort Wood, now Liberty Island.

The figure is sheathed in 62,000 lbs. of copper with a thickness of two pennies and the concrete foundation weighs 27,000 tons. 25 windows in the crown represent the Earth's gemstones. The seven rays of the statue's spiked crown represent the seven seas and continents. The tablet in her left hand has the date of July 4, 1776 in Roman numerals. Lady Liberty functioned as a working lighthouse from 1886 to 1902. A one-quarter scale model in bronze was given to France in 1889 and is just north of the Eiffel Tower.

Emma Lazarus ended her 1883 poem *The New Colossus* with these words: "Send these, the homeless, tempest-tost to me, I lift my lamp beside the golden door!"

STL-1

❑ **STL-1. Early Statue Of Liberty Multicolor Button,**
1897. Whitehead & Hoag. 1.25" diameter. - **$30 $60 $125**

STL-2

STL-3

❑ **STL-2. Taft Statue Of Liberty Rare Jugate Button,**
1908. 1.75" diameter button considered to be one of the most desirable in the political hobby. - **$1200 $2500 $5000**

❑ **STL-3. "Lincoln-Douglas Debate" 50th Anniversary Pocket Mirror,**
1908. 1.75" diameter celluloid covered mirror with fabric loop. - **$350 $700 $1400**

STL-4

❑ **STL-4. Winsor McCay Political Cartoon Original Art,**
1910s. 11.25x14.5" on illustration board with pen and ink cross-hatching. Signed at lower right corner. Liberty's banner reads "Liberty of the Press" and storm caption is 'Futile Attacks." Unique - **$1750**

STL-5

❑ **STL-5. "I Am An American" Citizen Handbook,**
c. 1920. 4x5.5" handbook with black textured paper cover has 128 pages. Patriotic themes including speeches of Washington, Lincoln, T. Roosevelt and Wilson. - **$5 $10 $20**

STL-6

❑ **STL-6. "We Want Beer" With Statue Of Liberty,**
1932. 1.25" diameter button urging the end of Prohibition. - **$15 $30 $60**

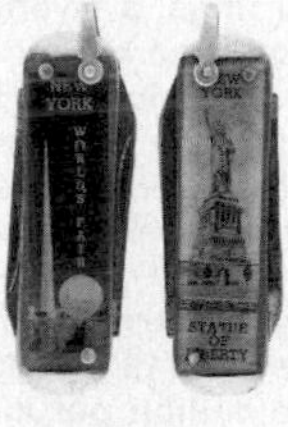

STL-7 STL-8

❑ **STL-7. "Help Spanish Refugees" Statue Of Liberty Pin,**
c. 1937. 5/16x1-1/8" brass pin on original card. Relates to Spanish Civil War 1936-1939. Near Mint Carded - **$100**
Pin Only - **$15 $30 $60**

❑ **STL-8. Rare New York World's Fair Logo And Statue Of Liberty Knife,**
1939. Knife is 2.25" long, two blades. - **$100 $225 $450**

STL-9

❑ **STL-9. Rare Large Victory Button,**
1942. 4" diameter, fraternal lodge issue. - **$30 $60 $125**

STL-10

STL-11

❑ **STL-10. Statue Of Liberty And Uncle Sam Patriotic Button,**
c. 1943. 1" diameter. - **$20 $45 $90**

❑ **STL-11. Statue Of Liberty Theme Large Victory Pin,**
c. 1943. 2.75" tall, 33 rhinestones. - **$50 $100 $150**

STL-12

❑ **STL-12. Family Dog Concert Poster FD-110,**
1968. 13-15/16x19-15/16" first and only printing for March 14-17, 1968 concert at Avalon Ballroom. Art by Stanley Mouse. - **$15 $35 $75**

STL-13

❑ **STL-13. "Soho News" Sign With John Lennon,**
c. 1975. 11x16.75" stiff paper sign advertising New York newspaper and feature story "Exclusive John Lennon's F.B.I. File." - **$30 $65 $125**

STL-14

❑ **STL-14. Suffrage And Equality Button With Statue Of Liberty Crown,**
1978. 3" diameter. - **$25 $50 $100**

STL-15

❑ **STL-15. Brian Campbell's Limited Edition Anti-Bush Button,**
2005. 4" diameter. Reverse sticker marked "49 of 100." Design based on the Monty Python inspired Broadway play Spamalot. Near Mint - **$100**

Steve Canyon

Following his success with *Terry and the Pirates*, Milton Caniff (1907-1988) created his *Steve Canyon* comic strip for distribution by Field Enterprises in 1947. Canyon, who runs a small airline, finds adventure and exotic women in all corners of the globe as he fights criminals and international spies. As the Cold War progresses, he sees service in Korea, Vietnam, and other hot spots, frequently doing battle with dangerous women. Comic books appeared in the late 1940s and 1950s, a radio adaptation with Barry Sullivan was syndicated in 1948, and a TV series with Dean Fredericks aired on NBC in 1958-1959 and was rerun on ABC in 1960. The newspaper strip ended publication in 1988. Items are copyrighted Field Enterprises Inc.

STV-1 STV-2

❑ **STV-1. "Steve Canyon" Newspaper Club Cello. Button,**
c. 1947. New Journal Comic. - **$25 $50 $100**

❑ **STV-2. "Copper Calhoon With Steve Canyon" Newspaper Club Cello. Button,**
c. 1947. New Journal Comic. From same series as preceding item with "Calhoon" name as spelled. - **$15 $35 $85**

STV-3

STV-4

❑ **STV-3. "P.I." Cello. Button,**
c. 1947. - **$45 $80 $150**

❑ **STV-4. "Daily Record/Sunday Advertiser" Cello. Button,**
c. 1950. Various newspapers. - **$50 $90 $160**

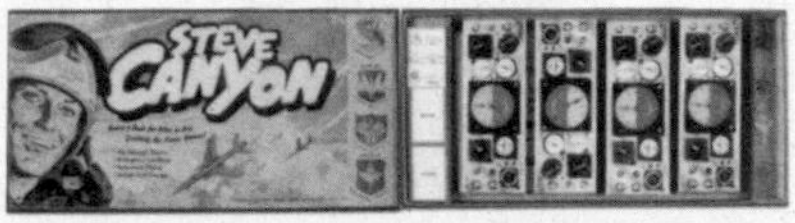

STV-5

❑ **STV-5. "Steve Canyon" Boxed Game,**
1959. Store item by Lowell Toy Mfg. Corp. - **$35 $65 $140**

STV-6

❑ **STV-6. "Steve Canyon And His Friends" Zippered Three-Ring Binder,**
1950s. Binder is 10.25x14" well-made and colorful with stitching along vinyl edges and around zipper. Art is by Milton Caniff. Plastic-coated cover. - **$30 $60 $100**

STV-7

❑ **STV-7. Chesterfield Cigarettes "Meet Steve Canyon-NBC TV" 21x22" Cardboard Store Poster,**
1950s. - **$60 $115 $165**

STV-8

STV-9

❑ **STV-8. "Steve Canyon's Airagers" Wings Litho. Tab,**
1950s. - **$15 $30 $50**

❑ **STV-9. Space Goggles On Picture Card,**
1950s. Store item by Rock Industries. Gold finish slitted plastic goggles of similar nature to sunglasses.
Carded - **$30 $60 $110**

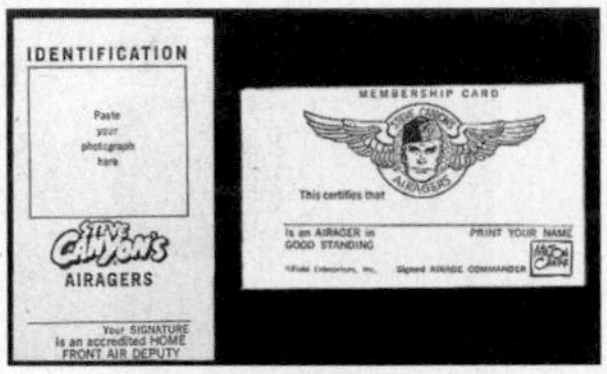

STV-10

❑ **STV-10. "Airager" Membership Card,**
1950s. Reverse has area for member's photograph. - **$15 $25 $50**

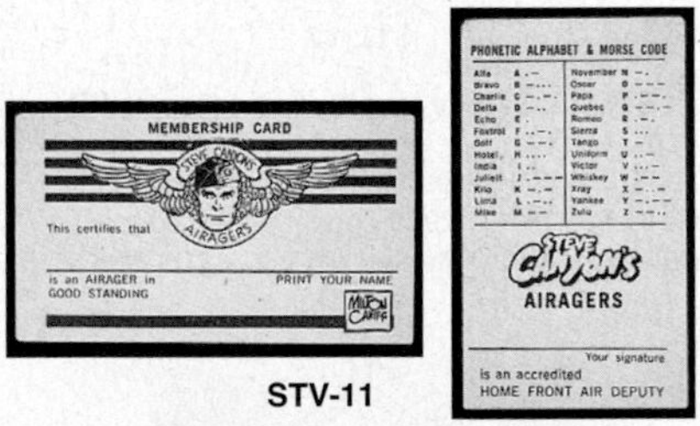

STV-11

❑ **STV-11. Airagers Membership Card,**
1950s. Variety with "Phonetic Alphabet & Morse Code" on reverse. - **$20 $30 $60**

STV-12

❑ **STV-12. Steve Canyon "Your United States" Milk Carton Bank,**
1960s. Sealtest for various school locations. Squared red, white and blue carton includes inscription urging "Stay In School." - **$25 $50 $100**

Straight Arrow

Straight Arrow **was a Western adventure radio series that was broadcast from 1948 to 1951, first on the Don Lee network on the west coast, and starting in 1949 on the Mutual network nationally. The series was created for the National Biscuit Company as a means of promoting Nabisco shredded wheat. Boxtop premiums, on-package items, and retail products were offered in impressive quantities, all related to his scripted adventures.**

Straight Arrow was actually young Steve Adams, owner of the Broken Bow Ranch, until innocent people were threatened or evil-doers plotted against justice. Then Adams would ride to his secret cave, mount his golden palomino Fury, and gallop out of the darkness as Straight Arrow, a Comanche warrior ready to fight for law and order. Howard Culver played Adams, and Fred Howard was his sidekick Packy McCloud.

Among the ***Straight Arrow*** **premiums were several rings, a Mystic Wrist Kit containing an arrowhead and cowrie shell, an arrowhead flashlight, Indian war drum, bandanna, patch, and feathered headband. Sets of Injun-Uity cards, originally packaged in the cereal boxes, were later reissued as bound volumes.**

Straight Arrow **comic books featuring Fred Meagher (1912-1976) art, with sales reaching one million per month, were published by Vincent Sullivan's Magazine Enterprises from 1950 to 1956, many containing advertisements for the program's premiums and other merchandise. A daily newspaper strip distributed by the Bell Syndicate and drawn by John Belfi (1924-1995) appeared from 1950 to 1952. "Kaneewah, Fury!"**

STA-1

❑ **STA-1. Large 20x36" Diecut Cardboard Store Sign,**
1948. Promotes radio series on Mutual Network. - **$800 $1700 $3000**

STA-2

❑ STA-2. Two-Red Feathered Headband With Mailer,
1948. Includes two feathers. A second version has a 1949 copyright and says "Nabisco Shredded Wheat" under portrait.
Near Mint With STA-3 In Mailer - **$300**
Headband Only - **$50 $80 $150**

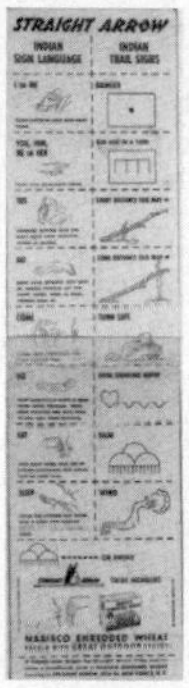

STA-3 STA-4

❑ STA-3. "Indian Sign Language/Indian Trail Signs" Paper,
1948. Came with headband. - **$30 $60 $125**

❑ STA-4. Standee,
1948. 5' 7" tall. Promotes Mutual Network Radio show. - **$1250 $2500 $4000**

STA-5

❑ STA-5. Nabisco Shredded Wheat 4x10" Cardboard Display Sign,
1949. - **$200 $350 $750**

STA-6

❑ STA-6. Radio Broadcast Reminder 12x15" Cardboard Store Sign,
1949. Diecut to extend feathers at top edge. - **$175 $325 $650**

STA-7

❑ STA-7. Store Display Framed Picture,
1949. Nabisco. Display promotion for set of 12 jigsaw puzzles of matching illustrations to the framed pictures. Example pictured is titled "Straight Arrow With Packy And Fury, To The Rescue." - **$50 $75 $165**

STA-8

❑ STA-8. "Book One" Box Insert Cards,
1949. Set of 36. Each - **$1 $2 $4**

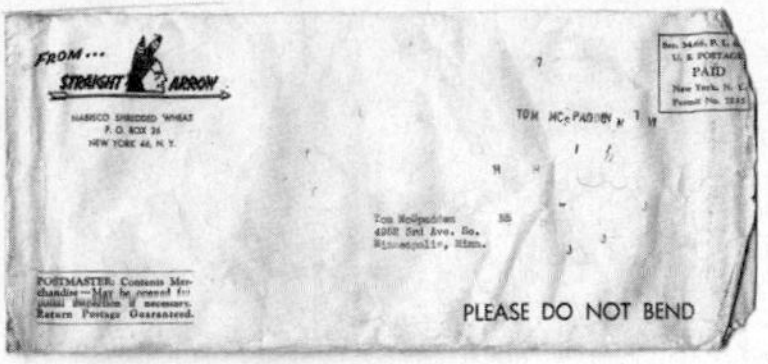

STA-9

❑ STA-9. Mailer For Bandanna and Gold Plated Slide,
1949. - **$30 $60 $90**

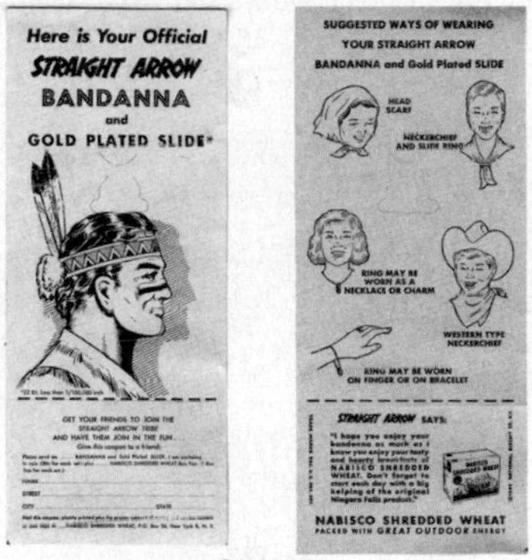

STA-10

❑ STA-10. Instructions For Bandanna and Gold Plated Slide,
1949. Has perforated card to rrecruit friends as club members. Complete - **$50 $100 $125**
Instructions Only - **$15 $30 $60**

STA-11

❑ STA-11. Bandanna,
1949. Near Mint With Mailer, Bandanna, Gold-Plated Slide And Instruction Card - **$400**
Bandanna Only - **$25 $50 $90**

(TOP VIEW)

STA-12

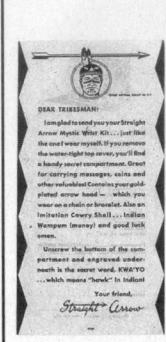

❑ **STA-12. Bandanna Gold Plastic Slide,**
1949. - **$25 $50 $175**

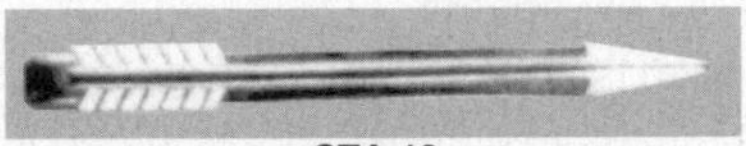

STA-13

❑ **STA-13. Gold Luster Metal Spring Tie Clip,**
1949. Bar image of arrow. - **$50 $100 $200**

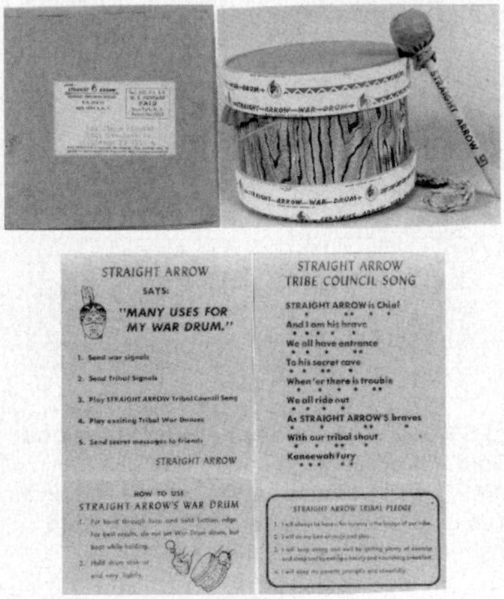

STA-14

❑ **STA-14. War Drum,**
1949. Complete Boxed - **$90 $185 $300**
Drum Only - **$30 $60 $125**

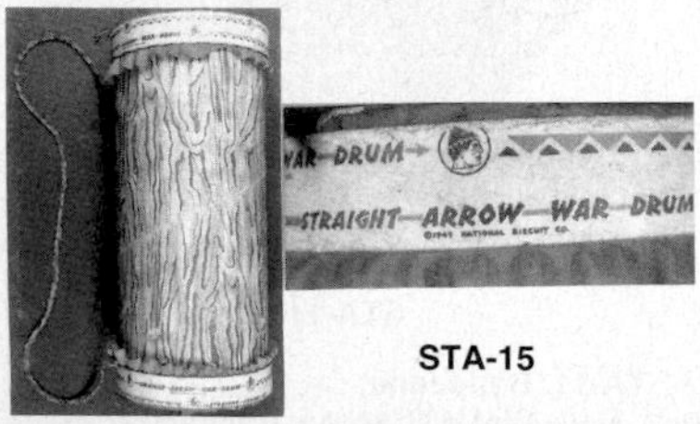

STA-15

❑ **STA-15. War Drum,**
1949. 12" tall cardboard/thin rubber with beater stick. Complete - **$75 $150 $300**

STA-16

❑ **STA-16. Jigsaw Puzzle,**
1949. Set of 12.
Each In Envelope - **$25 $50 $75**
Loose - **$5 $15 $30**
Box For 10 Puzzles (Rare) - **$50 $150 $300**

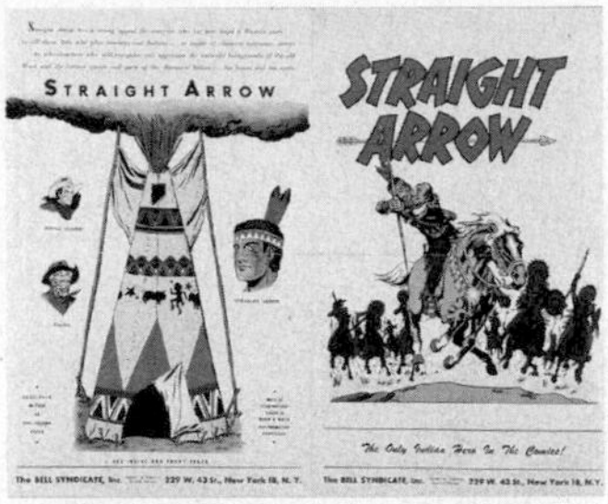

STA-17

❑ **STA-17. Radio/Comic Strip Pressbook,**
1950. Rare. Contains comic strips, list of premiums, sales information. - **$300 $600 $1200**

STA-18

❑ **STA-18. Straight Arrow Coloring Book,**
1950. Premium and store item. -
$40 $125 $250

STA-19

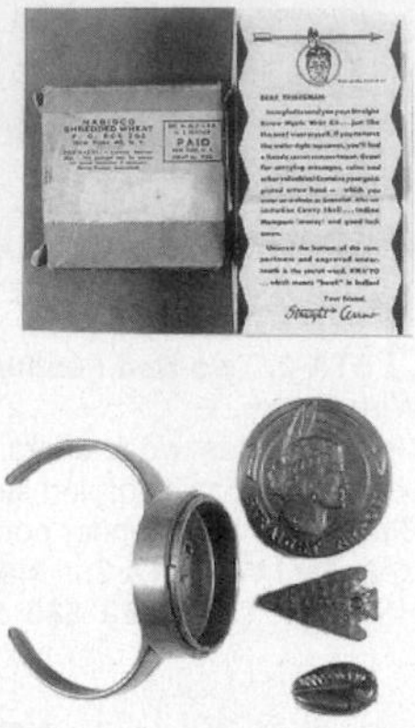

STA-20

❑ **STA-19. Mystic Wrist Kit Instructions,**
1950. Instructions on how to use kit also explains hidden secret word on bottom. -
$20 $40 $85

❑ **STA-20. Mystic Wrist Kit,**
1950. Gold plastic bracelet with container holding arrowhead and cowrie shell.
Near Mint Boxed - **$350**
Bracelet and Parts - **$65 $125 $225**
Insert - **$20 $40 $85**

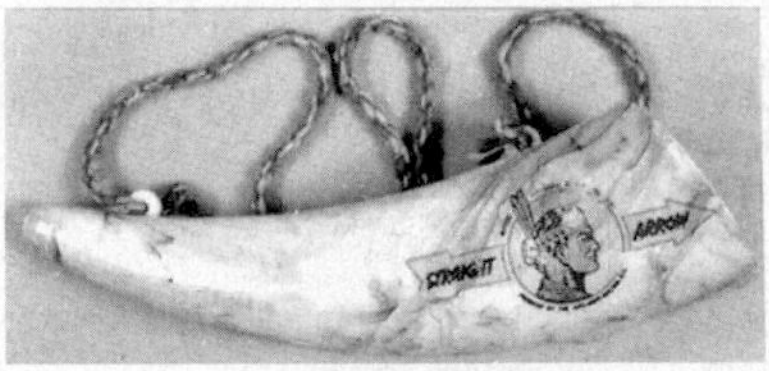

STA-21

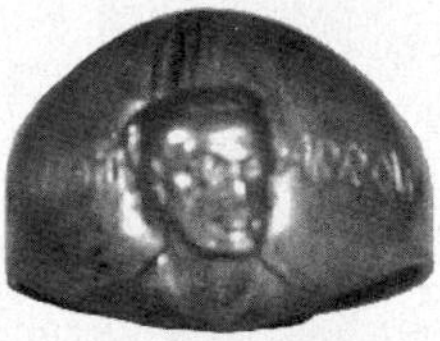

STA-22

❑ **STA-21. Plastic Powder Horn With String Cord,**
1950. - **$75 $160 $375**

❑ **STA-22. Brass Portrait Ring,**
1950. See STA-28. - **$20 $40 $85**

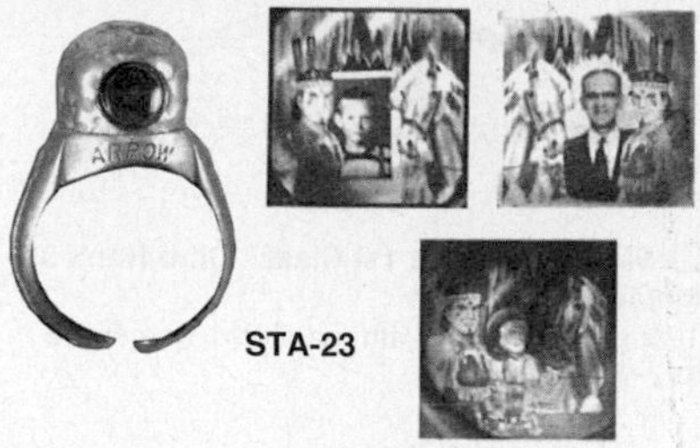

STA-23

❑ STA-23. Golden Nugget Picture Ring,
1950. Gold plastic with view lens holding picture scene within cave interior, also known as "Cave Ring". Four known versions. The adult photo version likely made for Nabisco executives. The Washington Crossing the Delaware painting scene (not shown) was likely a ringmaker's prototype. The other two were Nabisco premiums.
Adult version - **$100 $200 $300**
Washington version - **$65 $125 $250**
Child version - **$50 $100 $190**
Straight Arrow, Pack McCloud, Fury version - **$100 $200 $300**

STA-24

❑ STA-24. "Book 2" Box Insert Cards,
1950. Set of 36. Each - **$1 $2 $4**

STA-25

STA-26

❑ STA-25. Tribal Shoulder Patch,
1950. - **$15 $30 $60**

❑ STA-26. Patch Instructions,
1950. Rare. Tells about patch and how to become a big chief. - **$50 $100 $150**

STA-27

❑ STA-27. Target Game with Box,
1950. Store item. Metal target with bow-like wooden gun launcher to fire "magnetic arrows." - **$125 $225 $400**

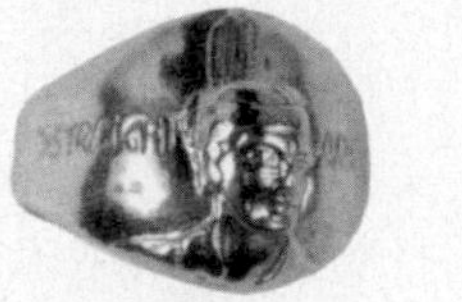

STA-28

❑ STA-28. Gold Plated Portrait Ring,
1950. Apparently the Robbins Co. produced a small number of the standard brass rings with a gold plated finish as the three examples we know of have all been traced back to Nabisco Co. executives. Rare. Near Mint - **$450**

STA-29

❑ STA-29. Straight Arrow Milk Glass Mug and Bowl,
c. 1950. Mug is 3" tall with wrap-around scene. No name or copyright but an exact likeness to Straight Arrow on horse. Second image is of cowboy on bucking bronco. Bowl is 2" tall with wrap-around scene with likeness of Straight Arrow on horse. Each - **$10 $18 $35**

STA-30

STA-31

❑ STA-30. "Injun-Uities" 21x27" Store Announcement Poster,
1951. Scarce. Pictures 12 "Injun-Uities" Nabisco cards from first series. - **$300 $600 $1200**

❑ STA-31. "Straight Arrow Injun-Uities Manual",
1951. Series 1 and 2 box inserts in book format. - **$20 $40 $75**

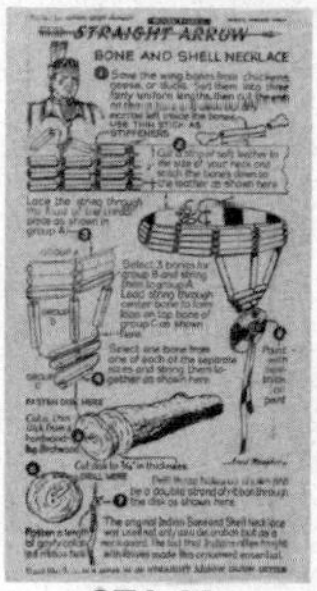

STA-32

STA-33

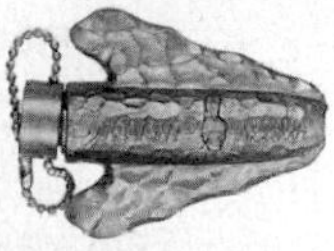

STA-34

❑ STA-32. "Book Three" Box Insert Cards,
1951. Set of 36. Each - **$2 $3 $6**

❑ STA-33. "Rite-A-Lite" Order Form,
1951. - **$20 $35 $70**

❑ STA-34. Rite-A-Lite Arrowhead With Cap On Bottom,
1951. Scarce. Gold heavy plastic battery operated light. Discontinued because of use of material for Korean War. End cap frequently missing. End cap has tiny lettering of club secret word TA-WATO-KO. - **$150 $250 $400**
Without End Cap - **$60 $90 $150**

STA-35

❑ STA-35. Rite-A-Lite Arrowhead Cancellation Letter,
1951. Rare. - **$125 $250 $400**

STA-36

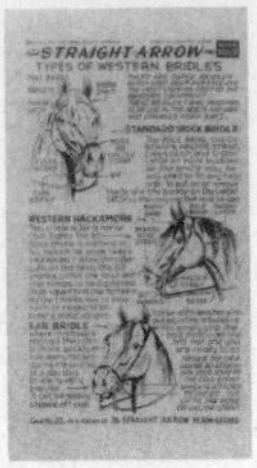
STA-37

❑ **STA-36. Glow-In-Dark Membership Card,**
1951. - **$75 $160 $275**

❑ **STA-37. "Book Four" Box Insert Cards,**
1952. Set of 36. Each - **$2 $3 $6**

STA-38

❑ **STA-38. Nabisco Shredded Wheat Box with Straight Arrow Finger Puppet Offer,**
1952. Package becomes paper toy TV set.- **$100 $200 $300**

STA-39

❑ **STA-39. Punch-Out Puppets Sheet,**
c. 1952. Comes with instruction card and two play script cards. See next item.
Unpunched - **$12 $20 $35**

STA-40

❑ **STA-40. Props,**
1952. Nabisco. Two pieces. For TV Puppet Theater. Goes with STA-38 and STA-39.
Each - **$5 $10 $15**

Strombecker Models Club

A model kit maker (principally aviation) from the 1930s onward, Strombecker Co. sponsored a model building club with a code book and series of badges to denote club ranks based on model building expertise. A similar club was sponsored by competitor Megow Co.

SMC-1

❑ **SMC-1. Club Manual,**
1930s. Includes secret code, photos of famous adult club members, photos of airplane and locomotive models. - **$30 $50 $85**

SMC-2

SMC-3

❑ **SMC-2. "Apprentice" Bronze Finish Badge,**
1930s. - **$10 $20 $40**

❑ **SMC-3. "First Class" Bronze Finish Badge,**
1930s. Awarded for building four models in four categories. - **$15 $30 $60**

SMC-4

❑ **SMC-4. "Master Model Builder" Gold Badge,**
1930s. This high rank is rare. Less than five known. - **$50 $175 $350**

SMC-5

❑ **SMC-5. "Airman 1st Class" Club Rank 3" Metal Wings Badge,**
1930s. Silver finish with red shield, one star. - **$12 $25 $50**

SMC-6

❑ **SMC-6. "Wing Leader" Club Rank 3" Metal Wings Badge,**
1930s. Gold finish, blue shield, two stars. - **$12 $25 $50**

SMC-7

❑ **SMC-7. "Captain" Club Rank Metal Wings Badge,**
1930s. Brass finish, green shield, three stars for highest rank. - **$20 $35 $70**

SMC-8

❑ **SMC-8. Strombecker Painted And Assembled Wood Ship Models,**
c. 1945. Eight different models, 9" to 11" long, all neatly assembled and painted in either solid gray, brown or black. Each - **$8 $12 $20**

SMC-9

❑ **SMC-9. Club Application Folder,**
c. 1949. Features "Captain 'Jet'" and pictures "Air Man 1st Class" tin badge to be received.
Folder - **$10 $20 $40**
Badge - **$20 $35 $70**

SMC-10

❑ **SMC-10. "Captain 'Jet' And The Strombecker Model-Makers Club" Comic,**
1953. 3-1/4x7-1/4" combination comic book and catalogue with 16 pages. - **$15 $25 $70**

Sunset Carson

Michael Harrison (1920-1990) took his cowboy name for a supporting role in the 1944 film *Call of the Rockies.* Carson starred in about 20 "B" Westerns for Republic Pictures from the mid-1940s to 1950, but his cowboy skills were demonstrated to greater advantage as an international rodeo star and trick rider in the Tom Mix Circus. Several Sunset Carson comic books were published in 1951, and adaptations of his films appeared in a number of issues of *Cowboy Western Comics* in the early 1950s.

SUN-1

❑ **SUN-1. "Republic Pictures" Felt Pennant,**
1940s. - **$30 $60 $110**

SUN-2

❑ **SUN-2. "Sunset Carson" Cello. Button,**
1940s. - **$20 $40 $85**

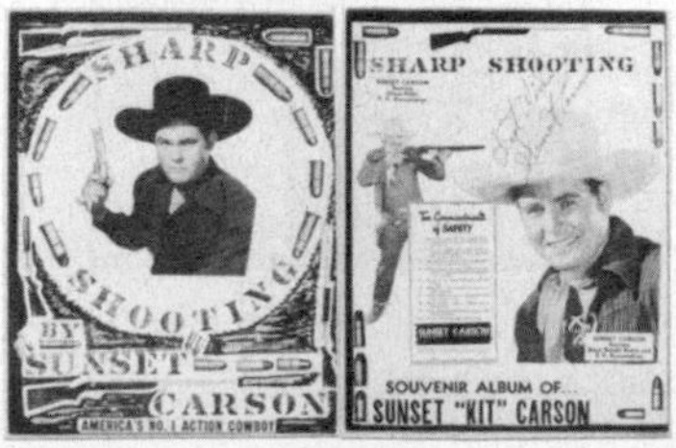

SUN-3

❑ **SUN-3. Sunset Carson Autographed "Sharpshooting" Brochure,**
c. 1950. Has photos of Carson with illustrations for Remington ammunition, likely sponsor.
Signed - **$25 $50 $100**
Unsigned - **$12 $25 $50**

SUN-4

❑ **SUN-4. Sunset Carson/Monte Hale Records Offer,**
c. 1950. Illinois Merchandise Mart. Paper sheet offering recorded adventures "Sunset Carson And The Black Bandit" and "Monte Hale And The Flaming Arrow." - **$12 $25 $55**

Super Circus

What started out as a kids' radio quiz program in Chicago became one of television's highest-rated children's shows. *Super Circus,* a weekly variety spectacular created by Fred Kilian (1911-1994), aired on ABC-TV from 1949 to 1956. Claude Kirchner acted as ringmaster, Mary Hartline--with dazzling blonde hair and miniskirt--twirled her baton, and clowns Cliffy, Nicky, and Scampy took care of the slapstick. Among the sponsors were Weather Bird shoes, Canada Dry, Kellogg's cereals, Quaker Oats, Mars candy, and Sunkist. Also, Mary Hartline Enterprises marketed a line of dolls, toys, children's clothes, food products, records, and books. The show moved to New York in 1955, and Jerry Colonna and Sandy Wirth replaced Kirchner and Hartline for the final season. *Super Circus* comic books appeared between 1951 and 1956.

SUC-1

❑ **SUC-1. "Super Circus Action Toy" Punch-Out Kit With Envelope,**
1950. Canada Dry. Set of 10 punch-out sheets.
Unused In Mailer - **$75 $150 $300**

SUC-2

SUC-3

❑ **SUC-2. "Weather-Bird Shoes" Photos,**
c. 1950. From a set. Each - **$12 $18 $35**

❑ **SUC-3. "Mary Hartline" Hand Puppet Premium,**
c. 1950. Three Musketeers candy. - **$20 $45 $75**

SUC-4

❑ **SUC-4. "Super Circus Side Show" Punch-Out Kit With Envelope,**
c. 1950. Milky Way candy bars. Punch-out sheet opens to 11x34".
Complete In Mailer - **$75 $150 $300**

SUC-5

SUC-6

❑ **SUC-5. "Super Circus Club" Member's Litho. Button,**
1951. Canada Dry. - **$10 $20 $40**

❑ **SUC-6. Spiral-Bound Photo Book,**
1951. - **$25 $75 $125**

SUC-7

SUC-8

❑ **SUC-7. Weather Bird Shoes Comic Book Vol. 1 #1,**
1951. - **$8 $24 $60**

❑ **SUC-8. Iron-On Transfer Sheets,**
1951. Weather-Bird shoes. Four tissue sheets in reverse image picturing Mary, Scampy, Nicky, Cliffy. Each - **$5 $10 $15**

SUC-9

❑ **SUC-9. "Super Circus Snickers Shack" Punch-Out With Mailer,**
c. 1951. Mars, Inc. Punch sheet opens to 11-1/2 x17". Complete In Mailer - **$55 $110 $225**

SUC-10

SUC-11

❑ **SUC-10. Mary Hartline Large Doll,**
1951. 16" tall with red dress and pink & white tassels. White boots. -
$200 $400 $700

❑ **SUC-11. Mary Hartline Doll with Photo Box,**
1951. From Ideal. Different face and dress design than giveaway version. Box is rare with cut-outs inside. Doll - **$60 $150 $275**
Picture Box - **$60 $150 $300**

SUC-12

SUC-13

❑ **SUC-12. Hard Plastic Premium Doll,**
1951. Giveaway doll has different design than store-bought item. Doll - **$50 $135 $225**
Picture Box - **$35 $65 $100**

❑ **SUC-13. Mary Hartline Cut-Out Dolls and Coloring Book,**
1952. Published by Whitman, #210425. Book is 11x15" with 28 pages and has 4 single-sided pages of costumes including Mary Hartline's signature costume for the show Super Circus. -
$50 $175 $300

SUC-14

❑ **SUC-14. "Super Circus Television Color Show" Boxed Set,**
1953. Store item by E. C. Kropp Co. -
$30 $60 $115

SUC-15

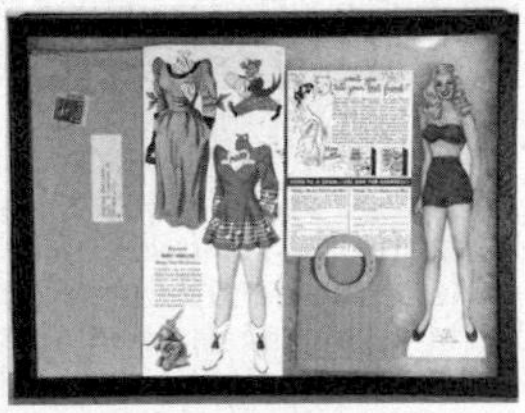

SUC-16

❑ **SUC-15. "TV Guide" With Cover Article,**
1953. Weekly issue for August 21 with color photo cover of Mary Hartline and Claude Kirchner plus two-page article. - **$15 $25 $50**

❑ **SUC-16. Mary Hartline Magic Doll,**
1955-56. Rare. Kellogg's premium from the show's last season. Has paper doll, cut-out dresses, stand, application and mailer. Ordered for 25¢ and 1 box top from Frosted Flakes or Sugar Smacks. Complete - **$135 $240 $400**

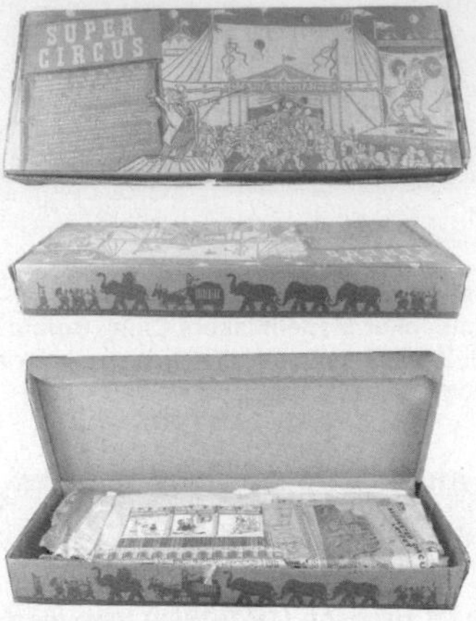

SUC-17

❑ **SUC-17. Super Circus Playset in Box,**
1950s. Playsets unused in box are rare.
- **$250 $500 $1000**

SUC-18

❑ **SUC-18. "Squeezem" Action Cards,**
1950s. Store item. Each is 3x4-1/2".
Each - **$10 $18 $35**

SUC-19

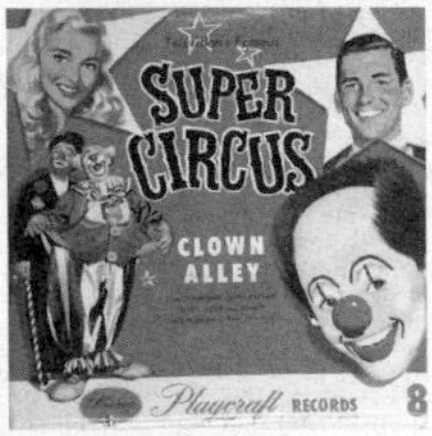

SUC-20

❑ **SUC-19. Punch-Out Puppets With Envelope,**
1950s. Snickers Candy Bars.
Unused In Mailer - **$50 $110 $200**

❑ **SUC-20. Clown Alley Record Album,**
1950s. Mercury Playcraft Records. With dust jacket. 78 RPM. Rare. - **$40 $75 $150**

SUC-21

❑ **SUC-21. Postcard,**
1950s. Premium from TV show, pictures 6 cast members - **$20 $35 $70**

SUC-22

❑ **SUC-22. Stiff Paper Standups,**
1950s. Weather Bird Shoes. 8.5" tall full color photo replicas of Claude Kirchner and Mary Hartline from set including Scampy, boy clown and Nickie, tramp clown and possibly others. Each - **$25 $50 $100**

SUC-23

❑ **SUC-23. "Super Circus Coloring Book,"**
1950s. - **$35 $75 $150**

Superman

Clark Kent's secret identity might just be the worst-kept secret ever. Consistently certified as one of the most recognized characters in the world, Superman is the very definition of a superhero (in fact, he's probably the reason for the word superhero). Not only was he dynamic and unlike anything anyone had seen before, but the marketing plan built around and executed for Superman was virtually a "how to" road map for future marketing executives.

When writer Jerry Siegel (1914-1996) and artist Joe Shuster (1914-1992) created Superman in 1933, they probably had no idea of the tremendous force they would unleash on an unsuspecting public. It wasn't until five years later, though, that *Action Comics* #1 (June 1938) was put together by editor Vincent Sullivan (1910-1999). It launched Superman into comic books and captured the attention of children. The daily newspaper strip first appeared seven months later (January 1939) and adults began to take notice. A companion comic, *Superman*, followed that summer and included the first mention of Supermen of America, the official Superman fan club. The club's first contest began December 1, 1939 and ended January 28, 1940; the prize became one of the most sought-after Superman collectibles ever, the Supermen of America patch (see entry in this section). Two weeks later, February 12, 1940, *The Adventures of Superman* radio show took to the airwaves for the first time and captured the imagination of entire families. Before long, characters Clark Kent and Lois Lane (and thanks to the radio show, several others) became fast friends with America's reading and listening public. The phenomenon had begun. Ghost artists in the golden age included Wayne Boring, Paul Cassidy, Leo Nowak, Fred Ray and Jack Burnley. Burnley's image of Superman waving, originally done for the cover of *World's Fair* comic in 1940 was used on several early premiums, and Fred Ray was likely the artist on the 1940 bubble gum cards. There have been thousands of Superman comic books, and daily and Sunday comic strips appeared from 1939 to 1967.

On radio *The Adventures of Superman* aired from 1940 to 1951, on the Mutual network from 1940 to 1949, then on ABC. Bud Collyer starred as Superman from 1940 to 1949. Force cereal sponsored in 1940, followed by Kellogg's Pep from 1943 to 1947. The series moved successfully to prime-time television syndication (1953-1958), mainly on ABC outlets, with George Reeves in the lead and Kellogg's Sugar Frosted Flakes as sponsor. *Lois and Clark: The New Adventures of Superman* ran on ABC-TV from 1993 to 1997 with Dean Cain as Clark/Superman and Teri Hatcher as Lois Lane. October 2001 marked Superman's return to television in a one hour drama on the WB network entitled *Smallville.* Tom Welling stars as the teenaged Clark Kent in a series that focuses on angst rather than adventure.

The first Superman cartoons were 17 six-minute theatrical shorts made by the Fleischer Studios for Paramount Pictures in 1941-1943. Television cartoons, with Bud Collyer returning as the voice of Superman, aired on CBS in the late 1960s under various titles: *The New Adventures of Superman* (1966-1967), *The Superman/Aquaman Hour of Adventure* (1967-1968), and *The Batman/Superman Hour* (1968-1969). Superman was also part of the *Superfriends* animated series on ABC in the 1970s, and a musical show, *It's a Bird...It's a Plane...It's Superman*, had a brief run on Broadway in 1966 and was shown on ABC-TV in 1975. Superman returned to the cartoon airwaves in 1996 on the WB network in *The New Batman/Superman Adventures.* He also appeared in *Justice League Unlimited* on Cartoon Network.

Superman's movie career began with two 15-episode chapter plays from Columbia Pictures, *Superman* (1948) and *Atom Man vs. Superman* (1950), with Kirk Alyn (1911-1999) in the lead role. *Superman and the Mole Men*, with George Reeves (1914-1959) starring, was released in 1951 and later served as a pilot for the TV series. *Superman - The Movie* (1978), with Christopher Reeve and Margot Kidder—a box office smash—was followed by *Superman II* (1981), *Superman III* (1983), and *Superman IV: The Quest for Peace* (1987). *Superman Returns* (2006) starred Brandon Routh as Clark/Superman, Kate Bosworth as Lois, and Kevin Spacey as Lex Luthor.

Superman marked his 60th anniversary in June 1998 (so his 70th is just around the corner). As of Spring 2008, he is regularly published in *Action Comics*, *Superman* (which retains the numbering of the original series, despite roughly two decades of being titled *Adventures of Superman*), *All Star Superman*, *Superman Confidential* and *Superman/Batman.* Various other titles have been published over the years. Please consult *The Official Overstreet Comic Book Price Guide* for further comic book titles. Superman also guest stars in many DC Comics titles and appears regularly with the Justice League of America.

In 2001, the 1978 feature film was released on DVD, including enhanced special effects, additional scenes, and some minor edits (including the impressive task of making the costume look the right color under the wide variety of lighting conditions in the movie). The release brought renewed interest to the '70s and '80s series and helped launch this year's movie revival. Over the course of his career he's been transformed, transmogrified and even killed, but Superman keeps coming back in his never-ending battle for truth, justice and the American way. Items are typically copyrighted National Comics Publications, Inc., National Periodical Publications, Inc. or DC Comics.

SUP-1

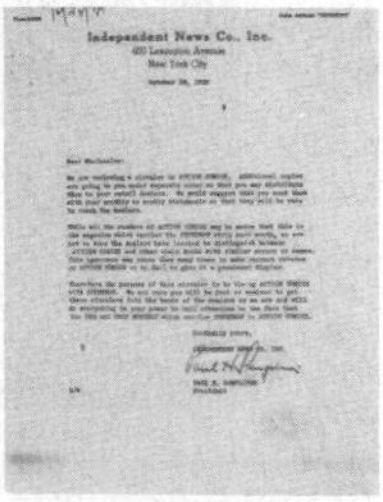

Independent News Co., Inc.

SUP-2

❑ **SUP-1. "Action Comics" Flier,**
1939. Sent to magazine wholesalers requesting they inform retailers Superman strip appears only in "Action Comics". - **$500 $1200 $2500**

❑ **SUP-2. "Action Comics" Cover Letter,**
1939. Came with flier above. - **$300 $600 $1000**

SUP-3

❑ **SUP-3. Action Comics "Superman" Litho. Button,**
1939. First button for Superman. 7/8" with back inscription "Read Superman/Action Comics Magazine". See SUP-80. - **$65 $135 $275**

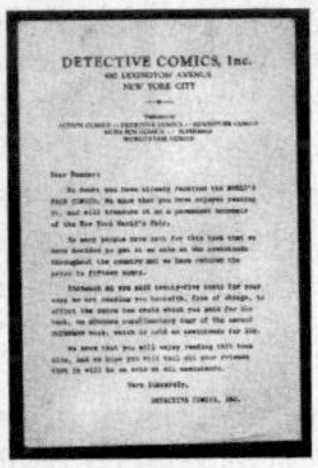
DETECTIVE COMICS, Inc.
480 LEXINGTON AVENUE
NEW YORK CITY

SUP-4

SUP-5

❑ **SUP-4. Detective Comics Stationery Letter,**
1939. N. Y. World's Fair. - **$175 $375 $750**

❑ **SUP-5. Action Comics Club Certificate, First Version,**
1939. Note bottom margin inscribed "Copyright 1939 by Detective Comics, Inc." - **$135 $300 $600**

SUP-6

❑ **SUP-6. Superman Contest Prize Ring,**
1940. Scarce. Inscribed "Supermen Of America, Member." Issued by DC Comics promoted in Superman and Action Comics. Believed to have been given away with candy and gum programs as well. Silver base, gold luster image, red accent on logo and around lettering. Reported 21 known: two in Poor grade, one in Fair, six in Good, three in Very Good, four in Fine, four in Very Fine, and one in Mint.
Good - **$4000**
Fine - **$10,000**
Very Fine - **$30,000**

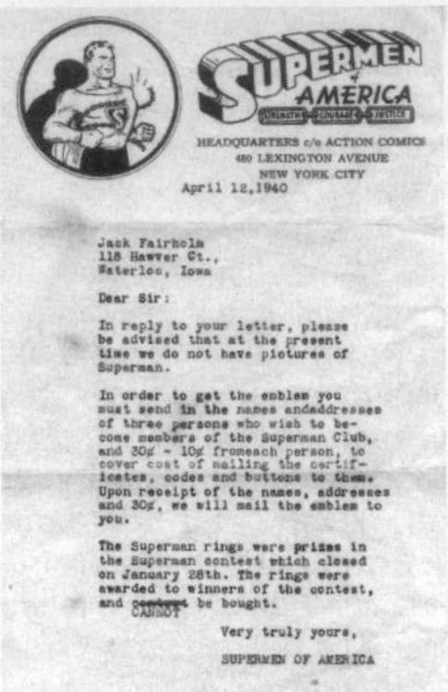
SUPERMEN of AMERICA
STRENGTH COURAGE JUSTICE
HEADQUARTERS c/o ACTION COMICS
480 LEXINGTON AVENUE
NEW YORK CITY

April 12,1940

Jack Fairholm
118 Hawver Ct.,
Waterloo, Iowa

Dear Sir:

In reply to your letter, please be advised that at the present time we do not have pictures of Superman.

In order to get the emblem you must send in the names andaddresses of three persons who wish to become members of the Superman Club, and 30¢ - 10¢ fromeach person, to cover cost of mailing the certificates, codes and buttons to them. Upon receipt of the names, addresses and 30¢, we will mail the emblem to you.

The Superman rings were prizes in the Superman contest which closed on January 28th. The rings were awarded to winners of the contest, and CANNOT be bought.

Very truly yours,

SUPERMEN OF AMERICA

SUP-7

❑ **SUP-7. Supermen of America Letter to Child,**
1940. Letter in response to letter sent to Superman. Discusses the requirements for membership in the club and the Superman of America Prize Ring. Unique. - **$2000**

SUP-8

❑ **SUP-8. "Superman Adventure" Poster,**
1940. Macy's department store. 7x17" in red, white and blue promoting their "Toyland-Fifth Floor" performance in which Superman "Comes Alive." - **$275 $450 $900**

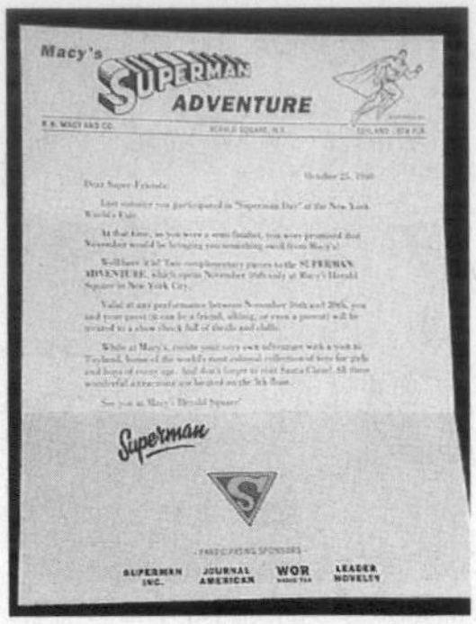
Macy's SUPERMAN ADVENTURE
Superman
SUPERMAN INC. JOURNAL AMERICAN WOR LEADER NOVELTY

SUP-9

❑ **SUP-9. "Superman Adventure" Letter To "Dear Super-Friends",**
1940. Macy's. Letter to participant semi-finalist in "Superman Day" at the New York World's Fair which was accompanied by two passes to the "Superman Adventure" event opening November 16. Letter lists participating sponsors as Superman Inc., Journal American, WOR Radio 710, Leader Novelty. - **$200 $350 $575**

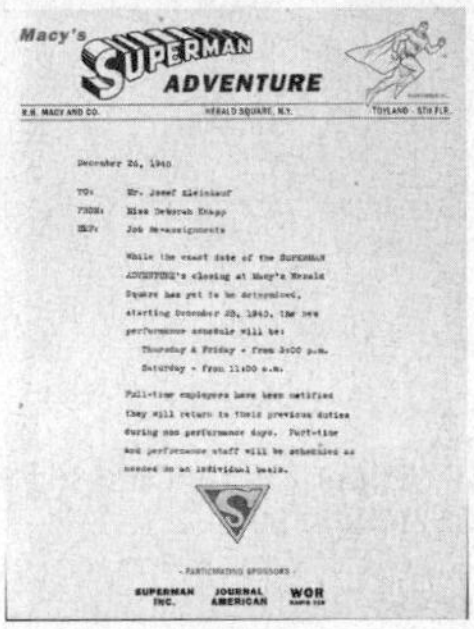
Macy's SUPERMAN ADVENTURE
R.H. MACY AND CO. HERALD SQUARE, N.Y. TOYLAND - 5TH FLR.

Thursday & Friday - from 3:00 p.m.
Saturday - from 11:00 a.m.

SUPERMAN INC. JOURNAL AMERICAN WOR

SUP-10

❑ **SUP-10. "Macy's Superman Adventure" Letter,**
1940. 8.5x11" typewritten letter dated December 26 from sponsoring New York department store in addition to Journal American and WOR Radio. Letter content is for Macy's employees, informing them of time changes and job reassignments due to upcoming "Superman Adventure's Closing At Macy's Herald Square" starting December 28. - **$500 $1000 $2000**

SUP-11

❑ SUP-11. Superman Thanksgiving Day Parade Ad Card,
1940. Similar in size to a postcard, promoted Macy's effort at Thanksgiving Day Parade. The Superman display was the largest balloon featured in the 1940 parade. - **$175 $350 $600**

SUP-12

❑ SUP-12. Macy's Advertisement in New York Times,
1940. New York Times late city edition paper dated November 15, 1940. Large ad promotion for the Macy's Superman In Toyland exhibit. - **$100 $200 $400**

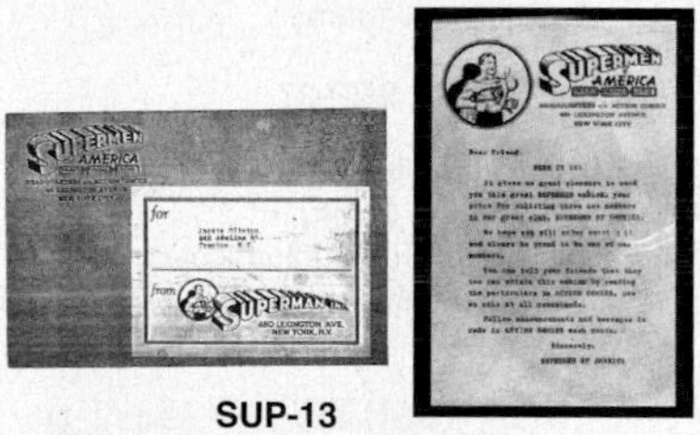

SUP-13

❑ SUP-13. Letter and Mailer,
1940. Came with Action Comics Patch. Each - **$600 $1550 $3000**

SUP-14

❑ SUP-14. Patch,
1940. Scarce. Has "Action Comics" at bottom of front side. A 3.75" fake patch has numerous small differences from the original. On the fake, the left breaking chain accent line touches his shoulder. - **$2000 $5500 $11,000**

SUP-15

❑ SUP-15. Patch,
1940. Rare. Prize same as the Supermen of America patch except has word "Leader" at bottom. - **$3300 $10,000 $20,000**

SUP-16

❑ SUP-16. Candy Patch,
1940. - **$1250 $3500 $9500**

SUP-17

❑ SUP-17. Handkerchief,
1940. Produced on several different color fabrics, including black and maroon. - **$850 $1750 $3750**

SUP-18

❑ SUP-18. Marx Wind-Up Tin Tank
1940. Store item. Body of tank in copper luster. - **$300 $600 $1200**

SUP-19

❑ SUP-19. Large Candy Box,
1940. - **$1150 $2250 $5000**

SUP-20

❑ SUP-20. "Superman In Movie Style" Boxed Viewer And Film Set,
1940. Store item by Acme Plastic Toys Inc. - **$300 $600 $1200**

(Red cover)

(Blue cover)

SUP-21

❑ SUP-21. Superman Cut-Out Book,
1940. Produced as #1502 by Saalfield Publishing Company of Akron, Ohio. There were two editions; one had a red cover and the other was blue, with different contents in each. Each - **$900 $2500 $4000**

SUP-22

❑ SUP-22. "Superman 6 Picture Puzzles" Rare Boxed Set,
1940. Box is 7.5x10.5x1.5" deep and contains six different 7.25x10" puzzles by Saalfield. Boxed set #1515.
Each Puzzle - **$65 $125 $250**
Box - **$150 $275 $500**
Complete - **$540 $1025 $2000**

SUP-23

❑ SUP-23. "The Adventures Of Superman" Game,
1940. Box is 9.75x19.25x1.5" deep and contains Milton Bradley game #4842. This is the first and rarest of the early board games which was also offered as a premium in the Superman Bubble Gum Club prize folder. Box includes matched pair of inserts with classic full figure Superman image. Board is 18.5x18.5" with similar but different and more detailed images than the "Speed" gameboard. - **$300 $650 $1150**

SUP-24

❑ SUP-24. "Superman Rollover Plane" Boxed Wind-Up,
1940. Marx. Issued with plane in three varieties - red, blue and this pictured version which is silver. Toy is 6x6.5x3.5" tall tin litho with built-in key and comes in illustrated box. Box art on four side panels is of aviator flying plane, no Superman images. However, the end flaps on right and left sides read "Superman Rollover Plane." Box - **$300 $600 $1000**
Silver Version - **$1000 $2000 $3000**
Red Or Blue Version - **$600 $1350 $2250**

SUP-25

SUP-26

❑ SUP-25. Figural Brass Pin Serially Numbered,
1940. Fleischer Studios. Shown in press book and available to movie exhibitors to promote the Superman cartoon. 1" tall with red and blue enamel paint. - **$800 $1600 $3000**

❑ SUP-26. "Superman's Magic Flight" Cardboard Mechanical Toy,
1940. - **$500 $1000 $2000**

(front)

(back)

SUP-27

❑ SUP-27. "Superman's Christmas Adventure" Comic Book,
1940. First superhero premium comic book. First issue, various stores. - **$382 $1146 $6300**

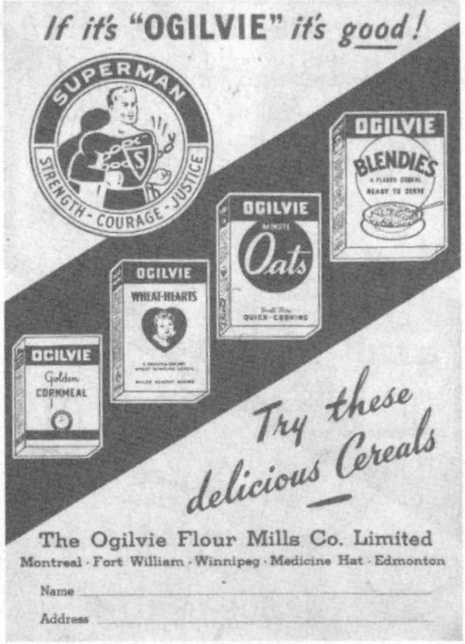

SUP-28

❑ SUP-28. Enameled Brass Badge Paper Order Form,
1940. Rare. Canadian badge (see next item). - **$175 $350 $700**

SUP-29

❑ **SUP-29. "Superman" Enameled Brass Badge,**
1940. Ogilvie premium. Canadian. - **$600 $1200 $2750**

SUP-30

❑ **SUP-30. Rectangular Fabric Patch,**
1940. Scarce. A recent unlicensed repro appeared on eBay and elsewhere. On the original, a black accent line on his neck is horizontal. On the repro, the largest accent line on his neck is more vertical.- **$500 $1500 $4000**

SUP-31

❑ **SUP-31. "Macy's Superman Adventure" Gummed Sticker,**
1940. Macy's department store, applied to purchased items. - **$175 $400 $900**

SUP-32

❑ **SUP-32. "Krypto-Raygun" With Box,**
1940. Store item by Daisy Mfg. Co. Came with seven filmstrips.
Complete Boxed - **$750 $1750 $3250**
Gun Only - **$150 $250 $500**
Filmstrip - **$12 $25 $50**

SUP-33 SUP-34

❑ **SUP-33. Wood And Composition Jointed Doll,**
1940. Store item by Ideal Toys. Includes cloth cape. Composition head frequently has restoration. - **$400 $800 $2250**
Near Mint With Box - **$7750**

❑ **SUP-34. Superman Die-Cut Sticker,**
1940. Promotes radio show on WHP radio station. About 4" tall. Other stickers feature different stations. - **$150 $300 $600**

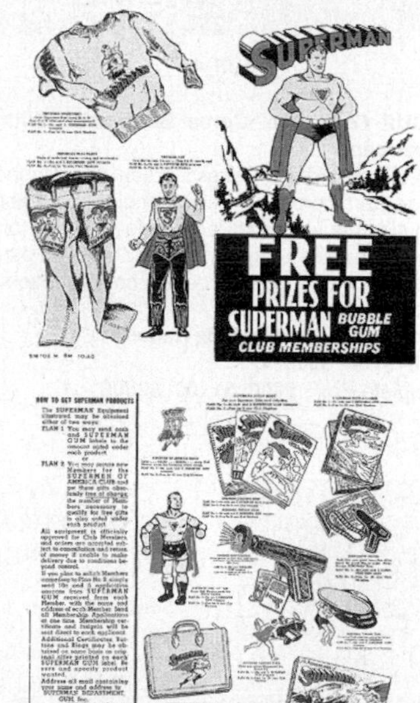

SUP-35

❑ **SUP-35. Superman Bubble Gum Club Prizes Folder,**
1940. Gum, Inc. Shows 15 items, most also available in stores, available for cash and Superman Gum labels or free of charge for securing new club members. The "Superman American" brass club badge was 10¢ and 5 wrappers or 10 new members. -
$300 $600 $1200

SUP-36

SUP-37

❑ **SUP-36. Bowman Bubble Gum Box,**
1940. - **$2750 $5500 $11,000**

❑ **SUP-37. "Democrat" Newspaper Cello. Button,**
1940. Rare newspaper premium. -
$750 $1650 $3500

SUP-38

❑ **SUP-38. Superman Christmas Adventure Ticket,**
1940. Admission ticket to Macy's Christmas Adventure play. This ticket has sponsor radio station WOR on the front. Other sponsors include Superman, Inc., Leader Novelty, and American Journal. Each - **$150 $300 $600**

SUP-39 SUP-40

❑ **SUP-39. Plaster "Carnival" Statue,**
1940. 1st of 4 varieties shown. With red and blue costume. - **$100 $250 $400**

❑ **SUP-40. Plaster "Carnival" Statue,**
1940. 2nd of 4 varieties shown. With red and green costume. - **$75 $225 $350**

SUP-41

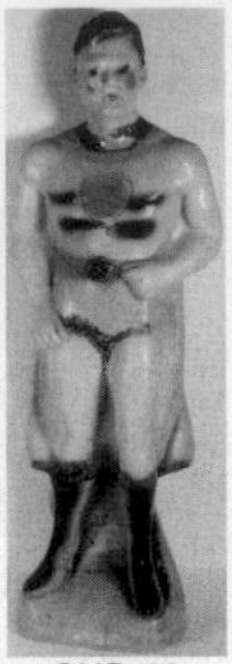

SUP-42

SUP-43

❑ SUP-41. Plaster "Carnival" Statue,
1940. 3rd of 4 varieties shown. With yellow and black costume. - **$75 $225 $350**

❑ SUP-42. Plaster "Carnival" Statue,
1940. 4th of 4 varieties shown. With red, yellow and black costume with emblem on chest. - **$75 $225 $350**

❑ SUP-43. "Superman/American" Brass Figural Badge,
1940. 1-5/8" tall with enamel paint. Gum Inc. for Superman Bubble Gum Club members. Also offered by Force cereal. - **$40 $75 $150**

SUP-44

❑ SUP-44. Superman Valentine,
1940. Valentine created by Quality Art Novelty Company in February, 1940. Many different. Each - **$30 $65 $150**

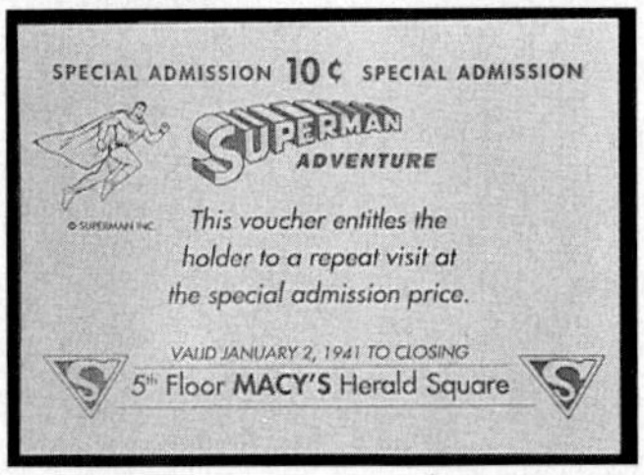

SUP-45

❑ SUP-45. "Superman Adventure Special Admission 10 Cent" Voucher,
1940. Macy's. 4x4-1/2" card for repeat visit at special price beginning January 2, 1941 to closing. - **$200 $275 $500**

SUP-46

❑ SUP-46. "Superman" Belt Slide,
1940. Metal plate about 1" square with rear flanges top and bottom. Silver luster finish accented by blue and red enamels. -
$150 $300 $600

SUP-47

❑ SUP-47. "Force" Cereal Box Panels With Superman,
1940. Force Wheat Flakes Cereal. Two clipped panels from cereal box, one complete front and both side panels. Featured is side panel ad for Superman radio program. Second panel is other half of back offering presidential coin set packaged individually.
Front With Superman Side Panel -
$100 $200 $500
Complete Box - **$600 $1200 $2500**

SUP-48

❑ SUP-48. Premium Package with Coin,
1940. Notice they used the slogan "New 1940 Super Force" since the Superman radio show was using Force as a sponsor.
Package with coin - **$200**
Coin only - **$10 $15 $20**

SUP-49

❑ SUP-49. "Superman" Gum Card Wrapper,
1940. Waxed paper wrapper is 4.5x6" by Gum Inc. Superman surrounded by illustrations of prizes, mostly Superman-related including sweatshirt, cut-out book, tie, belt, etc. Text reads "Join The Superman Supermen Of America Club And Compete For These Valuable Prizes." Wrapper design includes "Membership Application" coupon. Five coupons and 10 cents needed to order club ring or badge.
- **$150 $300 $750**

SUP-50

❑ SUP-50. Superman Wrist Watch In Box,
1940. New Haven Clock Co. Distributed by the Everbrite Watch Company Inc. Watch has a 1.25" chromed metal case which has raised and recessed rim accent design. This is the rectangular case version. Dial features color illustration of Superman from knee up with his name running across lower body.
Box with Insert - **$600 $1250 $2500**
Watch - **$300 $600 $1250**

SUP-51

❑ SUP-51. "Superman Comes To Cleveland" Newspaper Debut Sign,
1940. Cleveland Plain Dealer in hometown of Superman creators Siegel and Shuster. 11.5x14.5" cardboard. - **$1150 $2250 $4250**

(box)

(art used on *Action*

(art used on *Superman*

(art used on *Action*

SUP-52

❑ SUP-52. Boxed Set of Three Puzzles,
1940. Each Puzzle - **$65 $125 $250**
Box - **$125 $250 $400**
Complete - **$320 $625 $1150**

SUP-53

❑ SUP-53. "Candy & Surprise" Panel Cards,
1940. Leader Novelty Candy Co. Four 2.25x3" loose cards from set of 48 offered as perforated panels on candy boxes. Pictured is example front panel plus cards #5-7 from numbered set of back panels. Front Panel - **$20 $40 $65**
Each Card - **$30 $60 $120**
Complete Box - **$150 $300 $650**

SUP-54

❑ SUP-54. "Supermen Of America" Club Cello. Button In Two Sizes,
1940. Colorful button in 1.25" size issued with the earliest club kit. Same design but in 7/8" size used very briefly in 1941.
Small version - **$185 $375 $700**
Large version - **$20 $40 $85**

SUP-55

❑ SUP-55. Child's Sweatshirt,
1940. Store item and premium offer by Superman Bubble Gum. Heavy cotton sweatshirt featuring chest portrait of Superman breaking chains. Made by Norwich Knitting. - **$1000 $3000 $5000**

SUP-56

❑ SUP-56. "Supermen Of America" Color Variety Cello. Button,
c. 1940. DC Comics. Pictures him in white shirt with red/yellow chest symbol, rare variety from DC files, apparently for test purposes.
- **$250 $750 $1200**

SUP-57

❑ SUP-57. Christmas Card With Superman,
c. 1940. DC Comics. 5.25x8.25" folder card with cover art of Superman changing into Santa Claus costume. - **$400 $850 $1500**

SUP-58

❑ SUP-58. "Superman Speed Game,"
c. 1940. Milton Bradley. Several different size boxes, this example is 8.75x15.5x1.75" deep marked "Good Bradley Games" at top left corner. This version has die-cut cardboard Superman playing pieces, another version came with wooden pieces to represent Superman.
Cardboard Pieces Version - **$85 $185 $350**
Wooden Pieces Version - **$65 $135 $275**

SUP-59

❑ SUP-59. Supermen of America/Action Comics Prototype Ring,
c. 1940. DC Comics but manner of distribution is unknown. Silver luster with red paint around lettering and on chest logo. Inner surface of bands have letter "U" logo of maker Uncas and "Made In U.S.A." Ring base differs from 'contest' ring. Contest ring sides have lightning bolts and planet design. This ring has accent lines on sides that form a small diamond shape with pair of 1/16" raised circles above. This ring has adjustable bands. The 'contest' ring also has adjustable bands. Seven examples known. One in Good, three in Very Good, one in Fine, one in Very Fine and one in Near Mint.
- **$4000 $8000 $16,000**

SUP-60

❑ **SUP-60. "Superman" Fleischer Cartoons Rare Poster,**
1941. One-sheet is 27x41" by Paramount Pictures Inc. for series of 17 cartoons produced by Paramount Pictures and Fleischer Studios released in movie theaters from 1941-1943. Large text reads "Amazing! Startling! Superman Is Here In Technicolor." Additional text reads "A Fleischer Studios Cartoon By Arrangement By Action Comics And Superman Magazines/ Superman Comic Strip Created By Jerome Siegel And Joe Shuster."
- **$4500 $8500 $15,000**

SUP-61

❑ **SUP-61. Cartoon Movie 6' Standee,**
1941. From Fleischer cartoon film. -
$15,000 $30,000 $60,000

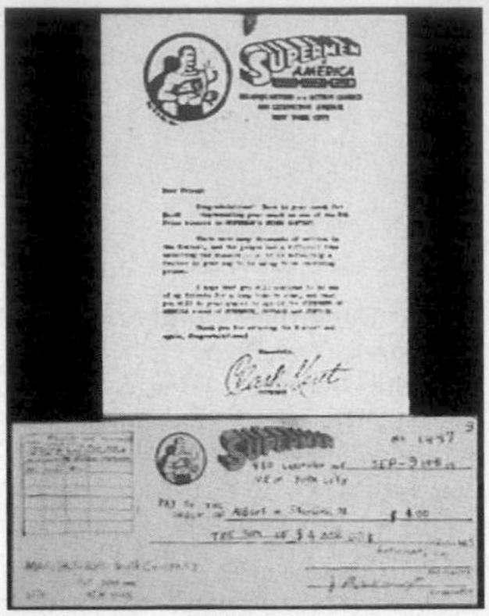

SUP-62

❑ **SUP-62. Contest Letter With Check Replica,**
1941. 7-1/4x10-1/2" letter congratulates winner of "Check For - $4 Representing Your Award As One Of The 8 Prize Winners In Superman's Super Contest." Original owner handmade a replica of the check prior to cashing it.
Letter Only - **$200 $375 $750**

SUP-63

SUP-64

❑ **SUP-63. Superman Secret Chamber Initial Brass Ring,**
1941. Produced by Ostby & Barton, Rhode Island. Sponsoring milk company's inital on top cover. First version with red/white/blue image of Superman glued on top of ring base, under the lift-off cover. Ring offered in conjunction with Defense Club Milk Program. Available for 2 bottle caps and 10¢. Ring must include the paper to obtain grade. 27 reported known: 4 in Good grade, 5 in Very Good, 5 in Fine, 5 in Very Fine and 3 in Near Mint. Five incomplete w/o paper. -
Good - **$1500**
Fine - **$5000**
Very Fine - **$10,000**
Near Mint - **$17,500**

❑ **SUP-64. Superman Secret Chamber Brass Ring With Superman Image on Top,**
1941. Produced by Ostby & Barton, Rhode Island. Pictures Superman, lightning bolt and letter "S". Top snaps off, Superman image was restamped over mystic eye on top, therefore rubbing exists on all rings. No Superman image under top. Ring offered in conjunction with Defense Club Milk Program. Available for 2 bottle caps and 10¢. 10 reported known: 4 in Good grade, 5 in Fine, 1 in Very Fine.
Good - **$2500**
Fine - **$8000**
Very Fine - **$20,000**

SUP-65

❑ **SUP-65. Superman Defense Club Twelve Numbered Milk Bottle Lids,**
1941. Each cardboard lid contains a number and a pledge. These lids were collected and redeemable with the milkman for a Superman American pin. These lids are rare. Each - **$65 $150 $300**

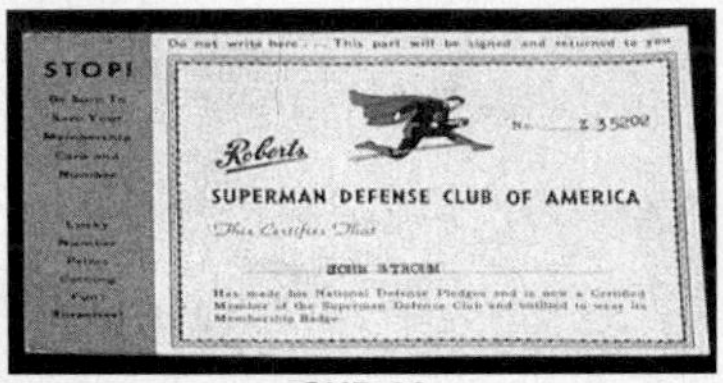

SUP-66

❑ **SUP-66. Superman Defense Club Milk Membership Card,**
1941. Roberts Milk sponsor. At the same time the Superman Junior Defense League of America bread campaign was going on, Superman was also promoting milk under this club name. Note the word "Junior" is deleted and "League" is changed to "Defense."
With Green Tab Notice Intact - **$200 $400 $800**
Without Tab - **$100 $200 $400**

SUP-67

❑ **SUP-67. Superman Defense Club Badge,**
1941. 1-5/8" tall enamel paint on brass. Same as SUP-43; 1940 badge offered again in conjunction with Defense Club milk program. Not to be confused with the Superman Junior Defense League bread program badge (see SUP-69). -
$40 $75 $150

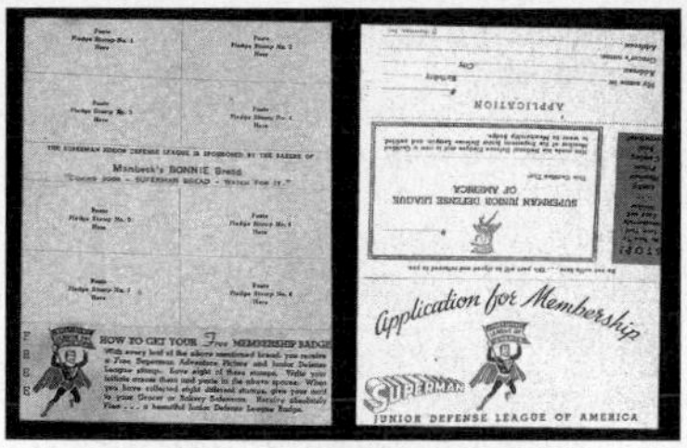

SUP-68

❑ **SUP-68. Superman Junior Defense League Bread Membership Folder,**
1941. Includes membership card and holder on back to paste membership pledge stamps. When the card was filled with eight stamps, it was redeemable at the local grocer for a Superman Junior Defense League pin.
Folder Complete - **$200 $400 $800**
Membership Card Only - **$100 $200 $400**
Superman Sticker Stamps Glued Each - **$10 $20 $40**

SUP-69

❑ **SUP-69. Superman Junior Defense League Bread Badge,**
1941. 1-1/8" tall enamel paint on brass. Premium for complete folder with stickers glued to back. - **$50 $75 $150**

SUP-70

❑ **SUP-70. Superman Adventure Cards With Stamps,**
1941. Rare. 24 adventure picture cards were issued in 1941 for the Superman bread campaign. The pledge stamps were detachable in order to paste them on the folder and receive the Junior Defense League pin. These cards are rare with the stamps still intact. Less than 25 exist.
Each With Stamp Attached - **$500 $1000 $2000**
Each Without Stamp - **$100 $200 $300**

Swan's
SUPERMAN
JUNIOR DEFENSE LEAGUE OF AMERICA
This Certifies That
NAME Betty McGloughan AGE 9
ADDRESS 12 Nokomis Cr. Knoxville, Tenn.
having duly pledged to do everything possible to aid SUPERMAN in NATIONAL DEFENSE, has been elected a member of the JUNIOR DEFENSE LEAGUE OF AMERICA
In Witness OF WHICH I HAVE THIS DAY SET MY SEAL AND SIGNATURE AS FOLLOWS:
Clark Kent
SUPERMAN

SUP-71

❑ **SUP-71. Bread Certificate,**
1941. Used to promote Junior Defense League of America. Rare. - **$500 $1000 $2000**

SUP-72

SUP-73

❑ **SUP-72. Cardboard Shield Badge,**
c. 1941. Rare. Badge for the promotion of Superman Bread. Worn by the grocery clerks and managers. Less than five known.
- $500 $1250 $2500

❑ **SUP-73. Bread Loaf Paper,**
c. 1941. Stroehmann's Bread. 4" tall diecut glossy paper, probably a loaf wrapper sticker listing call letters and broadcast times for "The Adventures Of Superman" radio program. - **$150 $300 $600**

SUP-74

SUP-75

❑ **SUP-74. Syroco-Style 5-1/2" Figure,**
1942. Wood composition in brown with red accents on logo and red cape. Promotional item from DC Comics for Superman comic books to distributors and retailers. Lois Boring, the wife of Superman artist Wayne Boring, states that Wayne told her he designed this figure for Detective Comics. We've also seen the figure offered in the 1943 catalog of wholesalers-jobbers Spors Company of Le Center, Minnesota. Superman, along with a soldier and sailor figure, were offered at $3.95 per dozen. Given the rarity of the Superman figure, it is unlikely the catalog company had inventory to fill orders. - **$800 $1800 $3600**

❑ **SUP-75. Syroco-Style 5-1/2" Painted Figure,**
1942. Full color, made of cellulose nitrate. See previous item. Rare. - **$1500 $3000 $6000**

SUP-76

❑ **SUP-76. Syroco-Style Superman Figure on Ashtray Base,**
1942. Rare. Full color 5-1/2" painted Superman figure. Promotional item from DC Comics for Superman comic books to distributors and retailers. Reported two known. - **$3500 $7000 $15,000**

SUP-77

SUP-78

❑ **SUP-77. "The Adventures Of Superman" Hardcover With Dust Jacket,**
1942. Store item published by Random House. 6x9-1/4" with 216 pages of text and black and white illustrations along with four color plates. Illustrations are by Joe Shuster, story is by George Lowther.
Wrapper Only - **$150 $300 $600**
Book Only - **$125 $225 $400**

❑ **SUP-78. "Schools At War/Help Smash The Axis" Poster,**
1942. Includes text "This Program Approved And Initiated By The U. S. Treasury Department And The U.S. Office Of Education." Red, white and blue 11x17". - **$400 $800 $1250**

SUP-79

❑ **SUP-79. Superman #18 With Pinback on Cover,**
1942. Premium pinback (SUP-80) was pinned to *Superman* #18 to promote *Action Comics*, the other Superman title.
Comic only - **$207 $621 $3000**

SUP-80

❑ **SUP-80. Action Comics "Superman" Litho. Button,**
1942. 7/8". Back inscription "Read Superman Action Comics Magazine". See SUP-3.- **$35 $65 $150**

SUP-81

❑ **SUP-81. "Salvage Speeds Victory" Sign,**
1942. 3 known. 18" x 12" sign has red, blue, black and yellow on white. - **$1000 $2000 $3500**

SUP-82

SUP-83

❑ **SUP-82. "The Adventures Of Superman/Armed Services Edition" Book,**
1942. Superman Inc. Paperback edition. - **$125 $250 $450**

❑ **SUP-83. DC Comics Portrait Sheet,**
c. 1942. Reverse shows covers of "Superman" #14, "World's Finest" #5, "Action Comics" #47. - **$125 $325 $650**

SUP-84

❑ **SUP-84. "The Adventures Of Superman" Comic Booklet,**
c. 1942. Py-Co-Pay tooth powder. Eight-page color booklet. - **$53 $159 $750**

SUP-85

❑ **SUP-85. "Superman Overseas Cap,"**
c. 1942. Issued by Skippy Peanut Butter. 5-1/4x11" fabric promoting also station KECA. - **$1200 $2750 $5000**

SUP-86 SUP-87

❑ **SUP-86. "Superman-Tim Club" Litho. Button,**
c. 1942. 7/8". Back slogan "Member In Good Standing". - **$15 $25 $60**

❑ **SUP-87. "Superman-Tim Club" Litho. Button,**
c. 1942. 7/8". Reverse has message in symbols to decode using member's code card. - **$20 $45 $90**

SUP-88

❑ **SUP-88. "Third War Loan" Card,**
1943. Rare. 11" x 11". - **$800 $1600 $2800**

SUP-89

❑ SUP-89. Decoder Folder,
1943. Scarce. Similar to one used in club kit. Pictures comics on the reverse. Given away at theaters. - **$150 $325 $550**

SUP-90

❑ SUP-90. Superman "Victory Kid" Handout,
1943. Stiff paper is 4-1/8x7" with image of Superman from chest up with art by Jack Burnley. Issued by the War Department in conjunction with Schools At War Activities League to be handed out by various groups. Text above Superman reads "Superman Says Knowledge Defends Our Future" and text below says "Quiet Please A Victory Kid Is Studying."
- **$135 $250 $500**

SUP-91

❑ SUP-91. War Savings Bond Poster,
1943. 12-1/2"x19-1/2". **$6000 $12,000 $25,000**

SUP-92

❑ SUP-92. Superman-Tim Birthday Postcards,
1943. Various designs. Each - **$30 $75 $150**

SUP-93

❑ SUP-93. "Superman Special Edition U.S. Navy" Comic Book,
1944. Similar to Superman Comic Book #33 but with alterations to the cover plus additional contents. - **$53 $159 $750**

SUP-94

❑ SUP-94. "Superman Transfers" Pack,
1944. Detective Comics. Store packet containing "A Whole Flock Of Honest-To-Goodness" water transfer pictures. - **$200 $400 $1000**

SUP-95

❑ SUP-95. "Superman's Christmas Adventure" Comic Book,
1944. Various stores. Example photo shows Christmas Tree variety cover and first page. - **$103 $309 $1500**

SUP-96 SUP-97

❑ SUP-96. "Superman's Christmas Play Book" Comic Book,
1944. Various stores. Candy cane and Superman cover. - **$97 $291 $1400**

❑ SUP-97. "Sincerely, Superman" Charity Reply Postcard,
1944. Response card for March of Dimes contribution. - **$250 $500 $1000**

SUP-98

❑ SUP-98. "Superman-Tim Club" Felt Patch,
1945. Various stores. Six different known. Each - **$250 $750 $1500**

SUP-99

❑ SUP-99. Superman Glow-In-The-Dark Picture,
c. 1945. Probable store item, at least four different known. Each - **$250 $500 $1000**

SUP-100

❑ SUP-100. Pep Cereal Box With Superman Button Pictured on Front,
1945. Rare. - **$250 $500 $750**

SUP-101

❑ SUP-101. Superman/Tim "Franco Club" Patch,
1946. "Franco" is likely name of boys' clothing store. - **$400 $800 $1350**

SUP-102

SUP-103

❑ SUP-102. Kellogg's "Superman Crusader" Silvered Brass Ring,
1946. Offered on "Adventures of Superman" radio show for 15 episodes beginning 10/28/1946 through 11/15/1946. One example seen with brass finish and no silvering. Perhaps taken home by worker prior to plating.
Standard Silvered Version - **$65 $150 $250**
Brass Version - **$150 $350 $700**

❑ SUP-103. Pep Monthly Calendar Card,
1946. - **$200 $400 $800**

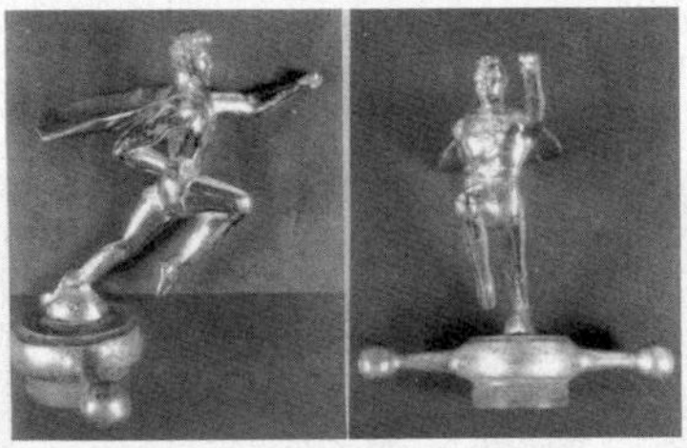

SUP-104

❑ SUP-104. Metal Hood Or Bicycle Ornament,
c. 1946. Store item by L. W. Lee Mfg. Co.
8" Tall Chrome Or Gold Finish - **$1000 $2000 $3000**
6" Tall Chrome Or Gold Finish - **$1250 $2650 $4750**
Box With Hardware - **$300 $600 $1000**

SUP-105

❑ SUP-105. "Superman-Tim Press Card",
c. 1946. Opens to 9" to hold 12 poster stamps.
No Stamps - **$100 $200 $300**
Each Mounted Stamp Add **$8 $15 $30**

SUP-106

❑ SUP-106. Grocer's Calendar Card,
1947. Kellogg's Pep. Very colorful 4-1/2x9-1/2" monthly card urging stock and display of cereal featuring Superman endorsement. Pictured example is for September. - **$600 $1300 $2200**

SUP-107

❑ SUP-107. Kellogg's Pep Box Back,
1947. #3 of at least 12. Text below story reads: For further exciting Adventures of Superman, read the backs of other Pep packages and follow the Superman radio program on the Mutual Network. Each Cut Panel - **$75 $150 $300**

SUP-108

SUP-109

❑ **SUP-108. Sterling Silver Full-Dimensional Charm,**
1947. Designed by Dell Weston of California. Only 1-1/8" tall with red enamel painted cape. - **$150 $300 $600**

❑ **SUP-109. "Superman-Tim Club Membership Card",**
1947. Various clothing stores.
- **$100 $200 $325**

SUP-110

❑ **SUP-110. Magic Record Set,**
1947. Musette Records. Color folder #1 or #2 with story and records. Each - **$50 $100 $185**

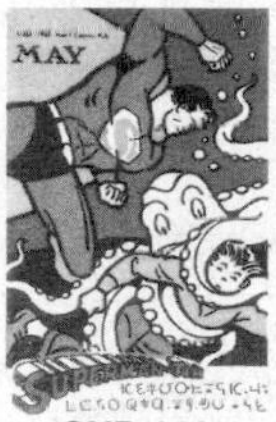

SUP-111

SUP-112

❑ **SUP-111. "Superman-Tim" Large Gummed Stamp,**
May 1947. Various participating stores. Issued monthly 1947-1950 to mount in club magazine. Each - **$20 $45 $100**

❑ **SUP-112. Australian Newspaper Superman Club Stickpin,**
1947. The Argus. 7/8" brass luster disk has embossed image of Superman in red along with newspaper name while below is a green panel surrounding inscription "Superman Club." - **$75 $150 $300**

SUP-113

❑ **SUP-113. Superman Super-Babe Composition Jointed Doll,**
1947. Imperial Crown Toy Company. Composition doll is 15" tall and manufactured by Imperial Crown Toy Company. Jointed at shoulders, hips and head, doll has sleep eyes. Comes with detailed costume including snap-on cape, shirt with felt Superman chest emblem, cloth pants with snap and snap vinyl belt, plus shoes and socks. - **$300 $600 $1200**

SUP-114

❑ **SUP-114. "Radio Quiz Master Games With Model Microphone" With Mailer Envelope,**
1948. National Comics. Superman name on envelope and game but no picture. Includes punch-out cardboard microphone.
Mailer - **$10 $35 $60**
Game - **$30 $100 $200**

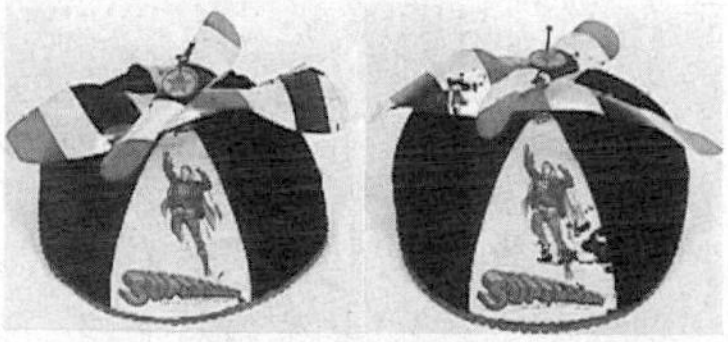

SUP-115

❑ **SUP-115. "Superman" Felt Beanie With Plastic Propellers,**
1948. Apparent store item with copyright of Nat'l Comics Pub. Inc. 7" diameter with alternating felt and leatherette panels plus metal rod at top holding three thin plastic propellers with small plastic star disk. Photo example is missing one propeller. - **$800 $1750 $3500**

SUP-116

❑ **SUP-116. DC Comics Picture,**
1948. Back pictures comic book covers. - **$65 $135 $275**

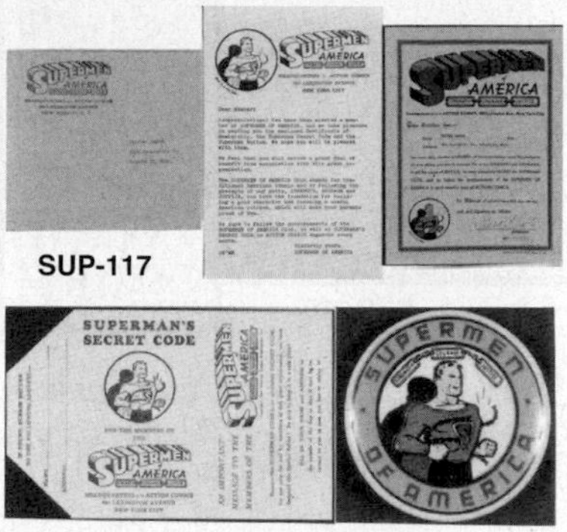

SUP-117

❑ **SUP-117. Membership Kit,**
1948. DC Comics. Includes envelope, letter, certificate, code folder, cello. button.
Complete With Envelope - **$150 $225 $425**
Letter - **$20 $40 $70**
Certificate - **$60 $80 $150**
Code Folder - **$20 $30 $60**
Button - **$20 $35 $70**

SUP-118

❑ **SUP-118. "Gilbert Hall Of Science" Catalogue,**
1948. A. C. Gilbert Co. - **$50 $115 $200**

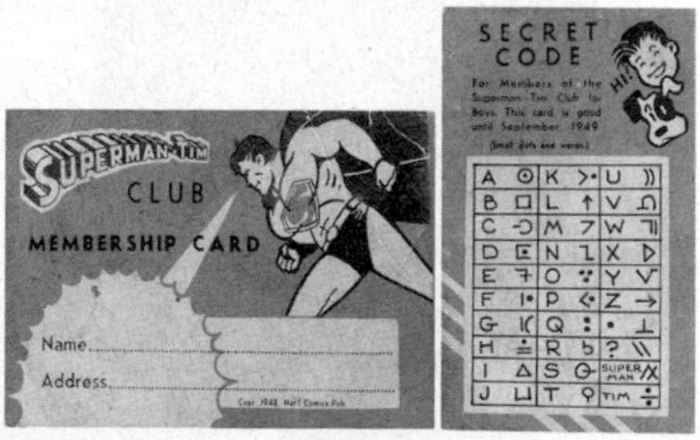

SUP-119

❑ **SUP-119. Superman-Tim Club Membership Card,**
1948. Paper card copyright by National Comics Publications. Front features Superman while back pictures Tim and has secret code to decipher stories in Superman-Tim magazines. - **$100 $200 $325**

SUP-120

❑ **SUP-120. "Superman-Tim Store" Birthday Postcard,**
1948. - **$25 $50 $125**

SUP-121

❑ **SUP-121. "Superman Film Serial" Australian Button,**
c. 1948. 1" cello in red/white/two shades of blue, likely promotion for serial starring Kirk Alyn with imprint for local "Hoyts Suburban Theaters." - **$100 $300 $600**

SUP-122

❑ **SUP-122. "Superman" Premium Enameled Brass Shield And Wallet,**
1949. Fo-Lee Gum Corp., Philadelphia. Reverse has two brass tabs to fold rather than bar pin. Issued attached to interior left of leather wallet by the Pioneer Co. which has embossed "Superman" figure enclosed by a chain circle on the front.
Badge - **$1650 $3750 $7500**
Wallet - **$1500 $3000 $6000**

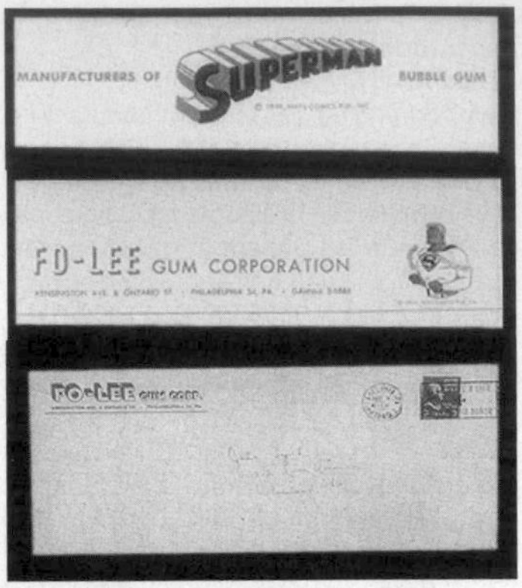

SUP-123

❑ **SUP-123. "Superman Bubble Gum" Maker's Stationery With Envelope,**
1949. Fo-Lee Gum Corp., Philadelphia. Stationery letterhead pictures Superman, bottom margin includes his name.
Envelope - **$50 $100 $225**
Stationery - **$100 $175 $375**

SUP-124

❑ **SUP-124. "Kellogg's Pep Real Photos" 22x32" Poster,**
1949. Folder that opens from 11x16" picturing movie and sports stars miniature photos offered individually as box inserts and in enlarged size as mail premiums. Superman image is pictured in two details. - **$300 $600 $900**

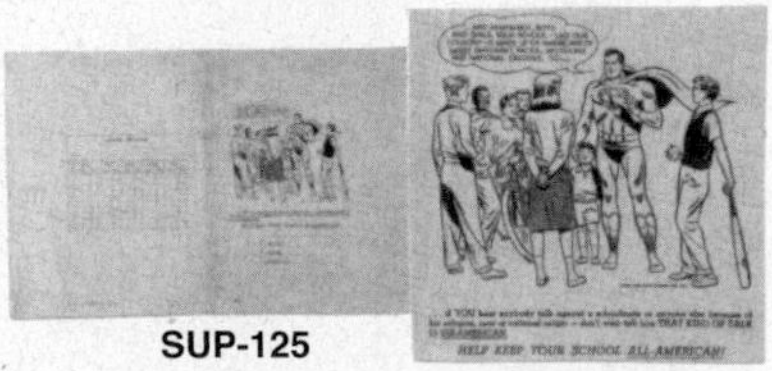

SUP-125

❑ **SUP-125. Superman Book Cover,**
1949. Nat'l Comics Pub. Inc. Distributed by Institute For American Democracy, Inc. 12x18" black on tan paper with text calling negative talk about religion, race or national origin "Un-American." - **$85 $165 $325**

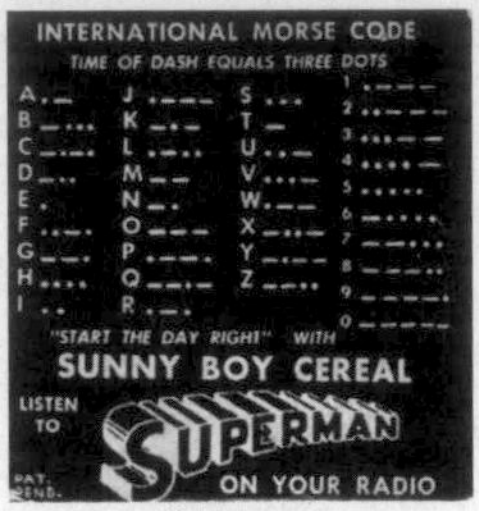

SUP-126

❑ **SUP-126. Sunny Boy Cereal Code Premium,**
1940s. Scarce. Canadian issue. - **$150 $400 $800**

SUP-127

❑ **SUP-127. Comic Book Rack Promo Photo,**
1940s. Central Wire Frame Co. 5-1/2x8-1/2" showing example books for Superman, King Comics, Feature Comics, Whiz Comics, Target Comics. - **$45 $85 $160**

SUP-128

❑ **SUP-128. Superman-Tim Bracelet,**
1940s. Scarce. - **$400 $800 $1600**

SUP-129 SUP-130

❑ **SUP-129. "Superman-Tim" Magazine,**
1940s. One of two examples shown. Issued monthly August 1942-May 1950. See next item for prices.

❑ **SUP-130. "Superman-Tim Magazine,**
1940s. Issued monthly August 1942-May 1950.
First Issue - **$750 $2000 $3000**
Other Issues - See *The Overstreet Comic Book Price Guide.*

SUP-131

❑ **SUP-131. Superman-Tim Shadow-Grams Booklet,**
Late 1940s. Giveaway book pictures 30 shadow puppets by the master of illusion Prince Hara. - **$175 $350 $700**

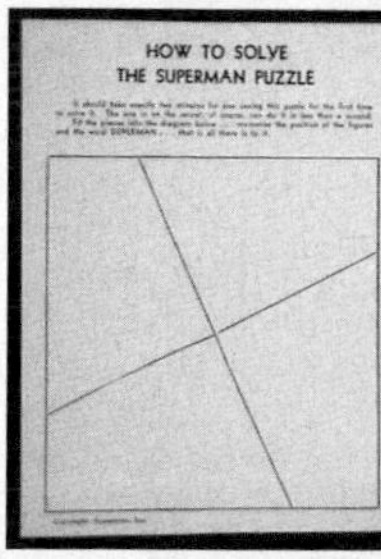

SUP-132

❑ **SUP-132. "Superman Magic Square Puzzle" Salesman's Sample Premium,**
1940s. Made by "Stunts! Inc." with blank area on envelope captioned "Imprint Here." Contains four cut puzzle pieces printed on both sides along with 5x6-1/4" diagram showing how to solve the puzzle by forming a square. Gordon Gold Archives. - **$750 $1500 $2750**

SUP-133

❑ **SUP-133. Metal Figural Pin,**
c. 1940s. Probable store item. 1-3/4" tall with painted features in fleshtone with small black and red accents and with traditional red and blue outfit. No markings. - **$150 $300 $600**

SUP-134

❑ **SUP-134. "Superman" Zippered Leather Billfold,**
1940s. Store item by Pioneer. -
$125 $250 $500

SUP-135

❑ **SUP-135. "Supermen Of Canada" Felt Patch,**
1940s. Issued by Oglivie Oats, sponsors of the radio program in Canada. 3-1/2" diameter blue on white. Rare. Three known examples.
- **$750 $1750 $4000**

SUP-136

❑ **SUP-136. Superman-Tim Club Card,**
1940s. Red, white and blue with Secret Code chart on reverse. - **$100 $200 $325**

SUP-137

SUP-138

❑ **SUP-137. Superman-Tim Celluloid Pin,**
1940s. - **$250 $500 $750**

❑ **SUP-138. Superman-Tim "Press Card",**
1940s. Reverse blocks for 12 code stamps.
Card - **$100 $200 $300**
Each Stamp Mounted Add - **$8 $15 $30**

SUP-139

❑ **SUP-139. Superman-Tim Silvered Brass Store Ring,**
1940s. Depicts Superman flying above initials "S T". 27 reported known: 2 in Good grade, 16 in Very Good, 5 in Fine, 2 in Very Fine and 2 in Near Mint. - **$450 $1000 $3000**

SUP-140

❑ **SUP-140. "Superman Silent Flame Lighter By Dunhill,"**
1940s. Battery operated lighter is 3x3x4.5" tall with Bakelite plastic base and attached solid cast metal 3" figure of Superman. Has pull-out cylindrical flame unit and underside panel featuring company information.
- **$1250 $2500 $4000**

SUP-141

❑ **SUP-141. "Superman-Tim Club" Large Patch,**
1940s. Felt patch is 5.5x6.75" with silk-screened design. From a series of at least six different patches issued by various stores with this being the largest and most impressive.
- **$400 $800 $1600**

SUP-142

SUP-143

❑ **SUP-142. "Superman-Tim" Felt Pennant,**
1940s. Scarce. Various clothing stores. Seen in yellow or red. Each - **$150 $300 $600**

❑ **SUP-143. Superman-Tim "Redback" Currency Bills,**
1940s. Each - **$5 $8 $20**

SUP-144

❑ **SUP-144. "Superman-Tim Club" Bat Toy,**
1940s. Various participating stores imprinted on back. Diecut masonite with very colorful litho. paper art from set that included rubber darts to strike at. - **$100 $200 $400**

SUP-145

❑ **SUP-145. "Superman-Tim Club" Bat Toy,**
1940s. Various participating department stores imprinted on back. Diecut masonite with very colorful litho. paper design. - **$100 $200 $400**

SUP-146

❑ **SUP-146. Superman Belt in Box,**
1940s. Belt by Pioneer has metal circular buckle with Superman on front and graphics on leather strap. Box - **$75 $125 $200**
Belt and Buckle - **$75 $125 $275**
Buckle Only - **$35 $65 $125**

SUP-147

❑ **SUP-147. Superman Pep Box,**
1940s. Promotes Pep comic character pinbacks. Back features an 8-panel Superman comic strip from series of at least 12.
Complete - **$500 $1000 $2000**

SUP-148

❑ **SUP-148. "Sunday Mail Comics Club" Australia Button,**
1940s. Newspaper sponsored club. Black, white, red, gray. - **$200 $400 $600**

SUP-149

❑ **SUP-149. "Sun-Times Comic Capers Club" Button,**
1940s. 2.25" cello centered by blue portraits of Superman, Nancy, Sluggo and parrot on white background rimmed in red. One of the rarest and most desirable comic character buttons. - **$750 $2000 $3750**

SUP-150

❑ **SUP-150. "Atom Man vs. Superman" 6' Movie Standee,**
1950. Columbia serial. - **$6000 $12,500 $25,000**

SUP-151

❑ **SUP-151. One-Sheet,**
1950. Promotes *Atom Man vs. Superman* serial. - **$1250 $2500 $4000**

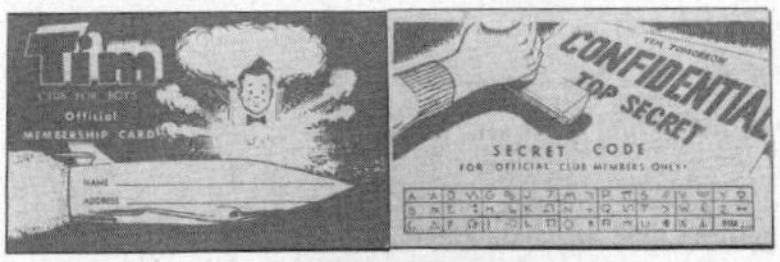

SUP-152

❑ **SUP-152. "Superman-Tim Club" Member Card,**
c. 1950. Stiff paper card picturing Superman on front. Back pictures Tim and has secret code. - **$50 $100 $200**

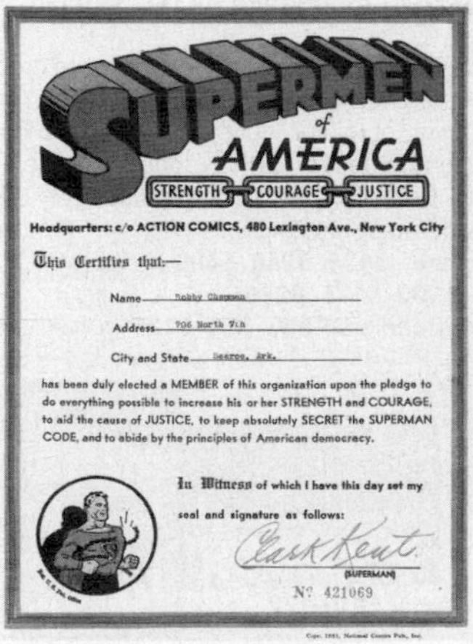

SUP-153

❑ **SUP-153. Superman Certificate,**
1951. - **$65 $90 $165**

SUP-154

SUP-155

❑ **SUP-154. Superman TV Guide,**
September 25, 1953. Featured George Reeves on the cover as Clark Kent and Superman. Inside was a story about the popular TV show. - **$100 $200 $500**

❑ **SUP-155. "Superman Muscle Building Club" Litho. Button,**
1954. Store item. Came with child's exercise set. - **$50 $100 $150**

SUP-156

❑ **SUP-156. "Superman" Premium Picture,**
1954. Issued by National Comics Publications. 4-7/8x6-7/8". - **$50 $125 $250**

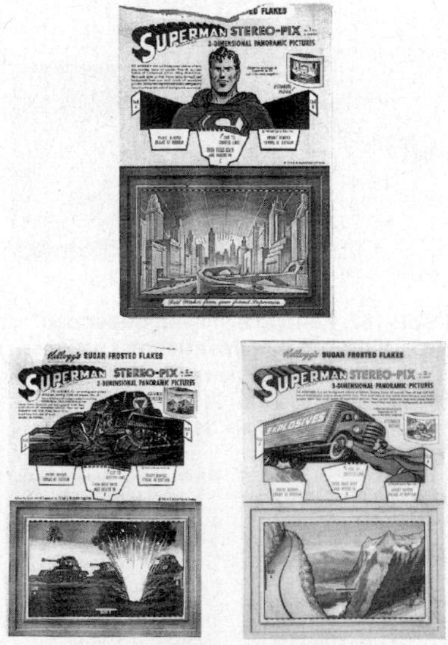

SUP-157

❑ **SUP-157. Kellogg's Stereo-Pix Box Back,**
1954. Sugar Frosted Flakes. Backs #1, #2, and #3 from series of 3-D assembly panels.
Uncut Box Back - **$40 $75 $150**

SUP-158

❑ **SUP-158. "Superman Golden Muscle Building Set" Boxed,**
1954. Peter Puppet Playthings. Large boxed set of youthful exercise equipment. Inner lid has seven-panel story of Superman teaching lad how to use the set. Equipment is accompanied by certificate, progress chart, litho button.
Complete With Button - **$300 $600 $1000**
Complete Except Button - **$250 $500 $850**

SUP-159

❑ **SUP-159. Playsuit & Fan Club Newspaper Ad,**
1954. Abraham & Straus Co., Brooklyn. Color ad picturing youth modeling example playsuit. Lower right pictures comic book, member card and I.D. card that accompanied each playsuit purchase. - **$20 $40 $85**

SUP-160

❑ **SUP-160. "Dangle-Dandies" Cereal Boxes Newspaper Ad,**
1955. Kellogg's Rice Krispies & Corn Flakes. Eight mobile character faces: Clarabell, pirate, skull, Tony the Tiger, Superman, Mr. Bluster, Indian, Howdy Doody. Ad Only - **$15 $30 $60**

(FRONT) **SUP-161** (BACK)

❑ **SUP-161. Kellogg's Sugar Smacks Cereal Box with Comic Book Offer,**
1955. Rare classic 1950's box which promotes free Superman comics inside the box. Comic books shown as **SUP 162, 163, 164.**
Near Mint Flat - **$6500**
Used Complete - **$500 $1150 $2250**

SUP-162

❑ **SUP-162 "The Superman Time Capsule" Comic Book,**
1955. Kellogg's Sugar Smacks. From set of three. Art by Win Mortimer. - **$34 $102 $420**

SUP-163

❑ **SUP-163. "Duel In Space" Comic Book,**
1955. Kellogg's Sugar Smacks. From set of three. - **$32 $96 $400**

SUP-164

❑ **SUP-164. "The Supershow Of Metropolis" Comic Booklet,**
1955. Kellogg's Sugar Smacks. From set of three. - **$32 $96 $400**

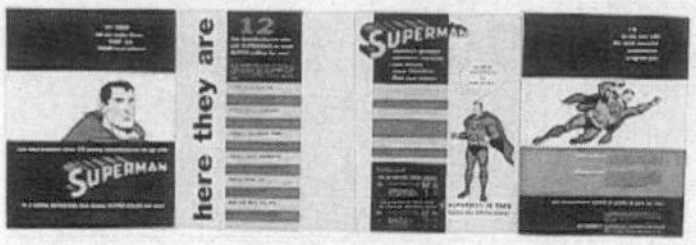

SUP-165

❑ **SUP-165. Sales Promotion Folder,**
1955. National Comics Publications Inc. 8-3/4x11-3/4" four-page glossy stiff paper folder with Superman appearing on three pages along with list of "12 Top Manufacturers" of Superman merchandise. Gordon Gold Archives. - **$300 $600 $1200**

SUP-166

❑ **SUP-166. Kellogg's "Flying Superman" Toy Offer Box,**
1955. Complete Box - **$250 $600 $1000**

SUP-167

❑ **SUP-167. Kellogg's "Flying Superman" Thin Plastic Toy With Instruction Leaflet,**
1955. Fragile premium flown by rubber band.
Instructions - **$50 $100 $135**
Figure And Plastic Stick - **$125 $250 $500**

SUP-168

❑ **SUP-168. Kellogg's Corn Flakes Cereal Box with Krypton Hydro-Jet Rocket Offer,**
1955. 12 ounce box with Norman Rockwell art on front. - **$225 $500 $900**

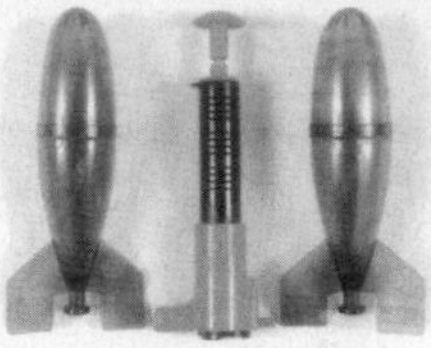

SUP-169

SUP-170

❑ **SUP-169. "Krypton Rocket" Plastic Set With Launcher,**
1955. Kellogg's. Rockets in red, blue, or green plastic with Superman logo.
Each Rocket - **$20 $45 $65**
Launcher - **$35 $75 $150**

❑ **SUP-170. Kellogg's Belt And Buckle,**
1955. Aluminum buckle with plastic belt.
Buckle - **$50 $100 $175**
With Belt - **$75 $150 $375**

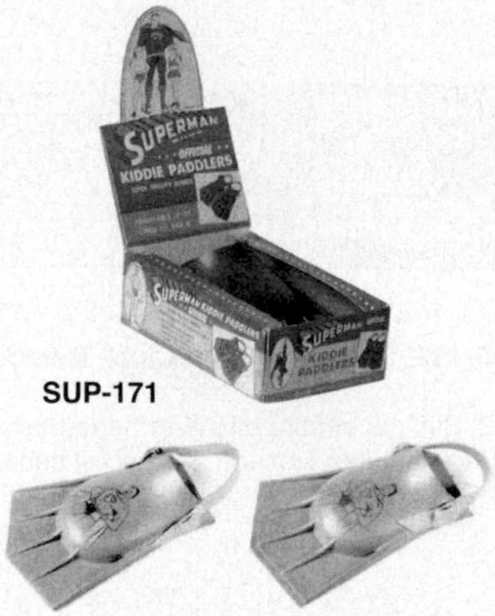

SUP-171

❑ **SUP-171. Superman Kiddie Paddlers in Box,**
1955. The popularity of the TV program prompted Super Swim Inc. to feature Superman on the packaging of this product. The boxes represent some of the best graphics produced in the 1950s. Each box also contained a Safety Swim Club membership card.
Complete - **$135 $240 $400**
Box - **$100 $175 $275**
Kiddie Paddlers - **$35 $65 $125**

SUP-172

❑ **SUP-172. "Sports Club" Membership Card,**
1955. Store item. Came with swim fins or goggles. - **$30 $60 $90**

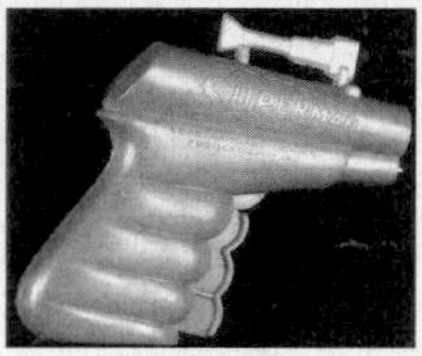

SUP-174

SUP-173

❑ SUP-173. Kellogg's Dangle-Dandy Box Back,
1955. Uncut Box Back - **$35 $65 $125**
Trimmed Out Figure - **$15 $30 $65**

❑ SUP-174. Kellogg's "Space Satellite Launcher Set",
1956. Came with two plastic spinners.
Complete With Spinners - **$200 $400 $800**
Box And Instructions - **$50 $100 $200**

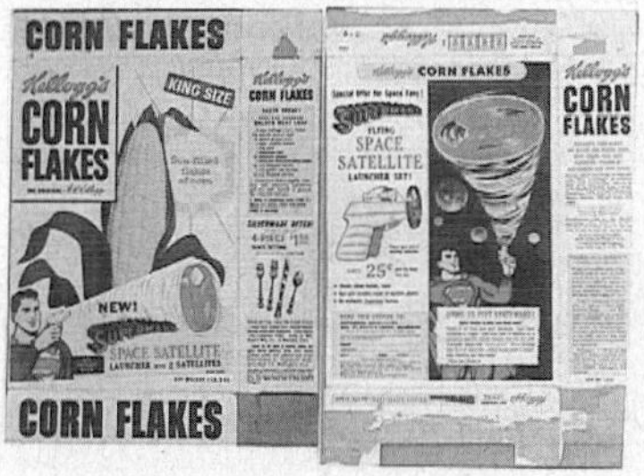

SUP-175

❑ SUP-175. Cereal Box With "Superman's Space Satellite Launcher" Offer,
1956. "King Size" box advertising "Superman's Flying Space Satellite Launcher Set" for 25 cents and one box top. Gordon Gold Archives.
Used Complete - **$250 $600 $1000**

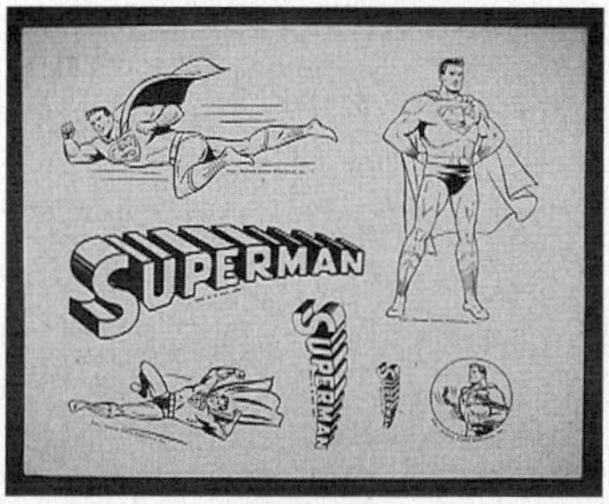

SUP-176

❑ SUP-176. Merchandiser's Guide,
1956. Glossy black and white sheet, 10 3/4 x 13" with 4 Superman images and 3 logos for use on products. Gordon Gold Archives. - **$85 $165 $325**

SUP-177

❑ SUP-177. "Superman Candy & Toy" Box,
1950s. Novel Packaging Corp. From same series as SUP-182 showing Superman. Photo shows back panel "Play Card." -
$150 $300 $700

SUP-178

❑ SUP-178. Life-Size Cardboard Store Display,
1956. Kellogg's Corn Flakes. Top diecut to hold jumbo display cereal box. Promotes Superman TV series.
Display Without Box - **$1250 $3000 $5500**
Display Box Only - **$150 $300 $600**

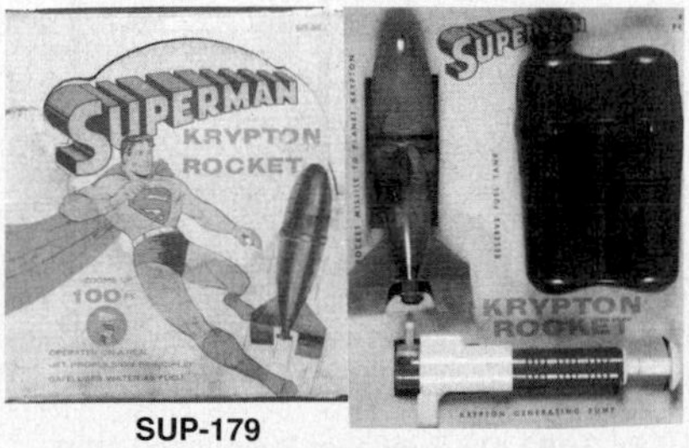

SUP-179

❑ SUP-179. "Superman Krypton Rocket" Boxed Set,
1956. Park Plastics Co. also issued as Kellogg's premium. Set consists of plastic fuel tank, pump unit, transparent rocket with Superman markings. Toy uses water as fuel. - **$135 $250 $500**

SUP-180

❑ SUP-180. "Superman" Hot Iron Transfer,
1950s. 8-3/4x9-1/4" tissue paper sheet. Gordon Gold Archives. **- $45 $85 $150**

SUP-181

❑ SUP-181. "Kellogg's Fun Catalog",
1950s. - **$40 $80 $150**

SUP-182

❑ SUP-182. "Superman Candy & Toy" Box,
1950s. Novel Package Corp. 1x2-1/2x4" long cardboard with "Play Card" back panel. One of a series. Also see SUP-177.
Each - **$150 $300 $700**

SUP-183

❑ SUP-183. Playsuit Mailing Folder,
1950s. Promotion to retailers from Funtime Playwear, Inc. - **$85 $175 $350**

SUP-184

❑ SUP-184. Fan Club Card,
1950s. Probably came with playsuit by Funtime Playwear. - **$30 $60 $110**

SUP-185

❑ SUP-185. George Reeves Fan Card,
1950s. DC Comics. - **$40 $80 $165**

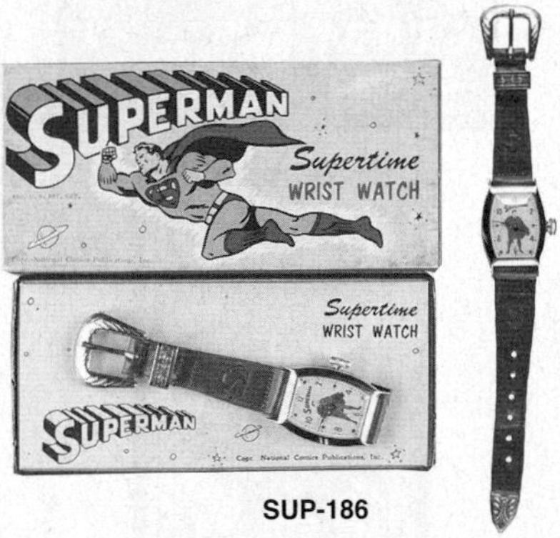

SUP-186

❑ SUP-186. Superman Supertime Wrist Watch,
c. 1950s. Ingraham. Chrome case watch. Full figure image in dial. "S" shield symbol on each band. Box insert has Superman name and space graphics. Box lid has nice image of Superman on two side panels and top panel. Box with insert - **$1000 $2000 $3000**
Watch - **$400 $800 $1200**

SUP-187

SUP-188

❑ SUP-187. Toy Watch,
1950s. Store item by Esco, West Germany. - **$65 $150 $325**

❑ SUP-188. "Supermen Of America" Cello. Button,
1950s. DC Comics. - **$25 $50 $75**

SUP-189 SUP-190

❑ SUP-189. "Supermen Of America" Color Variety Cello. Button,
1950s. DC Comics. Pictured in white shirt rather than blue with red/yellow chest symbol. Rare variety from DC files, apparently for test purposes. - **$250 $550 $1050**

❑ SUP-190. "Supermen Of America" Cello. Button,
1961. National Periodical Publications. Final version of series with 1961 copyright on rim edge. Same dated bottom was used for 1965 kit. - **$20 $35 $65**

SUP-191 SUP-192

❑ SUP-191. "Initiative Award" Poster 11x14",
c. 1963. Independent News Co. Inc. given to comic book retailers. - **$65 $125 $200**

❑ SUP-192. DC Publisher Response Letter To Fan Letter,
1964. National Periodical Publications Inc. Mentions upcoming Superboy television program and 80-page Giant DC Annuals. - **$35 $50 $80**

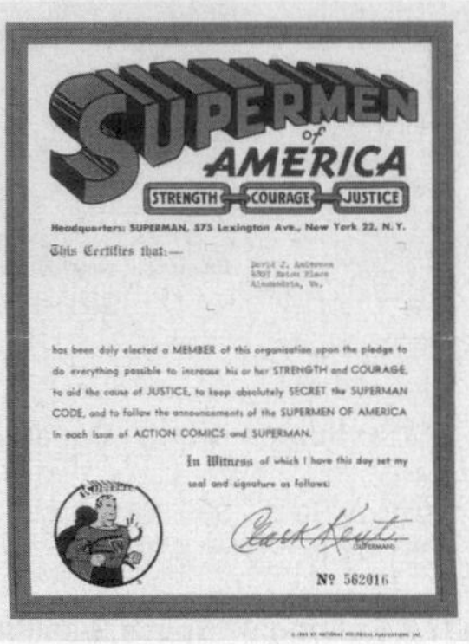

SUP-193

❑ SUP-193. Superman Membership Certificate,
1965. Last year for the Club. May be the rarest of all varieties of Superman Certificates since their beginning in 1939. Lack of participation in the Club was probably due to the strong market for Marvel Heroes which diverted interest from the DC Heroes. - **$200 $400 $600**

SUP-194

❑ SUP-194. "Superman Cards" Rare Test Box,
1965. Topps Gum. 3.75x8x1-1/8" deep countertop display box is a test issue with several notable differences from the standard box. Both boxes feature photo of George Reeves as Superman on the lid, however, this test box has portrait of him as Superman on front side panel only whereas the standard box has that portrait in addition to one of him as Clark Kent, and on the right and left side panels the text "Superman Cards" and price of 5-cents is positioned differently. - **$325 $650 $1100**

SUP-195

❑ SUP-195. "Superman Cards" Standard Issue Display Box,
1965. Box is 3.75x8x1-7/8" deep and originally contained 24 packs of cards issued by Topps. - **$125 $250 $400**

SUP-196

SUP-197

SUP-198

❑ **SUP-196. Superman Club 3-1/2" Cello. Button With Retail Box,**
1966. Store item. Box originally held quantity of buttons. Button - **$5 $10 $25**
Empty Box - **$40 $75 $150**

❑ **SUP-197. Superman Litho. Button,**
1966. N.P.P. Inc. Vending machine issue, set of eight. Each - **$10 $15 $25**

❑ **SUP-198. "New Adventures Of Superman" Gummed Paper Sticker,**
1966. CBS-TV. For introduction of Saturday morning animated series beginning September 10. Unused - **$15 $30 $60**

SUP-199

❑ **SUP-199. "Superman Golden Records" Boxed Set,**
1966. N.P.P. Inc. Includes comic book, LP record, iron-on patch, membership card with secret code, Supermen Of America litho. button. Complete - **$35 $75 $175**

SUP-200

SUP-200. Superman Pennant,
1966. 29" long. - **$75 $165 $325**

SUP-201

SUP-202

❑ **SUP-201. "Superman" Rare Flicker Rings,**
1966. Issuer unknown. Has tiny copyright symbol and word "Eppy." Gold plastic base holds flicker with yellow or blue background showing various images of Superman. Set of eight.
Each - **$85 $175 $300**

❑ **SUP-202. Eating Set,**
1966. Knife and fork, store bought.
On Card - **$60 $115 $200**
Each Utensil Loose - **$8 $12 $25**

SUP-203

❑ **SUP-203. "All Star Dairies" 1968 Calendar,**
1967. 8x10" complete 12-month calendar featuring cover page Christmas art of Superman and All Star Dairies Boy. Each calendar page has small illustration of them in activity related to the particular month. - **$85 $175 $350**

SUP-204

❑ **SUP-204. "Superman" & "Batman" Comic Book Display Rack Sign,**
1960s. 5.75x11.75" two-sided litho tin sign with wire frame for attachment to display rack. - **$115 $225 $450**

SUP-205

❑ **SUP-205. Superman Plastic Identification Label,**
1960s. These were logo ads attached to comic book racks in the early '60s.
Each - **$55 $85 $165**

SUP-206

SUP-207

❑ **SUP-206. "All Star Dairy Foods" Plastic Truck Bank,**
1960s. - **$50 $100 $200**

❑ **SUP-207. Vending Machine Header Card,**
c. 1971. Includes Marvel and DC characters in form of magnet, sticker, rubber figures and Wonder Woman/Diana Prince flicker picture. - **$75 $150 $250**

SUP-208

❑ **SUP-208. Metal Figure Sculpture,**
1972. 10.25" tall solid white metal figure casting in silver finish and also in bronze finish. An example has been seen with a plate set into base fron reading "Super Salesman October 1972." Detailing includes "S" chest emblem that also includes tiny "30" within the chest logo, possibly for an anniversary year. Sculpture weight is nearly five pounds.
- **$175 $350 $600**

SUP-209

❑ **SUP-209. Record,**
1972. Coca-Cola premium. - **$15 $35 $75**

SUP-210

❑ SUP-210. "Original Radio Broadcast" Vol. 1 Record Album,
1974. Kellogg's Corn Flakes. Issued as set of four.
Each - **$12 $30 $60**

SUP-211

❑ SUP-211. Superman 1 ounce Silver Ingot,
1974. Ingot proof. Copyright National Periodical Publications. - **$35 $60 $90**

SUP-212

❑ SUP-212. Post Sugar Crisp Cereal Box - 12 oz.,
1975. Offers mini comic books. Superman appears on front; Superman, Batman, Robin, and Wonder Woman on back of box -
$75 $150 $265

SUP-213

❑ SUP-213. Kellogg's Corn Flakes Cereal Box - 12 oz.,
1976. Offers record album. Superman appears on front and back of box - **$75 $150 $265**

SUP-214

SUP-215

❑ SUP-214. Nestle's Domed Ring With Mailer,
1976. Near Mint With Mailer - **$65**
Ring Only - **$10 $20 $40**

❑ SUP-215. "I Saw Superman" 3-1/2" Cello. Button,
1976. Issued for Albright-Knox Art Gallery exhibit. - **$20 $50 $100**

SUP-216

❑ SUP-216. "Kryptonite Rocks!!" Sign,
1977. 18.5x20" full color sign for toy rocks product that glow in dark. - **$30 $65 $140**

SUP-217

SUP-218

❑ SUP-217. Movie Sheet Music,
1978. "Can You Read My Mind?" love theme. -
$15 $30 $50

❑ SUP-218. Drake's Trading Cards 23x32" Store Sign,
1978. - **$20 $40 $80**

SUP-219

❑ SUP-219. "Super Heroes Fun Book And Check List",
1978. Various bread companies. Check list for sticker set. See next item. - **$20 $40 $75**

SUP-220

SUP-221

❑ SUP-220. Super Hero Stickers,
1978. Various bread companies. Set of 30. See SUP-219. Each Unused - **$2 $4 $6**

❑ SUP-221. "Superbank" 3-1/2" Cello. Button,
1970s. Garden State National Bank, probably others. - **$25 $45 $85**

SUP-222

❑ SUP-222. Post Honey-Comb Cereal Box,
1970s. Superman appears on front; offers Superman poster - set of 4 on back of box -
$75 $135 $250

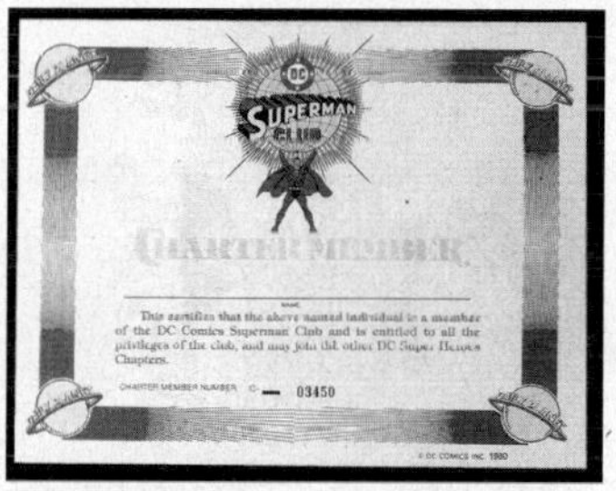

SUP-223

❑ SUP-223. DC Comics Superman Club Membership Kit,
1980. DC Comics. 8.75x11.75" mailing envelope containing serially numbered Charter Member Certificate, Welcome letter from newsletter editor Laurie Sutton, Superman Club bookcover, gold foil paper Official Membership card serially numbered, gold foil Superman Club sticker, large iron-on showing club logo image in reverse for application, 16.5x21" poster picturing Superman and other DC characters, Daily Planet Vol. 1 #1 newsletter from September-October 1980. Near Mint Complete - **$75**

SUP-224

❑ SUP-224. Rotary Dial Telephone,
1981. Character Phones Inc. Large 17.5" tall hard plastic figural phone in original but generic white cardboard box. Figure is accompanied by separate fabric cape attached by velcro strip. Mint In Generic Box - **$1000**

SUP-225

❑ SUP-225. "Superman Peanut Butter" 7x11" Paper Store Sign,
1981. Includes pad of t-shirt order forms. - **$35 $65 $100**

SUP-226

❑ SUP-226. "Superman's Kryptonite!" Card With Sample,
1983. 4x6" card with blister pack square holding Kryptonite samples to produce Superman qualities by user. - **$20 $35 $60**

SUP-227

❑ SUP-227. Super Powers Standee,
1984. 1st standee to promote Superboy. - **$125 $250 $400**

(Initial version shown with error listing of "Joe Siegel and Jerry Shuster" on the back)

SUP-228

❑ SUP-228. Superman 50th Birthday Coin,
1988. From a series devoted to different cartoon characters. When the coin was initially struck, the first names of Superman creators Jerry Siegel and Joe Shuster had been reversed. The error was fixed and the coin was struck properly.
Silver 1 oz. round with error - **$55 $85**
Silver 1 oz. round with correct names - **$18 $30**

SUP-229

❑ SUP-229. "Supergirl" Motion Picture Soundtrack Album,
1984. - **$10 $20 $40**

SUP-230

SUP-231

❑ **SUP-230. Super Powers Clark Kent Mail-In Action Figure,**
1986. Available only by mail with five proof-of-purchase seals from Super Powers figures.
Figure - **$15 $30 $65**
Generic Mailer Box - **$5 $10 $20**

❑ **SUP-231. Kryptonite Ring,**
1990. Toy Biz. Came packaged with Superman action figure. - **$10 $20 $30**

SUP-232

❑ **SUP-232. Vitamins Club Member Kit,**
1991. Pharmavite Corp. Large mailing envelope with "Kids Of Steel Team" logo holding Vol. 1 #1 newsletter and "Official Membership Certificate," both shown. Also included but not shown: personalized plastic membership card, Superman watch, two DC Comics super heroes cards (2-1/8x3-3/8", one card was also in each store-purchased vitamin package), comic book (example we've seen had issue #480 "The Adventures Of Superman"). Near Mint Complete - **$70**

SUP-233

❑ **SUP-233. "Mild-Mannered Sales Associate" Superman Logo Button,**
1992. Fossil Watch Co. Worn only by Fossil sales people, not intended as a giveaway. - **$15 $30 $60**

SUP-234

❑ **SUP-234. Superman Resin Figure,**
1993. Limited to 6,100. Shown many times on the "Seinfeld" TV show, causing great demand in the secondary market. Boxed - **$525**

SUP-235

❑ **SUP-235. Superman Statue,**
1993. By Ron Lee, limited to 750. Comes with tag. Statue and base are 12" high. - **$175**

SUP-236

❑ **SUP-236. Reign of the Supermen Watch,**
1993. Limited to 15,000. With instructions, insert and watch. Complete - **$200**

SUP-237

SUP-238

❑ **SUP-237. Syroco-Style Limited Edition Figure,**
1995. 4" tall, 250 made. Mint - **$100**

❑ **SUP-238. Superman Paper Tablecloth,**
1996. 54" x 84". Promotes animated TV show. - **$5 $10 $20**

(FRONT OF BOX)

(OPENED BOX)

SUP-239

❑ SUP-239. "The History of Superman" Action Figure Collection,
1996. Three action figures from different eras, in colorful display box. Boxed - **$135**

SUP-240

SUP-241

❑ SUP-240. "I Hate Superman" Hardback Children's Book,
1996. Unusual presentation. - **$5 $10 $20**

❑ SUP-241. Superman Costume Kit in Box,
1996. - **$8 $12 $35**

SUP-242

❑ SUP-242. Burger King Standee,
1997. Six foot tall standee promoting cartoon TV show. - **$75 $135 $275**

SUP-243

❑ SUP-243. Hallmark Resin Figure,
1997. Golden Age style. Limited edition of 1,450. Boxed - **$185**

SUP-244

SUP-245

❑ SUP-244. Hallmark Resin Figure,
1997. Figure is flying over the Daily Planet. Great example of Superman with long hair. Boxed - **$110**

❑ SUP-245. Bean Bag Figure,
1998. Warner Bros. store exclusive. - **$12**

SUP-246

❑ SUP-246. Kingdom Come Resin Statue,
1998. Sculpted by Alex Ross. Silver color. Limited to 5,000. Boxed - **$260**

SUP-247

SUP-248

❑ SUP-247. Superman Radio,
1999. Clock has the art deco style of the 1930s. Boxed. - **$175**

❑ SUP-248. Resin Figure,
1999. Warner Bros. store exclusive. - **$150**

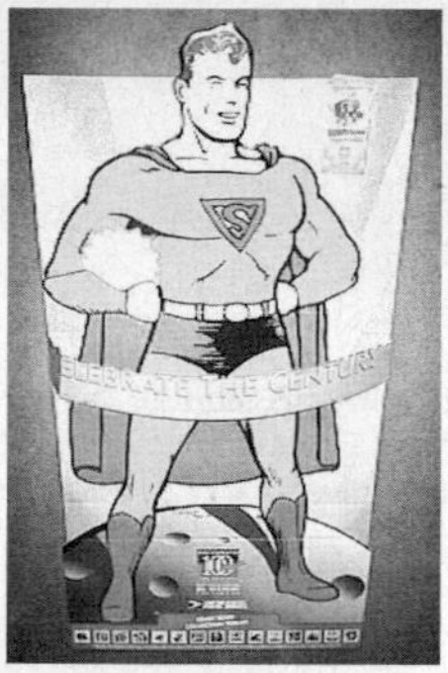

SUP-249

❑ SUP-249. Stamp Collecting Promotional Standee,
1998. U.S. Postal Service. About five feet tall titled "Celebrate The Century/Collect A Century In Stamps." - **$175**

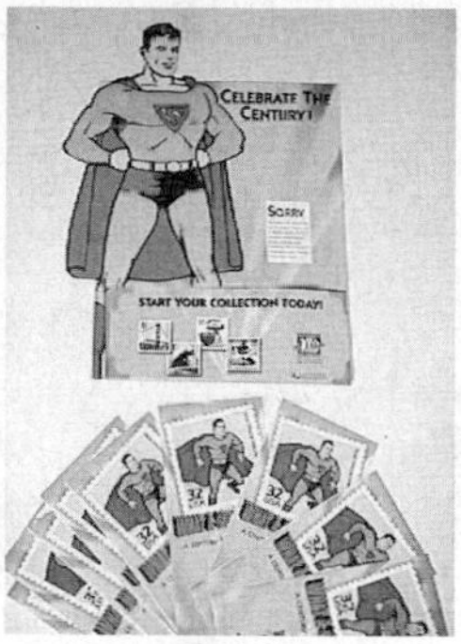

SUP-250

❑ SUP-250. Stamp Collecting Standee With Brochures,
1998. U.S. Postal Service. 15-1/2" tall standee designed to hold giveaway brochures.
Standee - **$110**
Brochure - **$1 $2 $5**

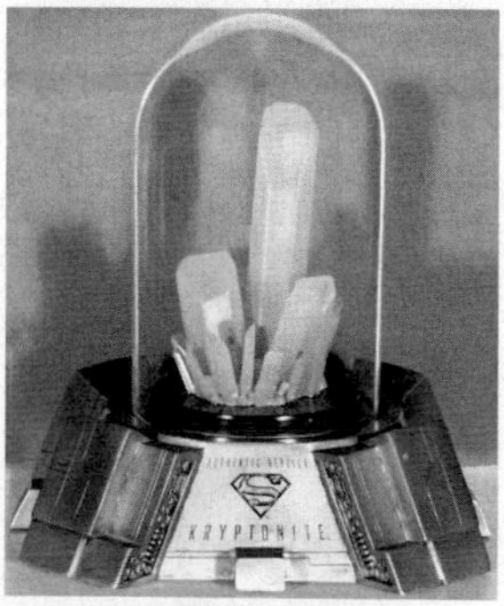

SUP-251

❑ SUP-251. Kryptonite Prop,
1999. Limited edition of 1,100. Mounted on base. Kryptonite glows green when the glass dome is lifted. - **$275**

SUP-252

❑ **SUP-252. Promo Sign for Burger King Toys,**
1990s. Shows 5 premium toys based on the animated series, given away at Burger King .-
$15 $30 $90

SUP-253

❑ **SUP-253. Lunch Box with Thermos,**
2000. - **$15**

SUP-254 (2nd view with lights on)

❑ **SUP-254. "Bottle City of Kandor" Prop,**
2000. Has mini-buildings inside that light up. Limited to 1,435. - **$250**

SUP-255

❑ **SUP-255. Superman Classic Rocket,**
2001. Schylling. Plastic rocket holding baby Kal-El. In a graphic-filled box - **$30**

SUP-256

❑ **SUP-256. Superman Classic Tin Carousel,**
2001. Schylling. Superman circling the Daily Planet. In a graphic-filled box. - **$30**

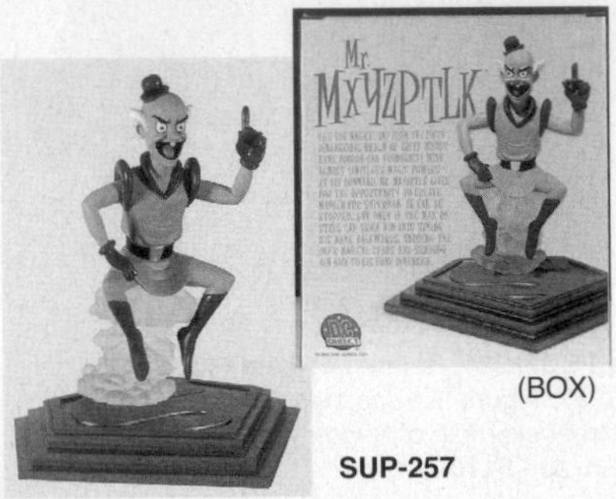

(BOX)

SUP-257

❑ **SUP-257. Mr. Mxyzptlk Statue,**
2001. The imp's cloud pedestal is resting on a Superman S-shield base. - **$65**

SUP-258

❑ **SUP-258. Supergirl's Arrival Statue,**
2001. Edition of 2,000. Resin re-creation of cover image from Action Comics #252, the first appearance of Supergirl. - **$250**

SUP-259

SUP-260

❑ **SUP-259. "Krypto" Soft Toy,**
2001. DC Direct. Plush figure of the Superdog. Boxed. - **$25**

❑ **SUP-260. Kingdom Come Full Color Statue,**
2001. Fully painted version of SUP-245. - **$175**

SUP-261

❑ **SUP-261. Smallville PVC Set,**
2001. DC Direct. - **$25**

SUP-262

❑ **SUP-262. *Superman* #14 Statue,**
2002. DC Direct. Sculpted by James Shoop, based on art by Fred Ray. Limited edition of 2,500. - **$175**

Syroco Figures

Adolph Holstein, a skilled European immigrant woodcarver, founded the Syracuse Ornamental Company in 1890, specializing in making hand-carved decorative components for the furniture industry. Demand for the company's intricate products soon exceeded production capacity, so Holstein developed a process to mass-produce replicas of the carvings by compressing a mixture of wood flour, waxes, and resins into molds. In the 1930s and 1940s the company changed its name to Syroco Inc. and manufactured a line of novelty items--cigarette boxes, pipe racks, plates, serving trays, and figurines of popular entertainers and public personalities, for sale in roadside souvenir shops. Syroco Inc. continues in business to this day, but production of the figures was discontinued by about 1950.

Syroco products of greatest interest to collectors are the 1941 Great American Series of historic personalities (about 6" tall). Previous edi-

tions of this guide pictured comic character figures copyrighted by King Features Syndicate. It is now known that this series was produced by the company, Multi-Products Inc. of Chicago. Those items are now listed in the Multi-Products category. Additional Multi-Products figures are pictured in the Captain Marvel and Pinocchio sections.

In 2000, Dark Horse Comics initiated its Syroco-like Classic Comic Characters line with Krazy Kat. Each of the figures depicts a famous character, thus far exclusively newspaper comic strips such as Li'l Abner, Blondie, and Terry and the Pirates. Each of the pieces was numbered, packaged in attractive custom tins, and comes with a descriptive booklet and a pinback. The figures are sculpted by Craig Yoe of Yoe Studios. In 2005, Dark Horse began two related lines featuring newer characters and Kellogg's spokescharacters.

The figures were initially offered in editions of 550, but after the phenomenal early success the edition size was increased to 750. It was increased again to 950, and then finally reduced to 600 copies, beginning with Felix the Cat.

SYR-1

❑ **SYR-1. Great American Series,**
1941. Five from series of historic personalities.
Teddy Roosevelt - **$50 $100 $175**
Lincoln - **$50 $100 $175**
Diamond Jim - **$65 $125 $200**
Steve Brodie - **$65 $125 $200**
John L. Sullivan - **$100 $200 $350**

SYR-2 SYR-3 SYR-4 SYR-5

❑ **SYR-2. Ben Franklin,**
1941. Great American Series. - **$40 $100 $225**

❑ **SYR-3. George Washington,**
1941. Great American Series. - **$40 $100 $225**

❑ **SYR-4. Will Rogers,**
1941. Great American Series. - **$50 $120 $275**

❑ **SYR-5. Buffalo Bill,**
1941.Great American series. - **$75 $150 $300**

SYR-6 SYR-7 SYR-8 SYR-9

❑ **SYR-6. "Stuyvesant,"**
1941. Great American series. - **$40 $100 $225**

❑ **SYR-7. First Sergeant Figure,**
1941. Figure is 5-7/8" tall. No name on base front but reverse has same "Copyright A 1941" low relief text as figures in The Great Americans Series. - **$30 $65 $125**

❑ **SYR-8. Krazy Kat Figure,**
2000. From Dark Horse. Limited to 550. - **$180**

❑ **SYR-9. Ignatz Figure,**
2000. From Dark Horse. Limited to 750. - **$95**

SYR-10 SYR-11 SYR-12

❑ **SYR-10. Prince Valiant Figure,**
2000. From Dark Horse. Limited to 550. - **$95**

❑ **SYR-11. Popeye Figure,**
2000. From Dark Horse. Limited to 550. - **$95**

❑ **SYR-12. Olive Oyl Figure,**
2000. From Dark Horse. Limited to 750. - **$70**

SYR-13 SYR-14 SYR-15 SYR-16

❑ **SYR-13. The Phantom Figure,**
2000. From Dark Horse. Limited to 750. - **$95**

❑ **SYR-14. Mandrake Figure,**
2000. From Dark Horse. Limited to 750. - **$70**

❑ **SYR-15. Li'l Abner Figure,**
2000. From Dark Horse. Limited to 950. - **$55**

❑ **SYR-16. Daisy Mae Figure,**
2000. From Dark Horse. Limited to 950. - **$55**

SYR-17 SYR-18 SYR-19 SYR-20

❑ **SYR-17. Dick Tracy Figure,**
2000. From Dark Horse. Limited to 950. - **$60**

❑ **SYR-18. Beetle Bailey Figure,**
2000. From Dark Horse. Limited to 950. - **$55**

❑ **SYR-19. Sarge Figure,**
2000. From Dark Horse. Limited to 950. - **$55**

❑ **SYR-20. Little Orphan Annie Figure,**
2000. From Dark Horse. Limited to 950. - **$60**

SYR-21 SYR-22 SYR-23 SYR-24

❑ **SYR-21. Flash Gordon Figure,**
2000. From Dark Horse. Limited to 950. - **$60**

❑ **SYR-22. Terry (and the Pirates) Figure,**
2000. From Dark Horse. Limited to 950. - **$55**

❑ **SYR-23. Dragon Lady Figure,**
2000. From Dark Horse. Limited to 950. - **$55**

❑ **SYR-24. Fearless Fosdick Figure,**
2001. From Dark Horse. Limited to 950. - **$55**

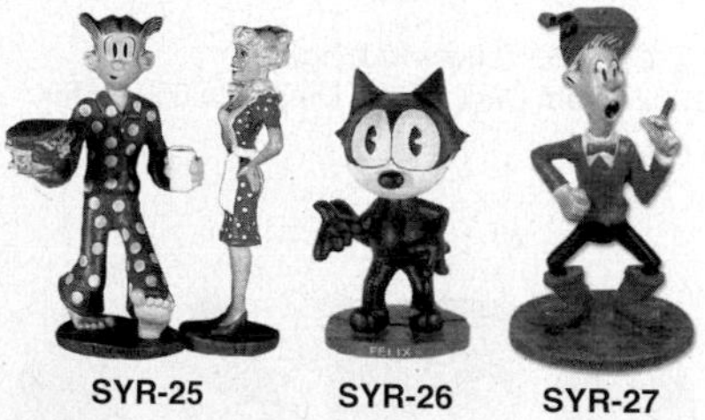

SYR-25 SYR-26 SYR-27

❑ **SYR-25. Blondie and Dagwood Figures,**
2001. From Dark Horse. Limited to 600.
Each - **$90**

❑ **SYR-26. Felix the Cat Figure,**
2001. From Dark Horse. Limited to 600. - **$120**

❑ **SYR-27. Smokey Stover Figure,**
2001. From Dark Horse. Limited to 600. - **$60**

SYR-28 SYR-29 SYR-30 SYR-31

❑ **SYR-28. Bluto Figure,**
2001. From Dark Horse. Limited to 600. - **$65**

❑ **SYR-29. Nancy Figure,**
2001. From Dark Horse. Sculpted by Yoe Studio. Limited to 600. - **$60**

❑ **SYR-30. Sluggo Figure,**
2001. From Dark Horse. Sculpted by Yoe Studio. Limited to 600. - **$60**

❑ **SYR-31. Wimpy Figure,**
2001. From Dark Horse. Limited to 600. - **$65**

SYR-32 SYR-33 SYR-34 SYR-35

❑ **SYR-32. Albert Figure,**
2001. From Dark Horse. Limited. - **$65**

❑ **SYR-33. Alley Oop Figure,**
2002. From Dark Horse. Limited. - **$60**

❑ **SYR-34. Little Nemo Figure,**
2002. From Dark Horse. Limited. - **$60**

❑ **SYR-35. Yellow Kid Figure,**
2002. From Dark Horse. Limited to 600. - **$60**

SYR-36 (tin box) SYR-37 SYR-38

❑ **SYR-36. The Spirit Figure,**
2002. From Dark Horse. Limited to 600. - **$65**

❑ **SYR-37. Tarzan Figure,**
2002. From Dark Horse. Limited to 600. - **$65**

❑ **SYR-38. Ming the Merciless Figure,**
2002. From Dark Horse. Limited to 600. - **$60**

SYR-39 SYR-40 SYR-41 SYR-42

❑ **SYR-39. Shmoo Figure,**
2002. From Dark Horse. Limited to 600. - **$85**

❑ **SYR-40. Offissa Pupp Figure,**
2003. From Dark Horse. Limited to 600. - **$60**

❑ **SYR-41. Buck Rogers Figure,**
2003. From Dark Horse. Limited to 600. - **$85**

❑ **SYR-42. Wilma Deering Figure,**
2003. From Dark Horse. Limited to 600. - **$70**

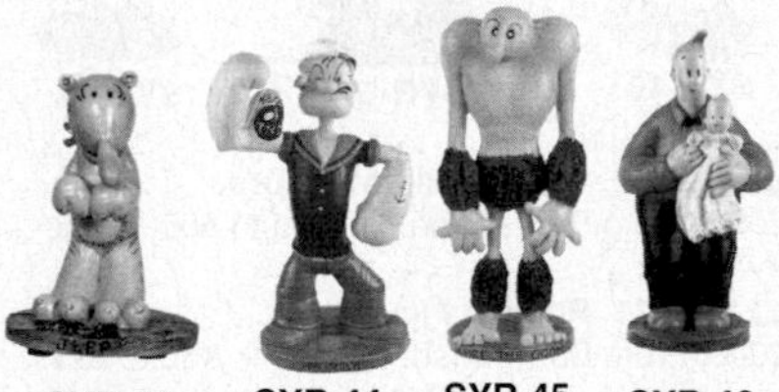

SYR-43 SYR-44 SYR-45 SYR-46

❑ **SYR-43. Eugene the Jeep Figure,**
2003. From Dark Horse. Limited to 600. - **$65**

❑ **SYR-44. Popeye II Figure,**
2004. From Dark Horse. Limited to 600. - **$55**

❑ **SYR-45. Alice the Goon Figure,**
2004. From Dark Horse. Limited to 600. - **$55**

❑ **SYR-46. Uncle Walt and Baby Skeezix Figure,**
2004. From Dark Horse. Limited to 600. - **$55**

SYR-47 SYR-48 SYR-49 SYR-50

❑ **SYR-47. Lone Ranger Figure,**
2004. From Dark Horse. Limited to 550. - **$55**

❑ **SYR-48. Tonto Figure,**
2004. From Dark Horse. Limited to 550. - **$55**

❑ **SYR-49. Dennis the Menace Figure,**
2004. From Dark Horse. Limited to 550. - **$55**

❑ **SYR-50. Barney Google Figure,**
2004. From Dark Horse. Limited to 550. - **$55**

Tailspin Tommy

Written by Glenn Chaffin and drawn by Hal Forrest, Tailspin Tommy debuted in 1928, just one year after Charles Lindbergh's historic nonstop flight across the Atlantic. Because American interest in aviation was at an all-time high, the strip about a teen who parlayed a job fixing planes into a career in piloting was a huge hit with newspaper readers, quickly expanding from its four debut newspapers to a list of 250 local newspapers. Within five years, Tailspin Tommy dominated a wide range of media including reprint books, a radio series, Big Little Books, a two-issue pulp magazine and even films. In 1934, Tailspin Tommy became the first comic strip character to spawn a movie serial. The 12-part series was released by Universal Studios with Maurice Murphy in the title role and Patricia Farr and Noah Beery, Jr. as Tommy's girlfriend Betty Lou and sidekick, Skeeter. Tommy was also the star of a Universal feature, Tailspin Tommy & the Great Air Mystery, with Clark Williams in the title role. But it was with Monogram Pictures that the character experienced his greatest cinematic success, with four features starring John Trent, Marjorie Reynolds and Milburn Stone. The strip and most of its multimedia ended in 1942. United Feature tried a short-lived Tailspin Tommy comic book, which began and ended in 1946.

TLS-1

TLS-2

❑ **TLS-1. "Tailspin Tommy In The Famous Pay-Roll Mystery" BLB,**
1933. #747. - **$14 $42 $95**

❑ **TLS-2. "Tailspin Tommy - The Dirigible Flight to the North Pole" BLB,**
1934. #1124. - **$14 $42 $95**

TLS-3

TLS-4

❑ **TLS-3. "Tailspin Tommy - The Famous Pay-Roll Mystery" Premium Book,**
1934. Premium version 3.5 x 5.25". - **$24 $72 $170**

❑ **TLS-4. Big Thrill Chewing Gum Premium Booklet,**
1934. Six different. Each - **$12 $36 $85**

TLS-5

TLS-6

❑ **TLS-5. Tailspin Tommy Scarce Serial Button,**
1934. 1.25" complete with Philadelphia Badge paper for first serial based on a comic strip and button reads "From The Hal Forrest Cartoon." - **$100 $200 $400**

❑ **TLS-6. "Tailspin Tommy In WIngs Over The Arctic" Cocomalt Premium Big Little Book,**
1935. Un-numbered Whitman softcover. - **$18 $54 $125**

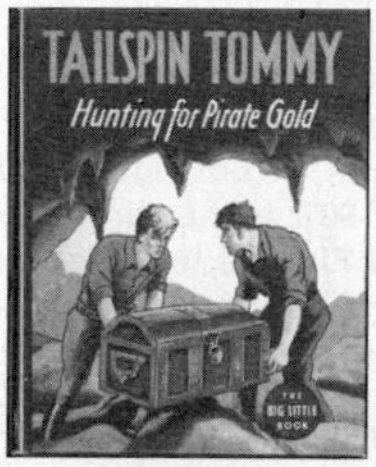

TLS-7

TLS-8

❑ **TLS-7. "Tailspin Tommy - Hunting For Pirate Gold" BLB,**
1935. #1172. - **$12 $36 $85**

❑ **TLS-8. "Tailspin Tommy In The Great Air Mystery/A Universal Picture " Cello. Button,**
1935. For movie serial picturing cast members Clark Williams, Noah Beery, Jr., Jean Rogers. - **$75 $150 $300**

TLS-9

TLS-10

❑ **TLS-9. "Tailspin Tommy Club" Cello. Button,**
c. 1935. Evening Sun newspaper. - **$60 $100 $200**

❑ **TLS-10. "Tailspin Tommy" Cello. Button,**
c. 1935. Newark Star-Eagle. From series of newspaper contest buttons. - **$12 $25 $50**

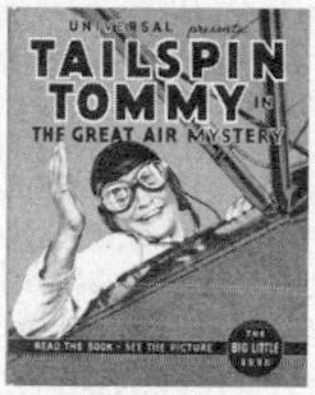

TLS-11

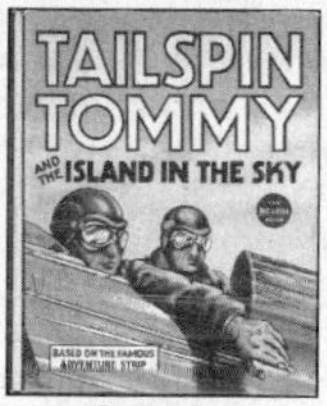

TLS-12

❑ **TLS-11. "Tailspin Tommy In The Great Air Mystery" BLB,**
1936. #1184. - **$14 $42 $95**

❑ **TLS-12. "Tailspin Tommy and the Island in the Sky" BLB,**
1936. #1110. - **$12 $36 $85**

TLS-13

TLS-14

❑ **TLS-13. "Tailspin Tommy - The Weasel and His Skywaymen" BLB,**
1937. All Pictures Comics #1410. - **$11 $33 $72**

❑ **TLS-14. "Tailspin Tommy and the Hooded Flyer" BLB,**
1937. #1423. - **$12 $36 $85**

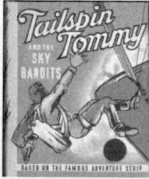

TLS-15

TLS-16

❑ **TLS-15. "Tailspin Tommy and the Sky Bandits" BLB,**
1938. #1494 - **$12 $36 $85**

❑ **TLS-16. "Tailspin Tommy and the Lost Transport" Better Little Book,**
1939. #1413. - **$11 $33 $72**

TLS-17

❑ **TLS-17. "Tail-Spin Tommy..Adventure" Newspaper Strip Promo Sign,**
1930s. 11x17" cardboard for strip "In The Chronicle Full-Sized Sunday Comics." - **$125 $200 $400**

TLS-18

❑ **TLS-18. "Tailspin Tommy" Wings Badge,**
1930s. Likely a newspaper sponsored club premium. Scarce. - **$35 $85 $160**

Tales of the Texas Rangers

With stories said to be based on the files of the Texas Rangers between the 1830s and the 1950s, this series aired on NBC radio from 1950 to 1952, with Joel McCrea as Ranger Jace Pearson. Created by Stacy Keach Sr., a television version was broadcast from 1955 to 1957 on CBS and from 1957 to 1959 on ABC, with Willard Parker and Harry Lauter as the leading lawmen. General Mills sponsored the radio series and Tootsie Rolls candy joined the cereal company in sponsoring the TV version. *Texas Ranger* and *Jace Pearson* comic books appeared in the 1950s. Items may be copyrighted Screen Gems Inc.

TXS-1

❑ **TXS-1. Membership Kit,**
c. 1955. Curtiss Candy.
Box Or Card - **$10 $25 $40**
Silvered Metal Badge - **$20 $45 $75**
Ring - **$35 $65 $125**

TXS-2

❑ **TXS-2. "Tales Of The Texas Rangers Deputy" Premium Ring,**
c. 1955. Aluminum from Curtiss Candy club membership kit. - **$35 $65 $125**

TXS-3 TXS-4

❑ **TXS-3. Candy Display Card,**
c. 1955. Curtiss Candy Co. - **$30 $60 $110**

❑ **TXS-4. Jace Pearson Fan Photo,**
c. 1955. - **$8 $12 $25**

TXS-5

TXS-6

❑ **TXS-5. "Baby Ruth" Candy Bar Box,**
c. 1955. Curtiss Candy Company. Pictured and named are stars Jace Pearson and Clay Morgan. 8x9-1/2x2" deep originally holding 24 bars. - **$30 $75 $150**

❑ **TXS-6. RCA 78 RPM Record With Sleeve,**
c. 1955. Store item. 10x10". - **$20 $40 $80**

Tarzan

Between 1911 and 1944 Edgar Rice Burroughs (1875-1950) wrote some 26 Tarzan novels, creating a world of adventure where justice and fair play triumph in the hands of an English orphan raised by apes in the African jungle. One of the most popular fictional characters of all time, Tarzan has thrilled readers and viewers throughout the world in print, in comics, in feature films and chapter plays, on radio, and on television. Tarzan's first appearance was in the October 1912 issue of *All Story Magazine*.

The first Tarzan movie was the 1918 silent *Tarzan of the Apes*, starring Elmo Lincoln, but the most remembered apeman is undoubtedly Johnny Weissmuller (1904-1984), who originated the abiding victory cry and made a dozen Tarzan films between 1932 and 1948. Notable among the many other cinema Tarzans: Buster Crabbe (1933), Herman Brix (1935), Lex Barker (1949-1953), and Gordon Scott (1955-1966). Including the silents and chapter plays, there have been more than 40 Lord of the Jungle movies.

The *Tarzan* comic strip, distributed by Metropolitan Newspaper Service, debuted in 1929. Metropolitan was absorbed by United Feature Syndicate in 1930, who continues to syndicate the strip. A Sunday version appeared in 1931. Noted artist Hal Foster (1892-1982) drew the first run of dailies, then did the Sunday pages taking over from Rex Maxon, from 1931 to 1937 when he left to do *Prince Valiant*. Burne Hogarth took the reins and continued as artist on the Sunday page until 1950, except for a two-year run drawn by Rubimor in 1945-1947. Other artists who worked on the strip include Rex Maxon, Bob Lubbers, Nick Cardy and Russ Manning.

There have been numerous *Tarzan* comic books, with reprints of the strips starting in 1929 and original material starting in 1947 by Western/Dell. Western/Dell published Tarzan until 1962 when Western split from Dell. Western/Gold Key published the comic until 1972, DC from 1972 until 1977, Marvel from 1977 until 1979. Malibu published a Tarzan comic book in 1992. Dark Horse has issued a Tarzan comic in a sporadic basis from 1996 to 1999. Dark Horse also published *Tarzan: The Lost Adventure*, a previously unreleased incomplete Burroughs manuscript, rewritten and completed by Joe R. Lansdale, in both serialized and novel formats.

Starting in 1932, various radio stations, or their advertising agencies, purchased Tarzan radio programs directly from American Radio Features Syndicate, who produced the first radio serial *Tarzan of the Apes*, starring Burroughs' daughter, Joan, and his son-in-law, James Pierce, in 286 episodes (episodes 1-131 were adapted from the novel *Tarzan of the Apes*, and episodes 132-286 were adapted from *The Return of Tarzan*). This serial, designated Serial No. 1, was syndicated by American Radio Features Syndicate (1932-1934) and Edgar Rice Burroughs, Inc. (1935-1940). Edgar Rice Burroughs purchased all rights to the Tarzan radio program in 1934, continuing to syndicate Serial No. 1 and produced two serials of 39 episodes each in 1935: *Tarzan and the Diamond of Asher*, Serial No. 2, syndicated from 1935-1940; and *Tarzan and the Fires of Thor*, Serial No. 3, syndicated from 1936-1940. Signal Oil purchased the rights to sponsor *Tarzan of the Apes*, Serial No. 1, on the west coast only; Signal Oil had stations only in the five Pacific coast states: California, Oregon, Washington, Idaho and Nevada. In other words, Signal Oil sponsored the Tarzan serial west of the Rocky Mountains only. World Broadcasting System, Inc. purchased rights from American Radio Features Syndicate to sell the serial east of the Rocky Mountains; however American Radio Features Syndicate also sold the serial to a few stations east of the Rocky Mountains. Among the 32 states in which the radio show was syndicated, New York's WOR, purchased Serial No. 1 and began broadcasting it in January 1933. From mid-January through mid-March 1933 the show was sponsored by Toddy, Inc. After a short hiatus, the serial continued from mid-June through early September 1933 sponsored by the H.J. Heinz Co. During 1952-1953, another radio program aired on CBS, sponsored by Post Toasties. Premiums from the 1930s series include membership material in Tarzan Clubs, a number of items from such sponsors as Foulds macaroni, Kolynos toothpaste, Bursley coffee, Hormel foods and the dairy industry.

A live-action TV adaptation starring Ron Ely was aired on NBC in 1966-1968 and rerun on CBS in 1969. Most recently Tarzan was seen in a weekly syndicated TV show, starring Wolf Larson, from 1991-1993 (on a few US stations, but seen mostly in Europe); *Tarzan: The Epic Adventures*, in 21 episodes, starring Joe Lara, in 1996-1997; and a short-lived show, starring Travis Fimmel, debuted on the WB channel in 2004, but was cancelled after only eight shows. Animated versions of Tarzan from Filmation studios were broadcast on CBS from 1976 to 1981, and from Walt Disney Studios on a syndicated basis beginning in 2001 and continuing in reruns on the Disney cable channel.

Edgar Rice Burroughs licensed Tarzan to Stephen Slesinger in 1932 to produce toys and games, but declined to renew the contract with him in 1938. Edgar Rice Burroughs, Inc. began to license the Tarzan name from 1938 on.

Disney opened *Tarzan The Broadway Musical* March 24, 2006.

TRZ-1

TRZ-2

❑ TRZ-1. Movie Premium,
1918. Photo of Tarzan actor Elmo Lincoln. - **$40 $90 $175**

❑ TRZ-2. "The Son Of Tarzan/The Mystic Order Of The Jungle" Early Serial Cello. Button,
1920. National Film Corp. 1-1/4" real photo partially tinted in yellow with surrounding pale blue rim. Tarzan was played by P. Dempsey Tabler. Also issued as a 2-1/4" pocket mirror.
Each - **$500 $1000 $3000**

TRZ-3

❑ TRZ-3. "The Son Of Tarzan" Movie Serial Cardboard Ad Blotter,
1920. Scarce. - **$75 $175 $375**

TRZ-4

❑ TRZ-4. "The Son Of Tarzan" First Movie Serial Doll,
1920. Premium from National Film Corporation. Meriem is a young girl in the movie who is kidnapped by Arab slavers. She is befriended by a black woman who gives her the "Geeka" doll which stays with Meriem until her eventual rescue by Korak, Son of Tarzan. "Geeka" doll is pictured in the campaign book for the serial and one actual example is known to us. Doll was to be cut out, stuffed with cotton or sawdust and then sewn into shape. - **$2000 $4000 $7500**

TRZ-5

❑ TRZ-5. Tarzan Story Fabric Store Banner,
c. 1920. Argosy All-Story Weekly. 29x40" banner with metal grommets at each corner and typed in red and blue on white background. Burroughs' first story appeared in this publication in 1912. - **$1250 $2500 $4000**

TRZ-6

❑ TRZ-6. "Elmo Lincoln In Adventures Of Tarzan" Movie Serial Paper Mask,
1921. Great Western Producing Co. 15-chapter serial imprinted on back for local theaters. - **$300 $600 $1200**

TRZ-7

TRZ-8

❑ TRZ-7. "Adventures Of Tarzan" Window Card,
1921. 14x20" movie card for 15-chapter serial starring Elmo Lincoln. Bottom margin is trimmed 2" from original.
Complete - **$750 $1500 $3000**

❑ TRZ-8. "The Son Of Tarzan" Movie Poster,
1927. 12x24" paper for 15-chapter serial reissue, only film version to star P. Dempsey Tabler. - **$50 $100 $200**

TRZ-9

❑ TRZ-9. "The Tarzan Twins" Book,
1927. Store item. - **$150 $300 $600**

TRZ-10

❑ TRZ-10. Book Store Advertising Stand-Up Promoting Tarzan,
1928. A.C. McClurg and Company. 10.5x13.5" featuring Burroughs' portrait and re-drawn rendition of J. Allen St. John's dust jacket illustration for "Tarzan, Lord of the Jungle." - **$3000 $6000 $9000**

TRZ-11

❑ TRZ-11. "Tarzan The Mighty" Lobby Card Set,
1928. Eight 11x14" greentone numbered cards for Universal Pictures serial starring Frank Merrill in title role. Title Card - **$75 $135 $400**
Each Chapter Card - **$50 $85 $175**

TRZ-12

❑ TRZ-12. "Tarzan The Mighty" Movie Serial Slide,
1928. 3.25x4" cardboard mount holding transparency for Universal 12-chapter serial starring Frank Merrill in title role. - **$85 $175 $300**

TRZ-13

❑ TRZ-13. "Tarzan The Mighty" Movie Serial Herald,
1928. 5.5x7" black and white folder for Universal 12-chapter serial starring Frank Merrill in title role. - **$250 $500 $750**

TRZ-14

TRZ-15

❑ TRZ-14. "Tarzan The Mighty Universal's Gigantic Chapter Play" Cello. Button,
1928. Universal. Known set of ten documented by book "*How To Make Money With Serials - A Universal Text Book for the Use of Motion Picture Exhibitors*". Examples known depict bird, coiled snake, crocodile, giraffe, lion, pangoline (scaled anteater) and zebra. Each - **$50 $100 $200**

❑ TRZ-15. "Tarzan The Tiger" Movie Serial Cello. Button,
1929. Universal. Set of fifteen consisting of: Anteater, Ape, Cape Buffalo, Crocodile, Dodo, Elephant, Giraffe, Hippopotamus, Ibex (long-horned mountain goat), Lion, Pangoline (scaled anteater), Parrot, Rhinocerous, Tiger, Zebra. Each - **$45 $90 $175**

TRZ-16

❑ TRZ-16. "Tarzan The Tiger" Cello Button,
1929. Promotion for Universal "Talking Serial" also printed for local movie house, likely San Francisco. - **$125 $225 $450**

TRZ-17

❑ TRZ-17. "Tarzan Lord of the Jungle" Store Advertising Stand-Up,
1929. Grosset & Dunlap. Full color, but dimensions unknown. - **$2500 $5000 $8000**

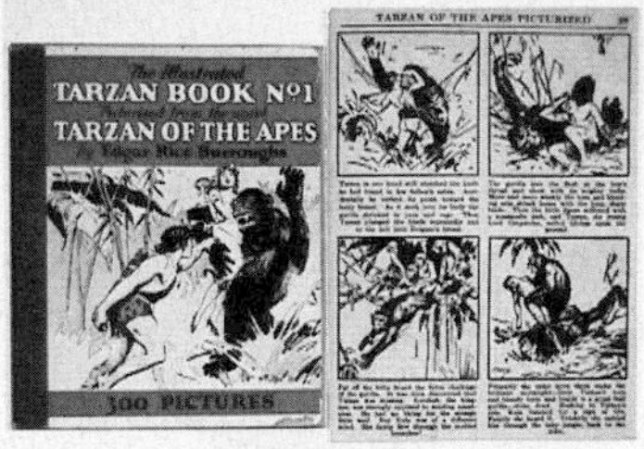

TRZ-18

❑ TRZ-18. "The Illustrated Tarzan Book No. 1" Hardcover First Edition,
1929. Store item by Grosset & Dunlap. 7x8-3/4" with 80 pages reprinting the first daily strips by Hal Foster.
With Dust Jacket: GD - **$86** FN - **$344**
VF - **$630**
Without Dust Jacket: GD - **$43** FN - **$172**
VF - **$315**

TRZ-19

❑ TRZ-19. "Tarzan Novels" Store Advertising Stand-Up,
1930. Grosset & Dunlap. 13x27" in full color.
- **$2500 $5000 $8000**

TRZ-20

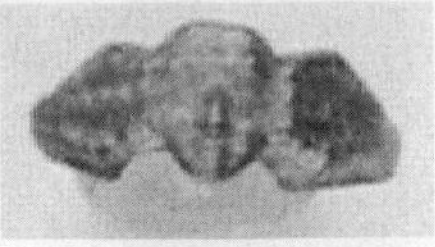

TRZ-21

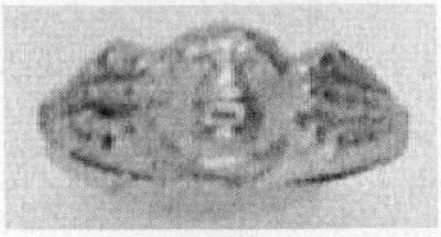

TRZ-22

❑ TRZ-20. Cardboard Bookmark,
1930. Grosset & Dunlap, publisher of Edgar Rice Burroughs novels. - **$25 $45 $85**

❑ TRZ-21. Tarzan Face Ring,
c. 1930. Issuer unknown. Non-adjustable white metal ring with silvery metallic finish. - **$125 $250 $400**

❑ TRZ-22. Kon-gah The Ape Ring,
c. 1930. A mate to the Tarzan ring. Non-adjustable white metal with silvery metallic luster. - **$100 $200 $300**

TRZ-23

TRZ-24

❑ TRZ-23. "Tarzan The Ape Man" Movie Theater Premium Flip Book,
1932. Book is 1.75x2.25" published by Moviebook Corp. Front cover reads "Tops Trader Horn For Thrills/Metro-Goldwyn-Mayer Tarzan The Ape Man With Johnny Weissmuller/Edgar Rice Burrough's New Tarzan Story." Reverse reads "Loew's State White Plains April 23-24-25-26." Pages feature actual bw photo scene of Tarzan wrestling a lion. - **$200 $400 $800**

❑ TRZ-24. Gift #1 And #2 Promo,
1932. Foulds Products. Paper sheet offering plaster statues. - **$125 $185 $375**

TRZ-25

❑ **TRZ-25. Promo Gift Sheet,**
1932. Toddy Malted Drink. Premium gift sheet for statues. Printed on unstapled paper. - **$125 $185 $375**

TRZ-26

❑ **TRZ-26. Plaster Statues,**
1932. Made by Gem Clay Forming Co. for distribution by both sponsors of the Tarzan radio show and others. The basic set of ten includes Tarzan with Cheetah (first version without base, later version with base), Kala holding the baby Tarzan, Jane Porter, Numa the lion, Sheeta the panther, Witch doctor, Pirate sitting on treasure chest, Lt. D'Arnot, Cannibal Warrior, and three monkeys (counted as a single item). Following the basic set of ten, six additional statues were issued. See following items for Leopard of Opar, Princess La, and Kerchak, the bull ape. The final three, with values similar to the preceding three, are: Esmeralda, French Sailor, and Lion Cubs (two counted as one).
Set Painted - **$200 $400 $600**
Set Unpainted - **$225 $450 $750**

TRZ-27

❑ **TRZ-27. Fould's Background For Plaster Statues,**
1932. Scarce. - **$1500 $3000 $5000**
Offer Blank - **$20 $40 $60**

TRZ-28

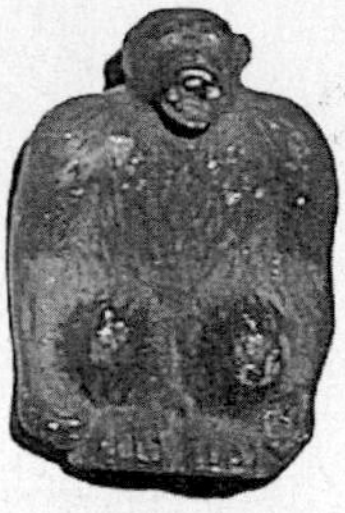

TRZ-29

❑ **TRZ-28. Plaster Statue Set Additions Order Coupons,**
c. 1932. Foulds' Macaroni, Spaghetti or Egg Noodles. Box insert papers for "Leopard Of Opar" and "Princess La, High Priestess Of Opar", later additions to the earlier set of ten.
Each Order Form - **$50 $125 $250**
Each Statue Painted - **$75 $125 $250**
Each Statue Unpainted - **$100 $200 $300**

❑ **TRZ-29. Kerchak Plaster Figure,**
c. 1932. A later addition to the earlier set of ten. Kerchak was the ape leader when Tarzan was adopted into the ape tribe. Later, Tarzan killed Kerchak to become King of the Apes. In addition to Foulds, these figures were given away by The Adlerika Co., Collin County Mill & Elevator, Grainger Bros., Heinz Foods, and Toddy, Inc.
Painted - **$75 $125 $250**
Unpainted - **$100 $200 $300**

TRZ-30

❑ **TRZ-30. "Signal Tarzan Club" Member Card,**
1932. Signal gasoline. Qualifies recipient as "Charter Member Of The Tribe Of Tarzan". - **$100 $300 $500**

TRZ-31

❑ **TRZ-31. "Signal Tarzan Club" Cello. Button,**
1932. Signal Oil Co. - **$35 $50 $85**

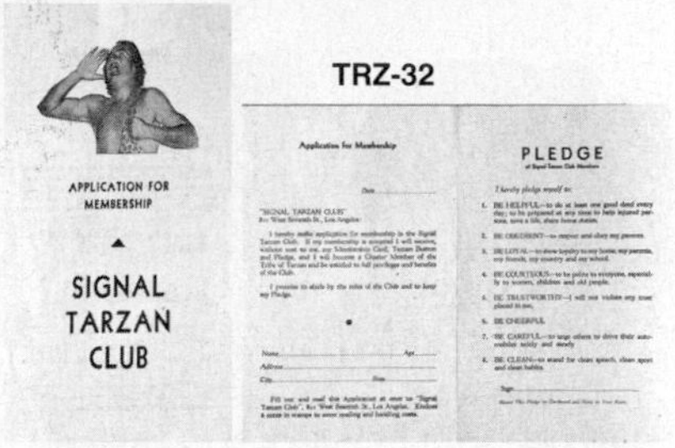

TRZ-32

❑ **TRZ-32. "Signal Tarzan Club" Application Folder,**
1932. Signal Oil Co. 5.5x8.5" four-page application for membership including pledge panel to be mounted on cardboard and hung in member's room. - **$135 $250 $400**

TRZ-33

❑ **TRZ-33. Tarzan Picture Puzzle,**
1932. Signal Oil Co. 13x18" black and white complete picture sheet guide plus set of six 8x10" paper sheets printed by full color puzzle pieces for scissoring and application to the guide picture.
Complete, Uncut - **$2000 $4000 $8000**

TRZ-34

❑ **TRZ-34. "Tarzan Of The Apes" Jigsaw Puzzle,**
c. 1932. Screen Book Magazine.
In Envelope, Sealed - **$700**
Near Mint With Envelope - **$500**
Loose - **$50 $100 $200**

TRZ-35

❑ **TRZ-35. "Tarzan The Fearless" 9x14" Cardboard Sign,**
1933. Rare. See next item. - **$400 $750 $1500**

TRZ-36

❑ **TRZ-36. "Tarzan The Fearless" Pair of Cardboard Signs,**
1933. Each 9x14", from same series as TRZ-35, showing Buster Crabbe as Tarzan.
Each - **$400 $750 $1500**

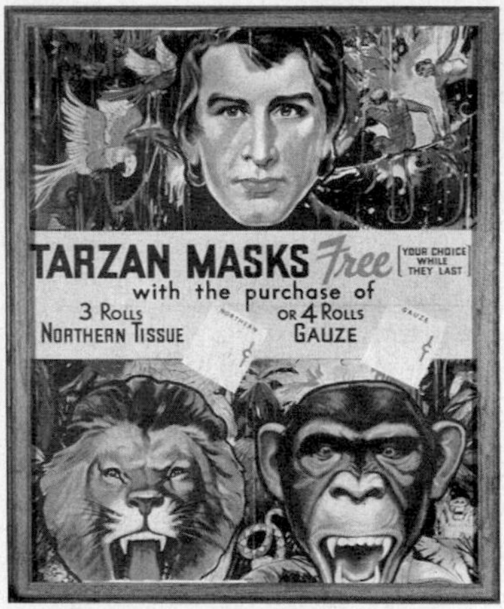

TRZ-37

❑ **TRZ-37. Northern Paper Mills Color Poster For Masks,**
1933. - **$400 $800 $2000**

TRZ-38

❑ **TRZ-38. Paper Masks,**
1933. Northern Paper Mills. Set of three picturing Tarzan, Numa the Lion, Akut the Ape.
Tarzan - **$40 $75 $150**
Each Animal - **$20 $40 $75**

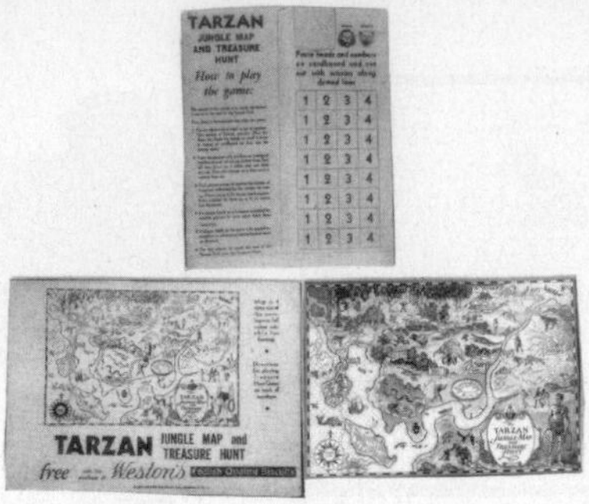

TRZ-39

❑ **TRZ-39. "Tarzan Jungle Map And Treasure Hunt" Game With Mailer Envelope,**
1933. Rare. Canadian version has "W" above logo for Weston's English Quality Biscuits. U.S. version has "T" above logo. Australian version has sponsor name of Pepsodent Toothpaste. Playing pieces printed on envelope back, except Australian version, which has separate sheet with perforated pieces.
Canada Near Mint In Mailer - **$900**
Canada Map Only - **$125 $325 $700**
U.S. Near Mint In Mailer - **$1100**
U.S. Map Only - **$150 $450 $900**
Australia Near Mint In Mailer - **$800**
Australia Map Only - **$125 $250 $650**
Australia Parts Sheet Only - **$25 $50 $125**

TRZ-40

❑ **TRZ-40. "Tarzan of the Apes" Picture Puzzle Boxed,**
1933. Saalfield Publishing Co. Scarce with all pieces included. - **$300 $600 $1200**

TRZ-41

❑ **TRZ-41. "Tarzan of the Apes" Picture Puzzles Boxed,**
1933. Saalfield Publishing Co. Three different puzzles included. Scarce with all three puzzles intact. - **$350 $700 $1500**

TRZ-42

❑ **TRZ-42. "Tarzan To Color" Coloring Book,**
1933. Saalfield Publ. Co. Two versions, each with some printed color inside. Un-crayoned examples are scarce.
#272 with 16 pgs. including cover
- **$90 $250 $700**
#988 with 26 pgs. including cover
- **$110 $300 $750**

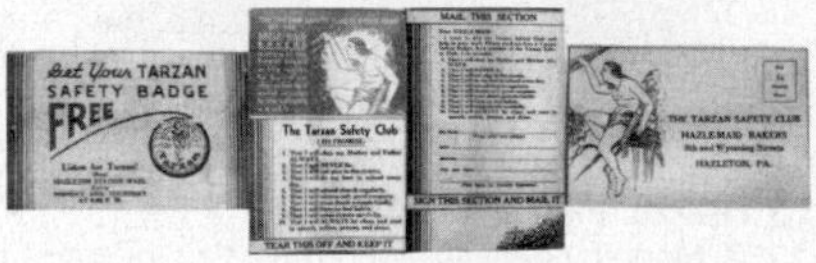

TRZ-43

❑ **TRZ-43. Safety Club Cards,**
1933. Various radio sponsors. Two cards printed each side, originally joined by perforation. One card to order badge, one card of safety pledges. Pair - **$180 $360 $700**

TRZ-44

❑ **TRZ-44. "Tarzan And The Crystal Vault Of Isis" Card #18,**
1933. Schutter-Johnson Candies. Card title "The Electric Menace" from numbered set of 50. Also produced in Canada, printed in English or French by Canadian Chewing Gum Company, Limited. Each - **$10 $30 $85**

TRZ-45

❑ **TRZ-45. "Tarzan" Club Cello. Button Variety,**
1933. 1-1/4" size but no sponsor name and without words "Safety Club." See next two items. - **$125 $300 $600**

TRZ-46

TRZ-47

❑ **TRZ-46. "Tarzan Safety Club" Cello. Button,**
1933. Issued in two sizes, 7/8" and 1-1/4". The 7/8" size is known to be a premium used by Power City Baking Co. who sponsored radio serial #1 "Tarzan of the Apes" on station WAZL in Hazelton, PA. Both sizes were made by M. Pudlin & Co., licensed by Stephen Slesinger, Inc. 7/8" Size - **$80 $200 $400**
1-1/4" Size - **$100 $250 $450**

❑ **TRZ-47. "Feldman's Tarzan Safety Club" Cello. Button,**
1933. 1-1/4" version of previous button with sponsor's name used by Feldman Baking Co. for Tarzan radio serials #2 and #3 over station WGBF in Evansville, IN. Made by M. Pudlin & Co., licensed by Stephen Slesinger, Inc. - **$200 $500 $750**

TRZ-48

TRZ-49

❑ **TRZ-48. Johnny Weissmuller Picture,**
1933. Rare. Wheaties premium for Jack Armstrong program. - **$75 $225 $400**

❑ **TRZ-49. Johnny Weissmuller Sport Kings Gum Card #21,**
1933. From same year that Wheaties issued his photo as Tarzan for the 1st Jack Armstrong premium. - **$150 $550 $1750**

TRZ-50

❑ **TRZ-50. Advertising Flip Booklet,**
c. 1933. Thom McAn shoes. Pages flipped one direction show Tarzan spearing an ape, reverse page sequence shows grateful child getting Thom McAn shoes from dad. - **$100 $200 $400**

TRZ-51

❑ **TRZ-51. "Tarzan 'Rescue'" Puzzle Game,**
1934. Store item by Einson-Freeman Co. - **$300 $600 $1200**

TRZ-52

❑ **TRZ-52. Paper Film For Cardboard Theater,**
1934. Scarce. Hormel Soups. - **$150 $350 $700**

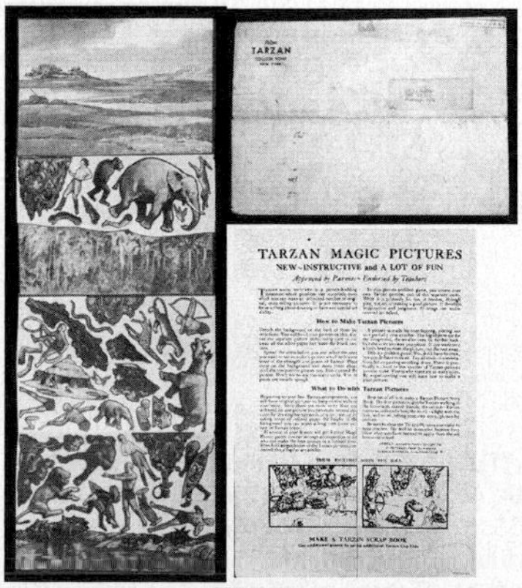

TRZ-53

❑ **TRZ-53. Tarzan Cup Magic Picture Cutouts,**
1934. Rare. Complete Uncut - **$275 $550 $900**

TRZ-54

❑ **TRZ-54. "Tarzan and His Mate" Movie Theater Window Card,**
1934. Untrimmed card measures 21 1/2" x 14". Features Johnny Weissmuller and Maureen O'Sullivan. Scarce. - **$500 $1000 $2000**

TRZ-55

❑ **TRZ-55. "Tarzan Treasure Land" Puzzle,**
1934. Einson-Freeman Co.
- **$350 $700 $1400**

TRZ-56

❑ **TRZ-56. Premium Movie Photo,**
1934. Promotes film "Tarzan and His Mate." Rare. - **$200 $400 $600**

TRZ-57

TRZ-58

❑ TRZ-57. Tarzan of the Air Promo with Mailer,
1934. - **$50 $125 $200**

❑ TRZ-58. "The Tarzan Twins" Whitman #770 Big Little Book,
1934 (1st printing). Rare. - **$107 $321 $750**
1935 version is the same except for date listed. - **$54 $162 $380**

TRZ-59

❑ TRZ-59. Club Member Cello. Button,
1935. Gano Downs Boys & Girls Shops. Issued by program sponsor of radio serial #2 "Tarzan and the Diamond of Asher" heard over station KLZ in Denver, CO. - **$300 $600 $1200**

TRZ-60

❑ TRZ-60. "Tarzan Series Tablet/ Composition Books/Notebooks/Fillers" Salesman's Sample Portfolio,
1935. Birmingham Paper Co. 10x12-1/4". Has tipped-in fold-out poster, various tipped-in tablet covers. - **$800 $1600 $2800**

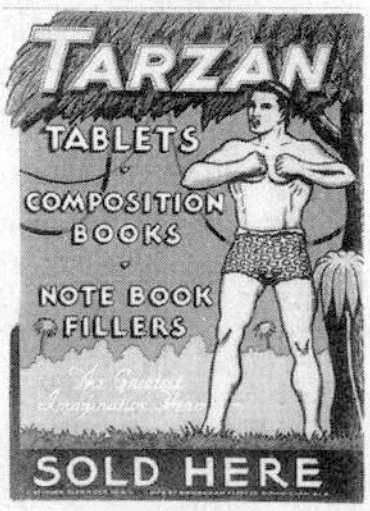

TRZ-61

❑ TRZ-61. School Paper Supplies 10x14" Cardboard Store Sign,
1935. Birmingham Paper Co. -
$165 $350 $700

TRZ-62

❑ TRZ-62. "Notebook Filler" Paper Wrapper Band,
1935. Store item, Birmingham Paper Company. Reverse pictures Mickey Mouse Ingersoll watch offered for saved bands. - **$10 $25 $60**

TRZ-63

❑ TRZ-63. "Tarzan Radio Club/Bursley Coffees" Enameled Brass Badge,
1935. Scarce. Issued by G.F. Bursley Co., makers of Burco Coffee, and sponsors of radio serial #1, "Tarzan of the Apes," on station WOWO-WGL, Ft. Wayne, IN in 1934-1935. Made by Etched Products Corp. and licensed by Stephen Slesinger, Inc. - **$250 $500 $1250**

TRZ-64

❑ TRZ-64. "Tarzan Radio Club/Drink More Milk" Enameled Brass Badge,
1935. Scarce. Issued by Milk Dealers & Distributors of Dayton, OH, sponsors of radio serial #1, "Tarzan of the Apes," on station WHIO in Dayton in 1936-1937. Made by Etched Products Corp., licensed by Stephen Slesinger. See related bracelet. - **$250 $500 $1250**

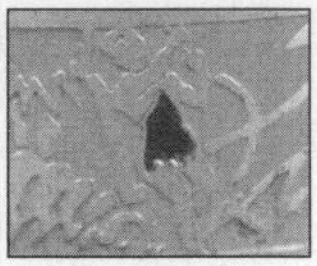
(SIDE DETAIL)

(SIDE DETAIL)

TRZ-65

❑ TRZ-65. "Tarzan Radio Club" Bracelet With Two Varieties,
1935. Brass with enamel paint. The variety reading "Drink More Milk" was used by Milk Dealers & Distributors of Dayton, OH in 1936-1937, sponsors of radio serial #1, "Tarzan of the Apes," on station WHIO in Dayton, OH.
The variety reading "Bursley Coffee" was used by G.F. Bursley Co., makers of Burco Coffee, and sponsors of radio serial #1, "Tarzan of the Apes," on station WOWO-WGL, Ft. Wayne, IN in 1934-1935. Both bracelets were made by Etched Products Corp. and licensed by Stephen Slesinger. Less than five known of both bracelets. Each - **$750 $1500 $3500**

TRZ-66

❑ TRZ-66. "Tarzan Of The Apes" Book,
1935. Various advertisers. 3.5 x 5.25".
- **$54 $162 $375**

TRZ-67

❑ TRZ-67. "Tarzan" Ice Cream Premium Booklet,
1935. 3 1/2" x 4" soft cover book. Pictured is a Whitman File copy. Rare. - **$124 $372 $980**

TRZ-68

❑ TRZ-68. "Tarzan of the Apes Exciting Jungle Game" Boxed,
1935. Lutz and Sheinkman. - **$350 $700 $1400**

(BOX) TRZ-69 (FILMS)

❑ TRZ-69. Box of Movie-Jecktor Films,
1935. Box of six paper film strips. Box is rare, films are usually found separately.
Box for Six Films - **$50 $100 $200**
Each Film Boxed - **$25 $50 $100**

TRZ-70

❑ TRZ-70. "Meadow Gold Custard" Tarzan Cup,
c. 1935. Beatrice Creamery Co. 3.25" tall waxed paper cup with lid offer for different Whitman books including Tarzan and others. -
$300 $750 $1250

TRZ-71

❑ TRZ-71. "Tarzan Ice Cream" Cup,
c. 1935. Cardboard cup is 2.25" tall with nice wrap-around art featuring two images of Tarzan along with jungle animals. Top rim text reads "Tarzan Ice Cream Builds Strong Bodies." Has imprint for "Hancock County Creamery."
- **$300 $750 $1250**

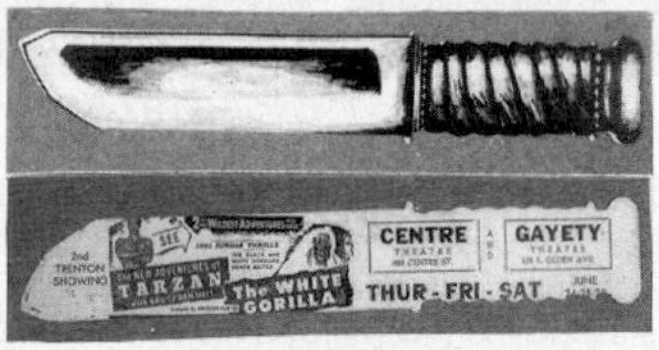

TRZ-72

❑ TRZ-72. "The New Adventures Of Tarzan" Cardboard Knife Movie Give-Away,
c. 1935. Various theaters. - **$50 $150 $300**

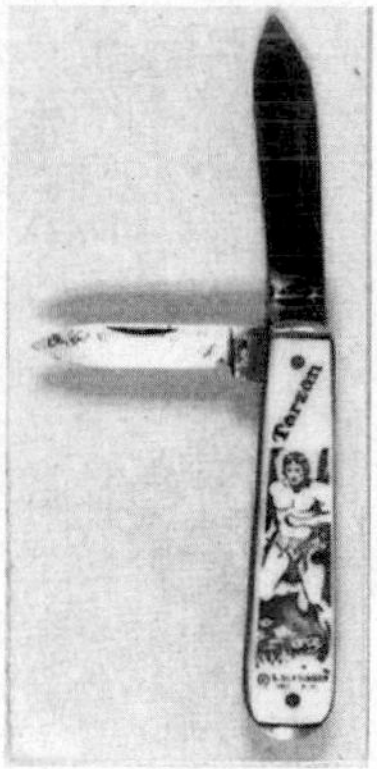

TRZ-73

❑ TRZ-73. Celluloid Pocketknife With Steel Blades,
1935. Store item made by Imperial. There are four different knives with the same image:
Single Blade - **$110 $325 $775**
Two Blades - **$135 $375 $850**
Three Blades - **$165 $450 $1100**
Boy Scout Version with Multiple Utilitarian Blades - **$200 $575 $1350**

TRZ-74

TRZ-75

❑ TRZ-74. "Tarzan Cups" 12x18" Paper Store Poster,
1935. - **$100 $300 $600**

❑ TRZ-75. "Tarzan Ice Cream Cup" 10x20" Paper Store Poster,
1935. - **$100 $300 $600**

TRZ-76

❑ TRZ-76. "Tarzan Cups" 6x19" Paper Store Poster,
1935. Offers premiums for lids saved. -
$90 $215 $425

TRZ-77

❑ TRZ-77. "Tarzan And His Jungle Friends" Booklet #1,
1936. Tarzan Ice Cream Cup. First of listed series of 12 featuring various characters. - **$102 $306 $715**

TRZ-78

TRZ-79

❑ TRZ-78. "Tarzan" Big Big Book,
1936. Whitman #4056. - **$105 $315 $735**

❑ TRZ-79. "Tarzan Escapes" Premium Card,
1936. Promo for the MGM movie. The task was to identify animals and receive free tickets to movies. Rare. - **$200 $400 $600**

TRZ-80

❑ **TRZ-80. Cartoon Adventures Cards Featuring "Tarzan Of The Apes,"**
1936. Eight 2.25x2-7/8" cards, a near sub-set, from this series. Other cards in this set feature Tailspin Tommy, Bronco Bill and Buck Rogers. The Tarzan sub-set is #409-416 and this group includes all but card #415. Our photo includes a duplicate card #410. Each - **$25 $50 $85**

TRZ-81

❑ **TRZ-81. "Tarzan And His Mate" Contest Award Medal,**
1936. Tarzan Ice Cream Cups. Sterling silver pendant known sponsored by at least Foremost Dairies and Beatrice Creamery (Meadow Gold). The medal has same title as 1934 M-G-M film, but the contest had no affiliation with M-G-M and they did not sanction it. The Lily-Tulip Cup Co. specifically told Edgar Rice Burroughs that the title had nothing to do with the film. Front includes finely detailed figures of Tarzan and Jane plus "Ice Cream For Health" slogan. Reverse inscription is "Awarded To" followed by name engraving area "For Physical Perfection And Outstanding Personality By The Makers Of Tarzan Cups." - **$400 $800 $1600**

TRZ-82

❑ **TRZ-82. "The Nielen Tarzan Club" Member's Cello. Button,**
1936. Used as a premium by the Nielen Co. on radio station WKRC, Cincinnati, OH to promote radio serial #2 "Tarzan and the Diamond of Asher." - **$325 $750 $1500**

TRZ-83

TRZ-84

❑ **TRZ-83. "Tarzan Escapes" Big Little Book #1182,**
1936. Johnny Weissmuller photo cover. Has scenes from the MGM movie. - **$31 $93 $220**

❑ **TRZ-84. "The Beasts of Tarzan" Big Little Book #1410,**
1937. 432 pages. - **$19 $57 $135**

TRZ-85

❑ **TRZ-85. "Tarzan: Gift Picture No. 1 Of A Series",**
1937. "Tarzan Appears Each Month In Tip Top Comics Magazine Copyright 1937 By United Feature Syndicate Inc." Art by Rex Maxon. - **$125 $275 $500**

TRZ-86

❑ **TRZ-86. "Tarzan And A Daring Rescue" Booklet,**
1938. Pan-Am gasoline and motor oils. Title page offers bow and arrow set plus school bag premiums. - **$43 $129 $300**

TRZ-87

TRZ-88

❑ **TRZ-87. "Tarzan In The Golden City" Premium Book,**
1938. Whitman softcover is 3.5x3.75" Edgar Rice Burroughs Inc. Issued for Pan-Am gasoline/motor oils. Has 64 pages in bw with story art on every other page. - **$125 $350 $700**

❑ **TRZ-88. "Tip Top Comics" 11x14" Store Sign,**
c. 1938. - **$175 $325 $650**

TRZ-89

❑ **TRZ-89. "Tarzan Big Little Book" Picture Puzzles,**
1938. Whitman Publ. Co. There are three variants, but all use the same box. Each variant uses one different puzzle from the others. Scarce. - **$150 $300 $600**

TRZ-90

❑ **TRZ-90. Tarzan Adventure Game Boxed,**
1939. Made by Parker Brothers.
- **$325 $600 $1200**

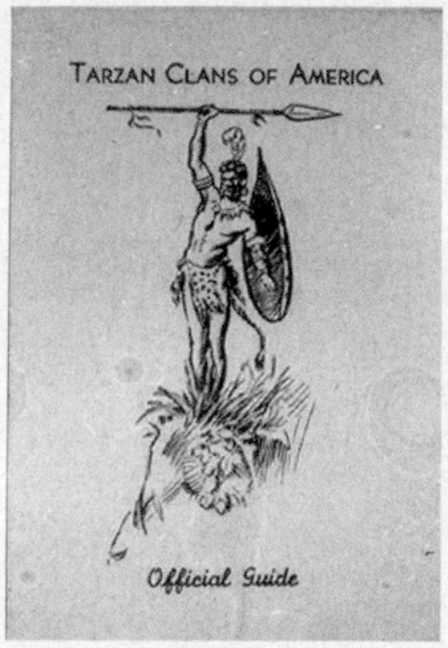

TRZ-91

❑ **TRZ-91. Clans Manual,**
1939. Tarzan Clans of America, Tarzana, California. Complete procedures and rituals for organizing and running a clan. - **$90 $175 $375**

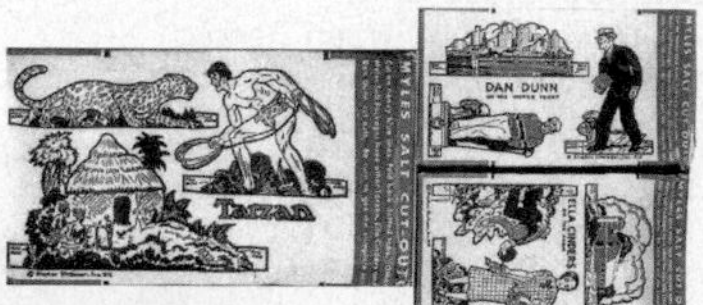

TRZ-92

❑ **TRZ-92. "Myles Salt Cut-Outs" Boxes,**
1930s. Panels picture Tarzan, Dan Dunn, Ella Cinders. Tarzan Box Uncut - **$200 $400 $800**
Others Uncut Each - **$50 $100 $200**

TRZ-93

❑ **TRZ-93. Tarzan Los Angeles Times Cello. Button,**
1930s. Rare. Los Angeles Times. Promotional newspaper button featuring Tarzan, Jimmy, and Perry. - **$400 $850 $1750**

TRZ-94

❑ **TRZ-94. "Tarzan Te Puro" Tea Canister With Lid,**
1930s. Litho. tin Spanish issue from Uruguay. A small quantity found in the 1990s.
- **$40 $65 $125**

TRZ-95

TRZ-96

❑ **TRZ-95. "Vita Hearts" Litho. Club Button,**
1930s. - **$350 $875 $2000**

❑ **TRZ-96. "Sons Of Tarzan Club" Cello. Button,**
1930s. Facsimile Johnny Weissmuller signature. Theater contest issue, match number to win prize. - **$50 $100 $200**

TRZ-97

TRZ-98

TRZ-99

❑ **TRZ-97. "Sons Of Tarzan Club" Second Variety Cello. Button,**
1930s. 1-1/4" green on yellow the same as the preceding item except without a contest serial number. - **$75 $150 $300**

❑ **TRZ-98. "Tarzan's Grip" Australian Cello. Button,**
1930s. 7/8" issued to promote glue product.
- **$35 $50 $100**

❑ **TRZ-99. "Tarzan Club" Cello. Button,**
1930s. K.L.S. Royal Bakers. 15/16" red, white and yellow with call letters of Salt Lake City, Utah radio station and company sponsor name. Scarce. - **$500 $1500 $3000**

TRZ-100

❑ **TRZ-100. Composition Figures,**
1930s. Store item by Belgian company Durso. Two Tarzan figures and Jane are about 2-1/2" tall, elephant is 3-1/2" tall and lion is 1-1/4" tall. Group As Pictured Near Mint - **$900**

TRZ-101

❑ **TRZ-101. "Tarzan" French Hardcover Book Set,**
1930s. Hatchette. Four books #1-4, all published in Paris between 1936-1938. Titles are Tarzan, Tarzan and Gloria, Tarzan and The Lion, Tarzan and The Elephants. Each includes Sunday reprint art by Foster. Contents are either 64 pages in #1 or 48 pages in the other three books. Each - **$135 $250 $500**

TRZ-102

❑ **TRZ-102. "Tarzan Of The Apes" Armed Services Edition Book,**
1940. 4x5.5" softcover 352-page complete novel published especially for members of U.S. Armed Forces. - **$185 $375 $775**

TRZ-103

❑ **TRZ-103. "The Return Of Tarzan" Armed Services Edition Book,**
c. 1940. 4.5x6.5" softcover 288-page complete novel published especially for members of U.S. Armed Forces. - **$225 $425 $850**

TRZ-104

❑ **TRZ-104. "Argosy Weekly" Issued With Complete Tarzan Story,**
1941. Three consecutive pulp issues #2-4 from Vol. 310 for August-September comprising complete Burroughs story "The Quest Of Tarzan."
First - **$50 $100 $200**
Second - **$30 $80 $150**
Third - **$30 $80 $150**

TRZ-105

❑ **TRZ-105. Tarzan Three-Record Set in Envelope,**
1941. Decca Records. Very scarce in original envelope with undamaged records.
- $125 $225 $350

TRZ-106

❑ **TRZ-106. Tarzan Three-Record Set in Envelope,**
1942. Decca Records. Very scarce in original envelope with undamaged records.
- $150 $250 $385

TRZ-107

❑ **TRZ-107. "Tarzan's New York Adventure" Spanish Movie Herald,**
1942. M-G-M. 3-1/2x5-1/4". - **$12 $25 $55**

TRZ-108

❑ **TRZ-108. "Tarzan And The Golden Lion" Better Little Book,**
1943. Whitman #1448**. - $20 $60 $140**

TRZ-109 TRZ-110

❑ **TRZ-109. "Tarzan and the Ant Men" Big Little Book #1444,**
1945. - **$16 $48 $115**

❑ **TRZ-110. "Tarzan Lord of the Jungle" Big Little Book #1407,**
1946. - **$16 $48 $115**

TRZ-111

❑ **TRZ-111. "Tarzan And The Mermaids" Australian Cello Disk,**
1948. A. W. Patrick. Based on RKO last movie starring Johnny Weissmuller. -
$210 $425 $650

TRZ-112

❑ **TRZ-112. Better Little Book Original Cover Art,**
1949. For #1467, *Tarzan in the Land of the Giant Apes.* - **$5750**

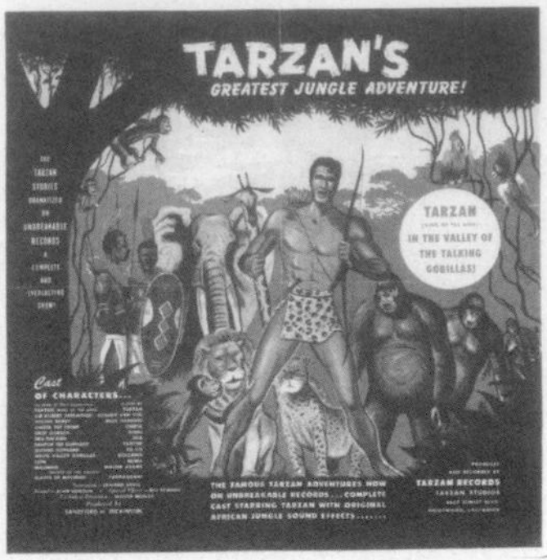

TRZ-113

❑ **TRZ-113. "Tarzan's Greatest Jungle Adventure" Record,**
1949. Produced by Tarzan Records.
- $65 $125 $250

TRZ-114

TRZ-115

❑ **TRZ-114. "I'm A Tarzan Fan" Valentine,**
c. 1940s. Store item with no copyright or maker's name. 4-1/2" tall diecut stiff paper. -
$65 $175 $350

❑ **TRZ-115. "Tarzan" Swim Meet Award,**
c. 1940s. Award is 3-3/8" tall with bar pin on back of fabric ribbon with loop suspending 1.5" tall very detailed award medal with text on top panel "Loew's Tarzan Meet" while below is image of young man swimming in the water accented by pair of leaf clusters left and right.
- $250 $500 $750

TRZ-116

❑ **TRZ-116. "Lex Barker Tarzan" Austalian Real Photo Cello. Button,**
1940s. 1". A.F. Patrick - **$50 $100 $200**

TRZ-117

❑ **TRZ-117. Dell Publishing Co. Pictures,**
1950. One sheet consisting of five photos.
Near Mint In Mailer - **$175**
Loose - **$25 $50 $125**

TRZ-118

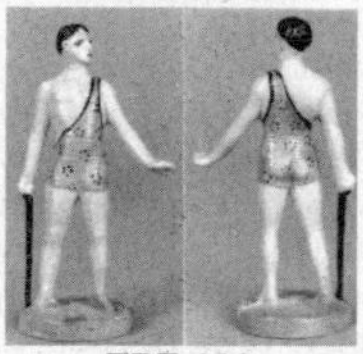

TRZ-119

❑ **TRZ-118. French Cello. Figure,**
1959. 2-1/2" tall marked "F Clairet". From a set of 15 figures, all marked "F. Clairet." The figures are: Tarzan, two apes holding sticks on a platform, one male lion, three female lions, tiger, adult elephant, baby elephant, black panther, zebra, ostrich, mountain goat, and kangaroo.
Tarzan - **$250 $500 $1000**

❑ **TRZ-119. "Westworld Tarzan Club" Badge,**
1950s. English 1-3/8" tall plastic badge in shield design with muted red background color at top and pale green tone on lower part.
- **$200 $400 $600**

TRZ-120

TRZ-121

❑ **TRZ-120. "Tarzan of the Apes" Hardcover Book with Ape-English Dictionary,**
1964. 285 pages. Tells story of Tarzan's birth and his growing up in Africa. Jesse Marsh art. -
$50 $100 $200

❑ **TRZ-121. "Tarzan and the Lost Safari" Hardcover Book,**
1966. Adapted from the movie. - **$25 $50 $90**
1957 edition with photo/art cover featuring Gordon Scott - **$30 $60 $100**

TRZ-122

TRZ-123

❑ **TRZ-122. "Tarzan" Lunch Box,**
1966. Store item by Aladdin. **- $85 $160 $350**

❑ **TRZ-123. "Tarzan/NBC" Promotional Book,**
1966. Advance information for 1966-1967 programming. **- $55 $110 $185**

TRZ-124

❑ **TRZ-124. "Tarzan And His Animals Magnetic Adventure Game" Boxed,**
1966. Merritt/J&L Randall Ltd. English game comprised of cardboard and plastic game parts for two players. Object is capture of animals drawn toward cage by magnetic action. -
$100 $250 $500

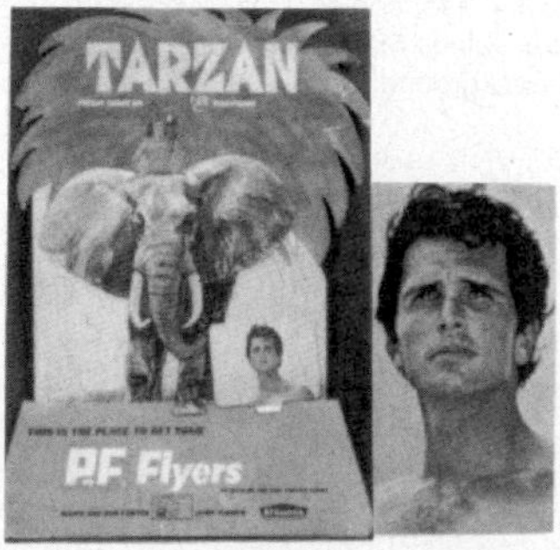

TRZ-125

❑ **TRZ-125. P.F. Flyer Store Display,**
1960s. Cardboard 20-1/2x28". Die-cut pieces create 3-D appearance.
Standee - **$150 $300 $700**

TRZ-126

❑ **TRZ-126. Plastic Flicker Picture Rings,**
1960s. Set of six. Gold plastic bases.
Each - **$10 $15 $25**

TRZ-127

TRZ-128

❑ **TRZ-127. "Tarzan" Portrait By Frazetta Button,**
1973. 3" full color cello with art by popular super hero and science-fiction illustrator. -
$18 $30 $60

❑ **TRZ-128. "Tarzan" Model Kit,**
1974. Store item by Auro ra.
Unused Near Mint - **$55**

TRZ-129

❑ **TRZ-129. Tarzan Resin Statue,**
1997. Last product worked on by the late Burne Hogarth. Limited to only 500.
Boxed - **$350**

Teenage Mutant Ninja Turtles

Donatello, Leonardo, Michaelangelo, and Raphael burst upon the scene in 1984 in issue #1 of *Teenage Mutant Ninja Turtles*, created by Kevin Eastman and Peter Laird. The first issue was self-published in black and white with a print run of 3,000 and quickly sold out. The pizza-loving sewer dwellers and their ninja master thrived not only in various comic books and collected editions, but in animated TV series (1988, 2003), premiums from Burger King, a concert tour sponsored by Pizza Hut, and hundreds of licensed items. Feature films were released in 1990, 1991, 1993 and 2007. All of this has combined to make the Turtles a billion dollar franchise. "Cowabunga!"

TMT-1

❑ **TMT-1. Fan Club Kit Ad and Coupon,**
1988. Playmates Toy Co. - **$12 $22 $35**

TMT-2

❑ **TMT-2. Fan Club Kit,**
1988. Playmates Toy Co. Envelope with bandanna, letter, story comic, sticker, charter member certificate with perforated membership card. Set - **$40 $65 $135**

TMT-3

❑ **TMT-3. "Teenage Mutant Ninja Turtles" Cereal Box with Cereal Bowl Attached,**
1989. - **$12 $30 $45**

TMT-4 TMT-5

❑ **TMT-4. Movie Promotion 2-1/8" Cello. Button,**
1990. Mirage Studios. - **$4 $8 $12**

❑ **TMT-5. Nabisco Shreddies Canadian Cereal Box,**
1990. Box offers first four of eight "Power Rings". Complete Box - **$200**
Turtles Rings - **$5 $10 $15**
Other Character Rings - **$8 $12 $20**

TMT-6

❑ **TMT-6. Animated Television Cel,**
c. 1990. Store item sold through retailers such as K-Mart in a bag with header card or through galleries in other formats. Backgrounds are usually color laser copies. Near Mint - **$30**
Higher Values May Apply Depending On Image And Background

TMT-7

❑ **TMT-7. Nabisco Shreddies Canadian Cereal Box,**
1991. Box offers last four of eight rings.
Complete Box - **$200**
Turtles Rings - **$5 $10 $15**
Other Character Rings - **$8 $12 $20**

TMT-8

❑ **TMT-8. Technodrome Scout Vehicle,**
1998. With box. - **$30**

Television Misc.

Television, only an experimental and isolated technical dream through the 1930s, would likely have erupted sooner if not for the World War II years. But erupt it did in the late 1940s to present day norm of scarcely any household in the United States without at least one TV set. Early TV programming could be much more easily sponsored by a single sponsor per show. It has been estimated that an early sponsor could well finance an entire season or more for the current cost, in equal dollars, of a 30-second advertising spot during recent Super Bowl telecasts. The basic cost of TV advertising, of course, is a prior consideration to the supplemental cost of premiums; thus the noticeable lack of mail premium offers so prevalent in the radio and earliest TV eras. Premiums associated to TV characters or shows are now most likely found as part of a retail item if indeed offered at all. This book section depicts a sampling of premium collectibles from a wide variety of shows.

TEL-1

TEL-2

❑ **TEL-1. Dumont "Small Fry Club" Cello. Button,**
1947. Among the earliest programs for children. Dumont television network 1947-1951, hosted by Big Brother Bob Emery. - **$30 $60 $125**

❑ **TEL-2. Big Brother "Small Fry Marionette" Historic TV Toy,**
1948. Small Fry Club. "Small Fry Girl" in box. "Big Brother Show" was on radio and converted over to TV. It was one of the first marionette TV shows. Boxed - **$150 $300 $600**

TEL-3

❑ **TEL-3. Early Children's TV Rare "The Magic Cottage" Brass Decoder,**
1949. Dumont Network. 2" tall badge issued for program aired 1949-1951. Bird depicted on front is Wilmer the Pigeon. Reverse has opening to insert paper with message. - **$125 $250 $500**

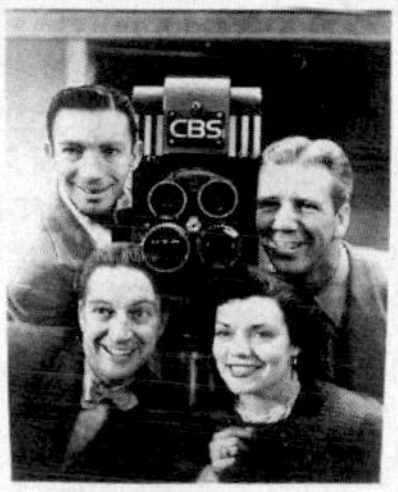

TEL-4

❑ **TEL-4. "The Garry Moore Show" Cast Photo,**
1949. Shows Ken Carson, Garry Moore, Denise Lor and Durward Kirby. - **$30 $60 $90**

TEL-5

❑ **TEL-5. "Crosley's House Of Fun" Comic Booklet,**
1950. Crosley Appliances. - **$5 $15 $30**

TEL-6

❑ **TEL-6. "4 Norge TV Comic Masks" With Envelope,**
1951. Norge Appliances. Paper masks of television's pioneering comedians Ed Wynn, Jack Carson, Danny Thomas, Jimmy Durante. Unpunched In Envelope - **$50 $100 $200**

TEL-7

TEL-8

❑ **TEL-7. "Kit Carson" Tie With Clasp,**
1953. 15" bolo tie with 1" brass slide clasp with TV portrayer Bill Williams portrait flanked by image of single Coca-Cola bottle. - **$40 $75 $150**

❑ **TEL-8. "Adventures of Kit Carson" Premium Pinback,**
1953. Probably sponsored Snyder's Potato Chips. Scarce. - **$30 $75 $165**

TEL-9

❑ **TEL-9. TV Guide #3,**
1953. April 17, 1953 cover features the stars of the top 4 shows of that time. - **$50 $100 $185**

TEL-10

TEL-11

❑ **TEL-10. "Kit Carson Kerchief" 16x24" Cardboard Store Poster,**
1953. Coca-Cola. - **$45 $115 $200**

❑ **TEL-11. "Kit Carson" Fabric Kerchief,**
1953. Picturing Bill Williams, TV series star. - **$15 $25 $60**

TEL-12

❑ **TEL-12. "See Kit Carson TV Show" Store Window Card,**
1953. Coca-Cola Co. 16x24" cardboard. - **$75 $150 $300**

TEL-13

❑ **TEL-13. TV Promo,**
1953. Four page Coca Cola premium. Tells about Old West and Kit Carson background. Talks about design of Kit Carson Kerchief premium. Promotes TV show "Adventures of Kit Carson." - **$15 $40 $75**

TEL-14

❑ **TEL-14. Kit Carson's Stage Coach,**
1953. Coca Cola TV premium. In mailer w/ complete instructions. - **$65 $125 $225**

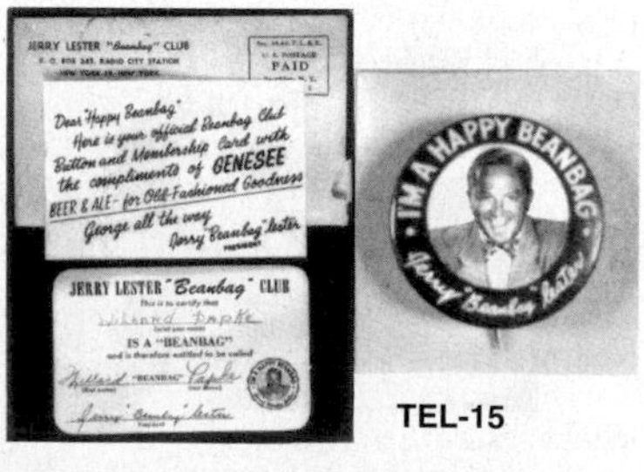

TEL-15

❑ **TEL-15. "Jerry Lester 'Bean Bag' Club" Kit,**
1953. Genesee Beer & Ale. Includes membership card, button, message card. Complete - **$40 $60 $120**

TEL-16

❑ **TEL-16. This is Your Life - Book Shaped Locket,**
1953. With coupon and ad.
Complete - **$60 $115 $200**
Locket Only - **$20 $35 $65**

TEL-17

❑ **TEL-17. Sid Caesar "Your Show of Shows" Cardboard Sign,**
1953. 10-1/2x13-1/2". - **$100 $200 $400**

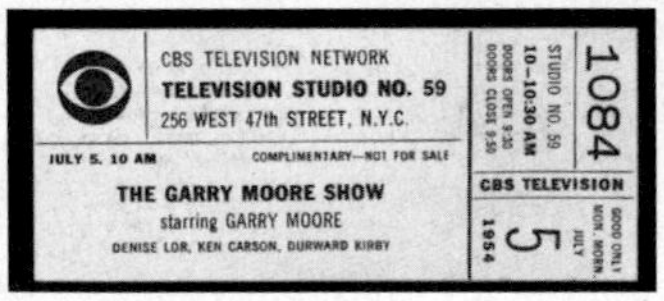

TEL-18

❑ **TEL-18. "The Garry Moore Show" Ticket,**
1954. Unused ticket for CBS Studios show. -
$20 $40 $75

TEL-19

❑ **TEL-19. "Father Knows Best" Cast Photo Postcard,**
c. 1954. Oversized 5-1/2x7" card picturing Anderson family of TV series. - **$10 $20 $40**

TEL-20

❑ **TEL-20. "Chester A. Riley" Fan Postcard,**
c. 1955. Cast photo of "Life Of Riley" series. -
$15 $30 $60

TEL-21

❑ **TEL-21. "'Kit Carson' Ranger" Membership Certificate,**
1956. Bar Bee meat products. 8-1/2x11" printed in black and white with gold engraving style inner border. - **$25 $50 $100**

TEL-22

❑ **TEL-22. "Hawaiian Eye" Song Sheet,**
1959. Star Bob Conrad pictured. - **$20 $35 $60**

TEL-23

❑ **TEL-23. TV Cameraman Plastic Pull Toy,**
1950s. Kraft Foods. - **$25 $60 $100**

TEL-24

❑ **TEL-24. "RCA TV Coloring Book",**
1950s. - **$10 $20 $40**

TEL-25

❑ **TEL-25. Television Bread Loaf End Label,**
1950s. Pictured example from set depicts "Television Demonstrated" in 1927.
Each - **$15 $25 $40**

TEL-26

❑ **TEL-26. "Million Sellers" Record Album With Mary Tyler Moore Cover,**
1950s. Store item on Tops Records label. Cardboard sleeve holds 33-1/3 rpm record. -
$12 $30 $60

TEL-27

TEL-28

❑ **TEL-27. Ding Dong School Bell,**
1950s. - **$25 $50 $100**

❑ **TEL-28. "Hollywood Off-Beat" TV Show Starring Melvyn Douglas - Dixie Cup Promo,**
1950s. - **$20 $40 $60**

TEL-29

TEL-30

❑ **TEL-29. Flying Turtle Club Beany TV,**
1950s. - **$40 $80 $150**

❑ **TEL-30. I Led Three Lives Promo,**
1950s. Small cardboard tag. Rare. - **$35 $75 $150**

TEL-31

❑ TEL-31. Dinah Shore Promo 2 1/2"x5",
1950s. Chevrolet TV premium. - **$12 $30 $50**

TEL-32

❑ TEL-32. Beat The Clock Brochure,
1950s. Sylvania promo for TV program. 10x15". 12 pgs. of great graphics of stars. -
$30 $60 $110

TEL-33

❑ TEL-33. "TV Bank" Litho. Bank,
1950s. Various companies. - **$12 $25 $35**

TEL-34

TEL-35

❑ TEL-34. "Farfel" Ceramic Mug,
1950s. - **$18 $30 $50**

❑ TEL-35. "Gene London Club" 3" Cello. Button,
1950s. Channel 10, Philadelphia TV station. -
$8 $15 $30

TEL-36

❑ TEL-36. "The Ghost Rider" Cello. Button,
1950s. WCAU-TV (Philadelphia). -
$12 $25 $50

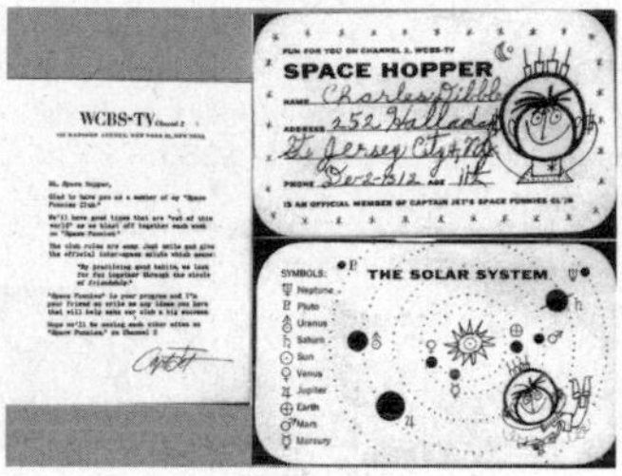

TEL-37

❑ TEL-37. "Space Hopper" Club Letter & Card,
c. 1960. WCBS-TV, New York City. Items for "Captain Jet" club. Letter - **$8 $15 $30**
Card - **$10 $15 $40**

TEL-38

❑ TEL-38. "Sea Hunt Underwater Adventure Game,"
1961. Lowell Toy Mfg. Corp. Copyright ZIV-United Artists Inc. Box has gameboard, 24 "Compressed Air" cards, four sets of colored plastic markers and an insert which has spinner, 20 "Treasure Gold" tokens.
- **$100 $200 $300**

TEL-39

❑ TEL-39. "The Untouchables" Playset,
1961. Marx #4676. Near Mint Boxed - **$2500**

TEL-40

❑ TEL-40. Charlie Weaver Mechanical Bartender,
1962. © Roy Rogers. Rosko Tested Toy.
Box - **$50 $100 $200**
Toy - **$25 $50 $100**

TEL-41

❑ TEL-41. "Chipmunks/Soaky" Cardboard Record,
1964. Colgate-Palmolive. - **$8 $15 $30**

TEL-42

TEL-43

❑ TEL-42. "Mr. Ed March Of Comics" #260,
1964. Various sponsors. - **$6 $12 $45**

❑ TEL-43. "Jimmy Nelson's Instant Ventriloquism" Record Album,
1964. Album also pictures Danny O'Day and Farfel. - **$15 $30 $60**

TEL-44

❑ **TEL-44. Magilla Gorilla Felt Doll,**
1964. Doll has cloth clothes. By Ideal with tag.
- **$100 $200 $400**

TEL-45

❑ **TEL-45. "The Dick Van Dyke Game,"**
1964. Standard Toycraft Copyright Calvada Productions. 9.25x18.5x1.75" deep box.
- **$125 $250 $400**

TEL-46

❑ **TEL-46. J. Fred Muggs 'Autographed' Photo,**
1965. Autographed inscription includes names of apparent owners/trainers "Bud Roy & Jerry." 8x10" black and white glossy signed to a restaurant "Where Show Folks Can Enjoy Good Food..." Similar Example - **$20 $35 $60**

TEL-47

❑ **TEL-47. "Mrs. Beasley" Talking Doll,**
1966. Store item by Mattel. Includes plastic glasses. Talking - **$75 $175 $350**
Not Talking - **$40 $80 $160**

TEL-48

❑ **TEL-48. Flipper "Magic Whistle" 5"x24" Paper Store Sign,**
c. 1966. P.F. Flyers footwear of B.F. Goodrich. -
$30 $60 $100

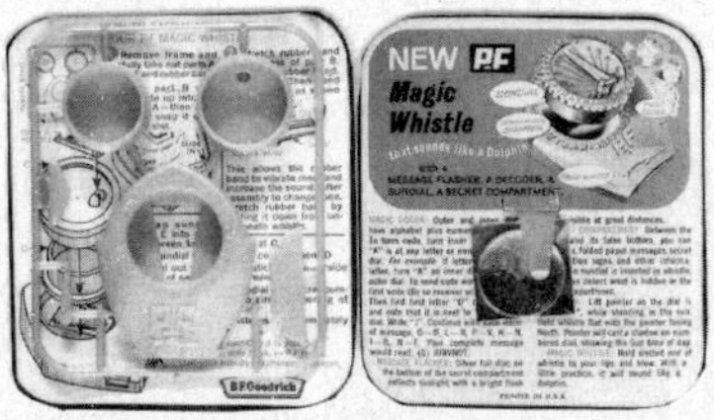

TEL-49

❑ **TEL-49. Dolphin "Magic Whistle" Plastic Assembly Parts On Card,**
c. 1966. P.F. footwear of B.F. Goodrich. "Flipper" not named but card pictures dolphin, assembled whistle is to produce tone "That Sounds Like A Dolphin".
Unassembled With Card - **$18 $35 $60**
Assembled - **$8 $15 $30**

TEL-50

❑ **TEL-50. Captain Scarlet Pinback on Card,**
1967. - **$50 $100 $200**

TEL-51

❑ **TEL-51. Captain Scarlet 12" Figure in Box,**
1967. Pedigree product. Much rarer than Captain Action doll of same period.
Boxed - **$1500**
Near Mint Figure without box - **$550**

TEL-52

❑ **TEL-52. Vulture Squadron Set Of Soft Rubber Figures,**
1969. Kellogg's Froot Loops. Typically about 1-1/2" tall. Each - **$5 $12 $25**

TEL-53

❑ **TEL-53. "Dastardly And Muttley" Kite Safety Booklet,**
1969. Color comic produced in association with Reddy Kilowatt with 16 pages of comics and activities involving electricity. - **$5 $15 $65**

TEL-54

❑ **TEL-54. "ABC Super Saturday Club" Membership Kit,**
1969. Contains 11 pieces. Club letter, litho tin buttons (2), 4" stickers (2), plastic membership card, iron-on transfer, stamp sheet (8-1/4x10-1/2"), stamp card, 11x16" poster and color booklet. Near Mint Complete **- $250**

TEL-55

❑ **TEL-55. "Maynard" G. Krebs Composition Bobbing Head,**
1960s. Store item. **- $100 $250 $500**

TEL-56

❑ **TEL-56. Danny Thomas Flicker Small Sign,**
1960s. Post Corn Flakes. **- $50 $100 $165**

TEL-57

❑ **TEL-57. "Wonderful World of Color" Wooden Blocks Set,**
1960s. Used to promote Disney's TV show. Box shows cartoon host Ludwig Von Drake.
Blocks in box **- $50 $100 $185**

TEL-58

❑ **TEL-58. "Family Affair/Mrs. Beasley" Pin On Card,**
1970. From series of "Buffy Jewelry" by Werthley. Near Mint Carded **- $230**
Card Only **- $18 $35 $70**
Pin Only **- $40 $80 $160**

TEL-59

TEL-60

❑ **TEL-59. "Dark Shadows/Josette's Music Box",**
1970. Store item by Dan Curtis Productions Inc. 2-1/2" diameter hard plastic with wind-up key on the underside and music box which plays Josette's Theme. **- $85 $150 $300**

❑ **TEL-60. "The Age of Television" Record Album with 32 Page Book,**
1972. RCA. A chronicle of the first 25 years of television, hosted by Milton Berle, Hugh Downs and the late Arlene Francis.
Album **- $30**
Book **- $20**

TEL-61

❑ **TEL-61. "This Is Your Life" Boxed Ashtray,**
1973. "Best Wishes from Ralph Edwards" printed in red on ashtray. **- $30 $55 $85**

TEL-62

❑ **TEL-62. "Flipper" Fan Postcard,**
1975. **- $10 $20 $40**

TEL-63

❑ **TEL-63. Gilda Radner Cut-Out Doll Book,**
1979. Scarce. 11 pages of cut-outs and a cardboard punch-out of Gilda. **- $20 $40 $70**

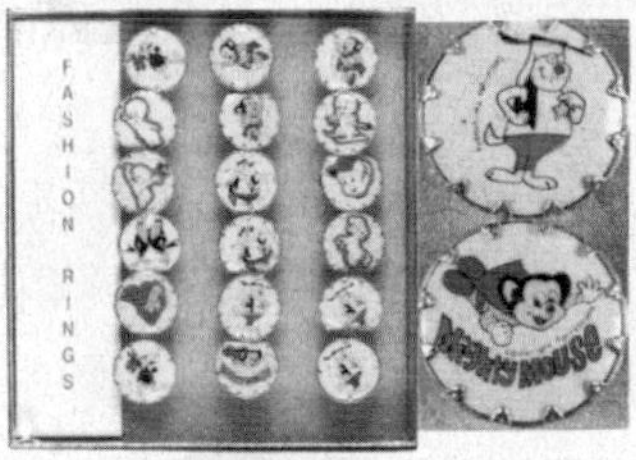

TEL-64

❑ **TEL-64. Animated TV Show Set Of 18 Character Rings In Box,**
c. 1980. Store item. Each has 7/8" diameter litho top. Various images of Mighty Mouse, Casper, Spooky, Wendy, Midnight, Heckle & Jeckle, Deputy Dawg. Near Mint Boxed **- $215**

TEL-65

❑ **TEL-65. "V" 45'er Pistol and Holster,**
1984. On card. **- $125**

TEL-66

TEL-67

❑ **TEL-66. "V" Enemy Visitor Figure,**
1984. With human mask, sunglasses and laser gun. In box. - **$65**

❑ **TEL-67. "V" Bop Bag in Box,**
1984. Copyright Warner Bros. - **$60**

TEL-68

❑ **TEL-68. Kellogg's Corn Flakes Cereal Box with "Captain Power" Mask of Lord Dread,**
1987. Cut out mask on back. - **$20 $40 $65**

TEL-69

❑ **TEL-69. Talking Cryptkeeper Doll,**
1994. In box. - **$30**

TEL-70

❑ **TEL-70. "Man Eating" Cow Figure,**
1995. From "The Tick". - **$50**

TEL-71

❑ **TEL-71. "Mr. Bill" Beanie,**
1998. 9" tall. TM Dreamsite Prod., Inc. - **$22**

TEL-72

❑ **TEL-72. "South Park" Wristwatch in Metal Box,**
1998. Features the kids on box. - **$20 $50 $90**

TEL-73

❑ **TEL-73. "South Park" Plush Doll Boxed Sets,**
1998. Each has two characters- Kenny and Kyle, or Cartman and Stan.
Each box - **$18**
Each Beanie - **$10**

TEL-74

TEL-75

❑ **TEL-74. "Crush Me Phil" Toonsylvania Toy in Box,**
1998. From Steven Spielberg's animated series. - **$20**

❑ **TEL-75. "Taunt Me Igor" Toonsylvania Toy in Box,**
1998. - **$20**

TEL-76

❑ **TEL-76. "Nickelodeon" Blimp Premium,**
1999. From Burger King. - **$2 $4 $10**

TEL-77

❑ **TEL-77. "Digimon" Pop-Up Ring Set,**
2000. Set of 3 pop-up rings. - **$20**

(Box) (Figure inside box)

TEL-78

❑ **TEL-78. "Bender" Robot Action Toy,**
2000. From the animated series "Futurama."
- **$25**

(Box) (Figure inside box)

TEL-79

❑ **TEL-79. "Nibbler" Robot Action Toy,**
2000. From the animated series "Futurama." - **$20**

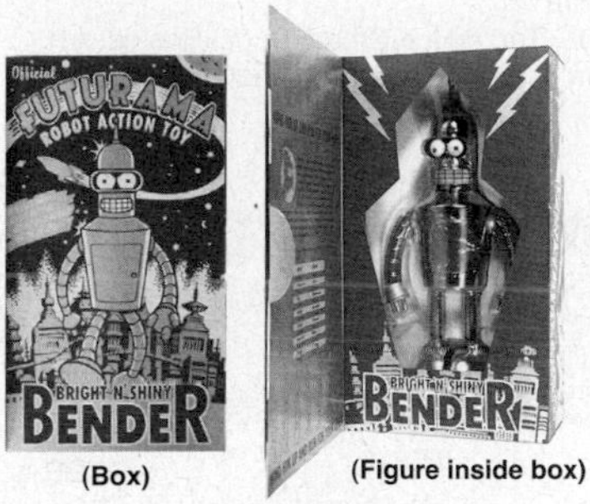

(Box) (Figure inside box)

TEL-80

❑ **TEL-80. "Bright 'N' Shiny Bender" Robot Action Toy with Box,**
2001. From the animated series "Futurama." - **$30**

TEL-81

❑ **TEL-81. Futurama "Bender" Mask,**
2001. 18" tall, 7 1/4" wide. - **$10**

(Punchouts)

TEL-82 (Background)

❑ **TEL-82. Futurama "Pop-Out People" Punchouts,**
2001. Cardboard punchouts of characters with background. - **$3**

TEL-83

TEL-84

❑ **TEL-83. "Muttley" Plush Doll,**
2001. From the show "Wacky Races." Includes glasses and tag. - **$20**

❑ **TEL-84. "Partridge Family" Bus Model,**
2001. Die-cast bus from the Johnny Lightning series. - **$12**

Tennessee Jed

The frontier adventures of Jed Sloan aired on ABC radio from 1945 to 1947. Acting as an undercover agent for General Grant in the period just after the Civil War, Sloan was a deadly marksman who daily did away with cattle rustlers and other villains of the Western Plains. John Thomas originally played Jed, followed by Don McLaughlin. Tip-Top bread and cakes was the sponsor. A single issue of a giveaway comic book was published in 1945.

TEN-1

❑ **TEN-1. Exhibit Card And Cardboard Dexterity Puzzle With Envelope,**
1945. Tip-Top Bread.
Near Mint In Mailer - **$110**
Card - **$10 $25 $45**
Puzzle - **$15 $35 $65**

TEN-2

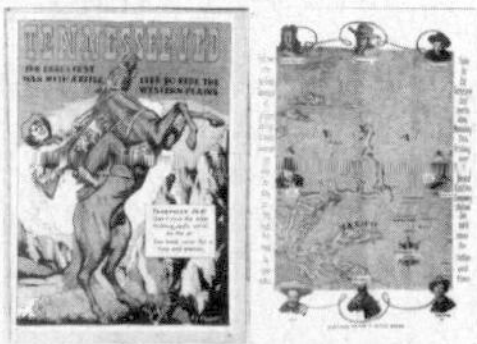

TEN-3

❑ **TEN-2. Oversized Cardboard Ear For Radio Broadcasts,**
1945. Tip-Top Bread. 3x5" with attachment tabs. - **$20 $45 $75**

❑ **TEN-3. Tip-Top Bread Comic Book,**
1945. Inside has adventure map keyed to radio broadcasts. - **$25 $45 $250**

TEN-4

❑ **TEN-4. Pumpkin Mask,**
1945. Tip-Top Bread. - **$45 $90 $185**

TEN-5

TEN-5. Tip-Top "Horse Puzzle" Cards With Envelope,
c. 1945. Three-card picture placement puzzle with solution on envelope back. - **$25 $55 $100**

TEN-6

TEN-7

❑ **TEN-6. Picture Card,**
1946. Tip-Top Bread. Radio premium. Jed kneeling on one knee. - **$10 $20 $40**

❑ **TEN-7. "Tennessee Jed Magic Tricks" Booklet,**
1940s. Tip-Top Bread. Sixteen pages of illustrated tricks using household products. - **$20 $35 $75**

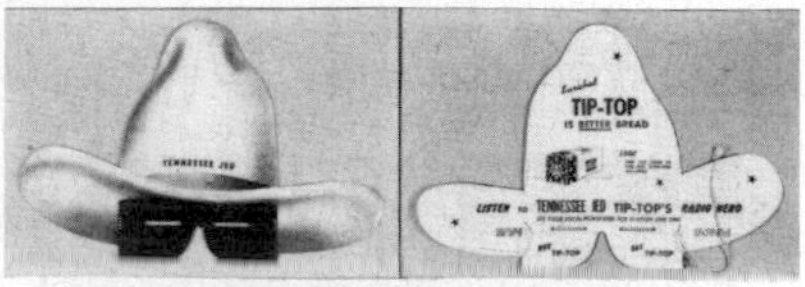

TEN-8

❑ **TEN-8. Paper Mask,**
1946. - **$30 $60 $115**

TEN-9

❑ **TEN-9. Tattoo Transfers With Mailer,**
1946. - **$85 $135 $275**

TEN-10

❑ **TEN-10. "Atom Gun" Cardboard Clicker,**
1946. Ward's Tip-Top Bread. - **$50 $100 $200**

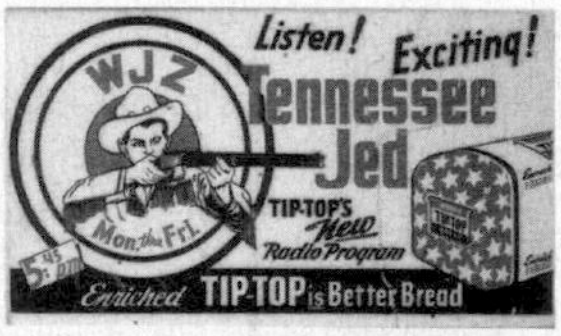

TEN-11

❑ **TEN-11. Cardboard Ink Blotter,**
c. 1946. - **$10 $25 $50**

TEN-12 TEN-13

❑ **TEN-12. Magnet Ring,**
c. 1946. Brass base with diecut arrowhead designs holding top magnet. - **$150 $300 $600**

❑ **TEN-13. Look-Around Brass Ring,**
c. 1946. - **$160 $350 $650**

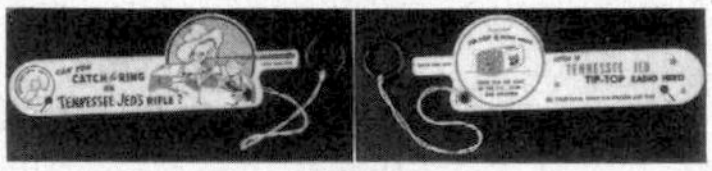

TEN-14

❑ **TEN-14. "Catch The Ring" Toy,**
1947. Cardboard with attached string and metal ring. - **$15 $35 $60**

Terry and the Pirates

Milton Caniff (1907-1988) created his *Terry and the Pirates* adventure comic strip in 1934 for the Chicago Tribune-New York News Syndicate. The scene of the action was China, and young Terry Lee and his pals Pat Ryan and comedic sidekick Connie were to come up against a variety of evil-doers and exotic women, notably the infamous Dragon Lady. The art on the strip greatly improved when Noel Sickles (1910-1982) began assisting on the strip in 1935, continuing on until 1939. During World War II Terry became an Air Force pilot and, along with Colonel Flip Corkin, battled the Axis. The strip ceased publication in 1973. A number of *Terry and the Pirates* comic books were published between 1939 and 1955, including giveaways from Sears & Roebuck, Buster Brown, Canada Dry, Libby Foods, Weather Bird shoes and others.

Radio adaptations aired on NBC from 1937 to 1939, sponsored by Dari-Rich chocolate drink, and on ABC from 1943 to 1948, sponsored by Quaker Oats, Puffed Wheat, and Puffed Rice. A 15-episode chapter play was released by Columbia Pictures in 1940 with William Tracy as Terry, and a syndicated television series aired in New York in 1952-1953 and had continued distribution through the 1950s. George Wunder was artist on the strip from 1946, when Caniff left to do *Steve Canyon* until 1973. In recent years the Hildebrandt Brothers and Dan Spiegle have attempted spirited revivals but the strip is not in production at the present time. Ohio State University in Columbus, Ohio has an extensive collection of Milton Caniff material including original art.

TER-1

❑ **TER-1. "Terry And The Pirates" Book,**
1935. Published by Whitman. 3-3/8x5-5/8" soft-cover format. Varieties with no ad, Sears ad or Perkins ad. Each - **$29 $87 $200**

TER-2

❑ **TER-2. "Terry And The Pirates Meet Again",**
1936. Tarzan Ice Cream Cups. Booklet #10 from series of various character titles. - **$54 $162 $380**

TER-3

TER-4

❑ **TER-3. "Terry And The Pirates" Game,**
1937. "Find the Hidden Treasure Game" from Whitman Publishing. - **$90 $190 $400**

❑ **TER-4. Quaker Puffed Wheat Comic Book,**
1938. 1938 strips, but issued in the 1940s. - **$2 $6 $12**

TER-5

❑ **TER-5. "Terry And The Pirates Ashore In Singapore" Premium Book,**
1938. Whitman BLB format with imprint for Stern & Co. - **$34 $102 $235**

TER-6

❑ **TER-6. "The Adventures Of Terry And The Pirates" Big Big Book,**
1938. Whitman #4073. - **$79 $237 $550**

TER-7 TER-8

❑ **TER-7. "Adventures Of Terry And The Pirates" Booklet,**
1938. From Whitman Penny Books series with inside ad for "Super-Comics" and "Crackajack Funnies" comic books. - **$10 $30 $62**

❑ **TER-8. "Terry And The Pirates" Big Little Book #1412,**
1938. Milton Caniff art. - **$14 $42 $95**

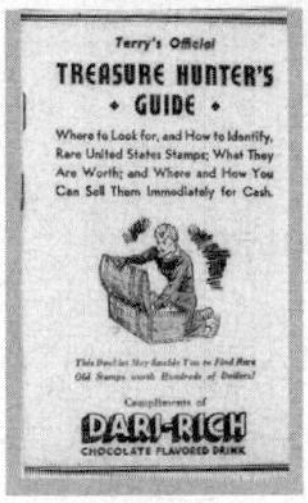

TER-9 TER-10

❑ **TER-9. "Treasure Hunter's Guide" Booklet,**
1938. Dari-Rich Chocolate Drink. Contents basically about stamp collecting. - **$35 $65 $110**

❑ **TER-10. "Terry And The Pirates And The Giant's Vengeance" Better Little Book,**
1939. Whitman #1446. - **$14 $42 $95**

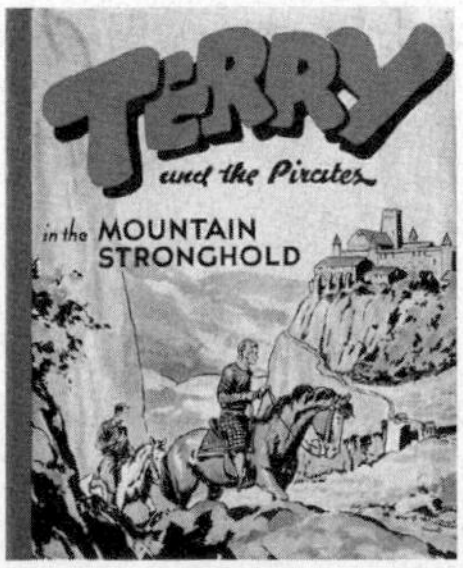

TER-11

❑ **TER-11. "Terry And The Pirates in the Mountain Stronghold" Big Little Book #1499,**
1941. - **$14 $42 $95**

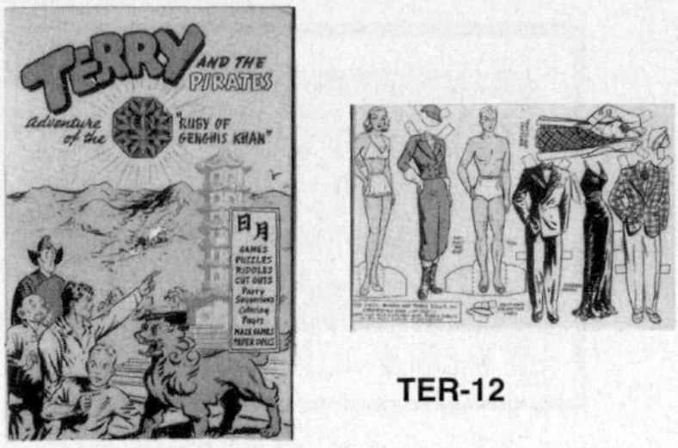

TER-12

❑ **TER-12. "Ruby Of Genghis Khan" Comic Activity Book,**
1941. Rare. Libby's fruit and vegetable juices. Contents include pencil puzzles, games, coloring pages, magic tricks, cut-out dolls.
GD - **$400** FN - **$1200** VF - **$2600**

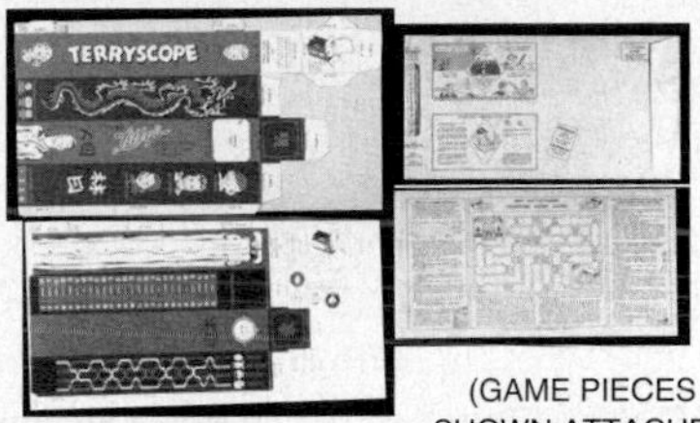

TER-13

(GAME PIECES SHOWN ATTACHED TO SCOPE AT BOTTOM LEFT)

❑ **TER-13. "Terryscope" Cardboard Assembly Kit,**
1941. Rare. Libby, McNeill & Libby. Pictures six characters, one side features secret code. Game pieces came attached on side of unassembled Terryscope.
Near Mint Terryscope Unassembled - **$800**
Terryscope Assembled - **$100 $300 $550**
Game Pieces (Four Different) - **$100**
Mailer - **$30 $60 $100**

TER-14

❑ **TER-14. Libby's Display Sign,**
1942. Shows Terry showing how to get plane spotter premium. 3 known. Gordon Gold Archives. - **$600 $1200 $2000**

TER-15

TER-16

TER-17

❑ **TER-15. "Victory Airplane Spotter" Cardboard Mechanical Disk With Envelope,**
1942. Libby, McNeill & Libby. Pictures Terry, Pat, April, Burma, Connie plus identifies 16 warplane silhouettes. - **$75 $175 $350**

❑ **TER-16. Quaker Oats B-25 Mascot Plane Photo,**
1943. - **$30 $60 $90**

❑ **TER-17. "Pilot's Mascot" Wooden Button,**
1943. Wire loop reverse for wearing with a safety pin. Came with Quaker Cereals B-25 airplane picture. - **$20 $40 $75**

TER-18

❑ **TER-18. Quaker Oats Pictures,**
c. 1944. Set of six. Pat Ryan, Burma, Terry, Phil Corkin, Dragon Lady, Connie. Near Mint In Mailer - **$525**
Each - **$20 $40 $80**

TER-19

❑ **TER-19. Quaker "Wings Of Victory" Box,**
c. 1945. Set of 12 warplane back pictures.
Each Complete Box - **$85 $200 $400**
Each Cut Picture Panel - **$10 $20 $35**

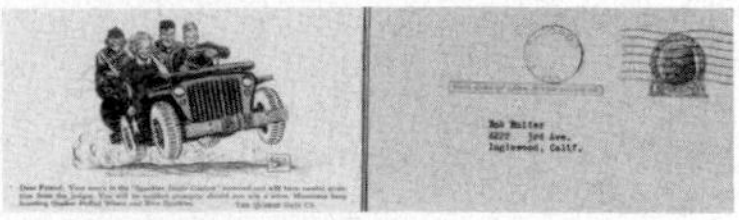

TER-20

❑ **TER-20. Quaker Cereals "Sparkies Jingle Contest" Postcard,**
1946. - **$20 $35 $75**

(PUZZLE BOX)

TER-21 (PUZZLE IMAGE)

❑ **TER-21. Jig Saw Puzzle in Box,**
1946. - **$60 $125 $225**

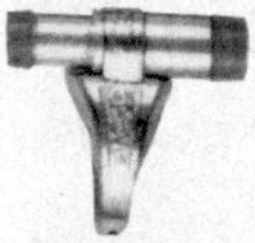

TER-22

TER-23

❑ **TER-22. Pirate's Gold Ore Detector Ring,**
1947. Quaker Cereals. Brass with aluminum/plastic telescope viewer holding tiny gold flakes. Documented by radio show episode titled "Quaker Puffed Wheat and Quaker Puffed Rice bring you Terry and the Pirates - the new and exciting adventure of Terry Lee and the Pirate Gold Detector Ring." The episode begins with Terry speaking about his long search for this ring. - **$40 $75 $150**

❑ **TER-23. "Tattoo Transfers" Set In Envelope,**
c. 1948. Coco-Wheats cereal. 22 water transfer pictures on two sheets, "Pack No. 9". - **$30 $60 $100**

TER-24

❑ **TER-24. Artist George Wunder Personal Christmas Card,**
c. 1948. - **$20 $40 $80**

TER-25

❑ **TER-25. "Terry Lee" Philadelphia School Graduation Button,**
1949. 3" button reads "Simon Gratz 41-49." Also has "Terry Lee" name on jacket of comic figure. Philadelphia Badge on edge curl. - **$40 $80 $160**

TER-26

❑ **TER-26. Terry & The Pirates Four Color Code-Writer,**
1940s. Libby McNeill & Libby. Partially used example is 2-3/4" long with silver luster metal cap holding red and yellow wood pencil with the lead a combination of four distinct colors. - **$125 $240 $480**

TER-27

❑ **TER-27. Character Stamps For Contest Entry,**
1940s. Quaker Oats. Awarded to entrants in bicycle contest announced in part by radio broadcasts. - **$50 $100 $200**

TER-28

TER-29

❑ **TER-28. "Terry Jingle" Contest Postcard,**
1940s. Quaker Puffed Wheat and Rice Sparkies. Acknowledgement card for entrant. - **$20 $35 $75**

❑ **TER-29. "Canada Dry" 13x17" Cardboard Ad Sign,**
1953. (Has 1952 copyright.) Offered a comic book with purchase of every carton of soda. - **$135 $210 $425**

TER-30

❑ **TER-30. "Hot Shot Charlie Flies Again" No. 1 Comic Book,**
1953. Canada Dry. From set of three. - **$15 $45 $165**

TER-31

TER-32

❑ **TER-31. "Terry And The Pirates In Forced Landing" Comic Book #2,**
1953. Canada Dry. Third book in set is "Dragon Lady In Distress". Each - **$15 $45 $165**

❑ **TER-32. Canada Dry "Chop-Stick-Joe" Litho. Button,**
1953. From set of five also including Terry, Burma, Dragon Lady, Hot Shot Charlie. Each - **$15 $30 $50**

TER-33

❑ **TER-33. "See Terry On TV" 3" Flicker Button,**
1953. Canada Dry. - **$35 $65 $120**

TER-34

❑ **TER-34. Prototype for "Hot Shot Charlie" Mask Ad,**
1953. Original art from the Gordon Gold Archives. Shown framed. - **$800**

TER-35

❑ **TER-35. "Canada Dry" Store Display For Contest,**
1953. Large 17.5x23.5" diecut cardboard for voting contest to select favorite Terry character and finish a jingle for cash prize winnings. - **$250 $500 $850**

TER-36

❑ **TER-36. Terry Mask Original Art Prototype,**
c. 1953. 8.5x10.5" stiff paper with watercolor art for proposed premium presented to Canada Dry. Mask has diecut openings for eyes, nostrils plus perforated lines along sides of head designed for removal although each hand-lettered "Free Terry And The Pirates Mask." Gordon Gold Archives. Unique. - **$800**

TER-37

TER-38

❑ **TER-37. Ad for Canada Dry Contest,**
1953. Promotes TV show. - **$8 $18 $30**

❑ **TER-38. Comic Book Ad,**
1950s. Canada Dry. - **$12 $25 $40**

Three Little Pigs

See Ted Hake's *Official® Price Guide to Disney Collectibles*, Second Edition, formatted identically to this book but in full color evaluating over 9,000 Disney company and character collectibles from 1924 through 2006.

Three Stooges

Slapstick and comic mayhem were the wacky hallmarks of the Three Stooges in their two dozen feature films and almost 200 two-reelers made between 1930 and 1965. The original trio--Moe Howard, his brother Curly, and Larry Fine--went from success in vaudeville to cult status in Hollywood and later to enduring popularity via television reruns in the late 1950s. (Another brother, Shemp, took over when Curly died; Joe Besser replaced Shemp on his death; and Joe DeRita later replaced Besser.) Animated cartoon series produced by Hanna-Barbera were syndicated on television--*The Three Stooges* in 1965 and *The Three Robonic Stooges* in 1978. Comic books appeared from the late 1940s to the 1970s. Will the Stooges' brand of comedy continue into the future? "Soitenly!"

THR-1

❑ **THR-1. "Moving Picture Machine" Newspaper Ad,**
1937. Pillsbury's Farina. - **$35 $85 $150**

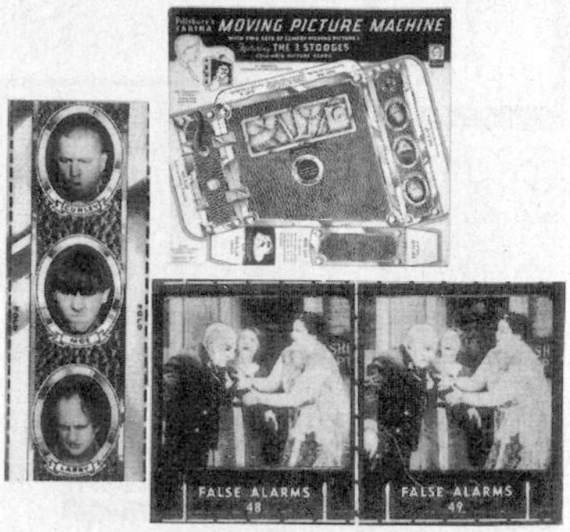

THR-2

❑ **THR-2. "Moving Picture Machine" Cardboard Punch-Out Kit,**
1937. Pillsbury's Farina. Came with films #5 and #6 based on actual movie "False Alarms," others available by purchasing more Farina. Scarce. Unpunched - **$500 $1200 $2500**
Assembled - **$300 $600 $1200**

THR-3

THR-4

❑ **THR-3. Photo With Ad Reverse,**
c. 1937. Pillsbury's Farina. Back offer is tied to Columbia Pictures promotion. - **$75 $150 $350**

❑ **THR-4. "Three Stooges" 3-D Comic V. 1 #2,**
1953. St. John Publishing Co. - **$48 $144 $675**

THR-5

❑ **THR-5. Vending Machine Display Paper For Picture Rings,**
1959. Same design on box which held rings.
Paper - **$20 $35 $70**
Empty Box - **$165 $325 $650**

THR-6

❑ THR-6. "Fan Club Of America" Membership Kit,
1959. Includes envelope, cover letter, sheet of stamps, "fan club franchise" certificate, sheet of four membership cards and two 5"x7" black and white photos. Complete - **$90 $175 $350**

THR-7

❑ THR-7. "Magic Re-Color Book",
1959. Store item by Fun Bilt Toys. 9x10-1/2" spiral-bound stiff cardboard covers and pages. - **$125 $275 $450**

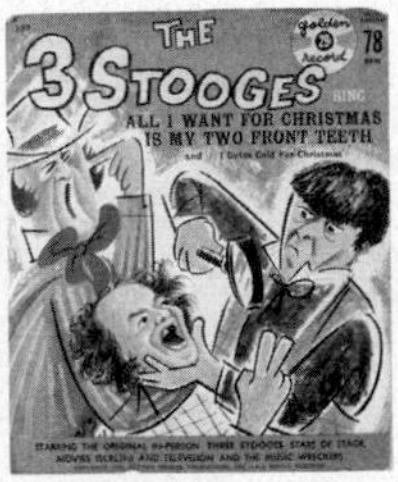

THR-8

❑ THR-8. Christmas Golden Record With Sleeve,
1959. 78 rpm 6" record by Stooges and The Music Wreckers titled "All I Want For Christmas Is My Two Front Teeth" and "I Gotta Cold For Christmas." - **$20 $30 $60**

THR-9

❑ THR-9. "Three Stooges Slap-Stick-On" Colorforms Set,
1959. Box is 13x16.75" and reads: "Here Are TV's Laughable Clowns In A Great New Toy That's Hilarious Fun! You Dress The Stooges In All Kinds Of Slap-Stick Clothes. Just Press Down The Plastic Clothing Parts; They Stick Like Magic. Then Lift To Remove. No Scissors, No Paste, No Muss. You Play Over And Over." - **$150 $250 $400**

THR-10

❑ THR-10. "The Three Stooges Candy & Toy" Box,
1959. Box is 2.5x3-5/8x7/8" deep copyright Norman Maurer Productions Inc. Box contained candy and a toy. Each - **$40 $80 $150**

THR-11

THR-12

❑ THR-11. "Three Stooges/I'm Curly" Ring,
1959. Gold plastic base with two flicker portraits. Also issued with Moe and Larry. Each - **$15 $20 $35**

❑ THR-12. "The Three Stooges On TV!" Large Rare Button,
c. 1959. Button is 4" diameter. If this pinback came from Phila. area, it had local WFIL TV ribbon attached. This one came from the midwest and never had an attached ribbon. With Or Without Ribbon Attached - **$150 $300 $600**

THR-13

❑ THR-13. Plastic Finger Puppets Set,
c. 1950s. Probable store item. Each stands 3-3/4" tall. Each - **$45 $90 $175**

THR-14

❑ THR-14. "The Nonsense Song Book" Record Album,
1950s. 33-1/3 rpm on Coral label. - **$30 $65 $135**

THR-15

THR-16

❑ THR-15. Home Movie Film,
c. 1950s. Store item by Excel Movie Products Inc. 4" square box holds 16mm black and white silent film of about 100' titled "All Hashed Up." - **$15 $30 $75**

❑ THR-16. Florida TV Station Promo Button,
1960. WEAT-TV, West Palm Beach. 2.25" litho. issue including cartoon art of local host Uncle Jim and his monkey Fuzzie. - **$185 $375 $600**

THR-17

THR-18

❑ **THR-17. Group Portrait 2-1/4" Cello. Button,**
c. 1960s. No sponsor, made by St. Louis Badge Co. - **$20 $35 $70**

❑ **THR-18. Movie/Fan Club Photo Card,**
1964. Black and white picturing them from movie "The 3 Stooges Go Around The World In A Daze" with facsimile signatures.
- $15 $30 $60
Each Real Autograph Add - **$30 $60 $90**

THR-19

❑ **THR-19. Triple Image Ceramic Bank,**
c. 1960s. Store item. - **$250 $500 $1000**

THR-20

THR-21

❑ **THR-20. Happy Birthday Record,**
1960s. Possible premium, personalized to individual first name. - **$12 $25 $50**

❑ **THR-21. Three Stooges Anti-Reagan Button,**
c. 1984. 3" diameter white printed in black portraits of the Stooges plus Ronald Reagan above inscription in red "Find The Dummy." - **$12 $25 $50**

THR-22

❑ **THR-22. "Clark/Collector Cups" 3" Cello. Button,**
1993. - **$8 $15 $30**

BOX FRONT

THR-23

❑ **THR-23. "The Three Little Beers" Doll Set,**
1997. 3 Dolls commemorate the 1935 movie. Boxed - **$150**

THR-24

❑ **THR-24. "The Three Little Beers" Resin Figures,**
1998. Classic golfing pose commemorates the 1935 movie. Set - **$100**

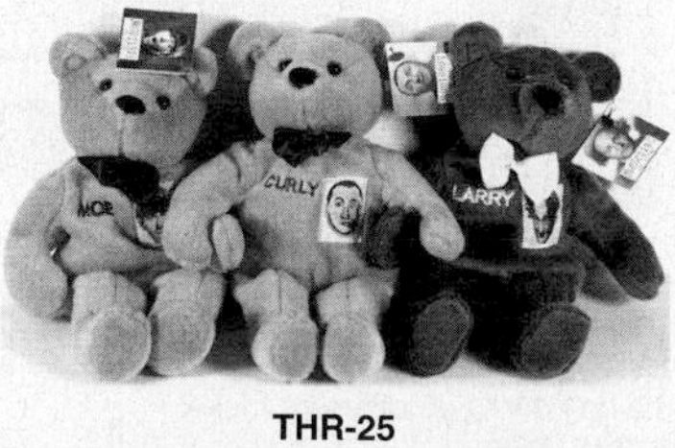

THR-25

❑ **THR-25. Bean Bear Set with Photo Tags,**
1990s. Bears each have embroidered names and pictures on chest and photo tags. Set - **$85**

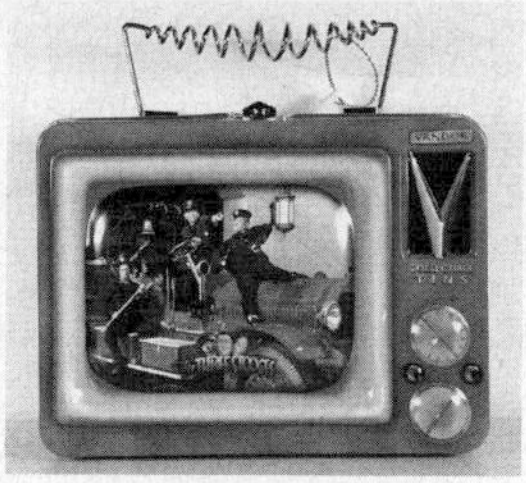

THR-26

❑ **THR-26. Three Stooges Lunch Box,**
2000. - **$35**

THR-27

THR-28

❑ **THR-27. "Larry Fine" Die-cast Metal Car,**
2000. From Team Lightning. - **$15**

❑ **THR-28. "Moe Howard" Die-cast Metal Car,**
2000. From Team Lightning. - **$15**

Thurston, the Magician

Howard Thurston (1869-1936) was a master magician who made a triumphant world tour in the early years of the 20th century, performing before royalty and notables. Walter Gibson, creator and writer of *The Shadow* was a ghost-writer for Thurston and wrote several of Thurston's magic trick books as well as his biography. Thurston's exploits and adventures were dramatized in a short-lived radio series on the NBC Blue network in 1932-1933. The program, known as *Thurston, the Magician* or *Howard Thurston, the Magician*, was sponsored by Swift & Co.

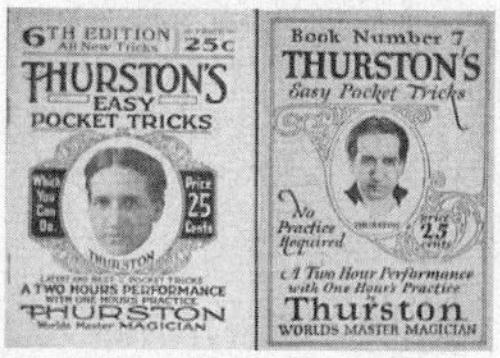

THU-1

THU-2

❑ **THU-1. "Thurston's Easy Pocket Tricks" Instructional Booklets,**
1918, 1923. Each 5x7-1/2" paperback has 48 pages. One is identified as "6th Edition" from 1918 and the other is "Book Number 7" from 1923. Each - **$12 $25 $50**

❑ **THU-2. "Good Luck/Thurston" Cello. Button,**
c. 1920. - **$40 $80 $175**

THU-3

❑ **THU-3. Magician Coin,**
1928. Good Luck Charm premium. Says "Thurston The Magician" on front. -
$20 $40 $60

THU-4

THU-5

❑ **THU-4. Magician Coin,**
1929. Rare. Says "Thurston The Magician" on front. - **$30 $60 $130**

❑ **THU-5. "Thurston's Dream Book",**
1920s. 32-page dream interpretation booklet sold for 25 cents through Thurston's Mystic Palace, Beechurst, Long Island, New York. -
$25 $50 $75

THU-6

❑ **THU-6. "Good Luck" Card,**
1920s. - **$20 $40 $60**

THU-7

THU-8

❑ **THU-7. "Thurston's Book Of Magic #1",**
1932. Swift & Company. Shows illustrations and explains how to do different tricks. -
$20 $40 $65

❑ **THU-8. "Thurston's Book Of Magic #2",**
1932. Swift & Company. Shows illustrations and explains how to do different tricks. -
$20 $40 $65

THU-9

THU-10

❑ **THU-9. "Thurston's Book Of Magic #3",**
1932. Swift & Company. Shows illustrations and explains how to do different tricks. -
$20 $40 $65

❑ **THU-10. "Thurston's Book Of Magic #4",**
1932. Swift & Company. Shows illustrations and explains how to do different tricks. -
$20 $40 $65

THU-11

THU-12

❑ **THU-11. "Thurston's Book Of Magic #5",**
1932. Swift & Company. Shows illustrations and explains how to do different tricks. -
$20 $40 $65

❑ **THU-12. Trick Packets,**
c. 1932. Swift & Co. At least 11 in set.
Each - **$15 $30 $60**

Tillie the Toiler

Russ Westover (1886-1966) started as a newspaper cartoonist in 1904. His first syndicated strip was *Snapshot Bill* in 1914. *Tillie The Toiler* began as a daily comic strip January 3, 1921 with a Sunday following on October 10, 1922. *The Von Swaggers* Sunday page topper started in 1926. Office worker and model Tillie Jones was joined with a cast including lovesick Clarence "Mac" MacDougall who was a co-worker at J. Simpkins womens' wear company. Noted creator of *Flash Gordon*, Alex Raymond (1909-1956) assisted Westover with the art chores in the early 1930s.

There were two live action feature films, both titled *Tillie The Toiler.* The MGM film, released June 5, 1927 was written by Agnes Johnstone and Edward Lowe. Directed by Hovart Henley, the film starred Marion Davies, Matt Moore and George Fawcett. The Columbia film, released August 7, 1941, was written by Karen DeWolf and Francis Martin. Sidney Salkow directed Kay Harris, William Tracy and George Watts.

Bob Gustafson took over as artist on the Tillie strip in 1951. The strip ended March 15, 1959 with Tillie and Mac getting married.

Dell published 14 *Tillie The Toiler* Four Color Comic books between 1941 and 1949.

TIL-1

❑ **TIL-1. "Comic Monthly - Tillie The Toiler" Platinum Age Comic Book,**
1922. Embee Distributing Co. Volume 1, No. 5 from May, 1922. - **$140 $490 $1000**

TIL-2

❑ **TIL-2. Tillie The Toiler Daily Comic Strip Original Art,**
1928. 5x20.25" thin art board with four panels done in India ink. Signed at bottom of last panel in ink by creator Russ Westover. Same Or Similar - **$50 $100 $185**

TIL-3

❑ **TIL-3. "Tillie The Toiler" Daily Strip Reprint Book,**
1929. Cupples & Leon. 10x10" with 48 pages. #4 in series of eight. - **$50 $175 $360**

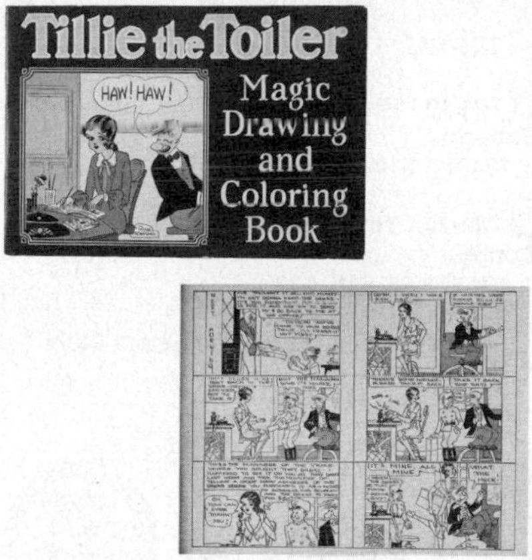

TIL-4

❑ **TIL-4. "Tillie The Toiler Magic Drawing And Coloring Book,**
1931. Gabriel Sons and Co. 8.5x12" with 32 pages. - **$30 $60 $100**

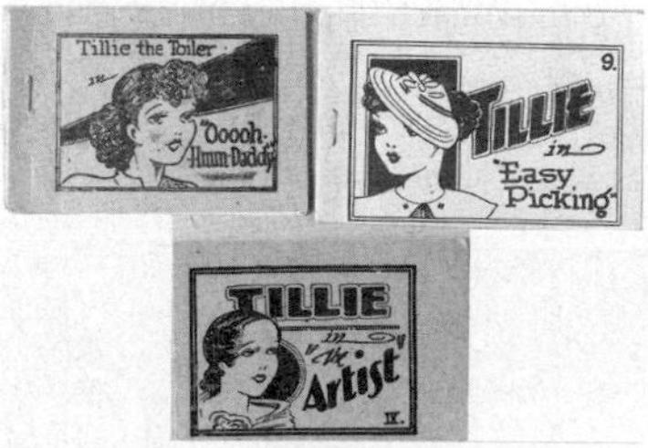

TIL-5

❑ **TIL-5. "Tillie The Toiler In Oooh-Hmm-Daddy/Easy Picking/The Artist" 8-Pagers,**
1930s. Three x-rated comic stories. First is 2-7/8x4.25", second is 3x4.5" and third is 2.75x4-1/8". Each - **$10 $20 $45**

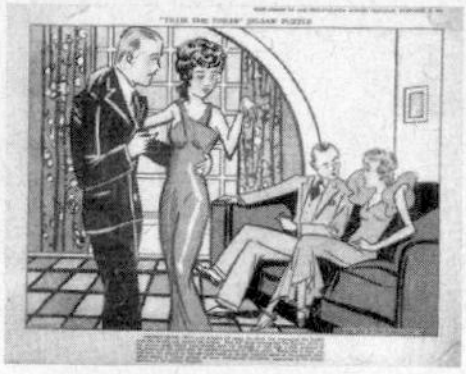

TIL-6

❑ **TIL-6. "Tillie The Toiler" Jigsaw Puzzle,**
1933. Various newspapers supplement. - **$12 $25 $45**

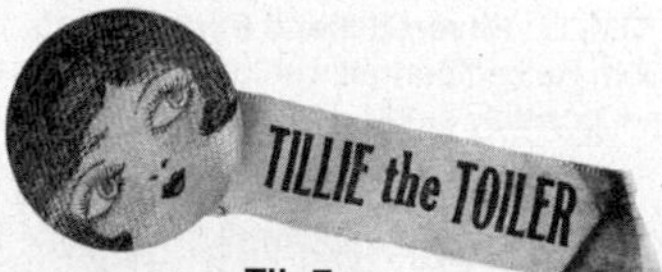

TIL-7

❑ **TIL-7. "Tillie The Toiler" Garter Button,**
1930s. 7/8" highly-domed, cloth-covered button. - **$15 $30 $60**

TIL-8

❑ **TIL-8. "Tillie The Toiler" Movie Window Card,**
1941. Columbia Pictures. 14x22". - **$65 $125 $200**

Tim Club

This club, headed by "Tim," a cartoon image lad with no surname, existed as early as 1929. Membership loosely consisted of youngsters that patronized clothing stores electing to join the "Tim" endorsement theme. Premiums included code books, stamp albums and pin-backs related to "Pie Eater" activities. Tim's merchandising clout was revitalized beginning in the early 1940s by addition of a super partner, Superman to be exact. Tim carried on his tradition but became the second banana in the new "Superman-Tim Store" promotion. Premiums continued, apparently free, including a monthly mailer newsletter/clothing catalogue/activities manual imprinted with local store name. Superman was prominently featured in each. Additional premiums were pin-back buttons, pennants, album stamps, Secret Code and other membership items. Superman-Tim currency was also available. The Club was still officially licensed to Tim Promotions, Inc. of New York City.

TIM-1

TIM-2

❑ **TIM-1. "Tim's Trip To Mars" Booklet,**
c. 1929. Tim's Store for Boys. 3-3/4x6-3/4" with 16 pages. - **$20 $30 $60**

❑ **TIM-2. Code Books,**
1930. Participating Tim stores. Pictured examples are for 1929, 1930, 1933.
Each - **$20 $30 $60**

TIM-3

❑ **TIM-3. Counter Display Sign,**
1930. Photo of "Our Gang," which promotes "The Knicker" magazine. 13-1/2 x 10". Tim shown on mat at bottom left. - **$200 $300 $500**

TIM-4

TIM-5

❑ **TIM-4. "The Knicker" Magazine,**
1930. Monthly publication, pictured example is for October. Each contains 12 pages with local store imprint on back cover.
Each Issue - **$15 $25 $40**

❑ **TIM-5. Tim Rancho Code Book,**
1935. Pie Eater's Club premium. 16 pages. - **$20 $30 $60**

TIM-6

❑ **TIM-6. Tim's Official Magazine & Folder,**
1935. With ads and mailer. Complete - **$20 $35 $75**

TIM-7

TIM-8

❑ **TIM-7. 1938 Franco Club Patch,**
1938. - **$60 $115 $190**

❑ **TIM-8. Tim Patch,**
1930s. Scarce. Comes in red, grey and brown. - **$30 $65 $125**

TIM-9

TIM-10

❑ **TIM-9. Pie-Eater Club Member Happy Birthday Letter,**
1930s. Metropolitan (clothing) store. Invites recipient to pick up free pie. - **$20 $35 $60**

❑ **TIM-10. "Tim's Official Stamps",**
1930s. Participating stores. For mounting in album supplied by store. Each - **$8 $15 $30**

TIM-11

TIM-12

❑ **TIM-11. Cello. Club Button,**
1930s. Red, white, blue and gold. - **$10 $20 $35**

❑ **TIM-12. Silvered Metal Portrait Ring,**
1930s. Raised portrait with dog portrait on each band, possibly sterling. - **$65 $135 $300**

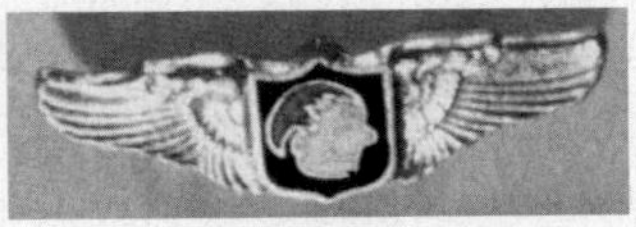
TIM-13

❑ **TIM-13. Tim Wings,**
1930s. Scarce. Store premium. - **$75 $135 $300**

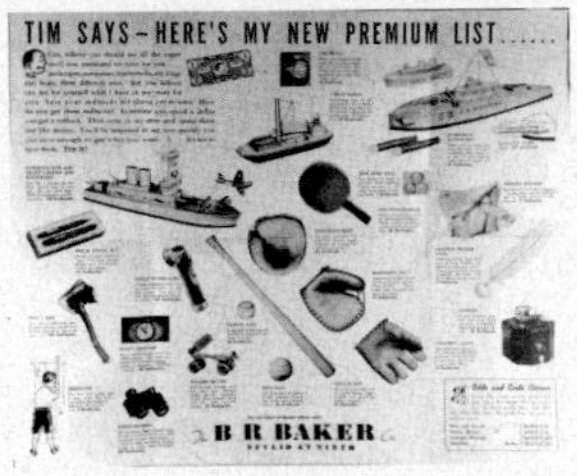

TIM-14

❑ **TIM-14. Premium Offer Display Poster,**
1930s. 14" x 17" poster features "Tim" ring and shows other items you can buy using special "redbacks" - play money received as a bonus for store purchases. - **$60 $120 $200**

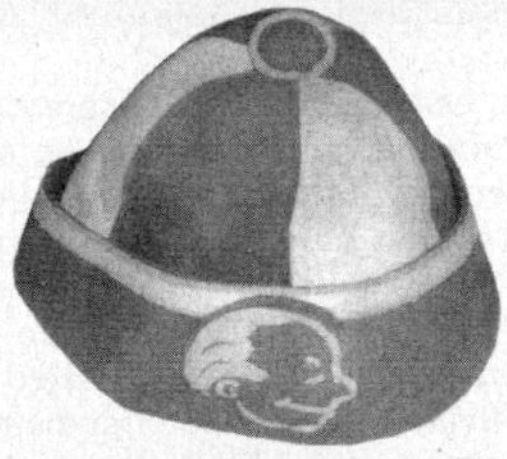
TIM-15

TIM-16

❑ **TIM-15. Felt Beanie,**
c. 1930s. - **$70 $145 $275**

❑ **TIM-16. Membership Card,**
c. 1940. - **$20 $40 $65**

TIM-17

TIM-18

❑ **TIM-17. "Tim's Magazine",**
1940. Participating stores. Issued monthly. Each - **$10 $20 $35**

❑ **TIM-18. Tim's "Redback" Currency,**
1940s. Various stores. Various denominations. Each - **$5 $8 $15**

TIM-19

TIM-20

TIM-21

❑ **TIM-19. "Pie Eaters Club/Tim" Litho. Button,**
c. 1940s. - **$10 $18 $35**

❑ **TIM-20. "Tim's Store For Boys" Cello. Button,**
c. 1940s. - **$8 $15 $30**

❑ **TIM-21. "Tim's Official Pie Eaters Club" Cello. Button,**
c. 1940s. - **$6 $12 $25**

TIM-22

TIM-23

TIM-24

❑ **TIM-22. "Pie Eaters Club/Tim" Cello. Button,**
c. 1940s. - **$6 $12 $25**

❑ **TIM-23. "Tim's Lucky Coin",**
c. 1940s. Front portrait, back inscription "From Tim's Official Store". Brass. - **$10 $20 $50**

❑ **TIM-24. "Tim's Club For Boys" Litho. Button,**
1950s. Rare. - **$20 $40 $60**

TIM-25

TIM-26

❑ **TIM-25. Membership Card,**
1950s. - **$30 $55 $110**

❑ **TIM-26. Litho. Tin Tab,**
1950s. Rare. - **$12 $25 $50**

Tim McCoy

Tim McCoy (1891-1978) became a Colonel in WWI, then went to Hollywood in the early 1920s, becoming a technical advisor for Jesse Lasky's 1923 silent western epic *The Covered Wagon*. By 1925, McCoy had become an actor and would go on to appear in some 90 films with a film career lasting into the mid-1960s. Most notable are his 1930s Columbia westerns and his 1941-42 *Rough Riders* series for Monogram which co-starred Buck Jones and Raymond Hatton. McCoy left films briefly for WWII, becoming a decorated aviator.

Most of the western life depicted in his films, particularly concerning Indians, was close to authentic rather than stereotyped. McCoy was fluent in various tribal languages. He was also known for his sharpshooting skills and quick draw. Between February 11, 1950 and October 8, 1953, he had two different TV shows in Los Angeles teaching children authentic history of the American West interspersed with old western films.

From the 1930s into the 1970s, McCoy performed in Wild West shows across the country bringing the westerns of the silver screen to life.

TMC-1

❑ **TMC-1. "The Indians Are Coming!" Promotional Headdress,**
1930. Universal. 30" wide by 16" tall. First all talking Universal serial. - **$75 $150 $250**

TMC-2

TMC-3

❑ **TMC-2. "Tim McCoy Police Car 17" Book,**
1934. 10-7/8x15" book with stiff paper covers and 32 pages. Based on Columbia picture, the first movie adaptation in a comic book format. - **$75 $300 $600**

❑ **TMC-3. "Col. Tim McCoy" Dixie Picture,**
1935. Dixie Ice Cream. 8x10" color photo. - **$10 $20 $45**

TMC-4

❑ **TMC-4. "Tim McCoy" Dixie Picture,**
1936. Puritan Pictures. 8x10". - **$30 $60 $125**

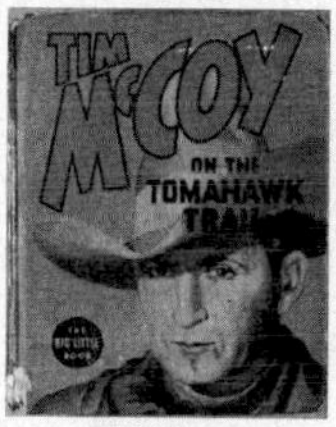

TMC-5

TMC-6

❑ **TMC-5. "Tim McCoy On The Tomahawk Trail" Big Little Book,**
1937. Whitman. Book No. 1436. - **$12 $36 $78**

❑ **TMC-6. "Tim McCoy" Dixie Picture,**
1938. Dixie Ice Cream. 8x10". - **$10 $20 $45**

TMC-7

TMC-8

❑ **TMC-7. "Tim McCoy And The Sandy Gulch Stampede" Better Little Book,**
1939. Whitman. Book No. 1490. - **$10 $30 $67**

❑ **TMC-8. Tim McCoy Color Button,**
1930s. 1.75" diameter. Likely rodeo or circus souvenir. - **$20 $40 $80**

TMC-9

TMC-10

❑ **TMC-9. Tim McCoy Black And White Button,**
1930s. 1.75" diameter. Likely rodeo or circus souvenir. - **$25 $50 $100**

❑ **TMC-10. "Tim McCoy's Vigilantes" Probable Movie Club Button,**
1930s. 7/8" diameter. - **$10 $20 $40**

TMC-11

❑ **TMC-11. "The Famous Carson And Barnes" Newspapers Featuring Tim McCoy,**
1959/1960. Two, each 16.25x22.5", four-page issues from "The Circus News." Each - **$10 $20 $35**

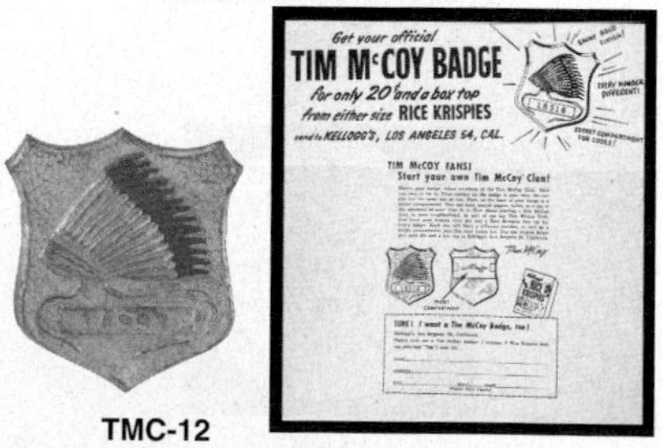

TMC-12

❑ **TMC-12. Tim McCoy Badge,**
1950s. Kellogg's Rice Krispies. 2" tall brass badge with serial number at center. Reverse has slide-off secret compartment. Also used by Lone Ranger as "Deputy Chief" badge. - **$100 $200 $400**

Tim Tyler

Cartoonist Lyman Young created *Tim Tyler's Luck* for the King Features Syndicate as a daily strip in 1928 and as a Sunday page in 1931. Alex Raymond assisted with the art on the Sunday pages in the early years before leaving to do *Flash Gordon* in 1934. Tim's adventures took him to Africa, where he joined the Ivory Patrol to help maintain law and order. A syndicated radio program aired in 1936-1937, a series of comic books appeared in the 1940s, and Universal Pictures released a 12-episode chapter play, also called *Tim Tyler's Luck*, in 1937, with Frankie Thomas as Tim.

TYL-1

TYL-2

❑ **TYL-1. "Tim Tyler's Luck/Ivory Patrol Club" Cello. Button,**
1937. Universal Pictures. For 12-chapter movie serial. - **$75 $150 $300**

❑ **TYL-2. "Tim Tyler Ivory Patrol Club/Viva" Cello. Button,**
c. 1937. - **$75 $150 $300**

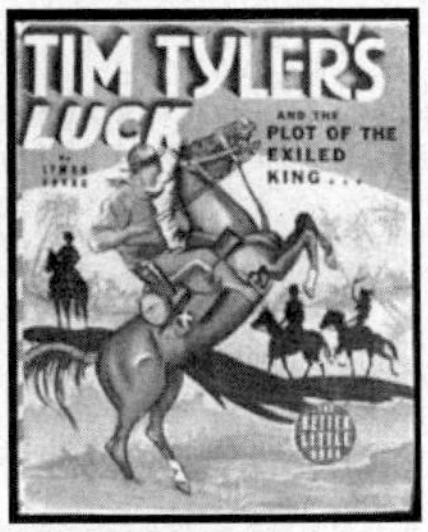

TYL-3

TYL-4

❑ **TYL-3. "Tim Tyler's Luck And The Plot Of The Exile King" Better Little Book,**
1939. Whitman #1479. - **$11 $33 $72**

❑ **TYL-4. "Tim Tyler" Newspaper Contest Cello. Button,**
1930s. New York Evening Journal. 1-1/4" in black and cream with shades of red. -
$15 $35 $70

Tom and Jerry

The classic helter-skelter cat-and-mouse rivalry between Tom and Jerry was brought to life in 114 theatrical cartoons created by the Hanna-Barbera team for MGM between 1939 and 1957. The animated superstars, with Tom generally chasing Jerry and with hardly ever a word of dialogue, won seven Oscars between 1943 and 1952. Noted animator Tex Avery directed several of their 1940s cartoons. MGM produced additional *Tom & Jerry* series in 1961-1962 and in 1963-1967. *Tom & Jerry: The Movie* ("They talk!") was released in 1993. Jerry danced with Gene Kelly in the 1945 feature film *Anchors Aweigh* and Tom and Jerry did a synchronized swim routine with Esther Williams in the 1953 MGM musical *Dangerous When Wet.*

The cartoon stars debuted on television when the Hanna-Barbera shorts aired on CBS Saturday mornings from 1965 to 1972. A made-for-TV series under a variety of names appeared starting in 1975. *Tom & Jerry Kids* premiered on the Fox Children's Network in 1990. The mischievous duo continues to win fans to this day. Licensing and merchandising of the characters has been extensive.

TMJ-1

❑ **TMJ-1. Movie Flip Booklets,**
1949. Grape-Nuts Flakes. Box inserts from series of 12 based on M-G-M or Walter Lantz cartoon characters. Each - **$10 $20 $40**

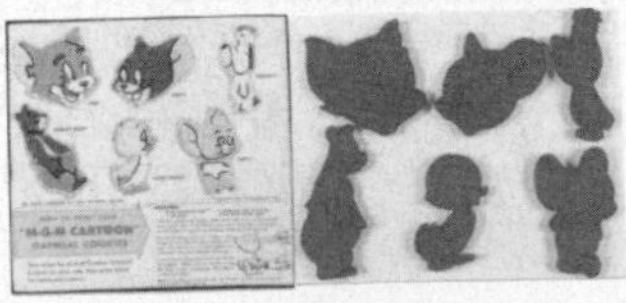
TMJ-2

❑ **TMJ-2. "M-G-M Cartoon Cookie Cutters" With Mailer,**
1956. Issued by Quaker Oats. Contains six different plastic figural cookie cutters.
Cutter Set - **$20 $40 $60**
Instructions - **$8 $12 $20**

TMJ-3

TMJ-4

❑ **TMJ-3. "Tom & Jerry Go For Stroehmann's Bread" Litho. Button,**
1950s. - **$10 $20 $30**

❑ **TMJ-4. "ABC Minors/M.G.M.'s Tom And Jerry" Cello. Button,**
c. 1960s. English Issue. - **$15 $30 $40**

TMJ-5

TMJ-6

❑ **TMJ-5. Glazed Ceramic English Mug,**
1960s. Store item. - **$15 $25 $50**

❑ **TMJ-6. "March Of Comics" Booklet,**
1970. Child Life Shoes. Issue #345 reprinting 1970 comic book story. - **$2 $6 $16**

TMJ-7

❑ **TMJ-7. Scooter Friction Drive Toy With Box,**
1972. Store item by Marx Toys. Plastic toy in image of Tom as operator and Jerry as sidecar passenger. Near Mint Boxed - **$150**
Loose - **$20 $40 $85**

TMJ-8

❑ **TMJ-8. "Tom Pulling Jerry's Cart" Plastic Wind-Up Toy,**
1977. Store item by Marx, Great Britain. 4-1/4" long. Near Mint Boxed - **$100**
Unboxed - **$20 $35 $65**

TMJ-9

❑ **TMJ-9. Boxed Vinyl Figure Banks,**
1978. Store item authorized figures packaged individually in matching "Money Box" cartons.
Near Mint Each Boxed - **$60**
Each Loose - **$12 $25 $40**

TMJ-10

❑ **TMJ-10. Ceramic Pencil Holder,**
1981. Store item made for Gorham Products. - **$10 $20 $45**

TMJ-11

❑ **TMJ-11. Tom and Jerry Figures,**
1989. 9" Tom and 5" Jerry. This set has Tom with a closed mouth grin. Set in box - **$45**

TMJ-12

❑ **TMJ-12. Tom and Jerry Figures,**
1989. 9" Tom and 5" Jerry. This set has Tom with an open mouth smile. Set in box - **$40**

TMJ-13

❑ **TMJ-13. Spike and Tyke Figures with Box,**
1989. 9" Spike and 5 3/4" Tyke. Set in box - **$40**

TMJ-14

TMJ-15

❑ **TMJ-14. "Tom" Bean Bag with Tag,**
1998. - **$12**

❑ **TMJ-15. "Jerry" Bean Bag with Tag,**
1998. - **$12**

Tom Corbett, Space Cadet

Set in the 24th century, this television space adventure followed the exploits of three young cadets as they trained in their spaceship Polaris to become officers of the Solar Guards. The series, based on Robert Heinlein's 1948 novel *Space Cadet* and scripted with the technical advice of rocket scientist Willy Ley, was distinguished by scientific accuracy and innovative camera effects. Corbett's unit at the Space Academy included Roger Manning (So what happens now, space heroes?) and Astro, a quick-tempered Venusian youth. Veteran actor Frankie Thomas played the part of Corbett.

Tom Corbett, Space Cadet **was one of the few series to appear on all four commercial TV networks, and on two of them simultaneously. The show, which was broadcast live, debuted on CBS in 1950, moved to ABC in 1951-1952, appeared on NBC in the summer of 1951, on the Dumont network in 1953-1954, and again on NBC in 1954-1955. Sponsors were Kellogg's cereals (1950-1952), Red Goose shoes (1953-1954), and Kraft Foods (1954-1955). The series also ran on ABC radio for six months in 1952, featuring the same cast as sponsored by Kellogg, and as a simulcast on NBC in 1954-1955, sponsored by Kraft.**

In print, a Corbett comic strip by Ray Bailey distributed by the Field Newspaper Syndicate appeared from 1951 to 1953, comic books with art by Al McWilliams, Paul Norris, John Lehti and Mort Meskin between 1952 and 1955, and a series of Corbett novels from Grosset & Dunlap between 1952 and 1956.

Merchandising of Tom Corbett material was extensive, including toys, a watch, lunch boxes, space goggles, and helmets. Kellogg's promoted a Space Academy membership club that offered badges, rings, patches, a cardboard decoder, ID cards, and autographed photos. Items are normally copyrighted Rockhill Productions.

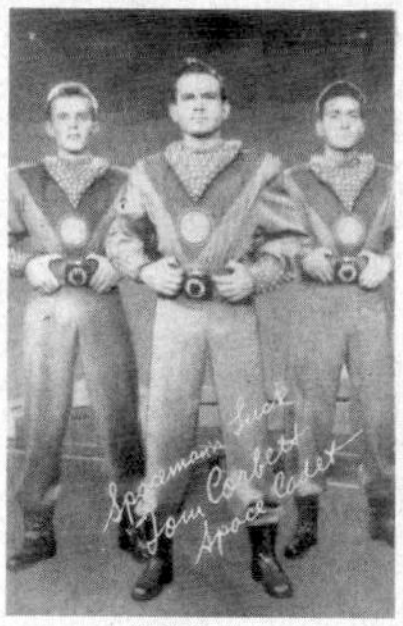
TCO-1

TCO-2

TCO-3

❑ **TCO-1. Membership Kit Cast Photo,**
1951. - **$20 $35 $75**

❑ **TCO-2. "Space Cadet" 2-1/8" Cello. Button,**
1951. Part of club membership kit. - **$50 $100 $200**

❑ **TCO-3. Fabric Patch,**
1951. Part of member's kit. - **$20 $40 $80**

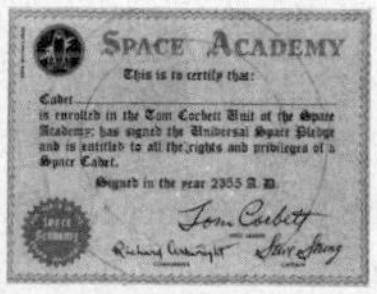

TCO-4

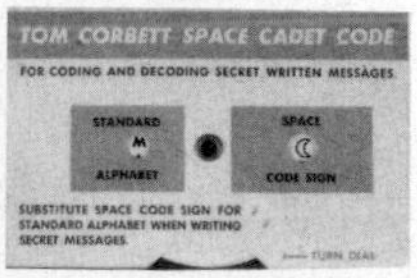

TCO-5

❑ **TCO-4. Certificate,**
1951. Part of member's kit. - **$25 $50 $100**

❑ **TCO-5. Kellogg's Cardboard Decoder,**
1951. Came with membership kit. -
$35 $90 $175

TCO-6

❑ **TCO-6. "Tom Corbett Space Cadet News" Vol. 1 #1,**
1951. Kellogg's. Part of member's kit. -
$50 $125 $200

TCO-7

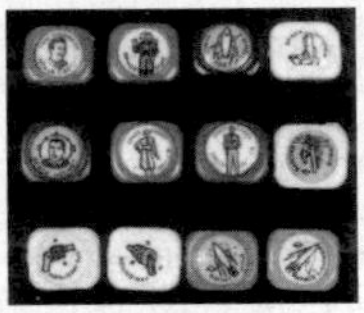
TCO-8

❑ **TCO-7. "Rocket Rings" Comic Book Ad,**
1951. Kellogg's Pep cereal. - **$2 $4 $6**

❑ **TCO-8. Kellogg's Plastic Rings With Insert Pictures,**
1951. Set of 12. Near Mint Set - **$250**
Each - **$5 $10 $20**

TCO-9

❑ **TCO-9. Cereal Box With "Tom Corbett Space Cadet Squadron" Back,**
1951. Also pictures "Rocket Launching Plane Catapulting Aircraft Carrier".
Complete Box - **$200 $400 $750**

TCO-10

❑ **TCO-10. Kellogg's "Space Cadet Rocketship" Action Picture Coin,**
1951. Plastic flicker disk from series picturing various Tom Corbett (and other) scenes. -
$10 $15 $35

TCO-11

❑ **TCO-11. "Space Cadet Song and March" Record Album with Sleeve,**
1951. Golden Record. - **$20 $35 $70**

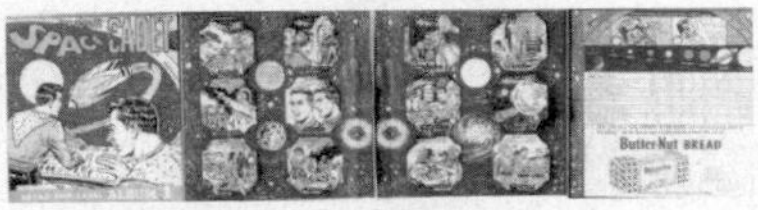
TCO-12

❑ **TCO-12. Butter-Nut Bread End Label Album #1,**
1952. Various sponsor imprints. Complete with 24 bread labels. Album #2 was also issued with additional set of 24 labels.
Near Mint Complete - **$1280**
Album Only - **$50 $100 $200**
Each Label - **$15 $25 $45**

TCO-13

❑ **TCO-13. Fischer's Buttercup Bread End Label Album No. 2,**
1952. Various sponsors. Holds labels #25-48.
Near Mint Complete - **$1280**
Album Only - **$50 $100 $200**
Each Label - **$15 $25 $45**

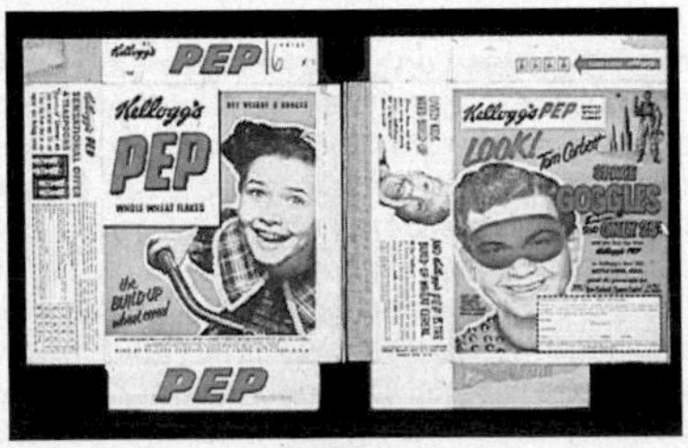

TCO-14

❑ **TCO-14. Cereal Box With "Tom Corbett Space Goggles" Offer,**
1952. Gordon Gold Archives.
Used Complete - **$225 $450 $800**

TCO-15

❑ **TCO-15. Cereal Box With Back Panel For Pin-Up Or For Mask,**
1952. Mask in full color with text promoting both radio and TV shows.
Used Complete - **$225 $450 $800**

TCO-16

❑ **TCO-16. Kellogg's Pep Flat - 8 oz. Cereal Box,**
1952. Astro "Space Cadet" pictured on back. Also promotes Tom Corbett TV show. -
$225 $450 $800

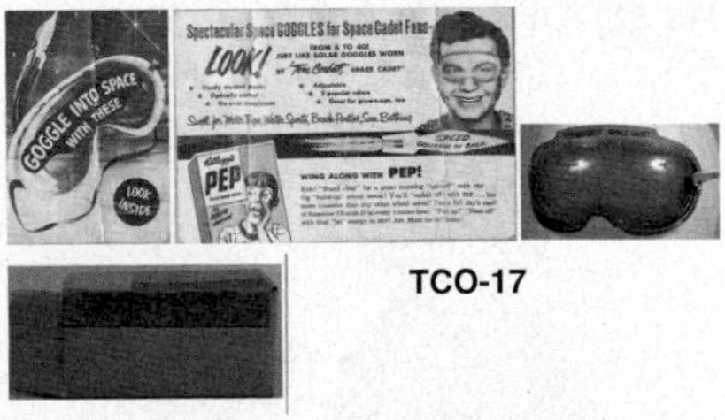

TCO-17

❑ **TCO-17. Space Goggles With Mailer And Instructions,**
1952. Kellogg's Pep. Molded thin plastic 5" wide goggles with elastic head strap premium for 25 cents and one box top. Instruction leaflet includes "Spectacular Space Goggles For Space Cadet Fans Just Like Solar Goggles Worn By Tom Corbett." Mailer - **$20 $40 $60**
Instructions - **$35 $65 $140**
Goggles - **$75 $150 $300**

TCO-18

TCO-19

TCO-20

❑ **TCO-18. "TV Digest" With Cover Article,**
1952. Weekly issue for August 23 with two-page article including photos. Front cover also pictures songstress Patti Page. - **$20 $40 $75**

❑ **TCO-19. "Tom Corbett/Space Cadet" Silvered Metal Ring,**
c. 1952. Came with membership kit. - **$55 $90 $175**

❑ **TCO-20. Rocket Ring,**
c. 1952. Silvered brass and white gold luster metal inscribed on underside "Space Cadet/Tom Corbett Unit". Solid metal top filled to steel expansion band. Exquisite construction. - **$100 $175 $400**

TCO-21

❑ **TCO-21. "Space Cadet" Bracelet,**
c. 1952. Aluminum bracelet measures 6" long with curved rectangular center plate showing spaceship design intended to be engraved with owner's name. Beautiful metallic finish. - **$50 $100 $200**

TCO-22

TCO-23

❑ **TCO-22. Official Emblem Metal Badge,**
c. 1952. - **$50 $125 $235**

❑ **TCO-23. "Electronic Inter Planet 2-Way Phone",**
1953. Store item. Cardboard box holding pair of plastic phones and coil of wire.
Boxed Set - **$200 $370 $600**
Each Phone - **$50 $85 $150**

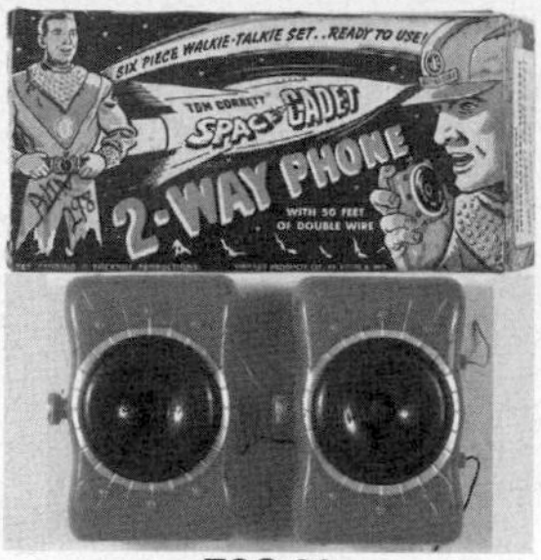

TCO-24

❑ **TCO-24. "Tom Corbett Space Cadet Game,"**
1953. Box is 10.25x21x1.25" deep and contains game by Peerless Playthings Co. Inc. The cardboard box insert serves as the gameboard with four small three-dimensional plastic spaceship playing pieces. Boxed - **$175 $350 $600**

TCO-25

❑ **TCO-25. "Tom Corbett Tru-Vue Stereo Film Card,"**
1954. Card is titled "The Secret From Space The Moon Pyramid." Near Mint Packet - **$50**
Loose - **$8 $12 $30**

TCO-26

❑ **TCO-26. View-Master Set,**
1954. Store item. - **$20 $35 $75**

TCO-27

TCO-28

❑ **TCO-27. Die-Cut Metal Pin,**
1954. In Sears catalogue, came on card with purchase of Corbett flashlight. - **$50 $100 $200**
Card Only - **$50 $100 $150**

❑ **TCO-28. Fiberboard Helmet,**
1950s. Scarce. Probable store item. Includes plastic badge on front. - **$90 $185 $300**

TCO-29

❑ **TCO-29. Rocket-Lite Plastic Pin,**
1950s. Store item by Usalite. Battery operated. - **$30 $60 $125**

TCO-30

❑ **TCO-30. Rocket-Lite Squadron Club Card,**
1950s. Reverse instructions for Space Cadet pin-on rocket light. - **$10 $30 $60**

TCO-31

TCO-32

❑ **TCO-31. Metallic Silver Fabric Cap with Sunglasses,**
1950s. Scarce. Probable premium. - **$100 $200 $350**

❑ **TCO-32. Official Hat,**
1950s. Scarce. Probable store item. Includes plastic badge on front. - **$115 $225 $400**

TCO-33

TCO-34

❑ **TCO-33. "Tom Corbett Space Cadet" Doll,**
1950s. Doll measures 7.5" tall and came in a space costume with two Tom Corbett Space Cadet decals, one on chest with rocket symbol and one on hat with smaller symbol and text.
- $65 $135 $200

❑ **TCO-34. "Tom Corbett Space Cadet" Girl Doll,**
1950s. Doll measures 7.5" tall in space costume and has Tom Corbett rocket logo on chest. Has sleep eyes. Example shown missing a pressed fabric hat accented by club emblem.
- $65 $135 $200

TCO-35

❑ **TCO-35. "Tom Corbett Kellogg's Corn Flakes" Cereal Box,**
1950s. From a 1950s series of boxes that featured cut-out "Space Cadet Equipment."
Complete **- $150 $300 $600**

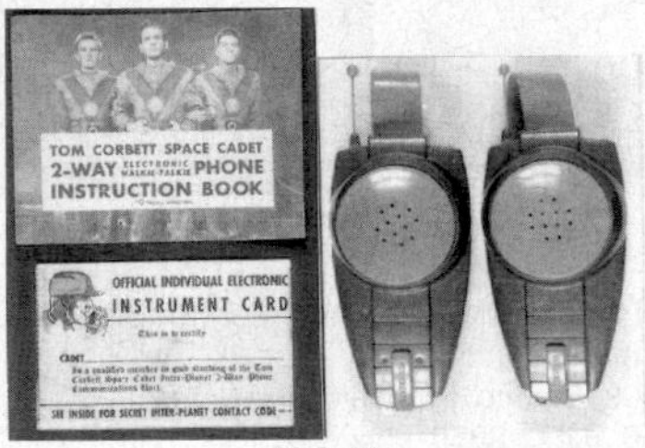

TCO-36

❑ **TCO-36. "Two-Way Electronic Walkie-Talkie Phone" Set,**
1950s. Store item by Remco.
Phone Set - **$50 $100 $200**
Instructions - **$30 $60 $100**
Code Card - **$30 $60 $100**

TCO-37

❑ **TCO-37. Visor,**
1950s. Cardboard cut-out from cereal box. -
$15 $25 $50

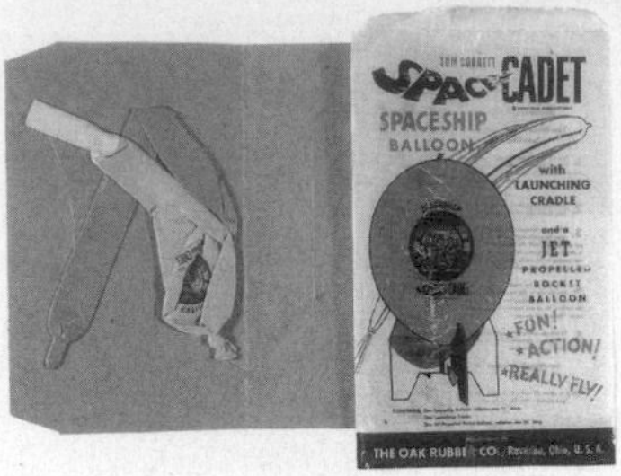

TCO-38

❑ **TCO-38. Spaceship Balloon With Mailer,**
1950s. Comes with unpunched cardboard base & two balloons. Probably store bought. -
$75 $125 $250

TCO-39

TCO-40

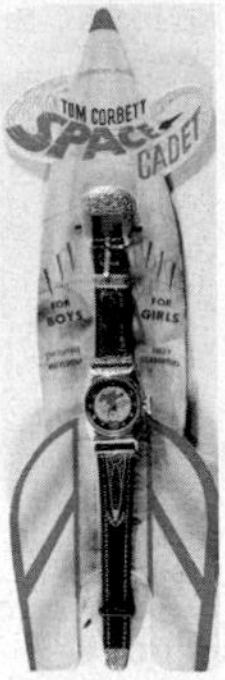

TCO-41

❑ **TCO-39. Space Cadet Patch,**
1950s. Cereal premium. One of several different.
Each - **$25 $50 $100**

❑ **TCO-40. Pinback,**
1950s. Metallic silver center with very bright blue outer border. Rare. - **$50 $100 $175**

❑ **TCO-41. Watch on Die Cut Rocket Card,**
1950s. Ingraham.
Card - **$200 $400 $800**
Watch only - **$75 $200 $300**

TCO-42

❑ **TCO-42. Model Craft Set,**
1950s. Box, powder, can, glue, paint set and 8 rubber molds. You could send off 10¢ for each extra mold. You could collect up to 350 different. Features molds for 7 Tom Corbett Space Cadet cast consisting of Tom, Roger, Astro, Captain Strong, Dr. Dale, and a Vesuvian as well as the logo for the TV show. - **$125 $265 $600**

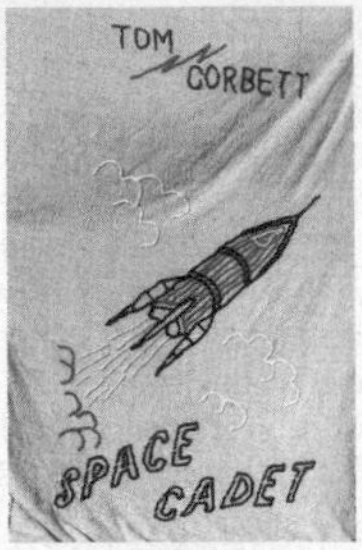

TCO-43

❑ **TCO-43. Chenille Bedspread,**
1950s. Large 6x8' bed covering centered by 32" tall raised chenille rocketship image between raised Tom Corbett and Space Cadet names. -
$75 $150 $300

TCO-44

❑ **TCO-44. "Tom Corbett Sparkling Space Ship" With Box,**
1950s. Polaris Space Ship - **$375 $750 $1500**
Box - **$350 $700 $1000**
Complete - **$725 $1450 $2500**

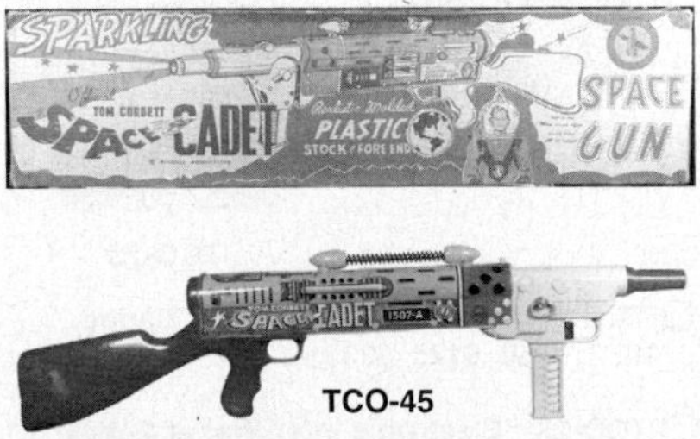

TCO-45

❑ **TCO-45. "Tom Corbett Space Cadet Sparkling Space Gun" in Box,**
1950s. Marx Toys. Gun - **$150 $300 $650**
Box - **$125 $300 $450**

TCO-46

❑ **TCO-46. Autographed Cast Photo,**
1990s. Signatures are of Jan Merlin, Al Markim, Frankie Thomas, Ed Bryce. Also signed by narrator Jackson Beck and director George Gould. Near Mint - **$250**

Tom Mix

Tom Mix (1880-1940), the greatest Western film star of the silent era, was born and grew up in rural DuBois, Pennsylvania. He enlisted in the Army at the outbreak of the Spanish-American war in 1898 and achieved the rank of first sergeant. His overseas military adventures are part of the legend, not reality, as he never left the United States. After leaving the Army in 1902 he moved to Oklahoma and found work as a drum major, bartender, and part-time ranch hand. In 1904 he attended the St. Louis World's Fair as a member of the Oklahoma Cavalry Band. In 1905 he went to work as a "cowboy" for the Miller Brothers' 101 Real Wild West Ranch, barnstormed in other Wild West shows, and served as a deputy sheriff and night marshal.

Tom Mix's movie career began in 1909 for the Selig Polyscope Company, first as an advisor and troubleshooter, then doubling as a stunt man, and ultimately starring in, writing, and directing some 64 silent shorts. By 1917, when he was hired by William Fox Productions, he was a star, and by 1921 he was one of the country's 10 top box office attractions. Over a period of 10 years he made 78 silent features for Fox, most of them as an idealized Western hero, doing his own stunts and riding his chestnut steed, Tony the Wonder Horse, to fame and fortune. He made another six silent features in 1928-1929 for the Film Booking Office, then left Hollywood to tour and star in Sells Floto Circus from 1929 to 1931.

Returning to films, he and Tony Jr. made his first talkies, nine features for Universal Pictures in 1931-1932, and his last movie, *The Miracle Rider*, a 15-episode chapter play, for Mascot Pictures in 1935. That same year he bought a circus, and from 1935 to 1938 the Tom Mix Circus toured the country and performed for crowds of admirers. In 1940 he was killed in an automobile accident in Arizona.

The Tom Mix radio program aired from 1933 to 1950, on NBC until 1944, then on the Mutual network. Ralston cereal was the exclusive radio program sponsor. Various actors played Tom in what was billed as a Western detective program. Tom and the Ralston Straight Shooters operated out of the T-M Bar Ranch, solving mysteries, crusading for justice, finding water for the cattle, even fighting saboteurs during the war years. Helping out, along with Tony, were young Jimmy and Jane, the Old Wrangler, Sheriff Mike Shaw, Wash the cook, and Pecos Williams, a singing sidekick played by Joe "Curley" Bradley until he took over the role of Tom in 1940.

Ralston offered hundreds of Tom Mix premiums--rings, flashlights, magnifiers, whistles, sirens, spurs, telescopes, wooden guns, comic books, photo albums, badges, anything that could carry the familiar Ralston checkerboard design or the T-M Bar brand. Tom's first comic book appearance was in issue #1 of *The Comics* in 1937, and he had his own books in the 1940s and 1950s. Ralston briefly revived the Straight Shooters in 1982-1983 as a 50th anniversary tribute, offering a comic book, patch, cereal bowl and watch in exchange for box tops. The Tom Mix Museum in Dewey, Oklahoma, opened in 1968. An annual "National Tom Mix Festival" in DuBois, Pennsylvania, began in 1980.

TMX-1

TMX-2

❑ **TMX-1. Tom Mix Real Photo Mirror,**
c. 1925. Mirror is 2.75" tall likely with scene from 1920s movie. - **$125 $275 $550**

❑ **TMX-2. "Tom Mix Fox Western Star" Pencil Tablet,**
c. 1925. Store item by Kay Co. Inc., New York City. 8x9-1/2". - **$40 $80 $175**

TMX-3

❑ **TMX-3. Coming Attractions Movie Theater Glass Slide,**
1927. For the movie "Tom Mix And Tony The Wonder Horse In The Arizona Wildcat." - **$45 $85 $160**

TMX-4

TMX-5

❑ **TMX-4. "Complete Novel Magazine" With Movie Story,**
1928. Pulp issue #35 for March featuring Tom Mix novel based on William Fox Production silent film "Daredevil's Reward." - **$100 $250 $500**

❑ **TMX-5. "Tom Mix" Real Photo Postcard,**
c. 1928. - **$15 $25 $50**

TMX-6

❑ **TMX-6. "Tom Mix Boys Mounted Troop Of America" Celluloid Blotter,**
1929. Celluloid is 2x6.25" with text below horses "Baxter Springs, Kansas Aug. 24, 1929." Tom Mix is seen in center of photo wearing large white hat and white coat riding Tony. Underside has two flat metal clips that hold 10 paper blotters. - **$250 $500 $750**

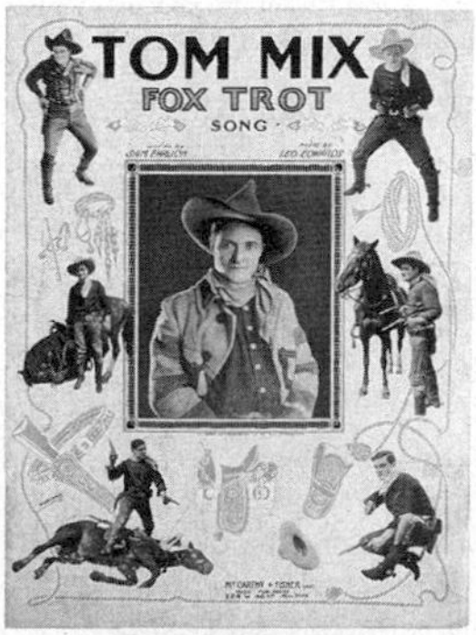

TMX-7

❑ **TMX-7. Photo Cover - Fox Trot Song Book,**
1929. Four pages. Store bought - **$25 $50 $125**

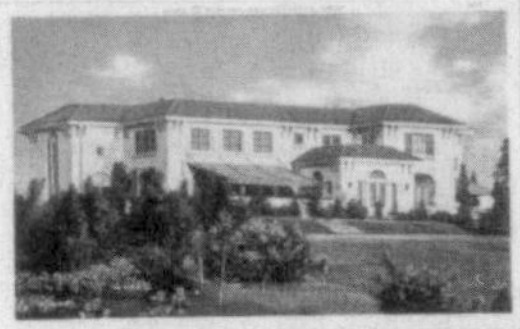

TMX-8

❑ **TMX-8. "Home Of Tom Mix" Postcard,**
1929. Pacific Novelty Company. - **$10 $20 $35**

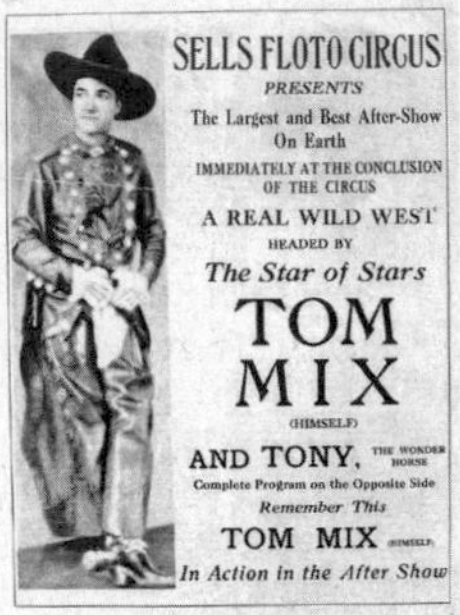

TMX-9

❑ **TMX-9. Sells Floto Circus Handbill,**
1929. Paper sheet listing seven events featuring Tom and Tony. - **$50 $100 $200**

TMX-10

❑ **TMX-10. "Sells Floto Circus" Cello. Button,**
c. 1929. Word "Sells" is part of circus proper name. Mix toured with circus 1929-1931. - **$30 $60 $130**

TMX-11

❑ **TMX-11. "Tom Mix" Rare Portrait Button,**
1920s. Button is 1.25" and likely shows him in a movie role. Reverse has union bug imprint. - **$300 $600 $1200**

TMX-12

❑ **TMX-12. "Tom Mix" Autographed Picture,**
1920s. The autograph reads "Best luck to my friend Fred Warrell." Warrell was the former manager of the Ringling Bros. and Barnum & Bailey Circus, and at the time of his death, he was the assistant manager of the Sells-Floto Circus where Mix was the star; the two were close friends. Warrell died on September 13, 1930. Typical 8x10" example - **$250 $500 $1000**

TMX-13

TMX-14

❑ **TMX-13. "Tom Mix For Sheriff" Cello. Button,**
c. 1930. - **$500 $1000 $2000**

❑ **TMX-14. "State Theatre" Contest Coupons,**
c. 1930. Series of 1-1/4x3-1/2" coupons inscribed with a single letter meant to be collected to spell out the phrase "Tom Mix Tickets" to obtain free admission. A free "Tom Mix Punching Ball" was awarded for a complete coupon set. Each Coupon - **$10 $20 $45**

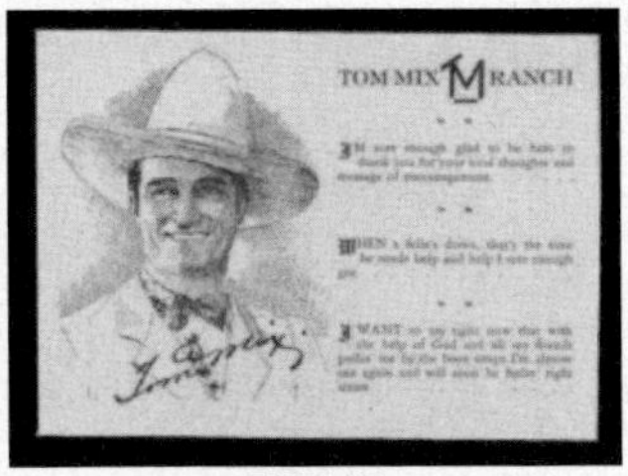

TMX-15

❑ **TMX-15. "Thank You" Card With Dated Envelope,**
1931. 4-3/4x6-1/4". Text includes "...with the help of God and all my friends pullin' me by the boot straps I'm almost out again and will soon be feelin' right smart." - **$75 $150 $300**

TMX-16

❑ **TMX-16. Circus Route Folder And Stationery,**
1931. Folder listing Sells Floto Circus season itinerary plus letterhead stationery for Sam B. Dill's Big Three Ring Circus, undated. Both featured Tom and Tony the Wonder Horse.
Route Book - **$40 $80 $150**
Stationery - **$35 $65 $125**

TMX-17 TMX-18

❑ **TMX-17. "Tom Mix With Tony/Universal Pictures" Cello. Button,**
1932. From his 1932-1933 years at Universal. - **$150 $300 $600**

❑ **TMX-18. Chewing Gum Wrapper With Deputy Ring Offer,**
1933. National Chicle Co. Product copyright is 1933. Ring offer expired June 30, 1935. - **$65 $125 $250**

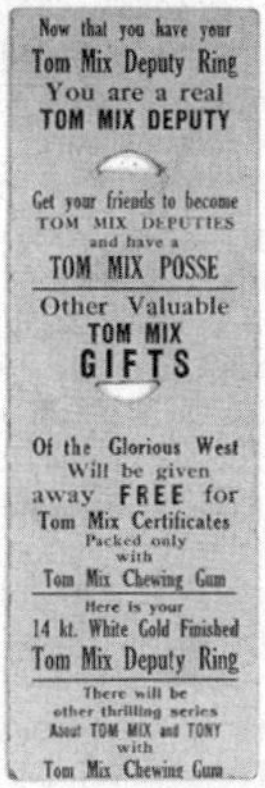

TMX-19

❑ **TMX-19. "Tom Mix Deputy Ring" Cardboard Mailing Holder,**
1933. National Chicle Gum. 2-5/8x8-1/8" red on cream. Designates ring owner as "a real Tom Mix Deputy." - **$200 $400 $800**

TMX-20

TMX-21

❑ **TMX-20. "Tom Mix Deputy" Gold And Silver Finish Brass Ring,**
1933. National Chicle Gum. Required 75 certificates clipped from gum wrappers. Offer expired June 30, 1935. See TMX-18, 19, and 25. - **$1500 $4000 $7500**

❑ **TMX-21. "The Life Of Tom Mix" First Club Manual,**
1933. Near Mint With Mailer - **$200**
Loose - **$50 $85 $160**

TMX-22

TMX-23

❑ **TMX-22. "Tom Mix Straight Shooters" Sheet Music,**
1933. Store item published by Shapiro, Bernstein & Co., New York. Shows two men, one in fancy outfit obviously representing Tom Mix along with young girl and young boy flanking "NBC" microphone. - **$20 $40 $80**

❑ **TMX-23. Exhibit Card,**
1933. - **$10 $20 $40**

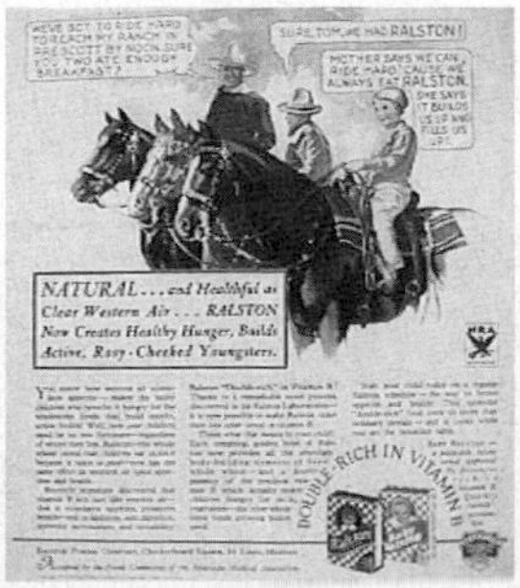

TMX-24

❑ **TMX-24. Premium Insert,**
1933. 5-3/4x6-1/4" full color insert included with the earliest premiums. - **$15 $25 $45**

TMX-25

❑ **TMX-25. "Tom Mix Gum" Advertising Folder Designed Like A Book,**
1933. National Chicle Co. 6x10-1/2" yellow, black and white stiff cardboard which folds to front and back covers with a 1" wide spine. Inside lists all 24 titles in the series of free booklets given with the gum and reverse promotes the "Deputy Ring." Probably packed in gum packet boxes for use as dealer display. Rare. - **$200 $500 $800**

TMX-26

❑ **TMX-26. "Straight Shooters" Fabric Patch,**
1933. Second version. Design is woven. See TMX-37. - **$25 $55 $100**

TMX-27

TMX-28

❑ **TMX-27. Club Manual "Enlarged Edition",**
1933. Near Mint With Mailer - **$150**
Loose - **$40 $75 $135**

❑ **TMX-28. Premium Catalogue Sheet,**
1933. - **$20 $40 $75**

TMX-29

TMX-30

❑ **TMX-29. Tom Mix & Tony Photo,**
1933. Sent with both 1933 club manuals. - **$15 $25 $45**

❑ **TMX-30. Paper Lario With Tricks And Stunts Sheet,**
1933. Tricks Sheet - **$35 $80 $150**
Lario - **$50 $125 $250**

TMX-31

TMX-32

❑ **TMX-31. Cigar Box Label,**
1933. - **$15 $30 $60**

❑ **TMX-32. Cigar Box Label,**
1933. - **$20 $40 $80**

TMX-33

❑ **TMX-33. Cowboy Hat,**
1933. Rare premium. Name is not on inside. - **$300 $650 $1300**

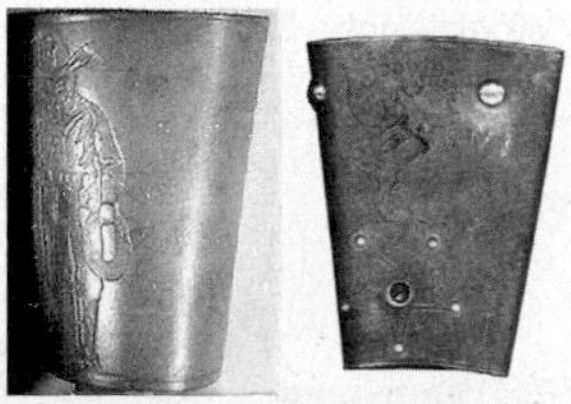

TMX-34

❑ **TMX-34. Leather Wrist Cuffs,**
1933. Shown at left, no Mix identification, depicts cowboy with lariat.
Set of Two - **$80 $160 $320**
With Mix Identification and Star (shown at right)
Set of Two Near Mint - **$475**

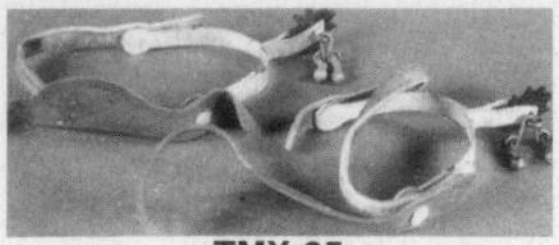
TMX-35

❑ TMX-35. Metal Spurs With Leather Straps,
1933. No Mix identification, horse head on top strap. Rubber rowels each have two metal jangle weights. - **$125 $225 $385**

TMX-36

TMX-37

❑ TMX-36. Fabric Bandanna,
1933. - **$40 $85 $175**

❑ TMX-37. First Version "Straight Shooters" Fabric Patch,
1933. The 1933 patch TMX-26 is 2-1/4x2-1/4" of woven fabric. This example is 2-1/2x2-1/2" with the design printed on the fabric rather than woven into it. Issued with the earliest 1933 club kit (see TMX-21) and used briefly until the club manual was "Enlarged" (TMX-27).
- **$65 $125 $250**

TMX-38

TMX-39

TMX-40

❑ TMX-38. "Good Luck/TM" Spinner,
1933. - **$20 $40 $90**

❑ TMX-39. Horseshoe Nail Ring,
1933. Generic horseshoe nail with silver luster. No Tom Mix markings. - **$20 $30 $40**

❑ TMX-40. "TM" Spinner Ring,
1933. Rare. Possibly a circus souvenir. -
$1750 $4500 $9000

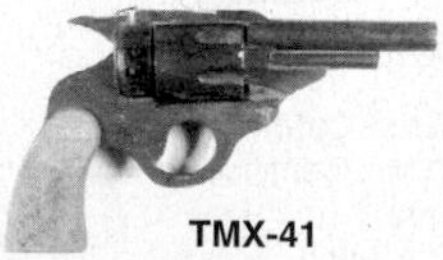
TMX-41

TMX-42

❑ TMX-41. Wooden Revolver,
1933. Earliest gun, opens and cylinder revolves. -
$85 $175 $300

❑ TMX-42. "Lucky Pocket Piece" Brass Medalet,
c. 1933 "Exhibit Supply Company/Chicago" on reverse inside with horseshoe design. -
$30 $60 $125

TMX-43

TMX-44

❑ TMX-43. Radio Program 15x24" Cardboard Sign,
c. 1933. Printed both sides. - **$175 $375 $650**

❑ TMX-44. "Tom Mix" Bisque 5" Figurine,
c. 1933. Rare. Store item. Only figural Mix item known. Made in Germany, marked #3509. At least three in series. Also see Charlie Chaplin and Harold Lloyd (in Movie Misc. section)-
$1000 $3000 $5500

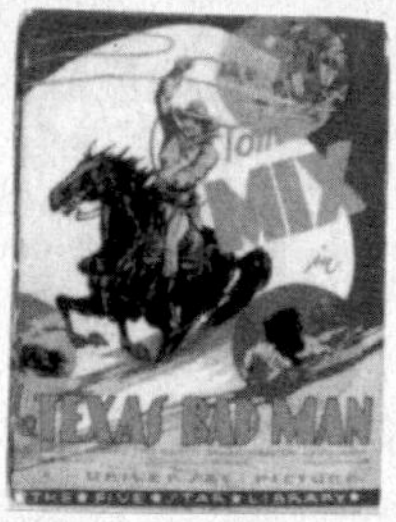

TMX-45

❑ TMX-45. "Tom Mix In The Texas Bad Man" Movie Book,
1934. Five Star Library book. 4-1/4x5" format. -
$21 $63 $145

TMX-46

❑ TMX-46. Rodeorope And Full Color Box,
1934. The Mordt Co. Store item. - **$250 $500 $1000**

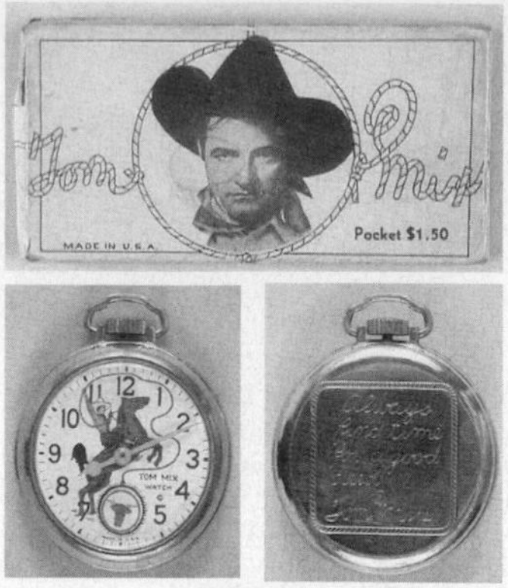

TMX-47

❑ TMX-47. Tom Mix Pocket Watch With Box,
1934. Store item by Ingersoll. Black and white box holds watch with color image of Tom on Tony. Hands are in yellow and reverse has inscription surrounded by rope design "Always Find Time For A Good Deed/Tom Mix."
Box - **$1000 $1750 $3500**
Watch - **$1500 $3000 $5000**

TMX-48

TMX-49

❑ TMX-48. National Chicle Co. Gum Booklet #2 Example,
1934. 48 numbered booklets.
Each - **$15 $30 $60**

❑ TMX-49. Ralston Radio Ad Cardboard Sign,
1934. Diecut cardboard 20x32" urging listenership over NBC Red Network. -
$400 $800 $1500

TMX-50

❑ TMX-50. Press Book,
1934. Rare. Elaborate 12 page book which features Tom Mix's first serial, "The Miracle Rider." Talks about Tom Mix's radio audience reaching 25 million listeners, his product line, and how to get premiums. Shows all 15 chapter lobby cards and posters. 16x 21" - **$400 $800 $1600**

TMX-51

❑ TMX-51. Premiums Catalogue Folder Sheet,
1934. Catalogue designated C 135 G. -
$20 $35 $75

TMX-52

❑ TMX-52. "Official Commission/Ranch Boss" Certificate,
1934. Promotion certification with facsimile signature of Tom Mix and "The Old Wrangler" as witness. - **$125 $325 $700**

TMX-53

❑ TMX-53. Paper Mask,
1934. Scarce. - **$150 $350 $750**

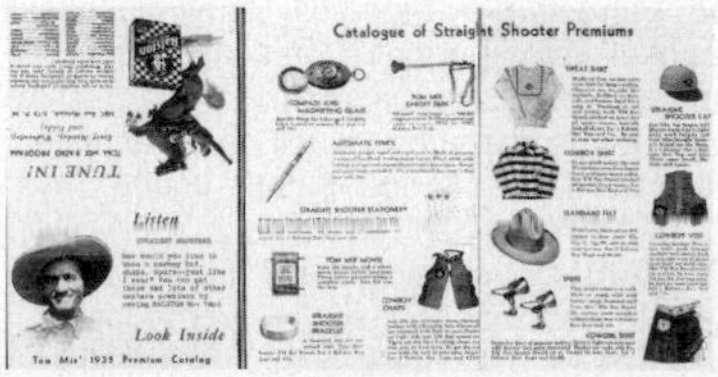

TMX-54

❑ TMX-54. Premiums Catalogue Folder Sheet,
1934. Catalogue designated C 135 O. -
$20 $35 $65

TMX-55

❑ TMX-55. "Series A" Photo Set,
1934. Set of five.
Each Photo Or Mailer - **$15 $35 $75**

TMX-56

❑ TMX-56. "Series B" Photo Set With Envelope,
1934. Set of five photos.
Each Photo Or Mailer - **$15 $35 $75**

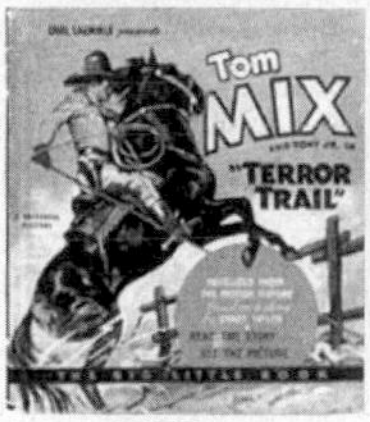

TMX-57

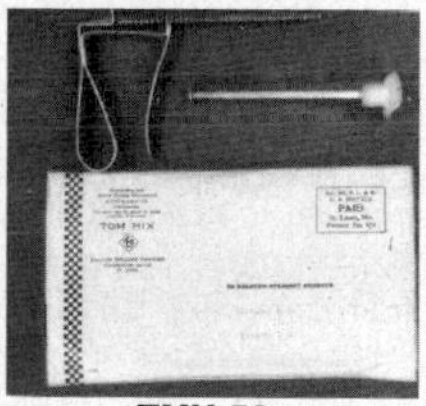

TMX-58

❑ TMX-57. "Tom Mix And Tony Jr. In Terror Trail" Photoplay Big Little Book,
1934. Whitman #762. - **$18 $54 $125**

❑ TMX-58. Zyp Gun With Mailer Envelope,
1934. Scarce. Metal spring gun with rubber cup dart. Also known as Tom Mix Target Gun.
Gun With Dart - **$100 $250 $500**
Mailer - **$20 $40 $75**

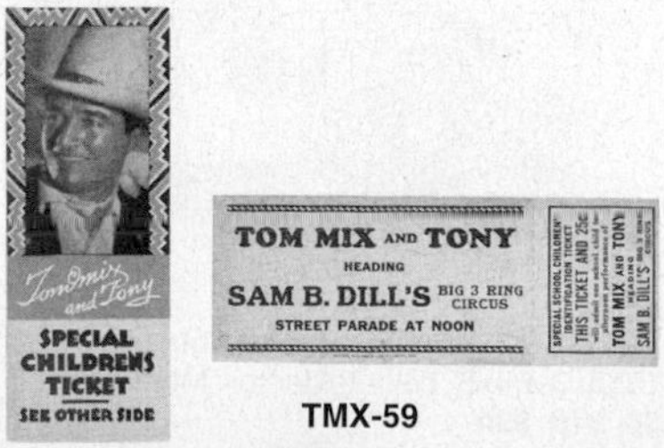

TMX-59

❑ TMX-59. "Tom Mix And Tony Special Childrens Ticket" For Sam B. Dill's Circus,
c. 1934. Weldon, Williams & Lick, Ft. Smith, Ark. 2x5.5" ticket with image of smiling Mix. Bright lightning bolt type margin. Mix joined Dill in 1934 by buying half interest in the circus. Dill died in Feb. 1935. Mix changed name to "Tom Mix Circus." - **$50 $100 $175**

TMX-60

❑ TMX-60. "TM" Ralston Logo Brass Ring,
1935. Named in ads "Tom Mix Lucky Ring". -
$50 $100 $150

TMX-61

❑ TMX-61. "Tom Mix In Flaming Guns" Movie Edition Book,
1935. Five Star Library Engle-Van Wiseman store item in BLB format with photos from Universal film. Scarce title. - **$18 $54 $125**

TMX-62

❑ TMX-62. Tom Mix Big Little Book Puzzles (Boxed),
1935. Store item. - **$150 $350 $650**

TMX-63

❑ **TMX-63. "Tom Mix Plays A Lone Hand" Big Little Book,**
1935. Whitman #1173. - **$12 $36 $78**

TMX-64

❑ **TMX-64. "Miracle Riders" Picture Folio,**
1935. Holds 15 bw numbered photo pages apparently corresponding to 15 serial chapters. Distributed by theaters, sponsored by Tootsie Rolls. Set - **$125 $250 $500**

TMX-65

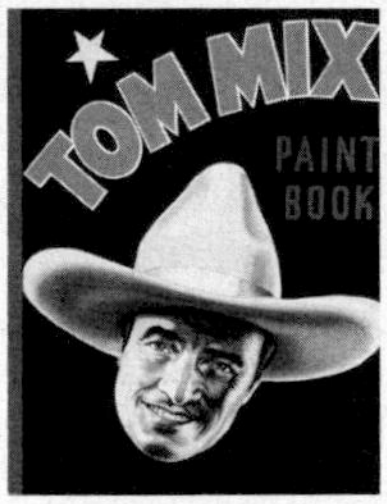

TMX-66

❑ **TMX-65. "Miracle Rider" Serial Club Cello. Button,**
1935. Mascot. - **$175 $300 $600**

❑ **TMX-66. Paint Book,**
1935. Store item. - **$125 $350 $700**

TMX-67

❑ **TMX-67. "Shooting Gallery" Cardboard Target With Box,**
1935. Store item by Parker Brothers. Includes rubber band gun. - **$150 $325 $650**

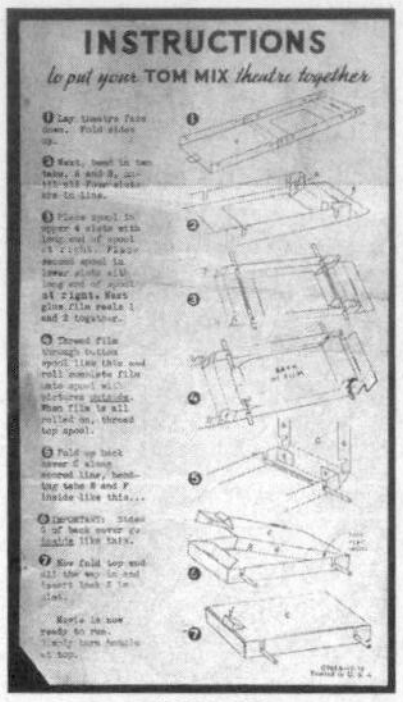

TMX-68

TMX-69

❑ **TMX-68. Theater Instructions,**
1935. 7-step instruction sheet. - **$50 $100 $200**

❑ **TMX-69. Portrait Button,**
1935. Canvas Products Co., St. Louis. Five buttons given with purchase of Tom Mix tent.
Litho. - **$35 $75 $150**
Cello. (Rare) - **$75 $150 $300**

TMX-70

TMX-71

❑ **TMX-70. Western Song Book,**
1935.Sixty-eight page book shows photos of Tom Mix and promotes his films. Includes letter from Tom Mix. - **$50 $100 $200**

❑ **TMX-71. "The Trail Of The Terrible 6" Booklet,**
1935. Ralston Premium. - **$20 $60 $140**

TMX-72

❑ **TMX-72. Premium Insert Folder,**
1935. 3-1/4x6" color folder for "Mother!" - **$8 $15 $30**

TMX-73

❑ **TMX-73. Humming Lariat,**
1935. Front text includes "Tom Mix and his Ralston Straight Shooters" along with promo for the radio show "5:45 Monday through Friday Mutual Network." However, we have not seen this item offered as a premium in Ralston catalogues so it may be a store item. - **$50 $125 $200**

TMX-74

❑ **TMX-74. Sunday Comics Color Ad For "2 In 1 Compass",**
1935. This example of the ad has expiration date of March 6, 1937. See TMX-93. - **$10 $20 $35**

TMX-75

TMX-76

❑ **TMX-75. Tom Mix Wristwatch,**
1935. Store item by Ingersoll. Same dial design as pocket watch but no reverse inscription. Came with metal link bands and the largest two closest to the case have black on silver luster portraits of Tom. - **$1500 $3000 $5000**

❑ **TMX-76. Dixie Ice Cream Picture,**
1935. Reverse has four scenes from Mascot serial "The Miracle Rider." - **$30 $75 $150**

TMX-77

❑ **TMX-77. Ralston Promotional Store Window Transfer,**
1935. 8-1/4x8-1/2" backing sheet holds superb color gummed front decal for placement on inner surface of window or door. Rare. - **$200 $400 $750**

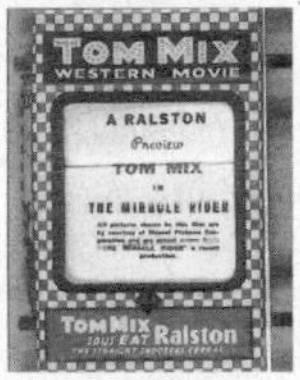

TMX-78

TMX-79

❑ **TMX-78. "Western Movie" Cardboard Mechanical Viewer,**
1935. Film scenes from "The Miracle Rider" Mascot Pictures serial. - **$85 $200 $350**

❑ **TMX-79. "Western Movie" Cardboard Box Viewer,**
1935. Film scenes from "Rustlers Roundup". - **$85 $200 $350**

TMX-80

❑ **TMX-80. "Miracle Rider" Dixie Ice Cream Lid,**
1935. - **$12 $25 $50**

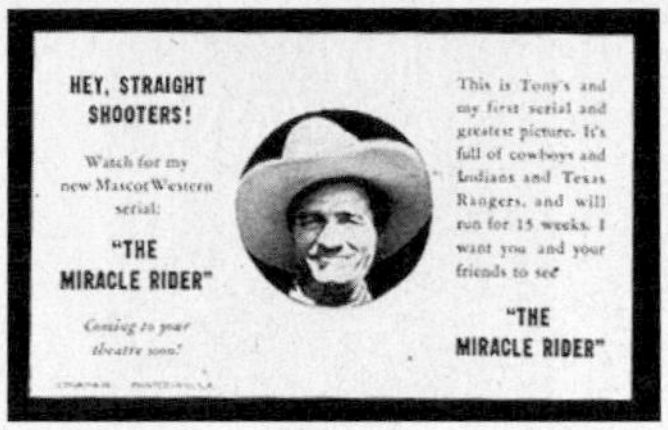

TMX-81

❑ **TMX-81. Promo,**
1935. Premium insert to promote Tom Mix film "The Miracle Rider." - **$25 $40 $80**

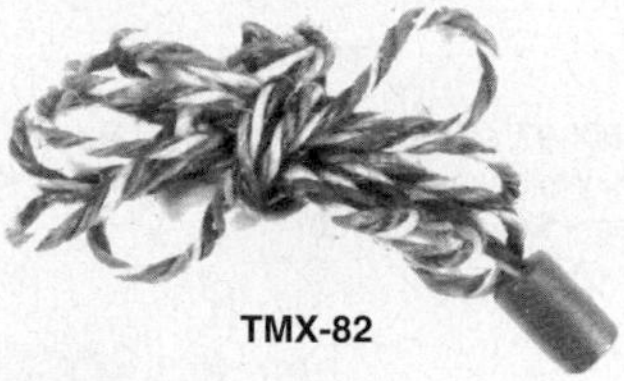

TMX-82

❑ **TMX-82. Spinning Rope,**
1935. Red, white and blue twine with Mix Ralston endorsement on wooden grip. - **$40 $80 $175**

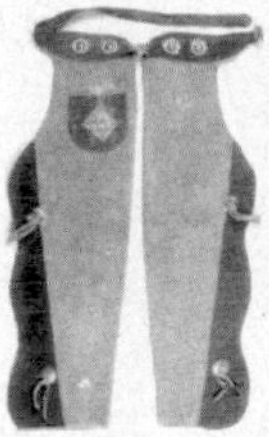

(ENLARGED VIEW)

TMX-83

❑ **TMX-83. Suede Leather Chaps,**
1935. - **$100 $300 $550**

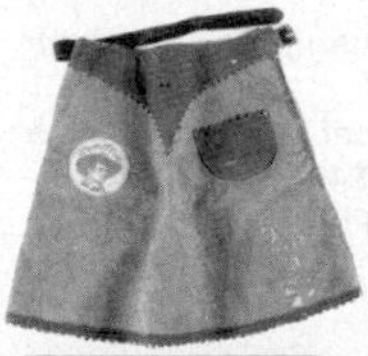

(ENLARGED VIEW)

TMX-84

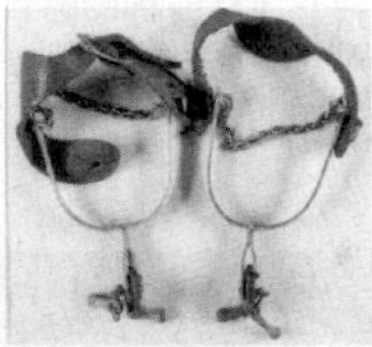

TMX-85

❑ **TMX-84. Suede Leather Cowgirl Skirt,**
1935. - **$110 $325 $600**

❑ **TMX-85. Metal Spurs With Leather Straps,**
1935. Straps have TM Bar Ranch symbol. - **$100 $200 $400**

TMX-86

❑ **TMX-86. Leather Wrist Cuffs,**
1935. Pair - **$80 $160 $350**

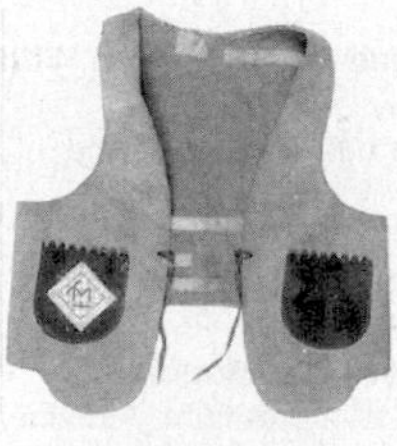

TMX-87

TMX-88

TMX-89

❑ **TMX-87. Suede Vest,**
1935. - **$75 $165 $325**

❑ **TMX-88. Brown Leather Holster,**
1935. Cover panel has Tom Mix Ralston logo.
Holster - **$135 $275 $550**
Belt - **$50 $100 $150**

❑ **TMX-89. Leather Bracelet With Foil On Brass Title Plate,**
1935. Tom Mix or Ralston markings on both front and back. Named in ads "Lucky Wrist Band".
Complete - **$30 $60 $135**
No Strap - **$15 $30 $60**

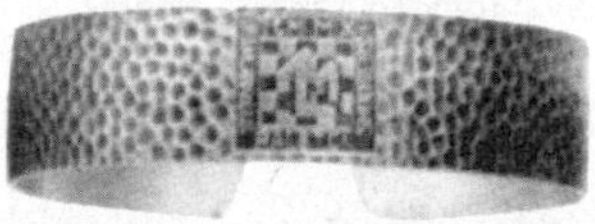

TMX-90

TMX-91

❑ **TMX-90. Straight Shooter Bracelet With Checkerboard Logo,**
1935. Silvered brass. - **$225 $400 $750**

❑ **TMX-91. Sun Watch,**
1935. - **$35 $75 $150**

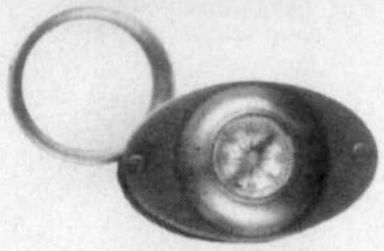

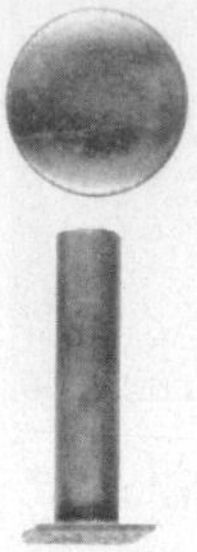

TMX-93

TMX-92

TMX-94

❑ **TMX-92. Bar Brand Branding Iron With Ink Pad Tin,**
1935. Brass stamper has TM initials and checkerboard design.
Branding Iron - **$35 $75 $125**
Ink Tin - **$30 $65 $115**

❑ **TMX-93. Compass With Magnifier,**
1935. Unmarked Ralston premium. Aluminum case with eyelet. See TMX-74. - **$15 $25 $45**

❑ **TMX-94. Lucky Charm Sterling Silver Horseshoe,**
1935. - **$115 $225 $400**

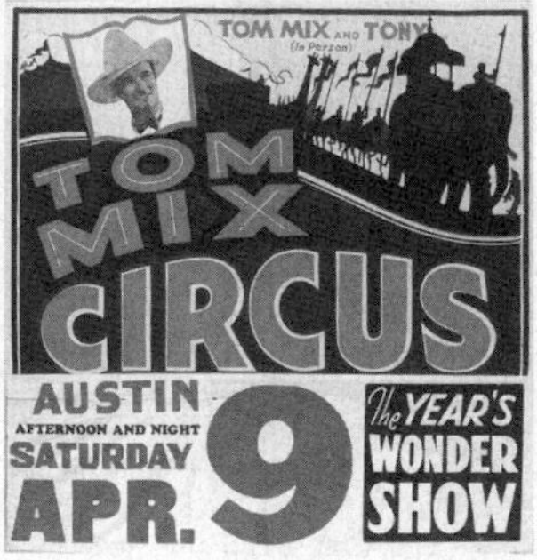

TMX-95

❑ **TMX-95. "Tom Mix Circus" Poster,**
c. 1935. Poster is 28x29" with text "Tom Mix And Tony In Person." - **$150 $275 $500**

TMX-96

❑ **TMX-96. "Tom Mix And Tony" Wood/Metal Riding Toy,**
c. 1935. Store item by Mengel Co. Inc. 5-3/4x17x16" tall. - **$135 $350 $750**

TMX-97

❑ **TMX-97. "Tony And His Pals" Book,**
1936. Whitman. Hardbound 6.75x8" with 144 pages. - **$40 $80 $160**

TMX-98

❑ **TMX-98. Premium Catalogue Folder,**
1936. - **$20 $40 $60**

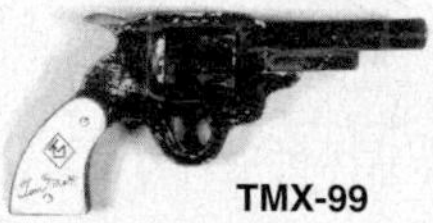

TMX-99

TMX-100

❑ **TMX-99. Wood Gun With Cardboard Handles,**
1936. Cylinder revolves but gun doesn't open. - **$300 $800 $1750**

❑ **TMX-100. Championship Cowboy Belt Buckle,**
1936. Brass with foil paper insert, also came with belt. Buckle Only - **$40 $80 $175**
Buckle And Belt - **$60 $135 $275**

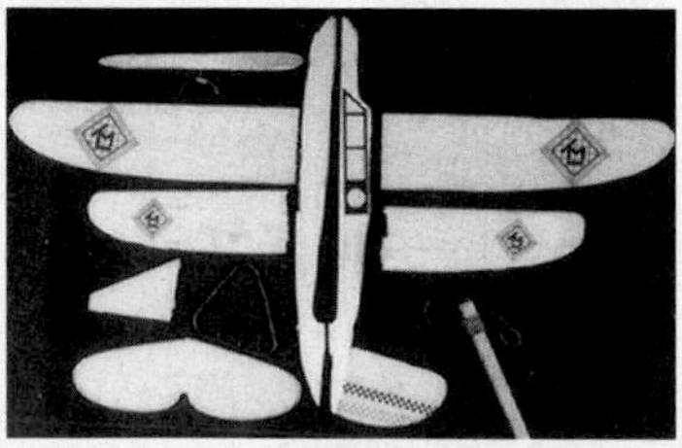

TMX-101

❑ **TMX-101. Flying Model Airplane Kit,**
1936. Scarce. Balsa wood with Ralston logo decals. - **$165 $325 $550**

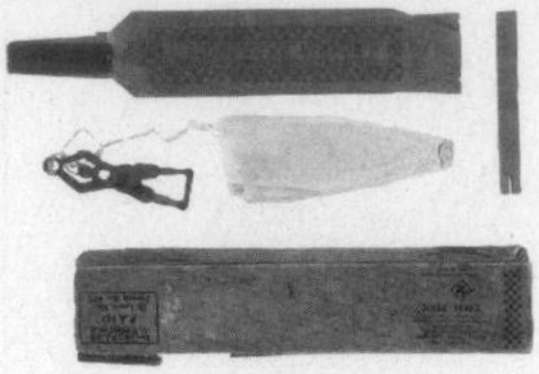

TMX-102

❑ **TMX-102. "Rocket Parachute",**
1936. Consists of balsa and cardboard launcher, wood stick with rubber band, metal figure string joined to paper parachute.
Mailer Only - **$25 $50 $100**
Toy - **$75 $150 $225**

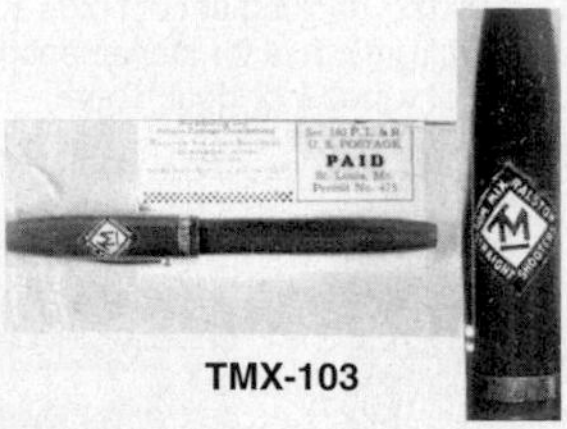

TMX-103

❑ **TMX-103. Fountain Pen With Mailer Envelope,**
1936. Pen cap has Tom Mix ranch brand symbol decal. Pen - **$40 $80 $175**
Mailer - **$15 $25 $40**

TMX-104

❑ **TMX-104. Girl's Brass Dangle Charm Bracelet,**
1936. Scarce. Charms depict ranch symbol, Tom on Tony, steer head, six-shooter. Also called "Championship Cowgirl Bracelet". - **$200 $400 $950**

TMX-105

❑ **TMX-105. Signet Ring Newspaper Advertisement,**
1936. - **$15 $25 $40**

TMX-106

❑ **TMX-106. Lucky Signet Ring,**
1936. Brass bands topped by raised personalized single initial designated by orderer. Ad mentions onyx-like black background around initial but ring was issued both with and without black background. - **$50 $85 $200**

TMX-107

❑ **TMX-107. "Tom Mix Circus" Season Tour Summary,**
1936. 7x10" with 24 pages issued "in-house" for employees. Rare. - **$125 $250 $400**

TMX-108

❑ **TMX-108. "Tom Mix Circus And Wild West" Poster,**
c. 1936. About 28x42". - **$125 $250 $400**

TMX-109

❑ **TMX-109. "Tom Mix Circus" Button,**
c. 1936. 1.75" black and white cello souvenir from his own circus tour that year and next. - **$75 $150 $300**

TMX-110

❑ **TMX-110. "Tom Mix Circus" Announcement Blotter,**
c. 1936. 3x6" cardboard ink blotter for coming appearance to be announced specifically by daily papers and billboards. - **$35 $75 $135**

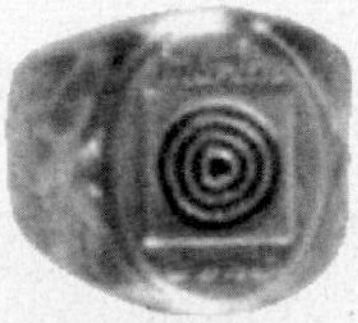

TMX-111

❑ **TMX-111. "Marlin Guns" Brass Target Ring,**
1937. Marlin Firearms Co. Tom Mix endorsed a Marlin rifle called the "Tom Mix Special .22 Caliber Rifle." The actual rifle is inscribed with his name. Mix appeared in Marlin ads promoting the rifle. The same ads offered a "simulated gold Military Type Ring" and a booklet by the National Rifle Association titled "How To Set Up A Rifle Range" for ten cents. Later, the rings were also offered as a "Gold Bull's Eye Ring" available to boys in lots of ten or more at 6 cents each with the suggestion that the rings be resold for 10 cents each and used as an insignia for members of a Marlin Club. Still later, in the 1950s, Marlin gave away the ring from their booths at National Rifle Association meetings and exhibits. - **$100 $175 $325**

TMX-112

❑ **TMX-112. Premium Catalogue Folder,**
1937. Pictured premiums include Signet Ring. - **$25 $50 $100**

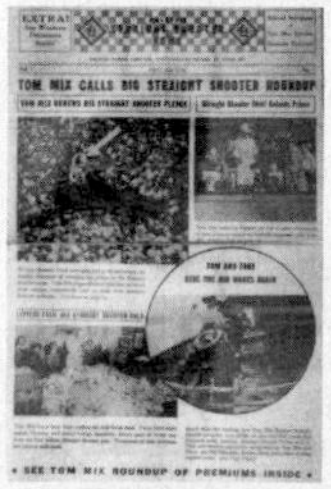

TMX-113 TMX-114

❑ **TMX-113. "Ralston Straight Shooter News" Vol. 1 #1 Issue,**
1937. - **$45 $85 $175**

❑ **TMX-114. "Ralston Straight Shooter News" #2,**
1937. - **$35 $75 $150**

TMX-115

❑ **TMX-115. Baby Turtle Newspaper Advertisement,**
1937. Premium was a real live baby turtle with Mix decal on its shell. - **$20 $40 $60**

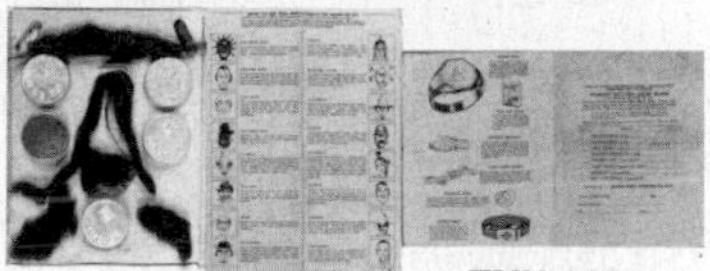

TMX-116

❑ **TMX-116. Movie Make-Up Kit With Paper,**
1937. Five tins with TM brand and words Clown, Indian, Chink, Mexican, Negro.
Complete - **$75 $150 $300**
Each Tin - **$8 $12 $25**

TMX-117

❑ **TMX-117. "Tom Mix Circus" 9x23" Felt Pennant,**
1937. - **$85 $165 $325**

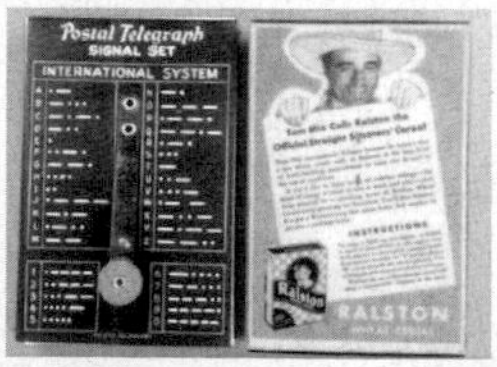

TMX-118

❑ **TMX-118. "Postal Telegraph Signal Set",**
1937. Cardboard box with metal tapper key. - **$60 $115 $225**

TMX-119 TMX-120

❑ **TMX-119. "Tom Mix And The Hoard Of Montezuma" Big Little Book,**
1937. Whitman #1462. - **$12 $36 $78**

❑ **TMX-120. "Tom Mix And The Scourge Of Paradise Valley" Book,**
1937. Whitman Big Big Book #4068. - **$63 $189 $445**

TMX-121

TMX-122

❑ **TMX-121. "Tom Mix In The Range War" Big Little Book,**
1937. Whitman #1166. - **$12 $36 $78**

❑ **TMX-122. Silver Frame Photo,**
1937. Photo is personalized by recipient first name. - **$40 $75 $160**

TMX-123

❑ **TMX-123. "Big Little Book" Cards,**
1937. Cards are 2-7/16x2-7/8" with 32 picturing Tom Mix although these are a subset from a larger set totaling seven different characters with 224 total cards.
Each Tom Mix Card - **$30 $70 $135**

TMX-124

❑ **TMX-124. Straight Shooters Badge Offer Flyer,**
1937. A three-fold sheet 5x7-3/4" that includes coupon. Scarce as these were typically sent into Ralston with one box top to acquire the badge. Has 1934 copyright but not used until 1937. Text refers to "silver plated" version of the badge. - **$100 $200 $400**

TMX-125

TMX-126

❑ **TMX-125. Straight Shooter Silver Luster Badge With Foil Paper Insert,**
1937. - **$25 $75 $150**

❑ **TMX-126. Straight Shooter Brass Badge,**
1937. Foil paper symbol. - **$35 $85 $165**

TMX-127

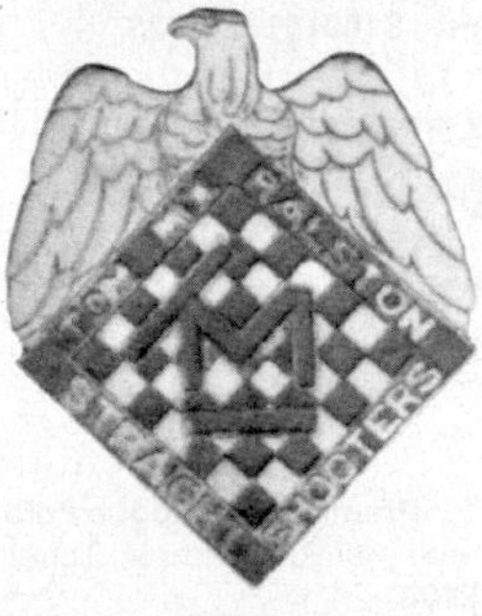

TMX-128

❑ **TMX-127. Straight Shooter Badge Lead Proof,**
c. 1937. Unique - **$1500**

❑ **TMX-128. Prototype "Ranch Boss" Enameled Brass Badge,**
c. 1937. Trial design for Ralston approval by Robbins Co., Massachusetts with enamel emblem rather than foil paper. Unique - **$7500**

TMX-129

❑ **TMX-129. Prototype "Tom Mix Ralston Straight Shooters" Star Brass Badge,**
c. 1937. Trial design for Ralston approval by Robbins Co., Massachusetts. Unique - **$7500**

TMX-130

TMX-131

❑ **TMX-130. Tom Mix "Wrangler" Robbins Company Prototype,**
c. 1937. One of four different trial designs produced in extremely limited quantity as test pieces for the badge to be offered by Ralston in 1938. 2-1/16" tall with reverse bar pin. The badge eventually decided upon for 1938 features this same design but in the Ralston logo area a metallic foil piece was added. This badge is in muted brass luster and has no other color. Possibly unique. Mint As Issued - **$1250**

❑ **TMX-131. Tom Mix Prototype Badge With Blue Accent,**
c. 1937. This piece is identical to previous item but the checkerboeard design has dark blue enamel accent paint. Possibly unique. Mint As Issued - **$1250**

TMX-132

TMX-133

❑ TMX-132. Tom Mix Red Logo With Blue Initials Prototype Badge,
c. 1937. Unlike the previous two items, this piece has bright golden brass luster. Also, the word "Wrangler" is in red. The Ralston logo area is in red and the "TM" initials are in dark blue. We've seen one additional example with this identical coloration. Mint As Issued - **$1500**

❑ TMX-133. Tom Mix Wrangler Prototype With Blue Border,
c. 1937. Like the previous item, the brass areas of this piece have brilliant luster rather than muted luster. On this piece the word "Wrangler" is in blue. Also on this piece the diamond border around the checkerboard logo is in dark blue rather than in red as on the previous item. Possibly unique. Mint As Issued - **$1500**

TMX-134

❑ TMX-134. "Tony" Hand-Painted Plaster Figure,
c. 1937. 4.75" tall replica of Tom's horse with name incised on each side below midsection. Likely circus souvenir. - **$85 $165 $300**

TMX-135

❑ TMX-135. Premium Catalogue Sheet,
1938. - **$20 $35 $65**

TMX-136

❑ TMX-136. Second Variety Wrangler Badge Folder,
1938. Item has 1934 Ralston copyright, but not used until 1938. 4x6" folder opens to 6x12" with slot for holding "Wrangler's Badge" which we believe refers to the version picturing him frontally rather than in partial profile. Includes offer to obtain "Ranch Boss" badge. See TMX 144 and 145. - **$85 $150 $300**

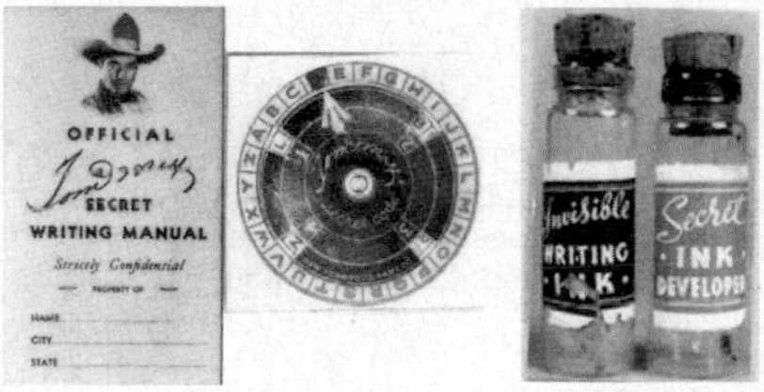

TMX-137

❑ TMX-137. Secret Ink Writing Kit,
1938. Includes: manual, cardboard decoder, two glass vials of ink and developer.
Manual - **$65 $135 $315**
Decoder - **$25 $60 $110**
Each Vial - **$20 $50 $75**

TMX-138

TMX-139

❑ TMX-138. Metal Telescope,
1938. Mailer Tube Only - **$15 $30 $50**
Telescope - **$50 $100 $200**

❑ TMX-139. Bullet Flashlight,
1938. 3" silvered brass tube with plastic end cap holding bulb. - **$55 $110 $175**

TMX-140

❑ TMX-140. Telephone Set,
1938. Litho. tin transmitter and receiver units joined by string. - **$30 $75 $115**

TMX-141

❑ TMX-141. Wrangler Badge Folder,
1938. - **$75 $150 $275**

TMX-142

TMX-143

❑ TMX-142. "Wrangler" Brass Badge,
1938. - **$50 $125 $225**

❑ TMX-143. Wrangler Badge Lead Proof,
c. 1938. Unique - **$1750**

TMX-144

TMX-145

❑ TMX-144. "Wrangler" Metal Badge With Foil Paper Insert,
1938. Version pictures him frontally rather than partial profile. Issued in either silver or gold luster. Either Version - **$75 $175 $350**

❑ TMX-145. "Ranch Boss" Brass Rank Badge,
1938. Centered by foil paper emblem. - **$150 $300 $600**

TMX-146

TMX-147

❑ **TMX-146. Ranch Boss Badge Lead Proof,**
c. 1938. Unique - **$3750**

❑ **TMX-147. Look-In Mystery Ring,**
1938. Brass with tiny view hole for inside portrait photo of Tom with Tony. - **$50 $100 $200**

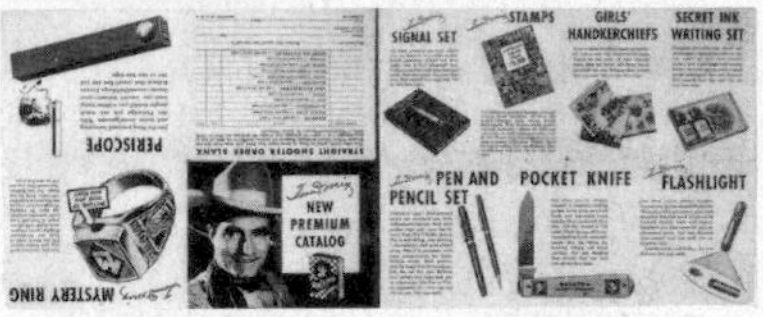

TMX-148

❑ **TMX-148. Premium Catalogue Folder Sheet,**
1939. - **$25 $40 $60**

TMX-149

❑ **TMX-149. Premium Catalogue,**
1939. 4x5" brown and white folded sheet. Contents picture three Tom Mix premiums plus generic premiums for adults. - **$25 $40 $60**

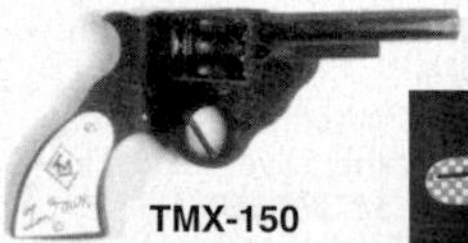

TMX-150

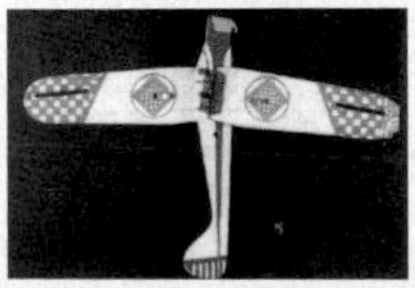

TMX-151

❑ **TMX-150. Wood Gun,**
1939. No moving parts. - **$85 $165 $325**

❑ **TMX-151. Streamline Parachute Plane,**
1939. Scarce. Balsa wood with designs in red and blue. Metal hinged wings. Came with parachutist and parachute. See next item.
Plane Only - **$125 $300 $500**

TMX-152

❑ **TMX-152. Streamline Plane Parachutist And Parachute,**
1939. Rare. Came with previous item. Metal figure smaller than 1936 Rocket Parachute and parachute is green or red. - **$75 $150 $250**

TMX-153

❑ **TMX-153. Signal Flashlight,**
1939. 3" metal tube with lens disk for red, green or clear light. Lens often missing and plastic end cap often cracked. Complete - **$30 $75 $165**

TMX-154

❑ **TMX-154. Cardboard Periscope,**
1939. Blue Tube - **$25 $50 $100**
Black Tube - **$50 $100 $150**
Instructions - **$25 $50 $75**

TMX-155

TMX-156

TMX-157

❑ **TMX-155. "Straight Shooters" Pocketknife,**
1939. - **$30 $75 $135**

❑ **TMX-156. Brass Compass And Magnifier,**
1939. Magnifying lens swings out. - **$25 $50 $100**

❑ **TMX-157. Pinback,**
1930s. Black and white 1 1/4". - **$65 $100 $200**

TMX-158

❑ **TMX-158. Leather Belt With "Tom Mix" Buckle,**
1930s. Store item**. - $75 $125 $250**

TMX-159

❑ **TMX-159. Wooden Gun Delay Card,**
1930s. Ralston. 4x8" with art of Tom in workshop sweating over gun saying "Gosh I'm Sorry To Be So Late With This Gun, But How'd I Know Everyone In America Was Gonna Want One Of 'Em!" Which of three premium guns this applied to is unspecified**. - $65 $135 $250**

TMX-160

TMX-161

❑ **TMX-160. Cinema Star Card #7,**
1930s. England. Wills Cigarettes premium. - **$10 $20 $30**

❑ **TMX-161. Event Cello. Button,**
1930s. Issuer unknown. Blue on white, 1 1/4". - **$30 $65 $135**

TMX-162

TMX-163

❑ **TMX-162. Hollywood Gum Card,**
1930s. - **$20 $40 $75**

❑ **TMX-163. "Wild West Club" Member Cello. Button,**
1930s. Rare. - **$500 $1500 $2500**

TMX-164

TMX-165

TMX-166

❑ **TMX-164. "Toledo Paramount Theater" Movie Cello. Button,**
1930s. Scarce issue from a single theater in Ohio. - **$200 $500 $750**

❑ **TMX-165. "Yankiboy Play Clothes" Cello. Button,**
1930s. Yellow rim 1-3/4" size. - **$50 $100 $175**

❑ **TMX-166. "Yankiboy Play Clothes" 2" Cello. Button,**
1930s. Orange rim. - **$35 $65 $125**

TMX-168

❑ **TMX-168. "Rodeo Box" Cardboard Pencil Case,**
1930s. Probably a store item or circus souvenir. Inscribed for "Tom Mix & Tony" with rodeo generic art. - **$45 $90 $200**

TMX-169

TMX-170

❑ **TMX-169. "My Own Confection" Candy Box,**
1930s. Casey Concession Co. Cardboard box for "Rare Sunshine Vitamin D" Candy probably sold at Tom Mix live performances. - **$60 $125 $200**

❑ **TMX-170. Cello./Steel Pocketknife,**
1930s. Store item by Imperial. - **$40 $100 $175**

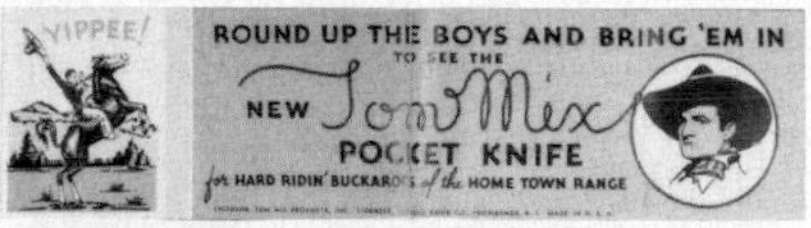

TMX-171

❑ **TMX-171. Pocketknife 6x24" Paper Store Sign,**
1930s. Scarce. - **$175 $350 $700**

TMX-167

❑ **TMX-167. Ralston Diecut Accordion Fold Display Sign,**
1930s. Rare. - **$750 $1500 $3500**

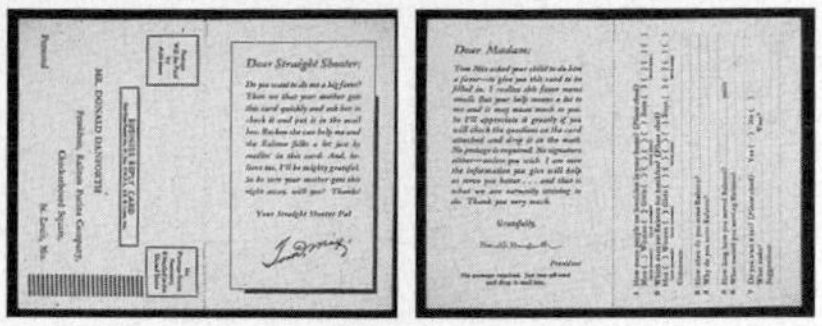

TMX-172

❑ **TMX-172. Ralston Purina Survey Folder,**
1930s. Perforated folder consisting of message from Tom asking child to pass the folder on to mother along with message addressed "Dear Madam" from company president Donald Danforth plus survey card on back of postpaid postcard. Complete - **$30 $45 $90**

TMX-173

❑ **TMX-173. Personal Christmas Card,**
1930s. 7x9" greeting card with front cover art of Indian blanket inscribed "A Blanket Message From The Mixes." Example we have seen was signed but not by Tom Mix.
With Mix Signature - **$150 $300 $500**
Secretarial Signature Or Unsigned - **$75 $125 $250**

TMX-174

❑ **TMX-174. "Radio Rifle" Promotional Brochure,**
1930s. Made by Rock-Ola. 8-3/4x11-1/2" four-sided folder in red, black and white aimed at "Operators." This large coin-operated device retailed for - $434.50. A licensed item although Tom's name does not appear on the artist renditions of the device. Folder - **$80 $150 $300**

TMX-175

❑ **TMX-175. Rexall Toothpaste Puzzle,**
1930s. In Envelope - **$50 $100 $185**
Loose - **$25 $50 $100**

TMX-176

❑ **TMX-176. Cardboard Headband With Feathers,**
1930s. Realto Theater and probably others. Total length of 18" marked "Made In Germany." - **$75 $165 $325**

TMX-177 TMX-178

❑ **TMX-177. "Capturing Outlaws In The Bad Lands",**
1930s. Compliments Ralston Corn Flakes. Paper photo with facsimile Mix inscription and signature. Reverse has short story "As Told By The Old Wrangler". - **$55 $100 $175**

❑ **TMX-178. Book And Album,**
1930s. Autograph book and birthday album. Theater premium, 20 pages. Has write-up on Tom Mix and promotes film "The Best Bad Man." - **$75 $150 $300**

TMX-179

❑ **TMX-179. "Purina Bread" Handbill,**
1930s. For various groceries. - **$35 $70 $100**

Bring this Ticket to
Schines State
Cortland, N. Y.
Nº 4451
MATINEE OF AUGUST 6th
You May Win a Beautiful Pony
"TONY" the 2nd
Given Away During the Showing of
TOM MIX and His Pony "Tony" in the
"TEXAS BAD MAN"

TMX-180

❑ **TMX-180. Pony Contest Movie Ticket,**
1930s. Ticket offering possibility prize of pony "Tony The 2nd" by attendance at local theater to see "Texas Bad Man" film. - **$20 $35 $60**

TMX-181 TMX-182

❑ **TMX-181. "Tom Mix Comics Book 1",**
1940. Ralston premium sent via mail so rarely found in top condition. Eleven additional issued between 1940-1942. - **$276 $828 $4000**

❑ **TMX-182. "Tom Mix Comics Book 2",**
1940. - **$69 $207 $1000**

TMX-183

❑ **TMX-183. "Stars Of Our Radio Program" Fan Card,**
1940. Back has form message for sending verses to contest song. - **$65 $125 $250**

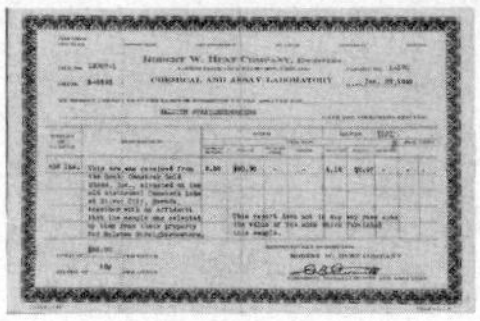

TMX-184 TMX-185

❑ **TMX-184. Gold Ore Assayer's Certificate,**
1940. Came folded with watch fob. - **$45 $85 $175**

❑ **TMX-185. Gold Ore Watch Fob,**
1940. - **$20 $50 $85**

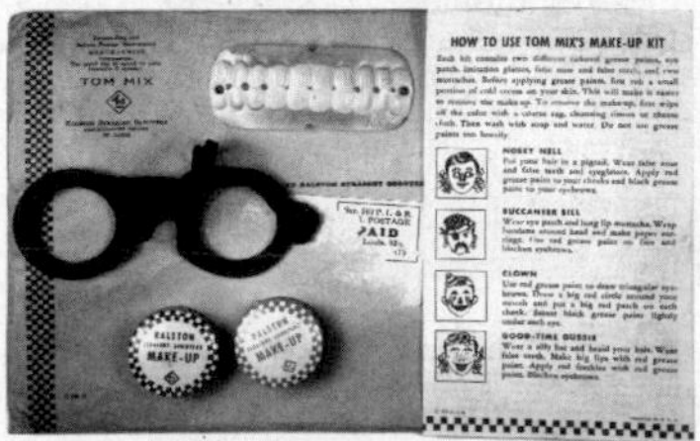

TMX-186

❑ **TMX-186. Tom Mix's Make-Up Kit,**
1940. Greasepaint in tin canisters of red or black checkerboard design. Other contents are instruction sheet, eye patch, imitation glasses, false nose and false teeth, and two moustaches.
Near Mint With Mailer - **$325**
Each Tin - **$8 $12 $20**
Nose or Teeth - **$20 $40 $75**
Other Pieces - **$5 $12 $20**

TMX-187

❑ **TMX-187. Indian Blow Gun Target Printer's Engraving Plate,**
1940. Unique - **$1500**

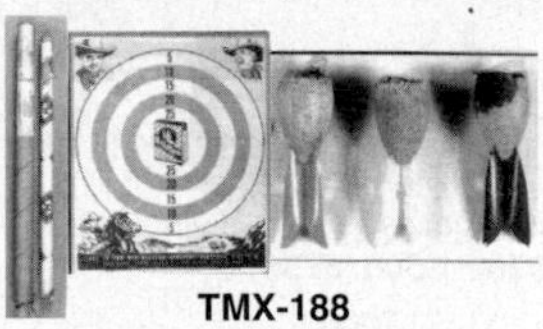

TMX-188

❑ **TMX-188. Indian Blow Gun Set,**
1940. Scarce. With paper target, four darts, mailer tube. Near Mint With Mailer - **$700**
Target - **$75 $125 $175**
Blow Gun - **$75 $125 $175**
Each Dart - **$15 $30 $60**

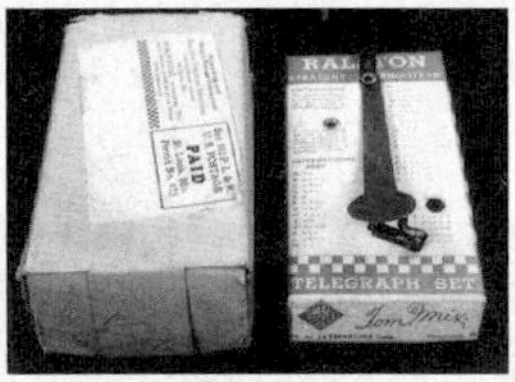

TMX-189

❑ **TMX-189. Telegraph Set With Box Mailer,**
1940. Cardboard with metal tapper key.
Telegraph - **$40 $80 $160**
Box - **$12 $25 $50**

TMX-190 TMX-191

❑ **TMX-190. Straight Shooters Manual,**
1941. - **$20 $50 $100**

❑ **TMX-191. "Tom Mix Comics" #3,**
1941. - **$50 $150 $700**

TMX-192

TMX-193

❑ **TMX-192. "Tom Mix Comics" #4,**
1941. - **$50 $150 $700**

❑ **TMX-193. "Tom Mix Comics" #5,**
1941. - **$50 $150 $700**

TMX-194

TMX-195

❑ **TMX-194. "Tom Mix Comics" #6,**
1941. - **$50 $150 $700**

❑ **TMX-195. "Tom Mix Comics" #7,**
1941. - **$50 $150 $700**

TMX-196

TMX-197

❑ **TMX-196. Six-Gun Brass Decoder Badge,**
1941. Gun turns brass pointer on reverse to one of nine code words. - **$40 $75 $150**

❑ **TMX-197. "Captain" Silvered Brass Spur Badge,**
1941. - **$50 $90 $185**

TMX-198

TMX-199

❑ **TMX-198. "Tom Mix Comics" #8,**
1942. - **$50 $150 $700**

❑ **TMX-199. "Tom Mix Comics" #9,**
1942. - **$50 $150 $700**

TMX-200

❑ **TMX-200. "Tom Mix Commandos Comics" Book #10,**
1942. - **$43 $129 $600**

TMX-201

TMX-202

❑ **TMX-201. "Tom Mix Commandos" Comic Book #11,**
1942. - **$43 $129 $600**

❑ **TMX-202. "Tom Mix Commandos" Comic Book #12,**
1942. - **$43 $129 $600**

TMX-203

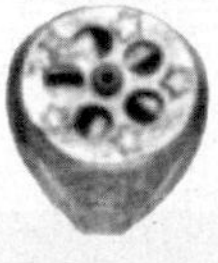

TMX-204

TMX-205

❑ **TMX-203. "Tom Mix" Signature Ring,**
1942. Brass with sterling silver top plate. - **$115 $225 $400**

❑ **TMX-204. Siren Ring,**
1944. Brass with enclosed siren disk wheel for blowing. - **$30 $80 $175**

❑ **TMX-205. "Secret Manual",**
1944. - **$30 $70 $115**

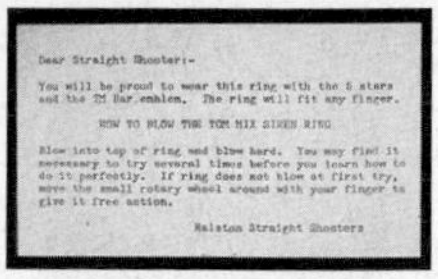

Dear Straight Shooter:-

You will be proud to wear this ring with the 5 stars and the TM Bar emblem. The ring will fit any finger.

HOW TO BLOW THE TOM MIX SIREN RING

Blow into top of ring and blow hard. You may find it necessary to try several times before you learn how to do it perfectly. If ring does not blow at first try, move the small rotary wheel around with your finger to give it free action.

Ralston Straight Shooters

TMX-206

❑ **TMX-206. Siren Ring Instruction Flyer,**
1944. - **$20 $35 $65**

TMX-207

❑ **TMX-207. "Curley Bradley" Photo With Mailer,**
1945. 8x10" glossy black and white with facsimile signature and title "The Tom Mix Of Radio."
Mailer - **$15 $25 $50**
Photo - **$60 $135 $225**

TMX-208

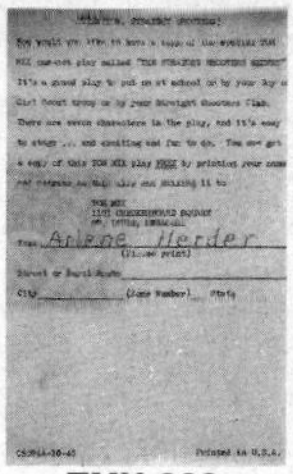

TMX-209

❑ **TMX-208. "Tom Mix Straight Shooters Album" Manual,**
1945. Near Mint With Envelope - **$150**
Manual Only - **$30 $65 $120**

❑ **TMX-209. "One-Act Play" Offer Sheet,**
1945. Offered script for play titled "The Straight Shooters Secret," issued with 1945 manual. No copy of the script is known. - **$35 $65 $100**

TMX-210

TMX-211

❑ **TMX-210. Cloth Patch,**
1945. Issued with 1945 club manual. Red flocking on white fabric. - **$25 $50 $100**

❑ **TMX-211. Straight Shooters Service Ribbon And Medal,**
1945. Fabric over metal bar pin suspending glow-in-dark plastic medal. - **$50 $100 $185**

TMX-212

❑ TMX-212. Fabric Patch No Flocking,
1945. Scarce version also likely issued with 1945 club manual. - **$40 $75 $135**

TMX-213

❑ TMX-213. "Curley Bradley The Tom Mix Of Radio" 78 RPM Three-Record Album,
c. 1945. Universal Recording Corp. -
$75 $150 $300

TMX-214

TMX-215

❑ TMX-214. Tom Mix And Tony "Last Picture" Photo,
1946. Black and white photo card captioned "This is the last picture taken of Tom and Tony together" prior to Mix death in 1940. Ralston premium with publication date on reverse of May, 1946. - **$75 $150 $300**

❑ TMX-215. Curley Bradley Fan Photo Card,
1946. Radio portrayer of Tom Mix, back has Safety Code, but also issued with blank back. Each - **$45 $90 $150**

TMX-216

❑ TMX-216. Glow Belt With Secret Compartment Buckle,
1946. Complete Near Mint With Mailer & Instructions - **$600**
Belt & Buckle - **$50 $100 $300**
Buckle Only - **$25 $65 $125**

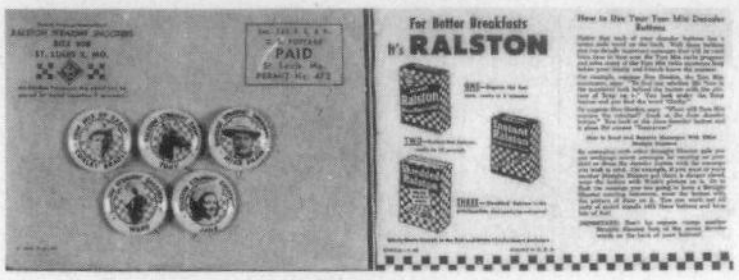

TMX-217

TMX-217. Decoder Buttons With Card,
1946. Set of five litho. buttons.
Complete Near Mint - **$150**
Each Button - **$8 $12 $20**

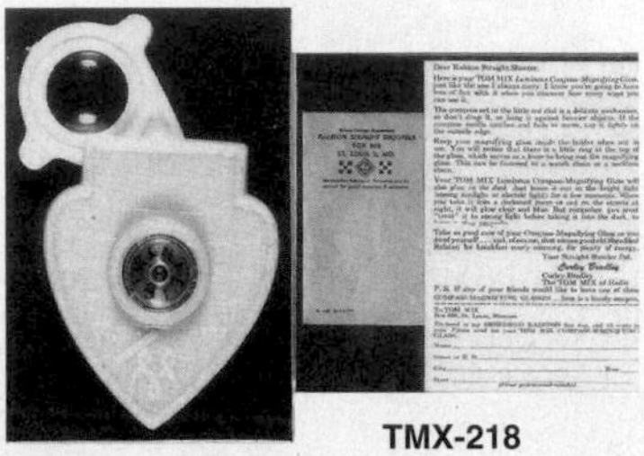

TMX-218

❑ TMX-218. "Luminous Compass-Magnifying Glass",
1946. Near Mint In Mailer - **$215**
Loose - **$30 $65 $115**

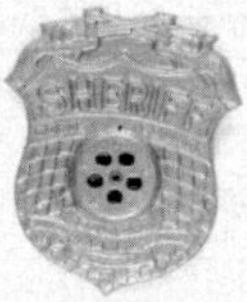

TMX-219

TMX-220

❑ TMX-219. Dobie County Sheriff Siren Badge,
1946. - **$30 $60 $100**

❑ TMX-220. Folder Mailed With Siren Badge,
1946. - **$35 $65 $125**

TMX-221

❑ TMX-221. "Look-Around" Ring,
1946. Near Mint In Mailer - **$200**
Ring Only - **$40 $75 $125**

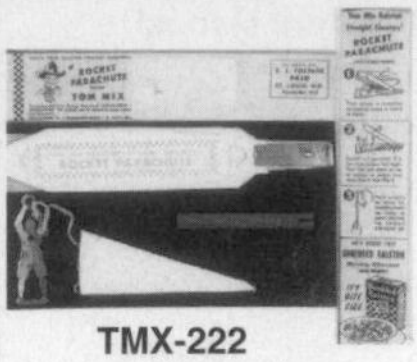

TMX-222

TMX-223

TMX-224

❑ TMX-222. "Rocket Parachute" Version #2 Re-issue With Box,
1947. Similar to original 1936 item with portrait added on mailer box. Boxed - **$75 $125 $225**

❑ TMX-223 "Tom Mix Bureau Of Identification File Card",
1947. Scarce as card was meant to be returned with member's fingerprints and ID bracelet number. - **$50 $100 $175**

❑ TMX-224. Identification Bracelet,
1947. Personalized by single initial designated by orderer. - **$15 $30 $60**

TMX-225

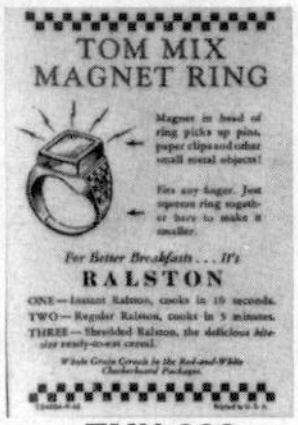

TMX-226

❑ TMX-225. Magnet Ring,
1947. Brass with silver finish magnet. -
$25 $50 $150

❑ TMX-226. "Magnet Ring" Paper Slip,
1947. - **$30 $60 $90**

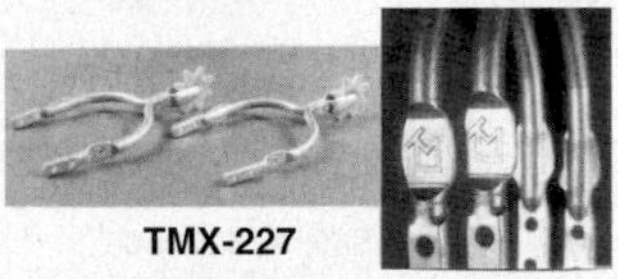

TMX-227

❑ TMX-227. Cowboy Spurs,
1947. Aluminum with glow in dark rowels.
Pair - **$50 $85 $175**

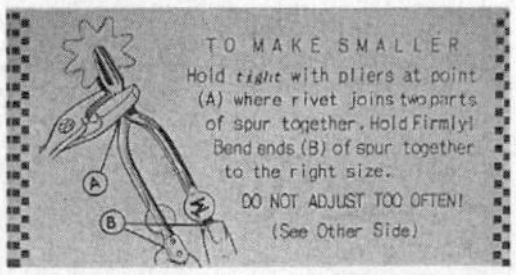

TMX-228

❑ TMX-228. Spurs Size Adjustment Instruction Flyer,
1947. 2-1/4x4-1/4" black on green. Reverse tells how to make spurs larger. - **$10 $20 $30**

TMX-229

❑ TMX-229. Spurs Offer Flyer,
1947. 3x6". This example has coded date of April 1948. - **$15 $25 $50**

TMX-230

❑ TMX-230. "Super-Magnetic Compass Gun And Signal Whistle" Instruction Sheet,
1948. Reverse offers five other premiums. - **$18 $35 $60**

TMX-231 TMX-232

❑ TMX-231. "Compass Gun" Dealer's Promotional Sheet,
1948. 8-1/2x11" sheet describing premium and advertising it receives on radio show as incentive for grocer to stock Ralston Cereals. - **$85 $175 $275**

❑ TMX-232. Super Magnetic Compass Gun And Whistle,
1948. Both gun and arrowhead whistle glow in dark. - **$50 $100 $200**

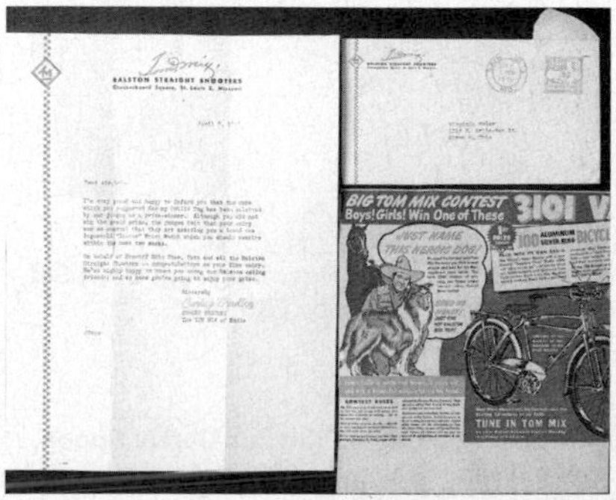

TMX-233

❑ TMX-233. Ralston Contest Winner Award Letter With Envelope & Descriptive Ad,
1948. Legal envelope holding 8.5x11" letter attributed to Curley Bradley notifying one of the winners of Ingersoll wristwatch resulting from entry to name collie dog. Notification is accompanied by Sunday newspaper comic section ad that publicizes the contest and its prizes.
Ad - **$10 $20 $30**
Mailer - **$25 $50 $100**
Letter - **$60 $115 $225**

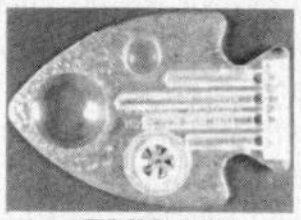

TMX-235

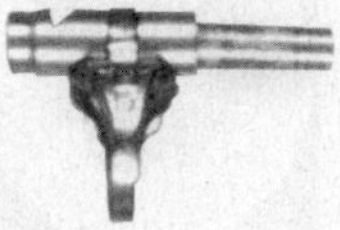

TMX-234 TMX-236

❑ TMX-234. "Tom Mix Safety Story" Poster,
1948. Yankee Network Station. Opens to 17x22". - **$20 $40 $75**

❑ TMX-235. "Signal Arrowhead" Plastic Whistle/Siren/ Magnifier,
1949. - **$30 $75 $135**

❑ TMX-236. Musical Ring,
1949. Aluminum slide whistle on brass base. - **$30 $65 $150**

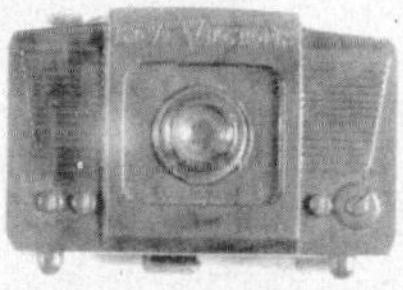

TMX-237

❑ TMX-237. "RCA Victor" Miniature TV Film Viewer,
1949. Brass back includes Tom Mix name. - **$20 $30 $50** (Add $10 Per Mix Film Disk)

TMX-238

❑ TMX-238. "Tom Mix Straight Shooter" T-Shirt,
c. 1949. Ralston premium offered on paper inserted with other premiums. Paper also offers spurs, signal arrowhead and others. - **$125 $300 $650**

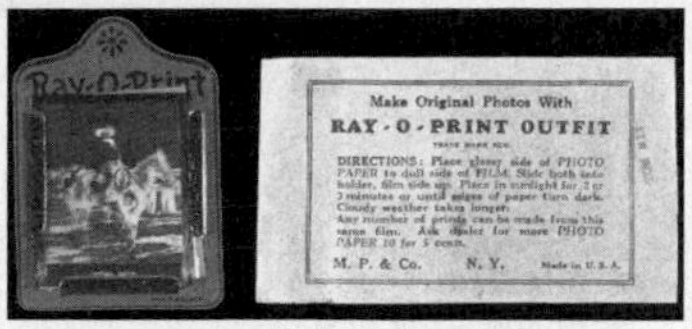

TMX-239

❑ TMX-239. Ray O Print Outfit,
1940s. With tin holder for negative and photo paper with envelope. - **$50 $125 $200**

TMX-240

❑ TMX-240. Ralston Cereal Box Picturing Boy In Tom Mix Hat And Neckerchief,
1940s. 6.5" tall box front panel pictures lad in premium hat and scarf. - **$125 $225 $450**

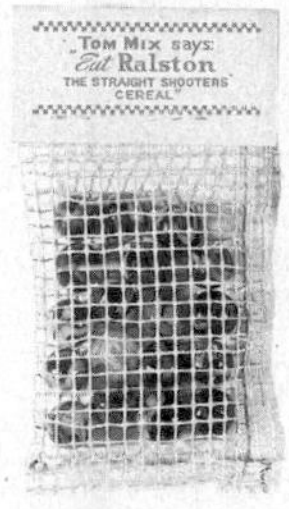

TMX-242

TMX-241

❑ TMX-241. Marbles,
1940s. Ralston premium with 18 marbles in bag. - **$25 $50 $100**

❑ TMX-242. Premiums Catalogue Sheet,
1950. Came with 1950 model TV and Tiger-Eye Ring as single package. - **$15 $25 $50**

TMX-243 TMX-244

❑ TMX-243. "RCA Victor" Miniature TV Film Viewer,
1950. Version without Mix name on reverse. - **$20 $35 $50** (Add $10 Per Mix Film Disk)

❑ TMX-244. Miniature Gold-Plated TV Viewer,
1950. Scarce. Only 200 made for executives. - **$50 $75 $150**

TMX-245

TMX-246

❑ **TMX-245. "2 For 1" Ralston Premium Offer Ad,**
1950. Comic book page picturing miniature RCA Victor television set and Magic-Light Tiger-Eye Ring as joint mail premiums. - **$1 $3 $5**

❑ **TMX-246. "Toy Television Set" Instruction Sheet,**
1950. - **$25 $50 $75**

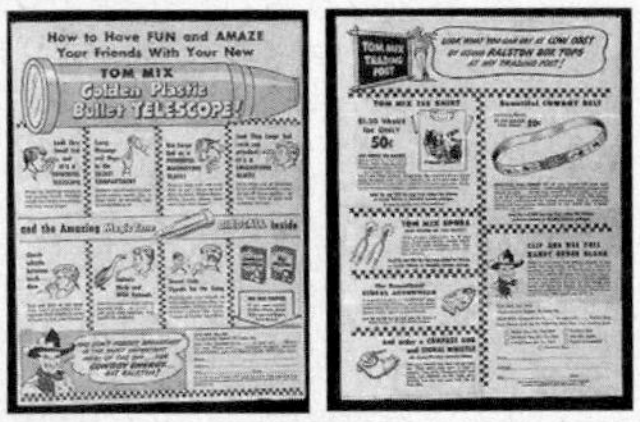

TMX-247

❑ **TMX-247. "Golden Plastic Bullet Telescope" Instruction Sheet,**
1950. Reverse side offers five other premiums. - **$15 $25 $50**

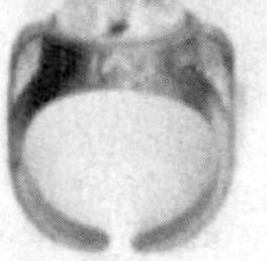

TMX-248

TMX-249

❑ **TMX-248. Magic-Light Tiger-Eye Ring,**
1950. Plastic with glow in the dark top. - **$50 $100 $200**

❑ **TMX-249. Golden Plastic Bullet Telescope & Birdcall,**
1950. Gold plastic holding inside bird call whistle. Complete - **$30 $60 $90**
Without Whistle - **$15 $25 $50**

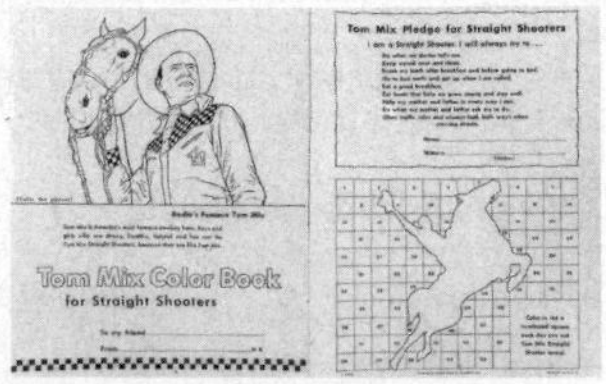

TMX-250

❑ **TMX-250. "Tom Mix Color Book",**
1950. - **$10 $20 $40**

TMX-251

❑ **TMX-251. "Tom Mix Ralston Straight Shooters Club" Revival Membership Kit,**
1982. 50-year membership card, fabric patch, comic booklet, early years photo reprint, current premium photo sheet.
Each - **$3 $5 $10**

TMX-252

❑ **TMX-252. "Tom Mix Ralston Straight Shooters" Revival Cereal Bowl,**
1982. - **$10 $15 $30**

TMX-253

TMX-254

❑ **TMX-253. Revival Wristwatch,**
1982. - **$60 $115 $265**

❑ **TMX-254. Tom Mix Festival Glass Mug,**
1982. Issued at 3rd annual festival in DuBois, PA. - **$10 $20 $40**

TMX-255

❑ **TMX-255. "It's A Stetson" Commemorative Hat Poster,**
1995. Stetson Hat Co. Large 28x40" heavy paper "Limited Edition Heritage Print" featuring black and white photo in black hat. Others known in series: Buffalo Bill Cody, Steve McQueen, James Stewart.
Each - **$20 $40 $75**

Tony the Tiger

Kellogg's, preparing to launch its new Sugar Frosted Flakes into the 1952 market, called on the Leo Burnett advertising agency to devise a quartet of appealing animals as spokescreatures. The agency's account executive, Jack Baxter, plus art director Jack Tolzein and copywriter John Matthews, are credited as the trio who created Tony the Tiger and his since-forgotten sidekicks Katy the Kangaroo, Elmo the Elephant and Newt the Gnu. Tolzein had Martin and Alice Provensen in mind to develop the characters, but their work on Golden Books prevented this and Tolzein gave the job to Pheobe Moore, a Chicago freelancer. Jack Baxter is credited as the first to growl Tony's signature slogan, "Sugar Frosted Flakes are GR-R-R-REAT!" Tony and his one-liner endorsement roar have been with us ever since, voiced mostly by basso singer and Kellogg employee Thurl Ravenscroft (1914-2005).

Tony himself has undergone some changes over the years, including adaptations to animation, live-action support by entertainment stars, and dozens of plastic figural premiums, but he remains your basic smiling, lip-smacking tiger icon.

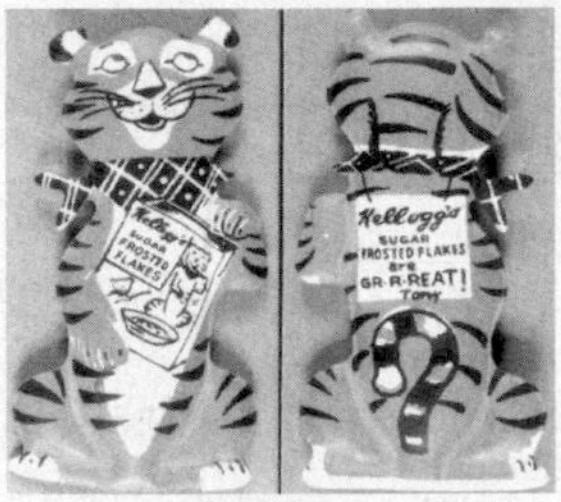

TNY-1

❑ **TNY-1. Vinyl Inflated Figure,**
1953. - **$25 $50 $100**

TNY-2

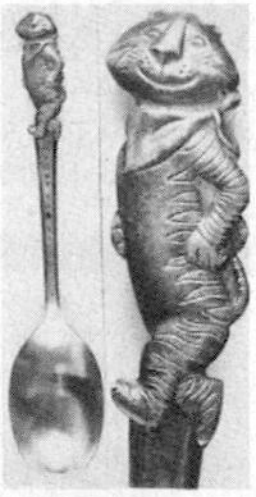

TNY-3

❑ **TNY-2. Tony The Tiger Mug And Bowl Set,**
1964. Kellogg's. Made by F&F Mold.
Mug - **$12 $25 $50**
Bowl - **$8 $15 $40**

❑ **TNY-3. Kellogg's Premium Cereal Spoon,**
1965. Silver finish marked "Old Company Plate" on reverse. - **$8 $12 $25**

TNY-4

❑ **TNY-4. Bicycle Noisemaker Attachment,**
1966. Hard plastic with attachment bracket for bicycle handlebar. Top disk wheel produces growling sound when turned. - **$25 $50 $100**

TNY-5

❑ **TNY-5. Cereal Box With "Tony The Tiger Beanie" Offer,**
1967. Beanie has image of Tony's face with attached 10" long tail. Gordon Gold Archives. Used Complete - **$100 $200 $300**

TNY-6

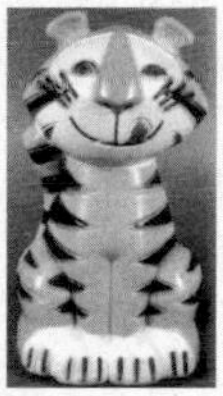
TNY-7

❑ **TNY-6. Tony The Tiger Swimmer Figure,**
1967. Kellogg's. 7-1/2" tall three-dimensional hard plastic with rubber bands holding arms which can be wound to make him swim. - **$60 $125 $175**

❑ **TNY-7. Plastic Bank,**
1968. - **$25 $45 $90**

TNY-8

❑ **TNY-8. Hard Plastic Cookie Jar With Box,**
1968. Jar Only - **$35 $65 $125**
Mailer Box - **$20 $30 $60**

TNY-9

❑ **TNY-9. Cereal Box With "Dick Dastardly Airplane-Telescope" Premium Offer,**
1969. Gordon Gold Archives.
Used Complete - **$100 $200 $300**

TNY-10

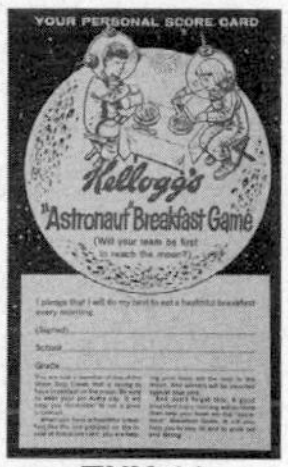

TNY-11

❑ **TNY-10. "Astronaut Breakfast Game" Litho. Button,**
1960s. White or blue background. - **$3 $8 $12**

❑ **TNY-11. "Astronaut Breakfast Game" Score Card,**
1960s. Multi-page scorecard - **$10 $20 $30**

TNY-12

TNY-13

❑ **TNY-12. Plush And Cloth Doll,**
1970. - **$20 $35 $60**

❑ **TNY-13. Vinyl Doll With Movable Head,**
c. 1974. - **$25 $50 $100**

TNY-14

❑ **TNY-14. Tony Premium Watch,**
1976. Kellogg's. Case is 1-5/8". - **$20 $40 $75**

TNY-15

❑ **TNY-15. Frosted Flakes TV Commercial Cel,**
1970s. Image is on pair of 10-1/2x12-1/2" acetate sheets. - **$35 $75 $100**

TNY-16

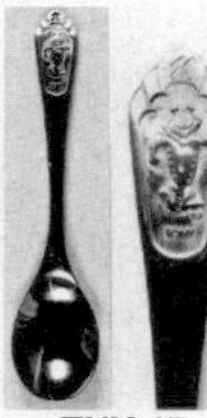
TNY-17

❑ **TNY-16. Plastic Radio,**
1980. Battery operated. Boxed - **$40 $60 $100**
Loose - **$20 $40 $75**

❑ **TNY-17. Stainless Steel Cereal Spoon,**
1983. - **$5 $10 $15**

TNY-18

❑ **TNY-18. Tony The Tiger Baseball,**
c. 1980s. Unmarked but a Kellogg's premium. Regulation-sized and constructed baseball picturing Tony portrait and also detailed by his paw print signature. - **$5 $10 $20**

TNY-19

❑ **TNY-19. Frosted Flakes Canadian Issue Box,**
1990. Offers Spider-Man and Tony The Tiger comic in English/French. Box - **$25 $40 $85**
Comic - **$10 $20 $40**

TNY-20

❑ **TNY-20. Large Stuffed Doll With Tag,**
1997. Sold at grocery stores. - **$10 $20 $35**

TNY-21

❑ **TNY-21. Cereal and Plush Doll Pack,**
1998. Large display with 2 boxes of cereal and a Tony the Tiger plush premium doll packaged in the center. - **$40**

TNY-22

❑ **TNY-22. Ring on Card,**
1998. Enameled. Copyright Kellogg's. - **$33**

Toonerville Folks

The comic cartoon panels of Fontaine Fox (1884-1964) apparently began appearing in newspapers in 1915. The following year the Toonerville Trolley was introduced, and in 1920 the Bell Syndicate began distributing Fox's Sunday page as *Toonerville Folks*. The ramshackle trolley and its Skipper, along with such Toonerville denizens as Mickey (himself) McGuire, the Powerful Katrinka, and the Terrible-Tempered Mr. Bang, delighted millions of readers for 40 years. Several collections of reprints were published in the early years, a series of two-reel live-action film comedies were released in the 1920s, starring Mickey Rooney as Mickey McGuire and Burt Gillett produced Toonerville animated shorts in 1936. The strip survived until 1955. Lilly Library at Indiana University in Bloomington, Indiana has an extensive collection of Fontaine Fox papers and original art.

TOO-1

❑ **TOO-1. "F. Fox's Funny Folks Cartoons" Toonerville Trolley Cartoon Book,**
1917. 8x10" hardcover published by George H. Duran Co. Probably the first Toonerville reprint book. - **$50 $250 $450**

TOO-2

TOO-3

❑ **TOO-2. Cartoon Book,**
1921. Store item published by Cupples & Leon Co. - **$60 $300 $550**

❑ **TOO-3. Litho. Tin Wind-Up Toy,**
1922. Store item by Nifty marked "Made In Germany." Box - **$300 $600 $1200**
Toy - **$450 $900 $1650**

TOO-4

❑ **TOO-4. Toonerville Trolley "The Powerful Katrina" German Wind-Up,**
1923. Fontaine Fox. 3.5x7.25x5.25" tall tin litho. Depicts Katrinka pushing a wheelbarrow that contains tin figure of Jimmy. When wound, she pushes the wheelbarrow forward stopping every so often to lift up the wheelbarrow before continuing on. - **$500 $1000 $2000**

TOO-5

❑ **TOO-5. Toonerville Trolley Aunt Eppie Hogg German Wind-Up Toy,**
c. 1923. Tin litho toy is 3.5x7x4.25" tall and marked "Made In Germany." Toy is of a flatbed truck driven by the Skipper and on back is the rather large Aunt Eppie Hogg. As the truck travels around, Eppie begins to "slide off" the back to the point where she causes the car to rear up. She then slides back and the truck levels off and continues on. - **$6000 $12,000 $20,000**

TOO-6

❑ **TOO-6. Toonerville Trolley's Mickey McGuire" Wind-Up Toy,**
1920s. Toy is 2x2.5x5.5" tall. Has painted composition head, metal cigarette, wood arms and legs, felt jacket and pants plus fabric bow at neck. Attached to jacket is 1" diameter cardboard tag marked "Mickey McGuire" along with Fontaine Fox copyright and "Germany."
Toy - **$250 $500 $1000**
Tag - **$50 $100 $200**

TOO-7

❑ TOO-7. Trolley With Skipper Toothbrush Holder,
c. 1930. 5.5" tall painted bisque with toothbrush slot in base. - **$250 $500 $1000**

TOO-8

❑ TOO-8. Coca-Cola Ad Folder,
1931. Thirteen different reported. Each - **$20 $40 $80**

TOO-9

❑ TOO-9. Cracker Box,
1931. Uneeda Crackers by Nabisco. - **$125 $250 $500**

TOO-10

❑ TOO-10. Toonerville Character Bisques,
c. 1931. Mickey Maguire, Powerful Katrinka, The Skipper. Mickey 2-1/2", others 3".
Each - **$30 $60 $90**

TOO-11

❑ TOO-11. Toonerville Trolley Bisque Figure,
c. 1931. 3-1/2" tall. Japan #5096. - **$50 $115 $200**

TOO-12

❑ TOO-12. "The Day The Big Wind Hit Toonerville" Magic Picture Folder,
1930s. Johnson & Johnson Red Cross products. Came with translucent red sheet for viewing bottom portion of scene in center of folder.
With Sheet - **$45 $85 $150**
No Sheet - **$25 $45 $75**

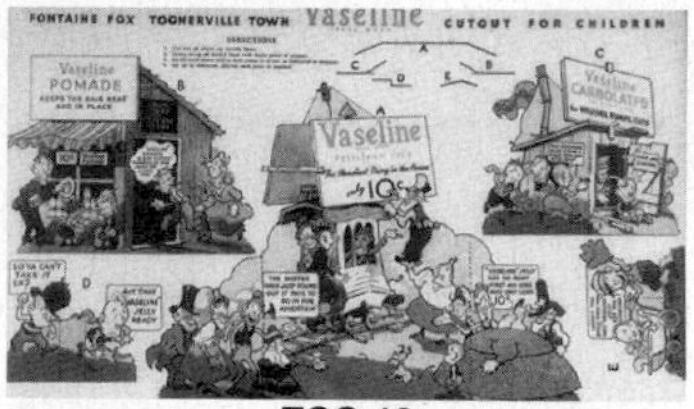

TOO-13

❑ TOO-13. Vaseline Petroleum Jelly Cut-Out Sheet,
1930s. Uncut - **$50 $100 $175**

TOO-14

❑ TOO-14. Paper Masks,
1930s. Westinghouse Mazda Lamps. Examples from set. Also seen with "Super Shell" gasoline ad on reverse.
Each - **$25 $50 $100**

TOO-15

TOO-16

❑ TOO-15. Comic Gum Wrapper,
1930s. Our Gang gum wrapper from Canada. Art by Fontaine Fox. - **$25 $50 $100**

❑ TOO-16. Mickey McGuire Bisque,
1930s. Store item, German made. - **$35 $65 $125**

TOO-17

TOO-18

❑ TOO-17. "Mickey McGuire Club" Cello. Button,
1930s. Probably a newspaper issue. Pictured is traditional derby hat with frayed crown. - **$20 $40 $75**

❑ TOO-18. "The Terrible Tempered Mr. Bang" Ad Poster,
1930s. Eveready Mazda automobile lamps. Paper is 20x30". - **$175 $350 $750**

TOO-19

❑ **TOO-19. "Mickey And His Pal" Premium Photo,**
1930s. Issuer unknown. About 5x7" black and white photo depicting Mickey Rooney as Mickey McGuire with derby apparently shredded by his dog. - **$20 $35 $70**

Toy Guns

It often amazes us when magazines and TV shows list the top 100 toys, guns are never mentioned. If you were a boy born between the mid 1930s through the 1950s you know generally the last plaything you would part with would be your toy gun. Children's guns have been very popular for the last 150 years. Boys and girls loved to play Cowboys and Indians and every once in a while enjoyed being a detective, pirate, army man or space guy as well. These toys were constantly played with and unfortunately many were dropped and broken. It is quite surprising that any survived in high grade much less in the original box. The biggest problem with this important segment of the toy market is supply. The high-grade, unused guns in the box have virtually disappeared off the market. Each time they appear it seems like a new record is set. Holster sets, generic or character related, are in high demand. New toy guns are starting to turn up at department stores and are selling well. Listed are prime examples of toy guns, we will continue to add more items with each update of our guide.

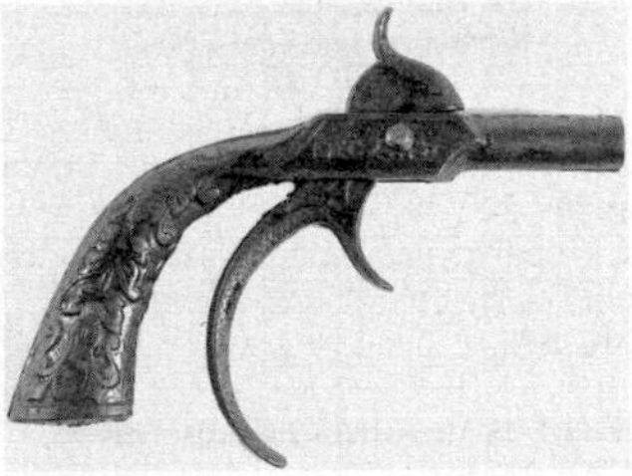

TGN-1

TGN-2

❑ **TGN-1. J. & E. Stevens Cap Gun,**
1870s. Cast iron. Rare. - **$200 $400 $775**

❑ **TGN-2. "Buffalo Bill" Cap Pistol,**
1890s. 11 3/4". Cast iron. - **$200 $350 $600**

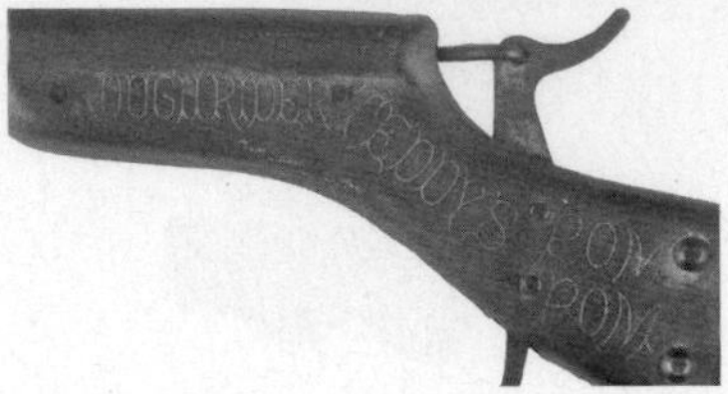

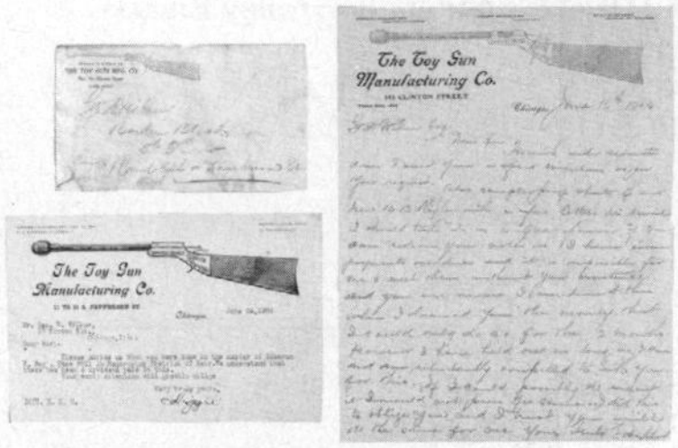

TGN-3

❑ **TGN-3. "Rough Rider Teddy's Pom-Pom" Toy Rifle With Letterheads,**
1902. Envelope is 3.75x6.5" and letterhead is 8.5x11". 24" long rifle stamped on side of chamber "Rough Rider Teddy's Pom Pom." Opposite side smaller type reads "Toy Gun Mfg. Co. Chicago Patent Allowed."
Envelope - **$25 $50 $100**
Letterhead - **$50 $100 $150**
Rifle - **$500 $1200 $2200**

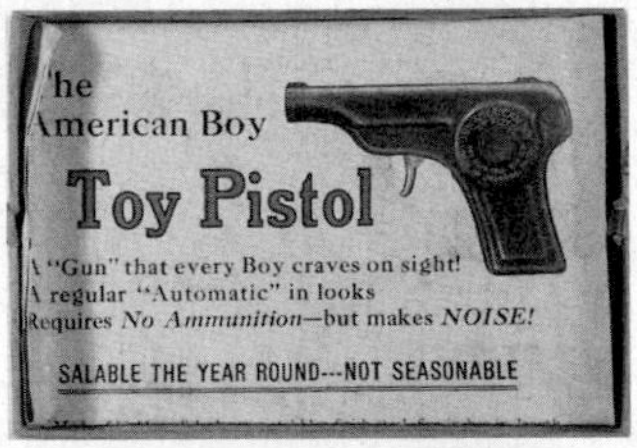

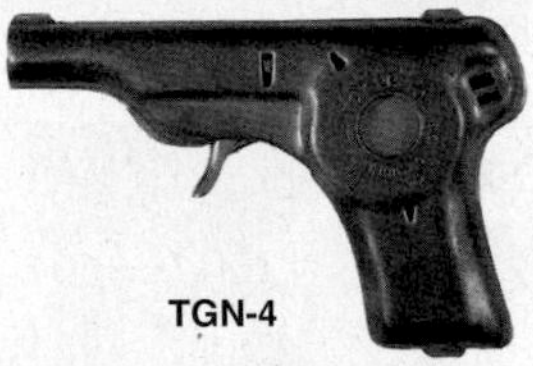

TGN-4

❑ **TGN-4. "American Boy" Pistol and Box,**
1919. With instructions. Rare.
Boxed - **$125 $200 $450**

TGN-5

TGN-6

❑ **TGN-5. The "Victor" Cap Gun,**
1920s. Cast iron. - **$100 $200 $300**

❑ **TGN-6. "Longboy" Cap Pistol,**
1920s. 11". Cast iron. - **$125 $225 $385**

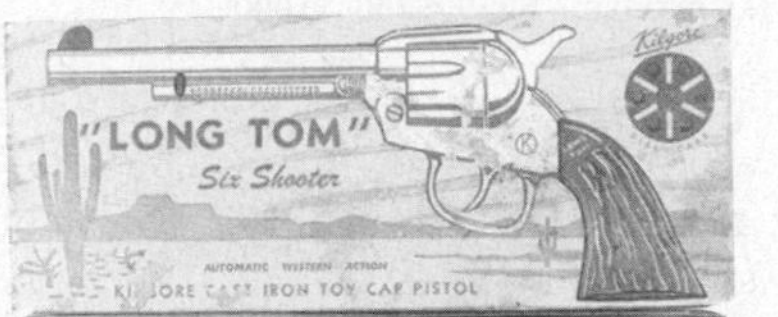

TGN-7

❑ **TGN-7. Long Tom Six Shooter By Kilgore Boxed,**
1938. Box is 1.5x4.25x10.5" and holds 10" long cast metal cap gun with plastic grips. First model with cast iron cylinder with nickle finish. "Long Tom" name on both grips.
Box - **$100 $300 $400**
Gun - **$200 $400 $875**

TGN-8

❑ **TGN-8. "Lone Ranger" Clicker Pistol,**
1938. Louis Marx gun. Was used as a giveaway on radio shows and sold at stores. Box is smaller than box for TGN-9. Scarce.
Pistol - **$125 $200 $375**
Box - **$100 $175 $300**

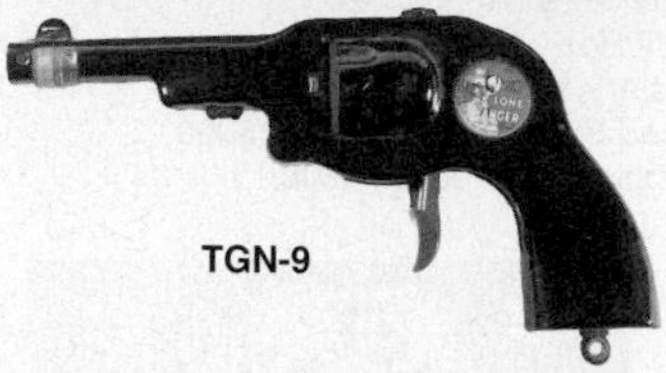

TGN-9

❑ **TGN-9. "Lone Ranger" Clicker Pistol,** 1938. Louis Marx gun. Gun is shiny black with silver trigger and clip on barrel. Colorful picture of the Lone Ranger above handle on side. Gun smokes when clicked. Powder was inserted inside gun. Box is 9 1/2" long.
Box - **$100 $175 $300**
Pistol - **$125 $200 $375**

TGN-10

❑ **TGN-10. G-Man Automatic Sparkler Gun,** 1938. Louis Marx Co. Metal gun with 4 3/4" box.
Boxed Near Mint - **$200**
Pistol - **$30 $60 $120**

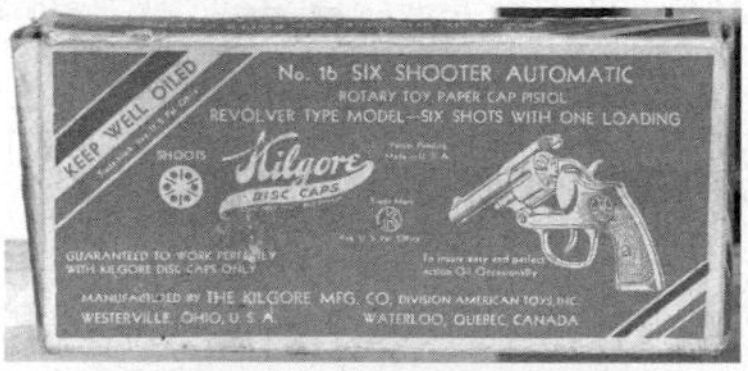

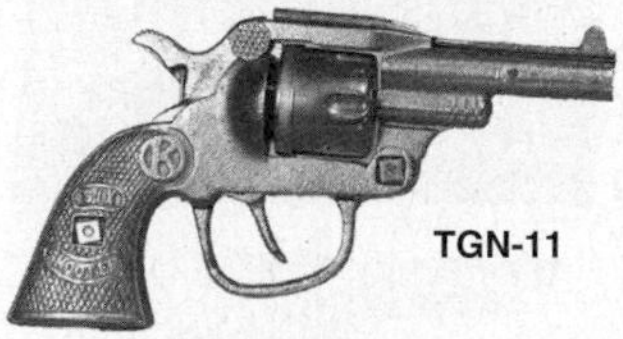

TGN-11

❑ **TGN-11. "Six Shooter" Cap Gun With Box,** 1938. Gun - **$35 $75 $175**
Box - **$75 $125 $175**

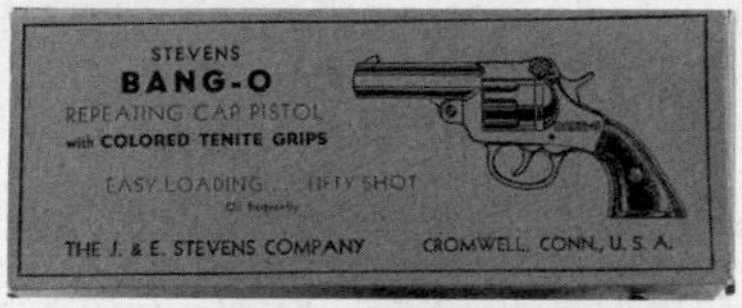

TGN-12

❑ **TGN-12. Bang-O Repeating Cap Pistol,** 1938. J. & E. Stevens product. Dark grey finish with white tenite grips. Box is orange colored with black print.
Pistol - **$40 $100 $200**
Box Near Mint - **$100**

TGN-13

❑ **TGN-13. Bang-O Repeating Cap Pistol,** 1930s. J. & E. Stevens product. With white tenite grips with red jewel on each side and scroll barrel. Cowboy pictured on one side, a horse on the other.
Pistol - **$50 $120 $260**
Box Near Mint - **$100**

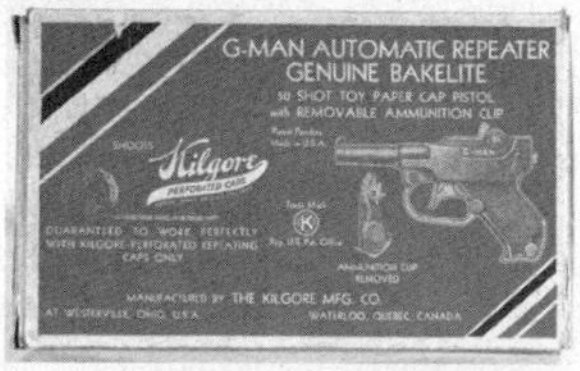

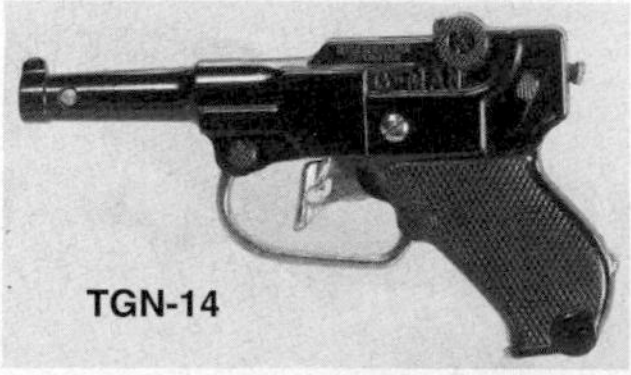

TGN-14

❑ **TGN-14. "G-Man" Automatic Bakelite Repeater With Removable Ammo Clip,** 1930s. Bakelite guns from this era are rare.
Gun - **$150 $300 $600**
Box - **$75 $150 $250**
Complete NM - **$850**

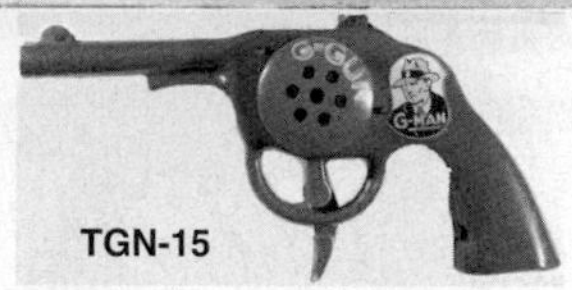

TGN-15

❑ **TGN-15. "G-Man" Gun with Siren Alarm,** 1930s. Louis Marx & Co. Colorful box.
Boxed Near Mint - **$550**

TGN-16

❑ **TGN-16. "Dick Tracy" Click Pistol,** 1930s. Louis Marx product in box.
Pistol - **$200**
Box Near Mint - **$75**

TGN-17

❑ **TGN-17. 25 Jr. Repeating Cap Pistol,** 1930s. J. & E. Stevens product in box. Bright silver-plate finish. Boxed Near Mint - **$175**

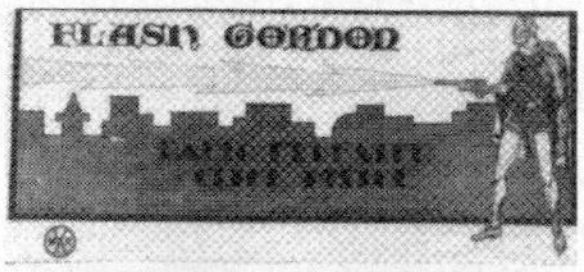

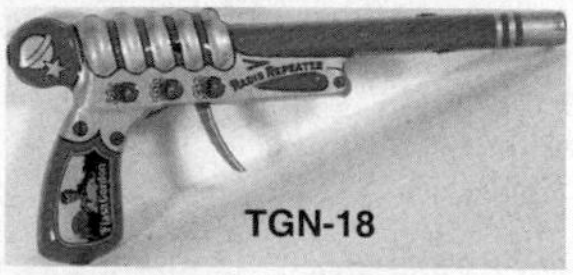

TGN-18

❑ **TGN-18. Flash Gordon Radio Repeater,** 1930s.
Gun - **$250 $500 $850**
Box - **$75 $200 $450**

TGN-19

❑ **TGN-19 "Popeye" Pirate Pistol in Box,**
1930s. Marx product. Tin clicker gun in colorful box.
Gun - **$150 $350 $600**
Box - **$75 $200 $450**

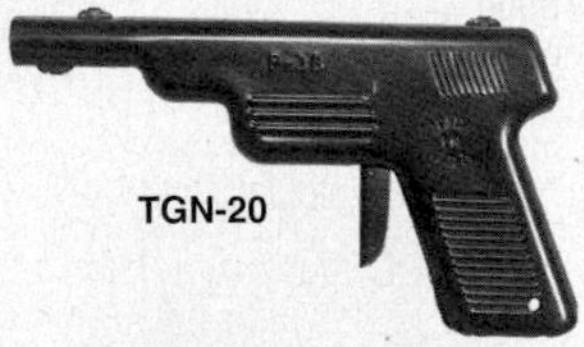

TGN-20

❑ **TGN-20. P-38 Clicker Pistol With Box,**
1945. By Meldon Bros. Boxed - **$150**
Gun - **$25 $50 $110**
Box - **$10 $20 $40**

TGN-21

TGN-22

❑ **TGN-21. "Dick" Cap Pistol with Box,**
1940s. Hubley product.
Boxed - **$50 $75 $175**

❑ **TGN-22. "Spit Fire" Toy Pistol with Box,**
1940s. Stevens 50 shot repeating pistol. Has two color-embossed tenite grips. Bright silver finish. Boxed Near Mint - **$275**

TGN-23

TGN-24

❑ **TGN-23. "G-Boy" Cap Pistol with Box,**
1940s. Rapid firing. White grips. Acme Novelty.
Boxed Near Mint - **$250**

❑ **TGN-24. "Army 45" 50 Shot Repeater in Box,**
1940s. By Hubley. Boxed Near Mint - **$350**

TGN-25

TGN-26

❑ **TGN-25. "Pow'r Pop" Pistol with Box,**
1940s. Comes with 5 corks.
Complete - **$50 $125 $200**

❑ **TGN-26. "Squirt-O- Matic" Water and Noise Pistol with Box,**
1940s. Double-barreled 8 1/2" metal water gun and noise pistol. Daisy No. 72 with box.
Gun - **$50 $150 $225**
Box - **$30 $50 $100**

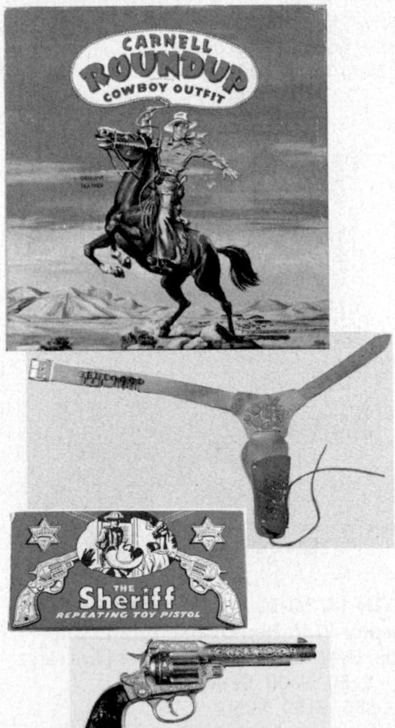

TGN-27

❑ **TGN-27. "Carnell Roundup" Cowboy Outfit and "The Sheriff" Packaged Pistol in Box,**
1940s. Roundup holster with six silver bullets. Has one "The Sheriff" pistol in red box. Gun has black handle with a red jewel on each side. This model gun is scarcer than the white handled model shown in TGN-28.
Outfit Box - **$40 $80 $150**
Holster - **$50 $100 $150**
Boxed Black Handled Gun - **$300**
Complete Near Mint - **$600**

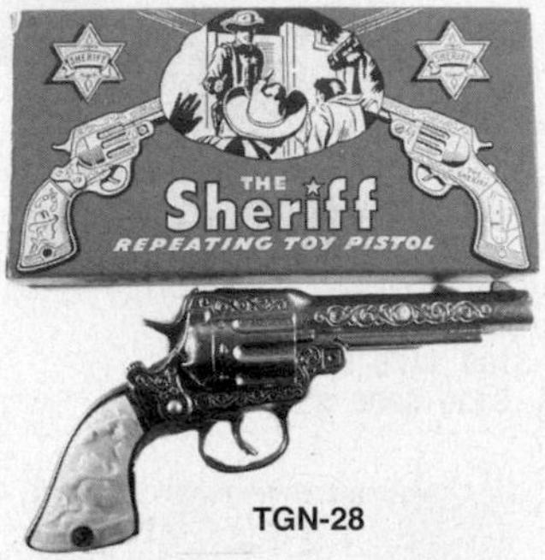

TGN-28

❑ **TGN-28. "The Sheriff" Repeating Toy Cap Pistol in Box,**
1940s. Similar to TGN-27 model gun but has white grips with a red jewel on each side.
Boxed Near Mint - **$300**

TGN-29

❑ **TGN-29. "The American" Toy Cap Pistol in Original Box,**
1940s. Made by Kilgore. 10" gun with moving cylinder.
Gun - **$175 $400 $850**
Original Box - **$150 $400 $500**

TGN-30

❑ TGN-30. "Ranger Gun" Boxed,
1940s. Leslie-Henry. 1.5x4x8" box with portrait of Ranger and text "Ranger Official Gun." Bottom notation is "M.A. Henry Co., New York." Box holds 8" long aluminum single-shot gun with red plastic horsehead grips.
Box - **$25 $50 $100**
Gun - **$25 $50 $100**

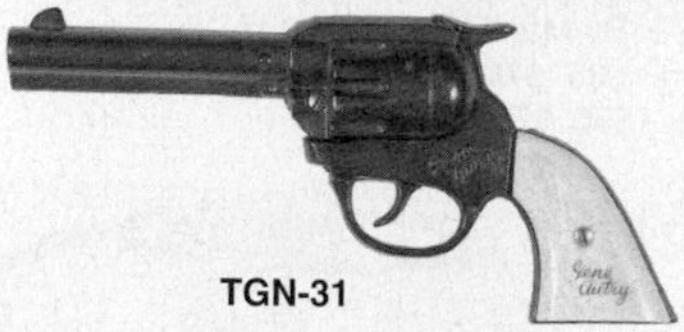

TGN-31

❑ TGN-31. "Public Cowboy #1" Gene Autry Cap Pistol,
1940s. Patterned after the movie gun.
Gun - **$135 $225 $475**
Box - **$100 $200 $300**

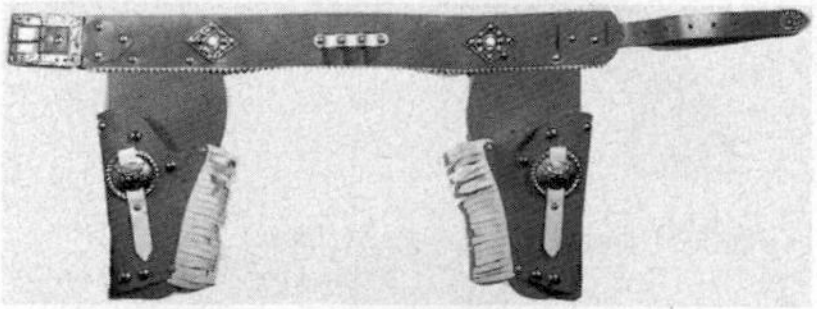

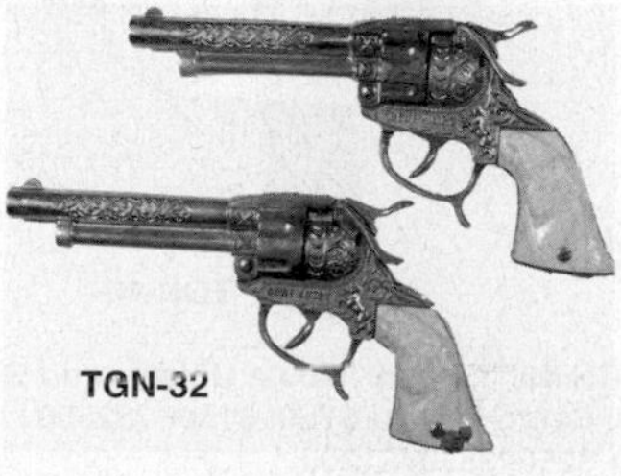

TGN-32

❑ TGN-32. Gene Autry Double Holster Set,
1940s. Guns are Leslie Stevens nickel-finish models with white grips embossed with a horse.
Box - **$150 $200 $300**
Double Holster - **$75 $150 $300**
Each Gun - **$85 $175 $375**
Complete Near Mint - **$1350**

TGN-33

❑ TGN-33. Gene Autry Cap Pistol -Jr. Model,
1940s. Black with white grips.
Gun - **$110 $200 $325**
Box - **$75 $135 $250**

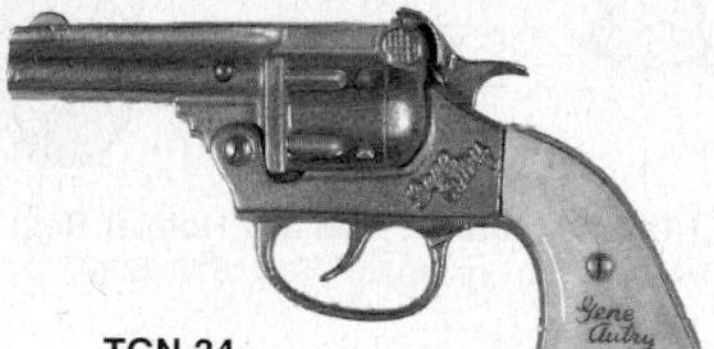

TGN-34

❑ TGN-34. Gene Autry Grey Cap Pistol,
1940s. Grey with white grips.- **$110 $200 $325**

TGN-35

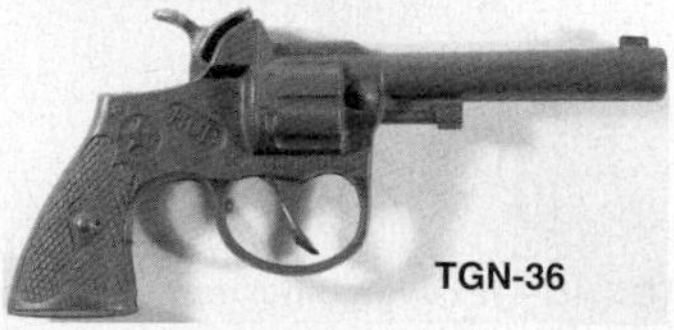

TGN-36

❑ TGN-35. "Teddy" Cap Gun,
1940s. Hubley. Cast iron. - **$25 $50 $100**

❑ TGN-36. "Hub" Cap Gun,
1940s. Hubley. Grey cast iron. - **$25 $50 $100**

TGN-37

❑ TGN-37. "Red Ranger" Metal Clicker Gun,
1940s. 8" Wyandotte Toy. - **$50 $100 $150**

TGN-38

❑ TGN-38. "Trooper" Cap Pistol in Box,
1940s. Hubley. Dull silver finish with black handle and red star. Box is darker red lettering on brown paper. Boxed Near Mint - **$275**

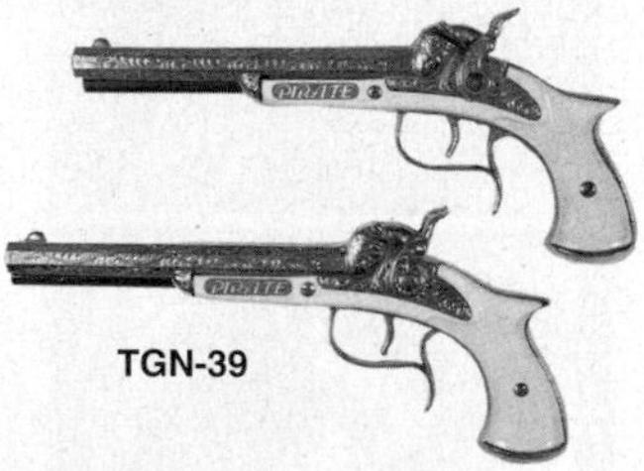

TGN-39

❑ TGN-39. "Pirate" Pistol in Original Box,
1940s. Hubley. Box is scarce.
Box - **$100 $200 $300**
Each Gun Pictured- **$75 $150 $300**

TGN-40

❑ **TGN-40. "Buffalo Bill" Repeating Toy Cap Pistol in Box,**
1940s. J. & E. Stevens product in box. With tenite embossed grips with red jewels. Has a cowboy design on one side, a horse on other.
Boxed Near Mint - **$400**

TGN-41

❑ **TGN-41. "Ranger" Repeating Toy Cap Pistol in Box,**
1940s. Kilgore product in box. Cast iron model. Bright silver color finish and scarce red grips.
Box - **$75 $100 $175**
Gun - **$125 $200 $375**

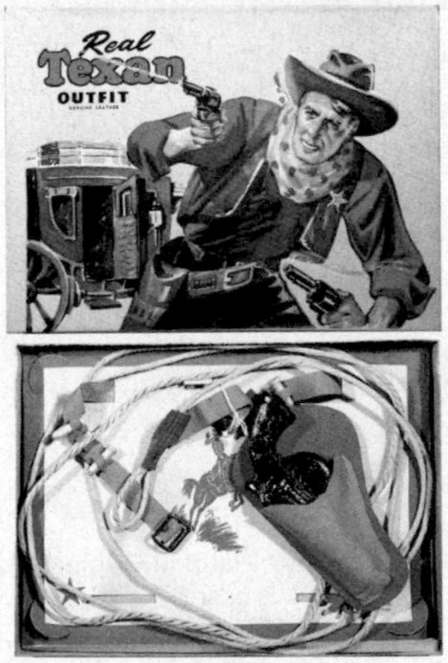

TGN-42

❑ **TGN-42. "Real Texan" Outfit in Box,**
1940s. "V" gun holster set with gun, lasso and belt. World War II era product.
Boxed Near Mint - **$350**

TGN-43

❑ **TGN-43. Stevens "49er" Cap Gun,**
1940s. Gold finish.
Box - **$75 $150 $300**
Gun - **$125 $250 $400**

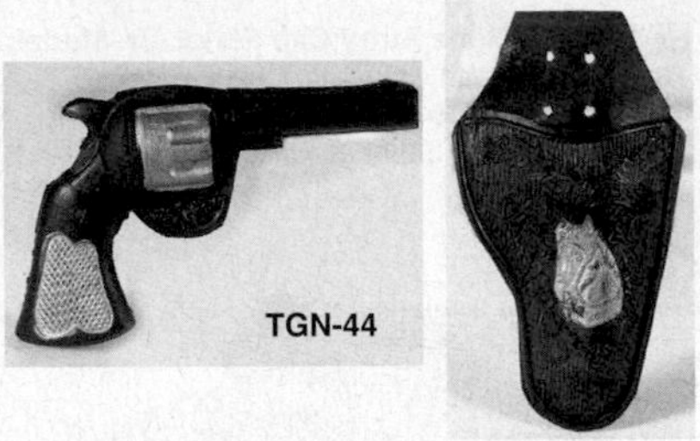
TGN-44

❑ **TGN-44. Rubber Gun and Holster Set,**
1940s. Made in Japan. - **$10 $15 $35**

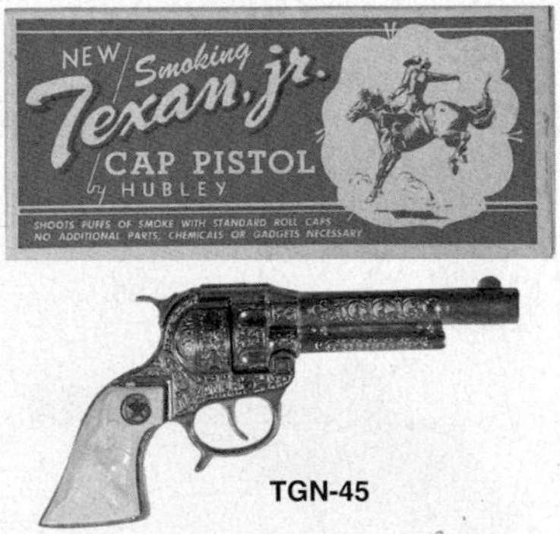

TGN-45

❑ **TGN-45. "Texan Jr. Smoking" Toy Cap Pistol in Box,**
1940s. Hubley product. White grips. Nickel-like finish, not shiny. Smokes when caps are used. Cylinder does not rotate.
Boxed Near Mint - **$325**

TGN-46

❑ **TGN-46. "Siren" Signal Pistol,**
1950. By Marx Toys. With box.
Gun - **$35 $75 $125**
Box - **$50 $75 $125**

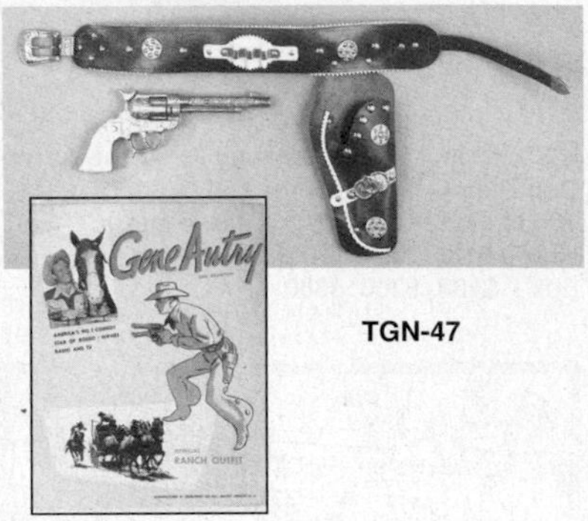

TGN-47

❑ **TGN-47. "Gene Autry And Champion Official Ranch Outfit,"**
c. 1950. Leslie-Henry Co. 2.5x11.25x14.5" box with color photo of Gene and Champion on lid. Comes with 10.5" die-cast gun with "44 Gene Autry" on side. Cap gun has revolving barrel. White plastic grips. Comes with 32" belt, 12" gun holster and three wood painted bullets.
Box - **$100 $200 $300**
Gun/Holster - **$200 $400 $600**

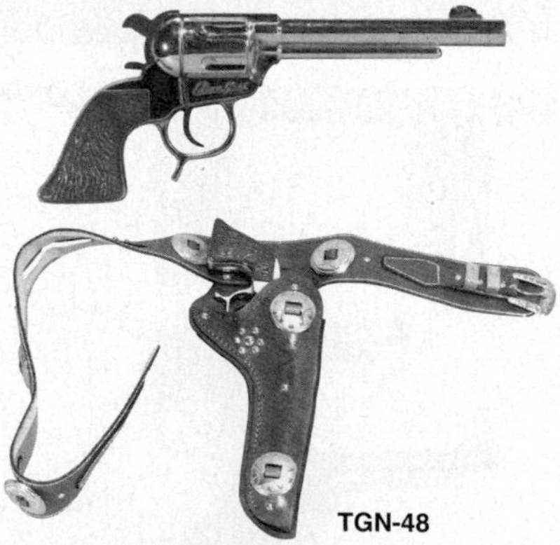
TGN-48

❑ **TGN-48. "Shane" Movie Holster and Gun,**
1953. Rare. Holster - **$750 $1500 $2500**
Gun - **$250 $850 $1200**

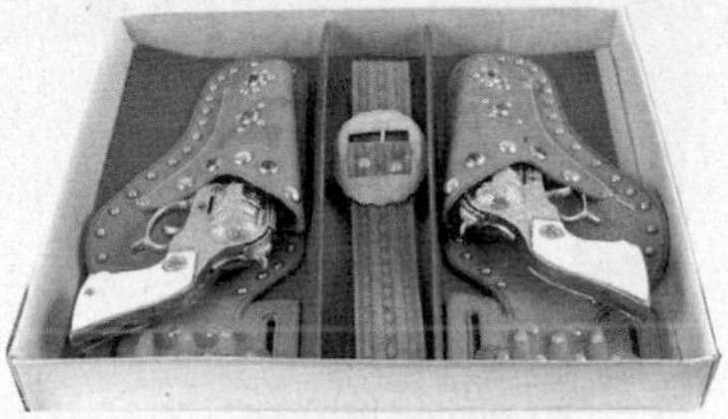

TGN-49

❑ **TGN-49. Star Ranger Boxed Set of Double Holster and Guns,**
1950s. Box - **$75 $100 $150**
Double Holster with 6 Bullets - **$75 $150 $250**
Each Texan Jr. Gun - **$50 $100 $225**
Complete - **$250 $450 $850**

TGN-50

❑ **TGN-50. "Texan Jr. " Gold Plated Pistol in Box,**
1950s. Hubley product. Black grips.
Boxed Near Mint - **$375**

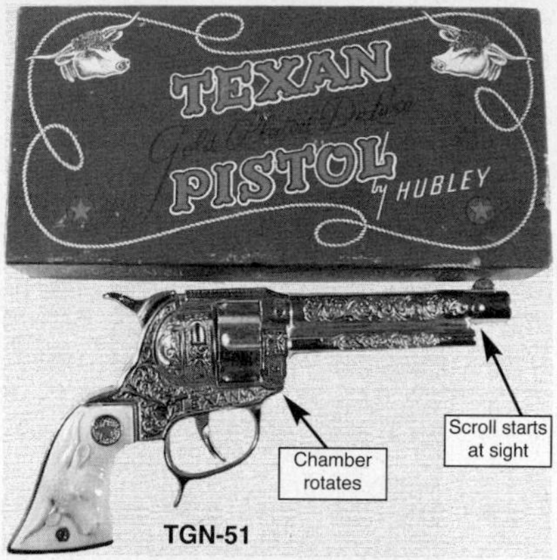

TGN-51

❑ **TGN-51. "Texan" Gold Plated Deluxe Pistol in Box,**
1950s. Hubley product. White grips.
Boxed Near Mint - **$575**

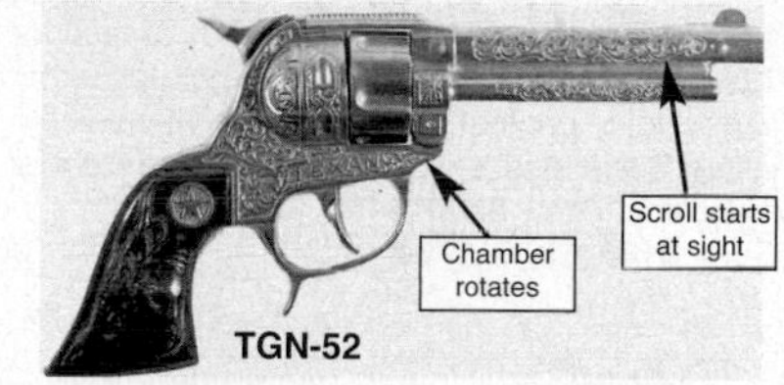

TGN-52

❑ **TGN-52. "Texan" Silver Plated Pistol,**
1950s. Hubley product. Black plastic grips.
Gun only - **$275**

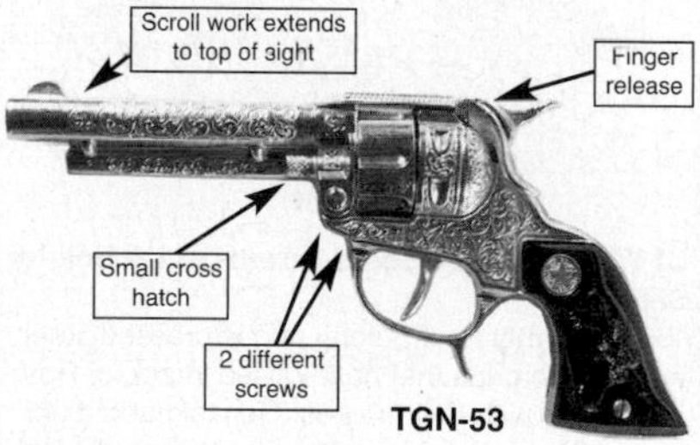

TGN-53

❑ **TGN-53. "Texan" Gold Plated Deluxe Pistol,**
1950s. Hubley product. Black grips. Revolving cylinder.
Gun only - **$75 $150 $375**

TGN-54

❑ **TGN-54. Smoking "Tex" Pistol in Box,**
1950s. With black grips. Shoots puff of smoke when caps are used.
Gun - **$25 $50 $150**
Box - **$25 $75 $125**

TGN-55

❑ **TGN-55. "Cowboy" Repeating Cap Pistol,**
May, 1950. Dull silver finish with white grips and black steer head on grips. Also comes in shiny silver finish with white grips and white steer head on grips (not pictured.)
Box - **$60 $125 $200**
Gun - **$75 $150 $300**

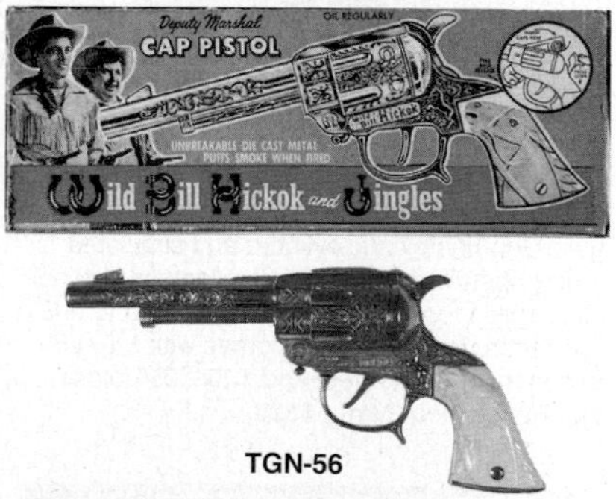

TGN-56

❑ **TGN-56. "Wild Bill Hickok" Cap Gun,**
1952. Bright silver finish with white grips. Toy produced to support popular TV series which began in 1951.
Box - **$100 $250 $350**
Gun - **$100 $200 $425**

TGN-57

❑ **TGN-57.**
Official Annie Oakley Cowgirl Holster Set,
1955. With guns, cuffs and spurs. Rare.
NM Boxed Complete - **$4200**

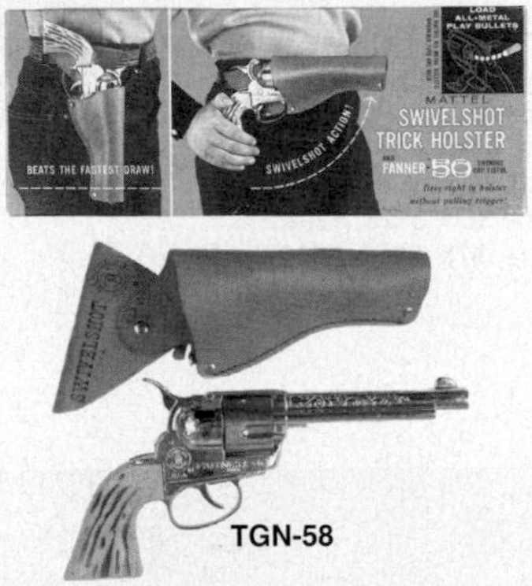

TGN-58

❑ **TGN-58. "Mattel Swivelshot Trick Holster And Fanner 50 Smoking Cap Pistol" Boxed,**
c. 1958. Mattel. 2.5x5x12" box holds 11" long gun. Gun has plastic cylinder and simulated horn grips. Comes with 9" long leather trick holster. Three foot nylon string is attached to end of pocket as designed. Also comes with 8.5x11" folded instruction sheet and 1.5x2.25" folded tag. Boxed Near Mint - **$325**

TGN-59

❑ **TGN-59. "Buck'n Bronc Shoot'n Iron" 50 Shot Cap Gun,**
1950s. Schmidt product.
Gun - **$90 $175 $325**
Box - **$60 $100 $175**

TGN-60

❑ **TGN-60. "Cowboy Classic Gold Plated Repeating Pistol By Hubley" Boxed,**
1950s. Paper-covered cardboard box measures 1.5x7.13.25" and holds 11.5" long gold-plated cap pistol in original packaging with velvet-like insert. Black plastic steerhead grips and red star medallion. Box - **$200 $450 $850**
Gun - **$150 $375 $700**

TGN-61

❑ **TGN-61. Roy Rogers Boxed Gun & Holster Set,**
1950. Balantyne. 9.5" long gun is pressed steel with plastic grips that have raised image of Roy on Trigger with their names. Gun is marked .45 Cal. although the original box is marked .38 Cal. Leather holster pictures Roy/Trigger and has simulated jewels. Boxed - **$500 $1200 $2500**

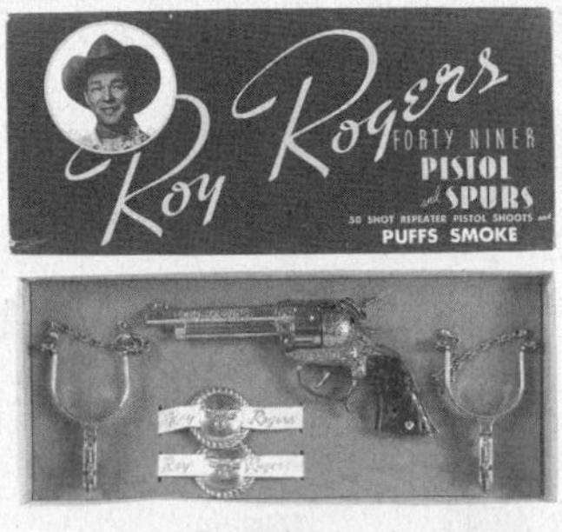

TGN-62

❑ **TGN-62. "Roy Rogers Forty-Niner Pistol And Spurs" In Original Box,**
c. 1950. Leslie-Henry Co. Inc. 7x16x2" deep box. Box holds 9" long two-piece cast metal cap gun that uses roll caps. Cast into each side is name "Roy Rogers." Black plastic grips have high relief of horse head. 3.25x5" spurs with 1.75" spinning rowels. Also included are two .75x8.25" leather straps with Roy's name in red. This is the gold luster version of the gun and spurs. Boxed - **$400 $800 $1000**
Gun Only - **$75 $200 $400**

(BOX FRONT) TGN-63 (SIDE OF BOX)

❑ **TGN-63. Roy Rogers Holster Set,**
1950-53. Belt holds 6 silver colored bullets. Roy's face and name printed at center of belt. "RR" embossed on each silver button and discs. Comes with official box with photo of Roy. Box has "Life Magazine" logo in upper left corner, distinguishing it from a similar box found with the TGN-71 set from 1954. Comes with 2 Schmidt cap guns each marked with Roy's name above the trigger. Guns have bronze colored grips and "RR & DE" embossed on barrel.
Double Holster - **$150 $325 $650**
Each Gun - **$125 $300 $625**
Box - **$175 $250 $450**
Boxed Complete- **$2325**

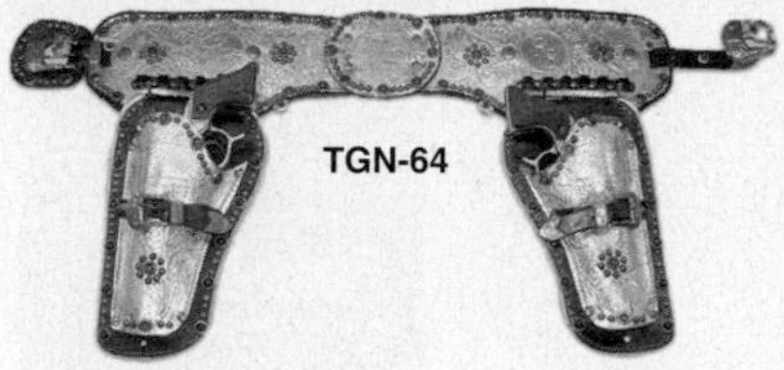
TGN-64

❑ **TGN-64. "Roy Rogers" Ornate Silver Color Holsters With Schmidt Cap Guns,**
1950-53. Double Holster - **$250 $650 $1000**
Each Gun - **$125 $250 $625**
Complete - **$500 $1150 $2250**

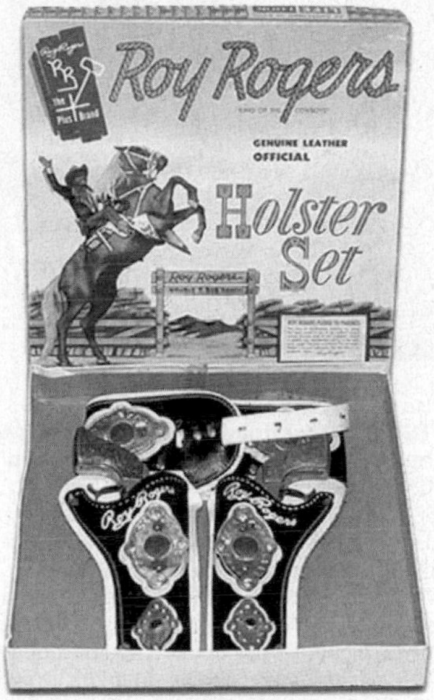

TGN-65

❑ **TGN-65. "Roy Rogers" Holster and Gun Set,**
1950-53. Complete in NM with box. - **$2750**

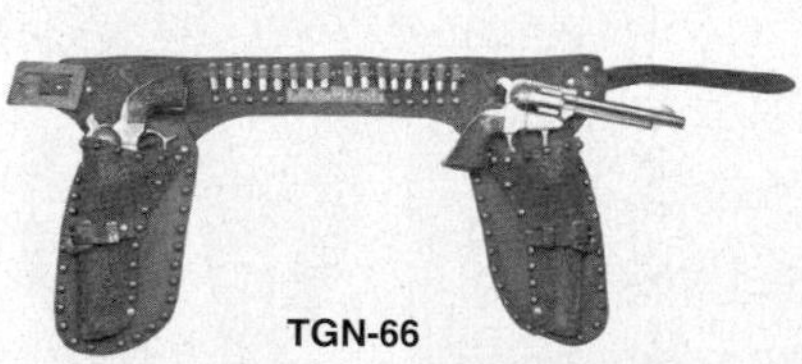
TGN-66

❑ **TGN-66. Roy Rogers Double Holster Gun Set,**
1953. Sold for $10.95 in 1953, the highest priced set that year. Exact duplicate of the holster worn by Roy on his TV program during this time. Guns are bronze colored with simulated bone handles. Model number 2399.
Double Holster - **$300 $425 $650**
Each Gun - **$175 $300 $625**

TGN-67

❑ **TGN-67. "Roy Rogers" Shootin' Iron,**
1953. Gold colored grips and polished nickel appearance. Comes in card with Roy's picture.
Gun on Card Near Mint - **$1250**

TGN-68

❑ **TGN-68. "Dale Evans Queen of the West" Cap Gun,**
1953. D-26 model. With initials in butterfly symbol on grips. If you have read any literature on toy guns, you know this item is highly sought after by collectors. Manufactured by George Schmidt. Very rare box included. Hammer and trigger are black and handle is gold colored.
Box - **$200 $600 $900**
Gun - **$300 $600 $1500**
Complete Unfired in Box - **$2400**

TGN-69

❑ **TGN-69. "Roy Rogers" Holster and Gun Set,**
1954. NM in box with 8x10 photo. Guns are made by Kilgore with white grips. - **$2800**

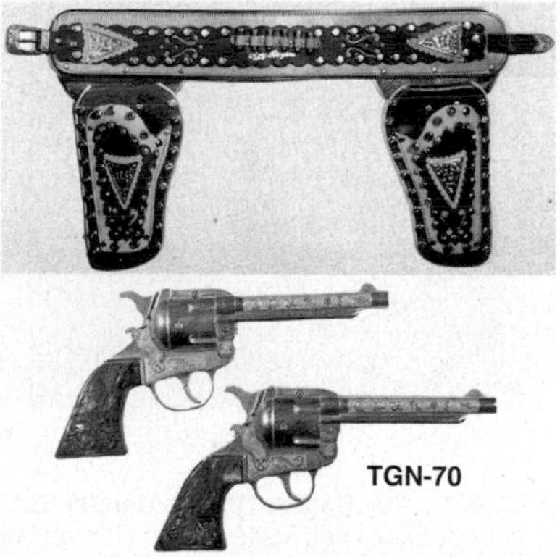
TGN-70

❑ **TGN-70. Roy Rogers Double Holster Set,**
1954. Belt holds 6 silver colored bullets. Belt is light brown and dark brown with many silver colored metal decorations and 2 red jewels. Comes with 2 Kilgore guns. Guns' grips are brown with caramel colored swirls and "RR" embossed on each grip. Each gun is marked with Roy's name above the trigger. Guns have "RR & DE" embossed on barrel.
Double Holster - **$200 $400 $900**
Each Gun - **$85 $175 $375**
Complete- **$1625**

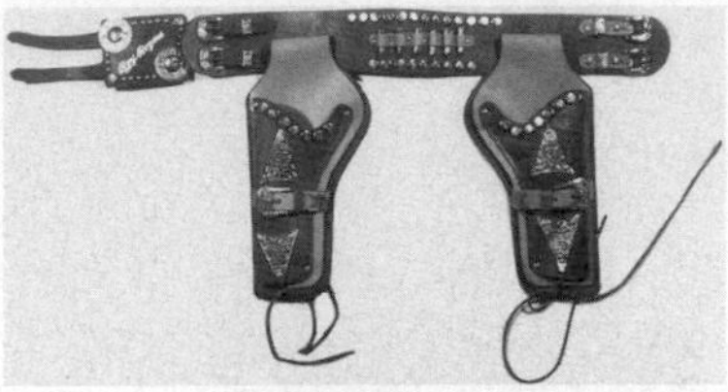

(SIDE OF BOX)

(BOX FRONT)

TGN-71

❑ **TGN-71. Roy Rogers Double Holster Set,**
1954. Dark brown belt holds 6 silver colored bullets. Roy's name printed on leather belt buckle with silver colored discs. Belt has silver colored decorations, no jewels, with "RR" embossed on silver triangular ornaments. Comes with official box with photo of Roy. Comes with 2 Kilgore cap guns each with dark brown horse head grips. Double Holster Set - **$175 $350 $750**
Each Gun - **$85 $175 $375**
Box - **$175 $300 $450**
Boxed Near Mint Complete - **$1925**

TGN-72

❑ **TGN-72. "Official Roy Rogers Combination Set",**
1959. 18" x 28" x 3" deep huge box with perforated lid. Includes leather wrist cuffs with name, leather/metal spurs, red cloth kerchief with metal clasp, rope lasso, 8x10" photo, sheriff badge and two white grip shooting irons.
Set in Box - **$1000 $2500 $4000**

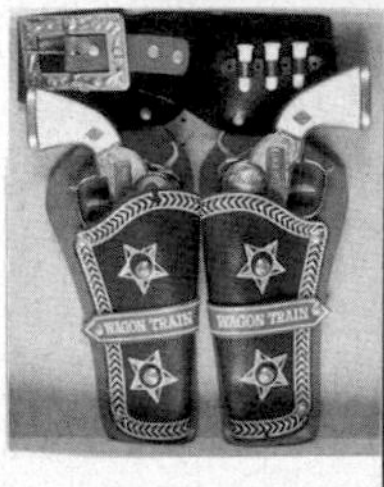

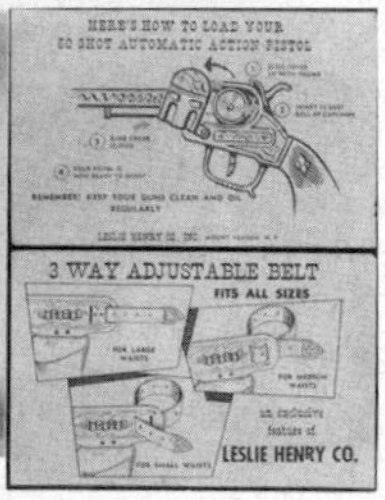

TGN-73

❑ **TGN-73. "Wagon Train" Gun And Holster Set Boxed,**
1958. Leslie-Henry Co. Illustrated and diecut lidded box holding double holster and gun set.
Box - **$100 $200 $350**
Double Holster - **$40 $65 $100**
Each Gun - **$40 $65 $125**
Near Mint Complete - **$700**

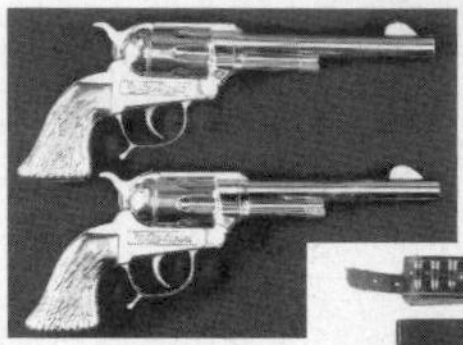

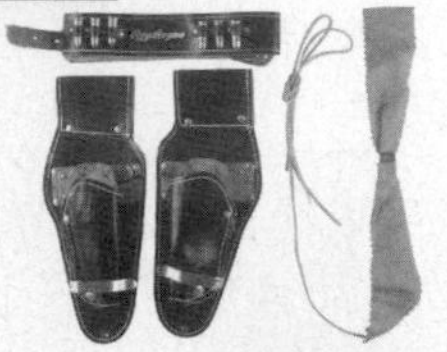

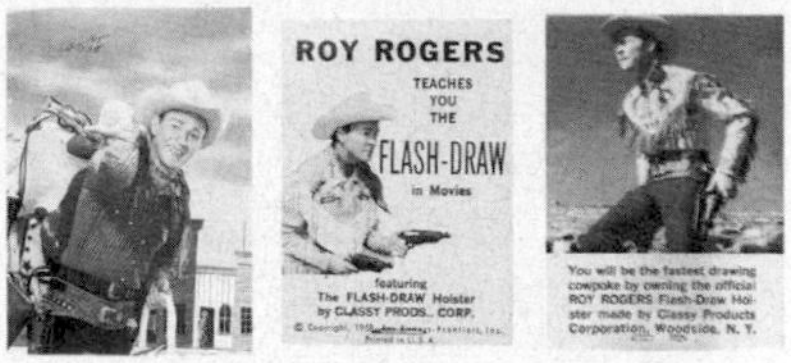

TGN-74

❑ **TGN-74. "Roy Rogers/Official Flash Draw Genuine Cowhide Holster With Swivel Hip Action" Boxed Gun Set,**
1958. Classy Products Corp. Box is 3.5x13x13" and comes with two 10" gold luster cap guns with facsimile signature on each. 35" long leather belt with two 2.5" long bullet clips hold three metal toy bullets each. Belt has 2.5" long facsimile signature gold printed and includes 16" cloth kerchief. 7.25x10" color pin-up picture of Roy with facsimile signature. Comes with 2x4" flip book copyright 1958.
Complete Boxed - **$1000 $2000 $3500**

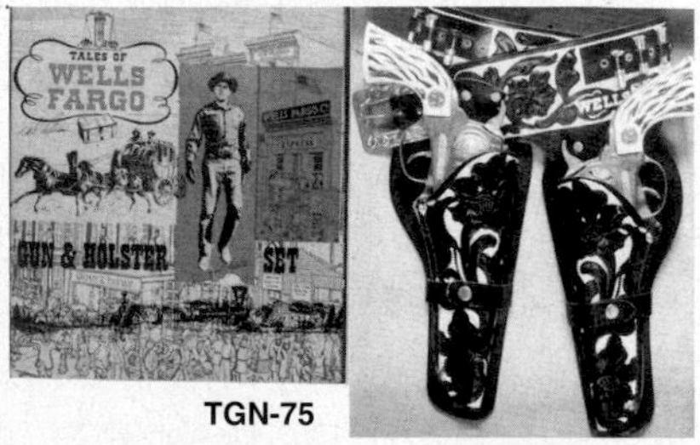

TGN-75

❑ **TGN-75. "Tales Of Wells Fargo" Gun And Holster Set Boxed,**
c. 1958. Carnell Roundup. Illustrated box holding double gun and holster set.
Box - **$100 $200 $350**
Double Holster - **$50 $100 $150**
Each Gun - **$40 $65 $125**
Near Mint Complete - **$750**

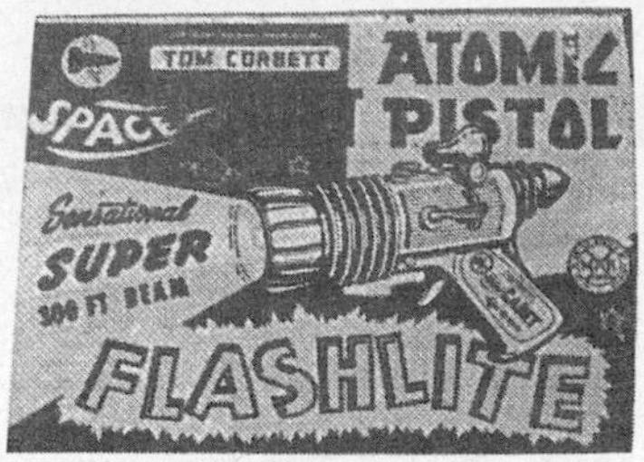

TGN-76

❑ **TGN-76. "Tom Corbett Atomic Pistol" Boxed,**
1950s. Marx Toys. Battery-operated flashlight gun. Gun - **$50 $150 $275**
Box - **$50 $150 $300**

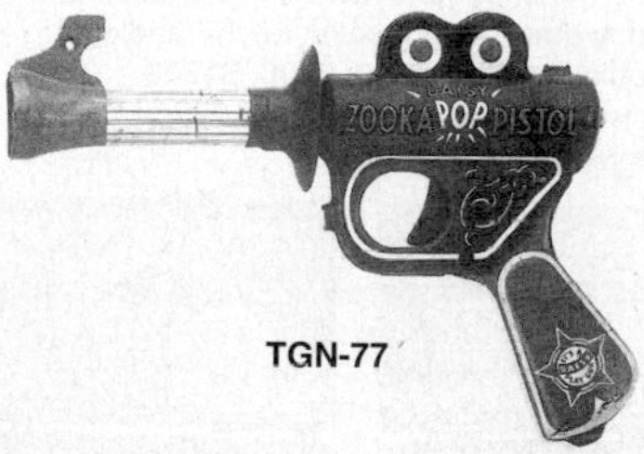

TGN-77

❑ **TGN-77. "Daisy Zooka 'Pop' Pistol" Boxed,**
1950s. Different graphics but same shape as the 1935 Buck Rogers Rocket Pistol XZ-35. Came in illustrated display box.
Also see TGN-117.
Pistol - **$100 $200 $400**
Box - **$75 $125 $250**

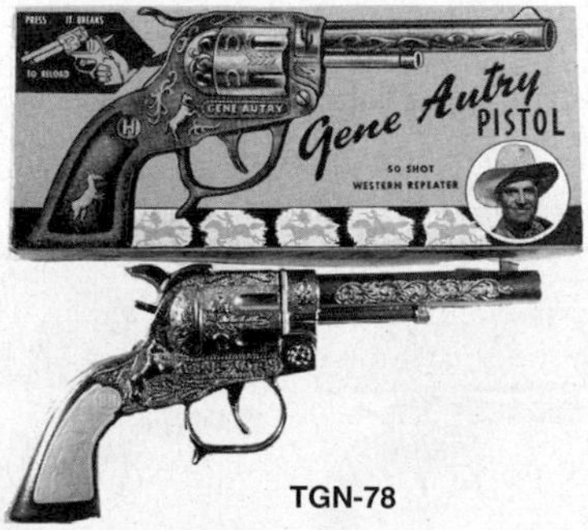

TGN-78

❑ **TGN-78. Gene Autry "50 Shot Western Repeater" Cap Gun,**
1950s. Leslie Henry model. Has white grips and a bright silver finish. Boxed Near Mint - **$475**

TGN-79

❑ **TGN-79. Gene Autry "50 Shot Western Repeater" Cap Gun,**
1950s. Leslie Henry model. Has white grips and a bright gold finish. Scarcer than silver finish model. Boxed Near Mint - **$575**

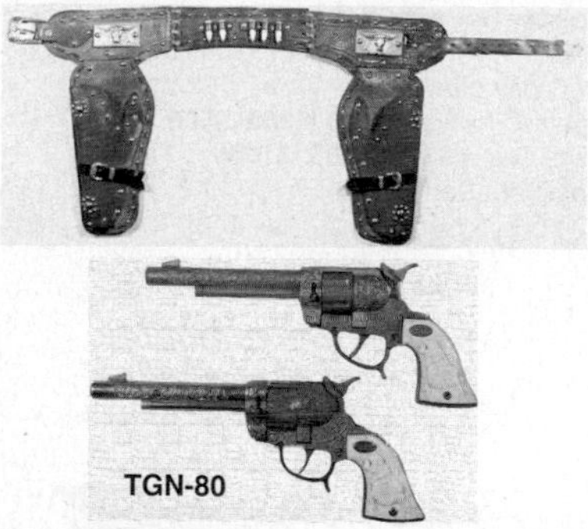

TGN-80

❑ **TGN-80. Gene Autry "Flying A" Double Holster Set,**
1950s. Has "Flying A" emblem pictured on each holster. Gene Autry's name is at the top of the emblem. Belt has 5 silver colored bullets. Set includes 2 "44" Leslie Henry cap guns with white horse head grips.
Holster - **$200 $300 $650**
Each Gun - **$125 $250 $450**
Complete - **$1550**

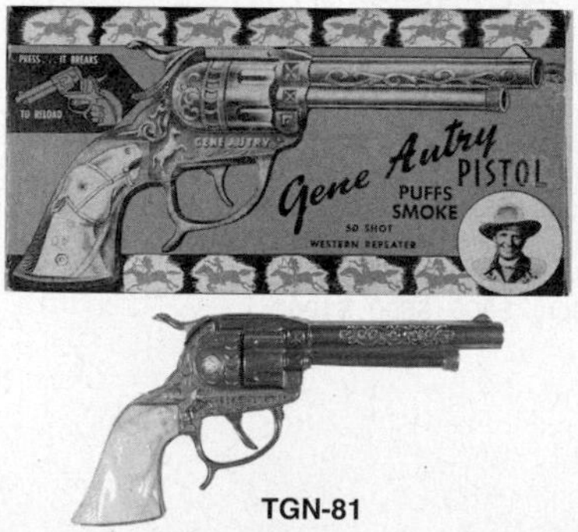

TGN-81

❑ **TGN-81. Gene Autry "50 Shot Western Repeater" Cap Gun with Box,**
1950s. Leslie Henry model. Puffs smoke.
Box - **$85 $175 $250**
Gun - **$85 $175 $350**

TGN-82

❑ **TGN-82. Gene Autry "Western Pistol" Cap Gun with Box,**
1950s. Rare 11" Box is colorful with photo of Gene on front. Gun is Leslie Henry model with nickel-plated finish. Comes with 6 removable copper bullets. See-through grips are copper colored. Box - **$500**
Gun with Bullets - **$150 $350 $750**

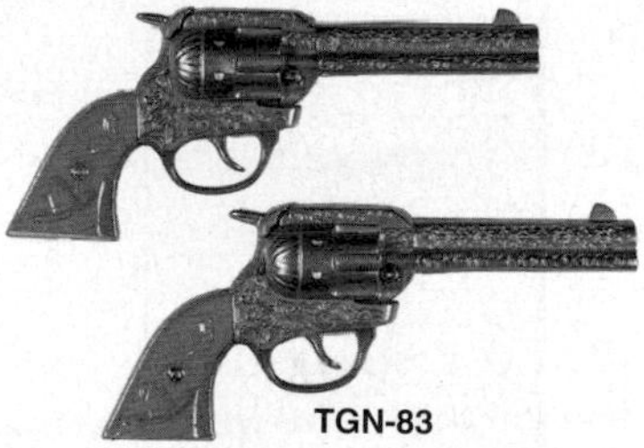

TGN-83

❑ **TGN-83. Set of Gene Autry Cast Iron Cap Guns,**
1950s. Engraving on guns was only used on later issues. Reddish grips. Scarce.
Each - **$275 $625 $1000**

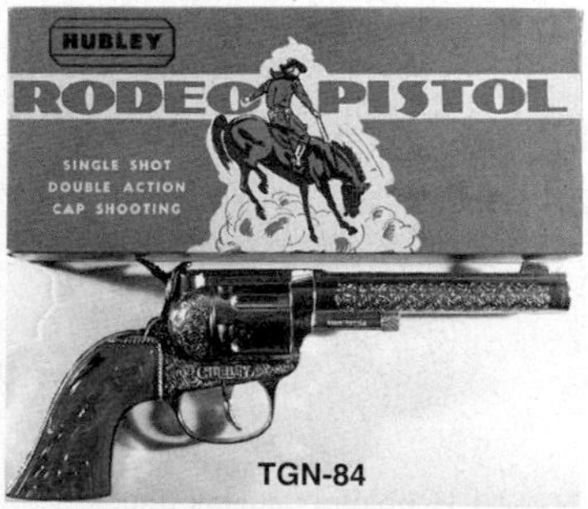

TGN-84

❑ **TGN-84. "Rodeo" Pistol with Box,**
1950s. Hubley product. Single shot cap shooting with double action.
Boxed Near Mint - **$185**

TGN-85

❑ **TGN-85. "Rodeo" Pistol with Box,**
1950s. Hubley product. Single shot repeating.
Boxed - **$30 $70 $180**

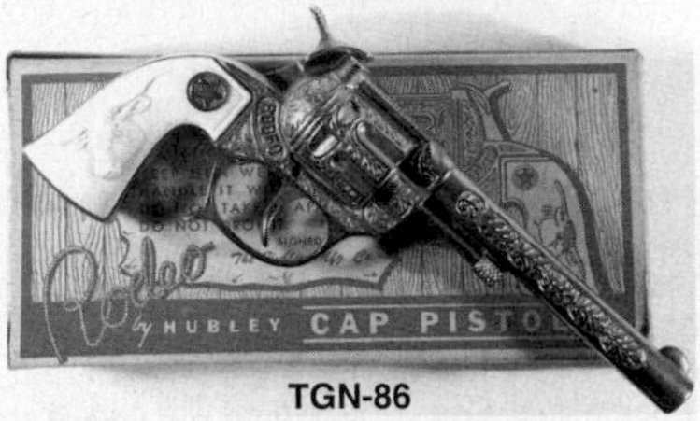

TGN-86

❑ **TGN-86. "Rodeo" Pistol with Box,**
1950s. Hubley product.
Boxed Near Mint - **$180**

TGN-87

❑ **TGN-87. Hopalong Cassidy Gun Box,**
1950s. Wyandotte product. - **$250 $600 $1000**

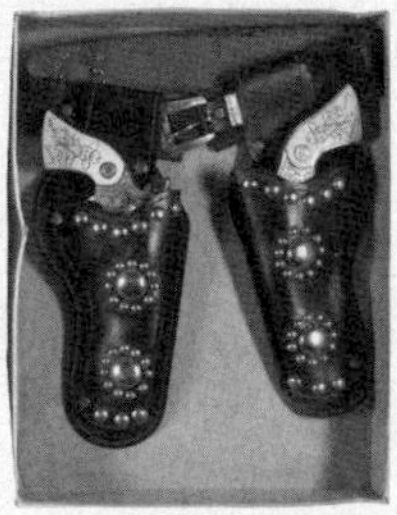

TGN-88

❑ **TGN-88. Hopalong Cassidy Double Holster Set With Guns,**
1950s. Wyandotte Products. Leather holster has "Hopalong Cassidy" printed in script on belt back with two Wyandotte Hoppy silver guns with white grips. Holster - **$125 $250 $500**
Each Gun - **$150 $250 $575**

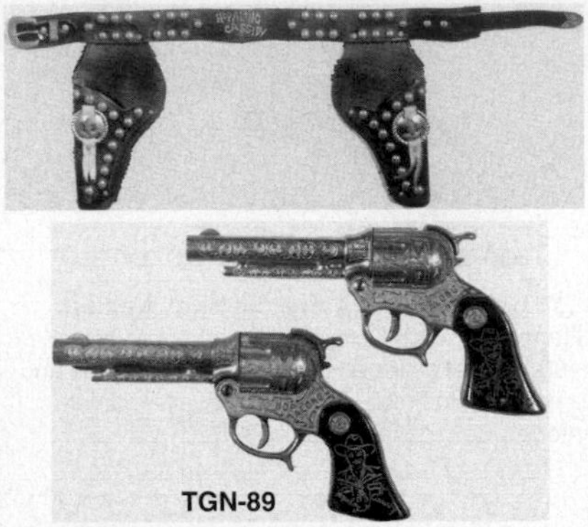

TGN-89

❑ **TGN-89. Hopalong Cassidy Double Holster Set with Guns,**
1950s. Wyandotte product. Guns are gold colored with black grips.
Double Holster - **$125 $250 $500**
Each Gun - **$300 $500 $1000**
Complete Set - **$2400**

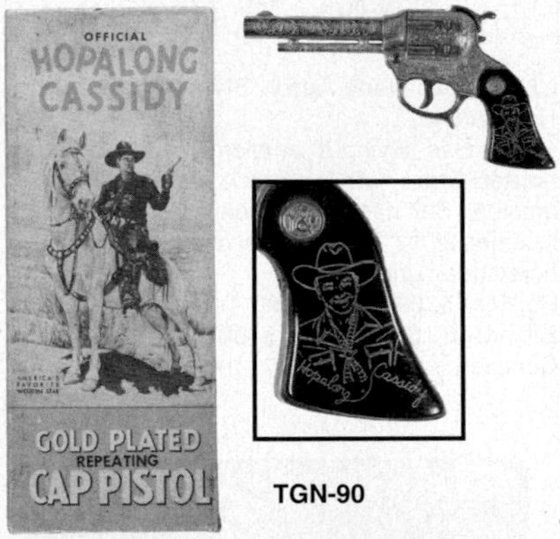

TGN-90

❑ **TGN-90. Hopalong Cassidy "Gold Plated Repeating Cap Pistol",**
1950s. Wyandotte Products. Black grips with Hoppy image and name in white.
Box - **$175 $350 $475**
Gun - **$300 $500 $1000**

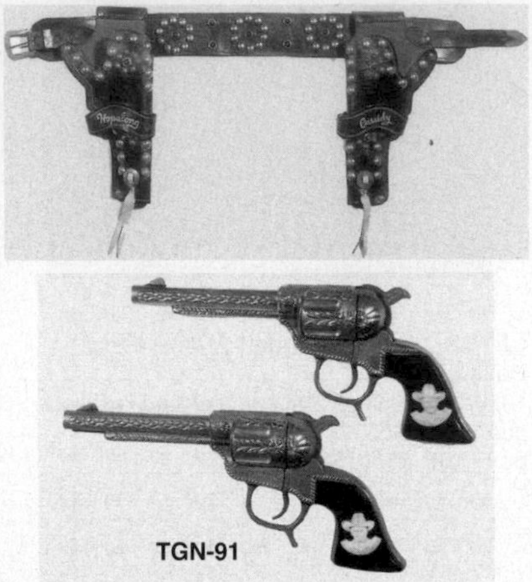

TGN-91

❑ **TGN-91. Hopalong Cassidy Variant Double Holster Set with Guns,**
1950s. Belt is decorated with red and blue jewels. 2 Schmidt guns have black grips with white Hoppy embossed face on each handle.
Double Holster - **$300 $800 $1200**
Each Gun - **$200 $375 $700**
Complete Set - **$2500**

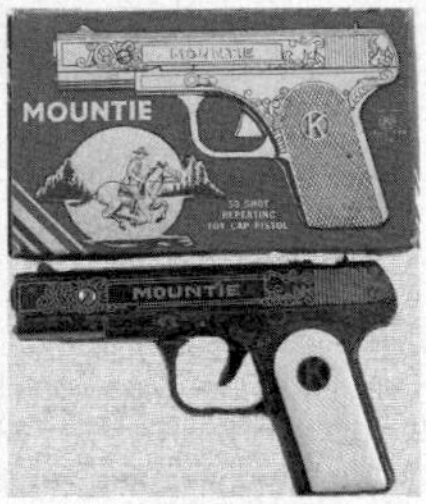

TGN-92 TGN-93

❑ **TGN-92. "Hawkeye" 50 Shot Cap Pistol with Box,**
1950s. Kilgore product. Boxed Near Mint - **$100**

❑ **TGN-93. "Mountie" 50 Shot Repeating Cap Pistol with Box,**
1950s. Kilgore product. Boxed Near Mint - **$95**

TGN-94 TGN-95

❑ **TGN-94. "Big Horn" Six Shooter with Box,**
1950s. Kilgore product #217. Silver metal grips.
Boxed Near Mint - **$225**

❑ **TGN-95. "Buck" Single Shot Pistol in Box,**
1950s. Kilgore product #407.
Boxed - **$75 $115 $190**

TGN-96

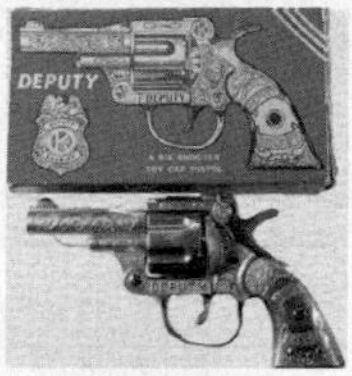

TGN-97

❑ **TGN-96. "Bronco" Six Shooter with Box,**
1950s. Kilgore product. Boxed Near Mint - **$200**

❑ **TGN-97. "Deputy Sheriff" Pistol in Box,**
1950s. Kilgore product #216. Boxed Near Mint - **$200**

TGN-98

❑ **TGN-98. Texas Star Ranger Cowboy Outfit Guns And Holster Boxed Set,**
1950s. Box is 2.5x11x14" and holds two 8.5" cast metal guns with plastic grips. Leather holster has two 12" deep pockets with pressed silver luster accents showing horse head inspired by Paladin TV show. Top of each pocket has 3 plastic bullets in clips. Comes with instructions for loading caps.
Boxed Complete - **$125 $225 $400**

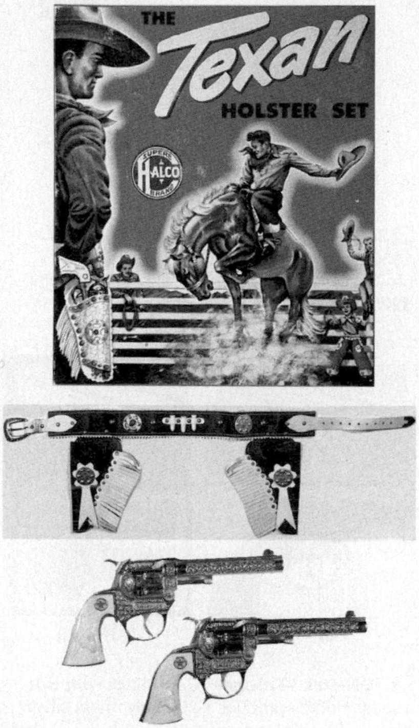

TGN-99

❑ **TGN-99. "Texan" Holster Set with Box,**
1950s. Halco. Includes 2 scarce Smokey Joe gold colored cap guns with white grips .
Box - **$50 $85 $125**
Double Holster - **$75 $150 $225**
Each gun - **$60 $120 $350**
Complete - **$1050**

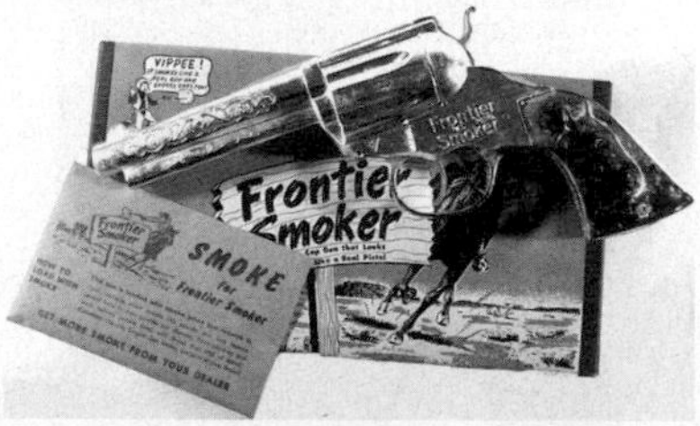

TGN-100

❑ **TGN-100. "Frontier Smoker" Cap Gun with Smoke Powder Packet in Box,**
1950s. Box is colorful.
Boxed Near Mint - **$300**

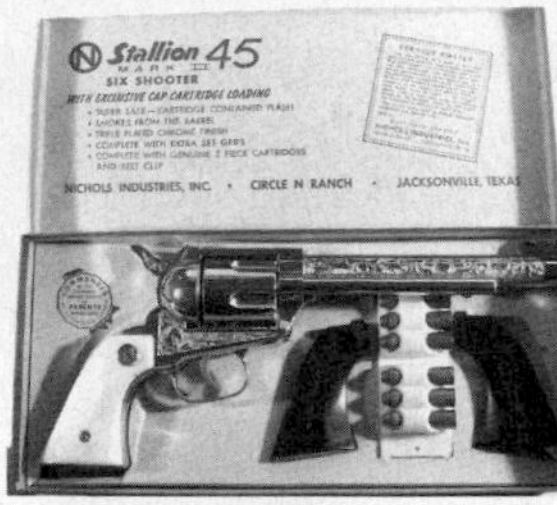

TGN-101

❑ **TGN-101. "Stallion 45 Mark II" Pistol with Box,**
1950s. Box and gun are silver color with 6 toy bullets in whote holder. Box is 12 1/2" long. There are white gun grips and extra black grips.
Boxed Near Mint - **$525**

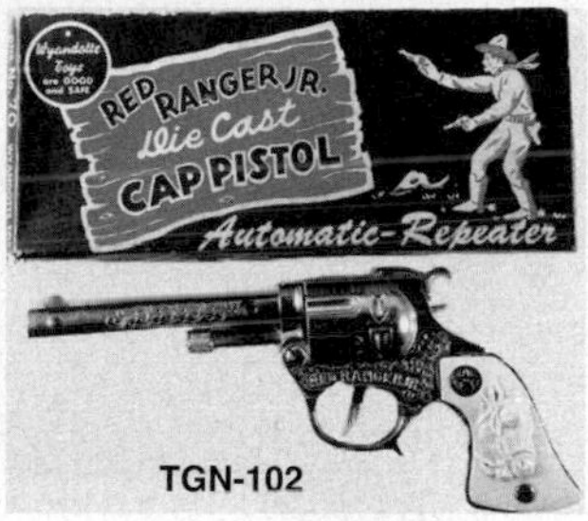

TGN-102

❑ **TGN-102. "Red Ranger Jr." Die Cast Cap Pistol in Box,**
1950s. Wyandotte product. Bright silver color.
Boxed Near Mint - **$160**

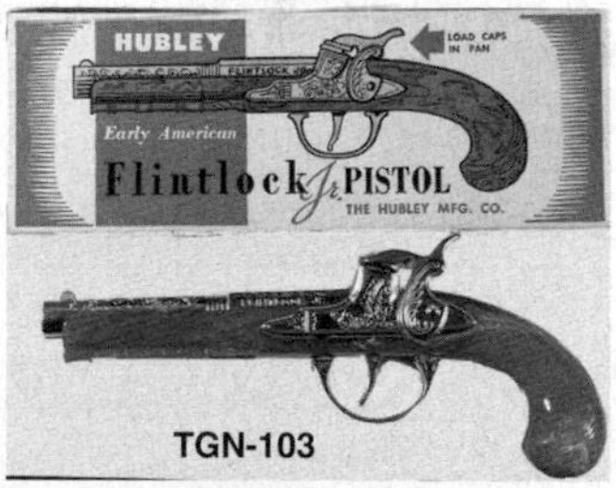

TGN-103

❑ **TGN-103. "Flintlock Jr." Cap Pistol in Box,**
1950s. Hubley product.
Boxed Near Mint - **$80**

TGN-104

❑ **TGN-104. "Kit Carson" Cap Gun on Card,**
1950s. Kilgore. - **$200**

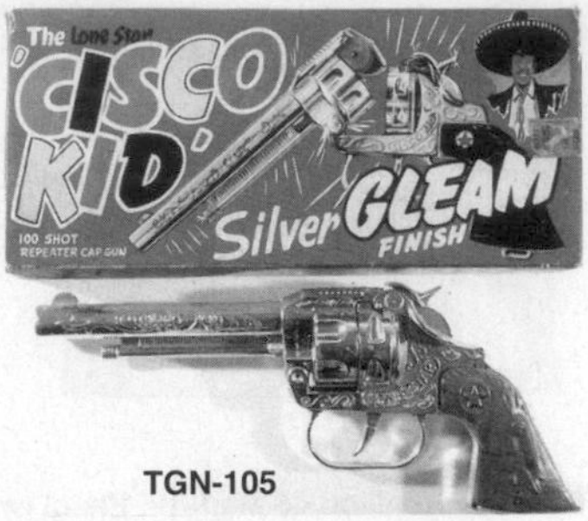

TGN-105

❑ **TGN-105. "Cisco Kid" 100 Shot Repeater in Box,**
1950s. Lone Star made in England. Has Cisco Kid name on barrel. Boxed Near Mint - **$650**

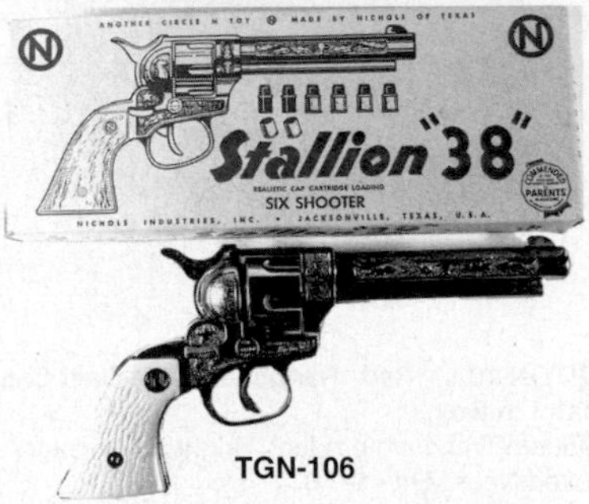

TGN-106

❑ **TGN-106. "Stallion 38" Pistol with Box,**
1950s. Nichols six shooter cap pistol with cap cartridge loading. Boxed Near Mint - **$250**

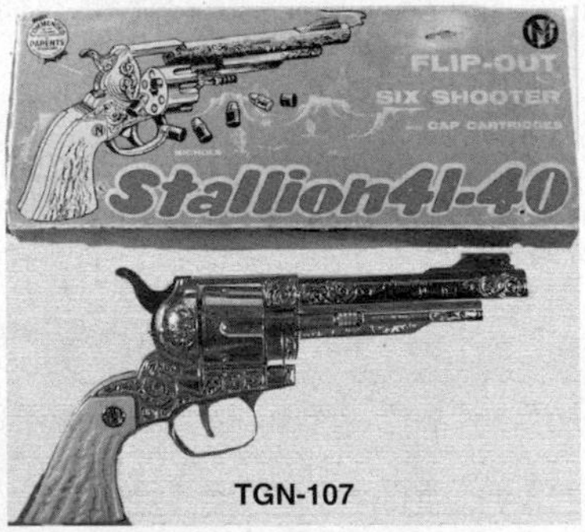

TGN-107

❑ **TGN-107. "Stallion 41-40" Pistol with Box,**
1950s. Nichols cap pistol with flip cylinder which holds 6 bullets. Boxed Near Mint - **$700**

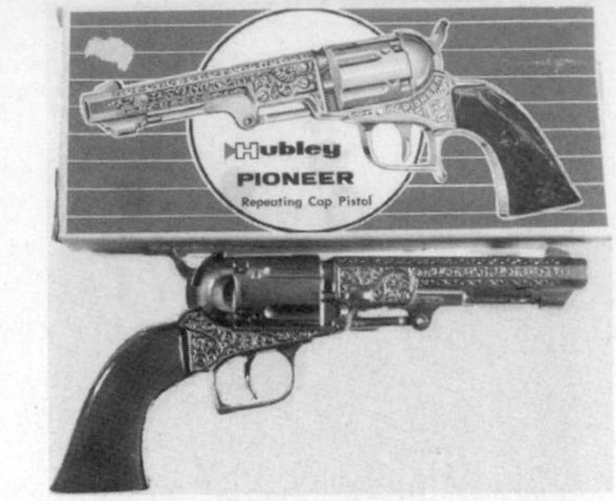

TGN-108

❑ **TGN-108. "Pioneer" Cap Pistol in Box,**
1950s. Hubley product. 9 1/2" gun has light brown plastic see-thru grips. Boxed Near Mint - **$225**

TGN-109 TGN-110

❑ **TGN-109. "Trooper" Cap Pistol with Box,**
1950s. Hubley product. Extremely bright silver finish with red star on handle. Gun is 6 3/4" long. Box is mostly bright red with white highlights.
Box - **$50**
Gun - **$100**

❑ **TGN-110. "Penguin Aurora 45" Butane Gas Lighter/Flashlight in Box,**
1950s.With 2 batteries. Boxed - **$15 $50 $100**

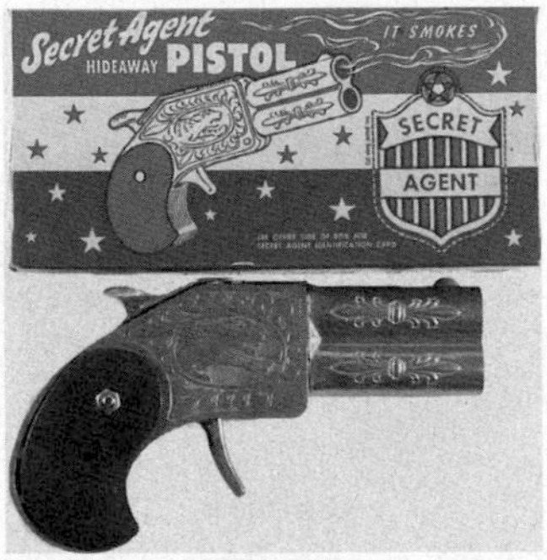

TGN-111

❑ **TGN-111. "Secret Agent" Hideaway Pistol in Box,**
1950s. Hamilton Specialties. Pistol has either blue, red, white, or black grips. Back of the box has a cut out Secret Agent I.D. card. Boxed Near Mint - **$60**

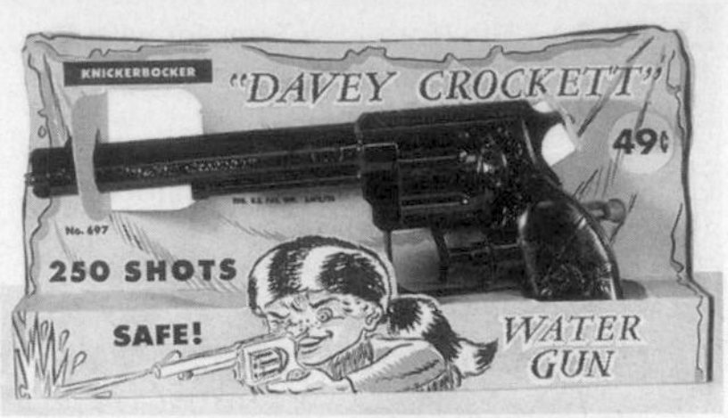

TGN-112

❑ **TGN-112. "Davey Crockett" Water Gun,**
1950s. By Knickerbocker. On card - **$25 $50 $100**

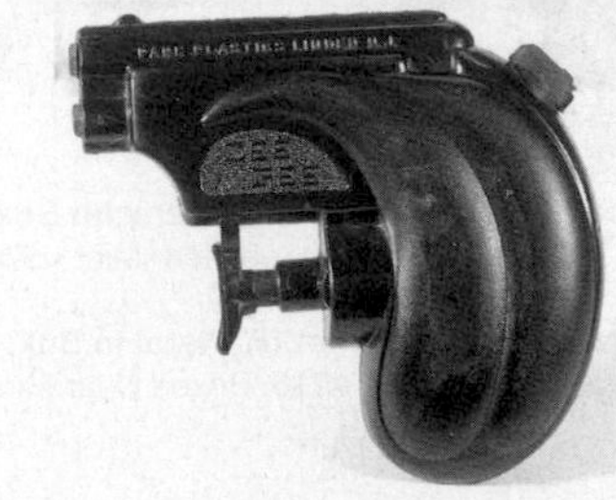

TGN-113

❑ **TGN-113. "Dee Gee" Water Gun,**
1950s. One of the most popular water guns from the 1950s fad. They're hard to find today. Water guns from the 40s and 50s all had metal tips on the end from where the water was forced. Later issues had plastic tips. - **$15 $30 $75**

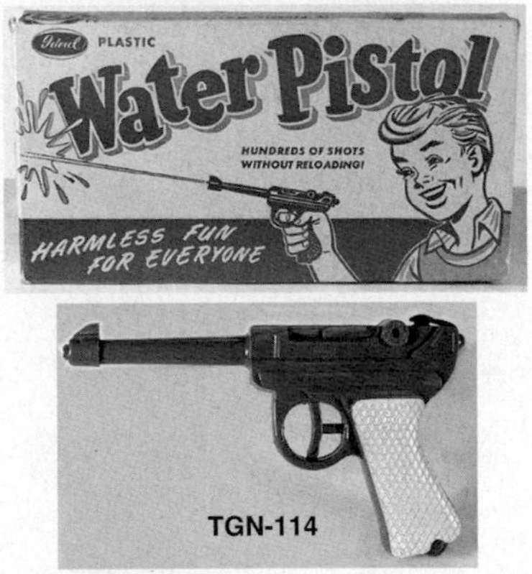

TGN-114

❑ **TGN-114. Ideal Water Pistol in Box,**
1950s. Luger style. - **$15 $30 $75**

TGN-115

❑ **TGN-115. "Space Jet" Water Gun,**
1950s. By Knickerbocker. Gun has metal tip. Three rockets are pictured on one side. Rare. -
$25 $50 $100

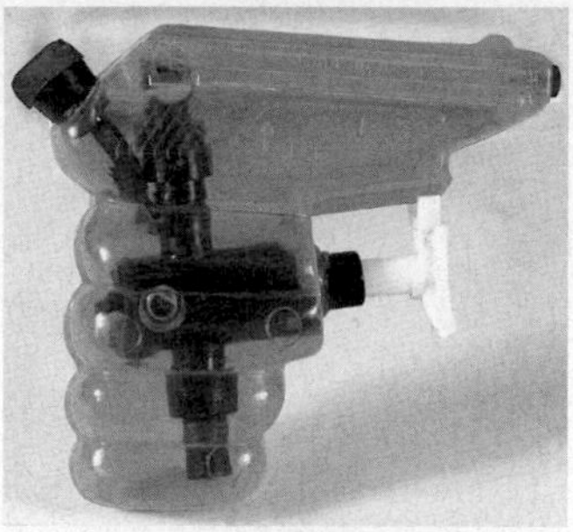

TGN-116

❑ **TGN-116. "Wee Gee" Salesman Sample Water Gun,**
1950s. The most popular water gun of the 1950s. Regular issue made in black and red. Must have metal tip.
Salesman sample (see-through red plastic) - **$50 $100 $175**
Regular black - **$15 $25 $45**
Regular red - **$20 $30 $50**

TGN-117

❑ **TGN-117. Rocket Dart Pistol in Box,**
1950s. Daisy product. Comes with 2 suction darts (1 green, 1 white) on colorful open box display. Box is 8 1/4" long and 6" high.
Also see TGN-77.
Metal Gun with 2 Darts - **$65 $125 $275**
Box - **$35 $75 $175**

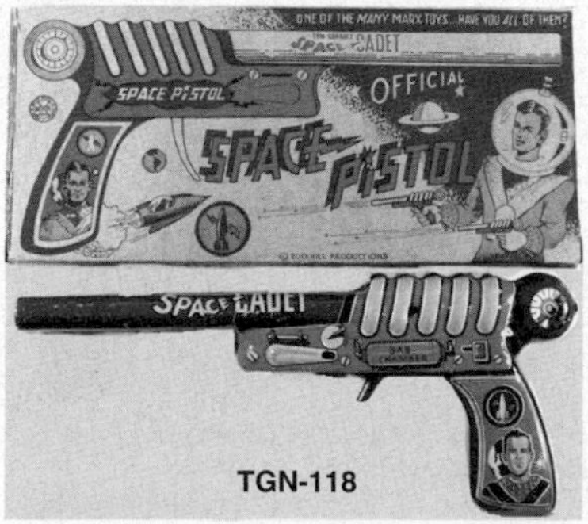

TGN-118

❑ **TGN-118. "Tom Corbett Space Cadet" Space Pistol in Box,**
1950s. Rockhill Productions.
Boxed Near Mint - **$1250**

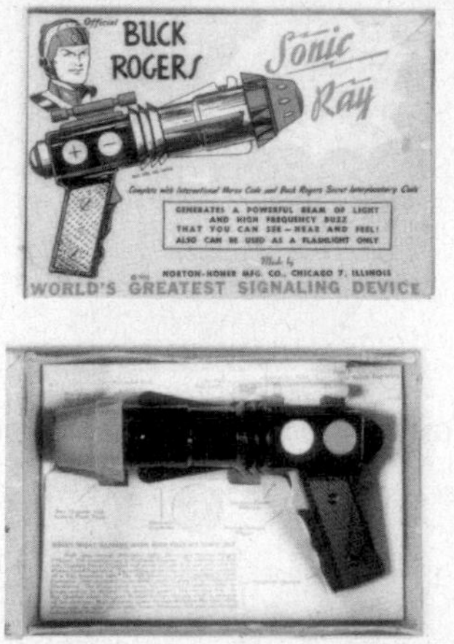

TGN-119

❑ **TGN-119. "Buck Rogers" Sonic Ray Gun in Box,**
1950s. Flashlight gun. In box with instructions.
Boxed - **$100 $300 $550**

TGN-120

❑ **TGN-120. "Flash Gordon" Water Pistol in Box,**
1950s. Boxed - **$125 $375 $750**

TGN-121

TGN-122

❑ **TGN-121. "Wyatt Earp Buntline Special" Cap Pistol on Card,**
1957. Card features Hugh O'Brian as TV's Wyatt Earp. On Card - **$100 $300 $550**

❑ **TGN-122. "Coyote" Cap Pistol on Card,**
1950s. Hubley product #237. Black handle.
Unfired on Card - **$175**

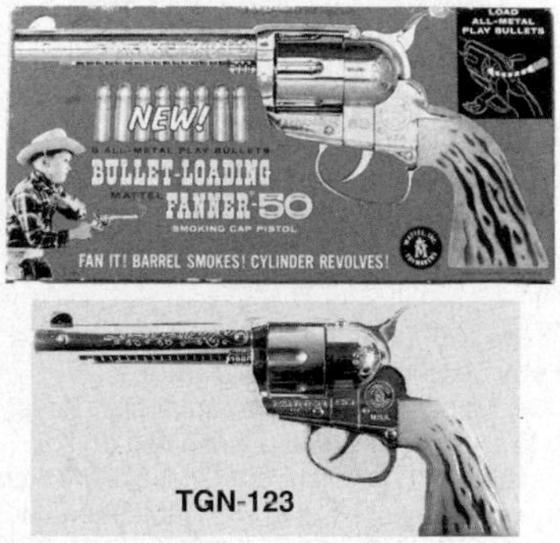

TGN-123

❑ **TGN-123. "Fanner-50" Pistol with Box,**
1950s. Mattel product. Has 8 all-metal play bullets. Boxed Near Mint - **$750**

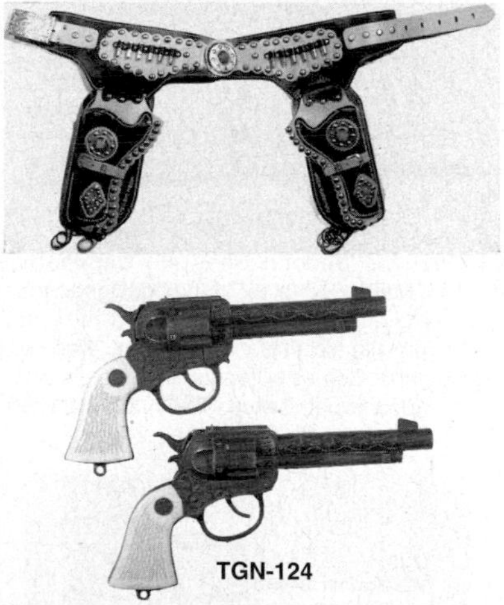

TGN-124

❑ **TGN-124. "Lone Ranger" Double Holster Set with Cap Pistols,**
1950s. Belt holds 12 silver colored bullets. Lone Ranger name appears on each side of holsters. Belt and holster are decorated with red jewels. Guns are bronze colored with white grips. Grips have small loops at bottom.
Double Holster - **$125 $250 $650**
Each Gun - **$95 $180 $350**
Complete - **$1350**

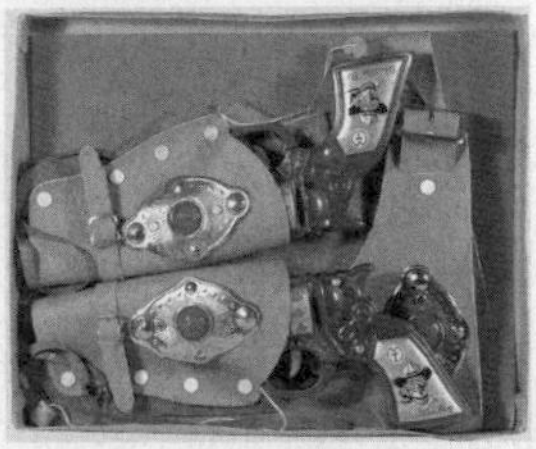

TGN-125

❑ **TGN-125. Lone Ranger Click Guns And Holster Set For Japanese Market,**
1960s. Marked "Made In Japan Aoshin Toys" and likely unlicensed. Japanese text on lid translates to "Lone Ranger." Grips show Clayton Moore-style masked man with caption below "Western Boy." Boxed Set - **$200**

TGN-128

❑ **TGN-128. "Secret Sam Bomb Binoculars,"**
1966. NM Boxed - **$135**
Unboxed Complete - **$20 $40 $75**

TGN-129 TGN-130

❑ **TGN-129. "Secret Sam Pipe Shooter,"**
1966. NM Boxed - **$135**
Pipe Only - **$20 $40 $75**

❑ **TGN-130. "Secret Sam Cane Shooter,"**
1966. On card by Topper Toys.
NM on Card - **$225**
Cane Only - **$25 $50 $100**

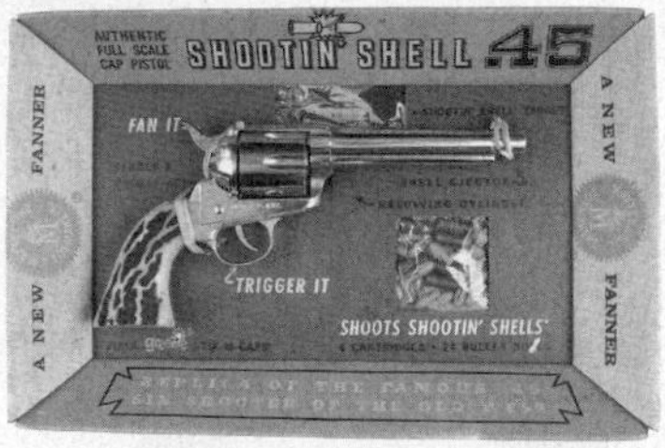

TGN-126

❑ **TGN-126. "Shootin' Shell .45" Cap Pistol,**
c. 1960. Mattel. 2x10x15.75" box designed to look like picture frame holds mounted 11" cast metal gun with nickel plating and simulated horn plastic grips. Comes with unopened shells and unpackaged target. Boxed - **$300 $650 $1350**

TGN-131

❑ **TGN-131. "Private Eye" Cap Gun,**
1960s. By Kilgore. NM On Card - **$100**
Gun Only - **$15 $25 $45**

TGN-127

❑ **TGN-127. "Outlaw Mustang" Cap Pistol With Box,**
1965. English. - **$75 $100 $250**
Gun - **$50 $65 $150**
Box - **$20 $40 $100**

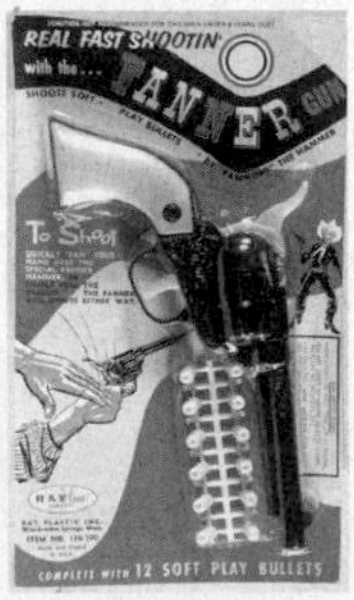

TGN-132 TGN-133

❑ **TGN-132. Padlock Pistol,**
1960s. By Hubley. Boxed - **$35 $75 $135**

❑ **TGN-133. Fanner Gun on Card,**
1960s. With plastic bullets. NM - **$150**

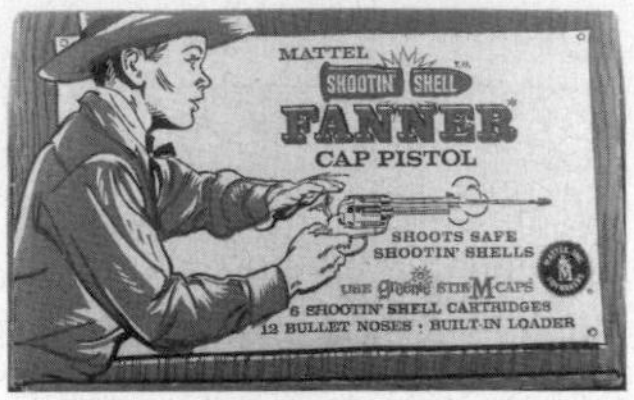

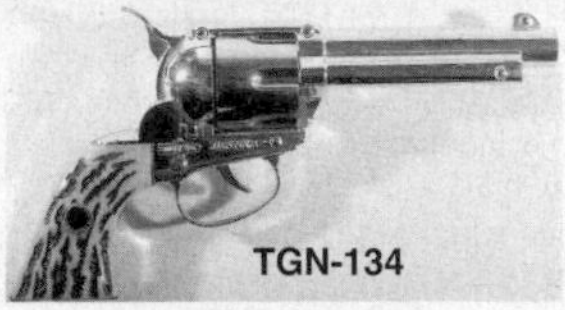

TGN-134

❑ **TGN-134. "Shootin' Shell Fanner" Pistol with Box,**
1960s. Mattel product. Boxed Near Mint - **$650**

TGN-135

❑ **TGN-135. "Wyatt Earp Buntline Special" Cap Pistol in Box,**
1960s. From Crescent Toys in England. Gun is bright silver with red grips. Box is 9 1/4" long.
Box Near Mint - **$150**
Gun - **$25 $75 $150**

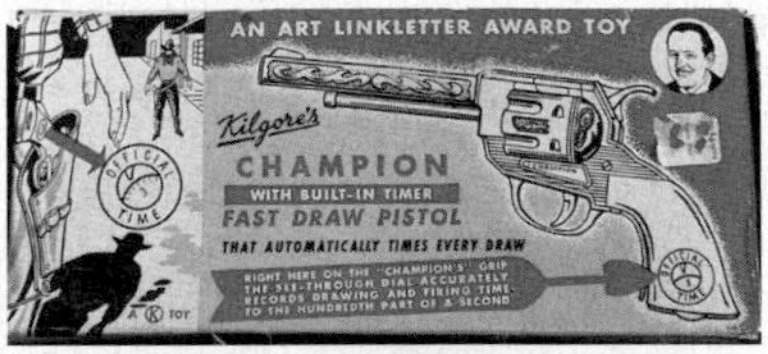

TGN-136

❑ **TGN-136. Kilgore's "Champion Fast Draw" Pistol with Box,**
1960s. Box is 11" long and very colorful. Has instructions for reading timer on back. Gun has bright silver finish and black handle.
Box - **$50 $125 $175**
Gun - **$50 $120 $225**

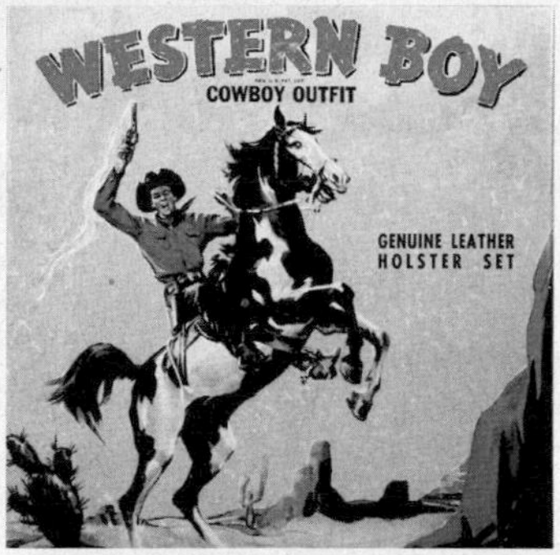

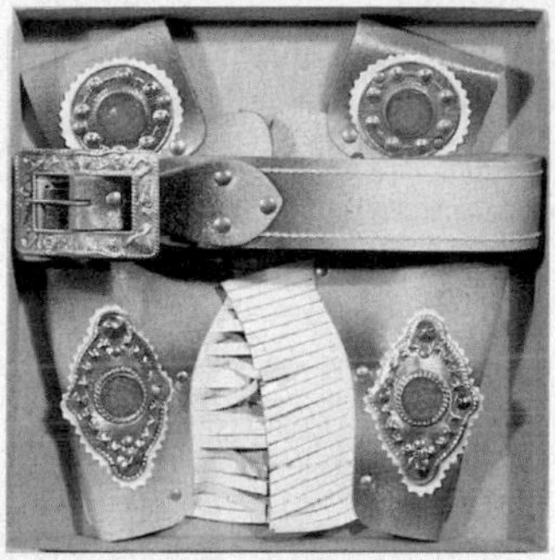

TGN-137

❑ TGN-137. "Western Boy" Double Holster in Box,
1960s. Grey and white with red jewels and silver colored buckles. No guns included.
Box - **$25 $50 $75**
Double Holster - **$50 $110 $175**
Complete - **$250**

TGN-138

❑ TGN-138. "Six Gun" with Bullets in Box,
1960s. Plastic six shooter which actually shot soft lightweight bullets. Set of 25 bullets came with the gun. Due to the popularity of the gun, most sets are now usually missing some or all of the bullets and the guns usually no longer work. There's also a target with a hole on the back of the box. Box - **$75 $100 $150**
Gun - **$25 $50 $100**
Set of 25 Bullets - **$50**

TGN-139

❑ TGN-139. "Indian Leather" Holster Set with "Ruf Rider" Cap Pistols and Box,
1960s. Belt and holsters have red jewels. Belt holds 8 silver colored bullets. Set comes with 2 guns which are die cast with bright chrome finish. "Ruf Rider" is embossed on guns.
Box - **$40 $65 $150**
Double Holster - **$75 $150 $250**
Each Gun - **$60 $120 $250**
Complete - **$900**

TGN-140

❑ TGN-140. "Deputy" Gun and Badge with Box,
1960s. Hubley product. Box - **$25 $50 $75**
Gun and Badge - **$75 $100 $175**

TGN-141

❑ TGN-141. "2 Guns in 1" Cap Pistol with Box,
1960s. Boxed - **$20 $75 $150**

TGN-142

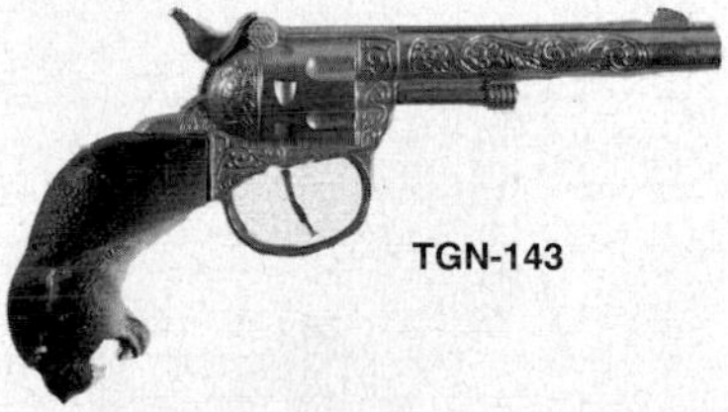

TGN-143

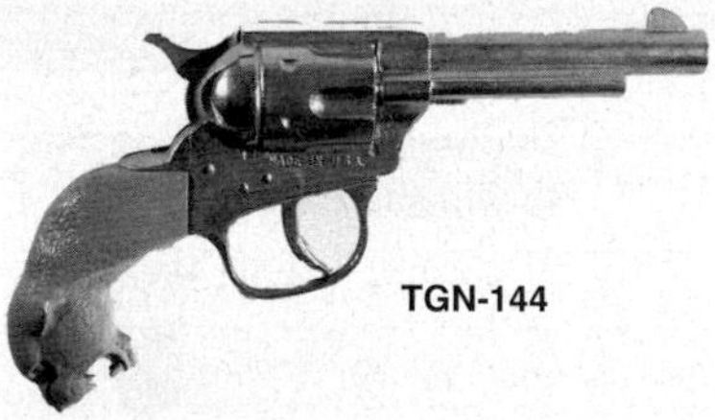

TGN-144

❑ TGN-142. Cap Gun with Horse Head Grip,
1960s. Hubley product. Horse is yellow with white mane. Unfired - **$250**

❑ TGN-143. Cap Gun with Panther Head Grip,
1960s. 6 1/2" Hubley product. Metal grip is black with white teeth and eyes. Prototype - **$750**

❑ TGN-144. Cap Gun with Puma Head Grip,
1960s. 7" Hubley product. Metal grip is tan with red eyes and mouth, and white teeth.
Prototype - **$750**

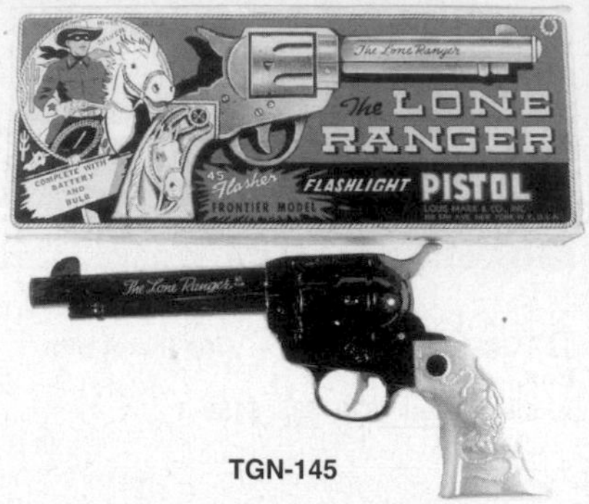

TGN-145

❑ **TGN-145. "Lone Ranger 45 Flasher" Frontier Model Flashlight Gun and Box,**
1960s. Complete with battery and bulb in box.
Boxed - **$750**

TGN-146

❑ **TGN-146. "State Ranger" Holster Set with "Cowpoke" Cap Pistols and Box,**
1960s. Belt holds 6 red bullets and a single holster. "Cowpoke" cap gun is brightly silver plated with plastic grips. Box - **$20 $40 $75**
Holster - **$50 $100 $175**
Gun - **$50 $100 $150**
Complete - **$400**

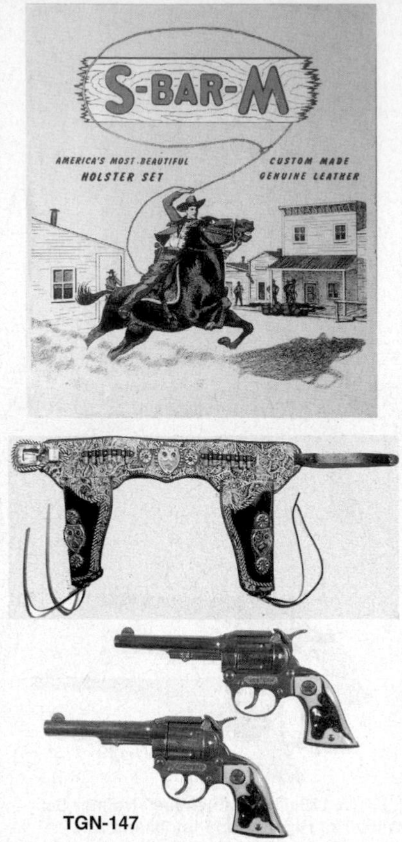

TGN-147

❑ **TGN-147. "S-Bar-M" Double Holster Set with "Western" Cap Pistols and Box,**
1960s. Belt holds 12 gold colored bullets. Holster has red and yellow jewels. Black and green designs on white. "Western" cap guns have black steer design on white grips.
Box - **$25 $60 $125**
Double Holster - **$75 $150 $250**
Each Gun - **$50 $100 $175**
Complete with unfired guns - **$725**

TGN-148

❑ **TGN-148. "Bonanza" Holster and Gun Set,**
1960s. Rayo product from Mexico. Plastic holster has 6 plastic bullets and cast photo buckle.
Gun and Holster - **$150**

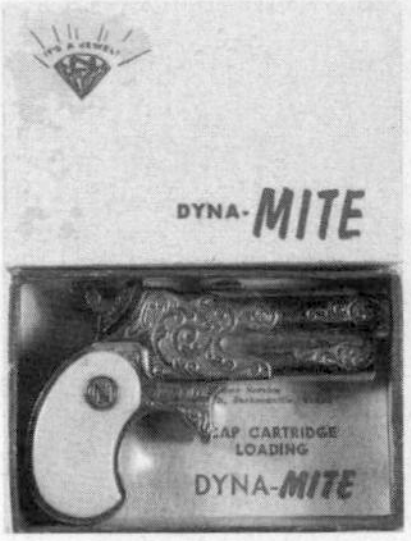

TGN-149

TGN-150

❑ **TGN-149. "Dyna-Mite" 3 1/2" Derringer,**
1960s. Nichols product. - **$20 $40 $100**

❑ **TGN-150. "Texas Ranger" Smoking Cap Gun on Card,**
1960s. Leslie Henry product. Die cast. - **$90**

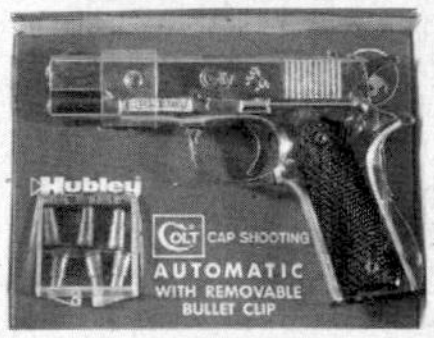

TGN-151

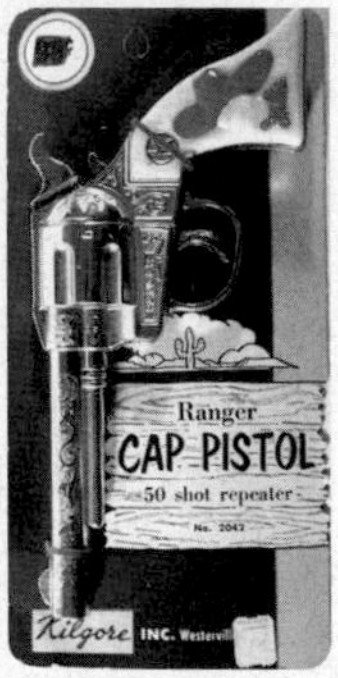

TGN-152

❑ **TGN-151. "Colt" Automatic Cap Pistol in Box,**
1960s. Hubley product. With toy bullets in box
Complete - **$15 $30 $75**

❑ **TGN-152. "Ranger" Cap Pistol on Card,**
1960s. Kilgore. 50 shot repeater has large white grips trimmed in red.
Carded - **$150**

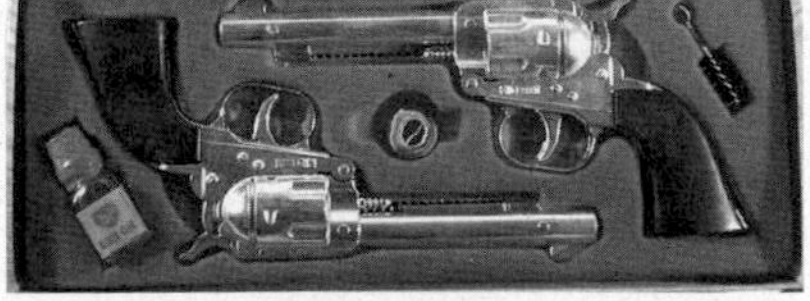

TGN-153

❑ **TGN-153. Set of "Kid MK II" Cap Guns with Gun Oil and Cleaner Brush in Box,**
1960s. BCM product from England. Guns have bright silver platings and specially-made brown grips. Box has insert.
Box - **$10 $25 $50**
Each Gun - **$10 $25 $50**
Complete - **$150**

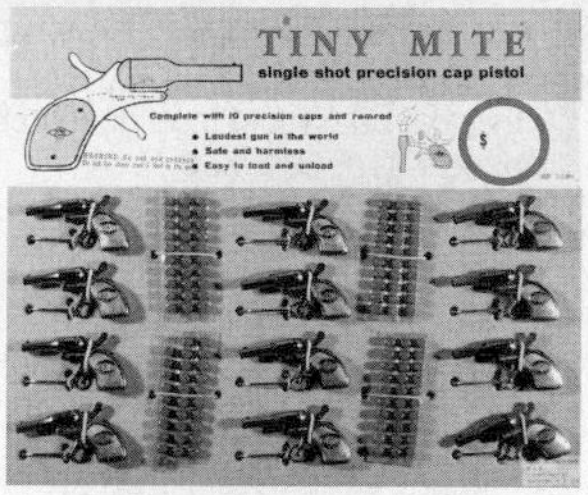

TGN-154

❑ **TGN-154. "Tiny Mite" Gun Set on Card,**
1960s. Made in Italy. 12 single shot precision guns per card.
Complete with Caps - **$100**
Each Gun with Caps - **$6**

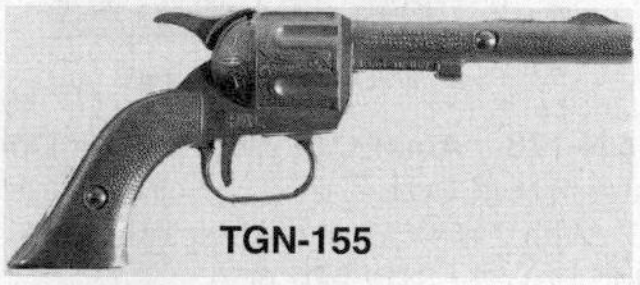

TGN-155

❑ **TGN-155. "Pal" Cap Pistol,**
1960s. - **$10 $20 $40**

TGN-156

❑ **TGN-156. "Mustang" Cap Pistols,**
1960s. Kilgore product. Set of gold plated cap guns in beautiful presentation box. Guns are referred to as "Tophand Twins." Deluxe gold finish with cameo grips. Each gun is approximately 9" long. Presentation box is cardboard made to look like wood. Insert is blue with felt-like finish. Gold finish on guns easily wears off.
Box - **$75 $150 $250**
Each Gun- **$50 $125 $250**

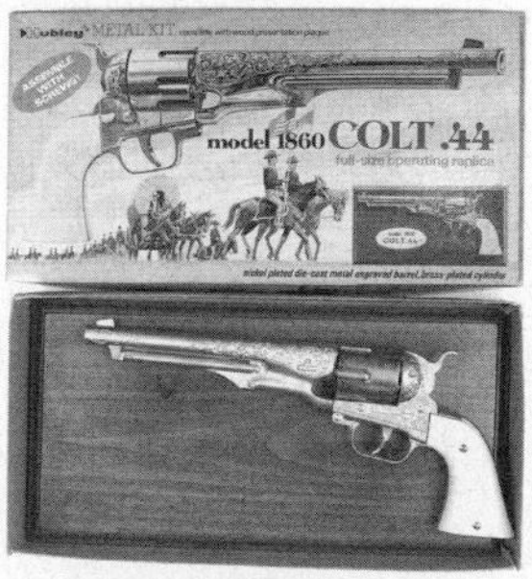

TGN-157

❑ **TGN-157. "Hubley Model 1860 Colt .44 Operating Replica" In Box,**
1971. Box measures 2.5x8x15.5" and holds 13" assembled die-cast metal gun model on wood plaque that has been assembled and finished.
Unused Boxed - **$100 $200 $300**
Assembled Boxed - **$50 $100 $200**

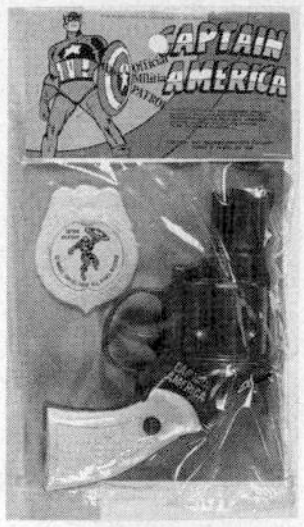

TGN-158 TGN-159

❑ **TGN-158. "Private Eye" Snub Nose Cap Gun on Card,**
1974. Kilgore product. Die cast metal.
On card - **$20 $60 $80**

❑ **TGN-159. "Captain America" Gun and Badge Set,**
1974. In display package. - **$20 $30 $50**

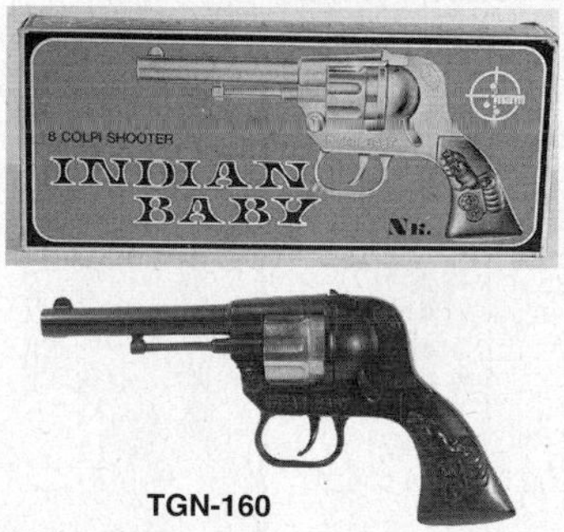

TGN-160

❑ **TGN-160. "Indian Baby" 8-Shot Toy Pistol in Box,**
1970s. Uses plastic cartridges. A smoker gun made in Italy. - **$25 $50 $80**

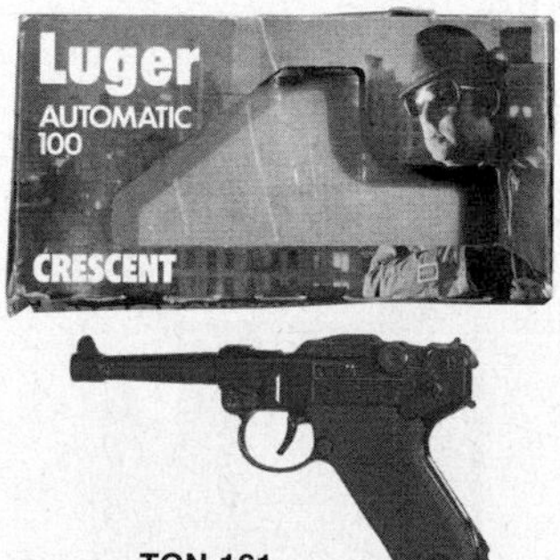

TGN-161

❑ **TGN-161. Luger Pistol and Box,**
1970s. By Crescent. Cap Gun. - **$50 $110 $160**
Gun - **$40 $80 $120**
Box - **$10 $30 $40**

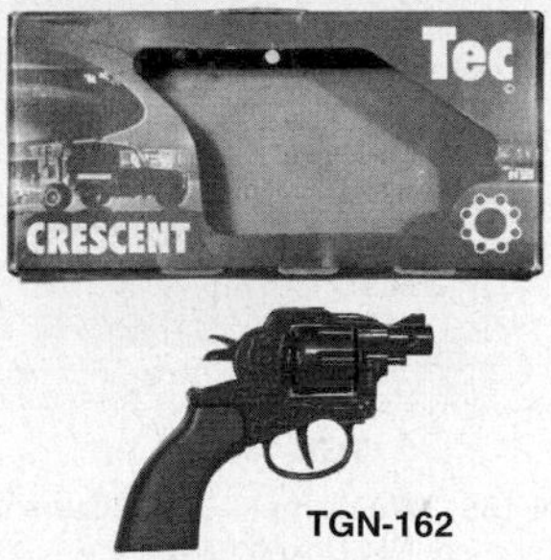

TGN-162

❑ **TGN-162. Snub Nose Cap Gun,**
1970s. By Crescent. England. Boxed - **$115**
Gun - **$15 $30 $75**
Box - **$10 $30 $40**

TGN-163

❑ **TGN-163. "Scout" Cap Gun,**
1970s. By Lone Star. England. NM Boxed - **$95**
Gun Only - **$15 $25 $60**

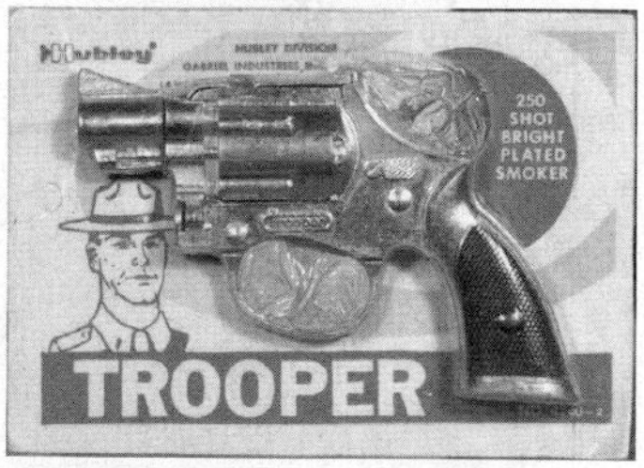

TGN-164

❑ **TGN-164. "Trooper" Cap Gun Smoker,**
1970s. By Hubley. NM Carded - **$145**
Gun Only - **$25 $40 $85**

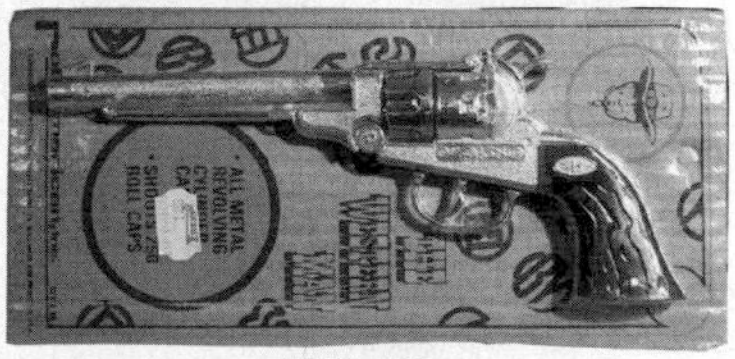

TGN-165

❑ **TGN-165. "Western Man" Cap Gun,**
1970s. NM Carded - **$150**
Gun Only - **$25 $40 $75**

TGN-166

❑ **TGN-166. "Westerner" Three Guns in One,**
1983. By Alco. NM Boxed - **$135**

TGN-167

❑ **TGN-167. "Browning Hi-Power" Cap Gun,**
1980s. Boxed - **$125**
Gun - **$20 $40 $90**
Box - **$10 $20 $35**

TGN-168

❑ **TGN-168. "Ranger" Cap Gun,**
1980s. Boxed - **$120**
Gun - **$20 $40 $90**
Box - **$10 $20 $35**

TGN-169

TGN-170

❑ **TGN-169. "Lost Frontier" Die Cast Metal Cap Gun on Card,**
1990. Esquire/Nichols product.
On Card - **$5 $10 $25**

❑ **TGN-170. "Masked Marshal" Set on Card,**
1990. Imperial product. Includes mask, badge, gun and bullets.
On Card - **$3 $6 $15**

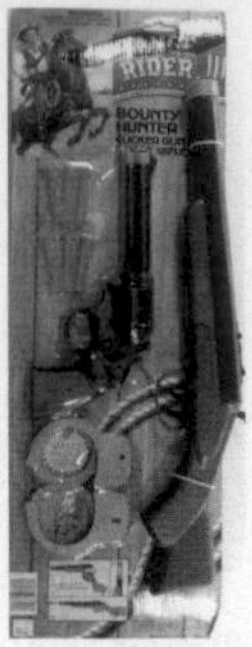

TGN-171

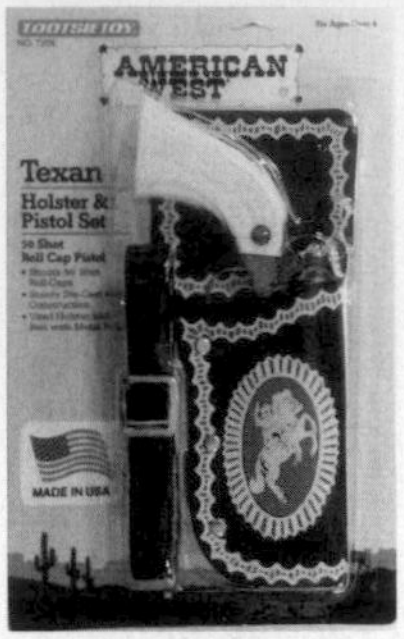

TGN-172

❑ **TGN-171. "Range Rider" Bounty Hunter Set on Card,**
1992. Includes clicker gun, shot gun and hand-cuffs on open card. - **$5 $10 $25**

❑ **TGN-172. "Texan" Holster and Pistol Set on Card,**
1992. 50 shot roll cap pistol. Die cast metal.
On Card - **$5 $10 $35**

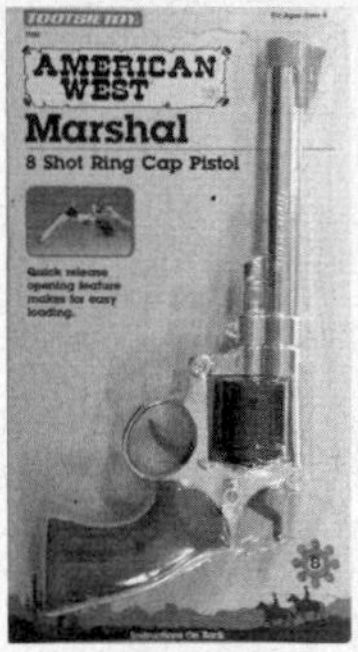

TGN-173

TGN-174

❑ **TGN-173. "Marshal" Cap Pistol on Card,**
1994. 8 shot cap pistol. Card is 6.75" x 12.75". - **$5 $10 $20**

❑ **TGN-174. "American West" Single Holster Set in Box,**
1995. Die cast metal cap gun in genuine leather holster. Boxed - **$5 $10 $20**

TGN-175

❑ **TGN-175. "American West" Brown Double Holster Set in Box,**
1995. With 2 die cast metal cap guns in brown holster. Boxed - **$10 $20 $50**

TGN-176

❑ **TGN-176. "American West" Black Double Holster Set in Box,**
1995. With 2 die cast metal cap guns in black holster. Boxed - **$10 $20 $50**

TGN-177

❑ **TGN-177. "American West" Leather Double Holster Set in Box,**
1995. With 2 die cast metal cap guns in leather holster. Boxed - **$10 $20 $50**

TGN-178

❑ **TGN-178. "American West" Carson Cap Gun on Card,**
1996. Die cast cylinder cap gun shoots 8 shot ring caps. On Card - **$3 $6 $15**

TGN-179

❑ **TGN-179. "American West" Snake Cap Gun on Card,**
1996. Die cast cylinder cap gun shoots strip caps. On Card - **$3 $6 $12**

TGN-180

❑ **TGN-180. "Electronic" Six Shooter in Box,**
1996. Western Gear product. What a kid wouldn't give for one of these in the 1950s. Has real sound and flashing barrel. Comes in black and brown grips. Boxed - **$5 $10 $15**

TGN-181

TGN-182

❑ **TGN-181. "Shiloh Kid" Double Gun and Holster Set on Card,**
1996. Die cast metal guns, holsters and belt. On Card - **$8 $12 $20**

❑ **TGN-182. "Cowboy Trail" Clicker Gun and Badge on Card,**
1997. On Card - **$3 $8 $15**

TGN-183

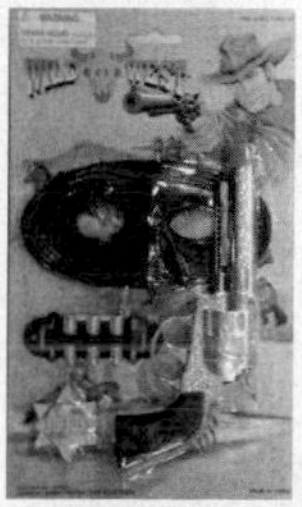
TGN-184

❑ **TGN-183. "Wild West" Gun and Knife Set on Card,**
1990s. Gun, 3 bullets, rubber knife and badge. On Card - **$3 $6 $12**

❑ **TGN-184. "Wild West" Gun and Mask Set on Card,**
1990s. Gun, 3 bullets, mask and badge. On Card - **$3 $6 $12**

TGN-185

❑ **TGN-185. "Electronic" Six Shooter with Holster in Box,**
2000. America Frontier product. Boxed - **$15**

Toy Story

See Ted Hake's *Official® Price Guide to Disney Collectibles*, Second Edition, formatted identically to this book but in full color evaluating over 9,000 Disney company and character collectibles from 1924 through 2006.

Transformers

Transformers came on the scene in 1984 and took the United States by storm. The toys were produced by Hasbro and featured robots that transformed into cars, planes, and other objects. Originally, Transformers were released by the Japanese toy company Takara. In 1983, Hasbro and Takara began a successful relationship in which Hasbro would release the toys internationally with Takara releasing the toys directly in Japan. In 1984, *Transformers* was also released as an animated cartoon which ran successfully from 1984-1987.

Marvel Comics brought Transformers to the pages of comic books in 1984 in what was originally intended to be only a four issue mini-series. *Transformers* #3 even featured a Spider-Man appearance (in his new black costume). The success of the comic mini-series prompted Marvel to continue the series for a total of eighty issues. Since their debut in comic books, the Transformers have been published by a wide range of publishers including Marvel Comics, Dreamwave Productions, and IDW Publishing.

The Transformers debuted on the silver screen in 1986 when the animated film *Transformers: The Movie* was released in theaters. The movie featured an incredible all-star cast including Orson Welles, Leonard Nimoy, Robert Stack, Michael Bell, Judd Nelson, Eric Idle, and Peter Cullen. The movie was a crucial event in the Transformers universe as numerous well-known original characters were tragically killed off in an ultimate battle between good and evil. Prior to the film, this type of transition in the world of cartoons had never been seen before. The film, interestingly enough, was rated PG. This was due to the film's level of violence and minor profanity. *Transformers: The Movie* in many ways was well ahead of its time and appeared to be marketed at two contradicting markets, adults and children. The film was also one of the final roles of famed actor Orson Welles who died shortly after completing his role as the voice of Unicron in the film.

A CGI-infused live action film titled *Transformers* was released in 2007, directed by Michael Bay. The film not only marked the return of the Transformers, but also featured voice actor Peter Cullen who was known as the voice of Autobot leader Optimus Prime in the animated features. The film's cast included Shia LaBeouf, Megan Fox, Josh Duhamel, Tyrese Gibson, Jon Voight, and John Turturro. A sequel to *Transformers* titled *Transformers 2* is scheduled for June 2009.

In the past 24 years, Hasbro has released and re-released Transformers in a variety of designs and character changes to both the toys as well as the several different incarnations of the animated programs. The characters have remained a success with both their new fans and those who grew up with the original characters in 1984.

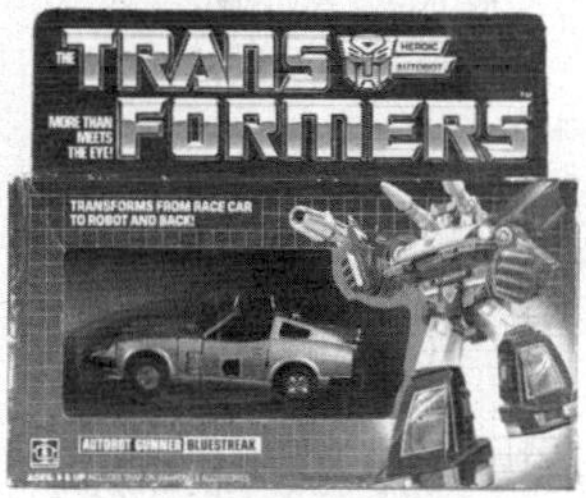

TRS-1

❑ **TRS-1. "Bluestreak" Figure In Box,**
1984. - **$125 $250 $500**

TRS-2

❑ **TRS-2. "Brawn" Figure On Card,**
1984. - **$50 $100 $200**

TRS-3

❑ **TRS-3. "Bumblebee" Figure On Card,**
1984. - **$100 $200 $400**

TRS-4

❑ **TRS-4. "Cliffjumper" Figure On Card,**
1984. - **$100 $200 $400**

TRS-5

❑ **TRS-5. "Frenzy" And "Laserbeak" Figures On Card,**
1984. - **$75 $125 $250**

TRS-6

❑ **TRS-6. "Gears" Figure On Card,**
1984. - **$50 $100 $125**

TRS-7

❑ **TRS-7. "Hound" Figure In Box,**
1984. - **$125 $250 $500**

TRS-8

❑ **TRS-8. "Huffer" Figure On Card,**
1984. - **$50 $100 $125**

TRS-9

❑ **TRS-9. "Iron-Hide" Figure In Box,**
1984. - **$125 $250 $500**

TRS-10

❑ **TRS-10. "Jazz" Figure In Box,**
1984. - **$125 $250 $500**

TRS-11

❑ **TRS-11. "Megatron" Figure In Box,**
1984. - **$250 $500 $1000**

TRS-12

❑ **TRS-12. "Mirage" Figure In Box,**
1984. - **$125 $250 $500**

TRS-13

❑ **TRS-13. "Optimus Prime" Figure In Box,**
1984. - **$250 $500 $1000**

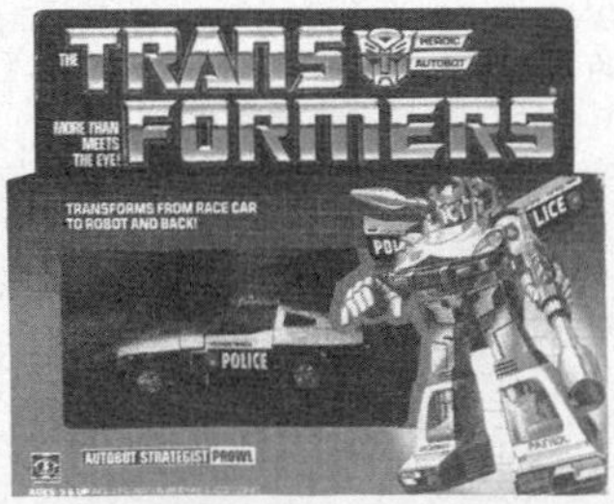

TRS-14

❑ **TRS-14. "Prowl" Figure In Box,**
1984. - **$125 $250 $500**

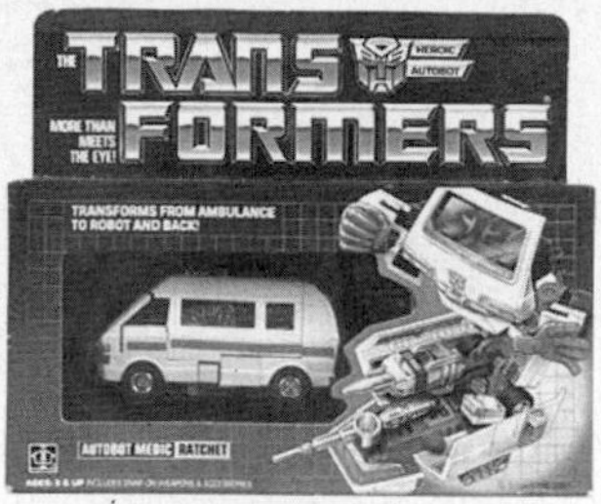

TRS-15

❑ **TRS-15. "Ratchet" Figure In Box,**
1984. - **$125 $250 $500**

TRS-16

❑ **TRS-16. "Ravage" And "Rumble" Figures On Card,**
1984. - **$75 $125 $250**

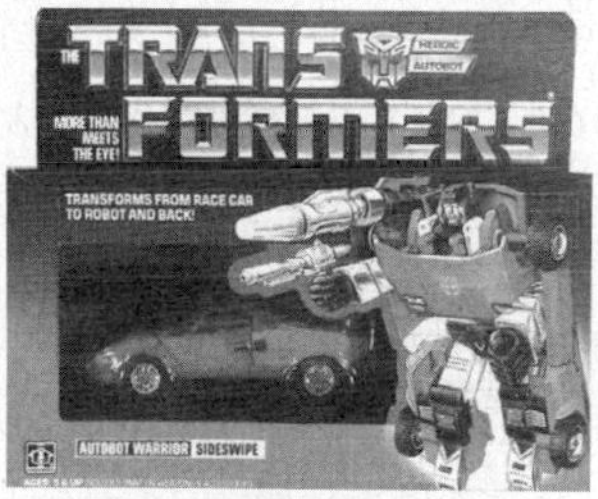

TRS-17

❑ **TRS-17. "Sideswipe" Figure In Box,**
1984. - **$125 $250 $500**

TRS-18

❑ **TRS-18. "Skywarp" Figure In Box,**
1984. - **$125 $250 $500**

TRS-19

❑ **TRS-19. "Soundwave" And "Buzzsaw" Figures In Box,**
1984. - **$150 $300 $600**

TRS-20

❑ **TRS-20. "Starscream" Figure In Box,**
1984. - **$150 $300 $600**

TRS-21

❑ **TRS-21. "Sunstreaker" Figure In Box,**
1984. - **$125 $250 $500**

TRS-22

❑ **TRS-22. "Thundercracker" Figure In Box,**
1984. - **$125 $250 $500**

TRS-23

❑ **TRS-23. "Trailbreaker" Figure In Box,**
1984. - **$125 $250 $500**

TRS-24

❑ **TRS-24. "Wheel-Jack" Figure In Box,**
1984. - **$125 $250 $500**

TRS-25

❑ **TRS-25. "Windcharger" Figure On Card,**
1984. - **$50 $100 $150**

TRS-26

❑ **TRS-26. "Transformers" Cookie Jar with Original Box,**
1984. This product was discontinued because of the ease of damage to top of jar. Boxed - **$600**

Trix

General Mills introduced Trix fruit-flavored corn puffs around 1955, and the distinctive Trix-loving rabbit made his debut on the cereal boxes and in animated television comercials in 1959. The original rabbit was a hand puppet that appeared in the introduction to *Rocky and His Friends, Captain Kangaroo*, and other General Mills-sponsored programs. Joe Harris created the rabbit and the slogan "Silly rabbit, Trix are for kids."

TRX-1

❑ **TRX-1. "Walky Squawky Talky" Cardboard Units In Envelope,**
1965. With Envelope - **$25 $50 $100**
Loose - **$20 $40 $80**

TRX-2

❑ **TRX-2. Cereal Box Flat With "Walkie-Squawky Talkies" Offer,**
1965. Gordon Gold Archives.
Near Mint Flat - **$400**
Used Complete - **$50 $100 $200**

TRX-3

❑ **TRX-3. "The Leaping Trix Rabbit" Box Flat,**
1969. Box contained 3" tall hard plastic premium of Rabbit figure and spring-loaded "Launching Tree Stump." Near Mint Flat - **$400**
Used Complete - **$50 $100 $200**
Complete Premium - **$15 $30 $60**

TRX-4

❑ **TRX-4. Tiddly Wink Miniature Plastic Game,**
c. 1960s. Lidded container holding small dexterity game featuring disks picturing Trix Rabbit. - **$8 $15 $25**

TRX-5

❑ **TRX-5. Harlem Globetrotters Premiums Cereal Box,**
1970. Back panel promotes series of four "Hot Shot Basketball Player" premiums. Gordon Gold Archives. Near Mint Flat - **$450**
Used Complete - **$75 $150 $250**

TRX-6

❑ **TRX-6. Vinyl Squeaker Figure,**
1978. - **$20 $40 $75**

TRX-7

❑ **TRX-7. Cereal Box Flat With "Rabbit Racer" Offer,**
1970s. Gordon Gold Archives.
Near Mint Flat - **$600**
Used Complete - **$100 $200 $300**

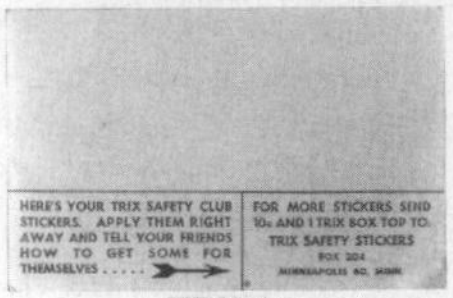

TRX-8

TRX-9

❑ **TRX-8. Club Stickers,**
1970s. Set Of Five - **$5 $10 $25**

❑ **TRX-9. Plastic Ramp Toy,**
1970s. Designed to walk on inclined surface. - **$15 $30 $50**

TRX-10

TRX-11

Dear Friend,

Thank you for sending in your vote. I see that you voted no – you must really believe that Trix are for kids! However, enough children voted yes so that I was able to eat a whole bowl of fruity, delicious Trix! I hope you are enjoying your Trix as much as I did. Thanks again, my friend!

Your Pal,

The Trix Rabbit

TRX-12

❑ **TRX-10. "Yes! Let The Rabbit Eat Trix!" 2-1/4" Litho. Button,**
1970s. For affirmative voter in contest, back has metal clip. - **$5 $15 $25**

❑ **TRX-11. "No! Trix Are For Kids!" 2-1/4" Litho. Button,**
1970s. For negative voter in contest, back has metal clip. - **$5 $15 $25**

❑ **TRX-12. Contest Vote Thank-You Letter,**
1970s. Accompaniment letter to litho. buttons for entrant in contest to determine if Trix Rabbit should be allowed to eat Trix cereal. - **$8 $15 $30**

TRX-13

❑ **TRX-13. "Trix Rabbit" Premium Doll With Mailer,**
1987. Issued by General Mills. Plush doll is 16" tall. Mailer - **$2 $4 $10**
Doll - **$12 $25 $50**

Twenty Thousand Years in Sing-Sing

This was a series of dramatized prison stories related by Sing-Sing Prison Warden Lewis E. Lawes. The show was sponsored by Sloan's Liniment and heard on the Blue Network from 1933 until 1939. The title was based on some 2,000 inmates each incarcerated for one year or more. Lawes, one of the era's more lenient wardens, related human interest stories, most with a positive theme, about men who overcame obstacles and returned to society to lead successful lives.

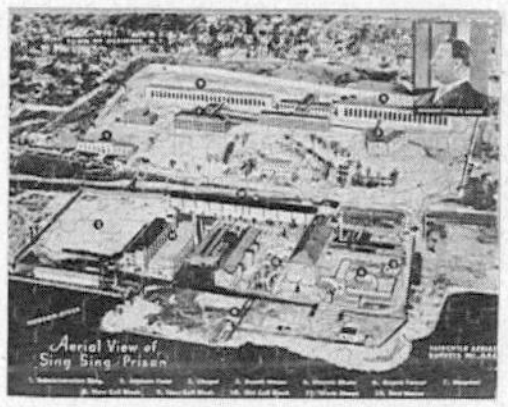

TWY-1

❑ **TWY-1. "Aerial View Of Sing-Sing Prison" Puzzle,**
1930s. Sloan's Liniment. 8x10" blue and white puzzle with inset black and white photo of Warden Lawes at top right.
Mailer (Not Shown) - **$10 $20 $30**
Puzzle - **$25 $45 $90**

TWY-2

❑ **TWY-2. "Strange Stories From Sing Sing!" Booklet,**
1930s. Has diecut front cover simulating jail bars. - **$20 $40 $85**

Uncle Don

Between 1928 and 1947, broadcasting regionally from New York radio station WOR, Uncle Don Carney entertained kids with stories, poems, jokes, songs, birthday announcements, and advice on health and behavior. Carney (1897-1954), whose real name was Howard Rice, started in vaudeville as a trick pianist and turned his air time into a classic children's program. Along with nonsense syllables, pig latin, and made-up words, Uncle Don promoted a number of "clubs" related to the products of his many commercial sponsors. The show was aired on the Mutual network for one season (1939-1940), sponsored by Maltex cereal. Uncle Don also read the comics on the air on Sunday mornings, and narrated *The Adventures of Terry and Ted* on CBS radio in 1935-1936. The often-told tale that Carney, after signing off one night, said "I guess that'll hold the little bastards" with the microphone still on, apparently never happened.

UDN-1

❑ **UDN-1. Engineers Club Cello. Button,**
1929. Lionel trains. 1-1/4" multicolor. -
$80 $175 $350

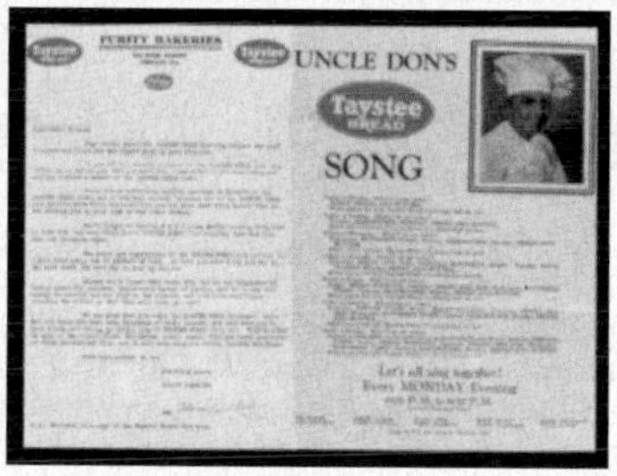

UDN-2

❑ **UDN-2. Letter And Song Sheet,**
1929. Taystee Bread, Chicago.
Letter - **$10 $20 $40**
Song - **$10 $20 $40**

UDN-3

UDN-4

❑ **UDN-3. Uncle Don Bank,**
1920s. Two types. Each - **$20 $40 $75**

❑ **UDN-4. "Lionel Engineers Club" Cello. Button,**
1930. - **$75 $160 $325**

UDN-5

❑ **UDN-5. Uncle Don's "Earnest Saver Club" Tin Bank,**
c. 1938. Various banks. Wrapper design of character with "Bank Book" body. - **$20 $40 $75**

UDN-6

UDN-7

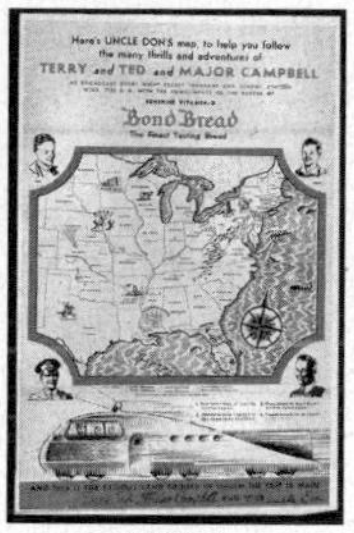

UDN-8

❑ **UDN-6. "Maltex 100% Breakfast Club" Litho. Button,**
c. 1939. - **$5 $10 $15**

❑ **UDN-7. Uncle Don Letter and Mailer,**
1930s. Savings Club. - **$20 $40 $65**

❑ **UDN-8. Uncle Don's "Terry And Ted And Major Campbell" 12x19" Map,**
1930s. Bond Bread. Map follows route of trio in their "Land Cruiser" pictured at bottom. -
$60 $110 $225

UDN-9

UDN-10

❑ **UDN-9. "Terry And Ted On The Trail Of The Secret Formula" Booklet,**
1930s. Bond Bread. Story told by Uncle Don with color pictures. - **$10 $15 $30**

❑ **UDN-10. Autogiro Theme Photo,**
1930s. Popsicle. Pictures Uncle Don as aviator with facsimile signature inscription for Popsicles. -
$10 $15 $30

UDN-11

UDN-12

❑ **UDN-11. "Borden Health Club" Cello. Button,**
1930s. - **$15 $20 $40**

❑ **UDN-12. "Ice Cream Club/Borden" Cello. Button,**
1930s. - **$15 $20 $40**

UDN-13

UDN-14

❑ **UDN-13. "Borden's Health Club Honor Prize",**
1930s. "Uncle Don" brass bar holding cloth ribbon suspending cello. pendant with reverse image of Borden milk bottle. - **$18 $35 $70**

❑ **UDN-14. "Bosco Club" Cello. Button,**
1930s. Pictured holding jar of chocolate drink syrup product. - **$15 $30 $60**

UDN-15

UDN-16

UDN-17

❑ **UDN-15. "Good Humor/G.H.H.C." Cello. Button,**
1930s. Pictured in Good Humor Ice Cream uniform. - **$20 $35 $75**

❑ **UDN-16. "I.V.C. Club" Cello. Button,**
1930s. - **$10 $15 $30**

❑ **UDN-17. "Mutual Grocery Club" Cello. Button,**
1930s. - **$10 $15 $30**

UDN-18

UDN-19

UDN-20

❑ **UDN-18. "Castles Ice Cream Club" Cello. Button,** 1930s. - **$10 $15 $30**

❑ **UDN-19. "Remitypers" Cello. Button,**
1930s. Remington Typewriters. - **$15 $30 $45**

❑ **UDN-20. "Taystee Bread Club" Cello. Button,**
1930s. - **$10 $15 $30**

UDN-21

❑ **UDN-21. "Song Game And Paint Book",**
1940. Store item by Melrose Music Corp., New York. 8-7/8x11-7/8" with 68 pages. Back cover promotes "Uncle Don" reading comics over the Mutual System on Sunday mornings and shows 17 King Features Syndicate characters all commenting on the show. Major characters shown are Phantom, Popeye, Jiggs and Maggie, Blondie and Dagwood. - **$20 $35 $70**

Uncle Sam

The name originated from meat packer Samuel Wilson (1766-1854) of Troy, New York who stamped meat which was going to American soldiers in the War of 1812 "US" for United States. First drawn as an elderly man with a goatee, noted political cartoonist Thomas Nast (1840-1902) refined his image in the 1870s to include a top hat and a stars and stripes costume which we recognize today.

Illustrator James Montgomery Flagg (1877-1960) first painted his iconic image of Uncle Sam pointing toward the viewer for the July 6, 1916 cover of *Leslie's Weekly Magazine*. The painting was then used as a WWI recruiting poster with text at the bottom "I Want You For U.S. Army" in 1917. Flagg used himself as a model for Uncle Sam. Four million posters were printed, making the poster the most famous in history. The poster was used again in WWII.

The 87th U.S. Congress adopted a resolution on September 15, 1961, crediting Samuel Wilson with the origination of Uncle Sam.

Quality Comics published eight issues of *Uncle Sam Quarterly* between Autumn, 1941 and Fall, 1943 and DC published two issues of *Uncle Sam* in 1997. "Hey Uncle Sam, Collectors Want You!"

UNS-1

UNS-2

❑ **UNS-1. "Yanko Spanko War" Uncle Sam Cartoon Button,**
1898. Whitehead & Hoag. 1.25" diameter. - **$50 $100 $200**

❑ **UNS-2. Uncle Sam Punching Spaniard Cartoon Button,**
1898. Whitehead & Hoag. 1.25" diameter. - **$50 $100 $200**

UNS-3

❑ **UNS-3. Spanish American War Figural Ashtray With Uncle Sam and Spanish Matador,**
1898. 4x8x3.25" tall Uncle Sam and Matador each pulling the end of a cigar inscribed "Cuba." - **$125 $250 $450**

UNS-4

❑ **UNS-4. "Cascade Beer" Tray With Uncle Sam And Foreign Friends,**
c. 1900. Bachrach & Co. San Francisco, Calif. 12.25x17.25" litho tin tray. - **$200 $400 $750**

UNS-5

UNS-6

❑ **UNS-5. Uncle Sam And Roosevelt "Welcome" Button,**
1904. Whitehead & Hoag. 1.25" diameter. Backpaper reads "Compliments of C.D. Kenny Co.," a Baltimore tea and coffee distributor. - **$600 $1200 $2400**

❑ **UNS-6. Uncle Sam With Firecrackers Button,**
1900s. Whitehead & Hoag. 1.25" button. - **$10 $20 $45**

UNS-7

UNS-8

❑ **UNS-7. "Union Leader Tobacco" Pocket Tin With Uncle Sam,**
1910. 3-3/8" wide by 4.5" tall tin with remnants of 1910 tax stamp. - **$40 $90 $150**

❑ **UNS-8. Uncle Sam Embraces TR Returning From Africa Pin,**
1910. Whitehead & Hoag. 1.75" diameter. - **$1500 $3000 $6000**

UNS-9

UNS-10

❑ **UNS-9. Uncle Sam Marches With Miss Liberty Button,**
c. 1916. 1.75" diameter. - **$35 $75 $165**

❑ **UNS-10. Wilson And Uncle Sam Calendar,**
1918. 15" wide by 25" tall with full calendar pad. - **$65 $125 $200**

UNS-11

❑ **UNS-11. "Uncle Sam Lenox" Pocket Watch In Box,**
c. 1940. 2.25x2.25x.75" deep box holds 2" diameter watch with Uncle Sam in center. Box - **$100 $200 $300**
Watch - **$100 $250 $400**

UNS-12

❑ **UNS-12. "The Love Of Freedom" Poster With Uncle Sam,**
1942. 16.25x20.25" poster with copyright from Max A. Stern, Chicago. - **$30 $60 $125**

UNS-13

❑ **UNS-13. "Put Another Nail In Hitler's Coffin!" Sheet Music,**
1942. Fanfare Music Co. N.Y. 9x12" with six pages. - **$20 $40 $75**

UNS-14

❑ **UNS-14. World War II Original Art With Uncle Sam And Teddy Bear,**
1942. 13-7/8x14-7/8" black wood frame holds India ink drawing signed by C.K. Berryman, one of the top political cartoonists of the 20th century. Same Or Similar - **$125 $250 $500**

UNS-15

❑ **UNS-15. WWII Uncle Sam Figure,**
c. 1942. Rare and large 9" wide by 9" deep by 24" tall painted plaster figure. - **$200 $400 $750**

UNS-16

❑ **UNS-16. "Go To Town With Uncle Sam" World War II Punchboard,**
c. 1943. 9.75x13.25x1" thick punchboard with original metal punch key attached on back. - **$75 $150 $300**

UNS-17

❑ **UNS-17. Uncle Sam "Victory" Pin By "Coro",**
c. 1943. 2.75" enamel paint on brass pin. - **$30 $60 $125**

UNS-18

❑ **UNS-18. James Montgomery Flagg Rare Uncle Sam Wants FDR Poster,**
1944. Poster issued by "Independent Voter's Committee Of The Arts And Sciences For Roosevelt." - **$150 $300 $500**

UNS-19

❑ **UNS-19. Uncle Sam Glazed Ceramic Planter,**
1940s. 4" diameter by 6" tall. - **$15 $30 $60**

UNS-20

❑ **UNS-20. Uncle Sam "Dime A Day Register Bank",**
1950s. 2.5x2.5x.5" deep tin litho bank. Two varieties, silver borders or red borders. Each - **$100 $200 $400**

Uncle Scrooge

See Ted Hake's *Official® Price Guide to Disney Collectibles*, Second Edition, formatted identically to this book but in full color evaluating over 9,000 Disney company and character collectibles from 1924 through 2006.

Uncle Wiggily

Uncle Wiggily Longears, an elderly rabbit in a tailcoat, was created by writer Howard R. Garis (1873-1962) for a nationally syndicated newspaper column of bedtime stories that began appearing in 1910. Drawings were added for a Sunday page that ran from 1919 through the 1920s, and a daily comic strip appeared in the mid-1920s, illustrated by various artists, most notably Lang Campbell. Wiggily comic books were published between 1942 and 1954, and there have been dozens of *Uncle Wiggily* story books. On radio, Albert Goris was Wiggily, telling bedtime stories to his young audience.

Uncle Wiggily may be the most underated character in comic character history today! The newspaper strip and the great stories told in books about the Bunny Rabbit Gentleman are legendary. Uncle Wiggily features were one of the first to include real name villains. What a line-up he had to face. First there was the "Skillery Scallery Alligator" followed by the "Pipsisewak" and his mean buddy "Skeezicks." Other villains were the bad old "Skuddlemagoon" and the Fox and Wolf known as the "Bad Chaps", "Old Bazumbers" and the "Bob Cat", these villians were always after one thing, Uncle Wiggily's ears which were referred to by these scoundrels as "souse."

What made Uncle Wiggily stories so interesting was the direct tie-in with children and adults use of personal free time. The author would place the bunny in natural settings like a picnic, fishing trip, at the beach swimming, visit to the farm, holiday trips, sports activities and others. On each trip he would run into the scheming bad guys and of course escaped the impossible traps set by each villain.

Uncle Wiggily also had a great supporting cast of friends that joined him on his great adventures. These included Nurse Jane Fuzzy Wuzzy, Sammie and Suzie Littletail, Jackie and Peetie Bow Wow, Johnnie and Billie Bushytail, Grandpa Goosey Gander, Nannie and Billy Wagtail, Mrs. Wibblewobble and her son Jimmie, Curly and Floppy Twistytail, Kittie Kat and a host of others.

UWG-1

❑ **UWG-1. "Put A Hat On Uncle Wiggily" Party Game Kit,**
1919. Store item by Milton Bradley. Game sheet is 22x27". Envelope - **$12 $25 $40**
Uncut Game - **$50 $100 $200**

UWG-2

UWG-3

❑ **UWG-2. "Uncle Wiggily's Travels" Book,**
1922. No. 6 in a series of 28 of which only 7 books feature Uncle Wiggily. Many colored pictures with text. Scarce. - **$75 $150 $260**

❑ **UWG-3. "Uncle Wiggily's Fortune" Book,**
1922. No. 8 in the same series as UWG-2. Scarce. - **$75 $150 $260**

UWG-4

UWG-5

❑ **UWG-4. "Uncle Wiggily and the Pirates",**
1922. - **$20 $60 $125**

❑ **UWG-5. "Uncle Wiggily's Apple Roast",**
1922. - **$20 $60 $125**

UWG-6

UWG-7

UWG-8

❑ **UWG-6. "Uncle Wiggily's Holidays",**
1922. - **$20 $60 $125**

❑ **UWG-7. "Uncle Wiggily's June Bug Friends",**
1922. - **$20 $60 $125**

❑ **UWG-8. "Uncle Wiggily's Picnic",**
1922. - **$20 $60 $125**

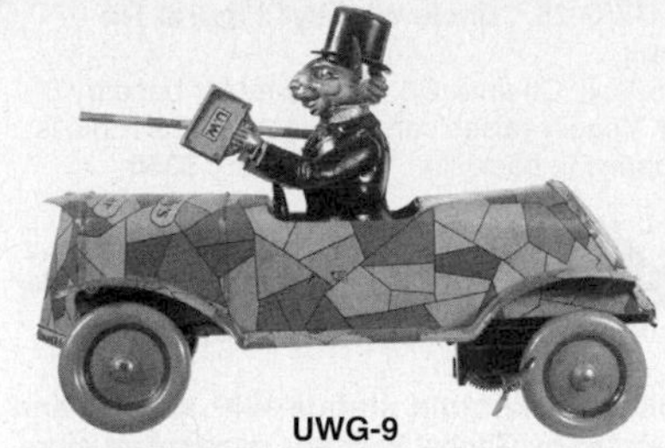

UWG-9

❑ **UWG-9. Uncle Wiggily's Crazy Car" German Wind-Up,**
c. 1922. Distler. 3.5x9.5x6.5" tall tin litho with built-in key. Toy bears name of Howard R. Garis, Uncle Wiggily's creator.
- **$2250 $4500 $7500**

UWG-10

UWG-11

UWG-12

❑ **UWG-10. China Mug,**
Copyright 1924. House named "Ovaltine House". Also came without name.
With Name - **$30 $60 $115**
No Name - **$40 $80 $165**
Two Handle Version - **$115 $225 $325**

❑ **UWG-11. China Plate,**
1924. Scarce. Store item by Sebring Pottery Co. Design matches mug. - **$60 $125 $250**

❑ **UWG-12. China Bowl With Silverplate Trim,**
1924. Rare store item by Sebring Pottery Co. Matches mug and plate. - **$150 $300 $500**

UWG-13

❑ **UWG-13. Two-Handle Mug Variety,**
1924. 3" tall china mug similar to single-handle Ovaltine version but without Ovaltine name and by different maker and copyright, possibly a store item. - **$115 $225 $325**

UWG-14

❑ **UWG-14. Uncle Wiggily and Grandpa Goosey Gander China Bowl,**
1924. Sebring Pottery Co. - **$125 $275 $450**

UWG-15

❑ **UWG-15. Boxed Game,**
c. 1920s. Milton Bradley #4817. - **$40 $75 $150**

UWG-16

UWG-17

❑ **UWG-16. "Hollow Stump Bungalow" Pressed Cardboard Toy With Figures,**
1920s. Store item by Androscoggin Pulp Co. 3-D residence and 10 diecut thin cardboard characters, each on wooden base.
Bungalow - **$100 $200 $400**
Each Figure - **$15 $30 $50**

❑ **UWG-17. "Animal Story Library" Box Set,**
1939. Box for 16 books, 8 of which were Uncle Wiggily. Books are 12 pages; 8" high and 6 7/8" wide. Other titles in the set are: Reddy Fox, Peter Rabbit (2), Babbling Coon, Flash the Deer, Three Little Bears, Paddy and Robber the Rat. Box - **$75 $150 $250**
Uncle Wiggily Books each - **$15 $25 $45**
Peter Rabbit Books each - **$10 $20 $35**
Other books each - **$5 $10 $20**

UWG-18

❑ **UWG-18. "Uncle Wiggily's Adventures" Boxed Set Of Four Storybooks,**
1939. Store item by Platt & Munk Co. with art by George Carlson. Set - **$50 $100 $200**

UWG-19

❑ **UWG-19. Color Relief Picture Framed,**
1930s. 9.75x11.75" framed painted image of strolling and smiling Uncle Wiggily. -
$30 $60 $125

(PUZZLE BOX)

Puzzle #1 shows some of the villains chasing Uncle Wiggily. The plot of many of his stories involved Wiggily's escapades with various villains who wanted to eat him, especially his ears.

Puzzle #2 shows Uncle Wiggily with many of his friends on a camping trip.

Puzzle #3 shows Uncle Wiggily with many of his friends at the beach.

UWG-20

❑ **UWG-20. "Uncle Wiggily" Picture Puzzles,**
1940. Scarce. Box contained three puzzles shown above. Box - **$35 $70 $150**
Each Puzzle- **$20 $30 $60**

UWG-21

UWG-22

❑ **UWG-21. Stuffed Doll,**
1943. Store item licensed by Georgine Averill. 20" tall stuffed cloth doll with fabric outfit including hat stitched to left hand. - **$225 $400 $800**

❑ **UWG-22. "Uncle Wiggily and the Red Monkey" Book,**
1943. From a series of 9 books, also used as a coloring book. There were 2 different sets- one with a slick cover and blank back cover and insides; the other had stiff cardboard covers, some with designs inside, some blank. Books measured 8 1/2" x 11". Each - **$8 $18 $35**

UWG-23

UWG-24

❑ **UWG-23. "Hollow Stump Club" Cello. Button,**
1946. WNJR Radio, Newark, New Jersey established by Newark Evening News. After Howard Garis retired from the newspaper, he read Uncle Wiggily stories over the air. Club membership and button distribution reached about 9,000 boys and girls. - **$50 $115 $250**

❑ **UWG-24. "Uncle Wiggily's Adventures" All Pictures Comics #1405,**
1946. - **$15 $45 $105**

UWG-25

❑ **UWG-25. "Uncle Wiggily" Figural Tin Bank,**
1950s. J. Chein & Co. 2.5" diameter base by 5" tall. Wiggily raises carrot to mouth when coin is dropped in back slot. - **$125 $225 $350**

Uncle Wip

Philadelphia radio station WIP, owned and operated by Gimbel Brothers department store, started broadcasting in March 1922. Uncle Wip's Kiddie Club was a late-afternoon children's program organized by the store which began within days of the station's first broadcast. Christopher Graham (1893-1930) was the first "Uncle Wip." In 1925 the show was so popular the city gave him an "Uncle Wip" license plate and a city vehicle. The show conitined with different hosts, winding up on TV in the 1950s.

UWP-1

UWP-2

❑ **UWP-1. "Uncle Wip And His Friends/Their Bed-Time Stories" Book,**
1923. - **$20 $60 $100**

❑ **UWP-2. "Uncle Wip's Kiddie Club" Certificate,**
1930s. Rare. - **$40 $85 $150**

UWP-3

UWP-4

UWP-5

❑ **UWP-3. "See Me At Gimbels" Cello. Button,**
1930s. Gimbels department store, Philadelphia. -
$20 $40 $75

❑ **UWP-4. "Uncle Wip's Kiddie Club At Gimbels" Cello. Button,**
1930s. Gimbels department store, Philadelphia. -
$10 $20 $35

❑ **UWP-5. "Uncle Wip's Kiddie Club/Listen In 6.45 P.M." Cello. Button,**
1930s. Gimbels department store, Philadelphia. -
$10 $20 $30

UWP-6

UWP-7

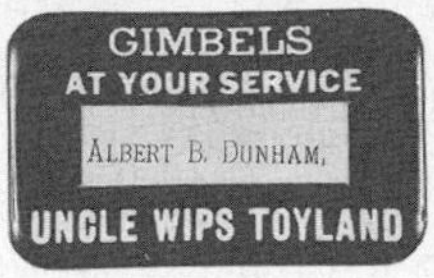

UWP-8

❏ **UWP-6. "Kiddie Klub/Gimbels" Cello. Button,**
1930s. Gimbels department store, Philadelphia. - **$5 $10 $15**

❏ **UWP-7. "Uncle Wip's Radio Girls" Cello. Buttons,** 1930s. - **$15 $30 $45**

❏ **UWP-8. "Uncle Wip's Toyland" Clerk Badge,**
1930s. Gimbels department store. 1-3/4x2-3/4" cello. slotted in rear for insertion of clerk's name paper. - **$25 $50 $100**

Underdog

Loveable, humble canine Shoeshine Boy was in actuality plucky superhero Underdog, whose magic cape and energy pills gave him the power to overcome mad scientists and villains, such as Simon Bar Sinister and Riff Raff, and rescue Sweet Polly Purebred, ace TV reporter. This animated series, with Wally Cox providing the voice of Underdog, aired on NBC from 1964 to 1966, moved to CBS from 1966 to 1968, then went back to NBC from 1968 to 1973. Noted Golden Age comic book artist Chad Grothkoff (1914-2005) was the main designer of the character. *Underdog* comic books appeared in the early 1970s. A live action feature film *Underdog* debuted in August 2007 with Jason Lee voicing the title character. Items are normally copyrighted Leonardo Productions.

UND-1

❏ **UND-1. "The Underdog Theme Song" Record With Sleeve,**
1965. LTY Records EP #1001. - **$15 $30 $60**

UND-2

❏ **UND-2. "Super Saturday Cavalcade" Cartoons Promotional Photo,**
1966. CBS-TV. Pictures stars of new Saturday morning lineup of animated color cartoons including Underdog. - **$15 $30 $50**

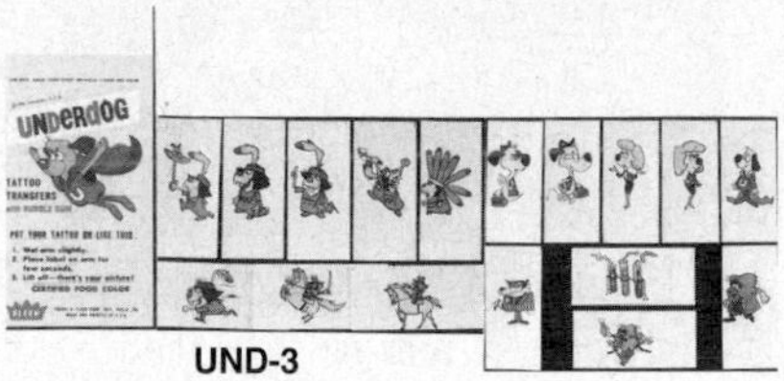

UND-3

❏ **UND-3. "Underdog Tattoo" Gum Wrappers,**
1966. Fleer's Gum. 17 different shown, each about 1.5x3.5" featuring same front design of flying Underdog. Reverses have different tattoo designs from both Underdog and Go-Go Gophers totaling nine different characters in variations from the two shows.
Each Unused Near Mint - **$20**
Each Used - **$3 $6 $12**

UND-4

❏ **UND-4. School Book Bag,**
1960s. 11.75" wide leatherette satchel featuring vinyl picture of Underdog rescuing Sweet Polly. - **$75 $150 $300**

UND-5

❏ **UND-5. Underdog Clock,**
1960s. Made in West Germany. Scarce. - **$80 $160 $275**

UND-6

UND-7

❏ **UND-6. Underdog Mug,**
1960s. Rare. Parents Magazine premium as well as Springmaid to promote their Underdog and Dudley Do-Right design sheets, bedspreads and towels. - **$60 $125 $250**

❏ **UND-7. Underdog Club Ring,**
1970. Charlton Comics. Silvered plastic expansion band with black on red paper picture. - **$20 $40 $60**

UND-8

❏ **UND-8. Fan Club Membership Card,**
1970. Charlton Comics. Part of fan club kit. - **$5 $10 $20**

UND-9

❏ **UND-9. T-Shirt,**
1970. Charlton Comics. - **$100 $200 $300**

UND-10

UND-11

❑ **UND-10. Sweatshirt,**
1970. Charlton Comics. - **$100 $200 $300**

❑ **UND-11. Color-Your-Own Giant Posters,**
1970. Charlton Comics. Set of six B&W 17x22" posters sent folded. Offered as "3 Good Guys/3 Funny Bad Guys" with pairs consisting of Underdog/Simon & Cad; Dudley Do-Right/ Snidely Whiplash; Bullwinkle & Rocky/Boris & Natasha. Each Uncolored - **$20 $40 $65**
Each Colored - **$10 $15 $30**

UND-12

❑ **UND-12. Wristwatch,**
1973. Store item by Lafayette with gold-tone case. Near Mint Boxed **- $500**
Loose **- $35 $100 $185**

UND-13 UND-14

❑ **UND-13. Premium Offer Poster,**
1974. Pacific Gas and Electric. 16x21". - **$20 $45 $80**

❑ **UND-14. "Kite Fun Book",**
1974. Pacific Gas and Electric. - **$5 $10 $30**

UND-15

❑ **UND-15. "Underdog Puzzler Squares" On Original Card,**
1975. Card is 6x7" and holds two 2.5x2.5" puzzles. Puzzles are of Underdog and Simon Bar Sinister. Carded - **$20 $40 $75**

UND-16

❑ **UND-16. "Save Sweet Polly" Game,**
1975. - **$40 $75 $150**

UND-17 UND-18

❑ **UND-17. Simon Bar Sinister Plastic Ring,**
1975. Vending machine. - **$75 $150 $225**

❑ **UND-18. "Saturday Cartoon Magnets",**
1975. Breaker Confections, Division of Sunline Inc., St. Louis. Set of four including Rocky, Bullwinkle, Speedy Gonzales, Underdog.
Order Folder - **$8 $15 $30**
Each Magnet - **$5 $10 $20**

UND-19

❑ **UND-19. Hard Vinyl Bank,**
1970s. Store item by Play Pal Plastics. 7-1/4" tall. **- $15 $35 $85**

UND-20 UND-21

❑ **UND-20. Pepsi Glass,**
c. 1970s. One of 5 Leonardo TTV characters in 16 oz. size. This one comes with and without Pepsi logo. - **$5 $10 $25**

❑ **UND-21. Plastic Cup And Bowl,**
1970s. Store item. Each - **$10 $20 $35**

UND-22

❑ **UND-22. Dakin Co. Vinyl Figure,**
1970s. Store item. Comes with blue felt cape. - **$35 $125 $225**
Near Mint Boxed - **$300**

UND-23 UND-24

❑ **UND-23. "Underdog" Plastic Ring,**
1970s. Vending machine item. Image in slight raised relief. - **$75 $150 $225**

❑ **UND-24. Underdog Rings Vending Machine Card,** 1970s. 5x7" insert display card diecut to hold six example plastic character image rings. - **$10 $20 $35**

UND-25 UND-26

❑ UND-25. "March Of Comics" Issue,
1981. No sponsor imprint on pictured example. Issue #479 by Western Publishing Co. - **$3 $9 $30**

❑ UND-26. "Macy's Thanksgiving Day Parade" Souvenir 3" Cello. Button,
1981. Pictures parade balloon figures of Underdog and Bullwinkle. - **$15 $30 $50**

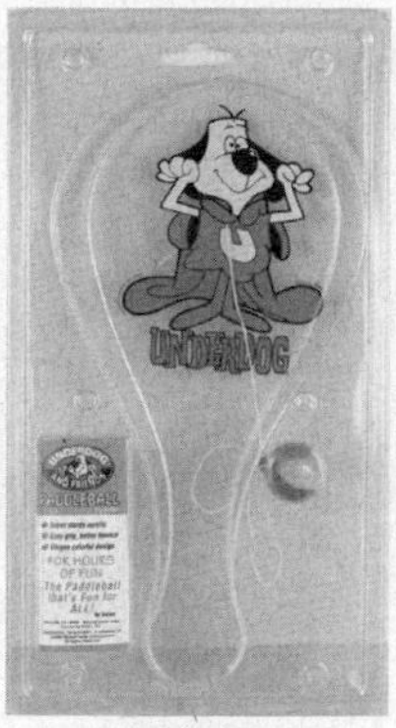

UND-27

❑ UND-27. Paddleball,
1997. With paper seal, in blister pack. - **$25**

UND-28

UND-29

❑ UND-28. Figures with "Power Pill" Ring in Box,
1998. - **$15 $25 $60**

❑ UND-29. Underdog Wacky Wobbler,
2000. - **$50**

Universal Monsters

It began in 1931 with the release of *Dracula*, starring Bela Lugosi (1882-1956) as the magnetic monster with a blood fetish. Universal had an enormous hit with the film version of Hamilton Deane's stage play based on Bram Stoker's novel. Originally intended for Lon Chaney (1883-1930), the film went to Lugosi after Chaney's death. *Frankenstein* followed that same year, directed by James Whale and featuring the macabre mastery of Boris Karloff (1887-1969) acting under heavy makeup designed by Jack Pierce. From these two films would spring an entire franchise of horror heroes who would reshape pop culture and make being scared something fun and exciting for generations of wide-eyed viewers.

As conflict around the globe escalated and America came closer to entering World War II, audiences turned increasingly to escapist fantasy in the theaters to embody and then vanquish their worst fears, and the Universal monsters were there to provide the catharsis. Universal launched a series based on *The Mummy* (again played by Karloff in its original appearance), blending Egyptian lore with fictional material. In 1941, Lon Chaney Jr. (1906-1973) portrayed the last of the major Universal monsters to be introduced, *The Wolf Man*. Universal then teamed these characters up in later installments to keep the excitement at a fever pitch and movie-goers in the theaters. *Frankenstein Meets the Wolf Man* (1943) brought Lugosi (now reduced to playing Frankenstein's monster after originally refusing the role) and Chaney Jr. together, and the final films in the Universal monster movie canon, *House of Frankenstein* (1944) and *House of Dracula* (1945), brought together all the major monsters and even resolved the Wolf Man's long-standing curse, allowing him to walk away with the girl at the end.

By the end of the 1940s, Universal Studios had established an extensive universe of scary stars who dominated the matinees and sparked a fan following that would ensure their immortality in the years to come (through the later publication of magazines like Forrest J. Ackerman's *Famous Monsters of Filmland*). Even when played for laughs, in movies like *Abbott and Costello Meet Frankenstein* (1948) (with Frankenstein, Dracula and the Wolf Man, also featuring Vincent Price in a closing Invisible Man cameo voice-over), or on television in guest appearances and parodies, the essential power of these characters did not diminish, and new generations of fans continued to discover the films.

By the 1950s, Frankenstein and the Wolf Man gave way to the Cold War and aliens from afar (none too subtle Communist metaphors invoked in many sci-fi and horror films). The era of the Universal monster appeared to be over, but Universal had a few more tricks up their sleeve with the release of the classic sci-fi film, *This Island Earth* (1954), featuring the Metaluna Mutant. *Creature From the Black Lagoon* (also 1954) brought us face to face with the misunderstood Gill-Man, an evolutionary throwback discovered in the Amazon and brought back in two sequels.

Decades later, countless reruns of all the old films on local television have made all the Universal monsters into cultural icons that remain potent and entertaining to this day. In the last few years, Sideshow Toys has sparked a renewal of collector interest in the venerable stars of the silver scream with an extensive line of merchandise, from action figures to polystone sculptures. Most items are copyright Universal Studios. The Universal Studios theme parks in North Hollywood, CA and Orlando, Florida help keep the thrills alive.

UVM-1

❑ UVM-1. "Frankenstein" Early Movie Theater Giveaway Photo,
1930s. 4x5-1/8" with inscription "I'll Be Scaring You-Frankenstein At Capitol Theater Newark N.J." - **$135 $300 $600**

UVM-2

❑ UVM-2. "Boris Karloff" Frankenstein Pennant,
1930s. Miniature brown felt pennant 2.25x4.25" long with profile of Frankenstein.
- **$40 $75 $150**

UVM-3

❑ UVM-3. "Aurora Frankenstein" Model,
1061. Universal Pictures Co. Inc.
5.25x13.25x2.25" deep box.
Near Mint Boxed - **$350**
Built (No Box) - **$20 $40 $100**

UVM-4

❑ **UVM-4. Wolf Man Model Kit,**
1962. Store item by Aurora.
Near Mint Boxed - **$350**
Built Unboxed - **$20 $40 $100**

UVM-5

❑ **UVM-5. Dracula Model Kit,**
1962. Store item by Aurora.
Near Mint Boxed - **$350**
Built No Box - **$15 $30 $80**

UVM-6

❑ **UVM-6. Frankenstein Battery Operated Figure Toy Boxed,**
1963. Marx Toys. 12.5" tall litho tin and vinyl remote control toy that grasps objects, walks forward, bends up and down.
Box - **$125 $300 $600**
Toy With Black Shoes- **$250 $500 $1200**
Toy With Brown Shoes- **$350 $700 $1400**

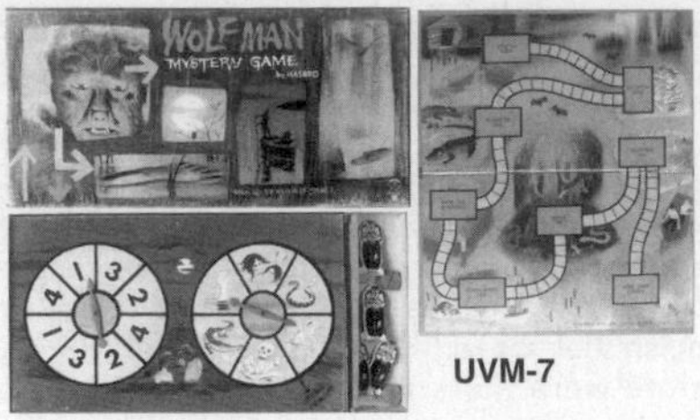

UVM-7

❑ **UVM-7. "Wolf Man Mystery Game" Boxed,**
1963. Hasbro. 9.5x19x1.5" boxed board game with accessory figures and pieces. -
$125 $275 $450

UVM-8

❑ **UVM-8. "The Mummy" Model Kit,**
1963. Store item by Aurora.
Near Mint Boxed - **$400**
Built No Box - **$25 $45 $110**

❑ **UVM-9. "Dracula" Three-Ring Binder,**
c. 1963. Vinyl over cardboard from binder series including Wolf Man and Frankenstein.
Each - **$100 $165 $300**

❑ **UVM-10. "The Phantom Of The Opera Mystery Game,"**
c. 1963. Hasbro, Universal Pictures Corp. 9.5x19x1.5" deep box. Parts are board, spinner, four die-cut cardboard Phantom playing pieces, wood bases, ten "Phantom Escape cards" and 20 "Phantom Cell Key" cards.
- **$400 $800 $1500**

UVM-11

❑ **UVM-11. "Gigantic Frankenstein" Model Kit,**
1964. Store item by Aurora. Large 14.5x18x5" deep box. Boxed Unbuilt - **$400 $800 $1600**

UVM-12

❑ **UVM-12. "Dracula's Dragster" Model Kit,**
1964. Store item by Aurora.
Near Mint Boxed - **$500**
Built No Box - **$50 $100 $200**

UVM-13

❑ **UVM-13. "Aurora Wolf Man's Wagon" Model,**
1964. Universal Pictures Co. Inc.
5.25x13.25x2.25" deep box.
Near Mint Boxed - **$500**
Built (No Box) - **$50 $100 $200**

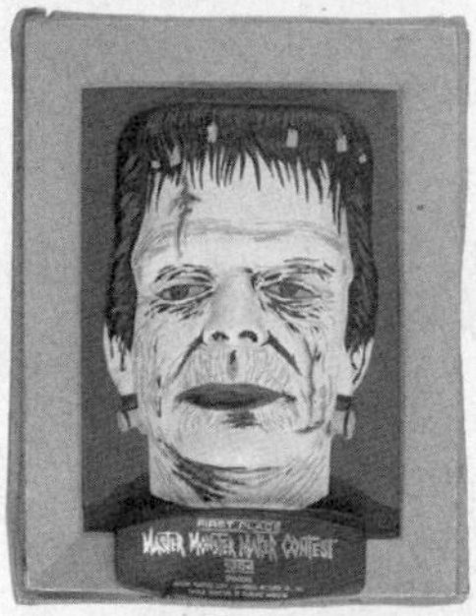

UVM-14

❏ UVM-14. Aurora Monster Model Contest Prize,
1964. 10x13x1" deep vacuform plastic with cardboard backing. Designed like a framed picture. Simulated plaque on front reads "First Place Master Monster Maker Contest 1964/Sponsors Aurora Plastics Corp./Universal Pictures Company Inc./Famous Monsters Of Filmland Magazine." Winning models were featured in Issue No. 32 Famous Monsters Magazine. - **$325 $650 $1300**

UVM-15

UVM-16

❏ UVM-15. "Bride Of Frankenstein/A Book-Box Paperdoll,"
1964. Store item by Merry Mfg. Co. Includes 15" tall diecut paperdoll. - **$40 $75 $150**

❏ UVM-16. Large Buttons,
c. 1965. Elwar Ltd. 3-1/2" full color button. Set includes Dracula, Frankenstein, Mummy, Wolf Man, Creature From Black Lagoon.
Each - **$20 $50 $100**

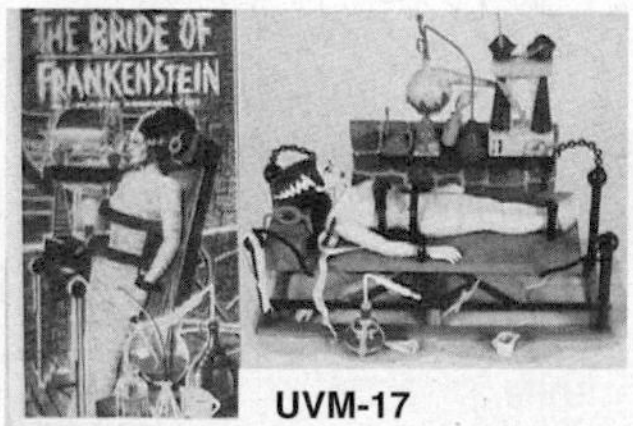

UVM-17

❏ UVM-17. The Bride Of Frankenstein Model Kit,
1965. Store item by Aurora.
Near Mint Boxed - **$1000**
Built No Box - **$100 $200 $400**

UVM-18

❏ UVM-18. Universal Monster Flicker Rings,
1960s. Vending machine issues. Each ring has two images of the character. Of those we've seen, all are black and white on green background except for the Mummy which is black and white on red background. Prices are for examples on silver plastic bases unmarked or marked "Hong Kong," not for flickers mounted on bases marked "China."
Dracula - **$60 $115 $200**
Frankenstein - **$60 $115 $200**
Wolf Man - **$85 $165 $300**
Mummy - **$60 $115 $300**
Phantom - **$60 $115 $300**

UVM-19

❏ UVM-19. Universal Monsters "Soaky" Bottles,
1960s. 10" tall soft vinyl and hard plastic soap bottle from series depicting him and three other Universal Pictures Co. monsters.
Frankenstein - **$30 $60 $115**
Creature - **$40 $85 $160**
Mummy - **$45 $90 $175**
Wolf Man - **$30 $60 $115**

UVM-20

❏ UVM-20. Monster Figures By Palmer Plastics,
1960s. Store item, unmarked. 3" tall in single color soft plastic. Pictured are: Creature From The Black Lagoon, Frankenstein, Wolf Man, Dracula, and It! from the movie *The Terror From Beyond Space*. Each - **$10 $18 $35**

UVM-21

❏ UVM-21. Universal Monsters Flicker Rings,
1960s. Probable vending machine issue. Soft plastic base with full color flicker featuring images taken from Don Post Universal Monster masks. Two images per ring: Creature From The Black Lagoon/Mr. Hyde, Phantom Of The Opera/Wolf Man, Mummy/Hunchback.
Each - **$25 $50 $85**

UVM-22

❏ UVM-22. Creature Action Aerating Aquarium Figure,
1971. Penn-Plax, 5-1/2" plastic figure.
Boxed - **$250 $500 $1000**
Loose - **$100 $200 $500**

UVM-23

❑ **UVM-23. "Universal's Movie Monsters" Lunch Box With Thermos,**
1979. Store item by Aladdin.
Box **- $85 $175 $400**
Bottle **- $15 $30 $60**

UVM-24

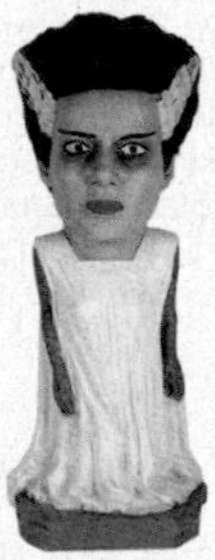

UVM-25

❑ **UVM-24. Dracula Figure,**
1980. **- $25 $45 $90**

❑ **UVM-25. Bride of Frankenstein Figure,**
1980. **- $25 $45 $90**

UVM-26

UVM-27

❑ **UVM-26. "Dracula" Glass Tumbler,**
1980. Universal City Studios. 5.5" from monster series of very limited distribution. -
$25 $50 $100

❑ **UVM-27. "Frankenstein" Glass Tumbler,**
1980. Universal City Studios. 5.5" from series of very limited distribution. **- $25 $50 $100**

UVM-28

UVM-29

❑ **UVM-28. "Creature From The Black Lagoon" Glass Tumbler,**
1980. Universal City Studios. 5.5" from monster series of very limited distribution. -
$20 $50 $100

❑ **UVM-29. "The Mutant" Glass Tumbler,**
1980. Universal City Studios. 5.5" from series of very limited distribution. **- $20 $50 $100**

UVM-30

UVM-31

❑ **UVM-30. Ball Puzzle Party Favors,**
1991. 8 ball puzzles featuring Frankenstein, Dracula, Wolfman and the Mummy on card.
Complete **- $50**
Each puzzle **- $5**

❑ **UVM-31. "The Mummy" Figure in Box,**
1998. Hasbro. **- $5 $15 $30**

UVM-32

UVM-33

❑ **UVM-32. "Frankenstein" Figure in Box,**
1998. Hasbro. **- $5 $15 $30**

❑ **UVM-33. "The Bride of Frankenstein" Figure in Box,**
1998. Hasbro. **- $5 $15 $30**

UVM-34

❑ **UVM-34. Collector Beans Box,**
1999. Green colored box for holding the limited edition bean bag figures. Box only **- $35**

UVM-35

UVM-36

❑ **UVM-35. "Frankenstein" Bean Figure,**
1999. Limited edition figure with tag. **- $10**

❑ **UVM-36. "The Bride of Frankenstein" Bean Figure,**
1999. Limited edition figure with tag. **- $10**

UVM-37

UVM-38

❑ **UVM-37. "Dracula" Bean Figure,**
1999. Limited edition figure with tag. **- $10**

❑ **UVM-38. "The Mummy" Bean Figure,**
1999. Limited edition figure with tag. **- $10**

UVM-39

UVM-40

❑ **UVM-39. "The Wolf Man" Bean Figure,**
1999. Limited edition figure with tag. - **$10**

❑ **UVM-40. "The Creature From the Black Lagoon" Bean Figure,**
1999. Limited edition figure with tag. - **$10**

UVM-41

UVM-42

❑ **UVM-41. "The Hunchback" Bean Figure,**
1999. Limited edition figure with tag. - **$10**

❑ **UVM-42. "The Phantom of the Opera" Bean Figure,**
1999. Limited edition figure with tag. - **$10**

UVM-43

UVM-44

❑ **UVM-43. "Sweet Crispers" Cookie Box,**
1999. Promotes Universal Monsters Prize trip to Universal Studios in Florida. Features the Creature on box front. Dracula is on the side of the box. - **$2 $3 $4**

❑ **UVM-44. "Monsters Cookies" Box,**
1999. Promotes Universal Studios in Florida. The main monsters are on the box. - **$2 $3 $4**

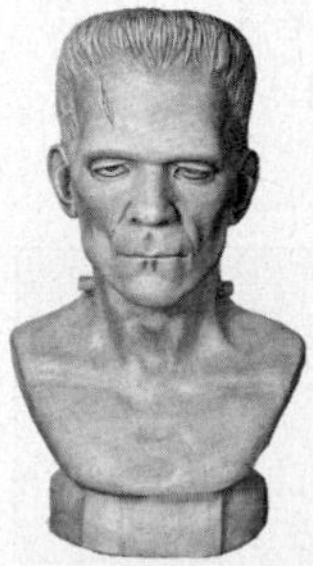

UVM-45

UVM-46

❑ **UVM-45. "Frankenstein" Bust,**
1990s. Very heavy 17 1/2" tall bust is an incredible likeness of Boris Karloff as the Monster. Limited edition of 50 from Karloff Studios. Production was supervised by Karloff's daughter. - **$650**

❑ **UVM-46. "The Mummy" Bust,**
1990s. Very heavy 17 1/2" tall bust is an incredible likeness of Boris Karloff as the Mummy. Limited edition of 50 from Karloff Studios. Production was supervised by Karloff's daughter. - **$650**

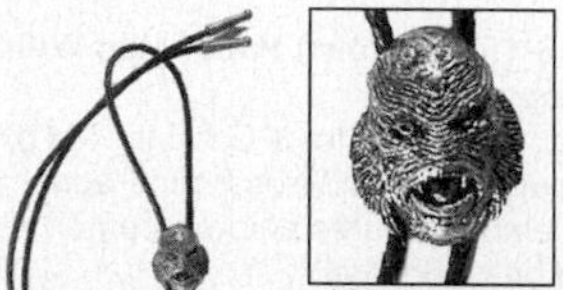

(Close-up of Creature face)

UVM-47

❑ **UVM-47. "The Creature" Bolo Tie,**
1990s. Only 10 made. By Randy Bowen. - **$275**

UVM-48

UVM-49

❑ **UVM-48. Bela Lugosi Resin Statue,**
1990s. Crafted by Randy Bowen. Limited edition of 1,000. Boxed - **$225**

❑ **UVM-49. "Dracula" Die-cast Metal Car,**
2000. Team Lightning. - **$5**

UVM-50

❑ **UVM-50. "Classic Movie Monsters" Boxed Set,**
2001. Features Frankenstein, the Mummy and the Wolf Man. - **$15 $30 $60**

UVM-51

❑ **UVM-51. Monster Figures Boxed Set,**
2001. 9 small figures boxed. - **$10 $20 $40**

U.S. Jones

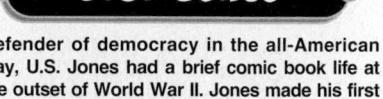

Defender of democracy in the all-American way, U.S. Jones had a brief comic book life at the outset of World War II. Jones made his first appearance in issue #28 of *Wonderworld Comics* in August 1941, and two issues of his own book appeared in 1941 and 1942. U.S. Jones Cadets received a decoder, a pinback button, and other membership material in the form of a "National Emergency Kit."

USJ-1

❑ **USJ-1. "U.S. Jones Cadets" Comic Book Club Cello. Button,**
1941. Rare. Part of member's kit. -
$1250 $3500 $6000

USJ-2

USJ-3

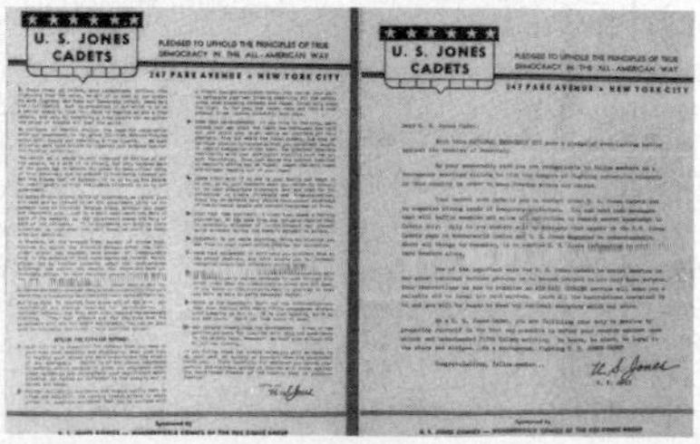

USJ-4

❑ **USJ-2. Secret Code Card,**
1941. Rare. Part of member's kit. Has instructions for use of 26 different code keys. -
$250 $500 $1000

❑ **USJ-3. Cadets Membership Card,**
1941. Rare. Part of member's kit. -
$200 $400 $800

❑ **USJ-4. Cadet Cover Letter And Cadet Civil Defense Sheet,**
1941. Rare. Part of member's kit. Explains kit and duties with pledge text.
Each - **$100 $200 $400**

USJ-5

❑ **USJ-5. U.S. Jones #1 Comic Book Ad,**
1941. Inside cover ad shown. - **$25 $50 $125**

Vic and Sade

Considered by many to be one of the greatest radio shows ever, *Vic and Sade* has been called a true original and the best American humor of its day. The series told of events in the daily lives of radio's home folks--Victor Gook, his wife Sade, their son Rush, and Sade's Uncle Fletcher--who lived in the little house halfway up in the next block in the town of Crooper, Illinois. Written by Paul Rhymer, *Vic and Sade* aired on the NBC, CBS, and Mutual networks from 1932 to 1946. The cast included Art Van Harvey, Bernadine Flynn, Billy Idelson and David Whitehouse. The show was the *Seinfeld* of it's day, a really interesting show about nothing. The program was supported by local advertisers the first two years until Crisco took over as longterm sponsor. Fitch's Cocoanut Shampoo sponsored in 1946.

VAS-1

❑ **VAS-1. Hometown Paper Map With Mailer Envelope,**
c. 1942. Rare. Procter & Gamble. 14x16" map of "Crooper, Illinois/40 Miles From Peoria" with cast member pictures at lower corner. Also issued on cardboard.
Envelope - **$20 $30 $60**
Map - **$150 $350 $700**

The Virginian

***The Virginian* 1902 novel by Owen Wister established many of the norms we associate with cowboy culture and inspired three Hollywood feature films: a 1914 version starring Dustin Farnum directed by C.B. DeMille; Paramount's 1929 version with Gary Cooper, Walter Huston, Richard Arlen and Mary Brian; and a 1946 version with Joel McCrea, Brian Donlevy and Sonny Tufts.**

NBC introduced *The Virginian* to prime time TV September 19, 1962. TV's first 90-minute western ran until March 24, 1971: nine seasons with 249 episodes.

Set at the Shiloh Ranch in Medicine Bow, Wyoming Territory, the series was written by Roy Huggins and Theodore Apstein. Percy Faith wrote the *Lonesome Tree* theme song.

The cast included: James Drury as ranch foreman and man with no name, Doug McClure as Trampas, Gary Clarke as Steve Hill, Lee J. Cobb as Judge Henry Garth, Roberta Shore as Betsy Garth and Pippa Scott as Molly Wood.

During the last season, the show's title changed to *The Men From Shiloh.*

Gold Key published one comic book in June, 1963.

VRG-1

❑ **VRG-1. "The Virginian" With Gary Cooper Lobby Cards,**
1929. Paramount Pictures. Two 14x17" linen-like lobby cards. Each - **$50 $100 $175**

VRG-2

❑ **VRG-2. "The Virginian" Hardcover With Gary Cooper Shown On Dust Jacket,**
1935. Grosset & Dunlap. 5.25x7.5" with 506 pages. Has illustrations by noted western artist Frederic Remington. May, 1935 edition.
Jacket - **$5 $10 $20**
Book - **$5 $10 $20**

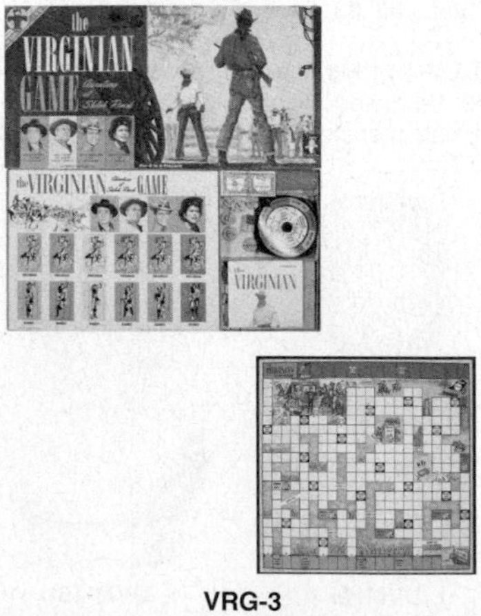

VRG-3

❑ **VRG-3. "The Virginian Game",**
1962. Transogram. 10x19.5x2" deep box contains playing pieces, spinner, play money and wooden peg bullets. - **$25 $50 $100**

VRG-4

❑ **VRG-4. "Universal City Studios" Four-Part Coloring Book Including Wagon Train And The Virginian,**
1964. MCA Enterprises. 8-3/8x10.75" with 128 pages. Other shows are "Karen" and "McHale's Navy." - **$10 $20 $40**

Wagon Train

Loosely based on the John Ford 1950 feature film *Wagon Master* which starred Ben Johnson, Joanne Dru, Harry Carey Jr., and Ward Bond, the TV show began on NBC September 18, 1957 and ran until September, 1962. The series moved to ABC in September, 1962 and ran until September, 1965: eight seasons, 442 episodes. Writers included Vince Giffon and Halsey Malone; directors included John English and Tay Garnett. The basic plot line was the journey of a wagon train heading west from post Civil War Missouri to California.

The notable cast included: Ward Bond (1903-1960) as wagon master Seth Adams, Robert Horton as Flint McCullough, Terry Wilson as Bill Hawks, Frank McGrath as Charlie Wooster and Robert Fuller as Cooper Smith. John McIntire took over as wagon master Christopher Hale when Ward Bond passed away in 1960. Guest stars included: Ronald Reagan, Bette Davis, Barbara Stanwyck and Lee Marvin.

Dell published 13 comics between March, 1958 and June, 1962 and Gold Key published four comics in 1964. All have photo covers. "Wagons Ho!"

WAG-1

❑ **WAG-1. "Wagon Train" First Edition Little Golden Book,**
1958. Revue Productions Inc. 6.5x8". - **$5 $15 $35**

WAG-2

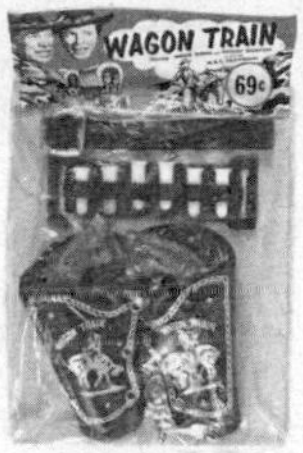

WAG-3

❑ **WAG-2. "Wagon Train" T-Shirt,**
1958. Revue Productions Inc. 15.25" tall child's size 8 t-shirt. - **$10 $25 $60**

❑ **WAG-3. "Wagon Train" Toy Clicker Gun In Holster Set With Badge On Store Card,**
1958. Revue Productions Inc. 7.25x11.75" card has attached clear vinyl bag holding holster set, pair of plastic clicking guns, gun belt with bullets and metal "Junior Marshal" badge. - **$50 $100 $150**

WAG-4

❑ **WAG-4. "Wagon Train Western Six Gun" With "Zing" Cap Gun,**
1958. Leslie-Henry Co. 9.5x16x1.75" deep cardboard packaging with tapered sides to give appearance of gun being in a frame. Gun is 4.5x11" cast metal with plastic grips. Includes 1.25x5" plastic bullet clip with six metal bullets
Packaged - **$125 $250 $500**
Gun Only - **$35 $65 $100**

WAG-5

❑ **WAG-5. Wagon Train Star Rare Button From "Robert Horton Fan Club",**
1958. 1" button made in England. - **$15 $30 $60**

WAG-6

❑ **WAG-6. "Wagon Train" Coloring Book,**
1959. Whitman. 8-3/8x10.75" with 128 pages. Book No. 1122. - **$10 $20 $40**

WAG-7

❑ **WAG-7. Nabisco Major Adams TV Sign 13x13",**
1950s. Promotes TV show, "Major Adams Trailmaster." Earlier TV program called Wagon Train. - **$55 $110 $225**

WAG-8

❑ **WAG-8. "Wagon Train" Frame Tray Puzzle,**
1961. Whitman. 11-3/8x14.5". #4427. - **$8 $15 $35**

Wanted-Dead or Alive

The pilot episode aired on the Robert Culp TV series *Trackdown* in March, 1958. The CBS show began September 6, 1958 and ran until March 29, 1961 with 94 episodes. Steve McQueen (1930-1980) played bounty hunter Josh Randall who had a sympathetic side. He was aided by his trusty Mare's Laig, a sawed-off Winchester Model 83 carbine. Co-stars included Wright King, Mort Mills and Olan Soule. Writers included D.D. and Mary Beauchamp and Ed Adamson. Directors included Thomas Carr and Don McDougall.

New World Pictures released a feature film sequel set in modern times on November 6, 1987 with Rutger Hauer as former CIA agent and bounty hunter Nick Randall who tracks down terrorists.

Dell published two *Wanted: Dead or Alive* comics with photo covers in 1960-61.

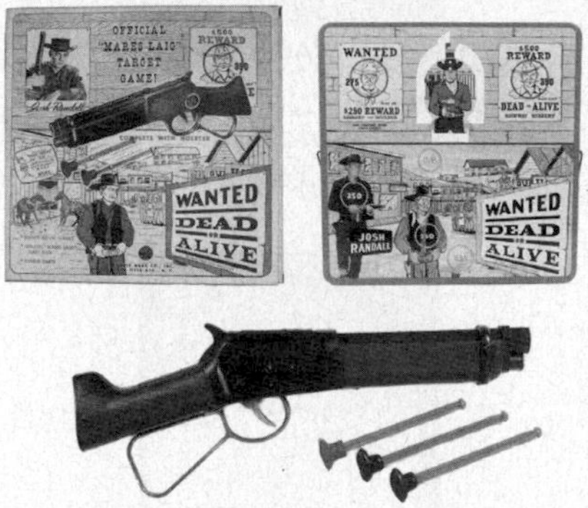

WDA-1

❑ **WDA-1. "Marx Wanted Dead Or Alive Official Mares Laig Target Game",**
1959. 15.5x15.5x2" deep box with cardboard insert that fits around target. Includes hard plastic and metal gun 13.5" with Marx logo that fires caps. Also comes with 4 suction cup darts and 15x15" tin litho target with wire easel attachment. - **$200 $400 $650**

WDA-2

❑ **WDA-2. "Wanted: Dead Or Alive/Mare's Laig" Miniature Rifle Cap Gun,**
c. 1959. Marx. 5.5" long dark metal and deep brown plastic replica of sawed-off rifle. Fires single cap. Card (not shown) - **$15 $25 $50**
Rifle Only - **$20 $40 $75**

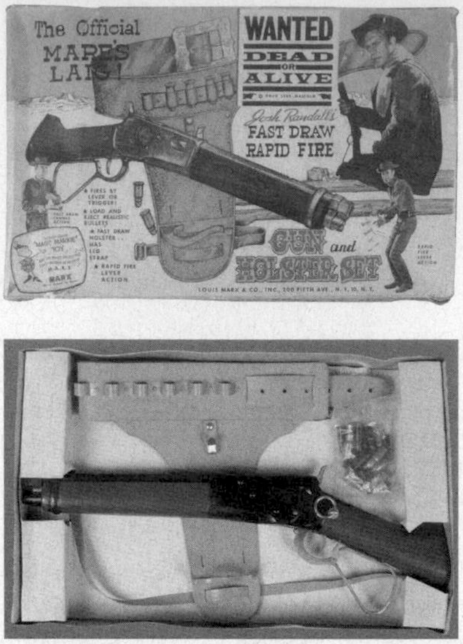

WDA-3

❑ **WDA-3. "The Official Mare's Laig!/Wanted Dead Or Alive Gun And Holster Set",**
c. 1959. Marx. 12x19x2" deep box holds 19" gun, the largest of three by Marx and this one ejects shells. - **$250 $500 $800**

WDA-4

❑ **WDA-4. "Wanted Dead Or Alive Game" By Lowell,**
c. 1959. 9x17.25x2" deep box. - **$40 $85 $175**

WDA-5

❑ **WDA-5. "Mares Laig" "Wanted Dead or Alive" Western Rifle Pistol on Card,**
1960. NM Carded - **$600**
Gun Only - **$85 $175 $325**

WDA-6

❑ **WDA-6. "Steve McQueen It's A Stetson" Poster,**
1990. Stetson. 27.5x39.5" heavy glossy stock with 24.25x33-7/8" black and white photo of McQueen. - **$25 $50 $125**

Wheaties Misc.

Wheaties, the Breakfast of Champions, was the result of a kitchen accident in 1921 when some gruel spilled on a hot stove and turned into crispy flakes. The Washburn Crosby Company in Minneapolis developed the cereal and began marketing it regionally in 1924. Advertising on radio, including the world's first singing commercial, proved successful and by 1928, when Washburn Crosby joined with other grain millers to form General Mills, Wheaties was an established product. Over the years sponsorship of such popular radio programs as *Jack Armstrong* and *Skippy*, as well as continuing promotion that linked the product to major figures in sports and the movies, has kept Wheaties an all-American favorite breakfast food. This section shows an assortment of their baseball and non-character premiums.

WHE-1

WHE-2

❑ **WHE-1. "Earl Averill" Box Back,**
1937. From a series of baseball stars described by their 1936 season statistics. - **$20 $30 $60**
Complete Box - **$200 $375 $750**

❑ **WHE-2. Knothole Drilling Insect 2-1/2" Cello. Button,**
c. 1930s. - **$25 $50 $100**

WHE-3

WHE-4

❑ **WHE-3. "Champs" Of The U.S.A. Box Back #1 Stamp Set,**
1930s. Shows 3 different cut-out stamps of Charles Ruffing, Lynn Patrick, and Leo Durocher. - **$20 $35 $70**

❑ **WHE-4. "Champs" Of The U.S.A. Box Back #2 Stamp Set,**
1930s. Shows 3 different cut-out stamps of Joe Dimaggio, Mel Ott, and Ellsworth Vines. - **$30 $60 $115**

WHE-5

WHE-6

❑ **WHE-5. "Champs" Of The U.S.A. Box Back #3 Stamp Set,**
1930s. Shows 3 different cut-out stamps of Jimmie Foxx, Bernie Bierman, and Bill Dickey. - **$25 $45 $85**

❑ **WHE-6. "Champs" Of The U.S.A. Box Back #5 Stamp Set,**
1930s. Shows 3 different cut-out stamps of Joe Medwick, Madison "Matty" Bell, and Ab Jenkins. - **$15 $20 $45**

WHE-7

WHE-8

❑ **WHE-7. "Champs" Of The U.S.A. Box Back #6 Stamp Set,**
1930s. Shows 3 different cut-out stamps of John Mize, Davey O'Brien, and Ralph Guldahl. - **$15 $20 $45**

❑ **WHE-8. "Champs" Of The U.S.A. Box Back #7 Stamp Set,**
1930s. Shows 3 different cut-out stamps of Joe Cronin, Cecil Isbell, and Byron Nelson. - **$15 $20 $45**

WHE-9

WHE-10

❑ **WHE-9. "Champs" Of The U.S.A. Box Back #8 Stamp Set,**
1930s. Shows 3 different cut-out stamps of Paul Derringer, Ernie Lombardi, and George I. Myers. - **$15 $20 $45**

❑ **WHE-10. "Champs" Of The U.S.A. Box Back #12 Stamp Set,**
1930s. Shows 3 different cut-out stamps of Hugh McManus, Luke Appling, and Stanley Hack. - **$15 $20 $45**

WHE-11

❑ **WHE-11. "Funny Stuff" Comic,**
1946. Books were taped to boxes.
Good - **$170**
Fine - **$500**

WHE-12

❑ **WHE-12. "Wheaties Hole-In-One Club" Member Certificate,**
c. 1949. 9x12" stiff paper with cartoon art, gold foil sticker, entry lines for name, date and course name for player achieving golf hole-in-one. - **$30 $45 $90**

WHE-13

❑ **WHE-13. Miniature Metal License Plates With Mailer,**
1953. Offered in four sets of 12 plus bonus District of Columbia if all ordered at same time.
Each License - **$5 $10 $15**

WHE-14

❑ **WHE-14. Box Flat - 1 oz.,**
1953. Has rare George Mikan basketball card on back - the key to the set. - **$75 $150 $300**

WHE-15

❑ **WHE-15. Box Back With Sports Cards,**
1950s. Has 7 sports cards. - **$50 $100 $150**

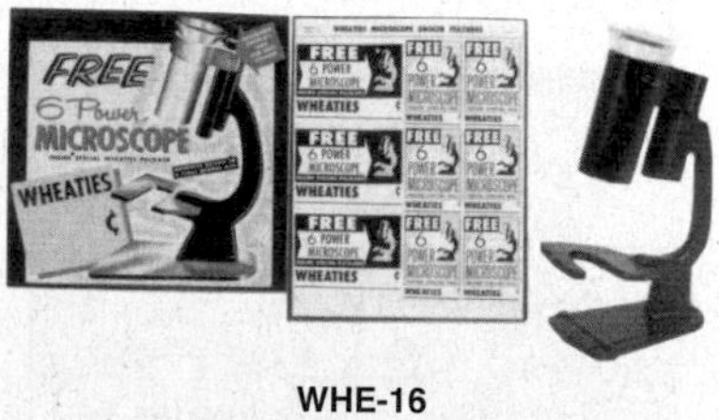

WHE-16

❑ **WHE-16. "Wheaties 6 Power Microscope" Store Display Sign, Shelf Stickers And Premium,**
1950s. Sign is 13-1/2x13-1/2". Gordon Gold Archives. Display - **$50 $100 $200**
Sticker Sheet - **$10 $15 $30**
Microscope - **$8 $12 $25**

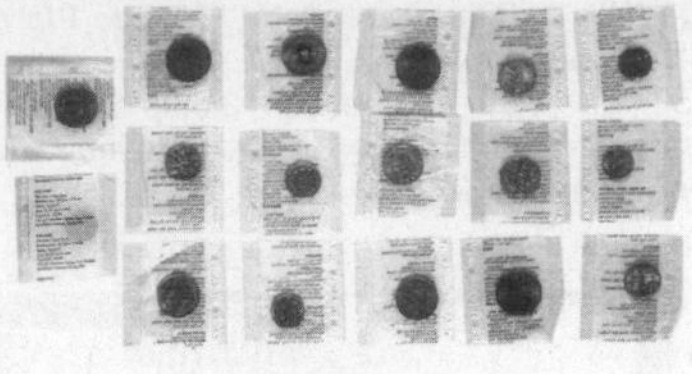

WHE-17

❑ **WHE-17. Wrapped Coins,**
1955. 17 international coins pictured with Wheaties wrapper. Each wrapper explains coin and facts about each country. Coin with wrapper was a premium given away in each box of Wheaties. Each - **$8 $15 $30**

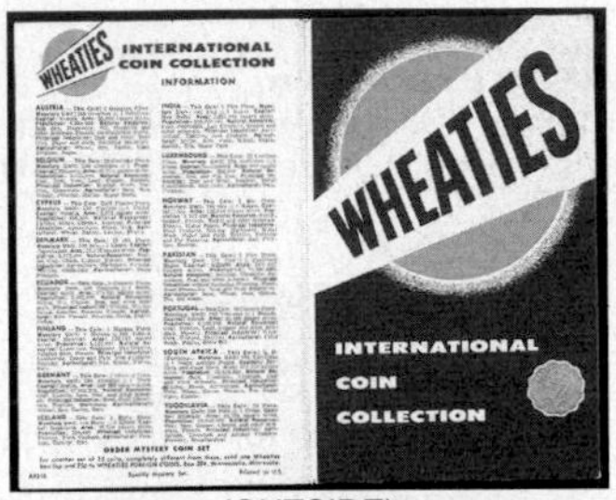

(OUTSIDE)

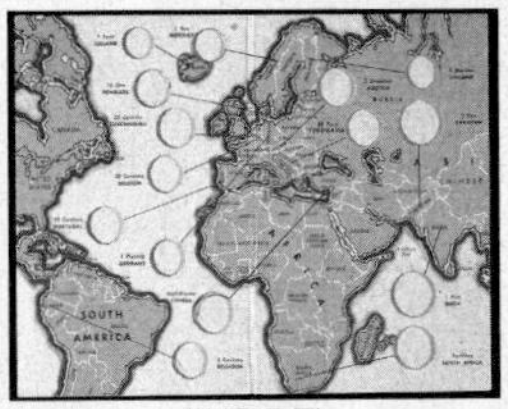

(INSIDE)

WHE-18

❑ **WHE-18. Coin Card,**
1955. Holder for 15 coins. International set. - **$20 $40 $65**

WHE-19

❑ **WHE-19. Cereal Box Featuring Champy And Mr. Fox Hand Puppets,**
1957. Side panel has order coupon for both puppets and the puppet theater. Gordon Gold Archives. Used Complete - **$115 $200 $350**

WHE-20

❑ **WHE-20. "Champy's Theatre" With Hand Puppets,**
1957. 17x44" theater assembly sheet offered as part of mail purchase of Champy and Mr. Fox puppets based on creation by Bill Baird for Mickey Mouse Club TV show.
Theater - **$25 $50 $100**
Each Puppet - **$25 $50 $100**

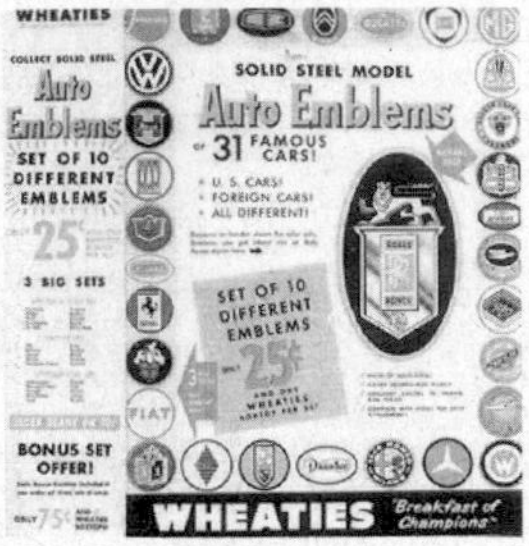

WHE-21

❑ **WHE-21. "Auto Emblems" Box,**
1950s. Shows all 31 emblems offered.
Complete - **$75 $150 $300**

WHE-22

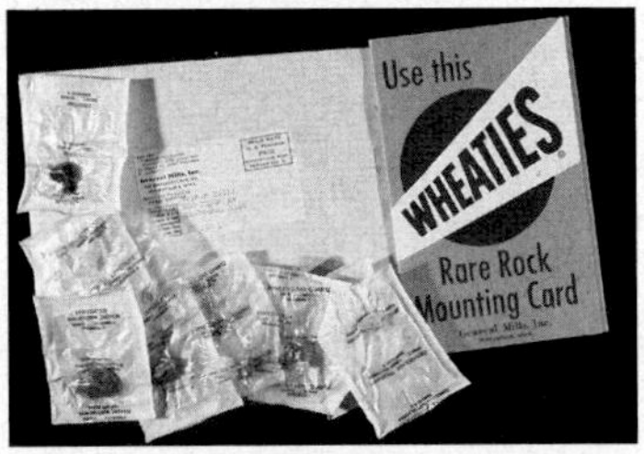

WHE-23

❑ **WHE-22. Hike-O-Meter,**
1950s. Pedometer with aluminum rim. - **$15 $25 $35**

❑ **WHE-23. Rare Rock Card,**
1950s. With 11 different rocks in descriptive mailers.
Display Card with Mailer - **$20 $40 $60**
Rocks in Packet Each - **$25**

WHE-24

❑ **WHE-24. Airline Stickers,**
1950s. Offered in each box of Wheaties. Stickers were 3"x3-1/2". 15 in the set.
Each - **$5 $10 $20**

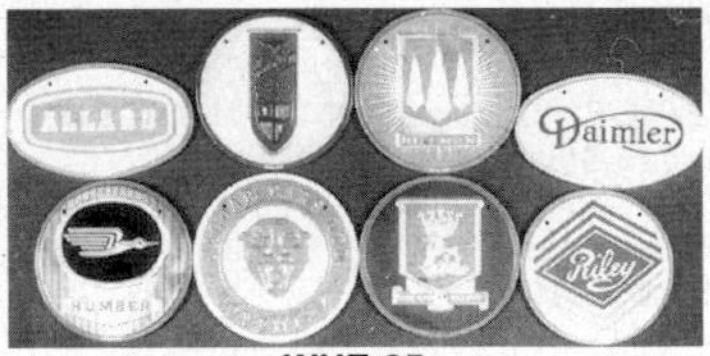

WHE-25

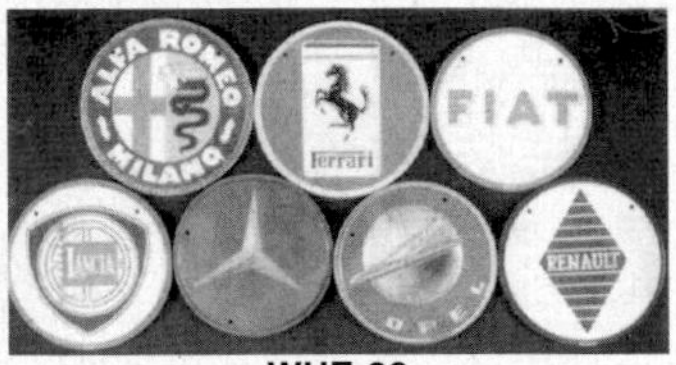

WHE-26

❑ **WHE-25. British Auto Metal Emblems,**
1950s. Set of 10, Bentley and MG not shown.
Each - **$5 $10 $20**

❑ **WHE-26. Continental Auto Metal Emblems,**
1950s. Set of 10. Volkswagen, Citroen, Bugati not shown. Each - **$5 $10 $20**

WHE-27

❑ **WHE-27. Auto Emblems,**
1950s. Ten different tin U.S. car emblems, mailer and instructions. Each - **$5 $10 $20**

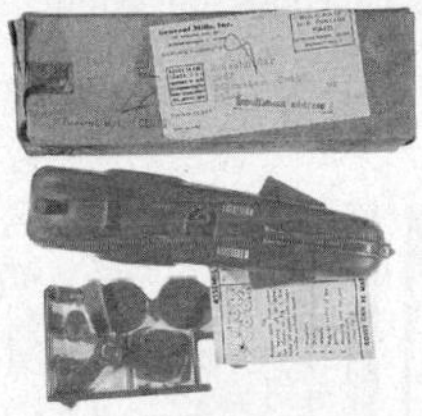

WHE-28

WHE-29

❑ **WHE-28. Land And Water Rover,**
1950s. General Mills. Red plastic car with propeller. Complete - **$45 $85 $200**

❑ **WHE-29. Red Records,**
1950s. Cereal premiums. Various popular folk, sea & traditional songs.
Each With Sleeve - **$4 $8 $12**
Each Without Sleeve - **$2 $4 $6**

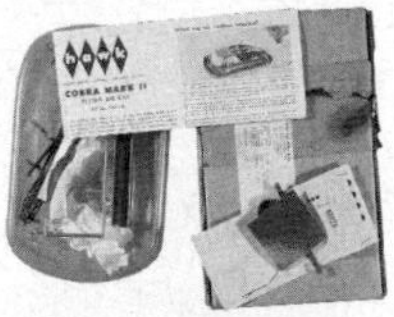

WHE-30

WHE-31

❑ **WHE-30. Flying Air Car,**
1960. Rare. General Mills. Large, wide, Cobra Mark II battery powered car.
With Instructions and Mailer. - **$60 $110 $200**

❑ **WHE-31. Miniature Reflective Paper License Plates With Mailer,**
1963. Wheaties Bran With Raisin Flakes. Probable set of 25 for scattered states in reflective flocked surface with peel-off back.
Each License - **$2 $4 $6**

WHE-32

❑ **WHE-32. Cereal Box With "Baseball Stamp Album" Offer,**
c. 1966. Gordon Gold Archives.
Near Mint Flat - **$200**
Used Complete - **$40 $75 $125**

WHE-33

❑ **WHE-33. Walter Payton Box,**
c. 1990. Complete Near Mint - **$28**

WHE-34

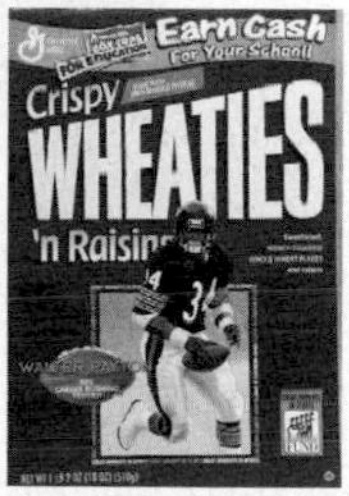

WHE-35

❑ **WHE-34. Christmas Ornament in Box,**
1994. In original box. - **$18**

❑ **WHE-35. Special Walter Payton Box,**
1998. "Great Moments in Sports" box salutes Walter Payton, the NFL career rushing leader. They called him "Sweetness" and he was a great man in and out of sports. A special tribute for the late Walter Payton because everything about him was sweet. - **$5 $10 $22**

Wild Bill Hickok

James Butler "Wild Bill" Hickok (1837-1876) was a U.S. Marshal in Kansas after the Civil War with a reputation as a marksman and a deadly lawman. Hollywood produced a number of fictionalized versions of the Hickok legend as portrayed by such stars as William S. Hart, Bill Elliott, Roy Rogers, Bruce Cabot, and Gary Cooper. In 1951, with Guy Madison (1922-1996) as Hickok and Andy Devine (1905-1977) as his sidekick Jingles, *The Adventures of Wild Bill Hickok* came to television and radio. The television series, sponsored by Kellogg's Sugar Corn Pops, aired until 1958, first in syndication, then on CBS (1955-1958), and on ABC (1957-1958). The radio version lasted until 1956, with Kellogg also sponsoring until 1954. Hickok comic books appeared from the late 1940s to the late 1950s. "Hey, Wild Bill, wait for me!"

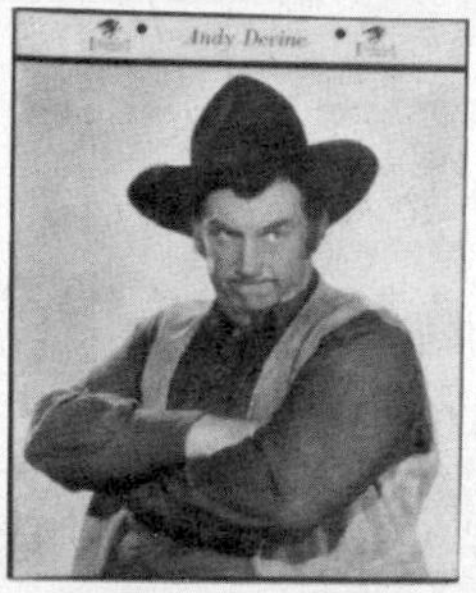

WLD-1

❑ **WLD-1. "Andy Devine" Dixie Picture,**
1948. - **$20 $40 $70**

WLD-2

❑ **WLD-2. "Sincerely Guy Madison" Studio Fan Postcard,**
c. 1948. Movie magazine promo. - **$10 $18 $35**

WLD-3

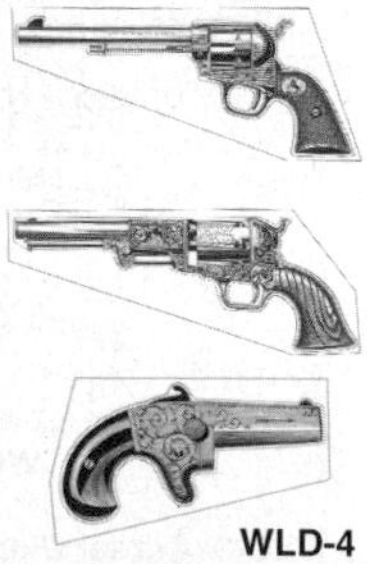

WLD-4

❑ **WLD-3. Kellogg's Sugar Pops Cereal Box With Cut-Outs,**
1952. Features Jingles and promotes "Famous Gun Series Cut-Outs." Back shows Wild Bill's gun "The Peacemaker."
Each Box - **$100 $175 $300**
Box Back Only - **$60**

❑ **WLD-4. Original Art For "Famous Gun Series" Cut-Outs,**
1952. 3 different shown. Each - **$160**

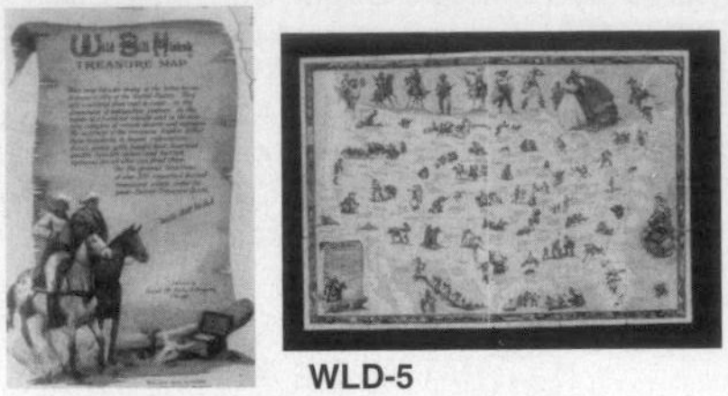

WLD-5

❑ WLD-5. "Secret Treasure Guide" And Treasure Map 25x36",
1952. Kellogg's Sugar Corn Pops.
Near Mint In Mailer - **$175**
Treasure Guide Booklet - **$12 $25 $50**
Treasure Map - **$25 $50 $100**

WLD-6

WLD-7

❑ WLD-6. Kellogg's Breakfast Game Score Card,
c. 1952. One side printed by game chart for entering daily breakfast diet over one-month period to be certified by school teacher and then presented to parents. - **$10 $20 $40**

❑ WLD-7. Cereal Mini-Box,
c. 1952. 4" tall "Kel-Bowl-Pac" one ounce individual serving box of Sugar Corn Pops with front panel art. - **$100 $175 $300**

WLD-8

❑ WLD-8. Cereal Display Box,
c. 1952. Kellogg of Canada. - **$150 $250 $500**

WLD-9

WLD-10

❑ WLD-9. Kellogg's Sugar Pops Box With "Beany Beanie" Offer,
c. 1952. Front panel shows Hickok and both front and back promote reflective beanie. Gordon Gold Archives.
Used Complete - **$100 $175 $300**

❑ WLD-10. Kellogg's Sugar Pops Box With "Airline Pilot's Wings" Offer,
c. 1952. Front panel shows Hickok with premium pictured on back panel. Gordon Gold Archives. Used Complete - **$100 $175 $300**

WLD-11

❑ WLD-11. "Guy (Wild Bill Hickok) Madison TV Guide Cowboy Album" Celluloid-Covered Wall Plaque,
c. 1953. Plaque is 6x9.25" from series of TV Guide promotional plaques sent to stations.
- **$75 $135 $250**

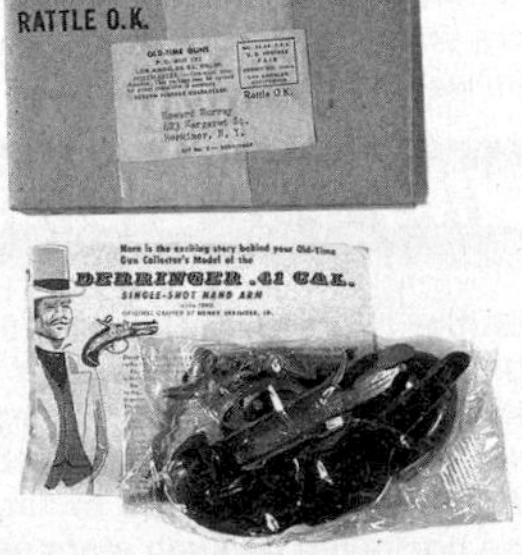

WLD-12

❑ WLD-12. Kellogg's "Old-Time Gun Series,"
1954. Kellogg's Sugar Corn Pops. Plastic old time gun series. Derringer, 41 cal.brown handle. With instructions and mailer. - **$30 $70 $150**

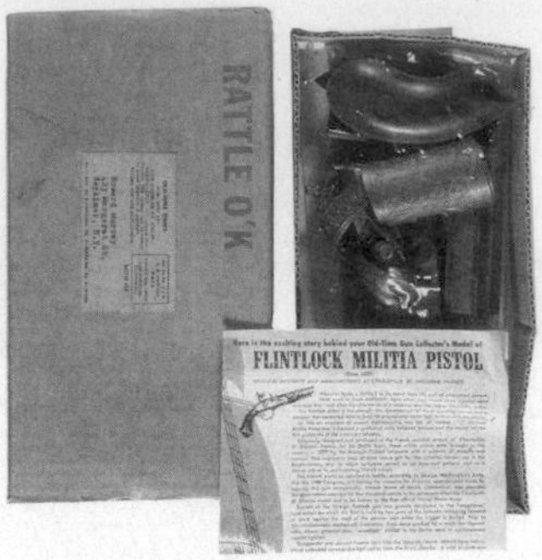

WLD-13

❑ WLD-13. Kellogg's "Old-Time Gun Series,"
1954. Kellogg's Sugar Corn Pops. Plastic old time guns. Flintlock Militia Pistol was originally offered for 1 box top and 50¢. That was a lot of money in those days, so the guns are all rare. With instructions and mailer. - **$30 $70 $150**

(front) (back)

WLD-14

❑ WLD-14. Kellogg's Sugar Pops Cereal Box Flat - 5 oz.,
1954. Jingles and his horse Joker pictured on front. Stereo-pix cut-out of the West on back. #1 of series. - **$100 $175 $300**

(FRONT) (BACK)

WLD-15

❑ WLD-15. Kellogg's Rice Krispies Cereal Box Flat with TV Promotion,
1954. Bilingual Canadian box. Contest awards a part in his TV show. - **$100 $200 $350**

WLD-16

WLD-17

❑ **WLD-16. Hickok/Guy Madison Fan Postcard,**
1954. - **$10 $15 $30**

❑ **WLD-17. "Jingles" Cello. Button With Attachment,**
c. 1954. Fabric ribbon holds miniature metal six-shooter. - **$30 $60 $100**

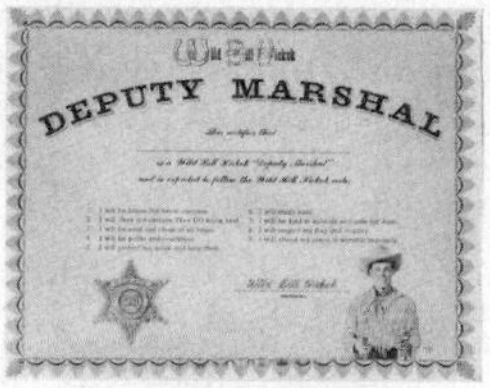

WLD-18

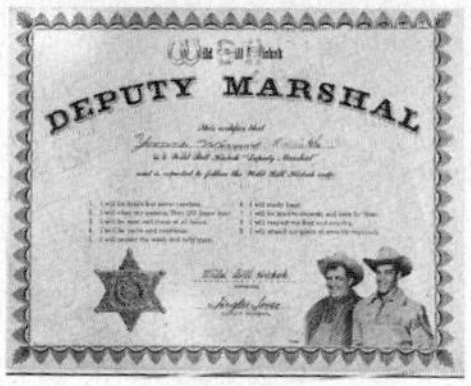

WLD-19

❑ **WLD-18. Deputy Marshal Certificate,**
1955. Probably a Kellogg's Sugar Corn Pops premium. - **$30 $60 $125**

❑ **WLD-19. Deputy Marshal Certificate,**
1955. Wild Bill & Jingles pictured. - **$35 $65 $135**

(FRONT)

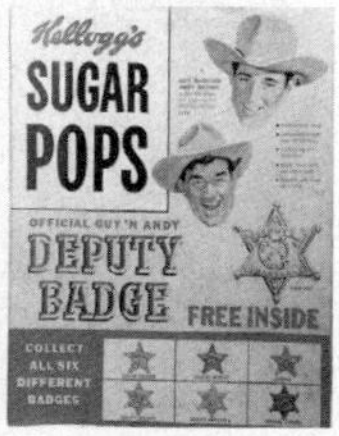

(BACK)

WLD-20

❑ **WLD-20. Kellogg's Sugar Pops Cereal Box with Badge Promotion,**
1956. Collection of 6 badges offered inside box. Wild Bill pictured on front. See WLD-21-24.
Box - **$125 $225 $400**

WLD-21

WLD-22

WLD-23

❑ **WLD-21. "Special Deputy" Copper Luster Tin Star Badge,**
1956. Kellogg's Sugar Pops. Set of six. Others without character name are: Deputy Marshall (sic), Deputy Sheriff, Junior Ranger, Sheriff. See next item. Each - **$12 $20 $30**

❑ **WLD-22. Kellogg's "Jingles/Deputy" 2-1/4" Copper Luster Tin Badge,**
1956. From Sugar Pops set of six, see previous item. - **$12 $20 $30**

❑ **WLD-23. Kellogg's "Wild Bill Hickok/ Deputy Marshal" 2-1/4" Silvered Tin Star Badge,**
1956. Similar to but not part of previous set. Finished in silver luster, not copper. -
$12 $20 $30

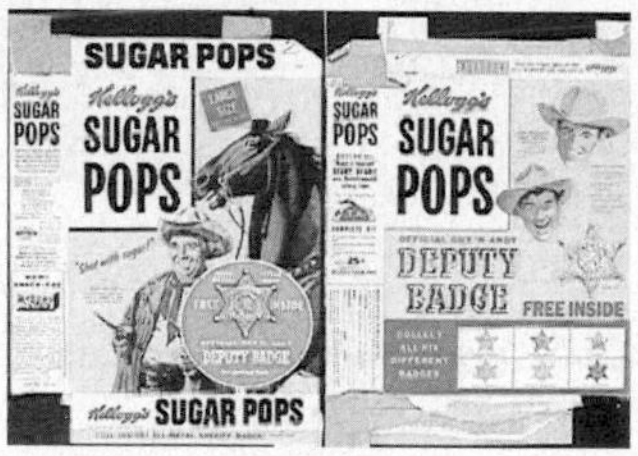

WLD-24

❑ **WLD-24. Cereal Box With "Deputy Badge" Offer,**
1956. Gordon Gold Archives. Jingles pictured on front.
Used Complete - **$125 $225 $400**

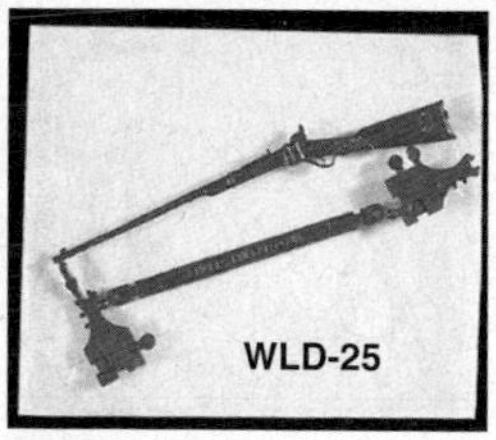

WLD-25

❑ **WLD-25. Rifle Series,**
1956. Sugar Corn Pops premium. Buffalo Sharps rifle in original package promoted by Jingles. Six different miniature rifles offered.
Each - **$10 $25 $40**

WLD-26

❑ **WLD-26. "Chris-Craft Speed Boat And Surfboard" Offer Cereal Box,**
1956. Gordon Gold Archives.
Used Complete - **$100 $175 $300**

WLD-27

❑ **WLD-27. "Andy Devine" Diecut Store Sign,**
c. 1956. 11x11" full color image of him as side-kick Jingles on radio and TV shows by unidentified sponsor, likely Kellogg's. - **$50 $100 $165**

WLD-28

❑ **WLD-28. Litho. Buttons,**
1957. Probable vending machine issue. 7/8" with browntone photo on single-color background. Part of a western TV star set probably totaling 14 different.
Wild Bill Or Jingles Each - **$12 $25 $50**

(front)

(back)

WLD-29

❑ **WLD-29. Kellogg's Sugar Pops Cereal Box Flat with Movie Outfit Promotion,**
1958. 8 oz. box has coloring contest to win a movie projector or 3-D camera.
Box - **$125 $225 $400**

WLD-30

❑ **WLD-30. "Kellogg's Sugar Corn Pops" Cereal Box,**
1950s. 16 "Famous Indian" drawings on back panels. Complete Box - **$100 $175 $300**

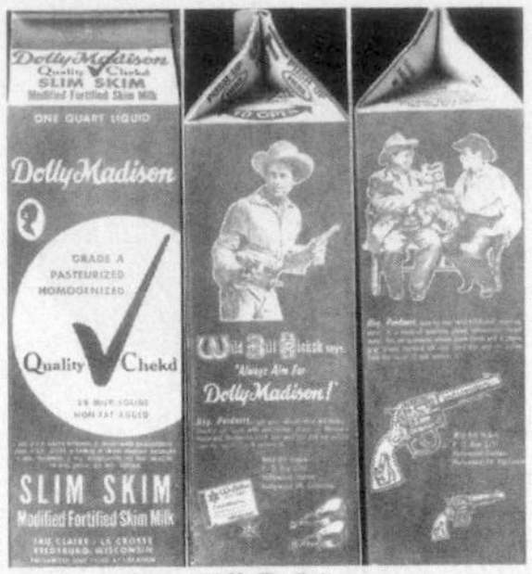

WLD-31

❑ **WLD-31. Hickok/Jingles Waxed Cardboard Milk Carton,**
1950s. Various dairies. - **$30 $60 $115**

WLD-32

WLD-33

❑ **WLD-32. "Drink Milk" Vinyl Tumbler,**
1950s. Various sponsors. -**$20 $50 $75**

❑ **WLD-33. Promo Press Kit & 10 Photos,**
1950s. Rare. - **$75 $150 $325**

WLD-34

❑ **WLD-34. Kellogg's Sugar Pops Cereal Box,**
1950s. The "Famous Guns of History" series is featured. Small plastic guns in each package. Box back was used for mounting guns. Eight guns pictured on back of box. Jingles pictured on front. Also offered generically in Pep cereal.
Complete Box - **$100 $175 $300**
Box Back Only - **$60**

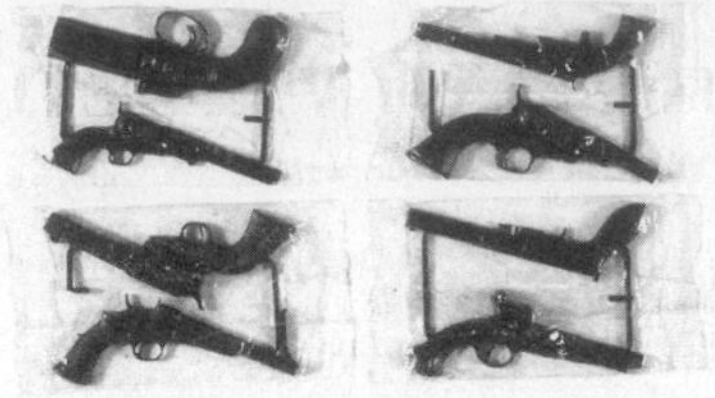

WLD-35

❑ **WLD-35. Kellogg's "Famous Guns of History" Series,**
1950s. Kellogg's Sugar Corn Pops. Four packages shown.
Each Package (Two Guns) - **$10 $25 $40**

WLD-36

WLD-37

❑ **WLD-36. Color Photo Litho. Button,**
1950s. - **$20 $50 $75**

❑ **WLD-37. Hickok & Jingles "We're Pardners" Litho. Button,**
1950s. - **$15 $40 $60**

WLD-38

WLD-39

❑ **WLD-38. "Wild Bill Hickok/Marshal" 2-1/4" Silvered Brass Badge,**
1950s. With insert paper photo, came with wallet and club member card.
Badge Only - **$20 $45 $90**
Three Piece Set - **$60 $125 $250**

❑ **WLD-39. "Marshal Wild Bill Hickok" Silvered Brass Badge On Metal Clip,**
1950s. Came with related wallet. - **$25 $50 $100**

The Wild, Wild West

Created by Michael Garrison as James Bond on horseback, the series ran on CBS-TV from September 17, 1965 through April 4, 1969: 4 seasons and 104 episodes. The show starred Robert Conrad as James West and Ross Martin (1920-1981) as Artemus Gordon, both special agents appointed by President U.S. Grant to fight crime in the old west. They traveled in a railroad car stocked with a vast array of equipment and devices to foil evil doers. CBS aired TV movies with original cast members on May 9, 1979 and October 7-8, 1980.

Warner Brothers released a feature film based on the series June 30, 1999 with Will Smith and Kevin Kline.

Gold Key published seven comics with photo covers between June, 1966 and October, 1969. Millennium published four comics between October 1990 and January 1991.

WWW-1

❑ **WWW-1. "TV Tab" Guide With "The Wild Wild West" Cover,**
1965. 7.5x10.5" newsprint supplement with 24 pages of TV listings August 1-7, 1965. - **$8 $15 $40**

WWW-2

❑ **WWW-2. "The Wild Wild West" First Issue Comic Book,**
1966. Gold Key. Standard - **$15 $40 $200**
Variety With Robert Conrad On Photo On Back Cover - **$20 $50 $225**

WWW-3

❑ **WWW-3. "Ross Martin" School Tablet,**
c. 1966. 8x10" lined paper tablet. - **$10 $20 $40**

WWW-4

❑ **WWW-4. "The Wild Wild West" Embossed Metal Lunch Box And Matching Plastic Thermos,**
1969. Aladdin Industries. 3.75x8x7" tall lunch box with 6.75" tall thermos.
Box - **$100 $200 $400**
Bottle - **$20 $40 $90**

WWW-5

❑ **WWW-5. 'The Wild Wild West" Paperback And TV Guides,**
1960s. First is paperback with 128 pages. Second is TV Guide for May 21, 1966 and third is TV Guide for Jan. 6, 1968. Each - **$5 $10 $20**

WWW-6

WWW-7

❑ **WWW-6. "Wild Wild West" Sunglasses,**
1999. Burger King premium. Artemus Gordon model has gold rims, with brown case.
Near Mint - **$12**

❑ **WWW-7. "Wild Wild West" Sunglasses,**
1999. Burger King premium. James West model has silver rims, with brown case.
Near Mint - **$12**

Will Rogers

Native American humorist, actor, political commentator and trick roper Will Rogers was born in 1879 on Dog Iron Ranch Indian Territory to parents of Cherokee ancestry. In the late 1890s, he became a trick roper in *Texas Jack's Wild West Circus*, going on to vaudeville. He married Betty Blake in 1908, and in the fall of 1915 was the star of Florenz Ziegfeld's *Midnight Frolics* at New York City's New Amsterdam Theatre leading to *Ziegfeld Follies* appearances from 1916 to 1925. His first film was MGM's *Laughing Bill Hyde* in 1918 and he would star in 71 movies (50 silent and 21 sound) including three Fox features directed by John Ford. Co-stars included: Billie Burke, Janet Gaynor, Lew Ayres and Hattie McDaniel. Rogers was #2 at the box office in 1933, #1 in 1934 and #2 in 1935.

Will Rogers wrote more than 4,000 syndicated newspaper columns and his radio show guests included presidents Coolidge and Hoover. An avid aviation booster, Rogers died in a plane crash with Wiley Post near Barrow, Alaska on August 15, 1935. Notable quotes: "We're all here for a spell, get all the good laughs you can;" "Be thankful we're not getting all the government we're paying for;" "I belong to no organized party, I'm a Democrat."

The Will Rogers Memorial Museum is located in Claremore, Oklahoma.

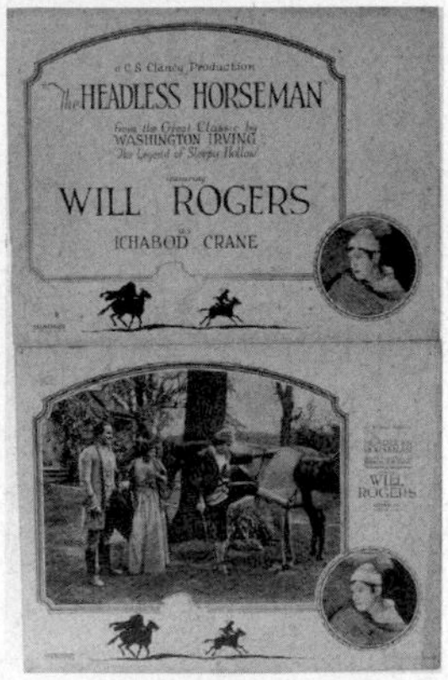

WRG-1

❑ **WRG-1. "The Headless Horseman" Will Rogers Lobby Card Set,**
1922. Hodkinson Pictures. Set of eight lobby cards, each 11x14" featuring Will Rogers as Ichabod Crane. Set - **$40 $100 $200**

WRG-2

❑ **WRG-2. "Will Rogers He Chews To Run" Button,**
1928. Button is 7/8" with backpaper reading "Read Will Rogers In Life." A reference to his satirical presidential campaign articles in Life magazine. - **$8 $15 $30**

WRG-3

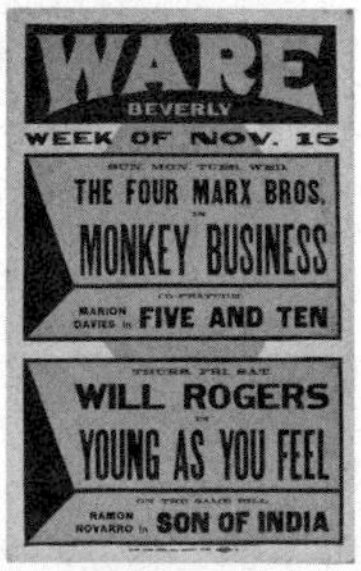

WRG-4

❑ **WRG-3. Will Rogers Oversized Autographed Photo,**
c. 1930. 11x14" photo with 4" long inscription "Yours For Fun - Will Rogers." Same Or Similar - **$100 $200 $400**

❑ **WRG-4. Marx Brothers "Monkey Business" Theatre Window Card,**
1931. 13.75x22" includes Will Rogers film "Young As You Feel." - **$65 $140 $250**

WRG-5

WRG-6

❑ **WRG-5. "I Vote For Will Rogers" Movie Promo Button,**
1935. 1.25" diameter for his 1935 movie "The County Chairman." - **$10 $20 $40**

❑ **WRG-6. "Will Rogers" Sebastian Miniature,**
1950. 3.25" tall figure with "Marblehead" foil label. - **$25 $50 $100**

WRG-7

❑ **WRG-7. "Will Rogers Never Met George McGovern" Button,**
1972. 1.5" diameter anti-McGovern button. - **$3 $6 $12**

William S. Hart

William Surrey Hart (1870-1946) began his career as a stage actor, gaining recognition in the role of Messala in the original stage production of *Ben Hur* in 1899, as well as *The Virginian* in 1907-1910 as part of a touring company.

Hart's first film, *His Hour of Manhood*, was released July 2, 1914 and he got his first major screen credit in *The Sagebrush Country* later in 1914. Recognized for depicting western adventure in accurate realism rather than contrived action, he often played roles as a good badman.

Hart appeared in some 76 films, directed 53 films and produced 19 films. Recognized as the greatest western actor of the silent film era, Hart's last film *Tumbleweeds* was released by Universal December 17, 1925. Directed by King Baggot, co-stars included: Barbara Bedford, Lucien Littlefield and J. Gordon Russell. He returned to the screen in 1939 to introduce the re-issue of the film, his first talking role.

The William S. Hart Ranch and Museum is located just north of Los Angeles in Newhall, California.

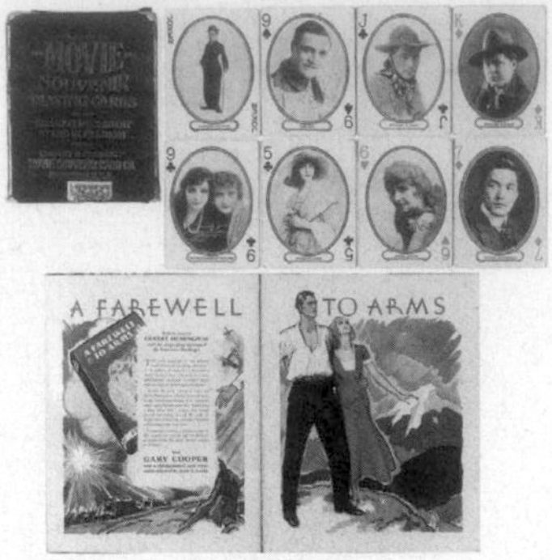

WSH-1

❑ **WSH-1. "Movie Souvenir Playing Cards"**
1916. Movie Souvenir Card Co., Cincinnati 3x3.5x1" deep slipcase box holds cards picturing "53 Most Prominent Stars In Filmdom." - **$125 $250 $500**

WSH-2

❑ **WSH-2. William S. Hart Autographed "Pinto Ben And Other Stories" First Edition Book,**
1919. 5x7.5" book with dust jacket and 96 pages. Autographed by William S. Hart. Same Or Similar - **$100 $200 $300**

WSH-3

❑ **WSH-3. William S. Hart Button,**
1920s. Button is 1.25". Issued to promote "'Sam Peck' Triple-Service Suit." One of only two buttons to picture this famous early western movie star. - **$25 $50 $100**

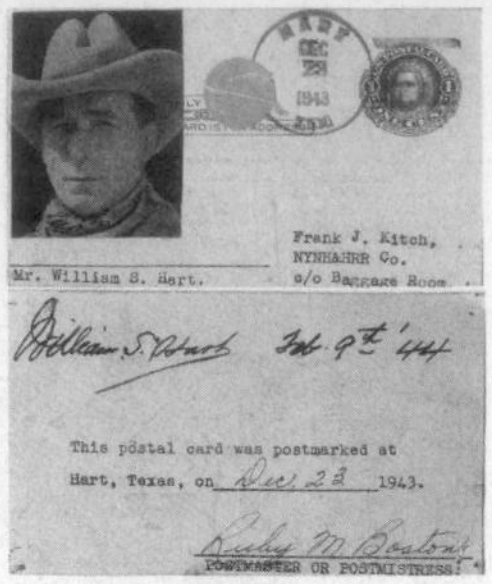

WSH-4

❑ **WSH-4. William S. Hart Autographed Postcard,**
1943. 3x5" postcard dated Dec. 23, 1943 has 2.25" wide signature at upper left of back by William S. Hart. Same Or Similar - **$75 $150 $225**

Willie Wiredhand

The National Rural Electric Cooperative Association was formed in 1942 as a support group for public power and rural electrification. In 1951 Andrew McLay, working for the National Rural Electric Cooperative Association (NRECA) created the figure of Willie Wiredhand to personify and characterize its aims. The smiling little fellow with an electric plug and cord for a torso has appeared on mugs, towels, Christmas ornaments, water bottles, magnets, pinback buttons, etc., and is still doing his job after almost 50 years.

WWH-1

❑ **WWH-1. "All-Electric Farm" Sign,**
1955. 9-1/2x13-1/2" tin litho. Issued by National Rural Electric Cooperative Assn. -
$35 $75 $160

WWH-2

WWH-3

❑ **WWH-2. Willie Wiredhand Cello. Button,**
1950s. Designated for "Director" of Rural Electrification program. - **$15 $25 $40**

❑ **WWH-3. Willie Wiredhand Cello. Button,**
1950s. For "Member" of Rural Electrification program. - **$10 $15 $20**

WWH-4

WWH-5

❑ **WWH-4. Willie Wiredhand Oval Cello. Button,**
1950s. - **$20 $40 $60**

❑ **WWH-5. Anniversary Event Button,**
1967. National Rural Electrical Cooperative Assn. About 2-1/2" issued for 25th annual meeting. - **$5 $10 $20**

WWH-6

WWH-7

❑ **WWH-6. Willy Wiredhand Night Light,**
1960s. National Rural Electric Cooperative Association. Plastic replica bulb with flat plane back pronged for insertion in household receptacle. Inscribed for local cooperative with initials copyright "NRECA." - **$15 $30 $50**

❑ **WWH-7. Glass Ashtray,**
c. 1960s. Dark translucent glass centered by figure image surrounded by other images of his household benefits. Imprinted for a local sponsoring company. - **$35 $75 $125**

WWH-8

WWH-9

❑ **WWH-8. Patriotic Cap,**
1960s. Flattened 4x12" garrison-style cardboard cap captioned "Minutemen For Rural Electrification." - **$10 $20 $40**

❑ **WWH-9. Iowa Rural Electric Co-Op Cello. Button,**
1970s. Colorful 2-1/4". - **$5 $10 $20**

Winky Dink

Created by Harry Prichett and Ed Wyckoff, *Winky Dink And You* aired on CBS-TV Saturday mornings from October 10, 1953 until April 27, 1957, then ran in syndication from 1969 to 1973. Hosted by Jack Barry (1918-1984) and his sidekick Mr. Bungle, played by Dayton Allen (1919-2004), the show was the first interactive television program. Young viewers ordered a kit through the mail that included crayons and a green vinyl "Magic Window" screen that stuck to the TV screen by static electricity. When cartoon characters Winky Dink (voiced by Mae Questel) or his dog Woofer (voiced by Dayton Allen) got in trouble, viewers could help them out by drawing a bridge as an escape route or other remedy. The highly innovative show was a boon to budding cartoonists, with the only drawback being kids who couldn't afford or couldn't wait for the kit and drew directly on the TV screen.

Dell published one comic in November, 1955 and Pines published one comic in March, 1957.

WDK-1

❑ **WDK-1. "Winky Dink Magic Set",**
1953. Pressman. 10.5x14.5x1.75" deep box contains many magic tricks, Winky Dink face mask, magic wand and instruction booklet. - **$60 $125 $200**

WDK-2

❑ **WDK-2. "Winky Dink Paint Set",**
1954. Standard Toykraft. 11.5x15.75x1.5" deep box contains paints, a basin, a brush, 6 crayons and six 8x11" coloring sheets. - **$25 $60 $125**

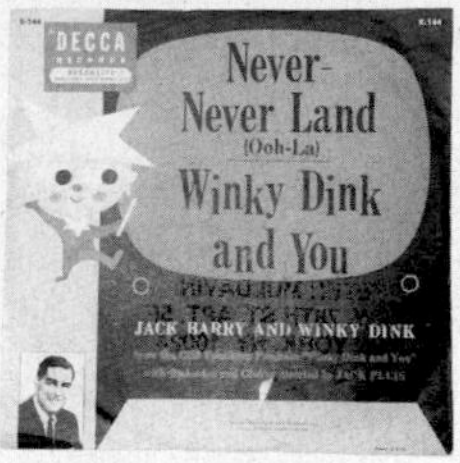

WDK-3

❑ **WDK-3. "Winky Dink And You" Record Album,**
1954. Decca Records. Release also featuring song title "Never-Never Land." - **$20 $40 $70**

WDK-4

❑ **WDK-4. Winky Dink Books,**
1955/1956. Whitman/Simon & Schuster. First is 8.25x11.25" with 80 pages. Second is first edition 6.75x8" Little Golden Book. Each - **$10 $20 $40**

WDK-5

WDK-6

❑ **WDK-5. "Winky Dink And You" TV Art Kit,**
1950s. Includes erasable "magic" window, crayons and erasing cloth. - **$45 $85 $175**

❑ **WDK-6. "Winky Dink" Litho. Button,**
1950s. - **$25 $45 $85**

WDK-7

WDK-8

❑ **WDK-7. "Winky Dink" Frame Tray Puzzle,**
1950s. Jaymar. 11x14" western theme puzzle showing Winky Dink. - **$20 $40 $75**

❑ **WDK-8. "Winky Dink" Frame Tray Puzzle,**
1950s. Jaymar. 11x14" puzzle with pirate theme picturing Winky Dink. - **$20 $40 $75**

WDK-9

❑ **WDK-9. "Official Super Winky Dink Television Game Kit",**
1950s. Standard Toykraft Products. 12.75x15.75x1" deep box contains 8 Magic Crayons, Official Magic Window, Deluxe Erasing Mitt, Winky Puzzle, 40 Plastic Winky Doodles, Magic TV Game Book. - **$100 $200 $300**

Winnie the Pooh

See Ted Hake's *Official® Price Guide to Disney Collectibles*, Second Edition, formatted identically to this book but in full color evaluating over 9,000 Disney company and character collectibles from 1924 through 2006.

Winnie Winkle

Martin Branner (1888-1970) titled his new comic strip about a working girl living with her parents *Winnie Winkle The Breadwinner*. The daily first appeared September 20, 1920, followed by a Sunday page in 1923. The cast included: Winnie's Dad Rip Winkle, Mother Ma Winkle and Winnie's office boss Mr. Bibbs. The Winkles adopted kid brother Perry Winkle in 1922 and he and his friends the Rinky Dinks, including Denny Dimwit were featured in many Sunday pages.

Over the years the strip evolved from humor to a soap opera theme. Winnie married Will Wright on June 14, 1937. She becomes pregnant with twins just as Will enters World War II and then Will goes missing making her a war widow. Years later, Will is found and Winnie begins a post-war career as a fashion designer.

Artclass Pictures Corporation released ten *Winnie Winkle* silent comedy shorts starring Ethelyn Gibson between September 1, 1926 and March 26, 1928. Martin Branner received the National Cartoonists Society award for Best Humor Strip in 1958. Max Von Bibber took over the strip from 1962 to 1980, followed by Frank Bolle. The strip ended July 28, 1996.

Dell published seven comics between 1941 and 1949.

WNW-1

❑ **WNW-1. "Winnie Winkle, The Breadwinner" Daily Comic Strip Original Art,**
1921. Chicago Tribune. 7-1/8x21" tan art board has 5x18" India ink image with Winnie on all 4 panels. Early, from the 9th month. Same Or Similar - **$100 $200 $400**

WNW-2

❑ **WNW-2. "Winnie Winkle" Boxed Board Game,**
c. 1930. Store item by Milton Bradley #4269. - **$75 $175 $300**

WNW-3

❑ **WNW-3. "Winnie Winkle By Branner" Comic Strip Reprint Book,**
1932. Cupples & Leon. 10x10". Book No. 3. - **$29 $116 $300**

WNW-4

❑ **WNW-4. "Winnie Winkle" Cigar Ad Sign,**
1930s. - **$65 $125 $200**

WNW-5

❑ **WNW-5. "Winnie Winkle" Cigar Box,**
1930s. - **$25 $50 $125**

WNW-6

❑ **WNW-6. "Denny Dimwit" From "Winnie Winkle" Boxed Figure,**
1948. Toy Craft Inc. 4x6x12" box holds 11" painted composition figure.
Box - **$25 $50 $100**
Toy - **$50 $100 $200**

WNW-7

❑ **WNW-7. "Denny Dimwit" Candy Box,**
1940s. Ma & Pa Winkle card on back of box. - **$45 $120 $200**

The Wizard of Oz

L. Frank Baum (1856-1919) wrote 14 Oz books, but it was the first, *The Wonderful Wizard of Oz*, published in 1900, that served as the basis of MGM's 1939 Technicolor spectacular, *The Wizard of Oz*. (A musical theatrical adaptation ran on Broadway in 1903, silent films were made as early as 1908; Oliver Hardy played the Tin Woodsman in a 1925 version and a radio version sponsored by Jell-O aired on NBC in 1933-1934.) The 1939 film, with an all-star cast headed by Judy Garland, has proved to be an enduring classic, repeated annually on television for millions of viewers since the 1950s. The cast included Ray Bolger as the Scarecrow, Jack Haley as the Tin Man, Bert Lahr as the Cowardly Lion, Margaret Hamilton as the Wicked Witch, Billie Burke as the Glinda the Good Witch and Frank Morgan as Oz. The "Munchkins" were a group of little people touring Vaudevillle known as "Leo Sinter's Midgets." It's estimated 124 of them were hired for the film. The film won an Oscar for the song *Over The Rainbow* by Harold Arlen and E.Y. Harburg and probably would have fared better but the main competition was *Gone With The Wind*. There have also been Oz theme parks and resorts, an exhibit at the Smithsonian, appearances in Macy's Thanksgiving Day parade, comic books, and extensive licensing in dozens of categories. "There's no place like home."

WIZ-1

❑ **WIZ-1. Music Supplement Newspaper Insert,**
1903. New York American and Journal. Four-page folder dated May 10, 1903 picturing singer Lottie Faust from New York's Majestic Theater. - **$30 $60 $125**

WIZ-2

WIZ-3

❑ **WIZ-2. "What Did The Woggle Bug Say?" Cello. Button,**
1905. Book advertising button. - **$35 $80 $160**

❑ **WIZ-3. Woggle Bug Cello. Button,**
1905. Book advertising button. Colors on coat vary from yellow to green. - **$35 $80 $160**

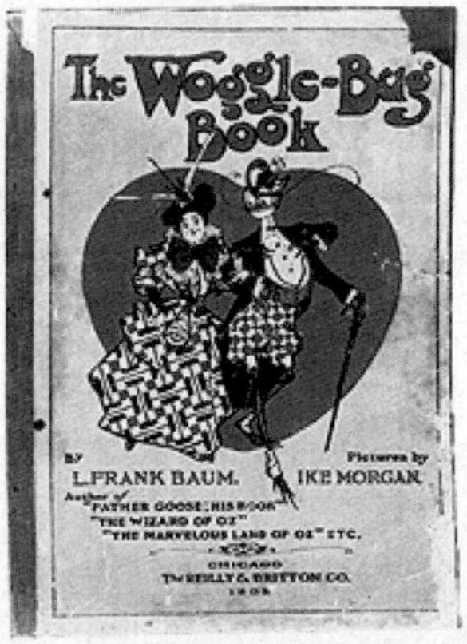

WIZ-4

❑ **WIZ-4. "The Woggle-Bug Book,"**
1905. Store item. 11x15" 48-page storybook by L. Frank Baum illustrated by Ike Morgan, published by Reilly & Britton Co., Chicago. - **$350 $750 $1800**

WIZ-5

❑ **WIZ-5. Magazine Story Poster 13x22",**
1905. For issue of St. Nicholas magazine with art by F. Richardson for Baum serial story "Queen Zixi Of Ix". - **$300 $750 $1500**

WIZ-6

❑ **WIZ-6. "Johnnie Johnston's Air Ship" Booklet With Art By Oz Illustrator Denslow,**
1909. Johnston Harvester Co. 16-page story about use of Johnston equipment around the world illustrated by W. W. Denslow, also noted for his Oz artistry. - **$75 $150 $300**

WIZ-7

❑ **WIZ-7. "Read The New Baum Book/The Scarecrow Of Oz" Cello. Button,**
1915. Early and rare book advertising release. - **$600 $1200 $2500**

WIZ-8

❑ **WIZ-8. "The Wonderful Game Of Oz,"**
1921. Parker Bros. 10x19.5x2" deep box. Board measures 19x19". Comes with 4x5" instruction booklet. Remarkably detailed pewter playing pieces include Dorothy, Scarecrow, Tin Man and Cowardly Lion. - **$500 $1000 $1500**

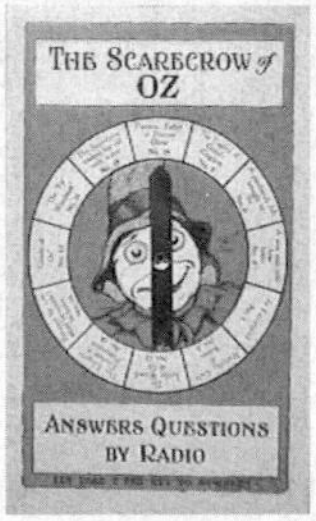

WIZ-9

❑ **WIZ-9. "The Scarecrow Of Oz Answers Questions By Radio" Book Promotional Leaflet,**
1924. J. B. Carroll Company, Chicago. Book sellers' give-away advertising the Oz books, incorporating a metal arrow and interior magnetic dial to ask and respond to questions. - **$250 $575 $1000**

WIZ-10

❑ **WIZ-10. First Known Oz Club Member Badge,**
1926. 1.75" wide brass wing design centered by stylized panel representing open book designated "Oz." Reverse names "The Ozmite Club" by Oz book publishers Reilly & Lee. Badge was obtained free by signing up in book department of select stores. - **$400 $900 $1850**

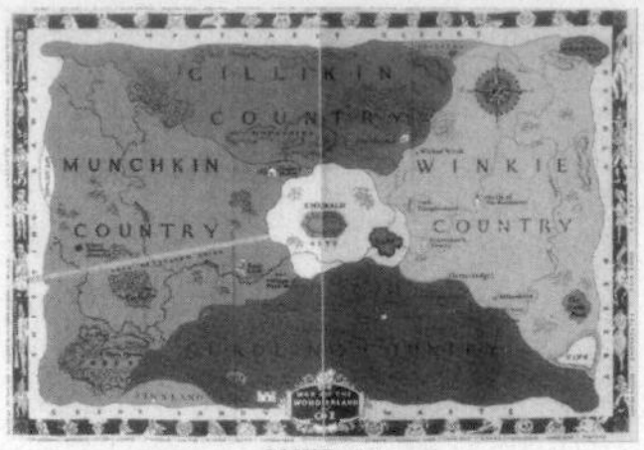

WIZ-11

❑ **WIZ-11. "Wonderland Of Oz" Map 16x22",**
1932. Philadelphia Evening Bulletin newspaper. - **$300 $700 $1200**

WIZ-12 WIZ-13

❑ **WIZ-12. Jackpumpkinhead And The Sawhorse,**
1933. Jell-O softbound book. - **$40 $100 $150**

❑ **WIZ-13. Tik Tok And The Nome King,**
1933. Jell-O softbound book. - **$40 $100 $150**

(FRONT) WIZ-14 (BACK)

❑ **WIZ-14. Ozma And The Little Wizard,**
1933. Jell-O softbound book. - **$40 $100 $150**

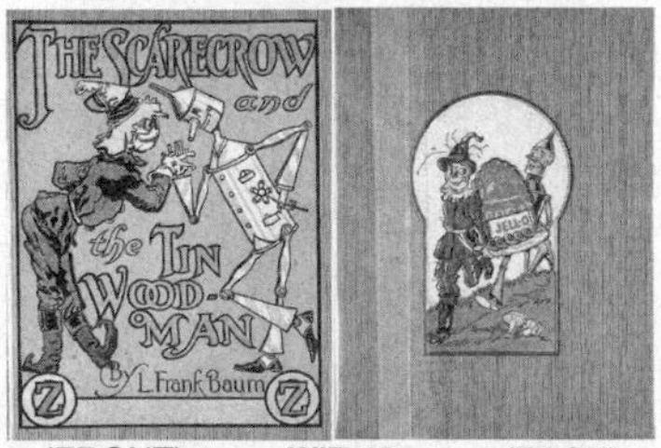

(FRONT) WIZ-15 (BACK)

❑ **WIZ-15. The Scarecrow And The Tin Woodman,**
1933. Jell-O softbound book. - **$40 $100 $150**

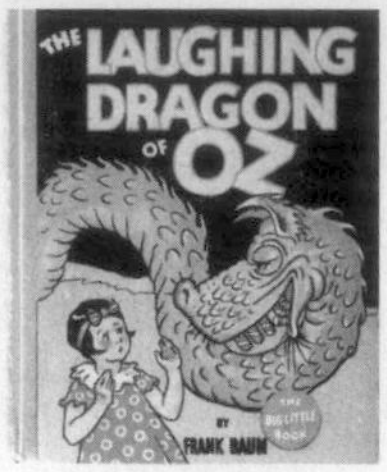

WIZ-16

❑ **WIZ-16. The Laughing Dragon of Oz,**
1934. Big Little Book #1126. Rare. 432 pages by Frank Baum. - **$93 $279 $650**

WIZ-17 WIZ-18

❑ **WIZ-17. Movie Advertising Cello. Button,**
1939. Scarce. Seen with "Loew's" (theater) and "Hecht's" (Baltimore and Washington DC department store) imprints. - **$100 $200 $400**

❑ **WIZ-18. Dorothy Mask,**
1939. Distributed by department stores and others. - **$20 $40 $80**

WIZ-19 WIZ-20

❑ **WIZ-19. Scarecrow Mask,**
1939. Distributed by department stores and others. - **$20 $40 $80**

❑ **WIZ-20. Cowardly Lion Mask,**
1939. Distributed by department stores and others. - **$20 $40 $80**

WIZ-21 WIZ-22

❑ **WIZ-21. Tin Woodman Mask,**
1939. Distributed by department stores and others. - **$20 $40 $80**

❑ **WIZ-22. Wizard Mask,**
1939. Distributed by department stores and others. - **$20 $40 $80**

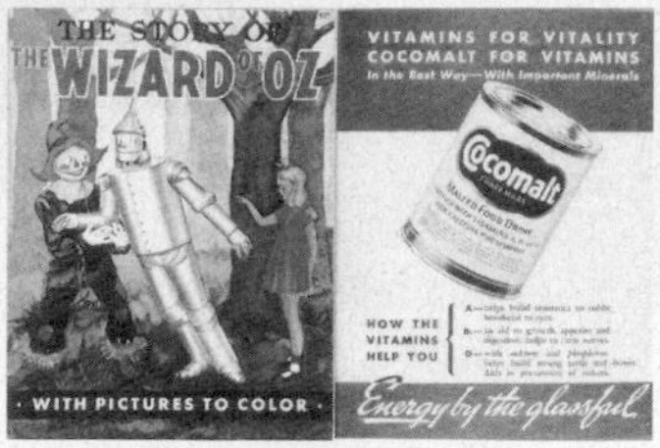

WIZ-23

❑ **WIZ-23. "The Story Of The Wizard Of Oz" Coloring Book,**
1939. Cocomalt. Premium Version - **$25 $50 $100**
Store Version Without Cocomalt Ad - **$15 $35 $75**

WIZ-24

❑ **WIZ-24. Pictorial Fabric Scarf,**
1939. Store item. Two different designs with numerous color variations. - **$75 $165 $350**

WIZ-25

❑ **WIZ-25. "The Wizard Of Oz" Movie Songs Folio,**
1939. Store item with 24 miniature illustrations for M-G-M film. - **$30 $60 $125**

WIZ-26

❑ **WIZ-26. "The Wizard Of Oz" Movie Score Record Album,**
1939. Decca Records. 10-1/2x12" with four records including "The Jitterbug" song that was cut from the movie. - **$50 $100 $250**

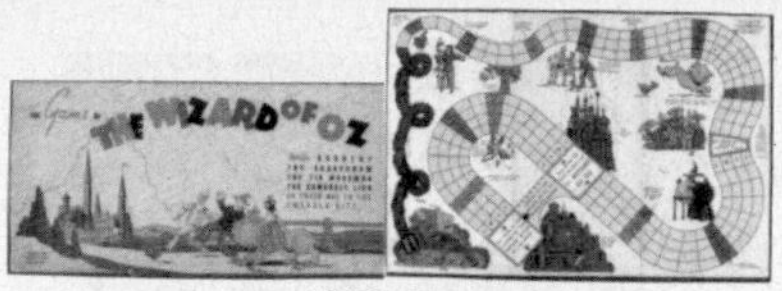

WIZ-27

❑ **WIZ-27. "Wizard of Oz" Boxed Board Game,**
1939. Store item by Whitman Publishing Co. Board in linen on 13x19" cardboard. Parts are wood die and four markers each in a single color. - **$150 $300 $600**

WIZ-28

WIZ-29

❑ **WIZ-28. Oz Dairy Product Glasses,**
1939. Sealtest Cottage Cheese. Set of eight: Dorothy, Toto, Scarecrow, Tin Woodman, The Cowardly Lion, The Good Witch, The Bad Witch and The Wizard. First example of the Wizard glass known to us sold on eBay in July 2007 for $2025. Each (except the Wizard) - **$50 $85 $150**

❑ **WIZ-29. Movie 3" Cello. Button,**
1939. M-G-M Studio. - **$50 $175 $350**

WIZ-30

WIZ-31

❑ **WIZ-30. "Frank Morgan" Movie Contest Cello. Button,**
1939. M-G-M Studios. 1-1/4" size, set of five also includes Judy Garland, Ray Bolger, Jack Haley, Bert Lahr. This size has serial number to match for winning prize.
Judy Garland - **$200 $400 $750**
Others - **$100 $250 $400**

❑ **WIZ-31. Title in Spanish Cello. Button,**
1939. From 7/8" series of five characters with Oz film title in Spanish.
Judy Garland - **$200 $400 $750**
Other Four - **$50 $100 $200**

WIZ-32

WIZ-33

❑ **WIZ-32. Full Color Paper Seal,**
1939. W. L. Stensgaard & Associates, Inc. 2-1/2" square designed for the Christmas 1939 department store promotion of the movie inscribed "Merry Christmas from The Merry Old Land of Oz." - **$135 $275 $500**

❑ **WIZ-33. Movie Premiere Souvenir Program,**
1939. Metro-Goldwyn-Mayer. Oversized 10-1/8x13-3/4" program titled "The Wizard of Oz Comes to Life," available only at the premiere screening held at Graumann's Chinese Theatre on August 15, 1939. - **$650 $1700 $3000**

WIZ-34

❑ **WIZ-34. Oz Soap Figure Set Boxed,**
1939. Outstanding set in 5.75x11x1.75" deep box with cellphane window beneath title "Kerk Guild's Soapy Characters From The Land Of Oz." Set consists of "The Scarecrow, The Tin Woodman, The Wizard, The Cowardly Lion And The Wicked Witch." Dorothy was sold separately but she is pictured on lid and panels along with Toto, Good Witch and other major characters. One side panel reads "For Fun in The Tub." Insert creates five compartments. Each soap is 4.5" tall.
Box And Insert - **$100 $200 $300**
Each Soap - **$25 $50 $100**

WIZ-35

❑ **WIZ-35. "The Wizard Of Oz" English Sheet Music,**
1940. Francis, Day & Hunter Ltd. 8.5x11" with eight pages. "Selection Of Melodies From The Wizard Of Oz." Songs include: The Merry Old Land Of Oz, We're Off To See The Wizard, If I Only Had A Brain, Ding Dong! The Witch Is Dead, Over The Rainbow And The Jitterbug (a song that was cut from the finished movie). Bw photo is outlined in white and placed on a red background that fades to black at bottom.
- **$40 $85 $160**

WIZ-36

WIZ-37

❑ **WIZ-36. Scarecrow Valentine,**
1940 Store item. From set of 12 picturing various characters by American Colortype Co. Each - **$25 $65 $125**

❑ **WIZ-37. "Magic Sand" Packet Envelope,**
c. 1940. Various theaters. Contains sand "From Along The Yellow Brick Road.." -
$200 $400 $1000

WIZ-38

❑ **WIZ-38. English Card Game Boxed,**
c. 1940. Movie scenes box containing deck of 44 cards, each different color art based on movie scenes. - **$100 $200 $400**

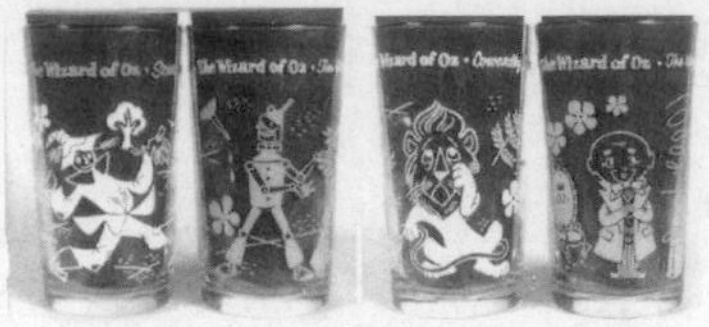

WIZ-39

❑ **WIZ-39. "S & Co." Glass Tumblers,**
1953. Swift Peanut Butter. Six designs with wavy, plain or fluted bases. Characters depicted are Dorothy, Toto, Scarecrow, Cowardly Lion, Tinman, and the Wizard. Each - **$12 $20 $30**

(FRONT)

(BACK)

WIZ-40

❑ **WIZ-40. "The Wizard Of Oz Coloring Book",**
1955. Swift & Company. Twelve page booklet retelling the Baum story and advertising Oz Peanut Butter tumblers on inside front and back covers. - **$60 $135 $275**

WIZ-41

❑ **WIZ-41. "Wizard Of Oz" Movie Soundtrack Album,**
1956. M-G-M. - **$20 $30 $60**

WIZ-42

❑ **WIZ-42. "The Land Of Make Believe" Map Poster Including Oz,**
1958. Large 26x38" glossy paper choice color and highly graphic illustration of land inhabited by numerous nursery rhyme or similar characters from children's story lore. Included at upper right corner is Emerald City of Oz. -
$75 $150 $300

WIZ-43

❑ **WIZ-43. Dorothy And Scarecrow Boxed Marionettes,**
1950s. Store item by Hazelle's Marionettes. Each is 13" tall. No Oz license but obvious likenesses. Each Box - **$25 $50 $75**
Each Marionette - **$35 $65 $100**

WIZ-44

❑ **WIZ-44. Oz Peanut Butter Mobile,**
c. 1960. Swift & Company. Thin cardboard punch-out of the Baum characters, advertising Oz Peanut Butter.
Unpunched - **$75 $150 $300**
Assembled - **$50 $100 $150**

(CLOSE-UP)

WIZ-45

❑ **WIZ-45. "Swift's Oz Peanut Butter" Ballpoint Pen,**
c. 1960. Plastic advertising pen issued in colors of red, beige, blue or yellow with lettering and Tin Man image in black. Also issued as a black pen with writing and Tin Man image printed in silver. - **$50 $100 $150**

WIZ-46

❑ **WIZ-46. View-Master Reel Set,**
1962. Envelope holding three stereo simulated view reels plus story leaflet.
Complete - **$15 $30 $55**

WIZ-47

❑ **WIZ-47. Vinyl Hand Puppets,**
1965. Procter & Gamble. Eight in set. Cardboard theater also issued.
Each Puppet - **$12 $20 $35**
Theater - **$40 $70 $125**

WIZ-48

❑ **WIZ-48. "Free Wizard Of Oz Hand Puppets" Store Display,**
1966. Procter & Gamble. Diecut standing display about five feet tall with plastic-bubble compartment at base holding seven samples of the eight available hand puppets. In 1966 the puppets were premiums for Top Job, Zest and Downy. When the promotion repeated in 1969, the products were Ivory Snow, Oxydol and Joy (the display was adjusted accordingly).
Originally the Wizard puppet was available only with the cardboard Emerald City theater as a mail-away premium.
Near Mint With Seven Puppets - **$3100**
Display Without Puppets - **$750 $1500 $2750**

WIZ-49

❑ **WIZ-49. Set Of 12 Litho. Buttons,**
1967. Samson Products. Vending machine distribution. Each - **$6 $12 $18**

WIZ-50

❑ **WIZ-50. "Wizard Of Oz" Premium Coloring Book,**
1967. M-G-M Inc. 4.25x4.75" coloring book with 16 pages. Inside front cover has ad for Baby Ruth and Butterfinger candy bars. Inside back cover has ad for three Oz books in this premium series. Each - **$150 $300 $550**

WIZ-51

❑ **WIZ-51. "Magic Kit",**
1967. Store item by Fun Inc. - **$40 $75 $125**

WIZ-52

❑ **WIZ-52. Iron-On Transfers,**
1967. Available through Morton Foods, Kitty Clover and others. Depicts images of Chuck Jones cartoon characters from the 1967-68 TV show, "Off to See the Wizard," issued in cellophane packets as a set of five (four main characters; the fifth was either "Wizard" or "Wicked Witch"). Each - **$15 $30 $60**

WIZ-53

❑ **WIZ-53. Oz Character Flicker Ring Set,**
c. 1967. Made by Vari-Vue and likely dispensed in vending machines. Set of 12 with two blue plastic rings for these characters: Cowardly Lion, Dorothy, Scarecrow, Tin Woodman, Witch, Wizard. One variety of the Lion ring and one of the Wizard ring includes inscription "Off To See The Wizard." Each - **$10 $20 $40**

WIZ-54

❑ **WIZ-54. "Wizard Of Oz Coloring Book",**
1968. Procter & Gamble. Captioned "Free! When You Buy One Regular-Size Bottle Of Top Job." - **$35 $75 $150**

WIZ-55

❑ **WIZ-55. Oz Characters Ceramic Music Box,**
c. 1969. Store item plays "Somewhere Over The Rainbow." **$50 $100 $175**

WIZ-56

❑ **WIZ-56. "M-G-M Classic-The Wizard Of Oz" Poster Autographed By Bolger And Haley,**
1977. 24x30" paper poster produced by Snuff Garrett, prominent Los Angeles record producer and owner of issuing company Nostalgia Merchant. Vivid color classic images from the original film highlighted by signatures of Ray Bolger (Scarecrow) and Jack Haley (Tin Woodman). Limited edition printing.
Near Mint - **$750**

WIZ-57

❑ **WIZ-57. "Emerald City Police" Badge,**
1980. Enameled metal marked on reverse for apparent maker "Fun House" plus year of issue. - **$20 $30 $55**

WIZ-58

WIZ-59

❑ **WIZ-58. Oz Promotional Wristwatch,**
1989. Macy's department store. 9-1/2" long plastic hinged case holds watch issued for 50th anniversary of original movie. 1-1/4" dial has color illustration of Dorothy and friends headed to Emerald City. Near Mint Boxed - **$125**
Unboxed - **$30 $50 $90**

❑ **WIZ-59. "It's Oz Time At Macy's" Store Clerk Button,**
1989. Macy's department store. 3" diameter beautifully colored cello. button used in conjunction with promotion for 50th year movie anniversary. - **$20 $35 $70**

WIZ-60

WIZ-61

WIZ-62

WIZ-63

❑ **WIZ-60. "Dorothy" Bean Bag with Tag,**
1998. Warner Brothers Studio Store. - **$18**

❑ **WIZ-61. "Cowardly Lion" Bean Bag with Tag,**
1998. Warner Brothers Studio Store. - **$15**

❑ **WIZ-62. "Scarecrow" Bean Bag with Tag,**
1998. Warner Brothers Studio Store. - **$25**

❑ **WIZ-63. "Tin Man" Bean Bag with Tag,**
1998. Warner Brothers Studio Store. - **$15**
Other bean bag figures exist for Glinda the Good Witch, Wicked Witch of the West, Lollipop Girl, Munchkin Boy, Flying Monkey and the Wizard -**$10-15 each**

(Figure) WIZ-64 (Box)

❑ **WIZ-64. "Glinda the Good Witch" Bobber Figure,**
2000. - **$25**

Wonder Woman

Wonder Woman **was created by psychologist/writer William Moulton Marston (1893-1947; pen name, Charles Moulton) and drawn by Harry G. Peter. Robert Kanigher took over the writing when Marston passed away in 1947. The comics' first major female superhero debuted in issue #8 of *All Star Comics* in December 1941 and had her own comic book by the next summer. Wonder Woman came from mysterious Paradise Island (no men allowed) to America as Diana Prince to help fight World War II. Over the years she has also battled aliens and terrorists, lost her flag-like costume and superpowers, regained them, dabbled in I Ching, and fallen in and out of love. A comic strip appearance in 1944 had a short life, and a hardback anthology was published in 1972. There have been two TV movies--*Wonder Woman* (1974) with Cathy Lee Crosby, and *The New, Original Wonder Woman* (1975) with Lynda Carter--and a TV series, also starring Carter, that aired on ABC (1976-1977) and CBS (1977-1979). The character was also featured in the *Superfriends* cartoon that aired on ABC in the 1970s, and the current *Justice League Unlimited* animated series on the Cartoon Network. Items are usually copyrighted DC Comics or Warner Bros. TV.**

WON-1

❑ **WON-1. "Sensation Comics" Litho. Button,**
1942. Rare. Offered in May issue of Sensation Comics. - **$350 $700 $1200**

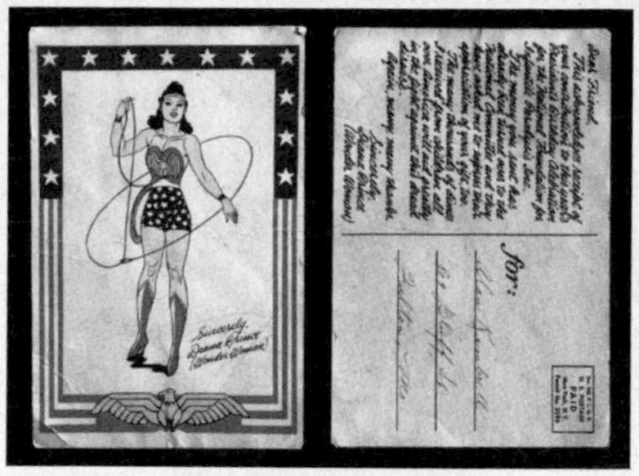

WON-2

❑ **WON-2. WWII Infantile Paralysis Comic Book Postcard Premium,**
1940s. Rare. - **$600 $1200 $2500**

WON-3

WON-4

❑ **WON-3. Valentine Card,**
1940s. Store item. Diecut stiff paper folder with inner message "For You, Valentine, I'd Move Heaven And Earth!" - **$30 $60 $135**

❑ **WON-4. "Wonder Woman" 3-1/2" Cello. Button,**
1966. #14 from the 1966 Super Hero Club button set from Button World Mfg. Co.
Near Mint Bagged - **$150**
Loose - **$22 $45 $85**

WON-5

WON-6

❑ **WON-5. Boxed Board Game,**
1967. Store item by Hasbro. Also features other Justice League of America characters. -
$50 $100 $200

❑ **WON-6. Ideal Super Queens Wonder Woman Doll,**
1967. NM in Box - **$3500**
Unboxed - **$300 $600 $1200**

WON-7

WON-8

❑ **WON-7. "Ms." Magazine First Issue With Wonder Woman Cover,**
1972. Vol. 1 #1 issue for July of feminist magazine fronted by color art by Murphy Anderson promoting "Wonder Woman For President." -
$15 $30 $60

❑ **WON-8. Proof Ingot,**
1974. Used as incentive to promote other DC Comics character ingots. Only 300 made.
Near Mint - **$250**

WON-9

WON-10

❑ **WON-9. "Wonder Woman" 2-1/4" Cello. Button,**
1975. Store item by Rainbow Designs. DC Comics copyright. - **$8 $15 $30**

❑ **WON-10. Metal Ring With Cello. Portrait,**
1976. N.P.P. Inc. Brass finish with copyright on underside. - **$50 $80 $150**

WON-11

WON-12

❑ **WON-11. TV Guide Weekly Issue,**
1977. Volume 25 #5 for week of January 29.
Without Mailing Label - **$8 $15 $25**
With Mailing Label - **$5 $10 $15**

❑ **WON-12. Blue Vinyl Lunch Box,**
1977. Store item by Aladdin Industries Inc.
Box - **$50 $100 $225**
Bottle - **$10 $20 $40**

WON-13

❑ **WON-13. Lynda Carter Autographed Photo,**
c. 1977. Glossy black and white. - **$10 $20 $50**

WON-14

❑ **WON-14. "Wonder Woman" Boxed Marionette,**
1977. Store item by Madison Ltd.
Near Mint Boxed - **$190**
Loose - **$25 $50 $80**

WON-15

❑ **WON-15. Watch,**
1977. Store item by Dabs.
Near Mint Boxed - **$175**
Loose - **$30 $60 $90**

WON-16

WON-17

❑ **WON-16. Pepsi Glass,**
1978. - **$5 $10 $15**

❑ **WON-17. "See The Superheroes At Sea World" Photo,**
1970s. Sea World appearance souvenir. Batman and Wonder Woman pictured with facsimile signatures. - **$15 $30 $60**

WON-18

WON-19

❑ **WON-18. Wonder Woman Feminist Cartoon Button,**
1970s. Button is 3" in full color with cartoon balloon reading "Never Under-Estimate The Power Of A Woman." - **$100 $200 $400**

❑ **WON-19. Resin Statue in Box,**
1995. Limited edition of 3000. Produced by Graphitti. Boxed - **$240**

WON-20

WON-21

❑ **WON-20. Hallmark Figure,**
1996. From DC Superheroes set. - **$55**

❑ **WON-21. Hallmark Figure,**
1996. 6" tall with base. - **$85**

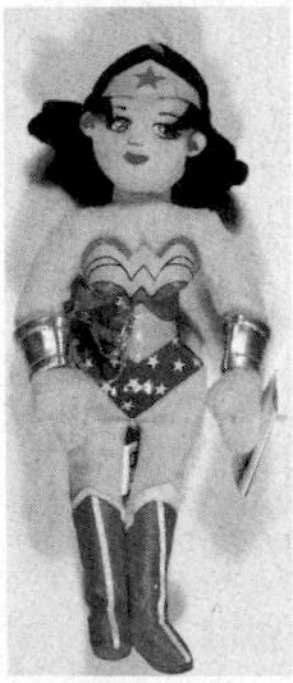
WON-22

WON-23

❑ **WON-22. Bean Bag Figure,**
1998. Warner Bros store exclusive. - **$8**

❑ **WON-23. Action Figure,**
1999. Variant with helmet and spear. - **$35**

WON-24

WON-25

❑ **WON-24. Resin Figure,**
1999. Warner Bros store exclusive. - **$125**

❑ **WON-25. Wonder Woman Statue,**
2000. DC Direct product. Hand painted, 9 1/2" tall. Limited to 5,000. - **$240**

WON-26

❑ **WON-26. "Spirit Of Truth" Graphic Novel,**
2001. Art by Alex Ross. - **$12**

WON-27

(Inside of bracelet is engraved)

(Box)

❑ **WON-27. Wonder Woman Prop Set,**
2001. DC Direct product. Set includes tiara, bracelets and earrings with a decorative base. Display base has a clear plastic removable lid. Limited to 1,200. Boxed - **$225**

WON-28

❑ **WON-28. Tin Dome Lunch Box,**
2001. Vandor. - **$15**

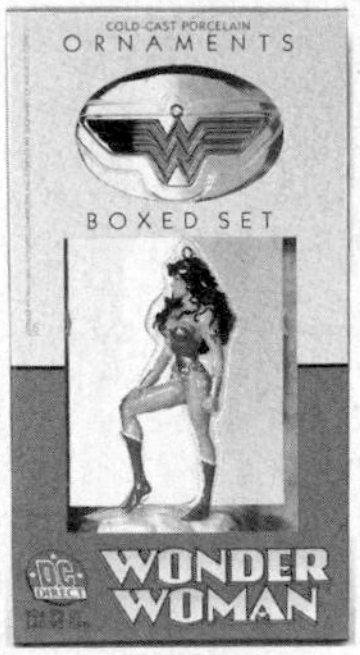

WON-29

WON-30

❑ **WON-29. Ornament Set in Box,**
2002. DC Direct. OPGN edition. Based on cover art to *Wonder Woman* (series 2) #72 by Brian Bolland. - **$30**

❑ **WON-30. Wonder Woman Maquette,**
2002. DC Direct. Sculpt by Karen Palinko. - **$110**

WON-31

❑ **WON-31. Burger King Figure,**
2002. NM - **$15**

WON-32

WON-33

❑ **WON-32. Pocket Super Heroes Figure,**
2002. Golden Age Wonder Woman figure was a retailer preview promotion. Also available in different packaging with a Solomon Grundy figure.
Figure in Promotional package - **$8**
Figure in Grundy box - **$5**

❑ **WON-33. Wonder Woman "Super Friends" Maquette,**
2003. DC Direct. Sculpt by Karen Palinko. - **$100**

WON-34

WON-35

❑ **WON-34. "Kingdom Come" Wonder Woman Action Figure in Box,**
2003. DC Direct. Part of the Kingdom Come Series 1 release. Based on art by Alex Ross. - **$20**

❑ **WON-35. Wonder Woman Mini-Bust,**
2003. DC Direct. Open edition. - **$50**

WON-36

❑ **WON-36. Wonder Woman Invisible Plane Replica,**
2005. DC Direct Gallery. Clear cold-cast porcelain replica on a hand-painted removable base. Approximately 4 1/2" tall X 15 1/2" long X 12 1 /2" wide. Limited to 1,250. Includes a non-removable Wonder Woman figure seated in the plane, a 4-color JLA charter membership document (11" X 8 1/2"), a blueprint of the plane (22" X 16") and a gold-plated JLA sanctuary key that measures 2 3/4" x 3" long x 1/4" deep. Packaged in a matte-black gift box with gold foil stamping. - **$250**

Woody Woodpecker

Between 1940 and 1972 Walter Lantz (1900-1994) created more than 200 animated shorts featuring the hyperactive woodpecker voiced by Ben Hardaway with the raucous laugh (supplied by Lantz's wife Grace who did his voice after 1956). Over the years Woody evolved from a multicolored lunatic into an appealing red-haired imp. His musical theme, *The Woody Woodpecker Song,* written by George Tibbles and Ramey Indries was nominated for an Academy Award in 1948. *The Woody Woodpecker Show* aired on the Mutual radio network in 1952-1954 and came to ABC television for the 1957-1958 season, then to NBC in 1971-1972 and 1976-1977. Woody made a number of comic book appearances starting in 1942. Items are normally copyrighted Walter Lantz Productions.

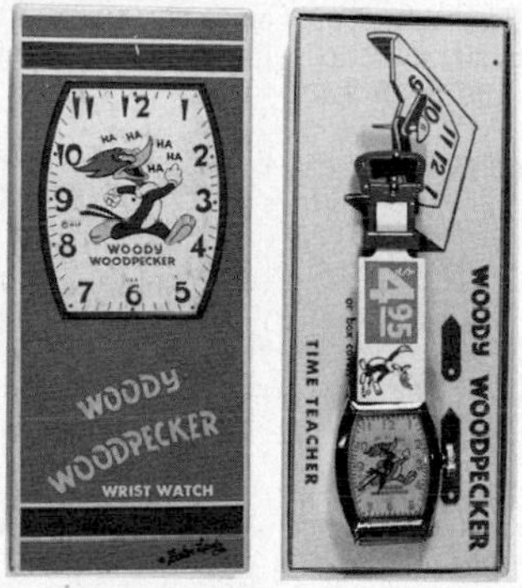

WDY-1

❑ **WDY-1. Wrist Watch with Box,**
1940s. Ingraham. Scarce.
Near Mint With Insert and Price Tag - **$2500**
Watch only - **$200 $425 $900**

WDY-2

WDY-3

❑ **WDY-2. Albers Quick Oats Container,**
1940s. Rare. Shows how to draw Woody and has a model sheet on back. Andy Panda is also featured. - **$175 $350 $700**

❑ **WDY-3. Promo,**
1951. Scarce. 6 pages (4 pages of comics). - **$125 $250 $500**

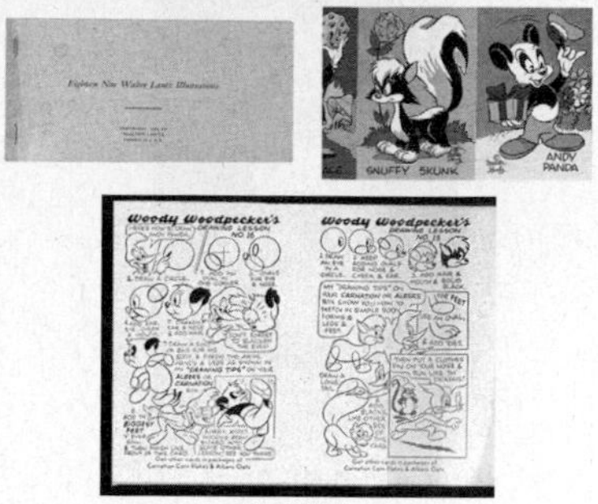

WDY-4

❑ **WDY-4. Cards With Folder,**
1953. Carnation Corn Flakes. Eighteen Walter Lantz character cards. Set - **$100 $200 $300**

WDY-5

❑ **WDY-5. "Woody Woodpecker Meets Scotty MacTape" Comic Book,**
1953. Scotch Tape sponsor. - **$18 $54 $220**

WDY-6

WDY-7

❑ **WDY-6. "Hi Pal!" Cello. Button,**
1957. Came on store bought doll. - **$25 $45 $90**

❑ **WDY-7. Premium Booklet,**
1958. Kellogg's Rice Krispies. 4 pages of recipes and a 1958 quarter. - **$25 $50 $100**

WDY-8

❑ **WDY-8. "Woody Woodpecker" Ceramic Toothbrush Holder,**
1950s. Figure is 2" diameter by 4" tall. Oval openings on either side of Woody with name below. WLP (Walter Lantz Productions) on back. High gloss glaze. - **$30 $60 $100**

WDY-9

❑ **WDY-9. "Woody Woodpecker" Figural Salt & Pepper Shakers,**
1950s. Glazed pottery figures are 2" diameter by 4" tall with name on front and WLP (Walter Lantz Productions) on back. Set - **$30 $60 $100**

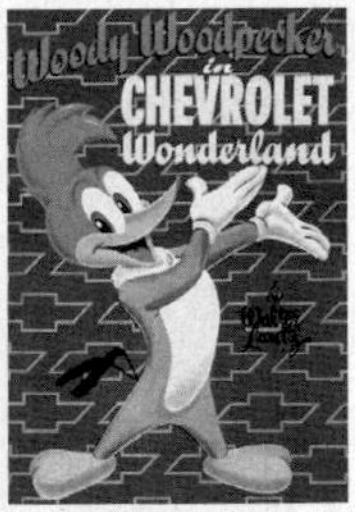

WDY-10

WDY-11

❑ **WDY-10. Premium Comic Chevrolet,**
1950s. - **$18 $54 $220**

❑ **WDY-11. Spoon,**
1950s. Cereal premium. - **$10 $20 $35**

WDY-12

WDY-13

❑ **WDY-12. Movie Label,**
1950s. - **$10 $20 $35**

❑ **WDY-13. Woody/Winnie Glazed Ceramic Salt And Pepper Set,**
1950s. Store item marked "Napco Originals By Guildcraft." Each is 3-7/8" tall from a series of pairs featuring Woody Woodpecker characters and other Lantz characters.
Each Pair - **$65 $125 $250**

(FRONT) (BACK)

WDY-14

❑ **WDY-14. Kellogg's Rice Krispies Cereal Box Flat with Fruit Promotion,**
1960. Woody fruit offer on back. Huck and Yogi spoon offer on side.
Box - **$60 $120 $225**

(FRONT) (BACK)

WDY-15

❑ **WDY-15. Kellogg's Raisin Bran Cereal Box Flat with Mug and Bowl Promotion,**
1963. Promotes mug and cereal bowl WDY-16.
Box - **$60 $120 $225**

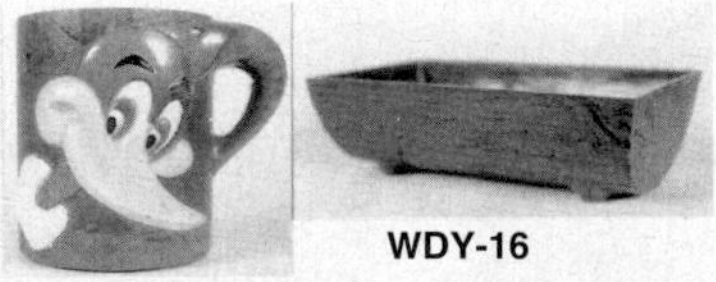

WDY-16

❑ **WDY-16. Kellogg's Plastic Mug And Cereal Bowl,**
1963. Bowl designed like a log trough.
Set - **$25 $40 $80**

WDY-17

WDY-18

❑ **WDY-17. Swimming Figure,**
1962. Kellogg's Cereals. Plastic jointed toy propelled by rubber band. Near Mint Boxed - **$150**
Unboxed - **$30 $65 $110**

❑ **WDY-18. Parking Pass,**
c. 1963. Lantz Studios. - **$30 $60 $100**

(FRONT) (BACK)

WDY-19

❑ **WDY-19. Kellogg's Rice Krispies 10 oz. Cereal Box Flat with Kazoo Promotion,**
1963. Promotes kazoo on back of box.
Box - **$60 $120 $225**

(FRONT) (BACK)

WDY-20

❑ **WDY-20. Kellogg's Rice Krispies 10 oz. Cereal Box Flat with Woody Crossword Puzzle,**
1963. Sports crossword on back of box.
Box - **$60 $120 $225**

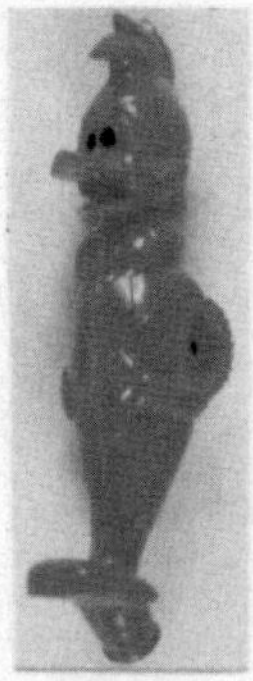

WDY-21

❑ **WDY-21. Figural Plastic Kazoo,**
c. 1965. 6-1/2" tall red plastic issued by Kellogg's. - **$12 $25 $55**

WDY-22

❑ **WDY-22. Kellogg's Plastic Door Knocker Assembly Kit,**
1966. Canadian issue. Boxed - **$25 $50 $85**
Built - **$15 $25 $50**

(FRONT) WDY-23 (BACK)

❑ **WDY-23. Rice Krispies Stuffed Toy Offer,**
1966. Cereal box flat. - **$60 $120 $225**

(FRONT) WDY-24 (BACK)

❑ **WDY-24. Stars Cereal Swimmer Offer,**
1967. Cereal box flat. - **$60 $120 $225**

WDY-25

WDY-26

❑ **WDY-25. Gum Box Display Card,**
1968. Fleer Gum. - **$10 $15 $30**

❑ **WDY-26. Figural Harmonica,**
c. 1960s. Possible Kellogg's premium. Plastic full figure with harmonica reed formed in tail.- **$18 $35 $75**

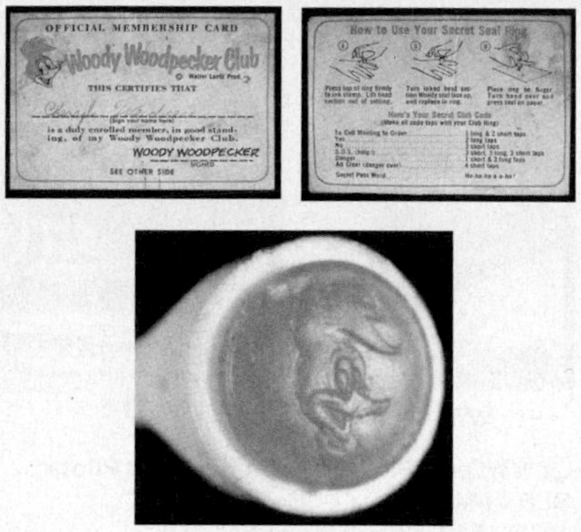

WDY-27

❑ **WDY-27. Club Card And "Secret Seal Ring",**
1960s. Kellogg's. Plastic ring in two color varieties has interior ink pad to stamp image of Woody. Card - **$15 $25 $50**
Ring - **$25 $50 $110**

WDY-28

❑ **WDY-28. "Woody's Cafe" Alarm Clock Varieties,**
c. 1970. Store item by Westclox, made in Hong Kong. This version has diecut hole on tree trunk to show alarm numerals. The original 1959 version by Columbia Time has a dial showing alarm numerals. Westclox - **$25 $50 $100**
Columbia Clock - **$50 $125 $250**
Columbia Box - **$50 $125 $250**

WDY-29

❑ **WDY-29. Woody And Winnie Woodpecker "Love" Leather Lunch Box,**
c. 1970s. Store item, maker unknown. Dark green leather with full color illustration on flap. Includes Walter Lantz Productions copyright. - **$175 $350 $650**

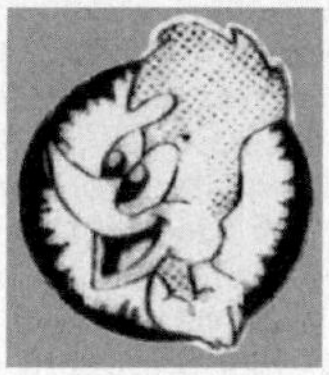
WDY-30

WDY-31

❑ **WDY-30. Plastic Portrait Ring,**
c. 1970s. Vending machine issue. - **$6 $10 $15**

❑ **WDY-31. Spoon,**
1970s. Store bought. - **$10 $25 $35**

WDY 32

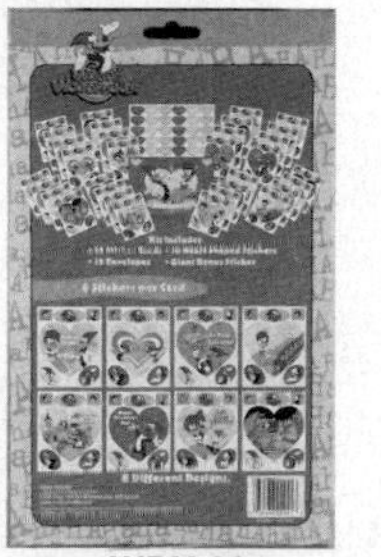
WDY-33

❑ **WDY-32. Replica Race Car on Card,**
1997. Revell diecast Wally Dallenbach car commemorates Universal Studios sponsorship of NASCAR Suzuka 100 held in Suzuka, Japan on Nov. 3, 1997. First in a series of proposed animated characters that Universal plans to feature on NASCAR Winston Cup cars. - **$45**

❑ **WDY-33. Valentine Kit,**
1999. Includes cards, stickers and envelopes. - **$2**

WDY-34

WDY-35

❑ **WDY-34. Premium Yo-Yo,**
1990s. Promotes new cartoons on the FOX Kids Network. Comes in yellow and blue.
Each - **$10 $20 $60**

❑ **WDY-35. Bobbing Head Figure,**
1990s. Boxed - **$65**

World War

Memorabilia was produced by various entities during World War I (1914-1919), setting a precedent for the huge volume of collectibles produced during World War II (1938-1945). American involvement in WWII began on December 7, 1941 and was intense on the home front as well as in the war zones. With millions of young men and women in uniform and far from home between early 1942 and 1945, family members and loved ones wanted to follow events as they occurred in Europe and in the Pacific. A number of advertisers answered the call by offering war maps and atlases and other print material that brought home details of the military movements and battles. V-E Day (Victory-Europe) was celebrated on May 8, 1945, and V-J Day (Victory-Japan) on August 15, 1945.

WWO-1

WWO-2

❑ **WWO-1. Victory Button 1.5" Size and Dated,**
1918. Features President Wilson and General Pershing. - **$50 $100 $200**

❑ **WWO-2. General Pershing Cast Iron Bank,**
1918. Cast iron bust. - **$100 $175 $425**

WWO-3

❑ **WWO-3. Pre-WWO Anti-War Button And Booklet,**
1936. Emergency Peace Campaign.
Button - **$10 $20 $30**
Booklet - **$15 $25 $50**

WWO-4

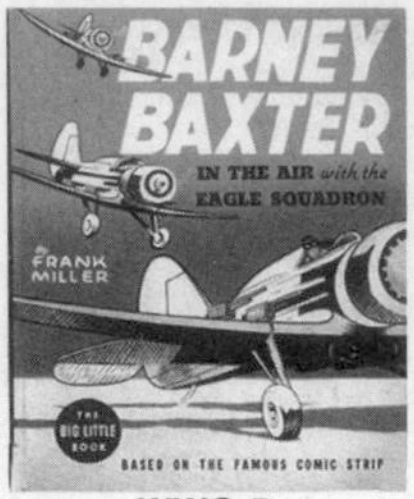

WWO-5

❑ **WWO-4. "Pat Nelson Ace of Test Pilots" BLB #1445,**
1937. - **$10 $30 $62**

❑ **WWO-5. "Barney Baxter In The Air With The Eagle Squadron" BLB #1459,**
1938. - **$11 $33 $72**

WWO-6

❑ **WWO-6. "Brad Turner In Transatlantic Flight" BLB #1425,**
1939. - **$10 $30 $62**

WWO-7

❑ **WWO-7. Anti-Hitler "Jackass Party Game" With Envelope,**
1939. Black/white envelope featuring caricature of Hitler as Nazi jackass. Contents include similar picture sheet plus uncut set of tails for "Pin The Tail On Adolf" blindfolded game. -
$75 $150 $300

WWO-8

WWO-9

❑ **WWO-8. "Don O'Dare Finds War" BLB #1438,**
1940. - **$10 $30 $62**

❑ **WWO-9. "Wings of the U.S.A." BLB #1407,**
1940. - **$10 $30 $62**

WWO-10

❑ **WWO-10. "Hit Hitler/Boycott Germany" Metal License Plate,**
c. 1940. Embossed tin plate measures 4.5x11.75". Made by "Motor Sign Co. 2737 Graybar Bldg." - **$200 $400 $650**

WWO-11

❑ **WWO-11. "Super-Defense Paper-Buster Gun,"**
c. 1940. Store item by Langson Mfg. Co. Metal gun is 6-1/4" long. Box - **$35 $75 $150**
Gun - **$25 $50 $100**

WWO-12

WWO-13

❑ **WWO-12. "Allen Pike of the Parachute Squad" BLB #1481,**
1941. - **$12 $36 $78**

❑ **WWO-13. "Air Fighters of America" BLB #1448,**
1941. - **$12 $36 $80**

WWO-14

WWO-15

❑ **WWO-14. "Pilot Pete Dive Bomber" BLB #1466,**
1941. - **$10 $30 $62**

❑ **WWO-15. "Uncle Sam's Sky Defenders" BLB #1461,**
1941. - **$10 $30 $62**

WWO-16

❑ **WWO-16. "Remember Pearl Harbor" Window Banner,**
c. 1941. 9x11" colorfully printed fabric with hanger cord and fringe tassel. - **$50 $100 $200**

WWO-17

❑ **WWO-17. "Remember Pearl Harbor" License Attachment,**
c. 1941. 3x10" diecut tin printed red, white and blue. - **$65 $150 $275**

WWO-18

WWO-19

❑ **WWO-18. Atlas Map,**
1942. Pure Oil premium. 16 pages. Edited by H. V. Kaltenborn. - **$20 $30 $50**

❑ **WWO-19. Atlas Map - 2nd Edition,**
1942. Pure Oil premium. 16 pages. - **$20 $30 $50**

WWO-20

❑ **WWO-20. Reading Kit - Boxed,**
1942. Says "Hours of entertainment for service men", included 5 different pulp magazines. - **$150 $300 $600**

WWO-21

WWO-22

❑ **WWO-21. H. V. Kaltenborn Photo,**
1942. Radio premium with Kaltenborn in uniform with "C" on sleeve for news correspondent. - **$10 $20 $40**

❑ **WWO-22. "Eat To Beat The Devil" Booklet,**
1942. Servel refrigerators. 32-page listing of health and nutrition tips with front cover caricature art of Hitler as the devil.
Booklet - **$15 $35 $75**
Button With Same Image - **$15 $35 $75**

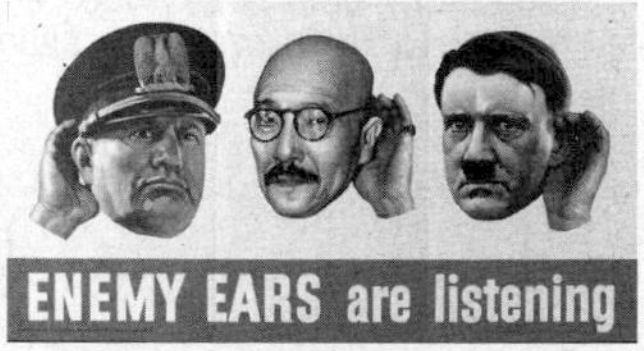

WWO-23

❑ **WWO-23. "Enemy Ears Are Listening" Anti-Axis Poster,**
1942. 14x26" paper black and white poster picturing Mussolini, Tojo and Hitler in stern expression while each holds a hand cupped to ear. - **$150 $275 $550**

WWO-24

❑ **WWO-24. License Plate Attachment,**
c. 1942. George Goode Garage and others. 5-1/2x10" metal finished in red, white and blue. - **$85 $150 $300**

WWO-25

❑ **WWO-25. Uncle Sam Large Punch Board,**
c. 1942. Issued by Hamilton Mfg. Co. 10x17". - **$85 $150 $300**

WWO-26

❑ **WWO-26. "Keep 'Em Flying! USA For America's Defense" Better Little Book #1420,**
1943. Whitman #1420. - **$10 $30 $62**

WWO-27

❑ **WWO-27. "7UP" Calendar for 1943,**
1943. The 12" x 7" calendar features an illustration of General MacArthur. - **$30 $60 $120**

WWO-28

❑ **WWO-28. "Girls In Uniform" Paperdoll Kit,**
1943. Store item by D. A. Pachter Co., Chicago. Unpunched **- $100 $200 $350**

WWO-29

❑ **WWO-29. "Capt. Ben Dix" Comic Book,**
1943. Bendix Aviation Corp. - **$8 $24 $65**

WWO-30 WWO-31

❑ **WWO-30. Flying Cadets Coloring Book,**
1943. Classic World War II cover by Fredric C. Madan. Book is filled with many pictures of U.S. planes. - **$50 $100 $220**

❑ **WWO-31. U.S. Marines Coloring Book,**
1943. Classic World War II cover by Fredric C. Madan. - **$50 $100 $220**

WWO-32 WWO-33

❑ **WWO-32. Submarine Coloring Book,**
1943. Cover by Fredric C. Madan. -
$50 $100 $220

❑ **WWO-33. Atlas Map - Victory Edition,**
1943. Pure Oil premium. 20 pages. -
$15 $30 $55

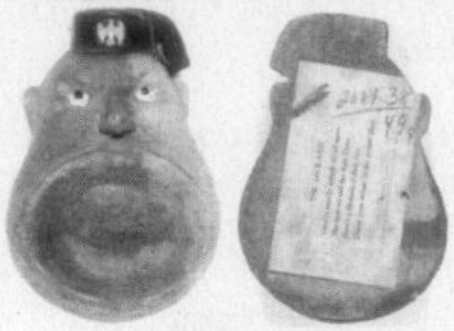

WWO-34

WWO-35

❑ **WWO-34. Anti-Mussolini Plaster Ashtray With Sticker Label,**
1943. - **$100 $200 $300**

❑ **WWO-35. "Kool Cigarettes" Poster,**
c. 1943. Issued by Brown & Williamson Tobacco Co. 12x18". - **$50 $100 $225**

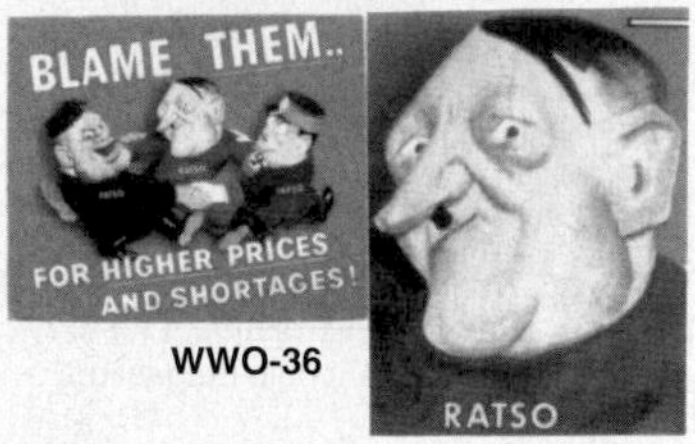

WWO-36

❑ **WWO-36. "Fatso-Ratso-Japso" Anti-Axis Easel Poster,**
c. 1943. 15-1/4x18" rigid cardboard. -
$200 $400 $650

WWO-37 WWO-38

❑ **WWO-37. "Radio At War Picture Book",**
c. 1943. Various sponsors. Depicts programs and stars of "Blue Network." - **$15 $25 $50**

❑ **WWO-38. Hitler Plaster Pin Cushion,**
c. 1943. Large Size - **$135 $225 $450**
Smaller "Hotzi Notzi" Size - **$75 $115 $200**

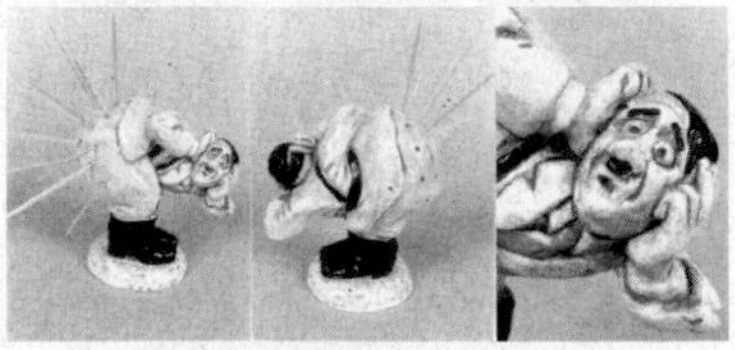

WWO-39

❑ **WWO-39. Anti-Hitler Plaster Toothpick Holder,**
c. 1943. - **$150 $275 $500**

WWO-40

❑ **WWO-40. "Radio For Victory" Picture Book,**
c. 1943. By WCBM, Baltimore. 36 pages including dozens of photos illustrating use of radio during WWII including examples of numerous popular radio and movie entertainment stars. -
$20 $35 $80

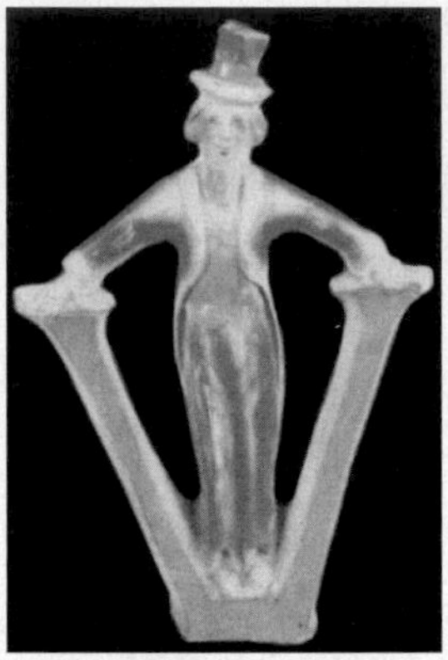

WWO-41

❑ **WWO-41. Uncle Sam Victory Statuette,**
c. 1943. 12-1/2" tall plaster store item by Turiddi Art. - **$75 $150 $265**

WWO-42

❑ **WWO-42. Anti-Hitler Matchbook Cover,**
c. 1943. Seat of Hitler is brown sandpaper for striking surface. Issued by Monogram.
Full Pack - **$30 $60 $100**
Cover Only - **$20 $40 $65**

WWO-43

❑ **WWO-43. "Target Tokyo" Cardboard Wheel Game,**
1944. Tip-Top Bread. - **$25 $50 $100**

WWO-44

WWO-45

❑ **WWO-44. Flying Forts Coloring Book,**
1944. Spectacular cover by Fredric C. Madan. Mentions loading eggs (bombs) heading for Hitler and Hirohito. - **$75 $125 $275**

❑ **WWO-45. Planes of Tomorrow Coloring Book,**
1944. Incredible look into the future. 50 different planes are shown, many of which look familiar 56 years later. It also talks about rocket ships going to the moon. - **$75 $125 $275**

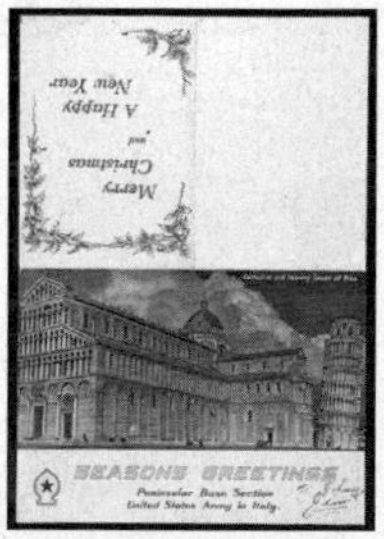

WWO-46

❑ **WWO-46. Christmas Card,**
1944. Christmas card from the United States Army in Italy. - **$10 $20 $40**

WWO-47

❑ **WWO-47. Pacific Map,**
1944. Pure Oil premium. Folds out to show battle areas in Pacific. - **$15 $30 $55**

WWO-48

WWO-49

❑ **WWO-48. Victory Map Set,**
1944. Pure Oil Co. Two sections fold out into huge wall map. - **$30 $60 $90**

❑ **WWO-49. Hitler Skunk,**
c. 1944. Glazed ceramic. - **$75 $150 $275**

WWO-50

❑ **WWO-50. Anti-Hitler Composition Pig Bank,**
c. 1944. Insert coin to make him squeak. Squeaking mechanism rarely works.
Not Working - **$100 $200 $400**
Box (Not Shown) - **$200 $400 $800**

WWO-51

❑ **WWO-51. "Sky Heroes" Stamp Album,**
c. 1944. Sinclair Oil Corp. Twenty stamps in set.
Complete - **$50 $100 $200**

WWO-52

❑ **WWO-52. "Victory Star Tumblers" Glasses Set In Carrier,**
c. 1944. Pillsbury's Flour. Set - **$50 $100 $200**

WWO-53

❑ **WWO-53. "A-Bomb Manhattan Project" Sterling Silver Award Pin,**
1945. 11/16" issue for October 16 when Gen. Leslie R. Groves presided over outdoor ceremony that awarded a pin and certificate to each of the employees involved in atom bomb tests at Los Alamos. The event also concluded Robert Oppenheimer's last day as director. -
$75 $135 $250

WWO-54

❑ **WWO-54. "Exide Batteries At War" Book,**
1946. Illustrations similar to Dixie Ice Cream series. - **$50 $100 $200**

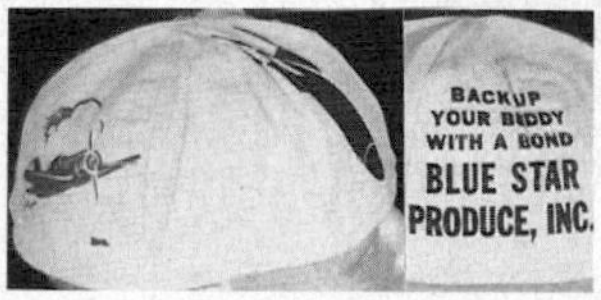

WWO-55

❑ **WWO-55. Bond Promotion Skull Cap,**
1940s. Blue Star Produce and others. Blue on white fabric reading "Backup Your Buddy With A Bond." - **$20 $35 $85**

WWO-56

❑ **WWO-56. War Bonds Dairy Milk Bottle,**
1940s. Fraim's Dairies and others. 9-1/2" tall glass quart bottle with image in maroon. -
$30 $60 $90

WWO-57

❑ **WWO-57. Esso War Maps,**
1940s. Periodic revisions in war years.
Each - **$10 $15 $30**

WWO-58

WWO-59

❑ **WWO-58. Lowell Thomas NBC War Map 16x20",**
1940s. Radio premium. Two sided colorful map of the World. - **$15 $25 $50**

❑ **WWO-59. Kaltenborn Campaign Book,**
1940s. Pure Oil premium. News editor for Roosevelt vs. Willkie election. - **$15 $30 $50**

WWO-60

WWO-61

❑ **WWO-60. Photo,**
1940s. "H. V. Kaltenborn Edits The News."
- **$5 $10 $20**

❑ **WWO-61. Radio Sign,**
1940s. Features Uncle Sam telling people to listen to updates on the War. - **$40 $75 $135**

WWO-62

❑ **WWO-62. Coca-Cola Air Insignia Cello. Buttons,**
1940s. Each is a full color 1" cello. from a set of 24. Manner of distribution is unknown. The numbered reverse back paper identifies the squadron and reads "Drink Coca-Cola."
Each - **$10 $25 $50**

WWO-63

❑ **WWO-63. Cartoon Slogan Matchbook,**
1940s. Topps Gum. Cover includes security slogan illustrated by cartoonist O. Soglow, creator of The Little King comic strip.
Complete - **$18 $35 $60**

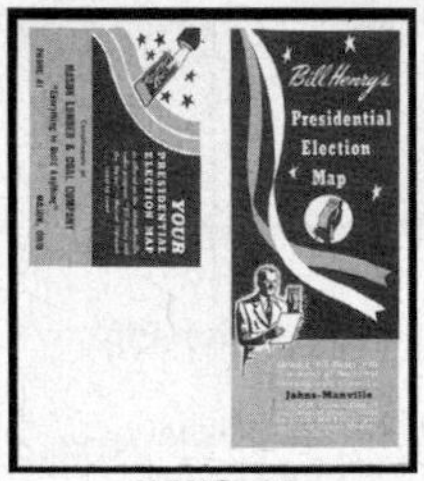

WWO-64

WWO-65

❑ **WWO-64. Bill Henry's Presidential Election Map,**
1940s. - **$25 $35 $60**

❑ **WWO-65. "Wanted for Murder" Hitler Pinback,**
1940s. Size of 1.25". On a reproduction, numerous tiny areas of the face that should be white are filled in by the black ink. - **$20 $35 $65**

WWO-66

❑ **WWO-66. "Fifth Columnist" Alert Folder,**
1940s. Diecut folder that changes portrait of masked subversive on front cover to inside cartoon of symbolic pig, snake, rat and skunk. - **$50 $100 $200**

WWO-67

❑ **WWO-67. "Uncle Sam" Tin Top Hat Bank,**
1940s. J. Chein Co. 4" diameter base, 3.25" diameter at top by 3.25" tall. Bright red, white and blue litho tin. - **$100 $200 $300**

WWO-68

❑ **WWO-68. "Hi-Speed Victory Club" Membership Letter And Button,**
1940s. Pinback button is 1". Green paper club letter 8.5x5.5" printed in black ink.
Letter - **$20 $35 $60**
Button - **$10 $20 $40**

WWO-69

❑ **WWO-69. Douglas MacArthur Figure/Salt & Pepper Shakers,**
1950. Plaster figure measures 5" tall with base reading "Copyright 1950 J.H. Miller." Hat shaker is 2" tall and pipe shaker is 3.5" long.
Figure - **$20 $35 $60**
Salt & Pepper - **$30 $60 $100**

WWO-70

❑ **WWO-70. "Wings Away" Plastic Plane Set,**
1950s. Box set of 32 different plastic planes. - **$150 $300 $600**

World's Fairs

International expositions blossomed into creative and technical spectacles in the 19th century, first in Europe and then in the United States, providing a mix of fine arts, industrial progress, and nationalist emotions. In addition to promoting international understanding, world's fairs produced an abundance of collectible souvenirs. Major American fairs include the Centennial Exposition (Philadelphia, 1876), World's Columbian Exposition (Chicago, 1893), Cotton Centennial (New Orleans, 1894), Pan-American (Buffalo, 1901), Louisiana Purchase (St. Louis, 1904), Panama-Pacific (San Francisco, San Diego and Seattle 1915), Sesquicentennial (Philadelphia, 1926) Century of Progress (Chicago, 1933-1934), California Pacific International (San Diego, 1935-1936), Great Lakes (Cleveland, 1936-1937), Golden Gate International (San Francisco, 1939-1940), The New York World's Fair, World of Tomorrow (New York, 1939-1940), Seattle Expo (1962), New York World's Fair (1964-1965), Expo '67 (Montreal 1967), Expo '74 (Spokane 1974), Knoxville World's Fair (1982), and Expo '86 (Vancouver, British Columbia 1986).

WFA-1

❑ **WFA-1. U.S. Centennial Pennant,**
1876. 18x24" vertical swallow-tail linen fabric including border design of 38 stars representing states admitted to the Union as of celebration year. - **$100 $250 $400**

WFA-2

❑ **WFA-2. Spoon ,**
1893. World's Fair spoon shows picture of Columbus and Administration Building. Sold at Fair. - **$10 $18 $30**

WFA-3

❑ **WFA-3. Giveaway Comic Booklet,**
1893. Features the story of "Bill an' Me" and their trip from Baltimore to Chicago to visit the Fair. Sponsored by Emerson's Bromo Seltzer. - **$25 $75 $150**

WFA-4

❑ **WFA-4. Ticket - Chicago 1893,**
1893. Unused 1893 child's ticket for World's Fair in Chicago. Children dreamed of the chance of attending the World's Columbian Exhibition in 1893. It is very rare to find an unused ticket that was bought at the Fair.
Complete - **$20 $40 $75**

WFA-5 WFA-6 WFA-7

❑ **WFA-5. Pan-American Exposition "Swift & Company" Cello. Button,**
1901. Advertising button for meat products. - **$15 $25 $60**

❑ **WFA-6. Pan-American Exposition Cello. Button,**
1901. Pictured is establishment and proprietor of "Cheyenne Joe's Rocky Mountain Tavern." - **$30 $60 $125**

❑ **WFA-7. Pan-American Exposition Cello. Button,**
1901. Full color 1-1/4" based on theme of North and South American continents joining hands, although depicting monkeys rather than the traditional two ladies of the official theme art design. - **$40 $80 $150**

WFA-8 WFA-9 WFA-10

❑ **WFA-8. St. Louis World's Fair Cello. Button,**
1904. Full color 1-3/4" depicting "The Home Of Jefferson." - **$35 $65 $135**

❑ **WFA-9. St. Louis World's Fair Cello. Button,**
1904. Pictured is Thomas Jefferson under alternate title of the fair "Universal Exposition." - **$30 $50 $100**

❑ **WFA-10. Sesquicentennial Cello. Button,**
1926. Mostly red, white and blue with bronze image of bell, 1-1/4". - **$15 $25 $50**

WFA-11 WFA-12

❑ **WFA-11. Sky Ride Promo ,**
1933. Chicago World's Fair premium came with Frank Buck Club material. - **$20 $30 $50**

❑ **WFA-12. Puzzle - Boxed ,**
1933. Chicago World's Fair 11x16" puzzle sold at Fair. - **$20 $40 $80**

WFA-13

❑ **WFA-13. "Radio Flyer" Replica Wagon,**
1933. Radio Steel & Mfg. Co., Chicago. Chicago Expo souvenir 3.75" long metal toy on rubber tires. Decals name the toy,
1933 Chicago event, sponsor. - **$50 $100 $200**

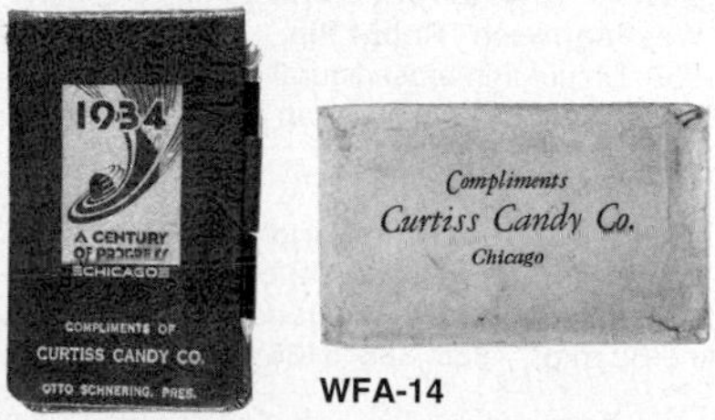

WFA-14

❑ **WFA-14. Notebook and Pen,**
1934. Chicago World's Fair premium from the Curtiss Candy Co. - **$30 $60 $90**
Mailer - **$10 $20 $30**

WFA-15

WFA-16

❑ **WFA-15. Salt And Pepper Shakers ,**
1934. Chicago World's Fair - Hall of Science pictured on each shaker. Sold at Fair. - **$25 $50 $85**

❑ **WFA-16. "Sears, Roebuck & Co." Chicago World's Fair Key Holder,**
1933. Cello. and brass 3" key case dated for opening year of the fair. - **$25 $50 $75**

WFA-17

❑ **WFA-17. "Century of Progress" Chicago World's Fair Ring,**
1934. Rare. Uncas. Ring has the same base with adjustable bands as the Supermen of America/Action Comics prototype ring. Base has also been found on one version of the Spider pulp ring. - **$50 $100 $150**

WFA-18 **WFA-19** **WFA-20**

❑ **WFA-18. New York World's Fair Enameled Brass Star Badge,**
1939. Souvenir issue for youthful "Safety Monitor." - **$50 $125 $210**

❑ **WFA-19. New York World's Fair "Westinghouse" Robot Pin,**
1939. Diecut thin brass figural pin of Robot Elektro giant mechanical man of Westinghouse Exhibit. - **$10 $20 $40**

❑ **WFA-20. New York World's Fair "Westinghouse" Robot Cello. Button,**
1939. Images of robot and robot dog "Elektro And Sparko." - **$35 $80 $135**

WFA-21

❑ **WFA-21. New York World's Fair Posterette,**
1939. 7x10-1/2" issued by Grinnell Litho Company. **- $40 $80 $150**

WFA-22 **WFA-23**

❑ **WFA-22. New York World's Fair "Abbott & Costello" Cello. Button,**
1939. Nomination of Costello for mayor and Abbott for "Commissioner Of Laffs" of "World's Fair Midway." A version with heads touching and no hat on Lou Costello is an altered reproduction of no value. - **$40 $80 $185**

❑ **WFA-23. "Guernseys" New York World's Fair Cello. Button,**
1939. Blue, white and brown 1-1/4" believed from exhibit by Guernsey Breeders Assn. - **$20 $35 $75**

WFA-24

❑ **WFA-24. Penny Bracelet 1939,**
1939. Boxed. 14 KT gold plated. Sold at the World's Fair. - **$35 $65 $100**

WFA-25

❑ **WFA-25. Jigsaw Puzzle Premium With Mailer,**
1939. Sloan's Liniment. 10-1/2x12-1/2" mailer holds 100-piece puzzle with color aerial view of the grounds identifying exhibit buildings by a numbered legend across the bottom.
Mailer - **$10 $20 $40**
Puzzle - **$40 $70 $135**

WFA-26

❑ **WFA-26. New York World's Fair Lunch Box And Bottle,**
1939. Store item by American Thermos Bottle Co. Both pieces are dark blue steel with the exposition logo in bright orange. The box was issued with a leather carrying strap.
Box - **$175 $275 $550**
Bottle - **$75 $150 $300**

WFA-27

❑ **WFA-27. "Today At The Fair" New York World's Fair Schedule Newspaper,** 1939.
Daily edition #118 for Monday, August 28 with eight pages of either daily or continuous events. Back page includes photo of "Elektro," the seven-foot tall robot of Westinghouse exhibit. - **$25 $50 $100**

WFA-28

❑ **WFA-28. "Wonder Bread" New York World's Fair Sticker Signs,** 1939. 11x18" and 9" diameter full color signs gummed on front for store window application. Both include image of "Wonder Bakery" exhibit building.
Each - **$40 $85 $175**

WFA-29 **WFA-30**

❑ **WFA-29. Bike Product New York World's Fair Ad Poster,**
1939. New Departure Coaster Brake. Photo endorsement by Grover Whalen, fair director, on 16x25" poster. - **$45 $85 $175**

❑ **WFA-30. "108 World's Fair Recipes" Booklet,**
1939. Souvenir of Borden Exhibit of New York World's Fair with 32 pages of recipes and Elsie illustrations. - **$15 $30 $60**

WFA-31

WFA-32

❑ **WFA-31. "Either World's Fair" Contest Paper Poster,**
1939. 16x25" by unidentifed sponsor offering prize of free trips for boys and girls to either Golden Gate Exposition of San Francisco or New York World's Fair. - **$85 $175 $300**

❑ **WFA-32. New York World's Fair Clown Doll,**
1939. 15" tall wood and composition doll in orange and blue fabric outfit. - **$150 $300 $600**

WFA-33

❑ **WFA-33. Fabric Flag With Logo,**
1939. Linen-like fabric in orange and blue with logo in white, 11x16". - **$65 $135 $225**

WFA-34

❑ **WFA-34. New York World's Fair Enamel Hat Badge,**
1939. Heavy brass badge is 1.75" with beautiful enamel center. Back has screw post and brass cap for use on a hat. - **$65 $125 $175**

WFA-35

❑ **WFA-35. Classic Die-Cut Sign,**
1939. 15"x19-1/2" sign features the skyline of New York City and the Golden Gate Bridge. Issued by Colgate-Palmolive Co. Promotes the "Golden Gate International" and "World of Tomorrow" Worlds' Fairs. Rare.
- $300 $500 $1000

WFA-36

❑ **WFA-36. "Boys' Life" Cover Article,**
1940. May issue with article "Scout Camp At The World's Fair." - **$15 $25 $50**

WFA-37

❑ **WFA-37. NYWF Banking Employee Jacket,**
1940. Has bakelite-like plastic chest buttons with relief images of Trylon and Perisphere. - **$75 $150 $300**

WFA-38

❑ **WFA-38. New York World's Fair Closing Day Pennant,**
1940. 4x9" felt fabric inscribed for visit on final day October 27th. - **$35 $65 $125**

WFA-39

❑ **WFA-39. "Futurama" Exhibit Booklet From Second Season,**
1940. General Motors. 7x8k-1/4" with 24 pages of black and white photos showing "The World Of Tomorrow." - **$15 $30 $65**

WFA-40

WFA-41

❑ **WFA-40. "Candy World's Fair Twin" Squeaker Doll,**
1964. 8-1/2" tall soft rubber made by Sun Rubber Co. Near Mint Packaged - **$200**
Loose - **$30 $60 $100**

❑ **WFA-41. New York World's Fair Flicker Ring,**
1964. Silvered plastic base topped by alternating image of Unisphere and souvenir text. - **$10 $15 $30**

WFA-42

WFA-43

❑ **WFA-42. Schaefer Center Sign,**
1964. Schaefer Beer. 15-1/2x18-1/2" full color stiff cardboard. - **$35 $75 $125**

❑ **WFA-43. Eastman Kodak Exhibit Glass,**
1964. Yellow and white images on 5-1/4" tall clear glass tumbler. - **$10 $18 $35**

WFA-44

❑ **WFA-44. "Sinclair Dinoland" Injection Molded Vinyl Dinosaur,**
1964. Sinclair Exhibit. From a series of at least six different, each about 5" to 9" long and produced in various single colors from a coin vending molding machine within the pavilion.
Each - **$15 $30 $50**

WFA-45

❑ **WFA-45. "World's Fair Twins" Kissing Bobbing Head Set,**
1965. Pair of composition symbolic twins with spring-mounted heads and inner magnet behind pursed lips. Box Only - **$25 $50 $85**
Pair Bobbing Heads - **$60 $120 $200**

Wyatt Earp

Legendary gunfighter and lawman Wyatt Earp (1848-1929) has been portrayed in at least two dozen Hollywood Westerns by such stars as George O'Brien, Randolph Scott, Richard Dix, Henry Fonda, Joel McCrea, Burt Lancaster and Kevin Costner. On television *The Life and Legend of Wyatt Earp* starred Hugh O'Brian in a serial drama that aired on ABC from 1955 to 1961. The series, written by Stuart N. Lake, was the first TV adult western and followed the romanticized adventures of Earp as a frontier marshal in Ellsworth and Dodge City, Kansas, and Tombstone, Arizona. Comic books appeared from 1955 onward. Most licensed items came from the TV series and are copyrighted Wyatt Earp Ent. Inc.

WYT-1

❑ **WYT-1. "Buntline Special" Gun On Card,**
c. 1955. Store item. 6x20" card holds 18" long plastic clicker replica gun popularized on TV series.
Card - **$50 $100 $300**
Gun - **$65 $125 $250**

WYT-2

❑ **WYT-2. Response Postcard To Fan With Real Photo,**
1956. Example shown has autograph.
Signed - **$25 $50 $85**
Unsigned - **$10 $20 $30**

(FRONT) **WYT-3** (BACK)

❑ **WYT-3. Cheerios Box,**
1957. Back panel has cut-out parts for "Peacemaker" gun on 10-1/2 oz. box; "Paterson" gun on 7 oz. box. A "Dragoon" gun was also issued on 15 oz. box.
Each Complete Box - **$115 $250 $400**

WYT-4

❑ **WYT-4. "Wyatt Earp Buntline Special" Plastic Pistol With Sunday Comic Ad Offer,**
1957. Gleem Toothpaste. 18" long black plastic clicker gun and newspaper ad dated February 3, 1957. Ad - **$10 $15 $30**
Gun - **$65 $125 $250**

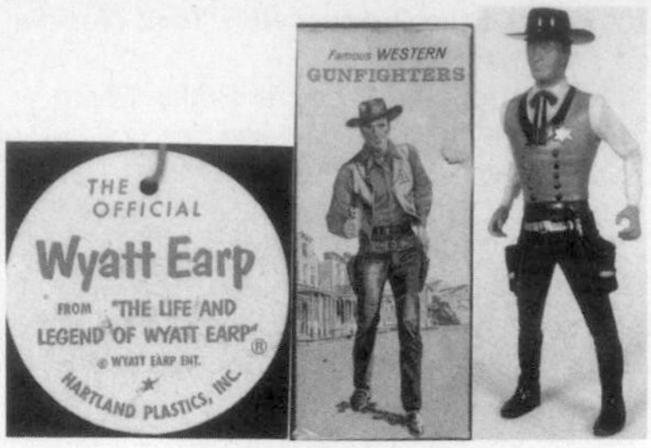

WYT-5

❑ **WYT-5. "Marshal Wyatt Earp" Hartland Gunfighter Figure Boxed With Tag,**
1957. Hartland Plastics. 7.5" tall replica figure with hat, two guns, string tag and portrait box.
Figure Complete - **$100 $200 $300**
Box - **$75 $150 $300**
Tag - **$25 $50 $150**

WYT-6

❑ **WYT-6. Photo Puzzle,**
1958. Large puzzle of Hugh O'Brian as Wyatt Earp. - **$25 $45 $90**

WYT-7 WYT-8

❑ **WYT-7. "Marshal Wyatt Earp" Sterling Silver Initial Ring,**
1958. Cheerios. Engraved personal initial, TV show copyright. - **$50 $85 $150**

❑ **WYT-8. "Marshal Wyatt Earp" Metal Badge On Card,**
c. 1958. Store item.
On Card - **$15 $25 $40**
Loose - **$10 $15 $30**

WYT-9

❑ WYT-9. "TV's Wyatt Earp" Hugh O'Brian Record Album,
c. 1958. 33-1/3 rpm. - **$10 $20 $40**

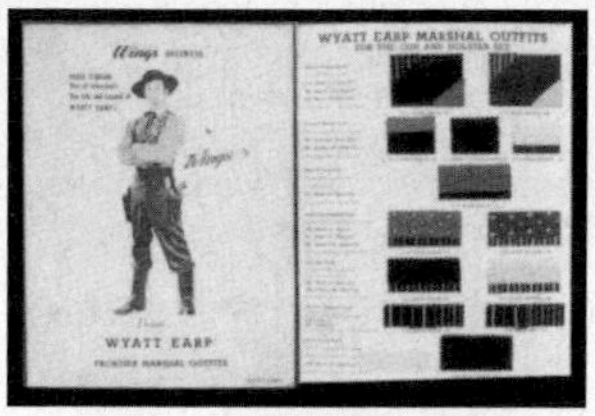

WYT-10

❑ WYT-10. "Wyatt Earp Frontier Marshal Outfit" Fabric Selection Brochure,
c. 1958. Issued by Wings Boyswear. 11x15" folder holds 34 different fabric swatches. - **$65 $125 $200**

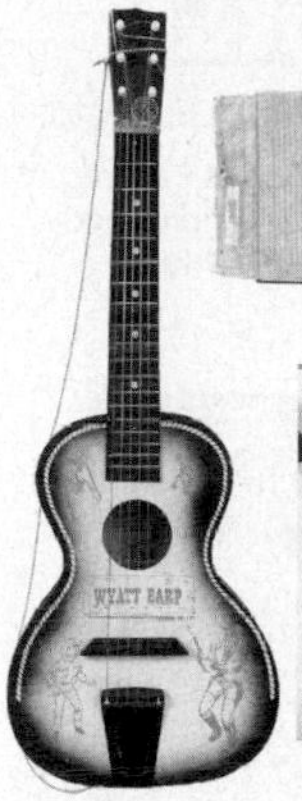

(BOX)

(CLOSE-UP OF ART)

WYT-11

❑ WYT-11. "Wyatt Earp" Toy Guitar In Box,
1959. Cardboard box is 3.5x11x30.5" long with red illustrations and text reading "Manufactured By Jefferson Villa 33, PA/Educator Approved Prestige Toy 1959" and contains 2.57x10.75" wide by 30" long wood/cardboard guitar.
Box - **$30 $60 $100**
Guitar - **$45 $65 $150**

WYT-12

WYT-13

❑ WYT-12. TV Guide with "Wyatt Earp" Cover,
1959. Hugh O'Brian featured. - **$10 $20 $50**

❑ WYT-13. "Wyatt Earp" Pinback,
1950s. Australian issue. - **$30 $60 $90**

X-Men

Stan Lee and Jack Kirby (1917-1994) created the X-Men, a band of superpower teenage mutant fighters crusading for justice and the acceptance of mutants in an increasingly prejudiced society. Introduced in issue #1 of *X-Men* in 1963, Cyclops, The Angel, The Beast, and Marvel Girl joined with Professor X to foil the evil schemes of arch-enemy Magneto. The book was suspended briefly in 1970, then revived with reprints and, starting in 1975, new adventures and new characters were introduced, sparking a run that has proliferated into numerous other titles and a huge surge in popularity. Including Specials and Annuals, Marvel has published well over 800 *X-Men* comic books. An animated version debuted on the Fox Children's Network in 1992, and two live-action feature films opened in July, 2000 and May, 2003. A third, *X-Men 3: The Last Stand*, was released in May 2006. A spin-off movie *X-Men Origins: Wolverine* starring Hugh Jackman is in production at press time.

XMN-1

XMN-2

❑ XMN-1. X-Men #1,
Sept. 1963. Marvel Comics. Origin and first appearance of the X-Men. -
$700 $2100 $19,000

❑ XMN-2. Plastic Badge With Reverse Needle Post/Clutch,
1988. Marvel. - **$4 $7 $12**

XMN-3

XMN-4

❑ XMN-3. Gold Ring,
1993. Diamond Comics Distribution seminar giveaway. 25 made. - **$900**

❑ XMN-4. Silver Ring,
1993. Diamond Comics Distribution seminar giveaway. - **$150**

(TOP) XMN-5 (SIDE)

❑ XMN-5. Xavier Institute Class Ring,
1994. 10k gold. - **$500**
Sterling Silver Version - **$100**
Bronze Finished Pewter Version - **$30**

(FRONT) XMN-6 (BACK)

❑ XMN-6. "Cookie Crisp" Cereal Box with X-Men Trading Card Promotion,
1994. Fleer trading card inside box and poster by Andy Kubert on back. - **$5 $10 $30**

XMN-7

❑ XMN-7. Gambit and the Shadow King Book,
1994. Has a hologram on the front cover. -
$5 $10 $30

(FRONT) XMN-8 (BACK)

❑ XMN-8. "Berry Berry Kix" Cereal Box with X-Men Overpower Card Promotion,
1995. Game offer on back. - **$5 $10 $30**

XMN-9

❑ **XMN-9. Xavier Institute Class Ring,**
2000. 1,000 made. Sterling silver. Boxed - **$250**

XMN-10

XMN-11

❑ **XMN-10. Electronic X-Jet in Box,**
2000. From the movie. - **$50**

❑ **XMN-11. "Wolverine" in Debut Costume Mini-Bust,**
2000. Limited to 2,000. - **$100**

The Yellow Kid

The Yellow Kid, **created by Richard F. Outcault (1863-1925), is generally considered to be the first true comic strip. After appearances as a minor character in *Truth* magazine in 1894 and in the *Hogan's Alley* gag panels in the *New York World* in 1895, the bald, jug-eared kid in a nightshirt grew in popularity and, by the beginning of 1896, his nightshirt was yellow. Although Outcault named him Mickey Dugan, readers referred to him as the yellow kid. William Randolph Hearst hired Outcault for his *New York Journal* later that year and titled his panels *McFadden's Flats*. The Yellow Kid only appeared in New York City newspapers through 1898. Outcault dropped the strip in 1898 and went on to other work, but the Kid made licensing history in promoting a wide range of products such as chewing gum, candy, cookies, games, puzzles, cigarettes, soap, bicycles, highchairs, and whiskey. George Luks (1867-1933) drew the character for a short period, then went on to greater fame as a realistic painter in the Ashcan School. Though he no longer retained any rights to the character, Outcault used the Yellow Kid several times in his Buster Brown Sunday pages.**

YLW-1

❑ **YLW-1. Yellow Kid And Lady 18x24" Paper Announcement Poster For New York Journal's Colored Sunday Supplement,**
1896. Scarce. Also reads "Wait For It-It Is Coming" including artists' names Archie Gunn and R. F. Outcault. - **$2000 $4000 $8000**

YLW-2

❑ **YLW-2. Wooden Cigar Box,**
1896. - **$300 $800 $1600**

YLW-3

❑ **YLW-3. Gum Card #11 Example,**
1896. Adams' Yellow Kid Chewing Gum. Set of 25, two styles: small number or large number (see YLW-7.)
Small Numbers Each - **$25 $50 $200**

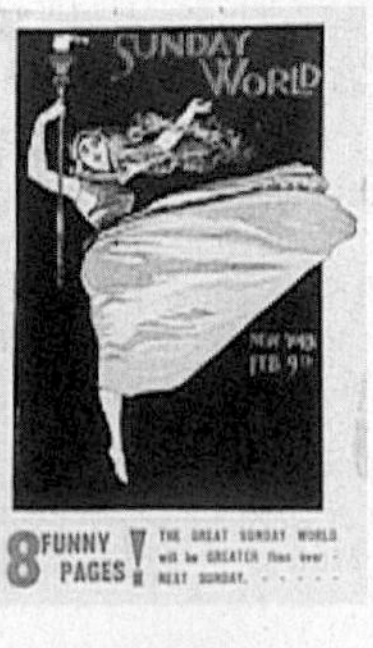

YLW-4

❑ **YLW-4. "Sunday World 8 Funny Pages!" Newspaper Advertising Poster,**
1896. 11x18-1/2" promoting the Sunday February 9th issue with facsimile signature of Outcault at lower left. A historic poster issued for what we believe was the first eight-page, color Sunday section. An unknown quantity of these were discovered about 1995. Over that time we've become aware of seven examples. - **$150 $300 $600**

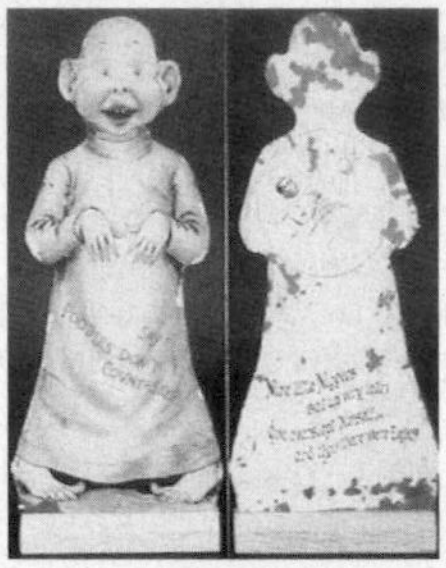

YLW-5

❑ **YLW-5. Diecut Wooden Target Figure,**
1896. Store item. 10-1/4" tall paper on wood part of a set. Each - **$200 $350 $750**

YLW-6

YLW-7

❑ **YLW-6. Soap Figure,**
c. 1896. Store item by D. S. Brown & Co.
Box - **$150 $275 $600**
Soap - **$150 $275 $600**

❑ **YLW-7. Gum Cards #6 and #21,**
1896. Adams' Yellow Kid Chewing Gum. Examples from set of 25 with large numbers.
Each - **$25 $50 $200**

YLW-8

YLW-9

YLW-10

❑ **YLW-8. Yellow Kid First Button In Set,**
1896. High Admiral cigarettes. The first 39 buttons in the set are the most frequently found. Each - **$15 $30 $60**

❑ **YLW-9. Cello. Button #35,**
1896. Buttons #40-94 become scarcer as the button number becomes higher. #90-94 are the scarcest. #95-100 were never issued.
#40-89 Each - **$25 $50 $100**
#90-94 Each - **$75 $150 $300**

❑ **YLW-10. Yellow Kid With Various Flags Cello. Button,**
1896. High Admiral Cigarette. Buttons numbered 101-160 depict him holding some type of flag, usually with the name of a country. Each - **$30 $60 $120**

YLW-11

YLW-12

❑ **YLW-11. Theatrical Production Cello. Button,**
1896. - **$30 $65 $125**

❑ **YLW-12. Yellow Kid For President McKinley Enameled Brass Lapel Stud,**
1896. Small figure inscribed "Hogan's Alley Is Out Fer McKinley". - **$350 $800 $1750**

YLW-13

❑ **YLW-13. "The Latest And The Greatest" Sheet Music Insert From Newspaper,**
c. 1896. Rare. - **$175 $350 $700**

YLW-14

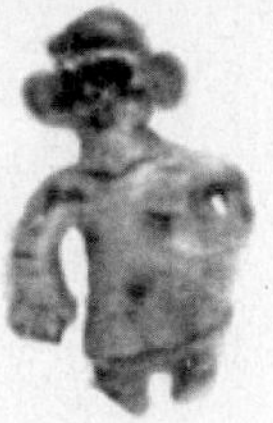

YLW-15

❑ **YLW-14. "The Original Yell-er Kid" Cello. Button,**
c. 1896. - **$300 $650 $1350**

❑ **YLW-15. Miniature Painted White Metal Figure Stickpin,**
c. 1896. - **$50 $100 $200**

YLW-16

YLW-17

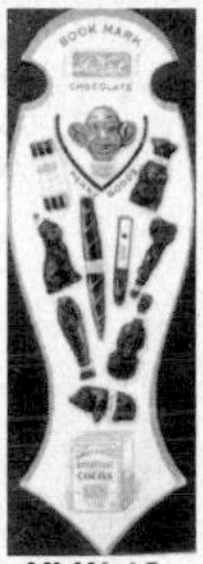

YLW-18

❑ **YLW-16. Pewter Candy Mold,**
c. 1896. - **$75 $150 $300**

❑ **YLW-17. Trade Card,**
c. 1896. Various advertisers. - **$45 $90 $175**

❑ **YLW-18. Chocolate Ad Paper Bookmark,**
c. 1896. Hawley & Hoops Breakfast Cocoa. Pictured are penny chocolate pieces in figural images including Yellow Kid. - **$50 $100 $200**

YLW-19

❑ **YLW-19. Toy Sand Pail,**
1896. 3-1/2" tall by 4-1/2" diameter full color litho tin including four perimeter cartoon images copyright by R. F. Outcault -
$850 $1750 $4000

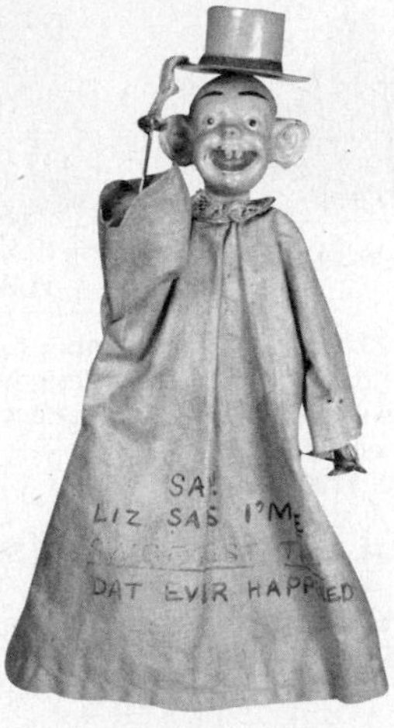

YLW-20

❑ **YLW-20. Yellow Kid Tipping Hat Doll,**
1896. Exceptional doll is 10" tall and wears glossy fabric outfit with lace collar. Hands/head are painted cast metal, hat is painted tin. Body is wood with 2.5" diameter base and attached to body is spring mechanism. Back of outfit reads "CAW Trademark/Sole Licensees And Manufacturers Under 1896 By R.F. Outcault Permission." Front reads "Say! Liz Says I'm De Sweetest Ting Dat Ever Happened." Attached to figure's back is a lever that when pressed causes him to tip his hat and move cane forward.
- **$2250 $4500 $6750**

YLW-21

YLW-22

❑ **YLW-21. "Yellow Kid Ginger Wafers" Pail With Lid,**
1896. 11" tall by 8" diameter tin pail in choice color paper label including tiny credits for R. F. Outcault, National Biscuit Co., maker Brinckerhoff & Co. - **$700 $1400 $3000**

❑ **YLW-22. "De Yeller Kid's High Ball" Whiskey Bottle With Paper Label,**
c. 1896. 6" tall clear glass pocket flask with label picturing him in nightshirt inscribed "Holy Gee! Dis Booze Is Great, See!" Rare, only several known examples. - **$350 $750 $1800**

YLW-23

YLW-24

❑ **YLW-23. Cast Iron Cap Bomb,**
c. 1896. 1.5x1.5" head likeness designed to fire single cap when tossed on hard surface. Top of head is looped for string or similar. - **$75 $150 $300**

❑ **YLW-24. Embossed Brass Long Shank Stickpin,**
c. 1896. Miniature likeness figure brass variety. - **$60 $150 $300**

YLW-25

❑ **YLW-25. Figural Glass Mustard Jar,**
c. 1896. Jar is 1-3/8" deep by 3.25" wide by 6.5" tall. Milk glass body has text embossed on back reading "Say, Ain't I Hot Stuff." Clear satin glass hea. - **$450 $900 $1500**

YLW-26

❑ **YLW-26. Yellow Kid Promotes High Admiral Cigarettes,**
c. 1896. Item is 8x11" thin cardboard cut from larger sheet most likely promoting High Admiral Cigarettes giveaway series of Yellow Kid pin-back buttons. Item realized $2481.00 in Hake's Auction #181, November 2005

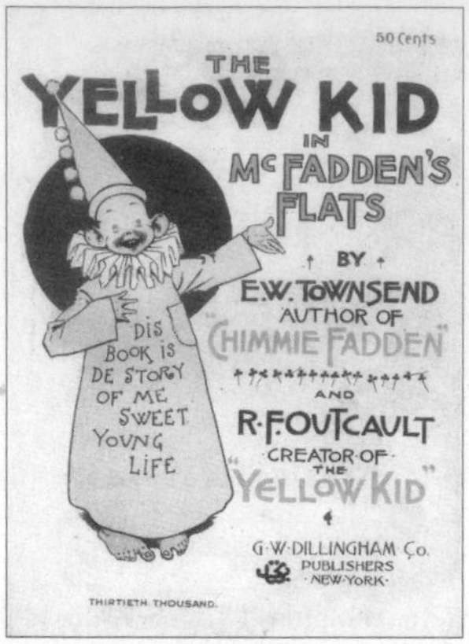

YLW-27

❑ **YLW-27. Yellow Kid In McFadden's Flats,**
1897. G.W. Dillingham Co. The first "comic" book featuring The Yellow Kid; E. W. Townsend narrative with R. F. Outcault Sunday comic page art reprints and some original drawings.
Good - **$6,000**
Fine - **$13,000**
No Near Mint copies known.

YLW-28

❑ **YLW-28. Flip Movie Book,**
1897. Has copyright by H. H. Willc. 1-1/2x2-1/4" with 84 pages printed on one side in black and white with his nightshirt in yellow against black background. Color page reads "Living Photograph Draw Thumb Over Top Edge And Pictures Appear As Alive." - **$250 $400 $800**

YLW-29

❑ **YLW-29. Advertising Card,**
1898. About 7" tall. Known in at least three versions. Seen without text on satchel and as we show with text for "Sweet Wheat Chewing Gum." Also seen with text covering his nightshirt promoting McCormick's Root Beer and satchel text designating him "Micky Dugan Salesman For McCormick & Co. Baltimore."
No text - **$110 $215 $375**
Sweet Wheat - **$135 $240 $475**
McCormick's - **$150 $265 $525**

YLW-30

❑ **YLW-30. Advertising Figure With Refrigerator White Metal Match Holder,**
c. 1898. Ranny-Refrigerator Co., Greenville, Mich. 1-3/4x4-3/4x6-1/2" tall heavy metal with brass luster. Text on shirt says "Say! Now I Can Keep Cool See." Front of refrigerator has additional product text. - **$600 $1200 $2000**

YLW-31

❑ **YLW-31. White Metal Figural Paperweight,**
c. 1898. Paperweight is 3" diameter by 6.75" tall. Shirt says "Say! Ain't I A Heavy Weight."
- **$500 $1000 $1600**

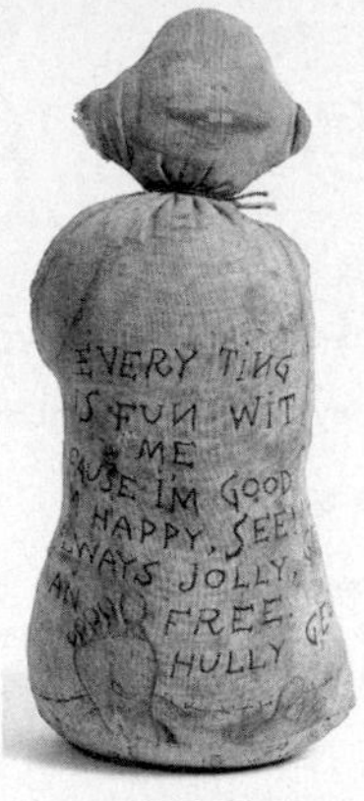

YLW-32

❑ YLW-32. Fabric Doll,
1899. 7" tall stuffed cloth doll by Arnold Print Works with Outcault copyright. Formed from original pattern sheet that includes earlier 1894 and 1896 copyrights by Outcault and New York Journal. Doll body includes printed remarks by Yellow Kid in his dialect. - **$350 $750 $1500**

YLW-33

❑ YLW-33. Yellow Kid High Chair,
1890s. Carved image of Yellow Kid on chair back. 45-1/2" x 17-1/2". -
$450 $900 $1750

YLW-34

❑ YLW-34. "The Sunday World Oct. 18" Newspaper Poster,
1890s. 12x16" with color portrait of Yellow Kid along with his dialogue promoting himself as the original Yellow Kid. Unsigned but art is probably by George Luks. At this time Outcault was drawing the Yellow Kid for the New York Journal. -
$800 $1600 $3500

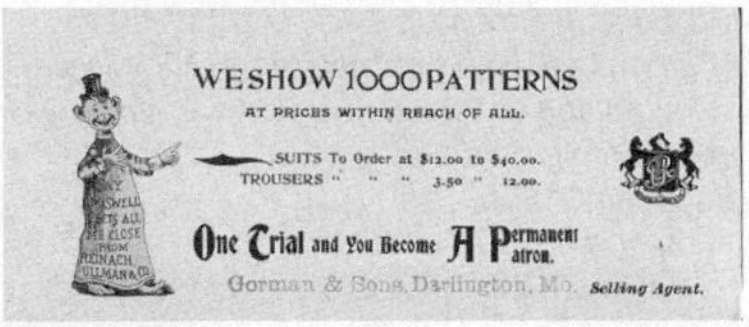

YLW-35

❑ YLW-35. Ink Blotter,
c. 1900. Rare. - **$100 $250 $500**

YLW-36

❑ YLW-36. "The Burr McIntosh-Monthly" Magazine With Yellow Kid As William Jennings Bryan,
1904. January issue, Vol. 3 #10. Shows Yellow Kid as William Jennings Bryan about to throw snowball at snowman of smiling Theodore Roosevelt in front of White House. -
$75 $150 $350

YLW-37

❑ YLW-37. Ad Printing Blocks in Box,
1910. Box with four blocks & four ad flyers. -
Box - **$50 $100 $150**
Each Block - **$50 $100 $150**
Each Ad - **$15 $30 $50**

YLW-38

YLW-39

❑ YLW-38. Cigarette Giveaway Button With Art By Tad,
c. 1912. Has back paper from either Hassen cigarette or Tokio cigarette. One of the scarcest buttons in the "I'm The Guy" series. -
$65 $125 $250

❑ YLW-39. Calendar Postcard,
January 1914. Various advertisers. Series of monthly calendar cards with 1911 Outcault copyright. Each - **$35 $70 $125**

YLW-40

❑ YLW-40. "Confectioner's Machinery And Tools" Catalogue,
1930. Pictures candy molds and shapers including one with Yellow Kid candy pattern. Thos. Mills & Brothers. - **$25 $50 $100**

(ENLARGED VIEW)

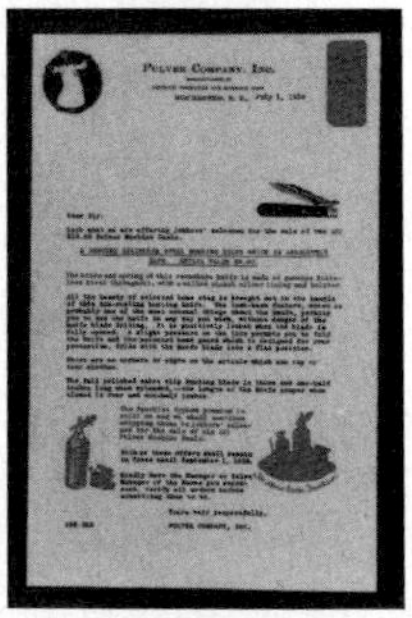

YLW-41

❑ YLW-41. Pulver Gum Co. With Yellow Kid Logo,
1930. 8-1/2x13" stationery sheet with typewritten message dated July 1 to Pulver salesmen offering prizes for sale of gum machines. Yellow Kid symbol is upper left. - **$35 $75 $125**

YLW-42

❑ **YLW-42. "Big Bubble Chewing Gum" Cello. Button,**
c. 1930. Full inscription "There Is Only One Yellow Kid Big Bubble Chewing Gum". - **$25 $50 $100**

YLW-43

❑ **YLW-43. Pulver's Chewing Gum,**
1930s. Complete - **$475 $950 $1850**
Outside Wrapper - **$150 $300 $600**
Each Stick with Gum Wrapper - **$75 $150 $250**

YLW-44

❑ **YLW-44. Richard Outcault's Yellow Kid Bronze Statue, Collectors' Ring & Lithograph,**
1995. Sculpted and produced by Randy Bowen. Limited edition of 100. The ring is complete with blue stones for eyes and fully articulated ears.
Complete - **$2250**
Ring only - **$850**
Lithograph - **$225**

YLW-45

❑ **YLW-45. Richard Outcault's Yellow Kid Gold Edition Statue,**
1995. Sculpted and produced by Randy Bowen. Limited edition of 25. Gold is 23 kt. Comes with a framed limited edition print.
Complete - **$4000**

Yogi Bear

Hanna-Barbera's Yogi Bear, a TV cartoon and merchandising superstar, was introduced in 1959 on *The Huckleberry Hound Show* and two years later was starring in his own series. Voiced by Daws Butler (1916-1988) and reminiscent of Art Carney's character Norton on the *Honeymooners* show, the genial bear in a porkpie hat, trailed by his diminutive pal Boo Boo, spent his time panhandling and swiping picnic baskets from visitors to Jellystone Park. Yogi's love interest was Cindy Bear (Ah do declare!). *The Yogi Bear Show* was syndicated from 1961 to 1963, sponsored by Kellogg cereals; *Yogi's Gang* with Yogi leaving the Park to crusade for the environment, was broadcast on ABC from 1973 to 1975; and *Yogi's Space Race* appeared on NBC from 1978 to 1979. The Yogi Bear comic strip began in 1961, drawn for many years by noted animator Gene Hazelton (1917-2005). Yogi has also appeared teamed with other Hanna-Barbera characters and in several TV specials. Yogi comic books began publication in 1959. His popularity continues to this day. Items are normally copyrighted Hanna-Barbera Productions.

YOG-1

YOG-2

❑ **YOG-1. Vinyl And Plush Doll,**
1960. Store item and Kellogg's premium. 19" tall. - **$35 $65 $150**

❑ **YOG-2. Ceramic Figurine,**
c. 1960. Store item. - **$25 $50 $75**

YOG-3

YOG-4

❑ **YOG-3. "Hey There, It's Yogi Bear" Litho. Button,**
c. 1960. - **$12 $25 $50**

❑ **YOG-4. Plastic Bank,**
c. 1960. Store item by Knickerbocker. - **$20 $30 $60**

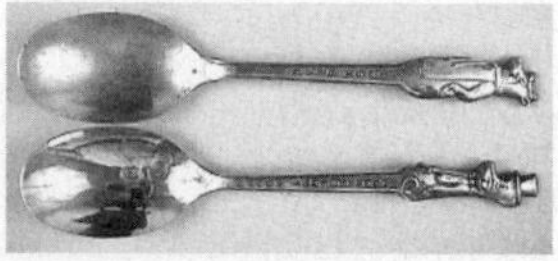

YOG-5

❑ **YOG-5. Cereal Spoon Set,**
1960. Kellogg's. Available for 50 cents and two box tops. Each - **$5 $10 $15**

YOG-6

❑ **YOG-6. "Mechanical Hopping Yogi Bear" Boxed By Line Mar,**
1961. Box is 2.5x3.25x4". Tin wind-up toy measures 4.5" tall when upright.
Box - **$75 $150 $300**
Toy - **$75 $150 $300**

YOG-7

❑ **YOG-7. Early Hanna-Barbera Probable Button Set,**
1961. Each is a 1" litho with studio copyright on curl. Characters are Yogi Bear, Huck Hound, Quick Draw McGraw, Touche Turtle, Lippy The Lion and Wally Gator. Each - **$15 $30 $50**

YOG-8

YOG-9

❑ **YOG-8. "Yogi's Mystery Message De-Coder" Newspaper Ad,**
1961. Kellogg's. Ad pictures cereal box and describes cut-out mechanical de-coder printed on box back.
Used Complete Box - **$100 $250 $425**
Assembled Decoder - **$35 $65 $150**
Advertisement - **$2 $5 $10**

❑ **YOG-9. Huck And Yogi Sweater Pins,**
1962. Kellogg's. Silver luster figures are joined by a chain and were advertised as "Pin-Mates" on the cereal box. - **$10 $20 $30**

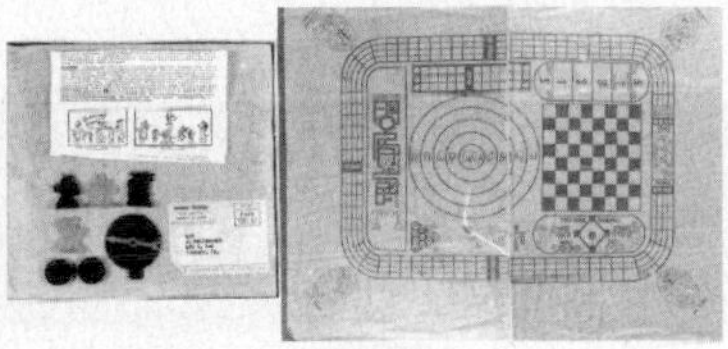

YOG-10

❑ **YOG-10. Yogi Bear Game Cloth,**
1962. Kellogg's Corn Flakes. 35x45" vinyl sheet; markers of Yogi, Huck, Quick Draw, Mr. Jinks; spinner; instructions; 24 red or black checkers picturing Yogi or Huck.
Near Mint In Mailer - **$60**
Complete/Loose - **$10 $20 $40**

YOG-11

❑ **YOG-11. Cereal Box With Printing Press Premium Offer,**
1963. Gordon Gold Archives.
Used Complete - **$100 $250 $425**

YOG-12

❑ **YOG-12. Movie Associated Premium Record,**
1964. Kellogg's. Features music and story from the feature length movie "Hey There It's Yogi Bear!" Came in illustrated mailer.
Mailer - **$5 $10 $20**
Record Jacket - **$5 $10 $20**
Record - **$5 $10 $20**

YOG-13

YOG-14

❑ **YOG-13. "Yogi Bear For President" Litho. Button,**
1964. Hanna-Barbera copyright. Comes in 2-1/4" or 3-1/2" size. Small - **$20 $40 $80**
Large - **$25 $50 $100**

❑ **YOG-14. "Yogi Bear For President" 3" Litho. Button,**
1964. - **$25 $50 $100**

YOG-15

YOG-16

❑ **YOG-15. Purex Bottle Bank With Wrapper,**
1967. Near Mint With Wrapper - **$90**
Bottle Only - **$15 $30 $60**

❑ **YOG-16. "Yogi Bear's Honey Fried Chicken" Restaurant Punch-Out Puzzle,**
c. 1969. - **$8 $15 $30**

YOG-17

YOG-18

❑ **YOG-17. Stamped Image Plastic Ring,**
1960s. Unknown sponsor. Hanna-Barbera copyright. - **$25 $50 $100**

❑ **YOG-18. Newspaper Strip Promotion Cello. Button,**
1960s. Sunday Tribune, possibly Chicago. - **$30 $60 $135**

YOG-19

❑ **YOG-19. "Yogi Bear" Vinyl Lunch Box,**
1960s. Store item. - **$150 $350 $700**

YOG-20

❑ **YOG-20. Yogi Bear Hat,**
1960s. Kellogg's premium. - **$12 $25 $45**

YOG-21

YOG-22

❑ **YOG-21. Yogi Bear Cereal Box,**
1960s. - **$100 $250 $425**

❑ **YOG-22. "Procter & Gamble Dividend Day '85" 2-1/4" Cello. Button,**
1985. From annual series going back at least to 1981. Each - **$10 $15 $30**

YOG-23

YOG-24

❑ **YOG-23. Yogi Bear Bean Bag with Tag,**
1999. - **$10**

❑ **YOG-24. Yogi Bear Plush on Card,**
1999. With Cartoon Network tag. - **$2 $4 $10**

Young Forty-Niners

Colgate's Ribbon Dental Cream sponsored this radio serial in the early 1930s, relating adventures in the California Gold Rush of 1849. Premiums included a map of the gold territory and punch-out versions of an Indian encampment and a wagon train. The program was apparently broadcast only regionally.

YFN-1

❑ **YFN-1. United States Adventure Map With Envelope,**
c. 1932. Colgate-Palmolive-Peet. Map opens to 20x31". Envelope - **$12 $25 $50**
Map - **$75 $150 $300**

YFN-2

YFN-3

❑ **YFN-2. Capt. Sam's Wagon Cardboard Punch-Out Folder,**
c. 1932. Rare. Colgate-Palmolive-Peet. Sheet opens to 19x37". Unpunched - **$60 $150 $250**

❑ **YFN-3. Indian Village,**
c. 1932. Rare. Colgate-Palmolive-Peet. Sheet opens to 19"x37". Unpunched - **$60 $150 $250**

YFN-4

❑ **YFN-4. "Young Forty-Niners" Punch-Out Sheet With Mailer,**
1933. Colgate-Palmolive-Peet Co. Mailing envelope holds thin cardboard opening to 16x22" holding figures of Captain Sam, Indian Jed Carson, Mustang pony, numerous accessory pieces. Mailer - **$12 $25 $50**
Unpunched - **$60 $150 $250**

Zorro

See Ted Hake's *Official® Price Guide to Disney Collectibles*, Second Edition, formatted identically to this book but in full color evaluating over 9,000 Disney company and character collectibles from 1924 through 2006.

This index covers the subject histories and most listed items. Actual people are entered alphabetically by last name. Characters and all other entries are alphabetical by the first word, disregarding articles A, An, and The.

-- A --

-- B --

-- C --

-- D --

-- H --

-- K --

-- L --

-- M --

-- Q --

-- R --

-- S --

ADVERTISERS' INDEX

Aikins, Larry. *Pictorial Price Guide to Metal Lunch Boxes & Thermoses.* Gas City, IN: L-W Book Sales, 1999.
Aikins, Larry. *Pictorial Price Guide to Vinyl & Plastic Lunch Boxes & Thermoses.* Gas City, IN: L-W Book Sales, 1992.
Blumberg, Arnold T. *The Big Big Little Book Book.* Timonium, MD: Gemstone Publishing, Inc. 2004.
Bordman, Gerald. *American Musical Theatre.* New York: Oxford University Press, 1978.
Brooks, Tim & Marsh, Earle. *The Complete Directory to Prime Time Network TV Shows.* 3rd ed. NY: Ballantine Books, 1985.
Brown, Hy. *Comic Character Timepieces: Seven Decades of Memories.* West Chester, PA: Schiffer Publishing, Ltd. 1992.
Bruce, Scott. *Cereal Box Bonanza: The 1950s.* Paducah, KY: Collector Books, 1995.
Bruce, Scott. *Cereal Boxes & Prizes 1960s.* Cambridge, MA: Flake World Publishing, 1998.
Bruce, Scott & Crawford, Bill. *Cerealizing America.* Boston: Faber & Faber, 1995.
Bruce, Scott. *Flake: The Breakfast Nostalgia Magazine.* Cambridge, MA: 1990-1995.
Bruegman, Bill. *The Aurora History and Price Guide.* Akron, OH: Cap'n Penny Productions, 1992.
Claggett, Tom, ed. *The Premium Exchange.* St. Clair Shores, MI: December 1976-January 1978.
Davis, Stephen. *Say Kids! What Time Is It? Notes From The Peanut Gallery.* Boston: Little, Brown and Company, 1987.
Dinan, John A. *The Pulp Western.* San Bernardino, CA: Borgo Press, 1983.
Douglas, George H. *The Early Days of Radio Broadcasting.* Jefferson, NC: McFarland & Co., 1987.
Dunning, John. *Tune in Yesterday.* Englewood Cliffs, NJ: Prentice-Hall, 1976.
Erickson, Hal. *Television Cartoon Shows: An Illustrated Encyclopedia 1949 Through 1993.* Jefferson, NC: McFarland & Co., 1995.
Eury, Michael. *Captain Action: The Original Super-Hero Action Figure.* Raleigh, NC: Twomorrows Publishing, 2002.
Fenin, George N. & Everson, William K. *The Western.* New York: Orion Press, 1962.
Fischer, Stuart. *Kids' TV: The First 25 Years.* New York: Facts on File, 1983.
Geissman, Grant. *Collectibly Mad: The Mad And EC Collectibles Guide.* Northhampton, MA: Kitchen Sink Press, 1995.
Goulart, Ron. *Cheap Thrills.* New Rochelle, NY: Arlington House, 1972.
Goulart, Ron, ed. *Encyclopedia of American Comics.* New York: Facts on File, 1990.
Goulart, Ron. *Great History of Comic Books.* Chicago: Contemporary Books, 1986.
Grossman, Gary H. *Saturday Morning TV.* New York: Dell, 1981.
Hake, Ted. *Hake's Americana & Collectibles Auction Catalogues Nos. 17-192.* York, PA: 1971-2007.
Hake, Ted. *Hake's Guide to Advertising Collectibles.* Radnor, PA: Wallace-Homestead, 1992.
Hake, Ted. *Hake's Guide to Comic Character Collectibles.* Radnor, PA: Wallace-Homestead, 1993.
Hake, Ted. *Hake's Guide to Cowboy Character Collectibles.* Radnor, PA: Wallace-Homestead, 1994.
Hake, Ted. *Hake's Guide to TV Collectibles.* Radnor, PA: Wallace-Homestead, 1990.
Hake, Ted. *Official Price Guide to Disney Collectibles.* 2nd Edition. New York: House of Collectibles, 2007.
Hake, Ted & King, Russell. *Collectible Pin-Back Buttons 1896-1986.* Radnor PA: Wallace-Homestead, 1991.
Halliwell, Leslie. *Halliwell's Film Guide.* 7th ed. New York: Harper & Row, 1990.
Hamilton, Bruce, ed. *Mickey Mouse in Color.* New York: Another Rainbow. 1988.
Heide, Robert & Gilman, John. *Cartoon Collectibles.* Garden City, NY: Doubleday, 1983.
Hickerson, Jay. *The Ultimate History of Network Radio Programming and Guide to All Circulating Shows.* 2nd ed. Hamden, CT: Presto Print II, 1992.
Hirschhorn, Clive. *The Warner Bros. Story.* New York: Crown, 1979.
Horn, Maurice, ed. *The World Encyclopedia of Comics.* New York: Avon Books, 1977.
Inman, David. *The TV Encyclopedia.* New York: Putnam, 1991.
Jacobs, Larry. *Big Little Books: A Collector's Reference & Value Guide.* Paducah, KY: Collector Books, 1996.
Keaton, Russell. *The Aviation Art of Russell Keaton.* Northampton, MA: Kitchen Sink Press, 1995.
Lenburg, Jeff. *The Encyclopedia of Animated Cartoon Series.* Westport, CT: Arlington House, 1981.
Levin, Marshall N. and Hake, Theodore L. *Buttons In Sets 1896-1972.* York PA: Hake's Americana & Collectibles Press, 1984.
Maltin, Leonard. *Of Mice and Magic.* New York: McGraw-Hill, 1980.
Maltin, Leonard. *TV Movies and Video Guide.* 1991 ed. New York: Penguin, 1990.
Mandelowitz, Hy. *The Premium Guide.* New York: November 1977-August 1979.
Matetsky, Amanda Murrah. *The Adventures Of Superman Collecting.* West Plains, MO: Russ Cochran, Ltd., 1988.
Melcher, Jack, ed. *Radio Premium Collectors Newsletter.* Waukegan, IL: January 1973-September 1975.
Miller, Francis. *Lindbergh–His Story in Pictures.* New York: Knickerbocker Press, 1929.
Milne, Tom and Willeman, Paul. *The Encyclopedia of Horror Movies.* New York: Harper & Row, Publishers, 1986.
Mix, Paul E. *The Life and Legend of Tom Mix.* South Brunswick & NY: A.S. Barnes, 1972.
Morgan, Hal. *Symbols of America.* New York: Viking Penguin, 1986.
Moskowitz, Milton, Levering, Robert & Katz, Michael. *Everybody's Business.* New York: Doubleday, 1990.
Murray, John J. & Bruce R. Fox. *The Fisher-Price 1931-1963 Toy Book.* Florence, AL: Books Americana, 1996. 3rd Edition.
Norris, M.G. "Bud." *The Tom Mix Book.* Waynesville, NC: The World Of Yesterday, 1989.
O'Brien, Richard. *Collecting Toys No. 8.* Florence, AL: Books Americana, 1997.
Olson, Richard D., ed. *Little Orphan Annie Reader.* New Orleans, LA: 1979-1980.
Olson, Richard D., ed. *The R.F. Outcault Reader: The Official Newsletter Of The R.F. Outcault Society.* Slidell, LA:1993.
Overstreet, Robert M. *The Overstreet Comic Book Price Guide.* 38rd ed. York, PA: Gemstone Publishing, Inc. 2008.
Overstreet, Robert M. *The Overstreet Toy Ring Price Guide.* 3rd ed. Timonium, MD: Gemstone Publishing, Inc. 1997.
Paquin, Mike. "Put on a 'Funny Face,'" *Collecting Figures,* pp. 74-75, June, 1995.
Penzler, Otto, Steinbrunner, Chris & Lachman, Marvin, eds. *Detectionary.* Woodstock, N.: Overlook Press, 1977.
Pinsky, Maxine A. *Marx Toys: Robots, Space, Comic, Disney & TV Characters.* Atglen, PA: Schiffer Publishing, 1996.
Renner, Eric. *American Disguise.* San Lorenzo, NM: Flying Monkey Press, 2007.
Rinker, Harry L. *Hopalong Cassidy King Of The Cowboy Merchandisers.* Atglen, PA: Schiffer Publishing, Ltd., 1995.
Santelmo, Vincent. *The Official 30th Anniversary Salute To GI Joe 1964-1994.* Iola, WI: Krause Publications, 1994.
Sarno, Joe, ed. *Space Academy Newsletter.* Chicago: July 1978-October, 1981.
Scarfone, Jay and Stillman, William. *The Wizard of Oz Collector's Treasury.* West Chester, PA: Schiffer Publishing, Ltd. 1992.
Selitzer, Ralph. *The Dairy Industry in America.* New York: Magazines for Industry, 1976.
Smilgis, Joel, ed. *Box Top Bonanza.* Moline, IL: December 1983-No. 49, 1991.
Stedman, Raymond William. *The Serials.* 2nd ed. Norman, OK: University of Oklahoma Press, 1977.
Swartz, Jon D. & Reinehr, Robert C. *Handbook of Old-Time Radio.* Metuchen, NJ: Scarecrow Press, 1993.
Terrace, Vincent. *Radio's Golden Years.* San Diego, CA: A.S. Barnes, 1981.
Thompson, Steve. *The Walt Kelly Collector's Guide: A Bibliography and Price Guide.* Richfield, MN: Spring Hollow Books.
Tumbusch, Tom. *Tomart's Price Guide to Radio Premium and Cereal Box Collectibles.* Dayton, OH: Tomart Publications, 1991.
Weiss, Ken & Goodgold, ed. *To Be Continued....* New York: Bonanza Books, 1972.
White, Larry. *Cracker Jack Toys.* Atglen, PA: Schiffer Publishing, Ltd. 1997.
Woolery, George W. *Animated TV Specials.* Metuchen, NJ: Scarecrow Press, 1989.
Woolery, George W. *Children's Television: The First Thirty-Five Years, 1946-1981. Part I.* Metuchen, NJ: Scarecrow Press, 1983.
Woolery, George W. *Children's Television: The First Thirty-Five Years, 1946-1981. Part II.* Metuchen, NJ: Scarecrow Press, 1985.
Young, S. Mark, Steve Duin, Mike Richardson. *Blast Off! Rockets, Robots, Ray Guns, and Rarities from the Golden Age.* Milwaukie, OR: Dark Horse Comics, 2001.

President's Note

As you have already no doubt noted by this point in the book, we are bullish on the market for vintage pop culture artifacts. In general, the world of toys and pop culture remains an area with tremendous growth potential, and the fact that it's so difficult to single out a specific category as out-performing the others is because so many of them are operating through periods of solid, sustained growth.

I'm sure you could name the categories just as easily as I can, but let's think about just a few of them: Buck Rogers, Flash Gordon, the early science fiction television shows like *Space Patrol* and *Tom Corbett*, the great western characters Hopalong Cassidy and Roy Rogers, classic, long-lived characters such as Popeye, Betty Boop, superheroes like Batman and Superman, promotional materials for clubs, club kits such as the Junior Justice Society of America, Spider-Man, and many others are all strong. Whether it's character watches, yo-yos, costumes, action figures, pop-up books, or any of the 350-plus other categories, this is a period of fantastic enthusiasm.

Right now we're seeing a renaissance of superb material coming on the market. Some of it is clearly following the successes of other recent sales in auctions, and that's only natural. Whenever an auction is successful and the publicity goes out, someone says "I have one of those," or something similar.

This is due in no small part to a healthy combination of information and timing. There's never been a better time for pop culture enthusiasts because society as a whole has finally started to realize that the history of popular culture is inexorably tied to mainstream history in this country. It seems like I say this all the time now, but take a look at the History Channel, A&E, The Learning Channel, your local PBS affiliate. Collectibles, those magnificent artifacts of days gone by, are everywhere. Whether it's a comic-themed movie sitting atop the box office charts or a top-selling video game or an actual comic book successfully utilizing well-known characters, this serves to reinforce the public's awareness of and comfort with this social acceptance.

And awareness is why our staff works so hard on books like this one, and why I opened Geppi's Entertainment Museum in 2006. The more people - both collectors and laymen - who know about this wonderful world of collecting, the more interesting it's going to get!

As always, we'd like to know what you think, so feel free to drop us a line at feedback@gemstonepub.com.

Stephen A. Geppi

Stephen A. Geppi
President and
Chief Executive Officer

P.S. Our "Top-Value" charts begin on the next page and offer some good insights into many of the specialties.

The following charts represent the top items in the categories noted. The prices reflected in these charts are for high grade items, generally in near mint condition except when there are no known examples in that grade, complete with all parts and packaging when applicable. Disney collectibles are not included in the following charts but can be referenced in the *Official Price Guide to Disney Collectibles*.

TOP PINBACK BUTTONS

U.S. Jones Cadets Comic Club Button	1941	$6,000
The Shadow Movie Club Button	1940	$5,500
Buck Rogers Strange World Adventures Club	1939	$4,000
The Shadow Is No More Button	1930s	$4,000
Buck Rogers 25th Century Acousticon Button	1936	$3,750
Sun-Times Comic Capers Club Button	1940s	$3,750
The Shadow Radio Club Button	1944	$3,600
Superman Democrat Newspaper Button	1940	$3,500
Buck Rogers Canadian Club Member Button	1937	$3,250
Follow Buck Rogers Button	1930s	$3,250

Buck Rogers Strange World Adventures Club Button

U.S. Jones Cadets Comic Club Button

TOP TOY MECHANICAL BANKS

Freedman's Bank	1880	$350,000
Darky and Watermelon Bank	1888	$250,000
Jonah And The Whale Pedestal Bank	1888	$250,000
Chinaman In Boat Bank	1881	$85,000
Girl Skipping Rope Bank	1890	$75,000
Merry-Go-Round Bank	1889	$65,000
Mama Katzenjammer Bank	1905	$50,000
Bread Winners Bank	1886	$45,000
Circus Bank	1888	$40,000
Calamity Bank	1905	$40,000
Confectionery Bank	1881	$38,000

Right: Girl Skipping Rope Bank

Far Right: Mama Katzenjammer Bank

TOP TOY RINGS

Superman Member Contest Prize Ring	1940	$30,000 VF
Little Orphan Annie Altascope Ring	1942	$22,500
Superman Secret Chamber Ring With Superman Image Top	1940	$20,000 VF
Superman Secret Chamber Initial Ring (With Paper Insert)	1940	$17,500
Sky King Kaleidoscope Prototype Ring	1950	$17,500
Operator 5 Ring	1934	$16,000
Supermen of America/Action Comics Prototype Ring	1940	$16,000
Cisco Kid Secret Compartment Ring	1950s	$13,000
Valric of the Vikings Magnifying Ring	1941	$10,000
Tom Mix Deputy Ring	1933	$7,500
Knights of Columbus Secret Compartment, Glow-In-Dark Ring	1940	$6,000

Above: Sky King Kaleidoscope Prototype Ring

Below: Little Orphan Annie Altascope Ring

TOP PROMOTIONAL COMICS

Motion Picture Funnies Weekly #1	1939	$29,000 VF/NM
Century of Comics	1933	$25,000 VF
Funnies on Parade	1933	$15,000
Lone Ranger Ice Cream	1947	$6,400 VF
Superman's Christmas Adventure #1	1939	$6,300
Terry and the Pirates Ruby of Genghis Khan	1941	$2,600 VF
Buster Brown Blue Ribbon Book of Jokes and Jingles Book 1	1904	$1,900
Captain Marvel and the Lieutenants of Safety Comic Book #1	1950	$1,600

Right: Century of Comics. Far Right: Funnies on Parade

TOP TOY TIMEPIECES

Tom Mix Pocketwatch	1934	$8,500
Betty Boop Pocketwatch	1934	$7,500
Popeye Pocketwatch	1935	$5,000
Tom Mix Wristwatch	1935	$5,000
Superman Supertime Wristwatch with Box	1950s	$4,200
Superman Wristwatch with Box	1940	$3,750
Buck Rogers Pocketwatch	1935	$3,500
Popeye Characters Alarm Clock (Unboxed)	1930s	$3,500
Babe Ruth Wristwatch with Display Case	1949	$3,500
Dizzy Dean Wristwatch with Box	1933	$3,500
Woody Woodpecker with Box	1940s	$3,400
Happy Hooligan Painted Figural Clock (No Box)	1910	$2,750
Joe Palooka with Box	1950s	$1,700
Capt. Marvel Jr.	1948	$1,350

Left: Buck Rogers Pocketwatch with Box
Above: Superman Wristwatch with Box

TOP TOY MAPS

Sherlock Holmes London Prototype Map (Original Art)	1955	$3,500
Sherlock Holmes Household Finance Map	1930s	$3,000
Buck Rogers Solar System Map	1933	$1,600
Sherlock Holmes London Prototype Map (Printed Version)	1955	$1,500
Buck Rogers School Map	1930s	$1,300
Wizard of Oz Wonderland of Oz Map	1932	$1,200
Black Flame of the Amazon Map (With Stamps)	1930s	$1,150
Tarzan Jungle Map USA Edition	1933	$1,100
Tarzan Jungle Map Canadian Edition	1933	$900
Jack Armstrong Map of the Hidden City and Surrounding Jungle	1930s	$900
Tarzan Jungle Map Australian Edition	1933	$800
Adventures of Og, Son of Fire Map	1935	$800
Vic and Sade Hometown Map	1942	$760
Captain Midnight Skelly Oil Flight Patrol Airline Map	1940	$700
Baron Munchausen Map of Radioland	1932	$650

Left: Tarzan Jungle Map Canadian Edition

Right: Captain Midnight Skelly Oil Flight Patrol Airline Map

TOP COMIC CHARACTER STATUETTES

Superman Syroco-Style Fully Painted Figure on Ashtray Base	1942	$15,000
Captain Marvel Syroco Statuette "Captain" Version	1945	$7,000
Captain Marvel Syroco Statuette "Capt." Version	1946	$7,000
Princess of Little Nemo Bisque Figure	1914	$6,000
Superman Syroco-Style Fully Painted	1942	$6,000
Tom Mix 5" Bisque Figure	1933	$5,500
Marvel Bunny 4 3/4" Statuette	1946	$5,250
Little Nemo Bisque Figure	1914	$5,000
Alley Oop Product Statuette (With Club)	1946	$4,150
Dr. Pill of Little Nemo Bisque Figure	1914	$4,000
Flip of Little Nemo Bisque Figure	1914	$4,000
The Imp of Little Nemo Bisque Figure	1914	$4,000
Marvel Bunny 6" Statuette	1946	$3,000
Mary Marvel 5" Figure (Red Dress, Red Lightning Bolt Version)	1946	$3,750
Superman Syroco-Style Brown with Red Accents	1942	$3,600
Phantom, Multi-Products Figure (Purple Costume)	1945	$1,950
Phantom, Multi-Products Figure (Brown Costume)	1945	$1,800
Captain Marvel 6.5" Figure	1946	$1,500
Captain Marvel, Jr. 5" Figure	1946	$1,500
Mary Marvel 5" Figure	1946	$1,500
Mary Marvel 6.5" Figure	1946	$1,300
Captain Marvel, Jr. 6.5" Figure	1946	$1,150
Rosie Multi-Products Figure	1945	$1,200
Flash Gordon Multi-Products Figure	1945	$1,000

Far Left: Superman Syroco-Style Fully Painted Figure on Ashtray Base
Left: Mary Marvel 5" Figure (Red Dress, Red Lightning Bolt Version)

TOP PROMOTIONAL DISPLAY ARTIFACTS

(The rare Disney posters and Disney promotional signs, which would fit in this category, are not included in this list since they are featured in *The Official Price Guide To Disney Collectibles* by Ted Hake, also available from Random House.)

Superman Fleischer Cartoon Standee	1941	$60,000
Superman War Savings Bond Poster	1943	$25,000
Atom Man vs. Superman 6' Movie Standee	1950	$25,000
The Day The Earth Stood Still 5' Movie Standee	1951	$22,500
Superman Fleischer Cartoon One Sheet Poster	1941	$15,000
Adventures of Captain Marvel One Sheet Poster Chapter 1	1941	$11,500
Adventures of Captain Marvel Six Sheet Movie Poster	1941	$11,000
Large Roy Rogers and Trigger Figural Store Display	1959	$10,500
New Adventures of Batman and Robin Movie Serial Three Sheet Poster	1949	$10,500
Spy Smasher Three Sheet Poster	1942	$10,000
The Phantom Three Sheet Poster	1940s	$8,000
Yellow Kid Announcement Poster New York Journal's Sunday Supplement	1896	$8,000
Captain Midnight Three Sheet Movie Serial Poster	1940s	$7,750
Captain America Movie Serial Three Sheet Poster	1944	$7,250
Hopalong Cassidy Timex Store Display	1950	$7,000
Flash Gordon's Trip to Mars Chapter Four One Sheet Poster	1938	$6,500
Captain Marvel Promotional Poster for Republic Pictures Serial	1941	$6,250
Superman Life-Size Cardboard Kellogg's Store Display	1956	$5,500
Captain Marvel Statuettes Store Sign	1946	$5,500
Pep Large Display Sign Featuring Character Pep Buttons	1945	$5,500
Kix Cereal "Name Silver Contest Poster"	1941	$5,000

The Day The Earth Stood Still 5' Standee

Atom Man vs. Superman 6' Movie Standee

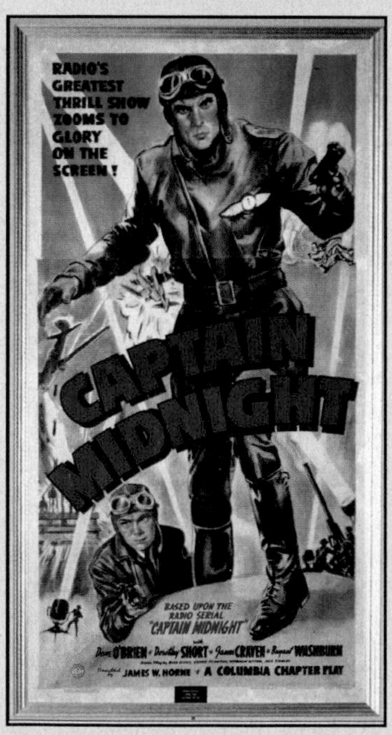

Captain Midnight Three Sheet Movie Serial Poster

TOP TOY CHARACTER ARTIFACTS (Categories Listed Previously Are Not Included)

Howdy Doody Marionette Promotional Photo Doll for Televison Show	1940s	$113,431
Popeye and Olive Oyl Tank	1950s	$20,000
Toonerville Trolley Aunt Eppie Hogg Wind-Up Toy	1923	$20,000
Batman Utility Belt	1966	$20,000
Supermen of America Leader Patch	1940	$20,000
Popeye Large Speed Boat Wind-Up	1935	$15,000
Popeye Heavy Hitter Tin Wind-Up	1930s	$14,500
Batman and Justice League of America Playset	1960s	$13,500
Buck Rogers Scientific Laboratory	1934	$13,000
Popeye Bag Puncher Wind-Up	1930s	$12,500
Captain Action Spider-Man Set	1967	$12,000
Wizard of Oz Waddle Book	1934	$11,500
Supermen of America Action Comics Patch	1940	$11,000
Bonzo Mechanical Bank	1930s	$10,000
Brownies The Dude 36" Tall Figure	1899	$9,500
Superman Candy Patch	1940	$9,500
Buck Rogers Cut-Out Adventure Book	1933	$9,000
Katzenjammer Kids Captain and the Kids Bell Ringer Toy	1910	$8,750
Sky King Secret Compartment Belt Buckle Prototype	1948	$8,500
Buck Rogers Solar Scouts Sweater Emblem	1936	$8,500
Buck Rogers Rocket Skates	1935	$8,500
Tarzan Picture Puzzle	1932	$8,000
The Shadow Dealer's Promotional Campaign Book	1945	$8,000
Superman Premium Enameled Brass Shield	1949	$7,500
Uncle Wiggily's Crazy Car	1922	$7,500
Barbie First Issued Doll	1959	$7,500
Tom Mix Ranch Boss Enameled Brass Badge Prototype	1937	$7,500
Tom Mix Straight Shooters Star Brass Badge Prototype	1937	$7,500
Harold Lloyd Mechanical Bank	1920s	$6,250
Bringing Up Father Jiggs Carnival Bumper Car Wind-Up	1920s	$6,000
Oswald the Lucky Rabbit Large Doll by Deans Rag Co.	1931	$5,500
Felix the Cat German Wind-Up Car	1920s	$5,500
Martian Wind-Up Toy	1950s	$5,000
Spider-Man Limited Edition Gibson Guitar Signed by Stan Lee	2000	$5,000
Supermans Child's Sweatshirt	1940	$5,000
Tarzan Background for Fould's Plaster Statues	1932	$5,000
Jack Armstrong Crocodile Glow in the Dark Plastic Whistle	1941	$5,000
Buck Rogers Solar Scouts Pennant	1936	$5,000
Superman Overseas Cap	1942	$5,000
Superman Metal Hood Ornament 4 1/2" Chrome Finish	1946	$4,750
Doc Savage Award "Bronze Medallion"	1930s	$4,500

Batman Utility Belt

Popeye Large Speed Boat Wind-Up

Buck Rogers Solar Scouts Sweater Emblem

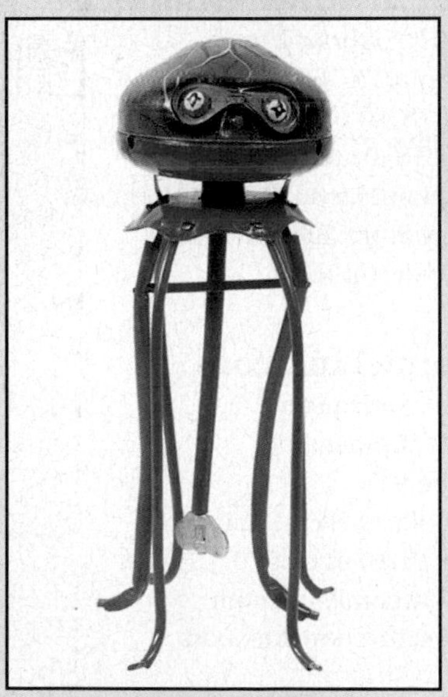
Martian Wind-Up Toy

Oswald The Lucky Rabbit Large Doll by Deans Rag Co.

Uncle Wiggily's Crazy Car

AUCTIONS, COLLECTORS, & RETAILERS

David J. Anderson, DDS
Seminary Professional Village
Alexandria, VA 22311
Tel: (703) 671-7422
Fax: (703) 578-1222
DJA2@cox.net
By appointment only.

B&D Comic Shop
Terry Baucom
802 Elm Avenue SW
Roanoke, VA 24016
Tel: (540) 342-6642
Fax: (540) 342-6694
www.banddcomics.com
bdcomics1@verizon.net

Barry's Collectors Corner
1826 S. Washington St.
Grand Cities Mall
Grand Forks, ND 58201
Tel: (701) 795-1386
UNDBK@aol.com

Bill 'n' Anne Campbell
3501 Foxbriar Lane
Cibolo, TX 78108
Tel: (830) 626-1077
Fax: (830) 626-8092
CaptainMarvel1940@satx.rr.com
eBay Store: Bill and Anne's
Wonderful Toys

ComicLink.com
Josh Nathanson
189 Montague St.
Suite 915
Brooklyn, NY 11201
Tel: (516) 466-2770
www.comiclink.com
buysell@comiclink.com

The Comics Club, Inc.
Duane Stamper
714 W. Lumsden Rd.
Brandon, FL 33511
Tel: (813) 653-4111
www.comicsclub.com
mail@comicsclub.com

Diamond International Galleries
3679 Concord Rd.
York, PA 17402
Tel: (888) 355-9800
www.DiamondGalleries.com
By appointment only.

Doodyville Historical Society
Jeff Judson
8 Hunt Court
Flemington, NJ 08822
Tel: (908) 782-1159
jtjudson@embarqmail.com

Dreamland
Rich Biedrzycki
1415 W. Schaumburg Rd.
Schaumburg, IL 60194
Tel: (847) 524-6060
Fax: (847) 524-6339
www.dreamlandcomics.com
Laurie@dreamlandcomics.com

Geppi's Entertainment Museum
301 West Camden Street
Baltimore, MD 21201
Tel: (410) 625-7060
Fax: (410) 625-7090
www.GeppisMuseum.com

Hake's Americana & Collectibles
P.O. Box 12001
York, PA 17402
Tel: (866) 404-9800
www.hakes.com
walex@hakes.com
By appointment only.

Harrison's
Larry Harrison
252 Essex St.
Salem, MA 01970
Tel: (978) 741-0786
Fax: (978) 741-0737
www.Harrisoncomicsltd.com
Harrisonscomics@Hotmail.com

Heritage Galleries & Auctioneers
Jim Halperin
3500 Maple Avenue, 17th Floor
Dallas, TX 75219
Tel: (800) 872-6467
www.HA.com

Jetpack Comics LLC
Ralph DiBernardo
112 Portland St.
Rochester, NH 03867
Tel: (603) 330-9636
www.jetpackcomics.com
info@jetpackcomics.com

Mahopac Cards & Comics
Gary Bailey
1000 Miller Road Plaza
P.O. Box 444
Mahopac, NY 10541
Tel: (845) 621-2699
Fax: (845) 621-6719
www.MahopacCards.com
MahopacCards@aol.com

Morphy Auctions
Dan Morphy
2000 North Reading Road
Denver, PA 17517
Tel: (717) 335-3435
Fax: (717) 336-7115
www.MorphyAuctions.com

Neat Stuff Collectibles
Mike Carbonaro
704 76th Street
North Bergen, NJ 07047
Tel: (201) 861-1414
Fax: (201) 861-1154
www.neatstuffcollectibles.com

The Paper Escape
Thomas McClain
205 W. 1st St.
Dixon, IL 61021
Tel: (815) 284-7567
www.paperescape.com
paperescape@paperescape.com

Serious Toyz
Tom Miano
82 Main St.
Cold Spring, NY 10516
Tel: (866) OLD-TOYZ
www.serioustoyz.com

ToyRing.com
Joe Statkus
www.toyring.com
yozi2@aol.com

Philip Weiss Auctions
1 Neal Court
Oceanside, NY 11572
Tel: (516) 594-0731
Fax: (516) 594-9414
www.philipweissauctions.com
info@philipweissauctions.com

Zipstoys.com
Toni Volk
2204 Darby Rd.
Havertown, PA 19083
Tel: (610) 536-9050
www.zipstoys.com
zips@zipstoys.com

MANUFACTURERS, PUBLISHERS, & SERVICES

Antique Toy World Magazine
Dale Kelley
PO Box 34509
Chicago, IL 06034
Tel: (773) 725-0633
www.AntiqueToyWorld.com
dale@AntiqueToyWorld.com

Collectors News
Ronda Jans
P.O. Box 306
506 2nd Street
Grundy Center, IA 50638
Tel: (800) 352-8039
Fax: (319) 824-3414
http://collectors-news.com
rjans@thepioneergroup.com

Comics Buyer's Guide
Brent Frankenhoff
700 E. State St.
Iola, WI 54990
Tel: (715) 445-4612
Fax: (715) 445-4087
www.cbgxtra.com
brent.frankenhoff@fwpubs.com

Diamond Comic Distributors
1966 Greenspring Drive, Suite 300
Timonium, MD 21093
Tel: (410) 560-7100
www.DiamondComics.com

Diamond Select Toys
1966 Greenspring Drive
Suite 402
Timonium, MD 21093
www.DiamondSelectToys.com
customerservice@
DiamondSelectToys.com

Gemstone Publishing
P.O. Box 12001
York, PA 17402
Tel: (888) 375-9800
www.Gemstonepub.com

PEANUTS
$151,534
$41,264
$11,550
AMAZING! STARTLING!
SUPERMAN
IS HERE!
TECHNICOLOR
AMERICANA &
HAKE'S
COLLECTIBLES
$19,898
7.5
Fantastic Four
THE GOERKE CO.
WELCOME
$10,350

We know who makes you smile.
SERIOUS TOYZ™
Vintage Toy & Collectible Auctions
REPEATEDLY NAMED AMONG THE LEADING TOY AUCTION HOUSES IN THE U.S.
We offer bidding by Phone, Mail, Fax, or LIVE on our Website
Always Seeking Quality Consignments
WE ALSO BUY · SELL · TRADE
CALL US TOLL FREE: 866-OLD TOYZ (866-653-8699)
ASK TO GET ON OUR MAILING LIST--IT'S FREE!
Visit our store: 82 Main St., Cold Spring, NY 10516
Online at: serioustoyz.com
© 2008 Serious Toyz™ ALL RIGHTS RESERVED
CAPTAIN AMERICA SCOOTER WITH FRICTION DRIVE BY MARX
DRAG NUT
FOXY GRANDPA PUZZLE
THE TWILIGHT ZONE
THE OUTER LIMITS
MAVERICK
GUN and HOLSTER SET
GIANT-SIZE X-MEN
SANTA CLAUS PUZZLE BOX
RIDERS OF THE DEADLINE
WILLIAM BOYD
HONEY WEST
STAR WARS
FRED FLINTSTONE
JONNY QUEST CARD GAME
WALT DISNEY'S DONALD DUCK DUET
GULLIVER'S TRAVELS
JAMES BOND 007 TEN MOVIE CHARACTERS
SUPERMAN SOCKS
PRESS ACTION TOYS
GREEN HORNET KITE
MAGIC INVISIBLE KITE
BAT MAN
Matt Dillon
MICKEY MOUSE ROCKING HORSE